American Fiction, 1901–1925

American Fiction, 1901–1925: A Bibliography is an invaluable record of first printings of American fiction for scholars of American literature, readers of fiction, and collectors of modern first editions. Over three hundred fifty print and online reference sources have been reviewed to approach, as nearly as possible, a comprehensive listing of titles that fit the bibliography's criteria. Each title entry includes rare book bibliographic description as prescribed by the Library of Congress's *Descriptive Cataloging of Rare Books*. Short story collections are included with complete listing of contents. When available, notation is made of copyright dates and publication announcements in *Publisher's Weekly*. Bibliographic notations for British printings of entries are acknowledged if they appear in the *British Library Catalogue*. Citations of standard authoritative sources (e.g., *Bibliography of American Literature*) are included.

The bibliography will assist all levels of research into the examination of the literary record of American cultural history and will augment, beyond literary studies, historical, political, religious and popular studies. The bibliography will also assist research in the growing areas of African-American, women's, and ethnic studies.

American Fiction, 1901–1925
A Bibliography

Geoffrey D. Smith
The Ohio State University Libraries

CAMBRIDGE
UNIVERSITY PRESS

PUBLISHED BY THE PRESS SYNDICATE OF THE UNIVERSITY OF CAMBRIDGE
The Pitt Building, Trumpington Street, Cambridge CB2 1RP, United Kingdom

CAMBRIDGE UNIVERSITY PRESS
The Edinburgh Building, Cambridge CB2 2RU, United Kingdom
40 West 20th Street, New York, NY 10011–4211, USA
10 Stamford Road, Oakleigh, Melbourne 3166, Australia

First published 1997

Printed in the United States of America

Typeset in Times Roman

Library of Congress Cataloguing-in-Publication Data has been applied for

*A catalogue record for this book is available from
the British Library*

ISBN 0 521 43469 6 hardback

For Lois,
Always and forever

Contents

Preface

American Fiction, 1901-1925: A Bibliography is a compilation of first printings of original fiction for adults by American authors published in the United States from 1901 through 1925. This current volume has been generally arranged and styled in the tradition of Lyle Wright's contribution to the earlier American fiction bibliography (*American Fiction, 1774-1900*, 3 vols.)[1], although the format and content have been altered to accommodate current scholarly research. For instance, publisher's and illustrator's indices have been added in response to the increased interest in the history of the book and the book arts. Still, the principal criteria for selection of titles in the bibliography remain true to Wright's and include "novels, novelettes, romances, short stories, tall tales, tract-like tales, allegories, and fictitious biographies and travels, in prose." (Exceptions are noted below.)

The first quarter of the twentieth century was, in many ways, a period of transition in American fiction. Among major authors, the period began with the late works of the nineteenth-century masters of realism (Howells, James, and Twain) and ended with the early works of the post-World War I, "lost generation" (Dos Passos, Fitzgerald, and Hemingway). Some writers flourished through most of the period (Cather, Dreiser, Glasgow, and Wharton), while the brilliant careers of others were cut short by death (Crane, Norris, and London). The period is particularly valuable for research in African-American studies, feminist criticism and the popular culture movement. Charles W. Chesnutt, W. E. B. DuBois, and Jean Toomer preceded the Harlem Renaissance and brought early national attention to black writers. Mary Wilkins Freeman, Dorothy Canfield Fisher, and Charlotte Perkins Gilman considered the problems of working women, marriage and divorce and female identity. David Graham Phillips, Robert Herrick, Upton Sinclair, and Jacob A. Riis were among the muckrakers and socialists who confronted the political, economic, and social issues of the period. Anna Katherine Green, Mary Roberts Rinehart, Jacques Futrelle, and Edgar Rice Burroughs were among the many early practitioners who developed the popular narrative genre of mystery and science fiction.

Of course, the majority of writers approached social and cultural issues with less insight, and often less tolerance, than most prominent writers, but knowledge of their views is equally important for a complete understanding of American beliefs and values. Arguably, many less recognized writers, as distinct from their more critically appreciated contemporaries, may have presented a more accurate assessment of the majority American view toward controversial political and social issues. The body of popular fiction, then, is an invaluable source of interdisciplinary and special studies of American culture history, in addition to its importance for the purely literary studies of particular authors and titles.

As noted above, every effort has been made to note the first printing of those titles that meet the selection criteria. Revised editions are listed if the work underwent extensive change, but not superficial additions, as in the proverbial added introduction or preface common to so many "revised" editions. The first, separate book publication of a short story is included, even if it appeared in an earlier collection or anthology. Retitled works are noted under the first title and cross-referenced accordingly in the bibliography and in the title index.

American Fiction, 1901-1925: A Bibliography omits many of the same classifications as Lyle Wright, including juveniles, folklore, collections of anecdotes, essays, and periodicals. Additionally, this volume omits series fiction on the grounds that series fiction is more a product of a manufacturer, i.e., carefully monitored, formula fiction, than the individual product of a creator or co-creator.

---

[1] *American Fiction, 1774-1850: A Contribution Toward a Bibliography* (2nd rev. ed., San Marino, Calif.: Huntington Library, 1969); *American Fiction, 1851-1975: A Contribution Toward a Bibliography* (San Marino, Calif.: Huntington Library, 1965); and *American Fiction, 1876-1900: A Contribution Toward a Bibliography* (San Marino, Calif.: Huntington Library, 1966).

BIBLIOGRAPHICAL COMMENT

The goal of the bibliography is to provide reliable research information for scholars of American cultural history, students of the book arts, and collectors. The bibliographic entries are arranged alphabetically by author. Anonymous works will be arranged alphabetically by title within the author sequence. Multiple titles by a single author will be arranged alphabetically by title under the author's name.

THE DESCRIPTIVE RECORD

Citation: each entry will be cited by the first letter of the main entry (author or title) and progressive, numerical indication of alphabetical order, e.g., A-1, A-2, A-3 . . . A-385, A-386; B-1, B-2, B-3 . . . B-700, B-701, B-702, etc.

Main entry: when available, author's names are listed according to the name authority as prescribed by The Program for Cooperative Cataloging of the Library of Congress; otherwise, name authority is established according to conventions of the *Anglo-American Cataloguing Rules, 2nd revised edition*. When available, birth and death dates are given. For each entry, the complete title, including sub-title, is recorded. The statement of responsibility (i.e., author's name) is recorded as printed on the title page and may vary from the author main entry. Illustrators' names or statements on illustrations are also recorded.

Imprint: the city of publication, publisher, and date of publication follow the statement of responsibility. Information derived from other than the title page will be bracketed (i.e., [ ]).

Pagination: the last numbered page of narrative text is recorded and may be followed by the bracketed notation of remaining unnumbered pages of narrative text, e.g., [1] or [2], etc. Frontispieces (front.), plates and illustrations are recorded. Particular note is made of photographic plates (photo. plates) and portraits (port.). Illustrators or photographers not acknowledged in the statement of responsibility are listed in brackets following illustration information, e.g., [Ill. by Edward C. Caswell.].

Copy specific notation: unless otherwise indicated, copies examined for this bibliography are from the William Charvat Collection of American Fiction at the Ohio State University Libraries. Examined copies from other libraries are designated by their OCLC (Online Computer Library Center) three letter code, e.g., DLC (Library of Congress), NYP (New York Public Library), etc. In some cases, copies are examined from both the Charvat Collection and another library and the dual examination is noted, e.g., OSU, DLC. A list of OCLC symbols appears in the prefatory matter. Unexamined copies are noted with reference to the source of the bibliographic description, e.g., "Unexamined copy, bibliographic data from NUC" (i.e., National Union Catalog).

Special notes: incidental information cited from the book, such as earlier periodical appearance, may be noted.

Cover titles: cover titles and other alternative titles used in the book are noted.

Contents: the entire contents are noted for short story collections by a single author and for most anthologies. Individual short story titles are listed in the title index. The first book appearance of a short story is cross-referenced in the bibliography.

Publishing history: the Library of Congress *Catalog of Copyright Entries* (LC), *Publishers' Weekly* weekly announcements (PW), and brief records from the *British Library Catalog* (BLC) are noted, e.g., LC: O 16, '23.

References: standard reference sources, which include additional descriptive information, appear at the end of the entry, e.g. BAL (Bibliography of American Literature). The list of references appears in the prefatory matter.

Cross references exist for name variants, joint authors, editors, title changes, and other variant editions. Pseudonym index, title index, illustrator index, and publisher index appear in the back matter.

7 January 1997   Geoffrey D. Smith

CITATION ↘
     K-221   King, Charles, 1844-1933. Norman Holt: a story of the
MAIN ENTRY→   Army of the Cumberland / by General Charles King . . . ; with
                illustrations by John Huybers and Seymour M. Stone. New York:
IMPRINT →   G. W. Dillingham Company, [c1901]. 346 p., front., [5] leaves ← PAGINATION
                of plates.   **TXU**←COPY SPECIFIC
SPECIAL NOTES→ Dornbusch notes other copies distributed by H. B. Claflin,
                publishers' agents.
COVER TITLE→ Cover title: *A story of the Army of Cumberland.*
CONTENTS→   Contents: A conquering corps badge -- Jack Royal -- Dove cote days -- A rival ally -- The senator's plight -- The luck of the horseshoe -- A camera capture -- The fate of Guadalupe -- The Manilla wire -- Betrayed by a button.
PUBLISHING   LC: Je 20, '01.
HISTORY→   PW: My 4, '01.
                BLC: London: T. Fisher Unwin; New York [printed], 1901.
REFERENCES→ References: Dornbusch 36.

*Note: This example is a composite descriptive record designed for illustration of bibliographic and informational components.

Acknowledgments

A major undertaking such as *American Fiction, 1901-1925: A Bibliography*, slight as it may seem in the long tradition of bibliographic scholarship, will ever remain the product of many contributors. Not least, are those who realized the importance of Lyle Wright's work in earlier American fiction and saw the potential for a similar undertaking at The Ohio State University Libraries: William J. Studer, Director of The Ohio State University Libraries; William J. Crowe, then Assistant to the Director; and Robert A. Tibbetts, then Curator of Rare Books and Manuscripts. Dedicated catalogers who have contributed to the bibliography over the years include Karen Smith, Biruta Osis, Nancy Alzo, Marija Dalbello-Lovrić and Carolyn Wahlmark. University Libraries is most fortunate to have Hannah Thomas, Head of Special Collections Cataloging, who has been a consistent, guiding force through the duration of the Bibliography's compilation, both for intellectual insights and technological expertise. Jane Witherspoon has been the consummate editorial and technical assistant who saw the manuscript through to its completion. Finally, I wish to thank Lois, Matthew and Justin who tolerate eccentricity.

This project could not have been accomplished without the personal contributions of many others too numerous to name, especially academic colleagues and faithful book dealers. We express our gratitude to the National Endowment for the Humanities (long may it live) and the Department of Education's Strengthening Research Resources Program for their tangible support and unflagging encouragement.

References

BAL. Blanck, Jacob, comp. *Bibliography of American Literature.* 9 vols. New Haven: Yale UP, 1955.

Bannister. Bannister, Henry S. *Donn Byrne: A Descriptive Bibliography, 1912-1935.* New York: Garland, 1982.

Brewer & Bruccoli. Brewer, Frances Joan. *James Branch Cabell.* 2 vol. Charlottesville: U of Virginia P, 1957.

Brewer & Bruccoli. Bruccoli, Matthew J. *Notes on the Cabell Collections at the University of Virginia.* Charlottesville: U of Virginia P, 1957. Vol. 2 of *James Branch Cabell.* 2 vols.

Bruccoli, Cozzens. ---. *James Gould Cozzens: A Descriptive Bibliography.* Pittsburgh, Pa.: U of Pittsburgh P, 1981.

Bruccoli, Fitzgerald. ---. *F. Scott Fitzgerald: A Descriptive Bibliography.* Rev. ed. Pittsburgh, Pa.: U of Pittsburgh P, 1987.

Bruccoli & Layman. Bruccoli, Matthew J. and Richard Layman. *Ring W. Lardner: A Descriptive Bibliography.* Pittsburgh: U of Pittsburgh P, 1976.

Brussel. Brussel, I. R. *A Bibliography of the Writings of James Branch Cabell: A Revised Bibliography.* 1932. Folcraft: Folcraft, 1970.

Clarkson. Clarkson, Paul S. *A Bibliography of William Sydney Porter (O. Henry).* Caldwell: Caxton, 1938.

Cohn. Cohn, Louis Henry. *A Bibliography of the Works of Ernest Hemingway.* New York: Random, 1931.

Crane. Crane, Joan. *Willa Cather: A Bibliography.* Lincoln: U of Nebraska P, 1982.

Cunningham. Cunningham, Scott. *A Bibliography of the Writings of Carl Van Vechten.* Philadelphia: Centaur, 1924.

Currie. Currie, Barton. *Booth Tarkington: A Bibliography.* Garden City: Doubleday, 1932.

Davis. Davis, Lavinia. *A Bibliography of the Writings of Edith Wharton.* Portland: Southworth, 1933.

Dornbusch. Dornbusch, C. E. *Charles King, American Army Novelist: A Bibliography from the Collection of the National Library of Australia, Canberra.* Cornwallville: Hope Farm, 1963.

Edel & Laurence. Edel, Leon and Dan H. Laurence. *A Bibliography of Henry James.* 3rd ed. Oxford: Clarendon, 1982.

Firmage. Firmage, George James. *E. E. Cummings: A Bibliography.* Middletown: Wesleyan UP, 1960.

Garrison. Garrison, Stephen. *Edith Wharton: A Descriptive Bibliography.* Pittsburgh: U of Pittsburgh P, 1990.

Gibson & Arms. Gibson, William M. and George Arms. *A Bibliography of William Dean Howells.* New York: New York Public Library, 1948.

Haas & Gallup. Haas, Robert Bartlett and Donald Clifford Gallup, comps. *A Catalogue of the Published and Unpublished Writings of Gertrude Stein, Exhibited in the Yale University Library, 22 February to 29 March, 1941.* New Haven: Yale U Library, 1941.

Hall. Hall, James N. *James Branch Cabell: A Complete Bibliography.* New York: Revisionist, 1974.

Hanneman. Hanneman, Audre, comp. *Ernest Hemingway: A Comprehensive Bibliography.* Princeton: Princeton UP, 1967.

Heins. Heins, Henry Hardy, ed. *A Golden Anniversary Bibliography of Edgar Rice Burroughs.* Complete ed., rev. West Kingston: Grant, 1964.

Holt. Holt, Guy. *A Bibliography of the Writings of James Branch Cabell.* Philadelphia: Centaur, 1924.

Johnson. Johnson, Merle. *A Bibliography of the Works of Mark Twain, Samuel Langhorne Clemens: A List of First Editions in Book Form and of First Printings in Periodicals and Occasional Publications of His Varied Literary Activities.* Rev. and enl. New York: Harper, 1935.

Kellner. Kellner, Bruce. *A Bibliography of the Work of Carl Van Vechten.* Westport: Greenwood, 1980.

Kelly. Kelly, William W. *Ellen Glasgow: A Bibliography.* Charlottesville: UP of Virginia, 1964.

Lee. Lee, Alfred P. *A Bibliography of Christopher Morley.* Garden City: Doubleday, 1935.

Lohf & Sheehy. Lohf, Kenneth A. and Eugene P. Sheehy, comps. *Frank Norris: A Bibliography.* Los Gatos: Talisman, 1959.

McDonald. McDonald, Edward D. *A Bibliography of the Writings of Theodore Dreiser.* Philadelphia: Centaur, 1928.

McElrath. McElrath, Joseph R. *Frank Norris: A Descriptive Bibliography.* Pittsburgh: U of Pittsburgh P, 1992.

Melish. Melish, Lawson McClung. *A Bibliography of the Collected Writings of Edith Wharton.* New York: Brick Row, 1927.

Orton. Orton, Vrest. *Dreiserana: A Book about His Books.* New York: Chocorua, 1929.

Perkins & Perkins. Perkins, P. D. and Ione Perkins. *Lafcadio Hearn: A Bibliography of His Writings.* Boston: Houghton, 1934.

Phillips. Phillips, Le Roy. *A Bibliography of the Writings of Henry James.* New York: Coward & McCann, 1930.

Pizer, Dowell, & Rusch. Pizer, Donald, Richard W. Dowell, and Frederic E. Rusch. *Theodore Dreiser: A Primary Bibliography and Reference Guide.* 2nd ed. Boston: Hall, 1991.

Potter. Potter, Jack. *A Bibliography of John Dos Passos.* Folcraft: Folcraft, 1976.

Quinby. Quinby, Henry Cole. *Richard Harding Davis: A Bibliography.* New York: Dutton, 1924.

Russo & Sullivan. Russo, Dorothy Ritter and Thelma L. Sullivan. *A Bibliography of Booth Tarkington, 1869-1946.* Indianapolis: Indiana Historical Society, 1949.

Russo & Sullivan, *Seven Authors*. ---. *Bibliographical Studies of Seven Authors of Crawfordsville, Indiana.* Indianapolis: Indiana Historical Society, 1952.

Russo. Russo, Dorothy Ritter. *A Bibliography of George Ade, 1866-1944.* Indianapolis: Indiana Historical Society, 1947.

Sanders. Sanders, David. *John Dos Passos: a Comprehensive Bibliography.* New York: Garland, 1987.

Sawyer. Sawyer, Julian. *Gertrude Stein: A Bibliography.* New York: Arrow, 1940.

Sheehy and Lohf. Sheehy, Eugene P. and Kenneth A. Lohf, comps. *Sherwood Anderson: A Bibliography.* Los Gatos: Talisman, 1960.

Sisson & Martens. Sisson, James E., III and Robert W. Martens. *Jack London First Editions: A Chronological Reference Guide.* Oakland: Star Rover, 1979.

Starrett. Starrett, Vincent. *Ambrose Bierce: A Bibliography.* Philadelphia: Centaur, 1929.

Swire. Swire, H. R. L. *A Bibliography of the Works of Joseph Hergesheimer.* Philadelphia: Centaur, 1922.

Weber & Weber. Weber, Clara Carter and Carl J. Weber, comps. *A Bibliography of the Published Writings of Sarah Orne Jewett.* Waterville: Colby, 1949.

Wetherbee. Wetherbee, Winthrop, Jr. *Donn Byrne: A Bibliography.* New York: New York Public Library, 1949.

Williams & Starrett. Williams, Ames W. and Vincent Starrett. *Stephen Crane: A Bibliography.* Glendale: Valentine, 1948.

Wilson. Wilson, Robert A., comp. *Gertrude Stein: A Bibliography.* New York: Phoenix, 1974.

Woodbridge, London, Tweney. Woodbridge, Hensley C., John London, and George H. Tweney, comps. *Jack London: A Bibliography.* Georgetown: Talisman, 1966.

OCLC Symbols

AAA	Auburn University, Auburn	COX	Univ of Colorado at Colorado Springs
ABC	Univ of Alabama at Birmingham	CPT	Point Loma Col, San Diego
AFU	Univ of Arkansas, Fayetteville	CRB	Corbit-Calloway Memorial Libr, Odessa, DE
AJB	Jacksonville State Univ, Jacksonville	CRL	Ctr for Res Libr, Chicago
AKO	Ouachita Baptist Univ, Arkadelphia	CRU	Univ of California, Riverside
AKP	Arkansas Tech Univ, Russellville	CSA	California State Univ, Sacramento
AKR	Univ of Akron Libr, Akron	CSB	California State Univ, San Bernardino
AKU	Univ of Arkansas, Little Rock	CSE	Col of St Elizabeth, Convent Station
ALK	Alaska State Libr, Juneau	CSF	San Francisco State Univ, San Francisco
ALL	Allentown Col of St Francis de Sales, Center Valley	CSH	California State Univ, Hayward
ALM	Univ of Alabama, University	CSJ	San Jose State Univ, San Jose
AMH	Amherst Col, Amherst, MA	CSL	Univ of Southern California, Los Angeles
ANC	Antioch Col Libr, Yellow Springs	CSU	Cleveland State Univ Libr, Cleveland
APL	Akron-Summit Cnty, Pub Libr, Akron	CS2	Culver-Stockton Col, Missouri
ASH	Spring Hill Col, Mobile	CUR	Univ of Redlands, Redlands
ASX	Southern Baptist Col Libr, Walnut Ridge, AR	CUY	Univ of California, Berkeley
ATO	Athenaeum of Ohio Libr, Cincinnati	CWL	Case Western Reserve Univ, Law Libr, Cleveland
AUM	Univ of Massachusetts at Amherst	CWR	Case Western Reserve Univ, Cleveland
AUU	Atlanta Univ Ctr, R W Woodruff Libr, Atlanta	CXP	Cuyahoga Cnty Pub Libr, Cleveland
AVL	Allegheny Col, Meadville	DAY	Univ of Dayton Libr, Dayton
AWE	Centre Cnty Libr, Harrisburg	DEF	Defiance Col Libr, Defiance
AWL	Clearfield Cnty Libr, Harrisburg	DGU	Georgetown Univ, Washington
AZN	Northern Arizona Univ, Flagstaff	DKC	Dickinson Col, Carlisle
AZS	Arizona State Univ, Tempe	DLC	Libr of Congress, Washington
AZU	Univ of Arizona, Tucson	DLM	Univ of Delaware, Newark
BAI	Balch Inst for Ethnic Studies Libr, Philadelphia	DMM	Dayton and Montgomery Cnty Pub Libr
BAT	Boston Athenaeum	DMP	Pathfinder Regional Libr Service Syst, Montrose
BBH	Bowdoin Col, Brunswick	DNU	Denison Univ Libr, Granville
BGU	Bowling Green State Univ Libr, Bowling Green	DPL	Denver Pub Libr
BHA	Harvard Divinity Sch, Cambridge	DRB	Dartmouth Col, Hanover
BKL	Brooklyn Public Libr	DRU	Drew Univ, Madison
BLC	Bluffton Col Libr, Bluffton	DTM	Dallas Theological Seminary, Dallas
BOS	Boston Univ, Boston	DVP	Univ of Denver, Denver
BRL	Boston Pub Libr	EAU	Am Univ, Washington
BSC	Cincinnati Bible Col & Seminary	EEA	Adrian Col, Adrian
BSF	North Dakota State Univ Libr, Bottineau	EEM	Michigan State Univ, East Lansing
BTS	Bates Col, Lewiston	EEX	Libr of Michigan, Lansing
BUF	SUNY at Buffalo	ELM	Univ of Michigan Libr, Ann Arbor
BYU	Brigham Young Univ, Hawaii Campus, Laie	ELZ	Elizabethtown Col, Elizabethtown
CBA	California State Col, Bakersfield	EMU	Emory Univ, Atlanta
CBC	Biola Univ Libr, La Mirada	ERE	East Carolina Univ, Greenville
CCO	Occidental Col, Los Angeles	EWF	Wake Forest Univ, Winston-Salem
CCT	California Lutheran Col, Thousand Oaks	EXA	Albion Col, Albion
CDC	Cedarville Col, Cedarville	EXG	Grand Valley State Univ, Allendale
CDS	San Diego State Univ, San Diego	EXN	Andrews Univ, Berrien Springs
CFI	California State Univ, Fullerton	EXS	Western Theological Seminary, Holland
CGP	Chicago Pub Libr	EYM	Univ of Michigan, Sch of Libr Sci, Ann Arbor
CGU	Univ of Chicago, Chicago	EYP	Detroit Pub Libr, Detroit
CHE	Chestnut Hill Col, Philadelphia	EYW	Wayne State Univ, Detroit
CIL	Cincinnati Law Libr Asn, Cincinnati	EZA	Alma Col, Alma
CIN	Univ of Cincinnati Libr, Cincinnati	EZC	Cent Michigan Univ, Mt Pleasant
CKM	Clark Univ, Worcester	FCE	Felician Col Libr, Lodi
CLE	Cleveland Pub Libr	FDA	Florida State Univ, Tallahassee
CLO	California State Univ, Long Beach	FHM	Univ of South Florida, Tampa
CLU	Univ of California Libr, Los Angeles	FOC	American Fiction, Edmond, OK
CNO	California State Univ, Northridge	FQG	Univ of Miami, Coral Gables
COD	Univ of Colorado at Boulder	FUG	Univ of Florida, Gainesville
COF	Colorado State Univ, Ft Collins	FXG	Florida Int Univ, Miami
COH	US Air Force Academy	GFC	George Fox Col, Newberg
COI	Iliff Sch of Theology, Denver	GGG	Gainesville Jr Col, John Harrison Hosch Libr, LRC, Gainesville
COP	Colorado Sch of Mines, Golden		
COS	Univ of Southern Colorado, Pueblo	GJG	Augusta Col, Reese Libr, Augusta

GPM	Georgia Southern Col, Henderson Libr, Statesboro		KBE	Berea Col, Berea
GSU	Georgia State Univ, Pullen Libr, Atlanta		KCC	Centre Col of Kentucky, Danville
GUA	Univ of Georgia, Athens		KCP	Kansas City Pub Libr
GZH	Univ of Wisconsin, Madison, Health Sci		KEU	Eastern Kentucky Univ, Richmond
GZM	Univ of Wisconsin, Madison		KFH	Ft Hays State Univ, Hays
GZN	Univ of Wisconsin, Milwaukee		KFP	Pittsburgh State Univ, Pittsburgh, KS
GZP	Univ of Wisconsin, Parkside, Kenosha		KGG	Georgetown Col, Cooke Memorial Libr, Georgetown
GZT	Univ of Wisconsin, Whitewater		KKR	Emporia State Univ, Emporia
GZU	Univ of Wisconsin, La Crosse		KKU	Univ of Kansas, Lawrence
GZW	Univ of Wisconsin, Green Bay		KLG	Univ of Louisville, Louisville
HCD	Col of the Holy Cross, Worcester		KMM	Morehead State Univ, Morehead
HDC	Claremont Col, Claremont		KRS	Kearney State Col, Kearney
HLS	Harvard Univ, Cambridge		KSL	Kentucky Dept of Libr & Archives, Frankfort
HSA	New Hampshire State Libr Proc Ctr, Concord		KSU	Kent State Univ Libr, Kent
HUC	Hebrew Union Col Libr, Cincinnati		KSW	Wichita State Univ, Wichita
HUH	Univ of Hawaii, Hamilton Libr, Honolulu		KTS	Southern Baptist Theological Seminary, Louisville
IAI	Illinois State Univ, Normal		KTU	Transylvania Univ, Lexington
IAK	Lake Forest Col, Lake Forest		KUK	Univ of Kentucky, Lexington
IAT	Southern Illinois Univ at Edwardsville		KWW	Asbury Col, Wilmore, KY
IAU	BARR Consortium, Inc, Sherman		LAS	La Salle Univ, Philadelphia
IAY	Univ of Illinois at Chicago Circle		LDL	Univ of Nebraska at Lincoln
IBA	Bradley Univ, Peoria		LFM	Franklin & Marshall Col, Lancaster
ICU	Texas Christian Univ, Ft Worth		LHA	McNeese State Univ, Lake Charles
ICY	Augustana Col, Rock Island		LKC	Lancaster Cnty Libr
IDG	Chicago Theological Seminary, Chicago		LNC	New Orleans Pub Libr
IDU	Depauw Univ, Greencastle		LNE	Northeast Louisiana Univ, Monroe
IFC	Franklin Col, Franklin		LNU	Univ of New Orleans, New Orleans
IFH	Judson Col Libr, Elgin		LPU	Los Angeles Pub Libr
IGA	Dallas Pub Libr		LQS	Lock Haven Univ of Pennsylvania, Lock Haven
IGR	Grace Col & Seminary Libr, Winona Lake		LRU	Tulane Univ, New Orleans
IIB	Butler Univ, Indianapolis		LUS	Louisiana State Univ in Shreveport Libr
ILU	Texas Tech Univ, Lubbock		LUU	Louisiana State Univ, Baton Rouge
IMC	Indiana Wesleyan Univ, Marion		LWA	Univ of Southwestern Louisiana, Lafayette
IMD	Indianapolis-Marion Cnty Pub Libr, Indianapolis		LZU	Lincoln Univ
IMF	Allen Cnty Pub Libr, Ft Wayne		MAA	Mount Angel Abbey Libr, St Benedict
IMI	Marian Col, Indianapolis		MBB	Brandeis Univ, Waltham
IMN	Manchester Col, North Manchester		MBS	Bethany Lutheran Theological
IMS	St Mary of the Woods Col, St Mary of the Woods			Seminary, Mankato
INA	Anderson Univ, Anderson		MCB	Cent Bible Col, Springfield
IND	Univ of Notre Dame, Notre Dame		MCD	Delta State Univ, Cleveland
INT	Univ of North Texas, Denton		MCF	Merced Cnty Libr, Merced
INU	Northwestern Univ, Evanston, IL		MCU	Ohioana Libr, Columbus
IOD	Drake Univ, Des Moines		MDS	St Mary's Col of Maryland, St Mary's City
IOG	Grinnell Col, Grinnell		MEU	Univ of Maine at Orono
IOH	Luther Col, Decorah		MFM	Mississippi State Univ, Mississippi State
IOL	Loras Col, Dubuque		MHS	Minnesota Hist Society, St Paul
IPL	Purdue Univ, West Lafayette		MIA	Miami Univ Libr, Oxford
IPU	Eastern New Mexico Univ, Portales		MLN	Minuteman Libr Network, Framingham
IQU	Univ of New Mexico, Albuquerque		MMM	Maine Maritime Acad, Castine
ISM	Southern Methodist Univ, Cent Libr, Dallas		MNC	Concordia Col, St Paul
ITU	Taylor Univ, Upland		MNL	Montgomery Cnty, Norristown Pub Libr
IUA	Univ of Texas at Arlington		MNU	Univ of Minnesota, Minneapolis
IUL	Indiana Univ, Bloomington		MOC	Morris Col, Sumter
IWA	Iowa State Univ, Ames		MOU	Southwest Missouri State Univ, Springfield
IWC	Wabash Col, Crawfordsville		MPI	Minneapolis Pub Libr & Info Ctr
IWU	Texas Woman's Univ, Denton		MTH	Mount Holyoke Col, South Hadley
IXA	Univ of Texas at Austin		MTU	Mount Union Col Libr, Alliance
IYU	Baylor Univ, Waco		MUB	Univ of Maryland, Baltimore Cnty
JBE	Olivet Nazarene Col, Kankakee		MUM	Univ of Mississippi, University
JET	United Libr of Garret Evangelical/Seabury West Theo		MUS	Univ of Southern Mississippi, Hattiesburg
	Seminary, Evanston		MUU	Univ of Missouri, Columbia
JFK	Illinois State Hist Libr, Springfield		NAM	SUNY at Albany
JFS	Loyola Univ of Chicago, Cudahy Libr, Chicago		NBU	Univ of Nebraska at Omaha
JNA	Northern Illinois Univ, De Kalb		NCS	North Carolina State Libr, Raleigh
KAT	Asbury Theological Seminary, Wilmore		NCU	Union Col, Lincoln

NDD	Duke Univ Libr, Durham	SRC	Richland Cnty Pub Libr, Columbia
NDO	Univ of North Carolina at Chapel Hill, Law Libr	STF	Stanford Univ Libr, Stanford
NEO	Elon Col Libr, Elon College	SUC	Univ of South Carolina, Columbia
NGU	Univ of North Carolina, Greensboro	SUR	Sul Ross State Univ Libr, Alpine, TX
NIC	Campbell Univ, Buies Creek	SVP	St Louis Pub Libr
NJB	Appalachian State Univ, Boone	TAW	Tacoma Pub Libr
NMI	Minot State Univ, Minot	TCT	Tennessee Temple Univ, Chattanooga
NMT	New Mexico Inst of Mining & Tech	TET	East Tennessee State Univ, Johnson City
NMW	Western Carolina Univ, Cullowhee	TJC	Vanderbilt Univ Libr, Nashville
NOC	Univ of North Carolina, Chapel Hill	TLM	Toledo-Lucas Cnty Pub Libr, Toledo
NOH	Univ of North Carolina, Health Sci Libr, Chapel Hill	TMA	Memphis State Univ, Memphis
NRC	North Carolina State Univ, Raleigh	TMN	Memphis and Shelby Cnty Pub Libr and Info Ctr, Memphis
NTH	Southern Baptist Hist Libr and Archives, Nashville	TNE	Baptist Sunday Sch Board, Nashville
NUI	Univ of Iowa Libr, Iowa City	TNS	Tennessee State Libr and Archives, Nashville
NWP	Northwestern Connecticut Commun Col, Winsted, CT	TNY	Trinity Univ Libr, San Antonio
NYG	New York State Libr, Albany	TOL	Univ of Toledo Libr, Toledo
NYP	New York Pub Libr, Res Libr, New York	TPN	Pan Am Univ Libr, Edinburg
OBE	Oberlin Col Libr, Oberlin	TSW	Southwestern Baptist Theological Seminary, Ft Worth
OCO	Columbus Metrop Libr, Columbus	TUL	Tulsa City Cnty Libr
OCP	Pub Libr of Cincinnati and Hamilton Co	TUS	Tuskegee Univ
ODL	Univ of Dayton, Law Libr, Dayton	TUU	Union Univ Libr, Jackson
OKA	Southern Nazarene Univ, Bethany	TWC	Texas Wesleyan Univ, Eunice and James L West Libr, Ft Worth
OKD	Oklahoma Dept of Libr, Oklahoma City		
OKG	Phillips Grad Seminary Libr, Enid	TXA	Texas A&M Univ, College Station
OKU	Univ of Oklahoma, Norman	TXH	Univ of Houston, Houston
ORE	Oregon State Univ, Corvallis	TXI	Southwest Texas State Univ, San Marcos
ORU	Univ of Oregon Libr, Eugene	TXS	Hardin-Simmons Univ, Abilene
OSO	Oregon State Libr, Salem	TXT	Texas Southern Univ, Houston
OSU	Ohio State Univ Libr, The, Columbus	TXU	Univ of Texas at El Paso
OUN	Ohio Univ Libr, Athens	TXX	Southwestern Univ, Georgetown
OUP	Univ of Portland, Portland	UAB	Univ of Alberta, Cameron Libr, Edmonton
OWK	Kent State Univ, Trumbull Campus, Warren, OH	UAF	Univ of Alaska, Fairbanks
OWL	Westerville Pub Libr, Westerville	UAG	Spokane Pub Libr
OWU	Ohio Wesleyan Univ Libr, Delaware	UAI	Everett Pub Libr, WA
OXZ	Toledo Pub Libr, Toledo	UBY	Brigham Young Univ Libr, Provo
PAU	Univ of Pennsylvania, Philadelphia	UCW	Univ of Connecticut, Storrs
PBA	Acad of the New Church, Bryn Athyn	UIU	Univ of Illinois, Urbana
PCJ	Pontifical Col, Josephinum, A T Wehrle Memorial Libr, Columbus	UMC	Univ of Maryland, College Park
		UMD	Univ Autonoma de Madrid
PFO	Pomona Pub Libr, Pomona	UND	Univ of North Dakota, Grand Forks
PGP	Univ of Southern Maine at Portland	UOK	Seattle Pub Libr
PLF	Free Libr of Philadelphia	UPM	Pennsylvania State Univ, University Park
PLT	Lutheran Theological Seminary, Philadelphia	UPP	Univ of Puget Sound Libr, Tacoma
PQA	Reeves Libr, Seton Hill Col, Greensburg	USD	Univ of South Dakota, Vermillion
PRE	Presbyterian Hist Society, Philadelphia	UTS	United Theological Seminary, Dayton, OH
PSC	Swarthmore Col, Swarthmore	UUA	Southern Utah State Col, Cedar City
PUL	Princeton Univ, Princeton	UUM	Univ of Utah, Salt Lake City
PVU	Villanova Univ, Villanova	UUO	Weber State Col, Ogden
RBN	Brown Univ, Providence	UWT	Freed Hardeman Col, Loden-Daniel Libr, Henderson
RCE	Rice Univ, Fondren Libr, Houston	VA@	Univ of Virginia, Charlottesville
RIU	Univ of Rhode Island, Kingston	VCV	Clinch Valley Col, Wise
RMC	Rosemont Col, Rosemont	VHB	Buffalo & Erie Cnty Pub Libr
RRR	Univ of Rochester, Rochester	VIC	Virginia State Libr, Richmond
SAP	San Antonio Pub Libr, San Antonio	VLR	Randolph-Macon Woman's Col, Lynchburg
SDA	Augustana Col, Sioux Falls	VLY	Lynchburg Col, Lynchburg
SDH	South Dakota State Archives, Pierre	VMI	Virginia Mil Inst Libr, Lexington
SDL	Stark Cnty Dist Libr, Canton	VPI	Virginia Polytechnic Inst and State Univ, Blacksburg
SDS	South Dakota State Libr, Pierre	VSL	Vermont State Dept of Libr, Montpelier
SEA	Clemson Univ, Clemson	VTP	Buffalo and Erie Cnty Hist Society Libr, Buffalo
SEM	Southeast Missouri State Univ, Cape Girardeau	VTU	Univ of Vermont, Bailey Libr, Burlington
SLG	Lander Col, Larry A Jackson Libr, Greenwood	VUT	Union Theological Seminary Libr, Richmond
SMI	Smithsonian Institution, Washington	VWM	Col of William & Mary, Williamsburg
SNN	Smith Col, Northampton	VXW	Vassar Col, Poughkeepsie
SOI	Southern Illinois Univ at Carbondale	VYL	Lehman Col Libr, Bronx
SPP	St Paul Pub Libr		

VYS	St Bonaventure Univ, St Bonaventure
WAU	Univ of Washington, Seattle
WDL	Warren Libr Asn, Warren
WEA	Eastern Washington Univ, Cheney
WIH	State Hist Society of Wisconsin, Madison
WII	Beloit Col Libr, Beloit
WIS	Univ of Wisconsin, Stevens Point
WLU	Wesleyan Univ, Middletown
WMC	Wilmington Col, Wilmington
WOO	Col of Wooster, Wooster
WPG	Worcester Polytechnic Inst, Worcester
WSM	Wright State Univ, Fordham Health Sci Libr, Dayton
WSU	Wright State Univ Libr, Dayton
WTU	Washington Univ, St Louis
WVA	Alderson-Broaddus Col, Philippi
WVB	Bethany Col, Bethany
WVF	Fairmont St Col, WV
WVH	Marshall Univ, Huntington
WVK	Kanawha Cnty Pub Libr, Charleston
WVU	West Virginia Univ Libr, Morgantown
WYU	Univ of Wyoming Libr, Laramie
XAV	Xavier Univ, Cincinnati
XQM	Queens Col, Flushing
YCP	York Col of Pennsylvania, Schmidt Libr, York
YNG	Youngstown State Univ Libr, Youngstown
YPM	SUNY, Col at Plattsburgh
YQR	Rochester Pub Libr
YU#	Yale Univ, Divinity Sch, New Haven
YUS	Yale Univ, Sterling Memorial Libr, New Haven
ZBK	Brooklyn Hist Society, Brooklyn
ZSJ	St John's Univ Libr, Jamaica
ZYU	New York Univ, New York

Bibliography

American Fiction
1901-1925

<u>A</u>

A-1   A. B. Travels of a lady's maid / by A. B. Boston:
L. C. Page & Company, 1908. 336 p.   **AZU**
LC: S 30, '08.

A-2   A. F. S. (Anita F. Silvani). The strange story of
Ahrinziman / by A. F. S. Chicago: R. R. Donnelley
& Sons Company, 1906. 284 p., front.

A. H., ed. <u>See</u> [Ward, Herbert D. (Herbert
Dickinson)]. *Lauriel: the love letters of an
American girl* **(1902), W-105.**

A-3   Abarbanell, Jacob Ralph, 1852-1922. The heart of the
people: a picture of life as it is to-day / by J. R.
Abarbanell . . . Boston, Massachusetts: The C. M.
Clark Publishing Company, 1908. 360 p., front. [Ill.
by William Kirkpatrick.]
PW: D 12, '08.

A-4   Abbath, *pseud.* The prodigal / by Abbath [pseud.].
Grand Rapids, Mich.: Eerdmans-Sevensma Co.,
[c1920]. 249, [1] p.
Unexamined copy: bibliographic data from NUC.
LC: Jl 3, '20.

A-5   Abbot, Alice Balch, b. 1867. A frigate's namesake /
by Alice Balch Abbot; with illustrations by George
Varian. New York: The Century Co., 1901.
204 p., front., [16] leaves of plates.
PW: O 12, '01.

A-6   Abbot, Prentice, b. 1889. The little gentleman across
the road / Prentice Abbot. Boston: Richard G.
Badger; Toronto: C. Clark, [1914]. 200 p.   **AMH**
LC: O 30, '14.
PW: N 7, '14.

Abbott, Aaron, b. 1867. <u>See</u> **Littleheart, Oleta,
pseud.**

A-7   Abbott, Austin, 1831-1896. A charming story:
(complete) / by Austin Abbott. [S. l.]: Issued by the
United States Express Company, 1908. 64 p. **NYP**
Cover title: *My chum's story.*

A-8   Abbott, Avery. Captain Martha Mary / Avery
Abbott. New York: The Century Co., 1912.
211 p., front. [Ill. by Remington Schuyler.]
LC: My 4, '12.
PW: Ap 27, '12.

A-9   Abbott, Eleanor Hallowell, b. 1872. The indiscreet
letter / by Eleanor Hallowell Abbott. New York:
The Century Co., 1915. 81 p.
LC: Je 29, '15.
PW: Jl 17, '15.

A-10   ____ Little Eve Edgarton / by Eleanor Hallowell
Abbott . . . ; with illustrations by R. M. Crosby.
New York: The Century Co., 1914. 210 p., front.,
[7] leaves of plates.
LC: S 18, '14.
PW: S 19, '14.
BLC: London: Hodder & Stoughton, [1917].

A-11   ____ Molly Make-Believe / by Eleanor Hallowell
Abbott; with illustrations by Walter Tittle. New
York: The Century Co., 1910. 211 p., front., 13 ill.
PW: O 1, '10.
BLC: London: William Heinemann, 1911.

A-12   ____ The ne'er-do-much / by Eleanor Hallowell
Abbott; with illustrations by James Montgomery
Flagg. New York: Dodd, Mead and Company,
1918. 144 p., front., [3] leaves of plates.
LC: Ap 2, '18.
PW: Mr 23, '18.
BLC: London: Hodder & Stoughton, [1919].

A-13   ____ Old-Dad / by Eleanor Hallowell Abbott. New
York: E. P. Dutton & Company, [c1919]. 241 p.
LC: F 14, '19.
PW: F 22, '19.

A-14   ____ Peace on earth, good-will to dogs / by Eleanor
Hallowell Abbott . . . New York: E. P. Dutton &
Company, [c1920]. 134 p.   **NYP**
PW: D 11, '19.

A-15   ____ Rainy week / by Eleanor Hallowell Abbott.
New York: E. P. Dutton & Company, [c1921].
227 p.
LC: Ag 1, '21.
PW: Jl 9, '21.

A-16   ____ The sick-a-bed lady: and also, Hickory Dock,
The very tired girl, The happy-day, Something that
happened in October, The amateur lover, Heart of the
city, The pink sash, Woman's only business:
illustrated / by Eleanor Hallowell Abbott . . . New
York: The Century Co., 1911. 371 p., front., [8]
leaves of plates. [Ill. by T. K. Hanna, Herman
Pfeifer, Dannenberg and Blanche Greer.]
PW: S 30, '11.
BLC: London: Hodder & Stoughton; New York
printed, 1911.

A-17   ____ Silver moon / by Eleanor Hallowell Abbott.
New York: E. P. Dutton & Company . . . , [c1923].
264 p.
LC: O 18, '23.
PW: N 3, '23.

A-18   ____ The stingy receiver / by Eleanor Hallowell
Abbott . . . ; with illustrations by Fanny Munsell.
New York: The Century Co., 1917. 162 p., front.,
ill.
LC: Mr 7, '17.
PW: Mr 10, '17.

A-19 _____ The white linen nurse / by Eleanor Hallowell Abbott . . . ; with illustrations by Herman Pfeifer. New York: The Century Co., 1913. 276 p., front., [5] leaves of plates.
LC: O 2, '13.
PW: S 27, '13.
BLC: London: Hodder & Stoughton, [1914]. (second edition)

A-20 Abbott, Frances M. (Frances Matilda), b. 1857. The simple single / by Frances M. Abbott . . . Concord, New Hampshire: The Rumford Press, 1909. 48 p.
LC: N 29, '09.
PW: Ap 9, '10.

Abbott, Helen Raymond. See Beals, Helen Abbott, b. 1888.

A-21 Abbott, Jane Ludlow Drake, b. 1881. Minglestreams / by Jane Abbott . . . ; with a frontispiece in color by H. Weston Taylor. Philadelphia; London: J. B. Lippincott Company, 1923. 320 p., front., [1] leaf of plates. Illustrated end papers.
LC: Ap 27, '23.
PW: My 12, '23.

A-22 Abbott, Keene, 1876-1941. A melody in silver / by Keene Abbott. Boston; New York: Houghton Mifflin Company, 1911. (Cambridge: The Riverside Press). 148 p.
LC: My 12, '11.
PW: My 6, '11.
BLC: London: G. P. Putnam's Sons, 1911.

A-23 _____ Wine o' the winds / by Keene Abbott. Garden City, N. Y.: Doubleday, Page & Company, 1920. 336 p., front., [3] leaves of plates.
PW: Je 26, '20.
BLC: London: Hodder & Stoughton; Garden City, N. Y. printed, [1921].

A-24 Abbott, Lucy Thurston, b. 1883. Naomi of the island / by Lucy Thurston Abbott; with a frontispiece in full colour from a painting by William Bunting. Boston: L. C. Page & Company, 1912. 368 p., [1] leaf of plates.

A-25 Abdullah, Achmed, 1881-1945. Alien souls / by Achmed Abdullah . . . New York: The James A. McCann Company, [c1922]. 248 p.
Contents: Feud -- Reprisal -- The home-coming -- The dance on the hill -- The river of hate -- The soul of a Turk -- Morituri -- The jester -- The strength of the little thin thread -- Grafter and master grafter -- The logical tale of the four camels -- The two-handed sword -- Black poppies -- The perfect way -- Tao.
LC: O 2, '22.
PW: N 18, '22.

A-26 _____ The blue-eyed Manchu / by Achmed Abdullah . . . New York: Robert J. Shores, [c1917]. 351 p., front. [Ill. by Eleanor Howard.]
LC: Mr 18, '18.
PW: Mr 16, '18.
BLC: London: Hutchinson & Co., [1923].

A-27 _____ Bucking the tiger / by Achmed Abdullah. New York: Robert J. Shores, 1917. 291 p.
LC: Je 5, '17.

A-28 _____ The honourable gentleman and others / by Achmed Abdullah. New York; London: G. P. Putnam's Sons, 1919. (New York: The Knickerbocker Press). v, 262 p.
Contents: The honourable gentleman -- The hatchetman -- A Pell Street spring song -- Cobbler's wax -- After his kind -- A simple act of piety -- Himself, to himself enough.
LC: N 4, '19.
PW: N 1, '19.

A-29 _____ The man on horseback / by Achmed Abdullah . . . New York: The James A. McCann Company, 1919. 340 p.
PW: Ja 17, '20.

A-30 _____ The mating of the blades / by Achmed Abdullah. New York: The James A. McCann Company, 1920. 281 p.
LC: N 9, '20.
PW: Ja 1, '21.
BLC: London: Hutchinson & Co., [1921].

A-31 _____ Night drums / by Achmed Abdullah . . . New York: The James A. McCann Company, [c1921]. 329 p.
LC: O 29, '21.
PW: O 29, '21.
BLC: London: Hutchinson & Co., [1922].

A-32 _____ The red stain / by Achmed Abdullah. New York: Hearst's International Library Co., 1915. 309 p., front.
PW: O 23, '15.
BLC: London: Simpkin, Marshall & Co, 1916.

A-33 _____ The remittance-woman / by Achmed Abdullah. Garden City, New York: Garden City Publishing Co., Inc., 1924. 120 p., front. ill., ill.
LC: Ap 2, '24.

A-34 _____ Shackled / by Achmed Abdullah. New York: Brentano's, [c1924]. 245 p.
LC: S 26, '24.
PW: O 4, '24.
BLC: London: Hutchinson & Co., [1925].

A simple act of piety. In *The best short stories of 1918 and the yearbook of the American short story* (1919), B-563.

A-35 _____ The swinging caravan / by Achmed Abdullah. New York: Brentano's, [c1925]. 311 p.
Contents: A gesture of no importance -- The great wife -- Slit-Eye -- The gates of Tamerlane -- Decadence -- Bred in the clay -- Most just among Moslims -- The rest is silence -- Victory -- Romance -- Dutiful grief.
LC: O 5, '25.
PW: O 17, '25.

An Indian jataka. In *The ten-foot chain, or, Can love survive the shackles?* (1920), T-108.

A-36 _____ The theif of Bagdad / by Achmed Abdullah . . . based on Douglas Fairbanks' fantasy of the Arabian nights; illustrated with scenes from the photoplay. New York: The H. K. Fly Company, [c1924]. 319 p., front., [3] leaves of plates, ill.

Unexamined copy: bibliographic data based on NUC.
P. 311-319: "Production sidelights on "The thief of
Bagdad", by Arthur J. Zellner"
LC: Jl 31, '24.
PW: Ag 2, '24.
BLC: London: Hutchinson & Co, [1924].

A-37 ____ The trail of the beast / by Achmed Abdullah
. . . New York: James A. McCann Company, 1919.
343 p.
LC: Je 30, '19.
PW: Jl 26, '19.
BLC: London: Hutchinson & Co., [1921].

A-38 ____ Wings: tales of the psychic / by Achmed
Abdullah . . . New York: The James A. McCann
Company, 1920. 239 p.
Contents: Wings -- Disappointment -- To be accounted for -- Tartar
-- Renunciation -- Krishnavana, destroyer of souls -- That haunting
thing -- The man who lost caste -- Silence -- Khizr -- Fear -- Light.
LC: Je 8, '20.
PW: Je 19, '20.

A-39 Abel Griscoms' letters. Boston: J. A. and W. Bird,
1905. 24 p., ill.   FOC (unexamined micro.)

A-40 Abernethy, Arthur Talmage, b. 1872. Moonshine:
being Appalachia's Arabian nights / by Arthur
Talmage Abernethy. Asheville, N. C.: The Dixie
Publishing Company, [c1924]. 219 p., front., [5]
leaves of plates.   SUC

A-41 Abet, Adam. Social conscience: or homocracy
versus monocracy in story, verse and essay / by
Adam Abet. Bridgeport, Conn.: Co-operative
Publishing Company, 1920. 474 p.   EYM
Contents: Part I. The problem of hope -- Part II. Broad view
[poetry] -- Part III. Omaria [nonfiction] -- Part IV. Humane humanity
[poetry] -- Part V. John Doe thought and his search for style -- Part
VI. Cabals of monocracy [poetry] -- Part VII. East and west [poetry]
-- Part VIII. Social tranquillity [essays] -- Part IX. Miscellaneous
[essays] -- Part X. From sunrise to sundown [poetry].

Abrahamson, Alma P. The Tomte Gubbe. In *The
Best college short stories, 1917-18* (1919), B-557.

A-42 Aces: a collection of short stories / by Dorothy
Canfield, Octavus Roy Cohen, Edna Ferber, F. Scott
Fitzgerald, Zona Gale, Bruno Lessing, Kathleen
Norris, Mary Roberts Rinehart, Benjamin J. Sher, G.
B. Stern, Thyra Samter Winslow, Israel Zangwill;
compiled by the Community Workers of the New
York Guild for the Jewish Blind. New York;
London: G. P. Putnam's Sons, 1924. ([New York]:
The Knickerbocker Press). 312 p.
Contents: What "really" happened / Dorothy Canfield -- Bass
ingratitude / Octavus Roy Cohen -- Old man Minick / Edna Ferber --
Gretchen's forty winks / F. Scott Fitzgerald -- Exit charity / Zona
Gale -- Love and cloaks and suits / Bruno Lessing -- The unbecoming
conduct of Annie / Kathleen Norris -- Twenty-two / Mary Roberts
Rinehart -- Abe's card / Benjamin R. Sher -- "The eleventh hat" / G.
B. Stern -- A love affair / Thyra Samter Winslow -- Noah's ark /
Israel Zangwill.
PW: N 1, '24.

A-43 Achorn, Edgar O. (Edgar Oakes). The unknown
quantity / by Edgar O. Achorn and Edward N. Teall.
Boston: Marshall Jones Company, 1919. 339 p.
LC: Ag 30, '19.
PW: Ag 30, '19.

A-44 Acosta, Mercedes de. Wind chaff / by Mercedes de
Acosta . . . New York: Moffat, Yard & Company,
1920. 255 p.
LC: N 9, '20.
PW: Ja 15, '21.

A-45 Adair, Ward W. (Ward William), b. 1870. The lure
of the iron trail / Ward W. Adair . . . New York;
London: Association Press, 1912. 201 p., front. [4]
leaves of plates (3 photo). [Ill. by Park Merrill.]
                                        NYP
Contents: The wood-passer of Doodletown -- The rawhider of the
Pan Handle -- The hiring switchman -- The plain, heroic breed -- The
open draw -- The Burlington stoker -- "Happy Jack" from Concord --
Roundhouse Tom -- Catskill Bill -- A member of the Owls' club --
Beating the wheel -- The chief conductor -- The "Y-man" at Twohy's
camp.
LC: D 31, '12.
PW: Ja 18, '13.

A-46 Adams, Adeline, 1859-1948. The Amouretta
landscape: and other stories / by Adeline Adams.
Boston; New York: Houghton Mifflin Company,
1922. (Cambridge [Mass.]: The Riverside Press).
248, [1] p.
Contents: The Amouretta landscape -- Bits of clay -- The young lady
in blue -- "C'est une taupe" -- Their appointed rounds -- Speaking of
angels -- The marquis goes donkey-riding -- The face called
forgiveness -- The artist's birthday.
PW: My 20 '22.

A-47 Adams, Andy, 1859-1935. Cattle brands: a
collection of western camp-fire stories / by Andy
Adams. Boston; New York: Houghton, Mifflin and
Company, 1906. (Cambridge: The Riverside Press).
316 p.
Contents: Drifting North -- Seigerman's per cent -- "Bad medicine"
-- A winter round-up -- A college vagabond -- The double trail --
Rangering -- At Comanche Ford -- Around the Spade wagon -- The
ransom of Don Ramon Mora -- The passing of Peg-leg -- In the hands
of his friends -- A question of possession -- The story of a poker
steer.
PW: Ap 7, '06.
BLC: London: A. Constable & Co.; Cambridge,
Mass. printed, 1903.

A-48 ____ The log of a cowboy: a narrative of the old
trail days / by Andy Adams; illustrated by E. Boyd
Smith. Boston; New York: Houghton, Mifflin and
Company, 1903. (Cambridge: The Riverside Press).
387 p., front., [6] leaves of plates.
PW: Je 6, '03.
BLC: London: A. Constable & Co.; Cambridge,
Mass. printed, 1903.

A-49 ____ The outlet / by Andy Adams . . . ; illustrated
by E. Boyd Smith. Boston; New York: Houghton,
Mifflin and Company, 1905. (Cambridge, Mass., U.
S. A.: The Riverside Press). 371 p., front., [5]
leaves of plates.
PW: Ap 15, '05.
BLC: London: A. Constable & Co., Cambridge,
Mass. printed, 1905.

A-50 ____ Reed Anthony, cowman: an autobiography /
by Andy Adams. Boston; New York: Houghton,
Mifflin and Company, 1907. (Cambridge, Mass.,
U. S. A.: The Riverside Press). 384 p., front.
LC: Ap 26, '07.
PW: Je 1, '07.

A-51   _____ A Texas matchmaker / by Andy Adams;
illustrated by E. Boyd Smith. Boston; New York:
Houghton, Mifflin and Company, 1904. (Cambridge,
Mass.: The Riverside Press). 355 p., front., [5]
leaves of plates.
PW: Je 4, '04.
BLC: London: Gay & Bird, Cambridge, Mass.
printed, 1904.

A-52   _____ Wells brothers: the young cattle kings / by
Andy Adams; with illustrations by Erwin E. Smith.
Boston; New York: Houghton Mifflin Company,
1911. (Cambridge, Mass., U. S. A.: The Riverside
Press). 356 p., front. [7] leaves of plates.
PW: Mr 18, '11.
BLC: London: Constable & Co.; Boston; New
York: Houghton Mifflin Co., 1911.

Adams, Bill. Way for a sailor. *In The best short
stories of 1923 and the yearbook of the American
short story*, (1924), B-568.

A-53   Adams, Carl B. (Carl Bruno), b. 1898. Mack / by
Carl B. Adams . . . Baltimore, Md.: Saulsbury
Publishing Company, [c1919]. 58 p.   **NYP**
PW: F 7, '20.

A-54   Adams, Charles A. (Charles Abel), b. 1854. Pete's
devils / by Charles A. Adams . . . Chicago: Scroll
Publishing Company, 1902. 239 p., ill.
PW: N 15, '02.

A-55   Adams, Charles Josiah, 1850-1924. How Baldy won
the county seat / by Charles Josiah Adams . . . New
York; London: F. Tennyson Neely, c1902. 383 p.
PW: D 20, '02.

A-56   Adams, Clayton, b. 1874. Ethiopia, the land of
promise: a book with a purpose / by Clayton Adams.
New York: The Cosmopolitan Press, 1917.
129 p.   **DLC**

A-57   Adams, Frank R. (Frank Ramsay), b. 1883. Five
Fridays / by Frank R. Adams; illustrated by Frank
Godwin. Boston: Small, Maynard & Company,
[c1915]. 339 p., front., [4] leaves of plates.
PW: Je 19, '15.

A-58   _____ Molly and I: or the silver ring / by Frank R.
Adams; illustrated by Frank Godwin. Boston: Small,
Maynard & Company, [c1915]. 310 p., front., [3]
leaves of plates.
PW: O 30, '15.

A-59   Adams, Frederick Upham, 1859-1921. The bottom
of the well / by Frederick Upham Adams; illustrations
by Alex O. Levy. New York: G. W. Dillingham
Company, [1906]. 352 p., col. front., [3] leaves of
col. plates.
PW: Je 2, '06.
BLC: London: T. Fisher Unwin; New York
[printed], 1906.

A-60   _____ John Burt / by Frederick Upham Adams . . .
Philadelphia: Drexel Biddle, 1903. 473 p., col.
front., [3] leaves of plates. [Ill. by Horace Taylor.]

PW: O 31, '03.
BLC: Toronto: Langton & Hall, 1905.

A-61   _____ John Henry Smith: humorous romance of
outdoor life / by Frederick Upham Adams; illustrated
for Mr. Smith by A. B. Frost. New York:
Doubleday, Page & Company, 1905. 346 p., incl.
front., ill.
PW: Je 3, '05.
BLC: London: Doubleday, Page & Co.; New York
printed, 1905.

A-62   _____ The kidnapped millionaires: a tale of Wall
Street and the tropics / by Frederick U. Adams.
Boston: Lothrop Publishing Company, [c1901].
504 p., incl. front.
LC: Je 5, '01.
PW: Jl 6, '01.
BLC: London: C. H. Kelly, 1901.

A-63   Adams, I. William. Kaiuolani: a Princess of Hawaii
/ by I. William Adams . . . New York: The
Mikilosch Press, 1912. 296 p.
LC: N 16, '12.

A-64   _____ Shibusawa, or, The passing of old Japan / by I.
William Adams; illustrated by E. Dalton Stevens.
New York; London: G. P. Putnam's Sons, 1906.
(New York: The Knickerbocker Press). 284 p.,
front., [3] leaves of plates.   **CLE**
PW: O 27, '06.

A-65   _____ Yodogima: in feudalistic Japan / by I. William
Adams . . . New York: The Mikilosch Press, 1911.
302 p.

A-66   Adams, J. Orville (James Orville), b. 1885. The
cruiser: a romance of the Idaho timber land frauds /
by J. Orville Adams; illustrated by Orrin C. Ross.
Spokane, Wash.: Published . . . J. Orville Adams,
December, 1909. 283 p., front., [3] leaves of plates.
LC: D 15, '09.

Adams, James Alonzo, 1842-1925. See **Grapho,
pseud.**

A-67   Adams, John Coleman, 1849-1922. Santa Claus's
baby: and other Christmas stories / by John Coleman
Adams. Boston: The Murray Press, 1911. 85 p.
                                          DLC
Contents: Santa Claus's baby -- The Christmas dinner of the
McCarty guards -- A belated Christmas -- Captain Wally's vision --
The Christmas tree of Kid McGiness -- Little Miss Santa Claus.
PW: Ja 6, '12.

Adams, Mary, pseud. See **Phelps, Elizabeth Stuart,
1844-1911.**

Adams, Minnie Barbour. Piers, the plowman, a story
of country life. *In Golden stories* **(1909), G-285.**

A-68   Adams, Samuel Hopkins, 1871-1958. Average Jones
/ by Samuel Hopkins Adams . . . ; illustrations by M.
Leone Bracker and P. Ford Harper. Indianapolis:
The Bobbs-Merrill Company, [c1911]. 345 p.,
front., [7] leaves of plates.

LC: O 18, '11.
PW: O 21, '11.
BLC: London: Frank Palmer, 1913.

A-69 ____ The beggar's purse: a fairy tale of familiar finance / by Samuel Hopkins Adams. Boston: Smith & Porter Press, Inc., 1918. 38 p.

A-70 ____ The clarion / by Samuel Hopkins Adams; with illustrations by W. D. Stevens. Boston; New York: Houghton Mifflin Company, 1914. (Cambridge: The Riverside Press). 417, [1] p., front., [3] leaves of plates.
LC: O 15, '14.
PW: S 26, '14.

A-71 ____ Common cause: a novel of the war in America: with illustrations / by Samuel Hopkins Adams. Boston; New York: Houghton Mifflin Company, 1919. (Cambridge, Mass., U. S. A.: The Riverside Press). 468 p., front., [1] leaf of plates. [Ill. by Arthur William Brown.]
PW: Ja 25, '19.

A-72 [____] Flaming youth / Warner Fabian [pseud.]. New York: Boni and Liveright, [c1923]. 336 p.
LC: Ap 20, '23.
PW: F 3, '23.

A-73 ____ The flying death / by Samuel Hopkins Adams . . . ; illustrated by C. R. Macauley. New York: The McClure Company, 1908. 239 p., front., [3] leaves of plates.
LC: Ja 25, '08.
PW: F 8, '08.

A-74 ____ From a bench in our square / by Samuel Hopkins Adams . . . Boston; New York: Houghton Mifflin Company, 1922. (Cambridge, Mass., U. S. A.: The Riverside Press). 307, [1] p.
LC: N 24, '22.
PW: D 2, '22.

The indissoluble bond. In *Marriage* (1923), M-457.

A-75 ____ Little Miss Grouch: a narrative based upon the private log of Alexander Forsyth Smith's maiden transatlantic voyage / by Samuel Hopkins Adams; with illustrations by R. M. Crosby. Boston; New York: Houghton Mifflin Company, 1915. (Cambridge, Mass., U. S. A.: The Riverside Press). 206, [1] p., front., [7] leaves of plates.
PW: S 25, '15.
BLC: London: John Murray; Cambridge, Mass. [printed], 1916.

____ jt. aut. The mystery (1905). See **White, Stewart Edward, 1873-1946, jt. aut., W-504.**

A-76 ____ Our square and the people in it / by Samuel Hopkins Adams; illustrated by J. Scott Williams. Boston; New York: Houghton Mifflin Company, 1917. (Cambridge, Mass., U. S. A.: The Riverside Press). 423, [1] p., front., [7] leaves of plates.
PW: N 10, '17.

A-77 [____] Sailors' wives / Warner Fabian [pseud.]. New York: Boni and Liveright, [c1924]. 316 p.
PW: S 13, '24.

A-78 ____ The secret of Lonesome Cove / by Samuel Hopkins Adams; illustrations by Frank E. Schoonover. Indianapolis: The Bobbs-Merrill Company, [c1912]. 339, [1] p., front., [5] leaves of plates.
LC: S 18, '12.
PW: S 21, '12.
BLC: London: Hodder & Stoughton, [1913].

A-79 ____ Siege / by Samuel Hopkins Adams. New York: Boni and Liveright, 1924. 402 p.
PW: F 23, '24.
BLC: London: Brentano's, [1927].

A-80 ____ Success: a novel / by Samuel Hopkins Adams. Boston; New York: Houghton Mifflin Company, 1921. (Cambridge, Mass.: The Riverside Press). 553, [1] p.
PW: O 15, '21.
BLC: London: Constable & Co.; Cambridge, Mass. [printed], 1921.

A-81 ____ The unspeakable perk / by Samuel Hopkins Adams; with frontispiece by George Ellis Wolfe. Boston; New York: Houghton Mifflin Company, 1916. (Cambridge, Mass., U. S. A.: The Riverside Press). 289, [1] p., front.
PW: Jl 29, '16.
BLC: London: Hodder & Stoughton; Cambridge, Mass. printed, 1916.

A-82 ____ Wanted . . . a husband: a novel / by Samuel Hopkins Adams; with illustrations by Frederic Dorr Steele. Boston; New York: Houghton Mifflin Company, 1920. (Cambridge, Mass., U. S. A.: The Riverside Press). 255, [2] p., front., [4] leaves of plates.
LC: Ap 27, '20.
PW: My 1, '20.

Adams, Will. The ghost that got the button. In *Humorous ghost stories* (1921), H-1018.

A-83 Addison, Julia de Wolf Gibbs, b. 1866. Florestane the troubadour: a mediæval romance of southern France / by Julia De Wolf Addison. Boston: Dana Estes & Company, [1903]. 307 p.
PW: O 3, '03.

A-84 ____ Mrs. John Vernon: a study of a social situation / Julia De Wolf Addison . . . ; frontispiece by Charles Dana Gibson. Boston: Richard G. Badger, 1909. ([Boston]: The Gorham Press). 205 p., front.

A-85 Addison, Thomas, b. 1861. Come-on Charley / by Thomas Addison. New York: G. W. Dillingham Company, [c1915]. 342 p.
PW: Mr 20, '15.

A-86   Ade, George, 1866-1944. Ade's fables / by George
        Ade . . . ; illustrated by John T. McCutcheon.
        Garden City, N. Y.: Doubleday, Page & Company,
        1914. 297, [1] p., front., [7] leaves of plates.
        Contents: The new fable of the private agitator and what he cooked
        up -- The new fable of the speedy sprite -- The new fable of the
        intermittent fusser -- The new fable of the search for climate -- The
        new fable of the father who jumped in -- The new fable of the uplifter
        and his dandy little opus -- The new fable of the wandering boy and
        the wayward parent -- The new fable of what transpires after the
        wind-up -- The dream that came out with much to boot -- The new
        fable of the toilsome ascent and the shining table-land -- The new
        fable of the aerial performer, the buzzing blondine, and the daughter
        of Mr. Jackson -- The new fable of Susan and the daughter and the
        granddaughter, and then something really grand -- The new fable of
        the scoffer who fell hard and the woman sitting by -- The new fable
        of the lonesome camp on the frozen heights -- The new fable of the
        marathon in the mud and the laurel wreath.
        LC: Ap 14, '14.
        PW: Ap 25, '14.
        References: Russo, p. 83-84.

A-87   ____ Breaking into society / by George Ade . . .
        New York; London: Harper & Brothers, 1904.
        208 p., front., ill. [Ill. by Harry Smith, Frank
        Holme, John McCutcheon and G. B. F.]
        References: Russo, p. 61-63.

        ____ Claudie. In *A book of American prose humor*
        (1904), B-731.

        ____ The fable of the preacher who flew his kite, but
        not because he wished to do so. In *International*
        short stories **(1910), I-29.**

        ____ The feud. In *More aces* **(1925), M-962.**

A-88   ____ Forty modern fables / by George Ade. New
        York: R. H. Russell, 1901, c1900-1901. 303 p.
        Contents: The fable of the undecided brunette and the two candidates
        -- The fable of the Boston biologist and the native with the blue
        hardware -- The fable of the knowing friend who tipped off her star
        recipe -- The fable of the people's choice who answered the call of
        duty and took seltzer -- The fable of the girl with a handicap who had
        to lock up her parents -- The fable of the good fellow who got the
        short end of it -- The fable of the husband who showed up and did the
        best he knew how -- The fable of the Bureau of Public Comfort and
        the man in charge -- The fable of Uncle Silas and the matrimonial
        game -- The fable of the old merchant, the sleuth and the tapioca --
        The fable of Springfield's fairest flower and Lonesome Agnes who
        was crafty -- The fable of the wise piker who had the kind of talk that
        went -- The fable of the two wives who talked about their husbands --
        The fable of the open champion, the veranda fixture and the once-a-
        weeker from town -- The fable of the cousin from down east who had
        his pick of the village lilacs -- The fable of the horse maniac and what
        caused the filing of the suit -- The fable of the household comedian
        and the lady's unexpected come back -- The fable of the hungry man
        from bird center and the Trans-Atlantic touch -- The fable of the
        brotherhood of states and the wife who was responsible for the jubilee
        -- The fable of the good fairy of the eighth ward and the dollar
        excursion of the steam-fitters -- The fable of the all-night seance and
        the limit that ceased to be -- The fable of the good people who rallied
        to the support of the church -- The fable of how Grandma shattered
        an idol and made it easy for the children -- The fable of the last day at
        school and the tough trustee's farewell to the young voyagers -- The
        fable of woman's true friend and the hopeful antique -- The fable of
        this year's St. George and the 800 microscopic dragons -- The fable
        of Alexander from up the road whose wife took him over the jumps --
        The fable of the general manager of the love affair who demanded a
        furlough -- The fable of the day's work and the morning after -- The
        fable of the sure-thing crook and the town of Nubbinville -- The fable
        of the foozle and the successful approach -- The fable of the old-time
        pedagogue who came down from the shelf and was sufficiently
        bumped -- The fable of the man who was going to retire -- The
        fable of the bookworm and the butterfly who went into the law -- The
        fable of the third and last call -- The fable of the crustacean who tried

to find out by reading a book -- The fable of the low-down expert
on the subject of babies -- The fable of the girl who could
compromise in a pinch -- The fable of the satiated globe-trotter who
found a new kind of nerve twister waiting for him at home -- The
fable of the skittish widower who tried to set himself back some thirty
years.
LC: O 26, '01
PW: D 14, '01.
References: Russo, p. 38-42.

A-89   ____ The girl proposition: a bunch of he and she
        fables / by George Ade. New York: R. H. Russell,
        1902. 192 p., front., ill. [Ill. by John T.
        McCutcheon, Frank Holme, Carl Werntz and Clyde
        J. Newman.]
        "The three fables concluding this volume are
        reprinted" . . . [from] "Fables in slang" and "More
        fables".
        Contents: The fable of the long-range lover, the lollypaloozer and the
        line of talk -- The fable of the crafty love-maker who needed a lady
        manager -- The fable of how Aggie had spells that the home remedies
        could not touch -- The fable of the parlor blacksmith who was unable
        to put it right over the plate -- The fable of the veteran club-girl who
        had no theories to offer -- The fable of the syndicate lover, the
        pickled papa and the rest of the bunch -- The fable of the misfit who
        lost his ticket because he got the wrong hold -- The fable of the balky
        boy who kept her marking time -- The fable of how Wisenstein did
        not lose out to Buttinsky -- The fable of the fatal album and the leap
        for life -- The fable of the young woman who had to have everything
        just so -- The fable of what befell the designing Chauncey who
        walked right up and spoke to her -- The fable of the he-flirt who was
        very jimpsy in the hotel office but a phoney piece of work when
        turned loose in a flat -- The fable of how Economical Edward got his
        quietus -- The fable of the married girl who ran the eating station for
        luminaries -- The fable of the girl who had her reasoning powers with
        her -- The fable of the fellow who had a friend who knew a girl who
        had a friend -- The fable of the roundabout way in which Gilbert
        made himself strong with Alice -- The fable of Eugene who walked
        the length of the counter before making his selection -- The fable of
        the reckless wife who had no one to watch her -- The fable of the cut-
        up who came very near to losing his ticket, but who turned defeat into
        victory -- The fable of the shower of blows that came down on Paw --
        The fable of how one brave Patsy worked himself into the king-row --
        The fable of Lutie, the false alarm, and how she finished about the
        time she started -- The fable of the two mandolin players and the
        willing performer -- The fable of the brash drummer and the peach
        who learned that there were others.
        PW: N 8, '02.
        References: Russo, p. 42-44.

A-90   ____ Hand-made fables / by George Ade . . . ;
        illustrated by John T. McCutcheon. Garden City, N.
        Y.: Doubleday, Page & Company, 1920. 332 p.,
        front., ill. [Ill. by John T. McCutcheon.]
        Reprinted from the Cosmopolitan magazine.
        Contents: The week-enders and the dreadful doings -- The compound
        fracture -- The two sensational failures -- The search for the holy grill
        -- The inside info -- All that triangle stuff -- The brand that was
        plucked and got cold -- The civic improver and the customary reward
        -- Almost getting back to nature -- The spotlights and the spotter --
        The man who wanted his Europe -- The kittenish superanns and the
        world-weary snipes -- The waist-band that was taut up to the moment
        it gave way -- The superguy and the double harness -- The lingering
        thirst and the boundless Sahara -- The hard-up yeoman -- Prince
        Fortunatas who lived in Easy Street and then moved away -- The
        straight and narrow path leading to the refreshment counter -- The
        film-fed family -- The ripe persimmon and the plucked flower -- What
        the best people are not doing -- Her birthday and the dwindling
        generosity -- The uplift that moved sideways -- The polite poison
        counter -- The ninny who swam away from the life preserver -- The
        twelve-cylinder speed of the leisure class -- The song-bird and the
        cyclone -- The bewildered maverick -- The rise and flight of the
        winged insect -- What they hankered for and what was delivered to
        them.
        PW: Mr 6, '20.
        References: Russo, p. 86-88.

A-91   ____ I knew him when--: a Hoosier fable dealing with the happy days of away back yonder / by George Ade. Chicago: Privately published by the Indiana Society of Chicago, Dec. 1910. (Chicago: Press of A. D. Weinthrop & Company). 127 p., ill. Marbled end papers. [Ill. by John T. McCutcheon.]
The work contains 177 illustrations, including reproductions of old photographs of Indiana celebrities and original character portraits by McCutcheon.
References: Russo, p. 76-77.

A-92   ____ In Babel: stories of Chicago / by George Ade. New York: McClure, Phillips & Co., 1903. 357, [1] p.
"These little stories and sketches have been rewritten from certain daily contributions to the Chicago record, now the Chicago record-herald." Pref.
Contents: "The dip" -- And Josephine Forgave -- The Barclay lawn party -- Why "Gondola" was put away -- Effie Whittlesy -- The feud -- "Tall-stoy" -- The other girl -- The judge's son -- House in Mercedes Street -- Hickey boy in the grip -- The set of Poe -- Dubley, '89 -- The money present -- Best of the Farleys -- Mr. Wimberley's trousers -- The former Kathryn -- Cupid in buttons -- The Buell cherry -- An incident in the "pansy" -- Miss Tyndall's picture -- Mr. Payson's satirical Christmas -- Life insurance -- Our private romance -- Mr. Lindsay on "San Jewan" -- The stenographic proposal -- The relatives' club -- George's return -- Harry and Ethel -- "Buck" and Gertie -- The scapegoat -- Willie Curtin-a man -- Opening of navigation -- No Clarence -- When father meets father.
PW: O 3, '03.
References: Russo, p. 59-61.

A-93   ____ Knocking the neighbors / by George Ade . . . ; illustrated by Albert Levering [sic]. Garden City, N. Y.: Doubleday, Page & Company, 1912. 229 p., front., ill.
Contents: The roystering blades -- The flat-dweller -- The advantage of a good thing -- The common carrier -- The heir and the heiress -- The undecided bachelors -- The wonderful meal of vittles -- The galloping pilgrim -- The progressive maniac -- Cognizant of our shortcomings -- The divine spark -- The philanthropic sons -- The juvenile and mankind -- The honeymoon that tried to come back -- The local Pierpont -- The life of the party -- The galumptious girl -- Everybody's friend and the line-bucker --The through train -- The long and lonesome ride -- Out of class b into the king row -- The boy who was told -- The night given over to revelry -- He should have overslept -- The dancing man -- The collision -- How Albert sat in -- The treasure in the strong box -- The old-fashioned prosecutor -- The unruffled wife and the gallus husband -- Books made to balance -- The two unfettered birds -- The telltale tintype.
LC: N 4, '12.
PW: N 16, '12.
References: Russo, p. 79-82.

      ____ Lafayette. In For France (1917), F-235.

      ____ Mary's little lamb. See Masson, Thomas Lansing, 1866-1934. A bachelor's baby: and some grownups (1907), M-587.

A-94   ____ People you know / by George Ade; illustrated by John T. McCutcheon and others. New York: R. H. Russell, 1903. 224 p., front., ill.
Contents: The periodical souse, the never-again feeling and the ride on the sprinkling cart -- The kind of music that is too good for household use -- The one or two points of difference between learning and learning how -- The night-watch and the would-be something awful -- The attenuated attorney who rang in the associate counsel -- What father bumped into at the culture factory -- The search for the right house and how Mrs. Jump had her annual attack -- The batch of letters, or one day with a busy man -- The sickly dream and how it was doctored up -- The two old pals and the call for help -- The

regular kind of place and the usual way it turned out -- The man who had a true friend to steer him along -- The young Napoleon who went back to the store on Monday morning -- The high art that was a little too high for the vulgarian who paid the bills -- Patient toiler who got it in the usual place -- The summer vacation that was too good to last -- How an humble beginner moved from one pinnacle to another and played the entire circuit -- The maneuvers of Joel and the disappointed orphan asylum -- Two young people, two photographers and the corresponding school of wooing -- The married couple that went to housekeeping and began to find out things -- The Samaritan who got paralysis of the helping hand -- The effort to convert the work horse into a high-stepper -- The self-made Hezekiah and his message of hope to this year's crop of graduates -- The girl who took notes and got wise and then fell down -- What they had laid out for their vacation -- The experimental couple and the three off-shoots.
PW: Ap 25, '03
References: Russo, p. 51-53.

A-95   ____ The slim princess / by George Ade . . . ; with illustrations by George F. Kerr. Indianapolis: The Bobbs-Merrill Company, [c1907]. 170 p., col. front., [15] leaves of col. plates.
"'The slim princess' has been elaborated and rewritten from a story printed in the Saturday evening post of Philadelphia late in 1906."
LC: My 6, '07.
PW: My 18, '07.
BLC: London: Gay & Hancock; printed in U. S. A., 1908.
References: Russo, p. 72-73.

      ____ "To make a hoosier holiday". In Short story classics (1905), S-466.

A-96   ____ True bills / by George Ade . . . ; illustrated. New York; London: Harper & Brothers, 1904. 154 p., front., ill. [Ill. by Harry Smith, Carl Werntz and John T. McCutcheon.]
Contents: The fable of the lonesome trolley-riders and their quest of harmless amusement -- The fable of the poor woman who had to live in a house that was over-run by anecdotes -- The fable of the divided concern that was reunited under a new management -- The fable of the family that worked overtime in taking care of Nellie -- The fable of successful Tobias and some of his happy new-years -- The fable of the red-letter night at Smartweed Junction -- The fable of what Horace stood for in order to land the Queen -- The fable of the boy with the steadfast ambition -- The fable of the unfortunate has-been and the sympathetic conductor -- The fable of another brave effort to infuse gentility into our raw civilization -- The fable of how Gertrude could keep it up until ten o'clock in the morning -- The fable of how the fearless favorite from St. Louis flagged the hot-looker across the way -- The fable of the one who got what was coming to him and then some more -- The fable of the society-trimmers and what broke up the experience meeting -- The fable of the girl who wanted to warm up when it was too late -- The fable of what our public schools and the primary system did for a poor but ambitious youth -- The fable of the two ways of going out after the pay envelope -- The fable of the misdirected sympathy and the come-back of the proud steam-fitter -- The fable of how the canny commercial salesman guessed the combination -- The fable of the taxpayers' friend who ran to an empty grand stand and finished outside the money -- The fable of the single-handed fight for personal liberty -- The fable of the never-to-be-benefactor who took a brand-new tack -- The fable of the old fox and the young fox.
PW: O 29, '04.
References: Russo, p. 67-69.

Adeler, Max, pseud. See Clark, Charles Heber, 1841-1915.

Ager, Carolus, pseud. See Field, Charles K. (Charles Kellogg), b. 1873.

A-97   Ager, Waldemar, 1869-1941. Christ before Pilate: an American story / by Waldemar Ager. Minneapolis: Augsburg Publishing House, [c1924]. 277 p., col. front.
PW: N 29, '24.

A-98   Agnus, Felix, 1839-1925. A woman of war and other stories / by Felix Agnus; illustrations by Willis H. Thorndike. Baltimore: Kohn & Pollock, Inc., 1908. 209 p., front., [6] leaves of plates, [8] ill.
Contents: Noel of 1864 -- A woman of war -- The gunner of "Lady Davis" -- The dead man's mark: a sacred trust.
Probable reprint of unexamined 1895 ed.
LC: Ap 11, '08.

A-99   Ahrens, Lillian Sincere. A child of sorrow / by Lillian Sincere Ahrens. New York: Broadway Publishing Company, [c1913]. 85 p., front. (port.)

A-100   Aiken, A. E., (Aaron Eugene). Exposure of Negro Society and Societies / by A. E. Aiken. [New York: J. P. Wharton, c1916]. 31 p.
Unexamined copy: bibliographic data from NUC.

A-101   Aiken, Conrad, 1889-1973. Bring! bring! and other stories / by Conrad Aiken. New York: Boni & Liveright, 1925. 240 p.
Contents: Bring! bring! -- Strange moonlight -- The disciple -- By my troth, Nerissa! -- Smith and Jones -- The escape from fatuity -- Hey, taxi! -- The dark city -- The orange moth -- The last visit -- The letter -- The anniversary -- Soliloquy on a park bench.
LC: My 8, '25.
PW: My 2, '25.
BLC: London: Martin Secker, 1925.

_____ The dark city. In *The best short stories of 1922 and the yearbook of the American short story* (1923), B-567.

_____ The disciple. In *The Harper prize short stories* (1925), H-233.

A-102   Aiken, Ednah. The hinges of custom / by Ednah Aiken. New York: Dodd, Mead and Company, 1923. 385 p.
PW: F 17, '23.

A-103   _____ If today be sweet / by Ednah Aiken. New York: Dodd, Mead and Company, 1923. 272 p.
LC: O 25, '23.
PW: N 3, '23.

A-104   _____ The river / by Ednah Aiken; illustrated by Sidney H. Riesenberg. Indianapolis: The Bobbs-Merrill Company, [c1914]. 423 p., col. front.
PW: O 31, '14.

Aikman, Henry G., pseud. See **Armstrong, Harold H. (Harold Hunter), b. 1884.**

A-105   Ailenrock, M. R., b. 1851, *pseud.* The white castle of Louisiana / by M. R. Ailenroc [pseud.]; illustrated. Louisville, Kentucky: John P. Morton & Company, 1903. 264 p., front., [4] leaves of plates.
                                    OSU, KUK
PW: Ja 23, '04.

A-106   Aix, *pseud.* Adventures of a nice young man: a novel / by Aix [pseud.]. New York: Duffield & Company, 1908. 407 p.
LC: S 14, '08.

A-107   _____ Thieves: a novel / by Aix [pseud.]. New York: Duffield & Company, 1911. 338 p., front., [3] leaves of plates. [Ill. by James Montgomery Flagg.]
LC: Mr 25, '11.
PW: Ap 1, '11.

A-108   Aker, J. W. The curse of Ham / by J. W. Aker. New York: Broadway Publishing Co., [c1909]. 190 p.   **DLC**
PW: S 4, '09.

A-109   Akin, Elizabeth Hall. Nina Hilt / by Elizabeth Hall Akin. [Princeton, Ky.?: s. n.], c1904. 182 p.
                                    KUK
PW: Je 24, '05.

A-110   Akins, Zoë, 1886-1958. Cake upon the waters / by Zöe [sic] Akins; illustrated by Lucius W. Hitchcock. New York: The Century Co., 1919. 224 p., front., [3] leaves of plates.
LC: S 2, '19.
PW: S 20, '19.

A-111   Albee, Helen R. (Helen Rickey), b. 1864. A kingdom of two: a true romance of country life / by Helen R. Albee; illustrated. New York: The Macmillan Company, 1913. 322 p., front., [11] leaves of plates.
PW: N 1, '13.

Alberg, Albert. See **Eaves, Catherine, pseud.**

A-112   Albert, Agnes Elnor. Alice Rayden, or, Weighed in the balance / by Agnes Elnor Albert. New York: Broadway Publishing Co., [c1910]. 233 p., front., [1] leaf of plates.
LC: D 24, '10.
PW: Mr 11, '11.

Alberton, Edwin, pseud. See **Philips, A. E. (Albert Edwin), b. 1845.**

A-113   Albertson, Augusta. Through gates of pearl: a vision of the heaven-life / by Augusta Alberton. New York; Chicago; Toronto; London; Edinburgh: Fleming H. Revell Company, [c1916]. 198 p.
PW: Je 17, '16.

A-114   Albery, F. F. D. (Faxon Franklin Duane), b. 1848. Michael Ryan, capitalist: a story of labor / by F. F. D. Albery. Columbus, Ohio: Rowfant Press and Bindery, 1913. 163 p.
LC: Je 2, '13.

A-115   Alborn, George C. (George Clarence). Ish Kerioth: the story of a traitor / by George C. Alborn. Boston, Mass.: Morning Star Publishing House, 1904, [c1903]. 262, [1] p., front. (port.)   **DLC**
PW: Jl 30, '04.

A-116   Albright, Ad. (Adam), b. 1862. My land. My
         country. My home. / by Ad. Albright. Albany, N.
         Y.: [Published by C. F. Williams & Son], 1915.
         427 p.

         Alden, Henry Mills, 1836-1919, jt. ed. See *Different
         girls* (1906), **D-383.**

         ____, jt. ed. See *The heart of childhood* (1906),
         H-441.

         ____, jt. ed. See *Life at high tide* (1907),
         L-281.

         ____, jt. ed. See *Quaint courtships* (1906), **Q-3.**

         ____, jt. ed. See *Shapes that haunt the dusk* (1907),
         S-339.

         ____, jt. ed. See *Southern lights and shadows*
         (1907), **S-718.**

         ____, jt. ed. See *Their husbands wives* (1906),
         T-161.

         ____, jt. ed. See *Under the sunset* (1906), **U-9.**

         Alden, Isabella Macdonald, 1841-1930. See **Pansy,
         pseud.**

A-117   Alden, W. L. (William Livingston), 1837-1908.
         Drewitt's dream: a story / W. L. Alden. New York:
         D. Appleton and Company, 1902. 321 p.
         PW: Ap 12, '02.
         BLC: London: Chatto & Windus, 1902.

A-118   Alder, W. F. (William Fisher). The Flying Fox / by
         W. F. Alder . . . illustrations and decorations by
         Howard Willard. [Los Angeles]: Wayside Press,
         1921. 141 p., ill.
         Unexamined copy: bibliographic data from NUC.
         LC: Mr 21, '21.

A-119   ____ The lagoon of desire / by W. F. Alder; with
         illustrations. Belle lettres ed. [Los Angeles]:
         Wayside Press, 1921. 132 p., [3] leaves of plates.
         [Ill. by Antonia Melvill.]
         LC: Mr 1, '21

A-120   Aldington, A. E. Love letters that caused a divorce /
         by A. E. Aldington. New York: G. W. Dillingham
         Company, 1906. 96 p.   **DLC**
         PW: F 24, '06.
         BLC: Dover: Standard office, [1905].

A-121   Aldis, Mary, 1872-1949. Drift / by Mary Aldis . . . ;
         etchings by Pierre Nuyttens. New York: Duffield &
         Company, 1918. 354, [1] p., front., [6] leaves of
         plates.
         LC: Ap 24, '18.
         PW: My 4, '18.

A-122   Aldrich, Bess Streeter, 1881-1954. Mother Mason /
         by Bess Streeter Aldrich. New York; London: D.
         Appleton and Company, 1924. 268, [1] p.

         LC: O 8, '24.
         PW: O 18, '24.

A-123   ____ The rim of the prairie / by Bess Streeter
         Aldrich. New York; London: D. Appleton and
         Company, 1925. 352 p.
         LC: O 6, '25.
         PW: O 24, '25.

         Aldrich, Clara Chapline (Thomas), 1884-1967. See
         Aldrich, Darragh, pseud.

A-124   Aldrich, Darragh, 1884-1967, *pseud.* Enchanted
         hearts / by Darragh Aldrich [pseud.]; frontispiece by
         Frances Rogers. Garden City, N. Y.: Doubleday,
         Page & Company, 1917. 406 p., front.   **NYP**
         PW: O 6, '17.

A-125   Aldrich, F. L. S. (Flora L. S.), 1859-1921. The one
         man / by Dr. (Mrs.) F. L. S. Aldrich. Boston: The
         Roxburgh Publishing Company, [c1910]. 287 p.,
         front. (port.)
         PW: O 22, '10.

A-126   Aldrich, G. A. (George Albert), b. 1863.
         Weatherton, Pacific islands and other stories: sonnets
         / by G. A. Aldrich. 1st ed. San Francisco: John R.
         McNicoll Printing Co., 1912. 130 p., photo. front.
         (port.).
         Cover title:Cover title: Short stories: poems.
         Contents: Weatherton, Pacific Islands -- Something about Orpington
         -- The Epitome Publishing Co. -- This time, it was Mufkins -- The
         hopelessness of Southby's case -- Sonnets [poetry] -- Epic of the
         South West [poem].

A-127   Aldrich, Mildred, 1853-1928. Told in a French
         garden, August, 1914 / by Mildred Aldrich . . .
         Boston: Small, Maynard & Company, 1916. 266 p.,
         front. (port.). [Ill. by Pierre-Emile Cornhillier.]
                                                      CWL
         PW: O 28, '16.

A-128   ____ A sea turn: and other matters / by Thomas
         Bailey Aldrich. Boston; New York: Houghton,
         Mifflin and Company, 1902. (Cambridge: The
         Riverside Press). 300 p.
         Contents: A sea turn -- His Grace the Duke -- Shaw's folly -- An
         untold story -- The case of Thomas Phipps -- The white feather.
         LC: S 8, '02.
         PW: O 4, '02.
         BLC: London: A. P. Watt & Son; Cambridge,
         Mass. printed, 1902.
         References: BAL 392.

A-129   Alein, Niela, b. 1867, *pseud.* H. C. of A.: a novel /
         by Niela Alein [pseud.] . . . Boston: The Roxburgh
         Publishing Company, Inc., 1922. 240 p.
         LC: D 20, '22.
         PW: Mr 31, '23.

A-130   Alexander, Arabel Wilbur. Light through darkened
         windows: a shut-in story / by Arabel Wilbur
         Alexander . . . Cincinnati: Jennings & Pye; New
         York: Eaton & Mains, [c1901]. 176 p.
         PW: Mr 23, '01.

Alexander, Charles, b. 1897. As a dog should. In
Prize stories of 1922 (1923), P-620.

A-131   The splendid summits / by Charles Alexander.
New York: Dodd, Mead and Company, 1925.
289 p.
LC: N 18, '25.
PW: N 21, '25.
BLC: London: Andrew Melrose, 1927.

Alexander, E. A. The prize-fund beneficiary. In
Different girls (1906), D-383.

Alexander, Elizabeth. Fifty-two weeks for Florette.
In *Thrice told tales (1924), T-219.*

A-132   Rôles / by Elizabeth Alexander; with
illustrations by Charles D. Mitchell. Boston: Little,
Brown, and Company, 1924. 310 p., front., [3]
leaves of plates.
PW: Ap 5, '24.

A-133 Alexander, Grace, 1872-1951. Judith: a story of the
candle-lit fifties / by Grace Alexander; with
illustrations by George Wright. Indianapolis: The
Bobbs-Merrill Company, [c1906]. 431 p., front., [5]
leaves of plates.
PW: Mr 10, '06.

A-134   Prince Cinderella / by Grace Alexander; with
frontispiece by W. B. King. Indianapolis: The
Bobbs-Merrill Company, [c1921]. 343 p., front.
LC: S 15, '21.

A-135 Alexander, James B. (James Bradun), b. 1831. The
Lunarian professor and his remarkable revelations
concerning the Earth, the moon, and Mars: together
with an account of the cruise of the Sally Ann / by
James B. Alexander . . . Minneapolis, Minn.:
[s. n.], 1909. 291 p.   **NYP**
PW: My 8, '09.

A-136 Alexander, Taylor, 1862-1952. Itoma: a forest
romance / by Taylor Alexander. Newport, N. Y.:
The Kuyahora Press, Inc., [c1909]. 193 p. Designed
end papers.   **MNC**
LC: F 28, '10.
PW: Ap 9, '10.

A-137 Alexander, Taylor, 1862-1952. Wina / by Taylor
Alexander. Chicago: M. A. Donohue & Company,
[c1904]. 94 p.
Unexamined copy: bibliographic data from NUC.
PW: Ap 8, '05.

Alfred, C. The white grave. In *Argonaut stories
(1906), A-298.*

A-138 Alien, b. 1858, *pseud.* Another woman's territory /
by "Alien" [pseud.] . . . New York: T. Y. Crowell
& Company, 1901. 315 p., front. [Ill. by Seymour
M. Stone.]   **AZU**
PW: My 11, '01.
BLC: Westminster: A. Constable & Co., 1901.

A-139   A maid of mettle / by "Alien" [pseud.] . . .
Philadelphia: G. W. Jacobs & Co., [1902]. 398 p.,
front., [4] leaves of plates. [Some signed by J.
Barnard Davis.]
Unexamined copy: bibliographic data from OCLC,
#24655424.
PW: D 6, '02.

A-140 Alla, Ogal, b. 1861, *pseud.* Blue Eye: a story of the
people of the plains / by Ogal Alla [pseud.].
Portland, Or.: The Irwin-Hodson Co., 1905. 245 p.
PW: Mr 10, '06.

A-141   A romance of the Sawtooth / by Ogal Alla
[pseud.] . . . Nampa, Idaho: Published and for sale
by the author, [c1917]. 153 p.
PW: S 15, '17.

A-142 Allegheny stories: a collection of stories of
Allegheny College life / contributed by certain of the
alumni and undergraduate body; compiled and edited
by Clyde H. Slease, '02, Buell B. Whitehill, '04.
Meadville, Pa.: McCoy & Calvin, 1902. 167 p.
Cover title: Allegheny College stories.
Contents: Timothy's day off / Leverne Alden Marsh -- A sophomore
picnic / Eli H. -- The new rules / M. J. Sweeney -- A paean of defeat
/ Grace Van Woert Henderson -- Simmons: a sketch -- A hulings
Thanksgiving dinner / Clara Campbell -- A bloom of evening / Alice
Crittenden Derby -- Four souls in Hades -- The blue and the gold /
Florence Mary Appleby -- A true son of Allegheny -- The return /
Frederick Palmer -- Why faculty objects to Θ N E [Theta Nu Epsilon]
/ J. C. Barkley -- Acknowledgement.

A-143 Allen, Anne Story. Merry hearts: the adventures of
two bachelor maids / by Anne Story Allen; with
frontispiece by Eliot Keen. New York: Henry Holt
and Company, 1903. 227 p., front.
PW: O 24, '03.

A-144 Allen, Anne Story. Tales of a terrier / by Anne Story
Allen; illustrations by Adelaide Magner. New York;
London; Montreal: The Abbey Press, [c1903].
144 p., front., ill.   **CLU**
Contents: Enter Sir Peter -- The best laid schemes -- The amende
honorable -- Down the road with Toto -- A close finish -- A
morning's experience -- Noblesse oblige -- One touch of nature -- A
yellow dog -- Stranger than fiction.

A-145 Allen, Clare. Ellen Ashe: a story / by Clare Allen.
Dayton, Ohio: Press of the U. B. Publishing House,
1905. 125 p., photo. front. [Ill. by R. D.
Beem.]   **DLC**

A-146 Allen, Constance M. The romance of a mystic ring /
by Constance M. Allen. Los Angeles: Baumgardt
Publishing Co., 1906. 211 p.

A-147 Allen, Edward, *pseud.* "Wayside": the waking
dream of a soul before an open wood fire / by
Edward Allen [pseud.]. Boston: Sherman, French &
Company, 1914. 159 p.   **CLE**
LC: N 6, '14.

A-148 Allen, Emma S. (Emma Sarah), b. 1859. Afterwards
/ by Emma S. Allen. New York: Edward J. Clode,
[c1914]. 447 p.
PW: Ja 16, '15.

A-149   _____ The awakening of the Hartwells: a tale of the San Francisco earthquake / by Emma S. Allen. New York: American Tract Society, [c1913]. 340 p., front., [3] leaves of plates.
Cover title: A tale of the San Francisco earthquake.
LC: D 22, '13.
PW: Ja 10, '14.

A-150   _____ The furnace for gold / by Emma S. Allen . . . New York: American Tract Society, [c1919]. 230 p., front., [3] leaves of plates. [Ill. by Robert Emmett Owen.]   **DLC**
LC: O 28, '19.
PW: D 6, '19.

A-151   _____ The high road / by Emma S. Allen . . . New York: The Meridian Press, [c1917]. 326 p., front., [2] leaves of plates. [Ill. by H. A. Weiss.]
PW: D 22, '17.

A-152   _____ The house of gladness / by Emma S. Allen. Philadelphia: George W. Jacobs & Company, [1915]. 334 p., front., [5] leaves of plates.
PW: S 18, '15.

A-153   [Allen, F. H.] Uncle Ned's cabin / by a son of the South [pseud.]. New Orleans, La.: E. S. Upton Printing Co., [1922]. 61p.
Unexamined copy: bibliographic data from OCLC, #5741246.

A-154   Allen, Frances Newton Symmes, b. 1865. Her wings / by Frances Newton Symmes Allen. Boston; New York: Houghton Mifflin Company, 1914. (Cambridge: The Riverside Press). 364 p.
PW: O 3, '14.

A-155   _____ The invaders / by Frances Newton Symmes Allen. Boston; New York: Houghton Mifflin Company, 1913. (Cambridge: The Riverside Press). 370, [2] p., front. [Ill. by George W. Gage.]
PW: Mr 29, '13.

A-156   _____ The plain path / by Frances Newton Symmes Allen. Boston; New York: Houghton Mifflin Company, 1912. (Cambridge: The Riverside Press). 344, [2] p., ill.
PW: Mr 9, '12.

Allen, Frances Orr. The Kis Khilim. In *West winds* **(1914), W-368.**

A-157   Allen, Frank Waller, b. 1878. Back to Arcady / Frank Waller Allen. Boston: Herbert B. Turner, 1905. 157 p., front., [3] leaves of plates. Illustrated end papers. [Ill. by I. B. Hazelton; book decorations by Theodore Brown Hapgood.]
Contents: My Lady o'roses -- After the silence of the years -- An orchard in Arcady -- My Lady and lovingkindness -- Back to Arcady.
PW: N 18, '05.
BLC: London: Ward Lock & Co., 1905.

A-158   _____ The golden road / by Frank Waller Allen . . . ; with illustrations and decorations by George Hood. New York: Wessels & Bissell Co., 1910. 228 p., front., [2] leaves of plates.

LC: N 28, '10.
PW: D 17, '10.

A-159   _____ The lovers of Skye / by Frank Waller Allen; illustrated by W. B. King. Indianapolis: The Bobbs-Merrill Company, [c1913]. 261 p., front., [5] leaves of plates.
PW: Mr 8, '13.

A-160   _____ The maker of joys / by Frank Waller Allen . . . Kansas City, Mo.: The Greyfriars' Shop Publishers, [c1907]. [43] p.   **DLC**
LC: O 21, '07.
PW: D 7, '07.

A-161   Allen, George Hoyt, 1857-1938. Uncle George's letters to the Garcia Club / by George H. Allen . . . Clinton, New York: Published by the Cedarine Allen Co., [c1902]. 194 p., photo. front., [6] leaves of plates, photo. ill.   **ABC**
PW: S 13, '02.

A-162   Allen, Irving R. (Irving Ross), b. 1887. The money-maker: the romance of a ruthless man / by Irving R. Allen; with illustrations by Robert W. Amick. New York: Dodd, Mead and Company, 1918. 371 p., front., [3] leaves of plates.

A-163   Allen, James Lane, 1849-1925. The alabaster box / by James Lane Allen. New York; London: Harper & Brothers, 1923. 64 p.
LC: N 9, '23.
PW: N 24, '23.
References: BAL 491.

A-164   _____ The bride of the mistletoe / by James Lane Allen. New York: The Macmillan Company, 1909. 190 p.
LC: Je 16, '09.
PW: Jl 3, '09.
References: BAL 475.

A-165   _____ A cathedral singer / by James Lane Allen . . . ; with frontispiece by Sigismond de Ivanowski. New York: The Century Co., 1916. 142 p., front.
LC: Mr 21, '16.
PW: Mr 18, '16.
BLC: London: Macmillan & Co., 1916.
References: BAL 484.

A-166   _____ The doctor's Christmas eve / By James Lane Allen. New York: The Macmillan Company, 1910. 304 p.
Originally announced under title: The brood of the eagle.
LC: D 1, '10.
PW: D 17, '10.
BLC: London: Macmillan & Co., 1910.
References: BAL 477.

A-167   _____ The emblems of fidelity: a comedy in letters / by James Lane Allen . . . Garden City, New York: Doubleday, Page & Company, 1919. 219 p.
LC: Mr 24, '19
PW: Ap 5, '19.
BLC: London: Curtis Brown, Garden City, N. Y. printed, 1919.
References: BAL 487.

A-168 ____ The heroine in bronze, or, A portrait of a girl: a pastoral of the city / by James Lane Allen. New York: The Macmillan Company, 1912. 281 p.
LC: O 31, '12.
PW: N 9, '12.
BLC: London: Macmillan & Co., 1912.
References: BAL 478.

A-169 ____ The Kentucky warbler / by James Lane Allen; with a frontispiece in colour. Garden City, N. Y.: Doubleday, Page & Company, 1918. 194, [1] p., col. front. [Ill. by Thomas Fogarty.]
LC: Ja 30, '18.
PW: Ja 19, '18.
BLC: London: Curtis Brown, 1918.
References: BAL 486.

A-170 ____ The landmark / by James Lane Allen. New York: The Macmillan Company, 1925. 200 p.
Contents: Introduction -- The landmark -- The ash-can -- The violet -- Miss Locke -- La Tendresse (play).
The title story has never before appeared in print.
LC: D 2, '25.
PW: D 12, '25.
References: BAL 492.

A-171 ____ The last Christmas tree: an idyl of immortality / by James Lane Allen. Portland, Maine: Thomas Bird Mosher, 1914. 33, [1] p., photo. front. (port.).
LC: N 23, '14.
PW: Ja 2, '15.
References: BAL 480.

A-172 ____ The mettle of the pasture / by James Lane Allen . . . New York: The Macmillan Company; London: Macmillan & Co., Ltd., 1903. 448 p.
PW: Ag 1, '03.
References: BAL 474.

____ The old mill on the Elkhorn. In *The Miller's holiday* **(1920), M-817.**

A-173 ____ The sword of youth / by James Lane Allen; with illustrations by John Wolcott Adams. New York: The Century Co., 1915. 261 p., front., incl. [20] leaves of plates.
LC: F 26, '15.
PW: F 27, '15.
BLC: London: Macmillan & Co., 1915.
References: BAL 481.

Allen, Mary Houston Anderson. See Allen, William, Mrs.

Allen, Maryland. The urge. In *Prize stories of 1921* **(1922), P-619.**

A-174 Allen, May V. Battling with love and fate / by May V. Allen. New York; London; Montreal: The Abbey Press, [c1902]. 167 p.
Contents: Battling with love and fate -- In duty bound, or, My summer blossom.
PW: Jl 19, '02.

A-175 Allen, Merritt Parmelee, 1892-1954. In Greenbrook / by Merritt P. Allen; illustrated by James H. Mather.

Boston: L. C. Page & Company, 1923. 309 p., front., [5] leaves of plates.

A-176 Allen, Robert, b. 1887, *pseud.* Captain Gardiner of the International Police / by Robert Allen [pseud.]. New York: Dodd, Mead and Company, 1916. 366 p.
Cover title: *Captain Gardiner.*
PW: Mr 18, '16.
BLC: London: Hodder & Stoughton, [1917].

A-177 Allen, Thomas N. (Thomas Newton), b. 1839. Chronicles of Oldfields / by Thomas N. Allen. Seattle, Washington: The Alice Harriman Company, 1909. 157 p., photo. front. (port.).　　**NYP**
LC: N 11, '09.

Allen, Will, pseud. See **Dromgoole, Will Allen, 1860-1934.**

A-178 Allen, William, Mrs. The love letters of a liar / by Mrs. William Allen. New York: Ess Ess Publishing Company, 1901, [c1900]. 67, [1] p.
PW: Ap 6, '01.

A-179 Allen, Willis Boyd, 1855-1938. The north Pacific: a story of the Russo-Japanese war / by Willis Boyd Allen. New York: E. P. Dutton & Company, 1905. 325 p., front., [7] leaves of plates. [Ill. by G. A. Traver.]
PW: D 9, '05.

A-180 Allgood, H. R. (Howard Ray). The Raynor-Moland feud / by H. R. Allgood. Baltimore: Saulsbury Publishing Company, 1918. 71 p., front. (port.).　　**DLC**

A-181 Alling, Bertha Baker. Dr. Stork and the garden of babes: a story / by Bertha Baker Alling; illustrated by the author. Lake Forest: Lakes Forester Press, 1907. 18 p., front., ill.　　**DLC**
PW: Ag 10, '07.

A-182 Allinson, Anne C. E. (Anne Crosby Emery), 1871-1932. Children of the way / by Anne C. E. Allinson. New York: Harcourt, Brace and Company, [c1923]. 193 p.
Contents: A lively hope -- The Good Shepherd -- The day star -- In their affliction -- For an helmet -- Not to the flesh -- Peaceable fruit -- A more excellent way -- Almost thou persuadest me.

A-183 ____ Roads from Rome / by Anne C. E. Allinson. New York: The Macmillan Company, 1913. 215 p.
PW: N 1, '13.

A-184 Allison, Irl Leslie. Through the years / by Irl Leslie Allison. New York: Schroeder and Gunther, Inc., 1925. 364 p.
LC: Ap 20, '25.

A-185 Allison, William. Alias Richard Power / by William Allison; frontispiece by Vera Claire. Garden City, N. Y.; Toronto: Doubleday, Page & Company, 1921. 333, [1] p., front.
LC: N 17, '21.
PW: N 12, '21.

A-186 ____ A secret of the sea / by William Allison; frontispiece by Rudolph F. Tandler. Garden City, N. Y.: Doubleday, Page & Company, 1920. 328 p., front.
PW: Mr 6, '20.

A-187 ____ The turnstile of night / by William Allison; frontispiece by John Newton Howitt. Garden City, N. Y.: Doubleday, Page & Company, 1920. 321, [1] p., col. front.
LC: O 21, '21.
PW: O 23, '20.

A-188 Allyn, Eunice Gibbs. The cats' convention / by Eunice Gibbs Allyn; illustrations from life by the author. New York: Cochrane Publishing Co., 1909. 255 p., photo. front., [11] leaves of plates, ill.   **DLC**
LC: D 17, '09.

A-189 Almirall, N. (Nina), b. 1877. The master-feeling: the story of Agatha Peynton / N. Almirall. Boston: Richard G. Badger, 1903. ([Boston]: The Gorham Press). 212 p.   **DLC**
PW: D 5, '03.

Alsberg, Henry G. Soirée Kokimono. *In Forum stories* **(1914), F-306.**

A-190 Alsbury, Edward Plummer. Guy Raymond: a story of the Texas revolution / by Edward Plummer Alsbury. Houston, Tex.: State Printing Co., Printers, 1908. 541 p., front. (port.).

Alsop, Gulielma Fell, b. 1881. The kitchen gods. *In The best short stories of 1919 and the yearbook of the American short story* **(1920), B-564;** *also Prize stories of 1919* **(1920), P-617.**

A-191 ____ My Chinese days / Gulielma F. Alsop; illustrated from photographs. Boston: Little, Brown, and Company, 1918. 271 p., front., [7] leaves of plates.
PW: S 21, '18.
BLC: London: Hutchinson & Co.; Norwold, Mass. [printed], [1920].

Alter, John E. <u>See</u> **Bat, Bill, pseud.**

Althouse, Daniel Whitman. <u>See</u> **Daniel, pseud.**

A-192 Altman, Addie Richman. The Harmons: a story of Jewish home life / by Addie Richman Altman. New York: Bloch Publishing Company, 1917. 166 p.
PW: N 10, '17.

A-193 ____ Before the dawn: a story of the fall of Richmond / by Joseph A. Altsheler. New York: Doubleday, Page & Company, 1903. 372 p.
PW: Mr 14, '03.
BLC: London: Hutchinson & Co.; New York printed, 1903.

A-194 ____ The candidate: a political romance / by Joseph A. Altsheler. New York; London: Harper &

Brothers, 1905. 428, [1] p.
PW: Mr 25, '05.

A-195 ____ Guthrie of the Times: a story of success / by Joseph A. Altsheler; illustrated by F. R. Gruger. New York: Doubleday, Page & Company, 1904. 338 p., front., [3] leaves of plates.   **KSU**
PW: D 17, '04.
BLC: London: Doubleday, Page & Co.; New York printed, 1904.

A-196 ____ The horsemen of the plains: a story of the great Cheyenne war / by Joseph A. Altsheler; illustrated by Charles Livingston Bull. New York: The Macmillan Company, 1910. 390 p., col. front., [7] leaves of col. plates.
PW: O 22, '10.

A-197 ____ The recovery: a story of Kentucky / by Joseph A. Altsheler . . . New York: Frank F. Lovell Company, [c1908]. 353 p.
LC: D 26, '08.
PW: Ap 10, '09.

A-198 Alvord, James Church. The iron cross / by James Church Alvord. West Medford, Mass.: The Christian Women's Peace Movement, [c1915]. 31 p. **WLU**
Also published in *Called to the colors and other stories*, 1915, C-50.

A-199 Amber, Miles, 1848-1914, *pseud.* Wistons: a story in three parts / by Miles Amber [pseud.]. New York: Charles Scribner's Sons, 1902. 346 p.

A-200 Ambrose, John Edward. Her guiding voice / by John Edward Ambrose . . . Boston, U. S. A.: The Christopher Publishing House, [c1923]. 310 p., front., [3] leaves of plates. [Ill. by Selden Irwin.]   **DLC**
LC: Ag 3, '23.
PW: S 15, '23.

A-201 American short stories / edited with an introduction by Fred Lewis Pattee . . . New York: Duffield and Company, 1925. 356 p.   **CSU**
Contents: The short story in America -- The rose of the Alhambra / Washington Irving -- The prophetic pictures / Nathaniel Hawthorne -- The great stone face / Nathaniel Hawthorne -- The black cat / Edgar Allan Poe -- The purloined letter / Edgar Allan Poe -- The outcasts of Poker Flat / Bret Harte -- A day of days / Henry James -- A struggle for life / Thomas Bailey Aldrich -- Madame Delicieuse / George W. Cable -- The lady or the tiger? / Frank R. Stockton -- A spring Sunday / Sarah Orne Jewett -- Hector / Henry Cuyler Bunner -- The leaser / Hamlin Garland -- Louisa / Mary Wilkins Freeman -- Polydore / Kate Chopin -- The third indgredient / O. Henry.

A-202 American short stories / edited for school use by James F. Royster . . . Chicago; Atlanta; New York: Scott, Foresman and Company, [c1925]. 342 p.
                                                                    TOL
Contents: Introduction -- His job / Grace Sartwell Mason -- Mr. Downey sits down / Leonard H. Robbins -- "They grind exceeding small" / Ben Ames Williams -- Down on their knees / Wilbur Daniel Steele -- Mary Smith / Booth Tarkington -- Long, long ago / Frederick Orin Bartlett -- Gold-mounted guns / Frederic Robert Buckley -- "The fat of the land" / Anzia Yezierska -- According to the code / Irvin S. Cobb -- Cobbler's wax / Achmed Abdullah -- Not wisely but too well / Octavus Roy Cohen -- The nature of an oath / Katherine Fullerton Gerould -- All or nothing / Charles Caldwell Dobie -- Footfalls / Wilbur Daniel Steele.
LC: Ag 7, '25.

Ames, Eleanor Maria (Eastbrook), 1831-1908. See **Kirk, Eleanor, pseud.**

A-203 Ames, Joseph Bushnell, 1878-1928. Curly Graham, cowpuncher / by Joseph B. Ames . . . ; illustrated by Remington Schuyler. New York; London: The Century Co., [c1924]. 321 p., front., [3] leaves of plates. **DLC**
LC: S 3, '24.
PW: S 6, '24.

A-204 ____ Loudon from Laramie / by Joseph B. Ames . . . New York; London: The Century Co., [c1925]. 374 p.
LC: Ja 27, '25.
PW: Ja 31, '25.

A-205 ____ The man from Painted Post / by Joseph B. Ames . . . New York; London: The Century Co., 1923. 336 p., front.
LC: S 18, '23.
PW: S 22, '23.

A-206 [____] Moran of Saddle Butte / by Lynn Gunnison [pseud.]. Chicago: A. C. McClurg & Co., 1924. 352 p., front. [Ill. by Remington Schuyler.]
LC: D 1, '24.
PW: D 13, '24.

A-207 ____ Shoe-Bar Stratton / by Joseph B. Ames; illustrated by G. W. Gage. New York: The Century Co., 1922. 354 p., front., [3] leaves of plates.
LC: Ap 29, '22.
PW: My 6, '22.
BLC: London: Hutchinson & Co., [1924].

A-208 [____] The valley of missing men / by Lynn Gunnison [pseud.]. Chicago: A. C. McClurg & Co., 1925. 410 p., front.
PW: O 10, '25.
BLC: London: Hutchinson & Co., [1926].

A-209 Ames narratives: romances of rural life / written by students of English, Agricultural Division, Iowa State College. Ames, Iowa: Published by J. M. Thurber for Alpha Chapter of Kappa Lambda Alpha, 1924. 128 p. **NYP**
Contents: College education -- Protecting the innocent -- Terry's story -- K. K. K.-a hanging -- Justice at Sprague's Landing -- The bur oak tragedy -- The wrong choice -- Lone tree -- Education plus -- The sheep killer -- The great lyceum venture -- A bit of evidence.

A-210 Amid, John. The distance back / by John Amid. [New York: The Winthrop Press], [c1914]. 31 p., col. front.

____ Prem Singh. In *The Bellman book of fiction* (1921), **B-485.**

A-211 Ammerman, Mary David. The White Rose of the Miami / by Mary David Ammerman. New York: Broadway Publishing Co., [c1911]. 154 p.
OSU, KUK

Amory, Harold. The lady in gray. In *Made to order* (1915), **M-352.**

A-212 Anderson, Ada Woodruff, b. 1860. The heart of the red firs: a story of the Pacific Northwest / by Ada Woodruff Anderson; illustrated by Charles Grunwald. Boston: Little, Brown and Company, 1908. 313 p., front., [3] leaves of plates.
LC: Mr 18, '08.
PW: Ap 11, '08.

A-213 ____ The rim of the desert / by Ada Woodruff Anderson . . . ; with frontispiece by Monte Crews. Boston: Little, Brown and Company, 1915. 402 p., front.
PW: Ap 17, '15.

A-214 ____ The strain of white / by Ada Woodruff Anderson; illustrated by Frances Rogers. Boston: Little, Brown, and Company, 1909. 300 p., front., [3] leaves of plates.
LC: Ap 16, '09.

A-215 Anderson, Antony E. Short stories / by Antony E. Anderson. Minneapolis, Minn.: Published by The Northland Press, [c1904]. 126 p., front. [Ill. by Antony E. Anderson.] **OSU, MNU**
Contents: The reign of Karl Johan -- A belated Valentine -- The admirable -- The "model" girl -- A newcomer hero -- One day at business -- The "mother" picture -- The Viking and the baby -- At Rocky Point Lighthouse -- "Handy" -- Miss Thankful's relations -- Patent leather tips -- "And this shall be a sign".

A-216 Anderson, David, 1878-1947. The blue moon: a tale of the Flatwoods / by David Anderson; frontispiece by W. B. King. Indianapolis: The Bobbs-Merrill Company, [c1919]. 313 p., front.
LC: O 10, '19.
PW: N 8, '19.
BLC: London: E. Nash Co., 1920.

A-217 ____ The red lock: a tale of the Flatwoods / by David Anderson; with frontispiece by W. B. King. Indianapolis: Bobbs-Merrill Company, [c1922]. 347 p., front.
LC: O 16, '22.
PW: N 11, '22.

Anderson, Florence Mary, Mrs. See **Bennett Florence Mary, b. 1883.**

A-218 Anderson, Frederick Irving. Adventures of the infallible Godahl / by Frederick Irving Anderson; with eight illustrations. New York: Thomas Y. Crowell Company, [1914]. 241 p., front., [7] leaves of plates. [Ill. by Fanny Munsell and Arthur Williams Brown, et al.]
LC: Mr 18, '14.

A-219 Anderson, Isabel, 1876-1948. The kiss and the queue: and other stories / by Isabel Anderson; with drawings by Larz Anderson. Boston: The Four Seas Company, [c1925]. 244 p., ill.
Contents: The kiss and the queue -- Maktub -- The Cape Cod mystery -- The great admiral's ghost -- Francois' bill -- The goddess Pele -- The white saint -- Porcupine camp -- The bat and the star -- Each in his own way -- Mr. Bosco -- My strange wanderings -- Enemies -- Perchance this time tomorrow -- The moon ball.
LC: My 15, '25.
PW: Ag 15, '25.

A-220   ____ Polly the pagan: her lost love letters / by Isabel Anderson; with a foreword by Basil King. Boston: The Page Company, 1922. 239 p., col. front. [Ill. by Dewitt Lockman.]
LC: S 16, '22.

Anderson, James A. <u>See</u> *The story of Alice* (1925), **S-986.**

A-221   Anderson, Kate. A fight against odds / by Kate Anderson. Chicago: Woman's temperance Publishing Association, [c1903]. 74 p., photo. front. (port.), [2] leaves of plates. [Ill. by F. J. Saunders.]   **ITU**

A-222   Anderson, Nephi, 1865-1923. Added upon: a story / by Nephi Anderson. Fifth and enlarged edition. Salt Lake City, Utah: The Deseret News, 1912. 228 p.

A-223   ____ The castle builder / by Nephi Anderson . . . Salt Lake City, Utah: Improvement Era, 1902.
188 p.   **UUA**
PW: F 14, '03.

A-224   ____ A daughter of the North / by Nephi Anderson . . . ; with five drawings by C. E. Tillotson. [Salt Lake City: Printed by De Utah-Nederlander Pub. Co.], c1915. 256 p., photo. front., ill.
      OSU, UUM
OSU copy: [S. l.: s. n.], 1905. 250 p., front., ill.

A-225   ____ Dorian / by Nephi Anderson . . . Salt Lake City, Utah: Bikuben Publishing Company, 1921. 223 p.
LC: D 17, '21.

A-226   ____ John St. John: a story of Missouri and Illinois / by Nephi Anderson . . . Independence, Jackson Co., Mo.: Zion's Printing and Publishing Company, 1917. 227 p.   **UUM**
PW: F 16, '18.

A-227   ____ Piney Ridge cottage: the love story of a "Mormon" country girl / by Nephi Anderson . . . Salt Lake City, Utah: The Deseret News, 1912. 237 p., front.   **OSU, UUM**
LC: Je 15, '12.

A-228   ____ Romance of a missionary: a story of English life and missionary experiences / by Nephi Anderson . . . Independence, Jackson County, Mo.: Zion's Printing and Publishing Company, 1919. 190 p., [10] leaves of plates.
LC: D 30, '19.

A-229   ____ Story of Chester Lawrence: being the completed account of one who played an important part in "Piney Ridge Cottage" / by Nephi Anderson. Salt Lake City, Utah: The Deseret News, 1913. 237 p.
LC: D 1, '13.

A-230   Anderson, Olof W. The treasure vault of Atlantis / by Olof W. Anderson; illustrated by Almira Alkire Burmaster. Minneapolis: Midland Publishing Co., 1925. 326 p., front.

Anderson, Robert Gordon, b. 1881, contributor. <u>See</u> *Bobbed hair* (1925), **B-700.**

A-231   ____ The cross of fire: a romance of love and war to-day / by Robert Gordon Anderson; with illustrations. Boston; New York: Houghton Mifflin Company, 1918. (Cambridge [Mass.]: The Riverside Press). 381, [1] p., front., [3] leaves of plates. [Ill. by Harold James Cue.]
LC: N 20, '18.
PW: N 23, '18.

A-232   ____ For love of a sinner: a tale with villain for hero / by Robert Gordon Anderson . . . New York: Minton, Balch & Company, 1924. 314 p.
LC: My 17, '24.
PW: My 17, '24.
BLC: London: Hutchison & Co., [1925].

A-233   ____ The isle of seven moons: a romance of unchartered seas and untrodden shores / by Robert Gordon Anderson. New York; London: G. P. Putnam's Sons, 1922. ([New York]: The Knickerbocker Press). 395 p. Illustrated (map) end papers.
LC: Ap 20, '22.
PW: Ap 22, '22.

A-234   ____ The little chap / by Robert Gordon Anderson; frontispiece by A. G. Peck. New York; London: G. P. Putnam's Sons, 1919. (New York: The Knickerbocker Press). 43 p., col. front.
LC: N 4, '19.
PW: N 1, '19.

A-235   ____ Not taps, but reveille / by Robert Gordon Anderson. New York; London: G. P. Putnam's Sons, 1918. (New York: The Knickerbocker Press). 33 p.
LC: N 14, '18.
PW: S 28, '18.

A-236   Anderson, Sherwood, 1876-1941. Dark laughter / Sherwood Anderson. New York: Boni & Liveright, 1925. 319 p. [Ill. end papers by G. T. Hartmann.]
LC: O 14, '25.
PW: S 12, '25.
BLC: London: Jarrolds, [1926].
Reference: Sheehy & Lohf 33.

A-237   ____ Horses and men: tales, long and short, from our American life / by Sherwood Anderson. New York: B. W. Huebsch, Inc., 1923. 347 p.
Contents: Foreword -- Dreiser -- I'm a fool -- The triumph of a modern -- "Unused" -- A Chicago Hamlet -- The man who became a woman -- Milk bottles -- The sad horn blowers -- The man's story -- An Ohio pagan.
LC: F 11, '24.
PW: N 24, '23.
BLC: London: Jonathan Cape; printed in U. S. A., 1924.
References: Sheehy & Lohf 21.

____ I'm a fool. <u>In</u> *The best short stories of 1922 and the yearbook of the American short story* (1923), **B-567.**

A-238   ____ Many marriages / Sherwood Anderson. New York: B. W. Huebsch, Inc., 1923. 264 p.
LC: Ap 13, '23.
PW: Mr 10, '23.
References: Sheehy & Lohf 25.

A-239   ____ Marching men / by Sherwood Anderson . . . New York: John Lane Company; London: John Lane, The Bodley Head; Toronto: S. B. Gundy, 1917. 314 p.
LC: S 18, '17.
PW: S 22, '17.
References: Sheehy & Lohf 4.

    ____ The other woman. In *The best short stories of 1920 and the yearbook of the American short story* (1921), B-565.

A-240   ____ Poor white: a novel / by Sherwood Anderson . . . New York: B. W. Huebsch, Inc., 1920. 371 p.
LC: Ap 4, '21.
PW: D 4, '20.
BLC: London: Jonathan Cape, 1921.
References: Sheehy & Lohf 13.

A-241   ____ The triumph of the egg: a book of impressions from American life in tales and poems / by Sherwood Anderson; in clay by Tennessee Mitchell; photographs by Eugene Hutchinson. New York: B. W. Huebsch, Inc., 1921. 269 p., [8] leaves of plates.
Contents: The dumb man -- I want to know why -- Seeds -- The other woman -- The egg -- Unlighted lamps -- Senility -- The man in the brown coat -- Brothers -- The door of the trap -- The New Englander -- War -- Motherhood -- Out of nowhere into nothing -- The man with the trumpet.
LC: D 8, '21.
PW: N 12, '21.
BLC: London: Jonathan Cape; printed in U. S. A., 1922.
References: Sheehy and Lohf 17.

A-242   ____ Windy McPherson's son / by Sherwood Anderson. New York: John Lane Company; London: John Lane, The Bodley Head, 1916. 347 p.
LC: S 22, '16.
PW: S 2, '16.
References: Sheehy & Lohf 1.

A-243   ____ Winesburg, Ohio: a group of tales of Ohio small town life / by Sherwood Anderson. New York: B. W. Huebsch, 1919. 303 p.
Contents: The book of the grotesque -- Hands -- Paper pills -- Mother -- The philosopher -- Nobody knows -- Godliness -- Surrender -- Terror -- A man of ideas -- Adventure -- Respectability -- The thinker -- Tandy -- The strength of God -- The teacher -- Loneliness -- An awakening -- "Queer" -- The untold lie -- Drink -- Death -- Sophistication -- Departure.
LC: N 17, '19.
PW: My 3, '19.
References: Sheehy & Lohf 9.

    Anderson, William Ashley. The end of the game. In *The Grim thirteen* (1917), G-537.

A-244   Anderson, William Lee, b. 1867. The legend of McNutt: a story of early home life and Christianity in the Yazoo and Mississippi Delta / by W. L. Anderson . . . Nashville, Tenn.; Dallas, Tex.: Publishing

House Methodist Episcopal Church, South: Bigham & Smith, Agents, 1902. 226 p.
PW: Ap 25, '03.

A-245   Anderton, Daisy. Cousin Sadie / by Daisy Anderton. Boston, Massachusetts: The Stratford Co., 1920. 236 p.
LC: Ag 3, '20.
PW: Ag 21, '20.

A-246   Andrews, Annulet, 1866-1943. The wife of Narcissus / by Annulet Andrews. New York: Moffat, Yard and Company, 1908. 250 p.
PW: F 15, '08.

A-247   Andrews, Charlton, 1878-1939. A parfit gentil knight / by Charlton Andrews; with 12 full-page drawings by J. H. Vanderpoel. Chicago: A. C. McClurg & Co., 1901. 414 p., front., [11] leaves of plates.
PW: N 9, '01.

A-248   Andrews, Isabella M. The failure of Cunningham / By Isabella M. Andrews. [Richmond, Va.: Hampton Institute Press, 1908]. 13 p., ill.   **VIC**

    Andrews, Mary Raymond Shipman. "American, Sir!". In *Short stories of various types* (1920), S-465.

A-249   ____ August first / by Mary Raymond Shipman Andrews and Roy Irving Murray; illustrated by A. I. Keller. New York: Charles Scribner's Sons, 1915. 179 p., front.
PW: Ap 3, '15.

A-250   ____ The better treasure / by Mary Raymond Shipman Andrews; with illustrations by H. M. Bunker. Indianapolis: The Bobbs-Merrill Company, [1908]. 72 p., front.
LC: O 19, '08.
PW: N 7, '08.

A-251   ____ Bob and the guides: illustrated / by Mary Raymond Shipman Andrews . . . New York: Charles Scribner's Sons, 1906. 351 p., front., [7] leaves of plates. [Ill. by F. C. Yohn.]
PW: Ap 7, '06.

A-252   ____ The counsel assigned / by Mary Raymond Shipman Andrews. New York: C. Scribner's Sons, 1912. 43 p., front.
LC: Mr 12, '12.
PW: Mr 16, '12.
BLC: London: Bickers & Son; New York printed, 1912.

A-253   ____ The courage of the commonplace / by Mary Raymond Shipman Andrews . . . New York: Charles Scribner's Sons, 1911. 82 p., front.
PW: O 7, '11.

A-254   ____ The eternal feminine: and other stories: illustrated / by Mary Raymond Shipman Andrews . . . New York: Charles Scribner's Sons, 1916. 369 p., front., [7] leaves of plates. [Ill. by W. D. Stevens, Alonzo Kimball, Irma Dérèmeaux.]

Contents: Her fling -- The eternal feminine -- Coals of fire -- The very lilac one -- A play to the gallery -- The fifth of October -- A political tip -- The healer -- The fugitive --Taki's career.
LC: N 1, '16.
PW: N 11, '16.

A-255 ____ The eternal masculine: stories of men and boys / by Mary Raymond Shipman Andrews; illustrated. New York: Charles Scribner's Sons, 1913. 430 p., front., [7] leaves of plates. [Ill. by Philip R. Goodwin.]
Contents: The scarlet ibis -- The campaign trout -- The reward of virtue -- The Sabine maiden -- The whistling of Zoètique -- The young man with wings -- Amici -- The captains -- Little Marcus.
LC: O 21, '13.
PW: N 1, '13.

A-256 ____ A good Samaritan / by Mary Raymond Shipman Andrews; illustrated by Charlotte Harding. New York: McClure, Phillips & Co., 1906. 51 p., front., [6] leaves of plates.
LC: S 19, '06.
PW: S 29, '06.

A-257 ____ Her country / by Mary Raymond Shipman Andrews. New York: Charles Scribner's Sons, 1918. 81 p.
PW: Je 1, '18.

A-258 ____ His soul goes marching on / by Mary Raymond Shipman Andrews. New York: Charles Scribner's Sons, 1922. 84 p., front. [Ill. by James Montgomery Flagg.]
LC: Mr 29, '22.
PW: My 13, '22.

A-259 ____ Joy in the morning / by Mary Raymond Shipman Andrews. New York: Charles Scribner's Sons, 1919.
345 p., front.
Contents: The ditch -- Her country too -- The swallow -- Only one of them -- The V. C. -- He that loseth his life shall find it -- The silver stirrup -- The Russian -- Robina's doll -- Dundonald's destroyer.
PW: N 1, '19.

A-260 ____ A kidnapped colony / by Mary Raymond Shipman Andrews; illustrated by E. M. Ashe. New York; London: Harper & Brothers, 1903. 175, [1] p., front., [3] leaves of plates.
PW: D 5, '03.

A-261 ____ The lifted bandage / by Mary Raymond Shipman Andrews . . . New York: Charles Scribner's Sons, 1910. 45 p.
LC: Mr 16, '10.

A-262 ____ The marshal / by Mary Raymond Shipman Andrews . . . ; illustrated by André Castaigne. Indianapolis: The Bobbs-Merrill Company, [c1912]. 423 p., front., [5] leaves of plates.
LC: O 2, '12.
PW: S 21, '12.

A-263 ____ The militants: stories of some parsons, soldiers and other fighters in the world: illustrated / by Mary Raymond Shipman Andrews. New York: Charles Scribner's Sons, 1907. 378 p., front., [7] leaves of plates. [Ill. by B. West Clinedinst, Arthur

Ignatius Keller . . . et al.]
Contents: The bishop's silence -- The witnesses -- The diamond brooches -- Crowned with glory and honor -- A messenger -- The aide-de-camp -- Through the ivory gate -- The wife of the governor -- The little revenge.
PW: My 18, '07.

A-264 ____ Old glory / by Mary Raymond Shipman Andrews. New York: Charles Scribner's Sons, 1916. 126 p., front.
Contents: The colors -- The stranger within the gates -- The star-spangled banner.
PW: Jl 29, '16.

A-265 ____ The perfect tribute / by Mary Raymond Shipman Andrews. New York: Charles Scribner's Sons, 1906.
47 p.
LC: S 12, '06.
PW: O 6, '06.

A-266 ____ Pontifex Maximus / by Mary Raymond Shipman Andrews. New York: Charles Scribner's Sons, 1925. 76 p.
PW: Mr 21, '25.

A-267 ____ The three things: the forge in which the soul of a man was tested / by Mary Raymond Shipman Andrews . . . Boston: Little, Brown and Company, 1915. 58 p.
PW: N 27, '15.

A-268 ____ Vive l'empereur / by Mary Raymond Shipman Andrews; illustrated by F. C. Yohn. New York: Charles Scribner's Sons, 1902. 159 p., front., [5] leaves of plates.
PW: N 22, '02.

____, contributor. See *The whole family* (1908), W-578.

A-269 ____ Yellow butterflies / by Mary Raymond Shipman Andrews. New York: Charles Scribner's Sons, 1922. 73 p.
LC: D 2, '22.
PW: D 16, '22.

Angell, Bryan Mary, b. 1877. See **Cromarsh, H. Ripley, pseud.**

A-270 Angellotti, Marion Polk. The Burgundian: a tale of old France / by Marion Polk Angellotti; illustrated by B. J. Rosenmeyer. New York: The Century Co., 1912. 363 p., front., [5] leaves of plates.
LC: Mr 25, '12.
PW: Mr 23, '12.

A-271 ____ The firefly of France / by Marion Polk Angellotti . . . ; illustrated by Grant T. Reynard. New York: The Century Co., 1918. 363 p., front., [3] leaves of plates.   **RBN**
LC: Ap 3, '18.

A-272 ____ Harlette / by Marion Polk Angellotti. New York: The Century Co., 1913. 162 p.
LC: Je 28, '13.
PW: Je 28, '13.

A-273   Sir John Hawkwood: a tale of the White Company in Italy / by Marion Polk Angellotti. New York: R. F. Fenno & Company, [c1911]. 298 p., front.
PW: My 20, '11.

A-274   Three black bags / by Marion Polk Angellotti. New York: The Century Co., 1922. 375 p., front. [Ill. by George W. Gage.]
LC: S 7, '22.
PW: S 9, '22.

A-275   Anne. The bachelor girl's colonial beau / by Anne. New York; Washington: The Neale Publishing Company, 1904. 63 p.

A-276   Annis, S. F. (Sarah Frances), b. 1844. The noble Earl of Fleetwood, or, Kathryn's promise / by Mrs. S. F. Annis. New York: Broadway Publishing Company, [c1913]. 575 p. **DLC**
LC: Je 13, '13.
PW: Ag 2, '13.

A-277   Anthon, Rose Reinhardt. Stories of India: moral, mystical, spiritual and romantic / by Rose Reinhardt Anthon. Los Angeles, Cal.: Times-Mirror Printing & Binding House, 1906. 136 p. **YCP**
Contents: The singer and his teacher -- The straight path -- The magic casket -- The saint and the snake -- The yogi and the housewife -- The Emperor and the sage -- The hermit and the householder -- All for the gooroo's books -- The yogi and the hunter -- Real renunciation -- The hermit and the villager -- Matching the pearl -- The oak and the vine -- The Moon-Maiden.
BLC: London: William Heinemann, [1914].

A-278   Anthony, Edward, b. 1895. "Razzberry!" / by Edward Anthony. New York: Henry Holt and Company, 1924. 340 p., front.
LC: Ap 26, '24.
PW: My 3, '24.

A-279   Anthony, Geraldine. Four-in-hand: a story of smart life in New York and at a country club / by Geraldine Anthony. New York: D. Appleton and Company, 1903. 377 p., front.
PW: O 17, '03.

A-280   A victim of circumstance: a novel / by Geraldine Anthony. New York; London: Harper and Brothers, 1901. 368, [1] p.
On cover: A story of Modern American Life.
PW: My 4, '01.

Anthony, H., pseud. See **Shands, Hubert Anthony, b. 1872.**

A-281   Anthony, Joseph, b. 1897. The gang / by Joseph Anthony . . . New York: Henry Holt and Company, 1921. 276 p., ill.
Cover title: The gang: 120th Street official.
LC: N 23. '21.
PW: D 10, '21.
BLC: London: Jonathan Cape; printed in U. S. A., 1922.

A-282   The golden village / by Joseph Anthony. Indianapolis: The Bobbs-Merrill Company, [c1924].

321 p.
LC: O 22, '24.
PW: O 25, '24.

A-283   Rekindled fires / by Joseph Anthony; frontispiece by J. Ormsbee. New York: Henry Holt and Company, 1918. 347 p., col. front.
LC: My 17, '18.
PW: My 11, '18.
BLC: London: Jonathan Cape; Rahway, N. J. [printed], 1918.

A-284   Anthony, Joseph H. Birds of a feather / Joseph H. Anthony. Lamoni, Iowa: Herald Publishing House, [19--?]. 325 p., photo. front., [8] leaves of plates.

A-285   Anthony, Wilder. Hidden gold / by Wilder Anthony; frontispiece by G. W. Gage. New York: The Macaulay Company, [c1922]. 290 p., front.
LC: Ap 25, '22.
PW: Jl 15, '22.
BLC: London: W. Collins Sons & Co., [1924].

A-286   Anthony, the joker / by George Barr McCutcheon. A great man's wife / by Booth Tarkington. The unpresentable appearance of Col. Crane / by G. K. Chesterton. Chicago; New York: The Chicago Tribune Newspaper Syndicate, [April 1924]. 125 p., front., ill.
Cover title: *Three yarns.*
References: BAL 13560.

Antin, Mary. The lie. In *Atlantic narratives*; **2nd series (1918), A-361.**

     Malinka's atonement. In *More aces* (1925), **M-962.**

A-287   Antrobus, Suzanne. The king's messenger: a novel / by Suzanne Antrobus. New York; London: Harper & Brothers, 1901. 347 p.
PW: S 14, '01.

A-288   Aplington, Kate A. (Kate Adele), b. 1859. Pilgrims of the plains: a romance of the Santa Fé trail / by Kate A. Aplington. Chicago: F. G. Browne & Co., 1913. 400 p., col. front.
LC: F 12, '13.
PW: F 8, '13.

A-289   Appel, John W., b. 1856. The light of Parnell / by John W. Appel. Philadelphia: The Heidelberg Press, 1916. 395 p., front.
PW: S 23, '16.

Appleby, Florence Mary. The blue and the gold. In *Allegheny stories* (1902), **A-142.**

A-290   Applegarth, Margaret T. (Margaret Tyson), 1886-1976. India inklings: the story of a blot / by Margaret T. Applegarth . . . ; with inklings drawn by the author. New York: George H. Doran Company, [c1922]. 170 p., front. ill., ill. **OSU, OKG**

Applegate, William Edward. See **Edward, William, pseud.**

A-291   Appleton, Alice. Milnwood in peace and in war, or, Love's labor's gained / by Alice Appleton. Mount Union, Pa.: [s. n.], [1907?]. 294 p., front. (port.).

A-292   Appleton, George. Beauacre: a bread and butter fact story / by George Appleton. Boston, Massachusetts: The C. M. Clark Publishing Co., [c1911]. 211 p.
LC: Mr 21, '12.
PW: My 11, '12.

A-293   Apthorp, F. Jay (Frank Jay), b. 1869. The little strike-breaker (a good unionist) / by F. Jay Apthorp and Will T. Henderson. Chicago: F. H. Jaenicken, Printer, c1915. 27 p.   **DLC**

Arbuckle, Mary. Wasted. In *Stories from the Midland (1924), S-984; also Thrice told tales (1924), T-219.*

A-294   Archer, F. M. (Frank Morton), b. 1862. The T N T cowboy . . . / by F. M. Archer. [Boston, 1919.] 65 p.
Unexamined copy: bibliographic data from NUC.
Another copy: "Second printing May, 1919, first printing March, 1919." Pagination: 81 p., incl. plates, front.
Unexamined copy: bibliographic data from NUC.

A-295   Arctander, Jno. W. (John William), 1849-1920. Guilty? / by Jno. W. Arctander . . . New York: Cochrane Publishing Company, 1910. 203 p., front., [3] leaves of plates. [Ill. by R. W. Amick.]
PW: My 14, '10.

A-296   ____ The lady in blue: a Sitka romance / by Jno. W. Arctander . . . ; illustrations by courtesy of Mr. W. H. Case . . . Seattle: Lowman & Hanford Co., [c1911]. 63 p., photo. ill.   **MHS**

A-297   Arfao, or, A Roland for an Oliver: the romance of a newspaper personal / by her and them; elaborately illustrated. New York: The Cosmos Publishing Club, 1906. 133 p., photo. front. (port.), [3] leaves of plates. [Ill. by A. Wolfson.]
PW: D 22, '06.

A-298   Argonaut stories / J. London, F. Norris, S. E. White . . . [et al.]; selected from the Argonaut; Jerome Hart, editor. San Francisco: Payot, Upham & Company, agents for Pacific Coast, 1906.
320 p.   **CLO**
Contents: Moon-face / Jack London -- A caged lion / Frank Norris -- The race bond / Gwendolen Overton -- The Rajah's nemesis / William C. Morrow -- The man-hunters' reward / Buckey O'Neill -- Conscience money / Geraldine Bonner -- The jack-pot / Charles Dwight Willard -- The seats of judgment / C. W. Doyle -- A double shot / Stewart Edward White -- Ten thousand years in ice / Robert Duncan Milne -- Leaves on the River Pasig / W. O. McGeehan -- The great euchre boom / Charles F. Embree -- The sorcery of Asenath / Maria Roberts -- Old "Hard Luck" / E. Munson -- The dotted trail / Will H. Irwin -- The white grave / C. Alfred -- The jewels of Bendita / Gilbert Cunyngham Terry -- The Man-Dog / Nathan C. Kouns -- The amateur revolutionist / John F. Wilson -- The blood of a comrade / Neil Gillespie -- Under flying hoofs / Bertrand W. Sinclair -- The Colonel and "The Lady" / Kathleen Thompson.
PW: Ap 21, '06.
References: BAL 11893.

A-299   Argyle, Harvey. As I saw it / by Harvey Argyle; stories illustrated. San Francisco, California: Home Publishing Company, 1902. 263 p., [23] leaves of plates (some photo.). Designed end papers. [Ill. by G. Staib.]
Contents: Incidents of the Civil War in Missouri -- The story of a blood-stained poem -- A story of the mines -- My first sweetheart and scenes of my childhood -- The commercial traveler -- A horse-race for a wife in the days of slavery.
PW: Jl 12, '02.

A-300   Arkins, Frank J. (Francis Joseph), b. 1866. The mystery of Bonanza Trail / by Frank J. Arkins; with illustrations by J. Richard Parry. Denver: The General Publishing Syndicate, [c1910]. 128 p., front., [2] leaves of plates. Designed end papers.

Arling, Emanie (Nahm). See Sachs, Emanie N.

A-301   Arlington, W. June. Fordwell Graham, or, Lost and won by the hand of the dead / by June W. Arlington. Philadelphia: Allen, Lane & Scott, [c1902]. 414 p.
PW: D 20, '02.

A-302   Armes, E. E. (Ellen Elizabeth), 1847-1904. John Varholm's heir, or, The Denwold Mills / by E. E. Armes. Fitchburg, [Mass.]: Sentinel Printing Company, 1905. 239 p.
PW: D 30, '05.

A-303   Armour, J. P. (John P.), b. 1856. Edenindia: a tale of adventure / by J. P. Armour. New York: G. W. Dillingham Company, [1905]. 317 p.
PW: O 21, '05.
BLC: London: T. Fisher Unwin; New York [printed], 1905.

A-304   Armstrong, Anne Wetzell, b. 1872. The seas of God: a novel. New York: Hearst's International Library Co., [c1915]. 384 p., col. front. [Ill. by T. K. Hanna.]
PW: Ap 24, '15.
BLC: London: Mills & Boon, 1916.

A-305   Armstrong, Estelle Aubrey. The Indian special / by Estelle Aubrey Armstrong. New York: Herman Lechner Publisher, [c1912]. 195 p.   **NYP**
PW: N 30, '12.

A-306   Armstrong, Everhardt. Foreordained: with other stories / by Everhardt Armstrong. Philadelphia: The John C. Winston Co., 1913. 270 p.   **DLC**
Contents: Foreordained -- Doubt -- The hat -- In October -- Ralston -- Stalled ox -- A summer reverie -- A white flower.
PW: Mr 29, '13.

A-307   Armstrong, Harold H. (Harold Hunter), b. 1884. For richer, for poorer / by Harold H. Armstrong. New York: Alfred A. Knopf, 1922. 308 p.
LC: S 8, '22.
PW: Ag 12, '22.

A-308   [____] The groper / by Henry G. Aikman [pseud.]. New York: Boni and Liveright, 1919. 282 p.

A-309   ____ The red-blood: a novel / by Harold H. Armstrong. New York; London: Harper &

Brothers, [c1923]. 479 p.
LC: S 7, '23.
PW: S 15, '23.

A-310   [____] Zell: a novel / by Henry G. Aikman
[pseud.]. New York: Alfred A. Knopf, 1921.
326 p.
BLC: London: Jonathan Cape; printed in U. S. A.,
1921.

A-311   Armstrong, Le Roy, 1854-1927. The outlaws: a
story of the building of the West / by Le Roy
Armstrong. New York: D. Appleton and Company,
1902. 320 p.
PW: Ap 26, '02.

A-312   Armstrong, Maurice McNeill. In the shadow of San
Juan / by Maurice McNeill Armstrong. Los Angeles,
Cal.: Pueblo Publishing Co., 1910. 207 p., photo.
front., [2] leaves of photo. plates.
PW: Jl 16, '10.

A-313   Armstrong, Willimina Leonora, 1866-1947. Incense
of sandalwood / by Willimina L. Armstrong. Los
Angeles, California: Baumgardt Publishing Co.,
[c1904]. 149 p., col. photo. front., [5] leaves of
plates (some col.). [Some ill. by N. G. Villa.]
PW: S 17, '04.

Armstrong, Willimina Leonora, 1866-1947, (Zamin
Ki Dost, pseud.), jt. aut. Son of power (1920). See
**Comfort, Will Levington, 1878-1932, jt. aut.,
C-629.**

A-314   Arnett, Lizzie, 'Mongst the hills of Kentucky / by
Lizzie Arnett; with illustrations by Tip Saunders.
Louisville, Ky.: Printed for the author by R. H.
Carothers & Son, 1909. 258 p., front., [5] leaves of
plates.   **NJB**
LC: F 20, '09.
PW: Ap 17, '09.

A-315   Arnold, Alexander Streeter, b. 1829. Hesper
Dalraven, heroine: a story for the times / by
Alexander Streeter Arnold . . . Boston: James H.
Earle Co., 1913. 320 p.

A-316   Arnold, Cornelia Minor. The hermit of Lover's Lane
/ By Cornelia Minor Arnold . . . Ossining, New
York: The Billington Press, 1912. 28 p., [1] leaf of
photo. plates.   **KSU**
LC: O 26, '12.

A-317   Arnold, Cornelia Minor. Stonefield silhouettes:
stories from a quainter day / by Cornelia Minor
Arnold. New York: Broadway Publishing Co.,
[c1911]. 228 p., front., [8] leaves of plates.
Contents: The apotheosis of Jeduthun -- The constancy of Constance
-- How 'Kiah "pervided" -- Cupid vs. Fate, Susan Tarbutton, et. al. --
The miraculous healing of Zenas Holsapple -- The short and simple
annals of Widder Abercrombie's second ventur' -- Doctor Bruin --
The gratitude of Miss Sarpeta -- Micajah Billop, marriage broker.

A-318   Arnold, Faith Stewart, b. 1860, pseud.
Emancipation: the key / by Faith Stewart Arnold
[pseud.]. Cambridge, Mass.: Printed at the
University Press, [c1922]. 267 p.   **EEM**

A-319   Arnold, Walter W. (Walter Watson), b. 1860. A
Missourian's honor / by Walter W. Arnold; 3
drawings by Hudson. New York: Broadway
Publishing Company, [c1904]. 79 p., front., [2]
leaves of plates.   **DLC**
PW: Mr 18, '05.

A-320   Arnold, Winifred, b. 1874. Mis' Bassett's matrimony
bureau / by Winifred Arnold. New York; Chicago;
Toronto; London; Edinburgh: Fleming H. Revell
Company, [c1912]. 196 p., front., [5] leaves of
plates. [Ill. by Harry C. Edwards, Robert L. Gray
and Adrien Claude Machefert.]   **FDA**
LC: N 18, '12.
PW: Ag 31, '12.

A-321   ____ Miss Emeline's kith and kin / by Winifred
Arnold . . . ; illustrated. New York; Chicago;
London; Edinburgh: Fleming H. Revell Company,
[c1919]. 224 p., front.
LC: D 3, '19.
PW: S 13, '19.

A-322   Aron, Blanche. Between ourselves: and other short
stories / by Blanche Aron; frontispiece from
photograph by the author. New York: Fifth Avenue
Printing Co., Inc., 1916. 72 p., photo. front. **DLC**
Contents: Old pals -- The cañon -- Mal entendu -- The orator in
embryo -- Entre nous.
PW: Mr 3, '17.

A-323   Arthur, Andrew J. From behind the veil / by Andrew
J. Arthur . . . Salem, Missouri: Gustin's Printery,
1901. 321, [3] p. Designed end papers.   **MOU**

A-324   Artinian, H. La rama / by H. Artinian. Baltimore,
MD.: Saulsbury Publishing Company, c1919. 63 p.

A-325   As we are: stories of here and now / collected by
Walter B. Pitkin. New York: Harcourt, Brace and
Company, [c1923]. 312 p.   **MUU**
Contents: Shif'less / James Boyd -- Railroad tracks / Emanie N.
Sachs -- Natural selection / Elizabeth Irons Folsom -- Excelsior /
Arthur Collard -- Mirage / Elaine Sterne -- Masters of ourselves and
ours / Walter B. Pitkin -- The harp and the triphammer / Paul Rand
-- "It's me, O Lord!" / Alma and Paul Ellerbe -- Berghita and the
Americans / Rolla Prideaux -- "Colonel, meet my mother" / Alma
and Paul Ellerbe -- The mask / Worth Tuttle -- The monument / Vara
M. Jones -- The case of Doctor Ford / Clement Wood.
LC: Ap 2, '23.

A-326   Asch, Nathan, 1902-1964. The office / by Nathan
Asch. New York: Harcourt, Brace and Company,
[c1925].
265 p.
LC: O 2, '25.
PW: O 3, '25.
BLC: London: R. Holden & Co.; printed in U. S.
A., 1926.

Asch, Shalom. A Jewish child. In Yiddish tales
(1912), Y-20.

____ A scholar's mother. In Yiddish tales (1912),
Y-20.
____ A simple story. In Yiddish tales (1912), Y-20.

____ The sinner. In Yiddish tales (1912), Y-20.

Ashby, Sara. Yesterday - a toast. In *California story book* **(1909), C-40.**

A-327 Ashby, William M. (William Mobile), b. 1889. Redder blood; a novel / by William M. Ashby. New York: The Cosmopolitan Press, 1915. 188 p. Unexamined copy: bibliographic data from NUC. PW: Jl 17, '15.

Ashe, Elizabeth. Blue reefers. In *Atlantic narratives*; **2nd series (1918), A-361.**

_____ The glory-box. In *Atlantic narratives*; **first series (1918), A-360.**

A-328 Ashmun, Margaret Eliza, 1875-1940. The lake / by Margaret Ashmun. New York: The Macmillan Company, 1924. 300 p. LC: S 17, '24. PW: S 13, '24. BLC: London: Macmillan & Co.; printed in U. S. A., 1924. [British title: *The lonely lake*.]

A-329 _____ Support / by Margaret Ashmun. New York: The Macmillan Company, 1922. 357 p. Unexamined copy: bibliographic data from NUC. LC: O 18, '22. BLC: London: Hurst & Blackwell, [1923].

A-330 _____ Topless towers: a romance of Morningside Heights / by Margaret Ashmun. New York: The Macmillan Company, 1921. 307 p. LC: O 21, '21. PW: N 26, '21.

A-331 Ashton, Mark. Azalim: a romance of Old Judea / by Mark Ashton; illustrated. Boston: L. C. Page & Company, 1904. 335 p., col. front., [8] leaves of plates. [Front. "reproduced in colour from the painting by G. Staal".] PW: My 14, '04. BLC: London: Eveleigh Nash, 1904. [British title: *Jezebel's husband: a romance of Old Judea*.]

A-332 _____ She stands alone: the story of Pilate's wife / by Mark Ashton; illustrated. Boston: L. C. Page & Company, 1901. 339 p., front., [11] leaves of plates. PW: Jl 13, '01. BLC: London: Hutchinson & Co., 1900.

A-333 Aspinwall, Alicia. The story of Marie de Rozel, Huguenot / by Alicia Aspinwall . . . New York: E. P. Dutton and Company, 1906. 82 p., front. LC: S 4, '06. PW: O 20, '06.

Aspray, Ruth Muriel. Foam-flowers. In *The best college short stories, 1924-1925* (1925), B-558.

Astro. See **Burgess, Gelett, 1866-1951.**

A-334 Atherton, Gertrude Franklin (Horn), 1857-1948. Ancestors: a novel / by Gertrude Atherton. New York; London: Harper & Brothers, 1907. 708 p. LC: S 25, '07.

PW: O 5, '07. BLC: London: John Murray, 1907.

A-335 _____ The aristocrats; being the impressions of the Lady Helene Pole during her sojourn in the Great north woods as spontaneously recorded in her letters to her friend in North Britain, the Countess of Edge and Ross. London; New York: J. Lane, 1901. 308, [1] p. Unexamined copy: bibliographic data from NUC. PW: Ap 20, '01. [Special limited edition: New York: B. W. Dodge, 1901.]

A-336 _____ The avalanche: a mystery story / by Gertrude Atherton. New York: Frederick A. Stokes Company, [c1919]. 229 p. PW: F 15, '19. BLC: London: John Murray, 1919.

A-337 _____ The bell in the fog: and other stories / by Gertrude Atherton . . . New York; London: Harper & Brothers, 1905. 300, [1] p., photo. front. (port.). Contents: The bell in the fog -- The striding place -- The dead and the countess -- The greatest good of the greatest number -- A monarch of a small survey -- The tragedy of a snob -- Crowned with one crest -- Death and the woman -- A prologue (to an unwritten play) -- Talbot of Ursula. PW: F 18, '05. BLC: London: Macmillan & Co., 1905.

A-338 _____ Black oxen / by Gertrude Atherton. New York: Boni and Liveright, [c1923]. 346 p. LC: F 5, '23. PW: F 3, '23. BLC: London: John Murray, 1923.

_____ Concha Arguello, Sister Dominica. In *The Spinners' book of fiction* **(1907), S-755.**

A-339 _____ The conqueror: being the true and romantic story of Alexander Hamilton / by Gertrude Franklin Atherton. New York: The Macmillan Company; London: Macmillan & Co., Ltd., 1902. 546 p. PW: Mr 29, '02.

A-340 _____ The crystal cup / by Gertrude Atherton. New York: Boni & Liveright, 1925. 315 p., front. (port.). LC: S 4, '25. PW: Ag 22, '25. BLC: London: John Murray, 1925.

A-341 _____ The gorgeous isle: a romance; scene: Nevis, B. W. I., 1842 / by Gertrude Atherton; illustrated by C. Coles Phillips. New York: Doubleday, Page & Company, 1908. 223 p., col. front., [3] leaves of plates. Illustrated end papers. LC: O 5, '08. PW: O 24, '08. BLC: London: John Murray, 1908.

A-342 _____ Julia France and her times: a novel / by Gertrude Atherton. New York: The Macmillan Company, 1912. 533 p. LC: Ap 18, '12. PW: My 4, '12. BLC: London: John Murray, 1912.

A-343 ____ Mrs. Balfame: a novel / by Gertrude
Atherton. New York: Frederick A. Stokes
Company, 1916. 335 p.   **CLE**
[CLE copy: Third printing.]
LC: F 28, '16.
PW: Mr 11, '16.
BLC: London: John Murray, 1916.

A-344 ____ Mrs. Pendleton's four-in-hand / by Gertrude
Atherton . . . New York: The Macmillan Company;
London: Macmillan & Co., Ltd., 1903. 89, [4] p.,
photo. front. (port.), [2] leaves of plates. Designed
end papers. [Ill. by Gordon H. Rant.]
PW: Jl 11, '03
BLC: London: Macmillan & Co., 1903.

A-345 ____ Perch of the devil / by Gertrude Atherton.
New York: Frederick A. Stokes Company, [1914].
373 p.
LC: Ag 31, '14.
PW: Ag 29, '14.
BLC: London: John Murray, 1914.

A-346 ____ Rezánov / by Gertrude Atherton; illustrated in
watercolors. New York; London: The Authors and
Newspapers Association, 1906. 320 p., col. front.,
[4] leaves of col. plates. [Ill. by Frank T. Merrill,
Frank Parker and Frank H. Desch.]
PW: D 15, '06.
BLC: London: John Murray, 1906.

A-347 ____ Rulers of kings: a novel / by Gertrude
Atherton. New York; London: Harper & Brothers,
1904. 412, [1] p.
PW: Ap 23, '04.
BLC: London: Macmillan & Co., 1904.

____ The sacrificial altar. *In The best short stories
of 1916 and the yearbook of the American short
story* (1917), **B-561.**

A-348 ____ The sisters-in law: a novel of our time / by
Gertrude Atherton. New York: Frederick A. Stokes
Company, [c1921]. 341 p.
LC: Ja 31, '21.
PW: Ja 22, '21.
BLC: London: John Murray, 1921.

A-349 ____ Sleeping fires: a novel / by Gertrude Atherton.
New York: Frederick A. Stokes Company, [c1922].
299 p.
British title: *Dormant fires.*
LC: F 2, '22.
PW: F 4, '22.

A-350 ____ The splendid idle forties: stories of old
California / by Gertrude Atherton; with illustrations
by Harrison Fisher. New York: The Macmillan
Comapny; London: Macmillan & Co., Ltd., 1902.
389 p., front., [7] leaves of plates.
Contents: The pearls of Loreto -- The ears of twenty Americans --
The wash-tub mail -- The conquest of Doña Jacoba -- A ramble with
Eulogia -- The isle of skulls -- The head of a priest -- La Pérdida --
Lukari's story -- Natalie Ivanhoff: a memory of Fort Ross -- The
vengeance of Padre Arroyo -- The bells of San Gabriel -- When the
devil was well.
PW: O 18, '02.

A-351 ____ Tower of ivory: a novel / by Gertrude
Atherton. New York: The Macmillan Company,
1910. 466 p.
LC: F 24, '10.
PW: Mr 5, '10.
BLC: London: John Murray, 1910.

A-352 ____ The travelling thirds / by Gertrude Atherton.
London; New York: Harper & Brothers, 1905. 294,
[1] p.
PW: O 21, '05.

____ Two heroines of France. *In For France*
(1917),F-235.

A-353 ____ The white morning: a novel of the power of
the German women in wartime / by Gertrude
Atherton. New York: Frederick A. Stokes
Company, [c1918]. 195 p., front.
LC: F 5, '18.
PW: F 2, '18.

A-354 Atkeson, William O. (William Oscar), b. 1854.
From the Marais des Cygnes: a novel / by William
O. Atkeson . . . ; Illustrated by Helen Walley.
Kansas City, Missouri: Burton Publishing Company,
[c1920]. 343 p., front.   **KFH**
PW: S 4, '20.

A-355 Atkins, E. H. (Elizabeth Helen), b. 1865. Chums /
by E. H. Atkins. Baltimore: Saulsbury Publishing
Company, 1918. 24 p.   **DLC**
LC: O 15, '18.

A-356 Atkinson, Eleanor, 1863-1942. Hearts undaunted: a
romance of four frontiers / by Eleanor Atkinson;
illustrated. New York; London: Harper & Brothers,
[1917]. 348, [1] p., front., [3] leaves of plates. [Ill.
by Frank T. Merrill.]
PW: N 24, '17.

A-357 ____ Johnny Appleseed: the romance of the sower /
by Eleanor Atkinson . . . ; with illustrations by Frank
T. Merrill. New York; London: Harper & Brothers,
1915. 340, [1] p., front., ill.
PW: Ap 3, '15.

A-358 ____ Mamzelle Fifine: a romance of the girlhood of
the Empress Josephine on the island of Martinique /
by Eleanor Atkinson. New York: D. Appleton and
Company, 1903. 396 p., front.
PW: O 31, '03.

A-359 ____ "Poilu": a dog of Roubaix / by Eleanor
Atkinson. New York; London: Harper & Brothers,
[1918]. 224, [1] p., front. [Ill. by Sophie Schneider.]
LC: N 4, '18.
PW: N 23, '18.

Atkinson, Grace Lucie, Mrs. See **Kimball,
Atkinson, jt. pseud. of Kimball, Richard Bowland
and Atkinson, Grace Lucia.**

A-360 Atlantic narratives; modern short stories; edited with
an introduction by Charles Swain Thomas . . .

Boston: The Atlantic Monthly Press, [1918]. 350 p.
Unexamined copy: bibliographic data from NUC.
On cover: First series

Contents: The preliminaries / Cornelia A. P. Comer -- Buttercup-night / J. Galsworthy -- Hepaticas / Anne D. Sedgwick -- Possessing Prudence / Amy W. Stone -- The glory-box / Elizabeth Ashe -- The spirit of the herd / D. L. Sharp -- In the pasha's garden / H. G. Dwight -- Little selves / Mary Lerner -- The failure / C. C. Dobie -- Business is business / H. S. Canby -- Nothing / Zephine Humphrey -- A moth of peace / Katharine F. Gerould -- In no strange land / Katharine Butler -- Little brother / Madeline Z. Doty -- What road goeth he / F. J. Louriet -- The clearer sight / E. Starr -- The garden of memories / C. A. Mercer -- The clearest voice / Margaret Sherwood -- The marble child / E. Nesbit -- The one left / E. V. Lucas -- The legacy of Richard Hughes / Margaret Lynn -- Of water and the spirit / Margaret P. Montague -- Mr. Squem / A. R. Taylor -- Biographical and interpretative notes.

A-361   Atlantic narratives; modern short stories; ed. with an introduction by Charles Swain Thomas . . . 2nd series. Boston: The Atlantic Monthly Press, [c1918]. 390 p.

Contents: The lie / Mary Antin -- Blue reefers / Elizabeth Ashe -- The debt / Kathleen Carman -- Seth Miles and the sacred fire / Cornelia A. P. Comer -- Buried treasure / Mazo De La Roche -- The princess of make-believe / Annie H. Donnell -- The two apples / J. E. Dunning -- The purple star / Rebecca H. Eastman -- Ruggs - R. O. T. C. / W. A. Ganoe -- The way of life / Lucy Huffaker -- A year in a coal-mine / J. Husband -- Woman's sphere / S. H. Kemper -- Babanchik / Christina Krysto -- Rosita / Ellen Mackubin -- Perjured / Edith R. Mirrielees -- What Mr. Grey said / Margaret P. Montague -- A soldier of the legion / E. Morlae -- The Boulevard of Rogues / M. Nicholson -- What happened to Alanna / Kathleen Norris -- Spendthrifts / Laura S. Porter -- Children wanted / Lucy Pratt -- The squire / Elsie Singmaster -- Gregory and the scuttle / C. H. Townsend -- In November / Edith Wyatt -- Biographical and interpretive notes.

Atwater, Caroline, 1853-1939. See **Brooke, Alison, pseud.**

A-362   Atwood, Alfred L. (Alfred Lucas). The Salvation Army girl: a novel / by Alfred L. Atwood. Austin, Minn.: Press of F. C. McCulloch Printing Co., c1914. 48 p.   **DLC**

Atwood, Anne. The aftermath. In *Castle stories* (1908), C-187.

____   For Rome. In *Castle stories* (1908), C-187.

____   An impromptu valentine. In *Castle stories* (1908), C-187.

____   Midsummer eve. In *Castle stories* (1908), C-187.

____   The wanderer. In *Castle stories* (1908), C-187.

Atwood, John Harrison, 1860-1934. See **J. A.**

A-363   Aubert, Marie. Dorothy / by Marie Aubert. Los Angeles: Edwin B. Hammack Printing Service, 1923. 159, [1] p., ill. [Ill. by Edwin Hammack.]   **CLU**

A-364   Augustin, George. The haunted bridal chamber, a romance of old-time New Orleans. By George Augustin . . . New Orleans, La.: The author, [1902]. 249 p.
Unexamined copy: bibliographic data from NUC.

Augustine, William Azariah. See **Frejolity, Azariah, b. 1885, pseud.**

Aumerle, Richard, pseud. See **Maher, Richard Aumerle.**

Aunt Rowena, pseud. See **Sullivan, Josephine Byrne.**

Austin, Benjamin Fish, b. 1850. See **Nitsua, Benjamin, pseud.**

A-365   Austin, John Osborne, 1849-1918. A modern love chase; Peggy Rogers; An incompetent / by John Osborne Austin . . . Rahway, N. J.: Privately printed for the author at The Quinn & Boden Co. Press, [1916]. 395 p., photo. front. (port.)   **NYP**

A-366   ____ Philip and Philippa: a genealogical romance of today / by John Osborne Austin. [Newport, R. I.: Press of Newport Daily News], 1901. 183 p.
LC: Ap 9, '01.
PW: Je 22, '01.

A-367   ____ A week's wooing; and, Dolph and Dolly / by John Osborne Austin . . . New York; London; Montreal: The Abbey Press, [c1902]. 206 p.
                                                                          DLC

A-368   Austin, Martha W. (Martha Waddill). Veronica / by Martha W. Austin. New York: Doubleday, Page & Company, 1903. 256 p.   **CWL**
PW: Mr 14, '03.
BLC: London: Isbister & Co, 1904.

A-369   Austin, Mary Hunter, 1868-1934. The ford / by Mary Austin; with illustrations by E. Boyd Smith. Boston; New York: Houghton Mifflin Company, 1917. (Cambridge: The Riverside Press). 440 p., col. front., [3] leaves of col. plates.
LC: Ap 16, '17.
PW: Ap 21, '17.

____   The ford of Crevecour. In *The Spinners' book of fiction* (1907), S-755.

A-370   ____ The green bough: a tale of the resurrection / by Mary Austin; decorations by Frank Bittner. Garden City, N. Y.: Doubleday, Page & Co., 1913. [40] p. front. Designed end papers.
LC: Mr 11, '13.
PW: Mr 22, '13.

A-371   ____ Isidro / by Mary Austin; illustrated by Eric Pape. Boston; New York: Houghton, Mifflin and Company, 1905. (Cambridge, Mass., U. S. A.: The Riverside Press). 424, [1] p., col. front., [3] leaves of col. plates. Designed end papers.
PW: My 6, '05.
BLC: London: A. Constable & Co.; Cambridge, Mass. printed, 1905.

A-372　　____ Lost borders: illustrated / by Mary Austin . . . New York; London: Harper & Brothers, 1909. 208 p., front., [6] leaves of plates. [Ill. by Denman Fink.]
Contents: The land -- The hood of the Minnietta -- A case of conscience -- The ploughed lands -- The return of Mr. Wills -- The last antelope -- Agua Dulce -- The woman at the Eighteen-mile -- The fakir -- The pocket-hunter's story -- The readjustment -- Bitterness of women -- The house of offence -- The walking woman.
LC: O 29, '09.
PW: N 6, '09.

A-373　　____ The lovely lady / by Mary Austin; frontispiece by Gordon Grant. Garden City, N. Y.: Doubleday, Page & Company, 1913. 272 p., col. front.
LC: N 4, '13.
PW: N 15, '13.

A-374　　[____] No. 26 Jayne Street / by Mary Martin [pseud.]. Boston; New York: Houghton Mifflin Company, 1920. (Cambridge: The Riverside Press). 353, [1] p.
LC: Je 8, '20.
PW: My 22, '20.

A-375　　____ Outland / by Mary Austin. New York: Boni and Liveright, 1919. 306 p.　　**DLM**
LC: D 15, '19.
PW: Ja 17, '20.
[First published in London (J. Murray, 1910) under pseudonym Gordon Stairs.]

A-376　　____ Santa Lucia: a common story / by Mary Austin. New York; London: Harper & Brothers, 1908. 345, [1] p.
LC: Ap 2, '08.
PW: Ap 11, '08.

____ The sturdy oak. In *The sturdy oak* (1917), **S-1101.**

A-377　　____ The trail book / by Mary Austin; with illustrations by Milo Winter. Boston; New York: Houghton Mifflin Company, 1918. (Cambridge: The Riverside Press). 304, [1] p., col. front., [3] leaves of col. plates, ill.　　**MUM**

A-378　　____ A woman of genius / by Mary Austin . . . Garden City, N. Y.: Doubleday, Page & Company, 1912. 510 p.
LC: Ag 30, '12.
PW: Ag 31, '12.

A-379　　Austin, Oscar P. (Oscar Phelps), 1848?-1933. Uncle Sam's children: a story of life in the Philippines / by Oscar Phelps Austin. New York: D. Appleton and Company, 1906. 258 p., front., [15] leaves of plates.　　**NDD**

A-380　　Austin, Walter, b. 1864. William Austin: the creator of Peter Rugg: being a biographical sketch of William Austin: together with the best of his short stories / collected and edited by his grandson, Walter Austin. Boston: Marshall Jones, 1925. 338 p., front., [10] leaves of plates.
Contents: Part I. Biographical sketch. Part II. Stories reproduced: Peter Rugg, the missing man -- The late Joseph Natterstrom -- Martha

Gardner, or moral reaction -- The man with the cloaks -- Appendices.
LC: Ap 24, '25.
PW: My 23, '25.

A-381　　Austrian, Joseph E., b. 1869. "We need the business" / by Joseph E. Austrian; being the letters of Philip Citron, head of the House of Citron, Gumbiner & Co.; with 25 illustrations in black-and-white by Stuart Hay. New York: Frederick A. Stokes Company, [c1919]. 74 p., front., ill.
PW: Ja 31, '20.

A-382　　The autobiography of a woman alone. New York; London: D. Appleton and Company, 1911. 376, [1] p.
PW: S 9, '11.

A-383　　Avery-Stuttle, Lilla Dale, 1855-1933. Shiloh: the man of sorrows / by Mrs. L. D. Avery-Stuttle . . . Boston: Richard G. Badger; Toronto: The Copp Clark Co., Limited, [c1914]. ([Boston]: The Gorham Press). 377 p., front., [7] leaves of plates.　　**EXN**

A-384　　Avirett, James Battle, 1837?-1912. The old plantation: how we lived in great house and cabin before the war / by James Battle Avirett. New York; Chicago; London: F. Tennyson Neely Co., [c1901]. 202 p., front. (port.).
PW: Je 1, '01.

A-385　　Axtell, A. G. (Archie Guy), b. 1868. The legends of the leaves / by A. G. Axtell. Blair, Neb.: The Courier Print, 1904. [28] p.　　**OBE**

A-386　　Ayres, Daisy Fitzhugh. The conquest / by Daisy Fitzhugh Ayres. New York; Washington: The Neale Publishing Company, 1907. 344 p.　　**NYP**
LC: F 26, '07.
PW: Ap 6, '07.

A-387　　Ayres, Mary Morgan. Four Christmases / by Mary Morgan Ayres. [Wilkes-Barre, Pennsylvania: Raeder Press, c1907]. 39 p.　　**NYP**
LC: N 20, '07.
PW: Ja 4, '08.

B

B. H. L. See **Coles, Bertha Horstmann Lippincott, 1880-1963.**

B. K. See **Kalisch, Burnham, 1867-1942.**

B-1　　Babcock, Bernie, 1868-1962. At the mercy of the state / by Bernie Babcock . . . Chicago: The New Voice Press, 1902. 125 p., ill.　　**CKM**
(CKM copy is National Prohibition Press, 1910.)

B-2　　____ Booth and the spirit of Lincoln: a story of a living dead man / by Bernie Babcock. Philadelphia; London: J. B. Lippincott Company, 1925. 320 p.
PW: N 28, '25.

B-3　　____ The coming of the King / by Bernie Babcock. Indianapolis: The Bobbs-Merrill Company, [c1921]. 359 p.

B-4   ____ The devil and Tom Walker-- / by Mrs. Bernie Babcock. Indianapolis, Ind.: Clean Politics Publishing Co., c1911. 15 p.

B-5   ____ Justice to the woman / by Bernie Babcock. Chicago: A. C. McClurg & Co., 1901. 373 p.   **NDD**
PW: S 14, '01.
Revised edition: New York: Broadway Publishing Company, 1903. 311 p., front., [5] leaves of plates. [Ill. by William Lincoln Hudson.]

B-6   ____ The soul of Abe Lincoln / by Bernie Babcock; with a frontispiece in color by Gayle Hoskins. Philadelphia; London: J. B. Lippincott Company, 1923. 328 p., col. front.
PW: Je 9, '23.

B-7   ____ The soul of Ann Rutledge: Abraham Lincoln's romance / by Bernie Babcock; with a frontispiece in color by Gayle Hoskins. Philadelphia; London: J. B. Lippincott Company, 1919. 322, [1] p., col. front.
LC: Jl 1, '19.
PW: Ap 26, '19.

B-8   Babcock, C. E. (Charles Edwin), b. 1840. The persecution of Stephen Strong / by Rev. C. E. Babcock, Ph.D. New York: Broadway Publishing Co., [c1908]. 145 p., front. [Ill. by William L. Hudson.]

Babcock, Edwina Stanton. Cruelties. In *The best short stories of 1918 and the yearbook of the American short story* (1919), **B-563.**

    ____ The excursion. In *The best short stories of 1917 and the yearbook of the American short story* (1918), **B-562.**

    ____ Gargoyle. In *The best short stories of 1920 and the yearbook of the American short story* (1921), **B-565.**

    ____ Mr. Cardeezer. In *The best short stories of 1923 and the yearbook of the American short story* (1924), **B-568.**

    ____ The strange flower. In *Short stories for class reading* (1925), **S-461.**

B-9   ____ Under the law / by Edwina Stanton Babcock; frontispiece by Ralph P. Coleman. Philadephia: The Penn Publishing Company, 1923. 359 p., front.
LC: Ja 15, '23.
PW: Ja 27, '23.

    ____ Wavering gold. In *The Harper prize short stories* (1925), **H-233.**

    ____ Willum's vanilla. In *The best short stories of 1919 and the yearbook of American short story* (1920), **B-564.**

B-10   Babcock, George. Yezad: a romance of the unknown / by George Babcock. Bridgeport, Conn.; New York, N. Y.: Co-operative Publishing Co., [c1922]. 463 p.
LC: N 28, '22.
PW: D 9, '22.

B-11   Babcock, William Henry, 1849-1922. Kent Fort Manor: a novel / by William Henry Babcock . . . Philadelphia: Henry T. Coates & Co., 1902. 393 p., front.
PW: D 20, '02; Ap 11, '03 [1903 printing]

B-12   ____ The tower of Wye: a romance / by William Henry Babcock. Philadelphia: Harry T. Coates & Co., 1901. 330 p., front., [3] leaves of plates. [Ill. by George Gibbs.]
PW: My 4, '01.

Babcock, Winnifred (Eaton), Mrs., b. 1879. See Watanna, Onoto, pseud.

Bachelder, Charlotte Carr, jt. aut. *Annals of Pollock's Cove* (1902). See **Eaton, Isabel Graham, b. 1845, jt. aut., E-16.**

B-13   Bacheller, Irving, 1859-1950. "Charge it", or, Keeping up with Harry: a story of fashionable extravagance and of the successful efforts to restrain it made by the Honorable Socrates Potter, the genial friend of Lizzie / by Irving Bacheller. New York; London: Harper & Brothers, 1912. 191, [1] p., front., [5] leaves of plates. [Ill. by W. H. D. Koerner.]
LC: S 7, '12.
PW: S 21, '12.

B-14   ____ Darrel of the Blessed Isles / by Irving Bacheller; illustrated by Arthur I. Keller. Boston: Lothrop Publishing Company, [1903]. 410 p., front.
PW: Ap 25, '03.
BLC: London: A. P. Watt & Co., 1903.

B-15   ____ D'ri and I: a tale of daring deeds in the second war with the British. Being the memoirs of Colonel Ramon Bell, U. S. A. / by Irving Bacheller; illustrated by F. C. Yohn. Boston: Lothrop Publishing Company, [c1901]. 362 p., front., [7] leaves of plates.
BLC: London: Grant Richards, 1901.

B-16   ____ Eben Holden's last day a-fishing / by Irving Bacheller. New York; London: Harper & Brothers, 1907. 60 p., front. [Ill. by H. S. Potter.]
LC: S 11, '07.
PW: S 21, '07.

B-17   ____ Father Abraham / by Irving Bacheller . . . Indianapolis: The Bobbs-Merrill Company, [c1925]. 419 p.
LC: Mr 2, '25.
PW: F 21, '25.
BLC: London: Hutchinson, [1925].

B-18   ____ The hand-made gentleman: a tale of the battles of peace / by Irving Bacheller. New York; London: Harper & Brothers, 1909. 331, [1] p., front., [1] leaf of plates.

LC: Ap 15, '09.
PW: Ap 24, '09.

B-19 ____ In the days of Poor Richard / by Irving Bacheller; illustrated by John Wolcott Adams. Indianapolis: The Bobbs-Merrill Company, [c1922]. 414 p., front., [5] leaves of plates.
LC: Jl 19, '22.
PW: Jl 8, '22.
BLC: London: Hutchinson & Co., [1923].

B-20 ____ Keeping up with Lizzie / by Irving Bacheller; illustrated by W. H. D. Koerner. New York; London: Harper & Brothers, 1911. 157, [1] p., front., [11] leaves of plates.
LC: Mr 4, '11.
PW: Mr 11, '11.

B-21 ____ Keeping up with William: in which the Honorable Socrates Potter talks of the relative merits of sense common and preferred / by Irving Bacheller; with cartoons by Gaar Williams. Ndianapolis: The Bobbs-Merrill Company, [c1918]. 144, [1] p., front., [7] leaves of plates.
LC: Je 24, '18.

B-22 ____ The light in the clearing: a tale of the North Country in the time of Silas Wright / by Irving Bacheller; illustrated by Arthur I. Keller. Indianapolis: The Bobbs-Merrill Company, [c1917]. 414, [1] p., front., [3] leaves of plates.
PW: Ap 14, '17.
BLC: London: W. Collins & Sons, [1918].

B-23 ____ A man for the ages: a story of the builders of democracy / by Irving Bacheller; illustrated by John Wolcott Adams. Indianapolis: Bobbs-Merrill Company, [c1919]. 416 p., front., [21] leaves of plates.
LC: D 6, '19.
PW: D 6, '19.
BLC: London: Constable & Co., 1920.

B-24 ____ The marryers: a history gathered from a brief of the Honorable Socrates Potter / by Irving Bacheller; illustrated. New York; London: Harper & Brothers, 1914. 216, [1] p., front., [3] leaves of plates. [Ill. by F. M. Spiegle.]
LC: Ap 22, '14.
PW: Ap 25, '14.

B-25 ____ The master: being in part copied from the minutes of the school for novelists, a round table of good fellows who, long since, dined every Saturday at the Sign o' the lanthorne, on Golden hill in New York City / by Irving Bacheller. New York: Doubleday, Page & Company, 1909. 302 p.
LC: O 22, '09.
PW: N 6, '09.
BLC: London: Doubleday, Page & Co; New York printed, 1909.

B-26 ____ The prodigal village: a Christmas tale / by Irving Bacheller. Indianapolis: The Bobbs-Merrill Company, [c1920]. 175, [1] p.
LC: N 26, '20.
PW: D 4, '20.

B-27 ____ The Scudders: a story of to-day / by Irving Bacheller. New York: The Macmillan Company, 1923. 201 p.
LC: My 2, '23.
PW: My 26, '23.
BLC: London: Mills & Boon, 1924.

B-28 ____ Silas Strong: emperor of the woods / by Irving Bacheller. New York; London: Harper & Brothers, 1906. 339, [1] p., incl. front.
PW: Mr 24, '06.
BLC: London: T. Fisher Unwin, 1906.

B-29 ____ The turning of Griggsby: being a story of keeping up with Dan'l Webster / by Irving Bacheller; illustrated by Reginald Birch. New York; London: Harper & Brothers, 1913. 150, [1] p., front., [3] leaves of plates.
LC: My 10, '13.
PW: My 17, '13.

B-30 ____ Vergilius: a tale of the coming of Christ / by Irving Bacheller. New York; London: Harper & Brothers, 1904. 278, [1] p.
PW: Ag 20, '04.

B-31 Bachman, Estella, b. 1860. The soul of the world / by Estella Bachman. Pasadena, California: Equitist Publishing House, 1909. 428 p.   **UUM**

B-32 Bachman, J. Fred., b. 1853. Adventures of Patsey Burns / by J. Fred. Bachman . . . Reading, Pa.: I. M. Beaver, 1919. 351 p., photo. front., [7] leaves of photo. plates.

B-33 ____ Charles Moser: a Pennsylvania German boy / by J. Fred. Bachman. Reading, Pa.: I. M. Beaver, 1916. 348 p., photo. front., [6] leaves of photo. plates.

B-34 Bachmann, Robert, b. 1879. The hand of a thousand rings: and other Chinese stories / by Robert Bachmann. New York: Cosmopolis Press, 1924. 252 p.
Contents: The hand of a thousand rings -- As collected by the Tao-Tai -- The comedy of the white rat -- The missing daughter of Chee Tong -- The man in the doorway -- The crimeful chromatics of Nam Sing -- Without consent of the Senate -- The oriental patience of Charlie Yip -- The little snake of the Great White Gods -- The man who never missed.
LC: N 12, '24.
BLC: London: Hutchinson & Co., [1925].

Backus, Emma Henriette Schermeyer. See Backus, Henry, Mrs.

B-35 Backus, Henry, Mrs. The career of Dr. Weaver / by Mrs. Henry Backus; illustrated by William Van Dresser. Boston: L. C. Page & Company, 1913. 379 p., col. front., [3] leaves of plates.
PW: Mr 22, '13.

B-36 Backus, Henry, Mrs. A place in the sun: a story of the making of an American / by Mrs. Henry Backus . . . ; illustrated by William Van Dresser. Boston: The Page Company, 1917. 410 p., col. front., [4] leaves of plates.
PW: My 5, '17.

B-37   Backus, Henry, Mrs. The rose of roses / by Mrs. Henry Backus. Boston: The Page Company, 1914. 356 p.
PW: Je 13, '14.

B-38   Bacon, Alice Mabel, 1858-1918. In the land of the gods: some stories of Japan / by Alice Mabel Bacon. Boston; New York: Houghton, Mifflin and Company, 1905. 273, [1] p.
Contents: The favor of Hachiman -- At the shrine of Fudō -- The blue flame -- The independence of Saburo -- Kitsuné yashiki -- Chokichi's pilgrimage -- The buyer of amé -- The peony lantern -- The lady of the scroll -- How Fumi remembered -- Glossary.
PW: O 21, '05.
BLC: London: A. Constable & Co.; Cambridge, Mass. printed, 1905.

B-39   Bacon, Dolores, 1870-1934, *pseud.* Crumbs and his times / by Dolores Bacon [pseud.]. New York: Doubleday, Page & Company, 1906. 173 p.
LC: Ag 27, '06
PW: O 13, '06.
BLC: London: Doubleday, Page & Co.; New York printed, 1906.

B-40   ____ The diary of a musician / edited by Dolores Marbourg Bacon [pseud.]; pictures by H. Latimer Brown, decorations by Chas. Edw. Hooper. New York: Henry Holt and Company, 1904. 276, [1] p.

B-41   ____ In high places / by Dolores Bacon [pseud.]; illustrated by George L. [i.e. T.] Tobin. New York: Doubleday, Page & Company, 1907. 347 p., front., [3] leaves of plates.
LC: S 28, '07.
PW: O 19, '07.
BLC: London: Doubleday, Page & Co., New York printed, 1907.

B-42   ____ King's divinity / by Dolores Bacon [pseud.] . . . ; with illustrations by Phillipps Ward. New York: Henry Holt and Company, 1906. 349 p., front., [3] leaves of plates.   **OSU, NYP**
LC: S 22, '06.
PW: O 20, '06.

B-43   Bacon, Edward, b. 1866, *pseud*. The last hurdle / by Edward Bacon [pseud.]. New York: The Knickerbocker Press, 1909. 272 p.   **DLC**
LC: Je 11, '09.

B-44   Bacon, Eugenie Jones, b. 1840. The red moon / by Mrs. Eugenie Jones-Bacon. New York; Washington: The Neale Publishing Company, 1910. 152 p.
                                                        DLC
LC: F 16, '10.
PW: Ap 2, '10.

B-45   Bacon, Frank, 1864-1922. Lightnin' / by Frank Bacon; after the play of the same name by Winchell Smith and Frank Bacon; with illustrations from photographs of the play. New York; London: Harper & Brothers, [c1920]. 292 p., front., [3] leaves of plates.
LC: Mr 12, '20.

PW: Mr 20, '20.
BLC: London: T. Fisher Unwin, 1925.

B-46   Bacon, John Harwood, B. 1875. The pursuit of Phyllis / by John Harwood Bacon; with two illustrations by H. Latimer Brown. New York: Henry Holt and Company, 1904. 230 p., front., [1] leaf of plates.
PW: O 1, '04.

B-47   Bacon, Josephine Dodge Daskam, 1876-1961. The biography of a boy / by Josephine Daskam Bacon; with illustrations by Rose O'Neill. New York; London: Harper & Brothers, 1910. 321, [1] p., front., [6] leaves of plates.
LC: Ja 17, '10.
PW: Ja 22, '10.

B-48   ____ Blind Cupid / by Josephine Daskam Bacon. New York; London: D. Appleton and Company, 1923. 352, [1] p.
Contents: Blind Cupid -- Nor iron bars on a cage -- The new Lochinvar -- Crossed wires -- The islanders -- Peter and the stage door -- In September.
LC: F 24, '23.
PW: Mr 10, '23.

B-49   ____ The domestic adventurers / by Josephine Daskam Bacon. New York: Charles Scribner's Sons, 1907. 221 p., front., [7] leaves of plates.
LC: S 12, '07.
PW: S 21, '07.

B-50   ____ Fables for the fair / by Josephine Dodge Daskam. New York: Charles Scribner's Sons, 1901. 125 p. Designed end papers.
Contents: I. The woman who was not athletic -- II. The woman who helped her husband -- III. The woman who used her theory -- IV. The woman who looked ahead -- V. The woman who fell between two figures -- VI. The woman who understood opera -- VII. The woman who made a conquest -- VIII. The woman who made a good wife -- IX. The woman who was too disinterested -- X. The woman who deliberated -- XI. The woman who believed in early rising -- XII. The woman who took advice -- XIII. The woman who took things literally -- XIV. The woman who had broad views -- XV. The woman who mourned her husband -- XVI. The woman who played "Cyrano" -- XVII. The woman who caught the idea -- XVIII. The woman who helped her sister -- XIX. The woman who could not sew -- XX. The woman who married her daughter -- XXI. The woman who could not help herself -- XXII. The woman who bribed her niece -- XXIII. The woman who knew too much -- XXIV. The woman who talked well -- XXV. The woman who adapted herself.
PW: O 19, '01.

B-51   ____ Her fiancé: four stories of college life / by Josephine Daskam (Mrs. Selden Bacon); with illustrations by Elizabeth Shippen Green. Philadelphia: Henry Altemus Company, [1904]. 164 p., front., [4] leaves of plates.
Contents: Her fiancé -- Her little sister -- The adventures of an uncle -- The point of view.
PW: N 12, '04.

B-52   ____ An idyll of All Fool's Day / by Josephine Daskam Bacon; with numerous illustrations by R. M. Crosby. New York: Dodd, Mead and Company, 1908. 120 p., front., [9] leaves of plates.
LC: Ag 21, '08.
PW: N 14, '08.

B-53   ____ The Imp and the Angel / by Josephine Dodge Daskam; illustrated by Bernard J. Rosenmeyer. New York: Charles Scribner's Sons, 1901. 168 p., front., [7] leaves of plates.
Contents: The Imp and the Angel -- The Imp and the drum -- The Imp and the author -- The Imp's matinée -- The Imp's Christmas dinner -- The Imp disposes -- The prodigal Imp.
PW: N 9, '01.
Another copy: Second edition, 1907. "First published in 1901. This edition has an additional story."   **KSU**
Contents: Same contents as 1901 ed. with the additional story *The Imp's Christmas visit.*
LC: S 14, '07.
PW: D 28, '07.

B-54   ____ In the border country / by Josephine Daskam Bacon; Clara Elsene Peck, decorator. New York: Doubleday, Page & Company, 1909. 130 p., front., [3] leaves of plates. Colored illustrated end papers.
PW: O 23, '09.
BLC: London: Doubleday, Page & Co.; New York printed, 1909.

B-55   ____ The inheritance / by Josephine Daskam Bacon; illustrated. New York; London: D. Appleton and Company, 1912. 347, [1] p., front., [3] leaves of plates.
PW: S 7, '12.

        ____ The little silver heart. In *Short stories for class reading* (1925), S-461.

B-56   ____ The luck o' Lady Joan: a fairy tale for women / by Josephine Daskam Bacon; illustrated by Clara Elsene Williams [sic]. Chicago: F. G. Browne & Co., 1913. 58 p., front.
LC: S 27, '13.
PW: O 4, '13.

B-57   ____ The madness of Philip: and other tales of childhood / by Josephine Dodge Daskam; illustrated by F. Y. Cory. New York: McClure, Phillips & Co., 1902. 222, [1] p.
Contents: The madness of Philip -- A study in piracy -- Bobbert's merry Christmas -- The heart of a child -- Ardelia in Arcady -- Edgar, the choir boy uncelestial -- The little god and Dicky.
BLC: London: Phillips & Co.; New York printed, 1902.

B-58   [____] Margarita's soul: the romantic recollections of a man of fifty / by Ingraham Lovell [pseud.]; with illustrations by J. Scott Williams and Whistler butterfly decorations. New York: John Lane Company; London: John Lane, The Bodley Head, 1909. 304 p., front., [15] leaves of plates.
LC: O 7, '09.

B-59   ____ The memoirs of a baby / by Josephine Daskam (Mrs. Selden Bacon); illustrated by F. Y. Cory. New York; London: Harper & Brothers, 1904. 271, [1] p. incl. front.
PW: Ap 16, '04.

B-60   ____ Middle aged love stories / by Josephine Daskam. New York: Charles Scribner's Sons, 1903. 290 p., photo. front. (port.).

Contents: In the valley of the shadow -- A philanthropist -- A reversion to type -- A hope deferred -- The courting of Lady Jane -- Julia the apostle -- Mrs. Dud's sister.
PW: My 2, '03.

B-61   ____ On our hill / by Josephine Daskam Bacon; with illustrations by T. M. and B. T. Bevans. New York: Charles Scribner's Sons, 1918. 336 p., col. front., [3] leaves of col. plates. Illustrated end papers.

B-62   ____ Open market / by Josephine Daskam Bacon; illustration by A. I. Keller. New York; London: D. Appleton Company, 1915. 333, [1] p., front.

B-63   ____ Square Peggy: illustrated / by Josephine Daskam Bacon . . . New York; London: D. Appleton and Company, 1919. 339, [1] p., [4] leaves of plates. [Ill. by Harry Russell Ballinger.]
Contents: Square Peggy -- Comrades in arms -- The ghost of Rosy Taylor -- Alice of the red tape -- The fruits of the Earth -- The film of fate -- Stepping stones -- Merry-go-round -- Quartermastery -- Ru of the reserves.
LC: S 25, '19.

B-64   ____ The strange cases of Dr. Stanchon / by Josephine Daskam Bacon. New York; London: D. Appleton and Company, 1913. 362 p., front. [Ill. by W. J. Aylward.]
Contents: The key -- The children -- The crystal -- The gospel -- The gypsy -- The warning -- The legacy -- The miracle -- The unburied -- The oracles.
LC: Ap 1, '13.
PW: Ap 5, '13.

B-65   ____ Ten to seventeen: a boarding-school diary / by Josephine Daskam Bacon; illustrated. New York; London: Harper & Brothers, 1908. 260 p., front., [13] leaves of plates. [Ill by Elizabeth Shippen Green, Florence Scovel Shinn, Jessie Wilcox Smith and Irma Dérèmeaux.]
LC: Ja 21, '08.

B-66   ____ To-day's daughter / by Josephine Daskam Bacon; illustrated by C. D. Williams. New York; London: D. Appleton and Company, 1914. 348, [1] p., front., [3] leaves of plates.
PW: S 19, '14.

B-67   ____ While Caroline was growing / by Josephine Daskam Bacon; illustrated. New York: The Macmillan Company, 1911. 330 p., [6] leaves of plates. [Ill. by B. J. Rosenmeyer and Maud Tousey.]
LC: Mr 2, '11.

B-68   ____ Whom the gods destroyed / by Josephine Dodge Daskam. New York: Charles Scribner's Sons, 1902. 236 p.
Contents: Whom the gods destroyed -- A wind flower -- When Pipps passed -- The backsliding of Harriet Blake -- A Bayard of Broadway -- A little brother of the books -- The maid of the mill -- The twilight guests.
PW: O 18, '02.

Bacon, Mary Applewhite. His sister. In *Different girls* (1906), D-383.

Bacon, Mary D., b. 1866. See **Bacon, Edward, pseud.**

Bacon, Mary Schell Hoke, 1870-1934. <u>See</u> **Bacon, Dolores, pseud.**

B-69   Bagby, Albert Morris, 1859-1941. Mammy Rosie / by Albert Morris Bagby . . . New York: Published by the author, 1904. 335 p.   **OUN**

B-70   Bagby, Arthur P. Peter Burling, pirate / by Arthur P. Bagby. Philadelphia: Dorrance Publishers, [c1924]. 219 p.   **NYP**
LC: F 27, '24.

B-71   Bagby, Francis Elizabeth Scott. Tuckahoe: a collection of Indian stories and legends / by Mrs. Thos. P. Bagby . . . ; frontispiece by Hudson. New York: Broadway Publishing Co., [c1907]. 83 p., front. [Ill. by William L. Hudson.]   **AZU**

Bagg, Helen F. <u>See</u> **Hall, Jarvis, pseud.**

Bailey, Alice Ward. <u>See</u> **Ward, A. B., b. 1857.**

Bailey, Edith Lawrence (Black). <u>See</u> **Lawrence, Edith, 1870-1912.**

B-72   Bailey, Mathilde Alpuente. Right or wrong: a tale of war and faith / by Mathilde Alpuente Bailey . . . New Orleans: The L. Graham Company, Ltd., 1912. 143 p., [1] leaf of plates.   **EMU**

B-73   Bailey, Paul, b. 1885. The man who turned Mex: and other stories / by Paul Bailey. Philadelphia: Dorrance & Company, [c1924]. 209 p.
Contents: The man who turned Mex -- For the old Bar Three -- That Pony Gulch holdup -- The man of the minute -- Two-hand Harris -- Bearcat Bob butts in.
LC: F 16, '25.
PW: Mr 28, '25.

B-74   Bailey, Temple, 1860?-1953. Contrary Mary / by Temple Bailey; illustrations by Charles S. Corson. Philadelphia: The Penn Publishing Company, 1914. 388 p., col. front., [4] leaves of plates.
LC: Ja 19, '15.
BLC: London: Duckworth & Co., [1916].

B-75   _____ The dim lantern / by Temple Bailey . . . illustrated by Coles Phillips. Philadelphia: The Penn Publishing Company, 1922. 344 p., col. front.   **IAI**
(IAI copy is 3rd printing; verso of t. p. reads "First printing Jan. 1923".)
LC: Ja 15, '23.
PW: Ja 20, '23.
BLC: London: Hurst & Blackett, [1923].

B-76   _____ The gay cockade / by Temple Bailey; frontispiece by C. E. Chambers. Philadelphia: The Penn Publishing Company, 1921. 398 p., col. front.
Contents: The gay cockade -- The hidden land -- White birches -- The emperor's ghost -- The red candle -- Returned goods -- Burned toast -- Petronella -- The canopy bed -- Sandwich Jane -- Lady Crusoe -- A rebellious grandmother -- Wait-for Prince Charming -- Beggars on horseback.
LC: N 3, '21.
PW: N 12, '21.

B-77   _____ Glory of youth / by Temple Bailey; illustrated by Henry Hutt & C. S. Corson. Philadelphia: The Penn Publishing Company, 1913. 331 p., front.   **CGP**
(CGP copy is fourth printing, 1924.)
LC: S 10, '13.
PW: N 29, '13.

B-78   _____ The holly hedge: and other Christmas stories / by Temple Bailey; frontispiece by Nat Little. Philadelphia: The Penn Publishing Company, 1925. 151 p., col. front.
Contents: The candle in the forest -- The tranquil beasts -- Three who stole at Christmas time -- The red candle -- The holly hedge.
LC: O 10, '25.

B-79   _____ Mistress Anne / by Temple Bailey . . . ; illustrations by F. Vaux Wilson. Philadelphia: The Penn Publishing Company, 1917. 307 p., col. front., [3] leaves of plates.   **EEM**
LC: Ap 13, '17.
PW: My 5, '17.

B-80   _____ Peacock feathers / by Temple Bailey; frontispiece by Coles Phillips. Philadelphia: The Penn Publishing Company, 1924. 340, [4] p., front.
LC: Ag 11, '24.
PW: S 20, '24.
BLC: London: Hurst & Blackett, [1925].

B-81   _____ The tin soldier / by Temple Bailey; illustrations by F. Vaux Wilson. Philadelphia: The Penn Publishing Company, 1918. 456 p., front., [3] leaves of plates.
LC: Ja 10, '19.
BLC: London: Skeffington & Son, [1919].

B-82   _____ The tranquil beasts: a Christmas story / Temple Bailey. Philadelphia: The Penn Publishing Company, [c1925]. 36 p.

B-83   _____ The trumpeter swan / by Temple Bailey; illustrated by Alice Barber Stephens. Philadelphia: The Penn Publishing Company, 1920. 386 p., front., [3] leaves of plates.
PW: S 11, '20.
BLC: London: Hurst & Blackett, [1921].

B-84   Baily, R. C. (Rebecca Chalkley). Mabel Thornley; or, The heiress of Glenwood and Glendinning / by R. C. Baily. New York; London; [etc.]: The Abbey Press, [1901]. 271 p.
Unexamined copy: bibliographic data rom NUC.
PW: Mr 29, '02.

B-85   Baily, Waldron, b. 1871. Heart of the Blue Ridge / by Waldron Baily; frontispiece by Douglas Duer. New York: W. J. Watt & Company, [c1915]. 275 p., front.
LC: My 21, '15.
PW: Je 26, '15.

B-86   _____ The homeward trail / by Waldron Baily; illustrations by George W. Gage. New York: W. J. Watt & Company, [c1916]. 314 p., front., [2] leaves of plates.
PW: N 25, '16.

B-87   ____ June gold / by Waldron Baily; frontispiece by Paul Stahr. New York: W. J. Watt & Company, [c1922]. 281 p., front.
LC: Mr 12, '23.
PW: Ag 25, '23.

B-88   ____ When the cock crows / by Waldron Baily; illustrated by G. W. Gage. New York: Bedford Publishing Co., 1918. 303 p., front., [2] leaves of plates.
LC: S 13, '18.
PW: N 30, '18.

B-89   [Baird, Edwin], b. 1886. The city of purple dreams / frontispiece by M. Wilson Craig. Chicago: F. G. Browne & Co., 1913. 411 p., col. front.   **NYP**
LC: S 10, '13.
PW: S 6, '13.
BLC: London: Ward, Lock & Co., 1916.

B-90   ____ Fay / by Edwin Baird. New York: E. J. Clode, [c1923]. 316 p.
LC: O 18, '23.

B-91   Baird, Jean K. (Jean Katharine), 1872-1918. The boy next door / by Jean K. Baird. New York: American Tract Society, [1910]. 214 p., photo. front., [1] leaf of photo. plates.   **OSU, DLC**
LC: S 16, '10.

B-92   ____ The heir of Barachah / by Jean K. Baird. Cincinnati: Monfort & Company, 1911. 164 p.
LC: S 13, '11.

B-93   ____ Sixty-five on time / by Jean K. Baird . . . ; halftones by Arthur De Bebian. Chicago; Akron, Ohio; New York: The Saalfield Publishing Company, [c1909]. 273 p., front., [3] leaves of plates.   **DLC**
LC: O 7, '09.

B-94   Baird, John C. (John Cramner), 1869-1922. Avenelle, or, The lone tree of Arlington / by John C. Baird. Boston: Mayhew Publishing Co., 1907. 187 p.   **DLC**
PW: Je 1, '07.

B-95   ____ The traveler and the grapes / by John C. Baird. New York: Broadway Publishing Co., [c1907]. 258 p., front., [3] leaves of plates. [Ill. by William L. Hudson.]   **CRU**
LC: D 20, '07.

B-96   Baisinger, Sara L. Nightshade; a story of an orphan boy and his sweetheart, who were not afraid, on the Platte, the southwest country, and Mexico / by Sara L. Baisinger. Chicago: W. B. Conkey Publishing Co., 1914. 389 p., incl. col. front.
Unexamined copy: bibliographic data from NUC.

Baker, Emma Eugene Hall. See **Hall, Eugene, pseud.**

B-97   Baker, Estelle. The rose door / by Estelle Baker. Chicago: Charles H. Kerr & Company, 1911.

202 p., front., [3] leaves of plates.
LC: My 29, '11.

B-98   Baker, Etta Iva Anthony. Miss Mystery: a novel / by Etta Anthony Baker; with frontispiece by Wilson C. Dexter. Boston: Little, Brown, and Company, 1913. 370 p., front.
PW: Mr 15, '13.

B-99   Baker, George K. (George Kline), b. 1884. Haliefa / by George K. Baker; illustrated. New York: The Neale Publishing Company, 1913. 94 p., front., [2] leaves of plates.

B-100   Baker, Hebron, Mrs. The Wynastons / by Mrs. Hebron Baker. New York: Broadway Publishing Co., [c1911]. 337 p.
LC: D 29, '11.

Baker, Horace C., jt. ed. See *The best college short stories, 1924-1925* **(1925), B-558.**

B-101   Baker, Josephine Turck. The burden of the strong / by Josephine Turck Baker. Evanston, Illinois: Correct English Publishing Company, [c1915]. 219 p.
PW: S 2, '16.

Baker, Julia Keim. See **Wetherill, J. K. (Julia Keim), b. 1858.**

B-102   Baker, Lorin Lynn, 1884-1934. The broken law: a novel; the story of the love-makers / by Lorin Lynn Baker . . . ; illustrated by Albert T. Reid. Boston: The Roxburgh Publishing Company Inc., [c1914]. 226 p., col. front.

Baker, Louise, Mrs., b. 1858. See **Alien**, pseud.

Baker, Ray Stannard, 1870-1946. See **Grayson, David, pseud.**

B-103   Baker, Robert Melville, b. 1868. The conspiracy / by Robert Baker and John Emerson; illustrated. New York: Duffield & Company, 1913. 327 p., photo. front., [6] leaves of photo. plates.
LC: My 1, '13.
PW: My 31, '13.

B-104   Baker, Solomon. The wisdom of Solomon / certain views as conceived and expressed by Mr. Solomon Baker, storekeeper, Hatch's Harbor. Boston: Privately printed, 1919. 78 p., front. (port.), [10] leaves of plates.

B-105   Balbach, Julia Anna Nenninger, b. 1852. Cupid intelligent / by Julia A. Balbach. New York: Press of J. J. Little & Ives Co., 1910. 198 p., front., [2] leaves of plates.
PW: My 7, '10.

B-106   Balch, Frank. A submarine tour / by Frank Balch. New York: Broadway Publishing Company, [c1905]. 179 p.

B-107 Balch, Mary G. (Mary Gertrude). The stronger light / by Mary G. Balch. Boston; New York: The Cornhill Publishing Company, [c1922]. 255 p., front.
LC: Je 2, '22.
PW: O 28, '22.

B-108 Baldwin, Aaron Dwight. The Gospel of Judas Iscariot / by Aaron Dwight Baldwin. Chicago: Jamieson-Higgins Co., 1902. 429 p.
PW: My 24, '02.

Baldwin, Eleanor. The white Zeppelin. In *Called to the colors and other stories* **(1915), C-50.**

B-109 Baldwin, Faith, 1893-1978. Laurel of Stonystream / by Faith Baldwin. Boston: Small, Maynard & Company, [c1923]. 334 p.

B-110 ____ Magic and Mary Rose / by Faith Baldwin. Boston: Small, Maynard & Company, [c1924]. 321 p.
PW: O 18, '24.

B-111 ____ Mavis of Green Hill / by Faith Baldwin (Mrs. Hugh Hamlin Cuthrell). Boston: Small, Maynard & Company, [c1921]. 272 p.
LC: S 1, '21.
PW: S 24, '21.
BLC: London: Hodder & Stoughton, [1923].

B-112 ____ Those difficult years / by Faith Baldwin . . . Boston: Small, Maynard & Company, [c1925]. 349 p.
LC: My 19, '25.
PW: My 2, '25.
BLC: London: Sampson Low & Co., [1926].

B-113 ____ Thresholds / by Faith Baldwin. Boston: Small, Maynard & Company, [c1925]. 301 p.
LC: O 1, '25.
PW: O 31, '25.
BLC: London: Sampson Low & Co., [1926].

B-114 Baldwin, James, 1841-1925. In my youth: from the posthumous papers of Robert Dudley. Indianapolis: The Bobbs-Merrill Company, [c1914]. 493 p. **OCP**

B-115 ____ The wonder-book of horses / by James Baldwin . . . New York: The Century Co., 1903. 249 p., front., ill. [Ill. by André Castaigne and Max F. Klepper.] **MBS**

B-116 Baldwin, Olivia A. (Olivia Artemisia), 1858-1931. Sita: a story of child-marriage fetters / by Olivia A. Baldwin. New York; Chicago; Toronto; London; Edinburgh: Fleming H. Revell Company, [c1911]. 353 p.
PW: S 16, '11.

B-117 Ball, Eustace Hale, 1881-1931. Traffic in souls: a novel of crime and its cure / Eustace Hale Ball; illustrations from scenes in the photoplay. New York: G. W. Dillingham Company, [c1914]. 289 p., photo. front., [5] leaves of photo. plates. **KFP**
PW: My 30, '14.

B-118 ____ The voice on the wire: a novel of mystery / by Eustace Hale Ball. New York: Hearst's International Library Co., 1915. 325 p., incl. front. [Ill. by Lee Thayer.]
PW: O 23, '15.

B-119 Ball, Frank P. My wondrous dream / by Frank P. Ball. [New York: published by Frank P. Ball, c1923]. 182 p.
LC: Ag 27, '23.

B-120 Ballard, Eva C. She wanted to vote, or, home influences / by Eva C. Ballard. Crawfordsville, Ind.: Brower Bros., 1901. 313 p., [7] leaves of plates. [Ill. by Chas. Dowden.] **KUK**
PW: Mr 8, '02.

B-121 Ballard, Harlan Hoge, 1853-1934. The tiler's jewel / by Harlan Hoge Ballard . . . ; with an ending by Captain William Haskell . . . Boston, Massachusetts: The Stratford Company, 1921. 134 p.
LC: F 19, '21.

Ballard, Ida H. The legend of the River Waste. In *Under Berkeley Oaks* **(1901), U-8.**

Ballard, Robert. See **Sabina, Poppaea, pseud.**

B-122 Ballin, Hugo, 1879-1956. The broken toy / by Hugo Ballin. New York: W. J. Watt & Co., [c1924]. 279 p.
PW: Mr 21, '25.

B-123 ____ The woman at the door / by Hugo Ballin. Hollywood, Calif.: Authors Publishing Corporation, 1925. 347 p.

B-124 Ballou, Clara E. Played on hearts / by Clara E. Ballou . . . New York: J. S. Ogilivie Publishing Company, 1902. 235 p.
Unexamined copy: bibliographic data from NUC.

B-125 Balmer, Edwin, 1883-1959. The achievements of Luther Trant / by Edwin Balmer [and] William MacHarg; illustrated by William Oberhardt. Boston: Small, Maynard & Company, [c1910]. 365 p., front., [8] leaves of plates.
LC: Ap 23, '10.
PW: Ap 16, '10.

____, jt. aut. *The blind man's eyes* (1916). See **MacHarg, William Briggs, b. 1872, jt. aut, M-245.**

B-126 ____ The breath of scandal / by Edwin Balmer; with frontispiece by Ralph P. Coleman. Boston: Little, Brown, and Company, 1922. 360 p., front.
LC: Ag 14, '22.
PW: Ag 26, '22.
BLC: London: E. Arnold & Co., 1923.

B-127 ____ Fidelia / by Edwin Balmer. New York: Dodd, Mead and Company, 1924. 368 p.
LC: Mr 27, '24.
PW: Mr 29, '24.

_____, jt. aut. *Indian drum* (1917). <u>See</u> **MacHarg, William Briggs, b. 1872, jt. aut, M-246.**

B-128   _____ Keeban / by Edwin Balmer. Boston: Little, Brown and Company, 1923. 295 p.
LC: Ap 26, '23.
PW: Ap 28, '23.
BLC: London: E. Arnold & Co., 1923.

B-129   _____ Resurrection rock / by Edwin Balmer; with frontispiece by Anton Otto Fischer. Boston: Little, Brown, and Company, 1920. 383 p., front.
PW: Ag 28, '20.
BLC: London: Hodder & Stoughton; Boston [printed], 1920.

B-130   _____ Ruth of the U. S. A. / by Edwin Balmer; illustratd by Harold H. Betts. Chicago: A. C. McClurg & Co., 1919. 361 p., front., [2] leaves of plates.
LC: Ap 3, '19.
PW: Ap 12, '19.

_____, jt. aut. *Surakarta* (1913). <u>See</u> **MacHarg, William Briggs, b. 1872, jt. aut, M-248.**

B-131   _____ That Royle girl / by Edwin Balmer. New York: Dodd, Mead and Company, 1925. 358 p.
LC: Ag 13, '25.
PW: Ag 15, '25.

B-132   _____ Waylaid by wireless: a suspicion, a warning, a sporting proposition, and a transatlantic pursuit / by Edwin Balmer; illustrated by Edmund Frederick. Boston: Small, Maynard and Company, [c1909]. 348 p., front., [6] leaves of plates.
LC: My 27, '09.
PW: Je 19, '09.

B-133   _____ A wild goose chase / by Edwin Balmer. New York: Duffield & Company, [c1915]. 290 p., front. [Ill. by Albert Matzke.]
LC: Ag 21, '15.
PW: S 11, '15.

B-134   Balmer, Helen Clark. Bellevue sketches and others / Helen Clark Balmer. Chicago: Press of Hollister Brothers, [c1901]. 78 p.
Contents: Bellevue sketches: An old mansion -- The gardens of Bellevue -- The Bellevue portraits -- Bellevue by moonlight -- A misplaced birthday -- A ghost at Bellevue -- A rejuvenation -- Rastus -- A broken reverie -- How the color-line was observed at Bellevue -- Ned's choice -- An aspect of slavery -- A proper perspective -- Ephraim the faithful -- A proxy baptism' -- How the secret became known -- Uncle Eph's release -- Aunt Mari's Easter bonnet -- The Governor's visit -- A judicial arrangement -- The defeat of the conquerors -- A humble philanthropist -- The vicissitude of a clothes line -- A vacation school -- The point of view -- A river scene. Other Virginia sketches: In the land of the sunbonnet -- A study of mountains -- Mandy Lu -- The ministration of Maud -- The case of Jane Emma -- The gypsy's grave -- My pickaninny -- Aunt Dinah's recipe for plum cake -- A fable about gems. Sketches for children: The discontented Fay -- To a belated fly -- The revolt of the fairy -- A legend -- A sage of the campus -- A humble Santa Claus -- Tom Flynn's revenge -- In a hospital -- "Besserheart" -- Pierrot -- A tragedy of Memorial Day -- The voice of the stairs.

B-135   Balshofer, Fred J. Over the Rhine: the world's greatest spy story / written by Fred J. Balshofer and Chas. A. Taylor. New York: Harpoon Publishing Co., Inc., c1918. 31 p.   **DLC**
Cover title: *Over the Rhine, an expose of the Kaiser's spy system.*

B-136   Baltzer, Frederick. Alma mater: a story of college life: written in commemoration of the fiftieth anniversary of Elmhurst College at Elmhurst, Illinois / by Frederick Baltzer . . . St. Louis, Mo.; Chicago, Ill.: Eden Publishing House, 1921. 192 p. **NYP**

B-137   Bancroft, Alberta, b. 1873. Royal rogues / by Alberta Bancroft; illustrated by Louis Betts. New York; London: G. P. Putnam's Sons, ([New York]: The Knickerbocker Press), 1901. 339 p., col. front., [8] leaves of plates.
PW: O 19, '01.

B-138   Bancroft, Griffing, b. 1879. The interlopers: a novel / by Griffing Bancroft; illustrations by Arthur D. Fuller. New York: The Bancroft Company, 1917. 397 p., front., [3] leaves of plates.
PW: Ag 4, '17.

B-139   Bangs, Ella Matthews. The King's mark: a story of early Portland / by Ella Matthews Bangs. Boston [Mass.]: The C. M. Clark Publishing Co., 1908. 344 p., front., [7] leaves of plates. [Ill. by John Goss.]
LC: O 20, '08.
PW: N 14, '08.

B-140   Bangs, John Kendrick, 1862-1922 Alice in Blunderland: an iridescent dream / by John Kendrick Bangs; illustrated by Albert Levering. New York: Doubleday, Page & Company, 1907. 124 p., ill.
LC: S 9, '07.
PW: S 21, '07.
References: BAL 775.

B-141   _____ The autobiography of Methuselah / ed. by John Kendrick Bangs; illustrated in color by F. G. Cooper. New York: B. W. Dodge & Company, 1909. 185 p., col. front., [11] leaves of col. plates.
LC: O 16, '09.
PW: D 25, '09.
References: BAL 781.

_____ Dawson's dilemma. <u>In</u> *A house party* (1901), **H-903.**

B-142   _____ Emblemland / by John Kendrick Bangs and Charles Raymond Macauley. New York: R. H. Russell, 1902. 164 p., front., ill.
LC: D 26, '02.
PW: F 14, '03.
References: BAL 759.

B-143   _____ The genial Idiot: his views and reviews / by John Kendrick Bangs. New York; London: Harper & Brothers Publishers, 1908. 214, [1] p.
LC: O 9, '08.
PW: O 17, '08.
References: BAL 778.

B-144 _____ Half hours with the Idiot / by John Kendrick Bangs. Boston: Little, Brown, and Company, 1917. 156 p.   **OSU, APL**
Contents: As to ambassadors' residences -- As to the fair sex -- He goes Christmas shopping -- As to the income tax -- A psychic venture -- On medical conservation -- The U. S. telephonic aid society -- For tired business men.
LC: My 29, '17.
PW: My 26, '17.
References: BAL 809.

B-145 _____ The inventions of the Idiot / by John Kendrick Bangs. New York; London: Harper & Brothers Publishers, 1904. 184, [1] p.
LC: Ap 14, '04.
PW: Ap 23, '04.
References: BAL 763.

B-146 _____ A little book of Christmas / by John Kendrick Bangs; with illustrations by Arthur E. Becher. Boston: Little, Brown, and Company, 1912. 173 p., col. front., [3] leaves of col. plates.
Contents: The conversion of Hetherington -- The child who had everything but - -- Santa Claus and Little Billee -- The house of the seven Santas.
LC: O 3, '12.
PW: O 26, '12.
References: BAL 793.

_____ Lost and found. In *Short stories from Life* **(1916), S-463.**

_____ Miss Tooker's wedding gift. In *International short stories* **(1910), I-29.**

B-147 _____ Mollie and the unwiseman / by John Kendrick Bangs; illustrations by Albert Levering and Clare Victor Dwiggins. Philadelphia: Henry T. Coates & Co., [1902]. 198 p., front., [7] leaves of plates., ill.
LC: N 10, '02.
PW: N 22, '02.
References: BAL 758.

_____, jt. aut. *Monsieur d'En Brochette* (1905). See **Taylor, Bert Leston, 1866-1921, jt. aut, T-68.**

B-148 _____ Mr. Munchausen: being a true account of some of the recent adventures beyond the Styx of the late Hieronymus Carl Friedrich, sometime Baron Munchausen of Bodenwerder, as originally reported for the Sunday edition of the Gehenna Gazette by its special interviewer the late Mr. Ananias formerly of Jerusalem and now first transcribed from the columns of that journal / by John Kendrick Bangs; embellished with drawings by Peter Newell. Boston: Printed for Noyes, Platt & Company, 1901. 180 p., col. front. (port.), [14] leaves of col. plates.
LC: N 18, '01.
PW: D 7, '01.
BLC: London: Grant Richards; Albany, N. Y. [printed 1903].
References: BAL 753.

B-149 _____ Mrs. Raffles: being the adventures of an amateur crackswoman, narrated by Bunny / edited by John Kendrick Bangs; illustrated by Albert Levering. New York; London: Harper & Brothers Publishers, 1905. 179, [1] p., front., [15] leaves of plates.
LC: O 5, '05.
PW: O 21, '05.
References: BAL 769.

B-150 _____ Olympian nights / by John Kendrick Bangs. New York; London: Harper & Brothers Publishers, 1902. 223, [1] p., front., [15] leaves of plates. [Ill. by Albert Levering.]
LC: Je 12, '02.
PW: Je 21, '02.
References: BAL 756.

B-151 _____ Over the plum-pudding / by John Kendrick Bangs; illustrated. New York; London: Harper & Brothers, 1901. 244, [1] p., front. (port.), [16] leaves of plates. Designed end papers. [Ill. Gustave Verbeck, et al.]
(Harper's portrait collection of short stories; v. 6.)
Contents: "Over the plum-pudding" -- Bills, M. D. -- The flunking of Watkins's ghost -- An unmailed letter -- The Amalgamated Brotherhood of Spooks -- A glance ahead -- Hans Pumpernickel's vigil -- The affliction of Baron Humpfelhimmel -- A great composer -- How Fritz became a wizard -- Rise and fall of the poet Gregory -- The loss of the "Gretchen B."
LC: O 26, '01.
PW: N 2, '01.
References: BAL 752.

B-152 _____ Potted fiction: being a series of extracts from the world's best sellers, put up in thin slices for hurried consumers / the United States Literary Canning Co.; edited by John Kendrick Bangs. New York: Doubleday, Page & Co., 1908. 132 p.   **EEM**
LC: Jl 27, '08.
PW: S 19, '08.
BLC: London: Doubleday, Page & Co.; printed in U. S. A., 1908.
References: BAL 777.

B-153 _____ R. Holmes & Co.: being the remarkable adventures of Raffles Holmes, Esq., detective and amateur cracksman by birth / by John Kendrick Bangs; illustrated by Sydney Adamson. New York; London: Harper & Brothers, 1906. 230, [1] p., front., [5] leaves of plates.
LC: Je 12, '06.
PW: Je 23, '06.
References: BAL 771.

_____, contributor. See *The whole family* (1908), **W-578.**

B-154 Bangs, Mary Rogers. High Bradford / by Mary Rogers Bangs; with illustrations. Boston; New York: Houghton Mifflin Company, 1912. (Cambridge: The Riverside Press). 222, [2] p., ill.
LC: My 1, '12.
PW: My 4, '12.

B-155 Banister, Corrilla. I'm a brick: a Congress of Religions / Corrilla Banister. Boston: Banner of Light Pub. Co., 1901. 155 p., front.   **BHA**
[Reprinted as A modern miracle: psychic power made plain, New York: The Grafton Press, [c1905].]

Bank, Carl, Mrs. Jane Ann, A ward of the state. <u>In</u> *West winds* **(1914), W-368.**

B-156   Banks, Charles Eugene, 1852-1932. John Dorn: promoter / by Charles Eugene Banks . . . ; illustrations by August Abelmann. Chicago: Monarch Book Company, [c1906]. 361 p., front., [16] leaves of plates.
PW: Mr 2, '07.

B-157   Banks, Edgar James, 1866-1945. An Armenian princess: a tale of Anatolian peasant-life / by Edgar James Banks. Boston: The Gorham Press; Toronto: The Copp Clark Co., Limited, [c1914]. 252 p.

B-158   Banks, Elizabeth L., 1870-1938. The autobiography of a "newspaper girl" / by Elizabeth L. Banks . . . New York: Dodd, Mead and Company, 1902. 317 p., photo. front. (port.).
BLC: London: Methuen & Co., 1902.

B-159   ____ The mystery of Frances Farrington / by Elizabeth Banks . . . New York: [s. n.], 1909. 77, [1] p.
Unexamined copy: bibliographic data from NUC.
LC: Mr 11, '09.
BLC: London: Hutchinson & Co., 1909.

B-160   ____ School for John and Mary: A story of caste in England / by Elizabeth Banks. London; New York: G. P. Putnam's Sons, 1924. 314 p.   **CWR**

B-161   Banks, Nancy Huston. The little hills / by Nancy Huston Banks. New York: The Macmillan Company; London: Macmillan & Co., Ltd., 1905. 325 p.
PW: Jl 1, '05.

B-162   ____ Oldfield: a Kentucky tale of the last century / by Nancy Huston Banks. New York: The Macmillan Company; London: Macmillan & Co., Ltd., 1902. 431 p.
[LC notes copy 2 with col. front. and col. plates.]
PW: Je 7, '02.

B-163   ____ Round Anvil Rock: a romance / by Nancy Huston Banks. New York: The Macmillan Company; London: Macmillan & Co., 1903. 356 p., front., [5] leaves of plates. [Ill. by Gordon H. Grant.]
PW: S 5, '03.

B-164   Banning, Margaret Culkin, b. 1891. Country club people / by Margaret Culkin Banning. New York: George H. Doran, [c1923]. 308 p.
LC: My 3, '23.
PW: Ap 28, '23.

B-165   ____ Half loaves / by Margaret Culkin Banning . . . New York: George H. Doran Company, [c1921]. 312 p.
LC: Ap 27, '21.
PW: Ap 16, '21.

B-166   ____ A handmaid of the Lord / by Margaret Culkin Banning. New York: George H. Doran Company,

[c1924]. 320 p.
LC: S 23, '24.
PW: S 20, '24.
BLC: London: Hurst & Blackett, [1925].

B-167   ____ Spellbinders / by Margaret Culkin Banning. New York: George H. Doran Company, [c1922]. 290 p.
LC: O 5, '22.
PW: S 9, '22.

B-168   ____ This marrying / by Margaret Culkin Banning. New York: George H. Doran Company, [c1920]. 290 p.
LC: Mr 27, '20.
PW: Ap 3, '20.
BLC: London: Hodder & Stoughton; printed in U. S. A., [1920].

____ Women come to judgment. <u>In</u> *The Harper prize short stories* **(1925), H-233.**

Banta, Adele Weber. <u>See</u> **Weber, Adele.**

Barbara, pseud. <u>See</u> **Wright, Mabel Osgood, 1859-1934.**

B-169   Barber, Eli. Home memories / by Eli Barber. Boston: Richard G. Badger, 1908. (Boston: The Gorham Press). 420 p.
LC: F 18, '08.
PW: Ap 18, '08.

B-170   ____ Margaret Ives / by Eli Barber. Boston: The Gorham Press; Toronto: The Copp Clark Co., Limited, [c1915]. 381 p.   **DLC**
LC: D 1, '15.
PW: N 27, '15.

B-171   Barber, Emma Spencer. Mildred Tucker / by Mrs. Emma Spencer Barber. Parkersburg [W. Va.]: Printed by the Baptist Banner Publishing Co., 1923. 130 p.

B-172   Barber, Marcin. Britz, of headquarters / by Marcin Barber. New York: Moffat, Yard and Company, 1910. 394 p.
LC: My 28, '10.
PW: Je 4, '10.

B-173   Barbour, A. Maynard (Anna Maynard), d. 1941 *pseud.* At the time appointed / by A. Maynard Barbour [pseud.]; with a frontispiece by J. N. Marchand. Philadelphia; London: J. B. Lippincott Company, 1903. 371 p., col. front.
PW: Je 6, '03.

B-174   ____ Breakers ahead / by A. Maynard Barbour [pseud.] . . . ; with frontispiece by James L. Wood. Philadelphia; London: J. B. Lippincott Company, 1906. 335 p., col. front.
PW: Je 16, '06.

B-175   ____ That Mainwaring affair / by A. Maynard Barbour [pseud.] . . . ; illustrated by E. Plaisted

Abbott. Philadelphia; London: J. B. Lippincott Company, 1901, [c1900]. 362 p., front., [3] leaves of plates.
PW: N 10, '00.
BLC: London: Ward, Lock & Co., 1901.

Barbour, Anna May. See **Barbour, A. Maynard (Anna Maynard), pseud.**

B-176   Barbour, Ralph Henry, 1870-1944. Cupid en route / Ralph Henry Barbour; illustrations by F. Foster Lincoln; decorations by Albert D. Blashfield. Boston: Richard G. Badger, [c1912]. (Boston, U. S. A.: The Gorham Press). 200 p., col. front., [7] leaves of plates. Illustrated end papers.
LC: S 19, '12.
PW: S 21, '12.

B-177   _____ Fortunes of war / by Ralph Henry Barbour and H. P. Holt . . . ; illustrated by C. M. Relyea. New York: The Century Co., 1919. 352 p., front., [3] leaves of plates.
LC: S 2, '19.
PW: S 20, '19.

B-178   _____ The golden heart / by Ralph Henry Barbour; with illustrations in color by Clarence F. Underwood and decorations by Edward Stratton Holloway. Philadelphia; London: J. B. Lippincott Company, 1910. 218 p., incl. col. front., [4] leaves of col. plates. Illustrated end papers.
LC: O 4, '10.
PW: N 12, '10.

B-179   _____ The harbor of love / by Ralph Henry Barbour; with illustrations in color by George W. Plank and decorations by Edward Stratton Holloway. Philadelphia; London: J. B. Lippincott Company, 1912. 161, [1] p., col. front., [3] leaves of col. plates.
LC: O 22, '12.
PW: N 9, '12.

B-180   _____ Heart's content / by Ralph Henry Barbour; with illustrations in color by H. Weston Taylor, and decorations by Edward Stratton Holloway. Philadelphia; London: J. B. Lippincott Company, 1915. 204 p., col. front., [3] leaves of col. plates.
LC: O 18, '15.
PW: O 23, '15.

B-181   _____ Holly: the romance of a southern girl / by Ralph Henry Barbour; with illustrations by Edwin F. Bayha. Philadelphia; London: J. B. Lippincott Company, 1907. 294, [1] p., col. front., [3] leaves of col. plates.
LC: O 16, '07.
PW: N 9, '07.

B-182   _____ The house in the hedge / by Ralph Henry Barbour; illustrated by Gertrude A. Kay. New York: Moffat, Yard and Company, 1911. 251 p., col. front., [3] leaves of plates.
LC: Je 3, '11.
PW: Je 3, '11.

B-183   _____ Joan of the island / by Ralph Henry Barbour and H. P. Holt. Boston: Small, Maynard & Company, [c1920]. 292 p.
LC: Mr 17, '20.
PW: My 8, '20.

B-184   _____ Joyce of the jasmines / by Ralph Henry Barbour; with illustrations in color by Clarence F. Underwood and decorations by Edward Stratton Holloway. Philadelphia; London: J. B. Lippincott Company, 1911. 204, [1] p., col. front., [4] leaves of col. plates. Designed end papers.
LC: N 6, '11.
PW: N 4, '11.

B-185   _____ Kitty of the roses / by Ralph Henry Barbour; with illustrations by Frederic J. von Rapp. Philadelphia; London: J. B. Lippincott, 1904. 173, [1] p., col. front., [4] leaves of col. plates.
PW: D 17, '04.

B-186   _____ Lady laughter / by Ralph Henry Barbour; with illustrations in color by Gayle Hoskins and decorations by Edward Stratton Holloway. Philadelphia; London: J. B. Lippincott Company, 1913. 176 p., col. front., [3] leaves of col. plates.
LC: D 3, '13.
PW: N 8, '13.

B-187   _____ The land of joy / by Ralph Henry Barbour. New York: Doubleday, Page & Company, 1903. 416 p.
PW: My 23, '03.
BLC: London: Hutchinson & Co.; New York printed, 1903.

B-188   _____ The lilac girl / by Ralph Henry Barbour; with illustrations in color by Clarence F. Underwood and decorations by Edward Stratton Holloway. Philadelphia; London: J. B. Lippincott Company, 1909. 236 p., col. front., [4] leaves of col. plates. Designed end papers.
LC: O 29, '09.
PW: N 6, '09.

B-189   _____ A maid in Arcady / by Ralph Henry Barbour; with illustrations by Frederic J. von Rapp. Philadelphia; London: J. B. Lippincott Company, 1906. 213, [1] p., col. front., [8] leaves of col. plates.
LC: O 1, '06.
PW: Ja 26, '07.

B-190   _____ My lady of the fog / by Ralph Henry Barbour; with twelve illustrations by Clarence F. Underwood and decorations by Edward Stratton Holloway. Philadelphia; London: J. B. Lippincott Company, 1908. 219, [1] p., front., [11] leaves of plates (some col.).
LC: S 8, '08.
PW: N 7, '08.

B-191   _____ An orchard princess / by Ralph Henry Barbour; with illustrations by James Montgomery Flagg. Philadelphia; London: J. B. Lippincott Company, 1905. 219 p., col. front., [3] leaves of col. plates.
PW: O 28, '05.

B-192 _____ Peggy-in-the-Rain / by Ralph Henry Barbour; illustrated. New York; London: D. Appleton and Company, 1913. 244, [1] p., front., [3] leaves of plates. [Ill. by Edmund Frederick.] **NYP**
LC: My 13, '13.
PW: My 17, '13.

_____ Soft ice. In *The Sporting spirit* (1925), S-770.

_____ Thicker than water. In *Short stories from Life* **(1916), S-463.**

B-193 Barcus, James S. The governor's boss / by James S. Barcus; novelized from the play "The governor's boss" by the author; frontispiece illustration by Lawrence Harris. New York: The Boss Publishing Co., 1914. 275 p., front., [5] leaves of plates.
LC: Ap 15, '14.

B-194 Bardeen, C. W. (Charles William), 1847-1924. The black hand: and other stories about schools / by C. W. Bardeen . . . Syracuse, N. Y.: C. W. Bardeen, c1914. 181 p. **GZT**
Cover title: *Stories of the school room.* Contents: The black hand -- Tide and untied -- Upper 12 -- A lost identity -- A sensitive plant -- By the campfire.
LC: D 21, '14.
PW: Ja 23, '15.

B-195 _____ Castiron Culver: and other stories about schools / by C. W. Bardeen . . . Syracuse, N. Y.: C. W. Bardeen Publisher, c1921. 245 p. **NYP**
PW: Ag 6, '21.

B-196 _____ The cloak room thief: and other stories about schools / by C. W. Bardeen . . . Syracuse, N. Y.: C. W. Bardeen, 1906. 226 p. **KEU**
"These stories appeared in the School bulletin during the year 1906."
Contents: The cloak room thief -- The verbs in mi -- Miss Ripley's point of view -- The bogus twenties -- The widow's might -- Commencement night -- Hopelessly heartless.
LC: Mr 25, '08.
PW: D 29, '06.

B-197 _____ Coykendall Webb: and other stories about schools / by C. W. Bardeen . . . Syracuse, N. Y.: C. W. Bardeen, [c1919]. 234 p. **DLC**
Cover title: *Stories of the school room, Coykendall Webb.* Contents: Coykendall Webb -- Agatha's prayer -- Fair warning -- Made in Germany -- A recovery -- Unconscious tuition -- The Trimble twins -- A superior woman.
LC: N 19, '19.
PW: F 7, '20.

B-198 _____ The false entry: and other stories about schools / by C. W. Bardeen . . . Syracuse, N. Y.: C. W. Bardeen, 1905. 244 p.
"These stories appeared in the School bulletin during the year 1905."
Contents: The false entry -- Debora's defeat -- The lightning calculator -- The Dunlap hat -- On the make.
PW: F 10, '06.

B-199 _____ Fifty-five years old: and other stories about teachers / by C. W. Bardeen . . . Syracuse, N. Y.: C. W. Bardeen, c1904. 216 p. **INT**

"These stories appeared in the successive monthly issues of the School bulletin from January to June, 1904."
Contents: Fifty-five years old -- Miss Fothergill's protest -- The new vice-principal -- The Alpha Upsilon Society -- The haunted schoolhouse -- Miss Trumbull's triumph.
PW: Jl 30, '04.

B-200 _____ Geraldine's saints: and other stories about schools / by C. W. Bardeen . . . Syracuse, N. Y.: C. W. Bardeen, c1915. 234 p. **DLC**
Cover title: *Stories of the school room, Geraldine's saints.* Contents: Geraldine's saints -- Around the world -- The Greenleaf mystery -- The president exaggerated -- A hot-house flower -- The stolen regents paper.
LC: Ag 9, '15.
PW: S 18, '15.

B-201 _____ The girl from Girton: and other stories about schools / by C. W. Bardeen. Syracuse, N. Y.: C. W. Bardeen, [c1914]. 235 p. **DLC**
Cover title: *Stories of the school room.* Contents: The girl from Girton -- Call no man happy -- The bully bewildered -- A fight to finish -- A story without names -- The man who couldn't.
LC: D 21, '14.
PW: D 26, '14.

B-202 _____ John Brody's astral body: and other stories about schools / by C. W. Bardeen . . . Syracuse, N. Y.: C. W. Bardeen, 1908. 195 p. **PAU**
"These stories appeared in the School bulletin during the years 1906-7-8."
Contents: John Brody's astral body -- The teacherette -- Her mother's daughter -- In the clouds -- When Greek meets Greek -- Bumptious Bill.
LC: D 31, '08.

B-203 _____ Little Bok: and other stories about schools / by C. W. Bardeen . . . Syracuse, N. Y.: C. W. Bardeen, [c1917]. 210 p. **DLC**
Cover title: *Stories of the school room, Little Bok.* Contents: Little Bok -- At the Biltmore -- The scientific spirit -- Two women's tongues -- In the laboratory -- Behind schedule -- The blank letter.
LC: O 22, '17.
PW: D 1, '17.

B-204 _____ Ruby Floyd's temptation: and other stories about schools / by C. W. Bardeen . . . Syracuse, N. Y.: C. W. Bardeen, [c1915]. 216 p. **NYP**
Contents: Ruby Floyd's temptation -- The tenth commandment -- The hold-up -- A merry soul -- A matter of marking -- Three months notice.
LC: Ja 3, '16.
PW: F 5, '16.

B-205 _____ The shattered halo: and other stories about schools / by C. W. Bardeen . . . Syracuse, N. Y.: C. W. Bardeen, c1913. 250 p. **GZT**
Cover title: *Stories of the school room, The shattered halo.* Contents: The shattered halo -- Colonel Bob's experiment -- Sandy Sam -- The block Y -- A strike and a spare -- The Rockingham rebellion -- Downright David -- The spirit summons.
LC: Ap 7, '13.
PW: Ap 12, '13.

B-206 _____ A single session: and other stories about schools / by C. W. Bardeen . . . Syracuse, N. Y.:

C. W. Bardeen, [c1916]. 208 p.   **DLC**
Cover title: *Stories of the school room, A single
session.* Contents: A single session -- The vanished check --
Eleven to one -- The poisoned pen -- Plot and counterplot -- The face
that followed.
LC: D 22, '17.
PW: D 1, '17.

B-207   ____ The trial balance: and other stories about
schools / by C. W. Bardeen . . . Syracuse, N. Y.:
C. W. Bardeen, c1913. 229 p.   **WAU**
Contents: The trial balance -- The Ossahinta scimitar -- The trouser-
pocket thief -- Put off at Buffalo -- Tried and found wanting -- The
cashier's prophecy.
LC: D 26, '13.
PW: My 2, '14.

B-208   ____ The woman trustee: and other stories about
schools / by C. W. Bardeen. Syracuse, N. Y.: C.
W. Bardeen, 1904. 259 p.
"These stories appeared in the successive monthly
issues of the School bulletin from July to December,
1904."
Contents: The woman trustee -- Without credentials -- Jot, the janitor
-- The masterful man -- On a pedestal -- Miss Dusinberrie's downfall.
PW: D 24, '04.

B-209   ____ The yellow streak: and other stories about
schools / by C. W. Bardeen . . . Syracuse, N. Y.: C.
W. Bardeen, Publisher, c1912. 255 p.   **UND**
Contents: The yellow streak -- Under arrest -- The January regents --
Miss Queroot -- How he became Professor Piper -- A hireling -- The
set of Tennyson.
LC: Ag 31, '12.
PW: S 21, '12.

B-210   Barker, Bruce, b. 1875, *pseud.* "Young Honesty" -
politician: being the story of how a young ranchman
helped to elect his father congressman / by Bruce
Barker [pseud.]; illustrated by John Goss. Boston;
Chicago: W. A. Wilde Company, [c1912]. 308 p.,
col. front.
LC: S 13, '12.
PW: S 21, '12.

B-211   Barker, Elsa, 1869-1954. Fielding Sargent: a novel /
by Elsa Barker. New York: E. P. Dutton &
Company, [c1922]. 319 p.
LC: O 30, '22.
PW: O 14, '22.

B-212   ____ Letters from a living dead man / written down
by Elsa Barker; with an introduction. New York:
Mitchell Kennerley, 1914. 291 p.
LC: Ap 29, '14.
BLC: London: W. Rider & Son, 1914.

B-213   ____ The son of Mary Bethel / by Elsa Barker.
New York: Duffield & Company, 1909. 549 p.
LC: S 8, '09.
BLC: London: Chatto & Windus, 1909.

B-214   ____ War letters from the living dead man: with an
introduction / written down by Elsa Barker. New
York: Mitchell Kennerley, 1915. 318 p., [1] leaf of
photo. plates (port.).
BLC: London: W. Rider & Son, [1915].

B-215   Barker, Laura Cooke. The immutable law / by Laura
Cooke Barker. East Aurora, N. Y.: The
Roycrofters, 1921. 75 p., front. [Ill. by Merle
James.]   **DLC**
LC: Ja 3, '22.

Barkley, J. C. Why faculty objects to ΘNε [Theta Nu
Epsilon]. <u>In</u> *Allegheny stories (1902), A-142.*

B-216   Barksdale, Emily Woodson. Stella Hope / by Emily
Woodson Barksdale. New York; Washington: The
Neale Publishing Company, 1907. 364 p.   **DLC**
LC: Je 4, '07.

B-217   Barksdale, George, b. 1869. Punch: a novel of
Negro life / by George Barksdale . . . New York;
Washington: The Neale Publishing Company, 1904.
484 p.   **EEM**
PW: D 10, '04.

B-218   Barmby, Beatrice. Betty Marchand / by Beatrice
Barmby. New York: George H. Doran Company,
[c1918]. 318 p.
LC: S 30, '18.
PW: S 28, '18.

B-219   ____ Sunrise from the hill-top / by Beatrice Barmby
. . . New York: George H. Doran Company, c1919.
308 p.
LC: N 10, '19.
PW: N 8, '19.

B-220   Barnaby, Horace T. (Horace Thomas), b. 1870. The
decade: a story of political and municipal corruption
/ by Horace T. Barnaby. Grand Rapids, Mich.:
Wolverine Book Publishing Company, 1908. 325 p.,
front.

B-221   Barnard, Annie E. My first cousin or myself / by
Annie E. Barnard. New York: Cochrane Publishing
Company, 1909. 86 p.   **TXA**

B-222   Barnard, Melville Clemens. The mystery of the
sandal-wood box: being an adventure of Harlan
Nims, the amateur American detective / by Melville
Clemens Barnard. Boston: Mayhew Publishing Co.,
1907. 116 p., front., [3] leaves of plates. [Ill. by A.
B. Hobbie.]   **DLC**
LC: Ap 3, '08.

B-223   Barnes, Annie Maria, b. 1857. An American girl in
Korea / by Annie M. Barnes; illustrated by Carl
Strehlau. Philadelphia: The Penn Publishing
Company, 1905. 392 p., front., [6] leaves of plates.
Illustrated end papers.
PW: O 7, '05.

B-224   ____ The lost treasure of Umdilla / by Annie M.
Barnes . . . New York; Chicago; London;
Edinburgh: Fleming H. Revell Company, [c1925].
224 p., front., [1] leaf of plates.
LC: My 2, '25.
PW: My 23, '25.

Barnes, Bruce. Gallilee and Hoolywood. <u>In</u> *The
rejected apostle (1924), R-164.*

_____ If thou have much. In *The rejected apostle* (1924), R-164.

_____ On the road to Damascus. In *The rejected apostle* (1924), R-164.

B-225   Barnes, Djuna. A book / by Djuna Barnes. New York: Boni and Liveright, [c1923]. 217 p., front. port, [5] leaves of plates.
Contents: A night among the horses -- Three from the Earth [play] -- The valet -- To the dogs [play] -- Beyond the end -- Pastoral [poem] -- Oscar -- Antique [poem] -- Katrina Silverstaff -- Hush before love [poem] -- The robin's house -- Paradise [poem] -- No man's mare -- Six songs of Khalidine [poem] -- The dove [play] -- Mother -- Song in autumn [poem] -- The nigger -- Lullaby [poem] -- Indian summer -- I'd have you think of me [poem] -- The rabbit -- The flowering corpse -- A boy asks a question of a lady -- First communion [poem] -- Finis [poem].
LC: O 12, '23.
PW: O 20, '23.

_____ A night among the horses. In *The best short stories of 1919 and the yearbook of the American short story* (1920), B-564.

B-226   Barnes, Edwin N. C. (Edwin Ninyon Chaloner), b. 1877. The reconciliation of Randall Claymore / by Edwin N. C. Barnes. Boston: James H. Earle & Company, 1902. 252 p., front. (port.).
PW: Je 28, '02.

B-227   Barnes, Howard McKent, 1884-1945. The little Shepherd of Bargain Row / by Howard McKent Barnes; illustrations from photographs of scenes in the play. Chicago: The Reilly & Britton Co., [c1915]. 315 p., front. (port.), [11] leaves of plates.

B-228   Barnes, James, 1866-1936. The clutch of circumstance / by James Barnes. New York: D. Appleton and Company, 1908. 385, [1] p., front., [3] leaves of plates. [Ill. by William L. Jacobs.]
LC: Ap 10, '08.
PW: Ap 11, '08.

B-229   _____ Outside the law / by James Barnes. New York: D. Appleton and Company, 1906, [c1905]. 281 p., front., [7] leaves of plates. [Ill. by Frederic Dorr Steele.]
PW: N 18, '05.

B-230   _____ The unpardonable war / by James Barnes . . . New York; London: The Macmillan Company, 1904. 356 p., front.
PW: N 5, '04.

B-231   Barnes, Julia Katherine. Annals of a quiet country town: other sketches from life / by Julia Katherine Barnes; illustrated by E. Warde Blaisdell. New York; London; Montreal: The Abbey Press, [c1902]. 424 p., front., [13] leaves of plates.
Contents: Our town -- My pastor -- Heaven on Earth -- Little vice-mother -- Billy Link's benefit -- Our comrade and Johnny -- Our political equality cranks; also, Their friend, the enemy -- The county fair -- A pastoral wedding -- My alter ego -- The ladies' baseball game -- Mendelssohn and others -- Her fête champetre -- Where clubs are trumps -- Aunty on the asphalt-a monologue -- A grand demonstration -- I. W. P. A. -- Hired maids and men -- A short tale -- That melodramatic funeral -- Auf wiedersehen -- Atavism -- A Mormon episode -- Golden Heights on sunset shores-a California itinerary -- Santa Catalina -- Little yellow slave girl -- Life's twilight [poem].
PW: Mr 28, '03.

Barnes, Lillian Corbett. By the light of the shooting star. In *Cuentos de California* (1904), C-962.

_____ A determined lover. In *From the old pueblo: and other tales* (1902), F-434.

B-232   Barnes, Will C. (William Croft), 1858-1936. Tales from the X-bar horse camp: The blue-roan "outlaw" and other stories / by Will C. Barnes . . . Chicago, Illinois: Published by the Breeders' Gazette, 1920. 217, [1] p., [17] leaves of photo. plates, ill.
Contents: Sunrise on the desert [poem] -- The blue-roan "outlaw" -- Campin' out -- Popgun plays Santa Claus -- "Just regulars" -- The stampede on the Turkey Track range -- The Navajo turquoise ring -- An Arizona etude -- Stutterin' Andy -- The passing of Bill Jackson -- The tenderfoot from Yale -- "Dummy" -- The mummy from the Grand Cañon -- Jumping at conclusions -- Lost in the petrified forest -- "Camel huntin" -- The Trinidad kid -- "Pablo" -- The shooting up of Horse Head.
LC: Jl 24, '20.
PW: D 23, '20.

B-233   Barnes, Willis. Doctor Josephine: a love story of profit sharing. New York: The Abbey Press, [1901]. 321 p.
Unexamined copy: bibliographic data from NUC.
PW: D 7, '01.

B-234   Barnett, Ada. The joyous adventurer / by Ada Barnett. New York; London: G. P. Putnam's Sons, 1924. (New York: The Knickerbocker Press). 497 p.
PW: F 16, '24.
BLC: London: G. Allen & Unwin, 1923.

B-235   _____ The man on the other side / by Ada Barnett. New York: Dodd, Mead and Company, 1922. 277 p.
LC: Ap 12, '22.
PW: Ap 15, '22.
BLC: London: G. Allen & Unwin, 1921.

B-236   Barnett, Evelyn Snead. The dragnet / by Evelyn Snead Barnett. New York: B. W. Huebsch, 1909. 383 p.
LC: D 31, '09.
PW: N 20, '09.

B-237   Barney, J. Stewart (John Stewart), 1868?-1925. L. P. M.: the end of the Great War / by J. Stewart Barney; with a frontispiece by Clarence F. Underwood. New York; London: G. P. Putnam's Sons, 1915. ([New York]: The Knickerbocker Press). 419 p., col. front.

B-238   Barnhill, Robert Gunkle. Mixed dates / by Robert Gunkle Barnhill; illustrated by Chelsea S. Stewart. [Indianapolis: The Neerman Press, [c1914]. 73 p., ill.   **DLC**

B-239   Barns, H. E. Naju of the Nile / by H. E. Barns; with sixteen full-page illustrations by Warwick Reynolds. Boston; New York: Houghton Mifflin Company, 1924. 277 p., front., [15] leaves of plates.
BLC: London; New York: G. P. Putnam's Sons, 1924.

B-240 Barnwell, R. Habersham (Robert Habersham), b. 1854. The gentle pioneers / by one of them, R. Habersham Barnwell. Boston: Richard G. Badger; Toronto: The Copp Clark Co., Limited, [c1915]. 363 p. **BRL**

B-241 Baron, *pseud.* The Marquis of Murray Hill / by the Baron [pseud.]. Boston: The Roxburgh Publishing Company, [c1909]. 360 p. **HLS**
LC: D 3, '09.

B-242 Baron, Edward David. The inscrutable woman: an autobiography, 1896-1910 / by Edward David Baron. New York: Broadway Publishing Company, [c1910]. 339 p. **CKM**

B-243 Barr, Amelia E. (Amelia Edith), 1831-1919. The belle of Bowling Green / by Amelia E. Barr . . . ; illustrated by Walter H. Everett. New York: Dodd, Mead & Company, 1904. 342 p., front., [5] leaves of plates.
PW: N 12, '04.
BLC: London: B. F. Stevens & Brown; New York printed, 1904.

B-244 _____ The black shilling: a tale of Boston towns / By Amelia E. Barr; illustrated. New York: Dodd, Mead & Company, 1903. 350 p., front., [3] leaves of plates. [Ill. by Stanley M. Arthurs.]
PW: O 10, '03.
BLC: London: T. Fisher Unwin, 1904.

B-245 _____ Cecilia's lovers / by Amelia E. Barr. New York: Dodd, Mead & Company, 1905. 389 p., col. front.
PW: O 7, '05.
BLC: London: T. Fisher Unwin; New York printed, [1905].

B-246 _____ Christine: a Fife fisher girl / Amelia Edith Huddleston Barr; frontispiece by Stockton Mulford. New York; London: D. Appleton and Company, 1917. 372, [1] p., col. front.
LC: Ag 27, '17.
PW: S 8, '17.

B-247 _____ The hands of compulsion / by Amelia E. Barr; frontispiece by Walter Everett. New York: Dodd, Mead & Company, 1909. 319 p., front.
LC: Mr 10, '09.
PW: Ap 10, '09.
BLC: London: Cassel & Co., 1910.

B-248 _____ The heart of Jessy Laurie / by Amelia E. Barr; frontispiece by Harrison Fisher. New York: Dodd, Mead & Company, 1907. 319 p., col. front.
LC: S 28, '07.
PW: O 19, '07.
BLC: London: Curtis Brown; printed in U. S. A., 1907.

B-249 _____ The house on Cherry Street / by Amelia E. Barr; frontispiece by Z. P. Nikolaki. New York: Dodd, Mead & Company, 1909. 375 p., col. front.
LC: N 5, '09.
PW: D 4, '09.

BLC: London: B. F. Stevens & Brown; printed in U. S. A., 1909.

B-250 _____ Joan: a romance of an English mining village / by Amelia E. Barr . . . ; frontispiece by Stockton Mulford. New York; London: D. Appleton and Company, 1917. 325 p., col. front.
LC: Ja 30, '17.
PW: F 17, '17.

B-251 _____ The lion's whelp: a story of Cromwell's time / by Amelia E. Barr; with illustrations by Lee Woodward Zeigler. New York: Dodd, Mead & Company, 1901. 383 p., front., [7] leaves of plates.
PW: O 5,'01.
BLC: London: T. Fisher Unwin, 1902.

B-252 _____ A maid of old New York: a romance of Peter Stuyvesant's time / by Amelia E. Barr. New York: Dodd, Mead and Company, 1911. 377 p.
LC: O 30, '11.
PW: N 4, '11.
BLC: London: B. F. Stevens & Brown; printed in U. S. A., 1911.

B-253 _____ The man between: an international romance / by Amelia E. Barr; illustrated in water-colors by Frank T. Merrill. New York; London: The Authors and Newspapers Association, 1906. 323 p., col. front., [3] leaves of col. plates.
PW: Jl 14, '06.
BLC: London: Chatto & Windus, 1907. [British title: *Love will venture in.*]

B-254 _____ The measure of a man / by Amelia E. Barr; illustrated by Frank T. Merrill. New York; London: D. Appleton and Company, 1915. 316, [1] p., front., [3] leaves of plates.
PW: S 4, '15.

B-255 _____ An Orkney maid / by Amelia E. Barr; illustated. New York; London: D. Appleton and Company, 1918. 307, [1] p., front. [Ill. by Stockton Mulford.]
LC: F 25, '18.
PW: Mr 2, '18.

B-256 _____ The paper cap: a story of love and labor / by Amelia E. Barr; frontispiece by Stockton Mulford. New York; London: D. Appleton and Company, 1918. 354, [1] p., col. front.
LC: O 9, '18.
PW: O 12, '18.

B-257 _____ Playing with fire / by Amelia E. Barr . . . ; illustrated by Howard Heath. New York; London: D. Appleton and Company, 1914. 329, [1] p., front., [3] leaves of plates.
LC: Ap 20, '14.
PW: My 2, '14.

B-258 _____ Profit & loss / by Amelia E. Barr . . . ; illustrated by Frank T. Merrill. New York; London: D. Appleton and Company, 1916. 307, [1] p., front., [3] leaves of plates. **OSU, SUC**
LC: S 5, '16.
PW: S 30, '16.

B-259   ____ A reconstructed marriage / by Amelia E. Barr; frontispiece by Z. P. Nikolaki. New York: Dodd, Mead and Company, 1910. 393 p., col. front.
LC: O 1, '10.
PW: O 15, '10.
BLC: London: T. Fisher Unwin, 1911.

B-260   ____ Sheila Vedder / by Amelia E. Barr; frontispiece by Harrison Fisher. New York: Dodd, Mead and Company, 1911. 341 p., front.
LC: Mr 18, '11.
PW: Mr 25, '11.
BLC: London: T. Fisher Unwin, 1912.

B-261   ____ A song of a single note: a love story / by Amelia E. Barr. New York: Dodd, Mead & Company, 1902. 330 p., front., [3] leaves of plates. [Ill. by Anna Whelan Betts.]
PW: N 1, '02.
BLC: London: B. F. Steevens [sic] & Brown; printed in U. S. A., 1902.

B-262   ____ Souls of passage / by Amelia E. Barr . . . ; with illustrations by Emlen McConnell. New York: Dodd, Mead, & Company, 1901. 327 p., col. front., [5] leaves of plates.
PW: Ap 6, '01.
BLC: London: T. Fisher Unwin, 1901.

B-263   ____ The strawberry handkerchief: a romance of The Stamp Act / by Amelia E. Barr. New York: Dodd, Mead & Company, 1908. 368 p., front. [Ill. by Harrison Fisher.]
LC: Ag 27, '08.
PW: O 10, '08.

B-264   ____ Thyra Varrick: a love story / by Amelia E. Barr; illustrated by Lee Woodward Zeigler. New York: J. F. Taylor & Company, 1903. 343 p., front., [11] leaves of plates.
PW: Ap 18, '03.
BLC: London: T. Fisher Unwin, 1904.

B-265   ____ The winning of Lucia: a love story / by Amelia E. Barr . . . ; illustrated by C. H. Taffs. New York; London: D. Appleton & Company, 1915. 334, [1] p., front., [3] leaves of plates.
PW: Ap 10, '15.

Barr, J., Mrs. See **Renfrew, Garroway, pseud.**

B-266 Barr, Martin W., 1860-1938. The king of Thomond: a story of yesterday / by Martin W. Barr. Boston: Herbert B. Turner & Company, 1907. 218 p., front.
LC: Ap 3, '07.
PW: Ap 20, '07.
BLC: London: Chatto & Windus, 1907.

Barr, Robert, 1850-1912. Dorothy of the mill. In *The Miller's holiday* (1920), M-817.

    ____ The mill on the Kop. In *The Miller's holiday* (1920), M-817.

    ____ , jt. aut. *The O'Ruddy* (1903). See **Crane, Stephen, 1871-1900, jt. aut, C-897.**

    ____ The pasha's prisoner. In *Comedy* (1901), C-614.

B-267 Barr, Walter, b. 1860. Shacklett: the evolution of a statesman / by Walter Barr. New York: D. Appleton and Company, 1901. 392 p.

B-268 Barrett, Harold James, b. 1885. Patricia's awakening / by Harold James Barrett. New York: Thomas Y. Crowell Company, [c1924]. 419 p.
PW: My 31, '24.

B-269 Barrett, James Francis, 1888-1934. The loyalist: a story of the American revolution / by James Francis Barrett. New York: P. J. Kenedy & Sons, [c1920]. 388 p.
LC: Ja 4, '21.

B-270   ____ The winter of discontent / by James Francis Barrett. New York: P. J. Kenedy & Sons, [c1923]. 420 p.
LC: Ja 10, '23.

B-271 Barrett, John E. (John Erigena), b. 1849. Red shadow: a romance of the Wyoming Valley in Revolutionary days / by John E. Barrett. Scranton, Pa.: The Colonial Press, 1913. 324 p., front.
                        UPM

B-272 Barrett, Lillian, b. 1884. Gibbeted gods / by Lillian Barrett. New York: The Century Co., 1921. 321 p., front.
LC: S 22, '21.

B-273   ____ The sinister revel / by Lillian Barrett. New York: Alfred A. Knopf, 1919. 364 p.
LC: O 2, '19.
PW: N 1, '19.

B-274 Barrett, R. E. (Robert Emmet). Here and there a man / by R. E. Barrett . . . Boston: The Roxburgh Publishing Company, Inc., [c1919]. 219 p. **DLC**
LC: S 25, '19.
PW: D 27, '19.

Barrett, Richmond Brooks, b. 1895. Art for art's sake. In *Prize stories of 1922* (1923), P-620.

B-275   ____ Rapture / by Richmond Brooks Barrett. New York: Boni and Liveright, [c1924]. 310 p.
LC: Ja 30, '24.
BLC: London: Jonathan Cape; printed in U. S. A., [1924].

B-276 Barretto, Larry, 1890-1971. A conqueror passes / by Larry Barretto. Boston: Little, Brown and Company, 1924. 309 p.
LC: Ja 7, '24.
PW: Ja 5, '24.

B-277   ____ To Babylon / by Larry Barretto. Boston: Little, Brown and Company, 1925. 322 p.
LC: F 7, '25.
PW: F 7, '25.

Barron, Edward, pseud. <u>See</u> **Potter, David, b. 1874.**

B-278 Barron, Elwyn Alfred, b. 1855. Marcel Levignet /
by Elwyn Barron. New York: Duffield & Company,
1906. 360 p.
LC: O 6, '06.
PW: N 17, '06.

B-279 Barrows, John Otis, 1833-1918. Boarding round:
interesting experiences of a young Yankee
schoolmaster / by John Otis Barrows. Boston: The
Roxburgh Publishing Company, Inc., [c1915]. 259 p.

B-280 Barrows, Wayne Groves, b. 1880. A child of the
plains / by Wayne Groves Barrows . . . illustrations
by Roland S. Stebbins. Boston, Mass.: The C. M.
Clark publishing co., 1910. 429 p., col. front.
DLC
"This is the second of three novels forming the "Way
out West" series."
PW: F 11, '11.

B-281 _____ The law of the range / by Wayne Groves
Barrows. Boston: The C. M. Clark Publishing
Company, 1909. 280 p., front., [7] leaves of plates.
[Ill. by John Goss.]
PW: N 20, '09.

B-282 Barry, Alfred Scott. The little girl who couldn't-get-
over-it / by Alfred Scott Barry. New York: E. P.
Dutton & Company, [c1918]. 317 p.   **NYP**
LC: Jl 11, '18.

B-283 Barry, John D. (John Daniel), 1866-1942. The
congressman's wife: a story of American politics /
by John D. Barry; illustrated by Rollin G. Kirby.
New York; London: The Smart Set Publishing Co.,
1903. 359 p., front., [3] leaves of plates.

B-284 _____ A daughter of Thespis: a novel / by John D.
Barry. Boston: L. C. Page and Company, 1903.
347 p.
PW: Ap 25, '03.
BLC: London: Chapman & Hall; Boston printed,
1903.

B-285 [_____] Our best society. New York; London: G. P.
Putnam's Sons, 1905. ([New York]: The
Knickerbocker Press). 362 p.   **DLC**

B-286 _____ Outlines: a collection of brief imaginative
studies related to many phases of thought and feeling,
and representing an effort to give an interpretation to
familiar human experiences / by John D. Barry. San
Francisco: Paul Elder and Company Publishers,
[c1913]. 179 p.   **NYP**

B-287 Barry, Richard Hayes, b. 1881. The bauble: a
novel: frontispiece / by Richard Barry . . . New
York: Moffat, Yard and Company, 1911. 342 p.,
col. front.
LC: N 11, '11.
PW: N 18, '11.

B-288 _____ Fruit of the desert / by Richard Barry;
frontispiece by Ralph Pallen Coleman. Garden City,
N. Y.; London: Doubleday, Page & Company, 1920.
245, [1] p., col. front.
LC: Ap 27, '20.
PW: Jl 3, '20.
BLC: London: Curtis Brown; Garden City, N. Y.,
printed 1920.

B-289 _____ Sandy from the Sierras / by Richard Barry;
illustrated by Fletcher C. Ransom. New York:
Moffat, Yard & Company, 1906. 318 p., front., [5]
leaves of plates.
LC: F 15, '07.
PW: Je 30, '06.
BLC: London: B. F. Steven & Brown; [New York
printed], 1906.

B-290 Barson, Robert Gale, b. 1883. Bill's mistake: a
story of the California redwoods / by Robert Gale
Barson. San Francisco, California: Harr Wagner
Publishing Co., 1921. 268 p.
LC: Je 20, '21.
PW: N 12, '21.

Bartch, Rae. By intuition of Cupid. <u>In</u> *Castle stories*
(1908), C-187.

B-291 Bartlett, Frederick Orin, b. 1876. Big Laurel / by
Frederick Orin Bartlett. Boston; New York:
Houghton Mifflin Company, 1922. (Cambridge: The
Riverside Press). 305 p.
LC: O 13, '22.
PW: O 14, '22.

B-292 _____ The guardian / by Frederick Orin Bartlett; with
a frontispiece by N. C. Wyeth. Boston: Small,
Maynard and Company, [c1912]. 470 p., col. front.
LC: F 28, '12.
PW: F 17, '12.

B-293 _____ Joan & co. / by Frederick Orin Bartlett.
Boston; New York: Houghton Mifflin Company,
1919. (Cambridge: The Riverside Press). 386 p.
LC: Jl 29, '19.
PW: Jl 26, '19.

B-294 _____ Joan of the alley / by Frederick Orin Bartlett;
with illustrations by Eleanor Winslow. Boston; New
York: Houghton, Mifflin and Company, 1904.
(Cambridge: The Riverside Press). 290 p., front.,
[7] leaves of plates.
PW: Mr 5, '04.
BLC: London: Gay & Bird; Cambridge, Mass.,
printed 1904.

_____ Long, long ago. <u>In</u> *The best short stories of
1919 and the yearbook of the American short story*
(1920), B-564.

B-295 _____ Mistress Dorothy / by Fred. O. Bartlett, illus.
by Sarah Noble-Ives. New York: E. P. Dutton &
Co., [1901]. 37 p., ill.
Unexamined copy: bibliographic data from NUC.
LC: S 4, '01.

B-296   [____] New lives for old / by William Carleton [pseud.] . . . Boston: Small, Maynard & Co., [c1913]. 222 p.
LC: F 19, '13.
PW: F 22, '13.

B-297   [____] One way out: a middle-class New-Englander emigrates to America / by William Carleton [pseud.]. Boston: Small, Maynard & Company, [c1911]. 303 p.   **CIN**
LC: F 4, '11.

B-298   [____] One year of Pierrot / by the mother of Pierrot [pseud.]. New York; London: G. P. Putnam's Sons, 1914. ([New York]: The Knickerbocker Press). 364 p.
LC: Ap 4, '14.
PW: Ap 4, '14.

B-299   ____ The prodigal pro tem / by Frederick Orin Bartlett; illustrated by Howard Chandler Christy. Boston: Small, Maynard and Company, 1910. 331 p., front., [2] leaves of plates.
LC: N 11, '10.
PW: N 5, '10.
BLC: London: Frank Palmer, 1912.

B-300   [____] The red geranium: together with My son and The case of Mathews / by William Carleton [pseud.] . . . ; illustrated by H. C. Wall and F. R. Gruger. Boston: Small, Maynard and Company, [c1915]. 395 p., front., [7] leaves of plates, 1 plan.
LC: Ag 16, '15.
PW: Je 5, '15.

B-301   ____ The seventh noon / by Frederick Orin Bartlett; with illustrations by Edmund Frederick. Boston: Small, Maynard and Company, [1910]. 350 p., col. front., [6] leaves of plates.
LC: F 10, '10.
PW: F 5, '10.

B-302   ____ The triflers / by Frederick Orin Bartlett; with illustrations by George Ellis Wolfe. Boston; New York: Houghton Mifflin Company, 1917. (Cambridge: The Riverside Press). 317, [1] p., front., [6] leaves of plates.
LC: Ap 4, '17.
PW: Ap 7, '17.
BLC: London: Methuen & Co., 1918.

B-303   ____ The Wall Street girl / by Frederick Orin Bartlett; with illustrations by George Ellis Wolfe. Boston; New York: Houghton Mifflin Company, 1916. (Cambridge: The Riverside Press). 333, [1] p., front., [6] leaves of plates.
LC: S 13, '16.
PW: S 16, '16.
BLC: London: Methuen & Co., 1918.

B-304   ____ The web of the golden spider / by Frederick Orin Bartlett . . . ; illustrated by Harrison Fisher and Charles M. Relyea. Boston: Small, Maynard and Company, 1909. 354 p., col. front., [3] leaves of plates.
LC: F 6, '09.

PW: F 27, '09.
BLC: London: Frank Palmer, 1912.

B-305   Bartley, Nalbro Isadorah, b. 1888. The bargain true / by Nalbro Bartley; with illustrations by Henry Raleigh. Boston: Small, Maynard & Company, [c1918]. 317, [1] p., front., [2] leaves of plates.
LC: Ja 8, '19.
PW: F 22, '19.

B-306   ____ Bread and jam / Nalbro Bartley . . . New York: George H. Doran Company, [c1925]. 341 p.
LC: O 1, '25.
PW: O 3, '25.

B-307   ____ Fair to middling / by Nalbro Bartley; frontispiece by Edward Ryan. Garden City, N. Y.; Toronto: Doubleday, Page & Company, 1921. 288 p., front.
LC: S 23, '21.
PW: O 1, '21.

B-308   ____ The gorgeous girl / by Nalbro Bartley; illustrated. Garden City, N. Y.: Doubleday, Page & Company, 1920. 331, [1] p., front., [3] leaves of plates. [Ill. by William L. Caffrey.]
LC: Ap 21, '20.
PW: Mr 27, '20.

B-309   ____ The gray angels / by Nalbro Bartley. Boston: Small, Maynard & Company, [c1920]. 420 p.
LC: S 18, '20.
PW: O 23, '20.

B-310   ____ Judd & Judd / by Nalbro Bartley. New York; London: G. P. Putnam's Sons, 1924. ([New York]: The Knickerbocker Press). 365 p.
LC: F 28, '24.
PW: F 23, '24.

B-311   ____ Paradise auction / by Nalbro Bartley; with illustrations by Ronald Anderson. Boston: Small, Maynard & Company, [c1917]. 501 p., col. front., [3] leaves of plates.
LC: S 7, '17.
PW: My 26, '17.

B-312   ____ Up and coming / by Nalbro Bartley. New York; London: G. P. Putnam's Sons, 1923. (New York: The Knickerbocker Press). 364 p.
LC: F 15, '23.
PW: F 10, '23.

B-313   ____ A woman's woman / by Nalbro Bartley; with illustrations by Henry Raleigh. Boston: Small, Maynard & Company, [c1919]. 428 p., front., [3] leaves of plates.
LC: Ag 15, '19.
PW: Ag 30, '19.

B-314   Bartnett, Harriet. Angelo, the musician / by Harriet Bartnett. New York: Godfrey A. S. Wieners, 1903. 340 p., front.
PW: My 9, '03.

B-315   ____ The enchanted sea-gull / by Harriet Bartnett

and Roxroy Keene. Boston: The Roxburgh Publishing Company, Incorporated, [c1917]. 320 p.
LC: O 19, '17.

Barto, Centennia. The fate of the four. In *Under Berkeley Oaks* (1901), U-8.

B-316   Barton, Bruce, 1886-1967. Just 100,000. A story. [New York]: n. d. [12] p.
Unexamined copy: bibliographic data from NUC.
[Poem by Dennis McCarthy on cover.]
OCLC lists: [New York: Stewardship Department, New Era Organization of the General Council of the Presbyterian Church, U. S. A., 1924?] #20783871.

B-317   ____ The making of George Groton / by Bruce Barton; illustrated by Paul Stahr. Garden City, N. Y.: Doubleday, Page & Company, 1918. 331 p., front., [3] leaves of plates.
LC: Ap 17, '18.

B-318   Barton, George, 1866-1940. The ambassador's trunk / by George Barton; illustrated by Charles E. Meister. Boston: The Page Company, 1919. 310 p., col. front., [4] leaves of plates.
LC: My 17, '19.
PW: Jl 5, '19.

B-319   ____ Barry Wynn; or, The adventure of a page boy in the United States Congress / by George Barton; illustrated by John Huybers. Boston: Small, Maynard and Company, [c1912]. 348 p., front, [3] leaves of plates. Unexamined data: bibliographic data from NUC.
LC: F 14, '12.

   ____ The Lady of the tower. In *The lady of the tower* (1909), L-13.

B-320   ____ The mystery of the red flame / by George Barton . . . ; illustrated by Charles E. Meister. Boston: The Page Company, 1918. 336 p., front., [5] leaves of plates.   **NYP**
PW: Ap 13, '18.

B-321   ____ The Pembroke Mason affair / by George Barton; illustrated by Charles E. Meister. Boston: The Page Company, 1920. 331 p., col. front., [4] leaves of plates.
PW: Mr 20, '20.

B-322   ____ The strange adventures of Bromley Barnes / by George Barton . . . ; illustrated by Charles E. Meister. Boston: The Page Company, 1918. 345 p., col. front., [5] leaves of plates.
Contents: Adventure of the thirteenth treaty -- Adventure of the bolted door -- Adventure of the scrap of paper -- Adventure of the stolen message -- Adventure of the burnt match stick -- Adventure of the French captain -- Adventure of the old chessplayer -- Adventure of the leather bag -- Adventure of the anonymous cards -- Adventure of the Cleopatra necklace -- Adventure of the baritone singer -- Adventure of the Amsterdam antiques.
LC: O 18, '18.

B-323   Barton, Marion T. D. An experiment in perfection / by Marion T. D. Barton. New York: Doubleday, Page and Company, 1907. 388 p.
BLC: London: Cassell & Co., 1907.

B-324   Barton, William Eleazar, 1861-1930. The romance of Rhoda: a New Testament love story / by William E. Barton. Chicago: Advance Publishing Company, 1917. 93 p.

B-325   Baskett, James Newton, b. 1849. Sweetbrier and thistledown: a story / by James Newton Baskett . . . ; with frontispiece illustration by W. F. Stecher. Boston; Chicago: W. A. Wilde, c1902. 340 p., front.

B-326   Bass, Edward Cary. Joseph and Judith, or, A bundle of old love letters / by Edward Cary Bass. Boston, Mass.: James H. Earle & Company, [c1906]. 124 p.

B-327   ____ Miss Marshall's boys / by Edward C. Bass . . . Boston: Richard G. Badger, 1909. (Boston: The Gorham Press). 62 p.   **VTU**
LC: D 28, '09.

B-328   Bassett, Hattie. Ethel Ernestine / by Hattie Bassett. Walnut Ridge, Ark: H. Bassett, [1924]. 122 p.
Unexamined copy: bibliographic data from NUC.
LC: S 23, '24.

B-329   Bassett, Mary E. Stone, 1857-1924. Judith's garden / by Mary E. Stone Bassett; illustrations by George Wright. Boston: Lothrop Publishing Company, [1902]. 337 p., col. front., [3] leaves of col. plates.
PW: Je 7, '02.

B-330   ____ The little green door: a novel / by Mary E. Stone Bassett; illustrations by Louise Clarke, decorations by Ethel Pearce Clements. Boston: Lothrop Publishing Co., [1905]. 341 p., front., [7] leaves of plates.
PW: S 2, '05.
BLC: London: Kegan Paul & Co., 1905.

B-331   ____ A midsummer wooing / by Mary E. Stone Bassett; illustrated by John Goss. Boston: Lothrop, Lee & Shepard Co., [1913]. 496 p., col. front., [3] leaves of col. plates.
PW: My 3, '13.

B-332   Bassett, Sara Ware, b. 1872. Flood tide / by Sara Ware Bassett; with frontispiece by M. L. Greer. Boston: Little, Brown and Company 1921. 328 p., front.
LC: Mr 22, '21.
PW: Ap 2, '21.

B-333   ____ Granite and clay / by Sara Ware Bassett; with frontispiece by M. L. Greer. Boston: Little, Brown, and Company, 1922. 305 p., front.
LC: Ag 15, '22.
PW: Ag 26, '22.

B-334   ____ The harbor road / by Sara Ware Bassett; illustrated by F. A. Anderson. Philadelphia: The Penn Publishing Company, 1919. 300 p., ill. "Illustrations not published in this edition."
LC: N 8, '19.
PW: S 20, '19.

B-335   ____   The taming of Zenas Henry / by Sara Ware Bassett. New York: George H. Doran Company, [c1915]. 288 p. [Illustrated end papers in colors, by Wm. L. Jacobs.]
PW: My 29, '15.
BLC: London: Hodder & Stoughton, printed in U. S. A., 1916.

B-336   ____   The wall between / by Sara Ware Bassett; with frontispiece by Norman Price. Boston: Little, Brown, and Company, 1920. 304 p., front.
LC: S 14, '20.
PW: S 4, '20.

B-337   ____   The wayfarers at the Angel's / by Sara Ware Bassett. New York: George H. Doran Company, [c1917]. 231 p.

B-338   Bat, Bill, *pseud.* Hoosier hunting grounds, or, The Beaver Lake trail / by Bill Bat [pseud.]. New York; Washington: The Neale Publishing Co., 1904. 324 p., photo. front. (port.).   **IMF**
PW: D 10, '04.

B-339   Batchelder, Roger, 1897-1947. Secrets: adapted from the Norma Talmadge picture / by Roger Batchelder; founded on the Sam H. Harris play "Secrets" by Rudolf Besier and May Edginton; illustrated with scenes from the photoplay, a First National picture. New York: Grosset & Dunlap, [c1924]. 217 p., front., [7] leaves of plates.

B-340   Batchelor, David O. (David Oren), b. 1865. The unstrung bow: a story of conquest / by David O. Batchelor. Boston: Sherman, French & Company, 1910. 286 p.
LC: O 20, '10.
PW: O 22, '10.

B-341   Bateman, M. Eugenie (Matilda Eugenie), b. 1867. The light that never fails / by M. Eugenie Bateman. New York: Cochrane Publishing Company, 1909. 61 p.   **DLC**
LC: F 5, '10.

Bateman, Victory, jt. aut. *By the stage door* (1902).
See **Patterson, Ada, jt. aut, P-158.**

B-342   Bates, Arlo, 1850-1918. The diary of a saint / by Arlo Bates. Boston; New York: Houghton, Mifflin and Company, 1902. (Cambridge: The Riverside Press). 310 p.
PW: N 1, '02.

B-343   ____   The intoxicated ghost: and other stories / by Arlo Bates. Boston; New York: Houghton, Mifflin and Company, 1908. (Cambridge: The Riverside Press). 303, [1] p.
Contents: The intoxicated ghost -- A problem in portraiture -- The knitters in the sun -- A comedy in crape -- A meeting of the Psychical club -- Tim Calligan's grave-money -- Miss Gaylord and Jenny -- Dr. Polnitzski -- In the Virginia room.
PW: Ap 25, '08.

B-344   Bates, Jimmie, *pseud.* It's all in the breakin' in / by Jimmie Bates [pseud.]. St. Louis: [s. n.], 1904. 98 p., front., [4] leaves of plates. [Ill. by George Ed. Brashear.]   **DLC**

B-345   Bates, Margaret Holmes, 1844-1927. In the first degree / by Margaret Holmes Bates . . . New York: Robert Grier Cooke, Inc., 1907. 289, [1] p., col. front.
LC: N 8, '07.

B-346   ____   Paying the Piper / by Margaret Holmes Bates . . . New York; Chicago; Norfolk; Baltimore; Atlanta; Washington; Florence, Ala.: Broadway Publishing Co., 1910. 344 p., front. [Ill. by William L. Hudson.]   **DLC**
LC: D 12, '10.

B-347   ____   Silas Kirkendown's sons / by Margaret Holmes Bates . . . Boston, Massachusetts: The C. M. Clark Pulishing Co., 1908. 324 p., front., [7] leaves of plates. [Ill. by R. Stebbins.]

B-348   Bates, Morgan. Martin Brook: a novel / by Morgan Bates. New York; London: Harper & Brothers Publishers, 1901. 364 p.
PW: Mr 30, '01.

B-349   Bates, Oric, 1883-1918. A madcap cruise / by Oric Bates. Boston; New York: Houghton, Mifflin & Company, 1905. (Cambridge: The Riverside Press). 329, [1] p.

B-350   Bates, Sylvia Chatfield. Andrea Thorne / by Sylvia Chatfield Bates . . . New York: Duffield & Company, 1925. 329 p.
LC: Mr 20, '25.
PW: Mr 7, '25.

B-351   ____   Elmira college stories / by Sylvia Chatfield Bates. New York; Washington; Baltimore; Indianapolis; Norfolk; Des Moines, Iowa: Broadway Publishing Co., [c1911]. 168 p., front., [1] leaf of plates.
Contents: Elmira "Alma mater" -- Prologue: Arrival -- The party with a point -- William, the conqueror -- The thirteenth prom man -- The table round -- An Elmira college boy -- "Recollection's magic sway" -- A freshman's diary -- A senior's diary -- The May queen -- "And I, for Rosalind" -- The greatest thing -- Commencement -- Epilogue: Departure -- L'envoi: Hymm to the campus.

B-352   ____   The geranium lady / by Sylvia Chatfield Bates; frontispiece by R. M. Crosby. New York: Duffield & Company, 1916. 279 p., front.   **OSU, NYP**
LC: F 2, '16.
PW: Mr 18, '16.

B-353   ____   The golden answer / by Sylvia Chatfield Bates. New York: The Macmillan Company, 1921. 289 p.
LC: Ap 27, '21.

B-354   ____   The vintage / by Sylvia Chatfield Bates . . . ; frontispiece by Paul Julien Meylan. New York: Duffield & Company, 1916. 55, [1] p., front.
LC: D 5, '16.
PW: D 23, '16.

B-355   Bateson, Carlen. The man in the camlet cloak / being an old writing transcribed and edited by Carlen Bateson; illustrated by W. Herbert Dunton. Akron, Ohio; Chicago; New York: The Saalfield Publishing Company, 1903. 320 p., front., [3] leaves of plates.

B-356   Battell, Joseph. Ellen; or The whisperings of an old pine / by Joseph Battell . . . Middlebury, Vermont: American Publishing Company, 1901. 471 p., incl. photo. front., incl. 70 photo. plates, ill. Index: pp. 461-471. Decorative end papers.
PW: Jl 20, '01.

B-357   The battle for the Pacific: and other adventures at sea / by Rowan Stevens, Yates Sterling, Jr., William J. Henderson, G. E. Walsh, Kirk Munroe, F. H. Spearman, and others; illustrated. New York; London: Harper & Brothers Publishers, 1908. 237, [1] p., front., [7] leaves of plates.
Contents: Part I. The dream of the guns: The battle for the Pacific / Rowan Stevens -- The bombardment of the Golden Gate / Yates Stirling, Jr. -- A fight in the fog / Yates Stirling, Jr. -- The battle off the hook / Yates Stirling, Jr. -- Harry Borden's naval monster / William J. Henderson -- The cruise of a commerce destroyer / Yates Stirling, Jr. -- Part II. Strange stories of the sea: Private or privateer? / George Ethelbert Walsh -- The mutiny on the swallow / William J. Henderson -- The scape-goat of *La Justicia* / Harold Martin -- Captain Sampson's queer cargo / George Ethelbert Walsh -- A warm corner in Sooloo / Owen Hall -- "Cap'n I's" closest call / Kirk Munro -- My borrowed torpedo boat / Julian Ralph -- The lost voice / F. H. Spearman -- Joe Griffin's great jump / William J. Henderson.

B-358   Bauch, Solomon, b. 1883. Whose fault? / by Solomon Bauch. New York: Published by Solomon Bauch, 1908. 20 p., photo. front. (port.).   **NYP**

B-359   Bauder, Emma Pow, b. 1848. The inhabitants of two worlds / by Emma Pow Bauder; illustrated in story. Chicago; Philadelphia: Monarch Book Company, [c1904]. 445 p., photo. front., [31] p. of plates (some photo.).

Bauer, Wright, pseud. See **Hobart, George Vere.**

B-360   Baugh, Birdie May. Genevieve, of Harris Hall. Richmond Va.: Hunter & Co., Inc., 1916. 189 p., photo. front. (port).   **EMU**

B-361   Baulsir, Edith. Within four walls / by Edith Baulsir. New York: The Century Co., 1921. 325 p., front. [Ill. by R. Van Buren.]
LC: S 12, '21.
PW: S 10, '21.

B-362   Baum, Emanuel M. (Emanuel Milton), b. 1882. The prince of passion / by Emanuel M. Baum. New York: Walter Neale, [c1924]. 220 p.
LC: N 10, '24.
PW: Mr 28, '25.

B-363   [Baum, L. Frank (Lyman Frank), 1856-1919]. Daughters of destiny / by Schuyler Staunton [pseud.]; illustrated with color reproductions of paintings by Thomas Mitchell Peirce and Harold DeLay. Chicago: The Reilly & Britton Co., [c1906]. 319 p., col. front., [7] leaves of col. plates.

B-364   [____] The fate of a crown / by Schuyler Staunton

[pseud.]. Chicago: The Reilly & Britton Co., [c1905]. 291 p., front. [Ill. by Hazel Roberts.]
PW: Je 17, '05.

B-365   [____] The flying girl / by Edith Van Dyne [pseud.] . . . ; illustrated by Joseph Pierre Nuyttens. Chicago: The Reilly & Britton Co., [c1911]. 232 p., front., [3] leaves of plates.
LC: Ag 28, '11.

B-366   [____] The last Egyptian: a romance of the Nile / illustrated by Francis P. Wightman. Philadelphia: Edward Stern & Co., Inc., 1908. 287 p., col. front., [7] leaves of col. plates.
LC: Mr 19, '08.
PW: Ap 18, '08.
BLC: London: Sisley's, 1908.

B-367   [____] Tamawaca folks: a summer comedy / by John Estes Cooke [pseud.]. [Chicago?]: The Tamawaca Press, [c1907]. 185 p.   **KUK**
LC: Ag 7, '07.

Bausman, Frederick. See **Aix, pseud.**

Baxter, George Owen, pseud. See **Brand, Max, pseud.**

B-368   Bay, J. Christian (Jens Christian), 1871-1962. The chalice of the chipped ruby / by J. Christian Bay. Chicago: Walter M. Hill, 1922. 91 p.
PW: Jl 15, '22.

B-369   Bayhan, Richard Seymour. Humorous tales of Bennington-on-the-hill: collected and written for her sons and daughters by one who was born near the site of the old continental store house. Cleveland: [Central Publishing House, c1918]. 68 p., photo. front. (port.), [8] leaves of plates.
Contents: Prologue -- Chapter I. Uncle Hi -- Chapter II. Granny Spiers -- Chapter III. Various people: Pussy Card -- One on Mr. Franklin Blackmer -- Munson and his poetry -- Hannah Haynes -- Nancy Black -- Liz Dibble -- How Aunt Sally Blatchford called on her dying(?) brother -- Aunt Mindy's cider mill -- Anecdote of Mrs. Benj. R. Sears (Mary Ann Waters) -- Anecdote of Colonel Martin Scott --Chapter IV. Various people (continued): Granny March's night-cap -- Mrs. Von Dorn, Aunt Betty Caslin and the bowl of tomato soup -- How Nora Flannigan testified at the county court -- How Colonel Sherill and Jacob Poole called on Mrs Hyde-- Aunt Betty Caslin's funeral -- Ann Brooks -- Occurrences personally recollected by the author -- L'Envoi: The old hill today -- Bennington Center.

Bayly, Charles, Jr. P'r'aps. *In The best college short stories (1917-1918), B-557.*

B-370   Beach, Alligood. A disciple of Plato / by Alligood Beach; illustrated by John Ward Dunsmore. Boston: Roberts Publishing Co., 1902. 353 p., front., [3] leaves of plates.
PW: N 15, '02.

B-371   Beach, David Nelson, 1848-1926. The Annie Laurie mine: a story of love, economics and religion / by David N. Beach; with illustrations by Charles Copeland. Boston; Chicago: The Pilgrim Press, [c1902]. 397 p., front., [6] leaves of plates.
PW: Je 6, '03.

B-372 Beach, Edgar Rice, b. 1841. Hands of clay: a great city's half--and the other half / by Edgar Rice Beach . . . St. Louis: Edward R. Eddins & Co., 1904. 348 p., photo. front. ill. (port.) **KLG**

B-373 Beach, Edward L. (Edward Latimer), 1867-1943. Midshipman Ralph Osborn at sea: a story of the U. S. Navy / by Commander Edward L. Beach, U. S. Navy; illustrated by Frank T. Merrill. Boston; Chicago: W. A. Wilde Company, [c1910]. 330 p., front., [4] leaves of plates.

B-374 Beach, Rex Ellingwood, 1877-1949. The auction block: a novel of New York life / by Rex Beach . . . ; illustrated by Charles Dana Gibson. New York; London: Harper & Brothers, 1914. 440, [1] p., incl. front., ill.
LC: S 14, '14.
PW: S 19, '14.
BLC: London: Hodder & Stoughton, [1914].

B-375 _____ The barrier: a novel / by Rex Beach; illustrated by Denman Fink. New York; London: Harper & Brothers, 1908. 309, [1] p., col. front., [5] leaves of col. plates.
LC: Mr 26, '08.
PW: Mr 28, '08.
BLC: London: Hodder & Stoughton, [1912].

B-376 _____ Big brother: and other stories / by Rex Beach. New York; London: Harper & Brothers, [c1923]. 367 p.
Contents: Big brother -- "The white brant" -- Recoil -- The obvious thing -- The talking vase -- Too fat to fight.
LC: O 12, '23.
PW: O 27, '23.
BLC: London: Hodder & Stoughton, [1924].

B-377 _____ The crimson gardenia: and other tales of adventure / by Rex Beach . . . ; illustrated. New York; London: Harper & Brothers, 1916. 377, [1] p., front., [3] leaves of plates. [Ill. by Charles Sarka and Anton Otto Fischer.]
Contents: The crimson gardenia -- Rope's end -- Inocenclo -- The wag-lady -- "Man proposes" -- Told in the storm -- The weight of obligation -- The stampede -- When the mail came in -- McGill -- The brand.
LC: Ap 14, '16.
PW: Ap 15, '16.
BLC: London: Hodder & Stoughton, [1916].

B-378 _____ Flowing gold / by Rex Beach. New York; London: Harper & Brothers, [c1922]. 377 p., front., [3] leaves of plates. [Ill. by W. H. D. Koerner.]
LC: S 9, '22.
PW: S 9, '22.
BLC: London: Hodder & Stoughton, [1922].

B-379 _____ Going some: a romance of strenuous affection / by Rex Beach; suggested by the play by Rex Beach and Paul Armstrong; illustrated by Mark Fenderson. New York; London: Harper and Brothers, 1910. 293, [1] p., ill.
LC: My 7, '10.
PW: My 14, '10.
BLC: London: Hodder & Stoughton, 1914.

B-380 _____ The goose woman: and other stories / by Rex Beach. First Edition. New York; London: Harper & Brothers, 1925. 266 p.
Contents: The goose woman -- Cave stuff -- Cool waters -- The Michigan Kid -- Powder.
LC: Jl 10, '25.
PW: Jl 18, '25.
BLC: London: Hodder & Stoughton, [1925].

B-381 _____ Heart of the sunset / by Rex Beach; with illustrations by M. Stockton Mulford. New York; London: Harper & Brothers, [1915]. 355, [1] p., col. front., [8] leaves of plates.
LC: S 22, '15.
PW: O 2, '15.

B-382 _____ The iron trail: an Alaskan romance / by Rex Beach . . . ; illustrated. New York; London: Harper & Brothers, 1913. 390, [1] p., front., [7] leaves of plates. [Ill. by Leone M. Bracker.]
LC: Ag 26, '13.
PW: Ag 30, '13.
BLC: London: Hodder & Stoughton, 1913.

B-383 _____ Laughing Bill Hyde: and other stories / by Rex Beach. New York; London: Harper & Brothers, [1917]. 392, [1] p., front. [Ill. by Douglas Duer.]
Contents: Laughing Bill Hyde -- The north wind's malice -- His stock in trade -- With bridges burned -- With interest to date -- The cub reporter -- Out of the night -- The real and the make-believe -- Running Elk -- The moon, the maid and the winged shoes -- Flesh.
PW: D 1, '17.
BLC: London: Hodder & Stoughton, [1918].

B-384 _____ The ne'er-do-well / by Rex Beach; illustrated by Howard Chandler Christy. New York; London: Harper & Brothers, 1911. 401, [1] p., front., [7] leaves of plates.
LC: Ag 21, '11.
PW: Ag 26, '11.
BLC: London: Hodder & Stoughton, 1911.

B-385 _____ The net: a novel / by Rex Beach; illustrated. New York; London: Harper & Brothers, [c1912]. 332, [1] p., front., [3] leaves of plates. [Ill. by Walter Tittle.]
LC: O 12, '12.
PW: O 26, '12.
BLC: London: Hodder & Stoughton, 1912.

B-386 _____ Pardners / by Rex E. Beach; illustrated. New York: McClure, Phillips & Co., 1905. 278 p., front., [7] leaves of plates. [Ill. by F. E. Schoonover, J. N. Marchand, Hy S. Watson, et al.]
PW: Ap 29, '05.
BLC: London: Hodder & Stoughton, 1912. (New Edition)

B-387 _____ Rainbow's end: a novel / by Rex Beach. New York; London: Harper & Brothers, [1916]. 375, [1] p., front., [3] leaves of plates. [Ill. by Stockton Mulford.]
LC: O 10, '16.
PW: O 14, '16.
BLC: London: Hodder & Stoughton, 1916.

B-388   ____ The silver horde: a novel / by Rex Beach; illustrated by Harvey T. Dunn. New York; London: Harper & Brothers, 1909. 389, [1] p., front., [7] leaves of plates.
LC: S 20, '09.
PW: S 25, '09.
BLC: London: Hodder & Stoughton, [1912].

B-389   ____ The spoilers / by Rex E. Beach; illustrated by Clarence F. Underwood. New York; London: Harper & Brothers, 1906. 313, [1] p., front., [3] leaves of plates.
LC: O 5, '07.
PW: Ap 7, '06.
BLC: New York; London: Harper & Brothers, 1906. British title: *The spoilers of the North.*

B-390   ____ Too fat to fight / by Rex Beach; with illustrations by T. D. Skidmore. New York: Harper & Brothers, [1919]. 54, [1] p., front., [3] leaves of plates.
LC: F 24, '19.
PW: Mr 1, '19.

B-391   ____ The winds of chance / by Rex Beach; illustrated. New York; London: Harper & Brothers, [1918]. 521, [1] p., front., [3] leaves of plates. [Ill. by J. Henry.]
LC: O 28, '18.
PW: N 9, '18.
BLC: London: Hodder & Stoughton, [1919].

B-392   Beachley, Elizabeth. Without the cross / by Elizabeth Beachley . . . Philadelphia: Dorrance and Company, 1925. 197 p.   **DLC**

B-393   Beadle, S. A. (Samuel Alfred). Adam Shuffler / by S. A. Beadle. Jackson, Miss.: Harmon Publishing Company, copyrighted September 16, 1901. 155, [1] p., [9] leaves of photo. plates.   **CLU**

B-394   Beadles, J. E. Robert Gordon: a story of the Mexican Revolution / by J. E. Beadles . . . ; illustrated. New York; London: F. Tennyson Neely, [c1902]. 444 p., front., [4] leaves of plates.

Beahan, Charles, jt. aut. *The island God forgot* (1922). See **Stilson, Charles B. (Charles Billings), jt. aut, S-936.**

B-395   Beal, Mary Barnes, b. 1844. A misunderstood hero / by Mary Barnes Beal. Boston; New York; [etc.]: The Pilgrim Press, [1905]. 333 p., front., plates. Unexamined copy: bibliographic data from NUC.

B-396   Beale, Will, b. 1878. Frontier of the deep: a tale of the great Northeast / by Will Beale. New York: Chelsea House, [c1925]. 320 p.
PW: Ag 22, '25.
BLC: London: T. Fisher Unwin, 1926.

B-397   Beall, St. Clair. The winning of Sarenne / by St. Clair Beall; with illustrations by Louis F. Grant. New York: The Federal Book Company, 1902. 343 p., front., [2] leaves of plates.

B-398   Beals, Christine. The winepress / by Christine Beals. New York: The Bookery Publishing Co., [c1912]. 254 p., front., [3] leaves of plates.

B-399   Beals, Helen Abbott, b. 1888. The merry heart / by Helen Raymond Abbott. New York: The Century Co., 1918. 351 p., front.   **CLE**

B-400   Beals, May. The rebel at large / by May Beals. Chicago: Charles H. Kerr & Company, 1906. 184 p.   **MNU**
Contents: A story of the lost -- The grit of Augusta -- A letter to Aristile -- In the bowels of the earth -- Two letters and a story -- The heresy of the child -- The altruism of the junior partner -- The quest of the wise world -- First revolt -- The victims -- The crushing of a strike -- First steps -- "Let them say" -- The things Claude did not notice -- Two tramps -- The sympathizin' of Mrs. Deacon Smith -- The aspirations of Mam'selle Reffold.

B-401   Bearden, George Steele, b. 1868. The prodigal father / by George S. Bearden. Boston, Massachusetts: The Stratford Company, 1920. 321 p., photo. front.

Beardsley, George. Cavalleria rusticana. In *Politics* **(1901), P-461.**

B-402   Beardsley, Mabel Baldwin. Her word and her bond / by Mabel Baldwin Beardsley. [Nutley, N. J.: The Ryan Press], c1914. 29 p.   **NYP**

B-403   Beatty, John, 1828-1914. The Acolhuans: a narrative of sojourn and adventure among the mound builders of the Ohio Valley: being a free translation from the Norraena of the memoirs of Ivarr Bartholdsson / by John Beatty. Columbus, Ohio: McClelland & Company Publishers, 1902. 423 p., [11] leaves of plates (some photo.).

B-404   ____ McLean: a romance of the war / by John Beatty. Columbus, Ohio: Press of Fred J. Heer, 1904. 237 p.

B-405   ____ Uncle Peter Sked / by John Beatty. Columbus, Ohio: F. J. Heer Printing Company, 1907. 236 p.

B-406   Beaumont, Gerald. Hearts and the diamond / by Gerald Beaumont. New York: Dodd, Mead and Company, 1921. 316 p.
Contents: With the help of God and a fast outfield -- The Crab -- Leave it to Angel-Face -- Rainbow -- Tin Can Tommy -- Kerrigan's kid -- The speed pill -- Pebble Pop -- Called an account of darkness -- His Honor, the umps -- Elephant.

B-407   ____ Riders up! / by Gerald Beaumont. New York; London: D. Appleton and Company, 1922. 330, [1] p.
Contents: Lil' ol' Red stockings -- Shooting Star -- Star of Isreal -- When Johnny comes marching home -- The Christmas handicap -- Oh, Susanna! -- Mud and ninety-five -- Thoroughbreds -- The king of the also-rans -- The empty stall.
LC: O 6, '22.
PW: O 28, '22.

B-408   Beazley, Rosalind. Virginia Rose: and other stories / by Rosalind Beazley. Chicago: [s.n.], [c1910]. 107 p., front., [4] leaves of plates.
Contents: Virginia Rose -- Among sylvan breezes -- Late love -- Fidelity -- Constance.
LC: D 16, '10.
PW: Mr 4, '11.

B-409 Bechdolt, Frederick R. (Frederick Ritchie), 1874-1950. The hard rock man / by Frederick R. Bechdolt. New York: Moffat, Yard and Company, 1910. 224 p.
LC: S 1, '10.
PW: S 3, '10.

_____, jt. aut. *9009* (1908). See **Hopper, James Marie, 1876-1956, jt. aut, H-837.**

B-410 _____ Tales of the old-timers / by Frederick R. Bechdolt . . . New York; London: The Century Co., [c1924]. 367 p., front. [Ill. by Frederic Remington.]
Contents: The warriors of the Pecos -- The warriors of the Canadian -- The law-bringers -- Tascosa -- Adobe walls -- Red blood and white -- The first cowboy -- The forgotten expedition to Santa Fé -- The Texans -- The most consummate villain -- Cassidy and the wild bunch -- The last of the open ranges.
LC: S 3, '24.
PW: S 6, '24.

B-411 Becker, Frederick W. Home rule of Eliza / by Frederick W. Becker; illustrated by H. C. Green. New York: The Platt [i. e. Pratt] & Peck Co., 1913. 279 p., front., [9] leaves of plates. **NYP**

B-412 Becker, William Templer. Larkin of Cotton Run / by William Templer Becker. New York: Helen Norwood Halsey, [c1913]. 329 p., front. (port.). [Also published by Broadway Publishing Co., [1913], apparent later printing.]

B-413 Beckley, Zoe. A chance to live / by Zoe Beckley; with a foreword by Kathleen Norris; illustration by Charles G. Voight. New York: The Macmillan Company, 1918. 329 p., ill. **DLC**
LC: N 14, '18.
PW: N 23, '18.

Beckman, Nellie Sims. See **Beckman, William, Mrs.**

B-414 Beckman, William, Mrs. Unclean and spotted from the world / by Mrs. William Beckman . . . San Francisco [Calif.]: The Whitaker & Ray Company (Incorporated), 1906. 400 p., photo. ill.

Beckwith, Carmelita, jt aut. *The lady of the dynamos* (1909). See **Shaw, Adèle Marie, jt aut, S-356.**

B-415 Beckwith, John Francis. Whose love was the greater?: undated leaves from a diary / by John Francis Beckwith. New York: The Shakespeare Press, 1913. 148 p., front. (port.). **DLC**

B-416 Beddow, Charles P., Mrs., b. 1860. The oracle of Moccasin Bend: a story of Lookout Mountain / by Mrs. Charles P. Beddow. New York; Washington: The Neale Publishing Co., 1903. 197 p., photo. front.

Beddow, Elizabeth Russell. See **Beddow, Charles P., Mrs., b. 1860.**

B-417 [Bedford-Jones, H. (Henry)], 1887-1949. Against the tide / by John Wycliffe [pseud.]. New York: Dodd, Mead, and Company, 1924. 279 p.
LC: Je 25, '24.
PW: Je 21, '24.

B-418 _____ Arizona argonauts / by H. Bedford-Jones. Garden City, New York: Doubleday, Page and Company, 1923, [c1920]. 122 p.
[Ill. paper cover by N. Ellen Hofer.]

B-419 _____ Bigfoot Joe and others: figments of fancy, written, hand-set in type, & printed / by H. Bedford-Jones. Lakeport [Michigan]: H. Bedford-Jones, 1920. [43] p. **ZYU**
Contents: Bigfoot Joe -- The clear word -- The naked man -- One night at Healy's -- The shepherd's failure.

B-420 _____ The conquest / by H. Bedford-Jones. Elgin [Ill.]; Chicago; New York; Boston: David C. Cook Publishing Company, [c1914]. 95 p., ill. [Ill. by I. Doseff.]
LC: D 4, '14.

B-421 _____ The cross and the hammer: a tale of the days of the Vikings / by H. Bedford-Jones. Elgin, Ill.: David C. Cook Publishing Co., [c1912]. 95 p., ill. [Ill. by E. H. Hartke.]
LC: O 14, '12.

B-422 _____ Flamehair the Skald: a tale of the days of Hardrede / by H. Bedford-Jones; illustrated by Dan Sayre Groesbeck. Chicago: A. C. McClurg & Co., 1913. 310 p., front., [3] leaves of plates.
LC: O 8, '13.
PW: N 1, '13.

B-423 _____ The Mardi Gras mystery / by H. Bedford-Jones; frontispiece by John Newton Howitt. Garden City, N. Y.; Toronto: Doubleday, Page & Company, 1921. 313, [1] p., front.
LC: Je 22, '21.
PW: My 21, '21.

B-424 _____ The mesa trail / by H. Bedford-Jones. Garden City [N. Y.]: Doubleday, Page & Company, 1920. 244 p., col. front.
LC: S 22, '20.
PW: S 18, '20.

B-425 _____ Mormon Valley / by H. Bedford-Jones. Garden City: Garden City Pub. Co., 1923. 120 p. Unexamined copy: bibliographic data from OCLC, #18650337.

B-426 _____ The second mate / by H. Bedford-Jones. Garden City, New York: Doubleday, Page & Company, 1923. 124 p.

B-427 [_____] A son of the Cincinnati / by Montague Brisard [pseud.]. Boston: Small, Maynard & Company, [c1925]. 294 p.
LC: Je 13, '25.
PW: Je 6, '25.

B-428   ____ The star woman / by H. Bedford-Jones. New York: Dodd, Mead and Company, 1924. 293 p. Illustrated end papers.
LC: S 4, '24.
PW: Ag 30, '24.

B-429   Beebe, Jessie Hollis. Red Sky's Annie: a story of the Bad Lands / by Jessie Hollis Beebe . . . ; illustrated. Boston: The Roxburgh Publishing Company, Inc., [c1911]. 161 p., photo. front., [4] leaves of photo. plates.
LC: D 23, '11.
PW: F 10, '12.

B-430   Beecham, John Charles. The argus pheasant / by John Charles Beecham; frontispiece by George W. Gage. New York: W. J. Watt & Company, [c1918]. 313 p., front.
LC: Je 22, '18.
PW: S 7, '18.
BLC: London: Methuen & Co., 1920.

B-431   ____ The yellow spider / John Charles Beecham. New York: W. J. Watt & Company, [c1920]. 301 p.
LC: Ap 14, '21.
PW: N 13, '20.
BLC: London: Methuen & Co., 1921.

B-432   Beecher, Carolyn. Maid and wife / by Carolyn Beecher. New York: Britton Publishing Co., [c1919]. 380 p., front., [3] leaves of plates.
LC: F 18, '18.
PW: Mr 29, '19.

B-433   ____ One woman's story: a novel / by Carolyn Beecher. New York: Britton Publishing Company, [c1919]. 401 p., front.
LC: S 19, '19.
PW: N 1, '19.

B-434   Beecher, May Howell, 1854-1923. The eighth husband / by May Howell Beecher. Boston: Sherman, French & Company, 1913. 210 p.
LC: O 1, '13.

B-435   ____ Jacqueminot: the romance of a rose / by May Howell Beecher . . . New York; London: F. Tennyson Neely Co., [c1901]. 103 p.   **DLC**

B-436   Beeckman, Ross. The last woman / by Ross Beeckman . . . ; frontispiece by Howard Chandler Christy; illustrations by Bert Knight. New York: W. J. Watt & Company, [c1909]. 317 p., col. front., [2] leaves of plates.   **CKM**
LC: S 20, '09.
PW: D 4, '09.
BLC: London: Greening & Co., 1912.

B-437   ____ Princess Zara / by Ross Beeckman; illustrations by Bert Knight. New York: W. J. Watt & Company, [1909]. 343 p., col. front., [3] leaves of plates. [Front. by Will Grefé.]
LC: Ja 30, '09.
PW: Ap 10, '09.
BLC: London: Greening & Co., 1912.

B-438   [Beekman, Helen]. Dainty devils: a novel. New York: William H. Young & Co.; London: R. & T. Washbourne, 1903. 361 p.   **DLC**
Afterwards issued under the title *Mrs. J. Worthington Woodward*.
PW: My 9, '03.

____ Mrs. J. Worthington Woodward. See **Beekman, Helen. *Dainty Devils* (1903), B-438.**

Beer, Abraham Rayfield. See **De Beer, A. R., pseud.**

Beer, Thomas, 1889-1940. Absent without leave. In *War stories* **(1919), W-94.**

B-439   ____ The fair rewards / Thomas Beer. New York: Alfred A. Knopf, 1922. 292 p. Decorated end papers.
LC: Mr 3, '22.
PW: F 11, '22.

____ Mummery. In *Prize stories of 1921* (1922), **P-619.**

____ Onnie. In *The best short stories of 1917 and the yearbook of the American short story* (1918), **B-562.**

B-440   ____ Sandoval: a romance of bad manners / by Thomas Beer. New York: Alfred A. Knopf, 1924. 219 p. Designed colored end papers.
LC: My 31, '24.
PW: My 31, '24.
BLC: London: William Heinemann, 1924.

____ Tact. In *Prize stories of 1922* (1923), **P-620.**

B-441   Beers, Frank. The green signal, or, Life on the rail / by Frank Beers. Kansas City, Mo.: Franklin Hudson Publishing Co., [c1904]. 238 p., front. (port.), [6] leaves of plates.
Contents: The brakeman -- The conductor -- The fireman -- The engineer -- The train dispatcher and operator -- To the public -- Conclusion -- Trains in the night.

B-442   Beers, H. Stewart (Herbert Stewart). Poppy venom / by H. Stewart Beers. Washington: Andrew B. Graham Company, [c1920]. 462 p., front. [Ill. by R. C. Boswell.]   **DLC**
LC: S 13, '21.

B-443   Beers, Lorna Doone. Prairie fires / by Lorna Doone Beers. New York: E. P. Dutton & Company, [c1925]. 367 p.   **UIU**
LC: My 4, '25.
PW: My 16, '25.
BLC: London: Jarrolds, [1927].

B-444   Beery, Jesse, 1861-1945. The story of "Kate and Queen": how "Kate" became an outlaw and how "Queen" became the family driver / As told by themselves; by . . . Jesse Beery. Pleasant Hill, Ohio: [s.n.], [c1908]. 93 p.

B-445   Beery, Jesse, 1861-1945. The thoroughbreds / Jesse Beery . . . [Piqua, Ohio: Printed by the Magee Brothers Company, c1912].

B-446   Behymer, Ida Holmes. The seal of destiny / by Ida Holmes Behymer. New York; London: F. T. Neely Co., [1901]. 258 p.
Unexamined copy: bibliographic data from NUC.
PW: My 10, '02.

B-447   Belasco, David, 1853-1931. The girl of the golden West / novelized from the play by David Belasco; with illustrations by J. N. Marchand. New York: Dodd, Mead and Company, 1911. 346 p., col. front., [3] leaves of col. plates.
LC: O 30, '11.
BLC: London: B. F. Stevens & Brown; printed in U. S. A., 1911.

B-448   _____ The return of Peter Grimm / novelised from the play by David Belasco; illustrations by John Rae. New York: Dodd, Mead and Company, 1912. 344 p., col. front., [2] leaves of col. plates.
LC: O 12, '12.
BLC: London: Andrew Melrose, 1912.

B-449   Belden, Jessie Perry van Zile, 1857-1910. Antonia / by Jessie Van Zile Belden; illustrated by Amy M. Sacker. Boston: L. C. Page & Company, 1901. 258 p., front., [4] leaves of plates.
PW: Je 8, '01.
BLC: London: John Murray, 1901.

B-450   Belk, G. W. (George W.). Floreen, or, The story of Mitchell: a legend of the "Land of the sky" / by G. W. Belk. Charlotte, N. C.: Stone Publishing Co., [c1916]. [24] p., ill., 1 port., some photo.   **NCS**
PW: D 2, '16.

B-451   Bell, Adelaide Fuller. The vassalage / by Adelaide Fuller Bell. Boston: The C. M. Clark Publishing Company, 1909. 318 p., front., [3] leaves of plates. [Ill. by Grace Perry.]
LC: N 17, '09.

B-452   Bell, Archie, 1877-1943. The Bermudian / by Archie Bell. New York: Broadway Publishing Company, [c1906]. 205 p., front. [Ill. by Sydney K. Hartman.]   **LRU**
Cover title: The Bermudian . . . a story of the land of the Easter lily.

B-453   _____ The Clevelanders: an exposé of high life in the Forest city / by Archie Bell. New York: Broadway Publishing Co., [c1907]. 151 p., front. (port.).
LC: Ap 4, '07.

B-454   _____ King Tut-ankh-Ámen: his romantic history, relating how, as Prince of Hermonthis, he won the love of Senpa, Priestess of the temple of Karnak, and through her interest achieved the throne of the pharaohs / by Archie Bell. Boston: The St. Botolph Society, 1923. 290 p., col. front., [4] leaves of plates.
LC: My 24, '23.

B-455   _____ Mary of Magdala: her romantic story / by Archie Bell; with a frontispiece in photogravure from a painting by W. St. J. Harper. Boston: L. C. Page & Company, [1925]. 310 p., front.
[Another printing: Boston: St. Boltoph Society, 1925.]
LC: Mr 24, '25.
PW: Ap 11, '25.

B-456   _____ A scarlet repentance / by Archie Bell. New York: Broadway Publishing Company, [c1905]. 134 p.
PW: Ag 18, '06.

Bell, Clara Ingraham. <u>See</u> **Ingraham, Frances C., pseud.**

Bell, Eric Temple, 1883-1960. <u>See</u> **Taine, John, pseud.**

B-457   Bell, Helen. The tang / by Helen Bell. Boston: Small, Maynard & Company, [c1921]. 303 p.
LC: Mr 25, '21.

B-458   Bell, John Calhoun, b. 1851. The pilgrim and the pioneer: the social and material developments in the Rocky Mountains / by John C. Bell . . . College View, Lincoln, Nebraska: Printed by the International Publishing Ass'n, [c1906]. 531 p., front., ill. [Some signed by Ned Hadley.]

B-459   Bell, Katherine Virginia. Stella Russell / by Katherine Virginia Bell. New York; Washington: The Neale Publishing Company, 1907. 289 p.
LC: Jl 10, '07.
PW: Ag 24, '07.

B-460   Bell, Lilian Lida, 1867-1929. About Miss Mattie Morningglory / by Lilian Bell. Chicago: Rand McNally & Company, [c1916]. 529 p.
LC: Ap 11, '16.
PW: Ap 8, '16.

B-461   _____ Abroad with the Jimmies / by Lilian Bell. Boston: L. C. Page & Company, 1902. 303 p., front. (port.).
Contents: I. Our house-boat at Henley -- II. Paris -- III. Strasburg and Baden-Baden -- IV. Stuttgart, Nuremberg, and Bayreuth -- V. The Passion play -- VI. Munich to the Achensee -- VII. Dancing in the Austrian Tyrol -- VIII. Salzburg -- IX. Ischi -- X. Vienna -- XI. My first interview with Tolstoy -- XII. At one of the Tolstoy receptions -- XIII. Shopping experiences.
PW: My 10, '02.
BLC: London: Lock & Co., [1902].

B-462   _____ Angela's quest / by Lilian Bell . . . ; with illustrations by A. B. Wenzel. New York: Duffield & Co., 1910. 275 p., front., [2] leaves of plates.   **OSU, NYP**
LC: N 5, '10.
PW: D 10, '10.

B-463   _____ At home with the Jardines / by Lilian Bell. Boston: L. C. Page & Company, 1904. 322 p.
PW: S 10, '04.

B-464 _____ A book of girls / by Lilian Bell; with a frontispiece by W. B. [sic] Stevens. Boston: L. C. Page & Company, 1903. 157 p., front. ill.
Contents: The last straw -- The surrender of Lapwing -- The penance of Hedwig -- Garrett Owen's little countess.

B-465 _____ Carolina Lee / by Lilian Bell; with a frontispiece in colour by Dora Wheeler Keith. Boston: L. C. Page & Company, 1906. 352 p., col. front.
PW: Mr 17, '06.

B-466 _____ The concentrations of Bee / by Lilian Bell; frontispiece by A. P. Button. Boston: L. C. Page & Company, 1909. 322 p., col. front. Illustrated end papers.
LC: O 12, '09.
PW: N 6, '09.

B-467 _____ The dowager countess and the American girl / by Lilian Bell. New York; London: Harper & Brothers, 1903. 204, [1] p.
PW: Je 27, '03.

B-468 _____ Hope Loring / by Lilian Bell . . . ; illustrated by Frank T. Merrill. Boston: L. C. Page & Company, 1903. 328 p., front., [4] leaves of plates.
PW: O 4, '02.
BLC: London: Ward, Locke & Co, 1902.

B-469 _____ The interference of Patricia / by Lilian Bell; with a frontispiece by Frank T. Merrill. Boston: L. C. Page & Company, 1903. 156 p., front.
PW: Jl 18, '03.

B-470 _____ Sir John and the American girl / by Lilian Bell. New York; London: Harper & Brothers Publishers, 1901. 256, [1] p., front. (port.).
[Harper's portrait collection of short stories; 2.]
Contents: Sir John and the American girl -- The pacifier of Pecos -- With Mamma away -- The Chattahoochee woman's club -- "Yessum" -- Miss Scarborough's point of view -- With feet of clay -- The junior prize at St. Mary's -- A pigeon-blood ruby.
PW: Je 29, '01.

B-471 Bell, Lucia Chase. Obil, keeper of camels: being the parable of the man whom the disciples saw casting out devils / by Lucia Chase Bell. San Francisco: Paul Elder & Company, [c1910]. 26 p.

Bell, Mary. The little maid's tragedy. In *Under Berkeley Oaks* (1901), U-8.

B-472 Bell, Mary E. Mammy's story and verses / by Mary E. Bell. Baltimore. Maryland: Printed by The Stockton Press, 19--. [9] p. **DGU** (photocopy)
Contents: Mammy's story -- [Remainder of text is poetry].

B-473 Bell, Narnie Harrison. Dry stories / by Narnie Harrison Bell. Temple [Tex.]: Telegram Publishing Company, 1915. 53 p., [1] leaf of photo. plates.
Contents: A woman's strategem -- The emancipation of Bill -- My friend, Dan Morgan -- A story of the cotton patch -- A tribute to Lee [poem].

B-474 Bell, O. G. The regeneration of Millicent. Norwich, N. Y.: Pharmacal Press, c1905. 32 p., ill.

B-475 Bell, Pearl Doles. The autocrat / by Pearl Doles Bell. New York: W. J. Watt & Company, [c1922]. 299 p.
LC: Mr 12, '23.
PW: S 1, '23.
BLC: London: Hutchinson & Co., [1925].

B-476 _____ Gloria Gray, love pirate / by Pearl Doles Bell; illustrated by John A. Hagstrom; frontispiece by the author. Chicago, Illinois: Roberts & Company, [c1914]. 333 p., front., [4] leaves of plates.
LC: Ja 8, '14.
PW: Ja 10, '14.

B-477 _____ Her elephant man: a story of the sawdust ring / by Pearl Doles Bell; illustrated by George Brehm. New York: Robert M. McBride & Company, 1919. 297 p., front., [2] leaves of plates.
LC: O 15, '19.
PW: N 1, '19.
BLC: London: J. Bale & Co., [1921].

B-478 _____ His harvest / by Pearl Doles Bell. New York: John Lane Company; London: John Lane, The Bodley Head; Toronto: S. B. Gundy, 1915. 319 p.
LC: O 26, '15.
PW: O 30, '15.

B-479 _____ The love link / by Pearl Doles Bell. New York: W. J. Watt & Co., [c1925]. 304 p.
LC: My 27, '25.
PW: Jl 25, '25.
BLC: London: Hutchinson & Co., [1926].

B-480 _____ Sandra / by Pearl Doles Bell. New York: W. J. Watt & Co., [c1924]. 328 p.
LC: F 18, '24.
PW: Ap 26, '24.
BLC: London: Hutchinson & Co., [1924].

Bell, William Mara. See **Marabell, William, pseud.**

B-481 Bellah, James Warner, 1899-1976. Sketch book of a cadet from Gascony / by James Warner Bellah. New York: Alfred A. Knopf, 1923. 148 p. **NYP**
"Alfred A. Knopf publication prize."
Contents: The last of the line -- The neophyte -- Bonfires and elms, 1919 -- Male bolge, 1920 -- The garden of Epicurus, 1921 -- The day, 1922 -- Scapa flow -- "Some dropped by the wayside," 1919 -- Flotsam -- The swashbackler -- The odyssey of Percival Fiske.

B-482 Bellamy, Francis R. (Francis Rufus), b. 1886. The balance: a novel / by Francis R. Bellamy; illustrated by Arthur Litle. Garden City, N. Y.: Doubleday, Page & Company, 1917. 347, [1] p., front., [3] leaves of plates.
LC: Ja 17, '17.
PW: Ja 20, '17.

B-483 _____ A flash of gold / by Francis R. Bellamy. -- 1st ed. -- Garden City, N. Y.: Doubleday, Page & Company, 1922. 293 p.
LC: S 25, '22.
PW: S 23, '22.
BLC: London: Curtis Brown; printed in U. S. A., 1922.

B-484　Bellinger, Martha, b. 1870. The stolen singer / by Martha Bellinger; with illustrations by Arthur William Brown. Indianapolis: The Bobbs-Merrill Company, [c1911]. 382 p., front., [4] leaves of plates.
PW: D 16, '11.

B-485　The Bellman book of fiction: 1906-1919 / chosen and edited by William C. Edgar . . . Minneapolis, Minn., U. S. A.: The Bellman Company, 1921.
254 p.　　　　　　　　　　　　　　　**MNU**
Contents: The mute / Robert W. Sneddon -- The laughing Duchess / Virginia Woodward Cloud -- Long, long ago / Frederick Orin Bartlett -- The right whale's flukes / Ben Ames Williams -- When Breathit went to battle / Lewis H. Kilpatrick -- The forgiver / Marjorie L. C. Pickthall -- Told to the parson / Eden Phillpotts -- Iron / Randolph Edgar -- The perfect interval / Margaret Adelaide Wilson -- The Archbishop of Rheims / Emily W. Scott -- The Trawnbeighs / Charles Macomb Flandrau -- The life belt / J. J. Bell -- Amina / Edward Lucas White -- The silver ring / Frank Swinnerton -- The surgeon / B. W. Mitchell -- The 'dopters / Aileen Cleveland Higgins -- Prem Singh / John Amid -- Even so / Charles Boardman Hawes -- The cask ashore / Sir Arthur Quiller-Couch.

B-486　Bement, Catherine Plumer, b. 1863. A spinner of webs / by Catherine Plumer Bement. Boston: The Four Seas Company, 1919. 389 p., front.
LC: D 1, '19.

B-487　Bement, Howard, b. 1875. Old man Dare's talks to college men / by Howard Bement; with an introduction by Marion LeRoy Burton. New York; Chicago; London; Edinburgh: Fleming H. Revell Company, [c1922]. 90 p.
Contents: "What are you here for?" -- "Why study?" -- "How to study" -- "The fraternity - a millstone or a milestone?" -- "Causes and effects".

B-488　Bencliff, Thomas. His American birthright: and other stories / by Thomas Bencliff. Saint Louis: Western Junior Publishing Company, 1903. 194 p., [5] leaves of plates. Decorated end papers.
Contents: His American birthright -- One clear call -- The decision.

Bend, Palmer, pseud. See **Putnam, George Palmer, 1887-1950.**

B-489　Bendele, Bertha. A girl of the West / by Bertha Bendele. Baltimore, Md.: Saulsbury Publishing Company, [c1919]. 87 p.　　　　**NYP**
LC: S 5, '19.

B-490　Benedict, Clare. A resemblance: and other stories / by Clare Benedict. New York; London: G. P. Putnam's Sons, 1909. ([New York]: The Knickerbocker Press). 378 p.　　　　**NYP**
"Partly reprinted from the Atlantic monthly, Harper's magazine and the Century magazine."
Contents: A resemblance -- An adventure at Lismore End -- His comrade -- Brand's guardian -- An interchange of courtesies -- The eternal masculine -- Love in the mist -- The end of "Donnelly" -- Roderick Eaton's children -- A portrait by Collyer.
LC: F 19, '09.

Benedict, Leopold, b.1856. See **Winchevsky, Morris, pseud.**

B-491　Benefield, Barry, b. 1883. The chicken-wagon family / by Barry Benefield. New York; London: The Century Co., [c1925]. 332 p.
PW: S 5, '25.

_____ Miss Willett. In *The best short stories of 1916 and the yearbook of the American short story* (1917), **B-561.**

B-492　Benét, Stephen Vincent, 1898-1943. The beginning of wisdom / by Stephen Vincent Benét. New York: Henry Holt and Company, 1921. 359 p.
LC: O 7, '21.
PW: O 22, '21.
BLC: London; Sydney: Chapman & Dodd, 1922.

B-493　_____ Jean Huguenot / by Stephen Vincent Benét. New York: Henry Holt and Company, 1923. 292 p.
LC: S 21, '23.
PW: O 13, '23.
BLC: London: Methuen & Co., 1925.

_____ Uriah's son. In *Prize stories of 1924* (1925), **P-622.**

B-494　_____ Young people's pride: a novel / by Stephen Vincent Benét; illustrations by Henry Raleigh. New York: Henry Holt and Company, 1922. 300 p., front., [5] leaves of plates.
LC: Ag 26, '22.
PW: Ag 26, '22.

B-495　Benét, William Rose, 1886-1950. The first person singular / by William Rose Benét. New York: George H. Doran Company, [c1922]. 300 p.
　　　　　　　　　　　　　　　　　OUN

B-496　Bengough, Elisa Armstrong. The talk of the town: a neighborhood novel / by Elisa Armstrong Bengough. New York: D. Appleton & Co., 1902. 232 p.
PW: N 8, '02.

Bennauer, Adolph. On trail, a story of the Northland. In *Golden stories* (1909), **G-285.**

B-497　Bennet, Robert Ames, 1870-1954. The blond beast / by Robert Ames Bennet. Chicago: The Reilly & Britton Co., [c1918]. 416 p.
LC: Je 26, '18.
PW: Je 1, '18.
BLC: London: Hutchinson & Co., [1919].

B-498　_____ Bloom of cactus / by Robert Ames Bennet; frontispiece by Ralph Pallen Coleman. Garden City, N. Y.: Doubleday, Page & Company, 1920. 248 p., col. front.
LC: My 4, '20.
PW: F 7, '20.

B-499　_____ Branded / by Robert Ames Bennet. Chicago: A. C. McClurg & Co., 1924. 307 p., front.
LC: N 4, '24.
PW: N 22, '24.

B-500　_____ The cattle baron / by Robert Ames Bennet . . . Chicago: A. C. McClurg & Co., 1925. 295 p., front. [Ill. by J. Allen St. John.]
LC: S 28, '25.
PW: O 10, '25.
BLC: London: W. Collins, Sons & Co., [1928]. British title: *The two-gun girl.*

B-501   For the white Christ: a story of the days of Charlemagne / by Robert Ames Bennet; having pictures and designs by Troy & Margaret West Kinney. Chicago: A. C. McClurg & Co., 1905. 474 p., col. front., [3] leaves of col. plates. Illustrated end papers.
PW: Mr 25, '05.
BLC: London: C. F. Cazenove; Cambridge, U. S. A. [printed], 1905.

B-502   [____] The forest maiden / by Lee Robinet [pseud.]; illustrated by George Brehm. Chicago: Browne & Howell Company, 1914. 349, [1] p., col. front. Unexamined copy: bibliographic data from NUC.
LC: My 6, '14.
PW: Ap 25, '14.

B-503   Into the primitive / by Robert Ames Bennet; with illustrations in color by Allen T. True. Chicago: A. C. McClurg & Co., 1908. 318 p., col. front., [3] leaves of col. plates.
LC: Ap 13, '08.
PW: Ap 11, '08.

B-504   Out of the depths: a romance of reclamation / by Robert Ames Bennet; with illustrations by George Brehm. Chicago: A. C. McClurg & Co., 1913. 399 p., col. front., [3] leaves of plates.
LC: Ap 2, '13.
PW: Ap 19, '13.
BLC: London: C. F. Cazenove; Coshocton [printed], 1913.

B-505   Out of the primitive / by Robert Ames Bennet; with illustrations in color by Allen T. True. Chicago: A.C. McClurg & Co., 1911. 378 p., col. front., [3] leaves of col. plates.
PW: O 21, '11.

B-506   The quarterbreed / by Robert Ames Bennet; illustrated by the Kinneys. Chicago: Browne & Howell Company, 1914. 347 p., col. front.
OSU, NYP
LC: My 6, '14.
PW: My 9, '14.

B-507   The rough rider / by Robert Ames Bennet . . . Chicago: A. C. McClurg & Co., 1925. 302 p., front. [Ill. by J. Allen St. John.]
LC: Mr 24, '25.
PW: Ap 18, '25.
BLC: London: W. Collins, Sons & Co., [1927].

B-508   The shogun's daughter / by Robert Ames Bennet; with 5 pictures in color by W. D. Goldbeck. Chicago: A. C. McClurg & Co., 1910. 420 p., col. front., [4] leaves of col. plates.
LC: O 3, '10.

B-509   Thyra: a romance of the Polar Pit / by Robert Ames Bennet; illustrated by E. L. Blumenschein. New York: Henry Holt and Company, 1901. 258 p., front., [6] leaves of plates, maps.
PW: N 23, '01.

B-510   The two-gun man: tells how a man is judged by his clothes and weapons, incidentally proving that two guns in the hands of an expert are better than one / by Robert Ames Bennet . . . Chicago: A. C. McClurg & Co., 1924. 348 p., front. [Ill. by James Allen St. John.]
LC: Ap 4, '24.
PW: My 17, '24.
BLC: London: T. Fisher Unwin, 1925. British title: *Two-Gun Sid.*

B-511   Tyrrell of the cow country / by Robert Ames Bennet; frontispiece by J. Allen St. John. Chicago: A. C. McClurg & Co., 1923. 355 p., front.
LC: S 29, '23.
PW: D 1, '23.
BLC: London: Cassell & Co., 1924. (Popular Edition.)

B-512   A volunteer with Pike: the true narrative of one Dr. John Robinson and of his love for the fair Señorita Vallois / by Robert Ames Bennet, with four illustrations in color by Charlotte Weber-Ditzler. Chicago: A. C. McClurg & Co., 1909. 453 p., col. front., [3] col. leaves of plates
LC: O 6, '09.
PW: O 9, '09.

B-513   Waters of strife / by Robert Ames Bennet. New York: W. J. Watt & Company, [c1921]. 295 p.
LC: Ja 28, '22.
BLC: London: W. Collins, Sons & Co., [1926]. British title: *Waters of conflict.*

B-514   Bennet, Robert Ames, 1870-1954. Which one? / by Robert Ames Bennet . . . ; with illustrations by J. V. McFall. Chicago: A. C. McClurg & Co., 1912. 403 p., col. front., [3] leaves of col. plates. **NYP**
LC: O 23, '12.
PW: D 21, '12.

B-515   Bennet-Thompson, Lilian, b. 1883. Without compromise / by Lilian Bennet-Thompson and George Hubbard. New York: The Century Co., 1922. 298 p.
LC: F 27, '22.

B-516   Bennett, F. I. (Francis I.). Glowing emeralds / by F. I. Bennett. New York: Hy. R. Wohlers, 1923. 300 p.
LC: Je 1, '23.

B-517   Bennett, Florence Mary, b. 1883. An off-islander: a story of Wesquo by the sea / by Florence Mary Bennett. Boston: The Stratford Company, 1921. 311 p., front.
LC: S 1, '21.

B-518   Bennett, H. (Harry), b. 1886. Mason of Bar X / by H. Bennett. Boston: Richard G. Badger, [c1920]. ([Boston, U. S. A.]: The Gorham Press). 215 p. **DLC**
LC: D 22, '20.
PW: Ja 1, '21.

B-519 Bennett, James Clark, 1866(or 7)-1942. Shedding the years / James Clark Bennett. New York: Capitol Book Company, 1925. 383 p.
LC: Je 10, '25.
PW: Jl 4, '25.

Bennett, James Gordon. Mary's little lamb. In **Masson, Thomas Lansing, 1866-1934.** *A bachelor's baby: and some grownups (1907), M-587.*

Bennett, James W. The kiss of the accolade. In *Prize stories of 1922 (1923), P-620.*

B-520 Bennett, Jennie. A light in the window: a story of the wanderings and sufferings of a wayward boy / by Jennie Bennett; illustrated. Chicago: Hammond Press, W. B. Conkey Company, 1913. 143 p.
DLC
LC: N 14, '13.

B-521 Bennett, John, 1865-1956. Barnaby Lee / by John Bennett; with illustrations by Clyde O. De Land. New York: The Century Co., 1902. 454 p., front., [33] leaves of plates.
PW: O 25, '02.

B-522 _____ Madame Margot: a grotesque legend of old Charleston / by John Bennett. New York: The Century Co., 1921. 110 p.
(The bat series.)
PW: N 16, '21.

B-523 _____ The treasure of Peyre Gaillard: being an account of the recovery, on a South Carolina plantation, of a treasure, which had remained buried and lost in a vast swamp for over a hundred years / arranged by John Bennett, after the ms. narrative by Buck Guignard, Esq. In the French manuscript entitled "Le monticule du Jude." New York: The Century Co., 1906. 370 p., front., [13] leaves of plates.
PW: N 3, '06.

B-524 Bennett, Johonnas, b. 1862. La belle San Antone / by Johonnas Bennett. New York; Washington: The Neale Publishing Company, 1909. 288 p.
LC: N 19, '09.
PW: N 13, '09.

B-525 Bennett, Mary Chapman. Finding the right path; The hand of love / by Mary Chapman Bennett. Baltimore, Md.: Saulsbury Publishing Company, [c1919]. 46 p., front., [1] leaf of plates. [Ill. by Will H. Chandlee.]
DLC
LC: Jl 28, '19.

B-526 Bennett, Mary E. (Mary Elizabeth). Reminiscences of Virginia life a century ago / by Mary E. Bennett. Baltimore, Md.: Thomas & Evans Printing Company, 1924. 145 p.
NYP
LC: Ap 20, '25.

B-527 Benson, B. K. (Blackwood Ketcham), b. 1845. Bayard's courier: a story of love and adventure in the cavalry campaigns / by B. K. Benson. New York: The Macmillan Company; London: Macmillan &

Co., Ltd, 1902. 402 p., front., [7] leaves of plates. [Ill. by Louis Betts.]

B-528 _____ A friend with the countersign / by B. K. Benson. New York: The Macmillan Company; London: Macmillan & Co., Ltd., 1901. 455 p., front., [11] leaves of plates, maps. [Ill. by Louis Betts.]
PW: S 21, '01.

B-529 _____ Old Squire: the romance of a black Virginian / by B. K. Benson. New York: The Macmillan Company; London: Macmillan & Co., Ltd., 1903. 431 p., maps.
PW: My 2, '03.

B-530 Benson, Ramsey, b. 1866. A knight in denim / by Ramsey Benson. New York: Charles Scribner's Sons, 1912. 307 p.

B-531 _____ A lord of lands / by Ramsey Benson. New York: Henry Holt and Company, 1908. 326 p.
WMC

B-532 _____ Melchisedec / by Ramsey Benson. New York: Henry Holt and Company, 1909. 301 p.

B-533 Bent, John J. (John Joseph). Stranger than fiction: a series of short stories / by John J. Bent. Boston, Mass.: Matthew F. Sheehan Co., [c1916]. 180 p., photo. front. (port.).
DLC
Contents: The supreme test -- The fulfillment of a prophecy -- The "call" of Caubeen Cassidy -- Margy's knight -- The temptation of "Billy" Blue -- The widow's might -- Anima remata -- A sick call from heaven -- The mission of a bookmark -- Golgotha to Olivet -- Sister Benizia's début -- Vita pro vita.
LC: N 27, '16.

B-534 Bentley, Robert Thomson. Forestfield: a story of the old South (in two periods) / by Robert Thomson Bentley. New York: The Grafton Press, [c1903]. 365 p., photo. front.
TNS
PW: F 13, '04.

B-535 Benton, Frank. Cowboy life on the sidetrack: being an extremely humorous and sarcastic story of the trials and tribulations endured by a party of stockmen making a shipment from the West to the East / by Frank Benton; illustrated by E. A. Filleau. Denver, Colo.: The Western Stories Syndicate, [c1903]. 207 p., ill., ports.
DLC

Bercovici, Konrad, b. 1882. The death of Murdo. In *The best short stories of 1922 and the yearbook of the American short story (1923), B-567.*

_____ The drought. In *More aces (1925), M-962.*

B-536 _____ Dust of New York / by Konrad Bercovici. New York: Boni and Liveright, 1919. 239 p., front., [3] leaves of plates. [Ill. by Samuel Cahan and Herb Roth.]
KSW
"A number of the stories included in this volume are reprinted from the New York World."
Contents: Theresa the vamp -- The troubles of a perfect type -- How the Ibanezes love -- The little man of Twenty-eighth Street -- The newly-rich Goldsteins -- All in one wild Roumanian song --

Expensive poverty -- Why her name is Marguerite V. L. F. Clement -- Luleika, the rich widow -- Because Cohen could neither read nor write -- The marriage broker's daughter -- The new secretary of the pretzel-painter's union -- The gypsy blood that tells -- When Stark's Café was closed -- Because of bookkeeping -- The strength of the weak -- Socialists! Beware of Mrs. Rosenberg -- A conflict of ideals -- The holy healer from Omsk -- Hirsh Roth's theory -- The tragedy of Afghan's living rug -- Babeta's dog -- The professor -- The pure motive.
LC: D 6, '19.
PW: D 6, '19.

B-537 ____ Ghitza: and other romances of gypsy blood / by Konrad Bercovici. New York: Boni and Liveright, [c1921]. 227 p.
Contents: Ghitza -- The law of the lawless -- Vlad's son -- Yahde, the proud one -- Tinka -- Fanutza -- Hazi, wife of Sender Surtuck -- The bear tamer's daughter -- Yancu Lautaru.
LC: S 30, '21.
PW: O 15, '21.

B-538 ____ Iliana: stories of a wondering race / by Konrad Bercovici. New York: Boni and Liveright, 1924. 324 p.
Contents: Muzio -- Seed -- The master -- Revenge -- The woman -- Wisdom of youth -- Happiness -- Jancu Gain -- Iliana -- The stranger -- Rutka.
LC: S 19, '24.
PW: S 6, '24.

B-539 ____ The marriage guest: a novel / by Konrad Bercovici. New York: Boni & Liveright, 1925. 285 p.
LC: O 14, '25.
PW: S 12, '25.

B-540 ____ Murdo / by Konrad Bercovici. New York: Boni and Liveright, [c1923]. 228 p.
LC: Ap 2, '23.
PW: Mr 31, '23.

____ Seed. In *The best short stories of 1923 and the yearbook of the American short story* (1924), **B-568.**

Berdyczewski, Micha Joseph. Military service. In *Yiddish tales* (1912), **Y-20.**

B-541 Bergengren, Ralph, b. 1871. Gentlemen all and merry companions / by Ralph Bergengren; with many illustrations by John Sloan. Boston: B. J. Brimmer Company, 1922. 247 p.
LC: Ja 2, '23.

B-542 Berger, Haddie Torrey. The days of the sons of God / by Haddie Torrey Berger. Boston, Massachusetts: The Stratford Company, 1924. 73 p.   **DLC**
LC: N 24, '24.

B-543 Berkeley, John. A modern revolt from Rome / by John Berkeley. Cincinnati: Jennings and Graham; New York: Eaton and Mains, [c1910]. 339 p.
LC: N 7, '10.

Berkowitz, Isaac Dob. Country Folk. In *Yiddish tales* (1912), **Y-20.**

____ The last of them. In *Yiddish tales* (1912), **Y-20.**

B-544 Berman, Henry. Gift bearers: a novel / by Henry Berman . . . New York: The Grafton Press, [c1907]. 212 p.   **BAI**
LC: O 26, '07.
PW: D 14, '07.

B-545 ____ The tyrant in white / by Henry Berman . . . New York: Frank F. Lovell Company, [c1909]. 320 p.   **UUM**
LC: S 24, '09.

B-546 ____ Worshippers: a novel / by Henry Berman. New York: The Grafton Press, [c1906]. 272 p.
PW: Mr 10, '06.

B-547 Bernstein, Herman, 1876-1935. Contrite hearts / by Herman Bernstein . . . New York: A. Wessels Company, [c1905]. 217 p.   **NYP**
PW: D 2, '05.

B-548 ____ In the gates of Israel: stories of the Jews / by Herman Bernstein. New York: J. F. Taylor & Company, 1902. 316 p., front. [Ill. by F. Lowenheim.]
Contents: Soreh Rivke's vigil -- The messenger of the community -- The awakening -- Alone -- The sinners -- The straight hunchback -- The marriage broker -- The artist -- A jealousy cure -- The disarmed reformer -- A Ghetto romance.

B-549 Berra, Matilde J. (Matilde Juana), b. 1846. The twentieth century woman toward the reconstructive movement / by Matilde J. Berra. Los Angeles, Calif.: [s. n.], [c1904]. 336 p., photo. front. (port.).   **ORU**
PW: D 17, '04.

B-550 Berrien, Katharine. Daddy Ben: (a study in black and white): being a story of the lives of real personages during the Civil War. Savannah, Ga.: The Savannah Morning News, 1906. 24 p.   **VIC**
Designed end papers.

B-551 Berry, Henry H. Hillside: a tale of New England country life / by Henry H. Berry . . . Lockport, Ill.: Will County Printing Co., 1904. 104 p., photo. ill.   **NYP**

B-552 Berry, Mary Anne. A woman of uncertain age / by Mary Anne Berry. New York: The Stuyvesant Press, 1909. 293 p.
LC: My 6, '09.

B-553 Berry, Robert Lee, 1874-1952. Around old Bethany: a story of the adventures of Robert and Mary Davis / by R. L. Berry . . . Anderson, Indiana: Gospel Trumpet Company, [c1925]. 111 p., ill. [Ill. by C. B. Millar.]   **INA**
LC: Je 25, '25.

Berschadski, Isaiah. Forlorn and forsaken. In *Yiddish tales* (1912), **Y-20.**

B-554 Berton, Guy, *jt. pseud.* Art thou the man? / by Guy Berton [jt. pseud.]; illustrations by Charles R. Macauley. New York: Dodd, Mead and Company, 1905. 288 p., front., [5] leaves of plates.

B-555 Bertrand, William T., b. 1858. Stories of doctors, for doctors, by a doctor / by Dr. W. T. Bertrand. Boston: The Roxburgh Publishing Company, Inc., [c1913]. 163 p.
"Some of these stories were read before medical societies."

B-556 The Best American humorous short stories / edited by Alexander Jessup . . . New York: Boni and Liveright, 1920. 276 p. Illustrated end papers.   **ANC**
(The modern library of the world's best books.)
Contents: The little Frenchman and his water lots / G. P. Morris -- The angel of the odd / E. A. Poe -- The schoolmaster's progress / Caroline M. S. Kirkland -- The Watkinson evening / Eliza Leslie -- Titbottom's spectacles / G. W. Curtis -- My double; and how he undid me / E. E. Hale -- A visit to the asylum for aged and decayed punsters / O. W. Holmes -- The celebrated jumping frog of Calaveras County / Mark Twain -- Elder Brown's backslide / H. S. Edwards -- The hotel experience of Mr. Pink Fluker / R. M. Johnston -- The nice people / H. C. Bunner -- The Buller-Podington compact / F. R. Stockton -- Colonel Starbottle for the plaintiff / B. Harte -- The duplicity of Hargraves / O. Henry -- Bargain day at the Tutt house / G. R. Chester -- A call / Grace M. Cooke -- How the widow won the deacon / W. J. Lampton -- Gideon / W. Hastings.
LC: Jl 21, '20.

B-557 The Best college short stories, 1917-18 / edited by Henry T. Schnittkind; introduction by Edward J. O'Brien. Boston, Massachusetts: The Stratford Company, 1919. 458 p.   **EYM**
Contents: Part I. Acadia University: Somewhere in France / Marguerite A. Woodworth -- Baldwin Wallace College: "The little white fool" / Allene M. Sumner -- Boston University: The career / Constance V. Frazier -- Brown University: The krotchet kid / Howard Shawcross -- Bryn Mawr College: The descending mantle / Monica Barry O'Shea -- College of the City of New York: The dead city / Isidor Schneider -- Columbia University: Pardise lost / Otis Peabody Swift -- Converse College: The potter's wheel / Sarah E. Glass -- Cornell University: Until Tomorrow / Leonard Wood, Jr. -- Harvard University: A butterfly in the fog / Latrobe Carroll -- Haverford College: Man or manners? / Colby V. Dam -- Hunter College: The "s" in fish means sugar / Mollie Grossman -- Macalester College: Greater love hath no man / Beatrice Walker -- Princeton University: P'r'aps / Charles Bayly, Jr. -- Radcliffe College: The way of peace / Ruth Otis Sawtell -- Verdict rendered / Louise F. Windle -- University of Minnesota: The Tomte Gubbe / Alma P. Abrahamson -- Vassar College: A question of method / Laura Scribner -- Invalid home / Catharine N. Wellington -- Washington University: Angéle / John J. Sharon -- Wellesley College: "Two parallel lines meet at infinity" / Helen B. Mitchell -- The return of Vach / Elizabeth Pickett. Part II. Other stories of distinction. Part III. The editor's attitude toward the young author. Part IV. How I have attained literary success.
LC: Ja 23, '19.

B-558 The Best college short stories, 1924-1925 / edited by Henry T. Schnittkind and Horace C. Baker. Boston, Massachusetts: The Stratford Company, 1925. 362 p.   **UND**
Contents: Part I. Barnard College: Michael of the mists / Madge Turner -- Boston College: A portrait in two panels / William F. Walsh -- Colorado College: The dream beautiful / Anne Sutton -- Columbia University: A comedy of manners / Norman Payson -- Converse College: Son Smith / Betty Clyce -- Cornell College: The Chinese lily / Thelma Lucile Lull -- Cornell College: Conformity / Winifred Mayne [i. e., Wayne] -- Depauw University: Paper bags / Alice Reeves -- Harvard University: The hanging of Kruscome Shanks / Walter D. Edmonds, Jr. -- Harvard University: The miracle of Ilderim Ali / "Essenz von Bierschaum" -- Hunter College: Communion / Aurora Joan La Guardia -- Marietta College: Marsh lanterns / Vernon Bowen -- Mount Holyoke College: Jealous gods / Ruth Muskrat -- University of California: The blue spider / Paul Woolf -- University of Idaho: Foam-flowers / Ruth Muriel Aspray -- University of Illinois: A game of billiards / Thornton C. McCune -- University of Michigan: The dark river / Hasseltine Bourland -- University of Richmond: A passage from the life of Francois Villon /

W. G. Richardson -- University of Utah: The spider / Phyllis McGinley -- University of Washington: The Samarkand sapphire / Babette Hughes -- University of Wisconsin: Ice carvings / J. McGrath. Part II. Stories of distinction -- Part III. Editor and author -- Part IV. Names and addresses of magazines publishing short stories -- Part V. How I have attained literary success.
LC: S 30, '25.
PW: N 28, '25.

B-559 The best love stories of 1924 / edited by Muriel Miller Humphrey. Boston: Small, Maynard & Company, [c1925]. 328 p.
Unexamined copy: bibliographic data from copyright records.
LC: Je 13, '25.
PW: Je 6, '25.

B-560 The best short stories of 1915 and the yearbook of the American short story / edited by Edward J. O'Brien. Boston: Small, Maynard & Company, publishers, [1916]. 386 p.   **OCO**
Contents: Introduction / The editor -- The water-hole / Maxwell Struthers Burt -- The wake / Donn Byrne -- Chautonville / Will Levington Comfort -- La dernière mobilisation / W. A. Dwiggins -- The citizen / James Francis Dwyer -- Whose dog -- ? / Frances Gregg -- Life / Ben Hecht -- T. B. / Fannie Hurst -- Mr. Eberdeen's house / Arthur Johnson -- Vengeance is mine / Virgil Jordan -- The weaver who clad the summer / Harris Merton Lyon -- Heart of youth / Walter J. Muilenburg -- The end of the path / Newbold Noyes -- The whale and the grasshopper / Seumas O'Brien -- In Berlin / Mary Boyle O'Reilly -- The waiting years / Katharine Metcalf Roof -- Zelig / Benjamin Rosenblatt -- The survivors / Elsie Singmaster -- The yellow cat / Wilbur Daniel Steele -- The bounty-jumper / Mary Synon -- The yearbook of the American short story for 1914 and 1915.
PW: Ap 22, '16.

B-561 The best short stories of 1916 and the yearbook of the American short story / edited by Edward J. O'Brien. Boston: Small, Maynard & Company, publishers, [1917]. 472 p.   **KSU**
Contents: Introduction / The editor -- The sacrificial altar / Gertrude Atherton -- Miss Willett / Barry Benefield -- Supers / Frederick Booth -- Fog / Dana Burnet -- Ma's pretties / Francis Buzzell -- The Great Auk / Irvin S. Cobb -- The lost Phœbe / Theodore Dreiser -- The silent infare / Armistead C. Gordon -- The cat of the cane-brake / Frederick Stuart Greene -- Making port / Richard Matthews Hallet -- "Ice water, pl--!" / Fannie Hurst -- Little selves / Mary Lerner -- The sun chaser / Jeanette Marks -- At the end of the road / Walter J. Muilenburg -- The big stranger on Dorchester Heights / Albert Du Verney Pentz -- The menorah / Benjamin Rosenblatt -- Penance / Elsie Singmaster -- Feet of gold / Gordon Arthur Smith -- Down on their knees / Wilbur Daniel Steele -- Half-past ten / Alice L. Tildesley -- The yearbook of the American short story for 1916.
LC: Ap 5, '17.

B-562 The best short stories of 1917 and the yearbook of the American short story / edited by Edward J. O'Brien . . . Boston: Small, Maynard & Company, publishers, [1918]. 600 p.
Contents: Introduction / The editor -- The excursion / Edwina Stanton Babcock -- Onnie / Thomas Beer -- A cup of tea / Maxwell Struthers Burt -- Lonely places / Francis Buzzell -- Boys will be boys / Irvin S. Cobb -- Laughter / Charles Caldwell Dobie -- The Emperor of Elam / H. G. Dwight -- The gay old dog / Edna Ferber -- The knight's move / Katharine Fullerton Gerould -- A jury of her peers / Susan Glaspell -- The bunker mouse / Frederick Stuart Greene -- Rainbow Pete / Richard Matthews Hallet -- Get ready the wreaths / Fannie Hurst -- The strange-looking man / Fanny Kemble Johnson -- The caller in the night / Burton Kline -- The interval / Vincent O'Sullivan -- "A certain rich man -" / Lawrence Perry -- The path of glory / Mary Brecht Pulver -- Ching, Ching, Chinaman / Wilbur Daniel Steele -- None so blind / Mary Synon -- The yearbook of the American short story for 1917.
LC: Mr 6, '18.
PW: Mr 9, '18.

B-563   The best short stories of 1918 and the yearbook of the American short story / edited by Edward J. O'Brien . . . Boston: Small, Maynard & Company, publishers, [1919]. 441 p.

Contents: Introduction / The editor -- A simple act of piety / Achmed Abdullah -- Cruelties / Edwina Stanton Babcock -- Buster / Katharine Holland Brown -- The open window / Charles Caldwell Dobie -- Blind vision / Mary Mitchell Freedley -- Imagination / Gordon Hall Gerould -- In Maulmain Fever-ward / George Gilbert -- The father's hand / G. Humphrey -- The visit of the master / Arthur Johnson -- In the open code / Burton Kline -- The willow walk / Sinclair Lewis -- The story Vinton heard at Mallorie / Katharine Prescott Moseley -- The toast to forty-five / William Dudley Pelley -- Extra men / Harrison Rhodes -- Solitaire / Fleta Campbell Springer -- The dark hour / Wilbur Daniel Steele -- The bird of Serbia / Julian Street -- At Isham's / Edward C. Venable -- De Vilmarte's luck / Mary Heaton Vorse -- The white battalion / Frances Gilchrist Wood -- The yearbook of the American short story, January to October, 1918.

PW: Ja 25, '19.

B-564   The best short stories of 1919 and the yearbook of the American short story / edited by Edward J. O'Brien . . . Boston: Small, Maynard & Company, publishers, [1920]. 414 p.

Contents: Introduction / The editor -- The kitchen gods / G. F. Alsop -- An awakening / Sherwood Anderson -- Willum's vanilla / Edwina Stanton Babcock -- A night among the horses / Djuna Barnes -- Long, long ago / Frederick Orin Bartlett -- Dishes / Agnes Mary Brownell -- The blood-red one / Maxwell Struthers Burt -- The wedding-jest / James Branch Cabell -- The wrists on the door / Horace Fish -- "Government goat" / Susan Glaspell -- The stone / Henry Goodman -- To the bitter end / Richard Matthews Hallet -- The meeker ritual / Joseph Hergesheimer -- The centenarian / Will E. Ingersoll -- Messengers / Calvin Johnston -- Mrs. Drainger's veil / Howard Mumford Jones -- Under a wine-glass / Ellen N. La Motte -- A thing of beauty / Elias Lieberman -- The other room / Mary Heaton Vorse -- "The fat of the land" / Anzia Yezierska -- The yearbook of the American short story, November, 1918, to September, 1919.

LC: F 14, '20.
PW: Mr 27, '20.

B-565   The best short stories of 1920 and the yearbook of the American short story / edited by Edward J. O'Brien . . . Boston: Small, Maynard & Company, publishers, [1921]. 500 p.

Contents: Introduction / The editor -- The other woman / Sherwood Anderson -- Gargoyle / Edwina Stanton Babcock -- Ghitza / Konrad Bercovici -- The life of five points / Edna Clare Bryner -- The signal tower / Wadsworth Camp -- The parting genius / Helen Coale Crew -- Habakkuk / Katharine Fullerton Gerould -- The judgment of Vulcan / Lee Foster Hartman -- The stick-in-the-muds / Rupert Hughes -- His job / Grace Sartwell Mason -- The rending / James Oppenheim -- The dummy-chucker / Arthur Somers Roche -- Butterflies / Rose Sidney -- The rotter / Fleta Campbell Springer -- Out of exile / Wilbur Daniel Steele -- The three telegrams / Ethel Storm -- The Roman bath / John T. Wheelwright -- Amazement / Stephen French Whitman -- Sheener / Ben Ames Williams -- Turkey red / Frances Gilchrist Wood -- The yearbook of the American short story, October, 1919, to September, 1920.

LC: Mr 2, '21.
PW: F 5, '21.

B-566   The best short stories of 1921 and the yearbook of the American short story / edited by Edward J. O'Brien . . . Boston: Small, Maynard & Company, publishers, [1922]. 506 p.

Contents: Introduction / The editor -- Brothers / Sherwood Anderson -- Fanutza / Konrad Bercovici -- Experiment / Maxwell Struthers Burt -- Darkness / Irvin S. Cobb -- An instrument of the gods / Lincoln Colcord -- The lizard god / Charles J. Finger -- Under the dome / Waldo Frank -- French Eva / Katharine Fullerton Gerould -- The past / Ellen Glasgow -- His smile / Susan Glaspell -- The harbor master / Richard Matthews Hallet -- Green gardens / Frances Noyes Hart -- She walks in beauty / Fannie Hurst -- The little master of the sky / Manuel Komroff -- The man with the good face / Frank Luther Mott -- Master of fallen years / Vincent O'Sullivan -- The shame dance / Wilbur Daniel Steele -- Kindred / Harriet Maxon Thayer -- Shelby /

Charles Hanson Towne -- The wallow of the sea / Mary Heaton Vorse -- The yearbook of the American short story, October, 1920, to September, 1921.

LC: F 9, '22.
PW: Ja 28, '22.

B-567   The best short stories of 1922 and the yearbook of the American short story / edited by Edward J. O'Brien. Boston: Small, Maynard & Company, publishers, [1923]. 389 p.

Contents: Introduction / The editor -- The dark city / Conrad Aiken -- I'm a fool / Sherwood Anderson -- The death of Murdo / Konrad Bercovici -- An unknown warrior / Susan M. Boogher -- The helpless ones / Frederick Booth -- Forest cover / Edna Bryner -- Natalka's portion / Rose Gollup [i. e., Gallup] Cohen -- The shame of gold / Charles J. Finger -- Two for a cent / F. Scott Fitzgerald -- John the Baptist / Waldo Frank -- Mendel Marantz-housewife / David Freedman -- Belshazzar's letter / Katharine Fullerton Gerould -- Winkleburg / Ben Hecht -- The token / Joseph Hergesheimer -- The resurrection and the life / William Jitro -- The golden honeymoon / Ring W. Lardner -- He laughed at the Gods / James Oppenheim -- In the Metropolis / Benjamin Rosenblatt -- From the other side of the south / Wilbur Daniel Steele -- The coffin / Clement Wood -- The yearbook of the American short story, October, 1921, to September, 1922.

LC: F 13, '23.
PW: F 3, '23.

B-568   The best short stories of 1923 and the yearbook of the American short story / edited by Edward J. O'Brien. Boston: Small, Maynard & Company, publishers, [1924]. 544 p.

Contents: Introduction / The editor -- Way for a sailor / Bill Adams -- The man's story / Sherwood Anderson -- Mr. Cardeezer / Edwina Stanton Babcock -- Seed / Konrad Bercovici -- Beyond the cross / Dana Burnet -- Ignition / Valma Clark -- The chocolate hyena / Irvin S. Cobb -- The samovar / John Cournos -- Reina / Theodore Dreiser -- Home girl / Edna Ferber -- The button / Henry Goodman -- My old man / Ernest Hemingway -- Seven candles / Fannie Hurst -- The today tomorrow / Margaret Prescott Montague -- The contract of Corporal Twing / Solon K. Stewart -- By due process of law / F. J. Stimson -- Renters / Ruth Suckow -- Blood-burning moon / Jean Toomer -- The promise / Mary Heaton Vorse -- Flora and Fauna / Harry Leon Wilson -- The yearbook of the American short story, October 1922, to September, 1923.

LC: F 8, '24.
PW: Ja 26, '24.

B-569   The best short stories of 1924 and the yearbook of the American short story / edited by Edward J. O'Brien. Boston: Small, Maynard & Company, publishers, [1925]. 367 p.

Contents: Introduction / The editor -- Champlin / Morgan Burke -- Billy / Mildred Cram -- Phantom adventure / Floyd Dell -- The cracked teapot / Charles Caldwell Dobie -- The last dive / Carlos Drake -- Adventures of Andrew Lang / Charles J. Finger -- The biography of Blade / Zona Gale -- Corputt / Tupper Greenwald -- The young men go down / Harry Hervey -- The lesser gift / Leonard L. Hess -- Grudges / Rupert Hughes -- A postscript to divorce / Gouverneur Morris -- Forgiveness / Lizette Woodworth Reese -- Nocturne: a red shawl / Roger Sergel -- The black laugh / A. B. Shiffrin -- Four generations / Ruth Suckow -- Two women and Hogback Ridge / Melvin Van den Bark -- The poet / Warren L. Van Dine -- In a thicket / Glenway Wescott -- Shoes / Frances Gilchrist Wood -- The yearbook of the American short story, October, 1923, to September, 1924.

LC: N 19, '24.
PW: Ja 17, '25.

B-570   Bethea, Jack, 1892-1928. Bed rock / by Jack Bethea. Boston; New York: Houghton Mifflin Company, 1924. (Cambridge: The Riverside Press). 355 p.
PW: N 1, '24.
BLC: London: Hodder & Stoughton, [1925].

B-571 Bethesda: the temperate life. New York: Moffat, Yard & Company, 1923. 299 p., front., [3] leaves of plates. [Ill. by Ray C. Strang.] **DLC**

B-572 Betiero, T. J. (Thomas Jasper). Nedoure, priestess of the Magi: an historical romance of white and black magic: a story that reveals wisdom of the ancient past / by T. J. Betiero. Seattle, Wash.: Published by W. F. Wohlstein & Co., [c1916]. 247 p.

B-573 Betten, J. C. That gal from Arkansaw . . . Eureka Springs, Ark: the author, c1906. 69 p. **NYP**

B-574 Betts, Lillian Williams. The story of an East-side family / by Lillian W. Betts. New York: Dodd, Mead and Company, 1903. 342 p.
PW: Ap 25, '03.

B-575 Betts, Nannie Deadrick. The flower of the season / by Nannie Deaderick Betts. New York: Broadway Publishing Co., 1912. 234 p., front. **DLC**
LC: Je 17, '12.

B-576 Betty comes to town: a letter home. New York: Robert L. Stillson Company, 1909. 30 p., ill. "A description of the Wanamaker's store."

Bevans, Neile, pseud. See **Van Slingerland, Mrs. Nellie Bingham.**

B-577 Beyerle, Lincoln Hamlin, b. 1860. The quitters / by Lincoln H. Beyerle. Illustrations by Will Carqueville. Chicago: W. B. Conkey Company, [c1910]. 261 p., front., [3] leaves of plates.
LC: Ag 18, '10.
PW: S 24, '10.

B-578 Biagi, L. D. The Centaurians; a novel / by Biagi. New York; Chicago [etc.]: Broadway Publishing Co., [c1911]. 339 p.
Unexamined copy: bibliographic data from NUC.
LC: O 21, '11.

B-579 Bianchi, Martha Dickinson, 1866-1943. A Cossack lover / by Martha Gilbert Dickinson Bianchi. New York: Duffield & Company, 1911. 363 p. **DLC**
LC: Ja 17, '11.
PW: Ja 28, '11.
BLC: London: Everett & Co., [1913].

B-580 _____ The cuckoo's nest / by Martha Gilbert Dickinson Bianchi . . . New York: Duffield and Company, 1909. 419, [1] p.
LC: Je 30, '09.
PW: Je 19, '09.

B-581 _____ The kiss of Apollo / by Martha Gilbert Dickinson Bianchi. New York: Duffield & Company, 1915. 408 p.
LC: My 5, '15.
PW: My 15, '15.

B-582 _____ A modern Prometheus / by Martha Gilbert Dickinson Bianchi. New York: Duffield & Company, 1908. 413 p., front.

B-583 _____ The point of view / by Martha Gilbert Dickinson Bianchi. New York: Duffield & Company, 1918. 330 p.
LC: Je 11, '18.
PW: Je 22, '18.

B-584 _____ The sin of angels / by Martha Gilbert Dickinson Bianchi. New York: Duffield & Company, 1912. 504 p.
LC: Ag 2, '12.
PW: Ag 17, '12.

B-585 Bianco, Margery Williams, 1880-1944. The late returning / by Margery Williams. New York: The Macmillan Company; London: Macmillan & Co., Ltd., 1902. 205 p.
PW: Je 7, '02.

B-586 _____ The price of youth / by Margery Williams. New York: The Macmillan Company; London: Macmillan & Co., Ltd., 1904. 312 p.
PW: Mr 26, '04.
BLC: London: Duckworth & Co., 1904.

Bibbins, Arthur Barneveld, Mrs. See **Bibbins Ruthella Mory, 1865-1942.**

B-587 Bibbins, Ruthella Mory, 1865-1942. Mammy 'mongst the wild nations of Europe / by Ruthella Mory Bibbins; illustrated by Francis P. Wightman. New York: Frederick A. Stokes Company, [1904]. 305 p., front., [7] leaves of plates. [Also ill. by T. P. Barclay.]
PW: O 22, '04.

Bickers, Daniel Garnett, b. 1873, ed. See **N. P. M.**

B-588 Bicknell, Frank M. (Frank Martin), 1854-1916. Blitzen the conjurer / by Frank M. Bicknell; with illustrations by Bart Haley. Philadelphia: Henry Altemus Company, [c1906]. 130 p., front., ill. **NYP**
LC: S 18, '06.

B-589 Biddle, Sarah. Some letters of an American woman concerning love and other things / by Sarah Biddle; drawings by Annetta Gibson McCall. Philadelphia: International Printing Company, 1902. 194 p., front., [15] leaves of plates.

B-590 Bidwell, Benson, b. 1835. Flying cows of Biloxi / by Benson Bidwell . . . ; illustrated. Chicago: The Henneberry Press, 1907. 44 p., photo. front. (port.), [1] leaf of col. plates, ill. **RRR**
LC: N 7, '07.

B-591 Bieder, Charles F. The sandalwood chest / by Charles F. Bieder. Cleveland, O.: Printed by the Britton Publishing Co., [c1919]. 24 p., front. [Ill. by Irma Detlefs.] **DLC**

Bienz, Mrs. Adah Viola (Rohrer), b. 1872. See **Searles, Jean Randolph, pseud.**

B-592 _____ My favorite murder / by Ambrose Bierce.

[S. l.: S. N., c1916?]. 16 p.
Unexamined copy: bibliographic data from OCLC,
#9073005.
First separate edition: reprinted from *Can such things
be*, [1893].
References: BAL 1131; Starrett, 25.

B-593   _____ A son of the gods; and, A horseman in the sky
/ by Ambrose Bierce; including an introduction by W.
C. Morrow; the photogravure frontispiece after a
painting by Will Jenkins. --1st ed.-- San Francisco;
New York: Paul Elder and Company, [c1907].
47 p., front.
Western Classics series No. 4. First book
appearance; reprinted from *Tales of soldiers and
civilians*, 1891.
LC: N 13, '07.
PW: D 21, '07.
References: BAL 1126; Starrett, 21.

Bierschaum, Essenz von. The miracle of Ilderim Ali.
See *The best college short stories, 1924-1925*, **B-558**.

Bigelow, Edith Evelyn Jaffray. See **Bigelow,
Poultney, Mrs., 1861-1932.**

B-594   Bigelow, Poultney, Mrs., 1861-1932. The middle
course / by Mrs. Poultney Bigelow; illustrated by C.
B. Currier. New York; London: The Smart Set
Publishing Co., 1903. 317 p., front., [4] leaves of
plates.

B-595   _____ While Charlie was away / By Mrs. Poultney
Bigelow. New York: D. Appleton & Co., 1901.
166 p.
BLC: London: William Heinemann, 1901.

B-596   Biggers, Earl Derr, 1884-1933. The agony column /
by Earl Derr Biggers; illustrated by Will Grefé.
Indianapolis: The Bobbs-Merrill Company, [c1916].
193, [1] p., front., [8] leaves of plates.
LC: N 1, '16.
PW: N 4, '16.

          _____ The apron of genius. In **Conrad, Joseph. *Il
conte* (1925), C-697.**

B-597   _____ The house without a key / by Earl Derr
Biggers. Indianapolis: The Bobbs-Merrill Company,
[c1925]. 316 p.
LC: Mr 19, '25.
PW: Mr 28, '25.
BLC: London: G. G. Harrap, 1926.

B-598   _____ Inside the lines / by Earl Derr Biggers and
Robert Welles Ritchie, founded on Earl Derr Biggers'
play of the same name. Indianapolis: The
Bobbs-Merrill Company, [c1915]. 331 p., front., [7]
leaves of plates
LC: O 8, '15.
PW: O 23, '15.

B-599   _____ Love insurance / by Earl Derr Biggers; with
illustrations by Frank Snapp. Indianapolis: The
Bobbs-Merrill Company, [c1914]. 402 p., front., [8]

leaves of plates.
LC: S 21, '14.
PW: S 26, '14.

B-600   _____ Seven keys to Baldpate / by Earl Derr Biggers;
illustrated by Frank Snapp. Indianapolis: The
Bobbs-Merrill Company, [c1913]. 408 p., front., [4]
leaves of plates.
LC: F 24, '13.
PW: F 15, '13.
BLC: London: Mills & Boon, 1914.

B-601   Bilbro, Mathilde. The middle pasture / by Mathilde
Bilbro; with illustrations by Frances Porter Pratt and
Christine Tucke Curtiss. Boston: Small, Maynard
and Company, [c1917]. 323, [1] p., col. front., [2]
leaves of plates.
LC: Ap 5, '17.

B-602   Bill, Alfred Hoyt, b. 1879. The clutch of the
Corsican: a tale of the days of the downfall of the
great Napoleon / by Alfred H. Bill; frontispiece by
Frank M. Rines. Boston: The Atlantic Monthly
Press, [c1925]. 241 p., front.
PW: Mr 28, '25.

Billings, Edith S. See **Billings, Maris, pseud.**

B-603   Billings, Maris, *pseud*. Cleomenes / by Maris
Warrington Billings [pseud.]. New York: John
Lane Company; London: John Lane, The Bodley
Head, 1917. 378 p.
PW: My 5, '17.
BLC: London: Jarrolds, [1920].

B-604   _____ An Egyptian love spell / by Maris Warrington
Billings [pseud.]. New York: The Central Publishing
Co., [1914]. 62 p., front., ill.
"Reprinted from the November, 1913, issue of "The
Word".

B-605   Billington, Addie B. Dear, my lady: the thrall of
conscience / by Addie B. Billington; illustrated by
Glen Geren. Des Moines: E. E. Evans Co., 1917.
95 p., photo. front. (port.), photo. ill. Decorated end
papers.

B-606   Bingham, Edfrid A. The heart of thunder mountain /
by Edfrid A. Bingham; with a frontispiece by Anton
Otto Fischer. Boston: Little, Brown and Company,
1916. 360 p., col. front.
PW: Mr 18, '16.

          _____ See also **Berton, Guy, jt. pseud. of Guy
Roberts La Coste and Eadfrid A. Bingham.**

B-607   Bingham, Frasier Franklin. Ashore at Maiden's
Walk / by F. F. Bingham. New York: Broadway
Publishing Company, [c1913]. 192 p., front., [4]
leaves of plates, ill.

B-608   Bingham, Kate Boyles, b. 1876. A daughter of the
Badlands / by Kate Boyles Bingham and Virgil D.
Boyles. Boston, Mass.: The Stratford Company,
1922. 259 p., front. [Ill. by G. Livingston.]
LC: Ap 3, '22.
PW: Ap 22, '22.

B-609　　＿＿＿　The homesteaders / by Kate and Virgil D. Boyles . . . ; with four illustrations in full color by Maynard Dixon. Chicago: A. C. McClurg & Co., 1909. 345, [1] p., col. front., [3] leaves of col. plates.
LC: S 13, '09.
PW: O 2, '09.

B-610　　＿＿＿　The Hoosier volunteer / by Kate and Virgil D. Boyles . . . ; illustrated by Troy and Margaret West Kinney. Chicago: A. C. McClurg & Co., 1914. 389 p., col. front., [3] leaves of col. plates.

B-611　　＿＿＿　Langford of the three bars / by Kate and Virgil D. Boyles; with illustrations in color by N. C. Wyeth. Chicago: A. C. McClurg & Co., 1907. 277, [1] p., col. front., [3] leaves of col. plates.
LC: Ap 17, '07.

B-612　　＿＿＿　The spirit trail / by Kate and Virgil D. Boyles . . . ; with four illustrations in full color by Maynard Dixon. Chicago: A. C. Mc Clurg & Co., 1910. 416 p., col. front., [3] leaves of col. plates.

B-613　　Bingham, Katharine. The Philadelphians: as seen by a New York woman / by Katharine Bingham; illustrated by Alice Barber Stephens and George Gibbs. Boston: L. C. Page & Company, 1903. 227 p., front., [15] leaves of plates.
(Page's commonwealth series; no. 7.)
"Originally appeared in the Ladies' home journal, 1902."
PW: F 21, '03.

B-614　　Binney, Alice Stead. The legend of Laddin's Rock / by Alice Stead Binney. [New York]: The Knickerbocker Press, 1902. 29 p., photo. front., [2] leaves of photo. plates, ill.
OSU's copy imperfect: lacks frontispiece.

B-615　　Binns, Jack, 1884-1959. The flying buccaneer: a novel of adventure in the skies / by Jack Binns. New York: Nicholas L. Brown, 1923. 311 p.
LC: N 9, '23.
PW: N 17, '23.

B-616　　Birch, White. Apache gold / by White Birch. New York: The H. K. Fly Company, [c1919]. 308 p., front.

Birge, William Spoford, 1857-1925, jt. aut. *No surrender* (1905). See **Swift, John Newton, b. 1854, jt. aut., S-1154.**

B-617　　＿＿＿　Senhor Antone: a tale of the Portuguese colony / by William S. Birge . . . New York; Chicago; London: F. Tennyson Neely Co., [c1901]. 146 p., [1] leaf of photo. plates.

B-618　　Birnbaum, Martin, 1878-1970. Prince Ulric's minstrel / by Martin Birnbaum. [S. l.: s. n.], c1916. 13 p.　　　　**NYP**

B-619　　Bishop, Ernest Franklin. The timber wolf: of the Yukon / Ernest Franklin Bishop. [Chicago: Digest Press, c1925]. 278 p., col. front., [1] leaf of photo. plates. [Ill. by Hal Bishop.]

B-620　　Bishop, John Peale, 1892-1944. The undertaker's garland / John Peale Bishop [and] Edmund Wilson, Jr.; decorations by Boris Artzybasheff. New York: Alfred A. Knopf, 1922. 192 p., ill.
Contents: Preface -- Prologue: Lucifer -- I. The death of the last centaur-- II. The funeral of St. Mary Magdalene -- III. The funeral of a romantic poet -- IV. The death of a dandy -- V. The death of an efficiency expert -- VI. The funeral of an undertaker -- VII. The death of a soldier -- VIII. The madman's funeral -- IX. Emily in Hades -- X. The death of God -- XI. Resurrection -- Epilogue: Apollo.
LC: O 11, '22.

B-621　　Bishop, William Henry, 1847-1928. Anti-babel: and other such doings / by William Henry Bishop. New York: The Neale Publishing Company, 1919. 251 p.
Contents: "Anti-babel" -- The man who made believe he had failed -- The Bric-a-brac mission -- The last of the fairy wands -- Insects I have met -- "Aleck," a sort of ghost story -- Yessamina -- The cruise of a drifted boat.
PW: Ja 24, '20.

B-622　　＿＿＿　Queer people , including The brown stone boy / by William Henry Bishop . . . New York; London: Street & Smith, [1902]. 282 p.
Unexamined copy: bibliographic data from NUC.
"Appeared originally in the `Century magazine', the `Atlantic monthly', `Harper's magazine', `Life', and similar periodicals."
Contents: The brown stone boy -- A little dinner -- Jerry and Clarinda -- A lunch at McArthur's -- Near the rose -- Betwixt and between -- A Christmas crime -- A domestic menagerie.
PW: My 17, '02.

B-623　　＿＿＿　Tons of treasure: a tale of adventure and honor: being a new and improved edition of "The yellow snake" / by William Henry Bishop . . . New York; London: Street & Smith, [c1902]. 274 p.
　　　　　　　MUM
PW: Je 7, '02.

B-624　　Bisland, Elizabeth. A candle of understanding: a novel / by Elizabeth Bisland. New York; London: Harper & Brothers, 1903. 305, [1] p.
PW: O 3, '03.

B-625　　＿＿＿　The case of John Smith: his heaven and his hell / by Elizabeth Bisland . . . New York; London: G. P. Putnam's Sons, 1916. ([New York]: The Knickerbocker Press). 244 p.　　　**CWR**
PW: My 13, '16.

B-626　　A bit of old ivory, and other stories / by Mary F. Nixon-Roulet, Mary T. Waggaman, Mary E. Mannix, Florence Gilmore, Marion Ames Taggart, P. G. Smyth, Anna T. Sadlier, Jerome Harte. New York; Cincinnati; Chicago: Benziger Brothers, 1910. 255 p.　　　　**DLC**
Contents: A bit of old ivory / Mary F. Nixon-Roulet -- The Tomkyns' telephone / Mary T. Waggaman -- Miss Hetty's tramp / Mary E. Mannix -- Bricks and mortar / Marion Ames Taggart -- Chilly con carney / P. G. Smith -- Widow Lavelle's lots / P. G. Smith -- The Rokeby ghost / Mary T. Waggaman -- When the dumb speak / Marion Ames Taggart -- "What God hath joined" / Anna T. Sadlier -- Helena's jewels / Mary E. Mannix -- A belated planet / Mary T. Waggaman -- The habit of Jerry / Marion Ames Taggart -- At the turn of the tide / Mary T. Waggaman -- The piebald nag / Anna T. Sadlier -- Bruin and her baby / Jerome Harte.

B-627　　Bittenbender, Ada M. (Ada Matilda Cole), b. 1848. Tedos and Tisod: a temperance story / by Ada M.

Bittenbender . . . Lincoln, Nebraska: Gilloa Book
Company, [c1911]. 361 p. **NYP**

B-628 Björkman, Edwin, 1866-1951. Gates of life / by
Edwin Björkman. New York: Alfred A. Knopf,
1923. 384 p. Designed end papers.
Sequel to "The soul of a child."
LC: Ap 25, '23.

_____ His own day. In *Forum stories* (1914), F-306.

B-629 _____ The soul of a child / by Edwin Björkman.
New York: Alfred A. Knopf, 1922. 321, [1] p.
LC: Mr 18, '22.

B-630 Black, Alexander, 1859-1940. The great desire / by
Alexander Black. New York; London: Harper &
Brothers, [1919]. 396 p.
LC: S 29, '19.
PW: N 1, '19.
BLC: London: Hodder & Stoughton, [1920].

B-631 _____ Jo Ellen / by Alexander Black. New York;
London: Harper & Brothers [c1923]. 325 p.
LC: S 25, '23.
PW: O 20, '23.
BLC: London: William Heinemann, 1923.

B-632 _____ Richard Gordon / by Alexander Black;
illustrated by Ernest Fuhr. Boston: Lothrop
Publishing Company, [1902]. 506 p., front., [5]
leaves of plates.
PW: O 18, '02.
BLC: London: C. H. Kelly; [printed in America],
1902.

B-633 _____ The seventh angel / by Alexander Black. New
York; London: Harper & Brothers, [c1921]. 360 p.
LC: F 18, '21.
PW: F 26, '21.

B-634 _____ Stacey / by Alexander Black. Indianapolis:
The Bobbs-Merrill Company, [c1925]. 343 p.
LC: Ja 8, '25.
PW: Ja 24, '25.

B-635 _____ Thorney / by Alexander Black; frontispiece by
Orson Lowell. New York: McBride, Nast &
Company, 1913. 306 p., col. front.
LC: Mr 15, '13.
PW: Jl 12, '13.

Black, J. D., Mrs. See **Potter, Margaret Horton,
1881-1911.**

B-636 Blackall, C. R. (Christopher Rubey), 1830-1924. The
son of the Timeus / by C. R. Blackall; decorations
and illustrations by Herbert Dixon Senat.
Philadelphia: George W. Jacobs & Co., 1914.
52 p., front., [1] leaf of plates, ill. **PLT**

Blackburn, Ivy (Chambers). See **Blackburn, W. S.,
Mrs.**

B-637 Blackburn, Mary Johnson. Folk Lore and Mammy
Days / by Mary Johnson Blackburn. Boston: Walter
H. Baker Company, 1924. 105 p., photo. front.
(port.). **WOO**
Contents: Foreword -- Into de wanderlan' [poetry] -- My white chile
[poetry] -- How come? [poetry] -- My Mammy [poetry] -- Dem
Jones's chil'un [poetry] -- Ole Aunt Lize [poetry] -- Mammy dreams
[poetry] -- The D. A. R. Buff-day celebration, or Mammy's tribute to
music -- Hol' my han' -- Lady bug -- Cramps -- [The remainder of
the book is poetry and music].

B-638 Blackburn, W. S., Mrs. In the toils of slavery / by
Mrs. W. S. Blackburn. Chicago: Published by the
American Baptist Publication Society, [c1906].
237 p. **DLC**
PW: N 3, '06.

B-639 Blackledge, Katharine Treat. The amulet: a tale of
the Orient / by Katharine Treat Blackledge. Los
Angeles, Cal.: Commercial Printing House, 1916.
267 p., [11] leaves of plates. [Ill. by Evelyn Hess and
W. A. Sharp.]

B-640 _____ Dorothea and travels in Europe / by Katharine
Treat Blackledge. Boston: The Cornhill Publishing
Company, [c1924]. 404 p., photo. front., [11] leaves
of photo. plates. **NYP**

B-641 _____ The jeweled serpent / by Katharine Treat
Blackledge. Boston: The Cornhill Publishing
Company, [c1922]. 258 p.
LC: My 11, '22.

B-642 Blacklock, Alaska, b. 1870, *pseud.* Nick of the
woods / by Alaska Blacklock [pseud.]. Portland,
Oregon: Jensen Publishing Company Press, 1916.
222 p., photo. ill.
On cover: *A tale of the Manistee.*

B-643 Blackstone, Valerius D., *pseud.* Auburn: a novel /
by Valerius D. Blackstone [pseud.]. New York;
Chicago; London: F. Tennyson Neely Co., [c1901].
147 p. **VA@**

B-644 Blackton, James Stuart, 1875-1941. The battle cry of
peace: a call to arms against war / by J. Stuart
Blackton. -- Limited souvenir ed. -- Brooklyn, N.
Y.: Published by the M. P. Publishing Co., [c1915].
73 p., photo. front. (port.), photo. Designed end
papers. **ZBK**

B-645 Blackwell, Florence Moss. The Black American / by
Florence Moss Blackwell. Augusta, Ga.: Phoenix
Printing Company, [1917?]. 85 p.
Unexamined copy: bibliographic data from OCLC,
#20395316.
LC: Mr 7, '19.

B-646 Blades, Leslie Burton. Claire / by Leslie Burton
Blades. New York: George H. Doran Company,
[c1919]. 269 p.
PW: My 31, '19.

B-647 Blades, Paul Harcourt. Don Sagasto's daughter: a
romance of southern California / Paul Harcourt
Blades. Boston: Richard G. Badger, [c1911].
([Boston]: The Gorham Press). 433 p.

B-648　Blair, Barbara. The journal of a neglected bull dog: being impressions of his master's love affairs / by Barbara Blair; drawings by Eugene A. Furman. Philadelphia: George W. Jacobs & Co., [1911]. 187 p., front., [5] leaves of plates. Illustrated end papers.
LC: Ag 10, '11.

B-649　Blair, Uncle, *pseud.* Changes of venue: fourteen stories and sketches of and from sundry places / by Uncle Blair [pseud.]. Oakland, California: Published by the author, J. E. Whinnery, 1919. 234 p. **NYP**
Contents: Juli-Ann's Dolly -- Hagar at Whisky Spit -- Martha of Alta Piedmont -- A sweetheart's voice -- Bill Jasper's first conversion -- The Vice President -- Mason Bell, deserter -- The senator's return -- Ezra Dalzell's substitute -- Vice President at Philadelphia -- The Duke of Medicine Hat -- Reported killed -- Last Bunker Hill oration -- Bill Jasper at New Orl'ans.
LC: My 12, '19.

B-650　Blake, Adam. The man with the hoe: a picture of American farm life as it is to-day / by Adam Blake. Cincinnati: The Robert Clarke Company, 1904. 431 p., front., [2] leaves of plates.
PW: Ja 2, '04.

B-651　Blake, Emily Calvin, b. 1882. Engaged girl sketches / by Emily Calvin Blake. Chicago: Forbes & Company, 1910. 156 p., front.　　　　**CLO**
Contents: An obscure situation -- The adorers of Anne -- In the face of reality -- A dreamer of dreams -- When all is fair -- Moonlight and roses -- Qualities of love.
LC: Jl 5, '10.

B-652　____ The great moments in a woman's life / by Emily Calvin Blake . . . Chicago: Forbes & Company, 1910. 88 p.　　　　**UBY**
LC: N 17, '10.

B-653　____ Suzanna stirs the fire / by Emily Calvin Blake; illustrations by F. V. Poole. Chicago: A. C. McClurg & Co., 1915. 358 p., front., [3] leaves of plates.
LC: S 27, '15.
BLC: London: Methuen & Co., 1918.

B-654　Blake, Forest, *pseud.* Saint Josephine / by Forest Blake [pseud.]. Cincinnati: Jennings and Graham; New York: Eaton and Mains, [c1909]. 359 p.
LC: O 22, '09.

B-655　Blake, Katharine Evans. Hearts' haven / by Katharine Evans Blake; illustrated by E. M. Ashe. Indianapolis: The Bobbs-Merrill Company, [c1905]. 496 p., col. front., [5] leaves of col. plates.
PW: O 14, '05.

B-656　____ The stuff of a man / by Katharine Evans Blake. Indianapolis: The Bobbs-Merrill Company, [c1908]. 423 p., col. front. [Ill. by Will Grefé.]
LC: Mr 7, '08.
PW: Mr 21, '08.

B-657　Blake, Margaret, 1875-1923, *pseud.* The greater joy: a romance / by Margaret Blake [pseud.]; illustrations by E. A. Furman. New York: G. W. Dillingham Company, [c1912]. 463 p., front., [3] leaves of plates.
LC: Mr 30, '12.

B-658　[____] The hyphen / by Lida C. Schem. New York: E. P. Dutton & Company, [c1920]. Vol. 1: 536 p.; Vol. 2: 539-1052 p.

B-659　____ Matthew Ferguson / by Margaret Blake [pseud.]; illustrations by E. A. Furman. New York: G. W. Dillingham Company, [c1914]. 538 p., front., [2] leaves of plates.
LC: Ap 29, '14.
PW: My 30, '14.

B-660　____ The voice of the heart: a romance / by Margaret Blake [pseud.] . . . ; illustrations by E. A. Furman. New York: G. W. Dillingham Company, [c1913]. 486 p., front., [3] leaves of plates.
LC: Ap 25, '13.
PW: Ap 26, '13.

B-661　Blake-Hedges, Florence Edythe. I am: a novel of psychotherapy / by Florence Edythe Blake-Hedges . . . ; illustrated. Boston: The Roxburgh Publishing Company (Incorporated), [c1910]. 283 p., front., [5] leaves of plates. [Ill. by Geo. A. McKew.]
LC: O 27, '10.

B-662　Blakeman, Wilbert C. The black hand / by Wilbert C. Blakeman. New York: Broadway Publishing Company, [c1908]. 316 p., front. [Ill. by Wm. L. Hudson.]　　　　**DLC**
LC: S 23, '08.

B-663　Blanchard, Amy Ella, 1856-1926. Because of conscience: being a novel relating to the adventures of certain Huguenots in old New York / by Amy E. Blanchard; with frontispiece by E. Benson Kennedy. Philadelphia; London: J. B. Lippincott Company, 1901. 355 p., front.
PW: N 2, '01.

B-664　____ The glad lady / by Amy E. Blanchard. Boston: Dana Estes & Company, [c1910]. 297 p., front., [6] leaves of plates.
LC: Je 25, '10.
PW: Ag 20, '10.

B-665　____ The house that Jack built: a story / by Amy E. Blanchard; illustrated by Frank T. Merrill. Boston; Chicago: W. A. Wilde Company, [c1925]. 320 p., front.
LC: Ja 22, '26.
PW: O 3, '25.

B-666　____ Talbot's angles / by Amy E. Blanchard. Boston: Dana Estes & Company, [c1911]. 291 p., col. front., [6] leaves of plates. [Ill. by L. J. Bridgman.]
LC: Jl 3, '11.
PW: S 9, '11.

B-667　Blanchard, Ferdinand Q. (Ferdinand Quincy), b. 1876. For the King's sake / by Ferdinand Q. Blanchard. East Orange, N. J.: [s. n.], 1909. 28 p.　　　　**DLC**
LC: Jl 8, '09.

B-668 Blanchard, Grace, d. 1944. The island cure / by Grace Blanchard; illustrated. Boston: Lothrop, Lee & Shepard Co., [c1922]. 186 p., front., [8] leaves of plates.
LC: Ap 1, '22.
PW: Ap 15, '22.

B-669 _____ Phillida's glad year: a story / by Grace Blanchard; with frontispiece by William F. Stecher. Boston; Chicago: W. A. Wilde Company, [c1913]. 299 p., col. front.
LC: N 29, '13.

B-670 _____ Phil's happy girlhood: a story / by Grace Blanchard; with illustrations by William F. Stecher. Boston; Chicago: W. A. Wilde Company, [c1910]. 357 p., front., [4] leaves of plates.
LC: N 22, '10.

B-671 Blanchard, J. L. (John L.), b. 1859. Who is my neighbor? / by J. L. Blanchard. Boston: Richard G. Badger, [c1913]. ([Boston]: The Gorham Press). 205 p.

B-672 Bland, T. A. (Thomas Augustus). "In the world celestial" / by T. A. Bland, M. D. . . . ; with an introduction by Rev. H. W. Thomas . . . New York: The Alliance Publishing Co.; Chicago: The Plymouth Publishing Co., 1901. 159 p., front. [Ill. by Hunter.]

B-673 Blanding, Hector. The door of the double dragon: a romance of China of yesterday and today / by Hector Blanding; frontispiece by George W. Gage. New York: W. J. Watt & Company, [c1920]. 289 p., front.
LC: Ap 14, '21.
PW: N 13, '20.

B-674 Blaney, Charles E., d. 1944. The millionaire detective: a novel: founded upon the great play of the same name / Chas. E. Blaney and Howard Hall. New York: J. S. Ogilvie Publishing Company, c1905. 123 p.

B-675 Blankman, Edgar G. (Edgar Gerritt), b. 1861. Deacon Babbitt: a tale of fact and fiction / by Edgar G. Blankman. Philadelphia: The John C. Winston Company, 1906. 334 p., front., [7] leaves of plates.
LC: Jl 20, '06.

B-676 Blease, Bessie Lee. Eilene; or, The invisible side of a visible character / by Bessie Lee Blease. New York; London: F. T. Neely [1901]. 160 p., front. (port.), plates.
Unexamined copy: bibliographic data from NUC.

B-677 Bleneau, Adele. The nurse's story: in which reality meets romance / by Adele Bleneau; illustrated by M. Leone Bracker. Indianapolis: The Bobbs-Merrill Company, [c1915]. 260 p., front., [4] leaves of plates.

B-678 Blessing-Eyster, Nellie, 1836?-1922. A Chinese Quaker: an unfictitious novel / by Nellie Blessing-Eyster. New York; Chicago; Toronto; London; Edinburgh: Fleming H. Revell Company, [c1902]. 377 p., front., [4] leaves of plates.

Blighton, Frank, jt. aut. *"Here's to the day!"* (1915). See **MacLean, Charles Agnew, jt. aut., M-304.**

Blinkin, Meyer. Women. In *Yiddish tales* (1912), **Y-20.**

B-679 Blinn, Edith. The ashes of my heart / by Edith Blinn; with illustrations by Andre Comte de Takacs. New York: Mark-Well Publishing Company Inc., 1916. 385 p., front., [10] leaves of plates.
LC: Mr 17, '16.
PW: Ap 8, '16.

B-680 _____ The edge of the world / by Edith Blinn; illustrations by Norma L. Virgin. New York: Britton Publishing Company, [c1919]. 306 p., front., [3] leaves of plates.
LC: F 18, '19.

Bliss, Alfonso. See **Linden, Edmund, pseud.**

B-681 Bliven, Mary A. L. (Mary Ann Lillibridge), b. 1934. The web of destiny / by Mary A. L. Bliven. New York: Broadway Publishing Co., [c1907]. 213 p., front. [Ill. by W. L. Hudson.]   **DLC**
LC: O 18, '07.

Block, Rudolph Edgar. See **Lessing, Bruno, pseud.**

Blomeyer, Edward. Ahead of date. In *Clever business sketches* (1909), **C-490.**

_____ Bill Sickles-Lazy Man. In *Clever business sketches* (1909), **C-490.**

_____ The truth prevails in Shadyville. In *Clever business sketches* (1909), **C-490.**

B-682 The blood of Venus: a romantic evolution of the story of the Roman Venus / modernized and specially adapted and abridged by the author of that strangest of modern romances, Cupid's mother. Akron, Ohio: The Star Rubber Company, c1910. 28 p., ill. "Copyrighted 1910 by J. LeRoy Tope."

B-683 Bloomer, J. M. (James M.), 1842-1923. D'Mars' affinity: romance of love's final test in time and tide / by J. M. Bloomer; illustrated by A. D. Condo. New York: J. S. Ogilvie Publishing Company, [c1903]. 342 p., front., [5] leaves of plates.

B-684 Bloomfield, Will J. The baron of the Barrens / by Will J. Bloomfield. Philadelphia: Dorrance, [c1923]. 297 p.

B-685 _____ Transplanting an old tree: a novel / by Will Bloomfield. New York: Isaac H. Blanchard Co., [c1901]. 141 p.
PW: Mr 22, '02.

B-686 Bloomingdale, Charles ("Karl"), Jr., 1868-1942. A failure / by Charles Bloomingdale, Jr. ("Karl"); illustrated by V. Floyd Campbell. Philadelphia; London: J. B. Lippincott Company, 1904. 276 p., front., [4] leaves of plates.
Contents: A failure -- Six lines of "news" -- The yellow streak -- A drive and a hazard or two -- A love affair -- An unwritten story.

B-687 Blow, Ben, b. 1868. Jefferson Davis Abraham Lincoln Bowe / by Ben Blow. San Francisco: Paul Elder & Company, 1917. 23 p., photo. front., [3] leaves of photo. plates. **NYP**
"Reprinted through the courtesy of the American magazine."

B-688 Blue, Guy, *pseud*. Persiflage: indulged by Guy Blue [pseud.]. [Gallatin, Mo., c1914.] 40 p.
Unexamined copy: bibliographic data from OCLC, #18058941.

B-689 Blum, Edgar C. Robert Emmet's wooing / by Edgar C. Blum . . . New York: Cochrane Publishing Company, 1910. 142 p., front. (port.), [3] leaves of photo. plates. [Ill. Underwood & Underwood, N. Y.]
LC: Mr 10, '10.

B-690 Blunt, Elizabeth Lee, b. 1839. When folks was folks / by Elizabeth L. Blunt. New York: Cochrane Publishing Company, 1910. 174 p.
LC: Je 28, '10.

B-691 Blunt, Hugh Francis. The dividers / by Hugh Francis Blunt . . . Manchester, N. H.: The Magnificat Press, 1920. 188 p.
Contents: The dividers -- The mills of God -- The defeat of Gloriannna McGinnis -- The waking of Madame Castelli -- Modern knight and lady fair -- Angels unawares -- "Held in derision" -- A pledge of love -- The sword -- The coming and going of Billy Maguire -- A mender of hearts -- The homeliest girl.

B-692 Bluntach, John Alexander. The greater emancipation: a story-study of mind / by John Alexander Bluntach. Rochester, N. Y.: The Charter Publisher, 1915. 216 p. **RRR**
LC: My 17, '15.

B-693 Blythe, Samuel G. (Samuel George), 1868-1947. The fakers / by Samuel G. Blythe . . . New York: George H. Doran Company, [c1914]. 388 p.
LC: O 27, '14.

B-694 _____ Hunkins / by Samuel G. Blythe. New York: George H. Doran Company, [c1919]. 365 p.
LC: O 21, '19.
PW: N 1, '19.

B-695 _____ The price of place / by Samuel G. Blythe. New York: George H. Doran Company, [c1913]. 359 p.
LC: O 23, '13.

B-696 _____ A western Warwick / by Samuel G. Blythe . . . New York: George H. Doran Company, [c1916]. 345 p.
LC: Je 23, '16.
PW: My 27, '16.
BLC: London: Headley Bros.; printed in U. S. A., [1916].

B-697 Boardman, Joseph. A perfect lady: a novelization of the Channing Pollock-Rennold Wolf play / by Joseph Boardman; illustrated from photographs of the play. New York: Edward J. Clode Publisher, [c1915]. 345 p., photo. front., [7] leaves of photo. plates. **NYP**
LC: Je 11, '15.
PW: Je 26, '15.

B-698 Boardman, N. S. (Normand Smith). The children of the saints: an early Christian romance / by N. S. Boardman. New York: Cochrane Publishing Company, 1911. 70 p.
LC: Ap 7, '11.

B-699 Boardman, William H. (William Henry), 1846-1914. The lovers of the woods / by William H. Boardman. New York: McClure, Phillips & Co., 1901. 239 p., col. front. [Ill. by G. Yeto.]
PW: My 11, '01.
BLC: London; New York: McClure, Phillips & Co., 1901.

Boas, Ralph Philip, ed. <u>In</u> *Short stories for class reading* **(1925), S-461.**

B-700 Bobbed hair / by twenty authors, Carolyn Wells, Alexander Woollcott, Louis Bromfield, Elsie Janis, Edward Streeter, Meade Minnigerode, Dorothy Parker, H. C. Witwer, Sophie Kerr, Robert Gordon Anderson, Kermit Roosevelt, Bernice Brown, Wallace Irwin, Frank Craven, Rube Goldberg, George Barr McCutcheon, Gerald Mygatt, George Agnew Chamberlain, John V. A. Weaver, George Palmer Putnam. New York; London: G. P. Putnam's Sons, 1925. ([New York]: The Knickerbocker Press). 357 p.
LC: Mr 24, '25.
PW: Mr 28, '25.
References: BAL 13562.

B-701 Boddy, E. Manchester (Elias Manchester). The strangle-hold / novelized by E. Manchester Boddy; from the book of the same title by H. C. Cutting; according to original ideas furnished by Eugene H. Kaufmann. [Los Angeles]: The Times-Mirror Press, c1924. 165 leaves **DLC**
LC: My 26, '24.

B-702 _____ The yellow trail: a story of Salmon River gold / by E. Manchester Boddy. Los Angeles, California: Times-Mirror Press, [c1922]. 296 p.
LC: D 26, '22.

B-703 Bodenheim, Maxwell, 1893-1954. Blackguard / by Maxwell Bodenheim; drawing by Wallace Smith. Chicago: Covici-McGee, 1923. 215, [1] p., front.
LC: Mr 26, '23.

B-704 _____ Crazy man / by Maxwell Bodenheim. New York: Harcourt, Brace and Company, [c1924]. 238 p.
LC: F 15, '24.
PW: F 9, '24.

_____, jt. aut. *Cutie* (1924). <u>See</u> **Hecht, Ben, 1893-1964, jt. aut., H-446.**

B-705   _____ Replenishing Jessica / Maxwell Bodenheim. New York: Boni and Liveright, [c1925]. 272 p.
LC: Je 22, '25.
PW: Je 13, '25.

B-706   Boggs, Robert, *pseud.* The man and his money; a novel / by Robert Boggs [pseud.] . . . New York: Broadway Publishing Company, 1913. 289 p.
Unexamined copy: bibliographic data from NUC.
LC: Ja 2, '15.

B-707   Boggs, S. E. (Sara Elizabeth), b. 1843. Sandpeep / by Sara E. Boggs; illustrated by May Bartlett. Boston: Little, Brown and Company, 1906. 421 p., front., [3] leaves of plates.
PW: My 5, '06.

B-708   Bogue, Herbert Edward. Dareford / by Herbert Edward Bogue; with illustrations by William Kirkpatrick. Boston, Massachusetts: The C. M. Clark Publishing Co., 1907. 363 p., front., [7] leaves of plates.
LC: Ap 22, '07.
PW: My 18, '07.

B-709   Bogue, Virgilia. The strength to yield: the psycholoy of a great temptation / by Virgilia Bogue. San Francisco: Cunningham, Curtiss & Welch, 1909. 269 p., col. front.
LC: S 9, '09.

B-710   Bohan, Elizabeth Baker. The drag-net: a prison story of the present day / by Elizabeth Baker Bohan; illustrated by Langdon Smith. Boston: The C. M. Clark Publishing Company, 1909. 332 p., front., [5] leaves of plates.
LC: N 22, '09.

B-711   Bohannon, Hattie Donovan. The light of stars / by Hattie Donovan Bohannon. New York: R. F. Fenno & Company, [c1909]. 351 p.
LC: Ap 19, '09.

B-712   Bolce, Harold, b. 1868. A romance of the orient: being a poem in prose regarding "high grade" / by Harold Bolce. Galveston, Texas: [s. n.], 1911. 30 p., col. ill. [Ill. by Raymond Nott.]   **DLC**

B-713   Bolling, Howard D. The mystery of the Cumberlands / by Howard D. Bolling. [Lynchburg VA.]: [Printed by J. P. Bell Company, Inc.], [192-]. 195 p., [2] leaves of photo. plates.   **VIC**

B-714   Bolton, Charles Edward, 1841-1901. The Harris-Ingram experiment / by Charles E. Bolton, M. A. Cleveland: The Burrows Brothers Company, 1905, [c1904]. 442 p.
PW: D 10, '04; D 24, '04.

Boltwood, Edward. The wedding Bob Dean ran. <u>In</u> *Greatest short stories* (1915), **G-424.**

B-715   Bond, O. J. (Oliver James), 1865-1933. Amzi: a novellette / by O. J. Bond. New York: Broadway Publishing Company, [c1904]. 81 p., front. [Ill. by S. Klarr.]   **IXA**
PW: F 25, '05.

B-716   Bond, William Sidney. His struggle magnificent / by William Sidney Bond. New York: Cochrane Publishing Company, 1910. 303 p.   **ALM**
LC: Ag 27, '10.

Bonesteel, Mary G. (Mary Greene), b. 1864, contributor. <u>See</u> *A double knot* (1905), **D-499.**

_____ The senior lieutenant's wager. <u>In</u> *The Senior lieutenant's wager: and other stories* (1905), **S-312.**

B-717   _____ The young color guard; or, Tommy Collins at Santiago / by Mary G. Bonesteel. New York; Cincinnati; Chicago: Benziger Brothers, 1902. 166 p., front.
Unexamined copy: bibliographic data from NUC.
LC: Mr 12, '04.

Bonneau, Jean Xavier. Eenna, the runner, a story of the woods. <u>In</u> *Golden stories* (1909), **G-285.**

B-718   Bonner, Geraldine, 1870-1930. The Black Eagle mystery / by Geraldine Bonner . . . ; illustrated by Frederic Dorr Steele. New York; London: D. Appleton and Company, 1916. 308, [1] p., front., [3] leaves of plates.
LC: F 16, '16.
PW: F 26, '16.

B-719   _____ The book of Evelyn / by Geraldine Bonner; with illustrations by Arthur William Brown. Indianapolis: The Bobbs-Merrill Company, [c1913]. 339 p., front., [5] leaves of plates.
LC: Ag 30, '13.
PW: Ag 30, '13.

_____ A Californian. <u>In</u> *The Spinners' book of fiction* (1907), **S-755.**

B-720   _____ The Castlecourt diamond case: being a compilation of the statements made by the various participants in this curious case now, for the first time, given to the public / by Geraldine Bonner . . . ; frontispiece illustration by Harrie F. Stoner. New York; London: Funk & Wagnalls Company, 1906, [c1905]. 223 p., front.
PW: Ja 20, '06.

_____ Conscience money. <u>In</u> *Argonaut stories* (1906), **A-298.**

B-721   _____ The emigrant trail / by Geraldine Bonner. New York: Duffield & Company, 1910. 496 p. col. front. [Ill. by John Rae.]
Contents: Part I.: The prairie -- Part II.: The river -- Part III.: The mountains -- Part IV.: The desert -- Part V.: The promised land.
LC: Ap 21, '10.
PW: My 7, '10.
BLC: London: Hutchinson & Co., 1910.

B-722   ____ The girl at central / By Geraldine Bonner; illustrated by Arthur William Brown. New York; London: D. Appleton and Company, 1915. 314, [1] p., front., [3] leaves of plates.
LC: Ap 30, '15.

B-723   ____ Miss Maitland, private secretary / by Geraldine Bonner; illustrated by A. I. Keller. New York; London: D. Appleton and Company, 1919. 353 p., front., [3] leaves of plates.
LC: Ap 2, '19.
PW: Ap 12, '19.

B-724   ____ The pioneer: a tale of two states / by Geraldine Bonner; with illustrations by Harrison Fisher. Indianapolis: The Bobbs-Merrill Company, [c1905]. 392 p., col. front., [5] leaves of plates.
PW: Ap 1, '05.

B-725   ____ Rich men's children / by Geraldine Bonner . . . ; with illustrations by C. M. Relyea. Indianapolis: The Bobbs-Merrill Company, [c1906]. 492 p., front., [5] leaves of plates.
LC: O 29, '06.
PW: D 1, '06.

____ The statement of Jared Johnson. In *Through the forbidden gates* (1903), **T-222**.

B-726   ____ Tomorrow's tangle / by Geraldine Bonner; illustrations by Arthur I. Kellar [sic]. Indianapolis: The Bobbs-Merrill Company, [1903]. 458 p., front., [4] leaves of plates.
LC: O 10, '03.
BLC: London: Cassell & Co., 1904. (Cassell edition: different preliminary pages and no illustrations.)

B-727   ____ Treasure and trouble therewith: a tale of California / by Geraldine Bonner; illustrated by Stockton Mulford. New York; London: D. Appleton and Company, 1917. 379, [1] p., front., [3] leaves of plates.
LC: Ag 20, '17.
PW: S 8, '17.

B-728   Bonner, John S. (John Sturgis). K. Lamity's Texas tales / by John S. Bonner (alias K. Lamity). Austin, Tex.: Press of Von Boeckmannn [sic] - Jones Company, [1904]. 256 p.
Unexamined copy: bibliographic data from NUC.

B-729   ____ The three adventurers: a thrilling tale of the early days of Texas / J. S. Bonner (K. Lamity). Austin, Texas: Harpoon Publishing Company, [c1911]. 354 p., ill. [Ill. by T. D. Bateman.]
NYP

B-730   Bonsteel, Abbie Benton. Hidden pearls / Abbie Benton Bonsteel. Nashville, Tennessee: Sunday School Board of Southern Baptist Convention, [c1925]. 71 p.   **IGR**

Boogher, Susan M. An unknown warrior. In *The best short stories of 1922 and the yearbook of the American short story* (1923), **B-567**.

B-731   A book of American prose humor: being a collection of humorous and witty tales, sketches, etc. / composed by the best known American writers. Chicago: Herbert S. Stone & Company, 1904. 249 p.
Cover title: *A book of American humor: prose.*
Contents: The shakers / Artemus Ward -- A business letter / Artemus Ward -- Oats / Josh Billings -- Our oldest inhabitants-two of them / Josh Billings -- The interviewer / Mark Twain -- Scotty Briggs and the clergyman / Mark Twain -- Milling in Pompeii / Bill Nye -- All about oratory / Bill Nye -- My mine / Bill Nye -- Samantha at Saratoga / Marietta Holley -- Chimmie meets the Duchess / E. W. Townsend -- Chimmie enters polite society / E. W. Townsend -- The genial idiot on the four hundred / John Kendrick Bangs -- "Checker's" letter / Henry M. Blossom, Jr. -- The fable of the two mandolin players and the willing performer / George Ade -- Claudie / George Ade -- On the French character / F. P. Dunne -- On the Victorian Era / F. P. Dunne -- On golf / F. P. Dunne -- In the country / Hayden Carruth -- John Henry on butting in / George V. Hobart -- Mr. and Mrs. Dinkelspiel discuss literary matters / George V. Hobart -- Dinkelspiel explains the Dreyfus case / George V. Hobart -- At the opera / Billie Baxter -- In love / Billie Baxter.

B-732   A book of Bryn Mawr stories / edited by Margaretta Morris and Louise Buffum Congdon. Philadelphia: George W. Jacobs and Company, 1901. 296 p.
Cover title: *Bryn Mawr stories.* Contents: Her masterpiece / Marian T. MacIntosh, '90 -- In maytime / Anne Maynard Kidder, 1903 -- Within four years / Elva Lee, '93 -- Free among the dead / Georgiana Goddard King, '96 -- Studies in college colour / L. S. B. S., '93, and G. E. T. S. '93 -- Epoch making / Cora Armistead Hardy, '99 -- A reminiscence / Clara Warren Vail, '97 -- Catherine's career / Harriet Jean Crawford, 1902 -- The apostasy of Anita Fiske / Ellen Rose Giles, '96 -- A diplomatic crusade / Edith Campbell Crane, 1900.

B-733   The book of Marjorie. New York: Alfred A. Knopf, 1920. 128 p.   **KSU**
PW: Mr 20, '20.

B-734   A book of narratives / edited by Oscar James Campbell, Jr. and Richard Ashley Rice. Boston; New York; Chicago: D. C. Heath & Co., Publishers, [c1917]. 497 p.   **DAY**
Contents: Part I. What is a story?: Introduction -- The piece of string / Guy de Maupassant -- Rhyolitic Perlite / Paul Palmerton -- Malachi's Cove / Anthony Trollope -- L'arrabbiata / Paul Heyse -- The cask of Amontillado / Edgar Allan Poe -- La Grande Bretèche / Honoré de Balzac. Part II. How to see a story in everyday life: Introduction -- The fiancée / Marguerite Audoux -- A page from the doctor's life / F. W. Stuart, Jr. -- The necklace / Guy de Maupassant -- To fool the ignorant / Ernest L. Meyer -- Wellington / Charles M. Flandreau -- Left behind / Arthur Ruhl -- The chaperon / Alta Brunt Sembower. Part III. How to see life imaginatively: Introduction -- In the firelight / Margaret Thomson -- City smoke / Booth Tarkington -- Scenes in factories / Margaret Richardson -- The spirit of a great city / Robert Herrick -- Thunder and lightning / Thomas Hardy -- Gerard and the bear / Charles Reade -- Tad Sheldon, second-class scout / John Fleming Wilson -- The Glenmore fire / Robert Herrick -- Part IV. How to describe character: Introduction -- The Brooke sisters / George Eliot -- The Baines sisters / Arnold Bennett -- Annixter / Frank Norris -- Bathsheba and Gabriel Oak / Thomas Hardy -- Eugénie and Old Grandet / Honoré de Balzac -- François Villon / R. L. Stevenson -- A lodging for the night / R. L. Stevenson -- Part V. How to present a moral issue: Introduction -- The greater love / Bartimeus -- Vis et vir / Victor Hugo -- A dead issue / Charles M. Flandreau -- The captain's vices / François Coppée -- A coward / Guy de Maupassant -- Bazarov's duel / Ivan Turgenev -- An unfinished story / O. Henry.
LC: Mr 3, '20.

B-735   A book of short stories: a collection for use in high schools / compiled and edited, with introduction and notes, and biographies of the authors, by Blanche Colton Williams . . . ; illustrated. New York; London: D. Appleton and Company, 1918. 291 p.,

front., [4] leaves of photo. plates, ill. [Ill. Jack
Flanagan.] **BGU, IPL**
(Apparent first book appearance of "The comforter"
by Elizabeth Jordan and "Molly McGuire, fourteen"
by Frederick Stuart Greene.)
Contents: Legend of the Moor's legacy / Washington Irving -- The
cask of Amontillado / Edgar Allan Poe -- Tennessee's partner / Bret
Harte -- The last lesson / Alphonse Daudet -- The Sire de Malétroit's
door / Robert Louis Stevenson -- The necklace / Guy de Maupassant
-- A gala dress / Mary Wilkins Freeman -- Under the lion's paw /
Hamlin Garland -- On the stairs / Arthur Morrison -- A blackjack
bargainer / "O. Henry" (William Sydney Porter) -- The well /
William Wydmark Jacobs -- The comforter / Elizabeth Jordan --
"Molly McGuire, fourteen" / Frederick Stuart Greene.

B-736   The Book of the prophet Wudro and the fifth book of
the kings of Eng being the hypocrypha / translated out
of the original tongues and with the former translation
diligently compared and revised. New York: The
Statesman Press, [1920]. 67 p., front., ill.
LNE (photocopy)

B-737   Boone, Henry Burnham. The career triumphant / by
Henry Burnham Boone. New York: D. Appleton
and Company, 1903. 279 p.

B-738   ____ Eastover Court House: a novel / by Henry
Burnham Boone and Kenneth Brown. New York;
London: Harper & Brothers, 1901. 317, [1] p.
Cover title: *Eastover Court House: a story of
modern American life.*
PW: F 9, '01.

B-739   ____ The Redfields succession: a novel / by Henry
Burnham Boone & Kenneth Brown. New York;
London: Harper & Brothers, 1903. 317, [1] p.
PW: My 16, '03.

B-740   Booth, Christopher B. The house of rogues: a
detective story / by Christopher B. Booth. New York
City: Chelsea House, [c1923]. 254 p.
BLC: London: Hutchinson & Co., [1927].

B-741   ____ The Kidnaping Syndicate: a detective story /
by Christopher B. Booth . . . New York City:
Chelsea House, [c1925]. 250 p.
PW: D 26, '25.
BLC: London: Skeffington & Son, [1926].

B-742   ____ A seaside mystery: a detective story / by
Christopher B. Booth. New York: Chelsea House,
[c1925]. 248 p.

Booth, Frederick. The helpless ones. In *The best
short stories of 1922 and the yearbook of the
American short story* (1923), **B-567.**

____ Supers. In *The best short stories of 1916 and
the yearbook of the American short story* (1917),
B-561.

B-743   Booth, George G., b. 1864. Cranbrook tales / by
George G. Booth. Detroit, Mich.: Printed at the
Cranbrook Press by George G. Booth, 1902. 99 p.,
ill.

"This is the end of the tales of Cranbrook as told by
George G. Booth and printed by him at the Cranbrook
Press, Detroit, Mich., U. S. A., and which were
finished on the 25th day of June, in the year 1902,
there being in all two hundred and eight copies . . ."
Contents: A pilgrimage to Cranbrook -- The landlord's tale -- The
grave-digger's tale -- The tale of the cloth-weaver -- The Viscount's
tale -- The cab-driver's tale.

B-744   Booth, Henry Spencer. The insurgent of St. Mark's /
by Henry Spencer Booth. Bristol, Tenn.: King
Printing Co., 1911. 419 p.
LC: Mr 24, '11.

B-745   [Booth, Maud Ballington], 1865-1948. The relentless
current / by M. E. Charlesworth [pseud.]. New
York; London: G. P. Putnam's Sons, 1912. ([New
York]: The Knickerbocker Press). 324 p.
LC: F 14, '12.
Later printing titled, *Was it murder, or, The relentless
current*, with introduction by the author and
frontispiece designed by Dalton Stevens. **NYP**

B-746   Booth, Venus G. As the Fates decree / by Venus G.
Booth. New York: Fifth Ave. Publishing Co. Inc.,
[c1916]. 309 p., photo. front., [1] leaf of plates.
LC: Je 19, '16.

B-747   ____ The mystery of Rachel / by Venus G. Booth.
Boston, Massachusetts: The Stratford Company,
[c1920]. 369 p., front.   **KFH**
LC: D 20, '20.
PW: D 25, '20.

B-748   ____ The wives of the deacon / by Venus G. Booth;
illustrated from photographs by the Author. New
York: Fifth Avenue Publishing Company, [1917].
321 p., front., [2] leaves of plates.
PW: N 24, '17.

B-749   Borchardt, Bernard F. (Bernard Fendig), b. 1889.
The way of the walking wounded / by B. F.
Borchardt. Philadelphia: Dorrance & Company,
[c1924]. 199 p.
LC: Je 25, '24.

B-750   Borden, Lucille Papin, b. 1873. The candlestick
makers / by Lucille Borden . . . New York: The
Macmillan Company, 1923. 513 p.
LC: O 3, '23.
PW: O 27, '23.
BLC: London: Hutchinson & Co., [1925].

B-751   ____ The gates of Olivet / by Lucille Borden. New
York: The Macmillan Company, 1922. 359 p.
DAY
LC: S 20, '22.
PW: S 30, '22.
BLC: London: Hutchinson & Co., [1924].

B-752   ____ Gentleman Riches / by Lucille Borden. New
York: The Macmillan Company, 1925. 377 p.
LC: S 24, '25.
PW: S 26, '25.
BLC: London: Hutchinson & Co., [1926].

B-753 Borders, Joe H. (Joseph H.). The queen --of-- Appalachia / by Joe H. Borders. New York; London; Montreal: The Abbey Press, [c1901]. 245 p., [1] leaf of photo. plates. (port.) **NJB**
PW: Jl 6, '01.

B-754 Boreham, Frank, 1871-1959. The home of the echoes / by F. W. Boreham. New York; Cincinnati: The Abingdon Press, [c1921]. 208 p.

B-755 Borland, James, H. A modern Socrates: a novel / by James H. Borland. Boston: Eastern Publishing Company, [c1904]. 340 p. **DLC**
PW: F 4, '05; Mr 4, '05.

B-756 Borne, Emily Hèloise. Poland: the public inn / by Emily Hèloise Borne. New York: Broadway Publishing Co., [c1907]. 121 p., front. [Ill. by Wm. L. Hudson.]
LC: Je 10, '07.

B-757 Borofsky, Samuel H. (Samuel Hyman), b. 1865. The wheel of destiny: a story of love and adventure / by Samuel H. Borofsky. Boston: Richard G. Badger; Toronto: The Copp Clark Co., Limited, [c1917]. 266 p., front., [3] leaves of plates. [Ill. signed by S. G.]

B-758 Bosch, Hermann, Mrs. Bridget / by Mrs. Hermann Bosch. New York: B. W. Dodge & Company, 1908. 390 p., front., [3] leaves of plates. [Ill. by Amy E. Hogeboom]
LC: Mr 30, '08.
PW: My 9, '08.

B-759 Bosher, Kate Lee Langley, 1865-1932. His friend Miss McFarlane: a novel / by Kate Langley Bosher. New York; London: Harper & Brothers, [1919]. 377, [1] p., front.
LC: Ap 14, '19.
PW: Ap 19, '19.

B-760 _____ The house of happiness / by Kate Langley Bosher. New York; London: Harper & Brothers, 1913. 304, [1] p., col. front. [Ill. by Walter Biggs.]
LC: O 18, '13.
PW: N 8, '13.

B-761 _____ How it happened / by Kate Langley Bosher; illustrated. New York; London: Harper & Brothers, 1914. 163, [1] p., front., [2] leaves of plates. [Ill. by Harriet Roosevelt Richards.]
LC: S 24, '14.
PW: S 26, '14.

B-762 _____ Kitty Canary: a novel / by Kate Langley Bosher. New York; London: Harper & Brothers, [1918]. 189, [1] p., col. front. [Ill. by Fanny Munsell.]
LC: F 16, '18.
PW: F 13, '18.
BLC: London: Hodder & Stoughton, [1918].

B-763 _____ The man in the lonely land / by Kate Langley Bosher. New York; London: Harper & Brothers, 1912. 181, [1] p., front. [Ill. by Harriet Roosevelt Richards.]
LC: Ap 5, '12.
PW: Ap 13, '12.

B-764 _____ Mary Cary "frequently Martha" / by Kate Langley Bosher; frontispiece by Frances Rogers. New York; London: Harper & Brothers, 1910. 167, [1] p., front.
LC: F 11, '10.
PW: F 19, '10.

B-765 _____ Miss Gibbie Gault: a story / by Kate Langley Bosher . . . ; frontispiece by Harriet Roosevelt Richards. New York; London: Harper & Brothers, 1911. 325, [1] p., front.
LC: My 6, '11.
PW: My 13, '11.

B-766 _____ People like that: a novel / by Kate Langley Bosher. New York; London: Harper & Brothers, [1916]. 299, [1] p., front., [1] leaf of plates. [Ill. by William Meade Prince.]
LC: Ap 27, '16.
PW: Ap 29, '16.

B-767 _____ When love is love: a novel / by Kate Langley Bosher. New York; Washington: The Neale Publishing Company, 1904. 318 p. **VLR**
PW: F 13, '04.

Bosanketh, Edward, pseud. See **Boyns, R. E. (Richard Edward), b. 1857.**

Boston, Ben, pseud. See **Magill, Harry Byron, b. 1872.**

B-768 Bosworth, Foster, Mrs., b. 1828. The Monteiths / by Mrs. Foster Bosworth "Colle Sands" . . . New York: The Knickerbocker Press, 1910. 124 p., front. (port.). **KSU**
LC: Ag 12, '10.

Bosworth, Jane. See **Bosworth, Foster, Mrs., b. 1828.**

B-769 Boteler, Mattie M. The evolution of Juliet / by Mattie M. Boteler . . . Cincinnati, Ohio: The Standard Publishing Company, Publishers of Christian literature, [c1903]. 228 p.

B-770 _____ Joe Binder's wild westing / by Mattie M. Boteler . . . Cincinnati, Ohio: The Standard Publishing Company, [c1903]. 241 p., ill. [Ill. by T. J. Willison.]
Contents: Joe Binder's wild westing -- The class of '88 -- How Hutson won the prize -- A belated Valentine -- How Sammy became a man -- Their star engagement.

B-771 _____ Like as we are / by Mattie M. Boteler . . . Cincinnati, Ohio: The Standard Publishing Company, [c1903]. 225 p. **VLY**

B-772 Boucicault, Ruth Holt. The rose of Jericho / by Ruth Holt Boucicault. New York; London: G. P. Putnam's Sons, 1920. ([New York]: The Knickerbocker Press). 485 p.
LC: Ap 19, '20.
PW: Mr 20, '20.

B-773 ____ The substance of this house / by Ruth Holt Boucicault; with illustrations by M. Leone Bracker. Boston: Little, Brown and Company, 1914. 392 p., front., [3] leaves of plates.
LC: F 16, '14.
PW: F 14, '14.
BLC: Toronto: Copp, Clark Co., 1914.

B-774 [____] The woman herself. New York: The Stuyvesant Press, 1909. 261 p.   **OSU, CLU**
LC: My 6, '09.

Bourland, Hasseltine. The dark river. *In The best college short stories* (1924-1925), B-558.

B-775 Bourn, Mary. The geese fly south / by Mary Bourn. -- First Edition. -- Garden City, N. Y.: Doubleday, Page & Company, 1923. 254 p.
LC: My 28, '23.
PW: Je 2, '23.
BLC: London: William Heinemann; printed in U. S. A., 1923.

B-776 Bouvet, Marguerite, 1865-1915. The smile of the sphinx / by Marguerite Bouvet; illustrated by H. S. De Lay. Chicago: A. C. McClurg & Co., 1911. 416 p., col. front., [3] leaves of col. plates.

B-777 Bow, J. G. (Jonathan Gaines), 1847-1932. Jessie Allen, or, The power of truth / by J. G. Bow . . . Louisville, Ky.: Baptist Book Concern, [c1916]. 259 p., photo. front., [7] leaves of plates (some photo.)   **ASX**

B-778 Bowdoin, William Goodrich, 1860-1947. The bunch of violets / by W. G. Bowdoin . . . Brooklyn, New York: Privately printed, 1907. (New York: Village Press). 19 p., front.   **ZBK**

B-779 ____ Jack and Jill according to the modern school of fiction / by W. G. Bowdoin . . . Brooklyn, New York: Privately printed, 1906. 15 p., front. **ZBK**
["Printed at the Village Press."]
Cover title: *Jack and Jill modernized.*

B-780 ____ The jewelled dagger / by W. G. Bowdoin . . . Brooklyn, New York: Privately printed, 1908. (New York: Tinsley Press). 19 p., col. front.   **OSU, NYP**

B-781 ____ The little girl and her doll / by W. G. Bowdoin . . . Brooklyn, New York: Privately printed, 1905. (New York: Gillis Press). 15 p., front.   **ZBK**

B-782 Bowen, L. P. (Littleton Purnell), 1833-1933. A daughter of the covenant: a tale of Louisiana / by Rev. L. P. Bowen . . . Richmond, Va.: The Presbyterian Committee of Publication, [c1901]. 281 p.   **VA@**
PW: D 21, '01.

B-783 Bowen, Robert Adger. Uncharted seas / by Robert Adger Bowen; with a frontispiece by Charles M. Relyea. Boston: Small, Maynard and Company, [c1913]. 401 p., front.
LC: Ap 1, '13.

Bowen, Vernon. Marsh lanterns. *In The best college short stories* (1924-1925), B-558.

B-784 Bower, B. M., *pseud.* The Bellehelen mine / by B. M. Bower [pseud.]; with frontispiece by Frank Tenney Johnson. Boston: Little, Brown and Company, 1924. 308, [1] p., front.
LC: Ag 16, '24.
PW: Ag 16, '24.
BLC: London: Hodder & Stoughton, [1925].

B-785 ____ Cabin fever: a novel / by B. M. Bower [pseud.]; with frontispiece by Frank E. Schoonover. Boston: Little, Brown and Company, 1918. 290, [1] p., front.
LC: Ja 11, '18.
PW: Ja 5, '18.

B-786 ____ Casey Ryan / by B. M. Bower [pseud.]; with frontispiece by Frank Tenney Johnson. Boston: Little, Brown and Company, 1921. 242 p., front.
LC: Ag 13, '21.
PW: Ag 13, '21.
BLC: London: Hodder & Stoughton, [1922].

B-787 ____ Chip, of the Flying U / by B. M. Bower [pseud.] (B. M. Sinclair) . . . ; illustrations by Charles M. Russell. New York: G. W. Dillingham Company, [c1906]. 264 p., col. front., [2] leaves of col. plates.
PW: Ap 14, '06.

B-788 ____ Cow-country / by B. M. Bower [pseud.]; with frontispiece by Frank Tenny Johnson. Boston: Little, Brown and Company, 1921. 249 p., front.
LC: Ja 11, '21.
PW: Ja 22, '21.
BLC: London: Hodder & Stoughton, [1921].

B-789 ____ Desert brew / by B. M. Bower [pseud.]; with frontispiece by Remington Schuyler. Boston: Little, Brown and Company, 1925. 311, [1] p., front.
LC: Ja 5, '25.
PW: Ja 3, '25
BLC: London: Hodder & Stoughton, [1925].

B-790 ____ The eagle's wing: a story of the Colorado / by B. M. Bower [pseud.]; with frontispiece by Frank Tenney Johnson. Boston: Little, Brown and Company, 1924. 296, [1] p., front.
LC: F 11, '24.
PW: F 9, '24.
BLC: London: Hodder & Stoughton, [1924].

B-791 ____ Flying U ranch / by B. M. Bower [pseud.] . . . ; illustrations by D. C. Hutchison. New York: G. W. Dillingham Company, [c1914]. 260 p., col. front., [2] leaves of plates.
LC: Mr 26, '14.
PW: Mr 28, '14.

B-792   ____ The Flying U's last stand / by B. M. Bower [pseud.] . . . ; with frontispiece by Anton Otto Fischer. Boston: Little, Brown and Company, 1915. 353 p., front.
LC: Mr 15, 15.
PW: Mr 13, '15.

B-793   ____ Good Indian / by B. M. Bower [pseud.]; with illustrations by Anton Otto Fischer. Boston: Little, Brown and Company, 1912. 372 p., front., [3] leaves of plates.
LC: S 18, '12.
PW: S 14, '12.

B-794   ____ The gringos: a story of the old California days in 1849 / by B. M. Bower [pseud.] . . . ; with illustrations by Anton Otto Fischer. Boston: Little, Brown and Company, 1913. 350 p., front., [3] leaves of plates.
LC: O 16, '13.
PW: O 18, '13.

B-795   ____ The happy family / by B. M. Bower [pseud.] (B. M. Sinclair). New York: G. W. Dillingham Company, [c1910]. 330 p., col. front. [Ill. by D. C. Hutchison.]
LC: Ap 18, '10.
PW: Ap 30, '10.

B-796   ____ Her prairie knight: and Rowdy of the "Cross L," / by B. M. Bower [pseud.] (B. M. Sinclair); illustrated in colors by W. Herbert Dunton. New York: G. W. Dillingham Company, [1907]. 314 p., col. front., [2] leaves of col. plates
LC: Je 29, '07.
PW: Ag 17, '07.

B-797   ____ The heritage of the Sioux / by B. M. Bower [pseud.]; with frontispiece by Monte Crews. Boston: Little, Brown and Company, 1916. 312, [1] p., front.
LC: S 28, '16.
PW: S 23, '16.

B-798   ____ Jean of the Lazy A / by B. M. Bower [pseud.]; with frontispiece by Douglas Duer. Boston: Little, Brown and Company, 1915. 322 p., front.
LC: O 18, '15.
PW: O 9, '15.
BLC: London: Methuen & Co., [1918].

B-799   ____ Lonesome land / by B. M. Bower [pseud.]; with illustrations by Stanley L. Wood. Boston: Little, Brown and Company, 1912. 322 p., front., [3] leaves of plates.
LC: F 13, '12.
PW: F 10, '12.
BLC: London: Stanley Paul & Co.; Cambridge, Mass. [printed], 1912.

B-800   ____ The lonesome trail / by B. M. Bower [pseud.] (B. M. Sinclair) . . . New York: G. W. Dillingham Company, [c1909]. 297 p., front. [Ill. by D. C. Hutchinson.]
LC: N 18, '08.
PW: Mr 20, '09.
BLC: London: T. Nelson & Co., [1920].

B-801   ____ The long shadow / by B. M. Bower [pseud.] . . . ; illustrations by Clarence Rowe. New York: G. W. Dillingham Company, [c1909]. 320 p., col. front., [3] leaves of col. plates.
LC: O 7, '09.
PW: O 30, '09.

B-802   ____ The lookout man / by B. M. Bower [pseud.]; with frontispiece by H. Weston Taylor. Boston: Little, Brown and Company, 1917. 321 p., front.
LC: Ag 23, '17.
PW: Ag 18, '17.

B-803   ____ The lure of the dim trails / by B. M. Bower [pseud.]; illustrations by C. M. Russell. New York: G. W. Dillingham Company, [1907]. 210 p., col. front., [2] leaves of col. plates.
LC: O 14, '07.
PW: N 2, '07.

B-804   ____ Meadowlark Basin / by B. M. Bower [pseud.]; with frontispiece by George W. Gage. Boston: Little, Brown and Company, 1925. 302 p., front.
LC: S 2, '25.
PW: S 5, '25.
BLC: London: Hodder & Stoughton, [1926].

B-805   ____ The Parowan bonanza / by B. M. Bower [pseud.]; with frontispiece by Frank Tenney Johnson. Boston: Little, Brown and Company, 1923. 305 p., front.
LC: Ag 20, '23.
PW: Ag 25, '23.
BLC: London: Hodder & Stoughton, [1924].

B-806   ____ The phantom herd / by B. M. Bower [pseud.] . . . ; with frontispiece by Monte Crews. Boston: Little, Brown and Company, 1916. 325 p., front.
LC: Ap 10, '16.
PW: Ap 8, '16.

B-807   ____ The Quirt / by B. M. Bower [pseud.]; with frontispiece by Anton Otto Fischer. Boston: Little, Brown and Company, 1920. 298 p., front.
LC: My 26, '20.
PW: Je 12, '20.

B-808   ____ The ranch at the Wolverine / by B. M. Bower [pseud.]; with frontispiece by Douglas Duer. Boston: Little, Brown and Company, 1914. 356 p., front.
LC: O 1, '14.
PW: S 26, '14.
BLC: London: Eveleigh Nash Co.; Boston [printed], 1916.

B-809   ____ The range dwellers / by B. M. Bower [pseud.] (B. M. Sinclair) . . . ; illustrated in colors by Charles M. Russell. New York; London: Street & Smith, 1907. 256 p., col. front., [2] leaves of col. plates.
LC: F 4, '07.
PW: Mr 2, '07.
BLC: London: T. Fisher Unwin; New York [printed], 1907.

B-810   ____ Rim o' the world / by B. M. Bower [pseud.]; with frontispiece by Anton Otto Fischer. Boston:

Little, Brown and Company, 1919. 349 p., front.
LC: N 11, '19.
PW: N 15, '19.
BLC: London: Hodder & Stoughton, [1922].

B-811   ____   Skyrider / by B. M. Bower [pseud.]; with frontispiece by Anton Otto Fischer. Boston: Little, Brown and Company, 1918. 317 p., front.
LC: O 31, '18.
PW: N 9, '18.
BLC: London: Methuen & Co., 1920.

B-812   ____   Starr, of the desert / by B. M. Bower [pseud.]; with frontispiece by Monte Crews. Boston: Little, Brown and Company, 1917. 312 p., front.
LC: My 1, '17.
PW: Ap 28, '17.

B-813   ____   The thunder bird / by B. M. Bower [pseud.]; with frontispiece by Anton Otto Fischer. Boston: Little, Brown and Company, 1919. 317 p., front.
LC: My 3, '19.
PW: Ap 19, '19.

B-814   ____   The trail of the white mule / by B. M. Bower [pseud.]; with frontispiece by Frank Tenney Johnson. Boston: Little, Brown and Company, 1922. 278 p., front.
LC: S 6, '22.
PW: Ja 20, '23.
BLC: London: Hodder & Stoughton, [1923].

B-815   ____   The uphill climb / by B. M. Bower [pseud.] . . . ; with illustrations by Charles M. Russell. Boston: Little, Brown and Company, 1913. 283 p., front., [3] leaves of plates.
LC: Ap 19, '13.
PW: Ap 5, '13.

B-816   ____   The voice at Johnnywater / by B. M. Bower [pseud.]; with frontispiece by Remington Schuyler. Boston: Little, Brown and Company, 1923. 300 p., front.
LC: F 9, '23.
PW: F 3, '23.
BLC: London: Hodder & Stoughton, 1923.

B-817   Bowers, Paul E., b. 1886. The pawns of fate / by Paul E. Bowers. Boston: The Cornhill Company, [c1918]. 210 p.
LC: N 17, '18; Mr 22, '19.

B-818   Bowes, Alpin M. (Alpin Marshall), b. 1881. The time to strike, or, Our nation's curse / by Rev. Alpin M. Bowes . . . ; foreword by Rev. Charles B. Allen. Louisville, Ky.: Pentecostal Publishing Company, [c1908]. 151 p.   **KKU**

B-819   Bowker, E. Vernon (Ernest Vernon). Daniel Ruben's partner / by E. Vernon Bowker . . . ; with an introduction by A. M. Starkweather; illustrated. Buffalo, N. Y.: Published by Condensed World Publishing Co., [c1904]. 160 p., front., ill.   **DLC**

B-820   Bowlan, Marian. City types: A book of monologues sketching the city woman / by Marian Bowlan. Chicago: T. S. Denison & Company Publishers, [c1916]. 276 p., front.   **MNU**
Contents: Teena Stars on Tag Day / [Marian Bowlan] -- Why shoe clerks go insane / [Eben Norris] -- Popular music hath charms / [Eben Norris] -- Sighs of a society editor -- The knight at the portal -- Chink! Chink! Chinee! -- The fashion show -- Tale of a tea shop -- Here comes the bride -- Teena at the opera -- Up in the air / [Eben Norris] -- The best seller -- "Movie-itis" -- In the life class / [Eben Norris] -- Mrs. McGovern prisints her daughter -- Twilight -- Elevating the drama / [Eben Norris] -- Minnie at the movies / [Eben Norris] -- A perfect fit -- The girl tourist -- An "a one" trimmer.
LC: N 13, '16.

B-821   Bowles, Mamie. The supreme sacrifice, or, Gillette's marriage / by Mamie Bowles . . . New York: G. W. Dillingham Company, 1901. 327 p.
BLC: London: William Heinemann, 1901. [British title: *Gillette's marriage.*]

B-822   Bowman, Earl Wayland, 1875-1952. The ramblin' kid / by Earl Wayland Bowman; illustrated by W. H. D. Koerner. Indianapolis: The Bobbs-Merrill Company, [c1920]. 323 p., front.
LC: My 5, '20.
PW: Je 12, '20.
BLC: London: Page & Co., 1921.

Bowman, James Cloyd, ed. See *The promise of country life* (1916), **P-624.**

Bowyer, Edith M. See **Nicholl, Edith M.**

B-823   Boyce, Frank M. (Frank Marcellus), b. 1879. Governor Jane: a story of the new woman / by Frank M. Boyce Jr. Niverville, New York: M. S. Boyce, 1913. 266 p., photo. front.
LC: Ag 25, '13.

B-824   Boyce, Neith, 1872-1951. The bond / by Neith Boyce . . . New York: Duffield & Company, 1908. 426 p.
LC: Mr 30, '08.
PW: D 2, '07.
BLC: London: Duckworth & Co.; New York printed, 1908.

B-825   ____   The eternal spring: a novel / by Neith Boyce; illustrations by Blendon Campbell. New York: Fox, Duffield & Company, 1906. 403 p., front., [5] leaves of plates.
PW: F 10, '06.
BLC: London: Hurst & Blackett, 1907.

B-826   ____   The folly of others / by Neith Boyce; with pictures by Horace T. Carpenter. New York: Fox, Duffield & Company, 1904. 232 p., front., [2] leaves of plates.
Contents: A provident woman -- Constancy -- The forbidden -- The mother -- Molly -- Two women -- Sophia -- The head of the house -- The sands of the Green River.
PW: Je 18, '04.

B-827   ____   The forerunner / by Neith Boyce. New York: Fox, Duffield & Company, 1903. 405 p.
PW: N 14, '03.

B-828   ____ Proud lady / Neith Boyce. New York: Alfred A. Knopf, 1923. 316 p.   **IUA**
LC: Ja 29, '23.
PW: F 10, '23.
BLC: London: Duckworth & Co., printed in U. S. A., [1923].

B-829   Boyd, James, 1888-1944. Drums / by James Boyd. New York: Charles Scribner's Sons, 1925. 490 p.
LC: Ap 7, '25.
PW: Ap 4, '25.
BLC: London: Unwin; New York printed, [1925].

Boyd, James, 1888-1944. Shif'less. In *As we are* **(1923), A-325.**

Boyd, Nancy, pseud. <u>See</u> **Millay, Edna St. Vincent, 1892-1950.**

B-830   Boyd, Thomas, 1898-1935. The dark cloud / by Thomas Boyd. New York: Charles Scribner's Sons, 1924. 267 p.
LC: S 9, '24.
BLC: London: Unwin's, 1925.

B-831   ____ Points of honor / by Thomas Boyd. New York; London: Charles Scribner's Sons, 1925. 328 p.
Contents: Unadorned -- The Kentucky boy -- Responsibility -- "Sound adjutant's call" -- Rintintin -- A little gall -- The ribbon counter -- The nine days' kitten -- The long shot -- Uninvited -- Semper fidelis.
LC: Mr 27, '25.
PW: Mr 21, '25.

B-832   ____ Samuel Drummond / by Thomas Boyd. New York: Charles Scribner's Sons, 1925. 308 p.
LC: Ag 26, '25.
PW: S 5, '25.
BLC: London: Jonathan Cape; printed in U. S. A., 1926.

B-833   ____ Through the wheat / by Thomas Boyd. New York: Charles Scribner's Sons, 1923. 266 p.
LC: Ap 30, '23.
PW: My 5, '23.

B-834   Boyd, Woodward, b. 1898, *pseud.* Lazy laughter / by Woodward Boyd [pseud.] . . . New York: Charles Scribner's Sons, 1923. 295 p.
LC: O 29, '23.
PW: N 17, '23.

B-835   ____ The love legend / by Woodward Boyd [pseud.]. New York: Charles Scribner's Sons, 1922. 329 p.
LC: O 7, '22.
PW: O 21, '22.

B-836   Boykin, Elizabeth Jones. Uncle Abe's Miss Ca'line / by Elizabeth Jones Boykin. Boston: The Roxburgh Publishing Company, Inc., [c1923]. 142 p.
LC: Ja 7, '24.

B-837   Boylan, Grace Duffie, 1861?-1935. The kiss of glory / by Grace Duffie Boylan; illustrations and cover by

J. C. Leyendecker. New York: G. W. Dillingham Company, [c1902]. 298 p., col. front.
PW: N 8, '02.
BLC: London: Unwin; New York [printed], 1902.

B-838   ____ The supplanter / by Grace Duffie Boylan; frontispiece by Stanley L. Wood. Boston: Lothrop, Lee & Shepard Co., [1913]. 362 p., front.
LC: Ag 18, '13.
PW: S 20, '13.

B-839   Boyle, Jack. Boston Blackie / by Jack Boyle; illustrated by W. H. D. Koerner. New York: The H. K. Fly Company, [c1919]. 318 p., front., [3] leaves of plates.
PW: S 6, '19.

B-840   Boyle, Virginia Frazer, 1863-1938. Serena: a novel / by Virginia Frazer Boyle . . . ; portrait of Serena by Elizabeth Gowdy Baker. New York: A. S. Barnes & Company, 1905. 377, [1] p., col. front. (port.).
    MUM
PW: My 13, '05.

Boyles, Kate. <u>See</u> **Bingham, Kate Boyles, b. 1876.**

Boyles, Virgil D. (Virgil Dillin), b. 1872, jt. aut. <u>See</u> **Bingham Kate Boyles, b. 1876.**

B-841   Boyns, R. E. (Richard Edward), b. 1857. A grass widow / by R. E. Boyns. San Francisco: Harr Wagner Publishing Company, 1919. 276 p.
LC: My 13, '19.
PW: Jl 5, '19.

B-842   [____] The Pharisee and the Publican / by Edward Bosanketh [pseud.] . . . New York; Baltimore; Atlanta: Broadway Publishing Co., 1910. 191 p.   **NYP**
LC: D 12, '10.
PW: Mr 4, '11.

Boynton, Helen (Mason), Mrs., b. 1841. <u>See</u> **Hall, Helene, pseud.**

B-843   Boyton, Neil, 1884-1956. In God's country: Catholic American stories / by Neil Boyton . . . New York; Boston; Cincinnati; Chicago; San Francisco: Benziger Brothers, Inc., [c1923]. 238 p.   **RMC**
Contents: The dream mother -- Golden Autumn -- Flowers -- The last lie -- The impotent powers -- The true captain -- Dora Dare's last success -- The other boy -- Much fruit -- The true blue star -- The night -- As the clock strikes -- The sin of Simon Gold -- Distinguished ancestry -- The last pew -- The right decision -- The kindly old gentleman -- The desired day -- A taste of jug -- The small angel -- Under the Ægis.
PW: D 8, '23.

B-844   Brace, Benjamin, *pseud.* The seventh person / by Benjamin Brace [pseud.]. New York: Dodd, Mead and Company, 1906. 321 p.
LC: S 28, '06.
PW: O 13, '06.

B-845   ____ Sunrise Acres / by Benjamin Brace [pseud.]. New York: Dodd, Mead and Company, 1905. 303 p.

B-846 Brace, Ernest. Commencement / by Ernest Brace. New York; London: Harper & Brothers, 1924. 366 p.
LC: Ag 21, '24.

B-847 Brackett, Charles, 1892-1969. The counsel of the ungodly / by Charles Brackett. New York; London: D. Appleton and Company, 1920. 266, [1] p.
LC: Jl 31, '20.
PW: Ag 28, '20.

B-848 _____ Week-end / by Charles Brackett. New York: Robert M. McBride & Company, 1925. 157 p.
LC: Jl 21, '25.
PW: Ag 1, '25.
BLC: London: Andrew Melrose, [1928].

Braden, Jenness Mae. See Ross, Betsey, pseud.

B-849 Bradford, Gamaliel, 1863-1932. Between two masters / by Gamaliel Bradford, Jr. Boston; New York: Houghton, Mifflin and Company, 1906. (Cambridge: The Riverside Press). 336 p.
PW: Ap 21, '06.

B-850 _____ Matthew Porter: a story of to-day / by Gamaliel Bradford, Jr. with a frontispiece in colour by Griswold Tyng. Boston: L. C. Page & Company, 1908. 419 p., col. front.
LC: Mr 27, '08.
PW: Ap 11, '08.

B-851 _____ The private tutor / by Gamaliel Bradford, Jr. Boston; New York: Houghton, Mifflin and Company, 1904. (Cambridge [Mass.]: The Riverside Press). 322 p.

Bradley, Harriet Lewis. The bringing of the rose. In *Shapes that haunt the dusk* (1907), S-339.

B-852 Bradley, Lillian Trimble. The dancing-master / by Lillian Trimble Bradley. New York: Minden-Burkert Printing Co., 1914. 56 p.   **DLC**
LC: My 9, '14.

B-853 Bradley, Mary Hastings. The favor of kings / by Mary Hastings Bradley; illustrated. New York; London: D. Appleton and Company, 1912. 387, [1] p., front., [7] leaves of plates. [Ill. by Schwankovsky.]   **KSU**

B-854 _____ The fortieth door / by Mary Hastings Bradley. New York; London: D. Appleton and Company, 1920. 323, [1] p.
LC: F 3, '20.
PW: F 14, '20.

B-855 _____ The innocent adventuress / by Mary Hastings Bradley. New York; London: D. Appleton and Company, 1921. 244, [1] p.
LC: Ja 24, '21.
PW: F 12, '21.

B-856 _____ The palace of darkened windows / by Mary Hastings Bradley; illustrated by Edmund Frederick. New York; London: D. Appleton and Company, 1914. 327, [1] p., front., [3] leaves of plates.
LC: Je 3, '14.
PW: S 5, '14.

B-857 _____ The splendid chance / by Mary Hastings Bradley; illustrated by Edmund Frederick. New York; London: D. Appleton and Company, 1915. 328, [1] p., front, [3] leaves of plates.
LC: Je 1, '15.
PW: Je 12, '15.

B-858 _____ The wine of astonishment / by Mary Hastings Bradley. New York; London: D. Appleton and Company, 1919. 312, [1] p.
LC: Ja 23, '19.
PW: Ja 11, '19.

B-859 Bradley, S. C. (Samuel Carlyle), b. 1842. Jesus of Nazareth: a life / by S. C. Bradley. Boston: Sherman, French & Company, 1908. 575 p. **KUK**
PW: N 14, '08.

B-860 Bradshaw, G. M. B. (George Monroe Brown), b. 1863. An appeal to the imagination in teaching science, illustrated by a story entitled: Seeing things in physiology / by G. M. B. Bradshaw. Youngsville, Pa.: Langdon Brothers, c1913. [52] p., ill. Cover title: *Seeing things in physiology.*

B-861 Bradshaw, Howard. The pasha's web / by Howard Bradshaw; frontispiece by George W. Gage. New York: W. J. Watt & Company, [c1921]. 281 p., front.
LC: Jl 13, '21.

B-862 Bradt, Charles Edwin, 1863?-1922. Problems of Pin-Hole Parish / by Charles Edwin Bradt. Wichita, Kansas, U. S. A.: The Missionary Press Co., [c1912]. 156 p.   **DLC**

B-863 Brady, Cyrus Townsend, 1861-1920. The adventures of Lady Susan / by Cyrus Townsend Brady; with frontispiece by C. Weber-Ditzler. New York: Moffat, Yard & Compnay, 1908. 372 p., col. front.
LC: O 10, '08.
PW: D 12, '08.
BLC: London: Greening & Co., 1909.

B-864 _____ And thus He came: a Christmas fantasy / by Cyrus Townsend Brady; pictures by Walter H. Everett. New York; London: G. P. Putnam's Sons, 1916. (New York: The Knickerbocker Press).
LC: O 25, '16.
PW: O 28, '16.

B-865 _____ Arizona: a romance of the great Southwest / by Augustus Thomas; made into a book from the play of the same name by Cyrus Townsend Brady; with illustrations by J. N. Marchand. New York: Dodd, Mead and Company, 1914. 326 p., col. front., [1] leaf of col. plates.   **CRL**
LC: O 1, '14.
PW: O 3, '14.
BLC: London: B. F. Stevens & Brown, [1913].

B-866   ____ As the sparks fly upward / by Cyrus Townsend Brady; with four illustrations by J. N. Marchand. Chicago: A. C. McClurg & Co., 1911. 386, [1] p., col. front., [3] leaves of col. plates.
LC: O 9, '11.
PW: S 23, '11.

B-867   ____ A baby of the frontier / by Cyrus Townsend Brady . . . ; illustrated. New York; Chicago; Toronto; London; Edinburgh: Fleming H. Revell Company, [c1915]. 286 p., front., [5] leaves of plates. [Ill. by Clark Fay and Gayle Hoskins.]   **UAB**
LC: O 14, '15.
PW: N 6, '15.

B-868   ____ The better man: with some account of what he struggled for and what he won / by Cyrus Townsend Brady; illustrated by F. Graham Cootes. New York: Dodd, Mead and Company, 1910. 305 p., col. front., [3] leaves of plates.
LC: O 1, '10.
PW: O 5, '10.
BLC: London: Greening & Co., 1911.

B-869   ____ The bishop: being some account of his strange adventures on the plains / by Cyrus Townsend Brady; illustrated. New York; London: Harper & Brothers, 1903. 303, [1] p., front., [7] leaves of plates. [Ill. by W. T. Smedley, E. Hering, and E. M. Ashe.]
PW: Ap 18, '03.

B-870   ____ The blue ocean's daughter / by Cyrus Townsend Brady. New York: Moffat, Yard & Company, 1907. 336 p., col. front., [4] leaves of plates. [Ill. by George Fort Gibbs.]
LC: S 7, '07.
PW: O 5, '07.
BLC: London: Greening & Co., 1908.

B-871   ____ Britton of the Seventh: a romance of Custer and the great Northwest / by Cyrus Townsend Brady . . . illustrated by the Kinneys. Chicago: A. C. McClurg & Co., 1914. 391, [1] p., front., [3] leaves of plates.
LC: O 19, '14.
PW: O 31, '14.
BLC: London: Cazenove; Chicago [printed], 1914.

B-872   ____ "By the world forgot": a double romance of the east and the west / by Cyrus Townsend Brady; frontispiece by Clarence F. Underwood. Chicago: A. C. McClurg & Co., 1917. 344 p., front.
LC: O 2, '17.
PW: O 27, '17.
BLC: London: Jarrolds, [1918].

B-873   ____ The chalice of courage: a romance of Colorado / by Cyrus Townsend Brady; with illustrations by Harrison Fisher and J. N. Marchand. New York: Dodd, Mead and Company, 1912. 382 p., col. front., [3] leaves of col. plates.
LC: F 23, '12.
PW: Mr 2, '12.

B-874   ____ A Christmas when the West was young / by Cyrus Townsend Brady . . . Chicago: A. C. McClurg & Company, 1913. 75 p., ill.
LC: S 30, '13.
PW: O 25, '13.

B-875   ____ The conquest of the Southwest: the story of a great spoliation: illustrated / by Cyrus Townsend Brady . . . New York: D. Appleton and Company, 1905. 293 p., front., [15] leaves of plates, maps, ports. [Ill. by Louis Betts, etc.] (Expansion of the republic series.)
PW: F 18, '05.

B-876   ____ The corner in coffee / by Cyrus Townsend Brady; illustrations by Gordon H. Grant. New York: G. W. Dillingham Company, [1904]. 298 p., front., [3] leaves of plates.
PW: F 20, '04.
BLC: London: Unwin; New York [printed], 1904; London: G. P. Putnam's Sons, 1904 (different title page).

B-877   ____ A doctor of philosophy / by Cyrus Townsend Brady. New York: Charles Scribner's Sons, 1903. 302 p.
PW: S 5, '03.
BLC: London: Harper & Bros.; New York [printed], 1903.

B-878   ____ The eagle of the empire: a story of Waterloo / by Cyrus Townsend Brady; illustrated by the Kinneys. New York: George H. Doran Company, [c1915]. 370 p., col. front., [3] leaves of plates.
LC: Ap 19, '15.
PW: Ap 10, '15.
BLC: London: Hodder & Stoughton; printed in U. S. A., 1915.

B-879   ____ The fetters of freedom / by Cyrus Townsend Brady; with illustrations by the Kinneys. New York: Dodd, Mead and Company, 1913. 399, [1] p., col. front., [3] leaves of col. plates.
LC: Ap 16, '13.
PW: Ap 12, '13.
BLC: London: Hurst & Blackett, [1914].

B-880   ____ Hearts and the highway: a romance of the road, first set forth by Lady Katherine Clanranald and Sir Hugh Richmond and now transcribed / by Cyrus Townsend Brady; illustrated by F. C. Yohn. New York: Dodd, Mead and Company, 1911. 321 p., col. front., [3] leaves of col. plates.
LC: Ap 10, '11.
PW: Ap 18, '11.

B-881   ____ Hohenzollern: a story of the time of Frederick Barbarossa / by Cyrus Townsend Brady; with illustrations by Will Crawford and decorations by Mills Thompson. New York: The Century Co., 1902. 288 p., front., [7] leaves of plates. [This book is an expansion of the story entitled "Barbarossa" which originally appeared in the Century magazine.]
PW: Ap 12, '02.

_____ A hazing interregnum. In *Stories of the colleges* (1901), S-984.

B-882 _____ The island of regeneration: a story of what ought to be / by Cyrus Townsend Brady . . . ; illustrations by the Kinneys. New York: Dodd, Mead and Company, 1909. 362 p., col. front., [3] leaves of col. plates.
LC: O 11, '09.
PW: O 23, '09.
BLC: London: Greening & Co., 1910.

B-883 _____ The island of surprise / by Cyrus Townsend Brady; illustrations by Walter Tittle. Chicago: A. C. McClurg & Co., 1915. 371 p., front., [14] leaves of plates.
LC: S 27, '15.
PW: O 9, '15.
BLC: London: C. F. Cazenove; Chicago: A. C. McClurg & Co.; Chicago [printed], 1915.

B-884 _____ The island of the stairs: being a true account of certain strange and wonderful adventures of Master John Hampdon, seaman, and teller of the tale, and Mistress Lucy Wilberforce, gentlewoman, in the great south seas / edited by Cyrus Townsend Brady; illustrated by the Kinneys. Chicago: A. C. McClurg & Co., 1913. 369, [1] p., front., [3] leaves of plates.
LC: N 22, '13.
PW: D 6, '13.
BLC: London: C. F. Cazenove; Chicago: A. C. McClurg & Co.; Binghamton, N. Y. [printed], 1913.

B-885 _____ The little angel of Canyon Creek / by Cyrus Townsend Brady; illustrated. New York; Chicago; Toronto; London; Edinburgh: Fleming H. Revell Company, [c1914]. 292 p., front., [5] leaves of plates. [Ill. by Gayle Hoskins and Clark Fay.]
LC: S 21, '14.
PW: S 5, '14.

B-886 _____ A little book for Christmas: containing a greeting, a word of advice, some personal adventures, a carol, a meditation, and three Christmas stories for all ages / by Cyrus Townsend Brady; with illustrations and decorations by Will Crawford. New York; London: G. P. Putnam's Sons, 1917. ([New York]: The Knickerbocker Press). 178 p., col. front., [4] leaves of plates, music.
Contents: A Christmas greeting -- From a far country -- On Christmas giving -- It was the same Christmas morning -- A Christmas carol -- The lone scout's Christmas -- Looking into the manger -- Christmas in the snows -- A Christmas wish.
LC: D 1, '17.
PW: D 1, '17.

B-887 _____ A little traitor to the South: a war-time comedy, with a tragic interlude / by Cyrus Townsend Brady; the illustrations are by A. D. Rahn; decorations by C. E. Hooper. New York: The Macmillan Company; London: Macmillan & Co., Ltd., 1904. 257 p., col. front., [5] leaves of col. plates.

B-888 _____ The man who won / by Cyrus Townsend Brady . . . Chicago: A. C. McClurg & Co., 1919. 243 p., photo. front., [15] leaves of photo. plates.
"By the courtesy of the Vitagraph Company of America, this book is illustrated by photographs of scenes taken from the picture play."
LC: N 17, '19.
PW: N 15, '19.

B-889 _____ The more excellent way: being the determinative episodes in the life of Chrissey De Sleden, hedonist / by Cyrus Townsend Brady. New York; London: G. P. Putnam's Sons, 1916. ([New York]: The Knickerbocker Press). 422 p., col. front. [Ill. by E. L. Crompton.]
Revised and enlarged edition. "First published as a serial under the title `Whom God hath joined.'"
LC: O 13, '16.
PW: S 23, '16.

B-890 _____ My lady's slipper / by Cyrus Townsend Brady; pictures by Charlotte Weber Ditzler. New York: Dodd, Mead & Company, 1905. 245 p., col. front., [3] leaves of col. plates.
PW: N 11, '05.

B-891 _____ The patriots: the story of Lee and the last hope / by Cyrus Townsend Brady; illustrations in colour by Walter H. Everett. New York: Dodd, Mead & Company, 1906.
348 p., col. front., [4] leaves of col. plates.
PW: Mr 24, '06.
BLC: London: Cassell & Co., 1906. (British title: *The patriots of the South.*)

B-892 _____ The Quiberon touch: a romance of the days when "the great Lord Hawke" was king of the sea / by Cyrus Townsend Brady. New York: D. Appleton and Company, 1901. 410 p., front.
PW: F 22, '02.
BLC: London: Greening & Co., 1908. (British title: *Little France; or, The Quiberon touch.*)

B-893 _____ The records: being truthful accounts, grave and gay, of the doings of certain real people hereinafter set down for the edification of the wise and the foolish, and the amusement of the tired and the unhappy / by Cyrus Townsend Brady; illustrations by Louis D. Arata. New York: G. W. Dillingham Company, [1904]. 321 p., front., [3] leaves of plates.
PW: D 10, '04.
BLC: London: Unwin; New York [printed], 1904.

B-894 _____ Richard the Brazen / by Cyrus Townsend Brady . . . and Edward Peple . . . ; illustrated. New York: Moffat, Yard & Company, 1906. 339 p., col. front., [5] leaves of col. plates. [Ill. by George Fort Gibbs.]
LC: Ag 16, '06.
PW: S 1, '06.

B-895   ____ The ring and the man: with some incidental relation to the woman / by Cyrus Townsend Brady; illustrated by George Gibbs. New York: Moffat, Yard and Company, 1909. 369 p., front., [5] leaves of plates.
LC: F 24, '09.
PW: Mr 13, '09.
BLC: London: Jarrold & Sons, 1916.

B-896   ____ Secret service: being the happenings of a knight in Richmond in the spring of 1865, done into book form from the play by William Gillette / by Cyrus Townsend Brady; illustrated by the Kinneys. New York: Dodd, Mead and Company, 1912. 331 p., col. front., [2] leaves of col. plates.
LC: Ja 24, '12.
PW: Ja 6, '12.
BLC: London: Hodder & Stoughton, [1916].

B-897   ____ Sir Henry Morgan, buccaneer: a romance of the Spanish Main / by Cyrus Townsend Brady; illustrations by J. N. Marchand and Will Crawford. New York: G. W. Dillingham Company, [1903]. 446, [1] p., col. front., [11] leaves of plates (1 col.).
PW: O 24, '03.
BLC: London: Unwin; New York [printed], 1903.

B-898   ____ The southerners: a story of the Civil War / by Cyrus Townsend Brady; illustrated by George Wright, with vignettes by Louis D. Arata. New York: Charles Scribner's Sons, 1903. 407, [1] p., col. front., [3] leaves of col. plates.
PW: Mr 21, '03.

B-899   ____ The sword hand of Napoleon: a romance of Russia and the great retreat / by Cyrus Townsend Brady; illustrated by the Reeses. New York: Dodd, Mead and Company, 1914. 357 p., front., [3] leaves of plates.
LC: Ap 16, '14.
PW: Ap 11, '14.
BLC: London: Hodder & Stoughton, 1915.

B-900   ____ Three daughters of the confederacy: the story of their loves and their hatreds, their joys and their sorrows, during many surprising adventures on land and sea / by Cyrus Townsend Brady; illustrated by J. N. Marchand. New York: G. W. Dillingham Company, [1905]. 440 p., col. front., [5] leaves of col. plates.
PW: O 7, '05.
BLC: London: Unwin; New York [printed], 1905.

B-901   ____ The two captains: a romance of Bonaparte and Nelson / by Cyrus Townsend Brady. New York: The Macmillan Company; London: Macmillan & Co., Ltd., 1905. 413 p., ill.
PW: F 11, '05.

B-902   ____ Under tops'ls and tents: illustrated / by Cyrus Townsend Brady . . . New York: Charles Scribner's Sons, 1901. 272 p., photo. front., [11] leaves of photo. plates.
PW: Ap 6, '01.

B-903   ____ Waif-o-the-sea: a romance of the great deep / by Cyrus Townsend Brady; illustrated by J. Allen St. John. Chicago: A. C. McClurg & Co., 1918. 316 p., front., [2] leaves of plates.
LC: O 17, '18.
PW: N 9, '18.
BLC: London: Jarrolds, [1919].

B-904   ____ Web of steel / by Cyrus Townsend Brady and Cyrus Townsend Brady, Jr.; illustrated by the Kinneys. New York; Chicago; Toronto; London; Edinburgh: Fleming H. Revell Company, [c1916]. 336 p., front., ill.
LC: Ap 11, '16.
PW: Ap 8, '16.

B-905   ____ The West Wind: a story of red men and white in old Wyoming / by Cyrus Townsend Brady . . . ; illustrated by Maynard Dixon. Chicago: A. C. McClurg & Co., 1912. 389 p., col. front., [3] leaves of col. plates.
LC: S 16, '12.
PW: O 12, '12.

B-906   ____ When blades are out and love's afield: a comedy of cross-purposes in the Carolinas / by Cyrus Townsend Brady; with illustrations by E. Plaisted Abbott, and decorations by Edward Stratton Holloway. Philadelphia; London: J. B. Lippincott Company, 1901. 305 p., front., [7] leaves of plates.
PW: Mr 30, '01.

B-907   ____ When the sun stood still / by Cyrus Townsend Brady . . . New York; Chicago; Toronto; London; Edinburgh: Fleming H. Revell Company, [c1917]. 308 p., front. [Ill. by Victor Pérard.]
LC: Ap 28, '17.
PW: Ap 28, '17.
BLC: London: Jarrold's, [1922].

B-908   ____ Woven with the ship: a novel of 1865, together with certain other veracious tales of various sorts / by Cyrus Townsend Brady; with many illustrations by Howard Chandler Christy, Frank X. Leyendecker, W. Glackens, Will Crawford, and H. L. V. Parkhurst. Philadelphia; London: J. B. Lippincott Company, 1902. 368 p., col. front., [9] leaves of plates.
Contents: Part I. Woven with the ship. Part II. Veracious tales of various sorts: A vaudeville turn -- The last tribute to his genius -- In Oklahoma -- Passing the love of a woman -- The final propositions -- The captain of H. B. M. ship Diamond Rock -- "When lovely woman stoops to folly" -- Saved by her slipper -- "Sonny Boy's" diary -- The amusing yarn of the bo's'n's mate -- The disembodied spirit.
PW: N 22, '02.

Brady, Cyrus Townsend, Jr., jt. aut. *Web of Steel* (1916) See **Brady, Cyrus Townsend, 1861-1920, jt. aut., B-904.**

B-909 Brady, Jasper Ewing. The case of Mary Sherman: a novel / by Jasper Ewing Brady; illustrated by Charles F. Lester, New York: Britton Publishing Company, [c1917]. 335 p., front., [3] leaves of plates.
LC: S 20, '17.
PW: S 8, '17.

B-910 Brady, John, b. 1864. Mrs. Featherweight's musical moments / by John Brady; illustrated by the author. New York: Printed and published at the Goerck Art Press, c1908. [52]p., ill.

B-911 Braendle, Rose Anne. Tales of many lands / by Rose A. Braendle . . . Washington, D. C.: Press of Gibson Bros., [c1906]. 187 p.
Contents: Nature's nobleman -- Chums -- A bluegrass romance -- Fidelia -- The ghost of Mereton Lodge -- Blind Benjamin -- Marie -- Madame de Benoit -- The flower girl of the Jockey Club -- Nanette -- The green banks of the Shannon -- Drilling recruits in the Bog of Allen -- Madame la Marquise -- The Jesuit's story -- Slumming -- The maniac wife -- The Count de Pirotto.
PW: Mr 9, '07.

Brainerd, Chauncey Cory, 1874-1922. See **Rath, E. J., jt. pseud. of Brainerd, Chauncey Cory and Brainerd, Edith Rathbone (Jacobs).**

Brainerd, Edith Rathbone (Jacobs). See **Rath, E. J., jt. pseud. of Brainerd, Chauncey Cory and Brainerd, Edith Rathbone (Jacobs).**

B-912 Brainerd, Eleanor Hoyt, 1868-1942. Bettina / by Eleanor Hoyt Brainerd; illustrated by Will Grefé. New York: Doubleday, Page & Company, 1907. 212 p., col. front., [4] leaves of plates.
LC: Ja 16, '07.
PW: Ja 26, '07.
BLC: London: Doubleday, Page & Company; New York printed, 1905. London: Cassell & Co.; New York printed, 1907 (with a different title page).

B-913 ____ Concerning Belinda / by Eleanor Hoyt Brainerd; illustrated by Harrison Fisher and Katharine N. Richardson. New York: Doubleday, Page & Company, 1905. 193 p., front., [11] leaves of plates.
PW: O 7, '05.
BLC: London: Doubleday, Page & Company; New York printed, 1905. London: Cassell & Co.; New York printed, 1908.

B-914 [____] Her golden hours; the confidences of a modern girl; illustrated by Lester Ralph. New York: Moffat, Yard & Company, 1916. 99 p., col. front., ill., col. plates.
Unexamined copy: bibliographic data from NUC.

B-915 ____ How could you, Jean? / by Eleanor Hoyt Brainerd; illustrated by James Montgomery Flagg. Garden City, N. Y.: Doubleday, Page & Company, 1917. 337, [1] p., front., [3] leaves of plates.
LC: O 18, '17.
PW: O 13, '17.
BLC: London: T. Nelson & Sons, [1920].

B-916 ____ The misdemeanors of Nancy / by Eleanor Hoyt; illustrated by Penrhyn Stanlaws. New York: Doubleday, Page & Co., 1902. 213 p., front., [15] leaves of plates.
"Most of the material in this book has appeared serially in the N. Y. Sun and Everybody's magazine."
BLC: London: Grant Richards, 1902.

B-917 ____ Nancy's country Christmas: and other stories / by Eleanor Hoyt; frontispiece by Anna Whelan Betts.

New York: Doubleday, Page & Company, 1904. 224 p., col. front.
Contents: Nancy's country Christmas -- In Oklahoma -- The little god and the machine -- In the light of the Christmas candles -- A visiting peer -- The vanishing boarder -- Gowns and a gobolink -- A disturber of the peace -- The littlest sister -- Women are made like that.
BLC: London: Doubleday, Page & Company; New York printed, 1904.

B-918 ____ Our little old lady / by Eleanor Hoyt Brainerd. Garden City, New York: Doubleday, Page & Company, 1919. 165, [1] p., front.
LC: D 1, '19.

B-919 ____ Pegeen / by Eleanor Hoyt Brainerd. New York: The Century Co., 1915. 295 p., col. front.
LC: S 15, '15.
BLC: London: Grant Richards, 1916.

B-920 ____ The personal conduct of Belinda / by Eleanor Hoyt Brainerd; illustrated by George Brehm. New York: Doubleday, Page & Company, 1910. 307 p., col. front., [4] leaves of col. plates.
LC: Mr 18, '10.
BLC: London: Hodder & Stoughton; New York printed, 1910.

____ The queer little thing. In *Prarie gold*, **(1917), P-588.**

B-921 Brainerd, Henry C., b. 1845. The old family doctor / by Henry C. Brainerd . . . Cleveland: The Arthur H. Clark Co., 1905, [c1904]. 117 p., front. **NOH**
PW: Ja 21, '05.

Braley, Berton, 1882-1966. Merely a case. In *The so-so stories* **(1914), S-715.**

B-922 ____ The sheriff of Silver Bow / by Berton Braley. Indianapolis: The Bobbs-Merrill Company, [c1921]. 338 p. **HLS**
LC: S 15, '21.
PW: O 1, '21.
BLC: London: Methuen & Co; printed in U. S. A., 1923.

B-923 Brand, Fern Tolley. Mme. Maimee / by Fern Tolley Brand. Glendale, California: Published by the West Publishing Company (not Inc.), c1922. 141 p.

B-924 Brand, Jack. By wild waves tossed: an ocean love story / by Captain Jack Brand; illustrations by the Kinneys. New York: The McClure Company, 1908. 310 p., front., [3] leaves of plates.
LC: Ap 5, '08.
PW: My 9, '08.
BLC: London: McClure Co.; printed in U. S. A., 1908.

B-925 Brand, Max, 1892-1944, *pseud.* Alcatraz / by Max Brand [pseud.] . . . New York; London: G. P. Putnam's sons, 1923. ([New York]: The Knickerbocker Press). 325 p. **SOI**
LC: Ja 30, '23.
PW: Mr 7, '25.

B-926 [____] Beyond the outpost / by Peter Henry Morland [pseud.]. New York; London: G. P. Putnam's Sons, 1925. ([New York]: The Knickerbocker Press). 354 p.
PW: O 31, '25.

B-927 [____] The bronze collar: a romance of Spanish California / by John Frederick [pseud.]. New York; London: G. P. Putnam's Sons, 1925. ([New York]: The Knickerbocker Press). 337 p.
LC: F 20, '25.

B-928 [____] Bull Hunter: a western story / by David Manning [pseud.]. . . New York City: Chelsea House, [c1924]. 247 p.   CRL
LC: D 31, '24.
PW: D 26, '25.

B-929 [____] Bull Hunter's romance: sequel to Bull Hunter: a western story / by David Manning [pseud.]. New York: Chelsea House, [c1924]. 251 p.
LC: D 31, '24.
PW: My 9, '25.

____ Bulldog. In *"Dawgs!": an anthology of stories about them* (1925), D-184.

B-930 ____ Dan Barry's daughter / by Max Brand [pseud.] . . . New York; London: G. P. Putnam's Sons, 1924. ([New York]: The Knickerbocker Press). 353 p.
LC: Ja 21, '24.
PW: Ja 26, '24.

B-931 [____] Donnegan: a western story / by George Owen Baxter [pseud.] . . . New York City: Chelsea House, [c1923]. 320 p., front.
LC: Ja 18, '23.
PW: Je 2, '23.

B-932 [____] Free Range Lanning: a western story / by George Owen Baxter [pseud.]; frontispiece by Edgar Wittmack. New York City: Chelsea House, 1921. 303 p., col. front.
LC: O 20, '21.
PW: Ja 7, '22.

B-933 [____] Jerry Peyton's notched inheritance: a western story / by David Manning [pseud.]. New York: Chelsea House, [c1920]. 255 p.

B-934 [____] Jim Curry's test: a western story / by David Manning [pseud.]. New York City: Chelsea House, [c1925]. 256 p.
PW: My 16, '25.

B-935 [____] King Charlie's Raiders: a western story / by David Manning [pseud.]. New York: Chelsea House, [c1925]. 256 p.
PW: My 16, '25.

B-936 [____] The long, long trail: a western story / by George Owen Baxter [pseud.] . . . New York City: Chelsea House, [c1923]. 320 p.
LC: S 19, '23.
PW: O 27, '23.

B-937 ____ The night horseman / by Max Brand [pseud.] . . . New York; London: G. P. Putnam's Sons, 1920. (New York: The Knickerbocker Press). 379 p.
LC: N 20, '20.
PW: N 13, '20.

____ Out of the dark. In *The ten-foot chain, or Can love survive the shackles?* (1920), T-108.

B-938 ____ The range-land avenger: a western story / by George Owen Baxter [pseud.] . . . New York City: Chelsea House, [c1924]. 319 p.
LC: O 7, '24.
PW: O 25, '24.

B-939 [____] Riders of the silences / by John Frederick [pseud.]; illustrated by Frank Tenney Johnson. New York: The H. K. Fly Company, [c1920]. 310 p., front.   BGU
PW: S 25, '20.

B-940 ____ The seventh man / by Max Brand [pseud.]. New York; London: G. P. Putnam's Sons, 1921. ([New York]: The Knickerbocker Press). 332 p.
LC: O 31, '21.
PW: O 22, '21.

B-941 [____] The shadow of Silver Tip: a western story / by George Owen Baxter [pseud.]. New York City: Chelsea House, [c1925]. 311 p.
Unexamined copy: bibliographic data from NUC.
PW: Je 6, '25.

B-942 ____ Trailin'! / by Max Brand [pseud.] . . . New York; London: G. P. Putnam's Sons, 1920. (New York: The Knickerbocker Press). 375 p.
LC: Ap 19, '20.
PW: Mr 27, '20.

B-943 ____ The untamed / by Max Brand [pseud.]. New York; London: G. P. Putnam's Sons, 1919. ([New York]: The Knickerbocker Press). 374 p.
LC: Mr 20, '19.
PW: Mr 1, '19.

B-944 [____] Wooden guns: a western story / by George Owen Baxter [pseud.]. New York City: Chelsea House. [c1925]. 318 p.
Unexamined copy: bibliographic data from NUC.
PW: D 26, '25.

B-945 Branham, Adelia Pope, 1861-1917. A daughter of April / by Adelia Pope Branham. New York; London; Montreal: The Abbey Press, [c1903]. 164 p., photo. front. (port.), ill.   DLC
Contents: A daughter of April -- When lights burn blue -- Told by the sea -- When Cupid procrastinates -- The renovation of Mr. Stubbs.

B-946 Brannan, Louisa. Two villages / by Louisa Brannan. New York: Everywhere Publishing Co., [c1911]. 52 p.   DLC

B-947 Brannon, Ada Cornelius, Mrs. A noble girl: a book devoted to the uplifting of character and modern

80

society / Mrs. Ada Cornelius Brannon . . . Cisco, Texas: Collie Printing Company, [c1906]. 219 p., photo. front., [1] leaf of photo. plates.　　**SUR**
LC: Je 26, '06.

B-948　Brant, John Ira, b. 1872. The new regime: A. D. 2202 / by John Ira Brant. New York: Cochrane Publishing Co.; London, England: T. Werner Laurie, 1909. 122 p.　　**OKU**
PW: Jl 31, '09; Ag 7, '09.

B-949　Brass, Theophilus. A chapter from the story of Pauline Parsons / by Theophilus Brass. Ashland, Mass.: William P. Morrison, 1916. 72 p.

B-950　Brassington, Viola. The message of Christmas: and other stories / by Viola Brassington. New York: The Metropolitan Press, 1910. 55, [1] p.　　**DLC**
Contents: The message of Christmas -- Our pilgrim fathers -- The soldier's message -- Elvin Adair's poetry -- The fair -- Camping -- At the brook -- School days.
LC: D 29, '10.
PW: F 11, '11.

B-951　Brasted, Fred. The gang: a story of the Middle West / by Fred Brasted . . . Philadelphia; Boston; Chicago; St. Louis: The Griffith & Rowland Press, 1910. 320 p., col. front., [7] leaves of plates. [Ill. by G. A. Newman.]
LC: Ap 8, '10.
PW: Ap 9, '10.

B-952　Bratton, Arno. The redemption of Arthur True: a rural school story / by Arno Bratten; with an introduction by E. G. Lentz. Marion, Illinois: The Stafford Publishing Company, 1909. 139, [1] p., photo. front. (port.).　　**MNU**
LC: Jl 12, '09.

Braudes, Reuben Asher. The misfortune. In *Yiddish tales* (1912), **Y-20.**

B-953　Bray, Blanche A. (Blanche Alice), b. 1873. His ward / by Blanche A. Bray . . . New York: The Cosmopolitan Press, 1911. 349 p.
PW: Ja 6, '12.

B-954　Bray, Mary Matthews, b. 1837. A romance of Barnstable / Mary Matthews Bray. Boston: Richard G. Badger, 1909. (Boston: The Gorham Press). 295 p.
PW: Je 19, '09.

Brean, S. C. Margaret Kelly's wake. In *Through the forbidden gates* (1903), **T-222.**

Breckenridge, Bertha Anna Kelsey. See **Breckenridge, John, Mrs., b. 1852.**

B-955　Breckenridge, John, Mrs., b. 1852. Mahanomah / by Mrs. John Breckenridge. New York: Cochrane Publishing Company, 1910, [c1911]. 128 p.
LC: Ja 28, '11.

B-956　Bredenbek, Magnus. The ingrate / by Magnus Bredenbek. Rahway, N. J.: The Cheston Publishing

Co., 1915. 250 p.
PW: Jl 10, '15.

B-957　Breen, A. E. (Andrew Edward), 1863-1938. A daughter of Mexico: a historical romance founded on documentary evidence / by Dr. A. E. Breen. Rochester, N. Y.: John P. Smith Printing Company, 1916. 342 p.
LC: O 21, '16.

B-958　Breese, Kathryn. Mine is the judgment / by Kathryn Breese. Boston: B. J. Brimmer Company, 1925. 342 p.　　**DLC**
PW: Je 13, '25.

Brenan, Florence McCarthy, b. 1854. See **Guest, Gilbert, pseud.**

B-959　Brenholtz, Edwin Arnold, b. 1859. Fate: the story of a study of a human life / by Edwin Arnold Brenholtz. New York; London; Montreal: The Abbey Press, [c1902]. 222 p.　　**ORE**

B-960　_____ In the last degree / by Edwin Arnold Brenholtz. Westwood, Mass.: Published at the Ariel Press, [c1904]. 138 p.
Contents: Dedicatory foreword -- In the last degree -- Al Harrad and his love -- The one-storied house -- Philista -- Baffled destiny -- When we awake -- Trinity.
LC: Ag 1, '06.

B-961　_____ The recording angel: a novel / by Edwin Arnold Brenholtz. Chicago: Charles H. Kerr & Company, 1905. 287 p.　　**KSU**
PW: My 6, '05.

B-962　Brenn, George J., b. 1888. Voices / by George J. Brenn. New York; London: The Century Co., 1923. 317 p., front. [Ill. by A. D. Rahn.]
LC: S 7, '23.
PW: S 22, '23.
BLC: London: Herbert Jenkins, 1925.

B-963　Brennan, George H. (George Hugh), b. 1865. Anna Malleen / by George H. Brennan. London; New York: Mitchell Kennerley, 1911. 377 p.
LC: Jl 22, '11.

B-964　_____ Bill Truetell: a story of theatrical life / by George H. Brennan; with frontispiece in color and twenty-three drawings in the text by James Montgomery Flagg. Chicago: A. C. McClurg & Co., 1909. 280 p., col. front.

B-965　Brent, John. A man's game / by John Brent. New York: The Century Co., 1921. 302 p., front.
LC: S 1, '21.

B-966　Brenton, Hilda. Uncle Jed's country letters / by Hilda Brenton . . . ; illustrated. Boston; New York: Henry A. Dickerman & Son, [c1902]. 73 p., front. [Ill. by W. Herbert Dunton.]
Contents: New Year's Day at Pine Hollow, 19-- -- The spellin' match at the Ridge -- Uncle Jed buys a stage coach -- Jed and Betsey at the White Mountains -- A case of jim-jams -- Uncle Jed's dream of the White House -- Uncle Jed's experience with lawyers.
PW: Je 7, '02.

B-967   Breuning, Margaret. You know Charles / by Margaret Breuning. New York: Henry Holt and Company, 1921. 202 p.
LC: N 19, '21.
PW: D 3, '21.

B-968   Brewer, Charles Louis. The elder brother: a dawn of thought sketch / by C. L. Brewer. Chicago: To-morrow Publishing Co., 1907. 64 p.

Brewer, Estelle H. M. See **Manning-Brewer, Estelle Hempstead, b. 1882.**

B-969   Brewster, Frances Stanton, b. 1860. Rhody / by Frances S. Brewster . . . Philadelphia: George W. Jacobs & Company, [c1912]. 230 p., col. front., [3] leaves of col. plates. [Ill. by Florence Scovel Shinn.]   **OSU, COD**
LC: S 24, '12.
PW: O 5, '12.

B-970   Brewster, S. W. (Samuel Wheeler). Retribution, a Kansas romance / by S. W. Brewster. [Independence, Kan.: Tribune Press, 1912?] [18] p. Unexamined copy: bibliographic data from NUC.

B-971   Briarly, Mary, *pseud.* In his own image / by Mary Briarly [pseud.]. New York: The Macmillan Company, 1921. 419 p.
PW: Ap 16, '21.

B-972   Bridges, Soule Jones, Mrs. A story founded on fact and verse / by Mrs. Soule Jones Bridges. Memphis, Tenn.: Southern Pub. Co., Printers, 1903. 32 p. Unexamined copy: bibliographic data from OCLC, #18356644.

B-973   Bridgman, Helen Bartlett, 1855-1935. The last passion / by Helen Bartlett Bridgman. New York: Cloister Publishing Company, [c1925]. 223 p.
LC: D 9, '25.

B-974   Bridgman, Raymond L. (Raymond Landon), 1848-1925. Loyal traitors: a story of friendship for the Filipinos / by Raymond L. Bridgman. Boston: James H. West Company, [c1903]. 310 p.
PW: F 7, '03.

Briggs, Anna Lansing. The weariness of Jane. In **Pacific Coast Women's Press Association. *La copa de oro* (1905), P-2.**

B-975   Briggs, Olive M. (Olive Mary), b. 1873. The bachelor dinner / by Olive M. Briggs. New York: Charles Scribner's Sons, 1912. 292 p., front., [1] leaf of plates.
LC: Ap 30, '12.
PW: My 4, '12.

B-976   _____ The black cross / by Olive M. Briggs; frontispiece by Sigismond de Ivanowski. New York: Moffat, Yard and Company, 1909. 420 p., col. front.
LC: Ja 23, '09.
PW: F 20, '09.

B-977   _____ The courting of Miss Parkina / by Olive M. Briggs. [New York: The Winthrop Press], c1914. 31 p., 1 col. ill. "Previously published in Munsey's magazine."

B-978   _____ The fir and the palm / by Olive M. Briggs. New York: Charles Scribner's Sons, 1910. 324 p., ill.
LC: Mr 16, '10.
PW: Mr 19, '10.

Brigham, Johnson, 1846-1936. See **Johnson, Wolcott, pseud.**

B-979   Brightman, Virginia Hudson. Sonny / by Virginia Brightman; frontispiece by George W. Gage. New York: W. J. Watt & Co., [c1923]. 284 p., col. front.
LC: F 21, '24.
BLC: London: Geoffrey Bles, 1926.

B-980   Brinley, Jay, *pseud.* The miner's tears; or, The Red cross beauty of the coal region / by Jay Brinley [pseud.]. [Scranton]: The Laurel Press, [c1916]. 425 p.
Unexamined copy: bibliographic data from NUC.

B-981   Brinsmade, Herman Hine. For the good of the party, or, The fortunes of "the Blackville star" / by Herman Hine Brinsmade . . . Boston: Sherman, French & Company, 1916. 195 p.   **DLC**
LC: Ja 2, '17.

B-982   _____ Utopia achieved: a novel of the future / by Herman Hine Brinsmade; cover by Maurer. New York: Broadway publishing Co., [c1912]. 177 p.
LC: Ap 10, '12.

B-983   Brinton, Davis. Trusia: a princess of Krovitch / by Davis Brinton; with illustrations by Walter H. Everett. Philadelphia; London: George W. Jacobs and Company, [1906]. 301 p., col. front., [3] leaves of plates.
PW: O 13, '06.

Brisard, Montague, pseud. See **Bedford-Jones, H. (Henry), 1887-1949.**

B-984   Briscoe, Margaret Sutton, b. 1864. The change of heart: six love stories / by Margaret Sutton Briscoe . . . New York; London: Harper & Brothers, 1903. 171, [1] p.
Contents: The assistant bishop -- Red tassels -- "Whither thou goest" -- Creating a vacuum -- Debtors -- Oscar and Louise.
PW: S 12, '03.

B-985   _____ The image of Eve: a romance with alleviations / by Margaret Sutton Briscoe. New York; London: Harper & Brothers, 1909. 227, [1] p., front.
LC: N 6, '09.
PW: N 13, '09.

B-986   Britt, Albert, b. 1874. The wind's will / Albert Britt. New York: Moffat, Yard and Company, 1912. 400 p.
LC: D 24, '12.

B-987   Britt, Gisela Dittrick. In the King's country / by Gisela Dittrick Britt. Boston: The Christian Endeavor World, [c1919]. 197 p., front., [3] leaves of plates. [Ill. by Sears Gallagher.]
LC: O 13, '19.

B-988   Britton, Frederic H. Teddie: a simple, little out-of-door story about a child, in the telling of which a promise to a friend is redeemed / by Frederic H. Britton. Detroit: F. B. Dickerson Co., 1910. 315 p.   **EEM**
LC: Jl 11, '10.

Britton, Rollin J., 1864-1931. See **Blue, Guy, pseud.**

B-989   Britton, Sumner Charles, b. 1902. Dreamy Hollow / by Sumner Charles Britton; a Long Island romance. New York: World Syndicate Company, Inc., [c1921]. 307 p., front., [2] leaves of plates.
LC: S 13, '21.

B-990   Broadus, Thomas Andrew. Serena Fair / by Thomas Andrew Broadus; illustrated. Louisville: The Baptist Argus, 1906. 238 p., front., [2] leaves of plates. [Ill. by Rosco R. Binkley.]
LC: D 22, '06.

B-991   Broaker, Frank, Mrs., b. 1864. The younger Mrs. Courtney: a novel / by Mrs. Frank Broaker; illustrations by Mr. Freeland A. Carter. New York: Alwood Company, 1903. 319 p., front., [6] leaves of plates.
PW: Ja 9, '04.

B-992   Brobston, Olivia Munnerlyn. Letters from the south / by Olivia Munnerlyn Brobston. Copyright 1912 by Olivia Munnerlyn Brobston. 23 p.   **FQG**
Contents: "Letters from Elizabeth Loring who is visiting in the country to her mother in New York City" -- "When 13 proved a real hoo-doo, or, The undoing of Bess".

B-993   Brock, Charles E. M. Let the world judge: a romance of the Pacific / by Charles E. M. Brock. New York: Broadway Publishing Co., 1904. 195 p. Unexamined copy: bibliographic data from The Publishers' Weekly.
PW: Je 11, '04.

B-994   Brock, Hanson. Down Miami / by Hanson Brock; illustrations from photographs by the Claude C. Matlack Company. Miami, Florida: The Tropic Press, [c1920]. 79, [1] p., col. photo. front., [5] leaves of photo. plates.   **NYP**
LC: Ag 2, '20.

B-995   Brock, Hanson. Primrose paradise / by Hanson Brock. [Miami: Strange Printing Co., c1921.] 88 p.   **MUS**

B-996   Broderick, Therese, b. 1870. The brand: a tale of the Flathead Reservation / by Therese Broderick (Tin Schreiner.) Seattle, Wash.: The Alice Harriman Company, 1909. 271 p., front., [1] leaf of plates.
LC: D 2, '09.

Brokaw, Estella (Bachman). See **Bachman, Estella, b. 1860.**

Bromfield, Louis, 1896-1956, contributor. See *Bobbed hair* **(1925), B-700.**

B-997   _____ The green bay tree: a novel / by Louis Bromfield. New York: Frederick A. Stokes Company, 1924. 341 p.
LC: Mr 31, '24.
PW: Mr 22, '24.
BLC: London: Unwin, 1924. [First novel library.]

B-998   _____ Possession: a novel / by Louis Bromfield . . . New York: Frederick A. Stokes Company, 1925. 493 p.
LC: O 2, '25.
PW: O 10, '25.
BLC: London: Unwin, 1926.

Bronner, Harriet. Renunciation. In *Castle stories* **(1908), C-187.**

_____ Santa Marghuerita. In *Castle stories* **(1908), C-187.**

B-999   Bronson, Clark H. (Clark Henry), b. 1845. Twice a man: a psychological romance / by Clark H. Bronson; illustrated by French. Chicago: Bronson & Co., 1904. 316 p., photo. front.

B-1000   Bronson, Edgar Beecher, 1856-1917. The love of loot and women / by Edgar Beecher Bronson . . . New York: Privately printed, 1917. 288, [1] p., photo. front. (port.). [Ill. by Doris T. Jaeger.]
    KSU

B-1001   _____ The red-blooded / by Edgar Beecher Bronson; with many illustrations. Chicago: A. C. McClurg & Co., 1910. 342 p., front., [18] leaves of plates.
Contents: Loving's bend -- A cow-hunters' court -- A self-constituted executioner -- Triggerfingeritis -- A juggler with death -- An aerial bivouac -- The evolution of a train robber -- Circus day at Mancos -- Across the border -- The three-legged doe and the blind buck -- The Lemon County hunt -- El Tigre -- Bunkered -- They who must be obeyed -- Djama Rout's heroism -- A modern Cœur-de-lion.
LC: S 12, '10.
PW: S 24, '10.

B-1002   _____ The vanguard / by Edgar Beecher Bronson. New York: George H. Doran Company, [c1914]. 316 p.
LC: Ap 14, '14.
PW: Ap 4, '14.
BLC: London: Hodder & Stoughton; printed in U. S. A., 1914.

Bronson-Howard, George, 1883-1922, jt. aut. *All in the night's work* (1924). See **Mumford, Ethel Watts, 1878-1940, jt. aut, M-1119.**

B-1003   _____ Birds of prey: being pages from the Book of Broadway / by George Bronson-Howard; illustrations by Wallace Morgan. New York: W. J. Watt & Company Publishers, [c1918]. 392 p., front., [2] leaves of plates.
LC: S 13, '18.
PW: O 12, '18.

B-1004   ____ The black book: being the full account of how the Book of the Betrayers came into the hands of Yorke Norroy, secret agent of the Department of State / by George Bronson-Howard; frontispiece by Paul Stahr. New York: W. J. Watt & Company, [c1920]. 294 p., front.
LC: Ag 14, '20.
PW: Ap 2, '21.

B-1005   ____ The devil's chaplain / by George Bronson-Howard . . . New York: W. J. Watt & Company, [c1922]. 313 p.   **OSU, COD**
LC: Mr 12, '23.
PW: S 1, '23.
BLC: London: Stanley Paul & Co., [1924].

B-1006   ____ An enemy to society: a romance of New York of yesterday and to-day / by George Bronson Howard; illustrated by Arthur S. Covey. Garden City, New York: Doubleday, Page & Company, 1911. 350 p., col. front., [3] leaves of col. plates.
LC: O 21, '11.
PW: N 11, '11.
BLC: London: T. Werner Laurie; Garden City, New York [printed, 1911].

B-1007   ____ God's man: a novel / by George Bronson-Howard; illustrated initials by Will Vawter. Indianapolis: The Bobbs-Merrill Company, [c1915]. 475 p.
LC: S 30, '15.
PW: O 9, '15.

B-1008   ____ Norroy, diplomatic agent / by George Bronson-Howard; illustrated by Gordon Ross. New York; Akron, O.; Chicago: The Saalfield Publishing Co., [c1907]. 433 p., col. front.   **OSU, COD**
LC: Ja 28, '07.
PW: Mr 9, '07.

B-1009   ____ Scars on the southern seas: a romance / by George Bronson-Howard. New York: B. W. Dodge & Company, 1907. 313 p., col. front., [2] leaves of col. plates. [Ill. by Nella Fontaine Binckley.]
LC: D 6, '07.
PW: D 21, '07.

B-1010   ____ Slaves of the lamp: being the adventures of Yorke Norroy in his quest of the four jade plates a Manhattan nights' entertainment / by George Bronson-Howard; illustrations by Arthur E. Becher. New York: W. J. Watt & Company, [c1917]. 309 p., col. front., [2] leaves of col. plates.
LC: N 14, '17.
PW: N 24, '17.

B-1011 Brooke, Alison, *pseud.* When she came to herself / by Alison Brooke [pseud.]. Philadelphia: American Baptist Publication Society, [c1901]. 180 p., front., [5] leaves of plates. [Ill. By Frank McKernan.]
   DLC

B-1012 Brooks, Alden. Escape / by Alden Brooks. New York: Charles Scribner's Sons, 1924. 309 p.
LC: Ap 29, '24.
PW: My 17, '24.

BLC: London: Unwin, 1924. (British title: *The enchanted land*.) [First novel library.]

B-1013   ____ The fighting men / by Alden Brooks. New York: Charles Scribner's Sons, 1917. 302 p.
Contents: The Parisian -- The Belgian -- The odyssey of three Slavs -- The man from America -- The Prussian -- An Englishman.
LC: Ag 16, '17.
PW: Ag 18, '17.

    ____ Out of the sky. In *War stories* (1919), W-94.

B-1014 Brooks, Allen. The silken cord and other stories / by Allen Brooks. Boston: Fleming-Hughes-Rogers Co., [c1919]. 76 p., photo. front., [3] leaves of photo. plates.   **ELM**
Contents: The silken cord -- "Some fish" -- "Another fish story" -- "No snake at all" -- Swan Island and the boys from the Grand Caymans -- In "49" -- Injun Pete.
PW: Ag 23, '19.

B-1015 Brooks, Amy. At the sign of the three birches / by Amy Brooks; with frontispiece by author. Boston: Lothrop, Lee & Shepard Co., [1916]. 419 p., front.
PW: S 9, '16.

B-1016 Brooks, Asa P. (Asa Passavant), b. 1868. The reservation: a romance of the pioneer days of Minnesota and of the Indian Massacre of 1862 / Asa P. Brooks. [Comfrey?, Minn.: s. n.], 1907. 235 p.   **NYP**
LC: O 8, '07.

B-1017 Brooks, Charles Stephen, 1878-1934. Luca Sarto: a novel: a history of his perilous journey into France in the year fourteen hundred and seventy-one / by Charles S. Brooks. New York: The Century Co., 1920. 360 p., front.
PW: Mr 6, '20.

B-1018 Brooks, Elisabeth W. (Elisabeth Willard). As the world goes by / by Elisabeth W. Brooks. Boston: Little, Brown and Company, 1905. 375 p.
PW: My 6, '05.

B-1019 Brooks, Geraldine, b. 1875. Romances of colonial days / by Geraldine Brooks. New York: Thomas Y. Crowell & Company, [1903]. 180 p., front., [8] leaves of plates. [Ill. by Arthur E. Becher.]
Contents: In Mayflower time (1621) -- Beside the water-gate (1690) -- The secret of the trees (1735) -- A crown that stung (1744) -- The serving of a laggard lover (1751) -- The wooing of a governor (1760) -- The passing of a sweetheart (1773) -- A strain from the Mischianza (1778) -- In the ambassador's garden (1785).

B-1020 Brooks, Hildegard, b. 1875. Daughters of desperation / by Hildegard Brooks; illustrated by Charlotte Harding. New York: McClure, Phillips & Company, 1904. 161 p., front., [13] leaves of plates.
PW: Ap 9, '04.
BLC: Edinburgh; London: W. Blackwood & Sons, 1904.

B-1021   ____ The larky furnace: and other adventures of Sue Betty / by Hildegard Brooks . . . ; with cover and illustrations by Peter Newell. New York: Henry Holt and Company, 1906. 202 p., [5] leaves of plates.   **ERE**

Contents: The larky furnace -- Pirates -- The white night -- The fish picture -- Work without wages -- One of Plutarch's lives.
PW: Mr 3, '06.

B-1022 ____ The master of Caxton / by Hildegard Brooks. New York: Charles Scribner's Sons, 1902. 411 p.
PW: Ap 12, '02.

B-1023 ____ Without a warrant / by Hildegard Brooks. New York: Charles Scribner's Sons, 1901. 292 p.
PW: Ap 6, '01.

B-1024 Brooks, Mary Wallace. A prodigal / by Mary Wallace Brooks. Boston: Richard G. Badger, 1907. ([Boston]: The Gorham Press). 187 p.   **RBN**
LC: Je 24, '07.

B-1025 Brooks, Sarah Warner, 1822-1906. Alamo ranch: a story of New Mexico / by Sarah Warner Brooks . . . Cambridge [Mass.]: Privately printed, 1903. 148 p., photo. front.   **BAT**

B-1026 Brooks, Virginia, b. 1886. Little lost sister / by Virginia Brooks; illustrations by Frank J. Hoban. Chicago: Gazzolo and Ricksen, 1914. 363 p., front. (port.), [3] leaves of col. plates.

B-1027 ____ Tilly from Tillamook / by Virginia Brooks. Portland, Or.: A. E. Kern & Co., [c1925]. 127 p.

B-1028 Brookshire, W. C. (William Chauncey), b.1885. The lost treasure restored / by W. C. Brookshire. [Austin, Tex.: Printed by Von Boeckmann-Jones Co., c1912]. 271 p.

Brother Jabez. See **Jabez, Brother.**

B-1029 [Broughton, Ida May], b. 1863. A modern Becky Sharp / by May Lincoln [pseud.]. Boston: Richard G. Badger; [Toronto: The Copp Clark Co., Limited, c1916]. 225 p., photo. front., [7] leaves of plates.

B-1030 Broun, Heywood, 1888-1939. The boy grew older / by Heywood Broun. New York; London: G. P. Putnam's Sons, 1922. ([New York]: The Knickerbocker Press). 291 p.
LC: O 21, '22.
PW: O 21, '22.

B-1031 ____ The sun field / by Heywood Broun . . . -- [1st ed.] -- New York; London: G. P. Putnam's Sons, 1923. ([New York]: The Knickerbocker Press). 204 p.
LC: O 16, '23.
PW: O 20, '23.

B-1032 Browder, J. C. (John Caldwell), b. 1876. Nisi prius / J. C. Browder. New York: The Neale Publishing Company, 1912. 275 p.

B-1033 Brower, James Hatton, b. 1867. The mills of Mammon / by James H. Brower; with illustrations by F. L. Weitzel and Henderson Howk. Joliet, Ill.: P. H. Murray & Company, 1909. 491 p., front., [7] leaves of plates.
LC: O 11, '09.

B-1034 Brower, Lorraine Catlin. The vale of illusion / by Lorraine Catlin Brower; illustrations by Grant Tyson Reynard. Chicago: The Reilly & Britton Co., [c1915]. 423 p., front., [3] leaves of plates.
PW: Ap 17, '15.

B-1035 Brown, Abbie Farwell, d. 1927. The gift: a Christmas story / by Abbie Farwell Brown. Boston: Massachusetts Charitable Eye and Ear Infirmary, [1920]. 31 p.
"Issued for private distribution only by the Massachusetts Charitable Eye and Ear Infirmary as a holiday greeting to its friends 1827-1919."

B-1036 Brown, Alice, 1857-1948. The black drop / by Alice Brown. New York: The Macmillan Company, 1919. 392 p.
LC: O 22, '19.
PW: N 1, '19.

B-1037 ____ Bromley neighborhood / by Alice Brown. New York: The Macmillan Company, 1917. 418 p.
LC: Jl 12, '17.
PW: Jl 21, '17.

B-1038 ____ The buckets in the sea / by Alice Brown. Boston: Massachusetts Charitable Eye and Ear Infirmary, [1920?]. 28 p.

B-1039 ____ Country neighbors / by Alice Brown. Boston; New York: Houghton Mifflin Company, 1910. (Cambridge: The Riverside Press). 361 p.
Contents: The play house -- His first wife -- A flower of April -- The auction -- Saturday night -- A grief defferred -- The challenge -- Partners -- Flowers of paradise -- Gardener Jim -- The silver tea-set -- The other Mrs. Dill -- The advocate -- The masquerade -- A poetess in spring -- The master minds of history.
LC: Ap 14, '10.
PW: Ap 16, '10.

B-1040 ____ The county road / by Alice Brown. Boston; New York: Houghton, Mifflin and Company, 1906. (Cambridge, Mass., U. S. A.: The Riverside Press). 341, [1] p.
Contents: A day off -- Old Immortality -- Bachelor's fancy -- The cave of Adullam -- A winter's courting -- Rosy balm -- A sea change -- The tree of a thousand leaves -- The pilgrim chamber -- The twisted tree -- The looking-glass -- A hermit in Arcadia -- A crown of gold.
LC: S 17, '06.
PW: O 13, '06.

B-1041 ____ The court of love / by Alice Brown. Boston; New York: Houghton, Mifflin and Company, 1906. (Cambridge: The Riverside Press). 210, [2] p.
PW: Je 2, '06.

B-1042 ____ The flying Teuton: and other stories / by Alice Brown . . . New York: The Macmillan Company, 1918. 321 p.
Reprinted in part from various periodicals.
Contents: The flying Teuton -- The island -- The empire of death -- The man and the militant -- A citizen and his wife -- The torch of life -- The tryst -- Waves -- The flags on the tower -- The trial at Ravello -- The mid-Victorian -- Father -- Nemesis.
LC: Ap 4, '18.
PW: Ap 13, '18.

_____ The girl in the tree. <u>In</u> *The Harper prize short stories* **(1925), H-233.**

B-1043 _____ High noon / by Alice Brown. Boston; New York: Houghton, Mifflin and Company, 1904. (Cambridge: The Riverside Press). 308 p.
Contents: A meeting in the market-place -- The book of love -- There and here -- His enemy -- Natalie Blayne -- A runaway match -- Rosamund in heaven -- The end of the game -- The miracle -- The map of the country -- The tryst -- A dream in the morning.
PW: Ap 23, '04.
BLC: London: Eveleigh Nash, 1904.

B-1044 _____ Homespun and gold / by Alice Brown. New York: The Macmillan Company, 1920. 301 p.
Contents: The wedding ring -- Mary Felicia -- A homespun wizardry -- Red poppies -- Ann Eliza -- The return of father -- The deserters -- The house of the bride -- A question of wills -- A brush of paint -- The path of stars -- The widow's third -- White pebbles -- Confessions -- Up on the mountain.
LC: N 4, '20.
PW: N 13, '20.

B-1045 _____ John Winterbourne's family / by Alice Brown. Boston; New York: Houghton Mifflin Company, 1910. (Cambridge, Mass.: The Riverside Press). 454 p.
LC: O 3, '10.
PW: O 1, '10.

B-1046 _____ Judgment: a novel / by Alice Brown; illustrated by W. T. Smedley. New York; London: Harper & Brothers, 1903. 194, [1] p., front., [5] leaves of plates.
PW: O 3, '03.

B-1047 _____ King's End / by Alice Brown. Boston; New York: Houghton, Mifflin and Company, 1901. (Cambridge, Mass.: The Riverside Press). 246 p.
Originally published in Lippincott's magazine under title: *April showers*.
PW: Mr 23, '01.
BLC: Westminster: A. Constable & Co.; Cambridge, Mass. printed, 1901.

B-1048 _____ The Mannerings / by Alice Brown. Boston; New York: Houghton, Mifflin and Company, 1903. (Cambridge: The Riverside Press). 382 p.
PW: Ap 4, '03.
BLC: London: Eveleigh Nash; Cambridge, Mass printed, 1903.

B-1049 _____ Margaret Warrener / by Alice Brown. Boston; New York: Houghton, Mifflin and Company, 1901. (Cambridge: The Riverside Press). 501, [1] p.
PW: N 23, '01.

B-1050 [_____] My love and I / by Martin Redfield. New York: The Macmillan Company, 1912. 377 p.
LC: S 12, '12.
PW: S 28, '12.

B-1051 _____ The mysteries of Ann / by Alice Brown. New York: The Macmillan Company, 1925. 274 p.
LC: Ap 8, '25.
PW: Ap 18, '25.

B-1052 _____ Old Crow / by Alice Brown. New York: The Macmillan Company, 1922. 534 p.
LC: O 4, '22.
PW: N 11, '22.
BLC: London: E. Nash & Grayson, printed in U. S. A., 1923.

B-1053 _____ Paradise / by Alice Brown. Boston; New York: Houghton, Mifflin and Company, 1905. (Cambridge: The Riverside Press). 388 p.
PW: N 4, '05.
BLC: London: A. Constable & Co., 1905.

B-1054 _____ The prisoner / by Alice Brown. New York: The Macmillan Company, 1916. 471 p.
LC: Je 16, '16.
PW: Je 17, '16.

B-1055 _____ Robin Hood's barn / by Alice Brown. New York: The Macmillan Company, 1913. 225 p., col. front., [6] leaves of col. plates. [Ill. by Horace T. Carpenter.]
LC: S 25, '13.
PW: O 18, '13.

B-1056 _____ Rose MacLeod / by Alice Brown; with a frontispiece by W. W. Churchill, Jr. Boston; New York: Houghton, Mifflin and Company, 1908. 406, [2] p., front.
LC: Ap 11, '08.
PW: Ap 25, '08.
BLC: London: A. Constable & Co.; Boston; New York: Houghton, Mifflin; Cambridge, Mass. [printed], 1908.

B-1057 _____ The story of Thyrza / by Alice Brown; with a frontispiece by Alice Barber Stephens. Boston; New York: Houghton Mifflin Company, 1909. (Cambridge, Mass.: The Riverside Press). 326, [2] p., col. front.
LC: F 19, '09.
PW: Mr 20, '09.
BLC: London: A. Constable & Co.; Boston; New York: Houghton, Mifflin Company; Cambridge, Mass. [printed], 1909.

B-1058 _____ Vanishing points / by Alice Brown. New York: The Macmillan Company, 1913. 352 p.
Contents: The man in the cloister -- Mother -- The story of Abe -- A guarded shrine -- The discovery -- The master -- The interpreter -- The hands of the faithful -- The wizard's touch -- A man of feeling -- The lantern -- The private soldier -- The clue -- Golden Baby -- The flight of the Mouse -- The queen of Arcady.
LC: F 27, '13.
PW: Mr 1, '13.
BLC: London: Constable & Co.; Greenfield, Mass. [printed], 1913.

_____, contributor. <u>See</u> *The whole family* **(1908), W-578.**

B-1059 _____ The wind between the worlds / by Alice Brown. New York: The Macmillan Company, 1920. 258 p.
LC: Je 30, '20.
PW: Ag 7, '20.
BLC: London: Eveleigh Nash Co.; printed in U. S. A., 1921.

_____ The wizard's touch. In *Different girls* (1906), **D-383.**

Brown, Anna Robeson. <u>See</u> **Burr, Anna Robeson Brown, 1873-1941.**

Brown, Bernice, contributor. <u>See</u> *Bobbed hair* **(1925), B-700.**

B-1060 _____ Men of earth / by Bernice Brown. New York; London: G. P. Putnam's Sons, 1924. (New York: The Knickerbocker Press). 357 p.
Contents: Miracle -- In April -- The cross-beam -- April floods -- Johnny Geraldy -- Freda Waldensen -- Big clumsy Swede -- Making a man of him -- No message.
LC: My 2, '24.

B-1061 _____ The shining road: a novel / by Bernice Brown. New York; London: G. P. Putnam's Sons, 1923. (New York: The Knickerbocker Press). 284 p.
LC: F 15, '23.

B-1062 Brown, Caroline, *pseud*. Dionis of the white veil / by Caroline Brown [pseud.] . . . ; illustrated by Henry Roth. Boston: L. C. Page & Company, 1911. 291 p., front., [5] leaves of plates.
References: Russo & Sullivan, *Seven Authors*, p. 9-10.

B-1063 _____ On the We-a Trail: a story of the great wilderness / by Caroline Brown [pseud.] . . . ; with illustrations by Max Klepper. New York: The Macmillan Company; London: Macmillan & Co., Ltd., 1903. 351 p., front., [7] leaves of plates.
LC: O 7, '03.
PW: O 24, '03.
References: Russo & Sullivan, *Seven Authors*, p. 6-7.

B-1064 Brown, Charles Platt. A great game / by Charles Platt Brown (the man behind the counter). New York: Broadway Publishing Company, 1914. 154 p.

B-1065 Brown, Charlotte Hawkins, 1883-1961. "Mammy": an appeal to the heart of the South / by Charlotte Hawkins Brown. [Boston: The Pilgrim Press, c1919]. 18 p., front. **OSU, NEO**
LC: Je 7, '20.

B-1066 Brown, Clinton Giddings. Ramrod Jones, hunter and patriot: a tale of the Texas revolution against Mexico / written by Robert Blalock; and now set forth by Clinton Giddings Brown; illustrated by E. S. Paxson. Akron, Ohio; New York; Chicago: The Saalfield Publishing Co., [c1905]. 321 p., front., [3] leaves of plates. **TNY**

Brown, Demetra Vaka. <u>See</u> **Vaka, Demetra, 1877-1946.**

Brown, E. Levi. At the hermitage. <u>In</u> *Shapes that haunt the dusk* **(1907), S-339.**

B-1067 Brown, Edna Adelaide, 1875-1944. Journey's end / by Edna A. Brown. Boston: Lothrop, Lee & Shepard Co., [1921]. 414 p.
PW: Ap 30, '21.

B-1068 _____ That affair at St. Peter's / by Edna A. Brown; illustrated by John Goss. Boston: Lothrop, Lee & Shepard Co., [1920]. 243 p., front., [3] leaves of plates.
PW: My 8, '20.

B-1069 Brown, Edwin, b. 1857. House of strength / by Edwin Brown . . . Boston: The Four Seas Company, 1922. 140 p., front., [9] leaves of plates.
PW: S 16, '22.

B-1070 Brown, Egbert. The final awakening / by Egbert Brown. Brunswick, Ga.: Overstreet & Co., c1923. 160 p. **UUM**
LC: Je 2, '23.

B-1071 Brown, Elizabeth Jewett, b. 1868. Nell Beverly, farmer: a story of farm life / by Elizabeth Jewett Brown and Susan Jewett Howe. New York: The Rural Publishing Co., [c1908]. 190 p.
[Distributed as a gift to subscribers by "The Rural New-Yorker".]
LC: D 14, '08.

Brown, Elsie. A shady plot. <u>In</u> **Humorous ghost stories (1921), H-1018.**

Brown, Elwood S. The bookkeeper: his accuracy. <u>In</u> *Clever business sketches* **(1909), C-490.**

_____ The promoter: his genius. <u>In</u> *Clever business sketches* **(1909), C-490.**

B-1072 Brown, Frederick Walworth, b. 1875. Dan McLean's adventures / by Frederick Walworth

Brown; illustrated. New York: The Baker & Taylor Company, [c1911]. 311 p., front., [1] leaf of plates.
[Ill. by William F. Taylor.]
LC: Mr 20, '11.
PW: Mr 25, '11.

B-1073 Brown, George Alfred, b. 1876. Harold the klansman / by George Alfred Brown. Kansas City, Mo.: The Western Baptist Publishing Company, 1923. 303 p.
LC: N 8, '23.
PW: F 23, '24.

B-1074 Brown, George Rothwell. Beyond the sunset: a tale of love and pirate gold / by George Rothwell Brown; illustrated by Reginald F. Bolles. Boston: Small, Maynard & Company, [c1919]. 319 p., col. front.
LC: S 24, '19.
PW: Ag 30, '19.

B-1075 _____ My country: a story of today / by George Rothwell Brown; with illustrations by Chase Emerson. Boston: Small, Maynard & Company, [c1917]. 359, [1] p., col. front., [2] leaves of plates.
LC: S 17, '17.
PW: Je 16, '17.

B-1076　Brown, H. N. (Handy Nereus), b. 1857. The necromancer; or, Voo-doo doctor: a story based on facts / by Rev. H. N. Brown . . . [Opelika, Ala.], c1904. 101, [1] p., front. (port.).
Unexamined copy: bibliographic data from NUC.
"The nations in song and other songs": p. [81]-101.

B-1077　Brown, Helen Dawes, b. 1857. Orphans / by Helen Dawes Brown. Boston; New York: Houghton Mifflin Company, 1911. (Cambridge: The Riverside Press). 286 p.　**ASH**
PW: My 20, '11.

B-1078　Brown, H. Collins (Henry Collins), 1862-1961. Mr. Goggles / by H. Collins Brown; with illustrations by Eliot Keen and from photographs. New York: B. W. Dodge & Company, 1907. 231 p., front., [28] leaves of plates.
PW: Je 22, '07.

B-1079　Brown, Hypkin. Farmer Bibbins / by Hypkin Brown. Boston: Richard G. Badger; Toronto: The Copp Clark Co., Limited, [c1914]. 319 p.

Brown, J. E. Driver of the band wagon. *In Clever business sketches (1909), C-490.*

B-1080　Brown, Jennie Comrie. Seventy times seven / by Jennie Comrie Brown. New York: Broadway Publishing Co., 1913. 243 p.

B-1081　Brown, John T. (John Thomas), b. 1869. Bruce Norman / by John T. Brown . . . Louisville, Ky: Jno T. Brown Pub. House, 1901. 215 p.　**WVH**

B-1082　Brown, John Young, 1858-1921. To the moon and back in ninety days: a thrilling narrative of blended science and adventure / by John Young Brown . . . Providence, Kentucky: Lunar Publishing Company, 1922. 214 p., front., [39] leaves of photo.

B-1083　Brown, Joseph M., 1851-1932. Astyanax: an epic romance of Ilion, Atlantis & Amaraca / by Joseph M. Brown . . . ; illustrated by William Lincoln Hudson. New York: Broadway Publishing Co., 1907. Book I: 336 p., Book II: 275 p., Book III: 286 p., xii, [2] p., [53] leaves of plates (some folded), ill., maps, music, ports.
LC: Ap 4, '07.
PW: My 4, '07.

Brown, Katharine Holland. Buster. *In The best short stories of 1918 and the yearbook of the American short story (1919), B-563.*

B-1084　____ Dawn / by Katharine Holland Brown; illustrated by F. Walter Taylor. New York: T. Y. Crowell & Co., [c1907]. 52, [1] p., front., [5] leaves of plates.
Unexamined copy: bibliographic data from NUC.
LC: Je 10, '07.
PW: S 7, '07.

B-1085　____ Diane: a romance of the Icarian settlement on the Mississippi River / by Katharine Holland Brown;

illustrated by S. J. Dudley. New York: Doubleday, Page & Company, 1904. 440 p., photo. front. (port.).　**CWR**
PW: D 17, '04.
BLC: London: Doubleday, Page & Co.; New York printed, 1904.

B-1086　____ The Hallowell partnership / by Katharine Holland Brown; illustrated. New York: Charles Scribner's Sons, 1912. 241 p., front., [3] leaves of plates. [Ill. by Clara Elsene Peck.]
LC: N 5, '12.
PW: N 9, '12.

B-1087　____ The messenger / by Katharine Holland Brown. New York: Charles Scribner's Sons, 1910. 38 p., col. front. [Ill. by James Montgomery Flagg.]
LC: Mr 16, '10.
PW: Mr 19, '10.

____ Those scars. *In Short stories for class reading (1925), S-461.*

B-1088　____ Uncertain Irene / by Katharine Holland Brown . . . New York: Duffield & Company, 1911. 236 p., front. [Ill. by Alonzo Kimball.]
LC: O 28, '11.
PW: N 11, '11.

B-1089　____ The wages of honor: and other stories / by Katharine Holland Brown; illustrated. New York: Charles Scribner's Sons, 1917. 309 p., front., [6] leaves of plates.
Reprinted in part from various periodicals.
Contents: The wages of honor -- The master strategist -- "Crabbed age and youth" -- Brewster blood -- The ragged edge of forty -- Raw prose -- Briarley's real woman -- Billy Foster and the snow queen -- Millicent, maker of history -- On a brief text from Isiah.
LC: S 19, '17.
PW: S 22, '17.

B-1090　____ White roses / by Katharine Holland Brown; illustrated by James Montgomery Flagg. New York: Duffield and Company, 1910. 333 p., front.
LC: O 18, '10.
PW: N 5, '10.

Brown, Kenneth, b. 1868., jt. aut. *The duke's price* (1910). See **Vaka, Demetra, 1877-1946, jt. aut., V-4.**

____, jt. aut. *Eastover Court House* (1901). See **Boone, Henry Burnham, jt. aut., B-738.**

____, jt. aut. *The first secretary* (1907). See **Vaka, Demetra, 1877-1946, jt. aut., V-5.**

____, jt. aut. *In pawn to a throne* (1919). See **Vaka, Demetra, 1877-1946, jt. aut., V-8.**

B-1091　____ Putter Perkins / by Kenneth Brown; with illustrations by E. W. Kemble. Boston; New York: Houghton Mifflin Company, 1923. (Cambridge [Mass.]: The Riverside Press). 126 p., front., [9] leaves of plates.
LC: F 27, '23.
PW: Mr 3, '23.

_____, jt. aut. *The Redfields succession* (1903). See **Boone, Henry Burnham, jt. aut., B-739.**

B-1092   _____ Sirocco: a novel / by Kenneth Brown. New York: Mitchell Kennerley, [c1906]. 292 p.
BLC: London: Cassell & Co.; New York [printed], 1907.
PW: Je 9, '06.

B-1093   Brown, M. V. (Merton Volney), b. 1869. The Burton manor / by M. V. Brown. New York: Broadway Publishing Company, [c1905]. 165 p.
DLC

B-1094   Brown, Martin. Cobra / by Martin Brown and Russell Holman; a novelization of the famous stage success by Martin Brown; illustrated with scenes from the photo play, a Ritz-Parmount picture, starring Rudolph Valentino. New York: Grosset & Dunlap, [c1925]. 281 p., front., [7] leaves of plates.
LC: S 14, '25.

B-1095   Brown, Nancy Keen. A broken bondage / by Nancy Keen Brown. Boston: The Roxburgh Publishing Company (Incorporated), [c1911]. 311 p., photo. front., [4] leaves of plates (1 photo port.). [Ill. by George W. Colby.]   **VIC**
LC: Ag 29, '11.
PW: S 9, '11.

B-1096   Brown, Paula, *pseud.* The Mormon girl / by Paula Brown [pseud.]. Lamoni, Iowa: Herald Publishing House, 1912. 205 p., front., [6] leaves of plates.   **OSU, NYP**
LC: D 14, '12.

B-1097   Brown, Philetus, 1868-1959, *pseud.* The lovers' club / by Philetus Brown [pseud.]. Chicago; New York; Boston: The Old Greek Press, [c1907]. 155 p.
LC: Ap 1, '07.

B-1098   Brown, Ritter. When dreams come true / by Ritter Brown; illustrated by W. M. Berger. New York: Desmond FitzGerald, Inc., [c1912]. 379 p., col. front., [4] leaves of plates.
PW: N 9, '12.

B-1099   Brown, Robert Carlton, 1886-1959. The remarkable adventures of Christopher Poe / by Robert Carlton Brown; illustrated by M. Wilson Craig. Chicago: F. G. Browne & Co., 1913. 399 p., col.

B-1100   _____ What happened to Mary: a novelization from the play and the stories appearing in the Ladies' world / by Robert Carlton Brown. New York: Edward J. Clode, [c1913]. 309 p., front., [7] leaves of plates, (2 port).

B-1101   Brown, S. W. (Stirling Wilson). Deacon White's idees / S. W. Brown. Boston, Mass.: Mayhew Publishing Company, 1905. 214 p.   **IUA**

Brown, Stirling Wilson. See **Brown, S. W.**

B-1102   Brown, Theron, 1832-1914. Under the mulberry trees: a romance of the old 'forties / by Theron Brown . . . Boston: Richard G. Badger, 1909. ([Boston, Mass.]: The Gorham Press). 504 p., front. [Ill. by Sears Gallagher.]
LC: N 27, '09.

B-1103   Brown, William Garrott, b. 1868. A gentleman of the South: a memory of the black belt, from the manuscript memoirs of the late Colonel Stanton Elmore / edited without change by William Garrott Brown. New York: The Macmillan Company; London: Macmillan & Co., Ltd., 1903. 232 p., front., [1] leaf of plates.
BLC: Toronto: G. M. Morang & Co., 1903.

B-1104   Brown, William H. (William Herbert), 1864-1929. The call of service / by Will H. Brown . . . Cincinnati, O.: The Standard Publishing Company, c1913. 258 p., photo. ill.
Contents: I. Troy Dixon's response -- II. The call of the hills.

B-1105   _____ The legacy of the golden key / by Will H. Brown . . . Cincinnati: The Standard Publishing Company, [c1914]. 321 p.

Browne, Alice Harriman. See **Harriman, Alice, 1861-1925.**

B-1106   Browne, Anna C., b. 1874. The prophet's wife / by Anna C. Browne. New York; Cincinnati; Chicago: Benziger Brothers, 1914. 248 p., front. [Ill. by Frank McKernan.]
PW: O 31, '14.

B-1107   Browne, George Waldo, 1851-1930. Ruel Durke: master of men / by George Waldo Browne. Boston: Richard G. Badger, 1910. ([Boston]: The Gorham Press). 304 p., front. [Ill. by Leslie L. Benson.]
LC: O 7, '10.
Browne, Porter Emerson, 1879-1934. The courtship of Miles Sheehan. In **Conrad, Joseph.** *Il conte* **(1925), C-697.**

B-1108   _____ A delegation from "de ate" / Porter Emerson Browne. [New York: The Winthrop Press, c1914]. 31 p., col. front. [Ill. by G. Hollrock.] Previously published in The American magazine.

B-1109   _____ A fool there was / by Porter Emerson Browne; illustrated by Edmund Magrath and W. W. Fawcett. New York: The H. K. Fly Company, [c1909]. 303 p., col. front., [3] leaves of col. plates.
LC: N 19, '09.
PW: Ja 8, '10.
BLC: London: Greening & Co., [1911].

B-1110   _____ Peace--at any price / by Porter Emerson Browne; illustrations by Peter Newell. New York; London: D. Appleton and Company, 1916. 69, [1] p., front., [5] leaves of plates.
LC: Ap 4, '16.
PW: Ap 15, '16.

B-1111 ____ Scars and stripes / by Porter Emerson Browne; frontispiece by Peter Newell. New York: George H. Doran Company, [c1917]. 208 p., front.
LC: Mr 13, '17.
PW: Mr 10, '17.

B-1112 ____ Someone and somebody / by Porter Emerson Browne; illustrated by Clarence F. Underwood. Indianapolis: The Bobbs-Merrill Company, [c1917]. 328 p., front., [4] leaves of plates.
LC: My 26, '17.
PW: My 26, '17.

B-1113 ____ The spendthrift / by Porter Emerson Browne; a story of American life, novelized from the play by Edward Marshall; illustrations from scenes in the play. New York: G. W. Dillingham Company, [c1910]. 333 p., front., [3] leaves of plates.
LC: N 8, '10.
PW: N 5, '10.
BLC: London: Unwin; New York [printed], 1910.

B-1114 Browne, Sara Elizabeth. Currents and undercurrents, or, Life as we see it to-day / by Sara Elizabeth Browne. New York; London; Montreal: The Abbey Press, [c1902]. 242 p.   **ABC**

B-1115 Browne, Walter Scott. The rose of the wilderness, or, Washington's first love / taken and revised from authentic sources by Walter Scott Browne. [Vineland, N. J.: s. n., 1901.] 456 p., front., [3] leaves of plates.
PW: Mr 1, '02.
(Apparent later printing: Camden, N. J.: Published by A. C. Graw, [c1901].)

B-1116 Browne, William Trevelyan. The way of peace / by W. T. Browne . . . New York: Printed for private circulation by Wynkoop Hallenbeck Crawford Co., 1905. 186 p.   **KKU**

Brownell, Agnes Mary. Dishes. *In The best short stories of 1919 and the yearbook of the American short story* (1920), **B-564.**

____ Doc Greer's practice. *In Stories from the Midland* (1924), **S-984.**

B-1117 ____ The thankful Spicers / by Agnes Mary Brownell; illustrated by F. R. Gruger. New York: Charles Scribner's Sons, 1921. 177 p., front., [3] leaves of plates.   **NYP**
PW: Ag 13, '21.

Brownell, Amanda Benjamin Hall. See **Hall, Amanda Benjamin, b. 1890.**

Brownell, Gertrude Hall. See **Hall, Gertrude, 1863-1961.**

B-1118 Brownson, Mary W. His sister / by Mary W. Brownson . . . Chicago: The Winona Publishing Company, 1904. 37 p., [3] leaves of plates. [Ill. by Marshall D. Smith.]   **IWU**
PW: O 8, '04.

B-1119 Broyles, C. E., Mrs., b.1865. The Jessamines: (a new story of the old South) / by Mrs. C. E. Broyles. Boston, Mass.: The Stratford Company, Publishers, 1921. 245 p.   **NYP**
LC: Jl 18, '21.

Broyles, Lester Everret. See **Terreve, Retsel, pseud.**

Broyles, Sallie Hightower. See **Broyles, C. E., Mrs., b. 1865.**

B-1120 Brubaker, Howard, 1882-1957. Ranny, otherwise Randolph Harrington Dukes: a tale of those activities which made him an important figure in his town, in his family--and in other families / by Howard Brubaker; with illustrations by F. Strothmann. New York; London: Harper & Brothers, [1917]. 325, [1] p., front., [7] leaves of plates.

Bruce, Andasia Kimbrough. See **Bruce, William Liddell, Mrs., b. 1868.**

B-1121 Bruce, Jerome. Studies in black and white: a novel in which are exemplified the lights and shades in the friendship and trust between black and white-- master and slave-- in their intercourse with each other in antebellum days / by Jerome Bruce . . . New York; Washington: The Neale Publishing Company, 1906. 472 p.   **LZU**
LC: N 27, '06.

B-1122 Bruce, John Edward. The awakening of Hezekiah Jones; a story dealing with some of the problems affecting the political rewards due the negro / by John Edward Bruce, "Bruce Grit". Hopkinsville, Ky.: P. H. Brown, [c1916]. 62 p.
Unexamined copy: bibliographic data from NUC.
LC: Ap 17, '16.

B-1123 Bruce, Magnus A. Max of the North: a novel / by Magnus A. Bruce. Milwaukee: Diederich-Schaefer Co., 1915. 345 p., front. [Ill. by R. A. Walter.]

B-1124 Bruce, Stewart E. The world in 1931 / by Stewart E. Bruce. New York: F. L. Searl & Co., 1921. 192 p.

B-1125 Bruce, Tydance. Tennessee Lee / by Tydance Bruce. New York; London: F. Tennyson Neely, [c1902]. 94 p.

B-1126 Bruce, William Cabell, 1860-1946. Below the James: a plantation sketch / by William Cabell Bruce . . . New York: The Neale Publishing Company, 1918. 157 p., photo. front.
LC: N 18, '18.

B-1127 Bruce, William Liddell, Mrs., b. 1868. Uncle Tom's cabin of to-day / by Mrs. William Liddell Bruce. New York; Washington: The Neale Publishing Company, 1906. 244 p., photo. front., [2] leaves of photo. plates.   **NYP**
LC: Ap 1, '07.

B-1128 Brudno, Ezra S. (Ezra Selig), b. 1877. The fugitive: being memoirs of a wanderer in search of a home / by Ezra S. Brudno. New York: Doubleday, Page & Company, 1904. 392 p.
PW: Mr 19, '04.
BLC: London: Heinemann; New York printed, 1904.

B-1129 _____ The jugglers / by Ezra Brudno. New York: Moffat, Yard & Company, 1920. 258 p.
LC: N 29, '20.
PW: F 26, '21.

B-1130 _____ The little conscript: a tale of the reign of Nicholas I / by Ezra S. Brudno. New York: Doubleday, Page & Company, 1905. 325 p.
PW: Je 3, '05.

B-1131 _____ One of us / by Ezra Brudno . . . Philadelphia; London: J. B. Lippincott Company, 1912. 359 p.   **OSU, NYP**
LC: Ap 30, '12.
PW: Jl 6, '12.

B-1132 _____ The sublime jester / by Ezra Brudno. New York: Nicholas L. Brown, 1924. 364 p.
LC: Mr 19, '25.
PW: N 15, '24.

B-1133 _____ The tether / by Ezra S. Brudno . . . Philadelphia; London: J. B. Lippincott Company, 1908. 334, [2] p.
LC: Jl 10, '08.
PW: S 26, '08.

B-1134 Bruère, Martha Bensley, b. 1879. Mildred Carver, U. S. A. / by Martha Bensley Bruère. New York: The Macmillan Company, 1919. 289 p.

B-1135 Brumbaugh, H. B. (Henry Boyer), 1836-1919. Onesimus: the runaway slave / by H. B. Brumbaugh. Elgin, Ill.: Brethren Publishing House, 1909. 159 p.   **ELZ**
LC: F 14, '10.

B-1136 Brummitt, Dan B. (Dan Brearley), 1867-1939. John Wesley, Jr.: the story of an experiment / by Dan B. Brummitt. New York; Cincinnati: The Methodist Book Concern, [c1921]. 281 p., front., [7] leaves of photo. plates (one copyrighted by Underwood & Underwood).

B-1137 Brunkhurst, Harriet. The window in the fence / by Harriet Brunkhurst. New York: George H. Doran Company, [c1916]. 318 p., col. front. [Ill. by Harold M. Sichel.]
BLC: London: Hodder & Stoughton, printed in U. S. A., 1916.

B-1138 Brunner, Emma Beatrice. The personal touch / by Emma Beatrice Brunner. New York: Brentano's, [c1922]. 312 p.
BLC: London: Brentano's; printed in U. S. A., [1923].

B-1139 Bruno, Guido, 1884-1942. Eternal moments: stories of life and love / By Guido Bruno; illustrations by Clara Tice. New York: [s. n.], 1920. 24 p.
Contents: Eternal moments -- In a doorway -- Intermezzo -- But the world is ours, Beloved! -- Memories -- The sorrow of the little violet -- Ave Maria -- Adultery on Washington Square -- The nun and the prostitute -- Jesus on Main Street.

B-1140 _____ A night in Greenwich Village: the story of a marriage / By Guido Bruno. New York: [s. n.], 1921. 19 p., ill. [Ill. by Coulton Waugh.]   **NYP**

B-1141 _____ Sentimental studies: stories of life and love / by Guido Bruno. New York: [s. n.], 1920. 32 p.
Contents: The madonna of our square -- Midnight in a pawnshop -- Tragedy in a birdhouse -- A woman's revenge -- Dead man's eyes -- Three dollars and sixty cents -- Liars.

B-1142 _____ Teaspoons and tealeaves / written by Guido Bruno in his garret on Washington Square. [Washington Square, N. Y.: s. n., ca. 1915.] 20 p.
Contents: A woman's revenge -- Dead man's eyes -- Three dollars and sixty cents -- Four dollars and ninety-five cents -- Liars.

B-1143 Bryan, Julian Scott, b. 1890. The garden of Luzon / Julian Scott Bryan. Boston: Richard G. Badger, [c1912]. ([Boston]: The Gorham Press). 159 p.
VA@

B-1144 Bryant, Francis A. A romance of two lives / by Francis A. Bryant. Boston: Mayhew Publishing Company, [c1903]. 321 p., front. (port.).
Another printing: Chicago: Scroll Publishing Co., 1903.

B-1145 Bryant, H. E. C. (Henry Edward Cowan), b. 1873. Tar heel tales / by H. E. C. Bryant, "Red Buck". Charlotte, N. C.: Stone & Barringer Co., 1910. 218 p., photo. front., [9] leaves of photo. plates.   **EMU**
Contents: Uncle Ben's last fox race -- Forty acres and a mule -- The spaniel and the cops -- A hound of the old stock -- Minerva-the owl -- Uncle Derrick in Washington -- And the sign failed not -- The Irishman's game cock -- Strange vision of Arabella -- A negro and his friend -- Faithful unto death -- "Red Buck": where I came by it -- Until death do us part -- Uncle George and the Englishman -- She didn't like my yellow shoes -- Afraid of the frowsy blonde -- Jan Pier-the shoeshine -- William and appendicitis.

B-1146 Bryant, Rose Cullen. Ruth Anne / by Rose Cullen Bryant; with illustrations by Will Grefé. Philadelphia; London: J. B. Lippincott Company, 1913. 320 p., front., [2] leaves of plates.
LC: O 4, '13.
PW: O 11, '13.

B-1147 Bryce, C. A. (Clarence Archibald), 1849-1928. Kitty Dixon, belle of the South Anna: a wee bit of love and war / By C. A. Bryce . . . [Richmond, Va.: The "Southern Clinic" Press, 1907.] 102 p., front., [1] leaf of plates. [Ill. by Mildred Bryce.]   **VIC**
"A Jamestown-year souvenir of old Virginia."
LC: Jl 12, '07.
PW: S 14, '07.

B-1148   ____ "Ups and downs" of a Virginia doctor / by his lifelong and personal friend Clarence A. Bryce . . . Ashland, Va.: Ashland Printing Company, 1904. 137, [1] p., photo. front., [16] leaves of plates. [Ill. by Mildred Bryce.]   **NYP**

Bryce, Ronald, pseud. <u>See</u> **Rockey, Howard, 1886-1934.**

Bryner, Edna Clare. Forest cover. <u>In</u> *The best short stories of 1922 and the yearbook of the American short story* **(1923), B-567.**

____ The life of five points. <u>In</u> *The best short stories of 1920 and the yearbook of the American short story* **(1921), B-565.**

B-1149   Buchanan, Benjamin Franklin. Bogus Hollow: a tale of the blue jeans town and vicinity / --by-- Benjamin Franklin Buchanan. [Souvenir ed.]. Dayton, Ohio: The Walker Litho. & Printing Co., 1901. 134, [2] p., photo. front., [3] leaves of photo. plates, photo. ill. Decorated end papers.

B-1150   Buchanan, Thompson, 1877-1937. The castle comedy / by Thompson Buchanan; illustrated and decorated by Elizabeth Shippen Green. New York; London: Harper & Brothers, 1904. 235, [1] p., col. front., [3] leaves of col. plates.
PW: S 17, '04.

B-1151   ____ Judith triumphant / by Thompson Buchanan. New York; London: Harper & Brothers, 1905. 254, [1] p.
PW: Ap 15, '05.

B-1152   ____ Making people happy / by Thompson Buchanan; frontispiece by Harrison Fisher. New York: W. J. Watt & Company, [1911]. 298 p., col. front., ill. [Ill. by W. W. Fawcett.]
LC: O 10, '11.
PW: N 18, '11.
BLC: London: Greening & Co., [1912].

B-1153   ____ The second wife / by Thompson Buchanan; frontispiece by Harrison Fisher; illustrations by W. W. Fawcett. New York: W. J. Watt & Company, [c1911]. 318, [1] p., col. front., [1] leaf of plates, ill.
LC: F 27, '11.
PW: Mr 4, '11.
BLC: London: Greening & Co., [1911].

B-1154   Buck, Charles Neville, b. 1879. Alias Red Ryan / by Charles Neville Buck; frontispiece by Walter De Maris. Garden City, N. Y., Doubleday, Page & Company, 1923. 298 p., front.
LC: My 26, '23.
PW: My 12, '23.

B-1155   ____ The battle cry / by Charles Neville Buck; illustrations by Douglas Duer. New York: W. J. Watt & Company, [c1914]. 356 p., front., [2] leaves of plates.
LC: Jl 11, '14.
PW: O 31, '14.
BLC: London: Hodder & Stoughton, [1921].

B-1156   ____ The call of the Cumberlands / by Charles Neville Buck; illustrations by Douglas Duer. New York: W. J. Watt & Company, [c1913]. 348 p., front., [3] leaves of plates.
LC: Ap 16, '13.
PW: My 10, '13.
BLC: London: G. Allen & Unwin, 1915.

B-1157   ____ The code of the mountains / by Charles Neville Buck; illustrations by G. W. Gage. New York: W. J. Watt & Company, [1915]. 303 p., front., [2] leaves of plates.
LC: My 21, '15.
PW: Je 26, '15.
BLC: London: Methuen & Co., 1920.

B-1158   ____ Destiny / by Charles Neville Buck; illustrations by R. F. Schabelitz. New York: W. J. Watt & Company, [c1916]. 444 p., col. front., [4] leaves of plates (2 double-leaf).
At end: Charles Neville Buck - The man. [7] p., photo. ill. (ports.).
LC: F 19, '16.
PW: F 19, '16.
BLC: London: Hodder & Stoughton, [1922].

B-1159   ____ A gentleman in pajamas / by Charles Neville Buck. New York; London: The Century Co., [c1924]. 312 p., front. [Ill. by A. D. Rahn.]
LC: F 23, '24.
PW: Mr 8, '24.

B-1160   ____ The key to yesterday / Charles Neville Buck; illustrations by R. Schabelitz. New York: W. J. Watt & Company, 1910. 339 p., front., [4] leaves of plates.
LC: Ag 11, '10.
PW: S 24, '10.
BLC: London: Greening & Co., 1912.

B-1161   [____] The law of Hemlock Mountain / by Hugh Lundsford [pseud.]; frontispiece by Douglas Duer. New York: W. J. Watt & Company, [c1920]. 308 p., front.
LC: O 23, '20.
PW: N 13, '20.

B-1162   ____ The lighted match / by Charles Neville Buck, illustrations by R. F. Schabelitz. New York: W. J. Watt & Company, [1911]. 307 p., front., [3] leaves of plates (1 double-leaf). At end: Two popular authors & something about them. [6] p., [2] leaves photo. plates (port.).
LC: Je 12, '11.
PW: N 18, '11.

____ The one-goal man. <u>In</u> *The Sporting spirit* **(1925), S-771.**

B-1163   ____ A pagan of the hills / by Charles Neville Buck . . . ; frontispiece by George W. Gage. New York: W. J. Watt & Company, [c1919]. 299 p., front.
LC: My 16, '19.
PW: My 10, '19.

B-1164   ____ The portal of dreams / by Charles Neville Buck; illustrated by Frank Snapp. New York: W. J. Watt & Company, [c1912]. 303 p., front., [3] leaves of plates.
LC: S 9, '12.
PW: N 9, '12.

B-1165   ____ Portugese silver / by Charles Neville Buck. New York; London: The Century Co., [c1925]. 309 p.
LC: F 16, '25.
PW: F 14, '25.

B-1166   ____ The rogue's badge / by Charles Neville Buck. -- First edition. -- Garden City, N. Y.: Doubleday, Page & Company, 1924. 280 p.
LC: S 25, '24.
PW: S 27, '24.
BLC: London: William Heinemann; printed in U. S. A., 1924.

B-1167   ____ The roof tree / by Charles Neville Buck; illustrated by Lee F. Conrey. Garden City, N. Y.; Toronto: Doubleday, Page, & Company, 1921. 341, [1] p., front., [3] leaves of plates.
LC: Mr 19, '21.
PW: Mr 5, '21.
BLC: London: Curtis Brown; Garden City, New York printed, 1921.

B-1168   ____ The tempering / by Charles Neville Buck; frontispiece by Ralph Pallen Coleman. Garden City, N. Y.: Doubleday, Page & Company, 1920. 416 p., col. front.
LC: Ap 5, '20.
PW: Mr 27, '20.

B-1169   ____ The tyranny of weakness / by Charles Neville Buck; frontispiece by Paul Stahr. New York: W. J. Watt & Company, [c1917]. 316 p., front.
PW: Ag 25, '17.
BLC: London: Robert Hayes [1920].

B-1170   ____ When 'Bear Cat' went dry / by Charles Neville Buck; illustrations by George W. Gage. New York: W. J. Watt & Company, [c1918]. 311 p., front., [2] leaves of plates.
LC: Mr 22, '18.
PW: Ap 6, '18.

B-1171   Buck, Charles W. (Charles William). Colonel Bob and a double love: a story from the civil side behind the southern lines / by Chas. W. Buck . . . ; illustrated by Plaschke. Louisville, Kentucky: The Standard Press, [c1922]. 433 p., [5] leaves of plates.   **NYP**
LC: D 26, '22.

B-1172   ____ Under the sun, or, The passing of the Incas: a story of old Peru / by Charles W. Buck. Louisville, Ky.: Sheltman & Company, [c1902]. 413 p., front.

B-1173   Buck, Mitchell S. (Mitchell Starrett), b. 1887. Afterglow: pastels of Greek Egypt, 69 B. C. / by Mitchell S. Buck; with a preface by Arthur Machen. New York: Nicholas L. Brown, 1924. 97 p.

LC: Mr 19, '25.
PW: Mr 21, '25.

B-1174   Buckingham, Emma May. Modern ghost stories: a medley of drama, impressions and spectral illusions / by Emma May Buckingham . . . New York: Fowler & Wells Co.; London: L. N. Fowler & Co., [c1906]. 139 p.   **CRU**
Contents: Are we naturally superstitious? -- Was it a spirit telegram? -- What was it? -- Spectral illusions -- The spectral hound -- Was it a spirit? -- Who was she? -- Psychological impressions -- How he found his ideal -- That shadow in the park -- A young wife's trial -- Tongueless voices -- The weird musician -- Irresistible impulse -- The phantom child -- A dream warning -- Dreams fulfilled -- A vision of heaven -- A dream over bride cake -- The haunted chamber -- The mystery of Riverford -- Elucidation.
PW: N 10, '06

B-1175   Buckland, Ralph Kent. "Worry" / by Ralph Kent Buckland . . . Boston: Sherman, French & Company, 1914. 95 p.   **NYP**
PW: Mr 28, '14.

B-1176   Buckley, Edith E. The snare of circumstance / by Edith E. Buckley; with illustrations by Arthur E. Becher. Boston: Little, Brown and Company, 1910. 367 p., front., [3] leaves of plates.

    Buckley, F. R. (Frederic Robert), b. 1896. Gold-mounted guns. In *Prize stories of 1922 (1923)*, **P-620.**

B-1177   ____ The sage hen / by F. R. Buckley. Indianapolis: The Bobbs-Merrill Company, [c1925]. 295, [1] p.
PW: Mr 7, '25.

B-1178   Buckley, Richard Wallace. The last of the Houghtons: a novel / by Richard Wallace Buckley. New York; Washington: Neale Publishing Company, 1907. 280 p.
LC: D 16, '07.
PW: Ja 4, '08.

    Budgett, Frances Elizabeth Janes, 1873-1928. See **Dejeans, Elizabeth, pseud.**

B-1179   Buffum, George T. (George Tower), 1846-1926. On two frontiers / by George T. Buffum; frontispiece by Maynard Dixon; pen-and-ink illustrations by Frank T. Merrill. Boston: Lothrop, Lee & Shepard Co., [1918]. 375 p., front.
Contents: East: The low-burned candle -- Kaluwo's uncut diamond -- The coveted lobola -- On the Kalahari -- Wazharo's blue clay -- Khama. West: The whitest man in Leadville -- Newannee-a sketch -- Breaking into Denver -- Our husband -- A lost city -- The Vigilantes of Bonanza Gulch -- The mine of the Humpback mule -- Wild Bill -- "A brown rug" -- "All set".
LC: Ap 13, '18.

B-1180   ____ Smith of Bear City: and other frontier sketches / by George T. Buffum; illustrated with six photogravures from original drawings by F. T. Wood. New York: The Grafton Press, 1906. 248, [1] p., [6] leaves of plates.
Contents: Smith of Bear City -- The death of Curly Bill -- Soapy Smith -- The cook from Texas -- Satan, the Burro -- Mother Corbett and her table -- Gentle Annie -- The queen of the bull-whackers -- The evolution of Clay Allison -- A trip through New Mexico -- Reminiscences of frontier hotels and their proprietors -- The man

under the bed -- The story of "Lost Charlie Kean" -- A race for life --
Some inmates of Las Vegas Jail -- Vehicles for the living and dead --
A night at Rincon -- Some incidents of early days in New
Albuquerque, New Mexico -- A night ride in the Deadwood coach --
Seven up and life or death.

B-1181 Buffum, J. H. (Jesse Howard), b. 1881. The garden
of pleasure / by J. H. Buffum. Springfield, Mass.:
Authors' Press, c1922. 32 p.   **DLC**

B-1182 Buford, Edward Powhatan. An earthen mold: the
evolution of a girl / Edward Powhatan Buford.
Boston: The Gorham Press; Toronto: The Copp
Clark Co., Limited, [c1914]. 314 p.   **NYP**

B-1183 Bugbee, Lucius H. The man who was too busy to
find the child. N. Y. Abingdon Press, 1915. 21 p.
Unexamined copy: bibliographic data from OCLC,
#13818789.
PW: O 16, '15.

B-1184 Bull, Alfred, b. 1851. The reckoning of heaven / by
Alfred Bull . . . Irving Park, Ill.: Alfred Bull,
Publisher, 1912. 129 p., front., ill.   **OSU, CSA**
PW: Mr 2, '12.

        Bullard, Arthur, 1879-1929. See **Edwards, Albert,
        pseud.**

B-1185 Bullock, William, b. 1876. In the current / by
William Bullock. New York: William Rickey &
Company, 1911. 274 p.

B-1186 Bumlong, George. George's letters home / by
George Bumlong. [Saranac Lake, N. Y.: A. I.
Vosburgh, 1903.]
Unexamined copy: bibliographic data from OCLC,
#26827026.

B-1187 Bump, Charles Weathers, 1872-1908. His Baltimore
madonna: and other stories / by Charles Weathers
Bump. Baltimore: Nunn & Company, 1906. 140 p.,
front.   **DLC**
Contents: His Baltimore madonna -- Imprisoned -- The girl in garnet
-- His little nest for two -- The woman's soul had changed -- The
Clytie's passenger -- A half-tone flirtation -- Chased by the Barye lion
-- "My violet" -- The surrender of Adoniram J. -- "The same old
story" -- The rosary from Montmartre.
LC: O 5, '06.
PW: N 10, '06.

B-1188 ____ The mermaid of Druid lake: and other stories /
by Charles Weathers Bump . . . Baltimore: Nunn &
Company, 1906. 148 p.   **NYP**
Contents: The mermaid of Druid Lake -- The goddess of truth -- A
daughter of Cuba libre -- A two-party line -- Timon up to date -- The
night that Patti sang -- An island on a jamboree -- Alexander the
Great -- Breaking into medecine -- The pink ghost of Franklin square
-- The vanished mummy -- "Mount Vernon 1-0-0-0".
LC: D 12, '06.

B-1189 Bunker, Alonzo. Soo Thah: a tale of the making of
the Karen nation / by Alonzo Bunker . . . , for thirty
years a resident among the Karens; with an
introduction by Henry C. Mabie . . . New York;
Chicago; Toronto; London; Edinburgh: Fleming H.
Revell Company, [c1902]. 280 p., photo. front., [11]
leaves of photo. plates.
BLC: London; Edinburgh: Oliphant, Andersen &
Ferrier; printed in U. S. A., 1902.

B-1190 Bunker, Annie Crosby, b. 1865. Crowning an ideal:
a story of the world war / by Annie Crosby Bunker
. . . Boston: Christopher Publishing House, [c1920].
95 p.
PW: My 8, '20.

B-1191 Bunker, Ira S. (Ira Sweet), b. 1848. A thousand
years hence, or, Startling events in the year A. D.
3000: a trip to Mars, incidents by the way / by Ira S.
Bunker. Portland, Ore.: Ira S. Bunker, c1903.
32 p., port.
Unexamined copy: bibliographic data from OCLC,
#15662525.

B-1192 Bunker, Jane. Diamond cut diamond / by Jane
Bunker; illustrated by M. Leone Bracker.
Indianapolis: The Bobbs-Merrill Company, [c1913].
387 p., front., [3] leaves of plates.

B-1193 Bunts, Frank Emory, 1861-1928. The soul of Henry
Harrington and other stories / by Frank Emory Bunts;
illustrated by Wm. J. Brownlow. Cleveland, Ohio:
[Press of the Gardner Printing Co.], 1916. 128 p.,
front., [6] leaves of plates, ill.
Contents: The soul of Henry Harrington -- Idolized -- A Japanese
hell -- A Christmas story -- Pete -- An old story with a new ending --
Jess of the hills.

B-1194 Burbridge, Juanita Cassil. Cheating the devil / by
Juanita Cassil Burbridge. New York: Nicholas L.
Brown, 1925, [c1924]. 272 p.
LC: Mr 19, '25.

B-1195 Burdette, Robert J. (Robert Jones), 1844-1914.
Alpha and omega: (a little cluster of Easter blossoms)
/ by Robert J. Burdette. [Pasadena, Cal.: Clara
Vista Press, c1914]. 23 p.   **DLC**
LC: Ap 13, '14.
References: BAL 2023.

        ____ , ed. See *Masterpieces of wit and humor*
        (1902), **M-590.**

B-1196 ____ A minute of time / by Robert J. Burdette.
[Chicago: 1902.] 11, [1] p.
Unexamined copy: bibliographic data from NUC.
Printed at the Press of Hollister Brothers, Chicago.
References: BAL 2012.

B-1197 ____ Old time and young Tom / by Robert J.
Burdette . . . Indianapolis: The Bobbs-Merrill
Company, [c1912]. 324, [1] p.
Contents: The rise and fall of the mustache -- My kindergarten of
fifty years -- A minute of time -- Favorites -- "Rounded with a sleep"
-- A day in Motley -- Taking account of stock -- The relief of the
slamrack -- Just for luck -- In the slave market -- Wasting other
people's time -- As it is written -- Talking with the mouth -- The six-
fingered man -- The average man.
LC: S 11, '12.
References: BAL 2021.

B-1198 Burdick, Annie M. (Annie Mabelle), b. 1868.
Furnished room houses: a tale of New York City / by
Silas Wright's widow (Annie M. Burdick); fully
illustrated. New York; London: F. Tennyson Neely,
[c1902]. 183 p., front., [5] leaves of plates. [Ill. by
William Cubitt Cooke.]

Cover title: *Furnished rooms to let.*
PW: Mr 14, '03.

B-1199   Burgess, Gelett, 1866-1951. Ain't Angie awful! . . .
/ by Gelett Burgess . . . illustrated by Rea Irvin.
Philadelphia: Dorrance & Co., [c1923]. 116 p.,
front., ill.   **KKU**
LC: S 15, '23.
PW: O 13, '23.

B-1200   ____ Find the woman / by Gelett Burgess;
illustrations by Hanson Booth. Indianapolis: The
Bobbs-Merrill Company, [c1911]. 342 p., front., [5]
leaves of plates.
LC: N 15, '11.
PW: N 18, '11.

____ The ghost-extinguisher. In *Humorous ghost
stories* **(1921), H-1018.**

B-1201   ____ The heart line: a drama of San Francisco / by
Gelett Burgess; with illustrations by Lester Ralph.
Indianapolis: The Bobbs-Merrill Company, [1907].
584 p., front., [11] leaves of plates.
LC: O 12, '07.
PW: N 2, '07.
BLC: London: Grant Richards, 1908.

B-1202   ____ Lady Méchante, or, Life as it should be: being
divers precious episodes in the life of a naughty
nonpareille, a farce in filigree / by Gelett Burgess;
with illustrations by the author. New York:
Frederick A. Stokes Company, [1909]. 393 p.,
front., ill.
LC: O 30, '09.
PW: N 13, '09.

B-1203   ____ A little sister of destiny / by Gelett Burgess.
Boston; New York: Houghton, Mifflin & Company,
1906. (Cambridge, Mass.: The Riverside Press).
258, [1] p.
PW: Ap 21, '06.

B-1204   ____ Love in a hurry / by Gelett Burgess; illustrated
by R. M. Brinkerhoff. Indianapolis: The
Bobbs-Merrill Company, [c1913]. 345, [1] p., front.,
[6] leaves of plates.
LC: S 11, '13.
PW: S 6, '13.

B-1205   [____] The master of mysteries: being an account of
the problems solved by Astro, seer of secrets, and his
love affair with Valeska Wynne, his assistant / with
illustrations by Karl Anderson and George Brehm.
Indianapolis: The Bobbs-Merrill Company, [c1912].
480 p., front., [24] leaves of plates.
LC: O 9, '12.
PW: O 12, '12.

B-1206   ____ Mrs. Hope's husband / by Gelett Burgess;
illustrated by Henry Raleigh. New York: The
Century Co., 1917. 161 p., front., [7] leaves of
plates
LC: Ag 30, '17.
PW: S 1, '17.

B-1207   ____ The picaroons / by Gelett Burgess and Will
Irwin. New York: McClure, Phillips & Company,
1904. 284 p.
PW: Ap 23, '04.

B-1208   ____ The reign of Queen Isyl / by Gelett Burgess
and Will Irwin. New York: McClure, Phillips &
Company, 1903. 255 p.
PW: D 5, '03.

B-1209   ____ The white cat / by Gelett Burgess; with
illustrations by Will Grefé. Indianapolis: The
Bobbs-Merrill Company, [1907]. 389, [1] p., front.,
[5] leaves of plates.
LC: Mr 7, '07.
PW: Mr 16, '07.
BLC: London: Chapman Hall, 1908.

B-1210   Burgess, W. Watson (William Watson), b. 1855. A
life sentence, or, Duty in dealing with crime / by W.
Watson Burgess. Boston: Richard G. Badger, 1905.
([Boston]: The Gorham Press). 210 p.

B-1211   Burgundy, Billy, *pseud.* Billy Burgundy's letters.
New York: J. F. Taylor & Company, 1902. 74 p.,
front., [11] leaves of plates. [Ill. by C. Marriner,
Jimmy Swinnerton, J. A. Lemon, Bert Cobb, and
Gene Carr.]   **TXA**
PW: Jl 12, '02.

B-1212   ____ Billy Burgundy's opinions / by Billy Burgundy
[pseud.]. New York: J. S. Ogilvie Publishing
Company, c1902. 91 p., ill.   **NYP**
Contents: Tale of a damsel who carried a fad too far -- Tale of a
damsel who didn't wed a duke -- Tale of a gumpish geezer who
finally made good -- Tale of a damsel who carried flashing to a finish
-- Tale of a guy who placed a heavy discount on dope -- Tale of a
chaperone.

B-1213   ____ Toothsome tales told in slang / by Billy
Burgundy [pseud.]. New York: Street & Smith,
1901. 127 p., front., ill. [Ill. by P. A. L., Richard
Felton Outcault, W. F. Marriner, J. A. Lemon, J. K.
Bryans, C. R. McAuley, C. Rigby, Bert Cobb, and
James Swinnerton.]
Contents: Tale of a soubrette and a scribe -- Tale of Alexander and
an actress -- Tale of a song -- Tale of a fairy and her fanciers -- Tale
of two poets -- Tale of two authors -- Tale of Estelle and her stable of
Bohemians -- Tale of a fair damsel and a fine dancer -- Tale of a
baritone.

B-1214   ____ The villagers, comprising humorous sketches
by Billy Burgundy [pseud.] . . . illustrated. New
York: J. S. Ogilvie Publishing Company, c1904.
88 p., ill.   **NYP**
Contents: Tale of the girl who couldn't stand the sight of him -- Tale
of a guy who got stung badly -- Tale of the heart-breaker who went
lame in the stretch -- Tale of the geezer who finally struck the right
key -- Tale of the busy-body who forced his own finish -- Tale of the
dame who got wise too late -- Tale of a book-worm who found a
change of diet.

B-1215   Burhans, Viola. The Cave-woman: a novel of to-day
/ by Viola Burhans. New York: Henry Holt and
Company, 1910. 339 p.   **DLC**
LC: Je 20, '10.
PW: Je 18, '10.

B-1216 ____ The conflict / by Viola Burhans; illustrations & cover by Wm. L. Hudson. New York: Broadway Publishing Co., [c1907]. 292 p., front., [4] leaves of plates.
LC: Ap 4, '07.
PW: My 4, '07.

B-1217 Burke, Adam J. Too much brother-in-law / by Adam J. Burke. Los Angeles, Cal.: Press of The Times-Mirror Printing and Binding House, [c1901]. 223 p., front.
[This book is a true story of real life. Only the names of people and places mentioned herein are fictitious.]

B-1218 Burke, Kenneth, b. 1897. The white oxen: and other stories / by Kenneth Burke. New York: Albert & Charles Boni, 1924. 297 p.
Contents: The white oxen -- The excursion -- Mrs. Maecenas -- Olympians -- Scherzando -- Portrait of an arrived critic -- David Wassermann -- After hours -- My dear Mrs. Wurtelbach -- The death of tragedy -- The book of Yul -- A progression -- In quest of Olympus -- First pastoral -- Prince Lian.
LC: Ja 10, '25.

Burke, Morgan. Champlin. In *The best short stories of 1924 and the yearbook of the American short story* (1925), B-569.

B-1219 Burleigh, Cecil. The parts of the puzzle / by Cecil Burleigh. Philadelphia: The Bailey, Banks & Biddle Company, 1913. [25] leaves.

B-1220 Burleigh, Grace Worrall. Mandy Wilkins' vision / by Grace Worrall Burleigh. Cincinnati: Jennings and Graham; New York: Eaton and Mains, [c1911]. 170 p., [4] leaves of plates. [Ill. by C. A. Lord.]
LC: N 13, '11.

B-1221 Burleigh, William Grant, 1866-1937. Matoaka: a story of the fight for Americanism / by William Grant Burleigh. Philadelphia: Dorrance & Company, [c1924]. 192 p.   **NYP**

B-1222 Burleson, Adele Steiner. Every politician and his wife / by Adele S. Burleson (Mrs. Albert Sidney Burleson); with an introduction by Thomas R. Marshall, Vice President of the United States. Philadelphia: Dorrance and Company, Inc., [c1921]. 177 p.   **NYP**
PW: Ap 9, '21.

B-1223 Burlingame, Roger, 1889-1967. You too / by Roger Burlingame. New York: Charles Scribner's Sons, 1924. 302 p.

Burmeister, José Bergin (King), Mrs., b. 1882. See **Crane, Mary, pseud.**

Burnet, Dana, 1888-1962. Beyond the cross. In *The best short stories of 1923 and the yearbook of the American short story* (1924), B-568.

____ The Christmas fight of X 157. In *War stories* **(1919), W-94.**

____ Fog. In *The best short stories of 1916 and the yearbook of the American short story* (1917), B-561.

____ Goliath. In *The Sporting spirit* **(1925), S-771.**

B-1224 ____ The lark / by Dana Burnet; with frontispiece by Jim Allen. Boston: Little, Brown and Company, 1921. 308 p., front.
LC: O 13, '21.
PW: O 15, '21.

____ Rain. In *The Grim thirteen* (1917), **G-537.**

____ "Red, white, and blue." In *War stories* (1919), **W-94.**

B-1225 ____ The shining adventure / by Dana Burnet. New York; London: Harper & Brothers, [c1916]. 266, [1] p., col. front.
LC: O 27, '16.
PW: N 4, '16.

B-1226 Burnett, Frances Hodgson, 1849-1924. The dawn of a to-morrow / by Frances Hodgson Burnett; illustrated. New York: Charles Scribner's Sons, 1906. 155, [1] p., col. front., [7] leaves of col. plates. [Ill. by F. C. Yohn.]
LC: F 23, '06.
PW: Mr 3, '06.
BLC: London: F. Warne & Co., 1907.
References: BAL 2102.

B-1227 ____ The head of the house of Coombe / by Frances Hodgson Burnett. New York: Frederick A. Stokes Company, [c1922]. 374 p.
LC: F 13, '22.
PW: F 4, '22.
BLC: London: William Heinemann, 1922.
References: BAL 2127.

B-1228 ____ In the closed room / by Frances Hodgson Burnett . . . ; illustrations by Jessie Willcox Smith. New York: McClure, Phillips & Co., 1904. 129, [1] p., col. front., [7] leaves of col. plates.
                                        OSU, YNG
LC: O 10, '04.
PW: O 15, '04.
BLC: London: Hodder & Stoughton; printed in U. S. A., 1904.
References: BAL 2100.

B-1229 ____ The land of the blue flower / by Frances Hodgson Burnett; with a frontispiece by Sigismond de Ivanowski. New York: Moffat, Yard and Company, 1909. 67 p., col. front.
LC: S 27, '09.
PW: O 16, '09.
BLC: London: G. P. Putnam's Sons, 1912.
References: BAL 2110.

B-1230 ____ The little hunchback Zia / by Frances Hodgson Burnett; with illustrations by Spencer Baird Nichols and W. T. Benda. New York: Frederick A. Stokes Company, [c1916]. 55 p., front., [3] leaves of plates.
LC: Ag 28, '16.
PW: Ag 26, '16.
BLC: London: William Heinemann, 1916.
References: BAL 2123.

B-1231 ____ The lost prince / by Frances Hodgson Burnett . . . ; with illustrations by Maurice L. Bower. New York: The Century Co., 1915. 415 p., front., [15] leaves of plates.
LC: O 22, '15.
PW: O 16, '15.
BLC: London: Hodder & Stoughton, 1915.
References: BAL 2122.

B-1232 ____ The making of a marchioness / by Frances Hodgson Burnett; illustrated by C. D. Williams. New York: Frederick A. Stokes Company Publisher, [1901]. 187 p., front., [3] leaves of plates.
LC: S 13, '01.
PW: O 5, '01.
BLC: London: Smith, Elder & Co., 1901.
References: BAL 2096.

B-1233 ____ The methods of Lady Walderhurst / by Frances Hodgson Burnett; illustrated by C. D. Williams. New York: Frederick A. Stokes Company, [c1901]. 303, [1] p., front., [3] leaves of plates.
PW: F 22, '02.
References: BAL 2097.

B-1234 ____ Robin / by Frances Hodgson Burnett. New York: Frederick A. Stokes Company, [c1922]. 343 p.
Sequel to *The head of the house of Coombe.*
LC: Jl 24, '22.
PW: Jl 29, '22.
BLC: London: William Heinemann, 1922.
References: BAL 2128.

B-1235 ____ The shuttle / by Frances Hodgson Burnett . . . New York: Frederick A. Stokes Company Publisher, [c1907]. 512 p., col. front. [Ill. by Clarence F. Underwood.]
LC: S 13, '07.
PW: O 5, '07.
BLC: London: William Heinemann, 1907.
References: BAL 2107.

B-1236 ____ T. Tembarom / by Frances Hodgson Burnett; illustrated by Charles S. Chapman. New York: The Century Co., 1913. 518 p., front., [7] leaves of plates.
LC: O 30, '13.
PW: O 25, '13.

BLC: London: Hodder & Stoughton, [1913].
References: BAL 2119.

B-1237 ____ The white people / by Frances Hodgson Burnett; with illustrations by Elizabeth Shippen Green. New York; London: Harper & Brothers Publishers, [1917]. 111, [1] p., front., [3] leaves of plates.
LC: F 17, '17.
PW: F 17, '17.
BLC: London: William Heinemann, 1920.
References: BAL 2125.

B-1238 Burnett, Irwin. The heretic; a story of New Jersey love and Puritanism in 1799 / by Irwin Burnett. New York; London; Montreal: The Abbey Press, [c1902].

347 p.   **UIU**
PW: Ag 30, '02.

B-1239 Burnett, Julia Marie. "True": and other stories / by Julia M. Burnett. Redondo Beach, California: Press of the Reflex Publishing Company, 1908. 168, [1] p.
Contents: "True" -- Bertie's Snowball -- Charlie's Messenger -- Joch -- The new hippodrome -- Crooked Charlie -- A Christmas vision.

B-1240 Burnett, Lemuel P. (Lemuel Payton). Two wives, or, The marital and other experiences of Lammy Browning / by Lemuel P. Burnett. New York; London; Montreal: The Abbey Press, [c1902].
556 p.   **DLC**

B-1241 Burnette, Harry Lascelles. Sons of Elohim / by Harry Lascelles Burnette. Chicago, U. S. A.: Randolph, Sterling & Van Ess, [c1922]. 419, [1] p., photo. front. (port.).   **CLU**

B-1242 Burnham, Clara Louise, 1854-1927. Clever Betsy: a novel / by Clara Louise Burnham; with illustrations by Rose O'Neill. Boston; New York: Houghton Mifflin Company, 1910. (Cambridge, Mass.: The Riverside Press). 401, [1] p., col. front., [2] leaves of plates.
LC: S 29, '10.
PW: S 17, '10.

B-1243 ____ Hearts' Haven: a novel / by Clara Louise Burnham; with illustrations. Boston; New York: Houghton Mifflin Company, 1918. (Cambridge: The Riverside Press). 342 p., col. front., [3] leaves of plates. [Ill. by Helen M. Gross.]
LC: O 28, '18.
PW: N 9, '18.
BLC: London: Constable & Co.; Cambridge, Mass. [printed], 1919.

B-1244 ____ In apple-blossom time: a fairy-tale to date / by Clara Louise Burnham; with illustrations. Boston; New York: Houghton Mifflin Company, 1919. (Cambridge, Mass.: The Riverside Press). 316, [2] p., front., [2] leaves of plates. [Ill. by B. Morgan Dennis.]
LC: O 7, '19.
PW: N 1, '19.

B-1245 ____ The inner flame: a novel / by Clara Louise Burnham. Boston; New York: Houghton Mifflin Company, 1912. (Cambridge: The Riverside Press). 500, [2] p., col. front. [Ill. by Orson Lowell.]
LC: S 30, '12.
PW: O 5, '12.
BLC: London: Constable & Co.; Cambridge, Mass. [printed], 1912.

B-1246 ____ Instead of the thorn: a novel / by Clara Louise Root Burnham. Boston; New York: Houghton Mifflin Company, 1916. (Cambridge: The Riverside Press). 389, [1] p., front. [Ill. by Joseph Pierre Nuyttens.]
LC: Ap 10, '16.
PW: Ap 15, '16.

B-1247   ____ Jewel: a chapter in her life / by Clara Louise Burnham; with illustrations by Maude and Genevieve Cowles. Boston; New York: Houghton, Mifflin and Company, 1903. (Cambridge: The Riverside Press). 340 p., front., [7] leaves of plates.
PW: O 3, '03.
BLC: Westminster: A. Constable & Co.; Cambridge, Mass. [printed], 1904.

B-1248   ____ Jewel's story book / by Clara Louise Burnham; with illustrations. Boston; New York: Houghton, Mifflin and Company, 1904. (Cambridge: The Riverside Press). 343 p., front., [4] leaves of plates. [Ill. by Albert Schmitt.]
PW: D 10, '04.
BLC: London: Gay & Bird; Cambridge, Mass. [printed], 1905.

B-1249   ____ The key note: a novel / by Clara Louise Burnham. Boston; New York: Houghton Mifflin Company, 1921. (Cambridge: The Riverside Press). 363, [1] p.
LC: O 26, '21.
PW: O 22, '21.

B-1250   ____ The Lavarons: a novel / by Clara Louise Burnham. Boston; New York: Houghton Mifflin Company, 1925. (Cambridge: The Riverside Press). 287 p.
LC: S 21, '25.
PW: O 3, '25.

B-1251   ____ The leaven of love: a novel / by Clara Louise Burnham. Boston; New York: Houghton, Mifflin Company, 1908. (Cambridge: The Riverside Press). 329, [1] p., col. front. [Ill. by Harrison Fisher.]
LC: Ag 20, '08.
PW: S 12, '08.
BLC: London: A. Constable & Co.; Cambridge, Mass. [printed], 1908.

B-1252   ____ Miss Pritchard's wedding trip: a novel / by Clara Louise Burnham. Boston; New York: Houghton, Mifflin and Company, 1901. (Cambridge, [Mass.]: The Riverside Press). 366 p.
PW: Ap 27, '01.

B-1253   ____ The opened shutters: a novel / by Clara Louise Burnham; with frontispiece by Harrison Fisher. Boston; New York: Houghton, Mifflin and Company, 1906. (Cambridge: The Riverside Press). 344 p., col. front.
LC: O 11, '06.
PW: N 17, '06.

B-1254   ____ The queen of Farrandale: a novel / by Clara Louise Burnham. Boston; New York: Houghton Mifflin Company, 1923. (Cambridge: The Riverside Press). 315, [1] p.
LC: O 8, '23.
PW: O 20, '23.

B-1255   ____ The right princess / by Clara Louise Burnham. Boston; New York: Houghton, Mifflin and Company, 1902. (Cambridge: The Riverside Press). 361, [1] p.

PW: O 4, '02.
BLC: London: A. P. Watt & Son; Cambridge, Mass. [printed], 1902.

B-1256   ____ The right track / by Clara Louise Burnham; with frontispiece by Mary Greene Blumenschein. Boston; New York: Houghton Mifflin Company, 1914. (Cambridge: The Riverside Press). 421, [1] p., col. front.
LC: S 8, '14.
PW: S 19, '14.
BLC: London: Costable & Co.; Cambridge, Mass. [printed], 1914.

B-1257 Burnham, S. M. (Sarah Maria), 1818-1901. A choice in the gathering, or, Sowing and waiting / by S. M. Burnham . . . Boston: A. I. Bradley & Company, [c1901]. 359 p., front. [Ill. by Victor R. Searles.] **DLC**
PW: S 21, '01.

Burns, Ella, b. 1861. See Desmond, Dionne, pseud.

B-1258 Burns, John H. Memoirs of a cow pony, as told by himself / by John H. Burns; illustrated. Boston: Eastern Publishing Co., [c1906]. 178 p., photo. front., photo. ill. [Ill. by B. Grossbeck.] **NYP**

B-1259 Burns, W. C. (William Crawford). Pleading for justice / by W. C. Burns. New York: Justice Publishing Company, 1920. 316 p., front., [2] leaves of plates. [Ill. by Ralph Pallen Coleman.]

Burns, William J. (William John), 1861-1932, jt. aut. *The Argyle case* (1913). See **Hornblow, Arthur, 1865-1942, jt. aut., H-841.**

B-1260   ____ The crevice / by William J. Burns and Isabel Ostrander; illustrations by Will Grefé. New York: W. J. Watt & Company, [c1915]. 315 p., front., [3] sets of double-leaf plates.
LC: Ag 9, '15.

B-1261 Burr, Amelia Josephine, 1878-1941. A dealer in empire: a romance / by Amelia Josephine Burr; illustrated. New York; London: Harper & Brothers, 1915. 297, [1] p., front. (port.), [1] leaf of plates (port.).
LC: Mr 13, '15.
PW: Mr 20, '15.

B-1262   ____ The three fires: a story of Ceylon / by Amelia Josephine Burr. New York: The Macmillan Company, 1922. 260 p.
BLC: London: Hurst & Blackett, [1923].

B-1263 [Burr, Anna Robeson Brown], 1873-1941. The great house in the park / by the author of "The house on Charles Street" and "The house on Smith Square". New York: Duffield & Company, 1924. 425 p.
LC: My 16, '24.

B-1264 [____] The house on Charles Street. New York: Duffield & Company, 1921. 283 p.
LC: D 13, '21.

B-1265 [____] The house on Smith Square / by the author of The house on Charles Street. New York: Duffield & Company, 1923. 316 p.
LC: Mr 13, '23.

B-1266 ____ The Jessop bequest / by Anna Robeson Burr. Boston; New York: Houghton Mifflin and Company, 1907. (Cambridge: The Riverside Press). 401, [1] p., col. front.
LC: O 23, '07.
PW: N 16, '07.

B-1267 ____ The millionaire's son / by Anna Robeson Brown . . . ; illustrated by Arthur E. Becher. Boston: Dana Estes & Company, 1903. 397 p., front., [5] leaves of plates.
PW: Ag 29, '03.

B-1268 ____ St. Helios / by Anna Robeson Burr. New York: Duffield & Company, 1925. 373 p.
PW: S 19, '25.
BLC: London: Brentano's, [1926].

B-1269 ____ Truth and a woman / by Anna Robeson Brown. Chicago: Herbert S. Stone & Company, 1903. 206 p.
PW: My 23, '03.

B-1270 ____ The wine-press / by Anna Robeson Brown. New York: D. Appleton and Company, 1905. 390 p.

B-1271 ____ The wrong move: a romance / by Anna Robeson Burr. New York: The Macmillan Company, 1923. 368 p.
LC: Mr 14, '23.
PW: Mr 31, '23.
BLC: London: Brentano's, 1924.

B-1272 Burr, Hanford M. (Hanford Montrose), b. 1864. Around the fire: stories of beginnings / Hanford M. Burr . . . ; illustrations from old wood-cuts. New York; London: Association Press, 1912. 238 p., front., ill. **KLG**
Contents: The Fire Spirit -- The first potter -- The first gang -- The first chief -- The smoke way -- The first milkman -- Rang, the red man -- Rang of the thinking hand -- The first sailor -- The garden of Ulma -- Let, the first artist -- Sax, the first musician -- The call of the Great Water -- The story of Lup -- The wooing of Senna -- Hune, the hunter of white men -- The lake dwellers -- How men found the Great Spirit.

B-1273 ____ The calling of Boyman / H. M. Burr . . . New York; London: Association Press, 1916. 143 p.

B-1274 ____ Donald McRea / by Hanford M. Burr . . . Springfield, Mass.: The Seminar Publishing Co., 1911. 172 p., photo. front. **DLC**

B-1275 ____ Handicapped / by H. M. Burr. Springfield, Mass.: Seminar Publishing Co., [c1912]. 46 p. **DLC**

B-1276 ____ Tales of Telal / by Hanford M. Burr . . . Springfield, Mass.: The Seminar Publishing Company, 1914. 116 p., ill. [Ill. by Gilbert N. Jerome.] **DLC**

Contents: Accad the swordmaker -- Akki the irrigator -- Nubta and Ardi, builders -- Gimil the scribe -- Nidinti and the magic crystal -- Tamal the tamer of wild asses -- Asta the star-gazer -- Adapa the fisherman -- Sargani the gardner -- Tera worshiper of Yahve (Jehovah).
LC: S 8, '14.

Burr, Helen. The ten wishes. *In When God walks the road and other stories* **(1924), W-445.**

B-1277 Burr, Jane, *pseud.* The glorious hope: a novel / by Jane Burr [pseud.]. Croton-on-Hudson, New York: Jane Burr, 1918. 248, [1] p. **DLC**
LC: O 22, '18.
PW: N 19, '21.
BLC: London: Duckworth & Co., 1921.

B-1278 ____ Letters of a Dakota divorcee / by Jane Burr [pseud.]. Boston: The Roxburgh Publishing Co., [c1909]. 148 p.

B-1279 ____ Married men / by Jane Burr [pseud.]. New York: Frank-Maurice, Inc., 1925. 274 p.
PW: Je 20, '25.

B-1280 ____ The passionate spectator / by Jane Burr [pseud.]. New York: Thomas Stelzer, 1921. 197 p.
PW: F 5, '21.
BLC: London: Duckworth & Co., 1920.

B-1281 Burr, Lucretia P. The copy-cats / by Lucretia P. Burr. Lyme, Conn.: [Privately printed by the Yale University Press], 1922. 77, [1] p.
Contents: The copy-cats -- Old home day -- Cook's summer school -- The vacuum-cleaner -- The Boston rocker -- The rummage sale -- Silver lustre -- The paper doll.
LC: Mr 24, '22.

B-1282 Burrell, David De Forest, b. 1876. Belligerent Peter / by David DeForest Burrell . . . ; a prize story. Philadelphia: American Sunday-School Union, [c1920]. 242 p. **DLC**
LC: Ag 4, '20.
PW: S 4, '20.

B-1283 ____ The hermit's Christmas / David De Forest Burrell. New York: American Tract Society, [c1912]. 28 p.

B-1284 ____ The lost star: an idyll of the desert / by David De Forest Burrell. New York; Chicago; Toronto; London; Edinburgh: Fleming H. Revell Company, [c1916]. 32 p., front. [Ill. by F. A. Mutz.]
PW: O 21, '16.

B-1285 Burrell, William Richard. From out of the flame; a story of the re-creation / by William Richard Burrell. Autograph ed. New York: Burr Printing House, 1905. 476 p., front. (port.).
Unexamined copy: bibliographic data from OCLC, #11691062.

B-1286 Burroughs, Burt E. (Burt Edward). Legends and tales of homeland on the Kankakee / by Burt E. Burroughs. Chicago: Regan Printing House, 1923. 277 p., front., [3] leaves of plates.
Contents: The trail of the king's highway -- The coming of the French to the Valley of Kankakee -- Pioneer life on the Kankakee

eighty years ago -- Mark Beaubien's story of the man who burned up -- The first threshing machine brought to Kankakee County -- "Shaw-wa-na-see's" Village of Little Rock -- An old-time "turkey shoot" on the Kankakee -- Hunting wolf on horseback -- A double wedding at Limestone in the year 1842 -- The forge on the prairie -- Early-day dances at the Davis Home -- The old Rinosa Post office -- Taxation a burden on the early settler -- The "Bogus Island" horse thief ring -- Limestone votes bonds for war bounties -- The cholera epidemic of 1851 -- The county-seat election of 1853 -- The letter that never came -- Removing a kiss with soft soap -- The eccentric Dan Parmlee -- A notable war-time dance and oyster supper -- The first shopper on Court Street -- When the first locomotive came to Kankakee -- Billy Caldwell "The Sau-ga-nash" -- Chief "Shaub-e-nee," The Grand Old Man -- The exodus of the Pottawattomie Nation -- The Old Hubbard Trail -- Kankakee County's first Fourth of July celebration -- A death and burial at "Leggtown" -- Kankakee's first Sunday School excursion -- Dominick Bray, voyageur, trader, citizen -- The story of "Little Canada" -- When young folks danced over in Little Canada -- Walking as a lost art -- The papoose's cradle -- The coming together of the 76th Regiment and Tommy Gorman -- When the first buggy came to Kankakee County -- "For they were jolly good fellows" -- A tale of Old Kankakee -- Outliving a shroud -- In the good old days of the ox team -- Hubbard's fight with Chief yellow head -- "Watch-e-kee's" prophecy -- "As it was in the beginning" -- Pioneers three and a horse trade -- A unique pioneer character -- The recollections of a nonagenarian -- Historical Flotsam and Jetsam.
LC: Ag 13, '23.

B-1287   Burroughs, Edgar Rice, 1875-1950. At the earth's core / by Edgar Rice Burroughs . . . ; illustrated by J. Allen St. John. Chicago: A. C. McClurg & Co., 1922. 277 p., front., [8] leaves of plates.
LC: Ag 25, '22.
PW: Ag 12, '22.
BLC: London: Methuen & Co., 1923.
References: Heins, p. 134-135.

B-1288   _____ The bandit of Hell's Bend / by Edgar Rice Burroughs . . . Chicago: A. C. McClurg & Co., 1925. 316 p., front. [Ill. by Modest Stein.] **NYP**
LC: Je 6, '25.
PW: Jl 18, '25.
BLC: London: Methuen & Co., 1926.
References: Heins, p. 164.

B-1289   _____ The beasts of Tarzan / by Edgar Rice Burroughs; with illustrations by J. Allen St. John. Chicago: A. C. McClurg & Co., 1916. 336, [1] p., front., ill.
LC: Mr 6, '16.
PW: Mr 25, '16.
BLC: London: C. F. Cazenove; Chicago: A.C. McClurg & Co.; Chicago [printed], 1916.
References: Heins, p. 42-44.

B-1290   _____ The cave girl / Edgar Rice Burroughs . . . Chicago: A. C. McClurg & Co., 1925. 323 p., front. [Ill. by J. Allen St. John.]   **OSU, FHM**
LC: Mr 23, '25.
PW: Ap 25, '25.
BLC: London: Methuen & Co., 1927.
References: Heins, p. 162-163.

B-1291   _____ The chessmen of Mars / by Edgar Rice Burroughs . . . ; illustrated by J. Allen St. John. Chicago: A. C. McClurg & Co., 1922. 375 p., front., [7] leaves of plates.
LC: D 4, '22.
PW: D 23, '22.
BLC: London: Methuen & Co., 1923.
References: Heins, p. 119-120.

B-1292   _____ The eternal lover / by Edgar Rice Burroughs . . . Chicago: A. C. McClurg & Co., 1925. 316 p., front. [Ill. by J. Allen St. John.]
LC: O 5, '25.
PW: O 24, '25.
BLC: London: Methuen & Co., 1927.
References: Heins, p. 165.

B-1293   _____ The girl from Hollywood / by Edgar Rice Burroughs; frontispiece by P. J. Monahan. New York: The Macaulay Company, [c1923]. 320 p., front.
LC: Ag 21, '23.
PW: S 8, '23.
BLC: London: Methuen & Co., 1924.
References: Heins, p. 158-159.

B-1294   _____ The gods of Mars / by Edgar Rice Burroughs; frontispiece by Frank E. Schoonover. Chicago: A. C. McClurg & Co., 1918. 348 p., front.
LC: O 2, '18.
PW: O 26, '18.
BLC: London: Methuen & Co., 1920.
References: Heins, p. 112-113.

B-1295   _____ Jungle tales of Tarzan / by Edgar Rice Burroughs . . . ; illustrated by J. Allen St. John. Chicago: A. C. McClurg & Co., 1919. 319 p., front., [4] leaves of plates, ill.
Contents: Tarzan's first love -- The capture of Tarzan -- The fight for the balu -- The god of Tarzan -- Tarzan and the black boy -- The witch-doctor seeks vengeance -- The end of Bukawai -- The lion -- The nightmare -- The battle for Teeka -- A jungle joke -- Tarzan rescues the moon.
LC: Mr 31, '19.
PW: Ap 12, '19.
BLC: London: Methuen & Co., 1919.
References: Heins, p. 51-53.

B-1296   _____ The land that time forgot / by Edgar Rice Burroughs . . . ; illustrated by J. Allen St. John. Chicago: A. C. McClurg & Co., 1924. 422 p., front., [3] leaves of plates.
LC: Je 19, '24.
PW: Jl 5, '24.
BLC: London: Methuen & Co., 1925.
References: Heins, p. 160-161.

B-1297   _____ The mucker / by Edgar Rice Burroughs; illustrated by J. Allen St. John. Chicago: A. C. McClurg & Co., 1921. 414 p., front., [4] leaves of plates.
LC: N 4, '21.
PW: N 26, '21.
BLC: London: Methuen & Co., 1921.
References: Heins, p. 156-157.

B-1298   _____ Pellucidar: a sequel to "At the earth's core", relating the further adventures of David Innes in the land underneath the earth's crust / by Edgar Rice Burroughs; illustrated by J. Allen St. John. Chicago: A. C. McClurg & Co., 1923. 322 p., front., [3] leaves of plates, map.
LC: S 8, '23.
PW: S 29, '23.
BLC: London: Methuen & Co., 1924.
References: Heins, p. 136-137.

B-1299　　＿＿＿ A princess of Mars / by Edgar Rice Burroughs; illustrated by Frank E. Schoonover. Chicago: A. C. McClurg & Co., 1917. 326, [1] p., front., [4] leaves of plates.
LC: O 13, '17.
PW: O 27, '17.
BLC: London: Methuen & Co., 1919.
References: Heins, p. 108-111.

B-1300　　＿＿＿ The return of Tarzan / by Edgar Rice Burroughs . . . ; with decorations by J. Allen St. John. Chicago, A. C. McClurg & Co., 1915. 365 p., ill.
LC: Mr 13, '15.
PW: Mr 20, '15.
BLC: London: C. F. Cazenove; Chicago: A. C. McClurg & Co.; Chicago [printed], 1915.
References: Heins, p. 39-41.

B-1301　　＿＿＿ The son of Tarzan / by Edgar Rice Burroughs . . . ; with illustrations by J. Allen St. John. Chicago: A. C. McClurg & Co., 1917. 394 p., front., ill
LC: Mr 12, '17.
PW: Mr 24, '17.
BLC: London: Methuen & Co., 1919.
References: Heins, p. 45-47.

B-1302　　＿＿＿ Tarzan and the ant men / by Edgar Rice Burroughs . . . Chicago: A. C. McClurg & Co., 1924. 346 p., front.
Contains "a 4-page supplement entitled: *How Burroughs wrote the `Tarzan Tales,' by Robert H. Davis:" Heins, p. 64.*
LC: O 3, '24.
PW: N 1, '24.
BLC: London: A. C. McClurg & Co., 1924.
References: Heins, p. 64-65.

B-1303　　＿＿＿ Tarzan and the golden lion / by Edgar Rice Burroughs . . . ; illustrated by J. Allen St. John. Chicago: A. C. McClurg & Co., 1923. 333 p., front., [7] leaves of plates.
LC: Mr 31, '23.
PW: Ap 28, '23.
BLC: London: Methuen & Co., 1924.
References: Heins, p. 58-63.

B-1304　　＿＿＿ Tarzan and the jewels of Opar / by Edgar Rice Burroughs . . . ; with illustrations by J. Allen St. John. Chicago: A. C. McClurg & Co., 1918. 350 p., front., [7] leaves of plates.
LC: Ap 23, '18.
PW: My 4, '18.
BLC: London: Methuen & Co., 1919.
References: Heins, p. 48-50.

B-1305　　＿＿＿ Tarzan of the apes / Edgar Rice Burroughs. Chicago: A. C. McClurg & Co., 1914. 400, [1] p., front. ill.
LC: Je 20, '14.
PW: S 5, '14.
BLC: London: Methuen & Co., 1917.
References: Heins, p. 31-38.

B-1306　　＿＿＿ Tarzan the terrible / by Edgar Rice Burroughs; illustrated by J. Allen St. John. Chicago: A. C. McClurg & Co., 1921. 408 p., front., [8] leaves of plates.
LC: Je 27, '21.
PW: Jl 16, '21.
BLC: London: Methuen & Co., 1921.
References: Heins, p. 56-57.

B-1307　　＿＿＿ Tarzan the untamed / by Edgar Rice Burroughs . . . ; illustrated by J. Allen St. John. Chicago: A. C. McClurg & Co., 1920. 428 p., front., [8] leaves of plates.
LC: My 4, '20.
PW: My 29, '20.
BLC: London: Methuen & Co., 1920.
References: Heins, p. 54-55.

B-1308　　＿＿＿ Thuvia, maid of Mars / by Edgar Rice Burroughs . . . ; illustrated by J. Allen St. John. Chicago: A. C. McClurg & Co., 1920. 256 p., front., [9] leaves of plates.
LC: N 4, '20.
PW: D 4, '20.
BLC: London: Methuen & Co., 1921.
References: Heins, p. 116-118.

B-1309　　＿＿＿ The warlord of Mars / by Edgar Rice Burroughs: frontispiece by J. Allen St. John. Chicago: A. C. McClurg & Co., 1919. 296 p., col. front.
LC: S 29, '19.
PW: N 1, '19.
BLC: London: Methuen & Co., 1920.
References: Heins, p. 114-115.

B-1310　　Burroughs, Joseph Birkbeck. Titan, son of Saturn: the coming world emperor / Joseph Birkbeck Burroughs. Oberlin, Ohio: The Emeth publishers, 1905. 450 p.

B-1311　　Burt, Katharine Newlin, b. 1882. The branding iron / by Katharine Newlin Burt; with illustrations. Boston; New York: Houghton Mifflin Company, 1919. (Cambridge, Mass.: The Riverside Press). 310 p., front., [4] leaves of plates. [Ill. by Charles Sarka.]
LC: Ag 21, '19.
PW: Ag 16, '19.
BLC: London: Constable & Co.; Cambridge, Mass. printed, 1919.

B-1312　　＿＿＿ Hidden Creek / by Katharine Newlin Burt; with illustrations by George Giguère. Boston; New York: Houghton Mifflin Company, 1920. (Cambridge: The

Riverside Press). 311, [1] p., front., [7] leaves of plates.
LC: S 7, '20.
PW: Ag 28, '20.
BLC: London: Constable & Co., 1921.

B-1313　　＿＿＿ "Q" / by Katharine Newlin Burt. Boston; New York: Houghton Mifflin Company, 1922. (Cambridge, Mass.: The Riverside Press). 312 p.
LC: Ap 19, '22.
PW: Ap 29, '22.
BLC: London: Hutchinson & Co., [1923].

B-1314 ____ Quest: a novel / by Katharine Newlin Burt. Boston; New York: Houghton Mifflin Company, 1925. (Cambridge, Mass.: The Riverside Press). 376 p.
LC: O 23, '25.
PW: O 31, '25.

B-1315 ____ The red lady / by Katharine Newlin Burt. Boston; New York: Houghton Mifflin Company, 1920. (Cambridge: The Riverside Press). 241, [1] p.
LC: Mr 29, '20.
PW: Ap 17, '20.
BLC: London: Constable & Co., 1920.

B-1316 ____ Snow-blind / by Katharine Newlin Burt. Boston; New York: Houghton Mifflin Company, 1921. (Cambridge, Mass.: The Riverside Press). 186 p.
PW: S 3, '21.
BLC: London: Constable & Co.; Cambridge, Mass. printed, 1922.

Burt, Maxwell Struthers, 1882-1954. The blood-red one. In *The best short stories of 1919 and the yearbook of the American short story* (1920), B-564.

B-1317 ____ Chance encounters / by Maxwell Struthers Burt; with a frontispiece by N. C. Wyeth. New York: Charles Scribner's Sons, 1921. 287 p., front.
Contents: The scarlet hunter -- Experiment -- Shining armor -- Devilled sweetbreads -- "A dream or two" -- The blood-red one -- "Bally old" Knott -- Each in his generation.
LC: O 6, '21.
PW: O 15, '21.

____ A cup of tea. In *The best short stories of 1917 and the yearbook of the American short story* (1918), B-562.

____ Each in his generation. In *Prize stories of 1920* (1921), P-618.

B-1318 ____ The interpreter's house / by Struthers Burt. New York: Charles Scribner's Sons, 1924. 445 p.
LC: F 18, '24.
PW: F 16, '24.
BLC: London: Hodder & Stoughton, [1924].

B-1319 ____ John O'May and other stories / by Maxwell Struthers Burt; illustrated. New York: Charles Scribner's Sons, 1918. 250 p., front., [7] leaves of plates.
Contents: John O'May -- Wings of the morning -- A cup of tea -- Closed doors -- The water-hole -- Le panache -- The glory of the wild green earth.
LC: S 13, '18.
PW: S 28, '18.

____ The water-hole. In *The best short stories of 1915 and the yearbook of the American short story* (1916), B-560.

B-1320 Burton, Beatrice, b. 1894. The flapper wife / by Beatrice Burton. New York: Grosset & Dunlap, [c1925]. 344 p.
LC: O 2, '25.
PW: O 17, '25.

B-1321 Burton, C. Francis. The call of the mate / by C. Francis Burton. Boston: Sherman, French & Company, 1917. 338 p.
LC: Ja 4, '18.
PW: Ja 5, '18.

B-1322 Burton, Frederick R. (Frederick Russell), 1861-1909. Her wedding interlude / by Frederick R. Burton. New York; London: Street & Smith, Publishers, [c1902]. 239 p.
PW: S 27, '02.

B-1323 ____ Redcloud of the lakes: a novel / by Frederick R. Burton; illustrations by Elfrieda Burton. New York: G. W. Dillingham Company, [c1909]. 374 p., col. front., [4] leaves of plates.
LC: My 22, '09.
PW: Jl 31, '09.
BLC: London: Unwin; New York [printed], 1909.

B-1324 ____ The song and the singer: a setting forth, in words, of certain movements in a latter-day life: prelude-allegro; andante con moto; scherzo; presto con brio-coda / by Frederick R. Burton. New York; London: Street & Smith, [c1902]. 383 p., front., [7] leaves of plates.
[Ill. by Charles Grunwald.]
PW: O 4, '02.
BLC: London: Shurmer Sibthorp, [1902].

B-1325 ____ Strongheart: a novel / by Frederick R. Burton; founded on William C. de Mille's play; illustrations by Clarence Rowe. New York: G. W. Dillingham Company, [c1908]. 393 p., front., [3] leaves of plates.
LC: Ag 31, '08.
PW: S 19, '08.
BLC: London: T. Fisher Unwin; New York [printed], 1908.

B-1326 Burton, George Lee. Tackling matrimony: to the men and girls who love each other more than ease and show and sham / by George Lee Burton; illustrated. New York; London: Harper & Brothers, 1913. 218, [1] p., front., [5] leaves of plates. [Ill. by Will Grefé.]

B-1327 Burton, Richard, 1861-1940. Three of a kind: the story of an old musician, a newsboy and a cocker dog / by Richard Burton; illustrated from drawings by Frank T. Merrill. Boston: Little, Brown and Company, 1908. 267 p., front., [3] leaves of plates.

B-1328 Burtscher, William J. (William John), b. 1878. Yellow Creek humor: a book of Burtscher drolleries / by William J. Burtscher. Baltimore: The Lord Baltimore Press, [c1909]. 107 p.

B-1329 Busch, Bonnie, b. 1884. His mortgaged wife / by Bonnie Busch. Philadelphia: Dorrance, [c1923]. 223 p.
LC: Ag 3, '23.
PW: S 8, '23.

B-1330 ____ Morality court / by Bonnie Melbourne Busch. Kansas City, Missouri: Burton Publishing Company, [c1921]. 286 p. **KCP**

B-1331　　____　Out of the Middle West / by Bonnie Melbourne Busch. Kansas City, Mo.: Burton Publishing Company, [c1922]. 293 p.
PW: My 6, '22.

B-1332　　Busch, William. A triple smile from cupid. [Saint Louis, Mo.?: s. n., 1904.] 40 p., ill.
Unexamined copy: bibliographic data from OCLC, #26829016.

B-1333　　Bush, Clara Goodyear Boise. The grinding: a Louisiana story / by Clara Goodyear Boise Bush. New York: Henry Holt and Company, 1921. 315 p.
LC: Jl 20, '21.
PW: Jl 23, '21.

Bush, Florence Lilian, jt. aut. *Goose Creek folks* (1912). See **Bush, Isabel Graham, jt. aut., B-1335.**

B-1334　　Bush, Harold Montfort, b. 1872. The diary of an enlisted man / by Captain Harold M. Bush. Columbus, Ohio: Edward T. Miller, 1908. 211 p.

B-1335　　Bush, Isabel Graham. Goose Creek folks: a story of the Kentucky mountains / by Isabel Graham Bush and Florence Lilian Bush. New York; Chicago; Toronto; London; Edinburgh: Fleming H. Revell Company, [c1912]. 224 p., front.
LC: Ja 2, '13.
PW: D 21, '12.

B-1336　　Bush, Olivia Ward, b. 1869. Driftwood / by Olivia Ward Bush. [Providence, R. I.: Atlantic Printing Co.], c1914. 86 p., photo. front. (port.).　　**AUU**
Contents: [Mostly poetry; one story:] The yule-tide song: a Christmas legend.

B-1337　　Bushnell, Belle Johnston, b. 1859. John Arrowsmith-planter / by Belle Bushnell; with illustrations by Walter Biggs. Cedar Rapids, Iowa: The Torch Press, 1910. 466 p., front., [2] leaves of plates.
LC: N 15, '09.

B-1338　　Bushnell, Charles Edwin. An Indian paradise: a first class true story / Charles Edwin Bushnell, author. [New York?: s. n., 1906?] 26 p.　　**NYP**

B-1339　　Buskett, Nancy. Fingers that see / by Nancy Buskett; editor Cynthia Grey . . . Seattle, U. S. A.: The Stuff Printing Concern, 1914. 138 p., front.

B-1340　　Bussenius, Luellen Teters. The honorable Miss Cherry Blossom: a novel / by Luellen Teters Bussenius. New York: Nicholas L. Brown, 1924. 245 p.

B-1341　　Bute, Currer, *pseud.* Her naked soul / by Currer Bute [pseud.]. New York: Broadway Publishing Company, [c1905]. 214 p., front., plates.
Unexamined copy: bibliographic data from NUC.
LC: Mr 28, '07.

B-1342　　Butler, Bion H., 1857-1935. The church on Quintuple mountain: a story of Pennsylvania oil country life, possibly a trifle exaggerated in spots / Bion H. Butler. Southern Pines, N. C.: Foss, Stradley & Butler, 1912. 271, [1] p., front.

B-1343　　Butler, Ellis Parker, 1869-1937. The adventures of a suburbanite / by Ellis Parker Butler; illustrations by A. B. Phelan. Garden City, N. Y.: Doubleday, Page & Company, 1911. 224 p., front., [15] leaves of plates.
LC: N 10, '11.
PW: N 18, '11.

B-1344　　____　The cheerful smugglers / by Ellis Parker Butler; with illustrations by May Wilson Preston. New York: The Century Co., 1908. 277 p., front., [7] leaves of plates.
LC: Mr 31, '08.
PW: Ap 18, '08.

B-1345　　____　The confessions of a daddy / by Ellis Parker Butler; with illustrations by Fanny Y. Cory. New York: The Century Co., 1907. 107 p., front., 8 leaves of plates.
LC: My 8, '07.
PW: My 18, '07.
BLC: London: Hodder & Stoughton, [1907].

____　"Dey ain't no ghosts." In *Humorous ghost stories* (1921), H-1018.

B-1346　　____　Dominie Dean: a novel / by Ellis Parker Butler. New York; Chicago; Toronto; London; Edinburgh: Fleming H. Revell Company, [c1917]. 302 p., front. [Ill. by Victor Pérard.]
LC: Jl 11, '17.
PW: Je 23, '17.

B-1347　　____　An experiment in gyro-hats / by Ellis Parker Butler . . . ; illustrations by Albert Levering. -- Special ed. -- New York; Chicago: The Q and C Co., [1910?]. 31, [1] p., ill.

B-1348　　____　The great American pie company / by Ellis Parker Butler . . . ; illustrated by Will Crawford. New York: McClure, Phillips & Co., 1907. 43, [1] p., col. front., [2] leaves of col. plates. [Ill. by Frederic Dorr Steele.]
LC: Ap 25, '07.
PW: My 4, '07.

B-1349　　____　In pawn / by Ellis Parker Butler; with illustrations. Boston; New York: Houghton Mifflin Company, 1921. (Cambridge: The Riverside Press). 272, [2] p., front., [3] leaves of plates. [Ill. by R. L. Lambdin.]
LC: O 26, '21.
PW: O 1, '21.

B-1350　　____　The incubator baby / by Ellis Parker Butler; illustrations by May Wilson Preston. New York; London: Funk & Wagnalls Company, 1906. 111 p., col. front., [3] leaves of col. plates.
LC: S 24, '06.
PW: D 8, '06.

B-1351   ____ The jack-knife man / by Ellis Parker Butler; illustrated by Hanson Booth. New York: The Century Co., 1913. 318 p., front., [3] leaves of plates.
LC: S 18, '13.
PW: S 13, '13.

B-1352   ____ Kilo: being the love story of Eliph' Hewlitt, book agent / by Ellis Parker Butler. New York: The McClure Company, 1907. 279 p., front., [6] leaves of plates.
LC: O 28, '07.
PW: N 2, '07.
BLC: London: Hodder & Stoughton, [1908].

B-1353   ____ Mike Flannery on duty and off / by Ellis Parker Butler; illustrations by Gustavus C. Widney. New York: Doubleday, Page & Company, 1909. 101 p., front., [3] leaves of plates.
LC: My 15, '09.
PW: Je 12, '09.
BLC: London: Doubleday, Page & Co.; New York printed, 1909.

B-1354   ____ Millingham's cat-fooler. [Cambridge, Ma.: Boston woven hose & rubber co., c1920.] [23] p., ill.   VA@

B-1355   ____ Perkins of Portland: Perkins the Great / by Ellis Parker Butler . . . Boston: Herbert B. Turner & Co., 1906. 135 p., front., [5] leaves of plates.
LC: S 7, '06.
PW: O 6, '06.

B-1356   ____ Philo Gubb: correspondence-school detective: with illustrations / by Ellis Parker Butler. Boston; New York: Houghton Mifflin Company, 1918. (Cambridge, Mass., U. S. A.: The Riverside Press). 352, [2] p., front., [19] leaves of plates. [Ill. by Rea Irvin.]
Contents: The hard-boiled egg -- The pet -- The eagle's claws -- The oubliette -- The un-burglars -- The two-cent stamp -- The chicken -- The dragon's eye -- The progressive murder -- The missing Mr. Master -- Waffles and mustard -- The anonymous wiggle -- The half of a thousand -- Dietz's 7462 Bessie John -- Henry -- Buried bones -- Philo Gubb's greatest case.
LC: O 2, '18.
PW: O 5, '18.

B-1357   ____ Pigs is pigs / by Ellis Parker Butler; illustrations by Will Crawford. New York: McClure, Phillips & Co., 1906. 37 p., front., [2] leaves of plates.
PW: Ap 21, '06.
BLC: London: Hodder & Stoughton, 1906. [2nd ed.]

B-1358   ____ Red Head and Whistle Breeches / by Ellis Parker Butler; with illustrations by Arthur D. Fuller. New York: The Bancroft Company, [c1915]. 48 p., ill.
LC: N 26, '15.
PW: D 18, '15.

____ The tenth Mrs. Tulkington. In *Marriage* (1923), M-457.

B-1359   ____ That pup / by Ellis Parker Butler; illustrated. New York: The McClure Company, 1908. 61 p., front., [7] leaves of plates.   Published in Harper's Monthly Magazine, August, 1908, under title: *Getting rid of Fluff.*
LC: O 17, '08.
PW: N 14, '08.

B-1360   ____ The thin Santa Claus: the chicken yard that was a Christmas stocking / by Ellis Parker Butler; illustrated by May Wilson Preston. New York: Doubleday, Page & Company, 1909. 35 p., front., [1] leaf of plates.
LC: S 29, '09.
PW: O 16, '09.
BLC: London: Doubleday, Page & Co.; New York printed, 1904.

B-1361   ____ The water goats: and other troubles / by Ellis Parker Butler; illustrations by Harrison Cady, Gustavus C. Widney and Irma Dérèmeaux. New York: Doubleday, Page & Company, 1910. 101 p., front., [3] leaves of plates.
Contents: The water goats -- Mr. Billing's pockets -- Our first burglar.
LC: Je 17, '10.
PW: Je 25, '10.

B-1362   Butler, George Frank, 1857-1921. The exploits of a physician detective / by Geo. F. Butler . . . Chicago: Clinic Publishing Co., 1908. 332 p., ill.
Contents: The Hautover case -- The mystery of the governess -- The tin box --The tragedy at the colonial -- Mrs. Worthley's secret -- The Wetchell job -- The missing bride -- The strange sickness of Mr. Whittaker -- Ransome -- The man with the glass eye -- The kleptomaniac -- The lodging house mystery -- The spirit club.

Butler, Katharine. In no strange land. In *Atlantic narratives*; first series (1918), A-360.

B-1363   Butler, Louise, 1866-1951. Red heart: a story of West Feliciana / by Louise Butler. [S. l.: s. n., 1921?]. 32 p., front.   LUU

B-1364   Butt, Archibald Willingham, 1865-1912. Both sides of the shield / by Major Archibald W. Butt, U. S. A., late military aid to the President; with a foreword by William H. Taft, and a short account of the author's life. Philadelphia; London: J. B. Lippincott Company, 1912. 155 p., front. (port.).

B-1365   Butt, Mary. An old time tragedy / by Mary Butt. New York; London; Montreal: The Abbey Press, [c1901]. 50 p.   DLC

B-1366   Butterworth, Hezekiah, 1839-1905. A heroine of the wilderness: the story of Lincoln's mother / by Hezekiah Butterworth . . . ; illustrated by Clare Victor Dwiggins. Philadelphia: The John C. Winston Co., 1906. 273 p., col. front., [4] leaves of plates.   EYW
PW: D 8, '06.

Buzzell, Francis. Lonely places. In *The best short stories of 1917 and the yearbook of the American short story* (1918), B-562.

_____ Ma's pretties. In *The best short stories of 1916 and the yearbook of the American short story* **(1917), B-561.**

Byers, F. K. Under the tricolor. In **Seattle Writers' Club.** *Tillicum tales* **(1907), S-248.**

B-1367   Byloff, Forrest G. The hero of the West: a romance of the valley, the prairie and the mountain / by Forrest G. Byloff. Boyers, Pa.: Hassler-DeAtley Pub. Co., c1919. 89 p.   **DLC**

B-1368   Byrd, Evie Sartor. A modern evil / by Evie Sartor Byrd. N. Y.: Broadway Publishing Co., 1907. 256 p., front. [Ill. by Wm. L. Hudson.]
LC: Ap 17, '07.
PW: Je 29, '07.

B-1369   Byrd, John Walter. The born fool / by John Walter Byrd. New York: George H. Doran Company, [1919]. 448 p.
PW: Je 14, '19.
BLC: London: Chatto & Windus, 1917.

B-1370   Byrne, Donn, 1889-1928, *pseud.* Blind Raftery and his wife, Hilaria / by Donn Byrne [pseud.]; illustrated by John Richard Flanagan. New York; London: The Century Co., [c1924]. 175 p., front., [3] leaves of plates.
LC: S 17, '24.
PW: S 20, '24.
BLC: London: Sampson Low & Co., [1925].
References: BAL 2294; Bannister, 7; Wetherbee, p. 17-19.

B-1371   _____ Changeling: and other stories / by Donn Byrne [pseud.]. New York; London: The Century Co., [c1923]. 418 p.
Contents: Changeling -- The barnacle goose -- Belfasters -- The keeper of the bridge -- In praise of Lady Margery Kyteler -- Reynardine -- Dramatis personæ -- Wisdom buildeth her house -- The parliament at Thebes -- Delilah, now it was dusk -- A quatrain of Ling Tai Fu's -- "Irish" -- By ordeal of justice.
LC: O 3, '23.
PW: O 13, '23.
BLC: London: Sampson Low & Co., [1924].
References: BAL 2293; Bannister, 6; Wetherbee, p. 13-17.

B-1372   _____ The foolish matrons / by Donn Byrne [pseud.]. New York; London: Harper & Brothers, 1920. 383, [1] p.
LC: O 2, '20.
PW: O 16, '20.
BLC: London: Sampson Low & Co., [1923].
References: BAL 2289; Bannister, 3; Wetherbee, p. 6-7.

B-1373   _____ Messer Marco Polo / by Donn Byrne [pseud.]; illustrated by C. B. Falls. New York: The Century Co., 1921. 147 p., front., [3] leaves of plates.
LC: S 22, '21.
PW: O 8, '21.
BLC: London: Sampson Low & Co.,

[1921].
References: BAL 2291; Bannister, 4; Wetherbee, p. 8-11.

B-1374   _____ O'Malley of Shanganagh / by Donn Byrne [pseud.] . . . ; illustrated by John Richard Flanagan. New York; London: The Century Co., [c1925]. 207 p., front., [3] leaves of plates.
LC: Mr 19, '25.
PW: Mr 21, '25.
References: BAL 2296; Bannister, 8; Wetherbee, p. 19-21.

B-1375   _____ Stories without women: (and a few with women) / by Donn Byrne [pseud.]; illustrated. New York: Hearst's International Library Co., 1915. 330 p., front. [Ill by T. D. Skidmore.]
Contents: Biplane no.2 -- Slaves of the gun -- In a cellar -- Bow Sing Low and the two who were thieves -- Donoghu's hour -- An African epic -- A man's game -- Jungle bulls -- The wake -- Out of Egypt -- Black medicine -- Panic -- The story of Suleyman Bey.
LC: N 5, '15.
PW: N 13, '15.
References: BAL 2286; Bannister, 1; Wetherbee, p. 1-5.

B-1376   _____ The strangers' banquet / by Donn Byrne [pseud.]. New York; London: Harper & Brothers Publishers, [1919]. 351, [1] p.
LC: D 11, '19.
PW: D 20, '19.
References: BAL 2288; Bannister, 2; Wetherbee, p. 5-6.

_____ Triangle. In *"Dawgs!": an anthology of stories about them* **(1925), D-184.**

_____ Underseaboat F-33. In *War stories* **(1919), W-94.**

B-1377   _____ The wind bloweth / by Donn Byrne [pseud.] . . . ; illustrated by George Bellows. New York: The Century Co., 1922. 393 p., front., [7] leaves of plates.
LC: O 2, '22.
PW: S 30, '22.
BLC: London: Sampson Low & Co., [1922].
References: BAL 2292; Bannister, 5; Wetherbee, p. 11-13.

B-1378   Byrne, Emma Beaver. The song beneath the keys / by Emma Beaver Byrne. Boston: Roxburgh Publishing Company, Inc., [c1916]. 234 p., front. [Ill. by A. W. Jones.]

B-1379   Byrne, Lawrence. The American ambassador / by Lawrence Byrne. New York: Charles Scribner's Sons, 1917. 301 p.

Byrnes, Francis X. A brief reunion. In *The Tragedy that wins and other short stories* **(1905), T-343.**

_____ The escape of Captain Neville. In *The Tragedy that wins and other short stories* **(1905), T-343.**

B-1380　Byrnes, Joseph (William Joseph). Justus Devine: or, the story of the sappers and the serfs (an allegory of state) / by Joseph Byrnes. Chicago: Byrnes, [c1904]. 60 p.
Unexamined copy: bibliographic data from OCLC, #26829099.

C

C-1　C. J. J. Otis Grey, bachelor / by C. J. J. ; illustrations by E. Jep. Boston: The Mutual Book Company, 1902. 95 p., front., ill.
Contents: Scotchy and I -- Bal-masque at the casino -- Skating carnival -- Ice yachting -- A trip through the tenderloin -- Following the hounds -- Golf -- Yachting -- A quiet poker game -- Cricket -- Whist -- Skiing.
PW: Je 7, '02.

C-2　Cabeen, F. von A. (Francis von Albede). The colonel and the Quaker / by F. von A. Cabeen . . . Philadelphia: Done into a book by Goodman's Sons & Co., 1906. 192 p.
Half-title: *The colonel and the Quaker, or, The return of the forefathers.*

C-3　Cabell, James Branch, 1879-1958. The certain hour (Dizain des poëtes) / by James Branch Cabell . . . New York: Robert M. McBride & Company, 1916. 253 p.　**BGU**
Contents: "Ballad of the double-soul" [poem] -- Auctorial induction -- Belhs cavaliers -- Balthazar's daughter -- Judith's creed -- Concerning Corinna -- Olivia's pottage -- A brown woman -- Pro Honoria -- The irresistible Ogle -- A princess of Grub Street -- The lady of all our dreams -- "Ballad of plagiary" [poem].
LC: O 21, '16.
PW: O 28, '16.
BLC: London: McBride, Nast & Co., 1917.
References: Brewer & Bruccoli 12; Brussel 11; Hall 12; Holt 11.

C-4　____ Chivalry: illustrated / by James Branch Cabell . . . New York; London: Harper & Brothers, 1909. 223, [1] p., col. front., [11] leaves of col. plates.
[Ill. by Howard Pyle, William Hurd Lawrence, and Elizabeth Shippen Greene.]
Contents: Precautional -- The prologue -- The story of the sestina -- The story of the tenson -- The story of the rat-trap -- The story of the choices -- The story of the housewife -- The story of the satraps -- The story of the heritage -- The story of the scabbard -- The story of the navarrese -- The story of the fox-brush -- The epilogue.
LC: O 22, '09.
PW: N 6, '09.
References: Brewer & Bruccoli 6; Brussel 6; Hall 6; Holt 6.
Revised edition: *Chivalry: dizaine des reines*, with an introduction by Burton Roscoe, published, 1921. (Brussel 6a; Holt 23.)

C-5　____ The cords of vanity / by James Branch Cabell. New York: Doubleday, Page & Company, 1909. 341 p., col. front. [Ill. by C. Coles Phillip.]
LC: F 6, '09.
PW: Mr 27, '09.
BLC: London: Doubleday, Page & Co.; New York printed, 1909. Another edition with a different title page: London: Hutchinson & Co.; New York printed, 1909.
References: Brewer & Bruccoli 13; Brussel 5; Hall 13; Holt 5.
Revised edition: *The cords of vanity: a comedy of shirking*, with an introduction by Wilson Follett, published 1920. (Brussel 5a; Holt 16.)

C-6　____ The cream of the jest: a comedy of evasions / by James Branch Cabell . . . New York: Robert M. McBride & Company, 1917. 280 p.
LC: S 21, '17.
PW: O 6, '17.
References: Brewer & Bruccoli 18; Brussel 13; Hall 18; Holt 13.
Revised edition: *The cream of the jest: a comedy of evasions*, with an introduction by Harold Ward, published 1922. (Brussel 13a; Holt 27.)

____ Domnei (1920). See **Cabell, James Branch. *The soul of Melicent* (1913), C-15.**

C-7　____ The eagle's shadow / by James Branch Cabell; illustrated by Will Grefé; decorated by Blanche Ostertag. New York: Doubleday, Page & Company, 1904. 256 p., front., [7] leaves of plates.
PW: O 8, '04.
BLC: London: William Heinemann; New York [printed], 1904. Another issue: London: William Heinemann; Norwood, Mass. printed, 1904.
References: Brewer & Bruccoli 17; Brussel 1; Hall 17; Holt 1.
Revised edition: *The eagles's shadow: a comedy of purse-strings*, with an introduction by Edwin Björkman, published 1923. Includes "An Appendix: About Morals" pp. 253-280. (Brussel 1a; Holt 28.)
LC: O 19, '23.
PW: O 20, '23.

C-8　____ Figures of earth: a comedy of appearances / by James Branch Cabell . . . New York: Robert M. McBride & Co., 1921. 356 p.
LC: Mr 7, '21.
PW: F 26, '21.
BLC: London: John Lane, 1921.
References: Brewer & Bruccoli 2; Brussel 17; Hall 2; Holt 19.

C-9　____ Gallantry: an eighteenth century dizain in ten comedies, with an afterpiece / by James Branch Cabell . . . ; illustrated in color by Howard Pyle. New York; London: Harper & Brothers, 1907. 333, [1] p., col. front., [3] leaves of col. plates.
Contents: The epistle dedicatory -- The prologue -- Simon's hour -- Love at Martinmas -- The casual honeymoon -- The rhyme to Porringer -- Actors all -- April's message -- In the second April -- Heart of gold -- The scapegoats -- The ducal audience -- Love's alumni -- The epilogue.
LC: O 10, '07.
PW: O 26, '07.
References: Brewer & Bruccoli 10; Brussel 4; Hall 10; Holt 4.
Revised edition: *Gallantry: dizain de têtes galantes*, with introduction by Louis Untermeyer, published 1922. (Brussel 4a; Holt 26.)

C-10　____ The high place: a comedy of disenchantment / by James Branch Cabell; with illustrations and decorations by Frank C. Papé. New York: Robert

M. McBride & Company, 1923. 312 p., front., [7] leaves of plates.
LC: D 19, '23.
PW: D 8, '23.
BLC: London: John Lane, 1923.
References: Brewer & Bruccoli 9; Brussel 22; Hall 9; Holt 29.

C-11   The judging of Jurgen / by James Branch Cabell. Chicago: The Bookfellows, 1920. 13, [1] p.
References: Brewer & Bruccoli 42; Brussel 16; Hall 7a; Holt 17.

C-12   Jurgen: a comedy of justice / by James Branch Cabell . . . New York: Robert M. McBride & Co., 1919. 368 p.
LC: S 30, '19.
PW: S 27, '19.
BLC: London: John Lane, 1921.
References: Brewer & Bruccoli 7; Brussell 15; Hall 7; Holt 15.

C-13   The line of love / by James Branch Cabell; illustrated in color by Howard Pyle . . . New York; London: Harper & Brothers, 1905. 290, [1] p., col. front., [9] leaves of col. plates. Illustrated end papers.
Contents: Epistle dedicatory -- The episode called Adhelmar at Puysange -- The episode called love-letters of Falstaff -- The episode called "Sweet Adelais" -- The episode called in necessity's mortar -- The episode called the castle of content -- The episode called in Ursula's garden -- Envoi.
PW: O 14, '05.
References: Brewer & Bruccoli 8; Brussel 2; Hall 8; Holt 2.
Revised ed.: *The line of love: dizain des mariages*; with an introduction by H. L. Mencken . . . New York: Robert M. McBride & Company, 1921. 261 p.
Contents: Epistle dedicatory -- The episode called the wedding jest -- The episode called Adhelmar Puysange -- The episode called love-letters of Falstaff -- The episode called "Sweet Adelais" -- The episode called in necessity's mortar -- The episode called the castle of content -- The episode called in Ursula's garden -- The episode called porcelain cups -- The envoi called semper idem.
LC: N 25, '21.
PW: N 26, '21.
References: Brussel 2a; Hall 8; Holt 22.

     Procelain cups. In *Prize stories of 1919 (1920), P-617.*

C-14   The rivet in grandfather's neck: a comedy of limitations / by James Branch Cabell . . . New York: Robert M. McBride & Company, 1915. 368 p.
Contents: Propinquity -- Renascence -- Tertius -- Appreciation -- Souvenir -- Byways -- Yoked -- Harvest -- Relics -- Imprimis.
LC: O 16, '15.
PW: O 23, '15.
BLC: London; New York: McBride, Nast & Co.; printed in U. S. A., 1916.
References: Brewer & Bruccoli 16; Brussel 9; Hall

16; Holt 9.

C-15   The soul of Melicent / by James Branch Cabell; illustrated in colour by Howard Pyle. New York: Frederick A. Stokes Company, [c1913]. 216 p., col. front., [3] leaves of col. plates. **MIA**
LC: S 15, '13.
PW: S 27, '13.
References: Brewer & Bruccoli 5; Brussel 8; Hall 5; Holt 8.
Revised edition: *Domnei: a comedy of woman-worship, 1920.* (Brussel 8a; Hall 5a; Holt 18.)
LC: N 10, '20.
PW: N 27, '20.

     The wedding-jest. In *The best short stories of 1919 and the yearbook of the American short story (1920), B-564.*

Cable, George Washington, 1844-1925. The angel of the Lord. In *A house party: an account of stories told at a gathering of famous American authors (1901), H-903.*

C-16   Bylow Hill / by George W. Cable; with illustrations in color by F. C. Yohn. New York: Charles Scribner's Sons, 1902. 215 p., col. front., [5] leaves of col. plates.
LC: My 20, '02.
PW: Je 7, '02.
BLC: London: Hodder & Stoughton; New York printed, 1902.
References: BAL 2371.

C-17   The cavalier / by George W. Cable; with illustrations by Howard Chandler Christy. New York: Charles Scribner's Sons, 1901. 311 p., front., [7] leaves of plates.
LC: O 4, '01.
PW: O 12, '01.
BLC: London: John Murray, 1901.
References: BAL 2368.

C-18   The flower of the Chapdelaines / by George W. Cable; with frontispiece by F. C. Yohn. New York: Charles Scribner's Sons, 1918. 339 p., col. front.
LC: Ap 4, '18.
PW: Ap 6, '18.
BLC: London: W. Collins, Sons & Co., [1918].
References: BAL 2384.

C-19   Gideon's band: a tale of the Mississippi / By George W. Cable; illustrated by F. C. Yohn. New York: Charles Scribner's Sons, 1914. 500 p., col. front., [3] leaves of col. plates.
LC: S 23, '14.
PW: S 26, '14.
References: BAL 2381.

C-20   ____ Kincaid's battery / by George W. Cable; illustrated by Alonzo Kimball. New York: Charles Scribner's Sons, 1908. 396 p., col. front., [6] leaves of plates.
LC: N 9, '08.
PW: N 21, '08.
BLC: London: Hodder & Stoughton; New York printed, 1909.
References: BAL 2376.

C-21   ____ Lovers of Louisiana (to-day) / by George W. Cable. New York: Charles Scribner's Sons, 1918. 351 p.
LC: Ag 31, '18.
PW: Ag 31, '18.
References: BAL 2385.

     ____ Père Raphaël. <u>See</u> Cable, George **Washington, 1844-1925. *"Posson Jone" and Père Raphaël* (1909), C-22.**

C-22   ____ "Posson Jone" and Père Raphaël: with a new word setting forth how and why the two tales are one / by George W. Cable; illustrated by Stanley M. Arthurs. New York: Charles Scribner's Sons, 1909. 162 p., incl. 2 leaves of col. plates, [6] leaves of col. plates.
BAL 2370 records private printing (4 copies) of *Père Raphaël*, 1901.
LC: O 27, '09.
PW: N 6, '09.
References: BAL 2377.

C-23   Cabot, Oliver. The man without a shadow / by Oliver Cabot; illustrated. New York: D. Appleton and Company, 1909. 339, [1] p., front., [3] leaves of plates. [Ill. by John Cassel.]
LC: Ap 23, '09.
PW: Ap 24, '09.

C-24   Caden, Arthur Brooke. An imaginary story / by Arthur Brooke Caden. Chicago: [s. n.], 1903. 239 p.
Unexamined copy: bibliographic data from OCLC, #26829177.

C-25   Cadmus, *pseud.* The island of sheep / by Cadmus [pseud.] and Harmonia [pseud.]. Boston; New York: Houghton Mifflin Company, 1920. 170 p.
LC: Mr 29, '20.
PW: Ap 3, '20.

C-26   Cady, Jay. The moving of the waters: a novel / by Jay Cady; with illustrations by H. Richard Boehm. New York: The John McBride Company, 1909. 318 p., col. front., [4] leaves of col. plates.
LC: O 21, '09.
PW: N 13, '09.

C-27   ____ The stake: a story of the New England coast / by Jay Cady. Philadelphia: George W. Jacobs & Company, [1912]. 331 p., col. front. [Ill. by Elenore Plaisted Abbott.]
LC: Mr 21, '12.
PW: Ap 6, '12.

C-28   Cahan, Abraham, 1860-1951. The rise of David Levinsky: a novel / by Abraham Cahan. New York; London: Harper & Brothers, [1917]. 529, [1] p.
LC: S 11, '17.

C-29   ____ The white terror and the red: a novel of revolutionary Russia / By A. Cahan. New York: A. S. Barnes & Company, 1905. 430 p.
PW: F 25, '05.
BLC: London: Hodder & Stoughton, 1905.

C-30   Cahill, James Semple. Behind the scenes of destiny / by James Semple Cahill. Philadelphia: Dorrance & Company, [c1924]. 293 p.
LC: My 28, '24.

     Cain, George M. A. One "Hail Mary". <u>In</u> *The friendly little house: and other stories* (1910), **F-432.**

C-31   ____ The perfect nurse / George M. A. Cain. New York: The Winthrop Press, c1914. 31, [1] p., col. ill.
Previously published in Munsey's magazine.
LC: O 23, '14.

     ____ The test. <u>In</u> *The friendly little house: and other stories* (1910), **F-432.**

C-32   Caldwell, George W. (George Walter), b. 1866. The Wizzywab / by George W. Caldwell . . . San Francisco, Cal.: Published by Phillips & Van Orden Co., [c1919]. 120 p., photo. front. (port.), ill.
LC: D 24, '19.

C-33   Caldwell, J. F. J. (James Fitz James). The stranger / by J. F. J. Caldwell. New York: The Neale Publishing Company, 1907. 520 p.
LC: F 28, '07.

C-34   Caldwell, W. W. (Willie Walker), 1860-1946. Donald McElroy, Scotch Irishman / by W. W. Caldwell; illustrated by Frank T. Merrill. Philadelphia: George W. Jacobs & Company, [c1918]. 351 p., front., [3] leaves of plates.
LC: O 19, '18.
PW: O 26, '18.

C-35   Caldwell, William A. (William Alexander), 1862-1903. Ten thousand on a life; a novel / by William A. Caldwell, M. D. New York; Washington: The Neale Publishing Company, 1905. 187 p., front. (port.).
Unexamined copy: bibliographic data from NUC.
PW: Je 3, '05.

C-36   Calhoun, Alice J. When yellow jasmine blooms: a story of the southland / by Alice J. Calhoun. New York; Washington: The Neale Publishing Company, 1904. 272 p.   **NDO**
PW: Je 3, '05.

C-37   Calhoun, Charles W. --Until proven guilty / by Charles W. Calhoun. San Francisco; Berkeley, Calif.: Western Publishing Company, 1917. 277 p.
LC: My 21, '17.

C-38 Calhoun, Dorothy Donnell. Blue gingham folks / by Dorothy Donnell Calhoun. New York; Cincinnati: The Abingdon Press, [c1915]. 221 p., front. ill. [Ill. by Frank R. Southard.]
LC: D 8, '15.

C-39 Calhoun, Frances Boyd, 1867-1909. Miss Minerva and William Green Hill / By Frances Boyd Calhoun; illustrated by Angus MacDonall. Chicago: The Reilly and Britton Co., 1909. 212 p., front., ill.
LC: F 1, '09.

C-40 California story book. Berkeley, California: Published by the English Club of the University of California, 1909. 195 p., photo. front.
Contents: Mater Gloria [poem] / Isabel McReynolds Gray, '07 -- The passing of Cock-eye Blacklock / Frank Norris, '94 -- Yesterday - a toast / Sara Ashby, '10 -- The idealist / James Hopper, '98 -- The history of Chop-Suey and Fan Tan / Gurden Edwards, '07 -- Phil / Christina Krysto, '09 -- The record quarter / Grace Torrey, '97 -- Values / Marguerite Ogden, '10 -- All in the play / Richard Walton Tully, '01 -- Steve / Francis Steel, '10 -- Buck Du Spain / Helen Duncan Queen, '07 -- Bernice, Patrice and Clarice / Elizabeth F. Young, '10 -- Billy-Too / Abby L. Waterman, '04 -- The spotted dawg / Eleanor Gates, '01.
LC: D 27, '09.

C-41 Calkins, Franklin Welles, 1857-1928. My host the enemy and other tales: sketches of life and adventure on the border line of the West / by Franklin Welles Calkins. Chicago; New York; Toronto: Fleming H. Revell Company, 1901. 302 p., front., [14] leaves of plates. [Some ill. by W. A. McCullough and William F. Stecher.]
Contents: A pair of Chapparejos -- Our celebration at Two-Owe-Tee -- The picked seven at Hat-Band -- The Owl Creek bighorn -- California Joe's partner -- The exploit of Antoine and Pierre -- Sandvig and St. Xavier -- The bullet-maker's strategy -- An adventure with a cougar -- "Go": an episode of invasion -- Those Gordon girls -- My host the enemy -- A pioneer woman's peril -- Tauk-Sok and Ook-Jook -- The professor's gun -- Michaud's exploit -- The blind cougar (adapted) -- Our uninvited guest -- Beaupre's tale of Bolerat -- A trapper's protégés -- The trader's dilemma -- In the scrogs.

C-42 _____ Two wilderness voyagers: a true tale of Indian life / by Franklin Welles Calkins. Chicago; New York; Toronto: Fleming H. Revell Company, 1902. 359 p.

C-43 _____ The wooing of Tokala: an intimate tale of the wild life of the American Indian drawn from camp and trail / by Franklin Welles Calkins . . . New York; Chicago; Toronto; London; Edinburgh: Fleming H. Revell Company, [c1907]. 340 p.
LC: My 1, '07.

C-44 Calkins, Harvey Reeves, 1866-1941. The centenary at Old first / by Harvey Reeves Calkins. New York; Cincinnati: The Methodist Book Concern, [c1919]. 361 p., front., [2] leaves of plates.
LC: Je 14, '19.

C-45 _____ Ganga Dass: a tale of Hindustan / by Harvey Reeves Calkins. New York; Cincinnati: The Abingdon Press, [c1917]. 79 p.
LC: F 24, '17.

C-46 _____ The victory of Mary Christopher: a story of to-morrow / by Harvey Reeves Calkins . . . Cincinnati: Jennings and Graham; New York: Eaton

and Mains, [190-?]. 163 p.   **EXS**
PW: N 1 '02.

C-47 Call, William Timothy, 1856-1917. Blackmail: an episode in finesse / by William Timothy Call. Brooklyn, N. Y.: W. T. Call, 1915. 57 p.   **BGU**
LC: Ag 24, '15.

C-48 Callahan, Charles Edward, 1845-1917. Fogg's ferry: a thrilling novel / by C. E. Callahan from his drama of the same name; illustrated. Chicago: Laird & Lee, [1902]. 331 p., front., ill. [Ill. by John C. Gilbert.]   **DLC**
PW: Mr 15, '02.

C-49 Callaway, Frances Bennett, d. 1905. Bee's flower children / by Frances Bennett Callaway; illustrations by Caroline B. Shay. New York; Boston; Chicago: American Tract Society, [c1905]. 254 p., photo. front., [12] leaves of photo. plates.   **DLC**
PW: S 30, '05.

C-50 Called to the colors: and other stories. West Medford, Mass.: Christian Women's Peace Movement, [c1915]. 198, [1] p.   **OSU, COD**
Contents: Called to the colors / Caroline A. Mason -- The white Zeppelin / Eleanor Baldwin -- On the field of honor / Ruth M. Rice -- Companions of the desert / Elizabeth Perkins -- The Red cross lady / Mary S. Stover -- The king's code / C. A. Miles -- The iron cross / J. C. Alvord.
LC: O 26, '15.

C-51 Callender, Romaine, 1857-1930. The prison-flower: a romance of the consulate and empire / Romaine Callender. Boston: Richard G. Badger, [c1912]. (Boston: The Gorham Press). 264 p., front.
"The prison-flower is partly founded on incidents in a tale from the French of X. B. Saintine."
LC: My 3, '12.

C-52 Calver, Vic. Romances of Mobile / issued by Louisville & Nashville R. R. [s. l.]: Issued by Louisville & Nashville R. R., [c1921]. 63, [1] p., ill. (some col., some photo.), map.
Contents: Mobile, the heart of the storied south -- The shining towers of El Dorado -- In the shadow of Fort St. Louis -- In the king's name -- The heart of Tuscaloosa -- Madame La Vergne smiles -- The last slave -- An epic of the sea -- Modern Mobile -- The Gulf Coast -- En route to Mobile.

C-53 Calvert, Elizabeth. The two houses / by Elizabeth Calvert. Boston: The Roxburgh Publishing Company Inc., [c1918]. 284 p.
LC: O 5, '18.

C-54 Calvin, Emily Ruth. A Jewish carol and The insuperable barrier / by Emily Ruth Calvin; with preface by Emil G. Hirsch. Chicago: Westminster Publishing Company, 1902. 56 p., photo. front. (port.), [3] leaves of plates.   **VYL**
"Two brief sketches written with a view of illustrating some phases of Jewish life."

C-55 Camden, John. The hundredth acre / by John Camden. Boston: Herbert B. Turner & Co., 1905. 321 p., front.
PW: Je 3, '05.
BLC: London: Ward, Lock & Co., 1905.

C-56   Cameron, Margaret, 1867-1947. The bachelor and the baby / by Margaret Cameron; illustrated. New York; London: Harper & Brothers, 1908. 42 p., front., [3] leaves of plates. [Ill. by W. D. Stevens.]
LC: O 2, '08.
PW: O 10, '08.

C-57   ____ The cat and the canary / by Margaret Cameron; illustrations by W. D. Stevens, decorations by Bertha Stuart. New York; London: Harper & Brothers, 1908. 62 p., front., [5] leaves of plates.
LC: F 12, '08.
PW: F 22, '08.

C-58   ____ The Golden rule Dollivers / by Margaret Cameron; illustrated by May Wilson Preston. New York; London: Harper & Brothers, 1913. 187, [1] p., col. front., [7] leaves of col. plates.
LC: S 13, '13.
PW: S 27, '13.

C-59   ____ The involuntary chaperon / by Margaret Cameron. New York; London: Harper & Brothers, 1909. 347, [1] p., front., [16] leaves of plates, map. [Ill. by H. Richard Boehm.]
LC: O 9, '09.
PW: O 23, '09.

C-60   ____ Johndover / by Margaret Cameron. New York; London: Harper & Brothers, [c1924]. 483 p.
LC: Ap 21, '24.
PW: Ap 19, '24.

C-61   ____ The pretender person / by Margaret Cameron; illustrated. New York; London: Harper & Brothers, 1911. 382, [1] p., front., [17] leaves of plates, double map.
LC: O 21, '11.

C-62   ____ Tangles: tales of some droll predicaments / by Margaret Cameron . . . ; illustrated. New York; London: Harper & Brothers, 1912. 367, [1] p., front., [7] leaves of plates. [Ill. by W. D. Stevens and Will Foster.]   **OBE**
Contents: "Who laughs last" -- The woman and the law -- The price of the past participle -- The thing that couldn't -- The pipes o' Pan -- The dénouement -- "The little white hin" -- The ultimate moment -- Wainwright and the little gods -- A chance Samaritan -- The mighty trifle -- The way to the wedding -- When the turtle turned loose -- Who killed Cock Robin? -- The forlorn hope.
LC: O 12, '12.
PW: O 19, '12.

C-63   Cameron, Myrtle. White supremacy / by Myrtle Cameron. Elliott, Illinois: Published by the author, 1925. 36 p.
LC: S 19, '25.

C-64   Camp, Wadsworth, 1879-1936. The abandoned room / by Wadsworth Camp . . . ; illustrated by Robert McCaig. Garden City, New York: Doubleday, Page & Company, 1917. 348 p., front., [3] leaves of plates.
LC: O 31, '17.
PW: O 27, '17.
BLC: London: Jarrolds, [1919].

C-65   ____ The barbarian / by Wadsworth Camp; frontispiece by John Lagatta. Garden City, N. Y.: Doubleday, Page & Company, 1925. 362 p., front.
LC: Mr 23, '25.
PW: F 28, '25.
BLC: London: William Heinemann; printed in U. S. A., 1925.

C-66   ____ The communicating door / by Wadsworth Camp; frontispiece by M. Leone Bracker. Garden City, N. Y.: Doubleday, Page & Company, 1923. 297 p., front.
Contents: The communicating door -- Hate -- The dangerous tavern -- The haunted house -- Defiance -- Open evidence -- The obscure move.
LC: My 28, '23.
PW: Ap 4, '25.

    ____ The draw-keeper. In *The Grim thirteen* **(1917), G-537.**

C-67   ____ The gray mask / by Wadsworth Camp . . . ; frontispiece by Walter De Maris. Garden City, New York: Doubleday, Page & Company, 1920. 301, [1] p., front.
LC: F 5, '20.
PW: F 7, '20.

C-68   ____ The guarded heights / by Wadsworth Camp; frontispiece by C. D. Mitchell. Garden City, N. Y.; Toronto: Doubleday, Page & Company, 1921. 363, [1] p., front.
LC: Ap 29, '21.
PW: Ap 2, '21.

C-69   ____ The hidden road / by Wadsworth Camp; frontispiece by C. Allan Gilbert. Garden City, N. Y.; Toronto: Doubleday, Page & Company, 1922. 334 p., front.
LC: My 19, '22.
PW: My 6, '22.

C-70   ____ The house of fear / by Wadsworth Camp; illustrated by Arthur I. Keller. Garden City, N. Y.: Doubleday, Page & Company, 1916. 342 p., front., [3] leaves of plates.
LC: S 8, '16.
PW: S 9, '16.
BLC: London: Hodder & Stoughton; Garden City printed, [1917].

    ____ The signal tower. In *The best short stories of 1920 and the yearbook of the American short story* **(1921), B-565.**

C-71   ____ Sinister Island / by Charles Wadsworth Camp; illustrated by W. C. Dexter. New York: Dodd, Mead & Company, 1915, [c1914]. 309 p., front., [4] leaves of plates.
LC: Mr 11, '15.
PW: Mr 13, '15.

    Campbell, Clara. A Hulings Thanksgiving dinner. In *Allegheny stories* **(1902), A-142.**

C-72 Campbell, Daisy Rhodes, b. 1845. The fiddling girl: the story of Virginia Hammond / by Daisy Rhodes Campbell; illustrated by John Goss. Boston: The Page Company, 1914. 304 p., front., [5] leaves of plates.
LC: Ap 6, '14.
PW: Ap 11, '14.

C-73 ____ The proving of Virginia / by Daisy Rhodes Campbell . . . ; illustrated by John Goss. Boston: The Page Company, 1915. 340 p., front., [5] leaves of plates.   **OSU, AKU**
LC: Ap 5, '15.

C-74 ____ The violin lady / by Daisy Rhodes Campbell . . . ; illustrated by John Goss. Boston: The Page Company, 1916. 322 p., col. front., [6] leaves of plates.
LC: F 24, '16.
PW: Mr 25, '16.

C-75 Campbell, Emma C. The rose parlor / by Mrs. Emma C. Campbell. Cincinnati [Ohio]: Monfort & Company, 1916. 275 p.

C-76 Campbell, Evelyn. The knight of lonely land / by Evelyn Campbell; with frontispiece by George W. Gage. Boston: Little, Brown, and Company, 1921. 302 p., front.
LC: Mr 24, '21.
PW: Ap 2, '21.

C-77 ____ The threshold: a novel / by Evelyn Campbell. New York: Robert M. McBride & Company, 1921. 309 p.
LC: N 18, '21.
PW: D 3, '21.

C-78 Campbell, Harriette Russell, b. 1883. Is it enough?: a romance of musical life / by Harriette Russell Campbell. New York; London: Harper & Brothers Publishers, 1913. 264, [1] p., front. [Ill. by Armand Both.]
LC: Je 14, '13.
PW: Je 21, '13.

C-79 Campbell, Helen, 1839-1918. Ballantyne: a novel / by Helen Campbell. Boston: Little, Brown and Company, 1901. 361 p.
PW: Ap 20, '01.

Campbell, Oscar James, Jr., jt. ed. See *A book of narratives* (1917), **B-734.**

C-80 Campbell, Scott, *pseud.* Below the dead-line / by Scott Campbell [pseud.]. New York: G. W. Dillingham Company, [1906]. 313 p.
Contents: The case of the vanished bonds -- The case of Dickson's diamonds -- The case of the stolen cipher -- The case of the man who vanished -- The case of the big finger -- The case of the banker's double -- The case of the missing magnate -- The case of the under-secretary -- The case of the boss mason -- The case of the vacant office -- The case of the convict code -- The case of the tan glove.

C-81 Campbell, W. P. (William Parker), 1843-1924. Neenie: the Coffeyman's daughter / by W. P. Campbell. Waukomis, Oklahoma: Address the

Hornet, c1907. 56, [1] p.   **OKD**
LC: O 14, '07.

C-82 Campbell, William Carey. A Colorado colonel: and other sketches / by William Carey Campbell. Topeka, Kan.: Crane & Company, 1901. 402 p., front., ill., music.
Contents: A Colorado colonel -- The bucking bronco -- "Quien sabe?" -- The eagle and the jack-rabbit -- A Cat Creek conversion -- The backsliding at Cat Creek -- In Arizona -- Soda Springs Smith -- Governor for five minutes -- Pike's Peak by moonlight -- Colonel Jackson of Colorado -- The medicine-man -- The passing of Jack Thompson -- The opening of the Cherokee Strip -- Christmas on the Huerfano -- Heap big injun -- Fables of the desert -- A Kansas emigrant -- At the Bright Angel Trail -- The cow-catcher.
PW: F 8, '02.

Canby, Henry Seidel, 1878-1961. The best bait for mosquitos. In *Representative short stories* (1917), **R-176.**

____ Business is business. In *Atlantic narratives; first series* (1918), **A-360.**

C-83 ____ Our house / by Henry Seidel Canby. New York: The Macmillan Company, 1919. 308 p.
LC: My 7, '19.
PW: My 10, '19.

C-84 Candee, Helen Churchill, 1861-1949. An Oklahoma romance / by Helen Churchill Candee. New York: The Century Co., 1901. 331 p.

C-85 Candler, Pat. Testore: the romance of an Italian fiddle-maker / by Pat Candler. New York: E. P. Dutton & Company, 1916. 264 p., front. [Ill. by A. G. Holman.]
Printed in Great Britain by Richard Clay & Sons, Limited.
BLC: London; Toronto: J. M. Dent & Sons, 1916.

C-86 Canfield, Chauncey L., 1843-1909. The city of six / by Chauncey L. Canfield; with five illustrations by John W. Norton. Chicago: A. C. McClurg & Co., 1910. 365, [1] p., front., [4] leaves of plates, map.
LC: Mr 21, '10.
PW: Ap 9, '10.

C-87 ____ The diary of a forty-niner / edited by Chauncey L. Canfield. New York; San Francisco: Morgan Shepard Company, 1906. 231 p., front., map.
LC: O 31, '06.

C-88 Canfield, Dorothy, 1879-1958. The bent twig / by Dorothy Canfield. New York: Henry Holt and Company, 1915. 480 p.   **DEF**
LC: N 9, '15.
PW: O 30, '15.
BLC: London: Constable and Co., 1916.

C-89 ____ The brimming cup / by Dorothy Canfield. New York: Harcourt, Brace and Company, 1921. 409 p.
LC: Mr 18, '21.
PW: Mr 5, '21.
BLC: London: Jonathan Cape, 1921.

_____ The cage. In *More aces* (1925), M-962.

C-90 _____ The day of glory / by Dorothy Canfield. New York: Henry Holt and Company, 1919. 149 p.
Contents: On the edge -- France's fighting woman doctor -- Lourdes -- Some confused impressions -- "It is rather for us to be here dedicated" -- The day of glory.
LC: Ap 21, '19.
PW: Ap 12, '19.

_____ Dr. Burke's cure. In **Conrad, Joseph.** *Il conte* (1925), C-697.

_____, jt. aut. *Fellow captains* (1916). See **Cleghorn, Sarah Norcliffe, 1876-1959, jt. aut., C-477.**

C-91 _____ Gunhild: a Norwegian-American episode / by Dorothy Canfield. New York: Henry Holt and Company, 1907. 342 p.
LC: O 12, '07.
PW: O 26, '07.

_____ The heyday of the blood. In *Short stories* (1925), S-460.

C-92 _____ Hillsboro people / by Dorothy Canfield; with occasional Vermont verses, by Sarah N. Cleghorn. New York: Henry Holt and Company, 1915. 346 p.
LC: Ap 10,'15.
PW: Ap 3, '15.

C-93 _____ Home fires in France / by Dorothy Canfield. New York: Henry Holt and Company, 1918. 306 p.
Contents: Notes from a French village in the war zone -- The permissionaire -- Vignettes from life at the rear -- A fair exchange -- The refugee -- A little Kansas leaven -- Eyes for the blind -- The first time after -- Hats -- A honeymoon . . . Vive l'Amérique! -- La pharmacienne.
LC: O 4, '18.
PW: S 14, '18.
BLC: London: Constable and Co., 1919.

C-94 _____ The home-maker / by Dorothy Canfield. New York: Harcourt, Brace and Company, [c1924]. 320 p.
LC: My 23, '24.
PW: My 17, '24.
BLC: London: Jonathan Cape, 1924.

C-95 _____ Raw material / by Dorothy Canfield. New York: Harcourt, Brace and Company, [c1923]. 302 p.
LC: Ag 25, '23.
PW: Ag 18, '23.

C-96 _____ The real motive / by Dorothy Canfield; with three poems by Sarah N. Cleghorn. New York: Henry Holt and Company, 1916. 334 p.
Contents: But this is also everlasting life [poem] -- The pragmatist -- The conviction of sin -- An April masque -- A sleep and a forgetting -- The lookout [poem] -- A good fight and the faith kept -- From across the hall -- Vignettes from a life of two months -- An academic question -- Fortune and the fifth card -- The city of refuge -- An untold story -- A thread without a knot -- There was a moon, there was a star [poem] -- The great refusal -- The sick physician.
LC: My 25, '16.
PW: My 27, '16.

BLC: London: Constable & Co.; Rahway, N. J. [printed], 1916.

C-97 _____ Rough-hewn / by Dorothy Canfield. New York: Harcourt, Brace and Company, [c1922]. 504 p.
LC: O 5, '22.
PW: O 28, '22.
BLC: London: Jonathan Cape, 1923.

C-98 _____ The secret of serenity / by Dorothy Canfield. Illustrations by Falls. [s. n., c1908] [16] p., ill.
VTU

C-99 _____ The squirrel-cage / by Dorothy Canfield; with illustrations by John Alonzo Williams. New York: Henry Holt and Company, 1912. 371 p., front., [3] leaves of plates.
LC: Ap 6, '12.
PW: Ap 6, '12.

_____, contributor. See *The sturdy oak* (1917), **S-1101.**

_____ A thread without a knot. See *Short stories of various types* (1920), **S-465.**

_____ What "really" happened. In *Aces* (1924), **A-42.**

C-100 Canfield, H. S. (Henry Spofford), b. 1858. Fergy the guide, and his moral and instructive lies about beasts, birds, and fishes / by H. S. Canfield; with illustrations by Albert D. Blashfield. New York: Henry Holt and Company, 1904. 342 p., ill. Unexamined copy: bibliographic data from NUC.
PW: O 1, '04.
BLC: London: David Nutt, 1905.

C-101 _____ A paladin in khaki / by H. S. Canfield. Chicago: Jamieson-Higgins Co., 1901. 322 p.

C-102 Canfield, William W. (William Walker), 1855-1937. Along the way / by William W. Canfield . . . New York: R. F. Fenno & Company, [c1909]. 329 p., col. front., [4] leaves of col. plates. [Ill. by Sydney K. Hartman.]
LC: S 2, '09.

C-103 _____ At Seneca Castle / William W. Canfield; illustrated by G. A. Harker. New York: E. P. Dutton & Company, [c1912]. 274 p., front., [3] leaves of plates.
LC: Jl 10, '12.

C-104 _____ The sign above the door / by William W. Canfield. Philadelphia: The Jewish Publication Society of America, 1912. 325, [1] p..
LC: Jl 3, '12.
PW: Jl 6, '12.

C-105 _____ The spotter: a romance of the oil region / by William W. Canfield . . . New York: R. F. Fenno & Company, [c1907]. 360 p.
LC: Ag 27, '07.
PW: S 14, '07.

Cannon, Alanson B. <u>See</u> **Fontaine, Felix, pseud.**

C-106   Canty, Charlotte, b. 1875. The whimsy girl / by Charlotte Canty; frontispiece by Robert W. Amick. New York: Dodd, Mead and Company, 1913. 180 p., front.
LC: O 2, '13.

C-107   Capwell, Irene Stoddard, b. 1854. Mrs. Alderman Casey / by Irene Stoddard Capwell; drawings by W. Herbert Dunton. New York: R. F. Fenno & Company, [c1905]. 175 p., col. front., [4] leaves of col. plates.
PW: S 30, '05.

Carden, W. Thomas. <u>See</u> **Noodle, Major Tom, pseud.**

C-108   Carew, Roger M., b. 1873, *pseud.* The contralto / Roger M. Carew [pseud.]. Boston: Richard G. Badger, [c1912]. (Boston: The Gorham Press). 339 p.
LC: Ag 6, '12.
PW: Ag 10, '12.

Carey, Charles. <u>See</u> **Waddel, Charles Carey, 1868-1930.**

C-109   Carey, George W. (George Washington), 1845-1924. Road to the moon: a great occult story / by Dr. George W. Carey. Los Angeles, Cal.: The Chemistry of Life Co., [1924]. 24 p.
"This story contains the omitted part of the original manuscript."

C-110   Carhart, Alfreda Post. Masoud the Bedouin / by Alfreda Post Carhart; illustrated by Jessie Gillespie. New York: Missionary Education Movement of the United States and Canada, 1915. 249 p., front., [5] leaves of plates.
Contents: Preface -- The way of them that dwell in tents: Masoud the Bedouin -- Honor in the desert -- The mourning for Sigr. -- Springs in a dry land: For the sake of Sheffaka -- The mark of the Cross -- Beshara, the Bearer of tidings -- Glances through the lattice: A life behind a veil -- The Child of a vow -- Haijeh Fatmeh the wise -- Ensigns upon the mountains: A Lebanon Rachel -- A village iconoclast -- Hid treasure -- Nimr's kussis -- Where East and West meet: The night at Ibil -- Luciyeh of the brave heart -- Transplanted children.
LC: S 15, '15.

C-111   Carleton, Marjorie Chalmers. Their dusty hands / by Marjorie Chalmers Carleton. Boston: B. J. Brimmer Company, 1924. 311 p.
LC: F 5, '25.
PW: D 13, '24.

C-112   Carleton, Monroe Guy, 1833-1918. Autobiography of a disembodied soul / by Monroe Guy Carleton; illustrated. New York: Vreeland Publishing Company, [1910, c1907]. 293 p., front., [5] leaves of plates. [Ill. by I. B. Beals.]
LC: Jl 7, '10.

C-113   Carleton, R. W. Will o' the wisp: a romance of the Mississippi / by R. W. Carleton. Chicago: Scroll Publishing Company, 1901. 206 p., incl. front., [4] leaves of plates.
PW: Ag 23, '02.

Carleton, William, pseud. <u>See</u> **Bartlett, Frederick Orin, b. 1876.**

C-114   Carlin, George A. He who gets slapped: a novel / by George A. Carlin; adapted from Leonid Andreyev's drama and the Victor Seastrom photoplay; illustrated with scenes from the photoplay, a Metro-Goldwyn-Mayer production. New York: Grosset and Dunlap, [c1925]. 273 p., photo. front., [7] leaves of photo. plates.
PW: Ag 15, '25.

C-115   Carling, George, b. 1852, *pseud.* Richard Elliott, financier / by George Carling [pseud.]; illustrated by Henry S. Watson. Boston: L. C. Page & Company, 1906. 348 p., front., [6] leaves of plates.
LC: S 28, '06.

C-116   Carling, John R. By Neva's waters: being an episode in the secret history of Alexander the First, Czar of all the Russias / by John R. Carling. Boston: Little, Brown and Company, 1907. 319 p., front., [2] leaves of plates. [Ill. by Howard Somerville.]
LC: Je 14, '07; O 17, '07.
PW: O 26, '07.
BLC: London: Ward, Lock & Co., 1908.

C-117   ____ The doomed city / by John R. Carling; illustrations by A. Forestier. New York: Edward J. Clode, [c1910]. 376 p., front., [2] leaves of plates.
LC: Jl 28, '10.
PW: S 24, '10.
BLC: London: Ward, Lock & Co., 1910.

C-118   ____ The shadow of the czar / by John R. Carling; illustrated. Boston: Little, Brown and Company, 1902. 419 p., front., [1] leaf of plates. [Ill. by Edward Read.]
PW: O 4, '02.
BLC: London: Ward, Lock & Co., 1902.

C-119   ____ The viking's skull / by John R. Carling. Boston: Little, Brown and Company, 1904. 349 p., front., [3] leaves of plates. [Ill. by Cyrus Cuneo.]
PW: Mr 26, '04.
BLC: London: Ward, Lock & Co., 1904.

C-120   ____ The weird picture / by John R. Carling . . . ; illustrated by Cyrus Cuneo. Boston: Little, Brown and Company, 1905. 283 p., front., [3] leaves of plates.
PW: My 20, '05.
BLC: London: Ward, Lock & Co., 1905.

C-121   Carlsen, C. L. (Carl Laurence), b. 1880. The son of Pio / C. L. Carlsen. New York: E. P. Dutton & Company, [c1919]. 279 p.
LC: Mr 24, '19.
PW: Ap 5, '19.

C-122   ____ The taming of Calinga / by C. L. Carlsen. New York: E. P. Dutton & Company, [c1916]. 239 p.
LC: N 4, '16.
PW: N 11, '16.

C-123   Carman, Albert R. (Albert Richardson), 1865-1939.
The pensionnaires: the story of an American girl who
took a voice to Europe and found-many things.
Boston: Herbert B. Turner & Co., 1903. 314 p.

C-124   Carman, Dorothy Walworth, 1900-1953. Faith of our
fathers / by Dorothy Walworth Carman. New York;
London: Harper & Brothers, 1925. 311 p.
PW: Mr 7, '25.

Carman, Kathleen. The debt. In *Atlantic narratives*;
2nd series (1918), A-361.

C-125   Carmichael, Ida. Beware! or, Irma's life. Houston,
Tex.: The author, [1901]. 183 p., front. (port.).
Unexamined copy: bibliographic data from NUC.

C-126   Carothers, Rose. Mother's Walter and Walter's
mother: a story from incidents of real life / by Mrs.
Rose Carothers. [Toledo, Oh.: The Studio Press
Company], c1906. 123 p., front. (port.), [2] leaves
of plates, photo. ill.
LC: D 24, '06.

C-127   Carpenter, Benjamin Fowler. The kingdom of gold:
dedicated to "Whomsoever", November 1888,
rejected by the builders of books for a quarter of a
century / by Benjamin Fowler Carpenter. Boston,
Mass.: The Christopher Press, 1913. 244 p.,
front.   **DLC**
LC: N 7, '13.

C-128   Carpenter, Edward Childs, 1872-1950. Captain
Courtesy / by Edward Childs Carpenter; five
illustrations in color by Elenore Plaisted Abbot.
Philadelphia; London: George W. Jacobs & Co.,
[1906]. 299 p., col. front., [4] leaves of col. plates.
LC: S 24, '06.

____, jt. aut. *The chasm* (1903). See **Kauffman,
Reginald Wright, 1877-1959, jt. aut., K-15.**

C-129   ____ The code of Victor Jallot: a romance of old
New Orleans / by Edward Childs Carpenter;
illustrations by Elenore Plaisted Abbott. Philadelphia:
George W. Jacobs & Company, [1907]. 334 p., col.
front., [4] leaves of col. plates.
LC: S 30, '07.

Carpenter, Frank G. Laundering in Asia. In *Second
suds sayings* **(1919), S-266.**

C-130   Carpenter, Grant. Long sweetening: a romance of
the red woods / by Grant Carpenter. New York:
Robert M. McBride & Company, 1921. 306 p.
LC: N 18, '21.
PW: D 3, '21.
BLC: London: Stanley Paul & Co., printed in U. S.
A., [1924].

C-131   ____ The night tide: a story of old Chinatown / by
Grant Carpenter; illustrations by J. A. Cahill. New
York: The H. K. Fly Company, [c1920]. 319 p.,
front., [4] leaves of plates.

C-132   Carpenter, Helen K. (Helen Knipe). The Cinderella
man: a romance of youth / by Helen K. Carpenter
and Edward Childs Carpenter. New York: The H.
K. Fly Company, [c1916]. 314 p., photo. front., [3]
leaves of plates.
LC: O 27, '16.
PW: O 28, '16.

C-133   Carpenter, Richard Thomas Devall, b. 1878. My
brother's keeper / by R. T. D. Carpenter . . .
Crowley, La.: R. T. D. Carpenter, [1914]. 145 p.,
[1] leaf of photo. plates (port.).   **DLC**

C-134   Carr, Clark E. (Clark Ezra), 1836-1919. The Illini:
a story of the prairies / by Clark E. Carr; with twenty
full-page portraits. Chicago: A. C. McClurg & Co.,
1904. 468 p., photo. front. (port.), [19] leaves of
photo. plates (port.).
PW: D 31, '04.

Carr, Sarah Pratt, b. 1850. A Gordian knot. In
Seattle Writers' Club. *Tillicum tales* (1907), S-248.

C-135   ____ The iron way; a tale of the West by Sarah Pratt
Carr; with four illustrations by John W. Norton.
Chicago, A. C. McClurg & Co., 1907. 367 p.,
front., [3] plates.   **ORU**
LC: Mr 28, '07.
PW: Mr 16, '07.

C-136   Carr, Stella. Stella's roomers: the astonishing story
of a New York rooming-house / by Stella Carr. New
York: Brandu's, [c1911]. 283 p.
LC: S 16, '11.
PW: S 2, '11.

C-137   Carradine, Beverly, b. 1848. Mississippi stories / by
B. Carradine . . . Chicago: The Christian Witness
Co., c1904. 254 p.
Contents: A church yard story -- The Ballantynes -- A strange
homestead -- Judge Dalrymple -- The two cronies.
Another printing: *A church yard story.* Chicago,
Boston, [c1904]. Cover title: Mississippi stories.

C-138   ____ People I have met / by Beverly Carradine.
Chicago; Boston: The Christian Witness Co.,
[c1910]. 265 p.
LC: Ag 11, '10.

C-139   ____ Yazoo stories / by Beverly Carradine.
Chicago; Boston: The Christian Witness Co.,
[c1911]. 244 p.
Contents: Major Rosser -- Charlie Goodfellow -- Stories around a
campfire -- A conversation in Hades -- A misunderstood man.
LC: D 18, '11.

Carrington, Carroll. Through the forbidden gates. In
Through the forbidden gates **(1903), T-222.**

C-140   Carrington, J. Timothy. Banished for reformation;
or, August's "coming back." Kansas City, Mo.:
Burton Publishing Co., [c1916]. 208 p.
Unexamined copy: bibliographic data from The
Publishers' Weekly.
PW: Ja 27, '17.

C-141   Carrol, George S., *pseud.* Notturno: a romance / by George S. Carrol [pseud.]. New York; London; Montreal: The Abbey Press, [c1903]. 280 p., front.
PW: Ap 25, '03.

Carroll, H. J. Father James' snuff box. In *The Senior lieutenant's wager: and other stories* (1905), **S-312.**

Carroll, Latrobe. A butterfly in the fog. In *The best college short stories, 1917-18* (1919), **B-557.**

C-142   Carroll, Mary Tarver, b. 1885. The renewal / by Mary Tarver Carroll. New York: Broadway Publishing Company, [c1905]. 76 p.   **DLC**
PW: My 20, '05.

C-143   Carroll, Robert S. (Robert Sproul), b. 1869. The grille gate / by Robert S. Carroll . . . Boston: Richard G. Badger, [c1922]. ([Boston]: The Gorham Press). 401 p., front.   **NYP**
LC: Je 21, '22.

C-144   Carruth, Frances Weston, b. 1867. The way of Belinda / by Frances Weston Carruth. New York: Dodd, Mead & Company, 1901. 310 p.
PW: Mr 30, '01.

Carruth, Hayden, 1862-1932. In the country. In *A book of American prose humor* (1904), **B-731.**

C-145   _____ Track's End: being the narrative of Judson Pitcher's strange winter spent there . . . : including an accurate account of his numerous adventures, and the facts concerning his several surprising escapes from death now first printed in full / as told by himself and edited by Hayden Carruth; illustrated by Clifford Carleton; with a correct map of Track's End drawn by the author. New York; London: Harper & Brothers, 1911. 229, [1] p., front., map, [7] leaves of plates, ill. Blue end papers with map illustration.
LC: S 8, '11.

C-146   Carruthers, Frank. Terror Island: an adventure story / by Frank Carruthers. New York: Chelsea House, [c1925]. 319 p.
PW: D 5, '25.

C-147   Carry, Mabel D. Betty Moore's journal / Mabel D. Carry. Chicago; New York; London: Rand McNally & Company, 1912. 183 p.
LC: F 8, '12.
PW: Mr 9, '12.

C-148   Carryl, Guy Wetmore, 1873-1904. Far from the maddening girls / by Guy Wetmore Carryl. New York: McClure, Phillips & Co., 1904. 185, [1] p., front., [7] leaves of plates. [Ill. by Peter Newell.]
LC: N 28, '04.
PW: D 3, '04.
References: BAL 2787.

C-149   _____ The lieutenant-governor: a novel / by Guy Wetmore Carryl. Boston; New York: Houghton, Mifflin and Company, 1903. (Cambridge: The Riverside Press). 269 p.
LC: Mr 10, '03.
PW: Mr 21, '03.
References: BAL 2784.

C-150   _____ The transgression of Andrew Vane: a novel / by Guy Wetmore Carryl . . . New York: Henry Holt and Company, 1904. 326 p., photo. front. (port.).
LC: Ap 22, '04.
PW: My 7, '04.
BLC: London: William Heinemann, 1904.
References: BAL 2786.

C-151   _____ Zut: and other Parisians / Guy Wetmore Carryl. Boston; New York: Houghton, Mifflin and Company, 1903. (Cambridge [Mass.]: The Riverside Press). 304 p.
Contents: Zut -- Caffard, deus ex machina -- The next corner -- The only son of his mother -- The tuition of Dodo Chapius -- Le Pochard -- A Latter-day Lucifer -- Poire! -- Papa Labesse -- In the absence of Monsieur -- Little Tapin.
References: BAL 2785.

C-152   Carson, Norma Bright, b. 1883. Rosemary--for remembrance / by Norma Bright Carson. New York: George H. Doran Company, [c1914]. 124 p. Designed end papers.
LC: O 19, '14.
BLC: London: Hodder & Stoughton, [1916].

C-153   _____ Trueheart Margery / by Norma Bright Carson . . . New York: George H. Doran Company, [c1917]. 274 p.
Unexamined copy: bibliographic data from NUC.
LC: N 12, '17.
PW: N 24, '17.

C-154   Carson, Shirley. The motto of Mrs. McLane: the story of an American farm / by Shirley Carson. New York: George H. Doran Company, [1913?]. 220 p.
No publication date in book; putative publication date from PW and NUC.
PW: Ja 25, '13.
BLC: London: Edward Arnold, 1911.

C-155   Carson, William Henry, b. 1859. Evelyn Van Courtland / by William Henry Carson. New York: R. F. Fenno & Company, [c1907]. 373 p.
LC: S 11, '07.

C-156   _____ The fool / by William H. Carson . . . ; illustrations by W. H. Worrall. New York: G. W. Dillingham Company, 1902. 334 p., front., [3] leaves of plates.
PW: Je 7, '02.
BLC: London: T. Fisher Unwin; New York [printed], 1902.

C-157   _____ Hester Blair: the romance of a country girl / by William Henry Carson; with illustrations by Charles H. Stephens. Boston: C. M. Clark Publishing Company, 1902. 348 p., [6] leaves of plates.
PW: Mr 1, '02.

C-158 ____ Tito / by William Henry Carson; illustrations by Charles H. Stephens. Boston: C. M. Clark Publishing Company, [c1903]. 363 p., front., [2] leaves of plates.
PW: Mr 14, '03.

C-159 Carter, Charles Franklin. Rafael: a story of Nueva California / by Charles Franklin Carter. Los Angeles: Press of Grafton Publishing Corporation, 1923. 368 p., [1] leaf of plates.
LC: N 2, '23.

C-160 ____ Stories of the old missions of California / by Charles Franklin Carter. San Francisco: Paul Elder & Company, 1917. 184 p. [Decorated by William H. Wilke.]
Contents: The Indian Sibyl's prophecy -- The flight of Padro Peyrl -- Father Zalviden's money -- La Beata -- Juana -- Father Uria's saints -- Pomponio.
LC: D 10, '17.
PW: O 29, '17.

C-161 Carter, Charles M. Romance of races; or, The genesis of nations / by Charles M. Carter . . . Washington: The Neale Publishing Company, 1901. 150 p.
Unexamined copy: bibliographic data from OCLC, #15053376.

C-162 Carter, Edward Champe. "A Marine, Sir!" / by Edward Champe Carter; with a foreword by John A. Lejeune, Major General Commandant, U. S. Marine Corps. Boston, Mass.: The Cornhill Publishing Company, [c1921]. 173 p.

C-163 Carter, John F., b. 1881. The destroyers / by John F. Carter, Jr. New York; Washington: The Neale Publishing Company, 1907. 350 p.   VIC
LC: D 31, '07.
PW: Ja 11, '08.

C-164 Carter, John Henton. Mississippi Argonauts: a tale of the South / by John Henton Carter; illustrated by L. Berneker. New York: Dawn Publishing Company, 1903. 291, [1] p., [9] leaves of plates.

C-165 Carter, Marion Hamilton. Souls resurgent / by Marion Hamilton Carter. New York: Charles Scribner's Sons, 1916. 407 p.
LC: S 28, '16.
PW: S 30, '16.

C-166 Carter, Mary Leland. An instrument in His hands / by Mary Leland Carter. The minister who was different / by Elbert A. Smith. Lamoni, Iowa: Herald Publishing House, 1908. 80 p; 122 p. On cover and at head of title: *The two-story book*.

Carter, R. G. The dice decide. In *Made to order* **(1915), M-352.**

Carter, Russell Kelso. See **Kenyon, Orr.**

C-167 Carter, Thomas Lane. Out of Africa: a book of short stories / by Thomas Lane Carter. New York; Washington: The Neale Publishing Company, 1911.

288 p.   **OSU, LUS**
Contents: The pity of it -- Up a tree -- "The Cauliflower" -- The comforting phonograph -- First lady of the land -- KCN -- A Kaffir Christmas -- Ah Sin's sin -- How like a soldier -- Me and Rhodes -- The miner.
LC: Jl 31, '11.
PW: Ap 29, '11.

C-168 Cartmell, F. Sydnor (Fannie Sydnor). Two demands / by F. Sydnor Cartmell. East Aurora, New York: Done into a book by the Roycrofters, 1909. 151, [1] p., photo. front., [1] leaf of photo. plates. **DLC**
LC: N 17, '09.

C-169 Carton, Hugh. The grand assize: as reported by a humble clerk / by Hugh Carton. Garden City, N. Y.: Doubleday, Page & Company, 1914. 279 p.
LC: N 18, '14.
BLC: London: William Heinemann, 1914.

C-170 Cartrette, Anna Gaskill. The awakening / by Anna Gaskill Cartrette. Wilmington, N. C.: Printed by Wilmington Printing Company, [c1921]. 167 p.
     NCS
LC: Ag 24, '21.

C-171 Carus, Paul, 1852-1919. Amitabha: a story of Buddhist theology / by Paul Carus. Chicago: The Open Court Publishing Company, 1906. 121 p., photo. front.
LC: Ag 16, '06.
PW: S 22, '06.

C-172 ____ The chief's daughter: a legend of Niagara / by Paul Carus; with illustrations by E. Biedermann. Chicago: The Open Court Publishing Company; London: Kegan Paul, Trench, Trübner & Co., 1901. 54 p., front., [6] leaves of plates, ill.
PW: Je 29, '01.

Carver, Ada Jack. Redbone. In *The Harper prize short stories* **(1925), H-233.**

Carver, George. The scarlet one. In *Stories from the Midland* **(1924), S-984.**

C-173 Case, Carleton B. (Carleton Britton), b. 1857. A batch of smiles: selected from many sources / by Craleton B. Case. New York: Shrewsbury Publishing Co., [c1914]. 160 p.

Case, Clarence Edwards. A false idol. In *A little book of Rutgers tales* **(1905), L-378.**

Case, Frances Powell. See **Powell, Frances.**

C-174 Case, John Homer. Jean Carroll: a tale of the the Ozark hills / by John Homer Case. New York: Broadway Publishing Co., 1911. 388 p., front., [5] leaves of plates.
LC: N 2, '11.
PW: S 9, '11.

C-175 Case, Louise Crittenden. Uncle Sam / by Louise Crittenden Case . . . New York: Broadway Publishing Co., [c1912]. 351 p., front., plates.

Unexamined copy: bibliographic data from OCLC, #8527838.
Cover title: *Uncle Sam: a tale of rural New York.*
LC: D 7, '12.

C-176   Casey, Patrick, b. 1893. The Gay-cat: the story of a road-kid and his dog / by Patrick and Terence Casey. New York: The H. K. Fly Company, 1921. 305 p., front.   **OSU, NYP**
PW: Ja 14, '22.

C-177   ____ Sea plunder / by Patrick Casey. Boston: Small, Maynard & Company, [c1925]. 343 p.
LC: Mr 20, '25.
PW: F 14, '25.
BLC: London: Brentano's; printed in U. S. A., [1925].

C-178   ____ The strange story of William Hyde / by Patrick and Terence Casey. New York: Hearst's International Library Co., 1916. 317 p.
LC: Mr 25, '16.

C-179   ____ The wolf-cub: a novel of Spain / by Patrick and Terence Casey; with frontispiece by H. Weston Taylor. Boston: Little, Brown and Company, 1918. 334 p., front.
LC: Ja 11, '18.
PW: Ja 5, '18.

Casey, Terence, jt. aut. *The strange story of William Hyde* (1916). See **Casey, Patrick, b. 1893, jt. aut., C-178.**

____, jt. aut. *The wolf-cub* (1918). See **Casey, Patrick, b. 1893, jt. aut., C-179.**

C-180   Caskie, Jacquelin Ambler. The figure in the sand / by Jaquelin Ambler Caskie. New York: American Library Service, [c1924]. 107 p., front. [Ill. by C. Balmer.]
LC: Je 30, '24.

C-181   ____ Nabala: (Nä-bä-lä) / by Jaquelin Ambler Caskie. Lynchburg, Va.: J. P. Bell Company, Inc., 1922. 172 p., col. front.
LC: O 7, '22.

C-182   Casparian, Gregory. An Anglo-American alliance: a serio-comic romance and forecast of the future / by Gregory Casparian; illustrated and published by the author. Floral Park, N. Y.: Mayflower Presses, 1906. 144 p., front., [11] leaves of plates.

C-183   Cassander, Verus. The delicious life-saving kiss, the quasi-miraculous kiss, or, See what a seasonable well-applied kiss may do: a story of the Spanish-American war and of all time / by Verus Cassander. [San Francisco?: s. n., c1904]. 91 p.   **DLC**
BLC: [London], 1904.

C-184   Castaigne, André. The bill-toppers / by André Castaigne; with illustrations by the author. Indianapolis: The Bobbs-Merrill Company, [c1909].

386 p., front., [5] leaves of plates.
LC: Jl 22, '09.
BLC: London: Mills & Boon, 1909.

C-185   ____ Fata Morgana: romance of art student life in Paris / by André Castaigne, with illustrations by the author. New York: The Century Co., 1904. 486 p., incl. 50 leaves of plates, front.

C-186   Castello, A. M. (Almeda Merchant), Mrs., b. 1856. Four in hand / by Mrs. A. M. Castello. Boston; Chicago: The Pilgrim Press, [c1901]. 477 p., front., plates.
Unexamined copy: bibliographic data from OCLC, #26829465.

C-187   Castle stories / by Castle girls. [Tarrytown, N. Y.]: Van Tassell-Odell Press, 1908. 130 p., ill.   **KSU**
Contents: The aftermath / Anne Atwood -- Santa Marghuerita / Harriet Bronner -- Laddie / Naomi Gillespie Smith -- Hotspur / Florence Vorpé -- By intuition of Cupid / Rae Bartch -- For Rome / Anne Atwood -- An impromptu valentine / Anne Atwood -- Renunciation / Harriet Bronner -- Midsummer eve / Anne Atwood -- A colonial valentine / Florence Vorpé -- The wanderer / Anne Atwood -- The soul of a musician / Florence Vorpé.
LC: Ag 24, '08.
PW: N 7, '08.

C-188   Castle, William Richards, 1878-1935. The green vase / by William R. Castle, Jr. New York: Dodd, Mead and Company, 1912. 406 p.
LC: Mr 26, '12.
PW: Mr 30, '12.

C-189   ____ The pillar of sand / by William R. Castle, Jr. New York: Dodd, Mead and Company, 1914. 403 p.
LC: Mr 5, '14.

C-190   Castleman, Virginia Carter, b. 1864. Roger of Fairfield / by Virginia Carter Castlemen [sic]; illustrated. New York; Washington: The Neale Publishing Company, 1906. 269 p., front., [2] leaves of plates.
LC: Ag 31, '06.

C-191   Cather, Willa, 1873-1947. Alexander's bridge / by Willa Sibert Cather. Boston; New York: Houghton Mifflin Company, 1912. (Cambridge, Mass., U. S. A.: The Riverside Press). 174, [1] p., front., [3] leaves of plates.
LC: Ap 25, '12.
PW: Ap 13, '12.
BLC: London: William Heinemann, 1912. Another edition: London: Constable & Co.; Boston and New York: Houghton Mifflin Company; Cambridge, Mass. [printed], 1912.
References: Crane, A5.

C-192   ____ A lost lady / by Willa Cather . . . New York: Alfred A. Knopf, 1923. 173, [1] p.
LC: S 22, '23.
PW: S 29, '23.
BLC: London: William Heinemann, 1924.
References: Crane, A13.

C-193   ____ My Ántonia / by Willa Sibert Cather . . . ; with illustrations by W. T. Benda. Boston; New York: Houghton Mifflin Company, 1918. (Cambridge, Mass., U. S. A.: The Riverside Press). 418, [1] p., [8] leaves of plates.
LC: S 28, '18.
PW: O 5, '18.
BLC: London: William Heinemann; Cambridge, Mass. printed, 1919.
References: Crane, A9.

C-194   ____ O pioneers! / by Willa Sibert Cather . . . Boston; New York: Houghton Mifflin Company, 1913. (Cambridge: The Riverside Press). 308, [1] p., col. front. [Ill. by Clarence F. Underwood.]
LC: Jl 2, '13.
PW: Jl 5, '13.
BLC: London: William Heinemann; Cambridge, Mass. printed, 1913.
References: Crane, A6.

C-195   ____ One of ours / Willa Cather . . . New York: Alfred A. Knopf, 1922. 459 p. "Second printing, September 1922." [First trade edition preceded by limited edition.]
LC: O 11, '22.
PW: S 9, '22.
BLC: London: William Heinemann, 1923.
References: Crane, A11.

C-196   ____ The professor's house / by Willa Cather . . . New York: Alfred A. Knopf, 1925. 283, [1] p.
LC: S 11, '25.
PW: S 5, '25.
BLC: London: William Heinemann, 1925.
References: Crane, A14.

C-197   ____ The song of the lark / by Willa Sibert Cather . . . Boston; New York: Houghton Mifflin Company, 1915. (Cambridge: The Riverside Press). 489, [1] p.
LC: O 4, '15.
PW: O 2, '15.
BLC: London: John Murray; Cambridge, Mass. [printed], 1916.
References: Crane, A8.

C-198   ____ The troll garden / by Willa Sibert Cather . . . New York: McClure, Phillips & Co., 1905. 253 p.
Contents: Flavia and her artists -- The sculptor's funeral -- The garden lodge -- "A death in the desert" -- The marriage of Phædra -- A Wagner matinee -- Paul's cake.
LC: Ap 5, '05.
PW: Ap 15, '05.
References: Crane, A4.

C-199   ____ Youth and the bright Medusa / by Willa Cather . . . New York: Alfred A. Knopf, 1920. 303 p.
Contents: Coming, Aphrodite! -- The diamond mine -- A gold slipper -- Scandal -- Paul's case -- A Wagner matinée -- The sculptor's funeral -- "A death in the desert".
LC: O 1, '20.
PW: O 2, '20.
BLC: London: William Heinemann; printed in U. S. A., 1921.
References: Crane, A10.

C-200 Catherwood, Mary Hartwell, 1847-1902. Lazarre / by Mary Hartwell Catherwood; with illustrations by André Castaigne. Indianapolis: The Bowen-Merrill Company, [c1901]. 436 p., front., [5] leaves of plates.
PW: O 5, '01.
BLC: London: B. F. Stevens & Brown, [1901]; Another edition: with illustrations by André Castaigne. London: Grant Richards, 1902.
References: BAL 2978 (BAL 2976, 2977 notes copyright printings).

C-201 Cauffman, Stanley Hart, 1880-1947. At the sign of the Silver Ship / by Stanley Hart Cauffman; illustrated by Frank E. Schoonover. Philadelphia: The Penn Publishing Company, 1924. 333 p., front.
LC: My 15, '25.
PW: Ja 17, '25.

C-202 Cautela, Giuseppe. Moon Harvest / Giuseppe Cautela. New York: Lincoln MacVeagh, The Dial Press, 1925. 253 p. Designed end papers.
LC: Ap 22, '25.
PW: My 9, '25.

Cavazza, Elisabeth, pseud. See **Pullen, Elisabeth.**

C-203 Caver, Mamie Jordan. As it is; or, The conditions under which the race problem challenges the white man's solution / by Mamie Jordan Caver. Washington, D. C.: Printed by Murray Bros., Inc., [c1919]. 102 p., port.
Unexamined copy: bibliographic data from NUC.

C-204 Chadwick, Charles. The cactus: a novel / by Charles Chadwick. New York: Thomas Y. Crowell Company, [c1925]. 314 p.
LC: Mr 9, '25.
PW: Mr 14, '25.

Chadwick, Francis. The dream warning. In *The Senior lieutenant's wager: and other stories* (**1905**), **S-312.**

C-205 Chaffey, M. Ella. To Cariboo and back / by M. Ella Chaffey. Columbus, Ohio: The Book Concern, [19--?]. 244 p.

Chalmers, Margaret Piper. See **Piper, Margaret Rebecca, b. 1879.**

C-206 Chalmers, Stephen, b. 1880. Footloose and free: illustrated / by Stephen Chalmers . . . New York: Outing Publishing Company, 1912. 265 p., incl. front., ill. [Some ill. by T. D. Skidmore.]
LC: O 18, '12.
PW: S 28, '12.

C-207   ____ The greater punishment / by Stephen Chalmers; frontispiece by Ralph Pallen Coleman. Garden City, N. Y.: Doubleday, Page & Company, 1920. 238 p., col. front.
LC: Je 30, '20.
PW: Je 26, '20.
BLC: London: J. Bale & Co., 1923, [c1922].

C-208 _____ A prince of romance / by Stephen Chalmers; illustrated by Charles B. Falls. Boston: Small, Maynard and Company, [c1911]. 340 p., front.
LC: Ja 31, '11.
PW: Mr 4, '11.
BLC: London: Grant Richards; Cambridge, Mass. printed, 1912.

C-209 _____ The trail of a tenderfoot / by Stephen Chalmers; illustrations by H. T. Dunn, C. F. Peters and J. M. Gleeson. New York: Outing Publishing Company, 1911. 234 p., incl. front., ill.
LC: F 6, '11.
PW: F 11, '11.

C-210 _____ The vanishing smuggler / by Stephen Chalmers; illustrations by Nesbitt Benson. New York: Edward J. Clode, [c1909]. 256 p., col. front., [3] leaves of col. plates.
LC: S 17, '09.
PW: O 23, '09.
BLC: London: Mills & Boon, [1910].

C-211 _____ When love calls men to arms: an autobiography of love and adventure, truthfully set down by Rorie Maclean, Laird of Kilellan, in the seventeenth century, and here rewritten from the original ms. into clearer English / by Stephen Chalmers; illustrated by Howard Chandler Christy. Boston: Small, Maynard & Company, [c1910]. 352 p., col. front., [4] leaves of plates.
LC: Jl 9, '10.
PW: Jl 9, '10.
BLC: London: Grant Richards; Cambridge, U. S. A. printed, [1912].

C-212 Chamberlain, Esther. The coast of chance / by Esther and Lucia Chamberlain; with illustrations by Clarence F. Underwood. Indianapolis: The Bobbs-Merrill Company, [1908]. 464 p., front., [3] leaves of plates.
LC: Ap 21, '08.

C-213 _____ Mrs. Essington: the romance of a house-party / by Esther and Lucia Chamberlain. New York: The Century Co., 1905. 248 p., col. front., [5] leaves of col. plates. [Ill. by Henry Hutt.]
PW: My 20, '05.

Chamberlain, George Agnew, 1879-1966, contributor. See *Bobbed hair* **(1925), B-700.**

C-214 _____ Cobweb / by George Chamberlain. New York; London: Harper & Brothers Publishers, [c1921]. 312, [1] p.
LC: O 1, '21.
PW: O 1, '21.
BLC: London: Mills & Boon, 1922.

C-215 _____ The great Van Suttart mystery / by George Agnew Chamberlain . . . New York; London: G. P. Putnam's Sons, 1925. (New York: The Knickerbocker Press). 315 p.
LC: Ag 13, '25.
PW: Ag 15, '25.

C-216 _____ Highboy rings down the curtain / by George Agnew Chamberlain. Bridgeton, New Jersey: Published by the Evening News Company, 1923. 55 p.
LC: D 29, '23.

C-217 [_____] Home: a novel / illustrated by Reginald B. Birch. New York: The Century Co., 1914. 337 p., front. Illustrated end papers.
LC: F 2, '14.
PW: Ja 17, '14.

C-218 _____ John Bogardus / by George Agnew Chamberlain; illustrated by W. T. Benda. New York: The Century Co., 1916. 344 p., front., [3] leaves of plates.
LC: F 24, '16.
PW: F 19, '16.

C-219 _____ The lantern on the plow / by George Agnew Chamberlain. New York; London: Harper & Brothers, 1924. 409 p.
[First Edition.]
LC: Ag 21, '24.
PW: Ag 30, '24.
BLC: London: Mills & Boon, 1925.

C-220 _____ Lip Malvy's wife: a novel / by George Agnew Chamberlain. New York; London: Harper & Brothers, 1923. 307 p.
[First Edition.]
LC: S 25, '23.
PW: Ag 1, '25.
BLC: London: Mills & Boon, 1924.

C-221 _____ Not all the king's horses: a novel / by George Agnew Chamberlain. Indianapolis: The Bobbs-Merrill Company, [c1919]. 309, [1] p.
LC: O 11, '19.
PW: N 1, '19.

C-222 _____ Pigs to market / by George Agnew Chamberlain. Indianapolis: The Bobbs-Merrill Company, [c1920]. 319 p.
Contents: Lovely reason -- Simon Simon -- The door to freedom.
LC: N 26, '20.
PW: D 4, '20.

C-223 _____ Rackhouse: a novel / by George Agnew Chamberlain. New York; London: Harper & Brothers, 1922. 302 p.
[First Edition.]
LC: O 23, '22.
PW: O 28, '22.
BLC: London: Mills & Boon, 1923.

C-224 _____ Taxi: an adventure romance / by George Agnew Chamberlain; ill. by Lejaren A. Hiller. Indianapolis: The Bobbs-Merrill Company, [c1920]. 222, [1] p., front., [5] leaves of plates.
LC: F 9, '20.
PW: Mr 13, '20.

C-225 _____ Through stained glass: a novel / by George Agnew Chamberlain. New York: The Century Co., 1915. 359 p.
LC: Mr 17, '15.
PW: Mr 13, '15.
BLC: London: G. Allen & Unwin, 1915.

C-226 _____ White man / by George Agnew Chamberlain; illustrated by W. H. D. Koerner. Indianapolis: The Bobbs-Merrill Company, [c1919]. 299, [1] p., front., [6] leaves of plates.
LC: F 5, '19.
PW: F 15, '19.
BLC: Toronto: G. J. McLeod, [1919].

Chamberlain, Lucia, jt. aut. *The coast of chance* (1908). See **Chamberlain, Esther, jt. aut., C-212.**

_____, jt. aut. *Mrs. Essington* (1905). See **Chamberlain, Esther, jt. aut., C-213.**

C-227 _____ The other side of the door / by Lucia Chamberlain . . . ; with illustrations by Herman Pfeifer. Indianapolis: The Bobbs-Merrill Company, [c1909]. 276 p., front., [5] leaves of plates.
LC: My 6, '09.
PW: My 8, '09.

C-228 _____ Son of the wind / by Lucia Chamberlain; with illustrations by Herman Pfeifer. Indianapolis: The Bobbs-Merrill Company, [c1910]. 411, [1] p., front., [4] leaves of plates.
LC: N 9, '10.
PW: N 12, '10.

C-229 Chamberlayne, E. S. (Edward Schuyler), b. 1873. The little back room: being the social and political adventures of Peter Cadogan / by E. S. Chamberlayne. New York: Frederick A. Stokes Company, [c1921]. 340 p.
LC: Ap 1, '21.
PW: N 12, '21.

C-230 Chamberlin, Aldin, Mrs. Whitewing: an Indian story / by Mrs. Aldin Chamberlin . . . [Charlevoix, Mich.]: Published by the author, 1911. 180 p.
EEX
LC: Jl 29, '11.

C-231 Chamberlin, Frederick Carleton, b. 1870. In the shoe string country: a true picture of southern life / by Frederick Chamberlin; illustrated. Boston: C. M. Clark Publishing Co., Inc., 1906. 353 p., front., [9] leaves of plates. [Ill. by A. B. Shute.]

Chamberlin, Mary Jane. See **Chamberlin, Aldin, Mrs.**

C-232 Chamberlin, Susie M. Three moral girls / by Susie M. Chamberlin. [S. l.: s. n., c1910]. 140, [10] p.
DLC
Contents: Three moral girls -- Sunshine in the shadows.
LC: Jl 2, '10.

Chambers, E. Whitman, jt. aut. *Garber of Thunder Gorge* (1924). See **Mersereau, John, b. 1898, jt. aut., M-697.**

C-233 Chambers, Robert W. (Robert William), 1865-1933. The adventures of a modest man / by Robert W. Chambers; illustrated by Edmund Frederick. New York; London: D. Appleton and Company, 1911. 325, [1] p., front., [5] leaves of plates, ill.

LC: F 27, '11.
PW: Mr 11, '11.

C-234 _____ Ailsa Paige: a novel / by Robert W. Chambers; illustrated. New York; London: D. Appleton and Company, 1910. 501, [1] p., front., [7] leaves of plates. [Ill. by Charles Dana Gibson.]
LC: S 2, '10.
PW: S 10, '10.

C-235 _____ America, or, The sacrifice: a romance of the American revolution / by Robert W. Chambers; illustrated with scenes from the photoplay. New York: Grosset & Dunlap, [c1924]. 399 p., photo. front., [7] leaves of photo. plates.
LC: Ap 22, '24.
PW: Jl 19, '24.

C-236 _____ Anne's bridge / by Robert W. Chambers; with illustrations by Henry Hutt. New York; London: D. Appleton and Company, 1914. 160, [1] p., front., [3] leaves of plates.
LC: N 27, '14.
PW: D 12, '14.

C-237 _____ Athalie / by Robert W. Chambers; with illustrations by Frank Craig. New York; London: D. Appleton and Company, 1915. 404, [1] p., front., [29] leaves of plates.
LC: Jl 26, '15.
PW: Jl 31, '15.

C-238 _____ Barbarians / by Robert W. Chambers; illustrated by A. I. Keller. New York; London: D. Appleton and Company, 1917. 353, [1] p., front., [3] leaves of plates.
LC: O 25, '17.
PW: O 27, '17.

C-239 _____ The better man / by Robert W. Chambers; illustrated by Henry Hutt. New York; London: D. Appleton and Company, 1916. 343, [1] p., front., [5] leaves of plates.
Contents: The progress of Janet -- A Lynx Peak pastoral -- Wildrick's dump -- Hell's ashes -- The fire-bird -- The better man -- The germ of madness -- Lucille's legs -- A nursery tale -- Number seven -- Down and out -- Carondelet -- Owl's Head -- Ole Hawg -- The real thing.
LC: Mr 28, '16.
PW: Ap 8, '16.

C-240 _____ Between friends / by Robert W. Chambers; with illustrations by Henry Hutt. New York; London: D. Appleton and Company, 1914. 142, [1] p., col. front., [3] leaves of plates.
LC: N 27, '14.
PW: D 12, '14.

C-241 _____ Blue-bird weather / by Robert W. Chambers; with illustrations by Charles Dana Gibson. New York; London: D. Appleton and Company, 1912. 140, [1] p., front. ill., ill.
LC: O 29, '12.
PW: N 9, '12.

C-242 _____ The business of life / by Robert W. Chambers; with illustrations by Charles Dana Gibson. New

York; London: D. Appleton and Company, 1913.
517, [1] p., incl. front.
LC: S 25, '13.
PW: S 20, '13.

C-243 ____ Cardigan: a novel / by Robert W. Chambers;
illustrated. New York; London: Harper & Brothers,
1901. 512, [1] p., front., [7] leaves of plates. [Ill.
by Philip R. Goodwin and F. E. Schoonover.]
PW: S 21, '01.
BLC: Westminster: A. Constable & Co., 1902,
[1901].

C-244 ____ The common law / by Robert W. Chambers;
with illustrations by Charles Dana Gibson. New
York; London: D. Appleton and Company, 1911.
535, [1] p., front., ill.
LC: Ag 31, '11.
PW: S 2, '11.

C-245 ____ The crimson tide: a novel / by Robert W.
Chambers; illustrated by A. I. Keller. New York;
London: D. Appleton and Company, 1919. 366,
[1] p., front., [3] leaves of plates.
LC: D 6, '19.
PW: Ja 17, '20.

C-246 ____ The danger mark / by Robert W. Chambers;
with illustrations by A. B. Wenzell. New York;
London: D. Appleton and Company, 1909. 495,
[1] p., front., [7] leaves of plates.
LC: S 20, '09.
PW: O 9, '09.

C-247 ____ The dark star / by Robert W. Chambers;
illustrated by W. D. Stevens. New York; London:
D. Appleton and Company, 1917. 420, [1] p., front.,
[31] leaves of plates.
LC: My 14, '17.
PW: My 26, '17.

C-248 ____ Eris / by Robert W. Chambers. New York:
George H. Doran Company, [c1922]. 323 p.
LC: S 25, '23.
PW: F 7, '25.
BLC: London: Hodder & Stoughton, 1923.

C-249 ____ The fighting chance / by Robert W. Chambers;
with illustrations by A. B. Wenzell. New York: D.
Appleton and Company, 1906. 499 p., front., [7]
leaves of plates.
LC: Ag 24, '06.
PW: S 1, '06.
BLC: London: A. Constable & Co., 1907.

C-250 ____ The firing line / by Robert W. Chambers.
New York: D. Appleton and Company, 1908.
498 p., front., [7] leaves of plates. [Ill. by Will
Foster.]
LC: Ag 21, '08.
PW: Ag 22, '08.

C-251 ____ The flaming jewel / by Robert W. Chambers.
New York: George H. Doran Company, [c1922].
273 p.
LC: Ag 3, '22.

PW: Je 24, '22.
BLC: London: Hodder & Stoughton, [1922].

C-252 ____ The gay rebellion / by Robert W. Chambers;
illustrated by Edmund Frederick. New York;
London: D. Appleton and Company, 1913. 299 p.,
front., [3] leaves of plates.
LC: F 27, '13.
PW: Mr 1, '13.

C-253 ____ The girl Philippa / by Robert W. Chambers;
illustrated by Frank Craig. New York; London: D.
Appleton and Company, 1916. 514, [1] p., front.,
[31] leaves of plates.
LC: Jl 18, '16.
PW: Jl 29, '16.

C-254 ____ The green mouse / by Robert W. Chambers;
illustrated in color by Edmund Frederick. New York;
London: D. Appleton and Company, 1910. 281 p.,
col. front., [5] leaves of col. plates.
LC: Ap 19, '10.
PW: Ap 23, '10.

C-255 ____ The hidden children / by Robert W. Chambers;
with illustrations by A. I. Keller. New York;
London: D. Appleton and Company, 1914. 650,
[1] p., col. front., [3] leaves of plates.
LC: S 3, '14.
PW: S 19, '14.

C-256 ____ In search of the unknown / by Robert W.
Chambers. New York; London: Harper & Brothers,
1904. 285, [1] p., col. front.
PW: Je 11, '04.
BLC: London: A. Constable & Co., 1905.

C-257 ____ In secret / by Robert W. Chambers. New
York: George H. Doran Company, [c1919]. 322 p.
LC: Je 23, '19.
PW: Je 14, '19.
BLC: London: Hodder & Stoughton; printed in U.
S. A., 1919.

C-258 ____ Iole / by Robert W. Chambers. New York:
D. Appleton & Co., 1905. 142 p., col. front., [3]
leaves of col. plates. [Ill. by Arthur C. Becker (i. e.
Becher), J. C. Leyendecker, and Karl Anderson.]
PW: Je 3, '05.
BLC: London: A. Constable & Co.; New York
printed, 1906.

C-259 ____ Japonette / by Robert W. Chambers; with
illustrations by Charles Dana Gibson. New York;
London: D. Appleton and Company, 1912. 384,
[3] p., incl. front.
"Copyright, 1911, 1912, by International Magazine
Company under the title *The turning point.*"
LC: Ap 2, '12.
PW: Ap 6, '12.

C-260 ____ The laughing girl: a novel / by Robert W.
Chambers; illustrated by Henry Hutt. New York;
London: D. Appleton and Company, 1918. 360,
[1] p., front., [3] leaves of plates.
LC: N 15, '18.
PW: N 16, '18.

C-261   ____ The little red foot / by Robert W. Chambers. New York: George H. Doran Company, [c1921]. 351 p.
LC: Je 10, '21.
PW: Je 4, '21.
BLC: London: Hodder & Stoughton; printed in U. S. A., [1921].

C-262   ____ The maid-at-arms: a novel / by Robert W. Chambers; illustrated by Howard Chandler Christy. New York; London: Harper & Brothers, 1902. 342, [1] p., front., [7] leaves of plates.
PW: O 4, '02.
BLC: Westminster: A. Constable & Co., 1902.

C-263   ____ The maids of Paradise: a novel / by Robert W. Chambers; illustrated. New York; London: Harper & Brothers, 1903. 387, [1] p., front., [7] leaves of plates.
PW: S 12, '03.
BLC: London: A. Constable & Co., [1903].

C-264   ____ The moonlit way: a novel / by Robert W. Chambers; illustrated by A. I. Keller. New York; London: D. Appleton and Company, 1919. 412, [1] p., front., [3] leaves of plates.
LC: Ap 25, '19.
PW: Ap 26, '19.

C-265   ____ Police !!! / By Robert W. Chambers; illustrated by Henry Hutt. New York; London: D. Appleton and Company, 1915. 292, [1] p., col. front., [5] leaves of col. plates.
Contents: The third eye -- The immortal -- The ladies of the lake -- One over -- Un peu d'amour -- The eggs of the silver moon.
LC: N 30, '15.
PW: D 4, '15.

C-266   ____ Quick action / by Robert W. Chambers; illustrated by Edmund Frederick. New York; London: D. Appleton and Company, 1914. 315, [1] p., front., [3] leaves of plates.
LC: Mr 28, '14.
PW: Je 27, '14.

C-267   ____ The reckoning / by Robert W. Chambers. New York: D. Appleton and Company, 1905. 386 p., front., [5] leaves of plates.
LC: O 7, '05.
BLC: London: A. Constable & Co., 1905.

C-268   ____ The restless sex / by Robert W. Chambers; illustrated by W. D. Stevens. New York; London: D. Appleton and Company, 1918. 419, [1] p., front., [31] leaves of plates.
LC: Ap 3, '18.
PW: Ap 6, '18.

C-269   ____ The slayer of souls / by Robert W. Chambers. New York: George H. Doran Company, [c1920]. 301 p.
LC: My 20, '20.
PW: My 22, '20.

C-270   ____ Some ladies in haste / by Robert W. Chambers. New York: D. Appleton and Company, 1908. 242 p., front., [3] leaves of plates. [Ill. by W. Morgan.]
LC: Ap 24, '08.
PW: Ap 18, '08.
BLC: London: A. Constable & Co., 1908.

C-271   ____ Special messenger / by Robert W. Chambers. New York: D. Appleton and Company, 1909. 260 p., front., [7] leaves of plates. [Ill. by George Fort Gibbs.]
LC: Mr 26, '09.
PW: Ap 3, '09.
BLC: London: T. Werner Laurie, [1909].

C-272   ____ The streets of Ascalon: episodes in the unfinished career of Richard Quarren, esq. / by Robert W. Chambers; with illustrations by Charles Dana Gibson. New York; London: D. Appleton and Company, 1912. 440, [1] p., incl. front. and 57 ills.
LC: S 25, '12.
PW: S 21, '12.

C-273   ____ The talkers / by Robert W. Chambers. New York: George H. Doran Company, [c1923]. 291 p.
LC: Mr 5, '23.
PW: F 24, '23.
BLC: London: T. Fisher Unwin, 1925.

C-274   ____ The tracer of lost persons / by R. W. Chambers. New York: D. Appleton and Company, 1906. 293 p., front., [5] leaves of plates. [Ill. by Edmund Frederick.]
PW: Je 16, '06.
BLC: London: John Murray, 1907.

    ____ The tree of heaven. In *Short story classics* **(1905), S-466.**

C-275   ____ The tree of heaven / by Robert W. Chambers. New York: D. Appleton and Company, 1907. 325 p., front., [3] leaves of plates. [Ill. by Henry Hutt, Howard Chandler Christy, and A. B. Wenzell.]
Contents: The carpet of Belshazzar -- The sign of Venus -- The case of Mr. Helmer -- The tree of dreams -- The bridal pair -- Excuria -- The golden pool -- Out of the depths -- The swastika -- The ghost of chance.
LC: My 8, '07.
PW: My 11, '07.
BLC: London: A. Constable & Co., 1908.

C-276   ____ Who goes there! / by Robert W. Chambers; with illustrations by A. I. Keller. New York; London: D. Appleton and Company, 1915. 339, [1] p., col. front., [8] leaves of plates.
LC: Mr 23, '15.
PW: Mr 27, '15.

C-277   ____ A young man in a hurry: and other short stories / by Robert W. Chambers; illustrated. New York; London: Harper & Brothers, 1904. 283, [1] p., front., [7] leaves of plates. [Ill. by Henry Hutt, Howard C. Christy, and W. T. Smedley.]
Contents: A young man in a hurry -- A pilgrim -- The shining band -- One man in a million -- The fire-warden -- The market hunter -- The path-master -- In Nauvoo -- Marlitts' shoes -- Pasque Florida.
PW: N 5, '04.
BLC: London: A. Constable & Co., 1905.

C-278 _____ The younger set / by Robert W. Chambers; with illustrations by G. C. Wilmshurst. New York: D. Appleton and Company, 1907. 513 p., front., [7] leaves of plates.
LC: Ag 9, '07.
PW: Ag 24, '07.
BLC: London: A. Constable & Co., 1907.
Chambers, Rosa, Mrs., b. 1886. See **Hayward, Rachel, pseud.**

C-279 Chamblin, Jean. Lady Bobs, her brother, and I: a romance of the Azores / by Jean Chamblin; illustrated. New York; London: G. P. Putnam's Sons, 1905. (New York: The Knickerbocker Press). 212 p., col. front., [15] leaves of photo. plates. [Ill. by Frederick Simpson Coburn.]
PW: N 18, '05.

C-280 Chambliss, Paul. At the heart of old Pelee / by Paul Chambliss; illustrated from full page drawings by the author. New York; London: F. Tennyson Neely, [c1903]. 162 p., front., [9] leaves of plates.
PW: Je 6, '03.

C-281 Chambrun, Clara Longworth, Comtesse de, 1873-1954. Pieces of the game: a modern instance / by the Countess de Chambrun. New York; London: G. P. Putnam's Sons, 1915. ([New York]: The Knickerbocker Press). 259 p., front. [Ill. by Ullise Caputo.]
LC: Jl 7, '15.
PW: Je 12, '15.

C-282 _____ Playing with souls: a novel / by Countess de Chambrun, née Clara Longworth. New York: Charles Scribner's Sons, 1922. 368 p. **OSU, NYP**
LC: S 16, '22.
PW: S 30, '22.

Champion, May Kelsey. An unskilled laborer. In *The heart of childhood* (1906), H-441.

C-283 Champney, Elizabeth Williams, 1850-1922. A daughter of the Huguenots / by Elizabeth W. Champney . . . ; with illustrations. -- 1st ed., published October, 1901. -- New York: Dodd, Mead and Company, 1901. 315 p., front., [11] leaves of plates. [Some photographic plates by Sir John Millais and George H. Boughton.]
LC: O 14, '01.
PW: O 26, '01.

C-284 _____ Margarita: a legend of the fight for the great river / by Elizabeth W. Champney; with illustrations. New York: Dodd, Mead & Company, 1902. 341 p., front. (port.), [8] leaves of plates, ill.
PW: S 20, '02.

C-285 _____ Romance of old Belgium: from Cæsar to Kaiser / by Elizabeth W. Champney and Frère Champney; with 90 illustrations. New York; London: G. P. Putnam's Sons, 1915. (New York: The Knickerbocker Press). 432 p., [94] p. of plates. **WAU**
LC: D 7, '15.
PW: D 11, '15.

C-286 Chance, Frank L. (Frank Leroy), b. 1877. The bride and the pennant: the greatest story in the history of America's national game . . . / by Frank L. Chance . . . ; with a preface by Charles A. Comiskey . . . Chicago: Laird & Lee, [1910]. 182 p., photo. front. (port.), ill.
LC: My 9, '10.

C-287 Chancellor, Louise Beecher, 1871-1908. The Players of London: a tale of an Elizabethan smart set / written by Louise Beecher Chancellor; decorations by Harry B. Matthews. New York: B. W. Dodge, [c1909]. 236 p., [4] leaves of plates.
LC: O 26, '09.

C-288 Chandler, Izora C. (Izora Cecilia), d. 1906. Told in the gardens of Araby: (untranslated until now) / by Izora Chandler and Mary W. Montgomery. New York: Eaton & Mains; Cincinnati: Jennings & Graham, [c1905]. 230 p.
Contents: Prelude -- The emerald roc -- The story of the beautiful girl who had her wish -- The story of the beautiful one who did not have her desire -- Story of the crying pomegranate and the laughing bear -- Story of the bird of affliction -- Story of the water-carrier -- Story of the coffee-maker's apprentice -- Story of the candy-maker's apprentice -- The crystal kiosk and the diamond ship.

C-289 Chandler, Mae G. Tangles / by Mae G. Chandler. [Kelso, Wash.: s. n.], [c1925]. 91 p. **DLC**

C-290 Chandler, St. Lawrence. A human note / by St. Lawrence Chandler, Marquis of Eckersley; illustrated by Jay La Brun Jenkins. [Kansas City, Mo.: Hudson Press, c1908]. 208 p., photo. front. (port.), [4] leaves of plates.

Channing, Grace Ellery. The end of the journey. In *Under the Sunset* (1906), U-9.

_____ Keepers of a charge. In *Life at high tide* (1907), L-281.

_____ "The marriage question." In *Their husband's wives* (1906), T-161.

C-291 Chansky, Lou W. Forbidden chances: short stories / of Lou W. Chansky. Omaha: Huntington, [c1925]. 71 p. **DLC**
Contents: Forbidden chances -- Early morn -- Proposal worries.

C-292 Chapeau, Ellen Chazal. Under the darkness of the night: historical romance / by Ellen Chazal Chapeau. Washington [D. C.]: The Neale Publishing Company, 1901. 217 p. **EWF**
LC: Ag 1, '01.
PW: O 12, '01.

Chapin, Anna Alice, 1880-1920, jt. aut. *The deserters* (1911). See **Jenks, George C., jt. aut., J-73.**

C-293 _____ Discords / Anna Alice Chapin. New York: Printed at the Pelham Press, 1902. 208 p., ill.
PW: Ja 17, '03.

C-294 ____ The eagle's mate / by Anna Alice Chapin; illustrations by Douglas Duer. New York: W. J. Watt & Company, [c1914]. 300 p., front., [2] leaves of plates.
LC: Ja 13, '14.
PW: F 14, '14.

C-295 ____ Jane / by Anna Alice Chapin. New York; London: G. P. Putnam's Sons, 1920. ([New York]: The Knickerbocker Press). 363 p.
LC: My 6, '20.
PW: Ap 24, '20.

C-296 ____ Mountain madness / by Anna Alice Chapin; illustrations by George W. Gage. New York: W. J. Watt & Company, [c1917]. 312 p., front., [2] leaves of plates.
LC: F 8, '17.
PW: F 24, '17.

C-297 ____ The under trail / by Anna Alice Chapin; with illustrations by Martin Justice. Boston: Little, Brown and Company, 1912. 374 p., front., [3] leaves of plates.
LC: My 1, '12.
PW: Ap 27, '12.
BLC: London: Sir I. Pitman & Sons; Boston [printed], 1912.

C-298 Chapin, Harry Lorenzo, 1872-1917. The adoption: and other sketches, poems and plays / by Harry Lorenzo Chapin. [Huron, Ohio?]: Privately printed for the author in an edition of three hundred copies, 1909. 196 p., photo. front. (port.).
Contents: Preface -- Autobiography -- Prefatory note to "The adoption" -- The adoption -- Infinite love -- The Aztecs and the lost Atlantis -- The Napoleon dynasty -- An epitome of four deceivers. [The remainder is poetry and plays.]
LC: Ag 11, '09.

C-299 Chapin, Maud H. (Maud Hudnut), b. 1872. Rush-light stories / by Maud H. Chapin. New York: Duffield & Company, 1918. 218 p.
Contents: The Ushebti's love story -- The Rose of Jericho -- The house of Father Snail -- The weather cock -- The tapissier of Notre Dame -- The golden chrysalis -- The windmill -- The marionettes -- The zodiac -- The potter -- The sea horses -- Abdhil Rahman -- The clock of St. Gudula -- The legend of the river -- Ars longa.
LC: N 29, '18.

C-300 ____ A stone in the path / by Maud H. Chapin. New York: Duffield and Company, 1922. 251 p.
LC: S 23, '22.

C-301 Chapman, Arthur, 1873-1935. Apache Valley / by Arthur Chapman. Garden City, New York: Garden City Publishing Co., Inc., 1923, [c1922]. 117 p.

C-302 ____ Mystery Ranch / by Arthur Chapman. Boston; New York: Houghton Mifflin Company, 1921. (Cambridge: The Riverside Press). 305, [1] p.
LC: O 26, '21.
PW: N 12, '21.

C-303 Chapman, Ervin S., b. 1838. Particeps criminis: the story of a California rabbit drive; with full page half-tone cuts from photographs taken upon the field during different stages of the drive / by Ervin S.

Chapman; illustrated by Harry Graydon Partlow. New York; Chicago; Toronto; London; Edinburgh: Fleming H. Revell Company, [c1910]. 106, [1] p., front. (port.), [7] leaves of photo. plates.
LC: D 13, '10.

C-304 Chapman, H. J. (Harry James), b. 1856. Lords of Acadia / by H. J. Chapman. Boston: Small, Maynard & Company, [c1925]. 356 p.
LC: Mr 31, '25.
PW: Ap 25, '25.

C-305 Chapman, Katharine Hopkins, 1872-1930. The fusing force: an Idaho idyl / by Katharine Hopkins Chapman; illustrated by W. Herbert Dunton. Chicago: A. C. McClurg & Co., 1911. 416 p., col. front.
LC: O 9, '11.
PW: S 23, '11.

C-306 ____ Love's way in Dixie: some short stories from Cupid's favorite field / by Katharine Hopkins Chapman. New York; Washington: The Neale Publishing Company, 1905. 144 p. **TNS**
Contents: The penitent passenger -- A willing victim -- Misdirected -- The peanut prince -- A pink cravat -- "The top o' the morning" -- Whose picture?
PW: S 16, '05.

C-307 Chapman, Marian, b. 1873. Poor Pinney / by Marian Chapman. New York: Boni and Liveright, [c1923]. 302, [1] p.
LC: F 27, '23.

Chappell, George Shepard, 1877-1946. See **Traprock, Walter E., pseud.**

C-308 Chappelle, L. L. The diverging paths: a story of the pioneer days of Missouri / by L. L. Chappelle. New York; Chicago; Washington; Baltimore; Atlanta; Norfolk; Florence, Ala.: Broadway Publishing Co., [c1911]. 214 p., front., [2] leaves of plates. [Ill. by Wm. L. Hudson.]
LC: Mr 18, '11.
PW: My 20, '11.

C-309 Chapple, Joseph Mitchell, 1867-1950. The heart chord: a story that just grew, unfolding widely-varied phases of American life as viewed in editorial work on a country weekly, daily newspaper and magazine / by Joe Mitchell Chapple. Boston: The Chapple Publishing Company, Ltd., 1916. 300 p., col. front., [12] leaves of plates. [Ill. Arthur Hutchins.]

C-310 Charles, Cecil. Miss Sylvester's marriage / by Cecil Charles; illustrated by W. Sherman Potts. New York; London: The Smart Set Publishing Co., 1903. 254 p., front., [3] leaves of plates.
PW: S 5, '03.

C-311 Charles, Frances Asa, b. 1872. The awakening of the Duchess / by Frances Charles . . . ; illustrated by I. H. Caliga. Boston: Little, Brown and Company, 1903. 227 p., col. front., [3] leaves of col. plates.
PW: O 31, '03.

C-312   ____ In the country God forgot: a story of to-day / by Frances Charles. Boston: Little, Brown & Company, 1902. 328 p.
PW: My 3, '02.

C-313   ____ Pardner of Blossom Range / by Frances Charles. Boston: Little, Brown and Company, 1906. 311 p.
LC: O 25, '06.
PW: N 3, '06.

C-314   ____ The siege of youth / by Frances Charles; illustrated by Harry E. Townsend. Boston: Little, Brown & Company, 1903. 293 p., front., [4] leaves of plates.
PW: Je 6, '03.

C-315   Charles, T. Owen (Thomas Owen), b. 1866. Dear old Wales: a patriotic love story / by T. Owen Charles . . . Pittsburgh, Pa.: Press of American Printing Co., [c1912]. 189 p., ill., music, ports. Decorated end papers. [Some ills. by Sarah Farley Allan.]   **SAP**
LC: Jl 17, '12.

Charlesworth, M. E., pseud. <u>See</u> **Booth, Maud Ballington, 1865-1948.**

Charlton, C. C. The taming of the barons. <u>In</u> **Seattle Writers' Club.** *Tillicum tales* **(1907), S-248.**

C-316   Charlton, Emanuel C. (Emanuel Carlson), b. 1849. A Puritan captain / by Emanuel C. Charlton . . . Dayton, Ohio: Christian Publishing Association, 1908. 268 p.

Chase, Amanda Mathews. <u>See</u> **Mathews, Amanda, b. 1866.**

C-317   Chase, Charles Wathen. Life, or, Unto the third and fourth generation / by Charles Wathen Chase and Eugene Francis. New York: Charles Montgomery Benton, [c1904]. 417 p.   **DLC**

C-318   Chase, Daniel, b. 1890. Flood tide / by Daniel Chase; frontispiece by W. B. King. New York: The Macmillan Company, 1918. 358 p., front.
LC: Mr 8, '18.
PW: Mr 23, '18.

C-319   ____ The middle passage / by Daniel Chase. New York: The Macmillan Company, 1923. 273 p.
LC: O 17, '23.

C-320   Chase, Edward E. (Edward Everett). Tales of Bolivar's children / by Edward E. Chase. Augusta, Me.: Kennebec Journal Company, 1914. 124 p.
Stories of the University of Maine.
Contents: The conception of Bolivar -- A matter of definition -- The story of Mr. Spear's pig -- Ideal conditions -- The best he had -- The reward of valor -- A corpseless funeral -- Mike Mahoney's reform movement -- The way to lose -- Fractional fabrication -- Who's a piker?
LC: Ja 20, '15.

Chase, F. E. The white brick. <u>In</u> *Through the forbidden gates* **(1903), T-222.**

C-321   Chase, J. Smeaton (Joseph Smeaton), 1864-1923. The penance of Magdalena: and other tales of the California missions / by J. Smeaton Chase; with illustrations. Boston; New York: Houghton Mifflin Company, [c1915]. [80] p., ill. [Ill. by Herbert Davis.]
Contents: The penance of Magdalena -- Padre Urbano's umbrella -- The bells of San Gabriel -- The buried treasure of Simí -- Love in the Padres' garden.

C-322   Chase, Jessie Anderson, b. 1865. Chan's wife: a story / by Jessie Anderson Chase. Boston: Marshall Jones Company, 1919. 223 p.
LC: O 4, '19.
PW: N 1, '19.

C-323   Chase, Mary Ellen, 1887-1973. The girl from the Big Horn country / by Mary Ellen Chase; illustrated by R. Farrington Elwell. Boston: The Page Company, 1916. 319 p., col. front., [6] leaves of plates.
LC: Ja 28, '16.

C-324   ____ Virginia of Elk Creek Valley / by Mary Ellen Chase . . . ; illustrated by R. Farrington Elwell. Boston: The Page Company, 1917. 297 p., front.
LC: Ap 9, '17.
PW: Ap 28, '17.

C-325   Chater, Melville, b. 1878. The eternal rose: a story without a beginning or an end / by Melville Carter. New York; Chicago; Toronto, etc.: Fleming H. Revell Company, [c1910]. 288 p.
LC: S 21, '10.

C-326   ____ Little love stories of Manhattan / by Melville Chater. New York: The Grafton Press, [c1904]. 225 p.
Contents: Cupid kidnapper -- Cupid skyscraper -- Cupid train announcer -- Cupid blue ribboner -- Cupid chaplain -- Cupid quick luncher -- Cupid silent partner -- Cupid castaway -- Cupid war correspondent -- Cupid refugee -- Cupid flower boy -- Cupid highwayman -- Cupid lion tamer -- Cupid bank robber -- Cupid swashbuckler -- Cupid masquerader -- Cupid trespasser -- Cupid motorman -- Cupid understudy -- Cupid and Western preferred -- Elevated Cupid.
PW: D 10, '04.

C-327   Chatfield-Taylor, H. C. (Hobart Chatfield), 1865-1945. The crimson wing / by H. C. Chatfield-Taylor. Chicago; New York: Herbert S. Stone & Company, 1902. 356 p.
PW: Mr 22, '02.
BLC: London: Grant Richards; Chicago [printed], 1902.

C-328   ____ Fame's pathway: a romance of a genius / by H. C. Chatfield-Taylor; illustrations by "JoB." New York: Duffield & Company, 1909. 341 p., front., [11] leaves of plates.
LC: Mr 24, '09.

C-329   Chatterton, A. L. (Augustus Leonard), b. 1852. The strange story of the Quillmores / by A. L. Chatterton. New York: Stitt Publishing Company, 1905. 272 p., front., [3] leaves of plates.
PW: D 2, '05.

C-330   Chauffeur chaff, or, Automobilia: anecdotes, stories, bon-mots: also a history of the evolution of the automobile / edited by Charles Welsh. Boston: H. M. Caldwell Co., [c1905]. 99 p.   **KSU**
Includes *The evolution of the automobile* by Charles Welsh, on p. 81-99.

C-331   Cheatham, Carrie V. Beatrice Sumpter / by Corrie V. Cheatham. Boston, Massachusetts: C. M. Clark Publishing Company, 1908. 333 p., front., [7] leaves of plates.   **NDD**
LC: D 9, '08.

C-332   Cheever, Harriet A. (Harriet Anna). Elmcove / by Mrs. Harriet A. Cheever. New York: American Tract Society, [c1902]. 334 p., front., [4] leaves of plates. [Ill. by H. Bockmeyer.]

C-333   Cheley, F. H. (Frank Hobart), 1889-1941. The adventure of a prodigal father / F. H. Cheley. New York; London: Association Press, 1916. 132 p.
LC: Ja 6, '17.
PW: Ja 13, '17.

C-334   ____ A big brother investment / F. H. Cheley . . . New York: Association Press, 1917. 101 p.
"This little story was first printed serially in the American motherhood magazine."
LC: Je 30, '17.
PW: Jl 7, '17.

C-335   ____ Buffalo Roost: a story of a Young Men's Christian Association boys' department / by F. H. Cheley; illustrations by the author. Cincinnati: Jennings and Graham; New York: Eaton and Mains, [c1913]. 363 p., front., [10] leaves of plates.
LC: Ap 17, '13.
PW: Ap 26, '13.

C-336   ____ The mystery of Chimney Rock: being a story of the search for gold in the land of the Ute Indians in "the days of '49" / by Frank H. Cheley; illustrated by Frank T. Merrill. Boston: W. A. Wilde, 1924. 300 p., ill.
Unexamined copy: bibliographic data from OCLC, #19840206.
LC: O 31, '24.
PW: O 18, '24.

C-337   ____ Overland for gold / by F. H. Cheley. New York; Cincinnati: The Abingdon Press, [c1920]. 272 p.
LC: Mr 20, '20.
PW: Mr 20, '20.

C-338   Chenault, Fletcher. Children of destiny / by Fletcher Chenault. New York; London: F. Tennyson Neely, [1902]. 152 p.
Unexamined copy: bibliographic data from OCLC, #26832684.

C-339   Chenery, Susan, *pseud*. As the twig is bent: a story for mothers and teachers / by Susan Chenery [pseud.]. Boston; New York: Houghton Mifflin Company, 1901. (Cambridge: The Riverside Press). 164 p.   **CWR**
PW: N 2, '01.

C-340   Cheney, Elizabeth. The house of love / by Elizabeth Cheney. New York; Cincinnati: The Abingdon Press, [c1914]. 314 p., front., [1] leaf of plates. [Ill. by George T. Tobin.]
LC: S 24, '14.
PW: O 3, '14.

C-341   Cheney, Frank J. A life of unity: and other stories / by Frank J. Cheney. Toledo: [Blade Printing and Paper Company], 1901. 185 p., front.
Contents: A life of unity -- Aunt Betsy and the ghost -- A Christmas incident -- The story of a kodak -- How a reporter "got even" with a chief of police -- Aunt Polly's kiss -- The old homestead -- The peculiar experiences of a railroad man -- What is happiness?
PW: F 22, '02.

C-342   [Cheney, Walter Thomas.] Miss Incognita: a novel by "Don Jon" [pseud.]. New York; Chicago; London: F. Tennyson Neely Co., [1901]. 321 p.

C-343   Cheney, Warren, 1858-1921. The challenge / by Warren Cheney; with illustrations by N. C. Wyeth. Indianapolis: The Bobbs-Merrill Company, [1906]. 386 p., front., [3] leaves of plates.
PW: Mr 10, '06.

C-344   ____ His wife / by Warren Cheney; with a frontispiece by Frank E. Schoonover. Indianapolis: The Bobbs-Merrill Company, [c1907]. 395 p., col. front.
LC: S 30, '07.

C-345   ____ The way of the North: a romance of the days of Baranof / by Warren Cheney. New York: Doubleday, Page & Company, 1905. 320 p.
PW: Mr 25, '05.

C-346   Cher, Marie, *pseud*. The immortal gymnasts / by Marie Cher [pseud.]. New York: George H. Doran Company, [c1915]. 338 p.
LC: N 30, '15.
PW: F 5, '16.
BLC: London: William Heinemann, 1915.

C-347   Cheshire, Ella Miller. The romance of Jessamine Place: and other stories / by Ella Miller Cheshire . . . Boston, U. S. A.: The Christopher Publishing House, [c1924]. 67 p., front. (port.).   **DLC**
Contents: Por' Brer' Wiley (poem) -- The romance of Jessamine Place -- An Alabama romance -- His great temptation.
LC: Ap 9, '24.
PW: Je 7, '24.

C-348   Chesnutt, Charles Waddell, 1858-1932. The colonel's dream / by Charles W. Chesnutt. New York: Doubleday, Page & Company, 1905. 294 p.
PW: S 16, '05.
BLC: London: Doubleday, Page & Co.; New York [printed], 1905. Another copy with a different title page: London: A. Constable & Co., 1905.

C-349   ____ The marrow of tradition / by Charles W. Chesnutt. Boston; New York: Houghton, Mifflin and Company, 1901. (Cambridge: The Riverside Press). 329, [1] p.
PW: N 2, '01.

C-350   Chester, George Randolph, 1869-1924. The ball of fire / by George Randolph Chester and Lillian Chester. New York: Hearst's International Library Co., 1914. 370 p., front., [3] leaves of plates. [Ill. by Will Foster, M. Leone Bracker, and George Gibbs.]
LC: S 30, '14.
PW: F 6, '15.

_____ Bargain day at the Tutt house. In *The best American humorous short stories* **(1920), B-556.**

C-351   _____ Cordelia Blossom / by George Randolph Chester; illustrated by Henry Raleigh. New York: Hearst's International Library Co., 1914. 384 p., front., [3] leaves of plates.
LC: Ap 3, '14.
PW: My 9, '14.

C-352   _____ The early bird: a business man's love story / by George Randolph Chester; with illustrations by Arthur William Brown. Indianapolis: The Bobbs-Merrill Company, [c1910]. 280 p., front., [5] leaves of plates.
LC: My 18, '10.
PW: Je 4, '10.

C-353   _____ The enemy / by George Randolph Chester & Lillian Chester; illustrated by A. B. Wenzell. New York: Hearst's International Library Co., [c1915]. 362 p., front., [7] leaves of plates.
LC: Ap 29, '15.
PW: My 15, '15.

C-354   _____ Five thousand an hour: how Johnny Gamble won the heiress / by George Randolph Chester; illustrated by Henry Raleigh. Indianapolis: The Bobbs-Merrill Company, [c1912]. 366, [1] p., front., [11] leaves of plates.
LC: Mr 19, '12.
PW: Mr 16, '12.

C-355   _____ Get-rich-quick Wallingford: a cheerful account of the rise and fall of an American business buccaneer / by George Randolph Chester. -- [1st ed.] -- Philadelphia: Henry Altemus Company, 1908. 448 p., front., [5] leaves of plates. [Ill. by F. R. Gruger, Widney and H. Raleigh.]   **KSU**
LC: Ap 14, '08.
PW: Ap 25, '08.
BLC: London: A. P. Watt, [1908]. Another edition: London: Grant Richards, 1908.

C-356   _____ The Jingo / by George Randolph Chester; with illustrations by F. Vaux Wilson. Indianapolis: The Bobbs-Merrill Company, [c1912]. 393, [1] p., front., [10] leaves of plates.
LC: S 24, '12.
PW: S 28, '12.

C-357   _____ The making of Bobby Burnit / by George Randolph Chester; with illustrations by James Montgomery Flagg and F. R. Gruger. Indianapolis: The Bobbs-Merrill Company, [c1909]. 416 p., front., [7] leaves of plates.
LC: Je 14, '09.
PW: Je 19, '09.

C-358   _____ On the lot and off / by George Randolph Chester and Lilian [sic] Chester. New York; London: Harper & Brothers, [c1924]. 328 p.
LC: Ap 5, '24.
PW: Ap 5, '24.

_____ The peanut hull. In *Saturday Evening Post* **(1919), S-90.**

C-359   _____ Runaway June / by George Randolph Chester & Lillian Chester . . . ; illustrated from photographs. New York: Hearst's International Library Co., [c1915]. 310 p., photo. front., [15] leaves of photo. plates.
LC: My 21, '15.
PW: Je 5, '15.

C-360   _____ The son of Wallingford / By Mr. and Mrs. George Randolph Chester. Boston: Small, Maynard & Company, [c1921]. 269 p.
LC: Ag 22, '21.
PW: O 1, '21.

C-361   _____ A tale of red roses / George Randolph Chester. Indianapolis: The Bobbs-Merrill Company, [c1914]. 296 p.
LC: O 14, '14.
PW: O 10, '14.

_____ The triple cross. In *Representative American short stories* **(1923), R-175.**

C-362   _____ Wallingford and Blackie Daw / by George Randolph Chester . . . Indianapolis: The Bobbs-Merrill Company, [c1913]. 400, [1] p.
LC: O 9, '13.
PW: O 25, '13.
BLC: London: Hodder & Stoughton, [1918].

C-363   _____ Wallingford in his prime / by George Randolph Chester. Indianapolis: The Bobbs-Merrill Company, [c1913]. 424 p.
LC: My 14, '13.
PW: My 10, '13.

C-364   _____ Young Wallingford / by George Randolph Chester; with illustrations by F. R. Gruger & Henry Raleigh. Indianapolis: The Bobbs-Merrill Company, [c1910]. 348 p., front., [5] leaves of plates.
LC: O 19, '10.
BLC: London: Hodder & Stoughton, 1917.

Chester, Lillian Gimblin, jt. aut. *The ball of fire* (1914). See **Chester, George Randolph, 1869-1924, jt. aut., C-350.**

_____, jt. aut. *The enemy* (1915). See **Chester, George Randolph, 1869-1924, jt. aut., C-353.**

_____, jt. aut. *On the lot and off* (1924). See **Chester, George Randolph, 1869-1924, jt. aut., C-358**

_____, jt. aut. *Runaway June* (1924). See **Chester, George Randolph, 1869-1924, jt. aut., C-359.**

_____, jt. aut. *The son of Wallingford* (1921). See

Chester, George Randolph, 1869-1924, jt. aut., C-360

C-365 ____ Taming a vaquero / by Lillian Gimblin Chester. San Francisco: Press Whitaker & Ray-Wiggin Co., 1909. 97 p.
LC: Ag 16, '09.

C-366 Chester, Lord, *pseud.* The great red dragon, or, The flaming devil of the Orient / by Lord Chester [pseud.]. Estero, Florida: The Guiding Star Publishing House, 1909. 48 p. **LPU**

Chetwood, Edith. <u>See</u> **Thompson, Edith Chetwood.**

C-367 Chetwood, John, b. 1859. Our search for the missing millions (of Cocos Island): being an account of a curious cruise and a more than curious character / by one of the searchers. [San Francisco?]: South Sea Bubble Company, [c1904]. 210 p., photo. front., [11] leaves of photo. plates. **CLO**

C-368 Chichester, John Jay. The bigamist: a detective story / by John Jay Chichester. New York: Chelsea House, [c1925]. 314 p.
PW: Je 27, '25.
BLC: London: Hutchinson & Co., [1927].

C-369 ____ The porcelain mask: a detective story / by John Jay Chichester. New York City: Chelsea House, [c1924]. 320 p.
LC: My 5, '24.
PW: My 3, '24.
BLC: London: Herbert Jenkins, 1925.

C-370 Chideckel, Maurice, b. 1876. The letters, musings and romance of a greenhorn / by Maurice Chideckel. Boston: The Roxburgh Publishing Company, Inc., [c1925]. 311 p.
PW: Je 13, '25.

C-371 Child, Richard Washburn, 1881-1935. The blue wall / by Richard Washburn Child; a story of strangeness and struggle. Boston; New York: Houghton Mifflin Company, [c1912]. 377, [1] p., col. front., [4] leaves of plates. [Ill. by E. Coles Phillips and Harold J. Cue.]
LC: Jl 2, '12.
PW: Je 22, '12.
BLC: London: Constable & Co.; Cambridge, Mass. [printed], 1912.

C-372 ____ Bodbank / by Richard Washburn Child. New York: Henry Holt and Company, 1916. 437 p.

C-373 ____ Fresh waters and other stories / by Richard Washburn Child. New York: E. P. Dutton & Company, [c1924]. 296 p.
Contents: Fresh waters -- The lure -- Here's how -- The man with the metal face -- The gorilla -- The screen -- Keats Shadd -- The playthings -- A thirty thousand dollar slap -- A strain of blood -- A story of a certain lady -- The eyes of the gazelle.
LC: N 8, '24.
BLC: London: Hodder & Stoughton; printed in U. S. A., [1925].

C-374 ____ The hands of Nara / by Richard Washburn Child. New York: E. P. Dutton & Company,

[c1922]. 326 p.
LC: Mr 15, '22.
PW: Mr 11, '22.

C-375 ____ Jim Hands / by Richard Washburn Child; frontispiece by J. A. Williams. New York: The Macmillan Company, 1910. 358 p., front.
LC: N 10, '10.
PW: D 3, '10.

____ Lassiter. <u>In</u> **Conrad, Joseph.** *Il conte* (1925), **C-697.**

C-376 ____ The man in the shadow / by Richard Washburn Child; illustrated. New York: The Macmillan Company, 1911. 372 p., front., [5] leaves of plates. [Ill. by Gayle Porter Hoskins, F. C. Yohn, George Hardin, Denman Fink, et al.]
Contents: The man in the shadow -- The quitters -- Shark -- Fight -- Service -- The white hand -- Civilized -- Unregenerate -- Among the nameless -- A glimmer of truth -- The final score -- The man as well -- "They was women" -- George Bond -- The decent average -- "J. P. J." -- Jenks and Julianna -- The one with red-brown hair.
LC: S 28, '11
PW: O 14, '11.

C-377 ____ The vanishing men / by Richard Washburn Child. New York: E. P. Dutton & Company, [c1920]. 324 p.
LC: Ap 30, '20.
PW: My 22, '20.

C-378 ____ The velvet black / by Richard Washburn Child. New York: E. P. Dutton & Company, [c1921]. 387 p.
Contents: The velvet black -- Identified -- The nightingale -- A whiff of heliotrope -- The cracking knee -- Fiber -- An experiment in rescue -- The avenger -- Pode -- In dancing shadows -- Foxed.
LC: Mr 28, '21.
PW: Mr 26, '21.
BLC: London: Hodder & Stoughton; printed in U. S. A., 1921.

Childe, Crispin, pseud. <u>See</u> **Schieren, Harrie Victor, b. 1881.**

Childs, Eleanor Stuart Patterson. <u>See</u> **Stuart, Eleanor, b. 1876.**

C-379 Childs, Jessie H. (Jessie Hopkins), b. 1867. The sea of matrimony: a novel / by Jessie H. Childs. New York; Baltimore: Broadway Publishing Company, [c1909]. 324 p.
LC: D 9, '09.
PW: Ja 15, '10.

C-380 Childs, Laura Clark. More Johanna stories / by Laura Clark Childs; illustrated by Walter Craft Stevens. Burlington, Vermont: Free Press Printing Co., [c1922]. 71, [1] p., ill.
Contents: Johanna and the fresh air children -- A wedding -- Johanna at sea -- Choosing a site -- -And Leery?
LC: D 11, '22.

C-381 Childs, Lysander D. The rights of a man / by Lysander D. Childs. Indianapolis: Enquirer Printing and Publishing Co., [c1918]. 222 p.
LC: Ja 25, '19.

C-382 Childs, Mary Fairfax. De namin' ob de twins: and other sketches from the cotton land / by Mary Fairfax Childs; illustrated by Edward H. Potthast. New York: B. W. Dodge & Company, 1908. 139 p., front., [6] leaves of plates.

Contents: De namin' ob de twins -- Roos' high, chicken -- Marse Linkum's mistek -- De baptizin' o' Black Betty -- "Down Souf" -- Aunt Glory's marriage certificate -- Mah honey -- De ole banjo-a Christmas memory -- De barn dance -- The "Old Masters" -- Little Abe's soliloquy -- Parson Pete's sermon -- Mandy and "Ole Miss"; Or, After many days -- When ebenin' comes -- Ole Joe an' de yaller mule; Or, "Faithful unto death" -- "Name this child" -- Ole 'Lijah's weddin'-a plantation episode -- Aunt 'Liza's visit North -- De "Yankee" buckeye -- De fambly tree -- De las' "will an' testimint" -- Mammy Sukey's buryin'.
LC: My 1, '08.

Chilton, Leila O. See **Ollie, pseud.**

C-383 Chipman, Charles Phillips, b. 1878. The page and the prince, or, A fight for a throne / by Charles Phillips Chipman; illustrated by John Goss. Boston: The Ball Publishing Co., 1908. 350 p., incl. front., [2] leaves of plates.
LC: N 23, '08.
BLC: London: Chatto & Windus, 1908.

C-384 ____ Through an unknown isle: a story of New Guinea / by Charles P. Chipman . . . ; illustrated by F. Gilbert Edge. Akron, Ohio; New York; Chicago: The Saalfield Publishing Company, 1903. 360 p., front., [3] leaves of plates. **OSU, CLU**
PW: D 5, '03.

C-385 Chipp, Elinor, b. 1898. Doubting castle / Elinor Chipp. New York: Boni and Liveright, [c1922]. 278 p. **UAG**
LC: S 23, '22.
BLC: London: W. Collins , Sons & Co., [1923].

C-386 ____ Many waters / by Elinor Chipp . . . New York; London: D. Appleton and Company, 1924. 330, [1] p. **OSU, KSU**
LC: Ag 1, '24.

Chipperfield, Robert Orr, pseud. See **Ostrander, Isabel Egenton, 1883-1924.**

C-387 Chisholm, A. M. (Arthur Murray), b. 1872. The boss of Wind River / by A. M. Chisholm; illustrations by Frank Tenney Johnson. Garden City, N. Y.: Doubleday, Page & Company, 1911. 340 p., col. front., [3] leaves of col. plates.
LC: S 21, '11.

C-388 ____ The land of big rivers: a story of the Northwest / by A. M. Chisholm. New York: Chelsea House, [c1924]. 305 p.
LC: N 18, '24.
BLC: London: Hodder & Stoughton, [1924].

C-389 ____ The land of strong men / by A. M. Chisholm; illustrated by Frank Tenney Johnson. New York: The H. K. Fly Company, [c1919]. 432 p., front., [3] leaves of plates.

C-390 ____ Precious waters / by A. M. Chisholm; illustrated by Clarence Rowe. Garden City, N. Y.: Doubleday, Page & Company, 1913. 422 p., col.

front., [3] leaves of col. plates. Pictorial end papers.
LC: F 20, '13.
BLC: London: Gay & Hancock; Garden City, N. Y., printed, [1915].

C-391 ____ The red-headed kids: an adventure story / by A. M. Chisholm. New York City: Chelsea House, [c1925]. 320 p. **RIU**
PW: O 31, '25.
BLC: London: Hodder & Stoughton, [1926].

C-392 ____ When Stuart came to Sitkum: a western story / by A. M. Chisholm. New York: Chelsea House, [c1924]. 320 p.
LC: Jl 19, '24.

C-393 Chittenden, Gerald, b. 1882. The anvil of chance / by Gerald Chittenden; with a frontispiece in color by W. C. Rice. New York; London; Bombay: Longmans, Green, and Co., 1915. 304 p., col. front.
LC: O 21, '15.
BLC: London: Longman's Co., 1915.

____ The victim of his vision. In *Prize stories of 1921* **(1922), P-619.**

C-394 Chittenden, Lulu Brower, b. 1877. At the end of the woods path / by Lulu Brower Chittenden. New York: Nicholas L. Brown, 1924. 190 p. **OSU, NYP**
LC: Mr 19, '25.
PW: N 15, '24.

C-395 Chitwood, Mary Morrison. All for the love of money / by Mary Morrison Chitwood. [Aurora, Mo.: Printed by Combination Card Co.], c1917. 204 p., photo. front. (port.). **AKP**
LC: Ap 9, '17.

C-396 ____ Saved for a purpose / by Mary Morrison Chitwood . . . Boston: The Christopher Publishing House, [c1921]. 228 p. **DLC**
LC: D 14, '21.

Christian, Mary, jt. aut. *Peggy-Elise* (1919). See **Kummer, Frederic Arnold, 1873-1943, jt. aut., K-410.**

Christian, Mary, jt. aut. *The pipes of yesterday* (1921). See **Kummer, Frederic Arnold, 1873-1943, jt. aut., K-411.**

C-397 Christian, W. Asbury (William Asbury), 1866-1936. Marah: a story of old Virginia / by W. Asbury Christian . . . Richmond, Va.: L. H. Jenkins, printers and binders, 1903. 386 p., front., [2] leaves of plates. **NOC**

C-398 Christianson, Barbara. A triumphant defeat / by Barbara Christianson; with introduction by Joseph Tyler Butts. New York; London: F. Tennyson Neely Co., [c1901]. 192 p., photo. front. (port.).
LC: O 30, '01.
PW: O 5, '01.

C-399 Christie, May. The gilded rose: a novel / by May Christie. New York; London: G. P. Putnam's Sons, 1925. ([New York]: The Knickerbocker Press).

379 p.   **DLC**
LC: Ag 25, '25.
PW: Ag 29, '25.
BLC: London: Hodder & Stoughton, [1924].

C-400   ____ The rebel bride / by May Christie . . . New York: Grosset & Dunlap, [c1925]. 308 p.   **VA@**
LC: F 27, '25.
PW: Mr 14, '25.
BLC: London: Hodder & Stoughton, [1924].

C-401   Christie, Nimmo. The black chanter: and other Highland stories / by Nimmo Christie. New York: The Macmillan Company; London: Macmillan & Co., Ltd., 1903. 226 p.
Contents: The black chanter -- The chieftain's duties -- The king's touch -- The dirk of Ewan -- The Craven's Craig -- The man of the paths -- The chief's portrait -- Fairy Ferlie -- The "wise woman" -- The bard.
BLC: Edinburgh; Glasgow: Scots Pictorial Publishing Co., 1903.

C-402   Christopher, Edgar Earl. The invisibles: a novel / by Edgar Earl Christopher; illustrated. Akron, Ohio; New York; Chicago: The Saalfield Publishing Company, 1903, [c1902]. 329 p., front., [3] leaves of plates. [Ill. by Winfield S. Lukens.]
PW: O 4, '02.

C-403   Church, J. W. Deep in piney woods / by J. W. Church; illustrated by M. Power O'Malley. New York: Thomas Y. Crowell & Co., [1910]. 354 p., col. front., [3] leaves of col. plates.
LC: Ag 24, '10.

C-404   Church, Samuel Harden. Flames of faith: a novel / by Samuel Harden Church . . . New York: Boni and Liveright, [c1924]. 358 p.   **NYP**
LC: Ap 4, '24.
PW: Mr 22, '24.

C-405   ____ Penruddock of the White Lambs: a tale of Holland, England and America / By Samuel Harden Church . . . ; with frontispiece by Frank T. Merrill. New York: Frederick A. Stokes Company, [1902]. 329 p., front.
PW: N 15, '02.

C-406   Church, Virginia, b. 1880. Commencement days: a novel / by Virginia Church; illustrated. Boston: L. C. Page & Company, 1910. 321 p., front., [14] leaves of plates.
PW: My 14, '10.

Churchill, Eugenia (Kellogg) Holmes. See **Kellogg, Eugenia.**

C-407   Churchill, Lida A. (Lida Abbie). A grain of madness: a romance / by Lida A. Churchill . . . New York; London; Montreal: The Abbey Press, [c1902]. 228 p.   **DLM**
PW: D 6, '02.
Another edition: New York City: New Tide Publishing House, [c1902]. 228 p.   **OSU**

C-408   Churchill, William, 1859-1920. An assisted idolator. Unexamined copy: bibliographic data from NUC.

C-409   Churchill, Winston, 1871-1947. Coniston / by Winston Churchill; with illustrations by Florence Scovel Shinn. New York: The Macmillan Company; London: Macmillan & Co., ltd., 1906. 543 p., ill.
BLC: London: Macmillan & Co., 1916.

C-410   ____ The crisis / by Winston Churchill; with illustrations by Howard Chandler Christy. New York: The Macmillan Company; London: Macmillan & Co., ltd., 1901. 522 p., front., [7] leaves of plates.
PW: Jl 2, '04.
BLC: London: Macmillan & Co., 1901.

C-411   ____ The crossing / by Winston Churchill; with illustrations by Sydney Adamson and Lilian Bayliss. New York: The Macmillan Company; London: Macmillan & Co., Ltd., 1904. 598 p., col. front., [6] leaves of col. plates.
PW: Je 4, '04.

C-412   ____ The dwelling-place of light / by Winston Churchill. New York: The Macmillan Company, 1917. 462 p., front. [Ill. by A. I. Keller.]
LC: O 11, '17.
PW: O 13, '17.
BLC: London: Macmillan & Co., 1917.

C-413   ____ The faith of Frances Craniford / by Winston Churchill. [New York: Church Pension Fund], 1917. 34 p.   **EEM**

C-414   ____ A far country / by Winston Churchill; illustrated by Herman Pfeifer. New York: The Macmillan Company, 1915. 509 p., front., [7] leaves of plates.
LC: Je 3, '15.
BLC: London: Macmillan & Co., 1915.

C-415   ____ The inside of the cup / by Winston Churchill; with illustrations by Howard Giles. New York: The Macmillan Company, 1913. 513 p., front., [5] leaves of plates.
LC: My 29, '13.
PW: Je 14, '13.
BLC: London: Macmillan & Co., 1913.

C-416   ____ A modern chronicle / by Winston Churchill; illustrated by J. H. Gardner Soper. New York: The Macmillan Company, 1910. 524 p., front. ill., [1] leaf of plates (port.), ill.
PW: Ap 9, '10.
BLC: London: Macmillan & Co., 1910.

C-417   ____ Mr. Crewe's career / by Winston Churchill . . . ; illustrated. New York: The Macmillan Company, 1908. 498 p., front., [7] leaves of plates. [Ill. by The Kinneys and A. J. Keller.]
LC: Ap 22, '08.
PW: My 16, '08.
BLC: London: Macmillan & Co., 1908.

C-418   ____ Mr. Keegan's elopement / by Winston Churchill. New York: The Macmillan Company; London: Macmillan & Co., Ltd., 1903. 73 p., front. (port.), [2] leaves of plates. Designed end papers. (Little novels by favourite authors.)

PW: Je 20, '03.
BLC: London: Macmillan & Co., 1903.

C-419   Cipriani, Lisi Cecilia. A Tuscan childhood / by Lisi Cipriani. New York: The Century Co., 1907. 269 p.   **OCP**
LC: S 20, '07.

C-420   Clancy, Eugene A. Watched out: an adventure story / by Eugene A. Clancy. New York City: Chelsea House, [c1925]. 250 p.
PW: My 16, '25.

C-421   Clancy, Louise Breitenbach. Christine of the young heart: a novel / by Louise Breitenbach Clancy . . . Boston: Small, Maynard & Company, [c1920]. 341 p.
LC: S 18, '20.

C-422   Clapp, H. Watson (Henry Watson). The daughter's portion / by H. Watson Clapp. [Springfield, Massachusetts: Phelps Publishing Co., c1924]. 333 p.   **DLC**
LC: Ag 23, '24.

C-423   ____ The triple alliance / by H. Watson Clapp. [s. l.: Phelps Service Press, c1922]. 369 p.   **NYP**
LC: Ag 23, '24.

C-424   Clare, W. H., *pseud.* The rattle of his chains / by W. H. Clare [pseud.]. Boston: Eastern Publishing Co., [c1905]. 370 p.   **DLC**
PW: F 24, '06.

C-425   Clark, Adelbert G. (Adelbert Gilroy), b. 1870. A heart of oak / by Adelbert Clark. Lakeport, N. H.: [s. n.], 1916. 267 p.
Contents: A heart of oak -- Heliotrope -- Mebema's opal -- A silver ring -- Her mother's sin.

C-426   ____ John Martin of Martin's Corner / by Adelbert Clark. Lakeport, N. H.: [s. n.], 1917. 337 p.
                                                DLC
LC: Je 11, '17.

C-427   Clark, Anna Taggart. The quest of "little Blessing" / by Anna Taggart Clark; cover design and illustrations by Howard Willard; typography by Taylor's Printery. Los Angeles, Cal.: Warren T. Potter, publisher and bookmaker, [c1916]. 55 p., ill.   **NYP**

         Clark, Arthur March, b. 1853. See **Duncan, James A., pseud.**

C-428   Clark, Badger, 1883-1957. Spike / Badger Clark . . . Boston: Richard G. Badger, [c1925]. ([Boston]: The Gorham Press). 215 p., front., [6] leaves of plates. [Some ills. by Harold Schmidt.]   **MNU**
Contents: The little widow -- In the natural -- The sacred salt -- A great institution -- Don't spoil his aim -- Tuck's quiet wedding -- The chronic hero -- The price of liberty -- Scat!
LC: Ap 13, '25.
PW: Ap 11, '25.

C-429   Clark, Charles Heber, 1841-1915. By the bend of the river: tales of Connock old and new / by Charles Heber Clark (Max Adeler); illustrated. Philadelphia:

The John C. Winston Company, [c1914]. 307 p., photo. front., [7] leaves of plates. [Ill. by W. R. Leigh and Will Owen.]
Reprinted in part from various periodicals.
Contents: Grandma Pevey -- The millionaires -- The great natural healer -- Frictional electricity -- The rally at the forge -- The fortunate island -- The reform campaign in Meriweather County -- An old fogy -- The Flying Dutchman -- Mr. Skinner's night in the underworld -- Jinnie.
LC: O 13, '14.

C-430   ____ Captain Bluitt: a tale of old Turley / by Charles Heber Clark (Max Adeler). Philadelphia: Henry T. Coates & Co., 1901. 463 p., front., [3] leaves of plates. [Ill. by John Henderson Betts.]
LC: N 1, '01.
PW: N 16, '01.
BLC: London: Ward, Lock & Co., 1901.

         [____] Frictional electricity. In *Short story classics* **(1905), S-466.**

C-431   ____ The great natural healer / by Charles Heber Clark (Max Adeler). Philadelphia: George W. Jacobs & Co., [1910]. 82 p., front., [4] leaves of plates.
LC: My 2, '10.
PW: My 14, '10.

C-432   ____ In Happy Hollow / by Max Adeler [pseud.] (Charles Heber Clark); illustrated by Clare Victor Dwiggins and Herman Rountree. Philadelphia: Henry T. Coates & Co., 1903. 337 p., front., ill.
PW: Jl 18, '03.
BLC: London: Ward, Lock & Co., 1903.

C-433   ____ The Quakeress: a tale / by Charles Heber Clark (Max Adeler); with illustrations in color by George Gibbs. Philadelphia: The John C. Winston Co., 1905. 392 p., col. front., [7] leaves of plates (some col.).

C-434   Clark, Charles Sumner. The tyranny of power: a romance of two notable wars of the United States, before the rebellion: an American story for Americans / by Charles Sumner Clark. Boston: The C. M. Clark Publishing Company, 1910. 375 p., front., [5] leaves of plates. [Ill. by D. S. Ross.]
LC: F 3, '10.

C-435   Clark, E. Marie. First wed, then won / by E. Marie Clark . . . Oneonta, N. Y.: The Oneonta Press, 1901. 182 p., photo. front., [9] leaves of photo. plates.

C-436   Clark, Ella M. The Ramoth / by Ella M. Clark. North Adams, Mich.: Published by Louis V. Harvey, 1918. 129 p., photo. ill.

C-437   Clark, Ellery H. (Ellery Harding), 1874-1949. The camp at Sea Duck Cove / by Ellery H. Clark; with illustrations by Lucy Fitch Perkins. Boston; New York: Houghton Mifflin Company, 1912. (Cambridge: The Riverside Press). 276, [1] p., front., [9] leaves of plates.
LC: S 23, '12.
PW: S 21, '12.

C-438 _____ The Carleton case / by Ellery H. Clark; with illustrations by George Brehm. Indianapolis: The Bobbs-Merrill Company, [c1910]. 345, [1] p., front., [4] leaves of plates.
LC: Mr 23, '10.
PW: Ap 16, '10.

C-439 _____ Daughters of Eve / by Ellery H. Clark. Philadelphia: Dorrance & Company, [c1924]. 287 p.   **NYP**
LC: S 24, '24.
BLC: London: Hurst & Blackett, [1925].

C-440 _____ Loaded dice / by Ellery H. Clark; with illustrations by F. Graham Cootes. Indianapolis: The Bobbs-Merrill Company, [c1909]. 375 p., front., [4] leaves of plates.
LC: Mr 10, '09.
PW: Mr 13, '09.

C-441 _____ The money gods / by Ellery H. Clark . . . Boston; New York: The Cornhill Publishing Company, 1922. 253 p.   **BGU**
LC: N 21, '22.

C-442 _____ Pharos / Ellery H. Clark. Boston: Richard G. Badger, [c1913]. (Boston: The Gorham Press). 375 p.
LC: O 6, '13.
PW: O 18, '13.

C-443 _____ Putting it over / by Ellery H. Clark. Boston: The Cornhill Publishing Company, 1923. 292 p., col. front., [1] leaf of plates. [Ill. by J. Malcolm Milne.]
LC: Je 14, '23.

C-444 Clark, Felicia Buttz, b. 1862. Beppino / by Felicia Buttz Clark. New York: Eaton & Mains; Cincinnati: Jennings & Pye, [c1901]. 68 p., front., [5] leaves of plates. [Ill. by George T. Tobin.]   **DLC**

C-445 _____ David Golding / by Felicia Buttz Clark. Cincinnati: Jennings and Pye; New York: Eaton and Mains, [c1903]. 201 p.
PW: O 31, '03.

C-446 _____ The Jesuit / by Felicia Buttz Clark. New York: Eaton & Mains; Cincinnati: Jennings & Graham, [c1908]. 282 p.
LC: N 20, '08.
PW: D 5, '08.

C-447 _____ The sword of Garibaldi / by Felicia Buttz Clark. New York: Eaton & Mains; Cincinnati: Jennings & Pye, [c1903]. 274 p., front., [21] leaves of plates.
PW: O 31, '03.

C-448 _____ That Ketron streak / by Felicia Butts [sic] Clark. Col., O. [i.e. Columbus, Ohio]: L. B. C. [i.e. Lutheran Book Concern], [191-?]. 128 p.
No publication date appears in book.

C-449 _____ Under the stars and stripes / by Felicia Buttz Clark. Col., O. [i.e., Columbus, Ohio]: L. B. C., [192-?]. 64 p.
No publication date appears in book.

C-450 _____ Virgilia, or, Out of the lion's mouth / by Felicia Buttz Clark. [Columbus, Ohio?]: L. B. C., 1917. 91 p., front., [2] leaves of plates.

C-451 Clark, Helen F. A child of the slums / by Helen F. Clark; with full-page illustrations by C. Pym. Boston: James H. Earle, Publisher, 1901. 158 p., front., [9] leaves of plates.   **DLC** (photocopy)
LC: Mr 10, '03.
PW: Je 13, '03.

Clark, Hugh A. <u>See</u> **Boggs, Robert, pseud.**

C-452 Clark, Imogen. A charming humbug / by Imogen Clark. New York: E. P. Dutton & Company, 1909. 290 p.
LC: Je 29, '09.
PW: Jl 17, '09.
BLC: London: Methuen & Co., 1911.

C-453 _____ God's puppets: a story of old New York / by Imogen Clark. New York: Charles Scribner's Sons, 1901. 381 p.
PW: Mr 30, '01.
BLC: Toronto: W. J. Gage & Co., [1901].

C-454 Clark, J. Mat. (James Madison), b. 1847. Luella Blassingame, or, The blue and the gray / by J. Mat. Clark. Nashville, Tenn.: McQuiddy Printing Company, 1903. 221 p.   **SUC**

C-455 Clark, Jacob Wendell, b. 1878. In the sight of God / by Jacob Wendell Clark; with an introduction by E. C. Dudley. Chicago: Covici-McGee Co., 1924. 369 p.
LC: My 17, '24.

C-456 Clark, James Bayard, b. 1869. Doctors, entre nous: short stories / by James Bayard Clark; illustrations by Joseph St. Amand. New York: The Medical Times Company, [c1922]. 66 p., ill.
Contents: An unlooked for conclusion -- How Dr. Jones came back -- The narrow-minded layman.

C-457 [Clark, Joseph], b. 1854. Fishin' fer men, or, The redemshun of Jeriko kort house / by Timothy Stand-by [pseud.] (Joseph Clark); drawings by Marie Grace Clark. Cincinnati: Jennings and Graham; New York: Eaton and Mains, [c1911]. 244 p., front., [15] leaves of plates.
"The twenty-four Timothy Stand-by letters combined in this volume were originally published as a serial in the Adult Bible class monthly . . . under the title `The redemshun of Jeriko kort house'."

C-458 _____ Timothy Stand-by: the Sunday-school man / by Joseph Clark . . . Philadelphia: The Sunday School Times Co., 1904. 142 p., front., ill. [Ill. by Frank Beard.]
"A compilation and revision of the first series of Timothy Stand-by letters published in The Ohio Sunday school worker."

C-459 Clark, Kate Upson, 1851-1935. Up the Witch Brook Road: a summer idyl / by Kate Upson Clark. New York: J. F. Taylor & Company, 1902. 366 p.

C-460   Clark, S. R. Graham (Susanna Rebecca Graham), b. 1848. The cry of the two-thirds / by Mrs. S. R. Graham Clark. Boston: James H. Earle & Company, 1901. 678 p., front. (port.).
PW: D 28, '01.

C-461   ____ Forty-eight Bernard Street / by Mrs. S. R. Graham Clark . . . Chicago: The Bible Institute Colportage Ass'n . . . , [c1924]. 128 p., incl. front.   **NEO**
LC: D 20, '24.

C-462   ____ Gail Weston / by S. R. Graham Clark . . . Philadelphia: Griffith & Rowland Press, [c1907]. 431 p., front., [5] leaves of plates. [Ill. by Franz de Merlier.]   **DLC**
LC: O 4, '07.

C-463   ____ Janet Vardoff / by Mrs. Graham Clark . . . Philadelphia; Boston; Chicago; St. Louis: The Griffith & Rowland Press, 1910. 455 p., col. front., [7] leaves of col. plates. [Ill. by Helen Pettes.]
LC: N 12, '10.

C-464   ____ Phyllis Burton: a tale of New England / by S. R. Graham Clark. Philadelphia: The Griffith & Rowland Press, 1905. 489 p., front., [11] leaves of plates. [Ill. by Walter Cooper Bradley.]
PW: S 30, '05.

C-465   Clark, Susie C. (Susie Champney), b. 1856. All that man should be unto woman: a psychic story / by Susie C. Clark . . . Boston, Massachusetts: The C. M. Clark Publishing Company, 1910. 255 p.
LC: S 12, '10.

Clark, Valma. Ignition. In *The best short stories of 1923 and the yearbook of the American short story* (1924), B-568.

C-466   Clark, W. Chester. Wade Maples: a tale of the cow country / by W. Chester Clark. [Koshonong, Mo.: Oregon County Leader Press, c1909]. 187 p.

C-467   Clarke, Albert G. (Albert Gallatin), Jr. The Arickaree treasure: and other brief tales of adventurous Montanians / by Albert G. Clarke, Jr. New York; London; Montreal: The Abbey Press, [c1901]. 232 p., front.
Contents: The Arickaree treasure -- Too Enterprising Bill -- There was John Smith -- That Sun River stampede -- Harrup's big sapphire -- 'Twas company orders -- Old Glass Eye's instinct -- Lost their ton of gold -- 'Tis an ill wind -- The missing match -- Unprofessional conduct of Dr. McCall -- Two men of the Marias -- Infernal luck of Mr. Brown.

C-468   Clarke, Francis H. Morgan Rockefeller's will: a romance of 1991-2 / by Francis H. Clarke. Portland, Oregon: Clarke-Cree Publishing Co., c1909. 306 p.

C-469   Clarke, Herman D. (Herman Devillo), b. 1850. The great test, or, The struggles and triumph of Lorna Selover / by Rev. Herman D. Clarke. Plainfield, N. J.: The American Sabbath Tract Society, 1916. 275 p., photo. front. (port.).   **NYP**
"This story was published as a serial in the Sabbath recorder in 1916."
LC: O 25, '16.

C-470   Clarke, Ida Clyde, b. 1878. Record no. 33 / by Ida Clyde Clarke; illustrated by Stockton Mulford. New York; London: D. Appleton and Company, 1915. 317, [1] p., front., [3] leaves of plates.
LC: S 14, '15.

Clarke, William James Patmore, b. 1847. See **Patmore, William J.**

C-471   Claussen, Ida von. "Forget it" / by Ida von Claussen. New York: Broadway Publishing Co., [c1910]. 277 p., photo. front. (port.), [6] leaves of photo. plates.   **DLC**
LC: D 3, '10.
PW: F 25, '11.

C-472   Clay, Grover. Hester of the hills: a romance of the Ozark Mountains / by Grover Clay; with a frontispiece in colour by Griswold Tyng. Boston: L. C. Page and Company, 1907. 410 p., col. front.
LC: O 1, '07.
PW: O 19, '07.

C-473   Clay, John M., Mrs. Frank Logan: a novel / by Mrs. John M. Clay. New York; London; Montreal: The Abbey Press, [c1901]. 223 p., [1] leaf of plates.
PW: F 22, '02.

C-474   ____ The sport of kings: racing stories / by Mrs. John M. Clay . . . New York: Broadway Publishing Co., [c1912]. 90 p.   **VPI**
Contents: Who rode La Sylphide? -- Why there was no sermon at Mount Gilead -- The bishop's daughter -- Honors are easy -- The Mexican empire steeplechase -- My kingdom is not of this world.
LC: My 24, '12.
PW: Jl 20, '12.

Clay, Josephine Russell. See **Clay, John M., Mrs.**

Cleaveland, Agnes Morley. The greatest of these. In *West winds* (1914), W-368.

C-475   [Cleaveland, Frank Edward], b. 1853. A rift in the cloud: a novel / written by one who sees only with the eyes of the mind. Washington, D. C.: Columbia Polytechnic institute for the blind, c1904. 159 p.
Unexamined copy: bibliographic data from OCLC, #26832851.

C-476   Cleaves, Charles Poole, b. 1869. A case of sardines: a story of the Maine coast / by Charles Poole Cleaves. Boston; New York; Chicago: The Pilgrim Press, [c1904]. 322 p., front., [5] leaves of plates.
PW: Jl 16, '04.

C-477   Cleghorn, Sarah Norcliffe, 1876-1959. Fellow captains / by Sarah N. Cleghorn and Dorothy Canfield Fisher. New York: Henry Holt and Company, 1916. 153 p.
LC: N 16, '16.

C-478   ____ The spinster: a novel wherein a nineteenth century girl finds her place in the twentieth / by Sarah N. Cleghorn. New York: Henry Holt and Company, 1916. 326 p.
LC: Ap 19, '16.
PW: Ap 8, '16.

C-479 ____ A turnpike lady: Beartown, Vermont, 1768-1796 / by Sarah N. Cleghorn. New York: Henry Holt and Company, 1907. 257 p.
LC: S 18, '07.

C-480 Cleland, Mabel Goodwin. Early days in the fir tree country / by Mabel Goodwin Cleland. Seattle, Washington: Published by Washington Printing Co. Inc., 1923. 212 p., ill. **MHS**
LC: Je 19, '23.

Clemens, Samuel Langhorn, 1835-1910. See **Twain, Mark, pseud.**

C-481 Clemens, William Montgomery, 1860-1931. The gilded lady: being the true story of a crime against the United States government as recorded by Henry V. Chardon, late of the secret service / by Will M. Clemens; illustrations by Louis F. Grant. New York: G. W. Dillingham Company, [1903]. 268 p., front., [3] leaves of plates.
BLC: London: T. Fisher Unwin; New York [printed], 1903.

C-482 ____ The house of the hundred doors / by Will M. Clemens . . . New York; London: The Hawthorne Press, [c1906]. 41 p.
LC: D 29, '06.

C-483 Clementia, b. 1878, *pseud.* The Selwyns in Dixie / by Clementia [pseud.]. Chicago: Matre & Co., [c1923]. 261 p., front. (port.).
LC: D 10, '23.

C-484 Clements, M. E., Mrs. The den of the sixteenth section / by Mrs. M. E. Clements. New York; Washington; Baltimore; Indianapolis; Norfolk; Des Moines, Iowa: Broadway Publishing Co., [c1911]. 332 p., photo. front. **DLC**
LC: N 2, '11.

C-485 Clements, Wib. F. What the Sam hill / by Wib. F. Clements. New York; Chicago; Washington; Baltimore; Atlanta; Norfolk [Va.]; Florence, Ala.: Broadway Publishing Co., [c1911]. 60 p., front., [9] leaves of plates.
LC: Ap 17, '11.

C-486 Cleugh, Sophia. Ernestine Sophie / by Sophia Cleugh . . . New York: The Macmillan Company, 1925. 451 p.
LC: O 24, '25.
BLC: London: Thornton Butterworth, 1926.

C-487 ____ Matilda: governess of the English / by Sophia Cleugh. New York: The Macmillan Company, 1924. 469 p.
LC: O 29, '24.
BLC: London: Thornton Butterwoth, 1925.

C-488 Cleveland, Philip Jerome, b. 1903. Her master: a religious romance / by Philip Jerome Cleveland. [S. l.]: Plainville Press, [192-?]. 150 p. **YUS**

C-489 Cleveland, Treadwell, b. 1872. A night with Alessandro: an episode in Florence under her last Medici / by Treadwell Cleveland, Jr.; with three views in color by Eliot Keen. New York: Henry Holt and Company, 1904. 188 p., col. front., [2] leaves of col. plates.
BLC: London: Chapman & Hall, 1904.

C-490 Clever business sketches. Detroit, Michigan, U. S. A.: Published by the Business Man's Publishing Co. Ltd., 1909. 252 p., ill. [Ill. by D. Parkinson and Ernest Adams]. **MNU**
Contents: The lure of the unspoken word / Charlton Lawrence Edholm -- The business spy / F. B. Linton -- The striped tourists / Montague Glass -- Bill Sickles-Lazy Man / Edward Blomeyer -- The truth prevails in Shadyville / Edward Blomeyer -- The progress of a gentleman / George Mahon -- The bookkeeper: his accuracy / Elwood S. Brown -- The phantom bookkeeper / Charles A. Sweetland -- John Davis, Manager, and the New President's policy / F. B. Linton -- The strange case of Clement Zent / George Rockhill Craw -- The promoter: his genius / Elwood S. Brown -- Brothers / S. Roland Hall -- Celestine and Coralie / Montague Glass -- Ahead of date / Edward Blomeyer -- John Hake, business gambler / B. P. Owie -- The strike at La Place's / Edgar Matthew Keator -- Driver of the band wagon / J. E. Brown -- The sixth floor elephants / Edgar Dayton Price -- Mixing the grades / M. W. Foshay -- The trapping of Bomb-proof Smith / Edgar Dayton Price -- Stover, the resourceful / Lincoln M. Stearns -- The best policy after all / W. W. Woodbridge -- How Jack closed the deal; The sticker; The Wyandotte shares / Edgar Dayton Price.
LC: My 5, '09.

C-491 Cliffe, A. A. (Alfred Allen). The wizard's wife; or, Dora's return to the kitchen / by A. A. Cliffe. [Canton, Ohio: A. A. Cliffe, c1919.] 64 p. Unexamined copy: bibliographic data from OCLC, #14087951.

C-492 Clifton, Richard. The miller and the toad / by Richard Clifton. Boston: Sherman, French & Company, 1909, [c1908]. 220 p.
LC: N 13, '08.

C-493 Clifton, Wallace, *pseud.* Three paths: biography of a man who tried them all: an allegorical romance / by Wallace Clifton [pseud.]. Los Angeles: The Typosium Publishers, 1925. 141 p.
LC: D 11, '25.

C-494 Cline, Leonard, 1893-1929. God head / by Leonard Cline. New York: The Viking Press, 1925. 221 p.
LC: O 20, '25.
PW: O 24, '25.

C-495 Clinkscales, J. G. (John George), 1855-1942. How Zach came to college / by J. G. Clinkscales. Spartanburg, S. C.: W. F. Barnes, 1904. 175 p., front., [3] leaves of plates. [Ill. by Glen Dening.]

C-496 Clinton, Major, *pseud.* Barbara: a romance of the Lower Sandusky Valley: a tale of the War of 1812 and 1813 / by Major Clinton [pseud.]; pen drawings by Louis Kindt. Kenosha, Wis.: Frank C. Culley, [c1901]. 384 p., front., ill.
PW: Mr 8, '02.

C-497 Cloninger, Margaret D. Breathing driftwood: a clean, gripping story of love and adventure . . . / by Margaret D. Cloninger and August Vogt; (illustrated). Dallas, Texas: Reilly Publishing Company, [c1925].

309 p., photo. front., [5] leaves of plates.
LC: Je 4, '25.

C-498 Closser, Myla Jo. At the gate / by Myra [sic] Jo
Closser. [s. l.]: Privately printed for Arthur B.
Lisle, [1915]. 23, [1] p.
Reprinted from the Century Magazine, March, 1915.
Another edition: At the gate / by Myla Jo Closser.
Emma / by Louise Closser Hale. [s. l.]: [s. n.],
[1917]. 40 p.

Cloud, Virginia Woodward. The laughing Duchess.
In *The Bellman book of fiction* (1921), **B-485.**

C-499 Clough, Fred M. The golden age; or, The depth of
time / by Fred M. Clough. Boston: Roxburgh,
[c1923]. 192 p.
Unexamined copy: bibliographic data from OCLC,
#22073566.
PW: D 1, '23.

C-500 Clouston, Adella Octavia, b. 1864. The lady of the
robins: a romance of some of New York's 400 / by
Adella Octavia Clouston . . . Boston: Published by
The American Humane Education Society, [c1910].
194 p.
LC: Ja 27, '11.

C-501 A clown's romance, or, Won in the big tent. Lowell,
Mass.: C. I. Hood & Co., [19--]. 32 p., ill.
DLC

C-502 Club stories / Washington State Federation of
Women's Clubs. Seattle, Wash.: Lowman &
Hanford Co., 1915. 94 p.
Hassell, S. W. (Susan Whitcomb) - Copyright holder,
presumably editor and compiler.
Contents: Rhododendrons / Sophie M. C. Fisher -- Susan's mountain
/ Elizabeth Jane Haring -- Old Jud Watkins / Lula Shortridge Stewart
-- The other kind / Caroline Field Williams -- Reconciled / Sara
Byrne Goodwin -- "Rock of Ages" / Gertrude Allen Knapp --
Deserted / Louise Monroe Walton -- The new word / Jessie Hopkirk
Davis -- Tod's "Santy" / Gertrude Allen Knapp -- Her birthright /
Gertrude Fulton Tooker -- The disciplinarian / Maude Farrar -- "The
fine country" / Anna Brabham Osborn.
LC: D 13, '15.

Clyce, Betty. Son Smith. In *The best college short
stories, 1924-1925* (1925), **B-558.**

C-503 Clyde, Margaret Horner, b. 1877. The thread that is
spun / by Margaret Horner Clyde. Boston:
Sherman, French & Company, 1915. 159 p.
OSU, NYP
LC: D 17, '15.

C-504 Coates, Joseph Hornor, 1849-1930. The counterpart
/ by Hornor Coates; frontispiece by George Gibbs.
New York: The Macaulay Company, 1909. 324 p.,
col. front.
LC: S 27, '09.

C-505 ____ The spirit of the Island / by Joseph Hornor
Coates; illustrated by Sidney M. Chase. Boston:
Little, Brown and Company, 1911. 273 p., front.,
[2] leaves of plates.
LC: My 16, '11.
PW: My 20, '11.

C-506 Cobb, Benjamin F. (Benjamin Franklin), b. 1844. A
country boy in the city, or, The adventures of Sandy
Pike / by Benj. F. Cobb. Kansas City, Missouri:
The Lumber Review Company, Publishers, 1906.
362 p., front., ill.

C-507 ____ Jack Henderson down East / by Benj. F. Cobb;
illustrations by Marshall D. Smith. New York:
Hurst and Company, [c1902]. 113 p., front., [6]
leaves of plates.

C-508 ____ Jack Henderson down South / by Benj. F.
Cobb; illustrations by Marshall D. Smith. New York:
Hurst and Company, [c1905]. 116 p., front., [6]
leaves of plates.

C-509 ____ Jack Henderson on experience / by Benj. F.
Cobb; illustrations by Marshall D. Smith. New York:
Hurst & Company, [c1905]. 115 p., front., [6]
leaves of plates.

C-510 ____ Jack Henderson on matrimony / by Benj. F.
Cobb; illustrations by Marshall D. Smith. New York:
Hurst and Company, [c1905]. 114 p., front., [6]
leaves of plates.

C-511 ____ Jack Henderson on tipping / by Benj. F. Cobb;
illustrations by Marshall D. Smith. New York:
Hurst and Company, [c1905]. 116 p., front., [6]
leaves of plates. **BGU**
Contents: Tipping as she is tipped -- To tip or not to tip -- Merry
Christmas -- Swearing off -- Grafting -- The long salesman -- At the
mission school.

C-512 ____ Jack Henderson out West / by Benj. F. Cobb;
illustrations by Marshall D. Smith. New York:
Hurst and Company, [c1905]. 126 p., incl. [6] leaves
of plates, front.

C-513 ____ Richard Vaughn / by Benj. F. Cobb;
illustrated. Chicago; New York: The Henneberry
Company, [c1901]. 358 p., front.

C-514 Cobb, Bertha B. (Bertha Browning), 1867-1951.
Anita: a story of the Rocky Mountains / by Bertha B.
and Ernest Cobb . . . ; color plates by L. J.
Bridgman; photographs by L. C. McClure; line
drawings by Anita Pettibone. Boston; New Upper
Fall, Mass.: The Arlo Publishing Company, [c1920].
285 p., photo. front., [11] leaves of plates, ill.

C-515 ____ Arlo / by Bertha B. and Ernest Cobb . . . ;
with illustrations by Charles Copeland. Boston: The
Riverdale Press, Brookline, 1915. 206 p., [5] leaves
of plates. Illustrated end papers.
LC: Ag 17, '15.
BLC: New York; London: G. P. Putnam's Sons,
1918.

Cobb, Ernest, b. 1877, jt. aut. See **Cobb, Bertha B.
(Bertha Browning), 1867-1951, jt. aut.**

C-516 Cobb, Irvin S. (Irvin Shrewsbury), 1876-1944. The
abandoned farmers / by Irvin S. Cobb; his humorous
account of a retreat from the city to the farm. New
York: George H. Doran Company, [c1920]. 247 p.,
front. [Ill. by Tony Sarg.] Illustrated end papers.
LC: O 20, '20.
PW: O 30, '20.

C-517 _____ Alias Ben Alibi / by Irvin S. Cobb. New
York: George H. Doran Company, [c1925]. 382 p.
OSU, MIA
LC: Ap 11, '25.
PW: F 21, '25.

C-518 _____ Back home: being the narrative of Judge Priest
and his People / by Irvin S. Cobb. New York:
George H. Doran Company, [c1912]. 348 p., front.,
[9] leaves of plates.
Reprinted from the Saturday Evening Post.
LC: N 8, '12.
PW: N 30, '12.
BLC: London: William Heinemann; Norwood,
Mass. [printed], 1912.

_____ Boys will be boys. In *The best short stories of
1917 and the yearbook of the American short story
(1918)*, **B-562.**

_____ The chocolate hyena. In *The best short stories
of 1923 and the yearbook of the American short
story (1924)*, **B-568.**

_____ Darkness. In *The best short stories of 1921
and the yearbook of the American short story (1922)*,
B-566.

C-519 _____ The escape of Mr. Trimm: his plight and other
plights / by Irvin S. Cobb . . . New York: George
H. Doran Company, [c1913]. 279 p.
Contents: The escape of Mr. Trimm -- The belled buzzard -- An
occurrence up a side street -- Another of those cub reporter stories --
Smoke of battle -- The exit of Anse Dugmore -- To the editor of the
Sun -- Fish-head -- Guilty as charged.
LC: O 23, '13.
PW: N 1, '13.
BLC: London: Hodder & Stoughton; [printed in U.
S. A.], 1914.

C-520 _____ Fibble, D. D. / by Irvin S. Cobb; illustrated by
Tony Sarg. New York: George H. Doran Company,
[c1916]. 279 p., front., [6] leaves of plates.
Illustrated end papers.
LC: N 15, '16.
PW: N 11, '16.

C-521 _____ From place to place / by Irvin S. Cobb . . .
New York: George H. Doran Company, [c1920].
407 p.
Contents: The gallowsmith -- The thunder of silence -- Boys will be
boys -- The luck piece -- Quality folks -- John J. Coincidence -- When
August the second was April the first -- Hoodwinked -- The bull
called Emily.
LC: F 11, '20.
PW: Ja 31, '20.

C-522 _____ Goin' on fourteen: being cross-sections out of
a year in the life of an average boy / by Irvin S.
Cobb; illustrated by Worth Brehm. New York:
George H. Doran Company, [c1924]. 357 p., front.,
[11] leaves of plates. Illustrated end papers.
LC: O 2, '24.
PW: S 20, '24.

_____ The great oak. In *The best short stories of
1916 and the yearbook of the American short story
(1917)*, **B-561.**

C-523 _____ J. Poindexter, colored / by Irvin S. Cobb.
New York: George H. Doran Company, [c1922].
270 p. [Ill. by Tony Sarg.]
LC: O 5, '22.
PW: Ag 5, '22.

C-524 _____ The life of the party / by Irvin S. Cobb;
illustrated by James M. Preston. New York: George
H. Doran Company, [c1919]. 66 p., incl. front., [2]
leaves of plates. Decorated end papers.
LC: Je 23, '19.
PW: Je 14, '19.

C-525 _____ Local color / by Irvin S. Cobb. New York:
George H. Doran Company, [c1916]. 460 p.
LC: N 15, '16.
PW: N 11, '16.

C-526 _____ Old Judge Priest / by Irvin S. Cobb. New
York: George H. Doran Company, [c1916]. 401 p.
Contents: The Lord provides -- A blending of the parables -- Judge
priest comes back -- A chapter from the life of an ant -- Sergeant
Jimmy Bagby's feet -- According to the code -- Forrest's last charge
-- Double-barrelled justice -- A beautiful evening.
LC: Ap 24, '16.
PW: Ap 29, '16.
BLC: London: Hodder & Stoughton, 1916.

C-527 _____ One third off / by Irvin S. Cobb . . . ;
illustrated by Tony Sarg. New York: George H.
Doran Company, [c1921]. 148 p., front., [3] leaves
of plates. Illustrated end papers.
LC: Ag 30, '21.

C-528 _____ A plea for old Cap Collier / by Irvin S. Cobb;
frontispiece by Tony Sarg. New York: George H.
Doran Company, [c1921]. 56 p., front. Decorated
end papers.
LC: Ag 30, '21.

C-529 _____ Snake doctor: and other stories / by Irwin S.
Cobb. New York: George H. Doran Company,
[c1923]. 343 p.
Contents: Snake doctor -- One block from Fifth avenue -- "-That
shall he also reap" -- Red-handed -- Otherwise Sweet William -- His
mother's apron strings -- This hero business -- The eminent Dr.
Deeves -- The second coming of a first husband.
LC: Jl 20, '23.
PW: S 22, '23.

C-530 _____ "Speaking of operations--" / by Irvin S. Cobb;
illustrations by Tony Sarg. New York: George H.
Doran Company, [c1915]. 64 p., front., [3] leaves of
plates. Illustrated end papers.
LC: D 1, '15.
PW: D 11, '15.
BLC: London: Hodder & Stoughton; U. S. A.
[printed], 1916.

C-531 _____ Sundry accounts / by Irvin S. Cobb. New
York: George H. Doran Company, [c1922].
435 p.
Contents: Darkness -- The cater-cornered sex -- A short natural
history -- It could happen again tomorrow -- The ravelin' wolf --
"Worth 10,000" -- Mr. Lobel's apoplexy -- Alas, the poor Whiffletit!
-- Plentiful Valley -- A tale of wet days.
LC: Ap 28, '22.
PW: My 6, '22.

C-532   _____ Those times and these / by Irvin S. Cobb. New York: George H. Doran Company, [c1917]. 374 p.
LC: Je 19, '17.
PW: Je 16, '17.

C-533   _____ The thunders of silence / by Irvin S. Cobb; illustrated. New York: George H. Doran Company, [c1918]. 61 p., front., [3] leaves of plates. Illustrated end papers.
LC: Ap 15, '18.
PW: Ap 20, '18.

_____ Who's who at the zoo. In **Conrad, Joseph. _Il conte_ (1925), C-697.**

C-534   Cobb, Margaret Smith. Blaxine: halfbreed girl / by Margaret Cobb Smith. New York; Washington: The Neale Publishing Company, 1910. 253 p.
LC: Ap 2, '10.

Cobb, Percival Bartlett, b. 1883. See **Wells, Percival W., pseud.**

C-535   Cobb, Stanwood, b. 1881. Ayesha of the Bosphorus: a romance of Constantinople / by Stanwood Cobb. Boston: Murray and Emery Company, 1915. 157 p., front. [Ill. by Darius Cobb.]
LC: S 2, '15.

Cobden, Ellen Melicent, 1848-1914. See **Amber, Miles, pseud.**

Coburn, Fordyce, Mrs. See **Abbott, Eleanor Hallowell, b. 1872.**

C-536   Coburn, G. F. (George Francis), b. 1841. Life in the Wabash Valley: a story of the pioneers and their descendants, 1860-1907 / by G. F. Coburn. Danville, Ill.: [s. n., ca. 1907]. 365 p.   **MIA**

C-537   Cocayne, Edith K. Sue McFarland, schoolmarm / by Edith K. Cocayne. Baltimore, Md.: Saulsbury Publishing Company, [c1918]. 55 p.   **PAU**
LC: Ja 6, '19.

C-538   Cochran, Jean Carter, b. 1876. The bells of the blue pagoda: the strange enchantment of a Chinese doctor / by Jean Carter Cochran. Philadelphia: The Westminster Press, 1922. 281 p., front., [4] leaves of plates.
LC: Jl 12, '22.

C-539   _____ Church Street: stories of American village life / by Jean Carter Cochran. Philadelphia: The Westminster Press, 1922. 227 p., front., [5] leaves of plates.
Contents: Home -- Oral traditions -- Old John -- Clerical notes -- Neighbors -- Poverty and riches -- The day we celebrate -- A hilltop idyl -- Our mother's passion -- Peculiar people -- An evergreen woman -- Everybody's uncle -- Dooryards -- His own people.
LC: My 17, '23.

C-540   Cochran, John S. (John Salisbury), 1841-1926. Bonnie Belmont: a historical romance of the days of slavery and the Civil War / by Judge John S. Cochran. [Wheeling, W. Va.: Press of Wheeling

News Lith. Co., c1907]. 291, [1] p., [16] leaves of plates (one folded). Designed end papers.
LC: N 6, '07.

C-541   Cocke, Sarah Johnson. The master of the hills: a tale of the Georgia Mountains / by Sarah Johnson Cocke. New York: E. P. Dutton & Co., [c1917]. 327 p.
LC: Jl 6, '17.
PW: Jl 21, '17.

C-542   Coddington, Fred M. (Frederick Miron). As they did it, or, The first church of Warden / by Fred M. Coddington. Cincinnati: Jennings & Graham; New York: Eaton and Mains, [c1901]. 450 p.

Codman, Anna Kneeland. See **Codman, Russell, Mrs., b. 1869.**

C-543   Codman, Russell, Mrs., b. 1869. An ardent American / by Mrs. Russell Codman; frontispiece by James Montgomery Flagg. New York: The Century Co., 1911. 411 p., col. front., ill. [Ill. by Haygarth Leonard.]
LC: My 26, '11.

Cody, Sherwin, 1868-1959. See **Brown, Philetus, pseud.**

C-544   Coffey, W. H. (William Harrison), b. 1862. Sis: a Missouri Valley story / by W. H. Coffey . . . Kansas City, Mo.: Press of Burton Publishing Company, [c1909]. 92 p., front.   **DLC**
LC: Ja 24, '10.

C-545   _____ Tim, a Kentucky mountain story / by W. H. Coffey . . . ; illustrated by Herman P. Keusch. Kansas City, Mo.: The Press of Burton Publishing Company, [c1908]. 93 p., ill.   **KSL**
LC: Ja 2, '09.

C-546   Coffin, Julia H. (Julia Haskell). The vendor of dreams / by Julia H. Coffin; illustrations by Haskell Coffin; decorations by John O'Neill. New York: Dodd, Mead and Company, 1917. 108 p., col. front., [2] leaves of col. plates, ill.   **NYP**
LC: S 11, '17.

C-547   Coggs, Dr., _pseud._ Teddy in darkest Africa, or, The daring exploits of Bwana-Tumbo: an exciting narrative of thrilling adventures, and a song to nature / by Dr. Coggs [pseud.], hunter, scholar and explorer. -- First edition. -- [S. l.: s. n.], 1910. 345 p., ill.   **CRU**

C-548   Coghlan, Lida L. (Lida Lavinia), b. 1860. The valley of peace / by Lida L. Coghlan . . . St. Louis, Mo.; London: B. Herder Book Co., 1925. 275 p.
LC: D 24, '24.
PW: F 7, '25.

C-549   _____ The waters of Lethe / by Lida L. Coghlan; with illustrations by Clara M. Coghlan. Baltimore, Md.; New York: John Murphy Company, [c1904]. 310 p., front., [7] leaves of plates.
PW: D 10, '04.

C-550 Cohan, Charles Cleveland. Born of the crucible / by Charles Cleveland Cohan. Boston: The Cornhill Company, [c1919]. 321 p.
LC: Ap 23, '20.
PW: Je 26, '20.

Cohen, Alfred J., 1861-1928. See **Dale, Alan, pseud.**

C-551 Cohen, Octavus Roy, b. 1891. Assorted chocolates / by Octavus Roy Cohen . . . ; frontispiece by J. J. Gould. New York: Dodd, Mead and Company, 1922. 330 p., front.
Contents: Noblesse obliged -- The evil lie -- Bird of prey -- The night-blooming serious -- Gravey -- Oft in the silly night -- H₂O boy -- Chocolate grudge.
LC: S 13, '22.
PW: S 9, '22.
BLC: London: Hodder & Stoughton, [1925].

_____ Bass ingratitude. In *Aces* (1924), A-42.

C-552 _____ Bigger and blacker / by Octavus Roy Cohen. Boston: Little, Brown and Company, 1925. 313 p.
Contents: Every little movie -- Double double -- The bathing booty -- A little child shall feed them -- Inside inflammation -- Miss Directed -- The lion and the uniform -- Write and wrong.
LC: My 11, '25.
PW: My 16, '25.

C-553 _____ Come seven / by Octavus Roy Cohen . . . ; with illustrations by H. Weston Taylor. New York: Dodd, Mead and Company, 1920. 423 p., front., [3] leaves of plates. **OSU, BGU**
Contents: Without benefit of Virgie -- The fight that failed -- The quicker the dead -- Alley money -- Twinkle, twinkle, movie star -- The light bombastic toe -- Cock-a-doodle-doo.
LC: S 28, '20.
PW: O 16, '20.

C-554 _____ The crimson alibi / by Octavus Roy Cohen . . . New York: Dodd, Mead and Company, 1919. 285 p.
LC: Ja 28, '19.
PW: F 1, '19.
BLC: London: E. Nash Co., 1919.

C-555 _____ Dark days and black knights / by Octavus Roy Cohen; frontispiece by J. J. Gould. New York: Dodd, Mead and Company, 1923. 335 p., front.
Contents: Music hath harms -- Presto change -- The widow's bite -- The B. V. demon -- Focus pokus -- His bitter half -- Far better than worse -- Completely done in oils.
LC: S 20, '23.
PW: S 15, '23.

C-556 _____ Gray dusk / by Octavus Roy Cohen . . . New York: Dodd, Mead and Company, 1920. 262 p.
LC: F 10, '20.
PW: Ap 3, '20.
BLC: London: E. Nash Co., 1920.

C-557 _____ Highly colored / by Octavus Roy Cohen . . . ; with frontispiece by H. Weston Taylor. New York: Dodd, Mead and Company, 1921, [c1920]. 331 p., front.
Contents: Auto-intoxication -- All's swell that ends swell -- The survival of the fattest -- The ultima fool -- Mistuh Macbeth -- Here comes the bribe.

LC: N 2, '21.
PW: N 12, '21.

C-558 _____ The iron chalice / by Octavus Roy Cohen. Boston: Little, Brown and Company, 1925. 290, [1] p.
LC: S 2, '25.
PW: S 5, '25.
BLC: London: Cassell & Co., 1926.

C-559 _____ Jim Hanvey, detective / by Octavus Roy Cohen. New York: Dodd, Mead and Company, 1923. 283 p.
Contents: Fish eyes -- Homespun silk -- Common stock -- Helen of Troy, N. Y. -- Caveat emptor -- The knight's gambit -- Pink bait.
LC: O 4, '23.
PW: O 6, '23.
BLC: London: E. Nash & Grayson; [printed in U. S. A.], [1924].

C-560 _____ Midnight / by Octavus Roy Cohen; frontispiece by Lee Thayer. New York: Dodd, Mead & Company, 1922. 281 p., front.
LC: Ja 31, '22.
PW: F 4, '22.
BLC: London: E. Nash & Grayson; printed in U. S. A., 1922.

C-561 _____ The other woman / by Octavus Roy Cohen and J. U. Giesy . . . ; illustrated by Albert Matzke. New York: The Macaulay Company, 1917. 268 p., front., [3] leaves of plates.
LC: Mr 19, '17.
PW: Mr 24, '17.

C-562 _____ Polished ebony / by Octavus Roy Cohen; illustrated by H. Weston Taylor. New York: Dodd, Mead and Company, 1919. 309 p., front., [3] leaves of plates.
Contents: All that glitters -- Pool and ginuwine -- The amateur hero -- Tempus fugits -- Not wisely but too well -- Backfire -- A house divided -- Poppy passes -- Painless extraction.
LC: S 18, '19.
PW: S 20, '19.

C-563 _____ Six seconds of darkness / by Octavus Roy Cohen . . . New York: Dodd, Mead and Company, 1921, [c1918]. 299 p.
LC: Ja 19, '21.
PW: Ja 22, '21.
BLC: London: E. Nash Co., 1921.

C-564 _____ Sunclouds / by Octavus Roy Cohen; frontispiece by J. J. Gould. New York: Dodd, Mead and Company, 1924. 303 p., front.
Contents: The law and the profits -- His wild notes -- His children's father -- The birth of a notion -- The late lamented -- The wild and wooly vest -- Measure for pleasure -- The battle of sedan -- The spider and the lie.
LC: S 20, '24.
PW: S 20, '24.
BLC: London: Hodder & Stoughton, [1925].

Cohen, Rose Gallup. Natalka's portion. In *The best short stories of 1922 and the yearbook of the American short story* (1923), B-567.

C-565 Cohn, Joseph, b. 1859. True stories: attractive, dramatic, amusing and moral aspect / by Joseph Cohn

... Yonkers, N. Y.: Printed by Gazette Press, c1924. 83 p.
Contents: Voice of conscience -- Reward for benefaction -- The Goldsmith -- A soul's destiny -- Jokai Maurus -- The little Chajim at the Melamed -- Love [poem] -- Supplement.

C-566   Colbert, Vesalius. Jewel Goldsmith's fight of faith, or, What saith my Lord? [Collinsville. ill.: s. n., c1903]. 59 p., photo. ill.   **JFK**

C-567   Colbron, Grace Isabel, 1869-1948. Joe Muller: detective: being the account of some adventures in the professional experience of a member of the imperial Austrian police / by Grace Isabel Colbron and Augusta Groner. New York: Duffield and Company, 1910. 334 p.   **VA@**
Contents: The case of the lamp that went out -- The case of the registered letter -- The case of the pocket diary found in the snow -- The case of the pool of blood in the pastor's study -- The case of the golden bullet.
LC: My 17, '10.

_____, jt. aut. *The lady in blue* (1922). See **Groner, Augusta, 1850-1922, jt. aut., G-551.**

Colburn, Frona. See **Wait, Frona Eunice, 1859-1946.**

C-568   Colcock, Annie T. Her American daughter / by Annie T. Colcock. New York; Washington: The Neale Publishing Company, 1905. 357 p.

C-569   _____ Margaret Tudor: a romance of old St. Augustine / by Annie T. Colcock; illustrated by W. B. Gilbert. New York: Frederick A. Stokes Company, [c1901]. 169 p., front., [2] leaves of plates.   **IXA**
PW: Ap 19, '02.

C-570   _____ Short stories / by Annie T. Colcock ... Charleston, S. C.: Walker, Evans & Cogswell Company, 1924. 283 p.   **NDD**
Contents: The revenge of "copper" kettle -- Fairy gold -- The humming bird of the zantee -- Just a looker-on -- A subterranean entanglement -- The price of her freedom -- A place in the sun -- The mysterious houseboat -- At the house of dreams -- Love's manifold altars -- White carnations -- A castle that crumbled -- The serpent ring -- New furrows -- Via amoris -- The stranger with the keys.

C-571   Colcord, Lincoln, 1883-1947. The drifting diamond / by Lincoln Colcord; with frontispiece by Anton Fischer. New York: The Macmillan Company, 1912. 279 p., col. front.
LC: O 10, '12.
PW: N 2, '12.

C-572   _____ The game of life and death: stories of the sea / by Lincoln Colcord; with frontispiece. New York: The Macmillan Company, 1914. 289 p., front. [Ill. by M. L. Bower.]
Reprinted from various periodicals.
Contents: The game of life and death -- The measure of a man -- The leak -- The voice of the dead -- De Long: a story of Sunda Straits -- Carrying sail -- Thirst: an incident of the Pacific -- The moths -- The final score -- The captain's son -- Home -- Envoy [poem].
LC: S 24, '14.
BLC: London: Macmillan, 1914.

C-573   _____ An instrument of the gods: and other stories of the sea / by Lincoln Colcord. New York: The Macmillan Company, 1922. 321 p.
Contents: An instrument of the gods -- Outward bound -- The uncharted isle -- Servant and master -- Rescue at sea -- Good-bye, Cape Horn! -- Under sail -- Anjer -- Moments of destiny -- Cape St. Roque -- A friend -- Ballad of master mariners.
LC: S 13, '22.

C-574   Cole, C. F. (Charles Foster). Donald McLane: a religious novel / by C. F. Cole. Dowagiac, Mich.: Republican Printing Company, 1907. 433 p., front. (port.).   **DLC**
LC: My 8, '07.

C-575   Cole, Charles. Visitors from Mars: a narrative / by Charles Cole. [Portland, Or.: Printed by Beattie & Hoffman], c1901. 99 p.
Unexamined copy: bibliographic data from OCLC, #12616650.
LC: Ag 6, '01.

C-576   Cole, Cyrenus, 1863-1939. Back to Four Corners, a story of politics in 1924 / by Cyrenus Cole ... Cedar Rapids, Iowa: The Torch Press, 1924. 47, [1] p.   **DLC**
Cover title.
LC: S 22, '24.

C-577   _____ From Four Corners to Washington: a little story of home, love, war, and politics / by Cyrenus Cole. Cedar Rapids, Iowa: Torch Press, 1920. 80 p.
Unexamined copy: bibliographic data from OCLC, #15585601.
Cover title.

C-578   _____ From Washington to Four Corners: a second story of home, love, war, and politics / by Cyrenus Cole. Cedar Rapids, Iowa: The Torch Press, 1922. 64 p.
Cover title.
LC: S 1, '22.

Cole, Donna Rieta. See **D. R. C.**

C-579   Cole, Horace L. The flesh and the devil: a novel / by Horace L. Cole. New York; London: F. Tennyson Neely, [c1902]. 328 p.
PW: Ap 26, '02.

C-580   Cole, Patience Bevier, b. 1883. Dave's daughter: a novel / by Patience Bevier Cole. New York: Frederick A. Stokes Company, [c1913]. 256 p.
LC: S 15, '13.
PW: S 27, '13.

C-581   Colean, Miles Lanier, b. 1898. Quest / by Miles Lanier Colean. New York: E. P. Dutton & Company, [c1923]. 287 p.
LC: Ag 25, '23.
PW: S 1, '23.

Coleman, Gilbert P., jt. aut. *Brown of Harvard* (1907). See **Young, Rida Johnson, jt. aut., Y-40.**

C-582   Coleman, Glenn. M. Golden mud / Glenn. M. Coleman ... [s. l.]: L. McCutcheon, printer, 1921. [24] p.   **NYP**
Contents: The outlaw -- What an explosion will do.

C-583 Coleman, John, b. 1864. The cruise of the "Odin" / by John Coleman. Boston: The Cornhill Publishing Company, 1923. 314 p., front., [2] leaves of plates. [Ill. by Carl E. Larcrest.]
LC: O 1, '23.

Coleman, McAlister. See McAlister, Frank A, jt. pseud. of McAlister Coleman and Frank Davis Halsey.

C-584 Coleman, Sara Lindsay. Wind of destiny / by Sara Lindsay Coleman. Garden City, New York: Doubleday, Page & Company, 1916. 111 p.
LC: N 2, '16.

C-585 [Coles, Bertha Horstmann Lippincott], 1880-1963. Chevrons: a story of West Point / by B. H. L.; illustrated by the author. Philadelphia; London: J. B. Lippincott Company, [c1901]. 267 p., front., [3] leaves of plates.
PW: N 16, '01.

C-586 Coles, Bertha Horstmann Lippincott, 1880-1963. Wound-stripes: stories of after the war / by Bertha Lippincott Coles. Philadelphia; London: J. B. Lippincott Company, 1921. 186 p.
Contents: Mrs. Copeland's convalescents -- Polly's protégé -- The need of being needed -- Silver chevrons -- "Semper fidelis", a story of Quantico.
LC: D 15, '21.

C-587 Colestock, Henry Thomas. The ministry of David Baldwin: a novel / by Henry Thomas Colestock. New York: Thomas Y. Crowell & Co., [c1907]. 369 p., front., [3] leaves of plates. [Ill. by E. Boyd Smith.]
LC: Mr 8, '07.

Collard, Arthur. Excelsior. In As we are (1923), A-325.

C-588 Colleton, Arthur Stanley. The isle of temptation / by Arthur Stanley Colleton. New York: The Stuyvesant Press, 1909. 292 p.
LC: Je 1, '09.

Collier, Nick Sherlock, pseud. See Davis, J. Frank (James Francis), 1870-1942.

Collin, Grace Lathrop, jt. aut. A crazy angel (1901). See Noble, Annette Lucile, 1844-1932, jt. aut., N-104.

C-589 ____ Putnam Place / by Grace Lathrop Collin. New York: Harper & Brothers, 1903. 261, [1] p.
PW: Mr 7, '03.

____ The seeds of time. In The heart of childhood (1906), H-441.

C-590 [Collingwood, Herbert W. (Herbert Winslow)], 1857-1927. "The child" / by "The Hope Farm Man" [pseud.]. New York: The Rural Publishing Company, [c1912]. 192 p.
LC: D 20, '12.

C-591 Collins, Charles Terry, Mrs., 1852-1914. A college courtship and other stories / by Mrs. Charles Terry Collins. Cambridge, [Mass]: Printed at the Riverside Press, 1915. 222 p., photo. front. (port.).
Contents: A college courtship -- The parson's butterfly -- Monsieur le Bébé.

C-592 Collins, Charles William, b. 1880. The natural law / by Charles Collins; based on the drama of Howard Hall and Charles Summer. New York: The Macaulay Company, 1916. 256 p., front., [5] leaves of plates.
LC: S 20, '16.

C-593 ____ The sins of Saint Anthony: tales of the theatre / by Charles Collins, with an introduction by Henry Kitchell Webster. Chicago: Pascal Covici, 1925. 265 p.
Contents: The pride of Iris: a tragic story -- One of our daughters: a cynical story -- When Marcia fell: a romantic story -- Up stage and down: a back stage story -- The marvelous Marco: a vaudeville story -- That girl on the end: a dancer's story -- The sins of Saint Anthony: an impertinent story.
LC: Ap 11, '25.
PW: Ap 4, '25.

C-594 Collins, Christine Leete, 1849-1912. Prose sketches and verse: a memorial collection / Christine Leete Collins. San Francisco [Calif.]: The Blair-Murdock Company, 1913. 62 p., photo. front. (port.).
Contents: In memory of a friend -- Memory's offering [poem] -- Only [poem] -- That summer ray [poem] -- My bungalow [poem] -- The future -- In memoriam-McKinley -- Betsy Bumble -- An April day's reflection -- The conversion of an unbeliever -- Over the mountains -- The critic's guillotine [poem] -- An Alaskan outing.

Collins, Frederick Lewis, b. 1882. See Lewis, Frederick, pseud.

C-595 Collins, George. A strange railroad wreck / by George Collins. New York: Broadway Publishing Company, c1904. 40 p., front. (port.).

C-596 Collins, Henry Albert. Ice-cream alley: a novel / by Henry Albert Collins, "the life annuity man." Peoria, Ill.: J. W. Franks & Sons, 1918. 221 p., photo. front.
LC: N 21, '18.

C-597 Collins, Hilda C. My guardian: a novel / by Hilda C. Collins. San Antonio, Tex.: W. L. Winter, 1902, [c1899]. 252 p.

C-598 ____ Nadia Grey: a novel / by Hilda C. Collins. [San Antonio: s. n.], 1909. 211 p.
LC: Ja 22, '10.

Collins, Mary Abby Wood. See Collins, Charles Terry, Mrs., 1852-1914.

Collins, Percy, jt. aut. A parish of two (1903). See McVickar, Henry Goelet, jt. aut., M-346.

C-599 Colter, Alice Marguerite, b. 1891. Tumbleweed / by Alice M. Colter; with illustrations by Archie Gunn. Indianapolis: The Bobbs-Merrill Company, [c1916]. 275 p., front., [5] leaves of plates.
LC: S 12, '16.
PW: S 2, '16.
BLC: London: Hodder & Stoughton, [1917].

C-600 Colton, Abigail. The tale of Christopher: a fantasia / by Abigail Colton. [Chicago: Purdy Publishing Company, c1917]. 144 p.   **KLG**
LC: O 19, '17.

C-601 Colton, Arthur Willis, 1868-1943. The belted seas / by Arthur Colton. New York: Henry Holt and Company, 1905. 312 p.
PW: Ap 1, '05.
BLC: London: Chatto & Windus, 1907.

C-602 _____ The cruise of the Violetta / by Arthur Colton. New York: Henry Holt and Company, 1906. 313 p.
LC: O 13, '06.
PW: O 27, '06.

C-603 _____ "The debatable land": a novel / by Arthur Colton. New York; London: Harper & Brothers Publishers, 1901. 312 p.
On cover: *A story of modern American life*.
PW: D 14, '01.

C-604 _____ The delectable mountains / by Arthur Colton. New York: Charles Scribner's Sons, 1901. 236 p.
Contents: The place of abandoned gods -- The leather hermit -- Black Pond clearing -- Joppa -- The elders' seat -- The romance of the Institute -- Nausicaa -- Sanderson of Back Meadows -- Two roads that meet in Salem -- A visible judgment -- The emigrant east -- Tobin's monument.
PW: Ap 27, '01.

C-605 _____ Port Argent: a novel / by Arthur Colton; with a frontispiece by Eliot Keen. New York: Henry Holt and Company, 1904. 340 p., front.

C-606 _____ Tioba: and other tales / by Arthur Colton; with a frontispiece by A. B. Frost. New York: Henry Holt and Company, 1903. 231 p., front.
Contents: Tioba -- A man for a' that -- The green grasshopper -- The enemies -- A night's lodging -- On Edom Hill -- Sons of R. Rand -- Conlon -- St. Catherine's -- The spiral stone -- The Musidora sonnet.
PW: Mr 21, '03.

C-607 Colum, Padraic, 1881-1972. Castle conquer. New York: The Macmillan Company, 1923. 376 p.
Unexamined copy: bibliographic data from OCLC, #1571765.
LC: Je 13, '23.
BLC: London: Macmillan & Co.; printed in U. S. A., 1923.

C-608 Colver, Alice Ross, b. 1892. The dear pretender / by Alice Ross Colver; illustrated by Charles Hargens, Jr. Philadelphia: The Penn Publishing Company, 1924. 292 p., front.
LC: Mr 10, '24.
PW: F 23, '24.
BLC: London: Hodder & Stoughton, [1925].

C-609 _____ If dreams come true / by Alice Ross Colver; illustrated by Frances Kratz. Philadelphia: The Penn Publishing Company, 1925. 364 p., front.
LC: Mr 13, '25.
PW: F 14, '25.
BLC: London: Hodder & Stoughton, [1926].

C-610 Colville, Fulton. The black mantle: a novel / by Fulton Colville. New York: The Cosmopolitan Press, 1911. 319 p.
LC: D 18, '11.
PW: Ja 6, '12.

Colvin, Addison Beecher, b. 1858. <u>See</u> **Hiram, Harvester, pseud.**

C-611 Colvin, Mary Kroh. Ironica; a romance of the Rockies / by Mary Kroh Colvin; illustrated by Isabella Morton. New York: H. Lechner, [c1911]. 245 p., front.
Unexamined copy: bibliographic data from NUC.
PW: F 10, '27.

C-612 Colwell, James. After the ball: a romance of youth today; illustrated with scenes from the photoplay "After the ball" as produced by Renco Film Company; from the widely popular song-story of the same name by Charles K. Harris / by James Colwell. Los Angeles, California: The Times-Mirror Press, c1924. 339 p., photo. front., [9] leaves of photo. plates.
LC: Ap 8, '24.
PW: Jl 12, '24.

C-613 Combs, A. Gail. The silver sphinx / by A. Gail Combs. Boston: The Roxburgh Publishing Company, Inc., [c1921]. 319 p.   **NYP**
LC: Jl 15, '21.

C-614 Comedy. New York: McClure, Phillips & Co., 1901. 174 p., front. [Ill. by Henry Hutt.]
Contents: The pasha's prisoner / Robert Barr -- At the Dovelys' / Sewell Ford -- The metamorphosis of Corpus Delicti / J. H. Cranson -- Sheriff of Elbert / Chauncey Thomas -- The saving grace / Stewart Edward White -- A chance shot / Henry Wallace Phillips -- The horse thief / E. Hough.
LC: O 2, '01.
PW: O 26, '01.
References: BAL 9317.

C-615 Comer, Cornelia A. P. (Cornelia Atwood Pratt). The preliminaries: and other stories / by Cornelia A. P. Comer. Boston; New York: Houghton Mifflin Company, 1912. (Cambridge [Mass.]: The Riverside Press). 211, [1] p.
LC: S 19, '12.
Contents: The preliminaries -- The long inheritance -- Clarissa's own child.

_____ Seth Miles and the sacred fire. In *Atlantic narratives*; 2nd series (1918), A-361.

C-616 Comfort, Benjamin F. (Benjamin Freeman), 1863-1941. Arnold's tempter / by Benjamin F. Comfort. Boston: The C. M. Clark Publishing Co., 1908. 447 p., front., [7] leaves of plates.
LC: O 20, '08.

Comfort, Will Levington, 1878-1932. Back o' the yards. In *The Grim thirteen* (1917), G-537.

_____ Chautonville. In *The best short stories of 1915 and the yearbook of the American short story* (1916), B-560.

C-617 _____ Down among men / by Will Levington
Comfort. New York: George H. Doran Company,
[c1913]. 287 p.
LC: N 11, '13.
PW: N 8, '13.
BLC: London: Hodder & Stoughton, [1914].

C-618 _____ Fate knocks at the door: a novel / by Will
Levington Comfort; with a frontispiece by M. Leone
Bracker. Philadelphia; London: J. B. Lippincott
Company, 1912. 374 p., col. front.
LC: Ap 30, '12.
PW: My 11, '12.

C-619 _____ The lady of Fallen Star Island / by Will
Levington Comfort . . . New York; London: Street
& Smith, [c1902]. 221 p., front., [3] leaves of
plates.   **KSU**
BLC: London: Shurmer Sib Thorp, [1902].

C-620 _____ The last ditch / by Will Levington Comfort.
New York: George H. Doran Company, [c1916].
360 p.
LC: N 15, '16.
PW: N 11, '16.

C-621 _____ Lot & company / by Will Levington Comfort.
New York: George H. Doran Company, [c1915].
341 p.
LC: N 10, '15.
PW: O 30, '15.

C-622 _____ The public square / by Will Levington
Comfort. New York: D. Appleton and Company,
1923. 319, [1] p.
LC: Ap 18, '23; My 7, '23.
PW: My 5, '23.

C-623 _____ Red fleece / by Will Levington Comfort. New
York: George H. Doran Company, [c1915]. 287 p.
(p. 283-287, advertisements.)
LC: Mr 3, '15.
PW: Mr 6, '15.
BLC: London: William Heinemann; printed in U. S.
A., 1916.

C-624 _____ The road of living men: a novel / by Will
Levington Comfort.; with a frontispiece by M. Leone
Bracker. Philadelphia; London: J. B. Lippincott
Company, 1913. 322 p., col. front.
LC: Ap 2, '13.
PW: Mr 29, '13.

C-625 _____ Routledge rides alone / by Will Levington
Comfort; with a frontispiece by Martin Justice.
Philadelphia; London: J. B. Lippincott Company,
1910. 310 p., col. front.   **EEM**
LC: Mr 31, '10.
PW: Ap 9, '10.

C-626 _____ She buildeth her house / by Will Levington
Comfort; with a frontispiece by Martin Justice.
Philadelphia; London: J. B. Lippincott Company,
1911. 352 p., col. front.
LC: Je 9, '11.
PW: Je 3, '11.

C-627 _____ The shielding wing / by Will Levington
Comfort; with a frontispiece by Howard E. Smith.
Boston: Small, Maynard & Company, [c1918].
381 p., col. front.
LC: D 28, '18.
PW: D 21, '18.

C-628 _____ Somewhere south in Sonora: a novel / by Will
Levington Comfort. Boston; New York: Houghton
Mifflin Company, 1925. (Cambridge: The Riverside
Press). 236, [1] p.
LC: S 4, '25.
PW: S 5, '25.

C-629 _____ Son of power / by Will Levington Comfort and
Zamin Ki Dost [pseud.]. Garden City, N. Y.:
Doubleday, Page & Company, 1920. 350 p.
LC: N 19, '20.
PW: N 20, '20.
BLC: London: Thornton Butterworth, 1922.

C-630 _____ Sport of kings / by Will Levington Comfort
. . . [Philadelphia: J. B. Lippincott Company,
c1913]. 48 p.   **DLC**
LC: N 4, '13.

C-631 _____ This man's world / by Will Levington
Comfort; frontispiece by Walter de Maris. Garden
City, N. Y.; Toronto: Doubleday, Page & Company,
1921. 324 p., front.
LC: N 12, '21.

C-632 _____ The yellow lord / by Will Levington Comfort.
New York: George H. Doran Company, [c1919].
311 p.
LC: My 19, '19.
PW: My 24, '19.

C-633 Commander. Clear the decks!: a tale of the
American Navy to-day / by "Commander"; with 20
illustrations. Philadelphia; London: J. B. Lippincott
Company, 1918. 302, [1] p., photo. front., [15]
leaves of plates.
"Several chapters appeared originally in *Sea power*."
LC: N 22, '18.

C-634 Commodore, b. 1859, *pseud*. Dilson's key / by the
Commodore [pseud.]. Wichita, Kansas, U. S. A.:
The Goldsmith-Woolard Publishing Co., 1916.
145 p., [5] leaves of photo. plates.   **KSW**
LC: D 26, '16.

Community Workers of the New York Guild for the
Jewish Blind. See *Aces* (1924), **A-42**.

Community Workers of the New York Guild for the
Jewish Blind. See *More aces* (1925), **M-962**.

Commuter's wife, A., pseud. See *Twenty miles out*
(1925), **T-442.**

C-635 Compton, D. R. (David Rinaldo), b. 1872. The
Longdens / by D. R. Compton. Philadelphia:
Dorrance & Company, [c1924]. 283 p.   **DLC**
LC: Mr 26, '24.

C-636 Compton, Hannibal Albert, b. 1890. A moonshiner's folly: and other stories / by Hannibal Albert Compton. Boston: The Roxburgh Publishing Company, [c1915]. 186 p. **VCV**
Contents: A moonshiner's folly -- A pauper's rise -- The husking bee that decided -- A spook chimney -- The legend of Oakview -- Mountain worshipers.
LC: F 26, '16.
PW: Ap 8, '16.

C-637 Comrie, Margaret S. (Margaret Simpson), b. 1851. A loyal Huguenot maid / by Margaret S. Comrie. Philadelphia: George W. Jacobs & Co., [1902]. 354 p., front., [3] leaves of plates. [Ill. by Arthur A. Dixon.] ·

Comstock, Anna Botsford, 1854-1930. See **Lee, Marian, pseud.**

C-638 Comstock, Harriet T. (Harriet Theresa), b. 1860. At the crossroads / by Harriet T. Comstock; frontispiece by Walter De Maris. Garden City, N. Y.; Toronto: Doubleday, Page & Company, 1922. 283 p., col. front.
LC: My 25, '22.
PW: Je 3, '22.

C-639 _____ Janet of the dunes / by Harriet T. Comstock; illustrated by Carle Michel Boog. Boston: Little, Brown and Company, 1908, [c1907]. 297 p., front., [3] leaves of plates.
LC: D 31, '07.
PW: Ja 18, '08.
BLC: London: Thomas Nelson & Sons, [1920].

C-640 _____ Joline / by Harriet T. Comstock. Garden City, N. Y.: Doubleday, Page & Company, 1925. 381 p.
LC: N 16, '25.
PW: O 31, '25.
BLC: London: William Heinemann; printed in U. S. A., 1925.

C-641 _____ Joyce of the North Woods / by Harriet T. Comstock; illustrated by John Cassel. Garden City, N. Y.: Doubleday, Page & Company, 1911. 390 p., front., [3] leaves of plates.
LC: Mr 22, '11.
PW: Ap 1, '11.
BLC: London: Hodder & Stoughton; New York printed, 1911.

C-642 _____ Mam'selle Jo / by Harriet T. Comstock; illustrated by E. F. Ward. Garden City, N. Y.: Doubleday, Page & Company, 1918. 367 p., front., [3] leaves of plates.
LC: O 3, '18.
PW: O 26, '18.
BLC: London: Hodder & Stoughton, [1924].

C-643 _____ The man thou gavest / by Harriet T. Comstock; illustrated by E. F. Ward. Garden City, N. Y.: Doubleday, Page & Company, 1917. 363 p., col. front., [1] leaf of col. plates.
LC: Ap 19, '17.
PW: Ap 21, '17.

C-644 _____ The place beyond the winds / by Harriet T. Comstock; illustrated by Harry Spafford Potter.

Garden City, N. Y.: Doubleday, Page & Company, 1914. 386 p., front., [4] leaves of plates.
LC: S 29, '14.
PW: O 3, '14.
BLC: London: Curtis Brown; Garden City, N. Y. printed, 1914.

C-645 _____ The queen's hostage / by Harriet T. Comstock; illustrated from drawings by Clyde O. Deland. Boston: Little, Brown, and Company, 1906. 319 p., front., [3] leaves of plates.
LC: Ag 27, '06.

C-646 _____ The shield of silence / by Harriet T. Comstock; frontispiece by George Loughridge. Garden City, N. Y.; Toronto: Doubleday, Page & Company, 1921. 292 p., front.
LC: Ap 25, '21.
PW: Ap 2, '21.
BLC: London: Hodder & Stoughton, [1921].

C-647 _____ Smothered fires / by Harriet T. Comstock. Garden City, N. Y.: Doubleday, Page & Company, 1924. 301 p.
LC: O 30, '24.
PW: O 18, '24.
BLC: London: William Heinemann; printed in U. S. A., 1924. Another edition: London: Hodder & Stoughton, printed in U. S. A., [1925] (with a different title page).

C-648 _____ A son of the hills / by Harriet T. Comstock. Garden City, N. Y.: Doubleday, Page and Company, 1913. 409, [1] p., front.
LC: N 5, '13.
PW: N 15, '13.

C-649 _____ The tenth woman / by Harriet T. Comstock; frontispiece by George W. Gage. Garden City, N. Y.: Doubleday, Page & Company, 1923. 341 p., front.
LC: My 24, '23.
PW: Je 9, '23.
BLC: London: William Heinemann; printed in U. S. A., 1923. Another edition: London: Hodder & Stoughton, [1924].

C-650 _____ Unbroken lines / by Harriet T. Comstock; illustrated by E. F. Ward. Garden City, N. Y.: Doubleday, Page & Company, 1919. 361, [1] p., front., [2] leaves of plates.
LC: D 1, '19.
PW: N 15, '19.

C-651 _____ The vindication / by Harriet T. Comstock; illustrated by Thomas Fogarty. Garden City, N. Y.: Doubleday, Page & Company, 1916. 375, [1] p., col. front., [3] leaves of plates.
LC: F 29, '16.
PW: My 27, '16.
BLC: London: Curtis Brown; Garden City, N. Y. printed, 1916. Another edition: London: Eveleigh Nash Co.; Garden City, N. Y., printed, 1916.

_____ The whitest gift of all. In *When God walks the road and other stories* **(1924), W-445.**

C-652 Comstock, Sarah, d. 1960. The daughter of Helen Kent / by Sara Comstock; frontispiece by John Alonzo Williams. Garden City, N. Y.; Toronto: Doubleday, Page & Company, 1921. 393, [1] p., front.
LC: O 22, '21.
PW: O 22, '21.

C-653 _____ The soddy / by Sarah Comstock. Garden City, N. Y.: Doubleday, Page & Company, 1912. 370 p.
LC: O 1, '12.
PW: O 12, '12.

C-654 _____ The valley of vision / by Sarah Comstock; frontispiece by Herman Pfeifer. Garden City, N. Y.: Doubleday, Page & Company, 1919. 424 p., col. front.
LC: Ap 10, '19.
PW: Ap 5, '19.
BLC: London: Eveleigh Nash Co., 1919. (British title: *Maria rebels; or The valley of vision*.)

C-655 Comstock, Seth Cook. Marcelle the mad / by Seth Cook Comstock. New York: D. Appleton and Company, 1906. 339 p.
PW: Mr 10, '06.

C-656 Conard, Howard Louis. Reconstructing Eden / by Howard Louis Conard; illustrations by W. A. Ireland. Columbus, Ohio: New Eden Publishing Co., 1909. 66 p., front., [4] leaves of plates.   **OCO**

C-657 Condict, Anna Yeaman. "My Li'l' Angelo" / by Anna Yeaman Condict. New York: D. Appleton and Company, 1904. 182 p., col. front. [Ill. by Benson Knipe.]

C-658 Condon, Frank, 1882-1940. The fifty dollar bill / by Frank Condon. New York: The Winthrop Press, c1914. 31, [1] p., col. front. ill.
Previously published in *The all-story magazine*.

C-659 Cone, Andrew Jackson, b. 1844? The Rock: a story of the war / by a rebel [pseud.]. New York: Broadway Publishing Company, [c1913]. 149 p., front. (port.), [4] leaves of plates.   **VIC**
LC: My 21, '13.

C-660 Cone, Joe, b. 1869. The waybackers / Joe Cone; full page illustrations by Eliot Keen; portrait studies by Horace Dummer. Boston: The Colonial Press Inc., [1905]. 379 p., front., [4] leaves of plates, ill.

C-661 The confessions of a débutante / with illustrations by R. M. Crosby. Boston; New York: Houghton Mifflin Company, 1913. 140 p., incl. front.

C-662 The confessions of a princess. New York: C. H. Doscher & Co., [c1908]. 269 p.   **DLC**
LC: Je 10, '08.
PW: Je 13, '08.
BLC: London: John Lane, 1906. [Third impression]

C-663 The confession of a rebellious wife. Boston: Small, Maynard and Company, [c1910]. 64 p.
LC: N 11, '10.
PW: N 5, '10.

C-664 The confessions of an inconstant man / illustrated. New York; London: D. Appleton and Company, 1914. 178, [1] p., front., [3] leaves of plates, ill. [Ill. by Graham F. Cootes.]
LC: Ap 3, '14.

Congdon, Louise Buffum, ed. <u>See</u> *A book of Bryn Mawr stories* **(1901), B-732.**

C-665 Conkley, Ralph, b. 1867, *pseud.* Kitty Knight / by Ralph Conkley [pseud.]. Richmond, Va.: Whittet & Shepperson, 1913. 313 p., front. (port.)
LC: Je 6, '13.

C-666 Conklin, David Bruce. Russell Ryder / by David Bruce Conklin; with illustrations by the author. New York: A. Wessels Company, 1902. 333 p., front., [4] leaves of plates.

C-667 Conklin, Edward J. Love blossoms / by Edward J. Conklin. Wichita, Kansas: Published by The Plaindealer Press, [1924]. 44 p., [3] leaves of plates.   **DLC**
Cover title.
LC: F 13, '24.

C-668 Conklin, Mary. The love emerald of Colombia / by Mary Elizabeth Conklin. Baltimore: Saulsbury Publishing Company, 1918. 63 p., [2] leaves of plates. [Ill. by F. L. Bryant.]   **VA@**
LC: O 26, '18.

C-669 Conley, John Wesley. The church at Libertyville: as seen by Thomas Bradley / edited by John Wesley Conley. Philadelphia: The Griffith and Rowland Press, 1907. 204 p.
LC: F 4, '07.

C-670 Conly, Ella Madge Smith, b. 1873. A lady of France / Ella Madge Conly. Chicago: Homewood Publishing Company, [c1908]. 245 p., front., plates. Unexamined copy: bibliographic data from OCLC, #29418802.

C-671 Connell, Richard Edward, 1893-1949. Apes and angels / by Richard Connell . . . New York: Minton, Balch & Company, 1924. 312 p.
                                        OSU, NYP
Contents: A friend of Napoleon -- A reputation -- Son of a sloganeer -- The wronging of Edwin Dell -- The unfamiliar -- A house in the country -- Shoes -- The prince has the mumps -- The battle of Washington square -- The last of the Flatfeet -- The man who could imitate a bee.
LC: My 17, '24.
PW: My 17, '24.

_____ Champions all. <u>In</u> *The Sporting spirit* **(1925), S-771.**

_____ A friend of Napoleon. <u>In</u> *Prize stories of 1923* **(1924), P-621.**

_____ The most dangerous game. <u>In</u> *Prize stories of 1924* **(1925), P-622.**

C-672 _____ The sin of Monsieur Pettipon: and other humorous tales / by Richard Connell. New York: George H. Doran Company, [c1922]. 287 p.

Contents: The sin of Monsieur Pettipon -- Mr. Pottle and the South-Sea cannibals -- Mr. Pottle and culture -- Mr. Pottle and the one man dog -- Mr. Pottle and pageantry -- The cage man -- Where is the Tropic of Capricorn? -- Mr. Braddy's bottle -- Gretna Greenhorns -- Terrible Epps -- Honor among sportsmen -- The $25,000 jaw.
LC: Jl 24, '22.

C-673   _____ Variety / by Richard Connell. New York: Minton, Balch & Company, 1925. 322 p.   **MNU**
Contents: Big Lord Fauntleroy -- Sssssssssshhhh -- Spring flow'rets; or Womanhood eternal -- The most dangerous game -- And the night shall be filled with music -- Neighbors -- All wrong -- The second egg -- Pieces of silver -- The hero of the devil's kitchen -- The great American game -- Isles of romance -- Six reasons why.
LC: Mr 28, '25.
PW: Mr 28, '25.
BLC: London: Leonard Parsons; printed in U. S. A., 1925.

C-674   Conners, W. F. (William Fuller). James Lee / by W. F. Conners. [Chicago: The Clinic Publishing Company, c1906]. 238, [1] p.   **ORU**
LC: D 1, '06.

C-675   Connolly, Arthur Leicester. The poet: (from "Sketches") / by Arthur Leicester Connolly. [Boston: Buchanan Co.], 1909. 15 p.   **NYP**

C-676   Connolly, James, b. 1842. The magic of the sea, or, Commodore John Barry in the making / by Captain James Connolly. St. Louis, Mo.; Freiburg (Baden), Germany; London: Published by B. Herder, 1911. 554 p.
LC: Je 23, '11.

C-677   Connolly, James B. (James Brendan), 1868-1957. The crested seas / by James Brendan Connolly; with illustrations. New York: Charles Scribner's Sons, 1907. 311 p., front., [7] leaves of plates. [Ill. by C. W. Ashley, W. J. Aylward, George Harding, and N. C. Wyeth.]
Contents: The dance -- On the bottom of the dory -- The blasphemer -- The commandeering of the Lucy Foster -- The illimitable senses -- The joy of a Christmas passage -- The drawn shutters -- The smugglers -- Between shipmates -- The ice-dogs -- The Americanization of roll-down Joe -- The harsh word -- The magnetic hearth.
LC: S 26, '07.
PW: O 5, '07.
BLC: London: Duckworth & Co; New York [printed], 1907.

C-678   _____ The deep sea's toll / by James B. Connolly; with illustrations by W. J. Aylward & H. Reuterdahl. New York: Charles Scribner's Sons, 1905. 315 p., front., [7] leaves of plates.
Contents: The sail-carriers -- The wicked "Celestine" -- The truth of the Oliver Cromwell -- Strategy and seamanship -- Dory-mates -- The salving of the bark Fuller -- On Georges Shoals -- Patsie Oddie's black night.
PW: O 14, '05.
BLC: London: Bickers & Son; New York [printed], 1906.

C-679   _____ Head winds / by James B. Connolly; illustrated. New York: Charles Scribner's Sons, 1916. 299 p., front., [5] leaves of plates. [Ill. by F. C. Yohn and N. C. Wyeth.]   **OXZ**
Contents: The adoption -- Chavero -- Quiltem -- The trawler -- Mother Machree -- Down river -- Colors! -- The camera man.
LC: S 14, '16.
PW: S 16, '16.
BLC: London: Thomas Nelson & Sons, [1920].

C-680   _____ Hiker joy / by James B. Connolly; with illustrations by N. C. Wyeth. New York: Charles Scribner's Sons, 1920. 244 p., front., [3] leaves of plates.
LC: My 24, '20.
PW: My 22, '20.

C-681   _____ Jeb Hutton: the story of a Georgia boy / by James B. Connolly; illustrated by M. J. Burns. New York: Charles Scribner's Sons, 1902. 289 p., front., [7] leaves of plates.
PW: S 20, '02.

C-682   _____ An Olympic victor: a story of the modern games / by James Brendan Connolly; with illustrations by A. Castaigne. New York: Charles Scribner's Sons, 1908. 186 p., front., [7] leaves of plates.
LC: Ag 27, '08.
PW: S 5, '08.

C-683   _____ On Tybee knoll: a story of the Georgia coast / by James B. Connolly; illustrated by Ch. Weber-Ditzler. New York: A. S. Barnes & Company, 1905. 285 p., col. front., [3] leaves of col. plates.
PW: My 13, '05.

C-684   _____ Open water / by James Brendan Connolly; with illustrations. New York: Charles Scribner's Sons, 1910. 322 p., front., [7] leaves of plates. [Ill. by F. C. Yohn, W. J. Aylward, and Maynard Dixon.]
Contents: The emigrants -- Tshushima Straits -- The consuming flame -- Gree Gree Bush -- The venture of the "Flying Hind" -- The cruise of the "Bounding Boy" -- The sea-faker -- Heroes -- The Christmas handicap.
LC: O 5, '10.
PW: O 8, '10.

C-685   _____ Out of Gloucester / by James B. Connolly; with illustrations. New York: Charles Scribner's Sons, 1902. 276 p., front., [7] leaves of plates. [Ill. by M. J. Burns.]
Contents: A chase overnight -- On the echo o' the morn -- From Reykjavik to Gloucester -- A fisherman of Costla -- Tommy Ohlsen's western passage -- Clancy.
PW: O 18, '02.
BLC: London: Hodder & Stoughton; New York [printed], 1906.

C-686   _____ Running free: with illustrations / by James B. Connolly. New York: Charles Scribner's Sons, 1917. 302 p., front., [5] leaves of plates. [Ill. by W. J. Enright and F. C. Yohn.]
Contents: The strategists -- The weeping Annie -- The bull-fight -- A bale of blankets -- Breath o' dawn -- Peter stops ashore -- The sea-birds -- The medicine ship -- One wireless night -- Dan Magee: white hope.
LC: S 19, '17.
PW: S 22, '17.
BLC: London: Thomas Nelson & Sons, [1921].

C-687   _____ The seiners / by James B. Connolly. New York: Charles Scribner's Sons, 1904. 314 p., front.
PW: Je 4, '04.
BLC: London: Hodder & Stoughton; New York [printed], 1904.

C-688   ____ Sonnie-Boy's people: illustrated / by James B. Connolly. New York: Charles Scribner's Sons, 1913. 363 p., front., [7] leaves of plates. [Ill. by Anton Otto Fischer, C. W. Ashley, and others.]
Contents: Sonnie-Boy's people -- Tim Riley's touch -- In the anchor watch -- Cross courses -- Leary of the "Ligonier" -- How they got the "Hattie Rennish" -- Killorin's Caribbean days -- The battle-cruise of the "Svend Foyn" -- The last passenger.
LC: S 30, '13.
PW: O 11, '13.

C-689   ____ Steel decks / by James B. Connolly. New York: Charles Scribner's Sons, 1925. 265 p.
LC: O 14, '25.
PW: O 10, '25.
BLC: London: Hodder & Stoughton, [1926].

C-690   ____ Tide rips: with illustrations / by James B. Connolly. New York: Charles Scribner's Sons, 1922. 246 p., front., [3] leaves of plates. [Ill. by W. B. King.]
Contents: His three fair wishes -- What price for fish? -- Not down in the log -- The sugar ship -- Beejum's progress -- The munition ship -- A port in France -- The rakish brigantine -- Rolling on to Athens.
LC: Mr 22, '22.
PW: Ap 1, '22.

C-691   ____ The trawler / by James B. Connolly. New York: Charles Scribner's Sons, 1914. 70 p.
LC: N 10, '14.

C-692   ____ Wide courses / by James Brendan Connolly; with illustrations. New York: Charles Scribner's Sons, 1912. 336 p., front., [7] leaves of plates. [Ill. by N. C. Wyeth, Gordon M. McCouch, Anton Otto Fischer, Howard Pyle, et al.]
Contents: The wrecker -- Laying the hose-pipe ghost -- The seizure of the "Aurora Borealis" -- Light-ship 67 -- Captain Blaise -- Don Quixote Kieran, pump-man -- Jan Tingloff -- Cogan capeador.
LC: Ap 16, '12.
PW: Ap 20, '12.
BLC: London: Duckworth & Co.; New York [printed], 1912.

C-693   Connor, Jean. Bond and free / by Jean Connor . . . New York; Cincinnati; Chicago: Benziger Brothers, 1913. 273 p.   **MUU**
LC: O 18, '13.

C-694   ____ So as by fire / by Jean Connor. New York; Cincinnati; Chicago: Benziger Brothers, 1909. 299 p.   **DLC**
LC: D 23, '09.
PW: Ja 1, '10.

Connor, Torrey. The quest. In *West winds* (1914), **W-368.**

C-695   Conover, W. Rockwood (Warren Rockwood), b. 1862. Sallie Blue Bonnet / by W. Rockwood Conover. Boston: The C. M. Clark Publishing Co., [c1911]. 369 p., col. front., [7] leaves of plates.
LC: Mr 27, '12.

C-696   Conrad, C. F. (Charles Fecker), b. 1863. Mute Island: a novel / by C. F. Conrad . . . New York, N. Y.: Published by The University Book Co., 1917. 231, [1] p., photo. front. (port.)   **DLC**
LC: Ja 12, '17.

C-697   Conrad, Joseph, 1857-1924. Il conte / by Joseph Conrad; with other stories by famous American authors; edited by Charles Donald Fox. New York City: The Charles Renard Co., 1925. 312 p.
    OSU, WSU
"The stories in this volume were first published in 1908 and 1909, in various issues of Hampton's magazine and the Broadway magazine."
Contents: Il conte / Joseph Conrad -- The snow man / O. Henry -- Salvatore Schneider / Ernest Poole -- The argonauts / Morgan Robertson -- The Holy City quartette / Emerson Hough -- The things they saw / Zona Gale -- Holding hands / Gouverneur Morris -- The breeze kid's big tear-off / Damon Runyon -- "The will of the Gods" / S. Ten Eyck Bourke -- Commander Jim Wickson's "habit" / Holman F. Day -- The thing in the hall / E. F. Benson -- The apron of genius / Earl Derr Biggers -- The new Earth / Mrs. Wilson Woodrow -- Who's who at the zoo / Irvin S. Cobb -- John Jones comes to life / Harris Merton Lyon -- The Pied Piper of One-Track Gulch / Francis Lynde -- Dr. Burke's cure / Dorothy Canfield -- The courtship of Miles Sheehan / Porter Emerson Browne -- The light in her eyes / Marguerita Spalding Gerry -- Lassiter / Richard Washburn Child.
LC: Ap 18, '25.

C-698   Conrad, Lawrence H. (Lawrence Henry), b. 1898. Temper / by Lawrence H. Conrad. New York: Dodd, Mead and Company, 1924. 305 p.
LC: F 12, '24.

C-699   Conrad, Stephen, 1875-1918. Mrs. Jim and Mrs. Jimmie: certain town experiences of the second Mrs. Jim as related to Jimmy's wife / by Stephen Conrad; with a frontispiece in colours from a drawing by Arthur W. Brown. Boston: L. C. Page & Company, 1905. 296 p., col. front.
PW: Ag 5, '05.

C-700   ____ The second Mrs. Jim / by Stephen Conrad; with a frontispiece by Ernest Fosbery. Boston: L. C. Page & Company, 1904. 164 p., front.

C-701   Conrard, Harrison, 1869-1930. The golden bowl: a Western story / by Harrison Conrard. New York City: Chelsea House, [c1925]. 256 p.
PW: S 26, '25.

Consolation club. See *The misfit Christmas puddings* **(1906), M-850.**

Conval, Ronleigh de. See **De Conval, Ronleigh, b. 1844.**

C-702   Converse, Florence, b. 1871. The children of light / by Florence Converse. Boston: Houghton Mifflin Company, 1912. 308 p.
BLC: London: J. M. Dent & Sons, 1912.

C-703   ____ Long Will: a romance / by Florence Converse. Boston; New York: Houghton, Mifflin and Company, 1903. (Cambridge: The Riverside Press). 377, [1] p., front., [5] leaves of plates. [Ill. by Garth Jones.]
PW: O 24, '03.
BLC: London; Bombay: Longman's, Green & Co.; Cambridge, Mass. printed, 1903.

C-704   Conway, Katherine E. (Katherine Eleanor), 1853-1927. Lalor's maples / by Katherine E. Conway. Boston: The Pilot Publishing Company, 1901. 329 p.

C-705 _____ The woman who never did wrong, and other stories / by Katherine E. Conway . . . Boston: T. J. Flynn & Company, [c1909]. 140 p.
Unexamined copy: bibliographic data from NUC.
Contents: The woman who never did wrong -- A Christmas rescue -- The place that was kept -- A marriage of self-respect -- The tragedy of a broken word -- An Atlantic liner episode -- The vocation of Veronica Melvin -- An Easter sunset -- Two women friends.
LC: N 13, '09.
PW: D 11, '09.

Cook, Burr, jt. aut. *"The plot concerns--"* (1925). See **Kaye, Joseph, jt. aut., K-33.**

C-706 [Cook, Fred H.] Prof. Hugo Shakenutts: the white-handed, pink-fingered gent: a parody on advertising. [Dayton, Ohio: The Drury Printing Co., c1918]. 127 p., ill.
LC: F 13, '19.

C-707 Cook, George Cram, 1873-1924. The chasm: a novel / by George Cram Cook . . . New York: Frederick A. Stokes Company, 1911. 379 p.
LC: F 13, '11.
PW: F 25, '11.

C-708 _____ Roderick Taliaferro: a story of Maximilian's empire / by George Cram Cook; with illustrations by Seymour M. Stone. New York: The Macmillan Company; London: Macmillan & Co., Ltd., 1903. 482 p., front., [5] leaves of plates.

C-709 Cook, Grace Louise. Wellesley stories / by Grace Louise Cook. Boston: Richard G. Badger & Company (Incorporated), 1901, [c1900]. 340 p.
Contents: Clorinda -- President Jefferson -- Professor Lamont -- Submerged -- Lyrical interlude -- Sir Toby's career -- Initiated into love.
PW: F 9, '01.

C-710 Cook, Marion, b. 1875. The child and the dream: a Christmas story / by Marion Cook. Portland, Oregon: The Metropolitan Press, 1908. 22 p., photo. front.
LC: D 14, '08.

C-711 Cook, Metta Horton. Helen's choice: a tale of Long Island / by Metta Horton Cook. New York: J. S. Ogilvie Publishing Co., c1913. 96 p.   **DLC**
LC: O 2, '13.

C-712 _____ Yennycott folks: an historical romance of the pioneer days of Long Island, touching upon such well-known families as the Hallock, Terry, Yonges, Horton, Tuttle, Salmon, Conkelyne, Goldsmith, Moore, Akerly, Booth, Herbert, Benjamin, Miller, King, Brown, Elton, Case, Tucker, Wines, Haynes, Corey and Payne families / by Metta Horton Cook. New York: J. S. Ogilvie Publishing Company, [c1910]. 128 p., photo. front. (port.), [5] leaves of photo. plates.

C-713 Cook, Richard Yerkes, 1845-1917. The manuscript "Pray for me". Philadelphia: Printed privately, 1908. 43 p., photo. front., [2] leaves of photo. plates.

C-714 Cook, Samuel Newton. Norma Lane: the daughter of an "absent Brother" / by Samuel Newton Cook.

Columbus, Ohio: Wayne-Cook Publishing Co., 1909. 245 p., front.
Also published under title: *Norma Lane, the daughter of an Elk.*
LC: S 4, '09.

C-715 Cook, William Wallace, 1867-1933. Around the world in eighty hours: an adventure story / by William Wallace Cook. New York City: Chelsea House, [c1925]. 249 p.
PW: D 19, '25.

C-716 [_____] The fiction factory: being the experience of a writer who, for twenty-two years, has kept a story-mill grinding successfully / by John Milton Edwards [pseud.]. Ridgewood, New Jersey: The Editor Company, [c1912]. 180 p.
LC: My 29, '12.

C-717 _____ Wilby's Dan / by William Wallace Cook; illustrated by C. B. Falls. New York: Dodd, Mead & Company, 1904. 325 p., col. front., [7] leaves of col. plates.   **IUA**

C-718 Cooke, Edmund Vance, 1866-1932. A morning's mail / Edmund Vance Cooke . . . Philadelphia: Pearson Brothers, 1907. 47, [1] p., ill.   **IUL**
"Originally printed in *Truth*."
LC: My 29, '07.

C-719 Cooke, Frances. Her journey's end / by Frances Cooke . . . New York; Cincinnati; Chicago: Benziger Brothers, 1911. 307 p.   **LUU**
LC: Mr 31, '11.

C-720 _____ "My lady Beatrice" / by Frances Cooke . . . New York; Cincinnati; Chicago: Benziger Brothers, 1908. 244 p.
LC: F 1, '08.
PW: F 15, '08.

C-721 _____ The secret of the green vase / by Frances Cooke. New York; Boston; Cincinnati; Chicago; San Francisco: Benziger Brothers, Inc., 1907. 248 p.   **RMC**
LC: N 23, '07.
PW: D 14, '07.

C-722 _____ The unbidden guest / by Frances Cooke . . . New York; Cincinnati; Chicago: Benziger Brothers, 1909. 255 p.
LC: N 19, '09.
PW: D 4, '09.

Cooke, Grace MacGowan, 1863-1944. A call. In *The best American humorous short stories* (1920), **B-556.**

_____ The capture of Andy Proudfoot. In *Southern lights and shadows* (1907), **S-718.**

C-723 _____ A gourd fiddle / by Grace MacGowan Cooke; illustrations by E. Lynn Mudge and E. B. Miles. Philadelphia: Henry Altemus Company, [c1904]. 118 p., front., [8] leaves of plates.
PW: D 3, '04.

C-724   ____ The grapple: a story of the Illinois coal region / by Grace MacGowan Cooke; with a frontispiece in colour from a drawing by Arthur W. Brown. Boston: L. C. Page & Company, 1905. 415 p., col. front.
PW: S 16, '05.

C-725   ____ Huldah: proprietor of the Wagon-Tire House and genial philosopher of the cattle country / by Grace MacGowan Cooke and Alice MacGowan; illustrated by Fanny Y. Cory. Indianapolis: The Bobbs-Merrill Company, [c1904]. 316 p., front., [7] leaves of plates.
PW: My 14, '04.

C-726   ____ The joy bringer: a tale of the painted desert / by Grace MacGowan Cooke. Garden City, N. Y.: Doubleday, Page & Co., 1913. 338 p., front., ill. [Ill. by Robert A. Graef.]
LC: Mr 27, '13.
PW: Ap 26, '13.

C-727   ____ Mistress Joy: a tale of Natchez in 1798 / by Grace MacGowan Cooke and Annie Booth McKinney. New York: The Century Co., 1901. 370 p., front., [5] leaves of plates. [Ill. by Charles M. Relyea.]
PW: O 26, '01.

C-728   ____ The power and the glory / by Grace MacGowan Cooke; illustrated by Arthur I. Keller. New York: Doubleday, Page & Company, 1910. 373 p., front., [3] leaves of plates.
LC: Ag 5, '10.
PW: Ag 6, '10.
BLC: London: Hodder & Stoughton; New York printed, 1910.

C-729   [____] The straight road / with illustrations by C. E. Chambers. New York: George H. Doran Company, [c1917]. 356 p., front., [7] leaves of plates. By Grace MacGowan Cooke and Alice MacGowan.
LC: Ap 24, '17.
PW: Ap 21, '17.

C-730   ____ Their first formal call / Grace MacGowan Cooke; illustrated by Peter Newell. New York; London: Harper & Brothers, 1906. 55 p., col. front., [13] leaves of col. plates.
First published in Harper's magazine, Aug., 1906, under title: A call.
LC: S 27, '06.
PW: O 20, '06.

C-731   [____] Wild apples: a California story / by the author of "The straight road"; with illustrations by C. E. Chambers. New York: George H. Doran Company, [c1918]. 346 p., front., [7] leaves of plates.
By Grace MacGowan Cooke and Alice MacGowan.
LC: S 30, '18.
PW: S 28, '18.

C-732   ____ William and Bill / by Grace MacGowan Cooke and Caroline Wood Morrison. New York: The Century Co., 1914. 295 p.
LC: Ja 23, '14.
PW: Ja 17, '14.

C-733   Cooke, Jane Grosvenor. The ancient miracle / by Jane Grosvenor Cooke. New York: A. S. Barnes & Company, 1906. 364 p., col. front. [Ill. by E. Shinn.]
LC: S 17, '06.

C-734   ____ An interrupted honeymoon / by Jane Grosvenor Cooke . . . New York: A. S. Barnes & Company, 1907. 351 p.   **NYP**
LC: D 23, '07.

Cooke, John Estes, pseud. <u>See</u> **Baum, L. Frank (Lyman Frank), 1856-1919.**

C-735   Cooke, Marjorie Benton, 1876-1920. Bambi / Marjorie Benton Cooke; illustrated by Mary Greene Blumenschein. Garden City, N. Y.: Doubleday, Page & Company, 1914. 366 p., col. front., [8] leaves of plates.
LC: S 29, '14.
PW: S 19, '14.
BLC: London: Jarrold Sons; Garden City, New York [printed], 1915.

C-736   ____ Cinderella Jane / by Marjorie Benton Cooke. Garden City, N. Y.: Doubleday, Page & Company, 1917. 307, [1] p., col. front.
LC: Ap 19, '17.
PW: Ap 28, '17.

C-737   ____ The clutch of circumstance / by Marjorie Benton Cooke. New York: George H. Doran Company, [c1918]. 230 p.
LC: O 10, '18.
PW: O 19, '18.
BLC: London: Skeffington & Son, [1919].

C-738   ____ The cricket / by Marjorie Benton Cooke; illustrated by J. Scott Williams. Garden City, N. Y.: Doubleday, Page & Company, 1919. 277, [1] p., front., [3] leaves of plates.
LC: Ap 21, '19.
PW: Ap 26, '19.
BLC: London: Curtis Brown; Garden City, New York [printed], 1919. Another edition: [London]: Jarrold's, [1919].

C-739   ____ Dr. David / by Marjorie Benton Cooke . . . ; illustrated in color by Monte Crews. Chicago: A. C. McClurg & Co., 1911. 365 p., col. front., [3] leaves of col. plates.
LC: Ag 21, '11.
PW: S 23, '11.

C-740   ____ The dual alliance / by Marjorie Benton Cooke; illustrated by Mary Greene Blumenschein. Garden City, N. Y.: Doubleday, Page & Company, 1915. 164, [2] p., col. front., [3] leaves of plates.
LC: O 18, '15.
PW: O 16, '15.

C-741   ____ The girl who lived in the woods / by Marjorie Benton Cooke; with five illustrations in colors by The Kinneys. Chicago: A. C. McClurg & Co., 1910. 430 p., col. front., [3] leaves of col. plates.
LC: O 3, '10.
PW: O 8, '10.
BLC: [London]: Jarrolds, 1917.

C-742　　____ Married? / by Marjorie Benton Cook; frontispiece by Reginald F. Bolles. Garden City, N. Y.; Toronto: Doubleday, Page & Company, 1921. 282 p., front.
LC: O 12, '21.
PW: O 15, '21.

____, contributor. See *The sturdy oak* (1917), **S-1100.**

C-743　　____ The threshold / Marjorie Benton Cooke. Garden City, N. Y.: Doubleday, Page & Company, 1918. 353, [1] p., col. front.
LC: Mr 28, '18.
PW: Mr 30, '18.
BLC: [London]: Jarrold's, [1918].

C-744　　Cooley, Stoughton, b. 1861. The captain of the Amaryllis / by Stoughton Cooley. Boston, Mass.: The C. M. Clark Publishing Company, [c1910]. 416 p., front., [5] leaves of plates. [Ill. by Leslie L. Benson.]
LC: F 10, '11.

C-745　　Coolidge, Asenath Carver. Between two rebellions / by Asenath Carver Coolidge. Watertown, N. Y.: [Hungerford-Holbrook Co.], 1909. 221, [1] p., photo. front. (port.), [1] leaf of photo. plates (port.). [Ill. by the author.]
LC: D 26, '08.
PW: Mr 6, '09.

C-746　　____ Cherry feasts for barbarous Fourths / by Asenath Carver Coolidge . . . Watertown, New York: [Hungerford-Holbrook Co.], 1909. 36 p., [1] leaf of photo. plates.　　**VHB**
PW: Jl 31, '09.

C-747　　____ Christmas vs. Fourth of July / by Asenath Carver Coolidge . . . Watertown, New York: [Printed by Hungerford-Holbrook Co.], 1908. 39 p.　　**STF**
"Published in `Boston Ideas' July, 1901."
LC: Jl 1, '08.

C-748　　____ Human beings vs. things / by Asenath Carver Coolidge . . . Watertown, N. Y.: Hungerford-Holbrook Company, 1910, [c1909]. 222 p., photo. front., [8] leaves of plates (incl. ports.).
LC: D 1, '09.

C-749　　____ The Independence Day horror at Killsbury / by Asenath Carver Coolidge . . . ; illustrated by Cassius M. Coolidge. Watertown, N. Y.: Hungerford-Holbrook Company, 1905. 244 p., front., [4] leaves of plates.

C-750　　____ The modern blessing fire / by Asenath Carver Coolidge . . . New York; London; Montreal: The Abbey Press, [c1902]. 152 p.

C-751　　____ Our nation's altar / by Asenath Carver Coolidge . . . Watertown, New York: Hungerford-Holbrook Co., 1910. 47 p., [1] leaf of photo. plates (port.).　　**NYP**
LC: Je 8, '10.

C-752　　____ Prophet of peace / penned by Asenath Carver Coolidge; pictured by Cassius M. Coolidge. Watertown, N. Y.: Hungerford-Holbrook Company, 1907. 226 p., front., [15] leaves of plates.
LC: Mr 7, '08.

C-753　　____ Reciprocity: a story of love and mining / by Asenath Carver Coolidge; illustated by the author. Watertown, N. Y.: Hungerford-Holbrook Company, 1911. 279 p., front., [7] leaves of plates.
LC: O 16, '11.
PW: F 10, '12.

C-754　　Coolidge, Dane, 1873-1940. Bat Wing Bowles / by Dane Coolidge; illustrated by D. C. Hutchison. New York: Frederick A. Stokes Company, [1914]. 296 p., col. front., [3] leaves of plates.
LC: Mr 9, '14.
PW: Mr 14, '14.

C-755　　____ The desert trail / by Dane Coolidge; illustrations by Douglas Duer and P. J. Monahan. New York: W. J. Watt & Company, [c1915]. 279 p., front., [2] leaves of plates.
LC: My 21, '15.
PW: Je 26, '15.

C-756　　____ The fighting fool: a tale of the western frontier / by Dane Coolidge. New York: E. P. Dutton & Company, [c1918]. 291 p.
LC: My 13, '18.
PW: My 25, '18.

C-757　　____ Hidden water / by Dane Coolidge; with four illustrations in color by Maynard Dixon. Chicago: A. C. McClurg & Co., 1910. 483 p., col. front., [3] leaves of col. plates.
LC: N 2, '10.
PW: D 3, '10.

C-758　　____ Lorenzo the Magnificent: (The riders from Texas) / by Dane Coolidge. New York: E. P. Dutton & Company, [c1925]. 320 p.
LC: Je 4, '25.
PW: Je 20, '25.

C-759　　____ Lost wagons / by Dane Coolidge . . . New York: E. P. Dutton & Company, [c1923]. 256 p.
LC: Ja 27, '23.
PW: F 3, '23.

C-760　　____ The man-killers / by Dane Coolidge . . . New York: E. P. Dutton & Company, [c1921]. 243 p.　　**NYP**
LC: Ap 6, '21.
PW: Ap 30, '21.

C-761　　____ Rimrock Jones / by Dane Coolidge; illustrations by George W. Gage. New York: W. J. Watt & Company, [c1917]. 311 p., front., [2] leaves of plates.
LC: My 5, '17.
PW: Je 16, '17.
BLC: London: Methuen & Co., 1920.

C-762　　____ The scalp-lock / by Dane Coolidge. New York: E. P. Dutton & Company, [c1924]. 253 p.

LC: Ja 28, '24.
PW: F 16, '24.
BLC: London: Hodder & Stoughton, [1924].

C-763   ____ Shadow Mountain / by Dane Coolidge . . . ; frontispiece by George W. Gage. New York: W. J. Watt & Company, [c1919]. 311 p., front.
LC: My 17, '19.
PW: Jl 5, '19.
BLC: London: Methuen & Co., 1921.

C-764   ____ Silver and gold: a story of luck and love in a western mining camp / by Dane Coolidge . . . New York: E. P. Dutton & Company, [c1919]. 260 p.
LC: Ag 29, '19.
PW: Ag 2, '19.

C-765   ____ The Texican / by Dane Coolidge . . . ; with illustrations in color by Maynard Dixon. Chicago: A. C. McClurg & Co., 1911. 368, [1] p., col. front., [4] leaves of col. plates.   **OSU, RCE**
LC: S 25, '11.
PW: S 23, '11.

C-766   ____ Wunpost / by Dane Coolidge . . . New York: E. P. Dutton & Company, [c1920]. 273 p.
LC: Je 28, '20.
PW: Jl 3, '20.
BLC: London: Hodder & Stoughton, [1921].

C-767   Coolidge, Emma Downing, 1884-1968. At the King's pleasure / by Emma Downing Coolidge. Boston, Massachusetts: The C. M. Clark Publishing Co., [c1911]. 242 p., col. front., [3] leaves of plates.
LC: Mr 21, '12.

C-768   ____ The dreamer / by Emma Downing Coolidge. Boston; New York; Chicago: The Pilgrim Press, [c1915]. 57 p.
LC: S 22, '15.
PW: D 4, '15.

C-769   Coolidge, Grace. Teepee neighbors / by Grace Coolidge. Boston: The Four Seas Company, 1917. 225 p.
Contents: Author's preface -- The man with the axe -- Ghosts -- The gift -- Shadows -- Civilization -- "By any other name" -- An Indian victory -- The passing of Felix runs behind -- The pot and the kettle -- Mothers -- A boy's mother -- The dead bird -- A venture in hard hearts -- The thrown-away baby -- The capture of Edmund Goes-in-Lodge -- "In the kingdom of the blind" -- Little things -- A man -- Lazarus -- At the end of his rope -- The love woman -- The agriculturalist -- The informers -- A matter of custom -- The day dream -- The unborn -- The man's part -- Tit for tat -- The other mad man.
LC: Ja 17, '18.
PW: Ja 19, '18.

C-770   Coolidge, Herbert, b. 1874. Pancho McClish / by Herbert Coolidge; with illustrations by J. N. Marchand. Chicago: A. C. McClurg & Co., 1912. 341 p., col. front., [3] leaves of col. plates.
LC: N 1, '12.
PW: N 16, '12.

C-771   Coom, Charles S. (Charles Sleeman), b. 1851. The baronet rag-picker: a story of love and adventure / by Charles S. Coom. Boston: C. M. Clark Publishing Co., Inc., 1905. 261 p., col. front. [Ill. by C. H. Richert.]

C-772   ____ Owl tower: the true story of a family feud in Old England / by Charles S. Coom; illustrations by William Kirkpatrick. Boston: The C. M. Clark Publishing Co., 1906. 368 p., front., [7] leaves of plates.
LC: D 10, '06.

C-773   Cooney, Dotia Trigg. A study in ebony / by Dotia Trigg Cooney. New York; Washington: The Neale Publishing Company, 1911. 284 p.
LC: Jl 31, '11.
PW: My 6, '11.

C-774   Cooper, Courtney Ryley, 1886-1940. The cross-cut / by Courtney Ryley Cooper; with frontispiece by George W. Gage. Boston: Little, Brown and Company, 1921. 321 p., front.
LC: My 4, '21.
BLC: London: W. Collins, Sons & Co., [1922].

____ Driftwood. In *Marriage* (1923), M-457.

C-775   ____ The eagle's eye; a true story of the imperial German government's spies and intrigues in America from facts furnished by William J. Flynn, recently retired chief of the U. S. Secret Service, novelized by Courtney Ryley Cooper . . . illustrated. New York: Prospect Press, Inc. [c1919]. 377 p., photo. front., [7] leaves of plates.   **VIC**
LC: Ja 8, '19.

C-776   ____ The last frontier / by Courtney Ryley Cooper; with frontispiece by Remington Schuyler. Boston: Little, Brown and Company, 1923. 304 p., front.
LC: O 29, '23.
PW: F 16, '24.

____, jt. aut. Martin Gerrity gets even. In *Prize stories of 1921* (1922), P-619.

C-777   ____ The white desert / by Courtney Ryley Cooper; with frontispiece by Anon (sic) Otto Fischer. Boston: Little, Brown and Company, 1922. 301 p., front.
LC: F 3, '22.
PW: F 18, '22.
BLC: London: Hurst & Blackett, [1923].

C-778   Cooper, Edward H. (Edward Herbert), 1867-1910. A fool's year / by E. H. Cooper. New York: D. Appleton & Company, 1902. 289 p.
BLC: London: Methuen & Co., 1901.

C-779   ____ The Marquis and Pamela / by Edward H. Cooper; pictures by Julia Roper. New York: Duffield & Company, 1908. 364 p., front., [5] leaves of plates.
LC: Mr 6, '08.
BLC: London: Chatto & Windus, 1908.

C-780   Cooper, Elizabeth, 1877-1945. Drusilla with a million / by Elizabeth Cooper. New York: Frederick A. Stokes Company, [c1916]. 317 p., front.
LC: F 8, '16.

C-781   ____ The heart of O Sono San / by Elizabeth Cooper; with thirty-one illustrations in duo tone from photographs. New York: Frederick A. Stokes

Company, [c1917]. 269 p., front., [15] leaves of plates. (Plates, except front., printed on both sides.)
LC: O 17, '17.
PW: O 27, '17.

C-782   _____ Living up to Billy / by Elizabeth Cooper. New York: Frederick A. Stokes Company, [1915]. 202 p., col. front.
LC: S 13, '15.
PW: S 11, '15.

C-783   Cooper, Francis L. (Francis Le Roy). Captain Pott's Minister / Francis L. Cooper; illustrated by John Goss. Boston: Lothrop, Lee & Shepard Co., [c1922]. 392 p., front., [3] leaves of plates.
LC: S 7, '22.

C-784   Cooper, J. C. (Jacob Calvin), 1845-1937. The Yamhills: an Indian Romance / J. C. Cooper; illustrated with sketches by Fred G. Cooper. M'Minnville, Oregon: J. C. Cooper, 1904, [c1902]. 187 p., front., ill.

C-785   Cooper, James A. Cap'n Abe, storekeeper: a story of Cape Cod / by James A. Cooper; illustrated by A. O. Scott. New York: Sully and Kleinteich, [c1917]. 340 p., front., [3] leaves of plates.
LC: My 29, '17.
PW: My 26, '17.

C-786   _____ Cap'n Jonah's fortune: a story of Cape Cod / by James A. Cooper; illustrated by A. O. Scott. New York: George Sully and Company, [c1919]. 340 p., front., [3] leaves of plates.
LC: Ja 2, '19.
PW: Ja 25, '19.

C-787   Cooper, James A. Sheila of Big Wreck Cove; a story of Cape Cod / by James A. Cooper . . . illustrated by R. Emmett Owen. New York: George Sully & Company [c1922]. 373 p., front., plates. Unexamined copy: bibliographic data from NUC.
LC: Mr 30, '22.

C-788   _____ Tobias o' the light: a story of Cape Cod / by James A. Cooper; illustrated by Joseph Wykoff. New York: George Sully & Company, [c1920]. 338 p., front., [3] leaves of plates.
LC: My 28, '20.
PW: Je 12, '20.

Cooper, Jeanette Wheeler. See Wheeler-Cooper, Jeanette.

C-789   Cope, Henry F. (Henry Frederick), 1870-1923. The Bonanza Bible class / by Henry F. Cope. Chicago: The Winona Publishing Company, 1904. 263 p., photo. front., [5] leaves of photo. plates.   CLE "Certain short sketches originally published in the Baptist union contained some part of the material which has gone to the making of this book . . . "

C-790   Copeland, Elliott. His father's wife / by Elliott Copeland. Baltimore, Md.: The McLean Company, c1916. 37 p.   DLC
LC: D 29, '16.

C-791   Copenhaver, Laura Scherer. An adventurous quest: a story of three boys as told by the friend in whom they confided / by Laura Scherer Copenhaver. Philadelphia, Pa.: Lutheran Publication Society, [c1903]. 405 p.
PW: Ap 25, '03.

C-792   Copley, Frank Barkley. The impeachment of President Israels / by Frank Barkley Copley; illustrated. New York: The Macmillan Company, 1913. 124 p., front., [2] leaves of plates. [Ill. by Stanley M. Arthurs.]

C-793   Copus, J. E. (John Edwin), 1854-1915. Andros of Ephesus: a tale of early Christianity / by the Rev. J. E. Copus. Milwaukee; New York: The M. H. Wiltzius Co., [c1910]. 277 p., front., [2] leaves of plates. [Ill. by Alexander J. Van Leshout.]
LC: D 12, '10.

C-794   _____ The son of Siro: a story of Lazarus: with illustrations / by J. E. Copus . . . New York; Cincinnati; Chicago: Benziger Brothers . . ., 1909. 367 p., front., [2] leaves of plates. [Ill. by E. Cadmus.]
LC: D 23, '08.

C-795   Corbett, Elizabeth Frances, b. 1887. Cecily and the wide world: a novel of American life today / by Elizabeth F. Corbett. New York: Henry Holt and Company, 1916. 344 p.
LC: S 1, '16.
PW: S 16, '16.
BLC: London: Hurst & Blackett, 1918.

C-796   _____ Puritan and pagan / by Elizabeth F. Corbett. New York: Henry Holt and Company, 1920. 347 p.
LC: N 11, '20.

C-797   _____ The vanished Helga / by Elizabeth F. Corbett. New York: George H. Doran Company, [c1918]. 334 p.
LC: O 10, '18.
PW: O 26, '18.

C-798   Corbin, John, 1870-1959. The cave man / by John Corbin. New York: D. Appleton and Company, 1907. 365 p., front., [3] leaves of plates. [Ill. by Harrison Fisher.]
LC: Ap 5, '07.

C-799   _____ The edge: a novel / by John Corbin; frontispiece in color by Katharine Gassaway. New York: Duffield & Company, 1915. 403 p., col. front.
PW: Mr 13, '15.

C-800   Corbin, John, 1870-1959. The first loves of Perilla / by John Corbin, with a frontispiece in color by C. Allan Gilbert. New York: Fox, Duffield and Company, 1903. 61 p., col. front. Unexamined copy: bibliographic data from OCLC, #16905835.

C-801   Corbyn, Clara A. B. La Gran Quibira: a musical mystery; opera historique; a romanza in five acts, with overture, prelude and interlude / by Clara A. B.

Corbyn. -- The Author's edition. -- [Los Angeles? 1904]. 533 p., front., [7] leaves of plates (one port.).

C-802   Corcoran, Brewer, b. 1877. The bantam / Brewer Corcoran. New York; London: Harper & Brothers, 1912. 253, [1] p., front. [Ill. by Charles F. Neagle.]
LC: Ap 20, '12.

C-803   _____ The Princess Naida / by Brewer Corcoran; illustrated by H. Weston Taylor. Boston: The Page Company, 1921. 296 p., front., [4] leaves of plates.
LC: Jl 25, '21.
PW: S 3, '21.

C-804   _____ The road to Le Rêve / by Brewer Corcoran; illustrated by H. Weston Taylor. Boston: The Page Company, 1916. 328 p., col. front., [4] leaves of plates.
LC: O 19, '16.
PW: N 11, '16.

C-805   Cork, Charles F. A Yankee interlude: a story of a New England farm / by Charles Farner Cork. Boston: The Roxburgh Publishing Company, Inc., [c1923]. 291 p.

C-806   Corkey, Alexander, 1871-1914. For conscience sake / by Alexander Corkey . . . Omaha: Forward Publishing Company, [c1912]. 317 p., photo. front.

C-807   _____ The testing fire / by Alexander Corkey. New York: The H. K. Fly Company, [c1911]. 303 p., front., [3] leaves of plates. [Ill. by John Goss.]
LC: Ja 23, '12.

C-808   _____ The victory of Allan Rutledge: a tale of the Middle West / by Alexander Corkey; photogravure illustrations by Florence Rutledge Wilde. New York: The H. K. Fly Company, [c1910]. 319 p., front., [3] leaves of plates.
LC: F 7, '11.

C-809   _____ The vision of joy, or, When "Billy" Sunday came to town: a sequel to "The victory of Allan Rutledge" / by Alexander Corkey; illustrated by Raymond L. Thayer. New York: The H. K. Fly Company, [c1913]. 319 p., front., [3] leaves of plates.
LC: D 29, '13.

C-810   Corlies, Margaret L. (Margaret Longstreble), b. 1867. Shreds / by Margaret L. Corlies; illustrated. Philadelphia: Press of J. B. Lippincott Company, 1905. 138, [1] p., front., [7] leaves of plates. [Ill. by A. B. Frost, Louise Wood, and M. Theodora Burt]
Contents: Giardino Reale -- The old diligence -- Misjudged -- The riderless roan -- Luscious fruit -- A mystery -- On the dock -- Trapped -- High life in my garden -- A reminiscence of Constantinople -- Aurora -- Snap -- Transition -- Signorina Camille Mina -- Phantom ships.

C-811   Cornelius, John, b. 1838, _pseud._ Along the King's highway: or, The invisible route: a romance of the southern United States / by John Cornelius [pseud.]; illustrated by the author. [San Antonio: Press of Maverick-Clarke Litho. Co., c1912]. 506 p., front., [6] leaves of plates.
LC: My 6, '12.

C-812   Cornelius, Mary Ann Mann, 1827-1918. Why? or, A Kansas girl's query . . . Chicago: Authors' and Writers' Union, 1903. 290 p.
Unexamined copy: bibliographic data from OCLC, #29075465.

C-813   Cornelius, Olivia Smith, b. 1882. The eyes at the window / by Olivia Smith Cornelius. New York; Washington; Baltimore, etc.: Broadway Publishing Co., [c1911]. 265 p.
LC: Ag 25, '11.
PW: S 9, '11.

C-814   _____ The Persian tassel / by Olivia Smith Cornelius. New York: The Neale Publishing Company, 1914. 238 p.
Unexamined copy: bibliographic data from NUC.
LC: F 16, '14.

C-815   Cornell, Hughes, _pseud._ Born Rich / by Hughes Cornell [pseud.]. Philadelphia: George W. Jacobs & Company, [c1924]. 307 p., col. front.
LC: Ap 28, '24.
PW: My 3, '24.

C-816   _____ Kenelm's desire / by Hughes Cornell [pseud.]. Boston: Little, Brown and Company, 1906. 388 p.

Cornell, Sarah (Hughes), Mrs. See **Cornell, Hughes, pseud.**

Cornish, Sam. Greater love hath no man than this. In _Minnesota stories_ (1903), **M-842.**

C-817   Corrothers, James David, 1869-1917. The black cat club: Negro humor & folk-lore / by James D. Corrothers; illustrated by J. K. Bryans. New York; London: Funk & Wagnalls Company, 1902. 264 p., incl. front.
PW: Mr 22, '02.

Corson, Geoffrey, pseud. See **Sholl, Anna McClure.**

C-818   Corstvet, Alexander. Elling: and some things that helped to shape his life / Alexander Corstvet. Milwaukee: S. Y. Gillan & Co., [c1901]. 273 p.

C-819   Cortez, Dolores. Mary of Magdala, or, The Magdalene of old: an interpretation / by Dolores Cortez . . . [Los Angeles]: Privately printed in the city of Los Angeles; 1905. 26 p.

C-820   Corwin, Minnie Lahr. Ethel Wright, or, Only a music teacher / by Minnie Lahr Corwin. New York: Cochrane Publishing Co., 1909. 135 p.   **DLC**
LC: O 13, '09.

C-821   Cory, Abe, 1873-1952. Out where the world begins: a story of a far country / by Abe Cory. New York: George H. Doran Company, [c1921]. 225 p., front., [3] leaves of plates.
LC: N 23, '21.

C-822   _____ The trail to the hearts of men: a story of east and west / by Abe Cory. New York; Chicago; Toronto; London; Edinburgh: Fleming H. Revell

Company, [c1916]. 332 p., incl. front., [2] leaves of plates. [Ill. by Victor Pérard.]
LC: O 16, '16.

C-823 [Coryell, John Russell], 1851-1924. A child of love: a startling story of the struggles of a girl born out of wedlock against the sins and perversions of to-day / by Margaret Grant [pseud.]. New York; London, England: Published by Physical Culture Publishing Co., [c1904]. 407 p. **OSU, FDA**

C-824 [____] The old homestead / novelized from Denman Thompson's great play; with illustrations from scenes in the play. -- Rev. ed. -- New York: G. W. Dillingham Company, [c1908]. 312 p., photo. front., [5] leaves of photo. plates.
LC: F 1, '08.

____, jt. aut. A strenuous lover (1904). See **Macfadden, Bernarr, 1868-1955, jt. aut., M-167.**

C-825 ____ Tommy's money: adventures in New York and elsewhere / by John R. Coryell; illustrated by W. A. Rogers. New York; London: Harper & Brothers Publishers, 1911. 218, [1] p., front., [3] leaves of plates. **OSU, NYP**
Contents: Tommy's money -- That Christmas dinner -- "The only Pietro" -- The champion bareback rider -- "Fulkee" -- "Poor Harry!" -- The presents Bert did not give -- Bob and Alec.
LC: O 16, '11.
PW: O 28, '11.

C-826 Cosgrove, J. J. (John Joseph), b. 1869. The twin gods: a novel / by John Joseph Cosgrove. New York: Published by The Technical Book Publishing Company, [c1917]. 184 p.
LC: Mr 2, '17.
PW: Mr 31, '17.

C-827 Costello, A. M. (Almeda Merchant), b. 1856. Four in hand / by A. M. Costello. Boston; Chicago: The Pilgrim Press, [c1901]. 477 p., front., [5] leaves of plates. [Ill. by Amy Brooks.] **DLC**

C-828 Costello, F. H. (Frederick Hankerson), 1851-1921. The girl with two selves / by F. H. Costello. Chicago: A. C. McClurg & Co., 1913. 335 p.
LC: My 3, '13.
PW: Jl 12, '13.

C-829 ____ Morgan's youngest rifleman / by F. H. Costello . . . ; a story of stirring adventures; original illustration by H. S. DeLay. Chicago: Laird & Lee, [c1913]. 292 p., col. front., [8] leaves of col. plates. **DLC**
LC: My 31, '13.

C-830 ____ Sure-dart: a story of strange hunters and stranger game in the days of monsters / by Frederick H. Costello . . . with five illustrations by Walter J. Enright. Chicago: A. C. McClurg & Co., 1909. 320 p., front., [4] leaves of plates.
LC: S 27, '09.
PW: O 9, '09.

C-831 Cotten, Bruce. The mirrors of Bensboro / by Bruce Cotten. Cylburn, [N. C.]: [s. n.], Christmas 1925. 36 p. **KUK**

C-832 Cotter, Joseph Seamon, b. 1861. Negro tales / by Joseph S. Cotter. New York: The Cosmopolitan Press, 1912. 148 p., photo. front. (port.). **NYP**
Contents: The author -- Caleb -- Rodney -- Tesney, The Deceived -- Regnan's anniversary -- "Kotchin' de nines" -- A town sketch -- The stump of a cigar -- A rustic comedy -- The jackal and the lion -- The king's shoes -- How Mr. Rabbit secures a pretty wife and rich father-in-law -- The little boy and Mister Dark -- Observation -- The boy and the ideal -- The negro and the automobile -- Faith in the white folks -- The cane and the umbrella.
LC: Ja 2, '13.

C-833 Cotter, Winifred. Sheila and others: the simple annals of an unromantic household / by Winifred Cotter. New York: E. P. Dutton & Company, [c1920]. 196 p. **ABC**
LC: O 13, '20.
PW: O 23, '20.

C-834 Cotton, Howard Preble. We three: a tale of the Erie Canal / by Howard Preble Cotton; with illustrations by R. I. Conklin. Boston, Mass.: The C. M. Clark Publishing Company, [c1910]. 297, [1] p., front., [3] leaves of plates.
LC: F 11, '11.
PW: Ja 21, '11.

C-835 Cotton, Jane Baldwin. Wall-eyed Caesar's ghost: and other sketches / by Jane Baldwin Cotton; illustrated by Frederic J. Cotton, M. D. Boston: Marshall Jones Company, [c1925]. 117 p., incl. front., ill.
Contents: Wall-eyed Caesar's ghost -- Another marriage of convenience -- An Elizabethan revival -- The end of the feud.
LC: O 5, '25.
PW: O 17, '25.

C-836 Cottrell, Marie, b. 1879, pseud. In the land of extremes / by Marie Cottrell [pseud.]. New York: Cochrane Publishing Company, 1909. 360 p.
LC: My 19, '09.

C-837 Cottrell, Minnie Creighton. Norton Hardin, or, The knight of the XX. century / by Minnie Creighton Cottrell. Boston: Mayhew Publishing Co., 1907. 328 p., front. (port.). **DLC**
LC: F 6, '07.

C-838 Coughlin, Hanorah. Strange fates, or, Detta / by Hanorah Coughlin. New York: Broadway Publishing Company, [c1904]. 241 p. **DLC**

C-839 Cournos, John, 1881-1966. Babel / John Cournos. New York: Boni and Liveright, [c1922]. 431 p. **KSU**
LC: S 23, '22.
PW: S 23, '22.
BLC: London: William Heinemann, 1923.

C-840 ____ The mask / by John Cournos. New York: George H. Doran, [c1919]. 320 p.
LC: D 31, '19.
PW: Ja 31, '20.
BLC: London: Methuen & Co., 1919.

C-841 ____ The new Candide / by John Cournos. New York: Boni and Liveright, 1924. 328 p.
LC: My 7, '24.
PW: My 17, '24.

_____ The samovar. In *The best short stories of 1923 and the yearbook of the American short story* (1924), B-568.

C-842 _____ The wall / by John Cournos . . . London: Methuen & Co. Ltd.; New York: George H. Doran Company, [1921?]. 286 p.
PW: O 22, '21.

C-843 Coursey, O. W. (Oscar William), b. 1873. Shorts: a volume of short stories and essayettes / by O. W. Coursey . . . Mitchell, South Dakota: Published by the Educator Supply Company, [c1925]. 156 p., photo. ill. (some ports.). **SDA**
Contents: Fiction series: Dewey understood -- A family reunited -- Red hair triumphant.

C-844 _____ The woman with a stone heart: a romance of the Philippine War / by O. W. Coursey . . . Mitchell, South Dakota: The Educator Supply Company, [c1914]. 178 p., [10] leaves of plates, ill., map. [Ill. by W. K. Leigh.] **NYP**
LC: Je 15, '14.

Courtney, Gerald. Good-bye, Vera. In *Made to order* (1915), M-352.

C-845 Courtney, Mary King. The pictures of Polly / by Mary King Courtney; illustrated. New York: Harper & Brothers, 1912. 106, [1] p., front., [5] leaves of plates. [Ill. by Will Foster.]
LC: S 27, '12.

C-846 Courtney, Ray. Object: adventure: a western story / by Ray Courtney. New York City: Chelsea House, [c1925]. 254 p.
PW: D 19, '25.

C-847 Coverdale, Harry. The seventh shot: a detective story / by Harry Coverdale. New York: Chelsea House, [c1924]. 318 p.
LC: Ag 19, '24.
PW: S 6, '24.
BLC: London: Skeffington & Son, [1926].

C-848 _____ The unknown seven: a detective story / by Harry Coverdale. New York City: Chelsea House, [c1923]. 320 p.
LC: Ag 2, '23.
PW: Ag 18, '23.
BLC: London: T. Fisher Unwin, 1924.

C-849 Covert, William Chalmers, 1864-1942. Glory of the pines: a tale of the Ontonagon / by William Chalmers Covert. Philadelphia: The Westminster Press, 1914. 245 p., col. front., [2] leaves of plates. [Ill. by Gertrude A. Kay.]
LC: Jl 7, '14.

C-850 Cowan, Louise Henry. Trapped / by Louise Henry Cowan (Mrs. James Craig Cowan). Boston: The Christopher Publishing House, [c1924]. 260 p.
PW: D 6, '24.

C-851 Cowen, Kittie Skidmore. An unconditional surrender / by Kittie Skidmore Cowen. Chicago: M. A. Donohue & Co., [c1904]. 458 p., ill.

C-852 Cowles, George Matthews. Winter bloom: a novel / by George Matthews Cowles. Valley, Nebraska: [s. n.], c1925. 15 p. **DLC**
LC: Ag 10, '25.

C-853 Cox, Carolyn. Stand by / Carolyn Cox. New York; London: Harper & Brothers, 1925. 351 p.
LC: Ag 17, '25.
PW: Ag 22, '25.

C-854 Cox, Florence Tinsley, 1877-1940. The chronicles of Rhoda / by Florence Tinsley Cox; illustrated by Jessie Willcox Smith. Boston: Small, Maynard & Company, [c1909]. 287 p., col. front., [1] col. leaf of plates.
Contents: A dethroned queen -- Lily-Ann -- The old major -- The fireside god -- The hottentot -- A social event -- Auntie May -- The green door -- The hidden talent.
LC: O 28, '09.

C-855 _____ The epic of Ebenezer: a Christmas story / by Florence Tinsley Cox . . . ; with illustrations by John Rae. New York: Dodd, Mead and Company, 1912. 72 p., ill.
LC: S 14, '12.

C-856 Cox, John E., b. 1850. Sang Sammy: a story of the mountain people / by John E. Cox. Providence, Ky.: Press of the Enterprise, [1903]. 112 p., ill. [Ill. by W. E. Harden.] **DLC**

C-857 Cox, Leland Dolph. Stolen from a duchy's throne: a romance of Tuscany / by Leland Dolph Cox; with illustrations by A. G. Heaton. Washington: The Neale Publishing Company, 1903. 191 p., front., [2] leaves of plates. [Ill. by A. G. Heaton.]
PW: Je 6, '03.

C-858 Cox, Marian, b. 1882. The crowds and the veiled woman / by Marian Cox. New York; London: Funk & Wagnalls Company, 1910. 413 p.
LC: Ap 27, '10.
PW: Ap 2, '10.

Cox, Marian. A honeymoon Christmas. In *Forum stories* (1914), F-306.

C-859 _____ Spiritual curiosities / by Marian Cox. New York: Mitchell Kennerley, 1911. 354 p.
Contents: Ars amoris -- Conscience -- Women in profile.
LC: Ja 22, '12.

C-860 Cozzens, James Gould, b. 1903. Confusion: a novel / by James Gould Cozzens. Boston: B. J. Brimmer Company, 1924. 404 p.
LC: Jl 12, '24.
PW: Ap 26, '24.
References: Bruccoli, *Cozzens* A2.

C-861 _____ Michael Scarlett: a history / by James Gould Cozzens. New York: Albert & Charles Boni, 1925. 318 p.
LC: N 11, '25.
PW: N 14, '25.
BLC: London: Robert Holden & Co., 1927.
References: Bruccoli, *Cozzens* A4.

C-862 Crabb, Arthur. Ben Thorpe / by Arthur Crabb. New York: The Century Co., 1921. 332 p., front. LC: S 22, '21.

C-863 ____ Ghosts: a Samuel Lyle mystery story / by Arthur Crabb. New York: The Century Co., 1921. 261 p., front. LC: Mr 23, '21. PW: Mr 19, '21.

C-864 ____ Samuel Lyle, criminologist / by Arthur Crabb; illustrated by S. C. Coll. New York: The Century Co., 1920. 347 p., front, [3] leaves of plates. LC: O 5, '20. PW: O 9, '20.

C-865 Craddock, Charles Egbert, *pseud.* The amulet: a novel / by Charles Egbert Craddock [pseud.]. New York: The Macmillan Company; London: Macmillan & Co., Ltd., 1906. 356 p. LC: O 23, '06. PW: N 17, '06. References: BAL 14819.

C-866 ____ The champion / by Charles Egbert Craddock [pseud.]. Boston; New York: Houghton, Mifflin and Company, 1902. (Cambridge: The Riverside Press). 257 p., front. [Ill. by Alice Barber Stephens.] LC: Je 10, '02. PW: Ag 2, '02. References: BAL 14815.

C-867 ____ The fair Mississippian: a novel / by Charles Egbert Craddock [pseud.]. Boston; New York: Houghton Mifflin Company, 1908. (Cambridge [Mass.]: The Riverside Press). 428, [1] p., col. front. (port.). LC: O 9, '08. PW: O 24, '08. References: BAL 14821.

C-868 ____ The frontiersmen / by Charles Egbert Craddock [pseud.]. Boston; New York: Houghton, Mifflin and Company, 1904. (Cambridge: The Riverside Press). 364 p.
Contents: The linguister -- A victor at chungke -- The captive of the ada-wehi -- The fate of the cheere-taghe -- The bewitched ball-sticks -- The visit of the turbulent grandfather -- Notes.
LC: Mr 29, '04. PW: Ap 9, '04. References: BAL 14817.

C-869 ____ The ordeal: a mountain romance of Tennessee / by Charles Egbert Craddock [pseud.]; with a frontispiece in color by Douglas Duer. Philadelphia; London: J. B. Lippincott Company, 1912. 280, [1] p., front. LC: O 23, '12. PW: O 19, '12. References: BAL 14823.

C-870 ____ The raid of the guerilla: and other stories / by Charles Egert Craddock [pseud.]; with illustrations by W. Herbert Dunton and Remington Schuyler. Philadelpia; London: J. B. Lippincott Company, 1912. 334 p., front., [3] leaves of plates.
Contents: The raid of the guerilla -- Who crosses Storm Mountain? -- The crucial moment -- Una of the hill country -- The lost guidon -- Wolf's head -- His unquiet ghost -- A Chilhowee lily -- The phantom

of Bogue Holauba -- The Christmas miracle.
LC: Je 24, '12. PW: Je 1, '12. References: BAL 14822.

C-871 ____ A spectre of power / Charles Egbert Craddock [pseud.]. Boston; New York: Houghton, Mifflin and Company, l903. (Cambridge: The Riverside Press). 415 p. LC: My 21, '03. PW: Je 6, '03. References: BAL 14816.

C-872 ____ The storm centre: a novel / by Charles Egbert Craddock [pseud.]. New York: The Macmillan Company; London: Macmillan and Co., Ltd., 1905. 351 p. LC: Je 19, '05. PW: Jl 1, '05. References: BAL 14818.

C-873 ____ The story of Duciehurst: a tale of the Mississippi / by Charles Egbert Craddock [pseud]. New York: The Macmillan Company, 1914. 439 p. LC: Jl 9, '14. PW: Ag 15, '14. References: BAL 14824.

C-874 ____ The windfall: a novel / by Charles Egbert Craddock [pseud.]. New York: Duffield & Company, 1907. 450 p. LC: Ap 12, '07. PW: Ap 27, '07. BLC: London: Chatto & Windus, 1907. References: BAL 14820.

C-875 Craddock, Irving. The Yazoo mystery: a novel / by Irving Craddock. New York: Britton Publishing Company, [c1919]. 302 p., incl. col. front. LC: N 4, '19.

C-876 Craig, Benjamin H., Mrs., b. 1861. Was she: a novel / by Mrs. Benjamin H. Craig. New York; Washington: The Neale Publishing Company, 1906. 176 p. PW: Mr 9, '07.

Craig, Cola Amanda Barr. See **Craig, Benjamin H., Mrs., b. 1861.**

C-877 Craig, Florence S. The Barnes family: a smile on every page / by Florence S. Craig. Los Angeles: The Neuner Company Press, 1910. 73 p.

C-878 Craig, Katherine L. (Katherine Lee), b. 1862. Judge Greyburn and Kathlene Lee / by Katherine L. Craig. New York; London; Montreal: The Abbey Press, [c1902]. 184 p., front., [2] leaves of plates. PW: Ap 25, '03.

C-879 Craig, Matthew. Maktoub: a romance of French North Africa / by Matthew Craig. New York; London: G. P. Putnam's Sons, 1918. ([New York]: The Knickerbocker Press). 417 p. LC: Mr 28, '18. PW: Mr 23, '18.

C-880 Craig, Violet. The fruit of folly / by Violet Craig. New York: The Macaulay Company, 1913. 278 p., front. **DLC**
LC: Ag 4, '13.

C-881 Cram, George F. (George Franklin), 1842-1928. Minette: a story of the First Crusade / by George F. Cram; with illustrations by Waldo Bowser and F. D. Schook. Chicago: John W. Iliff & Company, 1901. 397 p., front., [8] leaves of plates.
PW: D 7, '01.

Cram, Mildred, b. 1889. Billy. In *The best short stories of 1924 and the yearbook of the American short story* **(1925), B-569.**

C-882 ____ Lotus salad / by Mildred Cram; illustrated by F. C. Yohn. New York: Dodd, Mead and Company, 1920. 305 p., front., [3] leaves of plates.
LC: Je 24, '20.
PW: Je 26, '20.

C-883 ____ Stranger things / by Mildred Cram . . . New York: Dodd, Mead and Company, 1923. 314 p.
Contents: Stranger things -- The yellow one -- The dryad -- Anna -- The amulet -- The gaudy little fish -- The bridge -- The lotus at Mitchell house -- Exhibit B -- Odell -- The precious certitude.
LC: O 25, '23.
PW: N 3, '23.
BLC: London: Cassel & Co., 1923.

C-884 ____ The tide / Mildred Cram. New York: Alfred A. Knopf, 1924. 321 p.
LC: N 10, '24.
PW: N 15, '24.
BLC: London: Jonathan Cape, 1925.

C-885 Cramp, Walter S. (Walter Samuel), b. 1867. Across the arid zone / by Walter S. Cramp. Boston: The C. M. Clark Publishing Company, [c1910]. 315 p.
LC: F 10, '11.
PW: D 3, '10.

C-886 ____ The biter / by Walter S. Cramp. Boston: The C. M. Clark Publishing Company, 1909. 250 p.
LC: N 12, '09.
PW: N 20, '09.

C-887 ____ Down in the canyon / by Walter S. Cramp. Boston: Richard G. Badger, [c1913]. (Boston: The Gorham Press). 239 p., front., [15] leaves of plates.
LC: D 5, '13.
PW: D 6, '13.

C-888 ____ The heart of silence / by Walter S. Cramp. Boston, Mass.: C. M. Clark Publishing Company, 1909. 325 p.
LC: Jl 7, '09.

C-889 ____ An heir to empire / Walter S. Cramp . . . ; illustrated by L. Pogliaghi. Boston: Richard G. Badger, [c1913]. ([Boston]: The Gorham Press). 237 p., front., [4] leaves of plates. **DLC**
LC: S 29, '13.
PW: Ag 16, '13.

C-890 ____ Myrta / by Walter S. Cramp; illustrated by Ludivico Pogliaghi. Boston: Richard J. Badger; Toronto: The Copp Clark Co., Limited, [c1915]. 303 p., front., [4] leaves of plates.
LC: Ag 23, '15.
PW: Ag 21, '15.

C-891 ____ Psyche / by Walter S. Cramp; with illustrations from drawings by W. T. Benda. Boston: Little, Brown and Company, 1905. 323 p., front., [3] leaves of plates.
PW: Ap 15, '05.

C-892 ____ The two gods / Walter S. Cramp . . . Boston: Richard G. Badger, [c1912]. (Boston, U. S. A.: The Gorham Press). 297 p.
LC: D 2, '12.
PW: N 30, '12.

C-893 Crandall, C. E. Z; a boy / by C. E. Crandall. Cincinnati: printed for the author by Jennings and Graham, [c1905]. 249 p., photo. front. (port.).

C-894 Crane, Clarkson, 1894-1971. The western shore / by Clarkson Crane. New York: Harcourt, Brace and Company, [c1925]. 303 p.
LC: Mr 12, '25.
PW: Mr 14, '25.

Crane, Edith Campbell. A diplomatic crusade. In *A book of Bryn Mawr stories* **(1901), B-732.**

C-895 Crane, Mary, b. 1882, *pseud.* Sara of Upper Dam / by Mary Crane [pseud.] (José King Burmeister). New York: George H. Doran Company, [c1924]. 315 p.
PW: S 27, '24.

C-896 Crane, Stephen, 1871-1900. Men, women and boats / by Stephen Crane; edited, with an introduction by Vincent Starrett. New York: Boni and Liveright, [c1921]. 245 p. Illustrated end papers signed by Horace Brodzky.
Contents: Stephen Crane: an estimate -- The open boat -- The reluctant voyagers -- The end of the battle -- The upturned face -- An episode of war -- An experiment in misery -- The duel that was not fought -- A desertion -- A dark-brown dog -- The pace of youth -- Sullivan County sketches: A tent in agony -- Four men in a cave -- The mesmeric mountain -- The snake -- London impressions -- The Scotch express.
PW: S 24, '21.
References: BAL 4100; Williams & Starrett 36.

C-897 ____ The O'Ruddy: a romance / by Stephen Crane . . . and Robert Barr . . . ; with frontispiece by C. D. Williams. New York: Frederick A. Stokes Company, [c1903]. 356 p., col. front. **VA@**
LC: N 2, '03.
PW: D 5, '03.
BLC: London: Methuen & Co., 1904.
References: BAL 4097; Williams & Starrett 34.

C-898 Cranke, J. P. In the land of to-morrow / by J. P. Cranke. New York; Baltimore; Atlanta: Broadway Publishing Co., [c1910]. 266 p.
LC: Je 28, '10.

Cranson, J. H. The metamorphosis of Corpus Delicti. In *Comedy* **(1901), C-614.**

Cranston, Ruth. See Warwick, Anne, pseud.

156

C-899 Crapsey, Algernon Sidney, 1847-1927. The greater love / by Algernon Sidney Crapsey. New York; London; Montreal: The Abbey Press, [c1902]. 453 p.

Crary, Agnes. The second edition. In *Under Berkeley Oaks* (1901), U-8.

C-900 Crater, George E., Jr. The forge of destiny / by George E. Crater, Jr. [New York?]: Owned, published and copyrighted . . . by The Dominion Publishing Company, Limited (a corporation), 1914. 222 p.
LC: Ag 6, '14.

C-901 Craveison, Ollis. Fun on the farm: in old Kentucky / by Ollis Craveison. [Newport, N. Y.: The Kuyahora Press, c1909]. 184 p., [3] leaves of photo. plates. **KTS**
LC: Ja 5, '10.

Craven, Frank, contributor. See *Bobbed hair* (1925), **B-700.**

C-902 Craven, Roger Carey. In the twilight zone / by Roger Carey Craven. Boston, Massachusetts: The C. M. Clark Publishing Company, 1909. 327 p., front., [5] leaves of plates. [Ill. by D. S. Ross.]
LC: N 17, '09.

C-903 Craven, Thomas, 1889-1969. Paint / by Thomas Craven. New York: Harcourt, Brace and Company, [c1923]. 229 p.
LC: F 12, '23.
PW: Mr 3, '23.

Craw, George Rockhill. The strange case of Clement Zent. See *Clever business sketches* (1909), **C-490.**

C-904 Crawford, F. Marion (Francis Marion), 1854-1909. Arethusa / by F. Marion Crawford; with illustrations by Gertrude Demain Hammond. New York: The Macmillan Company; London: Macmillan & Co., 1907. 355 p., front., [15] leaves of plates.
LC: O 12, '07.
PW: O 26, '07.
BLC: London: Methuen & Co., 1907.
References: BAL 4231 (BAL 4229: copyright issue).

C-905 _____ Cecilia: a story of modern Rome / by F. Marion Crawford. New York: The Macmillan Company; London: Macmillan & Co., Ltd., 1902. 421 p.
LC: O 25, '02.
PW: N 8, '02.
BLC: London: Methuen & Co., 1902.
References: BAL 4213.

C-906 _____ The diva's ruby: a sequel to "Primadonna" and "Fair Margaret," / by F. Marion Crawford; with illustrations by J. Montgomery Flagg. New York: The Macmillan Company, 1908, [c1907]. 430 p., front., [11] leaves of plates.
LC: D 19, '07. (BAL notes S 18, '08.)
PW: O 17, '08.
BLC: London: Macmillan; Norwood, Mass.

[printed], 1908.
References: BAL 4238.

C-907 _____ Fair Margaret: a portrait / by F. Marion Crawford; with illustrations by Horace T. Carpenter. New York: The Macmillan Company; London: Macmillan & Co., Ltd., 1905. 383 p., front., [5] leaves of plates.
PW: N 18, '05.
BLC: British title: *Soprano: a portrait.*
References: BAL 4224.

C-908 _____ The heart of Rome: a tale of the "lost water" / by Francis Marion Crawford. New York: The Macmillan Company; London: Macmillan & Co., 1903. 396 p.
LC: O 13, '03.
PW: O 31, '03.
References: BAL 4218.

C-909 _____ A lady of Rome / by F. Marion Crawford. New York: The Macmillan Company; London: Macmillan & Co., Ltd., 1906. 383 p.
LC: O 11, '06.
PW: O 27, '06.
References: BAL 4227.

C-910 _____ The little city of hope: a Christmas story / by F. Marion Crawford; with illustrations by W. Benda. New York: The Macmillan Company, 1907. 209 p., incl. front. and [7] leaves of plates.
LC: N 21, '07.
PW: D 14, '07.
References: BAL 4233.

C-911 _____ Man overboard! / By F. Marion Crawford. New York: The Macmillan Company; London: Macmillan & Co., 1903. 96 p., front. (port.), [2] leaves of plates. [Ill. by A. I. Keller.]
(Little novels by favourite authors.)
LC: My 22, '03.
PW: Je 20, '03.
References: BAL 4216 (BAL 4215: copyright issue).

C-912 _____ Marietta: a maid of Venice / by F. Marion Crawford. New York: The Macmillan Company; London; Macmillan & Co., Ltd., 1901. 458 p.
LC: O 26, '01.
PW: N 9, '01.
References: BAL 4209.

C-913 _____ The primadonna: a sequel to "Fair Margaret" / by F. Marion Crawford. New York: The Macmillan Company; London: Macmillan & Co., Ltd., 1908. 396 p., front. [Ill. by the Kinneys.]
LC: D 27, '07. (BAL also notes Ap 18, '08.)
PW: My 2, '08.
References: BAL 4235.

C-914 _____ Stradella / by F. Marion Crawford. New York: The Macmillan Company, 1909. 415 p., front., [7] leaves of plates. [Ill. by J. C. Leyendecker and Frank Craig.]
LC: S 5, '08; S 24, '09.
PW: O 9, '09.
References: BAL 4246 (BAL 4239: copyright issue).

C-915　　____　The undesirable governess / by F. Marion Crawford; illustrated. New York: The Macmillan Company, 1910. 227 p., [14] leaves of plates.
LC: Ap 22, '10.
PW: Ap 30, '10.
References: BAL 4247 (BAL 4244: copyright issue).

C-916　　____　Wandering ghosts: with frontispiece / by F. Marion Crawford . . . New York: The Macmillan Company, 1911. 302 p., front. [Ill. by M. Leone Bracker.]
Contents: The dead smile -- The screaming skull -- Man overboard! -- For the blood is the life -- The upper berth -- By the waters of paradise -- The doll's ghost.
LC: Mr 23, '11.
PW: Ap 1, '11.
BLC: London: T. Fisher Unwin, 1911. British title: *Uncanny tales*.
References: BAL 4249.

C-917　　____　The white sister / by F. Marion Crawford. New York: The Macmillan Company, 1909. 335 p., front., [1] leaf of plates.
LC: Ap 17, '09.
PW: My 8, '09.
BLC: London: Macmillan, 1909.
References: BAL 4242.

C-918　　____　Whosoever shall offend / by F. Marion Crawford; with eight illustrations drawn in Rome with the author's suggestions, by Horace T. Carpenter. New York: The Macmillan Company; London: Macmillan & Co., Ltd., 1904. 388 p., front., [7] leaves of plates.
LC: O 6, '04.
PW: O 22, '04.
References: BAL 4221.

C-919　　Crawford, Gloria. The little book / Gloria Crawford; a fable disclosing the true meaning of the mission of Jesus of Nazareth on earth. San Francisco: Published by the Comforter League of Light, [c1922]. 22 p.

Crawford, Harriet Jean. Catherine's career. In *A book of Bryn Mawr stories* (1901), B-732.

C-920　　Crawford, Jack Randall, 1878-1968. I walked in Arden / Jack Crawford. New York: Alfred A. Knopf, 1922. 295 p.
LC: My 12, '22.

C-921　　Crawford, Lewis F. (Lewis Ferandus), 1870-1936. Badlands and broncho trails / by Lewis F. Crawford. Bismarck, N. D.: Capital Book Co., [c1922]. 114, [1] p., photo. front., [5] leaves of photo. plates. Designed end papers.
Contents: Idyl to Sentinel Butte -- A range tragedy -- The old regular -- Vesuvius -- Nugget -- Horse Thief Springs -- The banker's plot -- By-products of the day's work -- A tenderfoot, a cowboy and a truth.
LC: Ja 2, '23.

C-922　　Crawford, M. D. C. (Morris De Camp), 1882-1949. The come-back / by M. D. C. Crawford. New York: Minton, Balch & Company, 1925. 309 p.
OSU, DLC
LC: Mr 3, '25.

PW: F 28, '25.
BLC: London: Geoffrey Bles, 1925.

C-923　　Crayon, Diedrick, 1876-1916. The return of the Half Moon / by Diedrick Crayon, Jr. New York; Baltimore: Broadway Publishing Co., 1909. 147, [1] p., front., [5] leaves of plates. [Ill. by William L. Hudson.]
LC: O 6, '09.
PW: N 20, '09.

Creagan, Leo F., jt. aut. Martin Gerrity gets even. In *Prize stories of 1921 (1922)*, **P-619**.

C-924　　Crean, Mildred Corning. A daughter of to-day / by Mildred Corning Crean. Boston: The C. M. Clark Publishing Company, [c1910]. 122 p., front., [1] leaf of plates.
LC: O 17, '10.

C-925　　[Creel, George], 1876-1953. Uncle Henry / Anonymous. New York: Reynolds Publishing Company, Inc., [c1922]. 256 p., front., [4] leaves of plates. [Ill. by Frank Goodwin.]
Contents: Love, marriage and other perils -- The irreconcilables -- Catch-as-catch-can healing -- Passing of the old guard -- The poor little rich man -- The yellow peril -- Dehoovering Herbert -- Millionaires' sons -- The trouble with Congress -- Knee length dramas -- The Harding honeymoon -- Overmanufacture in judges -- Too booze or not to booze -- Pants across the sea -- Freedom's shriek -- The Newberry case -- The nude in literature -- Bull-jawed brutes -- Dumdums and diaries -- The Four-Power Pact -- Mr. Ruth and Mr. Dempsey -- Humanizing science -- The yellow kids -- The Missouri spree -- Freedom's faults -- America's famous mud baths -- Fishes and fishing -- Our international policy.
LC: S 28, '22.

C-926　　Creelman, James, 1859-1915. Eagle blood / by James Creelman; illustrated by Rose Cecil O'Neill. Boston: Lothrop Publishing Company, [1902]. 470 p., front., [5] leaves of plates.
PW: O 18, '02.
BLC: London: Charles H. Kelly, 1902.

C-927　　Cressy, Will, 1863-1940. The hills o' Hampshire / by Will H. [sic] Cressy and James Clarence Harvey; colored frontispiece by J. W. F. Kennedy. Boston: Dana Estes & Company, [c1913]. 302 p., col. front.
LC: N 11, '13.

C-928　　Cretcher, Mack. The Kansan: a novel / by Mack Cretcher . . . Philadelphia: Dorrance, [c1923]. 341 p.　　　　　　　　　　**KKR**
LC: N 5, '23.
PW: N 10, '23.
BLC: London; New York: Andrew Melrose, [1924].

Crew, Helen Coale. The parting genius. In *The best short stories of 1920 and the yearbook of the American short story* (1921), **B-565**.

C-929　　Crewdson, Charles N., Mrs., b. 1869. An American baby abroad: how he played Cupid to a Kentucky beauty / by Mrs. Charles N. Crewdson; illustrated by R. F. Outcault and Modest Stein. Boston: Little, Brown and Company, 1910. 327, [1] p., front., [6] leaves of plates.
LC: My 12, '10.

C-930　Crewdson, Charles N. (Charles Newman), b. 1870. Building business / Charles N. Crewdson . . . New York: D. Appleton and Company, 1907. 291 p.
LC: Mr 2, '07.

C-931　_____ Tales of the road / by Charles N. Crewdson; illustrated by J. J. Gould. Chicago: Thompson & Thomas, 1905. 352 p., incl. front., [15] leaves of plates.
Contents: The square deal wins -- Clerks, cranks and touches -- Social arts as salesmen's assets -- Tricks of the trade -- The helping hand -- How to get on the road -- First experiences in selling -- Tactics in selling-I -- Tactics in selling-II -- Tactics in selling-III -- Cutting prices -- Canceled orders -- Concerning credit men -- Winning the customer's good will -- Salesmen's dont's -- Merchants the salesman meets -- Hiring and handling salesmen -- Hearts behind the order book.

Crewdson, Lula (Cox). See Crewdson, Charles N., Mrs., b. 1869.

C-932　Crissey, Forrest, 1864-1943. The country boy / by Forrest Crissey; illustrated by Griselda Marshall McClure. Chicago; New York; Toronto; London; Edinburgh: Fleming H. Revell Company, [c1903]. 300 p., front., [14] leaves of plates.
Reprinted from the Saturday Evening Post, the Woman's Home Companion, and the Chicago Evening Post.

C-933　_____ Tattlings of a retired politician / by Forrest Crissey . . . ; with fifty-eight illustrations by John T. McCutcheon. -- Special limited political edition. -- Chicago: Thompson & Thomas, 1904. 487 p., incl. front., ill.
Contents: Still hunts and stolen marches -- Parable of the widow's mite -- A million-dollar bribe -- Political spanks and spankers -- A woman in it -- How the dear people forget -- Puppets and pulls -- Grafters and stingers -- Quitters and stayers -- Eleventh hour surprises -- Paying the fiddler -- Landslide and storm centers -- The Glad-Hand Brigade -- Fights and feuds -- Trail of the serpent -- Fruits of victory -- Love at first sight -- At the drop of the hat -- The graft and the gaff -- Flirting with the fixer -- Kissing by favor -- The game and the candle.

C-934　Crockett, George Langtry, 1870-1923. The Plunderer: a political story of Maine, exposing the piratical system and explaining the remedy / by George Langtry Crockett . . . Boston, Massachusetts: The J. K. Waters Company, 1907. (Boston, Massachusetts: The Waters Press). 272 p.
LC: Jl 16, '07.

C-935　Crockett, Ingram, b. 1856. A brother of Christ: a tale of western Kentucky / by Ingram Crockett; illustrated in colors by Hartman. New York: Broadway Publishing Company, [c1905]. 309 p., col. front., [3] leaves of plates. Designed end papers.

C-936　Cromarsh, H. Ripley, b. 1877, pseud. The secret of the Moor cottage / by H. Ripley Cromarsh [pseud.]. Boston: Small, Maynard & Company, 1906. 284, [1] p.
LC: O 10, '06.
BLC: London: Ward, Lock & Co., 1907.

C-937　Cronyn, George W. (George William), b. 1888. '49: a novel of gold / by George W. Cronyn. Philadelphia: Dorrance & Company, [c1925]. 278 p.　　　　　CLO

LC: F 16, '25.
PW: F 28, '25.

C-938　Crosby, Edward Harold. The evolution of Fredda / by Edward Harold Crosby . . . ; with illustrations by H. Boylston Dummer. Boston, Massachusetts: The C. M. Clark Publishing Co., [c1911]. 382 p., front., [4] leaves of plates.　　　　　DLC
LC: F 10, '11.

C-939　_____ Radiana: a novel / by Edward Harold Crosby; illustrations by P. B. Dakyn. Boston: Published by The Ivy Press, 1906. 427 p., front., [2] leaves of plates.
LC: N 17, '06.
PW: Ja 19, '07.

C-940　Crosby, Ernest Howard, 1856-1907. Captain Jinks: hero; By Ernest Crosby; illustrations by Dan Beard. New York; London: Funk & Wagnalls Company, 1902. 393 p., front., [8] leaves of plates.
PW: Mr 8, '02.

C-941　Crosby, Kingsland. The strange case of Eleanor Cuyler / by Kingsland Crosby; with frontispiece in colour by Harrison Fisher. New York: Dodd, Mead and Company, 1910. 339 p., col. front.
LC: O 1, '10.

C-942　Cross, Ruth, b. 1887. The golden cocoon: a novel / by Ruth Cross. New York; London: Harper & Brothers, 1924. 341 p.
LC: Mr 15, '24.
PW: Mr 22, '24.

C-943　Cross, Sidney Arthur. Dominicana: being some of Joe Wilson's reminiscences. New York: [s. n.], 1904. 62 p.　　　　　DLC

C-944　Crouch, Frances. Feminine Finance / by Frances Crouch; drawings by Amy E. Hogeboom. New York: B. W. Dodge & Company, 1907. 347 p., front., [3] leaves of plates.
LC: N 1, '07.

C-945　Crouch, Haden. The guides' story: a Filipino romance / Haden Crouch. Columbus, O.: [s. n.], 1910. 44, [1] p.
Unexamined copy: bibliographic data from OCLC, #29605220.

Crounse, Avery J. St. Joseph. In Minnesota stories (1903), M-842.

_____ Within and without the curriculum. In Minnesota stories (1903), M-842.

C-946　Crowe, Pat, 1869-1938. Society's prodigal: a novel / by Pat Crowe. Chicago: [s. n.], 1907, [c1906]. 242 p., front., [1] leaf of plates. [Ill. by Adrien Claude Machefert.]

C-947　Crowell, Bertha. Wings of the cardinal / by Bertha Crowell. New York: George H. Doran Company, [c1917]. 329 p.
PW: S 1, '17.

Crowell, Chester T. Margaret Blake. In *Prize stories of 1924* (1925), P-622.

C-948　Crowley, Mary Catherine. A daughter of New France: with some account of the gallant Sieur Cadillac and his colony on the Detroit / by Mary Catherine Crowley; illustrated by Clyde O. De Land. Boston: Little, Brown and Company, 1901. 409 p., front., [5] leaves of plates.
PW: My 11, '01.

C-949　_____ The heroine of the Strait: a romance of Detroit in the time of Pontiac / by Mary Catherine Crowley; illustrated by Ch. Grunwald. Boston: Little, Brown and Company, 1902. 373 p., front., [5] leaves of plates.
PW: Ap 19, '02.

C-950　_____ In treaty with honor: a romance of old Quebec / by Mary Catherine Crowley; illustrated from drawings by Clyde O. De Land. Boston: Little, Brown and Company, 1906. 291, [1] p., front., [4] leaves of plates.
LC: S 17, '06.
PW: O 27, '06.

C-951　_____ Love thrives in war: a romance of the frontier in 1812 / by Mary Catherine Crowley; illustrated by Clyde O. De Land. Boston: Little, Brown and Company, 1903. 340 p., front., [5] leaves of plates.
PW: Je 6, '03.

C-952　_____ Valencia's garden / by Mrs. Schuyler Crowninshield. New York: McClure, Phillips & Co., 1901. 303 p.
PW: Je 1, '01.
BLC: London; New York: McClure, Phillips, 1901.

C-953　Croy, Homer, 1883-1965. Boone Stop / by Homer Croy. New York; London: Harper & Brothers, [1918]. 320, [1] p., front. [Ill. by John Frost.]
LC: Jl 20, '18.
PW: Jl 27, '18.

_____ Casting bread on the waters of imagination. In *The so-so stories* (1914), S-715.

_____ It's all in a name. In *The so-so stories* (1914), S-715.

_____ The pink of imagination. In *The so-so stories* (1914), S-715.

C-954　_____ R. F. D. No. 3 / by Homer Croy. New York; London: Harper & Brothers, 1924. 349 p.
LC: O 3, '24.
PW: O 11, '24.

C-955　_____ Turkey Bowman / by Homer Croy. New York; London: Harper & Brothers, [1920]. 274, [1] p., front. [Ill. by Arthur G. Dorr.]
LC: S 27, '20.
PW: O 2, '20.

C-956　_____ West of the water tower. New York; London: Harper & Brothers, [c1923]. 367, [1] p.

_____ When a feller needs a friend. In *The so-so stories* (1914), S-715.

C-957　_____ When to lock the stable / by Homer Croy; with illustrations by Monte Crews. Indianapolis: The Bobbs-Merrill Company, [c1914]. 361 p., front., [11] leaves of plates.
LC: S 10, '14.
PW: S 12, '14.

C-958　Crozier, Alfred Owen, 1863-1939. The magnet: a romance of the battles of modern giants / by Alfred O. Crozier; illustrated by Wallace Morgan. New York; London: Funk & Wagnalls Company, 1908. 497 p., front., [5] leaves of plates.
LC: Ja 6, '08.
PW: S 28, '07.

C-959　Crozier, R. H. (Robert Haskins), 1836-1918. The end of the world: a tale of trial / by R. H. Crozier. Palestine, Tex.: R. H. Crozier, c1908. (Palestine: Palestine Printing Co.). 133 p.
Unexamined copy: bibliographic data from OCLC, #21362106.

C-960　_____ Kirk Ward's ghost, or, a modern miracle / by Rev. R. H. Crozier. Palestine, Tex.: Palestine Printing Co., 1909. 139 p.

Cruger, Van Rensselaer, Mrs., d. 1920. See **Gordon, Julien, pseud.**

Crutch, Phinneas A., pseud. See **Minnigerode, Meade, 1887-1967.**

C-961　Crutcher, Philip. Wings and no eyes: a comedy of love / by Philip Crutcher; with illustrations by Virginia Hargraves Wood. New York: The Grafton Press, [c1904]. 289 p., front., [3] leaves of plates.　**BGU**

C-962　Cuentos de California. Los Angeles: [s.n.], 1904. 77 p., front.
Contents: "The woman of dreams" / Henry S. Kirk -- Christmas at Seven Devils / Catherine Markham -- By the light of the shooting star / Lillian Corbett Barnes -- The way of a woman / Olive Percival -- Susy / Nancy K. Foster -- The spiritual wooing of Peter Hance / Gertrude Henderson.

Cuffee, Nathan J. (Nathan Jeffrey), b. 1852, jt. aut. *"Lords of the soil"* (1905). See **Smith, Annie L. (Annie Lydia), b. 1836, jt. aut., S-583.**

C-963　Culbert, Denny Cullingsworth, b.1892. Musty corn / by Denny Culbert. Philadelphia: Dorrance and company, 1925. 243 p.　**DLC**
LC: N 21, '25.
PW: D 12, '25.

C-964　Cull, John Augustine. The bride of Mission San José: a tale of early California / by John Augustine Cull. New York: The Abingdon Press, [1920]. 448 p., front.
LC: D 24, '20.
PW: D 18, '20.

C-965　Cullaton, Harriet C. (Harriet Carpenter), b. 1861. Firm of Nan & Sue, stenographers / by Harriet C.

Cullaton. New York: Broadway Publishing Co., 1904. 156 p., front. **VA@**

C-966 Cullen, Clarence Louis, d. 1922. The eddy: a novel of to-day / by Clarence L. Cullen; illustrations by Ch. Weber Ditzler. New York: G. W. Dillingham Company, [c1910]. 352 p., col. front., [4] leaves of plates.
LC: Mr 30, '10.
PW: Ap 2, '10.

C-967 _____ More ex-tank tales / By Clarence Louis Cullen, with introduction by the author. New York: J. S. Ogilvie Publishing Company, c1902. 245 p. These sketches originally appeared in the New York Sun.

C-968 Cullens, F. B. (Frederic Bacon), b. 1863. "Luce the foundling": an Anglo-American tale . . . / by F. B. Cullens . . . [Richmond, Va.: Published by Lewis Printing Co., 1925]. 208 p. **ALM**
LC: Jl 14, '25.

C-969 _____ The serpent's trail, or, Memoirs of Harold Bagote, physician: a tale of the South and of Cuba / by F. B. Cullens. New York; Baltimore: Broadway Publishing Company, [c1910]. 168 p. **ALM**
LC: Mr 31, '10.

C-970 _____ Where the magnolias bloom: a tale of Southern life / by Frederic Bacon Cullens. New York; London; Montreal: The Abbey Press, [c1901]. 79 p.
Cover title: *Where magnolias bloom.*
PW: Mr 1, '02.

Culley, Frank Clinton. See **Clinton, Major, pseud.**

C-971 Culter, Mary McCrae, b. 1858. The girl who kept up / by Mary McCrae Culter; illustarted by C. Louise Williams. Boston: Lee and Shepard, 1903. 301 p., front., [6] leaves of plates.
Unexamined copy: bibliographic data from OCLC, #29743815.

C-972 _____ A prodigal daughter / by Mary McCrae Culter. Cincinnati: Monfort & Co., 1908. 184, [1] p.
Unexamined copy: bibliographic data from OCLC, #29607510.

C-973 Culver, R. K. The range rivals / by R. K. Culver. [New York: The Winthrop Press, c1914]. 29 p., col. front.

C-974 Cumberland, Edward. Stubs of time / by Edward Cumberland; illustrations by the author. [St. Louis: Press of Nixon-Jones, 1904]. 288 p., front., [12] leaves of plates, ill.
Contents: Apology -- Dedication: To Clara, a rhapsody -- The seal of De Burleyville -- Uncle Billy's advice -- November -- Mistress Carrington of Virginia -- After all.

C-975 Cummings, E. E. (Edward Estlin), 1894-1962. The enormous room / by E. E. Cummings. New York: Boni and Liveright, [c1922]. 271 p.
LC: My 1, '22.
PW: My 13, '22.
References: Firmage, A 2.

C-976 Cummings, Edward, b. 1871. Marmaduke of Tennessee / by Edward Cummings; illustrated by Frank E. Schoonover. Chicago: A. C. McClurg & Co., 1914. 371, [1] p., front., [4] leaves of plates.
BLC: London: C. F. Cazenove; Chicago: A. C. McClurg & Co.; Chicago [printed], 1914.

C-977 Cummings, Lettie M. Professor Huskins / by Lettie M. Cummings. Boston: Richard G. Badger; Toronto: The Copp-Clark Co., Limited, [c1916]. 306 p.
LC: Ap 28, '16.
PW: Ap 29, '16.

C-978 Cummings, Maria S. Lopez de (Maria Sacramenta Lopez de), b. 1852. Claudio and Anita: a historical romance of San Gabriel's early mission days / by Maria S. Lopez de Cummings. Los Angeles: J. F. Rowny Press, 1921. 142 p., front., [2] leaves of plates (1 port.). Designed end papers.

C-979 Cummings, May. The threshold of Nirvana / by May Cummings. Baltimore, Md.: The McLean Company, [c1916]. 29 p. **DLC**
LC: Mr 4, '16.

C-980 _____ Transplanted / by May Cummings . . . Baltimore: Saulsbury Publishing Company, 1918. 141 p. **DLC**
LC: Ap 9, '18.

C-981 Cummings, Ray. The girl in the golden atom / by Ray Cummings. New York; London: Harper & Brothers, 1923. 341 p.
PW: N 24, '23.
BLC: London: Macmillan, 1922.

C-982 Cummings, Scott. The Rexworth mystery / by Scott Cummings; illustrated by Anna W. Speakman. Philadelphia: Philadelphia Suburban Publishing Company, [c1911]. 272 p., front., [4] leaves of plates.
LC: Je 15, '11.
PW: Jl 29, '11.

C-983 Cummings, William G., b. 1885. An island chronicle / by William Cummings. New York: Alfred A. Knopf, 1924. 302 p.
LC: My 14, '24.
PW: My 24, '24.

C-984 _____ Passion and glory / by William Cummings. New York: Alfred A. Knopf, 1925. 278 p.
LC: O 30, '25.
PW: O 31, '25.

C-985 Cummins, Harle Oren. Welsh rarebit tales / by Harle Oren Cummins; illustrated by R. Emmett Owen; cover and decorations by Bird. Boston: The Mutual Book Company, [c1902]. 173 p., front., [5] leaves of plates.
Partially reprinted from various periodicals.
Contents: The man who made a man -- In the lower passage -- The fool and his joke -- The man and his beast -- At the end of the road -- The space annihilator -- A question of honor -- The wine of Pantinelli -- The strangest freak -- The false prophet -- A study in psychology -- The painted lady and the boy -- The palace of sin -- The man who was not afraid -- The story the doctor told.

C-986   Cummins, Mary Hornibrook. The awakening / by Mary Hornibrook Cummins. Boston: Davis & Bond, [c1912]. 187 p.
LC: O 17, '13.

C-987   ____ A little child / by Mary Hornibrook Cummins. Boston: Davis & Bond, [c1913]. 41 p.   **DLC**

C-988   ____ Renatus: (a man reborn) / by Mary Hornibrook Cummins. Boston: Davis & Bond, [c1914]. 157 p.
LC: S 30, '14.

C-989   ____ The story of Richard Trent / by Mary Hornibrook Cummins. Boston: Davis & Bond, 1915. 221 p.
LC: Ag 23, '15.

C-990   Cummins, R. E. (Robert Emmet), b. 1849. A perfect score / by R. E. Cummins. Boston, Massachusetts: The Stratford Company, 1925. 317 p.
PW: Ag 22, '25.

C-991   Cummins, Ralph. Sky-high corral / by Ralph Cummins. -- First edition. -- Garden City, New York: Garden City Publishing Co., Inc., 1923. 119 p.

C-992   Cunningham, A. B. (Albert Benjamin), 1888-1962. The chronicle of an old town: a novel / by Albert Benjamin Cunningham. New York; Cincinnati: The Abingdon Press, [c1919]. 326 p.
LC: O 3, '19.

C-993   ____ The manse at Barren Rocks / by Albert Benjamin Cunningham. New York: George H. Doran Company, [c1918]. 301 p.
LC: O 10, '18.

C-994   ____ Singing mountains / by Albert Benjamin Cunningham . . . New York: George H. Doran Company, [c1919]. 315 p.
LC: S 12, '19.

C-995   Cunningham, Caroline, b. 1844. Too fit for the unfit / by Caroline Cunningham. Topeka, Kansas: [s. n.], 1913. 122 p.

C-996   Cunningham, Eugene, 1896-1957. The regulation guy / by Eugene Cunningham . . . Boston; New York: Cornhill Publishing Company, 1922. 266 p.   **MCF**
Contents: The regulation guy -- Over there -- Pirate Wilson-deserter -- The rebound -- The hard guy -- The good hater -- Mickey and the manicure -- The man he was -- On the god's knees -- A salt water Lothario -- Luck to order -- The masquerade -- Paid in full -- Lifting the restriction -- The yellow streak -- The standing luck of the U. S. N.
LC: N 27, '22.

C-997   ____ The trail to Apacaz / by Eugene Cunningham. New York: Dodd, Mead and Company, 1924. 292 p.
LC: S 4, '24.
PW: Ag 30, '24.
BLC: London: T. Fisher Unwin, 1924.

C-998   Cunningham, Frances Berkeley. Priest or pretender: a novel / by Frances Berkeley Cunningham. Boston, Mass.: The C. M. Clark Publishing Company, 1908. 274 p., front., [7] leaves of plates.
LC: D 22, '08.
PW: Ap 3, '09.

C-999   Cunningham, Francis A. (Francis Aloysius), 1862-1935. The awakening / by Francis A. Cunningham. Boston: Marlier and Company, 1901. 289 p.   **DLC**

C-1000   Cunningham, William Bennett. Legends of Lost River Valley / as related by Joseph Pontus; arranged by William B. Cunningham. Chicago: Champlin & Carlisle, [c1903]. 187, [1] p., [4] leaves of plates.   **DLC**
Contents: Joseph Pontus -- Lost River-The Great Springs -- The wolves -- Dave and Tige -- Fanny Dilbro-The Indian bride -- The pigeons-migration of birds -- Indian religion -- The Garners-Cupid's pranks -- Carrie Lee-The bridge -- The Houcks-The reindeer -- The great toboggan -- Court stories of early times -- Jim Cummings' speech -- Two girls -- Jumping glory -- Rebekah-"The camels are coming" -- Orange County-Its people -- Indiana-The past-The future.

C-1001   Cuppy, Will, 1884-1949. Maroon tales: University of Chicago stories / by Will J. Cuppy. Chicago: Forbes & Company, 1910. 337 p.
Contents: The extra major -- The wisdom of Hawkins -- Some odes and some episodes -- The indiscretions of Yvonne de La Plaisance -- Big boys and little boys -- Including the doctorate -- The great paste-pot handicap -- Honors in diplomacy.
LC: D 20, '09.
PW: D 18, '09.

C-1002   Curnick, Edward T. The Kentucky ranger / by Edward T. Curnick . . . Chicago, Ill.: The Christian Witness Co., [c1922]. 198 p.   **NDD**
LC: Ja 14, '24.

C-1003   Curran, Charles, H. Through lands of yesterday: a story of romance and travel / by Charles H. Curran . . . Boston: Chapple Publishing Company, Limited, 1911. 421 p., photo. front., [12] leaves of photo. plates.

C-1004   Curran, Henry H. (Henry Hastings), b. 1877. Van Tassel and Big Bill / by Henry H. Curran. New York: Charles Scribner's Sons, 1923. 311 p., front., [3] leaves of plates. [Ill. by Thomas Fogarty.]
LC: S 17, '23.
PW: O 6, '23.

Curran, John H., Mrs., (medium). <u>See</u> **Worth, Patience, (spirit).**

C-1005   Curran, John Joseph. Mr. Foley of Salmon: a story of life in a California village / by J. J. Curran. [San Jose]: Published by the author, 1907. (San Jose, California: Printed by Melvin, Hillis & Black). 186 p.
LC: Jl 29, '07.

Curran, Pearl Lenore Pollard, 1883-1937. *Hope Trueblood* (1918). <u>See</u> **Worth, Patience, (Spirit), W-896.**

_____ *The sorry tale* (1917). See **Worth, Patience, (Spirit), W-897.**

C-1006   Currie, Barton, 1878-1962. Officer 666 / Barton W. Cvrrie & Avgvstin Mc Hvgh. New York: The H. K. Fly Company, [c1912]. 308 p., col. front., [3] leaves of col. plates. Colored illustrated end papers.
LC: D 5, '12.

C-1007   Currier, Charles Elliott. In the early days: Philippine sketches / by Charles Elliott Currier. New York: Broadway Publishing Company, 1914. 89 p. **DLC**
Contents: The passing of Nelson -- The fighting chaplain -- An unnamed battle -- The coward -- The cholera fight -- Pete, a battle winner -- "Padre del monte" -- A yellow hero -- The redeeming feature -- Balangiga -- How Foley won his star.
LC: Ja 2, '15.

C-1008   Curry, Z. M. (Zodie Mae). Visions of the trenches / by Z. M. Curry. Baltimore, Md.: Saulsbury Publishing Company, [c1919]. 19 p.   **DLC**
LC: S 5, '19.

C-1009   Curtin, D. Thomas (Daniel Thomas), b. 1886. The tyranny of power / by D. Thomas Curtin. Boston: Little, Brown and Company, 1923. 377 p.
LC: Mr 15, '23.
PW: Mr 10, '23.

Curtis, Alice Turner. See **Curtis, Irving, Mrs.**

C-1010   Curtis, Charles Albert, 1835-1907. Captured by the Navajos / by Captain Charles A. Curtis; illustrated. New York; London: Harper & Brothers Publishers, 1904. 290, [1] p., front., [6] leaves of plates. [Ill. by W. P. Snyder.]

C-1011   Curtis, David A., b. 1846. Old man Greenhut and his friends / by David A. Curtis. New York: Duffield and Company, 1911. 339 p., front., [7] leaves of plates. [Ill. by Gordon H. Grant.]
LC: S 14, '11.

C-1012   _____ Stand pat, or, Poker stories from the Mississippi / by David A. Curtis; illustrated by Henry Roth. Boston: L. C. Page & Company, 1906. 269 p., front., [5] leaves of plates.
Partly reprinted from The New York Sunday Sun.
Contents: A new poker deck -- Three kings -- Finish of the one-eyed man -- Looking for Gallagher -- Stumpy's dilemma -- Gallagher's return -- Gallagher stripped -- A trial of skill -- A social call -- Stumpy violates etiquette -- The new poker rule made in Arkansas -- A stranger and fond of poker -- On hand just once -- It was a great deal -- He sat in there with a V -- His queer system -- An extra ace -- Played by the book -- Only one sure way to win -- Kenny's royal flush.
PW: Je 2, '06.

C-1013   Curtis, Earl G. Saturday nights / by Earl G. Curtis. Chicago: Reilly & Lee, Co., [c1922]. 255 p.
"An American novel that deals with the emotions that lie below the surface of life - emotions that sway the masses that toil."

C-1014   Curtis, Edward S., 1868-1952. In the land of the head-hunters / by Edward S. Curtis . . . ; illustrated with photographs by the author. Yonkers-on-Hudson, New York: World Book Company, 1915. 112, [1] p., photo. front., photo. ill.
At head of title: *Indian life and Indian lore.*

Curtis, G. W. Titbottom's spectacles. In *The best American humorous short stories* (1920), B-556.

Curtis, George DeClyver, b. 1870. See **Marword, Gregory, pseud.**

C-1015   Curtis, Georgina Pell, 1859-1922. Trammelings: and other stories / by Georgina Pell Curtis . . . St. Louis, Mo.; Freiburg, (Baden): Published by B. Herder; London; Edinburgh: Sands & Co., 1909. 580 p.   Reprinted from various periodicals.
Contents: Trammelings -- Castle walls -- A romance of the Guadalupe -- A romance of the San Rafael Canon -- The Christ Child of Norumbega -- The sign of Orion -- Catarina -- A little child shall lead them -- The vow of Tir-na-N'oge -- The love gift -- A modern utopia -- Gabrielle -- The quest of Magdalena -- Ramon -- Conchita -- The story of Santos -- In Paradisum -- "One of the least" -- The bells of San Juan Capistrano -- A story of the holy vase -- Valentine -- A madonna of the Casa Grande -- The strife obscure -- An episode of the present struggle in France -- The Waters of Trembling -- Azrael.
LC: D 14, '09.

C-1016   Curtis, Henry Ellsworth. Elizabeth Crane: a novel / by Henry Ellsworth Curtis. New York: Broadway Publishing Co., [c1910]. 204 p.   **WSU**
LC: D 19, '10.

C-1017   Curtis, Irving, Mrs. A challenge to adventure / by Mrs. Irving Curtis. Boston: Marshall Jones Company, 1919. 330 p., front.
LC: S 29, '19.

C-1018   Curtis, Isabel Gordon, 1863-1915. The congresswoman / by Isabel Gordon Curtis. Chicago: Browne & Howell Company, 1914. 505 p.
LC: Ap 3, '14.
PW: Mr 28, '14.

C-1019   _____ The lapse of Enoch Wentworth / by Isabel Gordon Curtis; with frontispiece by Alonzo Kimball. Chicago: F. G. Browne & Co., 1913. 359 p., col. front.
LC: Ja 22, '13.
PW: Ja 18, '13.

C-1020   _____ The woman from Wolverton: a story of Washington life / by Isabel Gordon Curtis. New York: The Century Co., 1912. 342 p.
LC: Mr 1, '12.
PW: F 24, '12.

C-1021   Curtis, Louisa Cutler Francis. The violin solo, and other stories / by Louisa Cutler Francis Curtis. Newport, R. I.: The Milne Printery, 1906. 62 p.   **DLC**
Contents: The violin solo -- Her Billie -- The three roses -- Not guilty -- The awakening of Anthony -- A dining-room romance -- The best is yet to come -- The Samanthy Mine -- A bunch of Golden Rod -- Love or art.
PW: D 1, '06.

C-1022   Curtis, Marion. The note of discord / by Marion Curtis. New York: Broadway Publishing Co., [c1907]. 180 p.   **DLC**
LC: O 14, '07.

C-1023   _____ The shadow of the scarlet sin: a novel of "real life" / by Marion Curtis. New York: Broadway

Publishing Co., [c1910]. 714 p.
Unexamined copy: bibliographic data from OCLC, #29616106.
LC: D 24, '10.
PW: F 25, '11.

C-1024   Curtis, May Belle. "Kathi" of Skenesborough / by May Belle Curtis. Glens Falls, N. Y.: Champlain Publishing Company, [c1914]. 255 p.

C-1025   Curtis, Wardon Allan, 1867-1940. The strange adventures of Mr. Middleton / by Wardon Allan Curtis. Chicago: Herbert S. Stone & Company, 1903. 311 p.
PW: O 24, '03.

C-1026   Curtiss, Philip, 1885-1964. Between two worlds: a novel / by Philip Curtiss. New York; London: Harper & Brothers, [1916]. 351, [1] p., front.
LC: S 9, '16.
PW: S 16, '16.

C-1027   ____ Crater's gold: a novel / by Philip Curtiss; with illustrations by W. C. Dexter. New York; London: Harper & Brothers, [1919]. 325 p., front., [3] leaves of plates.
LC: Ap 11, '19.
PW: Ap 19, '19.
BLC: London: Thornton Butterworth, [1920]. (without ills.)

C-1028   ____ The gay conspirators / by Philip Curtiss. New York; London: Harper & Brothers, 1924. 324 p.
LC: S 23, '24.
PW: O 4, '24.

C-1029   ____ The ladder: the story of a casual man / by Philip Curtiss. New York; London: Harper & Brothers, 1915. 302, [1] p., front.
LC: F 20, '15.
PW: Mr 6, '15.

C-1030   ____ The man who knew life / by Philip E. Curtiss. New York: The Winthrop Press, c1914. 31, [1] p., col. front. ill.
Previously published in The American magazine.

C-1031   ____ Mummers in Mufti / By Philip Curtiss. New York: The Century Co., 1922. 370 p.
LC: S 19, '22.
PW: S 30, '22.
BLC: London: Leonard Parsons; printed in U. S. A., 1923.

C-1032   ____ Wanted, a fool: a novel / by Philip Curtiss ... New York; London: Harper & Brothers, 1920. 227, [1] p., front.
LC: O 25, '20.
PW: N 20, '20.

C-1033   Curwood, James Oliver, 1878-1927. The Alaskan: a novel of the North / by James Oliver Curwood; with illustrations by Walt Louderback. New York: Cosmopolitan Book Corporation, 1923. 326 p., front., [3] leaves of plates.
LC: Ag 2, '23.
PW: Ag 4, '23.
BLC: Toronto: Copp Clark Co., [1923].

C-1034   ____ The ancient highway: a novel of high hearts and open roads / by James Oliver Curwood; illustrations by Walt Louderback. New York: Cosmopolitan Book Corporation, 1925. 373 p., front., [3] leaves of plates.
LC: Jl 25, '25.
PW: Jl 25, '25.
BLC: London: Hodder & Stoughton, [1925].

C-1035   ____ Back to God's country: and other stories / by James Oliver Curwood . . . ; illustrated with scenes from the photoplay, a first national production. New York: Grosset & Dunlap, [c1920]. 274 p., photo. front., [3] leaves of photo. plates.
Contents: Back to God's country -- The yellow-back -- The fiddling man -- L'Ange -- The case of Beauvais -- The other man's wife -- The strength of men -- The match -- The honor of her people -- Bucky Severn -- His first penitent -- Peter God -- The mouse.
LC: Je 18, '20.
PW: Je 12, '20.

C-1036   ____ Baree, son of Kazan / by James Oliver Curwood; illustrated by Frank B. Hoffman. Garden

City, N. Y.: Doubleday, Page & Company, 1917. 303, [1] p., front., [5] leaves of plates. (2 double-leaf plates.)
LC: O 3, '17.
PW: O 20, '17.

C-1037   ____ The country beyond: a romance of the wilderness / by James Oliver Curwood; with illustrations by Walt Louderback. New York: Cosmopolitan Book Corporation, 1922. 340 p., front., [3] leaves of plates.
LC: Ag 2, '22.
PW: Ag 5, '22.
BLC: London: Hodder & Stoughton, [1922].

C-1038   ____ The courage of Captain Plum / by James Oliver Curwood; with illustrations by Frank E. Schoonover. Indianapolis: The Bobbs-Merrill Company, [1908]. 319, [1] p., front., [3] leaves of plates.
LC: O 15, '08.
PW: O 24, '08.
BLC: London: Hodder & Stoughton, [1924].

C-1039   ____ The courage of Marge O'Doone / by James Oliver Curwood; frontispiece by Lester Ralph. Garden City, New York: Doubleday, Page & Company, 1918. 309, [1] p., col. front.
LC: Mr 2, '18.
PW: Mr 2, '18.

C-1040   ____ The danger trail / by James Oliver Curwood; with illustrations by Charles Livingston Bull. Indianapolis: The Bobbs-Merrill Company, [c1910]. 305, [1] p., col. front., [4] leaves of col. plates.
LC: Mr 14, '10.
PW: Mr 19, '10.
BLC: London: Hodder & Stoughton, [1924].

C-1041   ____ The flaming forest: a novel of the Canadian northwest / by James Oliver Curwood; with illustrations by Walt Louderback. New York: Cosmopolitan Book Corporation, 1921. 296 p., front., [3] leaves of plates.

LC: Ag 12, '21.
PW: Ag 13, '21.
BLC: London: Hodder & Stoughton, [1921].

C-1042 ____ Flower of the North: a modern romance / by
James Oliver Curwood . . . New York; London:
Harper & Brothers, 1912. 307, [1] p., front. [Ill. by
Douglas Duer.]
LC: Mr 14, '12.
PW: Mr 23, '12.
BLC: London: Hodder & Stoughton, [1920].

C-1043 ____ A gentleman of courage: a novel of the
wilderness / by James Oliver Curwood; with
illustrations by Robert W. Stewart. New York:
Cosmopolitan Book Corporation, 1924. 342 p., col.
front., [1] double col. plate.
LC: Jl 19, '24.
PW: Jl 19, '24.
BLC: London: Hodder & Stoughton, [1924].

C-1044 ____ God's country-- and the woman / by James
Oliver Curwood; illustrated by William Oberhardt and
Norman Borchardt. Garden City, N. Y.: Doubleday,
Page & Company, 1915. 347 p., col. front., [9]
leaves of col. plates (1 double).
LC: Ja 19, '15.
PW: Ja 23, '15.
BLC: London: Cassell & Co., 1915.

C-1045 ____ The gold hunters: a story of life & adventure
in the Hudson Bay wilds / by James Oliver Curwood
. . . ; with illustrations by C. M. Relyea.
Indianapolis: The Bobbs-Merrill Company, [c1909].
328 p., front., [5] leaves of plates.
LC: Ag 13, '09.
PW: F 5, '10.

C-1046 ____ The golden snare / by James Oliver Curwood
. . . ; illustrated with scenes from the photoplay--
David M. Hartford's production. A first national
attraction. New York: Grosset & Dunlap, [c1921].
257 p., photo. front., [4] leaves of photo. plates.
EYM
LC: My 12, '21.
PW: Jl 16, '21.
BLC: London: Cassell & Co., 1918.

C-1047 ____ The grizzly king: a romance of the wild / by
James Oliver Curwood; illustrated by Frank B.
Hoffman. Garden City, N. Y.: Doubleday, Page &
Company, 1916. 234, [1] p., front., [3] leaves of
plates.
LC: S 8, '16.
PW: S 9, '16.
BLC: London: Curtis Brown; Garden City, New
York printed, 1916.

____ His first pentinent. In *Greatest short stories*
(1915), G-424.

C-1048 ____ The honor of the big snows / by James Oliver
Curwood . . . ; with illustrations by Charles
Livingston Bull. Indianapolis: The Bobbs-Merrill
Company, [c1911]. 317, [1] p., col. front., [4]
leaves of col. plates.
LC: Mr 8, '11.

PW: Mr 11, '11.
BLC: London: Hodder & Stoughton, 1924.

C-1049 ____ The hunted woman / by James Oliver
Curwood; illustrated by Frank B. Hoffman. Garden
City, New York: Doubleday, Page & Company,
1916. 324 p., col. front., [3] leaves of col. plates.
LC: F 29, '16.
PW: My 27, '16.

C-1050 ____ Isobel: a romance of the northern trail / by
James Oliver Curwood . . . New York; London:
Harper & Brothers, 1913. 280, [1] p., col. front.
[Ill. by John Newton Howitt.] **GGG**
LC: My 10, '13.
PW: My 17, '13.

C-1051 ____ Kazan / by James Oliver Curwood . . . ;
illustrated by Gayle Hoskins and Frank Hoffman.
Indianapolis: The Bobbs-Merrill Company, [c1914].
340 p., front., [4] leaves of plates.
LC: Mr 19, '14.
PW: Mr 21, '14.
BLC: London: Cassel & Co., 1914.

C-1052 ____ Nomads of the North: a story of romance and
adventure under the open stars / by James Oliver
Curwood; illustrated by Charles Livingston Bull.
Garden City, New York: Doubleday, Page &
Company, 1919. 318 p., front., [3] leaves of plates.
LC: Ap 5, '19.
PW: Ap 5, '19.
BLC: London: Hodder & Stoughton, [1919].

C-1053 ____ Philip Steele of the Royal Northwest mounted
police / by James Oliver Curwood; illustrations by
Gayle Hoskins. Indianapolis: The Bobbs-Merrill
Company, [c1911]. 306, [1] p., front., [4] leaves of
plates.
LC: N 8, '11.
PW: N 11, '11.
BLC: London: Everett & Co., 1912.

C-1054 ____ The river's end: a new story of God's country
/ by James Oliver Curwood; illustrated by Dean
Cornwell. New York: Cosmopolitan Book
Corporation, 1919. 303 p., front., [3] leaves of
plates.
LC: S 30, '19.
PW: N 1, '19.
BLC: London: Hodder & Stoughton, [1920].

____ Thomas Jefferson Brown. In *Greatest short
stories* **(1915), G-424.**

C-1055 ____ The valley of silent men: a story of the Three
River Country / by James Oliver Curwood; illustrated
by Dean Cornwell. New York: Cosmopolitan Book
Corporation, 1920. 298 p., front., [3] leaves of
plates.
LC: S 10, '20.
PW: Ag 28, '20.
BLC: London: Hodder & Stoughton, [1921].

C-1056 ____ The wolf hunters: a tale of adventure in the
wilderness / by James Oliver Curwood; with
illustrations by C. M. Relyea. Indianapolis: The

Bobbs-Merrill Company, c1908. 318, [1] p., front.,
[5] leaves of plates.
LC: Jl 10, '08.
PW: D 12, '08.
BLC: London: Cassell & Co., [1917].

Cushing, Paul, pseud. See Wood-Seys, Roland A.
(Roland Alexander), 1854-1919.

Cuthrell, Faith Baldwin. See Baldwin, Faith, 1893-1978.

C-1057   Cutler, Hal L., b. 1873. Ne-bo-shone: (at the bend
of the river) / by Hal L. Cutler; in which is
incorporated an Indian lullaby "Ne-bo-shone"
composed by Lexie Woodruff Abbott; illustrated by
Herbert Morton Stoops. Chicago: The Reilly &
Britton Co., [c1917]. 315 p., front., [3] leaves of
plates.

C-1058   Cutler, Robert, 1895-1974. Louisburg square / by
Robert Cutler; illustrated by Elise Ames. New York:
The Macmillan Company, 1917. 322 p., front., [4]
leaves of plates.
LC: Ap 5, '17.

C-1059   ____ The speckled bird / by Robert Cutler. New
York: The Macmillan Company, 1923. 422 p.
LC: F 8, '23.
PW: F 24, '23.

C-1060   Cutting, Elizabeth. Behold the magnet / by Elizabeth
Cutting. [Hollywood, California: Gillett Service
League, c1923]. 39 p., [1] leaf of plates.   DLC
LC: Jl 3, '23.

C-1061   Cutting, Mary Stewart Doubleday, 1851-1924. The
blossoming rod / by Mary Stewart Cutting;
frontispiece. Garden City, New York: Doubleday,
Page & Company, 1914. 51, [1] p., col. front. [Ill.
by Walter De Maris.] Illustrated end papers.
LC: N 2, '14.
PW: N 7, '14.

C-1062   ____ Heart of Lynn / by Mary Stewart Cutting . . . ;
illustrated by Helen Stowe. Philadelphia; London: J.
B. Lippincott Company, 1904. 264 p. front., [4]
leaves of plates.
PW: Ap 2, '04.

C-1063   ____ Just for two / by Mary Stewart Cutting;
illustrated by Edmund Frederick, A. I. Keller and
Robert Edwards. New York: Doubleday, Page &
Company, 1909. 243 p., front., [3] leaves of plates.
Contents: The enchantment -- The path to Spain -- The wife -- Miss
Dream -- A clear field -- The Cloisonné vase.
LC: S 28, '09.
PW: O 16, '09.

C-1064   ____ Little stories of courtship / by Mary Stewart
Cutting. New York: McClure, Phillips & Co., 1905.
232, [1] p., front. [Ill. by Frederic Dorr Steele.]
Contents: Paying guests -- Henry -- When love is kind -- Latimer's
mother -- In Cinderella's shoes -- In regard to Josephine -- The
coupons of fortune -- The perfect tale.
BLC: London: Hodder & Stoughton; New York
printed, 1906.

C-1065   ____ Little stories of married life / by Mary Stewart
Cutting. New York: McClure, Phillips & Co., 1902.
260 p., front. [Ill. by Alice Barber Stephens.]
Contents: Their second marriage -- A good dinner -- The strength of
ten -- In the reign of Quintilia -- The happiest time -- In the married
quarters -- Mrs. Atwood's outer raiment -- Fairy gold -- A
matrimonial episode -- Not a sad story -- Wings.
BLC: London: Hodder & Stoughton; New York
printed, 1906.

C-1066   ____ The lovers of Sanna: a novel / by Mary
Stewart Cutting; illustrated by Robert Edwards. New
York: McBride, Nast & Company, 1912. 226 p.,
front., [3] leaves of plates.   DLC
LC: My 16, '12.
PW: Je 1, '12.

C-1067   ____ More stories of married life / by Mary Stewart
Cutting. New York: McClure, Phillips & Co., 1906.
260 p., front. [Ill. by Alice Barber Stephens.]
Contents: A little surprise -- At the sign of the rubber plant -- The
terminal -- The hinge -- A symphony in coal -- The triumph of father
-- The portion of the youngest -- Polly Townsend's rebellion --

The mother of Emily -- Madonna of the toys: a Christmas story --
The name of the firm.
PW: Ap 21, '06.

____ Really married. In Marriage (1923), M-457.

C-1068   ____ Refractory husbands / by Mary Stewart
Cutting. Garden City, N. Y.: Doubleday, Page &
Company, 1913. 232, [2] p., front. [Ill. by George
Brehm.]
Contents: When Aunt Mary came -- A friend of the married --
Father's little joke -- Marie twists the key -- Meeting the dog --
Marrying Willow -- Thursday -- Bunny's bag -- The blossoming rod.
LC: S 23, '13.
PW: S 27, '13.

C-1069   ____ Some of us are married / by Mary Stewart
Cutting; frontispiece by William Caffrey. Garden
City, N. Y.; London: Doubleday, Page & Company,
1920. 380 p., front.
Contents: The purveyor of the funds -- An opening for Mariana -- As
Lochinvar -- Leslie's friend -- The wonder-worker -- Boogybrae --
Benson's day -- Dance-mad Billy -- Clytie comes back -- The shell --
Child of the heart -- Her job -- Two autobiographical stories: The
man who went under -- The song of courage.
LC: Ap 19, '20.
PW: Ap 10, '20.

C-1070   ____ The suburban whirl: and other stories of
married life / by Mary Stewart Cutting; illustrated by
Alice Barber Stephens. New York: The McClure
Company, 1907.
202 p., front., [6] leaves of plates.
Contents: The suburban whirl -- The measure -- On the ridge -- Mrs.
Tremley.
LC: O 16, '07.
PW: O 26, '07.

C-1071   ____ The unforeseen / by Mary Stewart Cutting;
illustrated by Will Foster. New York: Doubleday,
Page & Company, 1910. 273 p., front., [3] leaves of
plates.
LC: O 22, '10.
PW: O 29, '10.
BLC: London: Hodder & Stoughton; New York
printed, 1910.

C-1072 ____ The wayfarers / by Mary Stewart Cutting; illustrations by Alice Barber Stephens. New York: The McClure Company, 1908. 374 p., front., [15] leaves of plates.
LC: Je 20, '08.
PW: Jl 4, '08.

____, contributor. See *The whole family* **(1908), W-578.**

D

D-1 D. R. C. (Donna Rieta Cole). Chums, or, An experiment in economics / by D. R. C. New York: Edited and published by Gertrude Ogden Tubby, [c1908]. 315 p. **DLC**
LC: D 16, '08.

D-2 ____ Faith-Hope: child of the slums / by D. R. C. . . . New York: Edited and published by G. O. Tubby, 1909. 300 p. **DLC**
LC: Mr 2, '10.

D-3 ____ Sue Chuc / by D. R. C. . . . New York: Goodyear Book Concern, 1913. 230 p. **NYP**
LC: Jl 16, '13.

D-4 Daffan, Katie, 1875-1951. The woman on the Pine Springs Road / by Katie Daffan . . . New York; Washington: The Neale Publishing Company, 1910. 296 p. **TXI**
LC: D 19, '10.
PW: Ja 7, '11.

D-5 Daggett, Mary Stewart, 1856-1922. The higher court / by Mary Stewart Daggett. Boston: Richard G. Badger, [c1911]. (Boston: The Gorham Press). 213 p.
LC: D 4, '11.
PW: D 9, '11.

D-6 ____ The Yellow Angel / by Mary Stewart Daggett; illustrated. Chicago: Browne & Howell Company, 1914. 235 p., front., [15] leaves of plates.
Reprinted in part from the Outlook and the Los Angeles Times Magazine.
Contents: The Yellow Angel -- Three heathen tales of the quarter: The redemption of Hop Lee -- The awakening of the dragon -- The black lily.
LC: My 6, '14.
PW: My 9, '14.

D-7 Dague, R. A. (Robert Addison), b. 1841. Henry Ashton: a thrilling story and how the famous co-operative commonwealth was established in Zanland / by R. A. Dague . . . Alameda, California: Published by the author, 1903. 235 p., photo. front. (port.).

D-8 Dahl, Dorthea. Returning home / by Dorthea Dahl. Minneapolis, Minn.: Augsburg Publishing House, 1920. 133 p.
Contents: The old book case -- The talking machine -- Only a little thing -- Grandmother -- The dedication -- The choir in Hancock.
LC: F 1, '21.

D-9 Dahlinger, Charles William, b. 1858. Where the red volleys poured / by Charles W. Dahlinger . . . ; illustrations by Charles Grunwald. New York: G. W. Dillingham Company, [c1907]. 375 p., front., [3] leaves of plates.
LC: Je 22, '07.
BLC: London: T. Fisher Unwin; New York printed, 1907.

D-10 Daingerfield, Henrietta G. Our mammy: and other stories / Henrietta G. Daingerfield. Lexington, Kentucky: [s. n.], 1906. 143 p., photo. front. (port.), [11] leaves of photo. plates (ports.).
Contents: "Our Mammy" -- Uncle Billy's mo'ners -- The new cooking stove -- A cup of cold water -- Little Margaret -- A personal devil -- "Tim" -- Little Christopher -- Our Amy -- Uncle Levi's free papers.

D-11 Daingerfield, Nettie Gray, b. 1844. Frescati: a page from Virginia history / by N. G. Daingerfield. New York; Washington: The Neale Publishing Company, 1909. 71 p.
LC: Ap 17, '09.

D-12 ____ That dear old sword / by Nettie Gray Daingerfield. Richmond, Virginia: Presbyterian Committee of Publication, [c1903]. 99 p., front., [1] leaf of plates. **KUK**
PW: F 28, '03.

D-13 Dake, Laura M. In the crucible / by Laura M. Dake; illustrated by the author. New York: The Alliance Publishing Company, 1901. 142 p., front. ill., ill. **DLC**
PW: D 21, '01.

D-14 ____ A man o' wax / by Laura M. Dake . . . San Francisco: The Whitaker and Ray Company, 1902. 122 p.
Unexamined copy: bibliographic data from OCLC, #14477084.
PW: N 1, '02.

D-15 Dale, Alan, 1861-1928, *pseud.* A girl who wrote / by Alan Dale [pseud.]. New York: Quail & Warner, 1902. 375 p., front. [Ill. by Clare Angell.]
PW: Jl 19, '02.

D-16 ____ Wanted: a cook: domestic dialogues / by Alan Dale [pseud.]. Indianapolis: The Bobbs-Merrill Company, [1904]. 381, [1] p.
BLC: London: G. P. Putnam's; Brooklyn [printed], 1905.

D-17 Dale, Mary, *pseud.* Bottled sunshine / by Mary Dale [pseud.]; illustrated. New York: The Bookery Publishing Co., [c1912]. 140 p., front., [7] leaves of plates. **NYP**
LC: D 24, '12.

D-18 Dale, Mary, *pseud.* Miss Eagle, the suffragette / by Mary Dale [pseud.]; illustrated. New York City: Aberdeen Publishing Company, 1909. 44, [2] p., front., [2] leaves of plates. [Ill. by Isabella Morton.] **DLC**
LC: My 19, '09.

D-19 Daley, Joseph Gordian. A cassock of the pines: and other stories / by Joseph Gordian Daley. New York: William H. Young and Company, 1901. 311 p., front., [3] leaves of plates.
Contents: A cassock of the pines -- Ex-Ottawans -- Madcaps -- When farms were abandoned -- Sophomores adrift -- The names in Nig's handwriting -- The donative of Mr. Gallagher -- Not a Gregory -- Her experiment -- A wayside belligerency -- A mother's affirmative -- A soldier from Underhill.
PW: Ap 12, '02.

D-20 _____ The rose and the sheepskin / by Joseph Gordian Daley . . . New York: Wiliam H. Young and Company, 1902. 389 p., front., [3] leaves of plates.

D-21 Daley, Myra. Jerd Cless / by Myra Daley. New York: Cochrane Publishing Co., 1909. 484 p. **DLC**
LC: N 19; '09.

D-22 Dallas, Richard, *pseud*. A master hand: a story of a crime / by Richard Dallas [pseud.]. New York; London: G. P. Putnam's Sons, 1903. ([New York]: The Knickerbocker Press). 257 p., front., ill. [Ill. by G. W. Peters.]

D-23 Dallett, Morris. A new Salome: a story for educated persons / Morris Dallett; with designs by the author, and an introduction by Ludwig Behren. -- Private ed. -- [Philadelphia?]: Paul W. Gibbons, 1922. 93 p., ill. Marbled end papers.
LC: S 23, '22.

D-24 _____ Star of earth / Morris Dallett. New York: Alfred A. Knopf, 1923. 183 p.
LC: Ja 29, '23.
PW: F 10, '23.
BLC: London: William Heinemann; printed in U. S. A., 1923.

D-25 Dalrymple, Leona, b. 1884. Diane of the green van / by Leona Dalrymple; illustrations by Reginald Birch. Chicago: The Reilly & Britton Co., [c1914]. 441 p., col. front., [3] leaves of col. plates.
LC: Mr 16, '14.
PW: Mr 7, '14.

D-26 _____ Fool's hill / by Leona Dalrymple. New York: Robert M. McBride & Company, 1922. 352 p.
LC: O 6, '22.
PW: O 21, '22.

D-27 _____ In the heart of the Christmas pines / by Leona Dalrymple; frontispiece by Norman Price. New York: McBride, Nast & Company, 1913. 51 p., col. front.
LC: O 20, '14.
PW: N 29, '13.

D-28 _____ Jimsy, the Christmas kid / by Leona Dalrymple . . . decorations by Charles Guischard. New York: Robert M. McBride & Company, 1915. 64 p., col. front. **MPI**
LC: N 10, '15.
PW: N 13, '15.

D-29 _____ Kenny / by Leona Dalrymple; illustrated by Joseph Pierre Nuyttens. Chicago: The Reilly & Britton Co., [c1917]. 479 p., front., [3] leaves of plates.
LC: Ag 13, '17.
PW: Ag 4, '17.

D-30 _____ The lovable meddler / by Leona Dalrymple; illustrations by Grant Tyson Reynard. Chicago: Reilly & Britton Co., [c1915]. 381 p., col. front., [3] leaves of col. plates.
LC: Jl 23, '15.
PW: Ag 7, '15.

D-31 _____ Träumerei / by Leona Dalrymple . . . ; illustrations by C. F. Peters. New York: Published by McBride, Nast & Company, 1912. 379 p., front., [3] leaves of plates.
LC: My 16, '12.

D-32 _____ Uncle Noah's Christmas inspiration / by Leona Dalrymple . . . ; illustrations by F. C. Yohn. New York: McBride, Nast & Company, 1912. 62 p., front.
LC: N 13, '12
Another copy: "Third printing, September, 1914." 123, [1] p., col. front., col. plates.
Unexamined copy: bibliographic data from DLC.
LC: O 20, '14.

D-33 _____ Uncle Noah's Christmas party / by Leona Dalrymple . . . ; illustrations by Charles L. Wrenn; decorations by Charles Guischard. New York: McBride, Nast & Company, 1914. 133, [1] p., incl. col. front., [3] leaves of col. plates.
LC: O 20, '14.

D-34 _____ When the yule log burns: a Christmas story / by Leona Dalrymple . . . New York: Robert M. McBride & Company, 1916. 58 p., col. photo. front.
LC: N 18, '16.
PW: D 2, '16.

D-35 Dalrymple, Penelope. That wager of Dot's / by Penelope Dalrymple. New York; London; Montreal: The Abbey Press, [c1901]. 361 p. **DLC**
PW: O 12, '01.

D-36 Dalton, Test, 1877-1945. The role of the unconquered / by Test Dalton. New York: G. W. Dillingham Co., [c1901]. 329 p.
PW: F 8, '02.
BLC: London: T. Fisher Unwin, 1902.

Dam, Colby V. Man or manners? In *The best college short stories, 1917-18* **(1919), B-557.**

Dam, H. J. W. The diamond drill and Mary. In *Through the forbidden gates* **(1903), T-222.**

Dana, Duncan. That day in Africa. In *Made to order* **(1915), M-352.**

D-37 Dana, Francis. The decoy / by Francis Dana. London; New York: John Lane The Bodley Head, 1902. 314 p.
PW: Mr 8, '02.

D-38   Dana, M. Cumming (Mercedes Cumming).
        According to her light / by M. Cumming Dana.
        Philadelphia: Dorrance, [c1922]. 298 p.   **NYP**
        LC: S 9, '22.

D-39   Dana, Marvin, b. 1867. The lake mystery / by
        Marvin Dana . . . ; frontispiece by J. Allen St. John.
        Chicago: A. C. McClurg & Co., 1923. 375 p.,
        front., ill. (music).
        LC: S 29, '23.
        PW: D 22, '23.

D-40   ____ The master mind / by Marvin Dana; from the
        play by Daniel D. Carter; illustrated by Frank Tenney
        Johnson. New York: The H. K. Fly Co., [c1913].
        320 p., front., [3] leaves of plates.   **NYP**
        LC: D 29, '13.
        PW: Jl 18, '14.

D-41   ____ The mystery of the third parrot: relates how a
        mystery that baffled the New York City police gave
        an eminent psychologist an opportunity to test his skill
        / by Marvin Dana . . . Chicago: A. C. McClurg &
        Co., 1924. 309 p., front.
        LC: Ap 30, '24.
        PW: My 17, '24.
        BLC: London: Hodder & Stoughton, [1925].

D-42   ____ A Puritan witch: a romance / by Marvin
        Dana; illustrated by P. R. Audibert. New York;
        London: The Smart Set Publishing Co., 1903.
        266 p., incl. front., [3] leaves of plates.
        PW: My 2, '03.

D-43   ____ The shooting of Dan McGrew: a novel / by
        Marvin Dana; based on the famous poem of Robert
        W. Service; profusely illustrated with scenes from the
        photoplay. New York: Grosset & Dunlap, [c1915].
        317 p., photo. front., [15] leaves of photo. plates.
        LC: Ag 18, '15.
        PW: Ja 15, '16.

D-44   ____ Within the law / by Marvin Dana from the play
        of Bayard Veiller. New York: The H. K. Fly
        Company, [c1913]. 344 p., col. front., [3] leaves of
        col. plates.
        LC: Je 5, '13.
        PW: Ap 5, '13.

D-45   Dane, Joan. Prince Madog, discoverer of America:
        a legendary story / by Joan Dane; illustrated by A. S.
        Boyd. Boston, Mass.: Everett Publishing Co.,
        [between 1901 and 1916]. 222, [1] p., col. front., [2]
        leaves of col. plates.   **NYP**
        BLC: London: Elliot Stock, [1909].

D-46   Dane, John Colin. Champion / by John Collin Dane
        . . . ; illustrations by W. E. Webster. New York: G.
        W. Dillingham Company, [1907]. 310 p., front., [7]
        leaves of plates.
        LC: Ap 20, '07.
        PW: My 18, '07; Je 8, '07

D-47   Danford, H. Edmund (Harry Edmund), 1879-1972.
        Soakum: a story / by H. Edmund Danford; illustrated
        by Donald Ross. [Caldwell, Ohio]: The author,

1912. [Bellows Falls, Vt.: The P. H. Gobie Press].
222 p., col front., plates.
Unexamined copy: bibliographic data from OCLC,
#11535557.

D-48   Danger. Boston: R. G. Badger, [c1912]. 198 p.
        Unexamined copy: bibliographic data from NUC.

D-49   Daniel, *pseud.* Crystal heavens / by Daniel [pseud.].
        The United States: Printed therein by the author,
        1921. 305 p., front.   **NYP**

D-50   Daniel, F. E. (Ferdinand Eugene), 1839-1914. The
        strange case of Dr. Bruno / by F. E. Daniel . . .
        Austin, Texas: Von Boeckmann-Jones Company,

        [c1906]. 235 p., photo. front., [1] leaf of plates. [Ill.
        by J. L. Brooks.]
        LC: N 28, '07.
        Another edition: New York: Guarantee Publishing
        Co., [c1906], with 14 ills. by J. L. Brooks.
        Unexamined copy: bibliographic data from NUC.

D-51   Daniel, Hawthorne, b. 1890. In the favour of the
        king / by Hawthorne Daniel; frontispiece by Gordon
        Stevenson. Garden City, N. Y.; Toronto:
        Doubleday, Page & Company, 1922. 293 p., col.
        front.
        LC: Ap 21, '22.

D-52   Daniel, J. W. (James Walter), b. 1856. The bottom
        rail / by James Walter Daniel. Boston: The
        Roxburgh Publishing Company, Incorporated,
        [c1915]. 239 p., photo. front., [5] leaves of photo.
        plates.
        LC: F 9, '15.

D-53   ____ A maid of the foot-hills, or, Missing links in
        the story of reconstruction / by J. W. Daniel. New
        York; Washington: The Neale Publishing Company,
        1905. 248 p.

D-54   Daniel Hovey: supposed to be a posthumous
        romance, of unknown authorship, the manuscript of
        which was discovered in a very peculiar --manner-- /
        edited by T. B. Morton. Little Rock, Ark.: Fred.
        W. Allsopp, Publisher, 1901. 311 p. Designed end
        papers.   **AKU**

D-55   Daniels, A. G. (Abraham Getzel), b. 1856. Potash
        and Perlmutter issue a catalog / by A. G. Daniels
        (after Montague Glass). Boston: Published by the
        author, [c1914]. 37 p.

D-56   Daniels, Gertrude Potter. Eshek, the oppressor / by
        Gertrude Potter Daniels; illustrations by G. C.
        Widney. Chicago: The Madison Book Co., [c1902].
        378 p., col. front., [7] leaves of col. plates. Note:
        [PW: D 6, '02: rights secured by the Madison Book
        Co. Originally published Nov. 10 by Rand McNally;
        withdrawn "beacause of its bitter and thinly disguised
        attack upon the Standard Oil Co. and the several
        railroad corporations allied with that company."
        Present publisher's book printed from original plates.]

D-57   ____ The Warners: an American story of today / by Gertrude Potter Daniels. Chicago: Jamieson-Higgins Co., 1901. 252 p.
PW: Ap 6, '01.

D-58   Danziger, Adolphe, b. 1866. Children of fate: a story of passion / by Adolphe Danziger . . . New York: Brentano's, 1905. 340 p.   **DLC**

D-59   ____ Helen Polaska's lover, or, The merchant prince / by Adolphe Danziger . . . New York: Adolphe Danziger, [c1908]. 381 p.   **DLC**
LC: Ap 2, '09.

D-60   [D'Apery, Ellen], 1842-1915. Letters of an American countess to her friend / by the countess herself. New York: J. S. Ogilvie Publishing Company, [c1902]. 128 p.   **DLC**

D'Apery, Helen (Burrell), Mrs., 1842-1915. <u>See</u> **Harper, Olive, pseud.**

D-61   Darby, Sarah. That affair in Philadelphia / by Mrs. Darby. New York: Broadway Publishing Co., [c1909]. 75 p.
LC: Ap 22, '09.
PW: My 8, '09.
<small>Contents: That affair in Philadelphia -- Mr. Ambassador -- Madam Marcot, milliner -- The highways of trolleydom -- Old St. John's -- The President's trip.</small>

D-62   Dare, Gloria. Out of the mist / Gloria Dare. San Francisco, California: California Press, [c1925]. 146, [2] p., photo. front. (port.).
LC: Je 5, '25; Je 17, '25.
PW: Ag 1, '25.

D-63   Dargan, Olive Tilford, 1869-1968. Highland annals / by Olive Tilford Dargan. New York: Charles Scribner's Sons, 1925. 286 p.
LC: S 9, '25.

D-64   Daring, Hope, b. 1860, *pseud.* An abundant harvest / by Hope Daring [pseud.]. Cincinnati: Jennings and Graham; New York: Eaton and Mains, [c1904]. 281 p.
PW: Ja 28, '05.

D-65   ____ The appointed way; a tale of the Seventh-day Adventists / by Hope Daring [pseud.]. Philadelphia: The Griffith & Rowland Press, 1905. 336 p., front. Unexamined copy: bibliographic data from OCLC, #2519596.
PW: O 14, '05.

D-66   ____ Entering into his own / by Hope Daring [pseud.]. New York: American Tract Society, [c1903]. 279 p., photo. front., [4] leaves of photo. plates.
PW: D 12, '03.

D-67   ____ Father John, or, Ruth Webster's quest / by Hope Daring [pseud.] . . . New York: American Tract Society, [c1907]. 270 p., front., [7] leaves of plates. [Ill. by Wm. S. Nortenheim.]
LC: O 12, '07.

D-68   ____ The Gordons / by Hope Daring [pseud.]. New York: American Tract Society, [c1912]. 180 p., col. front. [Ill. by Clinton Pettee.]
LC: S 25, '12.
PW: N 2, '12.

D-69   ____ Madeline: the island girl / by Hope Daring [pseud.]. New York: Eaton & Mains; Cincinnati: Jennings & Graham, [c1906]. 282 p., [4] leaves of photo. plates.

D-70   ____ Paying the price! / by Hope Daring [pseud.] . . . New York: American Tract Society, [c1914]. 236 p., front.   **DLC**
LC: D 19, '14.
PW: Ja 16, '15.

D-71   ____ To the third generation / by Hope Daring [pseud.]. New York: American Tract Society, [c1901]. 298 p., front., [1] leaf of plates.
PW: O 5, '01.

D-72   ____ Valadero ranch / by Hope Daring [pseud.]. New York: American Tract Society, [c1911]. 288 p., front., [2] leaves of plates.
LC: O 30, '11.
PW: N 18, '11.

D-73   ____ A Virginian holiday / by Hope Daring [pseud.]. New York: American Tract Society, [c1909]. 300 p., front., [3] leaves of plates. [Ill. by Frank Lloyd Rose et al.]
LC: D 8, '09.

D-74   Darley, George M. The pastor / George M. Darley. Boston: The Gorham Press; Toronto: The Copp Clark Co., Limited, [c1916]. 239 p.   **COD**
LC: D 2, '16.
PW: D 2, '16.

D-75   Darling, Mary Greenleaf, b. 1848. A girl in this century: a continuation of " We four girls" / by Mary Greenleaf Darling . . . ; illustrated by Lilian Crawford True. Boston: Lee and Shepard, 1902. 264 p., front., [3] leaves of plates. [Ill. by Lilian Crawford True.]

D-76   Darrow, Clarence, 1857-1938. An eye for an eye / by Clarence S. Darrow. New York: Fox, Duffield & Company, 1905. 213 p.
PW: O 28, '05.

D-77   ____ Farmington / By Clarence S. Darrow. Chicago: A. C. McClurg & Co., 1904. 277 p.
BLC: London: C. F. Cazenove; Cambridge, U. S. A. [printed], 1904.

D-78   Dart, Harry Grant. The sprightly adventures of Mr. Homesweet Home / by Harry Grant Dart. New York: Moffat, Yard & Company, 1914. 121 p.
LC: N 7, '14.

Dashiell, Landon R. *Aunt Sanna Terry.* <u>In</u> *The Great modern American stories* **(1920), G-422.**

Daskam, Josephine Dodge. <u>See</u> **Bacon, Josephine Dodge Daskam, 1876-1961.**

D-79   Datchet, Charles. Morchester: a story of American Society, politics, and affairs / by Charles Datchet. New York; London: G. P. Putnam's Sons, 1902. ([New York]: The Knickerbocker Press). 480 p. PW: Ap 26, '02.

Daugherty, E. C. Laying the ghost. <u>In</u> **Seattle Writer's Club.** *Tillicum tales* (1907), S-248.

D-80   Davenport, Arnold. By the ramparts of Jezreel / by Arnold Davenport. New York; London; Bombay: Longmans, Green, and Co., 1903. 388 p., front. [Ill. by Lancelot Speed.] PW: F 28, '03. BLC: London: Longman's Green & Co., 1903.

D-81   Davenport, Benjamin Rush. Blood will tell: the strange story of a son of Ham / by Benjamin Rush Davenport; illustrations by J. H. Donahey. Cleveland: Caxton Book Co., 1902. 340 p., front., [3] leaves of plates. PW: Je 14, '02.

D-82   Davenport, Delbert Essex. High girl, or, Genius in oblivion; and The first of his family; two stories of the Minute / by Delbert Essex Davenport. New York: The Mantup Publishing Company, [c1919]. 239 p., front., [2] leaves of plates. [Ill. by Roy Namsorg.]

D-83   Davenport, Willard Goss, b. 1843. Milton Blairlee and the Green Mountain Boys: a story of the New Hampshire grants / by Willard Goss Davenport; illustrated by Fanny Knights Ide. New York: The Grafton Press, [c1904]. 304 p., front., [4] leaves of plates.

D-84   [David, K.], *pseud.* Black butterflies: a novel / by Berthe St. Luz [pseud.]. New York: R. F. Fenno & Company, 1905. 337 p., incl. front., [5] leaves of plates. [Ill. by W. E. B. Starkweather.] PW: Jl 22, '05.

D-85   [____] Tamar Curze / by Berthe St. Luz [pseud.] . . . New York: R. F. Fenno & Company, [c1908]. 206 p., col. front. [Ill by R. Sherman-Kidd.] **EYM**

D-86   Davidge, Frances. The game and the candle / by Frances Davidge . . . New York: D. Appleton and Company, 1905. 371 p.

D-87   ____ The misfit crown / by Frances Davidge. New York: D. Appleton & Company, 1904. 342 p.

Davidson, Charles Lock, b. 1859. <u>See</u> **Commodore, pseud.**

D-88   Davidson, George Trimble. The moderns: a tale of New York / by George Trimble Davidson. New York: Frederick A. Stokes Company, [c1901]. 364 p. LC: Je 11, '01.

PW: Je 22, '01.
BLC: London: Grant Richards, 1901.

D-89   Davidson, Laura Lee. Isles of Eden / by Laura Lee Davidson. New York: Minton, Balch & Company, 1924. 200 p. LC: S 12, '24.

D-90   Davidson, P. (Peter), 1842-1916. The queen of the isles: a legend of the isles of the sea in prehistoric times / by [star]; translated from the French by P. Davidson; illustrated with engraving of the Menai Straits and the Island of Mona. Louisville, White County, Ga., U. S. A.: Peter Davidson, 1907. 67 p., photo. front. Author's name represented on t. p. by a six-pointed star with a flower in the center. LC: D 18, '07.

D-91   Davies, Acton, 1870-1916. The first lady in the land, or, When Dolly Todd took boarders / by Acton Davies & Charles Nirdlinger; illustrated by Howard Giles. New York: The H. K. Fly Company, [c1912]. 309 p., col. front., [4] leaves of plates. LC: D 5, '12.

D-92   ____ Romance: a novel / by Acton Davies; from the drama by Edward Sheldon; with pictures from the play.   New York: The Macaulay Company, 1913. 320 p., incl. photo. front., [5] leaves of photo. plates. LC: My 21, '13. PW: My 31, '13. BLC: London: Mills & Boon, 1915.

D-93   Davies, Mary Carolyn. The husband test / by Mary Carolyn Davies; frontispiece by Elizabeth Pilsbry. Philadelphia: The Penn Publishing Company, 1921. 259 p., front. LC: Ap 12, '21.

D-94   Davies, Zelda Edloe. Her sacrifice / by Zelda Edloe Davies. New York: Broadway Publishing Company, 1913. 152 p., front. (port.).   **DLC** LC: N 8, '13.

D-95   Daviess, Maria Thompson, 1872-1924. Andrew the Glad / by Maria Thompson Daviess; illustrated by R. M. Crosby. Indianapolis: The Bobbs-Merrill Company, [c1913]. 357 p., front., [4] leaves of plates. LC: Ja 30, '13. PW: Ja 25, '13.

D-96   ____ Blue-grass and Broadway / by Maria Thompson Daviess . . . New York: The Century Co., 1919. 373 p., front. [Ill. by Leslie L. Benson.] LC: My 27, '19. PW: My 24, '19.

D-97   ____ The daredevil / by Maria Thompson Daviess; frontispiece from painting by E. Sophonisba Hergesheimer. Chicago: The Reilly & Britton Co., [c1916]. 344 p., col. front. LC: Mr 20, '16. PW: Ap 22, '16.

D-98   ____ The elected mother: a story of woman's equal rights / by Maria Thompson Daviess. Indianapolis: The Bobbs-Merrill Company, [c1912]. 31 p. "Reprinted from a volume of short stories."
LC: Jl 22, '12.
PW: O 12, '12.

D-99   ____ The golden bird / by Maria Thompson Daviess; illustrated by Edward L. Chase. New York: The Century Co., 1918. 267 p., front., [3] leaves of plates.
LC: S 5, '18.
PW: S 28, '18.

D-100   ____ The heart's kingdom / by Maria Thompson Daviess; illustrated by W. B. King. Chicago: The Reilly & Britton Co., [c1917]. 367 p., front., [3] leaves of plates.
LC: O 8, '17.
PW: S 15, '17.

D-101   ____ The matrix / by Maria Thompson Daviess. New York: The Century Co., 1920. 260 p., front. [Ill. Sarah E. Cowan.]
LC: Mr 3, '20.
PW: Mr 6, '20.

D-102   ____ The melting of Molly / by Maria Thompson Daviess; illustrated by R. M. Crosby. Indianapolis: The Bobbs-Merrill Company, [c1912]. 200, [1] p., front., [11] leaves of plates.
LC: My 22, '12.
PW: My 4, '12.

D-103   ____ Miss Selina Lue and the soap-box babies / by Maria Thompson Daviess; with illustrations by Paul J. Meylan. Indianapolis: The Bobbs-Merrill Company, [c1909]. 221, [1] p., front., [5] leaves of plates.
LC: O 9, '09.
PW: O 9, '09.

D-104   ____ Out of a clear sky: a novel / by Maria Thompson Daviess. New York; London: Harper & Brothers, [1917]. 155, [1] p., front. [Ill. by E. F. Ward.]
LC: My 5, '17.
PW: My 5, '17.

D-105   ____ Over Paradise ridge: a romance / by Maria Thompson Daviess; illustrated. New York; London: Harper & Brothers, [1915]. 160, [1] p., col. front., [1] leaf of col. plates.
LC: O 25, '15.
PW: N 6, '15.

D-106   ____ Phyllis / by Maria Thompson Daviess; with illustrations by Percy D. Johnson. New York: The Century Co., 1914. 286 p., front., ill.
LC: S 30, '14.
PW: S 26, '14.

D-107   ____ The road to Providence / by Maria Thompson Daviess; with illustrations by W. B. King. Indianapolis: The Bobbs-Merrill Company, [c1910]. 274 p., front., [4] leaves of plates.

LC: N 2, '10.
PW: N 5, '10.

D-108   ____ Rose of Old Harpeth / by Maria Thompson Daviess; with illustrations by W. B. King. Indianapolis: The Bobbs-Merrill Company, [c1911]. 312 p., front., [5] leaves of plates.
LC: S 23, '11.
PW: S 30, '11.
BLC: London: Religious Tract Society, [1914].

D-109   ____ The tinder-box / by Maria Thompson Daviess; with illustrations by John Edwin Jackson. New York:

The Century Co., 1913. 312 p., front., [7] leaves of plates.
LC: N 8, '13.
PW: N 8, '13.

D-110   Davis, Beale, 1866-1929. The goat without horns / by Beale Davis. New York: Brentano's, [c1925]. 318 p.
LC: S 19, '25.
PW: O 10, '25.

D-111   ____ One way street / by Beale Davis. New York: Brentano's, [c1924]. 317 p.
LC: S 17, '24.
PW: S 13, '24.
BLC: London: Stanley Paul & Co., 1926.

D-112   Davis, Caesar, b. 1892. A tragedy in whiskers / by Caesar Davis . . . ; illustrated by Fred H. Shantz. [Colorado Springs, Colo.]: Apex Book Co., 1917. 69 p., incl. front., ill.   **DLC**
LC: Ja 17, '18.

D-113   Davis, Charles Belmont, 1866-1926. Her own sort and others / by Charles Belmont Davis; illustrated. New York: Charles Scribner's Sons, 1917. 332 p., front., [5] leaves of plates. [Ill. by F. R. Gruger, James Montgomery Flagg, and William Van Dresser.]
Contents: Her own sort -- The octopus -- God's material -- The joy of dying -- When Johnny came marching home -- The professor -- The twenty-first reason -- Side-tracked -- The men who would "die" for her -- Her man.
LC: Mr 14, '17.
PW: Mr 17, '17.

D-114   ____ In another moment / by Charles Belmont Davis; with illustrations by Wallace Morgan. Indianapolis: The Bobbs-Merrill Company, [c1913]. 372 p., front., [5] leaves of plates.
LC: My 14, '13.
PW: My 10, '13.

D-115   ____ The lodger overhead and others / by Charles Belmont Davis; illustrated. New York: Charles Scribner's Sons, 1909. 370 p., front., [7] leaves of plates. [Ill. by A. I. Keller and James Flagg.] Reprinted from various periodicals.
Contents: The lodger overhead -- The essential sense -- "The band" -- Tommy -- The girl with the green toque -- The white light of publicity -- The dancing man -- The greatest of these -- The executors -- The beggar at your gate.
LC: Ap 13, '09.
PW: Ap 24, '09.

D-116 _____ Nothing a year: a novel / by Charles Belmont Davis. New York; London: Harper & Brothers, [1916, c1915]. 291, [1] p., front. [Ill. by Will Foster.]
LC: F 23, '16.
PW: Mr 4, '16.

D-117 _____ The stage door: illustrated / by Charles Belmont Davis. New York: Charles Scribner's Sons, 1908. 360 p., front., [7] leaves of plates. [Ill. by Alonzo Kimball, Albert Sterner, and John Wolcott Adams.] Reprinted from various periodicals.
Contents: Everyman's riddle -- "Beauty" -- Kerrigan -- Coccaro the clown -- "Sedgwick" -- A modern Cleopatra -- The cross roads, New York -- The kidnappers -- The flawless emerald -- Carmichael's Christmas spirit -- The road to glory.
LC: My 7, '08.
PW: My 16, '08.

D-118 _____ Tales of the town / Charles Belmont Davis . . . New York: Duffield and Company, 1911. 339 p., front., [7] leaves of plates. [Ill. by David Robinson.]
Contents: The gray mouse -- The romance of a rich young girl -- Once to every man -- The conquerors -- The most famous woman in New York -- Where ignorance was bliss -- The extra girl -- The rescue -- Marooned -- The song and the Savage.
LC: Ag 10, '11.
PW: Ag 26, '11.

D-119 Davis, Charles E. (Charles Edward), b. 1853. Paul Leonard's sacrifice / by Charles E. Davis. Boston, Mass.: Published by H. Loranus Davis, [c1902]. 264 p., front. (port.).
A New England story read at the Sunday evening services of the First Methodist Episcopal Church in Lynn, Massachusetts, and the Tremont Street Methodist Episcopal Church in Boston, Massachusetts.

D-120 Davis, Edith M. Allah kerim / by Edith M. Davis . . . Boston: The Roxburgh Publishing Company, Inc., [c1920]. 118 p.
LC: Mr 29, '20.
PW: My 29, '20.

D-121 Davis, Elizabeth S. Ropes of sand / by Elizabeth S. Davis; illustrated by Wm. L. Hudson. New York: Guarantee Publishing Co., [c1906]. 196 p., front., [5] leaves of plates. Decorated end papers.

D-122 Davis, Elmer Holmes, 1890-1958. Friends of Mr. Sweeney / by Elmer Davis. New York: Robert M. McBride & Company, 1925. 282 p.
LC: N 18, '25.
PW: N 21, '25.
BLC: London: Methuen & Co., 1926.

D-123 _____ I'll show you the town / by Elmer Davis. New York: Robert M. McBride & Company, 1924. 373 p.
LC: Ap 12, '24.
PW: Ap 5, '24.

D-124 _____ The keys of the city / by Elmer Davis. New York: Robert M. McBride & Company, 1925. 305 p.
LC: F 14, '25.

PW: F 21, '25.
BLC: London: Methuen & Co., 1926.

D-125 _____ The Princess Cecilia / by Elmer Davis; illustrated by C. H. Taffs. New York; London: D. Appleton and Company, 1915. 332, [1] p., front.
LC: Ap 30, '15.
PW: My 1, '15.

D-126 _____ Times have changed / by Elmer Davis. New York: Robert M. McBride & Company, 1923. 300 p.   **AZU**
LC: Ap 26, '23.
PW: Ap 7, '23.
BLC: London: Hodder & Stoughton, [1924].

Davis, Frederick William, 1858-1933. See **Campbell, Scott, pseud.**

Davis, Foxcroft, pseud. See **Seawell, Molly Elliot, 1860-1916.**

D-127 Davis, Garrett Morrow, b. 1851. In the footsteps of Boone; an historical romance of pioneer days in Kentucky / Garrett M. Davis. Washington, D. C.: The Neale Publishing Company, 1903. 291 p. **KGG**

Davis, George M., jt. aut. *Firebrands* (1911). See **Martin, Frank E. (Frank Eugene), jt. aut., M-507.**

D-128 Davis, George Wesley, b. 1861. Alone: (a beautiful land of dreams) / by George Wesley Davis. Los Angeles: Times-Mirror Press, [c1922]. 166 p., front.
LC: D 27, '22.

D-129 _____ A morphine tablet / by George Wesley Davis . . . New York: W. F. Brainard . . . , [c1914]. 207 p.   **NYP**
LC: N 28, '14.

D-130 _____ Sulphur fumes, or, In the garden of hell / by George Wesley Davis. Los Angeles: The Times-Mirror Press, 1923. 289 p.
LC: O 1, '23.

Davis, Harold Thayer, b. 1892. See **Davis, Caesar, pseud.**

D-131 Davis, J. Frank (James Francis), 1870-1942. Almanzar / by J. Frank Davis; frontispiece by Hanson Booth. New York: Henry Holt and Company, 1918. 227 p., front.
LC: O 17, '18.
PW: N 9, '18.
BLC: London: Thomas Nelson & Sons, [1922].

D-132 _____ Almanzar Evarts, hero / by J. Frank Davis . . . ; illustrated by John Bob Payne. Macon, Georgia: The J. W. Burke Company, 1925. 163 p., front.
LC: N 14, '25.
PW: Ja 9, '26.

D-133   ____ The Chinese label / by J. Frank Davis; with illustrations by Ralph P. Coleman. Boston: Little, Brown & Company, 1920. 296 p., front., [3] leaves of plates.
LC: Ap 14, '20.
PW: Ap 10, '20.

D-134   [____] Frenological finance: being a true history of the life and adventures of Mortimer Kensington Queen / by Nick Sherlock Collier [pseud.]. Boston, Massachusetts: The C. M. Clark Publishing Company, 1907. [62] p., ill.   **DLC**
LC: Ap 9, '07.
PW: Ap 27, '07.

Davis, Jessie Hopkirk. The new word. In *Club stories* **(1915), C-502.**

D-135   Davis, Kate. A perilous path, or, Apples of Sodom / by Kate Davis. New York; London; Montreal: The Abbey Press, [c1901]. 161 p.
PW: Je 22, '01.

Davis, Leslie. Caught in the web, a summer tale. In *Golden stories* **(1909), G-285.**

Davis, M. E. M. (Mollie Evelyn Moore), 1844-1909. At La Glorieuse. In *Shapes that haunt the dusk* **(1907), S-339.**

D-136   ____ Jaconetta: her loves / by M. E. M. Davis. Boston; New York: Houghton, Mifflin and Company, 1901. (Cambridge: The Riverside Press). 152 p., front., [3] leaves of plates. [Ill. by Ethel Franklin Betts.]
PW: O 5, '01.

D-137   ____ The little chevalier / by M. E. M. Davis; with illustrations. Boston; New York: Houghton, Mifflin and Company, 1903. (Cambridge: The Riverside Press). 317, [1] p., front., [3] leaves of plates. [Ill. by H. J. Peck.]

D-138   ____ The price of silence / by M. E. M. Davis; with illustrations by Griswold Tyng. Boston; New York: Houghton, Mifflin and Company, 1907. (Cambridge, Mass.: The Riverside Press). 280 p., front., [5] leaves of plates.
LC: Mr 14, '07.
PW: Ap 13, '07.

   ____ A snipe hunt. In *Southern lights and shadows* **(1907), S-718.**

D-139   Davis, Mary L. K., *pseud.* Results / by Mary L. K. Davis [pseud.]. Puyallup, Washington: Owl Press, 1922. 48 p.   **DLC**

D-140   [Davis, Morgan Lewis], b. 1862. The gas offis / by the offis boy; illustrated by Wm. L. Hudson. New York: Broadway Publishing Co., [c1906]. 102 p., front., [4] leaves of plates.   **VA@**
LC: Ag 17, '06.

D-141   Davis, Norah, b. 1878. The northerner / by Norah

Davis. New York: The Century Co., 1905. 324 p.
PW: O 14, '05.

D-142   ____ The other woman / by Norah Davis. New York: The Century Co., 1920. 398 p.
LC: Je 1, '20.
PW: Je 12, '20.

D-143   ____ Wallace Rhodes: a novel / by Norah Davis. New York; London: Harper & Brothers, 1909. 334 p.
LC: Ap 1, '09.
PW: Ap 10, '09.

D-144   ____ The world's warrant / by Norah Davis; with a frontispiece by F. C. Yohn. Boston; New York: Houghton, Mifflin and Company, 1907. (Cambridge: The Riverside Press). 293, [1] p., col. front.
LC: Ap 4, '07.
PW: My 11, '07.
BLC: London: Archibald Constable & Co., 1907.

D-145   Davis, Oscar King, b. 1866. At the Emperor's wish: a tale of the new Japan / by Oscar King Davis. New York: D. Appleton and Company, 1905. 149 p., col. front., [3] leaves of col. plates. [Ill. by Charles M. Relyea.] Illustrated end papers.

   ____ See also **Davis, Schroeder, jt. pseud. of Davis, Oscar King and Schroeder, Reginald.**

D-146   Davis, Owen, 1874-1956. The family cupboard: a novel / from the play by Owen Davis. New York: The Macaulay Company, [c1914]. 301 p., photo. front., [5] leaves of photo. plates.
LC: F 25, '14.
PW: Mr 28, '14.

D-147   ____ Lola / by Owen Davis . . . ; illustrated with scenes from the photo-play produced and copyrighted by the World Film Corporation. New York: Grosset & Dunlap, [c1915]. 304 p., photo. front., [15] leaves of photo. plates.
LC: Ag 4, '15.
PW: S 18, '15.

D-148   Davis, Pearl Ulilla. Ignorance unveiled / by Pearl Ulilla Davis. New York: Broadway Publishing Company, [1904]. 149 p., front. (port.).
Unexamined copy: bibliographic data from OCLC, #26833976.
PW: D 12, '03.

D-149   Davis, Rebecca Harding, 1831-1910. Bits of gossip / by Rebecca Harding Davis . . . Boston; New York: Houghton, Mifflin & Company, 1904. (Cambridge, [Mass.]: The Riverside Press). 233 p.   **KSU**
Contents: In the old house -- Boston in the sixties -- In the far South -- The Scotch-Irishman -- The Civil War -- The shipwrecked crew -- A peculiar people -- Above their fellows.
BLC: Westminster: Archibald Constable; Cambridge, Mass. printed, 1904.

D-150   Davis, Richard Harding, 1864-1916. The bar sinister / by Richard Harding Davis; illustrated by E. M. Ashe. New York: Charles Scribner's Sons, 1903.

108 p., col. front., [6] leaves of col. plates.
First separate printing: see *Ranson's folly* (1902) for
first book appearance.
LC: S 30, '03.
PW: D 12, '03.
References: BAL 4540; Quinby, 26 (p. 56-58).

D-151   _____ Captain Macklin: his memoirs / by Richard
Harding Davis; illustrated by Walter Appleton Clark.
New York: Charles Scribner's Sons, 1902. 328,
[1] p., front., [6] leaves of plates.
LC: S 11, '02.
PW: O 4, '02.
BLC: London: William Heinemann, 1902.
References: BAL 4539; Quinby, 25 (p. 53-56).

D-152   _____ The consul / by Richard Harding Davis. New
York: Charles Scribner's Sons, 1911. 62 p., front.
[Ill. by F. D. Steele.]
LC: My 12, '11.
PW: My 13, '11.
References: BAL 4554; Quinby, 36 (p. 71-72).

D-153   _____ The deserter / by Richard Harding Davis; with
an introduction by John T. McCutcheon. New York:
Charles Scribner's Sons, 1917. 43 p. First separate
printing: see *The man who had everything* (1916) for
first book appearance.
LC: O 17. '17.
PW: O 20, '17.
References: BAL 4577; Quinby, 49a (p. 90-91).

D-154   _____ Her first appearance / by Richard Harding
Davis . . . ; illustrated by C. D. Gibson and E. M.
Ashe. New York; London: Harper & Brothers,
1901. 52, [1] p., col. front., [2] leaves of col. plates.
Illustrated end papers.
First separate printing: first book appearance in *Van
Bibber, and others* (1892).
LC: N 26, '01.
PW: D 7, '01.
References: BAL 4536.

D-155   _____ In the fog / by Richard Harding Davis;
illustrated by Thomas Mitchell Pierce & F. D. Steele.
New York: R. H. Russell, 1901. 155 p., front., [15]
leaves of plates (some col.).
LC: N 22, '01.
PW: D 21, '01.
BLC: London: Ward Lock & Co., 1901. Another
edition: London: William Heinemann, 1902.
References: BAL 4537; Quinby, 23 (p. 50-51).

D-156   _____ The lost road / by Richard Harding Davis;
illustrated by Wallace Morgan. New York: Charles
Scribner's Sons, 1913. 266 p., front., [5] leaves of
plates.
Contents: The lost road -- The miracle of Las Palmas -- Evil to him
who evil thinks -- The man [i. e. men] of Zanzibar -- The long arm --
The god of coincidence -- The buried treasure of Cobre.
LC: O 14, '13.
PW: O 25, '13.
BLC: London: Duckworth & Co.; New York
printed, 1914.
References: BAL 4560; Quinby, 39 (p. 75).

D-157   _____ The lost road / by Richard Harding Davis with
an introduction by John T. McCutcheon; illustrated.
New York: Charles Scribner's Sons, 1916. 330 p.,
front., [5] leaves of plates.   **KSU**
The novels and stories of Richard Harding Davis, vol.
12. Reprints save for *The man who had everything*,
pp. 308-330, which was issued as a separate printing
(1917), and retitled *The deserter* (q. v.).
References: BAL 4574; Quinby, 47 (p. 84-85).

D-158   _____ The man who could not lose / by Richard
Harding Davis; illustrated. New York: Charles
Scribner's Sons, 1911. 254 p., front., [7] leaves of
plates. [Ill. by George Wright, Wallace Morgan, F.
D. Steele, and J. N. Marchand.]
Contents: The man who could not lose -- My buried treasure --The
consul -- The nature faker -- The lost house.
LC: S 20, '11.
PW: S 23, '11.
References: BAL 4555.; Quinby, 37 (p. 72-73).

D-159   _____ The man who could not lose / by Richard
Harding Davis. New York: Charles Scribner's Sons,
1911. 65 p.   **NOC**
First separate printing (see previous entry).
References: BAL 4556.

D-160   _____ The man who could not lose / by Richard
Harding Davis, with an introduction by Leonard
Wood; illustrated. New York: Charles Scribner's
Sons, 1916. 365 p., front., [4] leaves of plates. [Ill.
by Wallace Morgan, George Wright, and F. D.
Steele.]   Bibliographic data from BAL.
The novels and stories of Richard Harding Davis, vol.
10. Reprints save for first book appearance of *The
log of the Jolly Polly*, pp. 312-365.
References: BAL 4574.

D-161   _____ The novels and stories of Richard Harding
Davis, illustrated. New York: Charles Scribner's
Sons, 1916. 12 vols. Reprints save for single stories
in vol. 10, *The man who could not lose*; vol. 11, *The
red cross girl*; and vol. 12 *The lost road* (q. v.).
Bibliographic data from BAL.
References: BAL 4574; Quinby, p. 96-97.

D-162   _____ Once upon a time / by Richard Harding Davis.
New York: Charles Scribner's Sons, 1910. 280 p.,
front., [7] leaves of plates.
Contents: A question of latitude -- The spy -- The messengers -- A
wasted day -- A charmed life -- The amateur -- The make-believe man
-- Peace manoeuvres.
LC: Ag 26, '10.
PW: S 24, '10.
BLC: London: Duckworth & Co., New York
printed, 1911.
References: BAL 4552; Quinby, 35 (p. 70-71).

D-163   _____ Ranson's folly / by Richard Harding Davis;
with illustrations by Frederic Remington, Walter
Appleton Clark, Howard Chandler Christy, E. M.
Ashe & F. Dorr Steele. New York: Charles
Scribner's Sons, 1902. 345 p., front., [15] leaves of
plates.
Contents: Ranson's folly -- The bar sinister -- A derelict -- La lettre
d'amour -- In the fog.

PW: Jl 12, '02.
BLC: London: Ward, Lock & Co., 1902. Another edition: London: William Heinemann, 1903.
References: BAL 4538; Quinby, 24 (p. 52-53).

D-164   ____ The Red Cross girl / by Richard Harding Davis; illustrated by Wallace Morgan. New York: Charles Scribner's Sons, 1912. 270 p., front., [7] leaves of plates. [Ill. also by Chase Emerson and Frederic Rodrigo Gruger.]
Contents: The Red cross girl -- The Grand Cross of the Crescent -- The invasion of England -- Blood will tell -- The sailorman -- The mind reader -- The naked man.
LC: S 12, '12.
PW: S 14, '12.
BLC: London: Duckworth & Co.; New York printed, 1912.
References: BAL 4557; Quinby, 38 (p. 73).

D-165   ____ The red cross girl / by Richard Harding Davis with an introduction by Gouverneur Morris; illustrated. New York: Charles Scribner's Sons, 1916. 296 p., front., [4] leaves of plates. [Ill. by Wallace Morgan, Chase Emerson, and F. R. Gruger.] Bibliographic data from BAL.
The novels and stories of Richard Harding Davis, vol. 11. Reprints save for first book appearance of *The boy who cried wolf*, pp. 251-276.
References: BAL 4574.

D-166   ____ The scarlet car / by Richard Harding Davis; illustrated by Frederic Dorr Steele. New York: Charles Scribner's Sons, 1907. 166 p., front., [11] leaves of plates.
Contents: The jail breakers -- The trespassers -- The kidnappers.
LC: Je 27, '07.
PW: Jl 13, '07.
References: BAL 4546; Quinby, 30 (p. 64-65).

D-167   ____ "Somewhere in France" / by Richard Harding Davis. New York: Charles Scribner's Sons, 1915. 224 p., col. front. [Ill. by Henry Raleigh.]
Contents: "Somewhere in France" -- Playing dead -- The card-sharp -- Billy and the big stick -- The boy scout -- The frame-up.
LC: Ag 31, '15.
PW: S 4, '15.
BLC: London: Duckworth & Co.; New York printed, 1916.
References: BAL 4570; Quinby, 46 (p. 82-83).

D-168   ____ Vera the medium / by Richard Harding Davis . . . ; illustrated by Frederic Dorr Steele. New York: Charles Scribner's Sons, 1908. 216 p., front., [5] leaves of plates.
LC: Je 3, '08.
PW: Je 13, '08.
References: BAL 4548; Quinby, 32 (p. 67-68).

D-169   ____ The white mice / by Richard Harding Davis; illustrated by George Gibbs. New York: Charles Scribner's Sons, 1909. 309 p., front., [7] leaves of plates.
LC: My 12, '09.
PW: Je 5, '09.
References: BAL 4549; Quinby, 33 (p. 68-69).

Davis, Robert H. (Robert Hobart), 1869-1942, jt. aut.

The bugler of Algiers (1916). See **Sheehan, Perley Poore, 1875-1943, jt. aut., S-372.**

____, jt. aut. *We are French!* (1914). See **Sheehan, Perley Poore, 1875-1943, jt. aut., S-378.**

D-170   Davis, Sam P. (Sam Post), 1850-1918. The first piano in camp / by Sam Davis; with an appreciation by Sam C. Dunham; with drawings by H. Fisk. New York; London: Harper & Brothers Publishers, [c1919]. 30, [1] p., col. front., [2] leaves of plates.
LC: S 23, '19.

D-171   Davis, Schroeder, *jt. pseud.* The storm birds / by Schroeder Davis [jt. pseud.]. New York: Moffat, Yard and Company, 1910. 376 p.
LC: My 28, '10.

D-172   Davis, See Barham. The power of conscience / by See Barham Davis. New York: The Stuyvesant Press, 1911. 225 p.
LC: Je 12, '11.

D-173   Davis, W. H. (William Henry), b. 1843. Something worth reading, or, A checkered life / by W. H. Davis . . . [Oregon City, Oregon: [s. n.], c1905]. 128 p.
                                                              DLC

D-174   Davis, William Stearns, 1877-1930. The beauty of the purple: a romance of imperial Constantinople twelve centuries ago / by William Stearns Davis. New York: The Macmillan Company, 1924. 570 p.
LC: S 24, '24.
PW: S 27, '24.
BLC: London: Leonard Parsons; printed in U. S. A., 1925.

D-175   ____ Belshazzar: a tale of the fall of Babylon / by William Stearns Davis; with illustrations by Lee Woodward Zigler [sic], decorations by J. E. Laub. New York: Doubleday, Page & Co., 1902. 427 p., front., [7] leaves of plates.
PW: Jl 5, '02.
BLC: London: Grant Richards, 1902.

D-176   ____ Falaise of the blessed voice: a tale of the youth of St. Louis, king of France / by William Stearns Davis. New York: The Macmillan Company; London: Macmillan & Co., Ltd., 1904. 360 p.
PW: O 8, '04.

D-177   ____ The friar of Wittenberg / by William Stearns Davis. New York: The Macmillan Company, 1912. 433 p.
LC: My 23, '12.
PW: Je 8, '12.

D-178   ____ "God wills it!": a tale of the first crusade / by William Stearns Davis; with illustrations by Louis Betts. New York: The Macmillan Company; London: Macmillan & Co., Ltd., 1901. 552 p., front., [7] leaves of plates.
PW: N 23, '01.

D-179   ____ The saint of the Dragon's Dale; a fantastic tale / by William Stearns Davis. New York: The

Macmillan Company; London: Macmillan & Co., Ltd., 1903. 129 p., front. (port.), [2] leaves of plates. [Ill. by The Kinneys.] Designed end papers. (Little novels by favourite authors.)
PW: Ag 15, '03.

D-180 _____ A victor of Salamis: a tale of the days of Xerxes, Leonidas and Themistocles / by William Stearns Davis . . . New York: The Macmillan Company; London: Macmillan & Co., Ltd., 1907. 450 p.
LC: Ap 20, '07.
PW: My 4, '07.

D-181 Davis, Yorke. The green cloak / by Yorke Davis; with illustrations by E. C. Caswell. New York: Sturgis & Walton Company, 1910. 307 p., front., [3] leaves of plates.
LC: Ap 15, '10.
PW: Je 25, '10.
BLC: London: Sidgwick & Jackson, 1910.

D-182 Davison, Charles Stewart, 1855-1942. "Selling the bear's hide": and other tales / by Charles Stewart Davison. Richmond Hill, Long Island, N. Y.: The Nassau Press, [c1902]. 131 p., front., [1] leaf of plates.
Contents: Selling the bear's hide -- A slip on the Ortler -- Up Clevedale and down again -- How I sent my aunt to Baltimore -- John O'Conor goes a-fishing -- A winter wedding at Weldon.
PW: Jl 19, '02.

D-183 Davisson, Ralph Boardman. The yokefellow / by Ralph Boardman Davisson. Boston, Massachusetts: The C. M. Clark Publishing Co., 1908. 311 p., front., [7] leaves of plates.
LC: D 18, '08.

D-184 "Dawgs!": an anthology of stories about them / edited by Charles Wright Gray. New York: Henry Holt and Company, 1925. 342 p. Illustrated end papers. [Signed by Morgan Stinemetz.]
Contents: As a dog should / by Charles Alexander -- Being a public character / by Don Marquis -- Bulldog / by Max Brand -- Fox terrier or something / by Booth Tarkington -- The grudge / by Albert Payson Terhune -- Justice in the painted hills / by Alexander Hull -- Memoirs of a yellow dog / by O. Henry -- Old Duke / by Arthur Train -- Pair of lovers / by Elsie Singmaster -- Rex / by D. H. Lawrence -- Shag of the pack / by Edison Marshall -- Such as walk in darkness / by Samuel Hopkins Adams -- The soul of Caliban / by Emma-Lindsay Squier -- Triangle / by Donn Byrne -- White Monarch and the gas-house pup / by R. G. Kirk -- Bibliography.
LC: S 17, '25.
PW: O 3, '25.

D-185 Dawson, Coningsby, 1883-1959. Christmas outside of Eden / by Coningsby Dawson . . . ; illustrations by Eugene Francis Savage. New York: Dodd, Mead and Company, 1922. 87 p., [2] leaves of plates (1 folded). **GZN**
LC: O 17, '22.
PW: O 28, '22.

D-186 _____ The coast of folly: a novel / by Coningsby Dawson; illustrations by C. D. Mitchell. New York: Cosmopolitan Book Corporation, 1924. 341 p., front., [3] leaves of plates.

LC: Ja 5, '24.
PW: Ja 19, '24.
BLC: London: Hutchinson & Co., [1924].

D-187 _____ The garden without walls / by Coningsby Dawson. New York: Henry Holt and Company, 1913. 491 p., front. (port.). Illustrated end papers.
LC: S 20, '13.
PW: S 13, '13.
BLC: London: William Heinemann, 1913.

D-188 _____ The kingdom round the corner: a novel / by Coningsby Dawson; illustrated by W. D. Stevens. New York: Cosmopolitan Book Corporation, 1921. 364 p., front., [3] leaves of plates.
LC: My 14, '21.
PW: My 14, '21.
BLC: London: John Lane, 1921.

D-189 _____ The little house / by Coningsby Dawson; with illustrations by Stella Langdale. London: John Lane, The Bodley Head; New York: John Lane Company, 1920. 127 p., front., [7] leaves of plates. Illustrated end papers.
LC: S 22, '20.
PW: S 18, '20.
BLC: London: John Lane, 1920.

D-190 _____ Murder Point: a tale of Keewatin / by Coningsby William Dawson. New York: Hodder & Stoughton: George H. Doran Company, [c1910]. 349 p.
LC: Mr 15, '10.
PW: Ap 2, '10.

D-191 _____ Old youth: a novel / by Coningsby Dawson; illustrations by Charles D. Mitchell. New York: Cosmopolitan Book Corporation, 1925. 365 p., front., [3] leaves of plates.
LC: S 8, '25.
PW: S 5, '25.
BLC: London: Hutchinson & Co., [1926].

D-192 _____ The raft / by Coningsby Dawson; with illustrations by Orson Lowell. New York: Henry Holt and Company, 1914. 460 p., front., [7] leaves of plates.
LC: O 1, '14.
PW: S 12, '14.
BLC: London: Constable & Co., 1914.

D-193 _____ The road to Avalon / by Coninsby Dawson. New York: Hodder & Stoughton: George H. Doran Company, [c1911]. 284 p.
Unexamined copy: bibliographic data from NUC.
LC: Mr 28, '11.
PW: Ap 1, '11.
BLC: London: Hodder & Stoughton, 1911.

D-194 _____ The seventh Christmas / by Coningsby Dawson. New York: Henry Holt and Company, 1917. 60 p. Illustrated end papers. [Signed by Herbert Deland Williams.]
LC: N 2, '17.
PW: O 20, '17.

D-195   ____ Slaves of freedom / by Coningsby Dawson. New York: Henry Holt and Company, 1916. 472 p. Illustrated end papers.
LC: N 16, '16.
PW: O 14, '16.
BLC: London: Constable & Co.; New York [printed], 1916.

D-196   ____ The test of scarlet: a romance of reality / by Coningsby Dawson. New York: John Lane Company; London: John Lane, The Bodley Head, 1919. 313 p.
LC: O 20, '19.
PW: N 1, '19.

D-197   ____ The unknown country / by Coningsby Dawson; with illustrations by W. C. Rice. New York: Hearst's International Library Co., [c1915]. 62 p., front., [3] leaves of plates.
LC: Mr 6, '15.
PW: Mr 27, '15.

D-198   ____ The vanishing point / by Coningsby Dawson . . . ; illustrated by James Montgomery Flagg. New York: Cosmopolitan Book Corporation, 1922. 350 p., front., [3] leaves of plates.
Half title: *The vanishing point: a modern novel.*
LC: Ap 3, '22.
PW: Ap 15, '22.
BLC: London: Hutchinson & Co., [1922].

D-199 Dawson, Elinor. Merciful unto me, a sinner / by Elinor Dawson. Chicago: Thompson & Thomas, 1905. 446 p.

D-200 Dawson, Emma Frances. A gracious visitation / written by Emma Frances Dawson; with an appreciation by Ambrose Bierce. San Francisco: The Book Club of California, 1921. 69, [1] p., music.

Dawson, Frances Warrington. <u>See</u> **Dawson, Warrington, 1878-1962.**

Dawson, Marjorie. <u>See</u> **Dale, Mary, pseud.**

D-201 Dawson, Minnie T. The Stillwell murder, or, A society crime / Minnie T. Dawson. Hannibal, Missouri: [s. n.], 1908. 154 p.   **KCP**

D-202 Dawson, Warrington, 1878-1962. Adventures in the night / by Warrington Dawson. Garden City, New York: Doubleday, Page & Company, [1924]. 253 p. "Printed in Great Britain."
PW: S 13, '24.
BLC: London: T. Fisher Unwin, 1924.

D-203   ____ The gift of Paul Clermont / Warrington Dawson. Garden City, N. Y.; Toronto: Doubleday, Page & Company, 1921. 332 p.
LC: O 12, '21.
PW: O 15, '21.
BLC: London: William Heinemann; Garden City, New York printed, 1921.

D-204   ____ The green moustache: a fantasy of modernism / by Warrington Dawson. Chicago: The Bernard Publishing Co., 1925. 315 p.
LC: Ja 29, '26.

D-205   ____ The scar / by Warrington Dawson. Boston: Small, Maynard & Company, 1910. 381 p.
LC: Mr 19, '10.
PW: Ap 2, '10.
BLC: London: Methuen & Co., 1906.

D-206   ____ The scourge / by Warrington Dawson. Boston: Small, Maynard & Company, 1910. 384 p.
LC: N 11, '10.
PW: N 12, '10.
BLC: London: Methuen & Co., 1908.

D-207   ____ The sin: an allegory of truth / by Warrington Dawson. Chicago: The Honest Truth Publishing Co., [c1923]. 118 p.
Contents: A few plain facts -- Characters -- Pause -- The sin.
LC: D 5, '23.
PW: Ap 19, '23.

D-208 Dawson, William James, 1854-1928. The Borrowdale tragedy / by W. J. Dawson . . . New York: John Lane Company; London: John Lane, The Bodley Head, 1920. 308 p.
LC: N 8, '20.
PW: N 20, '20.

D-209   ____ Chalmers comes back / by W. J. Dawson . . . New York: John Lane Company; London: John Lane, The Bodley Head, 1919. 316 p.
LC: S 29, '19.
PW: N 1, '19.

D-210   ____ Masterman and son / by W. J. Dawson . . . New York; Chicago; Toronto; London; Edinburgh: Fleming H. Revell Company, [c1909]. 365 p.
LC: O 2, '09.
PW: O 23, '09.
BLC: London: Hodder & Stoughton, 1909.

D-211   ____ One night in Bethlehem: a Christmas story / by W. J. Dawson. New York: Hodder and Stoughton: George H. Doran Company, [c1910]. 54 p., col. front., [3] leaves of col. plates.   **VUT**
LC: N 12, '10.
BLC: London: Hodder & Stoughton; Cambridge, U. S. A. [printed], 1910.

D-212   ____ A prophet in Babylon: a story of social service / by W. J. Dawson . . . New York; Chicago; Toronto; London; Edinburgh: Fleming H. Revell Company, [c1907]. 366 p.   **CLE**
LC: O 2, '07.
PW: O 19, '07.
BLC: London: Hodder & Stoughton, 1907.

D-213   ____ Robert Shenstone: a novel / by W. J. Dawson . . . New York: John Lane Company; London: John Lane, The Bodley Head; Toronto: S. B. Gundy, 1917. 411 p.
LC: S 18, '17.
PW: S 15, '17.

D-214 _____ A soldier of the future / by William J. Dawson . . . New York; Chicago; Toronto; London; Edinburgh: Fleming H. Revell Company, [c1908]. 360 p.
LC: S 1, '08.
PW: S 12, '08.
BLC: London: Hodder & Stoughton, 1908.

D-215 _____ The war eagle: a contemporary novel / by W. J. Dawson . . . New York: John Lane Company; London: John Lane, The Bodley Head, 1918. 313 p.
LC: S 6, '18.
PW: Ag 31, '18.

D-216 Day, Charles H. Actress and clerk: a story of stage and store: a blending of professional and commercial life: an original theme / by Chas. H. Day. Chicago;

New York: Will Rossiter, c1905. 288 p., ill. [Ill. by S. F. Crews.] Decorated end papers.

D-217 Day, Clarence, 1874-1935. This simian world / by Clarence Day, Jr.; with illustrations by the author. New York: Alfred A. Knopf, 1920. 95 p., ill. Reprinted in part from various periodicals.
LC: Je 11, '20.
PW: Je 12, '20.
BLC: London: Jonathan Cape, [1921].

D-218 Day, Cora S., b. 1873. Round the circle / by Cora S. Day . . . New York: American Tract Society, [c1904]. 152 p., front., [10] leaves of plates.
LC: Ag 11, '06.

D-219 Day, Dorothy, 1897-1980. The eleventh virgin / by Dorothy Day. New York: Albert & Charles Boni, 1924. 312, [1] p.
LC: Ap 9, '24.

D-220 Day, Dorothy S. The ventures of Connie, or, Being married / by Dorothy S. Day. Boston, Massachusetts: The Stratford Company, 1922. 85 p., front.   **DLC**
LC: Mr 31, '22.

D-221 Day, Ernest Everett. Adventures of an enthusiast / by Ernest Everett Day. Excelsior, Minnesota: The Tri-State Publishing Co., 1907. 136 p.   **MHS**
[Advertisements on p. [134]-136.]
LC: Ag 2, '07.
BLC: London; Melbourne: Ward, lock & Co., 1907.

D-222 Day, George Edward, 1864-1919. A wilderness cry: the story of a great sacrifice / by George Edward Day; illustrations by William Kirkpatrick. Boston: The C. M. Clark Publishing Co., 1906. 381 p., front., [7] leaves of plates.
LC: N 7, '06.

D-223 Day, Holman, 1865-1935. All-wool Morrison: time: today, place: the United States, period of action: twenty-four hours / by Holman Day. New York; London: Harper & Brothers, 1920. 324, [1] p.
LC: Ag 12, '20.
PW: O 2, '20.

D-224 _____ Blow the man down: a romance of the coast / by Holman Day. New York; London: Harper & Brothers, [1916]. 461, [1] p., front. [Ill. by Perc. E. Cowen.]
LC: Jl 1, '16.
PW: Jl 8, '16.

D-225 _____ Clothes make the pirate / by Holman Day; containing thirty-four chanties and ballads. New York; London: Harper & Brothers, 1925. 310 p.
LC: Mr 7, '25.
PW: Mr 7, '25.

_____ Commander Jim Wickson's habit. In **Conrad, Joseph.** *Il conte* (1925), C-697.

D-226 _____ The eagle badge, or, The Skokums of the Allagash / by Holman Day; illustrated. New York; London: Harper & Brothers, 1908. 289, [1] p., front., [3] leaves of plates. [Ill. by Thomas Fogarty.]
LC: O 9, '08.
PW: O 17, '08.

D-227 _____ Joan of Arc of the north woods / by Holman Day. -- [1st ed.]. -- New York; London: Harper & Brothers, [c1922]. 349, [1] p.
LC: O 23, '22.
PW: O 28, '22.

D-228 _____ King Spruce: a novel / by Holman Day; illustrated by E. Roscoe Shrader. New York; London: Harper & Brothers, 1908. 371, [1] p., col. front., [3] leaves of col. plates.
LC: Ap 2, '08.
PW: Ap 11, '08.

D-229 _____ The landloper: the romance of a man on foot / by Holman Day. New York; London: Harper & Brothers, [1915]. 333, [1] p., col. front. [Ill. by Vincent Lynch.]
LC: Jl 3, '15.
PW: Jl 10, '15.

D-230 _____ Leadbetter's luck / by Holman Day. New York: Duffield and Company, 1923. 263 p., front., [3] leaves of plates. [Ill. by Chase Emerson.]
LC: O 20, '23.
PW: O 20, '23.

D-231 _____ The loving are the daring / by Holman Day. New York: Harper & Brothers, [c1923]. 422 p.
LC: S 25, '23.
PW: O 13, '23.

D-232 _____ The ramrodders: a novel / by Holman Day. New York; London: Harper & Brothers, 1910. 352 p., front. [Ill. by Harold Matthews Brett.]
LC: Ap 23, '10.
PW: Ap 30, '10.

D-233 _____ The red lane: a romance of the border: illustrated / by Holman Day . . . New York; London: Harper & Brothers, 1912. 398, [1] p., front., [3] leaves of plates. [Ill. by Denman Fink and Douglas Duer.]
LC: Jl 26, '12.
PW: Ag 3, '12.

D-234 _____ The rider of the king log: a romance of the northeast border / by Holman Day; with a frontispiece by Harold Brett. New York; London: Harper & Brothers, 1919. 499 p., front.
LC: S 23, '19.
PW: N 1, '19.

D-235 _____ The skipper and the skipped: being the shore log of Cap'n Aaron Sproul / by Holman Day; illustrated. New York; London: Harper & Brothers, 1911. 416 p., front. [Ill. by Frances Rogers.]
LC: F 11, '11.
PW: F 18, '11.

D-236 _____ Squire Phin: a novel / by Holman F. Day; with frontispiece. New York: A. S. Barnes & Company, 1905. 393 p., front. [Ill. by John Rae.]
PW: O 21, '05.

D-237 _____ When Egypt went broke: a novel / by Holman Day. New York; London: Harper & Brothers, 1921. 362, [1] p., front.
LC: Jl 11, '21.
PW: Jl 16, '21.

D-238 _____ Where your treasure is: being the personal narrative of Ross Sidney, diver / by Holman Day. New York; London: Harper & Brothers, [1917]. 460, [1] p., col. front. [Ill. by Chase Emerson.]
LC: Je 28, '17.
PW: Jl 7, '17.

Day, Raymond Pue, b. 1886. See Shields, D., pseud.

D-239 Day, Thomas Fleming, 1861-1927. The adventures of two yachtsmen: transcribed from the note-book of the late John Gordon Falcon / by Thomas Fleming Day . . . New York; London: The Rudder Publishing Company, 1907. 118 p.   DLC
LC: Ja 2, '08.

D-240 _____ The four and the fire, or, Five nights in a yacht club / by Thomas Fleming Day . . . ; illustrations by J. W. Sheppard. New York; London: The Rudder Publishing Company, 1907. 167, [1] p., front., ill.   COD
LC: F 12, '08.

D-241 The Daysman. New York: Cochrane Publishing Company, 1909. 420 p.   CSJ
LC: Ja 20, '10.

Dazey, Charles Turner, b. 1855, jt. aut. *In old Kentucky* (1910). See Marshall, Edward, 1870-1933, jt. aut., M-491.

_____, jt. aut. *The old flute-player* (1910). See Marshall, Edward, 1870-1933, jt. aut., M-495.

D-242 Dean, John Marvin, 1875-1935. The miracle on Hermon: a story of the Carpenter / by John Marvin Dean. New York; Chicago; London; Edinburgh: Fleming H. Revell Company, [c1921]. 64 p., front.
LC: D 12, '21.

D-243 _____ The promotion: a story of the Philippine War / by John Marvin Dean . . . Philadelphia: The Griffith and Rowland Press, 1906. 207 p., ill. (some photo).
LC: S 13, '06.

D-244 _____ Rainier of the last frontier / by John Marvin Dean. New York: Thomas Y. Crowell Company, [1911]. 373 p., col. front.
LC: Ag 10, '11.
PW: S 2, '11.

D-245 Dean, S. Ella Wood. Love's purple / by S. Ella Wood Dean. Chicago: Forbes & Company, 1911. 343 p.
LC: O 31, '11.

D-246 Dean, Sara, b. 1870. A disciple of chance: an eighteenth century love story / by Sara Dean. New York: Frederick A. Stokes Company, [1910]. 409 p.
LC: Mr 17, '10.

D-247 _____ Travers: a story of the San Francisco earthquake / by Sara Dean; with illustrations in colour by W. Herbert Dunton. New York: Frederick A. Stokes Company, [1908]. 287 p., col. front., [2] leaves of col. plates.
LC: Jl 25, '07.

D-248 Deane, Ethel. "None so blind" / by Ethel Deane. Boston, Mass.: Reid Publishing Company, 1910. 332 p., front., [2] leaves of plates. [Ill. by John Goss.]
LC: My 3, '10.

D-249 Dear, William C. My chum, Pres.: by a former Pittsburgh newsboy / William C. Dear, author. Pittsburgh, Pa.: Pittsburgh Printing Company, [c1925]. 102 p.   DLC
LC: S 1, '25.

D-250 Dearborn, Malcolm. Bethsaida: a story of the time of Christ / by Malcolm Dearborn. New York: G. W. Dillingham Company, [1903]. 301 p.
PW: O 24, '03.
BLC: London: T. Fisher Unwin, 1903.

D-251 _____ Lionel Ardon: a tale of chivalry in the days of Queen Mary, Elizabeth, and Lady Jane Grey / by Malcolm Dearborn. New York: G. W. Dillingham Company, [1902]. 326 p.
PW: N 8, '02.

De Bardeleben, Mary. The story of a great choice. In *When God walks the road and other stories* (1924), W-445.

D-252 De Barrios, Adelaide. The shepherdess of to-day / by Adelaide De Barrios. New York: Aberdeen Publishing Company, [c1910]. 101 p. Decorated end papers.
PW: My 21, '10.

D-253 De Beer, A. R., *pseud.* "Old Noo'leans": a novelization of the dramatic playlet of the same name; Midnight: a dramatic playlet of Parisian life / by A. R. De Beer [pseud.]. [S. l.: Published by the author, 192-?]. 62 p.

D-254   De Bet, William. Philip Worthy / By William De Bet . . . Nashville, Tenn.: McQuiddy Printing Company, 1904. 109 p. **IIB**

De Bra, Lemuel. A life-a bowl of rice. In *Twenty-three stories* **(1924), T-445.**

D-255   ____ Ways that are wary / by Lemuel De Bra. New York: Edward J. Clode, Inc., [c1925]. 320 p.
Contents: Ways that are wary -- Mock Don Yuen meditates -- The wedding of Chan Fah -- Mock Don Yuen and the Tongs -- A life-a bowl of rice -- The strategy of Ah Lo -- The mystery of the missing hands -- The Buddha twins -- The filial piety of Wong Kee Lim -- The strange slaying of Bock Gee -- The testing of Ah Toy -- The queer fortune of Duck Yoan.
LC: Ap 1, '25.
PW: Ap 4, '25.
BLC: London: Thornton Butterworth, 1924.

DeCamp, Charles B. The bitter cup. In *Different girls* **(1906), D-383.**

D-256   De Camp, Etta, b. 1866. Return of Frank R. Stockton: . . . stories and letters which cannot fail to convince the reader that Frank R. Stockton still lives and writes through the instrumentality of Miss Etta de Camp. -- 1st ed. -- London: William Rider & Son, Ltd.; New York, U. S. A.: Macoy Publishing & Masonic Supply Co., 1913. 314, [1] p., front. (port.). [Ill. by Edwin J. Prittie.]
Contents: Five little maids from afar -- A married man's deception -- Thompkin's blunder -- What became of the ghost of Mike O'Flynn -- The man who always turned up -- What Amos Jones drew in the great lottery -- The widow he lost -- Letters from Mr. Stockton -- Why I know Frank R. Stockton writes through me.
LC: Mr 14, '13.

D-257   De Carrick, William. The King's coming: a story of the happy end / by William De Carrick; frontispiece by J. E. Brown. New York: The Sherwood Company, 1919. 447 p., front.
LC: Je 6, '19.

DeCastro, Adolphe Danziger. See **Danziger, Adolphe, b. 1866.**

De Chambrun, Clara (Longworth). See **Chambrun, Clara Longworth, contesse de, 1873-1954.**

D-258   Decker, Ida Smith. Patience and her garden / Ida Smith Decker. San Francisco: Paul Elder & Company, Publisher, [c1910]. 7 p., [1] leaf of plates. Unexamined copy: bibliographic data from OCLC, #10394392.

D-259   De Conval, Ronleigh, *pseud*. The fair lady of Halifax, or, Colmey's six hundred / by Ronleigh de Conval [pseud.]. Raleigh, N. C.: Edwards & Broughton Printing Co., 1920. 408 p., photo. front. **NDD**
LC: Mr 11, '20.

D-260   De Courcy, M. B. (Matthias Bodine), 1859-1906. Sons of the Red Rose: a story of the rail in the early '80's / by M. B. De Courcy. Washington, D. C.: J. William Cannon, c1905. 234 p., front., [7] leaves of plates. [Ill. by Elliott Brewer and John E. Sheridan.]

De Esque, Jean Louis, b. 1879. See **Stewart, pseud.**

D-261   De Forest, Jean Louise. The love affair of a homely girl / by Jean Louise DeForest; frontispiece by H. Richard Boehm. New York: Sully and Kleinteich, 1914. 213 p., front.
LC: Ja 16, '14.
PW: Ja 24, '14.

D-262   ____ Molly / by Jean Louise de Forest. New York: Sully and Kleinteich, 1915. 304 p., col. front.
LC: F 24, '15.
PW: Mr 6, '15.

D-263   De Fremery, Edna. The greater mystery / by Edna De Fremery; with frontispiece illustration by the author. San Francisco: Sunset Press, 1920. 207 p., col. front.

De Galvez, Helen Bell. See **Bell, Helen.**

D-264   De Groot, John H. The man in the bearskin / by John H. De Groot. Rock Island, Illinois: Augustana Book Concern, [c1925]. 191 p., front., [1] leaf of plates.
LC: S 4, '25.
PW: S 12, '25.

D-265   Dejeans, Elizabeth, *pseud*. The double house / by Elizabeth Dejeans [pseud.]. Garden City, N. Y.: Doubleday, Page & Company, 1924. 273 p.
LC: Ap 21, '24.
PW: Ap 12, '24.
BLC: London: Hutchinson & Co., [1924].

D-266   ____ The far triumph / by Elizabeth Dejeans [pseud.] . . . ; with illustrations in color by Martin Justice. Philadelphia; London: J. B. Lippincott Company, 1911. 374 p., col. front., [2] leaves of col. plates. **NYP**
LC: O 11, '11.
PW: O 21, '11.

D-267   ____ The heart of desire / by Elizabeth Dejeans [pseud.] . . . ; with illustrations in color by The Kinneys. Philadelphia; London: J. B. Lippincott Company, 1910. 365 p., col. front., [2] leaves of col. plates.
LC: Mr 30, '10.
PW: Ap 9, '10.

D-268   ____ The house of Thane / by Elizabeth Dejeans [pseud.]; with illustrations in color by Frederick C. Yohn. Philadelphia; London: J. B. Lippincott Company, 1913. 309 p., col. front., [2] leaves of col. plates.
LC: Je 13, '13.
PW: Je 7, '13.

D-269   ____ The life-builders: a novel / by Elizabeth Dejeans [pseud.]. New York; London: Harper & Brothers, 1915. 409, [1] p., front.
LC: Ap 17, '15.
PW: Ap 24, '15.

D-270   ____ The Moreton mystery / by Elizabeth Dejeans [pseud.] . . . ; illustrated by W. H. D. Koerner. Indianapolis: The Bobbs-Merrill Company, [c1920]. 345 p., front., [3] leaves of plates.
LC: Ag 19, '20.
PW: S 11, '20.

D-271   ____ Nobody's child / by Elizabeth Dejeans [pseud.]; frontispiece by Arthur I. Keller. Indianapolis: The Bobbs-Merrill Company, [c1918]. 340 p., front.
LC: Mr 12, '18.

D-272   ____ The romance of a million dollars / by Elizabeth Dejeans [pseud.]. Indianapolis: The Bobbs-Merrill Company, [c1922]. 364 p.
LC: Ag 31, '22.
PW: S 2, '22.

D-273   ____ The tiger's coat / by Elizabeth Dejeans [pseud.]; with illustrations by Arthur I. Keller. Indianapolis: The Bobbs-Merrill Company, [c1917]. 428 p., front., [5] leaves of plates.
LC: Mr 10, '17.
PW: Mr 10, '17.
BLC: London: Thornton Butterworth, 1923.

D-274   ____ The winning chance / Elizabeth Dejeans [pseud.]; with a frontispiece by Gayle Porter Hoskins. Philadelphia; London: J. B. Lippincott Company, 1909. 317, [1] p., front.
LC: My 1, '09.
PW: My 22, '09.
BLC: London: John Milne, 1909.

D-275   ____ The winning game / by Elizabeth Dejeans [pseud.]. Garden City, N. Y.: Doubleday, Page & Company, 1925. 329 p.
LC: Mr 2, '25.
PW: F 14, '25.
BLC: London: William Heinemann; printed in U. S. A., 1925.

De Koven, Anna Farwell. See **De Koven, Reginald, Mrs., 1862-1953.**

D-276   De Koven, Reginald, Mrs., 1862-1953. By the waters of Babylon / Mrs. Reginald De Koven. Chicago: Herbert S. Stone and Company, 1901. 349 p.
PW: Je 1, '01.

D-277   De Kroyft, Helen Aldrich, 1818-1915. The foreshadowed way / by . . . Helen Aldrich De Kroyft. New York; London: F. Tennyson Neely Co., [c1901]. 182 p.

D-278   Delamare, Henriette Eugénie, 1858-1937. The adventures of four young Americans / by Henriette Eugénie Delamare . . . Philadelphia: H. L. Kilner & Co., [c1912]. 187 p.
Unexamined copy: bibliographic data from NUC.

D-279   ____ Her heart's desire / by Henriette Eugénie Delamare. Philadelphia: H. L. Kilner & Co., [c1915]. 301 p.
LC: Mr 29, '15.

D-280   ____ The little ambassadors / by Henriette Eugénie Delamare. Philadelphia: H. L. Kilner & Co., [c1915]. 299 p.
LC: N 26, '15.

D-281   ____ The little apostle on crutches / by Henriette Eugénie Delamare. New York; Cincinnati; Chicago; San Francisco: Benziger Brothers, Inc., 1912. 165 p., front.   **FCE**
LC: Ja 31, '12.

D-282   ____ Nellie Kelly; or, The little mother of five / by Henriette Eugénie Delamare . . . Philadelphia: H. L. Kilner & Co., [c1912]. 189 p.
Unexamined copy: bibliographic data from NUC.

D-283   ____ Ronald's mission / by Henriette Eugénie Delamare . . . Philadelphia: H. L. Kilner & Co., [c1913]. 220 p.   **ABC**
LC: Jl 19, '13.

D-284   De Land, Charles Edmund, b. 1854. The psychic trio, or, Nations reconciled / by Charles Edmund De Land . . . Boston: Richard G. Badger, [c1919]. ([Boston, U. S. A.]: The Gorham Press). 426 p.   **NYP**

D-285   ____ Tragedy of the white medicine: a story of Indian mystery, revenge, and love / by Charles Edmund DeLand. New York: The Neale Publishing Company, 1913. 135 p.
LC: D 31, '13.

D-286   Deland, Margaret Wade Campbell, 1857-1945. Around old Chester / by Margaret Deland; illustrated. New York; London: Harper & Brothers, [1915]. 377, [1] p., front., [7] leaves of plates. [Ill. by Alice Barber Stephens, W. H. D. Koerner, and H. Pyle.]
Contents: "Turn about" -- The harvest of fear -- The voice -- An encore -- The third volume -- The thief -- Miss Clara's Perseus.
LC: S 18, '15.
PW: O 2, '15.

D-287   ____ The awakening of Helena Richie / by Margaret Deland; illustrated by Walter Appleton Clark. New York; London: Harper & Brothers, 1906. 356, [1] p., col. front., [8] leaves of plates.
LC: Jl 12, '06.
PW: Jl 21, '06.
Another edition: Half-title: Margaret Anglin edition; with pictures of scenes in the play.

D-288   ____ Dr. Lavendar's people / by Margaret Deland: illustrated by Lucius Hitchcock. New York; London: Harper and Brothers, 1903. 369, [1] p., front., [11] leaves of plates.
Contents: The apotheosis of the Reverend Mr. Spangler -- The note -- The grasshopper and the ant -- Amelia -- "An exceding high mountain" -- At the stuffed-animal house.
PW: O 24, '03.

D-289   ____ An encore / by Margaret Deland; illustrated by Alice Barber Stephens. New York; London: Harper & Brothers, 1907. 78 p., front., [2] leaves of plates. Illustrated end papers.
LC: O 2, '07.
PW: O 12, '07.

_____ An encore. In *Quaint courtships* (1906), **Q-3.**

D-290 _____ The hands of Esau / by Margaret Deland; illustrated. New York; London: Harper & Brothers, 1914. 85, [1] p., front., [1] leaf of plates.
LC: O 24, '14.
PW: S 19, '14.

_____ The immediate jewel. In *Life at high tide* **(1907), L-281.**

D-291 _____ The iron woman / by Margaret Deland; with illustrations by F. Walter Taylor. New York; London: Harper & Brothers, 1911. 477, [1] p., front., [7] leaves of plates.
LC: S 21, '11.
PW: S 30, '11.

_____ "Many waters". In *Short story classics* (1905), **S-466.**

D-292 _____ New friends in Old Chester / by Margaret Deland. New York; London: Harper & Brothers, [c1924]. 271, [1] p., front.
Contents: The Eliots' Katy -- An Old Chester secret -- "How could she!"
LC: My 15, '24.
PW: My 24, '24.
BLC: London: John Murray, 1924.

D-293 _____ An Old Chester secret / by Margaret Deland; illustrations by F. Walter Taylor. New York; London: Harper & Brothers, [1920]. 125, [1] p., front., [3] leaves of plates.
LC: O 25, '20.
PW: N 13, '20.

D-294 _____ Partners / by Margaret Deland; illustrated by Charles Dana Gibson. New York; London: Harper & Brothers, 1913. 114, [1] p., front., [3] leaves of plates.
LC: O 4, '13.
PW: O 11, '13.

D-295 _____ The promises of Alice: the romance of a New England parsonage / by Margaret Deland; with illustrations by Harold Brett. New York; London: Harper and Brothers, [1919]. 130, [1] p., front., [3] leaves of plates.
LC: Ag 20, '19.
PW: Ag 30, '19.

D-296 _____ R. J.'s mother: and some other people / by Margaret Deland; illustrated. New York; London: Harper & Brothers, 1908. 312 p., front., [7] leaves of plates.
Contents: R. J.'s mother -- The Mormon -- Many waters -- The house of Rimmon -- A black drop -- The white feather.
LC: My 7, '08.
PW: My 16, '08.

D-297 _____ The rising tide / by Margaret Deland; illustrated by F. Walter Taylor. New York; London: Harper & Brothers, [1916]. 292, [1] p., front., [3] leaves of plates.
LC: Ag 29, '16.
PW: S 2, '16.
BLC: London: John Murray, 1916.

D-298 _____ The vehement flame: a novel / by Margaret Deland; with frontispiece by C. E. Chambers. New York; London: Harper & Brothers, [c1922]. 378 p., front.
LC: Je 3, '22.
PW: Je 3, '22.
BLC: London: John Murray, 1922.

D-299 _____ The voice / by Margaret Deland; illustrated by W. H. D. Koerner. New York; London: Harper & Brothers, 1912. 84, [1] p., front., [2] leaves of plates.
LC: S 21, '12.
PW: O 5, '12.

D-300 _____ The way to peace / by Margaret Deland; illustrated by Alice Barber Stephens. New York; London: Harper & Brothers, 1910. 93, [1] p., front., [6] leaves of plates. Illustrated end papers.
LC: O 1, '10.
PW: O 8, '10.

D-301 _____ Where the laborers are few / by Margaret Deland; illustrated by Alice Barber Stephens. New York; London: Harper & Brothers, 1909. 85, [1] p., front., [2] leaves of plates. Designed end papers.
LC: O 16, '09.
PW: O 23, '09.

D-302 De Laney, Paul, d. 1946. The toll of the sands / by Paul De Laney . . . ; illustrated by Paul Gregg. -- 1st ed. -- Denver: The Smith-Brooks Printing Company, [c1919]. 333 p., front., [3] leaves of plates.
Half title: *The toll of the sands: a story of love and adventure in the Great Gold Rush into the Death Valley country.*
LC: D 27, '19.
PW: F 28, '20.
BLC: London: T. Fisher Unwin, 1921.

D-303 Delano, Edith Barnard, 1875-1946. The colonel's experiment / by Edith Barnard Delano; illustrated. New York; London: D. Appleton and Company, 1913. 315, [1] p., col. front., [3] leaves of col. plates. [Ill. by Florence Storer.]
LC: O 13, '13.
PW: N 1, '13.

_____ For value received. In *Marriage* **(1923), M-457.**

D-304 _____ June / by Edith Barnard Delano; with illustrations. Boston; New York: Houghton Mifflin Company, 1916. (Cambridge: The Riverside Press). 234, [2] p., front., [7] leaves of plates. [Ill. by Florence Storer.]
LC: S 13, '16.
PW: S 9, '16.
BLC: London: Methuen & Co., 1917.

D-305 _____ The land of content / by Edith Barnard Delano. New York; London: D. Appleton and Company, 1913. 333, [1] p., front., [3] leaves of plates. [Ill. by J. Henry.]
LC: F 27, '13.
PW: Mr 1, '13.

D-306 ____ Rags / by Edith Barnard Delano; illustrated by C. H. Taffs. New York; London: D. Appleton and Company, 1915. 335, [1] p., front., [3] leaves of plates.
LC: Mr 10, '15.
PW: S 4, '15.

D-307 ____ To-morrow morning: chronicle of the new Eve and the same old Adam / by Edith Barnard Delano; with illustrations. Boston; New York: Houghton Mifflin Company, 1917. (Cambridge: The Riverside Press). 292, [2] p., front., [3] leaves of plates. [Ill. by John Alonzo Williams.]
LC: O 8, '17.
PW: O 13, '17.

D-308 ____ The way of all earth / by Edith Barnard Delano. New York: Boni and Liveright, 1925. 283 p. **RBN**
LC: Ap 21, '25.
PW: Ap 18, '25.
BLC: London: Hodder & Stoughton, [1925].

D-309 ____ When Carey came to town / by Edith Barnard Delano . . . ; illustrations by W. B. King. New York: Dodd, Mead and Company, 1916. 280 p., front., [3] leaves of plates.
LC: Mr 21, '16.
PW: Mr 18, '16.

D-310 ____ Zebedee V. / by Edith Barnard Delano; illustrated. Boston: Small, Maynard and Company, [c1912]. 274 p., front., [3] leaves of plates. [Ill. by H. Burgess, Thomas Fogarty et al.]
LC: N 8, '12.
PW: O 12, '12.

D-311 Delanoy, M. Frances Hanford (Mary Frances Hanford). Afterclaps of fortune / by Frances Hanford Delanoy . . . New York; London; Montreal: The Abbey Press, [c1902]. 146 p.

D-312 ____ Coals of fire / by M. Frances Hanford Delanoy . . . New York; London; Montreal: The Abbey Press, [c1901]. 204 p., [1] leaf of photo. plates (port.).
PW: Je 15, '01.

D-313 De la Vergne, George H. (George Harrison), b. 1868. At the foot of the Rockies: (stories of mountain and plain), or, Boy life on the old ranche / by George H. de la Vergne. New York; London; Montreal: The Abbey Press . . . , [c1901]. 209 p.
Contents: I. A day's adventures in the mountains -- II. When we went hunting -- III. "Pike's Peak or bust" -- IV. Some military episodes -- V. The story of the diminutive pine -- VI. On the plains -- VII. Our Saturday at home -- VIII. My grandfather's ghost stories -- IX. The Fourth of July -- X. Among our books.

D-314 Dell, Berenice V. The silent voice / by Berenice V. Dell. Boston: The Four Seas Company, [c1925]. 474 p.
LC: My 5, '25.
PW: Ag 22, '25.

D-315 Dell, Floyd, 1887-1969. The briary-bush: a novel / by Floyd Dell. New York: Alfred A. Knopf, 1921.

425 p.
LC: N 25, '21.
PW: N 12, '21.
BLC: London: William Heinemann, 1922.

D-316 ____ Janet March: a novel / by Floyd Dell. New York: Alfred A. Knopf, 1923. 457 p.
LC: O 11, '23.
PW: O 20, '23.

D-317 ____ Moon-calf: a novel / by Floyd Dell. New York: Alfred A. Knopf, 1920. 394 p.
LC: N 5, '20.
PW: O 30, '20.
BLC: London: William Heinemann, 1922.

____ Phantom adventure. In *Prize stories of 1923 (1924), P-621.*

D-318 ____ Runaway: a novel / by Floyd Dell. New York: George H. Doran Company, [c1925]. 304 p.
LC: O 1, '25.
PW: O 3, '25.
BLC: London: Cassell & Co., 1926.

D-319 ____ This mad ideal: a novel / by Floyd Dell. New York: Alfred A. Knopf, 1925. 246 p.
LC: Mr 31, '25.
PW: F 28, '25.

D-320 The Dells of the Wisconsin: America's most beautiful summer home. Kilbourn, Wisconsin: The Wisconsin Dells Co., [c1903]. [40] p., ill. [Some photographs by H. H. Bennett.] **NYP**

D-321 De Long, Allen Percy. When the lilacs bloom / by Allen Percy De Long . . . [Fowler, Ind.: Benton Publishing Company, c1908.] 412 p., plates (partly col.).
Unexamined copy: bibliographic data from OCLC, #25859562.

D-322 De Long, Arthur H. (Arthur Hamilton), 1862-1919. It is not lawful: a romance / by Arthur H. De Long. New York: Eaton & Mains; Cincinnati: Jennings & Graham, [c1913]. 353 p., front.
LC: S 12, '13.
PW: S 27, '13.

D-323 Demarest, Virginia. The fruit of desire: a novel / by Virginia Demarest. New York; London: Harper & Brothers, 1910. 331, [1] p.
LC: Jl 22, '10.
PW: Jl 30, '10.

D-324 ____ Nobody's: a novel / by Virginia Demarest; with frontispiece. New York; London: Harper & Brothers, 1911. 336 p., front. [Ill. by Alice Barber Stephens.]
LC: Jl 22, '11.
PW: Jl 29, '11.

D-325 Demens, Inna. He who breaks / by Inna Demens. New York: Dodd, Mead and Company, 1918. 349 p. **DLC**
LC: Ap 13, '18.

DeMercado, J. See **Noel, Jean, pseud.**

D-326　De Meyer, Mahrah, b. 1875. Nadine Narska / by Mahrah de Meyer (Baroness de Meyer). New York: Wilmarth Publishing Company, 1916. 287 p.
LC: Ja 27, '17.

D-327　Deming, P. (Philander), 1829-1915. The story of a pathfinder / by P. Deming. Boston; New York: Houghton, Mifflin and Company, 1907. (Cambridge [Massachusetts], U. S. A.: The Riverside Press). 259, [1] p., photo. front. (port.). **NYP**
Partly reprinted from various periodicals.
Contents: The story of a pathfinder -- A lover's conscience -- A stranger in the city -- Mr. Green's promise -- In slavery days -- The secret story.
LC: My 2, '07.
PW: Je 1, '07.

D-328　De Montville, T. B. (Telesphore Boucher), b. 1867. The eternal quest / by T. B. de Montville. Boston: The Roxburgh Publishing Company, Inc., [c1915]. 212 p.
LC: Ja 17, '17.

D-329　Dendron, Bertram, *pseud.* The man in the moon, or, The unexpected / by Bertram Dendron [pseud.]. New York: Bonnell, Silver & Company, [c1901]. 100 p., ill.　　　　　　　　　　　　　**COH**
PW: My 10, '02.

D-330　Denio, Louise Coddington. The purple butterfly / by Louise Coddington Denio. N. Y. [i. e. New York]: Broadway Publishing Co., [c1907]. 187 p., front., [2] leaves of plates. [Ill. by Wm. L. Hudson.]
LC: Je 19, '07.

D-331　Denison, Webster, b. 1878. Fine feathers / novelized from Eugene Walter's drama by the same name by Webster Denison; with ten illustrations from photograhs. Chicago: A. C. McClurg & Co., 1914. 311, [1] p., double photo. front., [9] leaves of photo. plates.
LC: F 4, '14.

D-332　____ Help wanted: a novel of today done from Jack Lait's great play / by Webster Denison. New York: The Macaulay Company, [c1914]. 320 p., front., [3] leaves of plates.
Another edition: The H. K. Fly Company, [c1914].

D-333　Dennen, G. A. (Grace Atherton), 1874-1927. The dawn meadow / G. A. Dennen. Boston: Richard G. Badger, 1911. ([Boston]: The Gorham Press). 181 p.
LC: Ap 17, '11.
PW: Je 3, '11.

D-334　Denny, Mary Louise. The doctor and the parson / by Mary Louise Denny. New York; Washington: The Neale Publishing Company, 1905. 137 p.　**BGU**
PW: My 20, '05.

D-335　Denny, Mary Putnam. The chimes of freedom / Mary Putnam Denny . . . Boston: Richard G. Badger, [c1913]. ([Boston, U. S. A.]: The Gorham

Press). 121 p., photo. front.　　　　　　　**NYP**
LC: N 28, '13.

D-336　Dentinger, Willett E. "The false conviction": a vision: founded upon a foreign military drama of the first rank / by Willett E. Dentinger. Washington, D. C.: [s. n.], 1907. 62 p., photo. front. (port.). **NYP**
LC: D 5, '07.

D-337　De Packh, M. Twenty years in Siberia; and Leaves from my Russian diary / by baroness M. de Packh; seven startling illustrations. New York: Guarantee Publishing Co., [c1907]. 200 p., photo. front. (port.), [6] leaves of plates, photo. ill. (port.). [Ill. by Gustavus A. Haist.]　　　　　　　　　　**KKU**

De Plume, Icarus. See **Plume, Icarus de.**

D-338　Deppen, Anna Chase. Our right to love / by Anna Chase Deppen. New York: J. S. Ogilvie Publishing Company, [c1905]. 274 p., front., [10] leaves of plates. Decorated end papers.

D-339　Deprend, Jeffrey. Embers: a novel / by Jeffrey Deprend. Chicago: J. W. Wallace and Company, 1919. 340 p.
LC: N 18, '18.
BLC: London: Hurst & Blackett, [1920].

D-340　____ The golden poppy: a novel / by Jeffrey Deprend . . . Chicago: J. W. Wallace & Company, 1920. 313 p.　　　　　　　**OSU, NYP**
PW: Ja 31, '20.

D-341　De Puy, E. Spence (Edward Spence), b. 1872. Dr. Nicholas Stone / by E. Spence De Pue [sic]; illustrated by Frank X. Chamberlin. New York: G. W. Dillingham Company, [1905]. 251, [1] p., front., [11] leaves of plates.
PW: F 25, '05.
BLC: London: T. Fisher Unwin; New York [printed], 1905.

Derby, Alice Crittenden. A bloom of evening. See *Allegheny stories* (1902), A-142.

Derieux, Samuel A. Comet. In *Prize stories of 1921 (1922),* P-619.

____ The destiny of Dan IV. In *Thrice told tales (1924),* T-219.

____ The sixth shot. In *Prize stories of 1922 (1923),* P-620.

____ The trial in Tom Belcher's store. In *Prize stories of 1919 (1920),* P-617.

D-342　De Rodyenko, S. P. R. (Stephen Piero Sergius), b. 1888. Small Me: a story of Shanghai life / by S. P. R. de Rodeynko. New York: The James A. McCann Company, [c1922]. 217 p.
LC: Ja 23, '22.

D-343   Derville, Leslie. The other side of the story: a novel / by Leslie Derville. New York: G. W. Dillingham Company, 1904. 318 p.   **DLC**
PW: My 21, '04.
BLC: London: T. Fisher Unwin; New York [printed], 1904.

D-344   Dery, D. George (Desiderius George), b. 1867. Under the Big Dipper / by D. George Dery. New York: Brentano's, 1916. 398 p., col. front.
LC: Je 30, '16.

D-345   De Ryee, William, b. 1887. Truth unadorned: a romance of realism / by William De Ryee . . . ; frontispiece illustration by J. C. Terry. [San Francisco]: Overland Monthly Publishing Co., 1916. 325, [1] p., col. front. [Ill. by J. C. Terry.]
LC: O 2, '16.

D-346   De Saix, Tyler. The man without a head / by Tyler De Saix; illustrated by M. Leone Bracker. New York: Moffat, Yard and Company, 1908. 352 p., front., [3] leaves of plates.
LC: Ag 11, '08.

De Sélincourt, Basil, Mrs. <u>See</u> **Sedgwick, Anne Douglas, 1873-1935.**

Desmond, Arthur. <u>See</u> **Dilg, Desmond, jt. pseud. of Arthur Desmond and Will H. Dilg.**

D-347   Desmond, Dionne, b. 1861, *pseud.* New Ireland / by Dionne Desmond [pseud.]. Boston: Angel Guardian Press, [c1912]. 186 p., front.   **DLC**
LC: N 27, '12.

D-348   Desmond, Harry W. The heart of woman: the love story of Catrina Rutherford contained in writings of Alexander Adams / transmitted to Harry W. Desmond. New York: J. F. Taylor & Company, 1902. 311 p., front. [Ill. by Dee Woodward Zeigler.]
PW: S 13, '02.

D'Esque, Jean Louis, b. 1879. <u>See</u> **Stewart, pseud.**

D-349   Detzer, Karl, b. 1891. True tales of the D. C. I. / by Karl W. Detzer. Indianapolis: The Bobbs-Merrill Company, [1925]. 343 p.
Contents: Introduction -- The girl of the star-bright eyes -- The music of Robert the devil -- The viaduct buccaneers -- M'seer Sharley -- A matter of evidence -- The magic cloak -- "Feenish, M. P." -- The masquerader -- Camouflage -- Duds! A comedy -- The deadly hobnail -- Come among friends -- Cherchez le cop -- Through bolted doors -- Neglect of duty -- Number 52 Rue Nationale -- The guilty party.
LC: O 24, '25.

D-350   De Vane, I. C. (Isabella Cornelia), *pseud.* Doctor Carrington / by I. C. de Vane [pseud.]; illustrated by the author. New York; London; Montreal: The Abbey Press, [c1901]. 237 p., [17] leaves of plates.   **DLC**
PW: O 5, '01.

D-351   De Vere, Tom, *pseud.* Pointed pickings from the Arkansaw traveler . . . / by Tom De Vere [pseud.]; with original cartoons and illustrations. Chicago:

Laird & Lee, [c1913]. 255 p., front., ill.   **MNU**
LC: Je 20, '13.
PW: Jl 5, '13.

Devereaux, Thomas H. <u>See</u> **De Vere, Tom, pseud.**

D-352   Devereux, Margaret. Plantation sketches / by Margaret Devereux. Cambridge: Privately printed at The Riverside Press, 1906. 168, [1] p., photo. front. (port.), [1] leaf of photo. plates.   **YNG**
Contents: Letter to my grandchildren -- Plantation life -- Going to the plantation -- My own early home -- Two bob whites -- Little Dave -- The hog-feeder's day -- The junior reserve -- Mammy -- War reminiscences.
PW: Jl 7, '06.

D-353   Devereux, Mary, d. 1914. Lafitte of Louisiana / by Mary Devereux; illustrated by Harry C. Edwards. Boston: Little, Brown and Company, 1902. 427 p., front., [4] leaves of plates.
PW: Je 21, '02.

D-354   ____ Up and down the sands of gold / by Mary Devereux. Boston: Little, Brown and Company, 1901. 425 p.

D-355   Devinne, Paul. The day of prosperity: a vision of the century to come / by Paul Devinne. New York: G. W. Dillingham Company, [1902]. 271 p.
PW: Ag 30, '02.
BLC: London: T. Fisher Unwin; New York [printed], 1902.

D-356   Devinny, V. The story of a pioneer: an historical sketch in which is depicted some of the struggles and exciting incidents pertaining to the early settlement of Colorado / by V. Devinny. Denver, Colorado: The Reed Publishing Company, 1904. 164 p., photo. front. (port.), [6] leaves of photo. plates (some ports.).

D-357   Devney, R. S. (Raymond Smith), b. 1876. A brand new doctor / by R. S. Devney. Lexington, Ky.: James E. Hughes, Printer, 1908. 176 p., front. (port.), [3] leaves of plates. [Ill. by F. O. Putnam.]   **DLC**
LC: N 23, '08.

D-358   De Vore, J. W. (James William). Somewhat of a liar myself / by J. W. De Vore; with an introduction by Joseph Tyler Butts. New York; London: F. Tennyson Neely, [c1901]. 85 p., front. (port.)

D-359   De Vore, L. (Leonard). The fatal gun; or, The romance of Reasoners' Run / by Dr. L. De Vore . . . Girard, Kan.: Appeal Publishing Company, 1902. 88 p., front. (port.).
Unexamined copy: bibliographic data from NUC.
PW: N 8, '02.

D-360   De Voto, Bernard Augustine, 1897-1955. The crooked mile / by Bernard De Voto. New York: Minton, Balch & Company, 1924. 432 p.
LC: S 26, '24.
PW: S 27, '24.

D-361 [DeVries, Gerber M.] Chasco: Queen of the Calusas. New Port Richey, Fla.: New Port Richey Press, c1922. [18] p., ill.
Unexamined copy: bibliographic data from OCLC, #22974911.

D-362 [De Waters, Lillian], b. 1883. Glad tidings / by the author of "Journeying onward," "Thinking heavenward." Stamford, Conn.: Mrs. Lillian De Waters, [c1909]. 307 p.
Unexamined copy: bibliographic data from OCLC, #6243899.
Another edition: Boston, Mass.: Davis & Bond, [c1909].

D-363 _____ Journeying onward / by Lillian De Waters . . . Boston: Davis & Bond, [c1908]. 47 p.
LC: D 30, '07.

D-364 _____ A life illumined / by Lillian De Waters . . . Boston: Published by Davis & Bond, [c1913]. 256 p., front.
LC: S 10, '13.

D-365 _____ The regeneration of Martin Stone / by Lillian DeWaters. Boston, Mass.: Davis & Bond, [c1917]. 61 p.

D-366 _____ Within the veil / by Lillian De Waters . . . Boston: Davis & Bond, [c1911]. 57 p.
LC: S 27, '11.

D-367 [Dewey, Byrd, Spilman, Mrs.], b. 1856. The tale of Satan. [2nd ed., n. p. c1913.] 19 p., ill.
Unexamined copy: bibliographic data from OCLC, #1730170.

D-368 Dewhurst, Frederic Eli. The Magi in the west and their search for the Christ: a tale for the Christmas-tide / by Frederic E. Dewhurst. Indianapolis: The Sketching Club, 1903. 26 p.   **FUG**

D-369 Dewing, E. B., b. 1885. A big horse to ride / by E. B. Dewing. New York: The Macmillan Company, 1911. 505 p.
LC: Je 15, '11.
PW: Je 24, '11.

D-370 _____ Other people's houses / by E. B. Dewing. New York: The Macmillan Company, 1909. 369 p.
LC: O 21, '09.
PW: N 6, '09.

Dey, Frederic Van Rensselaer, 1856-1922. See **Vanardy, Varick, pseud.**

D-371 Dibble, Henry C. The sequel to a tragedy: a story of the far West / by Henry C. Dibble. Philadelphia; London: J. B. Lippincott Company, 1901. 276 p.

Dickey, Paul, 1885-1933, jt. aut. *The ghost breaker* (1915). See **Goddard, Charles W. (Charles William), 1879-1951, jt. aut., G-271.**

Dickinson, Hester A. The phantom coach. In *West winds* (1914), W-368.

D-372 Dickinson, Marion, d. 1909. The 'cello and other stories / by Marion Dickinson. Springfield, Mass.: Press of Loring-Axtell Company, 1910. 214 p., photo. front., [1] leaf of plates.
Contents: Preface -- The 'cello -- The captain's charge -- Billy and the tulip -- Paul's New Year's gift -- 'Tilda's enemy -- Granny's last Easter -- Heart's delight -- With Flossy's assistance -- 'Twixt friend and foe -- The awakening garden -- Arabella's great day -- The flowering currant -- The garden of forgotten flowers.

D-373 Dickson, Harris, 1868-1946. Duke of Devil-May-Care / by Harris Dickson . . . New York: D. Appleton and Company, 1905. 295 p., front., [3] leaves of plates. [Ill. by Harry C. Edwards.] **MNU**

D-374 _____ Gabrielle transgressor / by Harris Dickson; with frontispiece by Walter H. Everett. Philadelphia; London: J. B. Lippincott Company, 1906. 374 p., col. front.
LC: O 16, '06.

D-375 _____ The house of luck / by Harris Dickson . . . ; with illustrations by E. M. Ashe. Boston: Small, Maynard & Company, [c1916]. 452 p., front., [2] leaves of plates.
LC: N 15, '16.
PW: O 28, '16.

D-376 _____ Old Reliable / by Harris Dickson . . . ; with illustrations by Emlen McConnell and H. T. Dunn. Indianapolis: The Bobbs-Merrill Company, [c1911]. 341 p., front., [5] leaves of plates.
LC: My 18, '11.
PW: My 13, '11.

D-377 _____ Old reliable in Africa / Harris Dickson. New York: Frederick A. Stokes Company, [1920]. 340 p.
LC: O 11, '20.
PW: O 16, '20.

D-378 Dickson, Harris, 1868-1946. The Ravanels: a novel / by Harris Dickson; illustrated by Seymour M. Stone. Philadelphia; London: J. B. Lippincott Company, 1905. 420 p., front., [3] leaves of plates.
PW: Mr 25, '05.

D-379 _____ She that hesitates / by Harris Dickson; the illustrations by C. M. Relyea. Indianapolis: The Bobbs-Merrill Company, [1903]. 404 p., front., [5] leaves of plates.
BLC: London: Ward, Lock & Co., 1904.

D-380 _____ The siege of Lady Resolute: a novel / by Harris Dickson. New York; London: Harper & Brothers, 1902. 378, [1] p.
PW: Mr 1, '02.

D-381 Dickson, S. O'H. (Sallie O'Hear). Grandma Bright's Q. P.'s. Richmond: Presbyterian Committee of Publication, [1901]. 123 p.
Unexamined copy: bibliographic data from OCLC, #7235544.
PW: D 21, '01.

D-382 _____ Ralph Fabian's mistakes / by Miss S. O'H. Dickson. New York: Broadway Publishing Co., [c1908]. 175, [1] p.
LC: F 29, '08.
PW: Ap 11, '08.

D-383   Different girls / edited by William Dean Howells and Henry Mills Alden. New York; London: Harper & Brothers, 1906. 271 p.

Contents: The little joys of Margaret / Richard Le Gallienne -- Kittie's sister Josephine / Elizabeth Jordan -- The wizard's touch / Alice Brown -- The bitter cup / Charles B. De Camp -- His sister / Mary Applewhite Bacon -- The perfect year / Eleanor A. Hallowell -- Editha / William Dean Howells -- The stout Miss Hopkins's bicycle / Octave Thanet -- The marrying of Esther / Mary M. Mears -- Cordelia's night of romance / Julian Ralph -- The prize-fund beneficiary / E. A. Alexander.

LC: Ag 17, '06.
References: BAL 9772; Gibson & Arms, 06-D.

D-384   Diggs, Clara Morris. The curse at the door / by Clara Morris Diggs. Boston; New York: The Cornhill Publishing Company, 1922. 193 p.
LC: N 21, '22.
PW: Ja 20, '23.

D-385   Dilg, Desmond, *jt. pseud.* Rival Caesars: a romance of ambition, love and war: being the tale of a Vice-President, a Major-General and three brilliant and beautiful women / by Desmond Dilg [jt. pseud.]. Chicago: Thurland & Thurland, 1903. 302 p., front. [Ill. by Walter J. Enright.]
PW: Mr 28, '03.

Dilg, Will H. <u>See</u> **Dilg, Desmond, jt. pseud. of Arthur Desmond and Will. H Dilg.**

D-386   Dillenback, George P. The fascinating sin / by George P. Dillenback . . . New York City: Helen Norwood Halsey, [c1914]. 338 p.   **NYP**
LC: Jl 22, '14.

D-387   _____ The mills of the gods / by George P. Dillenback. New York: Broadway Publishing Co., [c1912]. 291 p.
LC: My 24, '12.
PW: Jl 20, '12.
Another edition: with photographic reproductions of scenes from the moving picture play as produced by the Vitagraph Company of America. New York: Grosset & Dunlap, c1912. 291 p., photo. front., [7] leaves of photo. plates.   **KGG**

D-388   Dilley, Edgar M. (Edgar Meck), b. 1874. The Red Fox's son: a romance of Bharbazonia / by Edgar M. Dilley; with a frontispiece in colour by John Goss. Boston: L. C. Page & Company, 1911. 363 p., col. front.
LC: Jl 7, '11.

Dillingham, Robert Barclay, pseud. See **Foulke, William Dudley, 1848-1935.**

D-389   Dillon, Mary C. Johnson. The American / by Mary Dillon . . . ; with illustrations by R. M. Brinkerhoff. New York: The Century Co., 1919. 300 p., front., [3] leaves of plates.
LC: Mr 24, '19.
PW: Mr 22, '19.

D-390   _____ Comrades / by Mary Dillon . . . ; with illustrations by R. M. Brinkerhoff. New York: The Century Co., 1918. 396 p., front., [3] leaves of plates.
LC: Ja 24, '18.

D-391   _____ The farmer of Roaring Run / by Mary Dillon . . . New York: The Century Co., 1920. 431 p., front. [Ill. by Hubert Mathews.]   **CWR**
LC: Ja 30, '20.
PW: Ja 31, '20.

D-392   _____ In old Bellaire / by Mary Dillon; with illustrations by C. M. Relyea. New York: The Century Co., 1906. 363 p., front., [5] leaves of plates.
PW: F 3, '06.

D-393   _____ The leader / by Mary Dillon; illustrated by Ruth M. Hallock. New York: Doubleday, Page & Company, 1906. 362 p., front., [3] leaves of plates.
LC: O 2, '06.
PW: S 8, '06.
BLC: London: Doubleday, Page & Co., 1906.

D-394   _____ Miss Livingston's companion: a love story of old New York / by Mary Dillon; with illustrations by E. A. Furman. New York: The Century Co., 1911. 434 p., front., [7] leaves of plates.
LC: Ap 24, '11.
PW: Ap 15, '11.

D-395   _____ The patience of John Morland / by Mary Dillon; illustrated by C. M. Relyea. New York: Doubleday, Page & Company, 1909. 406 p., col. front., [3] leaves of col. plates.
LC: Je 15, '09.
PW: Jl 17, '09.
BLC: London: Eveleigh Nash; New York printed, 1909.

D-396   _____ The rose of old St. Louis / by Mary Dillon; with illustrations by André Castaigne and C. M. Relyea. New York: The Century Co., 1904. 460 p., front., [7] leaves of plates.
PW: Jl 16, '04.

D-397   Dillon, Nell C. Love's toll: a novel / by Nell C. Dillon. New York: International Authors' Association, [c1917]. 208 p.
LC: My 7, '18.

D-398   Dimmitt, Della. The stairway to happiness: the story of a Christmas eve / by Della Dimmitt; decorations by Norma L. Virgin. Chicago: The Little Book Press, 1919. 39 p., front., ill.   **DLC**

Dinsmore, Dorothy Starr, ed. <u>See</u> **Smith, Margaret B. *The best of people* (1922), S-656.**

D-399   Dix, Beulah Marie, 1876-1970. The battle months of George Daurella / by Beulah Marie Dix. New York: Duffield & Company, 1916. 320 p.
LC: Mr 28, '16.
PW: Ap 8, '16.

D-400   _____ The beau's comedy / by Beulah Marie Dix & Carrie A. Harper. New York; London: Harper &

Brothers, 1902. 319, [1] p., front.
PW: Mr 29, '02.

D-401   _____ The fair maid of Graystones / by Beulah Marie
Dix . . . New York: The Macmillan Company;
London: Macmillan & Co., Ltd., 1905. 351 p.
PW: O 7, '05.

D-402   _____ The fighting blade / by Beulah Marie Dix; with
frontispiece by George Varian. New York: Henry
Holt and Company, 1912. 328 p., front.
LC: Ap 6, '12.
PW: My 4, '12.
BLC: London: Hodder & Stoughton, 1913.

D-403   _____ The gate of horn / by Beulah Marie Dix . . .
New York: Duffield & Company, 1912. 329 p.
LC: Ag 2, '12.
BLC: London: Methuen & Co., [1913].

D-404   _____ Hands off! / by Beulah Marie Dix . . . New
York: The Macmillan Company, 1919. 321 p.,
front. [Ill. by D. C. Hutchison.]   **BAI**
LC: O 22, '19.
BLC: London: Eveleigh Nash Co., 1920.

D-405   _____ Kay Danforth's camp / by Beulah Marie Dix.
New York: Duffield and Company, 1917. 153 p.,
front., plates.
Unexamined copy: bibliographic data from NUC.
LC: O 15, '17.

D-406   _____ The life, treason, and death of James Blount of
Breckenhow / compiled from the Rowlestone papers
and edited by Beulah Marie Dix. New York: The
Macmillan Company; London: Macmillan & Co.,
Ltd, 1903. 345 p.

D-407   _____ The little god Ebisu / by Beulah Marie Dix . . .
New York: Duffield & Company, 1914. 201 p.,
front., [2] leaves of plates.   **NYP**
LC: O 2, '14.
PW: O 10, '14.

D-408   _____ Maid Melicent / by Beulah Marie Dix . . . ;
illustrated in color by Lucius W. Hitchcock. New
York: Hearst's International Library Co., 1914.
202 p., col. front., [7] leaves of col. plates.   **NYP**
LC: S 30, '14.
PW: F 6, '15.

D-409   _____ The making of Christopher Ferringham / by
Beulah Marie Dix. New York: The Macmillan
Company; London: Macmillan & Co., Ltd., 1901.
453 p.
PW: Mr 23, '01.

D-410   _____ Merrylips / by Beulah Marie Dix; with
illustrations by Frank T. Merrill. New York: The
Macmillan Company; London: Macmillan & Co.,
Ltd., 1906. 307 p., front., [7] leaves of plates.
LC: S 25, '06.
PW: O 13, '06.

D-411   _____ Mother's son: a novel / by Beulah Marie Dix.
New York: Henry Holt and Company, 1913. 331 p.

LC: O 21, '13.
PW: N 8, '13.

D-412   Dix, Dorothy, 1861-1951, *pseud*. Fables of the elite /
by Dorothy Dix [pseud.]; illustrated by James A.
Swinnerton. New York: R. F. Fenno & Company,
1902. 261 p., front., ill.
"These sketches originally appeared in the columns of
The New York Journal."
Contents: The bear who loved the tigress -- The goat who played the
races -- How the owl became an oracle -- The female goose and the
silly hens -- The colt who had a college education -- The bear who
tried to be truthful -- The lion who was a prize -- The bearess whose
indifference charmed -- The bearess who was too good -- The donkey
who learned to kick -- The donkey who arbitrated society -- The hen
who understood the game -- The bearess who wanted a career -- The
goat who was a shining light -- The elephantess who tried to be cute --
The bear who was happy though married -- The lion who knew it all
-- The bear who travelled on his nerve -- The donkey who admired
his own perspicacity -- The bears who solved the divorce problem --
The bear who found nothing in economy -- The bearess who had
money -- The bear whose name was Willie Wisdom -- The lion who
tackled public office -- The bears who butted in on a strange game.
PW: My 3, '02.

D-413   _____ Hearts à la mode: illustrated / by Dorothy Dix
[pseud.] . . . New York: Hearst's International
Library Co., 1915. 157 p., front., [14] leaves of
plates. [Ill. by E. E. Ackley.]
Contents: Family stew -- To can a wife -- To preserve husbands --
Scrambled brains -- To roast a friend -- Cold cuts -- To pickle a
husband -- Mock husband -- Deviled mother-in-law -- Chicken-town
style -- Minced neighbor -- Frappés -- Shellfish-clams and lobster --
To put up peaches -- How to make dough.
LC: Ag 24, '15.
PW: O 23, '15.

D-414   _____ Mirandy / by Dorothy Dix [pseud.]; with
illustrations by E. W. Kemble. New York: Hearst's
International Library Co., 1914. 256 p., incl. front.,
incl. [19] leaves of plates.
LC: Ap 13, '14.
PW: My 9, '14.

D-415   _____ Mirandy exhorts / by Dorothy Dix [pseud.];
illustrated by E. W. Kemble. Philadelphia: The
Penn Publishing Company, 1922. 300 p., front., [4]
leaves of plates.
LC: O 6, '22.
PW: D 23, '22.

D-416   Dix, Edwin Asa, 1860-1911. Old Bowen's legacy: a
novel / by Edwin Asa Dix. New York: The Century
Co., 1901. 289 p.
PW: Ap 20, '01.

D-417   _____ Prophet's Landing: a novel / by Edwin Asa
Dix. New York: Charles Scribner's Sons, 1907.
254 p.
LC: Mr 22, '07.
PW: Ap 13, '07.

D-418   Dix, William Frederick, b. 1867. The face in the
girandole: a romance of old furniture / by William
Frederick Dix. New York: Moffat, Yard &
Company, 1906. 154 p., col. front., [3] leaves of
col. plates. [Ill. by Charlotte Weber-Ditzler.]
LC: O 27, '06.
PW: N 10, '06.

D-419   The lost princess / by William Frederick Dix.
New York: Moffat, Yard & Company, 1907.
297 p., col. front. [Ill. by Carle J. Blenner.]
LC: Ag 13, '07.
PW: S 14, '07.
BLC: London: Everett & Co., 1908.

D-420   Dixon, J. Qallan (James Qallan), b. 1851. Genevieve
de Brabant: an original novel of fact and fiction; a
romance of love, travel, self-sacrifice, adventure and
war in France, England, Italy, Malta and South
Africa / by J. Qallan Dixon. [Chicago: Donohue,
c1904]. 219 p., front. (port.).

D-421   Dixon, Royal, 1885-1962. Signs is signs / by Royal
Dixon; with illustrations by L. S. Geer. Philadelphia:
George W. Jacobs & Company, [1915]. 209 p.,
front., [11] leaves of plates, ill. Illustrated end
papers.
LC: Je 9, '15.

D-422   Dixon, Thomas, 1864-1946. The black hood / by
Thomas Dixon. New York; London: D. Appleton
and Company, 1924. 336 p., front. [Ill. by William
Fisher.]
LC: Je 19, '24.
PW: Je 21, '24.

D-423   The clansman: an historical romance of the Ku
Klux Klan / by Thomas Dixon, Jr.; illustrated by
Arthur I. Keller. New York: Doubleday, Page &
Company, 1905. 374 p., front., [7] leaves of plates.
"*The clansman* is the second book of a series of
historical novels planned on the race conflict."
PW: Ja 21, '05.
BLC: London: William Heinemann; New York
printed, 1905.

D-424   Comrades: a story of social adventure in
California / by Thomas Dixon, Jr.; illustrated by C.
D. Williams. New York: Doubleday, Page &
Company, 1909. 319 p., col. front., [3] leaves of
col. plates.
LC: Ja 12, '09.
PW: Ja 23, '09.
BLC: London: Doubleday, Page & Co.; New York
printed, 1909.

D-425   The fall of a nation: a sequel to The birth of a
nation / by Thomas Dixon; illustrated by Charles
Wrenn. New York; London: D. Appleton and
Company, 1916. 361, [1] p., front., [5] leaves of
plates.
LC: Je 3, '16.
PW: Je 10, '16.

D-426   The foolish virgin: a romance of today / by
Thomas Dixon; illustrated by Walter Tittle. New
York; London: D. Appleton and Company, 1915.
352, [1] p., front., [5] leaves of plates.
LC: S 23, '15.
PW: S 11, '15.

D-427   The leopard's spots: a romance of the white
man's burden--1865-1900 / by Thomas Dixon, Jr.;
illustrated by C. D. Williams. New York:

Doubleday, Page & Co., 1902. 465 p., front., [7]
leaves of plates. (some ports.).
PW: Mr 22, '02.
BLC: London: Doubleday, Page & Co., 1902.

D-428   The love complex / by Thomas Dixon. New
York: Boni & Liveright, 1925. 287 p.
LC: Je 22, '25.
PW: Je 20, '25.

D-429   The man in gray: a romance of North and
South / by Thomas Dixon. New York; London: D.
Appleton and Company, 1921. 427 p., front.
LC: N 3, '21.
PW: N 19, '21.

D-430   The one woman: a story of modern Utopia /
by Thomas Dixon, Jr.; illustrated by B. West
Clinedinst. New York: Doubleday, Page &
Company, 1903. 350 p., front., [7] leaves of plates.
PW: Ag 8, '03.
BLC: London: Doubleday, Page & Co.; New York
printed, 1903.

D-431   The root of evil: a novel / by Thomas Dixon;
illustrated by George Wright. Garden City, N. Y.:
Doubleday, Page & Company, 1911. 407 p., col.
front., [4] leaves of col. plates.
LC: Ja 27, '11.
PW: Ja 28, '11.

D-432   The sins of the father: a romance of the South
/ by Thomas Dixon; illustrated by John Cassel. New
York; London: D. Appleton and Company, 1912.
462 p., front., [15] leaves of plates.
LC: Ap 2, '12.
PW: Ap 13, '12.

D-433   The southerner: a romance of the real Lincoln
/ by Thomas Dixon; illustrated by J. N. Marchand.
New York; London: D. Appleton and Company,
1913. 543, [1] p., front., [5] leaves of plates.
LC: Je 17, '13.

D-434   The traitor: a story of the fall of the invisible
empire / by Thomas Dixon, Jr.; illustrated by C. D.
Williams. New York: Doubleday, Page &
Company, 1907. 331 p., col. front., [3] leaves of
col. plates.
"This volume closes . . . `The trilogy of
reconstruction.'"
LC: Jl 24, '07.
PW: Ag 3, '07.
BLC: London: Doubleday, Page & Company; New
York printed, 1907.

D-435   The victim: a romance of the real Jefferson
Davis / by Thomas Dixon; illustrated by J. N.
Marchand. New York; London: D. Appleton and
Company, 1914. 510, [1] p., front., [5] leaves of
plates.
LC: Jl 2, '14.
PW: Jl 11, '14.

D-436   The way of a man: a story of the new woman
/ by Thomas Dixon; illustrated by Stockton Mulford.

New York; London: D. Appleton and Company, 1919. 294, [1] p., front., [5] leaves of plates.
LC: Mr 5, '19.
PW: Mr 1, '19.

D-437 Dobbins, Douglas. Quarrytown / by Douglas Dobbins. Westerville, Ohio: Published by American Issue Publishing Company, [c1915]. 273 p., [6] leaves of plates. [Ill. by Russell Henderson.]
LC: Je 1, '15.

Dobie, Charles Caldwell, 1881-1943. All or nothing. In *Representative American short stories* (1923), **R-175.**

D-438 _____ The blood red dawn / by Charles Caldwell Dobie. New York; London: Harper & Brothers, [1920]. 357, [1] p.
LC: Je 11, '20.
PW: Je 5, '20.

D-439 _____ Broken to the plow: a novel / by Charles Caldwell Dobie. New York; London: Harper & Brothers, [c1921]. 315 p.
LC: Ag 27, '21.

_____ The cracked teapot. In *The best short stories of 1924 and the yearbook of the American short story* (1925), **B-569.**

_____ The failure. In *Atlantic narratives*; first series (1918), **A-360.**

_____ The hands of the enemy. In *The Harper prize short stories* (1925), **H-233.**

_____ Horse and horse. In *Prize stories of 1924* (1925), **P-622.**

_____ Laughter. In *The best short stories of 1917 and the yearbook of the American short story* (1918), **B-562.**

_____ The open window. In *The best short stories of 1918 and the yearbook of the American short story* (1919), **B-563.**

_____ Wild geese. In *The Harper prize short stories* (1925), **H-233.**

Dobree, Louisa Emily. The invitation. In *The Senior lieutenant's wager: and other stories* (1905), **S-312.**

D-440 Dodd, Anna Bowman, 1855-1929. The American husband in Paris / by Anna Bowman Dodd. Boston: Little, Brown & Company, 1901. 156 p., front. [Ill. by H. C. Ireland.]
PW: My 18, '01.

D-441 _____ In and out of a French country-house / by Anna Bowman Dodd; with illustrations by Robert Demachy. New York: Dodd, Mead & Company, 1910. 243 p., front., [14] leaves of plates.
LC: O 15, '10.
PW: O 22, '10.

D-442 _____ On the knees of the gods / by Anna Bowman Dodd. New York: Dodd, Mead & Company, 1908. 429 p.
LC: Ja 24, '08.
PW: F 8, '08.
BLC: London: B. F. Stevens & Brown; printed in U. S. A., 1908.

D-443 Dodd, Lee Wilson, 1879-1933. The book of Susan: a novel / By Lee Wilson Dodd. New York: E. P. Dutton & Company, [c1920]. 289 p.
LC: Jl 1, '20.
PW: Jl 31, '20.

D-444 _____ The girl next door: being the crabbed chronicle of a misanthrope / by Lee Wilson Dodd . . . New York: E. P. Dutton & Company, [c1923]. 224 p.
PW: Mr 10, '23.

D-445 _____ Lilia Chenoworth / by Lee Wilson Dodd. New York: E. P. Dutton & Company, [c1922]. 289 p.
LC: Ap 18, '22.
PW: Ap 15, '22.

D-446 _____ Pegeen and the potamus, or The sly giraffe, with some account of the wise old man who dwells in Tai-poo / by Lee Wilson Dodd, illustrated by Clarence Day. New York: E. P. Dutton & Co., [c1925]. 187 p., front., ill. Designed end papers. Cover title: *The sly giraffe with some account of the wise man who dwells in Tai Poo.*
LC: Jl 30, '25.
PW: Ag 22, '25.

Dodd, Robert Allen, b. 1887. See **Allen Robert, pseud.**

D-447 Dodds, Minnie Milbank. In this world of ours / by Minnie Milbank Dodds. New York: The Shakespeare Press, 1912. 432 p.   **DLC**
LC: My 10, '12.

D-448 Dodge, Henry Irving, 1861-1934. The hat and the man: an allegorical tale / by Henry Irving Dodge . . . ; illustrations by Dan Beard. New York: G. W. Dillingham Company, [1906]. 128 p., front., [5] leaves of plates.
LC: O 8, '06.
PW: D 1, '06.
BLC: London: T. Fisher Unwin; New York [printed], 1906.

D-449 _____ He made his wife his partner / by Henry Irving Dodge . . . ; illustrated by William Shewell Ellis. New York; London: Harper & Brothers . . . , 1919. 79 p., photo. front., [3] leaves of photo. plates.
     NYP
LC: Mr 21, '19.
PW: Ap 5, '19.

D-450 _____ The other Mr. Barclay / by Henry Irving Dodge; drawings by Nella Fontaine Binckley. New York: Consolidated Retail Booksellers, 1906. 373 p., front., [3] leaves of plates.
PW: Ap 21, '06.

D-451 _____ Skinner makes it fashionable / by Henry Irving Dodge . . . New York; London: Harper & Brothers, 1920. 111 p., front. **CLE**
LC: Ap 6, '20.
PW: Ap 10, '20.

D-452 _____ Skinner's baby / by Henry Irving Dodge. Boston; New York: Houghton Mifflin Company, 1917. (Cambridge: The Riverside Press). 243, [1] p.
LC: O 8, '17.
PW: O 20, '17.
BLC: London: Jarrolds, [1920].

D-453 _____ Skinner's big idea / by Henry Irving Dodge. New York; London: Harper & Brothers, [1918]. 79, [1] p.
LC: Mr 9, '18.

D-454 _____ Skinner's dress suit / by Henry Irving Dodge; with illustrations. Boston; New York: Houghton Mifflin Company, 1916. (Cambridge: The Riverside Press). 164, [2] p., front., [5] leaves of plates. [Ill. by F. Vaux Wilson.]
LC: O 3, '16.
PW: O 7, '16.
BLC: London: Jarrolds, [1919].

D-455 _____ The yellow dog / by Henry Irving Dodge. New York; London: Harper & Brothers, [1918]. 77, [1] p., front.
LC: My 27, '18.
PW: Je 8, '18.

D-456 Dodge, Louis, b. 1870. Bonnie May / by Louis Dodge; illustrations by Reginald Birch. New York: Charles Scribner's Sons, 1916. 356 p., front., [11] leaves of plates.
LC: Ag 30, '16.
PW: Ag 26, '16.

D-457 _____ Children of the desert / by Louis Dodge. New York: Charles Scribner's Sons, 1917. 312 p.
LC: Mr 14, '17.

D-458 _____ Nancy: her life and death / by Louis Dodge. New York: Charles Scribner's Sons, 1921. 66 p., front., [2] leaves of plates.
LC: O 6, '21.
PW: O 15, '21.

D-459 _____ Rosy / by Louis Dodge. New York: Charles Scribner's Sons, 1919. 331 p.
LC: My 1, '19.
PW: My 10, '19.

D-460 _____ A runaway woman / by Louis Dodge; illustrated by George Wright. New York: Charles Scribner's Sons, 1918. 394 p., front., [2] leaves of plates.
LC: O 15, '18.
PW: S 21, '18.

D-461 _____ Tawi Tawi / by Louis Dodge. New York: Charles Scribner's Sons, 1921. 348 p.
LC: Mr 31, '21.
PW: Ap 2, '21.

D-462 _____ Whispers / by Louis Dodge. New York: Charles Scribner's Sons, 1920. 261 p.
LC: Ap 23, '20.
PW: Ap 24, '20.

Dodge, Mary Mapes. The crow-child. In *Modern short stories* (1918), M-879.

D-463 Doling, Anna Mooney, b. 1875. Brilla / by Anna M. Doling. New York: The Neale Publishing Company, 1913. 201 p.

D-464 Dolly Winter: the letters of a friend which Joseph Harald is permitted to publish. New York: J. Pott & Co., 1905. 205 p.
Unexamined copy: bibliographic data from OCLC, #26835258.

D-465 Dolman, Maria, *pseud.* The pegsticks / by Maria Dolman [pseud.]. New York, N. Y.: Hermann Lechner, [c1911]. 114 p., front., [2] leaves of plates. [Ill. by Isabella Morton.] **DLC**
LC: D 30, '11.

D-466 Don-Carlos, Cooke, b. 1874. A bottle in the smoke / Cooke Don-Carlos. Boston, Mass.: Mayhew Publishing Company, 1907. 243 p., photo. front. [Ill. by Soule Art Co.] **DLC**
LC: S 23, '07.

D-467 _____ Virginia's inheritance / by Cooke Don-Carlos. Boston: Davis & Bond, [c1915]. 205 p.
LC: Ag 23, '15.

Don Jon, pseud. See Cheney, Walter Thomas.

Donn-Byrne, Brian Oswald, 1889-1928. See **Byrne, Donn, pseud.**

Donnell, Annie Hamilton, b. 1862. The feel doll. In *The heart of childhood* (1906), H-441.

_____ The minister. In *Quaint courtships* (1906), **Q-3.**

D-468 _____ Miss Theodosia's heartstrings / by Annie Hamilton Donnell; with illustrations by William Van Dresser. Boston: Little, Brown, and Company, 1916. 186, [1] p., front., [3] leaves of plates.
LC: O 2, '16.

_____ The princess of make-believe. In *Atlantic narratives,* 2nd series (1918), **A-361.**

D-469 _____ Rebecca Mary / by Annie Hamilton Donnell; with illustrations by Elizabeth Shippen Green. New York; London: Harper & Brothers, 1905. 193, [1] p., col. front., [8] leaves of plates.
PW: O 7, '05.
BLC: London: Hodder & Stoughton; printed in U. S. A., 1906.

D-470 _____ The very small person / by Annie Hamilton Donnell . . . ; illustrated by Elizabeth Shippen Green. New York; London: Harper & Brothers Publishers,

1906. 192, [1] p., col. front., [7] leaves of col. plates.
Contents: Little blue overalls -- The boy -- The adopted -- Bobby unwelcome -- The little girl who should have been a boy -- The lie -- The princess of make-believe -- The promise -- The little lover -- The child -- The recompense.
LC: O 25, '06.

D-471 Donnelly, Anna Foss. Honest hearts / by Anna Foss Donnelly. New York; London; Montreal: The Abbey Press, [c1902]. 221 p.

Donnelly, Eleanor C. (Eleanor Cecilia), 1838-1917. Little Nightengale's strange story. In *The Senior lieutenant's wager: and other stories* (1905), S-312.

D-472 ____ Miss Varney's experience: and other stories / by Eleanor C. Donnelly and Mary Genevieve Kilpatrick. Philadelphia: H. L. Kilner & Co., [c1901]. 184 p., front. (port.). **IUA**
Contents: Miss Varney's experience -- The wolf-gatherers -- The tragedy in the garden -- Hadrian Monreale -- Jaspar's wraith.
PW: D 7, '01.

D-473 [Donnelly, H. Grattan (Henry Grattan)], 1850-1931. Fairhaven: a story of pilgrim land / by Justis Henry G. D. [pseud.]. Boston: Christopher Publishing House, [c1917]. 177 p., front., [3] leaves of plates.
LC: Jl 10, '18.

D-474 Donoho, M. H. (Milford Hill), b. 1844. Circle-Dot: a true story of cowboy life forty years ago / by M. H. Donoho. Topeka: Monotyped and printed by Crane & Company, 1907. 256 p., photo. front. [Ill. by R. B. Hanford, Kansas City, Kansas.] **NYP**

D-475 Donovan, C. F. (Cornelius Francis), b. 1876. The left hander: a novel / by Rev. C. F. Donovan. Chicago: Joseph H. Meier, Publisher, [c1925]. 301, [1] p., front., [3] leaves of plates. [Ill. by J. T. Armbrust.]
LC: Ag 31, '25.
PW: O 3, '25.

D-476 Donworth, Grace. Down home with Jennie Allen / by Grace Donworth; with illustrations by Frederic R. Gruger. Boston: Small, Maynard and Company, [c1910]. 336 p., front., [5] leaves of plates, music.
LC: S 10, '10.

D-477 ____ The letters of Jennie Allen to her friend Miss Musgrove / by Grace Donworth; with sixteen illustrations by Frederick R. Gruger. Boston: Small, Maynard and Company, 1908. 291 p., front., [15] leaves of plates.
LC: O 24, '08.

D-478 Dooley, James H., Mrs. Dem good ole times / by Mrs. James H. Dooley; illustrated by Suzanne Gutherz; decorated by Cora Parker. New York: Doubleday, Page & Company, 1906. 150 p., col. front., [15] leaves of col. plates.
LC: O 20, '06.

Dooley, Sallie May. See **Dooley, James H., Mrs.**

Doonan, Grace Wallace, Mrs. See **Keon, Grace, b. 1873, pseud.**

D-479 Dorée, Nadage. The Sinful bachelor: and his sinful doings, a novel / by Nadage Dorée. New York; Philadelphia; Chicago: The News Company, 1908. 334 p., front. (port.).

D-480 Dorley, David, b. 1884, *pseud.* My ain Laddie / edited by David Dorley [pseud.]. Boston: The Stratford Publishing Co., 1922. 106 p.

D-481 Dorman, C. T. (Caroline Trotti), b. 1853. Under the magnolias / by C. T. Dorman. New York; London; Montreal: The Abbey Press, [c1902]. 251 p. **NDD**
PW: Ja 31, '03.

D-482 Dorr, Henry G. Mohawk Peter: legends of the Adirondacks and Civil War memories / by Henry G. Dorr; illustrations by Nellie L. Thompson. Boston: The Cornhill Publishing Co., [c1921]. 275 p., front., [7] leaves of plates. **NYP**

D-483 Dorrance, Ethel Arnold Smith, b. 1880. Back of beyond: an adventure story / by Ethel Smith Dorrance and James French Dorrance. New York: Chelsea House, [c1925]. 256 p.

D-484 [____] Damned: the intimate story of a girl / anonymous. New York: The Macaulay Company, [c1923]. 352 p.
LC: Mr 17, '23.
PW: F 10, '23.

D-485 ____ Flames of the Blue Ridge / by Ethel and James Dorrance. New York: The Macaulay Company, [c1919]. 342 p., front. [Ill. by George W. Gage.]
LC: N 1, '19.

D-486 ____ Get your man: a Canadian mounted mystery / by Ethel and James Dorrance; frontispiece by G. W. Gage. New York: The Macaulay Company, [c1921]. 302 p., front.
Unexamined copy: bibliographic data from OCLC, #11096484.

D-487 ____ Glory rides the range / by Ethel and James Dorrance . . . New York: The Macaulay Company, [c1920]. 308 p., front. [Ill. by George W. Gage.]
LC: Ap 1, '20.
PW: Mr 20, '20.

D-488 ____ His robe of honor / by E. S. and J. F. Dorrance. New York: Moffat, Yard & Company, 1916. 324 p. **OSU, NYP**
LC: O 11, '16.
PW: My 27, '16.

D-489 ____ Lonesome town / by Ethel and James Dorrance; frontispiece by G. W. Gage. New York: The Macaulay Company, [c1922]. 310 p., front.
LC: S 2, '22.
PW: S 16, '22.

D-490 ____ A maid and a man / by Ethel Smith Dorrance; with illustrations by Ch. Weber-Ditzler. New York: Moffat, Yard & Company, 1909. 243 p., col. front., [3] leaves of col. plates.
LC: S 17, '09.
PW: S 25, '09.

Dorrance, James French, b. 1879, jt. aut. *Back of beyond* (1925). <u>See</u> **Dorrance, Ethel Arnold Smith, b. 1880, jt. aut., D-483.**

_____, jt. aut. *Flames of the Blue Ridge* (1919). <u>See</u> **Dorrance, Ethel Arnold Smith, b. 1880, jt. aut., D-485.**

_____, jt. aut. *Get your man* (1921). <u>See</u> **Dorrance, Ethel Arnold Smith, b. 1880, jt. aut., D-486.**

_____, jt. aut. *Glory rides the range* (1920). <u>See</u> **Dorrance, Ethel Arnold Smith, b. 1880, jt. aut., D-487.**

_____, jt. aut. *His robe of honor* (1916). <u>See</u> **Dorrance, Ethel Arnold Smith, b. 1880, jt. aut., D-488.**

_____, jt. aut. *Lonesome town* (1922). <u>See</u> **Dorrance, Ethel Arnold Smith, b. 1880, jt. aut., D-489.**

D-491   _____ Never fire first: a Canadian Northwest mounted story / by James French Dorrance; frontispiece by Charles Durant. New York: The Macaulay Company, [c1924]. 309 p., front.
LC: Mr 21, '24.
PW: Mr 8, '24.
BLC: London: I. Nicholson & Watson, 1936.

D-492   Dorset, G. A successful wife: a story / by G. Dorset; illustrated. New York; London: Harper & Brothers, 1910. 304 p., front., [3] leaves of plates. [Ill. by James Montgomery Flagg.]
LC: Ag 23, '10.
PW: S 3, '10.
BLC: London: William Heinemann, 1910. British title: *The confessions of a successful wife.*

D-493   Dorsey, George Amos, 1868-1931. Young Low / by George A. Dorsey. New York: George H. Doran Company, [c1917]. 377 p.
LC: Je 19, '17.
PW: Je 16, '17.

D-494   Dorsey, John T. The lion of Judah / by John T. Dorsey . . . illustrated by Clovis E. J. Fouché and W. E. Scott. Chicago: Fouché Company, Inc., [c1924]. 207 p., ill.
Unexamined copy: bibliographic data from NUC.

D-495   Dos Passos, John, 1896-1970. Manhattan transfer / by John Dos Passos. New York; London: Harper & Brothers, 1925. 404 p.
LC: N 12, '25.
PW: N 21, '25.
References: Potter 7; Sanders A25-1.

D-496   _____ One man's initiation-- 1917 / by John Dos Passos. New York: George H. Doran Company, 1922. 128 p.   **MNU**

BLC: London: G. Allen & Unwin, 1920.
References: Potter 4; Sanders A20-1.

D-497   _____ Streets of night / by John Dos Passos. New

York: George H. Doran Company, [c1923]. 311 p.
LC: N 30, '23.
PW: N 24, '23.
BLC: London: Martin Secker, 1923.
References: Potter 6; Sanders A23-1.

D-498   _____ Three soldiers / John Dos Passos. New York: George H. Doran Company, [c1921]. 433 p.
LC: S 29, '21.
PW: S 24, '21.
BLC: London: Hurst & Blackett, [1922].
References: Potter 2; Sanders A21-1.

Dost, Zamin Ki, pseud. <u>See</u> **Armstrong, Willimina Leonora, 1866-1947.**

Doty, Madeline Z. Little brother. In *Atlantic narratives*; first series (1918), A-360.

D-499   A double knot, and other stories / by Mary T. Waggaman, Anna T. Sadlier, Magdalen Rock, Mary E. Mannix, Mary G. Bonesteel, Eugenie Uhlrich, S. M. O'Malley, Mary F. Nixon-Roulet, Maurice F. Egan, Grace Keon, Jerome Harte, Julia C. Walsh, Mary Boyle O'Reilly, Katharine Jenkins. New York; Cincinnati; [etc.]: Benziger Brothers, 1905. 212 p.
Unexamined copy: bibliographic data from NUC.
PW: D 2, '05.

D-500   Doubleday, Roman, 1862-1927, *pseud.* The green tree mystery / by Roman Doubleday [pseud.] . . . ; illustrated by Charles L. Wrenn. New York; London: D. Appleton and Company, 1917. 319, [1] p., front., [3] leaves of plates.   **MNU**
LC: S 17, '17.
PW: S 29, '17.

D-501   _____ The Hemlock Avenue mystery / by Roman Doubleday [pseud.]; illustrated from drawings by Charles Grunwald. Boston: Little, Brown and Company, 1908. 276 p., front., [3] leaves of plates.
LC: F 24, '08.
PW: F 29, '08.

D-502   _____ The red house on Rowan Street / by Roman Doubleday [pseud.] . . . ; with illustrations by William Kirkpatrick. Boston: Little, Brown and Company, 1910. 313 p., front., [3] leaves of plates.
LC: Mr 22, '10.
PW: Mr 26, '10.

D-503   _____ The Saintsbury affair / by Roman Doubleday [pseud.] . . . ; with illustrations by J. V. McFall. Boston: Little, Brown and Company, 1912. 296 p., front., [3] leaves of plates.
LC: F 13, '12.
PW: F 10, '12.

D-504   Dougherty, Harry V. (Harry Vincent), b. 1873. Well-- who killed him? / by Harry V. Dougherty. Boston: Richard G. Badger, [c1922]. ([Boston]: The Gorham Press). 173 p.   **VIC**
Contents: Well-- who killed him? -- The railroad mystery -- The blackmailer outwitted -- The police and the crime -- Crime knows no flag: a Mexican

detective story -- Crooks and others in tight places --
You mean Sherlock Holmes -- Marie Deval sings
"Martha" -- The underworld -- The visitor of mystery
-- The hidden romance -- Some reminiscences -- The
new London jewel robbery -- The nickel-plated
wrench -- The "Lamaser" or the man you are looking
for -- Seeing is not believing -- Problems the world
must face -- The eyes of the criminal -- Would you
have done likewise?
LC: S 25, '22.

D-505   Dougherty, Jeannette M. The secret name; a story
. . . by Jeannette M. Dougherty . . . Cincinnati:
Jennings and Pye; New York: Eaton and Mains,
[1903]. 240 p., front., [4] leaves of plates.
Unexamined copy: bibliographic data from NUC.
PW: Ja 2, '04.

Doughty, William Milton Sherwood. See **Millwood,
Sherman, pseud.**

D-506   Douglas, Amanda M. (Amanda Minnie), 1831-1916.
Honor Sherburne / by Amanda M. Douglas. New
York: Dodd, Mead & Company, [1904]. 340 p.
(The Sherburne series / Amanda M. Douglas.)
PW: O 15, '04.

D-507   ____ A question of silence / by Amanda M.
Douglas. New York: Dodd, Mead & Company,
1901. 365 p.
PW: Mr 9, '01.

D-508   ____ Sherburne inheritance / by Amanda M.
Douglas. New York: Dodd, Mead & Company,
1901. 383 p.
PW: O 26, '01.

D-509   ____ A Sherburne quest / by Amanda M. Douglas.
New York: Dodd, Mead & Company, [c1902].
369 p.
PW: D 6, '02.

D-510   Douglas, Charles Noel, 1863-1920. Uncle Charlie's
story book: fun, fact, and fancy. (Fiftieth birthday
souvenir) / Lovingly dedicated to old friends and new
by Charles Noel Douglas. Brooklyn: Charles Noel
Douglas, [c1913]. 157 p., photo. front. (port.), [1]
leaf of photo. plates (port.). Contents: The romance of Helen
Blackford -- How Uncle Charlie became a hero of the Spanish War --
The story of a rose -- The ghosts of the Mississippi -- Woman against
woman -- Lily, or Help wanted! -- A terrifying experience -- How
Maria met Uncle Charlie -- How Billy the Goat met Uncle Charlie --
The glorious Fourth and how we got it [play] -- "Stranded" [play].
LC: S 15, '13.

D-511   Douglas, Donald. The grand inquisitor / Donald
Douglas. New York: Boni and Liveright, [c1925].
318, [1] p. Designed end papers.
LC: F 18, '25.
PW: F 21, '25.

Douglas, Helen Cooper. Unseen hands. In *Greatest
short stories* **(1915), G-424.**

D-512   Douglas, James McKenzie. The black water o'Dee /
by James McKenzie Douglas; illustrated. Newton, N.
J.: The Nelson E. Barton Publishing Co., [c1922].

304 p., front., [2] leaves of plates. [Ill. by D.
Lubell.]
LC: Ja 8, '23.

D-513   Douglas, Malcolm, 1888-1968. He would be an
actor: a story of the stage / by Malcolm Douglas.
New York: The Metropolis Publishing Co., [c1903].
241 p.   **OSU, EAU**

D-514   Douglas, Mary. The husks of life: a love story / by
Mary Douglas. New York: Chelsea House, [c1925].
246 p.
PW: D 26, '25.

D-515   Douglass, James M., b. 1860. The riding master:
and other stories / by James M. Douglass. New
York; London: F. Tennyson Neely, [c1902]. 135 p.
Contents: Introduction -- The riding master -- A rare specimen --
Cypress Hedge Ranch -- Smith's promotion, and what it cost him --
The race for the seniors.
PW: S 13, '02.

D-516   Douglass, John Jordan. The girdle of the great: a
story of the new South / by John Jordan Douglass.
New York: Broadway Publishing Co., [c1908].
197 p., front., [1] leaf of plates. [Ill. by Wm L.
Hudson.]
LC: Mr 5, '08.

D-517   Dounce, Harry Esty. Cliartho philanders: a very
ancient idyll newly refurbished for another spring / by
Harry Esty Dounce. Clinton, New York: George
William Browning, 1909. 26 p.   **DLC**
LC: D 27, '09.

D-518   Dow, J. C., Mrs. The blue and the grey, or, After
many days / by Mrs. J. C. Dow, Sr. Chicago: M.
A. Donohue & Company, [c1904]. 188 p., [8] leaves
of plates (ports.).   **RCE**
PW: Jl 16, '04.

D-519   Dowd, Emma C., d.1938. Polly of Lady Gay
Cottage / by Emma C. Dowd; with illustrations.
Boston; New York: Houghton Mifflin Company,
1913. (Cambridge: The Riverside Press). 257,
[1] p., col. front., [3] leaves of col. plates. [Ill. by
Irma Dérèmeaux.]
LC: My 5, '13.
BLC: London: Constable & Co.; Cambridge, Mass.
[printed], 1913.

D-520   ____ Polly of the hospital staff / by Emma C. Dowd;
with illustrations. Boston; New York: Houghton
Mifflin Company, 1912. (Cambridge: Riverside
Press). 289, [1] p., col. front., [3] leaves of col.
plates. [Ill. by Irma Dérèmeaux.]
LC: Ap 4, '12.
BLC: London: Constable & Co.; Cambridge, Mass.
[printed], 1912.

D-521   ____ When Polly was eighteen / by Emma C. Dowd.
Boston; New York: Houghton Mifflin Company,
1921. (Cambridge: Riverside Press). 276, [2] p.,
front.
LC: S 12, '21.

D-522   Dowding, Henry Wallace. The man from Mars, or, Service, for service's sake / by Henry Wallace Dowding (Dunraven). New York: Cochrane Publishing Company, 1910. 385 p.
LC: N 17, '10.
PW: D 3, '10.

D-523   Downie, Vale, b. 1883. Robin the Bobbin / by Vale Downie; illustrated. New York; London: Harper & Brothers, [1915]. 96, [1] p., front., [1] leaf of plates. [Ill. by Denman Fink.]
LC: S 25, '15.

D-524   Downing, Hall. Nell Gwynne of old Drury: our lady of laughter: a romance of King Charles II and his court / by Hall Downing. Chicago; New York: Rand, McNally & Company, [1901]. 310 p.
PW: F 9, '01.

D-525   Downing, Henry Francis, b. 1851. The American cavalryman: a Liberian romance / by Henry F. Downing. New York: The Neale Publishing Company, 1917. 306 p.   **XQM**
LC: S 20, '17.

Downs, Sarah Elizabeth Forbush (Mrs. George Sheldon Downs). <u>See</u> **Sheldon, Georgie, Mrs., b. 1843.**

Dowst, Charles O., 1853-1919. Good advice. <u>In</u> *Second suds sayings* **(1919), S-266.**

____ , ed. <u>See</u> *Second suds sayings* **(1919), S-266.**

D-526   Dowst, Henry Payson, 1876-1921. Bostwick's budget / by Henry Payson Dowst. Indianapolis: The Bobbs-Merrill Company, [c1920]. 94 p., front., [2] leaves of plates. [Ill. by Frank Crerie.]
   OSU, NYP
LC: O 9, '20.
PW: O 30, '20.

D-527   ____ The man from Ashaluna / by Henry Payson Dowst. Boston: Small, Maynard & Company, [c1920]. 278 p.
LC: O 26, '20.

D-528   Doyen, E. Grattan (Edward Grattan). Satan of the modern world / E. Grattan Doyen. New York: Broadway Publishing Company, 1904. 291 p. Unexamined copy: bibliographic data from OCLC, #26835307.
PW: F 18, '05.

Doyle, C. W. The seats of judgment. <u>In</u> *Argonaut stories* **(1906), A-298.**

Doyle, Martha Claire (MacGowan), Mrs., b. 1868. <u>See</u> **James, Martha, pseud.**

D-529   Doyle, Mary Berry. The dead quickened / by Mrs. Mary Berry Doyle. New York: Broadway Publishing Company, [c1913]. 45 p.
LC: Ag 15, '13.

D-530   Drachman, Bernard, 1861-1945. From the heart of

Israel: Jewish tales and types / by Bernard Drachman; illustrated by A. Warshawsky. New York: James Pott & Company, 1905. 294 p., front., [15] leaves of plates.   **EEM**
Contents: Apologia pro libro suo -- The village Kehillah -- The little horseradish woman -- The general -- Too late, but on time -- The proselyte of righteousness -- Isaac and Alice -- The scissors-grinder -- The shlemihl -- A victim of prejudice -- The Rabbi's game of cards -- Glossary of Hebrew and other non-English terms.

D-531   Drago, Harry Sinclair, 1888-1979. Following the grass / by Harry Sinclair Drago; frontispiece by E. F. Ward. New York: The Macaulay Company, [c1924]. 320 p., front.
LC: Ag 8, '24.
PW: Ag 23, '24.
BLC: London: Hutchinson & Co., [1925].

D-532   [____] The hidden things / by J. Wesley Putnam [pseud.]. . . New York: The Macaulay Company, 1915. 245 p.   **DLC**
LC: D 13, '15.
PW: D 11, '15.

D-533   ____ Out of the silent North / by Harry Sinclair Drago; frontispiece by Frank Tenney Johnson. New York: The Macaulay Company, [c1923]. 304 p., front.
LC: Mr 17, '23.
PW: My 5, '23.
BLC: London: Hutchinson & Co., [1924].

D-534   [____] Playthings of desire / by J. Wesley Putnam [pseud.]; frontispiece by Delos Palmer, Jr. New York: The Macaulay Company, [c1924]. 317 p., front.
LC: O 8, '24.
PW: N 8, '24.

D-535   ____ Smoke of the .45 / by Harry Sinclair Drago; frontispiece by Frank Tenney Johnson. New York: The Macaulay Company, [c1923]. 311 p., front.
LC: O 9, '23.
PW: O 6, '23.
BLC: London: Hutchinson & Co., [1924].

D-536   ____ The snow patrol / by Harry Sinclair Drago; frontispiece by E. F. Ward. New York: The Macaulay Company, [c1925]. 255 p., front.
LC: S 2, '25.
PW: Ag 8, '25.
BLC: London: Hutchinson & Co., [1926].

D-537   ____ Suzanna: a romance of early California / by Harry Sinclair Drago; frontispiece by G. W. Gage. New York: Macaulay Company, [c1922]. 286 p., incl. front.
LC: D 16, '22.
PW: D 2, '22.
BLC: London: Hutchinson & Co., [1924].

D-538   ____ Whispering sage / by Harry Sinclair Drago and Joseph Noel. New York: The Century Co., 1922. 304 p., front.
LC: S 19, '22.
PW: S 30, '22.

D-539　[____] Whoso findeth a wife / by J. Wesley Putnam [pseud.]. New York: The Macaulay Company, 1914. 248 p.
LC: Jl 10, '14.

D-540　[____] The woman thou art / by Grant Sinclair [pseud.]. New York: The Macaulay Company, [c1925]. 320 p.
LC: S 17, '25.
PW: S 26, '25.

D-541　Drake, Alexander W. (Alexander Wilson), 1843-1916. Three midnight stories / by Alexander W. Drake. New York: The Century Co., 1916. 117 p., front. (port.), [7] leaves of plates (some ports.).
Contents: A memory / A. B. Paine -- The yellow globe -- Interlude-Kensal Green [poem] -- The curious vehicle -- Interlude-Paderewski [poem] -- The loosened cord -- Alexander W. Drake-The man: A brief biography / Clarence Clough Buel -- An appreciation / William Fayal Clarke -- A word of tribute / Robert Underwood Johnson.
LC: D 6, '16.

D-542　Drake, Austin Mann. The vial of Vishnu: the report of a cycle of events following the violation of the command that the vial must always remain in the possession of its rightful owner / by Austin Mann Drake. Chicago: Percy Roberts, 1915. 400 p.
LC: D 20, '15.

Drake, Carlos. The last dive. In *The best short stories of 1924 and the yearbook of the American short story* (1925), B-569.

D-543　Drake, Hoke S. (Hoke Smith). The corduroy prince / by Hoke S. Drake. [Johnson City, Tenn.: Muse-Whitlock Co., c1921.] 43 p.　　　**DLC**

Drake, Jeanie. On pigeon river. In *Through the forbidden gates* (1903), T-222.

D-544　Drake, Nicholas, author of The grey valley. Triangles / by Nicholas Drake . . . Richmond, Virginia: Southern Progress Publishing Co., [c1922]. 136 p.
Contents: The man with the scar -- Three letters -- Beyond the horizon -- The graphophone girl -- Among those missing -- Four dollars -- It will come out right -- The Hunt murder -- On a park bench -- The picture -- Four o'clock -- The hand of Nemesis -- Reincarnation -- The letter -- A lesson in contrast -- The son of Rachel.
LC: D 4, '22.

D-545　Drane, Hamilton. Madison Hood / by Hamilton Drane; illustrations by H. von Hofsten. Chicago: The Hamming Publishing Co., [c1913]. 314 p., front., [3] leaves of plates.
LC: Ja 6, '13.
PW: F 15, '13.

D-546　Dreer, Herman, b. 1889. The immediate jewel of his soul; a romance / by Herman Dreer. St. Louis, Mo.: St. Louis Argus Publishing Company, 1919. 317 p., photo. front., [3] leaves of photo. plates. Bibliographic data from 1969 facsimile.
PW: Ap 24, '20.

D-547　Dreisbach, George. The mystery of "the devil's kitchen": and other stories / by George Dreisbach. [Philadelphia: Printed by G. Dreisbach], c1921. 48 p.　　　**DLC**
Contents: The mystery of "The devil's kitchen" -- Impressions -- "I got you" -- The lumberman's daughter -- A young hero -- Tresckow falls -- The first settlers -- The ford's feat -- "The pulpit rock" -- "The slide" -- Roy's awakening -- A girl worth while -- The little slate picker.

D-548　Dreiser, Theodore, 1871-1945. An American tragedy / by Theodore Dreiser. New York: Boni & Liveright, 1925. 2 v.; Vol. I: 431 p. Vol. II: 409 p.
LC: D 23, '25.
BLC: London: Constable & Co., 1926. (2 vol.)
References: McDonald 18A; Orton 34; Pizer, Dowell & Rusch A25-1.

D-549　____ The financier: a novel / by Theodore Dreiser . . . New York; London: Harper & Brothers, 1912. 779, [1] p.
LC: O 26, '12.
PW: N 2, '12.
References: McDonald 4; Orton 8; Pizer, Dowell & Rusch A12-1.

D-550　____ Free: and other stories / by Theodore Dreiser . . . New York: Boni and Liveright, 1918. 369 p.
Contents: Free -- McEwen of the shining slave makers -- Nigger Jeff -- The lost Phoebe -- The second choice -- A story of stories -- Old Rogaum and his Theresa -- Will you walk into my parlor -- The cruise of the "Idlewild" -- Married -- When the old century was new.
LC: F 6, '19.
PW: Ag 24, '18.
References: McDonald 11; Orton 18; Pizer, Dowell & Rusch A18-1.

D-551　____ The "genius" / by Theodore Dreiser. New York: John Lane Company; London: John Lane, The Bodley Head; Toronto: S. B. Gundy, 1915. 736 p.
LC: O 7, '15.
PW: O 2, '15.
References: McDonald 7; Orton 12; Pizer, Dowell & Rusch A15-1.

D-552　____ Jennie Gerhardt: a novel / by Theodore Dreiser . . . New York; London: Harper & Brothers, 1911. 432, [1] p., front.
LC: O 21, '11.
PW: O 28, '11.
References: McDonald 3; Orton 6; Pizer, Dowell & Rusch A11-1.

____ The lost Phœbe. In *The best short stories of 1916 and the yearbook of the American short story* (1917), B-561.

____ Marriage-For one. In *Marriage* (1923), M-457.

____ Reina. In *The best short stories of 1923 and the yearbook of the American short story* (1924), B-568.

D-553   ____   The Titan / by Theodore Dreiser . . . New
York: John Lane Company; London: John Lane,
The Bodley Head; Toronto: Bell & Cockburn, 1914.
551, [1] p.
LC: My 26, '14.
PW: My 30, '14.
References: McDonald 6; Orton 10; Pizer, Dowell &
Rusch A14-1.

D-554   Drew, Anna Atwood. The Karls of Karltonville: and
their new thought or the life beautiful / by Anna
Atwood Drew. Boston: James H. Earle &
Company, 1905. 244 p., front.(port.), [6] leaves of
plates.

D-555   Drew, Reginald. Anne Boleyn / by Reginald Drew.
Boston: Sherman, French & Company, 1912. 364 p.
LC: Ja 8, '13.

D-556   ____   By the king's command / by Reginald Drew.
New York: Broadway Publishing Company, 1903.
328 p., front. [Ill. by Arthur Wiiliam Brown.]
PW: D 12, '03.

D-557   Driggs, Howard R. (Howard Roscoe), 1873-1963.
Wild roses: a tale of the Rockies / by Howard R.
Driggs. Chicago; Lincoln: University Publishing
Company, [c1916]. 248 p., front.
LC: O 26, '16.

D-558   Driggs, Laurence La Tourette, b. 1876. The
adventures of Arnold Adair, American ace / by
Laurence LaTourette Driggs; with illustrations from
drawings by Henry S. Watson and from photographs.
Boston: Little, Brown and Company, 1918. 335 p.,
front., [7] leaves of plates.   **AZS**
LC: My 6, '18.

D-559   Driscoll, Clara, 1881-1945. The girl of La Gloria /
by Clara Driscoll; illustrated by Hugh W. Ditzler.
New York; London: G. P. Putnam's Sons, 1905.
297 p., col. front., [5] leaves of col. plates.   **ILU**
PW: F 25, '05.

D-560   ____   In the shadow of the Alamo / illustrated by
Florence Eagar. New York; London: G. P.
Putnam's Sons, 1906. (New York: The
Knickerbocker Press). 205 p., incl. front., ill.
Contents: The custodian of the Alamo: I. The past. II. The present
-- Sister Genevieve -- Juana of the Mission de la Concepcion -- The
old priest of San Francisco de la Espada -- Tommy Huntress --
Phillipa, the Chili Queen -- The red rose of San José.

D-561   Driscoll, David A. From the melting pot into the
mold / by David A. Driscoll. Boston: The
Christopher Publishing House, [c1923]. 382 p.
                                                 DLC
LC: Ag 3, '23.

D-562   Driver, John Merritte, 1858-1918. Americans all: a
romance of the great war / by John Merritte Driver.
Chicago: Forbes & Company, 1911. 537 p.
LC: Mr 27, '11.
PW: Ap 8, '11.

D-563   ____   A modern tragedy; a romance of Italy and
America / by John Merritte Driver . . . Chicago:
Laird & Lee, [c1906]. 418 p., incl. plates, front.
Unexamined copy: bibliographic data from OCLC,
#26137368.

D-564   ____   Purple peaks remote: a romance of Italy and
America / by John Merritte Driver . . . ; illustrated.
Chicago: Laird & Lee, [c1905]. 418 p., col. front.,
ill. [Ill. by Farkas.]

D-565   Droke, Anna Elizabeth Scott. At the foot of No-Man
/ by Anna Elizabeth Scott Droke. Cincinnati:
Monfort & Company, [c1906]. 146 p.
LC: D 12, '06.
PW: F 9, '07.

D-566   ____   The diary of a minister's wife / by Anna E. S.
Droke; illustrations by George Avison. New York:
Eaton & Mains; Cincinnati: Jennings & Graham,
[c1914]. 259 p., front., [7] leaves of plates.   **YNG**
LC: Ap 13, '14.

D-567   Dromgoole, Will Allen, 1860-1934. The island of
beautiful things: a romance of the South / by Will
Allen Dromgoole . . . ; illustrated in color from
paintings by Edmund H. Garrett. Boston: L. C.
Page & Company, 1912. 302 p., col. front., [3]
leaves of col. plates.
LC: O 5, '12.
PW: O 19, '12.
BLC: London: Sir Isaac Pitman & Sons; Boston, U.
S. A. [printed], 1913, [1912].

Drum, Blossom. See **Oliphant, Blossom Drum.**

D-568   Drummond, Dale. The evolution of Peter Moore / by
Dale Drummond. New York: Britton Publishing
Company, [c1919]. 307 p., front., [3] leaves of
plates. [Ill. by Thelma Gooch.]
LC: F 18, '19.

D-569   ____   A man and a woman: a human story of life /
by Dale Drummond. New York: Britton Publishing
Co., [c1918]. 460 p., front., [3] leaves of plates.
[Ill. by Harold A. Van Buren.]
LC: S 20, '18.

D-570   ____   A woman who dared; a novel by Dale
Drummond . . . New York: Britton Publishing
Company, [c1919]. 312 p., col. front.
Unexamined copy: bibliographic data from NUC.
LC: S 15, '19.
PW: N 1, '19.

D-571   Drummond, Florence. An American wooing / by
Florence Drummond. Boston; New York: Houghton
Mifflin Company, 1912. 301 p.
BLC: London: Grant Richards, 1912.

D-572   Dryden, Charles. On and off the breadwagon: being
the hard luck tales, doings and adventures of an
amateur hobo / by Charles Dryden . . . ; illustrated
by Hy. Gage. Chicago: Star Publishing Company;
Chicago: Trade supplied by The Reilly & Britton
Company, [c1905]. 266 p., incl. front., ill.   **DLC**

D-573 Dryden, Henry Francis. A financial fiction / by Henry Francis Dryden . . . San Francisco: [s. n.], 1919. 38 p.
Caption title: *The new cashier's thrift campaign.*

D-574 ____ Jimmy's gentility / by Henry Francis Dryden. Boston: Sherman, French & Company, 1915. 379 p.
LC: Jl 28, '15.
PW: Jl 31, '15.

D-575 Drysdale, William, 1852-1901. Pine Ridge plantation, or, The trials and successes of a young cotton planter / by William Drysdale . . . New York: Thomas Y. Crowell & Co., [c1901]. 320 p. front., [7] leaves of plates (some photo.). [Ill. by Charles Copeland.]
PW: O 19, '01.

D-576 DuBois, James T., 1851-1920. Fun and pathos of one life / by James T. Du Bois. New York; Washington: The Neale Publishing Company, 1908. 187 p.
LC: Je 25, '08.

D-577 Du Bois, Mary Constance, 1879-1959. Elinor Arden: royalist / by Mary Constance Du Bois; with illustrations by W. Benda. New York: The Century Co., 1904. 283 p., front., [17] leaves of plates.

D-578 Du Bois, W. E. B. (William Edward Burghardt), 1868-1963. The quest of the Silver Fleece: a novel / by W. E. Burghardt DuBois . . . ; illustrated by H. S. DeLay. Chicago: A. C. McClurg & Co., 1911. 434 p., front., [3] leaves of plates.
LC: N 6, '11.
PW: D 2, '11.

D-579 Du Bose, Horace M. (Horace Mellard), 1858-1941. The men of Sapio ranch / by Horace M. Du Bose. Nashville, Tenn.: Publishing House of the M. E. Church, South; Dallas, Tex.: Smith & Lamar, agents, 1909. 221 p., front., [6] leaves of plates. [Ill. by Latimer J. Wilson.]
LC: My 12, '09.

D-580 Du Bosque, Francis. Carlotta Cortina / by Francis Du Bosque. New York: Benj. R. Tucker, 1906. 28 p. **NYP**

D-581 ____ Johann Schmidt / by Francis Du Bosque . . . New York: Benj. R. Tucker, 1907. 44 p. **NYP**

D-582 Dudley, Carl Hermon. And this is war / by Carl Hermon Dudley. New York: Cochrane Publishing Company, 1910. 150 p. **TJC**
LC: Ap 21, '10.
PW: My 21, '10.

D-583 Dudley, E. Lawrence (Edward Lawrence), b. 1879. The Isle of Whispers: a tale of the New England seas / by E. Lawrence Dudley. New York: Henry Holt and Company, 1910. 297 p.
LC: F 24, '10.

D-584 ____ Spriggles: a tale of youth / by E. Lawrence Dudley . . . ; frontispiece by George Gibbs. New York; London: D. Appleton and Company, 1919. 465, [1] p., front. **NYP**
LC: Ag 12, '19.
PW: S 6, '19.

Dudman, Ada, Mrs. See **Dolman, Maria, pseud.**

Duer, Alice. See **Miller, Alice Duer, 1874-1942.**

D-585 Duer, Caroline King, 1865-1956. Unconscious comedians / by Caroline Duer. New York: Dodd, Mead & Company, 1901. 317 p. **AZU**
Contents: An unaccountable countess -- The aloofness of Lucy -- My niece, Mrs. Dove -- An unfinished elopement -- Rumours.
PW: O 5, '01.

D-586 Duer, Elizabeth. The prince goes fishing / Elizabeth Duer. New York: D. Appleton and Company, 1906. 299 p., front., [3] leaves of plates. [Ill. by Arthur E. Becher.] **VA@**
LC: S 28, '06.
PW: O 6, '06.

D-587 Duffus, R. L. (Robert Luther), 1888-1972. The coast of Eden / by Robert L. Duffus. New York: The Macmillan Company, 1923. 281 p.
LC: Ja 31, '23.
PW: F 10, '23.

D-588 ____ Roads going south / by Robert L. Duffus. New York: The Macmillan Company, 1921. 292 p.
LC: S 21, '21.
BLC: London: Eveleigh Nash & Co.; printed in U. S. A., 1923.

D-589 Duffy, James O. G. (James Oscar Greeley), 1864-1933. Glass & gold: a novel / by James O. G. Duffy. Philadelphia; London: J. B. Lippincott Company, 1901. 374 p.
PW: N 2, '01.

D-590 Duffy, Richard, b. 1873. An adventure in exile: a sentimental comedy / by Richard Duffy. New York: B. W. Dodge & Company, 1908. 359 p.
LC: N 12, '08.

D-591 Duganne, Phyllis. Prologue / by Phyllis Duganne. New York: Harcourt, Brace and Howe, 1920. 304 p.
LC: Ag 28, '20.
PW: S 18, '20.

D-592 Duggan, Janie Prichard. An isle of Eden: a story of Porto Rico / by Janie Prichard Duggan . . . Philadelphia: The Griffith & Rowland Press, 1912. 346 p., col. front., [10] leaves of plates.
LC: D 28, '12.

D-593 Duke, Mary Kerr. The mystery of Castlegreen; a Louisiana romance / by Duke. New York: Broadway Publishing Co., 1913. 175 p.
Unexamined copy: bibliographic data from OCLC, #5820230.
LC: Mr 6, '13.

D-594   Dunbar, Aldis, b. 1870. The sons o' Cormac, an'
        tales of other men's sons / by Aldis Dunbar. New
        York: E. P. Dutton & Company [c1920]. 233 p.
        Unexamined copy: bibliographic data from OCLC,
        #5740562.

        Dunbar, Olivia Howard. The shell of sense. In
        Famous modern ghost stories (1921), F-18.

D-595   Dunbar, Paul Laurence, 1872-1906. The fanatics /
        by Paul Laurence Dunbar . . . New York: Dodd,
        Mead and Company, 1901. 312 p.
        LC: Mr 11, '01.
        PW: Mr 30, '01.
        References: BAL 4936.

D-596   _____ The heart of Happy Hollow / by Paul Laurence
        Dunbar . . . illustrated by E. W. Kemble. New
        York: Dodd, Mead and Company, 1904. 309 p.,
        front., [5] leaves of plates.   **MIA**
        LC: O 25, '04.
        PW: N 12, '04.
        References: BAL 4950.

D-597   _____ In old plantation days / by Paul Laurence
        Dunbar . . . ; illustrated. New York: Dodd, Mead
        and Company, 1903. 307 p., front., [9] leaves of
        plates. [Ill. by Martin Justice.]
        Contents: Aunt Tempe's triumph -- Aunt Tempe's revenge -- The
        walls of Jericho -- How Brother Parker fell from grace -- The trousers
        -- The last fiddling of Mordaunt's Jim -- A supper by proxy -- The
        trouble about Sophiny -- Mr. Groby's slippery gift -- Ash-cake
        Hannah and her Ben -- Dizzy-headed Dick -- The conjuring contest --
        Dandy Jim's conjure scare -- The memory of Martha -- Who stand
        for the Gods -- A lady slipper -- A blessed deceit -- The brief cure of
        Aunt Fanny -- The Stanton coachman -- The Easter wedding -- The
        finding of Martha -- The defection of Maria Ann Gibbs -- A judgment
        of Paris -- Silent Sam'el -- The way of a woman.
        LC: S 23, '03.
        PW: O 10, '03.
        References: BAL 4946.

D-598   _____ The sport of the gods / by Paul Laurence
        Dunbar . . . New York: Dodd, Mead and Company,
        1902. 255 p.
        LC: Ap 14, '02.
        PW: My 10, '02.
        References: BAL 4939.

D-599   Dunbar, Ruth. The Swallow: a novel based upon the
        actual experiences of one of the survivors of the
        famous Lafayette escadrille / by Ruth Dunbar. New
        York: Boni and Liveright, 1919. 246 p.
        LC: My 29, '19.
        PW: My 10, '19.

D-600   Duncan, Frances, b. 1877. My garden doctor / by
        Frances Duncan. Garden City, N. Y.: Doubleday,
        Page and Company, 1914. 192 p.
        LC: Mr 28, '14.
        PW: Ap 4, '14.

D-601   _____ Roberta of Roseberry Gardens / by Frances
        Duncan . . . ; illustrated by Jane Donald. Garden
        City, New York: Doubleday, Page & Company,
        1916. 265, [1] p., col. front., [1] leaf of col. plates.
        LC: Ap 18, '16.
        PW: Ap 29, '16.

D-602   Duncan, Georgia Elizabeth. Samanthy Billins of
        Hangin'-Dog / by Georgia Elizabeth Duncan;
        illustrated by Rosine Raoul. Atlanta, Georgia:
        Mutual Publishing Company, December, 1905.
        199 p.   **GSU**

D-603   Duncan, James A., b. 1853, *pseud.* It's mighty
        strange, or, "The older, the newer" / by James A.
        Duncan [pseud.]. Boston: The Stratford Company,
        1918. 319 p.
        LC: Ja 16, '18.

D-604   Duncan, Norman, 1871-1916. Battles royal down
        North / by Norman Duncan . . . ; with an
        appreciation by Wilfred T. Grenfell . . . ; illustrated.
        New York; Chicago; London; Edinburgh: Fleming
        H. Revell Company, [c1918]. 269 p., photo. front.
        (port.), [3] leaves of plates. [Ill. by Walt
        Louderback.]
        Contents: The rose of great price -- The long arm -- The last Lucifer
        -- White water -- The wreck of the Rough-an'-Tumble.
        LC: D 31, '18.
        PW: Ag 24, '18.

D-605   _____ The best of a bad job: a hearty tale of the sea /
        by Norman Duncan . . . New York; Chicago;
        Toronto; London; Edinburgh: Fleming H. Revell
        Company, [c1912]. 204 p., front., [3] leaves of
        plates. [Ill. by George Harding.]
        LC: Ja 2, '13.
        PW: N 9, '12.

D-606   _____ The bird-store man: an old-fashioned story /
        Norman Duncan; illustrated by C. H. Taffs. [New
        York]: Fleming H. Revell Company, [c1914].
        136 p., front., [4] leaves of plates.
        LC: S 21, '14.
        PW: S 5, '14.

D-607   _____ Christmas Eve at Swamp's End / Norman
        Duncan . . . [New York]: Fleming H. Revell
        Company, [c1911-1915]. 32 p., front., ill.
        Contents: The wistful heart -- A gift neglected -- The making of a
        man -- Christmas Eve at Swamp's End.

D-608   _____ Christmas Eve at Topmast Tickle / by Norman
        Duncan. [New York]: Fleming H. Revell Company,
        [c1910]. 32 p., front.   **BBH**

D-609   _____ The cruise of the Shining Light / by Norman
        Duncan . . . New York; London: Harper &
        Brothers, 1907. 343, [1] p.
        LC: Ap 11, '07.
        PW: Ap 20, '07.

D-610   _____ Doctor Luke of the Labrador / by Norman
        Duncan. [New York; Chicago; Toronto; London;
        Edinburgh]: Fleming H. Revell Company, [c1904].
        327 p. Illustrated end papers.
        PW: N 19, '04.
        BLC: London: Hodder & Stoughton, 1904.

        _____ Dr. Grenfell's parish. In *The joy in work*
        (1920), J-229.

D-611   _____ Every man for himself / by Norman Duncan
. . . New York; London: Harper & Brothers, 1908.
304, [1] p., front., [5] leaves of plates. [Ill. by
George Harding and William Hurd Lawrence.]
LC: S 17, '08.
PW: S 26, '08.

D-612   _____ Finding his soul / by Norman Duncan . . . ;
illustrated. New York; London: Harper & Brothers,
1913. 61, [1] p., front., ill.
LC: O 4, '13.
PW: O 11, '13.

D-613   _____ Harbor tales down north / by Norman Duncan
. . . ; with an appreciation by Wilfred T. Grenfell
. . . ; illustrated. New York; Chicago; London;
Edinburgh: Fleming H. Revell Company, [c1918].
282 p., photo. front. (port.), [4] leaves of plates. [Ill.
by Jay Hambidge.]
Contents: I. Madman's luck -- II. The siren of Scalawag Run -- III.
The art of Terry Lute -- IV. The doctor of Afternoon Arm -- V. A
Crœsus of Gingerbread Cove -- VI. A madonna of Tinkle Tickle --
VII. The little nipper o' Hide-an'-seek Harbor -- VIII. Small Sam
Small -- IX. An idyl of Rickity Tickle.
LC: D 31, '18.
PW: Ag 24, '18.

D-614   _____ The measure of a man: a tale of the big woods
/ by Norman Duncan . . . New York; Chicago;
Toronto; London; Edinburgh: Fleming H. Revell
Company, [c1911]. 356 p., front., [2] leaves of
plates. [Ill. by George Harding.]
LC: O 21, '11.
PW: S 9, '11.
BLC: London: Hodder & Stoughton, [1912].

D-615   _____ The mother / by Norman Duncan. [New
York; Chicago; Toronto]: Fleming H. Revell
Company, [c1905]. 220 p., col. front. [Ill. by H. E.
Fritz.]
PW: O 21, '05.
BLC: London: Hodder & Stoughton, [1905].

_____ A romance of Whooping Harbor. In *Quaint
courtships* (1906), Q-3.

D-616   _____ The suitable child / by Norman Duncan;
illustrated by Elizabeth Shippen Green. New York;
Chicago; Toronto; London; Edinburgh: Fleming H.
Revell Company, [c1909]. 96 p., front., [4] leaves of
plates. Illustrated end papers.
LC: O 30, '09.
PW: O 23, '09.

D-617   _____ The way of the sea / by Norman Duncan . . . ;
frontispiece by Howard Pyle. New York: McClure,
Phillips & Co., 1903. 332 p., front.
Contents: The chase of the tide -- The strength of men -- The raging
of the sea -- The breath of the north -- Concerning Billy Luff and
Master Goodchild -- The love of the maid -- The healer from Far-
away Cove -- In the fear of the Lord -- A beat t' harbour -- The fruits
of toil.
"The stories are reprinted [from] . . . `McClure's
magazine' . . . `Ainslie's magazine,' the `Atlantic
monthly,' the `Evening post' (New York), and
`Harper's monthly magazine'".
PW: O 3, '03.
BLC: London: Hodder & Stoughton, [1904].

D-618   Duncan, Walter, b. 1884. The fourth at bridge: and
other stories / by Walter Duncan. New York: The
Shakespeare Press, 1912. 168 p.   **SUC**
Contents: The fourth at bridge -- The gray hour -- Fair exchange or
robbery? -- The man that didn't come back -- By freight-collect -- The
parallel -- Kenny's debt -- "Zeek'yel" -- The climax -- It pays to
advertise -- The other scare head -- Blind baggage.
LC: D 21, '12.

D-619   Dunckel, John. The Mollyjoggers: tales of the
camp-fire: a brief history of the origin and
experiences of an old James River fishing and hunting
club, and a collection of stories, poems, etc., as told
and recited around the camp-fire / by John Dunckel;
illustrated. Springfield, Missouri: Published by H.
S. Jewell, [190-]. 83 p., ill. [Ill. by F. Finch.]
Designed end papers.   **KCP**
Contents (fiction only): First night: A trip with the Mollyjoggers --
The paper story -- The noodle factory story -- The raft story -- The
conjured fishing hole. Second night: McLarty's new saloon -- Wid
Krumpley's letter -- The diver's story -- High explosives -- The load
of hay. Third night: The rat story -- Moving hell -- Monkey wrench
-- Aeronaut in Mississippi -- The Swede juror -- The Dutchman's
advice to his dog -- The ginger snap. Fifth night: Dutch political
speech -- Who would not vote for a brewer? -- The bull story. Last
night: Dutch politician -- Minneapolis and St. Paul -- Polar bear.

D-620   Dungan, D. R. (David Roberts), 1837-1920. Rosa
Gray: a story taken from real life / by D. R. Dungan
. . . Cincinnati, O.: The Standard Publishing Co.,
[c1904]. 424 p., front., [5] leaves of plates.
PW: Ap 22, '05.

D-621   Dunham, Anna C. (Anna Cross), b. 1846. The
corduroy road: a tale of pioneer life in the Middle
West in the early 40's / by Anna C. Dunham;
illustrations by E. N. Clark. Akron, Ohio: The
Werner Company, [c1909]. 234 p., front., [3] leaves
of plates.
LC: O 29, '09.

D-622   Dunham, Curtis. Gamboling with Galatea: a bucolic
romance / by Curtis Dunhamn; with illustrations by
Oliver Herford. Boston; New York: Houghton
Mifflin Company, 1909. (Cambridge: Riverside
Press). 185, [1] p., col. front., [5] leaves of col.
plates.
LC: My 15, '09.

D-623   Duniway, Abigail Scott, 1834-1915. From the West
to the West: across the plains to Oregon / by Abigail
Scott Duniway; with frontispiece in color. Chicago:
A. C. McClurg & Co., 1905. 311 p., col. front. [Ill.
by The Decorative Designers.]

D-624   Dunlap, Fanny E. The gift of the Nile; Jephthah's
daughter; Stephen / by Fanny E. Dunlap; with
introduction By Alice Hegan Rice. New York: The
Knickerbocker Press, 1904. 56 p.

D-625   [Dunlap, Roberta K.] Mabel Gordon: a novel / by
R. K. D. New York: J. S. Ogilvie Publishing
Company, c1901. 250 p.   **DLC**
PW: Ap 6, '01.

D-626   Dunn, Ella H. (Ella Heustis), b. 1851. The castle of
many mirrors and their sequel / by Ella H. Dunn.
Chicago: M.A. Donohue & Company, [c1906].

287 p., [4] leaves of plates. [Ill. by Linda M. Jensen.]   **DLC**
LC: D 22, '07.

D-627   Dunn, J. Allan (Joseph Allan Elphinstone), 1872-1941. Dead man's gold / by J. Allan Dunn; frontispiece by Ralph Pallen Coleman. Garden City, N. Y.: Doubleday, Page & Company, 1920. 246 p., col. front.
LC: Ag 12, '20.
PW: Jl 17, '20.
BLC: London: Hurst & Blackett; Garden City, N. Y. [printed, 1921].

D-628   _____ The girl of Ghost Mountain / by J. Allan Dunn. Boston: Small, Maynard & Company, [c1921]. 273 p.
LC: D 21, '21.

D-629   _____ Jim Morse gold-hunter / by J. Allan Dunn . . . Boston: Small, Maynard & Company, [c1920]. 266 p.
LC: O 30, '20.

D-630   _____ Jim Morse, south sea trader / by J. Allan Dunn . . . Boston: Small, Maynard & Company, [c1919]. 239 p., front., plates.
Unexamined copy: bibliographic data from OCLC, #17610925.
LC: S 24, '19.

D-631   _____ A man to his mate / J. Allan Dunn . . . illustrated by Stockton Mulford. Indianapolis: The Bobbs-Merrill Company, [c1920]. 335 p., front., [3] leaves of plates.   **OSU, CLU**
LC: O 25, '20.
PW: O 30, '20.
BLC: London: Hurst & Blackett, [1921].

D-632   _____ The man trap / by J. Allan Dunn; frontispiece by Ralph Pallen Coleman. Garden City, N. Y.; Toronto: Doubleday, Page & Company, 1921. 294 p., front.
LC: Mr 19, '21.
BLC: London: Hurst & Blackett, [1922].

D-633   _____ Rimrock trail / by J. Allan Dunn; illustrated by Modest Stein. Indianapolis: The Bobbs-Merrill Company, [c1922]. 397 p., front., [3] leaves of plates.
LC: Ap 3, '22.
BLC: London: Hurst & Blackett, [1924]

D-634   _____ Turquoise Cañon / by I. [sic] Allan Dunn; frontispiece by Ralph Pallen Coleman. Garden City, New York: Doubleday, Page & Company, 1920. 241 p., col. front.
LC: Mr 23, '20.
PW: Mr 6, '20.

D-635   _____ The water-bearer / by J. Allan Dunn. New York: Dodd, Mead and Company, 1924. 312 p.
LC: F 12, '24.
BLC: London: Hurst & Blackett, [1924].

D-636   Dunn, Martha Baker, 1848-1915. 'Lias's wife: an island story / by Martha Baker Dunn; illustrated by Albert F. Schmidt [sic]. Boston: L. C. Page & Company, 1901. 263 p., front., [7] leaves of plates.

D-637   Dunn, Robert. The youngest world: a novel of the frontier / by Robert Dunn. New York: Dodd, Mead and Company, 1914. 492 p.
LC: Mr 23, '14.
PW: Mr 21, '14.
BLC: London: G. Bell & Sons, 1914.

D-638   Dunn, Waldo Hilary, 1882-1969. The vanished empire: a tale of the Mound builders / by Waldo H. Dunn; with an introduction by J. P. MacLean . . . Cincinnati: The Robert Clarke Company, 1904. 180 p., front., ill., maps. [Ill. by W. J. Baer.]
PW: My 7, '04.

D-639   [Dunne, Finley Peter], 1867-1936. Dissertations by Mr. Dooley / by the author of "Mr. Dooley's philosophy." New York; London: Harper & Brothers, 1906. 312, [1] p.
Contents: The king in his shirt-sleeves -- Royal doings -- Oratory -- Banting -- The pursuit of riches -- Short marriage contracts -- The bringing up of children -- The labor troubles -- The automobile -- The comforts of travel -- Our representatives abroad -- Diplomatic uniforms -- The intellectual life -- The vice-president -- A lenten sermon -- The Irish question -- The American family -- The Carnegie-Homer controversy -- Gambling -- An international police force -- Oats as a food -- The Carnegie libraries -- The race question -- Senatorial courtesy -- The candidate -- War -- The "Anglo-Saxon" triumph -- Corporal punishment -- Hotels and hotel life -- The simple life -- The food we eat -- National housecleaning -- Socialism -- Business and political honesty -- Sieges -- Mr. Carnegie's hero fund -- Banks and banking -- The bar.
LC: O 25, '06.
PW: D 1, '06.

[_____] Mary's little lamb. See **Masson, Thomas Lansing, 1866-1934.** *A bachelor's baby: and some grownups* (1907), M-587.

_____ "Mr. Dooley on corporal punishment." In *International short stories* (1910), I-29.

D-640   [_____] Mr. Dooley on making a will and other necessary evils . . . / by the same author of Mr. Dooley says, Mr. Dooley in peace and in war, etc. New York: Charles Scribner's Sons, 1919. 221 p.
Contents: On making a will -- Famous men -- At a summer resort -- Drink and politics -- On home life -- On food in war -- On old age -- On the power of music -- On the descent of man -- On the higher baseball -- On heroes and history -- On going to see the doctor -- On "the gift of oratory" -- On golf -- On "the game of cards" -- On the Orange Revolution of 1914 -- On St. Patrick's Day -- On past glories -- On criminal trials.
LC: Ag 26, '19.
PW: Ag 23, '19.
BLC: London: William Heinemann, 1920.

D-641   _____ Mr. Dooley on timely topics of the day: on the life insurance investigation, on business and political honesty, on national housecleaning. Compiled and distributed on Behalf of the Advertising Department of Collier's. [n. p.], 1905. 31 p.
Unexamined copy: bibliographic data from OCLC, #14627226.

D-642 [____] Mr. Dooley says / by the author of "Mr. Dooley in peace and in war," "Mr. Dooley in the hearts of his countrymen," etc. New York: Charles Scribner's Sons, 1910. 239 p.

Contents: Divorce -- Glory -- Woman suffrage -- The bachelor tax -- The rising of the subject races -- Panics -- Ocean travel -- Work -- Drugs -- A broken friendship -- The army canteen -- Things spiritual -- Books -- The tariff -- The big fine -- Expert testimony -- The call of the wild -- The Japanese scare -- The Hague Conference -- Turkish politics -- Vacations.

LC: S 23, '10.
PW: S 17, '10.
BLC: London: William Heinemann, 1910.

D-643 ____ Mr. Dooley's opinions / by Peter Finley Dunne. New York: R. H. Russell, Publisher, 1901. 212 p.

Contents: Christian science -- Life at Newport -- The Supreme Court's decisions -- Disqualifying the enemy -- Amateur ambassadors -- The city as a summer resort -- An editor's duties -- On the poet's fate -- The yacht races -- On athletics -- On lying -- Discusses party politics -- The truth about Schley -- Fame -- Cross-examinations -- Thanksgiving -- On the midway -- Mr. Carnegie's gift -- The crusade against vice -- The New York Custom House -- Some political observations -- Youth and age -- On Wall Street -- Colleges and degrees -- The Booker Washington incident.

PW: D 21, '01.
BLC: London: William Heinemann, 1902.

D-644 ____ Observations / by Mr. Dooley. New York: R. H. Russell, 1902. 279 p.

Contents: A little essay on books -- The law's delays -- Sherlock Holmes -- International amenities -- Art patronage -- Immigration -- White House discipline -- Money and matrimony -- Prince Henry's visit -- Prince Henry's reception -- Cuba vs. beet sugar -- Bad men from the West -- European intervention -- The Philippine peace -- Soldier and policeman -- King Edward's coronation -- One advantage of poverty -- The fighting word -- Home life of geniuses -- Reform administration -- Work and sport -- The news of a week -- The end of the war -- Newport -- Arctic exploration -- Machinery -- Swearing -- The war game -- Newspaper publicity -- Adventure -- Rights and privileges of women -- Avarice and generosity -- The end of things -- Hypocrisy -- History -- Enjoyment -- Gratitude.

BLC: London: William Heinemann, 1903.

D-645 Dunning, Eva L. (Eva Louise), b. 1861. Della Dare: and other stories / by Eva L. Dunning . . . Columbus, Ohio: Eva L. Dunning, c1916. 80 p. **DLC**

Contents: Della Dare -- Belvidere -- The soldier's daughter -- A jewel in the rough.

LC: S 21, '16.

D-646 ____ Trosy, or, The wreck of the Chesapeake / by Eva L. Dunning. Columbus, Ohio: Eva L. Dunning, c1914. 77 p.
LC: N 11, '14.

D-647 Dunning, James Edmund, b. 1873. The master builders / by James Edmund Dunning; illustrated. New York: D. Appleton and Company, 1909. 339, [1] p., front., [3] leaves of plates. [Ill. by F. B. Masters.]
LC: Je 11, '09.
PW: Je 19, '09.

____ The two apples. In *Atlantic narratives*; **2nd series (1918), A-361.**

D-648 Dunseth, W. H. (William Henry), b. 1860. Seven days in spirit garb, or, With the seen and the unseen / by W. H. Dunseth; with an introduction by Thomas J.

Burrill. [Pittsburgh]: Pittsburgh Printing Company, [c1903]. 156 p.

D-649 Dunton, James G. (James Gerald), b.1899. Wild asses / by James G. Dunton. Boston: Small, Maynard & Company, [c1925]. 333, [1] p.
LC: Mr 19, '25.
PW: Ap 11, '25.

D-650 DuPuy, William Atherton, 1876-1941. Uncle Sam, detective / by William Atherton DuPuy; with four illustrations by S. Edwin Megargee, Jr. New York: Frederick A. Stokes Company, [c1916]. 247 p., front., [3] leaves of plates.
LC: Ag 17, '16.

D-651 Durant, H. R. (Harry R.), b. 1871. Wallops / by H. R. Durant . . . ; illustrated by George Wright. Hartford, Conn.: Dissell Publishing Co., 1907. 264 p., front., [2] leaves of plates. Reprinted from various periodicals.

Contents: The unknown -- The double cross -- A quitter -- Buffalo -- The champion goes home -- Red Kelly's revolution -- A sucker -- The abduction of Red Kelly -- When Campbell cried -- How Moriarty escaped.

LC: D 3, '07.

D-652 Durham, Robert Lee, 1870-1949. The call of the South / by Robert Lee Durham; illustrated by Henry Roth. Boston: L. C. Page & Company, 1908. 439 p., front., [5] leaves of plates.
LC: Mr 14, '08.
PW: Ap 4, '08.

D-653 Durley, Ella Hamilton. My soldier lady / by Ella Hamilton Durley. Boston, Massachusetts: The C. M. Clark Publishing Company, 1908. 228 p., front., [7] leaves of plates.
LC: D 4, '08.
PW: D 12, '08.

D-654 ____ The standpatter: a chronicle of democracy / by Ella Hamilton Durley . . . ; illustrated by Burr Giffen. New York City: The Herald Square Publishing Company, [c1912]. 158 p., front., [4] leaves of plates.

D-655 Duryea, Nina Larrey, 1874-1951. The house of the seven gabblers / by Nina Larrey Duryea; illustrated by Hermann Heyer. New York; London: D. Appleton and Company, 1911. 271, [1] p., front.
LC: Je 13, '11.
PW: Je 24, '11.

D-656 ____ A sentimental dragon / by Nina Larrey Duryea. New York: George H. Doran Company, [c1916]. 328 p. Illustrated end papers. [Signed by F. Rogers.]
LC: Ap 24, '16.
PW: Ap 1, '16.

D-657 Dushaw, Amos I. (Amos Isaac), b. 1877. Proselytes of the Ghetto: time: the present: place: New York / by Amos I. Dushaw . . . New Brunswick, N. J.: J. Heidingsfeld . . . , [c1909]. 128 p. **NYP**
LC: Ag 27, '09.

D-658 Dutton, Charles J. (Charles Judson), 1888-1964. The house by the road / by Charles J. Dutton . . . New York: Dodd, Mead and Company, 1924. 313 p.
LC: Mr 27, '24.
PW: Mr 29, '24.
BLC: London: John Lane, 1924.

D-659 _____ Out of the darkness / by Charles J. Dutton . . . New York: Dodd, Mead & Company, 1922. 282 p.
LC: Mr 22, '22.
PW: Ap 8, '22.
BLC: London: John Lane; printed in U. S. A., 1922.

D-660 _____ The second bullet / by Charles J. Dutton. New York: Dodd, Mead and Company, 1925. 301 p.
LC: Ap 1, '25.
PW: Ap 4, '25.

D-661 _____ The shadow on the glass / by Charles J. Dutton . . . New York: Dodd, Mead and Company, 1923. 251 p.
LC: Ja 16, '23.
PW: Ja 13, '23.
BLC: London: Herbert Jenkins, 1925.

D-662 _____ The Underwood mystery / by Charles J. Dutton. New York: Dodd, Mead and Company, 1921. 305 p.   **DPL**
LC: Ja 19, '21.
BLC: London: G. H. Robinson & J. Birch, 1922.

D-663 Dutton, Louise Elizabeth. The goddess girl / by Louise Elizabeth Dutton. New York: Moffat, Yard and Company, 1915. 385 p.
PW: O 30, '15.

D-664 _____ Going together / by Louise Dutton . . . ; frontispiece by James H. Crank. Indianapolis: The Bobbs-Merrill Company, [c1923]. 311 p., front.
LC: Mr 5, '23.

_____ Judgment. In *Forum stories* (1914), **F-306.**

D-665 _____ The wishing moon / by Louise Dutton; illustrated by Everett Shinn. Garden City, N. Y.: Doubleday, Page & Company, 1916. 335 p., col. front.
LC: O 30, '16.
PW: N 4, '16.

D-666 Duval, G. R. Written in the sand / by G. R. Duval . . . Philadelphia: The John C. Wilson Company, 1913. 335 p., col. front. [Ill. by George Gibbs.]
LC: F 6, '13.
BLC: London: W. J. Ham-Smith, 1912.

D-667 Duvall, Thomas Jeffries. Better than divorce / by Rev. Thomas J. Duvall . . . Louisville, Ky.: Pentecostal Publishing Company, [c1914]. 288 p.
Unexamined copy: bibliographic data from OCLC, #12497609.
LC: Ap 16, '14.

D-668 Duxbury, C. Richmond, Mrs. New England folk / by Mrs. C. Richmond Duxbury. New York; London;

Montreal: The Abbey Press, [1901], [c1900]. 295 p., [1] leaf of plates (port.).
PW: Ag 31, '01.

Dwiggins, W. A. La dernière mobilisation. In *The best short stories of 1915 and the yearbook of the American short story* (1916), **B-560.**

D-669 Dwight, C. A. S. (Charles Abbott Schneider), 1860-1956. Cruising for the cross / Rev. C. A. S. Dwight . . . New York: American Tract Society, [c1903]. 201 p., front., [9] leaves of plates.   **RBN**

D-670 _____ Railroading with Christ / by Rev. Charles A. S. Dwight. New York: American Tract Society, [1902]. 77 p., ill.
Unexamined copy: bibliographic data from OCLC, #26835419.

D-671 Dwight, H. G. (Harrison Griswold), 1875-1959. The emperor of Elam: and other stories / by H. G. Dwight. Garden City, N. Y.: Doubleday, Page & Company, 1920. 387, [1] p.
Contents: Like Michael -- Henrietta Stackpole, rediviva -- The pagan -- White bombazine -- Unto the day -- Mrs. Derwall and the higher life -- The bathers -- Retarded bombs -- Susannah and the elder -- The emerald of Tamerlane (in collaboration with John Taylor) -- Studio smoke -- Behind the door -- The bald spot -- The emperor of Elam.
LC: O 28, '20.
PW: N 13, '20.

D-672 _____ Stamboul nights / by H. G. Dwight; frontispiece by W. T. Benda. Garden City, N. Y.: Doubleday, Page & Company, 1916. 371, [1] p., front.
Contents: The leopard of the sea -- Mortmain -- Mehmish -- The glass house -- The house of the giraffe -- The golden javelin -- His beatitude -- The place of martyrs -- Under the arch -- For the faith -- Mill valley -- The regicide -- The river of the moon -- In the Pasha's garden.
LC: Mr 29, '16.
PW: Mr 25, '16.

D-673 Dwight, Henry Otis, 1843-1917. A Muslim Sir Galahad: a present day story of Islam in Turkey / by Henry Otis Dwight . . . New York; Chicago; Toronto; London; Edinburgh: Fleming H. Revell Company, [c1913]. 188 p., photo. front., [3] leaves of photo. plates.   **OSU, NYP**
LC: Je 10, '13.

Dwyer, James Francis. The citizen. In *The best short stories of 1915 and the yearbook of the American short story* (1916), **B-560.**

_____ The little man in the smoker. In *War stories* (1919), **W-94.**

Dyar, Alice E. The Barker twins. In *Minnesota stories* (1903), **M-842.**

_____ A Christmas prodigal. In *Minnesota stories* (1903), **M-842.**

_____ The French grandmother. In *Minnesota stories* (1903), **M-842.**

_____ Misunderstood. In *Minnesota stories* (1903), **M-842.**

D-674　Dyar, Muriel Campbell, b. 1876. Davie and Elisabeth: wonderful adventures / Muriel Campbell Dyar. New York; London: Harper & Brothers, 1908. 130 p., front. [Ill. by Rachael Robinson.]
LC: O 9, '08.

_____ Elizabeth and Davie. In *Life at high tide* **(1907), L-281.**

D-675　Dye, Eva Emery, 1855-1947. The conquest: the true story of Lewis and Clark / by Eva Emery Dye . . . Chicago: A. C. McClurg & Company, 1902. 443 p., photo. front. (port.).
BLC: London: C. F. Cazenove; Cambridge, U. S. A. [printed], 1902.

D-676　_____ McDonald of Oregon: a tale of two shores / by Eva Emery Dye; illustrated by Walter J. Enright. Chicago: A. C. McClurg & Co., 1906. 395 p., front., [5] leaves of plates.
LC: S 20, '06.
BLC: London: C. F. Cazenove & Son; Chicago: A. C. McClurg & Co., 1906.

Dye, Elisabeth F. Hans Kremler's anniversary. In *Through the forbidden gates* **(1903), T-222.**

D-677　Dyer, Edward O. (Edward Oscar), b. 1853. The camp on Poconnuck / Edward O. Dyer. [Hartford, Conn.: The Case, Lockwood & Brainard Co., 1910]. 48 p.

D-678　Dyer, Walter A. (Walter Alden), 1878-1943. Gulliver the Great: and other dog stories / by Walter A. Dyer. New York: The Century Co., 1916. 317 p., front., incl. [8] leaves of plates. Reprinted in part from various periodicals.
Contents: Gulliver the Great -- The twa dogs o' Glenfergus -- Maginnis -- The madness of Antony Spatola -- Justice at Valley Brook -- Ishmael -- The strike at Tiverton Manor -- Spider of the newsies -- The blood of his fathers -- The regeneration of Timmy -- Wotan, the Terrible -- The hound of my Lady Blanche -- Lorna of the black eye -- Tom Sawyer of the movies -- The return of the champion -- Prayer for a pup.
LC: S 14, '16.

D-679　_____ Pierrot, dog of Belgium / by Walter A. Dyer . . . ; illustrated by Gordon Grant. Garden City, New York: Doubleday, Page & Company, 1915. 112 p.
COX
LC: Mr 30, '15.
PW: Ap 3, '15.
BLC: London: Curtis Brown; Garden City, New York printed, 1915. Another edition: London: Duckworth & Co.; Garden City, N. Y., printed 1915.

D-680　_____ The vision of Anton / by Walter A. Dyer. Riverside, Cal.: Published for Frank A. Miller, 1911. [32] p.
Unexamined copy: bibliographic data from OCLC, #14115211.

D-681　Dyke, Watson. The hunter / by Watson Dyke. New York; London: G. P. Putnam's Sons, 1918. ([New York]: The Knickerbocker Press). 387 p. **DLC**
LC: Mr 28, '18.

Dykes, Pauline Browning. <u>See</u> **Brown Paula, pseud.**

D-682　Dyson, Verne, b. 1879. Black cloth: a novel / by Verne Dyson. New York, Clandoin, Gale & Co., 1925. 303 p.
[Far Eastern Edition.]

E

E-1　Eager, James Henry Lovell. Courtship under contract: the science of selection: a tale of woman's emancipation / by James Henry Lovell Eager. New York; Passaic, N. J.: The Health-Culture Company; London, England: L. N. Fowler & Co., [c1910]. 440 p., photo. front. (port.).

Eakins, J. J. The courtship of Colonel Bill. <u>In</u> *Southern lights and shadows* **(1907), S-718.**

E-2　Earle, Mary Tracy, b. 1864. The flag on the hilltop / Mary Tracy Earle . . . ; with illustrations. Boston; New York: Houghton, Mifflin and Company, 1902. (Cambridge: The Riverside Press). 125, [1] p., front., [3] leaves of plates. [Ill. by Winfield S. Lukens.]　　**TJC**

_____ The glass door. In *Life at high tide* **(1907), L-281.**

E-3　Earls, Michael, 1873-1937. Marie of the House d' Anters / by Micheal Earls. New York; Cincinnati; Chicago: Benziger Brothers, 1916. 444 p., front. [Ill. by Frank McKernan.]　　**JFS**
LC: Ap 13, '16.
PW: Ap 29, '16.

E-4　_____ Melchior of Boston / by Michael Earls. New York; Cincinnati; Chicago: Benziger Brothers, 1910. 176 p., front., [2] leaves of plates.
LC: N 14, '10.
PW: D 3, '10.

E-5　_____ Stuore / by Michael Earls. New York; Cincinnati; Chicago: Benziger Brothers, 1911. 251 p.
Contents: Preface -- The apparition to Ernest Marcy -- For assessor: John Desmond -- The place of purgatory -- Dasey -- The message of the burglar's letter -- Norry Donlan, benefactress -- Old Captain. Partly reprinted from the Ave Maria and Benziger's magazine.
LC: O 11, '11.
PW: O 21, '11.

E-6　_____ The wedding bells of Glendalough / by Michael Earls. New York; Cincinnati; Chicago: Benziger Brothers, 1913. 388 p.
LC: My 31, '13.
PW: Je 14, '13.

E-7　Earp, James W. Boomer Jones / by James W. Earp . . . ; illustrations by "Bugs" Hardaway. Kansas City, Missouri: Burton Publishing Company Publishers, [c1921]. 94, [2] p., ill.　　**OKD**
Contents: It's a bear -- Hitting the high ones with Jones -- Watch 'em explode -- Nicknames he has met and acquired -- Salome's rival -- He wins the championship belt -- Love is a disease like the mumps -- On jay towns -- Jones on the local -- Boomer Jones-pugilist -- The Boomer's girl -- Old Hard-Luck Jones -- Alibi Mike -- Back to the farm.

Eastland, Florence Martin, b. 1866. The duchess of Rattlesnake Priarie. In **Seattle Writers' Club.** *Tillicum tales* **(1907), S-248.**

E-8   ____ Matt of the water-front / by Florence Martin Eastland. Cincinnati: Jennings and Graham; New York: Eaton and Mains, [c1909]. 153 p., front. [Ill. by B. C. Bubb.]
LC: My 3, '09.

Eastman, Charles Alexander, 1858-1939. The Gray Chieftain. In *Under the Sunset* **(1906), U-9.**

E-9   ____ Old Indian days / by C. A. Eastman (Ohiyesa) . . . ; illustrations in color by Dan Sayre Groesbeck. New York: The McClure Company, 1907. 279 p., col. front., [3] leaves of col. plates.   Reprinted from various periodicals.
Contents: The love of Antelope -- The madness of Bald Eagle -- The singing spirit -- The famine -- The chief soldier -- The white man's errand -- The grave of the dog -- Winona, the woman-child -- Winona, the child-woman -- Snana's fawn -- She-who-has-a-soul -- The peace-maker -- Blue Sky -- The faithfulness of Long Ears -- The war maiden.
LC: O 15, '07.

E-10   ____ Red hunters and the animal people / by Charles A. Eastman (Ohiyesa) . . . New York; London: Harper & Brothers, 1904. 248, [1] p., front. **IUA**
Contents: The great cat's nursery -- On Wolf Mountain -- The dance of the little people -- Wechah the provider -- The mustering of the herds -- The sky warrior -- A founder of ten towns -- The gray chieftain -- Hootay of the Little Rosebud -- The river people -- The challenge -- Wild animals from the Indian stand-point -- Glossary of Indian words and phrases.

E-11   Eastman, E. R. (Edward Roe), b. 1885. The trouble maker / by E. R. Eastman. New York: The Macmillan Company, 1925. 315 p.
LC: S 30, '25.
PW: O 10, '25.

E-12   Eastman, Elaine Goodale, 1863-1953. Little Brother o' Dreams / by Elaine Goodale Eastman. Boston; New York: Houghton, Mifflin Company, 1910. (Cambridge, [Mass.]: The Riverside Press). 191, [1] p.
LC: Mr 19, '10.

E-13   Eastman, Rebecca Hooper. The big little person: a romance / by Rebecca Hooper Eastman. New York; London: Harper & Brothers, 1917. 345, [1] p., front. [Ill. by Fanny Munsell.]
LC: S 20, '17.
PW: S 29, '17.

    ____ The purple star. In *Atlantic narratives*; **2nd series (1918), A-361.**

E-14   Eastwood, Carlin. The master road / by Carlin Eastwood; frontispiece by Blanche Letcher. New York; Seattle: The Alice Harriman Company, 1910. 251 p., front.
LC: O 24, '10.
PW: O 22, '10.

E-15   Eaton, G. D. (Geoffrey Dell), b. 1894. Backfurrow / by G. D. Eaton. New York; London: G. P.

Putnam's Sons, 1925. (New York: The Knickerbocker Press). 332 p.
LC: S 14, '25.
PW: F 14, '25.

E-16   Eaton, Isabel Graham, b. 1845. Annals of Pollock's Cove: some idyls of the Maine sea-coast / by Isabel Graham Eaton and Charlotte Carr Bachelder. New York; London: F. Tennyson Neely, [c1902]. 110 p., front. [Ill. by I. G. Eaton.]
PW: Ja 17, '03.

E-17   ____ By the shores of Arcady / by Isabel Graham Eaton; decorations by W. G. Krieghoff. New York: The Outing Publishing Company, 1908. 325 p., ill.
LC: Ja 22, '09.
PW: D 12, '08; F 6, '09.

E-18   Eaton, Paul W. (Paul Webster), b. 1861. The treasure / by Paul W. Eaton. New York: R. F. Fenno & Company, [c1909]. 410 p., col. front., [4] leaves of plates. [Ill. by Sydney K. Hartman.]
LC: N 17, '09.
PW: N 13, '09.

E-19   Eaton, Seymour, 1859-1916. Dan Black: editor and proprietor: a story / by Seymour Eaton. Philadelphia: The Library Publishing Company, [c1904]. 53, [1] p., front., ill.

E-20   Eaton, Walter Prichard, 1878-1957. The bird house man / by Walter Prichard Eaton; illustrated by Thomas Fogarty. Garden City, N. Y.: Doubleday, Page & Company, 1916. 347, [1] p., front., [2] leaves of plates.
LC: S 8, '16.
PW: S 9, '16.
BLC: London: Hodder & Stoughton; Garden City, N. Y. printed, [1917].

E-21   ____ The idyl of Twin Fires / by Walter Prichard Eaton; illustrated by Thomas Fogarty. Garden City, N. Y.: Doubleday, Page & Company, 1915. 304 p., front., [3] leaves of plates, ill.
LC: Mr 30, '15.
BLC: London: Hodder & Stoughton; Garden City, N. Y. printed, [1916].

E-22   ____ The man who found Christmas / by Walter Prichard Eaton . . . ; frontispiece by Walter King Stone. New York: McBride, Nast & Company, 1913. 57 p., col. front., [1] leaf of plates.
LC: D 3, '13.
PW: N 29, '13.

E-23   ____ The runaway place: a May idyl of Manhattan / by Walter Prichard Eaton and Elise Morris Underhill. New York: Henry Holt and Company, 1909. 257 p.
LC: My 22, '09.

Eaton, Winnifred, b. 1879. See **Watanna, Onoto, pseud.**

E-24   Eatough, Harry. Jim Morgan's last chance / by Harry Eatough. Baltimore, Md.: Saulsbury

Publishing Company, [1918]. 26 p., front. (port.).
LC: Ja 6, '19.

E-25   Eaves, Catherine *pseud*. How I twice eloped: an
Indiana idyll / suggested by Abraham Lincoln;
elaborated by Catherine Eaves [pseud.]. Chicago:
Oak Printing and Publishing Co., [c1901]. 88 p.,
ill.   **IBA**

E-26   Eberhardt, Walter F., 1891?-1935. Classmates: a
story of West Point / by Walter F. Eberhardt; based
on the play by Wm. C. DeMille and Margaret
Turnbull; illustrated with scenes from the photoplay
produced by Inspiration Pictures, Inc., a First
National picture. New York: Grosset & Dunlap,
[c1925]. 303 p., photo. front., [7] leaves of photo.
plates.
LC: Ja 23, '25.

E-27   _____ Sundown: an epic drama of to-day / by Earl J.
Hudson; novelized by Walter F. Eberhardt; with
illustrations from the First National Picture produced
with an all star cast. New York: Grosset & Dunlap,
[c1924]. 274 p., photo. front., [7] leaves of photo.
plates.
LC: Jl 19, '24.

E-28   Eby, Anson D. (Anson Doner), b. 1867. By their
fruits / by Anson D. Eby. Lancaster, Pa.: Conestoga
Publishing Co., Inc., [c1925]. 135 p.   **LKC**
LC: Ag 24, '25.

E-29   _____ Showers of blessing / by Anson D. Eby.
Lancaster, Pa.: [The Examiner Printing House],
1908. 268 p.   **LFM**
LC: N 14, '08.

E-30   Eckstorm, Fannie Hardy, 1865-1946. The Penobscot
man / by Fannie Hardy Eckstorm. Boston; New
York: Houghton, Mifflin and Company, 1904.
(Cambridge: The Riverside Press). 326 p., front.
PW: Je 4, '04.

E-31   Eddy, Arthur Jerome, 1859-1920. Ganton & Co.: a
story of Chicago commercial and social life / by
Arthur Jerome Eddy; illustrated by Thomas Fogarty.
Chicago: A. C. McClurg & Co., 1908. 415 p., col.
front., [4] leaves of col. plates.
LC: S 25, '08.

E-32   _____ Tales of a small town / by one who lived there.
Philadelphia; London: J. B. Lippincott Company,
1907. 336 p.
Contents: Hugh Doring -- The corner saloon -- Blind Izra -- A
jailbird -- The village bully -- Old Canahan's occupation -- The
rector's conversion -- The judge's story -- Mrs. Dummerford's niece.
LC: S 28, '07.

E-33   Edes, Robert T. (Robert Thaxter), 1838-1923.
Parson Gay's three sermons, or, Saint Sacrement / by
Robert T. Edes. New York: Cochrane Publishing
Co., 1908. 151 p.   **NYP**
LC: Ap 22, '08.

Edgar, Randolph. Iron. In *The Bellman book of
fiction* **(1921), B-485.**

_____, ed. See *The Miller's holiday* **(1920), M-817.**

Edholm, Charlton Lawrence. The lure of the
unspoken word. In *Clever business sketches* **(1909),
C-490.**

E-34   Edhor, I. Hearts of gold / by I. Edhor; illustrated.
New York; Cincinnati; Chicago: Benziger Brothers,
1903, [c1902]. 234 p., front., [2] leaves of
plates.   **DLC**
PW: D 5, '03.

Edmonds, Walter D., Jr. The hanging of Kruscome
Shanks. In *The best college short stories, 1924-1925*
(1925), B-558.

Edson, Harold, pseud. See **Hall, Asa Zadel.**

E-35   Edward, William, *pseud*. Colonel Rockinghorse: a
book of paraphrases / by William Edward [pseud.].
New York: Hastings & Baker, [c1919]. 103 p., ill.
LC: Je 30, '19.

E-36   Edwards, Albert, 1879-1929, *pseud*. Comrade Yetta
/ by Albert Edwards [pseud.] . . . New York: The
Macmillan Company, 1913. 448 p.
LC: F 27, '13.
PW: Mr 8, '13.

E-37   _____ A man's world / by Albert Edwards [pseud.].
New York: The Macmillan Company, 1912. 312 p.
LC: S 12, '12.

E-38   [_____] The stranger / by Arthur Bullard. New
York: The Macmillan Company, 1920. 332 p.
LC: My 12, '20.
PW: Je 5, '20.
BLC: London: Macmillan & Co.; printed in U. S.
A., 1920.

E-39   Edwards, David W. (David William), b. 1849. Up
the grade / by David W. Edwards. Boston: The C.
M. Clark Publishing Company, 1909. 406 p., front.,
[5] leaves of plates. [Ill. by E. Ellis Swift.]
LC: N 22, '09.

Edwards, E. B. Ye tithe mint and rue. In **Seattle
Writers' Club.** *Tillicum tales* **(1907), S-248.**

E-40   Edwards, Eugene. A million dollar jack pot: and
other poker stories / by Eugene Edwards; with
numerous illustrations by Ike Morgan. Chicago:
Jamieson-Higgins Co., 1901. 188 p., ill.
Contents: What is poker? -- The early days of poker -- Poker in
Washington -- Poker in London and Paris -- Poker and jurisprudence
-- All about jack pots -- Scheme for a national jack pot -- Women and
poker -- Old time poker in The South -- Poker and hypnotism -- A
life-long game -- About bluffing.
PW: Mr 2, '01.

E-41   Edwards, Fern. Learning to live / by Fern Edwards.
Yakima, Wash.: Washington Office Supply Co.,
[c1922]. 119 p., [4] leaves of plates.
LC: D 14, '22.

Edwards, Gurden. The history of Chop-Suey and Fan

Tan. In *California story book* (1909), C-40.

E-42   Edwards, Harry Stillwell, 1855-1938. The adventures of a parrot / by Harry Stillwell Edwards . . . Macon, Georgia: Published by the J. W. Burke Company, [c1920]. 37, [1] p.

_____ The answer. In *Short stories from Life* (1916), S-463.

E-43   _____ The blue hen's chicken / by Harry Stillwell Edwards . . . Macon, Georgia: The J. W. Burke Company, 1924. 51 p., ill.   **NYP**

E-44   _____ Brother Sims's mistake / by Harry Stillwell Edwards . . . Macon, Georgia: Publishfd [sic] by the J. W. Burke Company, [c1920]. 35 p.
          OSU, KUK

E-45   _____ Eneas Africanus / by Harry Stillwell Edwards. Published at Macon, Georgia: By the J. W. Burke Company, [c1920]. 47 p., front., [6] leaves of plates.   Another edition: [Macon, Georgia: The J. W. Burke Co., printers, 19--]. 38 p.   **NYP**
Another edition: [Macon, Georgia: The J. W. Burke Co., c1919]
Unexamined copy: bibliographic data from DLC.

E-46   _____ How Sal came through / by Harry Stillwell Edwards . . . Macon, Georgia: Published by the J. W. Burke Company, [c1920]. 30, [1] p.

E-47   _____ Isam's spectacles / by Harry Stillwell Edwards . . . Macon, Georgia: Published by the J. W. Burke Company, [c1920]. 22, [1] p.

E-48   _____ Just sweethearts; a Christmas love story / by Harry Stillwell Edwards . . . Macon, Georgia: The J. W. Burke Company, [c1920]. [93] p.   **NDD**
LC: D 12, '19.
PW: F 14, '20.

E-49   _____ Madelon passes; and, Mam'selle Delphine: a story of the Christmas / by Harry Stillwell Edwards. Macon, Ga.: Issued by The Holly Bluff Publishing Co.; Atlanta: The Martin & Hoyt Co., [c1922]. 39 p.

E-50   _____ Mam'selle Delphine: a story of the Christmas / by Harry Stillwell Edwards . . . Macon, Georgia: Issued by the Holly Bluff Publishing Co., [c1921]. (Chattanooga, Tennessee: From the press of Purse Printing Co.). 30 p.   **KUK**

E-51   _____ Shadow: a Christmas story / by Harry Stillwell Edwards . . . Macon, Georgia: Published by the J. W. Burke Company, [c1920]. 19, [1] p.

E-52   Edwards, Jeannette Llewellyn. A girl and the devil; a novel / by Jeannette Llewellyn Edwards . . . New York: Broadway Publishing Company, [1903]. 270 p., front. (port.), [11] leaves of plates. Unexamined copy: bibliographic data from OCLC, #6474204.
PW: Je 27, '03.

Edwards, John Milton, pseud. See **Cook, William Wallace, 1867-1933.**

E-53   Edwards, Louise Betts. The Tu-tze's tower: a novel / by Louise Betts Edwards. Philadelphia: Henry T. Coates & Co., 1903. 418 p., front., [3] leaves of plates. [Ill. by John Sloan.]
PW: My 16, '03.

E-54   Edwards, Robert T. (Robert Thomas), b. 1868. Short Methodist stories / by Robert T. Edwards. New York: Cochrane Publishing Company, 1909. 139, [1] p.   **JET**
Contents: A story of a Methodist bishop -- The superannuated preacher -- Aid for freedom -- Bible society -- The prodigal church -- A story of foreign missions.
LC: Ap 6, '09.
PW: Je 26, '09.

E-55   Edwards, Sue. Jewels of paste / by Sue Edwards. New York; London; Montreal: The Abbey Press, [c1901]. 116 p., [1] leaf of plates (port.).   **VA@**
Contents: By the power of his will -- Rebecca -- To slow music -- The gallant defense of Miss Sarah -- The Rev. Mr. Smeak -- The story of Storey Hastings.
PW: D 14, '01.

E-56   Eells, Edward. A mission to hell / by Edward Eells . . . Boston: Sherman, French & Company, 1909. 403 p.
LC: O 9, '09.

E-57   Egan, Joseph B. (Joseph Burke), b. 1879. The beaten path: a novel of the great Northwest / by Joseph Burke Egan. Boston: The Gorham Press, 1918. 300 p., front., [2] leaves of plates. [Ill. by J. B. Egan.]
LC: Ag 8, '18.
PW: Ag 3, '18.

E-58   _____ Little people of the dust: a novel / by Joseph Burke Egan. Boston; New York; Chicago: The Pilgrim Press, [c1913]. 284 p., col. front., [2] leaves of col. plates. [Ill. by Grace Hackett.]   **JFS**
LC: N 6, '13.
PW: N 8, '13.

E-59   Egan, Maurice Francis, 1852-1924. Amelie in France / by Maurice Francis Egan . . . Philadelphia: H. L. Kilner & Co., [c1912]. 202 p.   **DLC**
"Part of this story appeared with great success in the Ave Maria some time ago."
LC: N 29, '12.

_____, contributor. See *A double knot* (1905), D-499.

_____ The heart of hearts. In *The Senior lieutenant's wager: and other stories* (1905), S-312.

E-60   _____ The ivy hedge / by Maurice Francis Egan. New York; Cincinnati; Chicago: Benziger Brothers, 1914. 331 p.
LC: N 21, '14.
PW: D 5, '14.

E-61   _____ The wiles of Sexton Maginnis / by Maurice Francis Egan; with illustrations by Arthur I. Keller.

New York: The Century Co., 1909. 380 p., front, incl. [20] plates.
LC: Mr 12, '09.
PW: Ap 3, '09.

E-62   Egan, Pierce, b. 1885. Namaqua / by Pierce Egan. Cedar Rapids, Iowa: Torch Press, 1925. 197 p., front., [6] leaves of photo. plates. [Ill. by Harold M. Dunning.]   **KSU**
LC: O 16, '25.

E-63   _____ A struggle for justice / by Pierce Egan. Bismarck: Tribune Company, 1913. 157 p., [1] leaf of photo. plates (port.).
LC: F 14, '13.

Egbert, H. M., pseud. See **Emanuel, Victor Rousseau, b. 1879.**

E-64   Egerton, Charles. The coming dawn / by Charles Egerton. New York: John Lane Company; London: John Lane, The Bodley Head, 1906. 304 p.
LC: S 28, '06.

E-65   Eggleston, George Cary, 1839-1911. Blind alleys: a novel of nowadays / by George Cary Eggleston; illustrated by E. Pollak. Boston: Lothrop, Lee & Shepard Co., [1906]. 414 p., front., [5] leaves of plates.
LC: Jl 9, '06.
PW: S 22, '06.

E-66   _____ A captain in the ranks: a romance of affairs / by George Cary Eggleston; with frontispiece by Charles D. Williams. New York: A. S. Barnes & Co., 1904. 337 p., col. front.
PW: O 29, '04.
BLC: London; United States: Author's Syndicate.

E-67   _____ A Carolina cavalier: a romance of the American revolution / by George Cary Eggleston; illustrated by C. D. Williams. Boston: Lothrop Publishing Company, [c1901]. 448 p., front., [5] leaves of plates.
PW: Mr 30, '01.

E-68   _____ A daughter of the South: a war's end romance / by George Cary Eggleston; illustrated by E. Pollak. Boston: Lothrop Publishing Company, [1905]. 403 p., front., [5] leaves of plates.
PW: Ag 26, '05.

E-69   _____ Dorothy South: a love story of Virginia just before the war / by George Cary Eggleston . . . ; illustrated by C. D. Williams. Boston: Lothrop Publishing Company, [c1902]. 453 p., front., [5] leaves of plates.   **CWR**
PW: Mr 29, '02.

E-70   _____ Evelyn Byrd / by George Cary Eggleston . . . ; illustrated by Charles Copeland. Boston: Lothrop Publishing Company, [1904]. 438 p., front., [4] leaves of plates.
PW: Je 4, '04.

E-71   _____ Irene of the mountains: a romance of old Virginia / by George Cary Eggleston; illustrated by

Frank T. Merrill. Boston: Lothrop, Lee, and Shepard Company, [1909]. 437 p., front., [5] leaves of plates.
LC: My 21, '09.
PW: S 11, '09.

E-72   _____ Jack Shelby: a story of the Indiana backwoods / by George Cary Eggleston . . . ; illustrated by G. W. Picknell. Boston: Lothrop, Lee & Shepard Co., [1906]. 338 p., front., [5] leaves of plates.   **CWR**
LC: Je 13, '06.
PW: Jl 21, '06.

E-73   _____ Love is the sum of it all: a plantation romance / by George Cary Eggleston; illustrated by Hermann Heyer. Boston: Lothrop, Lee & Shepard Co., [1907]. 387 p., front., [5] leaves of plates.
LC: Jl 10, '07.
PW: S 14, '07.

E-74   _____ The master of Warlock: a Virginia war story / by George Cary Eggleston; illustrated by C. D. Williams. Boston: Lothrop Publishing Company, [1903]. 433 p., front., [5] leaves of plates.
PW: F 7, '03.
BLC: London: Charles H. Kelly, 1903.

E-75   _____ Two gentlemen of Virginia: a novel of the old regime in the old dominion / by George Cary Eggleston; illustrated by Frank T. Merrill. Boston: Lothrop, Lee & Shepard Co., [1908]. 456 p., front., [5] leaves of plates.
LC: Ag 6, '08.
PW: S 5, '08.

E-76   _____ The Warrens of Virginia: a novel / by George Cary Eggleston . . . founded on the play of William C. De Mille; illustrations from scenes in the play. New York: G. W. Dillingham Company, [c1908]. 344 p., front., [2] leaves of plates.
LC: Ag 12, '08.
PW: Ag 29, '08.
BLC: London: T. Fisher Unwin; New York [printed], 1908.

E-77   _____ Westover of Wanalah: a story of love and life in old Virginia / by George Cary Eggleston; illustrated by Emil Pollak Ottendorff. Boston: Lothrop, Lee & Shepard Co., [1910]. 451 p., front., [5] leaves of plates.
LC: Jl 29, '10.
PW: Ag 20, '10.

E-78   _____ What happened at Quasi: the story of a Carolina cruise / by George Cary Eggleston; illustrated by H. C. Edwards. Boston: Lothrop, Lee & Shepard Co., [1911]. 368 p., front., [5] leaves of plates.
LC: Mr 29, '11.
PW: Ap 15, '11.

E-79   Eggleston, Joseph William, 1844-1927. Tuckahoe: an old-fashioned story of an old-fashioned people / by Joseph William Eggleston. New York; Washington: The Neale Publishing Company, 1903. 305 p., front., [1] leaf of plates.
PW: Ja 16, '04.

Eggleston, Richard Beverley, b. 1867. <u>See</u> **Conkley, Ralph, pseud.**

E-80   Egleston-Hinman, Elizabeth, b. 1881. Naya: a story of the Bighorn Country / by Elizabeth Egleston-Hinman; with illustrations by F. De Forest Schook. Chicago; New York; London: Rand, McNally & Company, 1910. 326 p., col. front., [5] leaves of plates.
LC: N 19, '10.

E-81   Ehrmann, Max, 1872-1945. A fearsome riddle / by Max Ehrmann; illustrated by Virginia Keep. Indianapolis: The Bowen-Merrill Company, [c1901]. 192 p., col. front., [3] leaves of col. plates.
PW: O 5, '01.
BLC: London: B. F. Stevens & Brown, [1901].

E-82   Eickemeyer, Carl. Cinderilla / Carl Eickemeyer . . . New York: [s. n.], 1906. 16 p., front.   **NYP**
LC: F 5, '07.

E-83   Eiker, Mathilde. Mrs. Mason's daughters / by Mathilde Eiker. New York: The Macmillan Company, 1925. 367 p.
LC: Mr 11, '25.
PW: Mr 14, '25.
BLC: London: T. Werner Laurie; printed in U. S. A., 1927.

E-84   Eilshemius, Louis M. (Louis Michel), 1864-1941. The devil's diary / by Louis M. Eilshemius. New York; London; Montreal: The Abbey Press, [c1901]. 271 p., [1] leaf of photo. plates (port.).   **KSU**

E-85   Elbow Lane / by the author of "Altogether Jane". New York: Mitchell Kennerley, 1915. 214 p. **DLC**
LC: Mr 31, '15.

E-86   Elder, Orville, b. 1866. The Frank stories / by Orville Elder. [Chicago: Rogers and Smith Company, printers, 1905]. 77, [1] p., ill.   **DLC**
Contents: A post-mortem bouquet -- Our darling -- Cubby walks -- A hop scotcher -- A kind of a time -- A deferred wedding -- The home comers -- One on Frank -- The discard.
LC: F 23, '05.
PW: Ap 1, '05.

E-87   ____ Mickey Peck: a novel / by Orville Elder. Boston: The Roxburgh Publishing Company, Inc., [c1918]. 208 p.   **DLC**
LC: F 14, '19.

E-88   Elder, Robert Dull. The sojourner / by Robert Dull Elder . . . ; illustrated. New York; London: Harper & Brothers, 1913. 334, [1] p., front., [3] leaves of photo. plates. [Ill. by Walter Biggs.]
LC: Ap 5, '13.
PW: Ap 12, '13.

E-89   Eldonrek, Louise, b. 1866, *pseud.* "Princess" Mae: a romance / by Louise Eldonrek [pseud.]; illustrated by E. J. Winn; cover design and title page by John Randolph Talbert. Richmond, Va.: Central Publishing Co., Inc., 1914. 114, [1] p., photo. front. (port.), [3] leaves of plates.
LC: O 7, '14.

E-90   Eldredge, Anna Wayne. Bennie Brighton / by Anna Wayne Eldredge. Los Angeles, Calif.: Published and for sale by Anna Wayne Eldredge, [c1923]. 250 p., photo. front. (port.), ill.
LC: Ja 5, '24.

E-91   Eldridge, Clement. Rescued by a prince / by Clement Eldridge (Captain Nautilus) . . . ; illustrated. Akron, O.; New York; Chicago: The Saalfield Publishing Co., 1901. 299 p., front., [4] leaves of plates. [Ill. by W. H. Fry.]
PW: Jl 20, '01.

E-92   Eldridge, E. F. (Edward Fayette), b. 1855. The Sinbad mines: a tale of the Rockies / by E. F. Eldridge. Denver: The Reed Publishing Company, [c1905]. 252 p., front. (port.).

E-93   Eldridge, Edward. A California girl / by Edward Eldridge. New York; London; Montreal: The Abbey Press, [c1902]. 247, [1] p.
PW: Ag 30, '02.

E-94   Eldridge, Frederick W. A social cockatrice / Frederick W. Eldridge. Boston: Lothrop Publishing Company, 1903. 412 p.
PW: Mr 21, '03.

E-95   Eldridge, George Dyre, b. 1848. I will repay: a novel / by George Dyre Eldridge. New York: Lewis, Scribner & Co., 1902. 313 p.
PW: O 4, '02.

E-96   ____ In the potter's house / by George Dyre Eldridge. New York: Doubleday, Page & Company, 1908. 338 p.
LC: F 5, '08.
PW: Mr 28, '08.
BLC: London: Doubleday & Co.; New York printed, 1908.

E-97   ____ The Millbank case: a Maine mystery of to-day / by George Dyre Eldridge; with a frontispiece in colour by Eliot Keen. New York: Henry Holt and Company, 1905. 297 p., col. front.
PW: Je 10, '05.

E-98   Eldridge, Paul, b. 1888. And the sphinx spoke / by Paul Eldridge; introduction by Benjamin De Casseres; cover design by Carlo De Fornaro. Boston, Massachusetts: The Stratford Company, [c1921]. 99 p.
LC: S 1, '21.

E-99   Eldridge, William Tillinghast. An American princess / by William Tillinghast Eldridge . . . ; with a frontispiece by E. Pollak Ottendorff. New York: Sturgis & Walton Company, 1909. 255 p., col. front.   **DLC**
LC: S 27, '09.

E-100   ____ Hilma / by William Tillinghast Eldridge; illustrations by Harrison Fisher and Martin Justice. New York: Dodd, Mead and Company, 1907. 331 p., front., [3] leaves of plates.
LC: F 27, '07.

BLC: London: B. F. Stevens & Brown; printed in U. S. A., 1907.

E-101 ____ Meryl / by William Tillinghast Eldridge; frontispiece by John Rae. New York: Dodd, Mead & Company, 1908. 323 p., col. front.
LC: Mr 17, '08.
BLC: London: B. F. Stevens & Brown; printed in U. S. A., 1908.

E-102 Elias, So. P. (Solomon Philip), b. 1868. Dreams come true / by Sol. P. Elias . . . Modesto, California: Press of the L. M. Morris Company, 1923. 54 p.   **DLC**

E-103 Elkin, Heiman J. (Heiman Jacob), b. 1864. The triangle / Heiman J. Elkin. New Orleans: Steeg Printing and Publishing Company, [c1911]. 141 p.   **NYP**
LC: Ap 14, '11.

Elkins, George W., 1858-1919. See **Space, M. T., pseud.**

Ellerbe, Alma. "Colonel, meet my mother". In *As we are* (1923), **A-325.**

____ "It's me, O Lord!" In *As we are* (1923), **A-325.**

Ellerbe, Paul, jt. aut. See **Ellerbe, Alma, jt. aut.**

E-104 Ellerbe, Rose L. (Rose Lucile), 1862-1928. Tales of California yesterdays / by Rose L. Ellerbe; cover design and illustrations by Howard Willard. Los Angeles, Calif.: Warren T. Potter, [c1916]. 205 p., incl. front., ill.
Reprinted in part from various periodicals.
Contents: Three cooks of San Gabriel -- The faith of his mother -- Padre Salvador's miracle -- In the shadow of the mission -- A tooth-and a tooth -- The bluff of Don José Morales -- The word of a Californian -- Siege of La Cajetin -- For lack of a peachblow silk -- "The hawk and the chickens" -- The fate of his race -- Simple Tony -- Ambitious Marta -- Faith triumphant -- The candle of good San Antonio -- The boss of the ranch -- The departure of José Juan -- The grave of Señora Valdez.
LC: D 30, '16.

E-105 Ellerson, C. C., Mrs. The vigilantes / by Mrs. C. C. Ellerson; illustrated by Ethel Palin. New York: Walker-Ellerson Publishing Company, [c1903]. 254 p., front., [9] leaves of plates.

E-106 Ellett, Frank Gates, b. 1860. A modern Hamilton / by Frank Gates Ellett . . . Detroit, Mich.: Press of Frank H. West, [c1912]. 217 p., photo. front. (port.). Designed end papers.
LC: Je 5, '12.

E-107 Elliott, Delia Buford. Adele Hamilton / by Delia Buford Elliott. New York; Washington: The Neale Publishing Company, 1907. 125 p.
LC: Ap 5, '07.
PW: Ag 03, '07.

E-108 Elliott, Francis Perry, 1861-1924. The gift of Abou Hassan / by Francis Perry Elliot; with illustrations by

Hanson Booth. Boston: Little, Brown and Company, 1912. 314 p., front., [3] leaves of plates.
LC: S 7, '12.
PW: Ag 24, '12.
BLC: Toronto: McClellend & Goodchild; Boston, U. S. A. [printed], 1912.

E-109 ____ The haunted pajamas / by Francis Perry Elliott; with illustrations by Edmund Frederick. Indianapolis: The Bobbs-Merrill Company, [c1911]. 355 p., col. front., [4] leaves of col. plates.
LC: Je 1, '11.
PW: Je 3, '11.

E-110 ____ Lend me your name! / by Francis Perry Elliott . . . ; illustrated by Carman Thomson. Chicago: The Reilly & Britton Co., [c1917]. 282 p., col. front. (ports.).
LC: Je 22, '17.

E-111 ____ Pals first: a romance of love and comradery / by Francis Perry Elliott. New York; London: Harper & Brothers, 1915. 331, [1] p., col. front. [Ill. by H. T. Fisk.]
LC: Mr 29, '15.
PW: Ap 3, '15.

E-112 Elliott, James T. (James Thomas). Elizabeth: a novel / by James T. Elliott; illustrated by Dearborn Melvill. Chicago: International Press Association, 1905. 281 p., front., ill.   **DLC**
PW: Je 3, '05.

E-113 Elliott, Mary King. Pretty Peggy O: a novel / by Mary King Elliott. New York: Broadway Publishing Co., 1913. 397 p.   **DLC**
LC: N 12, '13.

Elliott, Maud Howe. See **Howe, Maud, 1854-1948.**

E-114 Elliott, Nina Miller. Every woman's right: a novel / by Nina Miller Elliott . . . Chicago: Thos. W. Jackson Publishing Co., [c1919]. 203 p., front., [3] leaves of plates. [Ill. by Frank J. Meserow.]
LC: D 1, '19.

E-115 ____ Helen Blair: a novel / by Nina Miller Elliott. Chicago: Thos. W. Jackson Publishing Co., [c1915]. 181 p., ill.
LC: D 27, '15.

E-116 ____ Peggy Kip: a novel / by Nina Miller Elliott . . . Chicago: Thos. W. Jackson Publishing Co., [c1920]. 216 p., front., [3] leaves of plates.   **DLC**
LC: N 29, '20.

E-117 ____ When the heart is young: a novel / by Nina Miller Elliott . . . Chicago: Thos. W. Jackson Publishing Co., [c1917]. 206 p., front., [3] leaves of plates.
LC: N 30, '17.

E-118 Elliott, Nina Mills. The accused / by Nina Mills Elliott. New York: [Saxonia Press, c1913]. 159 p.   **DLC**
LC: N 18, '13.

E-119   ____ Paisano: (my blood) / by Nina Mills Elliott. New York: The Shakespeare Press, 1912. 96 p., front., [4] leaves of plates. [Ill. by R. J. Dean.]
LC: O 11, '12.
PW: D 28, '12.

E-120   Elliott, Robert. The wrong way: a story / by Robert Elliott. New York: The M. W. Hazen Company, [c1904]. 209 p.
PW: Ja 21, '05.

Elliott, Sarah Barnwell, 1848-1928. An incident. In *Southern lights and shadows* (1907), S-718.

E-121   ____ The making of Jane: a novel / by Sarah Barnwell Elliott. New York: Charles Scribner's Sons, 1901. 432 p.
PW: N 2, '01.

E-122   Ellis, Edward Sylvester, 1840-1916. High twelve: a sequel to Low twelve: "By their deeds ye shall know them": a series of striking and truthful incidents illustrative of the fidelity of Free Masons to one another in times of distress and danger / Edward S. Ellis . . . New York: Macoy Publishing & Masonic Supply Co., 1912. 268 p., [12] leaves of plates. [Ill. by Edwin John Prittie.]   **LQS**
LC: O 16, '12.
PW: N 16, '12.

E-123   ____ Low twelve: "By their deeds ye shall know them," A series of striking and truthful incidents illustrative of the fidelity of free masons to one another in times of distress and danger / by Edward S. Ellis, A. M. New York: F. R. Niglutsch, 1907. 247 p., front., [15] leaves of plates. [Ill. by Edwin J. Prittie and John Steeple Davis.]
LC: Ap 25, '07.
PW: Je 8, '07.

E-124   Ellis, George W. (George Washington), 1875-1919. The leopard's claw: a thrilling story of love and adventure from a European castle through the West African jungle, disclosing a deep insight into the quality and spiritual influence of African social institutions and conditions, and revealing a profound psyschic [sic] interpretation of African inner life, all clustered about the mysterious function and significance of the leopard's claw / by George W. Ellis . . . New York: International Authors' Association, [c1917]. 172 p.   **IAY**
LC: Je 28, '18.

E-125   Ellis, J. Breckenridge (John Breckenridge), 1870-1956. Adnah: a tale of the time of Christ / by J. Breckenridge Ellis. Philadelphia: George W. Jacobs & Co., [1902]. 308 p.
PW: N 8, '02.

E-126   ____ Agnes of the Bad Lands / by J. Breckenridge Ellis. New York: The Macaulay Company, 1916. 305 p., front., [3] leaves of plates. [Ill. by Albert Matzke.]
LC: S 20, '16.
PW: S 16, '16.

E-127   ____ Arkinsaw cousins: a story of the Ozarks / by J. Breckenridge Ellis. New York: Henry Holt and Company, 1908. 328 p.
LC: F 17, '08.
PW: F 29, '08.

E-128   ____ Fated to win (the soul of a serf): intensely dramatic and true to life, a romance of love and valor / by J. Breckinridge Ellis . . . ; a graphic description of the hero's struggles and the triumph of a woman's diplomacy; ten superb illustrations by H. S. De Lay. Chicago: Laird & Lee, [c1910]. 346 p., col. front., [9] leaves of plates.   **DLC**
Contains three additional chapters to *The soul of a serf*, also published in 1910.
LC: D 10, '10.
PW: D 31, '10.

E-129   ____ Fran / by John Breckenridge Ellis; illustrations by W. B. King. Indianapolis: The Bobbs-Merrill Company, [c1912]. 380 p., front., [4] leaves of plates.
LC: Ap 2, '12.
PW: Mr 9, '12.

E-130   ____ Garcilaso / by J. Breckenridge Ellis. Chicago: A. C. McClurg & Co., 1901. 394 p.
PW: Ap 20, '01.

E-131   ____ His dear unintended / by J. Breckenridge Ellis . . . New York: The Macaulay Company, 1917. 313 p., front., [3] leaves of plates. [Ill. by W. L. Howes.]
LC: S 6, '17.
PW: S 8, '17.

E-132   ____ The Holland wolves / by J. Breckenridge Ellis; with six full-page illustrations by Troy and Margaret Kinney. Chicago: A. C. McClurg & Company, 1902. 395 p., front., [5] leaves of plates.
PW: O 4, '02.

E-133   ____ Lahoma / by John Breckenridge Ellis; with illustrations by W. B. King. Indianapolis: The Bobbs-Merrill Company, [c1913]. 360 p., front., [4] leaves of plates.
LC: D 3, '13.
PW: D 6, '13.

E-134   ____ The little fiddler of the Ozarks: a novel / by John Breckenridge Ellis . . . ; original illustrations by H. S. DeLay. Chicago: Laird & Lee, [c1913]. 308 p., col. front., [8] leaves of plates.
LC: My 31, '13.
PW: Ag 2, '13.

E-135   ____ The picture on the wall / by J. Breckenridge Ellis . . . Kansas City, Missouri: Burton Publishing Company, [c1920]. 253 p.   **OKD**
LC: O 10, '21.

E-136   ____ The red box clew: for the young, from seven to seventy / by J. Breckenridge Ellis . . . Chicago; New York; Toronto; London; Edinbur.h: Fleming H. Revell Company, 1902. 230 p.
PW: D 6, '02.

E-137　　____ Something else: a novel / by J. Breckenridge Ellis; with illustrations by Ernest L. Blumenschein. Chicago: A. C. McClurg & Co., 1911. 438 p., incl. col. front., [3] leaves of col. plates.
LC: S 25, '11.
PW: S 30, '11.

E-138　　____ The soul of a serf: a romance of love and valor among the Angles and Saxons / by J. Breckinridge Ellis . . . Chicago: Laird & Lee, [c1910]. 328 p., col. front., [9] leaves of plates. [Ill. by H. S. DeLay.]
LC: Je 22, '10.
PW: Jl 2, '10.

E-139　　____ Stork's nest / by J. Breckenridge Ellis; illustrated by Elizabeth Ingham. New York: Moffat, Yard & Company, 1905. 375 p., front., [3] leaves of plates.

E-140　　____ The third diamond / by John Breckenridge Ellis . . . Boston: Richard G. Badger, [c1913]. (Boston, U. S. A.: The Gorham Press). 376 p.
LC: S 29, '13.
PW: S 6, '13.

E-141　　____ Twin Starrs: a novel / by J. Breckenridge Ellis . . . Boston: Mayhew Publishing Company, 1908. 215 p., dbl. phot. front. (ports.).　　**OSU, OKD**
LC: Ap 3, '08.
PW: Ap 18, '08.

E-142　　____ The Woodneys, an American Family / by J. Breckinridge Ellis . . . New York: The Devin-Adair Company, 1914. 187 p., front. [Ill. by Mat Harben.]
　　　　　　NYP
LC: Je 18, '14.
PW: Ag 22, '14.

E-143　　Ellis, James Tandy, 1868-1943. Colonel Torkey Shabb / by James Tandy Ellis . . . Boston: The Christopher Publishing House, [c1925]. 47 p., front., [1] leaf of plates.
LC: D 30, '25.

E-144　　____ Shawn of Skarrow / by James Tandy Ellis . . . Boston, Massachusetts: The C. M. Clark Publishing Co., [c1911]. 140 p., front., [9] leaves of plates. [Ill. by H. Boylston Dummer.]　　**EXG**

E-145　　____ Sycamore Bend / by James Tandy Ellis . . . Macon, Georgia: The J. W. Burke Company, 1923. 89, [1] p.　　**NDD**

E-146　　____ The tang of the South: stories / James Tandy Ellis. Lexington, Kentucky.: Hurst & Byars Printing Company, [c1924]. 114 p., front. (port.).
　　　　　　OSU, KTU
Cover title. Contents: His move -- Not vague but striking -- The hot end -- The longest chase -- The dream -- The climax -- The boy we took along -- The way out -- Pap's way -- Not superstitious -- Following instructions -- The call -- The wild oats -- Old buddies -- The opinion -- Home ties -- The supper -- Missed a few -- The calm captain --With Governor McCreary -- The river that was -- The codicil -- An old melody -- Down the river -- The unvarnished truth -- Playing them out -- The change of the wind -- Worth the money -- The old eyes -- As seen through other eyes -- The first wild west

show -- When they walked home -- The ghostly arm -- Items of family interest -- Anything to be accommodating -- Let not our rambling dreams affright our souls -- The defense -- Too much prayer -- "Swift to its close ebbs out life's fleeting day." -- The price -- By rounds -- Some fat --The cause of it -- When he retired -- Changing front -- To meet old "Nosey" -- The light that failed -- The young lawyer -- Case dismissed -- Railroading in old days -- The law for it -- Some scripture -- The nose for it -- A matter of politics -- The claimer -- The old-timer -- The great tragedy -- She knew Tom -- A condition of nerves -- Pig or pup? -- The verdict -- The diplomat -- The promise -- The truly great -- Nothin' but the truth -- Not much respect for "jestice" -- Tom Tonyer -- They called and he answered -- When Moike came home -- A matter of weather -- A game one -- The glad hand -- The monitor -- The old path -- The church pillar -- The track -- The friendly sentinel -- The boy he raised -- The epistle -- The sweet repose -- When he departed -- The golden rule -- No serious reflection -- Not interested -- The adorable uncle -- A shattered ideal -- A day of dissipation -- The obstacle -- A matter of precedent -- The heart of it -- The old timer -- The L. & N. record run -- Saving Grace -- The return -- The absence of Bill -- The end of the war -- When he put him across -- The test -- Joe Mulhattan's cats -- The vision -- The battle of Perryville -- Signs wrong -- The phenomena -- "The givin' hand" -- When they laughed -- Spell-bound -- No ear for music -- When the road hog met his brother -- Home sweet home -- The end -- One sure conversion -- The argument closed -- The number 13 -- The good old days -- How he led them -- A night to be remembered -- When he went to war -- The private still -- Nothing doing -- Called his hand -- The efficacy of prayer -- They put them over -- He put one over -- The wearin' av the green -- He knew himself -- The toast -- Like wimmen -- Perambulating home -- The only "Bill" Thorne -- A change in the wind -- Clark Riley -- Not agreeable -- He didn't know much -- Too much rabbit -- His conscience -- Not before the footlights -- Stolen sweets -- Twice in the same place -- The bitter end -- Reconciliation -- Games is games -- The consultation -- Speaking of tenacity -- No ghost to sit beside him -- Dog-gone my cats! -- The judge fixed me -- A matter of genealogy -- The family tree -- Dogs and plain truths.

Ellis, John Breckenridge. See **Ellis, J. Breckenridge (John Breckenridge), 1870-1956.**

E-147　　Ellis, Ross. The spirit of service: and other stories / by Ross Ellis. Chicago: The Inland Trade Press Company, 1914. 219 p., ill.
Reprinted from the Inland Stationer and the Business Equipment Journal.
Contents: The spirit of service -- Plugging for profits -- The livest wire -- A question of ethics -- The inside game -- The intensive idea -- Service -- The miracle -- A family affair -- Jerry Lane grows up -- The old order changeth -- A problem of policy -- The bald spot.
LC: F 19, '15.

E-148　　Ellis, Salone. The last wilderness / by Salone Ellis. Boston: Small, Maynard & Company, [c1925]. 356 p.
LC: O 21, '25.
PW: N 7, '25.

E-149　　____ The logger / by Salone Ellis. Boston: Small, Maynard & Company, [c1924]. 377 p.
LC: N 18, '24.
PW: N 8, '24.
BLC: London: Sampson Low & Co., [1926].

E-150　　Ellis, William, b. 1866. Johnson, of the ninth / by William Ellis. Wausau, Wisconsin: The Philosopher Press, [c1901]. 26 p.　　**DLC**
Reprinted from The Saturday Evening Post of Philadelphia.

E-151　　Ellison, Edith Nicholl. The blossoming of the waste: by Edith Nicholl Ellison . . . New York: Calkins and Company, 1908. 428 p., front., [1] leaf of plates.　　**TXU**
PW: My 23, '08.

E-152   _____ The burnt-offering / --by-- Edith Nicholl
Ellison . . . New York: Broadway Publishing Co.,
[c1908]. 190 p.
LC: N 27, '08.
PW: Ja 2, '09.

E-153   _____ The human touch: a tale of the great
Southwest / by Edith M. Nicholl; illustrated by
Charles Copeland. Boston: Lothrop Publishing
Company, [c1905]. 409 p., front., [3] leaves of
plates.   **AZS**

E-154   _____ The upward trail / by Edith Nicholl Ellison . . .
New York: Rowland & Ives, [c1918]. 302 p.
LC: My 6, '18.

E-155   Ellison, Margaret. The hunger of souls / by Margaret
Ellison . . . [Los Angeles: Printed by J. A. Alles
Co., c1922.] 62 p.
Unexamined copy: bibliographic data from NUC.
LC: My 27, '22.

E-156   Ellsworth, Franklin F. (Franklin Fowler), 1879-1942.
The band-wagon: a political novel of middle-America
/ by Franklin F. Ellsworth. Philadelphia: Dorrance
and Company, Inc., [c1921]. 391, [1] p.
LC: Ag 5, '21.

E-157   Elmore, James Buchanan, 1857-1942. Twenty-five
years in Jackville: a romance in the days of "The
Golden Circle", and selected poems / by James
Buchanan Elmore. Alamo, Ind.: Published by the
author [J. B. Elmore], 1904.
215 p., front. (port.). Designed end papers.

E-158   Elwell, Ambrose. At the sign of the Red Swan / by
Ambrose Elwell; illustrated by Reginald F. Bolles.
Boston: Small, Maynard & Company, [c1919].
216 p., col. front., [2] leaves of plates.
LC: D 10, '19.
PW: Ja 17, '20.

E-159   Elwood, Walter, b. 1886. Guimó / by Walter
Elwood; frontispiece by Grant Tyson Reynard.
Chicago: The Reilly & Britton Co., [c1915]. 344 p.,
front.
LC: F 1, '15.

Ely, Margaret Roberta, b. 1875. See **Ely, R. M.,
pseud.**

Ely, Mary S., jt. aut. _Confidences_ (1912). See
O'Hara, Edith C. (Edith Cecilia), jt. aut., O-50.

E-160   Ely, R. M., b. 1875, _pseud._ Evangeline of Ole
Virginia / by R. M. Ely [pseud.]. Louisville,
Kentucky: John P. Morton & Company,
Incorporated, 1923. 192 p.   **TET**

E-161   Emanuel, Victor Rousseau, b. 1879. The Big
Muskeg / by Victor Rousseau . . . Cincinnati:
Stewart Kidd Company, 1921. 302 p.
LC: Je 4, '21.
BLC: London: Hodder & Stoughton, [1923].

E-162   _____ Jacqueline of Golden River / by H. M. Egbert
[pseud.]; frontispiece by Ralph Pallen Coleman.
Garden City, N. Y.: Doubleday, Page & Company,
1920. 248 p., col. front.
PW: N 13, '20.
BLC: London: Hodder & Stoughton, 1924.

E-163   _____ The messiah of the cylinder / by Victor
Rousseau; illustrated by Joseph Clement Coll.
Chicago: A. C. McClurg & Co., 1917. 319 p.,
front., [10] leaves of plates.
LC: O 30, '17.
PW: N 24, '17.
BLC: London: Curtis Brown; Chicago: A. C.
McClurg & Co. [printed], 1917.

E-164   _____ Middle years / by V. R. Emanuel. New York:
Minton, Balch & Company, 1925. 332 p.
LC: Mr 10, '25.
PW: Mr 21, '25.

E-165   _____ The Selmans / V. R. Emanuel. New York:
Lincoln MacVeagh, The Dial Press, 1925. 372 p.
LC: O 6, '25.
PW: O 10, '25.

E-166   _____ Wooden spoil / by Victor Rousseau. New
York: George H. Doran Company, [c1919]. 312 p.
LC: Ap 28, '19.
PW: My 31, '19.
BLC: London: Hodder & Stoughton, [1923].

Embree, Charles Fleming, 1874-1905. The great
euchre boom. In _Argonaut stories_ **(1906), A-298.**

E-167   _____ A heart of flame / by Charles Fleming Embree
. . . ; the illustrations by Dan Smith. Indianapolis:
The Bowen-Merrill Company, [c1901]. 380, [1] p.,
front., [5] leaves of plates.
PW: Ap 13, '01.
BLC: London: B. F. Stevens & Brown, [1901].

E-168   Embree, Emily Davant. A lesser light / by Emily
Davant Embree; illustrated by Grace Wilson. Belton,
Texas: Baylor College, [c1904]. 307 p., photo.
front., [5] leaves of plates.

E-169   _____ Mine inheritance / by Emily Davant Embree.
Belton, Texas: The Cottage Home, [c1906]. 312 p.,
photo. front., [4] leaves of plates. [Ill. by A. J.
Embree.]   **NTH**

E-170   Emerson, Alice B. Ruth Fielding of the red mill, or,
Jasper Parloe's secret / by Alice B. Emerson . . . ;
illustrated. New York: Cupples & Leon Company,
[c1913]. 204 p., front.
LC: Je 19, '24.
PW: Jl 19, '13.

E-171   Emerson, Evalyn. Sylvia: the story of an American
countess / by Evalyn Emerson. Boston: Small,
Maynard & Company, 1901. 312 p., [12] leaves of
plates. [Ill. by Albert D. Blashfield, Carle J.
Blenner, J. Wells Champney, Howard Chandler
Christy, Louise Cox, Joseph De Camp, John Elliott,
C. Allan Gilbert, Albert Herter, Henry Hutt, Alice
Barber Stephens, and A. B. Wenzell.]
PW: O 19, '01.

Emerson, John, jt. aut. *The conspiracy.* See **Baker, Robert Melville, b. 1868, jt. aut., B-103.**

E-172   Emerson, W. H. (William H.), b. 1833. Josiah: a story of the old South / by W. H. Emerson . . . Astoria, Ill.: Search Light Printing House, 1906. 412 p.
Unexamined copy: bibliographic data from NUC and OCLC, # 29674958.
OCLC records publishing date as 1905.
LC: Ag 30, '06.

E-173   [_____] The ole watah mill deserted by man and doomed to silence and decay. And Mellissy and tha chillens. As told by Josiah [pseud.]. The black woman's burden, 1840-1865. A story of human slavery in Kentucky. A veneere of fiction, a density of fact. Astoria, Ill.: Search Light Printing House, 1903. 426 p.
Unexamined copy: bibliographic data from NUC and OCLC, # 19920829.

E-174   Emerson, Willis George, 1856-1918. Buell Hampton / by Willis George Emerson. Boston; Chicago: Forbes & Company, 1902. 420 p.
PW: My 10, '02.

E-175   _____ The builders / by Willis George Emerson. Chicago: Forbes & Company, 1906. 361 p.
LC: Je 25, '06.
BLC: London: Brown, Longham & Co., 1907.

E-176   _____ The man who discovered himself / by Willis George Emerson; illustrated by A. Hutchins. Chicago: Forbes & Company, 1919. 341 p., incl. front., [3] leaves of plates.
LC: Jl 7, '19.
PW: Jl 19, '19.

E-177   _____ The smoky god, or, A voyage to the inner world / by Willis George Emerson . . . ; with illustrations by John A. Williams. Chicago: Forbes & Company, 1908. 186 p., col. front., col. ill.   **UWT**
LC: Ag 10, '08.
PW: Ag 22, '08.

E-178   _____ The treasure of Hidden Valley / by Willis George Emerson. Chicago: Forbes & Company, 1915. 431 p.
LC: Je 24, '15.
BLC: London: Cassell & Co., [1916].

E-179   _____ A vendetta of the hills / by Willis George Emerson . . . ; illustrations by A. Hutchins. Boston: The Chapple Publishing Company, Ltd., 1917. 388 p., front., [7] leaves of plates.
LC: Mr 24, '17.
PW: Ap 28, '17.

E-180   Emery, Clay, b. 1870, *pseud.* Cap'n Titus: sketches of New England country folk / by Clay Emery [pseud.]. New York: Doubleday, Page & Company, 1902. 87 p.   **OSU, LAS**
Contents: The Captain's ride -- A remarkable shot -- Captain Titus sells some apples -- Uncle Silas on baked beans -- Captain Titus's eel story -- A whaling yarn -- A deep sea yarn -- Captain Titus's horse

trade -- A stomach pump story -- Captain Titus's bread foot -- Captain Titus goes yachting.
PW: N 1, '02.

Emery, G. "Squads right." **In *War stories* (1919), W-94.**

E-181   Emery, Pat. The valley of the Colorado / by Pat Emery . . . Los Angeles, Cal.: Pat Emery . . . , 1915. 146 p., photo. front.   **OSU, NYP**

E-182   Emery Percy M. Ten wildcats / by Percy M. Emery. [Oakland?, Calif., c1909.] 95 p.
Unexamined copy: bibliographic data from NUC.
Contents: The latest news from Rainbow Canyon -- The revellers of Rainbow Canyon -- Trapper Wilson & co. -- How Dead Horse got the dough -- The lynching bee -- Peter Bundy's placer ranch -- Partners -- Jerry McGordon -- A deal in real estate -- Albo Linton of Rainbow Canyon -- The prisoners -- Our babies.

E-183   Emley, Mabel R. Her romance; and, The value of a trained mind / by Mabel R. Emley. Baltimore, Md.: Saulsbury Publishing Company, [c1919]. 31 p.   **DLC**
LC: S 2, '19.

Emmet, Rosina H. The yearly tribute. **In *Life at high tide* (1907), L-281.**

E-184   Emory, Frederic, 1853-1908. A Maryland manor: a novel of plantation Aristocracy and its fall / by Frederic Emory: with a frontispiece by B. West Clinedinst. New York: Frederick A. Stokes Company, [c1901]. 449 p., front.
PW: Ap 27, '01.

E-185   Empey, Arthur Guy, 1883-1963. The Madonna of the hills: a story of a New York cabaret girl / by Arthur Guy Empey. New York; London: Harper & Brothers, [c1921]. 403, [1] p.
LC: F 3, '21.
PW: F 5, '21.

E-186   _____ Tales from a dugout / by Arthur Guy Empey. New York: The Century Co., 1918. 269 p.
Contents: Jim -- Soldier of the King -- The pacifist -- Private Ginger -- The lone tree sentinel -- Christmas in a dugout -- A siren of the boches -- Winning a D. C. M. -- The fusilier giants under fire -- "Blighty - What hopes?" -- Rounding up spies -- "Horses for France".
LC: N 2, '18.

E-187   The empty house. New York: Macmillan, 1917. 301 p., ill. [Ill. by Edward C. Caswell.]
LC: Je 28, '17.
PW: Jl 7, '17.

E-188   Emrick, Sara Rebecca. The shadow of a curse, or, Under the lilac bush / by Sara Rebecca Emrick. New York: Broadway Publishing Co., 1913. 446 p., front., [10] leaves of plates.   **ABC**
LC: Jl 11, '13.

E-189   Endicott, Ruth Belmore. Carolyn of the Corners / by Ruth Belmore Endicott; with illustrations by Edward C. Caswell. New York: Dodd, Mead and Company, 1918. 318 p., front., [3] leaves of plates.
LC: F 4, '18.
BLC: London: Jarrolds, [1919].

E-190   Carolyn of the sunny heart / by Ruth Belmore Endicott . . . ; illustrated by Edward C. Caswell. New York: Dodd, Mead and Company, 1919. 304 p., front., [3] leaves of plates. LC: F 26, '19.

E-191   England, George Allan, 1877-1936. The air trust / by George Allan England; illustrations by John Sloan. St. Louis, Mo.: Published by Phil Wagner, [c1915]. 333 p., front., [5] leaves of plates. LC: D 13, '15. PW: Ja 29, '16.

E-192   The alibi / by George Allan England; with a frontispiece by Modest Stein. Boston: Small, Maynard & Company, [c1916]. 363 p., col. front. LC: My 1, '16. PW: Ja 29, '16.

E-193   Cursed / by George Allan England . . . ; frontispiece by Modest Stein. Boston: Small, Maynard & Company, [c1919]. 349 p., col. front. LC: Ag 18, '19. PW: Jl 12, '19.

E-194   Darkness and dawn: illustrated / by George Allan England. Boston: Small, Maynard and Company, [c1914]. 672 p., col. front., [3] leaves of plates. [Ill. by P. J. Monahan and George W. Gage.] Illustrated end papers. LC: F 26, '14. PW: F 14, '14.

E-195   The flying legion / by George Allan England; frontispiece by P. J. Monahan. Chicago: A. C. McClurg & Co., 1920. 394 p., front. [Ill. by P. J. Monahan.] LC: Jl 28, '20. PW: Ag 28, '20.

E-196   The gift supreme / by George Allan England . . . New York: George H. Doran Company, [c1916]. 352 p. Illustrated end papers. PW: O 6, '17.

E-197   The golden blight / by George Allan England . . . ; frontispiece by C. D. Williams. New York: The H. K. Fly Company, [c1916]. 350 p., front., [4] leaves of plates. [Ill. by John Sloan.] LC: Ja 24, '17. PW: Ja 27, '17.

E-198   Keep off the grass / by George Allan England . . . ; illustrated by the author. Boston: Small, Maynard & Company, [c1919]. 140 p., front., ill. LC: Je 23, '19.

E-199   Pod, Bender & Co. / by George Allan England. New York: Robert M. McBride & Company, 1916. 382 p. LC: O 21, '16. PW: O 28, '16. BLC: London: T. Werner Laurie; printed in U. S. A., 1916.

E-200   Enright, Maurice. The Ridgefield Tavern: a romance of Sarah Bishop, hermitess, during the American Revolution / by Maurice Enright; with illustrations by Katherine Enright. Brooklyn: Eagle Book and Job Printing Department, 1908. 229 p., front., [3] leaves of plates. Designed end papers.

E-201   Enright, Richard E. (Richard Edward), b. 1871. The borrowed shield: a detective story / by Richard E. Enright. New York: G. Howard Watt, 1925. 320 p. LC: D 7, '25.

E-202   Vultures of the dark / by Richard E. Enright. New York: Brentano's, [c1924]. 360 p. LC: O 29, '24. PW: N 1, '24. BLC: London: Brentano's; printed in U. S. A., [1926].

E-203   Enright, Thomas. The king of Nobody's Island / by Thomas Enright. New York: The Gibson Publishing Company, c1909. 202 p. LC: Jl 12, '09.

E-204   Ensign, H. L. (Hermon Lee), 1849-1899. Lady Lee: and other animal stories / by Hermon Lee Ensign; illustrated in photogravure from original drawings by Max F. Klepper, J. Carter Beard, Jay Hambidge and Will H. Drake. Chicago: A. C. McClurg & Co., 1901. 256 p., front., [16] leaves of plates. Contents: Introductory memoir -- Lady Lee -- Gentleman Jack -- Union Square Jim -- My friend the elephant -- Sallie Russell -- Little Byron -- Baby and the kitten -- Maxey -- Daniel Pratt -- A kindergarten experiment. PW: O 5, '01.

E-205   Entwisle, T. Walker (Thomas Walker). For the house of LaCromie: a story of piracy and the commune / by T. Walter Entwisle. New York: Broadway Publishing Company, [c1905]. 235 p., front., [3] leaves of plates. [Ill. by Sidney K. Hartman.]   **DLC**

E-206   Eparde, Tirza. Two ends of a houseboat / by Tirza Eparde. New York; Baltimore: Broadway Publishing Co., [c1909]. 282 p., front., [5] leaves of plates. [Ill. by Wm. L. Hudson.]   **DLC** LC: D 31, '09.

E-207   Epstein, A. J. Tarquinius Superbus, or, The last of the Roman kings / by A. J. Epstein. New York: Mutual Publishing Company, [c1901]. 221 p., front. [Ill. by F. B. Madan.] PW: My 24, '02.

E-208   Erixon, Alexandre. The vale of shadows / by Alexandre Erixon. New York: Broadway Publishing Company, [c1908]. 286 p., front., [3] leaves of plates. [Ill. by Alexandre Erixon and William L. Hudson.] LC: O 26, '08. PW: D 12, '08.

Ernest, Joseph. Episode of the black casquette. _In Master tales of mystery_ **(1915), M-588.5.**

Ernst, E. Z., ed. <u>See</u> **Lewis, Dewitt F.** *A trip to the North Pole . . .* **(1912), L-248.**

E-209   Erskine, John, 1879-1951. The enchanted garden / by John Erskine. Chicago: The Bookfellows, 1925. 75 p.   **OSU, DPL**
LC: N 19, '25.

E-210   ____ The private life of Helen of Troy / by John Erskine. Indianapolis: The Bobbs-Merrill Company, [c1925]. 304 p.
LC: O 28, '25.
PW: N 7, '25.

E-211   Erskine, Laurie York, b. 1894. The confidence man / by Laurie York Erskine. New York; London: D. Appleton and Company, 1925. 302, [1] p.
LC: Ja 28, '25.
PW: F 7, '25.

E-212   ____ The laughing rider / by Laurie York Erskine . . . New York; London: D. Appleton and Company, 1924. 306, [1] p.
LC: Mr 11, '24.
PW: Mr 22, '24.
BLC: London: Hodder & Stoughton, [1927].

E-213   ____ The river trail: romance of the Royal Mounted / by Laurie York Erskine. New York; London: D. Appleton and Company, 1923. 339, [1] p.
LC: Ag 24, '23.
PW: S 1, '23.

E-214   ____ Valor of the range / by Laurie York Erskine. New York; London: D. Appleton and Company, 1925. 282 p.
LC: S 10, '25.
PW: S 19, '25.

E-215   Erskine, Payne, 1854-1924. The eye of dread / by Payne Erskine; with frontispiece by George Gibbs. Boston: Little, Brown and Company, 1913. 508 p., front.
LC: O 23, '13.
PW: O 18, '13.
BLC: London: Sampson Low & Co.; Boston [Mass.] printed, [1913].

E-216   ____ A girl of the Blue Ridge / by Payne Erskine; with frontispiece by J. Duncan Gleason. Boston: Little, Brown and Company, 1915. 401 p., front.
LC: Ap 24, '15.
PW: Ap 17, '15.
BLC: London: S. Low & Co., 1915.

E-217   ____ Joyful Heatherby / by Payne Erskine; with illustrations by M. Leone Bracker. Boston: Little, Brown and Company, 1913. 449 p., front., [3] leaves of plates.
LC: Ja 7, '13.
PW: Ja 4, '13.
BLC: London: Sampson Low & Co.; Boston, U. S. A. [printed, 1913].

E-218   ____ The mountain girl / by Payne Erskine; with illustrations by J. Duncan Gleason. Boston: Little, Brown and Company, 1912. 312 p., front., [5] leaves of plates.
LC: Mr 12, '12.
PW: F 10, '12.
BLC: London: Sampson Low & Co., [1912].

E-219   ____ When the gates lift up their heads: a story of the seventies / by Payne Erskine. Boston: Little, Brown and Company, 1901. 445 p.
PW: Je 1, '01.

E-220   Eskew, Harry, b. 1863, *pseud.* Dolly's folly: a Saratoga convention story / by Harry Eskew [pseud.]. Bloomfield, N. J.: The H. B. Wiggin's Sons Co., 1903. 31 p., ill. (some photo.).   **DLC**

E-221   ____ A fair prize: a World's Fair story / by Harry Eskew. Bloomfield, N. J.: H. B. Wiggin's Sons Co., 1904. 64 p., ill. (some photo.)   **DLC**

E-222   ____ The house of the honeymoon: a story / by Harry Eskew. Bloomfield, N. J.: H. B. Wiggin's Sons Co., 1903. 62 p., front., [3] leaves of plates. [Ill. by F. A. Stevens.]   **OSU, NYP**

E-223   Espy, Ella Gray. What will the answer be? / by Ella Gray Espy. New York; Washington: The Neale Publishing Company, 1907. 162 p.   **NYP**
LC: My 31, '07.

E-224   Essary, J. T. (John Thurman), 1855-1919. Tennessee mountaineers in type: a collection of stories / by J. T. Essary. New York: Cochrane Publishing Company, 1910. 110 p., front. (port.).
Contents: Introductory -- Salutatory -- In contempt of court -- His first case -- "Died a Bornin" -- An eye for business -- Young America -- A dying request -- The Jew merchant -- His pet sermon -- Wanted to see a real live editor -- Inquired the way to Jones -- The moonshiner diplomat -- Married according to law -- Mr. Boozer -- Took up collection for foreign missions -- He lived the simple life -- An indiscreet juror -- The samboes -- The wag of the town -- He grew poetical -- Poet no. 2 -- A modern horse jock -- The power of oratory -- Dr. Banks first call -- A dago organ-grinder in court -- "Who hit Billy Patterson?" -- Amen Bill Jones -- Little president -- In conclusion.
LC: N 17, '10.

E-225   Estabrook, Alma Martin. The rule of three: a story of Pike's Peak / by Alma Martin Estabrook; illustrated by George Brehm. Boston: Small, Maynard and Company, [c1909]. 309, [1] p., front., [5] leaves of plates.
LC: Ap 22, '09.

E-226   Estabrook, William Chester. The tribute and other stories / by William Chester Estabrook. Greenfield, Indiana: The Press of the Wm. Mitchell Printing Company, [1915]. 122 p.
Contents: The tribute -- The lovelier road -- The mourner -- The magic of sourness -- Staufenhagen -- The savers -- Horses for kingdom come -- A night call -- The renaissance.

E-227   Estes, George. The Wayfaring Man: a tale of the Temple / by George Estes . . . Portland, Oregon: George Estes' Publishers (Incorporated), [c1922]. (Portland, Oregon: Press of Kilham Stationery & Printing Company). 225 p., front., [5] leaves of plates.
LC: Ag 15, '22.

E-228   Estes, Thomas Jerome. Liberty Island / by T. J. Estes . . . [Yellville, Ark.], 1923. 48 p.

                          IXA (photocopy)

Estill, Eugenia. <u>See</u> **Meredith, junior, pseud.**

Eton, Seymour. <u>See</u> **Eaton, Seymour, 1859-1916.**

E-229   Eubank, Lulu Katherine. Old glory: a romance of Baltimore / by Lulu Katherine Eubank. New York; London; Montreal: The Abbey Press, [c1901]. 245 p.
PW: S 7, '01.

E-230   Eustis, Edith, b. 1874. Marion Manning: a novel / by Edith Eustis. New York; London: Harper & Brothers, 1902. 338, [1] p.
PW: Je 7, '02.

E-231   Evangeline, *pseud.* The new Acadians / by Evangeline [pseud.]; illustrated by Kate Van Buskirk. Chicago: Hammond Press, W. B. Conkey Company, 1904. 394 p., photo. front., [3] leaves of photo. plates.

E-232   Evans, Anna D. It beats the Shakers: or, A new tune / by Anna D. Evans. London; New York: Anglo-American Corporation, [c1905]. 128 p. Unexamined copy: bibliographic data from OCLC, #26938881

Evans, Augusta J. (Augusta Jane). <u>See</u> **Wilson, Augusta J. (Augusta Jane) Evans, 1835-1909.**

Evans, Florence Wilkinson. <u>See</u> **Wilkinson, Florence.**

E-233   Evans, George S. (George Samuel), 1876-1904. Wylackie Jake of Covelo / by George S. Evans. San Francisco, Cal.: Press of the Hicks-Judd Company, [1904]. 107 p., front. (port.).
Contents: Written in the dust -- A matchmaker of the foothills -- When understanding cried aloud at "Frying Pan" -- Enter Lizard Bill -- A personally conducted elopement -- Why Wylackie Jake went to Tehama -- Exit of a tenderfoot -- Doyle, J. P. -- Beyond the realm of law.

E-234   Evans, Henry Ridgely, b. 1861. The house of the sphinx: a novel / by Henry Ridgely Evans . . . New York; Washington: The Neale Publishing Company, 1907. 219 p.
LC: D 18, '07.
PW: Ja 4, '08.

E-235   Evans, Larry, d. 1925. His own home town / by Larry Evans . . . ; illustrated by Harvey Dunn. New York: The H. K. Fly Company, [c1917]. 319 p., front.

E-236   ____ Once to every man / by Larry Evans; illustrated by Anton Otto Fischer. New York: H. K. Fly Company, [c1914]. 317 p., front., [3] leaves of plates.
LC: Mr 31, '15.

E-237   ____ The painted lady / by Larry Evans . . . ; illustrated with scenes from the photoplay, a William Fox production. New York: Grosset & Dunlap, [c1925]. 251 p., photo. front., [7] leaves of photo. plates.   **MUB**
LC: Mr 27, '24.
PW: F 7, '25.

E-238   ____ Then I'll come back to you / by Larry Evans; illustrated by Will Stevens. New York: The H. K. Fly Company, [c1915]. 372 p., front., [3] leaves of plates.
LC: D 1, '15.
PW: D 4, '15.

E-239   ____ Winner take all / by Larry Evans. New York: The H. K. Fly Company, [c1920]. 241 p.
BLC: London: Hodder & Stoughton, [1921].

E-240   Evans, Marian, b. 1884. Chronicles of the Marvilou Company "Just girls" / by Marian Evans. New York City: Helen Norwood Halsey, [c1913]. 314 p., incl. front., ill. (some photo.).

E-241   Evans, Mary Ruth. The story of Edah / by Mary Ruth Evans. New York: Broadway Publishing Co., 1914. 324 p.   **DLC**
LC: N 6, '14.

E-242   Evans, Zella. The tragedy of Montiville / by Zella Evans. Fort Wayne, Indiana: Published by the author, [c1905]. 104 p.   **IMF**
PW: Jl 22, '05.

E-243   Evarts, Hal G. (Hal George), 1887-1934. The bald face: and other animal stories / by Hal G. Evarts; with illustrations by Charles Livingston Bull. New York: Alfred A. Knopf, 1921. 317 p., front., [7] leaves of plates.
Contents: The bald-face (grizzly bear) -- The tawny menace (mountain lion) -- The palmated pioneer (moose) -- The vanished squadrons (white cranes) -- Traveling otter -- The black ram of sunlight (mountain sheep) -- Dog town (prarie dog) -- The black and cinnamon twins (bear) -- Savagery -- The last move (antelope).
LC: N 25, '21.
BLC: London: Hodder & Stoughton; printed in U. S. A., [1922].

E-244   ____ The cross pull / Hal G. Evarts. New York: Alfred A. Knopf, 1920. 273 p., incl. front.
LC: Mr 3, '20.
PW: Mr 20, '20.
BLC: London: Hodder & Stoughton, [1920].

E-245   ____ The passing of the old West / by Hal G. Evarts; with illustrations by Charles Livingston Bull. Boston: Little, Brown and Company, 1921. 234 p., front., [7] leaves of plates.
"Published serially as *Old-timer*."
LC: O 26, '21.
PW: O 29, '21.

E-246   ____ The settling of the sage / by Hal G. Evarts; with illustrations by Douglas Duer. Boston: Little, Brown and Company, 1922. 300 p., front., [3] leaves of plates.
LC: Ja 30, '22.
PW: F 18, '22.
BLC: London: Hodder & Stoughton, [1922].

E-247 _____ Spanish acres / by Hal G. Evarts. Boston: Little, Brown and Company, 1925. 303 p.
LC: Ag 14, '25.
PW: Ag 15, '25.

E-248 _____ Tumbleweeds / by Hal G. Evarts; with frontispiece by W. H. D. Koerner. Boston: Little, Brown and Company, 1923. 297 p., front.
LC: Ja 10, '23.
PW: Ja 6, '23.
BLC: London: Hodder & Stoughton, 1923.

E-249 _____ The yellow horde / by Hal G. Evarts; with illustrations by Charles Livingston Bull. Boston: Little, Brown and Company, 1921. 227 p., front., [3] leaves of plates.
LC: Ap 23, '21.
PW: Ap 16, '21.
BLC: London: Hodder & Stoughton, [1921].

E-250 Evarts, R. C. (Richard Conover), b. 1890. Alice's adventures in Cambridge / by R. C. Evarts; illustrated by E. L. Barron. Cambridge, Mass.: Published by The Harvard Lampoon, [c1913]. 67 p.
LC: Je 17, '13.

E-251 Everard, Florence. A noble fool / by Florence Everard. New York: Stitt Publishing Company, 1906. 300 p. **NYP**
PW: Je 9, '06.
BLC: Bristol: J. W. Arrowsmith, 1907.

E-252 Everett, Bert Noland, b. 1873. Accomplished through sacrifice / by Bert N. Everett . . . Decatur, Ill.: The Review Press, c1910. 120, [1] p., photo. front. (port.). **TXX**
LC: Je 13, '10.

E-253 Everett, Charles. Nano: a heart's story from the unseen world / by Charles Everett. New York; Washington: The Neale Publishing Company, 1904. 120 p.
PW: D 24, '04.

Everett, Elizabeth Abbey. Bufo, the mascot. In *West winds* (1914), W-368.

E-254 Everett, Lloyd T. (Lloyd Tilghman), b. 1875. For Maryland's honor: a story of the war for Southern independence / by Lloyd T. Everett. Boston: The Christopher Publishing House, [c1922]. 229 p., col. front., [1] leaf of plates.
LC: Ja 18, '22.

E-255 Everett, Ruth. That man from Wall street: a story of the studios / by Ruth Everett . . . New York: George Thiell Long, [c1908]. 360 p., front. **CKM**
LC: Je 11, '08.
PW: Je 20, '08.

E-256 Evinson, Elmer, b. 1872, *pseud.* An amateur performance / by Elmer Evinson [pseud.]. New York: Broadway Publishing Company, [c1909]. 164 p. **DLC**
LC: Je 16, '09.

E-257 Ewell, Alice Maude, 1860-1946. A long time ago: in Virginia and Maryland with a glimpse of old England / by Alice Maude Ewell. New York; Washington: The Neale Publishing Company, 1907. 246 p., front., [9] leaves of plates. [Ill. by George Wharton Edwards, Reginald Bathurst Birch, W. D. Stevens, et al.]
LC: Ag 19, '07.

E-258 Eyerman, John. Blankenbergne: a serio-comic detective tale in which no fire-arms are used and no one is killed, being a three days episode in the life of the Duke of Belleville / as related by Lord Edward Lyndon; with an introductory chapter by The Duke of Belleville; edited by John Eyerman. Easton, Pa: J. E., Private Press at Oakhurst House, 1910. 62 p. **DLC**

E-259 _____ Peachmonk: a serio-comic detective tale in which no fire-arms are used and no one is killed, being a three days episode in the life of the Duke of Belleville / as related by Lord Edward Lyndon; John Eyerman. New York: [s. n.], 1917. 26 p. **DLC**

E-260 Eyre, Archibald. The custodian / by Archibald Eyre; with illustrations by Penrhyn Stanlaws. New York: Henry Holt and Company, 1904. 359 p., front., [3] leaves of plates.
BLC: London: Ward, Lock & Co., 1904.

E-261 _____ The girl in waiting / by Archibald Eyre. Boston; London: J. W. Luce and Company, 1906. 325 p., front. [Ill. by G. F. Gray.]
BLC: London: Ward, Lock & Co., 1906.

E-262 _____ The trifler: a love comedy / by Archibald Eyre; illustrated by Archie Gunn. New York; London: The Smart Set Publishing Co., 1903. 334 p., front., [5] leaves of plates.
BLC: London: Ward, Lock & Co., 1903.

E-263 Eyre, Laurence, 1881-1959. The things that count / by Laurence Eyre; novelized from the play by the author; illustrated from scenes in the play. Boston: Little, Brown and Company, 1914. 282 p., front., [5] leaves of plates.
LC: O 14, '14.

Eyster, Nellie (Blessing), Mrs. See **Blessing-Eyster, Nellie, 1831?-1922.**

F

F. D. B., pseud. See **Warner, Anne, 1869-1913.**

F. Z. E., pseud. See **Warde, Reginald, b. 1878.**

F-1 Fa-El-La. The lost pearl / by Fa-El-La. New York; Cincinnati: The Lawriston Press, 1904. 54 p., front., [4] leaves of plates. **DLC**

F-2 Faber, Christine. The burden of honor / by Christine Faber. New York: P. J. Kenedy & Sons, [c1915]. 291 p. **DLC**
PW: O 9, '15.

F-3 _____ An original girl / by Christine Faber. New York: P. J. Kenedy, 1901. 767 p., front., [7] leaves of plates. [Ill. by W. V. Cahill.]
PW: Ag 3, '01.

F-4 _____ Reaping the whirlwind: a story of to-day / by Christine Faber . . . New York: P. J. Kenedy & Sons, 1905. 466 p.   **MNL**

F-5 Faber, Rix. Six mad men / by Rix Faber. New York; Chicago; Boston: The Old Greek Press, [c1907]. 405 p.
LC: Ap 6, '07.

F-6 Fabian, Joseph Warren. The tyranny of prohibition: a novel / by Joseph Warren Fabian. New York City: The Independent Authors' Library, Copyright, 1924. 94 p.

Fabian, Warner, pseud. See **Adams, Samuel Hopkins, 1871-1958.**

F-7 Fagan, George Henry Joseph. Eternal universal liberty / written by George Henry Joseph Fagan. [s. l.: s. n., 192-?]. 112 p.

Fagan, James O. The diary of a white kaffir. In *Through the forbidden gates* **(1903), T-222.**

F-8 Fagin, Myron Lawrence. Defiance: a narrative / by Myron Lawrence Fagin. [Chicago]: Imperial Press, [c1908]. 265 p.
LC: Je 6, '08.

F-9 Fagin, Nathan Bryllion, b. 1892. Of love and other trifles / by N. Bryllion Fagin. Washington, D. C.: Rossi-Bryn Company, 1925. 47 p.
Contents: To the gentle reader -- Of love -- Only a city -- Regret -- The martyr -- Successful methods -- The strange creature -- The epitaph -- Sailing on -- The autobiography of a kiss -- Magic -- Reformation -- Freedom -- Night in the garden -- Futility -- Their common bond -- Peculiarly made -- The fly and the bees -- The heartless ones -- Resurrection -- A game of angles -- They who are hard -- A summer romance -- Of the moon.

F-10 Fairbank, Janet Ayer. The Cortlandts of Washington Square / by Janet A. Fairbank. Indianapolis: The Bobbs-Merrill Company, [c1922]. 399 p.
LC: O 2, '22.
PW: O 7, '22.
BLC: London: Arrowsmith, 1926.

F-11 _____ The Smiths / by Janet A. Fairbank. Indianapolis: The Bobbs-Merrill Company, [c1925]. 433 p.
LC: Je 10, '25.
PW: My 30, '25.
BLC: London: Arrowsmith, 1925.

Fairbrother, Al, jt. aut. *Discovered!* (1910?) See **Hopkins, Lindsey, jt. aut., H-816.**

F-12 Fairman, Leroy. The blue calf: and other tales of Peter / by Leroy Fairman. Boston: Griffith-Stillings Press, 1908. 143 p., ill.
Contents: The blue calf -- A streak of luck -- When civic duty calls -- The Essex Falls Banner -- The Deacon's cat -- Peter's engagement.

LC: N 27, '08.

F-13 _____ The philosophy of Peter the printer / by Leroy Fairman. As told in six improving tales, of which this is the first. Boston, Mass.: The Griffith-Stillings Press, c1906. Col. front., ill.
Unexamined copy: bibliographic data from NUC.
LC: S 12, '06.
PW: Jl 14, '06.

F-14 Fairweather, Mary. The passion stroke: a tale of ancient Masonry / by Mary Fairweather. Boston: Richard G. Badger, 1906. (Boston: The Gorham Press). 255 p., col. ill.
LC: Je 12, '06.

F-15 Fales, William E. S. Bits of broken china / by Wm. E. S. Fales. New York; London: Street & Smith, [c1902]. 171 p., incl. front., ill.
Contents: Poor Doc High -- The Red Mogul -- The temptation of Li-Li -- A Mott street incident -- The end of the hall -- The mousetrap -- The turning of the worm.
PW: My 17, '02.

F-16 Fame, John. Witchery of an oriental lamp / by John Fame. New York, N. Y.: The Best Sellers Co., [c1923]. 348 p.   **DLC**
LC: Ap 26, '23.

F-17 Famous, William N. Colonel Crook stories / by William N. Famous; illustrated by Joseph A. Lemon. New York: Excelsior Publishing House, [c1909]. 95 p., ill.
Contents: Colonel Crook explains why -- Colonel Crook's practical joke -- Colonel Crook has lots -- Colonel Crook as a gyp -- Colonel Crook has pictures -- Colonel Crook supes -- Colonel Crook gets the hook -- Colonel Crook plays a week -- Colonel Crook spellbinds -- Colonel Crook exhorts -- Colonel Crook, temperance orator -- Colonel Crook masquerades -- Colonel Crook, railroader -- Colonel Crook joy-rides -- Colonel Crook, ardent lover.

F-18 Famous modern ghost stories / selected, with an introduction by Dorothy Scarborough . . . New York; London: G. P. Putnam's Sons, 1921. ([New York]: The Knickerbocker Press). 419 p.
Contents: Introduction: The imperishable ghost -- The willows / Algernon Blackwood -- The shadows on the wall / Mary E. Wilkins Freeman -- The messenger / Robert W. Chambers -- Lazarus / Leonid Andreyev -- The beast with five fingers / W. F. Harvey -- The mass of shadows / Anatole France -- What was it? / Fitz James O'Brien -- The middle toe of the right foot / Ambrose Bierce -- The shell of sense / Olivia Howard Dunbar -- The woman at Seven Brothers / Wilbur Daniel Steele -- At the gate / Myla Jo Closser -- Ligeia / Edgar Allan Poe -- The haunted orchard / Richard Le Gallienne -- The bowmen / Arthur Machen -- A ghost / Guy de Maupassant.
LC: My 24, '21.

F-19 Fane, Frances Gordon, b. 1867. Richard Wyndham: a novel / by Frances Gordon Fane . . . New York: G. W. Dillingham Company, [c1902]. 384 p.
PW: N 8, '02.

F-20 _____ The way of a man with a maid / by Frances Gordon Fane. New York: G. W. Dillingham, 1901, [c1900]. 301 p.
Unexamined copy: bibliographic data from OCLC, #17664719.
PW: Ap 20, '01.

Faragoh, Francis Edwards. The distant street. In *Prize stories of 1923 (1924), P-621.*

F-21 Faris, John Thomson, 1871-1949. How it was done in harmony: a story of adult class work / by John T. Faris. Cincinnati: The Standard Publishing Company, [c1916]. 132 p.

F-22 Fariss, Amy Cameron. The sin of Saint Desmond / by Amy Cameron Fariss. Boston: Richard G. Badger, 1905. (Boston: The Gorham Press). 351 p., front. [Ill. by C. F. Cobbledick.]
LC: My 8, '06.
PW: Ap 21, '06.

Farley, Eileen. St. Patrick and the pink gown. In *The lady of the tower (1909), L-13.*

F-23 Farley, J. Elizabeth (Judith Elizabeth), b. 1844. The world we do not see / by J. Elizabeth Farley. New York: Broadway Publishing Company, 1912. 110 p.   **DLC**

F-24 Farman, Emma Shogren. Where the Mississippi flows: and other stories / by Emma Shogren Farman. Chicago, Ill.: The Swedish M. E. Book Concern, [c1906]. 126 p., photo. front.
Contents: Where the Mississippi flows -- Darlig Sven -- When the railroad came -- Nils Kvarn's eternity machine -- Brother Swenson's call -- The old man's long walk -- Annie's gold ring.

F-25 Farmer, James Eugene, 1867-1915. Brinton Eliot: from Yale to Yorktown / by James Eugene Farmer . . . New York: The Macmillan Company; London: Macmillan & Co., Ltd., 1902. 395 p.

F-26 Farnsworth, F. F. (Floyd Forney), b. 1869. The man on horseback: a story of life among the West Virginia hills / by Dr. F. F. Farnsworth. Charleston, W. Va.: Tribune Printing Co., 1921. 264 p. **WVU**
LC: N 5, '21.

F-27 Farnum, Mabel Adelaide, b. 1887. The cry of the street: a novel / by Mabel A. Farnum . . . Boston, Mass.: Angel Guardian Press, [c1913]. 253, [1] p., photo. front., [3] leaves of plates.
LC: D 1, '13.

F-28 ____ The fruit of the tree: a novel / by Mabel A. Farnum. St. Louis, Mo.; Freiburg (Baden), Ger.; London: Published by B. Herder, 1914. 293 p.
LC: D 7, '14.
PW: D 19, '14.

F-29 ____ The town landing / by Mabel Farnum. New York: P. J. Kenedy & Sons, 1923. 227 p.
LC: Ja 10, '24.
PW: D 15, '23.

F-30 ____ The wounded face / by Mabel A. Farnum. Boston: Angel Guardian Press, 1911. 158 p., front. [Ill. by H. Hofmann.]
LC: D 16, '11.

F-31 Farquhar, Anna, b. 1865. The devil's plough: the romantic history of a soul conflict / by Anna Farquhar . . . ; with a frontispiece in colour by Frank T. Merrill. Boston: L. C. Page & Company, 1901. 342 p., col. front.
PW: Mr 9, '01.
BLC: London: John Macqueen, 1901.

F-32 ____ An Evans of Suffolk / by Anna Farquhar. Boston: L. C. Page & Company, 1904. 408 p.
PW: F 27, '04.

F-33 ____ Her Washington experiences: as related by a cabinet minister's wife in a series of letters to her sister / by Anna Farquhar; illustrated by T. De Thulstrup. Boston: L. C. Page & Company, 1902. 222 p., front., incl. [18] leaves of plates.

F-34 Farquhar, Franklin S. (Franklin Smith), b. 1865. Edith and John: a story of Pittsburgh / by Franklin S. Farquhar. [Tacoma, Wash.: Printed by Commercial Bindery & Printing Co., 1912]. 252 p.   **TAW**

F-35 Farr, Julia. The great experience / by Julia Farr . . . Salt Lake City, Utah: The Deseret News, 1920. 224 p., front., [4] leaves of plates. [Ill. by J. A. Baywater.]   **NYP**

F-36 ____ Venna Hastings: story of an eastern Mormon convert / by Julia Farr. Independence, Jackson County, Mo.: Zion's Printing and Publishing Company, 1919. 200 p.   **UUM**
LC: Ap 28, '19.

F-37 Farrar, John, b. 1848. Uncle Ike / by John Farrar. New York; London; F. Tennyson Neely, [c1902]. 235 p.

Farrar, Maude. The disciplinarian. In *Club stories (1915), C-502.*

F-38 Farrell, John Rupert. A change of opinion / by John Rupert Farrell. Boston: Richard G. Badger, [c1920]. ([Boston]: The Gorham Press). 243 p.
PW: Mr 13, '20.

Farrer, F. M. The recoil of circumstance. In **Seattle Writer's Club.** *Tillicum tales (1907), S-248.*

F-39 Farrington, Frank, b. 1872. John Martin's clerks: a tale of the store / by Frank Farrington . . . Delhi, N. Y.: Merchants' Helps Publishing Co., 1907, [c1906]. 92 p.   **DLC**
LC: Jl 8, '07.

F-40 Farrington, Franklin Fillmore. The mansion with one door / by Franklin Fillmore Farrington. Cincinnati, Ohio: Powell & White, [c1924]. 52 p.

F-41 Fauley, Wilbur Finley, 1872-1942. After midnight: a romantic story adapted from Lawrence Marston and Finley Fauley's play of the same name. New York: J. S. Ogilvie Publishing Company, [c1904]. 179 p.
Unexamined copy: bibliographic data from OCLC, #26939010.

F-42   ____ Fires of fate: a mystery novel / by Wilbur Finley Fauley; frontispiece by Frank Tenney Johnson. New York: Metropolitan Book Service, [c1923]. 310 p., front.
LC: Mr 12, '23.

F-43   ____ Jenny be good / by Wilbur Finley Fauley. New York: Britton Publication Company, [c1919]. 326 p., col. front.
LC: Ag 23, '19.

F-44   ____ Queenie: the adventures of a nice young lady / by Wilbur Finley Fauley . . . ; frontispiece by G. W. Gage. New York: The Macaulay Company, [c1921]. 306 p., front.
LC: My 3, '21.

F-45   Faulkner, Georgene, b. 1873. Sammy's service star; the story of a Christmas angel / by Georgene Faulkner, "the story lady." Chicago: Ralph Fletcher Seymour, [c1917]. 16 p., incl. front.   **PLF**
LC: F 2, '18.

F-46   Fauset, Jessie Redmon. There is confusion / by Jessie Redmon Fauset. New York: Boni and Liveright, 1924. 297 p.   **CLE**
BLC: London: Chatto & Windus, 1924.

     Faust, Frederick, 1892-1944. <u>See</u> **Brand, Max, pseud.**

F-47   Faversham, Julie Opp, 1873-1921. The squaw man: a novel / by Julie Opp Faversham; adapted from the play by Edward Milton Royle. New York; London: Harper & Brothers Publishers, 1906. 293, [1] p., front., [7] leaves of plates.
LC: D 13, '07.

F-48   Fawcett, Edgar, 1847-1904. The vulgarians / by Edgar Fawcett; illustrated by Archie Gunn. New York; London: The Smart Set Publishing Co., 1903. 213 p., front., [3] leaves of plates.
LC: My 19, '03.
PW: Je 6, '03.
References: BAL 5681.

F-49   Fay, John William, b. 1871. Muzzling the tiger / by John W. Fay. New York: Murray Hill Publishers, Inc., [c1924]. 390 p., front., [1] leaf of plates. [Ill. by Stockton Mulford.]
LC: Ap 10, '24.
PW: Ap 26, '24.

F-50   Fay, Mattie Talbert. The tables turned: a temperance story / by Mattie Talbert Fay. Boston: The Roxburgh Publishing Company, Inc., [c1914]. 160 p.   **DLC**

     Fedden, Katharine Waldo Douglas. <u>See</u> **Fedden, Romilly, Mrs., d. 1939.**

F-51   Fedden, Romilly, Mrs., d. 1939. The peacock's tail / by Mrs. Romilly Fedden. Boston; New York: Houghton Mifflin Company, 1925. (Cambridge: The Riverside Press). 243 p.

LC: O 12, '25.
PW: O 24, '25.
BLC: London: T. Nelson & Sons, 1926.

F-52   ____ Shifting sands / by Mrs. Romilly Fedden (Katherine Waldo Douglas). Boston; New York: Houghton Mifflin Company, 1914. (Cambridge: The Riverside Press). 336, [2] p.
LC: N 13, '14.
PW: F 20, '15.

F-53   ____ The sign / by Mrs. Romilly Fedden (Katharine Waldo Douglas). New York: Dodd, Mead and Company, 1912. 329 p.
LC: Jl 6, '12.
BLC: London: Macmillan & Co., 1912.

F-54   ____ The spare room / by Mrs. Romilly Fedden; with illustrations by Haydon Jones. Boston; New York: Houghton Mifflin Company, 1913. (Cambridge: The Riverside Press). 203 p., front., [3] leaves of plates.
PW: Ja 31, '14.
BLC: London: Duckwith & Co., 1913.

F-55   Fee, Mary H. (Mary Helen). The locusts' years / by Mary Helen Fee . . . ; illustrated by Charles Sarka. Chicago: A. C. McClurg & Co., 1912. 378 p., incl. col. front.
LC: O 7, '12.

     Feehan, (Sister) Mary Edward, b.1878. <u>See</u> **Clementia, pseud.**

F-56   Feld, Rose C. (Rose Caroline), b. 1895. Humanizing industry / by R. C. Feld. New York: E. P. Dutton & Company, [c1920]. 390 p.   **OBE**

     Felix, Harry. <u>See</u> **H. F.**

     Fell, Gulielma. <u>See</u> **Alsop, Gulielma Fell, b. 1881.**

F-57   Fellom, James. The rider of the Mohave: a western story / by James Fellom. New York: Chelsea House, [c1924]. 318 p.
LC: N 4, '24.
PW: N 22, '24.
BLC: London: Geoffrey Bles, [1926].

F-58   Fenger, Frederic A. (Frederic Abildgaard), b. 1882. The golden parrot / by Frederic A. Fenger; with illustrations by Harold Cue. Boston; New York: Houghton Mifflin Company, 1921. (Cambridge: The Riverside Press). 275, [1] p., front., ill.
LC: Ap 2, '21.
PW: Mr 12, '21.

F-59   Fenn, R. W. (Robert Wilson), b. 1867. The hidden empire: a tale of true deeds and great ones which the tropic sun witnessed / by R. W. Fenn; with illustrations by M. Leone Bracker. New York: Dodd, Mead and Company, 1911. 402 p., front., [4] leaves of plates, 1 map.
LC: S 16, '11.
PW: S 16, '11.

F-60   ____ Horacio: a tale of Brazil / by R. W. Fenn. San Francisco: [s. n.], 1911. 299 p.   **CSH**
LC: Jl 13, '11.

Fenollosa, Mary McNeil. See **McCall, Sidney, pseud.**

F-61   Fenwick, Frances De Wolfe. The arch-satirist / by Frances De Wolfe Fenwick; illustrated by Charles Copeland. Boston: Lothrop, Lee & Shepard Co., [c1910]. 358 p., col. front.
LC: Ap 9, '10.

Ferber, Edna, 1887-1968. April 25th, as usual. In *Prize stories of 1919* **(1920), P-617.**

F-62   ____ Buttered side down: stories / by Edna Ferber; with frontispiece in color by R. Ford Harper and other illustrations in black-and-white by Thomas Fogarty and Irma Dérèmeaux. New York: Frederick A. Stokes Company, [c1912]. 230 p., col. front., [4] leaves of plates.
Contents: The frog and the puddle -- The man who came back -- What she wore -- A Bush league hero -- The kitchen side of the door -- One of the old girls -- Maymeys from Cuba -- The leading lady -- That home-town feeling -- The homely heroine -- Sun dried -- Where the car turns at 18th.
LC: Ap 1, '12.

F-63   ____ Cheerful: by request / by Edna Ferber. Garden City, N. Y.: Doubleday, Page & Company, 1918. 366 p.
Contents: Cheerful-by request -- The gay old dog -- The tough guy -- The eldest -- That's marriage -- The woman who tried to be good -- The girl who went right -- The hooker-up-the-back -- The guiding Miss Gowd -- Sophy-as-she-might-have-been -- The three of them -- Shore leave.
LC: S 17, '18.
PW: S 14, '18.
BLC: London: Methuen & Co., 1919.

F-64   ____ Dawn O'Hara: the girl who laughed / by Edna Ferber; frontispiece in colors by R. Ford Harper. New York: Frederick A. Stokes Company, [c1911]. 302 p., col. front.
LC: My 16, '11.
PW: My 20, '11.

F-65   ____ Emma McChesney & Co. / by Edna Ferber; with four illustrations by J. Henry. New York: Frederick A. Stokes Company, [1915]. 231 p., front., [3] leaves of plates.
Contents: Broadway to Buenos Aires -- Thanks to Miss Morrissey -- A closer corporation -- Blue serge -- "Hoops, my dear!" -- Sisters under their skin - An étude for Emma.
LC: O 2, '15.
PW: O 2, '15.

F-66   ____ Fanny herself / by Edna Ferber; illustrated by J. Henry. New York: Frederick A. Stokes Company, [c1917]. 323 p., front., [3] leaves of plates.
LC: O 6, '17.
PW: O 6, '17.

____ The gay old dog. In *The best short stories of 1917 and the yearbook of the American short story* **(1918), B-562.**

F-67   ____ Gigolo / by Edna Ferber. Garden City, New York: Doubleday, Page & Company, 1922. 291 p. "First edition."
Contents: The afternoon of a faun -- Old man Minick -- Gigolo -- Not a day over twenty-one -- Home girl -- Ain't nature wonderful! -- The sudden sixties -- If I should ever travel!
LC: N 23, '22.
PW: N 11, '22.
BLC: London: Eveleigh Nash & Grayson; printed in U. S. A., 1923. (British Title: *Among those present*.)

F-68   ____ The girls / by Edna Ferber. Garden City, N. Y.; Toronto: Doubleday, Page & Company, 1921. 374 p.
LC: O 28, '21.
PW: O 8, '21.
BLC: London: William Heinemann, 1922.

F-69   ____ Half portions / by Edna Ferber. Garden City, N. Y.: Doubleday, Page & Company, 1920. 315, [1] p.
Contents: The maternal feminine -- April 25th, as usual -- Old lady Mandle -- You've got to be selfish -- Long distance -- Un morso doo pang -- One hundred per cent -- Farmer in the dell -- The dancing girls.
LC: My 26, '20.
PW: My 29, '20.

____ Home girl. In *The best short stories of 1923 and the yearbook of the American short story* **(1924), B-568.**

____ Old man Minick. In *Aces* **(1924),, A-42.**

____ One hundred percent. In *War stories* **(1919), W-94.**

F-70   ____ Personality plus: some experiences of Emma McChesney and her son, Jock / by Edna Ferber, with fifteen illustrations, by James Montgomery Flagg. New York: Frederick A. Stokes Company, [1914]. 161 p., front., [3] leaves of plates, ill.
LC: S 22, '14.
PW: S 19, '14.

F-71   ____ Roast beef medium: the business adventures of Emma McChesney / by Edna Ferber; with twenty-seven illustrations by James Montgomery Flagg. New York: Frederick A. Stokes Company, [c1913]. 296 p., front., [3] leaves of plates, ill.
Contents: Roast beef, medium -- Representing T. A. Buck -- Chickens -- His mother's son -- Pink tights and ginghams -- Simply skirts -- Underneath the high-cut vest -- Catching up with Christmas -- Knee-deep in knickers -- In the absence of the agent.
LC: Mr 29, '13.
PW: Ap 5, '13.
BLC: London: Methuen & Co., 1920.

F-72   ____ So big / by Edna Ferber. -- 1st ed. -- Garden City, New York: Doubleday, Page & Company, 1924. 360 p.
LC: Mr 7, '24.
PW: F 9, '24.
BLC: London: William Heinemann, 1924.

F-73   Ferguson, Esther Baldwin, b. 1842. The lump of gold / by Esther Baldwin Ferguson. San Francisco: Gilmartin Company, [c1910]. 229 p.

F-74 Ferguson, John W. The way to win / by John W. Ferguson. New York; Washington: The Neale Publishing Company, 1909. 358 p. **SUC**

F-75 Ferguson, Robert, b. 1845. Love tested in the fires of the sixties / by Rev. Robert Ferguson . . . New York: The Shakespeare Press, 1912. 235 p., front. (port.).
Unexamined copy: bibliographic data from NUC.
LC: N 21, '12.

F-76 Ferguson, W. B. M. (William Blair Morton), b. 1882. The black company: a mystery story / by W. B. M. Ferguson. New York: Chelsea House, [c1924]. 320 p.
LC: Ap 17, '24.
PW: Ap 19, '24.

F-77 _____ Garrison's finish: a romance of the race-course / by W. B. M. Ferguson; illustrations by Charles Grunwald. New York: Street & Smith, [c1906]. 282 p., front., [5] leaves of plates.
LC: Je 20, '07.

F-78 _____ A man's code / by W. B. M. Ferguson . . . ; illustrations by A. L. Bairnsfather. New York: G. W. Dillingham Company, [c1915]. 305 p., front., [2] leaves of plates.
LC: Je 1, '15.

F-79 _____ Zollenstein / by W. B. M. Ferguson. New York: D. Appleton and Company, 1908. 349, [1] p., front.
LC: My 1, '08.

F-80 Fergusson, Harvey, 1890-1971. The blood of the conquerors / by Harvey Fergusson. New York: Alfred A. Knopf, 1921. 265, [1] p.
LC: O 6, '21.
PW: O 22, '21.
BLC: London: Chapman Hall, 1922.

F-81 _____ Capitol Hill: a novel of Washington life / by Harvey Fergusson. New York: Alfred A. Knopf, 1923. 309 p.
LC: Ap 25, '23.
PW: Ap 14, '23.
BLC: London: John Lane, 1924.

F-82 _____ Women and wives / by Harvey Ferguson. New York: Alfred A. Knopf, 1924. 310 p.
LC: My 7, '24.
PW: Ap 26, '24.
BLC: London: John Lane; printed in U. S. A., 1924.

F-83 Fernald, Chester Bailey, 1869-1938. John Kendry's idea / by Chester Bailey Fernald . . . ; with frontispiece by C. D. Williams. New York: The Outing Publishing Company, 1907. 348 p., col. front.
LC: Jl 18, '07.

F-84 _____ Under the jack-staff / by Chester Bailey Fernald. New York: The Century Co., 1903. 262 p.

Contents: The lights of Sitka -- The spirit in the pipe -- The yellow burgee -- The transit of Gloria Mundy -- A hard road to Andy Coggin's -- Clarence's mind -- The proving of Lannigan -- Help from the hopeless -- Clarence at the ball -- The Lannigan system with girls -- A yarn of the pea-soup sea.
"The spirit in the pipe" reprinted from *The cat and the cherub* to complete this volume.
PW: O 17, '03.

F-85 Ferraro, Agnese, *pseud.* Private Angelo Ferraro, U. S. N. G. / by Agnese Ferraro [pseud.]. Pittsburgh, Pa.: Pittsburgh Printing Company, 1919. 176 p. **VWM**

F-86 Ferris, Anita B. (Anita Brockway), b. 1881. Across the threshold / by Anita B. Ferris. New York City: Missionary Education Movement, 1914. [38] p., front., ill. **CLE**
"Reprint from Everyland, September, 1914."
LC: N 24, '14.

F-87 _____ The magic box / by Anita B. Ferris. New York City: Published jointly by Council of Women for Home Missions and Missionary Education Movement of the United States and Canada, [c1922]. 103 p., photo. front., [5] leaves of photo. plates.
Contents: A dollar for college -- A ride for the doctor -- Up north -- The lost pocketbook -- Caroline's play -- The magic box.
LC: Jl 18, '22.

F-88 Ferris, Elmer E. (Elmer Ellsworth), b. 1861. The business adventures of Billy Thomas / by Elmer E. Ferris. New York: The Macmillan Company, 1915. 227 p., front. [Ill. by E. T. Caswell.] **NYP**

F-89 _____ Pete Crowther: salesman / by Elmer E. Ferris; illustrations by G. C. Widney. Garden City, N. Y.: Doubleday, Page & Co., 1913. 205 p., front., [7] leaves of plates.

F-90 Fessenden, Laura Dayton. Hatsu, a story of Egypt / by Laura Dayton Fessenden . . . [Highland Park, Ill.: The Canterbury Press], 1904. 102 p.
Unexamined copy: bibliographic data from NUC.
PW: Ap 22, '05.

F-91 _____ "2002": childlife one hundred years from now / book by Laura Dayton Fessenden; pictures by S. P. Campbell. Chicago: Jamieson-Higgins Co., [c1902]. 184 p., photo. front. (port.), ill. **CRU**
PW: N 1, '02.

F-92 _____ The white witch of a salem town / By Laura Dayton Fessenden. s. l.: s. n., Christmas, 1923. 90 p. **ILU**

Ficke, Arthur Davidson. At Kamakura: 1917. In *Prairie gold* (1917), P-588.

F-93 Field, Charles K. (Charles Kellogg), b. 1873. Stanford stories: tales of a young university / by Charles K. Field (Carolus Ager) and Will Irwin; illustrated. San Francisco: A. M. Robertson, 1913. 319 p., front., [5] leaves of plates. [Ill. by W. E. Worden or Robinson & Crandall.]
Contents: A midwinter madness -- Pocahontas, freshman -- His uncle's will -- The initiation of Dromio -- The substituted fullback -- Two pioneers and an audience -- For the sake of argument -- An

alumni dinner -- Boggs' election feed -- In the dark days -- Crossroads -- A song-cycle and a puncture -- Bannister's "scoop" -- A woodside idyl -- One commencement.

Bannister's "scoop" and *A woodside idyl* are additions to the 1900 edition.

F-94   Field, Edward Salisbury, 1878-1936. Cupid understudy / by Edward Salisbury Field . . . illustrations by Will Grefé. New York: W. J. Watt & Company, [1909]. 106, [1] p., col. front., [6] leaves of plates.   **MUU**
LC: N 4, '09.
PW: D 4, '09.

F-95   ____ In pursuit of Priscilla: a chronicle of the man willing and the woman wilful / by Edward Salisbury Field; with illustrations by Will Grefé. Philadelphia: Henry Altemus Company, [c1906]. 112 p., front., [3] leaves of plates.   **OSU, DLC**
LC: O 26, '07.
PW: D 21, '07.

F-96   ____ The purple stockings / by Edward Salisbury Field. New York: W. J. Watt & Company, [c1911]. 115 p., col. front., [3] leaves of plates. Illustrated end papers. [Ill. by Will Grefé.]
LC: O 10, '11.
PW: N 18, '11.

F-97   ____ The rented earl / by Edward Salisbury Field; frontispiece by Will Grefé. New York: W. J. Watt & Company, [c1912]. 215 p., col. front.
LC: O 24, '12.

F-98   ____ The sapphire bracelet / Edward Salisbury Field; illustrations by Will Grefé. New York: W. J. Watt & Company, [c1910]. 164 p., col. front., [4] leaves of plates. Illustrated end papers.
LC: O 6, '10.
PW: O 22, '10.

F-99   ____ A six-cylinder courtship / Edward Salisbury Field; frontispiece by Harrison Fisher; illustrations by Clarence F. Underwood. New York: The John McBride Company, [c1907]. 130 p., col. front., [6] leaves of plates.
LC: N 9, '07.
PW: D 21, '07.

F-100   ____ Twin beds / by Edward Salisbury Field. New York: W. J. Watt & Company, [c1913]. 176 p.
LC: Ag 18, '13.
PW: Ja 24, '14.

F-101   Field, Elaine L. A romance in meditation / by Elaine L. Field. New York; London; Montreal: The Abbey Press, [c1901]. 94 p.   **DLC**

F-102   Field, Eugene, 1850-1895. The complete Tribune primer / by Eugene Field; containing 75 original drawings by F. Opper. Boston, Massachusetts: Mutual Book Company, [1901]. 143 p., ill.
Reprint save for Conky Stiles; a concordance.
LC: Je 29, '01.
References: BAL 5788.

F-103   ____ Conky Stiles / by Eugene Field. Cleveland: The Rowfant Club, 1925. 14 p.
This story first appeared in The Wellspring, Sept. 16, 1899. Previously published in book form: *The complete Tribune primer*, 1901. (q. v.)
References: BAL 5888.

Field, Isobel (Osbourne). See **Strong, Isobel, b. 1858.**

F-104   Field, Louise Maunsell. Katherine Trevalyan / by Louise Maunsell Field. New York: The McClure Company, 1908. 347 p.
LC: Mr 25, '08.
PW: Ap 4, '08.

F-105   ____ The little gods laugh: a novel / by Louise Maunsell Field; with frontispiece by John Newton Howitt. Boston: Little, Brown and Company, 1917. 326 p., front.
LC: S 11, '17.

F-106   ____ Love and life / by Louise Maunsell Field. New York: E. P. Dutton & Company, [c1923]. 286 p.   **NYP**
LC: S 24, '23.
PW: O 20, '23.

F-107   ____ A woman of feeling / by Louise Maunsell Field . . . New York: Dodd, Mead and Company, 1916. 295 p.   **PAU**
LC: F 23, '16.
PW: F 19, '16.

F-108   Field, Roswell Martin, 1851-1919. The bondage of Ballinger / by Roswell Field. Chicago; New York; Toronto; London; Edinburgh: Fleming H. Revell Company, 1903. 214 p., incl. front. [Ill. by G. M. McClure.]
PW: O 24, '03.

F-109   ____ Little Miss Dee / by Roswell Field. Chicago; New York; Toronto; London; Edinburgh: Fleming H. Revell Company, 1904. 241 p., incl. front. (port.). [Ill. by Griselda McClure.]
PW: D 10, '04.

F-110   ____ Madeline / by Roswell Field. Chicago: Printed by the Prairie Press, 1906. 104 p.   **NOC**
LC: Je 18, '06.
PW: Ag 4, '06.

F-111   ____ The passing of mother's portrait / by Roswell Field. Evanston: William S. Lord, 1901. (Chicago: Printed by R. R. Donnelley and Sons Company, at the Lakeside Press). 63 p.   **IWC**
"First appeared in an abridged form, in a recent number of the Atlantic Monthly."

F-112   ____ The romance of an old fool / by Roswell Field. Evanston: William S. Lord, 1902. 144 p.
PW: O 18, '02.

F-113 Field, Samuel. It pays to advertise / by Roi Cooper Megrue and Walter Hackett; Novelized by Samuel Field. New York: Duffield & Company, 1915. 333 p., photo. front., [7] leaves of photo. plates. [Ill. by White, N. Y.] **NDD**
LC: Mr 2, '15.

F-114 ____ The white pearl: a romance / by Edith Barnard Delano and Samuel Field; illustrated. New York: Duffield & Company, 1916. 324 p., photo. front., [7] leaves of photo. plates. **NYP**
"This novel was written by Samuel Field, based upon `The white pearl,' by Edith Barnard Delano."
LC: Je 27, '16.

F-115 ____ Young America / by Fred Ballard; novelized by Samuel Field. New York: Duffield & Company, 1916. 280 p., photo. front., [7] leaves of photo. plates.
"This story is founded on the play of the same name by Fred Ballard."
LC: F 26, '16.

F-116 Field, Sylvester. Job Trotter seeks health: finds Negroes' earthly paradise is Africa / by Sylvester Field. New York: Broadway Publishing Company, [c1904]. 68 p. **DLC**

F-117 Fielding, Anna. Did she fail? / by Anna Fielding. New York; London; Montreal: The Abbey Press, [c1901]. 130 p.
Unexamined copy: bibliographic data from NUC.
PW: Jl 6, '01.

F-118 Fielding, Howard, 1861-1929. Equal partners / by Howard Fielding; illustrations by Seymour M. Stone. New York: G. W. Dillingham Company, [c1901]. 269 p., front., [3] leaves of plates.
PW: Ag 24, '01.

F-119 Fifty best stories from the People's home journal and Good literature. New York: F. M. Lupton, [c1904]. 192 p., ill.
Unexamined copy: bibliographic data from OCLC, #17168726
LC: My 11, '04.
References: BAL 553. BAL reports first book appearance of Jane G. Austin's "The little hair trunk," pp. 119-124.

F-120 Filcher, J. A. (Joseph Adams). Untold tales of California: short stories illustrating phases of life peculiar to early days in the West / by J. A. Filcher. [San Francisco: J. A. Filcher], 1903. 161 p., front., [2] leaves of plates (1 photo.).
Contents: Sam Aston -- Justice vs. law -- The imperiled miner -- Lost sheep -- Encountering wild animals -- Justice Jones -- Mountain holdups -- Teamster stories -- Hiram Hawkins -- The two verdicts -- Hearts were trumps -- A twelve-year-old hero.

F-121 Fillmore, Parker, 1878-1944. The hickory limb / by Parker H. Fillmore; illustrations by Rose Cecil O'Neill. New York: John Lane Company; London: John Lane, The Bodley Head, 1910. 70 p., ill.
LC: O 27, '10.

F-122 ____ The Rosie world / by Parker Fillmore; with illustrations by Maginel Wright Enright. New York: Henry Holt and Company, 1914. 354 p., col. front., [7] leaves of col. plates. Reprinted in part from Everybody's magazine and from Smith magazine.
LC: O 1, '14.

F-123 ____ The young idea: a neighborhood chronicle / by Parker H. Fillmore . . . ; illustrations by Rose Cecil O'Neill. New York: John Lane Company, 1911. 341 p. **MNL**
Partly reprinted from various periodicals.
LC: Je 20, '11.

Findlater, Jane Helen, 1866-1946, jt. aut. *The affair at the inn* (1904). <u>See</u> **Wiggin, Kate Douglas Smith, 1856-1923, jt. aut., W-595.**

____, jt. aut. *Robinetta* (1911). <u>See</u> **Wiggin, Kate Douglas Smith, 1856-1923, jt. aut., W-603.**

Findlater, Mary, 1865-1964, jt. aut. *The affair at the inn* (1904). <u>See</u> **Wiggin, Kate Douglas Smith, 1856-1923, jt. aut., W-595.**

____, jt. aut. *Robinetta* (1911). <u>See</u> **Wiggin, Kate Douglas Smith, 1856-1923, jt. aut., W-603.**

Finger, Charles J. Adventures of Andrew Lang. <u>In</u> *The best short stories of 1924 and the yearbook of the American short story* (1925), **B-569.**

____ The lizard god. <u>In</u> *The best short stories of 1921 and the yearbook of the American short story* (1922), **B-566.**

____ The shame of gold. <u>In</u> *The best short stories of 1922 and the yearbook of the American short story* (1923), **B-567.**

F-124 Finklea, A. B., Mrs. Col. Wilton's daughters / by Mrs. A. B. Finklea. New York; Baltimore: Broadway Publishing Co., [c1909]. 176 p.

F-125 Finley, Harry T., 1866-1940. Where the needle points / by Harry T. Finley. New York; London; Montreal: The Abbey Press, [c1902]. 300 p.

Finnegan, May. "The last shall be first." <u>In</u> *The lady of the tower* (1909), **L-13.**

Finnegan, Mulloy. Out of the storm. <u>In</u> *Greatest short stories* (1915), **G-424.**

Finney, Frank, jt. aut. *A bride and a bridle* (1903). <u>See</u> **Street, Julian, 1879-1947, jt. aut., S-1020.**

____, jt. aut. *A limited engagement* (1905). <u>See</u> **Street, Julian, 1879-1947, jt. aut., S-1024.**

____, jt. aut. *Merely a matter of matrimony* (1904). <u>See</u> **Street, Julian, 1879-1947, jt. aut., S-1025.**

____, jt. aut. *The treasure on the beach* (1906). <u>See</u> **Street, Julian, 1879-1947, jt. aut., S-1032.**

____, jt. aut. *Violets and vexation* (1904). <u>See</u>
Street, Julian, 1879-1947, jt. aut., S-1033.

F-126   Finney, Lewis Erwin. Dan's ministry / by Lewis
Erwin Finney. New York; Chicago; Washington;
Baltimore; Atlanta; Norfolk; Florence, Ala.:
Broadway Publishing Co., [c1911]. 279 p., front.,
[1] leaf of plates.   **TXI**
LC: Mr 18, '11.
PW: Ap 22, '11.

F-127   ____ Jim Miller's girls / by Lewis Erwin Finney . . .
Boston: The Roxburgh Publishing Company, Inc.,
[c1914]. 301 p.   **CLU**
LC: N 27, '14.

F-128   Finney, Marian MacLean. In Naaman's house / by
Marian MacLean Finney. New York; Cincinnati:
The Abingdon Press, [c1922]. 295 p.
LC: S 14, '22.
PW: S 30, '22.

F-129   Firebaugh, Ellen M. The story of a doctor's
telephone: told by his wife / by Ellen M. Firebaugh
. . . Boston, Mass.: The Roxburgh Publishing
Company (Incorporated), [c1912]. 239 p.   **WSM**

F-130   Fischer, George Alexander. This labyrinthine life: a
tale of the Arizona desert / by George Alexander
Fischer. New York: B. W. Dodge & Co., 1907.
382 p., front., [3] leaves of plates.
LC: Mr 16, '07.
PW: Mr 23, '07.

F-131   Fischer, William Joseph, 1879-1912. The years
between / by William J. Fischer. Techny, Illinois:
Printed and published by the Society of the Divine
Word, 1912. 242 p., photo. front. (port.).   **NYP**

F-132   Fisguill, Richard, *pseud*. Mazel / by Richard Fisguill
[pseud.]. Eldredge Court, Chicago: Herbert S. Stone
& Co., 1902. 321 p.
PW: Ap 26, '02.

F-133   ____ The Venus of Cadiz: an extravaganza / by
Richard Fisguill. New York: Henry Holt and
Company, 1905. 323 p.
PW: Je 17, '05.

F-134   Fish, Horace, 1885-1929. The great way: a story of
the joyful, the sorrowful, the glorious / by Horace
Fish. New York: Mitchell Kennerley, 1921.
482 p.   **NYP**
LC: Ag 25, '21.
BLC: London: Cassell & Co., 1921.

F-135   ____ The saint's theatre: a novel / by Horace Fish.
New York: B. W. Huebsch, Inc.: Mitchell
Kennerley, 1924. 386 p.
LC: Ap 14, '24.
PW: My 3, '24.
BLC: London: Cassell & Co., 1923.

F-136   ____ Terassa of Spain / by Horace Fish. New York:
Mitchell Kennerley, 1923. 356 p.

LC: My 31, '23.

F-137   ____ The wrists on the door / a short story by
Horace Fish. New York: B. W. Huebsch Inc. &
Mitchell Kennerley, 1924. 66 p., incl. front. (port.).
[Ill. by Ernest Haskell.]

Fisher, Dorothy Canfield. <u>See</u> **Canfield, Dorothy,
1879-1958.**

F-138   Fisher, Jacob, *pseud*. The cradle of the deep: an
account of the adventures of Eleanor Channing and
John Starbuck / by Jacob Fisher [pseud.]; with a
frontispiece in full color from a painting by Modest
Stein. Boston: L. C. Page & Company, 1912.
307 p., col. front.
LC: S 25, '12.

F-139   ____ The man who saw wrong / by Jacob Fisher
[pseud.]; frontispiece by George Gibbs. Philadelphia:
The John C. Winston Company, [c1913]. 357 p.,
col. front.
LC: O 2, '13.

F-140   ____ The quitter: a novel / by Jacob Fisher [pseud.]
. . . ; illustrated by H. Weston Taylor. Philadelphia:
The John C. Winston Company, [c1914]. 340 p.,
front., [3] leaves of plates.
LC: S 19, '14.
PW: O 3, '14.

F-141   Fisher, Mary, b. 1858. Gertrude Dorrance: a story /
by Mary Fisher. Chicago: A. C. McClurg & Co.,
1902. 430 p.
PW: Ap 12, '02.

F-142   ____ The journal of a recluse / translated from the
original French. New York: Thomas Y. Crowell &
Co., [c1909]. 334 p., front. [Ill. by C. Allori.]
                                        AZU
LC: S 11, '09.
PW: O 9, '09.

F-143   ____ Kirstie / by M. F.; author of "The journal of a
recluse". New York: Thomas Y. Crowell Company,
[1912]. 291 p.
LC: S 10, '12.

F-144   ____ The Treloars / by Mary Fisher. New York:
Thomas Y. Crowell Company, [c1917]. 358 p.
LC: My 24, '17.

F-145   Fisher, Mary A. (Mary Ann), b. 1839. Among the
immortals, in the Land of Desire; a glimpse of the
beyond / by Mary A. Fisher. New York: The
Shakespeare Press, [c1916]. 276 p.   **DLC**
LC: D 30, '16.

F-146   ____ The ghost in the garret: and other stories / by
Mary A. Fisher . . . New York: Aberdeen
Publishing Company, [c1910]. 147 p., front. **CRU**
Contents: The ghost in the garret -- The sealed jar -- The work or the
woman -- The man with an idea -- Minerva Knowlton -- How it came
back -- Helen Hamilton's hero.
LC: Ja 3, '11.
PW: Ag 27, '10.

F-147   ____ Louisa Forrester / by Mary A. Fisher. New York: [Printed and bound by J. J. Little & Co.], 1905. 206 p.

F-148   ____ Young doctor Hamilton / by Mary A. Fisher. New York: Cochrane Publishing Co., 1908. 64 p., front.
LC: D 1, '08.
PW: D 12, '08.

F-149   ____ Young Mrs. Morton / by Mary A. Fisher . . . New York: Cochrane Publishing Company, 1911. 159 p.   **NYP**
PW: F 10, '12.

F-150 Fisher, Sophie. The imprudence of Prue / by Sophie Fisher; with illustrations by Herman Pfeifer. Indianapolis: The Bobbs-Merrill Company, [c1911]. 357 p., front., [4] leaves of plates.

    ____ Rhododendrons. In *Club stories* (1915), **C-502.**

F-151 Fisk, Kenneth. Stories three / by Kenneth Fisk. New York: L. Middleditch Co., 1920. 48 p., front. (port.).
Unexamined copy: bibliographic data from NUC.
Contents: Temple bells -- Matty -- Harlequin's serenade.

F-152 Fisk, May Isabel. Monologues / by May Isabel Fisk. New York; London: Harper & Brothers, 1903. 189, [1] p., front. (port.).
Three of the monologues are reprinted from "Smart set."
Contents: Keeping a seat at the benefit -- Her first call on the butcher -- Hunting for an apartment -- The heart of a woman -- A bill from the milliner -- A woman in a shoe-shop -- Another point of view -- Mis' Deborah has a visitor -- The pudding -- The year after -- Heard on the beach.

F-153   ____ The silent sex / monologues by May Isabel Fisk. New York: Harper & Brothers, 1923. 279 p., front. (port.).
Contents: Dressing for the play -- The village dressmaker -- The woman investor -- An English lady marketing -- The way out -- Calling on the doctor -- Mrs. Meekey explains the "higher thought" -- Buying a hat -- The journey -- Her "night-thoughts" -- A busy woman -- Shopping.
LC: Mr 20, '23.
PW: Ap 21, '23.

    ____, jt. aut. *The stolen throne* (1907). See **Kaufman, Herbert, 1878-1947, jt. aut., K-30.**

Fisler, May Lewis, Mrs., b. 1866. See **Juneau, May, pseud.**

F-154 Fitch, A. H. (Abigail Hetzel). The breath of the dragon / by A. H. Fitch. New York; London: G. P. Putnam's Sons, 1916. ([New York]: The Knickerbocker Press). 447 p., col. front. [Ill. by Modest Stein.]
LC: O 13, '16.

F-155 Fitch, Albert Parker, b. 1877. None so blind / by Albert Parker Fitch. New York: The Macmillan Company, 1924. 366 p.
LC: F 20, '24.

F-156 Fitch, Clyde, 1865-1909. A wave of life: a novel / by Clyde Fitch. New York, Mitchell Kennerley, [1909?, c1891]. 292 p., front.
"This . . . was first published in `Lippincott's monthly magazine,' for February, 1891."
PW: D 25, '09.
References: BAL 6099.

F-157 Fitch, George Helgeson, 1877-1915. At good old Siwash / by George Fitch; illustrated. Boston: Little, Brown and Company, 1911. 309 p., front., [18] leaves of plates. [Ill. F. R. Gruger and May Wilson Preston.]
LC: S 28, '11.

F-158   ____ The big strike at Siwash / by George Fitch; illustrated by Frank Crerie and May Wilson Preston. New York: Doubleday, Page & Company, 1909. 56 p., front., [2] leaves of plates.
LC: O 16, '09.
PW: N 6, '09.
BLC: London: Doubleday, Page & Co., New York printed, 1909.

F-159   ____ Homeburg memories / by George Fitch; with illustrations by Irma Dérèmeaux. Boston: Little, Brown and Company, 1915. 301, [1] p., front., [3] leaves of plates.
LC: F 18, '15.

F-160   ____ Petey Simmons at Siwash / by George Fitch; illustrated by G. C. Widney. Boston: Little, Brown and Company, 1916. 244, [1] p., front., [3] leaves of plates.
LC: Ag 17, '16.
PW: Ag 12, '16.

Fitch, Wm. E. Evolution. In *Second suds sayings* (1919), **S-266.**

    ____ Her conscience troubled her. In *Second suds sayings* (1919), **S-266.**

    ____ If. In *Second suds sayings* (1919), **S-266.**

    ____ Laugh it off. In *Second suds sayings* (1919), **S-266.**

F-161 Fitzgerald, Denis Gerald. The quest of Coronado: an historical romance of the Spanish cavaliers in Nebraska / by Denis Gerald Fitzgerald . . . Baltimore, Md.; New York: John Murphy Company, [c1901]. 174 p.   **RRR**

F-162 Fitzgerald, F. Scott (Francis Scott), 1896-1940. The beautiful and damned / by F. Scott Fitzgerald. New York: Charles Scribner's Sons, 1922. 449 p.
LC: Mr 6, '22.
PW: Mr 11, '22.
BLC: London: W. Collins Sons & Co., [1922].
References: Bruccoli, *Fitzgerald* A8.

    ____ The camel's back. In *Prize stories of 1920* (1921), **P-618.**

F-163 _____ Flappers and philosophers / by F. Scott
Fitzgerald . . . New York: Charles Scribner's Sons,
1920. 269 p.
Contents: The offshore pirate -- The ice palace -- Head and shoulders
-- The cut-glass bowl -- Bernice bobs her hair -- Benediction --
Dalrimple goes wrong -- The four fists.
LC: S 14, '20.
PW: S 11, '20.
BLC: London: W. Collins Sons & Co., [1922].
References: Bruccoli, *Fitzgerald* A6.

F-164 _____ The great Gatsby / by F. Scott Fitzgerald . . .
New York: Charles Scribner's Sons, 1925. 218 p.
LC: Je 2, '25.
PW: Ap 18, '25.
BLC: London: Chatto & Windus, 1926.
References: Bruccoli, *Fitzgerald* A11.

_____ Gretchen's forty winks. In *Aces* (1924), A-42.

F-165 _____ Tales of the jazz age / by F. Scott Fitzgerald.
New York: Charles Scribner's Sons, 1922.
317 p.
Contents: My last flappers: The jelly-bean -- The camel's back --
May day -- Porcelain and pink. Fantasies: The diamond as big as
the Ritz -- The curious case of Benjamin Button -- Tarquin of
Cheapside -- O russet witch. Unclassified masterpieces: The lees of
happiness -- Mr. Icky -- Jemina.
LC: S 28, '22.
PW: O 7, '22.
BLC: London: W. Collins Sons & Co., [1923].
References: Bruccoli, *Fitzgerald* A9.

F-166 _____ This side of paradise / by F. Scott Fitzgerald
. . . New York: Charles Scribner's Sons, 1920.
305 p.
LC: Ap 6, '20.
PW: Ap 3, '20.
BLC: London: W. Collins Sons & Co., [1921].
References: Bruccoli, *Fitzgerald* A5.

_____ Two for a cent. In *The best short stories of
1922 and the yearbook of the American short story*
(1923), B-567.

F-167 Fitzgerald, John Tornrose. Bixby of Boston: being
the little story of a young railway office clerk / by
John Tornrose Fitzgerald; illustrated with twenty
drawings by the author. New York: Broadway
Publishing Co., 1906. 83 p., col. front., [19] leaves
of plates (some col.). **DLC**
LC: N 24, '06.

F-168 FitzGerald, Mary C. Lights and lilies / by Mary C.
FitzGerald. New York: Sturgis & Walton Company,
1917. 45 p. **DLC**

F-169 Fitzgerald, Michael, b. 1859. 1812: a tale of Cape
Cod / by Michael Fitzgerald. Yarmouthport, Mass.:
C. W. Swift, 1912. ([Yarmouthport, Mass.]: The
Register Press). 97 p. **WPG**
LC: O 2, '12.

F-170 Fitzgerald, Robert. The statesmen snowbound / by
Robert Fitzgerald; illustrated by Wad-el-Ward. New
York; Washington: The Neale Publishing Company,
1909. 217 p., front., ill. **KUK**
LC: Je 30, '09.

F-171 Fitzhugh, Percy Keese, b. 1876. The galleon
treasure / by Percy K. Fitzhugh. New York: T. Y.
Crowell, [c1908]. 278 p., front., [3] leaves of plates.
Unexamined copy: bibliographic data from OCLC,
#29694148.

F-172 Fitzpatrick, Catherine. Lizbeth / by Catherine
Fitzpatrick; frontispiece by Hudson. New York:
Broadway Publishing Co., [c1906]. 163 p., front.,
[1] leaf of plates.
LC: D 12, '07.

F-173 FitzSimons, Simon, b. 1853. How George Edwards
scrapped religion / by Rev. Simon FitzSimons . . .
Boston, Massachusetts: The Stratford Company
. . . ,1923. 319 p. **NYP**

F-174 Flagg, James Montgomery, 1877-1960. I should say
so / James Montgomery Flagg. New York: George
H. Doran Company, [c1914]. 202 p., ill. [Ill. by
James M. Flagg.] Illustrated end papers.
LC: Je 25, '14.
PW: Jl 4, '14.

F-175 _____ The mystery of the hated man and then some /
James Montgomery Flagg. New York: George H.
Doran Company, [c1916]. 265 p., ill. [Ill. by James
M. Flagg.] Illustrated end papers.
Contents: The mystery of the hated man -- Miss Sticky-Moufie-Kiss
-- The nut's automobile guide -- The care and feeding of husbands --
Whiskerculture -- Visiting -- A picnic -- A marriage vacation --
"Breaking into the art game" -- Being visited -- Is Christmas a bore?
-- What migentleman will wear -- Going away from here -- Frills and
Ednaferberlows -- A barely civil engineer -- Mrs. Pearl
Prunepincher's page in every lady's magazine.
LC: O 14, '16.
PW: S 30, '16.

F-176 Flandrau, Charles Macomb, 1871-1938. The diary of
a freshman / by Charles Macomb Flandrau . . . New
York: Doubleday, Page and Company, 1901.
335 p. **WSU**
First published in the "Saturday Evening Post."
PW: Je 1, '01.

_____ The Trawnbeighs. In *The Bellman book of
fiction* (1921), B-485.

F-177 Flandrau, Grace Hodgson. Being respectable / by
Grace H. Flandrau. New York: Harcourt, Brace and
Company, [c1923]. 336 p.
LC: F 8, '23.
BLC: London: Jonathan Cape, printed in U. S. A.,
1923.

F-178 _____ Cousin Julia / by Grace Hodgson Flandrau.
New York; London: D. Appleton and Company,
1917. 365, [1] p.
LC: Ag 27, '17.

F-179 _____ Entranced / by Grace Flandrau. New York:
Harcourt, Brace and Company, [c1924]. 323 p.
LC: O 29, '24.

Flannagan, Zoë, author. See *Grey Towers* (1923),
G-521.

F-180 Flatt, Anne McCallum. The dawn of a new era / by Annie McCallum Flatt. Boston: Richard G. Badger, [c1920]. ([Boston]: The Gorham Press). 278 p. **DLC**
PW: Mr 20, '20.

F-181 Fleharty, Clara Viola. The Radiance of the Morning Club / by Clara Viola Fleharty. Boston: Richard G. Badger, [c1911]. (Boston: The Gorham Press). 193 p.
LC: D 19, '11.

F-182 ____ A study in life tints / by Clara Viola Fleharty . . . Chicago, Ill.: M. A. Long Book and Publishing House, 1907. 481 p., ill.
Unexamined copy: bibliographic data from OCLC, #20619731.
Contains prose and poetry.

F-183 ____ A wild rose / by Clara Viola Fleharty . . . Chicago: Wm. Johnston Printing Co., 1902. 308, [1] p., photo. ill.
LC: Jl 3, '11.
PW: Jl 29, '11.

F-184 Fleming, George Elliott. A beggar in evening dress / by George Elliott Fleming. [S. l.: s. n., c1908.] 93 p. **DLC**
LC: Ap 28, '08.

F-185 Fleming, Sarah Lee Brown. Hope's highway: a novel / by Sarah Lee Brown Fleming. New York: The Neale Publishing Company, 1918. 156 p. **WLU**
LC: N 18, '18.
PW: N 16, '18.

Flick, Lawrence F. The houses of Husse and Montefort. In *The Tragedy that wins and other short stories* **(1905), T-343.**

F-186 Flint, Annie Austin, b. 1866. The breaking point: a novel / by Annie Austin Flint; frontispiece by Dora Wheeler Keith. N. Y. City: Broadway Publishing Co., 1915. 291 p., front.

F-187 ____ A girl of ideas / by Annie Flint. New York: Charles Scribner's Sons, 1903. 348, [1] p.
PW: Ap 4, '03.
BLC: London: Ward, Lock & Co.; New York printed, 1903.

F-188 Flint, Elizabeth L., 1855-1918. King Philip of Primrose Street / Elizabeth L. Flint. Boston: Richard G. Badger, [c1912]. ([Boston]: The Gorham Press). 48 p. **NYP**

F-189 Flint, Elliott. The short cut / by G. Elliot Flint. New York: The Romance Press, 1909. 292 p. **DLC**
LC: Ap 16, '09.

F-190 Flisch, Julia A. Old Hurricane: a novel / by Julia A. Flisch. New York: Thomas Y. Crowell Company, [c1925]. 356 p.
LC: F 27, '25.
PW: Mr 14, '25.

F-191 Flower, Elliott, 1863-1920. The best policy / by Elliott Flower; illustrated by George Brehm. Indianapolis: The Bobbs-Merrill Company, [c1905]. 268 p., front., [6] leaves of plates.

F-192 ____ Delightful Dodd / by Elliott Flower; illustrated by Frank T. Merrill. Boston: L. C. Page & Company, 1904. 295 p., front., [3] leaves of plates.
PW: N 12, '04.

F-193 ____ Policeman Flynn / by Elliott Flower; with illustrations by Frederic Dorr Steele. New York: The Century Co., 1902. 293, [1] p., front., ill.
PW: Mr 1, '02.
BLC: Toronto: Copp, Clark Co., 1902.

F-194 ____ Slaves of success / by Elliott Flower . . . ; illustrated by Jay Hambidge. Boston: L. C. Page & Company, 1905. 304 p., front., [7] leaves of plates.
PW: Ap 1, '05.

F-195 ____ The spoilsmen / by Elliott Flower. Boston: L. C. Page & Company, 1903. 324 p.
PW: Mr 21, '03.
BLC: London: G. P. Putnam's Sons, 1904.

F-196 Flowers, S. L. (Sumpter Lee), 1881-1945. The circuit rider, or, Suffering for Christ's sake / by Evangelist S. L. Flowers. Olivet-Georgetown, Ill.: Published by The Flowers Publishing Company, [c1912]. 183 p., photo. front. (port.), ill. (some photo.). **JBE**

F-197 Floyd, N. J. (Nicholas Jackson), b. 1828. The last of the cavaliers, or, The phantom peril: a historical romance dealing with the cause and conduct of the war between the sections of the American Union / by N. J. Floyd . . . New York: Broadway Publishing Company, [c1904]. 427 p., photo. front. (port.), [9] leaves of plates. [Ill. by Wm. L. Hudson.]
OSU, VA@

F-198 Flynn, William J. (William James), b. 1867. The barrel mystery / by William J. Flynn . . . New York: The James A. McCann Company, 1919. 265 p.
PW: Ja 17, '20.

____, jt. aut. The eagles eye (1919). See **Cooper Courtney Ryley, 1886-1940, jt. aut., C-775.**

F-199 Flynt, Josiah, 1869-1907. The little brother: a story of tramp life / by Josiah Flynt. New York: The Century Company, 1902. 254 p., col. front.
PW: Mr 29, '02.

F-200 ____ The rise of Ruderick Clowd / by Josiah Flynt. New York: Dodd, Mead & Company, 1903. 370 p., front., [5] leaves of plates. [Ill. by W. B. Cox.]
PW: Ap 25, '03.
BLC: London: Grant Richards; New York [printed], 1904.

Flynt, Joseph. Jamie the Kid. In *Under the Sunset* **(1906), U-9.**

Fogarty, Kate T. The making of a basket. In *The joy in work* **(1920), J-229.**

F-201   Fogg, Lawrence Daniel. The asbestos society of sinners: detailing the diversions of Dives and others on the playground of Pluto, with some broken threads of drop-stitch history, picked up by a newspaper man in Hades and woven into a Stygian nights' entertainment / by Lawrence Daniel Fogg. Boston, Mass.: Mayhew Publishing Company, [c1906]. 169 p.   **UUM**

F-202   Foley, James W. (James William), 1874-1939. The letters of William Green / by J. W. Foley . . . ; illustrations in line by Charles Guischard. New York: McBride, Nast & Co., 1914. 209 p., front., ill.
OSU, MNU

F-203   Follett, Marie L. (Marie Louise). Libra Dawn; or, Dawn of liberty, a sequel to Cupid's yokes / by Marie L. Follett . . . [Le Claire? Ia.], 1903.
Unexamined copy: bibliographic data from NUC.

F-204   Folsom, Elizabeth Irons, b. 1878. Free / by Elizabeth Irons Folsom. New York: The Macaulay Company, [c1925]. 320 p.
LC: S 2, '25.
PW: Ag 29, '25.

_____ Natural selection. In *As we are* **(1923), A-325.**

_____ Towers of fame. In *Prize stories of 1923* **(1924), P-621.**

Folwell, Arthur Hamilton, jt. aut. *Monsieur d'En Brochette* (1905). See **Taylor, Bert Leston, 1866-1921, jt. aut, T-68.**

Fones, Alice, jt. aut. *The man with the scar* (1911). See **Fones, Warren, jt. aut., F-205.**

F-205   Fones, Warren, *pseud.* The man with the scar / Warren & Alice Fones [pseud.]. Boston: Richard G. Badger, 1911. ([Boston]: The Gorham Press). 244 p., front.
LC: Ja 3, '11.
PW: Mr 4, '11.

F-206   Fontaine, Felix, *pseud.* Richard Gordon: an echo from the hills / by Felix Fontaine [pseud.]. Nashville: B. L. Foster Co., 1906. 253 p.   **TNS**

F-207   Foote, John Taintor, 1881-1950. Blister Jones / by John Tainter Foote; illustrated by Jay Hambidge. Indianapolis: The Bobbs-Merrill Company, [c1913]. 324 p., front., [5] leaves of plates.
LC: O 29, '13.
PW: N 1, '13.

F-208   _____ Dumb-Bell of Brookfield / by John Taintor Foote . . . ; frontispiece. New York; London: D. Appleton and Company, 1917. 261, [1] p., front.
LC: F 27, '17.

F-209   _____ The look of eagles / by John Taintor Foote; frontispiece by George Morris. New York; London: D. Appleton and Company, 1916. 71, [1] p., col. front.   **KSU**
LC: Ag 28, '16.
PW: Ag 26, '16.

F-210   _____ The lucky seven / by John Taintor Foote . . . New York; London: D. Appleton and Company, 1918. 308, [1] p.
Contents: Bolters -- Opus 43, number 6 -- Goldie May and the faithful servant -- Red fox furs -- Augusta's bridge -- A cake in the fourteenth round -- Old pastures.
LC: F 18, '18.
PW: Mr 2, '18.

F-211   _____ Pocono Shot: a dog story / by John Taintor Foote. New York; London: D. Appleton and Company, 1924. 142, [1] p.
LC: S 13, '24.
PW: S 27, '24.

F-212   _____ The song of the dragon / by John Taintor Foote. New York; London: D. Appleton and Company, 1923. 310, [1] p.
Contents: The song of the dragon -- Economic independence -- The white grouse -- Spirit dope -- Soft craws -- Cherries -- Shame on you.
LC: Ja 29, '23.
PW: F 17, '23.

F-213   _____ A wedding gift: a fishing story / by John Taintor Foote. New York; London: D. Appleton and Company, 1924. 62, [1] p.
LC: S 13, '24.
PW: S 27, '24.

F-214   Foote, Mary Hallock, 1847-1938. The desert and the sown / by Mary Hallock Foote. Boston; New York: Houghton, Mifflin and Company, 1902. (Cambridge: The Riverside Press). 313, [1] p.
PW: Je 7, '02.

F-215   _____ Edith Bonham / by Mary Hallock Foote. Boston; New York: Houghton Mifflin Company, 1917. (Cambridge [Mass.]: The Riverside Press). 342, [1] p.
LC: Mr 20, '17.
PW: Mr 31, '17.

_____ Gideon's knock. In *The Spinners' book of fiction* **(1907), S-755.**

F-216   _____ The ground-swell / by Mary Hallock Foote. Boston; New York: Houghton Mifflin Company, 1919. (Cambridge: The Riverside Press). 283, [1] p.
LC: O 13, '19.
PW: N 1, '19.

F-217   _____ A picked company: a novel / by Mary Hallock Foote. Boston; New York: Houghton Mifflin Company, 1912. (Cambridge: The Riverside Press). 416 p.
LC: O 14, '12.
PW: O 19, '12.

231

F-218   ____ The royal Americans / by Mary Hallock Foote. Boston; New York: Houghton Mifflin Company, 1910. (Cambridge: The Riverside Press). 386 p.
LC: Ap 14, '10.
PW: Ap 16, '10.
BLC: London: Constable & Co.; Boston; New York: Houghton Mifflin Co.; Cambridge, Mass, [printed], 1910.

F-219   ____ A touch of sun, and other stories / by Mary Hallock Foote. Boston; New York: Houghton, Mifflin and Company, 1903. (Cambridge: The Riverside Press). 273, [1] p.
Contents: A touch of sun -- The maid's progress -- Pilgrims to Mecca -- The Harshaw bride.
PW: N 21, '03.

F-220   ____ The valley road / by Mary Hallock Foote. Boston; New York: Houghton Mifflin Company, 1915. (Cambridge: The Riverside Press). 359, [1] p.
LC: S 13, '15.
PW: S 11, '15.

F-221   Footner, Hulbert, 1879-1944. The Deaves affair / by Hulbert Footner. New York: George H. Doran Company, [c1922]. 319 p.
LC: Ap 15, '22.
BLC: London: W. Collins Sons & Co., [1922].

F-222   ____ The fur bringers: a story of the Canadian Northwest / by Hulbert Footner. New York: The James A. McCann Company, 1920. 313 p.
LC: My 14, '20.
PW: Jl 17, '20.
BLC: London: Hodder & Stoughton, [1916].

F-223   ____ The huntress / by Hulbert Footner. New York: The James A. McCann Company, [c1922]. 312 p.
LC: O 2, '22.
BLC: London: Hodder & Stoughton, [1917].

F-224   ____ Jack Chanty: a story of Athabasca / by Hulbert Footner. Garden City, N. Y.: Doubleday, Page & Co., 1913. 337 p., col. front., [4] leaves of plates. [Ill. by William Sherman Potts.]
LC: S 23, '13.
PW: S 27, '13.
BLC: London: Hodder & Stoughton, 1917.

F-225   ____ Officer! / by Hulbert Footner. New York: George H. Doran Company, [c1924]. 279 p.
LC: S 6, '24.
PW: Ag 30, '24.
BLC: London: W. Collins Sons & Co., [1924].

F-226   ____ The owl taxi / by Hulbert Footner. New York: George H. Doran Company, [c1921]. 309 p.
LC: F 7, '21.
BLC: London: W. Collins Sons & Co., [1922].

F-227   ____ Ramshackle house / by Hulbert Footner. New York: George H. Doran Company, [c1922]. 311 p.
BLC: London: W. Collins & Sons, [1923].

F-228   ____ The sealed valley / by Hulbert Footner;

illustrated by W. Sherman Potts. Garden City, N. Y.: Doubleday, Page & Company, 1914. 356 p., front., [3] leaves of plates.
LC: O 15, '14.
PW: O 17, '14.
BLC: London: Hodder & Stoughton, 1915.

F-229   ____ The substitute millionaire / by Hulbert Footner . . . New York: George H. Doran Company, [c1919]. 350 p.
LC: O 2, '19.
BLC: London: W. Collins & Sons, [1921].

F-230   ____ Thieves' wit: an everyday detective story / by Hulbert Footner. New York: George H. Doran Company, [c1918]. 345 p.
LC: Mr 2, '18.
BLC: London: Hodder & Stoughton, [1919].

F-231   ____ Two on the trail: a story of the far Northwest / by Hulbert Footner; illustrated by W. Sherman Potts. Garden City, New York: Doubleday, Page & Company, 1911. 349 p., col. front., [3] leaves of col. plates.
LC: F 20, '11.
PW: F 25, '11.
BLC: London: Methuen & Co.; printed in New York, 1911.

F-232   ____ The under dogs / by Hulbert Footner. New York: George H. Doran Company, [c1925]. 325 p.
LC: O 1, '25.
PW: O 3, '25.

F-233   ____ The wild bird / by Hulbert Footner. New York: George H. Doran Company, [c1923]. 282 p.
PW: Ap 25, '25.
BLC: London: Hodder & Stoughton, 1923.

F-234   ____ The woman from "outside": (on Swan River) / by Hulbert Footner . . . New York: The James A. McCann Company, [c1921]. 268 p.   **DLC**
LC: O 26, '21.

F-235   For France. Garden City, New York: Doubleday, Page & Company, 1917. 412 p., front., ill. [Ill. by F. Walter Taylor, Victor Chapman, Charles Dana Gibson, John Wolcott Adams, Albert Sterner, Robert Henri, John Sloan, William Glackens, Oscar Cesare, F. R. Gruger, John Sargent, Randall Davey, Oliver Herford, James Montgomery Flagg, Wallace Morgan, Ernest Lawson, James Preston, Boardman Robinson, Rea Irvin, Sergeant, Walter Hale, Ernest Peixotto, and Arnold Brunner.]   **MIA**
Contents: The destroyers of Nuremberg / Booth Tarkington -- Lafayette / George Ade -- Two heroines of France / Gertrude Atherton -- Jim Mattison of wagon wheel gap / Hamlin Garland. [Also includes poetry, extracts from larger works, short stories.]
PW: O 20, '17.

F-236   Forbes, A. S. C., Mrs. Mission tales in the days of the dons / by Mrs. A. S. C. Forbes; with nine full page illustrations and decorative drawings by Langdon Smith. Chicago: A. C. McClurg & Co., 1909. 343, [1] p., front. (port.), [8] leaves of plates. Illustrated end papers.

Contents: Mission bells [poem] -- In the days of the Padres -- A story of San Juan Capistrano -- The ride of the neophytes [poem] -- Matilija -- Concepción Agüella -- The story of Little Rossiya -- The penance bell of Los Angeles -- Wana and Ahzi-papoose -- Pirate Joe -- Dos Hermanas (The two sisters) -- Terésa, the Popeloutechom neophyte -- El Molino Viéjo.

F-237   [Forbes, Alexander], 1882-1965. The radio gunner / with illustrations. Boston; New York: Houghton Mifflin Company, 1924. (Cambridge: The Riverside Press). 318 p., front., [3] leaves of plates. [Ill. by Heman Fay, Jr.]   **MNU**

Forbes, Esther. Break-neck hill. In *Prize stories of 1920* (1921), **P-618.**

Forbes, Harriet Rebecca Piper. See **Forbes, A. S. C., Mrs.**

F-238   Forbes, John Maxwell. Doubloons-and the girl / by John Maxwell Forbes; illustrated by Arthur O. Scott. New York: Sully and Kleinteich, [1917]. 342 p., front., [3] leaves of plates.
LC: Ap 5, '17.
PW: Ap 14, '17.

F-239   ____ Wilbur Crane's handicap / by John Maxwell Forbes . . . ; illustrated by A. O. Scott. New York: George Sully & Company, [c1918]. 288 p., front., [3] leaves of plates.
LC: S 26, '18.
PW: O 12, '18.

F-240   Forbes-Lindsay, C. H. (Charles Harcourt), b. 1860. Daniel Boone, backwoodsman / by C. H. Forbes-Lindsay . . . ; with illustrations by Frank McKernan. Philadelphia; London: J. B. Lippincott Company, 1909, [c1908]. 319, [1] p., col. front., [3] leaves of plates.
LC: S 2, '08.

F-241   ____ John Smith, gentleman adventurer / by C. H. Forbes-Lindsay; with illustrations in color by Harry B. Lachman. Philadelphia; London: J. B. Lippincott Company, 1907. 304 p., col. front., [3] col. leaves of plates.
LC: S 17, '07.

F-242   Ford, James L. (James Lauren), 1854-1928. The brazen calf / by James L. Ford; with illustrations by W. Glackens. New York: Dodd, Mead and Company, 1903. 323 p., front., [6] leaves of plates.
PW: O 24, '03.

F-243   ____ The great mirage: a novel of the city underneath it / by James L. Ford . . . New York; London: Harper & Brothers, 1915. 350, [1] p., col. front. [Ill. by May Wilson Preston.]
LC: Ja 16, '15.
PW: Ja 23, '15.

F-244   ____ Hot Corn Ike / by James L. Ford. New York: E. P. Dutton & Company, [c1923]. 300 p.
LC: F 13, '23.
PW: F 17, '23.

F-245   ____ Waitful watching, or, Uncle Sam and the fight in Dame Europa's school / by James L. Ford . . . ; illustrated by Reginald Birch. New York: Frederick A. Stokes Company, [c1916]. 56 p., front., [3] leaves of plates.
LC: Ag 28, '16.
PW: S 9, '16.

F-246   ____ The wooing of Folly / by James L. Ford. New York: D. Appleton and Company, 1906. 294 p.
LC: S 28, '06.
PW: O 6, '06.

F-247   Ford, James Tooker. The dying lamp: the glorious dawn: a tale of the fall of Jerusalem / by J. Tooker Ford. Freeport, Ill.: Brown & Dollmeyer, [c1902]. 260 p., photo. front., [5] leaves of plates, map.   **GZM**
PW: Ag 9, '02.

F-248   Ford, Paul Leicester, 1865-1902. A checked love affair: and "The Cortelyou feud" / by Paul Leicester Ford; with photogravures by Harrison Fisher and with cover and decorations by George Wharton Edwards. New York: Dodd, Mead and Company, 1903. 112 p., front., [4] leaves of plates.
LC: O 17, '03.
PW: N 14, '03.
References: BAL 6233. BAL notes: "The Cortelyou feud" had prior publication in *Tattle-tales of Cupid*, 1898.

____ A family tradition. In *A house party* (1901), **H-903.**

F-249   ____ His version of it / by Paul Leicester Ford; with illustrations by Henry Hutt and decorations by Theodore B. Hapgood. New York: Dodd, Mead & Company, 1905. 109 p., col. front., incl. [4] leaves of col. plates.
LC: S 18, '05.
PW: O 7, '05.
References: BAL 6236. BAL notes: reprinted from *Tattle-tales of Cupid*, 1898.

F-250   ____ Love finds the way / Paul Leicester Ford; with illustrations by Harrison Fisher; decorations by Margaret Armstrong. New York: Dodd, Mead & Company, 1904. 107, [1] p., front., [4] leaves of plates.
LC: O 22, '04.
PW: N 12, '04.
References: BAL 6235.

F-251   ____ Wanted--a chaperon / by Paul Leicester Ford; with illustrations by Howard Chandler Christy; decorations by Margaret Armstrong. New York: Dodd, Mead & Company, 1902. 109 p., col. front., [5] leaves of col. plates.
LC: O 1, '02.
PW: O 18, '02.
References: BAL 6232.

F-252   ____ A warning to lovers, &, "Sauce for the goose is sauce for the gander" / by Paul Leicester Ford; with illustrations by Henry Hutt and decorations by T.

M. Cleland. New York: Dodd, Mead & Company, 1906. 103, [1] p., col. front., [4] leaves of col. plates.
LC: S 15, '06.
PW: O 13, '06.
References: BAL 6237. BAL notes: reprinted from *Tattle-tales of Cupid*, 1898.

Ford, Sewell, 1868-1946. At the Dovelys'. In *Comedy* (1901), **C-614.**

F-253   Cherub Devine: a novel / by Sewell Ford. New York: Mitchell Kennerley, [c1909]. 395 p.
                                          EYM
LC: Ap 19, '09.
PW: My 8, '09.

F-254   Honk, honk !! Shorty McCabe at the wheel / by Sewell Ford; illustrations by F. Vaux Wilson. New York: Mitchell Kennerley, 1909. 43 p., front., ill.
LC: Mr 29, '10.
PW: D 4, '09.

F-255   Horses nine: stories of harness and saddle / by Sewell Ford; illustrated. New York: Charles Scribner's Sons, 1903. 270 p., front., [6] leaves of plates. [Ill. by Frederic Dorr Steele and L. Maynard Dixon.]
Contents: Skipper -- Calico -- Old Silver -- Blue Blazes -- Chieftain -- Barnacles -- Black Eagle -- Bonfire -- Pasha.
PW: Mr 21, '03
BLC: London: George Newnes; New York printed, 1903.

F-256   The house of Torchy / by Sewell Ford; illustrations by Arthur William Brown. New York: Edward J. Clode, [c1918]. 325 p., front., [7] leaves of plates.
LC: O 23, '18.
PW: N 9, '18.

F-257   Inez and Trilby May / by Sewell Ford; with illustrations by Marshall Frantz. New York; London: Harper & Brothers, 1921. 292, [1] p., front., [3] leaves of plates.
LC: N 28, '21.
PW: D 3, '21.

     Jane's gray eyes. In *Quaint courtships* (1906), **Q-3.**

F-258   Just horses / by Sewell Ford; illustrated. New York: Mitchell Kennerley, 1910. 198 p., incl. front., [3] leaves of plates. [Ill. by Karl Anderson and Henry Roth.]
Contents: Jerry -- Keno: a cayuse known to fame -- The life of the crowded way -- The story of Pericles of Spread Eagle battery -- Fiddler -- The straying of Lucifer -- Deacon: and how he took out the Christmas mail.
LC: My 5, '10.
PW: My 21, '10.

F-259   Meet 'em with Shorty McCabe / by Sewell Ford. New York: Edward J. Clode, [c1920]. 303 p.
LC: Ja 14, '21.
PW: F 12, '21.

F-260   Odd numbers: being further chronicles of Shorty McCabe / by Sewell Ford; illustrations by F. Vaux Wilson. New York: Edward J. Clode, [c1912]. 309 p., front., [5] leaves of plates.
Contents: Goliah and the purple lid -- How Maizie came through -- Where Spotty fitted in -- A grandmother who got going -- A long shot on DeLancey -- Playing Harold both ways -- Cornelia shows some class -- Doping out an odd one -- Handing Bobby a blank -- Marmaduke slips one over -- A look in on the goat game -- Mrs. Truckles' broad jump -- Heiney takes the gloom cure -- A try-out for Toodleism -- The case of the Tiscotts -- Classing Tutwater right -- How Hermy put it over -- Joy riding with aunty -- Turning a trick for Beany.
LC: F 7, '12.
BLC: London: T. Werner Laurie, [1912].

F-261   On with Torchy / by Sewell Ford; illustrations by Foster Lincoln. New York: Edward J. Clode, [c1914]. 317 p., front., [7] leaves of plates.
LC: Ja 8, '14.
PW: Ja 31, '14.

F-262   Shorty McCabe / by Sewell Ford . . . ; illustrated by Francis Vaux Wilson. New York: Mitchell Kennerley, [c1906]. 316 p., front., [5] leaves of plates.
LC: O 26, '06.
PW: O 6, '06.
BLC: London: T. Werner Laurie, [1908].

F-263   Shorty McCabe gets the hail / by Sewell Ford. New York: Edward J. Clode, [c1919]. 313 p.
LC: Ag 11, '19.
PW: Ag 30, '19.

F-264   Shorty McCabe looks 'em over / by Sewell Ford; illustrations by F. Vaux Wilson. New York: Edward J. Clode, [c1917]. 344 p., front., [7] leaves of plates.
LC: Ap 11, '18.

F-265   Shorty McCabe on the job / by Sewell Ford . . . ; illustrated by F. Vaux Wilson. New York: Edward J. Clode, [c1915]. 320 p., front., [7] leaves of plates.
LC: Mr 9, '15.
PW: Mr 27, '15.

F-266   Side-stepping with Shorty / by Sewell Ford; illustrated by Francis Vaux Wilson. New York: Mitchell Kennerley, [c1908]. 325 p., front., [5] leaves of plates.
LC: Ap 15, '08.
PW: My 9, '08.

F-267   Torchy / by Sewell Ford; illustrations by George Brehm and James Montgomery Flagg. New York: Edward J. Clode, [c1911]. 311 p., front., [5] leaves of plates.
LC: My 1, '11.
PW: My 20, '11.
BLC: London: T. Werner Laurie, [1911].

F-268   Torchy and Vee / by Sewell Ford. New York: E. J. Clode, [c1919]. 307 p.
Unexamined copy: bibliographic data from OCLC, #4891788.
LC: N 21, '19.
PW: Ja 17, '20.

F-269   ____ Torchy as a pa / by Sewell Ford. New York: Edward J. Clode, [c1920]. 306 p.
LC: Ja 27, '21.

F-270   ____ Torchy, private sec. / by Sewell Ford; illustrated by F. Foster Lincoln. New York: Edward J. Clode, [c1915]. 344 p., front., [5] leaves of plates. **OSU, LNU**
LC: D 4, '15.
PW: Ja 15, '16.

F-271   ____ Trilby May crashes in / by Sewell Ford; with illustrations by Marshall Frantz. New York; London: Harper & Brothers, 1922. 285, [1] p., front., [3] leaves of plates.
LC: S 23, '22.
PW: S 30, '22.

F-272   ____ Truegate of Mogador: and other Cedarton folks / by Sewell Ford. New York: Charles Scribner's Sons, 1906. 324 p., front., [7] leaves of plates. [Ill. by A. B. Frost, A. I. Keller and F. Walter Taylor.]
Contents: Truegate of Mogador -- Of such as spin not -- The king gander of Sea Dog shoal -- Captain's folly -- Across a picket fence -- "Shiner" Liddel's revel -- The impressing of Looney Fipps -- Seed to the sower -- Julius -- The romances of "Windy Bill" -- The ride of his life -- Through the needle's eye.
LC: Ja 12, '07.
PW: O 20, '06.

F-273   ____ Trying out Torchy / by Sewell Ford; illustrated by Foster Lincoln. New York: Edward J. Clode, [c1912]. 342 p., front., [5] leaves of plates.
LC: S 18, '12.
BLC: London: T. Werner Laurie, [1913].

F-274   ____ Wilt thou Torchy / by Sewell Ford; illustrations by Frank Snapp and Arthur William Brown. New York: Edward J. Clode, [c1917]. 311 p., front., [5] leaves of plates.
LC: F 10, '17.
PW: F 24, '17.

F-275 Forgione, Louis. Reamer Lou / by Louis Forgione. New York: E. P. Dutton & Company, [c1924]. 279 p.
PW: F 14, '25.

F-276 Forman, Henry James, 1879-1966. The captain of his soul / by Henry James Forman. New York: McBride, Nast & Company, 1914. 468 p.
LC: N 16, '14.
PW: N 7, '14.
BLC: London: Grant Richards; Binghampton [sic] & New York printed, 1915.

F-277   ____ The enchanted garden / by Henry James Forman; with frontispiece by A. D. Rahn. Boston: Little, Brown and Company, 1923. 310, [1] p., front.
LC: Ag 21, '23.
PW: Ag 25, '23.
BLC: London: Hodder & Stoughton, [1923].

F-278   ____ Fire of youth: a novel / by Henry James Forman; with frontispiece by Richard Culter. Boston: Little, Brown and Company, 1920. 364 p., front.
LC: Mr 1, '20.
PW: Mr 6, '20.

F-279   ____ Guilt: a mystery story / Henry James Forman. New York: Boni & Liveright, [c1924]. 252 p. Decorated end papers.
LC: Ap 4, '24.

F-280   ____ The man who lived in a shoe / by Henry James Forman. Boston: Little, Brown and Company, 1922. 334 p.
LC: S 18, '22.
PW: S 9, '22.
BLC: London: Hodder & Stoughton, [1922].

F-281   ____ The Pony Express: a romance / by Henry James Forman; illustrated with scenes from the photoplay; a James Cruze production; a Paramount picture. New York: Grosset & Dunlap, [c1925]. 306 p. photo. front., [7] leaves of photo. plates.
LC: N 9, '25.
PW: N 7, '25.
BLC: London: Hodder & Stoughton, [1926].

F-282   ____ Sudden wealth / by Henry James Forman. New York: Boni and Liveright, 1924. 414 p.
LC: O 4, '24.
PW: O 11, '24.
BLC: London: Jonathan Cape, 1924.

F-283 Forman, Justus Miles, 1875-1915. Bianca's daughter: a novel / by Justus Miles Forman. New York; London: Harper & Brothers, 1910. 337, [1] p., col. front.
LC: Ap 4, '10.
PW: Ap 9, '10.
BLC: London: Ward, Lock & Co., 1910.

F-284   ____ The blind spot: a novel / by Justus Miles Forman; illustrated. New York; London: Harper & Brothers, 1914. 323, [1] p., front., [3] leaves of plates. [Ill. by Herman Pfeifer.]
LC: O 3, '14.
PW: O 10, '14.

F-285   ____ Buchanan's wife: a novel / by Justus Miles Forman; illustrated by Will Grefé. New York; London: Harper & Brothers Publishers, 1906. 290, [1] p., front., [7] leaves of plates.
LC: Ag 9, '06.
PW: Ag 18, '06.
BLC: London: Ward, Lock & Co., 1906.

F-286   ____ The garden of lies: a romance / by Justus Miles Forman; with a frontispiece by William James Hurlbut. New York: Frederick A. Stokes Company, [1902]. 331 p., front.
PW: O 11, '02.
BLC: London: Ward, Lock & Co., 1904.

F-287   ____ The island of enchantment / by Justus Miles Forman; illustrated by Howard Pyle. New York; London: Harper & Brothers, 1905. 105, [1] p., col. front., [3] leaves of col. plates. Designed end papers.
PW: O 7, '05.

F-288   ____ Jason: a romance / by Justus Miles Forman;
with illustrations by W. Hatherell, R. I. New York;
London: Harper & Brothers Publishers, 1909.
356 p., front., [7] leaves of plates.
LC: My 14, '09.
PW: Jl 31, '09.

F-289   ____ Journeys end: a romance of to-day / by Justus
Miles Forman; illustrated by Karl J. Anderson. New
York: Doubleday, Page & Company, 1903. 240 p.,
2 front., [16] leaves of plates.
PW: F 28, '03.
BLC: London: Ward, Lock & Co., 1903.

F-290   ____ Monsigny: a novel / by Justus Miles Forman;
with drawings by Karl Anderson. New York:
Doubleday, Page & Company, 1903. 246 p., front.,
[3] leaves of plates.
PW: Ag 29, '03.
BLC: London: Ward, Lock & Co.; New York
printed, 1903.

F-291   ____ The opening door: a story of the woman's
movement / by Justus Miles Forman . . . New York;
London: Harper & Brothers, 1913. 328, [1] p.,
front. [Ill. by John Alonzo Williams.]
LC: Ap 19, '13.
PW: Ap 26, '13.

F-292   ____ A stumbling block / by Justus Miles Forman.
New York; London: Harper & Brothers Publishers,
1907. 309, [1] p.
LC: Jl 18, '07.
PW: Ag 3, '07.
BLC: London: Hutchinson & Co., 1907.

F-293   ____ Tommy Carteret: a novel / by Justus Miles
Forman; illustrations in color by H. H. Foley. New
York: Doubleday, Page & Company, 1905. 351 p.,
col. front., [3] leaves of col. plates.
PW: Mr 11, '05.
BLC: London: Ward, Lock & Co., 1905.

F-294   ____ The twin sisters: a novel / by Justus Miles
Forman. New York; London: Harper & Brothers,
[1916]. 332, [1] p.
PW: Mr 18, '16.

F-295   ____ The unknown lady: a novel / by Justus Miles
Forman. New York; London: Harper & Brothers
Publishers, 1911. 350 p., front.
LC: F 18, '11.
PW: F 25, '11.
BLC: London: Ward, Lock & Co., 1911.

F-296   Forrest, Arthur. ...The... Biddle boys and Mrs.
Soffel: the great Pittsburgh tragedy and romance:
with full description of their lives and crimes / by
Arthur Forrest (journalist); illustrated. Baltimore,
MD.: I.& M. Ottenheimer, [c1902]. 127, [1] p., ill.

F-297   Forrest, J. R. (Joshua Rhodes), b. 1847. Retribution:
a border mystery / by J. R. Forrest . . . New York:
J. S. Ogilvie Publishing Company, c1906. 262 p.,
front. Decorated end papers.

LC: N 3, '06.
PW: O 6, '06.

F-298   ____ The student cavaliers / by J. R. Forrest. New
York: R. F. Fenno & Company, [c1908]. 328 p.,
front.
LC: Ag 24, '08.
PW: S 5, '08.

Forrest, W. M. (William Mentzel), b. 1868. See
Mansfield, Laurence R., pseud.

F-299   Forrester, Izola L. (Izola Louise), 1878-1944. The
dangerous inheritance, or, The mystery of the Tittani
rubies / by Izola Forrester. Boston; New York:
Houghton Mifflin Company, 1920. (Cambridge: The
Riverside Press). 299, [1] p.
LC: O 29, '20.
PW: O 30, '20.

F-300   ____ "Us fellers" / text by Izola L. Forrester;
pictures by B. Cory Kilvert. Philadelphia: George
W. Jacobs & Company, 1907. 150 p., col. front., [6]
leaves of col. plates.   **IMI**
LC: O 3, '07.
PW: O 12, '07.

F-301   Forsslund, Louise, 1873-1910, *pseud.* Old lady
number 31 / by Louise Forsslund [pseud.]. New
York: The Century Co., 1909. 275 p.
LC: Mr 12, '09.
PW: Ap 3, '09.

F-302   ____ The ship of dreams: a novel / by Louise
Forsslund [pseud.]. New York; London: Harper &
Brothers, 1902. 306, [1] p.
PW: O 4, '02.

F-303   Forsslund, Louise, 1873-1910, *pseud.* The story of
Sarah / by M. Louise Forsslund [pseud.] (M. Louise
Foster). New York: Brentano's, 1901. 433 p.
PW: Mr 23, '01.
BLC: London: Grant Richards, 1901.

F-304   Fort, Charles, 1874-1932. The outcast manufacturers
/ by Charles Fort. New York: B. W. Dodge &
Company, 1909. 328 p.

F-305   Fortnightly Club. Garvanza prose and verse / by the
Fortnightly Club. Garvanza [Calif.]: [s. n.], 1906.
64 p.
Contents: Inez and Manda -- Annabella Gray [poem].

F-306   Forum stories / selected by Charles Vale. New York:
Mitchell Kennerley, 1914. 344 p.   **OSU, EEM**
"These stories have appeared in the Forum since it
passed under its present direction in July, 1910."
Contents: A honeymoon Christmas / Marian Cox -- At the height /
B. Russell Herts -- He came to Proveis / Edward Bedinger Mitchell --
Her child / Margaret Widdemer -- His immortality / Reginald Wright
Kauffman -- His own day / Edwin Björkman -- "I have borne my lord
a son" / Florence Kiper -- Judgment / Louise Elizabeth Dutton --
"Little darling" / Rose Strunsky -- Soirée Kokimono / Henry G.
Alsberg -- The brass candlestick / J. Nilsen Laurvik -- The difference
/ James Hopper -- The little golden shoes / Robert W. Sneddon -- The
pride of his calling / Donal Hamilton Haines -- The rolling stone /
Frank Chester Pease -- The swimmers / John S. Reed.

F-307 Fosdick, J. William (James William), 1858-1937.
The honor of the Braxtons: a novel / by J. William
Fosdick. New York: J. F. Taylor & Company,
1902. 305 p., front., [40] leaves of plates.
PW: Ap 12, '02.

Foshay, M. W. Mixing the grades. In *Clever
business sketches* (1909), C-490.

F-308 Foster, Ardeen. The reign of John Rudd: a novel /
by Ardeen Foster . . . New York: McElroy
Publishing Company, 1906. 207 p., photo. ill. **NYP**

F-309 Foster, Caroline H. W. (Holcombe Wright),
1864-1929. Little stories of yesterday / by Caroline
H. W. Foster (Army Elizabeth Leigh) . . . Los
Angeles, California: The Arroyo Press, 1906.
83 p. **NYP**
"All of these Little stories have been published before
in Outing, The argonaut, Short stories, and other
periodicals . . ."
Contents: The padre's cats -- The hand of St. Peter -- The day of the
dead -- Miguel -- The box of doublooms -- The beaded pouch -- Don
Frederico's crypt.

Foster, Charles Freeman, 1830-1912. See **Sealis,
Hatherly, pseud.**

F-310 Foster, David Skaats, 1852-1920. The divided medal
/ by David Skaats Foster . . . New York; London:
The Franklin Book Company, [c1914]. 359 p.
Contents: The divided medal. (The remainder of text is poetry.)

F-311 _____ Flighty Arethusa / by David Skaats Foster;
with three illustrations and cover design by Paul
Wilhelmi. [Philadelphia]: Press of J. B. Lippincott
Company, 1910. 326 p., col. front., [3] leaves of
plates, ill. **OSU, DLC**
LC: D 4, '10.

F-312 _____ The kidnapped damozel; The oval diamond;
Alraschid in petticoats / by David Skaats Foster.
New York; London: The Franklin Book Company,
[c1915]. 375 p. **DLC**
LC: Ap 12, '15.

F-313 _____ The lady of Castle Queer / by David Skaats
Foster. New York: The Franklin Book Company,
[c1919]. 308 p. **TXA**
LC: O 25, '19.

F-314 _____ Mademoiselle of Cambrai / by David Skaats
Foster. New York: The Franklin Book Company,
[c1920]. 340 p. **IUA**
LC: Ag 25, '20.

F-315 _____ The road to London / by David Skaats Foster.
New York; London: The Franklin Book Company,
[c1914]. 335 p.
LC: My 18, '14.

F-316 _____ Our Uncle William; also, Nate Sawyer / by
David Skaats Foster . . . New York; London: The
Franklin Book Company, [c1915]. 410 p. **DLC**
LC: Ap 12, '15.

F-317 Foster, Ethel Twycross. Little tales of the desert / by
Ethel Twycross Foster . . . ; illustrations by
Hernando G. Villa. Los Angeles, Cal.: Published by
the author, [c1913]. 23 p., [7] leaves of col. plates,
ill.
Contents: Christmas on the desert -- Trade rats -- A chat with Mrs.
Cottontail -- Rabbits and cactus burrs -- The dangerous pet -- A visit
to Palm Springs -- The road-runner -- A strange capture -- A desert
May party.

F-318 Foster, Frank Keyes, 1854-1909. The evolution of a
trade unionist / by Frank K. Foster . . . [Boston,
Mass.: Allied Printing Trades Council], 1901.
174 p. **VXW**

Foster, Josephine H. Glen Alpine. In **Pacific Coast
Women's Press Association.** *La copa de oro* **(1905),
P-2.**

F-319 Foster, Joshua H. (Joshua Hill), 1861-1947. The
Judgment Day: a story of the seven years of Great
Tribulation / Joshua H. Foster. Louisville, Ky.:
Baptist World Publishing Company, 1910. 139 p.,
front. [Ill. by Spearman.] **IYU**
LC: My 31, '10.

Foster, Julia B. Pals. In *West winds* **(1914), W-368.**

F-320 Foster, Mabel G. (Mabel Grace), b. 1869. The heart
of the doctor: a story of the Italian quarter / by
Mabel G. Foster. Boston; New York: Houghton,
Mifflin and Company, 1902. (Cambridge: The
Riverside Press). 255 p., front. [Ill. by Sears
Gallagher.]
PW: O 18, '02.

Foster, Mary Louise, 1873-1910. See **Forsslund,
Louise, pseud.**

F-321 Foster, Maximilian, b. 1872. Corrie who? / by
Maximilian Foster; illustrated by George Brehm.
Boston: Small, Maynard and Company, 1908.
482 p., front., [4] leaves of plates.
LC: O 24, '08.

F-322 _____ Humdrum house? / by Maximilian Foster.
New York; London: D. Appleton and Company,
1924. 306, [1] p.
LC: Ag 11, '24.
PW: Ag 23, '24.

F-323 _____ In the forest: tales of wood-life / by
Maximillian Foster. New York: Doubleday, Page &
Co., 1901. 318 p., front., [19] leaves of plates. [Ill.
by Carl Rungius.]
Contents: The conqueror -- Terror -- Legs -- Tragedy -- The
survivors -- On the snow -- At the end of the trail -- The Dungarvan
Whooper -- Liberty.
PW: O 12, '01.
BLC: London: Doubleday, Page & Co., 1901.

F-324 _____ Keeping up appearances / by Maximilian
Foster . . . ; illustrated by Lester Ralph. New York;
London: D. Appleton and Company, 1914. 284,
[1] p., front., [3] leaves of plates. **OSU, MUU**
LC: Ap 20, '14.
PW: My 2, '14.

_____ Mrs. Redmond's shame. In *Marriage* (1923), **M-457.**

F-325 _____ Rich man, poor man / by Maximilian Foster . . . ; illustrated by F. R. Gruger. New York; London: D. Appleton and Company, 1916. 322, [1] p., front., [3] leaves of plates.
LC: Ja 25, '16.
PW: F 5, '16.

F-326 _____ Shoestrings / by Maximilian Foster; illustrated by F. R. Gruger. New York; London: D. Appleton and Company, 1917. 325, [1] p., front., [3] leaves of plates.
LC: F 27, '17.
PW: Mr 3, '17.

F-327 _____ The trap / by Maximilian Foster. New York; London: D. Appleton and Company, 1920. 282, [1] p.
LC: Ag 25, '20.
PW: ·S 11, '20.

F-328 _____ The whistling man / by Maximilian Foster; illustrated. New York; London: D. Appleton and Company, 1913. 313, [1] p., front., [3] leaves of plates. [Ill. by Henry Raleigh.]
LC: Ag 1, '13.
PW: Ag 9, '13.

Foster, Nancy K. (Nancy Kier), b. 1865. *Monsieur La Tribe.* In *From the old pueblo: and other tales* (1902), **F-434.**

F-329 _____ Not of her race / Nancy K. Foster. Boston: Richard G. Badger, 1911. ([Boston]: The Gorham Press). 279 p., front.
LC: O 14, '10.

_____ Susy. In *Cuentos de California* (1904), **C-963.**

F-330 Foster, R. F. (Robert Frederick), 1853-1945. Cab no. 44 / by R. F. Foster. New York: Frederick A. Stokes Company, [1910]. 323 p.
LC: Ja 26, '10.

Foster, Theodosia Maria, 1838-1923. See **Huntington, Faye, pseud.**

F-331 Foster, W. Bert (Walter Bertram), b. 1869. The heron nest / by W. Bert Foster . . . New York: Published by the Rural Publishing Co., [c1909]. 192 p.

F-332 [Foulke, William Dudley], 1848-1935. The Quaker boy: a tale of the outgoing generation as it appears chronicled in the autobiography of Robert Barclay Dillingham. New York: Cochrane Publishing Company, 1910. 258 p., front.   **ANC**
LC: Ag 29, '10.
Later edition of The Quaker Boy retitled *Dorothy Day* / by William Dudley Foulke . . . New York: The Cosmopolitan Press, 1911. 297 p.
LC: D 18, '11.
PW: Ja 6, '12.

4-19-69, pseud. See **Mighels, Philip Verrill, 1869-1911.**

F-333 Fowler, Charles H. Historical romance of the American Negro / by Charles H. Fowler . . . Baltimore: Press of Thomas & Evans, 1902. 269 p., [31] leaves of plates (some photo.).   **RCE**

F-334 Fowler, Nathaniel C. (Nathaniel Clark), 1858-1918. Gumption: the progressions of Newson New / by Nathaniel C. Fowler, Jr. Boston: Small, Maynard and Company, 1905. 332 p., front., [5] leaves of plates. [Ill. by Charles Copeland.]

F-335 _____ The Knockers' club / by Nathaniel C. Fowler, Jr. New York: Sully and Kleinteich, 1913. 216 p.

F-336 Fox, C. A. (Charles Albert). Bud and Ella / by C. A. Fox. Taft, California: C. A. Fox, [c1922]. 57 p., ill.
"From the Press of Gem Publishing Company, Los Angeles, California."

F-337 _____ Silent / by C. A. Fox. Taft, California: C. A. Fox, [c1922]. 183 p.
"From the Press of Gem Publishing Company, Los Angeles, California."
LC: D 19, '22.
PW: Mr 24, '23.

Fox, Charles David, ed. See **Conrad, Joseph.** *Il conte* (1925), **C-697.**

F-338 Fox, Daniel Frederick, b. 1862. The vindication of Robert Creighton: a tale of the Southwest / by Daniel Frederick Fox. New York; Chicago; London; Edinburgh: Fleming H. Revell Company [c1921]. 272 p., front.

Fox, David, pseud. See **Ostrander, Isabel Egenton, 1883-1924.**

Fox, E. Lyttleton. The squaring up of Hoppy the roustabout. In *Yale Tales* (1901), **Y-1.**

F-339 Fox, Edward Lyell, b. 1887. The new Gethsemane / by Edward Lyell Fox; illustrations by C. G. Bigelow. New York: Robert M. McBride & Co., 1917. 73 p., front., [3] leaves of plates (1 double-leaf plate).   **VUT**
Reprinted from Woman's world.
PW: O 6, '17.

F-340 Fox, Frances Barton, b. 1887. The heart of Arethusa / by Frances Barton Fox; with a frontispiece by F. W. Read. Boston: Small, Maynard and Company, [c1918]. 333 p., col. front.
LC: My 6, '18.
PW: My 4, '18.

F-341 Fox, George R., b. 1880. The fangs of the serpent / by George R. Fox. New York: Minton, Balch & Company, 1924. 293 p.
LC: My 17, '24.

F-342   Fox, Henry C. (Henry Clay), 1836-1920. Uncle Zeek and Aunt Liza: a tale of episodes / by Hon. Henry C. Fox. Boston, Mass.: Mayhew Publishing Company, [c1905]. 221, [1] p.
PW: F 3, '06.

F-343   Fox, John, 1863-1919. Blue-grass and rhododendron: outdoors in old Kentucky / by John Fox, Jr. New York: Charles Scribner's Sons, 1901. 294 p., front., [19] leaves of plates. [Ill. by F. C. Yohn, H. L. Brown, and W. S. Rogers.]
Contents: The Southern mountaineer -- The Kentucky mountaineer -- Down the Kentucky on a raft -- After Br'er Rabbit in the Blue-grass -- Through the bad bend -- Fox-hunting in Kentucky -- To the breaks of Sandy -- Br'er Coon in ole Kentucky -- Civilizing the Cumberland -- Man-hunting in the Pound -- The Red Fox of the mountains -- The hanging of Talton Hall.
LC: S 21, '01.
PW: O 5, '01.
BLC: London: Archibald Constable & Co.,; New York printed, 1905.
References: BAL 6249.

F-344   ____ Christmas eve on Lonesome: and other stories / by John Fox, Jr.; illustrated. New York: Charles Scribner's Sons, 1904. 234 p., col. front., [7] leaves of col. plates. [Ill. by A. I. Keller, Fletcher Charles Ransom, Frank Earle Schoonover, William Sherman Potts.]
Contents: Christmas eve on Lonesome -- The army of the Callahan -- The last Stetson -- The pardon of Becky Day -- A crisis for the guard -- Christmas night with Satan.
LC: O 4, '04.
PW: O 29, '04.
BLC: London: Archibald Constable & Co.; New York printed, 1904.
References: BAL 6252.

F-345   ____ Erskine Dale, pioneer / by John Fox, Jr.; illustrated by F. C. Yohn. New York: Charles Scribner's Sons, 1920. 258 p., front., [7] leaves of plates.
LC: S 28, '20.
PW: O 9, '20.
BLC: London: Hodder & Stoughton, [1920].
References: BAL 6263.

F-346   ____ The heart of the hills / by John Fox, Jr.; illustrated by F. C. Yohn. New York: Charles Scribner's Sons, 1913. 396 p., front., [6] leaves of plates.
LC: Mr 12, '13.
PW: Mr 15, '13.
BLC: London: Constable & Co., 1913.
References: BAL 6259.

F-347   ____ In Happy Valley / by John Fox, Jr.; illustrated by F. C. Yohn. New York: Charles Scribner's Sons, 1917. 229 p., front., [7] leaves of plates.
Contents: The courtship of Allaphair -- The compact of Christopher -- The Lord's own level -- The Marquise of Queensberry -- His last Christmas gift -- The angel from Viper -- The Pope of the Big Sandy -- The goddess of Happy Valley -- The battle-prayer of Parson Small -- The Christmas tree on Pigeon.
LC: O 10, '17.
PW: S 29, '17.
BLC: London: Hodder & Stoughton, 1918.
References: BAL 6262.

F-348   ____ A knight of the Cumberland / by John Fox, Jr.; illustrated by F. C. Yohn. New York: Charles Scribner's Sons, 1906. 158 p., col. front., [3] leaves of col. plates.
LC: O 22, '06.
PW: N 10, '06.
BLC: London: Archibald & Co., 1906.
References: BAL 6255.

F-349   ____ The little shepherd of Kingdom Come / by John Fox Jr.; illustrated by F. C. Yohn. New York: Charles Scribner's Sons, 1903. 404 p., front., [7] leaves of plates.
LC: Jl 21, '03.
PW: S 5, '03.
BLC: Westminster: Archibald Constable & Co., 1903.
References: BAL 6250.

F-350   ____ The trail of the lonesome pine / by John Fox, Jr.; illustrated by F. C. Yohn. New York: Charles Scribner's Sons, 1908. 422 p., front., [7] leaves of plates.
LC: S 26, '08.
PW: O 17, '08.
BLC: London: Archibald Constable & Co., 1908.
References: BAL 6256.

F-351   France, Lewis B., 1833-1907. No stranger to my neighbor / by Lewis B. France; illustrated by Charles Edgar Shaw. Denver, Colorado: Outdoor Life Publishing Company, [c1906]. 129 p., [6] leaves of plates.   **DPL**
LC: D 1, '06.

Francis, Eugene, jt. aut. *Life; or, Unto the third and fourth generation* (1904). See **Chase, Charles Wathen, jt. aut., C-317.**

F-352   Francis, John, b. 1875. The triumph of Virginia Dale / by John Francis, Jr.; with a frontispiece in full color from a painting by W. Haskell Coffin; and other illustrations from drawings by John Goss. Boston: The Page Company, 1921. 357 p., col. front., [4] leaves of col. plates.

F-353   Francis, Joseph Thomas. The masonic city: a novel / by Joseph Thomas Francis. Morristown, N. J.: [Morris County Press], 1922. 87 p.   **DLC**
LC: Ja 19, '22.

F-354   Francis, Mary C. Dalrymple: a romance of the British prison ship, the Jersey / by Mary C. Francis . . . New York: James Pott & Company, 1904. 371 p.
PW: Ap 2, '04.

____, jt. aut. *Old Joe Prouty (1901).* See **Golden, Richard, jt. aut., G-284.**

F-355   ____ A son of destiny: the story of Andrew Jackson / by Mary C. Francis. New York: The Federal Book Company, 1902. 459 p., front. (port.).
PW: D 27, '02.

F-356   Frank, Waldo David, 1889-1967. Chalk face / by Waldo Frank. New York: Boni and Liveright, [c1924]. 252 p.
LC: O 4, '24.
PW: O 11, '24.

F-357   ____ City block. Darien, Conn.: Published by Waldo Frank, 1922. 320 p.
LC: O 20, '22.

F-358   ____ The dark mother: a novel / by Waldo Frank. New York: Boni and Liveright, [c1920]. 376 p.
TOL
LC: O 8, '20.
PW: O 16, '20.

F-359   ____ Holiday / by Waldo Frank. New York: Boni and Liveright, [c1923]. 233 p.
LC: S 13, '23.
PW: Ag 25, '23.

   ____ John the Baptist. In *The best short stories of 1922 and the yearbook of the American short story (1923)*, **B-567**.

F-360   ____ Rahab / by Waldo Frank. New York: Boni and Liveright, [c1922]. 250 p.
LC: Mr 13, '22.
PW: Mr 18, '22.

   ____ Under the dome. In *The best short stories of 1921 and the yearbook of the American short story (1922)*, **B-566**.

F-361   ____ The unwelcome man: a novel / by Waldo Frank. Boston: Little, Brown, and Company, 1917. 371 p.
LC: Ja 9, '17.
PW: Ja 6, '17.

F-362   Franken, Rose, 1895-1988. Pattern / by Rose L. Franken. New York: Charles Scribner's Sons, 1925. 348 p.
PW: Ap 18, '25.

F-363   Franklin, Annie. Billy Fairchild, widow, and other stories / by Annie Franklin. [San Francisco: Press of Bolte & Braden Co., c1917]. 161 p., front. **DLC**
Contents: Billy Fairchild, widow -- A romance at fifty -- A girl's heart -- Carmen.

F-364   Franklin, Edgar, b. 1879. In and out / by Edgar Franklin; frontispiece by Paul Stahr. New York: W. J. Watt & Company, [c1917]. 314 p., front.

F-365   ____ Mr. Hawkins' humorous adventures / by Edgar Franklin. New York: Dodge Publishing Company, [c1904]. 323 p., front., [4] leaves of plates. [Ill. by Bernhard Gutmann.]

F-366   Fraser, Cedric D. M'lord o' the white road / by Cedric Fraser. New York: D. Appleton and Company, 1922. 319 p.
LC: Ag 14, '22.
BLC: London: [1921].

F-367   Fraser, Georgia. Crow-Step / by Georgia Fraser. New York: Witter and Kintner, [1910]. 401 p., front. [Ill. by Florence J. Woolston.]
LC: O 12, '10.
PW: D 13, '10.

F-368   Fraser, Robert. The fire opal / by Robert Fraser . . . New York: Edward J. Clode, [c1911]. 311 p. Illustrated end papers.
LC: F 2, '11.
PW: Mr 4, '11.

F-369   ____ Three men and a maid / by Robert Fraser. New York: Edward J. Clode, 1907. 298 p.
LC: Ap 11, '07.
PW: My 4, '07.

F-370   Frayser, Nannie Lee, d. 1924. Little prodigals / by Nannie Lee Frayser. Cleveland, Ohio: F. M. Barton Company, 1910. 55 p. **KTS**
PW: Jl 2, '10.

F-371   Frazer, Elizabeth. The secret partner / by Elizabeth Frazer. New York: Henry Holt and Company, 1922. 206 p.
LC: Je 3, '22.
PW: Je 10, '22.

F-372   Frazer, William H. (William Henry), 1873-1953. The possumist: and other stories / by William H. Frazer; with an introduction by Julian S. Miller; illustrations by Donald A. Sprout. Charlotte, N. C.: The Murrill Press, 1924. 68 p.
Contents: The possumist -- "Jes complimentin' yo sermon" -- Out-Heroding Herod -- Real discernment -- Grasping an opportunity -- Honor to whom honor is due -- "Flyin'? Not me!" -- Taking time by the forelock -- Scotch precautions -- For a consideration -- The motive behind the act -- Superiority recognized -- Uncle Aaron's greeting.
LC: D 1, '24.
PW: F 21, '25.

   Frazier, Constance V. The career. In *The best college short stories, 1917-18 (1919)*, **B-557**.

F-373   Frazier, Esther Yates. Pearl: an ocean waif / by Esther Yates Frazier . . . Denver, Colorado: The Reed Publishing Company, 1903. 237 p. **COD**
PW: D 31, '04.

   Freck, Laura F., ed. <u>See</u> *Short stories of various types (1920)*, **S-465**.

F-374   Frederick, J. George (Justus George), b. 1882. Breezy / by J. George Frederick; illustrations by W. D. Stevens. New York: McClure, Phillips & Co., 1906. 37 p., front., [5] leaves of plates.
LC: S 19, '06.

F-375   ____ Two women / by J. George Frederick. New York: Nicholas L. Brown, 1924. 345 p.
LC: D 15, '23.
PW: F 16, '24.

   Frederick, John, pseud. <u>See</u> **Brand, Max, 1892-1944, pseud.**

F-376 Frederick, John T. (John Towner), 1893-1975.
Druida / John T. Frederick; with seven woodcuts by
Wilfred Jones. New York: Alfred A. Knopf, 1923.
286 p., front., ill. Designed end papers.
LC: Ja 15, '23.
PW: Ja 13, '23.

F-377 _____ Green Bush / John T. Frederick; with nine
drawings by George L. Stout. New York: Alfred A.
Knopf, 1925. 304 p.
LC: S 10, '25.
PW: S 26, '25.

_____, ed. See *Stories from the Midland* (1924),
S-984.

F-378 Frederick, Lemira. His own estate / by Lemira
Frederick. New York: Cochrane Publishing
Company, 1911. 144 p.   **DLC**

Fredericks, Arnold, pseud. See **Kummer, Frederic
Arnold, 1873-1943.**

Fredericks, Percy, pseud. See **Pierce, Frederick E.**

F-379 Freear, Robert Louis. Nancy Hart: an American
heroine / Robert Louis Freear. Boston: C. M. Clark
Publishing Company, 1908. 305 p., front. [Ill. by
N. K. Saunders.]
LC: O 20, '08.

F-380 _____ The shadow dwellers: a romance / by Robert
Louis Freear . . . New York: Isaac H. Blanchard
Co., [c1901]. 157 p.
PW: Mr 22, '02.
BLC: New York: Isaac H. Blanchard Co.; London:
R. McClure, [1901].

Freedley, Mary Mitchell. Blind vision. In *The best
short stories of 1918 and the yearbook of the
American short story* (1919), **B-563**; *see also War
stories* (1919), **W-94.**

F-381 Freedman, David, 1898-1936. Mendel Marantz / by
David Freedman; illustrations by M. Leone Bracker.
New York: The Langdon Publishing Company, Inc.,
1925. 301 p., col. front., [10] leaves of col. plates.
LC: F 4, '26.
PW: F 6, '26.

_____ Mendel Marantz-housewife. In *The best short
stories of 1922 and the yearbook of the American
short story* (1923), **B-567.**

F-382 Freeland, Holman. Trelawny / by Holman Freeland;
with illustrations by Arthur W. Brown. New York:
Edward J. Clode, 1903. 317, [1] p., front., [5]
leaves of plates. Designed end papers.
PW: D 5, '03.
BLC: London: Isbister and Co., 1902.

F-383 Freeman, Gladys. Mis' Melissa's baby / by Gladys
Freeman. New York: Isaac H. Blanchard Company,
1915. 61 p.   **DLC**

F-384 Freeman, Lewis R. (Lewis Ransome), b. 1878.
Hell's hatches / by Lewis R. Freeman. New York:
Dodd, Mead and Company, 1921. 291 p.
LC: Mr 17, '21.
PW: Ap 9, '21.
BLC: London: William Heinemann, 1921.

F-385 _____ Sea-hounds / by Lewis R. Freeman . . . ; with
illustrations from photographs by the author. New
York: Dodd, Mead & Company, 1919. 309 p.,
photo. front., [7] leaves of photo. plates.   **KSU**
BLC: London: Cassell & Co., 1919.

F-386 Freeman, Mary Eleanor Wilkins, 1852-1930. An
alabaster box / by Mary E. Wilkins Freeman and
Florence Morse Kingsley; illustrated by Stockton
Mulford. New York; London: D. Appleton and
Company, 1917. 310, [1] p., front., [3] leaves of
plates.
LC: Mr 26, '17.
PW: Ap 7, '17.
References: BAL 6400.

F-387 _____ The butterfly house / by Mary E. Wilkins
Freeman; with illustrations by Paul Julien Meylan.
New York: Dodd, Mead and Company, 1912.
292 p., front., [3] leaves of plates.
LC: F 23, '12.
PW: Mr 2, '12.
References: BAL 6395.

F-388 _____ By the light of the soul: a novel / by Mary E.
Wilkins Freeman; illustrations by Harold M. Brett.
New York; London: Harper & Brothers, 1907,
[c1906]. 497, [1] p., front., [7] leaves of plates.
LC: S 6, '06.
PW: Ja 26, '07.
References: BAL 6383.

F-389 _____ The copy-cat: & other stories / by Mary E.
Wilkins Freeman. New York; London: Harper &
Brothers, 1914. 350, [1] p., front., [7] leaves of
plates. [Ill. by Walter Biggs, Worth Brehm, and W.
H. D. Koerner.]
Contents: The copy-cat -- The cock of the walk -- Johnny in the
woods -- Daniel and little Dan'l -- Big sister Solly -- Little Lucy Rose
-- Noblesse -- Coronation -- The amethyst comb -- The umbrella man
-- The balking of Christopher -- Dear Annie.
LC: S 24, '14.
PW: S 26, '14.
References: BAL 6397.

F-390 _____ The debtor: a novel / by Mary E. Wilkins
Freeman . . . ; illustrations by W. D. Stevens. New
York; London: Harper & Brothers, 1905. 562,
[1] p., front., [7] leaves of plates.
PW: N 4, '05.
References: BAL 6377.

F-391 _____ "Doc." Gordon / by Mary E.
Wilkins-Freeman; illustrated in water-colors by Frank
T. Merrill. New York; London: The Authors and
Newspapers Association, 1906. 322 p., front., front.,
[3] leaves of plates.
LC: Jl 19, '06.
PW: O 20, '06.

BLC: London: T. Fisher Unwin, 1907.
References: BAL 6380, BAL Addendum: PBSA, 61:127.

F-392   ____ Edgewater people / by Mary E. Wilkins Freeman . . . New York; London: Harper & Brothers, [1918]. 314, [1] p., front. [Ill. by Edwin F. Bayha.] **OSU, CWR**
Contents: Sarah Edgewater -- The old man of the field -- The voice of the clock -- Value received -- The flowering bush -- The outside of the house -- The liar -- Sour sweetings --- Both cheeks -- The soldier man -- The ring with the green stone -- "A retreat to the goal".
LC: N 14, '18.
PW: N 30, '18.
References: BAL 6403.

F-393   ____ The fair Lavinia: and others / Mary E. Wilkins Freeman; illustrated. New York; London: Harper & Brothers, 1907. 307, [1] p., front., [7] leaves of plates. [Ill. by William Hurd Lawrence, A. I. Keller, and Alice Barber Stephens.]
Contents: The fair Lavinia -- Amarina's roses -- Eglantina -- The pink shawls -- The willow-ware -- The secret -- The gold -- The underling.
LC: O 24, '07.
PW: N 9, '07.
References: BAL 6386.

F-394   ____ The givers: short stories / by Mary E. Wilkins Freeman. New York; London: Harper & Brothers, 1904. 295, [1] p., front., [7] leaves of plates. [Ill. by William Hurd Lawrence, Fletcher Charles Ransom, W. E. Mears, and Lester Ralph.]
Contents: The givers -- Lucy -- Eglantina -- Joy -- The reign of the doll -- The chance of Araminta -- The butterfly -- The last gift.
LC: Je 9, '04.
PW: Je 18, '04.
References: BAL 6372.

F-395   ____ The green door / by Mary E. Wilkins-Freeman; illustrated by Mary R. Bassett. New York: Moffat, Yard and Company, 1910. 62 p., col. front., [3] leaves of col. plates. **IND**
LC: N 3, '10.
PW: D 3, '10.
BLC: London: Gay and Hancock, 1912.
References: BAL 6392.

    ____ The hall bedroom. In *Short story classics* (1905), S-466.

F-396   ____ The home-coming of Jessica . . . [by Mary E. Wilkins]; An idyl of Central Park . . . [by Brander Matthews]; The romance of a soul . . . [by Robert Grant]. Springfield, O.; New York; Chicago: The Crowell & Kirkpatrick Co., 1901. 50 p., ill.
Unexamined copy: bibliographic data from OCLC, #26825333.
"These stories and illustrations are reproduced from the . . . issues of the Woman's home companion" for Aug., Sept., Nov., 1901.
Cover title: *Three short stories* [by] Mary E. Wilkins . . . Brander Matthews . . . Robert Grant.
LC: D 23, '01.
References: BAL 6369.

    ____ Hyacinthus. In *Quaint courtships* (1906), Q-3.

F-397   ____ The portion of labor / by Mary E. Wilkins. New York; London: Harper & Brothers, 1901. 562, [1] p., front., [7] leaves of plates. [Ill. by Jay Hambidge and A. I. Keller.]
LC: N 8, '01.
PW: N 16, '01.
References: BAL 6366. BAL Addendum: PBSA 55: 152-53.

F-398   ____ The shoulders of Atlas: a novel / by Mary E. Wilkins Freeman. New York; London: Harper & Brothers, 1908. 293, [1] p., front.
LC: Je 10, '08.
PW: Je 20, '08.
References: BAL 6388.

F-399   ____ Six trees: short stories / by Mary E. Wilkins Freeman. New York; London: Harper & Brothers, 1903. 206, [1] p., front., [15] leaves of plates. [Ill. by Charles Broughton.]
Contents: The elm-tree -- The white birch -- The great pine -- The balsam fir -- The Lombardy poplar -- The apple-tree.
LC: F 19, '03.
PW: F 28, '03.
References: BAL 6370.

F-400   ____ Understudies: short stories / by Mary E. Wilkins . . . ; illustrated. New York; London: Harper & Brothers, 1901. 229, [1] p., front., [25] leaves of plates. [Some ill. by Charles Broughton.]
Contents: The cat -- The monkey -- The squirrel -- The lost dog -- The parrot -- The doctor's horse -- Bouncing Bet -- Prince's feather -- Arethusa -- Mountain-laurel -- Peony -- Morning-glory.
LC: Ap 16, '01.
PW: Ap 20, '01.
References: BAL 6365.

    ____, contributor. See *The whole family* (1908), W-578.

F-401   ____ The wind in the rose-bush: and other stories of the supernatural / by Mary E. Wilkins; illustrated by Peter Newell. New York: Doubleday, Page & Company, 1903. 237 p., front., [7] leaves of plates.
Contents: The wind in the rose-bush -- The shadows on the wall -- Luella Miller -- The southwest chamber -- The vacant lot -- The lost ghost.
LC: Mr 18, '03.
PW: Mr 28, '03.
BLC: London: John Murray; [New York printed], 1903.
References: BAL 6371.

F-402   ____ The winning lady: and others / by Mary E. Wilkins Freeman; illustrated. New York; London: Harper & Brothers, 1909. 327, [1] p., front., [7] leaves of plates.
Contents: The winning lady -- Little-girl-afraid-of-a-dog -- The joy of youth -- Billy and Suzy -- The selfishness of Amelia Lamkin -- The travelling sister -- Her Christmas -- Old woman Magoun -- Eliza Sam -- Flora and Hannah -- A New-Year's resolution.
LC: O 29, '09.
PW: N 13, '09.
References: BAL 6391.

F-403   ____ The Yates pride: a romance / by Mary E. Wilkins Freeman. New York; London: Harper & Brothers, 1912. 64, [1] p., front., [2] leaves of

plates.
LC: S 21, '12.
PW: O 5, '12.
References: BAL 6396.

F-404 Freeman, William Neely, b. 1860. Saint Mammon: a novel of American society. New York: The Broadway Publishing Co., 1908. 440 p., ill.
LC: O 26, '08.
PW: D 12, '08.

F-405 Frejolity, Azariah, b. 1855, *pseud*. The itinerary of Azariah Frejolity, or, What becomes of old barbers / by Azariah Frejolity [pseud.]. [Carey, Ohio?: s. n.], c1908. 232 p.

French, Alice, 1850-1934. See **Thanet, Octave, pseud.**

F-406 French, Allen, 1870-1946. At Plattsburg / by Allen French. New York: Charles Scribner's Sons, 1917. 310 p.
LC: My 2, '17.

F-407 _____ The barrier: a novel / by Allen French. New York: Doubleday, Page & Company, 1904. 316 p.
PW: Je 4, '04.
BLC: London: Doubleday, Page & Co.; New York printed, 1904.

F-408 _____ The colonials: being a narrative of events chiefly connected with the siege and evacuation of the town of Boston in New England / written by Allen French. New York: Doubleday, Page & Co., 1902. 504 p., front. Designed end papers.
PW: F 8, '02.
BLC: London: Doubleday & Co., 1902. Another copy: London: Grant Richards, 1902.

F-409 _____ The hiding-places: a novel / by Allen French. New York: Charles Scribner's Sons, 1917. 386 p.
LC: Mr 14, '17.
PW: Mr 17, '17.

French, Anne Warner. See **Warner, Anne, 1869-1913.**

F-410 French, Charles Sheldon. The worship of the golden calf: a story of wage-slavery in Massachusetts / by Charles Sheldon French. Dalton, Mass.: C. Sheldon French, 1908. (Pittsfield, Mass.: William J. Oatman). 189 p.

F-411 French, Davida. Not included in a sheepskin: Stanford stories / by Davida French, Esther Stevens, Laura Wells. Stanford University, California: Published by the Stanford Book Store, [c1907]. 242 p., front.
Contents: The three R's -- A girl and a nudibranc -- Prepdom on parade -- The arrogance of the second year -- Miss Johnston and the seminar system -- Dedicate to Plato -- The rulers of the realm -- Earthquake emergency -- Senior finalities.

F-412 [French, Francis F]. Skid Puffer: a tale of the Kankakee swamp / illustrated by F. T. Richards and Victor Perard and from photographs of scenery. New York: Henry Holt and Company, 1910. 382 p., front., [5] leaves of plates, maps. Preface signed:

Francis F. French.
LC: Mr 14, '10.
PW: Ap 16, '10.

F-413 French, Harry W. (Harry Willard), b. 1854. The devil's discharge / by Willard French. New York: The Neale Publishing Company, 1914. 173 p.

French, Joseph Lewis, b. 1858, ed. In *Masterpieces of mystery* (1920), M-589.

F-414 French, Lillie Hamilton, 1854-1939. Mrs. Van Twiller's salon / records by George Leake; expurgations by Lillie Hamilton French . . . New York: J. Pott & Company, 1905. 359 p.

F-415 _____ My old maid's corner / by Lillie Hamilton French. New York: The Century Co., 1903. 227 p.
PW: O 17, '03.

French, Willard. See **French, Harry W. (Harry Willard), b. 1854.**

F-416 Fretz, Lewis Barnett. Bennie, the Pythian of Syracuse: and other titles / by Lewis Barnett Fretz. Chicago: Scroll Publishing Company, 1901. 176 p., photo. ill. (port.).
Contents: Includes "Somebody's mother," a fictional piece.
PW: My 24, '02.

Fridy, Alliene. When God walks the road. In *When God walks the road and other stories* (1924), W-445.

F-417 Friedlander, Elsie Goerner. Her father's voice / by Elsie Goerner Friedlander. [Pittsburgh, Pa.: Published by Lincoln Printing Company, c1924]. 161 p.
LC: Mr 31, '24.

F-418 Friedman, I. K. (Isaac Kahn), b. 1870. The autobiography of a beggar: prefaced by some of the humorous adventures & incidents related in the Beggars' club / by I. K. Friedman; with eighteen illustrations by W. Glackens. Boston: Small, Maynard & Company, 1903. 350 p., front., [17] leaves of plates.

F-419 _____ By bread alone: a novel / by I. K. Friedman . . . New York: McClure, Phillips & Co., 1901. 481 p.
PW: N 2, '01.
BLC: London: McClure, Phillips, 1901.

F-420 _____ The radical / by I. K. Friedman . . . New York: D. Appleton and Company, 1907. 362 p., col. front. [Ill by Harrison Fisher.]
LC: S 27, '07.
PW: O 12, '07.

F-421 Friel, Arthur O. (Arthur Olney), 1885-1959. Cat o' mountain / by Arthur O. Friel . . . ; illustrated by Donald S. Humphreys. Philadelphia: The Penn Publishing Company, 1923. 333 p., front.
LC: Je 20, '23.
PW: S 15, '23.
BLC: London; New York: Andrew Melrose, 1924.

F-422   ____ Hard wood / by Arthur O. Friel . . . ; jacket and frontispiece by R. J. Cavaliere. Philadelphia: The Penn Publishing Company, 1925. 333 p., front.
LC: Ag 11, '25.
PW: Jl 25, '25.
BLC: London; New York: Andrew Melrose, 1926.

F-423   ____ King--of Kearsarge / by Arthur O. Friel; frontispiece by Joseph M. Clement. Philadelphia: The Penn Publishing Company, 1921. 368 p., front.
LC: S 20, '21.
PW: O 8, '21.
BLC: London; New York: Andrew Melrose, 1922.

F-424   ____ The king of No Man's Land / by Arthur O. Friel . . . New York; London: Harper & Brothers, 1924. 347 p.
LC: Ap 5, '24.
PW: Ap 5, '24.

F-425   ____ Mountains of mystery / by Arthur O. Friel. New York; London: Harper & Brothers, 1925. 399 p.
LC: Ap 4, '25.
PW: Ap 4, '25.

F-426   ____ The pathless trail / by Arthur O. Friel. New York; London: Harper & Brothers, 1922. 337 p. **GPM**
LC: Mr 21, '22.
PW: Ap 1, '22.

F-427   ____ Tiger River / by Arthur O. Friel . . . -- 1st ed. -- New York; London: Harper & Brothers, 1923. 352 p.
LC: F 16, '23.

F-428 Friend, Emil, 1865-1921. Masks: a novel / by Emil Friend. Chicago: Geo. W. Ogilvie & Co., 1905. 355 p., front., [2] leaves of plates. [Ill. by W. C. Both.] Designed end papers.

F-429 Friend, Oscar J. (Oscar Jerome), b. 1897. The Bullet Eater / by Oscar J. Friend . . . Chicago: A. C. McClurg & Co., 1925. 389 p., front. [Ill. by Herbert Bohnert.]
LC: S 22, '25.
PW: O 10, '25.

F-430   ____ Click of Triangle T / by Oscar J. Friend . . . Chicago: A. C. McClurg & Co., 1925. 370 p., front. [Ill. by Remington Schuyler.]
LC: Ap 25, '25.
PW: My 2, '25.

F-431   ____ The round-up: a story of ranchmen, cowboys, rustlers, and bad-men happening in the days when the great Southwest was being won for civilization / by Oscar J. Friend. Chicago: A. C. McClurg & Co., 1924. 373 p., front. [Ill. by J. Allen St. John.] **MNL**

F-432 The friendly little house: and other stories / by Marion Ames Taggart, George M. A. Cain, Nora Tynan O'Mahoney, Mary T. Waggaman, Mary E. Mannix, Jerome Harte, Norman Whiteside, Anna Blanche McGill, Richard Aumerle, Anna T. Sadlier, Magdalen Rock. New York; Cincinnati; Chicago: Benziger Brothers, 1910. 276 p. **DLC**
Contents: The friendly little house / Marion Ames Taggart -- The test / George M. A. Cain -- The killing of Barnaby Fox / Nora Tynan O'Mahony -- An expiation / Mary T. Waggaman -- The wanderer / Mary E. Mannix -- The fall of the year / Marion Ames Taggart -- The song of the Hurdy Gurdy / Jerome Harte -- Sister Angela's patient / Mary T. Waggaman -- The burglar of the West Grange Farm / Nora Tynan O'Mahony -- The voice of wilderness / Norman Whiteside -- Pro Patria / Marion Ames Taggart -- The force of habit / Anna Blanche McGill -- Dona Leanor De Bobadilla / Richard Aumerle -- One "Hail Mary" / George M. A. Cain -- Miss Milly and Mr. Willy / Anna Blanche McGill -- The way of the Lord / Anna T. Sadlier -- Pointing the moral / Jerome Harte -- The wrong basket trunk / Magdalen Rock -- Next of kin / Magdalen Rock.
PW: O 15, '10.

F-433 Frisbie, Henry S. (Henry Samuel). Prophet of the kingdom / by Henry S. Frisbie. Washington, [D. C.]: The Neale Publishing Company, 1901. 238 p. **BGU**
PW: Ap 12, '02.

Frischmann, David. Three who ate. In *Yiddish tales* **(1912), Y-20.**

F-434 From the old pueblo and other tales. Los Angeles: [s. n.], 1902. 82 p., front. [Ill. by Adeline Gish.] **CCO, CLU**
Contents: From the old pueblo -- The miracle of San Juanito / Amanda Mathews -- The reaping of vanity / Gwendolen Overton -- Monsieur La Tribe / Nancy K. Foster -- A determined lover / Lillian Corbett Barnes -- An Aztec biography / Amanda Mathews -- The story of Suey Ho Yee / Olive Percival.

F-435 Frooks, Dorothy, b. 1899. The American heart / by Dorothy Frooks . . . ; with an introduction by Henry Clews. Kansas City, Missouri: Burton Publishing Company, [c1919]. 218 p. **NYP**

F-436 Frost, Adelaide Gail, 1868-1928. By waysides in India / Adelaide Gail Frost. [Indianapolis, Ind.?: Christian Woman's Board of Missions?, c1902.] 58 p., front. (port.), [5] leaves of plates. [Ill. by J. E. Dean.] **AZS**

F-437 Frost, Margaret A. (Margaret Ann). Sunny / by Margaret A. Frost. Philadelphia: Griffith and Rowland Press, 1907. 200 p., front., [5] leaves of plates. [Ill. by Frank McKernan.] **VPI**
LC: Mr 25, '07.

F-438 Frost, Thomas Gold, 1866-1948. The man of destiny / by Thomas Gold Frost; with illustrations by S. Nemtzoff. New York: The Gramercy Publishing Company, 1909. 312 p., front., [2] leaves of plates.
LC: Jl 5, '09.

F-439 Frost, Walter Archer, 1876-1964. The man between / by Walter Archer Frost; illustrations by Howard McCormick. Garden City, N. Y.: Doubleday, Page & Company, 1913. 304 p., front., [3] leaves of plates.

F-440 Frothingham, Eugenia Brooks, b. 1874. The evasion / by Eugenia Brooks Frothingham. Boston; New York: Houghton, Mifflin and Company, 1906. (Cambridge: The Riverside Press). 414, [2] p.
PW: Ap 7, '06.

F-441 ____ The finding of Norah / by Eugenia Brooks
Frothingham. Boston; New York: Houghton Mifflin
Company, 1918. (Cambridge: The Riverside Press).
93, [1] p.
LC: F 25, '18.

F-442 ____ Her Roman lover / Eugenia Brooks
Frothingham. Boston; New York: Houghton Mifflin
Company, 1911. (Cambridge: The Riverside Press).
286, [2] p., front., [3] leaves of plates. [Ill. by Alice
Barber Stephens.]
LC: O 5, '11.
PW: S 23, '11.

F-443 ____ The turn of the road / Eugenia Brooks
Frothingham. Boston; New York: Houghton, Mifflin
and Company, 1901. (Cambridge: The Riverside
Press). 266 p.
PW: Mr 2, '01.

F-444 ____ The way of the wind / by Eugenia Brooks
Frothingham. Boston; New York: Houghton Mifflin
Company, 1917. (Cambridge: The Riverside Press).
333, [1] p.
LC: F 23, '17.
PW: F 24, '17.
BLC: London: Constable & Co., 1917.

F-445 Frothingham, Jessie Peabody, 1862-1949. Running
the gantlet: the daring exploits of Lieutenant
Cushing, U. S. N. / by Jessie Peabody Frothingham
. . . New York: D. Appleton & Company, 1906.
283 p., col. front., [3] leaves of col. plates. [Ill. by
H. C. Edwards.]

F-446 Fry, Lena Jane. Other worlds: a story concerning
the wealth earned by American citizens and showing
how it can be secured to them instead of to the trusts /
by Lena Jane Fry. Chicago: Lena Jane Fry, 1905.
199 p., photo. front. (port.), ill. (some photo.). [Ill.
by A. Peyton, E. H. Fry, or L. J. Fry.]   **DRB**

F-447 Fuessle, Newton A. (Newton Augustus), 1883-1924.
The flail / by Newton A. Fuessle. New York:
Moffat, Yard & Company, 1919. 328 p.
LC: Mr 20, '19.
PW: Mr 15, '19.

F-448 ____ Flesh and phantasy / by Newton A. Fuessle.
Boston: The Cornhill Company, [c1919]. 211 p.
Reprinted in part from various periodicals.
Contents: The leap -- The million heir -- The legal mind -- The
incredible pilgrimage -- The cough of the Spartan -- Direct action --
In the fourth dimension -- The lost woman -- A dialogue on
decadence -- The conversion of Hank Carlowe -- The love philtre --
The stroke of two -- The spoiled woman -- Ten minutes after six.
LC: Ap 24, '20.
PW: Jl 5, '19.

F-449 ____ Gold shod / by Newton Fuessle . . . New
York: Boni and Liveright, [c1921]. 243 p.
LC: S 13, '21.
PW: S 17, '21.
BLC: London: Leonard Parson's, 1922.

F-450 ____ Jessup / Newton Fuessle. New York: Boni
and Liveright, [c1923]. 280 p.

LC: Ap 2, '23.
PW: Mr 31, '23.

F-451 Fuhr, Lulu R. Tenderfoot tales: number two / by
Lulu R. Fuhr. Topeka, Kan.: Crane & Co., 1916.
28 p.
Unexamined copy: bibliographic data from OCLC,
#10838150.

F-452 Fuhrman, Karl, b. 1870. Little tales retold with a
Persian intermezzo. [San Francisco?]: Printed for
my dear friends of the Bohemian Club, San
Francisco, Karl Fuhrman, B. C., 1925. 24 p., photo.
ill. (port.).
Contents: "To the grove" [poem] -- The judgment of Ramigan, the
sage -- The corpse -- Adrienne -- A Persian intermezzo [poem] -- The
sewing machine -- Legend of the fifth day -- Take 'em as you find
'em.

Fulkerson, Etta. Dorothy finds a way. _In When God
walks the road and other stories_ **(1924), W-445.**

F-453 Fuller, Anna, 1853-1916. A bookful of girls / by
Anna Fuller. New York; London: G. P. Putnam's
Sons, 1905. (New York: The Knickerbocker Press).
262 p., front., [5] leaves of plates. [Ill. by Noble
Ives.]
Contents: Blythe Halliday's voyage -- Artful Madge -- The ideas of
Polly -- Nannie's theatre party -- Olivia's sun-dial -- Bagging a
grandfather.
PW: Ap 1, '05.

F-454 ____ Katherine Day / by Anna Fuller. New York;
London: G. P. Putnam's Sons, 1901. (New York:
The Knickerbocker Press). 613 p.
PW: Je 29, '01.

F-455 ____ Later Pratt portraits: sketched in a New
England suburb / by Anna Fuller; illustrated by Maud
Tousey Fangel. New York; London: G. P. Putnam's
Sons, 1911. (New York: The Knickerbocker Press).
415 p., front., [10] leaves of plates.
Contents: Old lady Pratt's spectacles -- The tomboy -- The downfall
of Georgiana -- William's Willie -- A brilliant match -- Jane --
Peggy's father -- The dean of the boarding house -- The dander of
Susan -- Ships in the air -- The passing of Ben.
LC: Ap 7, '11.
PW: Ap 1, '11.

F-456 ____ The thunderhead lady / by Anna Fuller and
Brian Read; picture headings by William J. Wilson.
New York; London: G. P. Putnam's Sons, 1913.
(New York: The Knickerbocker Press). 186 p., ill.
LC: Je 10, '13.
PW: Je 14, '13.

F-457 Fuller, Caroline M. (Caroline Macomber). The
bramble bush / by Caroline Fuller. New York;
London: D. Appleton and Company, 1911. 307,
[1] p., front. [Ill. by John Harmon Cassel.]
LC: Mr 29, '11.
PW: Ap 1, '11.

F-458 ____ Brunhilde's paying guest: a story of the South
to-day / by Caroline Fuller. New York: The Century
Co., 1907. 348 p., col. front.
LC: Ag 17, '07.

F-459   Fuller, Edward, b. 1860. John Malcolm, a novel / by Edward Fuller; illustrated. Providence: Snow & Farnham, 1902. (Providence: The Providence Press). 432 p., front., [5] leaves of plates. [Ill. by J. H. Appleton.]

F-460   Fuller, Grace Hadley. Too-Loo Byrd: the story of a little negro waif / by Grace Fuller. Macon, Georgia: Press of the J. W. Burke Company, 1924. 74 p., photo. front.   **NYP**

Fuller, Hamilton Brock, jt. aut. *On the firing line* (1905). See **Ray, Anna Chapin, 1865-1945, jt. aut., R-70.**

Fuller, Harry V. A freshman and his friends. In *Minnesota stories* (1903), **M-842.**

____ Out of Egypt. In *Minnesota stories* (1903), **M-842.**

____ The passing of Percival. In *Minnesota stories* (1903), **M-842.**

F-461   Fuller, Henry Blake, 1857-1929. Bertram Cope's year: a novel / by Henry B. Fuller. Chicago: Ralph Fletcher Seymour, 1919. (Chicago: The Alderbrink Press). 314 p.
LC: O 20, '19.
PW: N 1, '19.
References: BAL 6478.

F-462   ____ On the stairs / by Henry B. Fuller. Boston; New York: Houghton Mifflin Company, 1918. (Cambridge: The Riverside Press). 264, [1] p.
LC: Mr 21, '18.
PW: Mr 23, '18.
References: BAL 6476.

____ Striking an average. In *The Great modern American stories* (1920), **G-422.**

F-463   ____ Under the skylights / by Henry B. Fuller. New York: D. Appleton and Company, 1901. 382 p.
Contents: The downfall of Abner Joyce -- Little O'Grady vs. the grindstone -- Dr. Gowdy and the squash.
LC: N 25, '01.
PW: D 14, '01.
References: BAL 6471.

F-464   ____ Waldo Trench, and others: stories of Americans in Italy / by Henry B. Fuller . . . New York: Charles Scribner's Sons, 1908. 338 p.
"Several of the stories composing this volume have appeared in Scribner's magazine."
Contents: Waldo Trench regains his youth -- New wine -- A coal from the embers -- For the faith -- Eliza Hepburn's deliverance -- Addolorata's intervention -- The house-cat.
LC: Ag 22, '08.
PW: S 5, '08.
References: BAL 6473.

F-465   Fuller, Margaret, 1872-1954. One world at a time / by Margaret Fuller. New York: The Century Co., 1922. 322 p.

F-466   Fuller, Phoebe W. Shadows cast before / by Phoebe W. Fuller. New York; London; Montreal: The Abbey Press, [c1902]. 240 p.   **DLC**
PW: Ag 9, '02.

F-467   Fuller, Robert H. (Robert Higginson), 1865-1927. The golden hope: a story of the time of King Alexander the Great / by Robert H. Fuller. New York: The Macmillan Company; London: Macmillan & Co., Ltd., 1905. 402 p.

F-468   Fuller, Vincent. The long green gaze: a cross word puzzle mystery / by Vincent Fuller. New York: B. W. Huebsch Inc., 1925. 217 p., [6] leaves of plates.
LC: Mr 16, '25.
PW: Mr 14, '25.

F-469   Fuller, William O. (William Oliver), 1856-1941. What happened to Wigglesworth / by W. O. Fuller; illustrated by E. D. Allen. Boston: Henry A. Dickerman & Son, 1901. 369 p., incl. front. (port.), map.
[These sketches in their original form, first appeared in the New York *World*, New York *Recorder* and Boston *Globe*, but as here printed they have undergone extensive revision.]
PW: N 9, '01.

F-470   Fullerton, Hugh S., 1873-1945. Racing yarns / by Hugh S. Fullerton. New York City: A. R. De Beer, [c1924]. 63 p.   **IND**
Contents: Out of the Dope Book -- The mystery stakes -- The woodpile -- The five a. m. handicap.
LC: Ag 29, '24.

F-471   Fullerton, Hugh S., 1873-1945. Tales of the turf / by Hugh S. Fullerton. New York City: A. R. De Beer, [c1922]. 63 p.
Contents: "Hardshell" Gaines -- "Jaundice's" last race -- Toutin' Mistah Fox.
LC: Ag 2, '22.

Fullilove, Maggie Shaw. See **Shaw-Fullilove, Maggie, 1884-1918.**

F-472   Fulton, Charles C. Without the city / by Charles C. Fulton. Boston: The Christopher Publishing House, [c1924]. 84 p.
LC: Ap 9, '24.
PW: My 31, '24.

Fulton, David Bryant, b.1863. See **Thorne, Jack, pseud.**

F-473   Fulton, Samuel. The Stoner family [a novel]. New York; London; Montreal: The Abbey Press, [1901]. 275 p.
Unexamined copy: bibliographic data from OCLC, #18977187.

F-474   Furman, Lucy S. The glass window: a story of the quare women / by Lucy Furman. Boston: Little, Brown, and Company, 1925. 287 p.
LC: O 14, '25.
PW: O 17, '25.

F-475   ____ Mothering on Perilous / by Lucy Furman; with illustrations by Mary Lane McMillan and F. R. Gruger. New York: The Macmillan Company, 1913. 310 p., incl. front., ill.

F-476   ____ The quare women: a story of the Kentucky mountains / by Lucy Furman. Boston: The Atlantic Monthly Press, [c1923]. 219 p.
LC: My 10, '23.
PW: Ap 7, '23.

F-477   ____ Sight to the blind: a story / by Lucy Furman; with an introduction by Ida Tarbell. New York: The Macmillan Company, 1914. 92 p., front, ill. (some photo.). [Ill. by Mary Lane McMillan and F. R. Gruger.]
LC: N 19, '14.

F-478 Futrelle, Jacques, 1875-1912. The chase of the golden plate / by Jacques Futrelle; with illustrations by Will Grefé and decorations by E. A. Poucher. New York: Dodd, Mead & Company, 1906. 219 p., front., [10] leaves of plates, ill. Designed end papers.
LC: N 2, '06.
PW: D 1, '06.

F-479   ____ The diamond master / by Jacques Futrelle; illustrated by Herman Pfeifer. Indianapolis: The Bobbs-Merrill Company, [c1909]. 212 p., col. front.
LC: O 23, '09.
BLC: London: Holden and Hardingham, [1912].

F-480   ____ The diamond master / by Jacques Futrelle . . . ; with illustrations by Herman Pfeifer. New York: A. L. Burt Company, [c1909]. 304, [1] p., front.
Contents: The diamond master -- The haunted bell.

F-481   ____ Elusive Isabel / by Jacques Futrelle; with illustrations by Alonzo Kimball. Indianapolis: The Bobbs-Merrill Company, [c1909]. 273, [1] p., front., [5] leaves of plates.
LC: My 8, '09.
PW: My 8, '09.

F-482   ____ The high hand / by Jacques Futrelle; with illustrations by Will Grefé. Indianapolis: The Bobbs-Merrill Company, [c1911]. 295, [1] p., front., [8] leaves of plates.
LC: My 10, '11.
PW: My 13, '11.

F-483   ____ My lady's garter / by Jacques Futrelle; illustrated by F. R. Gruger. Chicago; New York: Rand, McNally & Company, [c1912]. 332 p., front. (port.), [12] leaves of plates.
LC: Ag 12, '12.
PW: Ag 31, '12.

F-484   ____ The simple case of Susan / by Jacques Futrelle. New York: D. Appleton and Company, 1908. 232 p., front.
LC: Ap 16, '08.
PW: My 2, '08.

F-485   ____ The thinking machine: being a true and complete statement of several intricate mysteries which came under the observation of Professor Augustus S. F. X. Van Dusen, Ph. D., L. D., F. R. S., M. D., etc. / by Jacques Futrelle; illustrations by the Kinneys. New York: Dodd, Mead & Company, 1907. 342 p., front., [3] leaves of plates.
LC: Mr 6, '07.
PW: Mr 23, '07.

F-486   ____ The thinking machine on the case / by Jacques Futrelle. New York: D. Appleton and Company, 1908. 337 p., front. [Ill. by the Kinneys.]
LC: Mr 20, '08.
PW: Mr 21, '08.

F-487 Futrelle, May, b. 1876. Lieutenant What's-his-name: elaborated from Jacques Futrelle's The simple case of Susan / by May Futrelle; frontispiece by Howard Chandler Christy. Indianapolis: The Bobbs-Merrill Company, [c1915]. 322 p., front.   **VA@**
LC: Mr 10, '15.
PW: Mr 13, '15.
BLC: London: George Newnes, [1916].

F-488   ____ Secretary of frivolous affairs / by May Futrelle. Indianapolis: The Bobbs-Merrill Company, [c1911]. 311 p., front., [5] leaves of plates. [Ill. by Frank Snapp.]
LC: Ag 2, '11.
PW: Ag 5, '11.

G

G. E. T. S., jt. aut. Studies in college colour. *In A book of Bryn Mawr stories* **(1901), B-732.**

G-1   G. E. X. Italian portraits in Engadine frames / G. E. X. Wausau, Wisconsin: The Philosopher Press: Van Vechten & Ellis, [c1904]. 190 p., front., [1] leaf of plates.   **CWR**

G-2   G. G. P. (Gertrude Gould Pickard), b. 1875. Hove up by the tide / by G. G. P. Portland: Smith & Sale, 1917. 51 p., col. ill.   **PGP**
LC: Je 18, '17.

G-3   Gabriel, Charles Hutchinson, 1856-1932. Dorothy Webb: a story of innocence, credulity, friendship, parental grief, and paternal love / by Chas. H. Gabriel. Nashville, Tenn.: McQuiddy Printing Company, 1924. 133 p.
Unexamined copy: bibliographic data from OCLC, #9950862.
LC: My 15, '24.

G-4   Gabriel, Charles Sumner. Jeremiah's Sammy / Charles Sumner Gabriel. Boston, Mass.: The C. M. Clark Publishing Co., [c1911]. 303 p., col. front. [Ill. by R. I. Conklin.]

G-5   Gabriel, Gilbert W. (Gilbert Wolf), 1890-1952. Brownstone front / by Gilbert W. Gabriel. New York; London: The Century Co., [c1924]. 365 p.
LC: S 3, '24.

G-6   ____ Jiminy / Gilbert W. Gabriel; decorations by Ada V. Gabriel. New York: George H. Doran Company, [c1922]. 270 p.
LC: Jl 24, '22.

G-7   Gaillard, Stephen. The pirates of the sky: a tale of modern adventure / by Stephen Gaillard; with illustrations by Leon D'Emo. Chicago: Rand McNally & Company, [c1915]. 351 p., [3] leaves of plates.

G-8   Gaines, Charles Kelsey, 1854-1943. Gorgo: a romance of old Athens / by Charles Kelsey Gaines . . . ; illustrated by George Varian. Boston: Lothrop, Lee & Shepard Co., [1903]. 507 p., front., [5] leaves of plates.
PW: S 12, '03.
BLC: London: A. P. Watt & Son, [1903].

G-9   Gaines, Miriam. Grandfather's love pie / by Miriam Gaines; illustrations by John Edward Whiting. Louisville, Kentucky: John B. Morton & Company, 1913. 70 p., front., [1] leaf of plates. **FDA**

G-10   Gaines, Ruth, 1877-1952. The village shield: a story of Mexico / by Ruth Gaines and Georgia Willis Read. New York: E. P. Dutton & Company, [c1917]. 264 p., col. front., [11] leaves of plates (some col). **AZS**

G-11   Gale, Forest, b. 1853. Five cousins in California: a sunny picture of a sunny land / by Gale Forest (Mrs. Robert C. Reinertsen). Boston, Massachusetts: The C. M. Clark Publishing Company, 1909. 287 p., photo. front., [7] leaves of plates (some photo.). [Some ill. by D. S. Ross.] **GZN**

G-12   Gale, James Scarth, 1863-1937. The vanguard: a tale of Korea / by James S. Gale . . . ; illustrated. New York; Chicago; Toronto; London; Edinburgh: Fleming H. Revell Company, [c1904]. 320 p., photo. front., [15] leaves of photo. plates. **CLE**
PW: Ap 2, '04.

G-13   Gale, Marie Josephine. Alice Brenton: a tale of old Newport in revolutionary days / by Marie Josephine Gale. Boston, Massachusetts: The C. M. Clark Publishing Company, 1909. 413 p., front., [7] leaves of plates. [Ill. by D. S. Ross.] **DLC**
LC: Ap 28, '09.

G-14   Gale, Oliver Marble, b. 1877. A knight of the wilderness / by Oliver Marble Gale and Harriet Wheeler; illustrated by Ivin Ney. Chicago: The Reilly & Britton Co., 1909. 338 p., front., [4] leaves of plates.
LC: Ja 10, '10.

     Gale, Zona, 1874-1938. The biography of Blade. In *The best short stories of 1924 and the yearbook of the American short story* **(1925), B-569.**

G-15   ____ Birth / by Zona Gale. New York: The Macmillan Company, 1918. 402 p.
LC: N 17, '18.
PW: N 16, '18.

G-16   ____ Christmas: a story / by Zona Gale; with illustrations by Leon V. Solon. New York: The Macmillan Company, 1912. 243 p., col. front., [5] leaves of col. plates.
LC: N 7, '12.
PW: N 30, '12.

     ____ The Clausons. In *Marriage* **(1923), M-457.**

G-17   ____ A daughter of the morning / by Zona Gale; illustrated by W. B. King. Indianapolis: The Bobbs-Merrill Company, [c1917]. 289 p., front., [4] leaves of plates.
LC: O 31, '17.
PW: N 10, '17.

G-18   ____ Faint perfume / by Zona Gale. New York: D. Appleton and Company, 1923. 217, [1] p.
LC: Mr 16, '23.
PW: Mr 24, '23.

G-19   ____ Friendship Village / by Zona Gale . . . New York: The Macmillan Company, 1908. 323 p.
LC: O 19, '08.
PW: N 14, '08.

G-20   ____ Friendship Village love stories / by Zona Gale. New York: The Macmillan Company, 1909. 321 p. Partly reprinted from various periodicals.
Contents: Open arms -- Inside June -- Miggy -- Splendour town -- Different -- The fond forenoon -- Afraid -- The java entertainment -- The cold shoulder -- Evening dress -- Undern -- The way the world is -- Householdry -- Postmarks -- Peter -- The new village -- Adoption -- At Peter's house -- The custodian.
LC: N 19, '09.
PW: D 4, '09.

G-21   ____ Heart's kindred / by Zona Gale . . . ; with frontispiece. New York: The Macmillan Company, 1915. 234 p., col. front. [Ill. by Clarence Rowe.] **CIN**
LC: O 7, '15.
PW: O 16, '15.

G-22   ____ The loves of Pelleas and Etarre / by Zona Gale. New York: The Macmillan Company; London: Macmillan & Co., Ltd., 1907. 341 p. Stories reprinted from various periodicals.
Contents: The odour of the ointment -- The matinée -- The path of In-the-spring -- The elopement -- The dance -- The honeymoon -- The other two -- A fountain of gardens -- The baby -- The marriage of Katinka -- The christening -- An interlude -- The return of Endymion -- The golden wedding -- "So the carpenter encouraged the Goldsmith" -- Christmas roses.
LC: S 23, '07.
PW: N 2, '07.

G-23   ____ Miss Lulu Bett / Zona Gale. New York; London: D. Appleton and Company, 1920. 264 p.
LC: Mr 9, '20.
PW: Ap 3, '20.
BLC: London: Hodder & Stoughton, [1922].

G-24   ____ Mothers to men / by Zona Gale. New York: The Macmillan Company, 1911. 327 p.
LC: O 5, '11.
PW: O 28, '11.

G-25   ____ Neighborhood stories / by Zona Gale . . . ; with frontispiece. New York: The Macmillan Company, 1914. 307 p., col. front. [Ill. by Arthur E. Becher.]

Contents: A great tree -- Exit charity -- The time has come -- The face of Friendship Village -- The flood -- The party -- The biggest business -- The prodigal guest -- Mr. Dombledon -- Human -- The homecoming.
LC: O 15, '14.
PW: O 31, '14.

G-26   ____ Peace in Friendship Village / by Zona Gale. New York: The Macmillan Company, 1919. 308 p.
LC: N 6, '19.
PW: D 13, '19.

G-27   ____ Romance Island / by Zona Gale; with illustrations by Hermann C. Wall. Indianapolis: The Bobbs-Merrill Company, [1906]. 394 p., col. front., [4] leaves of col. plates.
LC: O 17, '06.
PW: N 17, '06.

____ The things they saw. See **Conrad Joseph, 1857-1924.** *Il conte* (1925), C-697.

G-28   ____ When I was a little girl / by Zona Gale . . . with illustrations by Agnes Pelton. New York: The Macmillan Company, 1913. 390 p., col. front, [6] leaves of plates. **OWK**
LC: O 2, '13.

____ A winter's tale. In *More aces* (1925), M-962.

Gallagher, Katherine J. Wilhelmina. In *Minnesota stories* (1903), M-842.

G-29   Gallatin, Francis D. An unfinished divorce, or, Her better self / by Francis D. Gallatin. New York: Cochrane Publishing Co., 1909. 260 p.   **NYP, DLC**
PW: Ap 24, '09.

Gallegher, Marie, jt. aut. *Paulus Fy* (1924). See **Mullins, Helene, b. 1899, jt. aut, M-1108.**

G-30   Gallizier, Nathan, 1866-1927. Castel del Monte: a romance of the fall of the Hohenstaufen dynasty in Italy / by Nathan Gallizier; illustrated by H. C. Edwards. Boston: L. C. Page & Company, 1905. 443, [1] p., front., [5] leaves of plates.
PW: Mr 25, '05.
BLC: London: Dean & Son; printed in U. S. A., [1905].

G-31   ____ The court of Lucifer: a tale of the Renaissance / by Nathan Gallizier . . . ; pictures by the Kinneys; decorations by P. Verburg. Boston: L. C. Page &

Company, 1910. 464 p., col. front., [3] leaves of col. plates. Illustrated end papers.   **NYP**
LC: O 22, '10.
PW: N 5, '10.

G-32   ____ The crimson gondola: a tale of Venice and Constantinople at the beginning of the thirteenth century / by Nathan Gallizier . . . ; pictures by E. H.

Garrett; decorations by P. Verburg. Boston: The Page Company, 1915. 447 p., col. front., [3] leaves of col. plates.
LC: S 28, '15.

G-33   ____ The hill of Venus / by Nathan Gallizier; pictures by E. H. Garrett; decorations by P. Verburg. Boston: L. C. Page and Company, 1913. 335 p., col. front., [3] leaves of col. plates.
LC: Mr 31, '13.
PW: Jl 12, '13.

G-34   ____ The Leopard prince: a romance of Venice in the fourteenth century, at the period of the Bosnian conspiracy / by Nathan Gallizier; pictures by the Kinneys; decorations by P. Verberg. Boston: The Page Company, 1920. 407 p., col. front., [3] leaves of col. plates. Illustrated end papers.
LC: N 2, '20.

G-35   ____ The lotus woman: a romance of Byzantine Constantinople / by Nathan Gallizier; illustrated and decorated by Eric Pape. Boston: The Page Company, 1922. 470 p., col. front., [3] leaves of col. plates. Illustrated end papers.
LC: N 27, '22.

G-36   ____ The sorceress of Rome / by Nathan Gallizier; pictures by the Kinneys; decorations by P. Verburg. Boston: L. C. Page & Company, [1907]. 463 p., col. front., [3] leaves of col. plates. Illustrated end papers.
LC: N 4, '07.
PW: D 7, '07.

G-37   ____ Under the witches' moon: a romantic tale of mediaeval Rome / by Nathan Gallizier. Boston: The Page Company, 1917. 455 p., col. front., [3] leaves of col. plates. [Ill. by the Kinneys.]
LC: O 11, '17.

G-38   Gallup, Christobel. The inner secret / by Christobel Gallup. Aurora, Ill.: Published by Good Thoughts Press, [c1923]. 294 p.
LC: N 30, '23.

Galpin, J. A. See **Blackstone, Valerius D., pseud.**

G-39   Galvin, Antoinette E. The story of Swan-like / by Antoinete E. Galvin. Boston: Richard G. Badger, [c1912]. ([Boston]: The Gorham Press). 156 p.

Galvin, George W., jt. aut. *A thousand faces* (1915). See **Thompson, Florence Seyler, jt. aut., T-185.**

G-40   Gambier, Kenyon, 1858-1929, *pseud.* The girl on the hilltop / by Kenyon Gambier [pseud.]. New York: George H. Doran Company, [c1920]. 319 p.
LC: Je 18, '20.
PW: Je 19, '20.

G-41   ____ The princess of Paradise Island / by Kenyon Gambier [pseud.] . . . New York: George H. Doran Company, [c1925]. 305 p.
LC: Ap 29, '25.
PW: Ap 25, '25.

G-42   ____ The white horse and the red-haired girl / by Kenyon Gambier [pseud.]. New York: George H. Doran Company, [c1919]. 290 p.
LC: Mr 10, '19.
PW: Mr 1, '19.

Ganoe, W. A. Ruggs - R. O. T. C. In *Atlantic narratives*; **2nd series (1918), A-361.**

G-43   Garden, Alice. Ananias' daughter / by Alice Garden. Philadelphia: Dorrance, [c1923]. 262 p.
LC: O 19, '23.

Gardener, The. pseud. <u>See</u> **Wright, Mabel Osgood, 1859-1934.**

G-44   Gardenhire, Samuel M. (Samuel Major), 1855-1923. The long arm / by Samuel M. Gardenhire . . . New York; London: Harper & Bothers, 1906. 344, [1] p., front., [7] leaves of plates. [Ill. by W. E. Mears.]

G-45   ____ Lux crucis: a tale of the great apostle / by Samuel M. Gardenhire. New York; London: Harper & Brothers Publishers, 1904. 391, [1] p.
PW: F 6, '04.

G-46   ____ Purple and homespun: a novel / by Samuel M. Gardenhire. New York; London: Harper & Brothers, 1908. 370 p.
LC: Ap 16, '08.

G-47   ____ The silence of Mrs. Harrold / by Samuel M. Gardenhire. New York; London: Harper & Brothers, 1905. 461, [1] p.
PW: F 4, '05.

G-48   Gardiner, Ruth Kimball, 1872-1924. The world and the woman / by Ruth Kimball Gardiner . . . New York: A. S. Barnes & Company, 1907. 292 p.
                               OSU, ABC
PW: N 16, '07.

G-49   Gardner, Ethellyn. Letters of the motor girl / by Ethellyn Gardner. Boston, Mass.: Distributed to the trade by the New England News Co., c1906.
[104] p., front.
LC: D 5, '06.

G-50   Gardner, Gilson, 1869-1935. A new Robinson Crusoe: a new version of his life and adventures, with an explanatory note / by Gilson Gardner. New York: Harcourt, Brace and Howe, 1920. 109 p.

G-51   Gardner, James. The strange case of Pauline Wilton / by James Gardner. New York: Broadway Publishing Company, [c1915]. 117 p.
LC: AP 13, '17.

G-52   Gardner, Sarah M. H. Quaker idyls / by Sarah M. H. Gardner; . . . with a frontispiece. New York: Henry Holt and Company, 1910. 284 p., front.
Contents: Twelfth street meeting -- A Quaker wedding -- Two gentlewomen -- Our little neighbors -- Pamelia Tewksbury's courtship -- Some ante-bellum letters from a Quaker girl -- Uncle Joseph -- My grandame's secret -- An unconcious disciple of Thespis -- A homely tragedy.
LC: Mr 23, '10.

G-53   Garis, Howard Roger, 1873-1962. The king of Unadilla: stories of court secrets concerning His majesty / by Howard R. Garis. New York: J. S. Ogilvie Publishing Company, c1903. 124 p., incl. front., ill.
Unexamined copy: bibliographic data from OCLC, #3174493.
[Peerless series, no. 130.]
PW: Ja 24, '03.

G-54   ____ With force and arms: a tale of love and Salem witchcraft / by Howard R. Garis. New York; London: J. S. Ogilvie Publishing Company, [c1902]. 343 p., front., [2] leaves of plates.
PW: O 18, '02.

G-55   Garland, Hamlin, 1860-1940. The captain of the Gray-horse troop: a novel / by Hamlin Garland. New York; London: Harper & Brothers, 1902. 414, [1] p., front. (port.).
PW: Mr 29, '02.
BLC: London: Grant Richards, 1902.

G-56   ____ Cavanagh, forest ranger: a romance of the mountain West / by Hamlin Garland . . . New York; London: Harper & Brothers, 1910. 300 p., photo. front.
LC: Mr 26, '10.

G-57   ____ The forester's daughter; a romance of the Bear-Tooth Range / by Hamlin Garland . . . ; illustrated. New York and London: Harper & Brothers, 1914. 286, [1] p., front., [3] leaves of plates. [Ill. by Robert W. Amick.]   **MIA**
LC: F 9, '14.
PW: F 14, '14.

____ A graceless husband. In *The Miller's holiday* **(1920), M-817.**

____ The graven image. <u>In</u> *Prairie gold* **(1917), P-588.**

G-58   ____ Her mountain lover / by Hamlin Garland. New York: The Century Co., 1901. 396 p., front.
PW: Ap 6, '01.
BLC: Toronto: Copp, Clark Co., 1901.

G-59   ____ Hesper: a novel / by Hamlin Garland . . . New York; London: Harper & Brothers, 1903. 444, [1] p.
PW: O 17, '03.

____ Jim Mattison of wagon wheel gap. <u>In</u> *For France* **(1917), F-235.**

____ The last threshing in the Coulee. <u>In</u> *The joy in work* **(1920), J-229.**

G-60   ____ The light of the star: a novel / by Hamlin Garland . . . New York; London: Harper & Brothers, 1904. 277, [1] p., front. [Ill. by Harrison Fisher.]
PW: My 21, '04.

G-61 _____ The Moccasin Ranch: a story of Dakota / by Hamlin Garland . . . New York; London: Harper & Brothers, 1909. 136 p., front. [Ill. by John Newton Howitt.]
LC: S 11, '09.

G-62 _____ Money magic: a novel / by Hamlin Garland . . . ; illustrated by J. N. Marchand. New York; London: Harper & Brothers, 1907. 354 p., front., [7] leaves of plates.
LC: O 10, '07.
PW: O 19, '07.

G-63 _____ Other main-travelled roads / by Hamlin Garland . . . New York; London: Harper & Brothers, [c1910]. 349, [1] p.
"Compiled from . . . volumes which now go out of print."
Contents: William Bacon's man -- Elder Pill, preacher -- A day of grace -- Lucretia Burns -- Daddy Deering -- A stop-over at Tyre -- A division in the coolly -- A fair exile -- An alien in the pines -- Before the low green door -- A preacher's love story -- An afterword.
LC: S 21, '10.
PW: O 1, '10.

G-64 _____ The shadow world / by Hamlin Garland. New York; London: Harper & Brothers, 1908. 294, [1] p.
LC: O 9, '08.
PW: O 17, '08.

G-65 _____ They of the high trails / Hamlin Garland; illustrated. New York; London: Harper & Brothers, [1916]. 453 p., front., [3] leaves of plates.
Contents: The grub-staker -- The cow-boss -- The remittance man -- The lonesome man -- The trail tramp -- The prospector -- The outlaw -- The leaser -- The forest ranger -- The tourist.
PW: Ap 29, '16.

G-66 _____ The tyranny of the dark / by Hamlin Garland . . . London; New York: Harper & Brothers, 1905. 438, [1] p., front., [7] leaves of plates. [Ill. by W. E. Mears.]
PW: My 13, '05.

G-67 _____ Victor Ollnee's discipline / by Hamlin Garland. New York; London: Harper & Brothers, 1911. 307, [1] p.
LC: S 22, '11.

G-68 _____ Witch's gold: being a new and enlarged version of "The spirit of Sweetwater" / by Hamlin Garland . . . New York: Doubleday, Page & Company, 1906. 231 p., front., [2] leaves of plates. [Ill. by W. L. Taylor.]
LC: Ag 27, '06.
PW: S 8, '06.

G-69 Garland, Retta Augusta. One and all / by Retta Augusta Garland. Santa Barbara, [California]: The Schauer Printing Studio, 1922. 107 p., [1] leaf of plates (port.). **DLC**
LC: D 11, '22.

Garnett, Captain Mayn Clew, pseud. See **Hains, Thornton Jenkins, b.1866.**

G-70 Garretson, J. (John). The story of Billy Owen: an historical novel of the great oil industry / by John Garretson. New York: The Neale Publishing Company, 1918. 280 p. **OKU**
LC: N 18, '18.
PW: N 16, '18.

G-71 Garrett, Charles W. (Charles Walter), b. 1873. Aurilly, the virgin isle / by Charles W. Garrett. Boston: The Christopher Publishing House, [c1923]. 152 p., front.
LC: S 17, '23.

Garrett, Edward Peter, 1878-1954. See **Garrett, Garet, pseud.**

G-72 Garrett, Garet, 1878-1954, pseud. The blue wound / by Garet Garrett [pseud.]. New York; London: G. P. Putnam's Sons, 1921. (New York: The Knickerbocker Press). 184 p.
LC: Mr 5, '21.

G-73 _____ The cinder buggy: a fable in iron and steel / by Garet Garrett [pseud.] . . . New York: E. P. Dutton & Company, [c1923]. 357 p.
LC: O 11, '23.
PW: O 20, '23.
BLC: London: William Heinemann, 1925.

G-74 _____ The driver / by Garet Garrett [pseud.]. New York: E. P. Dutton & Company, [c1922]. 294 p.
LC: O 30, '22.
BLC: London: Constable & Co., 1924.

G-75 _____ Satan's bushel / by Garet Garrett [pseud.] . . . New York: E. P. Dutton & Company, [c1924]. 207 p.
PW: Ja 26, '24.

G-76 Garrett, Junie Candler. Janice / by Junie Candler Garrett. New York: Broadway Publishing Co., 1913. 115 p., front., [2] leaves of plates. **DLC**

G-77 Garrett, Luda Bell. Valda: a novel / by Luda Bell Garrett. St. Louis, Mo., U. S. A.: Published by Becktold Printing and Book Mfg. Co., 1904. 347 p. **DLC**
PW: O 22, '04.

G-78 Garrison, Adele. Revelations of a wife: the story of a honeymoon / by Adele Garrison; with frontispiece by M. W. Newberry. New York: Universal Press, [c1917]. 376 p., incl. front.

G-79 Garrison, Theodosia Pickering, 1874-1944. The story of a pencil: the Mongol speaks / by Theodosia Garrison. New York: W. E. Heim & Co., [c1910]. [16] p.

G-80 Gartland, Hannah. The Globe Hollow mystery / by Hannah Gartland. New York: Dodd, Mead and Company, 1923. 294 p.
LC: F 15, '23.

G-81 ____ The house of cards / by Hannah Gartland. New York: Dodd, Mead and Company, 1922. 327 p.
LC: Ja 10, '22.
PW: Ja 21, '22.
BLC: London: Herbert Jenkins, 1924.

G-82 Garvey, Ina. A comedy of Mammon / by Ina Garvey; illustrated by William Fuller Curtis. Boston: Dana Estes & Co.; London: E. Grant Richards, [c1908]. 322 p., front., [2] leaves of plates.
LC: My 2, '08.

G-83 Garvin, Martha Jane. A balance of destiny / by Martha Jane Garvin. Boston, Mass.: The C. M. Clark Publishing Co., [c1911]. 288 p., col. front., [3] leaves of plates.

G-84 Gates, Eleanor, 1875-1951. Apron-strings / by Eleanor Gates . . . a story for all mothers who have daughters and for all daughters who have mothers. New York: Sully and Kleinteich, 1917. 306 p.
OSU copy is 2nd printing.
PW: N 10, '17.

G-85 ____ Cupid, the cow-punch / by Eleanor Gates . . . ; illustrations by George Gibbs and Allen True. New York: The McClure Company, 1907. 316 p., front., [7] leaves of plates.
LC: N 16, '07.

G-86 ____ Good-night (Buenas noches) / by Eleanor Gates . . . illustrated by Arthur Rackham. New York: T. Y. Crowell & Co., [c1907]. 52, [1] p., col. front., [4] col. plates.
Unexamined copy: bibliograhic data from OCLC, #4691141.

G-87 ____ The justice of Gideon / by Eleanor Gates. New York: The Macaulay Company, 1910. 343 p., front. [Ill. by H. T. Dunn.]
Contents: The justice of Gideon -- Doc -- The boomerang -- Buenas noches -- Little watcher -- Missy and I -- The Genevieve epidemic -- Agatha's escort -- A yellow man and a white -- Yee Wing, powder-man -- The search for the spring -- The silver bell of Los Morales -- The revenge of Manuelita.
LC: O 18, '10.

G-88 ____ Phoebe / by Eleanor Gates. New York: George Sully and Company, [c1919]. 276 p.
LC: F 26, '19.

G-89 ____ The plow-woman / by Eleanor Gates . . . New York: McClure, Phillips & Co., 1906. 364 p.
LC: S 28, '06.
PW: O 13, '06.
BLC: London: Methuen & Co., 1907.
____ The spotted dawg. In *California story book* (1909), C-40.

____ A yellow man and a white. In *The Spinners' book of fiction* (1907), S-755.

G-90 Gates, H. L. (Henry Leyford), 1880-1937. The mystery of the Hope diamond / as set down by H. L. Gates . . . ; from the personal narrative of Lady Francis Hope (May Yohe); fully illustrated from the photoplay. New York: International Copyright Bureau, 1921. 255 p., photo. front., [10] leaves of photo. plates.
LC: Ag 30, '21.

G-91 Gates, Susa Young, 1856-1933. John Stevens' courtship: a story of the Echo Canyon War / by Susa Young Gates. Salt Lake City, Utah: The Deseret News, 1909. 377 p., photo. front.
LC: S 25, '09.

G-92 Gatlin, Dana. The full measure of devotion / by Dana Gatlin. Garden City, New York: Doubleday, Page & Company, 1918. 56 p.
First published in McClure's magazine.
LC: Ja 30, '18.

G-93 ____ Missy / by Dana Gatlin; frontispiece by W. B. King. Garden City; New York: Doubleday, Page & Company, 1920. 354 p., front.
LC: N 13, '20.
BLC: London: Curtis Brown; Garden City, N. Y., printed 1920.

Gattle, Caroline A., b. 1871. See **Gordon, Carol, pseud.**

G-94 Gaul, Avery, b. 1886, *pseud*. Five nights at the Five Pines / by Avery Gaul [pseud.]. New York: The Century Co., 1922. 280 p.
LC: S 7, '22.

Gaul, Hariette Lester (Avery), Mrs., b. 1886. See **Gaul, Avery, pseud.**

G-95 Gauss, Henry Colford, b. 1867. Floyd Ireson / by H. C. Gauss. Salem, Massachusetts: Newcomb & Gauss, 1901. 121 p.
PW: Ag 17, '01.

G-96 Gauss, Marianne, b. 1885. Danae / by Marianne Gauss. New York; London: Harper & Brothers, 1925. 335 p.
PW: O 10, '25.

G-97 Gaut, W. R. (William Robbins), b. 1866. The amateur man / W. R. Gaut. New York: Duffield & Company, 1918. 480 p.
LC: D 2, '18.

G-98 Gavf, Emma. A comedy of circumstance / by Emma Gavf; illustrated by Wallace Morgan. Garden City, N. Y.: Doubleday, Page & Company, 1911. 253 p., col. front., [4] leaves of plates.
BLC: London: Hodder & Stoughton; Garden City, N. Y., printed 1911.

G-99 Gay, Mary Ann Harris, b. 1827. The transplanted: a story of Dixie before the war / by Mary A. H. Gay . . . New York; Washington: The Neale Publishing Company, 1907. 233 p.   **VIC**
LC: S 16, '07.
PW: S 28, '07.

G-100 Gay, Maude Clark, b. 1876. The knitting of the souls: a tale of 17th century Boston / by Maude

Clark Gay; illustrated by Frank T. Merrill. Boston: Lee and Shepard, 1904. 395 p., col. front., [5] leaves of col. plates.

G-101   _____ Paths crossing: a romance of the plains / by Maude Clark Gay. Boston, Mass.: The C. M. Clark Publishing Company, 1908. 268 p., front., [7] leaves of plates. [Ill. by William Kirkpatrick.]

G-102   Gay, Robert M., b. 1879. The eight forty-five: extracts from the diary of John Skinner, a commuter / by Robert M. Gay; sketches by Wallis E. Howe. Boston: The Atlantic Monthly Press, [c1925]. 154 p., ill.   **MNU**
PW: Ap 4, '25.

G-103   Gaylord, Katherine. Tithes of talent: the story of a noble love / by Katherine Gaylord. New York: Broadway Publishing Company, [c1903]. 77 p., photo. front. (port.).

G-104   Geiermann, Peter, 1870-1929. Margaret's influence: a secret of the confessional / by Rev. Peter Geiermann. St. Louis: B. Herder, 1910. 224, [1] p. Unexamined copy: bibliographic data from OCLC, #29708232.

G-105   Gelzer, Jay, b. 1889. Compromise: a novel / by Jay Gelzer. New York: Robert M. McBride & Company, 1923. 273 p.
LC: O 6, '23.
PW: O 20, '23.

G-106   _____ The street of a thousand delights / by Jay Gelzer. New York: Robert M. McBride & Company, 1921. 269 p.
LC: Jl 28, '21.
BLC: London: Mills & Boon, 1922.

G-107   George, Francis. The only Nancy: a tale of the Kentucky mountains / by Francis George. New York; Chicago; Toronto; London; Edinburgh: Fleming H. Revell Company, [c1917]. 245 p.
                                                    OSU, TJC
LC: D 8, '17.
PW: S 22, '17.

G-108   George, Henry, b. 1812. The romance of John Bainbridge / by Henry George . . . New York; London: The Macmillan Company, 1906. 468 p.
LC: O 24, '06.

G-109   Gerberding, Elizabeth, b. 1857. The golden chimney: a boy's mine / by Elizabeth Gerberding. San Francisco: A. M. Robertson, 1902. 213 p., photo. front., [3] leaves of photo. plates.

G-110   Germaine, Quincy, *pseud.* The even hand / by Quincy Germaine [pseud.]. Boston; New York; Chicago: The Pilgrim Press, [c1912]. 276 p., col. front., [3] leaves of col. plates. [Ill. by Francis Yenwood.]
LC: S 24, '12.
PW: O 19, '12.

G-111   Gernsback, Hugo, 1884-1967. Ralph 124C 41+: a romance of the year 2660 / by Hugo Gernsback . . . Boston, Massachusetts: The Stratford Company, 1925. 293 p., front., [10] leaves of plates, ill.

Gerould, Gordon Hall, b. 1877. Imagination. In *The best short stories of 1918 and the yearbook of the American short story* (1919), B-563.

G-112   _____ A midsummer mystery / by Gordon Hall Gerould . . . New York; London: D. Appleton and Company, 1925. 256, [1] p.
LC: Mr 24, '25.
PW: Ap 4, '25.

G-113   _____ Peter Sanders, retired / by Gordon Hall Gerould. New York: Charles Scribner's Sons, 1917. 338 p.
LC: Ap 17, '17.
PW: Ap 21, '17.

G-114   _____ Sir Guy of Warwick / by Gordon Hall Gerould; illustrated by Bror. J. Olsson-Nordfeldt and Ben Cohen. Chicago; New York; London: Rand McNally & Co., [c1905]. 256 p., [1] leaf of plates, ill.   **CHE**
PW: Ag 5, '05.

G-115   _____ Youth in Harley / by Gordon Hall Gerould. New York: Charles Scribner's Sons, 1920. 409 p.
LC: Ag 25, '20.
PW: Ag 28, '20.

G-116   Gerould, Katherine Fullerton, 1879-1944. A change of air / by Katharine Fullerton Gerould; illustrated by H. J. Mowat. New York: Charles Scribner's Sons, 1917. 208 p., front., [3] leaves of plates.
LC: O 17, '17.
PW: O 20, '17.

G-117   _____ Conquistador / by Katharine Fullerton Gerould. New York: Charles Scribner's Sons, 1923. 205 p.
LC: Ap 9, '23.
PW: Mr 31, '23.
BLC: London: G. G. Harrap & Co., 1924.

_____ French Eva. In *The best short stories of 1921 and the yearbook of the American short story* (1922), B-566.

G-118   _____ The great tradition: and other stories / by Katharine [sic] Fullerton Gerould . . . New York: Charles Scribner's Sons, 1915. 353 p.
Contents: The great tradition -- Pearls -- The dominant strain -- The bird in the bush -- The miracle -- Wesendonck -- Leda and the swan -- The weaker vessel.
LC: Mr 30, '15.
PW: Ap 3, '15.
BLC: London: Methuen & Co., 1916.

_____ Habakkuk. In *The best short stories of 1920 and the yearbook of the American short story* (1921), B-565.

_____ The knight's move. In *The best short stories of 1917 and the yearbook of the American short story* (1918), B-562.

G-119 _____ Lost Valley: a novel / by Katharine Fullerton Gerould. New York; London: Harper & Brothers, 1922. 451, [1] p.
LC: Ja 20, '22.
PW: Ja 21, '22.

_____ A moth of peace. In *Atlantic narratives*; first series (1918), A-360.

_____ The nature of an oath. In *American short stories* (1925), A-202.

G-120 _____ Vain oblations / by Katharine Fullerton Gerould. New York: Charles Scribner's Sons, 1914. 324 p.
Contents: Vain oblations -- The mango-seed -- The wine of violence -- On the staircase -- The tortoise -- The divided kingdom -- The case of Paramore.
LC: Mr 13, '14.
PW: Mr 14, '14.
BLC: London: Sidgwick & Jackson, 1914.

G-121 _____ Valiant dust / by Katharine Fullerton Gerould. New York: Charles Scribner's Sons, 1922. 347 p.
Contents: An honest man -- Habakkuk -- Miss Marriott and the fawn -- Martin's Hollow -- The knight's move -- Blue bonnet -- East of Eden -- Sea green -- The penalties of Artemis -- Lonquier's third act -- The toad and the jewel -- Belshazar's letter.
LC: N 18, '22.
PW: N 18, '22.
BLC: London: G. G. Harrap & Co., 1925.

G-122 Gerry, Margarita Spalding, 1870-1939. As Caesar's wife: a novel / by Margarita Spalding Gerry; illustrated by James Montgomery Flagg. New York; London: Harper & Brothers, 1912. 315, [1] p., front., [7] leaves of plates.
LC: S 21, '12.
PW: O 5, '12.

_____ The flag factory. In *War stories* (1919), W-94.

G-123 _____ The flowers / by Margarita Spalding Gerry . . . ; with illustrations by Elizabeth Shippen Green. New York; London: Harper & Brothers Publishers, 1910. 39, [1] p., col. front., [2] leaves of col. plates. **RBN**
LC: Ap 4, '10.
PW: Ap 9, '10.

G-124 _____ Heart and chart / by Margarita Spalding Gerry; illustrated. New York; London: Harper & Brothers, 1911. 303, [1] p., front., [7] leaves of plates. [Ill. by Elizabeth Shippen Green and Frank E. Schoonover.]
Contents: The dress with the blue ribbons -- The gout -- The enemy -- A credit to Densmore -- The house of the five sisters -- Schlosser's wife -- The hero -- A message -- The island.
LC: O 21, '11.
PW: O 28, '11.

_____ The light in her eyes. In **Conrad, Joseph.** *Il conte* (1925), C-697.

G-125 _____ The masks of love: a novel / by Margarita Spalding Gerry; illustrated. New York; London: Harper & Brothers, 1914. 270, [1] p., front., [7] leaves of plates. [Ill. by E. C. Caswell.]
LC: F 9, '14.
PW: F 21, '14.

G-126 _____ The sound of water / by Margarita Spalding Gerry; illustrated. New York; London: Harper & Brothers Publishers, 1914. 183, [1] p., front., [7] leaves of plates. [Ill. by W. D. Stevens.]
LC: O 3, '14.
PW: O 10, '14.

G-127 _____ The toy shop: a romantic story of Lincoln the man / by Margarita Spalding Gerry. New York; London: Harper & Brothers, 1908. 50, [1] p., front.
LC: S 10, '08.
PW: S 19, '08.

G-128 Gerstenberg, Alice, 1885-1972. The conscience of Sarah Platt / by Alice Gerstenberg . . . Chicago: A. C. McClurg & Co., 1915. 325 p.
PW: Ap 10, '15.

G-129 _____ Unquenched fire: a novel / by Alice Gerstenberg. Boston: Small, Maynard and Company, [c1912]. 417 p.
PW: My 11, '12.
BLC: London: John Long, 1913.

G-130 Gher, A. M. (Alphonso Moser), b. 1858. The missing empire: a tale of "Kittatinnies" / by A. M. Gher. [Carlisle, Pa.: s. n., 1906]. 53 p. **NYP**

G-131 Ghosh, Sarath Kumar, b. 1883. The verdict of the gods / by Sarath Kumar Ghosh . . . New York: Dodd, Mead & Company, 1905. 307 p., front., [5] leaves of plates. **NYP**

G-132 Gibbons, J. J. (James Joseph). Slieve Bawn and the Croppy scout: a historical tale of seventeen ninety-eight in North Connaught / by the Rev. J. J. Gibbons. Denver, Col.: [The Kistler Press, c1914]. 283 p.

G-133 Gibbons, William Futhey, 1859-1936. Those black diamond men: a tale of the Anthrax Valley / by William Futhey Gibbons. New York; Chicago; Toronto: Fleming H. Revell Company, 1902. 389 p., front., [4] leaves of plates.

G-134 Gibbs, A. Hamilton (Arthur Hamilton), b. 1888. The hour of conflict / by Hamilton Gibbs . . . New York: George H. Doran Company, [c1914]. 296 p. Illustrated end papers.
BLC: London: Stanley Paul & Co., 1914.

G-135 _____ Soundings: a novel / by A. Hamilton Gibbs. Boston: Little, Brown, and Company, 1925. 320 p. Unexamined copy: bibliographic data from OCLC, #172502.
LC: Mr 11, '25.
PW: Mr 14, '25.

G-136 Gibbs, George Fort, 1870-1942. The black stone / by George Gibbs; illustrated by George Gibbs. New York; London: D. Appleton and Company, 1919. 357, [1] p., front., [4] leaves of plates.
LC: Mr 5, '19.
PW: Mr 1, '19.

G-137 _____ The bolted door: illustrated / by George Gibbs. New York; London: D. Appleton and Company, 1911. 346 p., col. front., [8] leaves of plates. [Ill. by the author.]
LC: F 1, '11.
PW: F 18, '11.

G-138 _____ Fires of ambition / by George Gibbs . . . New York; London: D. Appleton and Company, 1923. 442, [1] p., front.   **DPL**
LC: S 25, '23.
PW: O 6, '23.

G-139 _____ The flaming sword: illustrated / by George Gibbs. New York; London: D. Appleton and Company, 1914. 346, [1] p., front., [3] leaves of plates.
LC: S 29, '14.
PW: O 17, '14.

G-140 _____ The forbidden way / by George Gibbs. New York; London: D. Appleton and Company, 1911. 387, [1] p., col. front., [8] leaves of plates. [Ill. by George Fort Gibbs.]
LC: S 28, '11.
PW: S 30, '11.

G-141 _____ The golden bough / by George Gibbs; illustrated. New York; London: D. Appleton and Company, 1918. 385 p., col. front., [4] leaves of plates. [Some ill. by the author.]
LC: S 12, '18.

G-142 _____ The house of Mohun / by George Gibbs. New York; London: D. Appleton and Company, 1922. 355, [1] p., front. [Ill. by George Fort Gibbs.]
LC: Je 26, '22.

G-143 _____ How to stay married / by George Gibbs. New York; London: D. Appleton and Company, 1925. 241, [1] p.
LC: Mr 24, '25.
PW: Ap 4, '25.

G-144 _____ In search of Mademoiselle / by George Gibbs. Philadelphia: Henry T. Coates & Co., 1901. 373 p., front., [3] leaves of plates. [Ill. by George Fort Gibbs.]
PW: My 11, '01.

G-145 _____ The love of Monsieur: a novel / by George Gibbs. New York; London: Harper & Brothers, 1903. 296, [1] p., front. [Ill. by George Fort Gibbs.]
PW: Je 6, '03.

G-146 _____ Mad marriage / by George Gibbs. New York; London: D. Appleton and Company, 1925. 367 p.
LC: S 2, '25.
PW: S 12, '25.

G-147 _____ Madcap / by George Gibbs; illustrated. New York; London: D. Appleton and Company, 1913. 343, [1] p., front., [3] leaves of plates. [Ill. by George Gibbs.]
LC: N 8, '13.
PW: N 15, '13.

G-148 _____ The maker of opportunities / by George Gibbs; illustrated by Edmund Frederick. New York; London: D. Appleton and Company, 1912. 271, [1] p., front., [3] leaves of plates.
LC: Ap 20, '12.
PW: Ap 20, '12.

G-149 _____ The Medusa emerald / by George Gibbs . . . ; illustrated by the author. New York: D. Appleton and Company, 1907. 336 p., front., [3] leaves of plates.
LC: O 25, '07.
PW: N 2, '07.

G-150 _____ Paradise garden: the satirical narrative of a great experiment / by George Gibbs; illustrated by William A. Hottinger. New York; London: D. Appleton and Company, 1916. 359, [1] p., front., [3] leaves of plates.
LC: S 26, '16.

G-151 _____ Sackcloth and scarlet / by George Gibbs. New York; London: D. Appleton and Company, 1924. 330, [1] p., front.
LC: S 17, '24.
PW: S 27, '24.

G-152 _____ The secret witness / by George Gibbs; illustrated by George Brehm. New York; London: D. Appleton and Company, 1917. 402, [1] p., front., [5] leaves of plates.
LC: Ag 27, '17.
PW: S 8, '17.

G-153 _____ The silent battle / by George Gibbs; illustrated. New York; London: D. Appleton and Company, 1913. 361 p., front., [5] leaves of plates. [Ill. by George Fort Gibbs and F. Graham Cootes.]
LC: Ap 1, '13.

G-154 _____ The splendid outcast / by George Gibbs; illustrated by George Gibbs. New York; London: D. Appleton and Company, 1920. 352, [1] p., front., [3] leaves of plates.
LC: F 3, '20.
PW: F 14, '20.

G-155 _____ Tony's wife / by George Gibbs; illustrated by the author. New York; London: D. Appleton and Company, 1910. 311, [1] p., front., [7] leaves of plates.
LC: Ap 11, '10.
PW: Ap 9, '10.

G-156 _____ The vagrant duke / by George Gibbs. New York; London: D. Appleton and Company, 1921. 370, [1] p., front. [Ill. by George Fort Gibbs.]
LC: Ja 24, '21.

G-157　　____ The yellow dove / by George Gibbs. New York; London: D. Appleton and Company, 1915. 330, [1] p., front., [3] leaves of plates. [Ill. by George Gibbs.]
LC: O 26, '15.
PW: O 30, '15.

G-158　　____ Youth triumphant / by George Gibbs. New York; London: D. Appleton and Company, 1921. 418, [1] p., front. [Ill. by George Gibbs.]
LC: O 7, '21.
PW: O 22, '21.

G-159　　Gibbs, J. T. (Jesse Thomas), b. 1865. Tom Wilkins: a story of school management and supervision / by J. T. Gibbs. Okawville, Illinois: J. T. Gibbs, 1913. 224 p.　　**DLC**

G-160　　Gibbs, Josiah F. (Josiah Francis), b. 1845. Kawich's gold mine: an historical narrative of mining in the Grand Canyon of the Colorado and of love and adventure among the polygamous Mormons of southern Utah / by Josiah F. Gibbs . . . -- (Author's edition.) -- Salt Lake City: Century Printing Company, 1913. 228 p., ill.　　**MNU**
Gibbs, Ralph E. Shadows. In *Under Berkeley Oaks* **(1901), U-8.**

Giberga, Ovidio. See **Coggs, Dr., pseud.**

G-161　　Gibson, David, 1871-1945. After many years, and other sketches / by David Gibson. Cleveland: The David Gibson Company, 1912. 210 p.
Unexamined copy: bibliographic data from OCLC, #4208794.
"These sketches originally appeared, for the most part, in the Gibson magazines, a series of personally edited monthly publications devoted to industrial and commercial sociology."

Gibson, Peter. See **Malanotte, Mario, pseud.**

Gibson, W. C. (William Curtis), b. 1857, jt. aut. *The log of the water wagon* (1905). See **Taylor, Bert Leston, 1866-1921, jt. aut., T-67.**

G-162　　Gibson, Walter Ernest. A marital messenger / by W. E. Gibson. New York; Washington: The Neale Publishing Company, 1910. 291 p.　　**VIC**
LC: D 16, '10.

G-163　　Gidley, Will S. (William Selden), b. 1852. A Dicker in souls: and other stories / by Will S. Gidley; illustrated by C. L. Wrenn and Paul G. Rogers. New York: The M. W. Hazen Company, [c1905]. 302 p., [1] leaf of plates, incl. 7 leaves of plates.
Contents: A Dicker in souls -- Diedrich Van Dyckman's day in New York -- The great matrimonial conspiracy -- John Smith I - and last -- A corner in cats -- The voice in the night -- The mysterious birthday box -- Six bachelor maids -- Room 13 -- Winning a father-in-law -- An interrupted love-story -- A Christmas restitution -- A society soldier -- Wigglesby's wooing -- The blue silk umbrella -- Miss Toodles and the burglar -- A Petersburg Christmas present -- Lawyer Sharpe's escalator -- The Widow Mulligan hold-up.

G-164　　Gielow, Martha S. (Martha Sawyer), 1854?-1933. The light on the hill: a romance of the southern

mountains / by Martha S. Gielow . . . ; illustrated. New York; Chicago; Toronto; London; Edinburgh: Fleming H. Revell Company, [c1915]. 250 p., front., [5] leaves of plates.　　**NJB**

G-165　　____ Old Andy, the moonshiner / by Martha S. Gielow . . . [Washington, D. C.: W. F. Roberts Company, c1909]. 42 p., front. (port.), [1] leaf of plates.　　**SEA**
LC: Ja 31, '10.
PW: Mr 12, '10.
Also: New York; Chicago; Toronto; London; Edinburgh: Fleming H. Revell Company, [c1909]. 46 p., front., [3] leaves of plates.

G-166　　____ Old plantation days / by Martha S. Gielow . . . New York: R. H. Russell, 1902. 183 p., photo. front. (port.), [16] leaves of plates (incl. [2] leaves of music).
Contents: Mammy speaks -- Mammy Joe and the old home -- Lookin' fer Marse Willie -- Dat chile -- Uncle Tom's matrimonial difficulties -- Ole bline Hannah -- Plantation sermon -- A brief sketch of Mammy Joe and her account of the sinking of the Merrimac -- Mammy Tilly's visit to the city -- Aunt Roxy Ann, an' de apple-tree -- How sis' Mandy an' her dog Pinchey got 'ligion -- Mammy's receipt for making Alabama velvets -- Go ter sleep on mammy's bre's' -- Mammy's luck charm fer de bride -- Mammy's receipt fer aig-braid -- De Chris'mus baby -- Little sweet ladie -- On my journey home -- Come ring dem charmin' bells -- Wheel in de middle o' de wheel -- Plantation funeral song -- Oh, lawd, ain' dem lobely -- Oh, ma'y, don' you weep -- Note by the author.
PW: Ja 24, '03.

G-167　　____ Uncle Sam / by Martha S. Gielow. New York; Chicago; Toronto; London; Edinburgh: Fleming H. Revell Company, [c1913]. 61 p., front., [3] leaves of plates.
LC: O 22, '13.

G-168　　Giesy, J. U. (John Ulrich), 1877-1947. All for his country / by J. U. Giesy. New York: The Macaulay Company, 1915. 320 p., col. front.
PW: Ap 17, '15.

G-169　　____ Mimi: a story of the Latin quarter in war-time / by J. U. Giesy. New York; London: Harper & Brothers, [1918]. 87, [1] p.
PW: Je 22, '18.

____, jt. aut. *The other woman* (1917). See **Cohen, Octavus Roy, b. 1891, jt. aut., C-561.**

G-170　　Giffen, Lilian. The ghost of the Belle-Alliance Plantation: and other stories / by Lilian Giffen. [Baltimore?: Friedenwald Co.?], c1901. 64 p., photo. front.　　**KSU**
Contents: The ghost of the Belle-Alliance Plantation -- The fortunes of war -- A meeting of nations -- Her people.

G-171　　Gifford, Alice Sherman. A romance of Hellerism / by Alice Sherman Gifford. New York; London: F. Tennyson Neely Co., [c1901]. 145 p., photo. front. (port.).　　**DLC**
Contents: A romance of Hellerism -- La Casa Negra -- The cat's-eye of Koli Kahn.

G-172　　Gifford, Franklin Kent, 1861-1948. Aphrodite: the romance of a sculptor's masterpiece / by Franklin Kent Gifford; with a frontispiece drawn by Edwin H.

Blashfield. Boston: Small, Maynard & Company, 1901. 351 p., front.
LC: O 14, '01.
PW: O 26, '01.

G-173 [____] The Belle Islers: a novel / by Richard Brinsley Newman [pseud.]; illustrated by Wallace Goldsmith. Boston: Lothrop, Lee & Shepard Co., [1908]. 423 p., incl. front.
LC: Mr 23, '08.
PW: Ap 4, '08.

G-174 ____ The democratic Rhine-maid: a novel / by Franklin Kent Gifford. New York: The Devin-Adair Company, 1914. 372 p.
LC: Je 18, '14.
PW: Ag 22, '14.

Gift, Theo. "Not Mentioned in despatches." In *The Senior lieutenant's wager: and other stories* (1905), **S-312.**

G-175 Gilbert, Anne. The owl's nest: a vacation among isms / by Anne Gilbert. New York; Chicago; Toronto: Fleming H. Revell Company, [c1912]. 123 p.

G-176 Gilbert, Caroline Mortimer. A dictionary gentleman and his family / by Caroline Mortimer Gilbert. New York: Broadway Publishing Company, [c1905]. 196 p.

G-177 Gilbert, George, 1874-1943. Cow women: a western story / by George Gilbert. New York: Chelsea House, [c1924]. 320 p.
LC: Je 17, '24.
PW: Jl 19, '24.

____ In Maulmain fever-ward. In *The best short stories of 1918 and the yearbook of the American short story* (1919), **B-563.**

G-178 ____ Midnight of the ranges / by George Gilbert; with frontispiece by George W. Gage. Boston: Little, Brown and Company, 1920. 302 p., front.
LC: S 15, '20.
PW: S 4, '20.

G-179 Gilbert, Nelson Rust. The affair at Pine court: a tale of the Adirondacks / by Nelson Rust Gilbert; with illustrations in color by Frank H. Desch. Philadelphia; London: J. B. Lippincott Company, 1907. 391 p., col. front., [2] leaves of col. plates.
LC: S 23, '07.
PW: O 12, '07.

G-180 Gilbreath, Olive. Miss Amerikanka: a story / by Olive Gilbreath; illustrated by Sigismund de Ivanowski. New York; London: Harper & Brothers, [1918]. 296, [1] p., mounted front., [3] mounted plates, ill.
LC: Mr 21, '18.
PW: Mr 23, '18.

G-181 Gilchrist, Annie Somers. Katherine Somerville, or, The Southland before and after the civil war / by

Annie Somers Gilchrist . . . ; illustrated by Rena Bernal Roberts. Nashville, Tenn.: Press of Marshall & Bruce Co., 1906. 347 p., front., [3] leaves of plates.   **MNU**

G-182 ____ The night-rider's daughter / by Annie Somers Gilchrist . . . Nashville, Tenn.: Marshall & Bruce Company, [c1910]. 240 p., front., [2] leaves of plates. [Ill. by S. E. Staggs.]   **MUS**

G-183 Gilchrist, Rosetta Luce, 1851-1921. Tibby: a novel dealing with psychic forces and telepathy / by Rosetta Luce Gilchrist. New York; Washington: The Neale Publishing Company, 1904. 332 p.
PW: Je 3, '05.

G-184 Gilder, Jeannette L. (Jeannette Leonard), 1849-1916. The tomboy at work / by Jeannette Gilder; illustrated by Florence Scovel Shinn. New York: Doubleday, Page & Co., 1904. 252 p., front., [15] leaves of plates.
BLC: London: Doubleday, Page & Co., 1904.

Giles, Ellen Rose. The apostasy of Anita Fiske. In *A book of Bryn Mawr stories* (1901), **B-732.**

G-185 Giles, Rosena A. The closed road / by Rosena A. Giles. Boston; New York: The Cornhill Publishing Company, 1923. 388 p., [2] leaves of plates.
LC: My 7, '23.
PW: Ag 4, '23.

G-186 ____ Soil, the master / by Rosena A. Giles. Boston: The Cornhill Publishing Company, [c1924]. 315 p., front.
LC: N 14, '24.
PW: My 16, '25.

G-187 Gilfillan, Joseph Alexander, 1838-1913. The Ojibway: a novel of Indian life of the period of the early advance of civilization in the great Northwest / by Joseph A. Gilfillan. New York; Washington: The Neale Publishing Company, 1904. 457 p.
PW: D 3, '04.

Gilkyson, Phoebe H. The amateur. In *The Harper prize short stories* (1925), **H-233.**

G-188 Gilkyson, Walter, 1880-1969. Oil / by Walter Gilkyson. New York: Charles Scribner's Sons, 1924. 286 p.

G-189 Gill, George Creswell. Beyond the blue-grass: a Kentucky novel / by George Creswell Gill. New York; Washington: The Neale Publishing Company, 1908. 223 p. Designed end papers.
PW: Ag 1, '08.

Gill, Mary (Gill). See **Houmas, Mount, pseud.**

G-190 Gillespie, Foy. The defenders / by Foy Gillespie. New York: The Cosmopolitan Press, 1912. 395 p.
LC: Mr 20, '12.
PW: Ap 6, '12.

Gillespie, Marian Evans, b. 1884. See **Evans, Marian.**

Gillespie, Neil. The blood of a comrade. In *Argonaut stories* **(1906), A-298.**

G-191   Gilliam, Charles Frederic, 1853-1915. A victorious defeat: the story of a franchise / by Charles Frederic Gilliam; illustrated by Ted Ireland. Boston: The Roxburgh Publishing Company, [c1906]. 371 p., incl. 4 leaves of plates, front.
LC: O 22, '06.

G-192   Gilliam, David Tod, 1844-1923. Dick Devereux: a story of the Civil War / by David Tod Gilliam. Cincinnati: Stewart & Kidd Company, 1915. 304 p., front. [Ill. by Lois Lenore Lenski.]
LC: O 25, '15.

G-193   ____ The rose croix / by David Tod Gilliam; illustrated by Ted Ireland. New York; Akron, Ohio; Chicago: Saalfield Publishing Company, [c1906]. 369 p., front., [3] leaves of plates.
LC: Je 23, '06.

G-194   Gilliam, E. W. (Edward Winslow), 1834-1925. The foundling / by Edw. W. Gilliam . . . Lynchburg, Va.: J. P. Bell Company, printers, [c1911]. 268 p., photo. front. (port.).   **OSU, VIC**

G-195   ____ Ravenswood / by Edward W. Gilliam. New York; Washington: The Neale Publishing Company, 1908. 241 p.

G-196   ____ The rector of Hazlehurst and some others of the cloth / by E. W. Gilliam . . . Baltimore: John Murphy Company, 1903. 478 p.

G-197   ____ Uncle Sam and the Negro in 1920 / by E. W. Gilliam . . . Lynchburg, Virginia: J. P. Bell Company (Inc.), 1906. 469 p., photo. front. (port.), [2] leaves of plates. [Ill. by Fred A. Dabney.]
          OSU, KSU

Gillis, Adolph. See **Worth, Marc, pseud.**

Gillmore, Inez Haynes, 1873-1970. See **Irwin, Inez Haynes.**

G-198   Gillmore, Rufus, 1869-1935. The Alster case / by Rufus Gillmore . . . ; illustrated by Charles L. Wrenn. New York; London: D. Appleton and Company, 1914. 330, [1] p., front., [3] leaves of plates.
LC: S 3, '14.
PW: S 19, '14.

G-199   ____ The mystery of the second shot / by Rufus Gillmore; illustrated. New York; London: D. Appleton and Company, 1912. 299, [1] p. [Ill. by H. Heyer.]
PW: Ap 27, '12.

G-200   ____ The opal pin / by Rufus Gillmore; illustrated. New York; London: D. Appleton and Company,

1914. 317, [1] p., front., [3] leaves of plates. [Ill. by Dalton Stevens.]
LC: Mr 28, '14.
PW: Ap 4, '14.

G-201   Gilman, Bradley, 1857-1932. Back to the soil, or, From tenement house to farm colony: a circular solution of an angular problem / by Bradley Gilman; with an introduction by Edward Everett Hall. Boston: L. C. Page & Company, 1901. 242 p., incl. front.
PW: S 14, '01.

G-202   ____ A Christmas burglar / by Bradley Gilman. Canton Corner, Mass.: [s. n.], December 25th, 1908. 24 p.   **NYP**

G-203   ____ How Miles Morgan's chimney was swept / by Bradley Gilman. Springfield, Mass.: [s. n.], December 25th, 1901. 20 p.   **NYP**

G-204   ____ Parson Purdy's problem / by Bradley Gilman. Canton, Mass.: [s. n.], December 25th, 1911. 17 p.
          NYP

G-205   ____ Ronald Carnaquay: a commercial clergyman / by Bradley Gilman. New York: The Macmillan Company; London: Macmillan & Co., Ltd., 1903. 374 p.
PW: Ap 18, '03.

G-206   Gilman, Charlotte Perkins, 1860-1935. The Crux: a novel / by Charlotte Perkins Gilman. New York: Charlton Company, 1911. 311 p.

G-207   ____ Moving the mountain / by Charlotte Perkins Gilman. New York: Charlton Company, 1911. 290 p.
PW: Ja 13, '12.

G-208   ____ What Diantha did: a novel / by Charlotte Perkins Gilman. New York: Charlton Company, 1910. 250 p.   **MNU**
PW: Ja 14, '11.

G-209   Gilman, Dorothy Foster, b. 1891. The bloom of youth / by Dorothy Foster Gilman. Boston: Small, Maynard & Company, [c1916]. 341 p.
LC: My 1, '16.
PW: F 19, '16.

G-210   ____ Lorraine: a novel / by Dorothy Foster Gilman. New York: The Macmillan Company, 1923. 281 p.
LC: O 24, '23.
PW: N 3, '23.

G-211   ____ Surprising Antonia / by Dorothy Foster Gilman; illustrated by Thelma Gooch. Boston: L. C. Page and Company (incorporated), 1923. 269 p., front., [3] leaves of plates.
LC: My 16, '23.

G-212   Gilman, Mildred Evans. Fig leaves / by Mildred Evans Gilman. New York: Siebel Publishing Corporation, 1925. 328 p.
LC: O 23, '25.
PW: O 24, '25.

G-213 Gilman, Stella. A gumbo lily, and other tales / by Stella Gilman. New York; London; Montreal: The Abbey Press, [c1901]. 176 p., [1] leaf of plates (port.). **USD**
Contents: A gumbo lily -- Barbed wire -- One of the colony -- The person concerned -- A little daughter of Eve -- Locoed -- The little ring -- But the stars shone -- As prohibited -- When mother married.
PW: D 14, '01.

Gilmer, Elizabeth Merriwether, 1861-1951. See **Dix, Dorothy, pseud.**

G-214 Gilmore, F. Grant. "The problem": a military novel / by F. Grant Gilmore . . . [Rochester, N. Y.: Press of Henry Conolly Co., c1915]. 99 p., photo. front (port.).

Gilmore, Florence, 1880-1945. After twenty-five years. In *The lady of the tower* (1909), L-13.

G-215 ____ Dr. Dumont / by Florence Gilmore . . . St. Louis, Mo.; Freiburg (Baden), Germany; London: Published by B. Herder, 1911. 123 p. **DLC**

G-216 ____ The parting of the ways / by Florence Gilmore. St. Louis; London: B. Herder Book Company, c1914. 206 p.
Unexamined copy: bibliographic data from OCLC, #11642476.

G-217 ____ A romance of old Jerusalem / by Florence Gilmore. St. Louis, Mo.; Freiburg (Baden), Germany; London: B. Herder, 1911. 120 p. **DLC**
LC: D 19, '10.

Gilpatric, Guy. Black art and Ambrose. In *Prize stories of 1920* (1921), P-618.

G-218 Gilson, Roy Rolfe, 1875-1933. Ember light: a novel / by Roy Rolfe Gilson . . . New York: The Baker & Taylor Company, 1911. 299 p., front., [3] leaves of plates. [Ill. by Noble Ives.]
LC: O 20, '11.

G-219 ____ The flower of youth: a romance / by Roy Rolfe Gilson. New York; London: Harper & Brothers, 1904. 263, [1] p.
PW: O 1, '04.

G-220 ____ In the morning glow: short stories / by Roy Rolfe Gilson; illustrated. New York; London: Harper & Brothers, 1902. 186, [1] p., front., [15] leaves of plates. [Ill. by Alice Barber Stephens.]
Contents: Grandfather -- Grandmother -- While Aunt Jane played -- Little sister -- Our yard -- The toy grenadier -- Father -- Mother.
PW: O 18, '02.

G-221 ____ Katrina: a story / by Roy Rolfe Gilson. New York: The Baker & Taylor Company, [1906]. 316 p., col. front., [5] leaves of col. plates. [Ill. by Alice Barber Stephens.]
LC: O 2, '06.
PW: N 3, '06.

G-222 ____ The legend of Jerry Ladd / by Roy Rolfe Gilson. Garden City, N. Y.; Doubleday, Page &

Company, 1913. 238 p.
LC: Mr 27, '13.
PW: Ap 5, '13.

G-223 ____ Miss Primrose: a novel / by Roy Rolfe Gilson. New York; London: Harper & Brothers, 1906. 294, [1] p.
PW: Mr 10, '06.

G-224 ____ Mother and father: from "In the morning glow" / by Roy Rolfe Gilson; illustrated by Alice Barber Stephens. New York; London: Harper and Brothers, 1903. 63, [1] p., front., [7] leaves of plates. [Ill. by Alice Barber Stephens and Adrian J. Iorio.]

G-225 ____ When love is young: a novel / by Roy Rolfe Gilson. New York; London: Harper & Brothers Publishers, 1901. 283 p.

____ The wind of dreams. In *The heart of childhood* (1906), H-441.

G-226 ____ The wistful years / by Roy Rolfe Gilson. New York: The Baker & Taylor Company, 1909. 318 p., col. front., [3] leaves of col. plates. [Ill. by F. Graham Cootes.]
LC: O 21, '09.

Giltner, Leigh Gordon. Down the incline. In *The Senior lieutenant's wager; and other stories* (1905), S-312.

G-227 Girardeau, Claude M., b. 1860. The Scarlet wagon / by Claude M. Girardeau. New York: Henry Holt and Company, 1914. 270 p. **MNL**

G-228 The girl with the rosewood crutches: she tells some chapters of her life / illustration by Harrison Cady. New York: McBride, Nast & Company, 1912. 267 p., front.

G-229 Givins, Robert C. Jones abroad / by Robert C. Givins . . . ; illustrated. Chicago, Ill.: Published by the Jones Abroad Publishing Company, [c1911]. 520 p., ill. [Ill. by W. Timan and W. S. Stacey.] **DLC**

G-230 ____ "Mlle. L'Inconnue": the automatic vocalist / by Robert C. Givins . . . [Chicago: Bentley-Murray], 1909. 113 p., col. front. (port.), ill. [Ill. by Chas. Crowell.] **DLC**
LC: Ja 17, '10.

G-231 Givins, Robert C. A thousand miles an hour / by Robert C. Givins . . . Chicago: Maclear & Marcus, [c1913]. 103 p. **DLC**
Also: -- Railroad edition. -- Chicago, Ill.: Around the World Publishing Co., [c1913].

G-232 Gladden, Hope, *pseud*. The problem / Hope Gladden [pseud.]. Boston: Richard G. Badger, [c1913]. ([Boston, U. S. A.]: The Gorham Press). 248 p. **DLC**

G-233　Glasgow, Ellen Anderson Gholson, 1873-1945. The ancient law / by Ellen Glasgow. New York: Doubleday & Company, 1908. 485 p.
LC: Ja 21, '08.
PW: F 1, '08.
BLC: London: Archibald Constable & Co.; New York printed, 1908.
References: Kelly, p. 30-32.

G-234　_____ Barren ground / by Ellen Glasgow. Printed in Garden City, N. Y.: Doubleday, Page & Co., 1925. (Garden City, N. Y.: Country Life Press). 511 p., ill. title page.
"First Edition."
LC: Ap 27, '25.
PW: Ap 4, '25.
BLC: London: John Murray, 1925.
References: Kelly, p. 58-66.

G-235　_____ The battle-ground / by Ellen Glasgow; illustrated by W. F. Baer and W. Granville Smith. New York: Doubleday, Page & Co., 1902. 512 p., col. front., [3] leaves of plates.
PW: Mr 29, '02.
BLC: London: Archibald Constable & Co., 1902.
References: Kelly, p. 14-18.

G-236　_____ The builders / by Ellen Glasgow. Garden City, N. Y.: Doubleday, Page & Company, 1919. 379, [1] p.
LC: N 21, '19.
PW: N 1, '19.
BLC: London: Curtis Brown; Garden City, N. Y. [printed], 1919. Another edition: London: John Murray, 1919.
References: Kelly, p. 49-51.

G-237　_____ The deliverance: a romance of the Virginia tobacco fields / by Ellen Glasgow; with illustrations by Frank E. Schoonover. New York: Doubleday, Page & Co., 1904. 543 p., col. front., [3] leaves of col. plates, ill.
PW: Ja 23, '04.
BLC: London: Archibald Constable & Co.; New York printed, 1904.
References: Kelly, p. 21-26.

G-238　_____ Life and Gabriella: the story of a woman's courage / by Ellen Glasgow; frontispiece by C. Allan Gilbert. Garden City, N. Y.: Doubleday, Page & Company, 1916. 529, [1] p., col. front.
LC: Ja 19, '16.
PW: Ja 15, '16.
BLC: London: John Murray; Garden City, N. Y. printed, 1916.
References: Kelly, p. 44-49.

G-239　_____ The miller of Old Church / by Ellen Glasgow. Garden City, New York: Doubleday, Page & Company, 1911. 432 p.
LC: Je 1, '11.
PW: Je 10, '11.
BLC: London: John Murray, 1911.
References: Kelly, p. 36-40.

G-240　_____ One man in his time / by Ellen Glasgow . . . Garden City, New York; Toronto: Doubleday, Page & Company, 1922. 379 p.
LC: My 31, '22.
BLC: London: John Murray, 1922.
References: Kelly, p. 52-54.

_____ The past. In *The best short stories of 1921 and the yearbook of the American short story (1922),* **B-566.**

G-241　_____ The romance of a plain man / by Ellen Glasgow . . . New York: The Macmillan Company, 1909. 464 p.　　　OSU copy is 2nd printing.
LC: Ap 28, '09.
PW: My 22, '09.
BLC: London: John Murray, 1909.
References: Kelly, p. 32-35.

G-242　_____ The shadowy third: and other stories / by Ellen Glasgow; frontispiece by Elenore Plaisted Abbott. Garden City, N. Y.: Doubleday, Page & Company, 1923. 291 p., col. front.　Note British title: *Dare's gift and other stories.* London: John Murray, 1924.
Contents: The shadowy third -- Dare's gift -- The past -- Whispering leaves -- A point in morals -- The difference -- Jordan's end.
LC: N 14, '23.
PW: N 3, '23.
References: Kelly, p. 55-57.

G-243　_____ Virginia / by Ellen Glasgow. Garden City, N. Y.: Doubleday, Page & Company, 1913. 526 p., front.
LC: Ap 24, '13.
PW: Ap 19, '13.
BLC: London: William Heinemann, 1913.
References: Kelly, p. 40-44.

G-244　_____ The wheel of life / by Ellen Glasgow. New York: Doubleday, Page & Company, 1906. 474 p.
PW: F 3, '06.
BLC: London: Archibald Constable; New York printed, 1906.
References: Kelly, p. 26-29.

G-245　Glaspell, Susan, 1882-1948. Fidelity: a novel / by Susan Glaspell. Boston: Small, Maynard and Company, [c1915]. 422 p.
LC: My 12, '15.
PW: My 8, '15.
BLC: London: Jarrolds, 1924.

G-246　_____ The glory of the conquered: the story of a great love / by Susan Glaspell. New York: Frederick A. Stokes Company, [c1909]. 376 p. Illustrated end papers.
LC: Mr 1, '09.
PW: Mr 13, '09.
BLC: London: Sir Isaac Pitman & Sons; New York printed, [1909].

_____ "Government goat." In *The best short stories of 1919 and the yearbook of the American short story (1920),* **B-564.**

_____ His smile. In *The best short stories of 1921 and the yearbook of the American short story* **(1922), B-566.**

_____ A jury of her peers. In *The best short stories of 1917 and the yearbook of the American short story* **(1918), B-562.**

G-247 _____ Lifted masks / stories by Susan Glaspell. New York: Frederick A. Stokes Company, [1912]. 257 p.
Contents: "One of those impossible Americans" -- The plea -- For love of the hills -- Freckles M'Grath -- From A to Z -- The man of flesh and blood -- How the prince saw America -- The last sixty minutes -- "Out there" -- The preposterous motive -- His America -- The anarchist: his dog -- At twilight.
LC: S 18, '12.
PW: S 14, '12.

G-248 _____ The visioning: a novel / by Susan Glaspell. New York: Frederick A. Stokes Company, [1911]. 464 p.
LC: My 2, '11.
PW: My 6, '11.
BLC: London: John Murray, 1912.

G-249 Glass, A. Wellington (Arthur Wellington), b. 1865. A justifiable falsehood: a story of love and mystery / by A. Wellington Glass. Elgin, Illinois: Courier Publishing Company, 1909, [c1908]. 192 p.

G-250 Glass, Charles Wilder, Mrs., b. 1874. Romance in Starland: a scientific novel / by Mrs. Charles Wilder Glass. Los Angeles, Cal.: J. F. McElheney Printing Company, [c1915?]. 83 p., photo. front (port.).
DLC

G-251 _____ Ruth's marriage in Mars: a scientific novel / by Mrs. Charles Wilder Glass. [Los Angeles, Cal.: s. n., c1912]. 56 p., photo. front. (port.).

Glass, Kate Elizabeth (Perkins). See **Glass, Charles Wilder, Mrs., b. 1874.**

G-252 Glass, Montague Marsden, 1877-1934. Abe and Mawruss: being further adventures of Potash and Perlmutter / by Montague Glass; illustrated by J. J. Gould and Martin Justice. Garden City, N. Y.: Doubleday, Page & Company, 1911. 379 p., front., [3] leaves of plates.
LC: O 20, '11.
BLC: London: Hodder & Stoughton, 1914.

_____ Celestine and Coralie. In *Clever business sketches* **(1909), C-490.**

G-253 _____ The competitive nephew / by Montague Glass; illustrated. Garden City, N. Y.: Doubleday, Page & Company, 1915. 350 p., front., [3] leaves of plates. [Ill. by J. J. Gould and Martin Justice.]
Contents: The competitive nephew -- Opportunity -- The sorrows of Seiden -- Serpents' teeth -- Making over Milton -- Birsky & Zapp -- The moving picture writes -- Coercing Mr. Trinkmann -- "Rudolph where have you been" -- Caveat emptor.
LC: Ap 19, '15.
PW: Ap 24, '15.

G-254 _____ Elkan Lubliner: American / by Montague Glass. Garden City, N. Y.: Doubleday, Page & Company, 1912. 323, [1] p.

G-255 _____ Object: matrimony / by Montague Glass. Garden City, New York: Doubleday, Page & Company, 1912. 74, [1] p., front. Illustrated end papers.   **KSU**
LC: O 1, '12.
PW: O 12, '12.

G-256 _____ Potash & Perlmutter: their copartnerhip ventures and adventures / by Montague Glass; illustrated. Philadelphia: Henry Altemus Company, [c1910]. 419 p., front., [7] leaves of plates. [Ill. by Henry Raleigh.]
LC: My 20, '10.
PW: Ag 13, '10.

G-257 _____ Potash and Perlmutter settle things / by Montague Glass. New York; London: Harper & Brothers, [1919]. 259, [1] p., front., [3] leaves of plates. [Ill. by Albert Levering.]
LC: S 29, '19.
PW: N 1, '19.

_____ The striped tourists. In *Clever business sketches* **(1909), C-490.**

G-258 _____ The truth about Potash and Perlmutter: and five other stories / by Montague Glass. Racine, Wis.: Whitman Publishing Company, [c1924]. 122 p.
Contents: The truth about Potash and Perlmutter -- Two tales of ingratitude -- Something just as good -- "And the greatest of these" -- How education paid -- Shopping in Naples.

G-259 _____ Worrying won't win: illustrated / by Montague Glass. New York; London: Harper & Brothers, 1918. 229 p., [1] p., front., [7] leaves of plates. [Ill. by F. M. Follett and T. Westerman.]
Contents: Potash and Perlmutter discuss the Czar business -- Potash and Perlmutter on soap-boxers and peace fellers -- Potash and Perlmutter on financing the war -- Potash and Perlmutter on Bernstorff's expense account -- Potash and Perlmutter discuss on the front page and off -- Potash and Perlmutter on Hooverizing the overhead -- Potash and Perlmutter on foreign affairs -- Potash and Perlmutter on Lordnorthcliffing versus Colonelhousing -- Potash and Perlmutter on national music and national currency -- Potash and Perlmutter on revolutionizing the revolution business -- Potash and Perlmutter discuss the sugar question -- Potash and Perlmutter discuss how to put the spurt in expert -- Potash and Perlmutter on being an optician and looking on the bright side -- The liquor question-shall it be dry or extra dry? -- Potash and Perlmutter on peace with victory and without brokers, either -- Potash and Perlmutter on keeping it dark -- Potash and Perlmutter on the peace program, including the added extra feature and the supper turn -- Potash and Perlmutter on the new national holidays -- Mr. Wilson: That's all -- Potash and Perlmutter discuss the grand-opera business -- Potash and Perlmutter discuss the magazine in war-times -- Potash and Perlmutter on saving daylight, coal, and breath -- Potash and Perlmutter discuss why is a play-goer? -- Potash and Perlmutter discuss society-New York, human, and American -- Potash and Perlmutter discuss this here income tax.
LC: My 27, '18.
PW: Je 8, '18.

G-260 _____ Y'understand / by Montague Glass. Garden City, N. Y.: Doubleday, Page & Company, 1925. 317 p.
Contents: Blood is redder than water -- Cousins of convenience --

They will do it -- It's never too late -- You can't fool the camera -- Never begin with lions -- The sixth McNally -- Keeping expenses down.
LC: S 30, '25.
PW: S 19, '25.
BLC: London: William Heinemann; printed in U. S. A., 1925.

Glass, Sarah E. The potter's wheel. In *The best college short stories, 1917-18* (1919), B-557.

G-261   Glassmire, Samuel H. (Samuel Haven), b. 1873. Olea: a story of the Norsemen in Pennsylvania / by Samuel Haven Glassmire. New York; London: The Knickerbocker Press, 1913. 96 p., front. (port.), [7] leaves of plates (some photo.). [Ill. by F. O. C. Darley.]

G-262   Gleason, Arthur, 1878-1923. Young Hilda at the wars / by Arthur H. Gleason . . . New York: Frederick A. Stokes Company, [1915]. 213 p., photo. front. (port.).

G-263   Gleeson, William, b. 1843. Vice and virtue: a story of our times / by William Gleeson. [Chicago: W. F. Mecklenberg, c1913]. 603 p., photo. front. (port.), [12] leaves of plates. [Some ill. by F. A. Gibson.]

Glenn, Isa Urquhart. The wager. In *Prize stories of 1923* (1924), P-621.

G-264   Glenn, L. Mell (Laurence Mell), b. 1888. Harking back / by L. M. Glenn. Greenville, S. C.: Furman University, 1908. 80 p., photo. front. (port.). **DLC**

G-265   Glentworth, Marguerite Linton. The tenth commandment: a romance / by Marguerite Linton Glentworth . . . Boston: Lee and Shepard, 1902. 350 p., photo. front. (port.).
PW: O 25, '02.
BLC: London: Gay & Bird; Norwood, Mass. printed, 1902.

G-266   Gloria, F. M., *pseud.* A war bride's adventure: an interview with St. Peter / by F. M. Gloria [pseud.]. South Bend, Indiana: The Seemore Co., 1916. 95, [2] p., photo. front. (port.).   **PUL**

G-267   Gluck, Sinclair, b. 1887. The green blot / by Sinclair Gluck. New York: Dodd, Mead & Company, 1925. 294 p.
LC: S 24, '25.
PW: S 26, '25.
BLC: London: Mills & Boon, 1925.

G-268   ____ The house of the missing / by Sinclair Gluck . . . New York: Dodd, Mead and Company, 1924. 303 p.
LC: Je 25, '24.
PW: Je 21, '24.

G-269   ____ Thieves' honor / by Sinclair Gluck. New York: Dodd, Mead & Company, 1925. 290 p.
LC: Ja 30, '25.
PW: Ja 31, '25.
BLC: London: Mills & Boon, 1924.

G-270   Gluck, Sinclair, b. 1887. The white streak / by Sinclair Gluck. New York: Edward J. Clode, [c1924]. 319 p.
LC: F 12, '24.
PW: Mr 8, '24.
BLC: London: Mills & Boon, 1924.

G-271   Goddard, Charles W. (Charles William), 1879-1951. The ghost breaker: a novel based upon the play / by Charles Goddard and Paul Dickey. New York: Hearst's International Library Company, 1915. 280 p., front., [11] leaves of plates.
PW: O 23, '15.

____, jt. aut. *The goddess* (1915). See **Morris, Gouverneur, 1876-1953, jt. aut., M-1009.**

G-272   ____ The misleading lady / by Charles W. Goddard and Paul Dickey; illustrated. New York: Hearst's International Library Co., 1915. 286 p., front., [11] leaves of plates.
PW: O 23, '15.
BLC: London: Duckworth & Co., 1916.

G-273   ____ The perils of Pauline: a motion picture novel / by Charles Goddard. New York: Hearst's International Library Co., [1915]. 316 p., front., ill. (not incl. in pagination.)
PW: Je 5, '15.
BLC: London: Hodder & Stoughton, 1916.

G-274   Goddard, Dwight, 1861-1939. A nature mystic's clue / by Dwight Goddard. Thetford, Vermont: [s. n.], 1925. 282 p.
[Printed by the Vermont Printing Company, Brattleboro, Vermont.]

G-275   Godfrey, Hollis, 1874-1936. The man who ended war / by Hollis Godfrey; illustrated from drawings by Charles Grunwald. Boston: Little, Brown & Company, 1908. 301 p., front., [3] leaves of plates.
LC: S 25, '08.
BLC: London: Ward, Lock & Co., 1910.

Goetchius, Marie Louise, pseud. See **Rutledge, Maryse, pseud.**

G-276   Goetzinger, Clara Palmer. Glad Ray / by Clara Palmer Goetzinger. Chicago: Fisher Publishing Company, [c1923]. 407 p., front., [2] leaves of plates. [Ill. by Don Jones.]   **DLC**

G-277   Goff, E. S. Emmerton Mills / by E. S. Goff. Boston: The Roxburgh Publishing Company, Inc., [c1916]. 198 p.   **DLC**

G-278   Gogin, Oliver Woodruff, b. 1820. The country Jake, or, Recollections of a city boy who "lived, moved and had his being" with the Suckers in the backwoods of Illinois in the '40's / by Oliver Woodruff Gogin. New York; Montreal; London: Broadway Publishing Company, [c1903]. 129 p., photo. front. (port.).
PW: D 19, '03.

G-279   Gohdes, C. B. (Conrad Bruno), 1866-1952. John Schenck: a story of the Galveston flood / by C. B. Gohdes, A. M. Columbus, Ohio: Lutheran Book Concern, 1911. 56 p.

G-280   _____ The lily of Carlisle: a story of the days of Cromwell and Blake / by C. B. Gohdes. Columbus, Ohio: Lutheran Book Concern, 1913. 83 p., [1] leaf of plates.

G-281   Gold, Michael, 1894-1967, *pseud.* The damned agitator; Free; The coal breaker / by Michael Gold [pseud.]. Chicago: Published by The Daily Worker Publishing Co., [1924?]. 31 p.
Cover title: *The damned agitator and other stories.*

Goldberg, Israel, 1887-1964. See **Learsi, Rufus, pseud.**

Goldberg, Rube, contributor. See *Bobbed hair* **(1925), B-700.**

G-282   Golden, Harry. Unseen acres: a western story / by Harry Golden. New York City: Chelsea House, [c1924]. 250 p.
PW: My 9, '25.
BLC: London: T. Nelson & Jones, 1927.

G-283   Golden, John, 1874-1955. 7th heaven / by John Golden; based on the play by Austin Strong, illustrated with scenes from the play. New York: The H. K. Fly Company, [c1924]. 278 p., front, [7] leaves of plates.   OSU copy: reprint.

G-284   Golden, Richard, 1874-1936. Old Jed Prouty: a narrative of the Penobscot / by Richard Golden and Mary C. Francis. New York: G. W. Dillingham Company, [c1901]. 340 p.
PW: N 9, '01.
BLC: London: T. Fisher Unwin; New York [printed], 1901.

Golden Light, pseud. See **Hicks, William Watkin, 1837-1915.**

G-285   Golden stories: a selection of the best fiction by the foremost writers. New York: The Short Stories Company, 1909. [226] p., [8] pages of photo. plates.
Contents: When cheetahs fall, a tale of India / Albert Dorrington -- Rowan Island, the story of a poet's secretary / Alwin West -- Caelum non animum, a romance of the sea / Anonymous -- Blinkey, the story of a tenderfoot / Robert C. McElravy -- My strange neighbors, the story of an old house / Marie Thiery -- The stolen bacillus, the strange experience of a scientist / H. G. Wells -- The flight of fifty thousand, a tale of San Francisco / Richard S. Graves -- Such a walk in darkness, a tale of the streets / Samuel Hopkins Adams -- A question of bars, the story of a delayed letter / Cochran Wilson -- Who hath loved much, a story of the Milay Archipelago / C. Menzies Miller -- The plucking of the pears, the story of a suburban villa / Michael Thivars -- Piers, the plowman, a story of country life / Minnie Barbour Adams -- His day, a tale of Italy / Eleanor M. Ingram. -- The breadwinner, a tale of Sussex / Percival Gibbon -- In Skeleton Pool, the story of a raftsman / Frank H. Sweet -- Ruggles' first case, the story of a mine / Chauncey Thomas -- A wayside waif, a tale of the road / Christie Murray -- The dove o' peace, the story of a highwayman / Mary S. Watts -- Caught in the web, a summer tale / Leslie Davis -- Crowninshield's brush, a fox-hunting story / David Gray -- Eena, the runner, a story of the woods / Jean Xavier Bonneau -- Count Antonio and the wizard's drug, a chronicle of the Middle Ages / Anthony Hope -- The maiden's scarf, a legend of

Normandy / Jacques Avrilo -- Mr. Shamansky and the dapper young man, a tale of the ghetto / Rosalie Lange -- On trail, a story of the Northland / Adolph Bennauer.
References: BAL 16293. BAL notes 254 p. and a first printing of *The gold that glittered by O. Henry.*

G-286   Goldsberry, Louise Dunham. Ted: and some other stories / by Louise Dunham Goldsberry. Boston: The Gorham Press, 1918. 170 p.   **OSU, DLC**
Contents: Ted -- "We" -- The sweet P's -- Bob-for-short -- Bob-for-short's Christmas -- Mother -- On Christmas Eve -- A little Christmas story -- The imp -- Shaft no. 2 -- Sketch in charcoal -- The story of one woman's life -- Nelly -- A tenement-house saint -- Out of the depths -- Bob -- In the salvationists' tent -- Babe.
LC: Je 29, '18.

G-287   Goldsmith, Milton, 1861-1957. A victim of conscience: a novel / by Milton Goldsmith. Philadelphia: Henry T. Coates & Company, 1903. 318 p., front., [3] leaves of plates.
PW: Je 27, '03.

Gollmar, Arthur Howard, b. 1871. See **Julier, Arthur H. G., pseud.**

G-288   Gollomb, Joseph, 1881-1950. The girl in the fog: a mystery novel / by Joseph Gollomb. New York: Boni and Liveright, [c1923]. 255 p.
LC: S 14, '23.
PW: S 1, '23.
BLC: London: John Long, 1924.

G-289   Gone West: by a soldier doctor / edited by H. M. G. and M. M. H.; with a preface by Frederick W. Kendall. New York: Alfred A. Knopf, 1919. 103 p.
LC: Je 11, '19.

G-290   Gonzales, Ambrose Elliott, 1857-1926. The black border: Gullah stories of the Carolina coast: (with a glossary) / by Ambrose E. Gonzales. Columbia, S. C.: The State Company, 1922. 348 p.
Contents: Noblesse oblige -- My maussuh -- An antemortem demise -- The lion of Lewisburg -- The lion killer -- Old Barney -- Billybedam -- A short cut to justice -- Sam Dickerson -- Simon the "squerril" hunter -- The "cunjuh" that came back -- The raccoon hunter -- The turkey hunter -- The 'gator hunter -- The "wiles that in the women are" -- A ricefield idyll -- The Dower House -- At the cross roads store -- Mingo the drill master -- Old Harrison -- A marriage of convenience -- The plat-eye -- Old Pickett -- The lost buck -- Jim Moultrie's divorce -- Buh alligettuh en' buh deer -- Buh hawss en' buh mule (a fable) -- Liss "bin eensult" -- The retort courteous -- The cat was crazy -A congaree water-color -- Waiting till the bridegrooms come -- A Gullah's tale of woe -- The doctor didn't "exceed" -- The lady couldn't "specify" -- A question of privilege -- Conductor Smith's dilemma -- One was taken-the other left -- Egg-zactly -- An interrupted offertory -- A flaw in the "eenditement" -- Old wine-new bottles -- A glossary of the Gullah -- The tar-baby story, as told by Col. C. C. Jones and Joel Chandler Harris.
LC: S 14, '22.

G-291   _____ Laguerre: a Gascon of the black border / by Ambrose E. Gonzales. Columbia, S. C.: The State Company, 1924. 318 p., front., [3] leaves of plates.
Contents: Laguerre -- On the judgment seat -- Pa Tumbo at the bar -- A feud in the feathers -- "More deadly than the male" -- Clever Alice -- "The man in the case" -- The trials of Tumbo -- "Place aux dames!" -- The crusader and the cow -- The critic on the hearth -- The road called straight -- To have and to scold -- "Caesar . . . turned to clay" -- The law and the lady -- Bed and board -- The taming of the shrew -- A judgment of Solomon -- The tragedy of the marsh.
PW: F 14, '25.

G-292 Goodell, Charles, 1854-1937. The old Darnman: a story of New England / by Charles L. Goodell; illustrated by Charles Grunwald. New York; London: Funk & Wagnalls Company, 1906. 63 p., front., [2] leaves of plates.
Published in an abbreviated form in Success.
LC: D 19, '06.
PW: D 29, '06.

G-293 Goodloe, Carter, b. 1867. At the foot of the Rockies / by Carter Goodloe; illustrated. New York: Charles Scribner's Sons, 1905. 290 p., front., [3] leaves of plates. [Ill. by Martin Justice and Jay Hambidge.]
Contents: Rivers' gymkhana -- Jack -- The heart of Lamont -- A countess of the West -- A doubting Thomas -- The edge of the world -- The Bungalow Ranche -- Red magic.
PW: My 13, '05.

G-294 ____ Calvert of Strathore / by Carter Goodloe; frontispiece from a drawing by Howard Chandler Christy. New York: Charles Scribner's Sons, 1903. 376, [1] p., col. front.
PW: F 21, '03.

G-295 ____ The star-gazers / by A. Carter Goodloe. New York: Charles Scribner's Sons, 1910. 233 p., col. front. [Ill. by F. Graham Cootes.]
LC: S 29, '10.

Goodman, Blanche. Uncle Zeke's cemetery. See **Goodman, Blanche. _The Viney sketches_ (1918), G-296.**

G-296 ____ The Viney sketches / by Blanche Goodman. Franklin, Ohio; Denver, Colo.: Eldridge Entertainmemt [sic] House, c1918. 82 p. Designed end papers.   **NOC**
"Reprinted by permission from The Saturday evening post." Includes: _Uncle Zeke's cemetery_, with a special t. p.
Contents: Book raisin' -- Checkmating Miss Fanny -- A change of heart -- Educating Sally Ann -- The equalizing bug -- Helping Rosabel -- On matrimony -- Out on bail -- Rechristening Cornell -- Rockbottom and Miss Sally Baker -- The unaccountable sex -- Viney at the moving pictures -- Viney on conservation -- Viney on club doings.

G-297 Goodman, Daniel Carson, b. 1883. Hagar Revelly / by Daniel Carson Goodman. New York: Mitchell Kennerley, 1913. 428 p.

G-298 ____ The taker / by Daniel Carson Goodman. New York: Boni and Liveright, 1919. 346 p.
PW: Ag 2, '19.

G-299 ____ Unclothed: a novel / by Daniel Carson Goodman. New York; London: Mitchell Kennerley, 1912. 374 p.
LC: My 8, '12.
PW: Ap 20, '12.

Goodman, Henry. The button. In _The best short stories of 1923 and the yearbook of the American short story_ (1924), **B-568.**

____ The stone. In _The best short stories of 1919 and the yearbook of the American short story_ (1920), **B-564.**

____ Thomas. In _Stories from the Midland_ (1924), **S-984.**

G-300 Goodman, Jules Eckert, b. 1876. Mother / by Jules Eckert Goodman; with illustrations by John Rae. New York: Dodd, Mead and Company, 1911. 322 p., front., [2] leaves of plates.
LC: F 25, '11.
PW: Mr 4, '11.

G-301 Goodrich, Arthur Frederick, 1878-1941. The balance of power: a novel / by Arthur Goodrich; illustrated by Otto Toaspern. New York: The Outing Publishing Company, 1906. 413 p., front., [6] leaves of plates.
LC: Ag 31, '06.
PW: S 8, '06.
BLC: London: Hodder & Stoughton, [1907].

G-302 ____ Gleam o' dawn: a novel: illustrated / by Arthur Goodrich . . . New York: D. Appleton and Company, 1908. 307, [1] p., front., [3] leaves of plates. [Ill. by D. C. Hutchison.]
LC: Je 5, '08.
PW: Je 6, '08.

G-303 ____ The lady without jewels / by Arthur Goodrich . . . ; illustrated. New York: D. Appleton and Company, 1909. 360 p., front., [3] leaves of plates. [Ill. by John Cassel.]
LC: My 28, '09.
PW: Je 12, '09.

G-304 ____ The sign of freedom / by Arthur Goodrich; illustrated by William A. Hottinger. New York; London: D. Appleton and Company, 1916. 324 p., front., [3] leaves of plates.
LC: Ap 24, '16.
PW: Je 24, '16.

G-305 ____ The yardstick man / by Arthur Goodrich. New York; London: D. Appleton and Company, 1910. 325, [1] p., front.
LC: S 26, '10.
PW: O 1, '10.

G-306 Goodrich, Edna. Deynard's divorce / by Edna Goodrich. Boston: Richard G. Badger, [c1912]. ([Boston]: The Gorham Press). 218 p., photo. front. (port.).

G-307 Goodson, Russell A. The end of the trail / by Russell A. Goodson. Baltimore, Md.: The McLean Company, Publishers, 1916. 57 p.

G-308 Goodwin, Dora M. M. (Miranda Merrill), b. 1868. The daughter of Angy / by Dora M. M. Goodwin. Roxbury, Mass., U. S. A.: Published by the author, [c1911]. 266 p.
Another printing: Boston: Richard G. Badger. ([Boston]: The Gorham Press), [c1911].
LC: O 20, '11.
PW: O 4, '11.

G-309 Goodwin, J. Joseph. The "Sinker" stories of wit and humor / by J. Joseph Goodwin . . . New York: J. S.

Ogilvie Publishing Company, c1902. 250 p., ill. Designed end papers.

Contents: Sinkers makes a start -- Sinkers sends a telegram -- Sinkers hears about the canal -- Sinker's opinion of horses -- Sinkers and the Klondyke -- Sinkers was a cit, but quit -- Sinkers at the funeral -- Race feud in the beanery -- Sinkers hears about golf -- Sinkers goes raceboating -- "Don't let's vait," says Sinkers -- Sinkers at the birthday party -- Sinkers as master of ceremonies -- Sinkers needs a war map -- Sinkers at the races -- Sinkers works the Raines' law -- Sinkers hears of fighting -- Sinkers has a substitute -- Sinkers forms a trust -- Sinkers as a poet -- Sinkers has Typhoid Ammonia -- Sinkers hears about harmony -- Proverbs from the German -- Sinkers meditates Boxiana -- Sinkers saw the feetball -- Mrs. Sinkers has the clocks -- Talking machines and others -- Sinkers looking for a horse -- Glimpses back at youth -- Sinkers thinks of his mind -- Sinkers hears the legislation -- Sinkers hears of Marconi -- Sinkers on a hunting trip -- Sinkers sees baseball -- Over plate 16,903 of beef-and -- Sinkers gets the Finnegans -- Sinkers and the letters -- Sinkers as a critic -- Sinkers photographs Lena -- Sinkers turned sailorman.
PW: Je 28, '02.

G-310   Goodwin, Maud Wilder, 1856-1935. Claims and counterclaims / by Maud Wilder Goodwin. New York: Doubleday, Page & Company, 1905. 356 p.
PW: Ag 19, '05.
BLC: London: Doubleday, Page & Co.; New York printed, 1905.

G-311   ____ Four roads to paradise / by Maud Wilder Goodwin; with illustrations by Arthur I. Keller. New York: The Century Co., 1904. 347 p., incl. [5] leaves of plates, front.
PW: Ap 23, '04.

G-312   ____ Sir Christopher: a romance of a Maryland manor in 1644 / by Maud Wilder Goodwin; illustrated by Howard Pyle, and other artists. Boston: Little, Brown and Company, 1901. 411 p., front., [5] leaves of plates, music. [Also ill. by James E. McBurney, S. M. Palmer and S. M. Arthurs.]
PW: Ap 27, '01.
BLC: London: Ward, Lock & Co., 1904.

G-313   ____ Veronica Playfair / by Maud Wilder Goodwin . . . ; illustrated by Lester Ralph. Boston: Little, Brown and Company, 1909. 319 p., col. front., [3] leaves of col. plates.
LC: S 24, '09.
BLC: London: Frederick Warne & Co.; Boston, U. S. A. [printed, 1912].

G-314   Goodwin, Ralph A. The Stoenberg affair / by Ralph A. Goodwin; illustrated by H. Richard Boehm. New York: Sully and Kleinteich, 1913. 306 p., front., [5] leaves of plates (some col.).

Goodwin, Sara Byrne. Reconciled. In *Club stories (1915), C-502.*

G-315   Goodwin, Wilder, 1887-1955. The up grade / by Wilder Goodwin; with illustrations by Charles Grunwald. Boston: Little, Brown and Company, 1910. 321 p., front., [3] leaves of plates.
LC: Ja 11, '10.

G-316   Goold, Marshall N. (Marshall Newton), 1881-1935. The ship of destiny / by Marshall N. Goold. Boston; New York: Houghton Mifflin Company, 1924. (Cambridge: The Riverside Press). 304 p.
LC: O 20, '24.

G-317   The Goose Creek Church: a morbid tale. New York: Printed at the Sign of the Eagle, 1901. (New York: Pelham Press). 22 p.
Unexamined copy: bibliographic data from OCLC, #15628360.

G-318   Gorden, George. Twenty minute tales: a few short stories / by George Gorden. New York: The Welton Press, [c1901]. 112 p., photo. front.
Contents: Uncle Hiram's letters -- Lower 6 -- Jack's Marquita and Marquita's Jack -- Martha Stetson, of the chorus -- My Lady of the Gondola -- The priest of Marco -- From my notebook. [Contains poetry.]

G-319   Gordon, Anne Hamilton. The awakening / by Anne Hamilton Gordon . . . [Philadelphia: Marine Printing Bureau], 1914. 58 p. Designed end papers.   **NDD**

G-320   Gordon, Armistead C. (Armistead Churchill), 1855-1931. The gift of the morning star: a story of Sherando / by Armistead C. Gordon; frontispiece by George Senseney. New York; London: Funk & Wagnalls Company, 1905. 373 p., front.
PW: Jl 1, '05.

G-321   ____ Maje: a love story / by Armistead C. Gordon. New York: Charles Scribner's Sons, 1914. 119 p., col. front., [4] leaves of plates.
PW: Mr 7, '14.

G-322   ____ Ommirandy: plantation life at Kingsmill / by Armistead C. Gordon; illustrated by Walter Biggs. New York: Charles Scribner's Sons, 1917. 295 p., front., [15] leaves of plates.
Contents: Ommirandy -- The Shunway -- The silent infare -- Baytop -- The king's harnt -- The cockatrice den -- Mr. Bolster -- Pharzy.
LC: O 17, '17.

G-323   ____ Robin Aroon: a comedy of manners / by Armistead C. Gordon. New York; Washington: The Neale Publishing Company, 1908. 222 p.
PW: O 17, '08.

____ The silent infare. In *The best short stories of 1916 and the yearbook of the American short story (1917), B-561.*

G-324   Gordon, Carol, b. 1871, *pseud.* Inspiration: a story of today / by Carol Gordon [pseud.]. New York: G. W. Dillingham Company, [c1914]. 317 p., col. front.
PW: Ag 8, '14.

G-325   Gordon, Grant. Angelward / by Grant Gordon. New York: Broadway Publishing Co., [c1907]. 391 p., front., [1] leaf of plates. [Ill. by Wm. L. Hudson.]   **DLC**

G-326   [Gordon, Harry Morris]. The cho-fur: is a true automobile love story where the chauffeur gets engaged to his own sister and eventually marries her . . . New York: Harry Morris Gordon, [c1907]. 430 p., front., [5] leaves of plates.

G-327   Gordon, Helen Van-Anderson, b.1859. Carrol's conversion; a story of life by Helen Van-Anderson

. . . New York City: The New York Magazine of
Mysteries, [c1904]. 342 p.   **ORU**

G-328   Gordon, Hugh. The blind road / by Hugh Gordon.
New York: Moffat, Yard and Company, 1912.
285 p., col. front. [Ill. by R. Ford Harper.]
LC: Ap 5, '12.
PW: Ap 13, '12.

G-329   Gordon, Irwin Leslie, 1888-1954. What Allah wills:
a romance of the purple sunset / by Irwin Leslie
Gordon; illustrated by Modest Stein. Boston: The
Page Company, 1917. 395 p., col. front., [3] leaves
of plates.

Gordon, John, pseud. See **Munson, Gorham Bert,
1896-1969.**

G-330   Gordon, Julien, d. 1920, *pseud.* Mrs. Clyde: the
story of a social career / by Julien Gordon [pseud.].
New York: D. Appleton and Company, 1901. 362,
[1] p.
PW: F 2, '01.
BLC: London: Methuen & Co., 1902.

G-331   ____ The wage of character: a social study / by
Julien Gordon [pseud.]. New York: D. Appleton
and Company, 1901. 272 p., front. (port.).
LC: S 28, '01.

G-332   ____ World's people / by Julien Gordon [pseud.]
(Mrs. Van Rensselaer Cruger). New York: J. F.
Taylor & Company, 1902. 352 p.
Contents: Lady Star's apotheosis -- Escapade -- In palace gardens --
Underbrush -- At the villa -- Moonlight -- The black swan --
Redemption -- A lost line -- Why I remained a bachelor -- A Latin
solution -- A modern daughter -- A modern mother.
BLC: London: Methuen & Co., 1903.

G-333   Gordon, Leslie Howard. The house of night / by
Leslie Howard Gordon. Boston: Small, Maynard &
Company, [c1921]. 302 p.
LC: Je 4, '21.
BLC: London: Hodder & Stoughton, [1921].

G-334   Gordon, Nathaniel. Stella: a sketch / by Nathaniel
Gordon. [New York?: s. n.], c1905. 32 p., front.,
[8] leaves of plates. [Ill. by Henning Rydén.]
Another printing: [New York: s. n.], c1910. 56
[1] p., front., [8] leaves of plates. [Ill. by Henning
Rydén.]

G-335   Gordon, Terry Bockover. Oakford: the story of a
Virginia plantation / by Terry Bockover Gordon; with
an introduction by Joseph Tyler Butts. New York;
London: F. Tennyson Neely Co. . . . , [c1901].
176 p.

G-336   Gordon, William S. (William St. Clair), 1858-1924.
Recollections of the old quarter / by Wm. S. Gordon
. . . Lynchburg, Virginia: Published by Moose
Bros. Company, 1902. 142 p., photo. front., [12]
leaves of photo. plates.   **CLE**
Contents: I. Miss Judy an' de doctor -- II. Gab'el's epic -- III. Marse
Hubbut's frien' -- IV. Plantation rambles -- V. Uncle Jacob's lament
-- VI. Character sketches.
PW: Je 20, '03.

G-337   Gorman, Herbert Sherman, 1893-1954. Gold by gold
/ by Herbert S. Gorman. New York: Boni and
Liveright, 1925. 380 p.
LC: F 9, '25.
PW: F 7, '25.

Gore, Susan Frances Richards. See **Chenery, Susan,
pseud.**

G-338   Goss, Charles Frederic, 1852-1930. Little Saint
Sunshine / by Charles Frederic Goss; the illustrations
by Virginia Keep. Indianapolis; The Bobbs-Merrill
Company, [1902]. 153 p., col. front., [5] leaves of
col. plates.
BLC: London: B. F. Stevens & Brown, [1902].

G-339   ____ The loom of life / by Charles Frederic Goss.
Indianapolis: The Bowen-Merrill Company, [1902].
315 p.
BLC: London: B. F. Stevens & Co., [1902].

G-340   ____ That other hand upon the helm / by Charles
Frederic Goss. Cincinnati: Jennings and Graham;
New York: Eaton and Mains, [c1910]. 130 p.
LC: N 3, '10.

G-341   Goss, Herbert I. (Herbert Irvin), b. 1857. T.
Thorndyke, attorney-at-law: the romance of a young
lawyer / by Herbert I. Goss. Boston, Mass.: The C.
M. Clark Publishing Company, 1907. 496 p., front.
(port.), [9] leaves of plates (some port.).

G-342   Gould, Cora Smith. The nuisance / by Cora Smith
Gould . . . Chicago; New York: Privately printed by
Rogers & Company, 1919. 266 p., ill.   **DLC**
DLC copy lacks illustrations.

G-343   Gould, Elizabeth Lincoln, d. 1914. Cap'n Gid / by
Elizabeth Lincoln Gould; illustrated by Ralph L.
Boyer. [Philadelphia]: The Penn Publishing
Company, 1916. 244 p., incl. front, front.

G-344   ____ Grandma / by Elizabeth Lincoln Gould;
illustrated by Mary Pemberton Ginther.
[Philadelphia]: The Penn Publishing Company, 1911.
263 p., incl. front. (port.). Decorated end papers.

G-345   Gould, Elizabeth Porter, 1848-1906. A pioneer
doctor: a story of the seventies / by Elizabeth Porter
Gould. Boston: Richard G. Badger, 1904.
([Boston]: The Gorham Press). 270 p.

G-346   Gould, Katherine Clemmons. The crystal rood / by
Mrs. Howard Gould; with illustrations by Earl Stetson
Crawford. New York: John Lane Company;
Toronto: Bell & Cockburn, 1924. 306 p., col.
front., [3] leaves of plates.
PW: N 28, '14.

G-347   Gouraud, Aimée Crocker. Moon-madness: and
other fantasies / by Aimée Crocker Gouraud. New
York: Broadway Publishing Co., [c1910]. 91 p.,
photo. front. (port.).
Contents: Our Lady of Red Lips -- Paula loved pearls -- The dance
of the cobra -- The painted Mrs. Perry -- Kara the faithful -- Betty
and Buddha -- Mrs. Pepper in Paris -- Moon-madness.
LC: D 12, '10.

G-348　Gowen, Herbert H. (Herbert Henry), 1864-1960.
Hawaiian idylls of love and death / by . . . Herbert
H. Gowen . . . New York: Cochrane Publishing
Co., 1908. 109 p., photo. front.
Contents: The Poison Goddess of Molokai -- The story of the Kiha-
Pu -- The splintered paddle -- The slandered priest of Oahu -- Keala --
Pele declares for Kamehameha -- The City of Refuge -- Sweet
Leilehua -- The spouting Cave of Lanai -- Lono's last marytr --
Keour, a story of Kalawao.
LC: Ag 1, '08.
PW: Ag 29, '08.

G-349　Grace, Emma Marr. The hundredth sheep / by
Emma Marr Grace. [Boston: Printed by Advent
Christian Publication Society], 1918. 72 p.

G-350　Graetz, Anna. Pearl and Periwinkle / Anna Graetz.
Col. [i.e. Columbus], Ohio: L. B. C., 1917. 61 p.,
front., [1] leaf of plates.

G-351　Graeve, Oscar. The brown moth / by Oscar Graeve
. . . New York: Dodd, Mead and Company, 1921.
329 p.
PW: Ja 22, '21.

_____ It was May. In *Saturday Evening Post* (1919),
S-90.

G-352　_____ The keys of the city / by Oscar Graeve. New
York: The Century Co., 1916. 274 p.
PW: S 9, '16.

G-353　_____ Youth goes seeking / by Oscar Graeve. New
York: Dodd, Mead and Company, 1919. 297 p.
PW: S 16, '19.

G-354　Graham, Alan. Follow the little pictures! / by Alan
Graham. Boston: Little, Brown and Company, 1920.
298, [1] p.　　　　　　　　　　　　　　**NYG**
PW: Je 26, '20.
BLC: Edinburgh; London: W. Blackwood & Sons,
1920.

Graham, Dorothy Patricia. The guerdon of charity.
In *The rejected apostle* (1924), **R-164.**

G-355　Graham, Douglas. Mildred McElroy, or, A tale of
stenographic life / by Douglas Graham. Philadelphia:
Thomas MacTaggart, [c1903]. 240 p. Designed end
papers.

G-356　Graham, Effie. Aunt Liza's "praisin' gate" / by Effie
Graham; decorations by Fred J. Arting. Chicago: A.
C. McClurg & Co., 1916. 196 p.

G-357　_____ The "Passin'-on" party / by Effie Graham;
with illustrations by Dorothy Dulin. Chicago: A. C.
McClurg & Co., 1912. 183 p., front., [9] leaves of
plates.

G-358　Graham, Hugh F. (Hugh Finlay), b. 1865. The
Acadian exile / by Hugh F. Graham. Boston:
Richard G. Badger, [c1919]. ([Boston]: The Gorham
Press). 154 p.　　　　　　　　　　　　　**LWA**
LC: Jl 25, '19.
PW: Jl 12, '19.

G-359　Graham, James Chandler, b. 1868. It happened at
Andover: well most of it did, anyway / by James
Chandler Graham. Boston; New York: Houghton
Mifflin Company, 1920. (Cambridge: The Riverside
Press). 270 p., col. front.
Contents: The unappreciated -- The transformation -- The ringer -- A
new boy -- The infirmary -- The foreign born -- Fish -- A Napoleon
of finance -- The sport -- Parents -- The spy -- The landlady -- An
affair du coeur -- A relation -- The evolution of a star -- The manager
-- Taking a chance -- The mark -- The vamp.

Graham, John, pseud. See **Phillips, David Graham,
1867-1911.**

G-360　Graham, John Ellsworth, Mrs. The Toltec savior: a
historical romance of ancient Mexico / by Mrs. John
Ellsworth Graham. New York: G. W. Dillingham
Company, [c1901]. 298 p., front.
LC: Mr 21, '01.

G-361　Graham, Julia Frances. Emily Roe of Baltimore / by
Julia Frances Graham. Saint Louis: Fred T. Bordon,
1911. 403 p., incl. front. (port.). Designed end
papers.　　　　　　　　　　　　　　　　**DLC**
First edition statement with different publisher also
appears on t. p.: First Edition, February 15, 1911,
M. A. Donohue & Co., Chicago.

G-362　Graham, Margaret Collier, 1850-1910. The wizard's
daughter: and other stories / by Margaret Collier
Graham. Boston; New York: Houghton, Mifflin and
Company, 1905. (Cambridge: The Riverside Press).
230, [2] p.
Contents: The wizard's daughter -- Marg'et Ann -- At the foot of the
trail -- Lib -- For value received -- The face of the poor.

G-363　Graham, Oscar. A prince of his race: a college-bred
Indian romance / by Oscar Graham. St. Paul, Kan.:
W. W. Graves, 1913. 175 p., [2] leaves of plates (1
port.).
LC: Ag 4, '13.

Graham, Sarah Melissa Cary Downing. See
Graham, John Ellsworth, Mrs.

G-364　Grainger, Boyne, b. 1882. The hussy / by Boine [sic]
Grainger. New York: Boni and Liveright, 1924.
300 p.
LC: Mr 7, '24.
PW: Mr 1, '24.

G-365　Granger, Henry Francis, b. 1868. The gray gull / by
Henry Francis Granger. Garden City, N. Y.:
Garden City Publishing Company, 1924. 119 p.
Unexamined copy: bibliographic data from OCLC,
#20943164.
[Famous authors series, no. 48.]
LC: Ap 2, '24.

Granich, Irving, 1894-1967. See **Gold, Michael,
pseud.**

Grant, Douglas, pseud. See **Ostrander, Isabel
Egenton, 1883-1924.**

Grant, Ethel Watts Mumford, 1878-1940. See
Mumford, Ethel Watts.

G-366　Grant, J. George T. (Jack George Thomas), b. 1883.
The sins of-- / by J. George T. Grant. Philadelphia:
Dorrance & Company, [c1924]. 184 p.
LC: Mr 26, '24.

G-367　Grant, John Wesley, b. 1850. Out of the darkness;
or, Diabolism and destiny / by J. W. Grant . . .
Nashville, Tenn.: National Baptist Publishing Board,
1909. 316 p.　　　　　　　　　　　　　　**CSU**
LC: Je 2, '09.

　　　Grant, Margaret, pseud. See **Coryell, John Russell,
1851-1924.**

G-368　Grant, Mary Geary. Invisible wings / by Mary Geary
Grant. New York: Moffat, Yard & Company,
[c1923]. 269 p.　　　　　　　　　　　　　　**DLC**
LC: Jl 26, '23.
PW: Ag 11, '23.
BLC: .London: Stanley Paul & Co., [1924].

　　　Grant, Robert, 1852-1940. Against his judgment. In
Short story classics (1905), S-466.

G-369　_____ The bishop's granddaughter / by Robert Grant.
New York: Charles Scribner's Sons, 1925. 298 p.
LC: Mr 7, '25.
PW: Mr 7, '25.

G-370　_____ The Chippendales / by Robert Grant. New
York: Charles Scribner's Sons, 1909. 602 p.
PW: Ap 10, '09.
BLC: London: Stanley Paul & Co.; New York
printed, [1909].

G-371　_____ The convictions of a grandfather / by Robert
Grant. New York: Charles Scribner's Sons, 1912.
289 p.

G-372　_____ The high priestess / by Robert Grant. New
York: Charles Scribner's Sons, 1915. 530 p.
PW: S 11, '15.
BLC: Toronto: Copp Clark Co.; printed in U. S.
A., 1915.

G-373　_____ The law-breakers: and other stories / by
Robert Grant. New York: Charles Scribner's Sons,
1906. 277 p.
Contents: The law-breakers -- Against his judgment -- St. George
and the dragon -- The romance of a soul -- An exchange of courtesies
-- Across the way -- A surrender.
PW: My 5, '06.

G-374　_____ The orchid / by Robert Grant; illustrated by
Alonzo Kimball. New York: Charles Scribner's
Sons, 1905. 229 p., col. front., [3] leaves of col.
plates.
PW: Ap 15, '05.

　　　_____ The romance of a soul. See **Freeman, Mary
Eleanor Wilkins, 1852-1930.** *The home-coming of
Jessica* (1901), F-396.

　　　_____ A surrender. In *A house party* (1901), H-903.

G-375　_____ The undercurrent / by Robert Grant; with

illustrations by F. C. Yohn. New York: Charles
Scribner's Sons, 1904. 480 p., front., [10] leaves of
plates.
BLC: London: Hutchinson & Co., 1904.

　　　Granville-Barker, Helen Manchester. See
Huntington, Helen, pseud.

G-376　Grapho, *pseud.* A progressive preacher / by Grapho
[pseud.]. Chicago: The Goodspeed Press, 1917.
319 p.　　　　　　　　　　　　　　　　　　**IOG**

G-377　Gratacap, L. P. (Louis Pope), 1851-1917. Benjamin
the Jew / by L. P. Gratacap . . . New York:
Thomas Benton, 1913. 492 p., front., [5] leaves of
plates. [Ill. by A. Operti.]
LC: F 19, '14.

G-378　_____ The certainty of a future life in Mars: being
the posthumous papers of Bradford Torrey Dodd /
edited by L. P. Gratacap. New York; Paris;
Chicago; Washington: Brentano's, 1903. 266 p.
PW: Jl 4, '03.
Another printing: [New York]: Irving Press, 1903.
Unexamined copy: bibliographic data from OCLC,
#20916616.

G-379　_____ The end: how the great war was stopped: a
novelistic vagary / by L. P. Gratacap. New York:
Thomas Benton, 1917. 274 p.
LC: Mr 31, '17.

G-380　_____ The evacuation of England: the twist in the
Gulf Stream / by L. P. Gratacap . . . New York:
Brentano's, 1908. 321 p.　　　　　　　　　**KSU**
LC: Je 13, '08.

G-381　_____ The mayor of New York: a romance of days
to come / by L. P. Gratacap . . . New York: G. W.
Dillingham Company, [c1910]. 471 p., incl. front.,
[3] leaves of plates. [Ill. by Joseph Cummings
Chase.]
LC: N 25, '10.
PW: N 19, '10.

G-382　_____ The new northland / by L. P. Gratacap; with 16
designs by Albert Operti. New York: Thomas
Benton, 1915. 391 p., front., [15] leaves of
plates.　　　Added t. p.: Krocker Land: a romance of
discovery / by Alfred Erickson, Prof. Hlmath
Bjornsen, Antoine Goritz, Spruce Hopkins; the
narrative by Alfred Erickson; edited by Azaziel Link.

G-383　_____ A woman of the ice age / by L. P. Gratacap
. . . New York: Brentano's, 1906. 230 p.　　**NYP**
PW: Jl 7, '06.

G-384　Grattan, Francis W. (Francis William), b. 1854.
With those that were: stories of two wars / by
Francis W. Grattan; illustrated by Wm. L. Hudson.
New York: Broadway Publishing Co., [c1909].
318 p., front., [10] leaves of plates.　　**OSU, VMI**
Contents: Cleeter -- The Beaumann Home guards -- Lost sheep --
Mary O'Reilly -- The broken vow -- Hers was but a sister's love --
James Seawood -- Otto Brown -- Two stories as related by Bill Davis
-- Bears -- "On the Banks of the Shrewsbury" -- Introduction to the
deserter -- Retribution -- Sergt. White's story -- Author's note --

Early love -- Peconic insurrection -- The hunter's tale -- The British soldier's revenge.

Graves, Charlotte F., b. 1846. <u>See</u> **Jemimy, Aunt, pseud.**

G-385   Graves, Etta Merrick. The castle builder / by Etta Merrick Graves . . . Boston: Sherman, French & Company, 1916. 241 p.   **MNL**
PW: D 9, '16.

G-386   Graves, John Temple, 1892-1961. The shaft in the sky / by John Temple Graves, Jr. New York: George H. Doran Company, [c1923]. 295 p.
LC: Mr 5, '23.
PW: F 24, '23.

G-387   ____ Two bubbles / by John Temple Graves, Jr. Boston, Mass.: The Stratford Company, 1920. 90 p.
PW: Ap 3, '20.

Graves, Richard S. The flight of fifty thousand, a tale of San Francisco. <u>In</u> *Golden stories* **(1909), G-285.**

G-388   Gray, Carl, 1860-1931, *pseud.* A plaything of the gods / by Carl Gray [pseud.]. Boston: Sherman, French & Company, 1912. 260 p., front., [4] leaves of plates.
Cover title: *A plaything of the gods: a tale of old California.*
PW: Jl 6, '12.

Gray, Charles Wright, ed. <u>See</u> *"DAWGS!"* **(1925), D-184.**

____ His father's son. <u>In</u> *The Sporting spirit* **(1925), S-771.**

G-389   Gray, Charlotte E. (Charlotte Elvira), 1873-1926. As His mother saw Him / by Charlotte E. Gray. New York: The Meridian Press, [c1917]. 254 p.   **DLC**

G-390   ____ The inn by the sea / by Charlotte E. Gray. Cincinnati: Jennings and Graham; New York: Eaton and Mains, [c1914]. 302 p.   On spine: The Abingdon Press.
LC: F 20, '14.

G-391   ____ The Jericho road / by Charlotte E Gray . . . Cincinnati: Jennings and Graham; New York: Eaton and Mains, [c1912]. 357 p.
Unexamined copy: bibliographic data from NUC.
PW: N 16, '12.

G-392   ____ "Out of the mire" / by Charlotte E. Gray. Cincinnati: Jennings and Graham; New York: Eaton and Mains, [c1911]. 307 p.

G-393   Gray, David, b. 1870. The boomerang: a novel based on the play of the same name / by David Gray . . . ; illustrated by Norman Price. New York: The Century Co., 1918. 307 p., front., [6] leaves of plates.   **KLG**
LC: O 1, '18.
PW: O 5, '18.

____ Crowninshield's brush, a fox-hunting story. <u>In</u> *Golden stories* **(1909), G-285.**

G-394   ____ Ensign Russell / by David Gray . . . New York: The Century Co., 1912. 241 p., front.

G-395   ____ Gallops 2 / by David Gray. New York: The Century Co., 1903. 225 p., front.
Contents: Her first horse show -- Isabella -- Crowinshield's brush -- Ting-a-ling -- The Braybrooke baby's godmother -- The echo hunt -- The Reggie Livingstones' country life.

G-396   ____ Mr. Carteret and others / by David Gray. New York: The Century Co., 1910. 218 p., incl. [7] leaves of plates, front.
Contents: Mr. Carteret and his fellow Americans abroad -- How Mr. Carteret proposed -- Mr. Carteret's adventure with a locket -- The case of the Evanstons -- The matter of a mashie -- The medal of honor story.
LC: Ap 1, '10.
PW: Mr 26, '10.

G-397   ____ Smith: a novel based on the play by W. Somerset Maugham / by David Gray. New York: Duffield & Company, 1911. 307 p., front., [3] leaves of plates.
LC: S 14, '11.

G-398   Gray, Elizabeth H. Old ninety-nine's cave / by Elizabeth H. Gray. Boston, Mass.: The C. M. Clark Publishing Co., 1909. 314 p.
LC: Mr 18, '09.
PW: Je 12, '09.

G-399   Gray, George Arthur. Leatherstocking / by George Arthur Gray; suggested by J. Fenimore Cooper's Leatherstocking tales; illustrated with scenes from the photoplay, a Pathé serial. New York: Grosset and Dunlap, [c1924]. 303 p., photo. front., [7] leaves of photo. plates.   **CSL**
LC: Je 17, '24.

G-400   Gray, Isabel McReynolds. Florizel / by Isabel McReynolds Gray. Los Angeles, Calif.: The author, 1910. 139 p., [4] leaves of plates. Designed end papers.
". . . by Isabel McReynolds Gray, done into type for her by the Los Angeles Printing Company and published by her at Los Angeles in the month of March Anno Domini MCMX."

G-401   Gray, J. J. Reclaimed, or, The mountain castle mystery: an international romance / by J. J. Gray. New York: Broadway Publishing Co., [c1907]. 217 p.   **DLC**

G-402   Gray, James, b. 1899. The penciled frown / by James Gray. New York: Charles Scribner's Sons, 1925. 297 p.
PW: S 5, '25.

G-403   Gray, John Thompson. A Kentucky chronicle / by John Thompson Gray. New York; Washington: The Neale Publishing Company, 1906. 590 p.   **DAY**
LC: S 24, '06.

G-404 Gray, Joslyn. Fireweed / by Joslyn Gray. New York: Charles Scribner's Sons, 1920. 331 p.
LC: Mr 25, '20.
PW: Mr 20, '20.

G-405 Gray, Mary Agatha, b. 1868. Derfel the strong: a romance of the days of King Henry VIII / by Mary Agatha Gray . . . New York; Cincinnati; Chicago: Benziger Brothers, 1914. 347 p.
BLC: London: R. & T. Washbourne, 1914.

G-406 _____ "Like unto a merchant" / by Mary Agatha Gray. New York; Cincinnati; Chicago: Benziger Brothers, 1915. 277 p.
LC: Ap 7, '15.
PW: Ap 17, '15.

G-407 _____ The tempest of the heart / by Mary Agatha Gray . . . New York; Cincinnati [etc.]: Benziger Brothers, 1912. 417 p., incl. front., plates.
Unexamined copy: bibliographic data from NUC.
PW: D 16, '11.

G-408 _____ The towers of St. Nicholas: a story of the days of "good Queen Bess" / by Mary Agatha Gray . . . New York: P. J. Kenedy & Sons, [c1913]. 237 p.
LC: Ja 15, '14.
PW: N 29, '13.
BLC: London: Burns & Oates, [1914].

G-409 _____ The turn of the tide: a story of humble life by the sea / by Mary Agatha Gray. New York; Cincinnati; Chicago: Benziger Brothers, 1910. 387 p.
LC: O 10, '10.
PW: O 29, '10.

G-410 Gray, Phoebe. The golden lamp / by Phoebe Gray . . . ; frontispiece by Blanche Greer. Boston: Small, Maynard & Company, [c1916]. 409 p., col. front. **DLC**
PW: F 19, '16.
BLC: London: Jarrolds, [1917].

G-411 _____ Little Sir Galahad / by Phoebe Gray; illustrated by F. Liley Young. Boston: Small, Maynard & Company, [c1914]. 376 p., front., [4] leaves of plates.
LC: D 8, '14.
BLC: London: S. Paul & Co., [1915].

G-412 Gray, William Benson. The volunteer organist: a story founded on the famous temperance play of the same name / by William B. Gray; illustrated. New York: J. S. Ogilvie Publishing Company, [c1902]. 192 p., incl. photo. front., [3] leaves of photo. plates.
PW: Mr 28, '03.
BLC: New York: W. B. Gray & Co., [1902].

G-413 Graydon, J. Farrer. The German bracelet / by J. Farrer Graydon. New York; Washington: The Neale Publishing Company, 1908. 310 p. **BGU**

G-414 Graye, Dawn, *pseud.* A story within a story / by Dawn Graye [pseud.]. Washington: The Neale Publishing Company, 1903. 156 p. **DLC**

G-415 Grayson, David, 1870-1946, *pseud.* Adventures in contentment / by David Grayson [pseud.]; illustrated by Thomas Fogarty. New York: Doubleday, Page & Company, 1907. 249, [1] p., front., ill.
LC: D 3, '07.
PW: D 14, '07.
BLC: London: Doubleday, Page & Co.; New York printed, 1907.

G-416 _____ Adventures in friendship / by David Grayson [pseud.] . . . ; illustrated by Thomas Fogarty. Garden City, New York: Doubleday, Page & Company, 1910. 232 p., col. front., [4] leaves of plates (some col.), ill. Illustrated end papers. **CWR**
LC: N 5, '10.
PW: N 19, '10.
BLC: London: Hodder & Stoughton; New York printed, 1910.

G-417 _____ Adventures in understanding / by David Grayson [pseud.]; illustrated by Thomas Fogarty. Garden City, N. Y.: Doubleday, Page & Company, 1925. 273 p., incl. front. Illustrated end papers.
LC: O 16, '25.
PW: O 3, '25.
BLC: London: William Heinemann; U. S. A. printed, 1925; Also: London: Hodder & Stoughton, [1925].

G-418 _____ The friendly road: new adventures in contentment / by David Grayson [pseud.]; illustrated by Thomas Fogarty. Garden City, N. Y.: Doubleday, Page & Company, 1913. 342 p., col. front., [7] leaves of plates. Illustrated end papers.
LC: O 27, '13.
PW: N 8, '13.
BLC: London: Andrew Melrose; Garden City, N. Y. [printed], 1913.

G-419 _____ Great possessions: a new series of adventures / by David Grayson [pseud.]; illustrated by Thomas Fogarty. Garden City, New York: Doubleday, Page & Company, 1917. 208 p., col. front., [8] leaves of col. plates. Illustrated end papers.
LC: O 18, '17.
PW: O 13, '17.
BLC: London: Curtis Brown; Garden City, N. Y., printed, 1917; Also: London: Hodder & Stoughton, [1918].

G-420 _____ Hempfield: a novel / by David Grayson [pseud.]; illustrated by Thomas Fogarty. Garden City, N. Y.: Doubleday, Page & Company, 1915. 335 p., col. front., [8] leaves of plates, ill. Illustrated end papers.
LC: O 18, '15.
PW: O 30, '15.
BLC: London: Hodder & Stoughton; Garden City, N. Y. printed, [1916].

G-421 Grayson, Justine. A tenderfoot abroad / by Justine Grayson. Boston: W. A. Butterfield, 1907. 98, [2] p.
LC: D 26, '07.

G-422 The Great modern American stories: an anthology /

compiled and edited with an introduction by William Dean Howells. New York: Boni and Liveright, 1920. 432 p. **BLC**

(The great modern short stories series.)

Contents: A reminiscent introduction / William Dean Howells -- My double; and how he undid me / Edward Everett Hale -- Circumstance / Harriet Prescott Spofford -- The celebrated jumping frog of Calaveras County / Mark Twain -- A passionate pilgrim / Henry James -- Mlle. Olympe Zabriski / T. B. Aldrich -- A prodigal in Tahiti / Charles Warren Stoddard -- The outcasts of Poker Flat / Francis Bret Harte -- The Christmas wreck / Frank Stockton -- The mission of Jane / Edith Wharton -- The courting of Sister Wisby / Sarah Orne Jewett -- The revolt of mother / Mary E. Wilkins Freeman -- Told in the poorhouse / Alice Brown -- An occurrence at Owl Creek bridge / Ambrose Bierce -- The return of a private / Hamlin Garland -- Striking an average / Henry B. Fuller -- Effie Wittlesy / George Ade -- The lost Phoebe / Theodore Dreiser -- A failure / Edith Wyatt -- The yellow wall paper / Charlotte Perkins Stetson Gilman -- The little room / Madelene Yale Wynn -- Aunt Sanna Terry / Landon R. Dashiell -- The lotus eaters / Virginia Tracy

-- Jean-Ah Poquelin / G. W. Cable -- Brer Rabbit, Brer Fox, and the Tar Baby / Joel Chandler Harris.
LC: Jl 3, '20.

G-423   Great short stories / edited by William Patten; a new collection of famous examples from the literatures of France, England and America . . . New York: P. F. Collier & Son, [c1909]. 3 v. **OCP**

Contents: Vol I: The murders in the Rue Morgue / Edgar Allan Poe -- The mystery of Marie Roget / Edgar Allan Poe -- The purloined letter / Edgar Allan Poe -- The sign of the four / Sir Arthur Conan Doyle -- A scandal in Bohemia / Sir Arthur Conan Doyle -- The doctor, his wife and the clock / Anna Katharine Green -- The rajah's diamond / Robert Louis Stevenson -- The mystery of the steel disk / Broughton Brandenburg -- The chronicles of Addington Peace / B. Fletcher Robinson. Vol. II: La morte amoreuse / Theophile Gautier -- The red room / H. G. Wells -- The phantom 'rickshaw / Rudyard Kipling -- The roll-call of the reef / A. T. Quiller-Couch -- The house and the brain / Lord Edward Bulwer-Lytton -- The dream-woman / Wilkie Collins -- Green branches / Fiona Macleod -- A bewitched ship / W. Clark Russell -- The signal-man / Charles Dickens -- The four-fifteen express / Amelia B. Edwards -- Our last walk / Hugh Conway -- Thrawn Janet / Robert Louis Stevenson -- A Christmas carol / Charles Dickens -- The spectre bridegroom / Washington Irving -- The mysterious sketch / Erckmann-Chatrian -- Mr. Higginbotham's catastrophe / Nathaniel Hawthorne -- Wandering Willie's tale / Sir Walter Scott. Vol. III: The attack on the mill / Emile Zola -- The venus of Ilie / Prosper Merimee -- The pavilion on the links / Robert Louis Stevenson -- The prisoners / Guy de Maupassant -- The siege of Berlin / Alphonse Daudet -- The man who would be king / Rudyard Kipling -- The black pearl / Victorien Sardou -- The prisoner of Assiout / Grant Allen -- The smugglers of the clone / S. R. Crockett -- The mysterious mansion / Honore de Balzac -- A terribly strange bed / Wilkie Collins -- The capture of Bill Sikes / Charles Dickens -- The postmistress of Laurel Run / Bret Harte -- The captain's vices / Francois Coppee -- Rappaccini's daughter / Nathaniel Hawthorne -- Zodomirsky's duel / Alexandre Dumas -- The courting of T'nowhead's bell / James Matthew Barrie -- The Rynard Gold Reef Company, Ltd. / Sir Walter Besant.

G-424   Greatest short stories. New York: P. F. Collier & Son, [c1915]. 8 vols. **EEM**

Contents (apparent first book appearances only): Vol II.: Thomas Jefferson Brown / James Oliver Curwood. Vol. III. Out of the storm / Mulloy Finnegan. Vol. IV. The Silver Lake panic / Raymond S. Spears -- The tall one and the wee one / Ruth Sawyer -- Captain Pike / Theodore Goodridge Roberts -- Everett, Commissioner of Justice / Gordon McCreagh -- The polite horse / Henry Beach Needham -- The charge / W. Douglas Newton -- The wedding Bob Dean ran / Edward Boltwood -- His first pentinent / James Oliver Curwood -- Unseen hands / Helen Cooper Douglas -- The churching of Bankson / Samuel Scoville, Jr.
PW: O 9, '15.

Greaves, Richard, pseud. See **McCutcheon, George Barr, 1866-1928.**

G-425   Greddington, Frances. Fetters of freedom / by Frances Greddington. Boston: Small, Maynard & Co., [c1924]. 383 p., col. front.

G-426   Green, Anna Katharine, 1846-1935. The amethyst box / by Anna Katharine Green. Indianapolis: The Bobbs-Merrill Company, [1905]. 151 p., front.
On cover: The Pocket Books.
PW: Ap 29, '05.
BLC: London: Chatto & Windus, 1905.

G-427   _____ The chief legatee / by Anna Katharine Green; illustrated in water-colors by Frank T. Merrill. New York; London: The Authors and Newspapers Association, 1906. 319 p., col. front., [4] leaves of col. plates.
LC: D 3, '06.
PW: Mr 23, '07.
BLC: Toronto: McLeod & Allen; New York; London: The Authors and Newspapers Association, [1907].

G-428   _____ Dark hollow / by Anna Katharine Green; with illustrations by Thomas Fogarty. New York: Dodd, Mead & Company, 1914. 381 p., front., [3] leaves of plates.
LC: F 4, '14.
PW: F 7, '14.
BLC: London: Eveleigh Nash, 1914.

G-429   _____ The filigree ball: being a full and true account of the solution of the mystery concerning the Jeffrey-Moore affair / by Anna Katharine Green; illustrated by C. M. Relyea. Indianapolis: The Bobbs-Merrill Company, [1903]. 418 p., front.
PW: Mr 28, '03.
BLC: London: T. Fisher Unwin, 1904.

G-430   _____ The golden slipper: and other problems for Violet Strange / by Anna Katharine Green (Mrs. Charles Rohlfs); frontispiece by A. I. Keller. New York; London: G. P. Putnam's Sons, 1915. ([New York]: The Knickerbocker Press). 425 p., col. front.
Contents: The golden slipper -- The second bullet -- The intangible clew -- The grotto spectre -- The dreaming lady -- The house of clocks -- The doctor, his wife, and the clock -- Missing: page thirteen -- Violet's own.
LC: N 9, '15.
PW: N 27, '15.

G-431   _____ The house in the mist / by Anna Katharine Green. Indianapolis: The Bobbs-Merrill Company, [1905]. 149 p., front.
On cover: The Pocket Books.
Contents: The house in the mist -- The ruby and the caldron.
PW: My 13, '05.

G-432   _____ The house of the whispering pines / by Anna Katharine Green. New York; London: G. P. Putnam's Sons, 1910. ([New York]: The Knickerbocker Press). 425 p., col. front.
LC: Mr 9, '10.
PW: Ap 2, '10.
BLC: London: Eveleigh Nash, 1910.

G-433   _____ Initials only / by Anna Katharine Green; frontispiece in color by Arthur I. Keller. New York: Dodd, Mead & Company, 1911. 356 p., col. front.
PW: O 7, '11.
BLC: London: Eveleigh Nash, 1912.

G-434   _____ The mayor's wife / by Anna Katharine Green; with illustrations by Alice Barber Stephens. Indianaolis: The Bobbs-Merrill Company, [1907]. 389 p., front., [6] leaves of plates.
LC: My 6, '07.
PW: My 11, '07.

G-435   _____ The millionaire baby / by Anna Katharine Green; with illustrations by Arthur I. Keller. Indianapolis: The Bobbs-Merrill Company, [1905]. 358 p., front., [5] leaves of plates.
PW: Ja 21, '05.
BLC: London: Chatto & Windus, 1905.

G-436   _____ The mystery of the hasty arrow / by Anna Katharine Green; with illustrations by H. R. Ballinger. New York: Dodd, Mead and Company, 1917. 432 p., front., [7] leaves of plates, maps.
LC: N 15, '17.
PW: N 10, '17.

G-437   _____ One of my sons / by Anna Katharine Green (Mrs. Charles Rohlfs) . . . New York; London: G. P. Putnam's Sons, 1901. (New York: The Knickerbocker Press). 366 p., front., [5] leaves of plates, ill. [Ill. by Louis Betts.]
PW: N 23, '01.
BLC: London: Ward, Lock & Co., 1904.

G-438   _____ The step on the stair / by Anna Katherine Green . . . New York: Dodd, Mead and Company, 1923. 380 p., front. (plan).
PW: Ja 13, '23.
BLC: London: John Lane, 1923.

G-439   _____ Three thousand dollars / by Anna Katharine Green. Boston: Richard G. Badger, 1910. ([Boston]: The Gorham Press). 157 p., front., [7] leaves of plates.
LC: N 27, '09.
PW: O 30, '09.

G-440   _____ To the minute; Scarlet and black: two tales of life's perplexities / by Anna Katharine Green (Mrs. Charles Rohlfs). New York; London: G. P. Putnam's Sons, 1916. ([New York]: The Knickerbocker Press). 226 p., col. front. [Ill. by Edna L. Crompton.]
LC: O 13, '16.
PW: S 30, '16.

G-441   _____ The woman in the alcove / by Anna Katharine Green; with illustrations by Arthur I. Keller. Indianapolis: The Bobbs-Merrill Company, [1906]. 371, [1] p., front., [4] leaves of plates.
PW: My 5, '06.
BLC: London: Chatto & Windus, 1906.

G-442   Green, Fitzhugh, 1888-1942. ZR wins / by Fitzhugh Green. New York; London: D. Appleton and Company, 1924. 270, [1] p., front.
LC: Jl 21, '24.
PW: Jl 26, '24.

G-443   Green, Helen, b. 1882. At the actor's boarding house: and other stories / by Helen Green. New York: The Nevada Publishing Co., 1906. 380 p., [1] leaf of plates (port.).   These stories originally appeared in the New York Morning Telegraph.
Contents: The honeymoon of Sam and Caroline -- The disastrous bookmaking of red-cheeked Rudolph -- Emma, the slavey, makes good in vaudeville -- The doings of an amateur valet --Allen and Allen split, but come together again -- The unreality of realism -- The romance of the rearranged Paris -- The fickleness of Pugnose Grady's girl -- The fake eviction -- The rise and fall of Dooley's dog act -- Mr. De Shine's return -- The way of a music hall song bird -- Dopey Polly never reached the orchard -- Making a prince into a good sport -- The poker game in the Pullman smoker -- The troubles of two working girls -- When black Mose met his Waterloo -- The creating of a top line act -- The finish of Daffy the dip -- The code of the hills -- The political beginning of Solly McGee -- How the Soubrettes broke a lease -- The manager's new wife -- Mary had to have her Broadway -- Flatnose Ed takes his medicine -- The comedian's wives -- The Boston kid's last trip -- The rival landladies and the bridal party -- The Emperor's pipe -- Confession of a con man -- Pinafore and "The Duke" skin a corporation -- The lead dollar -- Mr. De Shine wins out -- Injun Billy's blonde -- New York Arabian nights -- Cap Brown's water treat -- The adventures of Clarence the messenger boy -- Topeka Thompson's educated dice -- In Habib's kitchen -- The love of one-arm Annie -- The way it goes on Broadway --Romance of an acrobat and a darning needle -- The further adventures of Clarence -- Mrs. Jimmy goes camping -- The weeping greaser's revenge -- The sultan's troupe -- The noodle's flat -- Out with the big top -- A woman of the hills -- The troubles of two working girls -- J. Wallace Barrington's troupe leave a board bill -- When the Thunder Mountain mail came in -- Old Peter -- Clancy, the Copper and the kid -- The fake hop fiends -- Roosevelt has a Christmas party -- Nat M. Wills and the "hairless mystery" -- Their first night in a sleeper.

G-444   _____ The maison de Shine: more stories of the actors' boarding house / by Helen Green. New York: B. W. Dodge & Company, 1908. 298 p.
Contents: A Christmas dinner -- The circus freaks come to board -- Gold eagle Charlie, Vaudeville's bad man -- A long-lost daughter comes to town -- An ex-husband saves the Emerys -- The scented letters -- The property man foils a suitor -- "The girl without booking" -- Mr. Mangle sidesteps trouble -- Fate finds Fido food -- The divorcees' party -- Two Salomes return to former ways -- The boarders go racing -- Mrs. Trippit gets back at Johnny -- The dancing Trippits again a team -- The landlady's benefit.

G-445   _____ Mr. Jackson / by Helen Green. New York: B. W. Dodge & Company, 1909. 299 p., front.
LC: O 16, '09.
PW: D 25, '09.

G-446   Greenberg, David S. (David Solon), b. 1887. A bunch of little thieves / by David S. Greenberg; with an introduction by . . . Frederick G. Bonser . . . ; illustrated by William Jackson Brownlow. New York: The Shakespeare Press, 1913. 336 p., front., [4] leaves of plates.

G-447   _____ Murder / by David S. Greenberg. New York: The Hour Publisher, 1916. 626 p.
LC: My 22, '16.

G-448   Greene, Anne Bosworth, 1877-1961. The lone winter / by Anne Bosworth Greene. New York; London: The Century Co., 1923. 379 p.

G-449   Greene, Frances Nimmo, 1850-1921. The devil to pay / by Frances Nimmo Greene. New York:

Charles Scribner's Sons, 1918. 285 p.
LC: Ap 30, '18.
PW: Ap 27, '18.

G-450 ____ Into the night: a story of New Orleans / by Frances Nimmo Greene; illustrated by C. F. Neagle. New York: Thomas Y. Crowell & Co., [1909]. 370 p., col. front., [3] leaves of col. plates. **MFM**
LC: S 11, '09.
PW: O 2, '09.
BLC: London: Methuen & Co., 1910.

G-451 ____ One clear call / by Frances Nimmo Greene; illustrated. New York: Charles Scribner's Sons, 1914. 329 p., front., [3] leaves of plates.
PW: O 17, '14.

G-452 ____ The right of the strongest / by Frances Nimmo Greene. New York: Charles Scribner's Sons, 1913. 401 p.
PW: Ap 19, '13.

G-453 ____ With spurs of gold: heroes of chivalry and their deeds / by Frances Nimmo Greene and Dolly Williams Kirk. Boston: Little, Brown and Company, 1905. 290 p., front., [5] leaves of plates.
PW: O 14, '05.

Greene, Frederick Stuart. The black pool. In *The Grim thirteen* (1917), **G-537.**

____ The bunker mouse. In *The best short stories of 1917 and the yearbook of the American short story* (1918), **B-562.**

____ The cat of the cane-brake. In *The best short stories of 1916 and the yearbook of the American short story* (1917), **B-561.**

____, ed. See *The Grim thirteen* (1917), **G-537.**

____ "Molly McGuire, fourteen." In *A book of short stories* (1918), **B-735.**

G-454 Greene, Harry Irving, b. 1868. Barbara of the snows / by Harry Irving Greene . . . ; illustrated by Harvey T. Dunn. New York: Moffat, Yard and Company, 1911. 358 p., col. front., [3] leaves of plates. **DLC**
LC: Mr 29, '11.
PW: Ap 1, '11.

G-455 ____ Yozondè of the wilderness / by Harry Irving Greene. New York: Desmond FitzGerald, Inc., [c1910]. 167 p., col. front. [Ill. by The Kinneys.]
LC: S 19, '10.

G-456 Greene, Homer, b. 1853. The Guardsmen / by Homer Greene. Philadelphia: George W. Jacobs & Company, [c1919]. 328 p., front., [2] leaves of plates.
LC: O 20, '19.

G-457 ____ Handicapped: the story of a white-haired boy / by Homer Greene; with illustrations. Boston; New York: Houghton Mifflin Company, 1914.

(Cambridge: The Riverside Press). 265, [1] p., front., [3] leaves of plates. [Ill. by B. J. Rosenmeyer.] **DLC**

G-458 ____ The unhallowed harvest / by Homer Greene. Philadelphia: George W. Jacobs & Company, [1917]. 390 p.
LC: Mr 15, '17.
PW: Mr 17, '17.

G-459 Greene, L. (Louis). The shepherd of the East / by L. Greene. Boston: The Roxburgh Publishing Company, Inc., [c1923]. 102 p. **DLC**

G-460 Greene, Mary E. (Mary Ellen), b. 1848. The door where the wrong lay / by Mary E. Greene. Boston, Mass.: The C. M. Clark Publishing Company, 1909. 317 p.
LC: Ap 26, '09.
PW: Je 26, '09.

G-461 Greene, Sarah Pratt McLean, 1856-1935. Deacon Lysander / by Sarah Pratt McLean Greene. New York: The Baker & Taylor Co., [1904]. 223, [1] p., front., [3] leaves of plates. [Ill. by H. J. Peck.]
PW: O 8, '04.

G-462 ____ Everbreeze / by Sarah P. McLean Greene. New York; London: D. Appleton and Company, 1913. 310 p., front., [3] leaves of plates. [Ill. by Charles M. Relyea.]
PW: F 8, '13.

G-463 ____ Flood-tide / by Sarah P. McLean Greene . . . New York; London: Harper & Brothers, 1901. 350 p.
PW: O 5, '01.

G-464 ____ The long green road / by Sarah P. McLean Greene . . . ; with frontispiece by P. J. Monahan. New York: The Baker & Taylor Company, 1911. 410 p., front.
LC: N 1, '11.
PW: N 18, '11.

G-465 ____ Power Lot / by Sarah P. McLean Greene. New York: The Baker & Taylor Co., [1906]. 396 p., front., [4] leaves of plates. [Ill. by Alex O. Levy.]

G-466 ____ Winslow Plain / by Sarah P. McLean Greene. New York; London: Harper & Brothers, 1902. 290 p., front. (port.).
PW: N 1, '02.

G-467 Greenfield, Will H. (William Henry). Ring and diamond / by Will H. Greenfield. Athol, Mass.: The Cook Publishing Company, 1921. 366 p. **NYP**
LC: Ap 13, '21.

G-468 Greenleaf, Saul G. The three knaves / by Saul G. Greenleaf. New York: R. F. Fenno & Company, [c1912]. 338 p.
PW: O 26, '12.

G-469　Greenleaf, Sue. Liquid from the sun's rays / by Sue Greenleaf. New York: The Abbey Press, [c1901]. 305 p.　**GUA**
LC: D 1, '06.

G-470　Greenlee, Maccowan. The lure of the purple star / by Maccowan Greenlee. Washington, D. C.: MacDaniel Publishing Company, [c1912]. 298 p., photo. front.
LC: Jl 25, '12.

Greenslet, Mrs. Ella (Holst), b. 1873. See **Stoothoff, Ellenor, pseud.**

Greenwald, Tupper. Corputt. In *The best short stories of 1924 and the yearbook of the American short story* **(1925), B-569.**

G-471　Greer-Petrie, Cordia. Angeline of the hill country / by Cordia Greer-Petrie; with illustrations by Carle Michel Boog. New York: Thomas Y. Crowell Co., 1925. 181 p., front., ill.
PW: Mr 14, '25.

Gregg, Frances. Whose dog -- ? In *The best short stories of 1915 and the yearbook of the American short story* **(1916), B-560.**

G-472　Gregory, Jackson, 1882-1943. The bells of San Juan / by Jackson Gregory; illustrated by Frank Tenney Johnson. New York: Charles Scribner's Sons, 1919. 337 p., front., [3] leaves of plates.
LC: O 16, '19.

G-473　_____ Desert Valley: by Jackson Gregory . . . ; with frontispiece by Frank Tenney Johnson. New York: Charles Scribner's Sons, 1921. 318 p., front. **UUO**
LC: My 9, '21.
PW: Ap 23, '21.

G-474　_____ The everlasting whisper: a tale of the California wilderness / by Jackson Gregory. New York: Charles Scribner's Sons, 1922. 375 p., front.
LC: Ja 30, '22.
PW: F 4, '22.

G-475　_____ The joyous trouble maker / by Jackson Gregory . . . ; with frontispiece in color by Frank Tenney Johnson. New York: Dodd, Mead and Company, 1918. 330 p., front.
LC: Ap 30, '18.
PW: Ap 27, '18.

G-476　_____ Judith of Blue Lake Ranch / by Jackson Gregory . . . ; illustrated by W. Herbert Dunton. New York: Charles Scribner's Sons, 1919. 393 p., front., [3] leaves of plates.
LC: My 24, '19.
PW: Ap 5, '19.

G-477　_____ Ladyfingers / by Jackson Gregory . . . ; illustrated by W. Herbert Dunton. New York: Charles Scribner's Sons, 1920. 368 p., front., [3] leaves of plates.
LC: My 18, '20.
PW: My 22, '20.

G-478　_____ The maid of the mountain: a romance of the California wilderness / by Jackson Gregory. New York: Charles Scribner's Sons, 1925. 331 p., front. [Ill. by James Reynolds.]
LC: Ag 8, '25.
PW: Ag 15, '25.

G-479　_____ Man to man / by Jackson Gregory; illustrated by J. G. Shepherd. New York: Charles Scribner's Sons, 1920. 367 p., front., [3] leaves of plates.
LC: O 18, '20.
PW: O 16, '20.

G-480　_____ The outlaw / by Jackson Gregory . . . ; with illustrations by J. N. Marchand. New York: Dodd, Mead and Company, 1916. 328 p., front., [3] leaves of plates.　**NYP**
LC: F 21, '16.
PW: F 19, '16.

G-481　_____ The short cut / by Jackson Gregory; with illustrations by Frank Tenney Johnson. New York: Dodd, Mead and Company, 1916. 383 p., col. front., [3] leaves of col. plates.
LC: O 16, '16.
PW: O 28, '16.

G-482　_____ Six feet four / by Jackson Gregory . . . ; with frontispiece in color by Frank Tenney Johnson. New York: Dodd, Mead and Company, 1918. 295 p., col. front.
LC: O 1, '18.
PW: O 19, '18.

G-483　_____ Timber-Wolf / by Jackson Gregory. New York: Charles Scribner's Sons, 1923. 333 p.
LC: S 10, '23.
PW: S 22, '23.

G-484　_____ Under handicap: a novel / by Jackson Gregory. New York; London: Harper & Brothers, 1914. 321, [1] p., front.
PW: Ap 4, '14.

G-485　_____ Wolf breed / by Jackson Gregory . . . ; with frontispiece in color by Frank Tenney Johnson. New York: Dodd, Mead and Company, 1917. 296 p., col. front.　**NYP**
LC: O 15, '17.
PW: O 20, '17.

G-486　Grendon, Felix, b. 1882. The love chase / by Felix Grendon . . . Boston: Small, Maynard & Company, [c1922]. 494 p.
LC: My 18, '22.
BLC: London: Hurst & Blackett, [1923].

G-487　_____ Nixola of Wall Street / by Felix Grendon. New York: The Century Co., 1919. 384 p., front. [Ill. by Leslie L. Benson.]
LC: Ap 22, '19.
PW: Ap 19, '19.

G-488　Grenell, Z. (Zelotes), 1841-1918. The sandals: a tale of Palestine / by Z. Grenell. New York; London: Funk & Wagnalls Company, 1902. 59 p.,

ill. [Ill. by F. A. Carter.]
(The hour-glass stories; 2.)

G-489   Gresham, Fanny Williams. The cowboy's courtship
and other courtships / by Fanny Williams Gresham.
New York; Washington: The Neale Publishing
Company, 1904. 81 p.   **KUK**
Contents: The cow-boy's courtship -- Norman's courtship -- The
Irish courtship -- Who won? or, The double courtship -- The old
maid's courtship.

G-490   Gresham, Robert Jesse, b. 1874. Sentiment and story
/ by Robert J. Gresham. New York; Washington:
The Neale Publishing Company, 1908. 276 p. **GUA**
LC: Ja 23, '08.

G-491   Grew, David. Beyond rope and fence / David Grew.
New York: Boni and Liveright, [c1922]. 240 p.,
front. [Ill. by Harold Sichel.]
LC: Ag 28, '22.
PW: S 2, '22.

G-492   Grew, David. The two coyotes / by David Grew.
New York: Thomas Seltzer, 1924. 289 p.
LC: Ap 7, '24.
BLC: London: T. Fisher Unwin, 1924.

        Grey, Cynthia, ed. See **Buskett, Nancy. *Fingers
        that see* (1914), B-1339.**

G-493   Grey, Douglas. The tracking of K. K.: a detective
story / by Douglas Grey. New York: Chelsea
House, [c1925]. 256 p.
PW: My 16, '25.

        Grey, John W., jt. aut. *The master mystery* (1919).
        See **Reeve, Arthur B. (Arthur Benjamin),
        1880-1936, jt. aut., R-138.**

G-494   Grey, Katharine. A little leaven / by Katharine Grey.
Philadelphia; London: J. B. Lippincott Company,
1922. 304 p.
LC: Mr 23, '22.

G-495   Grey, Marian E. Greselda / by Marian E. Grey.
Boston: Herbert B. Turner & Co., 1904. 120 p.,
front. [Ill. by Manton.]

G-496   Grey, Zane, 1872-1939. Betty Zane / by P. Zane
Grey; cover design, letters and illustrations by the
author. New York: Charles Francis Press, [c1903].
291 p., front. (port.), [5] leaves of plates.
PW: F 27, '04.

G-497   ____ The border legion / by Zane Grey . . . ;
illustrated by Lillian E. Wilhelm. New York;
London: Harper & Brothers, 1916. 365, [1] p.,
front., [3] leaves of plates.
LC: My 20, '16.
PW: My 27, '16.

        ____ Byme-by-tarpon. In *The Sporting spirit*
        (1925), S-771.

G-498   ____ The call of the canyon / by Zane Grey. New
York; London: Harper & Brothers, 1924. 291 p.,

front., [3] leaves of plates. [Ill. by H. R. Ballinger.]
LC: Ja 5, '24.
PW: Ja 12, '24.
BLC: London: Hodder & Stoughton, [1923].

G-499   ____ The day of the beast / by Zane Grey . . . New
York; London: Harper & Brothers Publishers,
[c1922]. 351 p.   **MNU**
LC: Ag 12, '22.
PW: Ag 26, '22.

G-500   ____ Desert gold: a romance of the border / by
Zane Grey . . . ; illustrated by Douglas Duer. New
York; London: Harper & Brothers, 1913. 325,
[1] p., front., [3] leaves of plates.
LC: Ap 19, '13.
PW: Ap 26, '13.

G-501   Grey, Zane, 1872-1939. The desert of wheat: a
novel / by Zane Grey . . . ; illustrated by W. H. D.
Koerner. New York; London: Harper & Brothers,
1919. 376 [1] p., front., [3] leaves of plates.
LC: Ja 18, '19.
PW: Ja 25, '19.
BLC: London: Hodder & Stoughton, [1919].

G-502   ____ The heritage of the desert: a novel / by Zane
Grey. New York; London: Harper & Brothers,
1910. 297, [1] p., front.   **CIN**
LC: S 10, '10.
PW: S 17, '10.

G-503   ____ The last of the plainsmen / by Zane Grey; with
illustrations from photographs by the author. New
York: The Outing Publishing Company, 1908.
314 p., photo. front., [25] leaves of photo.
plates.   **OSU, SDA**
LC: Ag 20, '08.
PW: S 5, '08.
BLC: London: Hodder & Stoughton, 1908.

G-504   ____ The last trail: a story of early days in the Ohio
Valley / by Zane Grey . . . ; with four half-tone
illustrations by J. Watson Davis. New York: A. L.
Burt Company, [c1909]. 300 p., front., [3] leaves of
plates.
LC: Ap 24, '09.
PW: Ap 10, '09.

G-505   ____ The light of western stars: a romance / by
Zane Grey . . . New York; London: Harper &
Brothers, 1914. 388, [1] p., col. front.
LC: Ja 17, '14.
PW: Ja 24, '14.

G-506   ____ The Lone Star ranger: a romance of the
border / by Zane Grey . . . New York; London:
Harper & Brothers, 1915. 372, [1] p., front. [Ill. by
Robert Amick.]
LC: Ja 9, '15.
PW: Ja 16, '15.

G-507   ____ The man of the forest: a novel / by Zane
Grey; illustrations by Frank Tenny Johnson. New
York; London: Harper & Brothers, [1920]. 382,
[1] p.
LC: F 3, '20.

G-508   ____ The mysterious rider: a novel / Zane Grey; illustrations by Frank Hoffman. New York; London: Harper & Brothers, [1921]. 335, [1] p., front., [3] leaves of plates.
LC: Ja 7, '21.
PW: Ja 8, '21.
BLC: London: Hodder & Stoughton, [1921].

G-509   ____ The rainbow trail: a romance / by Zane Grey . . . New York; London: Harper & Brothers, 1915. 372, [1] p., col. front.
LC: Ag 13, '15.
PW: Ag 21, '15.

G-510   ____ The redheaded outfield: and other baseball stories / by Zane Grey. New York: Grosset & Dunlap, [c1920]. 238 p.
Contents: The redheaded outfield -- The rube -- The rube's pennant -- The rube's honeymoon -- The rube's Waterloo -- Breaking into fast company -- The knocker -- The winning ball -- False colors -- The manager of Madden's Hill -- Old Well-well.
LC: Je 25, '20.
PW: Jl 17, '20.

G-511   ____ Riders of the purple sage: a novel / by Zane Grey . . . ; illustrated by Doug Duer. New York; London: Harper & Brothers, 1912. 334 p., front., [3] leaves of plates.
LC: Ja 22, '12.
PW: Ja 27, '12.

G-512   ____ The short-stop / by Zane Grey . . . ; illustrated by H. S. DeLay. Chicago: A. C. McClurg & Co., 1909. 310 p., front., [5] leaves of plates.   **OUN**
LC: Jl 2, '09.
PW: Jl 10, '09.

G-513   ____ The spirit of the border: a romance of the early settlers in the Ohio Valley / by Zane Grey . . . New York: A. L. Burt Company, [c1906]. 274 p., front., [3] leaves of plates. [Ill. by J. Watson Davis.]
PW: Mr 24, '06.

G-514   ____ Tappan's burro: and other stories / by Zane Grey . . . ; with illustrations in color by Charles S. Chapman and Frank Street. New York; London: Harper & Brothers, [c1923]. 253 p., col. front., [6] leaves of col. plates.
Contents: Tappan's burro -- The great slave -- Yaqui -- Tigre -- The rubber hunter.
LC: O 27, '23.
PW: N 10, '23.
BLC: London: Hodder & Stoughton, [1923].

G-515   ____ The thundering herd / by Zane Grey. New York; London: Harper & Brothers, 1925. 400 p., front., [3] leaves of plates. [Ill. by E. F. Ward.]
LC: Ja 8, '25.
PW: Ja 10, '25.
BLC: London: Hodder & Stoughton, [1925].

G-516   ____ To the last man: a novel / by Zane Grey; illustrations by Frank Spradling. New York; London: Harper & Brothers, [c1921]. 310, [1] p., front., [2] leaves of plates.
LC: Ja 7, '22.
PW: D 31, '21.

G-517   ____ The U. P. trail: a novel / by Zane Grey . . . New York; London: Harper & Brothers, [1918]. 408, [1] p., front. [Ill. by R. Farrington Elwell.]
LC: Ja 30, '18.
PW: Ja 26, '18.

G-518   ____ The vanishing American / by Zane Grey. New York; London: Harper & Brothers, 1925. 308 p., front., [3] leaves of plates.
PW: D 19, '25.
BLC: London: Hodder & Stoughton, [1926].

G-519   ____ Wanderer of the wasteland / by Zane Grey . . . ; with illustrations by W. Herbert Dunton. -- 1st. ed. -- New York; London: Harper & Brothers, [c1923]. 419 p., front., [2] leaves of plates.
LC: Ja 6, '23.
PW: Ja 6, '23.
BLC: London: Hodder & Stoughton, [1923].

G-520   ____ Wildfire / by Zane Grey; illustrated. New York; London: Harper & Brothers, [1917], [c1916]. 320, [1] p., front., [3] leaves of plates. [Ill. by Frank Tenney Johnson.]
LC: Ja 15, '17.
PW: Ja 20, '17.
BLC: London: T. Nelson & Sons, [1920].

G-521   Grey towers: a campus novel. Chicago: Covici-McGee Co., 1923. 286 p.
LC: Ag 15, '23.
PW: Ag 25, '23.

G-522   Griel, Cecile L. Carmela / by Cecile L. Griel. New York: Young Womens Christian Association, 1918. 33 p.   **NYP**
(Inch library. Third inch.)

G-523   Griffis, William Elliot, 1843-1928. In the Mikado's service: a story of two battle summers in China / by William Elliot Griffis; illustrated by William F. Stecher. Boston; Chicago: W. A. Wilde Company, [c1901]. 361 p., front., [4] leaves of plates.
PW: O 5, '01.

G-524   Griffith, Frank Carlos, b. 1851. The man from Maine: a humorous episode in the life of Asa King / by Frank Charles Griffith; pictures by A. B. Shute. Boston, Mass., U. S. A.: C. M. Clark Publishing Co., Inc., 1905. 255 p., front., [9] leaves of plates.

G-525   Griffith, Grace Kellogg. The mould / by Grace Kellogg Griffith; illustrated by Charles Hargens, Jr. Philadelphia: The Penn Publishing Company, 1923. 336 p., front.
LC: N 30, '23.

G-526   Griffith, Helen Sherman, b. 1873. The lane / by Helen Sherman Griffith; frontispiece by Elizabeth Pilsbry. Philadelphia: The Penn Publishing Company, 1925. 348 p., front.
LC: Mr 13, '25.
PW: F 28, '25.

G-527   ____ Rosemary for remembrance / by Helen Sherman Griffith . . . ; illustrated by Mary Pemberton

Ginther. Philadelphia: The Penn Publishing Company, 1911. 327, [1] p., col. front., [4] leaves of plates. Designed end papers. [Plates ill. by H. Devitt Welsh.] **VA@**
LC: O 3, '11.

G-528   Griffith, Susan M. Hazel Gray; or One little lamp / by Susan M. Griffith . . . Philadelphia: American Baptist Publication Society, [1902]. 318 p.
DLC (microfilm)
LC: Ap 11, '02.

Griffiths, Arthur, jt. aut. *One wonderful rose* (1920). See **Griffiths, Bertha, b. 1892, jt. aut., G-529.**

G-529   Griffiths, Bertha, b. 1892. One wonderful rose / by Bertha & Arthur Griffiths. Boston: Richard G. Badger, [c1920]. ([Boston]: The Gorham Press). 253 p., photo. front.

G-530   Griffiths, David Pugh. The last of the quills: a story of Welsh life / by David Pugh Griffiths. Binghampton, N. Y.: The Modern Press, Printers, 1902. 423 p., front. (port.), [6] leaves of plates.
PW: Ag 9, '02.

G-531   Griggs, George B. Norkoma: a novel. Houston, Texas: J. V. Dealy Company, 1906. 365 p., photo. front., [7] leaves of plates (some photo.). [Ill. by J. Moody Dawson.]
PW: Ap 28, '06.

G-532   Griggs, S. E. (Stephen Elind), b. 1880. Souls of the infinite: an outline of the truth / by S. E. Griggs . . . ; illustrated by the author. New York: The Metropolitan Press, 1911. 171 p., photo. front. (port.), [3] leaves of plates, ill.

G-533   Griggs, Sutton Elbert, b. 1872. The hindered hand, or, The reign of the repressionist / by Sutton E. Griggs. Nashville, Tenn.: The Orion Publishing Company, 1905. 303 p., [15] leaves of plates. [Ill. by Robert E. Bell.]
PW: F 24, '06.

G-534   ____ Overshadowed: a novel / by Sutton E. Griggs . . . Nashville, Tenn.: The Orion Publishing Co., 1901. 217 p. Designed end papers.   **TNS**

G-535   ____ Pointing the way / by Sutton E. Griggs. Nashville, Tenn.: The Orion Publishing Company, 1908. 233 p.
PW: S 19, '08.

G-536   ____ Unfettered: a novel; Dorlan's plan: (sequel to "Unfettered"): a dissertation on the race problem / by Sutton E. Griggs . . . Nashville, Tenn.: The Orion Publishing Company, 1902. 276 p.   **TUS**

G-537   The grim thirteen: short stories / by thirteen authors of standing; edited by Frederick Stuart Greene; with an introduction by Edward J. O'Brien . . . New York: Dodd, Mead and Company, 1917. 385 p.
Contents: The day of Daheimus / Vance Thompson -- Rain / Dana Burnet -- Old Fags / Stacy Aumonier -- The head of his house / Conrad Richter -- The Abigail Sheriff memorial / Vincent O'Sullivan

-- Easy / Ethel Watts Mumford -- The draw-keeper / Wadsworth Camp -- The razor of Pedro Dutel / Richard Matthews Hallet -- Knute Ericson's celebration / Robert Alexznder Wason -- The parcel / Mrs. Belloc Lowndes -- Back o' the yards / Will Levington Comfort and H. A. Sturtzel -- The end of the game / William Ashley Anderson -- The black pool / Frederick Stuart Greene.
LC: S 11, '17.
PW: S 8, '17.

G-538   Grimes, Edward Breene. A kettle of coin / by Edward Breene Grimes. Dayton, Ohio: United Brethren Publishing House, 1901. 126 p.   **UTS**

G-539   Grimm, George, 1859-1945. Pluck: being a faithful narrative of the fortunes of a little "greenhorn" in America / by George Grimm; illustrated by Mark Forrest. Milwaukee, Wis.: Germania Publishing Co., [c1904]. 284 p., front., [7] leaves of plates.

G-540   Grindell, Clara Froelich. Consider the lilies / by Clara Froelich Grindell . . . ; illustrations by Ida W. Prentice. New York: The Knickerbocker Press, 1906. 36 p., [3] leaves of plates.   **DLC**

G-541   Grinnell, George Bird, 1849-1938. The punishment of the stingy: and other Indian stories / by George Bird Grinnell; illustrated. New York; London: Harper & Brother Publishers, 1901. 234, [1] p., col. front. (port.), [16] leaves of plates. [Ill. by E. W. Deming.]   **NMI**
(Harper's portrait collection of short stories; v. 5.)
Contents: The stories and the story-tellers -- The Bluejay stories -- The punishment of the stingy -- Bluejay, the imitator -- Bluejay visits the ghosts -- The girl who was the ring -- The first corn -- The star boy -- The grizzly bear's medicine -- The first medicine lodge -- Thunder Maker and Cold Maker -- The blindness of Pi-wáp-ŏk -- Ragged Head -- Nothing Child -- Shield Quiver's wife -- The Beaver stick -- Little friend coyote.

G-542   Grisewood, R. Norman (Robert Norman), b. 1876. The drifting of the Cavashaws / by R. Norman Grisewood; illustrations by Warren Y. Cluff. New York: R. F. Fenno & Company, [c1913]. 339 p., front., [3] leaves of plates.   **DLC**

G-543   ____ The venture: a story of the shadow world / by R. Norman Grisewood . . . New York: R. F. Fenno & Company, [c1911]. 228 p.
LC: Mr 3, '11.
PW: Mr 25, '11.

G-544   ____ Zarlah the Martian / by R. Norman Grisewood. New York: R. F. Fenno & Company, [c1909]. 194 p., front.
LC: S 2, '09.

G-545   Grissom, Irene Welch, b. 1873. A daughter of the Northwest / by Irene Welch Grissom. Boston: The Cornhill Company, [c1918]. 225 p.
LC: Mr 20, '19.
PW: Ap 5, '19.

G-546   ____ The superintendent / by Irene Welch Grissom. New York; Seattle: The Alice Harriman Company, 1910. 288 p.
PW: D 17, '10.

G-547 [Griswold, Grace], d. 1927. Letters from G. G. New York: Henry Holt and Company, 1909. 223 p. LC: O 12, '09.

G-548 Griswold, Latta, 1876-1931. The Inn at the Red Oak / by Latta Griswold. New York: Robert J. Shores, [c1917]. 280 p., front. [Ill. by L. Krumel.]

G-549 Griswold, Lorenzo, b. 1847. Short stories / by Lorenzo Griswold. New York: Printed by the Trow Press, 1907. 259 p.
Contents: Restitution -- George Dale's ambition -- An unexpected witness / D. G. -- A regular popinjay -- Hontanita -- A dream -- Tsitha -- Two doctors - a story.

G-550 Griswold, Ruth Lee, b. 1889. Unknown from the skies / by Ruth L. Griswold. Boston: Richard G. Badger, [c1923]. ([Boston]: The Gorham Press). 230 p., front.

Groner, Augusta, 1850-1922, jt. aut. *Joe Muller: detective* (1910). See **Colbron, Grace Isabel, 1869-1948, jt. aut., C-567.**

G-551 ____ The lady in blue: a Joseph Muller story / by Augusta Groner and Grace Isabel Colbron . . . New York: Duffield and Company, 1922. 304 p. **DLC**

G-552 Grose, Parlee C. (Parlee Clyde), b. 1889. The five fairies / by Parlee C. Grose. New York: Fifth Avenue Publishing Co., [c1917]. 223 p., front., [2] leaves of plates. LC: Ja 29, '18.

G-553 Gross, Anna Goldmark. The gnomes of the Saline Mountains: a fantastic narrative / by Anna Goldmark Gross . . . New York: The Shakespeare Press, 1912. 181 p., front., [3] leaves of plates. [Ill. by I. T. Ballin.]
Contents: The gnomes of the Saline Mountains; a fantastic narrative -- The artist -- The street singer; a Viennese story -- Concetta; an Italian novelette.

G-554 Gross, Anton. Merchants of precious goods: and other stories / by Anton Gross. Boston: The Roxburgh Publishing Company, Inc., [c1920]. 185 p.
Contents: Merchants of precious goods -- Hazardous venture in plutonic region -- The idealist -- An unseen episode -- A victim of time -- The poet, the lady and the lamb -- A formented neighborhood -- The passing of Mme. Arlington -- Love.

G-555 ____ The musing wanderer / by Anton Gross. Boston: The Roxburgh Publishing Company, Inc., [c1923]. 238 p. LC: S 18, '23.

G-556 Gross, Josiah. Ondell and Dolee: a story of mysticism / by Josiah Gross. New York, London [etc.]: The Abbey Press, [c1902]. 260 p. Unexamined copy: bibliographic data from OCLC, #17568336.

G-557 Gross, Mark S. (Mark Stanislaus), b. 1889. To the dark tower: being Gerard Linton's account of all that happened at the house of Jacques Cournot in the summer of nineteen hundred and seven / by Mark S. Gross, S. J. New York: P. J. Kenedy & Sons, [c1922]. 356 p., [1] leaf of plates.

G-558 Gross, Myra Geraldine. The star of Valhalla: a romance of early Christianity in Norway / by Myra Gross; with illustrations in colour by Archie Gunn. New York: Frederick A. Stokes Company, [1907]. 355 p., col. front., [2] leaves of col. plates. LC: My 8, '07. PW: Je 1, '07.

G-559 Grossmann, Edith Searle. The heart of the bush / by Edith Searle Grossmann. New York: John Lane Company, 1911. 334 p., incl. col. front. Unexamined copy: bibliographic data from NUC.

Grossman, Mollie. The "s" in fish means sugar. In *The best college short stories, 1917-18 (1919), B-557.*

Grove, Harriet (McCrory), jt. ed as H.M.G. See *Gone West, (1919), G-289.*

G-560 Grueningen, Herman. Mundane: a story / by Herman Grueningen. San Francisco: The Tomoye Press, [c1918]. 31 p., photo. front. (port.). **NYP**

G-561 Grumbine, J. C. F. (Jesse Charles Fremont), 1861-1938. The great secret and other stories / by J. C. F. Grumbine . . . Boston, Mass.: Published by the Order of the White Rose, [c1906]. 107 p.
Contents: Ghosts in the White Tower -- The coach and the strange driver -- A bit of Old Boston -- Miss Windermere's country house -- The great secret.

G-562 Gue, Belle Willey, b. 1860. An American / by Belle Willey Gue. Boston: Richard G. Badger, [c1921]. (Boston: The Gorham Press). 268 p.

G-563 ____ The fugitives / by Belle Willey Gue . . . Philadelphia: Dorrance, [c1923]. 210 p. **OSU, CLU** LC: Ag 3, '23.

G-564 ____ Grounded / by Belle Willey Gue. Philadelphia: Dorrance, [c1922]. 176 p. LC: S 20, '22.

G-565 ____ The last ditch / by Belle Willey Gue. Boston: The Stratford Company, 1923. 296 p., front. (port.). LC: D 6, '23. PW: F 9, '24.

G-566 ____ The neutral ground / by Belle Willey Gue. Boston, Massachusetts: The Stratford Company, 1922. 289 p., front. (port.), [1] leaf of plates (port.). LC: D 11, '22.

G-567 Guernon, Charles. Choice / Charles Guernon. Philadelphia; London: J. B. Lippincott Company, 1925. 352 p. LC: Ap 2, '25. PW: Ap 18, '25.

G-568 ____ Titans / by Charles Guernon. New York: Duffield & Company, 1922. 306 p. LC: F 10, '23. PW: F 17, '23. BLC: London: Hodder & Stoughton; printed in U. S. A., [1923].

G-569 Guernsey, Alice Margaret, b. 1850. Home mission readings: for use in missionary meetings / by Alice M. Guernsey. New York; Chicago; Toronto; London; Edinburgh: Fleming H. Revell Company, [c1905]. 128 p. **DLC**
Contents: A package of letters -- Uncle Sam's "how d'y' do" -- The immigrant chapter -- With a nurse deaconess -- Everyday service -- A deaconess in the mining regions -- "It doesn't matter nothin'" -- "Such stuff as dreams" -- A personal investment -- Headlines -- Their adopted member -- Girls and girls -- Decoration day by proxy -- What was the use? -- Mrs. Winn's way -- Strategic points -- The problem of Robert -- The rummage barrel -- A bundle of fagots -- The burden of Mendon -- From Christmas to Easter -- Christmas gifts for the Christ-child.

G-570 Guernsey, D. Riley (Daniel Riley), b. 1849. Lost in the Mammoth cave / by D. Riley Guernsey; illustrated. New York: Broadway Publishing Company, [c1905]. 315 p., front., [1] leaf of plates. [Ill. by Sydney K. Hartman.]

G-571 Guest, Gilbert, *pseud.* A bridal trip in a prairie schooner: a novel / by Gilbert Guest [pseud.]. Omaha: Burkley Printing Company, 1921. 265 p.

G-572 _____ Daisy, or, A flower of the tenements of little old New York / Gilbert Guest [pseud.]. Omaha: Burkley Printing Company, 1921. 236 p. **DLC**

G-573 _____ Loretta, the sunshine of the convent: a novel / by Gilbert Guest [pseud.]. Omaha: Burkley Printing Company, 1921. 175 p. **DLC**

G-574 _____ Margaret, or, Was it magnetism? / by Gilbert Guest [psued.]. Omaha: Burkley Printing Company, 1920. 101 p.
LC: O 8, '20.

G-575 _____ Snapshots by the way / Gilbert Guest [pseud.]. Omaha, NE: Burkley Printing Company, 1920. 205 p.
Unexamined copy: bibliographic data from OCLC, #30815212.
Contents: A meeting of souls -- What Jack won -- A debt twice paid -- A farm house idyl -- A love story without a sweetheart -- A "deestrick" school idyl -- To him who waits.

Guilbeault, Zephirin J. See **Bates, Jimmie, pseud.**

Guilday, Peter K. Greater lover than this. In *The lady of the tower* (1909), L-13.

Gummere, Francis B. See **Heigh, John, pseud.**

G-576 Gundelfinger, George Frederick. The new fraternity: a novel of university life / by George Frederick Gundelfinger. Sewickley, Pa.: The New Fraternity, [1916]. 301 p.

G-577 Gunn, Robert A. (Robert Alexander), b. 1844. Bruce, Douglas: a man of the people: a novel / by Robert A. Gunn. Boston: Mayhew Publishing Company, 1909. 301 p., front. (port.).
LC: D 22, '09.

Gunnison, Lynn, pseud. See **Ames, Joseph Bushnell, 1878-1928.**

G-578 Gunter, Archibald Clavering, 1847-1907. The adventures of Dr. Burton / by Archibald Clavering Gunter. New York: The Home Publishing Company, [c1905]. 223 p., front., [5] leaves of plates. [Ill. by George Ryder and Herman Heyer.]
PW: D 2, '05.

G-579 _____ The changing pulse of Madame Touraine / by Archibald Clavering Gunter . . . New York: The Home Publishing Company . . . , [c1905]. 228 p.

G-580 _____ The city of mystery: (taken from the archives of ancient Paris, as found in the secret prison of the exempt, Pomereu in the Rue de la Tixeranderie when the buildings were torn down in 1851) / by Archibald Clavering Gunter . . . New York: The Home Publishing Company, [c1902]. 275 p. **ZSJ**
BLC: London: Samuel French, 1902.

G-581 _____ The conscience of a King: a novel / by Archibald Clavering Gunter. New York: The Home Publishing Company, [1903]. 278 p., front., [4] leaves of plates.
PW: My 23, '03.
BLC: London: Samuel French, 1903.

G-582 _____ The deacon's second wind: a story / by Archibald Clavering Gunter. New York: The Home Publishing Company, [c1901]. 253 p.
(The Welcome series, no. 72.)
LC: Jl 18, '01.
BLC: London: Frederick Routledge, 1901.

G-583 _____ The man behind the door: a novel / by Archibald Clavering Gunter. New York: The Home Publishing Company, [1904]. 281 p.
PW: My 7, '04.
BLC: London: Samuel French, 1904: Another edition: London: F. V. White & Co., 1904.

G-584 _____ Mr. Barnes, American: a sequel to "Mr. Barnes of New York" / by Archibald Clavering Gunter; illustrations by B. Martin Justice. New York: Dodd, Mead and Company, 1907. 329 p., col. front.
LC: Mr 6, '07.
PW: Mr 23, '07.
BLC: London: B. F. Stevens & Brown; printed in U. S. A., 1907.

G-585 _____ My Japanese prince: (being some startling excerpts from the diary of Hilda Patience Armstrong of Meriden, Connecticut, at present travelling in the Far East) / by Archibald Clavering Gunter. New York: The Home Publishing Company, [c1904]. 256 p.
PW: O 8, '04.
BLC: London: Samuel French, 1904.

G-586 _____ Phil Conway: a novel / by Archibald Clavering Gunter . . . New York: The Home Publishing Company, [1903]. 297 p.
Unexamined copy: bibliographic data from OCLC, #18807277.
PW: F 6, '04.
BLC: London: Samuel French, 1904.

G-587   ____ A prince in the garret: a novel / by Archibald Clavering Gunter. New York: The Home Publishing Company, [c1905]. 278 p., front., incl. [3] leaves of plates. [Ill. by Archie Gunn and Herman Rountree.]
PW: My 6, '05.
BLC: London: Samuel French, 1905.

G-588   ____ Prince Karl: novelized from the play / by Archibald Clavering Gunter. New York: G. W. Dillingham Company, [1907]. 215 p., col. front.
LC: O 21, '07.
BLC: London: Ward, Lock & Co., 1909.

G-589   ____ The surprises of an empty hotel: a novel / by Archibald Clavering Gunter. New York: The Home Publishing Company, [c1902]. 292 p., double-leaf front., [6] double-leaf plates. [Ill. by Archie Gunn.]
PW: Ap 5, '02.
BLC: London: Frederick Routledge, 1902.

G-590   Guthrie, Kenneth Sylvan, 1871-1940. A romance of two centuries: a tale of the year 2025 / Kenneth Sylvan Guthrie. Alpine, N. J.: The Platonist Press, [c1919]. 365, [3] p., front.

G-591   Guthrie, Patty. Eliza and Etheldreda in Mexico: notes of travel / by Patty Guthrie. New York: Broadway Publishing Co., [c1911]. 151 p.

G-592   Guy, Charles Warren. Whoa: New England stories for big and little folk / by Charles Warren Guy. Boston: Eastern Publishing Co., [c1905]. 273 p., photo. front., [11] leaves of plates.
Contents: Part One: Charlie and William Clapp at Grandpa's -- Skating at Grandpa's -- Thanksgiving at Grandpa's -- Making maple sugar at Grandpa's -- Helping Grandpa with his haying -- Second summer at Grandpa's -- Charlie and William go hunting -- The bee tree -- Finding crows' nests -- Finding ducks' nests -- The two girls -- The white mountains -- Seeing Dover -- Evening stories -- Visiting Quincy -- A Christmas Eve entertainment -- Christmas Day -- More evening stories -- Shopping -- Pickpockets -- Jimmie and Nellie, the newsboy and the girl -- How Grandpa caught a thief -- A lame horse -- Nat, the pop-corn boy -- A strange letter -- Grandpa's reply -- An evening chat -- Card playing -- Boston years ago -- Home again -- The ice boat -- Fishing. Part Two: Going to Grandpa Brown's -- Mary Brown at Grandpa's -- Mary goes a-strawberrying -- Mary's Fourth of July at Grandpa's -- Salting the sheep -- A rainy day -- Going to the mill -- Selling the bossy -- Mending the sheep pasture fence -- Going after high blueberries -- The lawn party -- Buying the cow -- Mary's Papa arrives at the farm -- Mary Brown goes fishing -- Going up the mountain -- Mary Brown goes home -- A doll party -- Grandpa and Grandma visit Boston -- Grandpa buying Christmas presents -- Mary Brown.

G-593   Guyse, Eleanor. A movable quartette / by Eleanor Guyse. New York; London; Montreal: The Abbey Press, [c1901]. 279 p.

H

H-1   H. B. K. Sutherland's Christmas: a chapter from two lives / by H. B. K. for E. D. L. Evanston, [Ill.]: William S. Lord, 1902. 79 p., front. [Ill. by Bud Buckerman.]
PW: N 1, '02.

H., Eli. A sophomore picnic. In *Allegheny stories* **(1902), A-142.**

H-2   H. F. (Harry Felix). "Je Suis Marsaudon": a tale of old Philadelphia / by H. F. Philadelphia: Privately Printed, distributed by The Domino Publishing Co., c1925. 14 p.
Cover title.

H. M. G., ed. <u>See</u> *Gone West* **(1922), G-289.**

H-3   Haas, Charles E. (Charles Edmund), b. 1873. A maid of Sonora / by Charles E. Haas. New York: Broadway Publishing Company, [1905]. 155 p., front., [2] leaves of plates.
PW: My 6, '05.

H-4   Habberton, John, 1842-1921. Caleb Wright: a story of the West / by John Habberton. Boston: Lothrop Publishing Company, [c1901]. 461 p.
PW: N 2, '01.
BLC: London: Charles H. Kelly, 1901.

____ Everybody's chance. In *Short story classics* **(1905), S-466.**

Hack, Oren S., Mrs. <u>See</u> **Miller, Elizabeth Jane, b. 1878.**

H-5   Hackathorn, Emma J. A little child shall lead them: a tale of every-day life that will be helpful to all / by Emma J. Hackathorn. E. Cleveland, O.: E. J. Hackathorn, 1907. 27 p. incl. front. [Ill. by C. A. Strong.]

H-6   Hackett, Francis, 1883-1962. That nice young couple / by Francis Hackett. New York: Boni & Liveright, 1925. 383 p.
PW: My 16, '25.
BLC: London: Jonathan Cape, 1925.

H-7   Hackley, Sarah Bell. The tobacco tiller: a tale of the Kentucky tobacco fields / by Sarah Bell Hackley. Boston: The C. M. Clark Publishing Company, 1909. 323 p., front., [3] leaves of plates. [Ill. by D. S. Ross.]
LC: S 10, '09.

H-8   Haeselbarth, Adam C. (Adam Christian), b. 1861. Patty of the palms: a story of Porto Rico / by Adam C. Haeselbarth. New York: The Kenny Publishing Co., [c1907]. 324 p., front. [Ill. by Dan Smith.]
LC: O 24, '07.

Haffey, Margaret Higgins, b. 1856, jt. aut. *Tract number 3377* (1909). <u>See</u> **Higgins, George H. (George Henry), 1852-1905, jt. aut., H-604.**

H-9   Haffner, Louise Von. The mystic phone: or, Winning a millionaire / by Louise von Haffner. New York: [s. n.], 1907. 236, [1] p.
Unexamined copy: bibliographic data from OCLC, #29750298.
LC: Ja 8, '07.

Hagboldt, Peter, 1886-1943, jt. aut. *Hammers of hell* (1921). <u>See</u> **Trautmann, W. E. (William Ernst), b. 1869, jt. aut., T-370.**

_____, jt. aut. *Riot* (1920). See **Trautmann, W. E. (William Ernst), b. 1869, jt. aut., T-371.**

H-10   Hagedorn, Hermann, 1882-1964. Barbara picks a husband: a comedy in narrative / by Hermann Hagedorn; frontispiece by J. Paul Verrees. New York: The Macmillan Company, 1918. 271 p., front.
LC: Je 26, '18.

H-11   _____ Faces in the dawn / by Hermann Hagedorn. New York: The Macmillan Company, 1914. 310 p.
LC: S 10, '14.

_____ The work of a ranchman. In *The joy in work* **(1920), J-229.**

Hageman, Drew Wyckoff. His nibs. In *A little book of Rutgers tales* **(1905), L-378.**

H-12   Haines, Alice Calhoun. Firecracker Jane: a novel / by Alice Calhoun Haines. New York: Henry Holt and Company, 1918. 327 p.
LC: O 14, '18.
BLC: London: Hurst & Blackett, [1919].

H-13   _____ Flower of the world / Alice Calhoun Haines. New York: E. P. Dutton & Company, [c1922]. 286 p.
LC: S 6, '22.

H-14   _____ The luck of the Dudley Grahams: as related in extracts from Elizabeth Graham's diary / by Alice Calhoun Haines; illustrations by Francis Day. New York: Henry Holt and Company, 1907. 300 p., front., [3] leaves of plates.
LC: O 5, '07.
BLC: London: Authors' Syndicate; New York: Henry Holt, 1907.

Haines, Donal Hamilton, 1886-1951. Bill. In *War stories* **(1919), W-94.**

H-15   _____ The last invasion / by Donal Hamilton Haines; illustrated. New York; London: Harper & Brothers, 1914. 339, [1] p., front., [6] leaves of plates. Illustrated end papers.   **OSU, TXA**
LC: O 24, '14.

_____ The pride of his calling. In *Forum stories* **(1914), F-306.**

H-16   _____ The return of Pierre / by Donal Hamilton Haines; with frontispiece from a painting by Édouard Detaille. New York: Henry Holt and Company, 1912. 307 p., front.
LC: F 23, '12.
BLC: London: Stanley Paul & Co., [1912].

H-17   _____ Sky-line Inn / by Donal Hamilton Haines; jacket in color by Harold Brett. Boston; New York: Houghton Mifflin Company, 1923. (Cambridge: The Riverside Press). 296 p.
LC: Ap 28, '23.
BLC: London: Eveleigh Nash; printed in U. S. A., [1923].

H-18   Hains, T. Jenkins (Thornton Jenkins), b. 1866. Bahama Bill: mate of the wrecking sloop Sea-horse / by T. Jenkins Hains; with a frontispiece in colour by H. R. Reuterdahl. Boston: L. C. Page & Company, 1908. 368 p., col. front.
LC: F 6, '08.

H-19   _____ The black barque: a tale of the pirate slave-ship, Gentle Hand, on her last African cruise / by T. Jenkins Hains; illustrated by W. Herbert Dunton. Boston: L. C. Page & Company, 1905. 322, [1] p., front., [4] leaves of plates.
PW: Mr 4, '05.
BLC: London: Dean & Son; printed in U. S. A., [1905].

_____ The chief mate's yarns: twelve tales of the sea (1912). See **Hains, T. Jenkins (Thornton Jenkins), b. 1866.** *The white ghost of disaster* **(1912), H-23.**

H-20   _____ The cruise of the Petrel: a story of 1812 / by T. Jenkins Hains. New York: McClure, Phillips & Co., 1901. 210 p.
PW: My 11, '01.
BLC: London: McClure, Phillips & Co.; New York [printed], 1901.

H-21   _____ The strife of the sea / T. Jenkins Hains . . . New York: The Baker & Taylor Co., [c1903]. 328 p., front., [3] leaves of plates. [Ill. by W. J. Aylward and C. W. Ashley.]
Contents: The old man of Sand Key -- The outcast -- The sea dog -- The Cape Horners -- The loggerhead -- The white follower -- King Albicore -- The Nibblers -- Johnny Shark -- A tragedy of the South Atlantic -- In the wake of the weather-cloth.
PW: O 24, '03.
BLC: London: Ward, Lock & Co.; printed in U. S. A., 1904.

H-22   _____ The voyage of the Arrow: to the China Seas: its adventures and perils, including its capture by Sea Vultures from the Countess of Warwick, as set down by William Gore, Chief Mate / by T. Jenkins Hains . . . ; with six illustrations by H. C. Edwards. Boston: L. C. Page & Company, 1906. 300 p., col. front., [5] leaves of col. plates.   **OSU, NYP**
Page's Library of famous sea stories.
BLC: London: Brown, Langham & Co.; Boston, Mass. printed, 1906.

H-23   [_____] The white ghost of disaster: the chief mate's yarn / by Captain Mayn Clew Garnett [pseud.]. New York: G. W. Dillingham Company, [c1912]. 352 p.
    KLG
Also published as *The chief mate's yarns: twelve tales of the sea.*
Contents: The white ghost of disaster -- The light ahead -- The wreck of the "Rathbone" -- The after bulkhead -- Captain Junard -- In the wake of the engine -- In the hull of the "Heraldine" -- A two-stranded yarn -- At the end of the drag rope -- Pirates twain -- The judgment of men -- On going to sea.
LC: My 24, '12.
PW: Je 1, '12.

H-24   Haldane, Joseph. Old Cronnak / by Joseph Haldane. New York: The Decker Publishing Company, [c1906]. 356 p.
LC: N 5, '06.

H-25 Haldeman-Julius, E. (Emanuel), 1889-1951. Caught and Dreams and compound interest / Mr. and Mrs. Haldeman-Julius. Girard, Kan.: Haldeman-Julius Company, [c1923]. 63 p.
Little blue book, no. 334; Five cent pocket series, no. 334.
"Reprinted from the Atlantic monthly."

H-26 _____ Dust / by Mr. and Mrs. Haldeman-Julius. New York: Brentano's, [1921]. 251 p.
LC: Mr 22, '21.
PW: Ap 16, '21.
BLC: London; New York: Andrew Melrose, [1922].

H-27 _____ The unworthy Coopers, and, Comtesse Du Jones / Mr. and Mrs. Haldeman-Julius. Girard, Kansas: Haldeman-Julius Company, [c1923]. 64 p.
Little blue book, no. 454. Reprinted from the Atlantic monthly.

Haldeman-Julius, Marcet, Mrs., 1887-1941, jt. aut. **See Haldeman-Julius, E. (Emanuel), b. 1889-1951, jt. aut.**

H-28 Hale, Anne Gardner, 1823-1914. The closed balcony / by Anne Gardner Hale; illustrated by John Goss and Lillian Hale. Boston, Massachusetts: The C. M. Clark Publishing Co., 1907. 334 p., front., [9] leaves of plates.
LC: S 7, '07.

H-29 Hale, Beatrice Forbes-Robertson, b. 1883. The nest-builder: a novel / by Beatrice Forbes-Robertson Hale; with a frontispiece by J. Henry. New York: Frederick A. Stokes Company, [c1916]. 376 p., front.

H-30 Hale, Lilian Walker. Friday in the basement; Rosemary; The fortunes of Little Phil; The Thanksgiving story / by Lilian Walker Hale. [Kansas City, Kan.: Printed by Cooper Journal Company, c1916]. 67 p.   **DLC**

H-31 Hale, Louise Closser, 1872-1933. The actress: a novel / by Louise Closser Hale; illustrated. New York; London: Harper & Brothers, 1909. 327, [1] p., front., [3] leaves of plates. [Ill. by William L. Jacobs et al.]
LC: F 18, '09.
PW: Mr 6, '09.
BLC: London: Archibald Constable & Co., 1909.

_____ Emma (1917). See **Closser, Myla Jo.** *At the gate* **(1917), C-498.**

H-32 _____ Her soul and her body / by Louise Closser Hale. New York: Moffat, Yard and Company, 1912. 288 p.
LC: O 11, '12.
PW: O 5, '12.
BLC: London: George Routledge & Sons, 1913.

H-33 _____ The married Miss Worth: a novel / by Louise Closser Hale. New York; London: Harper &

Brothers, 1911. 298 p., front. [Ill. by J. D. Gleason.]
LC: F 4, '11.
PW: F 11, '11.

H-34 _____ A motor car divorce / by Louise Closser Hale; with drawings by Walter Hale. New York: Dodd, Mead & Company, 1906. 319 p., col. front., [33] leaves of col. plates.
PW: Mr 24, '06.
BLC: London: Duckworth & Co., 1906.

H-35 _____ Oh, New York! New York!, or, The story of Jim / by Louise Closser Hale. [S. l.: s. n., 1925?]. 39 p.
"Through the courtesy of the Woman's home companion, this story is made into a book . . ."
Title from cover.

H-36 Hale, Mabel, b. 1879. The hero of Hill House / by Mabel Hale. Anderson, Indiana: Gospel Trumpet Company, [c1922]. 221 p.

H-37 _____ Martha Wilton's strong tower / by Mabel Hale . . . Anderson, Ind.: Gospel Trumpet Company, [c1925]. 112 p., ill.   **INA**
LC: N 9, '25.

Hale, Marice Rutledge (Gibson), b.1884. **See Rutledge, Maryse, pseud.**

H-38 Hale, Martha Ellen. Climbing the heights / by Martha Ellen Hale. Chicago: Scroll Publishing Company, 1902. 329 p.   **DLC**

H-39 Hale, William, b. 1856. A dauntless Viking / by William Hale. Boston: Richard G. Badger, [c1905]. ([Boston]: The Gorham Press). 332 p., front., ill. [Ill. by Mary Powell Helme Hale.]

Haley, Bart, jt. aut. *In the sweet dry and dry* (1919). **See Morley, Christopher, 1890-1957, jt. aut., M-975.**

H-40 Haley, Harry F. (Harry Franklin), b. 1883. Immortal Athalia / by Harry F. Haley. Philadelphia: Dorrance, [c1922]. 310 p.
LC: My 2, '22.

H-41 The half-smart set: a novel / with three illustrations in color by Armand Both. New York: Frederick A. Stokes Company, [1908]. 311 p., col. front., [2] leaves of col. plates.
LC: My 15, '08.

H-42 Hall, Agnes Bowes. Craigie / Agnes Bowes Hall. Boston: The Roxburgh Publishing Company, Inc., [c1914]. 450 p.
LC: S 9, '14.

H-43 Hall, Amanda Benjamin, b. 1890. Blind wisdom / by Amanda Benjamin Hall. Philadelphia: George W. Jacobs & Company, [c1920]. 381 p., col. front. [Ill. by Pearl L. Hill.]
LC: O 2, '20.
PW: O 23, '20.

H-44 ____ The heart's justice / by Amanda Hall. New York: George H. Doran Company, [c1922]. 316 p.
LC: O 25, '22.
PW: N 11, '22.
BLC: London: Stanley Paul & Co.; printed in U. S. A., [1924].

H-45 ____ The little red house in the hollow / by Amanda Benjamin Hall. Philadelphia: George W. Jacobs & Company, [c1918]. 295 p., col. front., [3] leaves of plates. [Ill. by A. I. Blankenberg.]   **ABC**
LC: Ap 10, '18.
PW: Ap 6, '18.
BLC: London: Hurst & Blackett, [1919].

H-46 Hall, Angelo, b. 1868. Forty-one thieves: a tale of California / Angelo Hall. Boston: The Cornhill Company, [c1919]. 133 p.   **KSU**

H-47 Hall, Asa Zadel. Stanton White: a romance of the new South / by Asa Zadel Hall . . . written under the pseudonym, Harold Edson. Cleveland: The Burrows Brothers Company, 1905. 297 p., front., [2] leaves of plates.   **IAY**

H-48 Hall, Austin. Unto the children: a story of the redwoods / by Austin Hall . . . San Jose, California: Semperviren's Club of California, 1924. 32 p., [2] leaves of photo. plates.

Hall, Bolton. See *The love letters of St. John (1917), L-526.*

H-49 Hall, Charles Everett. Some honeymoon! / by Charles Everett Hall; illustrated by Robert Gaston Herbert. New York: George Sully & Company, [c1918]. 280 p., front., [3] leaves of plates.
LC: Ap 1, '18.
PW: Ap 20, '18.

H-50 Hall, Edith. Behind the mask / by Edith Hall. New York; London; Montreal: The Abbey Press, [c1902]. 94 p.
Contents: What is love? -- An oriole lilted a song -- In the shadow of the palms -- Red roses.

H-51 Hall, Edith Macomber. The black trail / by Edith Macomber Hall. New York; London: Greaves Publishing Company, 1911. 173 p.
Contents: The price of silence -- Blue Jim -- A yellow slip of paper -- Florine's folly -- My Wild Rose -- The gleam of an opal -- The violet boy -- The spell of the evil eye -- The secret of the abalone shell -- Sebastian -- Dick Beebe, esq. -- Peaceful Hollow.
LC: Ja 2, '12.

Hall, Edward Allen, b. 1854. See **Allen, Edward, pseud.**

H-52 Hall, Eliza Calvert. Aunt Jane of Kentucky / by Eliza Calvert Hall, with a frontispiece and page decorations by Beulah Strong. Boston: Little, Brown, and Company, 1907. 283 p., col. front.
LC: Mr 28, '07.
PW: Ap 13, '07.
BLC: London: Cassell & Co., 1909.

H-53 ____ Clover and blue grass / by Eliza Calvert Hall [pseud]; with a frontispiece by H. R. Ballinger.

Boston: Little, Brown & Company, 1916. 239 p., col. front.
Contents: How Parson Page went to the circus -- Mary Crawford's chart -- Old mahogany -- Millstones and stumbling-blocks -- "One taste of the old time" -- One day in spring.
LC: S 28, '16.
PW: S 23, '16.

H-54 ____ The land of long ago / by Eliza Calvert Hall; illustrated by G. Patrick Nelson & Beulah Strong. Boston: Little, Brown & Company, 1909. 295 p., front., [7] leaves of plates.
LC: S 24, '09.
PW: S 18, '09.
BLC: London: Cassell & Co., 1910.

H-55 ____ Sally Ann's experience / by Eliza Calvert Hall . . . ; with frontispiece by G. Patrick Nelson and decorations by Theodore B. Hapgood. Boston: Little, Brown and Company, 1910. 45 p., front. Designed end papers.   **OSU, GZU**
LC: S 15, '10.
PW: S 10, '10.

H-56 ____ To love and to cherish / by Eliza Calvert Hall . . . ; illustrated by J. V. McFall. Boston: Little, Brown and Company, 1911. 205 p., front., [3] leaves of plates.
LC: My 16, '11.
PW: My 6, '11.

H-57 Hall, Emmett Campbell. The belovéd adventurer / written by Emmett Campbell Hall. Philadelphia: The Lubin Manufacturing Company, 1914. 155 p., front., [7] leaves of plates.
"Produced as a series of fifteen photoplays featuring Arthur V. Johnson and Lottie Briscoe."

H-58 Hall, Eugene, *pseud.* Vernal Dune, in which is shown the end of an era / by Eugene Hall [pseud.]. New York: The Neale Publishing Company, 1913. 251 [1] p.   **NDD**

H-59 Hall, Eva Holmes. Genevieve: a story of southern life before the war of the states / by Eva Holmes Hall. New York: The Neale Publishing Company, 1913. 403 p.

H-60 Hall, Frederick, b. 1873. A voice in the night: and other stories / by Frederick Hall. Philadelphia: The Sunday School Times Company, 1911. 194 p.
Contents: A voice in the night -- When the king arose -- The regicide -- The son of the desert -- The little girl up Damascus way -- A song of ascents -- The boy with the lunch -- The hour before the dawn -- The tie of blood -- Friends in waiting.

H-61 Hall, G. Stanley (Granville Stanley), 1844-1924. Recreations of a psychologist / by G. Stanley Hall. New York; London: D. Appleton and Company, 1920. 336 p.

H-62 Hall, Gertrude, 1863-1961. Aurora the magnificent / by Gertrude Hall; illustrated by Gerald Leake. New York: The Century Co., 1917. 437 p., front., [7] leaves of plates.
LC: Ap 4, '17.
PW: Mr 24, '17.

H-63   ____ Miss Ingalis / by Gertrude Hall . . . New York: The Century Co., 1918. 307 p., front.
LC: S 5, '18.
PW: S 7, '18.
BLC: London: Skeffington & Son, [1919].

H-64   ____ The truth about Camilla / by Gertrude Hall . . . New York: The Century Co., 1913. 494 p., front., ill.
LC: O 22, '13.
PW: O 18, '13.
BLC: London: William Heinemann, 1913.

H-65   ____ The unknown quantity / by Gertrude Hall. New York: Henry Holt and Company, 1910. 300 p.
LC: F 24, '10.
PW: Mr 5, '10.

Hall, Grace. <u>See</u> **Griswold, Grace, d. 1927.**

H-66   Hall, Helene, *pseud*. The song of a heart: Christmas mile-stones / Helene Hall [pseud.]. Cincinnati: The Robert Clarke Co., 1901. 196 p.   **DLC**
PW: Jl 13, '01.

H-67   Hall, Herschel S. (Herschel Salmon), 1874-1921. Steel preferred / by Herschel S. Hall. New York: E. P. Dutton & Company, [1920]. 305 p.
PW: Jl 24, '20.

H-68   Hall, Holworthy, 1887-1936, *pseud*. Dormie one: and other golf stories / by Holworthy Hall [pseud.] . . . New York: The Century Co., 1917. 349 p., front., ill. [Ill. by Arthur Little, Wallace Morgan, and C. H. Taffs.]
Contents: Alibi -- If you don't mind my telling you -- The runner-up -- The luck of the devil -- The last round -- If it interferes with business -- Dormie one -- "Consolation".
LC: S 20, '17.
PW: S 22, '17.

H-69   ____ Egan / by Holworthy Hall [pseud.] . . . New York: Dodd, Mead and Company, 1920. 380 p.
LC: S 16, '20.

H-70   ____ The gilded mean / by Holworthy Hall [pseud.]. [New York?: The Winthrop Press], [c1914]. 31, [1] p., col. ill.

H-71   ____ Henry of Navarre, Ohio / by Holworthy Hall [pseud.]. New York: The Century Co., 1914. 191 p.
LC: Je 17, '14.

H-72   ____ The man nobody knew / by Holworthy Hall [pseud.] . . . ; illustrations by Clarence F. Underwood. New York: Dodd, Mead and Company, 1919. 315 p., front., [3] leaves of plates.   **VA@**
LC: Ja 15, '19.
PW: Ja 18, '19.

H-73   ____ Paprika: being the further adventures of James P. McHenry, better known to the initiated connoisseurs of fiction as "Pepper" / by Holworthy Hall [pseud.]. New York: Privately published, 1916.

183 p.
Verso of t. p.: Press of William J. Clark, New York.
LC: S 8, '16.

H-74   ____ Pepper / by Holworthy Hall [pseud.]. New York: The Century Co., 1915. 316 p.
LC: Mr 17, '15.
PW: Mr 13, '15.

H-75   ____ Rope / by Holworthy Hall [pseud.]. New York: Dodd, Mead and Company, 1922. 303 p.
LC: O 17, '22.

H-76   ____ The six best cellars / by Holworthy Hall [pseud.] and Hugh Kahler; illustrated by May Wilson Preston. New York: Dodd, Mead and Company, 1919. 106 p., front.
LC: Ag 26, '19.

H-77   ____ What he least expected / by Holworthy Hall [pseud.] . . . ; illustrated by Frederic Dorr Steele. Indianapolis: The Bobbs-Merrill Company, [c1917]. 390 p., col. front., [9] leaves of col. plates.   **OSU, SOI**
"Copyright by Collier's weekly under the title *Help wanted*."
LC: Mr 19, '17.

Hall, Howard Girard, 1878-1921, jt. aut. *The millionaire detective*, (1905). <u>See</u> **Blaney, Charles E., d. 1944, jt. aut., B-674.**

H-78   ____ A soldier of the empire: a romance of the hundred days / by Howard Hall . . . New York; Washington: The Neale Publishing Company, 1903. 225 p., photo. front. (port.).   **VHB**
PW: Ag 15, '03.

H-79   Hall, Jarvis, *pseud*. Across the mesa / by Jarvis Hall [pseud.]; frontispiece by Henry Pitz. Philadelphia: The Penn Publishing Company, 1922. 319 p., front.
LC: Je 1, '22.

H-80   ____ Through Mocking Bird Gap / by Jarvis Hall [pseud.]; frontispiece by Joseph M. Clement. Philadelphia: The Penn Publishing Company, 1921. 303 p., front.
LC: Ap 12, '21.
PW: Ap 16, '21.

H-81   ____ Up the Rito / by Jarvis Hall [pseud.]; jacket and frontispiece by R. J. Cavaliere. Philadelphia: The Penn Publishing Company, 1925. 316 p., front.
LC: Ag 11, '25.
PW: Je 27, '25.

H-82   Hall, Leland, b. 1883. Sinister house / by Leland Hall: with illustrations by Haydon Jones. Boston; New York: Houghton Mifflin Company, 1919. (Cambridge: The Riverside Press). 226 p., front., [3] leaves of plates.   **NYP**
LC: F 10, '19.

H-83   Hall, Manly Palmer, b. 1901. Shadow forms: a collection of occult stories / by Manly P. Hall;

frontispiece by Homer Conant. -- 1st ed. -- Los Angeles, Calif.: The Hall Publishing Co., [c1925]. 165 p., col. front.

Contents: Black hat sorcery -- The witch doctor -- The teapot of Mandarin Wong -- Silver souls -- The third eye -- The spirit of the snows -- The lots of the great god Shiva -- The temple of sin -- The dance of the veils -- The emerald tablet -- Your God and my God -- The cave of the apes.

Hall, Margery Watson. See **Watson, Margery, b. 1864.**

H-84   Hall, Marshall R., 1889-1947. The valley of strife / by Marshall R. Hall. Boston: Small, Maynard & Company, [c1925]. 292 p.
LC: Je 13, '25.
PW: Je 6, '25.

Hall, Owen. A warm corner in Sooloo. In *The battle for the Pacific* (1908), **B-357.**

H-85   Hall, Ruth, b. 1858. A downrenter's son / by Ruth Hall. Boston; New York: Houghton, Mifflin and Company, 1902. (Cambridge: The Riverside Press). 304 p.
PW: O 4, '02.

H-86   _____ The golden arrow: a story of Roger Williams's day / by Ruth Hall . . . Boston; New York: Houghton, Mifflin and Company, 1901. (Cambridge: The Riverside Press). 316 p., front. [Ill. by Frank T. Merrill.]
PW: O 12, '01.

H-87   _____ The Pine Grove house / by Ruth Hall. Boston; New York: Houghton, Mifflin and Company, 1903. (Cambridge: The Riverside Press). 290 p.   **AZU**

Hall, S. Roland. Brothers. In *Clever business sketches* (1909), **C-490.**

H-88   Hall, Thomas. Twenty years a lumberjack: a tale of the pine woods / by Thomas Hall. Chicago: The Charles E. Thompson Co., [c1909]. 224 p., ill.
                      NYP

H-89   Hall, Violette. Chanticleer: a pastoral romance / by Violette Hall; illustrated by W. Granville Smith. Boston: Lothrop Publishing Company, [1902]. 304 p., col. front., [7] leaves of col. plates.
PW: Ag 23, '02.

Hall, Virginia, jt. aut. *Glint of wings* (1922). See **Moffett, Cleveland, 1863-1926, jt. aut., M-889.**

H-90   Hallet, Richard Matthews, b. 1887. The canyon of the fools / by Richard Matthews Hallet; with illustrations by W. H. D. Koerner. New York; London: Harper & Brothers, [c1922]. 409 p., front., [3] leaves of plates.
LC: Ap 4, '22.
PW: Ap 1, '22.

_____ The harbor master. In *The best short stories of 1921 and the yearbook of the American short story* (1922), **B-566.**

H-91   _____ The lady aft / by Richard Matthews Hallet; illustrated by Sidney M. Chase. Boston: Small, Maynard and Company, [c1915]. 352 p., front.
LC: Ag 24, '15.
PW: Je 19, '15.
BLC: London: T. Werner Laurie, [1915].

_____ Making port. In *The best short stories of 1916 and the yearbook of the American short story* (1917), **B-561.**

_____ Rainbow Pete. In *The best short stories of 1917 and the yearbook of the American short story* (1918), **B-562.**

_____ The razor of Pedro Dutel. In *The Grim thirteen* (1917), **G-537.**

_____ To the bitter end. In *The best short stories of 1919 and the yearbook of the American short story* (1920), **B-564.**

H-92   _____ Trial by fire: a tale of the Great Lakes / by Richard Matthews Hallet; with a frontispiece by O. E. Cesare. Boston: Small, Maynard and Company, [c1916]. 308, [1] p., col.front.
LC: Je 19, '16.
PW: My 27, '16.

H-93   Hallett, E. R. (Eldora Rodenbeek), b. 1861. Driven out by flame / by E. R. Hallett. Philadelphia: Dorrance, [1922?]. 333 p.
LC: N 1, '22.

H-94   Hallett, Rosa Kellen. Serena and Samantha: being a chronicle of events at the Torbolton home / by Rosa Kellen Hallett. Boston: Sherman, French & Company, 1912. 174 p.
Reprinted from Youth's companion.

H-95   Halloran, Edna Parthenia. The way out / Edna Parthenia Halloran. Boston: Richard G. Badger, [c1913]. ([Boston, U. S. A.]: The Gorham Press). 59 p.   **DLC**
PW: Ag 9, '13.

Hallowell, Eleanor A. The perfect year. In *Different girls* (1906), **D-383.**

H-96   Hallworth, Joseph. Arline Valère: a story of life / reproduced in facsimile from the original manuscript of Joseph Hallworth; with one hundred and eighty sketches by the author. Boston: L. C. Page & Company, 1901. 161 p., ill.
PW: Ag 17, '01.

H-97   Halphide, Alvan Cavala. The fulfilling of the law / by Alvin [sic] Cavala Halphide . . . 1st ed. Chicago: M. A. Donohue & Company, [c1907]. 256 p.
Unexamined copy: bibliographic data from OCLC, #18367502.

H-98   Halsey, Forrest. The bawlerout / by Forrest Halsey. New York: Desmond FitzGerald, Inc., [c1912]. 211 p., col. front.
LC: Je 4, '12.
PW: Je 15, '12.

H-99   ____ Fate and the butterfly / by Forrest Halsey. New York: B. W. Dodge & Company, 1909. 276 p., col. front. (port.), [3] leaves of plates. [Ill. by H. Richard Boehm.]
LC: Mr 31, '09.

H-100   ____ The shadow on the hearth / by Forrest Halsey. Westerville, Ohio: American Issue Pub. Co., [c1914]. 156 p., plates.
Unexamined copy: bibliographic data from OCLC, #11589383.

H-101   ____ The stain / by Forrest Halsey; with illustrations by Thomas Fogarty. Chicago: F. G. Browne & Co., 1913. 343 p., front., [3] leaves of plates.
LC: Mr 8, '13.
PW: Mr 8, '13.

H-102   ____ A term of silence / by Forrest Halsey. New York: Desmond Fitzgerald, Inc., [c1913]. 246 p.
LC: O 24, '13.

Halsey, Frank Davis. <u>See</u> **McAlister, Frank A., jt. pseud. of McAlister Coleman and Frank Davis Halsey.**

H-103 [Halsey, Mina Deane], b. 1873. A tenderfoot in southern California / by M. D. Yeslah. New York: Printed for the author by J. J. Little & Ives Co., 1908. 149, [1] p.
LC: S 28, '08.

H-104   ____ When east comes west / by Mina Deane Halsey. New York: Printed for the author by J. J. Little & Ives Co., 1909. 110 p.

H-105   ____ Whiskeretta / by Mina Deane Halsey . . . New York: Printed for the author by J. J. Little & Ives Co., 1911. 46 p.
LC: D 16, '11.

H-106 Halsted, Leonora B. A victorious life / by Leonora B. Halsted; frontispiece by H. Richard Boehm. New York: The Metropolitan Press, 1910. 320 p., col. front.

H-107 Hamblen, Herbert Elliott, b. 1849. The red-shirts: a romance of the old volunteer fire department / by Herbert E. Hamblen. New York; London: Street & Smith, [c1902]. 341 p., front., [7] leaves of plates.
BLC: London: Shurmer Sib Thorp, [1902].

H-108 Hamby, William H. (William Henry), 1876-1928. The desert fiddler / by William H. Hamby; frontispiece by Ralph Pallen Coleman. Garden City, N. Y.; Toronto: Doubleday, Page & Company, 1921. 232 p., front.
LC: My 2, '21.
PW: Ap 2, '21.

H-109   ____ The Ranch of the thorn: an adventure story / by William H. Hamby. New York: Chelsea House, [c1924]. 312 p.
LC: F 5, '24.
PW: F 2, '24.
BLC: London: Hutchinson & Co., 1924.

H-110   ____ The sound of the hammer: a story / by William H. Hamby. [S. l.: s. n., ca. 1914]. 23 p. "Reprinted from Ainslee's magazine."

H-111   ____ Tom Henry of Wahoo County: a story of the Ozarks / by William H. Hamby. Philadelphia: Westminster Press, 1911. 189 p., front., [11] leaves of plates. [Ill. by Sears Gallagher.]
Unexamined copy: bibliographic data from OCLC, #10347538.
PW: S 2, '11.

H-112 Hamill, Katherine B. (Katherine Bernie), b. 1877. A flower of Monterey: a romance of the Californias / by Katherine B. Hamill; with illustrations in full color by Jessie Gillespie and Edmund H. Garrett. Boston: The Page Company, 1921. 341 p., col. front., [1] leaf of col. plates.

H-113 Hamilton, Charles William. Shooting over decoys: and other tales / by Charles William Hamilton . . . Boston: David D. Nickerson & Co., 1923. 307 p., front., [15] leaves of plates.   **AUM**
Contents: Shooting over decoys -- A boy's gun -- A Thanksgiving turkey -- Stubble and prairie -- The scape of the snipe -- Birdo and Bobwhite -- Jumping mallards -- A wild goose chase -- The white flag -- Chasing a phantom -- A mountain pass -- Up in the hills -- A pair of antlers -- A little bear tale -- The Professor's lion.
LC: D 31, '23.

H-114 Hamilton, Ida Stuart. The passion flower: a romance / by Ida Stuart Hamilton. New York: Printing by the Irving Press, [c1918]. 132 p.   **DLC**
LC: Ag 12, '18.

H-115 Hamilton, J. C. M. (James Crawford McKinney), b. 1845. The golden key / by J. C. M. Hamilton. New York: Cosmopolitan Press, 1911. 235 p.
Unexamined copy: bibliographic data from OCLC, #18286478.

H-116 Hamilton, James Gilbert. " 'Twas ever thus": a novelette / by James Gilbert Hamilton . . . Litchfield, Ill.: Union Printing Co.; Hillsboro, Ill.: Montgomery News, [c1914]. 24 p., front., plates.
Unexamined copy: bibliographic data from NUC.

Hamilton, Robert W., pseud. <u>See</u> **Stratemeyer, Edward, 1862-1930.**

H-117 Hamilton, Sylla W. (Sylla Withers), 1883-1946. Forsaking all others: a story of Sherman's march through Georgia / by Sylla W. Hamilton. New York; Washington: The Neale Publishing Company, 1905. 197 p.   **BKL**

H-118 Hamilton, W. T. (William Thomas), 1822-1908. The three stages of Clarinda Thorbald / by William T. Hamilton, Jr. Philadelphia: Dorrance, [c1924]. 190 p.   **OSU, DLC**
LC: F 27, '24.

H-119 Hamlin, John H. (John Hamlin), b. 1880. Beloved acres / by John Hamlin; illustrated by Charles Lassell. New York; London: The Century Co., [c1925]. 228 p., front., [3] leaves of plates.
LC: S 1, '25.
PW: S 5, '25.

Hammond, Clara the Marquise. See **Lanza, Clara, b.1859.**

H-120 Hammond, Gilbert Romine. Wilfred Glenn, or, The struggle with wealth / by Gilbert Romine Hammond . . . ; with five illustrations. Dayton, Ohio: Printed by Drury Printing Co., [c1911]. 269 p., [5] leaves of plates (4 photo.).

H-121 Hammond, Harold, b. 1874. West Point: its glamour and its grind / by Captain Harold Hammond . . . New York: Cupples & Leon Company, [c1910]. 254 p., photo. front., [11] leaves of photo. plates, ill.
LC: Mr 18, '10.

H-122 Hammond, L. H. (Lily Hardy), 1859-1925. In the garden of delight / by L. H. Hammond. New York: Thomas Y. Crowell Company, [c1916]. 262 p.
LC: S 15, '16.

H-123 _____ The master-word: a story of the South to-day / by L. H. Hammond. New York: The Macmillan Company; London: Macmillan & Co., Ltd., 1905. 334 p.

H-124 Hammond, Thomas West, b. 1850. On board a whaler: an adventurous cruise through southern seas / by Thomas West Hammond; illustrated by Harry George Burgess. New York; London: G. P. Putnam's Sons, 1901. ([New York]: The Knickerbocker Press). 397 p., front., [5] leaves of plates. **BTS**

H-125 Hamrick, Gemes L'mon. Terressa, a thrilling western romance. Tuttle, Okla.: The Author, 1911. 280 p., [1] leaf of plates (port.).
Unexamined copy: bibliographic data from OCLC, #12654134.
Also: Tuttle, Okla.: [Times Print], 1911.
Unexamined copy: bibliographic data from OCLC, #25537188.

H-126 Hanaranda, Mulla, b. 1882. Cabriba: the garden of the gods / by Mulla Hanaranda. New York: American Library Service, 1925. 421 p.

H-127 Hancock, Albert Elmer, 1870-1915. Bronson of the rabble: a novel / by Albert E. Hancock; with a frontispiece by Stanley M. Arthurs. Philadelphia; London: J. B. Lippincott Company, 1909. 321 p., col. front.
LC: S 29, '09.

H-128 _____ Henry Bourland: the passing of the cavalier / by Albert Elmer Hancock. New York: The Macmillan Company; London: Macmillan & Co., Ltd, 1901. 409 p., front., [7] leaves of plates. [Ill. by Will Grefé.]
PW: Je 1, '01.

H-129 Hancock, Elizabeth Hazlewood. Betty Pembroke / by Elizabeth Hazlewood Hancock. New York; Washington: The Neale Publishing Company, 1907. 309 p.
PW: D 28, '07.

H-130 Hanford, C. H. (Cornelius Holgate), 1849-1926. General Claxton: a novel / by C. H. Hanford. New York: The Neale Publishing Company, 1917. 263 p., photo. front. (port.).
PW: D 1, '17.

H-131 _____ Halcyon days in Port Townsend: historical novel / By C. H. Hanford. Seattle, Washington: Printed by Apex Printing Co., c1925. 118 p., [11] leaves of plates. **UPP**
LC: S 1, '25.

H-132 [Hankins, Arthur Preston], 1880-1932. The boss of Camp Four: a western story / by Emart Kinsburn

[pseud.]. New York City: Chelsea House, [c1925]. 256 p.
PW: My 16, '25.

H-133 _____ Canyon gold / by Arthur Preston Hankins . . . ; frontispiece by Charles Durant. New York: The Macaulay Company, c1925. 312 p., front.
LC: S 2, '25.
PW: Ag 22, '25.

H-134 _____ Cole of Spyglass Mountain / by Arthur Preston Hankins. New York: Dodd, Mead and Company, 1923. 309 p.
LC: Mr 7, '23.
PW: Mr 17, '23.

H-135 _____ Falcon, of Squawtooth: a western story / by Arthur Preston Hankins. New York: Chelsea House, [c1923]. 318 p.
LC: O 6, '23.
PW: O 20, '23.

H-136 [_____] Gems of promise: a western story / by Emart Kinsburn [pseud.]. New York: Chelsea House, [c1924]. 252 p.

H-137 _____ The heritage of the hills / by Arthur P. Hankins. New York: Dodd, Mead and Company, 1922. 307 p.
LC: Mr 22, '22.
BLC: London: Methuen & Co., 1923.

H-138 _____ The Jubilee girl / by Arthur Preston Hankins; with frontispiece by Mead Schaeffer. New York: Dodd, Mead and Company, 1921. 320 p., col. front.
LC: O 12, '21.

H-139 _____ The she boss: a western story / by Arthur Preston Hankins. New York: Chelsea House, [c1922]. 318 p., front.
LC: D 22, '22.
PW: Je 2, '23.

H-140 [_____] Squatters at Dabchick Lake / by Emart Kinsburn [pseud.]. New York: Chelsea House, [c1925]. 256 p.
PW: My 16, '25.

H-141 _____ The valley of Arcana / by Arthur Preston Hankins. New York: Dodd, Mead and Company, 1923. 281 p.
LC: S 20, '23.
PW: S 15, '23.

H-142 Hanna, Elizabeth Heming. High mountain: an idyl of the old south / by Elizabeth Heming Hanna. New York; London; Montreal: The Abbey Press, [c1902]. 124 p., front., [3] leaves of plates.

H-143 Hannan, Charles. The elder MacGregor / by Charles Hannan . . . illustrated by James H. Lowell, jr. New York: R. F. Fenno & Company, [c1904]. 171 p., front., [3] leaves of plates. **NDD**
Contents: MacGregor on humor -- The Salvation Army -- The gipsies of the glen -- Mistress Mackie and the powders -- MacGregor attends a fire -- Jimmy of the hills -- MacGregor and the white cow -- Angus Macrae -- MacGregor and the button -- MacGregor and the minister's coat -- Going for a soldier -- MacGregor on writing a book.
BLC: London: R. A. Everett & Co., 1902.

Hannett, Arthur Thomas, b.1884. See **Thomas, Arthur, pseud.**

H-144 Hannibal, P. M. (Peter M.), 1849-1935. Protect our schools: a story with a ring to it / by P. M. Hannibal. Dannebrog, Neb.: Published by P. M. Hannibal, 1901. (Dannebrog, Neb.: Dannebrog News Printers). 154 p.

H-145 ____ Thrice a pioneer: a story of forests, plains, and mountains / by P. M. Hannibal . . . Dannebrog, Nebr.: Published for P. M. Hannibal, c1901. (Blair, Nebr.: Danish Luth. Pub. House). 202 p. **EEM**
PW: Mr 1, '02.

H-146 ____ Uncle Sam's cabin: a story of a mighty mystery / by P. M. Hannibal . . . Dannebrog, Nebraska: P. M. Hannibal, c1910. (University Place, Neb.: Claflin Printing Co.). 616 p.

H-147 Hannis, Margaret. The emancipation of Miss Susana / by Margaret Hannis; frontispiece by August Spaenkuch; text illustrations by George E. Hausmann. New York; London: Funk & Wagnalls Company, 1907. 73, [1] p., front., ill.
LC: Jl 29, '07.
PW: O 5, '07.

____, jt. aut. The law and the letter (1907). See **Winn, Mary Polk, jt. aut., W-751.**

H-148 Hannon, William Morgan. The leading lady: a novel with a preface / by William Morgan Hannon . . . New Orleans: Latin Quarter Publishing Co., 1916. 118 p. **ABC**
LC: D 28, '16.

H-149 Hans, Joseph M. (Joseph Marion). Euskal jai, or, In quest of health and happiness / by The Euskal Jai Company; author, Joseph M. Hans. [New York?: The Euskal Jai Company?], c1904. 63 p. **DLC**

H-150 Hansbrough, Henry Clay, 1848-1933. The second amendment / by Henry Clay Hansbrough. Minneapolis: The Hudson Publishing Company, 1911. 359 p., front.

Hanscombe, Walter Clarence. See **Clare, W. H., pseud.**

H-151 Hanshew, Mary E. The riddle of the amber ship / by Mary E. and Thomas W. Hanshew. Garden City, N. Y.: Doubleday, Page & Company, 1924. 319 p.
LC: Ap 28, '24.
PW: Ap 19, '24.

H-152 ____ The riddle of the frozen flame / by Mary E. and Thomas W. Hanshew; illustrated by Walter De Maris. Garden City, N. Y.: Doubleday, Page & Company, 1920. 284 p., front., [3] leaves of plates.
LC: Je 7, '20.
PW: My 29, '20.

H-153 ____ The riddle of the mysterious light / by Mary E. and Thomas W. Hanshew. Garden City, N. Y.; Toronto: Doubleday, Page & Company, 1921. 323, [1] p., front. [Ill. by Walter De Maris.] **DLC**
LC: Ja 31, '21.

____, jt. aut. The riddle of the Purple Emperor (1919). See **Hanshew, Thomas W., 1857-1914, jt. aut., H-161.**

H-154 ____ The riddle of the spinning wheel: being an exploit in the career of Hamilton Cleek, detective / by Mary E. and Thomas W. Hanshew; frontispiece by Walter de Maris. Garden City, N. Y.: Doubleday, Page & Company, 1922. 305 p., front.
LC: N 18, '22.

H-155 Hanshew, Thomas W., 1857-1914. Cleek: the Man of the Forty Faces / by T. W. Hanshew. New York: Cassell & Company, 1913. 305 p.
LC: F 10, '13; F 15, '13.
PW: F 15, '13.
BLC: London: Cassell & Co., 1913.

H-156 ____ Cleek of Scotland Yard: being the record of the further life and adventures of that remarkable detective genius, "the Man of the Forty Faces," once known to the police as "the Vanishing Cracksman" / by T. W. Hanshew . . . ; illustrated from photographs of the motion pictures . . . Garden City, New York: Doubleday, Page & Company, 1914. 358 p., photo. front., [7] leaves of photo. plates, ill.
LC: Mr 2, '14.
PW: Mr 14, '14.
BLC: London: Cassell & Co., 1914.

H-157 ____ Cleek of the forty faces / by T. W. Hanshew. Garden City, N. Y.: Doubleday, Page & Company, 1911. 158 p.
Unexamined copy: bibliographic data from LC.
LC: Ja 4, '12.

H-158 ____ Cleek, the master detective / by T. W. Hanshew . . . ; illustrated by Gordon Grant. Garden City, New York: Doubleday, Page & Company, 1918. 343, [1] p., front., [3] leaves of plates.
LC: Mr 2, '18.

H-159 ____ Cleek's government cases / by Thomas W. Hanshew . . . Garden City, New York: Doubleday, Page & Company, 1917. 330 p., front., [4] leaves of plates. [Ill. by Clarence Rowe.]
LC: F 23, '17.
PW: Mr 10, '17.

____, jt. aut. with Mary E. Hanshew. The rape of fear. See *Masterpieces of mystery* **(1920), M-589.**

____, jt. aut. *The riddle of the amber ship* (1924). See **Hanshew, Mary E., jt. aut., H-151.**

____, jt. aut. *The riddle of the frozen flame* (1920). See **Hanshew, Mary E., jt. aut., H-152.**

____, jt. aut. *The riddle of the mysterious light* (1921). See **Hanshew, Mary E., jt. aut., H-153.**

H-160   ____ The riddle of the night: being the record of a singular adventure of that remarkable detective genius, Hamilton Cleek, the man of the forty faces, once known to the police as the Vanishing Cracksman / by Thomas W. Hanshew . . . ; illustrated by Gordon Grant. Garden City, New York: Doubleday, Page & Company, 1915. 319, [1] p., front., [3] leaves of plates, ill.
LC: S 18, '15.

H-161   ____ The riddle of the Purple Emperor / by Thomas W. and Mary E. Hanshew; illustrated by Walter de Maris. Garden City, New York: Doubleday, Page & Company, 1919. 309, [1] p., front., [3] leaves of plates.
LC: Mr 22, '19.

____, jt. aut. *The riddle of the spinning wheel* (1922). See **Hanshew, Mary E., jt. aut., H-154.**

H-162   Hanson, Daniel Louis. The business philosophy of Moses Irons / by Daniel Louis Hanson; illustrated by Charles D. Mitchell. New York; Chicago; London: A. W. Shaw Company, [c1920]. 348 p., front., [2] leaves of plates.

H-163   Hanson, Joseph Mills, b. 1876. The trail to El Dorado / by Joseph Mills Hanson . . . ; illustrations by Dorothy Dulin. Chicago: A. C. McClurg & Co., 1913. 241, [1] p., incl. front., ill.   **SDS**
LC: Ag 1, '13.

H-164   ____ With Carrington on the Bozeman Road / by Joseph Mills Hanson . . . ; illustrated by John W. Norton. Chicago: A. C. McClurg & Co., 1912. 411 p., front., [4] leaves of plates.
(Among the Sioux series.)
LC: O 2, '12.

H-165   ____ With Sully into the Sioux land / by Joseph Mills Hanson . . . ; illustrated by John W. Norton. Chicago: A. C. McClurg & Co., 1910. 407 p., front., [4] leaves of plates.   **OSU, KLG**
(Among the Sioux series.)
LC: N 16, '10.

H-166   Hapgood, Hutchins, 1869-1944. An anarchist woman / by Hutchins Hapgood . . . New York: Duffield & Company, 1909. 308 p.
LC: Ap 30, '09.
PW: My 22, '09.

Hapgood, Neith (Boyce). See **Boyce, Neith, 1872-1951.**

H-167   Harband, Beatrice M. Daughters of darkness in sunny India / by Beatrice M. Harband . . . New York; Chicago; Toronto; London; Edinburgh: Fleming H. Revell Company, [c1903]. 302 p., photo. front.   **GFC**
PW: Je 20, '03.

H-168   Harbaugh, T. C. (Thomas Chalmers), 1849-1924. Middletown Valley in song and story / by T. C. Harbaugh. [S. l.: s. n.], [c1910]. 173 p., photo. front. (port.), [19] leaves of plates (some photo. by Marken & Bielfeld, Frederick, Md.).
Contents: When "Jim" came back -- The old valley mills [poem] -- The tanyard mystery -- When I come back to Middletown [poem] -- Left till called for -- The ballad of Nancy Crouse [poem] -- Witch Margery -- The bells of Middletown [poem] -- Sergeant Everhart's Christmas Eve -- Christmas on South Mountain [poem] -- The mysterious guests -- A dream of the daisies [poem] -- $5,000 reward -- From Braddock Heights [poem] -- Silver Star -- The march to South Mountain [poem] -- Polly Crumbine's Jake -- Before the trolley came [poem] -- "Turn me over" -- Where Catoctin seeks the sea [poem] -- At twelve o' the clock -- The old turnpike [poem] -- Mr. Grossnickle's ghost -- The old home [poem] -- Old Markley's spook -- The meadows of Catoctin [poem] -- The Valley in time of war -- When Betty came to Middletown [poem] -- The marked letter -- The old elm [poem] -- The hero of Highland -- Who has not heard? [poem] -- An uninvited Santa Claus -- Christmas in the Valley [poem] -- "A Catoctin mystery" -- In memoriam [poem] -- The stolen bride -- The death of Reno [poem] -- A matchless panorama -- The old school house [poem] -- Doctor Bear's patient -- Polly Snurr's elopement.

H-169   Harben, Will N. (William Nathaniel), 1858-1919. Abner Daniel: a novel / by Will N. Harben. New York; London: Harper & Brothers, 1902. 311, [1] p.
PW: Je 28, '02.

H-170   ____ Ann Boyd: a novel / by Will N. Harben. New York; London: Harper & Brothers, 1906. 389, [1] p., col. front.
LC: S 14, '06.
PW: S 22, '06.

H-171   ____ The cottage of delight: a novel / by Will N. Harben. New York; London: Harper & Brothers, [c1919]. 426, [1] p., front. [Ill. by R. Alston Brown.]
LC: S 9, '19.
PW: S 20, '19.

H-172   ____ The desired woman: a novel / by Will N. Harben. New York; London: Harper & Brothers, 1913. 406, [1] p., col. front. [Ill. by F. Rogers.]
LC: S 6, '13.

H-173   ____ The divine event / by Will N. Harben. New York; London: Harper & Brothers, [c1920]. 357, [1] p.
LC: S 25, '20.
PW: O 2, '20.

H-174   ____ Dixie Hart / by Will N. Harben. New York; London: Harper & Brothers, 1910. 339, [1] p., col. front. [Ill. by Harold Matthews Brett.]
LC: O 8, '10.

H-175   ____ The Georgians: a novel / by Will N. Harben. New York; London: Harper & Brothers, 1904. 337, [1] p.
PW: S 17, '04.

H-176   ____ Gilbert Neal: a novel / by Will N. Harben. New York; London: Harper & Brothers, 1908. 361, [1] p., col. front.
LC: S 24, '08.
PW: O 10, '08.

H-177   ____ The hills of refuge: a novel / by Will N. Harben. New York; London: Harper & Brothers, [1918]. 431, [1] p., front.
LC: O 29, '18.
PW: N 9, '18.

H-178   ____ The inner law: a novel / by Will N. Harben. New York; London: Harper & Brothers, [c1915]. 398, [1] p., front. [Ill. by Dexter C. Wilson.]
LC: S 9, '15.
PW: S 11, '15.

H-179   ____ Jane Dawson: a novel / by Will N. Harben. New York; London: Harper & Brothers, 1911. 363, [1] p., front.
LC: S 30, '11.
PW: O 14, '11.

H-180   ____ Mam' Linda: a novel / by Will N. Harben; illustrated by F. B. Masters. New York; London: Harper & Brothers, 1907. 387, [1] p., front., [7] leaves of plates.
LC: S 11, '07.
PW: S 21, '07.

H-181   ____ The New Clarion: a novel / by Will N. Harben. New York; London: Harper & Brothers, 1914. 374 p., front. [Ill. by Stockton Mulford.]
LC: S 5, '14.
PW: S 12, '14.

H-182   ____ Paul Rundel: a novel / by Will N. Harben. New York; London: Harper & Brothers, 1912. 411, [1] p., front. [Ill. by Walter Biggs.]
LC: S 27, '12.

H-183   ____ Pole Baker: a novel / by Will N. Harben. New York; London: Harper & Brothers, 1905. 357, [1] p.
PW: O 14, '05.

H-184   ____ The redemption of Kenneth Galt / by Will N. Harben. New York; London: Harper & Brothers, 1909. 352 p., front.
LC: S 25, '09.
PW: O 9, '09.

H-185   ____ Second choice: a romance / by Will N. Harben. New York; London: Harper & Brothers, [1916]. 367, [1] p., front. [Ill. by Wilson C. Dexter.]
LC: S 9, '16.
PW: S 16, '16.

H-186   ____ The substitute / by Will N. Harben . . . New York; London: Harper & Brothers Publishers, 1903. 329, [1] p.
PW: Mr 28, '03.

H-187   ____ The triumph: a novel / by Will N. Harben. New York; London: Harper & Brothers, [1917]. 396, [1] p., front. [Ill. by Wilson C. Dexter.]
LC: Ag 27, '17.
PW: S 1, '17.

H-188   ____ Westerfelt: a novel / by Will N. Harben. New York; London: Harper & Brothers, 1901. 329, [1] p.
PW: Je 29, '01.

H-189   ____ The woman who trusted: a story of literary life in New York / by Will N. Harben . . . Philadelphia: Henry Altemus Company, [c1901]. 257 p., photo. front. (port.).   **TXT**
"Originally published as a serial in The Saturday evening post."
PW: Mr 23, '01.

H-190   Harboe, Paul, d. 1907. The son of Magnus / by Paul Harboe. New York: J. F. Taylor & Company, 1902. 339 p., front. [Ill. by James E. McBurney.]
PW: O 18, '02.

    Hardart, Francis J. The two red lights. In *The Tragedy that wins and other short stories* **(1905), T-343.**

H-191   Hardin, Norma B. (Norma Bertha). Archdeacon Prettyman in politics / by Norma B. Hardin. Boston, Massachusetts: The Stratford Company, [c1921]. 215 p., front., [3] leaves of plates.   **NYP**

H-192   Harding, Ellison. The Demetrian / by Ellison Harding. New York: Brentano's, 1907. 315 p.
LC: Ap 9, '07.
PW: My 11, '07.

H-193   Harding, John W. (John William), b. 1864. The chorus lady / by James Forbes; novelized from the play by John W. Harding; illustrations from scenes of the play. New York: G. W. Dillingham Company, [1908]. 329 p., photo. front., [7] leaves of photo. plates.
LC: Mr 6, '08.
PW: Mr 28, '08.

H-194   ____ The city of splendid night / by John W. Harding . . . ; frontispiece by Carol Aus; other illustrations by Charles Grunwald. New York: G. W. Dillingham Company, [c1909]. 330 p., front., [4] leaves of plates.
LC: F 15, '09.
PW: Mr 13, '09.
BLC: London: T. Fisher Unwin; New York [printed], 1919.

H-195   ____ The gate of the kiss: a romance in the days of Hezekiah, king of Judah / by John W. Harding; illustrated by George Varian. Boston: Lothrop Publishing Company, [1902]. 403, [1] p., front., [3] leaves of plates.
PW: My 17, '02.
BLC: London: Charles H. Kelly, 1902.

H-196   The girl question: founded on the play of Will M. Hough and Frank R. Adams / by John W. Harding; illustrations by Gordon Grant. New York: G. W. Dillingham Company, [c1908]. 216 p., front., [5] leaves of plates.
LC: O 16, '08.
PW: N 14, '08.

H-197   Paid in full / by Eugene Walter; a story of modern American life, novelized from the play by John W. Harding; illustrations from scenes in the play. New York: G. W. Dillingham Company, [1908]. 333 p., front., [6] leaves of plates.
LC: My 21, '08.
PW: Je 6, '08.

H-198   The time, the place and the girl / from the play of Will M. Hough and Frank R. Adams; by John Harding; illustrations by Gordon Grant. New York: G. W. Dillingham Company, [c1908]. 166 p., front., [5] leaves of plates.
LC: Ag 4, '08.
PW: Ag 29, '08.

H-199 Harding, Lewis A. (Lewis Albert), 1880-1944. The call of the hour / by Lewis Albert Harding; with twelve illustrations by Eva M. Truesdell. Wichita, Kansas: The Sunflower Publishing Company, 1913. 183 p., ill.   **EYM**
Partly reprinted from various periodicals.

H-200 Harding, Robert Cosmo. O'Connor's career / by Robert Cosmo Harding. Baltimore, Md.: Saulsbury Publishing Company, [c1919]. 203 p.   **DLC**
LC: Jl 17, '19.

H-201 Harding, William Newman. Richard Neilson / by William Newman Harding. Baltimore, Md.: The McLean Co., 1917. 368 p.   **NYP**

H-202 Hardy, Arthur Lemuel, b. 1874. The clutch of circumstance / by Arthur Lemuel Hardy. Boston: Mayhew Publishing Co., 1909. 137 p., front. (port.). Unexamined copy: bibliographic data from OCLC, #16637916.
LC: O 15, '09.

H-203 Hardy, Arthur Sherburne, 1847-1930. Aurélie / by Arthur Sherburne Hardy; with illustrations by Elizabeth Shippen Green. New York; London: Harper & Brothers Publishers, 1912. 30, [1] p., col. front., [1] leaf of col. plates, ill.
LC: S 14, '12.
PW: S 21, '12.
References: BAL 7050.

H-204   Diane and her friends / by Arthur Sherburne Hardy; with illustrations by Elizabeth Shippen Green. Boston; New York: Houghton Mifflin Company, 1914. (Cambridge: The Riverside Press). 298, [1] p., front., [7] leaves of plates.
LC: O 19, '14
References: BAL 7051.

H-205   Helen / by Arthur Sherburne Hardy. Boston; New York: Houghton Mifflin Company, 1916.

(Cambridge: The Riverside Press). 314, [1] p., front. [Ill. by Elizabeth Shippen Green.]
LC: N 6, '16.
PW: N 25, '16.
References: BAL 7052.

H-206   His daughter first / by Arthur Sherburne Hardy. Boston; New York: Houghton, Mifflin and Company, 1903. 349 p.
LC: Ap 30, '03.
PW: My 16, '03.
References: BAL 7049.

H-207   No. 13, Rue du Bon Diable / by Arthur Sherburne Hardy; with illustrations. Boston; New York: Houghton Mifflin Company, 1917. (Cambridge: The Riverside Press). 212, [1] p., front., [9] leaves of plates, ill.
LC: O 20, '17.
PW: O 27, '17.
References: BAL 7054.

Hardy, Cora Armistead. Epoch making. In *A book of Bryn Mawr stories* (1901), **B-732.**

H-208 Hardy, Lowell, b. 1878. Frosty Ferguson, strategist / by Lowell Hardy; illustrations by Will Crawford. New York: John Lane Company; London: John Lane: The Bodley Head; Toronto: Bell & Cockburn, 1913. 80 p., front., [2] leaves of plates.

H-209 Hargrave, Will Loftin. Wallannah: a colonial romance / by Will Loftin Hargrave. Richmond: B. F. Johnson Publishing Company, 1902. 429 p., front., [7] leaves of plates. [Ill. by A. C. MaclLvain.]
PW: Mr 8, '02.

H-210 Hargreaves, William. The lost and found!, or, who is the heir? / by Wm. Hargreaves . . . New York; [Philadelphia, Pa.]: For sale by the National Temperance Society and Publication House, and the author . . . Philadelphia, Pa., [1901]. 168 p.

Haring, Elizabeth Jane. Susan's mountain. In *Club stories* (1915), **C-502.**

H-211 Harkins, E. F. (Edward Francis), b. 1872. The schemers: a tale of modern life / by Edward F. Harkins; with a frontispiece by Ernest Fosbery. Boston: L. C. Page & Company, 1903. 396 p., front.
BLC: London: Chatto & Windus, 1904.

H-212 Harl, Ruth. Lord Strathmore's ruby / by Ruth Harl; with frontispiece by Walter Wagner. Chicago: Albert H. King, 1915. 124 p., front.

Harlan, M.R., Mrs., b. 1879. **See Cottrell, Marie, pseud.**

H-213 Harland, Henry, 1861-1905. The lady paramount / by Henry Harland. London; New York: John Lane, 1902. 291, [1] p.
LC: Ap 9, '02.
PW: Ap 19, '02.
References: BAL 7085.

H-214   ____ My friend Prospero: a novel / by Henry Harland; frontispiece by Louis Loeb. New York: McClure, Phillips & Co., 1904. 317 p., front.
LC: Ja 20, '04.
PW: Ja 23, '04.
References: BAL 7089.

H-215   ____ The royal end: a romance / by Henry Harland . . . New York: Dodd, Mead & Company, 1909. 349 p.
LC: F 18, '09.
PW: Ap 10, '09.
References: BAL 7092.

H-216   Harland, Marion, *pseud.* The Carringtons of High Hill: an old Virginia chronicle / by Marion Harland [pseud.]. New York: Charles Scribner's Sons, 1919. 308 p.
LC: S 10, '19.

H-217   ____ The distractions of Martha / by Marion Harland [pseud.]; illustrated by R. Emmett Owen. New York: Charles Scribner's Sons, 1906. 223 p., front., [9] leaves of plates.
LC: S 27, '06.
PW: S 15, '06.

H-218   ____ In our county: stories of old Virginia life: illustrated / by Marion Harland [pseud.] . . . New York; London: G. P. Putnam's Sons, 1901. (New York: The Knickerbocker Press).
465 p., photo. front., [11] leaves of plates.
Contents: Dodder -- The big revival at Pine Creek -- Our family skeleton -- Samuella -- At the spa -- "V. V." -- The overseer's wife -- Marthy -- The desire of his eyes -- The Lethe mystery.
PW: S 28, '01.

H-219   ____ A long lane / by Marion Harland [pseud.]; frontispiece. New York: Hearst's International Library Co., 1915. 363 p., col. front. [Ill. by Welp.]
LC: N 5, '15.
PW: N 27, '15.

H-220   ____ When grandmamma was fourteen / by Marion Harland [pseud.] . . . ; illustrated by Etheldred B. Barry. Boston: Lothrop Publishing Company, [1905]. 399 p., front., [3] leaves of plates, ill. **VLR**
PW: S 23, '05.

H-221   Harley, Ella, b. 1887. The husband in Texas / by Ella Harley; illustrated by Pauline Harley. New York: The Neale Publishing Company, 1913. 190 p., front., [3] leaves of plates.
LC: N 19, '13.

H-222   Harman, B. Harrison. Business is business; the ruin of materialism and the hope of idealism in the interest of justice / by B. Harrison Harman. Boston: Richard G. Badger, [c1922]. (The Gorham Press, [Boston, U. S. A.]). 277 p.   **CS2**

Harmonia, pseud. jt. aut. *The island of sheep,* (1920). See **Cadmus, pseud. jt. aut., C-25.**

H-223   Harney, Will Wallace. The spirit of the South / Will Wallace Harney. Boston: Richard G. Badger, 1909. ([Boston]: The Gorham Press). 227 p.   **TJC**
Contents: Who won the pretty widow? -- Reverend Mr. Bland's wrestle with the Chester White hog -- A western seeress. [Poetry on p. 155-227.]
LC: Je 14, '09.
PW: Je 19, '09.

Harper, Carrie A., jt. aut. *The beau's comedy* (1902). See **Dix, Beulah Marie, 1876-1970, jt. aut., D-400.**

H-224   Harper, Henry Howard, b. 1871. Bob Hardwick: the story of his life and experiences / by Henry Howard Harper. New York: Issued privately by the De Vinne press and printed only on advance subscriptions from members of the Bibliophile Society, c1911. 303 p., front. (port.), [3] leaves of plates. [Ill. by W. H. W. Bicknell.]
LC: O 12, '11.

H-225   ____ The codicil: a novel / by Henry Howard Harper. New York: Issued privately by The Vail-Ballou Company, 1915. 293 p., front., [3] leaves of plates.
LC: Ap 27, '15.

H-226   ____ The devils' nest: (a novel) / by Henry Howard Harper; with etched frontispiece by W. H. W. Bicknell. Boston: Printed privately, 1923. 312 p., front.
LC: D 26, '23.

H-227   ____ The stumbling block: a novel / by Henry H. Harper. Boston: [s. n.], 1912. 253 p., front. [Ill. by W. H. W. Bicknell.]
"This volume is printed only in a limited edition, for complimentary distribution by the author."

H-228   ____ The tides of fate: a novel / by Henry Howard Harper; with original copperplate etchings by W. H. W. Bicknell. Boston: Privately printed, 1918, [c1919]. 324 p.
LC: Ap 18, '19.
PW: Je 7, '19.

H-229   ____ The unexpected Hodgkins: a novel / by Henry Howard Harper. New York: Issued privately by the Vail-Ballou Company and printed only on advance subscriptions from members of the Bibliophile Society, 1915. 316 p., front.
LC: Ap 27, '15.

H-230   Harper, Olive, 1842-1915, *pseud.* Fighting Bill, sheriff of Silver Creek: a romantic story based upon the great play of the same name / by Olive Harper [pseud.] . . . New York: J. S. Ogilvie Publishing Company, c1907. 187 p.
PW: O 5, '07.

H-231   ____ The sociable ghost: being the adventures of a reporter who was invited by the sociable ghost to a grand banquet, ball, and convention under the ground of old Trinity churchyard. A true tale of the things he saw and did not see while he was not there / written down by Olive Harper [pseud.] and another;

illustrated by Thomas McIlvaine and A. W. Schwartz. New York: J. S. Ogilvie Publishing Company, c1903. 235 p., front., [13] leaves of plates. Designed end papers.
PW: Je 27, '03.

Harper, Sarah Jane, b. 1863. See **Humphreys, Dean, pseud.**

H-232   Harper, Vincent. The mortgage on the brain: being the confessions of the late Ethelbert Croft, M. D. / by Vincent Harper; illustrated by Charles Raymond Macauley. New York: Doubleday, Page & Company, 1905. 293 p., front., [3] leaves of plates.
BLC: London: Hutchinson & Co.; New York printed, 1905.

H-233   The Harper prize short stories: the twelve prize-winning short stories in the 1924-25 short story contest conducted by Harper's magazine / the judges Meredith Nicholson, Zona Gale, Bliss Perry; the authors Conrad Aiken, Edwina Stanton Babcock, Margaret Wilkin Banning . . . [et al.]; with an introduction by Bliss Perry . . . New York; London: Harper & Brothers Publishers, 1925. 359 p.
Contents: Preface -- Introduction / Bliss Perry -- Loutré / Lisa Ysaye Tarleau -- Redbone / Ada Jack Carver -- The hands of the enemy / Charles Caldwell Dobie -- Legend / Fleta Campbell Springer -- Women come to judgment / Margaret Culkin Banning -- The girl in the tree / Alice Brown -- Wavering gold / Edwina Stanton Babcock -- Wild geese / Charles Caldwell Dobie -- When Hell froze / Wilbur Daniel Steele -- The amateur / Phoebe H. Gilkyson -- A captain out of Etruria / A. R. Leach -- The disciple / Conrad Aiken -- Biographical notes.
LC: S 18, '25.
PW: O 10, '25.

H-234   Harré, T. Everett (Thomas Everett), 1884-1948. Behold the woman!: a tale of redemption / by T. Everett Harré . . . Philadelphia; London: J. B. Lippincott Company, 1916. 400 p.
LC: Ap 21, '16.
PW: Ap 15, '16.

H-235   ____ The eternal maiden: a novel / by T. Everett Harré. New York: Published by Mitchell Kennerley, [c1913]. 279 p.

H-236   ____ One hour and forever: the story of a woman and a love supreme / (as told to and set down by) T. Everett Harré. New York: The Macaulay Company, [c1925]. 374 p.
LC: Mr 19, '25.
PW: Ja 31, '25.

H-237   Harrigan, Edward, 1845-1911. The Mulligans / by Edward Harrigan; illustrations by L. F. A. Lorenz. New York: G. W. Dillingham Company, 1901. 451 p., front., [3] leaves of plates.
PW: O 5, '01.
BLC: London: T. Fisher Unwin; New York [printed], 1901.

H-238   Harriman, Alice, 1861-1925. Chaperoning Adrienne: a tale of the Yellowstone national park / by Alice Harriman-Browne; with illustrations by Charles M. Russell, and photographs. [Seattle: Metropolitan Press, c1907]. 92, [4] p., inc. front., ill.

H-239   ____ A man of two countries / by Alice Harriman; chapter headings by C. M. Dowling. New York; Seattle: The Alice Harriman Company, 1910. 301 p.
LC: N 14, '10.

____ Old Bill's awkward squad. In **Seattle Writer's Club.** *Tillicum tales* **(1907), S-248.**

H-240   Harriman, Karl Edwin, 1875-1935. Ann Arbor tales / by Karl Edwin Harriman. Philadelphia: George W. Jacobs and Company, 1902. 322 p.
Contents: The making of a man -- The kidnapping -- The champions -- The case of Catherwood -- The door -- A nocturne -- A modern Mercury -- The day of the game -- The old professor.
PW: D 6, '02.

H-241   ____ The girl and the deal / by Karl Edwin Harriman; with illustrations by W. H. D. Koerner. Philadelphia: George W. Jacobs & Co., [c1905]. 349 p., front., [11] leaves of plates.

H-242   ____ The girl out there / by Karl Edwin Harriman; with illustrations by A. Russell. Philadelphia; London: George W. Jacobs & Co., [1906]. 356 p., front., [5] leaves of plates.

H-243   ____ The homebuilders / by Karl Edwin Harriman . . . Philadelphia: George W. Jacobs and Company, 1903. 329 p.   **CLE**
Contents: The homebuilders -- The casting of a stone -- The patriots -- The will of Anton Tschaeche -- The wage of his toil -- Daddy -- The day of the game -- The artist.
PW: F 6, '04.
BLC: London: S. C. Brown, Longham & Co., 1904.

H-244   ____ Sadie: the story of a girl, some men, and the eternal fitness of things / by Karl Edwin Harriman. New York: D. Appleton and Company, 1907. 309, [1] p., front., [3] leaves of plates. [Ill. by Charlotte Weber-Ditzler and Henry Raleigh.]
LC: O 25, '07.

H-245   Harriman, Miriam. Ah-Ling of Peking: a romance of old China / by Miriam Harriman. New York: George H. Doran Company, [c1923]. 87 p.   **KSU**

Harriman-Browne, Alice. See **Harriman, Alice, 1861-1925.**

Harrington, Eugune W., b. 1866. See **Stoddard, Cal, pseud.**

H-246   Harrington, George W. (George Wheaton), b. 1874. The plebian pestilence: a small-pox interlude / by George W. Harrington . . . Boston; New York: The Cornhill Publishing Company, [c1922]. 110 p.
         DLC
LC: Ag 7, '22.

H-247   ____ A reversion of form: and other horse stories / by George W. Harrington. Boston: Sherman, French & Company, 1911. 226 p.
Contents: A reversion of form -- In compatibility -- Found -- A coup d' état -- The renunciation -- "Peach" -- Separation -- Paragon Wilkes: Jack of all trades -- The misfit.
LC: Jl 12, '11.

Harrington, John Walker. Ottenhausen's coup. In *Love* (1901), L-525.

Harriott, Clara (Morris). See **Morris, Clara, 1848-1925.**

H-248   Harris, Albert W. (Albert Wadsworth), 1867-1958. Cracker tales / by Albert W. Harris. [s. l.]: Privately Printed, [c1912]. 93 p., col. front.
Contents: Henry gets started -- The Bensons -- Mark Mitchell, the swamp angel -- I get the answer to several questions -- The "Sunk Lands" -- The smoking compartment.
LC: D 19, '12.

H-249   Harris, Brady. The spirit of the West: a tale of the Ozarks / written, illustrated, edited and published by Brady Harris. West Plains, Mo.: Journal Press, c1904. 126 p., ill.
Unexamined copy: bibliographic data from OCLC, #15558856.

H-250   Harris, Clare Winger, b. 1891. Persephone of Eleusis: a romance of Ancient Greece / by Clare Winger Harris. Boston, Mass.: The Stratford Company, 1923. 219 p.
LC: Ja 12, '23.

H-251   Harris, Corra, 1869-1935. A circuit rider's widow / by Corra Harris; illustrated by Walter H. Everett. Garden City, N. Y.: Doubleday, Page & Company, 1916. 374 p., front., [5] leaves of plates.
LC: S 28, '16.
PW: N 4, '16.

H-252   _____ A circuit rider's wife / by Corra Harris; with illustrations by William H. Everett. Philadelphia: Henry Altemus Company, [c1910]. 336 p., front., [7] leaves of plates.
LC: Jl 15, '10.
PW: Ag 13, '10.
BLC: London: Constable & Co., 1911.

H-253   _____ The co-citizens / by Corra Harris; illustrated by Hanson Booth. Garden City, New York: Doubleday, Page & Company, 1915. 220 p., front., [3] leaves of plates.
LC: S 28, '15.
PW: S 11, '15.

H-254   _____ A daughter of Adam / by Corra Harris. New York: George H. Doran Company, [c1923]. 333 p.
LC: Mr 30, '23.
PW: Mr 31, '23.
BLC: London: Hodder & Stoughton; printed in U. S. A., [1923].

H-255   _____ Eve's second husband / by Corra Harris; illustrated. Philadelphia: Henry Altemus Company, [c1911]. 352 p., front., [3] leaves of plates.
LC: F 23, '11.
PW: Mr 11, '11.
BLC: London: Constable & Co., 1911.

H-256   _____ The eyes of love / by Corra Harris. New York: George H. Doran Company, [c1922]. 317 p.
LC: Jl 24, '22.
PW: Je 3, '22.

H-257   _____ From sunup to sundown / by Corra Harris and Faith Harris Leech. Garden City, New York: Doubleday, Page & Company, 1919. 363, [1] p.
MUM
LC: Mr 22, '19.
PW: Mr 22, '19.

H-258   _____ Happily married / by Corra Harris. New York: George H. Doran Company, [c1920]. 287 p.
LC: F 16, '20.
PW: F 21, '20.
BLC: London: Hodder & Stoughton; printed in U. S. A., [1920].

H-259   _____ In search of a husband / by Corra Harris . . . Garden City, New York: Doubleday, Page & Company, 1913. 328 p., col. front., [1] leaf of plates. [Ill. by C. H. Taffs and Howard Giles.]
LC: O 27, '13.
PW: N 8, '13.
BLC: London: Grant Richards; printed in the United States, [1913].

H-260   _____ Justice / by Corra Harris; illustrations by Gayle Hoskins. New York: Hearst's International Library Co., 1915. 53 p., front., [3] leaves of plates.
LC: O 12, '15.
PW: N 13, '15.

H-261   _____ Making her his wife / by Corra Harris; illustrated by W. B. King. Garden City, N. Y.: Doubleday, Page & Company, 1918. 283, [1] p., front., [3] leaves of plates.
LC: Mr 18, '18.
PW: Ap 20, '18.
BLC: London: T. Nelson Sons, [1924].

H-262   _____ My son / by Corra Harris . . . New York: George H. Doran Company, [c1921]. 274 p.
LC: Ap 26, '21.
PW: Ap 9, '21.
BLC: London: Hodder & Stoughton; printed in U. S. A., [1921].

H-263   _____ The recording angel / by Corra Harris; illustrated by W. H. Everett. Garden City, N. Y.: Doubleday, Page & Company, 1912. 331 p., col. front., [3] leaves of col. plates.
LC: My 8, '12.
PW: Ap 6, '12.
BLC: London: Constable & Co.; Garden City, N. Y. [printed], 1912.

H-264   Harris, Credo Fitch, 1874-1956. Sunlight Patch / by Credo Harris. Boston: Small, Maynard & Company, [c1915]. 392 p., front. [Ill. by G. W. Gage.]
LC: N 29, '15.
PW: N 27, '15.

H-265   _____ Toby: a novel of Kentucky / by Credo Harris. Boston: Small, Maynard and Company, [c1912]. 367 p.
LC: My 4, '12.

H-266   _____ Where the souls of men are calling / by Credo Harris; frontispiece by John R. Neill. New York:

Britton Publishing Company, [c1918]. 298 p., col. front.
LC: Ap 17, '18.
PW: My 25, '18.

H-267   ____ Wings of the wind / by Credo Harris. Boston: Small, Maynard & Company, [c1920]. 338 p.
LC: Jl 8, '20.
PW: Jl 3, '20.

H-268   Harris, Eleanor E. The game of Doeg: a story of the Hebrew people / with illustrations by Alfred Feinberg. Philadelphia: The Jewish Publication Society of America, 1914. 189 p., front., [4] leaves of plates.

H-269   Harris, Frances Allen. Among the meadows: a novel / by Frances Allen Harris. New York; Washington: The Neale Publishing Company, 1905. 384 p.   **KSL**

H-270   ____ The Cameo Lady / by Frances Allen Harris. Philadelphia: Dorrance, [c1922]. 114 p.
LC: My 6, '22.

H-271   Harris, Frank Burlingame, 1873-1897. The road to Ridgeby's / by Frank Burlingame Harris. Boston: Small, Maynard & Company, 1901. 334 p.
PW: Jl 20, '01.

H-272   Harris, Garrard, 1876-1927. Joe, the book farmer: making good on the land / by Garrard Harris; illustrated. New York; London: Harper & Brothers, 1913. 350, [1] p., front., [5] leaves of plates.

H-273   Harris, Henry E. The king of Andorra / by Henry E. Harris. New York; London; Montreal: The Abbey Press, [c1901]. 288 p.
PW: F 15, '02.

H-274   Harris, J. O. (Joanis Orlando). Colonel Johnson of Johnson's Corners / by J. O. Harris . . . ; illustrated by Buckton Nendick. Chicago: Published from the office of the Insurance Post of Chicago by Charles A. Hewitt, [c1901]. 249 p., front., ill.
PW: S 28, '01.

H-275   Harris, Joel Chandler, 1848-1908. Gabriel Tolliver: a story of reconstruction / by Joel Chandler Harris. New York: McClure, Phillips & Co., 1902. 448 p.
LC: Jl 11, '02. (BAL notes "a special printing was deposited for copyright . . .")
PW: O 4, '02.
References: BAL 7149.

H-276   ____ A little Union scout / by Joel Chandler Harris . . . ; illustrated by George Gibbs. New York: McClure, Phillips & Co., 1904. 181 p., col. front., [7] leaves of col. plates.
LC: Ap 15, '04.
PW: Ap 23, '04.
BLC: London: Duckworth; printed in U. S. A., 1904.
References: BAL 7153.

____ Major Perdue's bargain. **In** *International short stories* **(1910), I-29.**

H-277   ____ The making of a statesman: and other stories / by Joel Chandler Harris . . . New York: McClure, Phillips & Co., 1902. 246, [1] p.
Contents: The making of a statesman -- A child of Christmas -- Flingin' Jim and his fool-killer -- Miss Puss's parasol.
LC: Mr 25, '02.
PW: My 17, '02.
References: BAL 7148.

H-278   ____ The shadow between his shoulder-blades / by Joel Chandler Harris; with illustrations by George Harding. Boston: Small, Maynard and Company, [c1909]. 132 p., front., [3] leaves of plates.
LC: O 21, '09.
PW: S 25, '09.
References: BAL 7162.

H-279   Harris, Joseph D. (Joseph Daniel), b. 1854. Two practical heroines / by Joseph D. Harris; illustrated. New York: Broadway Publishing Company, [c1905]. 127 p., front., [2] leaves of plates. [Ill. by Sydney K. Hartman.]
PW: Ap 1, '05.

Harris, May. In the interests of Christopher. **In** *Quaint courtships* **(1906), Q-3.**

H-280   Harris, Kennett, b. 1864. Meet Mr. Stegg / by Kennett Harris. New York: Henry Holt and Company, 1920. 320 p., front. [Ill. by Rodney Thomson.]
Contents: The brachycephalic bohunkus -- Getting even -- Concerning cautious Clyde -- The bird in the hand -- The metamorphosis of Mary Ann -- Benny and her familee.
LC: D 27, '20.

H-281   Harris, Linnie Sarah, b. 1868. Sweet Peggy / by Linnie Sarah Harris . . . Boston: Little, Brown, and Company, 1904. 279 p., front., plates.
                                          NYP (micro.)
PW: O 22, '04.

H-282   Harris, Merton L. The golden mirage: a romance of the great Southwest / by Merton L. Harris. New York; Chicago; London; Edinburgh: Fleming H. Revell Company, [c1925]. 272 p.   **TNS**
LC: O 14, '25.
PW: Ag 15, '25.

H-283   Harris, Miriam Coles, 1834-1925. The tents of wickedness / by Miriam Coles Harris. New York: D. Appleton and Company, 1907. 474 p., col. front. [Ill. by Harrison Fisher.]
LC: O 4, '07.

H-284   Harris, Nick, b. 1882. In the shadows: thirty detective stories: showing "why crime doesn't pay": a series of famous cases / by detective Nick Harris. Los Angeles: The Times-Mirror Press, 1923. 361 p., photo. front. (port.), ill. [Some ill. by Helene Rico.]
Contents: The confession of a master burglar -- The suffering of the innocent -- Fight crime with advertising -- Mabel's mistake -- The Stockdale murder -- The calling of Johnny MacRay -- The secret cipher -- Circumstantial evidence -- The pal of "Jimmy the Rat" -- The phantom shot -- The cause of divorces -- The policeman's tryst -- The Cowards murder -- The yellow slip -- A pair of shoes -- The murder scoop -- The death of Desdemona -- "A mass of golden hair"

-- Just a little dog -- The jet earrings -- Queen of the safe crackers -- The trunk bandit -- The national swindle -- The mystery woman -- Witherell case -- The modern Bluebeard -- The old man's violin -- Murder of Father Heslin -- Friday, the thirteenth -- The passing of Sergeant Fitzgerald.

H-285   Harris, Virginia Fisher. Tillie, a love story / by Virginia Harris Fisher. [Tyler, Tex.: Lee & Burnett, printers, 1903]. 163 p.   **DLC (micro)**
LC: Je 5, '03.
PW: O 31, '03.

H-286   Harris, W. S. (William Shuler), b. 1865. Life in a thousand worlds / by Rev. W. S. Harris; illustrated. Dallas, Tex.: Published by Peter J. Talty, [c1905]. 344 p., [19] leaves of plates.
DLC copy: Cleona, Pa.: G. Holzapfel, [1905].

H-287   ____ Mr. World and Miss Church-Member: a twentieth century allegory / by Rev. W. S. Harris; with an introduction by Bishop R. Dubs . . . ; illustrations by Paul J. Krafft. Harrisburg, PA: Evangelical Press, c1901. 315 p., ill.

H-288   ____ The prince of Raccoon Fork / by Baxter Harrison. Boston: The Roxburgh Publishing Company, [c1917]. 188 p.   **NYP**
LC: Ap 17, '18.
PW: My 25, '18.

H-289   Harrison, Burton, Mrs., 1843-1920. The Carlyles: a story of the fall of the Confederacy / by Mrs. Burton Harrison. New York: D. Appleton and Company, 1905. 283 p.   **CLE**
LC: O 20, '05.
PW: N 4, '05.
References: BAL 7223.

H-290   ____ The count and the congressman / by Mrs. Burton Harrison . . . ; illustrated by Alex O. Levy. New York: Cupples & Leon Company, [c1908]. 300 p., front., [2] leaves of plates.   **GSU**
LC: My 5, '08. (BAL notes as advanced printing for copyright.)
PW: Ag 8, '08.
References: BAL 7228.

____ The fairy godmother's story. In *A house party* **(1901), H-903.**

H-291   ____ Latter-day sweethearts / by Mrs. Burton Harrison; illustrated in water-colors by Frank T. Merrill. New York; London: The Authors and News Association, 1907. 323 p., col. front., facsim., [4] leaves of col. plates.
LC: F 15, '07. (BAL 7225 notes "prepared for copyright purposes." Je 14, '06.)
PW: D 15, '06.
BLC: London: T. Fisher Unwin, 1906.
References: BAL 7227.

H-292   ____ A princess of the hills: an Italian romance / by Mrs. Burton Harrison . . . ; illustrated by Orson Lowell. Boston: Lothrop Publishing Company, [c1901]. 306 p., front., [3] leaves of plates.
LC: Je 19, '01.
PW: Je 29, '01.

BLC: London: Charles H. Kelly, 1901. Also, London: Methuen & Co., 1902.
References: BAL 7218.

H-293   ____ Sylvia's husband / by Mrs. Burton Harrison. New York: D. Appleton & Co., 1904. 221 p.   **GZM**
(Novelettes de luxe.)
LC: Ja 21, '04.
PW: F 6, '04.
References: BAL 7222.

H-294   ____ The unwelcome Mrs. Hatch / by Mrs. Burton Harrison. New York: D. Appleton & Co., 1903. 191 p., ill. [Ill. by Florence Pearl Nosworthy.] (Novelettes de luxe.)
LC: Je 20, '03.
PW: Je 27, '03.
References: BAL 7221.

Harrison, Constance Cary. See **Harrison, Burton, Mrs., 1843-1920.**

Harrison, Don. The mixing. In *Stories from the Midland* **(1924), S-984.**

H-295   Harrison, Edith Ogden. Clemencia's crisis / by Edith Ogden Harrison; illustrations by Fred J. Arting. Chicago: A. C. McClurg & Co., 1915. 257 p., front., ill.
LC: O 18, '15.

H-296   ____ The lady of the snows: a novel / by Edith Ogden Harrison; with illustrations and decorations by J. Allen St. John. Chicago: A. C. McClurg & Co., 1912. 290 p., col. front., [3] leaves of col. plates.
LC: O 28, '12.
PW: N 2, '12.

H-297   ____ Princess Sayrane: a romance of the days of Prester John / by Edith Ogden Harrison . . . ; with four pictures in color by Harold H. Betts. Chicago: A. C. McClurg & Co., 1910. 313, [1] p., col. front., [3] leaves of col. plates. Decorated end papers.
LC: O 19, '10.

H-298   Harrison, Ellanetta. The stage of life: a Kentucky story / by Ellanetta Harrison. Cincinnati: The Robert Clarke Company, 1903. 252 p., front., [5] leaves of plates.
PW: Ap 25, '03.

H-299   Harrison, Henry Sydnor, 1880-1930. Andrew Bride of Paris / Henry Sydnor Harrison. Boston; New York: Houghton Mifflin Company, 1925. 215 p., front., [3] leaves of plates. [Ill. by F. R. Gruger.]
LC: S 28, '25.
PW: S 26, '25.
BLC: London: Constable & Co., 1925.

H-300   ____ Angela's business / by Henry Sydnor Harrison; with illustrations by Frederic R. Gruger. Boston; New York: Houghton Mifflin Company, 1915. (Cambridge: The Riverside Press). 374, [2] p., front., [7] leaves of plates.
LC: Mr 29, '15.

PW: Mr 27, '15.
BLC: London: Constable & Co., 1915.

H-301   [____] Captivating Mary Carstairs / by Henry Second [pseud.]. Boston: Small, Maynard and Company, [c1910]. 346 p., front.
PW: Mr 4, '11
BLC: London: Constable Co., 1914.

____ Pursuit. In *Marriage* (1923), M-457.

H-302   ____ Queed: a novel / by Henry Sydnor Harrison; with a frontispiece by R. M. Crosby. Boston; New York: Houghton Mifflin Company, 1911. (Cambridge: The Riverside Press). 430 p., front.
LC: My 12, '11.
BLC: London: Constable & Co; Boston; New York: Houghton Mifflin Company, 1911.

H-303   ____ Saint Teresa: a novel / by Henry Sydnor Harrison. Boston; New York: Houghton Mifflin Company, 1922. (Cambridge: The Riverside Press). 455, [1] p.
LC: Ap 26, '22.
PW: Mr 18, '22.
BLC: London: Constable & Co.; Cambridge, Mass. printed, [1922].

H-304   ____ V. V.'s eyes / by Henry Sydnor Harrison; with illustrations. Boston; New York: Houghton Mifflin Company, 1913. (Cambridge: The Riverside Press). 508, [2] p., front., [3] leaves of plates. [Ill. by Raymond M. Crosby.]
LC: My 26, '13.
BLC: London: Constable & Co., 1913.

H-305   ____ When I come back / by Henry Sydnor Harrison. Boston; New York: Houghton Mifflin Company, 1919. (Cambridge: The Riverside Press). 68, [1] p.
LC: O 25, '19.
BLC: London: Constable & Co., 1920.

H-306   Harrison, Ida Withers, 1851-1927. Beyond the battle's rim: a story of the Confederate refugees / by Ida Withers Harrison. New York: The Neale Publishing Company, 1918. 247 p., photo. front.

H-307   Harrison, J. "Kind hearts and coronets" / J. Harrison. New York; Cincinnati; Chicago: Benziger Brothers, 1904, [c1903]. 279 p.
PW: Mr 26, '04.

H-308   ____ The way that led beyond / by J. Harrison . . . New York; Cincinnati; Chicago: Benziger Brothers, [c1904]. 222 p.   **ASH**
PW: O 22, '04.

H-309   Harrison, Mary Bennett. Shining windows / by Mary Bennett Harrison. Los Angeles: Harrison & Hathaway, [c1925]. 26 p.
LC: Ag 17, '25.

H-310   Harrison, T. Milner (Thomas Milner), b. 1865. Modern arms and a feudal throne: the romantic story of an unexplored sea / by T. Milner Harrison;

illustrations by W. E. Starkweather. New York: R. F. Fenno & Company, 1904. 376 p., front., [3] leaves of plates.

H-311   Harry, T. Everett (Thomas Everett), b. 1884. Infans amoris: the tale of a once sorrowful soul: a romance / by T. Everett Harry. New York; London; Montreal: The Abbey Press, [c1902]. 335 p. **BGU**

H-312   Hart, Edward, b. 1854. The silica gel pseudomorph: and other stories / by Edward Hart . . . Easton, Pa.: The Chemical Publishing Co.; London, England: Williams & Norgate; Tokyo, Japan: Maruzen Company, Ltd., 1924. 175 p.   **CLE**
Contents: The silica gel pseudomorph -- Peep-Chick Mountain -- Round Valley -- Mont L'Hery -- Death Valley -- The professor's story -- My friend Zahn -- Just Samuel Jones -- Fat and lean -- Woozy -- The hermit -- Sandy's story -- The hoboes -- Jumping steel -- All the way from Melbourne -- A defense of the wealthy -- The skin of the bear -- A visit from the Wileys -- In the days of the Roses -- The red devil.

H-313   Hart, Edwin Kirkman. Claire: a romance of American nursehood / Edwin Kirkman Hart. Philadelphia: Published by the author: for sale by the American Sunday-School Union, 1905. 280 p. incl. photo. front., [3] leaves of photo. plates.

H-314   Hart, Ethel Gertrude. The dream girl / by Ethel Gertrude Hart; illustrated by Gordon Grant. Garden City, New York: Doubleday, Page & Company, 1913. 274 p.

H-315   Hart, Frances Noyes, 1890-1943. Contact: and other stories / by Frances Noyes Hart. Garden City, N. Y.: Doubleday, Page & Company, 1923. 328 p.
Contents: "Contact" -- There was a lady -- Long distance -- Philip the Gay -- Green gardens -- Delilah -- Her Grace -- The honourable Tony.
LC: Je 6, '23.

____ The end of the path. In *The best short stories of 1915 and the yearbook of the American short story* (1916), B-560.

____ Green gardens. In *The best short stories of 1921 and the yearbook of the American short story* (1922), B-566.

H-316   ____ Mark / by Frances Newbold Noyes. New York: Edward J. Clode, [c1913]. 258 p., col. front., [9] leaves of plates. [Ill. by Fred Pegram.]

Hart, Jerome Alfred, 1854-1937, ed. See *Argonaut stories* (1906), A-298.

H-317   ____ The Golconda bonanza / by Jerome A. Hart. San Francisco: The Pioneer Press, [c1923]. 315 p., ill. [Ill. by Jules Tavernier, V. Nahl, and J. D. Strong.]
LC: N 8, '23.

H-318   ____ A vigilante girl / by Jerome Hart; illustrated by John W. Norton. Chicago: A. C. McClurg & Co., 1910. 397 p., front., [4] leaves of plates.
LC: Ap 4, '10.
PW: Ap 16, '10.

H-319   Hart, Mabel. Sacrilege farm / by Mabel Hart. New
         York: D. Appleton and Company, 1903. 333 p.
         (Appletons' Town and Country Library; no. 319.)
         PW: My 2, '03.
         BLC: London: William Heinemann, 1902.

         Hart, Mary, jt. aut. *Pinto Ben: and other stories*
         (1919). See **Hart, William Surrey, 1874-1946, jt.
         aut., H-321.**

         Hart, Nina, comp. See *Representative short stories*
         (1917), R-176.

H-320   Hart, William Surrey, 1874-1946. A lighter of
         flames / by William S. Hart. New York: Thomas Y.
         Crowell Company, [c1923]. 246 p., col. front., [3]
         leaves of col. plates. [Ill. by James Montgomery
         Flagg.]
         LC: O 3, '23.
         PW: O 20, '23.
         BLC: London: Brentano's, 1924.

H-321   _____ Pinto Ben: and other stories / by William S.
         Hart and Mary Hart; illustrations by R. L. Lambdin.
         New York: Britton Publishing Company, [c1919].
         95, [1] p., col. front., [7] leaves of plates (some
         col.).
         Reprinted from the New York morning telegraph and
         Lippincott's magazine.
         Contents: Pinto Ben -- a story in verse / William S. Hart -- The
         savage-a story / William S. Hart -- The last of his blood-a story /
         Mary Hart.
         LC: Ap 5, '19.

H-322   _____ Told under a white oak tree / by Bill Hart's
         pinto pony, edited by his master, William S. Hart;
         with illustrations by J. Montgomery Flagg. Boston;
         New York: Houghton Mifflin Company, [c1922].
         (Cambridge: The Riverside Press). 51 p., front., [7]
         leaves of plates.
         LC: S 16, '22.

H-323   Harte, Bret, 1836-1902. Condensed novels: second
         series; new burlesques / by Bret Harte. Boston; New
         York: Houghton, Mifflin and Company, 1902.
         (Cambridge: The Riverside Press). 236 p.
         Contents: Rupert the resembler -- The stolen cigar case -- Golly and
         the Christian, or, The minx and the manxman -- The adventures of
         John Longbowe, yeoman -- Dan'l Borem -- Stories three -- "Zut-ski".
         LC: S 29, '02.
         PW: O 11, '02.
         BLC: London: Chatto & Windus, 1903. (BAL notes
         1902.)
         References: BAL 7399.

         _____ A niece of Snapshot Harry's and other tales.
         See **Harte, Bret, 1836-1902.** *The writings of Bret
         Harte,* **H-331.**

H-324   _____ Openings in the old trail / by Bret Harte.
         Boston; New York: Houghton, Mifflin and
         Company, 1902. (Cambridge, Mass., U. S. A.: The
         Riverside Press). 332 p.
         LC: Ap 19, '02.
         PW: My 3, '02.
         References: BAL 7398. BAL 7397 notes: London:
         C. Arthur Pearson, Ltd., 1902. British title: *On the
         old trail.*

H-325   _____ Salomy Jane / by Bret Harte; with illustrations
         by Harrison Fisher and Arthur I. Keller. Boston;
         New York: Houghton Mifflin Company, 1910.
         (Cambridge: The Riverside Press). 78 p., [1] leaf of
         col. plates, ill. (some col.).
         First separate book appearance.
         LC: O 20, '10.
         PW: O 15, '10.
         BLC: London: Chatto & Windus; Cambridge, Mass.
         [printed], 1910.
         References: BAL 7546.

H-326   _____ Stories and poems and other uncollected
         writings / by Bret Harte; compiled by Charles Meeker
         Kozlay, with an introductory account of Harte's early
         contributions to the California press. Boston; New
         York: Houghton Mifflin Company, 1914.
         (Cambridge, Mass., U. S. A.: The Riverside Press).
         432 p., front. (port.), [3] leaves of plates.
         Also, Vol. 20. of *The writings of Bret Harte.*
         Contents: Bret Harte: dedication / by Ina Coolbrith -- Introduction --
         Early prose: Stories (1860-1865): My metamorphosis -- Boggs on
         the horse -- Story of the revolution -- A child's ghost story -- Facts
         concerning a meerschaum -- My otherself. A German-silver novel --
         "His wife's sister" -- A case of blasted affections -- "Ran away" --
         Madame Brimborion -- The lost heiress: a tale of the Oakland bar --
         The countess -- The petroleum fiend. A story of today -- Stories for
         little girls. Miscellaneous (1860-1870): Ships -- Wanted - a printer --
         Washington -- The Angelus -- Artemus Ward -- Fixing up an old
         house -- On a pretty girl at the opera -- Our last offering - (on the
         assassination of Abraham Lincoln) [nonfiction] -- Early Californian
         superstitions -- Popular biographies-Sylvester Jayhawk [nonfiction] --
         Stage-coach conversations -- The pioneers of "Forty-Nine" -- Lessons
         from the Earthquake [nonfiction] -- Charles Dickens [nonfiction] --
         Later prose: Stories: An American Haroun al-Raschid -- The first
         man -- Retiring from business -- A gentleman of La Porte.
         Miscellaneous: Washington in New Jersey -- What Bret Harte saw --
         American Humor [essay] -- The improved Æsop for intelligent
         modern children [fables] -- Confucius and the Chinese classics -- The
         great patent-office fire -- Longfellow [nonfiction] -- A few words
         about Mr. Lowell [nonfiction] -- My favorite novelist and his best
         book [nonfiction]. The remainder of the volume is poetry.
         LC: My 13, '14.
         PW: Jl 11, '14.
         References: BAL 7408.

H-327   _____ The story of Enriquez: Chu Chu, The devotion
         of Enriquez, The passing of Enriquez / by Bret Harte.
         San Francisco: [E. & R. Grabhorn], 1924. 194 p.
         Unexamined copy: bibliographic data from OCLC,
         #27426364.
         First separate book appearance. Issued in a case.
         References: BAL 7556.

H-328   _____ Tennessee's partner / by Bret Harte; including
         an introduction by William Dallam Armes; the
         frontispiece in photogravure from a painting by
         Albertine Randall Wheelan. San Francisco; New
         York: Paul Elder and Company, [c1907]. 38 p.,
         front.
         First separate book appearance. (Western classics,
         no. 3.)
         LC: O 7, '07.
         PW: D 21, '07.
         References: BAL 7542.

         _____ A treasure of the redwoods and other tales.
         See **Harte, Bret, 1836-1902.** *The writings of Bret
         Harte,* **H-331.**

H-329 _____ Trent's trust: and other stories / by Bret Harte. Boston; New York: Houghton, Mifflin and Company, 1903. (Cambridge, Mass., U. S. A.: The Riverside Press). 264 p.
Contents: Trent's trust -- Mr. MacGlowrie's widow -- A ward of Colonel Starbottle's -- Prosper's "old mother" -- The convalescence of Jack Hamlin -- A pupil of Chestnut Ridge -- Dick Boyle's business card.
LC: My 4, '03.
PW: My 16, '03.
BLC: London: Eveleigh Nash, 1903. (BAL 7403.)
References: BAL 7404.

H-330 _____ Under the redwoods / by Bret Harte. Boston; New York: Houghton, Mifflin and Company, 1901. (Cambridge, Mass., U. S. A.: The Riverside Press). 334 p.
Contents: Jimmy's big brother from California -- The youngest Miss Piper -- A widow of the Santa Ana Valley -- The mermaid of the Lighthouse Point -- Under the eaves -- How Reuben Allen "saw life" in San Francisco -- Three vagabonds of Trinidad -- A vision of the fountain -- A romance of the line -- Bohemian days in San Francisco.
LC: Ap 11, '01.
PW: Ap 27, '01.
BLC: London: Chatto & Windus, 1903. (BAL notes another London edition: Pearson, 1901.)
References: BAL 7396.

H-331 _____ The writings of Bret Harte. 20 vols. Reprints save for:
    Vol. 17: A niece of Snapshot Harry's and other tales / by Bret Harte. Boston; New York: Houghton, Mifflin Company, 1903. (Cambridge: The Riverside Press). 355 p. First book appearance of *The four guardians of Lagrange*.
    Vol. 18: A treasure of the redwoods and other tales / by Bret Harte. Boston; New York: Houghton, Mifflin Company, 1903. (Cambridge: The Riverside Press). 363 p. First book appearance of *How I went to the mines*.
    Vol. 20: Stories and poems and other uncollected writings. See separate entry above, H-326.
References: BAL 7384.

H-332 Harte, Emmet F. (Emmet Forrest), b. 1876. Honk & Horace, or, trimming the tropics / by Emmet F. Harte; illustrated by F. Fox. Chicago: The Reilly & Britton Co., [c1913]. 288 p., ill.

Harte, Jerome, b. 1883. Bruin and her baby. In *A bit of old ivory, and other stories* (1910), B-626.

_____, contributor. See *A double knot* (1905), D-499.

H-333 _____ The light of His countenance: a tale of Rome in the second century after Christ / by Jerome Harte. New York; Cincinnati; Chicago: Benziger Brothers, 1910. 276 p., front., [2] leaves of plates.
PW: Ap 30, '10.

_____ A midnight call. In *The Senior lieutenant's wager: and other stories* (1905), S-312.

_____ The picture in the fire. In *The lady of the tower* (1909), L-13.

_____ Pointing the moral. In *The friendly little house: and other stories* (1910), F-432.

_____ The song of the Hurdy Gurdy. In *The friendly little house: and other stories* (1910), F-432.

Hartman, Lee Foster, 1879-1941. The judgment of Vulcan. In *The best short stories of 1920 and the yearbook of the American short story* (1921), B-565; also *Prize stories of 1920* (1921), P-618.

H-334 _____ The white sapphire: a mystery romance / by Lee Foster Hartman; illustrated. New York; London: Harper & Brothers, 1914. 296, [1] p., front., [3] leaves of plates. [Ill. by John Newton Howitt.]

H-335 Hartmann, George, b. 1852. Tales of Aztlan: the romance of a hero of our late Spanish-American war: incidents of interest from the life of a western pioneer and other tales / by George Hartmann. -- Rev. ed. -- New York: Broadway Publishing Company, [c1908]. 163 p., photo. front. (port.)   AZU
First edition (1907) under title: *Wooed by a sphinx of Aztlan*.

H-336 _____ Wooed by a sphinx of Aztlan: the romance of a hero of our late Spanish-American war and incidents of interest from the life of a western pioneer / by George Hartmann. Prescott [Ariz.]: George Hartmann, 1907. 125 p., front. (port.)
Revised edition: *Tales of Aztlan*, 1908.

H-337 Hartshorn, Willard Lamonte. Short smokes / Willard Lamonte Hartshorn. [Evanston? Ill., 1903]. 157 p. Unexamined copy: bibliographic data from NUC.
Contents: The hand that filled it -- In a nurse's uniform -- Where teacher is pupil -- The man across the aisle -- The new rider -- The son of a hypnotist -- The five stages -- A compartment episode -- John Oaks.

H-338 Hartzell, Albert A. Alicia / by Albert A. Hartzell. Buffalo, N. Y.: Revere Publishing Company, [c1904]. 287 p., front., [3] leaves of plates. [Ill. by Percy Reeves.]   VTP

H-339 Harvey, Alexander, 1868-1949. Shelley's elopement: a study of the most romantic episode in literary history / by Alexander Harvey. New York: Alfred A. Knopf, 1918. 288 p.
LC: S 27, '18.

H-340 _____ The toe: and other tales / by Alexander Harvey. New York: Mitchell Kennerley, 1913. 251 p.
Reprinted in part from various periodicals.
Contents: The toe -- The raft -- The fools -- The finishing touch -- The finger of fate -- The measure of all things -- The mustache -- Miss Dix -- The forbidden floor -- The frou-frou -- The golden rat.
LC: D 18, '13.
PW: Ja 10, '14.

H-341 Harvey, Emma Bates, b. 1868. Greater than Caesar / by Emma Bates Harvey. Boston: James H. Earle & Company, 1902. 196 p., front.
PW: Je 13, '03.

Harvey, James Clarence, jt. aut. *The hills o' Hampshire* (1913). See **Cressy, Will, 1863-1940, jt. aut., C-927.**

H-342 Harvey, Louis V. The immortalizing of Texas: and other sketches / by Louis V. Harvey. New York: Every Where Publishing Company, [c1911]. 102 p., front.
Contents: The immortalizing of "Texas" -- The strontium crystal -- My closest shave -- The sign of the Magi -- A reminiscence of other days.

H-343 Harvey, Marion, b. 1900. The house of seclusion / by Marion Harvey. Boston: Small, Maynard & Company, [c1925]. 329 p.
LC: My 23, '25.
PW: My 2, '25.

H-344 ____ The mystery of the hidden room / by Marion Harvey. New York: Edward J. Clode, [c1922]. 312 p.   **CFI**
LC: O 9, '22.
BLC: London: Brentano's, 1923.

H-345 ____ The vengeance of the ivory skull / by Marion Harvey . . . New York: Edward J. Clode, [c1923]. 307 p.   **CLE**
LC: My 12, '23.
PW: Je 2, '23.

H-346 Harvey, William W. (William Wirt), b. 1866. Lige Golden: the man who twinkled / by William W. Harvey; illustrated by Thomas Hunt. Boston: B. J. Brimmer Company, 1924. 207 p., front., [5] leaves of plates.
LC: Jl 12, '24.

H-347 Harwell, Mary M. Friend. Almost an angel / by Mary M. Friend Harwell. New York; Washington: The Neale Publishing Company, 1908. 241 p. **DLC**
LC: Ag 19, '08.

H-348 Hasbrouck, Louise Seymour, b. 1883. The hall with doors / by Louise S. Hasbrouck; illustrated by Clinton Brown. New York: The Womans Press, 1920. 182 p., front., [3] leaves of plates.
PW: My 29, '20.

H-349 Haselden, Florence Taylor. Marion / by Florence Taylor Haselden. New York: Broadway Publishing Company, [c1908]. 104 p.   **DLC**
PW: Ja 23, '09.

H-350 Haskell, Oreola Williams, b. 1875. Banner bearers: tales of the suffrage campaigns / by Oreola Williams Haskell . . . ; with an introduction by Ida Husted Harper . . . Geneva, N. Y.: W. F. Humphrey, 1920. 350 p.   **KSU**
Contents: The invader -- Sizing up a boss -- Tenements and teacups -- Mrs. Rensling takes a rest -- The silent forces -- Stall-fed -- The nail -- Winds and weather-vanes -- A musical martyr -- When Hester hikes -- The yellow button -- A touch of romance -- A fallen star -- The greatest thing -- The poster -- The slogan -- Methods -- Sissies -- Switchboard suffrage -- The heart of a chief -- Four generations -- The great short cut.

Haskin, Sara Estelle. The story of a slave boy who became great. In *When God walks the road and other stories* (1924), W-445.

____, ed. See *When God Walks the Road and other stories* (1921), W-445.

H-351 Haslett, Harriet Holmes. Impulses: stories touching the life of Sandy, in the city of Saint Francis / by Harriet Holmes Haslett. Boston: The Cornhill Company, [c1920]. 259 p.
Contents: The case of Sandy -- The hobo dinner -- His first abduction -- The human lottery -- ...... "And a little child shall lead them" -- A lame dog -- The movie fan -- Pertaining to things spiritual -- The blue-eyed lady.
LC: Jl 2, '20.

____ The temptation of Ann O'Brien. In *West winds* (1914), W-368.

H-352 Hasley, Ida Frances. Jane Marvin / by Ida Frances Hasley . . . [Oklahoma City]: c1923. 19 p. Unexamined copy: bibliographic data from NUC.

Hassan, Abdul, pseud. See **Seymour, George Steele, b. 1878.**

Hassell, S. W. (Susan Whitcomb), ed. See *Club stories* (1915), C-502.

H-353 Hastings, Frank W. (Frank Warren), 1856-1925. The untamed philosopher: at home and with the Plugonians of Plugonia: being a tale of hens and some other people / by Frank W. Hastings. Boston, Mass.: The C. M. Clark Publishing Co., 1906. 258 p., incl. front., [8] leaves of plates. [Ill. by F. Gilbert Edge.]
The first thirteen chapters published in 1896 under title: *Wed to a lunatic.*

H-354 ____ Wed to a lunatic: a lie / by Frank W. Hastings. -- 2nd ed. -- St. Johnsbury, Vt.: Caledonian Press, 1901. 131 p.
"Enlarged and revised to meet the requirements of modern science." First ed., 1896.

H-355 Hastings, George Gordon. The first American king / by George Gordon Hastings. London; New York: The Smart Set Publishing Company, 1904. 354 p.
PW: Jl 2, '04.

H-356 Hastings, Henry. Mistress Dorothy of Haddon Hall: being the true love story of Dorothy Vernon of Haddon Hall / by Henry Hastings. New York: R. F. Fenno & Company, 1902. 296 p.
PW: Jl 5, '02.

H-357 Hastings, Milo, b. 1884. City of endless night / by Milo Hastings. New York: Dodd, Mead and Company, 1920. 346 p.
LC: S 16, '20.
PW: S 18, '20.

H-358 Hastings, Rosetta Butler, b. 1844. Coffin nails: the story of Jane McGregor / by Rosetta Butler Hastings . . . Clay Center, Kansas: The Dispatch Publishing Company, [c1908]. 264 p.   **DLC**

Hastings, Wells, 1879-1923. Gideon. In *The Best American humorous short stories* (1920), B-556.

H-359 ____ The man in the brown derby / by Wells Hastings; with illustrations by Herman Pfeifer. Indianapolis: The Bobbs-Merrill Company, [c1911]. 346 p., front., [4] leaves of plates.
LC: O 11, '11.

H-360   _____ The professor's mystery / by Wells Hastings and Brian Hooker; with illustrations by Hanson Booth. Indianapolis: The Bobbs-Merrill Company, [c1911]. 341 p., front., [4] leaves of plates.
LC: Mr 22, '11.

H-361   Haswell, A. M. (Alanson Mason), b. 1847. A daughter of the Ozarks / by A. M. Haswell. Boston: The Cornhill Company, [c1921]. 259 p.
LC: D 23, '21.

H-362   _____ A drama of the hills / by A. M. Haswell . . . Boston: The Cornhill Publishing Company, [c1923]. 348 p., front., [2] leaves of plates.   **KLG**
PW: Ap 12, '24.

Hatch, Samuel A. A baseball wager. In *Minnesota stories* **(1903), M-842.**

H-363   Hatcher, Eldridge B. (Eldridge Burwell), 1865-1943. Dorothy Page / by Eldridge B. Hatcher . . . Louisville, Ky.: Baptist World Publishing Co., 1912. 194 p.   **OSU, VIC**
PW: D 7, '12.

H-364   _____ The young professor: a story of Bible inspiration / Eldridge B. Hatcher. Nashville, Tennessee: Sunday School Board, Southern Baptist Convention, [c1901]. 503 p., photo. front., [7] leaves of plates.
(The Eva Garvey publishing fund; book no. 2.)

H-365   Hatfield, Clarence E. The echo of Union chapel: a tale of the Ozark low hill country / by Clarence E. Hatfield. New York: Broadway Publishing Co., [c1912]. 222 p.   **IAT**
LC: D 13, '12.

H-366   _____ The tug of the millstone / by Clarence E. Hatfield. Boston: Richard G. Badger; Toronto: The Copp Clark Co., Limited, [c1915]. 378 p.
LC: S 13, '15.
PW: S 18, '15.

H-367   Hatfield, Frank. The realm of light / by Frank Hatfield. Boston, Mass.: Reid Publishing Company; London: Arthur F. Bird, [1908]. 430 p.
PW: Ag 22, '08.

H-368   Hatfield, Richard, b. 1853. Geyserland: empiricisms in social reform / being data and observations recorded by the late Mark Stubble . . . ; edited by Richard Hatfield. Washington, D. C.: Printed for Richard Hatfield . . . , 1908. 451 p., front.
PW: Je 27, '08.

H-369   Hatkof, Judge. One summer at Lundy: a true history and not a summer idyl / by Judge Hatkof. [San Francisco, Calif.?: s. n., 1903]. 20 p., ill.
Unexamined copy: bibliographic data from OCLC, #26940190.

Hatton, Fanny Locke, jt. aut. *Years of discretion* (1913). See **Hatton, Frederic, 1879-1946, jt. aut., H-370.**

H-370   Hatton, Frederic, 1879-1946. Years of discretion / by Frederic Hatton and Fanny Locke Hatton; novelized from the play by the authors; with illustrations by Alonzo Kimball. New York: Dodd, Mead and Company, 1913. 349 p., col. front., [3] leaves of col. plates.
BLC: London: B. F. Stevens & Brown; printed in U. S. A., 1913. Another copy: Dublin; London: Maunsel & Co., 1914.

Haubold, Herman Arthur, 1867-1931. See **Trepoff, Ivan, pseud.**

H-371   Hauck, Darby. The death cry / by Darby Hauck; frontispiece by Eleanor Howard. New York: R. J. Shores, [c1917]. 275 p., incl. front.
Unexamined copy: bibliographic data from NUC and OCLC, #21106899.
LC: D 17, '17.

H-372   Hauck, Louise Platt, 1883-1943. Missouri yesterdays: stories of the romantic days of Missouri / by Louise Platt Hauck. Kansas City, Missouri: Burton Publishing Company, [c1920]. 207 p.   **LDL**
Contents: The ghost that walks in the full of the moon -- A Missouri apple blossom -- The tale of the freckled twins -- The little house of devotion -- His own rooftree -- Little lost love -- A black sheep -- During the night -- A little scandal -- The swamp fox of the Confederacy -- In Missouri -- Clarice.
"These stories first appeared in the St. Joseph Sunday gazette."
LC: O 28, '20.

H-373   _____ The mystery of Tumult Rock / by Louise Platt Hauck . . . Kansas City, Missouri: Burton Publishing Company, [c1920]. 277 p., incl. photo. front.   **SEM**
LC: O 10, '21.
PW: N 12, '21.

H-374   Hauser, I. L. Caste: a novel / by I. L. Hauser. Chicago: I. L. Hauser, 1908. 199 p.
Unexamined copy: bibliographic data from OCLC, #17124950.
LC: S 8, '08.

H-375   Haushalter, Walter M. (Walter Milton), b. 1889. The lotus thorne of Nirvana / by Walter M. Haushalter. Columbia, Mo.: Lucas Brothers, [c1924]. 272 p.

H-376   Havens, Munson Aldrich, 1873-1942. Old valentines: a love story / by Munson Havens; with illustrations. Boston; New York: Houghton Mifflin Company, 1914. (Cambridge: The Riverside Press). 224, [2] p., col. front., [3] leaves of col. plates. [Ill. by Griswold Tyng.]
PW: F 7, '14.
BLC: London: Constable & Co.; Cambridge, Mass. [printed], 1914.

H-377   Havermyer, Alfred. The conversion of John Stoneman / by Alfred Havermyer. [Berea, Ohio: Berea Printing Company, c1910.] 162 p.   **DLC**
LC: Ja 23, '11.

H-378   Hawes, Charles Boardman, 1889-1923. The dark frigate: wherein is told the story of Philip Marsham who lived in the time of King Charles and was bred a sailor but came home to England after many hazards by sea and land and fought for the King at Newbury and lost a great inheritance and departed for Barbados in the same ship, by curious chance, in which he had long before adventured with the pirates / by Charles Boardman Hawes; illustrated. Boston: The Atlantic Monthly Press, [c1923]. 247 p., front., [8] leaves of plates.
LC: N 5, '23.
BLC: London: William Heinemann, 1924.

____   Even so. In *The Bellman book of fiction* **(1921), B-485.**

H-379   ____ The great quest: a romance of 1826, wherein are recorded the experiences of Josia Woods of Topham, and of those others with whom he sailed for Cuba and the Gulf of Guinea / by Charles Boardman Hawes; illustrated by George Varian. Boston: The Atlantic Monthly Press, [c1921]. 359 p., front., [4] leaves of plates. Illustrated end papers.
LC: O 5, '21.
BLC: London: William Heinemann, 1922.

H-380   Hawes, George Edward. The fresh air child / by George Edward Hawes. New York; Chicago; Toronto; London; Edinburgh: Fleming H. Revell Company, [c1907]. 61 p., front., [1] leaf of plates. [Ill. by Griselda Marshall McClure.]   **NYP**

H-381   Hawkes, Clarence, 1869-1954. Piebald: king of bronchos: the biography of a wild horse / by Clarence Hawkes . . . ; illustrated by Charles Copeland. Philadelphia: George W. Jacobs & Co., 1912. 297 p., front., [4] leaves of plates. Illustrated end papers.
BLC: London: Hutchinson & Co., [1923].

Hawkins, Flora Legler. See **Legler-Hawkins, Flora.**

H-382   Hawkins, May Anderson, b. 1902. A wee lassie, or, A unique republic / by Mrs. May Anderson Hawkins . . . Richmond, Va.: Presbyterian Committee of Publication, [c1902]. 277 p., photo. front., [8] leaves of photo. plates.   **KUK**

Hawkins, Nehemiah, 1833-1928. See **Knight of Chillon of Switzerland and associates, pseud.**

H-383   Hawkins, Willis Brooks, 1852-1928. Andy Barr / by Willis B. Hawkins. Boston: Lothrop Publishing Company, [1903]. 472 p.

H-384   Hawks, Wells. Moonshine strategy: and other stories / by Wells Hawks . . . ; frontispiece by Harrison Fisher. Baltimore, Md.: I. & M. Ottenheimer, 1906. 137 p., front., [8] leaves of plates. [Additional ill. by E. V. Nadherny, F. C. Drake, W. H. Loomis, Clinton Peters, George McManus, Will R. Barnes, McKee Barclay, and E. Marcus.] Reprinted from various periodicals.
Contents: Moonshine strategy -- The orange obi -- Marse Arthur-- A blue pencil -- Amen -- The sidewalk spring -- His love and her's -- Franz -- Love's wreckage -- A penny in the slot -- The Lattimore Parker ball -- The girl with the beautiful shoulders.

LC: O 25, '06.
PW: D 1, '06.

H-385   ____ Red wagon stories, or, Tales told under the tent / by Wells Hawks. Baltimore, Md.: I. & M. Ottenheimer, [c1904]. 89, [1] p.
Contents: The press agent's story -- The Grafter's lament -- The Bill Poster's visit -- The Candy Butcher's dream of love -- The Boss Canvasman's yarn -- The side show Spieler speaks -- The band master's solo -- The Candy Butcher talks about a love affair and his encounter with the Buckwheat Man -- The concert manager gets reminiscent -- The hands at the window -- The concert manager tells the boys an elephant story.

H-386   Haworth, Paul Leland, 1876-1938. The path of glory / by Paul Leland Haworth; with illustrations by Harry C. Edwards. Boston: Little, Brown and Company, 1911. 348 p., front., [3] leaves of plates.
LC: Ap 27, '11.
PW: Ap 15, '11.
BLC: London: W. J. Ham-Smith, 1911.

Hawser, A. B., pseud. See **Muller, J. (Julius Washington), 1867-1930.**

H-387   Hawthorne, Hildegarde. A country interlude: a novelette / by Hildegarde Hawthorne. Boston; New York: Houghton, Mifflin and Company, 1904. (Cambridge: The Riverside Press). 161, [1] p.
PW: Mr 5, '04.

____   Perdita. In *Shapes that haunt the dusk* **(1907), S-339.**

Hawthorne, Julian, 1846-1934, ed. In *Library of the world's best mystery and detective stories* **(1908), L-277.**

H-388   ____ Lovers in heaven. New York: New Church Board of Publication, [1905]. 16 p.
Unexamined copy: bibliographic data from NUC.

H-389   Hay, Corinne. Light and shade 'round gulf and bayou / by Corinne Hay; illustrated. Boston: The Roxburgh Publishing Company, Inc., [c1921]. 222 p., front., [6] leaves of plates. [Ill. by Julia Ann Mountfort.]   **LNC**
Contents: The flaming sword -- Henrique Jacquard -- On James Creek -- Lone Grave Bluff -- Easter lilies -- The unwelcome tenant -- Alciphron.

H-390   Hay, Edwin Barrett, 1849-1906. The Vivians / by Edwin Barrett Hay. New York; Washington: The Neale Publishing Company, 1907. 315 p., photo. front. (port.).
PW: Ap 6, '07.

H-391   Hay, James, Jr., 1881-1936. The Bellamy case / by James Hay, Jr. . . . New York: Dodd, Mead and Company, 1925. 259 p.
LC: Ja 6, '25.
PW: Ja 10, '25.

H-392   ____ The man who forgot: a novel / by James Hay, Jr. Garden City, New York: Doubleday, Page & Company, 1915. 311 p.   **OSU, ABC**
LC: Ap 19, '15.
PW: Ap 10, '15.
BLC: London: Curtis Brown; Garden City, N. Y. printed, 1915.

H-393 ____ The Melwood mystery / by James Hay, Jr. . . New York: Dodd, Mead and Company, 1920. 323 p.
LC: Mr 23, '20.
PW: Ap 3, '20.

H-394 ____ Mrs. Marden's ordeal / by James Hay, Jr.; with frontispiece by Armand Both. Boston: Little, Brown and Company, 1918. 307 p., front.
LC: My 6, '18.
PW: Ap 27, '18.

H-395 ____ "No clue!": a mystery story / by James Hay, Jr. . . . New York: Dodd, Mead and Company, 1920. 288 p.
LC: S 16, '20.
PW: S 18, '20.
BLC: London: Herbert Jenkins, 1923 [1922].

H-396 ____ The unlighted house: a novel / by James Hay, Jr. . . . New York: Dodd, Mead and Company, 1921. 281 p.
LC: Mr 17, '21.
PW: Ap 23, '21.
BLC: London: Herbert Jenkins, 1922.

H-397 ____ The winning clue / by James Hay, Jr. New York: Dodd, Mead and Company, 1919. 298 p.
LC: Je 24, '19.
PW: Jl 12, '19.
BLC: London: Herbert Jenkins, 1920.

Hay, Timothy, pseud. <u>See</u> **Rollins, Montgomery, 1867-1918.**

H-398 Hayden, Clara R. A century of Tallahassee girls: as viewed from the leaves of their diaries / collected and compiled by Clara R. Hayden. [Atlanta: Foote & Davies Co., 1924?]. [36] p., ill. **NDD**
Cover title: *A century of Tallahassee girls, 1824-1924.*

H-399 Hayden, Eleanor G. From a thatched cottage / by Eleanor G. Hayden . . . New York: Thomas Y. Crowell & Co., Publishers, [1903?]. 309 p.
NYP (micro)
PW: Mr 7, '03.

H-400 Hayden, Sarah Marshall. Mr. Langdon's mistake: a novel / by Sarah Marshall Hayden . . . Washington, D. C.: John James Hayden, 1901. 383 p., photo. front., [7] leaves of plates (some photo., 1 port.).

H-401 Hayes, Cleburne Lee. The little schoolmistress / by Cleburne Lee Hayes. Nashville, Tennessee: The Claude J. Bell Company, [c1905]. 253 p.

H-402 Hayes, Ellen, 1851-1930. Two comrades / by Ellen Hayes . . . Boston: E. L. Grimes Company, 1912. 197 p. **SNN**

H-403 Hayes, Hiram W. (Hiram Wallace), b. 1858. Douglas / by Hiram W. Hayes . . . ; illustrated by Edmonston. Washington, D. C.: Published by The Howerton Press, [c1912]. 348 p., photo. front.
LC: O 31, '12.
PW: N 16, '12.

H-404 ____ The man of clay: (a tale of life) / by Hiram W. Hayes; illustrated by Alfred Russell. Boston: Published by Davis & Bond, [c1911]. 376 p., front., [2] leaves of plates.
LC: O 20, '11.
PW: D 16, '11.

H-405 ____ Matthew Brent / by Hiram W. Hayes. New York: The H. K. Fly Company, [c1923]. 285 p.
LC: D 31, '23.
PW: F 23, '24.

H-406 ____ Paul Anthony, Christian: a tale of truth / by Hiram W. Hayes. Boston, Mass.: Published by Reid Publishing Company, 1907. 415 p.
LC: D 13, '07.
PW: D 14, '07.
BLC: Boston, Mass.: Reid Publishing Co.; London: Arthur P. Bird, 1908.

H-407 ____ The peacemakers: a tale of love / by Hiram W. Hayes . . . Boston, Mass.: Published by Reid Publishing Co., [c1909]. 420 p., front.
LC: N 5, '09.
PW: N 13, '09.

H-408 ____ A prince of the realm / by Hiram W. Hayes . . . Boston, Mass.: Davis & Bond, [c1912]. 40 p.

H-409 ____ The Princess Sofia: a companion story to Paul Anthony, Christian and The man of clay / by Hiram W. Hayes. Boston, Mass.: Davis & Bond, [c1917]. 297 p., front.

H-410 ____ A royal good fellow / by Hiram W. Hayes. Washington, D. C.: Published by The Howerton Press, c1910. 200 p., front., [1] leaf of plates. [Ill. by Constance White.]
LC: S 16, '10.

H-411 ____ The starting point / by Hiram W. Hayes . . . Boston, Mass.: The Harmony Shop, [c1921]. 411 p.
LC: D 7, '21.
PW: Je 3, '22.

H-412 Hayes, J. W. (Jeff W.), 1853-1917. Paradise on earth / by Jeff W. Hayes. Portland, Ore.: F. W. Baltes and Company, 1913. 112 p., front. (port.).

H-413 ____ Portland, Oregon A. D. 1999: and other sketches / by Jeff W. Hayes . . . Portland, Oregon: F. W. Baltes and Company, 1913. 112 p., photo. front. (port.) **OSO**
Contents: Portland, Oregon, A. D. 1999 -- The bad man from Bodie -- He never came back -- Where did you get that oil -- A grapevine telegraph line -- Along the shore -- Showing off -- "Knifin' de dough" -- A musical aborigine -- "The gentleman of Havre" -- On the wing -- He knew a good thing -- Inadequate cuspidors -- No jobs, but vacancies -- Phenomenal telegraphing -- His old Kentucky -- The office at Spirit Lake -- The Indians were too loyal -- A governor for fifteen minutes took the bull by the horns -- The seven mounds -- When gold grew on sage brush.

H-414 Hayes, Mary Bassett. Alda's awakening: a story / by Mary Bassett Hayes. San Jose, California: The Mercury Herald Company, [192-?]. 144 p.

H-415 Haymond, Bruce. Borderland echoes: a West Virginia story / by Bruce Haymond; illustrated by twelve full page illustrations by the author. Boston: The Roxburgh Publishing Company, 1921, [c1922]. 264 p., front., [11] leaves of plates.

H-416   Haymond, W. E., Mrs. Agnes Cheswick: a novel / by Mrs. W. E. Haymond. New York: Isaac H. Blanchard Company, [c1901]. 128 p.   **DLC**
PW: Mr 22, '02.

H-417   Haynes, Williams, 1886-1960. Casco Bay yarns / by Williams Haynes . . . ; illustrated with photographs by the author. New York: D. O. Haynes & Co., [c1916]. 189 p., photo. front., [14] leaves of photo. plates.   **OSU, CSE**
Reprinted in part from various periodicals.
Contents: Live lobster -- Bewitched gold -- Tainted money -- The cruise of the Souse -- The story of Casco Bay: The land of Aucocisco ; The frontier of New England; 1776, 1812 and 1861 -- Casco myths and legends.
PW: Jl 29, '16.

H-418   Hays, Harold Melvin. Blighty / by Harold Hays . . . [New York City: Communal Prtg. Co., 1920]. 19 p.   **RBN**

H-419   Hays, Inda Barton. Dixie dolls: and other tales / by Inda Barton Hays; drawings by Hugh M. Eaton. New York: Broadway Publishing Company, 1904. 89 p., front. [6] leaves of plates.   **EMU**
Contents: Secessia Virginia -- Two war-time Christmas dolls -- The King's whirr -- A mountain blossom.
PW: F 4, '05.

H-420   Hays, Milton D. My grandfather's best brand, or, No, I thank you; and, A parent's mistake: two romances of the sixties / by Milton D. Hays; illustrated by F. R. Murray. Pittsburgh: Milton D. Hays Company, 1908. 320 p., incl. photo. front., [8] leaves of plates.

H-421   Hayward, Francis Sidney. Helen Ayr: a story of the square deal / by Francis Sidney Hayward. New York: Cochrane Publishing Co., 1908. 269 p., front., [2] leaves of plates.   **COD**
LC: D 11, '08.

H-422   Hayward, Laurence. The way hearts go: a social comedy / by Laurence Hayward. New York: E. P. Dutton & Company, [c1917]. 342 p.
LC: Ja 27, '17.
PW: F 3, '17.

H-423   Hayward, Rachel, b. 1886, *pseud*. The Hippodrome / by Rachel Hayward [pseud.]. New York: George H. Doran Comany, [c1913]. 295 p.
LC: Mr 26, '13.
PW: Ap 26, '13.
BLC: London: William Heinemann, 1913.

H-424   _____ Letters from Là-Bas / by Rachel Hayward [pseud.] . . . Boston: J. W. Luce and Company, 1914. 289 p.   **EMU**
BLC: London: William Heinemann, [1914].

H-425   Haywood, John Campbell. Driftwood and other tales / by John Campbell Haywood . . . Philadelphia: The United States Review Publishing Company, [c1905]. 119 p., photo. front., [1] leaf of photo. plates.

Contents: Driftwood -- One woman -- What happened at Harvey's -- The pyromaniac -- What happened at Cranston -- The yellow dog -- What happened at Hyslop's Grounded currents -- Okara Abdul Hassim -- An attic fantasy -- Bill Freeman, Chauffeur -- Bill Freeman's song.

H-426   _____ The silver cleek / by John Campbell Haywood; illustrations by Gordon Grant. New York: Mitchell Kennerley, [c1908]. 236 p., front., [2] leaves of plates.   **NYP**
LC: N 27, '08.

H-427   Hazard, R. H. The house on stilts: a novel / by R. H. Hazard; illustrations by J. A. Lemon. New York: G. W. Dillingham Company, [c1910]. 346 p., front., [3] leaves of plates.
LC: Ag 17, '10.
PW: Ag 20, '10.

Hazeltine, Horace, pseud. See **Wayne, Charles Stokes, b. 1858.**

H-428   Hazelton, Elizabeth C. Alaskan forget-me-nots, the northern garden that lured the Portland rose. [Seattle, c1921]. [26] p., ill.
Unexamined copy: bibliographic data from NUC.

H-429   Hazelton, George Cochrane, 1868-1921. Mistress Nell; a merry tale of a merry time ('twixt fact and fancy) by George C. Hazelton, jr. New York, C. Scribner's sons, 1901. 311, [1] p., front., [6] leaves of plates. [Some photo. by Byron, N. Y. and H. Marceau.]
PW: Ap 20, '01.
BLC: London: John Murray, 1901.

H-430   _____ The raven: the love story of Edgar Allan Poe ('twixt fact and fancy) / by George Hazelton. New York: D. Appleton and Company, 1909. 347, [1] p.
PW: F 27, '09.

H-431   Hazzard, John Edward, b. 1881. The four-flusher / by John Edward Hazzard . . . New York: G. W. Dillingham Company, [c1908]. 190 p., col. front.
LC: O 10, '08.
PW: N 14, '08.

H-432   Heady, Morrison, 1829-1915. The red moccasins: a story / by Morrison Heady. Louisville, Ky.: Courier-Journal Job Printing Co., 1901. 202 p. Designed end papers.   **KLG**

Healy, Thomas A. The drama that won the prize. In *The Tragedy that wins and other short stories (1905), T-343.*

H-433   Hearn, Lafcadio, 1850-1904. An American miscellany / by Lafcadio Hearn; articles and stories now first collected by Albert Mordell. New York: Dodd, Mead and Company, 1924. 2 v.; Vol. I: 227 p. Vol. II: 265 p.
Contents: V. 1: Introduction -- Ghost story: The cedar closet -- Mock Heroic Novelette: Giglampz -- Tan-yard murder story: Violent cremation -- Fantasy: Valentine vagaries -- Tales of the haunted: The restless dead -- Some strange experience. Essays in curious research: A bird store reverie -- Notes on the utilization of human remains -- The demi-monde of the antique world -- The poisoners. Songs of the roustabouts: Levee life -- Negro stories: Dolly-an idyll of the levee -- Banjo Jim's story. Prose poems: Butterfly fantasies -- Frost fancies. Autobiographical narratives:

Steeple climbers -- A romantic incident at the musical club. Life among the lowly: Some pictures of poverty. V. 2: Studies in human nature: Face studies -- Progressive living -- Frankness -- Frauds -- A Mephistophelian -- Something about success. Essay on the unconcious mind: Nightmare and nightmare legends -- Essay on the religious conditions of art: Philosophy of imaginative art -- Tales in poetical prose: Subhadra -- The dead wife -- St. Brandan's Christmas -- Bidasari -- Torn letters -- Three dreams. Historical tales: A lily in the mouth of hell -- The piper of Hamelin. Southern sketches: Saint Malo -- The garden of paradise. Art studies of Doré: Gustave Doré -- Doré's Raven. Cosmological speculation: The life of stars -- The destiny of solar systems. Speculations on life and death: The great "I AM" -- A Concord comprise. Studies in Creole: The Creole patois -- Some notes on Creole literature -- The scientific value of Creole -- A sketch of the Creole patois. Pictures of New Orleans: The scenes of Cable's romances -- The last of the New Orleans fencing masters. Studies of Negro life: The last of the voudoos -- New Orleans superstitions. Race studies in the West Indies: A study of half-breed races in the West Indies -- West Indian society of many colorings. American envoy: A winter journey to Japan.

LC: O 7, '24.

PW: O 4, '24.

References: BAL 7984. Perkins & Perkins, p. 95-97.

H-434   ____ The dream of a summer day / by Lafcadio Hearn. Boston; New York: Houghton Mifflin Company, 1922. (Cambridge: The Riverside Press) 27 p., front. (front. and t. p. are 1 sheet folded and pasted in.)

On cover: Merry Christmas booklets. First separate book appearance.

References: BAL 7978; Perkins & Perkins, p. 85.

H-435   ____ Fantastics: and other fancies / by Lafcadio Hearn; edited by Charles Woodward Hutson. Boston; New York: Houghton Mifflin Company, 1914. 241, [1] p.

First published in the New Orleans Item 1879-1881; and in the Times-Democrat, 1882-1884.

Contents: Introduction -- All in white -- The little red kitten -- The night of All Saints -- The devil's carbuncle -- Les coulisses -- The stranger -- Y porqué? -- A dream of kites -- Hereditary memories -- The ghostly kiss -- The black cupid -- When I was a flower -- Metempsychosis -- The undying one -- The vision of the dead Creole -- The name on the stone -- Aphrodite and the king's prisoner -- The fountain of gold -- A dead love -- At the cemetery -- "Aida" -- El vómito -- The idyl of a French snuff-box -- Spring phantoms -- A kiss fantastical -- The bird and the girl -- The tale of a fan -- A legend -- The gipsy's story -- The one pill-box -- A river reverie -- "His heart is old" -- MDCCCLIII -- Hiouen-thsang -- L'amour aprés la mort -- The post office.

LC: Ja 2, '15.

References: BAL 7955. Perkins & Perkins, p. 68-69

H-436   ____ A Japanese miscellany / by Lafcadio Hearn . . . Boston: Little, Brown and Company, 1901. 305 p., front., [4] leaves of plates (3 double-sided), ill.

Contents: Strange stories: Of a promise kept -- Of a promise broken -- Before the Supreme Court -- The story of Kwashin Koji -- The story of Umétsu Chūbei -- The story of Kōgi the priest -- Folklore gleanings: Dragon-flies -- Buddhist names of plants and animals -- Songs of Japanese children (In Japanese and English) [nonfiction] -- Studies here and there: On a bridge -- The case of O-Dai --Beside the sea -- Drifting -- Otokichi's Daruma -- In a Japanese hospital.

LC: O 17, '01.

PW: N 23, '01

BLC: London: Sampson Low & Co., 1901.

References: BAL 7936; Perkins & Perkins, p. 42-43.

H-437   ____ Karma / by Lafcadio Hearn. New York: Boni and Liveright, 1918. 163 p.

Contents: Karma -- A ghost -- The first Muezzin, Bilâl -- China and the Western world.

LC: Ja 3, '19.

PW: D 7, '18.

References: BAL 7961. Perkins & Perkins, p. 76.

H-438   ____ Kottō: being Japanese curios, with sundry cobwebs / collected by Lafcadio Hearn . . . ; with illustrations by Genjiro Yeto. New York: The Macmillan Company; London: Macmillan & Co., Ltd., 1902. 251 p., photo. front., [2] leaves of plates (1 photo.), col. ill.

The first "nine tales have been selected from the `Shin Chomon Shū', `Hyaku Monogatari', `Uji-Jūi-Monogatari-Shō', and other old Japanese books, to illustrate some strange beliefs".

Contents: The legend of Yurei-Daki -- In a cup of tea -- Common sense -- Ikiryō -- Shiryō -- The story of O-Kamé -- Story of a fly -- Story of a pheasant -- The story of Chūgorō -- A woman's diary -- Heiké-gani -- Fireflies -- A drop of dew -- Gaki -- A matter of custom -- Revery -- Pathological -- In the dead of the night -- Kusa-Hibari -- The eater of dreams.

LC: O 21, '02.

PW: N 1, '02.

References: BAL 7938; Perkins & Perkins, p. 45-46.

H-439   ____ Kwaidan: stories and studies of strange things / Lafcadio Hearn . . . Boston; New York: Houghton, Mifflin and Company, 1904. 240 p., front., [1] leaf of plates. [Ill. by Keichū Takénouche.]

Contents: Kwaidan: The story of Mimi-nashi-Hōīche -- Oshidori -- The story of O-Tei -- Ubazakura -- Diplomacy -- Of a mirror and a bell -- Jikininki -- Mujina -- Rokuro-Kubi -- A dead secret -- Yuki-Onna -- The story of Aoyagi -- Jiu-roku-zakura -- The dream of Akinosuké -- Riki-Baka -- Hi-mawari -- Hōrai -- Insect studies: Butterflies -- Mosquitoes -- Ants.

LC: Mr 17, '04.

PW: Ap 9, '04.

References: BAL 7940; Perkins & Perkins, p. 49-50.

H-440   ____ The romance of the Milky Way, and other studies & stories / by Lafcadio Hearn. Boston; New York: Houghton Mifflin and Company, 1905. 209 p.

Contents: The romance of the Milky Way -- Goblin poetry -- "Ultimate questions" -- The mirror maiden -- The story of Itō Norisuké -- Stranger than fiction -- A letter from Japan.

LC: O 9, '05.

PW: N 4, '05.

BLC: London: Archibald Constable & Co; Cambridge, Mass. printed, 1905.

References: BAL 7943; Perkins & Perkins, p. 53-54.

H-441   The heart of childhood / edited by William Dean Howells and Henry Mills Alden. New York; London: Harper & Brothers, [c1906]. 286 p. **CIN** (Harper's novelettes.)

Contents: The first pussy-willows / Annie Webster Noel -- The truce / Marie Manning -- État ten / Ethel Sigsbee Small -- An unskilled laborer / May Kelsey Champion -- A doll / Alice McGowan -- The seeds of time / Grace Lathrop Collin -- The feel doll / Annie Hamilton Donnell -- The wind of dreams / Roy Rolfe Gilson -- The amigo / William Dean Howells -- Adeline Thurston, poetess / Elizabeth Jordan -- "Dad's grave" / J. Elwin Smith -- A transplanted boy / Constance Fenimore Woolson -- Zan Zoo / George Heath.

LC: D 1, '06.

PW: F 23, '07.

References: BAL 9775; Gibson & Arms 06-G.

Heath, Gordon. Zan Zoo. In *The heart of childhood* (1906), H-441.

H-442 Heath, Oscar Morrill, b. 1872. Composts of tradition: a book of short stories dealing with traditional sex and domestic situations / Oscar Morrill Heath. Chicago: O. M. Heath and Co., [c1913]. 303 p., photo. front. (port.), [5] leaves of photo. plates.
Contents: The apology of an iconoclast -- The year the ice went out -- Theodora's retribution -- The maid of the Neptunian strand -- Jonathan Buck, his curse -- A Puritan's point of view -- An ordinary situation with the usual denouement.

H-443 Heath, Sarah Ritchie. The padre's little caretaker: a romance of the Carmel mission / by Sarah Ritchie Heath. [s. l.: s. n., c1913]. 34 p.

H-444 Heaven, Louise (Palmer), b. 1846. An idol of bronze. N. Y. Grafton Press, 1901. 244 p. Unexamined copy: bibliographic data from *The Publishers' Weekly*.
PW: D 21, '01.

H-445 Hecht, Ben, 1893-1964. Broken necks: and other stories / Ben Hecht. Girard, Kansas: Haldeman-Julius Company, [c1924]. 64 p. (Little blue book; no. 699.)
Contents: Broken necks -- Decay -- The bomb thrower -- Dog eat dog -- Fragments.

H-446 ____ Cutie: a warm mamma / by Ben Hecht and Maxwell Bodenheim . . . Chicago: privately printed by the Hechtshaw Press, 1924. 68, [1] p.

H-447 ____ Erik Dorn / by Ben Hecht. New York; London: G. P. Putnam's Sons, 1921. ([New York]: The Knickerbocker Press). 409 p.
LC: O 27, '21.
PW: S 3, '21.

H-448 ____ Fantazius Mallare: a mysterious oath / Ben Hecht; drawings, Wallace Smith. Chicago: Covici-McGee, 1922. 174 p., [10] leaves of plates.
LC: S 21, '22.

H-449 ____ The Florentine dagger: a novel for amateur detectives / by Ben Hecht. New York: Boni and Liveright, [c1923]. 256 p., front., [4] leaves of plates. [Ill. by Wallace Smith.] **KSU**
LC: O 12, '23.
BLC: London: William Heinemann, 1924.

H-450 ____ Gargoyles / by Ben Hecht. New York: Boni and Liveright, [c1922]. 346 p.
LC: S 23, '22.
PW: S 30, '22.

H-451 ____ Humpty Dumpty / by Ben Hecht. New York: Boni and Liveright, 1924. 383 p.
LC: N 14, '24.
PW: N 15, '24.

H-452 ____ The kingdom of evil: a continuation of the journal of Fantazius Mallare / by Ben Hecht; twelve full page illustrations by Anthony Angarola. Chicago: Pascal Covici, 1924. 211 p., ill.
LC: N 22, '24.

____ Life. In *The best short stories of 1915 and the yearbook of the American short story* (1916), **B-560.**

H-453 ____ Tales of Chicago streets / Ben Hecht. Girard, Kansas: Haldeman-Julius Company, [c1924]. 57 p. (Litlle blue book; no. 698.)
Contents: Life -- Depths -- Gratitude -- Nocturne -- Black umbrellas -- The yellow goat.

H-454 ____ A thousand and one afternoons in Chicago / Ben Hecht; design and illustrations by Herman Rosse. Chicago: Covici-McGee, [1922]. 288, [1] p., ill.
Contents: A self-made man -- An Iowa humoresque -- An old audience speaks -- Clocks and owl cars -- Confessions -- Coral, Amber and Jade -- Coeur de lion and the soup and fish -- Dapper Pete and the sucker play -- Dead warrior -- Don Quixote and his last windmill -- "Fa'n Ta Mig!" -- Fanny -- Fantastic lollypops -- Fog patterns -- Grass Figures -- Ill-humoresque -- Jazz band impressions -- Letters -- Meditation in E minor -- Michigan Avenue -- Mishkin's minyon -- Mottka -- Mr. Winkelberg -- Mrs. Rodjezke's last job -- Mrs. Sardotopolis' evening off -- Night diary -- Nirvana -- Notes for a tragedy -- On a day like this -- Ornaments -- Pandora's box -- Pitzela's son -- Queen Bess' feast -- Ripples -- Satraps at play -- Schopenhauer's son -- Sergt. Kuzick's Waterloo -- Sociable gamblers -- Ten-cent wedding rings -- The auctioneer's wife -- The dagger Venus -- The exile -- The great traveler -- The indestructible masterpiece -- The lake -- The little fop -- The man from yesterday -- The man hunt -- The man with a question -- The mother -- The pig -- The snob -- The soul of Sing Lee -- The sybarite -- The tattooer -- The thing in the dark -- The watch fixer -- The way home -- Thumbnail lotharios -- Thumbs up and down -- To Bert Williams -- Vagabondia -- Waterfront fancies -- Where the "blues" sound -- World conquerors.
LC: D 2, '22.
PW: D 16, '22.
BLC: London: Grant Richards; Chicago printed, 1923.

____ Winkleburg. In *The best short stories of 1922 and the yearbook of the American short story* (1923), **B-567.**

H-455 Hedges, M. H. (Marion Hawthorne), b. 1888. Iron City / by M. H. Hedges. New York: Boni and Liveright, 1919. 318 p.
LC: S 27, '19.
PW: S 27, '19.

H-456 Heermance, Edgar L. (Edgar Laing), b.1876. The Christ child: three Christmas stories / by Edgar L. Heermance. Mankato, Minn.: Endeavor Press, 1907. 32, [1] p.
Unexamined copy: bibliographic data from OCLC, # 29759956.
Contents: The shepherd and the Christ child -- The madonna of Devil's Creek -- A declaration of independence.

Heermann, Elizabeth Alexander. Fifty-two weeks for Florette. In *Prize stories of 1921* (1922), **P-619.**

Hegan, Alice Caldwell. See **Rice, Alice Caldwell Hegan, 1870-1942.**

H-457 Heigh, John, *pseud*. The house of cards: a record / by John Heigh [pseud.], sometime Major U. S. V. New York; The Macmillan Company; London: Macmillan & Co., Ltd., 1905. 370 p.
PW: Je 10, '05.

Hellman, Sam, 1885-1950. I am a pirate king. In *More aces* (1925), **M-962.**

H-458 ____ Low bridge and punk pungs / by Sam Hellman; with illustrations by Tony Sarg. Boston: Little, Brown and Company, 1924. 111, [1] p., front., [4] leaves of plates.

H-459   Helm, Benjamin. Allie in Beulah land, or,
Swanannoa camp-meeting: a Kentucky story / by
Rev. Benjamin Helm. Louisville, Ky.: Pentecostal
Publishing Co., [c1901]. 284 p., [2] leaves of plates.

H-460   Helm, Jeannette. Without clues / Jeannette Helm.
New York: Boni and Liveright, [c1923]. 319 p.
LC: S 24, '23.
PW: O 13, '23.
BLC: London: Brentano's, 1924.

H-461   Helm, Nellie Lathrop. When Jesus was here among
men / by Nellie Lathrop Helm. Chicago; New York;
Toronto; London; Edinburgh: Fleming H. Revell
Company, 1902. 205 p., front., [15] leaves of
plates.   **DLC**
PW: O 11, '02.

H-462   Hemenway, Hetty, 1890-1961. Four days: the story
of a war marriage / by Hetty Hemenway; with
frontispiece by Richard Culter. Boston: Little,
Brown and Company, 1917. 57, [1] p., front.
LC: S 12, '17.
PW: Ag 25, '17.

H-463   Hemingway, Ernest, 1899-1961. In our time: stories
/ by Ernest Hemingway. New York: Boni &
Liveright, 1925. 214, [1] p.
Contents: Indian camp -- The doctor and the doctor's
wife -- The end of something -- The three day blow --
The battler -- A very short story -- Soldier's home --
The revolutionist -- Mr. and Mrs. Elliot -- Cat in the
rain -- Out of season -- Cross country snow -- My old
man -- Big Two-hearted River, pt. I -- Big Two-
hearted River, pt. II -- L'envoi.
LC: O 14, '25.
PW: O 17, '25.
BLC: London: Jonathan Cape, 1926.
References: Hanneman 3; Cohn, p. 18-21.

             ____ My old man. _In The best short stories of 1923
and the yearbook of the American short story_ **(1924),
B-568.**

H-464   Hemphill, Vivia. Down the Mother Lode / by Vivia
Hemphill. Sacramento: Purnell's, 1922. 91 p.
Contents: Foreword -- "49" (poem) -- One Sunday in Stimson's bar
-- The Tom Bell stronghold -- The hanging of Charlie Price --
Rattlesnake Dick -- Indian vengeance -- Grizzly Bob of Snake Gulch
-- Curley Coppers, the jack -- The race of the shoestring gamblers --
The dragon and the tomahawk -- The Barstow lynching.
LC: My 23, '22.

H-465   Hempstead, Junius L. (Junius Lackland), b. 1842. A
chequered destiny / by Junius L. Hempstead . . .
New York City: Ben- Franklin Publishing Co.,
[c1905]. 315 p.   **DLC**

H-466   ____ The Deschanos: a thrilling romance / by
Junius L. Hempstead . . . New York City:
Ben-Franklin Publishing Co., [c1905]. 361 p., photo.
front. (port.).

H-467   ____ Thompson, the detective: a thrilling story of
adventure / by Junius L. Hempstead. New York:
Abbey Press, [c1902]. 368 p.
Unexamined copy: bibliographic data from OCLC,
#10774071.

H-468   Hemstreet, Charles, b. 1866. The Don Quixote of
America / by Charles Hemstreet . . . New York:
Dodd, Mead and Company, 1921. 238 p.
PW: F 26, '21.

H-469   Hemstreet, Charles, b. 1866. Flower of the fort / by
Charles Hemstreet. New York: James Pott & Co.,
1904. 240 p.
PW: Ap 2, '04.

H-470   Henderson, C. K. (Charles Kennon), b. 1846. The
countryman / by C. K. Henderson. New York;
Washington: The Neale Publishing Company, 1907.
208 p.   **EMU**
LC: Ag 7, '07.
PW: Ag 24, '07.

H-471   Henderson, Charles Hanford, 1861-1941. John
Percyfield: the anatomy of cheerfulness / by C.
Hanford Henderson. Boston; New York: Houghton,
Mifflin and Company, 1903. (Cambridge: The
Riverside Press). 382 p.
PW: Mr 28, '03.

H-472   ____ The lighted lamp: a novel / by C. Hanford
Henderson . . . Boston; New York: Houghton
Mifflin Company, 1908. (Cambridge: The Riverside
Press). 417, [1] p.
LC: S 26, '08.
PW: O 10, '08.

        Henderson, Gertrude. The singular experience of the
gilstraps. <u>See</u> _Under the Berkeley Oaks_ **(1901), U-8.**

        ____ The spiritual wooing of Peter Hance. <u>In</u>
Cuentos de California **(1904), C-962.**

        Henderson, Grace Van Woert. A paean of defeat.
<u>See</u> _Allegheny stories_ **(1902), A-142.**

H-473   Henderson, Howard A. M. (Howard Andrew Millet),
1836-1912. Diomede the centurion, or sowing scarlet
seed / by Howard A. M. Henderson. Cincinnati:
Jennings & Pye; New York: Eaton & Mains,
[c1901]. 422 p.

H-474   Henderson, W. J. (William James), 1855-1937. The
soul of a tenor: a romance / by W. J. Henderson;
frontispiece in color by George Gibbs. New York:
Henry Holt and Company, 1912. 366 p., col. front.
PW: O 19, '12.

        Henderson, Will T., jt. aut. The little strike breaker.
<u>See</u> **Apthorp, F. Jay, jt. aut., A-293.**

        Henderson, William J. Harry Borden's naval
monster. <u>In</u> _The battle for the Pacific_ **(1908), B-357.**

        ____ Joe Griffin's great jump. <u>In</u> _The battle for the
Pacific_ **(1908), B-357.**

        ____ The mutiny on The Swallow. <u>In</u> _The battle for
the Pacific_ **(1908), B-357.**

H-475   Hendricks, Grace. Lonesome trail / by Grace
Hendricks. Baltimore, Maryland: Saulsbury
Publishing Company, 1918. 38 p.   **DLC**
LC: My 23, '18.

H-476   Hendryx, James B. (James Beardsley), b. 1880. At the foot of the rainbow / by James B. Hendryx . . . New York; London: G. P. Putnam's Sons, 1924. (New York: The Knickerbocker Press). 331 p.
LC: S 16, '24.
PW: S 20, '24.

H-477   _____ The challenge of the North / by James Hendryx. Garden City, New York: Garden City Publishing Co., Inc., 1923. 119 p.

H-478   _____ The gold girl / by James B. Hendryx. New York; London: G. P. Putnam's Sons, 1920. ([New York]: The Knickerbocker Press). 349 p., front. [Ill. by P. J. Monahan.]
LC: Ap 19, '20.
PW: Mr 20, '20.

H-479   _____ The gun-brand / by James B. Hendryx. New York; London: G. P. Putnam's Sons, 1917. ([New York]: The Knickerbocker Press). 417 p., col. front. [Ill. by Clyde Forsythe.]
LC: My 5, '17.
PW: Ap 28, '17.

H-480   _____ North / by James B. Hendryx . . . New York; London: G. P. Putnam's Sons, 1923. (New York: The Knickerbocker Press). 334 p.
LC: Ja 30, '23.
PW: Ja 27, '23.

H-481   _____ Oak and iron: of these be the breed of the North / by James B. Hendryx . . . New York; London: G. P. Putnam's Sons, 1925. (New York: The Knickerbocker Press). 369 p.
LC: Ap 4, '25.
PW: Ap 18, '25.
BLC: London: Hutchinson & Co., [1925].

H-482   _____ The one big thing / by James B. Hendryx. -- First edition. -- Garden City, New York: Garden City Publishing Co., Inc., 1923. 122 p.

H-483   _____ Prairie flowers / by James B. Hendryx. New York; London: G. P. Putnam's Sons, 1920. ([New York]: The Knickerbocker Press). 315 p.
LC: F 5, '21.
PW: Ja 8, '21.
BLC: London: Jarrolds, [1923].

H-484   _____ The promise: a tale of the great Northwest / by James B. Hendryx. New York; London: G. P. Putnam's Sons, 1915. ([New York]: The Knickerbocker Press). 419 p.
LC: S 30, '15.
PW: O 2, '15.

H-485   _____ Snowdrift: a story of the land of the strong cold / by James B. Hendryx . . . New York; London: G. P. Putnam's Sons, 1922. (New York: The Knickerbocker Press). 381 p.
LC: F 17, '22.
PW: F 11, '22.

H-486   _____ The Texan: a story of the cattle country / by James B. Hendryx. New York; London: G. P.

Putnam's Sons, 1918. ([New York]: The Knickerbocker Press). 392 p. Illustrated end papers.
LC: D 4, '18.
PW: N 30, '18.

H-487   _____ Without gloves / by James B. Hendryx . . . New York; London: G. P. Putnam's Sons, 1924. (New York: The Knickerbocker Press). 389 p.
LC: Mr 28, '24.
PW: Mr 22, '24.
BLC: London: Hutchinson, [1924].

H-488   Henle, James. Sound and fury / James Henle. New York: Alfred A. Knopf, 1924. 267 p.
LC: S 15, '24.
PW: S 13, '24.

H-489   Hennessy, Roland Burke. Beautiful, bad Broadway / by Roland Burke Hennessy . . . ; illustrated by George Granby. Chicago, Ill.: Will Rossiter, 1901. 133 p., ill.   **DLC**

H-490   Henry, Alfred Hylas, b. 1865. By order of the prophet: a tale of Utah / by Alfred H. Henry; illustrated by E. S. Paxson. Chicago; New York; Toronto; London; Edinburgh: Fleming H. Revell Company, 1902. 402 p., front., [5] leaves of plates.
PW: S 20, '02.

H-491   Henry, Arthur, 1867-1934. The house in the woods / by Arthur Henry; illustrated. New York: A. S. Barnes & Company, 1904. 323 p., front., [9] leaves of plates.
PW: My 7, '04.
BLC: London: David Nutt, 1905.

H-492   _____ An island cabin / by Arthur Henry. New York: McClure, Phillips & Co., 1902. 286, [1] p.
PW: My 24, '02.
BLC: London: McClure, Phillips & Co.; New York, U. S. A. printed, 1901.

H-493   _____ Lodgings in town / by Arthur Henry; illustrated. New York: A. S. Barnes & Company, 1905. 327 p., incl. front., [15] leaves of plates. [Ill. by Everett Shinn and John Rae.]
PW: O 21, '05.

H-494   _____ The unwritten law: a novel / by Arthur Henry. New York: A. S. Barnes and Company, 1905. 401 p.
PW: Ap 1, '05.
BLC: London: David Nutt, 1905.

H-495   Henry, Barklie McKee. Deceit: a novel / by Barklie McKee Henry. Boston: Small, Maynard & Company, [c1924]. 314 p.
LC: Je 27, '24.
PW: Jl 19, '24.

H-496   Henry, Clyde A., b. 1873. The little black men / by Clyde A. Henry; illustrated. [Farson, Iowa: [s. n.], 1907]. 44, [1] p., front. (port.), ill.
Unexamined copy: bibliographic data from OCLC, #29761143.
LC: Je 22, '07.

H-497   Henry, Elizabeth Angela. Cloudy weather: a romance of Fenian days / by E. Angela Henry; foreword by Rev. Luke F. Sharkey and Rev. Thomas McMillan . . . Buffalo, New York: [Printed by the Union and Times Press?, c1921]. 131 p.

Henry, Justis, pseud. See **Donnelly, H. Grattan (Henry Grattan), 1850-1931.**

H-498   Henry, Lyman I. Paul, son of Kish / by Lyman I. Henry. Chicago, Illinois: The University of Chicago Press, [1923]. 356 p., front., [2] leaves of plates. [Ill. by Louis Grell.]

H-499   Henry, O., 1862-1910, *pseud.* Cabbages and kings / by O. Henry [pseud.]. New York: McClure, Phillips & Co., 1904. 344 p.
Contents: The proem: by the carpenter -- "Fox-in-the-morning" -- The lotus and the bottle -- Smith -- Caught -- Cupid's exile number two -- The phonograph and the graft -- Money maze -- The admiral -- The flag paramount -- The shamrock and the palm -- The remnants of the code -- Shoes -- Ships -- Masters of arts -- Dicky -- Rouge et noir -- Two recalls -- The vitagraphoscope.
LC: N 17, '04.
PW: D 3, '04.
BLC: London; New York: McClure, Phillips & Co., 1904.
References: BAL 16270; Clarkson.

H-500   ____ Calloway's code / by O. Henry [pseud.]. New York: The Winthrop Press, 1914. 31, [1] p., col. front.
Unexamined copy: bibliographic data from NUC.
First separate book appearance.
References: BAL 16313.

H-501   ____ Compliments of the season: a story of Christmas / by O. Henry [pseud.]. San Francisco: Haywood H. Hunt, 1919. [22] p., 1 ill.
Unexamined copy: bibliographic data from OCLC, #13642897.
"Privately printed." First separate book appearance.
References: BAL 16319.

H-502   ____ The ethics of pig / by O. Henry [pseud.]. New York: Winthrop Press, c1914. 31 p., col. front.
Unexamined copy: bibliographic data from OCLC, #12304799.
Originally published in *The gentle grafter.* First separate book appearance.
References: BAL 16314.

H-503   ____ The four million / by O. Henry [pseud.] . . . New York: McClure, Phillips & Co., 1906. 261 p.
Contents: Tobin's palm -- The gift of the magi -- A cosmopolite in a café -- Between rounds -- A skylight room -- A service of love -- The coming-out of Maggie -- Man about town -- The cop and the anthem -- An adjustment of nature -- Memoirs of a yellow dog -- The love-philtre of Ikey Schoenstein -- Mammon and the archer -- Springtime à la carte -- The green door -- From the cabby's seat -- An unfinished story -- The caliph, Cupid and the clock -- Sisters of the Golden Circle -- The romance of a busy broker -- After twenty years -- Lost on dress parade -- By courier -- The furnished room -- The brief début of Tildy.
PW: Ap 21, '06.
References: BAL 16271; Clarkson.

H-504   ____ The gentle grafter / by O. Henry [pseud.] . . . New York: The McClure Company, 1908. 235 p., ill. [Ill. by H. C. Greening and May Wilson Preston.]
Contents: The octopus marooned -- Jeff Peters as a personal magnet -- Modern rural sports -- The chair of philanthromathematics -- The hand that riles the world -- The exact science of matrimony -- A midsummer masquerade -- Shearing the wolf -- Innocents of Broadway -- Conscience in art -- The man higher up -- A tempered wind -- Hostages to Momus -- The ethics of pig.
LC: O 30, '08.
PW: N 14, '08.
References: BAL 16276; Clarkson.

H-505   ____ The gift of the wise men / by O. Henry [pseud.]. Illustrated by Charles M. Relyea. Garden City, N. Y.: Doubleday, Page & Company, 1911. [22] p., col. front., [3] leaves of col. plates.
"This story is reprinted from the larger volume, `The four million,' and first appeared in the New York World, 1905.
References: BAL 16310; Clarkson.

H-506   ____ Heart of the West / by O. Henry [pseud.] . . . New York: The McClure Company, 1907. 334 p.
Contents: Hearts and crosses -- The ransom of Mack -- Telemachus, friend -- The handbook of Hymen -- The pimienta pancakes -- Seats of the haughty -- Hygeia at the Solito -- An afternoon miracle -- The higher abdication -- Cupid à la carte -- The caballero's way -- The sphinx apple -- The missing chord -- A call loan -- The princess and the puma -- The Indian summer of Dry Valley Johnson -- Christmas by injunction -- A chapparral prince -- The reformation of Calliope.
LC: O 15, '07.
PW: O 19, '07.
References: BAL 16274; Clarkson.

H-507   ____ The hiding of Black Bill / O. Henry [pseud.]. O. Henry and me / Ethel Patterson; with an introduction by Mary Ely. New York: The Ridgway Company, 1908. 32 p.
First separate book appearance.
References: BAL 16312.

H-508   ____ Let me feel your pulse, by O. Henry [pseud.]; illustrations by W. W. Fawcett. New York: Doubleday, Page & Company, 1910. 38 p., front. and conjugate title-page, [6] leaves of plates.
At head of title: Adventures in neurasthenia.
"Published in the Cosmopolitan magazine under the title `Adventures in neurasthenia: some experiences of a nerve-sick man seeking health.'"
LC: O 11, '10.
PW: N 5, '10.
References: BAL 16296; Clarkson.

H-509   ____ A lickpenny lover / by O. Henry [pseud.]. New York: Winthrop Press, c1914. 31 p., col. front.
Unexamined copy: bibliographic data from OCLC, #12304783.
Originally published in *The voice of the city.* First separate book appearance.
References: BAL 16315.

H-510   ____ (Spirit). My tussle with the devil: and other stories / by O. Henry's ghost [pseud.]. New York: I. M. Y. Company, 1918. 197 p.
Contents: My tussle with the devil -- The contest -- Sleeping -- Yearning -- Animals -- Flowers -- Jewels -- Remembrances -- Munitions -- Going home -- My hearth -- The three h's -- The senses -- Fancies -- Yesterday, today -- Action, reaction -- A vision.
References: BAL References and Ana, v. 7, p.167; Clarkson.

H-511   O. Henryana: seven odds and ends, poetry and short stories / by O. Henry [pseud.]. Garden City, New York: Doubleday, Page & Company, 1920. 89 p.
Contents: The crucible [poem] -- A lunar episode -- Three paragraphs -- Bulger's friend -- A professional secret -- The elusive tenderloin -- The struggle of the outliers.
LC: D 6, '20.
References: BAL 16302; Clarkson.

H-512   Options / by O. Henry [pseud.]; illustrated. New York; London: Harper & Brothers, 1909. 323, [1] p., front., [7] leaves of plates. [Ill. by Charles Sarka, Horace Taylor, Gordon Grant, Arthur Little, and James Montgomery Flagg.]
Contents: "The Rose of Dixie" -- The third ingredient -- The hiding of Black Bill -- Schools and schools -- Thimble, thimble -- Supply and demand -- Buried treasure -- To him who waits -- He also serves -- The moment of victory -- The head-hunter -- No story -- The higher pragmatism -- Best-seller -- Rus in urbe -- A poor rule.
LC: O 22, '09.
PW: N 6, '09.
References: BAL 16292; Clarkson.

H-513   Roads of destiny / by O. Henry [pseud.]. New York: Doubleday, Page & Company, 1909. 376 p.
Contents: Roads of destiny -- The guardian of the accolade -- The discounters of money -- The enchanted profile -- "Next to reading matter" -- Art and the bronco -- Phoebe -- A double-dyed deceiver -- The passing of Black Eagle -- A retrieved reformation -- Cherchez la femme -- Friends in San Rosario -- The fourth in Salvador -- The emancipation of Billy -- The enchanted kiss -- A departmental case -- The renaissance of Charleroi -- On behalf of the management -- Whistling Dick's Christmas stocking -- The halberdier of the little Rheinschloss -- Two renegades -- The lonesome road.
LC: Ap 24, '09.
PW: My 15, '09.
References: BAL 16277; Clarkson.

H-514   Rolling stones / by O. Henry [pseud.]; illustrated with original photographs, drawings by the author, reproductions of letters, etc. Garden City, New York: Doubleday, Page & Company, 1912. 292 p., photo. front. (port.), [14] leaves of double-sided plates (incl. two double leaf plates).
Contents: Introduction -- The dream -- A ruler of men -- The atavism of John Tom Little Bear -- Helping the other fellow -- The marionettes -- The Marquis and Miss Sally -- A fog in Santone -- The friendly call -- A dinner at ----* -- Sound and fury -- Tictocq -- Tracked to doom -- A snapshot at the President -- An unfinished Christmas story -- The unprofitable servant -- Aristocracy versus hash -- The prisoner of Zembla -- A strange story -- Fickle fortune, or, How Gladys hustled -- An apology -- Lord Oakhurst's curse -- Bexar script no. 2692 -- Queries and answers -- The pewee [poem] -- Nothing to say [poem] -- The murderer [poem] -- Some postscripts: A contribution [poem] -- The old farm [poem] -- Vanity [poem] -- The lullaby boy [poem] -- Chanson de Bohéme [poem] -- Hard to forget [poem]. Drop a tear in this slot [poem] -- Tamales [poem] -- Some letters [reproductions].
LC: D 27, '12.
PW: Ja 4, '13
BLC: London: Hodder & Stoughton, [1916].
References: BAL 16299; Clarkson.

H-515   Sixes and sevens / by O. Henry [pseud.] . . . Garden City, New York: Doubleday, Page & Co., 1911. 283 p.
Contents: The last of the troubadours -- The sleuths -- Witches' loaves -- The pride of the cities -- Holding up a train -- Ulysses and the dogman -- The champion of the weather -- Makes the whole world kin -- At arms with Morpheus -- The ghost of a chance -- Jimmie Hayes and Muriel -- The door of unrest -- The duplicity of Hargraves -- Let me feel your pulse -- October and June -- The church with an

overshot wheel -- New York by campfire light -- The adventures of Shamrock Jolnes -- The lady higher up -- The greater Coney -- Law and order -- Transformation of Martin Burney -- The caliph and the cad -- The diamond of Kali -- The day we celebrate.
LC: O 20, '11. (BAL lists O 5, '11.)
PW: O 21, '11.
BLC: London: Hodder & Stoughton, [1916].
References:References: BAL 16298; Clarkson.

H-516   Strictly business: more stories of the four million / by O. Henry [pseud.]. New York: Doubleday, Page & Company, 1910. 310 p.
Contents: Strictly business -- The gold that glittered -- Babes in the jungle -- The day resurgent -- The fifth wheel -- The poet and the peasant -- The robe of peace -- The girl and the graft -- The call of the tame -- The unknown quantity -- The thing's the play -- A ramble in Aphasia -- A municipal report -- Psyche and the pskyscraper -- A bird of Bagdad -- Compliments of the season -- A night in New Arabia -- The girl and the habit -- Proof of the pudding -- Past one at Rooney's -- The venturers -- The duel -- "What you want".
LC: F 24, '10.
PW: Mr 5, '10.
References: BAL 16294; Clarkson.

H-517   The trimmed lamp: and other stories of the four million / by O. Henry [pseud.] . . . ; frontispiece by Alice Barber Stephens. New York: McClure, Phillips & Co., 1907. 260 p., front.
Contents: The trimmed lamp -- A Madison Square Arabian Night -- The Rubaiyat of a Scotch highball -- The pendulum -- Two Thanksgiving Day gentlemen -- The assessor of success -- The buyer from Cactus City -- The badge of Policeman O'Roon -- Brickdust Row -- The making of a New Yorker -- Vanity and some sables -- The social triangle -- The purple dress -- The foreign policy of Company 99 -- The lost blend -- A Harlem tragedy -- "The guilty party"-an East Side tragedy -- According to their lights -- A midsummer knight's dream -- The last leaf -- The Count and the wedding guest -- The country of Elusion -- The ferry of unfulfilment -- The tale of tainted tenner -- Elsie in New York.
LC: Ap 25, '07.
PW: My 4, '07.
References: BAL 16273; Clarkson.

H-518   The two women; The one: A fog in Santone; The other: A medley of moods / By O. Henry [pseud.] . . . Boston: Small, Maynard and Company, Publishers, [c1910]. 81 p.
Unexamined copy: bibliographic data from OCLC, #8254789.
A medley of moods had prior publication in *Whirligigs*, 1910, as "Blind man's holiday." *A fog in Santone* appears here first, collected in *Rolling stones*, 1912.
LC: D 21, '10.
References: BAL 16297; Clarkson.

H-519   The voice of the city: further stories of the four million / by O. Henry [pseud.] . . . New York: The McClure Company, 1908. 243 p. Stories originally appeared in: New York World; and, Ainslee's magazine.
Contents: The voice of the city -- The complete life of John Hopkins -- A lickpenny lover -- Dougherty's eye-opener -- "Little speck in garnered fruit" -- The harbinger -- While the auto waits -- A comedy in rubber -- One thousand dollars -- The defeat of the city -- The shocks of doom -- The Plutonian fire -- Nemesis and the candy man -- Squaring the circle -- Roses, ruses and romance -- The city of dreadful night -- The Easter of the soul -- The fool-killer -- Transients in Arcadia -- The rathskeller and the rose -- The clarion call -- Extradited from Bohemia -- A Philistine in Bohemia -- From each according to his ability -- The memento.
LC: My 28, '08.
PW: Je 13, '08.
References: BAL 16275; Clarkson.

H-520   ____ Waifs and strays: twelve stories / by O. Henry [pseud.] . . . ; together with a representative selection of critical and biographical comment. Garden City, New York: Doubleday, Page & Company, 1919, [c1917]. 305 p.

Reprinted in part from various sources. First trade edition preceded by a limited edition, 1917. 308 p. (BAL 16301; LC: N 19, '17.)

Contents: The red roses of Tonia -- Round the circle -- The rubber plant's story -- Out of Nazareth -- Confessions of a humourist -- The sparrows in Madison Square -- Hearts and hands -- The cactus -- The detective detector -- The dog and the playlet -- A little talk about mobs -- The snow man. Critical and biographical comments.

BLC: N. Y.: Doubleday, Page, & Co., New York [printed], 1919. London: Hodder & Stoughton, [1920].

References: BAL 16318; Clarkson.

H-521   ____ Whirligigs / by O. Henry [pseud.]. New York: Doubleday, Page & Company, 1910. 314 p.

Contents: The world and the door -- The theory and the hound -- The hypotheses of failure -- Calloway's code -- A matter of mean elevation -- "Girl" -- Sociology in serge and straw -- The ransom of Red Chief -- The marry month of May -- A technical error -- Suite homes and their romance -- The whirligig of life -- A sacrifice hit -- The roads we take -- A blackjack bargainer -- The song and the sergeant -- One dollar's worth -- A newspaper story -- Tommy's burglar -- A chaparral Christmas gift -- A little local colour -- Georgia's ruling -- Blind man's holiday -- Madame Bo-Peep, of the ranches.

LC: S 17, '10.
PW: O 8, '10.
References: BAL 16295; Clarkson.

H-522   Henry, Stuart Oliver, 1860-1953. Villa Elsa: a story of German family life / by Stuart Henry. New York: E. P. Dutton & Company, [c1920]. 354 p.
PW: F 14, '20.

H-523   Henry-Ruffin, M. E. (Margaret Ellen), d. 1941. The North Star: a tale of Norway in the tenth century / by M. E. Henry-Ruffin; illustrated by Wilbur Dean Hamilton. Boston: Little, Brown and Company, 1904. 356 p., front., [5] leaves of plates.
PW: Ap 23, '04.

H-524   ____ The shield of silence / by M. E. Henry-Ruffin. New York; Cincinnati; Chicago: Benziger Brothers, [c1914]. 463 p.   **SEM**

H-525   Henshaw, Nevil, 1880-1938. Aline of the Grand Woods: a story of Louisiana / by Nevil G. Henshaw. New York: The Outing Publishing Company, 1909. 491, [1] p.
PW: F 20, '09.

H-526   ____ The inheritance of Jean Trouvé / by Nevil Henshaw. Indianapolis: The Bobbs-Merrill Company, [c1922]. 391 p.
LC: F 27, '22.
PW: Mr 4, '22.
BLC: London: Hodder & Stoughton, [1922].

H-527   ____ The painted woods / by Nevil Henshaw. Indianapolis: The Bobbs-Merrill Company, [c1924]. 283, [1] p.
"A short version of this novel, under the title Jeanne of the Deep Swamp, ran serially in Outing during 1914 and 1915."

LC: Ap 5, '24.
PW: My 3, '24.

H-528   Hensley, Marie E. My life in two worlds / inspired by George Gordon Byron. [San Rafael, California?: s. n.], [c1917]. 384 p. On cover: My life in two worlds by Marie E. Hensley.

H-529   ____ Who and what am I? / by Marie E. Hensley . . . Boston, U. S. A.: The Christopher Publishing House, [c1922]. 183 p.   **DLC**

H-530   Hepburn, Elizabeth Newport. Fulfillment / by Elizabeth Newport Hepburn. New York: Henry Holt and Company, 1924. 362 p.
LC: My 10, '24.
PW: My 17, '24.
BLC: London: Mills & Boon, 1925.

H-531   ____ The wings of time / by Elizabeth Newport Hepburn. New York: Frederick A. Stokes Company, [c1921]. 325 p.
LC: O 10, '21.
PW: O 15, '21.
BLC: London: Eveleigh Nash & Grayson, 1922.

H-532   Her brother's letters: wherein Miss Christine Carson, of Cincinnati, is shown how the affairs of girls and women are regarded by men in general and, in particular, by her brother, Lent Carson, lawyer, of New York City / anonymous; drawings by F. Vaux Wilson and C. M. Relyea. New York: Moffat, Yard & Company, 1906. 217 p., front., [11] leaves of plates.
PW: O 13, '06.

H-533   Her Highness: an Adirondack romance. Boston: Richard G. Badger, 1910. ([Boston]: The Gorham Press). 309 p., front. [Ill. by Benson.]
LC: Jl 8, '10.
PW: O 15, '10.

H-534   Her other self / by the author of The search for a nose. Washington: The Neale Company, 1901. 184 p.

H-535   Herbert, F. Hugh (Frederick Hugh), b. 1897. There you are! / by F. Hugh Herbert; frontispiece by J. M. Clifton. New York: The Macaulay Company, [c1925]. 312 p.
LC: S 2, '25.
PW: Ag 8, '25.

H-536   Hereford, William Richard, 1871-1928. The demagog / by William Richard Hereford. New York: Henry Holt and Company, 1909. 364 p.
LC: N 2, '09.
PW: N 20, '09.

H-537   ____ When fools rush in / by William Richard Hereford; illustrated by George O. Baker. Indianapolis: The Bobbs-Merrill Company, [c1913]. 288, [1] p., front., [4] leaves of plates.
LC: S 25, '13.
PW: O 4, '13.

H-538 Heresford, Justin. A bridgeman of the crossways /
by Justin Heresford, Jr. Boston: Marshall Jones
Company, [c1925]. 290 p.
PW: F 28, '25.

H-539 Hergesheimer, Joseph, 1880-1954. Balisand / Joseph
Hergesheimer. New York: Alfred A. Knopf, 1924.
371 p.
LC: S 25, '24.
PW: S 6, '24
BLC: London: William Heinemann, 1924.

H-540 _____ The bright shawl / by Joseph Hergesheimer.
New York: Alfred A. Knopf, 1922. 220 p.
LC: O 11, '22.
PW: O 7, '22.
BLC: London: William Heinemann, 1923.
References: Swire, p. 22-23.

H-541 _____ Cytherea / Joseph Hergesheimer. New York:
Alfred A. Knopf, 1922. 371 p.
LC: Ja 24, '22.
PW: Ja 14, '22.
BLC: London: William Heinemann, [1922].
References: Swire, p. 19-20.

H-542 _____ The dark fleece / Joseph Hergesheimer. New
York: Alfred A. Knopf, 1922. 134 p.
"Published, April, 1918, in a volume now out of
print, entitled `Gold and iron,' and then reprinted
twice. First published separately March 1922."
PW: Je 3, '22.
References: Swire, p. 22.

H-543 _____ Gold and iron / by Joseph Hergesheimer. New
York: Alfred A. Knopf, 1918. 331, [1] p.
Contents: Wild oranges -- Tubal Cain -- The dark fleece.
LC: Jl 23, '18.
PW: My 25, '18.
BLC: London: William Heinemann, 1919.
References: Swire, p. 12.

H-544 _____ The happy end / by Joseph Hergesheimer.
New York: Alfred A. Knopf, 1919. 315 p.
Contents: Lonely valleys -- The Egyptian chariot -- The flower of
Spain -- Tol'able David -- Bread -- Rosemary Roselle -- The thrush in
the hedge.
LC: O 24, '19.
PW: N 1, '19.
BLC: London: William Heinemann, 1920.
References: Swire, p. 14.

H-545 _____ Java Head / by Joseph Hergesheimer . . . New
York: Alfred A. Knopf, 1919. 255 p.
LC: D 31, '18.
PW: Ja 11, '19.
BLC: London: William Heinemann, 1919.
References: Swire, p. 13.

H-546 _____ The lay Anthony: a romance / by Joseph
Hergesheimer. New York; London: Mitchell
Kennerley, 1914. 327 p.
LC: Ag 24, '14.
PW: Ag 22, '14.
References: Swire, p. 9-10.

H-547 _____ Linda Condon / by Joseph Hergesheimer. New
York: Alfred A. Knopf, 1919. 304 p.

LC: N 12, '19.
PW: N 8, '19.
BLC: London: William Heinemann, 1920.
References: Swire, p. 15.

_____ The meeker ritual. In *The best short stories of
1919 and the yearbook of the American short story*
(1920), B-564.

_____ Miss Conifee. In *Marriage* **(1923), M-457.**

H-548 _____ Mountain blood: a novel / by Joseph
Hergesheimer. New York; London: Mitchell
Kennerley, 1915. 312 p.
LC: My 27, '15.
PW: My 29, '15.
References: Swire, p. 10.
Revised edition: New York: Alfred A. Knopf, 1919.
368 p.
PW: D 6, '19.

H-549 _____ The three black Pennys: a novel / by Joseph
Hergesheimer. New York: Alfred A. Knopf, 1917.
408 p.
LC: O 4, '17.
PW: S 29, '17.
BLC: London: William Heinemann, 1918.
References: Swire, p. 10-11.

_____ The token. In *The best short stories of 1922
and the yearbook of the American short story* **(1923),
B-567.**

H-550 _____ Tol'able David / Joseph Hergesheimer. New
York: Alfred A. Knopf, 1923. 55 p., front. First
separate printing: appeared in *The happy end*, 1914.

H-551 _____ Tubal Cain / Joseph Hergesheimer. New
York: Alfred A. Knopf, 1922. 146 p.
"Published, April, 1918, in a volume now out of
print, entitled `Gold and iron,' and then reprinted
twice. First published separately, March, 1922."
PW: Je 3, '22.
References: Swire, p. 21.

H-552 _____ Wild oranges / Joseph Hergesheimer. New
York: Alfred A. Knopf, 1922. 128 p.   **BGU**
"Published, April, 1918, in a volume now out of
print, entitled `Gold and iron,' and then reprinted
twice. First published separately March, 1922."
PW: Je 3, '22.
References: Swire, p. 20-21.
Earlier "special edition of eighty-five copies of *Wild
oranges* printed Christmas 1919 on perusia hand-
made paper by Alfred A. Knopf for his bookseller
friends . . . ," 1919.
References: Swire, p. 17.

H-553 Herman, Paul H. (Paul Howard), b. 1871. The bear
and the lamb: a tale of ancient barbarity practised in
modern times / by Paul H. Herman. New York:
Cochrane Publishing Company, 1910. 122 p. **HUC**
LC: N 17, '10.

H-554 Herner, Mabel Cora Herner. The silent chord / by
Mabel Cora Herner. New York; London; Montreal:
The Abbey Press, [c1902]. 307 p., photo. front.

(port.), [4] leaves of plates (some photo.). [Ill. by Walter H. Shilrock.] **DLC**

H-555   Herr, Charlotte Bronte. San Pasqual: a tale of old Pasadena / by Charlotte Herr; with a preface by John Steven McGroarty; illustrations by Frances Creedon. [Pasadena [Calif.]: The Post Printing and Binding Co., c1924]. 120 p., front.
LC: Ag 21, '24.

H-556   ____ Their Mariposa legend: a romance of Catalina / by Charlotte Herr; illustration by Orrin White. [Pasadena, Calif.: Post Printing and Binding Co., c1921]. 106 p., col. front.
LC: My 8, '23.

H-557   Herrick, Robert, 1868-1938. Clark's field / by Robert Herrick. Boston; New York: Houghton Mifflin Company, 1914. (Cambridge: The Riverside Press). 477, [1] p.
LC: Je 18, '14.
PW: Je 20, '14.

H-558   ____ The common lot / by Robert Herrick. New York: The Macmillan Company; London: Macmillan & Co., Ltd., 1904. 426 p.
PW: O 15, '04.

H-559   ____ The conscript mother / by Robert Herrick. New York: Charles Scribner's Sons, 1916. 99 p., front.
LC: My 3, '16.
PW: My 6, '16.
BLC: London: Bickers & Son, 1916.

____ The Glenmore fire. In *A book of narratives* **(1917), B-734.**

H-560   ____ The healer / by Robert Herrick. New York: The Macmillan Company, 1911. 455 p.
LC: N 9, '11.
PW: N 18, '11.

H-561   ____ His great adventure / by Robert Herrick; with frontispiece. New York: The Macmillan Company, 1913. 408 p., col. front.
LC: S 5, '13.
PW: S 27, '13.
BLC: London: Mills & Boon, 1914.

H-562   ____ Homely Lilla / by Robert Herrick. New York: Harcourt, Brace and Company, [c1923]. 293 p.
LC: F 8, '23.
PW: Ja 27, '23.

H-563   ____ A life for a life / by Robert Herrick. New York: The Macmillan Company, 1910. 433 p.
LC: Je 2, '10.
PW: Je 11, '10.
BLC: London: Macmillan, 1910.

H-564   ____ The master of the inn / by Robert Herrick. New York: Charles Scribner's Sons, 1908. 84 p.
PW: My 2, '08.

H-565   ____ The memoirs of an American citizen / by Robert Herrick . . . New York: The Macmillan

Company; London: Macmillan & Co., Ltd., 1905. 351 p., front., ill. [Ill. by F. B. Masters.]
First published in Saturday evening post, 1905.
PW: Ag 5, '05.

H-566   ____ One woman's life / by Robert Herrick. New York: The Macmillan Company, 1913. 405 p.
LC: F 20, '13.
PW: Mr 1, '13.
BLC: London: Mills & Boon, 1913.

H-567   ____ The real world / by Robert Herrick. New York: The Macmillan Company; London: Macmillan & Co., Ltd., 1901. 358 p.
PW: N 23, '01.

____ The spirit of a great city. In *A book of narratives* **(1917), B-734.**

H-568   ____ Their child / by Robert Herrick. New York: The Macmillan Company; London: Macmillan & Co., Ltd, 1903. 95 p., front. (port.), [2] leaves of plates. [Ill. by Seymour M. Stone.] Designed end papers.

H-569   ____ Together / by Robert Herrick . . . New York: The Macmillan Company, 1908. 595 p.
                           OSU, AKR
LC: Jl 3, '08.
PW: Jl 18, '08.
BLC: London: Macmillan, 1908.

H-570   ____ Wanderings / by Robert Herrick. New York: Harcourt, Brace and Company, [c1925]. 317 p.
Contents: Magic -- The station of the cross -- The adventures of Ti Chatte -- The passions of Trotsky.
LC: Ag 24, '25.
PW: Ag 22, '25.
BLC: London: Jonathan Cape; printed in U. S. A., 1926.

H-571   ____ Waste / by Robert Herrick. New York: Harcourt, Brace and Company, [c1924]. 449 p.
LC: Ap 15, '24.
PW: Ap 5, '24.
BLC: London: Jonathan Cape; printed in U. S. A., 1924.

Herring, Donald Grant, jt. aut. *MacIvor's folly* (1925). See **Kahler, Hugh MacNair, b. 1883, jt. aut., K-4.**

H-572   Herring, J. L. (John Lewis), b. 1866. Saturday night sketches: stories of old wiregrass Georgia / by J. L. Herring; illustrated by Tom J. Nicholl. Boston: The Gorham Press, 1918. 303 p., front., [6] leaves of plates.
Contents: Saturday night -- The fire in Morris's wagon yard -- The song of the redeemed -- When the debaters met -- Cane grinding time -- "Running up" the bridegroom -- When we put Jim away -- When Stegall stopped growing -- Fodder-pulling time -- The conversion -- Uncle Wiley's turkey pen -- Grandma's spinning wheel -- Sunday at Obediah Gay's -- Carrying the cotton to market -- The Cape Jessamine -- A candy-pulling in the wiregrass -- Corn liquor and Tutt's pills -- A wiregrass Easter -- An old-time wiregrass frolic -- Cat-fishing in the olden time -- A county site removal election -- "Helping" Jim grind cane -- The old wash-hole -- With the rites of the order -- Cal Turner and the black runner -- "Big Court" in the olden time -- The community cotton picking -- Cutting a bee tree -- Friday afternoon in the old-time school -- Corn planting time -- Town ball on

the schoolhouse yard -- The old way of shelling peanuts -- At old China Grove -- Sol Drawhorn and the grey lizard -- Sheep-shearing time -- The singing school -- Helping Aunt Mary make sausage -- A deer drive in the old days -- The homefolks dance -- The revival's close -- The downfall of a millionaire -- Cane chewing time -- Carrying cotton to George Spring's gin -- Fourth of July in the olden time -- Helping Granny make soap -- An old time fire-hunt -- The Sunday School celebration -- When the wiregrass was ablaze -- The singing play -- Three watermelons an unhandy turn -- A house-raising and home building -- A nest of squirrels -- An old time circus day -- Going to mill with Bud -- A log-rollin', quiltin', and frolic -- The union sing -- Saturday night.
LC: F 18, '18.

H-573   Hersch, Alvin D. (Alvin David), b. 1888. Soul toys / by Alvin D. Hersch. Boston: Richard G. Badger, [c1923]. ([Boston]: The Gorham Press). 365 p.
OSU, GUA

Herts, B. Russell. At the height. In *Forum stories (1914), F-306.*

H-574   Hervey, Harry, b. 1900. The black parrot: a tale of the golden Chersonese / by Harry Hervey . . . New York; London: The Century Co., 1923. 337 p.
LC: S 18, '23.
PW: S 22, '23.

H-575   _____ Caravans by night: a romance of India / by Harry Hervey. New York: The Century Co., 1922. 400 p.
LC: F 27, '22.
PW: Mr 4, '22.

H-576   _____ Ethan Quest: his saga / by Harry Hervey. New York: Cosmopolitan Book Corporation, 1925. 334 p.
LC: My 18, '25.
PW: My 16, '25.

_____ The young men go down. In *The best short stories of 1924 and the yearbook of the American short story (1925), B-569.*

H-577   Herzig, Irwin M. The seekers / by Irwin M. Herzig. New York: Press of J. J. Little & Ives Company, [c1925]. 365 p.
LC: D 22, '25.

H-578   Hess, Frances Hardin, Mrs. Mammy: a memory, being a true history faithfully set down of one life that is a type of the many, that existed in the old South / by Mrs. Frances Hardin Hess ... San Francisco: [Printed by California Press], 1913. 84 p.
Unexamined copy: bibliographic data from OCLC, #14443178.
Advertising matter on p. 83-84.

H-579   Hess, Isabella R. (Isabella Rosa), b. 1872. Saint Cecilia of the Court / by Isabella R. Hess. New York; Chicago; Toronto; London; Edinburgh: Fleming H. Revell Company, [c1905]. 212 p., front., [5] leaves of plates. [Ill. by Fergus Kyle.]
PW: S 30, '05.
BLC: Edinburgh; London: Oliphant & Co.; printed in United States, [1905].

Hess, Leonard L. The lesser gift. In *The best short stories of 1924 and the yearbook of the American short story (1925), B-569.*

H-580   Hesser, Ethelda Daggett. Inner darkness / by Ethelda Daggett Hesser. New York: Harper & Brothers Publishers, 1924. 301 p.
LC: F 13, '24.
PW: F 16, '24.

H-581   Heston, Winifred. A bluestocking in India: her medical wards and messages home / by Winifred Heston. New York; Chicago; Toronto; London; Edinburgh: Fleming H. Revell Company, [c1910]. 226 p., front. [Ill. by Victor Pérard.]   **CIN**
PW: Jl 16, '10.
BLC: London: Andrew Melrose, 1910.

H-582   Heuser, Herman J. (Herman Joseph), 1851-1933. The chaplain of St. Catherine's / by Herman J. Heuser. New York: Longmans, Green and Co., 1925. 305 p.
LC: Ap 4, '25.

H-583   _____ In the workshop of St. Joseph / by Herman J. Heuser . . . New York; Cincinnati; Chicago: Benziger Brothers, 1925. 236 p., front., [6] leaves of plates. Illustrated end papers.   **XAV**
LC: D 23, '25.

H-584   Hevener, Oakley Prentice. Kathleen Rhodora: a novel / by Oakley Prentice Hevener . . . [Fairmont, W. Va.: Fairmont Printing Co. c1921]. 242 p., [1] leaf of photo. plates.   **OSU, WVK**
LC: Ap 26, '22.

H-585   Hewes, Charles Edwin. The theatre terrible: a creation, presenting various aspects of the greater drama / by Charles Edwin Hewes; illustrated. Chicago; Denver: The Egerton-Palmer Press, 1910. 543 p., col. front., [2] leaves of col. plates.
LC: O 26, '10.

H-586   Hewitt, Charles Edward. The house of Judah / by Charles Edward Hewitt. New York; Cincinnati: The Abingdon Press, [c1919]. 224 p., front., [1] leaf of plates.
LC: F 24, '19.

H-587   _____ The outcast: a tale of the mountain people / by Charles Edward Hewitt. New York: J. S. Ogilvie Publishing Company, c1913. 177 p., front., [1] leaf of plates. [Ill. by Isabella Morton.]
LC: Ag 20, '13.

H-588   _____ "The spirit of Penn": a tale founded upon the faith of the Quakers / told in two parts by Charles Edward Hewitt. New York: J. S. Ogilvie Publishing Company, c1909. 188 p., photo. front.
LC: Je 25, '09.

H-589   Heyward, DuBose, 1885-1940. Porgy / Du Bose Heyward; decorated by Theodore Nadejen. New York: George H. Doran Company, [c1925]. 196 p.
LC: S 15, '25.
PW: S 19, '25.
BLC: London: Hodder & Stoughton; printed in U. S. A., [1926].

H-590   Heyward, Jane Screven. Brown jackets / by Jane Screven Heyward. Columbia, S. C.: The State

Company, 1923. 64 p., photo. front. (port.), [1] leaf of photo. plates.
PW: Ja 19, '24.

Hibbard, G. The eyes of affection. *In Their husband's wives* (1906), **T-161.**

H-591   Hibler, Charles H. (Charles Henry), b. 1854. Down in Arkansas / by Charles H. Hibler. New York; London; Montreal: The Abbey Press, [c1902]. 285 p.   **MUM**
PW: O 4, '02.

H-592   Hichborn, Philip, 1882-1912. Hoof beats / by Philip Hichborn. Boston: Richard G. Badger, 1912. ([Boston]: The Gorham Press). 169 p., front., [9] leaves of plates. [Ill. by Irma Dérèmeaux and Wallace Morgan.]   **NYP**
Contents: The marquis -- Cleopatra -- Hammersley's pluck -- The brook -- The bishop of Barchester -- Mr. Leffington feels inspired -- When the marquis came into his own -- Brutus: cow pony -- Those who ride straight.
LC: O 16, '12.
PW: O 19, '12.

H-593   Hickman, Albert Scott. The two blondes / by Albert Scott Hickman. Boston: Richard G. Badger; Toronto: The Copp Clark Co., Limited, [c1915]. 355 p.
LC: Ap 27, '15.
PW: My 8, '15.

H-594   Hickman, Warren Edwin, b. 1861. An echo from the past; a first-hand narration of events of the early history of the Arkansas Valley of Colorado / by Dr. Warren Edwin Hickman. Denver, Col.: printed by the Western Newspaper Union, 1914. 179 p., photo. front. (port.).   **AZU**

H-595   Hickmott, Allerton Cushman. Fabric of dreams / Allerton Cushman Hickmott. Hartford: Press of Finlay Brothers, [c1925]. 60 p.
LC: Jl 30, '25.

H-596   Hicks, John, 1847-1917. Something about Singlefoot: chapters in the life of an Oshkosh man / by John Hicks . . . New York: Cochrane Publishing Company, 1910. 437 p.

H-597   Hicks, William C. (William Campbell), b. 1844. Joachim's daughter: a story of the time of Herod the Great, "King of the Jews" / by William C. Hicks. Benton Harbor, Mich.: Peters & Alger, 1903. 304 p.

H-598   [Hicks, William Watkin], b. 1837. Angels' visits to my farm in Florida / by Golden Light [pseud.]. New ed., May 1913 . . . Boston: The Sanctuary Publishing Company, [c1913]. 307 p.
Unexamined copy: bibliographic data from LC.
LC: Jl 17, '13.

Hidden, William Buffett. See **Physiopath, A., pseud.**

H-599   Hiemenz, Clara. Cress / by Clara Hiemenz; illustrations by H. E. Steinbruegge. [St. Louis:

Nixon-Jones Ptg. Co., c1906]. 74 p. col. front., [2] leaves of col. plates.
LC: D 3, '06.

H-600   Higgers, Jim. The adventures of Theodore: a humorous extravaganza / as related by Jim Higgers to one of the rough writers; illustrations by Henrich. Chicago: The H. J. Smith & Devereaux Co., [c1901]. 210 p., front., [8] leaves of plates.
PW: My 4, '01.

Higgins, Aileen Cleveland. The 'dopters. *In The Bellman book of fiction* (1921), **B-485.**

H-601   Higgins, Elizabeth, b. 1874. Out of the West: a novel / by Elizabeth Higgins. New York; London: Harper & Brothers, 1902. 315 p.
PW: S 13, '02.

H-602   Higgins, F. Marshall. Io: a narrative / by F. Marshall Higgins . . . Minneapolis, Minnesota: Goodyear Book Co., 1901. 122 p., [1] leaf of plates.   **NYP**
PW: D 7, '01.

H-603   Higgins, Francena Hill. Conquerors all: based on facts / by Francena Hill Higgins . . . San Diego, Cal.: Published by the Gnostic Press, 1917. 308 p., col. front.
LC: D 20, '17.

H-604   Higgins, George H. (George Henry), 1852-1905. Tract number 3377: a romance of the oil region / by George H. Higgins and Margaret Higgins Haffey. Boston, Massachusetts: The C. M. Clark Publishing Company, 1909. 382 p., front., [7] leaves of plates.
LC: S 10, '09.

H-605   Higginson, Ella, 1862-1940. Mariella; of out-west / by Ella Higginson. New York; London: The Macmillan Company, 1902. 435 p.
PW: N 15, '02.

H-606   Highland, Lawrence, b. 1891, *pseud.* Punishment: a novel / by Lawrence Highland [pseud.]. Boston: The Four Seas Company, [c1925]. 274 p.   **CLE**

H-607   The highroad: being the autobiography of an ambitious mother. Chicago: Herbert S. Stone & Company, 1904. 289 p.

H-608   Hightower, Clyde W. The redemption of Black Rock Ranch / by Clyde W. Hightower. Philadelphia: Dorrance & Company, [c1924]. 208 p.
LC: Mr 27, '24.

H-609   Hildebrand, Arthur Sturges, 1887-1924? The parlor begat Amos / by Arthur Sturges Hildebrand. New York: Harcourt, Brace and Company, [c1922]. 323 p.   **OSU, TJC**
LC: F 3, '22.
PW: F 18, '22.

H-610   Hildreth, J. H. The queen's heart / J. H. Hildreth. Boston: Marshall Jones Company, 1918. 325 p.
LC: Jl 27, '18.

H-611   Hile, William H. The ostrich for the defence / by William H. Hile. Boston: Press of Geo. H. Ellis Co., 1912. 324 p., photo. front., [2] leaves of photo. plates.
LC: S 12, '12.

H-612   Hill, A. A. (Arthur Asa). What's he to me? / by A. A. Hill; with illustrations. New York: Howard O. Bullard, 1914. 362 p., front., [4] leaves of plates.   **DLC**

H-613   Hill, Edwin C. (Edwin Conger), 1884-1958. The iron horse / novelized by Edwin C. Hill; from William Fox's great picture romance of the East and the West by Charles Kenyon and John Russell; illustrated with scenes from the photoplay. New York: Grosset & Dunlap, [c1924]. 329 p., photo. front., [7] leaves of photo. plates.
LC: N 8, '24.
PW: Ja 17, '25.

H-614   Hill, Everett Merrill, b. 1867. The story the crocus told / Everett M. Hill. Spokane: The Uplook Publishing Company, [c1909]. (Chicago: The Lakeside Press). 238 p., photo. front., (port.), [1] leaf of photo. plates.
LC: Ja 3, '10.

H-615   Hill, Francis. Once on the summer range / by Francis Hill. New York: The Macmillan Company, 1918. 328 p.   **MNL**
LC: O 10, '18.
PW: O 26, '18.

H-616   Hill, Frederick Trevor, 1866-1930. The accomplice / by Frederick Trevor Hill . . . New York; London: Harper & Brothers, 1905. 325, [1] p.
PW: My 13, '05.

H-617   ____ The minority: a novel / by Frederick Trevor Hill . . . New York: Frederick A. Stokes Company, [c1902]. 406 p.
PW: Ap 19, '02.
BLC: London: Grant Richards; Cambridge, U. S. A. [printed], 1902.

H-618   ____ Tales out of court / by Frederick Trevor Hill . . . New York: Frederick A. Stokes Company Publishers, [c1920]. 251 p.   **GZM**
Contents: Exhibit no. 2 -- The shield of privilege -- The woman in the case -- Two fishers of men -- The unearned increment -- The judgment of his peers -- Of disposing memory -- Submitted on the facts -- The personal equation -- In the presence of the enemy -- A debt of honor -- The weapons of a gentleman -- Pewee-gladiator -- Peregrine Pickle -- Charity suffereth long -- War.
LC: O 25, '20.
PW: N 13, '20.

H-619   ____ The thirteenth juror: a tale out of court / by Frederick Trevor Hill; illustrated by Gordon Grant. New York: The Century Co., 1913. 211 p., front., [7] leaves of plates.
LC: O 2, '13.
PW: O 4, '13.

H-620   ____ The web / by Frederick Trevor Hill; illustrated by A. J. Keller. New York: Doubleday, Page & Co., 1903. 344 p., front., [3] leaves of plates.

PW: D 5, '03.
BLC: London: William Heinemann; New York [printed], 1903.

H-621   Hill, George B. (George Bradbury), b. 1886. The young farmer / by George B. Hill; illustrated by Ralph L. Boyer. Philadelphia: The Penn Publishing Company, 1913. 384 p., front., [4] leaves of plates.   **OSU, ORE**
LC: Mr 27, '13.
PW: N 29, '13.

H-622   Hill, Grace Livingston, 1865-1947. According to the pattern / by Grace Livingston Hill . . . Philadelphia: The Griffith and Rowland Press, 1903. 280 p., front., [5] leaves of plates.   **KUK**
PW: O 31, '03.

H-623   ____ The angel of His presence / by Grace Livingston Hill . . . Gabriel the Acadian / by Edith M. Nicholl Bowyer. Philadelphia: American Baptist Publication Society, 1902. 80 p., ill.; 136 p., [8] leaves of plates. [Ill. by Joseph J. Ray.]   **DLC**
PW: N 15, '02.

H-624   ____ Ariel Custer / by Grace Livingston Hill. Philadelphia; London: J. B. Lippincott Company, 1925. 336 p.
LC: O 27, '25.
PW: N 7, '25.

H-625   ____ Aunt Crete's emancipation / by Grace Livingston Hill-Lutz . . . ; illustrations by Clara E. Atwood. Boston, Mass.: The Golden Rule Company, [c1911]. 143 p., front., [7] leaves of plates.
LC: Jl 14, '11.

H-626   ____ Because of Stephen / by Grace Livingston Hill. Boston: Published by The Golden Rule Co., [c1903]. 196 p., front.
"Appeared in the columns of the Christmas endeavor world."

H-627   ____ The best man / by Grace Livingston Hill Lutz . . . ; with illustrations in color by Gayle Hoskins. Philadelphia; London: J. B. Lippincott Company, 1914. 304 p., col. front., [2] leaves of col. plates.   **NYP**
LC: F 19, '14.
PW: F 7, '14.

H-628   ____ The big blue soldier / by Grace Livingston Hill (Mrs. Lutz) . . . Philadelphia; London: J. B. Lippincott Company, 1923. 176 p.
LC: Mr 6, '23.
PW: Mr 17, '23.

H-629   ____ The city of fire / by Grace Livingston Hill (Mrs. Lutz) . . . ; with a frontispiece in color by Ralph P. Coleman. Philadelphia; London: J. B. Lippincott Company, 1922. 333 p., col. front.
LC: Jl 13, '22.
PW: Je 3, '22.

H-630   ____ Cloudy Jewel / by Grace Livingston Hill (Mrs. Lutz) . . . ; with a frontispiece by H. Weston Taylor.

Philadelphia; London: J. B. Lippincott Company, 1920. 351, [1] p., col. front.
LC: N 15, '20.
PW: N 13, '20.

H-631 ____ Dawn of the morning / by Grace Livingston Hill Lutz . . . with illustrations in color by Anna Whelan Betts. Philadelphia; London: J. B. Lippincott Company, 1911. 320 p., col. front., col. plates.
Unexamined copy: bibliographic data from OCLC, #1811273.
LC: My 24, '11.

H-632 ____ The enchanted barn / by Grace Livingston Hill Lutz . . . ; with frontispiece by Edmund Frederick. Philadelphia; London: J. B. Lippincott Company, 1918. 313 p., col. front.
LC: My 22, '18.
PW: My 11, '18.

H-633 ____ Exit Betty / by Grace Livingston Hill (Mrs. Lutz) . . . ; with a frontispiece by H. Weston Taylor. Philadelphia; London: J. B. Lippincott Company, 1920. 247 p., col. front.
LC: Ag 18, '20.
PW: My 29, '20.

H-634 ____ The finding of Jasper Holt / by Grace Livingston Hill Lutz . . . ; with illustrations in color by Edwin F. Bayha. Philadelphia; London: J. B. Lippincott Company, 1916. 272 p., col. front., [2] leaves of col. plates.
LC: My 29, '16.
PW: My 13, '16.

H-635 ____ The girl from Montana / by Grace Livingston Hill-Lutz . . . ; illustrations by Sears Gallagher. Boston, Mass.: The Golden Rule Company, 1908. 211 p., front., [7] leaves of plates. First published in the Christian endeavor world.
LC: D 19, '08.
PW: Ja 30, '09.
Another edition: Philadelphia; London: J. B. Lippincott, [c1922]. 220 p., front. (New chapter at end).
LC: Mr 23, '22.

H-636 ____ Lo, Michael! / by Grace Livingston Hill Lutz . . . ; with illustrations in color by Gayle Hoskins. Philadelphia; London: J. B. Lippincott Company, 1913. 369 p., col. front., [2] leaves of col. plates.
LC: Je 13, '13.
PW: Je 7, '13.

H-637 ____ The man of the desert / by Grace Livingston Hill Lutz . . . ; illustrated. New York; Chicago; Toronto; London; Edinburgh: Fleming H. Revell Company, [c1914]. 289 p., front., [3] leaves of plates. [Ill. by Victor Pérard.]
LC: S 21, '14.
PW: S 5, '14.

H-638 ____ Marcia Schuyler / by Grace Livingston Hill Lutz; with a frontispiece in color by Anna Whelan Betts and six illustrations in tint by E. L. Henry. Philadelphia; London: J. B. Lippincott Company,

1908. 348 p., col. front., [6] leaves of plates.
LC: F 13, '08.
PW: Ap 4, '08.

H-639 ____ Miranda / by Grace Livingston Hill Lutz . . . ; with illustrations by E. L. Henry. Philadelphia; London: J. B. Lippincott Company, 1915. 344 p., col. front., [4] leaves of plates.
LC: My 20, '15.
PW: My 1, '15.

H-640 ____ The mystery of Mary / by Grace Livingston Hill Lutz . . . ; with a frontispiece by Anna W. Speakman. Philadelphia; London: J. B. Lippincott Company, 1912. 202, [1] p., col. front.   **NYP**
LC: Mr 13, '12.
PW: F 24, '12.

H-641 ____ Not under the law / by Grace Livingston Hill . . . Philadelphia; London: J. B. Lippincott Company, 1925. 336 p.
LC: My 15, '25.
PW: My 16, '25.

H-642 ____ The obsession of Victoria Gracen / by Grace Livingston Hill Lutz . . . ; with illustrations by Edwin F. Bayha. Philadelphia; London: J. B. Lippincott Company, 1915. 301 p., col. front., [2] leaves of col. plates.
LC: O 18, '15.
PW: O 9, '15.

H-643 ____ Phoebe Deane / by Grace Livingston Hill Lutz . . . ; with illustrations by E. L. Henry. Philadelphia; London: J. B. Lippincott Company, 1909. 330 p., col. front., [5] leaves of plates.
LC: S 18, '09.
PW: O 9, '09.
BLC: London: Hodder & Stoughton, [1921].

H-644 ____ Re-creations / by Grace Livingston Hill . . . Philadelphia; London: J. B. Lippincott Company, 1924. 376 p.   **OSU, KWW**
LC: My 17, '24.
PW: My 31, '24.

H-645 ____ The red signal / by Grace Livingston Hill (Lutz) . . . ; with a frontispiece by Edmund Frederick. Philadelphia; London: J. B. Lippincott Company, 1919. 304 p., col. front.
LC: Je 26, '19.
PW: Ap 26, '19.

H-646 ____ The search / by Grace Livingston Hill (Lutz) . . . ; with a frontispiece by Edmund Frederick. Philadelphia; London: J. B. Lippincott Company, 1919. 317 p., col. front.
LC: D 2, '19.
PW: N 15, '19.

H-647 ____ The story of a whim / by Grace Livingston Hill; illustrations by Etheldred B. Barry. Boston: The Golden Rule Co., [c1903]. 175 p.
"Appeared in the columns of the Christian endeavor world."
PW: Je 6, '03.

H-648   ____ Tomorrow about this time / by Grace Livingston Hill. Philadelphia; London: J. B. Lippincott Company, 1923. 345 p.
LC: Jl 28, '23.
PW: Jl 14, '23.

H-649   ____ The tryst / by Grace Livingston Hill (Mrs. Lutz); with a frontispiece in color by Ralph P. Coleman. Philadelphia; London: J. B. Lippincott Company, 1921. 350 p., col. front.
LC: Je 10, '21.
PW: My 14, '21.

H-650   ____ An unwilling guest / by Grace Livingston Hill. Philadelphia: American Baptist Publication Society, 1902. 327 p., front., [5] leaves of plates. [Ill. by V. Davisson.]
PW: Je 14, '02.

H-651   ____ A voice in the wilderness: a novel / by Grace Livingston Hill Lutz . . . New York; London: Harper & Brothers, 1916. 376, [1] p., col. front. [Ill. by Norman Rockwell.]   **WVB**
LC: S 23, '16.
PW: O 7, '16.

H-652   ____ The witness: a novel / by Grace Livingston Hill Lutz . . . New York; London: Harper & Brothers, 1917. 337, [1] p.
LC: N 5, '17.
PW: N 24, '17.

H-653   Hill, J. Wagley (John Wagley), b. 1839. Dadsie Dan / by J. Wagley Hill . . . Omaha, Neb.: Published by W. D. Poessnecker, [c1914]. 82 p., front. (port.), [19] leaves of plates (some photo.). Gilt end papers.   **TXS**

Hill, James A. An engineer's Christmas story. In *The railroad* (1901), **R-6.**

H-654   Hill, John L. The transition / by John L. Hill. New York: Broadway Publishing Company, [c1909]. 306 p., front., [2] leaves of plates. [Ill. by Wm. L. Hudson.]   **DLC**
LC: Je 16, '09.
PW: Jl 31, '09.

H-655   Hill, Marion, 1870-1918. Georgette / by Marion Hill . . . Boston: Small, Maynard and Company, [c1912]. 371, [1] p.
LC: My 16, '12.
PW: My 11, '12.
Also published as: The lure of crooning water; with a frontispiece by Arthur Hutchins, [c1913].
LC: S 20, '13.
BLC: London: John Long, 1913.

H-656   ____ McAllister's grove / by Marion Hill; frontispiece by Thomas Fogarty. New York: D. Appleton and Company, 1917. 317, [1] p., front.
LC: My 14, '17.
PW: My 26, '17.
BLC: London: John Long, 1917.

H-657   ____ The Pettison twins / by Marion Hill; illustrated by F. Y. Cory. New York: McClure, Phillips &

Co., 1906. 262, [1] p., ill.
LC: S 28, '06.
PW: O 6, '06.

____ The star spangled banner. In *Youth* (1901), **Y-51.**

H-658   ____ Sunrise Valley / by Marion Hill . . . ; illustrated by Robert Edwards. Boston: Small, Maynard and Company, [c1914]. 325 p., col. front., [2] leaves of plates.
PW: Mr 28, '14.
BLC: London: John Long, 1914.

H-659   ____ The toll of the road / by Marion Hill; frontispiece by Stockton Mulford. New York; London: D. Appleton and Company, 1918. 321 p., front.
LC: My 14, '18.
PW: My 25, '18.
BLC: London: John Long, 1918.

____ A tune in court. In *Youth* (1901), **Y-51.**

H-660   Hill, Walter S. (Walter Scott), b. 1871. The dominant power / by Walter S. Hill. Kansas City: Burton Publishing Company, [c1919]. 352 p.   **NYP**
LC: Je 17, '19.

H-661   Hill, William Laurie, b. 1835. The master of the Red Buck and the Bay Doe: a story of Whig and Tory warfare in North Carolina in 1781-83 / by William Laurie Hill. Charlotte, N. C.: Stone Publishing Co., 1913. 297 p., col. front., [4] leaves of plates.

H-662   Hill, William Stanley. What a man wishes: a novel / by William Stanley Hill; frontispiece by C. D. Williams. New York: The Morningside Press, [c1913]. 273 p., col. front.
LC: Ja 27, '13.

Hilliard, John Northern, 1872-1935, jt. aut. *The golden hope* (1916). See **Mason, Grace Sartwell, b. 1877, jt. aut., M-579.**

H-663   Hillier, Amelia Willard. Ebb and Flo: and other short stories / by Amelia Willard Hillier. Waunakee, Wisconsin: J. M. Williams & Son, c1908. 270 p.   **DLC**
Contents: Ebb and Flo -- Raising the dead -- Student's lark -- Deaf Auntie -- The minister's daughter -- The lost couple -- Peter Pringles plight -- Home again -- Etta Elder's unknown way -- Laura Louften's ideal -- The little traveler -- The silly girls -- Cold reason versus love -- Hugo, the hermit -- The light went out -- Hunting with a marriage license -- Pickled pansy -- Grandma's story -- Sale of the spotted calf -- Fresh air kids -- Martha Goodwin's help -- Mrs. Porter's April story -- On the waves -- Coy Cox -- A letter in the snow -- The jail birds -- The woman tramp -- Seeing him as he was -- The ring -- Dr. Dunham's adopted son -- The yellow dog -- On the track -- Her stratagem.
LC: O 12, '08.

H-664   Hillis, Newell Dwight, 1858-1929. The quest of John Chapman: the story of a forgotten hero / by Newell Dwight Hillis. New York: The Macmillan Company; London: Macmillan & Co., Ltd., 1904. 349 p.
PW: D 3, '04.

H-665 _____ The story of Phaedrus: how we got the greatest book in the world / Newell Dwight Hillis; with illuminations by George Willis Bardwell. New York: The Macmillan Company, 1914. 311 p., [3] leaves of plates (some col.).
LC: Ap 9, '14.
PW: Ap 24, '14.
BLC: London: Duckworth, 1915.

H-666 Hillman, H. W. (Harry W.), b. 1870. "The call of the farm" / by H. W. Hillman. New Haven: Valley View Publishing Company, 1911. 309 p.
LC: F 27, '11.

H-667 _____ Looking forward: the phenomenal progress of electricity in 1912 / by H. W. Hillman; illustrated by W. L. Greene. Northampton, Mass.: Valley View Publishing Company, 1906. 320 p., front., [5] leaves of plates. **AFU**

H-668 Hilton, Marian A. The garden of girls: a story / by Marian A. Hilton; illustrated. New York: The Tandy-Thomas Company, 1909. 360 p., front., [4] leaves of plates. [Ill. by W. O. Wilson.] **DLC**

H-669 Hilton-Turvey, Carol Brevoort, b. 1880. The Van Haavens / by C. Hilton-Turvey; with illustrations by H. R. Ballinger. Boston: Small, Maynard & Company, [c1916]. 400 p., front., [3] leaves of plates.
LC: S 18, '16.
PW: S 2, '16.

H-670 Hinckley, Henrietta R. From out of the West / by Henrietta R. Hinckley. Boston: Mayhew Publishing Company, 1905. 231, [1] p.

H-671 Hinckley, Julian, b. 1884. E: the complete and somewhat mad history of the family of Montague Vincent, Esq., gent. / by Julian Hinckley. New York: Duffield & Company, 1914. 387 p.
LC: Ap 27, '14.
PW: My 2, '14.
BLC: London: John Long, 1917.

H-672 Hincks, Reginald N. (Reginald Noton). Angel-face / by Reginald N. Hincks. Boston; New York: The Cornhill Publishing Co., [c1922]. 198 p.
LC: My 11, '22.

H-673 Hindley, Howard L. The gentleman from Hayville: extracts from the diary of a new member, originally published in the Rutland herald / by Howard L. Hindley. Rutland, Vermont: [s. n.], 1909. 76, [1] p., ill.
Cover title: The member from Hayville.

H-674 Hines, Jack, b. 1877. The blue streak / by Jack Hines . . . New York: George H. Doran Company, [c1917]. 270 p., front., [4] leaves of plates. [Ill. by Philip R. Goodwin.] **KSU**
Contents: The blue streak -- "Scar-face" -- "King of the Malamutes" -- Flying Arrow -- This aims to be a dog country -- Betcher-Boots -- Grey Cloud -- A one-man dog -- "A black wolfskin" -- June from Irish Hill.
LC: O 16, '17.
PW: O 6, '17.

H-675 _____ Seegar and Cigareet / by Jack Hines; with illustrations by Philip R. Goodwin. New York: George H. Doran Company, [c1912]. 56 p., front., [2] leaves of plates.
LC: My 7, '12.
PW: Je 8, '12.

H-676 Hines, Ruby E. Which hope we have / by Ruby E. Hines . . . [Pontiac, Ill., Printing Department of Illinois State Reformatory], 1913. 104 p.
Unexamined copy: bibliographic data from NUC.

H-677 Hingston, William Edward, b. 1851. The settling price / William E. Hingston. Boston: The Cornhill Company, [c1920]. 290 p.
PW: My 22, '20.

H-678 Hinman, Fidélité, 1867-1952. Love's confession / Fidélité Hinman. Oberlin, Ohio: [The Oberlin Print Shop], 1914. 36 p. **OBE**

H-679 Hinrichsen, William H., 1850-1907. Plots and penalties / by William H. Hinrichsen; fully illustrated. Chicago: Rhodes & McClure Publishing Company, 1902. 458 p., [1] leaf of plates (port.), ill. Designed end papers. **OSU, MNU**

H-680 Hiram, Harvester, b. 1858, *pseud.* Lumberman "Lew": a story of fact, fancy, and fiction / by Harvester Hiram [pseud.]. Glens Falls, N. Y.: Glens Falls Publishing Co., [19--]. 117 p. **CSB**

H-681 _____ "Stray steps" / by Harvester Hiram [pseud.] (Addison B. Colvin) . . . [Glens Falls, N. Y.]: The Glens Falls Publishing Company, c1920. 200 p.
LC: Ja 21, '21.

H-682 Hirsch, Leon D. (Leon David), b. 1881. The man who won, or, The career and adventures of the younger Mr. Harrison / by Leon D. Hirsch; illustrated by William Van Dresser. Boston: The Page Company, 1918. 395 p., front., [3] leaves of plates.
LC: O 14, '18.
PW: O 19, '18.

H-683 Hitchcock, Mary, b. 1865. The first soprano / by Mary Hitchcock. New York: Gospel Publishing House, [c1912]. 187 p.

H-684 Hoag, Rush M. The answering message: and other naval stories / by Rush M. Hoag. New York: Broadway Publishing Co., [c1911]. 106 p., front (port.).
Contents: The answering message -- The deserters -- No next of kin -- Without a country -- The thief -- Returned -- The dynamiter.
LC: D 14, '11.

H-685 [Hobart, George V. (George Vere)], 1867-1926. Back to the woods: the story of a fall from grace / by Hugh Mchugh [pseud.]. New York: G. W. Dillingham Co., [1903, c1902]. 116 p., front., [5] leaves of plates. [Ill. by Gordon H. Grant.]
PW: F 14, '03.

H-686 [____] Beat it! / by Hugh McHugh [pseud.](George V. Hobart); illustrations by Gordon H. Grant. New York: G. W. Dillingham Co., [1907]. 113 p., front., [5] leaves of plates.
LC: F 11, '07.
PW: Mr 2, '07.

H-687 [____] Cinders: (the diary of a drummer) / by Wright Bauer [pseud.]. New York: G. W. Dillingham Co., 1907. 117 p., front., [10] leaves of plates. [Ill. by Tom Barclay.]   **MNU**
LC: F 23, '07.
PW: Ap 6, '07.

H-688 ____ Dinkelspiel's letters to Looey / by George V. Hobart . . . ; illustrations by Tom Barclay. New York: G. W. Dillingham Co., [c1908]. 190 p., front., [5] leaves of plates.
LC: Ap 11, '08.
PW: My 2, '08.

H-689 [____] Down the line with John Henry / by Hugh McHugh [pseud.]; illustrations by McKee Barclay. New York: G. W. Dillingham Co., [c1901]. 110 p., incl. front., [6] leaves of plates.
PW: N 9, '01.

H-690 [____] Get next! / by Hugh McHugh [pseud.] . . . ; illustrations by Gordon H. Grant. New York: G. W. Dillingham Co., [1905]. 111 p., front., [5] leaves of plates.
PW: Ag 26, '05.

H-691 [____] Go to it / by Hugh McHugh [pseud.] (George V. Hobart) . . . ; illustrations by Gordon H. Grant. New York: G. W. Dillingham Co., [1908]. 113 p., front., [5] leaves of plates.
LC: Mr 16, '08.
PW: Mr 28, '08.

H-692 [____] I need the money / by Hugh McHugh [pseud.]; illustrated. New York: G. W. Dillingham Co., [1904]. 114 p., front., [5] leaves of plates. [Ill. by Gordon H. Grant.]
PW: F 20, '04.

H-693 ____ Ikey's letters to his father / by George V. Hobart. New York: G. W. Dillingham Company, [1907]. 73 p.
LC: My 2, '07.
PW: Je 22, '07.

H-694 [____]. I'm from Missouri: (they had to show me) / by Hugh McHugh [pseud.] . . . ; illustrations by Gordon H. Grant. New York: G. W. Dillingham Co., 1904. 107 p., front., [5] leaves of plates.
PW: Ag 20, '04.

H-695 [____] It's up to you: a story of domestic bliss / by Hugh McHugh [pseud.]; illustrations by Gordon H. Grant. New York: G. W. Dillingham Co., [1902]. 121 p., front., [5] leaves of plates.
PW: Je 28, '02.

H-696 ____ Jim Hickey: a story of the one-night stands / by George V. Hobart . . . ; illustrations by McKee Barclay. New York: G. W. Dillingham Company,

[1904]. 119 p., front., [5] leaves of plates.
PW: D 17, '04.
BLC: London: T. Fisher Unwin; New York [printed], 1904.

H-697 [____] John Henry / by Hugh McHugh [pseud.]; illustrations by Albert Hencke. New York: G. W. Dillingham Company, [c1901]. 96 p., front., [6] leaves of plates.
PW: Ap 20, '01.

H-698 [____] John Henry: and other stories / by Hugh McHugh [pseud.] (George V. Hobart); illustrations by Albert Hencke and Gordon Grant. New York: G. W. Dillingham Co., [c1903]. 246 p., front., [2] leaves of plates.   **YSM**
Contents: John Henry at the theatre -- John Henry in a street car -- John Henry on butting-in -- John Henry in literature -- John Henry plays pool -- John Henry on would-be actors -- John Henry plays progressive euchre -- John Henry's courtship -- John Henry's wedding -- John Henry's honeymoon trip -- John Henry's seashore visit -- John Henry hunts a flat -- John Henry entertains friends -- John Henry plays ping pong -- John Henry and Wall Street -- John Henry and the horse trainer -- John Henry and the souse thing -- John Henry and the two dippy boys -- John Henry and the orphan skates -- John Henry and the big race -- John Henry and the strong finish.

H-699 [____] Out for the coin / by Hugh McHugh [pseud.] . . . ; illustrations by Gordon H. Grant. New York: G. W. Dillingham Co., [1903]. 107 p., front., [5] leaves of plates.
PW: Ag 29, '03.

H-700 [____] Skidoo! / by Hugh McHugh [pseud.] (George V. Hobart); illustrations by Gordon H. Grant. New York: G. W. Dillingham Co., [1906]. 112 p., front., [5] leaves of plates.
PW: Mr 31, '06.

H-701 [____] You can search me / by Hugh McHugh [pseud.] . . . ; illustrations by Gordon H. Grant. New York: G. W. Dillingham Co., [1905]. 119 p., front., [5] leaves of plates.
PW: F 25, '05.

H-702 ____ You should worry says John Henry / by George V. Hobart; illustrations by Edward Carey. New York: G. W. Dillingham Company, [c1914]. 173 p., ill.   **MUU**
LC: Jl 27, '14.
PW: Ag 8, '14.

H-703 Hobbs, Roe R. (Roe Raymond), b. 1871. The court of Pilate: a story of Jerusalem in the days of Christ / by Roe R. Hobbs; illustrations by S. DiFranco. New York: R. F. Fenno & Company . . . , [c1906]. 332 p., front., [3] leaves of plates.
LC: S 26, '06.
PW: O 6, '06.

H-704 ____ Gates of flame / by Roe R. Hobbs . . . New York; Washington: The Neale Publishing Company, 1906. 286 p.
LC: O 22, '06.
PW: N 17, '06.

H-705 ____ Zaos: (a novel) / by Roe R. Hobbs. New York; Washington: The Neale Publishing Company,

1906. 269 p.
LC: Jl 19, '06.
PW: S 22, '06.

H-706 Hobday, William Alfred. Accessory after the fact / by William Alfred Hobday. Boston, Massachusetts: The C. M. Clark Publishing Company, [c1911]. 153 p., front., [5] leaves of plates.   **STF**
LC: Mr 21, '12.
PW: Ap 27, '12.

H-707 Hobson, Anne. In old Alabama: being the chronicles of Miss Mouse, the Little Black Merchant / by Anne Hobson; illustrated by Carol McPherson. New York: Doubleday, Page & Company, 1903. 237 p., photo. front., [7] leaves of plates.
PW: S 19, '03.
BLC: London: Grant Richards, 1904.

H-708 Hobson, G. A. (George A.). Reuel, the gideonite / by G. A. Hobson. [Fairfield, Neb.: s. n.], c1904. 64 p.   **DLC**

H-709 Hobson, Harriet Malone. The comrade of Navarre: a tale of the Huguenots / by Harriet Malone Hobson . . . Philadephia; Boston; Chicago; St. Louis; Toronto, Can.: The Griffith & Rowland Press, [1914]. 280 p., front. [Ill. by Ralph P. Coleman.]
LC: D 30, '14.
PW: D 12, '14.

H-710 ____ Sis within / by Harriet Malone Hobson. Philadelphia: George W. Jacobs & Company, [c1913]. 351 p.
LC: O 18, '13.
PW: N 1, '13.

H-711 Hobson, Richmond Pearson, 1870-1937. In line of duty / by Richmond Pearson Hobson . . . New York; London: D. Appleton and Company, 1910. 365 p., col. front., [3] leaves of col. plates. [Ill. by Rollin Crampton.]   **CLE**
LC: S 22, '10.
PW: O 8, '10.

H-712 Hochwalt, Albert Frederick, 1869-1938. Arrows of ambition: a romance of the Thirty Years' War / by Albert Frederick Hochwalt. Boston, Mass.: Mayhew Publishing Company, 1907. 295 p., front.   **DLC**
LC: Mr 18, '07.

H-713 ____ Greymist: a story founded on an actual episode in field trials / by Albert F. Hochwalt. New York: Charles Renard Corporation, [c1925]. 132 p., photo. front., [3] leaves of photo. plates.   **CLE**
LC: Ag 24, '25.
PW: N 21, '25.

Hocking, Lorena Winchell, jt. aut. *Raising Cain* (1912). See **Hosmer, Carolyn Elizabeth, jt. aut., H-863.**

H-714 Hodder, Alfred, 1866-1907. The new Americans / by Alfred Hodder. New York: The Macmillan Company; London: Macmillan & Co., Ltd., 1901. 472 p.
PW: O 26, '01.

H-715 Hodge, T. Shirby, 1841-1926, *pseud.* The white

man's burden: a satirical forecast / by T. Shirby Hodge [pseud.]. Boston: The Gorham Press; Toronto: The Copp Clark Co., Limited, [c1915]. 225 p.   **OKU**

H-716 Hodge, William T. (William Thomas), b. 1874. The guest of honor / by William Hodge. Boston: Chapple Publishing Company, Ltd., 1911. 352 p., photo. front., (port.), [12] leaves of plates (1 col.). [Ill. by Arthur Hutchins.]

H-717 ____ Eighteen miles from home / by William T. Hodge. Boston: Small, Maynard & Company, 1904. 230 p., front. [Ill. by Marion L. Peabody.]
PW: D 17, '04.

H-718 Hodges, Arthur, 1864-1949. The bounder: a vulgar tale / by Arthur Hodges . . . Boston; New York: Houghton Mifflin Company, 1919. (Cambridge, Mass., U. S. A.: The Riverside Press). 450 p.
LC: My 8, '19.
PW: My 3, '19.

H-719 ____ The essential thing / by Arthur Hodges; frontispiece by Harrison Fisher. New York: Dodd, Mead and Company, 1912. 379 p., col. front.
LC: F 23, '12.
PW: Mr 2, '12.
BLC: London: B. F. Stevens & Brown; New York printed, 1912.

H-720 ____ Pincus Hood / by Arthur Hodges; with illustrations by Frederic R. Gruger. Boston: Small, Maynard & Company, [c1916]. 438, [1] p., front., [2] leaves of plates.
LC: S 22, '16.
PW: S 30, '16.
BLC: London: Constable & Co., 1917.

H-721 Hodges, Henry Clay. Two thousand years in Celestial Life: introduction to science and key of life, manifestations of Divine Law (received through psychic telegraphy): autobiography of Clytina, born in Athens, 147 B.C., passed to Celestial Life, 131 B. C. / [compiled . . . by Henry Clay Hodges . . . ; revised and edited by Hamilton G. Howard . . .]. Detroit, Michigan, U. S. A.: Published by Astro Publishing Company, 1901. 201 p., front., [3] leaves of plates (1 col.; 1 photo.).
Spine title: *Clytina*.

H-722 Hodgkin, James B. Southland stories / by James B. Hodgkin. Manassas, Va.: The Journal Press, 1903. 175 p.
Contents: The Randolphs -- Chief -- Will Nedmund's Christmas -- Sam's courtship -- The story of a violet -- Christmas Eve -- De profundis -- The old choir-master.

H-723 Hodsdon, Helen Merrill. The little window / by Helen Merrill Hodsdon. New York: Thomas Y. Crowell Company, [c1913]. 87 p., incl. front., [2] leaves of col. plates. [Ill. by Emily Hall Chamberlain.]
PW: S 6, '13.

H-724 Hoerl, Arthur, 1892-1968. The force eternal / by Arthur Hoerl. [Brooklyn, N. Y.: Arthur Hoerl, c1923]. 30 p.   **DLC**
LC: Je 8, '23.

H-725   Hofer, Ernst, 1855-1934. Jack Norton / E. Hofer.
Boston: Richard G. Badger, [c1912]. (Boston: The
Gorham Press). 292 p.
PW: F 22, '13.

H-726   Hoff, John D., b. 1858. Tenderfoot and expert: a
true story and experience of a tenderfoot at Goldfield
and Tonopah. [San Francisco, Calif.: J. D. Hoff,
Mutual Pub. Co., c1905]. 32 p., ill.
Unexamined copy: bibliographic data from OCLC,
#21734906.

H-727   Hoffman, Aaron, b. 1880. The Cohens and Kellys:
a story of East-Side West-Side. New York: based on
the play Two blocks away / by Aaron Hoffman; with
illustrations . . . New York: Jacobsen-Hodgkinson
Corporation, [c1925]. 135 p., photo. ill.   **BAI**

H-728   Hoffman, Marie E. Lindy Loyd: a tale of the
mountains / by Marie E. Hoffman. Boston: Marshall
Jones Company, 1920. 263 p.
LC: Ap 29, '20.
PW: My 8, '20.

H-729   Hoffman, Robert Fulkerson. Mark Enderby,
engineer / by Robert Fulkerson Hoffman; with four
illustrations by William Harnden Foster. Chicago:
A. C. McClurg & Co., 1910. 372 p., col. front., [3]
leaves of col. plates.
Some material which appeared in various periodicals
is used in a revised form.
LC: O 25, '10.
PW: N 12, '10.

H-730   Hoffman, William Stanislaus. Richard Haddon: a
romance of old Fort Crawford / by William Stanislaus
Hoffman. Boston: The Stratford Co., 1920. 291 p.,
front.   **MHS**
LC: D 20, '20.
PW: Jl 9, '21.

H-731   Holbrook, Daisy G. S. A modern knight: (a trans-
Atlantic trifle) / Daisy G. S. Holbrook. Hartford,
Conn.: The Case, Lockwood & Brainard Co., 1911.
212 p.   **DLC**

Holbrook, Richard. A bachelor of arts. In *Stories of
the colleges* (1901), S-985.

H-732   [Holden, Marietta], b. 1845. Uncovered ears and
opened vision / by "The Princess" [pseud.]. New
York: Published by Broadway Publishing Company,
[c1904]. 151 p., photo. front. (port.).

H-733   Holder, Charles Frederick, 1851-1915. The
adventures of Torqua: being the life and remarkable
adventures of three boys, refugees on the island of
Santa Catalina (Pimug-na) in the eighteenth century /
by Charles Frederick Holder . . . ; illustrated.
Boston: Little, Brown & Company, 1902.
282 p., photo. front., [10] leaves of plates, ill.
PW: O 18, '02.

H-734   ____ The marooner / by Charles Frederick Holder
. . . New York: B. W. Dodge & Company, 1908.
305 p.
LC: N 6, '08.
PW: D 12, '08.

H-735   Holderness, Herbert O. (Herbert Owen). The
reminiscences of a Pullman conductor, or, Character
sketches of life in a Pullman car / by Herbert O.
Holderness. Chicago: [s. n.], 1901. 229, [1] p.,
incl. front., [4] leaves of plates, ill. Designed end
papers.   **EYM**
Contents: Our first few trips and what they taught us -- Some types
of passengers -- The young Hebrew commercial traveler -- The
chronic kicker -- The old lady and the parrot -- Newly married
couples -- Grand Dukes and Duchesses -- Grand Dukes and
Duchesses (cont.) -- Sleeping car morals and marriage certficates --
Millionaires -- Cats and dogs -- The old couple with the lunch basket
-- The man from out West -- The fascinating young lady -- The jolly
passenger -- Operatic artists -- Deadheads -- The pompous railroad
official -- Base ball and other college fiends -- The social ethics of a
sleeping car -- Inebriates -- The emigrant family -- Children -- The
commercial traveler -- The hog -- The invalid -- The Pullman
superintendent at home and abroad -- Pullman conductors -- The
Pullman car porter -- The spotter --Newsboys -- The Pullman ten
commandments (Respectfully dedicated to the Pullman Corporation).

H-736   Holding, Elisabeth Sanxay, 1889-1955. Angelica / by
Elisabeth Sanxay Holding. New York: George H.
Doran Company, [c1921]. 289 p.
PW: D 3, '21.

H-737   ____ Invincible Minnie / by Elisabeth Sanxay
Holding. New York: George H. Doran Company,
[c1920]. 320 p.
LC: Mr 27, '20.
PW: Ap 3, '20.
BLC: London: Hodder & Stoughton; printed in U.
S. A., [1920].

H-738   ____ Rosaleen among the artists / by Elizabeth
Sanxay Holding. New York: George H. Doran
Company, [c1921]. 290 p.
LC: Ag 30, '21.
PW: Jl 30, '21.

H-739   ____ The unlit lamp: a study of inter-actions / by
Elisabeth Sanxay Holding . . . New York: E. P.
Dutton & Company, [c1922]. 334 p.   **TOL**
LC: S 18, '22.
PW: O 7, '22.

H-740   Holding, Margaret A. "Why, Jimmy" / by Margaret
A. Holding. Baltimore, Md.: Saulsbury Publishing
Company, [c1919]. 42, [1] p.   **DLC**
LC: S 5, '19.

H-741   Hollabaugh, Andrew Newton. Room no. 879 / by
Andrew Newton Hollabaugh. Nashville, Tenn.:
Cokesbury Press, 1925. 261 p.   **TJC**
LC: S 26, '25.

H-742   Holland, Annie Jefferson. Talitha Cumi: a story of
freedom through Christian Science / by Annie J.
Holland. Boston: Lee and Shepard, 1904. 417 p.

H-743   Holland, Clarence Fowler. Playing the game / by
Clarence Fowler Holland. Little Rock, Arkansas:
Printed by the Democrat Printing & Litho. Co.,
[c1923]. 249 p.   **AKE**
LC: F 27, '23.

H-744   Holland, Josephine P. Calhoun Strout: psychic / by
Josephine P. Holland. Rochester, N. Y.: The Austin
Publishing Company, 1909. 70 p.

H-745   Holland, Rupert Sargent, 1878-1952. The Count at
Harvard: being an account of the adventures of a
young gentleman of fashion at Harvard University /
by Rupert Sargent Holland. Boston: L. C. Page
Company, 1906. 320 p., front. [Ill. by Frank T.
Merrill.]
PW: Ap 14, '06.

H-746   ____ Crooked lanes / by Rupert Sargent Holland.
Philadelphia: George W. Jacobs & Company,
[c1923]. 288 p.
LC: O 17, '23.

H-747   ____ The heart of Sally Temple / by Rupert Sargent
Holland. New York: McBride, Nast & Company,
1913. 281 p.
LC: N 4, '13.
PW: N 15, '13.

H-748   ____ The house of delusion / by Rupert Sargent
Holland. Philadelphia: George W. Jacobs &
Company, [c1922]. 302 p.
LC: N 13, '22.
PW: O 28, '22.

H-749   ____ The man in the moonlight / by Rupert S.
Holland. Philadelphia: G. W. Jacobs & Company,
[c1920]. 291 p.
LC: Je 14, '20.
PW: Jl 17, '20.
BLC: London: S. Paul & Co., 1925.

H-750   ____ The man in the tower / by Rupert S. Holland;
with illustrations by Frank H. Desch. Philadelphia;
London: J. B. Lippincott Company, 1909. 311 p.,
col. front., [3] leaves of plates.
LC: S 18, '09.
PW: O 9 '09.

H-751   ____ Minot's folly / by Rupert Sargent Holland.
Philadelphia: Macrae Smith Company, 1925. 277 p.
LC: O 14, '25.
PW: O 24, '25.

H-752   ____ The mystery of the "Opal" / by Rupert Sargent
Holland. Philadelphia: George W. Jacobs &
Company, [c1924]. 288 p.
LC: O 13, '24.
PW: O 11, '24.
BLC: London: S. Paul & Co., 1924.

H-753   ____ The panelled room / by Rupert Sargent
Holland. Philadelphia: George W. Jacobs &
Company, [c1921]. 275 p.
LC: O 31, '21.
PW: N 12, '21.

Holland, W. Bob (West Bob), 1868-1932, ed. See
Twenty-five ghost stories (1904), T-444.

H-754   Holley, Marietta, 1836-1926. Around the world with
Josiah Allen's wife / by Marietta Holley; illustrations
by H. M. Pettit. New York: G. W. Dillingham
Company, [1905]. 471 p., front., [11] leaves of
plates.
PW: O 7, '05.
BLC: London: T. Fisher Unwin,; New York
[printed], 1905.

H-755   ____ Josiah Allen on the woman question / by
Marietta Holley; illustrated. New York; Chicago;
Toronto; London; Edinburgh: Fleming H. Revell
Company, [c1914]. 187 p., front., [3] leaves of
plates. [Ill. by Chas. E. Searle.]
LC: N 7, '14.
PW: N 14, '14.

H-756   ____ Samantha at Coney Island and a thousand other
islands / by Josiah Allen's wife [pseud.](Marietta
Holley). New York: The Christian Herald, Bible
House, [c1911]. 349 p., front. (port.) ill.
LC: O 30, '11.

H-757   ____ Samantha at the St. Louis Exposition / by
Josiah Allen's wife [pseud.](Marietta Holley) . . . ;
illustrations by Ch. Grunwald. New York: G. W.
Dillingham Company, [1904]. 312 p., incl. front.,
[5] leaves of plates, ill.
PW: N 12, '04.
BLC: London: T. Fisher Unwin; New York
[printed], 1904.

H-758   ____ Samantha on children's rights / by Josiah
Allen's wife [pseud.](Marietta Holley); illustrations
by Charles Grunwald. New York: G. W.
Dillingham Company, [c1909]. 318 p., front., [5]
leaves of plates.
LC: O 7, '09.
PW: O 23, '09.

H-759   ____ Samantha on the woman question / by Marietta
Holley "Josiah Allen's wife" [pseud.]. New York;
Chicago; Toronto; London; Edinburgh: Fleming H.
Revell Company, [c1913]. 191, [1] p., front., [3]
leaves of plates. [Ill. by Chas. E. Searle.]
LC: D 22, '13.
PW: S 20, '13.

H-760   ____ Samantha vs. Josiah: being the story of a
borrowed automobile and what came of it / by
Marietta Holley; illustrations by Bart Haley. New
York; London: Funk & Wagnalls Company, 1906.
395 p., front., ill.
PW: Je 16, '06.

H-761   Holliday, Carl, 1879-1936. I sat at the gate beautiful:
(being the record of Jacob of Nazareth, who was
thrown to the lions in the Roman arena in the year 91
A. D.) / by Carl Holliday . . . Nashville, Tenn.:
Cokesbury Press, 1925. 72 p.

Holly, Ella, (real name of Alice Fones, jt. aut.). *The
man with the scar* (1911). See **Fones, Warren, jt.
aut., F-205.**

H-762   Holman, Irving B. (Irving Buckingham). The sign of
the morning / by Irving B. Holman. Cincinnati:
Jennings and Graham; New York: Eaton and Mains,
[c1912]. 133 p.   **OBE**
PW: O 12, '12.

H-763   Holman, Russell. The cheat / by Russell Holman;
based upon the story by Hector Turnbull; illustrated
from Paramount's new photoplay starring Tallulah
Bankhead. New York: Grosset & Dunlap, [c1923].
310 p., photo. front., [3] leaves of photo. plates.
LC: Ag 23, '23.

H-764   ____ The freshman / novelized by Russell Holman; based upon the great comedy starring Harold Lloyd . . . New York: Grosset & Dunlap, [c1925]. 345 p., photo. front., [7] leaves of photo. plates.
LC: O 8, '25.
PW: O 17, '25.

____, jt. aut. The story without a name (1924). See **Stringer, Arthur, S-1061.**

H-765   Holmburg, Charles K. Silverado: the story of a Colorado mining town / by Charles K. Holmburg. Chicago, 1923. 245 p., front., plates.
Unexamined copy: bibliographic data from OCLC, #1978949.
LC: D 5, '23.

H-766   Holmes, Charles B. (Charles Bassett), b. 1840. Elsieville: a tale of yesterday / by Charles B. Holmes. New York: Published by Charles B. Holmes, 1903. 183 p. Decorated end papers.
PW: Ja 16, '04.

H-767   Holmes, E. Proctor (Ellis Proctor). Oaky, the son of his dad: a humorous story of New England life / by . . . E. Proctor Holmes. Chicago: Scroll Publishing Company, 1901. 293 p., front.
LC: Jl 1, '01.
PW: Ag 24, '01.

H-768   Holmes, Harriet Emerson. Thornton Stanly, or, The rescue: a tale of Topsfield at the time of the War of 1812 / by Mrs. Harriet Emerson Holmes. Topsfield [Mass.]: The Topsfield Historical Society, 1919. 70 p., photo. front.

H-769   Holmes, Mary Caroline. The knock on the door: a story of to-day / by Mary Caroline Holmes . . . New York; Chicago; London; Edinburgh: Fleming H. Revell Company, [c1918]. 239 p., front.
LC: D 31, '18.
PW: O 5, '18.
BLC: London; Edinburgh: Oliphant; printed in U. S. A., [1919].

H-770   ____ "Who follows in their train?": a Syrian romance / by Mary Caroline Holmes; illustrated. New York; Chicago; Toronto; London; Edinburgh: Fleming H. Revell Company, [c1917]. 218 p., front. [Ill. by Victor Pérard.]
LC: D 8, '17.
PW: Ag 4, '17.

H-771   Holmes, Mary Jane, 1825-1907. The abandoned farm; and Connie's mistake / by Mrs. Mary J. Holmes. New York: G. W. Dillingham Company, [1905]. 319 p., front. [Ill. by Gordon Grant.]
LC: S 15, '05.
PW: O 7, '05.
References: BAL 8700.

H-772   ____ The Cromptons / by Mary J. Holmes. New York: G. W. Dillingham Company, [1902]. 384 p., front.
PW: Ag 30, '02.
BLC: London: T. Fisher Unwin, 1902.
References: BAL 8693.

H-773   ____ Lucy Harding: a romance of Russia / by Mary J. Holmes . . . New York: American News Company, Publisher's Agents, [c1905]. 266 p., front., [7] leaves of plates. [Ill. by Charles Grunwald.]   **MUM**
PW: D 30, '05.
References: BAL 8701.

H-774   ____ The Merivale banks / by Mary J. Holmes. New York: G. W. Dillingham Company, [1903]. 318 p., front. [Ill. by Gordon H. Grant.]
LC: S 11, '03.
PW: S 19, '03.
References: BAL 8694.

H-775   ____ Rena's experiment / by Mary J. Holmes. New York: G. W. Dillingham Company, [c1904]. 310 p., front. [Ill. by Gordon H. Grant.]
LC: Ag 4, '04.
PW: Ag 20, '04.
References: BAL 8696.

H-776   Holmes, Richard Sill, 1842-1912. Bradford Horton: Man: a novel / by Richard S. Holmes. New York; Chicago; Toronto; London; Edinburgh: Fleming H. Revell Company, [1913]. 306 p.
LC: N 10, '13.
PW: O 4, '13.

H-777   ____ The maid of honor / by Richard S. Holmes. New York; Chicago; Toronto; London; Edinburgh: Fleming H. Revell Company, [c1907]. 374 p.
                    MNL (3rd ed.)
LC: N 25, '07.
PW: D 7, '07.

H-778   ____ The victor / by Richard S. Holmes. New York; Chicago; Toronto; London; Edinburgh: Fleming H. Revell Company, [c1908]. 320 p.
LC: O 19, '08.
PW: N 14, '08.

Holmes, Roy J., jt. ed. See *War stories* **(1919), W-94.**

H-779   Holmes, Thomas K. The heart of Canyon Pass / by Thomas K. Holmes . . . ; illustrated by R. Emmett Owen. New York: George Sully & Company, [c1921]. 312 p., front., [3] leaves of plates.
LC: N 2, '21.
PW: N 26, '21.

H-780   ____ The man from tall timber / by Thomas K. Holmes; illustrated by R. Emmett Owen. New York: George Sully & Company, [c1919]. 434 p., front., [3] leaves of plates.
LC: D 30, '19.
PW: Ja 10, '20.

Holt, H. P., jt. aut. *Fortunes of war.* See **Barbour, Ralph Henry, 1870-1944, jt. aut., B-177.**

____, jt. aut. *Joan of the island.* See **Barbour, Ralph Henry, 1870-1944, jt. aut., B-183.**

H-781   Holt, Harrison Jewell. The calendared isles: a romance of Casco Bay / Harrison Jewell Holt.

Boston: Richard G. Badger, 1910. ([Boston]: The Gorham Press). 296 p.
LC: N 2, '10.
PW: Je 18, '10.

H-782 ____ Midnight at Mears house: a detective story / by Harrison Jewell Holt; illustrated by M. J. Spero. New York: Dodd, Mead and Company, 1912. 337 p., front., [3] leaves of plates.
LC: Ap 30, '12.
PW: My 11, '12.
BLC: London: Simpkin, Marshall & Co., 1916.

H-783 Holt, Henry, 1840-1926. Calmire: man and nature / by Henry Holt . . . -- Sixth edition, revised. -- Boston; New York: Houghton, Mifflin and Company, 1906. (Cambridge [Mass.]: The Riverside Press). 705 p.
PW: Mr 17, '06.

H-784 [____] Sturmsee: man and man / by the author of "Calmire". New York; London: The Macmillan Company, 1905. 682 p.   MNU
PW: Je 3, '05.

H-785 Holt, Isabella, 1892-1962. The low road / by Isabella Holt. New York: The Macmillan Company, 1925. 271 p.
LC: F 25, '25.
PW: Mr 7, '25.
BLC: London: Macmillan; printed in U. S. A., [1925].

H-786 ____ The Marriotts and the Powells: a tribal chronicle / by Isabella Holt. New York: The Macmillan Company, 1921. 328 p.
LC: O 19, '21.
PW: N 12, '21.

H-787 Holt, Matt. J. (Matthew Joseph), b. 1866. Voices; Birth-marks; The man and the elephant / Matt J. Holt . . . Louisville: The Standard Printing Co., Inc., 1922. 358 p.   OSU, EWF
Cover title: *Birth-marks*.

H-788 Holt-Lomax, R. H. A moment's mistake / by R. H. Holt-Lomax. New York; London: The Abbey Press, [c1901]. 200 p.   DLC
PW: D 28, '01.

H-789 Home, Marshall. The MacGregors / by Marshall Home. Chicago: Scroll Publishing Company, 1901. 285 p., front., [2] leaves of plates.   RCE
PW: S 7, '01.

H-790 Homer, N. Y., *pseud.* A slight indiscretion / by N. Y. Homer [pseud.]. New York: Cochrane Publishing Co., 1909. 228 p.   DLC
LC: Ag 13, '09.

H-791 Honeymoon confidences / by the bride herself. New York: The Hudson Press, [c1909]. 206 p., incl. front.
LC: Ag 28, '09.

Hood, Archer Leslie. See **Leslie, Lilian, jt. pseud. of Perkins, Violet Lilian and Hood, Archer Leslie.**

H-792 Hood, Frances A. The mystery of a pyramid / by Frances A. Hood. La Crosse, Wis.: Published by the author, [c1915]. 126 p.   KSU

H-793 Hood, Robert Allison. The chivalry of Keith Leicester: a romance of British Columbia / by Robert Allison Hood. New York: George H. Doran Company, [c1918]. 339 p.
LC: S 23, '18.
PW: S 21, '18.

H-794 ____ The quest of Alistair / by Robert Allison Hood . . . New York: George H. Doran Company, [c1921]. 328 p.   CLE
PW: O 29, '21.

H-795 Hoogstraat, M. E. (Moree E.), b. 1869. For bush or bonnet? / by M. E. Hoogstraat; illustrated by Robt. L. Stearns. New York; London; Montreal: The Abbey Press, [c1902]. 231 p., [3] leaves of plates.
PW: S 13, '02.

Hooker, Brian, 1880-1946, jt. aut. *The professor's mystery* (1911). See **Hastings, Wells, 1879-1923, jt. aut., H-360.**

H-796 ____ The right man / by Brian Hooker; illustrations by Alonzo Kimball. Indianapolis: The Bobbs-Merrill Company, [1908]. 149, [1] p., col. front., [6] leaves of col. plates.
LC: O 10, '08.
PW: O 17, '08.

H-797 Hooker, Forrestine C. (Forrestine Cooper), 1867-1932. The long dim trail / Forrestine C. Hooker. New York: Alfred A. Knopf, 1920. 364 p.   AZS
(Borzoi western stories.)
LC: O 1, '20.
PW: O 16, '20.
BLC: London: Milss & Boon, 1922.

H-798 ____ When Geronimo rode / by Forrestine C. Hooker. Garden City, N. Y.: Doubleday, Page & Company, 1924. 325 p.
LC: Mr 28, '24.
PW: Ap 5, '24.
BLC: London: Hodder & Stoughton; printed in U. S. A., [1925].

H-799 Hooker, William Francis, 1856-1938. Branded men and women: story of a western town / by William Francis Hooker. Boston: Richard G. Badger, [c1921]. ([Boston]: The Gorham Press). 305 p.
LC: Ja 4, '22.
PW: Ja 21, '22.

H-800 Hooper, C. Lauron (Cyrus Lauron), b. 1863. Gee-boy / by Cyrus Lauron Hooper. New York; London: John Lane, 1903. 271 p.

H-801 Hoover, Bessie Ray, b. 1874. Opal / by Bessie R. Hoover . . . ; illustrated. New York; London: Harper & Brothers Publishers, 1910. 330 p., front., ill.
LC: O 29, '10.
PW: N 5, '10.

H-802   Pa Flickinger's folks / by Bessie R. Hoover; illustrated. New York; London: Harper & Brothers, 1909. 273, [1] p., front., [6] leaves of plates. [Ill. by Fred Strothmann.] Partly reprinted from Harper's Magazine, Everybody's and The Ladies' World.
Contents: Opal and the parade -- Opal's half-holiday -- No merry-go-roundin' -- Bill's Budzbanowsky -- Cousin Mosely's money -- Mis' Hi Lundy's present -- Butch Panner's gold-mine -- Jed, the gentleman farmer -- A sure-enough Santy -- Grandpaw Peebles -- The social whirl -- Opal's chance.
LC: Ag 20, '09.
PW: Ag 28, '09.

H-803   Rolling acres / by Bessie R. Hoover. Boston: Small, Maynard & Company, [c1922]. 286 p.
LC: S 21, '22.

H-804 Hoover, Francis Trout, 1841-1921. Not in His steps: a story of the ministerial dead-line of fifty years / by Francis T. Hoover . . . ; introduction by Rev. William E. Park; illustrated. Cleona, Pa.: Holzapfel Publishing Company, [1911]. 360 p., photo. front. (port.), [18] leaves of plates, ill. [Ill. by William E. Park.]

H-805 Hope, Andrew J. Karel and Leida: a Christmas story. New York: The Lafayette Press, n. d. 46 p.
Unexamined copy: bibliographic data from NUC.

H-806   The wonderful adventures of Thomas Cresson, Esq., engineer: a Christmas story. New York: J. J. Little and Company, n. d. 48 p.
Unexamined copy: bibliographic data from NUC.

"The Hope Farm Man," pseud. See **Collingwood, Herbert W. (Herbert Winslow), 1857-1927.**

H-807 Hopkins, Alice K. (Alice Kimball), b. 1839. Mona the druidess, or, The astral science of old Britain / by Alice K. Hopkins . . . ; illustrations and cover design by Victor Q. [sic] Searles. Boston: Eastern Publishing Company, 1904. 345 p., front., ill.
CRU, CSA

H-808 Hopkins, Anna Gillilland. The tangled skein / by Anna Gillilland Hopkins; illustrated by Geo. A. Calley. Boston: The Roxburgh Publishing Company Inc., [c1914]. 209 p., front., [4] leaves of plates.
LC: Mr 28, '14.

H-809 Hopkins, Frances Stocker. Sara: a romance of the early nineteenth century / by Frances Stocker Hopkins. New York: The Neale Publishing Company, 1912. 194 p.
LC: D 4, '12.
PW: N 30, '12.

H-810 Hopkins, Herbert Müeller, 1870-1910. The fighting bishop / by Herbert M. Hopkins. Indianapolis: The Bowen-Merrill Company, [c1902]. 380 p.
PW: Mr 15, '02.
BLC: London: B. F. Stevens & Brown, 1902.

H-811   The mayor of Warwick / by Herbert M. Hopkins . . . Boston; New York: Houghton, Mifflin and Company, 1906. (Cambridge, Mass., U. S. A.: The Riverside Press). 435, [1] p., col. front. [Ill. by

Henry Hut.]
PW: My 5, '06.

H-812   Priest and pagan / by Herbert M. Hopkins. Boston; New York: Houghton, Mifflin and Company, 1908. (Cambridge: The Riverside Press). 372, [2] p., col. front. [Ill. by Martin Justice.]
PW: Mr 28, '08.

H-813   The torch / by Herbert M. Hopkins. Indianapolis: The Bobbs-Merrill Company, [1903]. 398 p.
PW: N 7, '03.

H-814 Hopkins, Isabella Pierpont. The Wingtown parson's linen duster / by Isabella Pierpont Hopkins. New York: Eaton & Mains; Cincinnati: Jennings & Pye, [c1903]. 89 p.
PW: S 26, '03.

H-815 Hopkins, J. Williams. Cross providences / by J. Williams Hopkins. Boston: The Roxburgh Publishing Company, [c1913]. 220 p.

H-816 Hopkins, Lindsey. Discovered!: the winning and giving of a $ million $ / Lindsey Hopkins, Al Fairbrother. [Greensboro, N. C.: s. n., 1910?]. [64] p., [1] leaf of photo. plates, ill.

H-817 Hopkins, Louise M. (Louise Martin), b. 1860. Signal lights: a story of life on the prairies / by Louise M. Hopkins. Boston, U. S. A.: The C. M. Clark Publishing Co., 1906. 336 p., front., [7] leaves of plates. [Ill. by Griswold Tyng.]
LC: Ag 24, '06.
PW: O 13, '06.

Hopkins, Margaret Sutton (Briscoe). See **Briscoe, Margaret Sutton, b. 1864.**

H-818 Hopkins, Nevil Monroe, 1873-1945. The Raccoon Lake mystery: further adventures of Mason Brant / by Nevil Monroe Hopkins; with four illustrations in color by Gayle Hoskins. Philadelphia; London: J. B. Lippincott Company, 1917. 319 p., col. front., [3] leaves of col. plates.
LC: S 20, '17.
PW: S 22, '17.

H-819   The strange cases of Mason Brant / by Nevil Monroe Hopkins; with four illustrations in color by Gayle Hoskins. Philadelphia; London: J. B. Lippincott Company, 1916. 304 p., col. front., [3] leaves of col. plates.
Contents: The mystery in the North case -- The Moyett case -- The investigation at Holman square.
LC: My 19, '16.
PW: My 13, '16.

H-820 [Hopkins, Pauline Bradford Mackie], b. 1873. The girl and the Kaiser / by Pauline Bradford Mackie . . . ; with drawings and decorations by John Cecil Clay. Indianapolis: The Bobbs-Merrill Company, [c1904]. 164 p., col. front., [5] leaves of col. plates.
PW: D 3, '04.

H-821   The voice in the desert / by Pauline Bradford Mackie (Mrs. Herbert Müeller Hopkins). New York:

McClure, Phillips and Company, 1903. 334 p.
PW: Ap 18, '03.

H-822   ____ The Washingtonians / by Pauline Bradford
Mackie (Mrs. Herbert Müeller Hopkins); with a
frontispiece by Philip R. Goodwin. Boston: L. C.
Page & Company, 1902. 357 p., front.
PW: N 23, '01.

H-823   Hopkins, Una Nixson. A winter romance in poppy
land / Una Nixson Hopkins. Boston: Richard G.
Badger, 1911. ([Boston]: The Gorham Press).
207 p., front., [5] leaves of plates. [Ill. by Warren
Rockwell.]
LC: D 12, '10.
PW: Mr 18, '11.

H-824   Hopkins, William B. Milliner to a mouse: a capital
chat / by William B. Hopkins . . . New York: The
Knickerbocker Press, [c1903]. 119 p.

H-825   Hopkins, William John, 1863-1926. The airship
Dragon-fly / by William J. Hopkins; illustrated by

Ruth M. Hallock. New York: Doubleday, Page &
Company, 1906. 346 p., front., [7] leaves of plates.
LC: Ag 17, '06.
PW: S 8, '06.
BLC: London: Doubleday, Page & Company, 1906.

H-826   ____ Burbury Stoke / by William John Hopkins.
Boston; New York: Houghton Mifflin Company,
1914. (Cambridge: The Riverside Press). 327,
[1] p.
LC: F 16, '14.
PW: F 28, '14.

H-827   ____ The clammer / by William John Hopkins.
Boston; New York: Houghton, Mifflin & Company,
1906. (Cambridge: The Riverside Press). 255,
[1] p.
Contents: The clammer -- A daughter of the rich -- Old Goodwin's
wife.
PW: Mr 24, '06.

H-828   ____ The clammer and the submarine / by William
John Hopkins. Boston; New York: Houghton Mifflin
Company, 1917. (Cambridge, Mass., U. S. A.: The
Riverside Press). 346 p.
LC: O 8, '17.
PW: O 6, '17.

H-829   ____ Concerning Sally / by William John Hopkins.
Boston; New York: Houghton Mifflin Company,
1912. (Cambridge: The Riverside Press). 390 p.
LC: S 23, '12.
PW: S 21, '12.
BLC: London: Constable & Co; Boston; New York:
Houghton Mifflin, 1912.

H-830   ____ The meddlings of Eve / by William John
Hopkins. Boston; New York: Houghton Mifflin
Company, 1910. (Cambridge: The Riverside Press).
297, [1] p.
Contents: I. Cecily -- II. Margaret.
LC: Ag 25, '10.
PW: Ag 20, '10.
BLC: London: Constable & Co; Boston; New York:
Houghton Mifflin, 1911.

H-831   ____ Old Harbor / by William John Hopkins.
Boston; New York: Houghton Mifflin Company,
1909. (Cambridge, Mass.: The Riverside Press).
388, [2] p.
LC: N 13, '09.
PW: N 20, '09.
BLC: London: Constable & Co.; Cambridge, Mass.
printed, 1910.

H-832   ____ She blows!: and sparm at that! / by William
John Hopkins . . . ; with illustrations from paintings
by Clifford W. Ashley. Boston; New York:
Houghton Mifflin Company, 1922. (Cambridge,
Mass., U. S. A.: The Riverside Press). 361 p.,
front., [7] leaves of plates.
LC: Mr 6, '22.
PW: Mr 18, '22.
BLC: London: Constable & Co.; Cambridge, Mass.
printed, [1922].

H-833   ____ Those Gillespies / by William John Hopkins;
illustrated by Lester G. Hornby. Boston; New York:
Houghton Mifflin Company, 1916. (Cambridge: The
Riverside Press). 324, [2] p., front., [4] leaves of
plates.
LC: My 12, '16.
PW: My 6, '16.

H-834   ____ Tumbleberry and Chick / by William John
Hopkins; with illustrations by Arthur G. Dove.
Boston; New York: Houghton Mifflin Company,
1925. (Cambridge: The Riverside Press). 287,
[1] p., front., [3] leaves of plates.
LC: F 16, '25.
PW: F 28, '25.

Hopper, James Marie, 1876-1956. The ants. In
Marriage (1923), **M-457.**

H-835   ____ Caybigan / by James Hopper. New York:
McClure, Phillips & Co., 1906. 340 p., front. [Ill.
by W. Hatherell.] Contents: The judgment of man -- The
Maestro of Balangilang -- Her reading -- The struggles and triumph
of Isidro de los Maestros -- The failure -- Some benevolent
assimilation -- A jest of the gods -- The coming of the maestra --
Caybigan -- The capture of Papa Gato -- The mañangete -- The past --
The prerogative -- The confluence -- The call.
LC: S 19, '06.
PW: D 1, '06.

____ Célestine. In *Prize stories of 1923 (1924)*,
P-621.

H-836   ____ Coming back with the spitball: a pitcher's
romance / by James Hopper; illustrated. New York;
London: Harper & Brothers, 1914. 69, [1] p.,
photo. front., [3] leaves of photo. plates. [Ill. by Paul
Thompson.]
LC: F 21, '14.
PW: Mr 7, '14.

____ The difference. In *Forum stories (1914)*,
F-306.

____ The idealist. In *California story book (1909)*,
C-40.

____ The judgment of man. In *Spinners' book of
fiction (1907)*, **S-755.**

327

H-837 ____ 9009 / by James Hopper and Fred R. Bechdolt. New York: The McClure Company, 1908. 195 p.
LC: S 22, '08.
PW: O 10, '08.
BLC: London: William Heinemann, 1909.

____ The proud dig and the lazy student. In *Under Berkeley Oaks* **(1901), U-8.**

H-838 ____ The trimming of Goosie / by James Hopper . . . New York: Moffat, Yard and Company, 1909. 216 p.
LC: S 17, '09.
PW: S 25, '09.

H-839 ____ What happened in the night: and other stories / by James Hopper. New York: Henry Holt and Company, 1913. 236 p.
Contents: What happened in the night -- A jumble in divinities -- The fishing of Suzanne -- The marvelous night -- The king's caprice -- The gift -- The black night -- White loves -- God's job.
LC: S 20, '13.
PW: O 11, '13.

H-840 Hopwood, Avery, 1884-1928. Sadie Love / by Avery Hopwood . . . New York: John Lane Company, 1915. 300 p., photo. front., [5] leaves of plates.
LC: D 8, '15.
PW: D 11, '15.

Horn, R. de S. The jinx of the "Shandon Belle." In *Prize stories of 1922* **(1923), P-620.**

H-841 Hornblow, Arthur, 1865-1942. The Argyle case / by Arthur Hornblow; founded on the play by Harriet Ford and Harvey J. O'Higgins; written in cooperation with Detective William J. Burns. New York; London: Harper & Brothers, 1913. 249, [1] p., photo. front., [4] leaves of photo. plates.
LC: S 6, '13.
PW: S 13, '13.

H-842 ____ Bought and paid for: a story of to-day / from the play of George Broadhurst, by Arthur Hornblow. New York: G. W. Dillingham Company, [c1912]. 339 p., front., [5] leaves of plates.
LC: F 24, '12.
PW: F 24, '12.
BLC: London; Leipsic: T. Fisher Unwin; New York [printed], 1912.

H-843 ____ By right of conquest: a novel / by Arthur Hornblow . . . ; illustrations by Archie Gunn and Charles Grunwald. New York: G. W. Dillingham Company, [c1909]. 353 p., col. front., [3] leaves of plates.
LC: My 1, '09.
PW: My 22, '09.
BLC: London: T. Fisher Unwin; New York [printed], 1909.

____, jt. aut. *The easiest way* (1911). See **Walter, Eugene, 1874-1941, jt. aut., W-81.**

H-844 ____ The end of the game: a novel / by Arthur Hornblow . . . ; illustrations by A. E. Jameson. New York: G. W. Dillingham Company, [c1907]. 464 p., front., [3] leaves of plates.

LC: Ap 8, '07.
PW: Ap 27, '07.
BLC: London: T. Fisher Unwin; New York [printed], 1907.

____, jt. aut. *The gamblers* (1911). See **Klein, Charles, 1867-1915, jt. aut., K-310.**

____, jt. aut. *John Marsh's millions* (1910). See **Klein, Charles, 1867-1915, jt. aut., K-311.**

H-845 ____ Kindling: (Margaret Illington's play) / adapted from the dramatization of Charles Kenyon by Arthur Hornblow; illustrations by William F. Taylor. New York: G. W. Dillingham, [c1912]. 375 p., front., [3] leaves of plates.
LC: My 24, '12.
PW: Je 1, '12.

____, jt. aut. *The lion and the mouse* (1906). See **Klein, Charles, 1867-1915, jt. aut., K-312.**

H-846 ____ The mask: a story of love and adventure / by Arthur Hornblow . . . ; illustrations by Paul Stahr. New York: G. W. Dillingham Company, [c1913]. 369 p., front., [2] leaves of plates.
LC: My 31, '13.
PW: Je 7, '13.

____, jt. aut. *The money makers* (1914). See **Klein, Charles, 1867-1915, jt. aut., K-314.**

H-847 ____ The price. Founded on the play by George Broadhurst. New York: G. W. Dellingham, [c1914]. 336 p.
Unexamined copy: bibliographic data from OCLC, #20851851.
PW: Mr 21, '14.

H-848 ____ The profligate: a novel / by Arthur Hornblow . . . ; illustrations by Charles Grunwald. New York: G. W. Dillingham Company, [c1908]. 383 p., front., [3] leaves of plates.
LC: My 20, '08.
PW: Je 13, '08.
BLC: London: T. Fisher Unwin,; New York [printed], 1908.

H-849 ____ The talker: a story of to-day / from the play of Marion Fairfax; by Arthur Hornblow. New York: G. W. Dillingham Company, [c1912]. 338 p., photo. front., [7] leaves of photo plates.
LC: S 16, '12.
PW: S 14, '12.

____, jt. aut. *The third degree* (1909). See **Klein, Charles, 1867-1915, jt. aut., K-316.**

H-850 ____ The watch dog: a story of to-day / by Arthur Hornblow; illustrations by Paul Stahr. New York: G. W. Dillingham Company, [c1915]. 319 p., front., [1] leaf of plates.
LC: Je 1, '15.
PW: My 29, '15.

H-851 Hornby, E. B. (Eliza Benedict), b. 1835. Under old rooftrees / Mrs. E. B. Hornby. Jersey City, N. J.: [Press of Redfield Brothers], 1908. 271 p.

H-852 Hornibrook, Isabel. Coxswain Drake of the Seascouts / by Isabel Hornibrook; with illustrations by Sears Gallagher. Boston: Little, Brown and Company, 1920. 281 p., front., [3] leaves of plates.
LC: O 23, '20.
PW: O 30, '20.

Horton, George, 1860-1942. Around the world. In *Second suds sayings* **(1919), S-266.**

H-853 ____ The edge of hazard / by George Horton . . . ; with pictures by C. M. Relyea. Indianapolis: The Bobbs-Merrill Company, [c1906]. 429 p., front., [5] leaves of plates.
PW: Mr 3, '06.

H-854 ____ Like another Helen / by George Horton; illustrated by C. M. Relyea. Indianapolis: The Bowen-Merrill Company, [1901]. 379 p., front., [6] leaves of plates.
PW: Ap 13, '01.
BLC: London: B. F. Stevens & Brown; Brooklyn, New York printed, [1901].

H-855 ____ The long straight road / by George Horton; illustrated by Troy and Margaret West Kinney. Indianapolis: The Bowen-Merrill Company, [1902]. 401 p., front., [5] leaves of plates.
PW: S 20, '02.
BLC: London: B. F. Stevens & Brown, [1912].

H-856 ____ Miss Schuyler's alias / George Horton . . . Boston: Richard G. Badger, [c1913]. (Boston: The Gorham Press). 33 p.
LC: Jl 18, '13.
PW: Je 27, '14.

H-857 ____ The monks' treasure / by George Horton; with a frontispiece by C. M. Relyea. Indianapolis: The Bobbs-Merrill Company, [1905]. 391 p., front.
PW: Mr 11, '05.
BLC: London: Ward, Lock & Co., 1907.

H-858 ____ The tempting of Father Anthony / by George Horton . . . ; with five full-page illustrations by Otto Schneider. Chicago: A. C. McClurg & Co., 1901. 246 p., front., [4] leaves of plates.
PW: O 5, '01.

H-859 Horton, Marcus, b. 1879. Bred of the desert: a horse and a romance / by Marcus Horton. New York; London: Harper & Brothers, 1915. 288, [1] p., front.
PW: Ap 17, '15.

Horton, Robert J. See **Roberts, James R.**

H-860 Hosford, Hester E. (Hester Eloise), b. 1892. A warning to wives / by Hester E. Hosford. Boston, Massachusetts: The Stratford Co., 1924. 461 p., photo. front. (port.).

H-861 Hoskins, Baker B., Jr. A great big grown-up love: a tale of Texas / by Baker B. Hoskins, Jr. New York: Broadway Publishing Company, [c1905]. 172 p.
LC: D 2, '07.
PW: Mr 25, '05.

H-862 Hoskins, Bertha Ladd. The double fortune / by Bertha Ladd Hoskins. New York; Washington: The Neale Publishing Company, 1909. 300 p.
PW: My 8, '09.

Hoskins, Jesse. See **Fones, Warren, pseud.**

H-863 Hosmer, Carolyn Elizabeth. Raising Cain / by Carolyn Elizabeth Hosmer and Lorena Winchell Hocking. Denver, Colo.: The W. H. Kistler Stationery Co., 1912. 173 p., photo. front. **DPL**

H-864 Hotchkiss, Chauncey C. (Chauncey Crafts), b. 1852. Betsy Ross: a romance of the flag / by Chauncey C. Hotchkiss . . . New York: D. Appleton and Company, 1901. 367 p.
PW: Ap 6, '01.

H-865 ____ For a maiden brave / by Chauncey C. Hotchkiss; illustrated in colors by Frank T. Merrill. New York: D. Appleton & Company, 1902. 373 p., col. front., [3] leaves of col. plates.
PW: Ja 17, '03.

H-866 ____ The ivory ball / by Chauncey C. Hotchkiss . . . ; illustrations by R. L. Rivera. New York: W. J. Watt & Company, [c1920]. 303 p., front., [3] leaves of plates.
LC: Ap 20, '20.
PW: Je 26, '20.

H-867 ____ Maude Baxter / by C. C. Hotchkiss . . . ; illustrations by Will Grefé. New York: W. J. Watt & Company, [c1911]. 319 p., front., [3] leaves of plates.
LC: F 27, 11.
PW: Mr 4, '11.

H-868 ____ Mistress Hetty / by Chauncey C. Hotchkiss. New York; London: Street & Smith, [c1902]. 200 p., front., [5] leaves of plates. [Ill. by H. P. Arms.]
PW: O 11, '02.
BLC: London: Shurmer Sib Thorpe, [1902].

H-869 ____ A prisoner of the sea / by Chauncey C. Hotchkiss . . . ; illustrated by Bert Knight. [New York]: The John McBride Co, 1908. 260 p., col. front., [4] leaves of col. plates.
LC: O 8, '08.
PW: O 31, '08.

H-870 ____ The red paper / by C. C. Hotchkiss; illustrations by Will Grefé. New York: W. J. Watt & Company, [c1912]. 299 p., front., [2] leaves of plates.
LC: S 9, '12.
PW: N 9, '12.

H-871 ____ The spur of danger / by C. C. Hotchkiss . . . ; illustrations by Will Grefé. New York: W. J. Watt & Company, [c1915]. 310 p., front., [2] leaves of plates.
LC: O 11, '15.
PW: F 5, '16.

H-872   ____ The strength of the weak: a romance / by Chauncey C. Hotchkiss. New York: D. Appleton and Company, 1902. 371 p.
PW: F 1, '02.

H-873   Houck, Ida Best. Steps toward heaven / by Ida Best Houck. Tiffin, Ohio: Published by Ida Best Houck, [c1912]. 69, [1] p.   **DLC**

H-874   Hough, Emerson, 1857-1923. The broken gate: a novel / by Emerson Hough; illustrated by M. Leone Bracker. New York; London: D. Appleton and Company, 1917. 348, [1] p., front., [3] leaves of plates.
LC: Ag 20, '17.
PW: S 8, '17.
References: BAL 9348.

H-875   ____ The covered wagon / by Emerson Hough . . . New York; London: D. Appleton and Company, 1922. 378, [1] p., front. [Ill. by W. H. D. Koerner.] Map on lining-paper.
LC: My 29, '22.
PW: Je 10, '22.
References: BAL 9359.

H-876   ____ 54-40 or fight / by Emerson Hough . . . ; with illustrations by Arthur I. Keller. Indianapolis: The Bobbs-Merrill Company, [c1909]. 402 p., front., [3] leaves of plates.
LC: Ja 20, '09.
PW: Ja 16, '09.
References: BAL 9330.

H-877   ____ Heart's desire: the story of a contented town, certain peculiar citizens, and two fortunate lovers: a novel: illustrated / by Emerson Hough . . . New York: The Macmillan Company; London: Macmillan & Co ., Ltd., 1905. 367 p., front., [7] leaves of plates. [Ill. by F. B. Masters and Howard Giles.]
LC: O 2, '05.
PW: O 28, '05.
BLC: London: Macmillan, [1905].
References: BAL 9323.

    ____ The Holy City quartette. <u>See</u> **Conrad, Joseph, 1857-1924.** *Il conte* **(1925), C-697.**

    ____ The horse thief. <u>In</u> *Comedy* **(1901), C-614.**

H-878   ____ John Rawn: prominent citizen / by Emerson Hough . . . ; with illustrations by M. Leone Bracker. Indianapolis: The Bobbs-Merrill Company, [c1912]. 385 p., front., [5] leaves of plates.
LC: Mr 6, '12.
PW: Mr 2, '12.
References: BAL 9336.

H-879   ____ The lady and the pirate: being the plain tale of a diligent pirate and a fair captive / by Emerson Hough . . . ; illustrated by Harry A. Mathes. Indianapolis: The Bobbs-Merrill Company, [c1913]. 436 p., front., [3] leaves of plates.
LC: Ag 1, '13.
PW: Ag 9, '13.
References: BAL 9339.

H-880   ____ The law of the land: of Miss Lady, whom it involved in mystery, and of John Eddring, gentleman of the South, who read its deeper meaning: a novel / by Emerson Hough . . . ; with illustrations by Arthur I. Keller. Indianapolis: The Bobbs-Merrill Company, [c1904]. 416 p., front., [5] leaves of plates.
PW: O 22, '04.
References: BAL 9322.

H-881   ____ The magnificent adventure: this being the story of the world's greatest exploration, and the romance of a very gallant gentleman: a novel / by Emerson Hough; illustrated by Arthur I. Keller. New York; London: D. Appleton and Company, 1916. 355, [1] p., front., [3] leaves of plates.
LC: Ag 30, '16.
PW: S 16, '16.
References: BAL 9344.

H-882   ____ The man next door / by Emerson Hough; illustrated by Will Grefé. New York; London: D. Appleton and Company, 1917. 309, [1] p., front., [3] leaves of plates.
LC: F 12, '17.
PW: F 17, '17.
References: BAL 9347.

H-883   ____ Maw's vacation: the story of a human being in the Yellowstone: illustrated / by Emerson Hough . . . Saint Paul [Minn.]: J. E. Haynes, 1921. 61 p., photo. front., [3] leaves of photo. plates.
LC: My 24, '21.
PW: S 24, '21.
References: BAL 9357.

H-884   ____ The Mississippi bubble: how the star of good fortune rose and set and rose again, by a woman's grace, for one John Law of Lauriston: a novel / by Emerson Hough; the illustrations by Henry Hutt. Indianapolis: The Bowen-Merrill Company, [c1902]. 452 p., front., [5] leaves of plates.
PW: My 3, '02.
BLC: London: B. F. Stevens & Brown, [1902].
References: BAL 9318.

H-885   ____ Mother of gold / by Emerson Hough. New York; London: D. Appleton and Company, 1924. 326, [1] p., front.
LC: F 12, '24.
PW: F 23, '24.
References: BAL 9363.

H-886   ____ North of 36 / by Emerson Hough; illustrated by W. H. D. Koerner. New York; London: D. Appleton and Company, 1923. 429 p., front., [3] leaves of plates.
LC: Jl 6, '23.
PW: Jl 21, '23.
References: BAL 9362.

H-887   ____ The purchase price: or, The cause of compromise / by Emerson Hough; with illustrations by M. Leone Bracker and Edmund Frederick. Indianapolis: The Bobbs-Merrill Company, [c1910]. 414, [1] p., front.
LC: N 29, '10.

PW: N 19, '10.
References: BAL 9333.

H-888   ____ The sagebrusher: a story of the West / by
Emerson Hough . . . ; illustrated by J. Henry. New
York; London: D. Appleton & Company, 1919.
318, [1] p., front., [3] leaves of plates.
LC: Ap 2, '19.
PW: Ap 12, '19.
References: BAL 9353.

H-889   ____ The ship of souls / by Emerson Hough . . .
New York; London: D. Appleton and Company,
1925. 291, [1] p., front. [Ill. by W. H. D. Koerner.]
LC: F 24, '25.
PW: Mr 7, '25.
References: BAL 9365.

H-890   ____ The singing mouse stories / by Emerson Hough
. . . ; with decorations by Mayo Bunker.
Indianapolis: The Bobbs-Merrill Company, [c1910].
235, [1] p., front., ill.
BAL: 1910 ed. contains 6 stories not present in 1895
ed.
Contents: The land of the singing mouse -- The burden of a song --
The little river -- What the waters said -- Lake Belle-Marie -- The
skull and the rose -- The man of the mountain -- At the place of the
oaks -- The birth of the hours -- The stone that had no thought -- The
tear and the smile -- How the mountains ate up the plains -- The
savage and its heart -- The beast terrible -- The passing of men -- The
house of truth -- Where the city went -- The bell and the shadows --
Of the greatest sorrow -- The shoes of the Princess -- The white
moths -- The house of dreams.
LC: N 28, '10.
PW: D 17, '10.
References: BAL 9334.

____ The unredeemed. In *Prairie gold* (1917),
P-588.

H-891   ____ The way of a man / by Emerson Hough . . . ;
with illustrations by George Wright. New York: The
Outing Publishing Company, 1907. 345 p., front.,
[4] leaves of plates.
LC: Ag 29, '07.
PW: O 12, '07.
BLC: London: Methuen & Co., [1910].
References: BAL 9327.

H-892   ____ The way out: a story of the Cumberlands
to-day / by Emerson Hough; illustrated by J. Henry.
New York; London: D. Appleton and Company,
1918. 312, [1] p., front., [3] leaves of plates.
LC: Je 3, '18.
PW: Je 1, '18.
References: BAL 9349.

H-893   Hough, Lynn Harold, b. 1877. The inevitable book /
by Lynn Harold Hough. New York; Cincinnati: The
Abingdon Press, [c1922]. 160 p.   **OSU, OKG**
Contents: A captain of industry -- "Silent, night, holy night"-- Doing
his bit at home -- "Like men" -- Tom Tilton in an empty church --
Behind the counter -- The great gloom and the shining light -- The
breaking and the making of a home -- Behind the plow -- "He went
back on his pal" -- Mark Snyder inherits the earth --The hatred of
Billy McKee -- The battle of Sentaro -- The fire in the heart of the
bishop.
LC: S 12, '22.

H-894   ____ The little old lady / by Lynn Harold Hough.
New York; Cincinnati: The Abingdon Press,

[c1917]. 133 p.   **OSU, TOL**
LC: Ag 24, '17.

H-895   Houghton, Beatrice York. The Shelleys of Georgia /
by Beatrice York Houghton; illustrated by J. Henry.
Boston: Lothrop, Lee & Shepard Co., [1917].
406 p., front., [3] leaves of plates.
PW: S 1, '17.

Houghton, G. Norhtbound by night. In **Seattle
Writers' Club.** *Tillicum tales* **(1907), S-248.**

H-896   Houghton, Jeanette. Fourthly; also The revenge of
Great Oak / by Jeanette Houghton . . . New York:
Broadway Publishing Company, 1904. 89 p.
NYP (micro)

H-897   Houghton, Lucile C. (Lucile Caplinger), b. 1881. A
venture in identity / by Lucile C. Houghton. Garden
City, N. Y.: Doubleday, Page & Company, 1911.
179, [1] p., front.
PW: N 11, '11.

H-898   Houk, Eliza, 1833-1914. Louisa Varena / Eliza
Houk. [Dayton, O.: Printed and bound by U. B.
Publishing House, c1905]. 322 p.
PW: Ag 12, '05.

H-899   Houk, L. C. Violett. The girl in question: a story of
not so long ago / by L. C. Violett Houk. New York:
John Lane Company, 1908. 261 p.

H-900   Houmas, Mount, *pseud.* A strange record / by Mount
Houmas [pseud.] . . . New York; Washington: The
Neale Publishing Company, 1908. 294 p.
LC: Je 3, '08.
PW: Je 27, '08.

H-901   House, Edward Mandell, 1858-1938. Philip Dru:
administrator: a story of tomorrow, 1920-1935. New
York: B. W. Huebsch, 1912. 312 p.

House, Grace Bigelow. Little foe of all the world. In
When God walks the road and other stories **(1924),
W-445.**

H-902   The house of deceit. New York: Henry Holt and
Company, 1914. 342 p.
PW: O 3, '14.

H-903   A house party: an account of stories told at a
gathering of famous American authors / the story
tellers being introduced by Paul Leicester Ford.
Boston: Small, Maynard & Company, 1901.
418 p.
The collection was presented in the form of a contest,
inviting readers to guess the authorship of each story.
Contents: Introduction -- A family tradition / [Paul Leicester Ford] --
Artemisia's mirror / [Bertha Runkle] -- Dawson's dilemma / [John
Kendrick Bangs] -- A surrender / [Robert Grant] -- Aunt Nancy's
annuity / [Frank R. Stockton]-- The messenger / [Octave Thanet] --
The green bowl / [Sarah Orne Jewett] -- The broken story / [Ruth
McEnery Stuart] -- Mother / [Owen Wister] -- The fairy godmother's
story / [Mrs. Burton Harrison] -- The angel of the Lord / [George
Washington Cable] -- The red oxen of Bonval / [Charles G. D.
Roberts].
PW: D 7, '01.
References: BAL 6229.

H-904 Houston, Allen Polk. Warfares of the heart: stories of the South / by Allen Polk Houston; illustrated. Chicago: The Branch Publishing Co., [c1917]. 128 p., ill. [Ill. by M. C. Loomis and C. O. Longabaugh.] **UIU**
Contents: My ole colored mammy -- Uncle Henry -- My southern mother -- A stormy courtship -- My little sister -- Did he rock the boat? -- Two brave men -- The world is truly small -- A thrice told tale -- I am in mourning to-day for an old friend -- Would you have lied? -- A southern belle.
LC: D 28, '17.

H-905 Houston, Margaret Belle. The little straw wife / by Margaret Belle Houston; illustrated by F. Graham Cootes. New York: The H. K. Fly Company, [c1914]. 217 p., front., [3] leaves of plates. **ICU**

H-906 _____ "The witch man" / by Margaret Belle Houston. Boston: Small, Maynard & Company, [c1922]. 255 p.
LC: Mr 3, '22.
PW: Mr 11, '22.
BLC: London: Hutchinson & Co., [1922].

H-907 Houston, Thomas W. (Thomas Watson), b. 1862. Mey Wing: a romance of Cathay / by Rev. Thomas W. Houston . . . Topeka, Kansas: Crane & Company, 1912. 191 p. **LLU**
LC: F 27, '12.
PW: Ap 6, '12.
Another printing: Lansing, Kansas: Thomas W. Houston, 1912. **OSU**

H-908 Hovey, Jean Edgerton. John o' Partletts': a tale of strife and courage / by Jean Edgerton Hovey; illustrated by Edmund H. Garrett. Boston: L. C. Page & Company, 1913. 313 p., col. front., [3] leaves of plates.
LC: O 8, '13.
PW: N 1, '13.

H-909 Howard, Arthur Platt, b. 1869. The man who bucked up: a fact story / by Arthur Howard. Garden City, New York: Doubleday, Page & Company, 1912. 279, [1] p.
PW: S 28, '12.

H-910 Howard, Bronson, 1842-1908. Kate: a comedy in four acts / by Bronson Howard. New York; London: Harper & Brothers, 1906. 210, [1] p.
PW: O 20, '06.

Howard, Clifford, b. 1868. The levitation of Jacob. In *Through the forbidden gates* (1903), T-222.

H-911 _____ The Passover: (an interpretation) / by Clifford Howard . . . New York: R. F. Fenno & Company, [c1910]. 260 p.
LC: Ag 18, '10.
PW: Ag 13, '10.

H-912 _____ What happened at Olenberg / by Clifford Howard . . . ; illustrated by Emile A. Nelson. Chicago: The Reilly & Britton Co., [c1911]. 204 p., col. front., [5] leaves of col. plates, ill.

Howard, Hamilton G., ed. See Hodges, Henry Clay. *Two thousand years in Ceslestial Life* (1901), **H-721.**

H-913 Howard, John Hamilton. In the shadow of the pines: a tale of Tidewater Virginia / by John Hamilton Howard. New York: Eaton & Mains; Cincinnati: Jennings & Graham, [c1906]. 249 p., front., [7] leaves of plates (map, ports.).

H-914 Howard, M. W. (Milford Wriarson), 1862-1937. The bishop of the Ozarks / by Milford W. Howard. Los Angeles, California: Times-Mirror Press, 1923. 232 p., photo. front. (port.), [4] leaves of photo. plates. **TXH**
LC: D 26, '22.
PW: My 19, '23.

H-915 _____ Peggy Ware / by M. W. Howard. Los Angeles, Cal.: Published by J. F. Rowny Press, 1921. 350 p.
LC: Ag 25, '21.

H-916 Howard, Maude Lesseur. Myriam and the mystic brotherhood / by Maude Lesseur Howard. New York: John Wurtele Lovell, [c1912]. 370 p. **CRU**
"The subject matter contained in this book was suggested by a short story appearing in the Cosmopolitan of March, 1903, entitled: The breed of the West, by J. N. Marchand."
LC: Je 7, '12.

H-917 Howard, Sidney Coe, 1891-1939. Three flights up / by Sidney Howard. New York: Charles Scribner's Sons, 1924. 286 p.
Contents: A likeness of Elizabeth -- Transatlantic -- Mrs. Vietch: a segment of biography -- The God they left behind them.
LC: O 29, '24.

H-918 Howard, William Lee, 1860-1918. Lila Sari / William Lee Howard. Boston: Richard G. Badger, 1908. ([Boston]: The Gorham Press). 225 p.
LC: O 29, '08.
PW: D 5, '08.

H-919 _____ The perverts / by William Lee Howard . . . New York: G. W. Dillingham Company, [c1901]. 388 p.
PW: F 15, '02.
BLC: London: T. Fisher Unwin, 1902.

H-920 Howard-Smith, Elise, b. 1893. A knight of today / by Elise Howard-Smith. Philadelphia: The John C. Winston Company, 1919. 364 p.
LC: Ap 19, '19.

H-921 Howe, E. W. (Edgar Watson), 1853-1937. The anthology of another town / by E. W. Howe. New York: Alfred A. Knopf, 1920. 181 p.
Contents: Doctor Gilkerson -- Jim and Dan Ayres -- George Coulter -- Sammy Hemingway -- Davis Straight -- Sam Harris -- Bart Wherry -- Pilson Blair -- Ben Barton -- Lige Banta -- Mary Mason -- Uncle Jimmy Haskins -- Gus Sanderson -- Tom Harrison -- Judge Terry -- The Wittwer boys -- Aunt Mahala -- Marie Taylor -- Bill Hall -- John Davis -- Hon. Martin Holbrook -- Ans Whitcomb -- Mart Towne -- Sarah Brownell -- Tom Marsh -- Jim Searles -- Sandy McPherson -- Joe Bush -- Cleve Hunt -- Michael Rafferty -- Joe Wells -- Tom Harper -- Asberry Morton -- Ben Bradford -- Pete Robidoux -- Bill Harmon -- Doc Robinson -- Jim Shields -- Ben Thompson -- Jerry Shackelford -- Cap. Hansen -- Henry Wulfburger -- George Pendleton -- Colonel Andy Miller -- Bud Moffett -- Milt Sayer -- Walt Williams -- Belle Davison -- Andrew Hackbarth -- Joe Stevens -- Gladys Hart -- Mrs. Joe Buey -- John Davis -- Taylor Ward -- Mary Ransom -- Charley Grover -- Thomas Lane Montgomery -- Old George Bennett -- Glen Barker -- Harvey King -- Vic Walker -- George Coleman --

Joe Ward -- Emanuel Strong -- Ed. Marsh -- Mrs. Mark Thompson -- W. T. Hawley -- Lawyer Bailey -- George Lawrence -- Mrs. John Hart -- George Hart -- Old Mr. Neal -- Bill Alvord -- Martha Wendell -- Chris Halleck -- Joe Allen.
PW: O 23, '20.

H-922   Howe, Frederic Clemson, 1867-1940. The confessions of a monopolist / by Frederic C. Howe . . . Chicago: The Public Publishing Company, [c1906]. 157 p.
"Portions of this volume have previously appeared in the World's Work, New York, under the title *The confessions of a commercial senator.*"

Howe, John Dicks, b. 1857, jt. aut. *Down on the old plantation* (1908). See **Scogin, Samuel Martha Caldwell, b. 1873, jt. aut., S-174.**

H-923   Howe, Maud, 1854-1948. Two in Italy / by Maud Howe . . . ; with illustrations from drawings by John Elliott. Boston: Little, Brown and Company, 1905. 274 p., front., [5] leaves of plates.   **KSU**
Contents: Anacrap' -- The inn of paradise -- Buona fortuna -- The castello -- Savonarola Finnerty (what I heard of him) -- Savonarola Finnerty (what I knew of him) -- The hermit of Pietre Ansieri -- In old Poland.
BLC: London: Kegan Paul & Co.; Cambridge, U. S. A. [printed], 1906.

Howe, Susan Jewett, jt. aut. *Nell Beverly, farmer* (1908). See **Brown, Elizabeth Jewett, b. 1868, jt. aut., B-1071.**

H-924   Howell, Whitfield G. Inheritance / by Whitfield G. Howell . . . Boston: The Roxburgh Publishing Company, Inc., [c1919]. 190 p.
PW: Ja 24, '20.

Howells, William Dean, 1837-1920. The amigo. In *The heart of childhood* (1906), **H-441.**

H-925   ____ Between the dark and the daylight: romances / by W. D. Howells. New York; London: Harper & Brothers, 1907. 184, [1] p., front., [5] leaves of plates.
Contents: A sleep and a forgetting -- The eidolons of Brooks Alford -- A memory that worked overtime -- A case of metaphantasmia -- Editha -- Braybridge's offer -- The chick of the Easter egg.
LC: O 24, '07.
PW: N 9, '07.
References: BAL 9783; Gibson & Arms 07-D.

____ Braybridge's offer. In *Quaint courtships* (1906), **Q-3.**

H-926   ____ Buying a horse / by William Dean Howells. Boston; New York: Houghton Mifflin Company, 1916. (Cambridge: The Riverside Press). 43, [1] p.
First separate book appearance.
LC: S 21, '16.
PW: S 23, '16.
References: BAL 9839; Gibson and Arms 16-D.

H-927   ____ The daughter of the storage: and other things in prose and verse / W. D. Howells. New York; London: Harper & Brothers, [1916]. 351, [1] p.
    OSU, CWR
Contents: The daughter of the storage -- A presentiment -- Captain

Dunlevy's last trip -- The return to favor -- Somebody's mother -- The face at the window -- An experience -- The boarders -- Breakfast is my best meal -- The mother-bird -- The amigo -- Black Cross farm -- The critical book store -- A feast of reason -- City and country in the fall -- Table talk -- The escapade of a grandfather -- Self-sacrifice: a farce-tragedy -- The night before Christmas.
LC: Ap 27, '16.
PW: Ap 29, '16.
References: BAL 9837; Gibson & Arms 16-C.
Another ed: The daughter of the storage, [1918]. 41, [1] p.
Unexamined copy: bibliographic data from OCLC, #5055048.

Gibson & Arms: "First separate edition. Reprinted from the plates of *The daughter of the storage: and other things in prose and verse* (q. v.).
References: BAL 9855; Gibson & Arms 18-D.

____, jt. ed. See *Different girls* (1906), **D-383.**

____ Editha. In *Different girls* (1906), **D-383.**

H-928   ____ Fennel and Rue: a novel / by W. D. Howells; illustrated by Charlotte Harding. New York; London: Harper & Brothers, 1908. 129, [1] p., front., [3] leaves of plates.
LC: Mr 13, '08.
PW: Mr 21, '08.
References: BAL 9787; Gibson & Arms 08-A.

____, ed. See *The Great modern American stories* (1920), **G-422.**

____, jt. ed. See *The heart of childhood* (1906), **H-441.**

H-929   ____ The Kentons: a novel / by W. D. Howells . . . New York; London: Harper & Brothers, 1902. 317 p.
LC: Ap 18, '02.
PW: Ap 26, '02.
References: BAL 9747; Gibson and Arms 02-A.

H-930   ____ The Leatherwood god / by William Dean Howells; with illustrations by Henry Raleigh. New York: The Century Co., 1916. 236 p., front., ill.
LC: N 2, '16.
PW: N 4, '16.
BLC: London: Herbert Jenkins, 1917, [1916].
References:References: BAL 9840; Gibson & Arms 16-E.

H-931   ____ Letters home / by W. D. Howells . . . New York; London: Harper & Brothers, 1903. 299 p.
LC: S 18, '03.
PW: O 3, '03.
References: BAL 9753; Gibson & Arms 03-C.

____, jt. ed. See *Life at high tide* (1907), **L-281.**

H-932   ____ Miss Bellard's inspiration: a novel / by W. D. Howells . . . New York; London: Harper & Brothers Publishers, 1905. 223, [1] p.
LC: Je 8, '05.
PW: Je 17, '05.
References: BAL 9760; Gibson & Arms 05-A.

H-933 ____ Mrs. Farrell: a novel / by William Dean Howells; with an introduction by Mildred Howells. New York; London: Harper & Brothers, [c1921]. 265, [1] p.
"This story . . . was first printed under the title of *Private theatricals* in the Atlantic monthly of 1875."
LC: S 3, '21.
PW: S 3, '21.
References: BAL 9864; Gibson & Arms 21-B.

H-934 ____ New leaf mills: a chronicle / W. D. Howells. New York; London: Harper & Brothers, 1913. 153, [1] p.
LC: F 21, '13.
PW: Mr 1, '13.
References: BAL 9825; Gibson & Arms 13-A.

H-935 ____ A pair of patient lovers / by W. D. Howells . . . New York; London: Harper & Brothers, 1901. 368 p., col. photo. front. (port.).
(Harper's portrait collection of short stories, v. 1.)
Contents: A pair of patient lovers -- The pursuit of the piano -- A difficult case -- The magic of a voice -- A circle in the water.
LC: My 23, '01.
PW: Je 1, '01.
References: BAL 9739; Gibson & Arms 01-B.

____, jt. ed. See *Quaint courtships* (1906), Q-3.

H-936 ____ Questionable shapes / by W. D. Howells . . . ; illustrated. New York; London: Harper & Brothers, 1903. 219 p., front., [3] leaves of plates.
Contents: His apparition -- The angel of the Lord -- Though one rose from the dead.
LC: My 19, '03.
PW: Je 6, '03.
References: BAL 9752; Gibson & Arms 03-B.

H-937 ____ The seen and unseen at Stratford-on-Avon: a fantasy / by W. D. Howells. New York; London: Harper & Brothers, 1914. 111, [1] p.
LC: My 11, '14.
PW: My 16, '14.
References: BAL 9829; Gibson & Arms 14-A.

____, jt. ed. See *Shapes that haunt the dusk* (1907), S-339.

H-938 ____ The son of Royal Langbrith: a novel / by W. D. Howells . . . New York; London: Harper & Brothers, 1904. 368, [1] p.
LC: O 6, '04.
PW: O 15, '04.
References: BAL 9758; Gibson & Arms 04-B.

____, jt. ed. See *Southern lights and shadows* (1907), S-718.

____, jt. ed. See *Their husbands wives* (1906), T-161.

H-939 ____ Through the eye of the needle: a romance / with an introduction, by W. D. Howells. New York; London: Harper & Brothers, 1907. 232, [1] p.
LC: Ap 18, '07.
PW: Ap 27, '07.
References: BAL 9779; Gibson & Arms 07-B.

____, jt. ed. See *Under the sunset* (1906), U-9.

H-940 ____ The vacation of the Kelwyns: an idyl of the middle eighteen-seventies / by William Dean Howells. New York; London: Harper & Brothers, [c1920]. 256, [1] p., photo. front. (port.).
LC: S 25, '20.
PW: O 9, '20.
References: BAL 9862; Gibson & Arms 20-D.

____, contributor. See *The whole family* (1908), W-578.

H-941 Howland, Legrand. Jacques of Bruges / by Legrand Howland. Wilmington, Del.: Published by Geo. A. Wolf, 1904. 59 p., ill. [Ill. by George A. Wolf.]

H-942 Hoy, Ella Compton. The church moths / by Ella Compton Hoy. Baltimore, Md.: Saulsbury Publishing Company, [c1919]. 54 p.   DLC
LC: Je 10, '19.

H-943 Hoy, Frank L., Mrs. Adrienne / by Mrs. Frank L. Hoy. New York; Washington: The Neale Publishing Company, 1906. 239 p.   DLC
LC: D 11, '06.
PW: F 2, '07.

Hoyt, Eleanor. See Brainerd, Eleanor Hoyt.

H-944 Hoyt, Francis Deming, 1843-1922. Catherine Sidney / by Francis Deming Hoyt. New York; London; Bombay; Calcutta: Longmans, Green, and Co., 1912. 347 p.
LC: S 28, '12.

H-945 ____ The coming storm / by Francis Deming Hoyt. New York: P. J. Kenedy & Sons, 1913. 283 p.
LC: Ja 15, '14.

H-946 ____ The Modernist / by Francis Deming Hoyt . . . Lakewood, N. J.: The Lakewood Press, 1915. 263 p., front., [5] leaves of plates. [Ill. by H. T. Fisk.]   NYP
LC: S 3, '15.

H-947 Hoyt, Laurel M. Onesimus the slave: a romance of the days of Nero / by Laurel M. Hoyt. Boston: Sherman, French & Company, 1915. 324 p.
          OSU, OSO
LC: D 7, '15.

H-948 Hoyt, T. C. Rimrock: a story of the West / by T. C. Hoyt. Boston: The Four Seas Company, [c1923]. 319 p., photo. front.
LC: Ja 14, '24.
PW: Je 7, '24.

H-949 Huard, Frances Wilson, b. 1885. Lilies, white and red / by Frances Wilson Huard. New York: George H. Doran Company, [c1919]. 268 p. Illustrated end papers.
Contents: Mademoiselle Prune -- The cockerel.
PW: My 3, '19.

H-950 Hubbard, Ethel Daniels. Ann of Ava / by Ethel Daniels Hubbard; illustrated by Jessie Gillespie.

Philadelphia; Boston; Chicago; St. Louis: Published for American Baptist Foreign Mission Society by American Baptist Publication Society, [c1913]. 245 p., front., [11] leaves of plates. (ports.).

Hubbard, George, jt. aut. *Without compromise* (1922). See **Bennet-Thompson, Lilian, b. 1883, jt. aut., B-515.**

H-951   Hubbard, Lindley Murray. An express of '76: a chronicle of the town of York in the War for Independence / by Lindley Murray Hubbard; illustrated by I. B. Beales. Boston: Little, Brown, and Company, 1906. 340 p., front., [4] leaves of plates.
LC; O 8, '06.
PW: O 27, '06.

H-952   Hubbard, Philip E. (Philip Egerton). Beside the tidewater: a collection of flotsam / by Philip E. Hubbard. Boston, Massachusetts: The Cornhill Publishing Company, 1922. 256 p.   **DLC**
Contents: Beside the tidewater -- Collector of the port -- On his majesty's service -- A bereavement -- Mrs. Blenker's windfall -- The breaking of the storm -- The war baby -- The "private" view -- When on active service -- A tour of the trenches -- Honours and distinctions -- Daylight saving -- The kiss of the bullet -- None but the brave -- Befo' de wo'.
PW: F 10, '23.

H-953   Hudgins, Charles Buckner. The convert / by Charles Buckner Hudgins. New York; Washington: The Neale Publishing Company, 1908. 333 p.   **NDD**
LC: Ja 25, '08.
PW: F 15, '08.

H-954   Hudson, Alan. A heritage of honor / Alan Hudson; illustrated by Roy Ives Conklin. Boston: Richard G. Badger, [c1912]. ([Boston, Mass.]: The Gorham Press). 395 p., [5] leaves of plates.
PW: Ap 12, '13.

H-955   Hudson, Charles B. The royal outlaw: a novel / by Charles B. Hudson. New York: E. P. Dutton & Co., [c1917]. 364 p.
LC: My 25, '17.
PW: Je 9, '17.

H-956   Hudson, Charles Bradford. The crimson conquest: a romance of Pizarro and Peru / by Charles Bradford Hudson; with frontispiece in full color by J. C. Leyendecker. Chicago: A. C. McClurg & Co., 1907. 454 p., col. front.
LC: O 9, '07.
PW: O 5, '07.
BLC: London: Grant Richards, 1908.

H-957   Hudson, Henry, 2d. Spendthrift town: a novel / by Henry Hudson, 2d. Boston; New York: Houghton Mifflin Company, 1920. (Cambridge: The Riverside Press). 402 p.
LC: N 12, '20.
PW: F 12, '21.

H-958   Hudson, Jay William, 1874-1958. Abbé Pierre / by Jay William Hudson. New York; London: D. Appleton and Company, 1922. 331 p. Illustrated end papers.

LC: Ap 25, '22.
PW: Ap 29, '22.

H-959   _____ The eternal circle / by Jay William Hudson. New York; London: D. Appleton and Company, 1925. 309, [1] p.
LC: O 26, '25.
PW: N 7, '25.

H-960   _____ Nowhere else in the world / by Jay William Hudson . . . New York; London: D. Appleton and Company, 1923. 383 p.
LC: O 17, '23.
PW: N 10, '23.

H-961   Hudson, Lillian (Row) b. 1860. Governor Thurmond's bird-house / by Lillian Hudson. San Francisco: John J. Newbegin, 1915. 32 p.

H-962   Hudson, William C. (William Cadwalader), 1843-1915. J. P. Dunbar: a story of Wall Street / by William Cadwalader Hudson. New York: B. W. Dodge and Company, 1906. 441 p.
LC: O 19, '06.

H-963   Huebner, Francis C. (Francis Christian), b. 1869. Charles Killbuck: an Indian's story of the border wars of the American revolution / by Francis C. Huebner; illustrated by W. F. Gilmore. Washington, D. C.: The Herbert Publishing Company, 1902. 315 p., photo. front. (port.), [4] leaves of plates.

H-964   Hueston, Ethel Powelson, b. 1887. Betty Gale on the mesa / by Ethel Hueston. Elgin, Ill.: David C. Cook Publishing Co., [c1919]. 48 p.

H-965   _____ Eve to the rescue / by Ethel Hueston . . . ; illustrated by Dudley Gloyme [sic] Summers. Indianapolis: The Bobbs-Merrill Company, 1920. 340 p., front., [3] leaves of plates.
LC: O 30, '20.
PW: D 4, '20.

H-966   _____ Leave it to Doris / by Ethel Hueston . . . ; illustrated by W. B. King. Indianapolis: The Bobbs-Merrill Company, [c1919]. 290, [1] p., front., [3] leaves of plates.
LC: S 27, '19.
PW: N 1, '19.
BLC: London: Methuen & Co., 1920.

_____ Masterpieces. In *Prairie gold* (1917), **P-588.**

H-967   _____ Merry O / by Ethel Hueston; illustrated by Edward C. Caswell. Indianapolis: The Bobbs-Merrill Company, [c1923]. 311, [1] p., front., [3] leaves of plates.
LC: Ap 4, '23.
PW: Ap 7, '23.
BLC: London: Hodder & Stoughton, [1923].

H-968   _____ Prudence of the parsonage / by Ethel Hueston; with illustrations by Arthur William Brown. Indianapolis: The Bobbs-Merrill Company, [c1915]. 347 p., col. front., [3] leaves of col. plates.
LC: Ag 23, '15.
PW: Ag 21, 15.
BLC: London: Eveleigh Nash Co., 1916.

H-969   ____ Prudence says so / by Ethel Hueston; with illustrations by Arthur William Brown. Indianapolis: The Bobbs-Merrill Company, [c1916]. 309 p., front., [3] leaves of plates.
LC: Ag 28, '16.
PW: S 2, '16.
BLC: London: Hodder & Stoughton, 1917.

H-970   ____ Prudence's daughter / by Ethel Hueston; illustrated by E. C. Caswell. Indianapolis: The Bobbs-Merrill Company, [c1924]. 309, [1] p., front., [3] leaves of plates.
LC: Ap 30, '24.
PW: My 3, '24.
BLC: London: Hutchinson & Co., [1926].

H-971   ____ Sunny slopes / by Ethel Hueston . . . ; illustrated by Arthur William Brown. Indianapolis: The Bobbs-Merrill Company, [c1917]. 356 p., front., [3] leaves of plates.
LC: Ag 22, '17.
PW: Ag 25, '17.
BLC: London: Skeffington & Son, [1918].

H-972   ____ Swedey / by Ethel Hueston. Indianapolis: The Bobbs-Merrill Company, [c1925]. 300 p.
LC: O 9, '25.
PW: O 3, '25.
BLC: London: Hutchinson & Co., [1926].

Huffaker, Lucy. The way of life. In *Atlantic narratives*; **2nd series (1918), A-361.**

Hughes, Babette. The Samarkand sapphire. In *The best college short stories, 1924-1925* **(1925), B-558.**

H-973 Hughes, Bruce. "The coveted inheritance" / by Bruce Hughes . . . Harrisburg, Pa.: Central Printing and Publishing House, 1907. 76 p.   **DLC** (micro)
LC: O 20, '07.

H-974 [____] Self-renunciation / by the author of "Nuggets of gold." [Philipsburg, Pa.: [s. n.], c1902]. 60 p.
                       DLC
PW: Ja 31, '03.

H-975 Hughes, Guy. A struggle of blood, or, Down and up / by Guy Hughes. New York; London; Montreal: The Abbey Press, [c1902]. 296 p.
PW: D 6, '02.

H-976 Hughes, Henry, b. 1876. The man without a church: the story of James Millbrook / by Henry Hughes. Boston: Sherman, French & Company, 1915. 329 p.

H-977 Hughes, Rupert, 1872-1956. The amiable crimes of Dirk Memling / by Rupert Hughes . . . ; illustrated. New York; London: D. Appleton and Company, 1913. 339 p., front., [3] leaves of plates. [Ill. by Charles L. Wrenn.]
LC: Ap 1, '13.
PW: Ap 12, 13.

H-978   ____ Beauty / by Rupert Hughes . . . ; with illustrations by W. T. Benda. New York; London: Harper & Brothers, [c1921]. 410 p., front., [3] leaves of plates.

LC: Je 3, '21.
PW: Je 4, '21.
BLC: London: E. Nash & Grayson, [1921].

H-979   ____ Clipped wings: a novel / by Rupert Hughes. New York; London: Harper & Brothers, [1916]. 403, [1] p., col. front.   Published serially as "The barge of dreams."
PW: Ja 15, '16.

H-980   ____ Colonel Crockett's co-operative Christmas / by Rupert Hughes. Philadelphia; London: George W. Jacobs and Company, [1906]. 66 p., col. front., [5] leaves of col. plates, ill. [Ill. by J. J. Gould.] Designed end papers.
LC: O 15, '06.

H-981   ____ The cup of fury: a novel of cities and shipyards / by Rupert Hughes . . . ; illustrated by Henry Raleigh. New York; London: Harper & Brothers, [1919]. 350 p., mounted front., mounted ills.
LC: My 19, '19.
PW: My 24, '19.

H-982   ____ Destiny / by Rupert Hughes . . . New York; London: Harper & Brothers, [c1925]. 385 p.
LC: My 18, '25.
PW: My 23, '25.
BLC: London: Hurst & Blackett, [1925].

H-983   ____ Empty pockets: a novel / by Rupert Hughes . . . ; with illustrations by James Montgomery Flagg. New York; London: Harper & Brothers, 1915. 606, [1] p., incl. front., ill.
LC: My 22, '15.
PW: Je 5, '15.

H-984   ____ Excvse me! / by Rvpert Hvghes. New York: The H. K. Fly Company, [c1911]. 313 p., col. front., [4] leaves of col. plates. [Ill. by James Montgomery Flagg.]
LC: S 18, '11.
PW: N 11, '11.
BLC: London: Frank Palmer, 1912.

H-985   ____ The gift-wife / by Rupert Hughes; illustrated. New York: Moffat, Yard and Company, 1910. 416 p., incl. front., [11] leaves of plates, ill. [Ill. by Sigurd Schou.]
LC: O 17, '10.
PW: O 22, '10.

H-986   ____ The golden ladder / by Rupert Hughes. New York; London: Harper & Brothers, [c1924]. 354 p.
LC: Je 5, '24.
PW: My 31, '24.
BLC: London: Hurst & Blackett, [1924].

     ____ Grudges. In *The best short stories of 1924 and the yearbook of the American short story* **(1925), B-569.**

     ____ The happiest man in I-O-Way. In *Prairie gold* **(1917), P-588.**

H-987   ____ In a little town / by Rupert Hughes. New

York; London: Harper & Brothers, [1917]. 382,
[1] p., front. [Ill. by James Montgomery Flagg.]
Contents: Don't you care! -- Pop -- Baby talk -- The mouth of the
gift horse -- The old folks at home -- And this is marriage -- The man
that might have been -- The happiest man in Ioway -- Prayers -- Pain
-- The beauty and the fool -- The ghostly counselors -- Daughters of
Shiloh -- "A" as in "father".
LC: Mr 17, '17.
PW: Mr 17, '17.

H-988   _____ The lady who smoked cigars / by Rupert
Hughes. New York: Desmond FitzGerald, Inc.,
[c1913]. 48 p., front., [3] leaves of plates.
"Illustrations by J. C. Chase."
LC: F 10, '13.
PW: F 22, '13.

H-989   _____ The last rose of summer / by Rupert Hughes.
New York; London: Harper & Brothers, 1914. 83,
[1] p., col. front.
LC: O 29, '14.
PW: N 7, '14.

H-990   _____ Long ever ago / by Rupert Hughes . . . ;
illustrated. New York; London: Harper & Brothers,
[1918]. 301, [1] p., front.
Contents: The Murphy that made America --
Michaleen! Michaelawn! -- Sent for out -- Except he
were a bird -- Long ever ago -- At the back of
Godspeed -- Canavan, the man who had his way --
The after-honor -- The bitterness of sweets --
Immortal youth.
LC: Mr 15, '18.
PW: Mr 23, '18.

H-991   _____ Miss 318: a story in season and out of season /
by Rupert Hughes. New York; Chicago; Toronto;
London; Edinburgh: Fleming H. Revell Company,
[c1911]. 128 p., incl. col. front., [8] leaves of plates.
[Ill. by V. S. Pérard.]
LC: O 3, '11.
PW: S 9, '11.

H-992   _____ Miss 318 and Mr. 37 / by Rupert Hughes . . .
New York; Chicago; Toronto; London; Edinburgh:
Fleming H. Revell Company, [c1912]. 128 p.,
front., [5] leaves of plates. [Ill. by Arthur William
Brown.]
LC: N 18, '12.
PW: S 14, '12.

H-993   _____ "Momma" and other unimportant people / by
Rupert Hughes . . . New York; London: Harper &
Brothers, 1920. 382, [1] p.
Contents: "Momma" -- The stick-in-the-muds -- Read it again -- The
father of waters -- Innocence -- The college Lorelei -- Yellow cords --
The split -- A story I can't write -- The butcher's daughter -- The
quick-silver window -- The dauntless bookkeeper -- You hadn't ought
to go.
LC: N 15, '20.
PW: N 27, '20.

H-994   _____ Mrs. Budlong's Christmas presents / by Rupert
Hughes. New York; London: D. Appleton and
Company, 1912. 120, [1] p.
LC: O 29, '12.
PW: N 9, '12.

H-995   _____ The old nest / by Rupert Hughes. New York:
The Century Co., 1912. 178 p., front.
LC: Mr 25, '12.

PW: Mr 23, '12.

_____ Peachblow. In *Marriage* (1923), M-457.

H-996   _____ The real New York / by Rupert Hughes;
drawings by Hy. Mayer. New York; London: The
Smart Set Publishing Company, 1904. 384 p., col.
front., [22] leaves of plates.
PW: Jl 2, '04.
BLC: London: Hutchinson & Co., 1905.

H-997   _____ Souls for sale / by Rupert Hughes . . . New
York; London: Harper & Brothers, [c1922]. 405 p.
LC: My 24, '22.
PW: Ap 22, '22.
BLC: London: Eveleigh Nash & Grayson, [1922].

H-998   _____ The thirteenth commandment: a novel / by
Rupert Hughes . . . ; with illustrations by James
Montgomery Flagg. New York; London: Harper &
Brothers, [1916]. 559, [1] p., front., ill.
LC: Jl 22, '16.
PW: Jl 29, '16.
BLC: London: Eveleigh Nash & Co., 1916.

H-999   _____ The unpardonable sin: a novel / by Rupert
Hughes . . . ; illustrated by James Montgomery
Flagg. New York; London: Harper & Brothers,
[1918]. 326, [1] p., front., [7] leaves of plates.
LC: Je 15, '18.
PW: Je 22, '18.

H-1000   _____ We can't have everything: a novel / by Rupert
Hughes; illustrated by James Montgomery Flagg.
New York; London: Harper & Brothers, [c1917].
636, [1] p., front.
LC: Ag 27, '17.
PW: S 1, '17.

H-1001   _____ What will people say?: a novel: illustrated /
by Rupert Hughes. New York; London: Harper &
Brothers, 1914. 510, [1] p., front., [3] leaves of
plates. [Ill. by H. Weston Taylor.]   **OSU, NOC**
LC: Ap 22, '14.
PW: My 2, '14.

H-1002   _____ What's the world coming to? / Rupert Hughes
. . . ; illustrated by Frank Snapp. New York;
London: Harper & Brothers, [1920]. 388, [1] p.,
front., [7] leaves of plates.
LC: My 22, '20.
PW: My 29, '20.

H-1003   _____ The whirlwind / by Rupert Hughes. Boston:
Lothrop Publishing Company, [1902]. 494 p.
PW: O 18, '02.
BLC: London: Charles H. Kelly, [printed in
America, 1902].

H-1004   _____ Within these walls / by Rupert Hughes . . .
New York; London: Harper & Brothers, 1923.
363 p., front., [3] leaves of plates. [Ill. by A. I.
Keller.]
LC: Je 2, '23.
PW: Je 19, 23.
BLC: London: E. Nash & Grayson, 1923.

H-1005 ___ Zal: an international romance / by Rupert Hughes. New York: The Century Co., 1905. 346 p.
PW: N 18, '05.

H-1006 Hulbert, Archer Butler, 1873-1933. The queen of Quelparte / by Archer Butler Hulbert; illustrated by Winfield S. Lukens. Boston: Little, Brown and Company, 1902. 329, [1] p., front., [5] leaves of plates.
PW: S 20, '02.

Hull, Alexander. The argosies. In *Prize stories of 1920* (1921), P-618.

___ Justice in the painted hills. In *"Dawgs!"* (1925), D-184.

H-1007 Hull, Caroline. The way: a story of today / by Caroline Hull. New York: Crown Publishing Co., [c1911]. 269 p.
LC: N 25, '11.

Hull, Helen R. (Helen Rose), 1888-1971. His sacred family. In *Prize stories of 1922* (1923), P-620.

H-1008 ___ Labyrinth / by Helen R. Hull. New York: The Macmillan Company, 1923. 343 p.
LC: O 10, '23.
PW: O 13, '23.

H-1009 ___ Quest / by Helen R. Hull. New York: The Macmillan Company, 1922. 353 p.
LC: O 25, '22.
PW: N 25, '22.

H-1010 ___ The Surry family / by Helen R. Hull. New York: The Macmillan Company, 1925. 333 p.
LC: N 11, '25.
PW: N 21, '25.

H-1011 Hull, William Harold. The reprisal / by William Harold Hull. Philadelphia: Dorrance and Company, [c1924]. 204 p.
Unexamined copy: bibliographic data from OCLC, #20699593.

H-1012 Hulsbuck, Solly, b. 1871, *pseud.* Penn'a-German stories / by Solly Hulsbuck [pseud.] . . . Elizabethville, Pa.: Published by the Hawthorne Press, [c1907]. 112 p., ill. **BAI**

H-1013 Hume, Cyril, 1900-1966. Cruel fellowship / by Cyril Hume. New York: George H. Doran Company, [c1925]. 306 p.
LC: Je 1, '25.
PW: My 30, '25.
BLC: London: Jonathan Cape; printed in U. S. A., [1926].

H-1014 ___ Wife of the centaur / by Cyril Hume. New York: George H. Doran Company, [c1923]. 372 p. Illustrated end papers.
LC: N 1, '23.
PW: N 24, '23.
BLC: London: Jonathan Cape, 1924.

Hume, Jean B. See **Viclare, Julien, pseud.**

H-1015 Hummel, George F. (George Frederick), 1882-1952. After all / by George F. Hummel. New York: Boni and Liveright, [c1923]. 350 p. **AUM**
LC: Je 12, '23.
PW: Je 16, '23.
BLC: London: Chapman & Hall, 1924.

H-1016 ___ A good man / by George F. Hummel. New York: Boni & Liveright, 1925. 317 p.
LC: Je 22, '25.
PW: Je 20, '25.
BLC: London: Geoffrey Bles; printed in U. S. A., 1926.

H-1017 ___ Subsoil: from the chronicle of a village / by George F. Hummel. New York: Boni and Liveright, [c1924]. 318, [1] p. Illustrated end papers.
LC: S 19, '24.
PW: Ag 30, '24.

H-1018 Humorous ghost stories / selected, with an introduction by Dorothy Scarborough . . . New York; London: G. P. Putnam's Sons, 1921. ([New York]: The Knickerbocker Press). 431 p.
Contents: Introduction: The humorous ghost -- The Canterville ghost / Oscar Wilde -- The ghost-extinguisher / Gelett Burgess -- "Dey ain't no ghosts" / Ellis Parker Butler -- The transferred ghost / Frank R. Stockton -- The mummy's foot / Théophile Gautier -- The rival ghosts / Brander Matthews -- The water ghost of Harrowby Hall / John Kendrick Bangs -- Back from that bourne / Anonymous -- The ghost-ship / Richard Middleton -- The transplanted ghost / Wallace Irwin -- The last ghost in harmony / Nelson Lloyd -- The ghost of Miser Brimpson / Eden Phillpotts -- The haunted photograph / Ruth McEnery Stuart -- The ghost that got the button / Will Adams -- The specter bridegroom / Washington Irving -- The specter of Tappington / compiled by Richard Barham -- In the barn / Burgess Johnson -- A shady plot / Elsie Brown -- The lady and the ghost / Rose Cecil O'Neill.
LC: My 24, '21.
PW: My 21, '21.

Humphrey, George, b. 1889. The father's hand. In *The best short stories of 1918 and the yearbook of the American short story* (1919), B-563.

Humphrey, Muriel Miller, ed. See *The best love stories of 1924* (1925), B-559.

H-1019 Humphrey, Zephine, 1874-1956. Grail fire / by Zephine Humphrey. New York: E. P. Dutton & Co., [c1917]. 285 p.
LC: Mr 15, '17.
PW: Mr 24, '17.

H-1020 ___ The homestead / by Zephine Humphrey. New York: E. P. Dutton & Company, [c1919]. 277 p.
LC: Jl 3, '19.
PW: Jl 12, '19.

___ Nothing. In *Atlantic narratives*; first series (1918), A-360.

H-1021 ___ Over against Green Peak / by Zephine Humphrey. New York: Henry Holt and Company, 1908. 276 p.
LC: Ap 10, '08.
PW: Ap 18, '08.

H-1022   The sword of the spirit / by Zephine Humphrey . . . New York: E. P. Dutton & Company, [c1920]. 300 p.
LC: My 20, '20.
PW: Jl 10, '20.

H-1023   Uncle Charley / by Zephine Humphrey. Boston; New York: Houghton Mifflin Company, (Cambridge: The Riverside Press), 1902. 226 p.
PW: O 4, '02.

H-1024 Humphreys, Dean, b. 1863, *pseud*. The black hand: a novelette / by Dean Humphreys [pseud.]. Albany, N. Y.: C. F. Williams and Son, 1911. 157 p. Unexamined copy: bibliographic data from NUC.
LC: Ja 4, '12.
PW: F 7, '12.

H-1025   Martha Mynheer: a novelette / by Dean Humphreys [pseud.]. Albany, N. Y.: C. F. Williams & Son, 1911. 179 p.
LC: D 26, '11.

H-1026 Humphreys, Ida F. Janse Douw's descendants / by Ida F. Humphreys. Philadelphia: Dorrance, [c1923]. 173 p.

H-1027 Huneker, James, 1857-1921. Melomaniacs / by James Huneker. New York: Charles Scribner's Sons, 1902. 350 p.
LC: F 21, '02.
PW: Mr 1, '02.
BLC: London: T. Werner Laurie, [1906].
References: BAL 9888.

H-1028   Painted veils / by James Huneker . . . New York: Boni and Liveright, [c1920]. 294, [4] p.
LC: Je 16, '21.
PW: Ja 8, '21.
References: BAL 9921.

H-1029   Visionaries / by James Huneker. New York: Charles Scribner's Sons, 1905. 342 p.
Contents: A master of cobwebs -- The eighth deadly sin -- The purse of Aholibah -- Rebels of the moon -- The spiral road -- A mock sun -- Antichrist -- The eternal duel -- The enchanted yodler -- The third kingdom -- The haunted harpsichord -- The tragic wall -- A sentimental rebellion -- Hall of the missing footsteps -- The cursory light -- An iron fan -- The woman who loved Chopin -- The tune of time -- Nada -- Pan.
LC: O 31, '05.
PW: O 28, '05.
BLC: London: T. Werner Laurie; New York printed, 1906.
References: BAL 9893.

H-1030 Hungerford, Edward, 1875-1948. The copy shop / by Edward Hungerford. New York; London: G. P. Putnam's Sons, 1925. (New York: The Knickerbocker Press). 342 p.
LC: Mr 6, '25.
PW: Mr 14, '25.

H-1031   Gertrude: a novel / by Edward Hungerford . . . ; frontispiece by George Brehm. New York: McBride, Nast & Company, 1913. 385 p., col. front. Partly reprinted from the Saturday Evenings Post.
LC: Ap 25, '13.

H-1032   Little Corky: a novel / by Edward Hungerford . . . ; with illustrations by M. Leone Bracker. Chicago: A. C. McClurg & Co., 1912. 405, [1] p., front., [5] leaves of plates.
LC: Mr 13, '12.
PW: Jl 6, '12.

H-1033 Hunt, Edward Eyre, 1885-1953. Haj, the law and the prophets / by Edward Eyre Hunt . . . Riverside, Connecticut: Hillacre Bookhouse, 1916. 71 p.

H-1034   Tales from a famished land: including The white island--a story of the Dardanelles / by Edward Eyre Hunt. Garden City, N. Y.: Doubleday, Page & Company, 1918. 193 p. Reprinted in part from various periodicals.
Contents: Saint Dympna's miracle -- Love in a barge -- The odyssey of Mr. Solslog -- Figures of the dance -- The saviour of Mont César -- Ghosts -- The deserter -- The glory of Tinarloo -- A Flemish fancy -- The swallows of Diest -- Pensioners -- Doña Quixote -- In the street of the spy -- The White Island-a story of the Dardanelles.
LC: Mr 28, '18.
PW: Mr 30, '18.

H-1035 Hunt, Frazier, b. 1885. Sycamore Bend: population 1300 / by Frazier Hunt. New York: Harcourt, Brace and Company, [c1925]. 293 p.
LC: S 11, '25.
PW: S 5, '25.

H-1036 Hunt, George D. Sophia Sidwell: an heiress: also narrations of tragedy and romance in farm life / by Geo. D. Hunt . . . Salem, Ohio: Press of the Thos. J. Walton Printing Co., 1904. 58 p., ill.
                              DLC (micro)
LC: Ag 8, '04.

H-1037 Hunt, Gertrude Breslau. An easy wheel and other stories / by Gertrude Breslau Hunt. Norwood Park, Ill.: G. B. Hunt, [ca. 1910]. 48 p.
Contents: An easy wheel -- The juggernaut's prey -- Blind Tekla' story -- Nero, a tale of a dog -- An eviction.

H-1038 Hunt, Laura Shellabarger. Ultra: a story of pre-natal influence / by Laura Shellabarger Hunt . . . Los Angeles: Times-Mirror Press, 1923. 365 p., [3] leaves of plates.

Hunt, Mattie Mitchell, jt. ed. as M. M. H. <u>See</u> ***Gone West (1919), G-289.***

H-1039 [Hunter, Alexander Stuart], 1857-1926. Different. Boston: The Gorham Press; Toronto: The Copp Clark Co., Limited, [1917]. 284 p.   **DLC**

H-1040 Hunting, Gardner, 1872-1958. A hand in the game / by Gardner Hunting; with frontispiece by J. N. Marchand. New York: Henry Holt and Company, 1911. 323 p., col. front.
LC: N 3, '11.
PW: D 2, '11.

H-1041 Huntington, Faye, 1838-1923, *pseud*. The opportunity circle / by Faye Huntington [pseud.]. New York: American Tract Society, [c1901]. 80 p., front.

H-1042 Huntington, Flora Clarke. The handkerchief and the sword: and other stories / by Flora Clarke Huntington. New York: Authors & Publishers Corporation, 1921. 105 p.
Contents: The handkerchief and the sword -- The chatelaine of Holden Lodge -- Under the shadows of Shiloh -- Uncle Ephraim -- The little rebel of Northington Manor -- The triumph of Mahaly Ann.

H-1043 Huntington, Helen, *pseud.* An apprentice to truth / by Helen Huntington [pseud.]. New York; London: G. P. Putnam's Sons, 1910. ([New York]: The Knickerbocker Press). 405 p. **ASH**

H-1044 ____ Eastern red / by Helen Huntington [pseud.] . . . New York; London: G. P. Putnam's Sons, 1918. ([New York]: The Knickerbocker Press). 289 p. **DLC**
LC: Mr 9, '18.
PW: F 9, '18.

H-1045 ____ Marsh lights / by Helen Huntington [pseud.] . . . New York: Charles Scribner's Sons, 1913. 395 p. **KLG**

H-1046 ____ The moon lady / by Helen Huntington [pseud.] . . . New York: Charles Scribner's Sons, 1911. 301 p.
LC: N 6, '11.

H-1047 ____ The sovereign good / by Helen Huntington [pseud.]. New York; London: G. P. Putnam's Sons, 1908. ([New York]: The Knickerbocker Press). 386 p.
LC: S 12, '08.
PW: S 26, '08.

 Huntley, F. Under the flatiron. In **Seattle Writer's Club.** *Tillicum tales* **(1907), S-248.**

H-1048 Huntley, Florence Chance, d. 1912. The gay Gnani of Gingalee, or, Discords of devolution: a tragical entanglement of modern mysticism and modern science / by Florence Huntley . . . Chicago: Indo-American Book Co., 1908. 206 p., front. (Harmonic fiction series; v. 2).

H-1049 Huntly, Hope. The way of the gods in Japan / by Hope Huntly. Boston: Richard G. Badger, 1911. ([Boston]: The Gorham Press). 339 p., front., [10] leaves of plates. **MBB**
Half title page reads: Kami-no-michi. The way of the gods in Japan.
PW: Mr 18, '11.

 Hurd, Marian Kent, jt. aut. *Miss Billy* (1905). See **Stokely, Edith Keeley, jt. aut., S-966.**

H-1050 Hurd, William E. Neta / by William E. Hurd. Boston: The Christopher Publishing House, [c1925]. 155 p.
LC: D 30, '25.

 Hurewitz, Israel. Manasseh. In *Yiddish tales* (1912), **Y-20.**

 ____ A picnic. In *Yiddish tales* (1912), **Y-20.**

 ____ Slack times they sleep. In *Yiddish tales* **(1912), Y-20.**

 ____ Yohrzeit for mother. In *Yiddish tales* **(1912), Y-20.**

H-1051 Hurlburt, R. Prentiss (Rufus Prentiss), b. 1864. At Cloudy Pass: a tale of love and adventure in Idaho / by R. Prentiss Hurlburt. Boston, Massachusetts: C. M. Clark Publishing Co., 1908. 269 p., front., [7] leaves of plates. [Ill. by John Goss.]
LC: D 9, '08.
PW: D 12, '08.

H-1052 Hurlbut, Edward H. Lanagan: amateur detective / by Edward H. Hurlbut; with illustrations by Frederic Dorr Steele. New York: Sturgis & Walton Company, 1913. 287 p., col. front., [3] leaves of plates.
LC: Jl 11, '13.

H-1053 Hurlbut, John E. (John Edwin), b. 1843. Above par / by John E. Hurlburt [i. e. Hurlbut]. Boston: Richard G. Badger, [c1913]. ([Boston, U. S. A.]: The Gorham Press). 274 p. **DLC**
LC: N 3, '13.
PW: N 8, '13.

H-1054 Hurlock, A. Stephens, Mrs. Darkness and dawn / by Mrs. A. Stephens Hurlock. [Philadelphia: Dukes, 1918.] 127 p. **DLC**
Cover title: *Janette.*

H-1055 Hurst, Edward Harry, b. 1868. Mystery Island / by Edward H. Hurst; with a frontispiece in colour by Griswold Tyng. Boston: L. C. Page and Company, 1907. 313 p., col. front.
LC: O 2, '07.
PW: O 19, '07.
BLC: London: Hurst & Blackett, 1908.

H-1056 Hurst, Fannie, 1889-1968. Every soul hath its song / by Fannie Hurst. New York; London: Harper and Brothers, [1916]. 376, [1] p., front. (port.).
Contents: Sea gullibles -- Rolling stock -- Hochenheimer of Cincinnati -- In memoriam -- The Nth commandment -- T. B. -- Summer resources -- Sob sister -- The name and the game.
LC: O 10, '16.

H-1057 ____ Gaslight sonatas / by Fannie Hurst . . . New York; London: Harper & Brothers, [1918]. 270, [1] p., front. [Ill. by T. D. Skidmore.]
Contents: Bitter-sweet -- Sieve of fulfilment -- Ice-water, pl-! -- Hers not to reason why -- Golden fleece -- Nightshade -- Get ready the wreaths.
LC: Ap 2, '18.
PW: Ap 13, '18.

 ____ Get ready the wreaths. In *The best short stories of 1917 and the yearbook of the American short story* (1918), **B-562.**

 ____ The gold in fish. In *More aces* (1925), **M-962.**

H-1058 ____ Humoresque: a laugh on life with a tear behind it / by Fannie Hurst . . . New York; London: Harper & Brothers, [1919]. 332, [1] p., front. [Ill. by Wilson C. Dexter.]
Contents: Humoresque -- Oats for the woman -- A petal on the current -- White goods -- "Heads" -- A boob spelled backward -- Even as you and I -- The wrong pew.
LC: Mr 21, '19.
PW: Ap 5, '19.

____ "Ice water, pl--!" In *The best short stories of 1916 and the yearbook of the American short story* **(1917), B-561.**

H-1059 ____ Just around the corner: romance en casserole / by Fannie Hurst . . . ; illustrated. New York; London: Harper and Brothers, 1914. 360, [1] p., front., [3] leaves of plates. [Ill. by Arthur William Brown and F. R. Gruger.]
Contents: Power and horse-power -- Other people's shoes -- The other check -- Marked down -- Breakers ahead -- The good provider -- Superman -- The paradise trail -- The squall.
LC: N 28, '14.
PW: S 26, '14.

H-1060 ____ Lummox / by Fannie Hurst. New York: Harper & Brothers, 1923. 329 p. Designed end papers.
LC: O 6, '23.
PW: O 27, '23.

____ Seven candles. In *The best short stories of 1923 and the yearbook of the American short story* **(1924), B-568.**

____ She walks in beauty. In *The best short stories of 1921 and the yearbook of the American short story* **(1922), B-566.**

H-1061 ____ Star-dust: the story of an American girl / by Fannie Hurst . . . New York; London: Harper & Brothers, [c1921]. 458 p., front.
LC: Mr 26, '21.
PW: Mr 26, '21.

____, contributor. See *The sturdy oak* (1917), **S-1101.**

____ T. B. In *The best short stories of 1915 and the yearbook of the American short story* (1916), **B-560.**

H-1062 ____ The vertical city / by Fannie Hurst . . . New York; London: Harper & Brothers, [c1922]. 280, [1] p.
Contents: She walks in beauty -- Back pay -- The vertical city -- The smudge -- Guilty -- Roulette.
LC: Mr 21, '22.
PW: Ap 1, '22.

H-1063 Hurst, S. B. H. (Samuel Bertram Haworth), b. 1876. Barney / by S. B. H. Hurst. New York; London: Harper & Brothers Publishers, 1923. 323 p.
LC: My 19, '23.
BLC: London: John Long, 1924.

H-1064 ____ Coomer Ali / by S. B. H. Hurst. New York; London: Harper & Brothers, 1922. 248 p., front. [Ill. by C. W. Woodruff.]
LC: F 2, '22.
PW: Ja 28, '22.
BLC: London: John Long, 1924.

H-1065 Hurt, Walter. The scarlet shadow: a story of the great Colorado Conspiracy / by Walter Hurt. Girard, Kansas: The Appeal to Reason, 1907. 416 p.
LC: D 9, '07.
PW: Ja 11, '08.

H-1066 Husband, Joseph, 1885-1938. Citadel: a novel / by Joseph Husband. Boston; New York: Houghton Mifflin Company, 1924. (Cambridge: The Riverside Press). 282 p.
LC: O 1, '24.
BLC: London: Hodder & Stoughton, [1925].

H-1067 ____ High hurdles / by Joseph Husband; with illustrations by M. Leone Bracker. Boston; New York: Houghton Mifflin Company, 1923. (Cambridge, Massachusetts, U. S. A.: The Riverside Press). 232 p., [5] leaves of plates.
LC: My 24, '23.
PW: My 12, '23.

____ A year in a coal-mine. In *Atlantic narratives;* **2nd series (1918), A-361.**

H-1068 Huselton, Estelle Zinkman. The tutored soul / by Estelle Zinkman Huselton. Boston: Sherman, French & Company, 1916. 263 p.
PW: S 16, '16.

H-1069 Husted, Lillia Shaw. The bride in black / by Lillia Shaw Husted. Boston: The Four Seas Company, 1920. 247 p., front.
LC: Ap 13, '20.
PW: Ap 24, '20.

H-1070 Huston, Ethelyn Leslie. The towers of Ilium / by Ethelyn Leslie Huston. New York: George H. Doran Company, [c1916]. 431 p. Illustrated end papers.
PW: S 23, '16.

H-1071 Huston, McCready, b. 1891. Hulings' quest / by McCready Huston. New York: Charles Scribner's Sons, 1925. 271 p.
LC: S 9, '25.
PW: S 12, '25.

H-1072 Hutcheson, Carl Franklin. The state's scandal: a political story based upon various actual municipal and state occurrences --- romance and tragedy playing vital parts / by Carl Franklin Hutcheson. Atlanta, Ga.: [s. n.], 1916. 143, [1] p., [1] leaf of photo. plates (port.). **MUS**

H-1073 Hutchings, Emily Grant. Indian summer / Emily Grant Hutchings. New York: Alfred A. Knopf, 1922. 296 p.
LC: Ag 5, '22.
PW: Jl 29, '22.

H-1074 [____] Jap Herron: a novel written from the ouija board; with an introduction, The coming of Jap Herron. New York: M. Kennerley, 1917. 230 p., front.
LC: O 23, '17.

H-1075 Hutchinson, Edith Stotesbury, b. 1877. A pair of little patent leather boots / by Edith Stotesbury Hutchinson; with 63 illustrations. Philadelphia; London: J. B. Lippincott Company, 1913. 260 p.
LC: Ap 2, '13.
PW: Mr 15, '13.

H-1076 Hutchinson, Hubbard. Chanting wheels: a novel / by Hubbard Hutchinson. New York; London: G. P. Putnam's Sons, 1922. (New York: The Knickerbocker Press). 293 p.
LC: Mr 25, '22.
PW: Mr 4, '22.

H-1077 Hyde, C. W. G. (Cornelius Willet Gillam), 1838-1920. The Green Valley school: a pedagogical story / by C. W. G. Hyde . . . Minneapolis: North-Western School Supply Co., 1907. 186 p., ill.

H-1078 Hyde, Henry M. (Henry Morrow), b. 1866. The buccaneers: a story of the Black Flag in business / by Henry M. Hyde; frontispiece by Bert Knight. New York; London: Funk & Wagnalls Company, 1904. 236 p., front.

H-1079 _____ One forty-two: the reformed messenger boy / by Henry M. Hyde. Eldridge Court, Chicago: Herbert S. Stone & Company, 1901. 204 p., ill. [Ill. by F. L. Young.]

H-1080 _____ The upstart / by Henry M. Hyde. New York: The Century Co., 1906. 332 p., front., [7] leaves of plates. [Ill. by W. Morgan.]
LC: S 28, '06.
PW: O 20, '06.

H-1081 Hyde, Jack. The Dreamer: the Man, the Devil and the Girl / by Jack Hyde. Boston: The Roxburgh Publishing Co., [191- ?]. 105 p., front. (port.).

H-1082 Hyde, John Dalison. The feet of the years / by John Dalison Hyde. New York: The Metropolitan Press, 1910. 298 p.
LC: D 5, '10.
BLC: London: Stanley Paul, [1910].

H-1083 Hyde, Mary Caroline, d. 1904. Hester Hyde: a colonial romance / by Mary Caroline Hyde . . . New York; London; Montreal: The Abbey Press, [c1902]. 120 p., photo. front., [2] leaves of photo. plates.
CLE

H-1084 Hyde, Mary Ellen Burke, b. 1854. The sins of the fathers / by Mary E. Hyde. Boston: Sherman, French & Company, 1914. 563 p.
PW: D 5, '14.

H-1085 Hyde, Miles G. (Miles Goodyear), b. 1842. The confessions and letters of Terence Quinn McManus / by Miles G. Hyde . . . Boston: Richard G. Badger, [c1911]. (Boston: The Gorham Press). 189 p.
DLC
LC: My 3, '12.
PW: Ja 6, '12.

I

I-1 I: in which a woman tells the truth about herself. New York: D. Appleton and Company, 1904. 363 p.
PW: Ap 2, '04.

I. S. See **Schneider, Isidor.**

I-2 Iglehart, Fanny Chambers Gooch, 1842-1913. The boy captive of the Texas Mier Expedition / by Fanny Chambers Gooch-Iglehart . . . ; illustrations by Bock. -- Revised, reprinted and republished by the author. -- [San Antonio, Tex.: Press of J. R. Wood Printing Co., c1909]. 331 p., col. front., [4] leaves of plates (1 port.), ill. (some photo., some port.).
LC: Ja 17, '11.

I-3 Iliowizi, Henry, 1850-1911. The Archierey of Samara: a semi-historic romance of Russian life / by Henry Iliowizi. Philadelphia: Henry T. Coates and Company, 1903. 337 p., front., [2] leaves of plates.

Illinois Girl, An, pseud. See **Owen, Belle, b.1866.**

I-4 Ilo, Wm. A. (William A.), b. 1861. Hazel Pierce / by Wm. A. Ilo. New York: A. Hograve & Co., 1902. 318 p., front.
PW: N 1, '02.

I-5 Imhaus, Elizabeth Vigoureux. Exiled by the world: a story of the heart / Elizabeth Vigoureux Imhaus; illustrations by Aug. Will. New York; London: Mutual Publishing Company, [1901]. 396 p., front., [11] leaves of plates.
This story is a novelization of the Celebrated Play of the same title, written in collaboration with Louise A. Imhaus.
PW: Mr 8, '02.
BLC: London: Gay & Bird, 1902.

I-6 _____ "Golden poppy": a romance of California / by Elizabeth Vigoureux Imhaus (Countess Neyts Cary) . . . New York: Broadway Publishing Co., [1915]. 261 p., photo. front. (port.).
NYP

I-7 In the house of her friends. New York: Robert Grier Cooke, 1906. 299 p.
LC: Jl 2, '06.

I-8 Ingalese, Isabella. Linked lives: a tale of yesterday and to-day / by Isabella Ingalese. New York: The Occult Book Concern, [c1903]. 232 p.

I-9 _____ Mata the magician: a romance of the new era / by Isabella Ingalese. New York: Abbey Press, [c1901]. 183 p.
Unexamined copy: bibliographic data from OCLC, #24586185.

I-10 Ingersoll, Ernest, 1852-1946. An island in the air: a story of singular adventures in the Mesa country / by Ernest Ingersoll . . . New York: The Macmillan Company; London: Macmillan & Co., Ltd., 1905. 303 p., col. front., [6] leaves of col. plates, ill. [Ill. by William A. McCullough and T. Cromwell Lawrence.]
PW: O 21, '05.

Ingersoll, Will E. The centenarian. In *The best short stories of 1919 and the yearbook of the American short story* (1920), B-564.

I-11 Ingham, Dorcas Helen, b. 1828. Passing pictures / by Dorcas Helen Ingham. Los Angeles: Printed for the author, Golden Press, 1913. 121 p., ill. (port.).

I-12   Ingham, Ellery Percy, 1856-1926. At the point of the sword; a romance of the Netherlands / by Ellery P. Ingham. New York; London; Montreal: The Abbey Press, [1902]. 379 p., front., ill. (map).
DLC (micro)
LC: Ag 2, '02.

I-13   Ingles, J. M. Back to the old trail / by J. M. Ingles. Boston, Mass.: Hamilton Brothers, [c1925]. 268 p.
LC: D 24, '25.

I-14   Ingraham, Charles A. Fact, fiction and reflection / by Charles A. Ingraham. Poughkeepsie, New York: Press of the A. V. Haight Company, 1909. 232 p., photo. front. (port.).   **AZU**
Contents: History: The advent of the Dutch -- The massacre at Schenectady -- The fame of Bennington -- Fort Stanwix -- Two lords of history -- Ireland and the Irish -- A backward glance at feudalism. Persons: John Brown of Ossawatomie -- Ellsworth -- Dr. T. De Witt Talmage -- Dr. Nott a great educator. Places: Willard's Mountain -- Bemis Heights -- Northern New York -- Historic grounds. Politics: A diagnosis of patriotism -- The party machine -- The waste of war. Nature: The flowers of the field --The birds of the air -- The stars of heaven -- Indian summer -- Sylvan shades -- Rural depopulation. Art: A brief review of art -- The power of the poet -- The evolution of music. Fiction: The vindication of a dog -- Black Dick -- The ferry girl -- The amendment of Caleb Storrs -- The good fortune of Fortunatus Paul. Reflection: Thoughts upon memory -- Know thyself -- The limitations of philosophy --The quality of humor -The days of old -- Time -- Past, present and future -- Iroquois' spiritual lesson -- Life is long. Religion: Infidelity -- Triune trunk of Christianity. Address: The higher orientation.

I-15   Ingraham, Frances C., *pseud.* Deborah Gray / by Frances C. Ingraham [pseud.]; illustrated by Harry B. Bradford and Eugenie De Land. New York; Washington: The Neale Publishing Company, 1903. 474 p., front., [5] leaves of plates.
PW: D 19, '03.

I-16   Ingraham, Prentiss, 1843-1904. The girl rough riders: a romantic and adventurous trail of fair rough riders through the wonderland of mystery and silence / by Prentiss Ingraham . . . ; illustrated by Bertha G. Davidson. Boston: Dana Estes & Company, 1903. 310 p., front., [7] leaves of plates.   **DLC**
PW: Jl 11, '03.

I-17   Ingram, Eleanor M. (Eleanor Marie), 1886-1921. The flying Mercury / by Eleanor M. Ingram; with illustrations by Edmund Frederick; decorations by Bertha Stuart. Indianapolis: The Bobbs-Merrill Company, [c1910]. 194 p., col. front., [6] leaves of col. plates.
LC: N 9, '10.
PW: N 12, '10.

I-18   _____ From the car behind / by Eleanor M. Ingram . . . ; with illustrations in color by James Montgomery Flagg. Philadelphia; London: J. B. Lippincott Company, 1912. 306 p., col. front., [2] leaves of col. plates.
LC: Mr 13, '12.
PW: F 24, '12.

I-19   _____ The game and the candle / by Eleanor M. Ingram; with illustrations by P. D. Johnson. Indianapolis: The Bobbs-Merrill Company, [c1909]. 327, [1] p., front., [4] leaves of plates.
LC: O 9, '09.
PW: O 16, '09.

_____ His day, a tale of Italy. In *Golden stories* **(1909), G-285.**

I-20   _____ A man's hearth / by Eleanor M. Ingram; with illustrations in color by Edmund Frederick. Philadelphia; London: J. B. Lippincott Company, 1915. 313 p., col. front., [2] leaves of col. plates.
LC: N 9, '15.
PW: N 6, '15.

1-21   _____ Stanton wins / by Eleanor M. Ingram; with illustrations by Edmund Frederick. Indianapolis: The Bobbs-Merrill Company, [c1911]. 256 p., col. front., [4] leaves of col. plates.
LC: My 18, '11.
PW: My 13, '11.

I-22   _____ The thing from the lake / by Eleanor M. Ingram . . . Philadelphia; London: J. B. Lippincott Company, 1921. 315 p.
LC: D 15, '21.
PW: Ag 13, '21.

I-23   _____ The twice American / by Eleanor M. Ingram . . . ; with illustrations in color by Edmund Frederick. Philadelphia; London: J. B. Lippincott Company, 1917. 336 p., col. front., [2] leaves of col. plates.
Copyright 1916, by Frank A. Munsey Company under the title of "The house of the little shoes".
LC: O 29, '17.
PW: N 3, '17.

I-24   _____ The unafraid / by Eleanor M. Ingram . . . ; with illustrations in color by Edmund Frederick. Philadelphia; London: J. B. Lippincott Company, 1913. 368 p., col. front., [2] leaves of col. plates.
LC: O 4, '13.
PW: O 18, '13.

Ink, Evangeline. See **Evangeline.**

I-25   Innes, Albert E. Tales of an optician: a collection of true stories of romance, adventure, comedy, by Mr. Frederick A. Airlie, spectacle maker / by Albert E. Innes. New York: Frederick Boger Publishing Co., 1903. 166 p.   **VXP**
Contents: My excuse -- The lady and the chatelaine bag -- A heavy penalty -- For love and money -- In the form of a man -- An epoch-maker -- A waiting game -- A case of circumstantial evidence -- The eye of fortune.

I-26   Innes, Norman. The lonely guard / by Norman Innes; frontispiece by J. C. Leyendecker. Philadelphia: George W. Jacobs & Company, [191-?]. 353 p., col. front.
PW: O 2, '09.
BLC: London: Ward, Lock & Co., 1908.

I-27   _____ My lady's kiss: a romance / by Norman Innes . . . ; illustrated. Chicago; New York: Rand, McNally & Company, [c1908]. 312 p., front., [2] leaves of plates.
LC: O 28, '08.
BLC: London: Ward, Lock & Co., 1908.

I-28   Inness, George, 1825-1894. Random thoughts / by George Inness, Jr. [S. l.]: Privately published, 1920.

139 p.

Contents: Burglars -- The suicide -- Frank Worthy and the circus -- The artist -- The Grand Cañon -- To describe a painting called "Sunrise" -- The storm -- To a white canvas -- My whiskey-flask -- The present -- My song -- The southern pine -- Loved An -- My brier pipe -- The passing of Peter Gross -- A temperance story -- Uriah and the hill lot -- The sealskin coat -- The colonel -- A fairy-tale -- The haunted house -- The piano stool -- The circus dog -- My stomach and I -- Three cronies -- Why should you mourn, dear -- My lady fair -- Camp comfort -- The kiss -- The portrait -- My father's son -- Frank Babcock -- The second Adventist -- Father Time -- The grain of wheat.

Innet, E. S. The pillow of justice. In *Through the forbidden gates* (1903), T-222.

I-29   International short stories / edited by William Patten: a new collection of famous examples from the literatures of England, France and America. New York: P. F. Collier & Son, [1910]. 3 v.

Contents: The prophetic pictures / by Nathaniel Hawthorne -- The legend of sleepy hollow / by Washington Irving -- The gold-bug / by Edgar Allen Poe -- Corporal Flint's murder / by J. Fenimore Cooper -- Uncle Jim and Uncle Billy / by Bret Harte -- The notary of Perigueux / by H. W. Longfellow -- The widow's cruise / by F. R. Stockton -- The count and the wedding guest / by O. Henry -- Miss Tooker's wedding gift / by John Kendrick Bangs -- The fable of the two mandolin players and the willing performer / by George Ade -- The fable of the preacher who flew his kite, but not because he wished to do so / by George Ade -- The shadows on the wall / by Mary E. Wilkins Freeman -- Major Perdue's bargain / by Joel Chandler Harris -- A Kentucky cinderella / by F. Hopkinson Smith -- By the waters of paradise / by F. Marion Crawford -- A memorable night / by Anna Katharine Green -- The man from red dog / by Alfred Henry Lewis -- Jean Michaud's little ship / by Charles G. D. Roberts -- Those old lunes! / by W. Gilmore Simms -- The chiropodist / by Bayard Taylor -- "Mr. Dooley on corporal punishment" / by F. P. Dunne -- Over a wood fire / by Donald G. Mitchell- "Ik Marvel".

References: BAL 782, 19793.

I-30   Ireland, Laura Isabel. Old love stories with new variations, or, The reward of a useful unselfish life / by Laura Isabel Ireland. Los Angeles, Calif.: Published by Austin Publishing Company, [1919]. 112 p.   **DLC**
LC: Je 18, '19.

I-31   Ireland, Mary E. (Mary Eliza), 1834-1927. Hilda's mascot: a tale of Maryland, my Maryland / by Mary E. Ireland; halftones by Donald Gardner. Chicago; Akron, Ohio; New York: The Saalfield Publishing Co., [1910]. 334 p., photo. front., [4] leaves of plates.
LC: Jl 9, '10.
PW: D 3, '10.

I-32   _____ Otterbrook parsonage / by Mary E. Ireland. Dayton, Ohio: United Brethren Publishing House, 1904. 207 p., photo. front., [4] leaves of photo. plates.
"Sequel to *Otterbrook's blessing*."

I-33   _____ Otterbrook people / by Mary E. Ireland. Dayton, Ohio: United Brethren Publishing House, 1907. 226 p.
Unexamined copy: bibliographic data from OCLC, #29780525.

I-34   _____ Otterbrook's blessing: a delightful story gleaned from a girl's diary / by Mary E. Ireland. Dayton, Ohio: United Brethren Publishing House, 1902. 195 p., photo. front., [7] leaves of photo. plates.   **DLC**

I-35   Irvine, Alexander, 1863-1941. The Magyar: a story of the social revolution / by Alexander Irvine. Girard, Kansas: The Socialist Publishing Company, [c1911]. 277 p.

I-36   _____ My lady of the chimney corner / by Alexander Irvine. New York: The Century Co., 1913. 221 p.
LC: Ag 19, '13.
PW: Ag 23, '13.
BLC: London: Eveleigh Nash, 1913.

I-37   Irvine, Leigh H. (Leigh Hadley), 1863-1942. An affair in the South Seas: a story of romantic adventure / by Leigh H. Irvine. London: T. Fisher Unwin; San Francisco, California: Payot, Upham & Co., 1901. 278 p., front.
PW: Je 1, '01.

I-38   Irving, Elizabeth. A new world, or, The way to win / by Elizabeth Irving (Leah M. Rike). Le Roy, Illinois: [s. n.], 1905. 432 p., front. (port.).   **JFK**

I-39   Irwin, Florence, b. 1869. The mask: a novel / by Florence Irwin; with frontispiece by Paul Stahr. Boston: Little, Brown and Company, 1917. 325 p., front.
LC: S 22, '17.
PW: S 26, '17.

I-40   _____ Poor dear Theodora! / by Florence Irwin. New York; London: G. P. Putnam's Sons, 1920. (New York: The Knickerbocker Press). 402 p.
LC: Ap 19, '20.
PW: Mr 6, '20.

I-41   _____ The road to Mecca / by Florence Irwin. New York; London: G. P. Putnam's Sons, 1916. ([New York]: The Knickerbocker Press). 422 p.
LC: My 9, '16.
PW: My 13, '16.

I-42   Irwin, Grace Luce. The diary of a show-girl / by Grace Luce Irwin; illustrated by Wallace Morgan. New York: Moffat, Yard and Company, 1909. 177 p., incl. front.
PW: Ap 10, '09.

I-43   [Irwin, Inez Haynes], 1873-1970. Angel Island / by Inez Haynes Gillmore; with two illustrations by John Rae. New York: Henry Holt and Company, 1914. 351 p., col. front., [1] leaf of plates.
LC: F 7, '14.
PW: F 7, '14.
BLC: London: G. Bell & Sons; [Rahway, New Jersey, printed], 1914.

I-44   _____ Gertrude Haviland's divorce / by Inez Haynes Irwin. New York; London: Harper & Brothers, 1925. 389 p.
"*Gertrude Haviland's divorce* was published serially under the title *Discarded*.
LC: O 20, '25.
PW: O 24, '25.

I-45   _____ The happy years / Inez Haynes Irwin; illustrations by R. M. Crosby, Gayle Porter Hoskins, and Harvey Dunn. New York: Henry Holt and

Company, 1919. 310 p., front., [3] leaves of plates. LC: O 8, '19.

I-46   [____] Janey: being the record of a short interval in the journey through life and the struggle with society of a little girl of nine, in which she repudiates her duties as an amateur mother, snares the most blundering of birds, successfully invades Grub Street, tracks the smallest and blindest of gods, peers behind the veil of the seen into the unseen, interprets the great bard, grubs at the root of all evil, faces the three great problems, birth, death, love, and finally, in passing through the laborious process of becoming ten, discovers the great illusion / by Inez Haynes Gillmore . . . ; with illustrations by Ada C. Williamson. New York: Henry Holt and Company, 1911. 320 p., front., [3] leaves of plates.   **CLE**
PW: N 4, '11.

I-47   [____] June Jeopardy / by Inez Haynes Gillmore. New York: B. W. Huebsch, 1908. 343 p.
LC: My 29, '08.
PW: Je 6, '08.

I-48   ____ The lady of kingdoms / by Inez Haynes Irwin . . . New York: George H. Doran Company, [c1917]. 494 p.
LC: O 8, '17.
PW: S 29,' 17.

I-49   [____] The Ollivant orphans / by Inez Haynes Gillmore . . . ; frontispiece by James Montgomery Flagg. New York: Henry Holt and Company, 1915. 313 p., front.   **OSU, CLE**
LC: N 9, '15.
PW: O 23, '15.
BLC: London: Methuen & Co.,; U. S. A. printed, 1915.

I-50   ____ Out of the air / by Inez Haynes Irwin. New York: Harcourt, Brace, and Company, 1921. 269 p.
LC: Mr 18, '21.
PW: Mr 26, '21.

I-51   [____] Phoebe and Ernest / by Inez Haynes Gillmore; with illustrations by R. F. Schabelitz. New York: Henry Holt and Company, 1910. 353 p., front. (integral leaf, not counted in pagination), ill.
LC: O 25, '10.
BLC: London: Constable & Co.; Rahway, New Jersey [printed], 1911.

I-52   [____] Phoebe, Ernest, and Cupid / by Inez Haynes Gillmore . . . ; with illustrations by R. F. Schabelitz. New York: Henry Holt and Company, 1912. 338 p., front., [7] leaves of plates.
LC: O 22, '12.

____ The spring flight. In *Prize stories of 1924* (1925), P-622.

I-53   Irwin, Violet Mary, b. 1881. The human desire / by Violet Irwin; with a frontispiece by James Montgomery Flagg. Boston: Small, Maynard and Company, [c1913]. 431 p., col. front.
LC: N 3, '13.
PW: O 18, '13.

I-54   ____ Wits and the woman / by Violet Irwin . . . ; illustrated by Christine T. Curtiss. Boston: Small, Maynard & Company, [c1919]. 330 p., front. [3] leaves of plates.
LC: S 24, '19.
PW: Ag 30, '19.

I-55   Irwin, Wallace, 1876-1959. The blooming angel / by Wallace Irwin . . . New York: George H. Doran Company, [c1919]. 285 p., front. [3] leaves of plates. [Ill. by May Wilson Preston.]
LC: Jl 24, '19.
PW: Jl 26, '19.

____, contributor. <u>See</u> *Bobbed hair* **(1925), B-700.**

I-56   ____ The golden bed / by Wallace Irwin. New York; London: G. P. Putnam's Sons, 1924. (New York: The Knickerbocker Press). 437 p.
LC: Ag 28, '24.
PW: Ag 16, '24.

I-57   ____ Letters of a Japanese schoolboy ("Hashimura Togo") / by Wallace Irwin . . . ; ilustrated by Rollin Kirby. New York: Doubleday, Page and Company, 1909. 370 p., front. [15] leaves of plates, ill.
LC: F 13, '09.
PW: Mr 20, '09.
BLC: London: Doubleday, Page and Company, New York printed, 1909.

I-58   ____ Lew Tyler's wives: a novel / by Wallace Irwin. New York; London: G. P. Putnam's Sons, 1923. (New York: The Knickerbocker Press). 384 p.
LC: S 11, '23.
PW: S 8, '23.

I-59   ____ More letters of a Japanese schoolboy / by Wallace Irwin; with illustrations by Ralph Barton. New York; London: G. P. Putnam's Sons, 1923. (New York: The Knickerbocker Press). 137 p., front. ill.
LC: O 11, '23.
PW: O 13, '23.

I-60   ____ Mr. Togo maid of all work / Wallace Irwin (Hashimura Togo). New York: Duffield & Company, 1913. 190 p., front. [Ill. by Rea Irvin.]
LC: O 17, '13.
PW: N 1, '13.

I-61   ____ Pilgrims into folly: romantic excursions / by Wallace Irwin . . . New York: George H. Doran Company, [c1917]. 342 p.
Contents: Wings -- He shot the bird of paradise -- The highest -- What became of Deegan Folk? -- You can't get away from your grandfather -- The torpedo -- The ideal gentleman.
LC: Je 19, '17.
PW: Je 16, '17.

I-62   ____ Seed of the sun / by Wallace Irwin . . . New York: George H. Doran Company, [c1921]. 352 p.
LC: Ja 21, '21.
PW: Ja 22, '21.
BLC: London: Hodder & Stoughton, printed in U.S.A., [1921].

I-63   _____ Suffering husbands / by Wallace Irwin . . .
New York: George H. Doran Company, [c1920].
376 p.
Contents: All front and no back -- Monkey on a stick -- Peaches and
cream -- Thunder -- The goat -- The light that paled -- Free -- Gasless
Sunday -- Mother's milk.
LC: Je 26, '20.
PW: Jl 3, '20.

        _____ The transplanted ghost. In *Humorous ghost
stories* **(1921), H-1018.**

I-64   _____ Trimmed with red / by Wallace Irwin. New
York: George H. Doran Company, [c1920]. 320 p.
LC: Ap 21, '20.
PW: Ap 17, '20.

I-65   _____ Venus in the East / by Wallace Irwin . . . ;
illustrated by May Wilson Preston. New York:
George H. Doran Company, [c1918]. 314 p., col.
front., [7] leaves of col. plates. Colored illustrated
endpapers.
LC: N 30, '18.
PW: D 14, '18.

I-66   Irwin, William Henry, 1873-1948. Columbine time /
by Will Irwin. Boston, Mass.: The Stratford
Company, [c1921]. 171 p., front., [2] leaves of
plates.
LC: N 4, '21.
PW: D 3, '21.

I-67   _____ The confessions of a con man / as told to Will
Irwin; illustrated by W. Glackens. New York: B.
W. Huebsch, 1909. 182 p., front. [6] leaves of
plates.
First published in the Saturday evening post of
Philadelphia.
LC: Ag 19, '09.
PW: Ag 14, '09.

        _____ The dotted trail. In *Argonaut stories* **(1906),
A-298.**

I-68   _____ The house of mystery: an episode in the career
of Rosalie Le Grange, clairvoyant / by Will Irwin.
New York: The Century Co., 1910. 252 p., front.,
[7] leaves of plates. [Ill. by F. C. Yohn.]
LC: Ap 1, '10.
PW: Mr 26, '10.

        _____, jt. aut. *The picaroons* (1904). **See Burgess,
Gelett, 1866-1951, jt. aut., B-1207.**

I-69   _____ The readjustment / by Will Irwin . . . New
York: B. W. Huebsch, 1910. 287 p.
LC: D 31, '10.
PW: D 10, '10.

I-70   _____ The red button / by Will Irwin; illustrated by
Max J. Spero. Indianapolis: Bobbs-Merrill
Company, [c1912]. 370 p., front., [5] leaves of
plates.
LC: O 24, '12.
PW: O 26, '12.

        _____, jt. aut. *The reign of Queen Isyl* (1903). **See
Burgess, Gelett, 1866-1951, jt. aut., B-1208.**

        _____, jt. aut. *Stanford stories* (1913). **See Field,
Charles K. (Charles Kellogg), b. 1873, jt. aut.,
F-93.**

I-71   _____ Warrior the untamed: the story of an
imaginative press agent / by Will Irwin; illustrations
by F. R. Gruger. New York: Doubleday, Page &
Company, 1909. 47 p., front., [3] leaves of plates.
LC: S 11, '09.
PW: S 11, '09.
BLC: London: Doubleday, Page & Company, New
York printed, 1909.

I-72   _____ Where the heart is: showing that Christmas is
what you make it / by Will Irwin. New York;
London: D. Appleton and Company, 1912. 72,
[1] p., front. [Ill. by Howard Heath.]
LC: O 29, '12.
PW: N 9, '12.

I-73   _____ Youth rides west: a story of the seventies / by
Will Irwin. New York: Alfred A. Knopf, 1925.
284 p.
LC: F 20, '25.
PW: F 14, '25.
BLC: London: Jonathan Cape, 1925.

I-74   Isaac, E. M. The hero of Trent, or, Saved from the
jaws of hell / by E. M. Isaac . . . Chicago; Boston:
The Christian Witness Co., [c1910]. 225 p.   **KAT**
LC: Ag 25, '10.

I-75   Isaacs, A. S. (Abram Samuel), 1852-1920. Step by
step: a story of the early days of Moses Mendelssohn
/ by Abram S. Isaacs. Philadelphia: The Jewish
Publication Society of America, 1910. 160 p., col.
front. (port.).   **CPE**
LC: D 13, '10.

I-76   _____ Stories from the rabbis / by Abram S. Isaacs.
2d and enl. ed. New York: Bloch Publishing
Company, 1911. 222 p.
Unexamined copy: bibliographic data from OCLC,
#2835290.
Partly reprinted from various periodicals. Reprinted
from 1893 edition, except for the addition of the last
two stories.
Contents: The Faust of the Talmud -- The wooing of the princess --
The Rip Van Winkle of the Talmud -- Rabbinical romance -- The
shepherd's wife -- The repentant rabbi -- The inheritance -- Elijah in
the legends -- When Solomon was king -- Rabbinical humor -- The
Munchausen of the Talmud -- The rabbi's dream -- The gift that
blessed -- In the sweat of thy brow -- A four-leaved clover -- The
expiation -- A string of pearls -- The vanished bridegroom -- The
lesson of the harvest.

I-77   _____ Under the Sabbath lamp: stories of our time
for old and young / by Abram S. Isaacs.
Philadelphia: The Jewish Publication Society of
America, 1919. 259 p.
Contents: Introduction -- The old shofar -- Born again -- Before
dawn -- The trendelé -- The children's gift -- The happy family -- A
voice for freedom -- From land to land -- A rabbi's wife -- How the
debt was paid -- Only a child -- The rabbi's romance -- Just from
Jerusalem -- The children's revolt -- At grandmother's school.
LC: Je 21, '19.

I-78   _____ The young champion: one year in Grace
Aguilar's girlhood / by Abram S. Isaacs . . .
Philadelphia: The Jewish Publication Society of

America, 1913. 196 p.
LC: Je 12, '13.

I-79   Isaman, Sara White. Sophisticating Uncle Hiram: a book of fun and laughter / by Sara White Isaman; illustrated. Chicago: The Reilly & Britton Co., [c1912]. 224 p., ill.

I-80   _____ Tourist tales of California / by Sara White Isaman. Los Angeles, Cal.: Published by the Author, 1907. 233 p., ill.
Contents: Los Angeles-That Good Old Tourist Town(poem) -- At Busch's Garden -- At Mt. Lowe -- At Los Angeles -- At Studio Steckell -- At Herman's -- At Long Beach -- Letters Home -- More Letters -- At Venice -- At the Ostrich Farm -- Apartment-House Life -- At La Fiesta -- At Catalina -- At Westlake Home.
LC: N 29, '07.
Another edition: Chicago: The Reilly & Britton Co., [1909]. 224 p., front., [5] leaves of plates.
LC: Je 10, '09.

I-81   _____ Uncle Hiram in California: more fun and laughter with Uncle Hiram and Aunt Phoebe / by Sara White Isaman. New York: H. K. Fly Company, [c1917]. 224 p.

I-82   Isham, Frederic Stewart, 1866-1922. Aladdin from Broadway / Frederic S. Isham; illustrated by William Thacher Van Dresser. Indianapolis: Bobbs-Merrill Company, [c1913]. 358 p., front., [5] leaves of plates.
LC: S 5, '13.
PW: S 6, '13.

I-83   _____ Black Friday / by Frederic S. Isham; with illustrations by Harrison Fisher. Indianapolis: The Bobbs-Merrill Company, [1904]. 409 p., front., [5] leaves of plates.
PW: O 15, '04.

I-84   _____ Half a chance / by Frederick S. Isham; with illustrations by Herman Pfeifer. Indianapolis: The Bobbs-Merrill Company, [c1909]. 383 p., front., [4] leaves of plates.
LC: S 25, '09.
PW: S 25, '09.

I-85   _____ The lady of the Mount / by Frederic S. Isham; with illustrations by Lester Ralph. Indianapolis: Bobbs-Merrill Company, [1908]. 389 p., front., [7] leaves of plates.
LC: F 10, '08.
PW: F 29, '08.

I-86   _____ A man and his money / by Frederic S. Isham . . . ; illustrations by Max J. Spero. Indianapolis: The Bobbs-Merrill Company, [c1912]. 368 p., front., [3] leaves of plates.
LC: Mr 27, '12.
PW: Mr 30, '12.

I-87   _____ Nothing but the truth / by Frederic S. Isham. Indianapolis: Bobbs-Merrill Company, [c1914]. 305 p.
LC: O 2, '14.
PW: O 3, '14.

I-88   _____ The nut cracker / by Frederic S. Isham; illustrated by Stockton Mulford. Indianapolis: Bobbs-Merrill Company, [c1920]. 248 p., front., [1] leaf of plates.
LC: Ap 19, '20.
PW: My 1, '20.

I-89   _____ The social bucaneer / by Frederic S. Isham . . . ; with illustrations by W. B. King. Indianapolis: The Bobbs-Merrill Company, [c1910]. 347 p., col. front., [5] leaves of plates.
LC: O 19, '10.
PW: O 22, '10.
BLC: London: Everett & Co., 1911.

I-90   _____ The strollers / by Frederic S. Isham; with illustrations by Harrison Fisher. Indianapolis: The Bowen-Merrill Company, [c1902]. 499 p., front., [3] leaves of plates.
PW: Mr 22, '02.
BLC: London: B. F. Stevens & Brown, [1902].

I-91   _____ This way out / by Frederic S. Isham . . . ; illustrated by Hanson Booth. Indianapolis: The Bobbs-Merrill Company, [c1917]. 297, [1] p., [4] leaves of plates.
LC: S 27, '17.
PW: S 29, '17.

I-92   _____ Three live ghosts / by Frederic S. Isham . . . Indianapolis: The Bobbs-Merrill Company, [c1918]. 250 p.
LC: D 9, '18.
PW: Ja 18, '19.

I-93   _____ Under the rose / by Frederic S. Isham; with illustrations by Howard Chandler Christy. Indianapolis: The Bowen-Merrill Company, [1903]. 427 p., col. front., [3] leaves of col. plates.
PW: Mr 14, '03.
BLC: London: Ward, Lock & Co.; printed in U. S. A., 1904.

I-94   Isham, Mary Keyt, b. 1871. Moonward and other orientations / Mary Keyt Isham. [S. l.: s. n., 19--]. 51 p.
Contents: Moonward -- Metamundane -- So are we -- Reductio and absurdum -- Frantic night in a jungle.

I-95   Ivey, Thomas N. (Thomas Neal), 1860-1923. Bildad Akers: his book: the notions and experiences of a quaint rural philosopher who thinks for himself / edited by Thomas N. Ivey . . . Raleigh, N. C.: Mutual Publishing Company, [c1909]. 205 p.
LC: D 27, '09.

J

J-1   J. A. The ash snake and the desert well / by J. A. [Kansas City, Mo.: Smith-Grieves Typesetting Co., c1918]. 44 p.   **DLC**

J-2   Jabez, Brother, *pseud.* A tale of the Kloster: a romance of the German Mystics of the Cocalico / by Brother Jabez [pseud.]; illustrations by Frank McKernan. Philadelphia: Griffith & Rowland Press, 1904. 336 p., front., [4] leaves of plates.

J-3   Jack, Ellen Elliott, b. 1842. The fate of a fairy / by Ellen E. Jack. Chicago: W. B. Conkey Company, [c1910]. 213 p., plates.
Unexamined copy: bibliographic data from OCLC, #1186399.
LC: Ja 3, '11.

J-4   Jackson, Birdsall. Pipe dreams & twilight tales, by Birdsall Jackson. New York: F. M. Buckles & Company, 1902. 257 p.
Contents: Little Cherry and Uncle Joel -- A true story of the revolution -- The question under discussion -- The life-saver -- The mysterious disappearance of Old Mayhew -- The wicked king and the good queen -- A bedtime fable -- The boat race -- The fox hunt -- The romance of the Dorothy -- Sister Liza's boy -- The cruise of the graduates -- The dream of power -- The scavenger -- The white man and the red man -- The dream of gold -- The old meeting house -- The yellow covered days -- When me an' Jim went fishin' -- The master's first day -- Under the cherry tree.
PW: Ja 3, '03.

J-5   Jackson, Charles Ross, 1867-1915. Quintus Oakes: a detective story / by Charles Ross Jackson. New York: G. W. Dillingham Company, [1904]. 318 p.
PW: Ap 2, '04.
BLC: London: T. Fisher Unwin; New York [printed], 1904.

J-6   _____ The sheriff of Wasco / by Charles Ross Jackson; illustrations by Louis F. Grant. New York: G. W. Dillingham Company, 1907. 318 p., front., [3] leaves of plates.
LC: Ap 13, '07.
PW: Ap 27, '07.

J-7   _____ The third degree / by Charles Ross Jackson. New York: G. W. Dillingham Company, [c1903]. 293 p.
PW: S 19, '03.
BLC: London, T. Fisher Unwin; New York [printed], 1903.

J-8   _____ Tucker Dan / by Charles Ross Jackson; illustrations by Gordon H. Grant. New York: G. W. Dillingham Company, [1905]. 199 p., front., [5] leaves of plates.
PW: My 13, '05.

J-9   Jackson, Charles Tenney, b. 1874. Captain Sazarac / by Charles Tenney Jackson . . . Indianapolis: The Bobbs-Merrill Company, [c1922]. 332 p.
LC: Ag 19, '22.
PW: Ag 5, '22.
Another edition: photoplay title, The Eagle of the sea; illustrated with scenes from the photoplay, a Paramount picture. New York: Grosset & Dunlap, [1922]. 332 p., photo. front., photo. plates.
Unexamined copy: bibliographic data from NUC.

J-10   _____ The day of souls: a novel / by Charles Tenney Jackson; with illustrations by Paul J. Meylan. Indianapolis: The Bobbs-Merrill Company, [c1910]. 390 p., front., [4] leaves of plates.
LC: Mr 12, '10.
PW: Mr 12, '10.

J-11   _____ The fountain of youth / by Charles Tenney Jackson; illustrated with photographs. New York: Outing Publishing Company, 1914. 343 p., photo. front., [31] leaves of photo. plates.
LC: O 17, '14.
PW: D 5, '14.

_____ The horse of hurricane reef. In Prize stories of 1922 (1923), P-620.

J-12   _____ John the fool: an American romance / by Charles Tenney Jackson . . . ; illustrated by Hazel Roberts. Indianapolis: The Bobbs-Merrill Company, [c1915]. 325 p., front., [5] leaves of plates.
LC: Mr 24, '15.
PW: Mr 27, '15.

J-13   _____ Loser's luck: being the questionable enterprises of a yachtsman, a princess, and certain filibusters in Central America / by Charles Tenney Jackson. New York: Henry Holt and Company, 1905. 327 p.
PW: N 18, '05.

_____ The man who cursed the liles. In Prize stories of 1921 (1922), P-619.

J-14   _____ The Midlanders / by Charles Tenney Jackson; illustrated by Arthur William Brown. Indianapolis: The Bobbs-Merrill Company, [c1912]. 386 p., front., [5] leaves of plates.
LC: O 16, '12.
PW: O 19, 12.

J-15   _____ My brother's keeper / by Charles Tenney Jackson; with illustrations by Arthur William Brown. Indianapolis: Bobbs-Merrill Company, [c1910]. 324 p., front., [5] leaves of plates.
LC: O 12, '10.
PW: O 22, '10.

J-16   [Jackson, Frederick], 1886-1953. Anne against the world: a love story / by Victor Thorne [pseud.]. New York City: Chelsea House, [c1925]. 255 p.
PW: My 23, '25.

J-17   _____ The hidden princess: a modern romance / by Fred Jackson. Philadelphia: George W. Jacobs & Co., [1910]. 263 p., incl. col. front. [Ill. by F. Graham Cootes.]
LC: Ag 30, '10.
PW: S 10, '10.

J-18   _____ The third act / by Fred Jackson. New York: Desmond Fitzgerald, Inc., [c1913]. 349 p., col. front. [Ill. by C. D. Williams.]   DLC
LC: N 13, '13.
PW: N 29, '13.

J-19   Jackson, Gabrielle E. (Gabrielle Emilie), b. 1861. The maid of Middies' Haven: a story of Annapolis life / by Gabrielle E. Jackson . . . ; illustrations by Norman P. Rockwell. New York: McBride, Nast & Company, 1912. 299 p., front., [3] leaves of plates.

J-20   Jackson, Loulia. The nameless woman: a story of my life / by Loulia Jackson. [Kansas City, Mo.: Press of Burd & Fletcher, c1910]. 675 p.   DLC
LC: Ap 2, '10.

J-21   Jackson, Margaret Doyle, b. 1868. A daughter of the pit / by Margaret Doyle Jackson. Boston; New York: Houghton, Mifflin and Company, 1903. (Cambridge: The Riverside Press). 351, [1] p.   **OSU, MEU**
PW: F 28, '03.
BLC: London: Cassell & Co.; Cambridge, Mass. printed, 1903.

J-22   ____ The Horse-Leech's daughters / by Margaret Doyle Jackson . . . Boston; New York: Houghton, Mifflin and Company, 1904. (Cambridge: The Riverside Press). 351, [1] p.
PW: Mr 26, '04.

J-23   ____ When love is king / by Margaret Doyle Jackson . . . ; illustrations by Ch. Grunwald. New York: G. W. Dillingham Company, 1905. 351, [1] p., front., [4] leaves of plates.   **VA@**
PW: Ap 1, '05.
BLC: London: T. Fisher Unwin; New York [printed], 1905.

J-24   Jackson, S. A. Among the maples / by S. A. Jackson. Pittsburgh: United Presbyterian Board of Publication, 1908. 204 p.

J-25   Jackson, Stephen, b. 1853, *pseud.* The magic mantle: and other stories / by Stephen Jackson [pseud.]; illustrated by W. F. Lamb. New York: M. S. Greene & Company, [c1903]. 333 p., front.
Contents: The magic mantle -- A dream with developments -- The eerie piper -- The end-of-the-week outing club.
PW: D 19, '03.

J-26   Jacobi, Mary Putnam, 1842-1906. Stories and sketches / by Mary Putnam Jacobi. New York; London: G. P. Putnam's Sons, 1907. (New York: The Knickerbocker Press). 443 p.
Previously published in various periodicals.
Contents: Found and lost -- Hair chains -- Imagination and language -- A study of still-life, Paris -- A sermon at Notre-Dame -- A martyr to science -- Concerning Charlotte -- Some of the French leaders.
PW: N 16, '07.

J-27   Jacobs, Allen, b. 1873. The quality of mercy / by Allen Jacobs. Cedar Rapids, Iowa: The Torch Press, 1924. 96 p.

J-28   Jacobs, Leon R. (Leon Ralph), b. 1885. Celibacy: a novel / by Leon R. Jacobs. New York: Broadway Publishing Co., [c1911]. 225 p., col. front., [3] leaves of col. plates.
LC: Jl 26, '11.

J-29   Jacobs, Lois Walker. The brown velvet house / by Lois Walker Jacobs. Chicago: The Bookfellows, 1924. 46 p.   **DLC**

J-30   Jacobs, Thornwell, 1877-1956. The law of the white circle / by Thornwell Jacobs . . . ; with illustrations by Gilbert Gaul. Nashville: Taylor-Trotwood Publishing Co., 1908. 253 p. incl. front., [1] leaf of plates.
LC: N 27, '08.

J-31   ____ Sinful Sadday: son of a cotton mill: a story of a little orphan boy who lived to triumph / by Thornwell Jacobs. Nashville, Tennessee: Smith & Lamar, 1907. 131 p., front., [11] leaves of plates,

ill. [Ill. by Jolley.]
LC: Ag 2, '07.
PW: S 21, '07.

Jacobsen, Norman, jt. aut. *Esmeralda* (1918). See **Putnam, Nina Wilcox, 1888-1962, jt. aut., P-651.**

____, jt. aut. *When the highbrow joined the outfit* (1917). See **Putnam, Nina Wilcox, 1888-1962, jt. aut., P-658.**

J-32   Jacobson, Millie Bock. Martha of India: a missionary story / by Millie Bock Jacobson. Rock Island, Ill.: Augustana Book Concern, [c1924]. 128 p., front., [3] leaves of plates. [Ill. by Jess Betlach.]   **DLC**
LC: O 16, '24.

Jaisohn, Philip, 1866-1951. See **Osia, N. H., pseud.**

J-33   James, Bushrod Washington, 1836-1903. The political freshman / by Bushrod Washington James. Philadelphia: Bushrod Library, 1902. 569 p. Designed end papers.
PW: Ap 19, '02.

James, Henry, 1843-1916. The altar of the dead; The beast in the jungle; The birthplace; and other tales (1909). See **James, Henry, 1843-1916. *The novels and tales of Henry James* (1907-09), J-43.**

J-34   ____ The ambassadors: a novel / by Henry James . . . New York; London: Harper & Brothers Publishers, 1903. 431, [1] p.
"First apppeared in the North American Review from January-December, 1903."
LC: N 6, '03.
PW: N 14, '03.
BLC: London: Methuen & Co., 1903.
References: BAL 10656; Edel & Laurence, A58; Phillips, p. 59.
BAL 10651 notes copyright deposits in nine parts.

____ The author of Beltraffio; The middle years; Greville Fane; and other tales (1909). See **James, Henry. *The novels and tales of Henry James* (1907-09), J-43.**

J-35   ____ The better sort / by Henry James. New York: Charles Scribner's Sons, 1903. 428, [1] p.
Contents: Broken wings -- The Beldonald Holbein -- The two faces -- The tone of time -- The special type -- Mrs. Medwin Flickerbridge -- The story in it -- The beast in the jungle -- The birthplace -- The papers.
LC: F 26, '03.
PW: Mr 7, '03.
BLC: London: Methuen & Co., 1903.
Reference: BAL 10652; Edel & Laurence A57; Phillips, p. 57-59.

J-36   ____ The finer grain / by Henry James. New York: Charles Scribner's Sons, 1910. 312 p.
Contents: The velvet glove -- Mora Montravers -- A round of visits -- Crapy Cornelia -- The bench of desolation.
LC: O 12, '10.
PW: O 15, '10.
BLC: London: Methuen & Co., 1916.
Reference: BAL 10671; Edel & Laurence A68; Phillips, p. 69-70.

J-37   Gabrielle de Bergerac / by Henry James. New York: Boni and Liveright, 1918. 153 p.
LC: Ja 3, '19.
PW: D 7, '18.
Reference: BAL 10701; Edel & Laurence A80; Phillips, p. 78.

J-38   The golden bowl / by Henry James. New York: Charles Scribner's Sons, 1904. 2 v.: 412 p.; 377 p.
LC: N 12, '04.
PW: N 19, '04.
BLC: London: Methuen & Co., 1905.
Reference: BAL 10659; Edel & Laurence A60; Phillips, p. 60.

J-39   The ivory tower / by Henry James. New York: Charles Scribner's Sons, 1917. 357 p.
LC: N 2, '17.
PW: N 3, '17.
BLC: London: W. Collins, Sons & Co., 1917.
Reference: BAL 10697; Edel & Laurence A77; Phillips, p. 75-76.

J-40   Julia Bride / by Henry James; illustrated by W. T. Smedley. New York; London: Harper & Brothers, 1909. 83, [1] p., front., [3] leaves of plates.   BAL notes prior publication in *The novels and tales of Henry James* (BAL 10665).
LC: S 25, '09.
PW: O 9, '09.
Reference: BAL 10780; Edel & Laurence A66; Phillips, p. 66.

J-41   A landscape painter / by Henry James. New York: Scott and Seltzer, 1919. 287 p.
"The four tales comprising this volume are printed now for the first time in America in book form. All of them were written by Henry James before he had attained his twenty-fifth year."
Contents: A landscape painter -- Poor Richard -- A day of days -- A most extraordinary case.
LC: D 22, '19.
PW: Ja 3, '20.
Reference: BAL 10704; Edel & Laurence A83; Phillips, p. 78-79.

     Mary's little lamb. See **Masson, Thomas Lansing, 1866-1934.** *A bachelor's baby: and some grownups* **(1907), M-587.**

J-42   Master Eustace / by Henry James. New York: Thomas Seltzer, 1920. 280 p.
Contents: Master Eustace -- Longstaff's marriage -- Théodolinde -- A light man -- Benvolio.
PW: N 20, '20.
Reference: BAL 10707; Edel & Laurence A85; Phillips, p. 80.

J-43   The novels and tales of Henry James. New York: Charles Scribner's Sons, 1907-09. 24 vols. Unexamined copy: bibliographic data from Edel & Laurence.
Reprints save for:
     Vol. XVI: The author of Beltraffio; The middle years; Greville Fane; and other tales / by Henry James. New York: Charles Scribner's Sons, 1909. 425, [1] p.

Edel & Laurence: "This was its [*Fordham Castle*] first book appearance."
     Vol. XVII: The altar of the dead; The beast in the jungle; The birthplace; and other tales / by Henry James. New York: Charles Scribner's Sons, 1909. 541, [1] p. Edel & Laurence: "*The friends of the friends* previously appeared under the title *The way it came. The jolly corner* and *Julia Bride* made their first book appearances here . . . "
References: Edel & Laurence A64.

J-44   The outcry / by Henry James. New York: Charles Scribner's Sons, 1911. 261 p.
LC: O 14, '11.
PW: O 14, '11.
BLC: London: Methuen & Co., 1911.
Reference: BAL 10674; Edel & Laurence A70; Phillips, p. 70-71.

J-45   The sacred fount / by Henry James. New York: Charles Scribner's Sons, 1901. 319 p.
LC: F 7, '01.
PW: F 16, '01.
BLC: London: Methuen & Co., 1901.
Reference: BAL 10644; Edel & Laurence A55; Phillips, p. 56.

J-46   The sense of the past / by Henry James. New York: Charles Scribner's Sons, 1917. 358 p.
"The second of the two novels which Henry James left unfinished."
LC: O 31, '17.
PW: N 3, '17.
BLC: London: W. Collins, Sons & Co., 1917.
Reference: BAL 10698; Edel & Laurence A78; Phillips, p. 76.

J-47   Travelling companions / by Henry James. New York: Boni and Liveright, 1919. 309 p.
"The seven stories in this volume were written and published . . . between 1868 and 1874 [in various American periodicals; not included in editions of his 'Works']"
Contents: Travelling companions -- The sweetheart of M. Briseux -- Professor Fargo -- At Isella -- Guest's confession -- Adina -- De Grey: a romance.
PW: My 3, '19.
Reference: BAL 10703; Edel & Laurence A82; Phillips, p. 79.

    , contributor. See *The whole family* **(1908), W-578.**

J-48   The wings of the dove / by Henry James. New York: Charles Scribner's Sons, 1902. 2 v.: 329 p.; 439 p.
LC: Ag 22, '02.
PW: S 6, '02.
BLC: Westminster: Archibald, Constable & Co., 1902.
Reference: BAL 10647; Edel & Laurence A56; Phillips, p. 56-57.

J-49   James, Howard. The wraith of Knopf: and other stories / by Howard James. New York: Broadway Publishing Co. . . . , [c1908]. 117 p., photo. front. (port.).

Contents: The wraith of Knopf -- The rehabilitation of Dabney -- The aftermath of battle -- The armistice -- The testimony of the sun -- Under the shadow of the poppy -- The redemption of Riley -- The dragon of Nansoong.
LC: Ag 11, '08.

J-50   James, Martha, b. 1868, *pseud.* Mint Julep / by Martha James [pseud.]; illustrated by Reginald F. Bolles. New York: W. D. Lane & Co., 1909. 345 p., front., [5] leaves of col. plates.
LC: O 18, '09.
PW: D 4, '09.

J-51   Jameson, Almus Day. A flesh and blood man / by Almus Day Jameson. Nashville; Richmond; Dallas; San Francisco: Cokesbury Press, [c1924]. 250 p., front. [Ill. by Charles Durant.]

J-52   Jamieson, Guy Arthur. At the edge of the yellow sky / by Guy Arthur Jamieson. New York: The M. W. Hazen Company, 1905, [c1904]. 125 p. [Ill. by Charles L. Wrenn.]
PW: Mr 18, '05.

J-53   ____ In the shadow of God / by Guy Arthur Jamieson . . . New York: R. F. Fenno & Company, [c1910]. 282 p.
LC: Mr 17, '10.
PW: Mr 26, '10.

Jane, Mary, pseud. <u>See</u> **Stine, Milton Henry, 1853-1940.**

Janes, Henry P., jt. aut. The second coming (1916). **See Kummer, Frederic Arnold, K-414.**

Janis, Elsie, 1889-1956, contributor. <u>See</u> *Bobbed hair* **(1925), B-700.**

J-54   ____ Love letters of an actress / by Janis Elsie. New York; London: D. Appleton and Company, 1913. 97 p. photo. front. (port.), [4] leaves of photo. plates, photo. ill.   **IMF**
LC: My 13, '13.
PW: My 31, '13.

J-55   ____ A star for a night: a story of stage life / by Elsie Janis; with pictures from the play taken especially for the book. New York: William Rickey & Company, 1911. 205 p., photo. front. (port.), [11] leaves of photo. plates.
LC: O 16, '11.
PW: O 28, '11.

Janvier, Margaret Thompson, 1845-1913. <u>See</u> **Vandegrift, Margaret, pseud.**

J-56   Janvier, Thomas Allibone, 1849-1913. At the Casa Napoleon / by Thomas A. Janvier; with portrait and illustrations. New York; London: Harper & Brothers, 1914. 225, [1] p., front. (port.), [8] leaves of plates. [ill. by W. T. Smedley.]
LC: Je 8, '14.
PW: Je 20, '14.
Reference: BAL 10868.

J-57   ____ From the south of France: The roses of Monsieur Alphonse, The poodle of Monsieur

Gáillard, The recrudescence of Madame Vic, Madame Jolicoeur's cat, A consolate giantess / by Thomas A. Janvier; illustrated. New York; London; Harper & Brothers, 1912. 234, [1] p., front., [7] leaves of plates. [Ill. by Elizabeth Shippen Green, James Montgomery Flagg, & Frank Craig.]
LC: My 11, '12.
PW: My 18, '12.
Reference: BAL 10867.

J-58   ____ In great waters: four stories / by Thomas A. Janvier; illustrated. New York; London: Harper & Brothers, 1901. 222, [1] p., front., [7] leaves of plates. [Ill. by Lucius Wolcott Hitchcock.]
Contents: The wraith of the Zuyder Zee -- A Duluth tragedy -- The death-fires of Les Martigues -- A sea upcast.
LC: N 8, '01.
PW: N 16, '01.
References: BAL 10857.

____ The sage-brush hen. <u>In</u> *Under the Sunset* **(1906), U-9.**

J-59   ____ Santa Fé's partner: being some memorials of events in a New-Mexican track-end town / by Thomas A. Janvier. New York; London: Harper & Brothers, 1907. 236, [1] p., front., [7] leaves of plates. [Ill. by Stanley M. Arthurs.]
LC: S 11, '07.
PW: S 21, '07.
Reference: BAL 10864.

J-60   Jarman, L. Gilbert (Lizzie Gilbert). Shadow of absent love / by Mrs. L. Gilbert Jarman . . . Memphis, Tenn.: Southern Publishing Co., 1903. 243 p., photo. front. (port.).
PW: F 20, '04.

J-61   Jarrold, Ernest, 1850-1912. Tales of the Bowery / by Ernest Jarrold; with an introductory poem by Gerald Brenan. New York: J. S. Ogilvie Publishing Company, c1903. 190 p., front. (caricature)
PW: Ap 25, '03.

J-62   Jay, Junius. Open-air politics and the conversion of Governor Soothem / by Junius Jay. Boston; New York: Houghton Mifflin Company, 1914. (Cambridge, Mass., U. S. A.: The Riverside Press). 235 p.
LC: O 26, '14.
PW: O 31, '14.

J-63   Jayhews, Thomas, 1865-1934. His better self: a novel / by Thomas Jayhews. Akron, Ohio: The Saalfield Publishing Company, [c1910]. 508 p.
LC: My 6, '10.
PW: D 10, '10.

J-64   Jemimy, Aunt, b. 1846, *pseud.* Uncle Jim and Aunt Jemimy in southern California / by Aunt Jemimy [pseud.]. Lincoln, Nebr.: The Woodruff Press, 1912. 208 p.
LC: D 23, '12.

J-65   Jenison, Sarah A. David Erenberg, healer / written by Sarah A. Jenison. New York: The Shakespeare Press, 1912. 183 p.   **DLC**

J-66   Jenkens, C. A. (Charles Augustus), 1850-1927. The bride's return, or, How Grand Avenue Church came to Christ: a story with a supreme purpose / by Rev. C. A. Jenkens . . . ; with illustrations by Hazel Robinson. Charlotte, N. C.: Published by C. H. Robinson & Company, [c1911]. 342 p., photo. front. (port.), [3] leaves of plates, ill.
LC: Je 19, '11.
PW: Jl 29, '11.

J-67   _____ Good gumption, or, The story of a wise fool . . . / by C. A. Jenkens . . . ; with illustrations. Nashville, Tenn.: The Southwestern Company, [c1907]. 400 p., incl. photo. front. (port.), ill.
LC: My 6, '07.
PW: Je 22, '07.

J-68   Jenkins, Burris, 1869-1945. The Bracegirdle / by Burris Jenkins; with a frontispiece in color by H. Weston Taylor. Philadelphia; London: J. B. Lippincott Company, 1922. 311 p., col. front.
LC: Mr 23, '22.
PW: Mr 4, '22.

J-69   _____ It happened "over there" / by Burris A. Jenkins . . . ; with illustrations by Burris A. Jenkins, Jr. New York; Chicago; London; Edinburgh: Fleming H. Revell Company, [c1918]. 192 p., front., [1] leaves of plates. **IPU**
LC: D 31, '18.
PW: S 21, '18.

J-70   _____ Princess Salome: a tale of the days of camel-bells / by Burris Jenkins; with a frontispiece by Gayle Hoskins. Philadelphia; London: J. B. Lippincott Company, 1921. 352 p., col. front.
LC: Ap 18, '21.
PW: Mr 5, '21.

Jenkins, Katharine, contributor. See _A double knot_ **(1905), D-499.**

_____ A Nürnberg treasure. In _The Senior lieutenant's wager: and other stories_ **(1905), S-312.**

_____ What influenced Jim. In _The lady of the tower_ **(1909), L-13.**

J-71   Jenkins, Stephen, 1857-1913. A princess and another / by Stephen Jenkins. New York: B. W. Huebsch, 1907. 405 p., front. [Ill. by Gertrude Huebsch.]
LC: N 19, '07.
PW: D 14, '07.

J-72   Jenks, George C. The climax / by George C. Jenks; from the celebrated play of the same name by Edward Locke; illustrated by W. W. Fawcett. New York: The H. K. Fly Company, [c1909]. 334 p., col. front., [3] leaves of col. plates.
LC: N 19, '09.

J-73   _____ The deserters / George C. Jenks & Anna Alice Chapin. New York: The H. K. Fly Company, [c1911]. 313 p., col. front., [3] col. leaves of plates.
LC: D 5, '12.

J-74   _____ Stop thief! / by George C. Jenks and Carlyle Moore. New York: The H. K. Fly Company, [c1913]. 301 p., col. front., [3] leaves of col. plates. [Ill. by Montgomery Flagg and Raymond L. Thayer.]
LC: O 9, '13.

J-75   Jerome, Annabell. Under the spell of the firs / by Annabell Jerome. New York: Broadway Publishing Co., [c1914]. 396 p., [6] leaves of photo. plates. **OSU, DLC**
LC: D 1, '14.

J-76   Jervey, Theodore D. (Theodore Dehon), b. 1859. The elder brother: a novel in which are presented the vital questions now confronting the South growing out of Reconstruction, and in which the author defines the true relations between the races now existing in the South / by Theodore D. Jervey. New York; Washington: The Neale Publishing Company, 1905. 522 p.
PW: Ja 12, '07.

J-77   Jessop, George Henry, d. 1915. Where the shamrock grows: the fortunes and misfortunes of an Irish family / by George H. Jessop . . . New York: The Baker & Taylor Company, [1912]. 212, [1] p.
BLC: London: Murray & Evender, [1911].

Jett, Ann Searcy, b. 1843. See **Se Arcy, Ann, pseud.**

J-78   Jetton, Robert H. Sue Ella: a historical romance: founded on incidents of the war between the states / by Robt. H. Jetton . . . ; illustrated by Thos. B. Woodburn; a Texas novel by a Texas editor. [Oakwood, Tex.: Printed by the author, c1915]. 160 p., photo. front., [14] leaves of plates, photo. ill. **RCE**
LC: S 20, '15.

J-79   Jewell, Edward Alden, 1888-1947. The charmed circle: a comedy / by Edward Alden Jewell. New York: Alfred A. Knopf, 1921. 291 p. **KSU**
LC: O 6, '21.

J-80   _____ The moth decides: a novel / by Edward Alden Jewell. New York: Alfred A. Knopf, 1922. 282 p.
LC: O 11, '22.
PW: O 7, '22.

J-81   _____ The White Kami: a novel / by Edward Alden Jewell. New York: Alfred A. Knopf, 1922. 326 p.
LC: Ap 13, '22.
PW: Ap 15, '22.

J-82   Jewett, Sarah Orne. An empty purse: a Christmas story / by Sarah Orne Jewett. Boston: Privately printed, 1905. 15, [1] p. **VA@** Weber & Weber note "The Merrymount Press, Boston." References: BAL 10919; Weber & Weber, p. 21.

_____ The green bowl. In _A house party_ **(1901), H-903.**

_____ A spring Sunday. In _American short stories_ **(1925), A-201.**

J-83   ____ The Tory lover / by Sarah Orne Jewett. Boston; New York: Houghton, Mifflin and Company, 1901. (Cambridge: The Riverside Press). 405 p., front., [3] leaves of plates. [Ill. by Marcia Oakes Woodbury and Charles H. Woodbury.]
LC: Ag 28, '01.
PW: O 5, '01.
BLC: London: Smith, Elder & Co., 1901.
Reference: BAL 10914; Weber & Weber, p. 21.

J-84   Jewett, Sophie, 1861-1909. Italian sketches / by Sophie Jewett. [Natick, Mass.: The Suburban Press, c1917]. 107 p.
Reprinted from various periodicals.
Contents: The land of Lady Poverty -- The fate of Francesco -- Bettina -- The boys of Italy: introduction to "Cuore" -- The lover of trees in Italy -- The altarpiece -- The eighth of December.

Jitro, William. The resurrection and the life. In *The best short stories of 1922 and the yearbook of the American short story (1923), B-567.*

J-85   Job, Herbert Keightley, 1864-1933. The blue goose chase: a camera-hunting adventure in Louisiana / by Herbert K. Job . . . ; illustrations by the author and William F. Taylor. New York: The Baker & Taylor Company, 1911. 331 p., photo. front., [7] leaves of plates (some photo.).   **RRR**

Jocelyn, Lydia A. See **Smith, Annie L. (Annie Lydia), B. 1836.**

J-86   Johanson, Bror Ulrick. The adventures of Hintala: memories of personal experiences / by Bror Ulrick Johanson. Seattle, Wash.: The Crucible Pub. Co., [c1922]. 129 p., front. [Ill. by Laing.]   **NYP**

J-87   John Van Buren, politician: a novel of to-day. New York; London: Harper & Brothers, 1905. 288, [1] p.
PW: Fe 25, '05.

J-88   Johns, Orrick. Blindfold / by Orrick Johns. New York: Lieber & Lewis, 1923. 259 p.
LC: Jl 16, '23.

Johns, W. D. The burglar's dilemma. In **Seattle Writer's Club.** *Tillicum tales (1907), S-248.*

Johnson, Adrian, jt. aut. *The game of the golden ball* (1910). See **Johnson, Elizabeth, jt. aut., J-99.**

J-89   Johnson, Alvin Saunders, b. 1874. John Stuyvesant Ancestor and other people / by Alvin Johnson. New York: Harcourt, Brace and Howe, 1919. 252 p.
LC: O 8, '19.
PW: N 1, '19.

J-90   ____ The professor and the petticoat / by Alvin Saunders Johnson. New York: Dodd, Mead and Company, 1914. 402 p.   **KRS**
LC: Ap 16, '14.
PW: Ap 11, '14.

J-91   Johnson, Amelia Etta Hall (Mrs. A. E. Johnson), 1858-1922. Martin Meriden: or, what is my motive / by Amelia Johnson. Philadelphia: American Baptist Publication Society, 1901. 176 p., front.   **DLC**
PW: O 5, '01.

Johnson, Anna, b. 1860. See **Daring, Hope, pseud.**

Johnson, Arthur. Mr. Eberdeen's house. In *The best short stories of 1915 and the yearbook of the American short story (1916), B-560.*

J-92   ____ Under the rose / by Arthur Johnson. New York; London: Harper & Brothers, [c1920]. 348, [1] p.
LC: S 11, '20.
PW: O 16, '20.

____ The visit of the master. In *The best short stories of 1918 and the yearbook of the American short story (1919), B-563.*

J-93   Johnson, Ben. Bettina Brown: a little child / by one of her subjects. New York: E. P. Dutton and Co., [c1917]. 104 p.
LC: N 28, '17.
PW: D 8, '17.

J-94   Johnson, Brita Elizabeth. Maher-shalal-hash-baz, or, Rural life in old Virginia / by Brita Elizabeth Johnson. Claremont, Va.: Sigfrid Olson, [c1923]. 328 p.

Johnson, Burgess. In the barn. In *Humorous ghost stories (1921), H-1018.*

J-95   Johnson, D. Powell. The accurséd Roccos: a tale of Dalmatia / by D. Powell Johnson. New York: Broadway Publishing Co., 1913. 455 p., front., [5] leaves of plates.
LC: Ja 30, '13.

J-96   Johnson, Daniel Harris, 1825-1900. The Hazel Green man's story: and other tales / by Daniel Harris Johnson . . . ; with a memoir by Electa Amanda Johnson. Milwaukee: The Young Churchman Co., 1904. 354 p., front. (port.). [Ill. by W. T. Bather.]
Contents: Memoir -- The hazel green man's story -- Our Paris letter -- Mr. Bridges nightmare -- Broke jail -- Muggins' holidays -- Captain Crosier retires from the lakes -- Widow Wortley -- The fat girl's jump -- Rankin brothers.
PW: D 3, '04.

J-97   Johnson, E. A. (Edward Augustus), 1860-1944. Light ahead for the Negro / by E. A. Johnson . . . New York: The Grafton Press, [c1904]. 132 p.
    MIA

J-98   Johnson, E. Joy. The foreman of the JA6: a novel / by E. Joy Johnson. New York: Wyoming Publishing Co., 1911. 282 p., [6] leaves of col. plates.
"Illustrations from original drawings by E. W. Grollings."
LC: O 23, '11.

J-99   Johnson, Elizabeth. The game of the golden ball / by Elizabeth and Adrian Johnson; illustrated by P. D. Johnson. New York: The Macaulay Company, 1910. 351 p., front., [3] leaves of plates.
PW: My 7, '10.

J-100   Johnson, Elizabeth Winthrop. One chance in a hundred: a novel / by Elizabeth Winthrop Johnson . . . Boston [Mass.]: Richard G. Badger, [c1911].

([Boston, Mass.]: The Gorham Press). 312 p.
LC: N 8, '11.
PW: D 2, '11.

J-101   Johnson, Enoch. A captain of industry / by Enoch Johnson. Boston, Massachusetts: The C. M. Clark Publishing Company, 1908. 509 p., front., [7] leaves of plates. [Ill. by John Goss.]
LC: S 9, '08.
PW: O 10, '08.

J-102   Johnson, Fanny Kemble. The beloved son / by Fanny Kemble Johnson; with a frontispiece by George W. Gage. Boston: Small, Maynard & Company, [c1916]. 407 p., front.
LC: O 2, '16.
PW: S 2, '16.

_____ The strange-looking man. In *The best short stories of 1917 and the yearbook of the American short story* (1918), B-562.

J-103   Johnson, Fenton, 1888-1958. Tales of darkest America / by Fenton Johnson. Chicago, Ill.: Published by the Favorite Magazine, [c1920]. 34 p.   **EYM**
Contents: The story of myself [non fiction] -- A very important business man -- A woman of good cheer -- The sorrows of George Morgan -- Trusting providence -- The sorrows of a stenographer -- The carnival.

J-104   Johnson, Franklin Pierce. To him that overcometh / by Rev. Franklin Pierce Johnson . . . Chicago: International Literary Bureau, [c1914]. 199 p., front. (port.).
Unexamined copy: bibliographic data from NUC.

J-105   Johnson, Gladys, 1891-1933. Moon country / by Gladys E. Johnson; illustrated by Charles Hargens, Jr. Philadelphia: The Penn Publishing Company, 1924. 301 p., front.
LC: Ag 11, '24.

J-106   _____ Wind along the waste / by Gladys E. Johnson. New York: The Century Co., 1921. 278 p., front. [Ill. by Robert E. Johnston.]
LC: Mr 23, '21.
PW: Mr 26, '21.

J-107   [Johnson, James Weldon], 1871-1938. The autobiography of an ex-colored man. Boston: Sherman, French & Company, 1912. 207 p.
LC: Je 6, '12.

J-108   Johnson, Laura. The home-coming in the Ozarks / by Laura Johnson. Chicago, Illinois: Glad Tidings Publishing Company, [c1922]. 191 p., front. **NYP**

J-109   Johnson, Owen, 1878-1952. Arrows of the Almighty / by Owen Johnson. New York: The Macmillan Company; London: Macmillan & Co., Ltd., 1901. 405 p.
PW: Ap 20, '01.

J-110   _____ Blue blood: a dramatic interlude / by Owen Johnson. Boston: Little, Brown and Company, 1924. 247 p.
LC: Mr 20, '24.
PW: Mr 15, '24.

J-111   _____ The eternal boy: being the story of the prodigious Hickey / by Owen Johnson. New York: Dodd, Mead & Company, 1909. 335 p., front., [9] leaves of plates, ill. [Ill. by Frederic D. Steele, Henry Raleigh, and May Wilson Preston.]
LC: Ja 21, '09.
PW: F 20, '09.
Also appeared as *The prodigious Hickey: a Lawrenceville story.* New York: The Baker and Taylor Company, 1910.
PW: Ag 13, '10.

J-112   _____ The humming bird / by Owen Johnson; illustrated. New York: The Baker & Taylor Company, 1910. 86 p., front., [2] leaves of plates. [Ill. by Frederic R. Gruger.]
LC: My 23, '10.
PW: Je 4, '10.

J-113   _____ In the name of liberty: a story of the terror / by Owen Johnson . . . New York: The Century Co., 1905. 406 p., front. [Ill. by André Castaigne.]
PW: Ja 21, '05.

J-114   _____ Making money / by Owen Johnson . . . ; with eight illustrations by James Montgomery Flagg. New York: Frederick A. Stokes Company, [c1915]. 327 p., front., [7] leaves of plates.
LC: O 4, '15.
PW: S 25, '15.
BLC: London: Martin Secker, 1916.

J-115   _____ Max Fargus / by Owen Johnson . . . New York: The Baker & Taylor Company, [1906]. 315 p., front., [4] leaves of plates. [Ill. by Fletcher Charles Ransom.]
LC: S 17, '06.
PW: S 22, '06.

J-116   _____ Murder in any degree; One hundred in the dark; A comedy for wives; The lie; Even threes; A man of no imagination; Larry Moore; My wife's wedding presents; The suprises of the lottery / by Owen Johnson; with illustrations by F. R. Gruger and Leon Guipon. New York: The Century Co., 1913. 305 p., front., [7] leaves of plates.
LC: My 23, '10.
PW: Ag 23, '13.

_____ The prodigious Hickey (1910). See **Johnson, Owen, 1878-1952.** *The eternal boy (1909),* **J-111.**

J-117   _____ The salamander / by Owen Johnson; with illustrations by Everett Shinn. Indianapolis: The Bobbs-Merrill Company, [c1914]. 529 p., front., [15] leaves of plates.
LC: My 13, '14.
PW: Ap 11, '14.
BLC: London: Martin Secker, 1915.

J-118   _____ The sixty-first second / by Owen Johnson . . . ; illustrated by A. B. Wenzell. New York: Frederick A. Stokes Company, [1913]. 383 p., double leaf front., [6] leaves of plates (1 double leaf).
LC: Mr 29, '13.
PW: Mr 29, '13.

J-119   ____ Skippy Bedelle: his sentimental progress from the urchin to the complete man of the world / by Owen Johnson; with illustrations by Ernest Fuhr. Boston: Little, Brown and Company, 1922. 316 p., front., [5] leaves of plates.
LC: O 23, '22.
PW: O 7, '22.

J-120   ____ Stover at Yale / by Owen Johnson; with eight illustrations in black-and-white by Frederick [sic] R. Gruger. New York: Frederick A. Stokes Company, [1912]. 386 p., front., [7] leaves of plates.
LC: Ap 6, '12.
PW: Ap 13, '12.

J-121   ____ The Tennessee Shad: chronicling the rise and fall of the firm of Doc Macnooder and the Tennessee Shad / by Owen Johnson. New York: The Baker & Taylor Company, 1911. 307 p., front., [7] leaves of plates. [Ill. by Frederic R. Gruger.] (Lawrenceville stories / Owen Johnson).
LC: My 20, '11.
PW: Je 3, '11.

J-122   ____ Virtuous wives / by Owen Johnson; with illustrations by C. H. Taffs. Boston: Little, Brown and Company, 1918. 352 p., front., [2] leaves of plates.
LC: Ag 17, '18.
PW: Ag 3, '18.
BLC: Toronto: McClelland & Co., [1918].

J-123   ____ The wasted generation / by Owen Johnson. Boston: Little, Brown and Company, 1921. 343 p.
LC: S 29, '21.
PW: S 10, '21.

J-124   ____ The woman gives: a story of regeneration / by Owen Johnson; with illustrations by Howard Chandler Christy. Boston: Little, Brown and Company, 1916. 458 p., front., [5] leaves of plates (2 double leaf).
LC: S 8, '16.
PW: S 23, '16.
BLC: Toronto: McClelland & Co., 1916.

J-125   Johnson, Samuel Paige, b. 1852. Zebadiah Sartwell: the miller of Whallonsburgh / by Dr. S. Paige Johnson; illustrated by William L. Hudson, foreword by Stepen G. Clow. New York: Broadway Publishing Company, 1903. 318 p., front. (port.), [10] leaves of plates.
PW: D 19, '03.

J-126   Johnson, Shirley Everton. The Cult of the Purple Rose: a phase of Harvard life / by Shirley Everton Johnson. Boston: Richard G. Badger, 1902. ([Boston]: The Gorham Press). 170 p.
PW: S 13, '02.

J-127   Johnson, Stanley. Professor / by Stanley Johnson. New York: Harcourt, Brace and Company, [1925]. 312 p.
PW: Mr 28, '25.

J-128   Johnson, Virginia W. (Virginia Wales), 1849-1916. A Bermuda lily / by Virginia W. Johnson . . . New York: The A. S. Barnes Company, 1912. 287 p.
DLC

J-129   ____ A lift on the road / by Virginia W. Johnson . . . New York: The A. S. Barnes Company, 1913. 160 p.
Contents: A lift on the road: an automobile rescue -- The lady from China -- A lost treasure: the servant problem -- Tying a knot: a sea romance -- The Duke's flight: a motor incident -- The luck of Friday.
LC: Mr 20, '13.

J-130   Johnson, William Franklin, b. 1856. Poco a poco: a novel / by William Franklin Johnson; illustrated by W. H. Fry. Akron, Ohio; New York; Chicago: The Saalfield Publishing Co., 1902. 307 p., front., [3] leaves of plates.
PW: Ag 9, '02.

J-131   Johnson, William Henry, 1845-1907. Sir Galahad of New France / by William Henry Johnson. Boston: Herbert B. Turner & Co., 1905. 356 p.
BLC: London: Ward, Lock, & Co., 1905.

J-132   Johnson, William Lyman. From Hawthorne Hall: an historical story, 1885 / by William Lyman Johnson. Dorchester, Boston, Mass.: The Homewood Press, [c1922]. 421 p., photo. front.

J-133   Johnson, William Samuel, b. 1859. Glamourie: a romance of Paris / by William Samuel Johnson. New York; London: Harper & Brothers Publishers, 1911. 294 p.
LC: Mr 18, '11.
PW: Mr 25, '11.

J-134   ____ Nothing else matters: a novel / by William Samuel Johnson . . . New York: Mitchell Kennerley, 1914. 306 p.
LC: Je 18, '14.
PW: Je 27, '14.

J-135   Johnson, Wolcott, 1846-1936, *pseud.* An old man's idyl / by Wolcott Johnson [pseud.]. Chicago: A. C. McClurg & Co., 1905. 264 p.

J-136   Johnston, Annie F. (Annie Fellows), 1863-1931. Asa Holmes, or, At the cross-roads / by Annie Fellows Johnston . . . ; with a frontispiece by Ernest Fosbery. Boston: L. C. Page & Company, 1902. 215 p., front.
PW: My 17, '02.

____ The family skeleton's wedding journey. In *Through the fobidden gates* **(1903), T-222.**

J-137   ____ Georgina's service stars / by Annie Fellows Johnston; illustrations by Thelma Gooch. New York: Britton Publishing Company, [c1918]. 313 p., col. front., [3] leaves of col. plates.
LC: O 8, '20.
PW: S 28, '18.

J-138   ____ The jester's sword: how Aldebaran, the king's son, wore the sheathed sword of conquest / by Annie Fellows Johnston . . . Boston: L. C. Page and Company, 1909. 84 p., front.
Unexamined copy: bibliographic data from OCLC, #602395.

J-139   ____ Miss Santa Claus of the Pullman / by Annie Fellows Johnson [i. e. Johnston]; with illustrations by Reginald B. Birch. New York: The Century Co., 1913. 172 p., col. front., [8] leaves of plates.
LC: O 30, '13.
PW: N 1, '13.

J-140   ____ The three weavers: a fairy tale for fathers and mothers as well as for their daughters / by Annie Fellows Johnston . . . Boston: L. C. Page & Company, 1905. 48 p., front. Illustrated end papers.   **EYM**
PW: S 16, '05.

J-141   ____ Travelers five along life's highway: Jimmy, Gideon Wiggan, the Clown, Wexley Snathers, Bap. Sloan / by Annie Fellows Johnston . . . ; with a foreword by Bliss Carman; frontispiece in full colour from a painting by Edmund H. Garrett. Boston: L. C. Page & Company, 1911. 199 p., col. front.
LC: N 9, '11.
PW: D 2, '11.

Johnston, Calvin. Messengers. In *The best short stories of 1919 and the yearbook of the American short story* **(1920), B-564.**

J-142 Johnston, Elizabeth Bryant, 1833-1907. The days that are no more / by Elizabeth Bryant Johnston; illustrated. New York; London; Montreal: The Abbey Press, [c1901]. 224 p., [10] leaves of plates, (1 photo. port.). [Ill. by C. Adele Fassett; photo. by Frances B. Johnston.]
Contents: A sho' nuf' case ob conjurin' -- Brudder Jim Crapp -- Dat buttahfly's Christmas gif' -- The story of a song -- Sweetlips-a blue grass her-o-wine -- Dat ole piece of chaany -- At de conference -- Plantation romance -- Mr. Ben Gordon.
PW: S 14, '01.

J-143 Johnston, J. Wesley (James Wesley), b. 1850. The house that Jack built / by Wesley Johnston . . . New York: Eaton & Mains; Cincinnati: Jennings & Graham, [c1905]. 253 p.   **IUA**
PW: Ap 8, '05.

J-144   ____ The mystery of Miriam / by J. Wesley Johnston. Boston: Herbert B. Turner & Co., 1904. 459 p.
PW: My 14, '04.
BLC: London: Grant Richards, 1904.

J-145   ____ Philip Yoakley: a story of today / by J. Wesley Johnston. Cincinnati: Jennings & Pye; New York: Eaton & Mains, [c1901]. 245 p.

J-146   ____ The riddle of life: a novel / by J. Wesley Johnston. Cincinnati: Jennings & Pye; New York: Eaton & Mains, [c1902]. 399 p.
PW: F 22, '02.

J-147   ____ A visit to the lie factory / by J. Wesley Johnston. New York, N. Y.: Charles C. Cook, [c1903]. 19 p.   **DLC**
PW: D 5, '03.

J-148 Johnston, James Perry, b. 1852. Told in the smoker / by J. P. Johnston; drawings by Howard Heath. Chicago: Thompson & Thomas, [c1908]. 338 p., ill.

"These stories are based on actual happenings, and give the author's personal experience during 35 years of hustling."
Contents: Visiting a farmer relative in Illinois -- A graduate of Yale College -- The pocket diamond case -- A family reared and educated on proceeds of graft -- The soap part of small consideration -- A Frenchman -- Bandit was run to Earth -- The first move in the game -- Contractor number one -- One of the oldest but most sucessful -- The backer a Chicago man -- No use for regular patrons -- Another envelope propsition -- Very old, but always successful -- A fifty dollar premium given with a five-dollar subscription -- Farmers made sub-agents -- The silent man and his reticent wife -- The laundryman flooded with business -- The "top and bottom" -- "Counterfeit money" shall be read instead of "cigars" -- Chromo gift enterprise -- New brand of wheat known as Canadian Red Line -- Silk hats and Prince Albert suits -- The "settler".

J-149 Johnston, Mary, 1870-1936. Audrey / by Mary Johnston; with illustrations by F. C. Yohn. Boston; New York: Houghton, Mifflin and Company, 1902. (Cambridge: The Riverside Press). 418 p., col. front., [5] leaves of col. plates.
PW: Mr 1, '02.
BLC: London: A. P. Watt & Son, 1901. Another edition with ills.: Westminster: Archibald, Constable and Co., 1902.

J-150   ____ Cease firing / by Mary Johnston; with illustrations by N. C. Wyeth. Boston; New York: Houghton Mifflin Company, 1912. 457, [1] p., col. front., [3] leaves of col. plates. Maps on lining papers.
LC: N 19, '12.
PW: N 16, '12.
BLC: London: Constable & Co., 1912.

J-151   ____ Croatan / by Mary Johnston. Boston: Little, Brown, and Company, 1923. 298 p. Maps on lining papers.
LC: O 29, '23.
PW: O 3, '25.
BLC: London: Thornton Butterworth, 1924.

J-152   ____ Foes: a novel / by Mary Johnston . . . New York; London: Harper & Brothers, [1918]. 358, [1] p.
LC: O 17, '18.
PW: N 9, '18.

J-153   ____ The fortunes of Garin / by Mary Johnston. Boston; New York: Houghton Mifflin Company, 1915. (Cambridge: The Riverside Press). 375, [1] p., col. front. [Ill. by A. I. Keller.]
LC: O 25, '15.
PW: O 23, '15.
BLC: London: Constable & Co., 1915.

J-154   ____ 1492 / by Mary Johnston. Boston: Little, Brown and Company, 1922. 315 p. Maps on lining papers.
PW: N 25, '22.

J-155   ____ Hagar / by Mary Johnston. Boston; New York: Houghton Mifflin Company, 1913. (Cambridge: The Riverside Press). 390 p.
LC: O 29, '13.
PW: N 8, '13.
BLC: London: Constable & Co., 1913.

J-156 _____ Lewis Rand / by Mary Johnston . . . ; with illustrations by F. C. Yohn. Boston; New York: Houghton Mifflin Company, 1908. (Cambridge: The Riverside Press). 510 p., col. front., [3] leaves of col. plates.
LC: Ag 20, '08.
PW: O 3, '08.
BLC: London: Archibald, Constable, & Co., 1908.

J-157 _____ The long roll / by Mary Johnston; with illustrations by N. C. Wyeth. Boston; New York: Houghton Mifflin Company, 1911. (Cambridge: The Riverside Press). 683, [1] p., col. front., [3] leaves of plates.
LC: Je 15, '11.
PW: Ap 29, '11.

J-158 _____ Michael Forth / by Mary Johnston. New York; London: Harper & Brothers, [c1919]. 363, [1] p.
LC: D 11, '19.
PW: D 20, '19.
BLC: London: Constable & Co., 1920.

J-159 _____ Silver cross / by Mary Johnston. Boston: Little, Brown and Company, 1922. 289 p.
LC: Mr 13, '22.
PW: Mr 18, '22.
BLC: London: Thorton Butterworth, 1922.

J-160 _____ Sir Mortimer: a novel / by Mary Johnston . . . New York; London: Harper and Brothers, 1904, [c1903]. 349, [1] p., col. front., [8] leaves of col. plates. [Ill. by F. C. Yohn.]
PW: Mr 26, '04.
BLC: London: Archibald, Constable, & Co., 1904.

J-161 _____ The slave ship / by Mary Johnston. Boston: Little, Brown and Company, 1924. 330 p.
LC: N 10, '24.
PW: N 8, '24.
BLC: London: Thorton Butterworth, 1925.

J-162 _____ Sweet rocket / by Mary Johnston . . . New York; London: Harper & Brothers, [1920]. 194, [1] p.
LC: O 25, '20.
PW: N 20, '20.
BLC: London: Constable & Co., 1920.

J-163 _____ The wanderers / by Mary Johnston. Boston; New York: Houghton Mifflin Company, [1917]. 426 p.
LC: S 18, '17.
PW: S 29, '17.
BLC: London: Constable & Co., 1917.

J-164 _____ The witch / by Mary Johnston. Boston; New York: Houghton Mifflin Company, 1914. (Cambridge [Mass.]: The Riverside Press). 441, [1] p., col. front.   **OSU, KSU**
LC: O 26, '14.
PW: O 31, '14.
BLC: London: Constable & Co., 1914.

J-165 Johnston, Ray R. (Raymond R. Carew). Maude Blackstone: the millionaire's daughter / by Ray R. Johnston. Chicago; New York: The Henneberry Company, [c1901]. 309 p., front., ill.

J-166 Johnston, William, 1871-1929. The apartment next door / by William Johnston; with illustrations by Arthur William Brown. Boston: Little, Brown and Company, 1919. 301 p., front., [3] leaves of plates.
LC: Ja 16, '19.
PW: Ja 11, '19.

J-167 _____ The house of whispers / by William Johnston; with illustrations by Arthur William Brown. Boston: Little, Brown and Company, 1918. 292 p., front., [3] leaves of plates.
LC: Ap 1, '18.
PW: Mr 30, '18.

J-168 _____ The innocent murderers / by William Johnston and Paul West. New York: Duffield and Company, 1910. 344 p., front.
LC: Ap 18, '10.
PW: My 7, '10.

J-169 _____ My own Main Street / by Wm. A. Johnston. Cincinnati: The Standard Publishing Company, [c1921]. 238 p., front., ill.
Includes poems (some adapted) by: James Whitcomb Riley, Will M. Maupin, Edgar A. Guest, G. S. Applegarth, Horace S. Keller, and Eugene Field.
LC: Ja 3, '22.
PW: Ja 21, '22.

J-170 _____ The mystery in the Ritsmore / by William Johnston; with illustrations by Harold James Cue. Boston: Little, Brown and Company, 1920. 293 p., front., [3] leaves of plates.
LC: Je 21, '20.
PW: Je 26, '20.

J-171 _____ The tragedy at the Beach Club / by William Johnston; with frontispiece by Marshall Frantz. Boston: Little, Brown and Company, 1922. 269 p., front.
LC: F 28, '22.
PW: Mr 18, '22.
BLC: London: Jarrolds, 1924.

J-172 _____ The Waddington cipher / by William Johnston. Garden City, N. Y.: Doubleday, Page & Company, 1923. 300 p.
LC: S 25, '23.
BLC: London: Stanley Paul & Co., 1925.

J-173 _____ The yellow letter / by William Johnston; with illustrations by Alexander Popini. Indianapolis: The Bobbs-Merrill Company, [c1911]. 301, [1] p., front., [5] leaves of plates.
LC: O 4, '11.
PW: N 11, '11.
BLC: London: Greening & Co., 1912.

J-174 Johnston, William Hamilton. When dreams came true: and other stories / by William Hamilton Johnston . . . Nashville, Tenn.; Dallas, Tex.: Publishing House of the M. E. Church, South, 1911. 196 p., front. ill., ill. [Ill. by E. M. Gardner.]
Contents: When dreams came true -- A foot race for a baby -- Salt-making time -- Crossing the swollen stream -- The squirrel hunt --

The circuit rider's first circuit -- A flood of buttermilk -- When Billy lost his head -- Piney on a rampage -- Old Shiney, the giant trout -- The beginning of the Big Flat revival -- Bandy's bad break -- The fight at Rainbow Falls -- An effective cure; or, nearly a tragedy -- A terrible accusation -- A strange place for an overcoat -- Brother Bayless's first sermon -- When Uncle Mose was challenged -- How old Ephraim was cured of the fits -- When the elder came to Roaring Oak -- Michael O'Harrity's toothache -- The hero of the wreck -- That treasury job.
PW: F 10, '12.

Jon, Don. See **Cheney, Walter Thomas.**

J-175   Jonas, Edward A. (Edward Asher), b.1865. Number thirty: being some relation of what happened to Chivvy / by Edward A. Jonas. Cincinnati: Stewart & Kidd Company, [1920]. 348 p.
LC: D 4, '20.
PW: D 18, '20.

J-176   Jones, C. (Caleb), b. 1851. Opisthophorus, or, The man who walked backward: a book of modern life / by C. and J. A. Jones. Chicago: W. B. Conkey Company, [c1909]. 199 p., photo. front., [7] leaves of photo. plates, ill. [Ill. by L. E. Brown.]

J-177   Jones, Claude Perry, b. 1870. Banduk jaldi banduk!: (Quick, my rifle) / By Claude P. Jones and A. L. Sykes; illustrations by Eliot Keen. New York: [Press of J. J. Little & Co., 1907]. 307 p., col. front.   **DLC**
LC: O 14, '07 (no publisher noted).
Another edition: . . . frontispiece by Eliot Keen. New York: Cortlandt Publishing Co., 1907. 313 p., col. front.   **OSU**
Reissued 1909, under title: The countersign: a story of Tibet / Claude P. Jones. Boston: Richard G. Badger, 1909. ([Boston]: The Gorham Press). 305 p., front.
LC: N 27, '09.
PW: N 20, '09.

_____ The countersign (1909). See **Jones, Claude Perry, b. 1870.** *Banduk jaldi banduk!* **(1907), J-177.**

J-178   Jones, Edgar De Witt, 1876-1956. Fairhope: the annals of a country church / by Edgar DeWitt Jones; frontispiece by Herbert Deland Williams. New York: The Macmillan Company, 1917. 212 p., [1] leaf of plates.   **OCP**
LC: Je 1, '17.
PW: Je 23, '17.

J-179   Jones, Edward Franc, 1828-1913. Richard Baxter: a story of New England life of 1830 to 1840 / by Edward F. Jones . . . ; illustrated. New York: The Grafton Press, [c1903]. 331 p., photo. front. (port.), [8] leaves of plates, ill., facsim., music.
PW: D 5, '03.

J-180   Jones, Erasmus W., b. 1817. The young captives: a story of Judah and Babylon / by Erasmus W. Jones. Elgin, Illinois: Published by David C. Cook Publishing Company, [c1907]. 94 p. incl. front., ill. [Ill. by Mark Hayne.]

J-181   Jones, Frederick William. A year at Brown / by Frederick William Jones; illustrated by Sydney R.

Burleigh. Providence: Snow & Farnham, 1903. 178 p., front., [4] leaves of plates.
Contents: The first night -- The freshman's first return home -- A rushing meeting -- Brown vs. Yale, a big game -- A gym ball -- "Her Brown salons" -- Class day -- Commencement.

J-182   Jones, Harry Waggenseller. A man in the making / by Harry Waggenseller Jones. Topeka: Crane & Company, 1912. 257, [1] p., front., [7] leaves of plates, ill. [Ill. by Lloyd L. Sargent.]

Jones, Howard Mumford. Mrs. Drainger's veil. In *The best short stories of 1919 and the yearbook of the American short story* **(1920), B-564.**

J-183   Jones, Ira L. The richer-- the poorer / by Ira L. Jones . . . ; illustrated by Th. B. Thompson. Chicago; New York: The Fiction Publishing Company, 1902. 321 p., front., [5] leaves of plates.
PW: F 28, '03.

Jones, J. A. (Julia Anna), b. 1862, jt. aut. *Opisthophorus* (1909). See **Jones, C. (Caleb), b. 1851, J-176.**

J-184   Jones, J. W. (John William), 1860-1930. The education of Robert, a deaf boy / by J. W. Jones . . . Columbus, Ohio: Printed at the State School for the Deaf, 1925. 157 p.

J-185   Jones, Jesse H. (Jesse Henry), 1836-1904. Joshua Davidson, Christian: the story of the life of one who, in the nineteenth century, was "like unto Christ;" as told by his body-servant / a parable by Jesse H. Jones; edited by Halah H. Loud. New York: The Grafton Press, [c1907]. 308 p., photo. front. (port.), [2] leaves of photo. plates (ports.).

J-186   Jones, Joshua Henry. By sanction of law / by Joshua Henry Jones, Jr. Boston: B. J. Brimmer Company, 1924. 366 p.   **CKM**

J-187   Jones, Katharine. The man who reaps: a story / by Katharine Jones. New York: Desmond FitzGerald, Inc., [c1912]. 273 p.
LC: Ja 30, '12.
PW: F 10, '12.

J-188   Jones, Leo Compton. The ruby necklace and other stories / Leo Compton Jones. [Memphis Tenn.?: Leo Compton Jones?, 1922]. 20 p.   **TMN**

J-189   Jones, Lillian B., Mrs. Five generations hence / by Mrs. Lillian B. Jones. Fort Worth, Tex.: Printed by Dotson-Jines Printing Company, 1916. 122 p.
Unexamined copy: bibliographic data from NUC.

J-190   Jones, Mabel Cronise. Achsah, the sister of Jairus / by Mabel Cronise Jones. New York; branch offices, Chicago, Washington, Baltimore, Atlanta, Norfolk, Florence, Ala.: Broadway Publishing Co., [c1911]. 76 p., col. front.   **DLC**
LC: My 27, '11.
PW: My 20, '11.

J-191   _____ In days of old when knights were bold / by Mabel Cronise Jones . . . New York: Broadway Publishing Company, [c1911]. 207 p.

J-192 ____ Rome's fool: and other tales / by Mabel Cronise Jones . . . New York: Broadway Publishing Company, 1914. 185 p.
Contents: Rome's fool -- The Worthington robbery -- When Cupid made laws for Rome -- A question of morals -- His calling -- The Haworth tragedy -- A diplomatic error -- When three hundred maidens swam the Tiber.

Jones, Marc Edmund. See **Reeve, Arthur B. (Arthur Benjamin), 1880-1936.** *The mystery mind* **(1921), R-139.**

J-193 Jones, Mary Tupper. The system's hand / by Mary Tupper Jones. Chicago: Mid-West Publishing & Producing Co., Inc., 1920. 276 p.

J-194 Jones, Morgan D., b. 1862. A nest of vipers / by Morgan D. Jones. N. Y. [i. e. New York]: Broadway Publishing Co., [c1910]. 328 p., incl. photo. front. (port.), [5] leaves of plates. [Ill. by William L. Hudson.]   **RCE**
LC: D 12, '10.
PW: D 31, '10.

J-195 Jones, Morgan P. The chiefs of Cambria: a Welsh tale of the eleventh century / by Morgan P. Jones. New York: The Abbey Press, [1901]. 250 p., photo. front. (port.), [7] leaves of plates (some photo.).
                                                                WEA
PW: My 3, '02.

J-196 Jones, Paul. The lady of the Lotos / written by Paul Jones. Cincinnati: Paul Jones, c1907. a-r [i. e. 18] p.
Unexamined copy: bibliographic data from OCLC, #20320840.
LC: O 16, '07.

Jones, Richard Morgan. See **Brinley, Jay, pseud.**

J-197 Jones, Robert Webster. Light interviews with shades / by Robert Webster Jones. Philadelphia: Dorrance, [c1922]. 151 p.   **OSU, UBY**
Contents: Bluebeard tells why he killed wives -- Queen Elizabeth discloses why she never married -- John Paul Jones and a grogless Navy -- Joshua advises daylight saving -- King Solomon's family vacation trip -- Brigham Young endorses woman suffrage -- Hippocrates on modern doctors -- Methuselah gives longevity secrets -- Jesse James talks on tipping -- Shakespeare mentions movies -- Adam condemns present fashions -- Captain Kidd speaks on tag days

-- Alfred the Great tries to find prosperous king -- Old King Cole gives views on prohibition -- King Henry VIII admits some matrimonial mistakes -- Don Quixote says he "wasn't so crazy as some modern performers" -- Pharaoh solves servant problem -- Nero discusses jazz -- Lord Bacon muses on ciphers.
LC: N 11, '22.
PW: S 23, '22.

J-198 Jones, T. E. (Theodore Elden), 1830-1907. Leaves from an Argonaut's note book: a collection of holiday and other stories illustrative of the brighter side of mining life in pioneer days / by T. E. Jones; illustrations by Laura Adams Armer. San Francisco, Cal.: The Whitaker & Ray Company (Incorporated), 1905. 304 p., front., [6] leaves of plates.
Contents: The milk pan -- The new leaf -- The Thanksgiving dinner -- The reservoirs -- The legend of Humbug Gulch -- The Joes --

Cyrus Billing's dream -- Bill's luck -- The ferry -- Simpson's Thanksgiving -- Stubbs' wooing -- The end of leap year -- Mrs. Crumpey's boarders -- Mr. Snively's vacation -- The story he told the prospectors.

J-199 Jones, V. C. (Victorine Clarisse Jacquet). Lady Moreland's mistake, or, Blood will tell / by V. C. Jones . . . Boston: Jamaica Publishing Co., 1916. 270 p.

Jones, Vara M. The monument. In *As we are* **(1923), A-325.**

J-200 Jones, Yorke, b. 1860. The climbers: a story of sun-kissed sweethearts / by Yorke Jones. Chicago, Ill.: Glad Tidings Publishing Company, [c1912]. 191 p. Unexamined copy: bibliographic data from OCLC, #10890683.

Jones-Bacon, Eugenie. See **Bacon, Eugenie Jones, b. 1840.**

J-201 Jonsson, Ivar, *pseud.* Joessa, or, So spins the flying world away / by Ivar Jonsson [pseud.] . . . New York; London: F. Tennyson Neely Company, 1901. 147 p.
PW: Jl 20, '01.

J-202 Joor, Harriet. A lover of the beautiful; and, The book of his youth / Harriet Joor. Boston: Richard G. Badger, [c1925]. ([Boston]: The Gorham Press). 35 p., ill.   **BGU**
LC: Ja 18, '26.
PW: F 13, '26.

J-203 Jordan, David Starr, 1851-1931. The fate of Iciodorum: being the story of a city made rich by taxation / by David Starr Jordan . . . New York: Henry Holt and Company, 1909. 111 p.
PW: Ap 17, '09.

Jordan, E. A. The chief's counterplot. In **Seattle Writer's Club.** *Tillicum tales* **(1907), S-248.**

Jordan, Elizabeth Garver, 1867-1947. Adeline Thurston, poetess. In *The heart of childhood* **(1906), H-441.**

J-204 ____ The blue circle: a novel / by Elizabeth Jordan . . . New York: The Century Co., 1922. 355 p., front., [3] leaves of plates. [Ill. by George W. Gage.]
LC: Ap 28, '22.
PW: My 6, '22.

____ The comforter. In *A book of short stories* **(1918), B-735.**

J-205 ____ Faith Desmond's last stand: a story of love, courage, and a miracle / by Elizabeth Jordan. Chicago: Extension Press, 1924. 268 p.
LC: N 10, '24.

J-206 ____ The girl in the mirror / by Elizabeth Jordan; illustrated by Paul Meylan. New York: The Century Co., 1919. 297 p., front., [3] leaves of plates.
LC: Ag 19, '19.
PW: Ag 16, '19.

_____ Kittie's sister Josephine. In *Different girls* (1906), D-383.

J-207 _____ The lady of Pentlands / by Elizabeth Jordan. New York; London: The Century Co., [c1924]. 375 p., front. [Ill. by Ralph Nelson.]
LC: Mr 24, '24.
PW: Ap 5, '24.

J-208 _____ Lovers' knots: the whimsical twists and tangles of a dozen youthful love affairs / by Elizabeth Jordan . . . New York; London: Harper & Brothers Publisher, [c1916]. 289, [1] p., front. [Ill. by F. Graham Cootes]. **CLE**
Contents: Man proposes -- The young man in Peacock alley -- A game of tag -- Mr. Brinkley to the rescue -- The far-away road -- Her man Friday -- Philip's "furnis man" -- A readjustment -- The girl who loved Herbert -- To meet Miss Pomeroy -- Bill Bates, preferred -- Thirty-three cents, plus -- An interlude -- Mr. Waldo amuses the baby.
LC: O 17, '16.
PW: O 21, '16.

J-209 _____ Many kingdoms / by Elizabeth Jordan . . . New York; London: Harper & Brothers, 1908. 311, [1] p., front. [Ill. by Dalton Stevens.]
Contents: Varick's lady o' dreams -- The exorcism of Lily Bell -- Her last day -- The simple life of Genevieve Maud -- His boy -- The community's sunbeam -- In memory of Hannah's laugh -- The quest of Aunt Nancy -- The Henry Smith's honeymoon -- The case of Katrina -- Bart Harrington, genius.
LC: O 22, '08.
PW: N 7, '08.

J-210 _____ May Iverson-- her book / by Elizabeth Jordan . . . ; illustrated. New York; London: Harper & Brothers, 1904. 281, [1] p., front., [7] leaves of plates. [Ill. by Charlotte Harding.]
Contents: The ordeal of Maude Joyce -- The redemption of Mabel Muriel -- Kittie's sister Josephine -- Love, the destroyer -- Sister Estelle to the rescue -- Adeline Thurston, poetess -- First aid to Kittie James -- The voice of truth -- The play's the thing -- What dreams may come.
PW: O 29, '04.

J-211 _____ May Iverson tackles life / by Elizabeth Jordan . . . ; illustrated. New York; London: Harper & Brothers, 1912. 245, [1] p., front., [7] leaves of plates. [Ill. by Charlotte Harding Brown.]
Contents: Foreword -- Woman suffrage at St. Catharine's -- I write a play -- The reduction cure for Kittie James -- When churchyards yawn -- I introduce beauty culture -- Mabel Blossom's pearl pin -- The call of spring -- I introduce motion study -- Our Grouchometer club -- The shadow of the angel.
PW: N 7, '14.

J-212 _____ May Iverson's career / by Elizabeth Jordan. New York; London: Harper & Brothers, 1914. 277, [1] p., front. [Ill. by James M. Flagg.]
LC: O 29, '14.
PW: N 7, '14.

J-213 _____ Red Riding Hood: a novel / by Elizabeth Jordan. New York; London: The Century Co., [c1925]. 356 p.
LC: Mr 19, '25.
PW: Mr 21, '25.
BLC: London: Hodder & Stoughton, [1926].

_____, ed. <u>See</u> *The sturdy oak* **(1917), S-1100.**

J-214 _____ Tales of destiny / by Elizabeth G. Jordan.

New York; London: Harper & Brothers, 1902. 292 p., front, [5] leaves of plates. [Ill. by Hermann Heyer.]
Contents: The voice in the world of pain -- An episode at Mrs. Kirkpatrick's -- The wife of a hero -- Victoria Delsaro, missing -- The one who intervened -- Her friend -- Miss Underhill's lesson -- The story of a failure -- In the case of Dora Risser -- A collaboration.
PW: Je 28, '02.

J-215 _____ Tales of the cloister / by Elizabeth G. Jordan . . . ; illustrated. New York; London: Harper & Brothers, 1901. 252, [1] p., photo. front. (port.), [12] leaves of plates. [Ill. by Bayard Jones and Arthur I. Keller.] Decorated end papers. (Harper's portrait collection of short stories; 4.)
Contents: From out of the old life -- The surrender of Sister Philomene -- As told by May Iverson -- Her audience of two -- The girl who was -- Belonging to the third order -- Under the black pall -- Between darkness and dawn -- The ordeal of Sister Cuthbert -- Saint Ernesta and the Imp.
PW: Ag 31, '01.

_____, contributor. <u>See</u> *The whole family* **(1908), W-578.**

J-216 _____ The wings of youth: a novel / by Elizabeth Jordan . . . New York; London: Harper & Brothers, [1918]. 319, [1] p., front. [Ill. by Paul Meylan.]
LC: Mr 21, '18.
PW: Mr 23, '18.

J-217 Jordan, Kate. Against the winds / by Kate Jordan; illustrated by Clark Fay. Boston: Little, Brown and Company, 1919. 348 p., front., [3] leaves of plates.
LC: My 6, '19.
PW: Ap 19, '19.
BLC: London: Hutchinson & Co., 1919.

J-218 _____ The creeping tides: a romance of an old neighborhood / by Kate Jordan . . . ; with frontispiece by Lucius Wolcott Hitchcock. Boston: Little, Brown and Company, 1913. 354 p., front.
LC: My 26, '13.
PW: My 10, '13.
BLC: London: S. Paul & Co., [1915].

J-219 _____ The next corner / by Kate Jordan; with a frontispiece by Wilson V. Chambers. Boston: Little, Brown and Company, 1921. 350 p., front.
LC: Ja 14, '21.
PW: D 25, '20.
BLC: London: Eveleigh Nash Co., 1921.

J-220 _____ Time the comedian / by Kate Jordan. New York: D. Appleton and Company, 1905. 333 p. **IUA**
PW: S 30, '05.

J-221 _____ Trouble-the-house / by Kate Jordan. Boston: Little, Brown and Company, 1921. 306 p.
LC: N 14, '21.
PW: S 19, '21.
BLC: London: Methuan & Co., 1922.

Jordan, Margaret E. In after years. In *The Senior lieutenant's wager: and other stories* **(1905), S-312.**

J-222 Jordan, Margaret Olive. God's smiles and a look into His face / by Maggie Olive Jordan. New York;

London: F. Tennyson Neely Co., [c1901]. 218 p.,
front. (port.).   **VA@**
PW: O 5, '01.

J-223   Jordan, Modeste Hannis. Sidney: a love story of the
         old South / by Modeste Hannis Jordan; frontispiece
         by Hermann Heyer. New York: The Cosmopolitan
         Press, 1912. 123 p., col. front.
         LC: Mr 20, '12.
         PW: My 11, '12.

J-224   ____ The studio baby: and some other children / by
         Modeste Hannis Jordan. New York: The
         Cosmopolitan Press, 1912. 171 p., col. front., ill.
         [Ill. by Hermann Heyer.]
         Contents: The studio baby -- The property baby -- The reformation
         of Valentine -- The mother o'dreams -- Lindy's Sam -- His righteous
         indignation -- The disciplinarians -- Constance.
         LC: Mr 20, '12.
         PW: Mr 2, '12.

J-225   Jordan, Moses. The meat man: a romance of life, of
         love, of labor / by Moses Jordan; illustrated with
         scenes from Wm. S. Scott Studio. Chicago: Judy
         Publishing Company, [c1923]. 96 p., front.   **DLC**
         LC: Ja 7, '24.
         PW: Ja 26, '24.

         Jordan, Virgil. Vengeance is mine. In *The best
         short stories of 1915 and the yearbook of the
         American short story* (1916), B-560.

         Jordan-Smith, Paul. See **Smith, Paul Jordan.**

J-226   Josaphare, Lionel, b. 1876. The man who wanted a
         bungalow; being the veracious account of an author
         who went back to nature to get inspiration and reduce
         expenses / by Lionel Josaphare. San Francisco:
         Press of W. S. Van Cott, [c1907]. 93 p.   **CUY**

J-227   ____ A tale of a town: or, the progress of the trust /
         by Lionel Josaphare. San Francisco: A. M.
         Robertson, [c1903]. 33 p.
         Unexamined copy: bibliographic data from OCLC,
         #15051362.
         PW: Ap 11, '03.

         Josenhans, Emma Parsons. Gulls. In **Seattle
         Writer's Club.** *Tillicum tales* (1907), **S-248.**

         Josiah, pseud. See **Emerson, W. H. (William H.),
         b. 1833.**

         Josiah Allen's Wife, pseud. See **Holley, Marietta,
         1844-1926.**

J-228   A Journal to Rosalind . . . New York: B. W.
         Huebsch, Inc., 1920. 157 p.   **NYP**
         LC: Mr 19, '21.
         PW: Mr 12, '21.

J-229   The joy in work: ten short stories of today / selected
         and edited by Mary A. Laselle . . . New York:
         Henry Holt and Company, 1920. 180 p.   **ORU**
         Contents: A fisherman of Costla / James B. Connolly -- France's
         fighting woman doctor / Dorothy Canfield -- The work of a ranchman
         / Hermann Hagedorn -- The Zadoc Pine labor union / H. C. Bunner

-- The thought and the stone / Mary E. Waller -- The rules of the
game / Stewart Edward White -- The last threshing in the Coulee /
Hamlin Garland -- Dr. Grenfell's parish / Norman Duncan -- The
making of a basket / Kate T. Fogarty -- From the depths of things /
Lawrence Perry.
         LC: N 11, '20.
         PW: Ap 16, '21.

J-230   Judson, Jeanne, b. 1890. Beckoning roads / by
         Jeanne Judson; illustrations by Grant T. Reynard.
         New York: Dodd, Mead and Company, 1919.
         259 p., front., [3] leaves of plates.
         "Copyright, 1918 . . . as *The call of life*."
         LC: F 26, '19.
         PW: Mr 15, '19.

J-231   ____ The stars incline / by Jeanne Judson. New
         York: Dodd, Mead and Company, 1920. 286 p.
         LC: F 10, '20.
         PW: F 14, '20.

J-232   Judson, Katharine Berry. When the forests are ablaze
         / by Katharine B. Judson . . . ; illustrated from
         photographs. Chicago: A. C. McClurg & Co., 1912.
         380 p., col. photo. front., [5] leaves of plates (some
         photo.).
         LC: S 16, '12.
         PW: O 5, '12.

J-233   Julier, Arthur H. G., *pseud.* The man with the face /
         by Arthur H. G. Julier [pseud.] . . . Boston,
         Massachusetts: The Stratford Co., Publishers, 1923.
         200 p., front., [1] leaf of plates. [Ill. by L. Rabin.]
                                                       GZM

J-234   Juneau, May, b. 1866, *pseud.* "Sylph": a nation's
         honor in a woman's hands: the romance and intrigue
         of a great political ring / by May Juneau [pseud.].
         Chicago, Ill.: W. R. Vansant, [c1911]. 214 p., col.
         front., [4] leaves of plates.   **DLC**
         PW: D 16, '11.

J-235   Jurgenson, G. Martin (Gerhard Martin), b. 1865.
         The little sufferers: a story of the abuses of
         children's societies / by G. Martin Jurgenson . . .
         New York: Broadway Publishing Co., [c1911].
         227 p.   **MNL**
         LC: O 21, '11.
         PW: Ja 20, '12.

         Justis Henry G. D., pseud. See **Donnelly, H.
         Grattan (Henry Grattan), 1850-1931.**

                               K

K-1   Kafka, Frederick P. Rummyniscences / by Frederick
         P. Kafka; with illustrations by Walt Lantz. Boston:
         The Cornhill Publishing Co., [c1921]. 174 p.
         LC: D 29, '21.

K-2   Kahler, Hugh MacNair, b. 1883. Babel / by Hugh
         MacNair Kahler. New York; London: G. P.
         Putnam's Sons, 1921. ([New York]: The
         Knickerbocker Press). 366 p.
         LC: Mr 11, '21.
         PW: F 19, '21.

K-3   ____ The east wind: and other stories / by Hugh MacNair Kahler . . . New York; London: G. P. Putnam's Sons, 1923. ([New York]: The Knickerbocker Press). 304 p.

Contents: The east wind -- The failure -- Like a tree -- In a hundred years -- Davy Corbutt's brother -- The torch.

LC: Ja 30, '23.
PW: Ja 27, '23.

K-4   ____ MacIvor's folly / by Hugh MacNair Kahler and Donald Grant Herring. New York; London: D. Appleton and Company, 1925. 286, [1] p.
LC: F 24, '25.
PW: Mr 14, '25.

    ____, jt. aut. *The six best cellars* (1919). See **Hall, Holworthy, 1887-1936, jt. aut., H-76.**

K-5   Kain, Kress, *pseud.* One heart that never ached / by Kress Kain [pseud.]. Boston: The Roxburgh Publishing Company, Inc., [c1911]. 234 p.
Unexamined copy: bibliographic data from OCLC, #27451050.

K-6   Kalfus, Anna. The honor of Breath Feather / by Anna Kalfus; illustrations by May Lessey. Berkeley, California: I. J. de Jarnette, [c1914]. 48 p., front., [3] leaves of plates.
LC: Mr 25, '14.

K-7   [Kalisch, Burnham], 1867-1942. Odd types: a character comedy / by B. K.; frontispiece and cover by Wm. L. Hudson. New York: Broadway Publishing Company, [c1906]. 443 p., front.

K-8   Kane, E. C. S., Mrs. A woman's protest / by Mrs. E. C. S. Kane. New York; London; Montreal: The Abbey Press, [c1901]. 213 p.   **DLC**

K-9   Kaneko, Josephine Conger. A little sister of the poor / by Josephine Conger Kaneko. Girard, Kansas: The Progressive Woman Publishing Co., 1909. 103 p.
    CSF

    Kaplan, De Witte, jt. aut. *Mothers of men* (1919). See **Warner, William Henry, jt. aut., W-147.**

K-10   Karger, Maxwell. Wilson or the kaiser?: a novel of to-day / after the story by Maxwell Karger. [New York: Terver Brothers Stationery Company], c1918. 43 p.   **DLC**
On cover: novelized by Janet Priest.
LC: N 29, '18.

    "Karl," pseud. See **Bloomingdale, Charles, Jr., 1868-1942.**

K-11   Karn, Oma, b. 1869. Milly and Mei Kwei: servants of the master / by Oma Karn. Elgin, Ill.: Brethren Publishing House, 1913. 95 p.
LC: Mr 17, '13.

K-12   Karr, Louise, b. 1857. Trouble: a pet dog / Louise Karr. New York; Bar Harbor: Himebaugh & Browne, [c1917]. 59 p.   **NYP**
PW: D 1, '17.

K-13   Katharine, *pseud.* Letters from an Oregon ranch / by "Katharine" [pseud.] . . . ; with twelve full-page illustrations from photographs. Chicago: A. C. McClurg & Co., 1905. 212 p., photo. front., [11] leaves of photo. plates.   Reissued in 1916 as *From an Oregon Ranch*, no photographic plates, but decorations by J. Allen St. John.   **ORE**

K-14   Kauffman, Reginald Wright, 1877-1959. The azure rose: a novel / by Reginald Wright Kauffman. New York: The Macaulay Company, 1919. 317 p., front.
LC: Ap 10, '19.
PW: Ap 12, '19.
BLC: London: T. Werner Laurie, [1918].

K-15   ____ The chasm: a novel / by Reginald Wright Kauffman . . . and Edward Childs Carpenter. New York: D. Appleton and Company, 1903. 302 p.
PW: N 7, '03.

K-16   ____ The free lovers: a novel of to-day / by Reginald Wright Kauffman. New York: The Macaulay Company, [c1925]. 241 p.
LC: Jl 22, '25.
PW: F 27, '26.
BLC: London: T. Werner Laurie, [1925].

    ____ His immortality. In *Forum stories* (1914), **F-306.**

K-17   ____ The house of bondage / by Reginald Wright Kauffman . . . New York: Moffat, Yard and Company, 1910. 466 p.
LC: S 1, '10.
PW: S 3, '10.

K-18   ____ Jarvis of Harvard / by Reginald Wright Kauffman; illustrated by Robert Edwards. Boston: L. C. Page & Company, 1901. 403 p., front., [5] leaves of plates.
PW: O 12, '01.

K-19   ____ Jim / by Reginald Wright Kauffman. New York: Moffat, Yard and Company, 1915. 413 p.
LC: My 14, '15.
PW: My 15, '15.

K-20   ____ The mark of the beast: a novel / by Reginald Wright Kauffman . . . New York: The Macaulay Company, 1916. 320 p., front., [4] leaves of plates. [Ill. by Albert Matzke.]
LC: S 20, '16.
PW: S 16, '16.
BLC: London: A. M. Gardner & Co., [1919].

K-21   ____ Miss Frances Baird, detective: a passage from her memoirs / as narrated to and now set down by Reginald Wright Kauffman . . . ; with a frontispiece in colour by William Kirkpatrick. Boston: L. C. Page & Company, 1906. 269 p., col. front.
LC: Je 20, '06.
PW: Je 30, '06.

K-22   ____ Money to burn: an adventure story / by Reginald Wright Kauffman. New York City: Chelsea House, [c1924]. 316 p.
LC: Je 3, '24.

PW: Je 28, '24.
BLC: London: Hurst & Blackett, [1927].

K-23   ____ My heart and Stephanie: a novel / by Reginald Wright Kauffman; with two portraits in colour from paintings by A. G. Learned. Boston: L. C. Page & Company, 1910. 233 p., col. front.
LC: Mr 19, '10.
PW: Mr 26, '10.
BLC: London: Sir Isaac Pitman & Sons; Boston, U. S. A. printed, 1910.

K-24   ____ Running sands / by Reginald Wright Kauffman. New York: Dodd, Mead and Company, 1913. 353 p.
LC: Mr 18, '13.
PW: Mr 22, '13.
BLC: London: B. F. Stevens & Brown, 1913.
Another edition: London: Eveleigh Nash, 1913.

K-25   ____ The sentence of silence / by Reginald Wright Kauffman. New York: Moffat, Yard and Company, 1912. 411 p.
LC: Ap 5, '12.
PW: Ap 13, '12.
BLC: London: Howard Latimer, 1913.

K-26   ____ Share and share alike: an adventure story / by Reginald Wright Kauffman. New York City: Chelsea House, [c1925]. 307 p.
PW: My 2, '25.
BLC: London: Hurst & Blackett, [1926].

K-27   ____ The spider's web / by Reginald Wright Kauffman; illustrated by Jean Paleologue. New York: Moffat, Yard and Company, 1913. 409 p., front., [2] leaves of plates.
LC: N 10, '13.
PW: N 29, '13.

K-28   ____ The things that are Caesar's: a novel / by Reginald Wright Kauffman . . . New York: D. Appleton and Company, 1902. 336 p.
PW: S 20, '02.

K-29   ____ Victorious: a novel / by Reginald Wright Kauffman. Indianapolis: The Bobbs-Merrill Company, [c1919]. 407 p.
LC: Ap 25, '19.
PW: Ap 26, '19.

K-30   Kaufman, Herbert, 1878-1947. The stolen throne / by Herbert Kaufman & May Isabel Fisk; illustrated by Howard Chandler Christy & Herman Rountree. New York: Moffat, Yard & Company, 1907. 303 p., col. front., [5] leaves of plates.
LC: Ap 4, '07.

K-31   Kaufman, Jessie. A jewel of the seas / by Jessie Kaufman; with illustrations in color by Gayle Porter Hoskins. Philadelphia; London: J. B. Lippincott Company, 1912. 327 p., col. front., [2] leaves of col. plates.
LC: O 9, '12.

Kaup, Elizabeth Bartol (Dewing), b. 1885. See Dewing, E. B.

Kavanagh, Herminie Templeton. See Templeton, Herminie.

Kay-Scott, C. See Scott, C. Kay.

K-32   Kayamar, *pseud.* Cornelia: a novel / by Kayamar [pseud.]. Sioux Falls, S. D.: Published by Sessions Printing Co., [c1918]. 411 p.
LC: O 2, '18.

K-33   Kaye, Joseph. "The plot concerns--": the stories of twelve famous contemporary plays told in a new way / by Joseph Kaye & Burr Cook; illustrated. New York; London: G. P. Putnam's Sons, 1925. ([New York]: The Knickerbocker Press). 309 p., front., [11] leaves of plates.
Contents: Conscience -- White cargo -- The show-off -- Dancing mothers -- Is zat so? -- Tarnish -- Expressing Willie -- Spring cleaning -- Mrs. Partridge presents -- Minnick -- The miracle -- In his arms.
LC: O 31, '25.

K-34   Kayme, Sargent. Anting-anting stories: and other strange tales of the Filipinos / by Sargent Kayme. Boston: Small, Maynard & Company, 1901. 235 p.
Contents: The anting-anting of Captain Von Tollig -- The cave in the side of Coron -- The conjure man of Siargao -- Mrs. Hannah Smith, nurse -- The fifteenth wife -- "Our lady of Pilar" -- A question of time -- The spirit of Mount Apo -- With what measure ye mete -- Told at the club -- Pearls of Sulu.

K-35   Kayser, Martha. The aerial flight to the realm of peace / by Martha Kayser . . . St. Louis, Mo.: Lincoln Press and Publishing Co., c1922. 54 p.
                                                            SMI

K-36   Kealing, Ethel Black. Desra of the Egyptians: a romance of earlier centuries / by Ethel Black Kealing. Indianapolis: Printed by Wheeler & Kalb, [c1910]. 212 p., front. (port.).   DLC
LC: Mr 1, '11.

K-37   ____ A princess of the Orient / by Ethel Black Kealing. [Boston]: The Christopher Press, [c1918]. 316 p., front. (port.).
LC: D 1, '18.

K-38   Kearney, Belle, 1863-1939. Conqueror or conquered, or, The sex challenge answered . . . / by Belle Kearney . . . Cincinnati, Ohio: The S. A. Mullikin Company, [c1921]. 576 p., front., [11] leaves of plates.   MMM
(The personal help library; v. 1.)
Title continues: A revelation of scientific facts from highest medical authorities, based upon the relations of sex life to the mental, moral and physical welfare of both sexes--young and old: a dramatic story of real life written in fascinating and entertaining style . . . : together with scientific instruction . . .
LC: Mr 18, '21.

Keating, Anne, Mrs. See Tequay, Anne, pseud.

K-39   Keating, Micheline. Fame / by Micheline Keating. New York; London: G. P. Putnam's Sons, 1925. ([New York]: The Knickerbocker Press). 252 p.
LC: My 22, '25.
PW: Jl 25, '25.

Keator, Edgar Matthew. The strike at La Place's. In *Clever business sketches* (1909), C-490.

K-40 Keays, H. A. Mitchell (Hersilia A. Mitchell), 1861-1910. He that eateth bread with me / by H. A. Mitchell Keays. New York: McClure, Phillips & Co., 1904. 351 p.
PW: Ap 2, '04.
BLC: London: McClure, Phillips & Co.; printed in U. S. A., 1904. Another edition: London: Methuen & Co., 1905.

K-41 ____ I and my true love / by H. A. Mitchell Keays; illustrated by Lester Ralph. Boston: Small, Maynard and Company, 1908. 353 p., col. front., [2] leaves of col. plates.
LC: O 6, '08.
PW: O 17, '08.

K-42 ____ The marriage portion: a novel / by H. A. Mitchell Keays. Boston: Small, Maynard & Company, [c1911]. 423, [1] p.
LC: O 27, '11.
PW: O 14, '11.
BLC: London: Grant Richards; U. S. A. printed, [1912].

K-43 ____ Mrs. Brand: a novel / by H. A. Mitchell Keays. Boston: Small, Maynard & Company, [c1913]. 375 p.
LC: Ja 2, '14.
PW: Mr 14, '14.

K-44 ____ The road to Damascus: a novel / H. A. Mitchell Keays. Boston: Small, Maynard, 1907. 447 p.
LC: O 2, '07.
PW: D 28, '07.
BLC: London: Grant Richards; Cambridge, Mass. printed, 1912.

K-45 ____ The work of our hands / by H. A. Mitchell Keays . . . New York: McClure, Phillips & Co., 1905. 319 p.
PW: O 14, '05.
BLC: London: McClure, Phillips & Co., New York [printed], 1905.

K-46 Keene, Roswell W. The blue diamond / by Roswell W. Keene. New York; London; Montreal: The Abbey Press, [c1902]. 477 p.
PW: Jl 5, '02.

Keene, Roxroy, jt. aut. *The enchanted sea-gull* (1917). See **Bartnett, Harriet, jt. aut., B-315.**

K-47 Keesing, Eldee, b. 1865. Before the war, or, The return of Hugh Crawford / by Eldee Keesing; illustrated by Robert J. Davison. Seattle, Wash.: Published by the author, 1915. 297 p., front., [2] leaves of plates.
Verso of t. p.: Press of Curtis-Johnson Printing Co., Chicago, Ill.
Cover title: *The return of Hugh Crawford.*
LC: Ap 7, '15.

K-48 ____ Gorham's gold / Eldee Keesing. Boston:

Richard G. Badger; Toronto: The Copp Clark Company, [c1915]. 357 p. **DLC**
LC: D 1, '15.

K-49 Keighton, R. E. (Robert Elwood), b. 1896. Along the Great South road: a Christmas story / by R. E. Keighton. [Philadelphia: Wetherill Printing Company, c1922]. [24] p. **DLC**

K-50 Keith, Katherine. The girl / by Katherine Keith. New York: Henry Holt and Company, 1917. 251 p.
LC: Ja 27, '17.

Keizer, Genet. See **Abbath, pseud.**

K-51 Kelland, Clarence Budington, 1881-1964. Conflict / by Clarence Budington Kelland. New York; London: Harper & Brothers, [c1922]. 330 p.
LC: Mr 21, '22.
PW: Ap 1, '22.

K-52 ____ Contraband / by Clarence Budington Kelland . . . --1st ed.-- New York; London: Harper & Brothers, [c1923]. 301, [1] p.
LC: Mr 1, '23.
PW: Mr 17, '23.

K-53 ____ Efficiency Edgar / by Clarence Budington Kelland . . . New York; London: Harper & Brothers, [1920]. 93, [1] p., col. front.
LC: Ap 30, '20.
PW: My 8, '20.

K-54 ____ The hidden spring: a novel / by Clarence B. Kelland; illustrated. New York; London: Harper & Brothers, [1916]. 295, [1] p., front., [3] leaves of plates. [Ill. by Gayle Hoskins.]
PW: Ap 15, '16.

K-55 ____ The highflyers / by Clarence Budington Kelland . . . New York; London: Harper & Brothers, [c1919]. 360, [1] p., col. front. [Ill. by Robert W. Amick.]
LC: Mr 8, '19.
PW: Mr 8, '19.

K-56 ____ Into his own: the story of an airedale / by Clarence B. Kelland . . . Philadelphia: David McKay, [c1915]. 46 p., front., [1] leaf of plates. **MUS**
LC: My 6, '15.
PW: Je 19, '15.

K-57 ____ The little moment of happiness / by Clarence Budington Kelland . . . New York; London: Harper & Brothers, 1919. 400 p., front. **AZU**
LC: S 9, '19.
PW: S 20, '19.

____ The mental hazard. In *Marriage* (1923), **M-457.**

K-58 ____ Miracle / by Clarence Budington Kelland. New York: Harper & Brothers, 1925. 295 p.
LC: F 4, '25.
PW: Ja 31, '25.
BLC: London: Hodder & Stoughton, [1925].

K-59 ____ Scattergood Baines / by Clarence Budington Kelland . . . New York; London: Harper & Brothers, [c1921]. 301 p., front.
LC: Mr 5, '21.
PW: Mr 12, '21.

K-60 ____ The source: a novel / by Clarence Budington Kelland . . . New York; London: Harper & Brothers, 1918. 311, [1] p., col. front.
LC: Mr 9, '18.
PW: Mr 23, '18.

K-61 ____ The steadfast heart / by Clarence Budington Kelland. New York; London: Harper & Brothers, [c1924]. 358, [1] p.
LC: Ja 19, '24.
PW: Ja 26, '24.

K-62 ____ Sudden Jim: a novel / by Clarence Budington Kelland. New York; London: Harper & Brothers, [1917, c1916]. 285 p., front.
LC: F 26, '17.
PW: Mr 3, '17.

K-63 ____ Thirty pieces of silver / by Clarence B. Kelland; illustrated. New York; London: Harper & Brothers, 1913. 31, [1] p., front., [2] leaves of plates.
LC: S 13, '13.
PW: O 4, '13.

K-64 ____ Youth challenges / by Clarence Budington Kelland . . . New York; London: Harper & Brothers, [c1920]. 345 p.
"This book appeared serially under the title of *The conflict*."
LC: O 20, '20.
PW: N 18, '22.

K-65 Keller, F. Engle. The inner life / by F. Engle Keller . . . Lancaster, Pa.: Commercial Printing House, 1914. 140 p.

K-66 [Kelley, Andrew Francis], b. 1876. The development of Dan / written by the Good wife's husband. [Cleveland: Printed by the J. B. Savage Co., c1915.] 66 p.   **CLE**
LC: Je 19, '15.

K-67 Kelley, Edith Summers. Weeds / by Edith Summers Kelley. New York: Harcourt, Brace and Company, [c1923]. 333 p.
LC: S 18, '23.
PW: O 6, '23.
BLC: London: Jonathan Cape; printed in U. S. A., 1924.

Kelley, Ellsworth. The little boy and his pa. <u>In</u> **Youth (1901), Y-51.**

K-68 Kelley, Ethel May, b. 1878. Beauty and Mary Blair: a novel / by Ethel M. Kelley. Boston; New York: Houghton Mifflin Company, 1921. (Cambridge: The Riverside Press). 282 p.
LC: Ap 4, '21.
PW: Mr 19, '21.
BLC: London: Duckworth & Co., 1921.

K-69 ____ Heart's blood / by Ethel M. Kelley. New York: Alfred A. Knopf, 1923. 205 p. Designed end papers.
LC: Ag 21, '23.
PW: S 1, '23.
BLC: London: Jarrold's, 1924.

K-70 ____ Outside Inn / by Ethel M. Kelley; with a frontispiece by W. B. King. Indianapolis: The Bobbs-Merrill Company, [c1920]. 310 p., front.
LC: My 1, '20.
PW: Ap 24, '20.

K-71 ____ Over here: the story of a war bride / by Ethel M. Kelley; frontispiece by Charles Dana Gibson. Indianapolis: The Bobbs-Merrill Company, [c1918]. 259 p., front.
LC: Ap 5, '18.
PW: Ap 20, '18.

K-72 ____ Turn about Eleanor / by Ethel M. Kelley; illustrated by F. Graham Cootes. Indianapolis: The Bobbs-Merrill Company, [c1917]. 310, [1] p., front., [3] leaves of plates.
LC: S 14, '17.
PW: S 29, '17.

K-73 ____ Wings / Ethel M. Kelley. New York: Alfred A. Knopf, 1924. 214 p. Designed end papers.
PW: S 6, '24.
BLC: London: Jarrold's, 1925.

K-74 [Kelley, Francis Clement, Bp.], 1870-1948. Charred Wood / by Myles Muredach [pseud.]; illustrated by J. Clinton Shepherd. Chicago: The Reilly & Britton Co., [c1917]. 316 p., front., [3] leaves of plates.
LC: N 19, '17.

K-75 ____ The city and the world: and other stories / by Francis Clement Kelley . . . Chicago: Extension Magazine, 1913. 155 p., front., [7] leaves of plates. [Ill. by Putnam Hall.] Reprinted in part from The Extension magazine.
Contents: The city and the world -- The flaming cross -- The Vicar-General -- The resurrection of Alta -- The man with a dead soul -- The autobiography of a dollar -- Le Braillard de la Magdeleine -- The legend of Deschamps -- The thousand dollar note -- The occasion -- The Yankee tramp -- How father Tom Connolly began to be a saint -- The unbroken seal -- Mac of the island.
LC: S 18, '13.

K-76 Kellock, Harold, b. 1879. "Mr. Hobby": a cheerful romance / by Harold Kellock; with illustrations by George C. Harper. New York: The Century Co., 1913. 334 p., front., ill.
LC: Ap 23, '13.
PW: Ap 19, '13.
References: BAL 13854.

K-77 Kellogg, Eugenia. The awakening of Poccalito: a tale of Telegraph Hill, and other tales / Eugenia Kellogg. San Francisco: The Unknown Publisher, 1903. 130 p., front. (port.).
Contents: The awakening of Poccalito -- A Mexican holiday -- Chief Skowl's revenge -- A heroine of diplomacy -- A sleuth of stowaways -- The story of a curse.

Kellogg, Grace. <u>See</u> **Griffith, Grace Kellogg.**

K-78　Kellogg, Jonathan, b. 1840. Beneath the stone: an historical romance / by Jonathan Kellogg. New York: The Neale Publishing Company, 1918. 176 p., photo. front (port.).
LC: My 14, '18.

K-79　Kelly, Allen. Bears I have met - and others / Allen Kelly; illustrations by Ernest Thomas Seton, W. H. Loomis, Homer Davenport, Walt McDougall, Charles Nelan, W. Hofacker, Will. Chapin and The Author. Philadelphia: Drexel Biddle, Publisher, 1903. 209 p., photo. front. (port.), [14] leaves of plates.　　　　　　　　　　　　　　　　　**CUY**
PW: S 5, '03.

Kelly, Denis E. Boschovich's stratagem. In *The Tragedy that wins and other short stories* (1905), **T-343**.

＿＿＿＿ A close shave. In *The Tragedy that wins and other short stories* (1905), **T-343**.

＿＿＿＿ The dead Indian. In *The Tragedy that wins and other short stories* (1905), **T-343**.

＿＿＿＿ "Teddy". In *The Tragedy that wins and other short stories* (1905), **T-343**.

Kelly, Eleanor Mercein. See **Mercein, Eleanor.**

K-80　Kelly, Florence Finch, 1858-1939. The Delafield affair / by Florence Finch Kelly; with four illustrations in color by Maynard Dixon. Chicago: A. C. McClurg & Co., 1909. 422 p., col. front., [3] leaves of col. plates.
LC: Mr 8, '09.
PW: Mr 13, '09.

K-81　＿＿＿＿ The Dixons: a story of American life through three generations / by Florence Finch Kelly . . . New York: E. P. Dutton & Company, [c1921]. 330 p.
LC: Ap 6, '21.
PW: Ap 16, '21.

K-82　＿＿＿＿ Emerson's wife: and other western stories / by Florence Finch Kelly . . . ; with illustrations in color by Stanley L. Wood. Chicago: A. C. McClurg & Co., 1911. 334 p., col. front., [3] leaves of col. plates.
Contents: Emerson's wife -- Colonel Kate's protégée -- The kid of Apache Teju -- A blaze on Pard Huff -- How Colonel Kate won her spurs -- Hollyhocks -- The rise, fall and redemption of Johnson Sides -- A piece of wreckage -- The story of a Chinese Kid -- Out of sympathy -- An old Roman of Mariposa -- Out of the mouth of babes -- Posey -- A case of the inner imperative.
LC: S 18, '11.
PW: S 23, '11.

K-83　＿＿＿＿ The fate of Felix Brand / by Florence Finch Kelly; illustrated by Edwin John Prittie. Philadelphia: The John C. Winston Company, [c1913]. 352 p., col. front., [3] leaves of plates.
LC: S 25, '13.
PW: O 4, '13.

K-84　＿＿＿＿ Rhoda of the Underground / by Florence Finch Kelly; with illustrations by The Kinneys. New York: Sturgis & Walton Company, 1909. 376 p., front., [3] leaves of plates.
LC: N 22, '09.
PW: D 4, '09.
BLC: London: Gay & Hancock, 1910.

K-85　Kelly, James Paul. Prince Izon: a romance of the Grand Canyon / by James Paul Kelly; five illustrations in color by Harold H. and Edwin Betts. Chicago: A. C. McClurg & Co., 1910. 398 p., col. front., [4] leaves of col. plates. Illustrated (map) end papers.
LC: Mr 28, '10.

K-86　Kelly, M. Agnes. His rebel sweetheart / by M. Agnes Kelly. New York; London; Montreal: The Abbey Press, [c1902]. 161 p., front.
PW: N 15, '02.

K-87　Kelly, Myra, 1876-1910. The golden season / by Myra Kelly; illustrated by R. M. Crosby, H. Heyer and W. Morgan. New York: Doubleday, Page & Company, 1909. 251 p., front., [7] leaves of plates.
LC: S 11, '09.
PW: Ja 22, '10.

K-88　＿＿＿＿ Her little young ladyship / by Myra Kelly. New York: Charles Scribner's Sons, 1911. 348 p., front. (port.).
LC: S 5, '11.
PW: Ag 26, '11.
BLC: London: Chapman & Hall, 1911.

K-89　＿＿＿＿ The isle of dreams / Myra Kelly. New York: D. Appleton & Co., 1907. 215 p.
LC: Ap 5, '07.
PW: Ap 6, '07.

K-90　＿＿＿＿ Little aliens / by Myra Kelly; illustrated. New York: Charles Scribner's Sons, 1910. 291 p., front., [7] leaves of plates. [Ill. by Frederic Dorr Steele, F. R. Gruger, and May Wilson Preston.]
Contents: "Every goose a swan" -- "Games in gardens" -- "A brand from the burning" -- Friends -- The magic cape -- "Bailey's babies" -- "The origin of species" -- The etiquette of Yetta -- A bent twig.
LC: Ap 13, '10.
PW: Ap 16, '10.
BLC: London: Longmans & Co.; New York printed, 1910.

K-91　＿＿＿＿ Little citizens: the humours of school life / by Myra Kelly; illustrated by W. D. Stevens. New York: McClure, Phillips & Co., 1904. 352, [1] p., front., [16] leaves of plates.
Contents: A little matter of real estate -- The uses of adversity -- A Christmas present for a lady -- Love among the blackboards -- Morris and the Honourable Tim -- When a man's widowed -- H. R. H., the prince of Hester Street -- The land of heart's desire -- A passport to paradise -- The touch of nature.
PW: O 29, '04.
BLC: London: Hodder & Stoughton; New York [printed], 1905.

K-92　＿＿＿＿ New faces / by Myra Kelly; illustrations by Charles F. Neagle. New York: G. W. Dillingham Company, [c1910]. 278 p., front., [5] leaves of plates.
Contents: The play's the thing -- There's danger in numbers -- Misery loves company -- The Christmas guest -- Who is Sylvia? -- The spirit of Cecelia Anne -- Theodora, gift of God -- Great oaks from little acorns.

LC: Ag 17, '10.
PW: Ag 20, '10.

K-93   _____ Rosnah / by Myra Kelly . . . ; illustrated by
Wallace Morgan. New York: D. Appleton and
Company, 1908. 398 p., front., [11] leaves of
plates.   **EMU**
LC: N 12, '08.
PW: N 21, '08.

K-94   _____ Wards of liberty / by Myra Kelly; illustrations
by Frederic Dorr Steele. New York: The McClure
Company, 1907. 310 p., front., ill.
Contents: Foreword -- In loco parentis -- A soul above buttons -- The
slaughter of the innocents -- A perjured Santa Claus -- Little Bo-peep
-- The wiles of the wooer -- The gifts of the philosophers -- Star of
Bethlehem.
LC: O 28, '07.
PW: N 2, '07.

K-95   Kelly, T. Howard (Thomas Howard), b. 1895. What
outfit Buddy? / By T. Howard Kelly . . . ; illustrated.
New York; London: Harper & Brothers, [1920].
211, [1] p., front., [4] leaves of plates.   **EYM**
LC: F 24, '20.

K-96   Kelly, Thomas, b. 1863. The Big Tree treaty, or,
The last council on the Genesee / by Thomas Kelly
. . . Geneseo, N. Y.: Published at Mt. Pleasant
Farm, 1916. 407 p.   **MHS**
LC: Je 5, '16.
"A sequel to General Sullivan's great war trail; or,
Heroes and heroines of 1779."

K-97   _____ 1779, General Sullivan's great war trail, or,
Heroes and heroines of 1779 / by Thomas Kelly . . .
Geneseo, N. Y.: Published at Mt. Pleasant Farm,
1913. 382 p.   **YPM**
LC: Mr 15, '13.

K-98   Kelly, Wayne Scott. Lariats and chevrons, or,
Corporal Jack, U. S. V. A., R. R. / by "Six Shot
Shortie" (Wayne Scott Kelly). Guthrie: The State
Capital Company, 1905. 620 p., photo. front. (port.).
[Photo by Vreeland Studio, Alva, Oklahoma.]

K-99   [Kelsey, Jeannette G. Washburn (Jeanette Garr
Washburn)], b. 1850. Clouded Amber / by Patience
Warren [pseud.]. Boston: Richard G. Badger;
Toronto: The Copp Clark Co., Limited, [c1915].
364 p.

K-100   [_____] A diverted inheritance. [Philadelphia]:
Printed for private circulation, 1904. 135 p., col.
front., [3] leaves of plates, map, genealogical table.

K-101   _____ Weathering the storm / by Jeannette G.
Washburn Kelsey (Patience Warren). [Philadelphia]:
[s. n.], 1920. 220 p.
LC: My 1, '20.

K-102   Kelton, Aryan. Dagmar / by Aryan Kelton. San
Francisco; Sacramento; Los Angeles: H. S. Crocker
Co., Inc., [1924]. 228 p., front.

K-103   Kelty, Richard Albert, b. 1878. Quaker Jim /
Richard A. Kelty. New York: Broadway Publishing
Company, [c1909]. 228 p.

Unexamined copy: bibliographic data from OCLC,
#12497511.
LC: O 20, '09.

Kemp, Leonora (Valdez). <u>See</u> **Davis, Mary L. K.,
pseud.**

K-104   Kemp, Matthew Stanley, b. 1874. Ande Trembath:
a tale of Old Cornwall England / by Matt. Stan.
Kemp. Boston: C. M. Clark Publishing Co., 1905.
383 p., col. front., [9] leaves of plates. [Ill. by C. H.
Reichert and Griswold Tyng.]
PW: S 2, '05.

K-105   _____ Boss Tom: the annals of an anthracite mining
village / by Matt. Stan. Kemp; illustrated by A. B.
Shute. Akron, Oh.; New York; Chicago: The
Saalfield Publishing Company, 1904. 412 p., front.,
[3] leaves of plates.
PW: N 5, '04.

K-106   Kemp, Randall H. (Randall Harold), b. 1852. A
half-breed dance, and other far western stories:
mining camp, Indian and Hudson's Bay tales based on
the experiences of the author / by Randall H. Kemp.
Spokane, Wash.: Inland Printing Company, c1909.
135 p., ill. [Ill. by Rache, H. Hodge, and F. B.
Cassid.]
Contents: A half-breed dance -- An original bear story -- Made an
odd clean-up -- Wanted, a partner -- Wealth in a glacier --
Underneath Spokane -- The enchanted valley -- Found and lost a
fortune -- A pot of gold -- Hee-hee stone -- He would take a check --
The barrel was not empty -- Was mistaken for Depew -- The prince
would not know him.
LC: My 10, '09.

Kemper, S. H. Woman's sphere. In *Atlantic
narratives*; **2nd series (1918), A-361.**

K-107   Kempshall, Julia Willis. Out of the ruts: a story for
girls and their elders / by Julia Willis Kempshall . . .
New York, N. Y.: Broadway Publishing Co.,
[c1912]. 173 p.
LC: My 24, '12.

K-108   Kempster, Aquila, b. 1864. The mark / by Aquila
Kempster; illustrated. New York: Doubleday, Page
and Co., 1903. 374 p., col. front., [3] leaves of col.
plates.
PW: N 14, '03.
BLC: London: Hutchinson & Co., 1904.

K-109   _____ Salvage / by Aquila Kempster. New York: D.
Appleton and Company, 1906. 353 p., front., [3]
leaves of plates. [Ill. by H. C. Edwards.]
LC: N 2, '06.

K-110   _____ The way of the gods / by Aquila Kempster.
New York: Quail & Warner, 1901. 264, [1] p.
                                            FQG
PW: Ag 3, '01.

K-111   Kencarden, Stuart. A mother of unborn generations:
a novel / by Stuart Kencarden. New York:
Broadway Publishing Company, [c1912]. 214 p.
                                            DLC
LC: My 29, '12.
PW: D 14, '12.

K-112 Kendall, Ezra, 1861-1910. Top Soil: rich in wit and humor relating the happenings to one "Sandy Loam" / by Ezra Kendall . . . ; illustrated. Cleveland, Ohio: The J. B. Savage Company: The Cleveland News Co., 1909. 192 p., ill. [Ill. by the Mugler Engraving Co.]
LC: Je 3, '09.

K-113 ____ The vinegar buyer: sharp sayings of sharp people / by Ezra Kendall; founded on James Whitcomb Riley's poem "Jap Miller"; illustrated. Cleveland, Ohio: The J. B. Savage Company: The Cleveland News Company, publishers' agents, 1909. 188 p.
At head of title: A sweet story full of fun.
LC: N 1, '09.

Kendall, Jane Anne Torrey, b. 1868. See Torrey, Jane Anne.

K-114 Kendrick, Élsie. The rip tide: and other stories / by Elsie Kendrick. Boston, Massachusetts: The Stratford Company, 1925. 201 p.   DLC
Contents: The rip tide -- On the stairs -- The transcendent marriage -- Married -- Sallie Sharpe -- Release -- March winds -- The Blairs -- The Ave Maria -- At sea -- Millinery -- An ultimatum -- Phantoms -- Stone walls.
LC: Ag 1, '25.
PW: Ag 22, '25.

K-115 Kennard, Joseph Spencer, 1859-1944. Memmo / by Joseph Spencer Kennard. New York: George H. Doran Company, [c1920]. 269 p.
LC: N 5, '20.
PW: N 13, '20.

K-116 Kennedy, Daniel Edwards. Philip the forester: a romance of the Valley of Gardens / by Daniel Edwards Kennedy . . . Brookline, Mass.: The Queen's Shop, 1909, [c1908]. 330, [2] p.
LC: My 18, '09.

K-117 Kennedy, Henry Clinton, b. 1871. A damphool in the Kentucky legislature / by H. C. Kennedy . . . Chicago: W. B. Conkey Company, [1909]. 190 p., incl. [6] plates.
Unexamined copy: bibliographic data from OCLC, #13421602.

Kennedy, Hugh. Delbart: timber cruiser. In *Saturday Evening Post* (1919), S-90.

K-118 Kennedy, Kathleen, *pseud.* Jack Eliot's senior year: a college romance / by Kathleen Kennedy [pseud.], illustrated by Bertha Davidson Hoxie. Boston: Printed for the author by the Rockwell and Churchill Press, [c1913]. 47 p., front., plates.
Unexamined copy: bibliographic data from OCLC, #18234093.

K-119 Kennedy, R. Emmet (Robert Emmet), 1877-1941. Black cameos / by R. Emmet Kennedy; decorations by Edward Larocque Tinker. New York: Albert & Charles Boni, 1924. 210 p., ill., music. Illustrated end papers.
LC: Ja 10, '24.

K-120 Kennedy, Sara Beaumont, d. 1921. Cicely: a tale of the Georgia march / by Sara Beaumont Kennedy; frontispiece by John Edwin Jackson. Garden City, N. Y.: Doubleday, Page & Company, 1911. 375 p., front.
LC: O 19, '11.
PW: O 7, '11.
BLC: London: Hodder & Stoughton; Garden City, N. Y., printed 1911.

K-121 ____ Joscelyn Cheshire: a story of revolutionary days in the Carolinas / by Sara Beaumont Kennedy. New York: Doubleday, Page & Co., 1901. 338 p., front., [7] leaves of plates. [Ill. by H. C. Edwards.]
PW: Je 1, '01.
BLC: London: Gay & Bird, 1901.

K-122 ____ The wooing of Judith / by Sara Beaumont Kennedy. New York: Doubleday, Page & Company, 1902. 399 p.
PW: O 4, '02.
BLC: London: Doubleday, Page & Co., 1902. Another edition: London: Hodder & Stoughton, 1903.

K-123 Kennedy, Sidney R. (Sidney Robinson), b. 1875. The lodestar / by Sidney R. Kennedy. New York: The Macmillan Company; London: Macmillan & Co., Ltd., 1905. 335 p., front., [5] leaves of plates. [Ill. by The Kinneys.]
PW: Mr 25, '05.

K-124 ____ White ashes / by Kennedy-Noble. New York: The Macmillan Company, 1912. 470 p.
LC: Ap 4, '12.
PW: My 4, '12.

K-125 Kennedy, William Antony. The invader's son / by William Antony Kennedy. New York: George Sully and Company, [c1919]. 387 p.
LC: Ag 23, '19.
PW: N 1, '19.
BLC: London: Stanley Paul & Co., [1923].

K-126 ____ The master of Bonne Terre / William Antony Kennedy. New York: Robert J. Shores, 1917. 587 p., ill.
LC: Je 5, '17.

K-127 Kennedy, Wm. G. (William G.). True love wins, or 'Midst war's alarms: a tale of love and war / by Wm. G. Kennedy. New York; London: F. Tennyson Neely Co., [c1901]. 259 p.   DLC
PW: O 5, '01.

Kennedy-Noble. See Kennedy, Sidney Robinson.

K-128 Kenner, Martha Ellis. Delphine, the little shrimp girl: a story intensified by fate's miraculous doings / by Martha Ellis Kenner. New Orleans, La.: Martha Ellis Kenner, [c1923]. 42 p., incl. col. front., ill. (some col.).   LHA
Note on t. p.: By permission of the author. A tribute to the beautiful women of the Southland by The gifted writer Charles Edgar De Anguérre will be found herein. Every daughter of the sunny South will read and treasure highly.

K-129 Kennerly, S. J. (Samuel Jackson), b. 1849. The story of Sam Tag: age from ten to fifteen: from 1860 to 1865 / by S. J. Kennerly. New York: The Cosmopolitan Press, 1911. 184 p. **RCE**
LC: D 18, '11.

K-130 Kennon, J. L. The planet Mars and its inhabitants: a psychic revelation . . . / by Iros Urides, (a Martian); written down and edited by J. L. Kennon. [S. l.: s. n.], [c1922]. 112 p., photo. front., map.
Title continues: Being a comprehensive outline of the planet's physical features, which includes its geographic, topographic and meteorologic aspects; a history of its people and the plan of their utopian, industrial and economic system; of their knowledge concerning our theories of relativity, constitution of matter, interatomic and cosmic energy, electricity, hyperspace, neutralization of gravity; including a history of the spiritual progress of the people of Mars and Christ's visit to their planet ten thousand years ago.

K-131 Kensington, Cathmer. Glenwood / by Cathmer Kensington. New York; London; Montreal: The Abbey Press, [c1901]. 393 p. **NYP**
PW: Ap 26, '02.

K-132 Kent, Elizabeth, 1875-1947. The house opposite: a mystery / by Elizabeth Kent. New York; London: G. P. Putnam's Sons, [c1902]. ([New York]: The Knickerbocker Press). 276 p. **ICY**
PW: S 20, '02.

K-133 ____ Who? / by Elizabeth Kent . . . New York; London: G. P. Putnam's Sons, 1912. ([New York]: The Knickerbocker Press). 360 p., col. front. [Ill. by John Cassel.]
LC: O 4, '12.

K-134 Kent, Oliver. Her heart's gift / by Oliver Kent . . . ; illustrations by Paul Stahr. New York: G. W. Dillingham Company, [c1913]. 334 p., front., [2] leaves of plates.
LC: Ag 30, '13.
PW: S 6, '13.

K-135 ____ Her right divine / by Oliver Kent; illustrations by Paul Stahr. New York: G. W. Dillingham Company, [c1913]. 340 p., front., [2] leaves of plates. **NYP**
LC: F 28, '13.
PW: Mr 1, '13.

K-136 Kenton, Edna, 1876-1954. Clem / by Edna Kenton. New York: The Century Co., 1907. 275 p., front. [Ill. by Charlotte Harding.]
LC: Ag 13, '07.
PW: Ag 24, '07.

K-137 ____ What manner of man / by Edna Kenton. Indianapolis: The Bowen-Merrill Company, [1903]. 291, [1] p.
PW: Mr 14, '03.

K-138 Kenyon, Camilla. Fortune at Bandy's Flat / by Camilla Kenyon . . . Indianapolis: The Bobbs-Merrill Company Publishers, [c1921]. 344 p.

LC: O 13, '21.
BLC: London: Hodder & Stoughton; printed in U. S. A., [1921].

K-139 ____ Spanish doubloons / by Camilla Kenyon; illustrated by Louis Rogers. Indianapolis: The Bobbs-Merrill Company, [c1919]. 311 p., front., [5] leaves of plates.
LC: O 10, '19.

K-140 Kenyon, James B. (James Benjamin), 1858-1924. Retribution: a tale of the Canadian border / [by] James B. Kenyon. Cincinnati: Jennings and Pye; New York: Eaton and Mains, [c1903]. 181 p.
PW: S 19, '03.

K-141 Kenyon, Orr, 1849-1928. Amor victor: a novel of Ephesus and Rome, 95-105 A. D. / by Orr Kenyon; illustrated. New York: Frederick A. Stokes Company, [1902]. 424 p., front., [11] leaves of plates. [Some ills. by W. B. Gilbert.]
PW: Je 7, '02.

K-142 ____ Caleb Koons: a'postle of common sense / by Russell Kelso Carter, M. D. (Orr Kenyon) . . . Boston, Massachusetts: The C. M. Clark Publishing Company, [c1910]. 440 p., col. front., [5] leaves of plates. [Some ills. by D. S. Ross.]
LC: F 11, '11.

K-143 ____ What God hath (not) joined / by Orr Kenyon . . . New York: Dodge Publishing Co., 1905. 377 p., col. front., [5] leaves of col. plates. [Ill. by Bernhard Gutmann.] **AZU**

K-144 Keon, Grace, b. 1873, *pseud.* Broken paths / by Grace Keon [pseud.]; illustrations by Frank H. (sic) Spradling. Chicago: Extension Press, 1923. 288 p., front., [7] leaves of plates.
LC: S 4, '23.
PW: O 6, '23.

____, contributor. See *A double knot* (1905), **D-499.**

____ How Dan went home. In *The Senior lieutenant's wager: and other stories* (1905), **S-312.**

K-145 ____ Just Happy: the story of a dog--and some humans / by Grace Keon [pseud.]. New York: The Devin-Adair Company, [c1920]. 267 p.
LC: Mr 24, '20.
PW: Ap 10, '20.

K-146 ____ "Not a judgement-" / by Grace Keon [pseud.] . . . New York; Cincinnati; Chicago: Benziger Brothers, [c1906]. 318 p. **BRL**
PW: Ap 28, '06.

K-147 [____] The ruby cross: a novel / by Mary Wallace. New York; Cincinnati; Chicago: Benziger Brothers, [c1917]. 303 p., front., [2] leaves of plates. [Ill. by Victor Pérard.]
LC: N 5, '17.

K-148 ____ The ruler of the kingdom: and other phases of life and character / by Grace Keon [pseud.]. New York; Cincinnati; Chicago: Benziger Brothers, 1904.

270 p. **HCD**
Contents: The ruler of the kingdom -- The greatest gift -- My Lady Hope -- The quest of Father Maurice -- The last of the Raeburns -- The distance between -- In the Love Country -- One man and a letter -- The angel of old memories -- Laelia -- By a baby's grace -- At the back of godspeed -- A lord of creation-and the lady -- With my own people: a sketch.
PW: D 3, '04.

K-149 ____ "When love is strong" / by Grace Keon [pseud.] . . . New York; Cincinnati; Chicago: Benziger Brothers, 1907. 241 p.
LC: Ap 29, '07.
PW: Je 1, '07.

K-150 Kepley, Ada H. (Ada Harriet), b. 1847. A farm philosopher: a love story / by Ada H. Kepley. Teutopolis, Ill.: Worman's Printery, [c1912]. 410 p., ill. (incl. ports.).
LC: Je 20, '12.

K-151 Kerfoot, Esidore. The Vatican, or The heir of Limerick / by Esidore Kerfoot. Chicago: [s. n.], 1904. 146 p., front. **DLC**

Kernodle, Louise Wellons Nurney, b. 1866. See **Eldonrek, Louise, pseud.**

K-152 Kerr, Alvah Milton, 1858-1924. The diamond key and how the railway heroes won it / by Alvah Milton Kerr; illustrated by F. B. Masters, Power O'Malley, Emlen McConnell, Jay Hambidge, and William J. Glackens. Boston: Lothrop, Lee & Shepard Co., [1907]. 376 p., front., [7] leaves of plates. [Also ill. by J. J. Gould.]
Partly republished from various periodicals.
Contents: Opening the throttle -- How Dreamy Meadows won -- Freckle Hogan's grit -- Destiny and a small boy -- The crêpe de chine torch -- The joining of the bonnets -- The mountain's voice -- The capture of Beaumont -- Saving the long house -- The president's son -- Dippy Hamilton's magic.
LC: F 23, '07.

K-153 Kerr, R. B. Up-to-date fables / by R. B. Kerr. New York: Published by Edwin C. Walker, 1905. 32 p.

K-154 Kerr, Sophie, 1880-1965. The blue envelope: a novel / by Sophie Kerr . . . ; frontispiece by Frances Rogers. Garden City, New York: Doubleday, Page & Company, 1917. 304 p., col. front.
LC: F 23, '17.
PW: F 24, '17.

____, contributor. See *Bobbed hair* (1925), **B-700.**

K-155 ____ The Golden block / by Sophie Kerr; frontispiece by Fanny Munsell. Garden City, N. Y.: Doubleday, Page & Company, 1918. 323, [1] p., front.
LC: Mr 2, '18.
PW: F 16, '18.

K-156 ____ Love at large: being the amusing chronicles of Julietta Carson / by Sophie Kerr; illustrated. New York; London: Harper & Brothers, [1916], [c1915]. 266, [1] p., front., [3] leaves of plates. [Ill. by Lucius Wolcott Hitchcock.]
"The first eight stories in this book were originally published in McClure's Magazine, and *Lonny puts one over* under the title *Kidnapped*, in Collier's Weekly."

Contents: Green-eyes -- The old-fashioned wife -- The poor working-girl -- Julietta-tired-of-her-husband -- Eggs chipolata -- Assisting George -- The gayest woman in Marchmont -- Julietta eats the canary -- Lonny puts one over.
PW: Ap 1, '16.

K-157 ____ One thing is certain: a novel / by Sophie Kerr. New York: George H. Doran Company, [c1922]. 336 p.
LC: O 6, '22.
PW: S 16, '22.

K-158 ____ Painted meadows / by Sophie Kerr . . . New York: George H. Doran Company, [c1920]. 320 p. **EYM**
LC: My 3, '20.
PW: My 8, '20.
BLC: London: Hodder & Stoughton; printed in U. S. A., [1920].

K-159 ____ The see-saw: a story of to-day / by Sophie Kerr; frontispiece. Garden City, New York: Doubleday, Page & Company, 1919. 360 p., col. front. **BGU**
LC: Mr 24, '19.
PW: Mr 22, '19.

____ Wild earth. In *Prize stories of 1921* (1922), **P-619.**

K-160 Kester, Paul, 1870-1933. His own country / by Paul Kester. Indianapolis: The Bobbs-Merrill Company, [c1917]. 692 p.
LC: Jl 9, '17.
PW: Je 30, '17.

K-161 Kester, Vaughan, 1869-1911. The fortunes of the Landrays / by Vaughan Kester; illustrated by the Kinneys. New York: McClure Phillips & Co., 1905. 481 p., front., [4] leaves of plates.
PW: O 14, '05.
BLC: London: McClure Phillips & Co.; New York [printed], 1905.

K-162 ____ The hand of the mighty: and other stories / by Vaughan Kester; with portrait, and a sketch of the author by Paul Kester. Indianapolis: The Bobbs-Merrill Company, [c1913]. 412 p., front. (port.). Reprinted in part from various periodicals.
Contents: The hand of the mighty -- The bad men of Las Vegas -- Mollie darling -- The blood of his ancestors -- When we have waited -- The deserter -- What Rearton saw -- How Mr. Rathburn was brought in -- Miss Caxton's father -- The half-breed -- Willie -- Mr. Feeney's social experiment -- All that a man hath.
LC: S 25, '13.
PW: N 1, '13.

K-163 ____ John o' Jamestown / by Vaughan Kester. New York: The McClure Company, 1907. 297 p.
LC: O 28, '07.
PW: N 2, '07.

K-164 ____ The just and the unjust / by Vaughan Kester; illustrations by M. Leone Bracker. Indianapolis: The Bobbs-Merrill Company, [c1912]. 390 p., front., [5] leaves of plates.
LC: My 28, '12.
PW: My 18, '12.

K-165　　____ The manager of the B & A: a novel / by
Vaughan Kester. New York; London: Harper &
Brothers, 1901. 274, [1] p.
PW: Ag 3, '01.

K-166　　____ The prodigal judge / by Vaughan Kester; with
illustrations by M. Leone Bracker. Indianapolis: The
Bobbs-Merrill Company, [c1911]. 448 p., front., [6]
leaves of plates.
LC: Mr 14, '11.
PW: Mr 11, '11.
BLC: London: Methuen & Co., [1911].

K-167　　Keyes, Frances Parkinson, 1885-1970. The career of
David Noble / by Frances Parkinson Keyes. New
York: Frederick A. Stokes Company, [c1921].
301 p.
LC: O 25, '21.
PW: N 12, '21.
BLC: London: Eveleigh Nash & Grayson; printed in
U. S. A., [1923].

K-168　　____ The old Gray homestead / by Frances
Parkinson Keyes; with illustrations by Florence
Gardiner. Boston; New York: Houghton Mifflin
Company, 1919. (Cambridge: The Riverside Press).
301, [1] p., front., [3] leaves of plates.　　**VIC**
LC: Mr 31, '19.
PW: Mr 29, '19.
BLC: London: Hodder & Stoughton; Cambridge,
Mass. printed, 1919.

K-169　　Keyser, Leander S[ylvester], b. 1856. The only way
out / by Leander S. Keyser . . . --2nd ed.-- Canal
Dover, Ohio: O. L. Younger & Company, 1906.
336 p.　　**NYP**
LC: Ag 24, '06.

Kidder, Anne Maynard. In Maytime. In *A book of
Bryn Mawr stories* **(1901), B-732.**

K-170　　Kiisel, Louise. Spirit gold / by Louise Kiisel.
Boston, Massachusetts: The Stratford Co., 1920.
196 p.　　**NYP**
LC: Ag 17, '20.
PW: Ag 28, '20.

K-171　　Kilbourne, Fanny, b. 1890. A corner in William / by
Fanny Kilbourne; with frontispiece by C. F.
Underwood. New York: Dodd, Mead and
Company, 1922. 268 p., col. front.
LC: S 13, '22.
PW: S 16, '22.

K-172　　____ The education of Sallie May / by Fanny
Kilbourne. New York; London: G. P. Putnam's
Sons, 1925. ([New York]: the Knickerbocker
Press). 157 p.
LC: O 3, '25.
PW: O 10, '25.

K-173　　____ Mrs. William Horton speaking / by Fannie
Kilbourne. New York: Dodd, Mead and Company,
1925, [c1924]. 276 p.
LC: F 11, '25.
PW: F 14, '25.

Kildare, Leita, jt. aut. *Such a woman* (1911). See
**Kildare, Owen Frawley, 1864-1911, jt. aut.,
K-175.**

K-174　　Kildare, Owen Frawley, 1864-1911. The good of the
wicked: and The party sketches / by Owen Kildare.
New York: The Baker & Taylor Co., [1904].
148 p.
Contents: The good of the wicked -- The responsibility of slang --
The party sketches -- Little stories from our streets.
PW: O 8, '04.

K-175　　____ Such a woman / by Owen and Leita Kildare;
illustrations by Joseph C. Chase. New York: G. W.
Dillingham Company, [c1911]. 316 p., front., [2]
leaves of plates.
LC: Ag 22, '11.

K-176　　____ The wisdom of the simple: a tale of lower
New York / by Owen Kildare . . . New York;
Chicago; Toronto; London; Edinburgh: Fleming H.
Revell Company, [c1905]. 353 p.
PW: D 2, '05.

K-177　　Killick, Arthur F. Fatty Lewis (x) his book / by
Arthur F. Killick; illustrated by Harry Wood. Kansas
City: The Lechtman Press, 1915. 158 p., ill.
Contents: Fatty and the dancers -- Fatty goes fishing -- Keeping up
with neighbors -- Mrs. Lewis "sees" a ball game -- The woes of
woman -- The worm turns -- The bright lights dimmed -- Fatty in the
role of satan -- Fatty on married life -- Fatty and the man tamers --
The new neighbor -- Some dope on fishing outfits -- Where
prohibition fails -- Fatty cuts expenses -- The servant problem -- The
Lewises plan a vacation -- Slicing the bank roll -- The why of Fatty
Lewis.

Kilpatrick, Lewis H. When Breathitt went to battle.
In *The Bellman book of fiction* **(1921), B-485.**

K-178　　Kilpatrick, Martha B. King Kavanaugh / by Martha
B. Kilpatrick; illustrated. New York: The Bookery
Publishing Company, [c1913]. 224 p., [3] leaves of
photo. plates.　　**TNS**

Kilpatrick, Mary Genevieve, jt. aut. *Miss Varney's
experience.* See **Donnelly, Eleanor C. (Eleanor
Cecilia), 1838-1917, jt. aut., D-472.**

K-179　　____ The test, or, Mother Bertrand's reward / by
Mary Genevieve Kilpatrick. Philadelphia: H. L.
Kilner & Co., [c1907]. 301 p.
LC: O 11, '07.

K-180　　Kimball, Atkinson, *jt. pseud.* The prince of Mercuria
/ by Atkinson Kimball [jt. pseud.]; drawings by Clara
Elsene Peck. New York: Hearst's International
Library Co, [c1914]. 184 p., incl. front.
LC: O 17, '14.

K-181　　Kimball, Edward N. The dominant chord / by
Edward Kimball; with a frontispiece in full colour
from a painting by William Bunting. Boston: L. C.
Page & Company, 1912. 319 p., col. front.
LC: Mr 6, '12.

K-182　　Kimball, George Selwyn, d. 1909. Jay Gould
Harmon with Maine folks: a picture of life in the
Maine woods / by George Selwyn Kimball . . .
Boston, U. S. A.: C. M. Clark Publishing Co., Inc.,

1905. 442 p., front., [9] leaves of plates. [Ill. by Griswold Tyng.]
PW: N 4, '05.

K-183 ____ The Lackawannas at Moosehead, or, The young leather stockings / by George Selwyn Kimball; illustrated by W. H. D. Koerner. Boston: The Ball Publishing Company, 1907. 320 p., front., [8] leaves of plates, map.
LC: N 9, '07.
PW: N 16, '07.

K-184 ____ Piney Home / by George Selwyn Kimball. Boston: Herbert B. Turner & Co., 1904. 371 p.
PW: N 5, '04.

K-185 Kimball, J. N. (James Newton). Bre'r Coon et al / by J. N. Kimball. [New York City: Underwood Typewriter Company, Inc., c1922]. 36 p. **DLC**

Kimball, Richard Bowland. See **Kimball, Atkinson, jt. pseud. of Mrs. Grace Lucie Atkinson and Richard Bowland Kimball.**

K-186 Kimberling, Hadley S. (Hadley Siegel), 1862-1920. Llewellyn: a novel / by Hadley S. Kimberling. New York: Broadway Publishing Company, [c1904]. 402 p., front., [4] leaves of plates. [Ill. by S. Klarr.]
PW: F 4, '05.

K-187 Kimmell, Mary Forward. Tantalus / by Mary Forward Kimmell. Boston: The C. M. Clark Publishing Company, 1909. 534 p.
LC: D 27, '09.

K-188 Kinder, Stephen. The sabertooth: a romance of Put-in-Bay / by Stephen Kinder; illustrated. Chicago: Laird & Lee, [c1902]. 270 p., front., [3] leaves of plates, ill. [Ill. by John C. Gilbert.]
PW: Ap 12, '02.

K-189 King, Basil, 1859-1928. Abraham's bosom / by Basil King. New York; London: Harper & Brothers, [c1918]. 53, [1] p., front.
LC: Je 15, '18.
PW: Je 22, '18.

K-190 ____ The city of comrades / by Basil King. New York; London: Harper & Brothers, [1919]. 405, [1] p., front., [3] leaves of plates.
LC: Mr 28, '19.
PW: Ap 5, '19.
BLC: London: Chapman Hall, 1919.

K-191 ____ The dust flower / by Basil King . . . ; with illustrations by Hibbard V. B. Kline. New York; London: Harper & Brothers, 1922. 349, [1] p., front., [3] leaves of plates. "First edition."
LC: O 23, '22.
PW: O 28, '22.
BLC: London: Hodder & Stoughton, 1922.

K-192 ____ The empty sack / by Basil King; illustrated. New York; London: Harper & Brothers, [c1921]. 445, [1] p., front., [2] leaves of plates. [Ill. by J. Henry.]
LC: S 16, '21.

PW: S 17, '21.
BLC: London: Hodder & Stoughton, [1921].

K-193 ____ The giant's strength / by Basil King . . . New York; London: Harper & Brothers, 1907. 341 p.
LC: Mr 14, '07.
PW: Mr 30, '07.

K-194 ____ Going west / by Basil King. New York: Harper & Brothers, [c1919]. 48, [1] p., col. front.
LC: Ag 20, '19.
PW: Ag 30, '19.

K-195 ____ The happy isles / by Basil King; with illustrations by John Alonzo Williams. New York; London: Harper & Brothers, 1923. 485 p., front., [3] leaves of plates.
LC: N 9, '23.
PW: N 24, '23.
BLC: London: Hodder & Stoughton, [1924].

K-196 ____ The high forfeit: a novel / by Basil King . . . New York; London: Harper & Brothers, 1925. 340 p.
LC: S 18, '25.
PW: O 10, '25.
BLC: London: Hodder & Stoughton, [1926].

K-197 ____ The high heart / by Basil King . . . ; illustrated. New York; London: Harper & Brothers, [1917]. 419, [1] p., col. front., [3] leaves of plates. [Ill. by Henry Raleigh.]
LC: S 20, '17.
PW: S 29, '17.

K-198 ____ In the garden of Charity / by Basil King. New York; London: Harper & Brothers, 1903. 319, [1] p.
PW: F 28, '03.

K-199 [____] The inner shrine: a novel of today / illustrated. New York; London: Harper & Brothers, 1909. 355, [1] p., front., [9] leaves of plates. [Ill. by Frank Craig.]
PW: My 15, '09.

K-200 ____ Let not man put asunder: a novel / by Basil King . . . New York; London: Harper & Brothers, 1901. 424, [1] p.
PW: N 2, '01.

K-201 ____ The letter of the contract / by Basil King. New York; London: Harper & Brothers, 1914. 209, [1] p., front., incl. [3] leaves of plates. [Ill. by James Montgomery Flagg.]
LC: Ag 14, '14.
PW: D 19, '14.
BLC: London: Methuen & Co., 1914.

K-202 ____ The lifted veil / by Basil King . . . ; illustrated by James Montgomery Flagg. New York; London: Harper & Brothers, 1917. 340, [1] p., front., [3] leaves of plates.
LC: Mr 17, '17.
PW: Mr 17, '17.
BLC: London: Methuen & Co., 1917.

K-203   The side of the angels: a novel / by Basil King; illustrated by Elizabeth Shippen Green. New York; London: Harper & Brothers, [1916]. 394, [1] p., front., [7] leaves of plates.
LC: F 21, '16.
PW: Mr 4, '16.
BLC: London: Methuen & Co., 1916.

K-204   The steps of honor / by Basil King. New York; London: Harper & Brothers, 1904. 285, [1] p.
PW: Ap 23, '04.

K-205 [   ] The street called Straight: a novel / by the author of "The inner shrine"; illustrated by Orson Lowell. New York; London: Harper & Brothers, 1912. 414, [1] p., col. front., [7] leaves of col. plates.
LC: My 23, '12.
PW: Je 1; '12.

K-206   The thread of flame / by Basil King. New York; London: Harper & Brothers, [1920]. 350, [1] p., front., [3] leaves of plates. [Ill. by John Alonzo Williams.]
LC: Ag 28, '20.
PW: S 4, '20.

K-207   The way home: a novel / by the author of "The inner shrine" (Basil King). Illustrated by W. H. D. Koerner. New York; London: Harper & Brothers Publishers, 1913. 546, [1] p., front., [3] leaves of plates.
LC: S 20, '13.
PW: N 1, '13.
BLC: London: Methuen & Co., 1914.

K-208 [   ] The wild olive: a novel / by the author of "The inner shrine"; illustrated by Lucius Hitchcock. New York; London: Harper & Brothers, 1910. 346 p., front., [7] leaves of plates.
LC: My 21, '10.
PW: Je 4, '10.

King, Bradley, jt. aut. *Her reputation* (1923). See **Mundy, Talbot, jt. aut., M-1129.**

K-209 King, Charles, 1844-1933. An Apache princess: a tale of the Indian frontier / by General Charles King . . . ; illustrations by Frederic Remington and Edwin Willard Deming. New York: The Hobart Company, 1903. 328 p., front., [7] leaves of plates.
PW: O 10, '03.
References: Dornbusch 1.

K-210   A broken sword: a tale of the Civil War / by General Charles King . . . New York: The Hobart Company, 1905. 301 p., front. (port.).
Dornbusch reports another printing with 314 p.: "The text of the last paragraph has been reset. Contents paged, 3-4. Text commences on p. 5."
References: Dornbusch 4.

K-211   Captured: the story of Sandy Ray / by General Charles King. New York: R. F. Fenno & Company, [c1906]. 349 p., front., [4] leaves of plates. [Ill. by William Edward Bloomfield Starkweather.]

Published also as: *Lieutenant Sandy Ray* and *The further story of Lieutenant Sandy Ray*.
LC: Ap 17, '07.
References: Dornbusch 11.

     The code of the corps. In *Stories of the colleges* **(1901), S-985.**

K-212   Comrades in arms: a tale of two hemispheres / by General Charles King; illustrations by George Gibbs and E. W. Deming. New York: The Hobart Company, 1904. 350 p., front., [3] leaves of plates.
PW: N 5, '04.
References: Dornbusch 14.

K-213   A conquering corps badge: and other stories of the Philippines / by General Charles King; with illustrations by Miss Alida Goodwin, B. Martin Justice and Stuart Travis. Cover designed by Miss Elinor Yorke King. Milwaukee: L. A. Rhoades & Company, 1902. 309 p., [16] leaves of plates.
Contents: A conquering corps badge -- Jack Royal -- Dove cote days -- A rival ally -- The senator's plight -- The luck of the horseshoe -- A camera capture -- The fate of Guadalupe -- The Manilla wire -- Betrayed by a button. PW: Ag 2, '02.
References: Dornbusch 15.

K-214   A daughter of the Sioux: a tale of the Indian frontier / by General Charles King; illustrations by Frederic Remington and Edwin Willard Deming. New York: The Hobart Company, 1903. 306 p., front., [7] leaves of plates.
PW: Ap 11, '03.
References: Dornbusch 16.

K-215   From the ranks / by Gen'l Charles King . . . Philadelphia; London: J. B. Lippincott Company, 1902, [c1901]. 317 p., front. [Ill. by E. M. Connelly.]   **TXU**
LC: O 19, '01.
References: Dornbusch 22.

K-216   In spite of foes, or, Ten years' trial / by General Charles King; with frontispiece by William T. Trego. Philadelphia; London: J. B. Lippincott Company, 1901. 331 p., front.
PW: Mr 9, '01.
References: Dornbusch 26.

K-217   The iron brigade: a story of the Army of the Potomac / by General Charles King; illustrations by R. F. Zogbaum. New York: G. W. Dillingham Company, [1902]. 379 p., front., [3] leaves of plates.
PW: O 4, '02.
References: Dornbusch 28.

K-218   A knight of Columbia: a story of the war / by General Charles King . . . ; illustrations by George Gibbs. New York: The Hobart Company, 1904. 348 p., front., [7] leaves of plates.
PW: Ap 2, '04.
References: Dornbusch 30.

K-219   Lanier of the cavalry, or, A week's arrest / by General Charles King; with illustrations by Frank McKernan. Philadelphia; London: J. B. Lippincott Company, 1909. 241, [1] p., front., [2] leaves of

plates.
LC: Mr 18, '09.
PW: Ap 24, '09.
References: Dornbusch 31.

K-220   The medal of honor: a story of peace and war / by General Charles King . . . ; illustrations by George Gibbs and E. W. Deming. New York: The Hobart Company, 1905, [c1904]. 348 p., front., [5] leaves of plates.
Dornbusch notes other copies distributed by H. B. Claflin, publishers' agents
PW: Ap 22, '05.
References: Dornbusch 34.

K-221   Norman Holt: a story of the Army of the Cumberland / by General Charles King . . . ; with illustrations by John Huybers and Seymour M. Stone. New York: G. W. Dillingham Company, [c1901]. 346 p., front., [5] leaves of plates.
Cover title: *A story of the Army of Cumberland*.
PW: My 4, '01.
References: Dornbusch 36.

K-222   Ray's daughter: a story of Manila / by General Charles King, U. S. V. Philadelphia; London: J. B. Lippincott Company, 1901. 320 p., front. [Ill. by William T. Trego.]
PW: N 3, '00.
References: Dornbusch 38.

K-223   The rock of Chickamauga / by General Charles King; illustrations by Gilbert Gaul and Chas. J. Post. New York: G. W. Dillingham Company, [1907]. 397 p., front., [4] leaves of plates.
LC: Je 20, '07.
PW: Jl 13, '07.
BLC: London: T. Fisher Unwin; New York [printed], 1907.
References: Dornbusch 40.

K-224   A soldier's trial: an episode of the canteen crusade / by General Charles King . . . New York: The Hobart Company, 1905. 333 p., photo. front. (port.).
PW: N 18, '05.
References: Dornbusch 42.

K-225   To the front: a sequel to Cadet days / by General Charles King; illustrated. New York; London: Harper & Brothers, 1908. 260, [1] p., front., [7] leaves of plates. [Ill. by Frederic Remington.]
LC: F 14, '08.
PW: F 22, '08.
References: Dornbusch 46.

K-226   Tonio: son of the Sierras: a story of the Apache War / by General Charles King . . . ; illustrations by Charles J. Post. New York: G. W. Dillingham Company, [1906]. 338 p., col. front., [3] leaves of col. plates.
PW: Je 30, '06.
BLC: London: T. Fisher Unwin, 1906.
References: Dornbusch 47.

K-227   The way of the west / by General Charles King. Chicago; New York: Rand, McNally & Company Publishers, [c1902]. 176 p., front.
BOS
PW: Je 7, '02.
References: Dornbusch 58.

K-228 King, Emma May. A race with fate, or, a double crime / by Emma May King. New York: The Shakespeare Press, 1913. 181 p.

King, Georgiana Goddard. Free among the dead. In *A book of Bryn Mawr stories* (1901), **B-732.**

K-229 King, Gertrude. The landlubbers / by Gertrude King; illustrated by Frank Stick. New York: Doubleday, Page & Company, 1909. 272 p., col. front., [3] leaves of col. plates.
LC: Mr 24, '09.
PW: Ap 10, '09.
BLC: London: Doubleday, Page & Company; New York printed, 1909.

K-230 King, Gordon, 1893-1930. Horatio's story / Gordon King. New York: Boni and Liveright, [c1923]. 272 p.
LC: O 12, '23.

K-231 King, Grace Elizabeth, 1852-1932. Balcony stories / by Grace King . . . New York: The Macmillan Company, 1925. 296 p., front., ill. [Ill. by Albert Sterner.]
Contents: The balcony -- A drama of three -- La grande demoiselle -- Mimi's marriage -- The miracle chapel -- The story of a day -- Anne Marie and Jeanne Marie -- A crippled hope -- "One of us" -- The little convent girl -- Grandmother's grandmother -- The old lady's restoration -- A delicate affair -- Pupasse -- Grandmama -- Joe.
LC: S 30, '25.
PW: O 10, '25.

K-232   La Dame de Sainte Hermine / by Grace King. New York: The Macmillan Company, 1924. 296 p.
LC: Ap 9, '24.
PW: Mr 8, '24.

K-233   The pleasant ways of St. Médard / by Grace King. New York: Henry Holt and Company, 1916. 338 p.
LC: S 1, '16.
PW: Ag 26, '16.
BLC: London: Constable & Co., 1916.

K-234 King, Homer A. (Homer Arthur), b. 1833. The bride of his palace, or, Love intwined with actual incidents in two lives: illustrated / by Homer A. King . . . Boston: The Chas. H. Woodman Press, 1903. 292, [1] p., ill.   **OSU, DLC**

K-235 King, Kenneth Kenelm, b. 1863, *pseud.* "100%" / by Kenneth Kenelm King [pseud.]. Washington, D. C.: The American Sentinel, [c1925]. 402 p.   **DLC**
LC: S 21, '25.

K-236 King, Mary R. H. (Mary Rayner Hyman), b. 1875. The judgment / by Mary R. H. King; illustrated by Julian Onderdonk. New York: Cochrane Publishing Co., 1911. 205 p., front., [5] leaves of plates.
DLC

LC: My 10, '11.
Another edition: New York: The Demille Publishing
Co., [c1911]. 266 p.
LC: Jl 28, '11.

K-237   King, Rufus, b. 1893. North Star: a dog story of the
Canadian Northwest / by Rufus King; frontispiece by
Charles Livingston Bull. New York: G. Howard
Watt, 1925. 302 p., col. front.
LC: Je 16, '25.

K-238   King, Scobe, b. 1866, *pseud.* The conquest of Ines
Ripley / by Scobe King [pseud.]; illustrated. Boston:
The Roxburgh Publishing Company, Incorporated,
[c1912]. 327 p., front., [6] leaves of plates.
LC: Ja 3, '13.

K-239   King, William Harvey, b. 1861. Medical Union
Number Six / by William Harvey King . . . [S. l.:
The Monograph Press, c1904]. 60 p.

K-240   Kingsbury, Carl Louis. In her father's place /
by Carl Louis Kingsbury. Elgin, Illinois: David C.
Cook Publishing Company, [c1906]. 96 p., ill. [Ill.
by G. A. Rieman.]

K-241   _____ The mystery at the Carrol ranch: a story of the
South-West / by Carl Louis Kingsbury. Elgin, Ill.:
David C. Cook Publishing Co., [c1910]. 94 p., ill.
[Ill. by E. H. Hartke and L. E. Dugger.]
LC: D 8, '10.
PW: Ja 14, '11.

K-242   Kingsbury, Sara, b. 1876. The atonement / by Sara
Kingsbury. Boston: Eastern Publishing Company,
[c1905]. 247 p.   **DLC**
PW: Mr 2, '07.

Kingsley, Florence Morse, 1859-1937, jt. aut. *An
alabaster box* (1917). <u>See</u> **Freeman, Mary Eleanor
Wilkins, 1852-1930, jt. aut., F-386.**

K-243   _____ And so they were married / by Florence Morse
Kingsley; with illustrations by W. B. King. New
York: Dodd, Mead & Company, 1908. 148 p.,
front., [3] leaves of plates.
LC: Ag 26, '08.
PW: O 3, '08.

K-244   _____ Balm in Gilead / by Florence Morse Kingsley.
New York; London: Funk & Wagnalls Company,
1907. 65 p., col. front. [Ill. by H. Benno
Reissman.]
LC: Ap 3, '07.
PW: My 11, '07.

K-245   _____ Francesca / by Florence Morse Kingsley.
Boston: Richard G. Badger, [c1911]. (Boston: The
Gorham Press). 216 p., col. front.
PW: O 28, '11.

K-246   _____ The glass house / by Florence Morse Kingsley;
illustrations by Alice Barber Stephens. New York:
Dodd, Mead and Company, 1909. 312 p., front., [3]
leaves of plates.
LC: Mr 10, '09.
PW: Ap 17, '09.

K-247   _____ The heart of Philura / by Florence Morse
Kingsley . . . ; frontispiece by Robert W. Amick.
New York: Dodd, Mead and Company, 1915.
362 p., front.
LC: S 22, '15.
PW: S 18, '15.

K-248   _____ Hurrying fate and Geraldine / by Florence
Morse Kingsley . . . New York: Franklin Bigelow
Corporation: The Morningside Press, [c1913].
288 p.
LC: S 18, '13.
PW: N 1, '13.

K-249   _____ The intellectual Miss Lamb / by Florence
Morse Kingsley. New York: The Century Co.,
1906. 100 p., front. [Ill. by Harrison Fisher.]
PW: Je 2, '06.

K-250   _____ Kindly light / by Florence Morse Kingsley
. . . ; illustrations by E. M. Nagel. Philadelphia:
Henry Altemus Company, [c1904]. 112 p., incl.
front., [1] leaf of plates.
Contents: Kindly light -- A June bride.
PW: My 14, '04.

K-251   _____ Miss Philura's wedding gown / by Florence
Morse Kingsley . . . ; with illustrations by Eugénie
Wireman. New York: Dodd, Mead and Company,
1912. 232 p., front., [4] leaves of plates.
LC: O 23, '12.
PW: O 26, '12.

K-252   _____ The needle's eye / by Florence Morse Kingsley
. . . ; illustrations by William E. Mears. New York;
London: Funk & Wagnalls Company, 1902. 386 p.,
front., [3] leaves of plates.
PW: S 20, '02.

K-253   _____ Neighbors / by Florence Morse Kingsley . . .
New York: Dodd, Mead and Company, 1917.
372 p.
LC: S 25, '17.
PW: S 29, '17.

K-254   _____ The princess and the ploughman / by Florence
Morse Kingsley. New York; London: Harper &
Brothers, 1907, [c1906]. 260, [1] p., col. front. [Ill.
by Lester Ralph.]
LC: My 16, '07.
PW: Je 1, '07.

K-255   _____ The resurrection of Miss Cynthia / by Florence
Morse Kingsley; with frontispiece by Martin Justice.
New York: Dodd, Mead & Company, 1905. 321 p.,
col. front.
PW: O 7, '05.
BLC: London: Hodder & Stoughton, 1905.

K-256   _____ The return of Caroline / by Florence Morse
Kingsley; frontispiece by Herman Methfessel. New
York; London: Funk & Wagnalls Company, 1911.
65 p., front.
LC: My 27, '11.
PW: My 6, '11.

K-257   _____ The singular Miss Smith / by Florence Morse Kingsley . . . ; with illustrations by Will Grefé. New York: The Macmillan Company; London: Macmillan & Co., Ltd., 1904. 208 p., front., [5] leaves of plates.
PW: My 14, '04.

K-258   _____ The star of love / by Florence Morse Kingsley; with eight illustrations in color by Arthur E. Becher. New York; London: D. Appleton and Company, 1909. 381, [1] p., col. front., [7] leaves of col. plates.
LC: O 12, '09.
PW: O 16, '09.

K-259   _____ Those Brewster children / by Florence Morse Kingsley . . . ; with illustrations by Emily Hall Chamberlain. New York: Dodd, Mead & Company, 1910. 214 p., front., [2] leaves of plates.
LC: Mr 12, '10.
PW: Mr 26, '10.

K-260   _____ Those queer Browns / by Florence Morse Kingsley . . . ; frontispiece by Harrison Fisher. New York: Dodd, Mead and Company, 1907. 282 p., col. front.
LC: Jl 25, '07.
PW: S 21, '07.

K-261   _____ To the highest bidder / by Florence Morse Kingsley; illustrated by John Rae. New York: Dodd, Mead and Company, 1911. 302 p., front.
LC: Ja 12, '11.
PW: Ja 28, '11.

K-262   _____ The transfiguration of Miss Philura / by Florence Morse Kingsley. New York; London: Funk & Wagnalls Company, 1901. 81 p., front.
PW: My 11, '01.

K-263   _____ Truthful Jane / by Florence Morse Kingsley . . . New York: D. Appleton and Company, 1907. 329 p.
LC: F 2, '07.
PW: F 2, '07.

K-264   _____ Veronica / by Florence Morse Kingsley . . . ; illustrated. New York; London: D. Appleton and Company, 1913. 312, [1] p., front., [3] leaves of plates. [Ill. by Arthur Becher.]
LC: Mr 17, '13.
PW: Mr 29, '13.

K-265   _____ Wilhelmina changes her mind / by Florence Morse Kingsley . . . ; illustrated by Robert A. Graef. Boston: Small, Maynard and Company, [c1912]. 192 p., front., [7] leaves of plates.
LC: Je 6, '12.
PW: Je 8, '12.

Kingsley, Maurice. Tio Juan. In *Under the Sunset* (1906), U-9.

K-266   Kingstandish, Silva. The colonel's jewels / by Silva Kingstandish. Philadelphia: The John C. Winston Co., 1914. 394 p.

K-267   Kinkade, Frederick. My lady's fortune hunt / by Frederick Kinkade. Boston, Mass.: The C. M. Clarke Publishing Co., 1908. 378 p., front., [7] leaves of plates. [Ill. by J. Armington.]
LC: D 4, '08.

K-268   Kinkaid, Mary Holland, b. 1861. The man of yesterday: a romance of a vanishing race / by Mary Holland Kinkaid; with illustrations in color by Volney A. Richardson. New York: Frederick A. Stokes Company, [1908]. 318 p., col. front., [2] leaves of plates.
LC: Mr 2, '08.
PW: Mr 28, '08.

K-269   _____ Walda: a novel / by Mary Holland Kinkaid. New York; London: Harper & Brothers, 1903. 311, [1] p.
PW: Mr 28, '03.

K-270   Kinkead, Eleanor Talbot. The courage of Blackburn Blair / by Eleanor Talbot Kinkead. New York: Moffat, Yard & Company, 1907. 478 p.
LC: O 23, '07.
PW: N 16, '07

K-271   _____ The invisible bond / by Eleanor Talbot Kinkead. New York: Moffat, Yard & Company, 1906. 513 p., double-leaf col. front. [Ill. by C. Allan Gilbert.]

K-272   _____ The spoils of the strong / by Eleanor Talbot Kinkead (Mrs. Thompson Short) . . . New York: The James A. McCann Company, 1920. 308 p.
LC: Ag 23, '20.

K-273   Kinney, Henry Walsworth, b. 1879. Broken butterflies / by Henry Walsworth Kinney. Boston: Little, Brown and Company, 1924. 323 p.
LC: F 12, '24.
PW: F 9, '24.
BLC: London: Eveleigh Nash & Co., 1924.

K-274   _____ The code of the Karstens / by Henry Walsworth Kinney. Boston: Little, Brown and Company, 1923. 359 p.
LC: Ja 15, '23.
PW: Ja 6, '23.
BLC: London: E. Nash & Grayson, 1923.

K-275   Kinney, Maud Kino-Ole, b. 1881. Between fate and Akuas / by Maud Kino-Ole Kinney. Philadelphia: Dorrance and Company, 1925. 216 p.

Kinney, W. R. Just a story. In *Yale tales* (1901), Y-1.

K-276   Kinnicutt, Grace. A story of Acadia / by Grace Kinnicutt . . . Chicago; New York: A. Flanagan Company, [c1903]. 55 p., photo. front., ill. **DLC**
PW: O 3, '03.

Kinsburn, Emart, pseud. See **Hankins, Arthur Preston.**

K-277   Kintzel, A. G. (Albert Gaston), Mrs., b. 1854. Lady Century / by Mrs. A. G. Kintzel. New York:

Broadway Publishing Company, [c1904]. 320 p.,
front., [3] leaves of plates. [Ill. by Sydney K.
Hartman.]
PW: Ja 7, '05.

K-278 _____ Leave me my honor / by Mrs. A. G. Kintzel.
New York: Broadway Publishing Company, [c1904].
247 p.   **DLC**
PW: Jl 16, '04.

Kiper, Florence. "I have borne my lord a son". In
Forum stories (1914), F-306.

Kirk, Dolly Williams, jt. aut. *With spurs of gold*
(1905). See **Greene, Frances Nimmo, 1850-1921,
jt. aut., G-453.**

K-279 Kirk, Eleanor, *pseud.* The Christ of the red planet /
Eleanor Kirk [pseud.] . . . New York: The
Publishers' Printing Company, [c1901]. 138 p.

K-280 Kirk, Ellen Olney, b. 1842. The apology of Ayliffe /
by Ellen Olney Kirk. Boston; New York: Houghton,
Mifflin and Company, 1904. (Cambridge: The
Riverside Press). 323, [1] p.
PW: O 1, '04.

K-281 _____ Good-bye, proud world / by Ellen Olney Kirk.
Boston; New York: Houghton, Mifflin and
Company, 1903. (Cambridge: The Riverside Press).
362 p.
PW: O 3, '03.

K-282 _____ Marcia: a novel / by Ellen Olney Kirk.
Boston; New York: Houghton, Mifflin and
Company, 1907. (Cambridge: The Riverside Press).
391, [1] p.
LC: Mr 4, '07.
PW: Mr 23, '07.

K-283 _____ Our Lady Vanity / by Ellen Olney Kirk.
Boston; New York: Houghton, Mifflin and
Company, 1901. (Cambridge: The Riverside Press).
353, [1] p.
PW: S 14, '01.

K-284 _____ A remedy for love / by Ellen Olney Kirk.
Boston; New York: Houghton, Mifflin and
Company, 1902. (Cambridge: The Riverside Press).
227, [1] p.
Originally published in Lippincott's magazine under
the title "An anticlimax."
PW: Je 7, '02.

Kirk, Henry S. "The woman of dreams". In
Cuentos de California (1904), C-962.

K-285 Kirk, Ralph G. b. 1881. Six breeds / by R. G. Kirk;
with illustrations by Charles Livingston Bull. New
York: Alfred A. Knopf, 1923. 266 p., front., [4]
leaves of plates.   **MNL**
Contents: Gun-shy -- MacRoman -- Fur chaser --
Zanoza -- White Monarch and the gas-house pup.
LC: My 9, '23.

K-286 _____ White Monarch and the gas-house pup / by R.
G. Kirk; with illustrations by William A. Kirkpatrick.

Boston: Little, Brown, and Company, 1917. 113 p.,
front., [3] leaves of plates.
LC: O 2, '17.

K-287 _____ Zanoza: a borzoi story / by R. G. Kirk;
pictures by Harvey Dunn. New York: Alfred A.
Knopf, 1918. 112 p., front., [3] leaves of plates.
LC: O 1, '18.

K-288 Kirkland, Winifred Margaretta, 1872-1943. The
Christmas bishop / by Winifred Kirkland; illustrated
by Louise G. Morrison. Boston: Small, Maynard
and Company, [c1913]. 153, [1] p., front., [1] leaf
of plates.
LC: N 26, '13.
PW: N 1, '13.

K-289 _____ The home-comers / by Winifred Kirkland; with
illustrations by Thomas Fogarty. Boston; New York:
Houghton Mifflin Company, [1910]. (Cambridge:
The Riverside Press). 326 p., front., [3] leaves of
plates.
LC: O 3, '10.
PW: O 1, '10.

K-290 _____ Polly Pat's parish / by Winifred Kirkland.
New York; Chicago; Toronto; London; Edinburgh:
Fleming H. Revell Company, [c1907]. 224 p.,
front., [7] leaves of plates. [Ill. by Griselda M.
McClure.]   **DLC**
LC: S 9, '07.
PW: S 7, '07.

K-291 Kirkman, Marshall Monroe, 1842-1921. The
emperor: a romance of the camp and court of
Alexander the Great: the love of Statira, the Persian
queen / by Marshall Monroe Kirkman; illustrated by
August Petrtyl. Chicago: Cropley Phillips Company,
[c1913]. 371 p., col. front., [15] leaves of plates,
ill.   **GZM**
A revision of the author's *The romance of Alexander
and Roxana*, published in 1909.
LC: O 18, '13.

K-292 _____ Iskander: a romance of the court of Philip of
Macedon and Alexander the Great / by Marshall
Monroe Kirkman . . . Chicago; New York; London:
The World Railway Publishing Company, 1903.
419 p., col. front., [1] leaf of col. plates, map. [Ill.
by August Petrtyl.]
BLC: London: Simpkin, Marshall & Co., 1903.

K-293 _____ The king: a romance of the camp and court of
Alexander the Great: the story of Theba, the
Macedonian captive / by Marshall Monroe Kirkman;
illustrated by August Petrtyl. Chicago: Cropley
Phillips Company, [c1913]. 349 p., col. front., [12]
leaves of plates, ill.   **GZM**
A revision of the author's *The romance of Alexander
the king*, published in 1909.
LC: O 18, '13.

K-294 _____ The prince: a romance of the camp and court
of Alexander the Great: the love story of Roxana, the
maid of Bactria / by Marshall Monroe Kirkman;
illustrated by August Petrtyl. Chicago: Cropley
Phillips Company, [c1913]. 502 p., col. front., [14]

leaves of plates, ill. **GZM**
A revision of the author's *The romance of Alexander the prince*, published 1909.
LC: O 18, '13.

K-295   ____ The romance of Alexander and Roxana: being one of the Alexandrian romances, "Alexander the prince," "Alexander the king" & " Alexander and Roxana" / by Marshall Monroe Kirkman . . . ; illustrated by August Petrtyl. Chicago; New York; London: Cropley Phillips Company, [c1909]. 398 p., col. front., [13] leaves of plates, map.
LC: O 29, '09.
PW: N 6, '09.

K-296   ____ The romance of Alexander the king: being one of the Alexandrian romances, "Alexander the prince", "Alexander the king" & "Alexander and Roxana" / by Marshall Monroe Kirkman . . . ; illustrated by August Petrtyl. Chicago; New York; London: Cropley Phillips Company, [c1909]. 348 p., front., [13] leaves of plates, ill.

K-297   ____ The romance of Alexander the prince: being one of the Alexandrian romances, "Alexander the prince," "Alexander the king" & "Alexander and Roxana" / by Marshall Monroe Kirkman; illustrated by August Petrtyl. Chicago; New York; London: Cropley Phillips Company, [c1909]. 469, [1] p., col. front., [13] leaves of plates.

K-298   Kiser, S. E. (Samuel Ellsworth), b. 1862. Charles the chauffeur / by S. E. Kiser. New York: Frederick A. Stokes Company, [1905]. 189 p., front.

K-299   Kitchell, Joseph Gray, b. 1862. The Earl of Hell / by Joseph Gray Kitchell. New York; London: The Century Co., [c1924]. 325 p.
LC: Ap 22, '24.
PW: Ap 19, '24.

K-300   Kitchell, Joseph Gray, b. 1862. The Kranbach Nocturne / by Joseph Gray Kitchell; illustrated by A. T. Farrell and W. M. Crocker. New York: The George Ethridge Company, [c1905]. 34, [1] p., ill.
DLC (micro)
LC: Ap 17, '05.

K-301   Kittredge, Charles Prentiss, 1867-1911. The missing link: a story of New England life / by Rev. Charles Prentiss Kittredge; revised and prepared for publication by Mrs. Chas. P. Kittredge. Westbrook, Maine: Safeguard Publishing Company, [c1913]. 265 p., [4] leaves of plates, ill.
LC: Je 23, '13.
Another edition: Brownville, Maine: [s. n.], [c1913].

K-302   Kittredge, Daniel Wright, 1879-1958. The memoirs of a failure: with an account of the man and his manuscript / by Daniel Wright Kittredge. Cincinnati: U. P. James, Bookseller, 1908. 199 p.
LC: D 7, '08.
PW: D 19, '08.
BLC: Toronto: Albert Britnell, 1908.

K-303   ____ A mind adrift / by Daniel Wright Kittredge.

Seattle: S. F. Shorey, 1920. (Seattle: Metropolitan Press). 83 p.
LC: D 9, '20.
PW: D 25, '20.

K-304   Kittrell, Norman G. (Norman Goree), b. 1849. Ned: nigger an' gent'man: a story of war and Reconstruction days / by Norman G. Kittrell . . . New York; Washington: The Neale Publishing Company, 1907. 257 p.
LC: Ag 3, '07.

K-305   Klarmann, Andrew Francis, 1866-1931. The fool of God: a historical novel / by Andrew Klarmann. New York; Cincinnati [etc.]: Frederick Pustet & Co., 1912. 533 p., col. front. (port.), [1] leaf of plates. [Ill. J. E. Biry.]
LC: Jl 16, '12.
PW: Ag 31, '12.

K-306   ____ Nizra: the flower of the Parsa: the visit of the wisemen / by Andrew Klarmann. St. Louis; Freiburg [Germany]: B. Herder, 1908. 303 p.
LC: O 8, '08.
PW: N 21, '08.

K-307   ____ The princess of Gan-Sar: (Mary Magdalen) / by Andrew Klarmann. Ratisbon [Regensberg]; Rome; New York; Cincinnati: Fr. Pustet & Co., 1907. 421 p.
LC: Ag 5, '07.
PW: Ag 24, '07.

Klaxton, Karl. The agnosticism of Dolly Rosa. In *The lady of the tower* (1909), L-13.

K-308   Kleber, John Christopher, b. 1861. The master spirit / by John C. Kleber . . . New York: Cochrane Publishing Company, 1909. 340 p.
LC: F 5, '10.

K-309   Kleberg, Alfred Leon, b. 1881. Slang fables from afar / by Al Kleberg. Baltimore, Md.: Phoenix Publishing Co., [c1903]. 94 p.
PW: Jl 18, '03.

K-310   Klein, Charles, 1867-1915. The gamblers: a story of to-day / by Charles Klein and Arthur Hornblow; illustrations by C. E. Chambers. New York: G. W. Dillingham Company, [c1911]. 351 p., front., [3] leaves of plates.
LC: Je 7, '11.
PW: Je 10, '11.

K-311   ____ John Marsh's millions: a novel / by Charles Klein and Arthur Hornblow . . . ; illustrations by Samuel Cahan. New York: G. W. Dillingham Company, [c1910]. 342 p., front., [3] leaves of plates.
LC: Ag 17, '10.
PW: Ag 20, '10.

K-312   ____ The lion and the mouse / by Charles Klein; a story of America life novelized from the play by Arthur Hornblow; illustrations by Stuart Travis. New York: G. W. Dillingham Company, [1906]. 399 p., front., [3] leaves of plates.

LC: Ag 4, '06.
PW: Ag 25, '06.
BLC: London: T. Fisher Unwin; New York [printed], 1906.

K-313 _____ Maggie Pepper / by Charles Klein . . . New York: H. K. Fly Company, [c1911]. 317 p., front., [3] leaves of plates.
LC: Ja 23, '12.
PW: F 17, '12.
BLC: London: W. J. Ham-Smith, [1912].

K-314 _____ The money makers: a story of today / by Charles Klein and Arthur Hornblow; illustrations by Paul Stahr. New York: G. W. Dillingham Company, [c1914]. 340 p., front., [2] leaves of plates.
LC: O 30, '14.
PW: O 24, '14.

K-315 _____ The music master / by Charles Klein, novelised from the play as produced by David Belasco; illustrations by John Rae. New York: Dodd, Mead and Company, 1909. 341 p., col. front., [3] leaves of col. plates.
LC: Mr 18, '09.
PW: Mr 27, '09.
BLC: London: B. F. Stevens & Brown; printed in U. S. A., 1909. Another edition: London: Hodder & Stoughton, [1909].

K-316 _____ The third degree: a narrative of metropolitan life / by Charles Klein and Arthur Hornblow; illustrations by Clarence Rowe. New York: G. W. Dillingham Co., [c1909]. 356 p., front., [5] leaves of plates.
LC: N 27, '09.
PW: N 20, '09.

K-317 Klein, Edwin G. The stolen automobile / by Edwin G. Klein. [New York: Lenz & Riecker], c1919. 22 p. **NYP**

K-318 Klette, C. H. B. (Charles Herman Bruno), b. 1861. The lost mine of the Mono: a tale of the Sierra Nevada / by C. H. B. Klette. New York: Cochrane Publishing Company, 1909, [c1908]. 215 p.

K-319 Klinck, Albert J. The lady in mauve / by Albert J. Klinck. Boston: Sherman, French & Company, 1911. 134 p.
LC: Jl 3, '11.
PW: Jl 1, '11.

K-320 _____ The quest for the Empress / by Albert J. Klinck. New York; London; Montreal: The Abbey Press, [c1901]. 93 p. **DLC**

Kline, Burton, b. 1877. The caller in the night. In *The best short stories of 1917 and the yearbook of the American short story* **(1918), B-562.**

K-321 _____ The end of the flight / by Burton Kline. New York: John Lane Company; London: John Lane, The Bodley Head, 1917. 441 p.
LC: Ap 17, '17.
PW: Ap 14, '17.

K-322 _____ The gallant rogue / by Burton Kline; with frontispiece by F. Vaux Wilson. Boston: Little, Brown and Company, 1921. 318 p., front.
LC: Ap 28, '21.
PW: Ap 16, '21.

_____ In the open code. In *The best short stories of 1918 and the yearbook of the American short story* **(1919), B-563.**

K-323 _____ Struck by lightening: the comedy of being a man / by Burton Kline. New York: John Lane Company; London: John Lane, The Bodley Head, 1916. 308 p.
LC: Ap 17, '16.
PW: Ap 22, '16.
BLC: London: John Lane; New York [printed], 1916.

K-324 Klingle, George. The Charlatan's prophecy / George Klingle. Boston: Richard G. Badger; Toronto: The Copp Clark Co., Limited, [c1915]. 399 p.
PW: Ag 7, '15.

K-325 Klinker, Lewis William. Winning a fortune / by Lewis Wm. Klinker; illustrations by Orpha Mae Klinker. [Hammond, Ind.; Chicago]: W. B. Conkey Company, [c1915]. 477 p., front., [4] leaves of plates.

K-326 Knapp, Adeline, 1860-1909. The well in the desert / by Adeline Knapp. New York: The Century Co., 1908. 329 p.
LC: Ag 19, '08.
PW: S 5, '08.

K-327 Knapp, George Leonard, b. 1872. The face of air / by George L. Knapp . . . New York: John Lane Company; London: John Lane, The Bodley Head; Toronto: Bell & Cockburn, 1912. 170 p.
LC: O 5, '12.

K-328 _____ The scales of justice / by George L. Knapp; with illustrations in color by the Kinneys. Philadelphia; London: J. B. Lippincott Company, 1910. 307, [1] p., col. front., [2] leaves of col. plates.
LC: S 26, '10.

Knapp, Gertrude Allen. "Rock of Ages". In *Club stories* **(1915), C-502.**

_____ Tod's "Santy". In *Club stories* **(1915), C-502.**

K-329 Knapp, Margaret Lizzie. But still a man / by Margaret L. Knapp. Boston: Little, Brown, and Company, 1909. 376 p.
LC: F 8, '09.
PW: F 13, '09.

K-330 Knapp, Shepherd, b. 1873. Old Joe: and other Vesper stories / by Shepherd Knapp. New York; Cincinnati: The Abingdon Press, [c1922]. 297 p.
Contents: Old Joe -- Repentance for a purpose -- The nurse -- Monsieur le Curé -- The head of the firm -- The garden -- The field -- The art of knowing how -- The mountain pass -- Doors -- The gift -- A successful experiment -- Goblins and fairies -- The waiter -- His conquerors -- The manger-a Christmas legend.
LC: Je 9, '22.

K-331   Knauss, Elizabeth. The conflict: a narrative based on the fundamentalist movement / by Elizabeth Knauss. California: Bible Institute of Los Angeles, c1923. 225 p.

K-332   Knevels, Gertrude, 1881-1962. Octagon house / by Gertrude Knevels. New York; London: D. Appleton and Company, 1925. 308 p.
PW: S 5, '25.

K-333   Knibbs, Henry Herbert, 1874-1945. Lost Farm camp / by Harry Herbert Knibbs; illustrated by Harold James Cue. Boston; New York: Houghton Mifflin Company, 1912. (Cambridge: Riverside Press). 354, [2] p., front., [3] leaves of plates.
LC: Mr 27, '12.
PW: Mr 30, '12.
BLC: London: Constable & Co.; Cambridge, Mass. [printed], 1912.

K-334   [____] Overland Red: a romance of the Moonstone Cañon trail; with illustrations by Anton Fischer. Boston; New York: Houghton Miffin Company, 1914. (Cambridge: The Riverside Press). 348, [2] p., col. front., [3] leaves of col. plates.
PW: Mr 7, '14.
BLC: London: Hodder & Stoughton, [1925].

K-335   ____ Partners of chance / by Henry Herbert Knibbs. Boston; New York: Houghton Mifflin Company, 1921. (Cambridge: The Riverside Press). 281 p.
LC: N 10, '21.
PW: N 19, '21.
BLC: London: Houghton Mifflin Company; Cambridge, Mass. printed, 1922.

K-336   ____ The ridin' kid from Powder River / by Henry Herbert Knibbs; with illustrations. Boston; New York: Houghton Mifflin Company, 1919. 457, [1] p., col. front., [4] leaves of plates. [Ill. by Stanley L. Wood and R. M. Brinkerhoff.]
LC: O 13, '19.
BLC: London: Hodder & Stoughton; Cambridge, Mass printed, [1921].

K-337   ____ Stephen March's way / by Harry Herbert Knibbs; illustrated by H. Weston Taylor. Boston; New York: Houghton Mifflin Company, 1913. (Cambridge, Mass.: The Riverside Press). 277, [1] p., front., [2] leaves of plates.
LC: Mr 12, '13.
PW: Mr 15, '13.

K-338   ____ Sundown Slim / by Henry Herbert Knibbs; with illustrations by Anton Fischer. Boston; New York: Houghton Mifflin Company, 1915. (Cambridge: The Riverside Press). 356, [2] p., col. front., [3] leaves of plates.
LC: My 24, '15.
PW: My 29, '15.
BLC: London: Hodder & Stoughton; Cambridge, Mass. [printed], 1917.

K-339   ____ Tang of life / by Henry Herbert Knibbs: with illustrations by E. Boyd Smith. Boston; New York: Houghton Mifflin Company, 1918. (Cambridge: The Riverside Press). 393, [1] p., col. front., [3] leaves

of col. plates.
LC: Ag 26, '18.
PW: Ag 17, '18.
BLC: London; New York: Andrew Melrose, 1922.

K-340   ____ Temescal / by Henry Herbert Knibbs. Boston; New York: Houghton Mifflin Company, 1925. (Cambridge: The Riverside Press). 369, [1] p.
LC: Ap 6, '25.
PW: Ap 11, '25.
BLC: London: Hutchinson & Co., [1925].

K-341   ____ Wild horses: a novel / by Henry Herbert Knibbs . . . Boston; New York: Houghton Mifflin Company, 1924. (Cambridge: The Riverside Press). 271, [1] p.
LC: F 27, '24.
PW: Mr 8, '24.
BLC: London: Hutchinson & Co., [1924].

Kniffin, Harry Anable. Per contra. In *Thrice told tales* (1924), T-219.

____ The tribute. In *Prize stories of 1921* (1922), **P-619.**

K-342   Kniffin, Thomas Henderson. Kentucky of Kentucky; a romance of the blue grass region / by H. Henderson Kniffin. New York: Cochrane Publishing Co., 1909. 163 p., ill.   **WVU**
LC: O 2, '09.

K-343   Knight of Chillon of Switzerland and associates, *pseud.* The Mormon of the Little Manitou Island: an historical romance / by the Knight of Chillon of Switzerland and associates [pseud.]. New York; London, England: Published by the Uplift Company, [c1916]. 526 p., front. (map), [26] leaves of plates. [Ill. by A.M. Clark.]   **UUM**

K-344   Knight, Adele Ferguson, b. 1867. Mademoiselle Celeste: a romance of the French Revolution / by Adele Ferguson Knight; frontispiece by Clarence F. Underwood. Philadelphia: George W. Jacobs & Company, [1910]. 322 p., col. front.
LC: My 2, '10.
PW: My 14, '10.
BLC: London: Hutchinson & Co., 1911.

K-345   ____ The right to reign: a romance of the kingdom of Drecq / by Adele Ferguson Knight; frontispiece by Clarence F. Underwood. Philadelphia: George W. Jacobs & Company, [1912]. 347 p., col. front.
LC: S 17, '12.

K-346   Knight, Gladys. Marriage for two / by Gladys Knight. New York: Boni and Liveright, [c1924]. 256 p.   **CLE**
LC: Jl 5, '24.
PW: Je 28, '24.

K-347   Knight, Reynolds. Tommy of the voices / by Reynolds Knight. Chicago: A. C. McClurg & Co., 1918. 374 p.
LC: S 13, '18.

K-348   Knight, William Allen, 1863-1957. At the crossing with Denis McShane / by William Allen Knight . . . ; drawings by Florence Scovel Shinn. Boston; New York; Chicago: The Pilgrim Press, 1912. 58 p., col. front., [4] leaves of col. plates.
LC: O 16, '12.
PW: O 19, '12.

K-349   ____ A Bedouin lover / by William Allen Knight. New York; Boston; Chicago: The Pilgrim Press, 1913. 54 p., col. front., [1] leaf of col. plates. Designed end papers.
LC: N 6, '13.
PW: N 8, '13.

K-350   ____ The love-watch / by William Allen Knight. Boston; New York; Chicago: The Pilgrim Press, [1904]. 55 p.
PW: D 17, '04.
BLC: London: Arthur F. Bird, [1904].

K-351   ____ No room in the inn / by William Allen Knight. Boston; New York; Chicago: The Pilgrim Press, [1910]. 58 p., col. front., [1] leaf of col. plates. [Ill. by Charles Copeland.] Designed end papers.
LC: S 3, '10.
PW: O 15, '10.
BLC: London: James Clarke & Co.; Norwood, Mass. [printed], 1910.

K-352   ____ Outside a city wall / by William Allen Knight . . . Boston; New York; Chicago: The Pilgrim Press, 1911. 63 p., front.
LC: Mr 28, '11.
PW: N 18, '11.
Contents: Gethsemane -- Calvary -- The garden tomb.

K-353   ____ Peter in the firelight / by William Allen Knight. Boston; New York; Chicago: The Pilgrim Press, 1911. 102, [1] p., front., [2] leaves of plates. [Ill. by Charles Copeland.]
LC: O 9, '11.
PW: N 18, '11.
BLC: London: James Clarke & Co.; Norwood, Mass. [printed], 1911.

K-354   ____ The pictureland of the heart / by William Allen Knight; illustrated by the photographers of the American colony in Jerusalem. New York; Boston; Chicago: The Pilgrim Press, 1916. 259 p., photo. front., [15] leaves of photo. plates, ill. Photographic illustrations on end papers.
LC: S 29, '16.
PW: S 16, '16.

K-355   ____ Saint Abigail of the pines / by William Allen Knight; frontispiece by George A. Williams. Boston; New York; Chicago: The Pilgrim Press, 1905. 185 p., front.
PW: O 28, '05.
BLC: London: Gay & Bird; Cambridge, U. S. A. [printed, 1905].

K-356   ____ The shepherd of Jebel Nur / by William Allen Knight. Boston; New York; Chicago: The Pilgrim Press, 1909. [34] p., front.
LC: Ag 21, '09.
PW: N 13, '09.

K-357   ____ The signs in the Christmas fire / by William Allen Knight. Boston; New York; Chicago: The Pilgrim Press, 1908. [32] p., front. Designed end papers.
LC: D 8, '07.
PW: O 10, '08.

K-358   ____ The song of our Syrian guest / William Allen Knight. Boston: The Pilgrim Press, [1903?]. 14 p. Reprinted from "The Congregationalist."
PW: My 7, '04.
Another edition: Illustrations and decorative designs by Charles Copeland. Boston; New York; Chicago: The Pilgrim Press, [1904]. [46] p., front., [2] leaves of plates.
LC: O 13, '06.
PW: My 7, '04.
BLC: Stirling: Drummond's Tract Depot, [1905].

K-359   ____ The well by Bethlehem's gate / by William Allen Knight . . . New York; Boston; Chicago: The Pilgrim Press, 1914. 55 p., photo. front., [3] leaves of photo. plates. [Ill. by the photographers of the American colony in Jerusalem.]
LC: Jl 9, '14.
PW: S 19, '14.
BLC: London: J. Clarke & Co., [1914].

Knipe, Alden Arthur, 1870-1950, jt. aut. See **Knipe, Emilie Benson, 1870-1958, jt. aut.**

K-360   Knipe, Emilie Benson, 1870-1958. A cavalier maid / by Emilie Benson Knipe and Alden Arthur Knipe . . . ; illustrated by Emilie Benson Knipe. New York: The Macmillan Company, 1919. 255 p., front., [5] leaves of plates.
LC: O 22, '19.
PW: N 8, '19.

K-361   ____ The flower of fortune / by Emilie Benson Knipe and Alden Arthur Knipe . . . ; illustrated by Emilie Benson Knipe. New York: The Century Co., [c1922]. 354 p., front., [3] leaves of plates.
LC: S 19, '22.
PW: S 30, '22.

K-362   ____ Girls of '64 / by Emilie Benson Knipe and Alden Arthur Knipe . . . ; illustrated by Emilie Benson Knipe. New York: The Macmillan Company, 1918. 262 p., front., [5] leaves of plates.
LC: O 30, '18.
PW: N 16, '18.

K-363   ____ A maid of '76 / by Emilie Benson Knipe and Alden Arthur Knipe; illustrated by Emilie Benson Knipe. New York: The Macmillan Company, 1915. 276 p., front., [5] leaves of plates.
LC: S 30, '15.
PW: O 23, '15.

K-364   ____ A Mayflower maid / by Emilie Benson Knipe and Alden Arthur Knipe; illustrated by Emilie Benson Knipe. New York: The Century Co., [c1920]. 287 p., front., [3] leaves of plates.
LC: S 22, '20.
PW: S 25, '20.

K-365   ____ Peg o' the ring: a maid of Denewood / by Emilie Benson Knipe and Alden Arthur Knipe; illustrations by C. M. Relyea. New York: The Century Co., 1915. 375 p., front., [15] leaves of plates.
LC: S 30, '15.
PW: S 25, '15.

K-366   ____ Powder, patches and Patty / by Emilie Benson Knipe and Alden Arthur Knipe . . . ; illustrated by Emilie Benson Knipe. New York; London: The Century Co., [c1924]. 305 p., front., [3] leaves of plates.
LC: S 17, '24.
PW: S 20, '24.

K-367   ____ The shadow captain: an account of the activities of one Christopher Rousby in the town of New Yorke during several months of the year of Our Lord 1703; the narrative compiled from notes gathered and set down by Launcelot dove, one time chief lieutenant to the famous Captain William Kidd. These, together with facts not well known to history, are here set forth / by Emilie Benson Knipe and Alden Arthur Knipe. New York: Dodd, Mead and Company, 1925. 347 p.
LC: Mr 3, '25.
PW: F 28, '25.

K-368   ____ Vive la France: a narrative founded on the diary of Jeannette de Martigny / by Emilie Benson Knipe and Alden Arthur Knipe; illustrated by Emilie Benson Knipe. New York: The Century Co., [1919]. 364 p., front., [7] leaves of plates.
LC: S 2, '19.
PW: S 20, '19.

Knister, Raymond. Mist-green oats. In *Stories from the Midland* (1924), S-984.

K-369 Knoppe, A. D., *pseud.* The De Wiltons of Virginia / by A. D. Knoppe [pseud.]. New York: Broadway Publishing Company, 1904. 196 p.

K-370 Knott, Henry. The destroyer: man to demon: the devastation of a life by strong drink / by Henry Knott. Chicago, Ill.: W. R. Vansant & Co., Copyright 1908. 222 p., incl. front., [7] leaves of plates. [Ill. by F. I. Wetherbee.]   **GZP**
LC: D 4, '08.

K-371 Knowles, Charles Edward. In quest of gold: being a romance dealing with the remarkable expedition of Ferdinand De Soto and his cavaliers to Florida in the year 1539 / by Charles E. Knowles; illustrations by Howard M. Nesmith. New York: John Lane Company, 1912. 228 p., front., [3] leaves of plates.
PW: Mr 23, '12.

K-372 Knowles, R. G. (Richard George), 1858-1919. Of stories- just a few / by R. G. Knowles. New York; Chicago; London: M. Witmark & Sons, [c1904]. 178 p., front. (port.), [1] leaf of plates, ill.
Contents: Dedication -- Note -- The kilted German -- A night in the bush -- The coal-black Egyptian -- Music as an aid to industry -- The city of three questions -- The added amendment -- Good dog, bad man, medium parson -- "Next" -- Over the rail -- The unrehearsed effect -- The modern buccaneer -- With the driver -- The last drink --

The joys of the sunny south -- Woman's heart -- Friendly enemies -- The boon of companionship -- Australia, ahoy! -- The cruise of the millionaires -- How to write a story.

K-373 Knowlton, J. A. (James Albert). Leeden's league, or, The voyager's quest / by James Albert Knowlton; the endeavors of resolute men, who through a hundred trials are led onward by an unseen hand to a desired goal, are herein related. Tipton, Indiana: J. Otto Lee, [1923]. 425 p.   **DLC**

K-374 Knox, Dorothea Heness. The heart of Washington / by Dorothea Heness Knox. New York; Washington: The Neale Publishing Company, 1909. 238 p.
LC: Ag 9, '09.

K-375 Knox, Janette Hill. Justa Hamlin's vocation / by Janette Hill Knox. New York; London; Montreal: Abbey Press, [1902]. 238 p.

K-376 Knox, Jessie Juliet. In the house of the Tiger / by Jessie Juliet Knox . . . Cincinnati: Jennings and Graham; New York: Eaton and Mains, [c1911]. 255 p., photo. front. (port.), [30] leaves of photo. plates.   **EYM**
LC: N 4, '11.

K-377 Kobbé, Gustav, 1857-1918. All-of-a-sudden Carmen / by Gustav Kobbé . . . ; illustated. New York; London: G. P. Putnam's Sons, 1917. ([New York]: The Knickerbocker Press). 278 p., front., [3] leaves of plates. [Ill. by William Van Dresser.]   **NYP**
LC: My 8, '17.

K-378   ____ Modern women / by Gustav Kobbé. New York: Moffat, Yard & Company, 1915. 130 p. Reprinted in part from various periodicals.
Contents: Clothes -- Speed -- News -- Love -- Man -- Show -- Horse -- Song -- Nerves -- Art -- Street -- End.
LC: S 30, '15.

K-379   ____ Signora: a child of the opera house / by Gustav Kobbé. New York: R. H. Russell, 1902. 205 p., photo. front., [15] leaves of plates (some photo.). [Ill. by Charles M. Relyea, A. Dupont, and E. W. Histed.]   **CIN**
PW: N 22, '02.

K-380 Koblegard, B. A. The mystery of the stone mill / by B. A. Koblegard. [Springfield, Ohio?: Herb Medicine Co.?, 191-?]. [32] p.

K-381 Koester, Frank, 1876-1927. Under the desert stars: a novel / by Frank Koester; illustrated by L. C. Van Benscoten. New York, N. Y.: Washington Square Publishing Company, c1923. 317 p., col. front., ill.

K-382 Kofoed, William H. Mirage / by William H. Kofoed. New York: Robert J. Shores, [c1917]. 379 p.   **NYP**
LC: Mr 18, '18.

K-383 Kohr, Herbert O. (Herbert Ornando), b. 1875. The escort of an emperor: a story of China during the great Boxer movement / by H. O. Kohr; dictated by a blind man who lost both eyes in a dynamite explosion. [Akron, Ohio?: s. n.], 1910. 268 p., photo. front. (port.).
LC: My 7, '10.

K-384   Kolle, Loretto E.   The blue lawn / by Loretto E.
         Kolle.   New York: R. F. Fenno & Company,
         [c1910].   278 p.
         LC: Ag 18, '10.
         PW: Ag 13, '10.

K-385   Komroff, Manuel, b. 1890.   The grace of lambs /
         stories by Manuel Komroff.   New York: Boni &
         Liveright, 1925.   221 p.
         Contents: The grace of lambs -- The little master of the sky -- The
         burning beard -- The dark cloak -- A union of beggars -- The beating
         of the reed -- Thumbs -- A Moscow rehearsal -- A wedding feast --
         Lady Lotto -- En route -- In a Russian tea-house -- The political horse
         -- How does it feel to be free?
         BLC: London: Jonathan Cape, 1926.

_____   The little master of the sky.   In *The best short
         stories of 1921 and the yearbook of the American
         short story* (1922), **B-566.**

         Koons, Ulysses Sidney.   See **Jabez, Brother, pseud.**

K-386   Koontz, Frederick Luther.   The dial of destiny / by
         Frederick Luther Koontz.   Boston, Mass.: The
         Roxburgh Publishing Company, [c1911].   323 p.,
         front., [5] leaves of plates.   [Ill. by Tinsley
         Mayer.]   **DLC**

K-387   Kortrecht, Augusta.   A Dixie rose / by Augusta
         Kortrecht; with a frontispiece by Ethel Pennewill
         Brown.   Philadelphia; London: J. B. Lippincott
         Company, 1910.   284 p., col. front.
         LC: S 26, '10.
         PW: O 26, '12.

         Kouns, Nathan C.   The Man-Dog.   In *Argonaut
         stories* (1906), **A-298.**

         Kozlay, Charles Meeker, comp.   See **Harte, Bret.**
         Stories and poems and other uncollected writings
         (1914), **H-326.**

K-388   Kramer, Harold Morton, 1873-1930.   The castle of
         dawn / by Harold Morton Kramer . . . ; illustrated by
         H. C. Edwards.   Boston: Lothrop, Lee & Shepard
         Co., [c1908].   409 p., front., [5] leaves of plates.
                                                        NYP
         LC: Mr 23, '08.
         PW: Ap 4, '08.

K-389   _____   The chrysalis / by Harold Morton Kramer
         . . . ; illustrated by H. C. Edwards.   Boston:
         Lothrop, Lee & Shepard Co., [1909].   419 p., front.,
         [5] leaves of plates.
         LC: Mr 11, '09.
         PW: Ap 10, '09.

K-390   _____   Gayle Langford: being the romance of a Tory
         belle and a patriot captain / by Harold Morton
         Kramer . . . ; illustrated by H. C. Edwards.   Boston:
         Lothrop, Lee & Shepard Co., 1907.   386 p., front.,
         [5] leaves of plates.
         LC: Ag 1, '07.
         PW: S 14, '07.

K-391   _____   Hearts and the cross / by Harold Morton
         Kramer; illustrated by Harold Matthews Brett.
         Boston: Lothrop, Lee & Shepard Co., [1906].

414 p. incl. front., [7] leaves of plates.
PW: S 22, '06.

K-392   _____   The rugged way / by Harold Morton Kramer;
         illustrated by F. Vaux Wilson.   Boston: Lothrop, Lee
         & Shepard Co., [1911].   428 p., front., [3] leaves of
         plates.
         LC: Ag 2, '11.
         PW: Ag 26, '11.

K-393   Kratzer, Elizabeth Cary.   Complete in Him / by
         Elizabeth Cary Kratzer. -- First edition. -- Chicago,
         Ill.: Published and for sale by Rev. G. A. Kratzer,
         [c1913].   235 p.   **OSU, COI**

         Krause, Lyda Farrington, 1864-1939.   See **Yechton,
         Barbara, pseud.**

K-394   Krausz, Sigmund.   The cameo of the empress / by
         Sigmund Krausz; illustrated by Lucile Patterson.
         Chicago: Laird & Lee, [c1912].   280 p., front., [4]
         leaves of plates.

         Krebs, Abbie E., ed.   See **Pacific Coast Women's
         Press Association.** *La copa de oro* (1905), **P-2.**

K-395   Kreymborg, Alfred, 1883-1966.   Erna Vitek / by
         Alfred Kreymborg.   New York: Albert and Charles
         Boni, 1914.   131 p.
         LC: Ag 1, '14.

K-396   Krishna, Kamala.   Torchbearers: a story of the
         realms of the mastersouls / by Kamala Krishna . . .
         Chicago: Solar Logos Publishing Co., 1925.   380 p.

K-397   Krooks, Jeremiah.   Them orfins / by Jeremiah
         Krooks.   [S. l.: s. n., 1913?].   [86] p., [4] leaves of
         photo. plates, ill.
         On cover: A story of Buckwheet Township.

         Krout, Caroline Virginia, 1852-1931.   See **Brown,
         Caroline, pseud.**

K-398   Krull, Vigilius H. (Vigilius Herman), b. 1874.   The
         test of love / by V. H. Krull.   Chicago: M. A.
         Donohue & Co., 1917.   38 p.   **DLC**

         Krysto, Christina.   Babanchik.   In *Atlantic
         narratives*; 2nd series (1918), **A-361.**

         _____   Phil.   In *California story book* (1909), **C-40.**

         Kubinyi, Florence Marie (Telmany) von, b. 1895.
         See **Gloria, F. M., pseud.**

K-399   Kubinyi, Victor von, b. 1875.   Mr. Man / by Victor
         de Kubinyi; decorations by the author.   New York:
         [s. n.], 1920.   160 p., [7] leaves of plates.   **NYP**
         PW: Mr 6, '20.

K-400   [Kuhn, Amanda Maria (Tiernan), Mrs.], 1841-1913.
         Patty Leroy . . .   Boston: R. G. Badger, [c1913].
         221 p.
         Unexamined copy: bibliographic data from NUC.

K-401 [Kummer, Frederic Arnold], 1873-1943. The blue lights / by Arnold Fredericks [pseud.] . . . ; illustrations by Will Grefé. New York: W. J. Watt & Company, [c1915]. 313 p., front., [2] leaves of plates.
Cover title: *The blue lights: a detective story.*
LC: Mr 2, '15.
PW: Ja 22, '16.

K-402 _____ The brute / by Frederic Arnold Kummer; illustrations by Frank Snapp. New York: W. J. Watt & Company, [1912]. 314 p., front., [3] leaves of plates.
LC: Ap 29, '12.
PW: Je 15, '12.

K-403 [_____] The film of fear / by Arnold Fredericks [pseud.]; frontispiece by Will Foster. New York: W. J. Watt & Company, [c1917]. 314 p., front., [1] leaf of plates.
LC: Jl 12, '17.
PW: Jl 28, '17.

K-404 _____ The green god / by Frederic Arnold Kummer; illustrations by R. F. Schabelitz. New York: W. J. Watt & Company, [1911]. 301 p., front., [3] leaves of plates.
LC: O 10, '11.
PW: N 18, '11.

K-405 [_____] The ivory snuff box / by Arnold Fredericks [pseud.]; illustrations by Will Grefé. New York: W. J. Watt & Company, [c1912]. 278 p., front., [2] leaves of plates.
LC: O 24, '12.
PW: N 9, '12.

K-406 [_____] The little fortune / by Arnold Fredricks [pseud.]; illustrations by Will Grefé. New York: W. J. Watt & Company, [c1915]. 301 p., front., [2] leaves of plates.
LC: N 20, '15.
PW: Ja 22, '16.

K-407 _____ A lost paradise / by Frederic Arnold Kummer; frontispiece by Will Grefé. New York: W. J. Watt & Company, [c1914]. 312 p., front.
LC: Ap 23, '14.
PW: O 24, '14.

K-408 [_____] One million francs / Arnold Fredericks [pseud.]; illustrations by Will Grefé. New York: W. J. Watt & Company, [c1912]. 305 p., front., [4] leaves of plates.
LC: Ap 29, '12.
PW: Je 15, '12.

K-409 _____ The painted woman / by Frederic Arnold Kummer; frontispiece by George W. Gage. New York: W. J. Watt & Company, [c1917]. 311 p., col. front.
LC: Jl 12, '17.
PW: Ag 25, '17.

K-410 _____ Peggy-Elise / by Frederic Arnold Kummer and Mary Christian. New York: The Century Co., 1919. 330 p., front.

LC: S 30, '19.
PW: S 27, '19.

K-411 _____ The pipes of yesterday: a novel / by Frederic Arnold Kummer and Mary Christian. New York: The Century Co., 1921. 224 p.
LC: F 21, '21.
PW: Mr 5, '21.

K-412 _____ Plaster saints / by Frederic Arnold Kummer; frontispiece by Joseph Franké. New York: The Macaulay Company, [c1922]. 318 p., front.
LC: Ap 25, '22.
PW: Je 10, '22.
Apparent later printing: . . . Illustrated with scenes from the photo-play screened as "The Spitfire." (with [3] additional plates).

K-413 _____ The road to fortune / by Frederic Arnold Kummer. New York: George H. Doran Company, [c1925]. 316 p.
PW: N 14, '25.
BLC: London: Hodder & Stoughton, [1926].

K-414 _____ The second coming: a vision / by Frederic Arnold Kummer and Henry P. Janes. New York: Dodd, Mead and Company, 1916. 96 p.   **DTM**
LC: Ap 18, '16.
PW: Ap 15, '16.

K-415 _____ A song of sixpence / by Frederic Arnold Kummer; illustrations by R. F. Schabelitz. New York: W. J. Watt & Company, [1913]. 285 p., front., [5] leaves of plates (2 double-leaf).
PW: Mr 15, '13.

K-416 _____ The web: a novel / by Frederic Arnold Kummer. New York: The Century Co., 1919. 280 p.
LC: F 7, '19.
PW: F 1, '19.

K-417 Kunst, Earle. The mystery of Evangeline Fairfax / by Earle Kunst; drawings by H. Richard Boehm. New York: The Metropolitan Press, 1910. 242 p., front., [3] leaves of plates.
LC: Mr 17, '10.

K-418 Kussy, Nathan, b. 1872. The abyss / by Nathan Kussy. New York: The Macmillan Company, 1916. 508 p.
LC: Mr 9, '16.
PW: Jl 1, '16.

K-419 _____ Grinmar: a novel / by Nathan Kussy; illustrated by Wm. L. Hudson. New York: Broadway Publishing Co., [c1907]. 174 p., front., [4] leaves of plates.
LC: Ap 4, '07.
PW: My 4, '07.

K-420 Kutchin, Victor. Love among the ruins / by Victor Kutchin. Stevens Point, Wis.: Worzalla Publishing Co., [c1925]. 397 p., photo. front. (port.), [4] leaves of plates.
LC: Ja 17, '25.
PW: Ap 18, '25.

K-421 Kyle, George A. (George Alexander), b. 1872. The Morning Glory club / by George A. Kyle; with a frontispiece in colours by Arthur O. Scott. Boston: L. C. Page and Company, 1907. 250 p., col. front.
LC: Mr 18, '07.
PW: Mr 30, '07.

K-422 Kyne, Peter B. (Peter Bernard), 1880-1957. Cappy Ricks, or, The subjugation of Matt Peasley / by Peter B. Kyne; illustrated by Harvey Dunn and Anton Otto Fischer. New York: The H. K. Fly Company, [c1916]. 349 p., front., [3] leaves of plates.
LC: My 26, '16.
PW: O 28, '16.
BLC: London: Hodder & Stoughton, [1919].

K-423 _____ Cappy Ricks retires: but that doesn't keep him from coming back stronger than ever / by Peter B. Kyne; illustrated by T. D. Skidmore. New York: Cosmopolitan Book Corporation, 1922. 442 p., front., [3] leaves of plates.
LC: S 2, '22.
PW: Ag 26, '22.
BLC: London: Hodder & Stoughton, [1922].

K-424 _____ The enchanted hill / by Peter B. Kyne; illustrations by Dean Cornwell. New York: Cosmopolitan Book Corporation, 1924. 369 p., col. front., [2] leaves of col. plates (double-leaf).
LC: O 24, '24.
PW: O 25, '24.
BLC: London: Hodder & Stoughton, [1924].

K-425 _____ The go-getter: a story that tells you how to be one / by Peter B. Kyne. New York: Cosmopolitan Book Corporation, 1921. 62 p.
LC: O 10, '21.
PW: N 12, '21.
BLC: London: Hodder & Stoughton, 1921.

K-426 _____ The Green-pea pirates / by Peter B. Kyne; illustrated by Gordon Grant. Garden City; New York: Doubleday, Page & Company, 1919. 308 p., front., [3] leaves of plates.
LC: N 21, '19.
PW: N 1, '19.
BLC: London: Hodder & Stoughton, [1920].

K-427 _____ Kindred of the dust / by Peter B. Kyne . . . ; illustrated by Dean Cornwell. New York: Cosmopolitan Book Corporation, 1920. 376 p., front., [3] leaves of plates.
LC: My 17, '20.
PW: My 22, '20.
BLC: London: Hodder & Stoughton, [1920].

K-428 _____ The long chance / by Peter B. Kyne; illustrated by Frank Tenny Johnson. New York: The H. K. Fly Company, [c1914]. 313 p., col. front., [3] leaves of col. plates.
PW: Ap 10, '15.

K-429 _____ Never the twain shall meet / by Peter B. Kyne . . . ; illustrations by Dean Cornwell. New York: Cosmopolitan Book Corporation, 1923. 375 p., front., [2] leaves of col. plates (double-leaf).
LC: O 22, '23.

PW: N 3, '23.
BLC: London: Hodder & Stoughton, [1923].

K-430 _____ The pride of Palomar / by Peter B. Kyne . . . ; illustrated by H. R. Ballinger and Dean Cornwell. New York: Cosmopolitan Book Corporation, 1921. 372 p., front., [3] leaves of plates (1 col. double-leaf).
LC: S 26, '21.
PW: O 1, '21.
BLC: London: Hodder & Stoughton, [1921].

K-431 _____ The three godfathers / by Peter B. Kyne; illustrated by Maynard Dixon. New York: George H. Doran Company, Publishers in America for Hodder & Stoughton, [c1913]. 95 p., col. front., [3] leaves of col. plates.
LC: N 24, '13.
PW: Ja 31, '14.
BLC: London: Hodder & Stoughton; printed in U. S. A., 1914.

K-432 _____ Valley of the giants / by Peter B. Kyne; illustrated by Dean Cornwell. Garden City, N. Y.: Doubleday, Page & Company, 1918. 388 p., col. front., [3] leaves of plates.
LC: O 3, '18.
PW: O 12, '18.
BLC: London: Hodder & Stoughton, [1919].

K-433 _____ Webster--man's man / by Peter B. Kyne . . . ; illustrated by Dean Cornwell. Garden City, New York: Doubleday, Page & Company, 1917. 384 p., col. front., [3] leaves of plates.   **EEM**
LC: O 3, '17.
PW: O 6, '17.
BLC: London: Hodder & Stoughton, 1919.

L

L-1 L. G. T. Three years behind the guns: the true chronicles of a "diddy-box" / by L. G. T.; illustrated by Chris Jörgensen and George Varian and with photographs. New York: The Century Co., 1908. 293 p., front., incl. [30] leaves of plates.

L. S. B. S., jt. aut. Studies in college colour. In *A book of Bryn Mawr stories* **(1901), B-732.**

L-2 L. T. T. L. Alice Carson's beggar / by "L. T. T. L." Richmond, Virginia: Whittet & Shepperson Printers, 1901. 15 p.   **WVU**

Lacey, Joseph Berry, b. 1842. See **Knoppe, A. D., pseud.**

La Coste, Guy Robert. See **Berton, Guy, jt. pseud. of Guy Robert La Coste and Eadfrid A. Bingham.**

L-3 Lacoste, Lucie. Fantine Avenel / by Lucie Lacoste . . . Boston; New York: The Cornhill Publishing Company, 1922. 382 p.   **DLC**
LC: N 21, '22.

L-4 _____ Miminetta / by Lucie Lacoste. New York: The Avondale Press, 1917. 127 p., front.   **DLC**
LC: O 18, '17.

L-5 La Croix, Arda. Billy the kid: a romantic story. Founded upon the play of the same name / by Arda LaCroix. New York: J. S. Ogilvie, c1907. 128 p., front. (port.), plate.
Unexamined copy: bibliographic data from OCLC, #13928718.
LC: S 25, '07.
PW: O 5, '07.

L-6 Ladd, Anna Coleman. The candid adventurer / by Anna Coleman Ladd. Boston; New York: Houghton Mifflin Company, 1913. (Cambridge: The Riverside Press). 307, [1] p., col. front.
LC: Mr 12, '13.

L-7 Ladd, Frederic Pierpont, 1870-1947. After: a novel / by Frederic Pierpont Ladd. New York: Duffield & Company, 1918. 311 p.
LC: Mr 14, '18.
PW: Mr 30, '18.

L-8 _____ The lady of Shenipsit: a novel of New England / by Frederic P. Ladd; with illustrations by Gordon Grant. New York: Sturgis & Walton Company, 1910. 335 p., front., [3] leaves of plates.
LC: S 1, '10.
PW: S 10, '10.

L-9 _____ The last of the Puritans: the story of Benjamin Gilbert and his friends / by Frederic P. Ladd; ten illustrations by M. S. Mulford. New York: F. M. Lupton, Publisher (Incorporated), [c1912]. 240 p., front., [9] leaves of plates.
LC: Ap 27, '12.
PW: Ap 27, '12.

L-10 _____ One fair daughter: a story / by Frederick P. Ladd . . . ; illustrations by Gordon Grant. New York: Mitchell Kennerley, [c1909]. 259 p., [2] leaves of plates.   **DLC**
LC: F 15, '09.
PW: Mr 13, '09.

L-11 _____ The woman pays / by Frederic P. Ladd; illustrations by Gordon Grant. New York: Mitchell Kennerley, [c1908]. 278 p., front., [3] leaves of plates.   **NYP**
LC: Je 6, '08.

L-12 Ladd, Horatio O. (Horatio Oliver), 1839-1932. Chunda: a story of the Navajos / by Horatio Oliver Ladd. New York: Eaton & Mains; Cincinnati: Jennings & Graham, [c1906]. 257 p., front., [6] leaves of photo. plates.
LC: O 20, '06.

L-13 The lady of the tower: and other stories / by George Barton, Peter K. Guilday, Marion Ames Taggart . . . [et al.]. New York; Cincinnati; Chicago: Benziger Brothers, 1909. 286 p.   **DLC**
Contents: The Lady of the tower / George Barton -- Greater love than this / Peter K. Guilday -- A woman's way / Marion Ames Taggart -- Major Bobby, peacemaker / Marion Ames Taggart -- We two and Miss Pamela / Maud Regan -- The bell of Santa Marta / Mary E. Mannix -- The picture in the fire / Jerome Harte -- At summer's close / Anna Blanche McGill -- The lady of the roses / Maud Regan -- Stephen Oxenham's mistake / Magdalen Rock -- The light fantastic / Marion Ames Taggart -- St. Patrick and the pink gown / Eileen Farley -- What influenced Jim / Katharine Jenkins --

The heir / Magdalen Rock -- The war of the roses / Marion Ames Taggart -- At the tolling of the Angelus / Sylvestre Perry -- "The last shall be first" / May Finnegan -- After twenty-five years / Florence Gilmore -- The agnosticism of Dolly Rosa / Karl Klaxton -- "Just a story" / Ursula Margaret Trainor.
LC: Ap 28, '09.
PW: My 8, '09.

L-14 Lagen, M. J. (Mary Julia). Daphne and her lad / by M. J. Lagen and Cally Ryland; with a frontispiece by Eliot Keen. New York: Henry Holt and Company, 1904. 237 p., front.

La Guardia, Aurora Joan. Communion. In *The best college short stories, 1924-1925* (1925), B-558.

L-15 La Guardia, Richard Dodge. The house of America / by Richard D. La Guardia. Boston: The Christopher Publishing House, [c1925]. 178 p.
LC: S 16, '25.

L-16 Laing, Herbert Greyson. Bob Carlton, American / by Herbert Greyson Laing; with illustrations by R. I. Conklin. Boston, Mass.: The C. M. Clark Publishing Company, [c1910]. 399, [1] p., col. front., [5] leaves of plates.
LC: F 10, '11.
PW: Ja 14, '11.

L-17 Laing, Sallie Wear. Her black body / by Sallie Wear Laing. Newark: The Essex Press, 1921. 324 p., incl. facsimile.   **NOC**
Contents: Her black body -- Her idol -- A row of old shoes -- Cameo bracelet -- Alice -- Her last sweetheart -- Miss Ann's beaux -- Love and life.
LC: F 24, '22.

L-18 Lait, Jack, 1882-1954. Beef, iron and wine / by Jack Lait. Garden City, N. Y.: Doubleday, Page & Company, 1916. 316 p.
Contents: The septagon -- "Charlie the Wolf" -- Felice o' the Follies -- Lars, the Useless, was a nuisance -- If a party meet a party -- Omaha Slim -- Jennie the imp of the night -- Taxi, mister -- The Canada kid -- Second from the end -- Heritage of the suffering brother -- One touch of art -- It wasn't honest, but it was sweet to save the dimes -- Ten dollars' worth -- The gangster's elegy -- Pies -- Annye's ma.
LC: S 30, '16.
BLC: London: William Heinemann, 1917.

L-19 _____ Gus the Bus and Evelyn, the exquisite checker / by Jack Lait . . . Garden City, New York: Doubleday, Page & Company, 1917. 342 p. Reprinted from the Chicago herald.
LC: O 18, '17.

L-20 Lake, Fred Perrine. Uncle Sim / by Fred Perrine Lake. Boston, Massachusetts: The C. M. Clark Publishing Co., 1909. 457 p., front., [7] leaves of plates. [Ill. by B. Goe Willis.]
LC: Je 23, '09.

L-21 Lake, Mary, b. 1873. The drug slave / by Mary Lake. London; New York; [etc.]: Cassell and Company, Ltd., 1913. 344 p.
Unexamined copy: bibliographic data from NUC.

L-22 Lake, Matalee T. As strong as the hills / by Matalee T. Lake. Washington: Terminal Press, Inc., 1921. 86 p., front.
LC: Je 13, '21.

L-23 Lamb, Harold, 1892-1962. The house of the Falcon / by Harold Lamb . . . New York; London: D. Appleton and Company, 1921. 286, [1] p., front. [Ill. by John A. Coughlin.]
LC: Mr 15, '21.

L-24 _____ Marching sands / by Harold Lamb. New York; London: D. Appleton and Company, 1920. 307, [1] p.
LC: Mr 27, '20.

L-25 Lamb, Mary E. (Mary Elizabeth), b. 1839. Irene Liscomb: a story of the old South / --by-- Mary E. Lamb . . . New York: Broadway Publishing Co., [c1908]. 264 p.   **IUA**
LC: D 19, '08.

L-26 Lambert, Mary. Mary Lambert's Raven takes periodical flights scattering the thoughts of its author over the world in verse, essay, story, drama and song, obeying the injunction of Kings III, XVII: "I have commanded the ravens to feed thee." Oakland, Calif.: The Raven Publishing Co., c1924. 64, [1] p., ill.

L-27 Lambourne, Alfred. A trio of sketches: being the reminiscences of The Theater green room and the scene-Painter's gallery from suggestions in "A Play-House" / Alfred Lambourne. [Salt Lake City?, 191-?]. 49 p.   **NYP**
Contents: Anna's wedding -- Beauty and the beast -- The music copyist.

Lamity, K., pseud. <u>See</u> **Bonner, John Sturgis.**

Lamont, Gordon. People don't do such things. <u>In</u> *Made to order* **(1915), M-352.**

L-27.5 Lamont, Watson, b. 1852. Abner Grimes / by W. L. New York: Broadway Publishing Company, 1913. 323 p.
Unexamined copy: bibliographic data from NUC.

L-28 La Motte, Ellen Newbold, 1873-1961. Civilization: tales of the Orient / by Ellen N. La Motte . . . New York: George H. Doran Company, [c1919]. 267 p. Reprinted in part from the Century magazine.
Contents: The yellow streak -- On the heights -- Homesick -- Civilization -- Misunderstanding -- Prisoners -- Canterbury chimes -- Under a wineglass -- Cholera -- Cosmic justice.
LC: Ap 28, '19.

L-29 _____ Snuffs and butters . . . / by Ellen N. La Motte . . . New York; London: Published by the Century Co., [c1925]. 256 p.
Contents: Snuffs and butters -- The Malay girl -- The golden stars -- The middle-class mind -- Proof -- Widows and orphans -- The Cardiff giant -- The onlookers -- In Mashonaland.
LC: Ap 21, '25.
PW: Ap 18, '25.

L-30 Lampton, William J. (William James), d. 1917. The confessions of a husband / by William J. Lampton . . . being a slight offset to "The confessions of a wife", by Mary Adams. New York: Cameron, Blake & Co., 1903. 25 p.   **COS**
PW: Je 6, '03.

_____ How the widow won the deacon. <u>In</u> *The best American humorous short stories* **(1920), B-556.**

L-31 _____ Tame animals I have known: with apologies to such wild animals as may feel aggrieved by comparison: being the personal histories of Algernon, an ass, Mary, a dove, Reuben, a lamb, Bessie, a bird, Ezra, a shark, Araminta, a spring chicken, Hiram, a hog, Maria, a cat, Simon, an orinthorhyncus, Hester, a militantrum, Hezekiah, a lobster, Eliza, a goose / by William J. Lampton. New York: The Neale Publishing Company, 1912. 150 p.

L-32 Lancaster, F. Hewes, 1871-1933. Marie of Arcady / by F. Hewes Lancaster; with a frontispiece by Rose O'Neill. Boston: Small, Maynard & Company, [c1909]. 343 p., front.
LC: O 21, '09.
PW: S 25, '09.

L-33 _____ The one and the other / by Hewes Lancaster . . . Boston: Small, Maynard and Company, [c1912]. 217 p.   **PUL**
LC: F 28, '12.
PW: Mr 2, '12.

L-34 _____ The wind in the garden / by Hewes Lancaster . . . Boston: The Stratford Company, 1919. 152 p.   **IMD**
LC: Ap 22, '19.
PW: My 10, '19.

L-35 Landau, Leo A., b. 1881. The big cinch: a society and financial novel / by Leo A. Landau; with illustrations by George Ed. Brashear. St. Louis: The Franklin Co., [1910]. (St. Louis: Press of Perrin & Smith). 304 p., front., [5] leaves of plates.
LC: Mr 2, '10.

L-36 Landis, D. R. (David Rogers), b. 1846. The pastorate of Martin Wentz: a segment of a consistent life / by D. R. Landis. Greenwood, Ind.: Greenwood Printing Co., [c1908]. 215 p.   **IFC**

L-37 Landis, Frederick, 1872-1934. The angel of Lonesome Hill: a story of a president / by Frederick Landis. New York: Charles Scribner's Sons, 1910. 40 p., front.
PW: My 7, '10.

L-38 _____ The glory of his country / by Frederick Landis. New York: Charles Scribner's Sons, 1910. 266 p.
LC: Mr 7, '10.
PW: Mr 12, '10.

L-39 Landon, Herman, b. 1882. Gray magic: a Gray Phantom mystery / by Herman Landon . . . New York: G. Howard Watt, 1925. 295 p.
LC: F 13, '25.
PW: My 2, '25.

L-40 _____ The Gray Phantom / by Herman Landon. New York: W. J. Watt & Company, [c1921]. 294 p.
LC: S 2, '21.
PW: Mr 25, '22.
BLC: London: John Long, 1923.

L-41   _____ The Gray Phantom's return / by Herman
Landon. New York: W. J. Watt & Company,
[c1922]. 297 p.
LC: Je 21, '22.
PW: Mr 25, '22.
BLC: London: John Long, 1926.

L-42   _____ Gray terror: a 'Gray Phantom' detective story
/ by Herman Landon. New York: G. Howard Watt,
1923. 330 p.
LC: Je 8, '23.
PW: My 5, '23.
BLC: London: John Long, 1925.

L-43   _____ Hands unseen / by Herman Landon. New
York: G. Howard Watt, 1924. 303 p.
On cover: A new Gray Phantom detective story.
LC: Ag 21, '24.
PW: Mr 15, '24.
BLC: London: Hutchinson & Co., [1926].

L-44   _____ The room under the stairs / by Herman
Landon. New York: G. Howard Watt, 1923. 310 p.
PW: D 29, '23.
BLC: London: Hutchinson & Co., [1925].

Lane, A. Earnest B. The vase of the Mikado. In
Through the forbidden gates **(1903), T-222.**

L-45   Lane, Cyrenus M. A heresy of yesterday / by
Cyrenus M. Lane. Boston: Davis & Bond, [c1913].
78 p.

L-46   Lane, Elinor Macartney, d. 1909. All for the love of
a lady / by Elinor Macartney Lane. New York: D.
Appleton and Company, 1906. 87 p., front., [5]
leaves of plates. [Ill. by Arthur E. Becher.]

L-47   _____ The apple-tree cottage / Elinor Macartney
Lane; illustrated by Frank Craig. New York;
London: Harper & Brothers, 1910. 51, [1] p., col.
front., [1] leaf of col. plates.
LC: Ap 9, '10.
PW: Ap 16, '10.

L-48   _____ Katrine: a novel / by Elinor Macartney Lane.
New York; London: Harper & Brothers, 1909.
314 p., front.
LC: Mr 19, '09.
PW: Mr 27, '09.

L-49   _____ Mills of God: a novel / by Elinor Macartney
Lane. New York: D. Appleton and Company, 1901.
337 p., front., [3] leaves of plates (ports.).
PW: Jl 13, '01.

L-50   _____ Nancy Stair: a novel / by Elinor Macartney
Lane. New York: D. Appleton and Company, 1904.
385 p., front.
PW: Je 4, '04.

L-51   Lane, J. Russell (John Russell), b. 1867. The house
between the trees: a novel / by J. Russell Lane.
Boston, Massachusetts: The C. M. Clark Publishing
Company, 1909. 356 p., front., [7] leaves of plates.
[Ill. by William Kirkpatrick.]
LC: Mr 5, '09.
PW: Ap 3, '09.

L-52   Lane, Jeremy. Yellow men sleep / by Jeremy Lane.
New York: The Century Co., 1919. 343 p., col.
front. [Ill. by George W. Gage.]
LC: S 2, '19.
PW: S 20, '19.

L-53   Lane, John Haden, b. 1835. The birth of liberty: a
story of Bacon's Rebellion / John H. Lane.
Richmond: The Hermitage Press, 1909. 181 p.

L-54   Lane, Rose Wilder, 1886-1968. Diverging roads / by
Rose Wilder Lane. New York: The Century Co.,
1919. 360 p.
LC: Mr 24, '19.

L-55   _____ He was a man / by Rose Wilder Lane. New
York; London: Harper & Brothers, 1925. 380 p.
LC: Mr 17, '25.

_____ Innocence. In *Prize stories of 1922* **(1923),
P-620.**

L-56   Lang, Lillian Lotus. Face to face: a practicable
novelette / by Lillian Lotus Lang. Los Angeles:
Times-Mirror Printing & Binding House, 1922.
313 p., photo. front (port.).

L-57   Lange, Frederick Charles. The industrial crisis, or,
Giant labor and giant capital face to face: a story of
the "toiling masses" and the "thrifty rich" / by F. C.
Lange. [S. l.: s. n.], 1903. 262 p., front., [20]
leaves of plates.   **CLE**

Lange, Rosalie. Mr. Shamansky and the dapper
young man, a tale of the ghetto. In *Golden stories*
(1909), G-285.

L-58   Langford, George, b. 1876. Kutnar, son of Pic / by
George Langford; illustrated by the author. New
York: Boni and Liveright, [c1921]. 221 p., incl.
front, ill.
(Long ages ago series.)
LC: S 30, '21.
PW: O 22, '21.

L-59   _____ Pic, the weapon-maker / by George Langford;
introduction by Henry Fairfield Osborn; illustrated by
the author. New York: Boni and Liveright, [c1920].
270 p., front. ill., ill. Illustrated end papers.
LC: Je 25, '20.
PW: Jl 3, '20.

L-60   Lanier, Henry Wysham, b. 1873. The romance of
Piscator / by Henry Wysham Lanier; with a
frontispiece by William Balfour Ker. New York:
Henry Holt and Company, 1904. 227 p., front.

L-61   Lanier, Louise. "The conqueror" / by Louise Lanier.
Atlanta: J. A. LaHatte Printing House, [c1914].
174 p.   **DLC**

L-62   Lanier, M. (Melissa), b. 1833. Woman's rights and
woman's mission / by Mrs. M. Lanier. Jackson,
Tenn.: McCowat-Mercer Printing Company, 1908.
146 p.
Unexamined copy: bibliographic data from OCLC,
#17773408.

L-63 Lanston, Aubrey. The harvesters / by Aubrey Lanston. New York: R. H. Russell, 1903. 306, [1] p.
PW: D 5, '03.

L-64 Lanza, Clara, b. 1859. The dweller on the borderland / by the Marquise Clara Lanza. Philadelphia: John Jos. McVey, 1909. 477 p.
LC: D 13, '09.

L-65 Lardner, Ring, 1885-1933. The big town: how I and the Mrs. go to New York to see life and get Katie a husband / by Ring W. Lardner; illustrations by May Wilson Preston. Indianapolis: The Bobbs-Merrill Company, [c1921]. 244 p., front., [4] leaves of plates.
LC: N 3, '21.
PW: N 19, '21.
References: Bruccoli & Layman A14.

_____ The golden honeymoon. In *The best short stories of 1922 and the yearbook of the American short story* (1923), B-567.

L-66 _____ Gullible's travels, etc. / by Ring W. Lardner . . . ; illustrated by May Wilson Preston. Indianapolis: The Bobbs-Merrill Company, [c1917]. 255, [1] p., col. front.
Contents: Carmen -- Three kings and a pair -- Gullible's travels -- The water cure -- Three without, doubled.
LC: F 14, '17.
PW: F 10, '17.
References: Bruccoli & Layman A5.

L-67 _____ How to write short stories: < with samples > / by Ring W. Lardner. New York; London: Charles Scribner's Sons, 1924. 359 p.
Contents: Preface: How to write short stories -- The facts -- Some like them cold -- Alibi Ike -- The golden honeymoon -- Champion -- My roomy -- A caddy's diary -- A frame-up -- Harmony -- Horseshoes.
LC: My 12, '24.
PW: My 31, '24.
BLC: London: Chatto & Windus, 1926.
References: Bruccoli & Layman A16.

L-68 _____ My four weeks in France / by Ring W. Lardner . . . ; illustrated by Wallace Morgan. Indianapolis: The Bobbs-Merrill Company, [c1918]. 187 p., front., [5] leaves of plates.
LC: My 25, '18.
PW: Je 15, '18.
References: Bruccoli & Layman A6.

L-69 _____ Own your own home / by Ring W. Lardner . . . ; illustrated by Fontaine Fox. Indianapolis: The Bobbs-Merrill Company, [c1919]. 123 p.
LC: O 10, '19.
PW: N 1, '19.
References: Bruccoli & Layman A9.

L-70 _____ The real dope / by Ring W. Lardner . . . ; illustrated by May Wilson Preston and M. L. Blumenthal. Indianapolis: The Bobbs-Merrill Company, [c1919]. 186 p., front., [4] leaves of plates.
LC: F 19, '19.
PW: F 22, '19.
References: Bruccoli & Layman A8.

L-71 _____ Say it with oil: a few remarks about wives / by Ring W. Lardner . . . Say it with bricks: a few remarks about husbands / by Nina Wilcox Putnam . . . Garden City, New York: Doubleday, Doran & Company, Inc., [c1923]. 25 p.; 33 p.
Bruccoli & Layman: ". . . an upside down book."
LC: Mr 30, '23.
PW: Mr 31, '23.
References: Bruccoli & Layman A15.

L-72 _____ Symptoms of being 35 / by Ring W. Lardner; silhouettes by Helen E. Jacoby. Indianapolis: The Bobbs-Merrill Co., [c1921]. 52, [1] p., front., ill.
LC: Ag 22, '21.
PW: S 10, '21.
References: Bruccoli & Layman A13.

L-73 _____ Treat 'em rough: letters from Jack the Kaiser killer / by Ring W. Lardner . . . ; illustrated by Frank Crerie. Indianapolis: The Bobbs-Merrill Company, [c1918]. 160 p., ill.
LC: S 21, '18.
PW: S 14, '18.
References: Bruccoli & Layman A7.

L-74 _____ What of it? / by Ring W. Lardner. New York; London: Charles Scribner's Sons, 1925. 220 p.
Contents: Preface -- The other side: The other side. Plays: Clemo uti-"The water lilies" -- I. Gaspiri -- Taxidea Americana. "Bed-time stories": How to tell a true princess -- Cinderella -- Red Riding Hood -- Bluebeard. Obiter dicta: "In conference" -- A close-up of Domba Splew -- What of it? -- The big drought -- In regards to geniuses -- Why authors? -- The dames -- Lay off the thyroid -- The Spulge Nine -- A visit to the Garrisons -- Sane Olympics -- Welcome to our suburb -- Polyglot bride -- Business is business -- Games for smart alecks-I -- Games for smart alecks-II -- Tennis by cable -- Who's it? -- Prohibition -- Segregate the fats -- Don't be a drudge -- That which we call a rose -- Who's who.
LC: Je 2, '25.
PW: Ap 18, '25.
References: Bruccoli & Layman A17.

L-75 _____ You know me Al: a busher's letters / by Ring W. Lardner. New York: George H. Doran Company, [c1916]. 247 p.
LC: Jl 27, '16.
PW: Jl 15, '16.
References: Bruccoli & Layman A4.

L-76 _____ The young immigrunts / by Ring W. Lardner, Jr.; with a preface by the father; portraits by Gaar Williams. Indianapolis: The Bobbs-Merrill Company, [c1920]. 86 p., front., ill.
LC: My 8, '20.
PW: Ap 24, '20.
References: Bruccoli & Layman A11.

L-77 Large, Mary Harriott. The twelfth juror / by Mary Harriott Large. Boston: The C. M. Clark Publishing Company, 1908. 298 p., front.

L-78 Larkin, Samuel Tilden. Old wine in new bottles / by Samuel Tilden Larkin. Cincinnati, Ohio: Monfort & Company Press, 1915. 230 p., front.   **UIU**

Larsson, Genevieve. Witch Mary. In *Prize stories of 1923* (1924), P-621.

L-79   Larus, John Ruse, b. 1858. The masque of death: a
        story of the terror / by John R. Larus. New York:
        The Neale Publishing Company, 1917. 375 p.

L-80   Lascelles, Ernita. The sacrificial goat / by Ernita
        Lascelles. New York: Boni and Liveright, [c1923].
        295 p.
        "Second printing, September, 1923."

        La Shelle, Kirke. And the woman? In *Second suds
        sayings* **(1919), S-266.**

L-81   Lasley, J. B. When dreams came true / by J. B.
        Lasley. Louisville, Kentucky: John P. Morton &
        Company, 1922. 31 p.   **KUK**

L-82   Latham-Norton, M. F. (Mary Franklin). The rose of
        Auzenburg / by M. F. Latham-Norton. New York:
        Broadway Publishing Co., [c1911]. 263 p.   **DLC**

        Lathrop, Annie Wakeman. See **Wakeman, Annie.**

        Lathrop, Lorin Andrews, 1858-1929. See **Gambier,
        Kenyon, pseud.**

L-83   Lathrop, Mabel C. The man that never grew up: a
        novel / by Mabel C. and William A. Lathrop. New
        York: Britton Publishing Company, [c1919]. 318 p.,
        front.
        LC: N 4, '19.
        PW: N 22, '19.

L-84   Lathrop, William Addison. Little stories from the
        screen / by William Addison Lathrop . . . ;
        illustrated. New York: Britton Publishing Company,
        [c1917]. 324 p., photo. front., [23] leaves of photo.
        plates. [Ill. by Lasky, Vitagraph, W. A. Brady,
        Edison, Pallas-Morosco.]
        Contents: The violin of m'sieur -- Janet of the chorus -- The treason
        of Anatole -- Mother's roses -- Captain Santa Claus -- Lily, of the
        valley -- Old good-for-nuthin' -- Tony -- Blade o' grass -- The house
        cat -- A caliph of the new Bagdad -- Fleur de lys -- The house next
        door -- The making-over of Geoffrey Manning -- The law and Peggy
        -- The passing of Dusty Rhodes -- The social adventures of Lord
        Nocastle -- A pair of queens -- Indiscretion --The parson of Pine
        Mountain -- Uncle John -- Lucia -- Circus Mary -- The last leaf --
        The heir of the ages.
        LC: Jl 28, '17.

L-85   _____ Love time in Picardy / by William Addison
        Lathrop. New York: Britton Publishing Company,
        [c1919]. 347, [1] p., col. front.
        LC: Ap 5, '19.

        Lathrop, William Anderson, jt. aut. *The man that
        never grew up* (1919). See **Lathrop, Mabel C., jt.
        aut., L-83.**

L-86   Latimer, Elizabeth Wormeley, 1822-1904. The
        prince incognito / by Elizabeth Wormeley Latimer.
        Chicago: A. C. McClurg & Co., 1902. 320 p.
        PW: Ap 12, '02.

L-87   Latin blood / by ?. Hollywood, California: Authors
        Publishing Corporation, 1925. 242, [1] p.
        [? is David Graham Fischer.]

L-88   Lauferty, Lilian, 1887-1958. A pair of sixes / by
        Edward Peple; novelized by Liliam Lauferty. New

York: Moffatt, Yard and Company, 1914. 327 p.,
front., [8] leaves of plates (ports.).
LC: N 7, '14.

L-89   Laughlin, Clara E. (Clara Elizabeth), 1873-1941.
        Children of to-morrow / by Clara E. Laughlin . . . ;
        illustrated by Lucius W. Hitchcock. New York:
        Charles Scribner's Sons, 1911. 445 p., col. front.,
        [3] leaves of col. plates.
        LC: S 5, '11.
        PW: Ag 26, '11.

L-90   _____ Divided: the story of a poem / Clara E.
        Laughlin. New York; Chicago; Toronto; London;
        Edinburgh: Fleming H. Revell Company, [c1904].
        92 p. Decorated end papers.
        (Art gift-book series.)
        PW: S 10, '04.

L-91   _____ Everybody's birthright: a vision of Jeanne
        d'Arc / by Clara E. Laughlin . . . New York;
        Chicago; Toronto; London; Edinburgh: Fleming H.
        Revell Company, [c1914]. 144 p., front., [2] leaves
        of plates. [Ill. by Victor Pérard.]
        LC: S 21, '14.
        PW: S 5, '14.

L-92   _____ Everybody's lonesome: a true fairy story / by
        Clara E. Laughlin . . . ; illustrated by A. I. Keller.
        New York; Chicago; Toronto; London; Edinburgh:
        Fleming H. Revell Company, [c1910]. 121 p.,
        front., [1] leaf of plates.
        LC: O 1, '10.
        PW: Jl 16, '10.

L-93   _____ The evolution of a girl's ideal: a little record
        of the ripening of the affections to the time of love's
        coming / by Clara E. Laughlin. Chicago; New York;
        Toronto: Fleming H. Revell Company, 1902. 73 p.
        PW: O 4, '02.

L-94   _____ Felicity: the making of a comédienne / by
        Clara E. Laughlin; illustrations by Alice Barber
        Stephens. New York: Charles Scribner's Sons,
        1907. 426 p., front., [3] leaves of plates.
        LC: Mr 18, '07.
        PW: Mr 23, '07.

L-95   _____ The gleaners: a novelette / by Clara E.
        Laughlin . . . ; illustrated. New York; Chicago;
        Toronto; London; Edinburgh: Fleming H. Revell
        Company, [c1911]. 155 p., front.
        LC: Ja 10, '12.
        PW: D 2, '11.

L-96   _____ The heart of Her Highness / by Clara E.
        Laughlin . . . New York; London: G. P. Putnam's
        Sons, 1917. ([New York]: The Knickerbocker
        Press). 383 p., col. front. [Ill. by D. C. Hutchison.]
        LC: O 9, '17.
        PW: S 22, '17.

L-97   _____ Jeanne-Marie's triumph / by Clara E.
        Laughlin. New York; Chicago; London; Edinburgh:
        Fleming H. Revell Company, [c1922]. 160 p.
        LC: Ja 6, '23.
        PW: S 9, '22.

L-98 _____ "Just folks" / by Clara E. Laughlin. New York: The Macmillan Company, 1910. 377 p.
LC: O 14, '10.
PW: O 29, '10.

L-99 _____ The keys of heaven / by Clara E. Laughlin. New York: George H. Doran Company, [c1918]. 417 p.
LC: Ja 28, '18.
PW: Mr 9, '18.

L-100 _____ The lady in gray: a story of the steps by which we climb / by Clara E. Laughlin. New York; Chicago; Toronto; London; Edinburgh: Fleming H. Revell Company, 1908. 60 p.
LC: S 26, '08.
PW: O 10, '08.

L-101 _____ "Miladi": being sundry little chapters devoted to your day-dreams, dear Miladi, and your realizations, harking back to your education, your experience in the industrial world and your decision in favor of the claims of home, and coming down to the development of your love, the building of your house o'dreams, and your motherhood / by Clara E. Laughlin . . . Chicago; New York; Toronto; London; Edinburgh: Fleming H. Revell Company, [c1903]. 199 p.
Contents: The heroines of Miladi -- Industrial Miladi -- Miladi and the "hand-made" woman -- The service problem of Miladi -- The education of Miladi -- The domestic relations of Miladi -- The foreign relations of Miladi -- Paying the price -- The fourfold love of Miladi -- Miladi's house o' dreams -- Conflicting tendencies -- The motherhood of Miladi.
PW: D 5, '03.

L-102 _____ The penny philanthropist: a story that could be true / by Clara E. Laughlin . . . New York; Chicago; Toronto; London; Edinburgh: Fleming H. Revell Company, [c1912]. 217 p., front. [Ill. by Victor Pérard.]
LC: N 18, '12.
PW: S 7, '12.

L-103 _____ When joy begins: a little story of the woman-heart / [by] Clara E. Laughlin. New York; Chicago; Toronto; London; Edinburgh: Fleming H. Revell Company, 1905. 96 p.
PW: D 30, '05.

L-104 _____ When my ship comes home / by Clara E. Laughlin. [New York; Chicago]: Fleming H. Revell Company, [c1915]. 143 p., front., ill. [Ill. by Samuel M. Palmer.]
LC: N 5, '15.
PW: N 6, '15.

Laurvik, J. Nilsen. The brass candlestick. In *Forum stories* (1914), F-306.

L-105 La Voie, Julia. A tale half told / Julia La Voie. New York: Broadway Publishing Company, [c1904]. 140 p., front. (port.), [3] leaves of plates. On spine: Illustrated by O. W. Waldo.
PW: Je 3, '05.

Law, Fannie Elizabeth, b. 1873. See **Fa-El-La.**

Law, Frederick Houk, 1871-1957, ed. See *Modern short stories* (1918), M-879.

L-106 _____ Sister Clementia: a novel / by Frederick Houk Law. New York: R. F. Fenno & Company, [c1910]. 277 p.
LC: N 17, '10.

L-107 Law, Hyram S., *pseud.* While hopes were kindling / by Hyram S. Law [pseud.]. [Buffalo, N. Y.: Peter, Paul & Co.], 1901. 117 p.

L-108 Lawler, James J. (James Joseph), b. 1856. From pit to palace: a romantic autobiography / by James J. Lawler. New York: The Palace Publishing Company; [London]: Kegan Paul, Trench, Trubner, London agents, [c1906]. 300 p., front., [5] leaves of plates. [Some ill. by E. V. Nadherny.]

L-109 Lawrance, William V. (William Vicars), 1834-1905. Under which master, or, the story of the long strike at Coverdale: a romance of labor / Wm. V. Lawrance. New York; London; Montreal: The Abbey Press, [c1901]. 443 p.

L-110 Lawrence, Albert, b. 1875, *pseud.* The travels of Phoebe Ann / by Albert Lawrence [pseud.]. Boston: C. M. Clark Publishing Co., 1908. 436 p., front., [7] leaves of plates.
LC: D 18, '08.

L-111 Lawrence, Albert Lathrop. Juell Demming: a story / by Albert Lathrop Lawrence. Chicago: A. C. McClurg & Co., 1901. 384 p.   **EEX**
PW: S 14, '01.

L-112 _____ The wolverine: a romance of early Michigan / by Albert Lathrop Lawrence; with illustrations from drawings by Arthur E. Becher. Boston: Little, Brown and Company, 1904. 337 p., front., [3] leaves of plates.
PW: O 29, '04.

Lawrence, Alberta (Chamberlin), b. 1875. See **Lawrence, Albert, pseud.**

L-113 Lawrence, Edith, 1870-1912. Crecy / by Edith Lawrence. New York: F. M. Buckles & Company, [c1904]. 221 p., front.

Lawrence, Elwell, pseud. See **Sullivan, Francis William, b. 1887.**

L-114 Lawrence, Josephine, 1897?-1978. Rainbow Hill / by Josephine Lawrence . . . ; illustrated by Thelma Gooch. New York: Cupples & Leon Company, [c1924]. 312 p., front., [3] leaves of plates.
LC: Je 11, '24.
PW: Ag 9, '24.

L-115 Lawrence, Lou, 1854-1932. The confessions of an old maid / Lou Lawrence. New York: Press of "The Rose-Jar," 1904. 223 p.   **NYP**

L-116 Lawson, Alfred William, b. 1869. Born again: a novel / by Alfred William Lawson. New York: Wox, Conrad Company, [c1904]. 287 p., front. (port.).

L-117 Lawson, Elsworth. Euphrosyne and her "golden book" / by Elsworth Lawson. Chicago: H. S. Stone & Company, 1901. 141 p.
LC: My 31, '01.

L-118 ____ From the unvarying star / by Elsworth Lawson . . . New York: The Macmillan Company; London: Macmillan & Co., Ltd., 1903. 292 p.
PW: Mr 14, '03.

L-119 Lawson, Laura Burnett. Leonora: a tale of the Great Smokies / by Laura Burnett Lawson. New York; Washington: The Neale Publishing Company, 1904. 247 p. **NOC**
PW: O 1, '04.

L-120 Lawson, Thomas W. (Thomas William), 1857-1925. Friday, the thirteenth: a novel / by Thomas W. Lawson; frontispiece in colour by Sigismond de Ivanowski. New York: Doubleday, Page & Company, 1907. 226 p., col. front.
LC: F 21, '07.
PW: Mr 2, '07.
BLC: London: Doubleday, Page & Co.; New York printed, 1907.

____ Mary's little lamb. See **Masson, Thomas Lansing, 1866-1934.** *A bachelor's baby: and some grownups* **(1907), M-587.**

L-121 Lawson, William Pinkney. The fire woman / by William Pinkney Lawson. New York: Boni & Liveright, 1925. 254 p.
LC: Je 22, '25.
PW: Je 20, '25.

L-122 ____ Lem Allen / by William Pinkney Lawson. New York: Boni and Liveright, [c1923]. 248 p.
LC: S 13, '23.
PW: S 8, '23.
BLC: London; New York: Andrew Melrose, [1925].

L-123 Lawson, X. Sydney Carrington's Contumacy / by X. Lawson. New York; Cincinnati, (etc.): Fr. Pustet & Co., [c1908]. 350 p.

L-124 Lazarre, Jacob. Beating sea and changeless bar / by Jacob Lazarre. Philadelphia: The Jewish Publication Society of America, 1905. 133 p.
Contents: "Wave and spar" -- "Once in some memorable before" -- "On some fortunate yet thrice blasted shore" -- "So hesitate and turn and cling- yet go".

L-125 Lea, Fanny Heaslip, 1884-1955. Chloe Malone / by Fannie Heaslip Lea; with illustrations by F. Graham Cootes. Boston: Little, Brown and Company, 1916. 292 p., front., [3] leaves of plates.
PW: S 9, '16.

L-126 ____ The dream-maker man / by Fanny Heaslip Lea . . . New York: Dodd, Mead and Company, 1925. 329 p.
LC: O 8, '25.
PW: O 10, '25.
BLC: London: Mills & Boon, 1926.

L-127 ____ Jaconetta stories / by Fannie Heaslip Lea . . . ; with illustrations by Will Foster. New York: Sturgis & Walton Company, 1912. 200 p., front., [2] leaves of plates. Partly reprinted from various periodicals. **TUL**
Contents: Jaconetta and the cynic -- Jaconetta and the memories -- Jaconetta and the celebrity -- Jaconetta and the Celt -- Jaconetta and the Captain -- Jaconetta and the monk -- Jaconetta and the poem -- Jaconetta and the conqueror.
LC: Ap 10, '12.
PW: Ap 20, '12.

L-128 ____ Quicksands / by Fannie Heaslip Lea; with illustrations by Clinton Balmer. New York: Sturgis & Walton Company, 1911. 331 p., front., [3] leaves of plates. **LUU**
LC: Ap 4, '11.
PW: Ap 22, '11.

L-129 ____ Sicily Ann: a romance / by Fannie Heaslip Lea; illustrated. New York; London: Harper & Brothers Publishers, 1914. 207, [1] p., col. front., [3] leaves of plates. [Ill. by F. Graham Cootes.] **INT**
LC: O 10, '14.

L-130 ____ With this ring / by Fanny Heaslip Lea. New York: Dodd, Mead and Company, 1925. 237 p. Unexamined copy: bibliographic data from OCLC, #6571233.
LC: F 11, '25.
PW: F 14, '25.
BLC: London: Mills & Boon, 1926.

L-131 Lea, Homer, 1876-1912. The vermilion pencil: a romance of China / by Homer Lea. New York: The McClure Company, 1908. 331 p., col. front.
LC: Mr 12, '08.
PW: Mr 21, '08.
BLC: London: McClure Company; printed in U. S. A., 1908.

Leach, A. R. A captain out of Etruria. In *The Harper prize short stories* **(1925), H-233.**

L-132 Leach, Le Roy. Tales of adventure / by Le Roy Leach. [S. l.: s. n.], 1903. 53 p. Unexamined copy: bibliographic data from OCLC, #26981212.

L-133 Leach, Valette Washburn. Jedediah Bascom / by . . . Valette Washburn Leach. New York; London; Montreal: The Abbey Press, [c1902]. 143 p.
PW: N 22, '02.

L-134 Leahy, Walter T. (Walter Thomas), 1858-1938. Columbanus, the Celt: a tale of the sixth century / by Walter T. Leahy. Philadelphia: H. L. Kilner & Co., [c1913]. 455 p.

L-135 Leamon, Sarah Cannon. Tom Morgan's farm / by Sarah Cannon Leamon . . . Cincinnati, Ohio: Press of Jennings & Pye, 1901. 104 p.
Contents: Tom Morgan's farm -- How to reform a young man -- Tossed about -- Our girls.

L-136 Learsi, Rufus, 1887-1964, *pseud.* Kasriel the watchman: and other stories / by Rufus Learsi [pseud.]. Philadelphia: The Jewish Publication

Society of America, 1925. 311 p., front., [7] leaves of plates. [Ill. by Reuben Leaf.]
Contents: Kasriel the Watchman -- Perl the Peanut Woman -- Benjy and Reuby -- Fievel the Fiddler -- Phantasies.

L-137   Leaverton, Ernest. In the garden of the heart / by Ernest Leaverton. New York: J. F. Tapley Co., [c1919]. 252 p., photo. front., [2] leaves of photo. plates.   **DLC**
LC: Ag 11, '19.

L-138   ____ In the valley of the Grand / by Ernest Leaverton. [New York, Printed by J. F. Tapley Co.], 1917. 47 p., front. (port.).   **DMP**
LC: D 19, '17.

L-139   LeBurke, Montgomery Hill. The she-devil: a romance of the Spanish-American War / by Montgomery Hill LeBurke. Philadelphia: Charles E. Apgar, 1910. 357 p.   **DLC**
LC: O 18, '10.

L-140   Le Cato, Nathaniel James Walter, b. 1835. The curse of caste / by N. J. W. Le Cato. New York: Walker-Ellerson Publishing Co., [c1903]. 320 p., front.
PW: Ap 2, '04.

L-141   Leckey, Phoebe Baker, b. 1882. The beckoning heights / by Phoebe Fabian Leckey; illustrated by Ashley Evelyn Baker. New York; Washington: The Neale Publishing Company, 1908. 327 p., front., [12] leaves of plates.   **VIC**
LC: Ap 6, '08.

L-142   Leddy, James. The new republic / by James Leddy. New York; London; Montreal: The Abbey Press, [c1902]. 109 p.
PW: Ja 10, '03.

Lederer, Charles. A Christmas invasion. In *Second suds sayings* (1919), **S-266.**

L-143   Lee, Albert, 1868-1946. The pie and the pirate / by Albert Lee; illustrated by Orson Lowell. New York: P. F. Collier and Son, [c1910]. 96 p., ill.
                                          OSU, MPI
LC: F 1, '10.

L-144   Lee, Alice Louise. Cap'n Joe's sister / by Alice Louise Lee; with a frontispiece in colors by Arthur Hutchins. New York: Frederick A. Stokes Company, [c1912]. 251 p., col. front.
LC: F 19, '12.
PW: F 24, '12.

____ The shout fiscal's prisoner. In *Stockman stories* (1913), **S-956.**

L-145   Lee, Amber. The woman I am / by Amber Lee. New York: Thomas Seltzer, 1925. 305 p.
LC: Mr 9, '25.
PW: Mr 21, '25.

L-146   Lee, Anne, b. 1871. A woman in revolt / by Anne Lee. New York: Desmond FitzGerald, Inc., [c1913]. 321 p.
PW: D 6, '13.

L-147   Lee, Charles C., *pseud.* Character building, or, The life of the college-bred woman / by Charles C. Lee [pseud.]. [S. l.: s. n.], 1906. 206 p.   **CWR**

Lee, E. M. A doubtful nationality. In **Seattle Writer's Club.** *Tillicum tales* **(1907), S-248.**

Lee, Elva. Within four years. In *A book of Bryn Mawr stories* **(1901), B-732.**

L-148   Lee, Frank, Mrs., 1849-1932. A boy and a box / by Mrs. Frank Lee. Elgin, Illinois: D. C. Cook Publishing Co., [c1909]. 93 p., ill.

L-149   ____ Little Boom No. 1 / by Mrs. Frank Lee . . . Boston; Chicago: The Pilgrim Press, c1902. 255 p., [2] leaves of plates. [Ill. by A. B. Shute.]   **OWL**
PW: D 27, '02.

L-150   ____ The making of Major / by Mrs. Frank Lee. Elgin, Illinois: David C. Cook Publishing Co., [c1913]. 93 p., incl. plates. [Ill. by I. Doseff.]

L-151   Lee, George Taylor, 1848-1933. A Virginia feud: the story of a mountain lassie / by George Taylor Lee. New York; Washington: The Neale Publishing Company, 1908. 341 p.   **TNS**
LC: Ja 25, '08.
PW: F 15, '08.

L-152   Lee, James Hampton, b. 1876. Gold from life's rainbows: short stories and sweet songs / by James Hampton Lee . . . ; illustrated by M. Power O'Malley. New York: Broadway Publishing Company, 1903. 206 p., photo. front. (port.), [14] leaves of plates.   **GUA**
Contents: The millionaire from Union Square -- Catawba castle circle -- Rockie's resurrection -- The soul of a singer -- The demon at Dutch Gap -- Mighty much of a man -- Her sister's brother -- The storm that stood still -- The horseman of seven nations -- A knight of the wire -- The phantom of Forest Hill -- The curse of cabin John Bridge -- The story of a story -- The ride of the black rat.
PW: D 19, '03.

L-153   ____ Letters of two, or, The true history of a late love affair / edited and compiled by James Hampton Lee . . . New York; London; Montreal: The Abbey Press, [c1901]. 149 p., [20] leaves of plates. (1 photo. port.).   **VIC**
PW: O 12, '01.

L-154   ____ The waist of the world: a circle into the great empyrean on the pinions of passion, and a little journey in the heart of things / by James Hampton Lee . . . N. Y. [i. e. New York]: Broadway Publishing Company, [c1906]. 161 p., photo. front. (port.), [3] leaves of plates.   **OSU, COP**
On cover: A romance of the Isthmus.
LC: D 27, '06.
PW: Mr 9, '07.

L-155   Lee, Janet. "Wild women": the romance of a flapper / by Miss Janet Lee (sophomore); with 25 illustrations. New York: Nicholas L. Brown, 1922. 136 p., ill.
PW: Je 24, '22.

L-156   Lee, Jennette, 1860-1951. The air-man and the tramp / by Jennette Lee. New York: Charles Scribner's Sons, 1918. 134 p.
PW: Ap 6, '18.

L-157   ____ Aunt Jane / by Jennette Lee. New York: Charles Scribner's Sons, 1915. 329 p.
LC: S 22, '15.
PW: S 25, '15.
BLC: London: Methuen & Co., 1916.

L-158   ____ The Chinese coat / by Jennette Lee. New York: Charles Scribner's Sons, 1920. 198 p.
LC: Ag 25, '20.
PW: Ag 28, '20.

L-159   ____ Dead right / by Jennette Lee. New York: Charles Scribner's Sons, 1925. 300 p.
LC: Mr 21, '25.
PW: Mr 21, '25.
BLC: London: Hurst & Blackett, [1925].

L-160   ____ The green jacket / by Jennette Lee. New York: Charles Scribner's Sons, 1917. 331 p.
LC: S 19, '17.
PW: S 22, '17.
BLC: London: Skeffington & Son, [1918].

L-161   ____ Happy Island: a new "Uncle William story" / by Jennette Lee. New York: The Century Co., 1910. 330 p., col. front. [Ill. by Frank Earle Schoonover.]
LC: Je 28, '10.
PW: Je 4, '10.

L-162   ____ Mr. Achilles / by Jennette Lee . . . ; with illustrations. New York: Dodd, Mead and Company, 1912. 261 p., front., [3] leaves of plates. [Ill. by John Rae.]
LC: S 30, '12.

L-163   ____ The mysterious office / by Jennette Lee. New York: Charles Scribner's Sons, 1922. 278 p.
LC: N 18, '22.
PW: N 25, '22.
BLC: London: Hurst & Blackett, [1922].

L-164   ____ The other Susan / by Jennette Lee. New York: Charles Scribner's Sons, 1921. 304 p.
LC: S 22, '21.
PW: O 1, '21.
BLC: London: Hurst & Blackett, [1922].

L-165   ____ A pillar of salt / by Jennette Lee. Boston; New York: Houghton, Mifflin and Company, 1901. (Cambridge: The Riverside Press). 255, [1] p.
PW: Mr 2, '01.

L-166   ____ The rain-coat girl / by Jennette Lee. New York: Charles Scribner's Sons, 1919. 330 p.
LC: O 16, '19.
BLC: London: Hurst & Blackett, [1921].

L-167   ____ Simeon Tetlow's shadow / by Jennette Lee. New York: The Century Co., 1909. 316 p., front.
LC: F 5, '09.
PW: Mr 6, '09.
BLC: London: Hodder & Stoughton, 1909.

L-168   ____ The son of a fiddler / by Jennette Lee. Boston; New York: Houghton, Mifflin and Company, 1902. (Cambridge: The Riverside Press). 286 p.
PW: Ap 5, '02.

L-169   ____ The taste of apples / by Jennette Lee; illustrations by F. Walter Taylor. New York: Dodd, Mead and Company, 1913. 345 p., front., [3] leaves of plates.
LC: S 16, '13.
PW: S 27, '13.

L-170   ____ Uncle Bijah's ghost / by Jennette Lee. New York: Charles Scribner's Sons, 1922. 187 p.
LC: Mr 27, '22.
PW: My 20, '22.

L-171   ____ Uncle William: the man who was shif'less / by Jennette Lee. New York: The Century Co., 1906. 298 p., front.
PW: Mr 24, '06.
BLC: London: Hodder & Stoughton, [1906].

L-172   ____ Unfinished portraits: stories of musicians and artists / by Jennette Lee. New York: Charles Scribner's Sons, 1916. 255 p., front.
Contents: There was in Florence a lady -- Thumbs and fugues -- A window of music -- Frederic Chopin - a record -- The man with the glove -- The lost monogram.
LC: S 28, '16.
PW: S 30, '16.

L-173   ____ The woman in the alcove / by Jennette Lee; illustrated by A. I. Keller and Arthur E. Becher. New York: Charles Scribner's Sons, 1914. 152 p., front., [3] leaves of plates.
LC: S 16, '14.
PW: S 19, '14.

L-174   Lee, Louisa Carter. Her desert lover: a love story / by Louisa Carter Lee. New York City: Chelsea House, [c1925]. 251 p.
PW: D 19, '25.

L-175   Lee, Margaret, 1841-1914. Separation / by Margaret Lee . . . New York: F. M. Buckles & Company, 1902. 271 p.
PW: Jl 12, '02.

L-176   Lee, Marian, 1854-1930, *pseud.* Confessions to a heathen idol / by Marian Lee [pseud.]; illustrated from photographs by Fred Robinson. New York: Doubleday, Page & Company, 1906. 351 p., front., [3] leaves of plates.
LC: S 22, '06.

L-177   Lee, Marion Beveridge. Barselma's kiss: a romance / by Marion Beveridge Lee . . . Boston, Massachusetts: The C. M. Clark Publishing Co., 1908. 332 p., photo. front. (port.), [7] leaves of plates. **AZU**

L-178   ____ The man with the rake / by Marion Beveridge Lee . . . New York; London; Montreal: The Abbey Press, [c1901]. 281 p.
PW: O 12, '01.

L-179 Lee, Mary Catherine, d. 1927. Lois Mallet's dangerous gift / by Mary Catherine Lee; with frontispiece. Boston; New York: Houghton, Mifflin and Company, 1902. (Cambridge: The Riverside Press). 116 p., front.
PW: O 4, '02.

Lee, Mary Choppel. See **Lee, Frank, (Mrs.), 1849-1932.**

L-180 Leech, Margaret, 1893-1974. The back of the book / by Margaret Leech. New York: Boni and Liveright, [1924]. 255 p.

L-181 Lees, Marie Grace D'Ungar, b. 1863. Lassita: in the land of mañana / by Marie Grace Lees. Chicago: Priv. print, 1911. 48 p.
Unexamined copy: bibliographic data from OCLC, #24837110.

Leete, Harley M. The confraternity of the holy agony. In *Under Berkeley Oaks* (1901), U-8.

L-182 Lefèvre, Edwin, 1871-1943. The golden flood / by Edwin Lefèvre; illustrated by W. R. Leigh. New York: McClure, Phillips & Co., 1905. 198, [1] p., front., [3] leaves of plates.
PW: Ap 29, '05.

L-183 _____ H. R. / by Edwin Lefèvre. New York; London: Harper & Brothers, 1915. 336, [1] p., front. [Ill. by F. Graham Cootes.]
LC: O 25, '15.
PW: N 6, '15.

L-184 _____ The plunderers: a novel / by Edwin Lefèvre. New York; London: Harper & Brothers, [1916]. 333, [1] p., front. [Ill. by M. Leone Bracker.]
Contents: The pearls of the Princess Patricia -- The panic of the lion -- As proofs of Holy Writ -- Cheap at a million.
PW: Je 17, '16.

L-185 _____ Sampson Rock of Wall Street: a novel / by Edwin Lefèvre . . . ; illustrated. New York; London: Harper & Brothers, 1907. 393, [1] p., front., [3] leaves of plates. [Ill. by The Kinneys.]
LC: F 20, '07.
PW: Mr 2, '07.

L-186 _____ Simonetta / by Edwin Lefèvre. New York: George H. Doran Company, [c1919]. 223 p.
LC: N 8, '19.

L-187 _____ To the last penny / by Edwin Lefèvre . . . New York; London: Harper & Brothers, 1917. 313, [1] p.
LC: Ap 7, '17.
PW: Ap 14, '17.

L-188 _____ Wall Street stories / by Edwin Lefèvre. New York: McClure, Phillips & Co., 1901. 224 p.
Contents: The woman and her bonds -- The break in turpentine -- The tipster -- A philanthropic whisper -- The man who won -- The lost opportunity -- Pike's Peak or bust -- A theological tipster.
PW: N 2, '01.
BLC: London: McClure, Phillips & Co., 1901.

Leffingwell, Albert F. The iron band. In *Made to order* (1915), M-352.

L-189 Legge, Clayton Mackenzie. Highland Mary: the romance of a poet: a novel / by Clayton Mackenzie Legge; illustrated by William Kirpatrick [i. e. Kirkpatrick]. Boston: C. M. Clark Publishing Co., 1906. 395 p., front., [8] leaves of plates.
LC: F 11, '07.

L-190 Legge, Ronald. The Hawk: a story of aerial war / by Ronald Legge. New York: The John McBride Co., 1909. 310 p.
LC: My 3, '09.

L-191 Legler-Hawkins, Flora. An unfinished melody / by Flora Legler-Hawkins. Chula Vista, Cal.: Denrich Press, [c1908]. 36 p.   **CDS**

L-192 Legum, John. Rachel and Leah: a Jewish story / by John Legum. Butler, Pa.: Ziegler Printing Co., 1901. 131, [1] p.   **DLC**
Another edition: Rachel and Leah: a tale of the Jewish pale in Russia . . . 2d and rev. ed. [Pittsburgh: Press of City Missions Publishing Co.], 1912. 101 p., ill.
Unexamined copy: bibliographic data from NUC.

L-193 Lehman, B. H. Wild marriage / by B. H. Lehman. New York; London: Harper & Brothers Publishers, 1925. 324 p.
LC: F 17, '25.
PW: F 21, '25.

L-194 _____ The man in black / by F. M. Lehman. Kansas City, Mo.: Publishing House of the Pentecostal Church of the Nazarene, 1913. 192 p., ill. [Ill. by C. W. Rosser.]

Lemmon, Robert S. The bamboo trap. In *Prize stories of 1923* (1924), P-621.

L-195 Le Moine, Weston J. The sacrifice: a true story / by Weston J. Le Moine; illustrated by W. E. Greer, Jr. New Orleans: Cox Printing and Publishing Co., Inc., [c1919]. 212 p., front., [4] leaves of plates.

L-196 Lemon, Mary Dyer. The Grimpy letters: a series of letters written by a young girl to her old lady chum / by Mary Dyer Lemon (Polly Dee). Indianapolis, Indiana: Indianapolis Book & Stationery Co., 1917. 201 p., photo. front.

L-197 LeNart, Marie. A child of divorce: a startling story of an amazing modern evil--its insidious warfare upon all that is high and holy in marrige and its lasting influence upon innocent lives / by Marie LeNart. Cincinnati: The Standard Publishing Company, [c1922]. 425 p., incl. front.

L-198 Lent, Edward B. (Edward Burcham), b. 1869. Cupid's middleman / by Edward B. Lent . . . ; illustrated by H. B. Matthews. New York: Cupples & Leon, [c1906]. 336 p., front., [4] leaves of plates.
LC: S 28, '06.

Leo, Brother Zachary, b. 1881. <u>See</u> **Scarlet, Will, pseud.**

L-199   Leonard, Elizabeth Jane. The mysterious trail: a story of mystery and romance in which the east and west meet / by Elizabeth Jane Leonard . . . ; illustrated. [York, Neb.]: Published by arrangement with the York Blank Book Company, [1925]. 209 p., photo. front. (port.), [1] leaf of photo. plates. **DLC**
LC: O 21, '25.

L-200   Leonard, Mary Finley, b. 1862. The little red chimney: being the love story of a candy man / by Mary Finley Leonard; illustrations in silhouette by Katharine Gassaway. New York: Duffield & Company, 1914. 164 p., front., [7] leaves of plates.
LC: Ag 21, '14.

L-201   _____ The ways of Jane: a story with which the wise and prudent have no concern / by Mary Finley Leonard . . . New York: Duffield and Company, 1917. 268 p.   **OSU, PFO**
LC: Mr 17, '17.

L-202   Leonard, Mary Hall, 1847-1921. The days of the Swamp Angel / by Mary Hall Leonard. New York: The Neale Publishing Company, 1914. 326 p.
LC: S 30, '14.
PW: D 26, '14.

Leonard, Ruth. J. Remington Victor. <u>In</u> *Minnesota stories* (1903), M-842.

_____ The passing of Quentin Dewey. <u>In</u> *Minnesota stories* (1903), M-842.

Lerner, Isaiah. Bertzi Wasserführer. <u>In</u> *Yiddish tales* (1912), Y-20.

_____ Ezrielk the scribe. <u>In</u> *Yiddish tales* (1912), **Y-20.**

_____ Yitzchok-Yossel Broitgeber. <u>In</u> *Yiddish tales* (1912), **Y-20.**

Lerner, Mary. Little selves. <u>In</u> *The best short stories of 1916 and the yearbook of the American short story* (1917), **B-561.**

L-203   Le Rossignol, James Edward, b. 1866. Little stories of Quebec / by James Edward Le Rossignol; decorations and illustrations by Laura Miller. Cincinnati: Jennings and Graham; New York: Eaton and Mains, [c1908]. [176] p., ill. (some col.).
Contents: The poor of this world -- Father Grandmaison -- The peacemaker -- Théophile -- The exile -- The miser.

L-204   Lerrigo, Charles Henry, 1872-1955. The castle of cheer / by Charles Henry Lerrigo. New York; Chicago; Toronto; London; Edinburgh: Fleming H. Revell Company, [c1916]. 304 p., front., [1] leaf of plates. [Ill. by Victor Pérard.]
LC: Ap 11, '16.
PW: Ap 8, '16.

L-205   _____ Doc Williams: a tale of the Middle West / by Charles H. Lerrigo. New York; Chicago; Toronto:

Fleming H. Revell Company, [c1913]. 329, [1] p., front. [Ill. by Victor Pérard.]
LC: Je 10, '13.
PW: My 3, '13.

L-206   Lesh, U. S. (Ulysses Samuel), b. 1868. A knight of the golden circle / U. S. Lesh. Boston: Richard G. Badger, 1911. ([Boston]: The Gorham Press). 282 p.

Leslie, Eliza. The Watkinson evening. <u>In</u> *The best American humorous short stories* (1920), **B-556.**

L-207   Leslie, Lilian, *jt. pseud.* The melody from Mars / by Lilian Leslie [jt. pseud.] . . . New York: Published by Authors' International Publishing Co., [c1924]. 206 p.   **CRU**
LC: D 5, '24.

L-208   Leslie, Scott. Flo's flop: a theatrical tale / (by Scott Leslie). [Tampa, Fla: S. Leslie, 19--?]. [16] p.   **NYP**

L-209   Lesser, Elizabeth. Just a little tag / Elizabeth Lesser; drawings by the author. New York: Broadway Publishing Company, [c1904]. 109 p., front., ill.   **NYP**

L-210   Lessing, Bruno, 1870-1940, *pseud.* Children of men / by Bruno Lessing [pseud.]. New York: McClure, Phillips & Co., 1903. 311 p., front.
Contents: The end of the task -- The Sader guest -- A rift in the cloud -- Out of his orbit -- The poisoned chai -- Urim and Thummim -- A Yiddish idyll -- The story of Sarai -- The Americanisation of Shadrach Cohen -- Hannukah lights -- A swallow-tailer for two -- Deborah -- An interruption -- The murderer -- Unconverted -- Without fear of God -- The sun of wisdom -- A daughter of Isreal -- The message of Acturus -- Queer Scharenstein -- The compact -- A song of songs -- A wedding in duress.
PW: O 24, '03.
BLC: Edinburgh; London: William Blackwood & Sons, printed in U. S. A., 1904.

L-211   _____ Jake - or Sam / by Bruno Lessing [pseud.]. New York: Desmond Fitzgerald, Inc., [c1909]. 44 p., ill. [Ill. by Arthur G. Dove.]   **UBY**
LC: S 27, '09.
PW: D 4, '09.

_____ Love and cloaks and suits. <u>In</u> *Aces* (1924), **A-42.**

L-212   _____ With the best intention / by Bruno Lessing [pseud.]; with illustrations by M. Leone Bracker. New York: Hearst's International Library Co., 1914. 348 p., front., [7] leaves of plates.

L-213   Lester, Leon. A son of the soil / by Leon Lester. Kinsley, Kan.: Minleon Shop, 1913. 81 p. Unexamined copy: bibliographic data from OCLC, #11280451.

L-214   Letters of an actress. New York: Frederick A. Stokes Co., 1903. 325 p.   **MEU**
BLC: London: Edward Arnold, 1902.

L-215   Leupp, Francis Ellington, 1849-1918. A day with father / by Francis E. Leupp. New York: Charles

Scribner's Sons, 1914. 67 p. The present story in a somewhat condensed form was written for the Woman's home companion.

L-216　Leverage, Henry. The ice pilot / by Henry Leverage; frontispiece by Rudolph Tandler. Garden City, N. Y.; Toronto: Doubleday, Page & Company, 1921. 294 p., front.
LC: F 12, '21.
PW: Ja 22, '21.

L-217　_____ The shepherd of the sea / by Henry Leverage; illustrated by Rudolph F. Tandler. Garden City, N. Y.: Doubleday, Page & Company, 1920. 303, [1] p., front., [3] leaves of plates.
LC: My 4, '20.
PW: Ja 17, '20.

L-218　_____ Where dead men walk / by Henry Leverage . . . New York: Moffat, Yard & Company, 1920. 315 p.
PW: Ja 24, '20.

L-219　_____ Whispering wires / adapted from the Saturday Evening Post story of the same title by Henry Leverage. New York: Moffat, Yard and Company, 1918. 299 p.
LC: O 2, '18.
PW: O 5, '18.

L-220　_____ The white cipher / by Henry Leverage. New York: Moffat, Yard & Company, 1919. 272 p., front. [Ill. by George Gibbs.]
LC: Je 23, '19.
PW: Jl 5, '19.

L-221　Levere, William C. (William Collin), 1872-1927. Vivian of Mackinac / by William C. Levere. Chicago: Forbes & Company, 1911. 299 p., col. front., [7] leaves of col. plates.
PW: Ag 12, '11.

L-222　Levinger, Elma Ehrlich, b. 1887. In many lands: stories of how the scattered Jews kept their festivals / by Elma Ehrlich Levinger . . . New York: Bloch Publishing Company, 1923. 143 p., ill.
Contents: Rosh Hashonah-The Jewish New Year -- The shofar call [poem] -- The man who came in late -- Yom Kippur-The day of atonement -- The atonement offering [poem] -- The day of return -- Succoth-The Jewish Thanksgiving -- Succoth in wartime [poem] -- Tent of Isreal -- Simchath Torah-The rejoicing over the Torah -- Simchath Torah [poem] -- The flag of My people -- Chanukah-The feast of lights -- Joseph's candle [poem] -- The Menorah of remembrance -- Purim-The feast of lots -- Unmasked [poem] -- The pruim players -- Passover-The feast of freedom -- The hills about Jerusalem [poem] -- The unwelcome guest -- The Sephira-days of remembrance -- A city gate in Palestine [poem] -- The long night -- Lag Baomer-The scholars' holiday -- The promise of spring [poem] -- The dove and the eagle -- Shabuoth-The festival of the first fruits -- The new harvest [poem] -- A rose for beauty -- Tisha B'ab-The day on which our temple fell -- O little land [poem] -- The vision that passed -- Sabbath-The Jewish rest day -- Sabbath peace [poem] -- The river of dreams.

L-223　_____ The new land: stories of Jews who had a part in the making of our country / by Elma Ehrlich Levinger . . . New York: Bloch Publishing Company . . . , 1920. 175 p.　**IUA**
Reprinted in part from The Hebrew standard and The Jewish child.

Contents: In the night watches -- When Katrina lost her way -- A place of refuge -- "Down with King George" -- The last service -- The generous giver -- Across the waters -- Three at grace -- The lucky stone -- The princess of Philadelphia -- A present for Mr. Lincoln -- The land Columbus found.
LC: Je 14, '20.

L-224　_____ The tower of David: a book of stories for the program of women's organizations / by Elma Ehrlich Levinger . . . ; published for the National Council of Jewish Women. New York: Bloch Publishing Company, 1924. 203 p.　**CRL**
Contents: The mother with nothing to give -- A Succoth table -- Vivian gets a booking -- More than bread -- The two-edged sword -- In the rabbi's study -- "Eight o'clock sharp!" -- Unhallowed candles -- Stairs -- A day in the Shushan -- "A star - for a night" -- Patchwork -- Birds of a feather -- A son of Pharaoh -- Dawn through the darkness -- Twenty years after -- A cemetery Jew -- The return of Akiba -- Intermarriage -- A mother of Bethlehem.

L-225　Levison, Eric. Ashes of evidence / by Eric Levison. Indianapolis: The Bobbs-Merrill Company, [c1921]. 360 p.
LC: O 3, '21.
PW: O 22, '21.

L-226　_____ The eye witness / by Eric Levison. Indianapolis: The Bobbs-Merrill Company, [c1921]. 355 p.
LC: F 28, '21.
PW: Mr 26, '21.

L-227　_____ Hidden eyes / by Eric Levison; with frontispiece by Sidney Riesenberg. Indianapolis: The Bobbs-Merrill Company, [c1920]. 344 p., front.
LC: Ag 27, '20.
PW: S 25, '20.

L-228　Levitan, M. (Michael). Their life in Russia and in America / by M. Levitan; with illustrations by E. Ladue. [Rome, N. Y.: The Citizen Press, c1914]. 34 p., front. (port.), [3] leaves of plates.　**HUC**

L-229　Levy, Melvin P., b. 1902. Matrix / by Melvin P. Levy. New York: Thomas Seltzer, 1925. 209 p.
LC: N 2, '25.
PW: N 14, '25.

L-230　Levy, Samuel Jacob. Broken bridges: a collection of short stories and plays of dental life / by S. J. Levy . . . Brooklyn, N. Y.: Published by the author, [c1924]. (Brooklyn, N. Y.: Alpert Press). 316 p.
Contents: To move or not to move -- An effectual antidote to bad business -- Doctor Maximilian Larov -- East, West, North, South--A chauffeur's dilemma -- Branching out -- Vacation in reality and imagination -- The vacation minus imagination -- My friend's wife and I -- A country romance -- The dental wizard -- Broken bridges [play] -- A successful dentist [play] -- A dentist in the making [play] -- A message from Heaven [play].

Lewin, Judah Löb. Earth of Palestine. In _Yiddish tales_ (1912), Y-20.

L-231　Lewis, Alfred Henry, 1857-1914. The Apaches of New York / by Alfred Henry Lewis; illustrated. New York: G. W. Dillingham Company, [c1912]. 272 p., front., [10] leaves of plates. [Ill. by Rodney Thomson, W. J. Enright, and James Daugherty.]
LC: Mr 30, '12.
PW: Ap 13, '12.
References: BAL 11763.

L-232   [____] The Black Lion Inn / illustrated by Frederic Remington. New York: R. H. Russell, 1903. 380, [1] p., front., [15] leaves of plates.
PW: My 16, '03.
References: BAL: 11749.

L-233   ____ The boss, and how he came to rule New York / by Alfred Henry Lewis. New York: A. S. Barnes & Company, 1903. 409 p., front., [9] leaves of plates. [Ill. by William J. Glackens.]
LC: O 26, '03.
PW: O 31, '03.
BLC: New York: A. S. Barnes & Co; London: Author's Syndicate, 1903.
References: BAL 11751.

L-234   ____ Confessions of a detective / by Alfred Henry Lewis; illustrated by E. M. Ashe. New York: A. S. Barnes & Company, 1906. 280 p., front., [7] leaves of plates. [Also ill. by Henry Raleigh.]
LC: F 9, '07.
PW: N 3, '06.
References: BAL 11757.

L-235   ____ The dismissal of Silver Phil / by Alfred Henry Lewis. New York: The Winthrop Press, c1914. 31, [1] p.
First separate printing: reprinted from *Wolfville nights*, [1902].
References: BAL 11767.

L-236   ____ Faro Nell and her friends: Wolfville stories / by Alfred Henry Lewis; illustrations by W. Herbert Dunton and J. N. Marchand. New York: G. W. Dillingham Company, [c1913]. 348 p., front., [11] leaves of plates.
Contents: Dead-Shot Baker -- Old man Enright's uncle -- Cynthiana, pet-named Original Sin -- Old Monte, official drunkard -- How the Mocking Bird was won -- That Wolfville-Red Dog Fourth -- Propriety Pratt, hypnotist -- That Turner person -- Red Mike -- How Tutt shot Texas Thompson -- The funeral of Old Holt -- Spelling Book Ben.
LC: My 7, '13.
PW: Ap 5, '13.
References: BAL 11764.

   ____ The man from Red Dog. In *International short stories* (1910), I-29.

L-237   ____ Peggy O'Neal / by Alfred Henry Lewis; illustrated by Henry Hutt. Philadelphia: Drexel Biddle, [1903]. 494 p., col. double front., [3] leaves of col. plates.
PW: Je 6, '03.
References: BAL 11750.

L-238   ____ The president: a novel / by Alfred Henry Lewis; illustrated. New York: A. S. Barnes and Company, 1904. 514 p., col. front., [7] leaves of col. plates. [Ill. by Jay Hambidge.]
LC: S 7, '04.
PW: S 17, '04.
References: BAL 11752.

L-239   ____ The story of Paul Jones: an historical romance / by Alfred Henry Lewis; illustrations by Seymour M. Stone and Phillipps Ward. New York: G. W. Dillingham Company, [1906]. 308 p., front., [7] leaves of plates.
LC: My 12, '06.
PW: Je 2, '06.
BLC: London: T. Fisher Unwin; New York [printed], 1906.
References: BAL 11756.

L-240   ____ The sunset trail / by Alfred Henry Lewis . . . ; illustrated. New York: A. S. Barnes & Co., 1905. 393 p., front., [7] leaves of plates. [Ill. by George Fort Gibbs, E. McConnell, and J. N. Marchand.]
LC: Ap 21, '05.
PW: My 13, '05.
References: BAL 11754.

L-241   ____ The throwback: a romance of the Southwest / by Alfred Henry Lewis . . . ; illustrated with a frontispiece in color and three other pictures from paintings by N. C. Wyeth. New York: The Outing Publishing Company, 1906. 347 p., col. front., [3] leaves of plates.
PW: Ap 14, '06.
BLC: London: Cassell & Co., 1907.
References: BAL 11755.

L-242   ____ Wolfville days / by Alfred Henry Lewis . . . ; with frontispiece by Frederic Remington. New York: Frederick A. Stokes Company, [c1902]. 311 p., front.
Contents: The great Wolfville strike -- The grinding of Dave Tutt -- The feud of pickles -- Johnny Florer's axle grease -- Toothpick Johnson's ostracism -- The Wolfville Daily Coyote -- Cherokee Hall plays poker -- The treachery of Curly Ben -- Colonel Sterett's reminiscences -- How the dumb man rode -- How Prince Hal got help -- How Wolfville made a jest -- Death; and the Donna Anna -- How Jack Rainey quit -- The defiance of Gene Watkins -- Colonel Sterett's war record -- Old Man Enright's love -- When Whiskey Billy died -- When the stage was stopped.
PW: F 22, '02.
BLC: London: Isbister & Co., 1902.
References: BAL 11747.

L-243   ____ Wolfville folks / by Alfred Henry Lewis. New York: D. Appleton and Company, 1908. 321, [1] p., front. [Ill. by W. Herbert Dunton.]
Contents: The widow dangerous -- The return of Rucker -- Cherokee Hall, gambler -- The looking out of Faro Nell -- The Off-Wheeler offends -- Wolfville's revival -- Bismark Dutch -- The canyon hold-up -- The popular sourness -- Doc Peets' error -- Jaybird Horne -- The heir of the Broken-O -- The Rose of Wolfville -- The Rose's thorns -- Sandy Carr, violinist -- Boggs and the ghost -- The guile of Cottonwood Wasson -- Top and bottom -- Texas receives a letter -- The false alarm -- The jest of Talky Jones -- The confusion of Talky -- Soap Suds Sal -- The wooing of Riley -- The copper head -- The salting of the golden rule -- The wisdom of Doc Peets -- The lecture in the Lady Gay -- Cash box and Mrs. Bill -- Mrs. Bill's protectorate.
LC: My 15, '08.
PW: My 16, '08.
References: BAL 11762.

L-244   ____ Wolfville nights / by Alfred Henry Lewis . . . New York: Frederick A. Stokes Company, [1902]. 326 p., front. [Ill. by E. S. Hall.]
Contents: Dedication -- Some cowboy facts -- The dismissal of Silver Phil -- Colonel Sterett's panther hunt -- How Faro Nell dealt bank -- How the raven died -- The queerness of Dave Tutt -- With the Apache's compliments -- The Mills of Savage Gods -- Tom and Jerry; wheelers -- The influence of Faro Nell -- The ghost of the Bar-B-8 -- Tucson Jennie's correction -- Bill Connors of the Osages -- When Tutt first saw Tucson -- The troubles of Dan Boggs -- Bowlegs and Major Ben -- Toad Allen's elopement -- The clients of Aaron Green -- Colonel Sterett's marvels -- The luck of Hardrobe -- Long ago on the Rio Grande -- Colonel Coyote Clubbs.

PW: O 11, '02.
References: BAL 11748.

L-245   _____ A Wolfville Thanksgiving / by Alfred H. Lewis
. . . New York: Frederick A. Stokes Company,
[1901, c1897]. 132 p.   **VA@**
(Half hour classics by modern masters of fiction.)
First separate printing: reprinted from *Wolfville*,
1897.
References:References: BAL 11746.

Lewis, Chas. Bertrand, 1842-1924. For the sake of
Lize. In *Through the forbidden gates* (1903), **T-222**.

L-246   _____ The humorous Mr. Bowser / by M. Quad . . .
with 16 illustrations and cover design by Merle
Johnson. New York: J. S. Ogilvie Publishing
Company, c1911. 253 p., front., plates, ill.
Unexamined copy: bibliographic data from NUC.

L-247   [_____] The life and troubles of Mr. Bowser: being a
veracious and authentic account of his doings at home
and abroad with Mrs. Bowser in the foreground to
assist in maintaining the interests of the general
narrative / by M. Quad <C. B. Lewis> . . .
Chicago: Jamieson-Higgins Company, 1902. 441 p.
incl. plates, front. (port.).
Unexamined copy: bibliographic data from NUC.

L-248   Lewis, DeWitt F. A trip to the North Pole and
beyond to civilization / written by DeWitt F. Lewis.
Edited and compiled by E. Z. Ernst. Linwood, Kan.:
The Industrial Exchange, 1912. 96 p., front.
Unexamined copy: bibliographic data from NUC.

L-249   Lewis, Edwin Herbert, 1866-1938. Sallie's
newspaper: a novel / by Edwin Herbert Lewis.
Chicago: Hyman-McGee Co., 1924. 294 p.
LC: Ag 1, '24.
PW: Ag 9, '24.

L-250   _____ Those about Trench / by Edwin Herbert Lewis.
New York: The Macmillan Company, 1916. 326 p.
LC: F 17, '16.
PW: F 26, '16.

L-251   _____ White lightning / by Edwin Herbert Lewis.
Chicago: Covici-McGee, 1923. 354 p.
LC: Je 4, '23.
PW: Je 30, '23.

L-252   Lewis, Elizabeth. Lorenzo of Sarzana / by Elizabeth
Lewis. Boston: Richard G. Badger, 1907.
([Boston]: The Gorham Press). 416 p.

L-253   Lewis, Florence J. (Florence Jane), b. 1881.
Climbing up to nature / by Florence J. Lewis.
Boston, Mass.: The C. M. Clark Publishing
Company, 1908. 353 p., front., [10] leaves of plates.
[Ill. by M. A. and W. A. J. Claus.]

L-254   Lewis, Frances McCall. The quest illusive: truth vs.
fiction / by Frances McCall Lewis. Chicago: The
Howell Company, 1916. 224 p.   **DLC**

L-255   Lewis, Frederick, *pseud.* The strange case of Mary
Page / by Frederick Lewis [pseud.] . . . illustrated by
Fanny Munsell. New York: E. J. Clode, [1916].
232 p., front. [6] leaves of plates.   **DLC**
LC: Ap 1, '16.

Lewis, George Edward, b. 1870. See **Blacklock,
Alaska, pseud.**

L-256   Lewis, Gertrude Russell. A designer of dawns and
other tales: little stories of the here and there / by
Gertrude Russell Lewis. Boston; Chicago: The
Pilgrim Press, [c1917]. 67 p.
Contents: The little old woman goes there -- The heaven of mother's
dreams -- The hall of waiting -- In the crown room -- In the counting
room -- The potter of Nazareth -- A designer of dawns.

L-257   Lewis, Graham, Mrs. Guyndine: a woman with a
conscience / by Mrs. Graham Lewis . . . ; a novel.
Guthrie, Okla.: State Capital Ptg. Co., 1901.
359 p., front. (port.). Designed end papers.
LC: Ag 27, '01.

L-258   Lewis, Harriett Graham. Beyond the menace / by
Harriett Graham Lewis. Boston, Massachusetts: The
Stratford Company, 1923. 224 p., front.   **NYP**
LC: My 26, '23.
PW: Jl 14, '23.

L-259   Lewis, Herbert P. (Herbert Pierce), b. 1874. Eb
Peechcrap and wife at the fair: being the experience
of residents of 'Possum Ridge, Arkansaw, in St.
Louis / by Herb Lewis. New York; Washington:
The Neale Publishing Company, 1906. 239 p.,
photo. front. (port.).   **IPL**

L-260   Lewis, Julius A. Sir Walter of Kent: a truthful
history of three centuries ago: printed with the
consent of Sir Walter's few living descendants /
edited by Julius A. Lewis. New York; London:
Bonnell, Silver & Co., 1902. 343 p.
PW: Ag 2, '02.

Lewis, O. F. Alma mater. In *Prize stories of 1920*
(1921), P-618.

_____ The get-away. In *Prize stories of 1921* (1922),
P-619.

_____ Old Peter takes an afternoon off. In *Prize
stories of 1922* (1923), **P-620.**

L-261   Lewis, Sinclair, 1885-1951. Arrowsmith / by
Sinclair Lewis . . . New York: Harcourt, Brace and
Company, 1925. 448 p.
LC: Mr 12, '25.
PW: Mr 7, '25.
BLC: London: Jonathan Cape, 1925. British title:
Martin Arrowsmith.

L-262   _____ Babbitt / by Sinclair Lewis . . . New York:
Harcourt, Brace and Company, [c1922]. 401 p.
LC: Jl 24, '22.
PW: S 16, '22.
BLC: London: Jonathan Cape, [1922].

L-263   ____ Free air / by Sinclair Lewis . . . New York: Harcourt, Brace and Howe, 1919. 370 p.
LC: N 7, '19.
PW: N 1, '19.

L-264   ____ The innocents: a story for lovers / by Sinclair Lewis . . . New York; London: Harper & Brothers, 1917. 216, [1] p., front. [Ill. by Worth Brehm.]
LC: S 20, '17.
PW: S 29, '17.

L-265   ____ The job: an American novel / by Sinclair Lewis . . . New York; London: Harper & Brothers, 1917. 326, [1] p.
LC: F 26, '17.
PW: Mr 3, '17.

L-266   ____ Main street: the story of Carol Kennicott / by Sinclair Lewis. New York: Harcourt, Brace and Howe, 1920. 451 p.
LC: O 27, '20.
PW: O 30, '20.
BLC: London: Hodder & Stoughton; Rahway, N. J. [printed], 1920.

L-267   ____ Our Mr. Wrenn: the romantic adventures of a gentle man / by Sinclair Lewis. New York; London: Harper & Brothers, 1914. 253, [1] p., front., ill.
LC: F 21, '14.
PW: Mr 7, '14.

L-268   ____ The trail of the hawk: a comedy of the seriousness of life / by Sinclair Lewis . . . New York; London: Harper & Brothers, [1915]. 408, [1] p., col. front. [Ill. by Norman Rockwell.]
LC: S 9, '15.
PW: S 11, '15.

        ____ The willow walk. *In The best short stories of 1918 and the yearbook of the American short story* **(1919), B-563.**

        ____ Young Man Axelbrod. *In Short stories* **(1925), S-460.**

L-269   Lewis, W. S. (Wilmarth Sheldon), 1895-1979. Tutors' lane / Wilmarth Lewis. New York: Alfred A. Knopf, 1922. 164 p.
LC: O 11, '22.

L-270   Lewis-Johnson, Annie. New dawn: a philosophical story of the unfolding of man through the power of evolution / by Annie Lewis-Johnson. New York: Roger Brothers; London: L. N. Fowler & Co., 1911. 332 p.
LC: Mr 25, '11.

L-271   Lewisohn, Ludwig, 1882-1955. The broken snare / by Ludwig Lewisohn. New York: B. W. Dodge & Company, 1908. 289 p.   **INA**
LC: S 28, '08.
BLC: London: S. Paul & Co.; [printed in U. S. A., 1908].

L-272   ____ Don Juan / by Ludwig Lewisohn. New York: Boni and Liveright, [c1923]. 305 p. Designed end papers.

L-273   Lewys, Georges. Georges Lewys' The "charmed American": (François, l'Américain): a story of the Iron Division of France. New York: John Lane Company; London: John Lane, The Bodley Head, 1919. 328 p., front.
LC: Ap 4, '19.

L-274   ____ The temple of Pallas-Athenæ: (Posterité) / by Georges Lewys. [Los Angeles?]: Privately printed for subscribers only, 1924. 416 p., front. [Ill. by Franz Geritz.]
LC: Jl 15, '24.

L-275   Libbey, Laura Jean, 1862-1924. The clutch of the marriage tie, or, Jilbett: a story of the second glass / by Laura Jean Libbey; a novel in seven parts. [Brooklyn]: Brooklyn Eagle Press, [c1920]. 63 p., front. (port.).   **DLC**

L-276   ____ Laura Jean Libbey's . . . latest and greatest romance, Wooden wives. Is it a story for philandering husbands? / by Laura Jean Libbey. [New York: Publishers Printing Company], c1923. 324 p.
Unexamined copy: bibliographic data from NUC.

L-277   Library of the world's best mystery and detective stories / edited by Julian Hawthorne. New York: The Review of Reviews Co., 1908, [c1907]. 6 v., front. (in each volume). [Ill. by Peter Newell, Power O'Malley, M. Walter Dunne, and S. L. Wood.]
Contents: English-Irish (Vol. 3) contains first book publication of *A terrible night* by Fitzjames O'Brien.
PW: S 19, '08.

L-278   Lichtenstein, Joy, b. 1874. For the blue and gold: a tale of life at the University of California / by Joy Lichtenstein. San Francisco: A. M. Robertson, 1901. 232 p., front., [12] leaves of plates.

L-279   Liebe, Hapsburg. The clan call / by Hapsburg Liebe; frontispiece by Ralph Pallen Coleman. Garden City, New York: Doubleday, Page & Company, 1920. 239, [1] p., col. front.
PW: N 13, '20.

    Lieberman, Elias. A thing of beauty. *In The best short stories of 1919 and the yearbook of the American short story* **(1920), B-564.**

L-280   Liesmann, Frederick J. White buffalo / by Frederick J. Liesmann. St. Louis, Mo.: Concordia Publishing House, 1918. 74 p., ill. [Ill. by Frederick J. Liesmann.]

L-281   Life at high tide / edited by William Dean Howells and Henry Mills Alden. New York; London: Harper & Brothers, 1907. 268 p.
(Harper's novelettes.)
Contents: The immediate jewel / Margaret Deland -- "And angels came-" / Anne O'Hagan -- Keepers of a charge / Grace E. Channing -- A working basis / Abby M. Roach -- The glass door / Mary T. Earle -- Elizabeth and Davie / Muriel C. Dyar -- Barney Doon, braggart / P. V. Mighels -- The reparation / E. Pottle -- The yearly tribute / Rosina H. Emmet -- A matter of rivalry / Octave Thanet.
LC: D 24, '08.
PW: Je 5, '09.
References: BAL 9786; Gibson & Arms 07-F.

L-282　The life within. Boston: Lothrop Publishing Company, [1903]. 385 p.
PW: F 14, '03.

L-283　Lightfoot, Richard. Must woman ever and man never forgive? / by Richard Lightfoot. Los Angeles: Angelus Publishing Company, [c1917]. 331 p., incl. front., [2] leaves of plates.

L-284　Lighton, William Rheem, 1866-1923. Billy Fortune / by William R. Lighton; illustrated. New York; London: D. Appleton and Company, 1912. 364, [1] p., front., [3] leaves of plates. [Ill. by Gayle Hoskins.]
LC: O 4, '12.
PW: O 12, '12.

L-285　____ Letters of an old farmer to his son / William R. Lighton. New York: George H. Doran Company, [c1914]. 212 p.
LC: O 27, '14.
PW: O 24, '14.

L-286　____ The Shadow of a great rock / by William R. Lighton. New York; and London: G. P. Putnam's Sons, 1907. (New York: The Knickerbocker Press). 276 p., col. front.
LC: My 11, '07.
PW: My 18, '07.

____ The state against Ellsworth. In *Love* (1901), **L-525.**

L-287　____ The ultimate moment / by William R. Lighton; illustrated by A. I. Keller. New York; London: Harper & Brothers, 1903. 310, [1] p., front., [7] leaves of plates.
PW: O 24, '03.

L-288　____ Uncle Mac's Nebrasky / by William R. Lighton; with frontispiece by W. Herbert Dunton. New York: Henry Holt and Company, 1904. 184 p., front.
PW: My 7, '04.

L-289　Liljencrantz, Ottilia Adelina, 1876-1910. Randvar the songsmith: a romance of Norumbega / by Ottilie A. Liljencrantz . . . New York; London: Harper & Brothers Publishers, 1906. 313, [1] p., col. front. [Ill. by The Kinneys.]
PW: F 17, '06.

L-290　____ The thrall of Leif the Lucky: a story of Viking days / written by Ottilie A. Liljencrantz; having pictures and designs by Troy & Margaret West Kinney. Chicago: A. C. McClurg & Co., 1902. 354 p., col. front., [5] leaves of col. plates.
PW: Mr 29, '02.
BLC: London: C. F. Cazenove; Cambridge, U. S. A. printed, 1902.

L-291　____ A Viking's love: and other tales of the North / by Ottilie A. Liljencrantz. Chicago: A. C. McClurg & Co., 1911. 74, [1] p., front., ill. [Ill. by Arthur E. Becher.]
Contents: A Viking's love -- The hostage -- As the Norns weave -- How Thor recovered his hammer.

LC: N 6, '11.
PW: D 2, '11.

L-292　____ The Vinland champions / by Ottilie A. Liljencrantz; illustrated by the Kinneys. New York: D. Appleton and Company, 1904. 255 p., front., [3] leaves of plates.
PW: N 12, '04.
BLC: London: Ward, Lock & Co., 1905.

L-293　____ The ward of King Canute: a romance of the Danish conquest / written by Ottilie A. Liljencrantz . . . ; having pictures by Troy & Margaret West Kinney. Chicago: Published by A. C. McClurg & Co., 1903. 382 p., col. front., [5] leaves of col. plates. Illustrated end papers.
PW: My 23, '03. [PW calls McClurg pbl. 2nd edition.]
BLC: London: Ward, Lock & Co., 1904. Printed from American plates. Another edition: Boston: Small, Maynard & Co., [1903]. [Small, Maynard edition notes A. C. McClurg as copyright holder].
Unexamined copy: bibliographic data from OCLC, #604256.

L-294　Lillibridge, Will, 1878-1909. Ben Blair: the story of a plainsman / by Will Lillibridge; with frontispiece in full color by Maynard Dixon. Chicago: A. C. McClurg & Co., 1905. 333 p., col. front.
PW: O 21, '05.
BLC: Chicago: A. C. McClurg & Co.; London: C. F. Cazenove, 1905.

L-295　____ The dissolving circle / by Will Lillibridge. New York: Dodd, Mead & Company, 1908. 314 p., col. front. [Ill. by The Kinneys.]
LC: Mr 30, '08.
PW: Ap 11, '08.

L-296　____ The dominant dollar / by Will Lillibridge; with four illustrations by Lester Ralph. Chicago: A. C. McClurg & Co., 1909. 349, [1] p., col. front., [3] leaves of col. plates.
LC: S 13, '09.
PW: S 25, '09.

L-297　____ The quest eternal / Will Lillibridge; frontispiece in color by the Kinneys. New York: Dodd, Mead and Company, 1908. 326 p., col. front.
LC: Ag 4, '08.
PW: O 10, '08.

L-298　____ Where the trail divides / by Will Lillibridge; with illustrations in color by The Kinneys. New York: Dodd, Mead and Company, 1907. 302 p., col. front., [3] leaves of col. plates.
LC: Mr 6, '07.
PW: Ap 13 '07.
BLC: London: B. F. Stevens & Brown; printed in U. S. A., 1907.

L-299　Lillibridge, William L. Edward Reynolds / by William L. Lillibridge. New York: The Grafton Press, [1902]. 419 p., front., [3] leaves of plates. [Ill. by F. A. Carter.]
PW: N 1, '02.

Limerick, Oliver Victor. See **Burgundy, Billy, pseud.**

Lin, Katherin Von der. See **Von der Lin, Katherin, b. 1878.**

L-300   Lincoln, Fred. S. An Indiana girl / by Fred. S. Lincoln. Washington: The Neale Publishing Company, 1901. 286 p.
PW: D 28, '01.

Lincoln, J. W. (John Willard), b. 1875. See **Barker, Bruce, pseud.**

L-301   Lincoln, Jeanie Gould, 1846-1921. A javelin of fate / by Jeanie Gould Lincoln . . . Boston; New York: Houghton, Mifflin and Company, 1905. (Cambridge: The Riverside Press). 295, [1] p.   **IUA**
PW: D 2, '05.

L-302   ____ The luck of Rathcoole: being the romantic adventures of Mistress Faith Wolcott (sometime known as "Miss Moppet") during her sojourn in New York at an early period of the republic / by Jeanie Gould Lincoln . . . Boston; New York: Houghton Mifflin Company, 1912. 262, [2] p., col. front., [3] leaves of col. plates. [Ill. by Douglas John Connah.]
LC: F 19, '12.
PW: F 17, '12.
BLC: London: Constable & Co; Cambridge, Mass. [printed], 1912. Another edition: London: Gay & Hancock; Cambridge, Mass., printed, [1912].

L-303   Lincoln, Joseph Crosby, 1870-1944. Cap'n Dan's daughter / by Joseph C. Lincoln . . . ; illustrated. New York; London: D. Appleton and Company, 1914. 389, [1] p., front., [2] leaves of plates. [Ill. by J. Henry.]
LC: Mr 5, '14.
PW: Mr 7, '14.

L-304   ____ Cap'n Eri: a story of the coast / by Joseph C. Lincoln; illustrated by Charlotte Weber. New York: A. S. Barnes & Company, 1904. 397 p., col. front., [3] leaves of col. plates.
PW: M 5, '04.
BLC: London: Author's Syndicate; New York: A. S. Barnes & Co., 1904.

L-305   ____ Cap'n Warren's wards / by Joseph C. Lincoln; illustrated by Edmund Frederick. New York; London: D. Appleton and Company, 1911. 379, [1] p., front., [3] leaves of plates.
LC: O 9, '11.
PW: O 14, '11.

L-306   ____ Cy Whittaker's place / by Joseph C. Lincoln . . . ; with illustrations by Wallace Morgan. New York: D. Appleton and Company, 1908. 402 p., front., [15] leaves of plates, ill.
LC: S 25, '08.
PW: O 10, '08.

L-307   ____ The depot master / by Joseph C. Lincoln . . . ; illustrated. New York; London: D. Appleton and Company, 1910. 379, [1] p., front., [3] leaves of

plates. [Ill. by Howard Heath.]
LC: My 25, '10.
PW: My 21, '10.

L-308   ____ Doctor Nye of North Ostable: a novel / by Joseph C. Lincoln . . . New York; London: D. Appleton and Company, 1923. 423 p.
LC: Ag 28, '23.
PW: S 8, '23.

L-309   ____ Extricating Obadiah / by Joseph C. Lincoln; illustrated by Walt Louderback. New York; London: D. Appleton and Company, 1917. 380, [1] p., front., [3] leaves of plates.
LC: O 15, '17.

L-310   ____ Fair Harbor: a novel / by Joseph C. Lincoln. New York; London: D. Appleton and Company, 1922. 379 p.
LC: O 11, '22.
PW: O 7, '22.

L-311   ____ Galusha the Magnificent: a novel / by Joseph C. Lincoln . . . New York; London: D. Appleton and Company, 1921. 407 p.
LC: Jl 1, '21.
PW: Jl 2, '21.

L-312   ____ Kent Knowles: quahaug / by Joseph C. Lincoln; illustrated by J. N. Marchand. New York; London: D. Appleton and Company, 1914. 450, [1] p., front., [3] leaves of plates.
LC: O 28, '14.
PW: N 7, '14.

L-313   ____ Keziah Coffin / by Joseph C. Lincoln; with illustrations by Wallace Morgan. New York; London: D. Appleton and Company, 1909. 386 p., front., 7 leaves of ill. (not included in pagination).
LC: S 16, '09.
PW: O 2, '09.

L-314   ____ Mary-'Gusta / by Joseph C. Lincoln; illustrated by H. M. Brett. New York; London: D. Appleton and Company, 1916. 410, [1] p., front., [3] leaves of plates.
LC: O 25, '16.
PW: N 4, '16.

L-315   ____ Mr. Pratt: a novel / by Joseph C. Lincoln; frontispiece by Horace Taylor. New York: A. S. Barnes and Company, 1906. 342 p., front.
PW: My 19, '06.

L-316   ____ Mr. Pratt's patients / by Joseph C. Lincoln; illustrated. New York; London: D. Appleton and Company, 1913. 344, [1] p., front., [3] leaves of plates. [Ill. by Howard Heath.]
LC: My 21, '13.
PW: My 31, '13.

L-317   ____ The "Old home house" / by Joseph C. Lincoln. New York: A. S. Barnes & Company, 1907. 291 p., front., ill. [Ill. by Martin Justice and Robert A. Graef.]
LC: Je 7, '07.
PW: Je 15, '07.

L-318 ____ Partners of the tide / by Joseph C. Lincoln
. . . ; frontispiece in colors by Charlotte Weber;
decorations by John Rae. New York: A. S. Barnes
& Co., 1905. 400 p., col. front., ill.
PW: My 13, '05.
BLC: London: Hodder & Stoughton, 1905.

____ The pie and the past. In *Marriage* (1923),
M-457.

L-319 ____ The Portygee: a novel / by Joseph C. Lincoln;
frontispiece by H. M. Brett. New York; London: D.
Appleton and Company, 1920. 361 p., col. front.
LC: Ap 12, '20.
PW: Ap 24, '20.

L-320 ____ The postmaster / by Joseph C. Lincoln;
illustrated. New York; London: D. Appleton and
Company, 1912. 316, [1] p., front., [3] leaves of
plates. [Ill. by Howard Heath.]
LC: My 11, '12.
PW: My 4, '12.

L-321 ____ Queer Judson / by Joseph C. Lincoln. New
York: D. Appleton and Company, 1925. 362 p.
LC: O 6, '25.
PW: O 17, '25.

L-322 ____ The rise of Roscoe Paine / by Joseph C.
Lincoln. New York; London: D. Appleton and
Company, 1912. 468, [1] p., front., [3] leaves of
plates. [Ill. by Edmund Frederick.]
LC: N 1, '12.
PW: N 9, '12.

L-323 ____ Rugged water / by Joseph C. Lincoln. New
York; London: D. Appleton and Company, 1924.
385 p.
LC: O 4, '24.
PW: O 11, '24.

L-324 ____ "Shavings": a novel / by Joseph C. Lincoln;
illustrated by H. M. Brett. New York; London: D.
Appleton and Company, 1918. 382 p., front., [3]
leaves of plates.
LC: N 15, '18.
PW: N 16, '18.

L-325 ____ Thankful's inheritance / by Joseph C. Lincoln;
illustrated by H. M. Brett. New York; London: D.
Appleton and Company, 1915. 382, [1] p., front., [3]
leaves of plates.
LC: Je 18, '15.
PW: Jl 3, '15.

L-326 ____ The woman-haters: a yarn of Eastboro
twin-lights / by Joseph C. Lincoln . . . ; illustrated.
New York; London: D. Appleton and Company,
1911. 338 p., front., [3] leaves of plates. [Ill. by
Howard Heath.]
LC: Je 13, '11.
PW: Je 24, '11.

Lincoln, May, pseud. See **Broughton, Ida May,
b.1863.**

L-327 Lincoln, Natalie Sumner, 1881-1935. C. O. D. / by
Natalie Sumner Lincoln; illustrated by Charles L.
Wrenn. New York: D. Appleton and Company,
1915. 328, [1] p., front., [3] leaves of plates.
LC: Mr 2, '15.
PW: Ap 3, '15.

L-328 ____ The cat's paw / by Natalie Sumner Lincoln.
New York; London: D. Appleton and Company,
1922. 303, [1] p., front. [Ill. by William Fisher.]
LC: S 19, '22.
PW: S 30, '22.

L-329 ____ I spy / by Natalie Sumner Lincoln . . . ;
illustrated by Charles L. Wrenn. New York: D.
Appleton and Company, 1916. 334 p., front., [3]
leaves of plates.
LC: My 23, '16.
PW: Je 3, '16.

L-330 ____ The lost despatch / by Natalie Sumner Lincoln
. . . ; illustrated. New York; London: D. Appleton
and Company, 1913. 309, [1] p., front., [3] leaves of
plates. [Ill. by Charles L. Wrenn.]   **OSU, VA@**
LC: F 27, '13.
PW: F 22, '13.

L-331 ____ The man inside / by Natalie Sumner Lincoln;
illustrated. New York; London: D. Appleton and
Company, 1914. 302, [1] p., front., [3] leaves of
plates. [Ill. by Charles L. Wrenn.]
LC: Mr 21, '14.
PW: Mr 21, '14

L-332 ____ The Meredith mystery / by Natalie Sumner
Lincoln. New York; London: D. Appleton and
Company, 1923. 279, [1] p., front.
LC: Mr 7, '23.
PW: Mr 31, '23.

L-333 ____ The missing initial / by Natalie Sumner Lincoln
. . . New York; London: D. Appleton and
Company, 1925. 290, [1] p.
LC: My 12, '25.
PW: My 23, '25.

L-334 ____ The moving finger / by Natalie Sumner Lincoln
. . . ; illustrated by Charles L. Wrenn. New York;
London: D. Appleton and Company, 1918. 363,
[1] p., front., [3] leaves of plates.   **WVH**
LC: Mr 27, '18.
PW: Mr 30, '18.

L-335 ____ The nameless man / by Natalie Sumner Lincoln
. . . ; illustrated by H. R. Ballinger. New York;
London: D. Appleton and Company, 1917. 320,
[1] p., front., [3] leaves of plates.
LC: S 17, '17.
PW: O 6, '17.

L-336 ____ The official chaperon / by Natalie Sumner
Lincoln . . . ; illustrated. New York; London: D.
Appleton and Company, 1915. 330, [1] p., front., [2]
leaves of plates. [Ill. by Edmund Frederick.]
LC: S 15, '15.
PW: S 25, '15.

L-337 _____ The red seal / by Natalie Sumner Lincoln. New York; London: D. Appleton and Company, 1920. 315, [1] p., front. [Ill. by Charles L. Wrenn.]
LC: Mr 9, '20.
PW: Mr 27, '20.

L-338 _____ The thirteenth letter / by Natalie Sumner Lincoln . . . New York: D. Appleton and Company, 1924. 289, [1] p., front.
LC: Mr 6, '24.
PW: Mr 15, '24.

L-339 _____ The three strings / by Natalie Sumner Lincoln . . . illustrated by Charles L. Wrenn. New York; London: D. Appleton & Company, 1918. 321, [1] p., incl. front., [3] leaves of plates. **DLC**
LC: N 15, '18.
PW: N 23, '18.

L-340 _____ The Trevor case / by Natalie Sumner Lincoln; illustrated by Edmund Frederick. New York; London: D. Appleton and Company, 1912. 332, [1] p., front., [3] leaves of plates.
LC: F 27, '12.
PW: Mr 16, '12.

L-341 _____ The unseen ear / by Natalie Sumner Lincoln. New York; London: D. Appleton and Company, 1921. 299, [1] p., front.
LC: F 25, '21.
PW: Mr 5, '21.

L-342 Lindelof, O. J. S., b. 1852. A trip to the north pole, or, The discovery of the Ten Tribes, as found in the Arctic Ocean / and published by O. J. S. Lindelof . . . Salt Lake City: Tribune Printing Company, 1903. 200 p., ill. **MNU**

L-343 Linden, Edmund, *pseud*. Sofia: a tale of the lower Rio Grande / by Edmund Linden [pseud.]. San Antonio, Tex.: T. Kunzman, printer, 1920. 29 p. Unexamined copy: bibliographic data from OCLC, #25662082.

L-344 Linderman, Frank Bird, 1869-1938. Lige Mounts: free trapper / by Frank B. Linderman; with illustrations by Joe De Yong. New York: Charles Scribner's Sons, 1922. 330 p., front., [2] leaves of plates.

L-345 _____ On a passing frontier: sketches from the Northwest / by Frank B. Linderman. New York: Charles Scribner's Sons, 1920. 214 p.
Contents: In the name of friendship -- Was Chet Smalley honest? -- The medicine keg -- The throw-away dance -- Jake Hoover's pig -- A gun trade -- The whiskey peddler -- The post-office at Wolftail -- Jew Jake's Monte -- At the bar -- Pap's pinto -- The bullet's proof -- The Indian's God -- Bravery -- What followed a sermon -- Cranks -- The flying Dutchmen.
LC: Je 15, '20.
PW: Je 12, '20.

L-346 Lindley, Elizabeth. The diary of a book-agent / by Elizabeth Lindley. New York: Broadway Publishing Co., 1912, [c1911]. 109 p. Includes *The modern philanthropist* on p. [76]-109.

L-347 Lindley, H. Esselstyn. Zula / by H. Esselstyn Lindley. New York: Broadway Publishing Company, [c1905]. 332 p., photo. front. (port.), [6] leaves of plates. [Ill. by Harry B. Matthews.]

Lindsay, C. H. (Charles Harcourt). See **Forbes-Lindsay, C. H. (Charles Harcourt), b. 1860.**

L-348 Lindsay, Flora Alice, b. 1861. A glimpse of love; or, The doctor's wooing / by Flora A. Lindsay . . . Seattle, Wash., and Portland, Ore.: Lindsay Publishing Company, c1910. 150 p., [1] leaf of plates (port.). **DLC**
LC: My 3, '10.
PW: Jl 2, '10.

L-349 Lindsay, Vachel, 1879-1931. The golden book of Springfield / by Vachel Lindsay. New York: The Macmillan Company, 1920. 329 p. **OSU, BGU**

L-350 Lindsey, William, 1858-1922. The backsliders / by William Lindsey. Boston; New York: Houghton Mifflin Company, 1922. (Cambridge: The Riverside Press). 362, [1] p.
LC: Mr 6, '22.
PW: Mr 18, '22.

L-351 _____ The severed mantle / by William Lindsey; with seven illustrations in color by Arthur I. Keller. Boston; New York: Houghton Mifflin Company, 1909. (Cambridge: The Riverside Press). 452, [2] p., col. front., [6] leaves of col. plates.
LC: O 20, '09.
PW: O 23, '09.
BLC: London: Methuen & Co., 1910.

L-352 [Linebarger, Paul Myron Wentworth], 1871-1939. Miss American Dollars: a romance of travel / by Paul Myron [pseud.] . . . ; with original pictures by François Olivier and other illustrations. Milwaukee, Wis.: Mid-Nation Publishers, 1916. 301 p., front., [5] leaves of plates (some photo.).
PW: Ap 22, '16.

Linfield, Mary Barrow, b. 1891. See **Highland, Lawrence, pseud.**

L-353 Lingen, Ernst. Forgive and forget / by Ernst Lingen. New York; Cincinnati; Chicago: Benziger Brothers, 1909. 349 p., front., [2] leaves of plates. [Ill. by E. Cadmus.] **DLC**
LC: F 5, '09.

L-354 Linn, James Weber, 1876-1939. The chameleon / by James Weber Linn . . . New York: McClure, Phillips, 1903. 418 p.
PW: Mr 7, '03.

_____ *The girl at Duke's*. In *Short stories of America* **(1921), S-464.**

_____ The head of the University of Chicago. In *Stories of the colleges* **(1901), S-984.**

L-355 _____ The second generation / by James Weber Linn. New York: The Macmillan Company; London:

Macmillan & Co., Ltd, 1902. 305 p.
PW: F 1, '02.

L-356 Linnet, Brown. Widow Wiley: and some other old
folk / by Brown Linnet. New York: E. P. Dutton
and Co., 1901. 307 p., photo. front., [19] leaves of
photo. plates.
Contents: Widow Wiley -- Sarah Ann's little girl -- Mrs. Shelly --
Ancient and modern -- Jack -- Bartlem -- The village shop -- Two old
women -- Social agonies -- A miner poet -- A tricycle tour for two --
The ghost in the chimney -- Well waters -- The settling of Tabitha --
Her little "ridicule" -- The tramp in the poultry-yard.

L-357 Linton, C. E. (Charles Ellsworth), 1865?-1930. The
earthomotor and other stories / by C. E. Linton;
illustrated by Murray Wade. Salem, Oregon: From
the press of Statesman Publishing Co., [1920?].
231 p., photo. front. (port.), ill.   **NYP**
Contents: The ocean cave at Heceta Head -- Rescue of the cave
woman -- Three weeks inside the earth -- The hermit of Chimaso
Island.
PW: Je 26, '20.

L-358 ____ The storm's gift / by C. E. Linton; illustrated.
Vancouver, Wash.: From the press of the Interstate
Bindery, [192-?]. 210 p., [7] leaves of plates (some
photo.).

Linton, F. B. The business spy. In *Clever business
sketches* **(1909), C-490.**

____ John Davis, Manager, and the New President's
policy. In *Clever business sketches* **(1909), C-490.**

L-359 Linton, Lulu. More than coronets: stories of kind
hearts / by Lulu Linton. Cincinnati, O.: Standard
Publishing Company, 1903. 143 p.   **BGU**
Contents: More than coronets -- A prophet in his own country -- A
cuffless professor -- Mary Farley's front -- The loyalty of number
thirteen -- As stars in their places.

Lippincott, Bertha Horstmann, 1880-1963. See
Coles, Bertha Horstmann Lippincott.

L-360 Lippmann, Julie Mathilde, b. 1864. "Burkeses Amy"
/ by Julie M. Lippmann . . . ; illustrations by Harriet
Mead Olcott. New York: Henry Holt and Company,
1915. 341 p., front., [2] leaves of plates.
LC: N 29, '15.
PW: D 4, '15.

L-361 ____ Flexible Ferdinand / by Julie M. Lippmann.
New York: George H. Doran Company, [c1919].
312 p.
LC: Ap 28, '19.
PW: Ap 26, '19.

L-362 ____ The interlopers / by Julie M. Lippmann;
illustrated by Ralph P. Coleman. Philadelphia: The
Penn Publishing Company, 1917. 325 p., front., [4]
leaves of plates. Designed end papers.
LC: N 3, '17.

L-363 ____ Making over Martha / by Julie M. Lippmann.
New York: Henry Holt and Company, 1913. 292 p.
LC: O 21, '13.
PW: N 8, '13.

L-364 ____ The mannequin / by Julie M. Lippmann. New
York: Duffield and Company, 1917. 227 p.

LC: Ap 25, '17.
PW: Ap 7, '17.

L-365 ____ Martha and Cupid / by Julie M. Lippmann.
New York: Henry Holt and Company, 1914. 197 p.
LC: N 23, '14.
PW: O 31, '14.

L-366 ____ Martha-by-the-day / by Julie M. Lippmann.
New York: Henry Holt and Company, 1912. 201 p.
LC: S 12, '12.
PW: S 7, '12.
BLC: London: Grant Richards, 1913.

L-367 Liscomb, Harry F. The Prince of Washington
Square: an up-to-the-minute story / by Harry F.
Liscomb. New York: Frederick A. Stokes
Company, 1925. 180 p.
PW: F 28, '25.

L-368 Lisle, Clifton. Diamond rock: a tale of the Paoli
massacre / by Captain Clifton Lisle; illustrations by
Charles Hargens, Jr. New York: Harcourt, Brace
and Howe, 1920. 301 p., front., [3] leaves of plates,
map.
LC: S 21, '20.

L-369 List, Single, Major. The battle of Booby's Bluffs / by
Major Single List. Washington: United States
Infantry Association, 1922. 134 p., [1] folded leaf of
plates.   **LUU**
"Reprinted from Infantry journal, 1921."

L-370 Litchfield, Grace Denio, 1849-1944. The burning
question / by Grace Denio Litchfield . . . New York;
London: G. P. Putnam's Sons, 1913. ([New York]:
The Knickerbocker Press). 307 p.
LC: F 20, '12.

L-371 ____ The letter D / by Grace Denio Litchfield. New
York: Dodd, Mead and Company, 1904. 322 p.
PW: O 8, '04.

L-372 ____ The supreme gift / by Grace Denio Litchfield;
with a frontispiece by Alice Barber Stephens.
Boston: Little, Brown and Company, 1908. 300 p.,
col. front.
LC: Mr 16, '08.

L-373 Litsey, Edwin Carlile, b. 1874. A bluegrass cavalier
/ by Edwin Carlile Litsey. Philadelphia: Dorrance,
[c1922]. 320 p.
LC: Mr 31, '22.
PW: Je 17, '22.
BLC: London; New York: Andrew Melrose, 1922.

L-374 ____ The love story of Abner Stone / by Edwin
Carlile Litsey. New York: A. S. Barnes and
Company, 1902. 170 p.
PW: Je 21, '02.

L-375 ____ A maid of the Kentucky hills / by Edwin
Carlile Litsey . . . ; illustrated by John Cassel.
Chicago: Browne & Howell Company, 1913.
380 p., col. front.
LC: N 21, '13.

L-376   ____ The man from Jericho / by Edwin Carlile Litsey. New York: The Neale Publishing Company, 1911. 290 p.   **KUK**
LC: D 18, '11.
PW: Ja 6, '12.

L-377   ____ The race of the swift / by Edwin Carlile Litsey; illustrated from drawings by Charles Livingston Bull. Boston: Little, Brown and Company, 1905. 151 p., front., [3] leaves of plates.
Contents: The race of the swift -- The robber baron -- The ghost coon -- The spoiler of the folds -- The fight on the tree-bridge -- The guardian of the flock -- The king of the northern slopes.
PW: O 14, '05.

L-378   A little book of Rutgers tales / perpetrated under the editorship of Augustus Hunt Shearer. New Brunswick, N. J.: The Rutgers Publishing Company, 1905. 140 p.
Contents: His nibs / Drew Wyckoff Hageman -- Tried twice and true / Augustus Hunt Shearer -- When '35 were sophs -- A false idol / Clarence Edwards Case -- The twins in college / Albert Leeds Stillman -- Where duty called -- The burglar / Conrad Orton Milliken -- A ruined life -- With elements of truth -- Life's demonology -- A successful pledge -- The point of view -- A mistake all around.

L-379   Little, Frances, 1863-1941, *pseud.* The house of the misty star: a romance of youth and hope and love in old Japan / by Frances Little [pseud.] (Fannie Caldwell Macaulay). New York: The Century Co., 1915. 270 p., front., [7] leaves of plates. [Ill. by Arthur E. Becher.]
LC: Ap 27, '15.

L-380   ____ Jack and I in Lotus Land / by the Lady of the Decoration, Frances Little [pseud.]. New York; London: Harper & Brothers, 1922. 260, [1] p., front. [Ill. by Gertrude A. Kay.]
LC: O 23, '22.
BLC: London: Hodder & Stoughton, [1922].

L-381   ____ The lady and Sada San: a sequel to The lady of the decoration / by Frances Little [pseud.]. New York: The Century Co., 1912. 225 p., col. front.
LC: O 4, '12.

L-382   ____ The lady of the decoration / by Frances Little [pseud.]. New York: The Century Co., 1906. 236 p.
PW: Ap 14, '06.

L-383   ____ Little Sister Snow / by Frances Little [pseud.]; with illustrations by Genjiro Kataoka. New York: The Century Co., 1909. 141 p., incl. [11] leaves of plates, col. front. Decorative end papers
LC: O 13, '09.

L-384   Little, Mary Wilson. Retrospection / Mary Wilson Little; cover drawing by Edith Tadd-Little. New York: Broadway Publishing Company, [c1909]. 88 p.   **NYP**
LC: Ap 22, '09.
PW: My 15, '09.

Little, Richard Henry. Getting laundry in war. <u>In</u> *Second suds sayings* **(1919), S-266.**

L-385   Littleheart, Oleta, b. 1867, *pseud.* The lure of the Indian country: and a romance of its great resort / by Oleta Littleheart [pseud.] . . . Sulphur, Okla.: by A. Abbott Publisher, c1908. 153 p., photo. ill.   **OKD** [Revised edition c1918].
LC: My 21 '09.

L-386   Livingston, Armstrong, b. 1885. The mystery of the twin rubies / by Armstrong Livingston. New York: Moffat Yard and Company, 1922. 330 p.
LC: F 3, '23.
BLC: London: S. Paul & Co., [1923].

L-387   Livingston, Florence Bingham. The custard cup / Florence Bingham Livingston. New York: George H. Doran Company, [c1921]. 297 p.
PW: Ap 16, '21.
BLC: London: Hodder & Stoughton; U. S. A. [printed], [1921].

L-388   ____ Under a thousand eyes / by Florence Bingham Livingston; illustrations by Maurice L. Bower. New York: Cosmopolitan Book Corporation, 1923. 456 p., front., [3] leaves of plates.
LC: Ap 23, '23.

L-389   Livingstone, Alice. A sealed book / by Alice Livingstone . . . ; with eight full page illustrations. New York: R. F. Fenno & Company, [c1906]. 384 p., front., [7] leaves of plates.   **ABC**
BLC: London: Ward, Lock & Co., 1906.

Livingstone, Rev. T. J., S. J. Pilgrims of the night. <u>In</u> *The Senior lieutenant's wager: and other stories* **(1905), S-312.**

L-390   Lloyd, Beatrix Demarest. The pastime of eternity / by Beatrix Demarest Lloyd. New York: Charles Scribner's Sons, 1904. 364 p.

L-391   Lloyd, Edward Mostyn. Tom Anderson, dare-devil: a young Virginian in the revolution / by Edward Mostyn Lloyd; with illustrations. Boston; New York: Houghton Mifflin Company, 1916. (Cambridge: The Riverside Press). 415 p., col. front., [3] leaves of col. plates. [Ill. by Harold Cue.]

L-392   Lloyd, John. The Captain's wife / by John Lloyd. New York: Mitchell Kennerley, [c1908]. 319 p., incl. col. front.
LC: Ap 18, '08.
PW: Ag 1, '08.

Lloyd, John, pseud. <u>See</u> **Morgan, Jacque Lloyd, b. 1873.**

L-393   Lloyd, John Uri, 1849-1936. Red Head / by John Uri Lloyd . . . ; illustrations and decorations by Reginald B. Birch. New York: Dodd, Mead and Company, 1903. 208 p., front., [9] leaves of plates.
PW: N 21, '03.

L-394   ____ Scroggins / by John Uri Lloyd; illustrations and decorations by Reginald B. Birch. New York: Dodd, Mead & Company, 1904. 119 p., front., [3] leaves of plates.
PW: D 3, '04.

L-395　　　　Warwick of the Knobs: a story of Stringtown County, Kentucky / by John Uri Lloyd . . . ; with photographic illustrations of Knob County. New York: Dodd, Mead & Company, 1901. 305 p., incl. [15] leaves of photo. plates, photo. front.
PW: O 12, '01.

L-396　　　Lloyd, John William, b. 1857. The dwellers in Vale Sunrise: how they got together and lived happy ever after. A sequel to "The natural man;" being an account of the tribes of him / by J. Wm. Lloyd. Westwood, Mass.: Ariel Press, 1904. 195 p. Unexamined copy: bibliographic data from OCLC, #7054615.

　　　　My Arizona bedroom. In **Robinson, William Henry, b. 1867.** *Yarns of the Southwest (1921),* **R-467.**

L-397　　　　The natural man: a romance of the golden age / by J. William Lloyd. Newark, N. J.: Benedict Prieth, [c1902]. 140 p.
PW: Ag 9, '02.

L-398　　　Lloyd, Marion. Four stories in the key of A flat. [S. l.: s. n., 19__]. 189 p. Designed end papers.
_{Contents: A medley -- The doctor's story -- Afterward -- A winter in Brambletown -- Saint and sinner.}

L-399　　　LLoyd, Nelson McAllister, 1873-1933. David Malcolm / by Nelson LLoyd. New York: Charles Scribner's Sons, 1913. 413 p.
LC: Ag 27, '13.
PW: S 6, '13.

L-400　　　　A drone and a dreamer / by Nelson Lloyd. New York: J. F. Taylor & Company, 1901. 259 p., incl. front., [3] leaves of plates. [Ill. by Florence Scovel Shinn.]
PW: Ag 10, '01.
BLC: London: William Heinemann; New York printed, 1901.

　　　　The last ghost in harmony. In *Humorous ghost stories (1921),* **H-1018.**

L-401　　　　Mrs. Radigan: her biography with that of Miss Pearl Veal, and the memoirs of J. Madison Mudison / by Nelson Lloyd . . . New York: Charles Scribner's Sons, 1905. 344 p.　　　　**AFU**
PW: S 23, '05.

L-402　　　　The Robberies Company, Ltd. / by Nelson Lloyd. New York: Charles Scribner's Sons, 1906. 404 p., front. [Ill. by F. C. Yohn.]
LC: S 24, '06.
PW: O 13, '06.

L-403　　　　Six stars / by Nelson Lloyd; illustrated. New York: Charles Scribner's Sons, 1906. 315 p., front., [7] leaves of plates. [Ill. by Howard Pyle, A. B. Frost, Fletcher C. Ransom, Albert Levering, and H. J. Peck.]
_{Contents: The third and a half generation -- The best gun in the valley -- The natural-born preacher -- The Snyder County gold-strike -- The Admirable Whoople -- The second venture -- The posy song -- The angels of Six Stars -- A bachelor of elements -- The man who studied continual -- Music hath charms -- The most determinedest}

_{man -- The uplifting power of pride -- The sentimental Miss Tubbs -- The modest man -- The contentedest man.}
PW: Ap 14, '06.

L-404　　　　The soldier of the valley / by Nelson Lloyd; illustrated by A. B. Frost. New York: Charles Scribner's Sons, 1904. 335 p., incl. [13] leaves of plates, front.
PW: O 8, '04.
BLC: London: Hodder & Stoughton, 1904.

L-405　　　Lloyd, Robert. The treasure of Shag Rock: an adventure story / by Robert Lloyd; illustrated by I. B. Hazelton. Boston: Lothrop Publishing Company, [c1902]. 344 p., front., [4] leaves of plates (1 photo.).
PW: Ag 30, '02.

L-406　　　Locke, G. E. (Gladys Edson), b. 1887. The house on the downs / by G. E. Locke; illustrated by Frank T. Merrill. Boston: L. C. Page & Company, [1925]. 305 p., front., [5] leaves of plates.
LC: My 1, '25.

L-407　　　　The purple mist / by G. E. Locke . . . ; illustrated by Charles E. Meister. Boston: L. C. Page & Company (Inc.), 1924. 363 p., front., [5] leaves of plates.
LC: Jl 25, '24.

L-408　　　　The Red Cavalier, or, The Twin Turrets mystery / by Gladys Edson Locke; with a frontispiece in full color from a painting by Charles E. Barnes. Boston: The Page Company, 1922. 372 p., col. front.
LC: My 5, '22.

L-409　　　　Ronald o' the moors / by Gladys Edson Locke . . . ; with illustrations by Nellie L. Thompson. Boston: The Four Seas Company, 1919. 332 p., front., [2] leaves of plates.　　　**NYP**
LC: D 22, '19.
PW: Ja 3, '20.

L-410　　　　The scarlet macaw / by G. E. Locke . . . ; illustrated by Charles E. Meister. Boston: L. C. Page & Company (Inc.), 1923. 315 p., col. front., [4] leaves of plates.
LC: Ag 17, '23.

L-411　　　　That affair at Portstead manor / by Gladys Edson Locke . . . Boston: Sherman, French & Company, 1914. 266 p.
Unexamined copy: bibliographic data from NUC.

L-412　　　Locke, James, 1869-1928. The plotting of Frances Ware / by James Locke . . . New York: Moffat, Yard and Company, 1909. 309 p.
LC: My 4, '09.
BLC: London: Everett & Co., [1911].

L-413　　　　The stem of the crimson dahlia / by James Locke; with frontispiece by Ch. Weber-Ditzler. New York: Moffat, Yard & Company, 1908. 342 p., col. front.
LC: Ja 24, '08.
BLC: London: T. Fisher Unwin, 1908.

L-414   Locke, Prescott. The conversion of Hamilton
Wheeler: a novelette of religion and love introducing
studies in religious psychology and pathology / by
Prescott Locke. Bloomington, Illinois: The Pandect
Publishing Company, 1917. 285 p.   **IIB**
"A voluntary contribution to the National Mental
Hygiene movement."
LC: Ag 27, '17.
PW: S 8, '17.

L-415   Lockett, Mary F. Christopher [a novel] / by "the
Princess" Mary F. Lockett. New York, London,
[etc.]: The Abbey Press, [1902]. 328 p., front.,
plates.
Unexamined copy: bibliographic data from NUC.
PW: My 3, '02.

L-416   Lockhart, Caroline, 1870-1962. The dude wrangler /
by Caroline Lockhart; frontispiece by Dudley Glyne
Summers. Garden City, N. Y.; Toronto:
Doubleday, Page & Company, 1921. 319, [1] p.,
front.
LC: My 20, '21.
PW: Jl 30, '21.

L-417   _____ The fighting shepherdess / by Caroline
Lockhart . . . ; with a frontispiece by M. Leone
Bracker. Boston: Small, Maynard & Company,
[c1919]. 373 p., col. front.
LC: Ag 8, '19.
PW: Ap 5, '19.

L-418   _____ The full of the moon / by Caroline Lockhart;
with illustrations by Charles H. Stephens.
Philadelphia; London: J. B. Lippincott Company,
1914. 267 p., col. front., [2] leaves of col. plates.
LC: Ap 21, '14.
PW: Mr 14, '14.

L-419   _____ The Lady Doc / by Caroline Lockhart; with
illustrations by Gayle Hoskins. Philadelphia; London:
J. B. Lippincott Company, 1912. 339 p., col. front.,
[3] leaves of plates.
LC: O 9, '12.
PW: O 12, '12.

L-420   _____ The man from the Bitter Roots / by Caroline
Lockhart . . . ; with illustrations in color by Gayle
Hoskins. Philadelphia; London: J. B. Lippincott
Company, 1915. 327 p., col. front., [2] leaves of
col. plates.
LC: N 10, '15.
PW: O 30, '15.

L-421   _____ "Me--Smith" / by Caroline Lockhart; with
illustrations by Gayle Hoskins. Philadelphia; London:
J. B. Lippincott Company, 1911. 315 p., col. front.,
[4] leaves of plates.
LC: F 23, '11.
PW: Mr 4, '11.

L-422   Lockwood, William Lewis. Trailers of the North /
by William Lewis Lockwood. New York: Broadway
Publishing Company, [c1905]. 197 p., front., [5]
leaves of plates. [Ill. by Wm. L. Hudson.]
Contents: In the great silence -- Fanshaw of the Northwest mounted
-- A kronikle of the trale -- The golden cache -- Skookum Jim --

Shipmates of the trail.
PW: F 10, '06.

L-423   Loeb, Harold A., b. 1891. Doodab / by Harold A.
Loeb. New York: Boni & Liveright, 1925. 287 p.
PW: Ag 22, '25.

L-424   Loeser, Joseph. Darting rays: and other stories / by
Joseph Loeser. Published in Milwaukee: by the
author, November, 1924. 179 p.
Contents: Darting rays or radiating charms -- Hate at first sight --
The picture in the locket -- Sunshine and darkness -- Heroism and
bravado -- Lively domestic scenes -- A married man and his typist --
Through a secret tunnel -- Thrilling happenings -- Brewster's
romantic experiences -- A journey around the world -- Hallucination
-- Donkey's eggs -- The Irishman and the big Swede -- Hansmichel
Nixcomeraus, the bully of the town -- Well of Mirth and the lost
glove.

Loevius, Frederick. See **Thaumazo, Fred, pseud.**

L-425   A log cabin romance: a pretty story of the early
pioneer life on the Western Reserve / written by five
members of The Ravenna Tuesday Club as a part of
their study of the early history of Ohio. Ravenna,
Ohio: The Republican Publishing Co., 1914. [38] p.

L-426   Lohn, Agnette Midgarden. The voice of the big firs /
Agnette Midgarden Lohn. [Fosston, Minn.: s. n.],
c1918. 428 p.
Unexamined copy: bibliographic data from OCLC,
#12073932.
"Copyrighted 1918 by Mrs. John Lohn, Fosston,
Minn."

L-427   Lombardi, Cynthia (Richmond). At sight of gold / by
Cynthia Lombardi . . . New York; London: D.
Appleton & Company, [c1922]. 341 p.   **INT**
LC: Ap 14, '22.
PW: My 2, '25.

L-428   _____ A cry of youth / by Cynthia Lombardi. New
York; London: D. Appleton and Company, 1920.
360 p.   **ABC**
LC: Ap 3, '20.
PW: Ap 17, '20.

L-429   Lonargan, John P. Cwan and Genevieve: a tale of
love and romance in the days of Roderick, last
monarch of all Ireland / by John P. Lonargan. New
York: T. J. Carey, [c1904]. 207 p.
Unexamined copy: bibliographic data from OCLC,
#26981001.

L-430   London, Jack, 1876-1916. The abysmal brute / by
Jack London . . . New York: The Century Co.,
1913. 169 p., front. [Ill. by Gordon Grant.]
LC: My 29, '13.
PW: My 31, '13.
BLC: London: G. Newnes, [1914].
References: BAL 11945; Woodbridge, London,
Tweney, 109; Sisson & Martens, p. 70, 127-128.

L-431   _____ Adventure / by Jack London . . . New York:
The Macmillan Company, 1911. 405 p.
LC: Mr 9, '11.
PW: Mr 18, '11.
BLC: London: Thomas Nelson & Sons,

1911.
References:References: BAL 11928; Woodbridge,
London, Tweney, 85; Sisson & Martens, p. 56.
Sisson & Martens records English edition, p. 54.

L-432   _____ Before Adam / by Jack London . . . ; with
numerous illustrations by Charles Livingston Bull.
New York: The Macmillan Company; London:
Macmillan & Co., Ltd., 1907. 242 p., incl. 7 leaves
of col. plates, col. front., ill., map.
PW: Mr 2, '07.
BLC: London: T. Werner Laurie, [1908].
References: BAL 11903; Woodbridge, London,
Tweney, 52; Sisson & Martens, p. 34, 123. BAL
11894 B notes copyright printing deposited Je 30, '06.

L-433   _____ Burning Daylight / by Jack London . . . New
York: The Macmillan Company, 1910. 361 p.,
front., [7] leaves of plates. [Ill. by Wallace Morgan.]
LC: O 6, '10.
PW: O 15, '10.
BLC: London: William Heinemann, 1911.
References: BAL 11918; Woodbridge, London,
Tweney, 75; Sisson & Martens, p. 48, 125. See also
BAL 11933 for use as promotional matter.

L-434   _____ The call of the wild / by Jack London;
illustrated by Philip R. Goodwin and Charles
Livingston Bull; decorated by Chas. Edw. Hooper.
New York: The Macmillan Company; London:
Macmillan & Co., Ltd., 1903. 231 p., incl. col.
front., [10] leaves of col. plates.
PW: Ag 1, '03.
BLC: London: William Heinemann; Norwood,
Mass. printed, 1903.
References: BAL 11876; Woodbridge, London,
Tweney, 19; Sisson & Martens, p. 14, 119-120.

L-435   _____ Children of the frost / by Jack London . . . ;
with illustrations by Raphael M. Reay. New York:
The Macmillan Company; London: Macmillan &
Co., Ltd., 1902. 261 p., front., [7] leaves of plates.
Contents: In the forests of the North -- The law of life -- Nam-Bok
the unveracious -- The master of mystery -- The sunlanders -- The
sickness of Lone Chief -- Keesh, the son of Keesh -- The death of
Ligoun -- Li Wan, the fair --The league of the old men.
References: BAL 11873; Woodbridge, London,
Tweney, 7; Sisson & Martens, p. 6. BAL 11871
notes copyright printing deposited My 28, '02.

L-436   _____ A daughter of the snows / by Jack London . . .
; with illustrations in color by Frederick C. Yohn.
Philadelphia: J. B. Lippincott Company, 1902.
334 p., front., [3] leaves of plates.
LC: O 11, '02.
PW: N 22, '02.
BLC: London: Ibister & Co., 1904.
References: BAL 11874; Woodbridge, London,
Tweney, 13; Sisson & Martens, p. 10.

L-437   _____ Dutch courage: and other stories / by Jack
London. New York: The Macmillan Company,
1922. 180 p., front. (port.), [7] leaves of plates. [Ill.
by G. M. Richards.]
Contents: Dutch courage -- Typhoon off the coast of Japan -- The
lost poacher -- The banks of the Sacramento -- Chris Farrington, able
seaman -- To repel boarders -- An adventure in the upper sea -- Bald-
face -- In Yeddo bay -- Whose business is to live.

LC: O 4, '22.
PW: N 11, '22.
BLC: London: Mills & Boon, 1923.
References: BAL 11985; Woodbridge, London,
Tweney, 164; Sisson & Martens, p. 105.

L-438   _____ The faith of men: and other stories / by Jack
London . . . New York: The Macmillan Company;
London: Macmillan & Co., Ltd., 1904. 286 p.
Contents: A relic of the Pliocene -- A hyperborean brew -- The faith
of men -- Too much gold -- The one thousand dozen -- The marriage
of Lit-lit --Bâtard -- The story of Jees Uck.
PW: Je 4, '04.
BLC: London: William Heinemann, [n. d.].
References: BAL 11878; Woodbridge, London,
Tweney, 26; Sisson & Martens, p. 18.

L-439   _____ The game / by Jack London . . . ; with
illustrations and decorations by Henry Hutt and T. C.
Lawrence. New York: The Macmillan Company;
London: Macmillan & Co., Ltd., 1905. 182 p., incl.
col. front., incl. [5] leaves of col. plates.
PW: Je 17, '05.
BLC: London: William Heinemann; Norwood, Mass
[printed], 1905.
References: BAL 11886; Woodbridge, London,
Tweney, 36; Sisson & Martens, p. 24, 121-22.

L-440   _____ The god of his fathers: & other stories / by
Jack London. New York: McClure, Phillips &
Company, 1901. 299 p.
Contents: The God of his fathers -- The great interrogation -- Which
make men remember -- Siwash -- The man with the gash -- Jan, the
unrepentant -- Grit of women -- Where the trail forks -- A daughter of
the aurora -- At the rainbow's end -- The scorn of women.
LC: My 15, '01.
PW: Je 1, '01.
BLC: London; New York: McClure, Phillips &
Company, 1901. Another edition: London: Isbister
& Co; Cambridge, U. S. A. [printed], 1902.
References: BAL 11870; Woodbridge, London,
Tweney, 4; Sisson & Martens, p. 4.

L-441   _____ Hearts of three / by Jack London. New York:
The Macmillan Company, 1920. 373 p.
LC: O 14, '20.
PW: O 30, '20.
BLC: London: Mills & Boon, [1918].
References: BAL 11982; Woodbridge, London,
Tweney, 158; Sisson & Martens, p. 104. BAL
11978, Woodbridge, London, Tweney 157, and
Sisson & Martens, p. 100, 129, record first English
edition.

L-442   _____ The house of pride: and other tales of Hawaii /
by Jack London . . . New York: The Macmillan
Company, 1912. 232 p., front. [Ill. by Mac M.
Pease.]
Contents: The house of pride -- Koolau the leper -- Good-by, Jack --
Aloha oe -- Chun Ah Chun -- The sheriff of Kona.
LC: Mr 21, '12.
PW: Ap 13, '12.
BLC: London: Mills & Boon, [1914].
References: BAL 11936; Woodbridge, London,
Tweney 96; Sisson & Martens, p. 62, 126.

L-443   _____ Iron heel / by Jack London . . . New York;
London: The Macmillan Company, 1908, [c1907].

354 p.
PW: F 29, '08.
BLC: London: Everett & Co., [1908].
References: BAL 11908; Woodbridge, London,
Tweney, 62; Sisson & Martens, p. 40, 123-24. BAL
11902 notes copyright printing deposited Ja 5, '07.

L-444   _____ Jerry of the islands / by Jack London . . .
New York: The Macmillan Company, 1917. 337 p.,
col. front.
LC: Ap 26, '17.
PW: Ap 28, '17.
BLC: London: Mills & Boon, 1917.
References: BAL 11973; Woodbridge, London,
Tweney, 147; Sisson & Martens, p. 94.

L-445   _____ John Barleycorn / by Jack London . . . ;
illustrated by H. T. Dunn. New York: The Century
Co., 1913. 343 p., front., incl. [7] leaves of plates.
LC: Ag 19, '13.
PW: Ag 23, '13.
BLC: London: Mills & Boon, 1914.
References: BAL 11946; Woodbridge, London,
Tweney, 113; Sisson & Martens, p. 72, 128. See
also BAL 11943.

L-446   [_____] The Kempton-Wace letters . . . / [by Jack
London and Anna Strunsky]. New York: The
Macmillan Company; London: Macmillan & Co.,
Ltd., 1903. 256 p.
LC: My 5, '03.
PW: Je 6, '03.
References: BAL 11875; Woodbridge, London,
Tweney, 16; Sisson & Martens, p. 12.

    _____ The league of the old men. In *Spinners' book
of fiction* (1907), S-755.

L-447   _____ The little lady of the big house / by Jack
London . . . New York: The Macmillan Company,
1916. 392 p., col. front. [Ill. by William Van
Dresser.]
LC: Ap 6, '16.
PW: Ap 15, '16.
BLC: London: Mills & Boon, 1916.
References: BAL 11966; Woodbridge, London,
Tweney, 138; Sisson & Martens, p. 88, 128.

L-448   _____ Lost Face / by Jack London . . . New York:
The Macmillan Company, 1910. 240 p., front., [5]
leaves of plates. [Ill. by Howard Giles and F. E.
Schoonover.]
Contents: Lost Face -- Trust -- To build a fire -- That Spot -- Flush
of gold -- The passing of Marcus O'Brien -- The wit of Porportuk.
LC: Mr 4, '10.
PW: Mr 12, '10.
BLC: London: Mills & Boon, [1915].
References: BAL 11915; Woodbridge, London,
Tweney, 70; Sisson & Martens, p. 44, 124.

L-449   _____ Love of life: and other stories / by Jack
London . . . New York: The Macmillan Company;
London: Macmillan & Co., Ltd., 1907, [c1906].
265 p.
Contents: Love of life -- A day's lodging -- The white man's way --
The story of Keesh -- The unexpected -- Brown wolf -- The sun-dog
trail -- Negore, the coward.

PW: O 5, '07.
BLC: London: Mills & Boon, 1907; London:
Everett & Co., 1908.
References: BAL 11904; Woodbridge, London,
Tweney, 56; Sisson & Martens, p. 36. BAL 11894A
notes copyright printing deposited My 9, '06.

L-450   _____ Martin Eden / by Jack London . . . ; with
frontispiece by the Kinneys. New York: The
Macmillan Company, 1909, [c1908]. 411 p., front.
PW: O 9, '09.
BLC: London: William Heinemann, 1910.
References: BAL 11912; Woodbridge, London,
Tweney, 66; Sisson & Martens, p. 42. BAL 11909
notes copyright printing deposited My 23, '08.

L-451   _____ Michael, brother of Jerry / by Jack London
. . . New York: The Macmillan Company, 1917.
344 p., col. front.
LC: N 8, '17.
PW: N 24, '17.
BLC: London: Mills & Boon, 1917.
References: BAL 11974; Woodbridge, London,
Tweney, 151; Sisson & Martens, p. 96.

L-452   _____ Moon-face: and other stories / by Jack London
. . . New York: The Macmillan Company; London:
Macmillan & Co., Ltd., 1906. 273 p.
Contents: Moon-face -- The leopard man's story -- Local color --
Amateur night -- The minions of Midas -- The shadow and the flash --
All Gold Canyon -- Planchette.
LC: S 11, '06.
PW: S 22, '06.
BLC: London: William Heinemann, 1914.
References: BAL 11895; Woodbridge, London,
Tweney, 43; Sisson & Martens, p. 28, 122. BAL
11894 notes copyright printing deposited Ap 27, '06.

L-453   _____ The mutiny of the Elsinore / by Jack London
. . . ; with frontispiece. New York: The Macmillan
Company, 1914. 378 p., col. front. [Ill. by Anton
Otto Fischer.]
LC: S 10, '14.
PW: O 3, '14.
BLC: London: Mills & Boon, 1915.
References: BAL 11956; Woodbridge, London,
Tweney, 124; Sisson & Martens, p. 78.

L-454   _____ The night-born: and also The madness of John
Harned; When the world was young; The benefit of
the doubt; Winged blackmail; Bunches of knuckles;
War; Under the deck awnings; To kill a man; The
Mexican / by Jack London . . . New York: The
Century Co., 1913. 290 p., col. front.
LC: F 26, '13.
PW: Mr 1, '13.
BLC: London: Mills & Boon, 1916.
References: BAL 11942; Woodbridge, London,
Tweney, 106; Sisson & Martens, p. 68, 127.

L-455   _____ On the Makaloa mat / by Jack London . . .
New York: The Macmillan Company, 1919.
229 p.
Contents: On the Makaloa mat -- The bones of Kahelili -- When
Alice told her soul -- Shin-bones -- The water baby -- The tears of Ah
Kim -- The Kanaka surf.
LC: O 22, '19.
PW: N 8, '19.

References: BAL 11981; Woodbridge, London, Tweney, 162; Sisson & Martens, p. 102, 130.

L-456   ____ The red one / by Jack London . . . New York: The Macmillan Company, 1918. 193 p., front. (port.).
Contents: The red one -- The hussy -- Like Argus of the ancient times -- The princess.
LC: O 24, '18.
PW: N 9, '18.
BLC: London: Mills & Boon, 1919.
References: BAL 11977; Woodbridge, London, Tweney, 154; Sisson & Martens, p. 98, 129.

L-457   ____ Revolution and other essays / by Jack London . . . New York: The Macmillan Company, 1910. 309 p.
Contains the short story "Goliah."
LC: Ap 14, '10.
PW: Ap 30, '10.
BLC: London: Mills & Boon, [1920].
References: BAL 11916; Woodbridge, London, Tweney, 72; Sisson & Martens, p. 46, 124.

L-458   ____ The scarlet plague / by Jack London . . . ; illustrated by Gordon Grant. New York: The Macmillan Company, 1915. 181 p., incl. front., ill.
LC: My 6, '15.
PW: My 15, '15.
BLC: London: Mills & Boon, [1915].
References: BAL 11960; Woodbridge, London, Tweney, 128; Sisson & Martens, p. 80. BAL 11940 notes copyright printing.

L-459   ____ The sea-wolf / by Jack London . . . ; with illustrations by W. J. Aylward. New York; London: The Macmillan Company, 1904. 366 p., front., [5] leaves of plates.
PW: N 19, '04.
BLC: London: William Heinemann, 1904.
References: BAL 11882; Woodbridge, London, Tweney, 29; Sisson & Martens, p. 20, 120-21.

L-460   ____ Smoke Bellew / by Jack London . . . ; illustrated by P. J. Monahan. New York: The Century Co., 1912. 385 p., incl. [7] leaves of plates, front.
LC: O 1, '12.
PW: O 5, '12.
BLC: London: Mills & Boon, 1913.
References: BAL 11939; Woodbridge, London, Tweney, 102; Sisson & Martens, p. 66, 127. See also BAL 11938.

L-461   ____ A son of the sun / by Jack London . . . ; illustrated by A. O. Fischer and C. W. Ashley. Garden City, N. Y.: Doubleday, Page & Company, 1912. 333 p., front., [3] leaves of plates.
Contents: A son of the sun -- The proud goat of Aloysius Pankburn -- The devils of Fuatino -- The jokers of New Gibbon -- A little account with Swithin Hall -- A Goboto night -- The feathers of the sun -- The pearls of Parlay.
LC: My 23, '12.
PW: Je 1, '12.
BLC: London: Curtis Brown & Co.; Garden City, New York printed, 1912. BAL records London: Mills & Boon, 1913.
References: BAL 11937; Woodbridge, London, Tweney, 99; Sisson & Martens, p. 64, 126.

    ____ The son of the wolf. In *West winds* (1914), **W-368.**

L-462   ____ South Sea tales / by Jack London . . . ; with frontispiece. New York: The Macmillan Company, 1911. 327 p., col. front. [Ill. by Anton Otto Fischer.]
Contents: The house of Mapuhi -- The whale tooth -- Mauki -- "Yah! Yah! Yah!" -- The heathen -- The terrible Solomons -- The inevitable white man -- The seed of McCoy.
LC: O 5, '11.
PW: O 28, '11.
BLC: London: Mills & Boon, 1912.
References: BAL 11932; Woodbridge, London, Tweney, 93; Sisson & Martens, p. 60, 126.

L-463   ____ The star rover / by Jack London . . . New York: The Macmillan Company, 1915. 329 p., col. front. [Ill. by James Hambidge.]
LC: O 7, '15.
PW: O 23, '15.
References: BAL 11963; Woodbridge, London, Tweney, 132; Sisson & Martens, p. 84. BAL 11962 and Sisson & Martens, p. 82 record first English edition with the title *The jacket*. London: Mills & Boon, Ltd., [1915].

L-464   ____ The strength of the strong / by Jack London . . . ; illustrated by Dan Sayer Groesbeck. Chicago: Charles H. Kerr & Company Co-operative, [c1911]. 29 p.   **DLC**
LC: Ag 1, '11.
PW: S 2, '11.
References: Bal 11931. BAL notes Charles H, [sic] Kerr & Company Co-operative; 30 p.

L-465   ____ The strength of the strong / by Jack London . . . ; with frontispiece. New York: The Macmillan Company, 1914. 257 p., front.
Contents: The strength of the strong -- South of the Slot -- The unparalleled invasion -- The enemy of all the world -- The dream of Debs -- The sea-farmer -- Samuel.
LC: My 21, '14.
PW: Je 20, '14.
BLC: London: Mills & Boon, [1917].
References: BAL 11955; Woodbridge, London, Tweney, 121; Sisson & Martens, p. 76.

L-466   ____ The turtles of Tasman / by Jack London . . . New York: The Macmillan Company, 1916. 268 p.
Contents: By the turtles of Tasman -- The eternity of forms -- Told in the drooling ward -- The hobo and the fairy -- The prodigal father -- The first poet [play] -- Finis -- The end of the story.
LC: S 28, '16.
PW: O 21, '16.
BLC: London: Mills & Boon, [1917].
References: BAL 11968; Woodbridge, London, Tweney, 142; Sisson & Martens, p. 90.

L-467   ____ The valley of the moon / by Jack London . . . ; with frontispiece in colors by George Harper. New York: The Macmillan Company, 1913. 530 p., col. front.
LC: O 30, '13.
PW: N 15, '13.
References: BAL 11947. BAL records London: Mills & Boon, 1913; Woodbridge, London, Tweney, 117; Sisson & Martens, p. 74. See also BAL 11944.

L-468 _____ When God laughs: and other stories / by Jack London . . . New York: The Macmillan Company, 1911. 319 p., front., [5] leaves of plates. [Ill. by G. Gibbs, W. R. Leigh, H. C. Wall, and E. M. Ashe.]
Contents: When God laughs -- The apostate -- A wicked woman -- Just meat -- Created He them -- The Chinago -- Make westing -- Semper idem -- A nose for the king -- The "Francis Spaight" -- A curious fragment -- A piece of steak.
LC: Ja 26, '11.
PW: F 4, '11.
BLC: London: Mills & Boon, [1912].
References: BAL 11926; Woodbridge, London, Tweney, 82; Sisson & Martens, p. 52, 125-26.

L-469 _____ White Fang / by Jack London . . . New York: The Macmillan Company; London: Macmillan & Co., Ltd., 1906. 327 p., col. front., [7] leaves of col. plates. [Ill. by Charles Livingston Bull.]
LC: O 2, '06.
PW: N 3, '06.
BLC: London: Methuen & Co., 1907.
References: BAL 11896; Woodbridge, London, Tweney, 46; Sisson & Martens, p. 30, 122. BAL 11888 notes copyright printing deposited N 15, '05.

L-470 _____ Wonder of woman: a "Smoke Bellew" story: in two parts / Jack London. New York: International Magazine Co., [c1912]. 32 p.
LC: O 1, '12.
References: BAL 11938.

L-471 Long, Helen Beecher. The girl he left behind / by Helen Beecher Long; illustrated by R. Emmett Owen. New York: George Sully & Company, [c1918]. 272 p., front., [3] leaves of plates.
LC: S 26, '18.
PW: O 12, '18.

L-472 _____ Janice Day / by Helen Beecher Long; illustrations by Walter S. Rogers. New York: Sully and Kleinteich, [c1914]. 308 p., front., [3] leaves of plates.
LC: S 26, '14.
PW: O 10, '14.

L-473 _____ The testing of Janice Day / by Helen Beecher Long; illustrated by Corinne Turner. New York: Sully and Kleinteich, [c1915]. 310 p., front., [3] leaves of plates.
LC: S 30, '15.
PW: S 25, '15.

L-474 Long, John Luther, 1861-1927. Baby Grand / by John Luther Long. Boston: Richard G. Badger, [c1912]. (Boston: The Gorham Press). 197 p. Partly reprinted from various periodicals.
Contents: Baby Grand -- Tom, Dick and Harry -- Et Caetera -- Spilled milk -- Dull Jim -- Dolly Jack -- The little old lady who wouldn't spoil Christmas.
LC: Je 22, '12.

L-475 _____ Billy-boy: a study in responsibilities / by John Luther Long . . . ; with illustrations by Jessie Willcox Smith and decorations by Robert McQuinn. New York: Dodd, Mead & Company, 1906. 74 p., col. front., ill. Illustrated end papers.   **PAU**
LC: S 26, '06.

L-476 _____ Felice / by John Luther Long; with frontispiece by James Montgomery Flagg. New York: Moffat, Yard & Company, 1908. 156 p., col. front.
LC: O 2, '08.

L-477 _____ Heimweh; The siren; The loaded gun; Liebereich; "Iupiter Tonans"; "Sis"; Thor's emerald; Guile / by John Luther Long; illustrated. New York: The Macmillan Company; London: Macmillan & Co., Ltd., 1905. 345 p., front., [6] leaves of plates. [Ill. by George Gibbs, John Wolcott Adams, W. L. Jacobs, Alice Barber Stephens, and Fred Strothmann.]
PW: O 7, '05.

L-478 _____ Naughty Nan / by John Luther Long . . . New York: Published by The Century Co., 1902. 418 p., col. front.
PW: Mr 1, '02.
BLC: London: Ward, Lock & Co., 1904.

L-479 _____ The prince of illusion; "Dolce"; Ein Nix-Nutz; The honorable Christmas; Gift of Yoshida Aramidzu; "Dizzy Dave"; The horse trade; "Jane an' me"; The dream woman / by John Luther Long. New York: The Century Co., 1901. 304 p.
PW: Ap 20, '01.

L-480 _____ Seffy: a little comedy of country manners / by John Luther Long; illustrations by C. D. Williams. Indianapolis: The Bobbs-Merrill Company, [c1905]. 143, [1] p., col. front., [7] leaves of col. plates.
PW: D 16, '05.

L-481 _____ Sixty Jane and The strike on the Schlafeplatz railroad, "Our Anchel," The lady and her soul, The beautiful graveyard, Lucky Jim, The outrageous Miss Dawn-Dream, The little house in the little street where the sun never came, The atonement / by John Luther Long . . . New York: The Century Co., 1903. 208 p., front. [Ill. by Albert Sterner.]
PW: O 17, '03.
BLC: London: Methuen & Co., 1904.

L-482 _____ War, or, What happens when one loves one's enemy / by John Luther Long . . . ; illustrations by N. C. Wyeth. Indianapolis: Bobbs-Merrill Company, [c1913]. 370, [1] p., col. front., [3] leaves of col. plates.
LC: Ap 19, '13.

L-483 _____ The way of the gods / by John Luther Long. New York: The Macmillan Company; London: Macmillan & Co., Ltd., 1906. 314 p.
PW: My 12, '06.

Long, Lily A. (Lily Augusta), 1862-1927. See **Doubleday, Roman, pseud.**

L-484 Long, Mae Van Norman. The wonder woman / by Mae Van Norman Long; illustrated by J. Massey Clement. Philadelphia: The Penn Publishing Company, 1917. 371 p., front., [4] leaves of plates.
LC: N 3, '17.
PW: N 24, '17.

L-485 Longley, Mary T. Nameless / by Mary T. Longley . . . Chicago: The Progressive Thinker Publishing House, 1912. 181 p., double-leaf front. (ports.).

L-486 Longstreet, Augustus B. (Augustus Baldwin), 1780-1870. Stories with a moral: humorous and descriptive of Southern life a century ago / by Augustus B. Longstreet, compiled and edited by Fitz R. Longstreet. Philadelphia: The John C. Winston Company, 1912. 396 p. Reprinted from various sources.
Contents: The village editor; or, The Natville gem -- The old soldiers - a narrative -- Darby, the politician -- Family government -- A family picture -- The old women - a tribute -- The matchmaker -- Julia and Clarissa -- A charming wife -- The ball -- William Mitten at school -- William Mitten at college.
References: BAL 12959.

Longstreet, Fitz Randolph, b. 1869, ed. and comp. *Stories with a moral* (1912). See **Longstreet, Augustus Baldwin, 1790-1870, L-486.**

L-487 Longstreth, T. Morris (Thomas Morris), b. 1886. Mac of Placid / by T. Morris Longstreth . . . New York: The Century Co., 1920. 339 p., front.
LC: Ap 23, '20.
PW: S 4, '20.

L-488 _____ The silent five / by T. Morris Longstreth . . . ; illustrated. New York; London: The Century Co., [c1924]. 293 p., front., [3] leaves of plates, maps. [Ill. by Courteney Allen.]
LC: Ag 19, '24.

L-489 Loomis, A. Perry, Mrs. The two R's: or, Stepping stones / by Mrs. A. Perry Loomis. Catskill, N. Y.: Enterprise Printing House, 1903. 283 p., front. (port.), ill.
Unexamined copy: bibliographic data from OCLC, #26980792.

Loomis, Annie Elisabeth, 1850-1940. See **Olmis, Elisabeth, pseud.**

L-490 Loomis, Charles Battell, 1861-1911. Araminta and the automobile / by Charles Battell Loomis; with illustrations by Otto Lang. New York: Thomas Y. Crowell & Co., [c1907]. 93, [1] p., front., [3] leaves of plates.
Contents: Araminta and the automobile -- The deception of Martha Tucker -- While the automobile ran down.
PW: S 7, '07.

L-491 _____ Cheerful Americans / by Charles Battell Loomis; with twenty-four illustrations by Florence Scovel Shinn, Fanny Y. Cory, F. L. Fithian, and F. R. Gruger. New York: Henry Holt and Company, 1903. 299 p., front., [23] leaves of plates.
Previously published in various periodials.
Contents: A man of putty -- Araminta and the automobile -- The man from Ochre Point, New Jersey -- "There's only one Noo York" -- Too much boy -- The cosmopolitanism of Mr. Powers -- An eastern Easter -- The man in the red sweater -- Little Miss Flutterly's dissertation on war -- The expatriation of Jonathan Taintor -- The memory of Carlotta -- Truman Wickwire's gloves -- The deception of Martha Tucker -- The minister's henhouse -- The men who swapped languages -- While the automobile ran down -- Veritable Quidors.
PW: Ag 15, '03.
BLC: London: William Heinemann, 1903.

L-492 _____ A holiday touch: and other tales of undaunted Americans / by Charles Battell Loomis; illustrated by Thomas Fogarty, F. R. Gruger, Peter Newell, Charles Battell Loomis, Hy. Mayer, H. G. Williamson and John Wolcott Adams. New York: Henry Holt and Company, 1908. 327 p., front., [6] leaves of plates.
Contents: A holiday touch -- The dinner to Paul -- The cannibals and Mr. Buffum -- The coat of Alpaca -- The unheard wedding march -- The only vice of Awful Adkins -- A study in optimism -- Enter the princess -- With a money king behind me -- Uncle Eli's induced ambergris -- A hurry call for Shakespeare -- The "come-on" -- The man who sang -- Prince Shamus of Ireland -- "Only an American".
PW: O 17, '08.

L-493 _____ I've been thinking / by Charles Battell Loomis. New York: James Pott & Company, 1905. 212 p., front. [Ill. by Robert A. Graef.]
PW: D 9, '05.

L-494 _____ Little Maude and her mamma / by Charles Battell Loomis . . . ; illustrated by the author. New York: Doubleday, Page & Company, 1909. 43 p., front., [3] leaves of plates.   **MNU**
LC: O 22, '09.
PW: O 23, '09.
BLC: London: Doubleday, Page & Co.; New York printed, 1909.

L-495 _____ Minerva's manoeuvres: the cheerful facts of a "return to nature" / by Charles Battell Loomis; illustrated by Frederic R. Gruger. New York: A. S. Barnes Company, 1905. 415 p., front., [3] leaves of plates.
PW: S 2, '05.

L-496 _____ More cheerful Americans / by Charles Battell Loomis; with illustrations by Florence Scovel Shinn, Fanny Y. Cory, F. R. Gruger, and May Wilson Watkins. New York: Henry Holt and Company, 1904. 284 p., front., [11] leaves of plates.
Previously published in various periodicals.
Contents: Poe's raven in an elevator -- A West Point start -- The song that sold -- The thousand dollar skates -- The widow Callahan's Christmas dinner -- Why the delegate walked -- 'Dam White -- The education of a butterfly -- How the cricket cricks -- Their wedding day -- Mrs. Smith's husband -- The bottle, the half brick and the lump of chalk -- For divers reasons -- Miss Flutterly on what is doing -- Miss Flutterly on politics and the drama -- My golf -- Mrs. Bidwell's tea -- A suburban Christmas -- How to write a novel for the masses.
PW: O 8 '04.

L-497 Looms, George. The Caraways / by George Looms. Garden City, New York: Doubleday, Page & Company, 1925. 311 p.
LC: Ap 16, '25.
PW: Ap 11, '25.

L-498 _____ John-no-Brawn / by George Looms . . . Garden City, New York: Doubleday, Page & Company, 1923. 320 p.
LC: N 3, '23.
PW: N 3, '23.
BLC: London: William Heinemann; printed in U. S. A., 1923.

L-499 _____ Stubble / by George Looms. -- 1st ed. -- Garden City, New York: Doubleday, Page & Company, 1922. 296 p.   **KUK**
LC: S 25, '22.
PW: S 30, '22.

L-500 Looney, Louisa Preston. Tennessee sketches / by Louisa Preston Looney. Chicago: A. C. McClurg & Co., 1901. 321 p.
Contents: The member from Tennessee -- In the face of the quarantine -- Aftermath of the old regime -- Jared Kerr's children -- Joe's last testament -- Places of power --Gray farm folk.

L-501 Loos, Anita, 1894-1981. "Gentlemen prefer blondes": the illuminating diary of a professional lady / by Anita Loos; intimately illustrated by Ralph Barton. New York: Boni & Liveright, 1925. 217 p., ill.
LC: N 14, '25.
PW: N 14, '25.
BLC: London: Brentano's, [1926].

L-502 Loose, Harry J. The shamus: a true tale of thiefdom and an expose of the real system in crime / by Detective Harry J. Loose . . . Boston: Christopher Publishing House, [c1920]. 296 p., photo. front. (port.)   **OSU, DVP**
LC: Jl 15, '20.

Loose, Katharine Riegel, b. 1877. See **Schock, Georg, pseud.**

L-503 Loraine, M. W. (Matie Whitney), b. 1871. The Lucky Chance: the story of a mine / by M. W. Loraine; illustrated by Haydon Jones. Boston: Small, Maynard and Company, [c1912]. 274 p., front., [3] leaves of plates.
LC: N 8, '12.

L-504 Lord, Mary E. Christobel's secret: a story of a young girl's premonitions / by Mary E. Lord. New York: The Grafton Press, [c1905]. 87 p., front. (port.).   **DLC**

L-505 Lorensen, Charles. Courtships in the air, or, The strange adventures of Hurry Harry: being a romance in two parts / written by himself and now set forth by Charles Lorensen. New York: Broadway Publishing Company, 1914. 325 p., [12] leaves of plates.
                                    HDC

L-506 Lorimer, George C. (George Claude), 1838-1904. The master of millions: a novel / by George C. Lorimer. New York; Chicago; Toronto; London; Edinburgh: Fleming H. Revell Company, [1903]. 588 p.
PW: Je 20, '03.

L-507 Lorimer, George Horace, 1869-1937. The false gods / by George Horace Lorimer . . . New York: D. Appleton and Company, 1906. 91 p., front., [3] leaves of plates. [Ill. by J. C. Leyendecker.]
PW: Ap 14, '06.

L-508 _____ Jack Spurlock--Prodigal / by George Horace Lorimer . . . ; illustrated by F. R. Gruger. New York: Doubleday, Page & Company, 1908. 333 p., front., [7] leaves of plates.
LC: My 22, '08.
PW: Je 6, '08.

BLC: London: John Murray, 1908.

L-509 [_____] Letters from a self-made merchant to his son: being the letters written by John Graham, head of the house of Graham & Company, pork-packers in Chicago, familiarly known on 'Change as "Old Gorgon Graham", to his son, Pierrepont, facetiously known to his intimates as "Piggy". Boston: Small, Maynard & Co., 1902. 312 p., front., [17] leaves of plates. [Ill. by F. R. Gruger and B. Martin Justice.] "Most of these letters were published serially in the *Saturday Evening Post* of Philadelphia, where they attracted much attention. New letters have been now added. The advice given is sound and genuine and the satire keen." --*The Publishers' Weekly*.
PW: O 25, '02.

L-510 _____ Old Gorgon Graham: more letters from a self-made merchant to his son / by George Horace Lorimer; with pictures by F. R. Gruger and Martin Justice. New York: Doubleday, Page & Company, 1904. 308 p., front., [15] leaves of plates.
PW: S 17, '04.
BLC: London: Methuen & Co.; New York printed, 1904.

L-511 Loring, Emilie Baker. A certain crossroad / by Emilie Loring . . . ; illustrated by R. Pallen Coleman. Philadelphia: The Penn Publishing Company, 1925. 319 p., front.
LC: Mr 13, '25.
PW: Ap 4, '25.

L-512 _____ Here comes the sun! / by Emilie Loring . . . ; illustrated by Paul Gill. Philadelphia: The Penn Publishing Company, 1924. 330 p., front.
LC: Mr 10, '24.
PW: F 23, '24.

L-513 _____ The trail of conflict / by Emilie Loring; frontispiece by W. V. Chambers. Philadelphia: The Penn Publishing Company, 1922. 325, [1] p., incl. front.
LC: O 6, '22.
PW: O 14, '22.

L-514 Lorraine, Elwin. The neutrals' portion: a romance of the Middle West / by Elwin Lorraine. New York: The Jackson Press, 1916. 272 p., front., [3] leaves of plates. [Ill. by Michael Petersham.]
PW: Ag 5, '16.

L-515 Lose, G. W. Theodore, or, The washerwoman's son / by Rev. G. W. Lose . . . Columbus, Ohio: Lutheran Book Concern, 1907. 136 p.

L-516 _____ A white field / by Rev. G. W. Lose. St. Louis, Mo.: Concordia Publishing House, 1918. 71 p.

Lothrop, Harriet Mulford Stone, 1844-1924. See **Sidney, Margaret, pseud.**

Loud, Halah H., ed. *Joshua Davidson, Christian* (1907). See **Jones, Jesse H. (Jesse Henry), 1836-1904, J-185.**

Louriet, F. J. What road goeth he. In *Atlantic narratives*; first series (1918), A-360.

L-517 Louthan, Hattie Horner, b. 1865. In passion's dragnet: a novel / by Hattie Horner Louthan . . . Boston: Richard G. Badger, 1903. (Boston: The Gorham Press). 229 p.
PW: Mr 5, '04.

L-518 _____ A Rocky Mountain feud / by Hattie Horner Louthan . . . Boston, Massachusetts: C. M. Clark Publishing Company, [c1910]. 210 p., photo. front., [5] leaves of plates.
LC: F 10, '11.
PW: Je 3, '11.

L-519 _____ "This was a man!": a romance / by Hattie Horner Louthan. Boston: The C. M. Clark Publishing Co., 1906. 499 p., front.
LC: D 10, '06.
PW: Ja 26, '07.

L-520 Louttit, George William, b. 1868. The Eddyite: a Christian Science tale / --by-- George W. Louttit . . . Fort Wayne, Indiana: Published by The Colonial Press, 1908. 223 p.
LC: O 23, '08.

L-521 _____ The gentleman from Jay / by George William Louttit . . . ; illustrations by Louis F. Grant. New York: G. W. Dillingham Company, [c1903]. 235 p., front., [5] leaves of plates.
PW: Ag 29, '03.

L-522 _____ A maid of the wildwood: a romance of the Middle West in early days / by George William Louttit. Fort Wayne, Indiana, U. S. A.: The Colonial Press, [c1901]. 351 p., col. front., [3] leaves of col. plates. Decorated end papers.
PW: Je 21, '02.

L-523 Loux, Du Bois H. (Du Bois Henry), b. 1867. Maitland Varne, or, The bells of De Thaumaturge / by Du Bois H. Loux. New York: De Thaumaturge Company, 1911. 396 p.
LC: Ja 7, '11.

L-524 _____ Ongon; a tale of early Chicago / by Du Bois H. Loux. New York: [Charles Francis Press], 1902. 182 p., front., [2] leaves of plates. **WOO**
PW: S 13, '02.

L-525 Love. New York: McClure, Phillips & Co., c1901. 172 p., front. [Ill. by Violet Oakley.] **KSU**
Contents: Love in a fog / Hester Coldwell Oakley -- The Captain of the "Aphrodite" / Elmore Elliott Peake -- The state against Ellsworth / William R. Lighton -- Ottenhausen's coup / John Walker Harrington -- Accordin' to Solomon / Mary M. Mears.
PW: F 23, '01; O 26, '01

L-526 The love letters of St. John. New York: Mitchell Kennerley, 1917. 155 p. **KSU**

L-527 The love toy / Anonymous. New York: The Macaulay Company, [c1925]. 253 p.
PW: Mr 28, '25.

Lovell, Ingraham, pseud. See **Bacon, Josephine Dodge Daskam, 1876-1961.**

L-528 Loveridge, Rose Taylor. Twins in twain / by Rose Taylor Loveridge. Marcellus, Michigan: F. W. Brown, 1909. 180 p.
PW: S 4, '09.

L-529 The Lover's replies to an Englishwoman's love-letters. New York: Dodd, Mead and Company, 1901. 196 p. **COD**

L-530 Lovett, Robert Morss, 1870-1956. Richard Gresham / by Robert Morss Lovett. New York: The Macmillan Company; London: Macmillan & Co., Ltd., 1904. 302 p.
LC: Je 18, '04.

L-531 _____ A wingéd victory / by Robert Morss Lovett . . . New York: Duffield & Company, 1907. 431 p.
LC: Mr 29, '07.
BLC: London: Cassell & Co., 1907.

L-532 Low, A. Maurice (Alfred Maurice), 1860-1929. The supreme surrender: a novel / by A. Maurice Low. New York; London: Harper & Brothers Publishers, 1901. 329, [1] p.
LC: Ag 20, '01.

Low, E. A. An extenuating circumstance. In **Seattle Writer's Club.** *Tillicum tales* (1907), S-248.

L-533 Lowe, Corinne, b. 1882. Confessions of a social secretary / by Corinne Lowe. New York; London: Harper & Brothers Publishers, [c1917]. 255, [1] p., front.
Published serially under the title, *This is the life*".
LC: F 17, '17.
PW: F 24, '17.

L-534 _____ Saul / by Corinne Lowe . . . New York: The James A. McCann Company, 1919. 347 p.
LC: Je 30, '19.
PW: Jl 26, '19.
BLC: London: Constable & Co., 1920.

L-535 Lowenberg, I., Mrs. The irresistible current / by Mrs. I. Lowenberg. New York: Broadway Publishing Co., [c1908]. 558 p., front., [3] leaves of plates. [Ill. by William L. Hudson.]
LC: Je 26, '08.
PW: Ag 8, '08.

L-536 _____ A nation's crime: a novel / by Mrs. I. Lowenberg . . . New York; Washington: The Neale Publishing Company, 1910. 378 p.
LC: D 16, '10.

L-537 _____ The voices / by Mrs. I. Lowenberg . . . San Francisco, California: Harr Wagner Publishing Co., 1920. 272 p.
LC: F 16, '20.
PW: Mr 13, '20.

L-538   Lowrance, Harvey C. Melvin Mace: a story of a zinc mine / by Harvey C. Lowrance. Kansas City, Missouri: Press of Franklin Hudson Publishing Company, [c1915]. 197 p., ill.   **DLC**
LC: O 4, '15.

L-539   Lowrie, Sarah Dickson, b. 1870. David the hero / by Sarah Dickson Lowrie . . . Philadelphia: The Westminster Press, 1903. 237 p.   **TUU**
PW: My 9, '03.

L-540   Luby, James, 1856-1925. The Black Cross Clove: a story and a study / by James Luby. New York: B. W. Huebsch, 1910. 368 p.
LC: D 31, '10.
PW: D 10, '10.

L-541   Luby, William Jeremiah, b. 1879. The vandal, or, Half a Christian: a novel on Irish-American life / by William J. Luby. Chicago: J. S. Hyland and Company, 1909. 344 p.
LC: S 20, '09.

L-542   Lucas, F. Alexander. Barnegat yarns: tales of Jersey's popular Barnegat Bay and shore / by F. Alexander Lucas. New York: Broadway Publishing Co., [c1911]. 219 p., front., [3] leaves of plates.
   VA@
Contents: Barnegat Bell -- Riley's pig -- A Barnegat romance -- A tale of a tide -- Mad Meg -- A Barnegat sleuth -- Love Lady's Island -- The Kittiwake gull -- A rich man's sorrow -- Smuggler's cove -- The wreck of the "Davy C" -- A lighthouse tragedy -- Swept by the sea -- Jack-Daw Jim -- A waif of the sea -- The old hawk toll -- Sea Hawk's score -- For love of gold -- An old man's darling.

Lucky Friday Club. See *The mysterious monogram (1911)*, **M-1183.**

L-543   Ludlow, James Meeker, 1841-1932. Avanti!: a tale of the resurrection of Sicily 1860 / by James M. Ludlow . . . New York; Chicago; Toronto; London; Edinburgh: Fleming H. Revell Company, [c1912]. 361 p., front.
LC: Ja 2, '13.

L-544   ____ Deborah: a tale of the times of Judas Maccabaeus / by James M. Ludlow. New York; Chicago; Toronto: Fleming H. Revell, [c1901]. 406 p., front., [3] leaves of plates.
PW: S 7, '01.
BLC: London: J. Nisbet & Co., [1901].

L-545   ____ Jesse ben David: a shepherd of Bethlehem / by James M. Ludlow. [Chicago]: Fleming H. Revell Company, [c1907]. 132 p., col. front., ill. [Ill. by Samuel M. Palmer.] Illustrated end papers.
LC: N 15, '07.

L-546   ____ Sir Raoul / James M. Ludlow; a tale of the theft of an empire. New York; Chicago; Toronto; London; Edinburgh: Fleming H. Revell Company, [c1905]. 370 p. front., [4] leaves of plates.
PW: O 21, '05.
BLC: London; Edinburgh: Oliphant & Co.; New York printed, 1905.

L-547   Ludlow, Louis, 1873-1950. In the heart of Hoosierland: a story of the pioneers, based on many actual experiences / by Louis Ludlow; illustrated by Clifford K. Berryman. Washington: Pioneer Book Company, [c1925]. 329, [1] p., ill.

L-548   Ludlow, Will Cumback, 1885-1907. Onawago, or, The betrayer of Pontiac / by Will Cumback Ludlow; illustrated by Irene Mull-Marquardt. Benton Harbor, Mich.: Antiquarian Publishing Company, 1911. 311 p., [6] leaves of plates (1 port.).

L-549   Luehrmann, Adele. The curious case of Marie Dupont / by Adele Luehrmann; illustrated by Frank Snapp. New York: The Century Co., 1916. 324 p., incl. [7] leaves of plates, front.
LC: Ag 19, '16.
PW: Ag 19, '16.

L-550   ____ The other Brown / by Adele Luehrmann; with illustrations by Lucius W. Hitchcock. New York: The Century Co., 1917. 354 p., incl. [7] leaves of plates, front.
LC: Ag 30, '17.
PW: S 1, '17.

L-551   ____ The triple mystery / by Adele Luehrmann . . . New York: Dodd, Mead and Company, 1920. 277 p.
LC: My 4, '20.
PW: My 8, '20.

L-552   Lull, Delos. Celestia / by Rev. D. Lull. New York: Press of the Reliance Trading Company, 1907. 238, [1] p.
Unexamined copy: bibliographic data from OCLC, #29851159.
LC: Ag 16, '07.

Lull, Thelma Lucile. The Chinese lily. In *The best college short stories, 1924-1925 (1925)*, **B-558.**

Lummis, Charles Fletcher, 1859-1928. The blue-corn witch. In *The Miller's holiday (1920)*, **M-817.**

____ The enchanted mesa. In *West winds (1914)*, **W-368.**

L-553   ____ My friend Will: including "The little boy that was" / by Charles F. Lummis . . . Chicago: A. C. McClurg & Co., 1911. 59 p., front., [6] leaves of plates.   **RCE**

____ The swearing enchiladas. In *The Miller's holiday (1920)*, **M-817.**

L-554   Lundberg, Holger. The midnight sun: a story of Russian court life, based on the motion-picture story adapted by Holger Lundberg, with illustrations produced and filmed by Universal Pictures Corporation . . . New York: Jacobsen-Hodgkinson Corporation, [1925]. 135 p., plates.
Unexamined copy: bibliographic data from NUC.

Lundsford, Hugh, pseud. See **Buck, Charles Neville, b. 1879.**

L-555 Lundy, J. H. (John Henary). Little Walter: a child from home guided by the unseen hand / J. H. Lundy. [Monterey, Calif.: Peninsula Herald Printing Co.], 1922. 357 p.

L-556 Lunt, Carroll Prescott, b. 1889. His Chinese idol / Carroll Prescott Lunt. London; New York: Lane, 1921. 227 p.
Unexamined copy: bibliographic data from NUC.

L-557 Lush, Charles K. (Charles Keeler). The autocrats: a novel / by Charles K. Lush . . . New York: Doubleday, Page & Company, 1901. 344 p.
PW: Je 1, '01.
BLC: London: Methuen & Co., 1902.

L-558 Lusk, Alice Freeman. A woman's answer to Roosevelt: a story on race suicide / Alice Freeman Lusk. [Los Angeles, Cal.: Commercial Printing House, 1908.] 108, [1] p.   **CUR**

L-559 Lusk, Fuzzy. Will it work? / by Fuzzy Lusk. [Moline, Ill.: Moline Press, c1924.] 26 p.   **STF**

L-560 Lutes, Della Thompson, d. 1942. Just away: a story of hope / by Della Thompson Lutes. Cooperstown, N. Y.: Published by Crist, Scott & Parshall, 1906. 76, [1] p.
LC: N 14, '06.
PW: D 22, '06.

L-561 _____ My boy in khaki: a mother's story / by Della Thompson Lutes. New York; London: Harper & Brothers, 1918. 193, [1] p., front. [Ill. by Stockton Mulford.]
LC: My 27, '18.
PW: Je 8, '18.

L-562 Luther, Mark Lee, b. 1872. The boosters / by Mark Lee Luther; frontispiece by Gerald Leake. Indianapolis: The Bobbs-Merrill Company, [c1924]. 352 p., front.
LC: Ja 24, '24.

L-563 _____ The crucible / by Mark Lee Luther . . . ; with illustrations by Rose Cecil O'Neill. New York: The Macmillan Company, 1907. 341 p., front., [5] leaves of plates.
LC: O 17, '07.

L-564 _____ The henchman / by Mark Lee Luther. New York: The Macmillan Company; London: Macmillan & Co., Ltd., 1902. 376 p.
PW: O 25, '02.

L-565 _____ The hope chest / by Mark Lee Luther; with frontispiece by James Montgomery Flagg. Boston: Little, Brown, and Company, 1918. 334 p., front.
LC: F 25, '18.
PW: F 23, '18.

L-566 _____ The mastery / by Mark Lee Luther. New York: The Macmillan Company; London: Macmillan & Co., Ltd., 1904. 402 p.
PW: O 1, '04.

L-567 _____ Presenting Jane McRae / by Mark Lee Luther; with illustrations by James Montgomery Flagg. Boston: Little, Brown, and Company, 1920. 333 p., front., [2] leaves of plates.
LC: Je 23, '20.
PW: Je 26, '20.

L-568 _____ The sovereign power / by Mark Lee Luther; with illustrations by Chase Emerson. New York: The Macmillan Company, 1911. 324 p., col. front., [8] leaves of plates.
LC: My 18, '11.

L-569 _____ The woman of it / by Mark Lee Luther. New York; London: Harper & Brothers, 1912. 343, [1] p.
LC: S 14, '12.

L-570 Lutton, Elizabeth Miller. The Cracker Box School / by Elizabeth Miller Lutton; illustrated by Herbert Morton Stoops. Chicago: The Reilly & Britton Co., [c1917]. 252 p., front., [3] leaves of plates.
PW: Ap 7, '17.

Lutz, Grace Livingston Hill. See **Hill, Grace Livingston, 1865-1947.**

L-571 Lydston, G. Frank (George Frank), 1858-1923. Poker Jim, gentleman: and other tales and sketches / by G. Frank Lydston. Chicago: Monarch Book Company, [c1906]. 396 p., front., [7] leaves of plates. [Ill. by August Abelmann.]
Contents: Poker Jim, gentleman -- Tommy the outcast -- Johnny -- My friend the undertaker -- A grim memento -- A wise child -- Leaves from a suicide's diary -- Chicquita -- A dead ideal -- A matter of professional secrecy -- A legend of the Yosemite -- A great city's shame.
PW: My 18, '07.

L-572 _____ Trusty five-fifteen / by G. Frank Lydston . . . Kansas City, Missouri: Burton Publishing Company, 1921. 564 p.
LC: Ja 3, '22.

L-573 Lyle, Eugene P. (Eugene Percy), b. 1873. Blaze Derringer / by Eugene P. Lyle, Jr.; illustrations by Morgan W. Eckley. New York: Doubleday, Page & Company, 1910. 314 p., col. front., [3] leaves of col. plates.
LC: Je 17, '10.
PW: Je 25, '10.
BLC: London: Hodder & Stoughton; New York printed, 1910.

L-574 _____ The Lone Star / by Eugene P. Lyle, Jr. . . . ; illustrated in colour by Philip R. Goodwin. New York: Doubleday, Page & Company, 1907. 431 p., col. front., [3] leaves of col. plates.
LC: Ag 2, '07.
PW: Ag 24, '07.
BLC: London: Doubleday, Page & Co.; New York printed, 1907.

L-575 _____ The Missourian / by Eugene P. Lyle, Jr.; illustrated by Ernest Haskell. New York: Doubleday, Page & Company, 1905. 519 p., col. front., [7] leaves of col. plates.

PW: Ag 5, '05.
BLC: London: Doubleday, Page & Co.; New York printed, 1905.

L-576   ____ The transformation of Krag / by Eugene P. Lyle, Jr. . . . ; illustrated by C. B. Falls. Garden City, New York: Doubleday, Page & Company, 1911. 321 p., col. front.
LC: O 21, '11.
PW: N 11, '11.

L-577   Lyman, Edward Branch, b. 1876. Me'ow Jones, Belgian refugee cat: his own true tale as written down by Edward Branch Lyman; illustrated by Julia Daniels. New York: George H. Doran Company, [c1917]. 91 p., col. front., plates (part col.), ill. Illustrated lining papers.
Unexamined copy: bibliographic data from NUC.
LC: N 2, '17.

L-578   Lyman, Olin L. (Olin Linus), b. 1873. The lash / Olin L. Lyman. Boston: Richard G. Badger, 1909. ([Boston]: The Gorham Press). 241 p.
LC: N 27, '09.

L-579   ____ Micky / by Olin L. Lyman. Boston: Richard G. Badger, 1905. (Boston: The Gorham Press). 241 p.

L-580   ____ The trail of the Grand Seigneur / by Olin L. Lyman; with colored illustrations from paintings by J. Steeple Davis and Clare Angell. New York: New Amsterdam Book Company, 1903. 432 p., col. front., [6] leaves of col. plates.
PW: Ap 4, '03.

L-581   Lynch, Gertrude. The fighting chance: the romance of an ingénue / by Gertrude Lynch; illustrated by Bayard Jones. New York; London: The Smart Set Publishing Co., c1903. 219 p., incl. front., [3] leaves of plates.
PW: S 5, '03.

Lynch, Jerome Morley, Mrs., 1864-1943. See **St. Felix, Marie, pseud.**

L-582   Lynch, Lawrence L., *pseud.* A blind lead: daring and thrilling adventures, clever detective work / by Lawrence L. Lynch [pseud.] (E. M. Van Deventer) . . . ; illustrated. Chicago: Laird & Lee, [c1912]. 324 p., front., [6] leaves of plates.
LC: Mr 1, '12.
PW: Mr 16, '12.

L-583   ____ The Doverfields' diamonds: the great gem mystery / by E. M. Van Deventer "Lawrence Lynch" . . . ; graphically illustrated by special artist. Chicago: Laird & Lee, [1906]. 359 p., front., [7] leaves of plates. [Ill. by Farkas.]
PW: Mr 10, '06.

L-584   ____ The woman who dared: a thrilling narrative / by Lawrence L. Lynch [pseud.] (E. Murdoch Vandeventer) . . . ; illustrated. Chicago: Laird & Lee, Publishers, [c1902]. 471 p., front., [8] leaves of plates. [Ill. by John C. Gilbert.]

PW: F 22, '02.
BLC: London: Ward, Lock & Co., [1902].

Lynch, Millard, jt. aut. *The crimson cross* (1913).
See **Walk, Charles Edmonds, b. 1875, jt. aut., W-37.**

L-585   Lynde, Francis, 1856-1930. After the manner of men / by Francis Lynde; illustrated by Arthur E. Becher. New York: Charles Scribner's Sons, 1916. 454 p., front., [3] leaves of plates.
LC: S 14, '16.

L-586   ____ Branded / by Francis Lynde; with frontispiece by Arthur E. Becher. New York: Charles Scribner's Sons, 1918. 370 p., col. front.
LC: Ap 18, '18.

L-587   ____ The city of numbered days / by Francis Lynde; illustrated by Arthur E. Becher. New York: Charles Scribner's Sons, 1914. 347 p., front., [3] leaves of plates.
LC: S 1, '14.

L-588   ____ David Vallory / by Francis Lynde; with a frontispiece by Arthur E. Becher. New York: Charles Scribner's Sons, 1919. 402 p., col. front.
LC: Ag 26, '19.
PW: Ag 23, '19.

L-589   ____ The Donovan chance / by Francis Lynde; illustrated by Thomas Fogarty. New York: Charles Scribner's Sons, 1921. 215 p., front., [7] leaves of plates.   **CRL**
LC: Ag 30, '21.

L-590   ____ Empire builders / by Francis Lynde . . . ; with illustrations by Jay Hambidge. Indianapolis: The Bobbs-Merrill Company, [c1907]. 377 p., front., [5] leaves of plates.
LC: Ag 12, '07.

L-591   ____ The fight on the standing stone / by Francis Lynde. New York: Charles Scribner's Sons, 1925. 248 p.
LC: Mr 27, '25.
PW: Mr 21, '25.
BLC: London: T. Nelson & Sons, [1927].

L-592   ____ The fire bringers / by Francis Lynde. New York: Charles Scribner's Sons, 1921. 284 p., front. [Ill. by Walter J. Enright.]
LC: Ag 27, '21.
PW: Ap 23, '21.

L-593   ____ A fool for love / by Francis Lynde . . . ; illustrated by George Brehm. Indianapolis: The Bobbs-Merrill Company, [c1905]. 204 p., front. (The pocket books).
PW: Ag 26, '05.

L-594   ____ The girl, a horse and a dog / by Francis Lynde; with frontispiece by Arthur E. Becher. New York: Charles Scribner's Sons, 1920. 381 p., col. front.
LC: Ag 25, '20.
PW: Ag 28, '20.

L-595 _____ The grafters / by Francis Lynde; illustrated by Arthur I. Keller. Indianapolis: The Bobbs-Merrill Company, [c1904]. 408 p., front., [5] leaves of plates.
PW: Ap 16, '04.

L-596 _____ The Honorable Senator Sage-brush / by Francis Lynde. New York: Charles Scribner's Sons, 1913. 411 p., front. [Ill. by Arthur E. Becher.]
LC: S 16, '13.
PW: O 11, '13.

L-597 _____ The king of Arcadia / by Francis Lynde. New York: Charles Scribner's Sons, 1909. 354 p., front., [3] leaves of plates. [Ill. by F. B. Masters.]
LC: F 27, '09.
PW: Mr 6, '09.

L-598 _____ The master of Appleby: a novel concerning itself in part with the great struggle in the two Carolinas; but chiefly with the adventures therein of two gentlemen who loved one and the same lady / by Francis Lynde; illustrations by T. de Thulstrup. Indianapolis: The Bowen-Merrill Company, [c1902]. 581 p., front., [5] leaves of plates.
PW: D 6, '02.
BLC: London: B. F. Stevens & Brown, [1902].

L-599 _____ Mellowing money / by Francis Lynde. New York: Charles Scribner's Sons, 1925. 293 p.
LC: Ag 8, '25.
PW: Ag 15, '25.

L-600 _____ Mr. Arnold: a romance of the revolution / by Francis Lynde; frontispiece by John Wolcott Adams. Indianapolis: The Bobbs-Merrill Company, [c1923]. 336 p., front.
LC: O 3, '23.
PW: O 13, '23.
BLC: London: Methuen & Co.; printed in U. S. A., 1924.

_____ The Pied Piper of One-Track Gulch. In **Conrad, Joseph. *Il conte* (1925), C-697.**

L-601 _____ Pirates' hope / by Francis Lynde. New York: Charles Scribner's Sons, 1922. 299 p.
LC: My 3, '22.
PW: My 6, '22.

L-602 _____ The price / by Francis Lynde. New York: Charles Scribner's Sons, 1911. 458 p.
LC: Je 3, '11.
PW: Je 10, '11.

L-603 _____ The quickening / by Francis Lynde; with illustrations by E. M. Ashe. Indianapolis: The Bobbs-Merrill Company, [1906]. 407 p., front., [4] leaves of plates.
PW: Mr 3, '06.

L-604 _____ The real man / by Francis Lynde; illustrated by Arthur E. Becher. New York: Charles Scribner's Sons, 1915. 450 p., front., [4] leaves of plates, map.
LC: Ag 31, '15.
PW: S 4, '15.

L-605 _____ Scientific Sprague / by Francis Lynde; illustrated by E. Roscoe Shrader. New York: Charles Scribner's Sons, 1912. 406 p., front., [3] leaves of plates.
LC: O 15, '12.

L-606 _____ Stranded in Arcady / by Francis Lynde; illustrated by Arthur E. Becher. New York: Charles Scribner's Sons, 1917. 257 p., front., [5] leaves of plates.
LC: My 31, 17.

L-607 _____ The taming of Red Butte western / by Francis Lynde; illustrated. New York: Charles Scribner's Sons, 1910. 410 p., front., [3] leaves of plates. [Ill. by Maynard Dixon.]
LC: Ap 13, '10.
PW: Ap 16, '10.

L-608 _____ The wreckers / by Francis Lynde; with a frontispiece by Arthur E. Becher. New York: Charles Scribner's Sons, 1920. 377 p., col. front.
LC: Mr 25, '20.
PW: Mr 20, '20.

L-609 Lyne, Moncure. From the Alamo to San Jacinto, or, The grito: a novel / by Moncure Lyne. New York: R. F. Fenno & Company, [c1904]. 320 p., front., [1] leaf of plates. [Ill. by F. B. Madan.]
Half-title page: *The grito, or from the Alamo to San Jacinto.*
PW: My 13, '05.
Another edition: The grito; or from the Alamo to San Jacinto. New York; Washington: The Neale Publishing Company, 1904.
Unexamined copy: bibliographic data from NUC.

L-610 Lyne, Moncure. The lone star: or, The grito: a novel dealing with the tyranny of Santa Anna: the triumph of Texas / by Moncure Lyne. [Richmond?, Va.], 1907. 320 p., incl. front.
Unexamined copy: bibliographic data from NUC.
LC: Jl 10, '07.

Lyng, Edward J. The mysterious apparitions. In *The Tragedy that wins and other short stories* (1905), **T-343.**

_____ The unlucky toreador. In *The Tragedy that wins and other short stories* (1905), **T-343.**

L-611 Lynn, Clara A. Tid bits: humorous stories of home people / by Clara A. Lynn. [Concord, N. H.: The Rumford Press, c1925.] 146 p.   **DLC**
LC: S 29, '25.

L-612 Lynn, Margaret. Free soil / by Margaret Lynn. New York: The Macmillan Company, 1920. 377 p.
PW: D 18, '20.

_____ The legacy of Richard Hughes. In *Atlantic narratives*; first series (1918), **A-360.**

L-613 Lyon, Doré, Mrs. Prudence Pratt / by Mrs. Doré Lyon; illustrated with eight original drawings by Malcolm A. Strauss. New York: Geo. V. Blackburne Co., 1903. 293 p., front., [7] leaves of plates.
PW: Je 27, '03.

L-614 Lyon, Harris Merton, 1883-1916. Graphics / by Harris Merton Lyon . . . St. Louis: William Marion Reedy, 1913. 319 p.

_____ John Jones comes to life. In **Conrad, Joseph.** *Il conte* **(1925), C-697.**

L-615 _____ Sardonics: sixteen sketches / by Harris Merton Lyon. New York: Metropolitan Syndicate, Inc., [c1908]. 225 p.
Contents: The father -- The singer's heart -- The comic relief -- In the black-and-tan -- The dog -- An incident in poison row -- The second motive -- Out of work -- The empty scope -- The girl who wouldn't marry -- Will's wife -- The right man -- For the good of the neighborhood -- The monarch -- Doctor miracle -- Into the fourth dimension.
LC: My 6, '09.
Another issue: New York: The Stuyvesant Press, 1909.

_____ The weaver who clad the summer. In *The best short stories of 1915 and the yearbook of the American short story* **(1916), B-560.**

L-616 Lyon, Lucile Grinnan. "The Greenwoods" / by Lucile Grinnan Lyon. New York: The Neale Publishing Company, 1915. 390 p.   **TWC**
PW: Ag 21, '15.

L-617 Lyons, Albert E. (Albert Edwin), b. 1866. Mister Bill: "a man" / by Albert E. Lyons. Boston: Richard G. Badger, 1905. (Boston: The Gorham Press). 319 p., front. [Ill. by E. Gordon.]
BLC: London: T. Fisher Unwin; Boston: Richard G. Badger; U. S. A. printed, 1906.

Lyons, Margaret Redic. See **Redic, Margaret.**

Lytle, Hal McLeod. Ella Gingles on trial. See **Lytle, H. M.** *Tragedies of the white slaves* **(1910), L-618.**

L-618 _____ Tragedies of the white slaves: true stories of the white slavery taken from actual life. Each one dealing with a different method by which white slaves have become innocent victims to destruction / by H. M. Lytle . . . [Chicago]: The Charles C. Thompson Co., [c1910]. 193 p.
Contents: The tragedy of the maternity homes -- The tragedy of the want ad -- The tragedy of the assignation house -- The tragedy of the immigrant girl -- The tragedy of the stage -- The tragedy of the five thousand -- The tragedy of the little lacemaker (Ella Gingles' own story) -- The first night -- Arrested -- The second orgy -- Ella Gingles on trial (by Hal McMeod Lytle) -- The return home.

L-619 Lytton, Legare Rogers, 1867?-1924. The last message / by L. Rogers Lytton. [New York, n. d.].
Unexamined copy: Bibliographic data from NUC.

M

M. E. S. See **Octave.**

M. F. See **Fisher, Mary, b. 1858.**

M. M. H., ed. See *Gone West* **(1922), G-289.**

M-1 Mabel, b. 1862, *pseud.* A soul's love letter / by Mabel [pseud.]. Westwood, Mass.: Published by the Ariel Press, 1904. 160 p.

M-2 Mabie, Hamilton Wright, 1846-1916. A child of nature / by Hamilton Wright Mabie; with illustrations and decorations by Charles Louis Hinton. -- 1st ed. -- New York: Dodd, Mead and Company, 1901. 127 p., front., [3] leaves of plates.
PW: N 2, '01.

M-3 Mabie, Louise Kennedy. The lights are bright: "Four bells and the lights are bright" <night call of lookout on the ore-boats of the Great Lakes>: a novel / by Louise Kennedy Mabie . . . New York; London: Harper & Brothers Publishers, 1914. 288, [1] p., front. [Ill. by Armand Both.]
LC: Jl 11, '14.
PW: Jl 18, '14.

M-4 _____ The wings of pride / by Louise Kennedy Mabie. New York; London: Harper & Brothers, 1913. 323, [1] p., front. [Ill. by Armand Both.]
LC: Mr 14, '13.
PW: Mr 22, '13.

M-5 Mabry, W. Dudley (William Dudley), b. 1848. When love is king: a story of American life / by W. Dudley Mabry. New York: R. F. Fenno & Company, 1902. 431 p.
PW: Ap 26, '02.

McAleese, Susan Elizabeth. See **Murray, Alice E., pseud.**

M-6 McAlilly, Alice. Hilda Lane's adoptions / by Alice McAlilly. Cincinnati: Jennings and Graham, 1905. 372 p.
Unexamined copy: bibliographic data from OCLC, #26978218.

M-7 _____ Hercules Carlson / by Alice McAlilly . . . Cincinnati: Jennings and Pye; New York: Eaton and Mains, [c1903]. 438 p.
PW: D 12, '03.

M-8 _____ The Larkins wedding / by Alice McAlilly; illustrated. New York: Moffat, Yard and Company, 1905. 192 p., front., [3] leaves of plates, ill. [Ill. by J. M. H. Williams.]   **DLC**
PW: O 7, '05.

M-9 _____ Terra Cotta: a study of life in the clay / by Alice McAlilly. Cincinnati: Jennings and Pye; New York: Eaton and Mains, [c1903]. 281 p.
PW: F 14, '03.

M-10 McAlister, Frank A., *jt. pseud.* The last mile / by Frank A. McAlister [jt. pseud.]. Garden City, New York: Doubleday, Page & Company, 1922. 355 p.   **IQU**
LC: O 13, '22.
PW: S 30, '22.

M-11 McAndrew, William, 1863-1937. Looking for trouble: a school story / by William McAndrew . . . Syracuse, N. Y.: C. W. Bardeen, c1907. 58 p.   **EYM**
(School bulletin publications.)

McAstocker, David Plante, b. 1884. See **Dorley, David, pseud.**

McAulay, Allan, b. 1863, jt. aut. *The affair at the inn* (1904). See **Wiggin, Kate Douglas Smith, 1856-1923, jt. aut., W-595.**

____ *Robinetta* (1911). See **Wiggin, Kate Douglas Smith, 1856-1923, jt. aut., W-603.**

Macaulay, Fannie Caldwell, 1863-1941. See **Little, Frances, pseud.**

Macauley, Charles Raymond, 1871-1934, jt. aut. *Emblemland* (1902). See **Bangs, John Kendrick, 1862-1922, jt. aut., B-142.**

M-12   ____ The Red tavern / by C. R. Macauley. New York; London: D. Appleton and Company, 1914. 413, [1] p., col. front.
LC: Mr 21, '14.

M-13   Macauley, Ward, 1879-1938. Two old cronies / by Ward Macauley . . . New York: Duffield & Company, 1914. 99 p.   **KLG**
LC: O 24, '14.

M-14   McBlair, Robert. Mister Fish Kelly: a novel / by Robert McBlair. New York: D. Appleton and Company, 1924. 347, [1] p., front.
LC: Ap 23, '24.
PW: My 3, '24.

M-15   MacBrayne, Lewis Edward, b. 1872. The men we marry / by Lewis MacBrayne; with illustrations by R. I. Conklin. Boston, Massachusetts: The C. M. Clark Publishing Co., [c1910]. 424 p., col. front., [5] leaves of plates.
LC: F 11, '11.

M-16   McBride, James L. (James Lloyd), 1882-1954. The innkeeper of Bethlehem / by James L. McBride. Philadelphia: The Westminster Press, 1913. 47 p.
                                                  DLC
PW: N 29, '13.

M-17   McCahan, Belle Travers. The preshus child / by Belle Travers McCahan. New York: Cochrane Publishing Co., 1909, [c1908]. 307 p.   **NYP**
LC: F 10, '09.

M-18   McCain, George Nox, b. 1856. The crimson dice / by George Nox McCain. Philadelphia: J. Murray Jordan, [c1903]. 310 p., front., [3] leaves of plates. [Ill. by Clarence Rowe.]
BLC: London: Ibister & Co., 1903.

M-19   McCaleb, Ida Harwood. Triumphs and failures / by Ida Harwood McCaleb. New York: Broadway Publishing Company, [c1905]. 293 p.
Unexamined copy: bibliographic data from NUC.

M-20   McCall, Sidney, *pseud.* Ariadne of Allan Water / by Sidney McCall [pseud.]; with frontispiece by C. H. Taffs. Boston: Little, Brown, and Company, 1914. 414 p., front.

LC: Ap 8, '14.
PW: Ap 4, '14.
BLC: London: Andrew Melrose, [1915].

M-21   ____ The breath of the gods / by Sidney McCall [pseud.]. Boston: Little, Brown, and Company, 1905. 431 p., [1] leaf of plates (plan).
PW: My 20, '05.
BLC: London: Hutchinson & Co., 1905.

M-22   ____ Christopher Laird / by Sidney McCall [pseud.]. New York: Dodd, Mead and Company, 1919. 338 p.
LC: S 30, '19.
PW: N 1, '19.

M-23   [____] The dragon painter / by Mary McNeil Fenollosa; illustrated by Gertrude McDaniel. Boston: Little, Brown, and Company, 1906. 261, [1] p., front., [5] leaves of plates.
LC: O 15, '06.
PW: O 27, '06.
BLC: London: Stanley Paul & Co.; Cambridge, U. S. A. [printed, 1910].

M-24   ____ Red horse hill / by Sidney McCall [pseud.]. Boston: Little, Brown, and Company, 1909. 361 p.
LC: Ap 28, '09.
PW: My 22, '09.

M-25   ____ The stirrup latch / by Sidney McCall [pseud.]; with frontispiece by William Van Dresser. Boston: Little, Brown and Company, 1915. 315 p., front.
LC: O 28, '15.

M-26   ____ The strange woman / by Sidney McCall [pseud.] . . . ; adapted from William J. Hurlbut's play of the same name. New York: Dodd, Mead and Company, 1914. 381 p., col. front. [Ill. by Edna L. Crompton.]
LC: N 20, '14.
PW: N 28, '14.

M-27   ____ Sunshine beggars / by Sidney McCall [pseud.]; with illustrations by William Van Dresser. Boston: Little, Brown, and Company, 1918. 302 p., front., [3] leaves of plates.
LC: F 26, '18.

M-28   ____ Truth Dexter / by Sidney McCall [pseud.]. Boston: Little, Brown and Company, 1901. 375 p.
PW: Mr 23, '01.
BLC: London: C. Arthur Pearson, [1902].

M-29   McCanne, Virginia (Yates). The MacGregors / by Marshall Home. Chicago: Scroll Publishing Company, 1901. 285 p., front.   **RCE**

M-30   McCants, Elliott Crayton, 1865-1953. In the red hills: a story of the Carolina country / by Elliott Crayton McCants. New York: Doubleday, Page & Company, 1904. 340 p., front., [2] leaves of plates.
PW: Ap 16, '04.

M-31   ____ One of the grayjackets: and other stories / by E. C. McCants. Columbia, S. C.: The State

Company, 1908. 160 p., front., [3] leaves of plates. [Ill. by Brantley Smith.] Reprinted from various periodicals.

Contents: One of the grayjackets -- The strategists -- Sons of the soil -- Vulp of the Carolina reds -- The recalling of George -- Almost home -- Visits to a fisherman.
LC: Jl 8, '09.
PW: O 2, '09.

M-32   McCardell, Roy L. (Roy Larcom), b. 1870. Conversations of a chorus girl / by Roy L. McCardell; illustrated by Gene Carr. New York; London: Street & Smith, [c1903]. 184 p., ill.
PW: Ag 15, '03.

M-33   ____ The diamond from the sky: a romantic novel / by Roy L. McCardell; sixteen illustrations by special permission of the North American Film Corporation. New York: G. W. Dillingham Co., [c1916]. 440 p., photo. front., [15] leaves of photo. plates.
LC: Ap 8, '16.

____ I'm cured. In *The so-so stories* (1914), S-715.

M-34   ____ Jimmy Jones: the autobiography of an office boy / by Roy L. McCardell . . . Boston: Dana Estes & Company, [c1907]. 310 p., front., ill.
LC: Jl 26, '07.
PW: Ag 10, '07.

M-35   ____ The show girl and her friends / by Roy L. McCardell . . . ; illustrated by Gene Carr. New York; London: Street & Smith, [c1904]. 200 p., incl. front., ill.

Contents: At the horse show -- Politics and society -- A typical Broadway first night -- Lonesome for home -- Beckoned from Brooklyn -- A New Year's Eve reception -- Amy back in town -- A pleasant party -- Old home week -- Dopey McKnight has presentiments -- How Harry Trimmers got stung -- The downfall of Dopey McKnight -- Why Dopey McKnight is still in jail for alimony -- Isn't it awful to be in jail in springtime -- The hero of Broadway.
PW: Ag 20, '04.

McCarron, Arthur E. The lawyer's story. In *The Tragedy that wins and other short stories* (1905), **T-343.**

____ A sad ending. In *The Tragedy that wins and other short stories* (1905), **T-343.**

____ A war-time tragedy. In *The Tragedy that wins and other short stories* (1905), **T-343.**

M-36   McCarter, Margaret Hill, 1860-1938. The candle in the window / by Margaret Hill McCarter . . . Chicago: A. C. McClurg & Co., 1925. 71 p., ill. [Ill. by James Allen St. John.]   **OSU, KFH**
PW: O 31, '25.

M-37   ____ The corner stone / by Margaret Hill McCarter . . . ; illustrated by J. Allen St. John. Chicago: A. C. McClurg & Co., 1915. 100 p., col. front.
LC: S 27, '15.
PW: O 9, '15.
BLC: London: C. F. Cazenove; Chicago: A. C. McClurg & Co. [printed], 1915.

M-38   ____ The cottonwood's story / by Margaret Hill

McCarter; illustrations by Lydia Wehe Crabill. Topeka, Kansas: Crane & Company, c1903. 100 p., ill.
PW: Mr 12, '04.

M-39   ____ Cuddy: and other stories / Margaret Hill McCarter. -- 4th ed. -- Topeka, Kansas: Crane & Company, 1908. 95 p., [3] leaves of plates. [Ill. by Carl Pierce Bolmar.]   **MNU**
[No earlier printing located. NUL and OCLC note 4th edition and none earlier.]

Contents: Cuddy -- Christmas Eve in the day coach -- Little Red Head.
LC: D 19, '08.
PW: Mr 13, '09.

M-40   ____ Cuddy's baby / by Margaret Hill McCarter . . . ; illustrated by J. Allen St. John. Chicago: A. C. McClurg & Co., 1917. 78 p., col. front., ill. Illustrated end papers.
LC: S 10, '17.
PW: S 29, '17.

M-41   ____ Homeland: a present-day love story / by Margaret Hill McCarter. New York; London: Harper & Brothers, [c1922]. 433 p.
LC: My 8, '22.
PW: My 13, '22.

M-42   ____ In old Quivira / Margaret Hill McCarter. Topeka, Kan.: Crane & Company, 1908. 139 p., front., ill. [Ill. by Carl Pierce Bolmar.]
LC: N 27, '08.

M-43   ____ A master's degree / by Margaret Hill McCarter; illustrations in color by W. D. Goldbeck. Chicago: A. C. McClurg & Co., 1913. 297 p., col. front., [1] leaf of col. plates.
LC: S 19, '13.
PW: O 11, '13.
BLC: London: C. F. Cazenove; Chicago [printed], 1913.

M-44   ____ Paying mother: the tribute beautiful / by Margaret Hill McCarter . . . ; illustrations and decorations by J. C. Gruelle. New York; London: Harper & Brothers, [1920]. 72 p., col. front., [2] leaves of plates. Illustrated end papers.
LC: S 27, '20.
PW: O 2, '20.

M-45   ____ The peace of the Solomon valley / Margaret Hill McCarter . . . Chicago: A. C. McClurg & Co., 1911. 91 p., col. front. [Ill. by Clara Powers Wilson.] Illustrated end papers.
LC: S 25, '11.

M-46   ____ The price of the prairie: a story of Kansas / by Margaret Hill McCarter; with five illustrations in color by J. N. Marchand. Chicago: A. C. McClurg & Co., 1910. 489 p., col. front., [4] leaves of col. plates.
LC: O 10, '10.
PW: O 29, '10.

M-47   ____ The reclaimers / by Margaret Hill McCarter. New York; London: Harper & Brothers, [1918].

362, [1] p., col. front. [Ill. by G. W. Gage.]
LC: N 2, '18.
PW: N 23, '18.

M-48   _____ Vanguards of the plains: a romance of the old Santa Fé trail / by Margaret Hill McCarter. New York; London: Harper & Brothers, [1917]. 397, [1] p., col. front. [Ill. by Frank Tenney Johnson.]
LC: N 5, '17.
PW: N 24, '17.

M-49   _____ A wall of men / by Margaret Hill McCarter . . . ; with illustrations in color by J. N. Marchand. Chicago: A. C. McClurg & Co., 1912. 494 p., col. front., [3] leaves of col. plates.
LC: O 23, '12.
PW: O 26, '12.

M-50   _____ Widening waters / by Margaret Hill McCarter . . . New York; London: Harper & Brothers, 1924. 400, [1] p.   **MNU**
LC: O 16, '24.
PW: O 25, '24.

M-51   _____ Winning the wilderness / by Margaret Hill McCarter; illustrations by J. N. Marchand. Chicago: A. C. McClurg & Co., 1914. 404 p., col. front., [3] leaves of plates.
LC: S 21, '14.
PW: O 10, '14.

M-52   Maccarthaigh, Inghin. My little kingdom / by Inghin Maccarthaigh. [New York]: Published by the author, [c1918]. 87 p. Printed on one side of leaf, on opposite pages.   **DLC**

M-53   McCarthy, Myles. The advance agent: first experience ahead of a show told in a musing anecdote and yarn / by Myles McCarthy; illustrated by J. H. Appleton. New York: Excelsior Publishing House, McKeon & Schofield, Proprietors, [c1908]. 92 p., front. (port.), ill.

M-54   McCarty, Ida Helen. Miriam'ne of the cedars / by Ida Helen McCarty. New York: The Shakespeare Press, c1911. 115 p., ill. (maps).   **DLC**

M-55   McCauley, Clarice Vallette. The garden of dreams / by Clarice Vallette McCauley. Chicago: A. C. McClurg & Co., 1912. 158 p.

M-56   McCausland, S. A. A. (Susan Austin Arnold). Shadowgraphs / by S. A. A. McCausland . . . New York: Authors & Publishers Corporation, [c1924]. 165 p.   **DLC**
Contents: As told by the Persian -- Invisible wings -- A flashlight of memory -- Aidu -- Evanice -- Did Lucifer laugh? -- A beautiful necessity -- The spinning of Lachesis.
LC: N 28, '24.

M-57   McClave, S. Wood (Stephen Wood). Fred Winsted: a college man / by S. Wood McClave. Boston: The Roxbury Publishing Company, [c1919]. 365 p.   **DLC**

LC: Je 23, '19.

M-58   McClellan, George Marion, 1860-1934. Old Greenbottom Inn: and other stories / by George Marion McClellan. [Louisville, Ky.?: s. n., 1906?] 210 p., front.   **KUK**
Contents: Old Greenbottom Inn -- For Annison's sake -- A creole from Louisiana -- Essie Dortch -- The death of Hanover.

M-59   _____ The path of dreams / by George Marion McClellan. Nashville, Tenn.: A. M. E. Sunday School Union, [c1916]. 206 p.
Contents: [Poetry] -- Gabe Yowl -- Old Greenbottom Inn -- For Annison's sake -- A Creole from Louisiana -- Essie Dortch.

M-60   McClelland, Marion. Kaleema / by Marion McClelland. New York: The Century Co., 1921. 292 p., front. [Ill. by G. W. Gage.]
LC: Ja 24, '21.
PW: Ja 8, '21.

McClumpha, Charles Flint, b. 1863, jt. ed. <u>See</u> *Minnesota stories* (1903), M-842.

McClure, Harvey Ross, b. 1886. <u>See</u> **Rosso, Harley, pseud.**

M-61   McClure, Marjorie Barkley, 1882-1967. A bush that burned / by Marjorie Barkley McClure. New York: Minton Balch & Company, 1925. 361 p.
LC: O 3, '25.
PW: S 26, '25.

M-62   _____ High fires / by Marjorie Barkley McClure. Boston: Little, Brown and Company, 1924. 358 p.
LC: Mr 21, '24.
BLC: London: Hodder & Stoughton, [1924].

M-63   McClure, Robert E. The dominant blood / by Robert E. McClure. Garden City, New York: Doubleday, Page & Company, 1924. 389 p.
PW: N 1, '24
BLC: London: William Heinemann; printed in U. S. A., 1924.

M-64   McClure, W. T. (Walter Tennant), 1856-1932. A betrayed trust: a story of our own times and country: a romance of the Middle West / by W. T. McClure. Nashville, Tenn.; Dallas, Tex.: Publishing House of the M. E. Church, South: Smith & Lamar, Agents, 1903. 214 p.

M-65   McCoid, Moses Ayers, 1840-1904. John Williamson of Hardscrabble / by M. A. McCoid; drawings by H. Shriner. Chicago: M. A. Donohue & Company, [c1902]. 341 p., photo. front. (port.), [9] leaves of plates.   **RCE**
PW: Ap 25, '03.

M-66   McConaughy, J. W. The boss / by J. W. McConaughy . . . & Edward Sheldon . . . New York: The H. K. Fly Company, [c1911]. 316 p., front., [3] leaves of plates.
LC: Ja 23, '12.
PW: F 17, '12.

M-67 _____ Madame X: a story of mother-love / by J. W. McConaughy; from the play of the same name by Alexandre Bisson; photogravure illustrations by Edward C. Volkert. New York: The H. K. Fly Company, [c1910]. 311 p., front., [4] leaves of plates.
LC: D 19, '10.
PW: Ja 22, '21.

M-68 _____ The typhoon: a story of new Japan / by J. W. McConaughy . . . ; from the Hungarian of Menyhert Lengyel. New York: The H. K. Fly Company, [c1912]. 306 p., col. front., [2] leaves of col. plates. [Ill. by Katsuji Makino.]
LC: Mr 6, '13.

McConn, Mac. A mutual scoop. In *Minnesota stories* (1903), **M-842.**

M-69 McConn, Max. Mollie's substitute husband / by Max McConn; with frontispiece by Edward C. Caswell. New York: Dodd, Mead and Company, 1920. 370 p., front.
LC: Ag 24, '20.
PW: Ag 21, '20.

M-70 McConnell, Charles Allen, 1860-1955. Caleb of the hill country / by Charles Allen McConnell. Kansas City, Missouri: Publishing House of the Pentecostal Church of the Nazarene, 1914. 163 p., front., [9] leaves of plates. [Ill. by C. W. Rosser.] **DLC**
LC: Ja 4, '15.

M-71 _____ Happy Day / by Charles Allen McConnell . . . Kansas City, Mo.: Nazarene Publishing House, [c1921]. 170 p. **OSU, OKA**

M-72 McConnell, Franz Marshall, b. 1862. The deacon's daughter / by F. M. McConnell. Nashville, Tenn.: Sunday School Board, Southern Baptist Convention, [c1918]. 128 p. **TNE**
LC reports: Oklahoma City, Okla.: Stealey Book and Publishing Company, [1918]. 144 p.

M-73 McConnell, Margaret Price. San Gabriel days / by Margaret Price McConnell. Kansas City, Mo.: Publishing House of the Pentecostal Church of the Nazarene, 1913. 186 p. **DLC**
LC: My 2, '14.

M-74 MacConnell, Sarah Warder. Many mansions / by Sarah Warder MacConnell. Boston; New York: Houghton Mifflin Company, 1918. (Cambridge: The Riverside Press). 345, [1] p.
LC: O 1, '18.
PW: O 5, '18.

M-75 _____ One / by Sarah Warder MacConnell. New York: The Macmillan Company, 1922. 280 p.
LC: Ja 18, '22.
PW: F 11, '22.

M-76 _____ Why, Theodora! / by Sarah Warder MacConnell; illustrated by Frank Godwin. Boston: Small, Maynard & Company, [c1915]. 294 p., front., [3] leaves of plates.
LC: D 10, '15.

M-77 McConnell, Walter C. (Walter Caruth), b. 1870. The nightriders' feud / by Walter C. McConnell. New York: The Cosmopolitan Press, 1912. 178 p.

M-78 McCook, Henry C. (Henry Christopher), 1837-1911. Prisca of Patmos: a tale of the days of St. John / by Henry C. McCook. Philadelphia: The Westminster Press, 1911. 318 p., col. front., [8] leaves of plates.
LC: S 27, '11.
PW: N 18, '11.

M-79 _____ Quaker Ben: a tale of colonial Pennsylvania in the days of Thomas Penn / by Henry C. McCook . . . Philadelphia: George W. Jacobs & Co., [1911]. 336 p., col. front., [3] leaves of plates. [Ill. by H. Devitt Welsh.]
LC: My 31, '11.
PW: Je 10, '11.

M-80 McCord, Lottie. Only a horse, or, Tom's reform / by Lottie McCord. Emporia, Kan.: M'Cord & M'Cord, 1905. 184 p., photo. front., [5] leaves of plates [some photo. by Gregg Photo.] **KSW**
Another edition: Chicago: A. Flanagan Company, [c1905]. 189 p., photo. front., [5] leaves of plates (some photo.).

M-81 McCord, P. B. (Peter B.) d. 1908. Wolf: the memoirs of a cave-dweller / by P. B. McCord; with drawings by the author. New York: B. W. Dodge & Company, 1908. 132 p., front., [11] leaves of plates.
LC: O 27, '08.

M-82 McCormack, P. J. Dennis Horgan, gentleman: and other sketches / by Rev. P. J. McCormack. Boston: DeWolfe and Fiske Company, 1911. 117 p., photo. front. (port.).
Contents: Dennis Horgan-gentleman -- The ancient owner of the modern store -- The colonel's man -- 'Twas on a market day -- A puzzling case -- The story the captain told -- The brute.

M-83 McCormick, Frank J. (Frank Joseph), 1871-1954. Four-in-hand: a group of short stories / by Frank J. McCormick, Jr. [Dayton, Oh.: Press of United Brethren Publishing House, 1906]. 129 p., front., [4] leaves of plates, ill. [Ill. by Hanson Booth and Albert Loose.]
Contents: Mr. Durbar's toast -- Mrs. Billy's baby and the professor -- From Dolly to Dick -- Poetry and life.
LC: N 19, '06.

M-84 [_____] Mr. Durbar's toast . . . [Dayton, O.: United Brethren Publishing House], 1905. [32] p.
DLC (photocopy)
LC: D 21, '05.
Marginal decorations in blue.

M-85 McCormick, William Bennett. The wanton: a story of the redlight / by William Bennett McCormick. Shreveport, Louisiana: Published by the author, 1925. 495 p.
LC: F 18, '25.

M-86 McCowan, Archibald. The prisoners of war: a reminiscence of the Rebellion / by Archibald McCowan. New York; London; Montreal: The Abbey Press, [c1901]. 187 p., photo. front. (port.).

M-87   McCowan, Hervey Smith, b. 1867. Flames of glory / by Hervey Smith McCowan. Grinnell, Iowa: The Character-Building Company, [c1919]. 307 p., [6] leaves of plates.
Contents: Embers and the flame -- The conquest -- The great adventure -- The storm -- Down the line -- When the world burns -- The Bowery boy in France -- The heart of a soldier -- Will the home line hold -- The priceless picture -- The nurse and the gambler -- The lovable lieutenant -- Mothers of the dead.
LC: Mr 1, '19.
PW: Ap 5, '19.

M-88   _____ The harvest of the highway / by Hervey Smith McCowan; cover design by Hervey Louis McCowan. Coeur d'Alene, Idaho: The Character Building Company, [c1924]. 346 p., front.

M-89   _____ The trail a boy travels and other stories / by Hervey Smith McCowan. New York; London: Association Press, 1916. 222 p., front., ill. [Ill. by Walt Louderback.]   **CLU**
Contents: The trail a boy travels -- The letter he was ashamed of -- The son thou gavest me -- The happiest woman in the world -- The guests of the house -- The stranger's story -- What will a father give for his sons? -- The doctor's fight -- The hunters -- The gardens of heaven.
LC: Ja 12, '17.
PW: D 30, '16.

M-90   McCoy, Samuel Duff, 1882-1964. Tippecanoe: being a true chronicle of certain passages between David Larrance & Antoinette O'Bannon of the battle of Tippecanoe in the Indiana wilderness, and of what befell thereafter in old Corydon and now first set forth / by Samuel McCoy; illustrated by Ralph P. Coleman. Indianapolis: The Bobbs-Merrill Company, [c1916]. 295 p., front., [4] leaves of plates.

M-91   McCoy, William M. The valley of the sun / by William M. McCoy. New York: The H. K. Fly Company, [c1921]. 308 p., front.
PW: Ja 14, '22.

McCue, Thomas F., b. 1866. See **King, Scobe, pseud.**

M-92   McCrackin, Josephine Clifford, b. 1838. The woman who lost him: and tales of the army frontier / by Josephine Clifford McCrackin; with introduction by Ambrose Bierce. Pasadena, Cal.: George Wharton James, 1913. 310 p., [4] leaves of plates (port.). "This story . . . is a reprint from the National Magazine, Boston, Mass."
Contents: Romantic history of Josephine Clifford McCrackin [nonfiction] / George Wharton James -- Her red hair -- The colonel's young wife -- The end of the song -- Drums -- Penitencia -- Desdemona -- A picture of the plains -- The priest and the soldier -- Pay day at the mine -- The woman who lost him -- One day in June -- Can dead men tell no tales? -- On the stroke of XII -- Where they found her -- What the white lady told me.

McCreagh, Gordon. Everett, Commissioner of Justice. In *Greatest short stories* (1915), **G-424.**

M-93   McCulley, Johnston, 1883-1958. The Black Star: a detective story / by Johnston McCulley; frontispiece by Edgar Wittmack. New York City: Chelsea House, 1921. 306 p., incl. front.
LC: Mr 21, '22.

PW: D 26, '25.
BLC: London: Hutchinson & Co., [1924].

M-94   _____ Black Star's campaign: a detective story / by Johnston McCulley . . . New York City: Chelsea House, [c1924]. 256 p.

M-95   [_____] The brand of silence: a detective story / by Harrington Strong [pseud.]. New York City: Chelsea House, [c1924]. 254 p.
PW: My 9, '25.

M-96   _____ Broadway Bab / by Johnston McCulley; frontispiece by George W. Gage. New York: W. J. Watt & Company, [c1919]. 314 p., front.
LC: O 9, '19.
PW: Ja 17, '20.

M-97   _____ The demon: a detective story / by Johnston McCulley. New York City: Chelsea House, [c1925]. 253 p.
PW: D 19, '25.

M-98   _____ John Standon of Texas: a western story / by Johnston McCulley. New York: Chelsea House, [c1924]. 256 p.
PW: My 9, '25.

M-99   _____ The mark of Zorro / by Johnston McCulley . . . illustrated with scenes from the photoplay. New York: Grosset & Dunlap, [c1924]. 300 p., photo. front., [3] leaves of photo. plates.   **CLE**
LC: D 13, '24.
PW: Ja 17, '25.

M-100   _____ The masked woman / by Johnston McCulley; frontispiece by Paul Stahr. New York: W. J. Watt & Company, [c1920]. 312 p., front.
LC: Ap 20, '20.
PW: Jl 24, '20.

M-101   _____ The rangers' code / by Johnston McCulley. New York: G. Howard Watt, 1924. 295 p.
LC: Ag 21, '24.
PW: Mr 15, '24.

M-102   _____ The Scarlet Scourge: a detective story / by Johnston McCulley. New York City: Chelsea House, [c1925]. 255 p.
PW: My 23, '25.

M-103   _____ The spider's den: a detective story / by Johnston McCulley. New York: Chelsea House, [c1925]. 253 p.
PW: D 19, '25.

M-104   [_____] Who killed William Drew?: a detective story / by Harrington Strong [pseud.]. New York City: Chelsea House, [c1925]. 256 p.
PW: My 9, '25.
BLC: London: Skattington & Son, 1926.

M-105   McCulloch, James E. (James Edward), 1873-1939. The mastery of love: a narrative of settlement life / by James E. McCulloch . . . New York; Chicago; Toronto; London; Edinburgh: Fleming H. Revell,

[c1910]. 272 p. **TJC**
LC: Ja 5, '11.
PW: F 11, '11

McCune, Thornton C. A game of billiards. In *The best college short stories, 1924-1925* **(1925), B-558.**

McCutcheon, Ben Frederick. See **Brace, Benjamin, pseud.**

M-106   McCutcheon, George Barr, 1866-1928. The alternative / by George Barr McCutcheon; with illustrations by Harrison Fisher and decorations by Theodore B. Hapgood. New York: Dodd, Mead & Company, 1909. 119, [1] p., col. front., [3] leaves of col. plates. Designed end papers.
LC: Ap 12, '09.
PW: Ap 17, '09.
References: BAL 13519.

M-107   ____ Anderson Crow, detective / by George Barr McCutcheon; illustrated by John T. McCutcheon. New York: Dodd, Mead and Company, 1920. 353 p., front., [23] leaves of plates.
LC: Mr 23, '20.
PW: Ap 3, '20.
References: BAL 13551.

____ Anthony, the joker. See *Anthony, the joker* **(1924), A-286.**

M-108   ____ Beverly of Graustark / by George Barr McCutcheon; with illustrations by Harrison Fisher. New York: Dodd, Mead & Company, 1904. 357 p., col. front., [4] leaves of col. plates.
PW: O 1, '04.
BLC: London: B. F. Stevens & Brown; [printed in U. S. A.], 1904.
References: BAL 13507.

M-109   ____ Black is white / by George Barr McCutcheon . . . ; with illustrations by A. I. Keller. New York: Dodd, Mead and Company, 1914. 389 p., col. front., [3] leaves of col. plates.
LC: Mr 23, '14.
PW: Mr 21, '14.
BLC: London: Everett & Co., [1915].
References: BAL 13533.

____, contributor. See *Bobbed hair* **(1925), B-700.**

M-110   [____] Brewster's millions / by Richard Greaves [pseud.]. Chicago: Herbert S. Stone & Co., 1903. 325 p.
LC: Ap 20, '03.
PW: My 9, '03.
BLC: London: Collier & Co., 1907.
References: BAL 13504.

M-111   ____ The butterfly man / by George Barr McCutcheon; with illustrations by Harrison Fisher and decorations by Theodore B. Hapgood. New York: Dodd, Mead & Company, 1910. 121 p., col. front., [3] leaves of col. plates. Designed end papers.
LC: My 9, '10.
PW: My 7, '10.
References: BAL 13521.

M-112   ____ Castle Craneycrow / by George Barr McCutcheon . . . Chicago: Herbert S. Stone and Company, 1902. 391 p.
LC: Ag 13, '02.
PW: Ag 23, '02.
BLC: London: Grant Richards; Chicago printed, 1903.
References: BAL 13502.

M-113   ____ The city of masks / by George Barr McCutcheon; with illustrations by May Wilson Preston. New York: Dodd, Mead and Company, 1918. 314 p., col. front. Col. illustrated end papers.
LC: S 19, '18.
PW: S 14, '18.
References: BAL 13546.

M-114   ____ Cowardice court / by George Barr McCutcheon; with illustrations by Harrison Fisher and decorations by Theodore B. Hapgood. New York: Dodd, Mead & Company, 1906. 140 p., col. front., [4] leaves of col. plates. Designed end papers.
PW: Ap 7, '06.
References: BAL 13511.

M-115   ____ The daughter of Anderson Crow / by George Barr McCutcheon . . . ; with illustrations by B. Martin Justice. New York: Dodd, Mead and Company, 1907. 346 p., col. front., [14] leaves of plates, ill.
LC: Ag 6, '07.
PW: S 21, '07.
BLC: London: Hodder & Stoughton, printed in U. S. A., 1907.
References: BAL 13515.

M-116   ____ The day of the dog / by George Barr McCutcheon; with illustrations by Harrison Fisher and decorations by Margaret & Helen Maitland Armstrong. New York: Dodd, Mead & Company, 1904. 137 p., col. front., [4] leaves of col. plates, ill.
LC: Mr 24, '04.
PW: Ap 9, '04.
References: BAL 13506.

M-117   ____ East of the setting sun: a story of Graustark / by George Barr McCutcheon. New York: Dodd, Mead and Company, 1924. 350 p.
LC: Ag 23, '24.
PW: O 4, '24.
BLC: London: G. G. Harrap & Co., 1925.
References: BAL 13561.

M-118   ____ The flyers / by George Barr McCutcheon; with illustrations by Harrison Fisher and decorations by Theodore B. Hapgood. New York: Dodd Mead & Company, 1907. 127 p., col. front., [4] leaves of col. plates.
LC: Mr 25, '07.
PW: Ap 13, '07.
BLC: London: B. F. Stevens & Brown; Cambridge, U. S. A. printed, 1907.
References: BAL 13514.

M-119   ____ A fool and his money / by George Barr McCutcheon; with illustrations by A. I. Keller. New

York: Dodd, Mead and Company, 1913. 373 p., col. front., [4] leaves of col. plates.
LC: S 16, '13.
PW: S 27, '13.
BLC: London: B. F. Stevens & Brown; printed in U. S. A., 1913.
References: BAL 13532. BAL notes large paper format.

M-120   ____ From the housetops / by George Barr McCutcheon . . . ; with illustrations by F. Graham Cootes. New York: Dodd, Mead and Company, 1916. 442 p., front., [4] leaves of plates.
LC: S 20, '16.
PW: S 23, '16.
BLC: London: B. F. Stevens & Brown; printed in U. S. A., 1916.
References: BAL 13537.

M-121   ____ Graustark: the story of a love behind a throne / by George Barr McCutcheon. Chicago: Herbert S. Stone and Company, 1901. 459 p.
LC: Ap 10, '01.
PW: Mr 23, '01.
BLC: London: Grant Richards, 1902.
References: BAL 13501.

M-122   ____ Green fancy / by George Barr McCutcheon; with frontispiece by C. Allan Gilbert. New York: Dodd, Mead and Company, 1917. 355 p., col. front.
LC: S 11, '17.
PW: S 8, '17.
BLC: London: Hodder & Stoughton, 1918.
References: BAL 13540.

M-123   ____ Her weight in gold / by George Barr McCutcheon; illustrated by H. Devitt Welsh. New York: Dodd, Mead and Company, 1912. 120, [1] p., front. ill., ill.
LC: Ap 30, '12.
PW: My 11, '12.
References: BAL 13528.
Also shorter version: Indianapolis: The Bobbs-Merrill Co., [c1911]. 77 p.
Contents: Her weight in gold -- The wrath of the dead.
References: BAL 13527.

M-124   ____ The hollow of her hand / by George Barr McCutcheon; with illustrations by A. I. Keller. New York: Dodd, Mead and Company, 1912. 422 p., col. front., [4] leaves of col. plates.
LC: Je 27, '12. BAL notes Je 26, '12. (copyright issue).
PW: O 5, '12.
BLC: London: B. F. Stevens & Brown; printed in U. S. A., 1912.
References: BAL 13529. BAL also notes copyright issue and large paper format.

M-125   ____ The husbands of Edith / by George Barr McCutcheon; with illustrations by Harrison Fisher and decorations by Theodore B. Hapgood. New York: Dodd, Mead & Company, 1908. 126, [1] p., col. front., [4] leaves of col. plates. Designed end papers.
LC: Ap 21, '08.
PW: My 2, '08.

BLC: London: Holden & Hardingham, 1912.
References: BAL 13516.

M-126   ____ Jane Cable / by George Barr McCutcheon; illustrations in color by Harrison Fisher. New York: Dodd, Mead & Company, 1906. 336 p., col. front., [4] leaves of col. plates.
LC: Ag 8, '06.
PW: S 22, '06.
BLC: London: Hodder & Stoughton, 1906.
References: BAL 13512.

M-127   ____ The light that lies / by George Barr McCutcheon . . . ; with illustrations by F. Graham Cootes. New York: Dodd, Mead and Company, 1916. 121 p., front., [4] leaves of plates.
LC: Ap 18, '16.
PW: Ap 15, '16.
BLC: London: Herbert Jenkins, [1917].
References: BAL 13536.

M-128   ____ The man from Brodney's / by George Barr McCutcheon; with illustrations by Harrison Fisher. New York: Dodd, Mead & Company, 1908. 355 p., col. front., [3] leaves of col. plates.
LC: Ag 26, '08.
PW: S 26, '08.
BLC: London: Hodder & Stoughton, 1908.
References: BAL 13517.

M-129   ____ Mary Midthorne / by George Barr McCutcheon . . . ; illustrations by Martin Justice. New York: Dodd, Mead and Company, 1911. 439 p., col. front., [3] leaves of col. plates.
LC: S 16, '11.
PW: S 16, '11.
BLC: London: B. F. Stevens & Brown; printed in U. S. A., 1911.
References: BAL 13526.

M-130   ____ Mr. Bingle / by George Barr McCutcheon; with illustrations by James Montgomery Flagg. New York: Dodd, Mead and Company, 1915. 357 p., front., [4] leaves of plates.
LC: S 22, '15.
PW: S 18, '15.
BLC: London: B. F. Stevens & Brown; printed in U. S. A., [1915].
References: BAL 13535.

M-131   ____ Nedra / by George Barr McCutcheon; illustrations by Harrison Fisher. New York: Dodd, Mead & Company, 1905. 343 p., col. front., [4] leaves of col. plates.
PW: S 30, '05.
BLC: London: B. F. Stevens & Brown; printed in U. S. A., 1905.
References: BAL 13509.

M-132   ____ Oliver October / by George Barr McCutcheon. New York: Dodd, Mead and Company, 1923. 337 p.
LC: Ag 30, '23.
PW: Ag 25, '23.
BLC: London: G. G. Harrap & Co., 1924.
References: BAL 13559.

M-133   ____ The Prince of Graustark / by George Barr McCutcheon; with illustrations by A. I. Keller. New York: Dodd, Mead and Company, 1914. 394 p., col. front., [3] leaves of col. plates.
LC: S 21, '14.
PW: S 12, '14; S 19, '14.
BLC: London: B. F. Stevens & Brown, 1914.
References: BAL 13534. BAL also notes adance printing and large paper format.

M-134   ____ The purple parasol / by George Barr McCutcheon . . . ; with illustrations by Harrison Fisher and decorations by Chas. B. Falls. New York: Dodd, Mead and Company, 1905. 108 p., col. front., [4] leaves of col. plates, ill. Designed end papers.
PW: Ap 22, '05.
References: BAL 13508.

M-135   ____ Quill's window / by George Barr McCutcheon; frontispiece by C. Allan Gilbert. New York: Dodd, Mead and Company, 1921. 335 p., col. front.
LC: S 20, '21.
PW: S 24, '21.
BLC: London: Eveleigh Nash & Grayson; printed in U. S. A., 1922.
References: BAL 13553.

M-136   ____ Romeo in Moon Village / by George Barr McCutcheon. New York: Dodd, Mead and Company, 1925. 344 p.
LC: S 24, '25.
PW: S 26, '25.
BLC: London: Eveleigh Nash & Grayson, 1926.
References: BAL 13563.

M-137   ____ The rose in the ring / by George Barr McCutcheon; with illustrations by A. I. Keller. New York: Dodd, Mead and Company, 1910. 425 p., col. front., [3] leaves of col. plates.
LC: S 17, '10.
PW: S 24, '10.
BLC: London: Everett & Co.; Cambridge, U. S. A. [printed], 1910.
References: BAL 13522.

M-138   ____ The Sherrods / by George Barr McCutcheon; with illustrations by C. D. Williams. New York: Dodd, Mead and Company, 1903. 343 p., front., [5] leaves of plates.
PW: S 19, '03.
BLC: London: Ward, Lock & Co.; printed from American plates, 1905.
References: BAL 13505.

M-139   ____ Sherry / by George Barr McCutcheon; frontispiece by C. Allan Gilbert. New York: Dodd, Mead and Company, 1919. 374 p., col. front.
LC: S 16, '19.
PW: S 20, '19.
References: BAL 13549.

M-140   ____ Shot with crimson / by George Barr McCutcheon; with illustrations by F. R. Gruger.

New York: Dodd, Mead and Company, 1918. 161 p., front., [3] leaves of plates.
LC: My 21, '18.
PW: My 25, '18.
References: BAL 13544.

M-141   ____ Truxton King: a story of Graustark / by George Barr McCutcheon; with illustrations by Harrison Fisher. New York: Dodd, Mead & Company, 1909. 369 p., col. front., [3] leaves of col. plates.
LC: S 13, '09.
PW: S 18, '09.
BLC: London: B. F. Stevens & Brown; printed in U. S. A., 1909.
References: BAL 13520.

M-142   ____ Viola Gwyn / by George Barr McCutcheon; frontispiece by E. C. Caswell. New York: Dodd, Mead and Company, 1922. 378 p., col. front.
LC: S 13, '22.
PW: S 9, '22.
BLC: London: E. Nash & Grayson; printed in U. S. A., 1922.
References: BAL 13557. BAL notes large paper format.

M-143   ____ West wind drift / by George Barr McCutcheon. New York: Dodd, Mead and Company, 1920. 368 p.
LC: O 27, '20.
PW: O 2, '20.
BLC: London: Eveleigh Nash Co.; printed in U. S. A., 1921.
References: BAL 13552.

M-144   ____ What's-his-name / by George Barr McCutcheon; with illustrations by Harrison Fisher. New York: Dodd, Mead and Company, 1911. 243 p., col. front., [3] leaves of col. plates.
LC: Ap 10, '11.
PW: Ap 8, '11.
BLC: London: B. F. Stevens & Brown; printed in U. S. A., 1911.
References: BAL 13525; BAL 13524: collected weekly newspaper appearances.

M-145   ____ Yollop / by George Barr McCutcheon; frontispiece by Edward C. Caswell. New York: Dodd, Mead and Company, 1922. 112 p., front.
LC: F 28, '22.
PW: Mr 4, '22.
References: BAL 13556.

M-146   McCutcheon, John T. (John Tinney), 1870-1949. Congressman Pumphrey: the people's friend / by John T. McCutcheon; with cartoons by the author. Indianapolis: The Bobbs-Merrill Company, [c1907]. 125, [1] p., front. ill., ill.
"The cartoons in this book are reprinted through the courtesy of the Chicago Tribune, where most of them first appeared."
LC: Mr 22, '07.
PW: Ap 13, '07.

M-147 ____ Dawson '11, fortune hunter / by John T. McCutcheon; pictured by the author. New York: Dodd, Mead and Company, 1912. 159 p., ill.
LC: O 23, '12.
PW: O 19, '12.

M-148 ____ An heir at large / by John T. McCutcheon; with illustrations by the author. Indianapolis: The Bobbs-Merrill Company, [c1923]. 302 p., incl. front., [4] leaves of plates.
LC: Mr 16, '23.
PW: Mr 10, '23.

M-149 ____ The restless age / by John T. McCutcheon . . . ; illustrated with cartoons by the author. Indianapolis: The Bobbs-Merrill Company, [c1921]. 218 p., ill.
LC: N 25, '21.
PW: Ja 21, '22.

McDermott, Francis J. Lost and found. In *The Tragedy that wins and other short stories* (1905), **T-343.**

____ A Japanese hero. In *The Tragedy that wins and other short stories* (1905), **T-343.**

M-150 McDermott-Stevenson, Myra E. Lariat letters / by Myra E. McDermott-Stevenson; illustrated by Zella Bey Mains. [Topeka?, Kan.: s. n., c1907]. 42 p., ill. **KFH**
LC: N 8, '07.

M-151 McDonald, D. D. Ned Collins the man and Mono his little Apache bride: a story filled with the deepest human interest / by D. D. McDonald . . . . [S. l.: s. n., c1924.] 46 p.

M-152 MacDonald, Edwina Levin. A lady of New Orleans / by Edwina Levin MacDonald. New York: The Macaulay Company, [c1925]. 314 p.
LC: S 2, '25.

M-153 MacDonald, Eleanor W. The winning of Walk-Over-the-Water: a story of Indian love / Eleanor W. MacDonald. [New York?: s. n., c1902]. 16 p., front., ill.

M-154 MacDonald, Everett. The red debt: echoes from Kentucky / by Everett MacDonald; illustrations from original drawings of William Oberhardt. New York: G. W. Dillingham Co., [1916]. 334 p., front., [4] leaves of plates.
LC: D 18, '16.
PW: Je 3, '16.

M-155 ____ Slimtonian Socker / by Everett MacDonald; illustrated by Ray Rohn. Philadelphia: George W. Jacobs & Company, [c1922]. 368 p., incl. [12] leaves of plates.
LC: Ap 27, '22.
PW: Je 3, '22.

M-156 MacDonald, Francis Charles. Sorcery / by Francis Charles MacDonald. New York: The Century Co., 1919. 215 p., front.

M-157 McDonald, Horace G. The white ribboner, or, How Paul Hamilton won the victory / by Horace G. McDonald . . . Portland, Oregon: Bethel Publishing Company, [c1919]. 503 p. **MAA**
LC: Ja 5, '20.
PW: Ap 10, '20.

M-158 McDonald, Irving T. (Irving Thomas), b. 1894. On his toes! / by Irving Thomas McDonald; with illustrations by Frank J. Rigney. New York: Dodd, Mead and Company, 1921. 320 p., front., [3] leaves of plates.

M-159 McDonald, Lucretia S. Checkerberry / by Lucretia S. McDonald. New York: Cochrane Publishing Co., 1908. 278 p. **NYP**
LC: D 26, '08.

M-160 MacDonald, Robert. The herr doctor / by Robert MacDonald; illustrations by W. E. Mears. New York; London: Funk & Wagnalls Company, 1902. 138 p., incl. front., ill.

M-161 McDonald, Samuel E. The other girl: with some further stories and poems / by Samuel E. McDonald. New York: Broadway Publishing Company, 1903. 79 p., front. (port.).
Contents: The other girl -- The upper current -- The downfall of woman -- The little clown -- Georgie's letters from Philip -- The will of two -- Franz Schubert [nonfiction] -- Franz Liszt [nonfiction] -- The fate of the greedy bear -- The chieftain sparrow -- His photo -- The uniting power -- The shortest day -- The love of Winnoa -- Jim -- The foolery of ping pong. [The remainder of the book is poetry.]
PW: D 19, '03.

M-162 McDonald, Stella Breyfogle. Clear shining after rain: and other stories / by Stella Bryfogle McDonald; illustrations by Lillian Marie Harmer. New York: Calkins and Company, 1907. 211 p., front., [4] leaves of plates. **DLC**
Reprinted from various periodicals.
Contents: Clear shining after rain -- A Wall Street incident -- Whom God hath joined -- An averted tragedy -- The heart of a bread-winner -- One man's summer -- A belle pro tem -- Wreckage -- The refining of Freddy -- Dalton's inspiration -- A man's loss -- Paranoia.
LC: D 12, '07.

M-163 Macdonald, Thomas A. Two lovers and two loves / by Thomas A. Macdonald . . . Paterson, New Jersey, U. S. A.: Published by the author, 1901. 472 p., [1] leaf of plates (col. map).
PW: Ap 27, '01.

M-164 McElrath, Frances. The rustler: a tale of love and war in Wyoming / by Frances McElrath; illustrations by Edwin Willard Deming. New York: Funk & Wagnalls Company, 1902. 425 p., front., [6] leaves of plates.
PW: My 3, '02.

McElravy, Robert C. Blinkey, the story of a tenderfoot. In *Golden stories* (1909), **G-285.**

M-165 McElroy, Lucy Cleaver, 1860-1901. Juletty: a story of old Kentucky / by Lucy Cleaver McElroy. New York: Thomas Y. Crowell & Co., [c1901]. 280 p., front., [15] leaves of plates. [Ill. by W. E. Mears.]
PW: My 11, '01.

M-166　　____ The silent pioneer / by Lucy Cleaver McElroy. New York: Thomas Y. Crowell & Co., [c1902]. 391 p., front., [3] leaves of plates. [Ill. by W. E. Mears.]
PW: Mr 8, '02.

M-167　　Macfadden, Bernarr, 1868-1955. A strenuous lover: a romance of a natural love's vast power / original story by Bernarr Macfadden; revised with the assistance of John R. Coryell. New York; London: Published by Physical Culture Publishing Co., [c1904]. 476 p.

M-168　　MacFadyen, Virginia. At the sign of the sun: a novel / by Virginia MacFadyen. New York: Albert & Charles Boni, 1925. 248 p.
LC: O 12, '25.
PW: O 17, '25.

M-169　　____ Windows facing west / by Virginia MacFadyen. New York: Albert & Charles Boni, 1924. 288 p.
LC: Ja 10, '25.
PW: Ja 3, '25.
BLC: London: Stanley Paul & Co., 1925.

M-170　　McFarland, Raymond, b. 1872. Skipper John of the Nimbus / by Raymond McFarland; with frontispiece in color by Anton Otto Fischer. New York; The Macmillan Company, 1918. 294 p., front.　**MEU**
LC: S 25, '18.

M-171　　____ Sons of the sea / by Raymond McFarland. New York; London: G. P. Putnam's Sons, 1921. ([New York]: The Knickerbocker Press). 425 p.
LC: Mr 11, '21.

M-172　　Macfarlane, Charles A. (Charles Albert), b. 1853. For old times' sake / by Charles A. Macfarlane. Methuen, Mass.: The Macfarlane Company, 1905. 220 p., front., ill. (some photo.).
PW: F 24, '06.

M-173　　____ Letitia: a thrilling novel of western life / by Charles A. Macfarlane. Boston, Massachusetts: The C. M. Clark Publishing Company, 1908. 287 p., front. [Ill. by N. K. Saunders.]
LC: N 21, '09. LC reports 7 plates.

M-174　　Macfarlane, Isabella. A royal knight: a tale of Nuremburg / by Isabella MacFarlane. New York: G. W. Dillingham Company, [1905]. 271 p.

M-175　　Macfarlane, Peter Clark, 1871-1924. The centurion's story / by P. C. Macfarlane. New York; Chicago; [etc.]: Fleming H. Revell Company, [c1910]. 45 p. Ornamental borders.
Unexamined copy: bibliographic data from OCLC, #19386898.
LC: Mr 17, '10.
PW: Mr 19, '10.

M-176　　____ The crack in the bell / by Peter Clark Macfarlane; illustrated by Leslie L. Benson. Garden City, New York: Doubleday, Page & Company,
1918. 458 p., front., [3] leaves of plates.
LC: O 3, '18.
PW: O 26, '18.

M-177　　____ The exploits of Bilge and Ma / by Peter Clark Macfarlane. Boston: Little, Brown, and Company, 1919. 300 p.
LC: S 26, '19.
PW: N 1, '19.

M-178　　____ Held to answer: a novel / by Peter Clark Macfarlane; with illustrations by W. B. King. Boston: Little, Brown and Company, 1916. 521 p., front., [5] leaves of plates.
LC: F 10, '16.
PW: F 5, '16.
BLC: London: Eveleigh Nash Co.; Boston [printed], 1916.

M-179　　____ Man's country: the story of a great love, of which business was jealous / by Peter Clark Macfarlane; with illustrations by Charles D. Mitchell. New York: Cosmopolitan Book Corporation, 1923. 343 p., front., [3] leaves of plates.
LC: Ja 8, '23.
PW: Ja 20, '23.
BLC: London: Hodder & Stoughton; printed in U. S. A., [1923].

M-180　　____ The quest of the yellow pearl / by P. C. Macfarlane. [New York]: Fleming H. Revell Co., [c1909]. 47 p., incl. photo. front., ill. [Ill. by H. J. Turner.]
PW: Ag 7, '09.

M-181　　____ Tongues of flame / by Peter Clark Macfarlane; ill. by Walt Louderback. New York: Cosmopolitan Book Corp., 1924. 405 p., front., [3] leaves of plates.
LC: My 21, '24.
PW: My 24, '24.
BLC: London: Brentano's; printed in U. S. A., [1925].

M-182　　McFaul, A. D. (Alexander D.), b. 1863. Ike Glidden in Maine: a story of rural life in a Yankee district / by A. D. McFaul; illustrated. Boston; New York: Dickerman Publishing Co., [c1903]. 297 p., front., [8] leaves of plates. [Ill. by D. F. Anderson.]

M-183　　McFee, William, b. 1881. Aliens / by William McFee . . . Garden City, New York: Doubleday, Page & Company, 1918. 416 p.
Rev. ed. of an earlier version.
LC: Mr 2, '18.
PW: Mr 2, '18.
BLC: London: Edward Arnold, 1914.

M-184　　____ Captain Macedoine's daughter / by William McFee. Garden City, N. Y.: Doubleday, Page & Company, 1920. 326 p.
LC: N 19, '20.
PW: O 16, '20.
BLC: London: Curtis Brown; Garden City, N. Y. printed, 1920.

M-185   ____ Casuals of the sea: the voyage of a soul / by William McFee. New York: Doubleday, Page & Co., 1916. 469, [1] p.
PW: Ag 26, '16.
BLC: London: Martin Secker, 1916.

M-186   ____ Command / by William McFee. Garden City, N. Y.: Doubleday, Page & Company, 1922. 337 p.
LC: N 25, '22.
PW: N 11, '22.
BLC: London: Martin Secker, 1922.

M-187   ____ An ocean tramp / by William McFee. Garden City, N. Y.; Toronto: Doubleday, Page and Company, 1921. 189 p.
LC: Mr 23, '21.
PW: Ap 30, '21.

M-188   ____ A Port Said miscellany / by William McFee. Boston: The Atlantic Monthly Press, [c1918]. 22 p.
IUL

M-189   ____ Race / by William McFee. Garden City, New York: Doubleday, Page & Company, 1924. 398 p.
LC: Ap 25, '24.
PW: Ap 19, '24.
BLC: London: Martin Secker, 1924.

M-190   McGaffey, Kenneth. The sorrows of a show girl: a story of the great "White way" / by Kenneth McGaffey. Chicago: J. I. Austen Company, 1908. 243 p.
"The stories were originally printed in the Morning Telegraph, New York."

M-191   McGarry, William Rutledge, 1872-1942. From Berlin to Bagdad: an historical romance / by William Rutledge McGarry, foreword and authorized German translation by Ernst Kroner. Portland: International Publishing Co., 1915. 167, [1] p.

M-192   McGee, Agnes Potter. Dorothy Angsleigh: a story of war times / by Agnes Potter McGee; illustrations by Max Bihn. Chicago: W. B. Conkey Company, 1907. 353 p., front., [7] leaves of plates.
Unexamined copy: bibliographic data from NUC.
LC: Ap 13, '07.
PW: My 11, '07.

    McGeehan, W. O. Leaves on the River Pasig. In *Argonaut stories* (1906), **A-298.**

M-193   McGeeney, Patrick Sylvester, 1873-1943. Down at Cross Timbers / by P. S. McGeeney . . . Boston, Mass.: Angel Guardian Press, 1909. 66 p., photo. front. (port.), [2] leaves of photo. plates.
LC: D 29, '09.

M-194   ____ Down at Stein's Pass: a romance of New Mexico / by P. S. McGeeney . . . Boston, Mass.: Angel Guardian Press, 1909. 114 p., photo. front. (port.), [1] leaf of photo. plates.
LC: D 29, '09.

M-195   McGhee, Zach. The dark corner / by Zach McGhee. New York: The Grafton Press, [c1908]. 206 p.
LC: D 1, '08.

M-196   McGibeny, Donald. Slag: a story of steel and stocks / by Donald McGibeny. Indianapolis: The Bobbs-Merrill Company, [c1922]. 311 p.
LC: Ap 14, '22.
PW: Ap 22, '22.

M-197   ____ 32 caliber / by Donald McGibeny; frontispiece by Hugh Mackey. Indianapolis: The Bobbs-Merrill Company, [c1920]. 249 p., front.
LC: O 25, '20.
PW: O 30, '20.

    McGill, Anna Blanche. At summer's close. In *The lady of the tower* **(1909), L-13.**

    ____ The force of habit. In *The friendly little house: and other stories* **(1910), F-432.**

    ____ A little romance in Avila. In *The Senior lieutenant's wager: and other stories* **(1905), S-312.**

    ____ Miss Milly and Mr. Willy. In *The friendly little house: and other stories* **(1910), F-432.**

    McGill, M. V. A letter to Cecilia. In **Seattle Writers' Club.** *Tillicum tales* **(1907), S-248.**

    McGinley, Phyllis. The spider. In *The best college short stories, 1924-1925* **(1925), B-558.**

M-198   McGirt, James E. (James Ephraim). The triumphs of Ephraim / by James E. McGirt . . . Philadelphia: The McGirt Publishing Co., 1907. 131 p., photot. front. (port.), [7] leaves of plates.   **MNU**

M-199   [MacGonigle, Jane Gracey], b. 1869. The blooming of the lilies. Pittsburgh: [s. n.], 1909. [28] p., ill.
Unexamined copy: bibliographic data from OCLC, #29867106.
LC: Ag 31, '09.

M-200   McGovern, Milton. Colette of the fields: and other short stories, and poems / by Milton McGovern. Washington: [s. n.], 1920. 221 p.
Contents: Colette of the fields -- The watcher by the sea [poem] -- The cross on old St. Mary's -- A disciple of Ingersoll -- St. Timothy's lighthouse -- A prayer to the sacred heart [poem] -- Just a little lad of ten -- The span of a minute -- Oh, eyes of God [poem] -- "Won't you come under my umbrella?" -- The call of the friend [poem] -- Oene -- Noble nuns -- A tale of by-gone days -- Sweetest of earthly sounds [poem] -- Friends -- In search of Nonie -- When the lights are low -- How did it happen? -- A wreath of holly.

M-201   ____ The twilight rendezvous / by Milton McGovern . . . Buffalo, N. Y.: Buffalo Catholic Publication Co., [c1925]. 255 p., photo. front.   **NYP**
PW: N 7, '25.

M-202   ____ When the moon became a Chinaman: and other stories / by Milton McGovern. New York: P. J. Kenedy & Sons, [c1924]. 326 p.
Contents: When the moon became a Chinaman -- Watchers in the night -- Elizabeth passes -- The tonic of friendship -- The son of Brancanini -- Tobio -- The house next door -- A spanish tale -- In search of Nonie -- The trick of tricks -- A romance of old France -- The man from Port Maurice.
LC: Ag 28, '24.

    MacGowan, Alice, 1858-1947. A doll. In *The heart of childhood* **(1906), H-441.**

____, jt. aut. *Huldah* (1904). See **Cooke, Grace MacGowan, 1863-1944, jt. aut., C-725.**

M-203   ____ Judith of the Cumberlands / by Alice MacGowan; with illustrations in colour by George Wright. New York; London: G. P. Putnam's Sons, 1908. ([New York]: The Knickerbocker Press). 406 p., col. front., [5] leaves of col. plates.
LC: O 1, '08.
PW: O 10, 08.

M-204   ____ The last word / by Alice MacGowan; illustrated. Boston: L. C. Page & Company, 1903, [1902]. 439 p., front., [6] leaves of plates.
PW: O 4, '02.
BLC: London: Hutchinson & Co.; Boston, Mass. [printed], 1903.

M-205   ____ The million-dollar suitcase / by Alice MacGowan and Perry Newberry. New York: Frederick A. Stokes Company, [c1922]. 326 p.
LC: Mr 13, '22.
PW: Mr 18, '22.

M-206   ____ The mystery woman / by Alice MacGowan and Perry Newberry. New York: Frederick A. Stokes Company, 1924. 303 p.
LC: F 4, '24.
PW: F 2, '24.

____ Pap Overholt. In *Southern lights and shadows* **(1907), S-718.**

M-207   ____ Shaken down / by Alice MacGowan and Perry Newberry . . . New York: Frederick A. Stokes Company, 1925. 309 p.
LC: F 9, '25.
PW: F 7, '25.

____, jt. aut. *The straight road* (1917). See **Cooke, Grace MacGowan, 1863-1944, jt. aut., C-729.**

M-208   ____ The sword in the mountains / by Alice MacGowan . . . ; illustrated. New York; London: G. P. Putnam's Sons, 1910. ([New York]: The Knickerbocker Press). 455 p., col. front., [5] leaves of col. plates. [Ill. by John Edwin Jackson and Robert Edwards.]
LC: N 2, '10.
PW: O 29, '10.

____, jt. aut. *Wild apples* (1918). See **Cooke, Grace MacGowan, 1863-1944, jt. aut., C-731.**

M-209   ____ The wiving of Lance Cleaverage / by Alice MacGowan . . . ; with illustrations in colour by Robert Edwards. New York; London: G. P. Putnam's Sons, 1909. (New York: The Knickerbocker Press). 398 p., col. front., [5] leaves of col. plates.
LC: O 18, '09.
PW: O 9, '09.

M-210   McGrady, Thomas, 1863-1907. Beyond the black ocean / by Rev. T. McGrady . . . . Chicago: Charles H. Kerr & Company, 1901, [c1900]. 304 p.

(Library of progress; no. 36.)
PW: Mr 23, '01.
Another edition: Terre Haute, Ind.: Standard Publishing Co., 1901. 304 p.

M-211   MacGrath, Harold, 1871-1932. The adventures of Kathlyn / by Harold MacGrath. Indianapolis: The Bobbs-Merrill Company, [c1914]. 375 p., front., ill.
LC: Je 25, '14.

M-212   ____ The best man / by Harold MacGrath with illustrations by Will Grefé, decorations by Franklin Booth. Indianapolis: The Bobbs-Merrill Company, [c1907]. 206 p., front., [7] leaves of plates.
Contents: The best man -- Two candidates -- The advent of Mr. "Shifty" Sullivan.
LC: S 18, '07.
PW: O 5, '07.

M-213   ____ Captain Wardlaw's Kitbags / by Harold MacGrath. Garden City, New York: Garden City Publishing Co., Inc., 1923. 119 p.   **DLC**
(Famous authors series; 36.)
LC: Mr 26, '24.

M-214   ____ The carpet from Bagdad / by Harold MacGrath; with illustrations by André Castaigne. Indianapolis: The Bobbs-Merrill Company, [c1911]. 390 p., col. front., [5] leaves of col. plates.
LC: S 1, '11.
PW: S 2, '11.

M-215   ____ The Cellini plaque / by Harold MacGrath. Garden City, N. Y.: Doubleday, Page & Company, 1925. 252 p.
LC: O 29, '25.
PW: O 10, '25.
BLC: London: Curtis Brown; printed in U. S. A., 1925.

M-216   ____ Deuces wild / by Harold MacGrath; illustrated by R. N. [i. e. M.] Crosby. Indianapolis: The Bobbs-Merrill Company, [c1913]. 143, [1] p., front., [9] leaves of plates.
LC: N 26, '13.
PW: N 29, '13.

M-217   ____ The drums of jeopardy / by Harold MacGrath; illustrated by Ralph Pallen Coleman. Garden City, N. Y.: Doubleday, Page & Company, 1920. 396 p., front., [3] leaves of plates.
LC: O 6, '20.
PW: O 2, '20.
BLC: London: Hodder & Stonghton, [1923].

M-218   ____ The enchanted hat / Harold MacGrath; with illustrations by Will Grefé; decorations by Franklin Booth. Indianapolis: The Bobbs-Merrill Company, [1908]. 219 p., col. front., [7] leaves of col. plates.
Contents: The enchanted hat -- The wrong coat -- A night's enchantment -- No Cinderella.
LC: N 13, '08.
PW: D 5, '08.

M-219   ____ Enchantment / by Harold MacGrath. Indianapolis: The Bobbs-Merrill Company, [c1905]. 198, [1] p.

Cover, spine and running title: *A night's
enchantment*.

Contents: The adventure of the lady in the closed carriage -- The
adventure of the golden louis -- The adventure of the satin slipper --
An adventure in love and politics -- The adventure of my lady's letter.
PW: My 6, '05.

Variant printing published simultaneously has front.
[Ill. by L. Ralph], series statement, The pocket
books, and supratitles for the same short stories as
other printing.

Contents: A night's enchantment . . . -- The blind madonna . . . --
No Cinderella . . . -- Two candidates . . . -- The enchated hat.

M-220   The girl in his house / by Harold MacGrath
. . . ; illustrated by Howard Giles. New York;
London: Harper & Brothers, [1918]. 148, [1] p.,
col. front., [2] leaves of col. plates.
LC: My 15, '18.
PW: My 25, '18.

M-221   The goose girl / by Harold MacGrath; with
illustrations by André Castaigne. Indianapolis: The
Bobbs-Merrill Company, [c1909]. 383 p., front., [5]
leaves of plates.
LC: Ag 16, '09.
PW: Ag 21, '09.

M-222   The green stone / by Harold MacGrath.
Garden City, N. Y.: Doubleday, Page & Company,
1924. 346 p.
LC: S 15, '24.
PW: S 27, '24.
BLC: London: Curtis Brown; printed in U. S. A.,
1924.

M-223   The grey cloak / by Harold MacGrath; the
illustrations by Thomas Mitchell Pierce. Indianapolis:
The Bobbs-Merrill Company, [1903]. 463 p., col.
front., [5] leaves of plates.
PW: My 9, '03.
BLC: London: Ward, Lock & Co.; printed in U. S.
A., 1904.

M-224   Half a rogue / by Harold MacGrath; with
illustrations by Harrison Fisher. Indianapolis: The
Bobbs-Merrill Company, [1906]. 448, [1] p., front.,
[3] leaves of plates.
LC: N 24, '06.
PW: D 15, '06.
BLC: London: Gay & Bird, 1907.

M-225   Hearts and masks / by Harold MacGrath; with
illustrations by Harrison Fisher; decorations by Ralph
Fletcher Seymour. Indianapolis: The Bobbs-Merrill
Company, [1905]. 186, [1] p., front., [9] leaves of
plates.
PW: N 18, '05.

M-226   The luck of the Irish: a romance / by Harold
MacGrath. New York; London: Harper & Brothers,
[1917]. 335, [1] p., col. front. [Ill. by W. H. D.
Koerner.]
LC: O 3, '17.
PW: O 13, '17.

M-227   The lure of the mask / by Harold MacGrath;
with illustrations by Harrison Fisher and Karl

Anderson. Indianapolis: The Bobbs-Merrill
Company, [c1908]. 401 p., col. front., [6] leaves of
plates.
LC: My 29, '08.
PW: Je 13, '08.
BLC: London: Stead's Publishing House; printed in
U. S. A., 1909.

M-228   The man on the box / by Harold MacGrath; the
illustrations by Harrison Fisher. Indianapolis: The
Bobbs-Merrill Company, [c1904]. 361 p., front., [6]
leaves of plates.
PW: N 19, '04.

M-229   The man with three names / by Harold
MacGrath; illustrated by Ralph Pallen Coleman.
Garden City, N. Y.: Doubleday, Page & Company,
1920. 284 p., front., [3] leaves of plates.
LC: Ja 29, '20.
PW: Ja 10, '20.
BLC: London: Hutchinson & Co., [1920].

M-230   The million dollar mystery / novelized from the
scenario of F. Lonergan, by Harold MacGrath . . . ;
profusely illustrated with scenes from the photoplay.
New York: Grosset & Dunlap, [c1915]. 298, [6] p.,
photo. front., [57] leaves of photo. plates.
"Harold MacGrath; a sketch of the author at work
and at play": p. [1]-[6] at end.
LC: Mr 15, '15.
PW: Jl 3, '15.

M-231   The pagan madonna / by Harold MacGrath;
frontispiece by W. H. D. Koerner. Garden City, N.
Y.; Toronto: Doubleday, Page & Company, 1921.
287, [1] p., col. front.
LC: My 23, '21.
PW: Ag 18, '23.

M-232   Parrot & co. / by Harold MacGrath;
illustrations in color by Andre Castaigne, and black
and white by Arthur William Brown. Indianapolis:
The Bobbs-Merrill Company, [c1913]. 305, [1] p.,
col. front., [20] leaves of plates (some col.).
LC: Je 4, '13.
PW: Je 7, '13.

M-233   Pidgin island / by Harold MacGrath; illustrated
by Arthur William Brown. Indianapolis: The
Bobbs-Merrill Company, [c1914]. 340, [1] p., front.,
[5] leaves of plates.
LC: Ap 2, '14.
PW: Ap 4, '14.

M-234   The place of honeymoons / by Harold
MacGrath . . . ; with illustrations by Arthur I. Keller.
Indianapolis: The Bobbs-Merrill Company, [c1912].
378 p., front., [3] leaves of plates.
LC: O 29, '12.
PW: O 19, '12.

M-235   The princess elopes / by Harold MacGrath.
Indianapolis: The Bobbs-Merrill Company, [1905].
207, [1] p., front. [Ill. by Harrison Fisher.]
On cover: The pocket books.
PW: Ap 29, '05.

M-236   ____ The private wire to Washington: the inside story of the great Long Island spy mystery that baffled the secret service / by Harold MacGrath; illustrated by C. H. Taffs. New York; London: Harper & Brothers, [1919]. 236, [1] p., col. front., [3] leaves of col. plates.
LC: Mr 8, '19.
PW: Mr 8, '19.

M-237   ____ The puppet crown / by Harold MacGrath; the illustrations by R. Martine Reay. Indianapolis: The Bowen-Merrill Company, [c1901]. 436 p., front., [3] leaves of plates.
PW: Ap 13, '01.
BLC: London: B. F. Stevens & Brown; Brooklyn, N. Y. printed, [1901].

M-238   ____ The ragged edge / by Harold MacGrath; frontispiece by George W. Gage. -- 1st ed. -- Garden City, N. Y.; Toronto: Doubleday, Page & Company, 1922. 313, [1] p., front.
LC: F 16, '22.
PW: F 18, '22.
BLC: London: Hodder & Stoughton; Garden City, N. Y. printed, [1922].

M-239   ____ A splendid hazard / by Harold MacGrath; with illustrations by Howard Chandler Christy. Indianapolis: The Bobbs-Merrill Company, [c1910]. 370 p., col. front., [4] leaves of col. plates.
LC: Je 4, '10.
PW: Je 4, '10.
BLC: London: Ward, Lock & Co., 1910.

M-240   ____ The voice in the fog / by Harold MacGrath . . . ; with illustrations by A. B. Wenzell. Indianapolis: The Bobbs-Merril Company, [c1915]. 278, [1] p., front., [6] leaves of plates.
LC: F 10, '15.
PW: F 13, '15.

M-241   ____ The world outside / by Harold MacGrath. Garden City, N. Y.: Doubleday, Page & Company, 1923. 332 p.
LC: Ap 26, '23.
BLC: London: John Long, 1924.

M-242   ____ The yellow typhoon / by Harold MacGrath; illustrated by Will Grefé. New York; London: Harper & Brothers, [c1919]. 294, [1] p., front., [1] leaf of plates.
LC: O 11, '19.
PW: N 1, '19.
BLC: London: Hodder & Stoughton, [1923].

McGrath, J. Ice carvings. In *The best college short stories, 1924-1925* (1925), **B-558**.

M-243   MacGregor, Hector. The Souter's lamp / by Hector MacGregor. Chicago; New York; Toronto, etc.: Fleming H. Revell Company, [1903]. 272 p.
Contents: The Souter's lamp -- The placing of Tammas Rattray, Beadle and grave-digger -- Mrs. Carment's new prayer -- Crookit Sol -- The De'il's bairn -- The English Gauger -- The Queen's Birthday -- The Candle on the Brae -- Stickit Saunie -- The Athole Gathering -- A year's revealing.
BLC: Edinburgh; London: Oliphant & Co., 1903.

M-244   McGregor, W. Burns (William Burns), b. 1856. Sowing and reaping / by W. Burns McGregor. New York: Peter G. Boyle . . . , [c1922]. 300 p. **WVK**
PW: Mr 24, '23.

MacHarg, William, b. 1872, jt. aut. *The achievements of Luther Trant* (1910). See **Balmer Edwin, 1883-1959, jt. aut., B-125.**

M-245   ____ The blind man's eyes / by William MacHarg and Edwin Balmer; with illustrations by Wilson C. Dexter. Boston: Little, Brown and Company, 1916. 368 p., front., [3] leaves of plates.
BLC: London: Eveleigh Nash Co.; Boston, U. S. A. [printed], 1916.

M-246   ____ The Indian drum / by William MacHarg and Edwin Balmer; with frontispiece by W. T. Benda. Boston: Little, Brown, and Company, 1917. 367 p., front.
LC: O 9, '17.
PW: O 6, '17.
BLC: London: Stanley Paul & Co., 1919.

M-247   ____ Peewee / by William MacHarg . . . Chicago: The Reilly & Lee Co., 1922, [c1921]. 276 p.
LC: Mr 24, '22.
PW: Mr 11, '22.

M-248   ____ The Surakarta / by William MacHarg and Edwin Balmer . . . ; illustrated by Lester Ralph. Boston: Small, Maynard & Company, [c1913]. 369 p., front., [4] leaves of plates.
LC: S 20, '13.
PW: S 13, '13.

McHenry, May. Deepwater politics. In *Politics* (1901), **P-461**.

McHugh, Hugh, pseud. See **Hobart, George Vere, 1867-1926.**

MacIntosh, Marian T. Her masterpiece. In *A book of Bryn Mawr stories* (1901), **B-732**.

M-249   McIntyre, John Thomas, 1871-1951. Ashton-Kirk, criminologist / by John T. McIntyre . . . ; illustrations by Ralph L. Boyer. Philadelphia: The Penn Publishing Company, 1918. 332 p., front., [3] leaves of plates.
LC: Jl 16, '18.
PW: O 26, '18.
BLC: London: G. H. Robinson & J. Birch, 1921.

M-250   ____ Ashton-Kirk, investigator / by John T, McIntyre . . . illustrations by Ralph L. Boyer. Philadelphia: The Penn Publishing Co., 1910. 336 p., col. front., [3] leaves of plates. **TXU**
LC: S 8, '10.
PW: D 3, '10.
BLC: London: G. H. Robinson & J. Birch, 1921.

M-251   ____ Ashton-Kirk, secret agent / by John T. McIntyre; illustrations by Ralph L. Boyer. Philadelphia: The Penn Publishing Company, 1912. 332 p., col. front., [3] leaves of plates.

LC: S 5, '12.
PW: Ag 3, '12.
BLC: London: C. Palmer & Hayward, 1916.

M-252 _____ Ashton-Kirk, special detective / by John T.
McIntyre; illustrations by Ralph L. Boyer.
Philadelphia: The Penn Publishing Company, 1914.
320 p., col. front., [3] leaves of plates.
LC: Jl 25, '14.
PW: O 10, '14.

M-253 _____ Blowing weather / by John T. McIntyre. New
York; London: The Century Co., 1923. 407 p.
LC: F 27, '23.
PW: Mr 3, '23.
BLC: London: Duckworth & Co., 1923.

M-254 _____ In the dead of night / by John T. McIntyre;
with illustrations by Frances Rogers. Philadelphia;
London: J. B. Lippincott Company, 1908. 292 p.,
col. front., [3] leaves of plates.
LC: Ap 13, '08.
PW: My 9, '08.
BLC: London: Ward, Lock & Co., 1909.

M-255 _____ The ragged edge: a tale of ward life & politics
/ by John T. McIntyre. New York: McClure,
Phillips & Co., 1902. 304 p.
(Lettered on cover: First novel series.)
PW: S 20, '02.

M-256 _____ A young man's fancy / by John T. McIntyre.
New York: Frederick A. Stokes Company, 1925.
174 p.
LC: Ap 11, '25.
PW: Ap 11, '25.

M-257 McIntyre, Robert, 1851-1914. A modern Apollos /
by Robert McIntyre. Cincinnati; Chicago; Kansas
City: Jennings & Pye; New York: Eatons & Mains,
[c1901]. 371 p.
PW: O 12, '01.

M-258 MacIntyre, William Irwin, b. 1882. Colored soldiers
/ by W. Irwin MacIntyre. Macon, Georgia: J. W.
Burke, 1923. 96 p., photo. front.

M-259 McIvor, Allan. The bride of Glendearg: a novel / by
Allan McIvor. New York: W. J. Ritchie, 1904.
318 p.
PW: Ap 16, '04.

M-260 _____ The mechanic / by Allan McIvor. New York:
William Ritchie, [c1906]. 300 p.
PW: My 19, '06.
BLC: London: Alexander Moring, [1906].

M-261 _____ The overlord: the story of the peons of Canada
/ by Allan McIvor . . . New York: William Ritchie,
[c1904]. 422, [1] p.
PW: D 3, '04.

M-262 MacIvor, Mary A. The upper trail / by Mary A.
MacIvor. Boston: Roxburgh Publishing Company
Incorporated, [c1912]. 326 p., photo. front., [3]
leaves of photo. plates.
LC: My 17, '12.

M-263 Mack, Thomas. The greatest man on earth / by
Thomas Mack . . . St. Louis, Mo.; London: B.
Herder Book Co., 1925. 261 p.
Contents: The greatest man on earth -- The watch invisible -- The
dark morass -- The final adjustment -- Sentimentalists -- The cheerless
giver.

M-264 Mack, Willard, 1878-1934. Anybody's property / by
Willard Mack . . . New York: The Macaulay
Company, 1917. 298 p.

M-265 Mackall, Lawton, b. 1888. Scrambled eggs / by
Lawton Mackall; with illustrations by Oliver Herford.
Cincinnati: Stewart & Kidd Company, [c1920]. 63,
[1] p., front., [4] leaves of plates.
PW: Ap 24, '20.

M-266 Mackay, Helen Gansevoort Edwards, 1876-1961.
Accidentals / by Helen Mackay. New York:
Duffield & Company, 1915. 320 p.
90 very short stories written in France at the advent
of World War I (1914).
LC: My 29, '15.
PW: Je 12, '15.
BLC: London: Andrew Melrose, [1915].

M-267 _____ Chill hours / by Helen Mackay. New York:
Duffield and Company, 1920. 191 p.   **IWA**
Contents: At the end -- Odette in pink taffeta -- Their places -- The
second hay -- One or another -- The cauldron -- Nostalgia -- Madame
Anna -- The little cousin of No. 12 -- "He cost us so much" -- "Here
are the shadows!" -- She who would not eat soup -- The vow --"I take
pen in hand" -- Footsteps -- The 9 and the 10 -- The moment.
LC: F 21, '20.
PW: My 1, '20.
BLC: London: Andrew Melrose, 1919.

M-268 _____ The cobweb cloak / by Helen MacKay . . . ;
frontispiece in color by Dugald Stewart Walker. New
York: Duffield & Company, 1912. 308 p., col.
front.
LC: Jl 20, '12.
BLC: London: Andrew Melrose, [1912].

M-269 _____ Half loaves: a story / by Helen Mackay. New
York: Duffield and Company, 1911. 377 p.
LC: Mr 11, '11.
PW: Mr 25, '11.
BLC: London: Chatto & Windus; Cambridge, Mass.
[printed], 1912.

M-270 _____ Houses of glass: stories of Paris / Helen
Mackay; illustrations by E. F. Folsom. New York:
Duffield & Company, [c1909]. 296 p., front.
Contents: Houses of glass -- Eleven ventures -- Thirteen little things
-- Steps of horn and of ivory.
LC: Mr 6, '09.
PW: Mr 20, '09.

M-271 _____ Stories for pictures / Dugald Stewart Walker,
Helen Mackay. New York: Duffield and Company,
1912. 167, [1] p., col. front., [7] leaves of col.
plates, ill. Illustrated end papers.
Stories by Helen Mackay; pictures by Dugald Stewart
Walker.
Contents: Pierrot -- The hills of solitude -- The villa of no name --
The death of a dream -- The painted fields -- White and scarlet -- The
red sun -- The jester and the bubbles -- The arrowy perfume --
Golden tears -- Kind grief -- May -- The white wild goose -- The
parrot and the jester -- The white peacock -- The glow on the

mountains -- The amber clouds -- The crickets -- The city garden -- The fisher of dreams -- Between two cypress trees -- August -- November second -- The little hour -- The dragon fly -- The clear shining -- The little bells -- The lost valley -- The fall and the dance of the leaves -- The gold and jasper key -- The little gray street -- Moon things.
LC: N 4, '12.

M-272 Mackay, Katherine. The stone of destiny / by Katherine Mackay. New York; London: Harper & Brothers, 1904. 111, [1] p.
PW: F 20, '04.

M-273 McKay-Smith, Virginia. The little grey lady / by Virginia MacKay-Smith. New York: Edwin S. Gorham, 1914. 54 p. **DLC**

M-274 MacKaye, Harold Steele, 1866-1928. The panchronicon / by Harold Steele MacKaye. New York: Charles Scribner's Sons, 1904. 350 p.
PW: Ap 23, '04.

M-275 ____ The winged helmet / by Harold Steele MacKaye . . . ; illustrated by H. C. Edwards. Boston: L. C. Page & Company, 1905. 389 p., front., [5] leaves of plates.
PW: Mr 4, '05.
BLC: London: Dean & Son, [1905].

M-276 McKean, Thomas, 1869-1942. The master influence: a novel / by Thomas McKean; with illustrations in color by Will Grefé. Philadelphia; London: J. B. Lippincott Company, 1908. 308 p., col. front., [2] leaves of col. plates.
PW: My 9, '08.

M-277 ____ The mercy of fate / by Thomas McKean. New York: Wessels & Bissell Co., 1910. 366 p.
LC: S 26, '10.
PW: O 8, '10.

M-278 ____ The vortex: a novel / by Thomas McKean. Philadelphia; London: J. B. Lippincott Company, 1905. 324 p.
PW: S 16, '05.

M-279 McKee, Mabel Anne, b. 1886. The heart of the rose / by Mabel A. McKee. New York; Chicago; Toronto; London; Edinburgh: Fleming H. Revell Company, [c1913]. 44 p.
LC: O 22, '13.

McKeehan, Irene P. A college play. In *Minnesota stories* (1903), **M-842**.

M-280 McKenna, John J. Stories of the Sun Worshipers Club of McKinley Park: in their political tales and reminiscences / by the original "Jawn" McKenna from "Archy Road." Chicago: [John F. Higgins], 1918. 246 p.
Contents: Fourth of July oration by Barney O'Flynn before the Sun Worshipers Club in McKinley Park -- A "grave" mistake -- A tribute to McKenna -- Mrs. Jim Kennedy attends a meeting at Baker's Hall and tells McKenna what she thinks of their goings on -- Nicholas Ryan, The club's statistician, induces Mrs. Jim Kennedy to address a meeting of the affiliated Republican clubs of the fifth ward at Baker's Hall, and she tells them something -Dennis Dwyer on the necessity of preparedness, practically demonstrated -- Conditions created by the war cloud plays havoc with Pat Price's 35th precinct club -- Danny McManus of the 41st precinct on the removal of the hyphen -- A war

reflection [poem] -- Old "Turrence" Dougherty's oration before the Sun Worshipper's Club at McKinley Park -- Continuance of Old Dougherty's oration -Conclusion of Old Dougherty's discourse -- The war is a bad omen for Pat English and his affiliated club -- The diplomacy of Tom Sheehan, the buffet keeper of Archer Road -- Jerry Duggan, president of the 40th precinct Republican club, in confab with McKenna -- Speech delivered by old man Anthony Devlin after taking two sups of Sheehan's whiskey -- Little Johnnie's inquiry [poem] -- Thoughts of the hour [poem] -- Young Dougherty, the lawyer, on practical government and Nicholas Ryan's views on a few other things -- More truth than poetry [poem] -- Ryan on loyalty to the flag -- Pat Price before the Sun Worshipers Club at the McKinley Park on his return from vacation. His fish story is good -- Ryan, the statistican, and McKenna in conversation -- Barney Mulligan, the far-down linen peddler, on the money question -- Ryan induces Mulligan to continue his discourse on the money question -- Lamentations of the pessimist members of the fifth ward Republican club [poem] -- The Eagle Society's picnic has its effect on Mac's orators. He tells his own story -- Ryan on press and politics -- Lamentations of the Old Friends' Club [poem] -- Pat Price and Barney O'Flynn on the good old days in politics -- The days of real sport [poem] -- Ryan and McKenna in conversation -- A few stories by members of the Sun Worshipers Club on old days in politics -- Toast to our flag [poem] -- McKenna in reminiscences of the Chicago fire of 1871 -- One of the Sun Worshipers gone to meet his reward -- Chicago as it looked in other days -- Nicholas Ryan in a patriotic mood -- Mind pictures [poem] -- Anthony Devlin on the old days in politics -- McKenna's candidacy for chaplain -- "Time's are changed" -- Dwyer to Mac -- Members of the Sun Worshipers Club in confab -- A Christmas wake story from the Brighton -- They have got Ryan guessing -- Old Anthony Devlin airs his views -- The old days in Halsted street -- Jerry Duggan airing his views -- Con O'Brien, the 41st precinct philosopher -- Dougherty's St. Patrick's Day -- Old Anthony Devlin in a reminiscent mood.

M-281 McKenzie, Alexander, b. 1872. A stage baby: the romance of a trouper / Alexander McKenzie; illustrated by R. G. Chandler. Worcester, Massachusetts: The Franklin Company, 1915. 96 p. **DLC**
LC: Jl 14, '15.

M-282 Mackenzie, Cameron, 1882-1921. The man who tried to be it / by Cameron Mackenzie; frontispiece by Alonzo Kimball. New York: George H. Doran Company, [c1917]. 146 p., col. front.
LC: Mr 13, '17.
PW: Mr 17, '17.

M-283 ____ Mr. and Mrs. Pierce: a story of youth / by Cameron Mackenzie; with illustrations by Alonzo Kimball. New York: Dodd, Mead and Company, 1916. 404 p., front., [7] leaves of plates.
LC: Ap 18, '16.
PW: Ap 15, '16.

M-284 Mackenzie, Jean Kenyon, 1874-1936. The story of a fortunate youth: chapters from the biography of an elderly gentleman / by Jean Kenyon Mackenzie. Boston: The Atlantic Monthly Press, [c1920]. 106 p.
LC: D 27, '20.

M-285 McKibbin, Julia Baldwin. Miriam / by Julia Baldwin McKibbin. Cincinnati: Jennings and Graham; New York: Eaton and Mains, [c1905]. 331 p.
PW: S 30, '05.

Mackie, Pauline Bradford. See **Hopkins, Pauline Bradford (Mackie)**.

M-286 Mackin, Marie. The sylvan portal / by Marie Mackin . . . -- Tourist edition. -- Bismarck, N. D.: Bismarck Book Company, 1925. 247 p., photo. front.

McKinney, Annie Booth, jt. aut. *Mistress Joy* (1901). See **Cooke, Grace MacGowan, 1863-1944, jt. aut., C-727.**

M-287   McKinney, Kate Slaughter, b. 1857. The silent witness: a tale of a Kentucky tragedy / by Kate Slaughter McKinney (Katydid). New York; Washington: The Neale Publishing Company, 1906. 263 p.
LC: D 15, '06.
PW: F 9, '07.

M-288   ____ The weed by the wall / Kate Slaughter McKinney (Katydid). Boston: Richard G. Badger, [c1911]. ([Boston]: The Gorham Press). 175 p.
LC: D 19, '11.
PW: D 23, '11.

M-289   [McKown, Mrs. T. D.] The devil's letters to Mary MacLane / by himself. Chicago: Inter-state Book Company, 1903. 217 p.   **DLC**

M-290   Mackubin, Ellen. A coward and other stories / by Ellen Mackabin. [s. l.]: Florence Mackubin, [191-?]. 252 p.
Reprinted from various periodicals.
Contents: A coward -- A nameless hero -- Texas -- His honor -- A perversion of justice -- Mrs. Jeff -- Rosita -- A public confession -- A life tenant -- The love story of a selfish woman -- The end of a story -- The ordeal of Isabel -- The man from Montana -- A derelict -- Jim Bassett's double -- Oscar Carlyn's job.

Mackubin, Ellen. Rosita. In *Atlantic narratives*; **2nd series (1918), A-361.**

M-291   McLane, Alice Belle. A mother's old love returned / by Alice Belle McLane. Carbondale. illinois: Henry Myers, 1915. 186 p.   **NYP**

M-292   MacLane, Mary, 1881-1929. I, Mary MacLane: a diary of human days / by Mary MacLane . . . New York: Frederick A. Stokes Company, [c1917]. 317 p., photo. front. (port.).

M-293   ____ My friend Annabel Lee / by Mary MacLane. Chicago: Herbert S. Stone and Company, 1903. 262 p., front. (port.).

M-294   [____] The story of Mary MacLane / by herself. Chicago: Herbert S. Stone and Company, 1902. 322 p., photo. front. (port.)

M-295   MacLaren, Edwin. The triangle of terror / by Edwin MacLaren. [Chicago: s. n., ca. 1922.] 64 p.
A reference in text implies the date of publication.
"Supplement to Detective tales, Chicago."

M-296   McLaughlin, Robert H. The eternal Magdalene / by Robert H. McLaughlin. New York: George H. Doran Company, [c1915]. 300 p.
LC: D 29, '15.
PW: Ja 8, '16.

M-297   McLaughlin, Robert W. (Robert William), 1866-1936. Caleb Matthews: an idyl of the Maine coast / by Robert W. McLaughlin . . . New York: Eaton & Mains; Cincinnati: Jennings & Graham,

[c1913]. 83 p., photo. front., [2] leaves of photo. plates.   **OSU, ZBK**
LC: Je 20, '13.
PW: Je 21, '13.

M-298   McLaughlin, W. J., Mrs. The diary of a Utah girl / by Mrs. W. J. McLaughlin. New York: Broadway Publishing Co., [c1911]. 159 p., front., [7] leaves of plates. [Ill. by Wm. L. Hudson.]

M-299   McLaurin, Kate L. The least resistance / by Kate L. McLaurin. New York: George H. Doran Company, [c1916]. 374 p. Illustrated end papers signed by May Wilson Preston.   **VA@**
PW: My 27, '16.

M-300   McLaws, Lafayette. Jezebel: a romance in the days when Ahab was king of Israel / by Lafayette McLaws; illustrated by Corwin K. Linson. Boston: Lothrop Publishing Company, [1902]. 490 p., front., [3] leaves of plates.
PW: Jl 5, '02.
BLC: London: Archibald Constable & Co., [1902].

M-301   ____ Maid of Athens / by Lafayette McLaws; with illustrations from drawings by Harry C. Edwards. Boston: Little, Brown, and Company, 1906. 285, [1] p., front., [3] leaves of plates.
PW: Mr 24, '06.

M-302   ____ The welding / by Lafayette McLaws . . . Boston: Little, Brown, and Company, 1907. 360 p.
LC: O 24, '07.
PW: N 2, '07.

M-303   ____ When the land was young: being the true romance of Mistress Antoinette Huguenin and Captain Jack Middleton in the days of the buccaneers / by Lafayette McLaws; illustrated by Will Crawford. Boston: Lothrop Publishing Company, [c1901]. 383 p., front., [6] leaves of plates.
PW: Ag 24, '01.
BLC: London: Archibald Constable & Co., [1901].

M-304   MacLean, Charles Agnew, 1880-1928. "Here's to the day!" / by Charles Agnew MacLean and Frank Blighton. New York: George H. Doran Company, [c1915]. 314 p.
LC: F 19, '15.
BLC: London: Hodder & Stoughton; U. S. A. printed, 1915.

M-305   ____ The mainspring / by Charles Agnew Maclean; with illustrations by Edmund Frederick. Boston: Little, Brown, and Company, 1912. 313 p., front., [3] leaves of plates.
LC: My 7, '12.
PW: My 4, '12.

M-306   McLean, Eddie. The sweet old days in Dixie / by Eddie McLean. Raleigh, N. C.: Edwards & Broughton Printing Company, 1907. 180 p.   **SUC**

MacLean, Malcolm A. The reason why. In *Minnesota stories* (1903), **M-842.**

M-307 Maclean, Stuart, b. 1872. Alexis: a story of love and music / by Stuart Maclean. New York; London: D. Appleton and Company, 1917. 307, [1] p.
LC: Ag 27, '17.
PW: S 8, '17.

M-308 McLeod, A. J. (Arthur James). The notary of Grand Pré: a historic tale of Acadia / by A. J. McLeod. Boston: Published by the author, 1901. 152 p. Designed end papers.

M-309 McLeod, Christian. The heart of the stranger: a story of Little Italy / by Christian McLeod. New York; Chicago; Toronto; London; Edinburgh: Fleming H. Revell Company, [c1908]. 221 p., photo. front., [7] leaves of photo. plates.

M-310 MacLeod, Della Campbell. A lantern of love: a novel in three parts / by Della MacLeod. Boston; New York: Houghton Mifflin Company, 1921. (Cambridge: The Riverside Press). 307, [1] p.
LC: Ag 1, '21.
PW: Jl 30, '21.

M-311 ____ The maiden manifest / by Della Campbell MacLeod; with illustrations by Harriet Roosevelt Richards. Boston: Little, Brown, and Company, 1913. 356 p., front., [3] leaves of plates.
LC: F 20, '13.
PW: F 15, '13.

M-312 ____ The swan and the mule: a novel / by Della MacLeod. Boston; New York: Houghton Mifflin Company, 1922. (Cambridge: The Riverside Press). 301 p.
LC: S 29, '22.
PW: Ap 28, '23.

M-313 McLintock, Minda A., b. 1856. Daddy Damm's kin-folks: Rx good for grouch / McLintock. Saint Louis, Mo.: [s. n.], [c1915]. 133 p., front., [9] leaves of plates. [Ill. by Robert A. McLintock.] **OSU, IMF**
LC: S 20, '15.

M-314 McMahan, Anna Benneson. Shakespeare's Christmas gift to Queen Bess in the year 1596 / by Anna Benneson McMahan. Chicago: A. C. McClurg & Co., 1907. 68 p., [18] leaves of plates.
PW: O 12, '07.

M-315 MacMahon, Henry. Orphans of the storm: a complete novel / from D. W. Griffith's motion picture epic on the immortal theme of The two orphans; novelized by Henry MacMahon; illustrated with scenes from the photo-play. New York: Grosset & Dunlap, [c1922]. 194 p., photo. front., [11] leaves of photo. plates.
LC: Ap 29, '22.

M-316 ____ The Ten commandments: a novel / by Henry MacMahon; from Jeanie MacPherson's story; produced by Cecil B. De Mille as the celebrated Paramount picture "The Ten commandments"; illustrated with scenes from the photoplay. New York: Grosset & Dunlap, [c1924]. 236 p., photo. front., [7] leaves of photo. plates. Illustrated end

papers.
LC: Ag 22, '24.

M-317 McMahon, John O. The million dollar prize / by John O. McMahon. Syracuse, N. Y.: s. n., 1901. 25 p.   **DLC** (photocopy)

M-318 McMahon, John Robert, b. 1875. Toilers and idlers: a novel / by John R. McMahon. New York: Published by Wilshire Book Company, [c1907]. 195 p., front.
LC: O 14, '07.
PW: D 7, '07.

M-319 McManus, Thomas J. L., b. 1852. The boy and the outlaw: a tale of John Brown's raid on Harper's Ferry / by Thomas J. L. McManus. New York: The Grafton Press, [1904]. 408 p., col. front., [1] leaf of plates. [Ill. by Edwin Betts.]

M-320 McMaster, John Bach, 1889-1915. The kidder: and other tales / by John Bach McMaster, Jr. Philadelphia: Printed by George W. Jacobs & Co., [c1915]. 343 p., front. (port.).
Contents: The kidder -- His own kind -- Dutch courage -- For better or worse -- The outcast -- The substitute -- On Gittings' farm -- The race -- The trial by fire -- Death us do part -- The wreck of the Alfred -- A wreck on the Great Lakes -- The man who didn't count -- Pierre Ranco, madman -- Bread upon the waters -- The scarred rifle -- Was he a coward? -- A chickadee's christmas.

M-321 McMasters, William Henry. Revolt: an American novel / by William H. McMasters; illustrated by Haydon Jones. Boston: David D. Nickerson & Company, [c1919]. 281 p., incl. front., [3] leaves of plates.

M-322 MacMillan, Georgette. The woman in mauve: a love story / by Georgette MacMillan. New York City: Chelsea House, [c1925]. 256 p.
PW: D 19, '25.

M-323 McMillan, Jennie. The mocking bird's breed / by Jennie McMillan. New York: Robert J. Shores, [c1918]. 293 p., front.   **EMU**

M-324 MacMillar, Jude, *pseud.* A random shaft . . . / by Jude MacMillar [pseud.]. Boston, Mass.: The C. M. Clark Publishing Co., 1908. 191 p., front., [7] leaves of plates.
Unexamined copy: bibliographic data from NUC.
LC: My 5, '08.
PW: Je 6, '08.

M-325 McMurdy, Robert, b. 1860. The upas tree / by Robert McMurdy; illustrations by William Ottman. Chicago: F. J. Schulte & Company; [London: B. F. Stevens & Brown, c1912]. 324 p., incl. front., [3] leaves of plates.
Includes *Beckwith's confession*, p. 297-324.

M-326 MacMurphy, Harriet Sherrill (Dakin), b. 1849. Meumbane; a story of the Fontenelles / by Harriet S. MacMurphy; illustrations by Robert F. Gilder . . . [Omaha: Festner Printing Co., c1915]. 15, [1] p., ill.   **WIH**

M-327　McMurtrie, Douglas C. (Douglas Crawford), 1888-1944. Dorothy's idea / by Douglas C. McMurtrie; illustrated by Marjorie Collins. New York City: [s. n.], 1910. 15 p., ill.

M-328　McNally, William James, b. 1891. The barb / by William J. McNally. New York; London: G. P. Putnam's Sons, 1923. ([New York]: The Knickerbocker Press). 389 p.
LC: Mr 27, '23.

M-329　McNealus, Virginia Q. (Virginia Quitman), b. 1856. The lay of the land: a collection of short stories / by Virginia Q. McNealus. New York: The Neale Publishing Company, 1916. 178 p.
Contents: An old coast idyl -- A vindication of home rules -- Sis Fluridy's cakewalk -- An apostle of a new dispensation -- In the hands of the Philistines -- From Dan to Beersheba -- A revolt of the quill -- Below the salt -- A premature fact.
PW: O 14, '16.

M-330　McNeely, Marian Hurd, 1877-1930. When she came home from college / by Marian Kent Hurd and Jean Bingham Wilson; with illustrations by George Gibbs. Boston; New York: Houghton Mifflin Company, 1909. (Cambridge: The Riverside Press). 272 p., front., [6] leaves of plates.　　**CLE**

M-331　McNeil, Everett, 1862-1929. Fighting with Fremont: a tale of the conquest of California / by Everett McNeil . . . New York: E. P. Dutton & Company, [c1910]. 348 p., front., [4] leaves of plates. [Ill. by D. C. Hutchison.]
LC: S 8, '10.
BLC: London; Edinburgh: W. & R. Chambers, 1911.

M-332　____ The lost nation / by Everett McNeil; illustrations by Hugh Spencer. New York: E. P. Dutton & Co., [c1918]. 335 p., incl. front., incl. [4] leaves of plates.
LC: O 30, '18.
BLC: London; Edinburgh: W. & R. Chambers, 1906.

M-333　____ The totem of Black Hawk: a tale of pioneer days in northwestern Illinois and the Black Hawk War / by Everett McNeil . . . ; illustrated by Henry S. Watson. Chicago: A. C. McClurg & Co., 1914. 369 p., front., [7] leaves of plates.　　**JFK**
LC: O 28, '14.

M-334　McNulty, William J. The north land / by William J. McNulty. Boston, U. S. A.: The Christopher Publishing House, [c1925]. 104 p.　　**DLC**

McPeak, Ival. Knowing dad. In *Stories from the Midland* (1924), S-984.

M-335　MacQueen, Glenroie. Where woman gleaned / by Glenroie MacQueen. Chicago, Ill.: The Winona Publishing Company, [c1907]. 604 p., front. (port.).

M-336　McRa, Duncan, b. 1863. The quaint family of three / by Duncan McRa. Charleston, W. Va., U. S. A.: Tribune Company Print, [1902]. 71, [1] p.　　**WVU**

M-337　McReynolds, Robert, d. 1928. He willed it so, or, The story of Rodney Wilkes / by Col. Robert McReynolds . . . [Lincoln, Neb.]: Press of Western Newspaper Union, 1901. 176 p., photo. front., incl. [9] plates (some photo. by App-Stott of Denver.)

M-338　____ Where strongest tide winds blew / by Robert McReynolds. Colorado Springs, Colo.: Gowdy-Simmons Publishing Co., 1907. 248 p., front., [4] leaves of plates, ill.
LC: My 17, '07.
PW: Jl 6, '07.

McTague, Stephen J. The romance of an inventor. In *The Tragedy that wins and other short stories (1905), T-343.*

M-339　Macvane, Edith, b. 1878. The adventures of Joujou / by Edith Macvane; with fifteen illustrations in color by Frank Ver Beck and decorations by Edward Stratton Holloway. Philadelphia; London: J. B. Lippincott Company, 1906. 302 p., col. front., [14] leaves of col. plates.
LC: O 1, '06.

M-340　____ The black flier / by Edith Macvane; with frontispiece by Howard Chandler Christy. New York: Moffat, Yard and Company, 1909. 382 p., col. front.
LC: My 19, '09.

M-341　____ The duchess of dreams / by Edith Macvane; with a frontispiece by Alonzo Kimball. Philadelphia; London: J. B. Lippincott Company, 1908. 307, [1] p., col. front.
PW: My 9, '08.
BLC: London: John Milne, 1908.

M-342　____ Her word of honor / by Edith Macvane; with illustrations by Frank Snapp. Boston: Little, Brown, and Company, 1912. 289 p., front., [5] leaves of plates.
LC: My 2, '12.
PW: Ap 27, '12.

M-343　____ Tarantella / Edith Macvane. Boston; New York: Houghton Mifflin Company, [1911]. (Cambridge: The Riverside Press). 255, [1] p., col. front. [Ill. by A. G. Learned.]
LC: O 18, '11.
BLC: London: Hurst & Blackett, 1912.

M-344　____ The thoroughbred / by Edith MacVane; illustrated by Charles Grunwald. New York: G. W. Dillingham Company, [c1909]. 303 p., front., [3] leaves of plates.　　**NYP**
LC: Mr 29, '09.
PW: Mr 20, '09.

McVickar, Harry Whitney, b. 1860. The reprisal. In *Shapes that haunt the dusk (1907), S-339.*

M-345　____ Reptiles / by Henry W. McVickar; illustrated by his own hand. [New York]: D. Appleton & Co., 1905. 208 p., front., [10] leaves of plates, ill.

M-346 McVickar, Henry Goelet. A parish of two; Douglas Dayton letters by Henry Goelet McVickar, Percy Dashiel letters by Percy Collins. Boston: Lothrop, Lee & Shepard Co., [1903]. 417 p.

M-347 McVoy, Ruth Shartel. The traitor's son: a novel / by Ruth Shartel McVoy. New York: The Neale Publishing Company, 1915. 306 p.
LC: N 15, '15.

M-348 McWhorter, J. C. (John Camillus), b. 1866. "The scout of the Buckhannon": an historical romance of western Virginia border: 1764-1782 / by J. C. McWhorter. [Buckhannon, W. Va.: s. n., c1924.] 143 p., front., [12] leaves of plates. [Ill. by Colista M. Dowling.]   **KUK**

M-349 McWilliams, Helen Hill. A bit o' silence / by Helen Hill McWilliams; illustrated from photographs by Frederick S. Franklin. Buffalo: The McDowell Press, 1912. 175 p., front., [7] leaves of plates.
PVU

M-350 Madden, Eva Annie, b. 1863. Two royal foes / by Eva Madden; illustrations by the Kinneys. New York: The McClure Company, 1907. 343 p., front., [3] leaves of plates.
LC: O 16, '07.

M-351 Maddox, Pearl Graves. The precipice / by Pearl Groves Maddox. Baltimore, Md.: The McLean Co., Publishers, 1917. 153 p., photo. front.   **NYP**

M-352 Made to order: short stories from a college course / selected by Howard Maynadier. New York: Lloyd Adams Noble, 1915. 309 p.
A collection of class-room stories written by students in English 22, Dr. Maynadier's course in composition at Harvard college.
Contents: The lady in gray / Harold Amory -- The dice decide / R. G. Carter -- Good-bye, Vera / Gerald Courtney -- That day in Africa / Duncan Dana -- People don't do such things / Gordon Lamont -- The iron band / Albert F. Leffingwell -- A young man in wrong / Philip R. Mechem -- Happily ever after / Edward C. Park -- The gran'son crew / Charles C. Petersen -- Our sphinx / William E. Shea -- The six twenties / George C. Smith, Jr. -- The balance / Richard B. Southgate -- The grip of the tropics / Leonard Wood, Jr.

M-353 Madison, Lucy Foster, 1865-1932. Bee and Butterfly: a tale of two cousins / by Lucy Foster Madison; illustrated by Adelia B. Beard. Chicago: M. A. Donohue & Co., [c1913]. 328 p., front.
LC: My 22, '13.

M-354 ____ A daughter of the Union / by Lucy Foster Madison . . . ; illustrated by Clyde O. Deland. Philadelphia: The Penn Publishing Company, 1903. 344 p., front., [6] leaves of plates.

M-355 ____ A maid of Salem towne / by Lucy Foster Madison . . . illustrated by Frank T. Merrill. Philadelphia: The Penn Publishing Company, 1906. 315 p., front., [6] leaves of plates.
Unexamined copy: bibliographic data from NUC.
PW: N 17, '06.

M-356 [Magill, Harry Byron], b. 1872. The time, the place and the girl / by Ben Boston [pseud.]. Chicago:

Yellowstone Park Publishing Company, 1908. 62 p., incl. front., plates, ill.
Unexamined copy: bibliographic data from OCLC, #18651166.

M-357 Magill, H. B. (Henry B.). The love confessions of a traveling man / by H. B. Magill. Chicago: The Chicago Press, 1906. 110 p., photo. front., [1] leaf of plates, ill. [Ill. by H. Putnam Hall.]

M-358 Magistrate, Mrs. When Teddy swings his stick / by Mrs. Magistrate. Houston, Tex.: Gulf Publishing Company, [c1905]. 79 p.
Unexamined copy: bibliographic data from OCLC, #2707365.

M-359 Magoun, Jeanne Bartholow. The light / by Jeanne Bartholow Magoun. New York: Mitchell Kennerley, 1911. 63 p.
PW: F 24, '12.

M-360 ____ The mission of Victoria Wilhelmenia / by Jeanne Barlow Magoun. New York: B. W. Huebsch, 1912. 146 p.   **CKM**
PW: My 11, '12.
BLC: London: G. P. Putnam's Sons; New York: B. W. Huebsch, 1912.

M-361 Magruder, Julia, 1854-1907. Her husband: the mystery of a man / by Julia Magruder; with illustrations by Lucius Wolcott Hitchcock. Boston: Small, Maynard and Company, [c1911]. 474 p., col. front., [5] leaves of plates.
LC: N 7, '11.
PW: D 30, '11.
BLC: London: Grant Richards; Cambridge, U. S. A. printed, 1912.

M-362 ____ A sunny southerner / by Julia Magruder. Boston: L. C. Page & Company, 1901. 194 p., front., [10] leaves of plates. [Ill. by Henry S. Hubbell.]
PW: Je 1, '01.

M-363 Magruder, Mary Lanier. Wages / by Mary Lanier Magruder. New York; London: Harper & Brothers, 1924. 308 p.

Maher, Richard Aumerle. Dona Leanor De Bobadilla. In *The friendly little house: and other stories* (1910), F-432.

M-364 ____ Gold must be tried by fire / by Richard Aumerle Maher . . . New York: The Macmillan Company, 1917. 303 p., front. [Ill. by J. Henry.]
LC: Ap 12, '17.
PW: Ap 21, '17.

M-365 ____ The heart of a man / by Richard Aumerle Maher. New York; Cincinnati; Chicago: Benziger Brothers, c1915. 414 p., front. [Ill. by Frank McKernan.]
LC: S 10, '15.
PW: S 25, '15.
BLC: London: Sir I. Pitman & Sons; printed in U. S. A., 1915.

M-366   ____ The hills of desire / by Richard Aumerle Maher. New York: The Macmillan Company, 1919. 257 p.
LC: Ap 30, '19.
PW: My 3, '19.

M-367   [____] The mantilla / by Richard Aumerle [pseud.]. St. Louis, Mo.; Freiburg (Baden), Germany; London: Published by B. Herder, 1913. 270 p.   **DLC**
LC: Ap 28, '13.
PW: Je 7, '13.

M-368   ____ The shepherd of the North / by Richard Aumerle Maher. New York: The Macmillan Company, 1916. 342 p.
LC reports col. front.
LC: Mr 2, '16.
PW: Mr 25, '16.
BLC: London: Macmillan & Co.; printed in U. S. A., 1916.

M-369   ____ While shepherds watched / by Richard Aumerle Maher; decorations by Charles R. Stevens. New York: The Macmillan Company, 1917. 159 p., col. front. Designed end papers.
LC: O 11, '17.
PW: N 3, '17.

M-370   ____ The works of Satan / by Richard Aumerle Maher. New York: The Macmillan Company, 1921. 370 p.
LC: S 7, '21.
PW: O 1, '21.

M-371   Maher, Stephen J. (Steven John), 1860-1939. The sister of a certain soldier / by Stephen J. Maher. New Haven: Press of the Tuttle, Morehouse & Taylor Company, 1918. 48 p.

Mahon, George. The progress of a gentleman. In *Clever business sketches* **(1909), C-490.**

M-372   Mahon, Shiela. Irish joy stories / by Shiela Mahon. New York: Mahon Press, 1918. 108 p., photo. front. (port.).   **NYP**
Contents: The unexpected letter -- The Blakes of Ballyvaughan -- The skirl of Irish pipes -- Lady Betty and the Gaelic -- Thady O'Dwyer and the widow -- The keeper of the fairy gold -- Dennis Blake and the leprahawn -- Jimmie Ryan and the fairies.

Mahoney, James. The hat of eight reflections. In *Prize stories of 1923* **(1924), P-621.**

M-373   Majette, Vara A. White-blood / by Vara A. Majette. Boston, Massachusetts: The Stratford Company, 1924. 336 p.   **NIC**
PW: Ja 17, '25.

M-374   Major, Charles, 1856-1913. Dorothy Vernon of Haddon Hall / by Charles Major . . . ; with illustrations by Howard Chandler Christy. New York: The Macmillan Company; London: Macmillan & Co., Ltd., 1902. 369 p., col. front., [7] leaves of plates.
LC: Ap 12, '02.
PW: My 3, '02.
BLC: London: Macmillan & Co., 1902.

References: BAL 13607. BAL also notes copyright printing.

M-375   ____ A forest hearth: a romance of Indiana in the thirties / by Charles Major; with illustrations by Clyde O. De Land. New York: The Macmillan Company; London: Macmillan & Co., Ltd., 1903. 354 p., incl. front., incl. [7] leaves of plates.
PW: O 31, '03.
References: BAL 13609.

M-376   ____ A gentle knight of old Brandenburg / by Charles Major . . . ; illustrated. New York: The Macmillan Company, 1909. 378 p., front., [7] leaves of plates. [Ill. by Howard Pyle.]   **IDU**
LC: O 1, '09.
PW: N 6, '09.
References: BAL 13613.

M-377   ____ Rosalie / by Charles Major. New York: The Macmillan Company, 1925. 331 p.
LC: Je 10, '25.
PW: Je 20, '25.
References: BAL 13619.

M-378   ____ The touchstone of fortune: being the memoir of Baron Clyde, who lived, thrived, and fell in the doleful reign of the so-called Merry Monarch, Charles II / by Charles Major. New York: The Macmillan Company, 1912. 299 p., col. front. [Ill. by Jay Hambidge.]
LC: Mr 22, '12.
PW: Ap 13, '12.
BLC: London: Macmillan & Co.; Norwood, Mass. [printed], 1912.
References: BAL 13617.

M-379   ____ Yolanda: maid of Burgundy / by Charles Major . . . ; with illustrations by Charlotte Weber Ditzler. New York: The Macmillan Company; London: Macmillan & Co., Ltd., 1905. 407 p., front., [4] leaves of plates.
References: BAL 13610.

M-380   Major, Gertrude Keene. The revelation in the mountain / by Gertrude Keene Major; with an introduction by Judge C. C. Goodwin. New York: Cochrane Publishing Co., 1909. 160 p., photo. front. (port.), [6] leaves of plates, ill.

M-381   [Major, Thomas Ambrose], 1875-1943. Suprest in formation: an extravaganza: the adventures of an intellectual hobo on the road to Damascus / written for the edification, enlightenment and entertainment of young ladies and their friends, by a Connoisseur of Universities. [Grand Rapids, Mich.: s. n., 1910?]. 357 p., front., [18] leaves of plates (some photo.), ill.

M-382   Mak, Klarenc Wade, b. 1861. Red Klover / by Klarenc Wade Mak (the fool killer) . . . Kansas City, Missouri, U. S. A.: Published by Dr. Mak & Himself, [c1922]. 432 p., incl. front. (port.).   **KKU**
Contents: The outlaw and suffrajet -- A strange case -- The end of a long trail -- Dr. Nobody from Nowhere -- Joe's baby.
LC: Jl 5, '22.

M-383 Makepeace, Carrie Jane, b. 1849. The whitest man / by Carrie J. Makepeace. Boston: Richard G. Badger, 1905. ([Boston]: The Gorham Press). 195 p.

M-384 Makin, Richard Lawrence. The beaten path: a novel / by Richard Lawrence Makin. New York; London: The Macmillan Company, 1903. 544 p.
PW: O 24, '03.

M-385 Malanotte, Mario, *pseud.* The Medici viola / by Mario Malanotte [pseud.]. New York: Privately Printed By the Author of "The Outer Parallel," "West Point", 1909. 201 p., front.
LC: My 28, '09.

M-386 Malcoskey, Edna Walker. The debutante / by Edna Walker Malcoskey. New York: E. P. Dutton & Company, [c1923]. 220 p.
LC: My 25, '23.
PW: Je 9, '23.

M-387 Malkiel, Theresa Serber. The diary of a shirtwaist striker: a story of the shirtwaist makers' strike in New York / by Theresa Serber Malkiel. New York: The Co-operative Press, [c1910]. 96 p.   **COD**
LC: S 21, '10.
PW: N 5, '10.

M-388 Mallette, Gertrude E. (Gertrude Ethel), b. 1887. Elsewhere land / by Gertrude E. Mallette. [Seattle: Press of the Department of Journalism, University of Washington], 1909. 98 p.
Unexamined copy: bibliographic data from OCLC, #18596081.

M-389 Malloch, Douglas, 1877-1938. Resawed fables / by Douglas Malloch. Chicago: American Lumberman, 1911. 128 p., front.
Contents: Of developing a specialty -- Of going up against the wrong proposition -- Of yielding to temptation -- Of Socrates and the man from Wisconsin -- Of piling it on -- Of the man who welches -- Of keeping the faith -- Of the moving of lumber in Kansas -- Of combining brains and capital -- Of the value of directness -- Of the straw that dislocated the camel's vertebrae -- Of the lumberman's derby -- Of the lumberman by proxy -- Of troubles -- Of the school of experience -- Of patriotism -- Of baseball and business -- Of the wisdom of keeping moving -- Of talking out in meeting -- Of getting an audience -- Of taking a few days off -- Of the point of view -- Of letting loose -- Of swinging back -- Of the gentle game of golf -- Of silence that isn't so golden -- Of what rip saw -- Of Bow Ling Ali and the man with the stump puller -- Of seeing the world -- Of helping others -- Of the light that failed -- Of the sense of touch -- Of the Savate expert and the man with the spiked boots -- Of the three sons who were put to the Arabian test -- Of the reformer reformed -- Of telling you so -- Of the man who was troubled with insomnia -- Of the man who wanted to borrow money -- Of the model young man and the jobs that lingered not -- Of the uses of experience.

M-390 Mallory, Herbert Samuel, 1872-1927. Tempered steel: a romance / by Herbert S. Mallory. New York: R. F. Fenno & Company, [c1909]. 426 p., front.
LC: My 13, '09.

M-391 Malone, Joseph S. Guided and guarded, or, Some incidents in the life of a minister-soldier / by Joseph S. Malone. New York; London; Montreal: The Abbey Press, [c1901]. 221 p.   **OSU, LUU**
PW: Ap 26, '02.

M-392 ____ Sons of vengeance: a tale of the Cumberland highlanders / by Joseph S. Malone. New York; Chicago; Toronto; London; Edinburgh: Fleming H. Revell Company, [c1903]. 299 p., front., [5] leaves of plates. [Ill. by S. M. Palmer.]
PW: O 24, '03.

Maloy, Charles Raymond, b.1873. <u>See</u> **Carew, Roger M., pseud.**

M-393 The man trap: a mystery story. Boston, Mass.: Published by The Riverton Press, 1909. 94 p., [1] p., front., [4] leaves of plates. [Ill. by Sears Gallagher.] "The publishers of this fascinating volume offer $1500 in prizes for the best endings to the story written and sent in by the purchasers of the book."
LC: D 9, '09.

M-394 Manchester, Leslie Clare. The funeral at Egg Hill / by Leslie Clare Manchester. Boston: Sherman, French & Company, 1911. 164 p.

M-395 Maniates, Belle Kanaris. Amarilly in love / by Belle K. Maniates; with illustrations by William Van Dresser. Boston: Little, Brown, and Company, 1917. 280 p., front., [3] leaves of plates.
LC: Ag 22, '17.
PW: Ag 18, '17.
BLC: London: Hodder & Stoughton, 1917.

M-396 ____ Amarilly of Clothes-Line alley / by Belle K. Maniates; with illustrations by J. Henry. Boston: Little, Brown and Company, 1915. 279 p., front., [3] leaves of plates.
LC: F 18, '15.
PW: Ap 24, '15.

M-397 ____ David Dunne: a romance of the Middle West / by Belle Kanaris Maniates; with illustrations by John Drew. Chicago; New York: Rand McNally & Company, [c1912]. 260 p., col. front., [6] leaves of plates.
LC: Je 21, '12.
PW: S 21, '12.

M-398 ____ Mildew manse / by Belle K. Maniates; with illustrations by William Van Dresser. Boston: Little, Brown, and Company, 1916. 240 p., front., [3] leaves of plates.
LC: Ja 21, '16.
PW: Ja 1, '16.

M-399 ____ Our next-door neighbors / by Belle Kanaris Maniates; with illustrations by Tony Sarg. Boston: Little, Brown, and Company, 1917. 280 p., front., ill.
LC: Mr 2, '17.
PW: F 17, '17.

M-400 ____ Penny of Top Hill trail / by Belle Kanaris Maniates; frontispiece by Philip Lyford. Chicago: The Reilly & Lee Co., 1919. 284, [1] p., front.
LC: Mr 3, '19.
PW: F 22, '19.

M-401 ____ Sand holler / by Belle Kanaris Maniates.

Chicago: The Reilly & Lee Co., [c1920]. 302 p.
LC: O 9, '20.
PW: O 23, '20.

M-402 Manlove, Margaret Isabel. Spiritual ship / by
Margaret Isabel Manlove. Los Angeles, California:
[s. n.], 1922. 108 p., front.
"Miscellaneous poems": p. [69]-108.

M-403 Manlove, Oliver Perry. The hospital cap / by Oliver
Perry Manlove. Manhattan: Broadway Publishing
Co., [c1906]. 230 p.   **DLC**
LC: D 12, '06.
PW: Mr 23, '07.

M-404 Mann, Chester. Jester men / by Chester Mann.
Albany, N. Y.: Weed-Parsons Printing Co., 1909.
292 p., front., [19] leaves of plates. [Ill. by Dorothy
Warren.]
LC: D 9, '09.

M-405 Mann, Florian A. (Florian Alexander). The story of
Ponce de Leon: soldier, knight, gentleman: whose
quest for the fountain of youth in the land of Bimini,
led to the discovery of Florida / by Florian A. Mann
. . . DeLand, Fla.: Printed for the author by E. O.
Painter & Company, 1903. 199 p., photo. front.

M-406 Mann, Henry, 1848-1915. Adam Clarke: a story of
the toilers: being a narrative of the experiences of a
family of British emigrants to the United States in
cotton mill, iron foundry, coal mine, and other fields
of labor / by Henry Mann . . . New York: Popular
Book Company, 1904. 280 p.

M-407 Mann, Horace. The world destroyer / by Horace
Mann. Washington, D. C.: The Lucas-Lincoln
Company, [c1903]. 235 p.
[Horace Mann is a pseudonym, real name unknown.]
PW: D 5, '03.

M-408 Mann, Mary Ridpath, b. 1867. The unofficial
secretary / by Mary Ridpath Mann; with illustrations
by F. J. Arting. Chicago: A. C. McClurg & Co.,
1912. 280, [1] p.

M-409 Mann, Oliver Edgecombe, b. 1869. Togo, the
missionary's dog, an autobiography / by Rev. Oliver
E. Mann. New York: Broadway Publishing
Company, [c1913]. 104 p.
Unexamined copy: bibliographic data from OCLC,
#15718521.

M-410 Manners, J. Hartley (John Hartley), 1870-1928. Peg
o' my heart: a comedy of youth / by J. Hartley
Manners . . . ; illustrations from photographs of the
play. New York: Dodd, Mead and Company, 1913.
381 p., photo. front., [5] leaves of photo. plates.
"This novel is founded by Mr. Manners on his play of
the same title."
LC: N 4, '13.
BLC: London: B. F. Stevens & Brown, 1913.

Manning, David, pseud. See **Brand, Max, 1892-
1944, pseud.**

Manning, Estelle Hempstead. See **Manning-Brewer,
Estelle Hempstead.**

M-411 Manning, Gloria. Improper Prue / by Gloria
Manning; with colored frontispiece by A. T.
Tornrose. New York: B. W. Dodge & Company,
1909. 314 p., front.
LC: F 17, '09.

M-412 Manning, Marie. Judith of the plains: a novel / by
Marie Manning. New York; London: Harper &
Brothers, 1903. 330, [1] p.
PW: O 31, '03.

M-413 ____ Lord Alingham, bankrupt / by Marie Manning.
New York: Dodd, Mead & Company, 1902. 288 p.
PW: Ap 12, '02.
BLC: London: B. F. Stevens & Brown; Cambridge,
U. S. A. printed, 1902.

____ The prophetess of the Land of No-Smoke. In
Under the Sunset (1906), U-9.

____ The truce. In *The heart of childhood* (1906),
H-441.

M-414 Manning-Brewer, Estelle Hempstead, b. 1882.
Háfiz: a story of adventure and romance, told from
old family love letters written during the exciting
events of the baronial feuds of seventeen hundred and
thirty-four, and now given to the world for the first
time / by Estelle Hempstead Manning. Washington,
D. C.: The Neale Publishing Company, 1902.
308 p., front., [4] leaves of plates. [Ill. by Felix
Mahoney.]   **IWA**

M-415 ____ Treason of the blood / by Estelle Hempstead
Manning-Brewer . . . Cedar Rapids, Iowa: The
Torch Press, 1911. 210 p., [3] leaves of plates. [Ill.
by Eva Manning.]   **NYP**
PW: N 4, '11.

Mannix, Madge. "Where laughter dies." In *The
Senior lieutenant's wager: and other stories* (1905),
S-312.

Mannix, Mary Ellen, 1846-1938. The bell of Santa
Marta. In *The lady of the tower* (1909), L-13.

____, contributor. See *A double knot* (1905), D-499.

____ Helena's jewels. In *A bit of old ivory, and
other stories* (1910), B-626.

M-416 ____ In quest of adventure / by Mary E. Mannix
. . . New York; Cincinnati; [etc.]: Benziger
Brothers, 1914. 173 p., front.
Unexamined copy: bibliographic data from NUC.

M-417 ____ A life's labyrinth / by Mary E. Mannix.
Notre Dame, Indiana: The Ave Maria, [c1901].
304 p.   **IMS**
"Intended to be a translation . . . of a German
romance by E. Wagner, entitled "Irrgänge des
lebens" . . . While it is suggested by the German
story, it is in no sense either an adaptation or
translation, and may justify claim . . . to be original.

_____ Miss Hetty's tramp. In *A bit of old ivory, and other stories* (1910), **B-626**.

M-418   _____ The peril of Dionysio / by Mary E. Mannix . . . New York; Cincinnati; [etc.]: Benziger Brothers, 1912. 183 p., front.
Unexamined copy: bibliographic data from NUC.

_____ The rich Miss Bannerman. In *The Senior lieutenant's wager: and other stories* (1905), **S-312**.

_____ The wanderer. In *The friendly little house: and other stories* (1910), **F-432**.

M-419   Mansfield, Laurence R., b. 1868, *pseud*. Fires of desire: a tragedy of modern India / by Laurence R. Mansfield [pseud.]; illustrations by F. Gilbert Edge. Boston: The C. M. Clark Publishing Co., 1907. 354 p., [8] leaves of plates.
LC: Ap 24, '07.

Mansfield, Shirley A. Shovelnose Kelly, master and owner. In *West winds* (1914), **W-368**.

M-420   Manson, Marsden, 1850-1931. The yellow peril in action: a possible chapter in history: dedicated to the men who train and direct the men behind the guns / by Marsden Manson. San Francisco, California: [Britton & Rey, printers], 1907. 28 p.

M-421   Mantle, Beatrice. Gret: the story of a pagan / by Beatrice Mantle. New York: The Century Co., 1907. 403 p., front. [Ill. by C. M. Relyea.]
LC: S 9, '07.
PW: S 28, '07.

M-422   _____ In the house of another / by Beatrice Mantle. New York: The Century Co., 1920. 318 p., front.
LC: O 5, '20.
PW: O 2, '20.

M-423   Manuel, F. G. Soul's redemption / by F. G. Manuel. Chicago, Ill., 1923. 25 p.
Unexamined copy: bibliographic data from NUC.

M-424   Mapes, Ella Stryker. Because of power / by Ella Stryker Mapes; illustrations by Latimer F. Wilson. New York: G. W. Dilingham Company, [c1903]. 269 p., front., [3] leaves of plates.
PW: My 23, '03.
BLC: London: T. Fisher Unwin; New York [printed], 1903.

M-425   Mapes, Victor, 1870-1943. The gilded way: a novel / by Victor Mapes . . . New York; Washington: Neale Publishing Company, 1910. 326 p.
LC: D 16, '10.
PW: D 3, '10.

M-426   _____ Partners three: a novel / by Victor Mapes. New York: Frederick A. Stokes Company, [1909]. 258 p.
LC: Mr 30, '09.
PW: Ap 10, '09.

M-427   Marabell, William, *pseud*. The heart of a rose: a narrative drama / by William Marabell [pseud.] . . . New York: The Klebold Press, [c1906]. 132 p.   **DLC**
PW: Ag 4, '06.

M-428   _____ Sherman Watterson: a novel of American life / by William Marabell [pseud.]. [New York]: Published by the author, [c1905]. 413 p.
PW: D 9, '05.

M-429   _____ The Wattersons: a novel of American life / by William Marabell [pseud.] . . . [San Francisco]: Published by the author, [c1907]. 654 p.   **DLC**
LC: My 20, '07.
PW: Jl 20, '07.

M-430   Marcin, Max, 1879-1948. Are you my wife? / by Max Marcin; illustrated by Z. P. Nikolaki. New York: Moffat, Yard and Company, 1910. 311 p., col. front., [3] leaves of col. plates.   **NYP**
LC : N 3, '10.

M-431   _____ The substitute prisoner / by Max Marcin; illustrated. New York: Moffat, Yard and Company, 1911. 304 p., col. front., [3] leaves of plates. [Ill. by R. Ford Harper.]
LC: N 4, '11.

M-432   Marcy, Mary, 1877-1922. Out of the dump / by Mary E. Marcy; illustrated by R. H. Chaplin. Chicago: Charles H. Kerr & Company, 1909. 123 p., front., [7] leaves of plates.
LC: D 17, '08.

M-433   Marean, Beatrice. Camilla / by Beatrice Marean. Boston: The Roxburgh Publishing Company, Inc., 1922. 208 p.
LC: S 30, '22.

M-434   Mariner-Scarritt, Elizabeth. Quid est / by Elizabeth Mariner-Scarritt. New York; London; Montreal: The Abbey Press, [c1902]. 172 p.   **NOC**
PW: S 20, '02.

Maring, F. Five dollars. In **Seattle Writer's Club.** *Tillicum tales* (1907), **S-248**.

M-435   Marion, Frances, 1888-1973. Minnie Flynn / by Frances Marion. New York: Boni and Liveright, 1925. 384 p.   **IMI**
LC: Ap 21, '25.
PW: Ap 18, '25.
BLC: London: Chatto & Windus, 1926.

Markham, Catherine. Christmas at Seven Devils. In *Cuentos de California* (1904), **C-962**.

M-436   Marks, Henry Kingdon, 1883-1942. Peter Middleton / Henry K. Marks. Boston: Richard G. Badger, [1919]. (Boston: The Gorham Press). 370 p.
LC: Ap 28, '19.
PW: Ap 26, '19.

M-437   ____ Undertow / by Henry K. Marks. New York; London: Harper & Brothers, [c1923]. 337 p.
LC: Ag 21, '23.
PW: O 27, '23.

M-438   Marks, Jeannette Augustus, 1875-1964. The end of a song / by Jeannette Marks. Boston; New York: Houghton Mifflin Company, 1911. 259, [1] p., col. front.
LC: Mr 15, '11.
PW: Mr 18, '11.

M-439   ____ Leviathan: the record of a struggle and a triumph / by Jeannette Marks. New York: Hodder & Stoughton: George H. Doran Company, [c1913]. 329 p.   **TOL**
LC: N 1, '13.
BLC: London: Hodder & Stoughton; U. S. A. [printed], 1914.

____ The sun chaser. In *The best short stories of 1916 and the yearbook of the American short story* (1917), **B-561.**

M-440   ____ Through Welsh doorways / by Jeannette Marks; with illustrations by Anna Whelan Betts. Boston; New York: Houghton Mifflin Company, 1909. 244, [2] p., col. front., [3] leaves of col. plates.
LC: Mr 19, '09.
PW: Ap 3, '09.
BLC: London: T. Fisher Unwin, 1910.

M-441   Marks, Percy, 1891-1956. Martha / by Percy Marks. New York; London: The Century Co., [c1925]. 338 p.
LC: Mr 2, '25.
PW: Mr 7, '25.

M-442   ____ The plastic age / by Percy Marks. New York; London: The Century Co., [c1924]. 332 p.
LC: Ja 29, '24.
BLC: London: Selwyn & Blount; printed in U. S. A., [1924].

M-443   Marks, William Dennis, 1849-1914. An equal opportunity: a plea for individualism / by W. Dennis Marks. Philadelphia: Patterson & White Co., 1905. 354 p.   **GUA**

M-444   Marmon, Willie Fain, b. 1878. A daughter of the hills / by Willie Fain Marmon. New York; Washington: The Neale Publishing Company, 1909. 246 p.
LC: Ja 5, '09.
PW: Ja 23, '09.

M-445   Marquand, John P. (John Phillips), 1893-1960. The black cargo / by J. P. Marquand. New York: Charles Scribner's Sons, 1925. 270 p.
LC: F 19, '25.
PW: F 21, '25.
BLC: London: Hodder & Stoughton, [1925].

M-446   ____ Four of a kind / by J. P. Marquand . . . New York: Charles Scribner's Sons, 1923. 331 p.
Contents: The right that failed -- Different from other girls -- Eight

million bubbles -- Only a few of us left.
LC: Mr 10, '23.
PW: Mr 17, '23.

M-447   ____ The unspeakable gentleman / by J. P. Marquand; with a frontispiece by A. I. Keller. New York: Charles Scribner's Sons, 1922. 265 p., front.
LC: My 16, '22.
PW: My 20, '22.
BLC: London: Hodder & Stoughton, [1922].

Marquis, Don, 1878-1937. Being a public character. In *"Dawgs!"* (1925), **D-184.**

M-448   ____ Carter and other people / by Don Marquis . . . New York; London: D. Appleton and Company, 1921. 311, [1] p.
Contents: Carter -- Old man Murtrie -- Never say die! -- McDermott -- Looney the Mutt -- Kale -- Bubbles -- The chances of the street -- The professor's awakening -- The penitent -- The locked box -- Behind the curtain -- Words and thoughts [a one-act play].
LC: Ag 25, '21.
PW: Ag 27, '21.

M-449   ____ The cruise of the Jasper B / by Don Marquis . . . New York; London: D. Appleton and Company, 1916. 318, [1] p.
LC: My 8, '16.
PW: My 27, '16.

M-450   ____ Danny's own story / by Don Marquis; illustrated by E. W. Kemble. Garden City, N. Y.: Doubleday, Page & Company, 1912. 333 p., front., [15] leaves of plates.
LC: Ja 20, '12.
PW: Ja 27, '12.

M-451   ____ The Old Soak; and, Hail and farewell / by Don Marquis; line drawings by Sterling Patterson. Garden City, N. Y.; Toronto: Doubleday, Page & Company, 1921. 141 p., front., [1] leaf of ill. (not incl. in pagination), ill.
LC: Je 22, '21.
PW: Je 4 , '21.

M-452   ____ The Old Soak's history of the world: with occasional glances at Baycliff, L. I., and Paris, France / by Don Marquis; with drawings by Stuart Hay. -- 1st ed. -- Garden City, New York: Doubleday, Page & Company, 1924. 144 p., front., ill.
LC: Je 5, '24.
PW: My 31, '24.
BLC: London: William Heinemann; printed in U. S. A., 1924.

____, jt. aut. *Pandora lifts the lid* (1924). See **Morley, Christopher, 1890-1957, jt. aut, M-976.**

M-453   ____ Prefaces / by Don Marquis . . . ; decorations by Tony Sarg. New York; London: D. Appleton and Company, 1919. 276 p., [4] p.
Contents: Preface to a book of literary reminiscences -- Preface to a cook book -- Preface to a book of fishhooks -- Preface to a book of cigarette papers -- Preface to the plays of Euripides -- Preface to a cat show catalogue -- Preface to the prospectus of a club -- Preface to a medium's dope book -- Preface to a treatise on a new art -- Preface to a memorandum book -- Preface to a hangman's diary -- Preface to a volume of poetry -- Preface to Old doctor Gumph's almanac --

Preface to a book of paragraphs -- Preface to a book of patterns -- Preface to the works of Billy Sunday -- Preface to a calendar -- Preface to a study of the current stage -- Preface to a book of safety pins -- Preface to the novels of Harold Bell Wright -- Preface to a book of statistics -- Preface to a moral book of arithmetic -- Preface to a book withheld -- Preface to Hoyt's rules -- Preface to the diary of a failure -- Foreward to a literary censor's autobiography -- Note to a chapter on journalism -- Foreward to a miser's autobiography -- Preface to a check book -- Preface to the autobiography of an old-fashioned anarchist -- Preface to an unpublished volume -- Preface to a book of prefaces.
LC: Je 25, '19.
PW: Je 28, '19.

M-454   ____ The revolt of the oyster / by Don Marquis. Garden City, N. Y.: Doubleday, Page & Company, 1922. 229 p.
LC: N 23, '22.
PW: D 2, '22.

M-455   Marquis, George H. (George Hersey). Fairview's mystery / by George H. Marquis. New York; London; Montreal: The Abbey Press, [c1901]. 84 p.
                                                                SDH
PW: Mr 1, '02.

M-456   Marquis, Reina Melcher, b. 1881. The torch bearer / by Reina Melcher Marquis. New York; London: D. Appleton and Company, 1914. 314, [1] p.
PW: Jl 11, '14.

M-457   Marriage: short stories of married life / by American writers Tarkington . . . [et al.]. Garden City, New York: Doubleday, Page & Company, 1923. 325 p.
                                                                EEM
Contents: "Us" / Booth Tarkington -- Really married / Mary Stewart Cutting -- Miss Conifee / Joseph Hergesheimer -- The house guest / Alice Duer Miller -- The lost columbine / Julian Street -- For value received / Edith Barnard Delano -- The perfect husband / Charles G. Norris -- The Clausons / Zona Gale -- Pursuit / Henry Sydnor Harrison -- The mental hazard / Clarence Budington Kelland -- The ants / James Hopper -- The indissoluble bond / Samuel Hopkins Adams -- The tenth Mrs. Tulkington / Ellis Parker Butler -- Mrs. Redmond's shame / Maximilian Foster -- Peachblow / Rupert Hughes -- Marriage-For one / Theodore Dreiser -- Driftwood / Courtney Ryley Cooper -- Birth stones / George Kibbe Turner -- His wife's visitor / Henry Kitchell Webster -- The pie and the past / Joseph C. Lincoln.
PW: Ap 28, '23.
BLC: London: Hodder & Stoughton; printed in U. S. A., [1923].

M-458   Marriott, Crittenden, 1867-1932. The isle of dead ships / by Crittenden Marriott; with illustrations by Frank McKernan. Philadelphia; London: J. B. Lippincott Company, 1909. 265 p., col. front., [3] leaves of plates.
LC: S 29, '09.
PW: O 23, '09.

M-459   ____ Out of Russia / Crittendon Mariott . . . ; with illustrations by Frank McKernan. Philadelphia; London: J. B. Lippincott Company, 1911. 258 p., col. front., [3] leaves of plates.   **RIU**
LC: Mr 21, '11.
PW: Ap 8, '11.

M-460   ____ Sally Castleton, southerner / by Crittenden Marriott . . . ; with illustrations by N. C. Wyeth. Philadelphia; London: J. B. Lippincott Company, 1913. 312 p., col. front., [5] leaves of plates.

LC: F 27, '13.
PW: F 8, '13.

M-461   ____ Via Berlin / by Crittenden Marriott . . . New York: R. J. Shores, [c1917]. 275 p., front. Unexamined copy: bibliographic data from OCLC, #9117784.

M-462   ____ The ward of Tecumseh / by Crittenden Marriott; with illustrations by Frank McKernan. Philadelphia; London: J. B. Lippincott Company, 1914. 336 p., col. front., [3] leaves of plates.
LC: O 15, '14.
PW: O 10, '14.

M-463   ____ The water devil / by Crittenden Marriott. Garden City, New York: Garden City Publishing Co., Inc., 1924. 117 p., ill. [Ill. by J. H. Litchfield.]
[Famous author series, no. 47.]
LC: Ap 2, '24.

M-464   Marschner, Harry. From death to life / by Harry Marschner. New York; London; Montreal: The Abbey Press, [c1901]. 392 p.

M-465   Marsden, John Pennington. Patrick Dunbar: or what came of a "Personal in the Times" / by John Pennington Marsden. Philadelphia: Hallowell Co., Ltd., 1909. 366, [1] p.
Unexamined copy: bibliographic data from OCLC, #29883750.

M-466   Marsh, Charles L. (Charles Leonard), 1854?-1930. Not on the chart: a romance of the Pacific / by Charles L. Marsh . . . ; with frontispiece and map. New York: Frederick A. Stokes Company, 1902. 336 p., front., [1] leaf of plates (map). [Ill. by Clarence F. Underwood.]
PW: Je 7, '02.
BLC: London: Ward, Lock & Co., 1904. Printed from American plates.

M-467   Marsh, George Cook, b. 1861. A singular will / by George C. Marsh; with an introduction by Joseph Tyler Butts. New York: F. T. Neely, [1901]. 283 p.
Unexamined copy: bibliographic data from OCLC, #26978523.
PW: Je 7, '02.

M-468   Marsh, George Tracy, b. 1876. Men marooned / by George Marsh. Philadelphia: The Penn Publishing Company, 1925. 314 p.
LC: O 16, '25.
PW: O 24, '25.

M-469   ____ Toilers of the trails / by George Marsh; illustrated by Frank E. Schoonover. Philadelphia: The Penn Publishing Company, 1921. 245 p., col. front., [8] leaves of plates.
Contents: For the Great Father -- Out of the mist -- A little tragedy at Coocoocache -- When the Prince came home -- With the winter mail -- The valley of the Windigo -- The quest of Narcisse Lablanche -- The land of his fathers -- The high brotherhood.
LC: Ja 5, '22.
PW: D 31, '21.

M-470   ____ The valley of voices / by George Marsh; illustrated by Frank E. Schoonover. Philadelphia: The Penn Publishing Company, 1924. 352, [5] p., front.
"George Marsh, an autobiography": 5 pages at end.
LC: O 3, '24.
PW: O 18, '24.

M-471   ____ The whelps of the wolf / by George Marsh . . . ; frontispiece by Frank E. Schoonover. Philadelphia: The Penn Publishing Company, 1922. 303 p., col. front.
LC: My 11, '22.
PW: S 2, '22.

M-472   Marsh, George Turner, b. 1857. The lords of dawn: a novel / by George Turner Marsh and Ronald Temple; with illustrations by Chiura Obata. San Francisco: John J. Newbegin, 1916. 304 p., ill.
"This tale aims to picture the awakening Japan-- the Japan of the period that begins with the year 1854, and ends with the year 1890."
LC: Jl 17, '16.
PW: S 2, '16.

Marsh, Leverne Alden. Timothy's day off. In *Allegheny stories* (1902), **A-142.**

M-473   Marsh, Marie L. (Marie Louise). Auburn and freckles / by Marie L. Marsh; illustrated by "Briggs." Chicago: F. G. Browne & Co., 1913. 144 p., front., [5] leaves of plates.

M-474   Marshall, Bernard, b. 1875. Redcoat and minuteman / by Bernard Marshall . . . ; illustrated by J. Scott Williams. New York; London: D. Appleton and Company, 1924. 277, [1] p., front. ill., 5 leaves of ill.
LC: O 20, '24.
PW: N 8, '24.

M-475   ____ The torch bearers: a tale of cavalier days / by Bernard Marshall . . . New York; London: D. Appleton and Company, 1923. 317, [1] p., front., ill. [Ill. by J. Scott Williams.]
LC: S 19, '13.
PW: O 13, '23.

M-476   ____ Walter of Tiverton / by Bernard Marshall . . . New York; London: D. Appleton and Company, 1923. 263 p., front. ill. [Ill. by J. Scott Williams.]
LC: My 9, '23.
PW: Je 2, '23.

M-477   Marshall, Edison, 1894-1967. The death bell / by Edison Marshall. -- 1st ed. -- Garden City, New York: Garden City Publishing Co., Inc., 1924. 120 p.   **DLC**
[Famous author series, no. 39.]
LC: Ap 2, '24.

  ____ The elephant remembers. In *Prize stories of 1919* (1920), **P-617.**

M-478   ____ The heart of Little Shikara: and other stories / by Edison Marshall. Boston: Little, Brown, and

Company, 1922. 298 p.
Contents: The heart of Little Shikara -- Never kill a porcupine -- Jungle justice -- Shag of the pack -- The son of the wild things -- Furs -- Little death -- The elephant remembers -- The serpent city -- Brother Bill the elk.
LC: O 18, '22.
PW: O 21, '22.
BLC: London: Hodder & Stoughton, [1924].

M-479   ____ The isle of retribution / by Edison Marshall; with frontispiece by Douglas Duer. Boston: Little, Brown, and Company, 1923. 322 p., front.
LC: F 10, '23.
PW: F 3, '23.
BLC: London: Hodder & Stoughton, [1923].

M-480   ____ The land of forgotten men / by Edison Marshall; with frontispiece by W. Herbert Dunton. Boston: Little, Brown, and Company, 1923. 306 p., front.
LC: Ag 22, '23.
PW: Ag 25, '23.
BLC: London: Hodder & Stoughton, [1924].

M-481   ____ Seward's folly / by Edison Marshall. Boston: Little, Brown and Company, 1924. 312 p.
LC: Jl 5, '24.
PW: Jl 12, '24.
BLC: London: Hodder & Stoughton, [1924].

M-482   ____ Shepherds of the wild / by Edison Marshall; with frontispiece by W. Herbert Dunton. Boston: Little, Brown, and Company, 1922. 300 p., front.
LC: Mr 1, '22.
PW: Mr 18, '22.
BLC: London: Hodder & Stoughton, [1922].

M-483   ____ The sky line of spruce / by Edison Marshall; with frontispiece by Douglas Duer. Boston: Little, Brown, and Company, 1922. 322 p., front.
LC: Ag 17, '22.
PW: Ag 26, '22.
BLC: London: Hodder & Stoughton, 1922.

M-484   ____ The sleeper of the moonlit ranges: a new novel / by Edison Marshall; illustrations by Jes W. Schlaikjer. New York: Cosmopolitan Book Corporation, 1925. 311 p., front., [2] leaves of plates (1 col. double).
LC: Ap 11, '25.
PW: Ap 11, '25.
BLC: London: Hodder & Stoughton, [1925].

M-485   ____ The snowshoe trail / by Edison Marshall; with frontispiece by Marshall Frantz. Boston: Little, Brown, and Company, 1921. 324 p., front.
LC: S 22, '21.
PW: S 10, '21.
BLC: London: Hodder & Stoughton, 1921.

M-486   ____ The strength of the pines / by Edison Marshall; with frontispiece by W. Herbert Dunton. Boston: Little, Brown and Company, 1921. 308 p., front.
LC: F 15, '21.
PW: F 5, '21.
BLC: London: Hodder & Stoughton, [1921].

M-487   The voice of the pack / by Edison Marshall; with frontispiece by W. Herbert Dunton. Boston: Little, Brown, and Company, 1920. 305 p., front.
LC: Ap 27, '20.
PW: Ap 10, '20.
BLC: London: Hodder & Stoughton; Norwood, Mass [printed], 1920.

M-488 Marshall, Edward, 1870-1933. Bat: an idyl of New York / by Edward Marshall; illustrations by Ike Morgan and Haygarth Leonard. New York: G. W. Dillingham Company, [c1912]. 288 p., col. front., ill.
LC: My 2, '12.
PW: My 11, '12.

M-489   Broadway Jones: from the play of George M. Cohan / by Edward Marshall; illustrations from scenes in the play. New York: G. W. Dillingham Company, [c1913]. 322 p., incl. photo. front., [7] leaves of photo. plates.
LC: Ag 30, '13.
PW: S 6, '13.

M-490   The family: a story of forgiveness / from the play of Robert Hobart Davis by Edward Marshall; illustrations from scenes in the play. New York: G. W. Dillingham Company, [c1911]. 348 p., photo. front., [7] leaves of photo. plates.
LC: O 28, '11.
PW: N 4, '11.

M-491   In old Kentucky: a story of the bluegrass and the mountains founded on Charles T. Dazey's play / by Edward Marshall and Charles T. Dazey; illustrations by Clarence Rowe. New York: G. W. Dillingham Company, [c1910]. 352 p., front., [5] leaves of plates.
LC: Mr 30, '10.
PW: Ap 2, '10.

M-492   Lizette: a story of the Latin quarter / by Edward Marshall; with illustrations by C. D. Williams and J. C. Fireman. New York: Lewis, Scribner & Co., 1902. 295 p., front., [3] leaves of plates.
PW: O 4, '02; N 22, '02.

M-493   The master of the house: a story of modern American life, adapted from the play of Edgar James / by Edward Marshall; illustrations from scenes in the play. New York: G. W. Dillingham Company, [c1913]. 363 p., photo. front., [7] leaves of photo. plates.
LC: Ap 25, '13.
PW: Ap 26, '13.

M-494   The middle wall / by Edward Marshall; illustrations by Louis F. Grant. New York: G. W. Dillingham Company, [1904]. 470 p., front., [5] leaves of plates.
PW: Ap 2, '04.

M-495   The old flute-player: a romance of to-day / by Edward Marshall and Charles T. Dazey; illustrations by Clarence Rowe; frontispiece by J. Knowles Hare, Jr. New York: G. W. Dillingham Company, [c1910]. 256 p., col. front., [3] leaves of plates.
LC: O 10, '10.
PW: O 8, '10.

M-496   The writing on the wall: a novel founded on Olga Nethersole's play by William J. Hurlbut / by Edward Marshall; illustrations by Clarence Rowe. New York: G. W. Dillingham Company, [c1909]. 350 p., front., [5] leaves of plates.
LC: N 27, '09.
PW: N 20, '09.
BLC: London: T. Fisher Unwin; New York [printed], 1909.

M-497 Marshall, Marguerite Mooers, 1887-1964. The drift / by Marguerite Mooers Marshall. New York; London: D. Appleton and Company, 1911. 255, [1] p.
PW: S 9, '11.

M-498 Marshall, Sidney J. (Sidney John), b. 1866. The king of Kor, or, She's promise kept: A continuation of the great story of "She", of H. Rider Haggard / by Sidney J. Marshall; with illustrations. Washington: Sidney J. Marshall, 1903. 258 p., front., [3] leaves of plates.
PW: My 23, '03.

M-499 Marshall, William Kennedy, b. 1835. Bud: a story of the Church of the New Humanity / by William Kennedy Marshall. Cincinnati: Jennings & Pye; New York: Eaton & Mains, [c1901]. 307 p.
PW: D 28, '01.

M-500   The entering wedge: a romance of the heroic days of Kansas / by William Kennedy Marshall. Cincinnati: Jennings & Graham; New York: Eaton & Mains, [c1904]. 274 p.
PW: O 1, '04.

M-501 Marsland, Cora, b. 1859. The angel of the Gila: a tale of Arizona / by Cora Marsland; with illustratins by S. S. Hicks and Gem Vaughn. Boston: Richard G. Badger, [c1911]. (Boston, U. S. A.: The Gorham Press). 292 p., front.
PW: D 16, '11.

M-502 Martin, Absalom. Kastle Krags: a story of mystery / by Absalom Martin. New York: Duffield and Company, 1922. 267 p.
LC: S 9, '22.
PW: S 30, '22.

Martin, Attwood R., Mrs. See **Martin, George Madden, 1866-1946.**

Martin, Dorothea (Knox). See **Knox, Dorothea Heness.**

M-503 Martin, Edward Sandford, 1856-1939. The courtship of a careful man, and a few other courtships / by Edward Sanford [sic] Martin. New York: London: Harper & Brothers, 1905. 184, [1] p., front., [7] leaves of plates. [Ill. by Howard Chandler Christy, T. K. Hanna and The Kinneys.]
Contents: The courtship of a careful man -- A party at Madeira's --

The making of a match -- A disguised providence -- Josephine --
Found: a situation.
PW: Ap 15, '05.

M-504   ____ Reflections of a beginning husband / by
Edward Sandford Martin . . . New York; London:
Harper & Brothers, 1913. 163 p. Designed end
papers.
LC: Ap 19, '13.

M-505   Martin, Elizabeth L. Only a factory girl: a story of
southern mill life / by Mrs. Elizabeth L. Martin.
Charlotte, N. C.: Mill News Printing Co., c1909.
98 p.
Unexamined copy: bibliographic data from OCLC,
#16617910.

M-506   ____ Only a factory girl: and other stories of
southern mill life / by Elizabeth L. Martin.
Charlotte, N. C.: Mill New Printing Co., c1909.
267 p.
Unexamined copy: bibliographic data from OCLC,
#9825230.
Contents: Only a factory girl -- Kate's terrible mistake -- Richard
Earle's sweetheart.

M-507   Martin, Frank E. (Frank Eugene). Firebrands / by
Frank E. Martin and George M. Davis; with
illustrations from photographs. Boston: Little,
Brown, and Company, 1911. 219 p., photo. front.,
[15] leaves of photo. plates (some signed by
Underwood & Underwood).

M-508   Martin, George Madden, 1866-1946. Children in the
mist / by George Madden Martin. New York;
London: D. Appleton & Company, 1920. 285,
[1] p., front. [Ill. by Paul Meylan.]
Contents: The flight -- The blue handkerchief -- An inskip niggah --
Pom -- The sleeping sickness -- Fire from heaven -- Malviney -- Sixty
years after.
LC: Jl 3, '20.
PW: Jl 31, '20.

M-509   ____ The house of fulfilment / by George Madden
Martin; illustrated by George Alfred Williams. New
York: McClure, Phillips & Co., 1904. 379 p.,
front., [7] leaves of plates.
PW: O 1, '04.
BLC: London: Hodder & Stoughton; New York
[printed], 1904.

M-510   ____ Letitia: nursery corps, U. S. A. / by George
Madden Martin. New York: The McClure
Company, 1907. 206 p., front., [15] leaves of plates.
[Ill. by Frederic Dorr Steele.]
LC: N 16, '07.
PW: D 7, '07.

____ A little feminine Casabianca. In Youth (1901),
Y-51.

M-511   ____ March on / by George Madden Martin. New
York; London: D. Appleton and Company, 1921.
351 p.
LC: N 3, '21.
PW: N 19, '21.

M-512   ____ Selina: her hopeful efforts and her livelier
failures / by George Madden Martin; illustrated by H.
D. Williams. New York: D. Appleton and
Company, 1914. 409, [1] p.
[LC records front., ill.]
LC: O 28, '14.
PW: N 7, '14.

Martin, Harold. The scape-goat of La Justica. In
The battle for the Pacific (1908), B-357.

M-513   Martin, Helen Reimensnyder, 1868-1939. Barnabetta
/ by Helen R. Martin. New York: The Century Co.,
1914. 340 p.
LC: Mr 25, '14.
PW: Mr 28, '14.

M-514   ____ The betrothal of Elypholate: and other tales of
the Pennsylvania Dutch / by Helen Reimensnyder
Martin; with illustrations by Charlotte Harding and
Alice Barber Stephens. New York: The Century
Co., 1907. 249 p., incl. [8] leaves of plates, front.
Contents: The betrothal of Elypholate -- The reforming of a
bridegroom -- The conversion of Elviny -- Ellie's furnishing -- Mrs.
Holzapple's convictions -- The narrow escape of Permilla -- The
courting of Pearly -- The disciplining of Mathias.
LC: S 20, '07.
PW: O 12, '07.

M-515   ____ Challenged: a novel / by Helen R. Martin.
New York: Dodd, Mead and Company, 1925.
284 p.
LC: Ja 30, '25.
PW: Ja 31, '25.

M-516   ____ The church on the avenue: a novel / by Helen
R. Martin. New York: Dodd, Mead and Company,
1923. 348 p.
LC: Ja 16, '23.
PW: Ja 13, '23.

M-517   ____ The crossways / by Helen Reimensnyder
Martin. New York: The Century Co., 1910. 311 p.
LC: F 24, '10.
PW: F 26, '10.

M-518   ____ Fanatic or Christian: a story of the
Pennsylvania Dutch / by Helen R. Martin. Garden
City, New York: Doubleday, Page & Company,
1918. 307, [1] p.
LC: Mr 13, '18.
PW: Mr 30, '18.

M-519   ____ The fighting doctor / by Helen Reimensnyder
Martin. New York: The Century Co., 1912. 242 p.
LC: Mr 1, '12.
PW: F 24, '12.

M-520   ____ Her husband's purse / by Helen R. Martin;
illustrated by John Newton Howitt. Garden City, N.
Y.: Doubleday, Page & Company, 1916. 343,
[1] p., front., [3] leaves of plates.
LC: Mr 29, '16.
PW: Mr 25, '16.
BLC: London: Curtis Brown; Garden City, N. Y.
printed, 1916.

M-521 ____ His courtship / by Helen R. Martin . . . ; illustrated by Alice Barber Stephens. New York: McClure, Phillips & Co., 1907. 322 p., front., [3] leaves of plates.
LC: Ap 22, '07.
PW: My 4, '07.
BLC: London; New York: McClure, Phillips & Co., 1907.

M-522 ____ Maggie of Virginsburg: a story of the Pennsylvania Dutch / by Helen R. Martin . . . New York: The Century Co., 1918. 406 p., front. [Ill. by F. McAnglly.]
LC: S 30, '18.
PW: O 5, '18.

M-523 ____ The marriage of Susan / by Helen R. Martin; frontispiece by Walter de Maris. Garden City, N. Y.; Toronto: Doubleday, Page & Company, 1921. 285, [1] p., front.
LC: S 22, '21.
PW: O 1, '21.

M-524 ____ Martha of the Mennonite country / by Helen R. Martin. Garden City, N. Y.: Doubleday, Page & Company, 1915. 317, [1] p., front. [Ill. by E. R. Lee Thayer.]
LC: Mr 3, '15.
PW: Mr 13, '15.
BLC: London: Curtis Brown; Garden City, N. Y. printed, 1915.

M-525 ____ The parasite: a novel / by Helen Reimensnyder Martin; with illustrations by James Montgomery Flagg. Philadelphia; London: J. B. Lippincott Company, 1913. 302 p., col. front., [1] leaf of col. plates.
LC: F 27, '13.
PW: F 8, '13.

M-526 ____ The revolt of Anne Royle / by Helen R. Martin. New York: The Century Co., 1908. 387 p.
LC: S 12, '08.
PW: O 3, '08.

M-527 ____ Sabina: a story of the Amish / by Helen Reimensnyder Martin. New York: The Century Co., 1905. 233 p.
PW: O 7, '05.

M-528 ____ The schoolmaster of Hessville / by Helen R. Martin. Garden City, N. Y.: Doubleday, Page & Company, 1920. 289, [1] p.
LC: S 22, '20.
PW: S 18, '20.

M-529 ____ The snob: the story of a marriage / by Helen R. Martin. New York: Dodd, Mead and Company, 1924. 391 p.
Unexamined copy: bibliographic data from OCLC, #2053950.
LC: Ja 15, '24.
PW: Ja 19, '24.

M-530 ____ Those Fitzenbergers / by Helen R. Martin; illustrated by Robert A. Graef. Garden City, N. Y.:

Doubleday, Page & Company, 1917. 363, [1] p., front., ill.
LC: Mr 14, '17.
PW: Mr 10, '17.

M-531 ____ Tillie, a Mennonite maid: a story of the Pennsylvania Dutch / by Helen Reimensnyder Martin; with illustrations by Florence Scovel Shinn. New York: The Century Co., [c1904]. 336 p., ill. **AZS**
PW: F 20, '04.
BLC: London: Hodder & Stoughton, 1905.

M-532 ____ When half-gods go: being the story of a brief wedded life as told in intimate and confidential letters written by a bride to a former college mate / by Helen Reimensnyder Martin. New York: The Century Co., 1911. 154 p.
LC: F 25, '11.
PW: F 18, '11.

M-533 Martin, J. L. (James Lee), b. 1873. Just a Missourian: the story of a Missouri pioneer / by J. L. Martin. Crowell, Texas: Published by the News Publishing Co., 1915. 167 p.   **KCP**

M-534 Martin, James, b. 1862. Jason Jones: the life story of an American politician: an autobiographical sketch found among the papers of a capitalist and political boss, recently deceased / edited by James Martin. Orange, New Jersey: The Chronicle Publishing Co., 1909. 245 p.
LC: Ja 18, '10.

M-535 Martin, John Andrew, 1868-1939. The Jayhawker / by John A. Martin. Boston, Massachusetts: The C. M. Clark Publishing Co., 1908. 344 p., front., [9] leaves of plates. [Ill. by John Goss.]
LC: Ag 29, '08.
PW: O 10, '08.

M-536 Martin, John F. The gypsy moth: a novel / by John F. Martin. New York: Broadway Publishing Company, [c1910]. 227 p.
LC: D 12, '10.

M-537 Martin, Leland S. Stern realities / by Leland S. Martin. San Francisco: Harr Wagner Publishing Company, 1916. 126, [1] p., photo. front. (port.).

M-538 Martin, M. C. The other Miss Lisle / by M. C. Martin. New York; Cincinnati; Chicago: Benziger Brothers, 1906. 282 p.   **DLC**
LC: O 10, '06.

M-539 ____ Rose of the world / by M. C. Martin. New York; Cincinnati; Chicago: Benziger Brothers, 1907. 328 p.
LC: N 30, '07.

M-540 Martin, M. T. (Marion Thomas), b. 1885. Babe Saunders: a story of the Oklahoma oil fields / by Rev. M. T. Martin . . . Excelsior Springs, Missouri: Christian Union Herald Print, [c1916]. 225 p., photo. front., [11] leaves of photo. plates.   **OKD**

M-541 Martin, Mabel Wood. The green god's pavilion: a novel of the Philippines / by Mabel Wood Martin. New York: Frederick A. Stokes Company, [c1920]. 353 p.

M-542 Martin, Marie Buxton. Within the rock / by Marie Buxton Martin. New York: Harold Vinal, 1925. 330 p.

Martin, Mary, pseud. See **Austin, Mary.**

M-543 Martin, Nettie Parrish. A pilgrim's progress in other worlds: recounting the wonderful adventures of Ulysum Storries and his discovery of the lost star "Eden" / by Nettie Parrish Martin . . . Boston: Mayhew Publishing Company, 1908. 482 p., photo. front. (port.). **CRU**

M-544 Martin, William. The lowland beauty, George Washington's first love: an historical novel / by William Martin. Loch Raven, Md.: The Raven Press, [c1914]. 100 p. Unexamined copy: bibliographic data from OCLC, #16795926.

M-545 Martin, William McChesney. Shoes of iron; A tale of witch town / by William McChesney Martin. Boston, Mass.: Mayhew Publishing Company, 1907. 186 p., [5] leaves of plates (some photo.). **WTU** LC: Ap 13, '07.

M-546 Martindell, Charlotte S. The diary of a bride. New York: Thomas Y. Crowell & Co., [c1905]. 162 p.

M-547 Martinez, Raymond J. (Raymond Joseph), b. 1889. In the parish of St. John / by Raymond J. Martinez. Thibodaux, La.; New Orleans: Geo. A. Martin & Co., 1925. 147 p., front., [1] leaf of plates. PW: Ag 15, '25.

M-548 Martyn, Wyndham, b. 1875. All the world to nothing / by Wyndham Martyn . . . ; with illustrations by H. H. Leonard. Boston: Little, Brown, and Company, 1912. 403 p., front., [3] leaves of plates. LC: S 16, '12. PW: S 7, '12. BLC: London: Sampson Low & Co.; Boston, U. S. A. [printed], [1913] (without ills.).

M-549 _____ Anthony Trent, master criminal / by Wyndham Martyn. New York: Moffat, Yard & Company, 1918. 316 p. LC: D 2, '18. PW: D 14, '18. BLC: London: Herbert Jenkins, 1922, [1921].

M-550 _____ The man outside / by Wyndham Martyn; illustrations by C. M. Relyea. New York: Dodd, Mead and Company, 1910. 312 p., front., [3] leaves of plates. LC: Ja 22, '10. PW: Ja 29, '10.

M-551 _____ The return of Anthony Trent / by Wyndham Martyn. New York, N. Y.; Newark, N. J.: Barse & Hopkins, [c1925]. 347 p.

Unexamined copy: bibliographic data from NUC. LC: Ag 5, '25. BLC: London: Herbert Jenkins, 1923.

M-552 _____ Under cover / by Roi Cooper Megrue; novelized by Wyndham Martyn; with illustrations by William Kirkpatrick. Boston: Little, Brown and Company, 1914. 300 p., front., [3] leaves of plates. LC: S 1, '14. PW: S 5, '14. BLC: London: Jarrold's, [1917].

M-553 Martzolff, Clement Luther, 1869-1922. The first service star / Clement Luther Martzolff. [S. l.: Martzolff, 1918?]. 21 p. Unexamined copy: bibliographic data from OCLC, #7888348. Reprinted from the American Lutheran Survey.

M-554 Marvel, Ik., 1822-1908, *pseud*. Noon: from Reveries of a bachelor / by Ik. Marvel [pseud.] (Donald G. Mitchell). New York: R. F. Fenno & Company, [c1907]. 38 p., front., [1] leaf of plates, ill. [Ill. by W. E. B. Starkweather.] **VHB** LC: Ag 24, '06.

_____ Over a wood fire. In *International short stories* (1910), I-29.

M-555 Marvin, Dwight Edwards, 1851-1940. The Christman / by Dwight Edwards Marvin . . . ; frontispiece by Hudson. New York: Broadway Publishing Company, [c1908]. 250 p., front. **DLC**

M-556 _____ Prof. Slagg, of London / by Dwight Edwards Marvin . . . New York: Broadway Publishing Company, [c1908]. 278 p., front., [4] leaves of plates. LC: N 9, '08.

M-557 Marword, Gregory, b. 1870, *pseud*. The wooing of a recluse / by Gregory Marword [pseud.]; with illustrations by Remington Schuyler. New York: The Devin-Adair Company, [c1914]. 115 p., front., [2] leaves of plates. Illustrated end papers.

Mary Jane, pseud. See **Stine, Milton H. (Milton Henry), 1853-1940.**

M-558 Mason, Abbie Daniels. The dawn of a new era / by Abbie Daniels Mason. Boston: James H. West Company, [1903]. 140 p. **MLN** PW: Mr 28, '03.

M-559 Mason, Arthur, 1876-1955. The cook and the captain bold / by Arthur Mason. Boston: The Atlantic Monthly Press, [c1924]. 217 p., front. LC: Ap 12, '24. BLC: [London]: William Heinemann, 1925.

M-560 _____ The flying bo'sun: a mystery of the sea / by Arthur Mason. New York: Henry Holt and Company, 1920. 241 p. LC: N 1, '20. BLC: London: Jonathan Cape; printed in U. S. A., [1921].

M-561   Mason, Carl Reutti. The clash of steel / by Carl Reutti Mason . . . New York; London; Montreal: The Abbey Press, [c1901]. 200 p., front. [Ill. by Geo. O. Sloneker.]   **CLU**

M-562   Mason, Caroline Atwater, 1853-1939. The binding of the strong: a love story / by Caroline Atwater Mason. New York; Chicago; Toronto; London; Edinburgh: Fleming H. Revell Company, [c1908]. 352 p., front. Illustrated end papers.
         LC: Ag 21, '08.
         PW: S 12, '08.
         BLC: London: Hodder & Stoughton, [1908].

         ____ Called to the colors. In *Called to the colors and other stories* **(1915), C-50.**

M-563   ____ Conscripts of conscience / by Caroline Atwater Mason . . . New York; Chicago; London; Edinburgh: Fleming H. Revell Company, [c1919]. 156 p.   **GZM**
         LC: F 5, '20.
         PW: Ja 17, '20.

M-564   ____ The high way / by Caroline Atwater Mason. New York; Chicago; London; Edinburgh: Fleming H. Revell Company, [c1924]. 382 p.
         LC: F 7, '24.
         PW: Ja 5, '24.

M-565   ____ Holt of Heatherfield / by Caroline Atwater Mason. New York: The Macmillan Company; London: Macmillan & Co., Ltd., 1903. 226 p., front., [3] leaves of plates. [Ill. by William L. Jacobs.]
         PW: O 31, '03.

M-566   ____ A lily of France / by Caroline Atwater Mason. Philadelphia: The Griffith & Rowland Press, 1901. 456 p., front., [3] leaves of plates. [Ill. by G. A. Newman.]
         PW: Ag 3, '01.

M-567   ____ The little green god / by Caroline Atwater Mason. New York; Chicago; Toronto: Fleming H. Revell Company, [1902]. 146 p.
         PW: Ag 2, '02; N 15, '02

M-568   ____ The mystery of Miss Motte / by Caroline Atwater Mason; with a frontispiece in colour by Albert R. Thayer. Boston: L. C. Page & Company, 1909. 244 p., col. front.
         LC: Ap 22, '09.
         PW: My 8, '09.

M-569   ____ Waxwing / by Caroline Atwater Mason . . . New York; Chicago; Toronto; London; Edinburgh: Fleming H. Revell Company, [c1905]. 48 p.
         PW: S 2, '05.

M-570   ____ The white shield / Caroline Atwater Mason. Philadelphia: The Griffith & Rowland Press, 1904. 160 p., front., [4] leaves of plates.
         PW: Ag 20, '04.

M-571   Mason, Edith Huntington. The great plan / by Edith Huntington Mason; illustrated by J. Allen St. John. Chicago: A. C. McClurg & Co., 1913. 308 p., front., [4] leaves of plates.
         LC: N 26, '13.
         PW: D 6, '13.
         BLC: London: C. F. Cazevone; Chicago: A. C. McClurg & Co.; Binghamton, N. Y. [printed], 1913.

M-572   ____ The politician / by Edith Huntington Mason . . . ; illustrated in full color by the Kinneys. Chicago: A. C. McClurg & Co., 1910. 409 p., col. front., [3] leaves of col. plates.
         LC: My 26, '10.
         PW: Ap 16, '10

M-573   ____ The real Agatha: the unusual adventures of two young men and an heiress / by Edith Huntington Mason; frontispiece by W. T. Smedley. Chicago: A. C. McClurg & Co., 1907. 165, [1] p., front., ill. "This story first appeared in `The Ladies' home journal', April, 1905."
         LC: N 25, '07.
         PW: D 7, '07.

M-574   Mason, Eveleen Laura, b. 1838. Mad? Which? Neither? / by Mrs. Eveleen Laura Mason. [s. l.: s. n.], 1904. 515 p., photo. ill.
         LC reports [Boston: G. H. Ellis].

M-575   ____ Who builds?: a romance: completed in the month of Addar (which is the last half of February and the first half of March) / Eveleen Laura Mason. Brookline, Massachusetts: Eveleen Laura Mason, c1903. 351 p., ill. (some photo.), music.

M-576   Mason, George Allen, b. 1870. The house of hearts in Eighty-Second St.: a novel / by G. Allen Mason; fully illustrated. New York: Broadway Publishing Company, [c1912]. 188 p., front., [5] leaves of plates. [Ill. by J. F. Leary.]   **DLC**

M-577   Mason, Grace Sartwell, b. 1877. The bear's claws / by Grace Sartwell Mason and John Northern Hilliard; with illustrations by W. D. Goldbeck. Chicago: A. C. McClurg & Co., 1913. 351 p., col. front., [3] leaves of col. plates.
         LC: Ap 3, '13.
         PW: Ap 19, '13.
         BLC: London: C. F. Cazenove; Chicago: A. C. McClurg & Co. [printed], 1913.

M-578   ____ The godparents / by Grace Sartwell Mason. Boston; New York: Houghton Mifflin Company, 1910. (Cambridge: The Riverside Press). 235, [1] p., front., [3] leaves of plates. [Ill. by F. Vaux Wilson.]
         LC: Ap 9, '10.
         PW: Mr 26, '10.

M-579   ____ The golden hope / by Grace Sartwell Mason and John Northern Hilliard; illustrated by W. A. Hottinger. New York; London: D. Appleton and Company, 1916. 362, [1] p., front., [3] leaves of plates.
         LC: Ap 24, '16.
         PW: My 6, '16.

_____ His job. In *The best short stories of 1920 and the yearbook of the American short story* (1921), **B-565.**

M-580 _____ His wife's job / by Grace Sartwell Mason . . . ; illustrated by Graham Coates. New York; London: D. Appleton & Company, 1919. 238, [1] p., front., [3] leaves of plates.   **NYP**
LC: Ap 21, '19.
PW: Ap 26, '19.

_____ Home-brew. In *Prize stories of 1923* (1924), **P-621.**

M-581 _____ The shadow of Rosalie Byrnes / by Grace Sartwell Mason . . . ; illustrated. New York; London: D. Appleton and Company, 1919. 235, [1] p., front., [3] leaves of plates. [Ill. by Will Foster and Arthur William Brown.]
LC: S 29, '19.

M-582 Mason, H. A. He conquered the Kaiser / by Capt. H. A. Mason. New York: The Macaulay Company, 1915. 311 p., col. front.
LC: Ap 10, '15.

M-583 Mason, Mai Rightor. The girl who loved the land / by Mai Rightor Mason. Nashville, Tenn.: The Central Book Co., [1917?]. 350 p.
LC: Mr 21, '17.

Mason, Roi M. The first night. In *Yale tales* (1901), **Y-1.**

Mason, Roi M. The prom concert. In *Yale tales* (1901), **Y-1.**

M-584 Mason, Roy, b. 1879. Judgment of the storm / by Roy Mason; based on the photoplay by Ethel Styles Middleton; as produced by Palmer Photoplay Corporation. Garden City, New York: Doubleday, Page & Company, 1923. 308 p., photo. front., [7] leaves of photo. plates. "Director's skeleton continuity, or studio scenario . . . by Ethel Styles Middleton."
LC: D 29, '23.
PW: D 29, '23.
BLC: London: William Heinemann; printed in U. S. A., 1923.

M-585 _____ When I am rich: a novel / by Roy Mason. New York: G. W. Dillingham Company, [c1909]. 343 p.
LC reports front. and [3] leaves of plates.
LC: Je 30, '09.
PW: Jl 31, '09.

Mason, Ruth Little, 1884-1927. On the field of honor. In *Called to the colors and other stories* (1915), **C-50.**

M-586 _____ The trailers: a novel / by Ruth Little Mason. New York; Chicago; Toronto; London; Edinburgh: Fleming H. Revell Company, [c1909]. 365 p. **CLE**
LC: F 17, '09.
PW: F 27, '09.

M-587 Masson, Thomas Lansing, 1866-1934. A bachelor's baby: and some grownups / by Thomas L. Masson; illustrated. New York: Moffat, Yard & Company, 1907. 332 p., front., [7] leaves of plates.
Partly reprinted from various periodicals.
Contents: To begin with -- A bachelor's baby -- The writing on the wall -- The decadence of husbands -- A boy and a girl story -- A modern conversation -- The foolish fool -- Diary of a world -- The only child -- As man to man -- Opinions -- The superfluous baby -- An American story -- Slaves -- The Children's Christmas Exchange Co., Limited -- All's well that begins well -- Mary's little lamb / Thomas W. Lawson -- Mary's little lamb / James Whitcomb Riley -- Mary's little lamb / Henry James -- Mary's little lamb / Rudyard Kipling -- Mary's little lamb / Mr. Dooley -- Mary's little lamb / George Ade -- Mary's little lamb / James Gordon Bennett -- Dimpleton stays at home -- A transaction in real estate -- Our habits -- Juniper Smith, president -- The culprit -- Barter -- The stork -- Governments -- The care of the mind -- A working subject -- Lying -- A kiss -- Christmas for two -- The art of conversation -- The kadoot of Lyssore -- An evening in Bohemia -- The before and after kiss -- A career -- Repartee -Their thoughts of her -- A labor of love -- Two women -- Select your wife with care -- Like father, like son -- A homely girl -- Arthur and his toys: I. The railroad -- II. The street-car line -- III. A set of slums -- IV. The killing -- V. The factory -- VI. The hotel.
LC: S 14, '07.
PW: O 19, '07.

M-588 _____ The Von Blumers / by Tom Masson . . . ; illustrated by Bayard Jones. New York: Moffat, Yard & Company, 1906. 330 p., col. front., [7] leaves of plates.
LC: N 8, '06.
PW: D 1, '06.

M-588.5 Master tales of mystery / by the world's most famous authors of to-day, collected and arranged by Francis J. Reynolds . . . New York: P. F. Collier & Son, [c1915.] 3 vol., front.
Apparent first book appearances: Vol. 1: A suspicious character / William Hamilton Osborne -- Angelo / John A. Moroso. Vol. 2: The border / Henry C. Rowland -- The mystery of seven minutes / Louis Joseph Vance. Vol. 3: The case of Mrs. Magnus / Burton E. Stevenson -- The episode of the black casquette / Joseph Ernest.

M-589 Masterpieces of mystery . . . ed. by Joseph Lewis French. Garden City, New York: Doubleday, Page & Company, 1920. 4 vol.
Contents: Vol. I. Detective stories (Contains first book appearance of *The rape of fear* by Mary E. and Thomas W. Hanshew.) -- Vol. II. Ghost stories -- Vol. III. Mystic-Humorous stories-- Vol IV. Riddle stories.
LC: D 2, '20.

M-590 Masterpieces of wit and humor: containing all that is best in the literature of laughter of all nations / with stories and an introduction by Robert J. Burdette . . . ; with illustrations by Frederick Opper, John T. McCutcheon, Robert L. Dickey, Charles Lederer, Ike Morgan, R. C. Bowman, G. W. Rehse, Bryan Walker, Hugh von Hafsten, Chas. Nelan and other famous cartoonists. [S. l.]: E. J. Long, [c1902]. 514 p., col. front., [1] leaf of plates, ill. (ports.).
   RRR
References: BAL 2013.

M-591 Masters, Edgar Lee, 1868-1950. Children of the market place / by Edgar Lee Masters. New York: The Macmillan Company, 1922. 469 p.
LC: Mr 1, '22.
PW: Ap 1, '22.
BLC: London: Hodder & Stoughton; printed in U. S. A., [1923].

M-592 ____ Mirage / by Edgar Lee Masters. New York: Boni and Liveright, [c1924]. 427 p.
LC: Ap 4, '24.
PW: Ap 12, '24.

M-593 ____ Mitch Miller / by Edgar Lee Masters; with illustrations by John Sloan. New York: The Macmillan Company, 1920. 262 p., ill.
LC: S 30, '20.
PW: O 9, '20.
BLC: London: Jonathan Cape; printed in U. S. A., 1921.

M-594 ____ The nuptial flight / Edgar Lee Masters. New York: Boni and Liveright, [c1923]. 376 p.
LC: S 13, '23.
PW: Ag 18, '23; Ag 25, '23.

M-595 ____ Skeeters Kirby: a novel / by Edgar Lee Masters. New York: The Macmillan Company, 1923. 394 p.
LC: F 14, '23.
PW: F 24, '23.

M-596 Mather, Frank Jewett, 1868-1953. The collectors: being cases mostly under the ninth and tenth commandments / by Frank Jewett Mather, Junr. New York: Henry Holt and Company, 1912. 193 p.
Contents: A ballade of art collectors -- Campbell Corot -- The del Puente Giorgione -- The Lombard runes -- Their cross -- The missing St. Michael -- The lustred pots -- The balaklava coronal -- On art collecting.

Mathews, Amanda, b. 1866. An Aztec biography. In *From the old pueblo: and other tales* (1902), **F-434.**

M-597 ____ The heart of an orphan / by Amanda Mathews; illustrations by W. T. Benda. New York: Desmond FitzGerald, Inc., [c1912]. 159 p., front., [7] leaves of plates.
Contents: The heart of an orphan -- The translation of Giovanna -- "Little sister in cage of gold" -- The Merry Christmas of Giovanna -- Giovanna's Italian renaissance -- Giovanna first remembers -- Giovanna as the wrong princess -- Giovanna's commencement.
LC: O 31, '12.

M-598 ____ The hieroglyphics of love: stories of Sonoratown and old Mexico / by Amanda Mathews. Los Angeles: The Artemisia Bindery, 1906. 112 p., photo. front., ill. [Ill. by Ralph Fullerton Mocine.]
Contents: The hieroglyphics of love -- The potter's wheel -- The Christmas of Esperanza -- The woman and the idol -- By the straggling cypress -- Manuela's lesson -- The kidnapping of Maria Luisa -- Cupid and the first reader -- An Aztec biography -- The taming of the twins -- The miracle of San Juanito -- A Guadalupe wooing.
LC: D 18, '06.

____ The miracle of San Juanito. In *From the old pueblo: and other tales* (1902), **F-434.**

M-599 Mathews, Frances Aymar. "Allee same" / by Frances Aymar Mathews; illustrated by C. F. Neagle. New York: Thomas Y. Crowell & Co., [c1907]. 63, [1] p., front., [3] leaves of plates.
"This story . . . originally appeared in `A little tragedy at Tien-Tsin," published . . . in 1904.

M-600 ____ Billy Duane: a novel / by Frances Aymar Mathews; illustrated. New York: Dodd, Mead and Company, 1905. 361 p., front., [3] leaves of plates. [Ill. by William Sherman Potts.]
PW: Mr 11, '05.

M-601 ____ A Christmas honeymoon / by Frances Aymar Mathews; illustrated in color by Herbert Bohnert. New York: Moffat, Yard and Company, 1912. 151 p., col. front., [3] leaves of col. plates.
LC: O 11, '12.
PW: N 2, '12.

M-602 ____ Fanny of the forty frocks / by Frances Aymar Mathews; frontispiece by George Gibbs. Philadelphia: The John C. Winston Company, [c1913]. 366 p., col. front.
LC: O 2, '13.
PW: N 1, '13.

M-603 ____ The flame dancer / by Frances Aymar Mathews; illustrations by C. F. Neagle. New York: G. W. Dillingham Company, [c1908]. 371 p., front., [3] leaves of plates.
PW: S 19, '08.
BLC: London: T. Fisher Unwin; New York [printed], 1908.

M-604 ____ If David knew: a novel / by Frances Aymar Mathews . . . ; illustrations by Joseph Cummings Chase. New York: G. W. Dillingham Company, [c1910]. 325 p., front., [3] leaves of plates.
LC: O 10, '10.
PW: O 8, '10.
BLC: London: T. Fisher Unwin; New York [printed], 1910.

M-605 ____ A little tragedy at Tien-Tsin / by Frances Aymer Mathews. New York: Robert Grier Cooke, 1904. 426 p., col. front.
Contents: A little tragedy at Tien-Tsin -- "Allee same" -- The elopement of the Princess Yu Tu -- The go-away child -- The lie that Yan Foo told -- Fifteen donkeys and a half -- The little blue cat from Malta -- The mystery of Piper's Ridge -- The man who was centuries old -- The story of a stable door -- At the sign of the shippe -- The lone house at Leith -- The brothers -- The lady of the sonnets.
PW: Ap 23, '04.

M-606 ____ The Marquise's millions: a novel / by Frances Aymar Mathews; frontispiece illustration by Charlotte Weber-Ditzler. New York; London: Funk & Wagnalls Company, 1905. 255 p., [1] leaf of col. plates.
PW: Ap 29, '05.

M-607 ____ My lady Peggy goes to town / by Frances Aymar Mathews; illustrated by Harrison Fisher. Indianapolis: Bowen-Merrill, [c1901]. 338, [1] p., front., [7] leaves of plates. Designed end papers. "The decorations designed by Virginia Keep, the cover designed by Francis Hazenplug."
PW: O 5, '01.

M-608 ____ My Lady Peggy leaves town / by Frances Aymar Mathews; frontispiece. New York: Moffat, Yard and Company, 1913. 372 p., front. [Ill. by Will Hammel.]
LC: Ap 9, '13.

M-609   _____ Pamela Congreve: a novel / by Frances
Aymar Mathews; with illustrations. New York:
Dodd, Mead and Company, 1904. 407 p., front., [5]
leaves of plates. [Ill. by A. D. Rahn.]
PW: My 7, '04.

M-610   _____ The staircase of surprise / by Frances Aymar
Mathews; illustrated. New York: D. Appleton and
Company, 1905. 311 p., front., [3] leaves of plates.
[Ill. by H. C. Edwards.]
PW: N 4, '05.

M-611   _____ The undefiled: a novel of to-day / by Frances
Aymar Mathews. New York; London: Harper &
Brothers, 1906. 277, [1] p.
LC: Ag 22, '06.
PW: S 1, '06.

M-612   Mathews, Robert Valentine. Child of the stars / by
Robert Valentine Mathews. New York: Edwin C.
Hill, 1904. 161 p.
PW: N 11, '05.

M-613   _____ The lost legion / by Robert Valentine Mathews
. . . New York: Published by Edwin C. Hill, 1909.
164 p.   **OSU, KSU**
LC: D 29, '09.
PW: F 19, '10.

M-614   _____ The song of the pines / by Robert Valentine
Mathews; illustrations by James Varrier. New York:
Edwin C. Hill Company, 1906. 350 p., front., [3]
leaves of plates.
LC: Ag 2, '06.
PW: My 18, '07.

M-615   Mathewson, Christy, 1880-1925. Pitcher Pollock / by
Christy Mathewson . . . ; with illustrations by Charles
M. Relyea. New York: Dodd, Mead and Company,
[c1914]. 335 p., front., [3] leaves of plates.   **KSU**
LC: Ap 16, '14.

M-616   Mathison, Volney G. The radiobuster: being some
of the adventures of Samuel Jones, deep sea wireless
operator / by Volney G. Mathison. New York:
Frederick A. Stokes Company, 1924. 182 p.

M-617   Matlack, Margaret Moore. Sergeant Jane / by
Margaret Moore Matlack; with illustrations by Nana
French Bickford. Boston: Little, Brown, and
Company, 1920. 278 p., front., [3] leaves of plates.

M-618   Mätter, John. Once / by John Mätter. New York:
Henry Holt and Company, 1910. 262 p.
LC: S 26, '10.
PW: O 15, '10.

M-619   _____ Three farms / by John Mätter . . . New York:
Henry Holt and Company, 1913. 262 p.   **CLE**
Contents: Provence: the desire -- Saskatchewan: the quest --
Indiana: the goal.
LC: Ap 2, '13.
PW: Ap 5, '13.

M-620   Matteson, H. H. The trap / by H. H. Matteson;
frontispiece by George W. Gage. New York: W. J.
Watt & Company, [c1921]. 293 p., front.
LC: Ja 28, '22.

Matthews, Brander, 1852-1929. An idyl of Central
Park. See Freeman, Mary Eleanor Wilkins,
1852-1930. *The home-coming of Jessica* (1901),
F-396.

M-621   _____ Vistas of New York / by Brander Matthews
. . . ; illustrated. New York; London: Harper &
Brothers Publishers, 1912. 242 p., front., [5] leaves
of plates.
Contents: A young man from the country -- On the steps of the City
Hall -- "Sisters under their skins" -- Under an April sky -- An idyl of
Central Park -- In a hansom -- The frog that played the trombone --
On an errand of mercy -- In a bob-tail car -- In the small hours -- Her
letter to his second wife -- The shortest day in the year.

M-622   Matthews, Dave S. America Kelsey: romance of the
great San Joaquin Valley / by Dave S. Matthews;
illustrated with reproductions of San Joaquin Valley
scenes. [Stockton, Calif.]: Stockton Record Print,
1915. 108 p., photo. front., [2] leaves of photo.
plates. [Photo. by Logan and Stockton Photo-
Engraving Co.] Designed end papers.

M-623   Matthews, Mary Anderson. Love vs. law / by Mary
Anderson Matthews. New York: Broadway
Publishing Company, [c1905]. 293 p., front.
Unexamined copy: bibliographic data from OCLC,
#26978636.

M-624   Matthews, Sue Froman. Grandmother: a tale of old
Kentucky / by Sue Froman Matthews. New York: J.
S. Ogilvie Publishing Company, [c1911]. 273 p.
Designed end papers.
LC: S 18, '11.

M-625   Maule, Mary K. (Mary Katherine), b. 1861. God's
anointed / by Mary Katherine Maule. New York:
The Century Co., 1921. 357 p., front.
LC: S 12, '21.

M-626   _____ The little knight of the X Bar B / by Mary K.
Maule; illustrated by Maynard Dixon. Boston:
Lothrop, Lee & Shepard Co., 1910. 461 p., front.,
[5] leaves of plates.
LC: F 2, '10.
PW: Ap 23, '10.
BLC: London: Hodder & Stoughton, [1925].

M-627   Maule, Mary K. (Mary Katherine), b. 1861. A
prairie-schooner princess / by Mary Katherine Maule;
illustrated by Harold Cue. Boston: Lothrop, Lee &
Shepard Co., 1920. 383 p., front., [3] leaves of
plates.
BLC: London: Hodder & Stoughton, [1927].

M-628   Mavity, Nancy Barr, b. 1890. Hazard / by Nancy
Barr Mavity. New York; London: Harper &
Brothers Publishers, 1924. 311 p.
LC: Mr 4, '24.

M-629   Maxwell, Claretta. We Brandons / by Claretta
Maxwell. New York: Broadway Publishing Co.,
[c1907]. 44 p., front. (port.).
LC: Ap 27, '07.

M-630   Maxwell, Hu, 1860-1927. Jonathan Fish and his
neighbors / by Hu Maxwell. Morgantown, W. Va.:
The Acme Publishing Company, 1902. 110 p.
Contents: Jonathan Fish -- The anarchist -- The fiddler of Polebridge
-- The deserter's child -- First impressions -- Isreal Thompson.
PW: Jl 19, '02.

M-631   Maxwell, Perriton. A third of life / by Perriton Maxwell. Boston: Small, Maynard & Company, [c1921]. 304 p., front., [7] leaves of plates.

M-632   May, Anna, *pseud.* Naomi Wentworth, or, "He leadeth me": a love story / by Anna May [pseud.]. Columbus, Ohio: A. M. Smith, [c1903]. 72 p. Unexamined copy: bibliographic data from OCLC, #15021616.

M-633   May, Earl Chapin, 1873-1960. Cuddy of the white tops / by Earl Chapin May. New York; London: D. Appleton and Company, 1924. 272, [1] p., front. LC: Je 19, '24. PW: Je 28, '24.

M-634   May, Emmet C. (Emmet Claire), b. 1875. The angelus of Sunset Hill / by Emmet C. May. Peoria, Illinois: W. F. Hall Printing Company, 1924. 223 p.   **DLC** LC: Ja 26, '25.

M-635   May, Florence Edna. The unmarried mother / by Florence Edna May. New York: J. S. Ogilvie, c1918. 125 p., front., plates. Unexamined copy: bibliographic data from OCLC, #27944643. On cover: Founded on the play of the same name.

M-636   ____ The unwanted child: a novel founded on the play of the same name / novelized by Florence Edna May . . . New York: J. S. Ogilvie Publishing Company, c1923. 128 p., photo. front., [3] leaves of photo. plates. [Some photo. by H. A. Atwell.] LC: S 10, '23.

M-637   ____ A wife's revelation, or, The revelations of a wife: a novel founded on the play of the latter title / by Florence Edna May . . . New York: J. S. Ogilvie Publishing Company, c1919. 121 p., photo. front., [3] leaves of photo. plates. [Some photo. by H. A. Atwell.]

M-638   May, Florence Land. The broken wheel / by Florence Land May. Boston, Massachusetts: The C. M. Clark Publishing Company, [c1910]. 438 p., front., [7] leaves of plates. [Ill. by D. S. Ross.] LC: Ap 9, '10.

M-639   May, Margery Land. To him that knocketh / by Margery Land May. [New York: Printed by Zincograph Company, c1925]. 315 p. Unexamined copy: bibliographic data from NUC. BLC: London: Hodder & Stoughton, [1925].

M-640   Mayer, Frank. The song of the wolf / by Frank Mayer. New York: Moffat, Yard and Company, 1910. 317 p. LC: My 7, '10. PW: My 14, '10.

Mayfield, Elizabeth. The higher law. In *The rejected apostle* (1924), **R-164.**

____ A mysterious disappearance. In *The rejected apostle* (1924), **R-164.**

____ The pearl of great price. In *The rejected apostle* (1924), **R-164.**

Mayhew, B. F. In the piny woods. In *Southern lights and shadows* (1907), **S-718.**

Maynadier, Howard, 1866-1960, ed. See *Made to order* (1915), **M-352.**

M-641   Maynard, Theodore, 1890-1956. The divine adventure: a novel / by Theodore Maynard . . . New York: Frederick A. Stokes Company, [c1921]. 315 p.   **NBU** LC: Ap 1, '21. PW: Mr 26, '21. BLC: London: Erskine Macdonald, 1921.

Mayo, Clayton. See **Emery, Clay, pseud.**

M-642   Mayo, Margaret, 1882-1951. Baby mine / by Margaret Mayo; with illustrations by Mayo Bunker. New York: Dodd, Mead and Company, 1911. 241 p., col. front., [7] leaves of col. plates. LC: O 30, '11. PW: N 4, '11. BLC: London: B. F. Stevens & Brown; New York printed, 1911.

M-643   ____ Polly of the circus / by Margaret Mayo; illustrated by Harry M. Bunker. New York: Dodd, Mead and Company, 1908. 184 p., col. front., [7] leaves of col. plates. LC: Ag 21, '08. PW: S 26, '08. BLC: London: Cassell & Co., 1909.

M-644   Mayo, Margery. Russians abroad: and other stories / by Margery Mayo. Boston, Massachusetts: The Stratford Co., 1922. 181 p.   **NYP** Contents: Russians abroad -- The peril of the sea -- An increase in the sale of soap -- The home ranch. LC: My 31, '22. PW: Je 10, '22.

Mayoe, Franklin, pseud. See Rosewater, Frank, b. 1856.

Mayoe, Marian, pseud. See **Rosewater, Frank, b. 1856.**

M-645   Mays, Julia Webb. Luda, the occult girl: a romance / by Julia Webb Mays. New York: Broadway Publishing Co., [c1912]. 280 p., [4] leaves of plates. [Ill. by Carolyn Smith.]   **DLC** LC: N 8, '12. PW: D 28, '12.

M-646   [Mays, Malie Eskie], b. 1864. The schoolma'ams of District 91 / by one of them. Topeka, Kansas: R. I. Palmer, [c1903]. 59 p.

M-647   Meacham, Allen. Belle Jones: a story of fulfilment / by Allen Meacham. New York: E. P. Dutton & Company, [c1916]. 102 p. PW: N 4, '16.

Meagher, Cathirine L. Old Bartley Bannim. In *The Senior lieutenant's wager: and other stories* (1905), **S-312.**

M-648   Means, E. K. (Eldred Kurtz), 1878-1957. E. K. Means . . . / illustrated by Kemble. New York; London: G. P. Putnam's Sons, 1918. ([New York]: The Knickerbocker Press). 385 p., front., [7] leaves of plates.
"Is this a title? It is not. It is the name of a writer of negro stories, who has made himself so completely the writer of negro stories that his book needs no title."
Contents: Forewood -- The late Figger Bush -- Hoodoo eyes -- The art of enticing labor -- The cruise of the Mud Hen -- Two sorry sons of sorrow -- Monarch of the manacle -- All is fair -- Hoodoo face.
LC: Jl 17, '18.
PW: Jl 13, '18.

M-649   ____ Further E. K. Means . . . / illustrated by Kemble. New York; London: G. P. Putnam's Sons, [c1921]. ([New York]: The Knickerbocker Press). 346 p., front.
"Is this a title? It is not. It is the name of a writer of negro stories, who has made himself so completely the writer of negro stories that this third book, like the first and second, needs no title."
Contents: The left hind foot -- The 'fraid cat -- The consolation prize -- The first high janitor -- Family ties -- The ten-share horse -- A chariot of fire.
LC: F 7, '21.
PW: Ja 29, '21.

M-650   ____ More E. K. Means . . . / illustrated by Kemble. New York; London: G. P. Putnam's Sons, 1919. ([New York]: The Knickerbocker Press). 369 p., front., ill.
"Is this a title? It is not. It is the name of a writer of negro stories, who has made himself so completely the writer of negro stories that this second book, like the first, needs no title." "First published in the All Story Weekly".
Contents: Diada, daughter of discord -- Getting ready to die -- A mascot jinx -- Messing with matrimony -- A corner in pickaninnies -- Idle dreams -- The gift of power -- Owner of Doodle-bug -- Every pose a picture -- D. D.
LC: My 31, '19.
PW: Je 7, '19.

____ Plumb nauseated. In *The ten-foot chain, or, Can love survive the shackles?* (1920), **T-108.**

M-651   Mearns, Hughes, b. 1875. I ride in my coach / by Hughes Mearns . . . ; illustrated by W. T. Schwarz. Philadelphia: The Penn Publishing Company, 1923. 362 p., front.
LC: Jl 12, '23.
PW: S 15, '23.

M-652   ____ Richard Richard / by Hughes Mearns; illustrated by Ralph L. Boyer. Philadelphia: The Penn Publishing Company, 1916. 446 p., front., [4] leaves of plates.
LC: Je 12, '16.
PW: S 30, '16.
BLC: London: Constable & Co., 1921.

M-653   ____ The vinegar saint / by Hughes Mearns . . . ;

illustrated by Ralph L. Boyer. Philadelphia: The Penn Publishing Company, 1920, [c1919]. 419 p., front., [3] leaves of plates.
LC: My 29, '19.
PW: Mr 1, '19.

M-654   Mearns, Lillian Hathaway. A Philippine romance / by Lillian Hathaway Mearns. New York: Aberdeen Publishing Company, [c1910]. 124 p., incl. front., [2] leaves of plates. [Ill. by Isabella Morton.]
LC: Ja 3, '11.
PW: F 11, '11.

M-655   Mears, Madge. The jealous goddess / by Madge Mears. London: John Lane; N. Y.: John Lane Company, 1915. 316 p.
Unexamined copy: bibliographic data from NUC.
PW: Je 26, '15.

Mears, Mary Martha, 1876-1943. According' to Solomon. In *Love* (1901), **L-525.**

M-656   ____ The bird in the box / by Mary Mears. New York: Frederick A. Stokes Company, [1910]. 376 p.
LC: N 14, '10.
PW: D 3, '10.

M-657   ____ The breath of the runners: a novel / by Mary Mears. New York: Frederick A. Stokes Company, [1906]. 293 p.
LC: O 8, '06.
PW: N 3, '06.

____ The marrying of Esther. In *Different girls* (1906), **D-383.**

M-658   ____ Rosamond the second: being the true record of the unparalleled romance of one Claudius Fuller / by Mary Mears . . . New York: Frederick A. Stokes Company, [c1910]. 163 p.
LC: My 3, '10.
PW: My 7, '10.

M-659   Mearson, Lyon. The whisper on the stair / by Lyon Mearson; frontispiece by George W. Gage. New York: The Macaulay Company, [c1924]. 311 p., front.
LC: Ag 8, '24.
PW: Ag 23, '24.
BLC: London: Hutchinson & Co., 1924.

Mechem, Philip R. A young man in wrong. In *Made to order* (1915), **M-352.**

Meeker, Nellie J., 1883-1902. See **Valentine, Jane, pseud.**

M-660   Meeker, Stella Colby. The valley people / Stella Colby Meeker. [Terre Haute, Ind.: The Viquesney Company, c1920]. 79 p.   **DLC**

M-661   Meekins, Lynn Roby, 1862-1933. Adam Rush: a novel / by Lynn Roby Meekins; with a frontispiece by Francis Day. Philadelphia; London: J. B. Lippincott Company, 1902. 352 p., incl. col. front.
PW: N 1, '02.

M-662 Megargel, Percy F. The car and the lady / by Percy F. Megargel and Grace Sartwell Mason. New York: The Baker and Taylor Company, 1908. 276 p.
LC: Ag 8, '08.

M-663 Meguire, Emma E. The makin's of a girl / Emma E. Meguire. Boston: Richard G. Badger, 1911. ([Boston]: The Gorham Press). 199 p. **OSU, DLC**
LC: D 20, 10.

M-664 Meherin, Elenore. "Chickie": a hidden, tragic chapter from the life of a girl of this strange "today" / by Elenore Meherin; illustrated with scenes from the photoplay, a First National picture, featuring Dorothy Mackaill. New York: Grosset & Dunlap, [c1925]. 529 p., front., plates.
Unexamined copy: bibliographic data from OCLC, #4453257.
PW: Jl 11, '25.

M-665 ____ "Chickie": a sequel / by Elenore Meherin. New York: Grosset & Dunlap, [c1925]. 308 p.
PW: N 28, '25.

M-666 Meigs, Cornelia, 1884-1973. Master Simon's garden: a story / by Cornelia Meigs; illustrated. New York: The Macmillan Company, 1916. 320 p., col. front., [3] leaves of col. plates. [Ill. by Frances White.]
PW: N 4, '16.

M-667 Meirovitz, Joseph M. (Joseph Moses), b. 1884. The path of error and other stories / by Joseph M. Meirovitz. Boston: Four Seas Company, 1918. 128 p.
"Many of these stories . . . were first printed in the New England socialist or the New England leader, in 1916 and 1917."
Contents: The path of error -- The artist's model -- "Cat and rat" -- Night work -- A citizen soldier's confession -- Resolutions -- Daughters of the underworld -- A torrid night -- His lost faith -- "Comrade Healy" -- A father's heart -- A Christian town -- War dogs -- A town editor -- Good friends -- Jack's dream -- At the restaurant -- Mary -- A deserted woman -- Alone.

M-668 Meixner, Anna. Life and love, in prose and rhyme / by Anna Meixner. New York: Broadway Publishing Company, 1903. 160 p., front. (port.).
Unexamined copy: bibliographic data from OCLC, #18420731.

M-669 Meloney, William Brown, 1878-1925. The girl of the Golden Gate / by William Brown Meloney. New York: Edward J. Clode, [c1913]. 313 p., col. front. [Ill. by H. Richard Boehm.]
LC: Mr 18, '13.
PW: Mr 29, '13.
BLC: London: Grant Richards; Rahway, N. J., printed 1913.

M-670 Melton, Frances Jones. A daughter of the highlanders / by Frances Jones Melton. Boston: The Roxburgh Publishing Company Incorporated, [c1910]. 376 p., photo. front. (port.).
LC: Je 22, '10.

M-671 Melville, Herman, 1819-1891. The apple-tree table and other sketches / by Herman Melville; with an introductory note by Henry Chapin. Princeton: Princeton University Press; London: Humphrey Milford: Oxford University Press, 1922. 329 p.
Contents: The apple-tree table -- Hawthorne and his Mosses -- Jimmy Rose -- I and my chimney -- Paradise of bachelors and the Tartarus of maids -- Cock-a-doodle-doo -- The fiddler -- Poor man's pudding and rich man's crumbs -- The happy failure -- The 'gees.
LC: Mr 28, '23.
PW: F 10, '23.
References: BAL 13681.

M-672 Mendes, H. Pereira (Henry Pereira), 1852-1937. In old Egypt: a story about the Bible but not in the Bible . . . / by H. Pereira Mendes; illustrated by Mabel L. Humphrey. New York: Frederick A. Stokes Company, 1903. 229 p., front., [11] leaves of plates.

M-673 Menke, Louis G. The fatal wedding: adapted from Theo. Kramer's great play of the same name / by Louis G. Menke. New York: J. S. Ogilvie Publishing Company, c1902. 125 p.

M-674 [Mercein, Eleanor], b. 1880. Kildares of Storm / by Eleanor Mercein Kelly; with frontispiece by Alonzo Kimball. New York: The Century Co., 1916. 435 p., front.
LC: O 25, '16.
PW: O 14, '16.

M-675 ____ The Mansion House / by Eleanor Mercein Kelly. New York; London: The Century Co., [c1925]. 339 p.
LC: Mr 30, '25.
PW: Ap 4, '25.

M-676 ____ Toya the unlike / by Eleanor Mercein Kelly; with a frontispiece by Arthur Hutchins. Boston: Small, Maynard and Company, [c1913]. 262 p., col. front.
LC: Je 24, '13.
PW: Jl 5, '13.

M-677 ____ Why Joan? / by Eleanor Mercein Kelly. New York: The Century Co., 1919. 407 p., col. front.
LC: Mr 24, '19.
PW: Mr 22, '19.

Mercer, C. A. The garden of memories. In *Atlantic narratives*; first series (1918), A-360.

M-678 Merchant, Mary Raymond. Alice Haines: a story of the retributive power of love / by Mary Raymond Merchant. Elmira, N. Y.: Frank A. Beach, printer, [1904?]. 108 p.

M-679 Meredith, Charlotte Hay. Mrs. Linthicum and Mary Jane / by Charlotte Hay Meredith; illustrated by C. A. Briggs . . . Chicago: M. A. Donohue & Co., [c1913]. 203 p., front., ill.

M-680 Meredith, Ellis, b. 1865. Heart of my heart / by Ellis Meredith. New York: McClure, Phillips & Co., 1904. 230 p.
PW: Ap 2, '04.
BLC: London: Methuen & Co., 1905.

____ The lost jurisdiction. In *Through the forbidden gates* (1903), T-222.

M-681   ____ The master-knot of human fate / by Ellis
Meredith. Boston: Little, Brown, and Company,
1901. 309 p.
PW: Ap 20, '01.

M-682   ____ Under the Harrow / by Ellis Meredith.
Boston: Little, Brown, and Company, 1907. 267 p.
LC: Mr 28, '07.
PW: Ap 13, '07.

M-683   Meredith, junior, *pseud.* The heiress of Cranham
Hall / by Meredith junior [pseud.]. New York;
Baltimore: Broadway Publishing Co., [c1910].
286 p., front., [3] leaves of plates. [Ill. by William
L. Hudson.]   **GZM**

M-684   Meredith, Katharine Mary Cheever. The wing of
love / by Katharine Mary Cheever Meredith. New
York: McClure, Phillips & Co., 1905. 162, [1] p.
PW: Ap 29, '05.

M-685   Merington, Marguerite. Scarlett of the Mounted / by
Marguerite Merington. New York: Moffat, Yard &
Company, 1906. 214 p., front., [5] leaves of plates.
[Ill. by A. duFord Piney.]
LC: Ag 20, '06.
PW: S 1, '06.

M-686   Meriwether, Elizabeth A., 1824-1917. The sowing of
swords, or, The soul of the 'sixties / by Hannah
Parting of New England; edited by Elizabeth A.
Meriwether . . . New York; Washington: The Neale
Publishing Company, 1910. 382 p.
LC: O 12, '10.

M-687   Merlinjones, Ivan Morgan. The reclamation of
Wales: a patriotic romance founded on facts: a
sequel to Dear Old Wales / by Ivan Morgan
Merlinjones . . . New York: Edwin S. Gorham,
1913. 188 p., [3] leaves of photo. plates.   **DLC**

   Merrick, Leonard. The laurels and the lady. In
More aces (1925), M-962.

M-688   Merrill, Harrison R. (Harrison Reuben), 1884-1938.
Bart of Kane County: and other stories / by Harrison
R. Merrill; illustrated; cover design by Ted Bushman;
frontispiece by George K. Lewis. Provo, Utah:
Published by Post Publishing Company, [c1925].
147 p., front., [3] leaves of plates.
Contents: Bart of Kane County -- The seer -- Speck's idol -- Eight
dollars worth -- Love's message -- The pig and the man -- Over
twenty-one -- The old trial -- "Too-re-kay" -- Shorty trades horses.

M-689   Merrill, Henry A. Alexander Gifford, or, Vi'let's
boy: a story of Negro life / by Rev. Henry A.
Merrill; illustrated. Salem, Mass.: Press of
Newcomb & Gauss, 1905. 331 p., front. (port.), [3]
leaves of plates.

M-690   Merrill, James Milford, 1847-1936. An American
sovereign / by James Milford Merrill. Boston: The
C. M. Clark Publishing Company, 1909. 307 p.,
front., [5] leaves of plates.
LC: D 27, '09.

M-691   Merrill, Orin S. "Mysterious Scott": the Monte
Cristo of Death Valley: and tracks of a tenderfoot: a
story of modern mystery of Western life and the real

experiences of a real tenderfoot, including a midsummer trip through Death Valley / by Orin S.
Merrill. Chicago, Ill.: Orin S. Merrill, Publisher,
[c1906]. 210 p., [1] leaf of plates (map), photo.
ill.   **CRU**

Merriman, Charles Eustace, jt. pseud. <u>See</u> **Tilton,
Dwight, jt. pseud. of W. D. Quint and G. T.
Richardson.**

M-692   Merrit, Edward A. The city of St. Anna: the story
of the man child / written by Edward A. Merrit. [Salt
Lake: Century, c1908]. 133 p.   **DLC**

M-693   Merritt, Abraham, 1882-1943. The moon pool / by
A. Merritt. New York; London: G. P. Putnam's
Sons, 1919. ([New York]: The Knickerbocker
Press). 433 p., front. [Ill. by J. C. Coll.]
LC: N 4, '19.

M-694   Merrow, Florenz S. The reconstruction of Elinore
Wood / by Florenz S. Merrow. New York;
Washington; Atlanta: Broadway Publishing Co.,
[c1910]. 321 p., front., [4] leaves of photo. plates.
      NYP
LC: Mr 18, '11.

M-695   The Merry Widow: a novel founded on Franz
Lehar's Viennese opera, Die lustige Witwe as
produced by Henry W. Savage; illustrations from
scenes in the American production. New York: G.
W. Dillingham Company, [c1909]. 331 p., photo.
front., [5] leaves of photo. plates.

M-696   Mersereau, John, b. 1898. The checkered flag / by
John Mersereau. Boston: Small, Maynard &
Company, [c1925]. 260 p.
LC: Je 13, '25.
PW: My 30, '25.
BLC: London: Brentano's; printed in U. S. A.,
[1925].

M-697   ____ Garber of Thunder Gorge / by John Mersereau
and E. Whitman Chambers. Boston: Small,
Maynard & Company, [c1924]. 305 p.
LC: Je 27, '24.
PW: Jl 19, '24.

M-698   Mertins, Gustave Frederick, b. 1872. The storm
signal / by Gustave Frederick Mertins; with
illustrations by Arthur I. Keller. Indianapolis: The
Bobbs-Merrill Company, [c1905]. 425 p., front., [5]
leaves of plates.
PW: D 23, '05.

M-699   ____ A watcher of the skies / Gustave Frederick
Mertins. New York: Thomas Y. Crowell Company,
[1911]. 376 p., col. front. [Ill. by Emlen
McConnell.]
PW: S 2, '11.

M-700   Merton, Madge. Confessions of a chorus girl / by
Madge Merton. New York: The Grafton Press,
[c1903]. 105 p., incl. front. [Ill. by Hal Canfield.]
PW: Ap 25, '03.

M-701   Merwin, Bannister. The girl and the bill / by Bannister Merwin; illustrations by Harrison Fisher and the Kinneys. New York: Dodd, Mead and Company, 1909. 371 p., col. front., [3] leaves of col. plates.
PW: Ap 10, '09.

M-702   Merwin, Samuel, 1874-1936. Anthony the absolute / by Samuel Merwin; illustrated by R. M. Crosby. New York: The Century Co., 1914. 360 p., incl. [8] leaves of plates, front.
LC: Mr 7, '14.
PW: Mr 7, '14.
BLC: London: Grant Richards; [printed in America, 1914.]

M-703   ____ Calumet "K" / by Merwin-Webster . . . ; with many illustrations by Harry C. Edwards. New York: The Macmillan Company; London: Macmillan & Co., Ltd., 1901. 345 p., front., [19] leaves of plates, plan.
PW: O 26, '01.
Another edition: 1903.
PW: Ap 18, '03.

M-704   ____ The charmed life of Miss Austin / by Samuel Merwin; forty illustrations by R. M. Crosby. New York: The Century Co., 1914. 323 p., front. ill., ill.
LC: S 18, '14.
PW: S 19, '14.
BLC: London: Grant Richards; New York printed, 1915.

M-705   ____ The citadel: a romance of unrest / by Samuel Merwin. New York: The Century Co., 1912. 409 p.
LC: Je 10, '12.
PW: Je 1, '12.

M-706   ____ Comrade John / by Merwin-Webster; with a frontispiece in color by George E. Burr. New York: The Macmillan Company, 1907. 370 p., col. front.
LC: O 17, '07.
PW: N 9, '07.

M-707   ____ Goldie Green / by Samuel Merwin. Indianapolis: The Bobbs-Merrill Company, [c1922]. 341 p., front.
LC: Ap 3, '22.
PW: Ap 15, '22.

M-708   ____ Henry is twenty: a further episodic history of Henry Calverly, 3rd / by Samuel Merwin; illustrated by Stockton Mulford. Indianapolis: The Bobbs-Merrill Company, [c1918]. 385 p., front., [4] leaves of plates.
Contents: The irrational animal -- In sand-fly time -- The stimulant -- The white star -- Tiger, Tiger! -- Aladdin on Simpson Street -- The bubble, reputation -- This bud of love -- What's money -- Love laughs.
LC: O 14, '18.
PW: O 12, '18.

M-709   ____ Hills of Han: a romantic incident / by Samuel Merwin; illustrated by Walt Louderback. Indianapolis: The Bobbs-Merrill Company, [c1920]. 365 p., front., [5] leaves of plates.
LC: Ap 12, '20.
PW: Ap 3, '20.
BLC: London: Hodder & Stoughton; printed in U. S. A., [1920].

M-710   ____ His little world: the story of Hunch Badeau / by Samuel Merwin; illustrated by Alonzo Kimball. New York: A. S. Barnes & Company, 1903. 201 p., front., [2] leaves of plates.
PW: O 3, '03.
BLC: N. Y.: A. S. Barnes & Company; London: Authors' Syndicate, 1903.

M-711   ____ The honey bee: a story of a woman in revolt / by Samuel Merwin; illustrated by R. M. Crosby. Indianapolis: The Bobbs-Merrill Company, [c1915]. 458 p., front., [6] leaves of plates.
LC: My 12, '15.
PW: My 15, '15.
BLC: London: Eveleigh Nash Co., 1916.

M-712   ____ In red and gold / by Samuel Merwin; illustrated by Cyrus Leroy Baldridge. Indianapolis: The Bobbs-Merrill Company, [c1921]. 352 p., front., [5] leaves of plates.
LC: Mr 23, '21.
PW: Ap 2, '21.
BLC: London: Hodder & Stoughton, [1921].

M-713   ____ The Merry Anne / by Samuel Merwin . . . ; with illustrations and decorations by Thomas Fogarty. New York: The Macmillan Company; London: Macmillan & Co., Ltd., 1904. 417 p., col. front., [5] leaves of col. plates, ill. Illustrated end papers.
PW: Ap 23, '04.

M-714   ____ The moment of beauty / Samuel Merwin. Boston; New York: Houghton Mifflin Company, 1925. (Cambridge: The Riverside Press). 312, [1] p., col. front.
LC: Mr 9, '25.
PW: Mr 14, '25.

M-715   ____ On Taku Bar / Samuel Merwin. New York: The Ridgway Company, [c1913]. 27 p.

M-716   ____ The passionate pilgrim: being the narrative of an oddly dramatic year in the life of Henry Calverly, 3rd / by Samuel Merwin; illustrated by Stockton Mulford. Indianapolis: The Bobbs-Merrill Company, [c1919]. 403 p., front., [4] leaves of plates.
LC: Ag 6, '19.
PW: Jl 26, '19.
BLC: London: G. Allen & Unwin, [1921].

M-717   ____ The road-builders / by Samuel Merwin; with illustrations by F. B. Masters. New York: The Macmillan Company; London: Macmillan & Co., ltd., 1905. 313 p., front., [10] leaves of plates. Illustrated end papers.
PW: O 21, '05.

M-718   ____ The road to Frontenac / by Samuel Merwin. New York: Doubleday, Page & Co., 1901. 404 p., front., [3] leaves of plates. [Ill. by E. L. Blumenschein.]

PW: O 12, '01.
BLC: London: John Murray, 1901.

M-719   ____ Silk: a legend as narrated in the journals and correspondence of Jan Po / by Samuel Merwin; illustrated by N. C. Wyeth. Boston; New York: Houghton Mifflin Company, 1923. (Cambridge: The Riverside Press). 266, [1] p., col. front. Map on end papers.
LC: O 24, '23.
PW: O 27, '23.
BLC: London: Constable & Co., 1924.

    ____, contributor. <u>See</u> *The sturdy oak* (1917), **S-1101.**

M-720   ____ Temperamental Henry: an episodic history of the early life and the young loves of Henry Calverly, 3rd / by Samuel Merwin; illustrated by Stockton Mulford. Indianapolis: The Bobbs-Merrill Company, [c1917]. 382 p., front., [4] leaves of plates.
LC: S 20, '17.
PW: S 29, '17.
BLC: London: G. Allen & Unwin, 1922.

M-721   ____ The trufflers: a story / by Samuel Merwin; illustrations by Frank Snapp. Indianapolis: The Bobbs-Merrill Company, [c1916]. 456 p., front., [4] leaves of plates.
LC: O 19, '16.
PW: O 14, '16.

M-722   ____ The whip hand: a tale of the pine country / by Samuel Merwin . . . New York: Doubleday, Page & Company, 1903. 299 p., front., [7] leaves of plates. [Ill. by F. R. Gruger.]
PW: N 14, '03.

M-723   Merz, Charles, b. 1893. Centerville, U. S. A. / by Charles Merz. New York; London: The Century Co., [c1924]. 275 p.
Contents: Grandpa Gilpin -- Cod Macy -- Henrietta Crosby -- Doctor Hodge -- Mrs. Henry Nesbit -- The brothers Tevis -- Madame Naida -- Captain Foley -- Lucy Wallis -- Myron Daw -- Millie Turner -- Harvey Burch -- Jim Lee -- Parson Todd -- Ernest Loring -- Peter Quigley.
LC: S 3, '24.

M-724   Messenger, F. M. (Frank Mortimer), b. 1852. Catacombs of worldly success, or, History of Coarsellor Dell: a glimpse of the interior workings of a large industrial concern, showing its social and religious sides, with relation to its business policies / by F. M. Messenger . . . Waukesha, Wisconsin: Published by Metropolitain Church Association, [c1910]. 235 p., [8] leaves of plates. Decorative end papers.

M-725   Metcalf, Arthur, b. 1864. The green devil: a romance of Thornton Abbey in the days of John Wyclif / by Arthur Metcalf. Boson; New York; Chicago: The Pilgrim Press, [1912]. 509 p., front., [3] leaves of plates. [Ill. by Frank T. Merrill.] Illustrated end papers.
LC: N 6, '12.
PW: N 16, '12.

M-726   Metcalf, Edwin Styles, b. 1843. Talien, a Spanish princess / by Edwin Styles Metcalf . . . Chicago: L'Ora Queta Publishing Company, [c1910]. 147 p., front.   **DLC**
LC: Jl 29, '10.

M-727   Metcalfe, Francis. Side show studies / by Francis Metcalfe; illustrated with many amusing drawings by Oliver Herford. New York: The Outing Publishing Company, 1906. 232 p., ill.   **MNU**

M-728   [Metcalfe, James Stetson], 1858-1927. Another three weeks / not by El-n-r Gl-n. New York: Life Publishing Company, 1908. 63 p.   **OSU, COD**
PW: F 1, '08.

M-729   [____] Jane Street of Gopher Prairie / by the author "Another three weeks." New York: The Probono Publishing Company, 1921. 54, [441]-449, [2] p.
PW: Ag 6, '21.

M-730   Metcalfe, Richard Lee, b. 1861. "Bishop Sunbeams": and other stories of service / by Richard L. Metcalfe . . . Lincoln, Nebraska, U. S. A.: The Woodruff-Collins Press, 1909. 192 p., col. front.
Contents: Bishop Sunbeams -- The master of Verbana Lodge -- The perfect tribute -- The invisible playmate -- "Comin' thro' the rye" -- The governor and the baby -- The surgeon of the Seventh Illinois -- Things that tell -- Dick -- The mother love -- Father and son -- Wayside literature -- Stories from life -- Man's trusted friend -- McGuffey and his pupils -- "Good, golden stuff" -- In the prison self -- Educating the heart -- "Cousin May" -- Flowers -- "I'm wishing for you".
LC: S 7, '09.
PW: O 16, '09.

M-731   ____ "Of such is the kingdom": and other stories from life / by Richard L. Metcalfe; illustrations by Franklin Booth. Lincoln, Nebraska: The Woodruff-Collins Press, 1907. 209 p., front., [6] leaves of plates.   **GZM**
"Tenth thousand."
LC: O 29, '07.
PW: Mr 9, '07.

M-732   Methven, Paul. Billy / by Paul Methven . . . New York: John Lane Company, 1911. 356 p.   **DLC**
BLC: London: Chatto & Windus, 1911.

M-733   Metour, Eugene Paul. In the wake of the Green banner / by Eugene Paul Metour; illustrated by E. M. Ashe. New York: Charles Scribner's Sons, 1909. 444 p., front., [3] leaves of plates.
BLC: London: William Heinemann, 1910.

M-734   Metz, Freda Virginia. Roselin, or, A ruby necklace / by Freda Virginia Metz. Hammond, Indiana: W. B. Conkey Company, 1913. 336 p.   **DLC**
PW: D 20, '13.

M-735   Meyer, Annie Nathan, 1867-1951. Robert Annys: poor priest: a tale of the great uprising / by Annie Nathan Meyer. New York: The Macmillan Company; London: Macmillan & Co., Ltd., 1901. 347 p.

    Meyer, B.Q. Bill Wayne, Esq. <u>In</u> *Yale tales* (**1901**), **Y-1.**

_____ Henrico Samuel-Smith, freshman. In *Yale tales* (1901), **Y-1**.

Meyer, Ernest L. To fool the ignorant. In *A book of narratives* (1917), **B-734**.

M-736   Meyer, George Homer. The nine swords of Morales: the story of an old-time California feud / by George Homer Meyer. Philadelphia: Henry Altemus Company, 1905. 264 p.

M-737   Meyer, John J. (John Joseph), b. 1873. The deer-smellers of Haunted Mountain: the almost unbelievable experiences of a cerebroic hunter in the hills of this world and the lowlands of the universe with a gypsy-eyed spirit adventurer: humorously tattle-taled / by John J. Meyer. New York: The Cerebroscope Company, 1921. 247 p., ill.
LC: Mr 14, '21.

M-738   _____ 20,000 trails under the universe with the cerebroscope: a tale of wonderful adventures / by John J. Meyer. New York: The Cerebroscope Company, [c1917]. 144 p., front., ill.
LC: Jl 6, '17.

M-739   Meyer, Lucy Rider, 1849-1922. Mary North: a novel / by Lucy Rider Meyer. New York; Chicago; Toronto; London; Edinburgh: Fleming H. Revell Company, 1903. 339 p.
PW: Mr 21, '03.

Meyer, Mahrah (Carsociolo) de, b. 1875. See **DeMeyer, Mahrah.**

M-740   Michaels, Janie Chase, 1864?-1959. Polly of the Midway-Sunset / by Janie Chase Michaels. San Francisco, Calif.: Harr Wagner Publishing Co., 1917. 104 p., front. Illustrated border. [Ill. by Mrs. Bertha Wenzlaff Janes.]
LC: My 5, '17.

M-741   [Micheaux, Oscar], b. 1884. The conquest: the story of a negro pioneer / by the pioneer. Lincoln, Nebr.: The Woodruff Press, 1913. 311 p., photo. front., [15] leaves of photo. plates.
LC: My 6, '13.
PW: My 31, '13.

M-742   _____ The forged note: a romance of the darker races / by Oscar Micheaux . . . ; illustrated by C. W. Heller. Lincoln, Nebraska: Western Book Supply Company, 1915. 521 p., ill.   Illustrated end papers.
LC: D 7, '15.
PW: Ja 8, '16.

M-743   _____ The homesteader: a novel / by Oscar Micheaux . . . ; illustrated by W. M. Farrow. Sioux City, Iowa: Western Book Supply Company, [c1917]. 533 p., col. front., [6] leaves of plates.

M-744   Michelson, Miriam, 1870-1942. Anthony Overman / by Miriam Michelson; illustrated by John Cecil Clay. New York: Doubleday, Page & Company, 1906. 330 p., front., [4] leaves of plates (1 double).

PW: Ag 18, '06.
BLC: London: Doubleday, Page & Co.; New York [printed], 1906.

M-745   _____ The awakening of Zojas / by Miriam Michelson. New York: Doubleday, Page & Company, 1910. 268 p.
Contents: The awakening of Zojas -- The cradle -- Peach blossoms -- Tares.
LC: Mr 11, '10.
BLC: London: Hodder & Stoughton; [printed in New York], 1910.

_____ The contumacy of Sarah L. Walker. In *Spinners' book of fiction* (1907), **S-755**.

M-746   _____ In the bishop's carriage / by Miriam Michelson; the illustrations by Harrison Fisher. Indianapolis: The Bobbs-Merrill Company, [1904]. 280 p., front., [5] leaves of plates.
"The first chapter of this book appeared as a short story in Ainslee's magazine."
PW: Mr 26, '04.
BLC: London: Archibald Constable & Co., 1904.

M-747   _____ The Madigans / by Miriam Michelson . . . ; with illustrations by Orson Lowell. New York: The Century Co., 1904. 361 p., incl. 22 plates, front.
PW: O 15, '04.

M-748   _____ Michael Thwaites's wife / by Miriam Michelson; illustrated by C. Coles Phillips. New York: Doubleday, Page & Company, 1909. 402 p., col. front. (double-leaf), [2] leaves of col. plates.
LC: My 28, '09.

M-749   _____ A yellow journalist / by Miriam Michelson. New York: D. Appleton and Company, 1905. 315 p., front., [3] leaves of plates. [Ill. by Gordon H. Grant.]
PW: N 4, '05.

M-750   Middleton, Cornelia Scribner. Polly for short / by Cornelia Scribner Middleton; drawings by Isabella Morton. New York City: Aberdeen Publishing Company, 1909. 31 p., ill.   **DLC**
LC: D 23, '09.

M-751   Middleton, George, b. 1880. His great play / George Middleton. New York: The Winthrop Press, c1914. 31 p., col. front. Previously published in Munsey's magazine.

M-752   Mighels, Ella Sterling, 1853-1934. Fairy tale of the white man: told from the gates of sunset / by Ella Sterling Mighels . . . ; cover and illustrations by W. Kimball Briggs. San Francisco: Pacific Publication Company, 1915. 72 p.
LC: Ja 17, '16.
PW: F 26, '16.

M-753   _____ The full glory of Diantha / by Mrs. Philip Verrill Mighels. Chicago: Forbes & Company, 1909. 432 p.
LC: My 10, '09.
PW: My 15, '09.

M-754   ____ Wawona: an Indian story of the Northwest / by Ella Sterling Mighels . . . San Francisco, California: Harr Wagner Publishing Co., [c1921]. 117 p., ill. (incl. map).
PW: Je 3, '22.

M-755   Mighels, Philip Verrill, 1869-1911. As it was in the beginning / by Philip Verrill Mighels . . . New York: Desmond FitzGerald, Inc., [c1912]. 373 p., col. front., ill. [Ill. by A. M. Froehlich.]
LC: My 25, '12.

     ____ Barney Doon, braggart. In *Life at high tide* **(1907), L-281.**

M-756   ____ Bruvver Jim's baby / by Philip Verrill Mighels. New York; London: Harper & Brothers, 1904. 264, [1] p.
PW: My 14, '04.

M-757   ____ The crystal sceptre: a story of adventure / by Philip Verrill Mighels. New York: R. F. Fenno & Company, 1901. 389 p.
LC: Jl 5, '01.
PW: Jl 20, '01.

M-758   ____ Dunny: a mountain romance / by Philip Verrill Mighels. New York; London: Harper & Brothers, 1906. 263, [1] p.
LC: S 27, '06.
PW: O 6, '06.

M-759   ____ The furnace of gold / by Philip Verrill Mighels; illustrations by J. N. Marchand. New York: Desmond FitzGerald, Inc., [c1910]. 402 p., front., [11] leaves of plates.
LC: Ja 12, '10.
PW: F 19, '10.

M-760   ____ Hearts of grace / by Philip Verrill Mighels . . . New York: Desmond FitzGerald, Inc., [c1913]. 442 p., col. front. [Ill. by John Innes.]
A revision of "When a witch is young."
LC: Mr 17, '13.
PW: Mr 22, '13.

M-761   ____ The inevitable: a novel / by Philip Verrill Mighels; with a frontispiece by John Wolcott Adams. Philadelphia: J. B. Lippincott Company, 1902. 361 p., col. front.
PW: N 1, '02.

     ____ A little pioneer. In *Under the Sunset* **(1906), U-9.**

M-762   ____ The pillars of Eden: a novel / by Philip Verrill Mighels. New York: Desmond FitzGerald, Inc., [c1909]. 350 p.
LC: S 7, '09.
PW: O 9, '09.

M-763   ____ Sunnyside Tad / by Phillip Verrill Mighels . . .; illustrated by Rachael Robinson. New York; London: Harper & Brothers, 1907. 323, [1] p., front., [3] leaves of plates.
LC: S 19, '07.
PW: O 5, '07.

M-764   ____ Thurley Ruxton / by Philip Verrill Mighels; illustrations by James Montgomery Flagg. New York: Desmond FitzGerald, Inc., 1911. 378 p., col. front., [5] leaves of plates.
LC: Ap 27, '11.
PW: My 20, '11.

M-765   ____ The ultimate passion: a novel / by Philip Verrill Mighels. New York; London: Harper & Brothers, 1905. 365, [1] p.
PW: Je 3, '05.

M-766   [____] When a witch is young: a historical novel / by 4-19-69 [pseud.]. New York: R. F. Fenno & Company, c1901. 442 p.
Published revision: *Hearts of grace*, (1913).
LC: Jl 5, '01.
PW: Jl 20, '01.

Mikels, Rosa M. R., ed. <u>See</u> *Short stories for high schools* **(1915), S-462.**

Miles, Carlton Wright. A special course in egotism. **In** *Minnesota stories* **(1903), M-842.**

Miles, Chester A. The king's code. <u>In</u> *Called to the colors and other stories* **(1915), C-50.**

Miles, Gertrude Elizabeth (Wilder), b. 1860. <u>See</u> **Arnold, Faith Stewart, pseud.**

M-767   Miles, N. H. Cragg's roost, or, Life among the cow-boys on the frontier / by N. H. Miles. New York: American Tract Society, [c1912]. 288 p., front. [Ill. by Clinton Pettee.]

M-768   Miles, R. H. P. (Robert Harrison Parker). Three men and a woman: a story of life in New York / by R. H. P. Miles. New York: G. W. Dillingham Co., 1901. 290 p.
PW: Mr 2, '01.

M-769   Milford, Dan. June of the cabins / by Dan Milford . . . Baltimore, Md.: Saulsbury Publishing Company, [c1919]. 54 p.   **DLC**

Millard, Bailey, 1859-1941. Down the flume with the sneath piano. **In** *Spinners' book of fiction* **(1907), S-755.**

M-770   ____ Jack Morning's treasure / by Bailey Millard; illustrations by Arthur William Brown. New York: Edward J. Clode, [c1909]. 247 p., incl. front., [5] leaves of plates.   **PAU**
LC: S 17, '09.
PW: N 20, '09.

M-771   ____ The lure o'gold / by Bailey Millard; drawings & decorations by Arthur William Brown. New York: Edward J. Clode, 1904. 247 p., front., [5] leaves of plates. Designed end papers.
PW: Je 25, '04.

M-772   ____ The Sea Hawk / by Bailey Millard. New York: Wessels & Bissell Co., 1910. 355 p.
LC: O 15, '10.
PW: O 22, '10.

M-773 [Millay, Edna St. Vincent], 1892-1950. Distressing dialogues / by Nancy Boyd [pseud.]; with a preface by Edna St. Vincent Millay. New York; London: Harper & Brothers, [c1924]. 290 p.
Contents: I like Americans -- Honor bright -- Our All-American Almanac and prophetic messenger -- The implacable Aphrodite -- The same boat -- No bigger than a man's hand -- The Greek dance -- Art and how to fake it -- Powder, rouge and lip-stick -- Out of reach of the baby -- Look me up -- For winter, for summer -- "Madame a Tort!" -- "Two souls with but a single thought" -- Knock wood -- Tea for the muse -- Rolls and salt -- How to be happy though good -- Here comes the bride -- Breakfast in bed -- Ships and sealing-wax -- Cordially yours.
PW: O 4, '24.

M-774 Miller, Addie L. (Addie Lettie Peck), b. 1867. Lettie, or, The whirlwind's reaper / by Addie L. Miller. Naugatuck, Conn.: Printed for the author, 1916. 278 p., front.

M-775 Miller, Alice Duer, 1874-1942. Are parents people? / by Alice Duer Miller. New York: Dodd, Mead and Company, 1924. 296 p.
Contents: Are parents people? -- The American husband -- Devoted women -- The return to normalcy -- The red carpet -- The widow's might -- Whose petard was it ? -- The new stoics -- Worse than married.
LC: F 27, '24.
PW: F 23, '24.

M-776 _____ The beauty and the bolshevist / by Alice Duer Miller; illustrated. New York; London: Harper & Brothers, [c1920]. 111, [1] p., front., [3] leaves of plates. [Ill. by Raymond M. Crosby.]
LC: O 20, '20.
PW: N 20, '20.

M-777 _____ The blue arch / by Alice Duer Miller. New York: Charles Scribner's Sons, 1910. 335 p.
LC: O 25, '10.
PW: O 29, '10.

M-778 _____ The burglar and the blizzard: a Christmas story / by Alice Duer Miller; with illustrations by Charlotte Harding. New York: Hearst's International Library Co., [c1914]. 92 p., front., [7] leaves of plates.
LC: O 30, '14.
PW: D 5, '14.

M-779 _____ Calderon's prisoner / by Alice Duer Miller. New York: Charles Scribner's Sons, 1903. 294 p.
Contents: Calderon's prisoner -- Cyril Vane's wife.
PW: O 24, '03.

M-780 _____ The charm school / by Alice Duer Miller. New York; London: Harper & Brothers, [c1919]. 169, [1] p., front., [3] leaves of plates. [Ill. by May Wilson Preston.]
LC: S 9, '19.
PW: S 20, '19.
BLC: London: Hodder & Stoughton, [1920].

M-781 _____ Come out of the kitchen!: a romance / by Alice Duer Miller; with illustrations by Paul Meylan. New York: The Century Co., 1916. 274 p., incl. 11 leaves of plates, front.
LC: Ap 28, '16.
PW: Ap 15, '16.
BLC: London: Hodder & Stoughton, [1916].

M-782 _____ The happiest time of their lives / by Alice Duer Miller . . . ; illustrated by Paul Meylan. New York: The Century Co., 1918. 368 p., front., [7] leaves of plates.
LC: My 24, '18.
PW: My 25, '18.
BLC: London: Hodder & Stoughton, [1919].

_____ The house guest. In Marriage (1923), M-457.

M-783 _____ Ladies must live / by Alice Duer Miller; illustrated by Paul Meylan. New York: The Century Co., 1917. 249 p., front., [7] leaves of plates.
LC: S 20, '17.
PW: S 22, '17.
BLC: London: Hodder & Stoughton, 1918.

M-784 _____ Less than kin / by Alice Duer Miller. New York: Henry Holt and Company, 1909. 230 p.
LC: My 17, '09.
PW: Je 12, '09.

M-785 _____ Manslaughter / by Alice Duer Miller . . . ; illustrated by F. R. Gruger. New York: Dodd, Mead and Company, 1921. 293 p., front., [3] leaves of plates.
LC: N 1, '21.
PW: N 12, '21.
BLC: London: Leonard Parsons, 1922.

M-786 _____ The modern obstacle / by Alice Duer Miller. New York: Charles Scribner's Sons, 1903. 273 p.
PW: My 9, '03.
BLC: London; New York: G. P. Putnam's Sons, 1904.

M-787 _____ The priceless pearl / by Alice Duer Miller. New York: Dodd, Mead & Company, 1924. 186 p.
LC: S 4, '24.
PW: Ag 30, '24.

M-788 _____ The reluctant duchess / by Alice Duer Miller. New York: Dodd, Mead & Company, 1925. 175 p.
LC: S 3, '25.
PW: S 5, '25.

_____ Slow poison. In Prize stories of 1920 (1921), P-618.

_____, contributor. See The sturdy oak (1917), S-1101.

M-789 _____ Things / by Alice Duer Miller. New York: Charles Scribner's Sons, 1914. 48 p.
LC: Ap 28, '14.
PW: My 2, '14.

M-790 Miller, Anne Archbold. Huldy's Whistle / by Anne Archbold Miller; illustrated by William Donahey. Chicago: The Reilly & Lee Co., [c1919]. 286, [1] p., front.
LC: Ag 7, '19.
PW: Ag 9, '19.

Miller, C. Menzies. Who hath loved much, a story of the Milay Archipelago. In Golden stories (1909), G-285.

M-791 Miller, Charles. The guardian / by Major-General Charles Miller; illustrated from drawings by Horatio R. Harper and G. Patrick Nelson. New York: [Printed by Robert Grier Cooke], 1903. [18] p., ill.

M-792 Miller, Daisye Kern. The year / by Daisye Kern Miller. Philadelphia: Dorrance and Company, 1925. 235 p.
LC: Je 27, '25.
PW: Jl 18, '25.

M-793 Miller, David Reed, 1846-1923. The Red Swan's Neck: a tale of the North Carolina mountains / by David Reed Miller. Boston: Sherman, French & Company, 1911. 328 p.   **EWF**
LC: O 12, '11.
PW: O 7, '11.

M-794 Miller, Delavan S. A drum's story: and other tales / by Delavan S. Miller . . . Watertown, N. Y.: Hungerford-Holbrook Company, [c1909].
229 p.   **OSU, TXA**
Contents: A drum's story -- A veteran and his grandchildren -- Lincoln and Tad -- The defenses of Washington -- Story of the second Bull Run -- Campaigning with Grant -- A drummer boy in gray -- War story told in churchyard -- An adventure on the East'n Sho' -- Heroines of '61 and Barbara Frietchie -- Down the Fairfax Pike -- Major Mallory of Malloryville -- The strange case of Geo. Murdstone -- Gypsy, my red roan -- Fighting their old battles o'er -- Six soldiers with seven legs off -- The grand review -- Whistling Pete -- Gov. Morgan's pets -- Jefferson County in the War for the Union -- Taps.
LC: N 8, '09.
PW: N 20, '09.

M-795 Miller, Edwin J. (Edwin Jabez), b. 1837. The adventures of Ned Minton: a story of fact and fiction / by Edwin J. Miller . . . Machias: A. R. Furbush, 1904. 240 p.

M-796 Miller, Elizabeth, b. 1878. The city of delight: a love drama of the siege and fall of Jerusalem / by Elizabeth Miller; with illustrations by F. X. Leyendecker. Indianapolis: The Bobbs-Merrill Company, [c1908]. 448 p., col. front., [5] leaves of plates.
PW: Mr 21, '08.
BLC: London: James Clarke & Co.; printed in U. S. A., 1908.

M-797 _____ Daybreak: a story of the age of discovery / by Elizabeth Miller (Mrs. Oren S. Hack). New York: Charles Scribner's Sons, 1915. 430 p.
LC: Ap 14, '15.

M-798 _____ Saul of Tarsus: a tale of the early Christians / by Elizabeth Miller . . . ; with illustrations by André Castaigne. Indianapolis: The Bobbs-Merrill Company, [c1906]. 442 p., front., [5] leaves of plates.
PW: N 3, '06.
BLC: London: Stead's Publishing House; printed in U. S. A., 1909.

M-799 _____ The yoke: a romance of the days when the Lord redeemed the children of Israel from the bondage of Egypt / by Elizabeth Miller. Indianapolis: The Bobbs-Merrill Company, [c1904]. 619 p.
PW: F 27, '04.

M-800 Miller, Elizabeth Gore. Romances of the California mission days / by Elizabeth Gore Miller . . . ; illustrated. Portland, Maine: Press of Lefavor-Tower Company, 1905, [c1903]. 231 p., photo. front., [13] leaves of photo. plates.
Contents: The warning bells of La Purisma -- The old Señora -- The tragedy at the old mill -- At the shrine of San Antonino de Pala -- The mystery of La Soledad -- The chapel ruins -- Sister Dolores -- The wedding ring -- The Angels' paradise -- A romance of San Juan Capistrano -- Bartolo's return -- The dream child's prophecy.

M-801 Miller, Elizabeth York. The blue aura / by Elizabeth York Miller; illustrations by Arthur I. Keller. New York: Edward J. Clode, [c1917]. 344 p., front., [5] leaves of plates.
LC: S 27, '17.
PW: O 20, '17.

M-802 _____ Obligations / by Elizabeth York Miller. New York; London: Published by The Century Co., [c1924]. 335 p., front.
LC: S 3, '24.
PW: S 6, '24.

Miller, George Amos, b. 1868. See Peggy Ann, pseud.

M-803 Miller, George E. (George Elmer), b. 1881. Prem Masih of Damoh / by George E. Miller . . . Cincinnati: Powell & White, [c1922]. 127, [3] p., photo. front., [2] leaves of photo. plates, ill.   **YU#**

M-804 Miller, George Ernest, b. 1855. Colonel Berry's challenge: a novel / by George Ernest Miller . . . Covington, South Cincinnati, Kentucky: George Ernest Miller, [c1915]. 319 p.
On cover: The book against prohibition that is startling the world.
LC: O 13, '15.

M-805 Miller, George Noyes, 1845-1904. The strike of a sex; and, Zugassent's discovery, or, After the sex struck / by George N. Miller (with author's preface). -- New and rev. ed. -- Chicago, Ill.: Stockham Publishing Co., [c1905]. 119, [9] p.   **CIN**
A birth control tract in story form. First ed. published anonymously in 1890.

Miller, Harvey Monroe, b. 1871. See Hulsbuck, Solly, pseud.

M-806 Miller, Henry Russell, 1880-1955. The ambition of Mark Truitt / by Henry Russell Miller. Indianapolis: The Bobbs-Merrill Company, [c1913]. 454 p.
LC: My 23, '13.
PW: My 31, '13.
BLC: London: C. Palmer & Hayward, 1916.

M-807 _____ His rise to power / by Henry Russell Miller . . . ; with illustrations by M. Leone Bracker. Indianapolis: The Bobbs-Merrill Company, [c1911]. 377 p., front., [6] leaves of plates.
LC: O 26, '11.
PW: O 28, '11.
BLC: London: C. Palmer & Hayward, 1916.

M-808 ____ The house of toys / by Henry Russell Miller; with frontispiece by Frank Snapp. Indianapolis: The Bobbs-Merrill Company, [c1914]. 301 p., front.
LC: N 18, '14.
PW: N 28, '14.

M-809 ____ The man higher up: a story of the fight, which is life and the force, which is love / by Henry Russell Miller; with illustrations by M. Leone Bracker. Indianapolis: The Bobbs-Merrill Company, [c1910]. 402 p., front., [3] leaves of plates.
LC: My 12, '10.
PW: My 21, '10.

Miller, James Marion, b. 1879. See MacMillar, Jude, pseud.

M-810 Miller, John Henderson, 1845-1923. Where the rainbow touches the ground / by John Henderson Miller; frontispiece by James A. Kempster. New York; London: Funk & Wagnalls Company, 1906. 253, [1] p., front.
LC: D 4, '06.
PW: D 22, '06.

M-811 Miller, Lewis B., b. 1861. A crooked trail; the story of a thousand-mile saddle trip up and down the Texas frontier in pursuit of a runaway ox, with adventures by the way / by Lewis B. Miller . . . Pittsburgh, Pa.: The Axtell-Rush Publishing Company, [c1908]. 184 p.   YUS (photocopy)
"Published originally as a serial story in the National stockman & farmer, Pittsburgh."

____ He visited his old home. In Stockman stories (1913), S-956.

____ A night in a log. In Stockman stories (1913), S-956.

M-812 ____ Saddles and lariats: the largely true story of the bar-circle outfit, and of their attempt to take a big drove of longhorns from Texas to California, in the days when the gold fever raged / by Lewis B. Miller . . . Boston: Dana Estes & Company, [c1912]. 285 p., front.
LC: O 3, '12.
PW: N 2, '12.

M-813 ____ The White River raft: the largely true story of a logging trip into the flooded forests of Arkansas, followed by an eventful voyage down the Mississippi / by Lewis B. Miller . . . Boston: Dana Estes & Company, [c1910]. 430 p., front., [7] leaves of plates. [Ill. by J. W. Kennedy.]
LC: O 19, '10.
PW: N 5, '10.
BLC: London: Sampson Low & Co., [1912].

M-814 Miller, Max, b. 1901. C +: a college commentary / by Max Miller. Seattle, U. S. A.: Sunset Publishing Co., c1922. 81 p.

M-815 Miller, Warren H. (Warren Hastings), b. 1876. Sea fighters: navy yarns of the Great War / by Warren H. Miller. New York: The Macmillan Company,

1920. 216 p., front.   MIA
Contents: Peace of the navy -- Brother to Icarus -- The salute -- His bit -- S.C.-1030 -- The defense -- The hands of the captain -- Live bait -- The plain path of duty.

M-816 Miller, Webb Rockefeller. Such things as dreams are made of / by Webb Rockefeller Miller; with his own illustrations and cover designs. Chicago: C. J. Lawrence Company Publishers, 1903. 163 p., ill.
PW: Ag 15, '03.

M-817 The Miller's holiday: short stories from the Northwestern Miller / by Edward Everett Hale, Charles F. Lummis, James Lane Allen . . . [et al.]; edited by Randolph Edgar. Minneapolis: The Miller Publishing Company, 1920. 217 p., front., [2] leaves of plates. [Ill. by R. Caton Woodville, Howard Pyle, and Frank X. Leyendecker.]
Contents: The church with an overshot wheel / O. Henry -- Captain Scarfield / Howard Pyle -- The wild western way / Octave Thanet -- Dorothy of the mill / Robert Barr -- Blueskin, the Pirate / Howard Pyle -- The miller's seal / Octave Thanet -- The blue-corn witch / Charles F. Lummis -- The old mill on the Elkhorn / James Lane Allen -- A graceless husband / Hamlin Garland -- The swearing enchiladas / Charles F. Lummis -- The labor question at Glasscock's / Octave Thanet -- The first grain market / Edward Everett Hale -- The mill on the Kop / Robert Barr -- The Christmas wreck / Frank R. Stockton.
LC: Ag 23, '20.
PW: O 30, '20.

Millet, F. D. A faded scapular. In Shapes that haunt the dusk (1907), S-339.

M-818 Millican, G. W. Revealed by fire / by G. W. Millican. New York: Broadway Publishing Co., 1912. 318 p.   DLC

M-819 Milligan, Blanche Margaret. Victories in the wildwood / by Blanche Margaret Milligan. Col., O.[i. e. Columbus, Ohio]: L. B. C., 1917. 96 p., [3] leaves of photo. plates.

Milliken, Conrad Orton. The burglar. In A liitle book of Rutgers tales (1905), L-378.

M-820 Mills, Jane Dearborn. Leaves from a life-book of today / by Jane Dearborn Mills. Germantown, Pa.: Swedenborg Publishing Association, 1901. 317 p.   PBA

M-821 Mills, Jessie. Ignazio: a drop from the melting pot / by Jessie Mills. Baltimore: Saulsbury Publishing Company, 1918. 34 p.   DLC

M-822 Mills, Mary Hampton. Be ye beggar or king / by Mary Hampton Mills. Asheville, N. C.: Advocate Publishing Co., [1925]. 176 p., front., ill.
LC: D 21, '25.

M-823 Mills, Weymer Jay, 1880-1938. Caroline of Courtlandt street / by Weymer Jay Mills; illustrations by Anna Whelan Betts; decorations by W. E. Mears. New York; London: Harper & Brothers, 1905. 290, [1] p., col. front., [5] leaves of col. plates. Illustrated end papers.
PW: N 4, '05.

M-824 ____ The ghosts of their ancestors / by Weymer Jay

Mills; pictures by John Rae. New York: Fox, Duffield & Co., 1906. 142, [1] p., col. front., [3] leaves of col. plates.
PW: Ap 28, '06.

M-825   _____ The girl I left behind me / by Weymer Jay Mills; pictures and decorations by John Rae. New York: Dodd, Mead & Company, 1910. 90 p., col. front., [10] leaves of col. plates.
LC: O 15, '10.
PW: O 22, '10.

M-826   _____ The old loves / by Weymer Mills . . . New York: Dodd, Mead & Company, 1912. 221 p.
Contents: His mother -- The grandmother -- Rebecca over the back fence -- The littlest girl -- Widow Poll -- The lark -- The heirass -- Barnum's lady -- Aurelia.
LC: O 23, '12.
PW: O 19, '12.

M-827   _____ Through the gates of old romance / by W. Jay Mills . . . ; with illustrations by John Rae. Philadelphia; London: J. B. Lippincott Company, 1903. 281, [1] p., incl. front., ill.
Contents: An unrecorded Philadelphia romance the Franklin family helped into flower -- The love-story of the noted Nathaniel Moore and "the heavenly Ellen," a belle of Chambers Street, New York City -- A true picture of the last days of Aaron Burr -- The poetic courtship of Philip Freneau, the poet of the revolution, and beautiful Eleanor Forman -- The Chevalier de Silly and his Newport Sally -- Susanna Rowson, of "Charlotte Temple" fame, and her British grenadier -- The ghosts of an old Staten Island manor -- Major André's last love -- Pinderina Scribblerus, an American Montagu.
PW: D 5, '03.

M-828   _____ The Van Rensselaers of old Manhattan: a romance / by Weymer Jay Mills; illustrated & decorated by John Rae. New York: Frederick A. Stokes Company, [1907]. 215 p., col. front., [4] leaves of col. plates.
LC: N 21, '07.
PW: D 14, '07.

M-829   Millwood, Sherman, *pseud.* The client: a novel / by Sherman Millwood [pseud.]. Philadelphia: [s. n.], 1904. 320 p.   **DLC**

Miln, George Crichton, Mrs. See **Miln, Louise Jordan, 1864-1933.**

M-830   Miln, Louise Jordan, 1864-1933. The feast of lanterns / by Louise Jordan Miln. New York: Frederick A. Stokes Company, [1921, c1920]. 304 p.
LC: F 26, '21.
PW: F 26, '21.
BLC: London: Hodder & Stoughton, [1920].

M-831   _____ The green goddess / by Louise Jordan Miln; based on the play, "The green goddess", by William Archer. New York: Frederick A. Stokes Company, [c1922]. 330 p.
LC: S 8, '22.
PW: S 23, '22.
BLC: London: Hodder & Stoughton, [1923].

M-832   _____ In a Shantung garden / by Louise Jordan Miln. New York: Frederick A. Stokes Company, 1924. 351 p.

LC: Jl 26, '24.
PW: Ag 2, '24.
BLC: London: Hodder & Stoughton, [1924].

M-833   _____ The invisible foe: a story adapted from the play by Walter Hackett / by Louise Jordan Miln (Mrs. George Crichton Miln). New York: Frederick A. Stokes Company, [c1920]. 279 p.
LC: Jl 8, '20.
PW: Jl 10, '20.
BLC: London: Jarrolds, [1918].

M-834   _____ Mr. & Mrs. Sên / by Louise Jordan Miln. New York: Frederick A. Stokes Company, 1923. 325 p.
LC: Mr 17, '23.
PW: Mr 24, '23.
BLC: London: Hodder & Stoughton, [1923].

M-835   _____ Mr. Wu / by Louise Jordan Miln (Mrs. George Crichton Miln); based on the play "Mr. Wu" by H. M. Vernon and Harold Owen. New York: Frederick A. Stokes Company, [1920]. 314 p.
LC: My 19, '20.
PW: Ap 24, '20.
BLC: London: Cassell & Co., 1918.

M-836   _____ The purple mask; adapted from the play "Le chevalier au masque" of M. M. Paul Armont and Jean Manoussi / by Louise Jordan Miln (Mrs. George Crichton Miln) . . . New York: Frederick A. Stokes Company, [1921]. 307 p.
"First published in The United States of America, 1921."
LC: Mr 21, '21.
PW: Mr 12, '21.
BLC: London: Hodder & Stoughton, [1918].

M-837   _____ Ruben and Ivy Sên / by Louise Jordan Miln. New York: Frederick A. Stokes Company, 1925. 360 p.
LC: S 10, '25.
PW: S 5, '25.
BLC: London: Hodder & Stoughton, [1925].

M-838   _____ The soul of China: glimpsed in tales of today and yesterday / by Louise Jordan Miln. New York: Frederick A. Stokes Company, 1925. 311 p.
Contents: The no-number wife -- The cat pagoda -- The tame dragon -- Weeping Willow -- Flower of luck -- The doll in the swing -- The sword of chastity -- The puppets of Mah Jong -- How music came to China -- Gratitude.
LC: Ja 6, '25.
PW: Ja 10, '25.
BLC: London: Hodder & Stoughton, [1925].

Milne, Robert Duncan. Ten thousand years in ice. In *Argonaut stories* (1906), A-298.

M-839   Miner, M. Annette Stillman (Mary Annette Stillman). Round Hill farm / by M. Annette Stillman Miner; with illustrations by H. Boylston Dummer. Boston, Massachusetts: The C. M. Clark Publishing Company, [c1911]. 208 p., front., [5] leaves of plates.   **DLC**
LC: Mr 20, '12.
PW: F 11, '11.

M-840   Mingins, Clara Wood. A new vote in the Christmas
         carol / by Clara Wood Mingins. New York City:
         Published by The Sherwood Company, 1913. 40 p.
                                                    DLC

M-841   Miniter, Edith, b. 1869. Our Natupski neighbors / by
         Edith Miniter. New York: Henry Holt and
         Company, 1916. 346 p.
         PW: O 21, '16.

M-842   Minnesota stories: a collection of twenty stories of
         college life / collected and arranged by Charles F.
         McClumpha . . . , and by W. I. Thomas.
         Minneapolis: The H. W. Wilson Company, 1903.
         327 p.
         Contents: A college play / Irene P. McKeehan -- That impossible
         thirteenth / Amy Oliver -- Wilhelmina / Katherine J. Gallagher --
         Greater love hath no man than this / Sam Cornish -- A special course
         in egotism / Carlton Wright Miles -- The passing of Quentin Dewey --
         J. Remington Victor / Ruth Leonard -- A mutual scoop / Mac
         McConn -- The passing of Percival -- Out of Egypt -- A freshman and
         his friends / Harry V. Fuller -- Misunderstood -- The Barker twins --
         A Christmas prodigal / Alice E. Dyar -- The French grandmother /
         Alice E. Dyar -- Within and without the curriculum -- St. Joseph /
         Avery J. Crounse -- The reason why / Malcolm A. MacLean -- A
         baseball wager / Samuel A. Hatch -- Mrs. West and some others.

M-843   Minnigerode, Meade, 1887-1967. The big year: a
         college story / by Meade Minnigerode. New York;
         London: G. P. Putnam's Sons, 1921. (New York:
         The Knickerbocker Press). 287 p., col. front. [Ill.
         by R. M. Crosby.]
         LC: Mr 18, '21.
         PW: Mr 19, '21.

         _____, contributor. See *Bobbed hair* (1925), B-700.

M-844   _____ Laughing house: a novel / by Meade
         Minnigerode. New York; London: G. P. Putnam's
         Sons, 1920. ([New York]: The Knickerbocker).
         283 p.
         LC: O 19, '20.
         PW: O 16, '20.

M-845   _____ Oh, Susanna!: a romance of the old American
         merchant marine / by Meade Minnigerode. New
         York; London: G. P. Putnam's Sons, 1922. (New
         York: The Knickerbocker Press). 401 p.
         LC: F 17, '22.
         PW: F 11, '22.

M-846   [_____] The Queen of Sheba: her life and times / by
         Phinneas A. Crutch [pseud.]; illustrated. New York;
         London: G. P. Putnam's Sons, 1922. (New York:
         The Knickerbocker Press). 191 p., photo. front., [3]
         leaves of plates.
         LC: Je 28, '22.
         PW: Je 17, '22

M-847   _____ The Seven Hills: a novel / by Meade
         Minnigerode. New York; London: G. P. Putnam's
         Sons, 1923. (New York: The Knickerbocker Press).
         308 p.
         LC: S 7, '23.
         PW: S 1, '23.

M-848   Minogue, Anna C. (Anna Catherine), b. 1874.
         Cardome: a romance of Kentucky / by Anna C.
         Minogue. New York: P. F. Collier & Son, [c1904].

306 p.
PW: Ap 15, '05.

M-849   _____ The waters of contradiction / by Anna C.
         Minogue . . . New York: P. J. Kenedy & Sons,
         [c1912]. 314 p.
         LC records front., plates.
         LC: D 31, '12.
         PW: F 1, '13.

         Mirrielees, Edith R. Perjured. In *Atlantic
         narratives*; 2nd series (1918), **A-361**.

         _____ Professor Boynton rereads history. In *Prize
         stories of 1924* (1925), **P-622**.

M-850   The misfit Christmas puddings / by the Consolation
         club; illustrated by Wallace Goldsmith. Boston;
         London: J. W. Luce & Company, 1906. 164 p.,
         front., [7] leaves of plates, ill.   **BUF**
         PW: Ja 5, '07.

         Mr. X. *See* **X, Mr.**

         Mitchell, B. W. The surgeon. In *The Bellman book
         of fiction* (1921), **B-485**.

M-851   Mitchell, C. C. (Charles Caldwell), b. 1868. The
         millionaire of Uz / by C. C. Mitchell. Boston:
         Richard G. Badger, [c1920]. (Boston, U. S. A.: The
         Gorham Press). 211 p.

         Mitchell, Edward Bedinger. He came to Proveis. In
         Forum stories (1914), **F-306**.

M-852   _____ The shadow of the crescent / by Edward
         Bedinger Mitchell. New York: Frederick A. Stokes
         Company, [c1909]. 270 p.
         LC: Je 19, '09.
         PW: Je 26, '09.

M-853   Mitchell, Frances Marian. Joan of Rainbow Springs /
         by Frances Marian Mitchell; illustrated by F. Vaux
         Wilson. Boston: Lothrop, Lee & Shepard Co.,
         [1911]. 480 p., incl. front., [3] leaves of plates.
         LC: My 25, '11.
         PW: Ag 26, '11.

         Mitchell, Helen B. "Two parallel lines meet at
         infinity." In *The best college short stories, 1917-18*
         (1919), **B-557**.

M-854   Mitchell, J. Calvin, b. 1859. Excerpts from The
         crater of gold: a mysterious manuscript / by J.
         Calvin Mitchell. Chicago, Ill.: Published by the
         Crater of Gold Publishing Co., [c1918]. 246 p.,
         photo. front. (port.), [5] leaves of plates. [Ill. by M.
         H. Natwick.]
         Contents: Pitiful man -- An air-castle -- War is murder -- Freedom of
         the seas -- Our flag's unfurled -- Uncle Sam must fight -- Jingo Land-
         a dream verbatim -- The law -- K. Zackley's statement -- The
         prospector's letter -- Mountain life song -- The struggle -- Something
         new -- Old custom -- The future government -- No chance for the old
         -- The homesteader's hope -- The cabin dwellers -- Found the way --
         The absolute faith -- Keep the law.

M-855   Mitchell, John Ames, 1845-1918. Dr. Thorne's idea:
         originally published as "Gloria victis" / by John Ames

Mitchell; illustrations by Balfour Ker. New York: Life Publishing Company, 1910. 244 p., front., [3] leaves of plates.
"This tale, inits original form, was published in 1899 as *Gloria Victis*. With the addition of certain passages and the revision of others - a belated duty to Stephen Wadsworth - the book is now presented under a clearer title."   No major revisions noted.
LC: Je 6, '10.
PW: Jl 2, '10.
References: BAL 14046.

M-856 ____ Drowsy / by John Ames Mitchell; with illustrations by Angus Macdonall and the author. New York: Frederick A. Stokes Company, [c1917]. 301 p., front., [18] leaves of plates (some col.).
LC: O 6, '17.
PW: O 6, '17.
References: BAL 14049.

M-857 ____ The last American: a fragment from the journal of Khan-Li, prince of Dimph-Yoo-Chur and admiral in the Persian navy / presented by J. A. Mitchell. New York: F. A. Stokes, [c1902]. 151 p., col. front., [7] leaves of col. plates, ill. [Ill. by F. W. Read, Albert D. Blashfield, and the author.]
PW: O 25, '02.
References: BAL 14042. BAL notes: "Revised for first edition; see under 1889."

M-858 ____ Pandora's box / by John Ames Mitchell; with four illustrations by the author. New York: Frederick A. Stokes Company, [c1911]. 390 p., front., [3] leaves of plates.
LC: S 11, '11.
PW: S 16, '11.
References: BAL 14047.

M-859 ____ The pines of Lory / by J. A. Mitchell; decorations by Albert D. Blashfield. New York: Life Publishing Company, 1901. 229, [1] p., incl. front.
LC: D 3, '01.
PW: D 7, '01.
References: BAL 14041.

M-860 ____ The silent war / by John Ames Mitchell; illustrations by William Balfour Ker. New York: Life Publishing Company, 1906. 222 p., incl. front., [3] leaves of plates.
LC: O 26, '06.
PW: D 8, '06.
References: BAL 14045.

M-861 ____ The Villa Claudia / by John Ames Mitchell; illustrations by A. D. Blashfield, by the author, and from ancient sources. New York: Life Publishing Company, 1904. 306 p., front., ill.
LC: My 7, '04.
PW: Jl 16, '04.
BLC: New York: Life Publishing Co.; London: James Henderson & Sons, 1904.
References: BAL 14043.

M-862 Mitchell, Ruth Comfort. Corduroy / by Ruth Comfort Mitchell. New York; London: D. Appleton and Company, 1923. 293, [1] p., front.
LC: Mr 6, '23.
PW: Mr 24, '23.

M-863 ____ Jane journeys on / by Ruth Comfort Mitchell. New York; London: D. Appleton and Company, 1922. 295, [1] p., front. [Ill. by Arthur William Brown.]
LC: Mr 2, '22.
PW: Mr 18, '22.
BLC: London: Hodder & Stoughton, [1925].

Mitchell, Ruth Comfort. Miss Kid. **In Pacific Coast Women's Press Association.** *La copa de oro* **(1905), P-2.**

M-864 ____ Play the game! / by Ruth Comfort Mitchell. New York; London: D. Appleton and Company, 1921. 243, [1] p., front. [Ill. by Arthur William Brown.]
LC: Mr 21, '21.
PW: Ap 2, '21.
BLC: London: Hodder & Stoughton, [1925].

M-865 ____ A white stone / by Ruth Comfort Mitchell. New York; London: D. Appleton and Company, 1924. 349, [1] p.
LC: N 14, '24.
PW: N 22, '24.
BLC: London: Hodder & Stoughton, [1925].

M-866 Mitchell, S. Weir (Silas Weir), 1829-1914. Circumstance / by S. Weir Mitchell. New York: The Century Co., 1901. 495 p.
LC: Jl 30, '01.
PW: O 12, '01.
BLC: London: Macmillan & Co.; U. S. printed, 1901.
References: BAL 14202.

M-867 ____ A comedy of conscience / by S. Weir Mitchell. New York: The Century Co., 1903. 129 p., incl. [4] leaves of plates, front.
LC: Mr 20, '03.
PW: Ap 4, '03.
BLC: Edinburgh; London: David Douglas, 1904.
References: BAL 14216.

M-868 ____ Constance Trescot: a novel / by S. Weir Mitchell . . . New York: The Century Co., 1905. 384 p., front. [Ill. by Charles M. Relyea.]
LC: Mr 1, '05.
PW: Mr 25, '05.
References: BAL 14228.

M-869 ____ A diplomatic adventure / by S. Weir Mitchell. New York: The Century Co., 1906. 166 p., front. [Ill. by Charles M. Relyea.]
LC: Mr 21, '06.
PW: Ap 14, '06.
References: BAL 14237.

M-870   ____ The guillotine club: and other stories / by S. Weir Mitchell . . . ; with illustrations by André Castaigne and F. R. Gruger. New York: The Century Co., 1910. 285 p., incl. [13] leaves of plates, front.
Contents: The guillotine club -- The fourteenth guest -- The mind-reader -- The house beyond Prettymarsh.
LC: O 27, '10.
PW: O 8, '10.
References: BAL 14263.

M-871   ____ John Sherwood, ironmaster / by S. Weir Mitchell. New York: The Century Co., 1911. 316 p.
LC: My 26, '11.
PW: My 20, '11.
References: BAL 14265.

M-872   ____ Little stories / by S. Weir Mitchell. New York: The Century Co., 1903. 109, [1] p.
Contents: A consultation -- Two men -- Haroun the caliph -- The waters of oblivion -- Conversion -- A man and a woman -- A ghost of glory -- The wise man's sack -- A dilemma -- The jewels of consistency -- "Thou art the soul of thy house" -- A step-son of knowledge -- The sins of the fathers.
LC: S 30, '03.
PW: O 17, '03.
References: BAL 14217.

M-873   ____ New Samaria; and, The summer of St. Martin / by S. Weir Mitchell . . . ; illustrated. Philadelphia; London: J. B. Lippincott Company, 1904. 168 p., photo. front. (port.), [4] leaves of plates. [Ill. Winfield S. Lukens.]
LC: S 9, '04.
PW: O 1, '04.
References: BAL 14222.

M-874   ____ The Red city: a novel of the second administration of President Washington / by S. Weir Mitchell; with illustrations by Arthur I. Keller. New York: The Century Co., 1908. 421 p., incl. [9] leaves of plates, front.
LC: O 22, '08.
PW: N 7, '08.
BLC: London: Macmillan & Co., 1908.
References: BAL 14249.

M-875   ____ A venture in 1777 / by S. Weir Mitchell. Philadelphia: George W. Jacobs & Company, [1908]. 120 p., col. front., [3] leaves of col. plates. [Ill. by J. J. Gould.] Designed end papers.
LC: O 1, '08.
PW: O 17, '08.
References: BAL 14247.

M-876   ____ Westways: a village chronicle / by S. Weir Mitchell . . . New York: The Century Co., 1913. 510 p.
LC: S 18, '13.
PW: S 13, '13.
BLC: London: T. Fisher Unwin; U. S. printed, 1914, [1913].
References: BAL 14272.

M-877   ____ The youth of Washington: told in the form of an autobiography / by S. Weir Mitchell. New York: The Century Co., 1904. 290 p.

LC: S 10, '04.
PW: O 15, '04.
BLC: London: T. Fisher Unwin; printed in U. S., 1904.
References: BAL 14223.

M-878   Mix, Jennie Irene. At fame's gateway: the romance of a pianiste / by Jennie Irene Mix. New York: Henry Holt and Company, 1920. 307 p.
PW: Ap 10, '20.

Mock, Fred, b. 1861. See Alla, Ogal, pseud.

M-879   Modern short stories: a book for high schools / edited with introduction and notes by Frederick Houk Law . . . New York: The Century Co., 1918. 303 p., front., [3] leaves of plates. [Ill. by Thomas Fogarty and W. T. Benda.]
Contents: The adventures of Simon and Susanna / Joel Chandler Harris -- The crow-child / Mary Mapes Dodge -- The soul of the great bell / Lafcadio Hearn -- The ten trails / Ernest Thompson Seton -- Where love is, there God is also / Count Leo Tolstoi -- Wood-ladies / Perceval Gibbon -- On the fever ship / Richard Harding Davis -- A source of irritation / Stacy Aumonier -- Moti Guj-Mutineer / Rudyard Kipling -- Gulliver the great / Walter A. Dyer -- Sonny's schoolin' / Ruth McEnery Stuart -- Her first horse show / David Gray -- My husband's book / James Matthew Barrie -- War / Jack London -- The battle of the monsters / Morgan Robertson -- A dilemma / S. Weir Mitchell -- The red-headed league / A. Conan Doyle -- One hundred in the dark / Owen Johnson -- A retrieved information / O. Henry -- Brother Leo / Phyllis Bottome -- A fight with death / Ian Maclaren -- The Dan-nan-Ron / Fiona Macleod.

M-880   Moffat, Edward S. (Edward Stewart), b. 1876. The desert and Mrs. Ajax / by Edward Moffat. New York: Moffat, Yard and Company, 1914. 334 p., front., [2] leaves of plates. [Ill. by O. T. Jackman.]
LC: My 7, '14.
PW: Ap 25, '14.

M-881   ____ Go forth and find / by Edward S. Moffat; illustrated by Lester Ralph. New York: Moffat, Yard & Company, 1916. 370 p., col. front., [1] leaf of col. plates.
LC: Ag 12, '16.
PW: My 27, '16.

M-882   ____ Hearts steadfast / by Edward S. Moffat . . . New York: Moffat, Yard & Company, 1915. 234 p.
LC: O 12, '15.
PW: O 9, '15.

M-883   Moffat, Jessie Emerson. A friend at court: a romance of the days of Louis XIV / by Jessie Emerson Moffat. New York: William Ritchie, [c1904]. 307 p., front., [4] leaves of plates. [Ill. by Charles Hope Provost.]

M-884   Moffat, R. N. (Robert Nethercoat), b. 1864. The messenger of Napoleon: a dramatic historical story / R. N. Moffat. Boston: The Roxburgh Publishing Company (Inc.), 1918. 353 p.

M-885   Moffatt, Adah Terrell. The Queen's gift: a fantasy / by Adah Terrell Moffatt; illustrations from drawings made and photographs posed by the author. Boston: The Roxburgh Publishing Company, Incorporated, [c1923]. 73 p., incl. [9] leaves of plates (some photo.), photo. front.

M-886   Moffett, Cleveland, 1863-1926. The battle / by Cleveland Moffett; illustrations from scenes in the play. New York: G. W. Dillingham Company, [c1909]. 303 p., front., [5] leaves of plates.
LC: Mr 10, '09.
PW: My 22, '09.
BLC: London: T. Fisher Unwin; New York printed, 1909.

M-887   ____ The bishop's purse / by Cleveland Moffett and Oliver Herford . . . ; illustrated. New York; London: D. Appleton and Company, 1913. 354 p., front., [3] leaves of plates. [Ill. by Charles L. Wrenn.]
LC: Mr 17, '13.
PW: Mr 29, '13.

M-888   ____ The conquest of America: a romance of disaster and victory: U. S. A., 1921 A. D.: based on extracts from the diary of James E. Langston, war correspondent of the "London times" / by Cleveland Moffett . . . New York: George H. Doran Company, [c1916]. 310 p., front., [7] leaves of plates. [Ill. by W. T. Benda.]
LC: Ap 24, '16.
PW: Ap 15, '16.
BLC: London: Hodder & Stoughton; printed in U. S., 1916.

M-889   ____ Glint of wings: the story of a modern girl who wanted her liberty--and got it / by Cleveland Moffett; and Virginia Hall; drawings by Anne Moffett. New York: The James A. McCann Company, [c1922]. 307 p., front., [7] leaves of plates.
LC: S 25, '22.
PW: N 11, '22.

M-890   ____ A king in rags / by Cleveland Moffett. New York: D. Appleton and Company, 1907. 333, [1] p.
LC: O 30, '07.
PW: N 2, '07.

M-891   ____ The land of mystery / by Cleveland Moffett; with sixty-nine illustrations from paintings and photographs. New York: The Century Co., 1913. 413 p., front., ill. [Ill. by A. Castaigne.]
LC: O 30, '13.
PW: N 1, '13.

M-892   ____ The mysterious card / by Cleveland Moffett. Boston: Small, Maynard and Company, [1912?, c1896]. 103 p.
"This story is reprinted from the issues of The black cat of February and August 1896." Includes: *The mysterious card unveiled* (sequel to the mysterious card) on p. 47-103.
PW: Je 8, '12.

M-893   ____ Possessed / by Cleveland Moffett. New York: The James A. McCann Company, 1920. 254 p.
LC: Ja 31, '20.
PW: F 14, '20.

M-894   ____ The Seine mystery / by Cleveland Moffett. New York: Dodd, Mead & Company, 1925. 288 p.
PW: Je 27, '25.
BLC: London; New York: Andrew Melrose, 1924.

M-895   ____ Through the wall / by Cleveland Moffett . . . New York; London: D. Appleton and Company, 1909. 408 p., incl. front., plates, ill.
Unexamined copy: bibliographic data from OCLC, #7537142.
LC: O 20, '09.

M-896   Mole, Marion. Vera of the Strong Heart / by Marion Mole. New York; London: G. P. Putnam's Sons, 1910. ([New York]: The Knickerbocker Press). 309 p.
LC: Je 21, '10.
BLC: London: Andrew Melrose, 1910.

M-897   Moles, Hunter Stephen. Ranger District Number Five / by Hunter Stephen Moles . . . Boston, Mass.: The Spencerian Press, [c1923]. 350 p., photo. front., [2] leaves of photo. plates, ill.

M-898   Molineux, Roland Burnham. The room with the little door / by Roland Burnham Molineux. New York: G. W. Dillingham Company, 1903. 263 p.
Sketches of the author's life in the Tombs prison, New York City, and in Sing Sing.
PW: Ja 24, '03.
BLC: London: T. Fisher Unwin; New York [printed], 1903.

M-899   ____ The vice admiral of the blue: a biographical romance: supposedly the chronicle left by Lord Nelson's friend, Thomas Masterman Hardy, Vice Admiral and Baronet / by Roland Burnham Molineux; illustrations by Troy and Margaret Kinney. New York: G. W. Dillingham Company, [1903]. 364 p., front., [3] leaves of plates.
PW: S 19, '03.
BLC: London: T. Fisher Unwin; New York [printed], 1903.

M-900   Molnar, Louis. Deka Parsec: shell-shocked views of life / by Louis Molnar. Los Angeles: Grafton Publishing Corporation, 1921. 196 p.
Contents: On the mountain -- Desert places -- Vicarious activities -- Charity -- Lizard Lodge -- The Count -- Ceremony -- Helping to build Rome -- Love murders -- The postman -- Walking -- The tourist -- From cellar to garret -- Caste -- Suicide -- The grab bag vision -- Thoughts -- The ideal the only real -- Five towns in one -- The poetic attitude.

Monday Afternoon Literary Circle. <u>See *A Romance of the Catskills*</u> (1903), R-519.

M-901   Monks, Minnie May. Three bachelor girls / by Minnie May Monks. New York: The Bookery Publishing Co., [c1914]. 141 p.   **DLC**

M-902   Monroe, Anne Shannon, 1877-1942. Behind the ranges / by Anne Shannon Monroe . . . Garden City, New York: Doubleday, Page & Company, 1925. 343 p.
LC: Ap 24, '25.
PW: Ap 25, '25.
BLC: London: William Heinemann; printed in U. S. A., 1925.

M-903   ____ Happy Valley: a story of Oregon / by Anne Shannon Monroe . . . ; illustrated by J. Allen St. John. Chicago: A. C. McClurg & Co., 1916. 347 p., front., ill.
LC: My 22, '16.
PW: Je 3, '16.

M-904   Monroe, Forest, *pseud.* Maid of Montauk / by Forest Monroe [pseud.]. New York: William R. Jenkins . . . , 1902. 164 p., front.
PW: Ap 26, '02

M-905   Montagu, Gordon. Glen Ellyn, paint maker: the original paint novel / by Gordon Montagu. St. Louis, Mo.: Press of Little & Becker Printing Co., [c1910]. 342 p.
LC: Ag 19, '10.

M-906   Montague, Elizabeth May. Beside a Southern Sea: a novel / by Elizabeth May Montague. New York; Washington: The Neale Publishing Company, 1905. 162 p.
PW: D 30, '05.

M-907   Montague, Joseph. The Crater of Kala: an adventure story / by Joseph Montague. New York City: Chelsea House, [c1925]. 253 p.
PW: D 19, '25.

M-908   Montague, Margaret Prescott, 1878-1955. Closed doors: studies of deaf and blind children / by Margaret Prescott Montague. Boston; New York: Houghton Mifflin Company, 1915. (Cambridge: The Riverside Press). 182, [2] p.
Contents: Why it was W-on-the-eyes -- Cain, the key -- Red Bird, he can see -- The little sign for friend -- Something big, like Red Bird -- What Mr. Grey said -- Marked for the unexpected.
LC: S 27, '15.
PW: O 2, '15.

M-909   ____ Deep channel / by Margaret Prescott Montague. Boston: The Atlantic Monthly Press, [c1923]. 289, [1] p.
LC: S 12, '23.
PW: S 8, '23.

M-910   ____ England to America / by Margaret Prescott Montague; with an introduction by John Drinkwater. Garden City, New York: Doubleday, Page & Company, 1920. 56 p.   **TOL**
LC: My 20, '20.
PW: My 22, '20.

M-911   ____ The gift / by Margaret Prescott Montague. New York: E. P. Dutton & Company, [c1919]. 59 p.
"This story originally appeared in the columns of the Atlantic monthly."
PW: Ap 19, '19.

M-912   ____ Her lovely thing / by Margaret Prescott Montague. Boston: Massachusetts Charitable Eye and Ear Infirmary, [1920?] 28 p.

M-913   ____ In Calvert's Valley / by Margaret Prescott Montague. New York: The Baker & Taylor Company, 1908. 419 p., front., [3] leaves of plates. [Ill. by V. A. Richardson.]
LC: N 2, '08.
PW: N 14, '08.

M-914   ____ Linda / by Margaret Prescott Montague . . . ; with illustrations. Boston; New York: Houghton Mifflin Company, 1912. (Cambridge [Mass.]: The Riverside Press). 396 p., col. front. [Ill. by Brett.]
LC: O 30, '12.
PW: N 2, '12.
BLC: London: Constable & Co; Cambridge, Mass. [printed], 1913.

M-915   ____ The man from God's country / by Margaret Prescott Montague. New York: E. P. Dutton & Company, [c1924]. 44 p.   **KSU**
PW: F 16, '24.

M-916   ____ Of water and the Spirit / by Margaret Prescott Montague. New York: E. P. Dutton & Company, [c1916]. 56 p.
"This story originally appeared in the columns of the Atlantic monthly . . . "
LC: D 5, '16.
PW: D 9, '16.

M-917   ____ The poet, Miss Kate and I / by Margaret P. Montague; decorations and illustrations by George W. Hood. New York: The Baker & Taylor Co., [1905]. 190 p., col. front. Ornamental borders.

M-918   ____ The sowing of Alderson Cree / by Margaret Prescott Montague; with frontispiece by W. T. Benda. New York: The Baker & Taylor Company, [1907]. 336 p., col. front.
LC: Mr 21, '07.
PW: Ap 20, '07.

____ The today tomorrow. In *The best short stories of 1923 and the yearbook of the American short story* (1924), B-568.

M-919   ____ Uncle Sam of Freedom Ridge / by Margaret Prescott Montague. Garden City, N. Y.: Doubleday, Page & Company, 1920. 60 p.
LC: Jl 17, '20.
PW: Jl 17, '20.

M-920   Montaigne, Marcia. A girl against odds: a love story / by Marcia Montaigne. New York: Chelsea House, [c1925]. 256 p.
PW: D 19, '25.

M-921   ____ Her wedding ring: a love story / by Marcia Montaigne. New York: Chelsea House, [c1925]. 254 p.
PW: D 26, '25.

M-922   Montanye, C. S. (Carleton Stevens), b. 1892. Some nephew!: a laugh movie in six reels / by C. S. Montanye. New York: Moffat, Yard and Company, 1920. 220 p., front., [2] leaves of plates. [Ill. by Stuart Hay.]
PW: My 8, '20.

M-923   Montgomery, Frances Trego. On a lark to the planets: a sequel to "The wonderful electric elephant" / by Frances Trego Montgomery . . . ; illustrated by Winifred D. Elrod. Akron, Ohio; New York; Chicago: The Saalfield Publishing Co., 1904. 180 p., col. front., [6] leaves of col. plates.

M-924　Montgomery, Louise, b. 1864. Mrs. Mahoney of the tenement / by Louise Montgomery; illustrated by Florence Scovel Shinn. Boston; New York; Chicago: The Pilgrim Press, [c1912]. 168 p., col. front., [4] leaves of col. plates.
PW: O 19, '12.

Montgomery, Mary W., jt. aut. *Told in the gardens of Araby* (1905). See **Chandler, Izora C. (Izora Cecilia), d. 1906, jt. aut., C-288.**

M-925　Montgomery, N. Ainsworth (Nellie Ainsworth), b. 1872. A modern patrician / by N. Ainsworth Montgomery. Boston: James H. Earle & Company, [c1903]. 444 p.
PW: Ag 8, '03.

Montross, Lois Seyster, jt. aut. *Town and gown* (1923). See **Montross, Lynn, 1895-1961, jt. aut., M-928.**

M-926　Montross, Lynn, 1895-1961. East of Eden / by Lynn Montross. New York; London: Harper & Brothers, 1925. 299 p.
LC: S 18, '25.
PW: O 10, '25.
BLC: London: Methuen & Co., 1926.

M-927　____ Half gods / by Lynn Montross . . . New York: George H. Doran Company, [c1924]. 296 p.
LC: Ag 22, '24.
PW: Ap 12, '24.

M-928　____ Town and gown / by Lynn Montross and Lois Seyster Montross. New York: George H. Doran Company, [c1923]. 283 p.
Contents: Peter Warshaw -- The faculty and the creaking shirt -- The fusser -- Girls who pet -- Yellow -- Dry as dust -- The first man -- Unity, coherence and emphasis -- Bass drums -- The strangest serenade -- Between the fours seas -- A blind date, Cousin Lottie and the cat -- When Greek meets barb.
LC: F 8, '23.

M-929　Moody, Helen Waterson, 1860-1928. A child's letters to her husband / by Helen Watterson Moody. New York: Doubleday, Page & Company, 1903. 125 p., photo. front.　**KSU**
BLC: London: William Heinemann; New York [printed], 1904.

M-930　Moody, R. N. (Robert Neill), b. 1851. Eunice Loyd, or, The struggle and triumph of an honest heart / by R. N. Moody . . . Cincinnati, Ohio: F. L. Rowe, 1909. 290 p., front. (port.).　**VA@**
LC: Ja 10, '10.

M-931　Moody, Winfield Scott, 1856-1931. The Pickwick ladle: and other collector's stories / by Winfield Scott Moody; illustrated. New York: Charles Scribner's Sons, 1907. 276 p., front., [6] leaves of plates. [Ill. by Walter Appleton Clark.]
Contents: The Pickwick ladle -- Buying a sideboard -- The E M I B Lowestoft -- The black hawthorn jar -- The disciplining of Peter -- The roseback plate.

M-932　Mooers, DeSacia. The blonde vampire / by DeSacia Mooers; fully illustrated. New York: Moffat, Yard & Company, 1920. 253 p., photo. front., [11] leaves

of photo. plates (2 double-leaf).
LC: N 18, '20.

M-933　Moon, Lorna. Doorways in drumorty / by Lorna Moon. Indianapolis: The Bobbs-Merrill Company, [c1925]. 157, [1] p.
Contents: The corp' -- Silk both sides -- The sinning of Jessie MacLean -- Wantin' a hand -- The tattie-doolie -- The courtin' of Sally Ann.
LC: O 24, '25.
BLC: London: Jonathan Cape, 1926.

M-934　Moore, Bertha Pearl. The love child / by Bertha Pearl Moore. New York: Thomas Seltzer, 1923. 253 p.
LC: S 4, '23.
PW: S 29, '23.

M-935　[____] Sarah and her daughter / by Bertha Pearl [pseud.]. New York: Thomas Seltzer, 1920. 521 p.
LC: Jl 12, '20.
PW: My 1, '20.

Moore, Carlyle, b. 1875, jt. aut. *Stop thief!* (1913). See **Jenks, George C., jt. aut., J-74.**

M-936　Moore, Charles Chilton, b. 1872. Tamám / by Charles Chilton Moore. New York; Washington: The Neale Publishing Company, 1908. 284 p.

M-937　Moore, Francis M. (Francis Marion), b. 1846. "Ghosts or devils" I'm done / by Francis M. Moore; the startling adventure of two officers of the 62nd Ohio infantry on Polly Island, S. C. during General Gilmore's seige [i.e., siege] of Fort Sumpter in the war of the rebellion and the story which incited their adventure. Deadwood, S. D.: Press of O. C. Cole & Son, [c1908]. 72 p.　**JFK**
LC: My 24, '09.

M-938　Moore, Frederick Ferdinand, b. 1877. The devil's admiral / by Frederick Ferdinand Moore; illustrated in color by Anton Otto Fischer. Garden City, N. Y.: Doubleday, Page & Co., 1913. 295, [1] p., col. front., [3] leaves of colored plates.
LC: F 21, '13.
BLC: London: Grant Richards; Garden City, N. Y., printed, 1913.

M-939　____ Isle o'dreams / by Frederick F. Moore; frontispiece by Ralph Pallen Coleman. Garden City, N. Y.: Doubleday, Page & Company, 1920. 234 p., col. front.
LC: Mr 23, '20.
PW: Mr 6, '20.

M-940　____ Sailor girl / by Frederick F. Moore . . . New York; London: D. Appleton and Company, 1920. 337, [1] p.　**DLC**
LC: Ap 3, '20.
PW: Ap 24, '20.

M-941　____ The samovar girl / by Frederick Moore . . . New York, London: D. Appleton and Company, 1921. 306, [1] p.
Unexamined copy: bibliographic data from NUC.
LC: Je 22, '21.

M-942 Moore, Idora McClellan, 1843-1929. Betsy Hamilton: Southern character sketches / by Idora McClellan Moore. Atlanta, Ga.: The Dickert Company, 1921. 204 p., photo. front. (port.).
TXA

Reprinted from various sources.
Contents: Betsy's first trip to town -- Ole Mis' Freshours -- Borrowing neighbors -- Betsy in a storm -- Hog killin' in Hillabee -- The surprise at Hun Tucker's -- The quiltin' at Mis' Roberson's -- Them chil'en of Nance's -- Zeke Scroggins, the embarrassed lover -- Pap -- Mrs. Pinkney's spring spell -- The Old Ingon Head's school -- Shooting in the snow -- The rivers of Georgia -- The rivers of Alabama -- My old log fire -- Between the two -- The rainbow trout -- My uncaged mockingbird -- Superstitions of the Alabama Negro -- "Huldy" -- "Ketchin' a chicken" -- Dat quarter -- "Babe" -- "Daddy Mose" on evolution -- "Daddy Mose" on darkness -- Mammy's baby -- Aunt Neely's first love -- "Trixie" -- Sis Lindy's busy day -- How Sis Lindy lost her job.

M-943 Moore, John Trotwood, 1858-1929. The bishop of Cottontown: a story of the southern cotton mills / by John Trotwood Moore; illustrated by the Kinneys. Philadelphia: The John C. Winston Company, 1906. 644 p., col. front., [4] leaves of plates.
PW: Je 2, '06.

M-944 ____ The gift of the grass: being the autobiography of a famous racing horse / by John Trotwood Moore; illustrated by G. Patrick Nelson. Boston: Little, Brown, and Company, 1911. 347, [1] p., col. front., [3] leaves of col. plates.
LC: Ja 17, '11.

M-945 ____ Jack Ballington, forester / by John Trotwood Moore; illustrations by George Gibbs. Philadelphia: The John C. Winston Co., [c1911]. 341 p., front., [3] leaves of plates.
LC: My 1, '11.

M-946 ____ A summer hymnal: a romance of Tennessee / by John Trotwood Moore. Philadelphia: Henry T. Coates & Company, 1901. 332 p., front., [4] leaves of plates. [Ill. by Stanley M. Arthurs.]
PW: Jl 6, '01.

M-947 ____ Uncle Wash: his stories / by John Trotwood Moore . . . ; illustrated. Philadelphia: The John C. Winston Co., 1910. 329 p., col. front., [4] leaves of plates. [Ill. by J. Lucas and C. H. Sykes.]
Contents: Sister Ca'line's enticement -- Brother Washington's consolidation -- The watermelon sermon -- A race for valentine -- Uncle Wash and his mothers-in-law -- How he played Santa Claus -- Spottycuss-his world beater -- Miss Ant'nette's provin' -- The resurrection of brother Washington -- How he captured a buck -- His balking mule -- His little preacher -- Miss Kitty -- The examination -- "Ho, every one that thirsteth" -- The mascot mule -- The ghost that saved three flushes -- The origin of the coon -- The nervous goats -- A contest in the King's English -- Phosphate Ike -- The reconstruction of Marse George -- His first Ku Klux -- At the fair -- Old Punch -- How Miss Celeste solved the negro problem -- How Jenny McGrew came to her own -- How he rode in an automobile -- Uncle Wash on the panic -- How Bigbyville went dry -- Uncle Wash on gambling -- How Uncle Wash married the widow.
LC: N 10, '10.
PW: Je 4, '10.

M-948 Moore, Julia A. (Davis), Mrs., 1847-1920. Sunshine and shadow: or, Paul Burton's surprise. A romance of the American revolution / by Julia A. Moore. [Cadillac, Mich., 1915]. 58 p.
Unexamined copy: bibliographic data from NUC.

M-949 Moore, Nancy, b. 1908. Mammy Dicey's philosophy, a story of yesterday / by Nancy Moore. Boston: The Roxburgh Publishing Company, Inc., [c1919]. 172 p.
Unexamined copy: bibliographic data from NUC.
LC: O 23, '19.
PW: Ja 10, '20.

M-950 Moore, Thomas Emmet. The haunted king / by Thomas Emmet Moore . . . Boston, Mass.: C. M. Clark Publishing Co. (Inc.), 1910. 348 p., col. front., [5] leaves of plates. [Ill. by R. I. Conklin.]
LC: S 12, '10.

M-951 ____ My Lord Farquhar: a romance / by Thomas Emmet Moore. New York; London; Montreal: The Abbey Press, [c1902]. 248 p.
PW: My 3, '02.

M-952 Moorehead, Warren King, 1866-1939. Tonda: a story of the Sioux / by Warren K. Moorehead. Cincinnati: The Robert Clarke Company, 1904.

309 p., incl. [17] leaves of plates, front. [Ill. by Francis West and Wm. H. Foster.]
PW: D 10, '04.

M-953 Moorer, Louisa Haynes. Sequoyah: a romance under western skies / by Louise Haynes Moorer. New York: Broadway Publishing Co., [c1911]. 180 p.
DLC
LC: D 29, '11.

M-954 Moose, Ethel Tompkins. The gifts divine / by Ethel Tompkins Moose. [Washington: The C. A. Brewton Press, c1925]. 290, [1] p.
VA@

M-955 Mootz, Herman Edwin, 1870-1949. Stripped to the hide / by Herman Edwin Mootz. Boston: The Roxburgh Publishing Company, [c1925]. 274 p., incl. photo. front. (port.).

M-956 Moran, Jeannie Blockburn, 1842-1929. Twin souls / by Jeannie Blackburn Moran . . . Boston, U. S. A.: The Christopher Publishing House, [c1922]. 80 p.
LC: Je 17, '22.
PW: S 30, '22.

M-957 Moran, Pearl van Antwerp. In a monk's cassock / by Pearl Van Antwerp Moran. Chicago: W. B. Conkey Company, [c1910]. 157 p., incl. front. (port.).
DLC
LC: N 12, '10.

M-958 Morath, Lelah Palmer. Romances of the Rockies / by Lelah Palmer Morath . . . Colorado Springs, Colorado: Published by The Gowdy-Simmons Printing Company, [c1907]. [132] p., ill. (1 photo. port.).
Contents: A book lover's dream -- The strike of the Bonnie Bell -- The wooing of Rose -- The ghost of Marchmont -- A campaign of Cupid -- A hat from heaven.
LC: Jl 25, '07.

M-959 More, E. Anson (Enoch Anson), 1854-1932. A captain of men / by E. Anson More; with frontispiece

474

by Henry W. Moore. Boston: L. C. Page &
Company, 1905. 356 p., col. front.
PW: Ap 8, '05.
BLC: London: Alston Rivers, 1905.

M-960   ____ A vision of empire / by E. Anson More . . .
Boston: Richard G. Badger; [Toronto: The Copp
Clark Co., Limited, c1915]. 275 p.   **COD**
LC: Je 12, '15.

M-961   More, Paul Elmer, 1864-1937. The Jessica letters:
an editor's romance. New York; London: G. P.
Putnam's Sons, 1904. ([New York]: The
Knickerbocker Press). 328 p.   **VTU**

M-962   More aces: a collection of short stories / by George
Ade, Mary Antin, Konrad Bercovici, Dorothy
Canfield, Willa Cather, Zona Gale, John Galsworthy,
Sam Hellman, Fanny Hurst, Leonard Merrick,
Kathleen Norris, G. B. Stern, Benjamin R. Sher, Rita
Weiman, Thyra Samter Winslow; compiled by the
Community Workers of the New York Guild for the
Jewish Blind. New York; London: G. P. Putnam's

Sons, 1925. ([New York]: The Knickerbocker
Press). 379 p.
Contents: The feud / George Ade -- Malinka's atonement / Mary
Antin -- The drought / Konrad Bercovici -- The cage / Dorothy
Canfield -- Scandal / Willa Cather -- A winter's tale / Zona Gale -- A
simple tale / John Galsworthy -- I am a pirate king / Sam Hellman --
The gold in fish / Fannie Hurst -- The laurels and the lady / Leonard
Merrick -- The masterpiece / Kathleen Norris -- "The beloved" /
G.B. Stern -- Rubber Heels / Benjamin Richard Sher -- The stage
door / Rita Weiman -- Her own room / Thyra Samter Winslow.
LC: O 14, '25.
PW: O 17, '25.

M-963   Morehouse, William Russell, 1879-1937. Mystica
Algooat: an Indian legend and story of Southern
California / by William Russell Morehouse.
Franklin, Ohio: The Editor Publishing Co., 1903.
200 p.

M-964   Moreland, Sinclair, b. 1885. The noblest Roman: a
story of political debauchery and prostituted
allegiance / by Sinclair Moreland; illustrated by Betty
Baugh. [Austin, Tex.: Noblest Roman Publishing
Company, 1910]. 384 p., front. (port.).
Unexamined copy: bibliographic data from OCLC,
#25662230.
LC: S 6, '10.
Second edition: c1911; 411 p.
LC: Ag 28, '11.

M-965   Morgan, Alice. The boy who brought Christmas / by
Alice Morgan; illustrated by John Jackson. Garden
City, New York: Doubleday, Page & Company,
1911. 139 p., col. front., [3] leaves of col. plates.
Illustrated end papers.   **OBE**
LC: N 1, '11.
PW: N 11, '11.

M-966   Morgan, Angela. The imprisoned splendor / by
Angela Morgan . . . New York: The Baker &
Taylor Company, 1915. 280 p.
Reprinted in part from various periodicals.
Contents: The imprisoned splendor -- The craving -- When the
woman invites -- What shall we do with mother? -- The price of
understanding -- Such is the love of woman -- The making of a man.

Morgan, Beatrice Burton, b. 1894. See **Burton,
Beatrice.**

M-967   Morgan, Byron. The roaring road / by Byron
Morgan. New York: George H. Doran Company,
[c1920]. 280 p.
PW: Je 5, '20.

____ Too much speed. In *The Sporting spirit*
(1925), S-771.

M-968   Morgan, George, 1854-1936. The issue / by George
Morgan . . . ; illustrated by George A. Williams.
Philadelphia; London: J. B. Lippincott Company,
1904. 419 p., photo. front., [5] leaves of plates.

M-969   Morgan, Jacque Lloyd, b. 1873. The coup d'etat / by
Jacque L. Morgan; illustrated by H. L. Grout. New
York: R. F. Fenno & Company, [c1913]. 320 p.,
front., [3] leaves of plates.
LC: Mr 24, '13.

M-970   [____] The invaders: a story of the
"Hole-in-the-wall" country / by John Lloyd [pseud.].
New York: R. F. Fenno & Company, [c1910].
452 p., front., [3] leaves of plates. [Ill. by Warren
Y. Cluff.]
LC: N 17, '10.

M-971   Moriarty, Helen, 1872?-1928. The hill people:
chronicles of insular community / by Helen Moriarty.
St. Louis, Mo.; London: B. Herder Book Co., 1925.
268 p.
Contents: A match for Manie -- Suseen Lomasney -- A rival over the
way -- The man from Dungarvan -- The pipes of Pod Fogarty --
Malachy Logan -- Jim Graney's wife -- Progress comes to the Hill --
The finger of scorn -- A twilight confidence -- The three Miss
Bannons -- Roaring Rob Scanlan -- Mrs. Garrigan's new carpet--
Mrs. Beatty takes offense -- Nor' Neilan's daughter -- The hill
influence.
LC: O 12, '25.

M-972   ____ Mrs. Strangeways: and seven other clever
stories / by Helen Moriarty. Cincinnati, Ohio: St.
Anthony Messenger, [c1922]. 140 p.
Contents: Mrs. Strangeways -- Christine's Valentine -- Woman are
queer -- The new parish hall -- Roses of today -- Back home --
Through the front door -- The shade of his hand.

Morlae, E. A soldier of the legion. In *Atlantic
narratives*; **2nd series (1918), A-361.**

Morland, Peter Henry, pseud. See **Brand, Max,
1892-1944, pseud.**

M-973   Morley, Christopher, 1890-1957. The haunted
bookshop / by Christopher Morley. Garden City,
New York: Doubleday, Page & Company, 1919.
289 p.
LC: Jl 8, '19.
PW: Je 28, '19.
BLC: London: Chapman Hall, 1920.
References: Lee 9.

M-974   ____ Hostages to fortune / by Christopher Morley; a
collection of poems, essays, and short stories, written
for the Haverfordian by Christopher Morley during
his college days. Haverford, Pa.: The Haverfordian,

[c1925]. 121 p.

Contents: The stargazer [poem] -- The limerick [nonfiction] -- To her [poem] -- Omna vincit amor -- To a skull [poem] -- The claret of Baccaral -- Skating song [poem] -- Episodes in the life of an Irish waitress: I. The undoing of Oliver Cromwell Jones; II. The katabasis of Xenophon; III. A temperance interlude; IV. Barbara's diary -- A ballad of midyears [poem] -- Pirates -- A grand opera incident -- To a grasshopper [poem] -- Letters of Robert Louis Stevenson [nonfiction].

LC: My 11, 25.
PW: Jl 4, '25.
References: Lee 49.

M-975   _____ In the sweet dry and dry / by Christopher Morley and Bart Haley; illustrated by Gluyas Williams. New York: Boni and Liveright, 1919. 168 p., front., ill.
LC: O 3, '19.
PW: S 13, '19.
References: Lee 10.

M-976   _____ Kathleen / by Christopher Morley; frontispiece by Wallace Morgan. Garden City; New York; London: Doubleday, Page & Company, 1920. 174 p., front.
LC: Ap 5, '20.
PW: Mr 27, '20.
BLC: London: Curtis Brown; Garden City, N. Y., printed, 1920.
References: Lee 13.

M-977   _____ Pandora lifts the lid / by Christopher Morley and Don Marquis. New York: George H. Doran Company, [c1924]. 299 p., front. Illustrated end papers.
LC: Je 6, '24.
PW: My 31, '24.
References: Lee 43.

M-978   _____ Parnassus on wheels / by Christopher Morley. Garden City, New York: Doubleday, Page & Company, 1917. 190 p.
LC: S 20, '17.
PW: S 22, '17.
BLC: London: William Heinemann; Garden City, N. Y. [printed], 1921.
References: Lee 5.

M-979   _____ Shandygaff: a number of most agreeable *Inquirendoes* upon *Life and Letters*, interspersed with *Short Stories* and *Skitts*, the whole Most Diverting to the Reader; accompanied also by some *Notes for Teachers* whereby the Booke may be made usefull in class-room or for private Improvement / by Christopher Morley . . . Garden City, N. Y.: Doubleday, Page and Company, 1918. (Garden City, New York: Country Life Press.) 326 p.

Contents: A question of plumage -- The man -- The head of the firm -- Rhubarb -- The haunting beauty of strychnine -- Ingo -- Housebroken -- Time to light the furnace -- A venture in mysticism -- An Oxford landlady -- A morning in marathon -- The American house of lords -- Cotswold winds -- Unhealthy -- Hay Febrifuge. The remainder of the text appears to be nonfiction.

LC: My 3, '18.
PW: My 11, '18.
References: Lee 7.

M-980   _____ The story of Ginger Cubes / by Christopher Morley. [New York: New York Evening Post, Inc.,

1922]. 37 p., ill. [Ill. by W. Gorman.]   **NYP**
"Reprinted from the Bowling Green of the New York Evening Post."
PW: Jl 22, '22.
References: Lee 28.

M-981   _____ Tales from a rolltop desk / by Christopher Morley; frontispiece by Walter Jack Duncan. Garden City, N. Y.; Toronto: Doubleday, Page & Company, 1921. 262 p., front.

Contents: The prize package -- Advice to the lovelorn -- The curious case of Kenelm Digby -- Gloria and the garden of Sweden -- The commutation chophouse -- The pert little hat -- Urn burial -- The battle of manila envelopes -- The climacteric -- Punch and Judy -- Referred to the author.

LC: Je 25, 21.
PW: Je 4, '21.
BLC: London: Curtis Brown; Garden City, N. Y., printed, 1921.
References: Lee 19.

M-982   _____ Thunder on the left . . . / by Christopher Morley. Garden City, New York: Doubleday, Page & Company, 1925. 273 p.
LC: Ja 2, '26.
BLC: London: William Heinemann; printed in U. S. A., 1925.
References: Lee 52.

M-983   _____ Where the blue begins / by Christopher Morley . . . Garden City, New York: Doubleday, Page & Company, 1922. 215 p.
"First edition." Lee notes large paper edition [32] and large- paper edition, limited, signed [33], 1924.
LC: N 3, '22.
PW: O 14, '22.
BLC: London: William Heinemann; printed in U. S. A., 1923.
References: Lee 34.

Moroso, John A. (John Antonio), b. 1874. Angelo. **In** *Master tales of mystery* **(1915), M-588.5.**

M-984   _____ The listening man / by John A. Moroso. New York: D. Appleton and Company, 1924. 273, [1] p., front.
LC: Ap 5, '24.

M-985   _____ The people against Nancy Preston / by John A. Moroso. New York: Henry Holt and Company, 1921. 257 p.
LC: O 5, '21.
BLC: London: Methuen & Co., 1922.

M-986   _____ The quarry / by John A. Moroso; with illustrations by Thomas Fogarty. Boston: Little, Brown, and Company, 1913. 324 p., front., [3] leaves of plates.
LC: Ap 19, '13.
PW: Ap 5, '13.
Also published as: *The city of silent men*. Photoplay edition. New York: The Macaulay Company, [1921, c1913]. [328] p., [1] leaf of plates.
BLC: London: Sampson Low & Co., [1922].

M-987   _____ The stumbling herd / by John A. Moroso. New York: The Macaulay Company, [c1923].

306 p.
LC reports front. by Harvey Dunn.
LC: Mr 17, '23.
PW: My 5, '23.

M-988   Morrill, Fred Brown, b. 1858. Beyond the horizon:
a novel / by Fred B. Morrill . . . New York: The
Neale Publishing Company, 1918. 296 p.
PW: N 16, '18.

M-989   ____ The campaign: a political novel / by Fred B.
Morrill. New York: The Neale Publishing
Company, 1917. 242 p.
LC: S 20, '17.

M-990   Morris, Anna Van Rensselaer. The apple woman of
the Klickitat / Anna Van Rensselaer Morris. New
York: Duffield & Company, 1918. 271 p., front.,
[3] leaves of plates.
PW: S 28, '18.

M-991   Morris, Clara, 1848-1925. Left in charge / by Clara
Morris. New York: G. W. Dillingham Company,
[1904]. 355 p.
PW: F 20, '04.
BLC: London: T. Fisher Unwin, 1904.

M-992   ____ The new "East Lynne": an entirely new and
original novel / by Clara Morris. [New York: C. H.
Doscher & Co., c1908]. 326 p., front.
PW: Jl 4, '08.

M-993   ____ A pasteboard crown: a story of the New York
stage / by Clara Morris; with a frontispiece from a
drawing by Howard Chandler Christy. New York:
Charles Scribner's Sons, 1902. 370 p., col. front.
PW: Je 7, '02.
BLC: London: Isbister & Co., 1902.

M-994   ____ The trouble woman / by Clara Morris . . .
New York; London: Funk & Wagnalls Company,
[c1904]. 58 p.
PW: Mr 26, '04.

M-995   Morris, Daniel Henry. As the gods decree: a novel
of the time of Augustus / by Daniel Henry Morris.
New York; Chicago; Washington; Baltimore; Atlanta;
Norfolk; Florence, Ala.: Broadway Publishing Co.,
[c1910]. 361 p.   **DLC**
LC: D 12, '10.

M-996   Morris, Edwin Bateman, b. 1881. Blue Anchor Inn /
by Edwin Bateman Morris. Philadelphia: The Penn
Publishing Company, 1912. 302 p., incl. col. front.,
[4] leaves of plates. [Ill. by A. Edwin Kromer.]
                                                   CLU
LC: S 5, '12.
PW: Ag 3, '12.

M-997   ____ The cresting wave / by Edwin Bateman Morris.
Philadelphia: The Penn Publishing Company, 1920.
417 p.
LC: Mr 13, '20.
PW: Ap 10, '20

M-998   ____ Mere man / by Edwin Bateman Morris . . . ;
illustrated by Ralph L. Boyer. Philadelphia: The
Penn Publishing Company, 1914. 226 p., front., [3]
leaves of plates.
LC: Jl 25, '14.
PW: O 10, '14.

M-999   ____ The millionaire / by Edwin Bateman Morris
. . . ; illustrated by Coles Phillips and Ralph L.
Boyer. Philadelphia: The Penn Publishing Company,
1913. 354 p., col. front., [4] leaves of plates.
LC: D 26, '13.
PW: N 29, '13.

M-1000   ____ The narrow street / by Edwin Bateman Morris
. . . ; illustrated by Nat Little. Philadelphia: The
Penn Publishing Company, 1924. 320 p., front.
LC: Ap 10, '24.
PW: Ap 19, '24.

M-1001   ____ Our Miss York / by Edwin Bateman Morris;
illustrated by Coles Phillips and Ralph L. Boyer.
Philadelphia: The Penn Publishing Company, 1916.
352 p., col. front., [4] leaves of plates.
LC: F 29, '16.
PW: Mr 25, '16.

Morris, Elisabeth, 1870-1964. See **Woodbridge,
Elisabeth.**

M-1002   Morris, George Van Derveer, 1867-1928. A man for
a' that / by George Van Derveer Morris. Cincinnati:
Jennings & Pye; New York: Eaton & Mains,
[c1902]. 403 p., front., [7] leaves of plates.
PW: S 13, '02.

M-1003   ____ Polly: being a fairy-tale of love, in which it is
shown that men love not so much the reality, the
substance, as they do their own ideals / by George
Van Derveer Morris . . . New York; Washington:
The Neale Publishing Company, 1906. 340 p. **KUK**
LC: D 21, '06.

M-1004   Morris, Gouverneur, 1876-1953. Aladdin O'Brien /
by Gouverneur Morris. New York: The Century
Co., 1902. 298 p.
PW: O 11, '02.
BLC: London: Cassell & Co; printed in the U. S.,
1903.

         ____ Behind the door. In *War stories* (1919), **W-94.**

M-1005   ____ The championship / by Gouverneur Morris.
New York: The Ridgway Company, [c1913]. 32 p.

M-1006   ____ The claws of the tiger / Gouverneur Morris.
New York: International Magazine Company,
[c1910]. 29 p.

         ____ Derrick's return. In *Prize stories of 1923*
(1924), P-621.

         ____ The despoiler. In *Short stories for class
reading* **(1925), S-461.**

M-1007   Ellen and Mr. Man / by Gouverneur Morris. New York: The Century Co., 1904. 189 p., front., [2] leaves of plates.
PW: O 22, '04.

M-1008   The footprint: and other stories / by Gouverneur Morris. New York: Charles Scribner's Sons, 1908. 336 p. Partly reprinted from various sources.
Contents: The footprint -- Paradise Ranch -- Captain England -- The execution -- Simon L'Ouvrier -- A Carolina night's dream -- The stowing away of Mr. Bill Ballad -- The explorers -- The little heiress, or, The hunted look -- The best man -- The crocodile.
LC: F 27, '08.
PW: Mr 7, '08.

M-1009   The goddess / by Gouverneur Morris . . . and Charles W. Goddard; illustrated. New York: Hearst's International Library Co., 1915. 402 p., photo. front., [15] leaves of plates.
LC: S 17, '15.
PW: O 23, '15.

M-1010   His daughter / by Gouverneur Morris; with frontispiece by C. Allan Gilbert. New York: Charles Scribner's Sons, 1918. 326 p., col. front.
LC: F 20, '18.
PW: F 9, '18.
BLC: London: W. Collins Sons & Co., 1919.

M-1011   If you touch them they vanish / by Gouverneur Morris; with illustrations by Charles S. Chapman. New York: Charles Scribner's Sons, 1913. 146 p., col. front., [7] leaves of col. plates.
LC: O 7, '13.
PW: O 11, '13.

     Ig's Amok. *In Prize stories of 1922* **(1923), P-620.**

M-1012   The incandescent lily: and other stories / by Gouverneur Morris. New York: Charles Scribner's Sons, 1914. 314 p.
Contents: The incandescent lily -- The custody of the child -- The championship -- Tango taught in ten teachings -- You can't get away with it -- A perfect gentleman of Pelham Bay Park -- Legay Pelham's headache -- The Bostonian -- Legay Pelham's Protégée -- The back seat.
LC: My 13, '14.
PW: My 9, '14.

M-1013   It: and other stories / by Gouverneur Morris. New York: Charles Scribner's Sons, 1912. 386 p.
Contents: It -- Two business women -- The trap -- Sapphira -- The bride's dead -- Holding hands -- The claws of the tiger -- Growing up -- The battle of Aiken -- An idyl of Pelham Bay Park -- Back there in the grass -- Asabri.
LC: Mr 26, '12.
PW: Mr 30, '12.

M-1014   Keeping the peace / by Gouverneur Morris. New York: Charles Scribner's Sons, 1924. 295 p.
LC: S 9, '24.
PW: S 13, '24.

     The little Frenchman and his water lots. *In The best American humorous short stories* **(1920), B-556.**

M-1015   The pagan's progress / by Gouverneur Morris; illustrated by John Rae. New York: A. S. Barnes & Company, 1904. 258 p., col. front., [5] leaves of plates.
PW: O 1, '04.
BLC: London: Authors' Syndicate; New Yrok: A. S. Barnes & Co., 1904.

M-1016   The penalty / by Gouverneur Morris; illustrated by Howard Chandler Christy. New York: Charles Scribner's Sons, 1913. 347 p., front., [46] leaves of plates (some double-leaf).
LC: Ap 2, '13.
PW: Ap 5, '13.

     A postscript to divorce. *In The best short stories of 1924 and the yearbook of the American short story* **(1925), B-569.**

M-1017   Putting on the screws / by Gouveneur Morris; illustrated by Paul Meylan. New York: Doubleday, Page & Company, 1909. 89, [1] p., col. front., [3] leaves of col. plates. Ornamental borders.
LC: O 22, '09.
PW: N 13, '09.
BLC: London: Doubleday, Page & Company; New York printed, 1909.

M-1018   The seven Darlings / by Gouverneur Morris; illustrated by Howard Chandler Christy. New York: Charles Scribner's Sons, 1915. 325 p., front., [15] leaves of plates.
LC: Mr 17, '15.
PW: Mr 20, '15.

M-1019   The spread eagle: and other stories / by Gouverneur Morris. New York: Charles Scribner's Sons, 1910. 357 p.
Contents: The spread eagle -- Targets -- The boot -- The despoiler -- One more martyr -- "Ma'am?" -- Mr. Holiday -- White muscats of Alexandria -- Without a lawyer -- The "Monitor" and the "Merrimac" -- The McTavish -- The parrot -- On the spot; or, The idler's house-party.
LC: O 12, '10.
PW: O 8, '10.

M-1020   Tom Beauling / by Gouverneur Morris. New York: The Century Co., 1901. 210 p.
PW: O 12, '01.

     The unsent letter. *In War stories* **(1919), W-94.**

M-1021   The voice in the rice / by Gouverneur Morris; with illustrations by J. C. Leydendecker and decorations by Bertha Stuart. New York: Dodd, Mead and Company, 1910. 158 p., col. front., [5] leaves of col. plates. Designed end papers.
LC: Ap 1, '10.
PW: Ap 2, '10.

M-1022   We three / by Gouverneur Morris; illustrated by Henry Hutt. New York; London: D. Appleton and Company, 1916. 318, [1] p., front., [3] leaves of plates.
LC: Ap 4, '16.
PW: Ap 15, '16.

M-1023 ____ When my ship comes in / by Gouverneur Morris; illustrated by Frank Snapp. New York: Charles Scribner's Sons, 1915. 361 p., front., [3] leaves of plates.
LC: S 14, '15.
PW: S 18, '15.

M-1024 ____ The wild goose / by Gouverneur Morris. New York: Charles Scribner's Sons, 1919. 340 p., front.
LC: O 1, '19.
PW: N 1, '19.

M-1025 ____ Yellow men and gold / by Gouverneur Morris; with illustrations by Charles B. Falls. New York: Dodd, Mead and Company, 1911. 244 p., col. front., [5] leaves of col. plates.
LC: Ap 10, '11.
PW: Ap 8, '11.
BLC: London: Eveleigh Nash, 1912; second edition.

M-1026 Morris, Harrison S. (Harrison Smith), 1856-1948. Hannah Bye / by Harrison S. Morris. Philadelphia: The Penn Publishing Company, 1920. 266 p.
LC: Ap 30, '20.
PW: My 22, '20.

M-1027 ____ The landlord's daughter / by Harrison S. Morris. Philadelphia: The Penn Publishing Company, 1923. 312 p., front.
LC: Je 20, '23.
PW: Mr 24, '23.

M-1028 Morris, James Walter. The old trail: a story of Rebekah / by James Walter Morris. Boston: Richard G. Badger, [c1913]. ([Boston]: The Gorham Press). 100 p.
LC: Ja 23, '14.

Morris, Margaretta, ed. See *A book of Bryn Mawr stories* **(1901), B-732.**

M-1029 Morrison, Adele Sarpy, b. 1842. Benvenuta: a romance of the Hudson River / by Adele Sarpy Morrison. [St. Louis]: Published by the Thompson Company, 1914. 232 p.   **KLG**
LC: N 25, '14.

M-1030 ____ A New England primrose / by Adele Sarpy Morrison; illustrated by C. O. Longabaugh. Chicago: The Branch Publishing Co., [c1918]. 165 p., col. front., ill.
LC: O 8, '18.

Morrison, Arthur. That brute Simmons. In *Short stories* **(1925), S-460.**

Morrison, Caroline Wood, jt. aut. *William and Bill* (1914). See **Cooke, Grace MacGowan, 1863-1944, jt. aut., C-732.**

M-1031 Morrison, John Arch, 1893-1965. The ministry of Rolla Clark / by J. A. Morrison . . . Anderson, Indiana: Gospel Trumpet Company, [c1925]. 112 p., ill. [Ill. by C. B. Millar.]   **INA**

M-1032 [Morrow, Honoré Willsie], 1880?-1940. Benefits forgot: a story of Lincoln and mother love / by Honoré Willsie; with illustrations by Charles E. Cartwright. New York: Frederick A. Stokes Company, [c1917]. 80 p., front., ill.
PW: O 13, '17.

M-1033 ____ The Devonshers / by Honoré Willsie Morrow. New York: Frederick A. Stokes Company, 1924. 354 p.
LC: S 20, '24.
PW: S 13, '24.
BLC: London: Hodder & Stoughton, [1924].

M-1034 [____] The enchanted canyon: a novel of the Grand Canyon and the Arizona desert / by Honoré Willsie. New York: Frederick A. Stokes Company, [c1921]. 346 p.
LC: Ap 12, '21.
PW: Ap 9, '21.
BLC: London: Thornton Butterworth, 1922.

M-1035 [____] The exile of the Lariat / by Honoré Willsie. New York: Frederick A. Stokes Company, 1923. 357 p.
LC: Ag 20, '23.
BLC: London: Hodder & Stoughton, [1924].

M-1036 [____] The forbidden trail / by Honoré Willsie; with a frontispiece in color by R. Emmet [sic] Owen. New York: Frederick A. Stokes Company, [1919]. 379 p., col. front.
LC: N 17, '19.
PW: N 15, '19.
BLC: London: Thornton Butterworth, 1920.

M-1037 [____] The heart of the desert (Kut-le of the desert) / by Honoré Willsie; with a frontispiece in colors by W. Herbert Dunton. New York: Frederick A. Stokes Company, 1913. 313 p., col. front.   **INU**

M-1038 [____] Judith of the godless valley / by Honoré Willsie. New York: Frederick A. Stokes Company, [c1922]. 354 p.
LC: Ag 28, '22.
PW: Ag 19, '22.
BLC: London: Hodder & Stoughton, [1923].

M-1039 ____ The lost speech of Abraham Lincoln: a story / by Honoré Willsie Morrow. New York: Frederick A. Stokes Company, 1925. 56, [1] p.
LC: Mr 28, '25.
PW: Mr 28, '25.

M-1040 [____] Lydia of the pines / by Honoré Willsie; with a frontispiece by Eric Pape. New York: Frederick A. Stokes Company, [c1917]. 357 p., col. front.
LC: Mr 3, '17.
PW: Mr 3, '17.

M-1041 [____] Still Jim / by Honoré Willsie . . . ; with a frontispiece in colors by W. Herbert Dunton and with illustrations in black and white by J. Scott Williams. New York: Frederick A. Stokes Company, [1915]. 369 p., col. front., [4] leaves of plates.
LC: Ap 26, '15.
PW: Ap 24, '15.
BLC: London: Grant Richards, 1916.

M-1042 ____ We must march: a novel of the winning of Oregon / by Honoré Willsie Morrow . . . New York: Frederick A. Stokes Company, 1925. 427 p. Illustrated end papers.
LC: O 17, '25.
PW: O 17, '25.

M-1043 Morrow, Lowell Howard. Atalantis: a novel / by Lowell Howard Morrow. Boston: Eastern Publishing Company, [c1902]. 285 p.
PW: D 5, '03.

Morrow, W. C. (William Chambers), 1853-1923. Breaking through. In *Spinners' book of fiction* **(1907), S-755.**

M-1044 ____ Lentala of the South Seas: the romantic tale of a lost colony / by W. C. Morrow; the illustrations from oil paintings by Maynard Dixon. New York: Frederick A. Stokes Company, [c1908]. 278 p., col. front., [6] leaves of col. plates.

____ The Rajah's nemesis. In *Argonaut stories* **(1906), A-298.**

M-1045 Morse, Harriet Clara. A cowboy cavalier / by Harriet C. Morse; illustrations by Samuel F. B. Morse . . . and John Goss. Boston, Massachusetts: The C. M. Clark Publishing Company, 1908. 294 p., front., [7] leaves of plates.
LC: My 19, '08.
PW: Je 20, '08.

M-1046 Morse, Margaret, b. 1877. On the road to Arden / by Margaret Morse; illustrated by Harold M. Brett. Boston; New York: Houghton Mifflin Company, 1909. (Cambridge: The Riverside Press). 251, [1] p., front., [4] leaves of plates.
PW: Ap 3, '09.

M-1047 ____ Scottie and his lady / by Margaret Morse; illustrated by Harold M. Brett. Boston; New York: Houghton Mifflin Company, 1910. (Cambridge [Mass.]: The Riverside Press). 276 p., front. and t. p. double-leaf, [3] leaves of plates.
LC: D 9, '10.

M-1048 ____ The spirit of the pines / by Margaret Morse. Boston; New York: Houghton, Mifflin & Company, 1906. (Cambridge: The Riverside Press). 158, [2] p.
PW: F 24, '06.

M-1049 Morten, W. H. (William Henry), b.1846. Haps and mishaps of Jack Haselton; a story of adventure / by W. H. Morten. New York; London; Montreal: The Abbey Press, [1902]. 264 p.   **NYP** (photocopy)
PW: S 13, '02.

M-1050 Mortimer, J. H. (James Howard), b. 1858. The dawn, or, The story of a British army officer in Ireland, England, Africa and America / by J. H. Mortimer; illustrated. [Chicago]: J. H. Mortimer, Publisher, [c1904]. 335 p., photo. front. (port.), [5] leaves of photo. plates.   **KKU**

M-1051 ____ A sprig of Plantagenet, or, The national debt of England: showing how it was contracted, and how tardily it is being paid, together with some legal advice regarding the manner in which it may be paid and collected, with the least possible amount of friction / by J. H. Mortimer . . . Chicago: The Independent Publishing Co.; London: G. W. Bacon & Company, Ltd., [c1909]. 461 p., photo. front. (port.), [5] leaves of photo. plates.

M-1052 Mortimer, Lillian. Bunco in Arizona: a novel founded upon the play of the same title / by Lillian Mortimer. Baltimore, Md.: I. & M. Ottenheimer, 1907. 85 p., photo. front. (port.).   **CLU**

M-1053 ____ No mother to guide her: a novel / founded upon the play of the same title by Lillian Mortimer. Philadelphia, Pa.: Royal Publishing Co., [c1906]. 91 p., photo. front. (port.).

M-1054 Morton, L. Curry. The hero and the man / by L. Curry Morton; illustrations by J. Allen St. John. Chicago: A. C. McClurg & Co., 1912. 459, [1] p., col. front., [3] leaves of col. plates.

M-1055 Morton, Martha, 1865-1925. Her lord and master / by Martha Morton; illustrated by Howard Chandler Christy and Esther MacNamara. Philadelphia: Drexel Biddle, [c1902]. 475 p., col. front., [4] leaves of plates.
PW: D 20, '02.

M-1056 ____ Val Sinestra / by Martha Morton. New York: E. P. Dutton & Company, [c1924]. 275 p.
PW: F 7, '25.

M-1057 Morton, Oren Frederic, 1857-1926. Land of the laurel: a story of the Alleghanies / by Oren F. Morton. Morgantown, W. Va.: The Acme Publishing Company, 1903. 240 p., [9] leaves of photo. plates. [Photo. by C. S. Rexroad and J. F. Christopher.]
(Arbor Lodge Series; III)
PW: D 5, '03.

M-1058 ____ Winning or losing?: a story of the West Virginia Hills / by Oren F. Morton . . . Kingwood, W. Va.: Published by the author, 1901. 365 p., photo. front., [6] leaves of photo. plates. [Photo. by C. S. Rexroad.]   **AFU**

Morton, T. B. (Thomas Bottomley), ed. See *Daniel Hovey* **(1901), D-54.**

M-1059 Morton, Victoria. The whirlpool / by Victoria Morton. New York: E. P. Dutton, c1916. 348 p. Unexamined copy: bibliographic data from OCLC, #21480872.
LC: N 4, '16.
PW: N 11, '16.

M-1060 ____ The yellow ticket / by Victoria Morton; from the play of the same name by Michael Morton; illustrated. New York: The H. K. Fly Company, [c1914]. 313 p., front., [3] leaves of plates. [Ill. by R. L. Thayer.]

M-1061 Morton, William Albert, b. 1866. The making of a "Mormon" / by William A. Morton. Salt Lake City, Utah: W. A. Morton, [c1915]. 47 p. Unexamined copy: bibliographic data from NUC.

M-1062 Mosby, James Logan. Paul Winslow: a novel / by James Logan Mosby. Columbia, Missouri: Press of E. W. Stephens Publishing Co., 1916. 320 p., front., [5] leaves of plates (Some photo.).

M-1063 Mosby, Thomas Speed, 1874-1954. Ben Blunt: his life and story; greatly abridged and truly told with much thrilling and ingenious comment thereon; an historical romance / by Speed Mosby. [St. Louis: Press of Commercial Printing Co., 1903.] 382 p.

M-1064 Moseley, Ella Lowery. The wonder lady / by Ella Lowery Moseley; illustrated by John Goss. Boston: Lothrop, Lee & Shepard Co., [1911]. 256 p., front., [7] leaves of plates. LC: Je 30, '11. PW: Ag 26, '11.

Moseley, Katharine Prescott. The story Vinton heard at Mallorie. In *The best short stories of 1918 and the yearbook of the American short story* (1919), B-563.

M-1065 Moses, Barr, b. 1874. Dreaming River / by Barr Moses. New York: Frederick A. Stokes Company, [1909]. 262 p. LC: Ja 13, '09.

Mosley, Jefferson. The secret at the crossroads. In *Prize stories of 1924* (1925), P-622.

M-1066 Moss, Catherine Winspear. The thousand leggers / by Catherine Winspear Moss. Boston, Massachusetts: The C. M. Clark Publishing Company, 1909. 92 p., front. (port.)   **DLC**

M-1067 Moss, Mary, b. 1864. The poet and the parish / by Mary Moss. New York: Henry Holt and Company, 1906. 326 p. LC: S 22, '06.

M-1068 ____ A sequence in hearts / by Mary Moss. Philadelphia; London: J. B. Lippincott Company, 1903. 333 p.   **GZM** PW: O 10, '03.

M-1069 A mother in exile. Boston: Little, Brown, and Company, 1914. 328 p. BLC: London: Everett & Co., [1914].

____ The mother of Pierrot, pseud. See **Bartlett, Frederick Orin, b. 1876, B-298**

M-1070 Mott, Frank Luther, 1886-1964. The man with the good face / by Frank Luther Mott. Iowa City, Iowa: The Midland Press, 1921. 60 p.   **IND**

____ The recruits' story. In *Prairie gold* (1917), **P-588.**

M-1071 Mott, Frederick B. (Frederick Blount). Before the crisis / by Frederick Blount Mott. New York; London: John Lane, The Bodley Head, 1904. 309 p. PW: D 3, '04.

M-1072 Mott, Lawrence, 1881-1931. Jules of the great heart: "free" trapper and outlaw in the Hudson Bay region in the early days / by Lawrence Mott; with frontispiece by F. E. Schoonover. New York: The Century Co., 1905. 303 p., col. front. **OSU, BYU** PW: O 28, '05. BLC: London: William Heinemann, 1905.

M-1073 ____ To the credit of the sea / Lawrence Mott; illustrated. New York; London: Harper & Brothers, 1907. 295, [1] p., front., [5] leaves of plates. [Ill. by George Harding and C. W. Ashley.] LC: My 2, '07. PW: My 11, '07.

M-1074 ____ The white darkness: and other stories of the great Northwest / by Lawrence Mott; illustrated by Frank E. Schoonover and Cyrus Cuneo. New York: The Outing Publishing Company, 1907. 308 p., front., [4] leaves of plates.
Contents: The white darkness -- Jaquette -- The silver fox -- Love in the wilderness -- Friends -- Wilkinson's chance -- The current of fear -- One of three -- A day's work in the mounted police -- Jean Baptiste's Christmas present -- The black thing of Hatchet Lake -- Wa-gush -- Follette -- The Indian's vengeance -- The taking of Almighty Voice -- The light of a match.
PW: F 9, '07. BLC: London: William Heinemann, 1907.

M-1075 Mountain, Lucena Belle Walker, b. 1877. Joy Delle / by Lucena W. Mountain. Cincinnati: Press of Jennings and Graham, [c1912]. 200 p.

M-1076 Mowbray, J. P., 1835-1903. The conquering of Kate / by J. P. Mowbray ("J. P. M.") New York: Doubleday, Page & Company, 1903. 315 p., col. front. [Ill. by Karl Anderson.] PW: Ap 25, '03.

M-1077 ____ A journey to nature / by J. P. Mowbray. New York: Doubleday Page and Co., A. D. 1901. 315 p. Illustrated end papers.   A series of papers originally contributed to the New York evening post.

M-1078 ____ The making of a country home / by J. P. Mowbray. New York: Doubleday Page and Co., 1901. 258 p. Illustrated end papers.

M-1079 ____ Tangled up in Beulah Land / by J. P. Mowbray. New York: Doubleday, Page & Co., 1902. 227 p.

M-1080 Moyer, Alice Curtice. A romance of the road: making love and a living / by Alice Curtice Moyer; illustrated with 41 half-tone portraits. Chicago: Laird & Lee, [c1912]. 279 p., front., [6] leaves of photo. plates.

Muckleston, Harold Struun, Mrs. See **Wherry, Edith, pseud.**

M-1081 Muenchgesang, Robert. In quest of truth: glimpses of Roman scenes during the reign of the Emperor Domitian / by Robert Muenchgesang; with an appendix explanatory of foreign expressions and historical names. St. Louis, Mo.: Published by B. Herder, 1905. 203 p., [1] leaf of plates.   **DLC**

Muilenburg, Frank Luther. The man with the good face. In *Stories from the Midland (1924)*, S-984.

Muilenburg, Walter John, b. 1893. At the end of the road. In *The best short stories of 1916 and the yearbook of the American short story (1917)*, B-561.

_____ Heart of youth. In *The best short stories of 1915 and the yearbook of the American short story (1916)*, B-560.

M-1082 _____ Prairie / Walter J. Muilenburg. New York: The Viking Press, 1925. 277 p.
PW: Ag 29, '25.
BLC: London: John Lane, 1926.

_____ The prairie. In *Stories from the Midland (1924)*, S-984.

M-1083 Mulder, Arnold, 1885-1959. Bram of the Five Corners / by Arnold Mulder . . . Chicago: A. C. McClurg & Co., 1915. 366 p.   **EXG**
PW: Ap 24, '15.

M-1084 _____ The dominie of Harlem / by Arnold Mulder. Chicago: A. C. McClurg & Co., 1913. 385 p.
LC: S 5, '13.
PW: S 20, '13.

M-1085 _____ The outbound road / by Arnold Mulder. Boston; New York: Houghton Mifflin Company, 1919. (Cambridge: The Riverside Press). 302 p.
LC: N 4, '19.
PW: N 8, '19.

M-1086 _____ The sand doctor / by Arnold Mulder. Boston; New York: Houghton Mifflin Company, 1921. (Cambridge: The Riverside Press). 317, [1] p.
LC: F 19, '21.

M-1087 Mulford, Clarence Edward, 1883-1956. Bar-20: being a record of certain happenings that occurred in the otherwise peaceful lives of one Hopalong Cassidy and his campanions on the range / by Clarence Edward Mulford; illustrated by N. C. Wyeth and F. E. Schoonover. New York: The Outing Publishing Company, 1907. 382 p., front., [6] leaves of plates.   **COF**
LC: Jl 11, '07.
PW: Ag 03, '07.

M-1088 _____ Bar-20 days / by Clarence E. Mulford; with illustrations in color by Maynard Dixon. Chicago: A. C. McClurg & Co., 1911. 412 p., col. front., [3] leaves of col. plates.
LC: Mr 29, '11.
PW: Ap 8, '11.

M-1089 _____ The Bar-20 three: relating a series of startling and strenuous adventures, in the cow-town of Mesquite, of the famous Bar-20 trio-Hopalong Cassidy, Red Connors, and Johnny Nelson / by Clarence E. Mulford; frontispiece by Frank E. Schoonover. Chicago: A. C. McClurg & Co., 1921. 353 p., front.
LC: My 2, '21.

PW: My 14, '21.
BLC: London: Hodder & Stoughton, [1921].

M-1090 _____ Black Buttes / by Clarence E. Mulford. Garden City, New York: Doubleday, Page & Company, 1923. 318 p.
LC: My 26, '23.
PW: My 12, '23.

M-1091 _____ "Bring me his ears" / by Clarence E. Mulford . . . ; frontispiece by J. Allen St. John. Chicago: A. C. McClurg & Co., 1922. 350 p., front.   **COF**
LC: O 31, '22.
PW: N 18, '22.

M-1092 _____ Buck Peters, ranchman: being the story of what happened when Buck Peters, Hopalong Cassidy, and their Bar-20 associates went to Montana / by Clarence E. Mulford and John Wood Clay; with four illustrations in color by Maynard Dixon. Chicago: A. C. McClurg & Co., 1912. 367 p., col. front., [3] leaves of col. plates.
LC: Ap 2, '12.
PW: Ap 13, '12.

M-1093 _____ The coming of Cassidy: --and the others / by Clarence E. Mulford; illustrations by Maynard Dixon. Chicago: A. C. McClurg & Co., 1913. 438 p., col. front., [4] leaves of col. plates.
LC: D 27, '13.
BLC: London: C. F. Cazenove; Chicago: A. C. McClurg & Co.; Binghamton, New York [printed], 1913.

M-1094 _____ Cottonwood Gulch / by Clarence E. Mulford. Garden City, N. Y.: Doubleday, Page & Company, 1925. 340 p.
LC: F 12, '25.
PW: Ja 24, '25.
BLC: London: Hodder & Stoughton, [1925].

M-1095 _____ Hopalong Cassidy / by Clarence E. Mulford; with five illustrations in color by Maynard Dixon. Chicago: A. C. McClurg & Co., 1910. 392 p., col. front., [4] leaves of col. plates.
LC: Mr 14, '10.
PW: Mr 26, '10.

M-1096 _____ Hopalong Cassidy returns / by Clarence E. Mulford. Garden City, New York: Doubleday, Page & Company, 1924. 310 p.
LC: S 13, '24.
BLC: London: Curtis Brown; printed in U. S. A., 1924. Another edition: London: Hodder & Stoughton, [1924].

M-1097 _____ Johnny Nelson: how a one-time pupil of Hopalong Cassidy of the famous Bar-20 ranch in the Pecos Valley performed an act of knight-errantry and what came of it / by Clarence E. Mulford . . . ; frontispiece by Robert W. Bierbrauer. Chicago: A. C. McClurg & Co., 1920. 354 p., front.
LC: Je 1, '20.
PW: Je 26, '20.
BLC: London: Hodder & Stoughton, [1921].

M-1098 ____ The man from Bar-20: a story of the cow-country / by Clarence E. Mulford . . . ; pictures by Frank E. Schoonover. Chicago: A. C. McClurg & Co., 1918. 319 p., col. front., [3] leaves of col. plates.
LC: Je 13, '18.
PW: My 25, '18.
BLC: London: Hodder & Stoughton, [1920].

M-1099 ____ The orphan / by Clarence E. Mulford . . . ; illustrations in color by Allen True. New York: The Outing Publishing Company, 1908. 399 p., col. front., [3] leaves of col. plates.
LC: F 21, '08.
PW: Mr 21, '08.

M-1100 ____ Rustlers' valley / by Clarence E. Mulford. Garden City, N. Y.: Doubleday, Page & Company, 1924. 333 p., ill.
LC: Ja 16, '24.
PW: Ja 12, '24.
BLC: London: Hodder & Stoughton, [1924].

M-1101 ____ "Tex": how Tex Ewalt, two-gun man, philosopher, poet, and one-time companion of Hopalong Cassidy turned a whole community upside down, and dealt retributive justice to several of Windsor's leading citizens, for the sake of a girl he loved / by Clarence E. Mulford . . . Chicago: A. C. McClurg & Co., 1922. 323 p., front.
LC: Mr 28, '22.
BLC: London: Hodder & Stoughton, [1922]. British title: Tex of Bar 20.

Mulholland, Clara. The ghost-chest of knockmarroon. In The Senior lieutenant's wager: and other stories (1905), S-312.

M-1102 Mülïer. Signor: a segment from the eternal cycle / by Mülïer. San Diego, Cal.: Published by The Gnostic Press, [c1917]. 219 p., front.
LC: F 12, '18.

M-1103 ____ Sojourners by the wayside: travelers on the long road / by Mülïer. San Diego, Cal.: Published by The Gnostic Press, [c1917]. 203 p.
LC: S 7, '17.
PW: D 29, '17.

M-1104 Mullany, Katherine F. (Katherine Frances). Miriam of Magdala; a study / by Katherine F. Mullany . . . New York: Magdala Co., [c1906]. 100 p. **DAY**
LC: Je 15, '06.

M-1105 Muller, Julius W. (Julius Washington), 1867-1930. The invasion of America: a fact story based on the inexorable mathematics of war / by Julius W. Muller . . . New York: E. P. Dutton & Company, 1916. 352 p., photo. front., [20] leaves of photo. plates, maps.
LC: D 27, '15.

M-1106 ____ Rulers of the surf: a story of the mysteries and perils of the sea / by J. W. Muller; illustrated. New York; London: D. Appleton and Company, 1910.

324 p., col. front., [3] leaves of col. plates. [Ill. by D. C. Hutchison.]
LC: S 22, '10.

M-1107 [____] Starboard lights: salt water tales / by A. B. Hawser [pseud]. New York: Quail & Warner, 1901. 255, [1] p. **CGU**
Contents: What happened at sea -- Strange yarns -- The cheerful derelict -- The friend that saved the ship -- Captain Hawser, fillibuster -- A suppressed sea fight -- Hennery and the cannibals -- An adventure of the bo's'n -- New styles in old salts -- His last storm -- A dream -- A mystery of New York Bay -- The professor's manuscript -- The little yellow man -- Of a mighty battle -- Fishing on the midnight sea -- From tide to tide -- The curse of the seigneur -- An eight-by-thirteen ocean.
Reissued as Fish yarns: and other salt water tales. Brooklyn, N. Y.: Knowlson & Muller, [c1904].

M-1108 Mullins, Helene, b. 1899. Paulus Fy: the history of an esthete / by Helene Mullins and Marie Gallegher. New York: Robert M. McBride & Company, 1924. 224 p.

M-1109 Mullins, Isla May Hawley, 1859-1936. Anne of the blossom shop, or, The growing up of Anne Carter / by Isla May Mullins . . . ; with a frontispiece in full color by Z. P. Nikolaki. Boston: The Page Company, 1914. 308 p., col. front. **KSL**
LC: S 8, '14.

M-1110 ____ Anne's wedding: a Blossom Shop romance / by Isla May Mullins . . . ; with a frontispiece in full color by Gene Pressler. Boston: The Page Company, 1916. 329 p., col. front.
LC: S 14, '16.
PW: S 30, '16.

M-1111 ____ The blossom shop: a story of the South / by Isla May Mullins; illustrated by John Goss. Boston: L. C. Page & Co., 1913. 223 p., front., [4] leaves of plates.
LC: Je 4, '13.
PW: Je 21, '13.

M-1112 ____ The boy from Hollow Hut: a story of the Kentucky mountains / by Isla May Mullins. New York; Chicago; Toronto; London; Edinburgh: Fleming H. Revell Company, [c1911]. 213 p., front., [3] leaves of plates.
LC: O 21, '11.

M-1113 ____ The Mt. Blossom girls, or, New paths from the Blossom shop / by Isla May Mullins . . . ; illustrated by John Goss. Boston: The Page Company, 1918. 338 p., col. front., [4] leaves of plates. **NGU**

M-1114 ____ Timothy's second wife / by Isla May Mullins . . . New York; Chicago; London; Edinburgh: Fleming H. Revell Company, 1922. 144 p.
LC: D 30, '22.

M-1115 ____ Tweedie: the story of a true heart / by Isla May Mullins . . . ; illustrated. Boston: The Page Company, 1919. 291 p., col. front., [4] leaves of plates. [Ill. by Gene Pressler and John Goss.]
LC: Mr 13, '19.
PW: Ap 12, '19.

M-1116   ____ Uncle Mary: a novel for young or old / by Isla May Mullins . . . ; with a frontispiece in full color from a painting by Gene Pressler and other illustrations from drawings by John Goss. Boston: The Page Company, 1922. 329 p., col. front., [4] leaves of plates.
LC: Je 9, '22.
PW: Ag 26, '22.

M-1117   Mullong, C. R. (Charles Robert), b. 1884. Beyond paradise / by C. R. Mullong. Philadelphia: Dorrance & Company, [c1924]. 288 p.

M-1118   Mumford, Claire. The undefended border: a story / by Claire Mumford. New York: York Kane York, 1917. 46 p.   **DLC**
(York's folk-book; no. 1)

M-1119   Mumford, Ethel Watts, 1878-1940. All in the night's work / by Ethel Watts Mumford and George Bronson-Howard. Garden City, N. Y.: Garden City Publishing Company, 1924. 120 p.
Unexamined copy: bibliographic data from OCLC, #20943181.
(Famous authors series; no. 37).

    ____ "Aurore." In *Prize stories of 1921* (1922), **P-619.**

M-1120   ____ Dupes / by Ethel Watts Mumford. New York; London: G. P. Putnam's Sons, 1901. (New York: The Knickerbocker Press). 288 p.
PW: Ap 13, '01.

    ____ Easy. In *The Grim thirteen* (1917), **G-537.**

M-1121   ____ Out of the ashes / by Ethel Watts Mumford. New York: Moffat, Yard and Company, 1913. 257 p.
LC: Je 23, '13.

    ____, contributor. See *The sturdy oak* (1917), **S-1101.**

M-1122   ____ The wedding song / by Ethel Watts Mumford. Garden City, New York: Doubleday, Page & Company, 1924. 292 p.
PW: O 4, '24.
BLC: London: William Heinemann; printed in U. S. A., 1924.

    ____ When time turned. In *Through the forbidden gates* (1903), **T-222.**

M-1123   ____ Whitewash / by Ethel Watts Mumford; illustrated by A. G. Learned. Boston: Dana Estes & Company, [1903]. 319 p., front., [5] leaves of plates.
PW: Ag 15, '03.
BLC: London: Ward, Lock & Co., 1905.

M-1124   Mumma, Rosa Meyers. Angela: a Salvation Army lassie / by Rosa Meyers Mumma . . . New York; Washington: The Neale Publishing Co., 1907. 144 p.   **DLC**

M-1125   ____ Fallina: a tale of modern American social life / by Rosa Meyers Mumma . . . Boston: The Roxburgh Publishing Company, 1906. 146 p. **DLC**
LC: O 10, '06.

M-1126   Mundy, Talbot, 1879-1940. Caves of terror / by Talbot Mundy. Garden City, New York: Garden City Publishing Co. Inc., 1924. 118 p., front., ill.

M-1127   ____ The eye of Zeitoon / by Talbot Mundy . . . ; illustrated by Dwight Franklin. Indianapolis: The Bobbs-Merrill Company, [c1920]. 354 p., front., [3] leaves of plates.
LC: Mr 22, '20.
PW: Mr 6, '20.
BLC: London: Hutchinson & Co., [1920].

M-1128   ____ Guns of the gods: a story of Yasmini's youth / by Talbot Mundy; illustrated by J. Clement Coll. Indianapolis: The Bobbs-Merrill Company, [c1921]. 359 p., front., [5] leaves of plates.
LC: Je 15, '21.
PW: Je 25, '21.
BLC: London: Hutchinson & Co., [1921].

M-1129   ____ Her reputation / by Talbot Mundy and Bradley King. Indianapolis: The Bobbs-Merrill Company, [c1923]. 333 p., photo. front., [3] leaves of photo. plates.   **OSU, TPN**
LC: S 14, '23.
PW: D 1, '23.

M-1130   ____ Hira Singh: when India came to fight in Flanders / by Talbot Mundy . . . ; illustrated by Joseph Clement Coll. Indianapolis: The Bobbs-Merrill Company, [c1918]. 308 p., front., [5] leaves of plates.
LC: S 16, '18.
BLC: London: Cassell & Co., 1918.

M-1131   ____ The ivory trail / by Talbot Mundy; illustrated by Joseph Clement Coll. Indianapolis: The Bobbs-Merrill Company, [c1919]. 411 p., front., [5] leaves of plates.
LC: Jl 5, '19.
PW: Jl 26, '19.
BLC: London: Constable & Co., 1920.

M-1132   ____ King--of the Khyber rifles: a romance of adventure / by Talbot Mundy . . . ; illustrated by Joseph Clement Coll. Indianapolis: The Bobbs-Merrill Company, [c1916]. 395 p., front., [12] leaves of plates (6 double-plate).
LC: N 22, '16.
PW: N 25, '16.
BLC: London: Constable & Co., 1917.

M-1133   ____ The nine unknown / by Talbot Mundy. Indianapolis: The Bobbs-Merrill Company, [c1924]. 353 p.
LC: Mr 26, '24.
PW: Mr 29, '24.
BLC: London: Hutchinson & Co., [1924].

M-1134   ____ Om: the secret of Ahbor Valley / by Talbot Mundy; jacket drawing by Leonard Lester.

Indianapolis: The Bobbs-Merrill Company, [c1924].
392 p.
LC: N 5, '24.
PW: N 8, '24.
BLC: London: Hutchinson & Co., [1924].

M-1135 _____ Rung ho! / by Talbot Mundy. New York:
Charles Scribner's Sons, 1914. 371 p.
LC: Mr 25, '14.
PW: Mr 28, '14.
BLC: London: Cassell & Co., 1914.

M-1136 _____ Told in The East / by Talbot Mundy.
Indianapolis: The Bobbs-Merrill Company Publisher,
[c1920]. 281 p. **UBY**
Contents: Hookum hai -- For the salt which he had eaten --
MacHassan Ah.
LC: N 26, '20.
PW: D 18, '20.

M-1137 _____ The winds of the world / by Talbot Mundy
. . . ; illustrated by Joseph Clement Coll.
Indianapolis: The Bobbs-Merrill Company, [c1917].
330 p., front., [3] leaves of plates.
LC: N 17, '17.
PW: D 1, '17.
BLC: London: Cassell & Co., [1916].

M-1138 Munger, Dell H., b. 1862. The wind before the
dawn / by Dell H. Munger; illustrated by Thomas
Fogarty. Garden City, New York: Doubleday, Page
& Company, 1912. 564, [2] p., col. front., [7] leaves
of col. plates, ill. Illustrated end papers.
BLC: London: Hodder & Stoughton; printed in
Garden City, New York, 1912.

M-1139 Munn, Charles Clark, 1848-1917. Boyhood days on
the farm: a story for young and old boys / by Charles
Clark Munn . . . ; illustrated by Frank T. Merrill.
Boston: Lothrop, Lee & Shepard Co., 1907. 403 p.,
front., [3] leaves of plates, ill.
LC: N 21, '07.
PW: D 7, '07.

M-1140 _____ The castle builders / by Charles Clark Munn;
illustrated by Frank T. Merrill. Boston: Lothrop,
Lee & Shepard Co., [1910]. 512 p., front., [7]
leaves of plates.
LC: Mr 28, '10.
PW: Ag 20, '10.

M-1141 _____ The girl from Tim's place / by Charles Clark
Munn . . . ; illustrated by Frank T. Merrill. Boston:
Lothrop, Lee & Shepard Co., 1906. 426 p., front.,
[7] leaves of plates.
PW: Mr 24, '06.

M-1142 _____ The heart of Uncle Terry / by Charles Clark
Munn . . . ; illustrated by W. L. Howes. Boston:
Lothrop, Lee & Shepard Co., [1915]. 480 p., front.,
[7] leaves of plates.
LC: Ap 5, '15.
PW: Ap 3, '15.

M-1143 _____ The hermit: a story of the wilderness / by
Charles Clark Munn; illustrated by A. Burnham
Shute. Boston: Lee and Shepard, 1903. 406 p.,

front., [7] leaves of plates.
PW: O 3, '03.

M-1144 _____ Myrtle Baldwin / by Charles Clark Munn;
illustrated by Henry Roth. Boston: Lothrop, Lee &
Shepard Co., [1908]. 510 p., front., [9] leaves of
plates.
LC: Je 6, '08.
PW: S 5, '08.

M-1145 _____ Rockhaven / by Charles Clark Munn;
illustrated by Frank T. Merrill. Boston: Lee and
Shepard, 1902. 384 p., front., [5] leaves of plates.
PW: Mr 29, '02.

M-1146 Munn, Margaret Crosby. The path of the stars / by
Margaret Crosby Munn. New York: Dodd, Mead &
Company, 1903. 289 p. **DLC**

M-1147 Muñoz, Anita Clay. In love and truth, or, The
downfall of Samuel Seele, healer / by Anita Clay
Muñoz. New York; London; Montreal: The Abbey
Press, [c1901]. 258 p. **DLC**
PW: Ap 27, '01.

M-1148 Munro, John. "Father Jack": a tale of the Rockies /
by John Munro. Fernande, Cal.: John Munro, 1904.
14 p.
Unexamined copy: bibliographic data from OCLC,
#26985920.

Munro, Kirk. "Cap'n I's" closest call. In *The battle
for the Pacific* (1908), B-357.

M-1149 Munsell, Ida Hamilton. Grandmother stories / by Ida
Hamilton Munsell . . . Chicago: Munsell Publishing
Company, 1915. 58 p., incl. front.
Unexamined copy: bibliographic data from NUC.
Contents: Grandmother's room -- Withered rose-leaves --
Grandmother's attic and a resurrected Stradivarius.

Munson, E. Old "Hard Luck". In *Argonaut stories*
(1906), A-298.

M-1150 [Munson, Gorham Bert], 1896-1969. Broken
shackles / by John Gordon [pseud.]. Philadelphia:
Dorrance and Company, Inc., [c1920]. 270 p. **CUY**
LC: N 15, '20.
PW: D 4, '20.

M-1151 Münsterberg, Margarete Anna Adelheid, b. 1889.
Anna Borden's career: a novel / by Margarete
Münsterberg. New York; London: D. Appleton and
Company, 1913. 362, [1] p., front. [Ill. by Stuart
Travis.]
LC: S 3, '13.
PW: S 6, '13.

M-1152 _____ Red poppies: a novel / by Margarete
Münsterberg . . . New York; London: D. Appleton
and Company, 1915. 336, [1] p.
LC: F 6, '15.
PW: F 6, '15.

M-1153 Murdoch, Louise S., b. 1872. Almetta of Gabriel's
Run / by Louise Murdoch; illustrated. New York:
The Meridian Press, [c1917]. 244 p., front., [2]
leaves of plates. [Ill. by H. A. Weiss.] **KUK**

M-1154   Murdock, Annie Gilchrist. Liang - from China: a
          story of a child widow / by Annie Gilchrist Murdock;
          third prize story. Nashville, Tennessee: The
          Cumberland Press, 1903. 78 p.   **DLC**
          PW: Je 13, '03.

M-1155   Murdock, Victor, 1871-1945. "Folks" / by Victor
          Murdock. New York: The Macmillan Company,
          1921. 220 p.
          Contents: Just folks -- The father of a town -- The bearded grain -- A
          flower that grew between -- A certain frontiersman -- The artist --
          The school teacher -- The boomer -- The lawyer -- The lady -- The
          actor -- The pure in heart -- The minister -- The doctor -- The scribe
          -- My mother -- My father -- The music master -- A friend -- The
          legislator -- "The prisoner-at-bar" -- The statistician -- A man apart --
          The torch -- "The reformer" -- The governor -- The conservative -- A
          princess -- The wizard -- A gentle man -- A rich man -- The ally --
          The rainmaker -- The car dispatcher -- A trader -- A cattle baron
          -- The salesman -- An Army officer -- The milliner -- The campaigner
          -- The optimist -- An impressario -- The veteran -- The contractor --
          The thinker -- A herald -- The crusader -- The captain -- The historian
          -- The railroader -- The farmer.
          PW: Ap 16, '21.

          Muredach, Myles, pseud. <u>See</u> **Kelley, Francis
          Clement, bishop, 1870-1948.**

          Murfree, Mary Noailles. <u>See</u> **Craddock, Charles
          Egbert, pseud.**

M-1156   Murphy, Clarence H. Terse tales / by Clarence H.
          Murphy. Point Pleasant, N. J.: Point Pleasant
          Printing and Publishing Co., 1917. 56 p.   **DLC**
          Contents: The Gothamite -- The legend of the straw man -- Jim Crow
          -- Rodman, buccaneer -- The oriental charm -- The heart breakers --
          Lights and shadows.

M-1157   Murphy, Edward F. (Edward Francis), b. 1892. Just
          Jack / by Edward F. Murphy. Baltimore, Md.:
          O'Donovan Bros., 1923. 256 p., ill.

M-1158   Murphy, Eva Morley, b. 1856. Lois Morton's
          investment / by Eva Morley Murphy . . . Topeka,
          Kansas: Crane & Company, 1912. 283 p.

M-1159   Murphy, Joseph Aloysius, b. 1884. An unknown
          master: and other stories / by Joseph A. Murphy.
          Boston: The Pilot Publishing Co., 1916. 193 p.,
          front., [4] leaves of plates.   **KSU**
          Contents: An unknown master -- The purloined story -- The
          misanthorpe -- Bread on the waters -- Called as Aaron -- The lost
          Gospel -- Reform of the Union church -- Denderah -- Unpatriotic
          Mrs. Dacey Cowardly Fra. Luis -- The double traitor -- The burying
          of uncle -- Noblesse oblige -- Ravelli.
          LC: My 23, '16.

M-1160   Murphy, Mabel Ansley, b. 1870. Timoleon, a friend
          of Paul: being the romantic adventures of a waif of
          Tarsus, together with a setting forth of the great
          Apostle's journeys / by Mabel Ansley Murphy . . .
          Philadelphia: American Sunday-School Union,
          [c1921]. 330 p., incl. front., [2] leaves of plates.
          [Ill. by F. A. Eckman.]   **DRU**

M-1161   Murray, Alice E, *pseud*. The ambitions of a worldly
          woman / by Alice E. Murray [pseud.]. New York;
          Chicago; London: F. Tennyson Neely Co., [c1901].
          168 p., photo. front. (port.)   **DLC**

PW: Ag 17, '01.

M-1162   Murray, Charles Theodore, b. 1843. Mlle. Fouchette
          / by Charles Theodore Murray; illustrated by W. H.
          Richardson, E. Benson Kennedy & Francis Day.
          Philadelphia; London: J. B. Lippincott Company,
          1902. 398 p., front. and t. p. on double-leaf plate,
          [3] leaves of plates.
          (OSU copy is "second edition".)
          PW: Mr 15, '02.
          BLC: London: Grant Richards, 1902.

M-1163   Murray, David Ambrose, b. 1861. His return: a
          story of the Second Coming / by David A. Murray
          . . . Chicago: The Stanley Publishing Company,
          1925. 212 p., front. [Ill. by William Holman Hunt.]

M-1164   Murray, John. The round-up: a romance of Arizona
          novelized from Edmund Day's melodrama / by John
          Murray and Mills Miller; illustrations from scenes in
          the play. New York: G. W. Dillingham Company,
          [c1908]. 344 p., photo. front., [5] leaves of photo.
          plates.
          LC: Mr 6, '08.
          BLC: London: T. Fisher Unwin; New York
          [printed], 1908.

          Murray, Roy Irving, jt. aut. *August first* (1915). <u>See</u>
          **Andrews, Mary Raymond Shipman, d. 1936, jt.
          aut., A-249.**

          Murrell, Cornelia Randolph. <u>See</u> **Ailenrock, M. R.,
          pseud.**

M-1165   Murtha, E. J. (Edward John), b. 1861. Sister-in-law:
          a story of fiction and friction / by E. J. Murtha.
          Baltimore, Md.: The McLean Company, [c1916].
          40 p.   **VA@**

M-1166   Musick, William Henry Harrison, b. 1840. Urlov,
          the wanderer: a realistic story of vicissitude and
          adventure, on sea and land / by W. H. H. Musick.
          [Hartville, Mo.?], c1904. 320 p.
          Unexamined copy: bibliographic data from NUC.

          Muskrat, Ruth. Jealous gods. *In The best college
          short stories, 1924-1925* (1925), B-558.

M-1167   Musser, Howard Anderson. Jungle tales: adventures
          in India / by Howard Anderson Musser; illustrated by
          Thomas Fogarty. New York: George H. Doran
          Company, [c1922]. 141 p., front., [3] leaves of
          plates.   **CLU**
          Contents: I. Gani -- II. Tigers-but especially bears -- III. Dahli the
          Manganese slave -- IV. Boys of the India jungle -- V. Trapped among
          crocodiles -- VI. Ballia and the bandit.
          LC: Jl 24, '22.

M-1168   ____ More jungle tales: adventures in India / by
          Howard Anderson Musser . . . ; illustrated from
          photographs and with drawings by Morgan Stinemetz.
          New York: George H. Doran Company, [c1923].
          196 p., front., [5] leaves of plates.   **AKO**

Contents: Shadrach-the dinner that four jungle dogs didn't eat -- Meshach-or fortunes in Kali Putr (Manganese) -- Giving the untainted leper child his chance -- Krishmarao, who fought the disease devil out of Manglewari -- Gangaram the mahar and his son Monkeyface -- Nandhi, the Ghond boy, sees civilization -- Nattu, the Bengali boy, who used to fight for goat-heads in Kali's temple -- Gopal Singh, the Brahmin convert, whose parents killed him -- Metapordu, the Telegu priest, and his heroic death -- Baji, the epileptic woman's son -- The untouchable boy who reached the heights -- Dennis Clancy's mud trial, or how to lose your temper -- A jungle Good Samaritan parable that Anton understood -- Some monkey shines in the jungle -- Wagh, the tiger -- Esther, the madman's unwilling bride -- Mungli, the girl who prayed the idol out of the village -- Snakes and snakes and then still more snakes! -- How Titus, the tiger-killer, was tamed -- Out of the jaws of a black man-eating panther -- When west goes east, or the lady and the tiger -- Some girls -- Papia Waghmari, the little temple Marli -- Blacking Atmaram's face -- Toe.
LC: O 4, '23.

M-1169 Musson, Bennet. Turn to the right / by Bennet Musson; from the play by Winchell Smith and John E. Hazzard. New York: Duffield and Company, 1917. 291 p.

M-1170 Muzzy, Alice M. Three fair philanthropists / by Alice M. Muzzy . . . New York; London; Montreal: The Abbey Press, [c1901]. 398 p.   **NYP**
PW: Ap 6, '01.

M-1171 My actor-husband: a true story of American stage life. New York: John Lane Company, 1912. 327 p.

My Sergeant, pseud. See **Sturgis, Granville Forbes, b. 1880.**

M-1172 My strange life: the intimate life story of a moving picture actress / illustrated with photographs of America's most famous motion picture actresses. New York: Edward J. Clode, [c1915]. 280 p., front., [11] leaves of plates.

M-1173 Myers, Alice Belle McLane. A mother's old love returned / by Alice Belle McLane. Carbondale, Illinois: Henry Myers, 1915. 186 p.
Unexamined copy: bibliographic data from OCLC, #26408935.

M-1174 Myers, Anna Balmer. Amanda: a daughter of the Mennonites / by Anna Balmer Myers; illustrated by Helen Mason Grose. Philadelphia: George W. Jacobs & Company, [c1921]. 311 p., front., [2] leaves of plates.
LC: O 19, '21.

M-1175 ____ The madonna of the curb / by Anna Balmer Myers; illustrated by Helen Mason Grose. Philadelphia: George W. Jacobs & Company, [c1922]. 336 p., front., [2] leaves of plates.
LC: O 28, '22.

M-1176 ____ Patchwork: a story of "the plain people" / by Anna Balmer Myers; illustrated by Helen Mason Grose. Philadelphia: George W. Jacobs & Company, [c1920]. 338 p., col. front., [3] leaves of plates.
PW: Mr 27, '20.

M-1177 Myers, Cora Estelle. Scot / by Cora Estelle Myers. [Candor, N. Y.]: Published by the author, 1923. 198 p., photo. front.   **DLC**

M-1178 Myers, Frank A., 1848-1930. Apologies for love / F. A. Myers. Boston: R. G. Badger, 1909. 401 p. Unexamined copy: bibliographic data from OCLC, #29916786.
PW: N 6, '09.

M-1179 Myers, Gertrude. Two no-trump: a novel of apartment-hotel life / by Gertrude Myers. Chicago: Covici-McGee Co., 1923. 241 p.   **OSU, DLC**
LC: N 3, '23.
PW: Ja 5, '24.

M-1180 Myers, Harriet Williams, b. 1867. The birds' convention / by Harriet Williams Myers . . . ; with illustrations from photographs by the author. Los Angeles, Calif.: Western Publishing Co., [c1913]. 81 p., photo. ill.

Myers, Walter L. In the uplands. In *Stories from the Midland* (1924), S-984.

M-1181 Myers, William Wilshire. Hotep: a dream of the Nile / by William Wilshire Myers. Cincinnati: The Robert Clarke Company, 1905. 356 p., front., [3] leaves of plates. [Ill. Tom Hall.]

Mygatt, Gerald, contributor. See *Bobbed hair* **(1925), B-700.**

M-1182 Mygatt, John Tracy. What I do not know of farming / by John Tracy Mygatt. New York: Broadway Publishing Company, [c1908]. 37 p.   **DLC**

M-1183 Myrick, Herbert, b. 1860. Cache la poudre: the romance of a tenderfoot in the days of Custer / by Herbert Myrick; illustrated from paintings by Charles Schreyvogel, Edward W. Deming and Henry Fangel, also by many photographs and numerous human documents. New York; Chicago: Orange Judd Company; London: Kegan Paul, Trench Trübner & Co., Ltd., 1905. 202 p., ill. [Some photos by Lee Moorehouse, D. F. Barry and W. G. Walker.] **KSU**

Myron, Paul, pseud. See **Linebarger, Paul Myron Wentworth, b. 1871.**

M-1184 The Mysterious monogram: a composite story / by The Lucky Friday Club. Quincy, Illinois: [Printed by Bradley & Anderson, c1911]. 153 p.   **DLC**

M-1185 Myth, M. Y. T. H., *pseud.* Dorothy of Angelwood / by M. Y. T. H. Myth [pseud.] . . . New York: Broadway Publishing Company, [c1909]. 46 p.   **DLC**
LC: Jl 29, '09.

M-1186 ____ An eastern lion in the West: or marvelous find of an ideal / by M. Y. T. H. Myth [pseud.]. New York: Broadway Publishing Company, 1909. 118 p., front., plates.
Unexamined copy: bibliographic data from OCLC, #29919022.

M-1187 [____] Eugenius: the star child / by Ludwig Nicolovius [pseud.] . . . New York: The Grafton Press, 1918. 45 p.   **DLC**

M-1188   Tales of enchantment / by M. Y. T. H. Myth [pseud.] . . . New York: Broadway Publishing Company, [c1908]. 276 p.   **DLC**
LC: D 19, '08.

M-1189   Unique tales / by M. Y. T. H. Myth [pseud.]. New York; London; Montreal: The Abbey Press, [c1901]. 158 p.   **DLC**
Contents: Wild roses and a happy family -- Embodiment of fragancy: Christmas story, narrative of adventures, and fairy tale -- Allotted for each other, or, A modern paradise.
PW: S 14, '01.

M-1190   The way to wings: and kindred sallies / by M. Y. T. H. Myth [pseud.] . . . Boston: Richard G. Badger, 1904. ([Boston, U. S. A.]: The Gorham Press). 103 p.   **DLC**
Contents: The way to wings -- Nature to the rescue -- My dog Schneider.

N

N-1   "N," *pseud.* The prophet: a novel / by "N" [pseud.]. New York; Washington; Baltimore; Indianapolis; Norfolk: Broadway Publishing Co., [c1912]. 260 p., front.
LC: Je 4, '12.

N-2   N. P. M., *pseud.* Printers' proofs: of The piece-makers / by the N. P. M. [pseud.]. Athens, Ga.: [s. n.], c1914. 82 leaves.   **GUA**

N-3   A nameless story. Chicago: Homewood Publishing Company, [c1902]. 179, 30 p.
Running title: *The story without a name.*
"A lodging for the night" (signed R. L. S., i. e. Robert Louis Stevenson): p. 3-30 at end.
Unexamined copy: bibliographic data from OCLC, #28360820.

N-4   Nantucket's first tea: an old-time romance. Nantucket, Mass.: The Inquirer and Mirror Press, [1907]. 24 p., ill. Designed end papers.   **BAT**

N-5   Narodny, Ivan. Echoes of myself: romantic studies of the human soul / by Ivan Narodny; illustrated by Eugene Higgins. -- Studio ed. -- New York; London: The Liberty Publishing Company, [c1909]. 231 p., front., [3] leaves of plates.   **OSU, CFI**
Contents: Studies of primitive man: The aeronaut of Ligova -- The suffragist of Durnova -- The Lamovoi letter. Studies of modern man: The empty grave -- Abaza -- The guest of the castle. Studies of truth and suffering: Father Feodosi -- The prisoner's friend -- The golden rules.
LC: N 2, '09.

N-6   Nash, Theodore Edward Delafayette, b. 1881. Love and vengeance, or, Little Viola's victory: a story of love and romance in the South; also society and its effects / by T. E. D. Nash. [Portsmouth, Va.: T. E. D. Nash, c1903]. 171, [1] p., front. (port.).   **UIU**

N-7   Nason, Frank Lewis, 1856-1928. The Blue Goose / by Frank Lewis Nason. New York: McClure, Phillips & Co., 1903. 295 p.
PW: Mr 28, '03.
BLC: London; New York: McClure, Phillips & Co., 1903.

N-8   To the end of the trail / by Frank Lewis Nason. Boston; New York: Houghton, Mifflin and Company, 1902. (Cambridge: The Riverside Press). 302 p.
PW: My 17, '02.

N-9   The vision of Elijah Berl / by Frank Lewis Nason. Boston: Little, Brown and Company, 1905. 290 p.
PW: Ap 22, '05.

N-10   Nassau, Robert Hamill, 1835-1921. In an elephant corral: and other tales of West African experiences / by Robert Hamill Nassau. New York: The Neale Publishing Company, 1912. 180 p.
Contents: The transformed matricide -- Nguva's chain -- In an elephant corral -- Upset by a hippopotamus -- My fight with Nyare -- Gorilla-hunting -- Uvengwa: a vampire -- A psychic mystery -- Voices of an African tropic night.

N-11   The youngest king: a story of the Magi / by Robert Hamill Nassau . . . Philadelphia: The Westminster Press, 1911. 95 p., front.   **MNU**
LC: S 20, '11.

N-12   Nathan, Robert, b. 1894. Autumn / by Robert Nathan. New York: Robert M. McBride & Company, 1921. 198 p.
LC: O 20, '21.

N-13   Jonah / by Robert Nathan. New York: Robert M. McBride & Company, 1925. 212 p.
LC: F 14, '25.
PW: F 14, '25.

N-14   Peter Kindred / by Robert Nathan. New York: Duffield and Company, 1919. 362 p.   **MNU**
LC: Ja 21, '20.
PW: F 28, '20.

N-15   The puppet master / by Robert Nathan. New York: Robert M. McBride & Company, 1923. 221 p.
LC: O 19, '23.
BLC: London: John Lane, 1924.

National Stockman and Farmer. See *Stockman Stories* 1913, S-956.

Naumberg, Hirsh David. The Rav and the Rav's son. In *Yiddish tales* (1912), **Y-20.**

Navillus, W. F., *pseud.* The godson of Jeanette Gontreau. In *War stories* (1919), **W-94, under real name, F. W. Sullivan.**

N-16   Hearts triumphant: a modern romance / by W. F. Navillus [pseud.] . . . Boston: The Roxburgh Publishing Company, Incorporated, [c1914]. 182 p.

N-17   Naylor, C. W. (Charles Wesley), 1874-1950. The redemption of Howard Gray / by C. W. Naylor . . . Anderson, Indiana: Gospel Trumpet Company, [c1925]. 111 p., ill. [Ill. by C. B. M.]   **INA**

N-18   Naylor, H. R., b. 1840. The mystery of Monastery farm / by H. R. Naylor. New York: Eaton &

Mains; Cincinnati: Jennings & Graham, [c1908].
135 p.
LC: Je 26, '08.

N-19   Naylor, J. B. (James Ball), 1860-1945. The cabin in the big woods / by James Ball Naylor . . ; illustrated by Fred A. Elliott. Akron, Ohio; New York; Chicago: The Saalfield Publishing Co., 1904. 239 p., photo. front., [3] leaves of photo. plates. **WVB**

PW: N 19, '04.

N-20   _____ In the days of St. Clair: a romance of the Muskingum valley / by Dr. James Ball Naylor; illustrated by W. H. Fry. Akron, Ohio; New York; Chicago: The Saalfield Publishing Co., 1902. 420 p., front., [3] leaves of plates. PW: S 13, '02.

N-21   _____ The Kentuckian: a thrilling tale of Ohio life in the early sixties / by James Ball Naylor . . . ; illustrations by A. B. Shute. Boston, U. S. A.: C. M. Clark Publishing Co., Inc., 1905. 385 p., front. LC reports 9 plates. PW: Mr 3, '06.

N-22   _____ The misadventures of Marjory / by James Ball Naylor . . . Boston, Massachusetts: The C. M. Clark Publishing Co., 1908. 394 p., front. [Ill. by William Kirkpatrick.] **OSU, MCU** PW: N 14, '08.

N-23   _____ Ralph Marlowe: a novel / by James Ball Naylor. Akron, Ohio; New York; Chicago: The Saalfield Publishing Company, 1901. 412 p. PW: Mr 9, '01.

N-24   _____ The scalawags / by James Ball Naylor; illustrated by Otto Lang. New York: B. W. Dodge and Company, 1907. 326 p., front., [3] leaves of plates. LC: Mr 16, '07. PW: Mr 23, '07.

N-25   _____ The sign of the prophet: a tale of Tecumseh and Tippecanoe / by James Ball Naylor. Akron, Ohio; New York; Chicago: The Saalfield Publishing Company, 1901. 416 p. PW: O 12, '01. BLC: London: Anthony Treherne and Co., 1901.

N-26   Neale, Walter, 1873-1933. The betrayal: a novel / by Walter Neale and Elizabeth H. Hancock. New York; Washington: The Neale Publishing Company, 1910. 500 p. LC: My 7, '10. PW: Jl 30, '10.

N-27   Nealy, Sid H. In the trail of the pack-mule / by Sid H. Nealy; illustrated from drawings by the author. New York; London: F. Tennyson Neely, [c1902]. 261 p., front., [31] leaves of plates.

N-28   Needham, Henry Beach, 1871-1915. The double squeeze / by Henry Beach Needham; with an introduction by Connie Mack; illustrations by Arthur

William Brown and George Wright. Garden City, New York: Doubleday, Page & Company, 1915. 248 p., front., [3] leaves of plates. **TUL**

_____ The polite horse. In *Greatest short stories* **(1915), G-424.**

N-29   Neff, Elizabeth Hyer. Altars to Mammon / by Elizabeth Neff; with illustrations by F. Dana Marsh. New York: Frederick A. Stokes Company, [1908]. 334 p., front., [2] leaves of plates. PW: F 22, '08.

N-30   _____ Miss Wealthy, deputy sheriff / by Elizabeth Neff; with a frontispiece in color by Arthur Hutchins. New York: Frederick A. Stokes Company, [1912]. 248 p., col. front. LC: S 16, '12. PW: S 14, '12.

Neff, Hepsy. The best decorator in the city. In *Stockman stories (1913)*, S-956.

_____ One Thanksgiving. In *Stockman stories* **(1913), S-956.**

N-31   Neff, M. A. (Mell A.) Paradise found / by M. A. Neff. Cincinnati, Ohio: Published by the author, 1914. 117 p., incl. photo. front. (port.), map, ill. **CIN**

N-32   Neidig, William J. (William Jonathan), 1870-1955. The fire flingers / by William J. Neidig. New York: Dodd, Mead and Company, 1919. 360 p. LC: Mr 25, '19. PW: Mr 22, '19.

Neidig, William J. The smile of Joss. In *Through the forbidden gates (1903)*, T-222.

N-33   Neihardt, John Gneisenau, 1881-1973. The dawn builder / John G. Neihardt. New York; London: Mitchell Kennerley, 1911. 335 p. **EYM** LC: Ja 14, '11.

N-34   _____ Life's lure / by John G. Neihardt. New York; London: Mitchell Kennerley, 1914. 277 p. LC: O 3, '14.

N-35   _____ The lonesome trail / by John G. Neihardt. New York: John Lane Company; London: John Lane, The Bodley Head, 1907. 303 p., front. [Ill. by F. E. Schoonover.] Reprinted from various periodicals. Contents: The alien -- The look in the face -- Feather for feather -- The scars -- The fading of Shadow Flower -- The art of hate -- The singer of the ache -- The white Wakunda -- The triumph of Seha -- The end of the dream -- The revolt of a sheep -- The mark of shame -- The beating of the war drums -- Dreams are wiser than men -- The smile of God -- The heart of a woman -- Mignon -- A political coup at Little Omaha -- The last thunder song -- The Nemesis of the deuces. LC: My 15, '07. PW: My 18, '07.

N-36   Neill, Esther W. (Esther Waggaman), b. 1874. Barbara's marriage and the Bishop / by Esther W. Neill. New York: The Macmillan Company, 1925. 243 p. LC: F 25, '25. PW: Mr 7, '25.

N-37 ____ The red ascent / Esther W. Neill. New York: P. J. Kenedy & Sons, 1914. 261 p., col. front. [Ill. by Victor Pérard.]
LC: N 27, '14.
PW: O 24, '14.

N-38 Neilson, Francis, b. 1867. Madame Bohemia / by Francis Neilson; illustrated by Charlotte Harding. Philadelphia: J. B. Lippincott Company, 1901 [c1900]. 3-410 p., front., [3] leaves of plates.
BLC: London: John Macqueen, 1901.

N-39 ____ A strong man's house / by Francis Neilson. Indianapolis: The Bobbs-Merrill Company, [c1916]. 360 p.

N-40 Nelson, Arthur A. Wings of danger: a novel / by Arthur A. Nelson . . . . New York: Robert M. McBride & Company, 1915. 448 p., col. front., [3] leaves of plates. [Ill. by G. W. Gage.]
LC: O 1, '15.
PW: O 9, '15.
BLC: London: McBride, Nast & Co.; Binghamton & N. Y. [printed], 1915.

N-41 Nelson, James Poyntz, b. 1849. Balla: and other Virginia stories / by James Poyntz Nelson. Richmond, Va.: The Bell Book and Stationery Co., 1914. 225 p.
Reprinted in part from Harper's weekly.
Contents: A recognition -- Balla -- Hugh and Betty -- Billy Hell Stanley -- On Slater circuit.

N-42 Nelson, John Arthur. The new disciple: a story of big business and a high ideal / by John Arthur Nelson. New York: F. P. Service, Inc., 1921. 374 p.

N-43 Nesbit, Wilbur D. (Wilbur Dick), 1871-1927. The gentleman ragman: Johnny Thompson's story of the Emigger / by Wilbur Nesbit. New York; London: Harper & Brothers, 1906. 311, [1] p.
LC: S 20, '06.
PW: O 6, '06.

N-44 Nesbitt, Marian. Lamps of fire / by Marian Nesbitt . . . Chicago: Franciscan Herald Press, [c1920]. 130 p.

N-45 Neuberger, Ruth Felicia Adams, b. 1870. His uncle's wife / by Ruth Neuberger. New York: The Alice Harriman Company, [c1912]. 175 p.
LC: Ag 31, '12.
PW: Ag 24, '12.

N-46 Neve, Condes. The house of Mendoza: a romance of modern Spain / by Condes Neve. Philadelphia: Dorrance and Company, 1925. 319 p.

N-47 Nevill, Florence. What dreams may come: a study in failure / by Florence Nevill; with preface by . . . T. K. Cheyne . . . Boston: Sherman, French & Company, 1910. 54 p.   **IOG**
LC: O 20, '10.
BLC: London: Robert Scott, 1914.

N-48 Neville, Elizabeth O'Reilly. Father Tom of Connemara / by Elizabeth O'Reilly Neville;

illustrated. Chicago; New York: Rand McNally & Company, [c1902]. 394 p., front., [7] leaves of plates, map.

N-49 Neville, Richard. A pirate of parts / by Richard Neville. New York: The Neale Publishing Company, 1913. 228 p., photo. front. (port.).

N-50 Nevin, Theodore W. (Theodore Williamson), 1854-1918. Confessions of a modern Midas / by Theodore W. Nevin. Pittsburg, Pa.: [s. n.], 1906. 189 p.   **AAA**

N-51 ____ Ralph Ranscomb, banker / by Theodore W. Nevin. New York; Washington: The Neale Publishing Company, 1908. 139 p.

N-52 New, Clarence Herbert, 1862-1933. The unseen hand: adventures of a diplomatic free lance / by Clarence Herbert New; illustrated by W. Clinton Pettee. Garden City, New York: Doubleday, Page & Company, 1918. 376 p., front., [3] leaves of plates.
First published in the Blue book magazine under the title *Free lances in diplomacy*.

N-53 Newberry, Fannie E. (Fannie Ellsworth), 1848-1942. The wrestler of Philippi: a tale of the early Christians / by Fannie E. Newberry. Elgin, Illinois: David C. Cook Publishing Company, [c1914]. 264 p., ill. [Ill. by G. A. Rieman.]
LC: My 26, '14.

Newberry, Perry, 1870-1938, jt. aut. *The million-dollar suitcase* (1922). See **MacGowan, Alice, 1858-1947, jt. aut., M-205.**

____, jt. aut. *Shaken down* (1925). See **MacGowan, Alice, 1858-1947, jt. aut., M-207.**

N-54 Newbigging, Anne C. (Anne Christena), b. 1869. A cry of the soul: a romance of 1862 / by Anne C. Newbigging. Boston: Sherman, French & Company, 1917. 323 p.   **USD**
PW: N 24, '17.

N-55 Newell, Arthur. A knight of the toilers / by Arthur Newell. Philadelphia, Pa.: F. L. Marsh & Co., [c1905]. 270 p.

N-56 Newgeon, Walter Bliss. Rhesa: a romance of Babylon / by Walter Bliss Newgeon. New Haven, Conn.: The Raymond Publishing Company, [c1922]. 383 p.
LC: Jl 15, '22.
PW: Ag 5, '22.

N-57 Newhall, Roberts DeSaussure. The discourses of Jimmy / by Roberts DeSaussure Newhall . . . Cincinnati: The Circular Advertising Co., 1908. 128 p.   **DLC**

N-58 Newkirk, Newton, 1870-1938. Back to nature / by Newton Newkirk ("Newt"); illustrations by the author. New York: Cassell & Company, Ltd., 1911. 172 p.

_____ The music of money. In *Through the forbidden gates* (1903), T-222.

N-59   _____ Stealthy Steve: the six-eyed sleuth: his quest of the big blue diamond: a satirical detective story / by Newton Newkirk; illustrations by the author. Boston: John W. Luce and Company, 1904. 170 p., front.
PW: D 17, '04.

Newlin, Katherine. See **Burt, Katherine Newlin.**

Newman, Elizabeth Murray. The revolt of Uncle Billy. In **Pacific Coast Women's Press Association.** *La copa de oro* (1905), **P-2.**

Newman, Frances. Rachel and her children. In *Prize stories of 1924* (1925), **P-622.**

Newman, H. E. See "N," pseud.

Newman, Richard Brinsley, pseud. See **Gifford, Franklin Kent, 1861-1948.**

N-60   Newton, Alma. The blue string: and other sketches / by Alma Newton . . . . New York: Duffield & Company, 1918. 169 p.
Contents: The blue string -- Lily Lee -- Little things -- Ashes -- The cottage door -- The satyr -- The subconscious entanglement -- The last summer -- The Huguenot -- The novena -- The dawn -- The artist and the materialist.
LC: D 27, '18.

N-61   _____ Dreaming true / by Alma Newton. New York: John Lane Company; London: John Lane, The Bodley Head, 1921. 122 p.

N-62   _____ A jewel in the sand / by Alma Newton. New York: Duffield and Company, 1919. 120 p.
LC: Ja 31, '20.
PW: F 28, '20.

N-63   _____ The love letters of a mystic / by Alma Newton; frontispiece. New York: John Lane Company, 1916, [c1915]. 109 p., col. front. [Ill. by August Leu.]
AZS
LC: D 22, '15.
PW: Ja 1, '16.

N-64   _____ Memories / by Alma Newton. New York: Duffield and Company, 1917. 98 p.
LC: O 15, '17.

N-65   _____ An old-fashioned romance / by Alma Newton. New York: Minton, Balch & Company, 1924. 248 p.
LC: My 17, '24.
PW: My 17, '24.

N-66   _____ Shadows / by Alma Newton . . . New York: John Lane Company; London: John Lane, The Bodley Head, 1921. 81 p.   **CGU**
LC: Mr 26, '21.

N-67   Newton, Emma Mersereau. The veil of Solana / by Emma Mersereau Newton. New York: Frank F. Lovell Book Company, [c1902]. 362 p.
PW: Ap 25, '03.

Newton, W. Douglas. The charge. In *Greatest short stories* (1915), **G-424.**

N-68   Nicholas, Anna. The making of Thomas Barton / by Anna Nicholas . . . Indianapolis: The Bobbs-Merrill Company, [c1913]. 335 p.
Contents: The making of Thomas Barton -- A race drama -- A Hawburg sensation -- Miss Lucyanna's eventful day -- Out of the past -- When Grandmother ran away -- A bit of human interest -- What could he do? -- A story without a moral -- Was it all a dream? -- The eternal feminine -- An ever-present help -- The postmistress -- Katharine Clark's story.
PW: My 10, '13.

N-69   Nicholas, Francis Child, b. 1862. The power supreme: a novel of church and state in South America / by Francis C. Nicholas; illustrated by William Kirkpatrick. Boston, R. E. Lee Company, 1908. 347 p., col. front.
LC: Jl 6, '08.

Nicholas, Griffith A., pseud. See **Worthington, Elizabeth Strong.**

N-70   Nicholl, Edith M. By their fruits / by Edith M. Nicholl (Mrs. Bowyer) . . . . New York; London; Montreal: The Abbey Press, [c1901]. 282 p. **DLC**
PW: Jl 6, 01

_____ Gabriel the Acadian. See **Hill, Grace Livingston, 1865-1947.** *The angel of His presence* (1902), **H-623.**

N-71   _____ The human touch, a tale of the great Southwest / by Edith M. Nicholl; illustrated by Charles Copeland. Boston: Lothrop Publishing Company, [c1905]. 409 p., front.
Unexamined copy: bibliographic data from OCLC, #20699599.

N-72   Nicholls, Josephine Hamilton. Bayou triste: a story of Louisiana / by Josephine Hamilton Nicholls. New York: A. S. Barnes and Company, 1902. 227 p., [4] leaves of plates. [Ill. by E. N. Clark.]
PW: N 22, '02.

Nichols, Lillian. How Miung Ja found her name. In *When God walks the road and other stories* (1924), **W-445.**

N-73   Nicholson, Meredith, 1866-1947. And they lived happily ever after! / by Meredith Nicholson. New York: Charles Scribner's Sons, 1925. 369 p.
LC: O 14, '25.
PW: O 3, '25.
References: Russo & Sullivan, *Seven Authors*, p. 128-129.

N-74   _____ Best laid schemes / by Meredith Nicholson . . . New York: Charles Scribner's Sons, 1922. 217 p.
Contents: The Susiness of Susan -- The girl with the red feather -- The Campbells are coming -- Arabella's house party -- The third man -- Wrong number.
LC: Ap 25, '22.
PW: My 6, '22.
References: Russo & Sullivan, *Seven Authors*, p. 122-123.

N-75   ____ Blacksheep! blacksheep! / by Meredith Nicholson; illustrated by Leslie L. Benson. New York: Charles Scribner's Sons, 1920. 346 p., front., [3] leaves of plates.
LC: Ap 29, '20.
PW: My 1, '20.
References: Russo & Sullivan, *Seven Authors*, p. 119-120.

____ The Boulevard of Rogues. *In Atlantic narratives*; **2nd series (1918), A-361.**

N-76   ____ Broken barriers / by Meredith Nicholson. New York: Charles Scribner's Sons, 1922. 402 p.
LC: S 16, '22.
PW: O 7, '22.
BLC: London: Hurst and Blackett, [1923].
References: Russo & Sullivan, *Seven Authors*, p. 124.

N-77   ____ A Hoosier chronicle / Meredith Nicholson; with illustrations by F. C. Yohn. Boston; New York: Houghton Mifflin Company, 1912. (Cambridge: The Riverside Press). 605, [1] p., front., [3] leaves of col. plates.
LC: Mr 19, '12.
PW: Mr 16, '12.
References: Russo & Sullivan, *Seven Authors*, p. 105-107.

N-78   ____ The hope of happiness / by Meredith Nicholson. New York: Charles Scribner's Sons, 1923. 358 p.
LC: O 9, '23.
PW: O 20, '23.
References: Russo & Sullivan, *Seven Authors*, p. 127-128.

N-79   ____ The house of a thousand candles / by Meredith Nicholson . . . ; with illustrations by Howard Chandler Christy. Indianapolis: The Bobbs-Merrill Company, [c1905]. 382 p., col. front., [6] leaves of col plates.
PW: N 18, '05.
BLC: Toronto: McLeod & Allen, 1907.
References: Russo & Sullivan, *Seven Authors*, p. 87-90.

N-80   ____ Lady Larkspur / by Meredith Nicholson. New York: Charles Scribner's Sons, 1919. 171 p.
LC: Mr 20, '19.
PW: Mr 29, '19.
References: Russo & Sullivan, *Seven Authors*, p. 118-119.

N-81   ____ The little brown jug at Kildare / by Meredith Nicholson; with illustrations by James Montgomery Flagg. Indianapolis: The Bobbs-Merrill Company, [c1908]. 422 p., front., [4] leaves of plates.
LC: S 14, '08.
PW: O 3, '08.
References: Russo & Sullivan, *Seven Authors*, p. 100-102.

N-82   ____ The lords of high decision / by Meredith Nicholson; illustrated by Arthur I. Keller. New York: Doubleday, Page & Company, 1909. 503 p., col. front., [3] leaves of col. plates.
LC: O 30, '09.
PW: N 13, '09.
BLC: London: Doubleday, Page & Company; New York printed, 1909.
References: Russo & Sullivan, *Seven Authors*, p. 102-103.

N-83   ____ The madness of May / by Meredith Nicholson; with illustrations by Frederic Dorr Steele. New York: Charles Scribner's Sons, 1917. 187 p., front., [3] leaves of plates.
LC: Ap 17, '17.
PW: Ap 21, '17.
References: Russo & Sullivan, *Seven Authors*, p. 114-115.

N-84   ____ The main chance / by Meredith Nicholson; illustrated by Harrison Fisher. Indianapolis: The Bobbs-Merrill Company, [c1903]. 419 p., col. front., [5] leaves of col plates.
LC: My 9, '03.
PW: Je 6, '03.
References: Russo & Sullivan, *Seven Authors*, p. 81-84.

N-85   ____ Otherwise Phyllis / by Meredith Nicholson. Boston; New York: Houghton Mifflin Company, 1913. (Cambridge: The Riverside Press). 397 p., front. [Ill. by Charles Dana Gibson.]
LC: S 8, '13.
PW: S 6, '13.
BLC: London: Constable & Co., Cambridge, Mass. [printed], 1913.
References: Russo & Sullivan, *Seven Authors*, 109-110.

N-86   ____ The poet / by Meredith Nicholson; with pictures by Franklin Booth and decorations by W. A. Dwiggins. Boston; New York: Houghton Mifflin Company, 1914. (Cambridge: The Riverside Press). 189, [1] p., col. front., [3] leaves of col. plates, ill.
LC: O 5, '14.
PW: O 10, '14.
References: Russo & Sullivan, *Seven Authors*, p. 111-112.

N-87   ____ The Port of missing men / by Meredith Nicholson . . . ; with illustrations by Clarence F. Underwood. Indianapolis: The Bobbs-Merrill Company, [c1907]. 399 p., front., [6] leaves of plates.
LC: Ja 28, '07.
PW: F 9, '07.
BLC: London: Gay & Bird, 1907.
References: Russo & Sullivan, *Seven Authors*, p. 94-97.

N-88   ____ The proof of the pudding / by Meredith Nicholson; with illustrations. Boston; New York: Houghton Mifflin Company, 1916. (Cambridge: The Riverside Press). 372, [1] p., front., [8] leaves of plates (2 double-leaf plates). [Ill. by C. H. Taffs.]
LC: My 15, '16.
PW: My 13, '16.

BLC: London: Hodder & Stoughton; Cambridge, Mass. [printed], 1916.
References: Russo & Sullivan, *Seven Authors*, p. 113-114.

N-89 ____ A reversible Santa Claus / by Meredith Nicholson; with illustrations by Florence H. Minard. Boston; New York: Houghton Mifflin Company, 1917. (Cambridge, Mass.: The Riverside Press). 176, [1] p., col. front., [3] leaves of col. plates. Decorated end papers.
LC: O 20, '17.
PW: O 27, '17.
References: Russo & Sullivan, *Seven Authors*, p. 115-116.

N-90 ____ Rosalind at Red Gate / by Meredith Nicholson; with illustrations by Arthur I. Keller. Indianapolis: The Bobbs-Merrill Company, [c1907]. 387 p., front., [8] leaves of plates.
LC: N 23, '07.
PW: D 14, '07.
BLC: London: Everett & Co., 1908.
References: Russo & Sullivan, *Seven Authors*, p. 97-100.

N-91 ____ The siege of the seven suitors / by Meredith Nicholson . . . ; illustrated by C. Coles Phillips and Reginald Birch. Boston; New York: Houghton Mifflin Company, 1910. (Cambridge: Riverside Press). 400, [1] p., col. front., ill.
LC: N 3, '10.
PW: N 5, '10.
References: Russo & Sullivan, *Seven Authors*, p. 104.

N-92 ____ Zelda Dameron / by Meredith Nicholson . . ; with drawings by John Cecil Clay. Indianapolis: The Bobbs-Merrill Company, [c1904]. 411 p., col. front., [7] leaves of col. plates.
LC: O 12, '04.
PW: N 5, '04.
References: Russo & Sullivan, *Seven Authors*, p. 84-86.

Nickerson, Herman, b. 1870, jt. aut. *The sword of Bussy* (1912). See **Stephens, Robert Neilson, 1867-1906, jt. aut., S-861.**

N-93 Nicolls, William Jasper, 1854-1916. Brunhilda of Orr's Island / by William Jasper Nicolls. Philadelphia: George W. Jacobs & Company, [1908]. 307 p., col. front.
LC: My 25, '08.

N-94 ____ The daughters of Suffolk / by William Jasper Nicolls; with twenty-four illustrations. Philadelphia; London: J. B. Lippincott Company, 1910. 332 p., front, [23] leaves of plates.
LC: My 7, '10.

N-95 ____ Graystone: a novel / by William Jasper Nicolls. Philadelphia; London: J. B. Lippincott Company, 1902. 338 p., incl. front.
PW: Mr 15, '02.

N-96 ____ Wild mustard: a seven days chronicle / by William Jasper Nicolls. Philadelphia; London: J. B. Lippincott Company, 1914. 288 p.
LC: S 26, '14.

Nicolovius, Ludwig, b. 1837. See **Myth, M. Y. T. H., pseud.**

N-97 Nigh, William. Blinky; a complete dramatic story of American life, condensed into tabloid form for the convenience of those busy readers whose imaginative gifts will permit them to paint their own scenes / by Wm Nigh. [New York: Federal Printing Company, c1920]. 43 p.
Unexamined copy: bibliographic data from NUC.

N-98 Nightshade: the confessions of a reasoning animal. New York: E. P. Dutton & Company, [c1924]. 288 p.
PW: Mr 29, '24.

N-99 Nineteen: a thrilling story of Western love and Eastern duplicity . . . Cincinnati: The Anderson-Ziegler Company, 1907.
Unexamined copy: bibliographic data from NUC.

N-100 Nirdlinger, Charles Frederic. The convalescents / by Charles Frederic Nirdlinger. New York; London: The Century Co., 1923. 312 p.
LC: F 27, '23.

____, jt. aut. *The first lady in the land* (1912). See **Davies, Acton, 1870-1916, jt. aut., D-91.**

N-101 Nirdlinger, D. Ella (Daisy Ella). Althea, or, The children of Rosemont plantation / by D. Ella Nirdlinger. New York; Cincinnati; Chicago: Benziger Brothers, 1908. 205 p., front. [Ill. by Egbert Cadmus.]
PW: N 22, '02.

N-101.5 Nitsua, Benjamin, *pseud.* The mystery of Ashton Hall / Benjamin Nitsua [pseud.]. Rochester, N. Y: The Austin Publishing Co., [c1910]. 321 p., including plan.
Unexamined copy: bibliographic data from NUC.
LC: O 19, '10.
PW: D 3, '10.

N-102 Nixdorff, Henry M. (Henry Morris), b. 1830. White rock: and other stories / by Henry M. Nixdorff . . . New York; London; Montreal: The Abbey Press, [c1903]. 113 p.
Contents: The Indian's home -- Lofty Mera -- Aunt Eliza -- Harry and Annie -- Elaine May -- Little Juda -- Uncle Daniel and Aunt Kitty.
PW: My 2, '03.

Nixon-Roulet, Mary F. See **Roulet, Mary F. (Nixon).**

Noble, Alden Charles, b. 1880, jt. aut. *Hold Redmere* (1901). See **Stevens, Thomas Wood, 1880-1942, jt. aut., S-894.**

____, jt. aut. *The parchment in the hollow hilt* (1904). See **Stevens, Thomas Wood, 1880-1942, jt. aut., S-895.**

N-103   ____ Scott who was nine: a tale of the joyous universe / by Alden Charles Noble. Chicago: Blue Sky Press, 1901. 21 p.   **OSU, TXH**
PW: Mr 2, '01.

N-104   Noble, Annette Lucile, 1844-1932. A crazy angel / by Annette L. Noble . . ; with the collaboration of Grace Lathrop Collin. New York; London: G. P. Putnam's Sons, 1901. ([New York]: The Knickerbocker Press). 343 p.
PW: O 5, '01.

N-105   ____ Under twelve flags / by Annette L. Noble. New York: American Tract Society, [c1903]. 293 p., front. [4] leaves of plates. [Ill. by Jos. J. Ray and A. de Mier.]
PW: N 7, '03.

Noble, Edmund, 1853-1937, jt. aut. *Before the dawn* (1901). See **Pimenoff, L. L. (Lydia Lvovna), jt. aut., P-421.**

Noble, Lydia Lvovna Pimenoff. See **Pimenoff-Noble, L. L.**

N-106   Noble, W. Arthur (William Arthur), b. 1866. Ewa: a tale of Korea / by W. Arthur Noble. New York: Eaton & Mains; Cincinnati: Jennings & Graham, [c1906]. 354 p., photo. front., [5] leaves of photo. plates.
LC: S 18, '06.
PW: S 29, '06.

N-107   Noblitt, Loren Scott, b. 1888. The lost song / Loren S. Noblitt. Zarephath, New Jersey: Pillar of Fire, 1921. 260 p., photo. front., [3] leaves of photo. plates, ill.
PW: Ja 21, '22.

Noel, Annie Webster. The first pussy-willows. In *The heart of childhood* (1906), H-441.

N-108   Noel, Jean, *pseud.* The courage of Paula / by Jean Noel [pseud.]. New York: Broadway Publishing Company, 1913. 160 p.
Unexamined copy: bibliographic data from NUC.
LC: My 13, '13.

Noel, Joseph, jt. aut. *Whispering sage* (1922). See **Drago, Harry Sinclair, 1888-1979, jt. aut., D-538.**

N-109   Noland, Stephen C. Sam Blick's diary / by Stephen C. Noland. New York; London: Harper & Brothers, 1922. 301 p.
PW: N 18, '22.

N-110   Noll, Arthur Howard, 1855-1930. In quest of Aztec treasure / by Arthur Howard Noll and Bourdon Wilson. New York; Washington: The Neale Publishing Company, 1911. 272 p.

N-111   Noodle, Major Tom, *pseud.* The Squash family; or A history of a Methodist preacher and his family, by Major Tom Noodle [pseud.] . . . Pulaski, Tenn: W. Thomas Carden, [c1905]. 175 p., incl. photo. front. (port.).   **IXA**

N-112   Noonan, William T., 1871-1952. Down and back: a railroad story. Boston: Privately Printed. [McGrath-Sherrill Press, Boston], 1917. 50 p.

N-113   Noot, J. (Judith). Lady Dean's daughter, or, The confession of a dying woman / by J. Noot; illustrated by R. W. Amick. New York: Cochrane Publishing Company, 1909. 219, [1] p., [4] leaves of plates.
    DLC
LC: Mr 8, '09.

N-114   Nordhoff, Charles, 1887-1947. The pearl lagoon / by Charles Nordhoff; illustrated by Anton Otto Fischer. Boston: The Atlantic Monthly Press, [c1924]. 224 p., front., [3] leaves of plates.
LC: O 17, '24.
BLC: London; Toronto: J. M. Dent & Sons; printed in U. S. A., 1926.

N-115   ____ Pícaro / by Charles Nordhoff. New York; London: Harper & Brothers Publishers, 1924. 299 p.
LC: S 23, '24.
PW: O 4, '24.

N-116   Nordling, Sophia. Toward the goal: a story / by Sophia Nordling. [Chicago, Ill.: Printed by Carlen & Jonsson, c1921]. 151 p.   **DLC**

N-117   Norman, English. Melvina Drew / by English Norman. New York: Broadway Publishing Company, [c1905]. 300 p., front. [Ill. by S. K. Hartman.]

N-118   Norman, M. E. Miss Pandora / by M. E. Norman. New York: George H. Doran Company, 1916. 316 p. Colophon reads: Billing and Sons, Ltd., printers, Guildford, England.
PW: Jl 29, '16.

N-119   Norman, Victor Louis. Chattooga Griffin: a heart story of the Blue Ridge Mountains / by Victor Louis Norman. Boston, Massachusetts: The Stratford Company, 1924. 302 p., photo. front., [2] leaves of photo. plates.

N-120   Norris, Charles Gilman, 1881-1945. The amateur / by Charles G. Norris. New York: George H. Doran Company, [c1916]. 379 p. Illustrated end papers.
LC: Mr 16, '16.
PW: Mr 11, '16.

N-121   ____ Brass; a novel of marriage / by Charles G. Norris . . . New York, E. P. Dutton & Co., [c1921]. 452 p.   **NYP**
LC: S 20, '21.
PW: Ag 20, '21.
BLC: London: William Heinemann, 1922.

N-122   ____ Bread / by Charles G. Norris . . . New York: E. P. Dutton & Company, [c1923]. 511 p.
LC: Ag 24, '23.
PW: S 1, '23.
BLC: London: T. Fisher Unwin, 1924.

____ The perfect husband. In *Marriage* (1923), M-457.

N-123   ____   Salt, or, The education of Griffith Adams / by Charles G. Norris . . . New York: E. P. Dutton and Company, [c1918]. 378 p.
LC: Je 10, '18.
PW: Je 15, '18.
BLC: London: Constable & Co., 1920.

Norris, Frank, 1870-1902. Annixter. In *A book of narratives* (1917), B-734.

____   A caged lion. In *Argonaut stories* (1906), **A-298.**

N-124   ____   A deal in wheat: and other stories of the new and old West / by Frank Norris; illustrated by Remington, Leyendecker, Hitchcock and Hooper. New York: Doubleday, Page & Company, 1903. 272 p., front., [3] leaves of plates.
Contents: A deal in wheat -- The wife of Chino -- A bargain with Peg-leg -- The passing of Cock-eye Blacklock -- A memorandum of sudden death -- Two hearts that beat as one -- The dual personality of Slick Dick Nickerson -- The ship that saw a ghost -- The ghost in the crosstrees -- The riding of Felipe.
LC: S 4, '03.
PW: S 19, '03.
BLC: London: Grant Richards, New York [printed], 1913.
References: BAL 15039; Lohf & Sheehy 33; McElrath A8.

N-125   ____   The joyous miracle / by Frank Norris. New York: Doubleday, Page & Company, 1906. 27 p., front.
LC: My 28, '06.
PW: O 20, '06.
BLC: London: Doubleday, Page & Co., printed in U. S. A., 1906.
References: BAL 15042; Lohf & Sheehy 37; McElrath A10.

____   A lost story. In *Spinners' book of fiction* (1907), **S-755.**

N-126   ____   The octopus: a story of California / by Frank Norris. New York: Doubleday, Page & Co., 1901. 652 p., map.
At head of title: *The epic of wheat.* (pt. 1 of the author's trilogy, The epic of the wheat; the other volumes are *The pit* and *The wolf.*)
LC: Ap 1, '01.
PW: Ap 6, '01.
BLC: London: Grant Richards, 1901.
References: BAL 15036; Lohf & Sheehy, 22; McElrath A6.

____   The passing of Cock-eye Blacklock. In *California story book* (1909), **C-40.**

N-127   ____   The pit: a story of Chicago / by Frank Norris. New York: Doubleday, Page & Co., 1903. 421 p., photo. front. (port.).
At head of title: *The epic of wheat.* (pt. 2 of the author's trilogy, The epic of the wheat; the other volumes are *The octopus* and *The wolf.*)
LC: N 29, '02.
PW: Ja 3, '03.
BLC: London: Grant Richards, 1903.

References: BAL 15038; Lohf & Sheehy 26; McElrath A7. BAL notes "no frontispiece" in five recorded printings.

N-128   ____   The third circle / by Frank Norris . . ; introduction by Will Irwin. New York: John Lane Company; London: John Lane, The Bodley Head, 1909. 298 p., photo. front. (port.).
Contents: The third circle -- The house with the blinds -- Little dramas of the curbstone -- Shorty Stack, pugilist -- The strangest thing -- A reversion to type -- "Boom" -- The dis-associated charities -- Son of a sheik -- A defense of the flag -- Toppan -- A caged lion -- "This animal of Buldy Jones" -- Dying fires -- Grettir at Drangey -- The guest of honour.
References: BAL 15045; Lohf & Sheehy 40; McElrath A11.

____   Travis Hallett's half-back. In *Under the Berkeley Oaks* (1901), **U-8.**

N-129   ____   Vandover and the brute / by Frank Norris. Garden City, New York: Doubleday, Page & Company, 1914. 354 p.
LC: Ap 14, '14.
PW: Ap 25, '14.
BLC: London: William Heinemann, 1914.
References: BAL 15046; Lohf & Sheehy, 44; McElrath A12.

N-130   Norris, Kathleen Thompson, 1880-1966. The beloved woman / by Kathleen Norris; frontispiece by C. Allan Gilbert. Garden City, N. Y.; Toronto: Doubleday, Page & Company, 1921. 359, [1] p., col. front.
LC: S 16, '21.
BLC: London: John Murray, 1921.

N-131   ____   Butterfly / by Kathleen Norris; frontispiece by C. Allan Gilbert. Garden City, N. Y.: Doubleday, Page & Company, 1923. 346 p., col. front.
LC: O 11, '23.
PW: S 8, '23.

N-132   ____   The Callahans and the Murphys / by Kathleen Norris; illustrations by James Montgomery Flagg. Garden City, N. Y.: Doubleday, Page & Company, 1924. 381 p., front. ill., [7] leaves of ill. (not incl. in pagination).
Contents: The Callahans of Clare --The Murphys of Mayo.
LC: Ap 21, '24.
PW: Ap 12, '24.
BLC: London: William Heinemann, 1924.

N-133   ____   Certain people of importance / by Kathleen Norris. Garden City, N. Y.: Doubleday, Page & Company, 1922. 486 p., front. (fold. double), a genealogy table.
LC: Ag 24, '22.
PW: Ag 19, '22.
BLC: London: William Heinemann, 1924.

N-134   ____   Harriet and the piper / by Kathleen Norris; illustrated by Arthur I. Keller. Garden City, N. Y.: Doubleday, Page & Company, 1920. 341, [1] p., front., [3] leaves of plates.
LC: Ag 12, '20.
PW: Ag 7, '20.
BLC: London: John Murray, 1920.

N-135 _____ The heart of Rachael / by Kathleen Norris;
frontispiece by Charles E. Chambers. Garden City,
N. Y.: Doubleday, Page & Company, 1916. 408 p.,
col. front.
LC: Ag 3, '16.
PW: Ag 19, '16.
BLC: London: John Murray, 1916.

N-136 _____ Josselyn's wife / by Kathleen Norris;
frontispiece by C. Allan Gilbert. Garden City, New
York: Doubleday, Page & Company, 1918. (Garden
City, N. Y.: The Country Life Press). 301, [1] p.,
col. front.
PW: S 28, '18.
BLC: London: John Murray, 1919.

N-137 _____ Little ships: a novel / by Kathleen Norris.
Garden City, N. Y.: Doubleday, Page & Co., 1925.
427 p.
LC: S 21, '25.
PW: S 12, '25.
BLC: London: John Murray, 1925.

N-138 _____ Lucretia Lombard / by Kathleen Norris;
illustrations by A. I. Keller. Garden City, N. Y.;
Toronto: Doubleday, Page & Company, 1922.
316 p., col. front., [3] leaves of plates.
LC: Ap 14, '22.
PW: Ap 1, '22.
BLC: London: Curtis Brown; Garden City, N. Y.,
printed, 1922.

N-139 _____ Martie, the unconquered / by Kathleen Norris;
illustrated by Charles E. Chambers. Garden City, N.
Y.: Doubleday, Page & Company, 1917. 376 p.,
col. front., [4] leaves of plates.
LC: Ag 18, '17.
PW: Ag 14, '17.
BLC: London: John Murray, 1918.

_____ The masterpiece. In *More aces* (1925),
M-962.

N-140 _____ Mother: a story / by Kathleen Norris. New
York: The Macmillan Company, 1911. 172 p.
LC: O 19, '11.
PW: N 18, '11.
BLC: London: John Murray, 1921.

N-141 _____ Poor, dear Margaret Kirby and other stories /
by Kathleen Norris . . ; with frontispiece. New
York: The Macmillan Company, 1913. 393 p., col.
front.
Contents: Poor, dear Margaret Kirby -- Bridging the years -- The
tide-marsh -- What happened to Alanna -- The friendship of Alanna --
"S is for Shiftless Susanna" -- The last Carolan -- Making allowances
for mamma -- The measure of Margaret Coppered -- Miss Mix,
kidnapper -- Shandon Waters -- Gayley the troubadour -- Dr. Bates
and Miss Sally -- The gay deciever -- The rainbow's end --
Rosemary's stepmother -- Austin's girl -- Rising water.
LC: Ja 30, '13.
PW: F 8 '13.

N-142 _____ The rich Mrs. Burgoyne / by Kathleen Norris;
illustrated by Lucius Henry Hitchcock. New York:
The Macmillan Company, 1912. 297 p., col. front.,
[4] leaves of col. plates.
LC: S 26, '12.
PW: O 12, '12.

N-143 _____ Rose of the world / by Kathleen Norris;
frontispiece in colour by C. Allan Gilbert. Garden
City, N. Y.: Doubleday, Page & Company, 1924.
423 p., col. front.
LC: Ag 30, '24.
PW: Ag 23, '24.
BLC: London: John Murray, 1924.

N-144 _____ Saturday's child / by Kathleen Norris . . ; with
frontispiece by F. Graham Cootes. New York: The
Macmillan Company, 1914. 531 p., col. front.
LC: Ag 30, '14.
PW: Ag 29, '14.
BLC: London: Macmillan, 1914.

N-145 _____ Sisters / by Kathleen Norris; illustrated by
Frank Street. Garden City, N. Y.: Doubleday, Page
& Company, 1919. 342 p., col. front., [4] leaves of
plates.
LC: O 2, '19.
PW: S 27, '19.
BLC: London: John Murray, 1919.

N-146 _____ The story of Julia Page / by Kathleen Norris;
frontispiece by C. Allan Gilbert. Garden City, N.
Y.: Doubleday, Page & Company, 1915. 421,
[1] p., col. front.
LC: S 18, '15.
PW: S 11, '15.
BLC: London: John Murray, 1915.

_____, contributor. See *The sturdy oak* (1917),
S-1101.

N-147 _____ The treasure / by Kathleen Norris . . .
illustrated. New York: The Macmillan Company,
1914. 186 p., incl. front., ill. [Ill. by F. R. Gruger.]
EYM
LC: F 5, '14.
PW: Mr 7, 14.

_____ The unbecoming conduct of Annie. In *Aces*
(1924), A-42.

N-148 _____ Undertow / by Kathleen Norris . . . Garden
City, New York: Doubleday, Page & Company,
1917. 248 p., col. front.
LC: Ap 4, '17.
PW: Mr 31, '17.
BLC: London: Curtis Brown, 1917.

N-149 _____ Uneducating Mary / by Kathleen Norris. . .
Garden City, N. Y., Garden City Publishing Co.,
Inc., 1923. 120 p., ill. (On cover: Famous author
series; no. 30.) Portrait of author on verso of cover.
COD
(lacks port. and series note.)
LC: Mr 26, '24.

N-150 Norris, Mary Harriott, 1848-1919. The grapes of
wrath: a tale of north and south / by Mary Harriott
Norris. Boston: Small, Maynard & Company, 1901.
345 p., col. front., [5] leaves of col. plates. [Ill. by
H. T. Carpenter.]
PW: Je 22, 01.

N-151 _____ The story of Christina / by Mary Harriott Norris. New York; Washington: The Neale Publishing Company, 1907. 438 p.
LC: Je 17, '07.
PW: Jl 6, '07.

N-152 _____ The veil: a fantasy / by Mary Harriott Norris. Boston: Richard G. Badger, 1907. ([Boston]: The Gorham Press). 309 p.
LC: D 30, '07.
PW: F 1, '08.

N-153 Norris, Zoé Anderson. The color of his soul / by Zoé Anderson Norris. New York: R. F. Fenno & Company, 1903. 220 p.

N-154 _____ The quest of Polly Locke / by Zoé Anderson Norris . . . New York: J. S. Ogilvie Publishing Company, c1902. 268 p., photo. front. (port.).
PW: S 13, '02.

N-155 _____ Twelve Kentucky colonel stories: describing scenes and incidents in a Kentucky colonel's life in the Southland / by Zoe Anderson Norris. New York: J. S. Ogilvie, [c1905]. 116 p., ill.   **NWP**
Contents: The Colonel gives the facts about a Kentucky shooting -- A mild-mannered Kentucky family -- The broken heart of Clabe Jones -- The Kentucky Colonel has a grievance -- The mother-in-law feud in Kentucky -- The Kentucky Colonel tells of the feud two women started -- The lonely old man who was the last survivor of a Kentucky feud -- Very set in his ways in the Kentuckian -- A school ma'am bred in old Kentucky -- A breach of Kentucky etiquette which was worse than laying down five aces at poker -- Mortifying blunder of a Kentucky gentleman -- There was once a Kentucky Masterson.

N-156 _____ The way of the wind / by Zoe Anderson Norris; drawings by Oberhardt. New York: Published by the author, 1911. 191 p., front. (port.).

N-157 North, Leigh, *pseud.* Love and labor: and other stories / by Leigh North [pseud.]. New Brunswick, N. J.: Press of J. Heidingsfeld Co., 1918. 125 p.
Contents: Love and labor -- Neith, the victorious -- The stairway -- The lady and the dragonman -- His Japanese wife -- Story of an hour -- The serpent -- The cuckoo clock -- Two Christmas Eves -- Nothing to do -- Which? Which? -- A Sicilian sketch -- The Cates pacificator.

N-158 North, Lillian A. Sheep of the shepherd: little idyls of a sheep farm / by Lillian A. North; illustrated by Lorenz C. Braren. New York: E. P. Dutton and Company, [c1923]. 173 p., front. ill., ill.

N-159 North, Mary M. A prairie-schooner: a romance of the plains of Kansas / by Mary M. North. Washington: The Neale Publishing Company, [c1902]. 117 p., front.
PW: Ap 25, '03.

N-160 [North, Nelson L.] Ask and receive. Including stories and folklore of the Adirondack and Lake Champlain region. Chicago: Scroll, 1901. 83 p. Unexamined copy: bibliographic data from OCLC, #28546299.

N-161 Northrop, Henry Davenport, 1836-1909. John Winslow / by Henry D. Northrop; illustrated by Jos. S. Moyer. New York: G. W. Dillingham Company, [c1901]. 383 p., front., [5] leaves of plates.
PW: Ap 20, '01.

N-162 Norton, Brayton. El diablo / by Brayton Norton; illustrated by Dan Sayre Groesbeck. Indianapolis: The Bobbs-Merrill Company, [c1921]. 362 p., front, [4] leaves of plates.
LC: N 5, '21.
BLC: London: Hodder & Stoughton, 1922.

N-163 Norton, Leigh. Arthur Norris, or, A modern knight / by Leigh Norton . . . ; illustrated by Donald S. Humphreys. Milwaukee: The Young Churchman Co., 1915. 117 p., front., [3] leaves of plates. **DLC**
PW: My 15, '15.

Norton, M. F. Latham. See **Latham-Norton, M. F.**

N-164 Norton, Roy, 1869-1942. The boomers / by Roy Norton; illustrations by W. Goldbeck. New York: W. J. Watt & Company, [c1914]. 384 p., front., [7] leaves of plates.
LC: Ap 23, '14.
BLC: London: Mills & Boon, 1914.

N-165 _____ Drowned gold: being the story of a sailor's life / by Roy Norton. Boston; New York: Houghton Mifflin Company, 1919. (Cambridge, Mass.: The Riverside Press). 268 p., front., [3] leaves of plates. [Ill. by J. D. Whiting.]
LC: O 7, '19.
PW: S 27, '19.
BLC: London: Skeffington & Son, 1919.

N-166 _____ The garden of fate / by Roy Norton; illustrations by Joseph Clement Coll. New York: W. J. Watt & Company, 1910. 349 p., col. front. [Ill. by Harrison Fisher.], [9] leaves of plates.
LC: Ag 11, '10.
PW: S 24, '10.
BLC: London: Everett & Co., 1911.

N-167 _____ Guilty: the magazine-gun tragedy: a strong moral graphically drawn / by Roy E. Norton and Wm. C. Hallowell; over thirty pen-drawings and half-tones from original photographs . . . Chicago: Laird & Lee, [c1904]. 259 p., [8] leaves of plates (ports.), ill.   **DLC**

N-168 _____ The mediator / by Roy Norton; illustrations by Douglas Duer. New York: W. J. Watt & Company, [1913]. 299 p., front., [2] leaves of plates.
LC: Ag 18, '13.
BLC: London: Mills & Boon, 1916.

N-169 _____ Mixed faces / by Roy Norton. New York: W. J. Watt & Company, [c1921]. 293 p.
LC: Je 27, '21.

N-170 _____ The plunderer / by Roy Norton; illustrations by Douglas Duer. New York: W. J. Watt & Company, [c1912]. 312 p., col. front., [3] leaves of plates.
LC: Jl 8, '12.
BLC: London: Mills & Boon, 1914.

N-171 _____ The toll of the sea / by Roy Norton. New York: D. Appleton and Company, 1909. 376 p., front., [3] leaves of plates. [Ill. by Beverly Towles.]
LC: Je 11, '09.
PW: Je 19, '09.

N-172   ____ The unknown Mr. Kent / by Roy Norton. New York: George H. Doran Company, [c1916]. 278 p. Illustrated end paper. [Ill. by F. Rogers.]
LC: O 23, '16.
PW: O 21, '16.
BLC: London: Mills & Boon, 1916.

N-173   ____ The vanishing fleets / by Roy Norton. New York: D. Appleton and Company, 1908. 349, [1] p., front., [3] leaves of plates. [Ill. by Jay Hambidge.]
LC: Ja 17, '08.
PW: Ja 25, '08.

N-174   Norton, Wm. H. (William Harrison), b. 1845. The ideal Christian life / by Wm. H. Norton . . . Atlanta, Ga.: The Index Printing Company, printers and binders, 1909. 263 p.   **EWF**
LC: Ja 14, '10.

N-175   Norton-Thomson, L., Mrs., b. 1836. Not to have and to hold / by Mrs. L. Norton-Thomson; illustrated by Hudson; author's portrait. New York; Baltimore: Broadway Publishing Co., 1909. 292 p., photo. front. (port.), [4] leaves of plates.   **OSU, EWF**
LC: D 9, '09.

N-176   Norvell, Joseph E. (Joseph Elgon), b. 1859. Jack of Deer Creek / by Joseph E. Norvell . . . Chicago, Ills.: The Christian Witness Co., [c1916]. 226 p.
LC: Je 29, '16.

N-177   ____ The lost guide / by Rev. Joseph E. Norvell . . . Chicago; Boston: The Christian Witness Co., [c1910]. 249 p., photo. front. (port.), [5] leaves of plates. [Ill. by C. Rosser.]
LC: Ag 8, '10.

N-178   Norwood, Joseph. Breaking the shell / by Joseph Norwood. Macon, Georgia: The J. W. Burke Company, 1923. 176 p., photo. front., [1] leaf of photo. plates.

N-179   Noto, Cosimo, b. 1871. The ideal city / by Cosimo Noto . . . New York: [s. n.], 1903. 377 p., front., [1] leaf of photo. plates (port.).   **LRU**

  Nott, Sarah Thurston. The mother. In *West winds* **(1914), W-368.**

N-180   Nourse, W. J. H. McCrohan and Slammin- "guides" / W. J. H. Nourse. New York: The Winthrop Press, c1914. 31 p., front.

N-181   Noyes, Charles Johnson, b. 1841. Patriot and Tory: a tale of stirring times and sturdy souls / by Charles Johnson Noyes. Boston; New York: Henry A. Dickerman & Son, [c1902]. 315 p., front. [Ill. by Herbert Dunton.]
PW: Mr 29, '02.

  Noyes, Frances Newbold. See **Hart, Frances Noyes, 1890-1943.**

N-182   Noyes, P. J. (Parker Jewitt), b. 1842. Why Doctor Dobson became a quack: and other stories / by P. J. Noyes. New York: Cochrane Publishing Company,

1910. 280 p.
Contents: Why Doctor Dobson became a quack -- An ameteur minstrel show -- An experimental telephone line -- The lost cap -- Tragedy of a needle -- The majesty of the law.
LC: Ap 28, '10.
PW: Jl 2, '10.

  Nutter, William Herbert, b. 1874. See **Witherspoon, Halliday, pseud.**

N-183   Nuverbis, *pseud.* Out of the beaten track: a story of the old South; love, hypnotism, and adventure / by "Nuverbis" [pseud.]. New York; London; Montreal: The Abbey Press, [c1901]. 212 p., front., [3] leaves of plates.
PW: Mr 22, '02.

N-184   Nyburg, Sidney L. (Sidney Lauer), 1880-1957. The chosen people / by Sidney L. Nyburg . . . Philadelphia; London: J. B. Lippincott Company, 1917. 362, [1] p.
LC: My 10, '17.
PW: Ap 14, '17.

N-185   ____ The conquest / by Sidney L. Nyburg . . . Philadelphia; London: J. B. Lippincott Company, 1916. 325, [1] p.
LC: Mr 2, '16.
PW: F 5, '16.

N-186   ____ The final verdict: six stories of men and women / by Sidney L. Nyburg. Philadelphia; London: J. B. Lippincott Company, 1915. 221 p.   **CIL**
Contents: The fruits of victory -- A study in blackmail -- With all her wordly goods -- A legal fiction -- The honor of the profession -- The ward of the court.
LC: F 27, '15.
PW: F 13, '15.

N-187   ____ The gate of ivory / by Sidney L. Nyburg. New York: Alfred A. Knopf, 1920. 375 p.
LC: N 5, '20.
PW: O 23, '20.

N-188   Nye, Ned, b. 1876. Nachette / by Ned Nye and Robt. A. Wason; illustrated by Andre De Takacs. New York; Detroit: Jerome H. Remick & Company, [c1909]. 447 p., front., [5] leaves of plates.   **OSU, CIL**
LC: Ag 11, '09.

N-189   Nygaard, A. (Andrea), b. 1854. Toleration: a novel / A. Nygaard. Boston: Richard G. Badger, 1909. (Boston, U. S. A.: The Gorham Press). 354 p.
PW: Je 12, '09.

N-190   Nylen, Irene. Man's highest duty: a story and a message / by Irene Nylen. New York City: Published by Alvin L. Schmoeger, [c1920]. 127 p.   **DLC**

O

O-1   Oakley, E. Clarence. Dyke's corners / E. Clarence Oakley. Boston: Richard G. Badger, 1909. (Boston, U. S. A.: The Gorham Press). 242 p.
LC: My 4, '09.
PW: Je 12, '09.

Oakley, Hester Coldwell. Love in a fog. In *Love* **(1901), L-525.**

O-2   Obear, Katherine Theus, b. 1852. Four months at Glencairn / Katherine T. Obear. New York: Broadway Publishing Company, [c1913]. 228 p. Unexamined copy: bibliographic data from OCLC, #6706604.

Obenchain, Eliza Caroline Calvert, Mrs., b. 1856. See **Hall, Eliza Calvert.**

O-3   Ober, Frederick A. (Frederick Albion), 1849-1913. The last of the Arawaks: a story of adventure on the Island of San Domingo / by Frederick A. Ober . . . ; with illustrations by William F. Stecher. Boston; Chicago: W. A. Wilde Company, 1901. 359 p., front., [4] leaves of plates.
PW: O 5, '01.

O-4   ____ The war chiefs: a story of the Spanish conquerors in Santo Domingo / by Frederick A. Ober. New York: E. P. Dutton and Company, 1904. 339 p., front. and t. p. double-leaf, [5] leaves of plates.
PW: S 10, '04.

O'Brien, Edward J., ed. See *The best short stories of . . .* **(1916-1924), B-560 - B-569.**

O'Brien, Fitz-James. A terrible night. In *Library of the world's best mystery and detective stories* **(1908), L-277.**

O-5   O'Brien, Frank M. (Frank Michael), 1875-1943. With accrued interest / by Frank M. O'Brien. [New York: The Winthrop Press], c1914]. 32 p., front. "The story . . . first appeared in Munsey magazine."

O-6   [O'Brien, Howard Vincent], 1888-1947. The green scarf: a business romance having to do with a man who is determined to win success without the help of wealth or family prestige / by Clyde Perrin [pseud.]. Chicago: A. C. McClurg & Co., 1924. 323 p., front.
LC: Mr 3, '24.
PW: Mr 22, '24.

O-7   ____ New men for old / by Howard Vincent O'Brien. New York: Mitchell Kennerley, 1914. 320 p.
LC: My 26, '14.
PW: My 30, '14.

O-8   ____ The terms of conquest / by Howard Vincent O'Brien. Boston: Little, Brown and Company, 1923. 357 p.
LC: N 22, '23.

O-9   ____ Thirty / by Howard Vincent O'Brien; illustrated by Robert W. Amick. New York: Dodd, Mead and Company, 1915. 336 p., col. front., [3] leaves of col. plates.
LC: S 2, '15.
PW: S 4, '15.

O-10   [____] The thunderbolt / by Clyde Perrin [pseud.]. Chicago: A. C. McClurg & Co., 1923. 283 p.
                                                                NYP

O-11   ____ Trodden gold / by Howard Vincent O'Brien; with frontispiece by Charles D. Mitchell. Boston: Little, Brown and Company, 1923. 316 p., front.
LC: F 27, '23.
PW: F 24, '23.
BLC: London: Hodder and Stoughton, 1923.

O-12   ____ What a man wants: a novel / by Howard Vincent O'Brien. Garden City, N. Y.: Doubleday, Page & Company, 1925. 344 p.
LC: S 21, '25.
PW: S 5, '25.

O-13   O'Brien, Joseph. The devil: a tragedy of the heart and conscience / by Ferenc Molnar; novelized by Joseph O'Brien from Henry W. Savage's great play. New York: J. S. Ogilvie Publishing Company, [c1908]. 189 p., photo. front., [7] leaves of photo. plates.
LC: O 2, '08.

O-14   O'Brien, Seumas, b. 1880. The whale and the grasshopper: and other fables / by Seumas O'Brien; with a frontispiece by Robert McCaig. Boston: Little, Brown, and Company, 1916. 302 p., front.
Contents: The whale and the grasshopper -- The house in the valley -- Peace and war -- The valley of the dead -- The king of Montobewlo -- The dilemma of Matty the goat -- Ham and eggs -- The white horse of Banba -- Rebellions -- Kings and commoners -- The folly of being foolish -- The lady of the moon -- A bargain of bargains -- Shauno and the shah -- The mayor of Loughlaurna -- The land of peace and plenty -- The linnet with the crown of gold -- The man with the wooden leg -- The hermit of the grove -- The king of Goulnaspurra.
BLC: Dublin: Talbot Press; London: T. Fisher Unwin, [1920].

O-15   O'Connell, Margaret Le B. (Margaret LeBoutillier), 1847-1910. The romance of reality / by Margaret LeB. O'Connell. Lancaster, Pa.: Press of the New Era Printing Company, 1912. 307 p.   **MNU**

O'Connor, Elizabeth Paschal. See **O'Connor, T. P., Mrs.**

O-16   O'Connor, Mary Hamilton. The "vanishing Swede": a tale of adventure and pluck in the pine forests of Oregon / by Mary Hamilton O'Connor. New York: Robert Grier Cooke, 1905. 209 p., front., map.
PW: My 13, '05.

O-17   O'Connor, T. P., Mrs., d. 1931. The hat of destiny / by Mrs. T. P. O'Connor. New York: Lieber & Lewis, 1923. 341, [1] p.
PW: Je 9, '23.
BLC: London: W. Collins Sons and Co., 1923.

O-18   ____ Little Thank You / by Mrs. T. P. O'Connor . . . . New York; London: G. P. Putnam's Sons, 1913. ([New York]: The Knickerbocker Press). 262 p., photo. front. (port.). [Ill. by Henry Spink]. Music on end papers.
PW: Ap 12, '13.

O-19 Octave, b. 1848. The stolen credentials: a tale of French chivalry / by Octave (M. E. S.). New York: Robert J. Shores, Publisher, [c1918]. 314 p., front. PW: S 28, '18.

O-20 O'Day, John Christopher. Oil wells in the woods / by John Christopher O'Day . . . ; with illustrations by Miss Ethel Farmer and photographs collected by the author. Deposit, N. Y.: The Oquaga Press, 1905. 359 p., col. photo. front., [14] leaves of photo. plates (1 col.). **VYS**

O-21 Odell, Eva Beede. Miss Prissy's diamond rings and other tales / by Eva Beede Odell . . . Cambridge, Mass.: Huntington Art Press, 1914. 112 p.
Contents: Miss Prissy's diamond rings -- Eleanor Raymond's story -- House-cleanin' in sappin' time.
LC: D 4, '14.

O-22 ____ The rivals: and other folklore tales / by Eva Beede Odell . . . Meredith, N. H.: The Meredith News Press, 1924. 88 p.
Contents: The rivals -- The album quilt -- Spoken for in the cradle -- The new minister -- Daniel Scruton's economy -- The hen party -- Betty's valentine.
LC: D 5, '24.

O-23 ____ Roxy's good angel: and other New England tales / by Eva Beede Odell. Concord, N. H.: The Rumford Printing Co., 1908. 111 p.
Contents: Roxy's good angel -- Silas Mason's will -- Caught in a cyclone -- Their other mother -- Nathan's wife -- Miss Harden's Christmas party.
LC: N 2, '08.

O-24 Odell, Samuel W. The Princess Athura: a romance of Iran / by Samuel W. Odell. New York: Thomas Y. Crowell Company, [1913]. 312 p., col. front. [Ill. by Jay Hambidge.]
LC: Mr 12, '13.
PW: Mr 29, '13.
BLC: London: George G. Harrays and Co., 1914.

O-25 Odenheimer, Cordelia Powell. The phantom caravan / by Cordelia Powell Odenheimer. New York; London; Montreal: The Abbey Press, [c1901]. 131 p.
PW: F 15, '02.

O-26 Oeland, Peter Joseph. The around town boys / by Peter Joseph Oeland. Charleston, S. C.: Press of Walker, Evans & Cogswell Co., 1910. 149 p. **MCD**
LC: My 16, '10.

O-27 Oemler, Marie (Conway), 1879-1932. His wife-in-law / by Marie Conway Oemler. New York; London: The Century Co., [c1925]. 370 p.
LC: Mr 2, '25.
PW: Mr 7, '25.

O-28 ____ The purple heights / by Marie Conway Oemler. New York: The Century Co., 1920. 381 p., front.
LC: O 5, '20.
PW: O 2, '20.

O-29 ____ Slippy McGee: sometimes known as the Butterfly man / by Marie Conway Oemler. New

York: The Century Co., 1917. 405 p.
LC: My 5, '17.
PW: Ap 28, '17.
BLC: London: William Heinemann, 1918.

O-30 ____ Two shall be born / by Marie Conway Oemler. New York: The Century Co., 1922. 411 p., front.
LC: O 2, '22.
PW: S 30, '22.
BLC: London: William Heinemann, 1923.

O-31 ____ Where the young Child was: and also The spirit of the house, The youngest officer, Linden goes home, The little brown house, That makes the world go round / by Marie Conway Oemler; illustrated by George Avison. New York: The Century Co., 1921. 242 p., front., [6] leaves of plates.
LC: O 3, '21.
PW: O 8, '21.
BLC: London: William Heinemann, 1921.

O-32 ____ A woman named Smith / by Marie Conway Oemler. New York: The Century Co., 1919. 375 p., front. [Ill. by Edward Ryan.]
LC: S 18, '19.
PW: S 13, '19.
BLC: London: William Heinemann, 1920.

Oeston, Agata Dolores Mercedes. <u>See</u> **Graye, Dawn, pseud.**

O-33 Ofloda, Dr. The pleasure of death: being the strange experiments and astonishing discoveries of a village doctor / by Dr. Ofloda. Toledo, Ohio: Dolfe Company, 1903. 87 p.
Unexamined copy: bibliographic data from NUC and OCLC, #16132149.

O-34 Ogden, George W. (George Washington), 1871-1966. The Baron of Diamond Tail / by G. W. Ogden . . . ; frontispiece by J. Allen St. John. Chicago: A. C. McClurg & Co., 1923. 311 p., front.
LC: S 8, '23.
PW: O 6, '23.
BLC: London: Hodder and Stoughton, 1923.

O-35 ____ The bondboy / by George W. Ogden. Chicago: A. C. McClurg & Co., 1922. 370 p. [Ill. by James Allen St. John.]
LC: O 31, '22.
PW: N 18, '22.
BLC: London: Hodder and Stoughton, 1923.

O-36 ____ Claim number one / G. W. Ogden . . . ; frontispiece by J. Allen St. John. Chicago: A. C. McClurg & Co., 1922. 352 p., front.
LC: Je 1, '22.
PW: Je 24, '22.
BLC: London: Hodder and Stoughton, 1923.

O-37 ____ The cow Jerry / by George W. Ogden . . . New York: Dodd, Mead & Company, 1925. 328 p.
LC: Ja 30, '25.
PW: Ja 31, '25.

O-38   ____ The Duke of Chimney Butte / by G.W. Ogden; frontispiece by P.V.E. Ivory. Chicago: A.C. McClurg & Co., 1920. 381 p., front.   **DLC**
LC: Ap 12, '20.
PW: My 1, '20.
BLC: London: Hodder and Stoughton, 1920.

O-39   ____ The flockmaster of Poison Creek / by G. W. Ogden; frontispiece by P. V. E. Ivory. Chicago: A. C. McClurg & Co., 1921. 315 p., front.
LC: Mr 29, '21.
PW: Ap 16, '21.
BLC: London: Hodder and Stoughton, 1922.

O-40   ____ Home place: a story of the people / by G. W. Ogden. New York; London: Harper & Brothers, 1912. 364, [1] p., front. [Ill. by W. Herbert Dunton.]
LC: O 12, '12.
PW: O 19, '12.

O-41   ____ The land of last chance / by G. W. Ogden . . . ; frontispiece by P. V. E. Ivory. Chicago: A. C. McClurg & Co., 1919. 338 p., col. front.
LC: S 29, '19.
PW: N 1, '19.
BLC: London: Hodder and Stoughton, 1921.

O-42   ____ The long fight / by George Washington Ogden. New York: Hearst's International Library Co., 1915. 297 p., front.
LC: S 27, '15.
PW: O 23, '15.
BLC: London: Hodder and Stoughton, 1924.

O-43   ____ The road to Monterey / by George W. Ogden . . . Chicago: A. C. McClurg & Co., 1925. 371 p., front. [Ill. by J. Allen St. John.]
PW: O 10, '25.
BLC: London: Hodder and Stoughton, 1924.

O-44   ____ The rustler of Wind River / by G. W. Ogden; frontispiece by Frank E. Schoonover. Chicago: A. C. McClurg & Co., 1917. 330 p., front.
LC: Mr 26, '17.
PW: Ap 7, '17.
BLC: Hodder and Stoughton, 1922.

O-45   ____ Tennessee Todd: a novel of the great river / by G. W. Ogden; with frontispiece by W. Herbert Dunton. New York: A. S. Barnes & Company, 1903. 344 p., front.
PW: O 31, '03.
BLC: New York: A. S. Barnes & Co.; London: Authors' Syndicate, 1903.

O-46   ____ The trail rider: a romance of the Kansas range / by George W. Ogden . . . New York: Dodd, Mead and Company, 1924. 365 p.   **CRL**
LC: F 27, '24.
PW: F 23, '24.
BLC: London: Hodder and Stoughton, 1924.

O-47   ____ Trail's end / by G. W. Ogden . . . ; frontispiece by P. V. E. Ivory. Chicago: A. C. McClurg & Co., 1921. 329 p., front.

LC: O 4, '21.
PW: O 22, '21.
BLC: London: Hodder & Stonghton, Chicago printed, 1922.

O-48   Ogden, Harriet V. C. (Harriet Verona Cadwalader). The sable cloud / by Harriet V.C. Ogden . . . ; illustrated by Ralph D. Dunkelberger. Philadelphia: The Penn Publishing Company, 1923. 310 p., incl. front.   **NYP**
LC: O 12, '23.
PW: O 27, '23.

O-49   ____ Then came Molly / by Harriet V. C. Ogden; frontispiece by Elizabeth Pilsbry. Philadelphia: The Penn Publishing Company, 1922. 318 p., front.
LC: My 11, '22.

Ogden, Marguerite. Values. In *California story book* (1909), **C-40.**

O'Hagan, Anne. "And angels came-." In *Life at high tide* (1907), **L-281.**

____, contributor. See *The sturdy oak* (1917), **S-1101.**

O-50   O'Hara, Edith C. (Edith Cecilia). Confidences / by Edith C. O'Hara and Mary S. Ely. New Orleans, La.: Press of Louisiana Printing Company, Limited, [c1912]. 142 p., [6] leaves of photo. plates.   **LHA**
PW: Mr 29, '13.

O-51   O'Higgins, Harvey Jerrold, 1876-1929. The adventures of Detective Barney / by Harvey J. O'Higgins; illustrations by Henry Raleigh. New York: The Century Co., 1915. 305 p., incl. 5 leaves of plates, front.
LC: Ja 26, '15.

O-52   ____ Don-a-dreams: a story of love and youth / by Harvey J. O'Higgins. New York: The Century Co., 1906. 412 p.
LC: Ag 24, '06.
BLC: London: Duckworth & Co., 1906.

O-53   ____ From the life: imaginary portraits of some distinguished Americans / by Harvey O'Higgins. New York; London: Harper & Brothers, [1919]. 334, [1] p., front. [Ill. by F. R. Gruger.]
Contents: Owen Carey -- Jane Shore -- Thomas Wales Warren -- Benjamin McNeil Murdock -- Conrad Norman -- W. T. -- Hon. Benjamin P. Divins -- Sir Watson Tyler -- District-Attorney Wickson.
LC: S 9, '19.
BLC: London: Jonathan Cape, 1922.

O-54   ____ A Grand army man / by Harvey J. O'Higgins, founded on the play by David Belasco, Pauline Phelps, and Marion Short; with illustrations by Martin Justice. New York: The Century Co., 1908. 253 p., incl. front., incl. [17] leaves of plates.
LC: S 3, '08.

O-55   ____ Julie Cane / by Harvey O'Higgins; with illustrations by Thomas Fogarty. New York; London: Harper & Brothers, 1924. 343 p., front., [3] leaves of plates. Decorated end papers.
LC: S 23, '24.
BLC: London: Jonathan Cape, 1924.

O-56   ____ Old Clinkers: a story of the New York Fire Department / by Harvey J. O'Higgins . . . ; with illustrations by Martin Justice. Boston: Small, Maynard & Company, [c1909]. 277 p., front., [10] leaves of plates (1 diagram, 1 plan).
LC: O 28, '09.

O-57   ____ Silent Sam: and other stories of our day / by Harvey J. O'Higgins. New York: The Century Co., 1914. 390 p.
Contents: Silent Sam -- His mother -- In the matter of art -- Tammany's tithes -- The clowns -- The devil's doings -- The hired man -- The honeymoon flat -- The old woman's story -- The hot-air harps -- The reporter -- The mother-in-law -- In the Musbee -- The exiles -- During the war -- In lover's meeting -- The two Mickeys -- Larkin.
LC: Mr 7, '14.
PW: Mr 7, '14.

O-58   ____ The smoke-eaters: the story of a fire crew / by Harvey J. O'Higgins. New York: The Century Co., 1905. 296, [1] p., front.   **BGU**
PW: F 18, '05.

O-59   ____ Some distinguished Americans: imaginary portraits / by Harvey O'Higgins. New York; London: Harper & Brothers, [c1922]. 335, [1] p.
Contents: Henri Anton -- Big Dan Reilly -- Mrs. Murchison -- Warden Jeff -- Peter Quale -- Dr. Adrian Hale Hallmuth -- Vance Cope.
LC: O 4, '22.

Ohiyesa, pseud. See **Eastman, Charles Alexander, 1858-1939.**

Older, Cora Miranda Baggerly. See **Older, Fremont, Mrs.**

O-60   Older, Fremont, Mrs., b. 1856. Esther Damon / by Mrs. Fremont Older. New York: Charles Scribner's Sons, 1911. 355 p.
LC: Je 3, '11.

O-61   ____ The giants / by Mrs. Fremont Older . . . New York: D. Appleton and Company, 1905. 385 p.
PW: O 7, '05.

O-62   ____ The socialist and the prince / by Mrs. Fremont Older; frontispiece by Harrison Fisher. New York; London: Funk & Wagnalls Company, 1903. 309 p., front.
PW: Mr 7, '03.

O-63   Oldham, Callie Bruce. Down south in Dixie / by Callie Bruce Oldham . . . ; illustrated by W. L. Sheppard. [Akron, Ohio: The Werner Co.], 1905. 107 p., incl. front. (port.), ill.
Contents: The awakening of Br'er Slufoot Mose -- Christmas at the quarters -- How Cindy war took down wid de style -- "Pity 'tis, 'tis true" -- Mammy in the rôle of peacemaker -- His uncle's legacy.
PW: Je 17, '05.

O-64   Olds, Charles Louis. Wood-pile recollections / by Charles Louis Olds. New York; London; Montreal: The Abbey Press, [c1901]. 140 p., photo. front., [5] leaves of photo. plates.
Contents: The why of it -- The law of recreation -- Aunts and other things -- How I discovered Jimmie -- Mr. Slate -- The Slate family, except Mr. Slate -- The sensation of "having been there before" -- Joyce -- Concerning sympathy -- My next-door neighbor -- Hasheesh

-- When the ice goes out -- Why Jones shrunk -- How Glenmore was cured of insomnia -- Mrs. Animule -- Tramps -- Similitudes -- When it snows -- My garden -- Jones Number Two -- The song of the saw -- Catching wood -- Of love -- The wood-pile and the wash-tub -- My study -- A night at the club -- Moods and antidotes -- The passing of Dutton.
PW: Ag 31, '01.

O-65   O'Leary, Agnes Marie. Beyond these voices: a novel / by Agnes Marie O'Leary. New York: Broadway Publishing Co., [1909]. 205 p., front., [2] leaves of plates. [Ill. by Wm. L. Hudson.]
LC: Ag 2, '09.

O-66   Olerich, Henry, b. 1851. Modern paradise: an outline or story of how some of the cultured people will probably live, work and organize in the near future / by Henry Olerich; fully illustrated. Omaha, Neb.: Equality Publishing Company, 1915. 198 p., front., [27] leaves of plates.   **AZS**

O-67   Oliphant, Blossom Drum. A dog-day journal / by Blossom Drum. New York; London; Montreal: The Abbey Press, [c1901]. 112 p.
PW: F 22, '02.

O-68   ____ Mrs. Lemon's neighbors / by Blossom Drum Oliphant . . . New York; Washington: The Neale Publishing Company, 1905. 65 p.   **DLC**

Oliver, Amy. That impossible thirteenth. In *Minnesota stories* (1903), M-842.

O-69   Oliver, Charles H. (Charles Henry), b. 1863. "646" and the troubleman / by Charles H. Oliver; illustrated by Harold S. DeLay. Chicago: Rand McNally & Company, 1916. 209 p., front., [2] leaves of plates.   **WDL**

O-70   Oliver, Edwin Austin. Holiday tales / by Edwin Austin Oliver . . . Yonkers, N. Y.: Yonkers Publishing Company, [1907?]. 123 p.
Contents: The night before Christmas -- The maid and the wolf -- Cranberry's Thanksgiving surprise -- Thirteen at table -- A joke on somebody -- A bright Christmas Eve -- Tattle of the toys -- The meek gobbler.

O-71   [Oliver, Frederick Spencer, 1866-1899]. A dweller on two planets, or, The dividing of the way / by Phylos, the Thibetan [pseud.]. Los Angeles, California: Baumgardt Publishing Company, 1905. 423 p., front., [7] leaves of plates, map.

O-72   [Oliver, John Rathbone], 1872-1943. The good shepherd / by John Roland [pseud.]. New York: Frederick A. Stokes Company, [1915]. 341 p.

O-73   [____] The six-pointed cross in the dust / by John Roland [pseud.]; with a frontispiece by J. Henry. New York: Frederick A. Stokes Company, [c1915]. 357 p., front.
BLC: Edinburgh; London: W. Blackwood and Sons, 1915. British title: *The adventures of cigarette.*

O-74   Oliver, Katherine Elspeth. The claw / by Katherine Elspeth Oliver. Los Angeles, Cal.: Out West Magazine, 1914. 384 p.

O-75   Oliver, Roland, *pseud.* Back stage: a story of the theater / by Roland Oliver [pseud.]. New York: The Macmillan Company, 1924. 285 p.
PW: Jl 19, '24.

Oliver, Temple, pseud. <u>See</u> **Smith, Jeanie Oliver Davidson, Mrs., 1830-1925.**

O-76   Ollie, *pseud.* Pet: a pony story / by Ollie [pseud.]. Austin, Tex.: Von Boeckmann-Jones Co., 1912. 74 p.

O-77   Olmis, Elisabeth, b. 1850, *pseud.* The Sylvester quarry: sequel to "Over at Little Acorns" / by Elisabeth Olmis [pseud.] . . . Richmond, Va.: Presbyterian Committee of Publication, [c1901]. 418 p.   **SUC**
PW: O 19, '01.

Olmstead, Emma K. Nance's dream doll. <u>In</u> *When God walks the road and other stories* **(1924), W-445.**

O-78   Olmstead, Florence. Anchorage / by Florence Olmstead. New York: Charles Scribner's Sons, 1917. 361 p.   **CLE**
LC: My 2, '17.
PW: My 5, '17.

O-79   ____ A cloistered romance / by Florence Olmstead. New York: Charles Scribner's Sons, 1915. 335 p.   **WLU**
LC: Ap 14, '15.
PW: Ap 17, '15.

O-80   ____ Father Bernard's parish / by Florence Olmstead. New York: Charles Scribner's Sons, 1916. 302 p.
LC: My 25, '16.
PW: My 27, '16.

O-81   ____ Madame Valcour's lodger / by Florence Olmstead. New York: Charles Scribner's Sons, 1922. 261 p.
LC: Ap 12, '22.
PW: Ap 15, '22.

O-82   ____ Mrs. Eli and Policy Ann / by Florence Olmstead. Chicago: The Reilly & Britton Co., [c1912]. 160 p., front. [Ill. by Irwin O. Myers.]
LC: Jl 29, '12.
PW: Ag 17, '12.

O-83   ____ On furlough / by Florence Olmstead. New York: Charles Scribner's Sons, 1918. 316 p.
LC: Ag 31, '18.
PW: Ag 31, '18.

O-84   ____ Stafford's Island / by Florence Olmstead. New York: Charles Scribner's Sons, 1920. 218 p.
LC: My 17, '20.
PW: My 22, '20.

O-85   ____ This little world / by Florence Olmstead. New York: Charles Scribner's Sons, 1921. 277 p.
LC: My 3, '21.
PW: Ap 23, '21.

O-86   Olmsted, Stanley. The emotionalist: the romance of an awakening to temperament / Stanley Olmsted. New York: D. Appleton & Company, 1908. 351, [1] p.
LC: O 16, '08.
PW: N 14, '08.

O-87   ____ The nonchalante: casual data touching the career of Dixie Bilton, Operettensängerin at Beilmar / by Stanley Olmsted. New York: Henry Holt and Company, 1906. 247 p.
PW: Mr 3, '06.

O'Loan, Charlotte A., d. 1929. <u>See</u> **Wynne, Joseph F., pseud.**

O'Mahony, Nora Tynan. The burglar of the West Grange Farm. <u>In</u> *The friendly little house: and other stories* **(1910), F-432.**

____ The killing of Barnaby Fox. <u>In</u> *The friendly little house: and other stories* **(1910), F-432.**

O'Malley, S. M., contributor. <u>See</u> *A double knot* **(1905), D-499.**

One of the Redeemed, pseud. <u>See</u> **Wheeler, Mary Sparkes, Mrs., 1835-1919.**

O'Neill, Bucky. The man-hunters' reward. <u>In</u> *Argonaut stories* **(1906), A-298.**

O-88   O'Neill, Fred. C. (Frederic Charles), b. 1872. Short talks to young toilers / by Rev. Fred. C. O'Neill. New York: Christian Press Association Publishing Company, 1905. 393 p., ill. [Ill. by C. Bartsch.]   **PCJ**
Contents: The scrap -- What happened to the Jins -- The wanderings of Agnes -- The young cavalier -- "Skinny and Freckles" -- Wrecks -- Jerry's glorious run -- The prince and the lambs -- Paddy and his dog -- The history of Rashna -- Ginggob and Gumalub the wicked Jins -- Chodorlahomar, the good giant -- Dan Pike's adventure -- The triumph of Ecclesie -- The war of the ants -- How Nibick and Slats saved the country -- The upheaval in animaldom -- How Muzma was changed -- What Paprika the imp did -- The old school-house -- The emerald isle -- The problem.

O-89   ____ Twenty-nine chats and one scolding / by Rev. Fred. C. O'Neill. New York: Christian Press Association Publishing Company, 1905. 291 p.   **OUP**

O-90   [O'Neill, Henry J.] The travels of John Wryland; being an account of his journey to Tibet, of his founding a kingdom on the island of Palti, and of his war against the Ne-ar-Bians. London: The International News Co.; Allentown, Pa.: The Equitable Publishing Co., 1903. 236 p.   **OKU**

O-91   O'Neill, John, b. 1869. Souls in hell: a mystery of the unseen / by John O'Neill. New York: Nicholas L. Brown, 1924. 383 p.
LC: D 15, '23.

O'Neill, Rose Cecil, 1874-1944. The lady and the ghost. <u>In</u> *Humorous ghost stories* **(1921), H-1018.**

O-92 ____ The lady in the white veil / by Rose O'Neill; with illustrations by the author. New York; London: Harper & Brothers, 1909. 350 p., col. front., [4] leaves of plates. **VHB**
LC: My 5, '09.
PW: My 22, '09.

O-93 ____ The loves of Edwy / tale and drawings by Rose Cecil O'Neill. Boston: Lothrop Publishing Company, [1904]. 432 p., front., [1] leaf of plates.
PW: Ag 27, '04.

O-94 The Opal: a novel. Boston; New York: Houghton Mifflin and Company, 1905. 173, [1] p., col. front. [Ill. by J. H. Gardner-Soper.]
PW: Mr 11, '05.

O-95 Oppenheim, James, 1882-1932. The beloved / by James Oppenheim. New York: B. W. Huebsch, 1915. 268 p.
LC: My 4, '15.

O-96 ____ Doctor Rast / by James Oppenheim; illustrated. New York: Sturgis & Walton Company, 1909. 321 p., front., [4] leaves of plates. [Ill. by Thomas Fogarty, Howard Giles, F. R. Gruger, and Rollin Kirby.]
LC: S 16, '09.
BLC: London: Andrew Melrose, 1910.

____ He laughed at the Gods. _In The best short stories of 1922 and the yearbook of the American short story_ (1923), B-567.

O-97 ____ Idle wives / by James Oppenheim. New York: The Century Co., 1914. 426 p.
LC: Ap 23, '14.

O-98 ____ The nine-tenths: a novel / by James Oppenheim. New York; London: Harper and Brothers, 1911. 319 p.
LC: S 22, '11.

O-99 ____ The Olympian: a story of the city / by James Oppenheim. New York; London: Harper & Brothers, 1912. 417 p., front., [1] leaf of plates. [Ill. by John Newton Howitt and John Alonzo Williams.]
LC: S 7, '12.

O-100 ____ Pay envelopes: tales of the mill, the mine and the city street / by James Oppenheim; illustrated by Harry Townsend. New York: B. W. Huebsch, 1911. 259 p., front., [2] leaves of plates. Previously published in various periodicals.
Contents: The great fear -- Meg -- Saturday night -- The cog -- Slag -- A woman -- Joan of the mills -- The empty life -- The young man -- The broken woman -- Stiny Bolinsky.
LC: Je 9, '11.

____ The rending. _In The best short stories of 1920 and the yearbook of the American short story_ (1921), B-565.

O-101 ____ Wild oats / by James Oppenheim; with a foreword by Edward Bok. New York: B. W. Huebsch, 1910. 261 p.

LC: Jl 18, '10.
PW: Jl 30, '10.

O-102 Orcutt, Emma Louise. The divine seal / by Emma Louise Orcutt. Boston, Massachusetts: The C. M. Clark Publishing Company, 1909. 315 p., front., [5] leaves of plates. [Ill. by A. S. Trueman.]
LC: N 15, '09.
PW: Ja 1, '10.

O-103 ____ Esther Mather: a romance / by Emma Louise Orcutt. New York: The Grafton Press, 1901. 298 p., front. [Ill. by L. F. A. Lorenz.] **DLC**
PW: D 21, '01.

O-104 Orcutt, William Dana, 1870-1953. The bachelors: a novel / by William Dana Orcutt. New York; London: Harper & Brothers, 1915. 428 p., front. [Ill. by H. Weston Taylor.]
LC: O 9, '15.
PW: O 23, '15.

O-105 ____ The balance: a novel of today / by William Dana Orcutt. New York: Frederick A. Stokes Company, [c1922]. 351 p.
LC: Mr 27, '22.
PW: Ap 1, '22.

O-106 ____ The flower of destiny: an episode / by William Dana Orcutt; illustrated by Charlotte Weber. Chicago: A. C. McClurg & Co., 1905. 277 p., incl. front., ill. Illustrated end papers. "Decorations and cover design by Mabel Harlow."
PW: Ap 15, '05.
BLC: London: C. F. Cazenove; Cambridge, U. S. A., printed, 1905.

O-107 ____ The lever: a novel / by William Dana Orcutt. New York; London: Harper & Brothers, 1911. 318 p., front.
LC: Ja 14, '11.
PW: Ja 21, '11.

O-108 ____ The Madonna of sacrifice: a story of Florence / by William Dana Orcutt; frontispiece by Gertrude Demain Hammond. Chicago: F. G. Browne & Co., 1913. 51 p., front.
LC: Mr 5, '13.
PW: Mr 8, '13.

O-109 ____ The moth: a novel / by William Dana Orcutt. New York; London: Harper & Brothers, 1912. 335 p., front. [Ill. by Lucius Wolcott Hitchcock.]
LC: Ag 19, '12.
PW: Ag 24, '12.

O-110 ____ Robert Cavelier: the romance of the Sieur de La Salle and his discovery of the Mississippi River / by William Dana Orcutt; illustrated by Charlotte Weber. Chicago: A. C. McClurg & Co., 1904. 313 p., col. front., [5] leaves of col. plates.
PW: Ap 16, 04.
BLC: London: William Heinemann; Cambridge, U. S. A. [printed], 1904.

O-111 ____ The spell / by William Dana Orcutt; illustrated by Gertrude Demain Hammond, R. I. New York; London: Harper & Brothers, 1909. 351, [1] p., front., [3] leaves of plates.
LC: Ja 20, '09.
PW: Ja 30, '09.

O-112 The ordeal of Elizabeth. New York: J. F. Taylor & Company, 1901. 412 p., front.
PW: D 14, '01.

O-113 Ordway, Samuel H. (Samuel Hanson), 1900-1971. Little Codfish Cabot at Harvard: true story of a life to which little folk may look forward and their elders may look back. Cambridge: The Little Codfish Cabot Publishing Co.; Boston: John W. Luce and Company, [c1924]. 62 p., ill. [Ill. by F. Wendevoth Saunders.]

O'Reilly, Mary Boyle, contributor. See *A double knot* (1905), **D-499.**

____ In Berlin. In *The best short stories of 1915 and the yearbook of the American short story* (1916), **B-560.**

____ Luigi of the bells. In *The Senior lieutenant's wager: and other stories* (1905), **S-312.**

O-114 Orgain, Kate Alma. A waif from Texas / by Kate Alma Orgain. Austin, Texas: Ben C. Jones & Co., 1901. 238 p., ill. [Some photographic and some signed by Western Studio or Success.] **TXH**

O-115 Organ, Margaret S. The last battle ground / by Margaret S. Organ . . . New York: George Thiell Long, [c1910]. 319 p.
LC: N 23, '10.
PW: Ja 14, '11.

Ormond, Frederic, pseud. See **Vanardy, Varick, pseud.**

O-116 [Ornitz, Samuel], 1890-1957. Haunch, paunch and jowel: an anonymous autobiography. New York: Boni and Liveright, [c1923]. 300 p. **FQG**
BLC: London: Wishart & Company, 1929.

O-117 O'Rourke, Kate Beirne. The noble and his daughter / by Kate Beirne O'Rourke. Los Angeles, Cal.: [J. B. Cummings], 1911. 160 p., photo. front. (port.).
Name of publisher from spine.
LC: D 1, '11.

O-118 Orthwein, Edith Hall. Love in the weaving / by Edith Hall Orthwein. New York: Broadway Publishing Co., [1910]. 198 p., col. front.
LC: Ag 23, '10.

O-119 O'Ryan, William Patrick. The plough and the cross: a story of new Ireland / by William Patrick O'Ryan. Point Loma, Cal.: The Aryan Theosophical Press, 1910. 378 p., incl. [8] photo. plates, photo. front., ill. Decorative end papers.
LC: S 6, '10.

Osborn, Anna Brabham. "The fine country." In *Club stories* (1915), **C-502.**

O-120 Osborn, Edwin Faxon. Onar / by Edwin Faxon Osborn . . . Kalamazoo, Mich.: Sylvan Press, [c1909]. 345 p., incl. front. (port.).
LC: S 2, '09.

O-121 Osborn, Stanley R. Red hair and blue sea / by Stanley R. Osborn. New York: Charles Scribner's Sons, 1925. 374 p., ill.
PW: My 23, '25.

O-122 Osborne, Duffield, 1858-1917. The angels of Messer Ercole: a tale of Perugia / by Duffield Osborne; with a frontispiece by F. Luis Mora and illustrations from photographs. New York: Frederick A. Stokes Company, [1907]. 230 p., front., [14] leaves of plates.
(Little novels of famous cities.)
LC: Ag 29, '07.

O-123 ____ The lion's brood / by Duffield Osborne; illustrated by Walter Satterlee. New York: Doubleday, Page & Co., 1901. 361 p., front.
PW: Ap 20, '01.

Osborne, George Randolph. Thicker than water. In *Short stories from Life* (1916), **S-463.**

O-124 Osborne, William Hamilton, 1873-1942. The blue buckle / by William Hamilton Osborne. New York: McBride, Nast & Co., 1914. 440 p.
LC: F 28, '14.
PW: Mr 14, '14.
BLC: London: Hodder and Stoughton, 1915.

O-125 ____ The boomerang / by William Hamilton Osborne . . . New York: Robert M. McBride & Co., 1915. 319 p.
LC: O 25, '15.
PW: O 30, '15.

O-126 ____ The catspaw / by William Hamilton Osborne; with illustrations by F. Graham Cootes. New York: Dodd, Mead and Company, 1911. 333 p., front., [3] leaves of plates.
LC: Mr 18, '11.
PW: Mr 25, '11.
BLC: London: Hodder and Stoughton, 1916.

____ Infamous inoculation. In *War stories* (1919), **W-94.**

____ Man snatchers. In *Saturday Evening Post* (1919), **S-90.**

O-127 ____ The red mouse: a mystery romance / by William Hamilton Osborne. New York: Dodd, Mead & Company, 1909. 321 p., front., [3] leaves of col. plates. [Ill. by the Kinneys.]
LC: Ja 5, '09.
PW: Ja 9, '09.
BLC: London: Hodder and Stoughton, [1916].

O-128 ____ The running fight / by William Hamilton Osborne; with illustrations by Harrison Fisher and George Brehm. New York: Dodd, Mead and Company, 1910. 378 p., front., [3] leaves of plates.
LC: My 9, '10.
PW: My 7, '10.

____ A suspicious character. In *Master tales of mystery* (1915), M-588.5.

O-129   Osbourne, Lloyd, 1868-1947. The adventurer / Lloyd Osbourne. New York: D. Appleton and Company, 1907. 396 p., front., [3] leaves of plates. [Ill. by L. A. Shafer.]
LC: S 27, '07.
BLC: London: William Heinemann, 1908.

O-130   ____ Baby bullet: the bubble of destiny / by Lloyd Osbourne. New York: D. Appleton and Company, 1906, [c1905]. 288 p., front., [3] leaves of plates. [Ill. by Martin Justice.]
PW: O 7, '05.
BLC: London: William Heinemann, 1905.

O-131   ____ Infatuation / by Lloyd Osbourne; with illustrations by Karl Anderson. Indianapolis: Bobbs-Merrill Company, [c1909]. 380 p., front., [4] leaves of plates.
LC: Mr 10, '09.

O-132   ____ Love, the fiddler / by Lloyd Osbourne. New York: McClure, Phillips & Company, 1903. 278 p.
Contents: The chief engineer -- Frenches first -- The golden castaways -- The awakening of George Raymond -- The mascot of Battery B.
PW: O 3, '03.
BLC: London: William Heinemann, 1903.

O-133   ____ The motormaniacs / by Lloyd Osbourne. Indianapolis: The Bobbs-Merrill Company, [1905]. 189 p., front.
On cover: The pocket books.
Contents: The motormaniacs -- The great bubble syndicate -- Coal oil Johnny -- Jones.
PW: My 20, '05.
BLC: London: William Heinemann, 1906.

O-134   ____ A person of some importance / by Lloyd Osbourne; with illustrations by A. B. Wenzell. Indianapolis: The Bobbs-Merrill Company, [c1911]. 328 p., front., [4] leaves of plates.
LC: S 13, '11.

O-135   ____ Schmidt / by Lloyd Osbourne . . . ; illustrated by Allen True. New York: Thomas Y. Crowell & Co., [c1907]. 43 p., front., [3] leaves of plates.
LC: Je 12, '07.

O-136   ____ Three speeds forward: an automobile love story with one reverse / by Lloyd Osbourne. New York: D. Appleton and Company, 1906. 100 p., front., [2] leaves of plates, ill. [Ill. by Karl Anderson and Henry Hutt.]
LC: Jl 14, '06.
BLC: London: Chatto and Windus, 1907.

O-137   ____ The tin diskers: the story of an invasion that all but failed / by Lloyd Osbourne; with illustrations by F. L. Fithian. Philadelphia: Henry Altemus Company, [c1906]. 127 p., front., incl. [5] leaves of plates. Designed end papers.
LC: S 7, '06.

O-138   ____ Wild justice / by Lloyd Osbourne. New York: D. Appleton and Company, 1906. 296 p., front., [3] leaves of plates.
Contents: The renegade -- The security of the high seas -- Forty years between -- O's head -- Professor No No -- Captain Elijah Coe -- Mr. Bob -- Old Dibs -- The labor captain.
PW: F 17, '06.
BLC: London: William Heinemann, 1906.

O-139   Osgood, Grace R. (Grace Rose), b. 1881. At the sign of the Blue Anchor: a tale of 1776 / by Grace R. Osgood. Boston: The C. M. Clark Publishing Company, 1909. 304 p., front., [5] leaves of plates. [Ill. by D. S. Ross.]
LC: S 10, '09.

O-140   Osgood, Irene, 1875-1922. A blood-moon: and other tales of divorce / by Irene Osgood . . . New York: Broadway Publishing Co., 1911. 207 p.
TJC
Contents: A blood-moon -- Stories from the buhl cabinet: The woman who wanted to be private. The woman who disliked the country. The woman who went on the stage. The woman who was fond of French cookery. The woman who regretted-the cat. The woman who had to divorce. The woman who had made up her mind. The woman who returned to her first love. -- Stories from Algiers: The pale witch-queen. Sabeehad. A little life-tragedy in brown. A murder in the garden of the mosque. The eyes behind the veil. A moorish fete in Algiers.
LC: O 2, '11.
BLC: London: Everett and Company, 1911.

O-141   ____ Servitude / by Irene Osgood . . . Boston: Dana Estes & Company, [c1908]. 421 p.
LC: Je 29, '08.
BLC: London: Sigley's, 1908.

O-142   O'Shaughnessy, Edith, 1870-1939. Married life / by Edith O'Shaughnessy. New York: Harcourt, Brace and Company, [c1925]. 299 p.
Contents: Mr. Crane's last wife -- You never can tell -- Seeing Edward again -- Arthur Albion Street's illness -- Mr. Bishop -- Souls in intaglio.
LC: S 24, '25.
PW: S 26, '25.
BLC: London: Jonathan Cope, 1925.

O-143   ____ Viennese medley / by Edith O'Shaughnessy. New York: B. W. Huebsch, Inc., 1924. 295 p.
LC: O 24, '24.
PW: O 11, '24.
BLC: London: Jonathan Cope, 1925.

O'Shaughnessy, James. The king of the subdivision. In *Through the forbidden gates* (1903), T-222.

O-144   O'Shea, John J. (John Joseph), 1842-1920. That scamp, or, The days of Decatur in Tripoli / by John J. O'Shea . . . Philadelphia: H. L. Kilner & Co., [1905]. 150 p., ill.

O'Shea, Monica Barry. The descending mantle. In *The best college short stories, 1917-18* (1919), B-557.

O-145   Osia, N. H., 1866-1951, *pseud.* Hansu's journey: a Korean story / by N. H. Osia [pseud.]. Philadelphia: Copyrighted by Philip Jaisohn & Co., [1922]. 69 p.
AZS

O-146 Oskison, John M. (John Milton), 1874-1947. Wild harvest: a novel of transition days in Oklahoma / by John M. Oskison. New York; London: D. Appleton and Company, 1925. 299, [1] p.
PW: Ag 29, '25.

O-147 Osmun, Leighton Graves. The clutch of circumstance / by Leighton Graves Osmun. New York: Sully and Kleinteich, 1914. 320 p.
LC: Ja 10, '14.
PW: F 7, '14.

O-148 Ostenso, Martha, b. 1900. Wild geese / by Martha Ostenso. New York: Dodd, Mead and Company, 1925. 356 p. Illustrated end papers.
LC: O 23, '25.
PW: O 10, '25.

O-149 [Ostrander, Isabel], 1883-1924. Above suspicion / by Robert Orr Chipperfield [pseud.]. New York: Robert M. McBride & Company, 1923. 302 p.
LC: F 15, '23.
PW: Ja 6, '23.
BLC: London: Hurst & Blackett, [1923].

O-150 _____ Annihilation / by Isabel Ostrander. New York: R. M. McBride & Company, 1924. 310 p.
LC: Mr 10, '24.
PW: F 9, '24.
BLC: London: Hurst & Blackett, [1923].

O-151 [_____] Anything once / by Douglas Grant [pseud.]; frontispiece by Paul Stahr. New York: W. J. Watt & Company, [c1920]. 147 p., front.
LC: Ag 14, '20.

O-152 _____ Ashes to ashes / by Isabel Ostrander . . . New York: Robert M. McBride & Co., 1919. 333 p.
OSU, OCP
LC: D 1, '19.
PW: D 27, '19.
BLC: London: Hurst & Blackett, [1921].

O-153 _____ At one-thirty: a mystery / by Isabel Ostrander; illustrations by W. W. Fawcett. New York: W. J. Watt & Company, [c1915]. 302 p., front., [3] leaves of plates.
LC: Mr 2, '15.
PW: Ja 29, '16.
BLC: London: Simpkin, Marshall, and Company, 1916.

O-154 _____ The black joker / by Isabel Ostrander. New York: Robert M. McBride & Company, 1925. 361 p.
LC: N 18, '25.
PW: N 21, '25.
BLC: London: Hurst and Blackett, 1926.

O-155 [_____] Booty / by Douglas Grant [pseud.]; frontispiece by George W. Gage. New York: W. J. Watt & Company, [c1919]. 318 p., front.
LC: My 17, '19.
PW: Jl 5, '19.
BLC: London: Hurst and Blackett, 1921.

O-156 [_____] Bright lights / by Robert Orr Chipperfield [pseud.]. New York: Robert M. McBride & Company, 1924. 269 p.
LC: Mr 10, '24.
PW: Mr 1, '24.
BLC: London: Hurst and Blackett, 1924.

O-157 _____ The clue in the air: a detective story / by Isabel Ostrander . . . ; frontispiece by Paul Stahr. New York: W. J. Watt & Company, [c1917]. 316 p., front.
LC: N 14, '17.
PW: D 15, '17.
BLC: London: Skeffington & Son, [1920].

_____, jt. aut. The crevice (1915). See Burns, William John, 1861-1932, jt. aut., B-1260.

O-158 _____ The crimson blotter / by Isabel Ostrander. New York: Robert M. McBride & Company, 1921. 300 p.
LC: My 13, '21.
PW: My 14, '21.
BLC: London: Hurst and Blackett, 1921.

O-159 [_____] The doom dealer: an exploit of The Shadowers, Inc. / by David Fox [pseud.]. New York: Robert M. McBride & Company, 1923. 343 p.
LC: Je 19, '23.
PW: Jl 14, '23.

O-160 _____ Dust to dust / by Isabel Ostrander. New York: Robert M. McBride & Company, 1924. 340 p.
LC: Jl 9, '24.
PW: Je 28, '24.
BLC: London: Hurst and Blackett, 1924.

O-161 [_____] Ethel opens the door: an exploit of The Shadowers, Inc. / by David Fox [pseud.]. New York: Robert M. McBride & Company, 1922. 337 p.
LC: Ja 20, '22.
PW: F 18, '22.

O-162 [_____] The fifth ace / by Douglas Grant [pseud.]; frontispiece by George W. Gage. New York: W. J. Watt & Company, [c1918]. 314 p., front.
LC: Je 22, '18.
PW: S 7, '18.
BLC: London: Hurst and Blackett, 1921.

O-163 [_____] The handwriting on the wall: an exploit of the Shadowers, Inc. / by David Fox [pseud.]. New York: Robert M. McBride & Company, 1924. 313 p.
LC: Je 7, '24.
PW: Je 21, '24.

O-164 _____ The heritage of Cain / by Isabel Ostrander; illustrations by George W. Gage. New York: W. J. Watt & Company, [c1916]. 310 p., front., [1] leaf of plates.
LC: Ag 25, '16.
PW: O 21, '16.

O-165 _____ How many cards? / by Isabel Ostrander. New York: Robert M. McBride & Co., 1920. 314 p.
LC: N 10, '20.
PW: N 13, '20.
BLC: London: Hurst and Blackett, 1922.

O-166 _____ Island of intrigue / by Isabel Ostrander . . . ; illustrated. New York: Robert M. McBride & Co., 1918. 303 p., front. [Ill. by Herman Pfeifer.]
LC: N 21, '18.
PW: N 23, '18.
BLC: London: Skeffington & Son, [1919].

O-167 _____ Liberation / by Isabel Ostrander. New York: Robert M. McBride & Company, 1924. 278 p.
LC: N 20, '24.
PW: N 22, '24.

O-168 _____ McCarty incog / by Isabel Ostrander. New York: Robert M. McBride & Company, 1922. 307 p.
LC: N 15, '22.
PW: Ja 6, '23.
BLC: London: Hurst and Blackett, 1923.

O-169 [_____] The man in the jury box / by Robert Orr Chipperfield [pseud.]. New York: Robert M. McBride & Co., 1921. 324 p.
LC: F 8, '21.
PW: Mr 5, '21.
BLC: London: Hurst and Blackett, 1921.

O-170 [_____] The man who convicted himself / by David Fox [pseud.]. New York: Robert M. McBride & Co., 1920. 308 p.
LC: O 18, '20.
PW: Ag 28, '20.
BLC: London: Hurst and Blackett, 1923.

O-171 _____ The neglected clue / by Isabel Ostrander. New York: Robert M. McBride & Company, 1925. 301 p.
LC: Ap 23,' 25.
PW: My 9, '25.
BLC: London: Hurst and Blackett, 1925.

O-172 _____ The primal law / by Isabel Ostrander. New York: Mitchell Kennerley, 1915. 342 p.
LC: Mr 6, '15.
PW: F 20, '15.

O-173 [_____] The second bullet / by Robert Orr Chipperfield [pseud.]. New York: Robert M. McBride & Company, 1919. 280 p.
LC: Ap 8, '19.
PW: Ap 17, '20.
BLC: London: Skeffington and Son, [1920].

O-174 [_____] The single track / by Douglas Grant [pseud.]; frontispiece by Douglas Duer. New York: W. J. Watt & Company, [c1919]. 290 p., front.
LC: F 2, '20.
PW: Ja 10, '20.
BLC: London: Hurst and Blackett, 1922.

O-175 _____ Suspense / by Isabel Ostrander . . . New York:

Robert M. McBride & Co., 1918. 352 p.
LC: My 6, '18.
PW: My 11, '18.
BLC: London: Skeffington and Son, 1919.

O-176 _____ The tattooed arm / by Isabel Ostrander. New York: Robert M. McBride & Company, 1922, [c1921]. 278 p.
LC: Jl 14, '22.
PW: Jl 15, '22.
BLC: London: Hurst and Blackett, 1922.

O-177 [_____] The trigger of conscience / by Robert Orr Chipperfield [pseud.] . . . New York: Robert M. McBride & Company, 1921. 313 p.
LC: S 14, '21.
PW: S 24, '21.
BLC: London: Hurst and Blackett, 1922.

O-178 _____ The twenty-six clues / by Isabel Ostrander . . . New York: W. J. Watt & Company, [c1919]. 277 p.
LC: Mr 4, '19.
PW: Ap 5, '19.
BLC: London: Hurst and Blackett, 1921.

O-179 [_____] Two-gun Sue / by Douglas Grant [pseud.]. New York: Robert M. McBride & Company, 1922. 316 p.
LC: My 24, '22.
PW: Je 3, '22.
BLC: London: Hurst and Blackett, 1922.

O-180 [_____] Unseen hands / by Robert Orr Chipperfield [pseud.] . . . New York: Robert M. McBride & Co., 1920. 307 p.
LC: Je 26, '20.
PW: Jl 3, '20.
BLC: London: Hurst and Blackett, 1921.

O-181 [Ó Súilleabháin, Pronnséas]. The portion of a champion / by Francis o Sullivan tighe. New York: Charles Scribner's Sons, 1916. 368 p.

O-182 O'Sullivan, Denis, Mrs. Mr. Dimock / by Mrs. Denis O'Sullivan. New York: John Lane Company; London: John Lane, The Bodley Head, 1920. 365 p.
VHB

O'Sullivan, Elizabeth Curtis. <u>See</u> **O'Sullivan, Denis, Mrs.**

O-183 O'Sullivan, F. Dalton (Frank Dalton). Under the yoke: a book with a purpose / by F. Dalton O'Sullivan. Chicago: Lansing, Ltd., [c1921]. 301 p.

O'Sullivan, Vincent, 1872-1940. The Abigail Sheriff memorial. <u>In</u> *The Grim thirteen* **(1917), G-537.**

O-184 _____ The good girl / by Vincent O'Sullivan. Boston: Small, Maynard & Company, [1917]. 417 p.
LC: S 7, '17.
PW: Jl 6, '12.
BLC: London: Constable and Company, 1912. Second impression.

Another edition: New York: E. P. Dutton & Co., 1912. 313 p. **SUC**

_____ The interval. In *The best short stories of 1917 and the yearbook of the American short story* **(1918), B-562.**

_____ Master of fallen years. In *The best short stories of 1921 and the yearbook of the American short story* **(1922), B-566.**

O-185 _____ Sentiment / by Vincent O'Sullivan. Boston: Small, Maynard & Company, [c1917]. 312 p.
Contents: Sentiment -- The end of a family -- The Mormon -- Mrs. Turner -- A case of conscience -- Anna Vaddock's fame -- War declared -- The dark day -- The speculation in Mrs. Catling -- She married the vicar.
LC: N 12, '17.
PW: O 13, '17.
BLC: London: Duckworth & Company, 1913.

O-186 Otis, Alexander, 1867-1939. Hearts are trumps / by Alexander Otis. New York: The John McBride Co., 1909. 333 p., col. front. [Ill. by Richard H. Boehm.]
LC: Ap 12, '09.

O-187 _____ The man and the dragon / by Alexander Otis; with illustrations by J. V. McFall. Boston: Little, Brown and Company, 1910. 323 p., front., [3] leaves of plates.
LC: S 27, '10.

O-188 Otterbein, Anna M. (Anna Mary), b. 1866. A victim of his duty, or, a hero of the confessional / by Anna M. Otterbein; illustrated by H. Horina. Techny, Illinois: Printed by The Society of the Divine Word, [191-?] 62 p., ill. **NYP**

Ouimet, Frances. Out of the bunker. In *The Sporting spirit* **(1925), S-771.**

O-189 Our sister republic: a single tax story. New York: Cochrane Publishing Co., 1911. 54 p.

O-190 Oursler, Fulton, 1893-1952. Behold this dreamer! / by Fulton Oursler; illustrated by Frank Tenney Johnson and Delos Palmer, Jr. New York: The Macaulay Company, [c1924]. 320 p., front., [1] leaf of plates.
LC: Mr 21, '24.
PW: Mr 8, '24.
BLC: London: T. Fisher Unwin, 1924.

O-191 _____ Sandalwood / by Fulton Oursler . . . New York: The Macaulay Company, [c1925]. 316 p.
LC: Ap 15, '25.
PW: Ap 4, '25.
BLC: London: William Heinemann, 1925.

O-192 Overton, Grant Martin, 1887-1930. The answerer / by Grant Overton. New York: Harcourt, Brace and Company, 1921. 373 p.
LC: N 3, '21.
PW: N 12, '21.

O-193 _____ Island of the innocent / by Grant Overton.

New York: George H. Doran Company, [c1923]. 332 p.
LC: Mr 5, '23.
PW: Mr 10, '23.
BLC: London: Gyldendal, printed in U. S. A., 1923.

O-194 _____ Mermaid / by Grant M. Overton; frontispiece by Henry A. Botkin. Garden City, New York: Doubleday, Page & Company, 1920. 295, [1] p., col. front.
LC: Ja 29, '20.
PW: Ja 17, '20.

O-195 _____ The thousand and first night / by Grant Overton. New York: George H. Doran Company, [c1924]. 331 p.
LC: F 1, '24.
PW: Ja 26, '24.

O-196 _____ World without end / by Grant Overton. Garden City, N. Y.; Toronto: Doubleday, Page & Company, 1921. 317, [1] p. **AZU**
LC: Mr 19, '21.
PW: F 26, '21.

O-197 Overton, Gwendolen, b. 1876. Anne Carmel / by Gwendolen Overton; with illustrations by Arthur I. Keller. New York: The Macmillan Company; London: Macmillian & Co., Ltd., 1903. 335 p., front., [5] leaves of plates.
PW: Je 20, '03.

O-198 _____ Captains of the world / by Gwendolen Overton. New York: The Macmillan Company; London: Macmillan & Co., Ltd., 1904. 376 p.
PW: N 5, '04.

O-199 _____ The golden chain / by Gwendolen Overton. New York; London: The Macmillan Company, 1903. 100 p., front., [1] leaf of plates.
(Little novels of favourite authors.)
PW: O 24, '03.

O-200 _____ The heritage of unrest: [a novel] / by Gwendolen Overton. New York: The Macmillan Company; London: Macmillan & Co., Ltd., 1901. 329 p.
PW: Mr 2, '01.

_____ The race bond. In *Argonaut stories* **(1906), A-298.**

_____ The reaping of vanity. In *From the old pueblo: and other tales* **(1902), F-434.**

O-201 Ovington, Mary White, 1865-1951. The shadow / by Mary White Ovington . . . New York: Harcourt, Brace and Howe, 1920. 352 p. **NOC**
PW: Ap 3, '20.

O-202 Owen, Alice. The root of all evil / by Alice Owen. Broadway, N. Y.: Broadway Publishing Co., [c1909]. 114 p., front. (port.). **OWU**
LC: O 6, '09.
PW: N 20, '09.

O-203 [Owen, Belle], b. 1866. A prairie winter / by an Illinois girl [pseud.]. New York: The Outlook Company, 1903. 164 p. **UUM**
PW: Ap 4, '03.

Owen, Caroline Dale, pseud. <u>See</u> **Snedeker, Caroline Dale (Parker), Mrs., 1871-1956.**

O-204 Owen, Frank, b. 1893. The actress / by Frank Owen; frontispiece by Benjamin Robinson. N. Y. City: Broadway Publishing Co., [c1915]. 101 p., front.
Contents: The actress -- Bernice of Constantine -- The doormat.

O-205 Owen, Nellie H. (Nellie Huggins), 1854-1916. Short stories and poems / by Nellie H. Owen. Richmond, Virginia: Whittet & Shepperson, [c1909]. 129 p. Designed end papers. **EWF**
Contents: Barbara Carlyle -- Valley Farm -- My sister Madge -- From tenement walls -- "Elmwood" during the war.

O-206 Owen, Rye. Red-headed gill / by Rye Owen. New York: Henry Holt and Company, 1903. 347 p.
PW: Mr 28, '03.
BLC: Bristol: J. W. Arrowsmith, 1903.

Owie, B. P. John Hake, business gambler. <u>In</u> *Clever business sketches* **(1909), C-490.**

O-207 Owings, Osmond Young, Mrs. David's heritage: a novel / by Mrs. Osmond Young Owings . . . New York: The Cosmopolitan Press, 1914. 203, [1] p. **SUC**

O-208 ____ Phoebe; a novel / by Mrs. Osmond Young Owings. New York: The Cosmopolitan Press, 1912. 248 p. **SRC**
LC: My 13, '12.

O-209 Oxnam, Lois. Lillian Johnson / by Lois Oxnam; illustrated by Bromley Oxnam. Los Angeles, Calif.: [s. n.], 1904. 37 p., photo. front. (port.).

O-210 Oyen, Henry, 1883-1921. Big Flat / by Henry Oyen. New York: George H. Doran Company, [c1919]. 311 p. **NMT**
LC: Ap 16, '19.
PW: Ap 19, '19.
BLC: London: Hodder and Stoughton, printed in U. S. A., [1920].

O-211 ____ Gaston Olaf / by Henry Oyen. New York: George H. Doran Company, [c1917]. 294 p.
LC: O 6, '17.
PW: S 29, '17.

O-212 Oyen, Henry, 1883-1921. Joey the dreamer: a tale of Clay Court / by Henry Oyen. Garden City, N. Y.: Doubleday, Page & Company, 1911. 318 p.
LC: S 21, '11.
PW: O 7, '11.
BLC: London: Hodder and Stoughton; Garden City, N. Y., printed, 1911.

O-213 ____ The man-trail / by Henry Oyen . . . New York: George H. Doran Company, [c1915]. 289 p. Illustrated end papers.

LC: O 4, '15.
PW: O 2, ' 15.
BLC: London: Hodder and Stoughton, printed in U. S. A., 1916.

O-214 ____ The plunderer / by Henry Oyen . . . New York: George H. Doran Company, [c1920]. 295 p. **AZU**
LC: Mr 17, '20.
PW: Mr 20, '20.
BLC: London: Hodder and Stoughton, printed in U. S. A., [1920].

O-215 ____ The snow-burner / by Henry Oyen. New York: George H. Doran Company, [c1916]. 336 p. Illustrated end papers.
LC: N 15, '16.
PW: N 11, '16.
BLC: London: Hodder and Stoughton, 1917.

O-216 ____ Tarrant of Tin Spout / by Henry Oyen. New York: George H. Doran Company, [c1922]. 304 p.
LC: Ap 28, '22.
PW: My 6, '22.
BLC: London: Hodder and Stoughton, printed in U. S. A., [1922].

O-217 ____ Twisted trails / by Henry Oyen . . . New York: George H. Doran Company, [c1921]. 304 p. **CLU**
LC: Ap 2, '21.
BLC: London: Hodder and Stoughton, printed in U. S. A., [1921].

P

P-1 Pace, Charles Nelson, 1877-1954. The passion of Herman: a story of Oberammergau / by Charles Nelson Pace. New York; Cincinnati: The Abingdon Press, [c1918]. 106 p. **BGU**

P-2 Pacific Coast Women's Press Association. La copa de oro (The cup of gold): a collection of California poems, sketches and stories / by the members of the Pacific Coast Women's Press Association; edited by Abbie E. Krebs. [San Francisco, Cal.: Press of Geo. Spaulding & Company], 1905. 118 p., ill. (some photo.). Designed end papers. [Ill. by Geo. F. Mannel.]
Contents: The redwoods of California [nonfiction] / Abbie E. Krebs -- Fra Junipero Serra [poem] / Ella M. Sexton -- The lost maid of Tuolumne / Laura Young Pinney -- Lines, (And what has a man when it is all attained) [poem] / Madge Morris -- Glen Alpine / Josephine H. Foster -- Emblem of our association (The Eschscholtzia) [poem] / Anna Morrison Reed -- Reciprocity [nonfiction] / Clare O. Southard -- The wail of the unappreciated one [poem] / Lenore Congdon Schutze -- Quatrain [poem] / Grace Hibbard -- Rachelle / Augusta Friedrich Von Eichen -- California [poem] / Florence Richmond -- Miss Kid / Ruth Comfort Mitchell -- The shadow of the cross [poem] / Elizabeth Vore -- The power of the press [nonfiction] / Sophie E. Skidmore Gardiner -- California eve in winter [poem] / Rose L. Bushnell Donnelly -- On San Francisco Bay [poem] / Grace Hibbard -- Woodman, spare those trees [nonfiction] / Nellie Blessing Eyster -- The daughter of the West [poem] / Minora Ellis Kibbe -- The weariness of Jane / Anna Lansing Briggs -- Oak of Paso De Robles [poem] / Auguste N. Cahill -- California's first emigrant ship [nonfiction] / Emily S. Loud -- Eschscholtzia (Copa de oro) [poem] / Harriet M. Skidmore, "Marie" -- Mystic Lore [nonfiction] / Abbie E. Krebs -- God's curtain [poem] / Julia Patterson Churchill -- Nostalgia [nonfiction] / Harriet Howe -- They called the city "Oakland" / Emily C. Scaddan -- A soul's desire [poem] / Alice Kingsbury Cooley --

Lights and shades of an astronomical journey [nonfiction] / Rose O'Halloran -- A question and answer [poem] / Mary Cameron Benjamin -- A change [poem] / Martha McKim -- The revolt of Uncle Billy / Elizabeth Murray Newman -- El Camino Real [poem] / Ella M. Sexton -- Reindeer farming in the Land of the Midnight Sun [nonfiction] / Mary E. Hart -- Under [poem] / Hester G. Benedict -- Press women abroad [nonfiction] / Mary Garton Foster -- The song at the wheel [poem] / Amelia Woodward Truesdell -- Notes by the historian [nonfiction] / Sarah E. Reamer.

Paddock, Charles W. The man on the mark. In *The Sporting spirit* (1925), S-771.

P-3   Padelford, Frederick Morgan, 1875-1942. Samuel Osborne: janitor / by Frederick Morgan Padelford. Boston: LeRoy Phillips Publisher, [c1913]. 37 p.

P-4   Padon, Ella F. (Ella Florence). In charge of the consul / by Ella F. Padon . . . Boston: Richard G. Badger, 1907. 133 p.   **DLC**

P-5   Pafflow, Charles W. The mysteries of the Zímniy dvóretz (Winter Palace): a Russian historical novel / by Charles W. Pafflow. New York; Washington: The Neale Publishing Company, 1905. 292 p. **MNU**

P-6   Page, Isaac Marshall, b. 1885. "The Kentuckian"; or, "A woman's reaping" / written by Isaac Marshall Page. Paducah: Billings Printing Company, [c1916]. 133 p., plates, port.
Unexamined copy: bibliographic data from OCLC, #4018322.
LC: Ja 18, '17.

P-7   Page, Kate Nelson. Tommy Atkins episode and other stories / by Kate Nelson Page. New York; London; Montreal: The Abbey Press, [c1902]. 133 p., photo. front., [20] leaves of plates (1 photo.).
Contents: Tommy Atkins episode -- Donn Sancha's ring -- The tales of a sideboard.
PW: Jl 19, '02.

P-8   Page, Thomas Nelson, 1853-1922. Bred in the bone / by Thomas Nelson Page; illustrated. New York: Charles Scribner's Sons, 1904. 274 p., front., [7] leaves of plates. [Ill. by Harrison Fisher, F. C. Yohn, Fletcher C. Ransom, A. B. Frost, and Thomas Fogarty.]
Contents: Bred in the bone -- The spectre in the cart -- The sheriff's bluff -- The long hillside -- Old Jabe's marital experiments -- The Christmas peace -- Mam' Lyddy's recognition.
PW: Je 4, '04.
References: BAL 15393.

P-9   ____ Gordon Keith / by Thomas Nelson Page; with illustrations by George Wright. New York: Charles Scribner's Sons, 1903. 548 p., front., [7] leaves of plates.
PW: Je 27, '03.
BLC: London: William Heinemann, 1903.
References: BAL 15391.

P-10   ____ John Marvel, assistant / by Thomas Nelson Page; illustrated by James Montgomery Flagg. New York: Charles Scribner's Sons, 1909. 573 p., front., [7] leaves of plates.
LC: O 21, '09.
PW: O 16, '09.
BLC: London: T. Werner Laurie, 1910.

References: BAL 15407.

P-11   ____ The land of the spirit / by Thomas Nelson Page; illustrated. New York: Charles Scribner's Sons, 1913. 257 p., front., [7] leaves of plates. [Some ill. by N. C. Wyeth or Walter Biggs.]
Contents: The stranger's pew -- The old planters -- The stable of the inn -- The shepherd who watched the night -- The bigot -- The trick-doctor -- The outcast.
LC: Ap 22, '13.
PW: Ap 26, '13.
BLC: London: T. Werner Laurie, 1913.
References: BAL 15415.

P-12   ____ The red riders / by Thomas Nelson Page. New York: Charles Scribner's Sons, 1924. 338 p.
LC: S 19, '24.
PW: S 27, '24.
References: BAL 15428.

P-13   ____ The shepherd who watched by night / by Thomas Nelson Page. New York: Charles Scribner's Sons, [1916]. 39 p., front. First separate book appearance: reprinted from *The land of the spirit* (q. v.).
LC: S 14, '16.
PW: S 16, '16.
References: BAL 15443.

P-14   ____ The stranger's pew / by Thomas Nelson Page. New York: Charles Scribner's Sons, 1914. 21 p., front. [Ill. by Blendon Campbell.] First separate book appearance: reprinted from *The land of the spirit* (q. v.).
LC: S 1, '14.
PW: S 5, '14.
References: BAL 15442.

P-15   ____ Under the crust / by Thomas Nelson Page; illustrated. New York: Charles Scribner's Sons, 1907. 307 p., front., [7] leaves of plates. [Ill. by J. N. Marchand, N. C. Wyeth, F. E. Schoonover, Harrison Fisher, and Herman Pfeifer.]
LC: N 7, '07.
PW: N 23, '07.
References: BAL 15401.

Page, Walter Hines, 1855-1918. See **Worth, Nicholas, pseud.**

P-16   Pahlow, Gertrude, 1881-1937. The cross of heart's desire / by Gertrude Pahlow. New York; Duffield and Company, 1916. 296 p.
LC: S 2, '16.
PW: S 23, '16.
BLC: London: Methuen and Company, 1918.

P-17   ____ The gilded chrysalis: a novel / by Gertrude Pahlow. New York: Duffield & Company, 1914. 308 p., front. [Ill. by G. Willam Breck.]
LC: Ag 21, '14.
PW: Ag 29, '14.

P-18   ____ The glory of going on / by Gertrude Pahlow. New York: Duffield & Company, 1919. 306 p.
LC: Ag 23, '19.
PW: S 20, '19.

P-19   Paine, Albert Bigelow, 1861-1937. The commuters: the story of a little hearth and garden / by Albert Bigelow Paine . . . New York: J. F. Taylor & Company, 1904. 300 p., front., [3] leaves of plates. [Ill. by Florence Scovel Shinn.]
PW: Ap 2, '04.

P-20   ____ Dwellers in Arcady: the story of an abandoned farm / Albert Bigelow Paine; with illustrations by Thomas Fogarty. New York; London: Harper & Brothers, [1919]. 241, [1] p., front., [7] leaves of plates. Illustrated lining-papers.
LC: Ap 24, '19.
PW: Ap 26, '19.

P-21   ____ From van dweller to commuter: the story of a strenuous quest for a home and a little hearth and garden / by Albert Bigelow Paine. New York; London: Harper & Brothers, 1907. 416 p., front., [7] leaves of plates. [Ill. by Florence Scovel Shinn.]
PW: O 5, '07.

P-22   ____ The great white way: a record of an unusual voyage of discovery, and some romantic love affairs amid strange surroundings / The whole recounted by one Nicholas Chase, promoter of the expedition, whose reports have been arranged for publication by Albert Bigelow Paine; with drawings by Bernard J. Rosenmeyer, sketches by Chauncey Gale, and maps, etc., from Mr. Chase's notebook. New York: J. F. Taylor & Company, 1901. 327 p., front., [5] leaves of plates, ill., map.
PW: D 7, '01.

P-23   ____ The lucky piece: a tale of the north woods / by Albert Bigelow Paine; frontispiece in color. New York: The Outing Publishing Company, 1906. 250 p., col. front. [Ill. by The Decorative Designers.]
PW: Ap 21, '06.

P-24   ____ "Peanut": the story of a boy / by Albert Bigelow Paine. New York; London: Harper & Brothers, 1913. 69, [1] p., col. front. [Ill. by William Van Dresser.]
LC: O 13, '13.
PW: O 25, '13.

P-25   ____ Single reels / by Albert Bigelow Paine. New York; London: Harper & Brothers, [c1923]. 254 p., front., [14] leaves of plates. [Ill. by Peter Newell, Fred Strothmann, Clarence Rowe, and Albert Levering.]
Contents: Mrs. Tumulty's hat -- The toy of fate -- Murphy's kitchen -- A thwarted Pygmalion -- An ordeal of art -- Englishman's luck -- A knave of keys -- Reforming Julius -- Thoroughbreds for three days -- The Don't hurry club -- Being a landlord -- The meanness of Pinchett -- An excursion into memory -- The united workman -- Reforming Vermy -- An adventure in decoration -- Northwest by north -- The great Roundup vegetable drive -- Reserved seats -- Getting square with the laundry -- Sunday morning recreation -- Mr. Rabbit's home brew (a bedtime reel).
LC: My 7, '23.
PW: My 12, '23.

P-26   ____ The tent dwellers / by Albert Bigelow Paine . . . ; with illustrations by Hy. Watson. New York: The Outing Publishing Co., 1908. 280 p., ill.

LC: O 5, '08.
PW: O 24, '08.
BLC: London: Hodder and Stoughton, 1908.

P-27   ____ The van dwellers: a strenuous quest for a home / Albert Bigelow Paine. New York: J. F. Taylor & Company, 1901. 191 p., front., [3] leaves of plates. [Ill. by Florence Scovel Shinn.]
PW: O 12, '01.

P-28   Paine, Ralph Delahaye, 1871-1925. The adventures of Captain O'Shea / by Ralph D. Paine. New York: Charles Scribner's Sons, 1913. 424 p.
LC: S 16, '13.
PW: S 20, '13.

P-29   ____ The call of the offshore wind / by Ralph D. Paine; with illustrations. Boston; New York: Houghton Mifflin Company, 1918. 373, [1] p., front., [9] leaves of plates. [Ill. by Sears Gallagher.]
LC: O 1, '18.
PW: S 14, '18.
BLC: London: Constable and Company, Cambridge, Mass., printed, [1920].

P-30   ____ College years / by Ralph D. Paine; illustrated by Worth Brehm. New York: Charles Scribner's Sons, 1909. 356 p., front., [5] leaves of plates.
Contents: Peter Burnham, pitcher -- The martyrdom of an oarsman -- A case of "professionalism" -- The honor of the game -- The mollycoddle -- The Casselbury twins -- The freshman full-back -- "For dear old Yale" -- A very commonplace hero -- How Hector won his "Y" -- The pretenders.
LC: S 13, '09.
PW: S 11, '09.

P-31   ____ Four bells: a tale of the Caribbean / by Ralph D. Paine; with a frontispiece by Frank E. Schoonover. Boston; New York: Houghton Mifflin Company, 1924. (Cambridge: The Riverside Press). 337 p., front.
LC: Mr 5, '24.
PW: Mr 15, '24.
BLC: London: Hodder and Stoughton, 1924.

P-32   ____ The head coach / by Ralph D. Paine . . . ; illustrated by George Wright. New York: Charles Scribner's Sons, 1910. 293 p., front., [5] leaves of plates.
LC: Mr 30, '10.
PW: Ap 2, '10.

P-33   ____ In Zanzibar / by Ralph D. Paine. Boston; New York: Houghton Mifflin Company, 1925. 327 p.
LC: Je 11, '25.
PW: My 30, '25.
BLC: London: Hodder and Stoughton, [1925].

P-34   ____ J. Archibald McKackney: (collector of whiskers) being certain episodes taken from the diary and notes of that estimable gentleman-student and now for the first time set forth / edited by Ralph D. Paine; with illustrations by Wallace Morgan. New York: The Outing Publishing Company, 1907. 180 p., front.
LC: N 15, '07.
PW: N 23, '07.

P-35 ____ The judgments of the sea: and other stories / by Ralph D. Paine; illustrated. New York: Sturgis & Walton Company, 1912. 327 p., front., [3] leaves of plates. [Ill. by Walter Appleton Clark, W. J. Aylward, and Sydney Adamson.] Partly reprinted from various sources.
Contents: The judgements of the sea -- Captain Arendt's choice -- The praying skipper -- The master of the Ping Yang -- The whistling buoy -- The last pilot schooner -- Shipmates -- Dick Floyd, mate -- Sealed orders -- The surfman's holiday -- John Janvin, shipmaster -- Corporal Sweeney, deserter -- The jade teapot.
LC: My 10, '12.
PW: My 18, '12.

P-36 ____ The long road home / by Ralph D. Paine; illustrations by Alonzo Kimball. New York: Charles Scribner's Sons, 1916. 344 p., front., [3] leaves of plates.
LC: Mr 15, '16.
PW: Mr 18, '16.

P-37 ____ The praying skipper and other stories / by Ralph D. Paine; illustrated. New York: The Outing Publishing Company, 1906. 292 p., col. front., [5] leaves of plates. [Ill. by Joseph Christian Leyendecker, William James Aylward, and Walter Appleton Clark.]
Contents: The praying skipper -- A victory unforeseen -- Corporal Sweeney, deserter -- The last pilot schooner -- The jade teapot -- Captain Arendt's choice -- Surfman Brainard's "day off".
PW: My 5, '06.

P-38 ____ Ships across the sea: stories of the American navy in the Great War / by Ralph D. Paine; with illustrations. Boston; New York: Houghton Mifflin Company, 1920. 347 p., front., [3] leaves of plates. [Ill. by Stanley Rogers.]
Contents: The orphan and the battle-wagon -- Ten fathoms down -- Too scared to run -- The quiet life -- On a lee shore -- The net result -- The last shot -- The silent service -- The red sector.
LC: Ap 27, '20.
PW: My 1, '20.

P-39 ____ Sons of Eli / by Ralph D. Paine; illustrated. New York: Charles Scribner's Sons, 1917. 295 p., front., [3] leaves of plates. [Ill. by Griswold Tyng, G. Heyendecker, and F. C Yohn.]   **TMA**
Contents: A victory unforeseen -- Follow the ball -- "Sleepy" Jordan -- The letter of the law -- Getting his goat -- The Indian -- The vengeance of Antonio -- A transaction with Shylock -- His code of honor.
PW: S 22, '17.

P-40 ____ The steam-shovel man / by Ralph D. Paine . . . ; illustrated by B. J. Rosenmeyer. New York: Charles Scribner's Sons, 1913. 212 p., col. front., [3] leaves of plates.
LC: Ag 27, '13.
PW: Ag 30, '13.

P-41 ____ The story of Martin Coe / by Ralph D. Paine . . . ; illustrated by Howard Giles. New York: The Outing Publishing Co., 1906. 404 p., col. front., [5] leaves of plates.
LC: S 15, '06.
PW: O 6, '06.
BLC: London: Hodder and Stoughton, 1907.

P-42 ____ The stroke oar / by Ralph D. Paine . . . ; illustrated by Walter J. Enright. New York: The

Outing Publishing Company, 1908. 245, [1] p., front., [3] leaves of plates.
LC: N 16, '08.
PW: D 12, '08.

P-43 ____ The twisted skein / by Ralph D. Paine; illustrated by H. Howland. New York: Charles Scribner's Sons, 1915. 311 p., front., [3] leaves of plates.
LC: S 14, '15.
PW: S 18, '15.

P-44 ____ The wall between / by Ralph D. Paine; illustrations by Alonzo Kimball. New York: Charles Scribner's Sons, 1914. 340 p., front., [3] leaves of plates.
LC: Ag 27, '14.
PW: Ag 29, '14.

Painter, Lydia Ethel (Farmer), Mrs. See G. E. X.

P-45 Palatianos, Dorothy. When he found himself / Dorothy Palatianos. Columbus, Ohio: The Heer Press, 1918. 233 p., photo. front.

P-46 Palen, Lewis Stanton, b. 1876. The White Devil of the Black Sea / by Lewis Stanton Palen. New York: Minton, Balch & Company, 1924. 298 p., front.
BLC: London: John Lane, 1924.

P-47 Pallen, Condé Bénoist, 1858-1929. Crucible Island: a romance, an adventure and an experiment / by Condé B. Pallen. New York: The Manhattanville Press, [c1919]. 215 p.
LC: Jl 12, '19.
BLC: London: Harding and More, 1920.

P-48 Palmer, Bell Elliott, b. 1873. The single-code girl: a novel / by Bell Elliott Palmer; frontispiece by Chase Emerson. Boston: Lothrop, Lee & Shepard, [1915]. 382 p., col. front.
LC: S 10, '15.
PW: S 18, '15.

P-49 Palmer, Frederick, 1873-1958. The big fellow / by Frederick Palmer . . . ; illustrated by M. Leone Bracker. New York: Moffat, Yard and Company, 1908. 513 p., front., [3] leaves of plates.
LC: S 2, '08.
PW: S 12, '08.
BLC: London: Everett and Company, Rahway, N. J. [printed], 1910.

P-50 ____ Danbury Rodd, aviator / by Frederick Palmer; illustrated. New York: Charles Scribner's Sons, 1910. 310 p., front., [7] leaves of plates. [Ill. by F. C. Yohn.]
LC: My 5, '10.
PW: My 7, '10.

P-51 ____ Invisible wounds / by Frederick Palmer. New York: Dodd, Mead and Company, 1925. 328 p.
LC: Mr 18, '25.
PW: Mr 21, '25.
BLC: London: John Lane, 1925.

P-52   ____ The last shot / by Frederick Palmer. New York: Charles Scribner's Sons, 1914. 517 p.
LC: Ap 28, '14.
PW: My 2, '14.
BLC: London: Chapman Hall, New York [printed], 1914.

P-53   ____ Lucy of the stars / by Frederick Palmer; illustrated by Alonzo Kimball. New York: Charles Scribner's Sons, 1906. 344 p., front., [3] leaves of plates.
PW: My 5, '06.
BLC: London: T. Werner Laurie, 1906.

P-54   ____ The old blood / by Frederick Palmer . . . New York: Dodd, Mead and Company, 1916. 390 p.
LC: O 23, '16.
PW: O 28, '16.
BLC: London: John Murray, 1916.

P-55   ____ Over the pass / by Frederick Palmer . . . New York: Charles Scribner's Sons, 1912. 438 p.
LC: Ap 30, '12.
PW: Ap 27, '12.

    ____ The return. In *Allegheny stories* (1902), **A-142.**

P-56   ____ The vagabond / by Frederick Palmer; illustrated by Harrison Fisher. New York: Charles Scribner's Sons, 1903. 476 p., front., [5] leaves of plates.
PW: S 5, '03.

P-57   ____ The ways of the service / by Frederick Palmer; illustrated by Howard Chandler Christy. New York: Charles Scribner's Sons, 1901. 340 p., front., [5] leaves of plates.
Contents: Ballard -- The romance of Private Saunders -- As man to man -- A battle and a quarrel -- Against his own people -- Marrying out of the army -- The taming of the captain -- Mrs. Gerlison's own story.
PW: Ap 20, '01.

P-58 Palmer, Katherine Stedman. The fat frog of Pau / by Katherine Stedman Palmer. New York: The Neale Publishing Company, 1919. 26 p.   **NGU**

P-59 Palmer, Mary A. (Mary Arleville), b. 1893. Marian: a story of the South / by Mary A. Palmer. New York: The Neale Publishing Company, 1917. 251 p.   **TNS**
LC: S 20, '17.
PW: S 15, '17.

P-60 Palmer, Olin Austin. At the mercy of fate: a tale of the Shenandoah Valley / by Olin Austin Palmer; with illustrations. Port Republic, Va.: Advance Press, [c1912]. 220 p., front., [3] leaves of plates. [Ill. by Ellwood Frey.]

P-61 Palmer, Sara C. (Sara Currie), b. 1880. The competing artists / by Sara C. Palmer . . . Chicago: The Bible Institute Colportage Ass'n., [c1918]. 126 p., ill.   **OSU, CBC**
LC: O 26, '18.

P-62   ____ Donald Campbell's loyalty / by Sara C. Palmer . . . Chicago: The Bible Institute Colportage Ass'n, [c1921]. 177 p., incl. [5] plates. [Ill. by D. Melvill.]   **TCT**
LC: D 27, '21.

Palmerton, Paul. Rhyolitic Perlite. In *A book of narratives* (1917), **B-734.**

P-63 Pancake, Edmund Blair. Miss New York / by Edmund Blair Pancake; illustrated by W. E. B. Starkweather. New York: R. F. Fenno and Company, [c1906]. 305 p., col. front., col. plates.
Unexamined copy: bibliographic data from OCLC, #19829432.

P-64 Pangborn, Frederic Werden, b. 1855. The silent maid: being the story of Stille Mægth, her strange bewitchment and her wondrous song, and how she came to love a mortal man / by Frederic Werden Pangborn. Boston: L. C. Page & Company, 1903. 223 p., incl. front. [Ill. by Frank T. Merrill.]
PW: Je 6, '03.

P-65 Pangborn, Georgia Wood, b. 1872. Interventions / by Georgia Wood Pangborn. New York: Charles Scribner's Sons, 1911. 410 p.
Contents: A tempered wind -- The rubber stamp -- Broken glass -- A dispensation -- The experimenter -- The gray collie -- Rasselas in the vegetable kingdom -- Martha -- E. Holbrook's patience -- The convalescence of Gerald -- Son of the woods -- Turned out to grass -- By the Sawyer method -- At Ephesus.
LC: O 14, '11.
PW: O 14, '11.

P-66   ____ Roman Biznet / by Georgia Wood Pangborn. Boston; New York: Houghton, Mifflin and Company, 1902. (Cambridge: The Riverside Press). 280 p., front. [Ill. by Alice Barber Stephens.]
PW: My 3, '02.

P-67 Pansy, 1841-1930, *pseud.* David Ransom's watch / by Pansy [pseud.] (Mrs. G. R. Alden) . . . ; illustrated. Boston: Lothrop, Lee & Shepard Co., [1905, c1904]. 354 p., front., [3] leaves of plates. [Ill. by Ernest Fosbery.]
PW: Je 10, '05.

P-68   ____ Four mothers at Chautauqua / by Pansy [pseud.] . . . ; illustrated from photographs. Boston: Lothrop, Lee & Shepard Co., [1913]. 408 p., photo. front. (port.), [15] leaves of photo. plates.
PW: Ag 9, '13.

P-69   ____ The long way home / by Pansy [pseud.] . . . ; illustrated by Elizabeth Withington. Boston: Lothrop, Lee & Shepard Co., [1912]. 428 p., front., plates.
Unexamined copy: bibliographic data from NUC.
LC: S 6, '12.
PW: Ag 31, '12.

P-70   ____ Lost on the trail / by Pansy [pseud.] . . . ; illustrated by Elizabeth Withington. Boston: Lothrop, Lee & Shepard Co., [1911]. 466 p., front., [3] leaves of plates.   **WOO**
LC: Mr 13, '11.
PW: Ap 15, '11.

P-71   ____ Mara / by Pansy [pseud.] (Mrs. G. R. Alden) . . . ; illustrated. Boston: Lothrop Publishing Company, [1903, c1902]. 341 p., front., [3] leaves of plates. [Ill. by Ernest Fosbery.]
PW: Je 13, '03.

P-72   ____ Ruth Erskine's son / by Pansy [pseud.] . . . ; illustrated by Louise Clark. Boston: Lothrop, Lee & Shepard Co., [1907], c1906]. 399 p., front., [3] leaves of plates.
LC: Ja 23, '08.
PW: O 5, '07.

P-73   ____ Unto the end / by Pansy [pseud.] (Mrs. G. R. Alden) . . . ; illustrated. Boston: Lothrop Publishing Company, [1902]. 365 p., front., [2] leaves of plates. [Ill. by Chase Emerson.]
PW: Je 7, '02.

P-74 Parish, John Carl, 1881-1939. The man with the iron hand / by John Carl Parish. Boston; New York: Houghton Mifflin Company, 1913. (Cambridge, [Mass.]: The Riverside Press). 288 p. (True tales of the Great valley).
LC: O 13, '13.
PW: O 18, '13.

Park, Charles Caldwell, 1860-1931. See **Gray, Carl, pseud.**

Park, Edward C. Happily ever after. In *Made to order* **(1915), M-352.**

P-75 Park, J. Edgar (John Edgar), 1879-1956. How I spent my million: a Christmas story / by J. Edgar Park. Boston; New York; Chicago: The Pilgrim Press, [c1913]. 65 p., ill.
PW: N 8, '13.

P-76   ____ The man who missed Christmas / by John Edgar Park. Boston; New York; Chicago: The Pilgrim Press, [c1911]. 31 p.   **IFH**

P-77   ____ The rejuvenation of Father Christmas / by J. Edgar Park. Boston; New York; Chicago: The Pilgrim Press, [c1914]. 67 p., ill. (some col.). [Ill. by H. Boylston Dummer.]   **BRL**
PW: O 24, '14.

P-78 Parke, J. Richardson (Joseph Richardson), 1854-1938. The wizard of the Damavant: a tale of the Crusades / by J. Richardson Parke; twenty-eight illustrations. Philadelphia: Professional Publishing Company, 1910. 445 p., [4] leaves of plates (1 port.).
LC: N 7, '10.

P-79 Parker, Austin. Here's to the gods / by Austin Parker. -- [1st ed.] -- New York; London: Harper & Brothers, [c1923]. 326 p.
LC: O 12, '23.
PW: O 27, '23.

Parker, C. A. The right Mr. Brown. In *Stockman stories* **(1913), S-956.**

P-80 Parker, Clarence Prentice. Angels unaware / by Clarence Prentice Parker. Louisville: Press of Geo. G. Fetter Company, [c1912]. 240 p.

P-81 Parker, Cornelia Stratton, b. 1885. Jenny the joyous / by Cornelia Stratton Parker . . . New York: Harcourt, Brace and Company, [c1924]. 330 p.
PW: My 24, '24.

Parker, Dorothy, contributor. <u>See</u> *Bobbed hair* **(1925), B-700.**

P-82 Parker, Dudrea. Pig iron: short stories / by Dudrea Parker (Mrs. Sumner Parker). Printed in the U. S. A. at Baltimore: The Norman Remington Company, 1921. 103 p.
Contents: An ephemeral love -- The white petal -- The reporter.
LC: F 7, '22.

P-83 Parker, Fitzgerald Sale, 1863-1936. Provincetown: a story: (for the most part true) / by Fitzgerald Sale Parker . . . Nashville, Tenn.: Cokesbury Press, 1924. 144 p.   **TJC**

P-84 Parker, Frances. Hope Hathaway: a story of western ranch life / by Frances Parker. Boston, Mass: C. M. Clark Publishing Co. (Inc.), 1904. 408 p., col. front., [9] leaves of plates.
PW: D 10, '04.

P-85   ____ Marjie of the lower ranch / by Frances Parker. Boston: C. M. Clark Publishing Co., 1903. 393 p., front., [7] leaves of col. plates. [Ill. by Victor A. Searles.]
PW: O 3, '03.

P-86   ____ Winding waters: the story of a long trail and stong hearts / by Frances Parker. Boston: The C. M. Clark Publishing Company, 1909. 398 p., front., [4] leaves of plates. [Ill. by John Goss.]
LC: O 30, '09.
PW: N 20, '09.

P-87 Parker, George A. (George Augustus), 1875-1915. Out of the depths / by George A. Parker; with illustrations by Alfredo L. Demorest. Boston, Massachusetts: Reid Publishing Company, [c1908]. 270 p., front., [2] leaves of plates.

P-88 Parker, Leslie. Big Jim Albright / by Leslie Parker. -- 1st. ed. -- Brooklyn, New York: C. F. Fraser Co., 1924. 435 p.   **DLC**
LC: Ag 29, '24.
PW: S 20, '24.

P-89 Parker, Lottie Blair. Homespun: a story of some New England folk / by Lottie Blair Parker. New York: Henry Holt and Company, 1909. 380 p.
LC: My 25, '09.
PW: Je 19, '09.

P-90 Parker, Mary Moncure. A girl of Chicago / by Mary Moncure Parker . . . New York; Chicago; London: F. Tennyson Neely Co., 1901. 140 p.   **IUA**
PW: Ag 17, '01.

P-91   Parker, Nellie Lowe. A woman of sorrows; an osteopathic novel, beginning at the time of the 1908 convention. Kirksville, Mo.: Journal Printing Company, 1913. 252 p.
Unexamined copy: bibliographic data from LC.
LC: Ag 5, '13.

P-92   Parker, Prescott Alphonson, b. 1860. Tom and Kitty, a story of Mobile Bay / by Prescott A. Parker. Volanta, Ala.: P. A. Parker [c1908]. 101 p., incl. plates.
Unexamined copy: bibliographic data from OCLC, #4913407.
LC: D 12, '08.

P-93   Parker, Richard. Just a woman / by Richard Parker; based on the drama by Eugene Walter . . . ; illustrated with scenes from the photoplay starring Conway Tearle, Clair Windsor, Percy Marmont, a First National Picture. New York: The Macaulay Company, [c1916]. 321 p., photo. front., [3] leaves of photo. plates.   **UMC**
LC: S 20, '16.
PW: S 9, '16.

P-94   _____ Three knots: a mystery / by Richard Parker. New York: The Macaulay Company, [c1924]. 314 p.
LC: O 8, '24.
PW: O 25, '24.

P-95   _____ Today: a novel / by Richard Parker; from the drama by George Broadhurst and Abraham S. Schomer. New York: The Macaulay Company, 1914. 304 p., col. front., [5] leaves of col. plates.
LC: Ap 27, '14.
PW: My 9, '14.

P-96   _____ Under fire / by Richard Parker; based on the drama of Roi Cooper Megrue. New York: The Macaulay Company, 1916. 317 p., photo. front., [7] leaves of photo. plates.
LC: Mr 20, '16.
PW: Ap 1, '16.

P-97   _____ The whip / by Richard Parker; novelized from Cecil Raleigh's great Drury Lane melodrama; illustrated with pictures from the play. New York: The Macaulay Company, 1913. 314 p., photo. front., [5] leaves of photo. plates.
LC: My 21, '13.
PW: My 31, '13.
BLC: London: Holden & Hardingham, [1916].

Parker, Sumner, Mrs. See **Parker, Dudrea.**

Parker, William Hendrix. See **Rekrap, pseud.**

P-98   Parkes, Anna L. The unconscious influence / by Mrs. Anna L. Parkes. Boston, Massachusetts: The Stratford Company, 1924. 224 p.

Parkinson, Robert Lincoln, jt. aut. _The Christian pirate_ (1911). See **Warren, Benjamin Clark, jt. aut., W-150.**

P-99   Parks, Leighton, 1852-1938. English ways and by-ways: being the letters of John and Ruth Dobson written from England to their friend, Leighton Parks. New York: Charles Scribner's Sons, 1920. 232 p.

Parks, Mabel E., b. 1862. See **Mabel, pseud.**

P-100   Parr, Walter Robinson, b. 1871. Unrest: a story of the struggle for bread / W. R. Parr . . . Boston: Richard G. Badger; Toronto: The Copp Clark Co., Limited. 191 p.

Parrack, J. B. See **Kain, Kress, pseud.**

P-101   Parrish, Anne, 1888-1957. Lustres / by Anne and Dillwyn Parrish. New York: George H. Doran Company on Murray Hill, [c1924]. 215 p.   **AZU**
Contents: The bishop and the butterfly -- The shopkeeper -- The snare -- The wood beyond the world -- The crab -- The big blue cap -- Star dust -- Of course -- Departure of the hero -- A picnic in Turkey -- Grubb -- Open the gates -- Fame -- "Whosoever shall receive this child" -- A few notes on my master by his gardener -- "Then cherish pity" -- The ferry-boat -- Modest Jones -- The little brothers.
LC: Ap 22, '24.
PW: Ap 19, '24.

P-102   _____ The perennial bachelor / by Anne Parrish . . . -- 1st ed. -- New York; London: Harper & Brothers, 1925. 334 p.
LC: Ag 26, '25.
PW: Ag 29, '25.
BLC: London: William Heinemann, 1926.

P-103   _____ A pocketful of poses / by Anne Parrish. New York: George H. Doran Company, [c1923]. 320 p.   **DLM**
LC: Mr 5, '23.
PW: Mr 17, '23.
BLC: London: Hodder & Stoughton, printed in U. S. A., [1923].

P-104   _____ Semi-attached / by Anne Parrish. New York: George H. Doran Company, [c1924]. 288 p.
LC: O 22, '24.
PW: O 25, '24.
BLC: London: Brentano's, printed in U. S. A., [1926].

Parrish, Dillwyn, b. 1894, jt. aut. _Lustres_ (1924). See **Parrish, Anne, 1888-1957, jt. aut., P-101.**

P-105   Parrish, Randall, 1858-1923. The air pilot: a modern love story / by Randall Parrish; illustrated by Clarence F. Underwood. Chicago: A. C. McClurg & Co., 1913. 318 p., col. front., [2] leaves of col. plates.
LC: Ap 23, '13.
PW: My 3, '13.
BLC: London: C. F. Cazenove; Chicago: A. C. McClurg & Co., 1913.

P-106   _____ Beth Norvell: a romance of the West / by Randall Parrish; with frontispiece in color by N. C. Wyeth. Chicago: A. C. McClurg & Co., 1907. 341 p., col. front.
LC: S 26, '07.
PW: S 21, '07.

BLC: London: G. P. Putnam's Sons; Cambridge, U. S. A. [printed], 1907.

P-107 _____ Beyond the frontier: a romance of early days in the Middle West / by Randall Parrish . . . ; illustrated by the Kinneys. Chicago: A. C. McClurg & Co., 1915. 406 p., front., [1] leaf of plates.
LC: O 12, '15.
PW: O 23, '15.
BLC: London: C. F. Cazenove; A. C. McClurg & Co., Chicago [printed], 1915.

P-108 _____ Bob Hampton of Placer / by Randall Parrish; illustrated by Arthur I. Keller. Chicago: A. C. McClurg & Co., 1906. 383 p., col. front., [3] leaves of col. plates.
LC: S 27, '06.
PW: S 22, '06.
BLC: London: G. P. Putnam's Sons; Chicago [printed], 1906.

P-109 _____ The case and the girl / by Randall Parrish. New York: Alfred A. Knopf, 1922. 343 p.
LC: Ap 13, '22.
PW: F 25, '22.
BLC: London: Stanley Paul & Co., [1923].

P-110 _____ Comrades of peril / by Randall Parrish . . . ; frontispiece by J. Allen St. John. Chicago: A. C. McClurg & Co., 1919. 349 p., col. front.
LC: O 27, '19.
PW: N 22, '19.

P-111 _____ "Contraband": a romance of the north Atlantic / by Randall Parrish. Chicago: A. C. McClurg & Co., 1916. 428, [1] p., front., [2] leaves of plates. [Ill. by the Kinneys.]
LC: O 23, '16.
PW: N 4, '16.
BLC: London: Curtis Brown, A. C. McClurg & Co.; Chicago [printed], 1916.

P-112 _____ The devil's own: a romance of the Black Hawk War / by Randall Parrish . . . ; illustrations by the Kinneys. Chicago: A. C. McClurg & Co., 1917. 356 p., front., [2] leaves of plates.
LC: O 30, '17.
PW: N 24, '17.

P-113 _____ Don MacGrath: a tale of the river / by Randall Parrish . . . ; illustrated by John W. Norton. Chicago: A. C. McClurg & Co., 1910. 269 p., front., [4] leaves of plates.
LC: O 3, '10.

P-114 _____ Gift of the desert / by Randall Parrish . . . ; frontispiece by J. Allen St. John. Chicago: A. C. McClurg & Co., 1922. 305 p., front.
LC: Ag 29, '22.
PW: S 9, '22.
BLC: London: T. Fisher Unwin, 1923.

P-115 _____ Gordon Craig, soldier of fortune / by Randall Parrish; illustrated by Alonzo Kimball. Chicago: A. C. McClurg and Co., 1912. 366 p., col. front., [3] leaves of col. plates.

LC: N 1, '12.
PW: N 16, '12.

P-116 _____ Keith of the border: a tale of the plains / by Randall Parrish . . . ; with four illustrations in full color by W. Herbert Dunton. Chicago: A. C. McClurg & Co., 1910. 362 p., col. front., [3] leaves of col. plates.   **UUO**
LC: S 26, '10.
PW: O 8, '10.

P-117 _____ The last voyage of the Donna Isabel; a romance of the sea / by Randall Parrish; illustrated in full color by Allen T. True. Chicago: A. C. McClurg & Co., 1908. 366 p., col. front., [3] leaves of col. plates. Illustrated end papers.
LC: S 14, '08.
PW: Ag 29, '08.
BLC: London: G. P. Putnam's Sons, Cambridge, U. S. A. [printed], 1908.

P-118 _____ Love under fire / by Randall Parrish; with five illustrations in full color by Alonzo Kimball. Chicago: A. C. McClurg & Co., 1911. 400 p., col. front., [4] leaves of col. plates. Designed end papers.
LC: Mr 29, '11.
PW: Ap 1, '11.

P-119 _____ The maid of the forest: a romance of St. Clair's defeat / by Randall Parrish; illustrated by Frank E. Schoonover. Chicago: A. C. McClurg & Co., 1913. 427, [1] p., col. front., [4] leaves of col. plates.
LC: S 29, '13.
PW: O 25, '13.
BLC: London: C. F. Cazenove, Chicago [printed], 1913.

P-120 _____ Molly McDonald: a tale of the old frontier / by Randall Parrish; with four illustrations by Ernest L. Blumenschein. Chicago: A. C. McClurg & Co., 1912. 403, [1] p., col. front., [3] leaves of col. plates.
LC: Ap 22, '12.
PW: My 11, '12.

P-121 _____ My lady of doubt / by Randall Parrish; with four illustrations in full color by Alonzo Kimball. Chicago: A. C. McClurg and Co., 1911. 381 p., col. front., [3] leaves of col. plates.
LC: O 18, '11.
PW: N 4, '11.

P-122 _____ My lady of the North: the love story of a gray-jacket / by Randall Parrish. Chicago: A. C. McClurg & Co., 1904. 362 p., col. front., [3] leaves of col. plates. [Ill. by E. M. Ashe.]
PW: O 22, '04.
BLC: London: C. F. Cazenove, Cambridge, U. S. A. [printed], 1904.

P-123 _____ My lady of the South: a story of the civil war / by Randall Parrish; illustrated in full color by Alonzo Kimball. Chicago: A. C. McClurg & Co., 1909. 360 p., col. front., [3] leaves of col. plates.
LC: O 6, '09.
PW: O 9, '09.
BLC: London: G. P. Putnam's Sons, printed in U. S. A., 1909.

P-124 _____ The mystery of the silver dagger / by Randall Parrish . . . New York: George H. Doran Company, [c1920]. 273 p.
LC: Je 9, '20.
PW: Mr 20, '20.
BLC: London: Hodder & Stoughton, printed in U. S. A., [1920].

P-125 _____ Prisoners of chance: the story of what befell Geoffrey Benteen, borderman, through his love for a lady of France / by Randall Parrish; illustrated in full color by the Kinneys. Chicago: A. C. McClurg & Co., 1908. 423 p., col. front., [3] leaves of col. plates.
LC: Mr 16, '08.
PW: Ap 4, '08.
BLC: London: G. P. Putnam's Sons, Cambridge, U. S. A. [printed], 1908.

P-126 _____ The red mist: a tale of civil strife / by Randall Parrish; illustrated by Alonzo Kimball. Chicago: A. C. McClurg & Co., 1914. 401 p., col. front., [3] leaves of col. plates.
LC: O 2, '14.
PW: O 10, '14.
BLC: London: C. F. Cazenove, Chicago [printed], 1914.

P-127 _____ Shea of the Irish brigade: a soldier's story / by Randall Parrish; frontispiece in color by Alonzo Kimball. Chicago: A. C. McClurg & Co., 1914. 342, [1] p., double col. front.
LC: Mr 27, '14.
PW: Ap 11, '14.
BLC: London: C. F. Cazenove; A. C. McClurg & Co.; Chicago [printed], 1914.

P-128 _____ The strange case of Cavendish / by Randall Parrish . . . New York: George H. Doran Company, [c1918]. 310 p.
PW: Mr 29, '19.
BLC: London: Hodder & Stoughton, printed in U. S. A., 1919.

P-129 _____ A sword of the old frontier: a tale of Fort Chartres and Detroit: being a plain account of sundry adventures befalling Chevalier Raoul de Coubert, one time captain in the Hussars of Languedoc, during the year 1763 / by Randall Parrish . . . ; illustrated by F. C. Yohn. Chicago: A. C. McClurg & Co., 1905. 407 p., col. front., [3] leaves of col. plates.
PW: N 4, '05.
BLC: London: C. F. Cazenove; Chicago: A. C. McClurg, 1905.

P-130 _____ When wilderness was king: a tale of the Illinois country / by Randall Parrish; with six pictures in full color and other decorations by Troy and Margaret West Kinney. Chicago: A. C. McClurg & Co., 1904. 387, [1] p., col. front., [5] leaves of col. plates. Illustrated end papers.
PW: Ap 2, '04.
BLC: London: C. F. Cazenove, Cambridge, U. S. A. [printed], 1904.

P-131 _____ Wolves of the sea: being a tale of the colonies from the manuscript of one Geoffry Carlyle, seaman, narrating certain strange adventures which befell him aboard the pirate craft "Namur" / by Randall Parrish; frontispiece by Frank E. Schoonover. Chicago: A. C. McClurg & Co., 1918. 355 p., front.
LC: O 2, '18.
PW: O 26, '18.

_____ Your lad, and my lad. In *Prairie gold* (1917), **P-588.**

P-132 Parrish-Wright, Clara, b. 1861. An up-to-date courtship / by Clara Parrish-Wright. New York: Cochrane Publishing, Co., 1909. 160 p., photo. front. (port.), [1] leaf of photo. plates.   **NYP**
LC: D 17, '09.

P-133 Parry, David Maclean, 1852-1915. The scarlet empire / by David M. Parry; with illustrations by Hermann C. Wall. Indianapolis: The Bobbs-Merrill Company, [c1906]. 400 p., col. front., [9] leaves of col. plates.
PW: Mr 17, '06.

P-134 Parry, Thomas Wood. When daddy was a boy / by Thomas Wood Parry; illustrated by H. Wood. Kansas City, Mo.: Franklin Hudson Publishing Company, 1907. 280 p., incl. front., ill.

P-135 Parshley, Matilda Clark (Allen), b. 1880. Letters to father / M. A. Parshley . . . [Marion?, Mass.: s.n.], c1911. 19 p.   photocopy
LC: F 24, '11.

P-136 Parson, Kirk. A fast game / by Kirk Parson. Boston: The Roxburgh Publishing Company (Incorporated), [c1910]. 343 p., photo. front.
LC: Jl 29, '10.
PW: Ag 6, '10.

P-137 _____ On the mountain division / by Kirk Parson. New York: Eaton & Mains; Cincinnati: Jennings & Graham, [c1903]. 255 p., front., [3] leaves of plates. [Ill. by Davis (i.e., W. B. Davis).]
PW: My 2, '03.

P-138 Parsons, Caroline. Esther Hills, housemaid / by Caroline Parsons. New York; London; Montreal: The Abbey Press, [c1901]. 198 p., front.
PW: D 28, '01.

P-139 Parsons, Cornelia Mitchell. The Quaker cross: a story of the old Bowne house / by Cornelia Mitchell Parsons . . . New York: National Americana Society, 1911. 342 p., front., [7] leaves of plates (some photo.).

P-140 Parsons, Marion Randall. A daughter of the dawn / by Marion Randall Parsons. Boston: Little, Brown, and Company, 1923. 287 p.
LC: Ap 30, '23.
PW: Ap 21, '23.
BLC: London: Geoffrey Bles, 1924.

P-141   Partridge, William Ordway, 1861-1930. The czar's
         gift / by William Ordway Partridge . . . ; illustrated
         by Victor Perard. New York; London: Funk &
         Wagnalls Company, 1906. 46 p., ill.
         LC: Jl 3, '06.

P-142   Parvis, Gladys. The street of the seven little sisters; a
         tale of old Cairo and the great desert / by Gladys
         Parvis. Chicago: R. F. Seymour, [c1925]. 104 p.,
         ill.
         Unexamined copy: bibliographic data from NUC.
         LC: Je 18, '25.
         PW: Je 27, '25.

P-143   Pascal, Ernest, 1896-1966. The dark swan / by
         Ernest Pascal. New York: Brentano's, [c1924].
         341 p.
         LC: F 11, '24.
         PW: F 23, '24.
         BLC: London: Brentano's, Binghamton [printed],
         1924.

P-144   _____ Hell's highroad / by Ernest Pascal . . . ;
         illustrated with scenes from the photoplay supervised
         by Cecil B. DeMille, starring Leatrice Joy, a
         Producers Distributing Corp. Release, directed by
         Rupert Julian. New York: Grosset and Dunlap,
         [c1925]. 297 p., photo. front., [7] leaves of photo.
         plates.   OSU, ALM
         LC: S 24, '25.
         PW: O 17, '25.

P-145   _____ The virgin flame: a novel / by Ernest Pascal.
         New York: Brentano's, [c1925]. 317 p.
         LC: F 12, '25.
         PW: F 21, '25.
         BLC: London: Brentano's, 1924. British title:
         Ragtime.

P-146   Patch, Kate Whiting, b. 1870. Because you are you /
         by Kate Whiting Patch; illustrations and decorations
         by John Rae. New York: Dodd, Mead and
         Company, 1913. 252 p., col. front., [3] leaves of
         col. plates.

P-147   Paterson, Isabel. The magpie's nest / by Isabel
         Paterson . . . New York: John Lane Company;
         Toronto: S. B. Gundy; London: John Lane, The
         Bodley Head, 1917. 303 p.   OCP
         LC: Mr 31, '17.
         PW: Mr 31, '17.

P-148   _____ The shadow riders / by Isabel Paterson. New
         York: John Lane Company; London: John Lane,
         The Bodley Head; Toronto: S. B. Gundy, 1916.
         379 p.
         LC: F 26, '16.
         PW: F 26, '16.

P-149   _____ The singing season: a romance of old Spain /
         by Isabel Paterson. New York: Boni and Liveright,
         [c1924]. 304 p.
         LC: Jl 5, '24.
         PW: Je 28, '24.
         BLC: London: Leonard Parsons, printed in U. S.
         A., 1925.

P-150   Deleted.

P-151   Patmore, William J. A happy night / by William J.
         Patmore. New York: Cochrane Publishing Co.,
         1908. 208 p.   DLC
         LC: N 14, '08.

         Pattee, Fred Lewis, 1863-1950, ed. See American
         short stories (1925), A-201.

P-152   _____ The breaking-point: a novel / by Fred Lewis
         Pattee. Boston: Small, Maynard & Company,
         [c1912]. 392 p.
         LC: F 14, '12.
         PW: F 10, '12.

P-153   _____ The house of the black ring / by Fred Lewis
         Pattee. New York: Henry Holt and Company, 1905.
         324 p., front. (map).
         PW: Ap 8, '05.

P-154   _____ Mary Garvin: the story of a New Hampshire
         summer / by Fred Lewis Pattee. New York:
         Thomas Y. Crowell & Co., [1902]. 383 p., front.,
         [3] leaves of plates. [Ill. by W. E. Mears.]
         PW: Ap 5, '02.

         Patten, Clinton A. See Rock, James, pseud.

P-155   Patten, Harrison, b. 1873. Three crimson days / by
         Harrison Patten. New York; Washington: The Neale
         Publishing Company, 1910. 67 p.   OSU, DLC
         LC: D 31 '10.
         PW: Ja 7, '11.

P-156   _____ The town and the trust: a novel / by Harrison
         Patten. New York; Washington: The Neale
         Publishing Company, 1910. 246 p.
         LC: O 12, '10.
         PW: D 31, '10.

P-157   Patten, Simon Nelson, 1852-1922. Mud Hollow:
         from dust to soul / by Simon N. Patten. Philadelphia:
         Dorrance, [c1922]. 384 p.
         PW: My 6, '22.

         Patten, William, 1868-1936, ed. See Great short
         stories (1909), G-423.

         _____, ed. See International short stories (1910),
         I-29.

P-158   Patterson, Ada. By the stage door / by Ada Patterson
         & Victory Bateman. New York: Grafton Press,
         [c1902]. 217 p.
         PW: S 13, '02.

P-159   Patterson, Arthur Willis, b. 1881. The heaviest pipe:
         a story of mystery and adventure / by Arthur M.
         Patterson. Philadelphia: George W. Jacobs &
         Company, [c1921]. 270 p.
         Lettered on cover: Arthur W. Patterson.
         PW: Ap 30, '21.

P-160   Patterson, Burd Shippen. "The head of iron": a
         romance of colonial Pennsylvania / by Burd Shippen

Patterson. Pittsburgh: T. M. Walker, 1908. 360 p., photo. front., [1] leaf of photo. plates. **OSU, YNG**

P-161 Patterson, Joseph Medill, b. 1879. A little brother of the rich: a novel / by Joseph Medill Patterson. Chicago: The Reilly & Britton Co., 1908. 361 p., col. front. [Ill. by Hazel Martyn Trudeau.], [5] leaves of plates. [Ill. by Walter Dean Goldbeck.]
LC: Ag 24, '08.
PW: S 12, '08.

P-162 ____ Rebellion / by Joseph Medill Patterson; illustrated by Walter Dean Goldbeck. Chicago: The Reilly & Britton Co., [1911]. 355 p., front., [3] leaves of plates.
LC: O 12, '11.
PW: O 7, '11.
BLC: London: Holden & Hardingham, [1914].

P-163 Patterson, Marjorie, d. 1948. The dust of the road / by Marjorie Patterson; with frontispiece in color by E. M. Woolfolk. New York: Henry Holt and Company, 1913. 321 p., col. front.
LC: Ag 30, '13.
PW: S 27, '13.
BLC: London: Chatto & Windus, 1913.

P-164 ____ Fortunata: a novel / by Marjorie Patterson. New York; London: Harper & Brothers, 1911. 334 p., front. [Ill. by A. Castaigne.]
LC: F 18, '11.
PW: F 25, '11.

P-165 ____ A woman's man / by Marjorie Patterson . . . New York: George H. Doran Company, [c1919]. 336 p.
LC: O 21, '19.
PW: N 1, '19.
BLC: London: William Heinemann, 1920.

P-166 Patterson, Reginald Heber. Eve, junior / by Reginald Heber Patterson. New York: The Macaulay Company, 1917. 347 p., front., [3] leaves of plates. [Ill. by Albert Matzke.]
LC: Je 16, '17.
PW: Je 9, '17.

P-167 ____ The girl from no. 13 / by Reginald Heber Patterson. New York: The Macaulay Company, 1915. 319 p., front., [3] leaves of plates. [Ill. by Clare Angell.]
LC: Ag 16, '15.
PW: Ag 14, '15.

P-168 Patton, Abel. "Har Lampkins": a narrative of mountain life on the borders of the two Virginias / by Abel Patton. New York; London; Montreal: The Abbey Press, [c1901]. 192 p.

P-169 Patton, Marion Oakman, b. 1860. The lighted taper: a novel / by M. Oakman Patton. Boston: Botolph Book Company, 1903, [c1902]. 285 p., front.
PW: N 22, '02.

P-170 Pattullo, George, 1879-1967. The sheriff of Badger: a tale of the southwest borderland / by George

Pattullo. New York; London: D. Appleton and Company, 1912. 312, [1] p., front., [3] leaves of plates. [Ill. by August Spaenkuch.]
Partly reprinted from various periodicals.
LC: Jl 24, '12.
PW: Je 22, '12.

____ The tie that binds. In *Prize stories of 1924* **(1925), P-622.**

P-171 ____ The untamed: range life in the Southwest / by George Pattullo. New York: Desmond Fitgerald, Inc., [c1911]. 288 p., col. front., [5] leaves of plates. [Ill. by Charles Livingston Bull, Haydon Jones, C. M. Russell, and H. T. Dunn.]
Partly reprinted from various periodicals.
Contents: Ol' Sam, a mule -- The marauder, a coyote -- Corazón, a roping horse -- The outlaw, a steer -- Shiela, a wolfhound -- Molly, a range cow -- The baby and the puma, mountain lion -- The mankiller, a jack -- Neutria, a mountain cowhorse.
LC: Ap 3, '11.
PW: Ap 15, '11.

P-172 Paul, Elliot, 1891-1958. Imperturbe: a novel of peace without victory / by Elliot H. Paul. New York: Alfred A. Knopf, 1924. 313 p. Designed end papers.
LC: My 7, '24.
PW: Ap 26, '24.

P-173 ____ Impromptu: a novel in four movements / by Elliot H. Paul. New York: Alfred A. Knopf, 1923. 356 p. Designed end papers.
LC: Ap 25, '23.
PW: Ap 14, '23.

P-174 ____ Indelible: a story of life, love, and music, in five movements / by Elliot H. Paul. Boston; New York: Houghton Mifflin Company, 1922. (Cambridge: The Riverside Press). 296, [1] p.
LC: Je 17, '22.
PW: Je 10, '22.
BLC: London: Jarrold's, 1924.

P-175 Paul, Henry. Mary's Yankee man / by Henry Paul. Columbus, O.: The Phillips Press, [c1920]. 177 p., incl. front.
Unexamined copy: bibliographic data from NUC.
LC: F 2, '20.

P-176 Paul, Willard A. (Willard Augustus), b. 1855. Don: his recollections / by Willard A. Paul; illustrated by Grace Loring Basset. Boston: The American Humane Education Society, 1914. 274 p., front., [5] leaves of plates, (some photo.).
Contents: I, myself -- I am named and broken in -- I become the doctor's assistant -- General history -- The sermon in the garden -- Rock Island Island -- A dog's appreciation -- I run away -- Rock Island arsenal -- Forty-five miles saved -- A youthful escapade -- Gyp -- Gyp takes part in the Easter service -- Gyp's last trip -- Black Hawk's watch tower -- Sears Park -- A hundred times at school -- A quick run -- The sewer horse -- Horses, like men, fear the unknown -- A long, cold night -- Bess is poisoned -- My master goes to jail -- The cyclone -- Noted people -- Bess stops the runaway -- Horses I have known, and their peculiarities -- The reunion -- Bess as a surgical patient -- A thousand miles in a private car -- Niagara -- On to Boston -- My first trip from Boston to Dorchester -- One of our best friends -- My master makes a mistake -- The gipsy camp -- Instinct or reason? -- Someone forgot -- We lose our Bess -- Accidents to others -- The disagreement between Master and myself -- Some things which I know from experience -- Bess, the black mare -- Grampian Way --

Character in horses -- Life in the stable -- The rescue -- The park system -- Children -- "Da' Foo'!" -- Teddy -- Thanksgiving -- The last word.

P-177   Paxson, W. A. (William Alpha). A Buckeye baron: a rural story of a Buckeye boy / by W. A. Paxson; illustrated by H. H. Walker, Dorothy Cole, W. Mock. Cincinnati: Robert Clarke Company, 1901. 375 p., front., [10] leaves of plates (some photo.).

P-178   Payne, Elisabeth Stancy. All the way by water / by Elizabeth Stancy Payne; frontispiece by Ralph D. [i. e. P.] Coleman. Philadelphia: The Penn Publishing Company, 1922. 377 p., front.
LC: Je 1, '22.
PW: Jl 1, '22.

P-179   ____ Fathoms deep / by Elizabeth Stancy Payne . . . ; illustrated by Charles Hargens, Jr. Philadelphia: The Penn Publishing Company, 1923. 329 p., front.
LC: Je 20, '23.

P-180   ____ Lights along the ledges / by Elisabeth Stancy Payne; illustrated by Ralph Pallen Coleman. Philadelphia: The Penn Publishing Company, 1924. 316 p., front.
LC: Ap 10, '24.
PW: Ap 19, '24.

P-181   ____ Singing waters / by Elizabeth Stancy Payne; frontispiece by R. Pallen Coleman. Philadelphia: The Penn Publishing Company, 1925. 311 p., front.
LC: My 15, '25.
PW: My 2, '25.

P-182   Payne, George Henry. A great part: and other stories of the stage / by George Henry Payne. New York: Continental Publishing Co., 1902. 220 p.
Contents: A great part -- Filby's boy -- Love letters of an actor -- A romance a la Russe -- Peter's fortune -- The horse that "starred" -- An eloping party.

P-183   Payne, Lamar Strickland. 20th century fables / by Lamar Strickland Payne; ten illustrations by O'Malley. Montreal; New York; London: Broadway Publishing Co., [c1904]. 64 p., front., [9] leaves of plates.   **EMU**
Contents: A newspaper episode -- The literary genius -- The modern courtships -- The title on the hunt for an heiress -- The fast pace which Rube tried to follow -- The modern wedding -- The millionaires and the socialist -- Tom, Dick and Harry, who each thought that he was it -- The millionaire -- The prodigal son -- The life assurer -- The university graduate -- The diplomat who missed his calling -- The newly wed.

P-184   Payne, Mary Elizabeth Riley, 1864-1936. Viola Livingstone, or, What's in a name ? / by Mary E. Payne. New York; London; Montreal: The Abbey Press, [c1901]. 107 p.   **DLC**
PW: Je 29, '01.

P-185   Payne, Odessa Strickland, b. 1857. Esther Ferrall's experiment / by Odessa Strickland Payne. Atlanta: Converse Publishing Co., 1909. 112 p.

P-186   Payne, Philip, b. 1867. Duchess of few clothes: a comedy / by Philip Payne . . . . Chicago; New York; London: Rand, McNally & Company, [c1904]. 340,

[1] p.
PW: Je 11, '04.
BLC: London: Hutchinson & Co., 1904.

P-187   ____ The mills of man: a novel / by Philip Payne. Chicago; New York: Rand, McNally & Co., 1903. 476 p.
PW: S 19, '03.
BLC: London: Ranl, McNally & Co., 1903.

P-188   Payne, Will, 1865-1954. The automatic capitalists / Will Payne; illustrated by Leslie L. Benson. Boston: Richard G. Badger, 1909. (Boston: The Gorham Press). 150 p., front., [4] leaves of plates.
LC: N 27, '09.

____ The best-laid plan. _In_ *Saturday Evening Post* **(1919), S-90.**

____ His escape. _In_ *War stories (1919)*, **W-94.**

P-189   ____ The losing game: a novel / by Will Payne; illustrations by F. R. Gruger. New York: G. W. Dillingham Company, [c1910]. 352 p., front., [7] leaves of plates.
LC: Mr 9, '10.

P-190   ____ Mr. Salt: a novel / by Will Payne; with illustrations by Charles H. White. Boston; New York: Houghton, Mifflin and Company, 1903. (Cambridge: The Riverside Press). 330 p., front., [3] leaves of plates.
PW: N 7, '03.

P-191   ____ On fortune's road: stories of business / by Will Payne . . . ; with eight full-page drawings by Thomas Fogarty. Chicago: A. C. McClurg & Co., 1902. 290 p., col. front., [7] leaves of plates.   **GZM**
Contents: In the panic -- A day in wheat -- The plant at High Grove -- The chairman's politics -- The lame boy -- The salt crowd's trade -- The end of the deal.
PW: S 20, '02.

P-192   ____ Overlook house / by Will Payne. New York: Dodd, Mead and Company, 1921. 373 p.
LC: Mr 17, '21.
PW: Ap 9, '21.

P-193   ____ The scarred chin / by Will Payne. New York: Dodd, Mead and Company, 1920. 310 p.
LC: F 25, '20.
PW: Mr 6, '20.

P-194   ____ The story of Eva: a novel / by Will Payne. Boston; New York: Houghton Mifflin, 1901. (Cambridge: The Riverside Press). 340 p.
PW: Ap 13, '01.
BLC: London: Archibald Constable & Co., 1901.

P-195   ____ When love speaks / by Will Payne. New York: The Macmillan Company; London: Macmillan & Co., Ltd., 1906. 370 p.
LC: N 6, '06.
PW: N 17, '06.

Payson, Norman. A comedy of manners. _See The best college short stories, 1924-1925 (1925)_, **B-558.**

P-196   Payson, William Farquhar, 1876-1939. Barry Gordon / by William Farquhar Payson; illustrations by Harry Townsend. New York: The McClure Company, 1908. 341 p., front., [5] leaves of plates.
LC: S 22, '08.
PW: O 10, '08.

P-197   ____ Debonnaire / by William Farquhar Payson; illustrations by Thomas Fogarty. New York: McClure, Phillips & Co., 1904. 227, [1] p., front., [5] leaves of plates. Illustrated end papers.
PW: O 1, '04.
BLC: London: McClure, Phillips, & Co., New York [printed], 1904.

P-198   ____ John Vytal: a tale of the lost colony / by William Farquhar Payson. New York; London: Harper & Brothers, 1901. 318 p., front.
PW: Mr 9, '01.

P-199   ____ Love letters of a divorced couple / William Farquhar Payson. Garden City, New York: Doubleday, Page & Company, 1915. 216 p. **GZM**
LC: Mr 30, '15.
PW: Mr 27, '15.
BLC: London: Curtis Brown, 1915.

P-200   ____ Periwinkle: an idyl of the dunes / by William Farquhar Payson; with illustrations by Thomas Fogarty. New York: Sturgis & Walton Company, 1910. 305, [1] p., incl. front., [3] leaves of plates.
LC: S 29, '10.
PW: O 15, '10.
BLC: London: Gay & Hancock, 1910.

P-201   ____ The triumph of life: a novel / by William Farquhar Payson. New York; London: Harper & Brothers, 1903. 424, [1] p.
PW: Ap 18, '03.

P-202   Peabody, Marian Lawrence. Polly's pension plans / by Marian Lawrence Peabody. [Boston]: Samuel Usher, 1917. (Boston: The Fort Hill Press). 73 p., front. [Ill. by the author.]

P-203   Peadro, Robert M. Idle hours of a busy lawyer / by Robert M. Peadro. Shelbyville, Illinois: Published by the Shelby County Leader, [c1910]. 129 p. **DLC**
LC: F 9, '10.

Peake, Elmore Elliott, b. 1871. Back to Indiana. In *Under the Sunset* (1906), U-9.

____ The Captain of the "Aphrodite." In *Love* (1901), L-525.

P-204   ____ The house of Hawley / by Elmore Elliott Peake . . . New York: D. Appleton and Company, 1905. 341 p.
PW: F 11, '05.

____ The night run of the "Overland". In *The railroad* (1901), R-6.

P-205   ____ The pride of Tellfair / by Elmore Elliott Peake. New York; London: Harper & Brothers, 1903. 390,

[1] p.
PW: F 14, '03.

P-206   Pearce, Eugene Lovick. The seventh wave / by Eugene L. Pearce. New York: Moffat, Yard & Company, 1921. 322 p.
LC: D 8, '21.

P-207   Pearce, John Irving. The strange case of Eric Marotté: a modern-historical problem-romance of Chicago / by John Irving Pearce, Jr. . . . ; frontispiece in colors by Carl J. Blenner; illustrated by Norman Tolson and numerous photographs. Chicago: P. F. Pettibone & Company, 1913. 366 p., col. front., [9] leaves of plates (some photo.). Designed end papers.

Pearl, Bertha, pseud. <u>See</u> **Moore, Bertha Pearl, 1894-1925.**

P-208   Pearson, Francis Bail, b. 1853. Uncle Danny's neighbors / by Francis B. Pearson . . . Indianapolis: The Bobbs-Merrill Company, [c1919]. 268 p.
LC: N 22, '19.
PW: Ja 24, '20.

Pease, Frank Chester. The rolling stone. <u>In</u> *Forum stories* (1914), F-306.

P-209   Peattie, Elia Wilkinson, b. 1862. The angel with a broom / by Elia W. Peattie. [Chicago]: Published by Ralph Fletcher Seymour for the Cordon, [c1915]. 29 p.

P-210   ____ Azalea's silver web / by Elia W. Peattie . . . ; illustrations by E. R. Kirkbride. Chicago: The Reilly & Britton Co., [c1915]. 284 p., front., [3] leaves of plates.
(The Blueridge series).
PW: Ag 21, '15.

P-211   ____ The beleaguered forest / by Elia W. Peattie. New York: D. Appleton and Company, 1901. 349 p.
PW: Ag 10, '01.

P-212   ____ Castle, knight & troubadour: in an apology and three tableaux / by Elia W. Peattie. Chicago: The Blue Sky Press, 1903. 65 p., front. [sic, see note below.] [Ill. by Harry Everett Townsend.]
OSU copy lacks front.; no other copy examined.
"Here endeth Castle, knight and troubadour, as written by Elia W. Peattie; the frontispiece was drawn by Harry Everett Townsend; and the whole made into this book and sold by the Blue Sky Press . . . Chicago. Of this first edition there were printed one hundred and seventy-five copies on paper and twenty-five copies on Japan vellum . . . "
PW: D 5, '03.

P-213   ____ The edge of things / by Elia W. Peattie. Chicago; New York; Toronto; London; Edinburgh: Fleming H. Revell Company, 1903. 255 p., [4] leaves of plates. [Ill. by E. S. Paxson.]
PW: D 26, '03.

P-214 ____ How Jacques came into the forest of Arden: an impertinence / by Elia W. Peattie. Chicago: The Blue Sky Press, [c1901]. [62] p., front., [4] leaves of plates. [Ill. by W. J. Enright.] **OSU, MBB**
PW: D 14, '01

P-215 ____ Lotta Embury's career / by Elia W. Peattie; with illustrations. Boston; New York: Houghton Mifflin Company, 1915. (Cambridge: The Riverside Press). 213, [1] p., front., [3] leaves of plates. [Ill. by Florence Storer.]
LC: S 27, '15.
PW: O 9, '15.

____ A madonna of the desert. In *Under the Sunset* **(1906), U-9.**

P-216 ____ The newcomers / by Elia W. Peattie; with illustrations by B. J. Rosenmeyer. Boston; New York: Houghton Mifflin Company, 1917. (Cambridge: The Riverside Press). 186, [1] p., front., [3] leaves of plates. **RBN**
LC: S 18, '17.
PW: S 22, '17.

P-217 ____ The precipice: a novel / by Elia W. Peattie. Boston; New York: Houghton Mifflin Company, 1914. (Cambridge: The Riverside Press). 417, [1] p., front. [Ill. by Howard E. Smith.]
LC: F 16, '14.

____ The Rubaiyat and the liner. In *Quaint courtships* **(1906), Q-3.**

P-218 Peck, Samuel Minturn, 1854-1938. Alabama sketches / by Samuel Minturn Peck. Chicago: A. C. McClurg & Co., 1902. 299 p.
Contents: The trouble at St. James's -- Sister Taylor's registered letter -- The dragon candlestick -- Pap's mules -- The old piano -- Mrs. McMurtrie's rooster -- The maid of Jasmindale -- The political split in Oakville -- Under the white rose-tree -- What became of Mary Ellen -- Far from the front.
PW: Mr 22, '02.

P-219 Peck, Theodora Agnes, 1882-1964. Hester of the Grants: a romance of old Bennington / by Theodora Peck. New York: Fox, Duffield & Co., 1905. 419 p., front. [Ill. by Thomas Mitchell Peirce.]
LC: Jl 12, '07.
PW: My 20, '05.

P-220 ____ The sword of Dundee: a tale of "bonnie Prince Charlie" / by Theodora Peck; pictures by John Rae. New York: Duffield & Company, 1908. 398 p., col. front., [6] leaves of plates.
LC: Je 4, '08.
PW: O 17, '08.

P-221 ____ White Dawn: a legend of Ticonderoga / by Theodora Peck . . . ; illustrated. New York; Chicago; Toronto; London; Edinburgh: Fleming H. Revell Company, [c1914]. 306 p., incl. front., [4] leaves of plates. [Ill. by S. M. Palmer.]
LC: S 21, '14.
PW: S 5, '14.

P-222 Pedrick, William R. Eminent respectability: a tale of love, politics and adventure / by William R. Pedrick. Philadelphia: Press of Alfred M. Slocum Co., 1902. 288 p. **DLC**

P-223 Peek, Comer L. (Comer Leonard), b. 1851. Lorna Carswell: a story of the South / by Comer L. Peek; fully illustrated by S. Mary Norton; foreword by May S. Gilpatric. New York: Broadway Publishing Company, 1903. 333 p., front. (port.), [7] leaves of plates.
LC: Jl 2, '06.

P-224 Peek, Tate W. Blind brothers / by Tate W. Peek. Philadelphia: Dorrance, [c1923]. 274 p. **DLC**
LC: O 19, '23.

P-225 Peggy Ann, b. 1868, *pseud.* Dear family / by Peggy Ann [pseud.]. New York; Cincinnati: The Abingdon Press, [c1925]. 107 p. **NUI**
LC: Je 6, '25.

P-226 Peirce, Grace Howard. Elizabeth's story / by Grace Howard Peirce. [Fond du Lac, Wis.: Printed by Haber Printing Co., c1910]. 120 p., incl. front. **DLC**
Contents: Elizabeth's story -- Anna Maria's visit to the minister -- Little Esther -- The children of the desert -- Uncle Joseph -- Lenchen's white dress.
LC: O 6, '10.

P-227 Pelley, William Dudley, b. 1890. Drag: a comedy / by William Dudley Pelley. Boston: Little, Brown, and Company, 1925. 359 p.
LC: F 21, '25.
PW: F 21, '25.
BLC: London; New York: Andrew Melrose, 1925. Second impression.

____ The face in the window. In *Prize stories of 1920 (1921)*, **P-618.**

P-228 ____ The fog: a novel / by William Dudley Pelley. Boston: Little, Brown, and Company, 1921. 500 p.
LC: S 27, '21.
PW: O 8, '21.
BLC: London; New York: Andrew Melrose, [1923].

P-229 ____ The greater glory / by William Dudley Pelley; with frontispiece by Norman Price. Boston: Little, Brown, and Company, 1919. 376 p., front.
LC: O 2, '19.
PW: N 1, '19.

____ The toast to forty-five. In *The best short stories of 1918 and the yearbook of the American short story (1919)*, **B-563.**

P-230 Pelton, Ben H. (Benjamin Hiram), b. 1854. Shelter Island, or, The power of God: a novel / by Ben H. Pelton; a story of truth. Denver, Colorado: The Pelton Publishing Company, [c1913]. 468 p., [1] leaf of photo. plates (port.).
LC: Ap 26, '13.
PW: My 31, '13.

P-231   ____ We called him Andy Grimes: the story of a contest of wits between the shrewdest of detectives and his quarry / by Ben H. Pelton. Denver, Colo.: Great Divide Publisher, [c1914]. 169 p., [1] leaf of photo. plates (port.).   **NYP**

P-232   Pelton, Mabell Shippie Clarke, 1864-1942. A tar-heel baron / by Mabell Shippie Clarke Pelton; with illustrations by Edward Stratton Holloway. Philadelphia; London: J. B. Lippincott Company, 1903. 354 p., front., [4] leaves of plates. PW: Mr 14, '03.

P-233   Pendexter, Hugh, 1875-1940. Gentlemen of the North / by Hugh Pendexter; frontispiece by Ralph Pallen Coleman. Garden City, New York: Doubleday, Page & Company, 1920. 243, [1] p., col. front. LC: O 28, '20. PW: N 13, '20.

P-234   ____ Kings of the Missouri / by Hugh Pendexter; illustrated by Kenneth M. Ballantyne. Indianapolis: The Bobbs-Merrill Company, [c1921]. 360 p., front., [5] leaves of plates. LC: Ag 8, '21. PW: Ag 13, '21.

P-235   ____ The mantle of Red Evans / Hugh Pendexter. New York: The Winthrop Press, c1914. 32 p., col. front. Previously published in Munsey's magazine.

P-236   ____ Old Misery / by Hugh Pendexter; illustrated by Remington Schuyler. Indianapolis: The Bobbs-Merrill Company, [c1924]. 389, [3] p., front., [3] leaves of plates. LC: Mr 8, '24. PW: Mr 22, '24.

P-237   ____ Pay gravel / by Hugh Pendexter . . . ; with frontispiece by Remington Schuyler. Indianapolis: The Bobbs-Merrill Company, [c1923]. 353 p., front. LC: Mr 16, '23. PW: Mr 31, '23.

P-238   ____ Red belts / by Hugh Pendexter; frontispiece by Ralph Pallen Coleman. Garden City, New York: Doubleday, Page & Company, 1920. 246 p., col. front. LC: F 5, '20. PW: F 7, '20.

P-239   ____ Tiberius Smith: as chronicled by his right-hand man, Billy Campbell / by Hugh Pendexter. New York; London: Harper & Brothers, 1907. 330, [1] p., front. [Ill. by Albert Levering.] LC: Mr 14, '07. PW: Mr 30, '07.

P-240   ____ The wife-ship woman / by Hugh Pendexter . . . Indianapolis: The Bobbs-Merrill Company, [c1925]. 338 p. LC: F 16, '25. PW: F 21, '25.

P-241   Pendleton, Louis, 1861-1939. A forest drama / by Louis Pendleton . . . Philadelphia: Henry T. Coates & Co., 1904. 272 p., front., [3] leaves of plates. [Ill. by James E. McBurney.] PW: Jl 2, '04.

P-242   ____ In Assyrian tents: the story of the strange adventures of Uriel / by Louis Pendleton . . . Philadelphia: The Jewish Publication Society of America, 1904. 248 p., front., [2] leaves of plates. [Ill. by E. M. Wireman.] PW: Je 18, '04.

P-243   Pengelly, John Bradford, b. 1880. A new Christmas legend / by J. Bradford Pengelly. Flint, MI: Flint Printing Company, 1916. 61, [1] p. Unexamined copy: bibliographic data from NUC.

P-244   Pennell, William W. (William Wesley), 1853-1930. The buckeye doctor: a tale for physicians and for physicians' patients / by William W. Pennell. New York: The Grafton Press, [1903]. 345 p. PW: Je 6, '03.

P-245   ____ Jonas Hawley / by William W. Pennell. Boston, Massachusetts: The C. M. Clark Publishing Company, [c1910]. 443, [1] p., col. front., [5] leaves of plates. [Ill. by David Bruce Conklin.] LC: F 10, '11.

P-246   Penniman, Paul. A campaign courtship / by Paul Penniman. Westerville, Ohio: The American Issue Publishing Company, c1914. 131 p., [5] leaves of plates (1 double). [Ill. by Westerman.]

P-247   Pennington, Jeanne G. (Jeanne Gillespie). The sea of circumstance / by Jeanne G. Pennington . . . New York; London; Montreal: The Abbey Press, [c1902]. 142 p.   **DLC** Contents: The beneficient teacher -- An unsolved problem -- Marcia Dunlap (a silhouette). PW: D 6, '02.

P-248   Pennoyer, Virginia E. Rodari, sculptor: a story of Pisa / by Virginia E. Pennoyer. San Francisco: D. Paul Elder and Morgan Shepherd, 1901. 43 p., front. Unexamined copy: bibliographic data from OCLC, #9553279. PW: Mr 9, '01.

Pentz, Albert Du Verney. The big stranger on Dorchester Heights. *In The best short stories of 1916 and the yearbook of the American short story* (1917), **B-561.**

P-249   Peple, Edward Henry, 1869-1924. An auto-biography: a tale of truth- and Ruth / by Edward Peple . . . New York: Moffat, Yard & Company, 1915. 151 p., front. [Ill. by Gordon Grant.] LC: D 13, '15. PW: D 11, '15.

P-250   ____ A broken rosary / by Edward Peple; illustrated by Scotson Clark. New York; London: John Lane, 1904. 313 p., col. front., [3] leaves of col. plates. PW: Mr 26, '04.

P-251   The cur and the coyote / by Edward Peple
. . . ; illustrated by R. L. Goldberg. New York:
Moffat, Yard, & Company, 1913. 64 p., incl. front.
LC: S 5, '13.
PW: S 20, '13.

P-252   The mallet's masterpiece / by Edward Peple;
illustrated by C. M. Burd. New York: Moffat, Yard
and Company, 1908. 69 p., front., [3] leaves of
plates. Ornamental border.
LC: N 16, '08.
PW: D 5, '08.

P-253   A night out / by Edward Peple; frontispiece by
R. L. Goldberg. New York: Moffat, Yard, and
Company, 1909. 44 p., front.   **NYP**
LC: N 30, '09.
PW: D 11, '09.

P-254   The prince chap: a story in three curtains and
several scenes / by Edward Peple . . . New York;
London: G. P. Putnam's Sons, 1904. (New York:
The Knickerbocker Press). 386 p., col. front. [Ill.
by Ch. Weber-Ditzler.]
PW: O 15, '04.

     ____, jt. aut. *Richard the Brazen* (1906). <u>See</u>
**Brady, Cyrus Townsend, 1861-1920, jt. aut.,
B-894.**

P-255   Semiramis: a tale of battle and of love / by
Edward Peple. New York: Moffat, Yard &
Company, 1907. 375 p., front.
LC: Ag 19, '07.
PW: S 14, '07.
BLC: London: Greening & Co., 1908.

P-256   The spitfire / by Edward Peple; illustrated by
Howard Chandler Christy and J. V. McFall. New
York: Moffat, Yard and Company, 1908. 346 p.,
col. front., [6] leaves of plates.
LC: S 2, '08.
PW: O 3, '08.
BLC: London: Greening & Co., 1909.

Percival, Olive. The story of Suey Ho Yee. <u>In</u> *From
the old pueblo: and other tales* (1902), F-434.

     The way of a woman. <u>In</u> *Cuentos de
California* (1904), C-963.

Perez, Isaac Löb. It is well. <u>In</u> *Yiddish tales* (1912),
Y-20.

     The treasure. <u>In</u> *Yiddish tales* (1912), **Y-20.**

     Whence a proverb. <u>In</u> *Yiddish tales* (1912),
Y-20.

     A woman's wrath. <u>In</u> *Yiddish tales* (1912),
Y-20.

Perkins, Elizabeth. Companions of the desert. <u>In</u>
Called to the colors and other stories (1915), **C-50.**

P-257 Perkins, John Willis, b. 1874. Fantassie, a strange
tale / by J. Willis Perkins . . . New York: Broadway
Publishing Company, 1906. 40 p., front.
Unexamined copy: bibliographic data from NUC.
LC: Ag 17, '06.

P-258 Perkins, Kenneth. The beloved brute / by Kenneth
Perkins; illustrated with scenes from Vitagraph
photo-play with Marguerite de la Motte, Victor
McLaglen, William Russell, Mary Alden, Stuart
Holmes. New York: The Macaulay Company,
[c1923]. 319 p., photo. front., [3] leaves of photo.
plates.
LC: Mr 17, '23.
PW: My 5, '23.
BLC: London: Hutchinson & Co., [1924].

P-259   The gun fanner / by Kenneth Perkins . . . New
York: The Macaulay Company, [c1924]. 318 p.
LC reports "frontispiece by Charles Durant" on t. p.
LC: Mr 27, '24.
PW: N 8, '24.
BLC: London: Hutchinson & Co., [1925].

P-260   Queen of the night / by Kenneth Perkins.
Chicago: A. C. McClurg & Co., 1925. 312 p.
LC: Ap 25, '25.
PW: My 30, '25.

P-261   Ride him, cowboy / by Kenneth Perkins . . . ;
frontispiece by Charles Durant. New York: The
Macaulay Company, [c1923]. 314 p., front.
LC: O 9, '23.
PW: O 6, '23.
BLC: London: Hutchinson & Co., [1924].

P-262 Perkins, Lawrence. The cross of Ares: and other
sketches / by Lawrence Perkins; with decoration by
Beatrice Stevens. New York: Brentano's, 1920.
119 p.
Contents: Civilization-a prologue -- The cross of Ares -- Une fille de
joie -- The winning of Denny McShea -- Shot at sunrise -- God is
love.
PW: O 30, '20.

Perkins, Margaret Mower. <u>See</u> **Richardson, Robert,
pseud.**

Perkins, Violet Lilian. <u>See</u> **Leslie, Lilian, jt. pseud.
of Violet Lilian Perkins and Archer Leslie Hood.**

P-263 Perrigo, James. The sheriff: a modern Maine story
in which pride and politics, romance and rum are
curiously intermingled / by James Perrigo. Portland,
Maine.: The Franklin Printing Company. [c1911].
85 p., incl. photo. front.
LC: Mr 8, '11.

Perrin, Clyde, pseud. <u>See</u> **O'Brien, Howard
Vincent, 1888-1947.**

Perrin, Lee James, b. 1884. <u>See</u> **Struly, Ewer,
pseud.**

Perry, Clair Willard, b. 1887. <u>See</u> **Perry, Clay,
pseud.**

P-264   Perry, Clay, b. 1887, *pseud.* Heart of Hemlock / by Clay Perry [pseud.]; with frontispiece by Gerard C. Delano. Indianapolis: The Bobbs-Merrill Company, [c1920]. 288 p., front.   **DLC**
LC: S 13, '20.
PW: O 16, '20.

P-265   ____ Roving river / by Clay Perry [pseud.] . . . Indianapolis: The Bobbs-Merrill Company, [c1921]. 301 p.
LC: N 3, '21.
PW: N 19, '21.

Perry, Edna, comp. <u>See</u> *Representative short stories* **(1917), R-176.**

P-266   Perry, Francis Foster. Their hearts' desire / by Frances Foster Perry; with illustrations by Harrison Fisher and decorations by Theodore B. Hapgood. New York: Dodd, Mead & Company, 1909. 152 p., col. front., [5] leaves of col. plates. Ornamental border.
LC: N 5, '09.
PW: D 4, '09.

P-267   Perry, Fred A. (Frederick Albertus), b. 1873. Cressy: a maid of Japan: a story of the conversion of a high class girl to Christianity, setting forth religious and social conditions in Japan / by Fred A. Perry . . . Lansing, Michigan: The Hammond Publishing Company, 1910. 318 p., photo. front. (port.), [7] leaves of photo. plates.   **EEA**

P-268   Perry, George B. (George Bone), 1846-1905. Slings and arrows: tales, sketches and verses, grave and gay: First series / by George B. Perry. Boston: The Dunscombe Publishing Co., 1901. 223 p., front. (port.), ill. [Ill. by C. W. Reed.]

Perry, Lawrence, 1875-1954. "A certain rich man - ". <u>In</u> *The best short stories of 1917 and the yearbook of the American short story* **(1918), B-562.**

P-269   ____ Dan Merrithew / by Lawrence Perry . . . ; illustrated by J. V. McFall. Chicago: A. C. McClurg & Co., 1910. 285, [1] p., col. front., [3] leaves of col. plates.
LC: Mr 14, '10.

____ From the depths of the things. <u>In</u> *The joy in work* **(1920), J-229.**

P-270   ____ Holton of the Navy: a story of the freeing of Cuba / by Lawrence Perry; illustrations by J. Allen St. John. Chicago: A. C. McClurg & Co., 1913. 390 p., col. front., [3] leaves of col. plates.
LC: Mr 29, '13.
PW: Ap 5, '13.
BLC: London: C. F. Cazenove; Chicago: A. C. McClurg & Co.; Coshocton, U. S. A. [printed], 1913.

____ A matter of loyalty. <u>In</u> *Prize stories of 1920* **(1921), P-618.**

P-271   ____ Prince or chauffeur?: a story of Newport / by Lawrence Perry; with four illustrations by J. V. McFall. Chicago: A. C. McClurg & Co., 1911. 382 p., col. front., [3] leaves of col. plates.
LC: Ap 12, '11.
PW: Ap 22, '11.

P-272   ____ The romantic liar / by Lawrence Perry. New York: Charles Scribner's Sons, 1919. 255 p.
LC: Ap 22, '19.
PW: My 10, '19.

P-273   Perry, Montanye. Blossomy cottage / by Montanye Perry. New York; Cincinnati: The Abingdon Press, [c1916]. 108 p., front., [1] leaf of plates. [Ill. by Frank R. Southard.]
LC: Mr 25, '16.
PW: F 12, '16.

P-274   ____ Where it touches the ground / by Montanye Perry. New York; Cincinnati: The Abingdon Press, 1917. 175 p.
LC: Ag 24, '17.
PW: Ag 4, '17.

P-275   ____ Zerah: a tale of old Bethlehem / by Montanye Perry. New York; Cincinnati: The Abingdon Press, [c1915]. 106 p., photo. front., [3] leaves of photo. plates.   **OSU, KSU**
LC: S 14, '15.
PW: S 11, '15.

P-276   Perry, Stella George Stern, b. 1877. The angel of Christmas: a vision of to-day / by Stella George Stern Perry . . . ; with four illustrations in colors by Maria L. Kirk. New York: Frederick A. Stokes Company, [c1917]. 112 p., col. front., [3] leaves of col. plates.   **PRE**
LC: S 22, '17.
PW: O 13, '17.

P-277   ____ Come home: a romance of the Louisiana rice-lands / by Stella G. S. Perry. New York: Frederick A. Stokes Company, 1923. 367 p., col. front. [Ill. by Alice Beard.]
LC: S 22, '23.
PW: Ja 12, '24.

P-278   ____ Melindy / by Stella George Stern Perry; frontispiece. New York: Moffat, Yard and Company, 1912. 250 p., front. [Ill. by Blanche Fisher Wright.]
LC: F 1, '13.
PW: Ja 17, '14.

P-279   ____ Palmetto: the romance of a Louisiana girl / by Stella G. S. Perry. New York: Frederick A. Stokes Company, [c1920]. 400 p.
LC: S 10, '20.
PW: S 4, '20.

Perry, Sylvestre. At the tolling of the Angelus. <u>In</u> *The lady of the tower* **(1909), L-13.**

P-280   Pesh-mal-yan, B. (Baruyr), b. 1865. The witch of Golgotha / by B. Pesh-mal-yan. Boston: Sherman, French & Company, 1913. 456 p.

P-281   Peterkin, Julia Mood, 1880-1961. Green Thursday: stories / by Julia Peterkin. New York: Alfred A. Knopf, 1924. 188 p.   **OSU, MNU**
Contents: Ashes -- Green Thursday -- Missile -- Meeting -- Mount Pleasant -- Finding peace -- The red rooster -- Teaching Jim -- Cat fish -- Son -- A Sunday -- Plum-blossoms.
LC: S 27, '24.
PW: S 20, '24.

   Petersen, Charles C. The gran'son crew. In *Made to order* (1915), M-352.

P-282   Petersilea, Carlyle, 1844-1903. Mark Chester, or, A mill and a million: a tale of southern California / by Carlyle Petersilea . . . Boston: Banner of Light Publishing Co., [c1901]. 196 p.

P-283   Peterson, Edmund Deacon. Log-cabin yarns of the Rocky Mountains / by Edmund Deacon Peterson. New York: The Cosmopolitan Press, 1912. 147 p.   **OCP**
Contents: The first night's yarns: Cap. White and the Indians -- Cap. White and the mountain-lion -- `Colorado's wonderful light air' -- `Th'cry-baby giant of Roarin' Fork' -- The second night's yarns: `Cap. White as a bulldozer' -- How Pete was saved by a squirrel -- `Beautiful Madeline, the big Swede's daughter; A tale of Cloud-Capped Leadville.' -- Which details the doings of the third night, which, because it is Sunday, they devote to letter-writing, and no stories are told -- Conclusion.

P-284   Peterson, Edward S. (Edward Sievers), b. 1876. When Santa came / by Edward S. Peterson. [S. l.: s. n., 1902?]. [14] p., photo. ill. (port.).   **NYP**
Cover title.

P-285   Peterson, Henry, 1818-1891. Dulcibel: a tale of old Salem / by Henry Peterson; illustrations by Howard Pyle. Philadelphia: John C. Winston Co., 1907. 402 p., col. front., [2] leaves of col. plates.
LC: Ap 1, '07.

P-286   Peterson, James A. (James Alsak), 1859-1928. Hjalmar, or, The Immigrant's son / by James A. Peterson. Minneapolis, Minnesota: K. C. Holter Publishing Company, 1922. 273, [1] p.
LC: N 23, '22.
PW: F 17, '23.

P-287   _____ Solstad: the old and the new; a story / by James A. Peterson. Minneapolis: Augsburg Publishing House, [c1923]. 344 p.
LC: N 15, '23.
PW: D 8, '23.

P-288   Peterson, Maud Howard. The commodore / by Maud Howard Peterson . . . ; illustrated by Alice Barber Stephens. Boston: Lothrop, Lee & Shepard Co., [1914]. 363 p., front., [6] leaves of plates.
Portions of this work have from time to time appeared in various periodicals under the nom de plume of Anna E. Finn.
Contents: The commodore -- The fighting blood -- The room of the trundle-bed -- On the high seas -- The sail and Siete Picos -- While the game was played -- The law's fulfilment.
LC: O 7, '14.
PW: O 31, '14.

P-289   [_____] The master-man. New York: John Lane Company; London: John Lane, the Bodley Head, 1906. 243 p.

P-290   _____ The potter and the clay: a romance of today / by Maud Howard Peterson; illustrated by Charlotte Harding. Boston: Lothrop Publishing Company, [c1901]. 348 p., front., [3] leaves of plates.
PW: My 18, '01.
BLC: London: C. H. Kelly, 1901. Another edition: London: Hodder & Stoughton, 1901.

P-291   _____ The sanctuary / by Maud Howard Peterson . . . Boston: Lothrop, Lee & Shepard, [c1912]. 469 p.
LC: Jl 30, '12.
PW: Ag 17, '12.
BLC: London: A. F. Bird, 1901.

P-292   Peterson, Peter Martin, b. 1872. The awakening of Jens Lyne / by P. M. Peterson. Minneapolis: Standard Press, 1914. 90 p.
Unexamined copy: bibliographic data from NUC.

P-293   Pettee, Florence Mae, b. 1888. White dominoes / by Florence M. Pettee. Chicago: The Reilly & Lee Co., [c1921]. 251 p.
LC: Mr 29, '21.

P-294   Pettersen, Rena Oldfield. Venus / by Rena Oldfield Pettersen. Philadelphia: Dorrance & Company, [c1924]. 248 p.   **GZT**
LC: F 27, 24.

P-295   Pettibone, Anita. The bitter country / by Anita Pettibone. Garden City, N. Y.: Doubleday, Page & Company, 1925. 318 p.
LC: F 16, '25.
PW: Ja 24, '25.
BLC: London: William Heinemann, printed in U. S. A., 1925.

P-296   Pettit, A. Judson (Alexander Judson), b. 1879. The last enemy / by A. Judson Pettit. Boston: Marshall Jones Company, 1918. 59 p.   **CSB**
PW: Ja 4, '19.

P-297   Pettit, Henry, b. 1842. A twentieth century idealist / by Henry Pettit. New York: The Grafton Press, [c1905]. 303 p., front., [1] leaf of plates.

P-298   Pettus, Maia, b. 1875. Meda's heritage / by Maia Pettus . . . New York; Washington: The Neale Publishing Company, 1906. 264 p.   **NDD**
PW: Je 23, '06.

P-299   _____ Princess of Glenndale: a story of the South / by Maia Pettus. Washington: The Neale Publishing Company, 1902. 314 p.
PW: F 28, '03.

P-300   Pezet, A. Washington (Alfonso Washington), b. 1889. Aristokia / by A. Washington Pezet; illustrated by Tony Sarg. New York: The Century Co., 1919. 214 p., front., [6] leaves of plates.

P-301   Phelan, Marion. The adventures of a young girl: a romance / by Marion Phelan. [Binghamton, N. Y.]: Published by the author, [c1914]. 88 p.   **DLC**

P-302 Phelon, William P. Our story of Atlantis: written down for the Hermetic Brotherhood / by W. P. Phelon . . . San Francisco, Calif.: Hermetic Book Concern, 1903. 217 p. Designed end papers.

P-303 Phelps, C. E. D. (Charles Edward Davis), 1851-1911. The accolade, or, The canon and his yeoman / by C. E. D. Phelps. Philadelphia; London: J. B. Lippincott Company, 1905. 352 p.

P-304 Phelps, Eleanor Gaylord. As a falling star / by Eleanor Gaylord Phelps. Chicago: A. C. McClurg & Co., 1901. 69 p., front. (port.).
PW: O 26, '01.

Phelps, Elizabeth Steward, Mrs. <u>See</u> **North, Leigh, pseud.**

P-305 Phelps, Elizabeth Stuart, 1844-1911. Avery / by Elizabeth Stuart Phelps. Boston; New York: Houghton, Mifflin and Company, 1902. (Cambridge: The Riverside Press). 122 p., front.
Issued under the title "His wife" in Harper's magazine, Sept.-Nov., 1901.
LC: O 16, '02.
PW: N 8, '02.
BLC: London: Grant Richards, 1903.
References: BAL 20980.

P-306 _____ A chariot of fire / by Elizabeth Stuart Phelps; illustrated. New York; London: Harper & Brothers, 1910. 44 p., front., [1] leaf of plates. [Ill. by William Hurd Lawrence.]
First separate book appearance.
LC: O 8, '10.
PW: O 15, '10.
References: BAL 21001.

P-307 _____ Comrades / by Elizabeth Stuart Phelps; illustrated by Howard E. Smith. New York; London: Harper & Brothers, 1911. 48, [1] p., front., [2] leaves of plates.
LC: S 30, '11.
PW: O 14, '11.
References: BAL 21003.

P-308 [_____] Confessions of a wife / by Mary Adams [pseud.]; with illustrations by Granville Smith. New York: The Century Co., 1902. 377 p., front., [5] leaves of plates.
LC: O 3, '02.
PW: O 25, '02.
References: BAL 20982.

_____ Covered embers. <u>In</u> *Their husband's wives* **(1906), T-161.**

P-309 _____ The empty house: and other stories / By Elizabeth Stuart Phelps; illustrated. Boston; New York: Houghton, Mifflin Company, 1910. (Cambridge: The Riverside Press). 326 p., front., [3] leaves of plates.
Contents: The empty house -- Twenty-four: four -- The presence -- The romance of the bill -- Fée -- His father's heart -- The rejected manuscript -- Sweet Home Road -- The joy-giver.
LC: N 3, '10.
PW: O 29, '10.
References: BAL 21002.

P-310 _____ Jonathan and David / by Elizabeth Stuart Phelps; with illustrations by W. T. Smedley. New York; London: Harper & Brothers, 1909. 47, [1] p., front., [2] leaves of plates.
LC: Ag 20, '09.
PW: Ag 28, '09.
References: BAL 20998.

P-311 _____ The man in the case / by Elizabeth Stuart Phelps; illustrated by Henry J. Peck. Boston; New York: Houghton, Mifflin and Company, 1906. (Cambridge [Mass.]: The Riverside Press). 265, [1] p., front., [5] leaves of plates.
LC: S 10, '06.
PW: S 29, '06.
BLC: London: Archibald Constable & Co.; Boston [Mass.]; New York: Houghton, Mifflin & Co., 1906.
References: BAL 20991.

P-312 _____ The oath of allegiance: and other stories / by Elizabeth Stuart Phelps; illustrated. Boston; New York: Houghton Mifflin Company, 1909. (Cambridge: The Riverside Press). 373, [1] p., col. front., [4] leaves of plates. [Ill. by William L. Jacobs and W. D. Stevens.]
Contents: The oath of allegiance -- Covered embers -- The autobiography of Aureola -- A chariot of fire -- His soul to keep -- A sacrament --"Tammyshanty" -- Unemployed -- The sacred fire -- Christophorus -- The chief operator.
LC: O 23, '09.
PW: S 25, '09.
BLC: London: Constable & Co., Cambridge, Mass. [printed], 1909.
References: BAL 20999.

P-313 _____ The successors of Mary the first / by Elizabeth Stuart Phelps. Boston; New York: Houghton, Mifflin and Company, 1901. (Cambridge: The Riverside Press). 267 p., front., [6] leaves of plates. [Ill. by A. I. Keller.]
LC: Ap 11, '01.
PW: Ap 27, '01.
References: BAL 20971.

P-314 _____ Though life us do part / by Elizabeth Stuart Phelps; with a frontispiece by Clarence F. Underwood. Boston; New York: Houghton Mifflin Company, 1908. (Cambridge: The Riverside Press). 323, [1] p., col. front.
LC: S 19, '08.
PW: O 17, '08.
References: BAL 20994.

P-315 _____ Trixy / by Elizabeth Stuart Phelps. Boston; New York: Houghton, Mifflin and Company, 1904. (Cambridge: The Riverside Press). 299 p., col. front. [Ill. by Etheldred Breeze Barry.]
LC: S 28, '04.
PW: O 15, '04.
BLC: London: Hodder & Stoughton, 1905.
References: BAL 20986.

P-316 _____ Walled in: a novel / by Elizabeth Stuart Phelps . . . ; illustrated by Clarence F. Underwood. New York; London: Harper & Brothers, 1907. 309, [1] p., front., [7] leaves of plates.
LC: O 15, '07.

PW: O 26, '07.
References: BAL 20993; BAL 20992: advanced issue.

____, contributor. See *The whole family* (1908), **W-578.**

P-317   Phelps, F. A. Joe Monigan: a tale of the early West / by F. A. Phelps. Chicago, Illinois: Published by The American Publishing House, [c1907]. 159 p.

P-318   Phelps, George L. A demon's scheme / by Geo. L. Phelps . . . Burlington, Colo.: Record, [19__].
1 folded sheet ([4] p.)

P-319   Phelps, George Olcott. One man power, plus / by G. Olcott Phelps; illustrated. Boston: The Roxburgh Publishing Company (Incorporated), [c1909]. 224 p., front., [6] leaves of plates. [Ill. by A. W. Jones.]
LC: N 10, '09.

P-320   Phelps, Guy Fitch, 1872-1933. The angel o' Deadman / by Guy Fitch Phelps . . . Cincinnati: The Standard Publishing Co., [c1917]. 374 p.; col. front., plates.
Unexamined copy: bibliographic data from OCLC, #6566200.
LC: My 21, '17.
PW: Je 16, '17.

P-321   ____ The black prophet / by Guy Fitch Phelps. Cincinnati [Ohio]: The Standard Publishing Company, [c1916]. 360 p.
LC: Ap 24, '16.
PW: My 6, '16.

P-322   ____ Ethel Vale: the white slave / by Rev. Guy F. Phelps. Chicago, Ill.: The Christian Witness Co., [c1910]. 217 p., [4] leaves of plates. [Ill. by C. Rosser.]
LC: Ag 25, '10.

P-323   ____ The moan of the Tiber / by Guy Fitch Phelps . . . Cincinnati: The Standard Publishing Company, [c1917]. 86 p.
LC: F 21, '17.

P-324   ____ The mountains of the morning / by Guy Fitch Phelps; illustrated by George T. Tobin. New York; Cincinnati: The Abingdon Press, [c1916]. 392 p., col. front., [2] leaves of plates.
LC: N 28, '16.
PW: N 25, '16.

P-325   Phelps, Sarah. Grandma Faithful's happy day / by Sarah Phelps. [Chicago?: s. n.], [c1907]. 46 p., front.   **DLC**
"A souvenir of the Puritanic faith."
LC: Ag 31, '07.

P-326   Phelps, William Lyon, 1865-1943. A dash at the Pole / by William Lyon Phelps . . . ; illustrations by John Goss. Boston: The Ball Publishing Company, 1909. [72] p., ill.
LC: N 27, '09.

P-327   Phifer, Charles Lincoln, 1860-1931. Diaz the dictator: a story of international intrigue and politics / by Charles Lincoln Phifer . . . Girard, Kansas: Published by C. L. Phifer, 1910. 123 p.   **WTU**

P-328   ____ The friar's daughter: a story of the American occupation of the Phillipines / by Charles Lincoln Phifer . . . Girard, Kansas: Published by C. L. Phifer, 1909. 108 p.   **DLC**

P-329   [Philips, A. E. (Albert Edwin)], b. 1845. The Florida wilds: being tales of adventure and romance from a land of romance with stories of plantation life / by Edwin Alberton [pseud.]. New York; Washington: The Neale Publishing Company, 1906. 245 p.   **TNS**
Contents: The fire-hunt and its sequel -- McLeod at the log-rolling -- A day of rare sport and an exciting conclusion -- Plantation scenes and incidents -- Lost, and an awful encounter -- A story of startling adventures -- The panther hunt -- The bee tree and the plan for a camp hunt -- Story and adventure of Billy McLeod -- The cracker -- A cracker courtship, or, Billy McLeod, the matchmaker.

P-330   ____ The romance of the Ten Thousand Islands: (a Florida story) / by A. E. Philips (Edwin Alberton). New York; Baltimore: Broadway Publishing Co., [c1909]. 311 p.
LC: D 31, '09.

P-331   Philips, Page. At bay: a novel / by Page Philips; based on the drama by George Scarborough. New York: The Macaulay Company, 1914. 253 p., photo. front., [4] leaves of photo. plates.
LC: Ap 15, '14.
PW: My 9, '14.
BLC: London: Hodder & Stoughton, 1916.

P-332   ____ The coast of opportunity / by Page Philips; illustrated by William L. Howes. New York: The Macaulay Company, 1917. 301 p., front., [3] leaves of plates.
LC: Mr 19, '17.
PW: Mr 24, '17.

P-333   ____ The trail of the waving palm / by Page Philips. New York: The Macaulay Company, 1915. 313 p., front., [3] leaves of plates. [Ill. by Howard Giles.]
LC: F 18, '15.
PW: F 6, '15.

P-334   Phillips, Charles Lincoln. Frederick Young: a novel / by Charles Lincoln Phillips; illustrated. Boston: Henry A. Dickerman & Son, [c1901]. 401 p., photo. front., [1] leaf of plates.
PW: My 11, '01.

P-335   Phillips, David Graham, 1867-1911. The conflict: a novel / David Graham Phillips. New York; London: D. Appleton and Company, 1911. 389, [1] p.
LC: S 21, '11.
PW: S 16, '11.
References: BAL 15976.

P-336   ____ The cost / by David Graham Phillips . . . ; illustrated by Harrison Fisher. Indianapolis: The Bobbs-Merrill Company, [c1904]. 402 p., col. front., [14] leaves of col. plates.
PW: My 14, '04.
BLC: London: T. Werner Laurie, [1905].
References: BAL 15959.

P-337   ____ Degarmo's wife: and other stories / David Graham Phillips. New York; London: D. Appleton and Company, 1913. 326 p.
<small>Contents: Degarmo's wife -- Enid -- Red roses and white.</small>
LC: Ag 1, '13.
PW: Jl 19, '13.
References: BAL 15979.

P-338   ____ The deluge / by David Graham Phillips; with illustrations by George Gibbs. Indianapolis: The Bobbs-Merrill Company, [c1905]. 482 p., col. front., [5] leaves of col. plates.
PW: N 4, '05.
References: BAL 15964.

P-339   ____ The fashionable adventures of Joshua Craig: a novel / by David Graham Phillips. New York: D. Appleton and Company, 1909. 365 p., front., [7] leaves of plates.
LC: Ja 16, '09.
PW: Ja 30, '09.
References: BAL 15971.

P-340   ____ The fortune hunter / by David Graham Phillips . . . ; with illustrations by E. M. Ashe. Indianapolis: The Bobbs-Merrill Company, [c1906]. 213, [1] p., front., [7] leaves of plates.
LC: My 19, '06.
PW: Je 2, '06.
References: BAL 15965.

P-341   ____ George Helm / David Graham Phillips. New York; London: D. Appleton and Company, 1912. 303 p.
LC: S 25, '12.
PW: O 5, '12.
References: BAL 15978.

P-342   ____ Golden fleece: the American adventures of a fortune hunting earl / by David Graham Phillips; illustrations by Harrison Fisher. New York: McClure, Phillips & Co., 1903. 326, [1] p., front., [15] leaves of plates.
PW: Ap 18, '03.
BLC: London: Grant Richards, printed in U. S. A., 1903.
References: BAL 15957.

P-343   ____ The grain of dust: a novel / David Graham Phillips; illustrated by A. B. Wenzell. New York; London: D. Appleton and Company, 1911. 427, [1] p., front., [7] leaves of plates.
"David Graham Phillips's place among modern American novelists:" pages 1-12 at end.
LC: Ap 13, '11.
PW: Ap 15, '11.
References: BAL 15975.

P-344   [____] The great god success: a novel / by John Graham [pseud.]. New York: Frederick A. Stokes Company, [c1901]. 299 p.
LC: Ag 30, '01.
PW: S 14, '01.
References: BAL 15954.

P-345   ____ Her Serene Highness: a novel / by David Graham Phillips. New York; London: Harper &

Brothers, 1902. 193, [1] p., front.
LC: My 2, '02.
PW: My 10, '02.
References: BAL 15955.

P-346   ____ The hungry heart: a novel / David Graham Phillips. New York; London: D. Appleton and Company, 1909. 501, [1] p.
LC: Ag 24, '09.
PW: Ag 21, '09.
BLC: London: William Heinemann, 1909.
References: BAL 15972.

P-347   ____ The husband's story: a novel / David Graham Phillips. New York; London: D. Appleton and Company, 1910. 467, [1] p.
LC: S 21, '10.
PW: S 24, '10.
References: BAL 15974.

P-348   ____ Light-fingered gentry / by David Graham Phillips . . . New York: D. Appleton and Company, 1907. 451 p., front., [3] leaves of plates. [Ill. by George Brehm.]
LC: S 20, '07.
PW: S 28, '07.
References: BAL 15968.

P-349   ____ The master-rogue: the confessions of a Croesus / by David Graham Phillips; illustrated by Gordon H. Grant. New York: McClure, Phillips & Co., 1903. 294 p., front., [5] leaves of plates.
PW: O 3, '03.
BLC: London: Grant Richards, 1904.
References: BAL 15958.

P-350   [____] The mother-light; a novel. New York: D. Appleton and Company, 1905. 296 p., front. **MNL**
LC: F 11, '05.
PW: F 25, '05.
References: BAL 15960.

P-351   ____ Old wives for new: a novel / David Graham Phillips. New York: D. Appleton and Company, 1908. 494, [1] p.
LC: Mr 6, '08.
PW: Mr 14, '08.
References: BAL 15969.

P-352   ____ The plum tree / by David Graham Phillips . . . ; illustrated by E. M. Ashe. Indianapolis: The Bobbs-Merrill Company, [c1905]. 389 p., front., [4] leaves of plates.
PW: Mr 11, '05.
References: BAL 15961.

P-353   ____ The price she paid: a novel / David Graham Phillips. New York; London: D. Appleton and Company, 1912. 378, [1] p.
LC: Je 19, '12.
PW: Je 8, '12.
References: BAL 15977.

P-354   ____ The second generation / David Graham Phillips. New York: D. Appleton and Company, 1907. 334 p., front., [3] leaves of plates. [Ill. by

Fletcher Charles Ransom.]
LC: Ja 21, '07.
PW: Ja 19, '07.
References: BAL 15967.

P-355   ____ The social secretary / by David Graham
Phillips . . . ; with illustrations by Clarence F.
Underwood; decorations by Ralph Fletcher Seymour.
Indianapolis: The Bobbs-Merrill Company, [c1905].
197, [1] p., front., [10] leaves of plates.
PW: S 30, '05.
References: BAL 15962.

P-356   [____] Susan Lenox: her fall and rise / with a
portrait of the author. New York; London: D.
Appleton and Company, 1917. 2 v.; vol. 1: 473,
[1] p., photo. front. (port.). ; vol. 2: 489, [1] p.,
photo. front. (port.).
LC: F 27, '17.
PW: Mr 3, '17.
References: BAL 15980. BAL notes: vol. 1:
<505> p.; vol. 2: <560> p.

P-357   ____ White magic: a novel / by David Graham
Phillips; illustrated by A. B. Wenzell. New York;
London: D. Appleton and Company, 1910. 392 p.,
front., [7] leaves of plates.
LC: Mr 22, '10.
PW: Ap 2, '10.
References: BAl 15973.

P-358   ____ A woman ventures: a novel / by David
Graham Phillips . . . ; with frontispiece by William
James Hurlbut. New York: Frederick A. Stokes
Company, [1902]. 331 p., front.   IWC
LC: S 19, '02.
PW: O 11, '02.
References: BAL 15956.

P-359   Phillips, Franklin Folsom, b. 1852. The white isles /
by Franklin F. Phillips. Boston, Mass.: The C. M.
Clark Publishing Co., [c1911]. 382 p., photo. front.
(port.), [3] leaves of plates.   DLC

P-360   Phillips, Henry Albert, 1880-1951. Other people's
lives / by Henry Albert Phillips. New York: Boni
and Liveright, [c1924]. 389 p.
LC: Ap 4, '24.
PW: Ap 12, '24.

Phillips, Henry Wallace, 1869-1930. A chance shot.
In *Comedy* (1901), C-614.

P-361   ____ The mascot of Sweet Briar Gulch / by Henry
Wallace Phillips . . . ; with illustrations by F. Graham
Cootes. Indianapolis: The Bobbs-Merrill Company,
[c1908]. 144 p., col. front., [8] leaves of col. plates.
LC: O 15, '08.
PW: N 7, '08.

P-362   ____ Mr. Scraggs: introduced by Red Saunders / by
Henry Wallace Phillips . . . New York: The Grafton
Press, [1906]. 188 p., col. front., [7] leaves of
plates. [Some signed by Martin Justice and N. C.
Wyeth.]
PW: Ja 20, '06.

P-363   ____ The pets / by Henry Wallace Phillips;
illustrations by A. B. Frost. New York: McClure,
Phillips & Co., 1906. 46, [1] p., incl. front., incl.
[4] leaves of plates.
LC: My 9, '06.

P-364   ____ Plain Mary Smith: a romance of Red Saunders
/ by Henry Wallace Phillips; with illustrations by
Martin Justice. New York: The Century Co., 1905.
318 p., incl. 8 plates, front.
PW: O 14, '05.

P-365   ____ Red Saunders: his adventures West & East /
by Henry Wallace Phillips. New York: McClure,
Phillips & Co., 1902. 210 p., front. [Ill. by Jay
Hambidge.]
Contents: A chance shot -- A red-haired cupid -- The golden Ford --
When the Chinook struck Fairfield.
PW: My 24, '02.
BLC: London & New York: McClure, Phillips, &
Co., U. S. A. printed, 1901.

P-366   ____ Red Saunders' pets: and other critters / by
Henry Wallace Phillips . . . ; illustrated. New York:
McClure, Phillips & Co., 1906. 231 p., front., [15]
leaves of plates, ill. [Ill. by A. B. Frost, Martin
Justice, A. Mattefert, and Will Crawford.]
Contents: The pets -- Oscar's chance, per Charley -- Billy the Buck
-- The demon in the canon -- The little bear who grew -- In the
absence of rules -- For sale, the golden queen -- Where the horse is
fate -- Agamemnon and the fall of Troy -- A touch of nature.
PW: My 19, '06.
BLC: London: Hodder & Stoughton, 1907.

P-367   ____ Trolley folly / by Henry Wallace Phillips . . . ;
illustrated. Indianapolis: The Bobbs-Merrill
Company, [c1909]. 257, [1] p., col. front., [7]
leaves of col. plates. [Ill. by The Kinneys, G. C.
Widney, and F. R. Gruger.]
LC: Mr 10, '09.
PW: Ap 3, '09.

P-368   Phillips, M. J. In our country's service / by M. J.
Phillips. Columbus: Edward T. Miller, 1909.
322 p.   NYP
PW: Ag 28, '09.

P-369   Phillips, Mary Elizabeth, 1857-1945. Tommy
Tregennis / by Mary E. Phillips. Boston: Small,
Maynard and Company, [1913]. 209 p.
BLC: London: Constable & Co., 1912.

P-370   Phillips, Maud Gillette, b. 1860. Law unwrit / by
Maud Gillette Phillips. New York: Frederick H.
Hitchcock, [c1925]. 345 p.

Phillips, Michael James. See **Phillips, M. J.**

P-371   Phillips, Roland Ashford. Golden Isle: an adventure
story / by Roland Ashford Phillips. New York City:
Chelsea House, [c1925]. 249 p.
PW: D 26, '25.

P-372   ____ Where the trail divides: an adventure story /
by Roland Ashford Phillips. New York: Chelsea
House, [c1925]. 248 p.
PW: D 26, '25.

P-373   Phillips, S. Harry. Dot / by S. Harry Phillips. Baltimore, Md.: The McLean Company, [c1916]. 50 p. **DLC**

P-374   Phipps, Isaac Newton, b. 1850. The forelopers: a romance of colonial days / by I. N. Phipps. New York: The Neale Publishing Company, 1912. 234 p.
LC: D 4, '12.
PW: N 30, '12.

P-375   Phipps, Sarah E. The angel of the pines / by Sarah E. Phipps . . . New York: Broadway Publishing Co., 1912. 133 p. **DLC**
LC: D 28, '12.

P-376   _____ The old house by the sea / by Sarah E. Phipps . . . New York: Broadway Publishing Company, [c1901]. 203 p., photo. front. (port.). Designed end papers.
PW: Ag 17, '01.

Physician, A. The strenuous life. In *The so-so stories* **(1914), S-715.**

Phylos the Thibetan, pseud. See **Oliver, Frederick Spencer, 1866-1899.**

P-377   Physiopath, A., *pseud.* Buff: a tale for the thoughtful / by a Physiopath [pseud.]. Boston: Little, Brown and Company, 1906. 255 p., photo. front. **VA@**

P-378   Picard, George H. (George Henry), 1850-1916. The bishop's niece / by George H. Picard . . . Boston: Herbert B. Turner & Co., 1905. 208 p., front. [Ill. by Alfredo Lutz Demorest.]

P-379   Pickard, Florence Willingham, b. 1862. Between scarlet thrones / by Florence Willingham Pickard. Boston, Massachusetts: The Stratford Company, 1919. 223 p., photo. front. **OSU, DNU**
PW: Ja 10, '20.

Pickard, Gertrude Gould. See **G. G. P., b. 1875.**

P-380   Pickard, William John. A spider phaeton and other stories / by William John Pickard. Chicago: Will Ransom, 1924. 163 p.
(Series of first volumes; no. 7).
Contents: A spider phaeton -- Too many flags -- Mr. Henry Shelfords' advice -- Queen of hearts -- A wise thing in the man -- Practical roses and sentimental shoes -- A wise thing in the girl -- Mr. Jeckel's wife -- A college hair-cut -- False teeth -- A bell and a battery -- Anna Marie.

P-381   Pickens, William, 1881-1954. The vengeance of the gods: and three other stories of real American color line life / introduction by Bishop John Hurst . . . Philadelphia, Pa.: The A. M. E. Book Concern, [c1922]. 125 p.
Contents: The vengence of the gods -- The superior race -- Passing the buck -- Tit for tat.
LC: Jl 17, '22.

P-382   Pickering, Abner, 1845-1940. As a soldier would: an army novel / by A. P. U. S. A. New York: Broadway Publishing Co., [c1911]. 187 p., col. front., [3] leaves of plates. [Ill. by Gail Converse.]
LC: O 21, '11.

P-383   Pickering, Sidney. The basket of fate. New York: Longmans, Green and Company, 1906. 343 p. Unexamined copy: bibliographic data from OCLC, #29967051.
BLC: London: Edward Arnold, 1906.

P-384   Pickering, Sidney. The key of paradise / by Sidney Pickering. New York: The Macmillan Company; London: Macmillan & Co., Ltd., 1903. 308 p.
BLC: London: Edward Arnold, 1903.

Pickett, Elizabeth. The return of Vach. In *The best college short stories, 1917-18* **(1919), B-557.**

Pickett, George E., Mrs. See **Pickett, La Salle Corbell.**

P-385   Pickett, LaSalle Corbell, 1848-1931. The bugles of Gettysburg / by LaSalle Corbell Pickett (Mrs. General George E. Pickett) . . . Chicago: F. G. Browne & Co., 1913. 163 p., front. **OSU, KSU**
LC: My 26, '13.
PW: My 31, '13.

P-386   _____ Ebil eye / by LaSalle Corbell Pickett . . . ; illustrated by Hattie E. Burdett, Harold L. Macdonald, Anna Sands and portrait of the author by Harold L. Macdonald. Washington: The Neale Co., 1901. 166 p., photo. front. (port.), [5] leaves of plates. **OSU, INU**
(In de miz series; v. 3).
Contents: Ebil eye -- Dat li'l' blue light -- Us -- Frenigike.
PW: Ag 3, '01.

P-387   _____ Jinny / by LaSalle Corbell Pickett . . . ; illustrated by Harold L. Macdonald, Max Weyl, R. N. Brooke, C. K. Berryman, and reprints by Sully. Washington: The Neale Co., 1901. 172 p., front. (port.), [8] leaves of plates. **KSU**
(In de miz series; v. 4).
Contents: Jinny -- Li'l'abrup -- The deforce X-mark -- De suppies' en de swif'es'.
PW: Ag 3, '01.

Pickthall, Marjorie L. C. The forgiver. In *The Bellman book of fiction* **(1921), B-485.**

_____ The men who climbed. In *The sporting spirit* **(1925), S-771.**

_____ The stove. In *Short stories* **(1925), S-460.**

P-388   Picton, Nina. The panorama of sleep, or, Soul and symbol / by Nina Picton . . . ; illustrations by Remington W. Lane. New York: The Philosophic Company, 1903. 160 p., front., [7] leaves of plates.

P-389   Pidgin, Charles Felton, 1844-1923. Blennerhassett, or, The decrees of fate: a romance founded upon events in American history / by Chas. Felton Pidgin . . . ; with illustrations by Charles H. Stephens. Boston: C. M. Clark Publishing Company, 1901. 442 p., front., [11] leaves of plates.
PW: S 7, '01.

P-390   _____ The chronicles of Quincy Adams Sawyer, detective / by Charles Felton Pidgin . . . and J. M.

Taylor; illustrated by Harold James Cue. Boston: L. C. Page & Company, 1912. 316 p., front., [5] leaves of plates.

Contents: The affair of the double thumb print -- The affair of the golden belt -- The affair of Unreachable Island -- The affair of Trimountain Bank -- The affair of Lamson's cook -- The affair of the Plymouth recluse -- The affair of William Baird, P.B.

LC: O 21, '12.
PW: O 26, '12.

P-391 _____ The climax, or, What might have been: a romance of the Great Republic / by Charles Felton Pidgin . . . Boston, Mass., U. S. A.: C. M. Clark Publishing Company, 1902. 335 p., front. [Ill. by C. W. Reed.]
PW: O 11, '02.

P-392 _____ The Corsican lovers: a story of the vendetta / by Charles Felton Pidgin; with eight illustrations by Malcolm Strauss. New York: B. W. Dodge & Company, 1906. 345 p., front., [7] leaves of plates.
PW: Mr 24, '06.

P-393 _____ The further adventures of Quincy Adams Sawyer and Mason Corner folks: a novel / by Charles Felton Pidgin . . . ; illustrated by Henry Roth. Boston: L. C. Page & Company, 1909. 385 p., front., [5] leaves of plates.
LC: My 11, '09.
PW: Je 19, '09.

P-394 _____ The hidden man: a novel / by Chas. Felton Pidgin . . . Boston: Mayhew Publishing Company, 1906. 215 p.
(Love and laughter library).
LC: S 27, '06.
PW: N 3, '06.

P-395 _____ The house of shame: a novel . . . / by Charles Felton Pidgin . . . New York: Cosmopolitan Press, 1912. 244 p.   **AFU**
LC: D 28, '12.
PW: F 15, '13.

P-396 _____ Labor; or, The money-god! Which?: A story of the times / by Charles Felton Pidgin . . . Boston: Mayhew Publishing Company, 1908. 232 p., front. (port.).   **EYM**
PW: My 16, '08.

P-397 _____ The letter H: a novel / by Charles Felton Pidgin . . . ; illustrations by Ch. Weber Ditzler. New York: G. W. Dillingham Company, 1904. 316 p., front., [5] leaves of plates.
PW: Ag 13, '04.
BLC: London: T. Fisher Unwin, New York [printed], 1904.

P-398 _____ Little Burr, the Warwick of America: a tale of the old revolutionary days / by Charles Felton Pidgin; illustrations by Issac Brewster Hazelton. Boston: The Robinson Luce Company, 1905. 396 p., front., [11] leaves of plates.
PW: Ap 1, '05.

P-399 _____ A nation's idol: a romance of Franklin's nine years of happiness at the Court of France / by Chas.

Felton Pidgin . . . Philadelphia: Henry Altemus Company, [c1904]. 348 p.
PW: N 12, '04.

P-400 _____ Quincy Adams Sawyer and Mason's Corner folks: a picture of New England home life / by Chas. Felton Pidgin. -- Rev. ed. -- Boston: C. M. Clark Publishing Company; New York: Grosset and Dunlap, sole agents . . ., [c1900,c1902]. 474 p., front., [11] leaves of plates (some photo.). [Ill. by C. W. Reed.]
Original edition published in 1900; Lyle Wright, 4240.

P-401 _____ Sarah Bernhardt Brown: and what she did in a country town: a dramatic novel / by Chas. Felton Pidgin . . . Boston, Mass.: The J. K. Waters Company, 1906. 436 p., front., [11] leaves of plates. [Ill. by Frank A. Lappen.]
PW: F 10, '06.

P-402 _____ Stephen Holton: a story of life as it is in town and country / by Charles Felton Pidgin; with a frontispiece by Frank T. Merrill. Boston: L. C. Page & Company, 1902. 312 p., front.
PW: My 10, '02.
BLC: London: Ward, Lock & Co., 1902.

P-403 _____ The toymakers / by Charles Felton Pidgin . . . Boston, Mass., U. S. A.: The C. M. Clark Publishing Co., 1907. 253 p., col. front., [9] leaves of plates.
LC: Ap 22, '07.
PW: My 18, '07.

P-404 Pier, Arthur Stanwood, 1874-1966. The ancient grudge / by Arthur Stanwood Pier. Boston; New York: Houghton, Mifflin and Company, 1905. (Cambridge [Mass.]: The Riverside Press). 477, [1] p.
PW: O 7, '05.
BLC: London: Dean & Son, printed in U. S. A., 1906.

P-405 _____ Confident morning: a novel / by Arthur Stanwood Pier. Boston; New York: Houghton Mifflin Company, 1925. (Cambridge: The Riverside Press). 325 p.
LC: Jl 13, '25.
PW: Jl 18, '25.

P-406 _____ Jerry / by Arthur Stanwood Pier; with illustrations by Christine Tucke Curtiss. Boston; New York: Houghton Mifflin Company, 1917. (Cambridge [Mass.]: The Riverside Press). 402 p., front., [3] leaves of plates.
LC: F 7, '17.
PW: F 17, '17.

P-407 _____ The sentimentalist: a novel / by Arthur Stanwood Pier. New York; London: Harper & Brothers, 1901. 424, [1] p.
PW: Mr 2, '01.

P-408   _____ The son decides: the story of a young German-American / by Arthur Stanwood Pier; with illustrations. Boston; New York: Houghton Mifflin Company, 1918. (Cambridge: The Riverside Press). 222, [1] p., front., [3] leaves of plates. [Ill. by Harold Cue.]   **IUA**
LC: My 1, '18.
PW: My 4, '18.

P-409   _____ The triumph / by Arthur Stanwood Pier. New York: McClure, Phillips & Co., 1903. 323 p., front., [7] leaves of plates. [Some ill. by W. D. Stevens.]
PW: Je 6, '03.

P-410   _____ The women we marry / by Arthur Stanwood Pier. Boston; New York: Houghton Mifflin Company, 1914. (Cambridge [Mass.]: The Riverside Press). 374, [1] p.
LC: Mr 30, '14.
PW: Ap 4, '14.
BLC: London: T. Werner Laurie, Cambridge, Mass. [printed, 1914].

P-411   Pier, Garrett Chatfield, b. 1875. Hanit the enchantress / by Garrett Chatfield Pier . . . New York: E. P. Dutton & Company, [c1921]. 283 p.
LC: Je 6, '21.
PW: Je 4, '21.

P-412   _____ Hidden valley / by Garrett Chatfield Pier. Boston, Massachusetts: The Stratford Company, 1925. 236 p.
LC: Ap 15, '25.
PW: Je 20, '25.

P-413   Pierce, Cornelia Boyden. Breath of the hills: tales of country life / by Cornelia Boyden Pierce . . . [Worcester, Mass.: Belisle Printing & Publishing Co.], [c1923]. 254 p., front., [1] leaf of plates.
Contents: What is success [poem] -- Keturah's gumption -- Sleep [poem] -- Fidelia's valentine -- Compensation [poem] -- Temperance's Thanksgiving turkey -- Snow-flakes [poem] -- A leap-year romance -- On Easter morning -- A prayer [poem] -- Jerusha's "risin' up" -- Thoughts of Easter [poem] -- For all time -- Her easter bonnet --The future [poem] -- The story of a wish-bone -- Lucinda's Christmas vision -- "Git up and git" [poem] -- Kesiah's independence -- The whip-poor-will [poem] -- A Hallowe'en romance -- My ideal [poem] -- A day for Thanksgiving -- Patience [poem] -- One soldier's grave -- The wind [poem] -- A mother's love -- Amost I doubted [poem] -- A Christmas jumble -- To Dorothy [poem] -- Aunt Calista's valentine -- True love [poem] -- Easter hopes -- Reconciliation [poem] -- The Pineville Woman's Club -- What happened to Hannah -- On the rocks [poem] -- How Tryphosia managed -- How Alvira went to the circus -- Messages of love [poem] -- Tildy Ann's mince pies -- St. Valentines Day [poem] -- The heart of her husband -- The lost manuscript -- Faithless [poem] -- Huldah's Christmas debt -- To thee [poem] -- The rummage sale at Pineville -- In thy good time [poem] -- Obadiah's auction -- Lift up thine eyes [poem] -- A baby's shoe -- Well done [poem] -- The greater hero [a memorial day story].

P-414   Pierce, Dexter Vinton. Caleb Abbott / by Dexter Vinton Pierce . . . Boston: Farrington Printing Company, 1904. 244 p., photo. front.

P-415   Pierce, Ernest Frederic. The traveller's joy / by Ernest Frederic Pierce. New York: E. P. Dutton & Company, 1907. 295, [1] p.
BLC: Bristol: J. W. Arrowsmith, 1906.

P-416   [Pierce, Frederick E.], b. 1877. The new goddess / by Percy Fredericks [pseud.]. New York, 1905. Unexamined copy: bibliographic data from NUC.

P-417   Pierce, George Winslow, 1841-1917. A select circle; with designs and songs / by George Winslow Pierce . . . [Boston?, 1904]. 175 p. Unexamined copy: bibliographic data from OCLC, #20717172.

P-418   Pierson, Jane Susanna Anderson, b. 1854. The coming of the dawn / by Jane A. Pierson; illustrations by Philip H. Pratt. Cincinnati: Standard Pub. Co., [c1917]. 299 p., front., [2] leaves of plates.
LC: S 26, '17.
PW: O 13, '17.

P-419   Pike, Florence Spaulding. The trail of the lost electric / by Florence Spaulding Pike. Jackson, Michigan: The Allen Publishing Company, [c1914]. 87, [2] p.   **DLC**

P-420   Pillars of smoke. -- new ed. -- New York: Sturgis & Walton Company, 1915. 252 p.
Ascribed to Kate Stephens.

P-421   Pimenoff, L. L. (Lydia Lvovna). Before the dawn: a story of Russian life / by Pimenoff-Noble. Boston; New York: Houghton, Mifflin and Company, 1901. (Cambridge: The Riverside Press). 401, [1] p. Written by Lydia Lvovna Pimenoff-Noble and Edmund Noble.

P-422   Pinckney, Sue, b. 1843. Darcy Pinckney / by Sue Pinckney . . . New York; Washington: The Neale Publishing Company, 1906. 379 p.   **DLC**
LC: O 24, '06.

P-423   _____ In the Southland / by Sue Pinckney. New York; Washington: The Neale Publishing Company, 1906. 207 p.   **NGU**
PW: Je 2, '06.

Pinckney, Susanna Hulrick Hayne, b. 1843. See **Pinckney, Sue.**

P-424   Pinkerton, Colin McKenzie, 1887-1967. The hidden fortune: an educational story / by Colin McKenzie Pinkerton . . . Des Moines, Iowa: Shissler-Chase Co., [c1902]. 259 p., incl. 5 plates (some photo.), photo. front.   **MNU**

P-425   Pinkerton, Kathrene Sutherland Gedney, b. 1887. The long traverse / by Kathrene and Robert Pinkerton; frontispiece by Ralph Pallen Coleman. Garden City; New York: Doubleday, Page & Company, 1920. 249, [1] p., col. front.
LC: Jl 28, '20.
PW: Jl 17, '20.

P-426   _____ Penitentiary post / by Kathrene and Robert Pinkerton; frontispiece by Ralph Pallen Coleman. Garden City, N. Y.: Doubleday, Page & Company, 1920. 245, [1] p., col. front.
LC: Je 21, '20.
PW: Je 26, '20.

P-427 Pinkerton, Robert Eugene, 1882-1970. The fourth
Norwood / by Robert E. Pinkerton. Chicago: The
Reilly & Lee Co., [c1925]. 351 p.
LC: S 14, '25.
PW: Ag 22, '25.
BLC: London: Hurst & Blackett, 1925.

_____, jt. aut. *The long traverse* (1920). See
**Pinkerton, Kathrene Sutherland Gedney, b. 1887,
jt. aut., P-425.**

_____, jt. aut. *Penitentiary post* (1920). See
**Pinkerton, Kathrene Sutherland Gedney, b. 1887,
jt. aut., P-426.**

P-428 _____ The test of Donald Norton / by Robert E.
Pinkerton. Chicago: The Reilly & Lee Co., [1924].
345 p., col. front.
LC: Ap 5, '24.
PW: My 24, '24.
BLC: London: Hurst & Blackett, [1924].

P-429 Pinkham, Edwin George, 1876-1948. Fate's a fiddler
/ by Edwin George Pinkham; illustrated by Lester
Ralph. Boston: Small, Maynard & Company, 1908.
417 p., col. front., [3] leaves of plates.
PW: Jl 11, '08.

P-430 Pinkston, Lady Lois, b. 1887. The earl of Rossville
Hall / by Lady L. Pinkston. New York; Washington:
The Neale Publishing Company, 1906. 306 p.
Unexamined copy: bibliographic data from OCLC,
#7678050.
LC: Jl 7, '06.

Pinney, Laura Young. The lost maid of Tuolumne.
In Pacific Coast Women's Press Association. *La
copa de oro* **(1905), P-2.**

P-431 Pinnix, Hannah C. (Hannah Courtney), 1851-1931.
Chaney's stratagem / by Hannah Courtenay Pinnix.
Boston, Massachusetts: The C. M. Clark Publishing
Company, 1909. 314 p., incl. front. [Ill. by R.
Stebbins.]
LC: N 12, '09.

Pinski, David, 1872-1959. Reb Shloimeh. **In** *Yiddish
tales* **(1912), Y-20.**

P-432 Pinski, David, 1872-1959. Temptations; a book of
short stories / by David Pinski; authorized translation
from the Yiddish by Dr. Isaac Goldberg. New York,
Brentano's, 1919. 325 p.
Contents: Introduction -- Beruriah -- The temptations of Rabbi Akiba
-- Johanan the high priest -- Zerubbabel -- Drabkin: a novelette of
proletarian life -- The black cat -- A tale of a hungry man -- In the
storm.
LC: My 17, '19.
BLC: London: G. Allen & Co., 1921.

P-433 Pinson, W. W. (William Washington), 1854-1930. In
white and black: a story / by W. W. Pinson;
illustrated by Bert Ball. Akron, O.: The Saalfield
Publishing Company, [c1902]. 357 p., front., [4]
leaves of plates.

Pioneer, The, [pseud.] <u>See</u> **Micheaux, Oscar.**

P-434 [Piper, Margaret Rebecca], b. 1879. Babbie: the
story of Babbie Lee, and some further doings of Peter
Loomis and Daphne / by Margaret Piper Chalmers;
illustrated by John Goss. Boston: L. C. Page &
Company, [1925]. 347 p., col. front., [3] leaves of
plates.
LC: S 14, '25.

P-435 _____ Sylvia Arden decides / by Margaret Rebecca
Piper . . . ; illustrated with a frontispiece in full color
by Haskell Coffin. Boston: The Page Company,
1917. 316 p., col. front.   **NYP**
LC: O 10, '17.
PW: N 10, '17.

P-436 _____ Sylvia of the hill top / by Margaret Rebecca
Piper . . . ; illustrated with a frontispiece in full color
by Gene Pressler. Boston: The Page Company,
1916. 311 p., col. front.   **CWR**
LC: My 11, '16.
PW: My 27, '16.

P-437 _____ Sylvia's experiment: the story of an unrelated
family / by Margaret Rebecca Piper; illustrated with a
frontispiece in full color by Z. P. Nikolaki. Boston:
The Page Company, 1914. 280 p., col. front.
                                    OSU, CUR
LC: S 8, '14.

P-438 _____ Wild wings: a romance of youth / by Margaret
Rebecca Piper . . . ; illustrated by John Goss.
Boston: The Page Company, 1921. 420 p., front.,
[3] leaves of plates.
LC: O 18, '21.
PW: N 19, '21; D 10, '21.

P-439 Pitblado, Charles Bruce, 1836-1913. Nareen / by the
late Rev. Charles Bruce Pitblado . . . and Rev. Edwy
Guthrie Pitblado . . . Toledo, Ohio: The Hadley
Press, [c1908]. 268 p.

Pitblado, Edwy Guthrie, jt. aut. *Nareen* (1908). See
**Pitblado, Charles Bruce, 1836-1913, jt. aut.,
P-439.**

P-440 Pitkin, Helen, b. 1877. An angel by brevet: a story
of modern New Orleans / by Helen Pitkin.
Philadelphia; London: J. B. Lippincott Company,
1904. 384 p., front.
PW: N 19, '04.

Pitkin, Walter B. (Walter Broughton), 1878-1953,
comp. In *As we are* (1923), A-325.

_____ Masters of ourselves and ours. In *As we are*
(1923), A-325.

P-441 Pitman, John. The detective story / John Pitman. [S.
l.: s. n., 1908]. 14 p. (Pages are numbered in
words).
Caption title.

P-442 Pitman, Norman Hinsdale, 1876-1925. The lady elect: a Chinese romance / by Norman Hinsdale Pitman; illustrated by Li Chu-T'ang. New York; Chicago; Toronto, etc.: Fleming H. Revell Company, [c1913]. 308 p., front., [9] leaves of plates.
LC: O 22, '13.

P-443 Pitman, William Dent. The Quincunx case / by William Dent Pitman. Boston: Herbert B. Turner & Co., 1904. 306 p.
PW: O 8, '04.
BLC: London: Grant Richards, [printed in U. S. A.], 1904.

P-444 Pitt, Chart. The law of the lean lands: a novel of the fur country / by Chart Pitt. New York: Frederick A. Stokes Company, 1925. 297 p.
BLC: London: Mills & Boon, 1925.

P-445 Pittman, H. D. (Hannah Daviess), 1840-1919. The belle of the Bluegrass Country: studies in black and white / by H. D. Pittman. Boston: The C. M. Clark Publishing Co., 1906. 424 p., col. front., [15] leaves of plates. [Some ill. by S. Y. Wendell; some photo. by Sanders Co., St. Louis.]
LC: Jl 26, '06.
PW: Ag 4, '06.

P-446 _____ Go forth and find / by H. D. Pittman . . . Boston: Richard G. Badger, 1910. ([Boston]: The Gorham Press). 382 p.
LC: N 29, '09.
PW: F 12, '10.

P-447 _____ The heart of Kentucky / by H. D. Pittman . . . New York; Washington: The Neale Publishing Company, 1908. 267 p.
LC: O 19, '08.
PW: D 5, '08.

P-448 _____ In dreamland: a story of living and giving / by Mrs. H. D. Pittman. Boston: Richard G. Badger; Toronto: The Copp Clark Co., Limited, [c1915]. 167 p., front., [3] leaves of plates. [Ill. by Isabella Morton.]
LC: O 26, '15.
PW: O 30, '15.

P-449 Planert, Harry. The last of the Templars / by Harry Planert. Cincinnati: The Standard Publishing Company, [c1919]. 112 p.   **NYP**

P-450 Plante, Louis. The shadow of the astral: a mystic narrative / by Louis Plante. Los Angeles, California: Published by the Austin Publishing Co., [c1921]. 330 p.

"Platinum Bill," pseud. See **Smith, Wilfrid Robert b. 1869.**

P-451 Plum, William Rattle. The sword and the soul: a romance of the Civil War / by William R. Plum . . . ; illustrated. New York: The Neale Publishing Company, 1917. 446 p., front., [3] leaves of plates. [Ill. by M. Gardner.]

P-452 Plumb, Albert H. (Albert Hale), b. 1863. When mayflowers blossom: a romance of Plymouth's first years / by Albert H. Plumb. New York; Chicago; Toronto; London; Edinburgh: Fleming H. Revell Company, [c1914]. 506 p., front.

P-453 Plume, Icarus de. The Island of Elcadar: a pilgrimage in novel-land / by Icarus de Plume; with introductory note by FitzHugh MontMorency. Boston: Marshall Jones Company, [c1921]. 111 p., front., ill.

P-454 Plummer, Charles Griffin, b. 1859. Gun-Grabbing Johnny / by Charles Griffin Plummer, M. D.; with a brief introduction by George Wharton James; illustrated with many bird and nature photographs. Pasadena, Calif.: The Radiant Life Press, 1923. 327 p., [11] leaves of photo. plates (plates printed on both sides).

P-455 Plunkett, Charles Hare. The letters of one: a study in limitations / by Charles Hare Plunkett. New York; London: G. P. Putnam's Sons, 1907. ([New York]: The Knickerbocker Press). 179 p.
BLC: London: Smith, Elder & Co., 1907.

P-456 Plympton, A. G. (Almira George), b. 1852. In the shadow of the black pine: a romance of the Massachusetts Bay Colony / by A. G. Plympton. Boston: Small, Maynard & Company, 1901. 369 p.
PW: O 26, '01.

P-457 Poate, Ernest M. Behind locked doors: a detective story / by Ernest M. Poate. New York: Chelsea House, [c1923]. 320 p.
LC: Ja 7, '24.

P-458 _____ Pledged to the dead: a detective story / by Ernest M. Poate. New York: Chelsea House, [c1925]. 320 p.
LC: Ja 6, '25.

P-459 _____ The trouble at Pinelands: a detective story / by Ernest M. Poate. New York City: Chelsea House, [c1922]. 310 p., front.
LC: D 13, '22.

P-460 Poling, Daniel A. (Daniel Alfred), 1884-1968. The furnace / by Dan Poling. New York: George H. Doran Company, [c1925]. 311 p.
PW: Jl 11, '25.
BLC: London: Hodder & Stoughton, printed in U. S. A., [1926].

P-461 Politics. New York: McClure, Phillips & Co., 1901. 178 p., front. [Ill. by W. R. Leigh.]   **SOI**
Contents: A manufacturer of history / C. Warren -- The member of the ninth / by J. G. Sanderson -- Deepwater politics / M. McHenry -- Cavalleria rusticana / G. Beardsley -- A temperance campaign / G. K. Turner.
PW: O 26, '01.

P-462 Politzer, Anthony P. (Anthony Philip). The rabbi of Liszka and the possibilities of Christian science in the twentieth century: a personal experience / by Anthony P. Politzer. [New York, Press of M. J. Roth, c1901.] 43 p., photo. front. (port.), [1] leaf of plates.   **HUC**

P-463 Pollard, Edward B. Paul Judson: a story of the Kentucky mountains / by Edward Bagby Pollard; illustrated. Louisville, Kentucky: The Baptist Argus, 1905. 448 p., front., [5] leaves of plates. [Some ill. by E. J. Bacon.] **KEU**

P-464 [Pollard, Percival], 1869-1911. The imitator: a novel. Saint Louis: William Marion Reedy, 1901. 196 p. **GZM**
PW: Ap 5, '02.

P-465 _____ Lingo Dan: a novel / by Percival Pollard . . . Washington, D. C.: The Neale Publishing Company, 1903. 174 p. **GSU**
PW: Ag 22, '03.

P-466 Pollock, Bernice McCally. Hortense: the romance of a year: a temperance novel / by Mrs. Bernice McCally Pollock. Morgantown, W. Va.: Acme Publishing Company, 1902. 154 p., photo. front. (port.). **WVF**

P-467 Pollock, Channing, 1880-1946. Behold the man: being a novel dealing with the dual personalities of the peasants who appear in the sacred performance at Ober-Ammergau / by Channing Pollock. Washington: The Neale Publishing Company, 1901. 104 p.
PW: N 16, '01.

P-468 _____ The fool: a novel from the play / by Channing Pollock; illustrated with scenes from the photoplay; a William Fox production. New York: Grosset & Dunlap, [c1925]. 300 p., photo. front., [7] leaves of photo. plates.
PW: F 7, '25.

Pollock, John Alfred, b. 1844. See **deConval, Ronleigh, pseud.**

Pollock, M. I. See **West, Emery, pseud.**

P-469 Pomeroy, Mary Shepardson. Love's crucible / by Mary Shepardson Pomeroy. Boston: Sherman, French & Company, 1911. 302 p. **DLC**
LC: N 29, '11.
PW: D 2, '11.

P-470 Pomeroy, Sarah Gertrude, b. 1882. A loyal little subject; a Christmas in Holland / by Sarah Gertrude Pomeroy; illustrated by Bertha Davidson Hoxie. Boston: D. Estes & Company, [c1908]. 31 p., incl. front., ill.
Unexamined copy: bibliographic data from NUC.
Running title: *Christmas in Holland*.

Pontus, Joseph. See **Cunningham, William Bennett.**

P-471 Pool, Bettie Freshwater, 1860-1928. The Eyrie: and other southern stories / by Bettie Freshwater Pool. New York: Broadway Publishing Company, [c1905]. 108 p., front. (port.). Designed end papers.
Contents: "The Eyrie" -- The Nag's Head picture of Theodosia Burr -- The shadow of the past -- Joe Pinetop's "Marse Jeemes" -- On the Amazon -- Divided -- Little Marse Hal -- Poems -- The monstrosity / Gaston Pool.
PW: S 2, '05.

P-472 _____ Under Brazillian skies / by Bettie Freshwater Pool . . . Elizabeth City, N. C.: Geo. P. E. Hart, 1908. 60 p.
Contents: Under Brazillian skies -- The hermit of South Mountains -- Foreshadowed -- The old brick house.
LC: N 28, '08.

P-473 Poole, Ernest, 1880-1950. The avalanche / by Ernest Poole. New York: The Macmillan Company, 1924. 344 p.
LC: My 29, '24.
PW: Je 7, 24.
BLC: London: Eveleigh Nash & Grayson, printed in U. S. A., 1925.

P-474 _____ Beggars' gold / by Ernest Poole. New York: The Macmillan Company, 1921. 234 p.
LC: O 29, '21.
PW: N 12, '21.

P-475 _____ Blind: a story of these times / by Ernest Poole. New York: The Macmillan Company, 1920. 416 p.
LC: O 20, '20.
PW: O 23, '20.
BLC: London: Macmillan, 1921.

P-476 _____ Danger / by Ernest Poole. New York: The Macmillan Company, 1923. 297 p.
LC: My 10, '23.
PW: Ap 28, '23.
BLC: London: Eveleigh Nash & Co., 1924.

P-477 _____ The harbor / by Ernest Poole. New York: The Macmillan Company, 1915. 387 p.
LC: F 4, '15.
PW: F 13, '15.

P-478 _____ His family / by Ernest Poole . . . New York: The Macmillan Company, 1917. 320 p. **OSU, CIN**
LC: My 17, '17.
PW: My 5, '17.
BLC: London: Macmillan, 1919.

P-479 _____ His second wife / by Ernest Poole . . . New York: The Macmillan Company, 1918. 302 p.
LC: My 16, '18.
PW: My 11, '18.
BLC: London: Macmillan, 1919.

P-480 _____ The hunter's moon / by Ernest Poole; illustrated by Decie Merwin; cover design by Abram Poole. New York: The Macmillan Company, 1925. 210 p., front., ill. Illustrated end papers.
LC: S 9, '25.
PW: O 10, '25.

P-481 _____ The little dark man: and other Russian sketches / by Ernest Poole. New York: The Macmillan Company, 1925. 141 p.
Contents: The dormeuse -- The little dark man -- Stories that his uncle told -- Mother Volga.
LC: Ap 22, '25.
PW: Ap 25, '25.

P-482 _____ Millions / by Ernest Poole. New York: The Macmillan Company, 1922. 279 p.
LC: S 20, '22.
PW: O 7, '22.

Poole, Ernest. Salvatore Schneider. See **Conrad, Joseph, 1857-1924.** *Il conte* (1925), C-697.

P-483 ____ The voice of the street / by Ernest Poole. New York: A. S. Barnes & Company, 1906. 285 p., front., [4] leaves of plates. [Some ill. by Joseph Stella.]   **FDA**

P-484 Poor, Agnes Blake, 1842-1922. Under guiding stars: a Massachusetts story of the century end / by Agnes Blake Poor. New York; London: G. P. Putnam's Sons, 1905. ([New York]: The Knickerbocker Press). 324 p.

P-485 Pope, Franklin. The stranger's visit / by Franklin Pope. Cleveland, Ohio: Zuriel Publishing Company, [c1908]. 61, [1] p.
LC: N 18, '08.

P-486 Pope, Martha Grace. Victoria. Boston: Sherman, French & Company, c1915. 243 p.
Unexamined copy: bibliographic data from OCLC, #21075208.

P-487 Popham, Florence. The housewives of Edenrise / by Florence Popham. New York: D. Appleton and Company, 1902. 285 p.
PW: O 25, '02.

P-488 Popham, William Lee, b. 1885. Garden of the gods romance: describing the Pike's Peak region, Crystal Park, Cripple Creek, Pike's Peak, the Royal Gorge, the Grand Canyon of the Arkansas, the mountain of the Holy Cross, Utah Desert, Castle Gate, the Great Salt Lake, the Mormon Tabernacle, and the Great Organ, etc., etc., description being from the author's observation / William Lee Popham. Louisville, Kentucky: The World Supply Company, [c1911]. (Louisville, Ky.: Mayes Printing Company). 110 p., [1] leaf of plates.   **KUK**
LC: D 18, '11.

P-489 ____ Grand Canyon of Arizona romance / William Lee Popham; description being from the author's observation. Louisville, Ky.: The World Supply Company, [1913]. 94 p., incl. plates.
Unexamined copy: bibliographic data from OCLC, #16152090.

P-490 ____ Love's rainbow dream / by William Lee Popham. [Louisville, Ky.: W. L. Popham, c1910]. 62 p.   **DLC**
LC: Ag 27, '10.

P-491 ____ Mammoth Cave romance / William Lee Popham; description being from the author's observation. Louisville, Kentucky: The World Supply Company, [c1911]. (Louisville, Ky.: Mayes Printing Company). 110, [1] p., photo. ill.   **KUK**
LC: D 18, '11.

P-492 ____ Natural Bridge romance: description being from the author's observation / William Lee Popham. Louisville, Kentucky: World Supply Company, [c1911]. (Louisville, Ky.: Mayes Printing Company). 109, [1] p., front.   **KUK**
LC: D 18, '11.

P-493 ____ Niagara Falls romance / William Lee Popham . . . Louisville, Kentucky: The World Supply Company, [c1911]. (Louisville, Ky.: Mayes Printing Company). 107, [1] p., incl. 2 p. of plates (1 photo.).
LC: D 18, '11.

P-494 ____ She dared to win / by William Lee Popham. [Louisville, Ky.: Westerfield-Bonte Co., [c1910]. 76 p.   **DLC**
LC: O 19, '10.

P-495 ____ A tramp's love / by William Lee Popham. [Louisville: s. n., c1910]. 79 p.
Unexamined copy: bibliographic data from OCLC, #29987745.
LC: Je 20, '10.

P-496 ____ The valley of love / by William Lee Popham. [Louisville, Ky.: Printed by Westerfield-Bonte Company, c1910]. 60 p.
Unexamined copy: bibliographic data from OCLC, #9117004.
LC: O 19, '10.

P-497 ____ The village by the sea / by William Lee Popham. [Louisville, Ky.: Printed by Westerfield-Bonte Co., [c1910]. 56 p., ill.   **DLC**
LC: O 19, '10.

P-498 ____ Washington Monument romance / William Lee Popham. Louisville, Kentucky: The World Supply Company, [c1911]. (Louisville, Ky.: Mayes Printing Company). 108, [1] p., front. (port.).   **OSU, VIC** (Seven wonders of the world series (American); 7).
LC: D 18, '11.

P-499 ____ Yellowstone park romance: description being from the author's observation. Being also a lasting souvenir and convenient guide for the tourist / William Lee Popham. Louisville, Kentucky: The World Supply Company, c1911. (Louisville, Ky.: Mayes Printing Company). 119 p., 1 p. of photo. plates.
LC: D 18, '11.

P-500 ____ Yosemite Valley romance / William Lee Popham; description being from the author's observation, including, besides Yosemite Valley description of the California "Big Tress", Long Beach--"The City by the Sea", and Santa Catalina Island--"The Magic Dream-Kissed Isle of the Pacific; being a permanent souvenir and convenient guide book for the tourist. Louisville, Kentucky: The World Supply Company, [c1911]. (Louisville, Ky.: Mayes Printing Company). 119 p., front., [1] leaf of plates.   **DLC**
LC: D 18, '11.

P-501 Porcher, Frances Cannon Smith. Mr. Perryman's Christmas eve: the story of a life of faithful service / by Frances S. Porcher. Chicago: The Reilly & Britton Co., [c1912]. 44 p., col. front. ill. [Ill. by Dan Sayre Groesbeck.]   **SPP**

P-502 Porte, R. T. (Roy Trewin), b. 1876. The printers of Chiapolis / by R. T. Porte . . . Salt Lake City, Utah: Published by Porte Publishing Company, [c1922]. 156 p., ill. [Ill. by Will Crawford.]
Contents: Preface -- Trading -- The partition -- Systems -- The strike -- Clothes -- Getting business -- Money -- The two bills -- Eats -- The feminine viewpoint -- Bicycles and printing -- Buying printing.

P-503 Porter, Albert Davis. The shepherd of Beth / by Albert Davis Porter. Waco, Tex.: N. H. Smith & Co., [c1921]. 58, [1] p.
Unexamined copy: bibliographic data from NUC.

P-504 ____ The shepherd of Beth, and other stories / by Albert Davis Porter. Nashville, Tenn.: Cokesbury Press, [c1924]. 98 p.   TXA
Contents: Shepherd of Beth -- The fisher lad of Gallilee -- The snow-white cross -- Stephen of Nain.
LC: Ja 12, '25.

P-505 Porter, Delia Lyman, 1858-1933. An anti-worry recipe: and other stories / by Delia Lyman Porter; drawings by N. E. Fritz. Boston; New York; Chicago: American Tract Society, [c1905]. 62 p., [5] leaves of plates.
Contents: An anti-worry recipe -- Ten investments for unemployed capital -- Through Lazarus glasses -- The Philiameter -- The beauty-blind.

P-506 Porter, Edward. Dennis McGrath--autocrat: and other horseless tales hanging thereby / by Edward Porter. Boston: Herbert B. Turner & Co., 1904. 211 p.
Contents: Dennis McGrath-autocrat -- An uncommon carrier -- A new view of a site -- In a blind-alley -- A divided house -- Two perfectly safe dummies -- A feast of reason -- A cooked-up scheme -- A midsummer nightmare-told in horseless stages: Prologue -- Stage I: The Governor and the red devil -- Stage II: The Lieutenant-Governor and the green fly -- Stage III: The Attorney-General and the white ghost -- Epilogue -- A whirligig of time-told in three whirls: Whirl I: A case of auto-hypnotism -- Whirl II: The progress of the three graces -- Whirl III: Between the red devil and the black type.
BLC: London: Grant Richards, Boston, U. S. A. [printed], 1904.

P-507 Porter, Eleanor H. (Eleanor Hodgman), 1868-1920. Across the years / by Eleanor H. Porter; with drawings by Helen Mason Grose. Boston; New York: Houghton Mifflin Company, 1919. ([Cambridge]: The Riverside Press). 315, [1] p., front., [8] leaves of plates, col. ill. title page. Reprinted in part from various periodicals.
Contents: When mother and father rebelled -- Jupiter Ann -- The Ax-minister path -- Phineas and the motor car -- The most wonderful woman -- The price of a pair of shoes -- The long road -- A couple of capitalists -- In the footsteps of Katy -- The bridge across the years -- For Jimmy -- The summons home -- The black silk gowns -- A belated honeymoon -- When Aunt Abby waked up -- Wristers for three -- The giving thanks of Cyrus and Huldah -- A New England idol.
LC: N 18, '19.
PW: N 15, '19.

P-508 ____ Dawn / by Eleanor H. Porter; with illustrations by Lucius Wolcott Hitchcock. Boston; New York: Houghton Mifflin Company, 1919. (Cambridge [Mass.]: The Riverside Press). 339, [1] p., front., [7] leaves of plates (1 double leaf).
LC: Ap 15, '19.
PW: Ap 5, '19.

P-509 ____ Hustler Joe: and other stories / by Eleanor H. Porter. New York: George H. Doran Company, [c1924]. 318 p.
Contents: The atonement of Hustler Joe -- Tangled -- A vacation exchange -- The twins' journey.
LC: S 6, '24.
PW: Ag 30, '24.

P-510 ____ Just David / by Eleanor H. Porter; with illustrations by Helen Mason Grose. Boston; New York: Houghton Mifflin Company, 1916. 323, [1] p., front., [11] leaves of plates.
LC: Mr 27, '16.
PW: Mr 25, '16.
BLC: London: Constable & Co., 1916.

P-511 ____ Mary Marie / by Eleanor H. Porter; with illustrations by Helen Mason Grose. Boston; New York: Houghton Mifflin Company, 1920. (Cambridge: The Riverside Press). 296 p., front., [3] leaves of plates.
LC: My 11, '20.
PW: My 8, '20.
BLC: London: Constable & Co., Cambridge, Mass. printed, [1920].

P-512 ____ Miss Billy / by Eleanor H. Porter; with a frontispiece in color from a painting by Griswold Tyng. Boston: L. C. Page & Company, 1911. 356 p., col. front.
Unexamined copy: bibliographic data from OCLC, #5132876.
LC: My 16, '11.
PW: Je 3, '11.
BLC: London: Stanley Paul & Co., 1914.

P-513 ____ Miss Billy--married / by Eleanor H. Porter; with a frontispiece in color from a painting by W. Haskell Coffin. Boston: The Page Company, 1914. 383 p., col. front.
LC: F 3, '14.
PW: Mr 7, '14.
BLC: London: Stanley Paul & Co., [1915].

P-514 ____ Miss Billy's decision / by Eleanor H. Porter; with a frontispiece in color from a painting by Henry Wadsworth Moore. Boston: L. C. Page & Company, 1912. 364 p., col. front.
LC: Jl 2, '12.
PW: Ag 3, '12.
BLC: London: S. Paul & Co., 1915.

P-515 ____ Money, love and Kate: together with the story of a nickel / by Eleanor H. Porter . . . New York: George H. Doran Company, [c1923]. 295 p.
LC: S 28, '23.
PW: N 3, '23.

P-516 ____ Oh, money! money!: a novel / by Eleanor H. Porter; with illustrations. Boston; New York: Houghton Mifflin Company, 1918. (Cambridge: The Riverside Press). 320, [2] p., front., [3] leaves of plates. [Ill. by Helen Mason Grose.]
LC: Mr 23, '18.
PW: Mr 23, '18.
BLC: London: Constable & Co., 1918.

P-517   _____ Pollyanna / by Eleanor H. Porter . . . ; illustrated by Stockton Mulford. Boston: L. C. Page & Company, 1913. 310 p., front., [7] leaves of plates.
At head of title: The first glad book.
LC: Mr 3, '13.
PW: Mr 29, '13.
BLC: London: Sir Isaac Pitman & Sons, Boston, U. S. A. [printed], 1913.

P-518   _____ Pollyanna grows up / by Eleanor H. Porter; illustrated by H. Weston Taylor. Boston: The Page Company, 1915. 308 p., front., [7] leaves of plates.
At head of title: The second glad book.
LC: Mr 11, '15.
PW: Ap 10, '15.
BLC: London: Sir Isaac Pitman & Sons, 1915.

P-519   _____ The road to understanding / by Eleanor H. Porter . . . Boston; New York: Houghton Mifflin Company, 1917. (Cambridge: The Riverside Press). 372 p., col. front., [3] leaves of col. plates. [Ill. by Mary Greene Blumenschein.] Illustrated end papers signed by Lewis E. Smith.
LC: Mr 26, '17.
PW: Mr 24, '17.
BLC: London: Constable & Co., 1917.

P-520   _____ Sister Sue / by Eleanor H. Porter; with illustrations. Boston; New York: Houghton Mifflin Company, 1921. (Cambridge: The Riverside Press). 310 p., front., [3] leaves of plates. [Ill. by Ernest Fuhr.]
LC: My 6, '21.
PW: Mr 19, '21.
BLC: London: Constable & Co., Cambridge, Mass. printed, [1921].

P-521   _____ The story of Marco / by Eleanor H. Porter. Cincinnati: Jennings and Graham; New York: Eaton and Mains, [c1911]. 326 p., front., [3] leaves of plates. [Ill. by Laura Miller.]
LC: N 8, '11.
PW: N 18, '11.
BLC: London: Stanley Paul & Co., [1920].

P-522   _____ The tangled threads / by Eleanor H. Porter; with drawings by Helen Mason Grose. Boston; New York: Houghton Mifflin Company, 1919. ([Cambridge]: The Riverside Press). 310, [1] p., front., [6] leaves of plates.
Reprinted from various periodicals.
Contents: A delayed heritage -- The folly of wisdom -- Crumbs -- A four-footed faith and a two -- A matter of system -- Angelus -- The apple of her eye -- A mushroom of Collingsville -- That angel boy -- The lady in black -- The saving of dad -- Millionaire Mike's Thanksgiving -- When mother fell ill -- The glory and the sacrifice -- The Daltons and the legacy -- The letter -- The indivisible five -- The elephant's board and keep -- A patron of art -- When Polly Ann played Santa Claus.
LC: N 8, '19.

P-523   _____ The tie that binds / by Eleanor H. Porter; with drawings by Helen Mason Grose. Boston; New York: Houghton Mifflin Company, 1919. ([Cambridge]: The Riverside Press). 360, [2] p., col. ill. t. p. and front. on inserted double-leaf (t. p. counted in pagination), [6] leaves of plates.

Reprinted from various periodicals.
Contents: The cat and the painter -- The heart of a hunchback -- Polly's Christmas surprise -- Nuts to crack and Mary Ellen -- To let-an apartment -- Her wedding journey -- The subjugation of Joan -- A matter of loyalty -- Jack -- A woman you know -- Escorting Harriet -- A case of the inevitable -- The angel of peace and Billy -- The second fiddle -- A quarantined squirrel -- A white rose -- The squaring of Jack -- Loosed.
LC: N 8, '19.
PW: N 15, '19.

P-524   _____ The turn of the tide: the story of how Margaret solved her problem / by Eleanor H. Porter; illustrated by Frank T. Merrill. Boston; Chicago: W. A. Wilde Company, [c1908]. 306 p., front., [3] leaves of plates.
LC: O 31, '08.
PW: O 17, 08.

P-525   Porter, Elizabeth Rachel (Cannon), b. 1885. The cities of the sun; stories of ancient America founded on historical incidents in Book of Mormon / by Elizabeth Rachel Cannon; illustrated from paintings by Geo. M. Ottinger and photogrphs by the author. Salt Lake City, Utah: The Deseret News, 1910. 118, [2] p., front., ill.
Unexamined copy: bibliographic data from NUC.

Porter, Frank W. Efficiency-your own. _In_ **Second suds sayings (1919), S-266.**

Porter, Gene Stratton, 1863-1924. **See Stratton-Porter, Gene.**

P-526   Porter, Grace B. (Grace Darling Burgdorf), b. 1874. The Perkinses / by Grace B. Porter. New York: Rand McNally & Co., 1912. 34 p., [3] leaves of plates.
LC: Jl 2, '12.

Porter, Harold Everett, 1887-1936. **See Hall, Holworthy, pseud.**

P-527   [Porter, Josephine Earl-Sheffield]. A white rose: and other stories. [New Haven, Conn.]: The Tuttle, Morehouse & Taylor Company, 1907. 92 p.
Designed end papers.   **DLC**
Contents: A white rose -- A clerk's idyl -- Kendrick's Sunday -- At Burrhampton Station -- Goliath of Gath -- Number four, Balzac Street -- Grandma Cameron's story -- The gift.
LC: O 7, '07.
PW: D 7, '07.

Porter, Laura S. The boy's mother. _In_ **War stories (1919), W-94.**

_____ Spendthrifts. _In_ **Atlantic narratives; 2nd series (1918), A-361.**

P-528   Porter, Linn Boyd, 1851-1916. Riverfall / by Linn Boyd Porter; illustrations by Louis F. Grant. New York: G. W. Dillingham Company, [1903]. 363 p., front., [5] leaves of plates.
BLC: London: T. Fisher Unwin, 1903.

P-529   Porter, Loas Lucina. Arranmoor: a novel / by Loas Lucina Porter. [s. l.: The Roxburgh Publishing Co., c1913]. 230 p.

P-530 Porter, M. E., Mrs. Captain Trueman's last prisoner: a tale of the sixties / by Mrs. M. E. Porter. Chicago: John N. Reynolds, [c1909]. 135 p. **NDD** At head of title: The novel of the century. LC: Jl 24, '09.

Porter, Rebecca N. (Rebecca Newman), b. 1883. The corner table. In *West winds* **(1914), W-368.**

P-531 _____ The girl from Four Corners: a romance of California to-day / by Rebecca N. Porter; with a frontispiece by Ada Williamson. New York: Henry Holt and Company, 1920. 373 p., front. LC: Ap 9, '20. PW: Ap 3, '20.

P-532 _____ The Rest Hollow mystery / by Rebecca N. Porter. New York: The Century Co., 1922. 301 p., front. [Ill. by George W. Gage.] LC: S 7, '22. PW: S 9, '22. BLC: London: John Long, 1924.

Porter, Sara Lindsay Coleman. See **Coleman, Sara Lindsay.**

Porter, William Sydney, 1862-1910. See **Henry, O, pseud.**

P-533 Portor, Laura Spencer. The shadow Christmas / by Laura Spencer Portor. New York; London: Harper & Brothers Publishers, 1925, [c1922]. 23 p. "Reprinted from Harper's Magazine".

P-534 _____ The story of the little angels / by Laura Spencer Portor. New York; London: Harper & Brothers, 1917. 94 p., ill. [Some ill. by Rhoda Chase.]   **OSU, CLE** LC: S 20, '17. PW: S 29, '17.

P-535 Post, Emily, 1873-1960. The eagle's feather / by Emily Post; illustrated by B. Martin Justice. New York: Dodd, Mead and Company, 1910. 305 p., front. LC: N 21, '10. PW: D 10, '10.

P-536 _____ The flight of a moth / by Emily Post; frontispiece by the author. New York: Dodd, Mead & Company, 1904. 253, [1] p., front. PW: O 1, '04.

P-537 _____ Parade: a novel of New York society / by Emily Post (Mrs. Price Post) . . . New York; London: Funk & Wagnalls Company, 1925. 382 p. LC: S 1, '25. PW: S 5, '25.

P-538 _____ Purple & fine linen / by Emily Post. New York: D. Appleton and Company, 1905. 346 p.

P-539 _____ The title market / by Emily Post . . . ; with illustrations by J. H. Gardner Soper. New York: Dodd, Mead and Company, 1909. 336 p., front., [5] leaves of plates.

LC: S 27, '09. PW: O 9, '09.

P-540 _____ Woven in the tapestry / by Emily Post. New York: Moffat, Yard and Company, 1908. 138 p. LC: Mr 10, '08. PW: Mr 21, '08.

P-541 Post, Melville Davisson, 1871-1930. The corrector of destinies: being tales of Randolph Mason as related by his private secretary, Courlandt Parks / by Melville Davisson Post . . . New York: Edward J. Clode, [c1908]. 302 p. LC: S 9, '08. PW: O 10, '08.

P-542 _____ Dwellers in the hills / by Melville Davisson Post. New York; London: G. P. Putnam's Sons, 1901. (New York: The Knickerbocker Press). 278 p. PW: Ap 6, '01.

_____ Five thousand dollars reward. In *Prize stories of 1919* **(1920), P-617.**

P-543 _____ The gilded chair: a novel / by Melville Davisson Post; illustrated by A. B. Wenzell and Arthur E. Becher. New York; London: D. Appleton and Company, 1910. 359, [1] p., col. front., [3] leaves of plates. PW: My 21, '10. LC: My 17, '10.

P-544 _____ Monsieur Jonquelle: prefect of police of Paris / by Melville Davisson Post . . . New York; London: D. Appleton and Company, 1923. 286, [1] p. LC: O 4, '23. PW: O 27, '23.

P-545 _____ The mountain school-teacher / by Melville Davisson Post. New York; London: D. Appleton and Company, 1922. 196, [1] p. Illustrated end papers. LC: Ag 29, '22. PW: S 30, '22.

P-546 _____ The mystery at the Blue Villa / by Melville Davisson Post . . . New York; London: D. Appleton and Company, 1919. 383, [1] p. Contents: The mystery at the Blue villa -- The new administration -- The great legend -- The laughter of Allah -- The stolen life -- The girl from Galacia -- The pacifist -- The sleuth of the stars -- The witch of the Lecca -- The miller of Ostend -- The girl in the villa -- The ally -- Lord Winton's adventure -- The wage-earners -- The sunburned lady -- The Baron Starkheim -- Behind the stars. LC: Ja 27, '20. PW: F 21, '20.

P-547 _____ The nameless thing / by Melville Davisson Post . . . New York; London: D. Appleton and Company, 1912. 337, [1] p., front., [3] leaves of plates. [Ill. by Arthur William Brown.] LC: My 17, '12. PW: Je 1, '12.

P-548 _____ The sleuth of St. James's Square / by Melville Davisson Post . . . New York; London: D. Appleton and Company, 1920. 337, [1] p.

Contents: The thing on the hearth -- The reward -- The lost lady --
The cambered foot -- The man in the green hat -- The wrong sign --
The fortune teller -- The hole in the mahogany panel -- The end of the
road -- The last adventure -- American horses -- The spread rails --
The pumpkin coach -- The yellow flower -- A satire of the sea -- The
house by the loch.
LC: O 25, '20.
PW: N 20, '20.

P-549   ____ Uncle Abner: master of mysteries / by
Melville Davisson Post . . . New York; London: D.
Appleton and Company, 1918. 342 p.
LC: Ag 23, '18.
PW: S 14, '18.

P-550   ____ Walker of the secret service / by Melville
Davisson Post . . . New York; London: D. Appleton
and Company, 1924. 287, [1] p.   **BGU**
LC: S 26, '24.
PW: O 4, '24.

P-551   Post, Van Zo. Diana Ardway / by Van Zo Post; with
illustrations in color by Gayle Hoskins. Philadelphia;
London: J. B. Lippincott Company, 1913. 327 p.,
col. front., [1] leaf of col. plates.
LC: O 4, '13.

P-552   ____ Retz / by Van Zo Post. New York: The
McClure Company, 1908. 334 p.

P-553   Postell, Catherine. On Toplecôte Bayou / by
Catherine Postell. New York: The Editor Publishing
Company, 1905. 126 p., photo. front.
Contents: On Toplecôte Bayou -- A gentleman of Bayou Pierre --
Yaller Rose -- Fidele -- Reform at Bienville -- An offering of candles
-- The defense of the house of d'Arcy -- O fond dove! -- The vortex.

Potter, A. K. Did you ever hire him? In *Second
suds sayings* **(1919), S-266.**

____ Down in old Mexico. In *Second suds sayings*
(1919), S-266.

____ A story from Cuba. In *Second suds sayings*
(1919), S-266.

Potter, Boardman (Squire). See **Squire, Frances.**

P-554   Potter, David, b. 1874. An accidental honeymoon /
by David Potter; with illustrations in color by George
W. Gage and decorations by Edward Stratton
Holloway. Philadelphia; London: J. B. Lippincott
Company, 1911. 147, [1] p., col. front., [7] leaves
of col. plates. Ornamental borders.
LC: N 6, '11.
PW: O 28, '11.

P-555   ____ The eleventh hour / by David Potter;
frontispiece in colour by the Kinneys. New York:
Dodd, Mead and Company, 1910. 298 p., col.
front.   **MUM**
LC: Mr 12, '10.
PW: Mr 26, '10.

P-556   ____ I fasten a bracelet / by David Potter . . . ; with
a frontispiece by Martin Justice. Philadelphia;
London: J. B. Lippincott Company, 1911. 273 p.,
col. front.   **NYP**

LC: O 4, '11.
PW: O 14, '11.

P-557   ____ The lady of the spur / by David Potter; with a
frontispiece by Clarence F. Underwood.
Philadelphia; London: J. B. Lippincott Company,
1910. 329 p., col. front.
LC: S 26, '10.
PW: O 1, '10.

P-558   [____] The lost goddess / by Edward Barron
[pseud.]. New York: Henry Holt and Company,
1908. 341 p., ill.
LC: F 17, '08.
PW: F 29, '08.

P-559   ____ The streak / by David Potter; with illustrations
by Gayle Hoskins and M. J. Spero. Philadelphia;
London: J. B. Lippincott Company, 1913. 348 p.,
col. front., [1] leaf of plates.
LC: O 4, '13.
PW: O 25, '13.

P-560   Potter, Margaret Horton, 1881-1911. The castle of
twilight / by Margaret Horton Potter; with six
illustrations by Ch. Weber. Chicago: A. C.
McClurg & Co., 1903. 428, [1] p., col. front., [5]
leaves of col. plates. Designed end papers.
"The decorations for title-page, end chapters and
chapter initials are by Miss Mabel Harlow."
PW: O 31, '03.
BLC: London: C. F. Cazenove, Cambridge, Mass.
[printed], 1903.

P-561   ____ The fire of spring / by Margaret Potter . . . ;
illustrated by Sydney Adamson. New York: D.
Appleton and Company, 1905. 357 p., front., [3]
leaves of plates.
PW: F 18, '05.

P-562   ____ The flame-gatherers / by Margaret Horton
Potter. New York: The Macmillan Company;
London: Macmillan & Co., Ltd., 1904. 417 p.
PW: My 21, '04.

P-563   ____ The genius / by Margaret Potter . . . London;
New York: Harper & Brothers, 1906. 488, [1] p.
PW: Mr 10, '06.

P-564   ____ The golden ladder: a novel / by Margaret
Potter . . . New York; London: Harper & Brothers,
1908. 433, [1] p.
LC: Ap 9, '08.
PW: Ap 18, '08.

P-565   ____ The house of de Mailly: a romance / by
Margaret Horton Potter; illustrated by A. I. Keller.
New York; London: Harper & Brothers, 1901.
468 p., front., [11] leaves of plates.
PW: Je 1, '01.

P-566   ____ Istar of Babylon: a phantasy / by Margaret
Horton Potter . . . New York; London: Harper &
Brothers, 1902. 494 p.
PW: O 4, '02.

P-567 ____ The princess / by Margaret Potter . . .
London; New York: Harper & Brothers, 1907. 385,
[1] p.
LC: Mr 7, '07.
PW: Mr 16, '07.

P-568 Potter, Mary Knight, d. 1915. Councils of Croesus /
by Mary Knight Potter; illustrated by W. H. Dunton.
Boston: L. C. Page & Company, 1903, [c1902].
232 p., front. [Ill. by W. B. Gilbert], [11] leaves of
plates.
(Page's commonwealth series, no. 6).
PW: S 13, '02.

P-569 ____ Ten beautiful years: and other stories / by
Mary Knight Potter. Philadelphia; London: J. B.
Lippincott Company, 1916. 239 p.
Reprinted in part from various periodicals.
Contents: Ten beautiful years -- The making of a prima donna --
Ultimately -- The wife -- The mother -- Socialism at The Larks -- The
triumph of failure -- In payment thereof -- The gift supreme -- Those
taught -- John Gorking's graft -- Needs must -- The scale -- The
greater call.
LC: Ag 30, '16.
PW: Jl 29, '16.

P-570 Potter, Mary Sargent, b. 1878. A little candle / by
Mary Sargent Potter. Boston: Marshall Jones
Company, [c1925]. 25 p.   **NYP**
LC: D 16, '25.
PW: D 26, '25.

Pottle, Emery, 1875-1945. The bond. _In Their
husband's wives_ **(1906), T-161.**

P-571 ____ Handicapped / by Emery Pottle. New York:
John Lane Company; London: John Lane, The
Bodley Head, 1908. 267 p.

____ The reparation _In Life at high tide_ **(1907),
L-281.**

P-572 Potts, Eugenia Dunlap. Idle hour stories / by Eugenia
Dunlap Potts . . . [Lexington, Ky?]: Published by
the author, 1909. 244 p.   **KUK**
Contents: A thrilling experience -- A cluster of ripe fruit -- The ghost
at Crestdale -- Her Christmas gift -- In a Pullman car -- In old
Kentucky -- His gratitude -- The singer's Christmas -- Turning the
tables -- How she helped him -- The iron box -- The girl farmers.

P-573 Pounds, Jessie Brown, 1861-1921. A popular idol /
by Jessie Brown Pounds . . . Cincinnati, O.: The
Standard Publishing Co., 1901. 130 p.   **DLC**

P-574 ____ Rachel Sylvestre: a story of the pioneers /
Jessie Brown Pounds . . . Cincinnati: The Standard
Publishing Company, [c1904]. 218 p.
PW: Je 10, '05.

P-575 ____ The young man from Middlefield / by Mrs.
Jessie Brown Pounds. St. Louis: Christian
Publishing Company, 1901. 257 p.   **ICU**
PW: D 7, '01.

P-576 Powell, Dawn, b. 1897. Whither / by Dawn Powell.
Boston: Small, Maynard & Company, [c1925].
305 p.
LC: Mr 2, '25.
PW: Mr 28, '25.

P-577 Powel(l), Elizabeth, _pseud._ That new world which is
the old / by Elizabeth Powel(l) [pseud.] . . .
Baltimore: The Norman, Remington Company,
1924. 171 p.
Unexamined copy: bibliographic data from NUC.

P-578 Powell, Frances. The by-ways of Braithe / by
Frances Powell. New York: Charles Scribner's
Sons, 1904. 361 p.
PW: Je 4, '04.
BLC: London: Harper & Bros., New York printed,
1904.

P-579 ____ The house on the Hudson / by Frances Powell.
New York: Charles Scribner's Sons, 1903. 416 p.
PW: Ap 4, '03.
BLC: London: Harper & Bros., New York printed,
1903.

P-580 ____ An old maid's vengeance / by Frances Powell.
New York: Charles Scribner's Sons, 1911. 330 p.
LC: Mr 23, '11.
PW: Mr 25, '11.

P-581 ____ Old Mr. Davenant's money / by Frances
Powell. New York: Charles Scribner's Sons, 1908.
328 p.
LC: Mr 27, '08.
PW: Je 20, '08.

P-582 ____ The prisoner of Ornith farm / by Frances
Powell. New York: Charles Scribner's Sons, 1906.
315 p.
PW: Mr 10, '06.

P-583 Powell, Ida Adaline. Driftwood / by Ida Adaline
Powell. [Chicago, Ill.: Printed by R. R. Donnelley
and Sons Company at the Lakeside Press, c1913].
189 p.
Contents: Driftwood -- Gold in the ashes -- The conquest of Anne --
Miss Mary -- Clever Peter -- The thirty days' siege -- His chance --
The front window -- Madonna of the brush -- The other little god --
When paths divide -- Following the gleam.
LC: Je 26, '13.

P-584 Powers, Carol H. The isle of whims / by Carol Hoyt
Powers. Boston: Richard G. Badger, [c1913].
([Boston]: The Gorham Press). 125 p.
PW: N 15, '13.

P-585 Powers, Frederick William. In the shadow of the
Cumberlands: a story of Kentucky mountain life / by
Frederick William Powers; illustrated. Columbus,
Ohio: The Champlin Printing Company, 1904.
(Columbus, Ohio: The Champlin Press). 192, [1] p.,
photo. front., [11] leaves of plates. [Ill. by LeRoy
Crigler and F. C. Price.]   **WVU**

P-586 Powers, T. J. (Thomas Jefferson), 1875-1940. The
garden of the sun: a novel / by . . . T. J. Powers.
Boston: Small, Maynard & Company, [c1911].
390 p., front., [2] leaves of plates.
LC: Jl 29, '11.

P-587 Powles, G. A. (George Albert). Oliver Langton / by
G. A. Powles. New York: R. F. Fenno &
Company, 1902. 471 p., photo. front., [2] leaves of
plates. [Ill. by Noble Ives.]   **DLC**
PW: D 6, '02.

P-588   Prairie gold / by Iowa authors and artists; jacket and frontispiece by J. N. Darling; decorations by Harriet Macy and Louise Orwig. Chicago: The Reilly & Britton Co., c1917. 352 p., front., ill. [Ill. by Frank Wing, Orson Lowell, C. L. Bartholomew.]
Contents: At Kamakura: 1917 / Arthur Davidson Ficke -- The captured dream / Octave Thanet -- The graven image / Hamlin Garland -- The happiest man in I-O-Way / Rupert Hughes -- Masterpieces / Ethel Hueston -- The queer little thing / Eleanor Hoyt Brainerd -- The recruits' story / Frank Luther Mott -- The unredeemed / Emerson Hough -- Woodrow Wilson and Wells, war's great authors / Honorae Willsie -- Your lad, and my lad / Randall Parrish.

P-589   Pratt, Agnes Louise. Aunt Sarah: a mother of New England / by Agnes Louise Pratt . . . Boston: Richard G. Badger, 1906. ([Boston]: The Gorham Press). 313 p.
LC: O 17, '06.
PW: N 3, '06.

Pratt, Charles Stuart. A celestial crime. In *Through the forbidden gates* (1903), T-222.

Pratt, Cornelia Atwood. See **Comer, Cornelia, A. P.**

P-590   Pratt, Grace Tyler. The Bainbridge mystery: the housekeeper's story / by Grace Tyler Pratt. Boston: Sherman, French & Company, 1911. 200 p.
LC: N 29, '10.
PW: D 17, '10.

P-591   Pratt, John Tinsley. In point of honor: a novel / by John Tinsley Pratt. Tiptonville, Tenn.: Pratt, painstaking printer, 1904. 175 p.
Unexamined copy: bibliographic data from OCLC: #26985722.

Pratt, Lucy. Children wanted. In *Atlantic narratives*; 2nd series (1918), A-361.

P-592   _____ Ezekiel / by Lucy Pratt; illustrated by Frederic Dorr Steele. New York: Doubleday, Page & Company, 1909. 254 p., front., [15] leaves of plates., ill.
LC: My 26, '09.
BLC: London: W. J. Ham-Smith, Garden City, N. Y. printed, 1911.

P-593   _____ Ezekiel expands / by Lucy Pratt; with illustrations by E. W. Kemble. Boston; New York: Houghton Mifflin Company, 1914. (Cambridge, Massachusetts, U. S. A.: The Riverside Press). 228 p., front., [5] leaves of plates.
LC: F 16, '14.

P-594   _____ Felix tells it / by Lucy Pratt; with illustrations by Gordon Grant. New York; London: D. Appleton and Company, 1915. 355 p., ill.
LC: Mr 2, '15.

P-595   Pratt, Magee. The orthodox preacher and Nancy: being the tale of the misfortunes of a minister who tried to do as Jesus would: a story of ministerial life as it is / by Magee Pratt . . . Hartford, Conn.: Connecticut Magazine Co., 1901. 191 p., front. (port.).   **IOG**

P-596   Prentis, John H. (John Harcourt), b. 1878. The case of Doctor Horace: a study of the importance of conscience in the detection of crime / by John H. Prentis. New York: The Baker and Taylor Company, 1907. 268 p., front. [Ill. by Rollin Crampton.]
LC: Mr 22, '07.

P-597   Presbrey, Eugene W. (Eugene Wiley), 1853-1931. New England folks: a love story / by Eugene W. Presbrey. New York: G. W. Dillingham Company, [c1901]. 230 p.
PW: Je 8, '01.

P-598   Prescott, Augusta. The stairway on the wall / by Augusta Prescott. New York: The Alice Harriman Company, 1911. 315, [1] p.
LC: Ap 8, '11.
PW: Ap 29, '11.

P-599   Preston, Laura Fitzhugh. Uncle Bob: his reflections / by Laura Fitzhugh Preston; with frontispiece by R. F. Outcault. New York: The Grafton Press, [1904]. 210 p., front.
Contents: The coat of many colors -- A little white soul -- Palm Sunday and Lent -- Marse Adam and Miss Eve -- How Jacob serbed seben yeahs for Rachel -- How Sis' July Ann come th'oo -- Foot washin' -- King Solomon Nebuchadnezzar Joy -- Double weddenses on de ole plantation -- The midnight visitor -- Aunt Molly and the twins -- The story of two valentines -- The visit to Palm Beach -- On 'count ob Miss Win'fred -- Uncle Bob at the circus -- In beharves ob Miss Lucy.

P-600   Preston, South G. The shadow of the king; or The unknown friend of Jesus; a story of interpretation / by South G. Preston (Stauros Stephanos); illustrated. Second edition. New York; London; Montreal: The Abbey Press Publishers, [c1901]. 253 p., photo. front. (port.), [7] leaves of plates.   **WVB**
LC: S 30, '01.
PW: D 14, '01.

P-601   Preston, W. M. (William Morton), b. 1863. Long draws: a short story of the day / by W. M. Preston. [Kansas City, Mo.: Press of Hudson-Kimberly Publishing Company, c1904]. 163 p.   **DLC**

Price, Clara Iza, pseud. See **Von Ravn, Clara Iza Tibbetts, Mrs., b. 1870.**

P-602   Price, E. D. (Edward D.). The letters of Mildred's mother to Mildred: satirical sketches of stage life / by E. D. Price ("The man behind the scenes"). New York: J. S. Ogilvie Publishing Company, [c1901]. 153 p.
These letters originally appeared in the New York Morning Telegraph.
Contents: Mother at the races -- Mother at a Chicago hotel -- Mother goes yachting -- Mother escapes matrimony -- Mother meets nature's noblemen -- Mother joins the repertoire company -- Mother in the one night stands -- Mother and the theatrical angel -- Mother returns to Mildred.

Price, Edgar Dayton. How Jack closed the deal. In *Clever business sketches* (1909), C-490.

_____ The sixth floor elephants. In *Clever business sketches* (1909), C-490.

_____ The sticker. In *Clever business sketches* **(1909), C-490.**

_____ The trapping of Bomb-proof Smith. In *Clever business sketches* **(1909), C-490.**

_____ The Wyandotte shares. In *Clever business sketches* **(1909), C-490.**

P-603　Price, Edith Ballinger, b. 1897. Garth, able seaman / by Edith Ballinger Price; illustrated by the author. New York; London: The Century Co., 1923. 244 p., front., [3] leaves of plates. LC: S 7, '23.

P-604　_____ My Lady Lee / by Edith Ballinger Price; with eighty illustrations by the author. New York: Greenberg, Publisher, Inc., 1925. 370 p., ill., music. LC: S 17, '25. PW: Jl 25, '25. BLC: London: Hodder & Stoughton, 1926.

P-605　_____ Silver Shoal light / by Edith Ballinger Price . . . ; illustrated by the author. New York: The Century Co., 1920. 351 p., front., [3] leaves of plates. LC: S 22, '20.

P-606　Price, Elizabeth Robinson. Frederica Dennison, spinster / by Elizabeth Price; frontispiece by Frank T. Merrill. Boston; New York; Chicago: The Pilgrim Press, [c1916]. 243 p., front. **VA@** LC: N 15, '16.

P-607　Price, Ella Perry. Her realm / by Ella Perry Price . . . Cincinnati: Jennings and Pye; New York: Eaton and Mains, [c1903]. 224 p., front., [4] leaves of plates. **DLC** PW: N 21, '03.

P-608　Price, Hannah J. (Hannah Julia), b. 1872. The closed door / by Hannah J. Price. Knoxville, Tenn.: Knoxville Lithographing Co., 1913. 212 p., front. LC: S 10, '13.

P-609　Price, Margaret Barnes. Daddy's widow; a Long Island story / by Margaret Barnes Price. New York, N. Y.: Broadway Publishing Co., [1916]. 366 p., front., plates. Unexamined copy: bibliographic data from NUC. PW: Ap 1, '16.

P-610　Prichard, Sarah J. (Sarah Johnson), 1830-1909. Shawnie Wade / by Sarah J. Prichard. Boston: Richard G. Badger, 1909. ([Boston]: The Gorham Press). 143 p. **MNL** PW: N 6, '09.

P-611　_____ The wonderful Christmas in Pumpkin Delight Lane / by Sarah J. Prichard. [New Haven, Conn.]: The Tuttle, Morehouse & Taylor Company, 1908. 185 p.

Prideaux, Rolla. Berghita and the Americans. In *As we are* (1923), A-325.

P-612　Priest, Ezra Fairbanks. Ashes of roses / by Ezra Fairbanks Priest. Wausau, Wis.: Philosopher Press, 1905. 173, [1] p., front. (port.). Unexamined copy: bibliographic data from OCLC, #26968565. Contents: Under the falling snow -- Resurgam -- Max -- Big Jim -- A bunch of violets -- His mother -- An idyl of boyhood -- Word pictures -- Only a society girl -- The flutter of angels' wings -- Heart throbs -- A hopeless quest -- A cup of cold water.

Priest, Janet. *Wilson or the kaiser?* (1918). See **Karger, Maxwell, K-10.**

P-613　Priest, John. Laurel Rock / by John Priest. West Chester, Pa.: Published by The Grove Publishing House, [c1904]. 266 p., photo. front., [2] leaves of photo. plates.

P-614　Prince, Helen Choate, b. 1857. The strongest master / by Helen Choate Prince. Boston; New York: Houghton Mifflin and Company, 1902. (Cambridge: The Riverside Press). 344 p.

"Princess, The," pseud. See **Holden, Marietta, b. 1845.**

P-615　Prindiville, Kate Gertrude. Two of the guests / by Kate Gertrude Prindiville. New York: James Pott & Company, 1905. 217 p. Designed end papers. **OSU, DLC**

Prindle, Frances Carruth. See **Carruth, Frances Weston, b. 1867.**

P-616　Prize stories from Collier's / selected by Henry Cabot Lodge, Theodore Roosevelt, Walter H. Page, William Allen White, Ida M. Tarbell, Mark Sullivan . . . [New York: P. F. Collier, 1916]. 5 v., fronts. Unexamined copy: bibliographic data from OCLC, #2922212.

P-617　Prize stories. O. Henry Memorial Award Prize stories of 1919 / chosen by the Society of Arts and Sciences; with an introduction by Blanche Colton Williams. Garden City, New York: Doubleday, Page & Co., 1920. 298 p. **AWE** Contents: England to America / by Margaret Prescott Montague -- "For they know not what they do / by Wilbur Daniel Steele -- They grind exceeding small / by Ben Ames Williams -- On strike / by Albert Payson Terhune -- The elephant remembers / by Edison Marshall -- Turkey red / by Frances Gilchrist Wood -- Five thousand dollars reward / by Melville Davisson Post -- The blood of the dragon / by Thomas Grant Springer -- "Humoresque" / by Fannie Hurst -- The lubbeny kiss / by Louise Rice -- The trial in Tom Belcher's store / by Samuel A. Derieux -- Porcelain cups / by James Branch Cabell -- The high cost of conscience / by Beatrice Ravenel -- The kitchen gods / by G. F. Alsop -- April 25th, as usual / by Edna Ferber.

P-618　Prize stories. Prize stories of 1920: O. Henry Memorial Award / chosen by the Society of Arts and Sciences; with an introduction by Blanche Colton Williams. Garden City, New York; Toronto: Doubleday, Page & Co., 1921. 322 p. Contents: Each in his generation / by Maxwell Struthers Burt -- "Contact!" / by Frances Noyes Hart -- The camel's back / by F. Scott Fitzgerald -- Break-neck hill / by Esther Forbes -- Black art and ambrose / by Guy Gilpatric -- The judgment of vulcan / by Lee Foster Hartman -- The argosies / by Alexander Hull -- Alma mater / by O. F. Lewis -- Slow poison / by Alice Duer Miller -- The face in the window / by William Dudley Pelley -- A matter of loyalty / by

Lawrence Perry -- Professor Todd's used car / by L. H. Robbins -- The thing they loved / by "Marice Rutledge" -- Butterflies / by "Rose Sidney" -- No flowers / by Gordon Arthur Smith -- Footfalls / by Wilbur Daniel Steele -- The last room of all / by Stephen French Whitman.

P-619   Prize stories. Prize stories of 1921: O. Henry Memorial Award / chosen by the Society of Arts and Sciences; with an introduction by Blanche Colton Williams . . . 1st ed. Garden City, New York; Toronto: Doubleday, Page & Co., 1922. 312 p.
Contents: The heart of little Shikara / by Edison marshall -- The man who cursed the liles / by Charles Tenney Jackson -- The urge / by Maryland Allen -- Mummery / by Thomas Beer -- The victim of his vision / by Gerald Chittenden -- Martin Gerrity gets even / by Courtney Ryley Cooper and Leo F. Creagan -- Stranger things / by Mildred Cram - Comet / by Samuel A. Derieux -- Fifty-two weeks for Florette / by Elizabeth Alexander Heermann -- Wild earth / by Sophie Kerr -- The tribute / by Harry Anable Kniffin -- The get-away / by O. F. Lewis -- "Aurore" / by Ethel Watts Mumford -- Mr. Downey sits down / by L. H. Robbins -- The marriange in Kairwan / by Wilbur Daniel Steele --Grit / by Tristram Tupper.
LC: Mr 31, '22.
PW: Mr 25, '22.

P-620   Prize stories. Prize stories of 1922: O. Henry Memorial Award / chosen by the Society of Arts and Sciences; with an introduction by Blanche Colton Williams . . . Garden City, New York: Doubleday, Page & Co., 1923. 260 p.
Contents: Snake doctor / by Irvin S. Cobb -- Innocence / by Rose Wilder Lane -- Gold-mounted guns / by F. R. Buckley -- As a dog should / by Charles Alexander -- Art for art's sake / by Richmond Brooks Barrett -- Tact / by Thomas Beer -- The kiss of the accolade / by James W. Bennett -- The sixth shot / by Samuel A. Derieux -- The jinx of the "Shandon Belle" / by R. de S. Horn -- His sacred family / by Helen R. Hull -- The horse of hurricane reef / by Charles Tenney Jackson -- Old Peter takes an afternoon off / by O. F. Lewis -- Ig's amok / by Gouverneur Morris -- The Anglo-Saxon / by Wilbur Daniel Steele -- "The writer-upward" / by Albert Payson Terhune -- Twilight of the god / by Mary Heaton Vorse.

P-621   Prize stories. Prize stories of 1923: O. Henry Memorial Award / chosen by the Society of Arts and Sciences; with an introduction by Blanche Colton Williams. 1st ed. Garden City, New York: Doubleday, Page & Co., 1924. 277 p.
Contents: Prelude / by Edgar Valentine Smith -- A friend of Napolieon / by Richard Connell -- Towers of fame / by Elizabeth Irons Folsom -- Phantom adventure / by Floyd Dell -- The distant street / by Francis Edwards Faragoh -- The wager / by Isa Urquhart Glenn -- Celestine / by James Hopper -- Witch Mary / by Genevieve Larsson -- The bamboo trap / by Robert S. Lemmon -- The hat of eight reflections / by James Mahoney -- Home-brew / by Grace Sartwell Mason -- Derrick's return / by Gouverneur Morris -- Shadowed / by Mary Synon -- The one hundred dollar bill / by Booth Tarkington -- Nice neighbours / by Mary S. Watts -- Not wanted / by Jesse Lynch Williams.
PW: Ap 5, '24.

P-622   Prize stories. Prize stories of 1924: O. Henry Memorial Award / chosen by the Society of Arts and Sciences; with an introduction by Blanche Colton Williams . . . 1st ed. Garden City, New York: Doubleday, Page & Co., 1925. 256 p.
Contents: Introduction / by Blanche Colton Williams -- The spring flight / by Inez Haynes Irwin -- Margaret Blake / by Chester T. Crowell -- Rachel and her children / by Frances Newman -- Uriah's son / by Stephen Vincent Benet -- The most dangerous game / by Richard Connell -- Horse and horse / by Charles Caldwell Dobie -- Professor Boynton rereads history / by Edith R. Mirrielees -- The secret at the crossroads / by Jefferson Mosley -- The tie that binds / by George Pattullo -- The courier of the czar / by Elsie Singmaster -- 'Lijah / by Edgar Valentine Smith -- A river combine-professional / by Raymond S. Spears -- What do you mean-Americans? / by Wilbur Daniel Steele -- One uses the handkerchief / by Elinore Cowan Stone -- Progress / by Harriet Welles.

P-623   Proctor, Gertrude Amelia. Gleams of scarlet: a tale of the Canadian Rockies / by Gertrude Amelia Proctor. Boston: Sherman, French & Company, 1915. 292 p.
PW: Ag 14, '15.

P-624   The Promise of country life: descriptions: narrations without plot: short stories / edited by James Cloyd Bowman . . . Boston; New York; Chicago: D. C. Heath & Co., [c1916]. 303 p.   **OSU, DAY**
Contents: The ploughman's horizon -- The habitants -- On the situation, feelings, and pleasures, of an American farmer -- The Platte and the desert -- Alone -- Solitude -- A wind-storm in the forests -- A night among the pines -- A barn-door outlook -- Dreams and disillusion -- The search and finding -- The valley -- After New York -- Hemp -- On the graces and anxieties of pig driving -- Horse magic -- The melancholy crane -- Rab and his friends -- Up the coolly -- Will o' the mill -- The father -- The piece of string -- Three arshins of land -- Solidarity -- Fame's little day -- The legend of Sleepy Hollow.
LC: My 24, '16.

P-625   Proppèr, A. H. (Albert Herschel), b. 1876. Tears & smiles: stories / by A. H. Proppèr. New York: Broadway Publishing Company, [c1909]. 126 p.
          DLC
Contents: The gentile -- An odd fellow -- Brother masons.
LC: Ag 2, '09.
PW: N 20, '09.

P-626   Prosper, John. Gold-killer: a mystery of the new underworld / by John Prosper. New York: George H. Doran Company, [c1922]. 283 p.
LC: Ap 18, '22.
PW: Mr 18, '22.

P-627   Prouty, Olive Higgins, b. 1882. Bobbie, general manager: a novel / by Olive Higgins Prouty. New York: Frederick A. Stokes Company, [c1913]. 354 p.
LC: F 24, '13.
PW: Mr 8, '13.
BLC: London: Eveleigh Nash, printed in U. S. A., 1913.

P-628   ____ The fifth wheel: a novel / by Olive Higgins Prouty . . . ; with four illustrations by James Montgomery Flagg. New York: Frederick A. Stokes Company, [c1916]. 300 p., front., [3] leaves of plates.
LC: Mr 24, '16.
PW: Mr 18, '16.
BLC: London: Cassell & Co., 1918.

P-629   ____ Good sports / by Olive Higgins Prouty. New York: Frederick A. Stokes Company, [c1919]. 236 p.
Contents: Catalogues -- Pluck -- "Why" -- From Mars -- Fifteen dollars' worth -- Broken ribs -- Unwanted -- Strategy -- War bride.
LC: Mr 31, '19.
PW: Mr 29, '19.

P-630   ____ The star in the window: a novel / by Olive Higgins Prouty . . . New York: Frederick A. Stokes Company, [c1918]. 345 p.
LC: S 16, '18.
PW: S 21, '18.
BLC: London: W. Collins, Sons & Co., [1920].

P-631   Stella Dallas: a novel / by Olive Higgins Prouty . . . Boston; New York: Houghton Mifflin Company, 1923. (Cambridge: Riverside Press). 304 p.
LC: Ap 28, '23.
PW: Ap 14, '23.

P-632   Prune, Nat, *pseud.* College chaps / by Nat Prune [pseud.] . . . ; illustrations by Hazelton. Boston: The Mutual Book Company, 1902. 95 p., front., ill.
DLC
Partly reprinted from the William and Mary college monthly and the Colonial echo.
PW: Je 14, '02.

P-633   Wedding bells: and other sketches / by Nat Prune [pseud.]. New York; London; Montreal: The Abbey Press . . . , [c1901]. 134 p.
Contents: Wedding bells -- The Buzzar at Hoggintown -- The pink party at Pathacket -- The county fair -- Doctor Silas -- Tobe Punkin on the Philippines -- Mr. Punkin dilates on wireless telegraphy -- Mr. Punkin talks on football -- The situation in the Transvall -- According to the code -- Tobe Punkin has his likeness took -- Cupid's lark at Smoky Gulch -- The last banquet -- My summer girl -- Monsieur Zero -- General principles -- Uncle William's will -- The bachelor's lament -- The modern Methuselah -- The man who sat with me -- The poetry club.
PW: Ag 3, '01.

P-634   Pryor, G. Langhorne (George Langhorne), b. 1857. Neither bond nor free: (A plea.) . . . / by G. Langhorne Pryor. New York: J. S. Ogilvie Publishing Company, [c1902]. 239 p. Designed end papers.

P-635   Pryor, Roger A., Mrs., 1830-1912. The colonel's story / Mrs. Roger A. Pryor . . . New York: The Macmillan Company, 1911. 387 p.
LC: Mr 23, '11.
PW: Ap 1, '11.

Pryor, Sara Agnes Rice. See **Pryor, Roger A., Mrs.**

P-636   Puddefoot, William G. (William George), b. 1842. Hewers of wood: a story of the Michigan pine forests / by William G. Puddefoot and Isaac Ogden Rankin; illustrated by Edith Browning Brand. Boston; Chicago: The Pilgrim Press, [c1903]. 352 p., front., [5] leaves of plates.

P-637   Pugh, Barbara Tucker. Chronicles of a country school teacher / by Barbara Tucker Pugh; illustrated by F. F. Beaufort. Baltimore, Md.: Saulsbury Publishing Company, [c1919]. 295 p., front., [4] leaves of plates.   **EEM**
PW: F 7, '20.

P-638   Pullen, Elizabeth. Mr. Whitman: a story of the brigands / by Elisabeth Pullen (Mrs. Stanley T. Pullen). Boston: Lothrop Publishing Company, [1902]. 352 p.

P-639   Pulsifer, Harold Trowbridge, 1886-1948. "Glory o' the dawn" / by Harold Trowbridge Pulsifer . . . Boston; New York: Houghton Mifflin Company, 1923. (Cambridge, Massachusetts: The Riverside Press). 70, [1] p.

Pulver, Mary Brecht. The path of glory. In *The best short stories of 1917 and the yearbook of the American short story* (1918), **B-562.**

P-640   The spring lady / by Mary Brecht Pulver; with frontispiece by Neysa McMein. Indianapolis: The Bobbs-Merrill Company, [c1914]. 298 p., front.
LC: S 15, '14.
PW: S 19, '14.

P-641   Pumphrey, Margaret Blanche, b. 1872. Pilgrim stories / by Margaret B. Pumphrey; illustrated by Lucy Fitch Perkins. Chicago; New York; London: Rand McNally & Company, [c1910]. 256 p., front., ill. Illustrated end papers.
LC: N 23, '10.

P-642   Pupin, Annie, b. 1840. The fairy stories that did not come true: containing also Miss Loomis' legacy; and The symphony in Q minor / by Madame A. Pupin. N. Y. C.: Published by Madame A. Pupin, [c1913]. 74 p.
Contents: The fairy stories that did not come true -- Miss Loomis' legacy -- The symphony in Q minor.

P-643   The fairy story that came true; showing that all modern inventions were foreshadowed in fairy stories; containing also "The three famous F's"; a story of the time of Chopin, Mendelssohn and Liszt / by Madame A. Pupin . . . N[ew] Y[ork]: Madame A. Pupin, [c1913]. 77 p., incl. front. (port.).
Unexamined copy: bibliographic data from NUC.

Purdy, Jennie Bouton. See **Shubael, pseud.**

P-644   Purinton, Annie E. At the shrine of the Madonna, and other stories / by Annie E. Purinton. Boston: Private printing, 1909. 198 p.
Unexamined copy: bibliographic data from NUC.
Partly reprinted from "Every other Sunday."
Contents: At the shrine of the Madonna -- The fate of a scudo -- A valentine -- A story of Epiphany -- Hans' Christmas -- Nello's temptation -- Raff -- The signora's cat -- On the mountain -- Trifles.
LC: D 20, '09.

P-645   Putnam, Effie Douglass. Cirillo: [a story] / by Effie Douglass Putnam. New York: Life Publishing Company, 1903. 234 p.
BLC: New York: Life Publishing Co.; London: Henderson & Co., 1903.

Putnam, George Palmer, 1887-1950, contributor. See *Bobbed hair* (1925), **B-700.**

     The sixth man. In *War stories* (1919), **W-94.**

P-646   [____] The smiting of the rock: a tale of Oregon / by Palmer Bend [pseud.]. New York; London: G. P. Putnam's Sons, 1918. (New York: The Knickerbocker Press). 328 p., col. front. [Ill. by Belmore Browne.]

P-647   Putnam, Israel, b. 1878. Daniel Everton, volunteer-regular: a romance of the Philippines / by Israel Putnam; illustrations by Sewell Collins. New York; London: Funk & Wagnalls Company, 1902. 407 p., front., [3] leaves of plates.
PW: My 3, '02.

Putnam, J. Wesley, pseud. <u>See</u> **Drago, Harry Sinclair, 1888-1979.**

P-648   Putnam, Nina Wilcox, 1888-1962. Adam's garden: a novel / by Nina Wilcox Putnam; with a frontispiece in color by H. Weston Taylor. Philadelphia; London: J. B. Lippincott Company, 1916. 328 p., col. front.
LC: Ap 21, '16.
PW: Ap 8, '16.

P-649   ____ Believe you me! / Nina Wilcox Putnam . . . New York: George H. Doran Company, [c1919]. 300 p.
LC: O 2, '19.

P-650   ____ Easy / by Nina Wilcox Putnam. New York; London: Harper & Brothers, [c1924]. 269 p.
LC: Mr 4, '24.
PW: Mr 8, '24.

P-651   ____ Esmeralda, or, Every little bit helps / by Nina Wilcox Putnam . . . and Norman Jacobsen; with illustrations by May Wilson Preston. Philadelphia; London: J. B. Lippincott Company, 1918. 172, [1] p., col. front., [4] leaves of plates.
LC: N 21, '18.
PW: N 16, '18.

P-652   ____ The impossible boy / by Nina Wilcox Putnam . . . ; illustrated by Arthur I. Keller. Indianapolis: The Bobbs-Merrill Company, [c1913]. 395 p., front., [3] leaves of plates.
LC: Mr 31, '13.
PW: Mr 29, '13.

P-653   ____ In search of Arcady / by Nina Wilcox Putnam; illustrations by J. Scott Williams. Garden City, N. Y.: Doubleday, Page, & Company, 1912. 361 p., front., [3] leaves of plates.
LC: Mr 5, '12.
PW: Mr 9, '12.

P-654   ____ It pays to smile / by Nina Wilcox Putnam . . . New York: George H. Doran Company, [c1920]. 286 p.
LC: N 5, '20.
PW: N 20, '20.

P-655   ____ Laughter limited / by Nina Wilcox Putnam . . . New York: George H. Doran Company, [c1922]. 341 p.
LC: O 5, '22.
PW: O 7, '22.
BLC: London; Sydney: Chapman & Dodd, Drogheda printed, 1923.

P-656   ____ The little missioner / by Nina Wilcox Putnam; illustrated by E. C. Caswell. New York; London: D. Appleton and Company, 1915. 321, [1] p., front., [3] leaves of plates.
LC: Mr 2, '15.
PW: Mr 13, '15.

____ Say it with bricks. <u>See</u> **Lardner, Ring, 1885-1933.** *Say it with oil* **(1923), L-71.**

P-657   ____ West Broadway / by Nina Wilcox Putnam . . . New York: George H. Doran Company, [c1921]. 250 p.
LC: N 2, '21.
PW: N 12, '21.

P-658   ____ When the highbrow joined the outfit / by Nina Wilcox Putnam and Norman Jacobsen. New York: Duffield & Company, 1917. 125 p.
LC: My 21, '17.
PW: My 26, '17.

Pyle, Howard, 1853-1911. Blueskin, the Pirates. <u>In</u> *The Miller's holiday* **(1920), M-817.**

____ Captain Scarfield. <u>In</u> *The Miller's holiday* **(1920), M-817.**

P-659   ____ Howard Pyle's Book of pirates: fiction, fact & fancy concerning the buccaneers & marooners of the Spanish Main / from the writing & pictures of Howard Pyle; compiled by Merle Johnson. New York; London: Harper & Brothers, 1921. 208 p., col. front., [12] leaves of plates (some col.), ill. Illustrated end papers.   **BGU**
Contents: Forward / by Merle Johnson -- Preface -- Buccaneers and marooners of the Spanish Main -- The ghost of Captain Brand -- With the buccaneers -- Tom Chist and the treasure box -- Jack Ballister's fortunes -- Blueskin, the pirate -- Captain Scarfield -- The ruby of Kishmoor.
LC: Ag 27, '21.
PW: S 3, '21.
References: BAL 16416. BAL notes: "Reprint with the exception of `Buccaneers and marooners of the Spanish Main.' Here first collected `Preface,' `Blueskin, the pirate,' and `Captain Scarfield.'"

____ In tenebras. <u>In</u> *Shapes that haunt the dusk* **(1907), S-339.**

P-660   ____ Rejected of men: a story of to-day / by Howard Pyle. New York; London: Harper & Brothers, 1903. 268, [1] p.
LC: Je 19, '03.
PW: Je 27, '03.
References: BAL 16403.

P-661   ____ The ruby of Kishmoor / by Howard Pyle; with illustrations by the author. New York; London: Harper & Brothers, 1908. 73, [1] p., col. front., [9] leaves of col. plates.
LC: O 29, '08.
PW: N 14, '08.
References: BAL 16412.

P-662   ____ Stolen treasure / by Howard Pyle; illustrated by the author. New York; London: Harper & Brothers, 1907. 253, [1] p., front., [7] leaves of plates.
Contents: With the buccaneers -- Tom Chist and the treasure-box -- The ghost of Captain Brand -- The devil at New Hope.
LC: My 9, '07.
PW: My 18, '07.
References: BAL 16408.

P-663   Pyrmont, Albert. "James Norris" / by Albert Pyrmont . . . Copyright edition. New York: C. Regenhardt, 1915. 560 p., ill.
Unexamined copy: bibliographic data from NUC.

548

Q

Q-1   Quackenbos, John Duncan, 1848-1926. Magnhild: a tale of psychic love / by John D. Quackenbos . . . Boston: Richard G. Badger, [c1918]. ([Boston]: The Gorham Press). 335 p.
LC: F 10, '19.
PW: F 15, '19.

Q-2   Quail, Joseph N. Brockman's maverick / by Joseph N. Quail; with illustrations by David F. Thomson. New York: Quail & Warner, 1901. 256 p., front., [5] leaves of plates.
PW: S 28, '01.

Q-3   Quaint courtships . . . / edited by William Dean Howells and Henry Mills Alden. London; New York: Harper & Brothers Publishers, 1906. 272 p. (Harper's novelettes.)
Contents: An encore / Margaret Deland -- A romance of Whooping Harbor / Norman Duncan -- Hyacinthus / Mary E. Wilkins Freeman -- Jane's gray eyes / Sewell Ford -- A stiff condition / Herman Whitaker -- In the interests of Christopher / May Harris -- The wrong door / Francis Willing Wharton -- Braybridge's offer / William Dean Howells -- The Rubaiyat and the liner / Elia W. Peattie -- The minister / Annie Hamilton Donnell.
LC: Ag 17, '06.
References: BAL 9773; Gibson & Arms 06-E.

Q-4   Quale, Carle C. Thrilling stories of white slavery / Carle C. Quale. [S. l.: s. n., 1912?]. 89 p., photo. ill. (port.).
Contents: Preface -- Introduction -- The judge who did not know his own daughter -- Lodges take the place of churches -- The escape of a girl -- The rambling talk of an old sport -- The road to hell -- Brother cutting up his own sister -- Did your curiosity lead you to your downfall? -- The suggested remedy -- Ignorance and disease mix well -- Faulty education the real cause of white slavery -- Are churches encouraging white slavery? -- Neglecting doing good is just as bad as doing evil -- The result of our present devouring politics -- He learned the truth at last -- Learning the language of the sinner -- "Keep out, or you'll be hurt" -- Chicago charity too costly -- Open the doors in winter -- Segregation is a misnomer -- Segregation does not segregate -- Living wages -- Attacking an ancient evil.

Quarles, M. D., Mrs. See **Powel(l), Elizabeth, pseud.**

Queen, Helen Duncan. Buck Du Spain. In *California story book* (1909), C-40.

Q-5   Quesenberry, Alice. The seven wheels / by Alice Quesenberry. San Antonio, Texas: Published by the Eagle Publishing Co., [c1919]. 142 p., incl. front., [3] leaves of plates.   **SAP**
LC: S 22, '19.

Q-6   Quick, Herbert, 1861-1925. Aladdin & co.: a romance of Yankee magic / by Herbert Quick . . . New York: Henry Holt and Company, 1904. 337 p.
LC: S 12, '07.
PW: O 12, '07.

Q-7   ____ The broken lance / by Herbert Quick; with illustrations by C. D. Williams. Indianapolis: The Bobbs-Merrill Company, [c1907]. 546 p., front., [4] leaves of plates.
LC: O 12, '07.
PW: N 9, '07.

Q-8   ____ The Brown Mouse / by Herbert Quick; with illustrations by John A. Coughlin. Indianapolis: The Bobbs-Merrill Company, [c1915]. 310 p., front., [7] leaves of plates.
LC: Ag 16, '15.

Q-9   ____ Double trouble, or, Every hero his own villain / by Herbert Quick . . . ; with illustrations by Orson Lowell. Indianapolis: The Bobbs-Merrill Company, [c1906]. 319 p., front., [15] leaves of plates.
PW: Ja 20, '06.

Q-10   ____ The Fairview idea: a story of the new rural life / by Herbert Quick . . . Indianapolis: The Bobbs-Merrill Company, [c1919]. 285 p.
LC: F 19, '19.
PW: Mr 1, '19.

Q-11   ____ The Hawkeye / by Herbert Quick; with illustrations by E. F. Ward. Indianapolis: The Bobbs-Merrill Company, [c1923]. 477 p., front., [7] leaves of plates.
LC: Ag 22, '23.

Q-12   ____ The invisible woman / by Herbert Quick. Indianapolis: The Bobbs-Merrill Company, [c1924]. 488 p.
LC: D 11, '24.
BLC: London: Brentano's, 1925.

Q-13   ____ Vandemark's folly / by Herbert Quick; with illustrations by N. C. Wyeth. Indianapolis: The Bobbs-Merrill Company, [c1922]. 420 p., front., [6] leaves of plates.
LC: F 9, '22.
PW: F 18, '22.
BLC: London: Hutchinson & Co; printed in U. S. A., 1922.

Q-14   ____ Virginia of the air lanes / by Herbert Quick . . . ; with illustrations by William R. Leigh. Indianapolis: The Bobbs-Merrill Company, [c1909]. 424 p., front., [4] leaves of plates.
LC: O 9, '09.
PW: O 16, '09.

Q-15   ____ Yellowstone nights / by Herbert Quick. Indianapolis: Bobbs-Merrill Company, [c1911]. 345 p.
LC: My 24, '11.

Quien, Sabe. See **Sabe, Quien, 1882-1943.**

Q-16   Quillen, Robert, 1887-1948. The path Wharton found / by Robert Quillen. New York: The Macmillan Company, 1924. 257 p.
LC: O 15, '24.

Quillin, Horace Stewart, b. 1863. See **Eskew, Harry, pseud.**

Q-17   Quimby, Alden W. (Alden Walker), b. 1854. Valley Forge: a tale / by Alden W. Quimby. New York: Eaton & Mains; Cincinnati: Jennings & Graham, [c1906]. 283 p., photo. front., [5] leaves of plates.
LC: O 8, '06.
PW: O 27, '06.

Quinby, Laurie J. See **Clifton, Wallace, pseud.**

Q-18 Quinn, Joseph J. Wolf moon: a romance of the great Southwest / by Joseph J. Quinn; coverpiece by Gene Stone; frontispiece by James C. Connery. Oklahoma City [Okla.]: The Little Flower Press, [c1924]. 265 p., incl. front.
LC: Ja 5, '24.

Quint, Wilder Dwight, 1863-1936. See **Tilton, Dwight, jt. pseud. of W. D. Quint and G. T. Richardson.**

Q-19 Quintard, C. T. (Charles Todd), 1824-1898. Nellie Peters' pocket handkerchief and what it saw: a story of the war / by Charles Todd Quintard . . . Sewanee, Tennessee: The University Press, 1907. 10 p.
NYP

Q-20 Quirk, Leslie W., b. 1882. Baby Elton, quarter-back / by Leslie W. Quirk; illustrated. New York: The Century Co., 1904. 201 p., front., ill. [Ill. by J. N. Marchand & Charles Relyea.]
PW: O 15, '04.

Q-21 _____ Playing the game / by Leslie W. Quirk; illustrated by Marjory H. Mason. Chicago: M. A. Donahue & Company, [c1915]. 312 p., incl. front. Unexamined copy: bibliographic data from OCLC, #18894795.
LC: Ap 10, '16.

R

R. K. D. See **Dunlap, Roberta K.**

R-1 Rabb, Kate Milner. A tour through Indiana in 1840: the diary of John Parsons of Petersburg, Virginia / edited by Kate Milner Rabb. New York: Robert M. McBride & Co., 1920. 391 p., front., [15] leaves of plates.

Rabinovitz, Shalom. The clock. In *Yiddish tales* **(1912), Y-20.**

_____ An easy fast. In *Yiddish tales* (1912), **Y-20.**

_____ Fishel the teacher. In *Yiddish tales* (1912), **Y-20.**

_____ Gymnasiye. In *Yiddish tales* (1912), **Y-20.**

_____ The passover guest. In *Yiddish tales* (1912), **Y-20.**

R-2 Rader, Paul, 1879-1938. The empty cottage at Silver Falls: and another story / by Paul Rader. New York: The Book Stall, [c1917]. 60 p. **DLC**
LC: Je 16, '17.

R-3 Ragsdale, Lulah, b. 1866. Miss Dulcie from Dixie / by Lulah Ragsdale; frontispiece by C. H. Taffs. New York; London: D. Appleton and Company, 1917. 285, [1] p., col. front. **NDD**
LC: Ag 20, '17.
PW: S 1, '17.

R-4 _____ Next-Besters / by Lulah Ragsdale. New York: Charles Scribner's Sons, 1920. 275 p., front. [Ill. by Wilson Dexter.]
LC: Jl 9, '20.
PW: Jl 3, '20.

R-5 Railey, Julia Houston. Show down / by Julia Houston Railey. New York; London: G. P. Putnam's Sons, 1921. ([New York]: The Knickerbocker Press).
348 p. **NRC**
LC: My 5, '21.
PW: Ap 9, '21.

R-6 The railroad. New York: McClure, Phillips & Co., 1901. 182 p., front. [Ill. by Jay Hambidge.]
OSU, OWU
Contents: The night run of the "Overland" / Elmore Elliot Peake -- The farmer's railroad / F.B. Tracy -- A million dollar freight train / Frank H. Spearman -- The winning of the Transcontinental / William McLeod Raine -- Conductor Pat Francis / Frank H. Spearman -- An engineer's Christmas story / James A. Hill.

Raimond, C. E., pseud. See **Robins, Elizabeth, 1862-1952.**

R-7 Raine, William MacLeod, 1871-1954. The big-town round-up / by William MacLeod Raine. Boston; New York: Houghton Mifflin Company, 1920. (Cambridge: The Riverside Press). 303, [1] p., col. front. [Ill. by George Giguère.]
LC: O 29, '20.
PW: N 13, '20.
BLC: London: Hodder & Stoughton, [1922].

R-8 _____ Brand blotters / by William MacLeod Raine . . . ; illustrations by Clarence Rowe. New York: G. W. Dillingham Company, [c1912]. 348 p., front., [1] leaf of plates.
LC: S 16, '12.
PW: S 14, '12.
BLC: London: Hodder & Stoughton, [1921].

R-9 _____ Bucky O'Connor: a tale of the unfenced border / by William MacLeod Raine . . . ; illustrations by Clarence Rowe. New York: G. W. Dillingham Company, [c1910]. 345 p., front., [3] leaves of plates.
LC: Ag 17, '10.
PW: Ag 20, '10.
BLC: London: Hodder & Stoughton, [1920].

R-10 _____ Crooked trials and straight / by William MacLeod Raine . . . ; illustrations by D. C. Hutchison. New York: G. W. Dillingham Company, [c1913]. 339 p., incl. front., [2] leaves of plates.
LC: Mr 19, '13.
PW: Mr 15, '13.

R-11 _____ A daughter of Raasay: a tale of the '45 / by William MacLeod Raine; illustrated by Stuart Travis. New York: Frederick A. Stokes Company, [1902]. 311 p., front., [3] leaves of plates.
PW: N 8, '02.

R-12 _____ A daughter of the dons: a story of New Mexico to-day / by William MacLeod Raine; illustrations by D. C. Hutchison. New York: G. W.

Dillingham Company, [c1914]. 320 p., front., [1] leaf of plates.
LC: O 2, '14.
PW: O 3, '14.

R-13 ____ The desert's price / by William MacLeod Raine. Garden City, N. Y.: Doubleday, Page & Co., 1924. 354 p.
LC: Ap 1, '24.
PW: Ap 5, '24.
BLC: London: Hodder & Stoughton, 1924. Another edition: London: Curtis Brown; printed in U. S. A., 1924.

R-14 ____ The fighting edge / by William MacLeod Raine . . . Boston; New York: Houghton Mifflin Company, 1922. (Cambridge, [Mass.]: The Riverside Press). 306 p.
LC: S 16, '22.
PW: S 30, '22.
BLC: London: Hodder & Stoughton, [1923].

R-15 ____ Gunsight Pass: how oil came to the cattle country and brought the new West / by William MacLeod Raine . . . Boston; New York: Houghton Mifflin Company, 1921. (Cambridge, [Mass.]: The Riverside Press). 331, [1] p.
LC: Ap 4, '21.
PW: Mr 19, '21.
BLC: London: Hodder & Stoughton, [1921].

R-16 ____ The highgrader / by William MacLeod Raine . . . ; illustrations by D. C. Hutchison. New York: G. W. Dillingham Company, [c1915]. 321 p., col. front., [2] leaves of plates.
LC: Je 1, '15.
PW: My 29, '15.

R-17 ____ Ironheart / by William MacLeod Raine. Boston; New York: Houghton Mifflin Company, 1923. (Cambridge: The Riverside Press). 288 p.
LC: Je 18, '23.
PW: Je 30, '23.
BLC: London: Hodder & Stoughton, 1923.

R-18 ____ A man four-square / by William MacLeod Raine. Boston; New York: Houghton Mifflin Company, 1919. (Cambridge: The Riverside Press). 286 p., col. front. [Ill. by George Gage.]
LC: Mr 31, '19.
PW: Mr 29, '19.
BLC: London: Jarrolds, [1921].

R-19 ____ Man-size / by William MacLeod Raine. Boston; New York: Houghton Mifflin Company, 1922. (Cambridge: The Riverside Press). 310 p.
LC: My 24, '22.
PW: My 20, '22.
BLC: London: Hodder & Stoughton, [1922].

R-20 ____ Mavericks / by William Macleod Raine . . . ; illustrations by Clarence Rowe. New York: G. W. Dillingham Company, [c1912]. 347 p., front., [3] leaves of plates.
LC: Mr 30, '12.
PW: Ap 13, '12.

R-21 ____ Oh, you Tex! / by William MacLeod Raine . . . Boston; New York: Houghton Mifflin Company, 1920. (Cambridge, [Mass.]: The Riverside Press). 340 p., front. [Ill. by Stanley Rogers.]
LC: Ap 19, '20.
PW: Ap 17, '20.
BLC: London: Hodder & Stoughton, [1923].

R-22 ____ The pirate of Panama: a tale of the fight for buried treasure / by William MacLeod Raine . . . New York: G. W. Dillingham Company, [c1914]. 316 p., front., [1] leaf of plates. [Ill. by D. C. Hutchison.]
LC: My 20, '14.
PW: My 30, '14.

R-23 ____ Ridgway of Montana: a story of to-day, in which the hero is also the villain / by William MacLeod Raine . . . ; illustrations by O. T. Jackman. New York: G. W. Dillingham Company, [c1909]. 318 p., front., [3] leaves of plates.
LC: Ap 20, '09.
PW: My 1, '09.

R-24 ____ Roads of doubt / by William MacLeod Raine. Garden City, New York: Doubleday, Page & Company, 1925. 327 p.
LC: Ap 6, '25.
PW: Mr 28, '25.
BLC: London: Hodder & Stoughton, [1925].

R-25 ____ The sheriff's son / by William MacLeod Raine; with illustrations by Harold Cue. Boston; New York: Houghton Mifflin Company, 1918. (Cambridge: The Riverside Press). 345, [1] p., front., [3] leaves of plates.
LC: My 29, '18.
PW: My 25, '18.
BLC: London: Andrew Montrose, 1919.

R-26 ____ Steve Yeager / by William MacLeod Raine. Boston; New York: Houghton Mifflin Company, 1915. (Cambridge, [Mass.]: The Riverside Press). 289, [1] p., front.
LC: N 1, '15.
PW: N 6, '15.

R-27 ____ Tangled trails: a western detective story / by William MacLeod Raine. Boston; New York: Houghton Mifflin Company, 1921. (Cambridge: The Riverside Press). 323, [1] p.
LC: N 1, '21.
PW: N 12, '21.
BLC: London: Hodder & Stoughton; Cambridge, Mass. [printed, 1921].

R-28 ____ A Texas ranger / by William MacLeod Raine . . . ; illustrations by W. Herbert Dunton and Clarence Rowe. New York: G. W. Dillingham Company, [c1911]. 337 p., front., [3] leaves of plates.
LC: Ag 3, '11.
PW: Ag 12, '11.

R-29 _____ Troubled waters / by William MacLeod Raine. Garden City, N. Y.: Doubleday, Page & Company, 1925. 309 p.
LC: S 5, '25.
PW: Ag 22, '25.
BLC: London: Hodder & Stoughton, [1924].

R-30 _____ The vision splendid: a story of to-day / by William MacLeod Raine; illustrations by D. C. Hutchison. New York: G. W. Dillingham Company, [c1913]. 331 p., incl. front., [2] leaves of plates.
LC: Ag 30, '13.
PW: S 6, '13.

_____ The winning of the Transcontinental. In *The railroad* **(1901), R-6.**

R-31 _____ Wyoming: a story of the outdoor West / by William MacLeod Raine . . . ; illustrations by Clarence H. Rowe. New York: G. W. Dillingham Company, 1908. 353 p., front., [3] leaves of plates.
LC: Jl 13, '08.
PW: Ag 29, '08.

R-32 _____ The Yukon trail: a tale of the North / by William MacLeod Raine; with illustrations by George Ellis Wolfe. Boston; New York: Houghton Mifflin Company, 1917. (Cambridge: The Riverside Press). 323, [1] p., front., [3] leaves of plates.
LC: My 17, '17.
PW: My 26, '17.
BLC: London: Jarrolds, [1919].

Raisin, Abraham. Avròhom the orchardkeeper. In *Yiddish tales* **(1912), Y-20.**

_____ The charitable loan. In *Yiddish tales* **(1912), Y-20.**

_____ The Kaddish. In *Yiddish tales* **(1912), Y-20.**

_____ Late. In *Yiddish tales* **(1912), Y-20.**

_____ Lost his voice. In *Yiddish tales* **(1912), Y-20.**

_____ Shut in. In *Yiddish tales* **(1912), Y-20.**

_____ The two brothers. In *Yiddish tales* **(1912), Y-20.**

R-33 Raleigh, Francis. Ralph Somerby at Panama / by Francis Raleigh; illustrated by H. C. Edwards and Charles Livingston Bull. Boston: L. C. Page & Company, 1913. 305 p., front., [9] leaves of plates.

Ralph, Julian, 1853-1903. Cordelia's night of romance. In *Different girls* **(1906), D-383.**

R-34 _____ The millionairess / by Julian Ralph; illustrated by C. F. Underwood. Boston: Lothrop Publishing Company, [1902]. 422 p., front., [5] leaves of plates.
PW: S 20, '02.

_____ My borrowed torpedo boat. In *The battle for the Pacific* **(1908), B-357.**

R-35 Ramage, Laeta Marion. Judith McNair / by Laeta Marion Ramage; with frontispiece by Wm. L. Hudson. New York: Broadway Publishing Co., 1907. 212 p., front. **DLC**
LC: Ap 4, '07.

R-36 Ramsay, F. P. (Franklin Pierce), 1856-1926. The question: a novel / by F. P. Ramsay. New York; Washington: The Neale Publishing Company, 1909. 178 p. **TJC**
LC: Je 30, '09.
PW: Jl 17, '09.

R-37 Ramsay, Janet, 1888-1940. High road / by Janet Ramsay. New York; London: The Century Co., [c1924]. 352 p.
LC: Mr 24, '24.

Ramsay, Robert L., 1880-1953, ed. In *Short stories of America* **(1921), S-464.**

R-38 Ranck, Carty. The doughboys' book / by Carty Ranck. Boston, Massachusetts: The Stratford Company, 1925. 380 p. **GUA**

R-39 Rand, Edward Augustus, 1837-1903. The Atlantic surfman / by Edward Augustus Rand. Cincinnati: Jennings and Graham; New York: Eaton and Mains, [c1904]. 285 p.
PW: D 10, '04.

R-40 _____ Ship ashore / by Edward A. Rand . . . . Cincinnati: Jennings and Pye; New York: Eaton and Mains, [c1903]. 235, [1] p., front., [2] leaves of plates. [Ill. by Amy Rand.]
PW: O 17, '03.

Rand, Paul. The harp and the triphammer. In *As we are* **(1923), A-325.**

R-41 Randall, John Herman, b. 1871. With soul on fire: a novel / by John Herman Randall. New York: Brentano's, [c1919]. 324 p.
PW: N 8, '19.

R-42 Randall, P. J. Clyde. The exodus / by P. J. Clyde Randall. Pittsburgh, Penn.: Peoples Printing Company, 1919. 119 p., front., [1] leaf of plates. [Ill. by Ed Winn.] **DLC**

R-43 Randolph, Mary. Because you love me / by Mary Randolph. New York: Broadway Publishing Company, [c1904]. 214 p. **DLC**

R-44 _____ Love letters from the Nile / by Mary Randolph. New York: The Knickerbocker Press, 1910. 205 p., col. front., [11] leaves of col. plates. [Ill. by F. Perlberg.] **KUK**
LC: D 6, '10.
PW: D 31, '10.

R-45 Rangeler, Harry H. Silenced by gold: the story of a wildcat well / by Harry H. Rangeler. New York; London; Montreal: The Abbey Press, [c1902]. 215 p. **ISM**

Rankin, Isaac Ogden, jt. aut. *Hewers of wood* (1903). <u>See</u> **Puddefoot, William G. (William George), b. 1842, jt. aut., P-636.**

R-46   Ranlett, S. Alice (Susan Alice), 1853-1942. The shepherd who did not go to Bethlehem / S. Alice Ranlett. Boston: Richard G. Badger, 1909. ([Boston, U. S. A.]: The Gorham Press). 115 p.
                         DLC
Stories reprinted from various periodicals.
Contents: The shepherd who did not go to Bethlehem -- Who loves gives -- The reflection of the star -- Altruda -- Pierre's part -- Mirza's pearl -- The stone angel -- The angel of the cathedral tower -- Hereward's offering.
LC: Ap 9, '09.

Ransom, Olive, pseud. <u>See</u> **Stephens, Kate, 1853-1938.**

R-47   Raphael, Alice Pearl, b. 1887. The fulfillment / by Alice P. Raphael; with a frontispiece from an etching by W. D. Steele. New York: Sturgis & Walton Company, 1910. 345 p., front.
LC: Mr 25, '10.

R-48   Rasmus, Minnie Miriam. Melody in F / Minnie Miriam Rasmus. [s. l.]: [s. n.], c1924. 40 p., ill.   **AZN**

R-49   Rath, E. J., *jt. pseud.* The brains of the family: a side-splitting domestic comedy / by E. J. Rath [jt. pseud.]. New York: G. Howard Watt, 1925. 284 p.
LC: F 5, '25.
PW: My 9, '25.
BLC: London: S. Low & Co., [1926].

R-50   _____ The dark chapter: a comedy of class distinctions / by E. J. Rath [jt. pseud.] . . . New York: G. Howard Watt, 1924. 306 p.
LC: Ag 21, '24.
PW: Je 14, '24.
BLC: London: Sampson Low & Co., [1925].

R-51   _____ Gas--drive in: a high-powered comedy-romance that hits on every cylinder / by E. J. Rath [jt. pseud.] . . . New York: G. Howard Watt, 1925. 302 p.
LC: S 28, '25.
PW: O 10, '25.

R-52   _____ Good references / by E. J. Rath [jt. pseud.]; frontispiece by Paul Stahr. New York: W. J. Watt & Company, [c1921]. 286 p., front.
LC: Mr 9, '21.
BLC: London: Sampson Low & Co., [1925].

R-53   _____ The mantle of silence / by E. J. Rath [jt. pseud.] . . . ; frontispiece by George W. Gage. New York: W. J. Watt & Company, [c1920]. 302 p., front.
LC: Ag 13, '20.
PW: Ag 2, '21.

R-54   _____ "Mister 44" / by E. J. Rath [jt. pseud.] . . . ; illustrations by George W. Gage. New York: W. J. Watt & Company, [c1916]. 326 p., front., [2] leaves of plates.

LC: Je 8, '16.
PW: Je 3, '16.
BLC: London: Methuen & Co., 1917.

R-55   _____ The nervous wreck / by E. J. Rath [jt. pseud.]. New York: G. Howard Watt, 1923. 326 p.
LC: N 1, '23.
PW: D 1, '23.

R-56   _____ Sam / by E. J. Rath [jt. pseud.]; illustrations by Will Grefé. New York: W. J. Watt & Co., [c1915]. 300 p., front., plates.
Unexamined copy: bibliographic data from OCLC, #3795727.
LC: N 20, '15.
BLC: London: Methuen & Co., 1918.

R-57   _____ The sixth speed / by E. J. Rath [jt. pseud.]; with frontispiece by C. Weber-Ditzler. New York: Moffat, Yard & Company, 1908. 408 p., col. front.   **OSU, BGU**
LC: F 28, '08.
BLC: London: Cassell & Co., 1910.

R-58   _____ Too many crooks / by E. J. Rath [jt. pseud.] . . . ; frontispiece by Paul Stahr. New York: W. J. Watt & Company, [c1918]. 294 p., front.
LC: D 11, '18.
PW: N 23, '18.

R-59   _____ Too much efficiency / by E. J. Rath [jt. pseud.]; frontispiece by Will Foster. New York: W. J. Watt & Company, [c1917]. 311 p., front.
LC: F 8, '17.
PW: F 24, '17.

R-60   Rathbone, Cornelia Kane. Darkened windows / by Cornelia Kane Rathbone. New York; London: D. Appleton and Company, 1924. 265 p.
LC: Ap 12, '24.
PW: My 31, '24.

R-61   Raum, Harry A. Affinity / by Harry A. Raum. Atlantic City, New Jersey: [s. n.]. 186 p.
Colophon reads: The Press Printing Co., Pleasantville, N. J.

Ravenel, Beatrice. The high cost of conscience. <u>In</u> *Prize stories of 1919* (1920), **P-617.**

R-62   Rawlings, Robert Cosby, b. 1861. A synopsis of the Yankee drummer abroad: a story of love and commerce / by R. C. Rawlings. [S. l.: Press of Punton-Clark Pub. Co., c1909]. 99 p.   **TNS**
Cover title: *The Yankee drummer abroad.*
LC: Je 21, '09.

R-63   Ray, Anna Chapin, 1865-1945. Ackroyd of the faculty / by Anna Chapin Ray. Boston: Little, Brown and Company, 1907. 311 p.
LC: Mr 28, '07.
PW: Ap 13, '07.

R-64   _____ The Brentons / by Anna Chapin Ray . . . ; with frontispiece by Wilson C. Dexter. Boston: Little, Brown and Company, 1912. 420 p., front.

LC: Ja 20, '12.
PW: Ja 13, '12.
BLC: London: W. J. Ham-Smith; printed in U. S.
A., 1912.

R-65   _____ The bridge builders / by Anna Chapin Ray.
Boston: Little, Brown and Company, 1909. 407 p.
LC: Ja 29, '09.
PW: F 20, '09.

R-66   _____ By the good Sainte Anne: a story of modern
Quebec / by Anna Chapin Ray . . . Boston: Little,
Brown, and Company, 1904. 286 p., front. [Ill. by
Alice Barber Stephens.]
PW: Ap 16, '04.

R-67   _____ The dominant strain / by Anna Chapin Ray . . .
; illustrated by Harry C. Edwards. Boston: Little,
Brown, and Company, 1903. 350 p., col. front., [4]
leaves of col. plates.
PW: Je 6, '03.

R-68   _____ Hearts and creeds / by Anna Chapin Ray . . . ;
illustrated from drawings by Alice Barber Stephens.
Boston: Little, Brown, and Company, 1906. 320 p.,
front., [3] leaves of plates.
PW: Mr 24, 06.

R-69   _____ On board the Beatic / by Anna Chapin Ray;
with frontispiece by Edmund Frederick. Boston:
Little, Brown and Company, 1913. 379 p., front.
LC: F 19, '13.
PW: F 15, '13.
BLC: Toronto: McClelland & Goudchild, 1913.

R-70   _____ On the firing line: a romance of South Africa /
by Anna Chapin Ray and Hamilton Brock Fuller.
Boston: Little, Brown and Company, 1905. 289 p.,
front. [Ill. by Alice Barber Stephens.]
PW: My 6, '05.
BLC: British title: *On the fighting line*.

R-71   _____ Over the quicksands / by Anna Chapin Ray
. . . ; frontispiece by Harriet Roosevelt Richards.
Boston: Little, Brown, and Company, 1910. 383 p.,
col. front.
LC: Mr 1, '10.
PW: Mr 5, '10.

R-72   _____ Quickened / by Anna Chapin Ray. Boston:
Little, Brown, and Company, 1908. 358 p.
LC: Mr 16, '08.
PW: Mr 21, '08.

R-73   _____ A woman with a purpose, / by Anna Chapin
Ray. Boston: Little, Brown, and Company, 1911.
338 p., col. front. [Ill by Frank Snapp.]
LC: F 14, '11.
PW: F 18, '11.
BLC: London: Stanley Paul & Co., [1911].

R-74   Ray, Ethelbert Sheb, b. 1865. The song of the pines
/ by E. S. Ray. Boston Mass.: The C. M. Clark
publishing Co., 1909. 354 p., photo. front., [5]
leaves of plates (some photo.).   **DLC**
LC: D 4, '09.

R-75   Ray, Frederick A. (Frederick Augustus), b. 1872.
The devil worshipper / by Frederick A. Ray . . .
Boston, Massachusetts: The C. M. Clark Publishing
Company, 1908. 469 p., col. front. [Ill. by John
Goss.]
LC: Jl 28, '08.
PW: N 14, '08.

R-76   _____ Maid of the Mohawk / by Frederick A. Ray.
Boston: The C. M. Clark publishing Co., 1906.
340 p., col. front., [7] leaves of plates. [Ill. by W.
Kirkpatrick.]   **FUG**
PW: N 17, '06.

R-77   Raymond, Allen. The heart of Salome / by Allen
Raymond. Boston: Small, Maynard & Company,
[c1925]. 320 p.
PW: Ag 22, '25.
BLC: London: Duckworth, 1925.

R-78   Raymond, Clifford, 1875-1950. Four corners / by
Clifford Raymond. New York: by George H. Doran
Company, [c1921]. 279 p.
LC: Je 21, '21.
PW: Je 4, '21.

R-79   _____ The mystery of the Hartley House / by Clifford
S. Raymond. New York: George H. Doran
Company, [c1918]. 292 p.
LC: S 23, '18.
PW: O 12, '18.

R-80   _____ One of three / by Clifford Raymond . . . New
York: George H. Doran Company, [c1919]. 285 p.

R-81   Raymond, Ibbie. S'ancrer / by Ibbie Raymond. New
York: [s. n.], 1906. 159 p.   **KSU**

R-82   Raymond, James F., b. 1826. The old mountain
hermit / by James F. Raymond. New York:
Broadway Publishing Company, [c1904]. 304 p.,
photo. front. (port.).

R-83   Raymond, Robert Lovejoy, b. 1874. At a dollar a
year: ripples on the edge of the maelstrom / by
Robert L. Raymond. Boston: Marshall Jones
Company, 1919. 239 p.

R-84   Raymond, Rossiter W. (Rossiter Worthington),
1840-1918. The feast of lights: comprising The
vision of Judas the Hammer, The story of Gaspar,
The epistle of Nicodemus, A night with Gamaliel / by
Rossiter W. Raymond. [Norwood, Mass: The
Plimpton Press], 1910. 96 p.   **KSU**
"Printed for private circulation" -- t. p.

R-85   Raymond, Walter Marion. Rebels of the new South /
by Walter Marion Raymond; illustrations by Percy
Bertram Ball. Chicago: Charles H. Kerr &
Company, 1905, [c1904]. 294 p. [5] leaves of plates.

R-86   Rayner, Emma. The dilemma of Engeltie: the
romance of a Dutch colonial maid / by Emma
Rayner; with a frontispiece in full colour by George
Gibbs. Boston: L. C. Page & Company, 1911.
402 p., col. front.

LC: Ag 4, '11.
PW: Ag 19, '11.
BLC: London: Cassell & Co., 1912.

R-87   Doris Kingsley: child and colonist / by Emma Rayner . . . ; illustrations by W. B. Davis. New York: G. W. Dillingham Company, [c1901]. 390 p., front., [5] leaves of plates.
LC: O 7, '01.
PW: O 26, '01.
BLC: London: T. Fisher Unwin; [N. Y. printed], 1901.

R-88   Handicapped among the free / by Emma Rayner . . . New York: Dodd, Mead & Company, 1903. 376 p.
PW: Mr 21, '03.
BLC: London: Hodder & Stoughton; N. Y. [printed], 1903.

Read, Brian, jt. aut. *The thunderhead lady* (1913). <u>See</u> **Fuller, Anna, 1853-1916, jt. aut., F-456.**

R-89   Read, Georgia Willis, 1819-1880. Médoc in the Moor / by Georgia Willis Read. Boston: Sherman, French & Company, 1914. 219 p.

_____, jt. aut. *The village shield* (1917). <u>See</u> **Gaines, Ruth, 1877-1952, jt. aut., G-10.**

R-90   Read, Opie Percival, 1852-1939. An American in New York: a novel of to-day / by Opie Read . . . ; illustrated by Emlen McConnell and Howard Heath. Chicago: Thompson & Thomas, 1905. 356 p., front., [7] leaves of plates.
PW: Ag 19, '05.

R-91   "By the eternal": a novel / by Opie Read; special illustrations. Chicago: Laird & Lee, [c1906]. 303 p., col. front., [6] leaves of plates.
LC: Ag 6, '06.
PW: S 8, '06.

R-92   [_____] Confessions of Marguerite: the story of a girl's heart / Anonymous. Chicago; New York: Rand, McNally & Company, [c1903]. 264 p.
PW: O 1, '04.

R-93   The Harkriders: a novel / by Opie Read. Chicago: Laird & Lee, [1903]. 353 p., incl. col. front., [7] leaves of col. plates. [Ill. by C. Schroeder.]
PW: Ag 1, '03.

R-94   The mystery of Margaret; a story of love, adventure and mystery. Written in the author's best style / by Opie Read . . . Chicago: Thompson & Thomas, [c1906]. 322 p.
Unexamined copy: bibliographic data from OCLC, #15359194.

R-95   The new Mr. Howerson / by Opie Read. Chicago: The Reilly & Britton Co., [c1914]. 460 p.
LC: Jl 18, '14.
PW: Ag 1, '14.

R-96   Old Lim Jucklin: the opinions of an open-air philosopher / by Opie Read. New York: Doubleday, Page & Co., 1905. 262 p.
PW: N 11, '05.
BLC: London: Doubleday, Page & Co.; N. Y. printed, 1905.

R-97   Our Josephine, and other tales / by Opie Read . . . New York; London: Street & Smith, [c1902]. 198 p., front., [3] leaves of plates. [Ill. by W. B. Bridge, Ch. Grunwald, and Furgher.]   **IUA**
Contents: Our Josephine -- A living mummy -- The blue "nigger"-- The incorporated bass -- A villain -- Hot horse to horse -- His neighbor's goods -- The 'tire wheat man -- Not with his boots on.
PW: O 11, '02.

_____ A rusher. <u>In</u> *Second suds sayings* (1919), **S-266.**

R-98   The son of the swordmaker: a romance / by Opie Read . . . ; illustrated. Chicago: Laird & Lee, [c1905]. 333 p., front., [6] leaves of plates, ill.
PW: Ag 19, '05.

R-99   The Starbucks: a novel / by Opie Read . . . ; illustrated. Chicago: Laird & Lee, [1902]. 322 p., incl. col. fornt., [7] leaves of photo. plates. "This book was written from the drama of `The Starbucks,' produced at the Dearborn theatre, Chicago. The illustrations . . . are made from photographs of the actual scenes and people of the play."
PW: Ag 2, '02.

R-100   "Turk": a novel / by Opie Read . . . ; illustrated. Chicago: Laird & Lee, [c1904]. 389 p., front., [7] leaves of plates. [Some ill. by C. Schroeder.]
(Opie Read's select works). Published later under title *"Turkey egg" Griffin*.
PW: Ag 20, '04.

R-101 Reade, Willoughby, 1865-1952. When hearts were true / by Willoughby Reade. New York; Washington: The Neale Publishing Company, 1907. 140 p.
Contents: His last song -- Forgive us our trespasses -- For the child's sake -- The ghost of Oak Ridge.

R-102 Reagan, Albert B., 1871-1936. Don Diego, or, The Pueblo Indian uprising of 1680 / by Albert B. Reagan. New York: The Alice Harriman Company, [c1914]. 352 p., col. front., [10] leaves of plates, ill., music, map. [Some ill. by A. B. Reagan.]
   AZU

Rebel, A., pseud. <u>See</u> **Cone, Andrew Jackson.**

R-103 Recht, Charles. Rue with a difference / by Charles Recht. New York: Boni and Liveright, 1924. 318 p.
PW: Ag 30, '24.

Redfield, Martin. <u>See</u> **Brown, Alice, 1857-1948.**

R-104   Redford, Elizabeth Adamson. Neither do I / by Elizabeth Adamson Redford; illustrated by Wm. L. Hudson. New York; Baltimore; Atlanta: Broadway Publishing Company, 1910. 254 p., front. (port.), [5] leaves of plates. **TNS**
LC: Je 28, '10.

R-105   Redic, Margaret. Trixey: the manicure girl / by Margaret Redic; cover by Wm. L. Hudson. New York: Broadway Publishing Co., [c1908]. 192 p.

R-106   Reed, Charles B. (Charles Bert), b. 1866. Four way lodge / by Charles B. Reed; illustrations by Earl H. Reed. Chicago: Pascal Covici, 1924. 238 p., [11] leaves of plates. **OSU, KSU**
LC: Ja 24, '25.

R-107   Reed, Cordelia Adelaide, b. 1853. The call / by Cordelia Adelaide Reed [and] Susan Russell. Chattanooga, Tennessee: Press of Hamilton Printing Co., [c1925]. 227 p.
LC: Ja 17, '25.
PW: F 21, '25.

R-108   Reed, Earl H. (Earl Howell), 1863-1931. The ghost in the tower: an episode in Jacobia / by Earl H. Reed. [Chicago]: Privately printed, 1921. 62 p., [10] leaves of plates. **NYP**
LC: D 20, '21.

R-109   _____ Tales of a vanishing river / by Earl H. Reed . . . ; illustrated by the author. New York: John Lane Company; London: John Lane, The Bodley Head, 1920. 266 p., front., [13] leaves of plates.
Contents: The Vanishing River -- The silver arrow -- The brass bound box -- The "Wether Book" of Buck Granger's grandfather -- Tipton Posey's store -- Muskrat Hyatt's redemption -- The Turkey Club -- The predicaments of Colonel Peets -- His unlucky star.
PW: D 18, '20.

R-110   Reed, Eleanor Caroline. The battle invisible: and other stories / by Eleanor C. Reed. Chicago: A. C. McClurg & Co., 1901. 336 p.
Contents: The battle invisible -- Patience and Prudence -- Transplanted -- Tolliver's fool -- The widow Perkins.
PW: S 21, '01.

R-111   Reed, Francis. Patrick Fitzpatrick / by Francis Reed . . . New York: Helen Norwood Halsey, [c1912]. 287 p., front.

Reed, John S. The swimmers. In *Forum stories* (1914), F-306.

R-112   Reed, Margery Verner. Futurist stories / Margery Verner Reed. New York: Mitchell Kennerley, 1919. 70, [1] p. **KSU**
Contents: Moonbeams -- The dream muff -- Rose petals -- In a field -- Incalculable -- A Neopolitan street song -- In Algiers -- Candles -- Igor -- Two had lived -- The fifth symphony -- The mad artist -- Old scores -- The last -- Ashes -- Nancy Turner -- The pawn shop keeper -- Something provincial -- Conflict -- That night his sorrow was lifted.
LC: Ap 22, '19.
PW: My 24, '19.

R-113   Reed, Myrtle, 1874-1911. At the sign of the Jack o'Lantern / by Myrtle Reed. New York; London: G. P. Putnam's Sons, 1905. (New York: The Knickerbocker Press). 353 p.
PW: S 9, '05.

R-114   _____ Flower of the dusk / by Myrtle Reed. New York; London: G. P. Putnam's Sons, 1908. (New York: The Knickerbocker Press). 341 p., col. front. [Ill. by Clinton Balmer.]
LC: S 3, '08.
PW: S 12, '08.

R-115   _____ Lavender and old lace / by Myrtle Reed. New York; London: G. P. Putnam's Sons, 1902. ([New York]: The Knickerbocker Press). 267 p.
PW: O 4, '02.

R-116   _____ Master of the vineyard / by Myrtle Reed. New York; London: G. P. Putnam's Sons, 1910. (New York: The Knickerbocker Press). 372 p., col. front. [Ill. by Blendon Campbell.]
LC: O 4, '10.
PW: S 24, '10.

R-117   _____ The master's violin / by Myrtle Reed. New York; London: G. P. Putnam's Sons, 1904. ([New York]: The Knickerbocker Press). 315 p.
PW: S 10, '04.

R-118   _____ Old rose and silver / by Myrtle Reed. New York: G. P. Putnam's Sons, 1909. (New York: The Knickerbocker Press). 364 p., col. front. [Ill by Walter Biggs.]
LC: O 18, '09.
PW: O 2, '09.

R-119   _____ The shadow of victory: a romance of Fort Dearborn / by Myrtle Reed. New York; London: G. P. Putnam's Sons, 1903. (New York: The Knickerbocker Press).
413 p., front. [Ill by W. E. Mears.]
PW: S 5, '03.

R-120   _____ A spinner in the sun / by Myrtle Reed. New York; London: G. P. Putnam's Sons, 1906. (New York: The Knickerbocker Press). 393 p.
LC: S 20, '06.
PW: S 29, '06.

R-121   _____ A weaver of dreams / by Myrtle Reed. New York; London: G. P. Putnam's Sons, 1911. (New York: Knickerbocker Press). 374 p., col. front. [Ill by Arthur Garfield Learned.]
LC: S 12, '11.
PW: S 16, '11.

R-122   _____ The white shield: stories / by Myrtle Reed; illustrations by Dalton Stevens. New York; London: G. P. Putnam's Sons, 1912. (New York: The Knickerbocker Press). 343 p., col. front., [4] leaves of plates.
Partly reprinted from various periodicals.
Contents: Preface -- Morning -- The white shield -- An international affair -- A child of silence -- The dweller in Bohemia -- A minor chord -- The madonna of the tambourine -- A mistress of art -- A rosary of tears -- The roses and the song -- A laggard in love -- Träumerei -- "Swing low, sweet chariot" -- The face of the master -- A reasonable courtship -- Elmiry Ann's valentine -- The knighthood of Tony -- Her volunteer -- In reflected glory -- The house beautiful -- From a human standpoint.
LC: O 4, '12.
PW: S 21, '12.

R-123 Reed, Sarah A. (Sarah Ann), 1838-1934. The belated passenger / by Sarah A. Reed. [S. l.: s. n., 19__?]. 83 p. Designed end papers.

R-124 ____ A romance of Arlington house / by Sarah A. Reed. Boston, Mass.: The Chapple Publishing Co., Ltd., [c1908]. 110 p., [7] leaves of plates. (1 col.). LC: Ja 15, '09.

R-125 Reel, Frederick. The bridge: a novel / by Frederick Reel, Jr. New York: Broadway Publishing Co., [c1915]. 211 p.

Reese, Lizette Woodworth. Forgiveness. In *The best short stories of 1924 and the yearbook of the American short story* (1925), **B-569.**

R-126 Reeve, Arthur B. (Arthur Benjamin), 1880-1936. The adventuress: a Craig Kennedy detective story / Arthur B. Reeve; frontispiece by Will Foster. New York; London: Harper & Brothers, [1917]. 342, [1] p., front. LC: N 19, '17. PW: D 8, '17.

R-127 ____ Atavar: a Craig Kennedy novel / by Arthur B. Reeve. New York; London: Harper & Brothers, [c1924]. 360 p. Cover title: *Atavar, the dream dancer.* LC: My 15, '24. PW: My 24, '24.

R-128 ____ Constance Dunlap, woman detective / by Arthur B. Reeve . . . New York: Hearst's International Library Company, 1916. 342 p. Unexamined copy: bibliographic data from OCLC, #29881518. LC: Mr 25, '16. PW: Ap 15, '16.

R-129 ____ Craig Kennedy listens in: adventures of Craig Kennedy, scientific detective / by Arthur B. Reeve . . . New York; London: Harper & Brothers, [c1923]. 391 p. Contents: The wireless phantom -- Buried alive! -- The brass key -- The boulevard of bunk -- The soul merchant -- Buccaneers of booze. LC: S 2, '25. PW: O 27, '23. BLC: London: Hodder & Stoughton, [1924].

R-130 ____ Craig Kennedy on the farm / by Arthur B. Reeve . . . , with an introduction by Loring Schuler . . . New York; London: Harper & Brothers, 1925. 359 p. LC: S 2, '25. PW: S 5, '25.

R-131 ____ The dream doctor: the new adventure of Craig Kennedy, scientific detective / by Arthur B. Reeve . . . ; illustrated by Will Foster. New York: Hearst's International Library Co., 1914. 379 p., front., [7] leaves of plates. LC: Ap 13, '14. PW: My 9, '14. BLC: London: Hodder & Stoughton, 1916.

R-132 ____ The ear in the wall / by Arthur B. Reeve . . . frontispiece by Will Foster. New York: Hearst's International Library Co., 1916. 341 p., front. LC: N 21, '16. PW: Ja 13, '17. BLC: London: Hodder & Stoughton, [1917].

R-133 ____ The exploits of Elaine: a detective novel / by Arthur B. Reeve . . . ; dramatized into a photo-play by Charles W. Goddard . . . New York: Hearst's International Library Co., [c1915]. 303 p., photo. front., [19] leaves of photo. plates. "Adapted from the `Craig Kennedy' series in the Cosmopolitan magazine." LC: My 21, '15. PW: Je 5, '15. BLC: London: Hodder & Stoughton, 1915.

R-134 ____ The film mystery / by Arthur B. Reeve . . . New York: Harper & Brothers, [c1921]. 379 p., front. (The Craig Kennedy series). On cover: A Craig Kennedy detective novel. LC: F 18, '21. PW: F 26, '21. BLC: London: Hodder & Stoughton, [1922].

R-135 ____ The fourteen points: tales of Craig Kennedy, master of mystery / by Arthur B. Reeve; with an introduction by Robert H. Davis. -- 1st ed. -- New York; London: Harper & Brothers, 1925. 456 p. Contents: Craig Kennedy and the compass: North. South. East. West -- Craig Kennedy and the elements: Air. Water. Earth. Fire. -- Craig Kennedy and the senses: Smell. Taste. Touch. Hearing. The sixth sense. LC: Mr 17, '25. PW: Mr 14, '25.

R-136 ____ The gold of the gods: the mystery of the Incas solved by Craig Kennedy -- scientific detective / by Arthur B. Reeve . . . ; frontispiece. New York: Hearst's International Library Co., 1915. 291 p., front. [Ill by Will Foster.] LC: N 5, '15. PW: D 25, '15. BLC: London: Hodder & Stoughton, 1916.

R-137 ____ Guy Garrick: an adventure with a scientific gunman / by Arthur B. Reeve . . . New York: Hearst's International Library Co., 1914. 326 p., front. [Ill. by Charles D. Mitchell.] LC: O 1, '14. PW: O 17, '14. BLC: London: Hodder & Stoughton, [1916].

R-138 ____ The master mystery / novelized by Arthur B. Reeve and John W. Grey; from scenarios by Arthur B. Reeve in collaboration with John W. Grey and C. A. Logue; profusely illustrated with photographic reproductions taken from the Houdini super-serial of the same name, a B. A. Rolfe production. New York: Grosset & Dunlap, 1919. 304 p., photo. front., [14] p. of photo. plates. LC: My 2, '19. PW: Je 14, '19.

R-139   ____ The mystery mind / by Arthur B. Reeve and John W. Grey; illustrated with photographic reproductions taken from the serial of the same name . . . ; novelization by Marc Edmund Jones. New York: Grosset & Dunlap, [c1921]. 356 p., photo. front., [3] leaves of photo. plates.   **EZC**
LC: F 3, '21.
PW: F 12, '21.

R-140   ____ The Panama plot: Pan-American adventures of Craig Kennedy, scientific dectective / by Arthur B. Reeve . . . ; frontispiece by Will Foster. New York; London: Harper & Brothers, 1918. 325 p., front.
Contents: The panama plot -- The love philter -- The black diamond -- The bitter water -- The nitrate king -- The green death -- The phantom parasite -- The door of dread -- The black cross -- The psychic scar.
LC: Ap 12, '18.
PW: Ap 20, '18.

R-141   ____ The poisened pen, further adventures of Craig Kennedy / by Arthur Benjamin Reeves. . . ; frontispiece by Will Foster. New York and London: Harper & Brothers, [1911]. 399 p., front.   **NYP**
LC: Mr 3, '13.
PW: Mr 1, '13.
BLC: London: Hodder & Stoughton, 1916.

R-142   ____ The romance of Elaine: sequel to "Exploits of Elaine" / by Arthur B. Reeve; illustrated with photos from film play. New York: Hearst's International Library Co., 1916. 352 p., photo. front., [7] leaves of photo. plates.
LC: Mr 25, '16.
PW: Ap 15, '16.
BLC: London: Hodder & Stoughton, [1916].

R-143   ____ The silent bullet; the adventures of Craig Kennedy, scientific detective / by Arthur B. Reeve . . . ; with illustrations by Will Foster. New York: Dodd, Mead and Company, 1912. 390 p., front., plates.   **MNU**
Contents: Craig Kennedy's theories -- The silent bullet -- The scientific cracksman -- The bacteriological detective -- The deadly tube -- The seismograph adventure -- The diamond maker -- The azure ring -- "Spontaneous combustion" -- The terror in the air -- The black hand -- The artificial paradise -- The steel door.
LC: F 9, '12.
PW: F 17, '12.
BLC: London: Hodder & Stoughton, [1916].

R-144   ____ The social gangster: adventures of Craig Kennedy, scientific detective / by Arthur B. Reeve . . . New York: Hearst's International Library Co., 1916. 342 p., front. [Ill. by Will Foster.]
LC: Ag 25, '16.
PW: S 9, '16.

R-145   ____ The soul scar: a Craig Kennedy scientific mystery novel / by Arthur B. Reeve . . . New York; London: Harper & Brothers, 1919. 298, [1] p., front. [Ill. by F. Graham Cootes.]
(The Craig Kennedy series).
LC: O 17, '19.
PW: N 1, '19.

R-146   ____ The treasure train: adventures of Craig Kennedy, scientific detective, which ultimately take him abroad / by Arthur B. Reeve . . . New York, London: Harper & Brothers, [1917]. 335 p., front.

Unexamined copy: bibliographic data from OCLC, #9103116.
LC: Je 11, '17.
PW: Je 16, '17.

R-147   ____ The war terror: further adventures with Craig Kennedy, scientific detective / by Arthur B. Reeve . . . New York: Hearst's International Library Co., [c1915]. 376 p., front. [Ill. by Will Foster.]
   OSU, CWR
LC: Mr 26, '15.
PW: Ap 24, '15.

R-148   Reeve, J. Stanley, b. 1878. "Rhubarb," the diary of a gentleman's hunter / by J. Stanley Reeve; with illustrations by the author. Philadelphia: Press of J. B. Lippincott Company, 1908. [58] p., front., [6] leaves of plates.
Unexamined copy: bibliographic data from OCLC, #6548643.

R-149   Reeve, Katharine Roosevelt. Covert-side courtship / by Katharine Roosevelt Reeve; with silhouettes by J. Stanley Reeve. Philadelphia: [Printed by J. B.

Lippincott Company], 1909. 98 p., front., [4] leaves of plates.   **KSU**
LC: D 23, '09.

Reeve, Winnifred Eaton. See **Watanna, Onoto, pseud.**

Reeves, Alice. Paper bags. In *The best college short stories, 1924-1925* **(1925), B-558.**

Regan, Maud. The lady of the roses. In *The lady of the tower* **(1909), L-13.**

____ We two and Miss Pamela. In *The lady of the tower* **(1909), L-13.**

R-150   Regis, Julius. The copper house: a detective story / by Julius Regis. New York: Henry Holt and Company, 1923. 296 p.
LC: O 12, '23.
PW: D 1, '23.
BLC: London: Hodder & Stoughton, [1923].

R-151   ____ No. 13 Toroni: a mystery / by Julius Regis. New York: Henry Holt and Company, 1922. 307 p.
LC: O 28, '22.
PW: N 11, '22.
BLC: London: Hodder & Stoughton, [1922].

Reid, Alberta Bancroft, Mrs. See **Bancroft, Alberta, b. 1873.**

R-152   Reid, Christian, 1846-1920, *pseud.* The coin of sacrifice / by Christian Reid [pseud.]. Notre Dame, Indiana: The Ave Maria Press, [1909?]. 57 p.   **NYP**
PW: Mr 27, 09.

R-153   ____ The daughter of a star / by Christian Reid . . . ; with frontispiece by John Campbell. New York: The Devin-Adair Company, [c1913]. 349 p., col. front.   **IMS**
LC: N 29, '13.
PW: D 27, '13.

R-154 _____ A daughter of the Sierra / by Christian Reid. St. Louis, Mo.: Published by B. Herder, 1903. 367 p. **SUC**
PW: Ap 4, '03.

R-155 _____ A far-away princess / by Christian Reid . . . New York: The Devin-Adair Company, [c1914]. 406 p., col. front. [Ill by John A. Campbell.] **SUC**
LC: D 7, '14.
PW: Ja 9, '15.

R-156 _____ The light of the vision / by Christian Reid . . . Notre Dame, Indiana: The Ave Maria, [c1911]. 324 p. Designed end papers. **CLE**
LC: D 21, '11.
PW: F 3, '12.

R-157 _____ Princess Nadine / by Christian Reid . . . New York; London: G. P. Putnam's Sons, 1908, [c1907]. (New York: The Knickerbocker Press). 340 p., col. front. [Ill by John E. Jackson.]
LC: D 14, '07.
PW: Ja 25, '08.

R-158 _____ The secret bequest / by Christian Reid . . . Notre Dame, Indiana, U. S. A.: The Ave Maria, [c1915]. 348 p.
LC: N 13, '15.

R-159 _____ Véra's charge / by Christian Reid . . . Notre Dame, Indiana, U. S. A.: The Ave Maria, [c1907]. 390 p.
LC: F 12, '08.
PW: Mr 7, '08.

R-160 _____ The Wargrave trust / by Christian Reid. New York; Cincinnati; Chicago: Benziger Brothers, [c1911]. 384 p.
LC: N 6, '11.
PW: D 2, '11.

R-161 Reid-Girardot, Marion. Red Eagle of the Medicine-way / by Marion Reid-Girardot . . . Boston: The Cornhill Publishing Company, 1922. 308 p.
LC: N 21, '22.

R-162 _____ Steve of the Bar Gee ranch: a thrilling story of life on the plains of Colorado / Marion Reid-Girardot. New York; London: Broadway Publishing Company, [c1914]. 287 p., [9] leaves of plates.
LC: Mr 10, '14.

R-163 Reilly, James M. Veldt, the lion hunter: a comic opera whirl / by James M. Reilly; illustrated. New York; Baltimore; Atlanta: Broadway Publishing Company, 1910. 173 p., front., [11] leaves of plates. [Ill. by Wm. L. Hudson.] **KFH**
LC: Je 28, '10.

Reinertsen, Robert C., Mrs., b. 1853. See **Gale, Forest.**

R-164 The rejected apostle: and other stories / by Helen Wainright, Elizabeth Mayfield, Bruce Barnes, Frances Thompson, Dorothy Patricia Graham, and Kathleen Welch. St. Louis, Mo.: The Vincentian Press, [c1924]. 161 p. **DLC**
Contents: The rejected apostle / Helen Wainright -- A mysterious disappearance / Elizabeth Mayfield -- If thou have much / Bruce Barnes -- The higher law / Elizabeth Mayfield -- Gallilee and Hollywood / Bruce Barnes -- The pearl of great price / Elizabeth Mayfield -- The ebony cross / Frances Thompson -- Madonna and child / Frances Thompson -- The guerdon of charity / Dorothy Patricia Graham -- Adeste fidelis / Frances Thompson -- On the road to Damascus / Bruce Barnes -- Thy kingdom come / Kathleen Welch.
LC: F 27, '24.

R-165 Reklaw, Irving. Brothers: a novel / by Irving Reklaw. New York: Broadway Publishing Company, [c1914]. 217 p. **DLC**

R-166 Rekrap, *pseud.* Malcomb Douglas: a work of fiction: the natural offspring of a fruitful imagination, that with the pen tries to build a beautiful and fantastic castle in the air / by Rekrap [pseud.]. Bessemer, Alabama: Herald-Journal . . . , 1901. 269 p.

R-167 Remington, Frederic, 1861-1909. John Ermine of the Yellowstone / by Frederic Remington; illustrated by the author. New York: The Macmillan Company; London: Macmillan and Co., Ltd., 1902. 271 p., incl. [7] leaves of plates, front. (port.), ill.
References: BAL 16497.

R-168 _____ The way of an Indian / written and illustrated by Frederic Remington . . . New York: Fox, Duffield & Company, 1906. 251, [1] p., col. front., [13] leaves of plates.
Unexamined copy: bibliographic data from OCLC, #1865001.
References: BAL 16498.

R-169 Renard, Paul, b. 1867. Dr. Morgan / by Paul Renard. Boston, Massachusetts: The C. M. Clark Publishing Company, [c1910]. 268 p.

R-170 René, J. Adelard (Joseph Adelard), b. 1868. Priest and man: a story of love and duty / by J. Adelard René. New York: The Editor Publishing Co., [c1904]. 179 p. **DLC**

R-171 Renfrew, Garroway, *pseud.* My old field / by Garroway Renfrew [pseud.]. Boston, Massachusetts: The Stratford Company, 1925. 118 p. **CLU**
PW: Ag 8, '25.

R-172 Rennie, Elizabeth Whitaker. A fiery sword / by Elizabeth Whitaker Rennie. New York; London; Montreal: The Abbey Press, [c1902]. 341 p., front., [7] leaves of plates. [Ill. by J. O'Neill.] **DLC**
PW: D 6, '02.

R-173 Rennolds, Harney. Out of the ashes: a possible solution to the social problem of divorce / by Harney Rennolds. Boston, Mass.: The C. M. Clark Publishing Company, 1906. 286 p., front. [Ill. by W. Kirkpatrick.] **CLU**

R-174 Repplier, Agnes, 1855-1950. In our convent days / by Agnes Repplier. Boston; New York: Houghton, Mifflin and Company, 1905. (Cambridge: The Riverside Press). 256, [2] p.
BLC: London: Archibald Constable & Co.; Cambridge, Mass [printed], 1905.

R-175 Representative American short stories / edited by Alexander Jessup. Boston; New York; Chicago; Atlanta; San Francisco; Dallas: Allyn and Bacon, [c1923]. 974 p., 209 p., front. (port.). **BGU**
Contents: The wife of Chino / Frank Norris -- Though one rose from the dead / William Dean Howells -- The case of Mr. Helmer / Robert William Chambers -- "Many waters" / Margaret Wade Deland -- Lovers in heaven / Julian Hawthorne -- The gift of the Magi / O. Henry -- The mind-reader / Silas Weir Mitchell -- The triple cross / George Randolph Chester -- Extra dry / Owen Wister -- The seed of the McCoy / Jack London -- The belled buzzard / Irvin Shrewsbury Cobb -- The penalties of Artemia / Katharine Fullerton Gerould -- The lost Phoebe / Theodore Dreiser -- The great legend / Melville Davisson Post -- The woman at Seven Brothers / Wilbur Daniel Steele -- All or nothing / Charles Caldwell Dobie.
LC: My 9, '23. .

R-176 Representative short stories / collected by Nina Hart and Edna M. Perry. New York: Macmillan, 1917. 304 p.
Unexamined copy: bibliographic data from OCLC, #2195713.
Macmillan's pocket American and English Classics.
Contents: Introduction -- Tennessee's partner / Bret Harte -- The fall of the house of Usher / Edgar Allan Poe -- White horse winter / Wilbur Daniel Steele -- Our Lady's juggler / Anatole France -- The constant tin soldier / Hans Christian Andersen -- Miss Youghal's sais / Rudyard Kipling -- The Sire de Malétroit's door / Robert Louis Stevenson -- The revolution at Satan's trap / Norman Duncan -- The ambitious guest / Nathaniel Hawthorne -- The lantern / Alice Brown -- Anna Mareea / Esther Tiffany -- The intervention of Peter / Paul Laurence Dunbar -- A Christmas present for a lady / Myra Kelly -- Wee Willie Winkie / Rudyard Kipling -- Miss Gunton of Poughkeepsie / Henry James -- The steamer child / Elsie Singmaster -- Uncle Reuben / Selma Lagerlöf -- The rout of the white hussars / Rudyard Kipling -- Perjured / Edith R. Mirrielees -- The best bait for mosquitos / Henry Seidel Canby.

R-177 The Rev. John Smith died- and went to Jupiter via hell. New York City: Published by The Juno Society, [c1908]. 318 p.
Cover title: *To Jupiter via hell.*

R-178 ReVere, Clifton E. The garden of faith / by Clifton E. ReVere. Baltimore, Md.: The McLean Company, [c1916]. 211 p., photo. front. (port.). **DLC**

R-179 Reyher, Ferdinand. The man, the tiger, and the snake / by Ferdinand Reyher. New York; London: G. P. Putnam's Sons, 1921. (New York: THe Knickerbocker Press). 232 p.
PW: Ag 20, '21.

R-180 Reynaert, John Hugh, b. 1843. The Eldorado of socialism, communism and anarchism; or, A trip to the planet Jupiter / by Rev. John H. Reynaert. [Orlando, Fla.: Reporter-Star Pub. Co., c1917]. 86 p.
Unexamined copy: bibliographic data from NUC.

R-181 Reynolds, Gerard A. The red circle / by Gerard A. Reynolds. New York City: P. J. Kennedy & Sons, [c1915]. 319, [1] p.
LC: D 30, '15.

R-182 Reynolds, Katharine Yirsa, b. 1883. Green Valley / by Katharine Reynolds; with frontispiece illustration by Nana French Bickford. Boston: Little, Brown, and Company, 1919. 287 p., col. front.
LC: Mr 26, '19.
PW: Mr 15, '19.

R-183 ____ Willow Creek / by Katharine Reynolds . . . ; illustrated by Hanson Booth. New York: Grosset & Dunlap, [c1924]. 292 p., front., [5] leaves of plates.
LC: N 13, '24.
PW: Ja 17, '25.

R-184 Reynolds, Minnie Josephine, b. 1865. The crayon clue / by Minnie J. Reynolds. New York: Mitchell Kennerley, 1915. 375 p.
LC: My 3, '15.

R-185 Reynolds, Robert R., (Robert Rice), b. 1887. Wanderlust / by Robert R. Reynolds. New York: Broadway Publishing Co., 1913. 98 p., front., [7] leaves of plates.

R-186 Reynolds, William H. (William Hampton), b. 1875. In the carbon hills: a romance of the land of coal / by W. H. Reynolds . . . Butler, Penna.: The Ziegler Publishing Co., [c1917]. 253, [1] p. **DLC**
LC: S 18, '17.

R-187 Reynolds, William H. (William Hampton), b. 1875. Our brother's child and other stories / by William H. Reynolds. Boston: Mayhew Publishing Company, 1906. 198, [5] p., photo. front. (port).
Unexamined copy: bibliographic data from OCLC, #29996552.
LC: Jl 2, '06.
Second revised edition, 1908. 121 p., photo. front. (port.).
Includes poems on p. 110-121.
LC: Je 22, '08.

R-188 ____ The tide of destiny; a story with a purpose / "to cheer the lonely, lift the frail, / And solace them that weep." A popular adaptation of the great fraternal story Our brother's child / by William H. Reynolds . . . ; Boston: Mayhew Publishing Company, 1910. 143 p., photo. ill. (port.). **SUC**
LC: Ag 20, '10.

R-189 Reynolds, Winifred M. Curly and others: stories and sketches for the Christmas-tide / by Winifred M. Renyolds. Concord, N. H.: The Rumford Press, [c1912]. 168 p., front., [3] leaves of plates.
Contents: Curly -- The little bisque dog -- The triumph of Thomas -- Miss Lizy's guest -- The sign that conquered -- Aunt Ju's Christmas rags -- Charles o' the woods.
LC: Je 9, '13.

R-190 Rhinow, Arthur B. "The devil" and other parables: truths for the times / by Arthur B. Rhinow. St. Louis, Mo.; Chicago, Ill.: Eden Publishing House, [c1923]. 142 p.
Contents: Foreword -- The devil -- Opium religion -- The minister of the church in the other block -- During the Brooklyn car strike -- The minister's malady -- The joy of service -- The ring -- Tradition -- "Even as a hen" -- From the diary of a modern minister -- The practical thing -- Brother Martin -- Making time -- Elijah -- The drummer's disappointment -- When he omitted Shadrach's oration -- The cure -- Going home -- A youthful fancy -- He felt the stars looking at him -- Cheap -- More time for herself -- The wise one -- The pale faith -- The boasters -- The church -- The spiritual man -- The smile -- Mr. Alberg's worry -- Covering ground.
LC: S 17, '23.

R-191 Rhoads, J. N. (John Neely), b. 1859. A thunderstorm / by J. N. Rhoads. . . ; Philadelphia:

Ferris & Leach, 1904. 296 p., front., [3] leaves of photo. plates (1 port.). **PLF**
PW: Mr 11, '05.

R-192   Rhodes, Albert Holland. The noble criminal: a strange tale taken from the notes and memoirs of Hadlock Jones by his friend, Dr. Lawrence L. Langdon / by Albert Holland Rhodes . . . ; illustrated by Roy Atherton Davidson. Boston: Holland Publishing Company, 1912. 67 p., front., [3] leaves of plates. **DLC**

R-193   Rhodes, Eugene Manlove, 1869-1934. Bransford in Arcadia, or, The little eohippus / by Eugene Manlove Rhodes . . . New York: Henry Holt and Company, 1914. 236 p., front. [Ill by H. T. Dunn.]
LC: F 7, '14.
PW: F 7, '14.

R-194   _____ Copper Streak Trail / by Eugene Manlove Rhodes . . . Boston; New York: Houghton Mifflin Company, 1922. (Cambridge [Mass.]: The Riverside Press). 318 p.
LC: My 24, '22.
PW: My 20, '22.
BLC: London: Hodder & Stoughton, [1923].

R-195   _____ The desire of the moth / by Eugene Manlove Rhodes . . . illustrations by H. T. Dunn. New York: Henry Holt and Company, 1916. 149 p., front., [1] leaf of plates. **AZS**

R-196   _____ The desire of the moth; and, The come on / by Eugene Manlove Rhodes; illustrations by H. T. Dunn. New York: Grosset & Dunlap, [c1920]. 282 p., front., [1] leaf of plates. Added novelette: *The come on.*
PW: My 22, '20.

R-197   _____ Good men and true / by Eugene Manlove Rhodes; illustrations by H. T. Dunn. New York: Henry Holt and Company, 1910. 177 p., front., [1] leaf of plates.
LC: Ag 29, '10.
PW: S 3, '10.

R-198   _____ Good men and true; and, Hit the line hard / by Eugene Manlove Rhodes; illustrations by H. T. Dunn. New York: Grosset & Dunlap Publishers, [c1920]. 315 p., front., [1] leaf of plates.
Hit the line hard: p. 179-315.

R-199   _____ Stepsons of light / by Eugene Manlove Rhodes; with illustrations. Boston: Houghton Mifflin Company, 1921. (Cambridge: The Riverside Press). 317 p.
LC: Je 9, '21.
PW: Je 11, '21.
BLC: London: Hodder & Stoughton; Cambridge, Mass. [printed], [1922].

R-200   _____ West is west / by Eugene Manlove Rhodes . . . ; illustrated by Harvey Dunn. New York: The H. K. Fly Company, [c1917]. 304 p., front.
BLC: London: Hodder & Stoughton, [1921].

R-201   Rhodes, H. Henry. Where men have walked: a story of the Lucayos / by H. Henry Rhodes. Boston, Mass.: The C. M. Clark Publishing Company, 1909. 294 p., front.
LC: O 30, '09.

R-202   Rhodes, Harrison, 1871-1929. The adventures of Charles Edward / by Harrison Rhodes; illustrated by Penrhyn Stanlaws. Boston: Little, Brown and Company, 1908. 288 p., front., [23] leaves of plates.
LC: Ap 25, '08.
PW: My 9, '08.

_____ Extra men. In *The best short stories of 1918 and the yearbook of the American short story* (1919), **B-563.**

R-203   _____ The flight to Eden: a Florida romance / by Harrison Rhodes. New York: Henry Holt and Company, 1907. 313 p.
LC: S 23, '07.
PW: O 26, '07.

R-204   _____ High life: and other stories / by Harrison Rhodes . . . New York: Robert M. McBride & Co., 1920. 249 p.
Contents: High life -- The little miracle at Tlemcar -- Fair daughter of a fairer mother -- The importance of being Mrs. Cooper -- The sad case of Quag -- Spring-time -- Vive l'Amerique!
LC: O 9, '20.
PW: N 13, '20.

R-205   _____ The lady and the ladder / by Harrison Garfield Rhodes; illustrated by Karl Anderson. New York: Doubleday, Page & Company, 1906. 231 p., front., [14] leaves of plates.
PW: F 24, '06.
BLC: London: Doubleday, Page & Co.; New York printed, 1905.

Rhodes, Hattie, H. See **Webb, Virginia, pseud.**

R-206   Rhodes, T. D. (Thomas Daniel), 1857-1937. The crest of the Little Wolf: a tale of "the young Lovell" and the wars of the roses / by T. D. Rhodes. Cincinnati: The Robert Blake Company, 1904. 181 p., front., [1] leaf of plates.

R-207   Rhodes, W. H. (William Henry), 1822-1876. The case of Summerfield / by W. H. Rhodes; with an introduction by Geraldine Bonner; the photogravure frontispiece from an oil painting by Galen J. Perrett. San Francisco; New York: Paul Elder & Company, [c1907]. 54 p., front.
(Western classics; no. 2).
LC: S 16, '07.

R-208   Rhone, Rosamond D. (Rosamond Dodson), b. 1855. The days of the Son of man: a tale of Syria / by Rosamond D. Rhone . . . New York; London: G. P. Putnam's Sons, 1902. (New York: The Knickerbocker Press). 373 p. **DPL**
PW: My 24, '02.

Ribeiro, Stella Carr. See **Carr, Stella.**

R-209   Rice, Alfred Ernest. An Oregon girl: a tale of American life in the new West / by Alfred Ernest Rice; illustrations by Colista M. Dowling. Portland, Oregon: Published by Glass & Prudhomme Co., 1914. 362 p., front., [5] leaves of plates.
LC: Ap 7, '14.

R-210   Rice, Alice Caldwell Hegan, 1870-1942. Calvary Alley / by Alice Hegan Rice . . . ; illustrated by Walter Biggs. New York: The Century Co., 1917. 413 p., col. front., [2] leaves of plates.
LC: O 3, '17.
PW: S 29, '17.
BLC: London: Hodder & Stoughton, [1917].

R-211   _____ The Honorable Percival / by Alice Hegan Rice. New York: The Century Co., 1914. 276 p., front., [13] leaves of plates. [Ill. by R. M. Crosby.]
LC: O 31, '14.
PW: O 24, '14.
BLC: London: Hodder & Stoughton, 1915 [1914].

R-212   _____ Lovey Mary / by Alice Hegan Rice . . . New York: The Century Co., 1903. 197 p., incl. front., ill. [Ill. by Florence S. Shinn.]
PW: Mr 7, '03.
BLC: London: Hodder & Stoughton, [1903].

R-213   _____ Miss Mink's soldier: and other stories / by Alice Hegan Rice. New York: The Century Co., 1918. 221 p., front.
Contents: Miss Mink's soldier -- A darling of misfortune -- "Pop" -- Hoodooed -- A matter of friendship -- The wild oats of a spinster -- Cupid goes slumming -- The soul of O Sana San.
LC: S 16, '18.
PW: S 14, '18.
BLC: London: Hodder & Stoughton, 1918.

R-214   _____ Mr. Opp / by Alice Hegan Rice; with illustrations by Leon Guipon. New York: The Century Co., 1909.
326 p., front., [5] leaves of plates.
LC: Mr 27, '09.
PW: My 1, '09.
BLC: London: Hodder & Stoughton, 1909.

R-215   _____ Mrs. Wiggs of the cabbage patch / by Alice Caldwell Hegan. New York: Published by The Century Co., 1901. 153 p.
PW: O 12, '01.
BLC: London: Hodder & Stoughton, 1902.

R-216   _____ Quin / by Alice Hegan Rice. New York: The Century Co., 1921. 393 p., front. [Ill. by G. W. Gage.]
LC: S 1, '21.
PW: Ag 20, '21.
BLC: London: Hodder & Stoughton, [1921].

R-217   _____ A romance of Billy-goat Hill / by Alice Hegan Rice . . . ; with illustrations by George Wright. New York: The Century Co., 1912. 404 p., incl. [7] leaves of plates, front.
LC: S 21, '12.
PW: S 21, '12.
BLC: London: Hodder & Stoughton, 1912.

R-218   _____ Sandy / by Alice Hegan Rice. New York: The Century Co., 1905. 312 p., incl. [6] leaves of plates, front. [Ill. by Wm. L. Jacobs.]
PW: Ap 29, '05.
BLC: London: Hodder & Stoughton, 1905.

R-219   _____ Turn about tales / by Alice Hegan Rice and Cale Young Rice. New York: The Century Co., 1920. 238 p., front. [Ill. by Robert E. Johnston.]
Contents: Beulah -- Lowry -- The nut -- Francella -- A partnership memory -- Archie's relapse -- Reprisal -- Under new moons -- The hand on the sill -- Aaron Harwood.
LC: S 21, '20.
PW: O 16, '20.
BLC: London: Hodder & Stoughton, [1920].

R-220   _____ Winners and losers / by Alice Hegan Rice and Cale Young Rice. New York; London: The Century Co., [c1925]. 300 p.
Contents: Phoebe -- Out of darkness -- Miss Gee -- The commonwealth's attorney -- Mourning a la mode -- Environment -- Between trains -- Heroes: two storiettes. 1. A hero de luxe. 2. A hero minus. -- In the day of resurrection -- Gull's nest.
LC: S 17, '25.
PW: S 19, '25.
BLC: London: Hodder & Stoughton, [1925].

R-221   Rice, Aurelia. The story of an old house; [and] The strategy of Grandma Terrence / by Aurelia Rice. Boston: Thomas Todd, [c1921]. 74 p.
LC: F 23, '22.

Rice, Cale Young, 1872-1943, jt. aut. *Turn about tales* (1920). See **Rice, Alice Caldwell Hegan, 1870-1942, jt. aut., R-219.**

_____, jt. aut. *Winners and losers* (1925). See **Rice, Alice Caldwell Hegan, 1870-1942, jt. aut., R-220.**

R-222   _____ Youth's way / by Cale Young Rice. New York; London: The Century Co., 1923. 217 p.
LC: Mr 27, '23.
PW: Ap 7, '23.
BLC: London: Hodder & Stoughton; printed in U. S. A., 1923.

R-223   Rice, Edward I. (Edward Irving). Old Jim Case of South Hollow / by Edward I. Rice. New York: Doubleday, Page & Company, 1909. 253, [1] p., front., ill.

R-224   Rice, Fannie Bond. A saint of the twentieth century / Fannie Bond Rice. Boston: Richard G. Badger, 1910. ([Boston]: The Gorham Press). 308 p.
LC: My 13, '10.
PW: My 21, '10.

R-225   Rice, Harry E. Eve and the evangelist: a romance of A. D. 2108 / by Harry E. Rice; illustrated by D. Orrin Steinberger. Boston: The Roxburgh Publishing Company, Incorporated, [c1908]. 223, [1] p., front., [3] leaves of plates.
LC: O 3, '08.

R-226   Rice, John Lovell. Rocher Fendu: the story of a twain parted from kin and country / John Lovell Rice. Boston: Richard G. Badger; Toronto: The Copp Clark Co., Limited, [c1915]. 501 p.
PW: Ja 15, '16.

R-227 Rice, Laban Lacy, b. 1870. The madonna of the slate: and other short stories / by Laban Lacy Rice . . . Nashville: The Baird-Ward Press, 1923. 228 p.
OSU, ALM
Contents: The madonna of the slate -- Bud Dalton gets religion -- Blondel's coup -- Etchings: Nicollo's way, Precious alternatives, Mrs. McTeague interposes -- The spirit wife -- Rose 'o the cove.

R-228 Rice, Louise Guest, b. 1880. The girl who walked without fear / by Louise Rice. New York; Chicago; Toronto; London; Edinburgh: Fleming H. Revell Company, [c1915]. 96 p.
LC: N 5, '15.

_____ The lubbeny kiss. In *Prize stories of 1919 (1920), P-617.*

R-229 _____ New blood: a story of the folks that make America / by Louise Rice; illustrated by Quin Hall. New York; Chicago; London; Edinburgh: Fleming H. Revell Company, [c1922]. 110 p.
LC: D 30, '22.

Rice, Richard. The white sleep of Auber Hurn. In *Shapes that haunt the dusk (1907), S-339.*

Rice, Richard Ashley, jt. ed. See *A book of narratives (1917), B-734.*

Rice, Ruth Little (Mason). See **Mason, Ruth Little, 1884-1927.**

R-230 Rich, Winifred. Tony's white room: and how the white rose of love bloomed and flourished there / by Winifred Rich. San Francisco: Paul Elder & Company, [1911]. 70 p., col. front., [9] leaves of col. plates. [Ill. by Elizabeth Ferrea.]

Richard, Benjamin. Rubber Heels. In *More aces (1925), M-962.*

Richard, Hetty Lawrence (Hemenway). See **Hemenway, Hetty Lawrence.**

R-231 Richard, Marie E. The knight in grey: a historical novel / by Marie E. Richard. Philadelphia: The Castle Press, [c1913]. 359 p.
LC: O 3, '13.

Richards, Annie Louise. See **Kennedy, Kathleen, pseud.**

R-232 Richards, Bernard Gershon, b. 1877. Discourses of Keidansky / by Bernard G. Richards. New York: Scott-Thaw Co., 1903. 228 p. "The majority of these papers have appeared in the Boston evening transcript."
Contents: Keidansky decides to leave the social problem unsolved for the present -- He defends the holy sabbath -- Sometimes he is a Zionist -- Art for Tolstoy's sake -- "Three stages of the game" -- "The badness of a good man" -- "The goodness of a bad man" -- "The feminine traits of men" -- The value of ignorance -- Days of atonement -- Why the world is growing better -- Home, the last resort -- A Jewish jester -- What constitutes the Jew? -- The tragedy of humor -- The immorality of principles -- The exile of the earnest -- Why social reformers should be abolished -- Buying a book in Salem street -- The purpose of immoral plays -- The poet and the problem -- "My vacation on the east side" -- Our rivals in fiction -- On enjoying one's own writings.
PW: Ap 18, '03.

R-233 Richards, Clarice E. A tenderfoot bride: tales from an old ranch / by Clarice E. Richards. New York; Chicago; London; Edinburgh: Fleming H. Revell Company, [c1920]. 226 p., photo. front., [7] leaves of photo. plates.
OSU, WSU
Contents: First impressions -- A surprise party -- The root cellar -- The great adventure progresses -- The government contract -- A variety of runaways --The measure of a man -- The sheep business -- The unexpected -- Around the Christmas fire -- Ted -- Blizzards -- Echoes of the past.
LC: N 11, '20.

R-234 Richards, Jarrett T. (Jarrett Thomas), 1843-1920. Romance on El Camino Real: reminiscences and romances where the footsteps of the padres fall / by Jarrett T. Richards; illustrations by Alexander F. Harmer. St. Louis, Mo.: B. Herder, 1914. 538 p., front., [12] leaves of plates.

R-235 Richards, John Wm. (John William). Grace Allen's minister, or, How a fine young man was constrained by charming Christian companions to become a minister / by John Wm. Richards . . . ; with a forward by George J. Congaware . . . Burlington, Iowa: The Lutheran Literary Board, 1923. 53 p.
DLC

R-236 Richards, Laura Elizabeth Howe, 1850-1943. A daughter of Jehu / by Laura E. Richards . . . ; illustrated. New York; London: D. Appleton and Company, 1918. 323, [1] p., front., [3] leaves of plates. [Ill. by Edward C. Caswell.]
LC: O 9, '18.
PW: O 12, '18.

R-237 _____ Geoffrey Strong / by Laura E. Richards. Boston: Dana Estes & Company, [c1901]. 217 p., front., [3] leaves of plates. [Ill. by Frank T. Merrill.]
PW: Ag 17, '01.

R-238 _____ Grandmother: the story of a life that never was lived / by Laura E. Richards. Boston: Dana Estes & Company, [c1907]. 155 p., front., [3] leaves of plates. [Ill. by Frank T. Merrill.]
(Handy volume editions of copyrighted fiction.)
LC: Jl 29, '07.
PW: O 12, '07.

R-239 _____ In blessed Cyrus / by Laura E. Richards. New York; London: D. Appleton and Company, 1921. 309, [1] p., front. [Ill. by Edward C. Caswell.]
LC: O 26, '21.
PW: N 19, '21.

R-240 _____ Miss Jimmy / by Laura E. Richards. Boston: Dana Estes & Company, [c1913]. 270 p., incl. col. front. [Ill. by Frank T. Merrill.]
LC: Ja 20, '13.
PW: My 31, '13.

R-241 _____ Mrs. Tree / by Laura E. Richards . . . Boston: Dana Estes & Company, [c1902]. 282 p., front., [3] leaves of plates. [Ill. by Frank T. Merrill.]
PW: Jl 12, '02.

R-242 _____ Mrs. Tree's will / by Laura E. Richards . . . Boston: Dana Estes & Company, [c1905]. 319 p., front., [3] leaves of plates. [Ill. by Frank T. Merrill.]
PW: O 7, '05.

R-243   ____ On board the Mary Sands / by Laura E. Richards . . . ; illustrated by Frank T. Merrill. Boston: Dana Estes & Company, [c1911]. 327 p., col. front., [3] leaves of plates. [Ill. by Frank T. Merrill.]
LC: O 17, '11.
PW: D 30, '11.

R-244   ____ Pippin: a wandering flame / by Laura E. Richards . . . ; frontispiece. New York; London: D. Appleton and Company, 1917. 304, [1] p., front.   **GZM**
LC: Mr 26, '17.
PW: Ap 14, '17.

R-245   ____ The silver crown: another book of fables / by Laura E. Richards. Boston: Little, Brown and Company, 1906. 105 p. Illustrated t. p. in black and red.
PW: O 20, '06.
BLC: London: H. R. Allenson; Boston, U. S. A. [printed], 1906.

R-246   ____ The squire / by Laura E. Richards. New York; London: D. Appleton and Company, 1923. 308, [1] p., front. [Ill. by Stockton Mulford.]
LC: O 20, '23.
PW: N 24, '23.

R-247   ____ "Up to Calvin's" / by Laura E. Richards; illustrated by Frank T. Merrill. Boston: Dana Estes & Company, [c1910]. 327 p., col. front., [3] leaves of plates.
LC: O 25, '10.
PW: N 5, '10.

R-248   ____ The wooing of Calvin Parks / by Laura E. Richards . . . ; illustrated. Boston: Dana Estes & Company, [c1908]. 276 p., front. (port.), [7] leaves of plates.
LC: Ag 24, '08.
PW: S 12, '08.

R-249   Richards, Marian Edwards. Zandrie / by Marion Edwards Richards. New York: Published by the Century Co., 1909. 386 p., col. front. [Ill. by author.]
LC: S 15, '09.

Richardson, Alice. A daughter of duty. In *The Senior lieutenant's wager: and other stories* (1905), **S-312.**

R-250   Richardson, Anna Steese Sausser, b. 1865. Adventures in thrift / by Anna Steese Richardson; illustrated by Charles S. Corson. Indianapolis: The Bobbs-Merrill Company, [c1916]. 229 p., front., [4] leaves of plates.
PW: Ap 8, '16.

R-251   Richardson, Charles. Tales of a warrior: sanguine but not sanguinary for old-time people / by Charles Richardson. New York; Washington: The Neale Publishing Company, 1907. 224 p.
Contents: The requital -- The little fifer -- The old general -- The light in the mountain -- Old Major Beverly -- "Meg" -- Meredith Jones, Esquire -- The conscript -- First Sergeant Ball, Co. B.
LC: Ap 5, '07.

R-252   Richardson, Dorothy, b. 1882. The book of Blanche / by Dorothy Richardson. Boston: Little, Brown, and Company, 1924. 358 p.
BLC: London: T. Fisher Unwin, 1924.

R-253   Richardson, Emma Sykes. An Armenian maiden / by Emma Sykes Richardson. [Garden City, N. Y.]: Private printing, [c1920]. 179 p.
Unexamined copy: bibliographic data from OCLC, #18424385.

Richardson, George Tilton. <u>See</u> **Tilton, Dwight, jt. pseud. of George Tilton Richardson and W. D. Quint.**

R-254   Richardson, James Hugh, 1894-1963. Spring Street: a story of Los Angeles / by James H. Richardson. Los Angeles, Calif.: Times-Mirror Press, 1922. 418 p.
LC: Ja 5, '23.

R-255   Richardson, James P. Whom the Romans call Mercury: a tale of the Jews / by James P. Richardson. Philadelphia: Dorrance, [c1922]. 96 p.   **TNY**
LC: My 10, '22.

R-256   Richardson, Lydia Bartlett. Ought we to care, or, Esther's opportunities / by Lydia Bartlett Richardson. New York: American Tract Society, [c1903]. 235 p., front., [3] leaves of plates.   **DLC**

Richardson, Margaret. Scenes in factories. <u>In</u> *A book of narratives* (1917), **B-734.**

R-257   Richardson, Norval, 1877-1940. The cave women / by Norval Richardson. New York: Charles Scribner's Sons, 1922. 268 p.
LC: S 16, '22.
PW: S 30, '22.
BLC: London: Eveleigh Nash & Grayson, 1923.

R-258   ____ George Thorne / by Norval Richardson . . . ; with a frontispiece in colour by John Goss. Boston: L. C. Page & Company, 1911. 333 p., col. front.
LC: My 4, '11.
PW: My 13, '11.
BLC: London: Sir Isaac Pitman & Sons; Boston, U. S. A., printed, 1911.

R-259   ____ The heart of hope / by Norval Richardson; illustrations by Walter H. Everett. New York: Dodd, Mead and Company, 1905. 361 p., front., [4] leaves of plates.   **BKL**
PW: Ap 8, 05.

R-260   ____ The honey pot, or, In the garden of Lelita / by Norval Richardson . . . ; drawings by Jessie Gillespie. Boston: L. C. Page & Company, 1912. 209 p., col. front., ill. at chapter headings. Illustrated end papers.
LC: O 2, '12.
PW: O 19, '12.

R-261   ____ The lead of honour / by Norval Richardson; with a frontispiece in colour by Frank T. Merrill.

Boston: L. C. Page & Company, 1910. 341 p., col. front.
LC: Jl 26, '10.
PW: N 12, '10.
BLC: London: Sir Isaac Pitman & Sons; Boston, U. S. A., printed, 1910.

R-262 _____ Pagan fire / by Norval Richardson . . . New York: Charles Scribner's Sons, 1920. 382 p.
LC: N 17, '20.
PW: N 27, '20.
BLC: London: Eveleigh Nash & Co., New York printed, 1921.

R-263 _____ That late unpleasantness / by Norval Richardson. Boston: Small, Maynard & Company, c1924. 314 p.
LC: O 20, '24.
PW: O 18, '24.

R-264 _____ The world shut out / by Norval Richardson. New York: Charles Scribner's Sons, 1919. 305 p.
LC: S 24, '19.
PW: S 20, '19.
BLC: London: Eveleigh Nash & Co.; New York printed, 1920.

R-265 Richardson, Robert, *pseud.* The greater Waterloo: a love story / by Robert Richardson [pseud.]. New York: G. W. Dillingham Company, [c1905]. 271 p.
BLC: London: T. Fisher Unwin; New York printed, 1905.

Richardson, W. G. A passage from the life of Francois Villon. In *The best college short stories, 1924-1925* (1925), B-558.

R-266 Richardson, Wallace Ruthven. Walworth: a novel / Wallace R. Richardson. New York: Press of Stettiner Brothers, 1902. 149 p.
Unexamined copy: bibliographic data from OCLC, #20500485.

R-267 Richberg, Donald R. (Donald Randall), 1881-1960. In the dark / by Donald Richberg . . . Chicago: Forbes & Company, 1912. 308 p. **JNA**
LC: S 3, '12.
PW: S 14, '12.

R-268 _____ A man of purpose / by Donald Richberg . . . New York: Thomas Y. Crowell Company, [c1922]. 329 p.
LC: Je 27, '22.
PW: Ap 15, '22.
BLC: London: Hurst & Blackett, [1923].

R-269 _____ The shadow men / by Donald Richberg. Chicago: Forbes & Company, 1911. 312 p.
LC: O 16, '11.
PW: O 28, '11.

R-270 Richmond, A. B. (Almon Benson). The Nemesis of Chautauqua Lake, or, Circumstantial evidence / by A. B. Richmond . . . Chicago: The Progressive Thinker Publishing House, 1901. 158 p. Designed end paper.

R-271 Richmond, Grace S. (Grace Smith), 1866-1959. The bells of St. John's / by Grace S. Richmond; frontispiece by Rudolph Tandler. Garden City, New York: Doubleday, Page & Company, 1920. 57, [1] p., col. front. Ornamental borders.
LC: Ja 3, '21.
PW: D 11, '20.

R-272 _____ Brotherly house / by Grace S. Richmond; frontispiece by Thomas J. Fogarty. Garden City, New York: Doubleday, Page & Co., 1912. 88, [2] p., col. front. Illustrated end papers.
LC: N 4, '12.
PW: N 9, '12.

R-273 _____ The Brown study / by Grace S. Richmond; illustrated by Herman Pfeifer. Garden City, New York: Doubleday, Page & Company, 1917. 196 p., col. front., [6] leaves of plates. Illustrated end papers.
LC: Ap 19, '17.
PW: Je 16, '17.
BLC: London: Hodder & Stoughton, [1920].

R-274 _____ A court of inquiry / by Grace S. Richmond; illustrated by R. M. Crosby and C. M. Relyea. New York: Doubleday, Page & Company, 1909. 177 p., front., [7] leaves of plates.
LC: S 23, '09.
PW: O 16, '09.
BLC: London: Doubleday, Page & Company; New York printed, 1909. Another edition: London: Methuen & Co., 1923.

R-275 _____ The enlisting wife / by Grace S. Richmond . . . ; frontispiece. Garden City, New York: Doubleday, Page & Company, 1918. 39, [1] p., front. [Ill. by R. M. Crosby.]
LC: Mr 2, '18.
PW: Mr 9, '18.

R-276 _____ Foursquare / by Grace S. Richmond; decorations by Lee Thayer, frontispiece by H. R. Ballinger. Garden City, N. Y.: Doubleday, Page & Company, 1922. 358 p., front. Illustrated end papers.
LC: S 29, '22.
PW: S 16, '22.
BLC: London: Methuen & Co., 1922.

R-277 _____ The indifference of Juliet / by Grace S. Richmond; illustrated by Henry Hutt. New York: Doubleday, Page & Company, 1905. 307 p., front., [8] leaves of plates.
PW: Ap 22, '05.
BLC: London: Hodder & Stoughton, [1919].

R-278 _____ Mrs. Red Pepper / by Grace S. Richmond; illustrated by W. H. D. Koerner. Garden City, New York: Doubleday, Page & Company, 1913. 339 p., front., [3] leaves of plates.
LC: My 19, '13.
PW: My 31, '13.

R-279   ____ On Christmas Day in the evening / by Grace S. Richmond; illustrated by Charles M. Relyea. New York: Doubleday, Page and Company, 1910. 76 p., col. front., [3] leaves of col. plates.
LC: N 1, '10.
PW: N 12, '10.

R-280   ____ On Christmas Day in the morning / by Grace S. Richmond; illustrated by Charles M. Relyea. New York: Doubleday, Page & Company, 1908. 40 p., col. front., [3] leaves of col. plates.
LC: O 13, '08.
PW: O 24, '08.
BLC: London: Doubleday, Page & Co.; New York printed, 1908.

R-281   ____ Red and black / by Grace S. Richmond; illustrated by Frances Rogers. Garden City, New York: Doubleday, Page & Company, 1919. 381, [1] p., front., [1] leaf of plates.
LC: D 1, '19.
PW: N 15, '19.
BLC: London: Methuen & Co., 1920.

R-282   ____ Red of the Redfields / by Grace S. Richmond. Garden City, New York: Doubleday, Page & Company, 1924. 314 p.
LC: N 25, '24.
PW: N 15, '24.
BLC: London: Curtis Brown, printed in U. S. A., 1924.

R-283   ____ Red Pepper Burns / by Grace S. Richmond; illustrated by C. M. Relyea and John Jackson. Garden City, New York: Doubleday, Page & Company, 1910. 229 p., col. front., [5] leaves of col. plates.
LC: O 22, '10.
PW: O 29, '10.
BLC: London: Hodder & Stoughton, 1910.

R-284   ____ Red Pepper's patients: with an account of Anne Linton's case in particular / by Grace S. Richmond . . . ; frontispiece. Garden City, New York: Doubleday, Page & Company, 1917. 285, [1] p., front. [Ill. by Gordon H. Grant.]
LC: S 20, '17.
PW: S 22, '17.
BLC: London: Methuen & Co., 1919.

R-285   ____ Round the corner in Gay street / by Grace S. Richmond; illustrated by Maud Thurston and Charles M. Relyea. New York: Doubleday, Page & Company, 1908. 346 p., front., [7] leaves of plates.
LC: Ag 22, '08.
PW: Ag 29, '08.
BLC: London: Doubleday, Page & Co; New York printed, 1908.
Another edition: London: Hodder & Stoughton, [1914].

R-286   ____ Rufus / by Grace S. Richmond; illustrated by Joseph Simont. -- 1st ed. -- Garden City, New York: Doubleday, Page & Company, 1923. 260 p., front., [7] leaves of plates.
LC: O 13, '23.

PW: O 13, '23.
BLC: London: Methuen & Co., 1924.

R-287   ____ Strawberry Acres / by Grace S. Richmond; illustrated by J. Scott Williams and Florence Storer. Garden City, New York: Doubleday, Page & Company, 1911. 366 p., front., [7] leaves of plates.
LC: O 20, '11.
PW: O 21, '11.
BLC: London: Hodder & Stoughton, [1919].

R-288   ____ The twenty-fourth of June, midsummer's day / Grace S. Richmond. Garden City, New York: Doubleday, Page & Company, 1914. 404 p., front., col. ill. Illustrated end papers.   **OSU, CIN**
LC: Ag 25, '14.
PW: Ag 29, '14.

R-289   ____ Under the Christmas stars / by Grace S. Richmond; illustrated by Alice Barber Stephens. Garden City, New York: Doubleday, Page & Company, 1913. 55, [1] p., col. front., [2] leaves of plates. Illustrated end papers.
LC: O 25, '13.
PW: N 15, '13.

R-290   ____ Under the country sky / by Grace S. Richmond; illustrated by Frances Rogers. Garden City, N. Y.: Doubleday, Page & Company, 1916. 350 p., col. front., [3] leaves of col. plates. [t. p. ill. by Decorative Designers.]
LC: Ap 28, '16.
PW: My 6, '16.
BLC: London: John Murray, 1916.

R-291   ____ The whistling mother / by Grace S. Richmond. Garden City, N. Y.: Doubleday, Page & Company, 1917. 31, [1] p., front.
LC: Ag 18, '17.
PW: Ag 4, '17.
BLC: London: Curtis Brown; Garden City, New York printed, 1917.

R-292   ____ With Juliet in England / by Grace S. Richmond; illustrated by Charles M. Relyea. New York: Doubleday, Page & Company, 1907. 315 p., col. front., [3] leaves of col. plates.
LC: N 12, '07.
PW: N 23, '07.
BLC: London: Doubleday, Page & Co.; New York printed, 1907.

R-293   Richter, Conrad, 1890-1968. Brothers of no kin: and other stories / by Conrad Richter. New York; Philadelphia; Chicago: Hinds, Hayden & Eldredge, Inc., [c1924]. 340 p.
Contents: Brothers of no kin -- The laughter of Leen -- Forest mould -- The old debt -- Wings of a swallow -- Tempered copper -- Over the hill to the rich house -- Suicide! -- Smokehouse -- Bad luck is good luck -- Swamson's "Home, sweet home" -- The sure thing.
LC: Ja 21, '24.
PW: F 2, '24.

____ The head of his house. In *The Grim thirteen* **(1917), G-537.**

566

R-294 Ricker, Sarah B. In the sixties / by Sarah Ricker. New York; London; Montreal: The Abbey Press Publishers, [1903]. 245 p. **BKL**
PW: Ap 25, '03.

R-295 Rickert, Edith, 1871-1938. The beggar in the heart / by Edith Rickert . . . New York: Moffat, Yard and Company, 1909. 348 p.
LC: O 6, '09.
PW: O 23, '09.
BLC: London: Edward Arnold, 1909.

R-296 ____ Folly / by Edith Rickert . . . ; with frontispiece by Sigismond De Ivanowski. New York: The Baker & Taylor Co., [c1906]. 368 p., col. front.
PW: Mr 17, '06.
BLC: London: Edward Arnold, 1906.

R-297 ____ The golden hawk / by Edith Rickert. New York: The Baker and Taylor Company, 1907. 349 p., front., [5] leaves of plates. [Ill. by Wladyslaw T. Benda.]
LC: Ap 15, '07.
PW: Ap 20, '07.
BLC: London: Edward Arnold, 1907.

R-298 ____ The reaper / by Edith Rickert. Boston; New York: Houghton, Mifflin and Company, 1904. (Cambridge: The Riverside Press). 341, [1] p.
PW: O 15, '04.
BLC: London: Edward Arnold, 1904.

R-299 Rideing, William Henry, 1853-1918. How Tyson came home: a story of England and America / by William H. Rideing. New York: John Lane; London: The Bodley Head, 1904. 303 p.

R-300 Rideout, Henry Milner, 1877-1927. Admiral's light / by Henry Milner Rideout; with illustrations. Boston; New York: Houghton, Mifflin and Company, 1907. (Cambridge: The Riverside Press). 241, [1] p., col. front., [11] leaves of plates. [Ill. by Martin Justice and Charles H. Woodbury.]

R-301 ____ Barbry / by Henry Milner Rideout. New York: Duffield and Company, 1923. 300 p.
LC: O 19, '23.
PW: O 27, '23.
BLC: London: Brentano's, 1925.

R-302 ____ Beached keels / by Henry Milner Rideout. Boston; New York: Houghton, Mifflin and Company, 1906. (Cambridge, [Mass.]: The Riverside Press). 300 p.
Contents: Blue Peter -- Wild justice -- Captain Christy.
LC: O 17, '06.
PW: N 17, 06.

R-303 ____ Dragon's blood / by Henry Milner Rideout; with illustrations by Harold M. Brett. Boston; New York: Houghton Mifflin Company, 1909. (Cambridge [Mass.]: The Riverside Press). 270 p., col. front., [3] leaves of col. plates.
LC: Ap 5, '09.
PW: Ap 24, '09.
BLC: London: Archibald Constable & Co.; Cambridge, Mass. [printed], 1909.

R-304 ____ Dulcarnon / by Henry Milner Rideout. New York: Duffield and Company, 1925. 230 p.
LC: S 8, '25.
PW: Ag 15, '25.
BLC: London: Hurst & Brackett, [1926].

R-305 ____ The far cry / by Henry Milner Rideout . . . New York: Duffield and Company, 1916. 273 p.
LC: O 28, '16.
PW: N 25, '16.
BLC: London: Jarrolds, [1919].

R-306 ____ Fern seed / by Henry Milner Rideout. New York: Duffield and Company, 1921. 199 p.
LC: Je 24, 21.
PW: Ag 6, '21.
BLC: London: Hurst & Blackett; printed in U. S. A., [1922].

R-307 ____ The foot-path way / by Henry Milner Rideout. New York: Duffield and Company, 1920. 420 p.
LC: Ap 16, '20.
PW: My 8, '20.
BLC: London: Jarrolds, 1924.

____ Hantu. In *Spinners' book of fiction* **(1907)**, **S-755.**

R-308 ____ The key of the fields; and Boldero / by Henry Milner Rideout. New York: Duffield and Company, 1918. 375 p.
LC: F 7, '18.
PW: Mr 2, '18.

R-309 ____ Man eater / by Henry Milner Rideout. New York: Duffield and Company, 1924. 239 p.
LC: N 10, '24.
PW: N 29, '24.
BLC: London: Hurst & Blackett, [1927].

R-310 ____ The Siamese cat / by Henry Milner Rideout; illustrations by W. F. Grefé. New York: McClure, Phillips & Co., 1907. 222, [1] p., front., [6] leaves of plates.
LC: Ap 10, '07.
PW: My 4, '07.
BLC: London: McClure, Phillips, & Co., 1907.

R-311 ____ Tin Cowrie Dass: a story / by Henry Milner Rideout . . . New York: Duffield & Company, 1918. 163 p.
LC: D 6, '18.
BLC: London: Jarrolds, [1919]. British title: *No man's money: The story of Tin Courie Dass.*

R-312 ____ The twisted foot / by Henry Milner Rideout; with illustrations by G. C. Widney. Boston; New York: Houghton Mifflin Company, 1910. (Cambridge [Mass.]: The Riverside Press). 248 p., front., [6] leaves of plates.
LC: My 16, '10.
PW: My 14, '10.

R-313 ____ White tiger / by Henry Milner Rideout; with a frontispiece by George Varian. New York: Duffield & Company, 1915. 168 p., front.
LC: O 12, '15.
PW: N 27, '15.

R-314   ____ The winter bell / by Henry Milner Rideout. New York: Duffield and Company, 1922. 178 p., front., [3] leaves of plates. [Ill. by F. R. Gruger.]
LC: Ap 11, '22.
PW: Ap 8, '22.

R-315   Ridgely, Newton. By law of might, or, The campaign in sunset: a romance of the real Wall Street / by Newton Ridgely. New York: H. A. Simmons & Co., [1908]. 398 p., front., ill. [Ill. by M. Jaediker.]
LC: Ag 4, '08.

R-316   Ridsdale, Knowles. The gate of fulfillment / by Knowles Ridsdale. New York; London: G. P. Putnam's Sons, 1920. ([New York]: The Knickerbocker Press). 215 p.
PW: Ap 17, '20.

R-317   Riesenberg, Felix, 1879-1939. P. A. L.: a novel of the American scene / by Felix Riesenberg . . . New York: Robert M. McBride & Company, 1925. 340 p.
LC: S 21, '25.
PW: S 12, '25.
BLC: London: Herbert Jenkins, 1926.

R-318   Rihani, Ameen Fares, 1876-1940. The book of Khalid / by Ameen Rihani. New York: Dodd, Mead and Company, 1911. 349 p., ill.

R-319   Riis, Jacob A. (Jacob August). Children of the Tenements: [stories] / by Jacob A. Riis. New York: Macmillan, 1903. 387 p., front., [7] leaves of plates (1 photo.). [Ill. by C. M. Relyea, Jay Hambidge, and Otto H. Bacher.]   **CSU**
Contents: The rent baby -- A story of Bleecker Street -- The kid hangs up his stocking -- The slipper-maker's fast -- Death comes to Cat Alley -- A proposal on the elevated -- Little Will's message -- Lost children -- Paolo's Awakening -- The little dollar's Christmas journey -- The kid -- When the letter came -- The cat took the kosher meat -- Nibsy's Christmas -- In the children's hospital -- Nigger Martha's wake -- What the Christmas sun saw in the tenements -- Midwinter in New York -- A chip from the maelstrom -- Sarah Joyce's husbands -- Merry Christmas in the tenements -- Abe's game of jacks -- A little picture -- A dream of the woods -- 'Twas 'Liza's doings -- Heroes who fought fire -- John Gavin, misfit -- A heathen baby -- The christening in Bottle Alley -- In the Mulberry Street Court -- Difficulties of a deacon -- Fire in the barracks -- War on the goats -- He kept his tryst -- Rover's last fight -- How Jim went to the war -- A backwoods hero -- Jack's sermon -- Skippy of Scrabble Alley -- Making a way out of the slum.
PW: N 14, '03.

R-320   ____ Christmas stories / by Jacob A. Riis. New York: The Macmillan Company, 1923. 190 p.
Contents: The kid hangs up his stocking -- Is there a Santa Claus? -- The Crogans' Christmas in the snowshed -- The old town -- His Christmas gift -- The snow babies' Christmas -- Jack's sermon -- Merry Christmas in the tenements -- What the Christmas sun saw in the tenements -- Nibsy's Christmas -- The little dollar's Christmas journey -- Little Will's message -- The burgomaster's Christmas.
LC: O 31 '23.
PW: N 10, '23.

R-321   ____ Is there a Santa Claus? / by Jacob A. Riis. New York: The Macmillan Company; London: Macmillan & Co., Ltd., 1904. 29, [1] p., ill.
PW: N 5, '04.

R-322   ____ Neighbors: life stories of the other half / by Jacob A. Riis . . . New York: The Macmillan Company, 1914. 209 p., front., [5] leaves of plates. [Ill. by W. T. Benda.]
Contents: The answer of Ludlow street -- Kin -- The wars of the Rileys -- Life's best gift -- Driven from home -- The problem from the widow Salvini -- Peter -- Kate's choice -- The mother's heaven -- Where he found his neighbor -- What the snowflake told -- The city's heart -- Chips from the maelstrom -- Heartsease -- His Christmas gift -- Our roof garden among the tenements -- The snow babies' Christmas -- As told by the rabbi -- The strand from above.
LC: O 29, '14.
PW: N 14, '14.

R-323   Riis, Stella E. (Asling), Mrs., b. 1877. Crowned at Elim / by Stella Eugenie Asling. New York: Smith & Wilkins, 1903. 263 p.
Unexamined copy: bibliographic data from NUC.

Rike, Leah M. See **Irving, Elizabeth.**

R-324   Riley, James, b. 1848. Christy of Rathglin: an entertaining and exciting story of the life of an Irish lad / by James Riley. Boston, Mass., U. S. A.: The C. M. Clark Publishing Co., 1907. 343 p., front., [9] leaves of plates. [Ill. by William Kirpatrick.]
PW: Ja 18, '08.

R-325   Riley, James Whitcomb, 1849-1916. Eccentric Mr. Clark: stories in prose / by James Whitcomb Riley. New York: The New York Book Co., [c1901]. 189 p.
Contents: Eccentric Mr. Clark -- Jamesy -- Tod -- A remarkable man -- A nest-egg -- Tale of a spider -- Where is Mary Alice Smith? -- An adjustable lunatic.

    ____ Mary's little lamb. See **Masson, Thomas Lansing, 1866-1934.** *A bachelor's baby: and some grownups* (1907), M-587.

R-326   ____ Riley Hoosier stories / James Whitcomb Riley; with pictures by Will Vawter. Indianapolis: The Bobbs-Merrill Company, [c1917]. 191 p., incl. front., plates.
Unexamined copy: bibliographic data from OCLC, #2684706.
Contents: Jamesy -- Tod -- A remarkable man -- A nest-egg -- Tale of a spider -- An adjustable lunatic.

R-327   Rinehart, Mary Roberts, 1876-1958. Affinities: and other stories / by Mary Roberts Rinehart. New York: George H. Doran Company, [c1920]. 282 p.
Contents: Affinities -- The family friend -- Clara's little escapade -- The borrowed house -- Sauce for the gander.
LC: My 29, '20.
PW: My 29, '20
BLC: London: Hodder & Stoughton; printed in U. S. A., 1920.

R-328   ____ The after house: a story of love, mystery and a private yacht / by Mary Roberts Rinehart; with illustrations by May Wilson Preston. Boston; New York: Houghton Mifflin Company, 1914. (Cambridge: The Riverside Press). 280, [2] p., front., [11] leaves of plates.
LC: F 5, '14.
PW: Ja 24, '14.
BLC: London: Simpkin, Marshall & Co., [1915].

R-329   ____ The amazing adventures of Letitia Carberry / by Mary Roberts Rinehart . . . ; illustrations by Howard Chandler Christy. Indianapolis: The Bobbs-Merrill Company, [c1911]. 344, [1] p., front., [9] leaves of plates.
LC: N 28, '11.
PW: D 2, '11.
BLC: London: Hodder & Stoughton, [1919].

R-330   ____ The amazing interlude / by Mary Roberts Rinehart . . . ; illustrations by the Kinneys. New York: George H. Doran Company, [c1918]. 317 p., front., [3] leaves of plates.
LC: My 11, '18.
PW: My 11, '18.
BLC: London: John Murray, 1918.

R-331   ____ Bab: a sub-deb / Mary Roberts Rinehart . . . ; illustrated by May Wilson Preston. New York: George H. Doran Company, [c1917]. 350 p., col. front., [7] leaves of col. plates.
LC: Je 7, '17.
PW: Je 2, '17.
BLC: London: Hodder & Stoughton, [1920].

R-332   ____ The breaking point / by Mary Roberts Rinehart; with a frontispiece by Thomas Fogarty. New York: George H. Doran Company, [c1922]. 356 p., col. front.
LC: O 5, '22.
PW: Jl 29, '22.
BLC: London: Hodder & Stoughton; printed in U. S. A., [1922].

R-333   ____ The case of Jennie Brice / by Mary Roberts Rinehart . . . ; illustrated by M. Leone Bracker. Indianapolis: The Bobbs-Merrill Company, [c1913]. 227, [1] p., front., [5] leaves of plates.
LC: Mr 6, '13.
PW: Mr 1, '13.

R-334   ____ The circular staircase / by Mary Roberts Rinehart; with illustrations by Lester Ralph. Indianapolis: The Bobbs-Merrill Company, [c1908]. 362 p., front., [6] leaves of plates.
LC: Ag 15, '08.
PW: Ag 15, '08.
BLC: London: Cassell & Co., 1909.

R-335   ____ Dangerous days / by Mary Roberts Rinehart . . . New York: George H. Doran Company, [c1919]. 400 p.
LC: Jl 3, '19.
PW: Jl 12, '19.
BLC: London: Hodder & Stoughton; printed in U. S. A., [1919].

R-336   ____ K. / by Mary Roberts Rinehart; with illustrations. Boston; New York: Houghton Mifflin Company, 1915. (Cambridge: The Riverside Press). 409, [1] p., front., [7] leaves of plates (1 double-leaf). [Ill. by Charles Edward Chambers.]
LC: Ag 9, '15.
PW: Ag 7, '15.
BLC: London: Smith, Elder & Co., 1915. Another edition: London: Hodder & Stoughton, 1917.

R-337   ____ Long live the king! / by Mary Roberts Rinehart; with illustrations by Arthur Becher. Boston; New York: Houghton Mifflin Company, 1917. (Cambridge [Mass.], The Riverside Press). 485, [1] p., col. front., [7] leaves of col. plates.
LC: S 26, '17.
PW: S 22, '17.
BLC: London: John Murray, 1917.

R-338   ____ Love stories / by Mary Roberts Rinehart . . . New York: George H. Doran Company, [c1919]. 352 p.   **AZS**
Contents: Twenty-two -- Jane -- In the pavilion -- God's food -- The miracle -- "Are we downhearted? No!" -- The game.
LC: Ap 28, '19.
PW: My 3, '19.

R-339   ____ The man in lower ten / by Mary Roberts Rinehart . . . ; with illustrations by Howard Chandler Christy. Indianapolis: The Bobbs-Merrill Company, [c1909]. 373 p., col. front., [4] leaves of col. plates.
LC: Mr 20, '09.
PW: Mr 20, '09.
BLC: London: Cassell & Co., 1909.

R-340   ____ More Tish / by Mary Roberts Rinehart . . . New York: George H. Doran Company, [c1921]. 280 p.
LC: N 23, '21.
PW: N 19, '21.
BLC: London: Hodder & Stoughton; printed in U.S.A., [1921].

R-341   ____ A poor wise man / by Mary Roberts Rinehart . . . New York: George H. Doran Company, [c1920]. 399 p.
LC: O 12, '20.
PW: O 16, '20.
BLC: London: Hodder & Stoughton; printed in U.S.A., [1920].

R-342   ____ The red lamp / by Mary Roberts Rinehart. New York: George H. Doran Company, [c1925]. 317 p.
LC: Ag 29, '25.
PW: Ag 15, '25.

R-343   ____ Sight unseen and The confession / by Mary Roberts Rinehart . . . New York: George H. Doran Company, [c1921]. 307 p.
LC: Ag 30, '21.
PW: Jl 30, '21.
BLC: London: Hodder & Stoughton; printed in U.S.A., [1921].

R-344   ____ The street of seven stars / by Mary Roberts Rinehart. Boston; New York: Houghton Mifflin Company, 1914. 377 p.
LC: N 27, '14.
PW: O 3, '14.
BLC: London: Cassell & Co., 1915.

R-345   ____ Temperamental people / by Mary Roberts Rinehart. New York: George H. Doran Company, [c1924]. 338 p.
Contents: Her Majesty, the queen -- The altar on the hill: the secretary -- Cynara: the sculptor -- The great success: the singer --

The secret house: the wife -- A midsummer knight's dream: the cowboy -- Lily: the philanderer -- "Ca ne fait rien": the dough boy.
LC: S 6, '24.
PW: Ag 30, '24.
BLC: London: Hodder & Stoughton; printed in U. S. A., [1924].

R-346   Tish / by Mary Roberts Rinehart; with illustrations by May Wilson Preston. Boston; New York: Houghton Mifflin Company, 1916. (Cambridge: The Riverside Press). 371, [1] p., col. front., [8] leaves of col. plates.
Contents: Mind over motor -- Like a wolf on the fold -- The simple lifers -- Tish's spy -- My country Tish of Thee.
LC: Ag 7, '16.
PW: Ag 5, '16.
BLC: London: Hodder & Stoughton, [1917].

R-347   The truce of God / by Mary Roberts Rinehart; decorations by Harold Sichel. New York: George H. Doran Company, [c1920]. 96 p., col. front., ill. Illustrated end papers in cream and purple.
LC: D 3, '20.
PW: D 4, '20.

R-348   Twenty-three and a half hours' leave / by Mary Roberts Rinehart . . . ; illustrated by May Wilson Preston. New York: George H. Doran Company, [c1918]. 86 p., col. front., [1] leaf of plates. Illustrated end papers.
LC: N 11, '18.
PW: N 23, '18.

     Twenty-two. In *Aces* (1924), A-42.

R-349   When a man marries / by Mary Roberts Rinehart . . . ; with illustrations by Harrison Fisher and Mayo Bunker. Indianapolis: The Bobbs-Merrill Company, [c1909]. 353, [1] p., [4] leaves of col. plates, ill.
LC: N 20, '09.
PW: D 4, '09.

R-350   Where there's a will / by Mary Roberts Rinehart . . . ; illustrations by F. Vaux Wilson. Indianapolis: The Bobbs-Merrill Company, [c1912]. 352 p., front., [5] leaves of plates.
LC: S 5, '12.
PW: Ag 17, '12.

R-351   The window at the White Cat / by Mary Roberts Rinehart . . . ; with illustrations by Arthur I. Keller. Indianapolis: The Bobbs-Merrill Company, [c1910]. 378 p., front., [3] leaves of plates.
LC: Ag 17, '10.
PW: Ag 20, '10.
BLC: London: Eveleigh Nash Co., 1911.

R-352 Rion, Hanna, 1875-1924. Fate and a marionette / by Hanna Rion. New York: Edward J. Clode, Inc., [c1924]. 320 p.
LC: S 27, '24.
BLC: London: Gyldendal, 1923.

R-353   The smiling road / by Hanna Rion . . . ; illustrations by Frank Ver Beck. New York: Edward J. Clode, [c1910]. 191 p., front., [9] leaves of plates.

Illustrated end papers.
LC: O 19, '10.

R-354 Ripley, Henry, 1847-1914. Hand-clasp of the East and West: a story of pioneer life on the western slope of Colorado / by Henry and Martha Ripley. [Denver, Colo.: Press of the Williamson-Haffner Engraving & Printing Co., 1914]. 471 p., incl. front., photo. ill.

Ripley, Martha, jt. aut. *Hand-clasp of the East and West* (1914). See **Ripley, Henry, 1847-1914, jt. aut., R-354.**

R-355 Rising, Lawrence. Proud flesh / Lawrence Rising. New York: Boni and Liveright, [c1924]. 317 p.
LC: Jl 5, '24.
PW: Jl 5, '24.
BLC: London: T. Fisher Unwin, 1925.

R-356   She who was Helena Cass / by Lawrence Rising. New York: George H. Doran Company, [c1920]. 320 p.
LC: O 5, '20.
PW: O 2, '20.
BLC: London: Hodder & Stoughton; printed in U.S.A., [1920].

R-357 Risley, R. V. (Richard Voorhees), 1874-1904. The life of a woman / by R. V. Risley . . . Chicago: Herbert S. Stone & Company, 1902. 325 p.
PW: N 1, '02.
BLC: London: Grant Richards; Chicago [printed], 1902.

Ritchie, Lily M., b. 1867. See **Briarly, Mary, pseud.**

R-358 Ritchie, Robert Welles, 1879-1942. Drums of doom / by Robert Welles Ritchie . . . New York: Dodd, Mead and Company, 1923. 270 p.
LC: Mr 20, '23.
BLC: London: Hutchinson & Co., [1923].

R-359   Dust of the desert / by Robert Welles Ritchie. New York: Dodd, Mead and Company, 1922. 300 p.
LC: S 13, '22.
PW: S 9, '22.
BLC: London: Hutchinson & Co., [1923].

    , jt. aut. *Inside the lines* (1915). See **Biggers, Earl Derr, 1884-1933, jt. aut., B-598.**

R-360   Stairway of the sun / by Robert Welles Ritchie . . . New York: Dodd, Mead and Company, 1924. 280 p.
LC: F 12, '24.
PW: F 16, '24.
BLC: Lodnon: Hutchinson & Co., [1924].

R-361   Trails to Two Moons / by Robert Welles Ritchie; with frontispiece by Frank Spradling. Boston: Little, Brown and Company, 1920. 308 p., front.
LC: S 30, '20.
PW: O 9, '20.

BLC: London: Hutchinson & Co.; printed in U.S.A., [1921].

R-362 Ritter, John P. The crossroads of destiny / by John P. Ritter . . . New York: G. W. Dillingham Company, [c1901]. 273 p., incl. front., [2] leaves of plates. [Ill. by John Huybers and Seymour Stone.] **IUA**

PW: My 4, '01.

R-363 Rivenburgh, Eleanor. Tales--in--Tapa: 1909 / Eleanor Rivenburgh. Honolulu, Hawaii: Paradise of the Pacific Publishers and Printers, 1909. 67, [1] p., [14] leaves of photo. plates, ill. **HUH**
Contents: Leialoha -- The widow McBryde -- The heart of Mona [i. e. Nona] -- A quiet game of whist -- Fineana -- Love's price.
LC: My 25, 10.

R-364 Rives, Amélie, 1863-1945. The ghost garden: a novel / by Amélie Rives (Princess Troubetzkoy) . . . ; with a frontispiece by George W. Hood. New York: Frederick A. Stokes Company, [c1918]. 299 p., col. front.
PW: Jl 27, '18.

R-365 _____ The golden rose: the romance of a strange soul / by Amélie Rives (Princess Troubetzkoy). New York; London: Harper & Brothers, 1908. 225, [1] p.
LC: My 7, '08.
PW: My 16, '08.

R-366 _____ Hidden house / by Amélie Rives (the Princess Troubetzkoy) . . . ; with a frontispiece by Gayle Porter Hoskins. Philadelphia; London: J. B. Lippincott Company, 1912. 151, [1] p., col. front. Colored, illustrated end papers.
LC: Mr 14, '12.
PW: Mr 9, '12.

R-367 _____ Pan's mountain / by Amélie Rives (Princess Troubetzkoy). New York; London: Harper & Brothers, 1910. 287, [1] p.
LC: O 1, '10.
PW: O 8, '10.

R-368 _____ Shadows of flames: a novel / by Amélie Rives (Princess Troubetskoy); with frontispiece in color by Alfred James Dewey. New York: Frederick A. Stokes Company, [1915]. 590 p., col. front.
LC: Ag 18, '15.
PW: S 4, '15.
BLC: London: Hurst & Blackett, 1915.

R-369 _____ Trix and Over-the-moon / by Amélie Rives (Princess Troubetzkoy); with illustrations by F. Walter Taylor. New York; London: Harper & Brothers, 1909. 164 p., front., [3] leaves of plates.
LC: O 16, '09.
PW: O 23, '09.

R-370 _____ World's-End / by Amélie Rives (Princess Troubetzkoy) . . . ; with four illustrations by Alonzo Kimball. New York: Frederick A. Stokes Company, [c1914]. 425 p., front., [3] leaves of plates.
LC: Ap 18, '14.
BLC: London: Hurst & Blackett, 1914. Sixth edition.

R-371 Rives, Hallie Erminie, 1876-1956. The castaway: three great men ruined in one year--a king, a cad, and a castaway / by Hallie Erminie Rives; illustrated by Howard Chandler Christy. Indianapolis: The Bobbs-Merrill Company, [1904]. 443 p., col. front., [7] leaves of plates.
PW: Je 4, '04.

R-372 _____ Hearts courageous / by Hallie Erminie Rives; illustrated by A. B. Wenzell. Indianapolis: The Bowen-Merrill Company, [1902]. 407 p., front., [5] leaves of plates.
PW: Je 7, '02.
BLC: London: B. F. Stevens & Brown, [1902].

_____ In the wake of war. In *Short story classics* **(1905), S-466.**

R-373 _____ The kingdom of slender swords / by Hallie Erminie Rives (Mrs. Post Wheeler); with a foreword by His Excellency baron Makino; illustrations by A. B. Wenzell. Indianapolis: The Bobbs-Merrill Company, [c1910]. 435, [1] p., col. front., [2] leaves of col. plates.
LC: Ja 29, '10.
BLC: London: Everett & Co., 1911.

R-374 _____ The long lane's turning / by Hallie Erminie Rives (Mrs. Post Wheeler) . . . ; with illustrations by Frances Rogers. New York: Dodd, Mead and Company, 1917. 391 p., col. front., [3] leaves of col. plates.
PW: Ag 25, '17.
BLC: London: Hurst & Blackett, 1918.

R-375 _____ Satan Sanderson / by Hallie Erminie Rives . . . ; with illustrations by A. B. Wenzell. Indianapolis: The Bobbs-Merrill Company, [c1907]. 399, [1] p., col. front., [4] leaves of col. plates.
LC: Ag 12, '07.
BLC: London: Hutchinson & Co., 1908.

R-376 _____ The Valiants of Virginia / by Hallie Erminie Rives (Mrs. Post Wheeler); illustrated by André Castaigne. Indianapolis: The Bobbs-Merrill Company, [c1912]. 432 p., col. front., [5] leaves of col. plates.
PW: D 7, '12.
BLC: London: Mills & Boon, 1913.

Roach, Abby Meguire. The level of fortune. In *Southern lights and shadows* **(1907), S-718.**

_____ Life's accolade. In *Their husband's wives* **(1906), T-161.**

R-377 _____ Some successful marriages / Abby Meguire Roach; illustrated by Alice Barber Stephens. New York; London: Harper & Brothers, 1906. 284, [1] p., front., [11] leaves of plates.
Contents: The inner imperative -- Life's accolade -- The right to martyrdom -- The level of fortune -- A working basis -- The spirit of partnership -- One of life's paradoxes -- His claim -- The vanished gods -- An epitaph and a ghost -- Unremembering June -- Nevertheless.

_____ A working basis. In *Life at high tide* **(1907), L-281.**

R-378 Roads, Ethel, b. 1890. The romance of a guardsman / by Ethel Roads . . . [Reading, Pa.: Press of Reading Eagle, c1917]. 180 p.
LC: Ag 11, '17.
PW: S 22, '17.

R-379 Robb, Carroll E. The lion tamer / by Carroll E. Robb. New York; London: Harper & Brothers, 1925. 321 p.
LC: Mr 2, '25.
PW: Mr 7, '25.

Robbins, Clarence Aaron. See Robbins, Tod.

R-380 Robbins, Emma Shelton. Oh, you English! / by Emma Shelton Robbins. New York: The Neale Publishing Company, 1915. 315 p.　　　DLC
PW: F 5, '16.

R-381 Robbins, John Williams. The witch of Tunthorne Gore / by John Williams Robbins; a souvenance of despoliation. [Hartford, Conn.: The Davidson Press, c1922]. 40 p., ill.　　　DLC

Robbins, L. H. Mr. Downey sits down. In Prize stories of 1921 (1922), P-619.

Robbins, L. H. Professor Todd's used car. In Prize stories of 1920 (1921), P-618.

R-382 Robbins, Leo. Mary the merry: and other tales / by Leo Robbins. Boston, Massachusetts: The Stratford Company, 1918. 84 p.　　　DLC, NYP
Contents: Mary the merry -- And yet- -- Pedigree -- Sisters -- Ades' "ad" for aid -- The price -- The Christmas gift -- The life of the dead -- Something to eat -- The pest -- Self-justified -- Quips of destiny.

R-383 Robbins, Mabel Hotchkiss. The genius of Elizabeth Anne / by Mabel Hotchkiss Robbins. Boston; New York; Chicago: The Pilgrim Press, [c1916]. 326 p., front. [Ill. by Frank T. Merrill.]　　　BGU
LC: N 15, '16.

R-384 _____ The heart of a mother-to-be / by Mabel Hotchkiss Robbins . . . Boston; Chicago: The Pilgrim Press, [c1917]. 145 p.　　　NYP
LC: S 19, '17.
PW: S 22, '17.

R-385 _____ Truant from heaven / Mabel Hotchkiss Robbins. Boston: Richard G. Badger, [c1912]. ([Boston, U. S. A.]: The Gorham Press). 139 p.　　　DLC
LC: F 19, '12.

R-386 Robbins, Tod, 1888-1949. Mysterious Martin; a fiction narrative setting forth the development of character along unusual lines / by Tod Robbins. New York: J. S. Ogilvie Publishing Company, [c1912]. 153 p., ill.
Unexamined copy: bibliographic data from OCLC: #6433098.
LC: Mr 28, '12.
PW: Ap 6, '12.

R-387 _____ Red of Surley: a novel / by Tod Robbins . . . New York; London: Harper & Brothers, [1919].

333, [1] p.
LC: Ap 24, '19.
PW: Ap 26, '19.

R-388 _____ Silent, white and beautiful: and other stories / Tod Robbins. New York: Boni and Liveright, [c1920]. 256 p.
Contents: Silent, white and beautiful -- Who wants a green bottle? -- Wild Wullie, the waster -- For art's sake.
LC: Ag 19, '21.
PW: D 11, '20.

R-389 _____ The spirit of the town: a novel presentation in fiction form of the impulse and desire which mould the lives of men / by Tod Robbins. New York: J. S. Ogilvie Publishing Company, [c1912]. 172 p., front. [Ill. by A. C. Gibbin.]
LC: D 10, '12.
PW: Ja 18, '13.

R-390 _____ The unholy three / by C. A. Robbins ("Tod" Robbins). New York: John Lane Company; London: John Lane, the Bodley Head; Toronto: S. B. Gundy, 1917. 310 p.　　　DLC
LC: S 18, '17.
PW: S 15, '17.

R-391 Roberson, Harriette Gunn. Mary of Magdala: a tale of the first century / by Harriette Gunn Roberson. Chicago; Akron, Ohio; New York: The Saalfield Publishing Company, [c1909]. 393 p.

R-392 Roberts, Brigham Henry, 1857-1933. Corianton; a Nephite story / by B. H. Roberts. [Salt Lake City?, 1902]. 111 p.
Unexamined copy: bibliographic data from OCLC, #7054767.
First published as a serial in the Contributor, 1889.

R-393 Roberts, Elbridge Gerry. A naval engagement: a marine narrative of love and war / by Elbridge Gerry Roberts. Red Bank, N. J.: [s. n.], 1918. 240 p.

R-394 Roberts, Everard. The jealous Mrs. Simkins / by Everard Roberts. New York: The Knickerbocker Press, [c1906]. 146 p.　　　DLC
PW: Je 23, '06.

Roberts, Goodridge E. Theodore, 1877-1953. Captain Pike. In Greatest short stories (1915), G-424.

_____, jt. aut. A soldier of Valley Forge (1911). See Stephens, Robert Neilson, 1867-1906, jt. aut., S-860.

R-395 Roberts, Ina Brevoort Deane, 1874-1941. The lifting of a finger / by Ina Brevoort Roberts. Philadelphia: J. B. Lippincott Company, 1901. 242 p.
PW: D 14, '01.

R-396 Roberts, J. L. (James Leslie). One of four / by J. L. Roberts . . . [Moberly, Mo.: s. n., c1924]. 157 p.　　　DLC

R-397 Roberts, James, b. 1881. The face of the king / by James Roberts. New York: Robert J. Shores,

[c1918]. 204 p., front.   **EMU**
LC: Je 22, '18.

R-398 Roberts, James R. The Cactus Kid: a western story /
by James Roberts. New York City: Chelsea House,
[c1925]. 254 p.
PW: D 19, '25.

R-399 ____ The cavalier of Rabbit Butte: a western story /
by James Roberts. New York: Chelsea House,
[c1925]. 254 p.
PW: D 19, '25.

R-400 ____ The coyote: a western story / by James
Roberts. New York City: Chelsea House, [c1925].
253 p.
PW: My 23, '25.

R-401 [____] The man of the desert: a western story / by
Robert J. Horton. New York: Chelsea House,
[c1925]. 320 p.
LC: Mr 5, '25.
PW: Mr 14, '25.

R-402 [____] The prairie shrine: a western story / by
Robert J. Horton. New York: Chelsea House,
[c1924]. 320 p.
PW: O 25, '24.

R-403 [____] Rider o' the stars: a western story / by R. J.
Horton. New York City: Chelsea House, [c1924].
306 p.
LC: Mr 18, '24.
PW: Ap 5, '24.

R-404 ____ Rovin' Redden: a western story / by James
Roberts . . . New York City: Chelsea House,
[c1925]. 250 p.
PW: D 26, '25.

R-405 [____] The spectacular kid: a western story / by
Robert J. Horton. New York: Chelsea House,
[c1925]. 256 p.
PW: My 9, '25.

R-406 ____ Unwelcome settlers: a western story / by
James Roberts. New York: Chelsea House, [c1925].
254 p.
PW: My 16, '25.

R-407 ____ Whispering cañon: a western story / by James
Roberts. New York: Chelsea House, [c1925].
252 p.
PW: My 16, '25.

Roberts, Maria. The sorcery of Asenath. In
Argonaut stories (1906), **A-298.**

R-408 Roberts, Octavia, b. 1875. The gates of light / by
Octavia Roberts. Boston: Massachusetts Charitable
Eye and Ear Infirmary, [1920?]. 27 p.

R-409 ____ My Lady Valentine / by Octavia Roberts.
Boston: The A. M. Davis Co., [c1916]. 118 p., col.
front.
LC: S 24, '17.

R-410 Roberts, Osseannah. Son of the north / by Osseannah
Roberts. Boston, Mass.: The C. M. Clark
Publishing Co., 1908. 270 p., front., [7] leaves of
plates.
PW: D 12, '08.

Roberts, Theodore Goodridge. Captain Pike. In
Greatest short stories (1915), **G-424.**

Robertson, Alice Alberthe. See **David, K., pseud.**

Robertson, Anna Adelia, b. 1875. See **Gladden,
Hope, pseud.**

R-411 Robertson, David Taylor. By paths they know not /
by David Taylor Robertson . . . Boston: The
Gorham Press, 1918. 201 p.   **DLC**
LC: Ag 10, '18.
PW: Ag 10, '18.

R-412 ____ The winning of the valley: a novel / by David
Taylor Robertson. Boston: The Roxburgh Publishing
Company, [c1915]. 287 p.
LC: S 14, '15.
PW: S 18, '15.

R-413 Robertson, Florence H. (Florence Henderson), b.
1849. Shadow land: stories of the South / by
Florence H. Robertson. Boston: Richard G. Badger,
1906. ([Boston]: The Gorham Press). 91 p., front.,
[5] leaves of plates.   **TJC**
Contents: Miss Tilly an' Marse Jeems -- Ubique fidelis -- Children of
the woods.
PW: Ap 21, '06.

R-414 Robertson, Frank C. (Frank Chester), b. 1890. The
foreman of the Forty-bar / by Frank C. Robertson.
New York, N. Y.; Newark, N. J.: Barse & Hopkins,
[c1925]. 319 p.
LC: Ag 1, '25.
PW: Ag 15, '25.
BLC: London: W. Collins Sons & Co., [1927].

R-415 Robertson, Harrison, 1856-1939. The inlander / by
Harrison Robertson . . . New York: Charles
Scribner's Sons, 1901. 320 p.
PW: Mr 30, '01.

R-416 ____ The opponents / by Harrison Robertson. New
York: Charles Scribner's Sons, 1902. 355 p.
PW: Ap 19, '02.

R-417 ____ The pink typhoon / by Harrison Robertson.
New York: Charles Scribner's Sons, 1906. 196 p.,
front. [Ill. by F. B. Masters.]
PW: My 19, '06.

Robertson, Morgan, 1861-1915. The argonauts. See
Conrad, Joseph. *Il conte* (1925), **C-697.**

R-418 ____ Down to the sea / by Morgan Robertson. New
York; London: Harper & Brothers, 1905. 311,
[1] p.
Contents: The closing of the circuit -- A cow, two men, and a parson
-- The rivals -- A chemical comedy -- A hero of the cloth -- The
subconscious Finnegan -- The torpedo -- The submarine -- Fifty
fathoms down -- The enemies -- The vitality of Dennis -- The helix --
The shark -- The mutiny.
PW: Mr 11, '05.

R-419 _____ The grain ship / by Morgan Robertson. [New York]: Published by McClure's Magazine and Metropolitan Magazine, [1914?]. 242 p. Reprinted from various periodicals.

R-420 _____ Land ho! / by Morgan Robertson . . . New York; London: Harper & Brothers, 1905. 321, [1] p.
Contents: The dollar -- The ship-owner -- The wave -- The cook and the captain -- The line of least resistance -- The lobster -- On board the "Athol" -- The magnetized man -- The mistake -- The submarine destroyer -- The dancer -- On the Rio Grande.

R-421 _____ Masters of men: a romance of the new navy / by Morgan Robertson . . . New York: Doubleday, Page & Company, c1901. 335 p., front., [3] leaves of plates. [Ill. by George Fort Gibbs.]
PW: My 11, '01.

R-422 _____ Over the border / by Morgan Robertson. [New York]: McClure's Magazine and Metropolitan Magazine, [1914?]. 263 p. Stories reprinted from various periodicals.

R-423 _____ Shipmates / by Morgan Robertson . . . New York: D. Appleton and Company, 1901. 347 p., front. [Ill. by H. C. Edwards.]
Contents: The nuisance -- The fool killer -- The devil and his due -- Polarity: a tale of two brunettes -- A tale of a pigtail -- The man at the wheel -- The day of the dog -- At the end of the man-rope -- A fall from grace -- The Dutch port watch -- On the forecastle deck.
PW: N 9, '01.

R-424 _____ Sinful Peck: a novel / by Morgan Robertson. New York; London: Harper & Brothers, 1903. 354, [1] p.
PW: Je 13, 03.

R-425 _____ The three laws and the golden rule / by Morgan Robertson. [New York]: McClure's Magazine and Metropolitan Magazine, [1914]. 249 p.
Reprinted from various magazines.

R-426 _____ The wreck of the Titan, or, Futility / by Morgan Robertson. [New York]: Published by McClure's Magazine and Metropolitan Magazine, [1914]. 243 p.

R-427 Robertson, Peter, 1847-1911. The seedy gentleman / by Peter Robertson; cover design and frontispiece by Gordon Ross. San Francisco: A. M. Robertson, 1903, [c1902]. 334 p., front.
Contents: Love -- Ourselves -- Woman's eyes -- Life is a fake -- Some human weaknesses -- Outlaws and opera -- The uselessness of things -- The morbid story -- Happiness -- More about love -- 'Is 'art was true to Poll -- Music -- The new woman -- Macbeth sees himself -- The club libre -- Weddings -- Life is never the same again -- Love ballads -- Ghosts -- The human orchestra -- A visitor from the shades -- The mode -- The comic opera of life -- Rag-time -- The last rose of summer -- Curiosity -- Man, get on to thyself -- The old life and the new -- Heartsease -- The love story of a Scot -- The devil -- Madam President -- In the brave days when we were twenty-one -- Poverty -- Christmas.

Robinet, Lee, pseud. See **Bennet, Robert Ames, 1870-1954.**

R-428 Robins, Elizabeth, 1862-1952. Camilla / by Elizabeth Robins; with frontispiece by C. Allan Gilbert. New York: Dodd, Mead and Company, 1918. 504 p., col. front.
LC: O 1, '18.
PW: O 19, '18.
BLC: London: Hodder & Stoughton, 1918.

R-429 _____ Come and find me / by Elizabeth Robins . . . ; with illustrations by E. L. Blumenschein. New York: The Century Co., 1908. 531 p., front., [10] leaves of plates.
LC: F 21, '08.
PW: F 29, '08.
BLC: London: William Heinemann, 1908.

R-430 _____ The convert / by Elizabeth Robins. New York: The Macmillan Company, 1907. 304 p.
LC: O 18, '07.
PW: N 9, '07.
BLC: London: Methuen & Co., 1907.

R-431 _____ A dark lantern: a story with a prologue / by Elizabeth Robins (C. E. Raimond). New York: The Macmillan Company; London: Macmillan & Co., Ltd., 1905. 400 p.
BLC: London: William Heinemann, 1905.

R-432 _____ The Florentine frame / by Elizabeth Robins . . . New York: Moffat, Yard and Company, 1909. 334 p.
LC: N 13, '09.
PW: N 20, '09.
BLC: London: John Murray, 1909.

R-433 _____ The magnetic north / by Elizabeth Robins (C. E. Raimond) . . . ; with a map. New York: Frederick A. Stokes Company, 1904. 417 p., [1] folded leaf of plates (map).
PW: Je 4, '04.
BLC: London: William Heinemann, 1904.

R-434 _____ The messenger / by Elizabeth Robins . . . ; with illustrations by George Giguére. New York: The Century Co., 1919. 426 p., front., [3] leaves of plates.
LC: S 30, '19.
PW: S 27, '19.
BLC: [London]: Hodder & Stoughton, [1919].

R-435 _____ The mills of the gods / by Elizabeth Robins. New York: Moffat, Yard & Company, 1908. 158 p.
LC: S 2, '08.
PW: O 17, '08.

R-436 _____ My little sister / by Elizabeth Robins. New York: Dodd, Mead and Company, 1913. 344 p.
LC: Ja 11, '13.
PW: Ja 25, '13.

R-437 _____ Time is whispering / by Elizabeth Robins. New York; London: Harper & Brothers, [c1923]. 378, [1] p.
LC: Ap 27, '23.
PW: Je 2, '23.
BLC: London: Hutchinson & Co., [1923].

R-438   _____ Under the southern cross / by Elizabeth Robins . . . ; illustrated & decorated by John Rae. New York: Frederick A. Stokes Company, 1907. 234 p., col. front., [3] leaves of col. plates. Illustrated end papers.
LC: O 28, '07.
PW: D 14, '07.

R-439   Robins, Sally Nelson. A man's reach / by Sally Nelson Robins; with illustrations in color by Edmund Frederick. Philadelphia; London: J. B. Lippincott Co., 1916. 333 p., col. front., [2] leaves of col. plates.
LC: Mr 2, '16.
PW: F 12, '16.

R-440   _____ Scuffles / by Sally Nelson Robins; illustrated by Harriotte Montague. New York: The Alice Harriman Company, 1912. 207 p., front., [2] leaves of plates.
LC: Ag 31, '12.
PW: Ag 24, '12.

R-441   Robinson, C. H. (Charles Henry), b. 1843. Hawk, the young Osage: a story of Indian life and adventures in the early times / by C. H. Robinson . . . ; illustrated and decorated by The Avery Studio. Boston: L. C. Page & Company, 1913. 272 p., front., [3] leaves of plates. Illustrated end papers.
                       CWR
LC: S 29, '13.

R-442   _____ Longhead: the story of the first fire / by C. H. Robinson . . . ; illustrated by Charles Livingston Bull. Boston: L. C. Page & Company, 1913. 127 p., front., [3] leaves of plates.
LC: Jl 26, '13.

R-443   Robinson, Charles Asbury. The roving red rangers, or, Laura Lamar, of the Susquehanna: a thrilling romance of the old colonial days / by C. A. Robinson . . . Greenfield, Ind.: Published by the author, 1902. 224 p.

R-444   _____ The trail of the white wolf, or, The doom of the Delawares: a thrilling story of early colonial days / by Charles Asbury Robinson . . . Greenfield, Ind.: Published by the author, 1903. 255 p., front., photo. ill. (1 port.).
PW: F 13, '04.

R-445   Robinson, Edwin Meade, 1878-1946. Enter Jerry / by Edwin Meade Robinson. New York: The Macmillan Company, 1921. 315 p.
LC: N 10, '21.

R-446   Robinson, Eliot Harlow, b. 1884. "Dee Dee": being the uncommon account of a commonplace crime: wherein the author has presented, in a simple, convincing manner, a story of romance and mystery . . . / by Eliot H. Robinson . . . Boston: Small, Maynard & Company, [c1925]. 318 p.
LC: O 21, '25.
PW: N 7, '25.
BLC: London: Hutchinson & Co., [1926].

R-447   _____ The maid of Mirabelle: a romance of Lorraine / by Eliot H. Robinson . . . ; illustrated with reproductions of sketches made by the author. Boston: The Page Company, 1920. 304 p., front., [5] leaves of plates. [Ill. by Eliot Harlow Robinson and Neale Ordayne.]
LC: Jl 28, '20.

R-448   _____ The man from Smiling Pass, or, The Honorable Abe Blount / by Eliot H. Robinson; with an illustration in color by H. Weston Taylor. Boston: L. C. Page & Company (incorporated), 1924. 359 p., col. front.
LC: S 12, '24.

R-449   _____ Man proposes, or, The romance of John Alden Shaw / by Eliot H. Robinson; illustrated by William Van Dresser. Boston: The Page Company, 1916. 359 p., col. front., [3] leaves of plates.
LC: S 7, '16.
PW: S 16, '16.

R-450   _____ Mark Gray's heritage / by Eliot H. Robinson. Boston: The Page Company, 1923. 381 p.
LC: Ap 14, '23.
PW: Je 14, '24.

R-451   _____ "Smiles," a Rose of the Cumberlands / by Eliot H. Robinson; illustrated by H. Weston Taylor. Boston: The Page Company, 1919. 377 p., front., [4] leaves of plates. OSU copy second impression.
LC: My 29, '19.
PW: Jl 5, '19.

R-452   _____ Smiling pass: being a further account of the career of "Smiles"; a Rose of the Cumberlands / by Eliot H. Robinson . . . ; illustrated by John Goss. Boston: The Page Company, 1921. 389 p., col. front., [4] leaves of plates.
LC: O 18, '21.
PW: N 19, '21.

R-453   Robinson, Frederick. The war of the worlds: a tale of the year 2,000 A. D. / by Frederick Robinson. [S. l.: s. n., c1914]. 111 p., photo. front. (port.), ill. (2 photo.). [Ill. by Frederick Robinson.]

R-454   Robinson, Harry Perry, Sir, b. 1859. Essence of honeymoon / by H. Perry Robinson . . . ; illustrated. New York; London: Harper & Brothers, 1911. 311, [1] p., front., [7] leaves of plates. [Ill. by Geo. Brehm.]   **OSU, NMW**
LC: My 15, '11.
BLC: London: William Heinemann, 1911.

Robinson, Katharine. See **Kayamar, pseud.**

R-455   Robinson, Mabel L. (Mabel Louise), 1874-1962. Dr. Tam O'Shanter / by Mabel L. Robinson. New York: E. P. Dutton & Company, [c1921]. 174 p., front., [3] leaves of plates. [Ill. by Loren Holmwood.]
LC: Jl 13, '21.
PW: Jl 2, '21.

R-456   Robinson, Margaret Blake. The left-side man / by Margaret Blake Robinson. New York: J. S. Ogilvie Publishing Company, c1902. 266 p.
PW: N 22, '02.

R-457   Robinson, Nellie G. (Nellie Grace), b. 1874. Philo's daughter: the story of the daughter of the thief with whom Christ was crucified / by Nellie G. Robinson. Cincinnati: Press of Jennings and Graham, [c1908]. 287 p.

R-458   Robinson, Nina Hill. The pillars of Rehoboth Church: a Glendower story / by Nina Hill Robinson. Nashville, Tenn.; Dallas, Tex.: Publishing House of the M. E. Church, South: Smith & Lamar, Agents, 1911. 160 p., front. (port.).   **EMU**
PW: Ja 27, '12.

R-459   [____] That boy o'mine / by the author of "Aunt Dice." Nashville, Tenn.; Dallas, Tex.: Publishing House M. E. Church, South: Smith & Lamar, Agents, 1908. 143, [1] p., front. [Ill. by W. A. Daniel.]   **EMU**
LC: O 8, '08.

R-460   Robinson, Ray. Twentieth century Athenians / by Ray Robinson. Boston: The Gorham Press, 1918. 300 p.   **NYP**

R-461   Robinson, Rowland Evans, 1833-1900. Hunting without a gun: and other papers / by Rowland E. Robinson; with illustrations by Rachael Robinson. New York: Forest and Stream Publishing Company, 1905. 381 p., front. (port.), ill.
Contents: Hunting without a gun -- In search of nothing -- In the spring woods -- The saved places -- Little Otter -- The path of boatless generations -- Down among the fishes--I -- Down among the fishes--II -- Landlord Dayton's shooting match -- How Elijah was fed at Christmas -- Uncle Gid's Christmas tree -- A new year's swearing off -- A brother-in-law of Antoine -- Antoine on the rail -- Antoine sugaring -- The gray pine: I -- The gray pine: II -- A bee hunter's reminiscences.
LC: Ap 28, '05.
PW: My 13, '05.
References: BAL 16892.

R-462   ____ Out of bondage: and other stories / by Rowland E. Robinson. Boston; New York: Houghton, Mifflin and Company, 1905. (Cambridge: The Riverside Press). 334 p.
Reprinted from various periodicals.
Contents: Out of bondage -- A letter from the 'Hio -- The shag back panther -- A story of the old frontier -- McIntosh of Vergennes -- A son of the revolution -- An old-time March meeting -- A September election -- Raspberrying in Danvis -- The Buttles gals -- Discovery of a new world -- Fourth of July at Highfield poorhouse -- What the November woods gave -- A housewife's calender -- The Goodwin spring -- The mole's path -- The purification of Cornbury.
LC: F 18, '05.
PW: Mr 11, '05.
References: BAL 16891.

R-463   ____ Sam Lovel's boy / by Rowland E. Robinson. Boston; New York: Houghton, Mifflin and Company, 1901. (Cambridge: The Riverside Press). 259 p.
LC: F 7, '01.
PW: F 23, '01.
References: BAL 16890.

Robinson, Suzanne Antrobus (Mrs. A. A. Robinson). **See Antrobus, Suzanne.**

R-464   Robinson, William Henry, b. 1867. Her Navajo lover / by W. H. Robinson. [Phoenix, Arizona: Bandar Log Press, c1903]. 19, [1] p., ill. (some photo).   **DLC**

R-465   ____ The man from yesterday / by Will Robinson; illustrated. Boston: The Roxburgh Publishing Co., Inc., [c1915]. 358 p., front., [4] leaves of plates. [Ill. by Charles D. Mitchell.]
LC: S 14, '15.
PW: S 11, '15.

R-466   ____ The witchery of Rita; and, Waiting for Tonti / by Will H. Robinson. Phoenix, Ariz.: The Berryhill Co., 1919. 71 p. [Ill. by W. H. James.]
LC: Mr 20, '20.
PW: Je 26, '20.

R-467   ____ Yarns of the Southwest / by Will H. Robinson. Phoenix, Arizona: Published by the Berryhill Company, [c1921]. (Chandler, Arizona: Chandler Arizonan Press). 86 p.
Contents: The desert -- The mule that died of too much imagination -- Southwestern justice -- The growing salve -- He wouldn't let her suffer -- Heaven, hell and heat -- With healing on its wings -- The grand bounce -- To the bitter end -- The way they grow at Salome -- Mythical animals -- The side-hill bear -- The Gilaopolis -- A bashful one -- Ostrich egg for one -- The greatful rattlesnake -- The lady and the lariat -- Little Bill's bandit -- My Arizona bedroom / J. William Lloyd.
LC: D 19, '21.

R-468   Robinson, William J. (William Josephus), 1867-1936. A clergyman's son and daughter / by William J. Robinson . . . New York: The Critic and Guide Company, 1922. 170 p.
LC: F 11, '22.

R-469   ____ Stories of love and life: of fact and fancy woven / by William J. Robinson, M. D. New York: The Critic and Guide Company, 1913. 179 p.
Contents: Margaret: a story of a radical couple -- They waited too long -- Was Selma justified? -- Love: a little story for free lovers -- The rise of Richard Martindale.
LC: Ap 12, '13.

R-470   Robison, William Michael, b. 1846. The scar / by Mike Robison. Nashville, Tenn.: The Cumberland Press, 1911. 96 p.
Unexamined copy: bibliographic data from NUC.
LC: Je 2, '11.

R-471   Roche, Arthur Somers, 1883-1935. The day of faith / by Arthur Somers Roche; with frontispiece by M. Leone Bracker. Boston: Little, Brown and Company, 1921. 361 p., front.
LC: O 27, '21.

____ The dummy-chucker. *In The best short stories of 1920 and the yearbook of the American short story* **(1921), B-565.**

R-472   ____ The eyes of the blind / by Arthur Somers Roche . . . New York: George H. Doran Company, [c1919]. 322 p.   **ABC**
LC: Mr 31, '19.

R-473 ____ Find the woman / by Arthur Somers Roche
. . . ; with four illustrations by Dean Cornwell. New
York: Cosmopolitan Book Corporation, 1921.
311 p., front., [3] leaves of plates.
LC: Mr 17, '21.
BLC: London: Hodder & Stoughton, [1921].

R-474 ____ Loot / by Arthur Somers Roche; illustrated by
M. Leone Bracker. Indianapolis: The Bobbs-Merrill
Company, [c1916]. 320 p., [6] leaves of plates.
Illustrated t. p. and end papers.
LC: Jl 20, '16.
PW: Jl 29, '16.

R-475 ____ A more honorable man / by Arthur Somers
Roche. New York: The Macmillan Company, 1922.
290 p.
LC: N 1, '22.
PW: D 2, '22.

R-476 ____ The pleasure buyers / by Arthur Somers
Roche. New York: The Macmillan Company, 1925.
321 p.
LC: Je 3, '25.
PW: Je 20, '25.

R-477 ____ Plunder / by Arthur Sommers Roche . . . ;
with illustrations by Will Foster. Indianapolis: The
Bobbs-Merrill Company, [c1917]. 322 p., front., [4]
leaves of plates. Illustrated end papers.
"Copyrighted by the Curtis Publishing Company
under the title *A scrap of paper*."
LC: Mr 26, '17.
PW: Mr 24, '17.

R-478 ____ Ransom! / by Arthur Somers Roche . . . New
York: George H. Doran Company, [c1918]. 312 p.
Illustrated end papers.
LC: My 20, '18.
PW: My 25, '18.

R-479 ____ The sport of kings / by Arthur Somers Roche
. . . ; illustrated by Arthur I. Keller. Indianapolis:
The Bobbs-Merrill Company, [c1917]. 324 p.,
front., [8] leaves of plates.
LC: Jl 16, '17.
PW: Je 30, '17.

R-480 ____ Uneasy street / by Arthur Somers Roche;
illustrated by James Montgomery Flagg. New York:
Cosmopolitan Book Corporation, 1920. 339 p.,
front., [3] leaves of plates.
LC: F 5, '20.
PW: Ja 31, '20.

R-481 Roche, James Jeffrey, 1847-1908. The sorrows of
Sap'ed: a problem story of the East / by James
Jeffrey Roche . . . ; illustrated by W. E. Mears.
New York; London: Harper & Brothers, 1904.
195 p., col. front., [7] leaves of col. plates, ill.

R-482 Rock, James, *pseud*. Thro' space / by James Rock
[pseud.]. Boston: New England Druggist Publishing
Co., 1909. 188 p.   **NYP**
LC: O 27, '09.

Rock, Magdalen. A broken engagement. In *The
Senior lieutenant's wager: and other stories* (1905),
S-312.

____, contributor. See *A double knot* (1905),
D-499.

____ The heir. In *The lady of the tower* (1909),
L-13.

____ Next of kin. In *The friendly little house: and
other stories* (1910), F-432.

____ Stephen Oxenham's mistake. In *The lady of
the tower* (1909), L-13.

____ The wrong basket trunk. In *The friendly little
house: and other stories* (1910), F-432.

R-483 [Rockey, Howard], 1886-1934. All that I want / by
Ronald Bryce [pseud.]; frontispiece by George W.
Gage. New York: The Macaulay Company,
[c1925]. 322 p. front.
LC: Mr 7, '25.
PW: Mr 14, '25.

R-484 ____ Daughters of luxury / by Howard Rockey;
frontispiece by Miriam Selss. New York: The
Macaulay Company, [c1925]. 307 p., front.
LC: Mr 27, '25.
PW: Ap 4, '25.

R-485 ____ This woman / by Howard Rockey; frontispiece
by P. J. Monahan. New York: The Macaulay
Company, [c1924]. 317 p., front.
LC: Mr 7, '24.
PW: Mr 1, '24.

R-486 Rodgers, Joseph F. Frank Boyle: simple annals of
the poor amid the maddening crowd's ignoble strife /
by Joseph F. Rodgers. New York: Broadway
Publishing Co., 1915. 193 p.   **NYP**

R-487 Rodney, George Brydges, b. 1872. Jim Lofton:
American / by George Brydges Rodney. New York:
The James A. McCann Company, 1920. 276 p.
LC: N 9, '20.
PW: Ja 29, '21.

R-488 Roe, Clifford Griffith, 1875-1934. The girl who
disappeared / by Clifford G. Roe . . . ; illustrations
by Walt Louderback. Naperville, Ill.: World's
Purity Federation, [c1914]. 352 p., front., [13]
leaves of plates.
LC: Ap 29, '14.
Another ed.: Chicago: American Bureau of Moral
Education, 1914.

R-489 Roe, George, b. 1861. Iblis in paradise: a story of
the temptation / by George Roe. Philadelphia: Henry
Altemus Company, [c1908]. [80] p., [4] leaves of
plates. [Ill. by Jean de Paleologue.] Ornamental
borders.   **OSU, SOI**

R-490 Roe, Mary Cheseldine. Polly to Peggy / by Mary
Cheseldine Roe. Cincinnati: Stewart & Kidd
Company, 1917. 58 p.   **NYP**
LC: Ap 13, '17.

R-491 Roe, Myrtle Louie Bodle, b. 1876. The predecessor / by Myrtle L. B. Roe . . . Priv. pub. [Binghamton and New York: Vail-Ballou Press, Inc., c1923]. 246 p., front. (port.).
Unexamined copy: bibliographic data from OCLC, #24448012.

R-492 _____ Through the narrows / Myrtle L. B. Roe; illustrated by Frank T. Merrill. Boston: Sherman, French & Company, 1912. 307 p., front., plates.
Unexamined copy: bibliographic data from OCLC, #8534907.

R-493 Roe, Vingie E. (Vingie Eve), 1879-1958. A divine egotist / by Vingie E. Roe . . . ; frontispiece by F. Rogers. New York: Dodd, Mead and Company, 1916. 348 p., front.
LC: O 3, '16.
PW: O 7, '16.

R-494 _____ The heart of Night Wind: a story of the great North West / by Vingie E. Roe . . . ; illustrated by George Gibbs. New York: Dodd, Mead and Company, 1913. 395 p., col. front., [3] leaves of plates.
LC: My 19, '13.
PW: My 17, '13.

R-495 _____ The maid of the whispering hills / by Vingie E. Roe; illustrations by George Gibbs. New York: Dodd, Mead and Company, 1912. 405 p., front., [3] leaves of plates (1 col.).
LC: Ja 24, '12.
PW: Ja 27, '12.
BLC: London: Gay & Hancock, 1915.

R-496 _____ Nameless river / by Vingie E. Roe . . . New York: Duffield and Company, 1923. 278 p.
LC: Ag 30, '23.
PW: S 22, '23.
BLC: London: Cassell & Co., 1923.

R-497 _____ The primal lure: a romance of Fort Lu Cerne / by V. E. Roe; illustrated by George Gibbs. New York: Dodd, Mead & Company, 1914. 350 p., front.
LC: Mr 5, '14.
PW: Mr 7, '14.
BLC: London: Gay & Hancock, [1915].

R-498 _____ The splendid road / by Vingie E. Roe . . . New York: Duffield and Company, 1925. 303 p.
LC: Mr 20, '25.
PW: Mr 28, '25.
BLC: London: Cassell & Co., 1925.

R-499 _____ Tharon of Lost Valley / by Vingie E. Roe . . . ; illustrations by Frank Tenney Johnson. New York: Dodd, Mead and Company, 1919. 299 p., front., [3] leaves of plates.   **OCP**
LC: S 30, '19.
PW: Ap 2, '21.
BLC: London: Cassell & Co., 1920.

R-500 _____ Val of Paradise / by Vingie E. Roe . . . New York: Dodd, Mead and Company, 1921. 253 p.,

col. front.
LC: Mr 17, '21.
PW: Ap 23, '21.

R-501 Rogers, Alice Ashmore. A waiting race / by Alice Ashmore Rogers. New York; London; Montreal: The Abbey Press; [c1902]. 164 p.   **NYP**
PW: Jl 12, '02.

R-502 Rogers, Anna A. (Anna Alexander), d. 1908. Peace and the vices / by Anna A. Rogers. New York: Charles Scribner's Sons, 1904. 310 p.
PW: Mr 26, '04.

R-503 Rogers, Bessie Story. As it may be: a story of the future / by Bessie Story Rogers. Boston: Richard G. Badger, 1905. ([Boston]: The Gorham Press). 83 p.

R-504 Rogers, Henry James. Jack Barnaby / by Henry James Rogers; illustrations by Ch. Weber Ditzler. New York: G. W. Dillingham Company, [1904]. 121 p., front., [3] leaves of plates.
PW: My 21, '04.
BLC: London: T. Fisher Unwin; New York [printed], 1904.

R-505 Rogers, James W., Mrs. A free lance of the streets: and other stories / by Mrs. James W. Rogers. New York; London; Montreal: The Abbey Press, [c1902]. 207 p., photo. front. (port.), [6] leaves of plates. [Ill. by Holland Wright.]
Contents: A free lance of the streets -- The house in the Fauborg -- The picker's relief -- Daddy Zeke's search for Lil Marse.
PW: F 7, '03.

R-506 Rogers, Joel Augustus. From Superman to man / by J. A. Rogers. [Chicago: M. A. Donahoe & Co., printers], c1917. 128 p.   **JNA**

R-507 Rogers, Joel Townsley. Once in a red moon / by Joel Townsley Rogers. New York: Brentano's, [c1923]. 347 p.
PW: O 20, '23.
BLC: London: Bretano's; [printed in U. S. A., 1923].

R-508 Rogers, Leigh. Wine of fury / by Leigh Rogers. New York: Alfred A. Knopf, 1924. 340 p.
BLC: London: Grant Richards, 1924.

R-509 Rogers, Mary Elizabeth. The gift and the debt / by Mary Elizabeth Rogers. [Cambridge, Ohio: Callihan and Stottlemire Company], 1916. 397 p., plates (1 col.).
Unexamined copy: bibliographic data from OCLC, #13175008.

R-510 Rogers, Mary Hulbert. Children of the night / by Mary Hulbert Rogers. New York: Duffield & Company, 1911. 271 p.

R-511 Rogers, Robert L., 1868-1935. Tom Johnson / by Robert L. Rogers. New York; London: F. Tennyson Neely, [c1903]. 171 p.   **AFU**

Rogers, Sara Edmundson. See **Rogers, James W., Mrs.**

R-512   Rogers, Willie Williamson. The house by the side of the road / by Willie Williamson Rogers. [Austin, Tex.: Printed by Von Boeckmann-Jones Company], [c1912]. 114 p.   **TXI**

Rohlfs, Anna Katharine, Mrs. See **Green, Anna Katharine.**

R-513   Roland, Alice Kate. Latter-day sinners / by Alice Kate Roland . . . New York; Washington: The Neale Publishing Company, 1906. 241 p. front. (port.).   **EEM**
LC: Ag 31, '06.

Roland, John, pseud. See **Oliver, John Rathbone, 1872-1943.**

R-514   Roll, William Frank. Falsely accused: a story of Russian intrigue / by William Frank Roll. Los Angeles, Cal.: Citizen Print Shop, c1919. 126 p., incl. 2 photo. plates (port.).   **DLC**

R-515   Rollins, Frank W. (Frank West), 1860-1915. Safe deposit box number 4016 / by Frank West Rollins. Boston: Printed for E. H. Rollins & Sons, 1913. 57 p.

R-516   Rollins, Montgomery, 1867-1918. The banker at the boarding-house / by Montgomery Rollins . . . ; illustrated by Frank T. Merrill. Boston: Lothrop, Lee & Shepherd, [1918]. 416 p., front., [3] leaves of plates.
LC: S 5, '18.
PW: Ag 31, '18.

R-517   [____] Over here stories / by Timothy Hay [pseud.] (Montgomery Rollins). Boston: Marshall Jones Company, 1918. 72 p.   **MTH**
LC: My 7, '18.
PW: My 25, '18.

R-518   ____ The village pest: a story of David / by Montgomery Rollins; illustrated by J. Henry. Boston: Lothrop, Lee & Shepard Co., [1917]. 360 p., front., [5] leaves of plates.
LC: S 7, '17.
PW: S 1, '17.

R-519   A Romance of the Catskills / by The Monday Afternoon Literary Circle. Paris, Tenn.: Press Parisian, [1903]. [58] p., photo. front. (port.).   **DLC**

R-520   Romberg, Shalah Silverman. The wanderer: and other stories / by Shalah Silverman Romberg. Chicago: Press of Rand McNally & Company, 1916. 64 p.
Contents: The wanderer -- A love story -- The story of the ring -- The stain of inheritance.
LC: Ag 24, '16.

Ronzone, Benjamin Anthony, b. 1848. See **Baron, pseud.**

R-521   Rood, Henry Edward, b. 1867. Hardwicke: a novel / by Henry Edward Rood. New York; London: Harper & Brothers, 1902. 311, [1] p.
PW: My 10, '02.

R-522   Roof, Katharine Metcalf. The great demonstration / by Katharine Metcalf Roof . . . New York; London: D. Appleton and Company, 1920. 334, [1] p.
LC: N 2, '20.
PW: D 11, '20.

R-523   ____ The stranger at the hearth / by Katharine Metcalf Roof. Boston: Small, Maynard & Company, [c1916]. 457 p.
LC: N 15, '16.
PW: O 28, '16.

____ The waiting years. In *The best short stories of 1915 and the yearbook of the American short story* (1916), B-560.

R-524   Rooker, William Velpeau, ca. 1860-1934. The weatherbeaten man: a tale of American patriotism / by William Velpeau Rooker. New York: Cochrane Publishing Company, 1911. 229 p.
PW: Ag 12, '11.

Roosevelt, Kermit, contributor. See *Bobbed hair* (1925), B-700.

R-525   Root, Edward Clary, b. 1877. Huntington, jr.: a romance of to-day / by Edward Clary Root; with illustrations in colour by Samuel M. Palmer. New York: Frederick A. Stokes Company, [1906]. 344 p., col. front., [3] leaves of col. plates.
PW: Je 9, '06.

R-526   ____ The unseen jury: a novel / by Edward Clary Root . . . ; with illustrations by Phillipps Ward. New York: Frederick A. Stokes Company, 1907. 339 p., front., [3] leaves of plates.
LC: Mr 2, '07.
PW: Mr 23, '07.

R-527   Root, Edward Tallmadge, 1865-1948. The redemption of Paradise Pond; Barbara: stories of Rhode Island life / by Edward Tallmadge Root. Providence: Remington Press, 1908, [c1909]. 66, 32 p., front., [3] leaves of plates.

R-528   Rose, Edward Everett, b. 1862. Father Kelly of the rosary / by Edward E. Rose; novelized from his beautiful play "The rosary". [S. l.]: Published by the Rosary Publishing Co., [1910]. 263 p., photo. front., [8] leaves of photo. plates.   **DLC**
LC: O 10, '10.

Rose, Henry Martin. See **Rose, Matt.**

Rose, Martha Emily (Parmelee), b. 1834. See **Lee, Charles C., pseud.**

R-529   Rose, Matt, 1858-1933. A streak of yellow / by Matt Rose. New York; Washington: The Neale Publishing Company, 1904. 266 p.

R-530   Rose, William Ganson, b. 1878. The ginger cure / by William Ganson Rose. Cleveland: Rose Publishing Company, 1911. 85 p.
LC: My 11, '11.
Another edition: New York: Duffield & Company, 1911.
PW: N 18, '11.

R-531 ____ Putting Marshville on the map / by William Ganson Rose .... New York: Duffield & Company, 1912. 83 p.
LC: Mr 1, '12.
PW: Mr 16, '12.

R-532 ____ Waking up Bolton / by William Ganson Rose ... New York: Duffield & Company, 1913. 73 p.
LC: Mr 1, '13.
PW: Mr 8, '13.

R-533 Roseboro, Viola. The joyous heart / by Viola Roseboro ... New York: Published by McClure, Phillips & Company, 1903. 327 p.
PW: My 2, '03.

R-534 ____ Players and vagabonds / by Viola Roseboro ... New York; London: The Macmillan Company, 1904. 334 p.
Contents: Where the ways crossed -- The embroidered robe -- Her mother's success -- Potent memories -- A bit of biography -- Our mantua-maker -- The clown and the missionary -- A marriage de covenance -- A glimpse of an artist.
PW: O 29, '04.

R-535 ____ Storms of youth / by Viola Roseboro. New York: Charles Scribner's Sons, 1920. 317 p.
LC: My 17, 20.
PW: My 22, '20.

R-536 Roselund, Doc, b. 1862. The ninety-ninth degree: Triscurria-Tremefaxio Order / by Doc Roselund. Chicago: Privately printed, 1917. 153 p., photo. front. (port.), [1] leaf of plates, ill. **DLC**

R-537 Rosenbach, Abraham Simon Wolf, b. 1876. The unpublishable memoirs / by A. S. W. Rosenbach. New York: M. Kennerley, 1917. 160 p., front. [Ill. by Oliver Herford.] **KSU**
Contents: The unpublishable memoirs -- The three trees -- The purple hawthorn -- The disappearance of Shakespeare -- The colonial secretary -- In deference of his name -- "The hundred and first story" -- The lady of the breviary -- The evasive pamphlet -- The great discovery -- The fifteen joys of marriage.

R-538 Rosenberger, Elizabeth D., 1863-1951. The scarlet line: and other Bible stories / by Elizabeth D. Rosenberger. Elgin, Ill.: Brethren Publishing House, 1903. 176 p., ill. **IGR**
Contents: The scarlet line -- The city of palms -- Pitchers and lamps -- A strong man -- The rose of Moab -- The home coming -- The boy priest -- Twenty years after -- Mizpeh -- Weighed and found wanting -- Another step downward -- David and Goliath -- The death of Saul -- The ark brought to Jerusalem.

Rosenblatt, Benjamin. In the Metropolis. In *The best short stories of 1922 and the yearbook of the American short story* (1923), **B-567.**

____ The menorah. In *The best short stories of 1916 and the yearbook of the American short story* (1917), **B-561.**

____ Zelig. In *The best short stories of 1915 and the yearbook of the American short story* (1916), **B-560.**

Rosenthal, Eliezer David. Sabbath. In *Yiddish tales* (1912), **Y-20.**

____ Yom Kippur. In *Yiddish tales* (1912), **Y-20.**

R-539 [Rosewater, Frank], b. 1856. Doomed: a startling message to the people of our day, interwoven in an antediluvian romance of two old worlds and two young lovers / by Queen Metel and Prince Loab of Atlo, re-incarnated in its editors, Marian and Franklin Mayoe [pseud.]; by the Atlon calendar, the year 14,009, by our calendar, the year 1920; illustrations by R. Emmett Owen. New York: Frank Rosewater, 1920. 282 p., front., [4] leaves of plates. **NYP**
LC: N 13, '20.

R-540 ____ The making of a millennium: the story of a millennial realm and its law / by Frank Rosewater ... Omaha, Nebr.: Century Publishing Co., [c1908]. 183 p., ill. **NYP**
LC: F 17, '08.

R-541 Ross, Betsey, *pseud.* Uncle Sam's star route: a romance of a rural mail route and the new parcel post, of Michigan's "Iron Country" and its southern sand hills, of the glorious farm lands to the south and the west of Lake Michigan, and of love, politics and personal efficiency everywhere / by Betsey Ross [pseud.]; with illustrations by H. Oliver Bodine. [Chicago]: The Twentieth Century Publishing Company of Chicago, 1913. 228 p., incl. front., 6 leaves of plates, music. [Ill. by Oliver H. Bodine.] **EEX**

R-542 Ross, Clinton, 1861-1920. Tale of the Capitolene Venus / Clinton Ross. Binghamton, N. Y.: C. Ross, c1909. 46 p.
Unexamined copy: bibliographic data from OCLC, #8530350.

R-543 Ross, Hendry Durie. From far Dakota, and otherwhere / by Hendry Durie Ross. New York: The Grafton Press, [c1905]. 96 p.
Contents: Clotilde -- Dale -- Desert born -- "Times ain't what they used to be" -- Vision.
BLC: London: T. C. & E. C. Jack, [1905].

R-544 Ross, H. M. (Henry Martin). Her blind folly / by H. M. Ross. New York; Cincinnati; Chicago: Benziger Brothers, Printers to the Holy Apostolic See, 1906. 200 p.
PW: F 24, '06.

R-545 ____ In god's good time: a novel / by H. M. Ross ... New York; Cincinnati; Chicago: Benziger Brothers, 1907. 238 p. **IOL**
IOL copy published 1913.
PW: Ap 6, '07.

R-546 ____ Out of bondage / by Martin Holt, pseud. New York, Cincinnati, [etc.]: Benziger Brothers, 1905. 188 p.
Unexamined copy: bibliographic data from OCLC, #26877351.
PW: S 30, '05.

R-547 ____ The test of courage / by H. M. Ross ... New York; Cincinnati; Chicago: Benziger Brothers, 1908. 266 p. **UMD**
PW: Ap 11, '08.

R-548 ____ "That man's daughter" / by Henry M. Ross. New York; Cincinnati; Chicago: Benziger Brothers, 1905. 190 p. **DLC**
PW: Ap 1, '05.

R-549 Ross, L. J. (Levi Judson). Eight years of his life a blank: a story of the pioneer days of South Dakota: a novel / written by L. J. Ross. [Watertown S. D.: Will R. Lambert, c1915]. 175 p., front.

R-550 Ross, Olin J., (Olin Jones), b. 1858. The sky blue: a tale of the iron horse and of the coming civilization / by Olin J. Ross . . . Columbus, Ohio.: Published by the author, [Linotype J. L. Trauger Ptg. Co.], 1904, [c1903]. 280 p. Designed end papers.

R-551 Rosso, Harley, *pseud.* Empty pews: the story of a weak unthinking people / by Harley Rosso [pseud.]. Saint Paul, Minn.; Hollywood, Cal.: McClure Publishing Co., [c1925]. 172 p.

R-552 Roth, Amelia M. A. An heiress in name only, or, The adventures of Gwendolyn / by Amelia M. A. Roth. Baltimore, Md.: Saulsbury Publishing Company, [c1919]. 106 p. **DLC**
LC: O 16, '19.
PW: F 7, '20.

R-553 Rothery, Agnes, 1888-1954. The high altar / by Agnes Edwards Rothery. Garden City, New York: Doubleday, Page & Company, 1924. 285 p.
LC: S 12, '24.
BLC: London: Curtis Brown; printed in U. S. A.. 1924.

R-554 ____ The house by the windmill / by Agnes Edwards Rothery. Garden City, New York: Doubleday, Page & Company, 1923. 286 p.
LC: My 28, '23.
BLC: London: Hutchinson & Co., [1924].

Roulet, Mary F. Nixon. A bit of old ivory. In *A bit of old ivory, and other stories* (1910), B-626.

____, contributor. See *A double-knot* (1905), D-499.

____ In mere Clichy's garden. In *The Senior lieutenant's wager: and other stories* (1905), S-312.

R-555 ____ The mirror / by Mary F. Nixon-Roulet . . . St. Louis, Mo.: Published by B. Herder, 1915. 168 p.

R-556 Rouse, Adelaide L. (Adelaide Louise), d. 1912. The letters of Theodora / by Adelaide L. Rouse . . . New York: The Macmillan Company; London: Macmillan & Co., Ltd., 1905. 307 p.
PW: Mr 4, '05.

R-557 ____ Under my own roof / by Adelaide L. Rouse; illustrations by Harrie A. Stoner. New York; London: Funk & Wagnalls Company, 1902. 291 p., front., [4] leaves of plates (1 double-leaf).
PW: Mr 8, '02.

Rousseau, Victor. See **Emanuel, Victor Rousseau, b. 1879.**

R-558 Roussel, Mamie A. Reaping the whirlwind / by Mamie A. Roussel. Los Angeles, Cal.: From the press of Gem Publishing Company, September, 1924. 83 p.

Rowe, Agnes M. "The Soggarth's curse." In *The Senior lieutenant's wager: and other stories* (1905), S-312.

R-559 Rowe, Clinton A. Moonlight and other stories / by Clinton A. Rowe, Jr. Baltimore, Md.: Saulsbury Publishing Company, [c1919]. 51 p., photo. front. (port.).
Contents: Moonlight -- Loyzelle -- The unsuspecting old goose.
LC: Ag 21, '19.

Rowe, Elizabeth Griswold. The crooked pine. In *West winds* (1914), W-368.

R-560 Rowe, Harlan P. The house of unfulfilled desire / Harlan P. Rowe. Boston: Richard G. Badger, 1911. ([Boston]: The Gorham Press). 91 p. **NYP**
PW: Mr 11, '11.

R-561 Rowe, Henriette G. (Henrietta Gould), 1835-1910. A maid of Bar Harbor / by Henrietta G. Rowe; illustrated from drawings by Ellen Wetherald Ahrens. Boston: Little, Brown and Company, 1902. 368 p., front., [4] leaves of plates.
PW: Je 21, '02.

R-562 Rowe, J. W. The secret of Stonehenge: a new thought story / by J. W. Rowe. New York, Baltimore, [etc.]: Broadway Publishing Company, 1913. 62 p.
Unexamined copy: bibliographic data from NUC.

R-563 Rowell, Harvey. Allan, son of a gunmaker / by Harvey Rowell. New York: Cochrane Publishing Company, 1909. 207, [1] p.

R-564 Rowland, Helen, b. 1876. The digressions of Polly / by Helen Rowland. New York: The Baker & Taylor Co., [c1905]. 262 p., col. front., [4] leaves of col. plates. [Ill. by Mary Peyton Gardner.] **KSU**
PW: Ap 1, '05.

R-565 ____ The widow: (to say nothing of the man) / by Helen Rowland; illustrated by Esther P. Hill. New York: Dodge Publishing Company, [c1908]. 179 p., front., [7] leaves of plates.
PW: Je 20, '08.
BLC: London: Stanley Paul & Co., [1909].

R-566 Rowland, Henry C. (Henry Cottrell), 1874-1933. The apple of discord: a novel / by Henry C. Rowland . . . ; with illustrations by Will Foster. New York: Dodd, Mead and Company, 1913. 225 p., front., [3] leaves of plates. **VA@**
LC: Mr 24, '13.
PW: Mr 22, '13.

____ The border. In *Master tales of mystery* (1915), M-588.5.

R-567 _____ The closing net / by Henry C. Rowland; with illustrations by A. C. Michael. New York: Dodd, Mead and Company, 1912. 335 p., front., [5] leaves of plates.
LC: O 23, '12.
PW: O 19, '12.
BLC: London: Hurst & Blackett, 1913.

R-568 _____ The Countess Diane / by Henry C. Rowland; illustrations & decorations by John Rae. New York: Dodd, Mead & Company, 1908. 149 p., col. front., [4] leaves of col. plates. Designed end papers.
LC: Jl 30, '08.
PW: N 14, '08.

R-569 _____ Duds / Henry C. Rowland. New York; London: Harper & Brothers, [c1920]. 332 p.
LC: Ja 26, '20.
PW: Ja 31, '20.

R-570 _____ Filling his own shoes / by Henry C. Rowland; with illustrations by George Ellis Wolfe. Boston; New York: Houghton Mifflin Company, 1916. (Cambridge: The Riverside Press). 345, [1] p., front., [3] leaves of plates.
LC: O 12, '16.
PW: O 21, '16.

R-571 _____ Hirondelle / by Henry C. Rowland. New York; London: Harper & Brothers, 1922. 321 p.
LC: S 23, '22.
PW: S 30, '22.

R-572 _____ In the service of the princess / by Henry C. Rowland; frontispiece in colour by John Rae. New York: Dodd, Mead and Company, 1910. 346 p., col. front.
LC: Ap 1, '10.
PW: Ap 2, '10.

R-573 _____ In the shadow / by Henry C. Rowland . . . New York: D. Appleton and Company, 1906. 316 p.
PW: Ap 28, '06.
BLC: London: William Heinemann; New York printed, 1906.

R-574 _____ The magnet: (published serially as "The pilot-fish"), a romance / by Henry C. Rowland; illustrations by Clarence F. Underwood. New York: Dodd, Mead and Company, 1911. 328 p., front., [15] leaves of plates.
LC: Ja 23, '11.
PW: Ja 28, '11.

R-575 _____ Mile high: a novel / by Henry C. Rowland . . . New York; London: Harper & Brothers, [c1921]. 266 p., front. [Ill. by Charles D. Mitchell.]
LC: Ag 10, '21.
PW: Ag 13, '21.

R-576 _____ The mountain of fears / by Henry C. Rowland; illustrated. New York: A. S. Barnes & Co., 1905. 301 p., front. [Ill. by Charles R. Macauley.]
Contents: The mountain of fears -- Oil and water -- The shears of Atropos -- Rosenthal the Jew -- Two savages -- Two gentlemen --- The bamboula -- Into the dark.
PW: N 18, '05.

R-577 _____ Of clear intent: a novel / by Henry C. Rowland . . . New York; London: Harper & Brothers, [c1923]. 282 p.
LC: S 14, '23.
PW: O 6, '23.

R-578 _____ Pearl Island / by Henry C. Rowland; illustrations by Henry Raleigh. New York: W. J. Watt & Company, [c1919]. 299 p., front., [6] leaves of plates.
LC: My 17, '19.
PW: My 10, '19.
BLC: London: W. Collins, Sons & Co., [1921].

R-579 _____ The peddler: a novel / by Henry C. Rowland . . . ; illustrated. New York; London: Harper & Brothers, [1920]. 275 p., front., [3] leaves of plates. [Ill. by James M. Preston.]
LC: S 18, '20.
PW: O 9, '20.

R-580 _____ The return of Frank Clamart / by Henry C. Rowland. New York; London: Harper & Brothers, [c1923]. 277 p.
LC: My 19, '23.
PW: Je 2, '23.

R-581 _____ Sea scamps: three adventurers of the East / by Henry C. Rowland. New York: McClure, Phillips & Co., 1903. 317 p.
Contents: Back tracks -- In the China Sea -- Jordan Knapp, trader -- Off Luzon -- The treasure box -- At the break of the monsoon -- In the whaleboat -- At the last of the ebb.
PW: O 17, '03.

R-582 _____ The sultana / by Henry C. Rowland . . . ; with illustrations by A. B. Wenzell. New York: Dodd, Mead and Company, 1914. 303 p., front., [3] leaves of plates.
LC: Ap 29, '14.
PW: Ap 18, '14.

R-583 _____ To windward: the story of a stormy course / by Henry C. Rowland . . . ; frontispiece in colors by Charlotte Weber. New York: A. S. Barnes & Company, 1904. 359 p., col. front.
PW: Mr 26, '04.
BLC: London: David Nutt, 1905.

R-584 _____ The wanderers: a novel / by Henry C. Rowland; frontispiece in colors by Charlotte Weber. New York: A. S. Barnes & Co., 1905. 392 p., col. front.
PW: Mr 11, '05.

R-585 Rowland, Joseph M. (Joseph Medley), 1880-1938. Blue Ridge breezes / Rev. J. M. Rowland . . . Richmond, Va.: Appeals Press, 1918. 535, [1] p.
VWM

R-586 _____ The Hill Billies / by Joseph M. Rowland . . . Nashville, Tennessee: Cokesbury Press, 1924. 298 p., front. **OSU, WVU**
LC: Je 6, '24.
PW: Ag 23, '24.

Rowland, Nelson F. The doctorine of pre-established harmony. In *The Tragedy that wins and other short stories* **(1905), T-343.**

_____ The game in the cars. In *The Tragedy that wins and other short stories* **(1905), T-343.**

R-587   Royce, George Monroe, b. 1850. The son of Amram / by G. Monroe Royce . . . New York: Thomas Whittaker, [1901]. 324 p.   **CLE**
PW: Ap 20, '01.

R-588   Royle, Edwin Milton, 1862-1942. Peace and quiet: a novel / by Edwin Milton Royle . . . New York; London: Harper & Brothers, [1916]. 378, [1] p., col. front. [Ill. by Harry C. Edwards.]
LC: S 23, '16.
PW: O 7, '16.

R-589   _____ The silent call / by Edwin Milton Royle . . . ; illustrated. New York: Charles Scribner's Sons, 1910. 392 p., photo. front., [7] leaves of photo. plates. [Photo. by Moffett Studio, Chicago and Rombach & Greene, Cincinnati.]
LC: Je 2, '10.
PW: Je 4, '10.
BLC: London: Harper & Brothers; New York [printed], 1910.

R-590   Roys, Cyrus D. Captain Jack: a story of Vermont, illustrating the struggles of the Green Mountain Boys during the most romantic period of their history / by Cyrus D. Roys. Chicago: The Lakeside Press, 1909. 359 p., front., [2] leaves of plates. [Ill. by Putnam Hall.]   **MNU**
LC: N 4, '09.

Royster, James F., ed. See *American short stories* **(1925), A-202.**

R-591   Ruben, Edward. Alvira: a story of the War of 1812 / by Edward Ruben . . . ; illustrations by F. Humphrey Woolrych. St. Louis, Mo.: Central Literary Publishing Co., 1911. 274 p., front., [7] leaves of plates.   **LUU**
LC: Ag 30, '11.

R-592   Rubin, Jacob H., b. 1870. The destruction of a nation: a fascinating and authentic account, in novel form, of the great Russian debâcle / J. H. Rubin, author; revised by Victor Rubin. [Harrisburg, Pa.: The Telegraph Printing Company], c1921. 60 p., incl. photo. front. (port.).   **DLC**

R-593   Rubin, Victor, b. 1892. Tar and feathers / by Victor Rubin. Philadelphia: Dorrance, [c1923]. 327 p.
LC: Ag 31, '23.
PW: S 8, '23.

R-594   Rud, Anthony M. (Anthony Melville), b. 1893. The devil's heirloom / by Anthony M. Rud. Garden City, New York: Garden City Publishing Co., Inc., 1924. 118 p.   **DRB**
LC: Ap 2, '24.

R-595   _____ The second generation / by Anthony M. Rud. Garden City, New York: Doubleday, Page &

Company, 1923. 318 p.
LC: N 3, '23.
PW: O 20, '23.
BLC: London: William Heinemann; printed in U.S.A., 1923.

R-596   Rudy, Jacob Marvin. Our nation's peril / by Jacob Marvin Rudy; illustrated by F. A. Hamilton. Chicago: L. W. Walter Company, 1918. 286 p., front., plates, ill. (some ports.).
Unexamined copy: bibliographic data from OCLC, #2041407.

Ruffin, Margaret Ellen. See **Henry-Ruffin, M. E.**

R-597   Ruger, Florence White. Constance d'Brolie / by F. White Ruger. New York; London; Montreal: The Abbey Press, [c1902]. 465 p.
PW: N 1, '02.

R-598   Ruggles, William N. (William Nelson), b. 1854. Out of the Ozarks / by William N. Ruggles. New York; Washington: The Neale Publishing Company, 1908. 352 p.
PW: Mr 27, '09.

R-599   Ruhl, Arthur, b. 1876. A break in training: and other athletic stories / by Arthur Ruhl; illustrated by a frontispiece in color by Howard Chandler Christy. New York: The Outing Publishing Company, 1906. 224 p., col. front.
PW: S 29, '06.

_____ Left behind. In *A book of narratives* **(1917), B-734.**

R-600   Rumsey, Frances. Ascent / by Frances Rumsey. New York: Boni and Liveright, 1922. 379 p.
LC: Ag 12, '22.
PW: Ag 5, '22.
BLC: London: John Lane; printed in U. S. A., [1923].

R-601   _____ Leonora: a novel / by Frances Rumsey. New York; London: D. Appleton and Company, 1910. 311, [1] p.
LC: S 26, '10.

R-602   _____ Mr. Cushing and Mlle. du Chastel / by Frances Rumsey. New York: John Lane Company; London: John Lane, The Bodley Head, 1917. 332 p.
LC: Ag 17, '17.
PW: Ap 14, '17.

Runkle, Bertha, 1879-1958. Artemisia's mirror. In *A house party* **(1901), H-903.**

R-603   _____ The helmet of Navarre / by Bertha Runkle; illustrations by André Castaigne. New York: The Century Co., 1901. 470 p., incl. front., ill.
Title within ornamental border.
PW: My 4, '01.
BLC: London: Macmillan & Co., 1901.

R-604   _____ The island / by Bertha Runkle . . . New York: The Century Co., 1921. 237 p., front.
LC: O 3, '21.
PW: O 15, '21.

R-605 ____ The scarlet rider / by Bertha Runkle . . . New York: The Century Co., 1913. 386 p., col. front. [Ill. by Armand Both.]
LC: My 29, '13.
PW: My 31, '13.
BLC: London: Andrew Melrose, 1913.

R-606 ____ Straight down the crooked lane / by Bertha Runkle; with a frontispiece by William Van Dresser. New York: The Century Co., 1915. 440 p., col. front.
LC: S 30, '15.
PW: S 25, '15.
BLC: London: Eveleigh Nash Co., 1916.

R-607 ____ The truth about Tolna / by Bertha Runkle . . . New York: The Century Co., 1906. 359 p., col. front., music.
PW: Mr 3, '06.

Runyon, Damon. The Breeze Kid's big tear-off. See Conrad, Joseph, 1857-1924. *Il conte* (1925), C-697.

R-608 Rupp, Frederick A. (Frederick Augustine), b. 1876. John Montcalm, heretic: a tale of the Maryland hills / by Frederick A. Rupp; illustrated. Reading, Pa.: I. M. Beaver, 1908. 272 p., photo. front., [5] leaves of photo. plates.
LC: D 14, '08.

R-609 Rush, Phil. A. (Philip Augustus), b. 1860. The teller's tale: a banking story for bankers: a law story for lawyers: a love story for lovers / by Phil. A. Rush. New York: The Knickerbocker Press, 1905. 217 p., front., [5] leaves of plates. [Ill. by John M. Burke.]   **OSU, KUK**

R-610 Russell, Andrew Lyle. The freighter: a tale of the Pittsburgh frontier / Andrew Lyle Russell. Boston: The Roxburgh Publishing Company, Inc., [c1915]. 518 p.

R-611 Russell, Charles M. (Charles Marion), 1864-1926. More Rawhides / by C. M. Russell . . . ; with illustrations by the author. Great Falls, Montana: Printed by Montana Newspaper Association, 1925. 59, [1] p., ill.   **DPL**
Contents: A gift horse -- A savage Santa Claus -- Bab's skees -- Broke buffalo -- Bullard's wolves -- Dog eater -- Dunc McDonald -- Fashions -- Hands up -- How Lindsay turned Indian -- Lepley's bear -- Longrope's last guard -- Mormon Murphy's confidence -- Night herd -- Ranches -- Range horses -- Safety first! but where is it -- The trail of the Reel Foot.
LC: D 16, '25.

R-612 ____ Rawhide Rawlins stories / by C. M. Russell; with illustrations by the author. Great Falls, Mont., Printed by Montana Newspaper Association, 1921. 60 p., ill.   **MNU**
Contents: A ride in a moving cemetery -- There's more than one David -- Highwood Hank quits -- Tommy Simpson's cow -- How Pat discovered the geyser -- How Louse Creek was named -- Some liars of the Old West -- Mormon Zack, fighter -- Johnny sees the big show -- When Mix went to school -- When Pete sets a speed mark -- Bill's Shelby Hotel -- A reformed cowpuncher at Miles City -- The story of the cowpuncher -- Bronc twisters -- Johnny reforms Landusky -- The horse.
LC: N 16, '21.

R-613 Russell, J. The judgment of God: an historical little novel / by J. Russell. New York: The Book Publishing House, [c1903]. 84 p.   **DLC**

R-614 Russell, John, 1885-1956. In dark places / by John Russell. New York: Alfred A. Knopf, 1923. 285 p. Maps on end papers.
Contents: The colour of the East -- The pagan -- The one-eyed devil -- The bird of paradise -- McKeon's graft -- The wreck on Deliverance -- The digger -- The slaver -- Jonah -- The winning hand -- The witch woman -- One drop of moonshine.
LC: My 17, '23.
PW: Je 2, '23.
BLC: London: Thorton Butterworth, 1923.

R-615 ____ The red mark: and other stories / by John Russell. New York: Alfred A. Knopf, 1919. 397 p.
Contents: The red mark -- Doubloon gold -- The wicks of Macassar -- The practicing of Christopher -- The passion-vine -- The adversary -- The slanted beam -- The lost god -- Meaning, chase yourself -- Jetsam -- East of eastward -- The fourth man -- The price of the head -- Amok.
LC: O 24, '19.
PW: N 8, '19.
BLC: London: Thornton Butterworth, [1921].
British title: *Where the payment ends* (stories arranged differently).

R-616 [____] The society wolf / by Luke Thrice [pseud.]; illustrated by W. H. Loomis and Modest Stein. New York: Cupples & Leon Company, [c1910]. 304 p., front., [5] leaves of plates.
LC: Mr 18, '10.
PW: Ap 16, '10.

R-617 Russell, Marion. The little church around the corner: a romantic story . . . / by Marion Russell. New York: J. S. Ogilvie Publishing Company, c1903. 192 p.

Russell, Susan, b. 1885, jt. aut. *The call* (1925). See Reed, Cordelia Adelaide, b. 1853, jt. aut., R-107.

R-618 Russell, Walter, 1871-1963. The bending of the twig / text and pictures by Walter Russell . . . New York: Dodd, Mead & Company, 1903. 297 p. incl. front., ill.

R-619 Russell, Wille Drennen. Dick / By Wille Drennen Russell; illustrated by Charles Sykes. New York; Washington: The Neale Publishing Company, 1905. 144 p. front., [5] leaves of plates.   **DLC**
LC: D 20, '05.

R-620 Rutherford, C. A. "Whiter than snow" / by C. A. Rutherford. New York: [s. n.], Copyright, 1922. 72 p. [Distributor Robert Rutter and Son, Inc.]

R-621 Rutledge, Archibald Hamilton, 1883-1973. Heart of the South / by Archibald Rutledge . . . Columbia, S. C.: The State Company, 1924. 391 p.   **OSU, UIU**
Contents: The Rose of Sharon -- Heart of the South -- Congaree -- The mystery of Romney -- The seamarsh buck -- Fenwick's ordeal -- Rodney's Bolio -- In the Promised Land -- Mobile's quest -- The old blood -- Poinsettia and Sparkplug -- Only one captain -- That night at Bowman's -- Terror of the twilight -- At the Blacktongue -- Lisbon's whoop -- A slip on the dome -- Caesar -- The last of the Ledyards -- A demon of the jetties -- Young Abel Yancey -- Benbow -- Christmas Eve on Wicklow -- Blood on the laurels -- The grim raider -- The King of Cherokee -- The white stag's tryst -- The terrible brink -- "Spurlos versenkt" -- The Kings of Curlew Island.
LC: N 10, '24.

R-622 _____ Old plantation days / by Archibald Rutledge; with eight illustrations. New York: Frederick A. Stokes Company, [c1921]. 344 p., front., [7] leaves of plates. [Ill. by Charles L. Bull, William F. Stecher, and John E. Jackson.]
Previously published in various periodicals.
Contents: Judge Napier's sentence -- What scared kitty -- The aim of the hunterman -- My colonel -- The whitehorn buck -- O ringing bells! -- Anyone's turkey -- The golden robber -- The haunted oak -- A monarch of the sky -- The duel in Cummings -- At low tide -- The strategy of Galboa -- The Romney spectre -- The lone bull of Maybank -- The token flood -- Joel's Christmas turkey -- The banded death -- The black mallard -- A fox and a conscience -- The fawn -- The secret killer -- Scipio makes a shot -- A pair of mallards -- Ghost point -- The silent champion -- Shadrach and the fiery furnace -- Margie has a man.
LC: S 3, '21.
PW: Ag 27, '21.

R-623 _____ Old plantation days / by Archibald Rutledge. [Cumberland, Md.: The Eddy Press Corporation, 19--]. 160 p., front., [1] leaf of plates. [Ill. by Charles L. Bull.]
Contents: The Romney spectre -- Ghost point -- The silent champion -- My colonel -- At low tide -- The egret's plumes -- Anyone's turkey -- The whitehorn buck -- Claws -- The duel in Cummings -- The banded death -- Scipio makes a shot -- The lone bull of Maybank -- The ocean's menace -- The heart of Regal -- A monarch in the sky -- The black mallard -- The doom of Ravenswood.

R-624 Rutledge, C. H. Flashes from the furnace / by C. H. Rutledge. [Mohawk, Mich.: Published by the Keweenaw Printing Co.], c1912. 221 p., [4] leaves of photo. plates (1 port.). **KAT**

R-625 Rutledge, Henry B. Romances of the rugged road / by Henry B. Rutledge . . . [Minneapolis?, Minn.: s. n., c1923]. 341 p., incl. photo. ill. (1 port.). **MHS**

R-626 [Rutledge, Maryse], b. 1884, *pseud.* Anne of Tréboul / by Marie Louise Goetchius [pseud.]. New York: Published by The Century Co., 1910. 298 p.
PW: My 21, '10.

R-627 [_____] The blind who see / by Marie Louise Van Saanen [pseud.]. New York: The Century Co., 1911. 411 p.
LC: O 31, '11.
PW: O 14, '11.

R-628 _____ Children of fate / by Marice [sic] Rutledge [pseud.]; with a frontispiece by J. Henry. New York: Frederick A. Stokes Company, [c1917]. 281 p., front.
LC: Mr 27, '17.
PW: Mr 31, '17.

R-629 _____ The sad adventurers: a novel / by Maryse Rutledge [pseud.]. New York: Frederick A. Stokes Company, 1924. 315 p.
LC: S 2, '24.
PW: Ag 23, '24.
BLC: London: Constable & Co., 1924.

_____ The thing they loved. In *Prize stories of 1920 (1921), P-618.*

R-630 [_____] Wild grapes / by Marie Louise Van Saanen [pseud.]. New York: Moffat, Yard and Company, 1913. 447 p.

LC: Je 23, '13.
PW: Ja 17, '14.

R-631 Rutzebeck, Hjalmar. Alaska man's luck: a romance of fact / by Hjalmar Rutzebeck. New York: Boni and Liveright, [c1920]. 260 p. Maps on lining papers. **CIN**
LC: O 18, '20.
BLC: London: T. Fisher Umwin, 1921.

R-632 _____ My Alaskan idyll / by Hjalmar Rutzebeck . . . New York: Boni and Liveright, [1922]. 296 p.
IOH
Colophon reads: Printed in Great Britain by Billing and Sons, Ltd., Guilford and Esher.
BLC: London: T. Fisher Unwin, 1922.

R-633 Ryan, Marah Ellis, 1866-1934. The dancer of Tuluum / by Marah Ellis Ryan; illustrated by René Kinga; decorations by Kay Roberts. Chicago: A. C. McClurg & Co., 1924. 210 p., [31] leaves of plates. T. P. is inserted plate counted in the pagination.
LC: Ja 9, '25.
PW: Mr 14, '25.

R-634 _____ The Druid path / by Marah Ellis Ryan; decorated by Will Vreeland. Chicago: A. C. McClurg & Co., [1917]. 321 p., incl. music. Decorated end papers.
Contents: The Druid path -- The enchanting of Doirenn -- Liadan and Kurithir -- Dervail Nan Ciar -- Randuff of Cumanac -- The dark rose.
LC: Ja 30, '17.
PW: F 3, '17.
BLC: London: Curtis Brown; Chicago [printed], 1917.

R-635 _____ The flute of the gods / by Marah Ellis Ryan . . . ; illustrated by Edward S. Curtis. New York: Frederick A. Stokes Company, [c1909]. 338 p., photo. front., [23] leaves of photo. plates.
LC: S 29, '09.
PW: O 9, '09.

R-636 _____ For the soul of Rafael / by Marah Ellis Ryan . . . ; with many illustrations from photographs taken expressly for this book, by Harold A. Taylor; decorative designs by Ralph Fletcher Seymour. Chicago: A. C. McClurg & Co., 1906. 378 p., photo. front., [16] leaves of photo. plates. Decorative end papers in tan.
PW: My 12, '06.
BLC: London: C. F. Cazenove, 1906.

R-637 _____ The house of the dawn / by Marah Ellis Ryan . . . ; illustrated and decorated by Hanson Booth. Chicago: A. C. McClurg & Co., 1914. 407 p., front., [3] leaves of plates. Decorative designs in tan throughout.
LC: N 2, '14.
PW: N 14, '14.

R-638 _____ Indian love letters / by Marah Ellis Ryan . . . Chicago: A. C. McClurg & Co., 1907. 122 p., photo. front., ill. [Photo. by Edward S. Curtis; Ill. by Ralph F. Seymour.]
LC: Mr 6, '07.
PW: Mr 16, '07.

R-639 _____ Miss Moccasins / by Marah Ellis Ryan. Chicago; New York: Rand, McNally & Company, [c1904]. 350 p.

R-640 _____ My Quaker maid / by Marah Ellis Ryan . . . Chicago; New York: Rand McNally & Company, [c1906]. 254 p.
PW: Mr 24, '06.

R-641 _____ That girl Montana / by Marah Ellis Ryan. Chicago; New York: Rand, McNally & Company, 1901. 357 p., front.
LC: O 21, '01.
PW: D 7, '01.

R-642 _____ The treasure trail: a romance of the land of gold and sunshine / by Marah Ellis Ryan; illustrated by Robert Amick. Chicago: A. C. McClurg & Co., 1918. 384 p., front., [3] leaves of plates.
LC: N 12, '18.
PW: N 30, '18.

R-643 _____ The woman of the twilight: the story of a story / by Marah Ellis Ryan; illustrations by Hanson Booth. Chicago: A. C. McClurg & Co., 1913. 424 p., front., [4] leaves of plates.
LC: My 5, '13.
PW: My 10, '13.
BLC: London: C. F. Cazenove, A. C. McClurg & Co.; Chicago [printed], 1913

R-644 Ryan, Margaret. Sue Terry, or, two hearts--two minds--two women's ways / by Margaret Ryan; with illustrations by prominent artists. New York: The M. W. Hazen Company, 1904. 358 p., front., [5] leaves of plates. [Ill. by W. Schaefer, Charles L. Wrenn, and Paul G. Rogers.]

R-645 Ryeman, Nora. The little lady of the Hall / by Nora Ryeman. New York; Cincinnati; Chicago: Benziger Brothers, 1915. 118 p. **DLC**

Ryland, Cally Thomas, b. 1871, jt. aut. *Daphne and her lad* (1904). See **Lagen, M. J. (Mary Julia), jt. aut., L-14.**

S

S-1 Sabe, Quién, 1882-1943. Daughter of the sun: a tale of adventure / by Quién Sabe. New York: Charles Scribner's Sons, 1921. 271 p., front.
PW: O 1, '21.

S-2 Sabin, Edwin Legrand, b. 1870. The circle K, or, Fighting for the flock / by Edwin L. Sabin . . . New York: Thomas Y. Crowell Company, [c1911]. 305 p., front., [7] leaves of plates. [Ill. by Clarence Rowe.]
LC: Ag 21, '11.
PW: S 2, '11.

S-3 _____ The city of the sun / by Edwin L. Sabin. Philadelphia: George W. Jacobs & Company, [c1924]. 316 p., front. (map).
LC: Ja 31, '24.
PW: F 23, '24.

S-4 _____ Desert dust / by Edwin L. Sabin . . . ; illustrated by J. Clinton Shepherd. Philadelphia: George W. Jacobs & Company, [c1922]. 313 p., col. front., [2] leaves of plates. **DPL**
LC: Ap 27, '22.
PW: Je 3, '22.
BLC: London: Hutchinson & Co., [1923].

S-5 _____ The great Pike's Peak rush, or, Terry in the new gold fields / by Edwin L. Sabin. New York: Thomas Y. Crowell Company, [c1917]. 253 p., front., [3] leaves of plates. [Ill. by H. T. Fisk.] **WYU**
Cover title: *The Pike's Peak rush.*
LC: S 14, '17.
PW: S 29, '17.

S-6 _____ How are you feeling now? / By Edwin L. Sabin; with illustrations by Tony Sarg. Boston: Little, Brown, and Company, 1917. 96 p., front., [3] leaves of plates.
LC: S 27, '17.
PW: S 22, '17.

S-7 _____ Loaded dice / by Edwin L. Sabin. Garden City, New York: Doubleday, Page & Company, 1923. 118 p.

S-8 _____ The magic mashie and other golfish stories / Edwin L. Sabin. New York: A. Wessels Company, 1902. 210 p., front., [1] leaf of plates. [Ill. by J. Campbell Phillips and Hatfield Shaw.] **KSU**
Contents: The magic mashie -- A spectre of the links -- The long game -- A November afternoon -- The way of it -- A mixed foursome -- Told by the caddie -- A twosome with conscience -- A rub of the green -- The great Moggins-Bumps match -- The supersensitive golf-ball -- Being a duffer -- Measure for measure -- The duffer.
PW: S 13, '02.

S-9 _____ The rose of Santa Fé / by Edwin L. Sabin . . . Philadelphia: George W. Jacobs & Company, [c1923]. 309 p., front. [Ill. by Joy Clinton Shepherd.]
LC: Ap 20, '23.
PW: Ap 21, '23.
BLC: London: Hutchinson & Co., [1923].

S-10 _____ When you were a boy / by Edwin L. Sabin; with pictures by Frederic Dorr Steele. New York: The Baker & Taylor Company, [1905]. 302 p., incl. front., ill. Reprinted from various periodicals.
Contents: The match game -- You at school -- Chums -- In the arena -- The circus -- When you ran away -- Goin' fishin' -- In society -- Middleton's hill -- Goin' swimmin' -- The Sunday-school picnic -- The old muzzle-loader -- A boy's loves -- Noon.
PW: N 11, '05.

S-11 _____ White Indian / by Edwin L. Sabin. Philadelphia: George W. Jacobs & Company, [c1925]. 320 p.
LC: F 11, '25.
PW: F 21, '25.
BLC: London: Hutchinson, [1926].

S-12 Sabina, Poppaea, *pseud.* Poppaeanum: the autobiography of a ghost / by Poppaea Sabina [pseud.]. Hawthorne, N. Y.: The Hawthorne Press, [c1904]. 54 p. **ORU**

Sabine, Martin, jt. aut. *The lotus lantern* (1911). See **Taylor, Mary Imlay, 1878-1938, jt. aut., T-97.**

S-13   Sabungi, Luigi Bari, b. 1838. Jehan Aftab: Abdul Hamid's last love . . . / by Luigi Bari Sabungi . . . Jersey City, New Jersey: The Real American Syndicate, [c1923]. 348 p., ill. (1 port., some photo.).
"A beautifully illustrated love story centered about the life of the famous late Sultan of Turkey, involving certain historical and political phases of his reign interwoven with an intimate glimpse into the life of the harem, with its intrigues and its crimes."
LC records: Detroit, Mich.: N. E. Khoury and J. David, c1923.

Sachs, Emanie N. Railroad tracks. In *As we are* **(1923), A-325.**

S-14   ____ Talk / by Emanie N. Sachs. New York: Harper & Brothers, 1924. 286 p.

S-15   Sadler, Cora G. The pendulum: a novel / by Cora G. Sadler. Boston: Sherman, French & Company, 1912. 386 p.
LC: Ap 27, '12.
PW: Ap 27, '12.

S-16   ____ Skoot: a story of unconventional goodness / by Cora G. Sadler. Cincinnati: Jennings & Pye; New York: Eaton & Mains, [c1902]. 141 p.
PW: Ag 2, '02.

S-17   Sadtler, William Augustus, b. 1864. Under two captains: a romance of history / by W. A. Sadtler. Philadelphia: Published for the author, [The General Council Press, Philadelphia, Pa., c1902]. 218 p., front. (port.).

S-18   Sage, Edmund. Masters of the city: a novel of to-day / by Edmund Sage. Philadelphia: The Madoc Publishing Co., [1909]. 127 p.
Unexamined copy: bibliographic data from LC.
LC: O 5, '09.

S-19   Sage, William, b. 1864. By right divine / by William Sage; with a frontispiece by Ch. Grunwald. Boston: Little, Brown, and Company, 1907. 370 p., col. front.
LC: Je 14, '07.
PW: Je 22, '07.

S-20   ____ The Claybornes: a romance of the civil war / by William Sage; with illustrations. Boston; New York: Houghton Mifflin Company, 1902. (Cambridge, Mass., U. S. A.: The Riverside Press). 404 p., front., [1] leaf of plates. [Ill. by Charles Copeland and Thulstrup.]
PW: Ap 26, '02.

S-21   ____ The district attorney / by William Sage. Boston: Little, Brown and Company, 1906. 296 p.
PW: Je 2, '06.

S-22   ____ Frenchy: the story of a gentleman / by William Sage; illustrated by L. L. Roush. New York: Scott-Thaw Company, 1904. 314 p., front.,

[7] leaves of plates.
PW: Je 11, '04.

S-23   ____ A maid of old Virginia: a romance of Bacon's rebellion / by William Sage; illustrated by Victor Pérard. New York; Chicago; Toronto (etc.): Fleming H. Revell Company, [c1915]. 367 p., incl. front., [3] leaves of plates.
LC: O 14, '15.
PW: S 4, '15.

S-24   Sager, Juliet G. (Juliet Gilman), b. 1873. Anne, actress: the romance of a star / by Juliet G. Sager. New York: Frederick A. Stokes Company, [1913]. 346 p.
LC: S 22, '13.
PW: O 4, '13.

S-25   Sain, Charles Macknight. The serpent / by Charles Macknight Sain . . . Chicago: Apollo Book Company, 1902. 239 p., front., [3] leaves of plates. [Ill. by F. I. Witherbee.]

S-26   St. Clair, Leo. Claris, a novel / by Leo St. Clair. Washington, D. C.: The Neale Publishing Company, 1903. 47 p., front.
Unexamined copy: bibliographic data from NUC.

S-27   St. Felix, Marie, *pseud.* 1864-1943. Told by two: a romance of Bermuda / by Marie St. Felix [pseud.] (Mrs. Jerome Morley Lynch). Chicago: M. A. Donohue & Co., [c1901]. 191 p., front., [6] leaves of plates. [Ill. by J. Greville Wilmot.]
PW: Ag 31, '01.

St. John, John Ferris, pseud. See **Whiteside, Guy Kenneth, b. 1879.**

S-28   St. Johns, Adela Rogers. The skyrocket: a new novel / by Adela Rogers St. Johns. New York: Cosmopolitan Book Corporation, 1925. 322 p.
LC: Mr 30, '25.
PW: Mr 28, '25.

St. Luz, Berthe, pseud. See **David, K., pseud.**

S-29   St. Morris, Charles, b. 1851. The law of love / by Charles St. Morris; illustrations by William Kirkpatrick. Boston, Mass.: The C. M. Clark Publishing Co., 1908. 375 p., front., [7] leaves of plates.

S-30   Sale, Edith Tunis. Red Rose Inn / by Edith Tunis Sale . . . ; with a frontispiece by Ethel Franklin Betts. Philadelphia; London: J. B. Lippincott Company, 1911. 175, [1] p., col. front.
LC: My 24, '11.

S-31   Salisbury, William, b. 1875. Adell Waltby / by William Salisbury. New Rochelle, N. Y.: The Independent Publishing Company, 1924. 311, [1] p.
                                                                    NYP
LC: Ap 15, '24.

S-32   ____ The American emperor: a novel / by William Salisbury. New York: The Tabard Inn Press, 1913. 398 p.
LC: Ap 17, '13.

S-33 Sallee, J. M. (John Milton), b. 1844. Mabel Clement / by J. M. Sallee . . . Fulton, Kentucky: Published by the National Baptist Publishing House, [c1903]. 282 p., front. (port.). **KUK**

S-34 Salmonsen, M. (Morris), 1843-1913. Among Jews: sketches / by M. Salmonsen . . . ; with a preface by Dr. Emil G. Hirsch; and a copy of an etching by the Danish painter Carl Bloch (1834-1890) . . . Chicago: Published by Meyer & Brother, [c1907]. 142 p., front. **ANC**
Contents: Preface -- Maaser -- Rabbi Benjamin -- A Passover evening -- Philosophy -- A fervent Zionist -- Sorrow -- A dinner party.

S-35 Salts, James D. (James David). The man from Missouri / by James D. Salts. New York City: Authors Co-operative Pub. Co., [c1916]. 238 p. **DLC**
LC: My 3, '16.

S-36 Saltus, Edgar, 1855-1921. Daughters of the rich / by Edgar Saltus. New York: Mitchell Kennerley, [c1909]. 259 p., col. front. [Ill. by Frank Haviland.]
LC: My 12, '09.
BLC: London: Grant Richards, [printed in U. S. A.], 1909.
References: BAL 17169.

S-37 _____ The ghost girl / by Edgar Saltus. New York: Boni and Liveright, [c1922]. 236 p.
LC: Ag 12, '22.
PW: Ag 12, '22.
References: BAL 17180.

S-38 _____ The monster / by Edgar Saltus. New York: Pulitzer Publishing Company, 1912. 240 p.
LC: S 24, '13.
PW: Je 28, '13.
References: BAL 17170. BAL notes publication date: 1912, [i. e. 1913].

S-39 _____ The Paliser case / by Edgar Saltus. New York: Boni and Liveright, 1919. 315 p.
LC: Ap 17, '19.
PW: Ap 19, '19.
References: 17174.

S-40 _____ The perfume of Eros: a Fifth Avenue incident / by Edgar Saltus. New York: A. Wessels Company, 1905. 222, [1] p.
"The perfume of Eros, in serial form, was entitled The yellow fay."
LC: N 7, '05.
PW: D 9, '05.
BLC: London: Grant Richards, 1905.
References: BAL 17164.

S-41 _____ Purple and fine women / by Edgar Saltus. New York; London: The Ainslee Publishing Company, 1903. 255 p. **RBN**
Contents: A bouquet of illusions -- Alma adorata -- The princess of the sun -- The dear departed -- The Princess of the Golden Isles -- The noose matrimonial -- A drama in a drawing room -- The top of the heap -- The elixir of love.
PW: Je 27, '03.
BLC: London: Shurmen Sibthorp, 1903.
References: BAL 17162.

Another edition: with an introduction by W. L. George. Chicago: Pascal Covici, 1925. 191 p.
Contents: same as 1903 ed.
LC: Ap 30, '25.
PW: Ap 25, '25.

S-42 _____ Vanity square: a story of Fifth Avenue life / by Edgar Saltus. Philadelphia; London: J. B. Lippincott Company, 1906. 304 p.
PW: Je 9, '06.
References: BAL 17165.

S-43 Salzscheider, F. Lucie. Pandora: a novel / by Mrs. Salzscheider. San Francisco: The Whitaker & Ray Company (Incorporated), 1901. 198 p., photo. front. (port.). **CLU**
PW: D 28, '01.

S-44 Samms, A. L. As it happened / by A. L. Samms. Chicago: Covici-McGee Co., 1924. 257 p. **STF**
LC: Jl 19, '24.
PW: Ag 2, '24.

S-45 Samms, A. L. Race: a novel of wives and others / by A. L. Samms. Chicago: Covici-McGee, 1923. 273 p.
LC: Ag 6, '23.
PW: Ag 11, '23.

S-46 Sampson, Emma Speed, 1868-1947. Billy and the Major / by Emma Speed Sampson . . . ; illustrated by William Donahey. Chicago: The Reilly & Britton Co., 1918. 299 p., front., ill.
LC: N 23, '18.
PW: S 14, '18.

S-47 _____ The comings of Cousin Ann / by Emma Speed Sampson . . . Chicago: Reilly & Lee Co., [c1923]. 266 p.
LC: S 1, '23.
PW: O 13, '23.

S-48 _____ Mammy's white folks / by Emma Speed Sampson . . . ; frontispiece by Irwin Myers. Chicago: The Reilly & Lee Co., [c1919]. 336 p., front.
LC: Mr 8, '20.

S-49 _____ Masquerading Mary / by Emma Speed Sampson . . . Chicago: Reilly & Lee Co., [c1924]. 297 p.
LC: S 22, '24.
PW: O 18, '24.

S-50 _____ Miss Minerva on the old plantation / by Emma Speed Sampson; illustrated by William Donahey. Chicago: The Reilly & Lee Co., [c1923]. 301 p., incl. front.
LC: Ap 24, '23.
PW: Je 9, '23.

S-51 _____ The shorn lamb / by Emma Speed Sampson . . . Chicago: The Reilly & Lee Co., [c1922]. 331 p.
LC: Je 12, '22.
PW: Jl 22, '22.

S-52   Sampson, Jane Felton. Chronicles of Old Riverby / by Jane Felton Sampson. Boston: Sherman, French & Company, 1913. 178 p.

Samson, Charles (spirit), jt. aut. *The angel's diary* (1903). <u>See</u> **Shirey, Effie M. (spirit), jt. aut., S-441.**

S-53   Samuel, Maurice, 1895-1972. The outsider / by Maurice Samuel. New York: Duffield and Company, 1921. 326 p.
LC: N 7, '21.
PW: N 19, '21.
BLC: London: Constable, 1922.

S-54   _____ Whatever gods / by Maurice Samuel . . . New York: Duffield and Company, 1923. 346 p.
LC: Jl 18, '23.
PW: Ag 11, '23.

S-55   Sanborn, Gertrude, 1881-1928. Blithesome jottings: a diary of humorous days / by Gertrude Sanborn. Boston: The Four Seas Company, 1918. 121 p.
                                                          DLC
LC: O 11, '18.
PW: O 26, '18.

S-56   _____ Toy / by Gertrude Sanborn . . . Chicago; New York: M. A. Donohue & Company, 1922. 413 p.
                                                          AWL
LC: N 11, '22.
PW: N 11, '22.

S-57   _____ Veiled aristocrats / by Gertrude Sanborn . . . Washington, D. C.: The Associated Publishers, [c1923]. 241 p.
LC: D 21, '23.

S-58   Sanborn, Mary Farley, b. 1853. The canvas door / by Mary Farley Sanborn . . . New York: B. W. Dodge & Company, 1909. 311 p., col. front. [Ill. by H. Richard Boehm.]
LC: N 30, '09.
PW: D 11, '09.
BLC: London: Alston Rivers, 1910.

S-59   _____ The first valley: a novel / by Mary Farley Sanborn . . . Boston: The Four Seas Company, 1920. 232 p.
LC: My 20, '20.
PW: Je 5, '20.

S-60   _____ Lynette and the congressman / by Mary Farley Sanborn. Boston: Little, Brown and Company, 1905. 396 p.

S-61   _____ The revelation of herself / by Mary Farley Sanborn. New York: Dodd, Mead and Company, 1904. 258 p.
PW: O 1, '04.

S-62   Sanders, Charles W. (Charles Wesley). Hill-bred Barton's code: a western story / by Charles Wesley Sanders. New York: Chelsea House, [c1925]. 254 p.
PW: My 16, '25.

S-63   _____ The man from Michigan: a Western story / by Charles Wesley Sanders. New York: Chelsea House, [c1924]. 252 p.
PW: My 9, '25.

S-64   _____ Ten thousand dollars reward / by Charles Wesley Sanders. Garden City, New York: Garden City Publishing Co., Inc., 1924. 116 p. (Famous author series; no. 46).
LC: Ap 2, '24.

S-65   _____ Trouble range / by Charles Wesley Sanders. New York: G. Howard Watt, 1925. 304 p.
LC: Je 16, '25.
PW: My 9, '25.

S-66   Sanders, Helen Fitzgerald, b. 1883. The dream maker / by Helen Fitzgerald Sanders . . . Boston: The Cornhill Company, [c1918]. 426 p.
LC: N 7, '18.

S-67   _____ Little Mother America / by Helen Fitzgerald Sanders . . . Boston: The Cornhill Company, 1919. 250 p.   **NYP**

S-68   _____ The white quiver / by Helen Fitzgerald Sanders . . . New York: Duffield & Company, 1913. 344 p., photo. front., [7] leaves of photo. plates.
LC: Je 27, '13.
PW: Jl 5, '13.

Sanderson, James Gardner. The member of the ninth. <u>In</u> *Politics* **(1901), P-461.**

_____ The personal equation. <u>In</u> *Stories of the colleges* **(1901), S-985.**

S-69   Sandford, Lionel E. Wilson of the Mounted / by Lionel E. Sandford. Lititz, Pa.: Published by Lionel E. Sandford through arrangement with The Express Printing & Publishing Co., [c1925]. 114 p., front., [1] leaf of plates.
LC: S 17, '25.

S-70   Sands, Beatrice. Weepers in playtime / by Beatrice Sands. New York: John Lane Company, 1908. 265 p.   **CLE**

S-71   Sandys, Edwyn. Sportsman "Joe" / by Edwyn Sandys . . . ; with illustrations by J. M. Gleeson and C. W. Pancoast. New York: The Macmillan Company; London: Macmillan & Co., Ltd., 1904. 338 p., front., [5] leaves of plates, ill.

S-72   Sandys, Miles. Michael Carmichael: a story of love and mystery / by Miles Sandys. Chicago: Laird & Lee, [1902]. 316 p., col. front., [9] leaves of ills., not counted in pagination.
PW: Ag 2, '02.

S-73   Sanger, William Cary, Jr., b. 1893. When hearts are young: and other stories / by William Cary Sanger, Jr. . . . Utica, N. Y.: Warren S. Purvis, Print., [c1921]. 28 p.   **NYP**
Contents: When hearts are young -- The great tides -- In the hands of the angels -- An Easter story.
LC: Je 5, '20.

S-74 Sangree, Allen. The jinx: stories of the diamond / by Allen Sangree; illustrations by F. R. Gruger, Archie Gunn, C. J. Taylor and Chase Emerson. New York: G. W. Dillingham Company, [c1911]. 311 p., col. front., [5] leaves of plates.
Contents: The jinx -- A break in training -- The ringer -- In Dutch -- The Indian sign -- A foul tip -- The post post-season game.
LC: O 12, '11.
PW: O 14, '11.

S-75 Sangster, Margaret Elizabeth, b. 1894. Friends o' mine: a book of poems and stories / by Margaret E. Sangster, Jr. New York: The Christian Herald, 1914. 232 p. **MNU**
"Some of the articles and poems . . . have been used in The Christian herald and . . . the New York times."
Contents: A talk of war -- The blue bowl -- About ideals -- A springtime fancy -- In the shadow of the mesquite -- Smiles and tears -- The gipsy spirit -- When trouble comes -- From twelve to one -- The onlooker -- Attractiveness -- A song of love -- At the dying of the year -- "Knee-deep in June" -- In search of vacationland -- Only a dog -- Commencement days -- In defense of the modern girl -- The moving finger -- The lady in the veil -- The spice of life -- Life's

signboards -- Flowers to the dead-- The punishment -- By love -- During a shower -- "An, you ha' seen what I ha' seen" -- The coming of "Mary Christmas" -- Adventure and achievement -- The Christmas spirit -- Good intentions -- The sleeping princess -- Following the star -- The eve o' Christmas.
LC: D 11, '14.

S-76 _____ The island of faith / by Margaret E. Sangster; illustrated. New York; Chicago; London; Edinburgh: Fleming H. Revell Company, [c1921]. 175 p., incl. front. [Ill. by Anne Brockman.]
LC: Jl 21, '21.
PW: Je 4, '21.

S-77 _____ Real people and dreams: a new book of stories and poems / by Margaret E. Sangster, Jr. New York: The Christian Herald Bible House, [c1915]. 244 p., photo. front. (port.), [4] leaves of plates.
Contents: The story of a smile -- The little girl at home -- The old china plate -- The city streets at night -- The Lincoln spirit -- The voice of Valley Forge -- In the dark -- The search for happiness -- A bit o' shamrock -- An Easter fable -- The joy of Easter -- The kind conductor -- In the apple tree -- House cleaning -- The mold of heroines -- A nation's birthday -- The girl who came back -- The things that are hard to get -- God's children -- The garden spot -- A mince pie Thanksgiving -- Count your blessings -- The fable of the poison ivy -- Love of people -- See something beautiful -- The miracle of the swamp -- On counting chickens -- Convict no. 66 -- The lonely lady's Christmas story -- The great gift.
LC: D 20, '15.

S-78 Sangster, Margaret Elizabeth Munson, 1838-1912. Eastover parish: a tale of yesterday / by Margaret E. Sangster. New York; Chicago; Toronto; London; Edinburgh: Fleming H. Revell Company, [c1912]. 224 p., front. (port.).
LC: N 18, '12.
PW: Ag 31, '12.

S-79 _____ Eleanor Lee: a novel / by Margaret E. Sangster. New York; Chicago; Toronto; London; Edinburgh: Fleming H. Revell Company, [c1903]. 322 p., front. [Ill. by Griselda Marshall McClure.]
PW: O 3, '03.

S-80 _____ Janet Ward: a daughter of the manse / by Margaret E. Sangster . . . New York; Chicago;

Toronto; London; Edinburgh: Fleming H. Revell Company, [c1902]. 301 p., photo. front.
PW: O 4, '02.

S-81 _____ My garden of hearts: a collection of the best short stories and essays written during a long literary lifetime / by Margaret E. Sangster. New York City: The Christian Herald, Bible House, [c1913]. 439 p., photo. front. (port.).
Contents: Complete stories: The revolution of Molly -- Mrs. Anthony -- The minister's wife -- Aunt Liddy -- The rejuvenation of mother -- A cherry pie -- At Lonesome Ford -- The waif's blessing -- A knight of Avenue A -- The trouble at Ingleside -- Miss Pamela's Easter bonnet -- Tom Hartwell's way -- A prodigal son -- Molly's change of scene -- On the master's service -- Barbara's lawn party -- One day in Maryland -- A little peacemaker -- Myrtle's treasure -- An old survivor -- The evolution of Blanche Titus -- A brave girl -- Molly Jenner's way -- The catnip woman -- Aleck Cameron's girl -- Bread upon the waters -- By way of contrivance -- Miss Rose -- The stumbling stone -- St. Valentine's eve -- An amateur in charity -- Under an August moon -- The "Spite Fence" -- The beautiful Miss Blarcom -- Elbert Ansel's Thanksgiving -- The homecoming of Nancy -- A glimpse of himself -- A life's harvest -- The next-door neighbor -- A Christmas pie -- Dorothy's test -- The album quilt -- The tribe of Reuben -- A stalled Christmas -- The little rift -- The critic -- The Christmas baby -- The first foot -- His fighting chance -- In Martin's alley -- Miss Eunice -- The little milliner -- Polly's beehive -- When Dorothy went home -- The senator's debt -- The little old lady -- Her new role -- The man of the house -- My visit to the Shakers -- The crocus bed -- Miss Jane -- A suset talk -- A little jaunt. Familiar talks: Long courtships -- Women who live in dread -- When love grows cold -- The stealing on of age -- The art of growing old -- Marrying for a home -- Concerning bores -- Second marriages -- The love that lasts -- Letters and love-letters -- The girl who does not want to marry -- When the ship comes in -- The large family or the small? -- On losing friends --A well-regulated household -- About hands and feet -- Essentials in home life -- Women's manners -- Little things of life.
LC: N 4, '13.
PW: D 20, '13.

S-82 _____ Twilight tales: twenty-four stories of love and romance from real life / by Margaret Sangster. New York: The Christian Herald, Bible House, [c1912]. 153 p., photo. front.
Contents: When buckwheat bloomed -- At Lonesome Ford -- The little old lady -- Mr. Warriner's transformation -- The romance of Marcia -- Letitia's first love -- A refrain in lilies -- Mrs. Christy's beginnings -- Sister Hannah -- The patience of hope -- One Easter Day -- Barbara Graham -- The saving of Benjamin Ray -- Cousin Mary -- Golden sunsets -- A bend in the road -- A midsummer meeting -- The peacemaker -- The new pupil -- A little corner -- A reparation -- A long lane -- The snowdrop's message -- The opposite shore.
LC: Jl 29, '12.

S-83 Sangster, Rena Urania Nott. The power of gold: a romance of London, England; in seven chapters / by (Rena) Urania Nott Sangster . . . Buffalo, N. Y.: The Matthews-Northrup Works, 1909. 150 p., photo. front. (port.).
LC D 6, '09.

S-84 Santmyer, Helen Hooven, b. 1895. Herbs and apples / by Helen Hoven Santmyer. Boston; New York: Houghton Mifflin Company, 1925. (Cambridge: The Riverside Press). 397 p.
LC: S 4, 25.
PW: S 5, '25.

S-85 Sappington, Joe. Joe Sap's tales / by himself; illustrated by Hal B. Crandall. Belton, Texas: Embree Printing Company, 1908. 255 p., incl. front. (port.), [2] leaves of plates. **IYU**
"Tenth thousand."

Contents: Pondering over the past -- Some fires I have attended -- The house I painted -- My visit to a great art gallery -- Some youthful fortunes I have made in my mind -- The fortune I made-almost by selling family rights -- A discourse on bald heads -- Some cats I have met -- The moving habit -- The old square dance -- Some speeches I never made -- Flattery -- Those pocketless trousers -- My experience in raising chickens -- The Sappington pie that exploded -- The phonograph's new field -- The major's bull run -- The old time country store -- The flag still waves -- Patient medicine -- The old time doctor -- Joe Sap's spring garden -- The old time school exhibition -- Some observations on society -- My race for Justice of the Peace in precinct 5 -- My first experience on a petit jury -- Some horse traders I once met -- Those old time country debates -- Whither are we drifting -- How I made a fortune drumming -- At the Texas Press Association -- The languages I have used most -- That Christmas turkey -- When I was judge of a baby show -- Some liars I have met -- My experience with a gypsy fortune teller -- The old time wagon circus -- My last shrubbery -- The butter that hung fire -- The milliner's graft -- The Yankee haters -- Fishing -- My teeth and toothache experiences.

S-86   Sargent, Gertrude W. (Gertrude Woodbury), b. 1859. The grand master's treasure / by Gertrude W. Sargent. Brooklyn, N. Y.: Published by the Gertreva Publishing Company, 1911. 289 p.

S-87   Sarver, Charles. The country boy / by Charles Sarver; from the play by Edgar Selwyn. New York: The H. K. Fly Company, [c1911]. 307 p., incl. col. front., [3] leaves of col. plates.

S-88   Sass, Herbert Ravenel, 1884-1958. The way of the wild / by Herbert Ravenel Sass; illustrations by Charles Livington Bull. New York: Minton, Balch & Company, 1925. 321 p., ill.
PW: S 19, '25.
BLC: London: T. Fisher Unwin, New York printed, 1926.

S-89   Satterlee, Anna Eliza Hickox, b. 1851. The wonder girl: a tourist tale of California / by Anna E. Satterlee . . . Boston: Sherman, French & Company, 1915. 202 p.

S-90   Saturday Evening Post. One issue: just one 52nd of a year: an object lesson in values. [Philadelphia, Pa.]: [The Curtis Publishing Company, c1919]. 382 p., ill. (1 col., some photo.). [Ill. by Norman Rockwell, Arthur William Brown, Will Grefe, E. F. Ward, May Wilson Preston, James M. Preston, Henry Raleigh, and H. Weston Taylor.]
"Pulbished exclusively for the use of authorized agents for the Saturday evening post."
Contents: Man snatchers / William Hamilton Osborne -- The peanut hull / George Randolph Chester -- As the British employer sees it [nonfiction] / Meyer Bloomfield -- Spineless leagues and faceless nations [nonfiction] / Gerald Stanley Lee -- Money / May Edginton -- A presidential potpourri [nonfiction] / Samuel G. Blythe -- The best-laid plan / Will Payne -- The blooming angel / Wallace Irwin -- Looking backward [nonfiction] / Henry Watterson -- Editorials -- A woman's woman / Nalbro Bartley -- A better scheme [nonfiction] / Will Payne -- Painless extraction / Octavus Roy Cohen -- It was May / Oscar Graeve -- Delbart: timber cruiser / Hugh Kennedy.

S-91   Saunders, Luke. The boy and the man: a story of a lawsuit / by Luke Saunders. New York: Published at the Bookery, [c1912]. 154 p., front., [2] leaves of plates.   WAU

S-92   Saunders, Marshall, 1861-1947. The girl from Vermont: the story of a vacation school teacher / by Marshall Saunders . . . Philadelphia; Boston; St. Louis; Chicago: The Griffith & Rowland Press,

[1910]. 248 p., col. front., [8] leaves of photo. plates (one ill. by Beals, N. Y.).   ISM
LC: Mr 7, '10.
PW: Mr 12, '10.

S-93   _____ Jimmy Gold-Coast, or, The story of a monkey and his friends / by Marshall Saunders . . . Philadelphia: David McKay Company, [c1924]. 319 p., front., ill. [Ill. by M. Sankey.]
LC: Ag 27, '24.
PW: O 25, '24.
BLC: London: Hodder & Stoughton, [1924].

S-94   Saunders, Ripley D. (Ripley Dunlap), b. 1856. Colonel Todhunter of Missouri / by Ripley D. Saunders; with illustrations by W. B. King. Indianapolis: The Bobbs-Merrill Company, Publishers, [c1911]. 327, [1] p., front., [5] leaves of plates.
LC: F 9, '11.
PW: F 11, '11.

S-95   _____ John Kenadie: being the story of his perplexing inheritance / by Ripley D. Saunders. Boston; New York: Houghton, Mifflin and Company, 1902. (Cambridge: The Riverside Press). 295, [1] p.
PW: My 17, '02.

S-96   Saunier, Bertha Seavey. The tree-pilot / by Bertha Seavey Saunier. Cincinnati: Jennings and Graham; New York: Eaton and Mains, [c1907]. 296 p., front., [4] leaves of plates.
LC: O 11, '07.

S-97   Savage, C. Maclean (Charles Maclean), b. 1884. The turn of the sword / by C. Maclean Savage; with frontispiece in colors and decorations by The Kinneys. Chicago: F. G. Browne & Co., 1913. 278 p., col. front. (double. leaf). Illustrated end papers.
LC: Mr 20, '13.
PW: Mr 22, '13.

Savage, Charles Woodcock. See **Woodcock-Savage, Charles.**

S-98   Savage, Richard Henry, 1846-1903. For a young queen's bright eyes; a novel / by Col. Richard Henry Savage . . . New York: The Home Publishing Company, [1902]. 320 p.
Unexamined copy: bibliographic data from NUC.
PW: My 24, '02.

S-99   _____ The golden rapids of high life: a novel / by Richard Henry Savage. New York: The Home Publishing Company, 1903, [c1902]. 274 p.   NUI
PW: Mr 28, '03.
BLC: London: Samuel French, 1903. Another edition: London: F. V. White & Co., 1903.

S-100   _____ The last traitor of Long Island: a story of the sea / by Richard Henry Savage . . . New York: The Home Publishing Company, 1903. 341 p.   NUI
PW: Ag 15, '03.
BLC: London: Samuel French, 1903. Another edition: London: F. V. White & Co., 1904.

S-101 _____ A Monte Cristo in khaki: the story of a self-made nobleman / by Richard Henry Savage . . . New York: The Home Publishing Company, 1903. 253 p.

                                         KSU

PW: D 5, '03.
BLC: London: Samuel French, 1903.

S-102 _____ Special orders for Commander Leigh: a story of the lower coast of Louisiana / by Col. Richard Henry Savage . . . New York: The Home Publishing Company . . . , [c1902]. 235 p. **VA@**
PW: S 13, '02.

S-103 Savile, Frank. Beyond the great south wall: the secret of the Antarctic / by Frank Savile . . . ; with sundry graphic illustrations painted by one Robert L. Mason. New York City: New Amsterdam Book Company, 1901. 322 p., front., [6] leaves of plates. **IPU**
PW: D 21, '01.
BLC: London: Sampson Low, & Co., 1899.

S-104 _____ The blessing of Esau: a romance on the marchlands / by Frank Savile . . . New York: A. Wessels Company, 1901. 324 p. **NYP**
PW: Je 1, '01.
BLC: London: Sampson Low & Co., 1900.

S-105 _____ The pursuit / by Frank Savile . . . ; with illustrations by Herman Pfeifer. Boston: Little, Brown, and Company, 1910. 317 p., front., [3] leaves of plates.
LC: Je 7, '10.
PW: Je 11, '10.
BLC: London: Edward Arnold, 1910.

S-106 _____ The road: a modern romance / by Frank Savile . . . ; with illustrations by Herman Pfeifer. Boston: Little, Brown, and Company, 1911. 313 p., front., [3] leaves of plates.
LC: Mr 1, '11.
PW: O 7, '11.

Sawtell, Ruth Otis. The way of peace. In *The best college short stories, 1917-18* **(1919)**, **B-557**.

S-107 Sawyer, Josephine Caroline, b. 1878. All's fair in love / by Josephine Caroline Sawyer; with illustrations and decorations by C. B. Falls. New York: Dodd, Mead & Company, 1904. 346 p., col. front., [7] leaves of col. plates.
PW: F 27, '04; Je 4, '04.
BLC: London: B. F. Stevens & Brown, 1904.

S-108 _____ Every inch a king: the romance of Henry of Monmouth, sometime Prince of Wales / by Josephine Caroline Sawyer. New York: Dodd, Mead & Company, 1901. 354 p.
PW: Ap 6, '01.

S-109 Sawyer, Kate H. Miss Penelope's Elopement: and other stories / by Kate H. Sawyer. New York; London; Montreal: The Abbey Press, [c1901]. 102 p. **DLC**
Contents: Miss Penelope's elopement -- Uncle Jeff's house -- Deputy sheriff -- Bob's trip abroad -- The embodiment of a thought -- Mrs. Brown -- Miss Scruggs -- Aunt Sallie's psychology.
PW: Ag 10, '01.

S-110 Sawyer, Nellie T. The Egyptian ring / by Nellie T. Sawyer. New York; London; Montreal: The Abbey Press, [c1901]. 105 p.
LC: My 25, '01.

S-111 Sawyer, R. H. (Reuben Herbert), b. 1866. The livery of heaven / by R. H. Sawyer. Boston, Massachusetts: The C. M. Clark Publishing Company, 1910. 422 p., front., [5] leaves of plates. **NDD**
LC: F 18, '10.

S-112 Sawyer, Ruth, 1880-1970. Doctor Danny / by Ruth Sawyer; illustrated by J. Scott Williams. New York; London: Harper & Brothers, 1918. 410, [1] p., front., [7] leaves of plates. Reprinted in part from various periodicals.
Contents: When Padraic came piping --The tinkers' Meg -- Sheila of the dunes -- Paddy the gander -- A lad from nowhere -- The unwakefulness of Timothy Baron -- Peter-Peter -- The coming o' the King -- The courting of Bridget -- The wee road to Bethlehem -- Road-menders -- The tall one and the wee one -- Doctor Danny -- The lifting of the promise -- As it was told by the lazy bush.
LC: N 29, '18.

S-113 _____ Gladiola Murphy / by Ruth Sawyer. New York; London: Harper & Brothers, 1923. 337 p.
LC: F 16, '23.
PW: Mr 3, '23.

S-114 _____ Herself, himself & myself: a romance / by Ruth Sawyer . . . New York; London: Harper & Brothers, [1917]. 286, [1] p., front.
LC: O 3, '17.
PW: O 13,'17.

S-115 _____ Leerie / by Ruth Sawyer; with illustrations by Clinton Balmer. New York; London: Harper & Brothers, [c1920]. 309, [1] p., front., [3] leaves of plates.
LC: Ag 3, '20.
PW: Ag 14, '20.

S-116 _____ The Primrose ring / Ruth Sawyer; illustrated. New York; London: Harper & Brothers, [1915]. 186, [1] p., front., [5] leaves of plates. [Ill. by Fanny Munsell.]
LC: My 8, '15.
PW: My 15, '15.

S-117 _____ Seven miles to Arden / by Ruth Sawyer . . . ; illustrated. New York; London: Harper & Brothers, 1916. 243, [1] p., col. front., [1] leaf of col. plates. [Ill. by Henry Raleigh.]
LC: Ap 27, '16.
PW: Ap 29, '16.

S-118 _____ The silver sixpence / by Ruth Sawyer; illustrated by James H. Crank. New York; London: Harper & Brothers, 1921. 331, [1] p., front., [3] leaves of plates.
LC: Mr 11, '21.
PW: Mr 19, '21.

_____ The tall one and the wee one. In *Greatest short stories* **(1915)**, **G-424**.

S-119 Saxby, Chester Leigh, b. 1891. A captain of the King / by Chester L. Saxby. Boston: Sherman, French & Company, 1914. 110 p. **DAY**

S-120 Saxon, William Andrew. Knight Vale of the K. K. K.: a fiction story of love, patriotism, intrigue and adventure / by William Andrew Saxon. [Columbus, Ohio: Patriot Publishing Company, c1924]. 160 p. Unexamined copy: bibliographic data from OCLC, #25488848.

S-121 Saxton, Evelyn. Droll stories of Isthmian life / by Evelyn Saxton. New Orleans, La.: The L. Graham Co., 1914. 242 p.
Contents: First part: Nine years ago at Panama -- Mr. Comstock's arrival -- The derelict -- The bounder -- Higgins' lady -- The gang in No. 10 -- The man from No. 9 -- The canal zone architect's wedding -- Graft -- Vere de vere -- An awful mystery -- A night off -- The district quartermasters -- Old Panama's renaissance -- Abe Lincoln, foundling -- Stranger than fiction -- Faction fights. Second part: The woes of the manly ones -- The flight of the manly ones -- The tango skirt and the woman -- An epic of the zone -- To the vultures on the zone -- A faker's farewell -- It's got 'em -- It's hell -- The loco germ -- An Isthmian wooer -- A word to the slandered ones -- Mrs. With's affinity -- Preserved peaches -- Eugenics -- Toboga -- Our uncle George.

S-122 Saylor, Emma R. (Emma Rosalyn), b. 1863. The last mile-stone / by Emma R. Saylor. San Francisco: Paul Elder & Company, 1917. 167 p., front. [Ill. by Norman D. Edwards.]
PW: O 27, '17.

S-123 Sayre, Theodore Burt. Tom Moore: an unhistorical romance, founded on certain happenings in the life of Ireland's greatest poet / by Theodore Burt Sayre . . . ; illustrated. New York: Frederick A. Stokes Company, [1902]. 341 p., photo. front., [9] leaves of photo. plates.
PW: S 13, '02.

Scala, Guglielmo, pseud. See **Schuyler, William, 1855-1914.**

Scarborough, Dorothy, 1878-1935, ed. See *Famous modern ghost stories* **(1921), F-18.**

S-124 ____ In the land of cotton / by Dorothy Scarborough . . . New York: The Macmillan Company, 1923. 370 p.
LC: Ap 11, '23.

S-125 [____] The wind / Anonymous. New York: Harper & Brothers, 1925. 337 p.
LC: S 18, '25.

S-126 Scarborough, George. The lure / by George Scarborough; illustrations from scenes in the play. New York: G. W. Dillingham Company, [c1914]. 300 p., photo. front., [5] leaves of photo. plates.

S-127 Scarborough, Harold E. (Harold Ellicott), 1897-1935. The immortals / by Harold E. Scarborough. New York: D. Appleton and Company, 1924. 279, [1] p.
LC: Ap 12, '24.
PW: Ap 19, '24.
BLC: London: T. Fisher Unwin, 1924.

S-128 ____ Stephen the well-beloved / by Harold E. Scarborough. New York: D. Appleton and Company, 1924. 323, [1] p.

S-129 Scarlet, Will, b. 1881, *pseud.* False gods: a novel / by Will Scarlet [pseud.]. New York; Cincinnati; Chicago: Benziger Brothers, 1924. 302 p.
LC: F 13, '24.

S-130 Schade van Westrum, Adriaan, b. 1865. The devil / founded on Ferenc Molnar's play, as produced by Harrison Grey Fiske at the Belasco Theatre, New York; by Adriaan Schade van Westrum; illustrations from scenes in the play. New York: G. W. Dillingham Company, [c1908]. 317 p., photo. front., [7] leaves of photo. plates.

S-131 Schaeffer, Evelyn Schuyler. Fortune's yellow / by Evelyn Schuyler Schaeffer . . . New York; London: Charles Scribner's Sons, 1925. 248 p.
LC: Mr 7, '25.
PW: Mr 7, '25.
BLC: London: Eveleigh Nash & Co., 1925.

S-132 ____ Isabel Stirling / by Evelyn Schuyler Schaeffer. New York: Charles Scribner's Sons, 1920. 409 p.
LC: O 16, '20.
PW: O 23, '20.
BLC: London: Eveligh Nash Co., New york [printed], 1921.

Schapiro, Löb. If it was a dream. In *Yiddish tales* **(1912), Y-20.**

S-133 Schauffler, Rachel Capen. The goodly fellowship / by Rachel Capen Schauffler. New York: The Macmillan Company, 1912. 325 p.
PW: My 11, '12.

S-134 Schauffler, Robert Haven, 1879-1964. Fiddler's luck: the gay adventures of a musical amateur / by Robert Haven Schauffler . . . Boston; New York: Houghton Mifflin Company, 1920. (Cambridge, Massachusetts, U. S. A.: The Riverside Press). 275 p.
LC: Je 8, '20.
PW: Je 19, '20.

S-135 ____ Where speech ends: a music maker's romance / by Robert Haven Schauffler; with a prelude by Henry Van Dyke; illustrated by E. W. [i. e. M.] Ashe, Frederic Dorr Steele and Leon Guipon. New York: Moffat, Yard & Co., 1906. 291 p., front., [6] leaves of plates.
BLC: London: B. F. Stevens & Brown, New York printed, 1906.

Schem, Lida C., 1875-1923. See **Blake, Margaret, pseud.**

S-136 Scherer, James A. B. (James Augustin Brown), 1870-1944. The tree of light / by James A. B. Scherer. New York: Thomas Y. Crowell Company, [c1921]. 125 p., incl. [4] leaves of plates, ill. [Ill. by Frank Craig.]

Scherr, Marie. See **Cher, Marie, pseud.**

Schertz, Helen Pitkin, b. 1877. See **Pitkin, Helen.**

S-137   [Schieren, Harrie Victor], b. 1881. Espeschilly Lem: a tale of a lonesome heart / by Crispin Childe [pseud.]. New York: McDevitt-Wilson's, 1925. 80 p., front., [3] leaves of plates.   **DLC**
LC: N 28, '25.

S-138   _____ The quitter / by Harrie Victor Schieren. Boston: Small, Maynard and Company, [c1924]. 285 p.
LC: Ag 13, '24.
PW: Ag 23, '24.

S-139   Schinke, Norma S. The Devil Wolf / by Norma S. Schinke. Boston: Small, Maynard & Company, [c1924]. 345 p.
LC: F 8, '24.
PW: Mr 22, '24.
BLC: London: T. Fisher Unwin, 1924.

S-140   Schleppey, Blanche Bloor. The soul of a mummy: and other stories / by Blanche Bloor Schleppey. [Indianapolis?: s. n.], 1908. 260 p.
Contents: The soul of a mummy -- Hearts and crafts -- The devil's sonata -- Just Jake -- Mrs. Mainwaring's second marriage -- The mad master -- The heart of Esculapius -- The nectar of a thousand years -- Marvin's ghost -- The Gnawbone culture club -- A house and a reincarnation.
LC: N 14, '08.
PW: Ja 16, '09.

Schmidt, Carl George, b. 1862. See **Carroll, George S., pseud.**

S-141   Schmidt, William, 1855-1931. Aethelburga: a story of Anglo-Saxon times / by William Schmidt. St. Louis, Mo.: Louis Lange Publishing Company, [c1923]. 290 p., ill. [Ill. by C. Adolph Glassgold.]

S-142   _____ The golden fountain / by William Schmidt; translated by Mary E. Ireland. Columbus, Ohio: W. Schmidt, 1916. 96 p.
Unexamined copy: bibliographic data from OCLC, #12570363.

S-143   _____ Saramanda: (Sri Ramuldu) / by W. Schmidt . . . Columbus, Ohio: Published by Fred J. Heer, 1903. 312 p. Title on t. p. in Telugu.

S-144   Schnebly, Frances M. The vital touch: a story of the power of love / by Frances M. Schnebly . . . ; illustrations by Harlan Tarbell. Chicago: Laird & Lee, [c1912]. 246 p., front., [3] leaves of plates.

Schneider, Charles W., Mrs. See **Schneider, Martha Lemon.**

Schneider, Isidor, 1896-1936. The dead city. In *The best college short stories, 1917-18 (1919), B-557.*

S-145   [_____] Doctor Transit / by I. S. New York: Boni & Liveright, 1925. 285 p.
PW: S 12, '25.

S-146   Schneider, Martha Lemon. A government countess: a novel of departmental life in Washington / by Martha Lemon Schneider (Mrs. Charles W. Schneider). New York; Washington: The Neale Publishing Company, 1905. 221 p.

Schnittkind, Henry T., ed. See *The best college short stories, 1917-18 (1919), B-557.*

Schnittkind, Henry T., jt. ed. See *The best college short stories, 1924-1925 (1925), B-558.*

Schock, Georg, b. 1877, *pseud.* The Christmas child. In *Shapes that haunt the dusk (1907), S-339.*

S-147   _____ Hearts contending: a novel / by Georg Schock [pseud.]; frontispiece by Denman Fink. New York; London: Harper & Brothers, 1910. 271, [1] p., col. front.
LC: Ap 9, '10.
PW: Ap 23, '10.

S-148   _____ The house of Yost / Georg Schock [pseud.]. New York: Boni & Liveright, [c1923]. 310 p.
LC: F 20, '23.
PW: F 24, '23.

S-149   Schoeler, William. The lie of the age / by Wm. Schoeler . . . Columbus, Ohio: The Book Concern, [c1922]. 260 p.   **OSU, IOH**
LC: Ag 27, '23.

S-150   _____ A strong man's defeat, or, the story of Samson / by William Schoeler. Columbus, Ohio: The Book Concern, [19--?]. 260 p.

S-151   _____ To the throne from the sheepcotes / by William Schoeler . . . Boston: The Roxburgh Publishing Company, Inc., [c1921]. 264 p.   **DLC**
LC: Ja 3, '22.

S-152   Schoolcraft, John. The bird of passage / by John Schoolcraft. New York: George H. Doran Company, [c1923]. 295 p.

S-153   Schoonmaker, M. (Moses), b. 1845. "Wayside gleanings": a religious novel / by M. Schoonmaker. Kansas City: The Joseph D. Havens Company, 1910. 184 p., photo. front. (port.).

S-154   Schoonmaker, Nancy Musselman, b. 1873. The eternal fires / by Nancy Musselman Schoonmaker. New York; Baltimore; Atlanta; Florence, Ala.: Broadway Publishing Company, [c1910]. 332 p.   **OSU, KMM**
LC: Ap 26, '10.

Schroeder, Reginald. See **Davis, Schroeder, jt. pseud. of Oscar King Davis and Reginald Schroeder.**

Scribner, Cornelia. See **Middleton, Cornelia Scribner.**

S-155   Schubert, Vernon E. (Vernon Edward), b. 1892. Cabin boy, or, The adventures of two American boys in foreign waters / by Vernon E. Schubert. Boston: The Roxburgh Publishing Company, Inc., [c1914]. 175 p., front. (port.).

S-156 Schuette, H. George, b. 1850. Athonia, or, The original four hundred / by H. George Schuette . . . Manitowoc, Wis.: The Lakeside Co., 1911. 479 p., front., [11] leaves of plates.

S-157 [Schuette, John]. The story of John and Rose: who began married life on an income of $900.00 a year, shows the comforting results attained by strict economy, systematic house and bookkeeping, and their accumulations to their olden age / by John Schuette. [Chicago: R. R. Donnelley & Sons Company], [c1914]. 254 p., [20] leaves of plates (1 col., port., some photo.).

S-158 Schuette, Walter E. (Walter Erwin), 1867-1955. The Birdstown bank / by Walter E. Schuette. Col., O. [i. e., Columbus, Ohio]: L. B. C. [i. e., Lutheran Book Concern], [1921?]. 64 p.

S-159 Schulder, Irene Dickson. Virginia Russell / by Irene Dickson Schulder. New York: Cochrane Publishing Company, 1908. 201 p., front., [3] leaves of plates. [Ill. by Robert Edwards.]
LC: Ag 6, '08.

S-160 Schultz, James Willard, 1859-1947. The gold cache / by James Willard Schultz; with illustrations by George Varian. Boston; New York: Houghton Mifflin Company, [c1917]. (Cambridge: The Riverside Press). 189, [1] p., front., [5] leaves of plates. **CLE**
LC: S 18, '17.
PW: S 22, '17.

S-161 _____ Lone Bull's mistake: a Lodge Pole chief story / by James Willard Schultz; with illustrations by George Varian. Boston; New York: Houghton Mifflin Company, 1918. (Cambridge: The Riverside Press). 207, [1] p., front., [3] leaves of plates.
PW: Ag 17, '18.

S-162 _____ On the warpath / by James Willard Schultz (Ap-i-kun-i); with illustrations by George Varian. Boston; New York: Houghton Mifflin Company, 1914. (Cambridge: The Riverside Press). 244, [2] p., front., [3] leaves of plates. **DRB**
LC: N 27, '14.

S-163 _____ The quest of the fish-dog skin / by James Willard Schultz (Ap-i-kun-i); with illustrations by George Varian. Boston; New York: Houghton Mifflin Company, c1913. (Cambridge: The Riverside Press). 218, [2] p., front., [3] leaves of plates. **CXP**
LC: O 8, '13.
PW: O 18, '13.

S-164 _____ Seizer of eagles / by James Willard Schultz . . . ; with illustrations by Frank E. Schoonover. Boston; New York: Houghton Mifflin Company, c1922. (Cambridge: The Riverside Press). 229, [1] p., front., [3] leaves of plates. **CLE**
LC: Je 17, '22.
PW: Je 10, '22.

S-165 _____ The trail of the Spanish horse / by James Willard Schultz; with illustrations by George Varian. Boston; New York: Houghton Mifflin Company, 1922. (Cambridge: The Riverside Press). 212, [1] p., front., [3] leaves of plates.
LC: S 11, '22.

S-166 _____ The war-trail fort: further adventures of Thomas Fox and Pitamakan / by James Willard Schultz; with illustrations by George Varian. Boston; New York: Houghton Mifflin Company, 1921. (Cambridge: The Riverside Press). 192, [2] p., front., [3] leaves of plates. **MUU**
LC: S 12, '21.

S-167 Schureman, J. F. Harold Ware: a story of passion, pathos and poultry: founded on the financial panic of 1907-1908 / by J. F. Schureman . . . ; illustrated. Marseilles, Illinois: Published by Commercial Poultry Publishing Co., 1908. 125 p., photo. front. (port.), ill.

S-168 Schuster, O. J. (Otto John), b. 1861. The treasures of Mayville / by O. J. Schuster. [Spring Grove, Va.: Little Pub., 1919]. 339 p.
Unexamined copy: bibliographic data based on PW.
PW: Mr 6, '20.
Another edition: Washington, D. C.: Hayworth Publishing House, 1919.

S-169 Schuyler, William, 1855-1914. The hope of glory: being part of a correspondence written in the Roman Empire between the years 52 and 66 A. D. / by William Schuyler. Boston: The Four Seas Company, 1915. 442 p., photo. front. (port.).
PW: Ja 15, '16.

S-170 [_____] Monna Lisa; or, The quest of the woman soul, transcribed by Guglielmo Scala [pseud.]. New York: Thomas Y. Crowell Company, [1911]. 206 p., col. front. **CIN**

S-171 _____ Under Pontius Pilate: being a part of the correspondence between Caius Claudius Proculus in Judea and Lucius Domitius Ahenobarbus at Athens in the years 28 and 29 A. D. / translated and edited by William Schuyler. New York; London: Funk & Wagnalls Company, 1906. 353 p., front., [7] leaves of plates.
LC: O 5, '06.
PW: O 13, '06.

Schweikert, H. C., ed. <u>See</u> *Short stories* (1925), **S-460.**

S-172 Scofield, Charles Josiah, b. 1853. Altar stairs / by Charles J. Scofield . . . ; illustrations by E. Bert Smith. Chicago: Christian Century Company, 1903. 320 p., front., [6] leaves of plates. Designed end papers.

S-173 Scoggins, C. E. (Charles Elbert), 1888-1955. The proud old name / by C. E. Scoggins. Indianapolis: The Bobbs Merrill Company, [c1925]. 137 p., front. [Ill. by W. H. D. Koerner.]
LC: Jl 18, '25.
PW: Ag 8, '25.

S-174   Scogin, Samuel Martha Caldwell, b. 1873. Down on the old plantation; original sketches of everyday life on a Mississippi cotton plantation / by Mrs. S. M. Scogin and John Dicks Howe. San Francisco, 1908. 154 p., incl. front. (port.), ill.
Unexamined copy: bibliographic data from OCLC, #14512660.

S-175   Scollard, Clinton, 1860-1932. The cloistering of Ursula: being certain chapters from the Memoirs of Andrea, Marquis of Uccelli, and Count of Castelpulchio / done into English by Clinton Scollard;

illustrated by Harry C. Edwards. Boston: L. C. Page & Company, 1902. 273 p., front., [4] leaves of plates, maps.
PW: F 15, '02.
BLC: London: Cassell & Co., 1902.

S-176   ____ Count Falcon of the Eyrie: a narrative wherein are set forth the adventures of Guido Orrabelli dei Falchi during a certain autumn of his career / by Clinton Scollard. New York: James Pott & Company, 1903. 263 p., front. [Ill. by A. M. Upjohn.]
PW: O 3, '03.

S-177   ____ A knight of the highway / by Clinton Scollard. Clinton, N. Y.: George William Browning, 1908. 228 p.
LC: O 6, '8.

S-178   ____ The son of a Tory: a narrative of the experiences of Wilton Aubrey in the Mohawk Valley and elsewhere during the summer of 1777 / now for the first time edited by Clinton Scollard . . . Boston: Richard G. Badger & Company (Incorporated), 1901. 307 p., front. [Ill. by I. B. Hazelton.]
PW: Ap 27, '01.

S-179   ____ The vicar of the marches / by Clinton Scollard . . . Boston: Sherman, French & Company, 1911. 230 p.   **CIN**
LC: D 12, '10.

S-180   Scott, C. Kay (Cyril Kay). Blind mice / by C. Kay Scott. New York: George H. Doran Company, [c1921]. 321 p.
LC: Ap 2, '21.
PW: Mr 12, '21.

S-181   ____ Sinbad: a romance / by C. Kay Scott. New York: Thomas Seltzer, 1923. 282 p.
LC: My 31, '23.
PW: Je 16, '23.

Scott, Emily W. The Archbishop of Rheims. In *The Bellman book of fiction* **(1921), B-485.**

S-182   Scott, Evelyn, b. 1893. Escapade / by Evelyn Scott . . . New York: Thomas Seltzer, 1923. 286 p.
                                                                   IPL
LC: Ag 1, '23.

S-183   ____ The golden door / by Evelyn Scott. New York: Thomas Seltzer, 1925. 275 p.

LC: Ap 13, '25.
PW: Mr 21, '25.

S-184   ____ Narcissus / by Evelyn Scott. New York: Harcourt, Brace and Company, [c1922]. 263 p.
LC: Je 17, '22.

S-185   ____ The narrow house / by Evelyn Scott . . . New York: Boni and Liveright, [c1921]. 221 p.
LC: Mr 18, '21.

S-186   Scott, Francina. The romance of a trained nurse / by Francina Scott; with three illustrations. New York: Cooke & Fry, 1901. 315 p., front., [2] leaves of plates.

S-187   Scott, George, b. 1838. Tamarack farm: the story of Rube Wolcott and his Gettysburg girl / by George Scott. New York: The Grafton Press, [c1903]. 236 p., photo. front., [1] leaf of photo. plates (port.).

S-188   Scott, Henry E. The alderman's wife / by Hon. Henry E. Scott . . . Chicago: H. E. Scott, 1904. 214 p., incl. front., ill.
Unexamined copy: bibliographic data from NUC.

S-189   Scott, J. W. (James Winfield), b. 1867. Jack Hardin's rendering of the Arabian nights: being a new translation in up-to-date English: with wise comments, explanations, & c., by this eminent linguist / by J. W. Scott. Boston: Herbert B. Turner & Co., 1903. 260 p., incl. front., [6] leaves of plates. [Ill. by Hugh Doyle.]
PW: My 9, '03.

S-190   Scott, Jessie. Runnymede: a romance of Australia / by Jessie Scott. San Francisco: The Whitaker and Ray Company, 1903. 144 p., front.   **DLC**
PW: Ap 11, '03.

S-191   Scott, John Reed, b. 1869. Beatrix of Clare / by John Reed Scott; with illustrations in color by Clarence F. Underwood. Philadelphia; London: J. B. Lippincott Company, 1907. 365 p., col. front., [3] leaves of col. plates.

S-192   ____ The cab of the sleeping horse / by John Reed Scott . . . New York; London: G. P. Putnam's Sons, 1916. ([New York]: The Knickerbocker Press). 361 p., col. front. [Ill. by William van Dresser.]
LC: O 10, '16.
PW: S 23, '16.

S-193   ____ The colonel of the Red huzzars / by John Reed Scott; with illustrations in color by Clarence F. Underwood. Philadelphia; London: J. B. Lippincott Company, 1906. 341 p., col. front., [2] leaves of col. plates.

S-194   ____ The Duke of Oblivion / by John Reed Scott; with a frontispiece in color by H. Weston Taylor. Philadelphia; London: J. B. Lippincott Company, 1914. 351 p., incl. col. front.
LC: S 26, '14.
PW: S 19, '14.

S-195   The first hurdle and others / by John Reed Scott . . . ; with a frontispiece in color by James Montgomery Flagg. Philadelphia; London: J. B. Lippincott Company, 1912. 305 p., incl. col. front.
Contents: The first hurdle -- The heel of Achilles -- Mrs. Randolph's nerve -- The testing of the Earls -- The affair of the protocol -- In the face of the enemy -- My lady -- The balance of power -- Five aces and an option -- A quarter to eight -- The poise of Plymington.
LC: N 21, '12.

S-196   The impostor: a tale of old Annapolis / by John Reed Scott . . . ; with illustrations in color by Clarence F. Underwood. Philadelphia; London: J. B. Lippincott Company, 1910. 330 p., col. front., [2] leaves of plates.
LC: S 26, '10.
PW: O 8, '10.

S-197   In her own right / by John Reed Scott; with illustrations in color by Clarence F. Underwood. Philadelphia; London: J. B. Lippincott Company, 1911. 336 p., col. front., [2] leaves of col. plates.
LC: Je 9, '11.
PW: Je 17, '11.

S-198   The last try / by John Reed Scott . . . ; with illustrations in color by Clarence F. Underwood. Philadelphia; London: J. B. Lippincott Company, 1912. 352 p., col. front., [2] leaves of col. plates.
LC: Ap 30, '12.
PW: Ap 13, '12.

S-199   The man in evening clothes / by John Reed Scott . . . New York; London: G. P. Putnam's Sons, 1917. ([New York]: The Knickerbocker Press). 387 p., col. front. [Ill. by E. L. Crompton.]
LC: My 31, '17.
PW: Je 2, '17.

S-200   The Princess Dehra / by John Reed Scott . . . ; with illustrations in color by Clarence F. Underwood. Philadelphia; London: J. B. Lippincott Company, 1908. 360 p., col. front., [3] leaves of col. plates.
OSU, EMU
LC: My 16, '08.
PW: Je 27, '08.
BLC: London: Archibald Constable & Co.; Philadelphia printed, 1908 (second edition).

S-201   The red emerald / by John Reed Scott . . . ; with illustrations in color by Edmund Frederick. Philadelphia; London: J. B. Lippincott Company, 1914. 352 p., col. front., [2] leaves of col. plates.
LC: F 19, '14.
PW: F 7, '14.

S-202   The unforgiving offender / by John Reed Scott . . . ; with illustrations in color by Clarence F. Underwood. Philadelphia; London: J. B. Lippincott Company, 1913. 388 p., col. front., [2] leaves of col. plates.
LC: My 1, '13.

S-203   The woman in question / by John Reed Scott . . . ; with illustrations in color by Clarence F. Underwood. Philadelphia; London: J. B. Lippincott Company, 1909. 346 p., col. front., [2] leaves of col. plates.
LC: My 12, '09.
PW: My 22, '09.

S-204 Scott, Leroy, 1875-1929. Children of the whirlwind / by Leroy Scott . . . Boston; New York: Houghton Mifflin Company, 1921. (Cambridge: The Riverside Press). 314 p.
LC: Ag 1, '21.

S-205   Cordelia the Magnificent / by Leroy Scott. New York: Henry Holt and Company, 1923. 395 p., front. [Ill. by Charles D. Mitchell.]
LC: My 2, '23.

S-206   Counsel for the defense / by Leroy Scott . . . ; frontispiece by Charles M. Chapman. Garden City, New York: Doubleday, Page & Company, 1912. 431 p., col. front.
LC: Mr 12, '12.

S-207   A daughter of two worlds: a novel of New York life / by Leroy Scott. Boston; New York: Houghton Mifflin Company, 1919. (Cambridge: The Riverside Press). 458 p.
LC: Mr 22, '19.
PW: Mr 8, '19.

S-208   The heart of Katie O'Doone / by Leroy Scott. Boston; New York: Houghton Mifflin Company, 1925. (Cambridge: The Riverside Press). 385, [1] p.
LC: N 2, '25.

S-209   Mary Regan / by Leroy Scott; with illustrations. Boston; New York: Houghton Mifflin and Company, 1918. (Cambridge: The Riverside Press). 384, [2] p., front., [7] leaves of plates. [Ill. by Dalton Stevens.]
LC: F 4, '18.
PW: Ja 26, '18.

S-210   No. 13 Washington Square / by Leroy Scott . . . ; with illustrations by Irma Dérèmeaux. Boston; New York: Houghton Mifflin Company, 1914. (Cambridge: Riverside Press). 280, [2] p., front., [5] leaves of plates.
LC: Je 24, '14.
PW: Je 27, '14.

S-211   Partners of the night / by Leroy Scott; illustrated by Dalton Stevens. New York: The Century Co., 1916. 361 p., incl. [7] leaves of plates, front.
LC: O 25, '16.
PW: O 14, '16.

S-212   The shears of destiny / by Leroy Scott; illustrated by Alexander Popini. New York: Doubleday, Page & Company, 1910. 333 p., front., [3] leaves of plates.
LC: S 17, '10.
PW: O 8, '10.
BLC: London: Hodder & Stoughton, New York printed, 1910.

____, contributor. See *The sturdy oak* (1917), **S-1101.**

S-213   ____ To him that hath / by Leroy Scott; illustrated from paintings by Sigurd Schou. New York: Doubleday, Page & Company, 1907. 401 p., front., [3] leaves of plates.
LC: Jl 1, '07.
PW: Ag 31, '07.
BLC: London: Doubleday, Page, & Co., New York printed, 1907.

S-214   ____ The walking delegate / by Leroy Scott; with frontispiece. New York: Doubleday, Page & Company, 1905. 372 p., front. [Ill. by the Kinneys.]
PW: My 20, '05.
BLC: London: William Heinemann, New York printed, 1905.

S-215   Scott, Mansfield. Behind red curtains / by Mansfield Scott; illustrated by George W. Gage. Boston: Small, Maynard & Company, [c1919]. 273 p., col. front.
LC: Ag 18, '19.
PW: Jl 12, '19.
BLC: London: Eveleigh Nash Co., 1920.

S-216   Scott, Martin J. (Martin Jerome), 1865-1954. For better for worse: a novel / by Martin J. Scott . . . New York; Cincinnati; Chicago: Benziger Brothers, 1923. 233 p.
LC: O 23, '23.

S-217   ____ Kelly: a novel / by Martin J. Scott. New York; Cincinnati; Chicago: Benziger Brothers, 1924. 232 p.
LC: S 17, '24.
PW: O 4, '24.

S-218   ____ Mother Machree: a novel / by Martin J. Scott, S. J. New York: The Macmillan Company, 1922. 177 p.
LC: N 1, '22.
PW: D 2, '22.

S-219   Scott, R. T. M. (Reginald Thomas Maitland), b. 1882. The black magician; another adventure of "Secret Service Smith" / by R. T. M. Scott . . . New York: E. P. Dutton & Company, [c1925]. 244 p.   **MIA**
LC: Jl 20, '25.
PW: Ag 8, '25.
BLC: London; William Heinemann, 1926.

S-220   ____ Secret Service Smith: wanderings of an American detective / by R. T. M. Scott. New York: E. P. Dutton & Company, [c1923]. 296 p.   **OCP**
LC: S 29, '23.
PW: D 8, '23.
BLC: London: Hodder & Stoughton, [1924].

Scoville, Samuel, Jr. The churching of Bankson. In *Greatest short stories* (1915), **G-424.**

S-221   Scribner, Frank Kimball, 1866-1935. The secret of Frontellac / by Frank K. Scribner; with a frontispiece

by Leon V. Solon. Boston: Small, Maynard and Company, [c1912]. 420 p., front.
LC: O 1, '12.
BLC: London: Gay & Hancock, Cambridge [Mass.] printed, 1912.

S-222   Scribner, Josephine Pittman. The Pilgrims' first Christmas / by Josephine Pittman Scribner. Boston; New York; Chicago: The Pilgrim Press, [c1913]. 30 p., col. front. Ornamental borders.   **IOD**

Scribner, Laura. A question of method. In *The best college short stories, 1917-18* (1919), **B-557.**

S-223   Scudder, Sam. A counterfeit citizen / by Sam Scudder. New York: Broadway Publishing Co., [c1908]. 346 p.
LC: Je 8, '08.
PW: Je 20, '08.

S-224   Scudder, Vida Dutton, 1861-1954. The disciple of a saint: being the imaginary biography of Raniero di Landoccio dei Pagliaresi / by Vida D. Scudder. New York: E. P. Dutton & Co., 1907. 383 p.
PW: My 4, '07.
BLC: London: J. M. Dent, 1907.

S-225   ____ A listener in Babel: being a series of imaginary conversations held at the close of the last century and reported / by Vida D. Scudder. Boston; New York: Houghton, Mifflin and Company, 1903. (Cambridge: The Riverside Press). 322 p.
PW: O 24, '03.

S-226   Seabrook, Phoebe Hamilton. A daughter of the Confederacy: a story of the old South and the new / by Phoebe Hamilton Seabrook. New York; Washington: The Neale Publishing Company, 1906. 290 p.
LC: N 23, '06.

S-227   Seabrooke, John Paul. The eyewitness: a detective story / by John Paul Seabrooke. New York: Chelsea House, [c1925]. 251 p.
PW: D 19, '25.
BLC: London: Jarrolds, [1926].

S-228   ____ Four knocks on the door: a detective story / by John Paul Seabrooke. New York: Chelsea House, [c1925]. 254 p.
PW: D 26, '25.
BLC: London: Jarrlods, [1927].

S-229   Seager, Frances Mead. Twentieth century goslings: a modern love story / by Frances Mead Seager. New York: Broadway Publishing Company, 1906. 340 p., front., plates.
Unexamined copy: bibliographic data from OCLC, #30049878.

S-230   Seagrave, Sadie Fuller. Saints' rest / by Sadie Fuller Seagrave. St. Louis: C. V. Mosby Company, 1918. 179 p., photo. front.   **GZH**

S-231   Sealis, Hatherly, 1830-1912, *pseud.* The veiled lady / Hatherly Sealis [pseud.]; illustrated by Hartman.

New York: Broadway Publishing Company, [c1905]. 114 p., [4] leaves of plates, ill.
Unexamined copy: bibliographic data from OCLC, #23129651.

S-232 Seaman, Augusta Huiell, b. 1879. Mamselle of the wilderness: a story of LaSalle and his pioneers / by Augusta Huiell Seaman; with drawings by George Wharton Edwards. [New York]: Sturgis & Walton Company, 1913. 405 p., front., [3] leaves of plates.
LC: Je 11, '13.

S-233 ____ Tranquillity house / by Augusta Huiell Seaman . . . ; illustrated by W. P. Couse. New York; London: The Century Co., [c1923]. 222 p., front., [3] leaves of plates.   **RRR**
LC: O 3, '23.

S-234 ____ When a cobbler ruled the king / by Augusta Huiell Seaman; with decoration and drawings by George Wharton Edwards. New York: Sturgis & Walton Company, 1911. 352 p., front., [3] leaves of plates.
LC: Ap 10, '11.

S-235 The seamy side: a story of the true condition of things theatrical / by one who has spent twenty years among them. Boston, Mass.: Percy Ives Publishing Co., [c1906]. 312 p., front. [Ill. by H. A. Dennison.]

S-236 Se Arcy, Ann, b. 1843, *pseud.* A Kentucky girl, or, A question unanswered / by Ann Se Arcy [pseud.]. Berea, Ky.: Printing Department, Berea College, 1909. 111 p., photo. front. (port.), [1] leaf of plates.   **OSU, ICU**
LC: O 21, '09.

S-237 Searles, Jean Randolph, b. 1872, *pseud.* Furthur annals of the girl in the slumber-boots / by Jean Randolph Searles [pseud.] . . . Cincinnati: Press of Jennings and Graham, [c1912]. 295 p., front. **DLC**
LC: O 31, '12.

S-238 ____ The girl in the slumber-boots / by Jean Randolph Searles [pseud.] . . . Cincinnati: Press of Jennings and Graham, [c1912]. 316 p., front. **DLC**
LC: O 24, '12.

S-239 Sears, Annie Lyman. The primary allegiance / by Annie Lyman Sears. Boston: B. J. Brimmer Company, 1924. 349 p.   **FDA**

S-240 Sears, Baldwin. The circle in the square: the story of a new battle on old fields / by Baldwin Sears. New York: A. S. Barnes & Company, 1903. 396 p.
BLC: New York: A. S. Barnes & Co.; London: Authors' Syndicate, 1903.

S-241 Sears, Clara Endicott, b. 1863. The bell-ringer: an old-time village tale / by Clara Endicott Sears; with illustrations. Boston; New York: Houghton Mifflin Company, 1918. 292 p., front., [3] leaves of plates. [Ill. by Genevieve Alameda Cowles.]
LC: S 28, '18.
PW: S 28, '18.

S-242 ____ The romance of Fiddler's green / by Clara Endicott Sears. Boston; New York: Houghton Mifflin Company, 1922. (Cambridge: The Riverside Press). 239 p.
LC: Mr 6, '22.
PW: Mr 18, '22.

S-243 Sears, Edmund Hamilton, 1852-1942. The son of the prefect: a story of the reign of Tiberius / by Edmund Hamilton Sears. Boston: R. G. Badger; Toronto: The Copp Clark Co., Limited, [c1914]. 449 p.
LC: O 30, '14.
PW: N 7, '14.

S-244 ____ Zatthu: a tale of ancient Galilee / by Edmund Hamilton Sears. Boston: The Cornhill Publishing Company, [c1925]. 467 p.
LC: My 25, '25.
PW: Ag 1, '25.

S-245 Sears, Joseph Hamblen, 1865-1946. A box of matches / by Hamblen Sears . . . ; illustrations by Will Grefé. New York: Dodd, Mead & Company, 1904. 369 p., incl. col. front., [4] leaves of plates. [Front. by Harrison Fisher.]
PW: O 15, '04.

S-246 ____ None but the brave / by Hamblen Sears. New York: Dodd Mead & Company, 1902. 309 p., col. front., [7] leaves of col. plates. [Ill. by Emlen McConnell.]
PW: Ap 12, '02.
BLC: London: B. F. Stevens & Brown, New York printed, [1912].

S-247 Sears, Margaret L. Menotomy: romance of 1776 / by Margaret L. Sears. Boston: Richard G. Badger, 1908. (Boston: The Gorham Press). 276 p.
LC: O 29, '08.

S-248 Seattle Writers' Club. Tillicum tales / by the Seattle Writers' Club; illustrated by original drawings and photographs. Seattle: Lowman & Hanford, 1907. 306 p., [12] leaves of plates (some photo.), ill. [Ill. by E. M. Lee and Margaret Josenhans.]
Contents: Laying the ghost / by E. C. Daugherty -- A Gordian knot / by S. P. Carr -- Gulls / by Emma Parsons Josenhans -- Northbound by night / by G. Houghton -- Under the flatiron / by F. Huntley -- The chief's counterplot / by E. A. Jordan -- A matrimonial epidemic at Skookum / by F. M. Eastland -- A letter to Cecilia / by M. V. McGill -- Five dollars / by F. Maring -- The taming of the barons / by C. C. Charlton -- Under the tricolor / by F. K. Byers -- A maker of violins / by K. Wilson -- An extenuating circumstance / by E. A. Low -- Ye tithe mint and rue / by E. B. Edwards -- On the edge of Death Valley / by A. M. Walden -- The recoil of circumstance / by F. M. Farrer -- A doubtful nationality / by E. M. Lee -- Old Bill's awkward squad / by A. H. Browne -- The burglar's dilemma / by W. D. Johns.
LC: N 15, '07.

S-249 Seavy, Tom. Dom Quick Jota / by Tom Seavy. Wantagh, New York: Bartlett Publishing Company, 1916. 281 p.   **DRB**

S-250 Seawell, Molly Elliot, 1860-1916. Betty at Fort Blizzard / by Molly Elliot Seawell . . . ; with illustrations in color and from pen drawings by Edmund Frederick. Philadelphia; London: J. B. Lippincott Company, 1916. 223, [1] p., col. front., [3] leaves of col. plates, ill.
Published serially in the Book news monthly under title: Colonel Fortescue's Betty.
LC: N 8, '16.

S-251   ____ Betty's Virginia Christmas / by Molly Elliot Seawell; with illustrations in color by Henry J. Soulen and decorations by Edward Stratton Holloway. Philadelphia; London: J. B. Lippincott Company, 1914. 213, [1] p., col. front., [3] leaves of col. plates, ill.
LC: O 15, '14.
PW: O 10, '14.

S-252   ____ The chateau of Montplaisir / by Molly Elliot Seawell. New York: D. Appleton and Company, 1906. 245 p., front., [3] leaves of plates. [Ill. by Gordon H. Grant.]
PW: Ap 7, '06.

S-253   [____] Despotism and democracy: a study in Washington society and politics. New York: McClure, Phillips and Company, 1903. 311 p.

S-254   ____ The diary of a beauty: a story / by Molly Elliot Seawell . . . ; with twelve illustrations by Frederick Dorr Steele. Philadelphia; London: J. B. Lippincott Company, 1915. 212 p., front., [11] leaves of plates.   **NDD**
LC: Ap 16, '15.
PW: Mr 27, '15.

S-255   ____ The fortunes of Fifi / by Molly Elliot Seawell; the illustrations by T. de Thulstrup. Indianapolis: The Bobbs-Merrill Company, [c1903]. 238, [1] p., col. front., [5] leaves of col. plates. Designed end papers.   **NDD**
PW: S 12, '03.

S-256   ____ Francezka / by Molly Elliot Seawell; illustrated by Harrison Fisher. Indianapolis: The Bowen-Merrill Company, [c1902]. 466 p., front., [6] leaves of plates.
PW: N 15, '02.
BLC: London: B. F. Stevens & Brown, 1902.

S-257   ____ The jugglers: a story / by Molly Elliot Seawell; with a frontispiece. New York: The Macmillan Company, 1911. 193 p., col. front. [Ill. by Charles S. Chapman.]   **CWR**
LC: O 19, '11.

S-258   ____ The last Duchess of Belgarde / by Molly Elliot Seawell. New York: D. Appleton and Company, 1908. 121, [1] p., col. front., ill. Title within ornamental border.
LC: Je 5, '08.
PW: Je 6, '08.

S-259   ____ The marriage of Theodora / by Molly Elliot Seawell. New York: Dodd, Mead and Company, 1910. 392 p., col. front. [Ill. by the Kinneys.]
LC: Ap 1, '10.
PW: Ap 2, '10.

S-260   [____] Mrs. Darrell / by Foxcroft Davis [pseud.]; with illustrations by William Sherman Potts. New York: The Macmillan Company; London: Macmillan & Co., 1905. 391 p., front., [5] leaves of plates.

S-261   ____ Papa Bouchard / by Molly Elliot Seawell; illustrated by William Glackens. New York: Charles Scribner's Sons, 1901. 261 p.
LC: O 4, '01.
PW: O 12, '01.

S-262   ____ The secret of Toni / Molly Elliot Seawell . . . ; illustrated by George Brehm. New York: D. Appleton and Company, 1907. 330, [1] p., front., [16] leaves of plates.   **WOO**
PW: F 2, '07.

S-263   ____ The son of Columbus / by Molly Elliot Seawell . . . ; illustrated. New York; London: Harper & Brothers, 1912. 236, [1] p., front., [3] leaves of plates. [Ill. by Victor Pérard.]
LC: S 14, '12.

S-264   ____ The victory / by Molly Elliot Seawell . . . New York: D. Appleton and Company, 1906. 405 p., front., [3] leaves of plates. [Ill. by John Wolcott Adams.]
LC: O 5, '06.
PW: O 13, '06.

S-265   [____] The whirl: a romance of Washington society / by Foxcroft Davis [pseud.]; with illustrations by Harrison Fisher and B. Martin Justice. New York: Dodd, Mead & Company, 1909. 306 p., col. front., [2] leaves of col. plates.
LC: Je 9, '09.
PW: Je 5, '09.

Second, Henry, pseud. <u>See</u> **Harrison, Henry Sydnor, 1880-1930.**

S-266   Second suds sayings: a collection of stories, sketches and articles regarding the laundry / by well known writers; selected by Charles Dowst . . . Chicago: Published by National Laundry Journal, Dowst Bros. Co., [c1919]. 204, [3] p., photo. front. (port.), [1] leaf of plates. [Ill. by T. J. Nicholl.]   **MUU**
Contents: A Christmas invasion / Charles Lederer -- Ahead of the world / Wolf van Shierbrand -- And the woman? / Kirke La Shelle -- Around the world / George Horton -- A rusher / Opie Read -- A story from Cuba / A.K. Potter -- A thrifty woman / Colonel Will Visscher -- Did you ever hire him? / A.K. Potter -- Down in old Mexico / A.K. Potter -- Efficiency-your own / Frank W. Porter -- Evolution / Wm. E. Fitch -- Getting laundry in war / Richard Henry Little -- Good advice / Charles Dowst -- Hard on the manager / H.H. Spencer -- Her conscience troubled her / Wm. E. Fitch -- If / Wm. E. Fitch -- Laugh it off / Wm. E. Fitch -- Laundering in Asia / Frank G. Carpenter.
LC: Mr 29, '19.

S-267   The Secret of Table Rock: a composite tale / written by members of the Winter Evening Reading Club, of Saint Albans, Vermont. Saint Albans, Vermont: Published by R. A. Brush, 1904. 71 p.   **VSL**

S-268   Sedberry, J. Hamilton (James Hamilton), b. 1863. Under the flag of the cross / by J. Hamilton Sedberry. Boston: C. M. Clark Publishing Co., 1908. 472 p., front., [9] leaves of plates. [Some ill. by W. Kirkpatrick.]

S-269   Sedgwick, Anne Douglas, 1873-1935. Adrienne Toner: a novel / by Anne Douglas Sedgwick (Mrs. Basil de Sélincourt). Boston; New York: Houghton

Mifflin Company, 1922. (Cambridge: The Riverside Press). 374 p.
LC: Ap 26, '22.
PW: Ap 22, '22.
BLC: London: E. Arnold & Co., 1921.

S-270   ____ Amabel Channice / by Anne Douglas Sedgwick. New York: The Century Co., 1908. 256 p.
LC: S 24, '08.
PW: O 10, '08.
BLC: London: Edward Arnold, 1908.

S-271   ____ Christmas roses: and other stories / by Anne Douglas Sedgwick (Mrs. Basil de Sélincourt) . . . Boston; New York: Houghton Mifflin Company, 1920. (Cambridge [Mass.]: The Riverside Press). 325, [1] p.
Contents: Christmas roses -- Hepaticas -- Daffodils -- Pansies -- Pink foxgloves -- Carnations -- Staking a larkspur -- Evening primroses -- Autumn crocuses.
LC: N 23, '20.
PW: D 11, '20.

S-272   ____ The encounter / by Anne Douglas Sedgwick (Mrs. Basil de Sélincourt). New York: The Century Co., 1914. 387 p.
LC: O 19, '14.
PW: O 10, '14.
BLC: London: Edward Arnold, 1914.

S-273   ____ A fountain sealed / by Anne Douglas Sedgwick (Mrs. Basil de Sélincourt) . . . Boston; New York: Houghton Mifflin Company, 1908, [c1907]. (Cambridge [Mass.]: The Riverside Press). 405 p.
"This book is published in England under the title of *Valerie Upton*.
LC: S 20, '07.
PW: O 12, '07.

S-274   ____ Franklin Winslow Kane / by Anne Douglas Sedgwick (Mrs. Basil de Sélincourt) . . . New York: The Century Co., 1910. 369 p.
LC: Ap 18, '10.
PW: Ap 23, '10.
BLC: London: Edward Arnold, 1910.

____ Hepaticas. In *Atlantic narratives*; first series **(1918), A-360.**

S-275   ____ The little French girl / by Anne Douglas Sedgwick (Mrs. Basil de Sélincourt). Boston; New York: Houghton Mifflin Company, 1924. (Cambridge: The Riverside Press). 508 p.
LC: S 2, '24.

S-276   ____ The nest; The white pagoda; The suicide; A forsaken temple; Miss Jones and the masterpiece / by Anne Douglas Sedgwick (Mrs. Basil de Sélincourt). New York: The Century Co., 1913. 302 p.
Partly reprinted from various periodicals.
LC: Ja 4, '13.
BLC: London: Edward Arnold, 1912.

S-277   ____ Paths of judgement / by Anne Douglas Sedgwick . . . New York: The Century Co., 1904. 346 p.

PW: O 15, '04.
BLC: London: Archibald Constable & Co., 1904.

S-278   ____ The rescue / by Anne Douglas Sedgwick. New York: The Century Co., 1902. 243 p., col. front. [Ill. by A. I. Keller.]
PW: My 10, '02.
BLC: London: John Murray, 1902.

S-279   ____ The shadow of life / by Anne Douglas Sedgwick . . . New York: The Century Co., 1906. 330 p.
PW: Mr 10, '06.
BLC: London: Archibald Constable & Co., 1906.

S-280   ____ Tante / by Anne Douglas Sedgwick (Mrs. Basil de Sélincourt). New York: The Century Co., 1911. 437 p.
LC: D 26, '11.
PW: Ja 20, '12.
BLC: London: Edward Arnold, 1911.

S-281   ____ The third window / by Anne Douglas Sedgwick (Mrs. Basil de Sélincourt). Boston; New York: Houghton Mifflin Company, 1920. (Cambridge: The Riverside Press). 154, [2] p.
LC: Je 8, '20.
PW: Je 5, '20.
BLC: London: Martin Secker, 1920.

S-282   Seebach, Julius, b. 1869. The singing weaver and other stories: hero tales of the Reformation / by Julius and Margaret Seebach; illustrations by Jessie Gillespie. Philadelphia, Pa.: The Lutheran Publication Society, 1917. 288 p., [2] leaves of plates. Illustrated title page on double leaf plate.
Contents: The singing weaver -- Her little Bible -- At the king's bidding -- The good little hen -- Lady Philippine's Easter gift -- At the turn of the tide -- His Majesty's potter -- The price of a book -- The courage of Grizel -- The glorious return.
LC: Jl 17, '17.
PW: Jl 21, '17.

Seebach, Margaret R. (Margaret Rebecca), 1875-1948, jt. aut. *The singing weaver and other stories,* (1917). See **Seebach, Julius, b. 1869, jt. aut., S-282.**

S-283   ____ That man Donaleitis: a story of the coal regions / by Margaret R. Seebach . . . Philadelphia, Pa.: The United Lutheran Publication House, [c1909]. 451 p., front.
LC: Ag 31, '09.

S-284   Seel, Earl Marion. Her wild oat / by Earl Marion Seel. Philadelphia: Dorrance & Company, [c1921]. 346 p.   **DLC**

S-285   Seelig, Rayner. The eternal huntress / by Rayner Seelig. New York: Alfred A. Knopf, 1924. 229 p.
LC: O 24, '24.
BLC: London: T. Fisher Unwin, 1926.

S-286   Seibel, George, 1872-1958. The fall: being a true account of what happened in paradise, for the benefit of all scandal-mongers, with a new interpretation of sacred history, vindicating snakes and apples / by

Geroge Seibel. Pittsburgh: Lessing Company, c1918. 62 p.
Unexamined copy: bibliographic data from OCLC, #6899029.

S-287   Seibert, Venita, b. 1875. The gossamer thread: being the chronicles of Velleda, who understood about "the different world" / by Venita Seibert; illustrated by W. T. Benda. Boston: Small, Maynard & Company, [c1910]. 224 p., front., [4] leaves of plates.
PW: Jl 9, '10.

S-288   Seitz, Howard Buckwalter, b. 1886. Stephen Mulhew: the making of a gentle man / by Howard B. Seitz . . . New York: The Cosmopolitan Press, 1912. 489 p., front.
Unexamined copy: bibliographic data from NUC.
LC: S 16, '12.

S-289   Selders, Adelbert. The native son who loses his identity / by A. Selders. [Albemarle, N. C.?]: Published by the Stanly Republican and Selders' Weekly, c1924. 128 p.   KSU
LC: O 8, '24.

S-290   Selkirk, Emily. The stigma / by Emily Selkirk. Boston: Herbert B. Turner & Co., 1906. 272 p.
PW: My 5, '06.

S-291   Selph, Fannie Eoline (Atkinson). Texas, or, The broken link in the chain of family honors: a romance of the Civil War / by Fannie Eoline Selph. West Nashville, Tenn.: [s. n., c1905]. 245 p., front., [5] leaves of plates. [Ill. by Burdette M. Phelps and Nancy Armistead.]

S-292   Seltzer, Charles Alden, 1875-1942. "Beau" Rand / by Charles Alden Seltzer; frontispiece by P. V. E. Ivory. Chicago: A. C. McClurg & Co., 1921. 311 p., front.
LC: N 1, '21.
PW: N 19, '21.

S-293   Seltzer, Charles Alden, 1875-1942. The boss of the Lazy Y / by Charles Alden Seltzer; illustrations by J. Allen St. John. Chicago: A. C. McClurg & Co., 1915. 346, [1] p., front., plates.
Unexamined copy: bibliographic data from OCLC, #6565538.
LC: Ap 12, '15.
PW: Ap 24, '15.
BLC: London: C. F. Cazonove; Chicago: A. C McClurg & Co., 1915.

S-294   _____ Brass commandments / by Charles Alden Seltzer. New York; London: The Century Co., 1923. 301 p., front. [Ill. by Modest Stein.]
LC: Ag 22, '23.
PW: S 1, '23.
BLC: London: Hodder & Stoughton, [1923].

S-295   _____ Channing comes through / by Charles Alden Seltzer . . . New York; London: Published by The Century Co., [c1925]. 429 p.
LC: O 2, '25.

PW: O 10, '25.
BLC: London: Hodder & Stoughton, [1926].

S-296   _____ The coming of the law / by Charles Alden Seltzer; frontispiece in color by R. W. Amick. New York: Outing Publishing Company, 1912. 378 p., col. front.
LC: O 18, '12.
BLC: London: T. Nelson & Sons, [1924].

S-297   _____ "Drag" Harlan / by Charles Alden Seltzer . . . ; frontispiece by P. V. E. Ivory. Chicago: A. C. McClurg & Co., 1921. 280 p., front.
LC: My 28, '21.
PW: Je 11, '21.

S-298   _____ "Firebrand" Trevison / by Charles Alden Seltzer . . . ; illustrated by P. V. E. Ivory. Chicago: A. C. McClurg & Co., 1918. 325 p., front., [2] leaves of plates.
LC: S 25, '18.
BLC: London: Methuen & Co., 1920.

S-299   _____ Last Hope ranch / by Charles Alden Seltzer. New York; London: Published by the Century Co., [c1925]. 335 p.
LC: Ap 21, '25.
PW: Ap 18, '25.

S-300   _____ The ranchman / by Charles Alden Seltzer . . . ; frontispiece by P. V. E. Ivory. Chicago: A. C. McClurg & Co., 1919. 319 p., col. front.
LC: S 22, '19.
PW: N 1, '19.

S-301   _____ The range boss / by Charles Alden Seltzer . . . ; illustrated by Frank E. Schoonover. Chicago: A. C. McClurg & Co., 1916. 333, [1] p., col. front., [3] leaves of col. plates.
LC: O 2, '16.
PW: S 30, '16.
BLC: London: Curtis Brown, Chicago: A. C. McClurg & Co., 1916.

S-302   _____ The range riders / by Charles Alden Seltzer; illustrated by Clarence Rowe. New York: Outing Publishing Company, 1911. 310 p., front., ill.
Contents: The double cross -- The trail of the serpent -- The kid and the cowboys -- The messenger from Conejos -- A tragedy on Little Elk -- The man who rode "Purgatory" -- The execution of Lanky -- The sixteeth man -- The nester of Carrizo -- The prince of the Z O.
LC: Ap 8, '11.
PW: Ap 15, '11.

S-303   _____ Square Deal Sanderson / by Charles Alden Seltzer; frontispiece by J. Allen St. John. Chicago: A. C. McClurg & Co., 1922. 323 p., front.
LC: Mr 28, '22.

S-304   _____ The trail horde / by Charles Alden Seltzer; frontispiece by P. V. E. Ivory. Chicago: A. C. McClurg & Co., 1920. 345 p., front.
LC: S 20, '20.
PW: O 16, '20.

S-305   _____ The trail to yesterday / by Charles Alden Seltzer . . . ; illustrated. New York: Outing

Publishing Company, 1913. 363 p., col. front., [2] leaves of plates. [Ill. by Robert W. Amick.]
LC: O 16, '13.
PW: N 8, '13.

S-306 _____ The Triangle cupid / by Charles Allen [i. e., Alden] Seltzer . . . ; illustrated. New York: Outing Publishing Company, 1912. 268 p., ill. [Ill. by V. C. Forsythe, Robert W. Amick, and Clarence Rowe.]
NBU
Partly reprinted from various periodicals.
Contents: The Triangle cupid -- The horse thief -- The man on the ridge -- The fear -- The special messenger -- The high card -- The thief at Circle Bar -- The reformation of "Two-Gun" Harlan.
LC: Je 10, '12.
PW: Jl 6, '12.

S-307 _____ The two-gun man / by Charles Alden Seltzer . . . ; illustrated with frontispiece by Robert W. Amick. New York: Outing Publishing Company, 1911. 349 p., col. front.
LC: N 3, '11.
PW: N 18, '11.

S-308 _____ The vengeance of Jefferson Gawne / by Charles Alden Seltzer . . . ; illustrated by P. V. E. Ivory. Chicago: A. C. McClurg & Co., 1917. 344 p., front., [3] leaves of plates.
LC: O 2, '17.
PW: O 27, '17.

S-309 _____ The way of the buffalo / by Charles Alden Seltzer . . . New York; London: Published by The Century Co., [c1924]. 318 p., front. [Ill. by Remington Schuyler.]
LC: Ag 19, '24.

S-310 _____ West! / by Charles Alden Seltzer; illustrated by W. M. Allison. New York: The Century Co., 1922. 312 p., front., [3] leaves of plates.
LC: Ag 24, '22.
PW: Ag 26, '22.

Sembower, Alta Brunt. The chaperon. In *A book of narratives* (1917), B-734.

S-311 Senger, Thomas B. It happened in Atlantic City / by Thomas B. Senger. Boston: Richard G. Badger; Toronto: The Copp Clark Co., Limited, [c1915]. 202 p.
LC: Ap 27, '15.

S-312 The Senior lieutenant's wager: and other stories / by Mary G. Bonesteel, H. J. Carroll, Mrs. Francis Chadwick . . . [et al.]. New York; Cincinnati; Chicago: Benziger Brothers . . . , [c1905]. 256 p.
UCW
"Stories by the foremost Catholic writers."
Contents: The senior lieutenant's wager / by Mary G. Bonesteel -- Father Jame's snuff box / by H. J. Carroll -- The dream warning / by Mrs. Francis Chadwick -- The invitation / by Louisa Emily Dobree -- Little Nightengale's strange story / by Eleanor C. Donnelly -- The heart of hearts / by Maurice Francis Egan -- " Not Mentioned in despatches" / by Theo. Gift. -- Down the incline / by Leigh Gordon Giltner -- A midnight call / by Jerome Hart -- A Nürnberg treasure / by Katharine Jenkins -- In after years / by Margaret E. Jordan -- How Dan went home / by Grace Keon -- Pilgrims of the night / by Rev T. J. Livingstone, S. J. A little romance in Avila / by Anna Blanche McGill -- "Where laughter dies" / by Madge Mannix -- The rich Miss Bannerman / by Mary E. Mannix -- Old Bartley Bannim / by

Cathirine L. Meagher -- The ghost-chest of knockmarroon / by Clara Mulholland -- In mere Clichy's garden / by Mary F. Nixon-Roulet -- Luigi of the bells Mary Boyle O'Reilly -- A daughter of duty / by Alice Richardson -- A broken engagement / by Magdalen Rock -- "The Soggarth's curse" / by Agnes M. Rowe -- John Lesperance, master / by Anna T. Sadlier -- From over the sea / by Teresa Stanton -- In passing / by Marion Ames Taggart -- An idle girl / by Katherine Tynan -- Breaking the news / by Eugenie Uhlrich -- The Bretherton bowl / by Mary T. Waggaman -- A piece of pink ribbon / by Emma Howard Wight.

Sergeant, My, pseud. <u>See</u> **Sturgis, Granville Forbes, b. 1880.**

S-313 Sergel, Roger L. Arlie Gelston / by Roger L. Sergel. New York: B. W. Huebsch, Inc., 1923. 420 p.
LC: F 11, '23.

_____ Glare of circumstance. In *Stories from the Midland* (1924), S-983.

_____ Nocturne: a red shawl. In *The best short stories of 1924 and the yearbook of the American short story* (1925), B-569.

S-314 Serl, Elmer Willis. Whillikins: a study in social hysteria / by Elmer Willis Serl . . . New York: The Neale Publishing Company, 1913. 131 p.
LC: Ja 10, '14.

S-315 Serviss, Garrett Putman, 1851-1929. A Columbus of space / by Garrett P. Serviss . . . ; illustrated. New York; London: D. Appleton and Company, 1911. 297, [1] p., front., [3] leaves of plates. [Ill. by Howard Heath.]
LC: S 21, '11.

S-316 _____ The second deluge / by Garrett P. Serviss . . . ; illustrations by George Varian. New York: McBride, Nast & Company, 1912. 399 p., front., [3] leaves of plates.
LC: Ap 13, '12.
BLC: London: Grant Richards, Rahway, N. J. printed, 1912.

Sessions, Archibald, jt. aut. *Building the union* (1917). <u>See</u> **Woodrow, Wilson, Mrs., 1875?-1935, jt. aut., W-855.**

S-317 Seton, Ernest Thompson, 1860-1946. Animal heroes: being the histories of a cat, a dog, a pigeon, a lynx, two wolves & a reindeer and in elucidation of the same over 200 drawings / by Ernest Thompson Seton . . . New York: Charles Scribner's Sons, 1905. 362 p.
"In this book the designs for cover, title-page, and general make-up were done by Grace Gallatin Seton."
Contents: The slum cat -- Arnaux: the chronicle of a homing pigeon -- Badlands Billy: the wolf that won -- The boy and the lynx -- Little warhouse: the history of a jackrabbit -- Snap: the story of a bull terrier -- The Winnipeg wolf -- The legend of the white reindeer.
BLC: London: Archibald Constable & Co., 1906.

S-318 _____ Monarch, the big bear of Tallac / with 100 drawings by Ernest Thompson Seton . . . New York: Published by Charles Scribner's Sons, 1904. 214 p.
PW: O 29, '04.
BLC: London: Archibald Constable & Co., 1905.

S-319 ____ The preacher of Cedar Mountain: a tale of the open country / by Ernest Thompson Seton; frontispiece by Clarence Rowe. Garden City, New York: Doubleday, Page & Company, 1917. 426 p., col. front.
LC: My 2, '17.
PW: My 5, '17.
BLC: London: Curtis Brown; Garden City, N. Y. printed, 1917.
Another edition: London: Hodder & Stonghton, [1917].

____ The ten trails. In *Modern short stories* **(1918), M-879.**

S-320 ____ Wild animal ways / by Ernest Thompson Seton . . . ; with 200 drawings by the author. Garden City, New York: Doubleday, Page & Company, 1916. 247, [1] p., front., [7] leaves of plates. **KSU**
Contents: Coaly Bay, the outlaw horse -- Foam, or the life and adventures of a razor-backed hog -- Way-Atcha, the coon-raccoon of Kilder Creek -- Billy, the dog that made good -- Atalapha, a winged brownie -- The wild geese of Wyndygoul -- Jinny, the taming of a bad monkey.
LC: My 27, '16.
PW: My 27, '16.
BLC: London: Hodder & Stoughton, Garden City, N. J. [sic], printed, [1916].

S-321 Seton, Julia, b. 1862. Destiny: a new-thought novel / by Julia Seton . . . New York: Edward J. Clode, [c1917]. 324 p.
PW: S 15, '17.

S-322 Severy, Melvin L. (Melvin Linwood), b. 1863. The Darrow enigma / by Melvin L. Severy; with illustrations by C. D. Williams. New York: Dodd, Mead & Company, 1904. 341 p., front., [4] leaves of plates.
PW: Ap 9, '04.
BLC: London: Grant Richards, New York [printed], 1904.

S-323 ____ Maitland's master mystery / by Melvin L. Severy . . . Boston: The Ball Publishing Company, 1912. 356 p.
LC: Ja 25, '13.

S-324 ____ The mystery of June 13th / by Melvin L. Severy . . . ; illustrated by The Kinneys. New York: Dodd, Mead and Company, 1905. 569 p., front., [5] leaves of plates, diagrams.
PW: N 11, '05.
BLC: London: B. F. Stevens & Brown, New York printed, 1905.

S-325 [Seymour, George Steele], b. 1878. Chronicles of Bagdad: an oriental fantasy / by Abdul Hassan [pseud.]. Chicago: The Bookfellows, 1923. 113 p.

S-326 Seymour, Jim. Hellaloo Pete o' Reno / by Jim Seymour; with an introduction by Upton Sinclair. [Pasadena, Calif.: U. Sinclair, c1919]. 17 p.
Unexamined copy: bibliographic data from OCLC, #21018909.

S-327 Seymour, Pliny Berthier. Woodhull / by Pliny Berthier Seymour; illustrations by William Kirkpatrick. Boston, Massachusetts: The C. M. Clark Publishing Co., 1907. 376 p., front., [9] leaves of plates.
LC: S 4, '07.
PW: O 5, '07.

S-328 Shackelford, Ethel. The jumping-off place / by Ethel Shackelford . . . New York: George H. Doran Company [c1913]. 307 p. **MPI**
LC: My 24, '13.
PW: My 17, '13.

S-329 ____ The life of me / by Ethel Shackelford; with illustrations by Harry L. Miller. Published in New York: Dodge Publishing Company, [c1910]. 286 p., double-leaf front. and t. p., [42] leaves of plates, ill.
LC: Jl 30, '10.

S-330 Shackelford, Henry. The lost king / by Henry Shackelford. New York; Paris; Chicago; Washington: Brentano's, 1903. 272 p., front., [5] leaves of plates, ill., map. [Ill. by HBM, i. e., Harry B. Matthews.]
PW: D 5, '03.

S-331 Shackelford, Otis M., b. 1871. Lillian Simmons; or, The conflict of sections; a story / by Otis M. Shackelford . . . illustrated by William Hamilton. Kansas City, Mo.: Burton Publishing Company [c1915]. 210 p., incl. front., ill. **NAM**

S-332 Shackleton, Robert, 1860-1923. The great adventurer / by Robert Shackleton. New York: Doubleday, Page and Co., 1904. 356 p.
PW: Mr 19, '04.

S-333 ____ Many waters: a story of New York / by Robert Shackleton . . . New York: D. Appleton and Company, 1902. 372 p.
PW: Ap 26, '02.

S-334 Shafer, Don Cameron, b. 1881. Barent Creighton: a romance / by Don Cameron Shafer. New York: Alfred A. Knopf, 1920. 327 p.
PW: Jl 17, '20.

S-335 Shafer, Sara Andrew, d. 1913. Beyond chance of change / by Sara Andrew Shafer. New York: The Macmillan Company; London: Macmillan & Co., Ltd., 1905. 295 p.
PW: Mr 11, '05.

S-336 Shaffner, Lillyan. Suzanne / by Lillyan Shaffner. Chicago: Monarch Book Company, [c1906]. 392 p., front., [11] leaves of plates. [Ill. by S. L. Holmes.]

S-337 Shands, Hubert Anthony, 1872-1955. The most foolish of all things / by Hubert Anthony Shands. Boston: Richard G. Badger, 1919. ([Boston]: The Gorham Press). 195 p. **ORE**
Another issue by H. Anthony, pseud.
LC: Mr 10, '19.

S-338 ____ White and black / by Hubert Anthony Shands. New York: Harcourt, Brace and Company, [c1922].

304 p.
LC: Mr 15, '22.
PW: Ap 1, '22.
BLC: London: Jonathan Cape, 1922.

Shane, Peggy (Smith), Mrs., b. 1898. See **Boyd, Woodward, pseud.**

S-339   Shapes that haunt the dusk / edited by William Dean Howells and Henry Mills Alden. New York; London: Harper & Brothers Publishers, [c1907]. 301 p.   **OSU, TOL**
(Harper's novelettes).
Contents: The Christmas child / Georg Schock -- The white sleep of Auber Hurn / Richard Rice -- In tenebras / Howard Pyle -- The little room / Madelene Yale Wynne -- The bringing of the rose / Harriet Lewis Bradley -- Perdita / Hildegarde Hawthorne -- At La Glorieuse / M. E. M. Davis -- A faded scapular / F. D. Millet -- At the hermitage / E. Levi Brown -- The reprisal / H. W. McVickar.
LC: Je 14, '07.
PW: D 21, '07.
References: BAL 9781; Gibson & Arms 07-C.

S-340   Shapiro, Anna Ratner. The birth of universal brotherhood / by Anna Ratner Shapiro. Kansas City, Mo.: Burton Publishing Co., [1916]. 268 p., col. front., [1] leaf of plates.   **NYP**
Another edition: Red Ruth: the birth of Universal Brotherhood; illustrated by Carl S. Junge. Chicago: Arc Publishing Co., 1917.
LC: O 30, '17.

S-341   Sharber, Kate Trimble, b. 1883. Amazing Grace: who proves that virtue has its silver lining / by Kate Trimble Sharber; illustrated by R. M. Crosby. Indianapolis: The Bobbs-Merrill Company, [c1914]. 327 p., front., [3] leaves of plates.
LC: N 11, '14.
PW: N 14, '14.

S-342   _____ The annals of Ann / by Kate Trimble Sharber; with illustrations by Paul J. Meylan. Indianapolis: The Bobbs-Merrill Company, [c1910]. 277, [1] p., front., [4] leaves of plates.
LC: N 2, '10.
PW: N 5, '10.

S-343   _____ At the age of Eve / by Kate Trimble Sharber . . . ; with illustrations by Paul Meylan. Indianapolis: The Bobbs-Merrill Company, [c1911]. 354 p., front.
LC: N 1, '11.
PW: N 4, '11.

Sharon, John Jones. Angéle. In *The best college short stories, 1917-18* **(1919), B-557.**

S-344   _____ The grey gander / by John Jones Sharon. New York: Duffield & Company, 1925. 311 p.

S-345   Sharp, Benjamin, 1858-1915? A captain of the vanished fleet / by Benjamin Sharp. Boston; New York; Chicago: The Pilgrim Press, [c1915]. 40 p.   **DRB**
"Published first in The Atlantic monthly of August, 1907."
LC: Jl 9, '15.

Sharp, D. L. The spirit of the herd. In *Atlantic narratives*; **first series (1918), A-360.**

S-346   Sharp, Katharine. Jocelyn West: a tale of the Grand Cañon / by Katharine Sharp. New York; London: The Goodhue Company, [c1912]. 189 p.
LC: S 20, '12.

S-347   Sharts, Joseph W. (Joseph William), b. 1875. The black sheep / by Joseph Sharts; pictures by John Rae. New York: Duffield & Company, 1909. 303 p., front., [3] leaves of plates.
LC: S 14, '09.
PW: O 2, '09.

S-348   _____ Ezra Caine / by Joseph Sharts. Chicago: Published by Herbert S. Stone & Company, 1901. 142 p.   **UCW**
LC: My 30, '01.
PW: Je 22, '01.

S-349   Sharts, Joseph William, b. 1875. The hills of freedom / by Joseph Sharts; illustrated by S. J. Dudley. New York: Doubleday, Page & Company, 1904. 296 p., front., [3] leaves of plates.
PW: D 3, '04.

S-350   _____ The king who came: a tale of the great revolt / by Joseph W. Sharts . . . New York: Duffield & Company, 1913. 298 p.
PW: Mr 28, '14.

S-351   _____ The romance of a rogue / by Joseph Sharts. Chicago: Herbert S. Stone & Company, 1902. 249 p., col. front. [Ill. by Frank Hazenplug.]
PW: Ap 5, '02.

S-352   _____ The vintage / by Joseph Sharts . . . New York: Duffield & Company, 1911. 299 p., col. front.
LC: Ap 27, '11.

S-353   Shastid, Thomas Hall, 1866-1947. Simon of Cyrene, dimachaerus splendens, or, The story of a man's (and a nation's) soul / by Thomas Hall Shastid. Ann Arbor, Michigan: George Wahr; London: Wheldon and Wesley, Ltd., 1923. 446 p.
LC: My 24, '23.

S-354   _____ Who shall command thy heart?: a starlight tale / by Thomas Hall Shastid . . . Ann Arbor, Michigan: George Wahr, Publisher to University of Michigan, 1924. 367 p.
LC: O 25. '24.

S-355   Shaw, Adèle Marie. The coast of freedom: a romance of the adventurous times of the first self-made American / by Adèle Marie Shaw. New York: Doubleday, Page & Company, 1902. 466 p. Written jointly with her brother Albert Judson Shaw.
BLC: London: Hodder & Stoughton, New York [printed], 1903.

S-356   _____ The lady of the dynamos / by Adèle Marie Shaw and Carmelita Beckwith. New York: Henry Holt and Company, 1909. 310 p.
LC: Mr 27, '09.

Shaw, Albert Judson, jt. aut. *The coast of freedom* (1902). See **Shaw, Adèle Marie, jt. aut., S-355.**

S-357 Shaw, Stanley, b. 1870. Hearts afire / by Stanley Shaw; frontispiece by Harold Denison. New York: The Macaulay Company, [c1924]. 320 p., front.
PW: N 8, '24.

S-358 ____ A siren of the snows / by Stanley Shaw; with illustration by Douglas Duer. Boston: Little, Brown, and Company, 1915. 328 p., front.
LC: Mr 15, '15.
BLC: London: Hodder & Stoughton, [1925].

S-359 ____ The woman tamer / by Stanley Shaw . . . ; frontispiece by Frank Tenney Johnson. New York: The Macaulay Company, [c1923]. 311 p., front.
LC: O 9, '23.
PW: O 6, '23.
BLC: London: Hodder & Stoughton, [1924].

S-360 Shaw-Fullilove, Maggie, 1884-1918. Who was responsible? / by Maggie Shaw Fullilove. Cincinnati: Printed for the author by the Abingdon Press, [1919?]. 181 p., photo. front. (port.). **IAY**

Shawcross, Howard. The krotchet kid. In *The best college short stories, 1917-18* **(1919), B-557.**

S-361 Shea, Cornelius, b. 1863. Love and lure; or, The heart of a "bad" man; a romance of Arizona / by Cornelius Shea; illustrated by O. W. Simons. New York: Broadway Publishing Company, 1912. 299 p., plates.
Unexamined copy: bibliographic data from OCLC, #20752654.
PW: D 21, '12.

Shea, William E. Our sphinx. In *Made to order* **(1915), M-352.**

S-362 Shear, Leah C. The radical millionaire / by Leah C. Shear. Boston, Massachusetts: The Stratford Company, 1923. 320 p., [3] leaves of plates. **UUM**
LC: Je 9, '23.
PW: Jl 14, '23.

Shearer, Augustus Hunt, 1878-1941, ed. See *A little book of Rutgers tales* **(1905), L-378.**

____ Tried twice and true. In *A little book of Rutgers tales* **(1905), L-378.**

S-363 Shearon, Lillian Nicholson. The little mixer / by Lillian Nicholson Shearon. Indianapolis: The Bobbs-Merrill Company, [c1922]. 55 p.
LC: N 20, '22.

S-364 Shedd, George Clifford, 1877-1937. Cryder / by George C. Shedd. Garden City, N. Y.: Doubleday, Page & Company, 1922. 388 p.
LC: O 27, '22.
BLC: London: Curtis Brown, printed in U. S. A., 1922.

S-365 ____ In the shadow of the hills / by George C. Shedd. New York: The Macaulay Company, [c1919]. 319 p.
LC reports incl. front.

LC: N 1, '19.
PW: N 1, '19.

S-366 ____ The incorrigible Dukane / by George C. Shedd . . . ; illustrated by Stanley L. Wood. Boston: Small, Maynard and Company, [c1911]. 359 p., col. front., [3] leaves of plates.
LC: O 11, '11.
PW: O 14, '11.
BLC: London: Stanley Paul & Co., Cambridge, Mass., prt., 1912.

S-367 ____ The invisible enemy / by George C. Shedd . . . New York: The Macaulay Company, 1918. 299 p.
LC: My 29, '18.
PW: Je 8, '18.

S-368 ____ The iron furrow / by George C. Shedd; frontispiece by Henry A. Botkin. Garden City, N. Y.: Doubleday, Page & Company, 1920. 277, [1] p., col. front.
LC: My 4, '20.
PW: Ja 17, '20.

S-369 ____ The isle of strife / by George C. Shedd; illustrated. Boston: Small, Maynard and Company, [c1912]. 375 p., col. front., [2] leaves of plates. [Ill. by George W. Gage.]
LC: Je 6, '12.
PW: Je 15, '12.

S-370 ____ The lady of mystery house / by George C. Shedd. New York: The Macaulay Company, 1917. 336 p., front., [3] leaves of plates. [Ill. by Albert Matzke.]
LC: Mr 19, '17.
PW: Mr 24, '17.
BLC: London: A. M. Gardner & Co., 1920.

S-371 ____ The princess of Forge / by George C. Shedd; illustrated by Howard Giles. New York: The Macaulay Company, 1910. 356 p., col. front., [4] leaves of col. plates.
LC: My 19, '10.
PW: My 14, '10.

S-372 Sheehan, Perley Poore, 1875-1943. The bugler of Algiers / by Perley Poore Sheehan and Robert H. Davis. New York: George H. Doran Company, [c1916]. 127 p., photo. front., [6] leaves of photo. plates.
"Formerly published under the title: *We are French!*, S-738."
LC: D 30, '16.
PW: J 13, '17.

S-373 ____ The house with a bad name / by Perley Poore Sheehan. New York: Boni and Liveright, [c1920]. 375, [1] p.
LC: Mr 18, '21.
PW: N 27, '20.
BLC: London: Brentano's, printed in U. S. A., 1923.

S-374 ____ If you believe it, it's so / by Perley Poore Sheehan; illustrated by Ada Williamson and Paul

Stahr. New York: The H. K. Fly Company, [c1919]. 346 p., front., [2] leaves of plates. **NYP**

S-375 _____ The passport invisible / by Perley Poore Sheehan . . . New York: George H. Doran Company, [c1917]. 241 p.
LC: F 28, '18.
PW: Mr 16, '18.

_____ Princess or Percheron. In *The ten-foot chain* **(1920), T-108.**

S-376 _____ The seer / by Perley Poore Sheehan. New York: Moffat, Yard and Company, 1912. 324 p.
LC: O 11, '12.
PW: O 12, '12.

S-377 _____ Those who walk in darkness / by Perley Poore Sheehan. New York: George H. Doran Company, [c1917]. 394 p.
LC: O 9, '17.
PW: S 29, '17.

S-378 _____ "We are French!" / by Perley Poore Sheehan and Robert H. Davis. New York: George H. Doran Company, [c1914]. 127 p.
LC: O 21, '14.
PW: O 31, '14.
BLC: London: Simpkin, Marshall & Co., 1915.

S-379 Sheehy, Julia Williams. William Winston / by Julia Williams Sheehy. New York: Broadway Publishing Company . . . , [c1913]. 239 p.
LC: N 26, '13.

S-380 Sheets, Emily Churchill Thompson, b. 1875. In Kali's country: tales from sunny India / by Emily T. Sheets; illustrations from drawings by Elma McNeal Childs. New York; Chicago; Toronto; London; Edinburgh: Fleming H. Revell Company, [c1910]. 208 p., front., [7] leaves of plates, ill.
Contents: Kalighat -- Shama Sahai -- Old Sarah -- A son of the law -- Mundra -- Of the tribe of Haunamon -- In ways mysterious -- The way to happiness -- Bachelor dreams -- The cost -- Among the clouds -- The infidel.
LC: Ja 5, '11.

S-381 Sheffield, A. Weber (Albert Weber), b. 1884. The noonday night: a romance of the weak and the strong / by A. Weber Sheffield; illustrations by Martha Fenner Skene. Oakland, Tennessee: The Southland Company, 1906. 325, [1] p., photo. front. (port.), [5] leaves of plates.

S-382 Sheffield, Andrew. Rose of Sharon / by Andrew Sheffield. Boston, Mass., U. S. A.: The C. M. Clark Publishing Co., 1908. 390 p., front., [7] leaves of plates. [Ill. by John Goss.]

S-383 Sheffield, Rena Cary. The Golden Hollow / by Rena Cary Sheffield; with a frontispiece in colour by Earl Stetson Crawford. New York: John Lane Company; London: John Lane, the Bodley Head; Toronto: Bell & Cockburn, 1913. 214 p., col. front.

S-384 Sheldon, Charles Monroe, 1857-1946. All the world / by Charles M. Sheldon . . . New York: George H.

Doran Company, [c1919]. 203 p. **IDG**
"Published in the Christian herald as a serial."
LC: Je 21, '19.

S-385 _____ A builder of ships: the story of Brander Cushing's ambition / by Charles M. Sheldon. New York: Hodder & Stoughton; George H. Doran Company, [c1912]. 282 p.
LC: N 8, '12.
BLC: London: Hodder & Stoughton, 1912.

S-386 _____ The heart of the world: a story of Christian socialism / by Charles M. Sheldon. New York; Chicago; Toronto; London; Edinburgh: Fleming H. Revell Company, [1905]. 265 p.
PW: My 20, '05.

S-387 _____ The high calling / by Charles M. Sheldon . . . New York: Hodder & Stoughton; George H. Doran Company, [c1911]. 352 p. **IMN**
LC: O 9, '11.
BLC: London: Hodder & Stoughton, 1911.

S-388 _____ His mother's prayers / by Charles M. Sheldon. Chicago: Advance Publishing Company, 1903. 29 p. Unexamined copy: bibliographic data from OCLC, #26877389.

S-389 _____ Howard Chase, Red Hill, Kansas / by Charles M. Sheldon. New York: George H. Doran, [c1918]. 291 p.
LC: Ja 28, '18; F 28, '18.
PW: Mr 9, '18.

S-390 _____ "Jesus is here!": continuing the narrative of In His steps (What would Jesus do?) / by Charles M. Sheldon . . . New York: Hodder & Stoughton; George H. Doran Company, [c1914]. 296 p.
LC: Ap 4, '14.

S-391 _____ Modern pagans / by Charles M. Sheldon . . . New York; Cincinnati: The Methodist Book Concern, [c1917]. 79 p. **OSU, IWA**
LC: Ag 24, '17.

S-392 _____ The narrow gate / by Charles M. Sheldon . . . Chicago: Advance Publishing Co., 1903. 230 p.

S-393 _____ Of one blood / by Charles M. Sheldon . . . Boston: Small, Maynard & Company, [c1916]. 339 p.
LC: Je 30, '16.
PW: Ap 22, '16.

S-394 _____ Paul Douglas-journalist / by Charles M. Sheldon . . . Chicago: Advance Publishing Company, 1909. 305 p.
LC: N 26, '09.

S-395 _____ The reformer / by Charles M. Sheldon . . . Chicago, U. S. A.: Advance Publishing Co.; London, England: Ward, Lock & Co., Ltd., 1902, [c1901]. 299 p., [5] leaves of photo. plates.
PW: Ap 11, '03.
BLC: London: Ward, Lock & Co., 1903.

S-396   ____ The richest man in Kansas / by Charles M. Sheldon . . . New York: The Christian Herald Bible House, [c1921]. 61 p., incl. front.
LC: Ag 12, '21.

Sheldon, Edward, 1886-1946, jt. aut. *The boss* (1911). See **McConaughy, J. W., jt. aut., M-66.**

S-397   Sheldon, Georgie, Mrs., b. 1843. Gertrude Elliot's crucible / by Mrs. George Sheldon Downs. New York: G. W. Dillingham Company, [1908]. 308 p., front., [3] leaves of plates. [Ill. by Ch. Grunwald.]
PW: Mr 14, '08.

S-398   ____ Katherine's sheaves / by Mrs. Georgie Sheldon Downs. New York; London: Street & Smith, [1904]. 370 p., front., plates.
Unexamined copy: bibliographic data from OCLC, #25381308.
PW: Je 25, '04.
BLC: London: Shurmer Sib Thorp, [1904].

S-399   ____ Redeemed / by Mrs. George Sheldon Downs; illustrations by Clarence Rowe. New York: G. W. Dillingham Company, [c1911]. 315 p., front., [3] leaves of plates.
LC: S 7, '11.
PW: S 16, '11.

S-400   ____ Step by step: a story of high ideals / by Mrs. George Sheldon Downs. New York: G. W. Dillingham Company, [1906]. 336 p., front., [3] leaves of plates.
LC: Jl 18, '06.
PW: Ag 25, '06.
BLC: London: T. Fisher Unwin, New York [printed], 1906.

S-401   Sheldon, Louise Vescelius. The soul of an organ / by Louise Vescelius-Sheldon. Boston, Mass.: The Christopher Publishing House, [c1916]. 90 p.
Unexamined copy: bibliographic data from OCLC, #30108410.

S-402   Sheldon, Mary Boardman. Coffee and a love affair: an American girl's romance on a coffee plantation / by Mary Boardman Sheldon. New York: Frederick A. Stokes Company, [1908]. 239 p.
LC: Jl 23, '08.

____ Missing. In *Through the forbidden gates* **(1903), T-222.**

S-403   Sheldon, Ruth Louise, 1846-1926. Dolly: a daughter of New England / by Ruth Louise Sheldon; illustrated by Wilhelmina Frederick. Akron, Ohio; Chicago; New York: Published by The Saalfield Publishing Co., [c1905]. 600 p., front., [2] leaves of plates. Designed end papers.

S-404   Shelton, William Henry, b. 1840. The three prisoners: a true story of adventure / by William Henry Shelton; illustrated by Jay Hambidge. New York: A. S. Barnes & Company, 1904. 292 p., front., [5] leaves of plates.

S-405   Shenton, Edward, b. 1895. The gray beginning / by Edward Shenton. Philadelphia: The Penn Publishing Company, 1924. 300 p.
LC: My 14, '24.

S-406   Shepherd, Charles Reginald, b. 1885. The ways of Ah Sin: a composite narrative of things as they are / by Charles R. Shepherd. New York; Chicago; London; Edinburgh: Fleming H. Revell Company, [c1923]. 223 p., photo. front.

S-407   Shepherd, Edith Woodell. A maid of moods: a tale of the Maine woods / by Edith Woodell Shepherd. Boston: The C. M. Clark Publishing Company, [c1910]. 284 p., front., [5] leaves of plates.
LC: O 17, '10.
PW: Ja 14, '11.

S-408   Shepherd, May F. Sadie, or, Happy at last / May F. Shepherd. New York: Broadway Publishing Co., [c1911]. 245 p.   **DLC**
LC: Mr 18, '11.

S-409   Shepherd, William G. (William Gunn), 1878-1933. The scar that tripled: a true story of the Great War / by William G. Shepherd. New York; London: Harper & Brothers, [1918]. 47, [1] p. This story relates the same incident told by Richard Harding Davis in *The deserter* with a continuation of the narrative.

S-410   Sheppard, Nathan Hoyt. Lucile of the vineyard: a temperance romance / by Nathan Hoyt Sheppard . . . Los Angeles, California: N. H. Sheppard . . , 1915. 212 p., photo. front. (port.).
LC: F 16, '16.

Sheppard, William L. My fifth in Mammy. In *Southern lights and shadows* **(1907), S-718.**

Sher, Benjamin R. Abe's card. In *Aces* **(1924), A-42.**

____ Rubber heels. In *More aces* **(1925), M-962.**

S-411   Sheridan, J. Alex. Bob Ryalls: clubman, lover, gambler: an Anglo-American story / by J. Alex Sheridan . . . Toledo, O.: Western Publishing Co., [c1913]. 568, [1] p.
LC: D 6, '13.

S-412   Sheridan, Ronnie A. Jess of Harbor Hill / by Ramie A. Sheridan . . . ; illustrated. New York: Cupples & Leon Company, [c1911]. 314 p., front., [3] leaves of plates.
(Harbor Hill romances).
LC: Ap 3, '11.

S-413   Sheridan, Sol. N. (Solomon Neill), b. 1859. The typhoon's secret / by Sol. N. Sheridan; frontispiece by Ralph Pallen Coleman. Garden City, New York: Doubleday, Page & Company, 1920. 250 p., col. front.
LC: My 4, '20.
PW: F 7, '20.

S-414 Sherlock, Charles Reginald, b. 1857. The red anvil: a romance of fifty years ago / by Charles Reginald Sherlock; with frontispiece by Walter Russel. New York: Frederick A. Stokes Company, [1902]. 342 p., front.
PW: Je 7, '02.

S-415 ____ Your Uncle Lew: a natural-born American: a novel / by Charles Reginald Sherlock; with a frontispiece by B. West Clinedinst. New York: Frederick A. Stokes Company, [c1901]. 305 p., front.
PW: Ap 6, '01.

S-416 Sherman, Andrew M. (Andrew Magoun), 1844-1921. Phil Carver: a romance of the war of 1812 / by Andrew M. Sherman. Morristown, New Jersey: George H. Sherman, [c1902]. 290 p.
PW: F 21, '03.

S-417 Sherman, Bryant Elihu, b. 1871. The bell cow / by Bryant E. Sherman. Boston, Mass.: The C. M. Clark Publishing Co., 1908. 286 p., front., [7] leaves of plates.   **MOC**
LC: D 18, '08.

S-418 Sherman, Charles, b. 1882. He comes up smiling / by Charles Sherman; with illustrations by Arthur William Brown. Indianapolis: The Bobbs-Merrill Company, [c1912]. 350 p., front., [5] leaves of plates.
LC: Ja 13, '12.
BLC: London: Hodder & Stoughton, [1913].

S-419 ____ Only relatives invited: a social and socialistic satire / by Charles Sherman . . . Indianapolis: The Bobbs-Merrill Company, [c1916]. 315 p.
LC: Mr 29, '16.

S-420 ____ The upper crust / by Charles Sherman . . ; with illustrations by Arthur William Brown. Indianapolis: The Bobbs-Merrill Company, [c1913]. 409, [1] p., front., [5] leaves of plates.
LC: My 7, '13.

S-421 ____ A wise son / by Charles Sherman . . . ; with frontispiece by Arthur William Brown. Indianapolis: The Bobbs-Merrill Company, [c1914]. 404 p., front.
LC: Mr 11, '14.
PW: Mr 14, '14.

S-422 Sherman, Homer. Brass tacks: the soul of New England turned wrong side out / by Homer Sherman. Boston: Published by Miller Publishing Company, 1918. 325 p.

S-423 Sherwen, Grayson N. The romance of St. Sacrement: a story of New France and the Iroquois / by Grayson N. Sherwen. Burlington, Vt.: Free Press Printing Company, 1912. 197 p., [6] leaves of photo. plates. [Photo. by Detroit Phot. Co.]
LC: My 3, '16.

Sherwood, Margaret Pollock, 1864-1955. The clearest voice. In *Atlantic narratives*; first series **(1918), A-360.**

S-424 ____ The coming of the tide / by Margaret Sherwood. Boston; New York: Houghton, Mifflin and Company, 1905. (Cambridge: The Riverside Press). 359 p., col. front.
PW: O 21, '05.
BLC: Archibald Constable & Co., Cambridge, Mass. printed, 1905.

S-425 ____ Daphne: an autumn pastoral / by Margaret Sherwood. Boston; New York: Houghton, Mifflin & Company, 1903. ([Boston]: The Riverside Press). 167, [1] p.
PW: N 7, '03.
BLC: London: Chatto & Windus, 1907.

S-426 ____ Nancy's pilgrimage / by Margaret Sherwood. Philadelphia: The Westminster Press, 1911. 165 p., front., [14] leaves of plates.
Unexamined copy: bibliographic data from OCLC, #10347420.
LC: Je 5, '11.

S-427 ____ The Princess Pourquoi / by Margaret Sherwood; illustrated. Boston; New York: Houghton, Mifflin & Company, 1907. 211, [1] p., front., [7] leaves of plates. [Ill. by Sarah S. Stillwell & J. J. Gould.]
Contents: The Princess Pourquoi -- The clever necromancer -- The princess and the microbe -- The seven studious sisters -- The gentle robber.
LC: O 1, '07.
PW: O 12, '07.

S-428 ____ The story of King Sylvain and Queen Aimée / by Margaret Sherwood; with illustrations and decorations by Sarah S. Stillwell. New York: The Macmillan Company; London: Macmillan & Co., Ltd., 1904. 240 p., col. front., incl. [15] leaves of plates.
PW: Ap 9, '04.

S-429 ____ A world to mend: the journal of a working man / by Margaret Sherwood. Boston: Little, Brown and Company, 1920. 335 p.
LC: S 30, '20.
PW: O 9, '20.

S-430 ____ The worn doorstep / by Margaret Sherwood. Boston: Little, Brown, and Company, 1916. 195 p.
LC: S 30, '16.
BLC: London: Hodder & Stoughton, 1917.

S-431 Sherwood, Walter James. The story of three / by Walter James Sherwood; illustrated by Edward James Carey. Evanston, Ill., William S. Lord, 1901. 15, [1] p., ill.   **DLC**
PW: Mr 29, '02.

S-432 Shields, D., *pseud*. The gentleman from Maryland / D. Shields [pseud.]. Boston: Richard G. Badger, [c1924]. ([Boston: U. S. A.]: The Gorham Press). 386 p.   **NYP**
PW: My 3, '24.

S-433 Shields, Gertrude M. Caste three / by Gertrude M. Shields; with frontispiece by Florence Gardner. New York: The Century Co., 1918. 450 p., col. front.

S-434 Shields, Samuel Jackson, b. 1848. A chevalier of
Dixie / by S. J. Shields. New York; Washington:
The Neale Publishing Company, 1907. 226 p.
LC: Ag 7, '07.
PW: Ag 24, '07.

S-435 Shields, Thomas Edward, 1862-1921. The making
and the unmaking of a dullard / by Thomas Edward
Shields . . . Washington, D. C.: The Catholic
Education Press, [c1909]. 296 p.

Shiffrin, A. B. The black laugh. In *The best short
stories of 1924 and the yearbook of the American
short story (1925)*, B-569.

Shipley, Hester E. See **Williams, Sarah Stone.**

S-436 Shipley, Joseph Twadell, b. 1893. King John / by
Joseph T. Shipley. New York: Greenberg, Publisher
Inc., 1925. 117 p.

Shipman, Helen (Barham), Mrs., 1892-1970. See
Shipman, Nell, pseud.

S-437 Shipman, Louis Evan, 1869-1933. The curious
courtship of Kate Poins: a romance of the regency /
Louis Evan Shipman . . . ; illustrated by A. I. Keller.
New York: D. Appleton and Company, 1901.
336 p., front., [5] leaves of plates.
PW: Je 1, '01.

S-438 ____ The quality of youth / by Louis Evan Shipman;
illustrated by L. L. Roush. New York: Scott-Thaw
Co., 1904. 195 p., [5] leaves of plates.

S-439 Shipman, Nell, *pseud.* Under the crescent / by Nell
Shipman [pseud.]; illustrated with scenes from the
photo play produced and copyrighted by the Universal
Film Manufacturing Company. New York: Grosset
& Dunlap, [c1915]. 277 p., photo. front., [62] leaves
of photo. plates.

S-440 Shipp, W. W. Wannaseska / W.W. Shipp. New
York: The Editor Company, [c1903]. 355 p. **GUA**

S-441 Shirey, Effie M. (Spirit). The angels' diary; and,
celestion study of man / by Effie M. Shirey and her
brother, Charles Samson from the celestial sphere.
[Denver, Colorado: The Merchants Publishing Co.],
1903. 223 p.
PW: My 9, '03.

S-442 Shively, George. Initiation / by George Shively.
New York: Harcourt, Brace and Company, [1925].
312 p.
LC: F 14, '25.
PW: F 14, '25.

S-443 Shoemaker, Henry W. (Henry Wharton), b. 1880.
Black Forest souvenirs: collected in northern
Pennsylvania / by Henry W. Shoemaker . . . ;
illustrated. Reading, Penn.: Published by
Bright-Faust Printing Co., 1914. 404, [2] p., front.,
[20] leaves of photo. plates, ill. [Ill. by Miss
Katherine H. McCormick; photo. by W. T. Clarke,
Betula, Pa.] **OSU, KSU**

Contents: John Decker's elk -- Why the senecas would not eat trout
-- Young woman's creek -- Conquering fate -- In the rafters -- The
winter of the wolves -- The three rivers -- The story of Regina -- The
death shout -- The healing spring -- A hunter's daughter -- The
moment the lights were lit -- Hugh Mitchell tree -- George Shover's
panther -- The tramper -- Little red riding hood -- The cursed woods
-- The screaming skull. Includes: Index to legends with locality and
informant's name.
LC: D 19, '14.

S-444 ____ In the Seven Mountains: legends collected in
central Pennsylvania / by Henry W. Shoemaker . . .
Reading, Pennsylvania: Published by the Bright
Printing Company, 1913. 433, [1] p., photo. front.,
[12] leaves of photo. plates (1 col.), ill. [Ill. by S.
W. Smith and W. W. Sholl.] **YNG**
Contents: Invocation -- Explanatory preface -- In the Seven
Mountains -- Dan Treaster's nights -- The ghost -- The canoe -- The
Logan brothers -- Dorman panther -- The token -- Pipsisseway's pine
-- Uncle Job -- Swartzell Panther -- A modern Petrarach -- The thread
-- On the ledge -- The Indian mound -- Lynz of Indianville Gap --
Turned to stone -- The devil's turnip patch -- Story of the cannon hole
-- The ghostly lights -- The old fort -- An episode of '65 flood -- At
the Gate of Dead.
LC: D 31, '13.

S-445 ____ The Indian steps: and other Pennsylvania
mountain stories / by Henry W. Shoemaker . . . ;
illustrated. Reading, Pa.: The Bright Printing
Company, 1912. 427 p., photo. front. (port.), [8]
leaves of photo. plates. [Photo. by Eliza Huntley, W.
T. Clarke and Fred Miller.] **DKC**
Contents: Introduction -- The Indian steps -- A redman's gratitude --
The fairy parks -- A hermit's secret -- The lonely grave -- The
jockey's sister -- The despatch rider -- On Black Moshannon -- The
dancing chairs -- My gipsey sweetheart -- The Harper -- In the
Blockhouse Country -- Shadows -- When ghosts walk -- The closed
house -- The giant horse-shoe -- Two crazy men -- The section house
on the hill -- An eternal feud -- Driving out of Rocky -- A rock of
ages -- She knew the poet -- Batallion days -- And the sword of Pine
Creek.
LC: S 4, '12.

S-446 ____ Juniata memories: legends collected in central
Pennsylvania / by Henry W. Shoemaker . . .
illustrated. Philadelphia, Pa.: John Joseph McVey,
[c1916]. 395 p., photo. front., [9] leaves of photo.
plates. **WVU**
Contents: Foreword -- Explanatory preface -- Old Dan -- The rede --
The snow image -- The shadow man -- The wolf tribe -- Candlemas --
The warlock -- Shaney John -- The hart's horn -- Nita-Nee -- The
original -- Lost Creek Valley -- The old tree -- The girl and the
panther -- The standing stone -- Warrior's Ridge -- Warrior's Mark --
Wild ducks -- A story of Black Jack -- Tom Fausett -- Aaron Hall --
Hallowe'en -- All Souls Night -- Merithew -- Green Gap -- The Rob
Roy.
LC: D 14, '16.

S-447 ____ More Pennsylvania mountain stories / by
Henry W. Shoemaker . . . Reading, Pennsylvania:
Published by the Bright Printing Company, 1912.
405 p., photo. front. (from painting by C. H.
Shearer), [3] leaves of photo. plates. **KSU**
Contents: Explanatory preface -- When the pigeons fly -- The last elk
-- The passing of a ghost -- The story of Lewis's Lake -- The last
pack -- Story of the sulphur spring -- The panther ride -- Marsh
marigold -- Story of the Picture Rocks -- Vindication of Fredrick
Stump -- The cross on the rock -- The fate of Georgie Dupre -- Billy
Anderson's ghost -- The dreamer -- The call of the track -- The ghost
of the pine -- A Pennsylvanian bison hunt -- McElhattan and his
springs -- The courage of Peter Pentz -- Tim Murphy's ghost -- The
last drive -- History of Tamarak Swamp -- Cora Pemberton's
biography -- The Vista -- The pitcher plant -- Meeting Hermionie.
LC: Mr 11, '12.

S-448 ____ North Mountain mementos: legends and

traditions gathered in northern Pennsylvania / by
Henry W. Shoemaker . . . Altoona, Pennsylvania:
Published by the Times Tribune Publishing Co.,
1920. 383, [1] p., front., [6] leaves of photo. plates.
[Ill. by J. Wesley Little and Katherine H.
McCormick.]   **LQS**
Contents: Preface -- Introduction -- Cornplanter at Wyoming --
Skanando, the geomancer -- The simpleton -- Oscaluwa -- Mariele --
Endermay -- John Hull -- Letty Logan -- Hunting feuds in the
mountains -- The beaver meadow -- The passing of the Martens -- Joe
Nelson's wolverene -- Wild life conservation -- The panther's path --
The Pennsylvania Indian reservation -- Wildmanuli -- The lady of
Pine Summit Manor -- Jack O' Lanthorn -- King Henry -- The Eagle
Rock -- The summons.
LC: Ap 10, '20.

S-449 _____ Pennsylvania mountain stories / by Henry W.
Shoemaker . . . Bradford, Pa.: Bradford Record
Publishing Company, 1907. 78 p., photo. front.
                                                    DLM
Contents: Why the Steiner House patient pulled through -- The story
of Altar Rock -- The spook of Spook Hill -- The romance of
Postoffice Rock -- The fate of Simeon Shaffer -- The legend of Penn's
Cave -- The hermit of the Knobs -- Prairie King -- Old Righter's
Ghost -- The mountain soldier's presentiment -- Granny Myers's
curse -- Witchcraft vs. mother-in-law -- The haunted tavern -- Fanny
Hedden's hotel -- The ghost walk -- Ole Bull's castle -- Booneville
Camp meeting -- The Bald Eagle Silver Mine.

S-450 _____ South Mountain sketches: folk tales and
legends collected in the mountains of southern
Pennsylvania / by Henry W. Shoemaker . . .
Altoona, Pennsylvania: Published by Times Tribune
Company, 1920. 332 p., photo. front., [16] leaves of
photo. plates, ill.   **OSU, KSU**
Contents: Aunt Tilly Henry's vision -- There were giants -- Love
beyond the grave -- Conestoga -- The white lady of Pomfret Castle --
The lost valley -- Whipporwill's shoes -- The star of the glen --
Ghosts of the living -- Fire for the ghosts -- The proof of Ossian -- A
ghost flower -- The wolf's glen -- The blue girl -- The black cat at
Peter Allen's -- The squaw man -- Woodpecker's head -- The timber
line -- The scalp bounty -- Mary Casselman, redemptioner -- The
north bastion -- The hunter's moon -- The lion's garden -- The man of
peace.
LC: O 18, '20.

S-451 _____ Susquehanna legends: collected in central
Pennsylvania / by Henry W. Shoemaker; illustrated.
Reading, Pennsylvania: Published by the Bright
Printing Company, 1913. 389 p., photo. front., [8]
leaves of photo. plates, ill. [Photo. by Fred C.
Miller, H. W. Swope, W. T. Clarke; ill. by Miss
Katherine H. McCormick.]   **MNU**
Contents: Teedyuscung's face -- The man who loved a fairy -- In the
foothills -- Killy, Killy, Killy -- Eleve -- Spiritually dead -- One hour
of happiness -- The play girl -- A frontiersman's diary -- The escape
-- The water witch -- The lonely ghost -- The horse-beater -- Queen
Elizabeth -- The headless man -- His rival's ghost -- Canoe place --
Golden hour in the camp -- The weather-vanes -- Elphe Soden -- The
white deer.
LC: Jl 24. '13.

S-452 _____ Tales of the Bald Eagle Mountains in Central
Pennsylvania / by Henry W. Shoemaker . . . ;
illustrated. Reading, Pa.: Published by the Bright
Printing Company, [c1912]. 490 p., photo. front.,
[10] leaves of photo. plates, ill. [Some photo. by H.
W. Swope, Charles W. Kimble, W. T. Clarke, and
C. H. Shearer; ill. by Miss Katherine H.
McCormick.]   **NOC**
Contents: Birth of the Bald Eagles -- The siren -- The red fox -- The
view tree -- The brown bear -- Old Philippe -- King Widaagh's spell
-- Caves of the Bald Eagles -- Pathfinder's child -- Conrad's broom --
The giantess -- Mary goes over the mountain -- The fate of Atoka --

For the glory of Indian summer -- The lost chord -- Bald Eagle's nest
-- The running race -- Two roses -- The sorceress -- Unrequited --
Before the fire -- Simpler's joy -- Ironcutter's cabin.
LC: D 31, '12.

S-453 [Sholl, Anna McClure]. Blue blood and red / by
Geoffrey Corson [pseud.]. New York: Henry Holt
and Company, 1915. 395 p.
LC: Mr 8, '15.

S-454 _____ The greater love / by Anna McClure Sholl . . .
New York: Outing Publishing Company, 1908.
390 p.
LC: My 26, '08.
PW: Je 13, '08.
BLC: London: T. Fisher Unwin, 1909.

S-455 _____ The law of life / by Anna McClure Sholl. New
York: D. Appleton and Company, 1903. 572 p.
PW: Ag 29, '03.
BLC: London: William Heinemann, New York
printed, 1904.

S-456 _____ The port of storms / by Anna McClure Sholl
. . . New York: D. Appleton and Company, 1905.
334 p.
PW: Mr 11, '05.

S-457 _____ This way out / by Anna McClure Sholl . . .
New York: Hearst's International Library Co., 1915.
299 p.
LC: N 5, '15.
PW: N 13, '15.

S-458 _____ The unclaimed letter / by Anna McClure Sholl.
Philadelphia: Dorrance and Company, Inc., [c1921].
291 p.
LC: S 10, '21.

Shook, Martha Caroline. See **Cornelius, John,
pseud.**

S-459 Shore, Viola Brothers. The heritage: and other
stories / by Viola Brothers Shore. New York:
George H. Doran Company, [c1921]. 293 p. **OSO**
Contents: The heritage -- Mary Mary -- Dimi and the double life -- If
you want a thing -- A mess of pottage -- We can't afford it --
Matzoths cast upon the waters -- O tempora! O mawruss!
LC: O 21, '21.
PW: O 22, '21.

Shores, Robert James, b. 1881. See **Roberts, James.**

Short, Thompson, Mrs. See **Kinkead, Eleanor
Talbot.**

S-460 Short stories / edited by H. C. Schweikert . . . New
York: Harcourt, Brace and Company, [c1925].
521 p.
Contents: Acknowledgments -- Preface -- A note to teachers --
Chronological list of authors -- Introduction-The short story -- A note
to pupils -- The token / Joseph Hergesheimer -- The third ingredient /
O. Henry -- Turkey red / Frances Gilchrist Wood -- The elephant
remembers / Edison Marshall -- The fall of the house of Usher /
Edgar Allan Poe -- The postmistress of Laurel Run / Bret Harte --
The ambitious guest / Nathaniel Hawthorne -- Penrod's busy day /
Booth Tarkington -- Young Man Axelbrod / Sinclair Lewis -- Ice
water, pl____! / Fannie Hurst -- The heyday of the blood / Dorothy
Canfield -- Hunger / Anzia Yezierska -- The remarkable wreck of the
Thomas Hyke / Frank R. Stockton -- Zenobia's infidelity / H. C.

Bunner -- The legend of Sleepy Hollow / Washington Irving -- The speckled band / A. Conan Doyle -- That brute Simmons / Arthur Morrison -- The monkey's paw / W. W. Jacobs -- The three strangers / Thomas Hardy -- The inn of the two witches / Joseph Conrad -- The stove / Marjorie L. C. Pickthall -- In the matter of a Private / Rudyard Kipling -- A letter home / Arnold Bennett -- Will o'the mill / Robert Louis Stevenson -- How Gavin Birse put it to Mag Lownie / James Matthew Barrie -- Happiness / Guy de Maupassant -- The bet / Anton Pavlovich Chekov -- The father / Björnstjerne Björnson -- Zodomirsky's duel / Alexandre Dumas -- Reading lists according to types -- A reading list of short stories -- Bibliography. LC: Mr 12, '25.

S-461   Short stories for class reading / edited by Ralph P. Boas . . . and Barbara M. Hahn. New York: Henry Holt and Company, [c1925]. 365 p.   **KEU**
Apparent first book appearance: Renfrew and the new generation, by Booth Tarkington.
Contents: Introduction -- A use for clods / Ben Ames Williams -- White birches / Temple Bailey -- The despoiler / Gouverneur Morris -- Van Bibber and the swan boats / Richard Harding Davis -- The gift of the magi / O. Henry -- The clearest voice / Margaret Sherwood -- The old pearl necklace / Mary Valentine Stanley -- Those scars / Katherine Holland Brown -- Renfrew and the new generation / Booth Tarkington -- The fat of the land / Anzia Yezierska -- The little silver heart / Josephine Daskam Bacon -- Humoresque / Fannie Hurst -- As a bird out of the snare / Dorthy Canfield -- Two for a cent / F. Scott Fitzgerald -- Moti guj-mutineer / Rudyard Kipling -- The strange flower / Edwina Stanton Babcock -- The doll's house / Katherine Mansfield -- Biographies and questions -- A list of short stories.

S-462   Short stories for high schools / edited with introduction and notes by Rosa M. R. Mikels . . . New York; Chicago; Boston: Charles Scribner's Sons, [c1915]. 453 p.   **WAU**
Apparent first book appearance: The triumph of night, by Edith Wharton.
Contents: Preface -- Introduction: Requirements for the short story -- How this book may be used -- The first Christmas tree / H. Van Dyke -- A French tar-baby / J. C. Harris -- Sonny's christenin' / Ruth M. Stuart -- Christmas night with Satan / J. Fox, jr. -- A nest egg / J. W. Riley -- Wee Willie Winkie / R. Kipling -- The gold bug / E. A. Poe -- The ransom of Red Chief / O. Henry -- The freshman full-back / R. D. Paine -- Gallegher / R. H. Davis -- The jumping frog / Mark Twain -- The lady or the tiger? / F. R. Stockton -- The outcasts of Poker Flat / F. B. Harte -- The revolt of mother / Mary E. W. Freeman -- Marse Chan / T. N. Page -- "Posson Jone" / G. W. Cable -- Our aromatic uncle / H. C. Bunner -- Quality / J. Galsworthy -- The triumph of night / Edith Wharton -- A messenger / Mary R. S. Andrews -- Markheim / R. L. Stevenson.

S-463   Short stories from Life: the 81 prize stories in "Life's" shortest story contest / with an introduction by Thomas L. Masson . . . Garden City, New York: Doubleday, Page & Company, 1916. 346 p.   **KSU**
Contents (first book appearance only): Thicker than water / Ralph Henry Barbour and George Randolph Osborne -- The answer / Harry Stillwell Edwards -- Collusion / Lincoln Steffens -- Lost and found / John Kendrick Bangs -- Strictly business / Lincoln Steffens -- A Po-lice-man / Lincoln Steffens.
LC: S 8, '16.
PW: S 9, '16.

S-464   Short stories of America / edited, with an introductory essay, course outline, and reading lists, by Robert L. Ramsay . . . Boston; New York; Chicago; Dallas; Atlanta; San Francisco: Houghton Mifflin Company, [c1921]. (Cambridge, [Mass.]: The Riverside Press). 348 p.
Contents: The luck of roaring camp / Bret Harte -- Taking the blue ribbon at the county fair / Mary N. Murfree -- Ben and Judas / Maurice Thompson -- Among the corn-rows / Hamlin Garland -- Ellie's furnishing / Helen R. Martin -- The arrival of a true southern lady / Francis Hopkinson Smith -- On the walpole road / Mary Wilkins Freeman -- At the 'Cadian ball / Kate Chopin -- The pearls of Loreto / Gertrude Atherton -- The windigo / Mary Hartwell Catherwood -- The girl at Duke's / James Weber Linn -- Love of life

/ Jack London -- By the rod of his wrath / William Allen White -- The making of a New Yorker / O. Henry -- A municipal report / O. Henry -- A local colorist / Annie Trumbull Slosson.

S-465   Short stories of various types / edited with an introduction and notes by Laura F. Freck. New York; Chicago: Charles E. Merrill Company, [c1920]. 327 p., front. (port.).   **MIA**
(Merrill's English texts). Apparent first book appearance: "American, Sir!", by Mary Raymond Shipman Andrews.
Contents: The gift of the Magi / O. Henry -- A reward of merit / Booth Tarkington -- "American, Sir!" / Mary Raymond Shipman Andrews -- John G. / Katherine Mayo -- Friends / Myra Kelly -- A camping trip / Hamlin Garland -- A thread without a knot / Dorothy Canfield Fisher -- Chu Chu / Francis Bret Harte -- Feathertop / Nathaniel Hawthorne -- The red-headed league / Arthur Conan Doyle -- The inconsiderate waiter / James Matthew Barrie -- The seige of Berlin / Alphonse Daudet -- The silver mine / Selma Lagerlof.

S-466   Short story classics (American) . . . / edited by William Patten; with an introduction and notes. New York: P. F. Collier & Son, [c1905]. 5 v. (1758 p.), front. in each volume, [10] leaves of plates.
Contents (first book appearance only): Volume I: The man in the reservoir / Charles Fenno Hoffman -- The diamond lens /Fitz-James O'Brien -- A brace of boys / Fitz Hugh Ludlow -- The man who stole a meeting-house / J. T. Trowbridge -- A ride with a mad horse in a freight-car / W. H. H. Murray -- Balacchi brothers / Rebecca Harding Davis. Volume II: The brigade commander / J. W. De Forest -- Who was she? / Bayard Taylor -- Mademoiselle Olympe Zabriski / Thomas Bailey Aldrich -- Brother sebastian's friendship / Harold Frederic -- The idyl of red gulch / Bret Harte -- Crutch, the page / George Alfred Townsend ("Gath") -- In each other's shoes / George Parsons Lathrop -- The Denver express / A. A. Hayes. Volume III: The soul of the great bell / Lafcadio Hearn -- A successful failure / J. C. Bunner -- The liar / Henry James -- Against his judgment / Robert Grant -- My terminal moraine / Frank R. Stockton -- The Indian's hand / Lorimer Stoddard -- The upper berth / F. Marion Crawford -- The old partisan / Octave Thanet -- The return / I. K. Friedman -- The tipster / Edwin Lefevre. Volume IV: After the battle / Joseph A. Altsheler -- Rosemary for remembrance / Henry Harland -- A red-haired Cupid / Henry Wallace Phillips -- The wild horse of Tartary / Clara Morris -- A derelict / Richard Harding Davis -- Such as walk in darkness / Samuel Hopkins Adams -- The lotus eaters / Virginia Tracy -- The hall bedroom / Mary E. Wilkins Freeman -- The damned thing / Ambrose Bierce -- Brother Rabbit's cradle / Joel Chandler Harris -- The tree of heaven / Robert W. Chambers. Volume V: "To make a hoosier holiday" / George Ade -- Mr. Dooley on the pursuit of riches / F. P. Dunne -- A Christmas present for a lady / Myra Kelly -- The spiral stone / Arthur Colton -- Mrs. Protheroe / Booth Tarkington -- How the raven died / Alfred Henry Lewis -- At the end of his rope / Florence Morse Kingsley -- Everybody's chance / John Habberton -- The run of the yellow mail / Frank H. Spearman -- Frictional electricity / Max Adeler -- In the wake of war / Hallie Erminie Rives -- While the automobile ran down / Charles Battell Loomis -- "Many waters" / Margaret Deland.

S-467   Shotland, Julia Eliza. Restdale / by Julia Eliza Shotland. New York: Burre Publishing Company, [c1906]. 277 p., photo. front. (port.), [5] leaves of photo. plates.
LC: Ja 12, '06.

S-468   Showerman, Grant, 1870-1935. A country chronicle / by Grant Showerman; illustrated by George Wright. New York: The Century Co., 1916. 349 p., front., ill.
LC: O 25, '16.

S-469   _____ With the professor / by Grant Showerman. New York: Henry Holt and Company, 1910. 360 p.
LC: Mr 1, '10.

S-470   Shubael, *pseud.* The dark strain / by Shubael [pseud.]. New York; London; Montrea[l]: The

Abbey Press, [c1903]. 253 p.
PW: Ap 25, '03.

S-471 Shugert, Fanny Alricks. The little Lady Bertha / by Fanny Alricks Shugert. New York: Every Where Publishing Company, [c1911]. 125 p. **DLC**
PW: O 4, '13.

S-472 Shuler, Marjorie. For rent, one pedestal / by Marjorie Shuler. New York City: Published by National Woman Suffrage Publishing Co., Inc., 1917. 126 p.

S-473 Shurts, J. Van der Veer (Jacob Van der Veer), b. 1849. Kedar Kross: a tale of the North country / by J. Van der Veer Shurts. Boston: Richard G. Badger, 1907. ([Boston]: The Gorham Press). 430 p.

S-474 Shute, Henry A. (Henry Augustus), 1856-1943. The country band / Henry A. Shute; illustrated by Bert [i. e. Dan] Sayre Groesbeck. Boston: Richard G. Badger, 1909 [c1908]. (Boston: The Gorham Press). 146 p., front., [3] leaves of plates.
LC: D 11, '08.
PW: D 12, '08.

S-475 _____ A country lawyer / by Henry A. Shute . . . ; with illustrations. Boston; New York: Houghton Mifflin Company, 1911. (Cambridge [Mass.]: The Riverside Press). 431 p., col. front., [7] leaves of plates. [Ill. by Irma Dérèmeaux.]
LC: N 3, '11.
BLC: London: Constable & Co., Cambridge, Mass. [printed], 1912.

S-476 _____ A few neighbors / by Henry A. Shute. New York: Doubleday, Page & Company, 1906. 214 p.
LC reports folded front.
PW: My 19, '06.
BLC: London: Doubledy, Page & Company, New York printed, 1906.

S-477 _____ The misadventures of three good boys: that is to say, fairly good boys / by Henry A. Shute; with illustrations by Sears Gallagher. Boston; New York: Houghton Mifflin Company, 1914. (Cambridge: The Riverside Press). 280 p., front., [16] leaves of plates.
LC: My 11, '14.
PW: My 16, '14.

S-478 _____ Plupy and old J. Albert / by Henry A. Shute; with silhouettes in miniature. Philadelphia: Dorrance & Company, [c1924]. 220 p., ill.
LC: Ag 5, '24.

S-479 _____ The real diary of the worst farmer / by Henry A. Shute; with illustrations by B. Morgan Dennis. Boston; New York: Houghton Mifflin Company, 1920. (Cambridge [Mass.]: The Riverside Press). 277, [1] p., front., [10] leaves of plates. **BGU**
LC: Ap 27, '20.
PW: My 1, '20.

S-480 _____ "Sequil", or, Things which aint finished in the first / by Henry A. Shute. Boston, Mass.: The

Everett Press, 1904. 189 p.
PW: N 5, '04.

S-481 _____ The youth Plupy, or, The lad with a downy chin / by Henry A. Shute; with illustrations by Reginald Birch. Boston; New York: Houghton Mifflin Company, 1917. (Cambridge: The Riverside Press). 253, [1] p., front., [5] leaves of plates.
LC: S 8, '17.
PW: S 1, '17.

S-482 Sibley, Edwin Day. Stillman Gott: farmer and fisherman / by Edwin Day Sibley. Boston: John S. Brooks & Company, 1902. 360, [1] p.
PW: Ag 30, '02.

S-483 Sibley, Frank P. (Frank Palmer), b. 1871. All by wire: a telegraphic explanation of a telepathic union of hearts / by Frank P. Sibley. Boston; London: John W. Luce & Company, 1905. 103 p. Illustrated t. p. [Ill. by Wallace Goldsmith.] Printed in the form of telegrams on one side of the leaf only.

S-484 Sibley, Frederick O. (Frederick Orrin). Zanee Kooran: a romance of India in the time of the great Sepoy rebellion / by Frederick O. Sibley. New York; London: F. Tennyson Neely Co., [c1901]. 244 p., front. (port.).

S-485 Sibley, Louise Lyndon. A lighthouse village / by Louise Lyndon Sibley. Boston; New York: Houghton, Mifflin and Company, 1901. (Cambridge: The Riverside Press). 152 p.

S-486 Sidner, Aurelia I. The price inevitable, or, The confessions of Irene: an autobiography / by Aurelia I. Sidner. New York: The Popular Publishing Co., 1902. 212 p., front., [2] leaves of plates. [Ill. by J. P. Rigby.]

S-487 Sidney, Margaret, *pseud.* A little maid of Boston town / by Margaret Sidney [pseud.]; illustrated by Frank T. Merrill. Boston: Lothrop, Lee & Shepard Co., [1910]. 423 p., front., [5] leaves of plates.
LC: S 2, '10.

S-488 _____ Sally, Mrs. Tubbs / by Margaret Sidney [pseud.] . . . Boston: Lothrop Publishing Company, [1903]. 180 p. **WIS**
PW: O 3, '03.

Sidney, Rose. Butterflies. In *The best short stories of 1920 and the yearbook of the American short story* (1921), B-565; *also Prize stories of 1920* (1921), P-618.

S-489 Siegel, Henrietta. The sign of ignorance / by Henrietta Siegel. New York: From the press of Broadway Publishing Co., [c1904]. 131 p., front., [3] leaves of plates. [Ill. by Chas. Dalton Cathcart.] **DLC**
PW: D 3, '04.

S-490 Sieghold, Kate P. (Kate Price), b. 1857. Old mission tales / by Kate P. Sieghold. San Francisco: John J. Newbegin, 1915. 20 p. Reprinted in part from the Overland Monthly.
PW: Ap 17, '15.

S-491 Siem, Conrad. The menace; a semi-scientific story of particular interest to the people of Nome. Dedicated to the miners on the Seward Peninsula / by Conrad Siem. Nome, Alaska: [s. n.], 1903. 22 p. **UAF**

S-492 Sigel, Franz. Llewellyn / by Franz Sigel; illustrated by Mark Dennis. Indianapolis: Wood-Weaver Printing Co., [c1903]. 518 p., front., [4] leaves of plates.

Silvani, Anita F. <u>See</u> **A. F. S.**

S-493 Silver, R. Norman. The golden dwarf: a sensational romance of to-day / by R. Norman Silver. Boston: L. C. Page & Company, 1903. 312 p.
PW: S 5, '03.
BLC: London: Jarrold & Sons, 1903.

Silvers, Earl Reed. Grandson. <u>In</u> *The Sporting spirit* **(1925), S-771.**

S-494 Simon, Robert A. (Robert Alfred), 1897-1981. "Our little girl" / by Robert A. Simon. New York: Boni and Liveright, [c1923]. 328 p.
LC: Mr 14, '23.
BLC: London: W. Collins Sons & Co., 1924.

S-495 Simonton, Ida Vera. Hell's playground / Ida Vera Simonton. New York: Moffat, Yard and Company, 1912. 447 p.
LC: Je 23, '13.
BLC: London: Gay & Hancock, 1915.

S-496 Sims, Mamie Hunt. Negro mystic lore / by Mamie Hunt Sims. Chicago: To-morrow Press, 1907. 149 p., photo. front. (port.). Designed end papers.

Sinclair, Bertha Muzzy, 1874-1940. <u>See</u> **Bower, B. M., pseud.**

S-497 Sinclair, Bertrand William, b. 1878. Big timber: a story of the Northwest / by Bertrand W. Sinclair . . . ; with frontispiece by Douglas Duer. Boston: Little, Brown and Company, 1916. 321 p., front.
LC: Ag 15, '16.
PW: Ag 12, '16.

S-498 _____ Burned bridges / by Bertrand W. Sinclair; with a frontispiece by Ralph P. Coleman. Boston: Little, Brown, and Company, 1919. 308 p., front.
LC: Ag 23, '19.
PW: Ag 16, '19.

S-499 _____ The hidden places / by Bertrand W. Sinclair; with frontispiece by Marshall Frantz. Boston: Little, Brown, and Company, 1922. 318 p.
LC: Ja 7, '22.
PW: Ja 14, '22.
BLC: London: Hodder & Stoughton, [1922].

S-500 _____ The inverted pyramid / by Bertrand W. Sinclair. Boston: Little, Brown, and Company, 1924. 339 p.
LC: Ja 7, '24.
PW: Ja 5, '24.

S-501 _____ The land of frozen suns: a novel / by Bertrand W. Sinclair. Illustrations by D. C. Hutchison. New York: G. W. Dillingham Company, [c1910]. 309 p., [2] leaves of plates.
LC: Ap 18, '10.
PW: Ap 23, '10.

S-502 _____ North of fifty-three / by Bertrand W. Sinclair . . . ; with illustrations by Anton Otto Fischer. Boston: Little, Brown, and Company, 1914. 345 p., front., [3] leaves of plates.
LC: Ap 7, '14.
PW: Ap 4, '14.

S-503 _____ Poor Man's Rock / by Bertrand W. Sinclair; with frontispiece by Frank Tenney Johnson. Boston: Little, Brown, and Company, 1920. 307 p., front.
LC: S 30, '20.
PW: O 9, '20.

S-504 _____ Raw gold: a novel / by Bertrand W. Sinclair; illustrations by Clarence H. Rowe. New York: G. W. Dillingham Company, [1908]. 311 p., front., [3] leaves of plates.
LC: Jl 13, '08.
PW: Ag 29, '08.

_____ Under flying hoofs. <u>In</u> *Argonaut stories* **(1906), A-298.**

Sinclair, Grant, pseud. <u>See</u> **Drago, Harry Sinclair, b. 1888.**

S-505 Sinclair, Upton, 1878-1968. A captain of industry: being the story of a civilized man / by Upton Sinclair . . . Girard, Kansas: The Appeal to Reason, 1906. 142 p.
LC: D 15, '06.
PW: Ap 20, '07.
BLC: London: William Heinemann, 1906.

S-506 _____ Damaged goods: the great play "Les avariés" of Brieux / novelized with the approval of the author by Upton Sinclair. Philadelphia: The John C. Winston Company, [c1913]. 194 p., front., [3] leaves of plates.
LC: O 30, '13.
PW: O 18, '13.

S-507 _____ Jimmie Higgins: a story / by Upton Sinclair . . . New York: Boni and Liveright, 1919. 282 p.
LC: My 29, '19.
PW: My 24, '19.
BLC: London: Hutchinson & Co., [1919].

S-508 [_____] The journal of Arthur Stirling: ("the valley of the shadow"): revised and condensed with an introductory sketch. New York: D. Appleton and Company, 1903. 356 p.
LC: O 18, '06.
PW: O 27, '06.
BLC: London: Doubleday, Page & Co., New York printed, 1906.

S-509 _____ The jungle / by Upton Sinclair. New York: Doubleday, Page & Company, 1906. 413 p.

PW: Mr 3, '06.
Another edition: New York: The Jungle Publishing
Co., 1906.

S-510 _____ King Coal: a novel / by Upton Sinclair; with
an introduction by Dr. Georg Brandes. New York:
The Macmillan Company, 1917. 396 p.
LC: S 20, '17.
PW: S 22, '17.
BLC: London: Hutchinson & Co., 1917.

_____ King Midas. See Sinclair, Upton, 1878-1968.
Springtime and harvest (1901), S-520.

S-511 _____ Love's pilgrimage: a novel / Upton Sinclair.
New York; London: Mitchell Kennerley, [c1911].
663 p.
LC: My 17, '11.
PW: Je 24, '11.
BLC: London: William Heinemann, 1912.

S-512 _____ Manassas: a novel of the war / by Upton
Sinclair. New York: The Macmillan Company;
London: Macmillan & Co., ltd., 1904. 412 p.
PW: O 8, '04.

S-513 _____ The metropolis / by Upton Sinclair. New
York: Moffat, Yard & Company, 1908. 376 p.
LC: F 15, '08.
PW: Mr 14, '08.
BLC: London: Edward Arnold, 1908.

S-514 _____ The millennium: a comedy of the year 2000 /
by Upton Sinclair . . . Pasadena, California: Upton
Sinclair, [1924?] 246 p.
Preface signed February, 1924.
Another ed.: Girard, Kan.: Haldeman-Julius Co.,
1924. Little blue book; no. 590-592.

S-515 _____ The moneychangers / by Upton Sinclair . . .
New York: B. W. Dodge & Company, 1908. 316 p.
LC: S 5, '08.
PW: S 19, '08.

S-516 _____ 100 %: the story of a patriot / by Upton
Sinclair. Pasadena, California: Published by The
author, [c1920]. 329 p.   **TOL**
LC: Ja 7, '21.
PW: N 20, '20.

S-517 _____ The overman / by Upton Sinclair; with
frontispiece. New York: Doubleday, Page &
Company, 1907. 90 p., front.
LC: S 25, '07.
PW: O 5, '07.
BLC: London: Doubleday, Page & Co., New York
printed, 1907.

S-518 _____ Prince Hagen: a phantasy: / by Upton
Sinclair. Boston: L. C. Page & Company, 1903.
249 p.
PW: Je 6, '03.
BLC: London: Chatto & Windus, 1903.

S-519 _____ Samuel the seeker / Upton Sinclair . . . New
York: B. W. Dodge & Company, 1910. 315 p.

LC: Mr 24, '10.
PW: Ap 2, '10.

S-520 _____ Springtime and harvest: a romance / by Upton
Sinclair. New York: The Sinclair Press, [c1901].
281 p., front.
Published later under title: *King Midas*, (1901).
PW: S 21, '01.

S-521 _____ Sylvia: a novel / by Upton Sinclair.
Philadelphia; Chicago: The John C. Winston
Company, [c1913]. 413 p.   **NOC**
LC: My 20, '13.
PW: My 17, '13.

S-522 _____ Sylvia's marriage: a novel / by Upton Sinclair.
Philadelphia; Chicago: The John C. Winston
Company, [c1914]. 348 p.   **OSU, IPL**
LC: O 13, '14.
PW: O 24, '14.

S-523 _____ They call me Carpenter: a tale of the second
coming / by Upton Sinclair . . . New York: Boni
and Liveright, [c1922]. 225 p.
LC: S 23, '22.
BLC: London: T. Werner Laurie, 1922.
Another edition: Chicago: The Paine Book Co.,
[c1922].

S-524 Sindell, Martin, b. 1867. Romance and reality / by
Martin Sindell . . . Eau Claire, Wis.: Issued by the
Paramount Publishing Company, 1919. 455 p.,
photo. front., photo. ill.
LC: O 8, '19.
PW: Ja 17, '20.

S-525 _____ Romance and revolution / by Martin Sindell
. . . Eau Claire, Wis.: Issued by the Paramount
Publishing Company, 1918. 555 p., photo. front.,
photo. ill.   **MNU**
LC: D 12, '18.

S-526 _____ Satisfied at last / by Martin Sindell; with
illustrations by Martin Sindell and Harold C. Dunbar.
Boston, Massachusetts: Reid Publishing Company,
[c1908]. 377 p., front., [3] leaves of plates.
LC: D 14, '08.
PW: Ja 16, '09.

S-527 Singleton, Esther, d. 1930. A daughter of the
revolution / by Esther Singleton. New York: Moffat,
Yard & Company, 1915. 309 p.
PW: N 27, '15.

S-528 Singmaster, Elsie, 1879-1958. Basil Everman / by
Elsie Singmaster. Boston; New York: Houghton
Mifflin Company, 1920. (Cambridge [Mass.]: The
Riverside Press). 305, [1] p.
LC: Mr 29, '20.
PW: Mr 6, '20.

S-529 _____ Bennett Malin / by Elsie Singmaster . . .
Boston; New York: Houghton Mifflin Company,
1922. (Cambridge [Mass.]: The Riverside Press).
328 p.
LC: Je 17, '22.
PW: Je 24, '22.
BLC: London: Hurst & Blackett, [1923].

S-530　　____ Bred in the bone: and other stories / by Elsie Singmaster; with illustrations by Elizabeth Shippen Green. Boston; New York: Houghton Mifflin Company, 1925. (Cambridge: The Riverside Press). 300 p., front., [5] leaves of plates.
"Stories reprinted from various periodicals."
Contents: The truth -- A sound in the night -- A man in the house -- The dreamer -- The end of the world -- Salt of the earth -- The Amishman -- Bred in the bone -- The courier of the czar -- Little and unknown.
LC: O 26, '25.
PW: N 7, '25.

____ The courier of the Czar. In *Prize stories of 1924 (1925), P-622.*

S-531　　____ Ellen Levis; a novel / by Elsie Singmaster. Boston; New York: Houghton Mifflin Company, 1921. (Cambridge: The Riverside Press). 284 p.
LC: F 19, '21.
PW: F 12, '21.

S-532　　____ Emmeline / by Elsie Singmaster; with illustrations. Boston; New York: Houghton Mifflin Company, 1916. (Cambridge [Mass.]: The Riverside Press). 154, [2] p., front., [3] leaves of plates. [Ill. by Bernard J. Rosenmeyer.]
LC: F 25, '16.
PW: F 26, '16.

S-533　　____ Gettysburg; stories of the red harvest and the aftermath / by Elsie Singmaster. Boston; New York: Houghton Mifflin Company, 1913. 190 p., front., [3] leaves of plates. [Ill. by Sidney H. Riesenberg, Frederic Dorr Steele, C. E. Chambers, and F. Walter Taylor.]
Partly reprinted from various periodicals.
Contents: July the first -- The homecoming -- Victory -- The battleground -- Gunner Criswell -- The substitute -- The retreat -- The great day -- Mary Bowman.
LC: My 5, '13.
PW: My 3, '13.

S-534　　____ The hidden road / by Elsie Singmaster . . . Boston; New York: Houghton Mifflin Company, 1923. (Cambridge [Mass.]: The Riverside Press). 333 p.
LC: My 24, '23.
PW: Je 2, '23.

S-535　　____ John Baring's house / by Elsie Singmaster. Boston; New York: Houghton Mifflin Company, 1920. (Cambridge: The Riverside Press). 156 p., col. front. [Ill. by Harold Cue.]
LC: N 1, '20.

S-536　　____ Katy Gaumer / by Elsie Singmaster. Boston; New York: Houghton Mifflin Company, 1915. (Cambridge: The Riverside Press). 336 p., front.
LC: F 25, '15.
PW: F 27, '15.

S-537　　____ The long journey / by Elsie Singmaster. Boston; New York: Houghton Mifflin Company, 1917. (Cambridge: The Riverside Press). 190 p., col. front.
LC: F 23, '17.
PW: F 24, '17.

____ Pair of lovers. In *"Dawgs!": an anthology of stories about them (1925), D-184.*

____ Penance. In *The best short stories of 1916 and the yearbook of the American short story (1917), B-561.*

____ The squire. In *Atlantic narratives; 2nd series (1918), A-361.*

____ The steamer child. In *Representative short stories (1917), R-176.*

____ The survivors. In *The best short stories of 1915 and the yearbook of the American short story (1916), B-560.*

S-538　　Sisson, Elizabeth. Dorothy: a tale of two lands / by Elizabeth Sisson . . . Cincinnati: Jennings and Graham; New York: Eaton and Mains, [c1906]. 333 p., front., [3] leaves of plates. [Ill. by Shafer.]
LC: O 20, '06.
PW: N 10, '06.

Sister Mary Imelda. See **Wallace, L. M.**

S-539　　Siviter, Anna Pierpont, 1858-1932. Nehe: a tale of the times of Artaxerxes / by Anna Pierpont Siviter; with illustrations by Chase Emerson. Boston; Chicago: W. A. Wilde Company, 1901. 318 p., front., [4] leaves of plates.

S-540　　Skiles, May Evelyn. A singular metamorphosis / by May Evelyn Skiles. New York; London; Montreal: The Abbey Press, [c1902]. 85 p.　　　**DLC**
PW: Ag 30, '02.

S-541　　Skinner, Constance Lindsay, 1882-1939. "Good-morning, Rosamond!" / by Constance Lindsay Skinner; illustrated by Thomas Fogarty. Garden City, New York: Doubleday, Page & Company, 1917. 384 p., col. front., [3] leaves of plates, ill. Illustrated end papers.　　　**LPU**
PW: Ap 21, '17.

S-542　　Skinner, Gertrude, b. 1880, *pseud*. A looking-glass / by Gertrude Skinner [pseud.]. Boston: Sherman, French & Company, 1913. 257 p.　　　**DLC**

S-543　　Skinner, Henrietta Dana, 1857-1928. Faith Brandon: a novel / by Henrietta Dana Skinner . . . New York; London: D. Appleton and Company, 1912. 423, [1] p., front.　　　**NYP**
LC: Ap 20, '12.
PW: Ap 20, '12.

S-544　　____ Heart and soul: a novel / by Henrietta Dana Skinner. New York; London: Harper & Brothers, 1901. 307, [1] p.
PW: Je 29, '01.

S-545　　____ Their choice: a novel / by Henrietta Dana Skinner . . . New York; Cincinnati; Chicago: Benziger Brothers, 1913. 180 p., col. front. [Ill. by Abbey Altson.]
LC: F 11, '13.
PW: Mr 1, '13.

S-546 Slade, A. F. Annie Deane: a wayside weed / by A. F. Slade. New York: Brentano's, 1901. 376 p.
PW: O 5, '01.

S-547 ____ Mary Neville: the history of a woman who attempted too much / by A. F. Slade . . . New York: Brentano's, 1902. 414 p. **NYP**
BLC: London: Hutchinson & Co., 1902.

S-548 Slade, J. W. (James William), b. 1877. The possum hunters: a story of the tobacco war in Kentucky / by J. W. Slade. Kansas City, Missouri: Burton Publishing Company, [c1920]. 376 p.
LC: Jl 30, '20.
PW: S 11, '20.

S-549 Slater, S., Jr., *pseud.* Via vitae / by S. Slater, Jr. [pseud.]; illustrator: Ruth Greene. Boston: The Roxburg Publishing Company Inc., [c1917]. 314 p., front., [1] leaf of plates.

S-550 Slattery, Margaret. The costly star / by Margaret Slattery; illustrated by Frank T. Merrill. Boston; Chicago: The Pilgrim Press, [c1917]. 32 p., col. front., [1] leaf of plates.

Slease, Clyde H., jt. ed. See *Allegheny stories* **(1902), A-142.**

S-551 Sleight, Mary Breck. At the manor: when the British held the Hudson / by Mary Breck Sleight. New York: R. F. Fenno & Company, [c1912]. 289 p., incl. front., [3] leaves of plates. [Some ill. by Miller.] **DLC**

S-552 Sloan, Annie L. (Annie Lee), b. 1861. The Carolinians: an old-fashioned love story of stirring times in the early colony of Carolina / by Annie L. Sloan. New York; Washington: The Neale Publishing Company, 1904. 375 p., front. (map).

S-553 Slosson, Annie Trumbull, 1838-1926. "And other folks": the story of a little girl and a little sermon / by Annie Trumbull Slosson. Philadelphia: Sunday School Times Co., [c1918]. 35 p., front. [Ill. by Charles D. Hubbard.] **NYP**

S-554 ____ Aunt Abby's neighbors / by Annie Trumbull Slosson. New York; Chicago; [etc.]: F. H. Revell Company, 1902. 170 p.
Unexamined copy: bibliographic data from OCLC, #5868304.

S-555 ____ A dissatisfied soul and A prophetic romancer / by Annie Trumbull Slosson . . . New York: Bonnell, Silver & Co., 1908. 89 p., photo. front., [3] leaves of plates.
PW: Jl 18, '08.

S-556 ____ A little sheherd of Bethlehem / by Annie Trumbull Slosson . . . Philadelphia: The Sunday School Times Company, 1914. 38 p., front. [Ill. by C. H. Stephens.] **MCB**
LC: Ja 3, '14.

S-557 ____ A local colorist / by Annie Trumbull Slosson. New York: Charles Scribner's Sons, 1912. 147 p.,

front. [Ill. by S. M. Chase.]
LC: Mr 7, '12.
PW: Mr 2, '12.

S-558 ____ Simples from the Master's garden / Annie Trumbull Slosson . . . Philadelphia: The Sunday School Times Company, [c1907]. 142 p., front. [Ill. by C. H. Stephens.] Text within ornamental borders. Contents: The Master's garden -- A simple cross-bearer -- A simple child trainer -- A simple Pentecost -- A simple dreamer -- A simple faith -- A simple expositor.

S-559 ____ White Christopher / by Annie Trumbull Slosson. New York: James Pott & Company, 1901. 66 p., front. Title within ornamental border.
PW: Mr 9, '01.
BLC: London: S. Bagster & Sons, 1901.

S-560 Sly, Winfield Scott. Anneeti, the gypsy artist / by Winfield Scott Sly . . . illustrated from life. Lansing, Mich.: The author, 1901. 179 p., incl. front., [5] leaves of plates.
Unexamined copy: bibliographic data from OCLC, #13881518.
PW: My 11, '01.

S-561 ____ Chronicles of a farm house / by Winfield Scott Sly. Lansing, Michigan: Published by Cere Root Specialty Company, 1923. 274 p., front. (port.), [5] leaves of plates (some photo.). **EXA**
LC: N 14, '23.

S-562 Small, Albert A. The children of union / by Albert A. Small . . . Tulsa, Oklahoma: The Union Publishing Co., [c1925]. 305 p. **OKD**

S-563 Small, Albion Woodbury, 1854-1926. Between eras from capitalism to democracy / by Albion W. Small. Kansas City, Mo.: Inter-Collegiate Press, [c1913]. 431 p.

S-564 Small, Charles Wilder. Poinsettia / Charles Wilder Small. [s. l.: s. n., c1907]. 106 p., photo. front., [3] leaves of photo. plates. **FXG**
LC: F 12, '08.

Small, Ethel Sigsbee. Ætat ten. In *The heart of childhood* **(1906), H-441.**

S-565 Small, Eugene L. (Eugene Lester). The awakening of Lesterville: a novel / by Eugene L. Small. Chicago Lawn, Illinois: [Englewood Print Shop], 1918. 250 p., incl. photo. front., [3] leaves of photo. plates. **DLC**

S-566 Small, Sidney Herschel, b. 1893. Both one / by Sidney Herschel Small . . . Indianapolis: The Bobbs-Merrill Company, [c1925]. 301, [1] p.
LC: S 28, '25.
PW: O 3, '25.

S-567 ____ Fourscore / by Sidney Herschel Small . . . Indianapolis: The Bobbs-Merrill Company, [c1924]. 376 p.
LC: S 29, '24.
PW: O 11, '24.

S-568 ____ The lord of Thundergate / by Sidney Herschel Small. Indianapolis: The Bobbs-Merrill Company, [c1923]. 337 p., front., [4] leaves of plates. [Ill. by Louis Rogers.]
LC: Mr 5, '23.
PW: F 17, '23.

S-569 Smart, Charles Alexander. A dream? / Charles Alexander Smart. [Oakland, Cal.: McCombs Print., 1905?]. 22 p.
Cover title.

S-570 Smart, Janie Sawyer. The vintage of Spain / by Janie Sawyer Smart. Boston, Massachusetts: The C. M. Clark Publishing Company, [c1910]. 358 p., col. front., [5] leaves of plates. [Some ill. by D. S. Ross.] **AZU**
LC: F 10, '11.

S-571 Smedberg, H. V. (Harold V.). The improprieties of Noah: and other stories / by H. V. Smedberg. New York; London; Montreal: The Abbey Press, [c1901]. 101 p.
Contents: The improprieties of Noah -- Priscilla's prisoner -- A cupid of the jimmy -- Misunderstood by the world -- Progress of a fib -- The summit of circumstance.
PW: F 15, '02.

S-572 Smeeth, Helen M. (Helen Marié), b. 1865. The log of three across the sea / by Helen M. Smeeth. Chicago: Manufactured by The Henneberry Company, 1910. 212 p.
LC: O 24, '10.
PW: Ja 21, '11.

S-573 Smiley, James Laurenson. Maud Muller's ministry, or, The claims of Christian socialism / by James Laurenson Smiley. Annapolis, Md.: [s. n., c1907]. 159 p. **DLC**

S-574 Smirnow, Louis. The last days of St. Pierre / by Louis Smirnow; with illustrations by R. I. Conklin. Boston, Massachusetts: The C. M. Clark Publishing Company, [c1910]. 604 p., front., [5] leaves of plates.

S-575 Smitch, Clara Evangeline. Above the clouds: and other tales / by Clara Evangeline Smitch. Leadville, Colo.: Leadville Publishing and Printing Co., 1906. 178 p.
Contents: The wooing of December -- Predestination -- The shadow -- The lost chord -- The forbidden law -- In the meshes -- Carroll branded a murderer -- Facing the inevitable -- The sacrifice -- The wedding day -- Condemned -- Parting -- Relenting -- The broken jardiniere -- Loyalty -- In twilight -- Maria Varga's revenge -- The hand of the dead -- Sleepy Hollow -- On the crest of the range -- The sighing of the pines.
LC: Jl 14, '06.
PW: Ag 25, '06.

S-576 Smith, Alice Prescott. Kindred / by Alice Prescott Smith . . . Boston; New York: Houghton Mifflin Company, 1925. (Cambridge [Mass.]: The Riverside Press). 344 p.
LC: Jl 27, '25.
PW: Ag 8, '25.
BLC: London: William Heinemann, 1926.

S-577 ____ The legatee / by Alice Prescott Smith. Boston;

New York: Houghton, Mifflin and Company, 1903. (Cambridge: The Riverside Press). 324 p.
PW: Ap 4, '03.

S-578 ____ Montlivet / by Alice Prescott Smith. Boston; New York: Houghton, Mifflin and Company, 1906. (Cambridge [Mass.]: The Riverside Press). 443, [1] p., front. (double map).
LC: S 19, '06.
PW: O 6, '06.

S-579 ____ Off the highway / by Alice Prescott Smith. Boston; New York: Houghton, Mifflin and Company, 1904. (Cambridge: The Riverside Press). 299 p. **CLE**
PW: N 5, '04.

Smith, Ann Eliza Brainerd. See **Smith, J. G., Mrs.**

Smith, Anna May. See **May, Anna, pseud.**

S-580 Smith, Annie H. Rosemary Leigh: a story of the South / by Annie H. Smith. New York; Washington: The Neale Publishing Company, 1905. 239 p. **GUA**

S-581 [Smith, Annie Laura, b. 1873]. Rosine; the story of a fair young girl / by Catherine Von Scyler [pseud.]. Montreal; New York; London; [etc.]: Broadway Publishing Company, 1903. 132 p., front. (port.). Unexamined copy: bibliographic data from OCLC, #17500642.

S-582 Smith, Annie L. (Annie Lydia), b. 1836. The black mask, or, Bonnie Orielle's lovers / by Annie L. Smith (Lydia A. Jocelyn) . . . Worcester, Mass.: Published by Edna I. Tyler, [c1906]. 349 p., photo. front. (port.) **KUK**
(Smith-Tyler library.)
LC: Ja 10, '07.

S-583 [____] "Lords of the soil": a romance of Indian life among the early English settlers / by Lydia A. Jocelyn and Nathan J. Cuffee. Boston, Mass., U. S. A.: C. M. Clark Publishing Co., Inc., 1905. 467 p., front. [Ill. by A. B. Shute.]
PW: S 16, '05.

S-584 Smith, Arthur Cosslett, 1852-1926. The turquoise cup, and, The desert / by Arthur Cosslett Smith; illustrated. New York: Charles Scribner's Sons, 1903. 208 p., col. front., [1] leaf of plates, ill.
PW: Mr 7, '03.
BLC: London: John Lane, Boston, U. S. A. [printed], 1913.

S-585 Smith, Arthur D. Howden (Arthur Douglas Howden), 1887-1945. The audacious adventures of Miles McConaughy: an epic of the merchant marine / by Arthur D. Howden Smith. New York: George H. Doran Company, [c1918]. 354 p. Illustrated end papers.
LC: Je 6, 18.
PW: Je 8, '18.
BLC: London: Skeffington & Son, [1919].

S-586 ____ Beyond the sunset / by Arthur D. Howden Smith . . . New York: Brentano's, [c1923]. 291 p.

Maps on end papers.
LC: F 14, '23.
PW: F 17, '23.
BLC: London: Brentano's, 1913.

S-587   ____ The doom trail / by Arthur D. Howden Smith. New York: Brentano's, [c1922]. 312 p. Maps on end papers.
LC: Mr 18, '22.
PW: Mr 4, '22.
BLC: London: Brentano's, printed in U. S. A., [1923].

S-588   ____ Porto Bello gold / by Arthur D. Howden Smith. New York: Brentano's, [c1924]. 330 p., col. front., [8] leaves of col. plates.
LC: N 24, '24.
LC notes another issue: No ills., maps on end papers.

S-589   ____ Spears of destiny: a story of the first capture of Constantinople / by Arthur D. Howden Smith. New York: George H. Doran Company, [c1919]. 342 p.
LC: Ap 6, '19.
PW: Ap 19, '19.
BLC: London: Skeffington & Son, printed in U. S. A., [1920].

S-590   ____ The treasure of the Bucoleon / by Arthur D. Howden Smith . . . New York: Brentano's, [c1923]. 292 p., ill.
LC: S 6, '23.
PW: N 17, '23.
BLC: London: Brentano's, 1924.

S-591   ____ The Wastrel / by Arthur D. Howden Smith. New York: Duffield and Company, 1911. 333 p., col. front.
LC: Mr 1, '11.
PW: Mr 25, '11.

S-592   Smith, Blanche Jane. Fresh from the Barrens / by Blanche Cox Smith; illustrations by Frank S. Bowers and Albert H. Smith. Indianapolis: Smith Printing Company, c1915. 253 p., [9] leaves of plates. Unexamined copy: bibliographic data from OCLC, #22967218.

S-593   Smith, Bridges, 1848-1903. 100 stories in black: a collection of bright, breezy, humorous stories of the colored race as seen in the sunny South / by Bridges Smith. New York: J. S. Ogilvie Publishing Company, [c1910]. 318 p., ill. [Ill. by C. Rigby, George B. Luks, & H. W. Phillips.]   **BUF**
"Originally appeared from day to day in the Macon Daily Telegraph."
Contents: A typical fight -- The tissue-paper ball -- Precious Jackson's last beau -- A scene in Yamacraw -- Fall styles -- Haslit Pete -- Before-day and littlebit -- The fortune teller -- The star boarder -- The rival societies -- Slowfoot Sal's outing -- Minerva's sister in Chicago -- Reconciliation -- Spiders -- The Mary Jane gown -- Parting of the ways -- The loiterers -- The spotter -- Cupid on matrimony -- The fight -- A chewing gum episode -- The linen shower -- Alley talk -- Why the board was raised -- Old Miss and Aunt Lou -- The little boy -- All mothers are alike -- Cross alley conversation -- Mind-reading in Yamacraw -- The bribe -- Uncle Isom's star -- Sleep sickness -- The cocaine sniffer -- The Tybee debating society -- A Tybee trick -- Poor Emma -- What fools these husbands be -- A first class funeral -- Taking the census -- The hook worm -- The educated daughter -- An Enoch Arden case -- The plum-colored kimono -- Mandy's country beau -- Who was scared the most -- The delivery boy's mistake -- The engagement ring -- The invalid -- The belated groom -- Out with the church -- In a Tybee backyard -- A fair exchange -- The slim girl -- The separation -- The ministering angels -- How she won her man -- The North Pole -- Back-boneless Mullet -- When the president comes -- The manicure artist -- The unwilling witness -- The card party -- The dinner hour -- Littlebit -- The lovers' quarrel -- Slowfoot Sal's fight -- The disagreement -- What the nurses said -- A chance meeting -- The vags -- The president's breakfast -- A wedding in Tybee -- The friend in court -- The sign of death -- The matrons' club -- The larceny of the rose -- The humming bird society -- The broken engagement -- Aunt Ann -- The eagle and the buzzard -- Slowfoot Sal's ride -- Sugar babe -- For sale: one goat -- The skeleton in the closet -- A Valentine party in Yamacraw -- Faith -- Reconciliation -- The accusation -- The waist-line party -- The trainman's revenge -- Fatty Fan's mistake -- The empire gown -- If I were pres'dent -- The fortune-teller -- The old couple -- The pure food law -- Swallowed a lightning bug -- Miss Jackson hypnotised -- The serenade -- A typical case.

S-594   Smith, Carolyn Scofield. The solution: a story of the new medication / by Carolyn Scoffield Smith. Boston: Richard G. Badger, [c1922]. ([Boston]: The Gorham Press). 134 p.   **AVL**

S-595   Smith, Charlotte Curtis. The old cobblestone house: a ghost story / by Charlotte Curtis Smith. Rochester, N. Y.: The Craftsman Press, 1917. 127 p.

S-596   Smith, Charlton Lyman. Gus Harvey: the boy skipper of Cape Ann / by Charlton Lyman Smith. Boston: Marshall Jones Company, 1920. 197 p., front., [3] leaves of plates.
LC: Ag 18, '20.

S-597   Smith, Chetwood, Mrs., 1872. Cranberry Cove stories / by Mrs. Chetwood Smith . . . ; illustrated by photographs. Boston: Richard G. Badger; Toronto: The Copp Clark Co., Limited, [c1915]. 213 p., photo. front., [7] leaves of photo. plates.   **VTU**
Contents: Scallop Island -- Robin Adair -- The wager -- Mademoiselle's holiday -- The world's sweet inn -- Diamonds and hearts -- Without benefit of doubt -- Merely actors -- Who only stand and wait -- Heart of gold -- The new library -- The nautilus.
LC: Mr 26, '15.
PW: Ap 17, '15.

S-598   ____ The god of the bees / by Mrs. Chetwood Smith; frontispiece by Mary Hamilton Frye. Boston: W. A. Butterfield, 1913. 204 p., front.

S-599   Smith, Clarke, b. 1857. About us and the deacon / by Clarke Smith. Philadelphia: The Literary Bureau, Inc., [c1911]. 319 p., front., [6] leaves of plates. [Ill. by J. Mains Rodgers.] Designed end papers.

S-600   Smith, D. B. (David Burson). Burson Adair: European letters of travel, essays, newspaper articles, poems and short stories / D. B. Smith. Bonham, Texas: [L. H. Jenkins, Inc., c1925]. 371 p., photo. front. (port.), [13] leaves of photo. plates.
Contents: Short stories [p. 213-371]: The haunted still -- The mail-rider of Fort Gates -- The homecoming of Susie -- The Comanche bride -- Washington's youngest commissary general -- The vigilant committee -- Love-making under difficulties -- The South bosque tragedy -- The Owl Creek romance -- The Eagle Springs tragedy -- General Nathan Forrest's youngest scout -- Annie Ross, or the angel of the bosques -- The coffee-mill bandit and the slave sleuth -- The new crisis.

S-601　　Smith, E. Palmer (Ella Palmer), b. 1855. Lydia of Lebanon / by E. Palmer Smith. Boston: The Roxburgh Publishing Co., [c1919]. 272 p.　**NYP**
LC: O 23, '19.

Smith, Edgar Valentine. 'Lijah. In *Prize stories of 1924* (1925), **P-622.**

____ Prelude. In *Prize stories of 1923* (1924), **P-621.**

S-602　　Smith, Elbert A., 1871-1959. Joe Pine / by Elbert A. Smith; illustrated by Paul N. Craig. Lamoni, Iowa: Herald Publishing House, 1916. 351, [1] p., front., [7] leaves of plates.

____ The minister who was different. See **Carter, Mary Leland.** *An instrument in His hands* (1908), **C-166.**

S-603　　Smith, Elliott, b. 1868. The land of lure: a story of the Columbia River Basin / by Elliott Smith . . . Tacoma, Wash.: Press of Smith-Kinney Company, 1920. 242 p., [4] leaves of photo. plates.
LC: N 6, '20.

S-604　　Smith, Elsie Rhea. Brother Luke / by Elsie Rhea Smith. Dallas, Texas: Johnston Company, 1909. 67 p.　　**DLC**
LC: D 18, '09.

S-605　　Smith, Emma Josephine, b. 1844. Unraveling a mystery / by Emma J. Smith . . . New York: The Cosmopolitan Press, 1911. 239 p.
Unexamined copy: bibliographic data from NUC.

S-606　　Smith, Ernest U. (Ernest Urial), b. 1866. Rachel: a story of the great deluge; with an introduction giving the results of the author's investigations into the question of the location of the lands of Eden and Nod, and incidentally explaining the origin of the American Indians / by Ernest U. Smith; illustrated by five maps. New York: The Grafton Press, [c1904]. 314 p., [5] leaves of plates (maps).　　**NYP**
PW: N 12, '04.

S-607　　Smith, F. Berkeley (Frank Berkeley), b. 1869. Babette: a novel / by F. Berkeley Smith. Garden City, N. Y.: Doubleday, Page & Co., 1916. 324 p., col. front. (port.). [Ill. by Oliver Herford.]
LC: Mr 29, '16.
PW: Mr 25, '16.

____, jt. aut. *Enoch Crane* (1916). See **Smith, F. Hopkinson (Francis Hopkinson), 1838-1915, jt. aut., S-615.**

S-608　　____ The lady of Big Shanty / by F. Berkeley Smith. New York: Doubleday, Page & Company, 1909. 323 p.
LC: O 16, '09.
PW: O 30, '09.
BLC: London: Doubleday, Page & Co., 1909.

S-609　　____ Madame Mésange / by F. Berkeley Smith. Garden City, New York: Doubleday, Page & Company, 1912. 44 p., col. front. Illustrated end papers.
LC: O 1, '12.
PW: O 12, '12.

S-610　　____ The Street of the Two Friends / by F. Berkeley Smith; illustrations by the author. Garden City, N. Y.: Doubleday, Page & Company, 1912. 406 p., ill.
LC: N 4, '12.
PW: N 16, '12.

S-611　　____ A village of vagabonds / by F. Berkeley Smith; color illustrations by F. Hopkinson Smith, pen drawings by the author. New York: Doubleday, Page & Company, 1910. 364 p., col. front., ill. Illustrated end papers in colors.
LC: My 21, '10.
PW: My 21, '10.
BLC: London: Hodder & Stoughton, 1910.

S-612　　Smith, F. Hopkinson (Francis Hopkinson), 1838-1915. The arm-chair at the inn / by F. Hopkinson Smith; with illustrations by A. I. Keller, Herbert Ward and the author. New York: Charles Scribner's Sons, 1912. 357 p., front., [7] leaves of plates.
LC: Ag 28, '12.
PW: Ag 31, '12.
BLC: London: T. Werner Laurie, [1912].
References: BAL 18251.

____ The arrival of a true Southern lady. In *Short stories of America* (1921), **S-464.**

S-613　　____ At close range / by F. Hopkinson Smith; illustrated. New York: Charles Scribner's Sons, 1905. 260 p., front., [5] leaves of plates. [Ill. by Charlotte Weber-Ditzler, F. C. Yohn, and Walter Granville Smith.]
PW: Mr 25, '05.
BLC: London: William Heinemann, New York printed, 1905.
References: BAL 18238.

S-614　　____ Colonel Carter's Christmas / by F. Hopkinson Smith; illustrated by F. C. Yohn. New York: Charles Scribner's Sons, 1903. 159 p., col. front., [7] leaves of col. plates.
LC: O 8, '03.
PW: D 5, '03.
References: BAL 18236.

S-615　　____ Enoch Crane: a novel / planned and begun by F. Hopkinson Smith and completed by F. Berkeley Smith; illustrated by Alonzo Kimball. New York: Charles Scribner's Sons, 1916. 337 p., front., [3] leaves of plates.
LC: S 20, '16.
PW: S 9, '16.
BLC: London: T. Werner Laurie, [1916].
References: 18263.

S-616　　____ Felix O'Day / by F. Hopkinson Smith; illustrated by George Wright. New York: Charles Scribner's Sons, 1915. 370 p., front., [3] leaves of plates.

LC: S 22, '15.
PW: S 18, '15.
BLC: London: T. Werner Laurie, [1916].
References: BAL 18261.

S-617   _____ The fortunes of Oliver Horn / by F. Hopkinson Smith; illustrated by Walter Appleton Clark. New York: Charles Scribner's Sons, 1902. 551, [1] p., front., [7] leaves of plates.
LC: Ag 21, '02.
PW: S 6, '02.
BLC: London: George Newnes, New York printed, 1902.
References: BAL 18234.

S-618   _____ Forty minutes late: and other stories / by F. Hopkinson Smith; illustrated. New York: Charles Scribner's Sons, 1909. 224 p., front., [7] leaves of plates (1 photo.). [Some ill. by S. M. Chase.]
Contents: Forty minutes late -- A gentleman's gentleman -- Abijah's bubble -- A list to starboard -- The little gray lady -- The man in the high-water boots -- Fiddles -- Homo -- The Parthenon by way of Papendrecht.
LC: S 29, '09.
PW: O 9, '09.
References: 18249.

S-619   _____ Kennedy Square / by F. Hopkinson Smith; illustrated by A. I. Keller. New York: Charles Scribner's Sons, 1911. 504 p., front., [5] leaves of plates.
LC: S 5, '11.
PW: Ag 26, '11.
BLC: London: T. Werner Laurie, [1911].
References: BAL 18250.

S-620   _____ Peter: a novel of which he is not the hero / by F. Hopkinson Smith; illustrated by A. I. Keller. New York: Charles Scribner's Sons, 1908. 482 p., front., [3] leaves of plates.
LC: Ag 22, '08.
PW: S 5, '08.
BLC: London: Hodder & Stoughton, New York, 1909.
References: BAL 18247.

S-621   _____ The romance of an old-fashioned gentleman / by F. Hopkinson Smith; illustrated by A. I. Keller. New York: Charles Scribner's Sons, 1907. 213 p., col. front., [4] leaves of col. plates.
LC: O 1, '07.
PW: O 19, '07.
References: BAL 18246.

S-622   _____ The tides of Barnegat / by F. Hopkinson Smith; illustrated by George Wright. New York: Charles Scribner's Sons, 1906. 422 p., front., [11] leaves of plates.
LC: Ag 9, '06.
PW: Ag 18, '06.
BLC: London: Hodder & Stoughton, New York printed, 1906.
References: BAL 18242.

S-623   _____ The under dog / by F. Hopkinson Smith; illustrated. New York: Charles Scribner's Sons, 1903. 332 p., front., [11] leaves of plates. [Ill. by Howard Chandler Christy, A. I. Keller, Thomas Fogarty, E. M. Ashe, William L. Jacobs, and Charles Grunwald.]
Contents: No respecter of persons -- Cap'n Bob of the Screamer -- A procession of umbrellas -- "Doc" Shipman's fee -- Plain Fin-paper hanger -- Long Jim -- Compartment number four, Cologne to Paris -- Sammy -- Marny's shadow -- Muffles-the bar-keep -- His last cent.
LC: My 22, '03.
PW: Je 27, '03.
References: BAL 18235.

S-624   _____ The veiled lady: and other men and women / by F. Hopkinson Smith; illustrated. New York: Charles Scribner's Sons, 1907. 295 p., front., [11] leaves of plates.
Contents: The veiled lady of Stamboul -- Loretta of the shipyard -- A coat of red lead -- Miss Murdock-"special" -- The beguiling of Peter Griggs -- Miss Jenning's companion -- Sam Joplin's epigastric nerve -- Miss Buffum's new boarder -- Captain Joe and the "Susie Ann" -- "Against orders" -- Muggles' supreme moment.
LC: Mr 26, '07.
PW: Ap 6, '07.
References: BAL 18244.

S-625   _____ The wood fire in no. 3 / by F. Hopkinson Smith; illustrated in colors by Alonzo Kimball. New York: Charles Scribner's Sons, 1905. 298 p., col. front., [8] leaves of col. plates.
LC: O 19, '05.
PW: N 4, '05.
BLC: London: Hodder & Stoughton, 1906.
References: BAL 18239.

S-626   Smith, Frederick Miller, b. 1870. The stolen signet / by Frederick M. Smith; pictures by F. R. Shaler. New York: Duffield & Company, 1909. 315 p., col. front., [2] leaves of plates.   **OSU, DLC**
LC: S 21, '09.
PW: N 6, '09.

Smith, George C., Jr. The six twenties. In *Made to order* (1915), **M-352.**

S-627   Smith, George Hoyt. Gray gull feathers / by George Hoyt Smith. Columbia, S. C.: The State Company, 1924. 106 p., photo. front. (port.).
Contents: Gray gull feathers -- A gate in the high wall -- When Elmville backslid -- Traumerei -- Trailing arbutus.
LC: Jl 9, '24.

S-628   _____ The Palmetto derby: and other stories / by George Hoyt Smith . . . New York: The Knickerbocker Press, 1925. 144 p.
Contents: The Palmetto derby -- Eugene, the eugenic -- Behind the scenes -- Peter van Vort -- A soft-hearted pole.
LC: D 9, '25.

S-629   Smith, Gordon Arthur, 1886-1944. The crown of life / by Gordon Arthur Smith. New York: Charles Scribner's Sons, 1915. 416 p.
LC: S 30, '15.
PW: O 2, '15.

_____ Feet of gold. In *The best short stories of 1916 and the yearbook of the American short story* (1917), **B-561.**

S-630   _____ Mascarose / by Gordon Arthur Smith. New York: Charles Scribner's Sons, 1913. 257 p., col. front. [Ill. by Frank Smith.]
LC: O 14, '13.
PW: O 25, '13.

No flowers. <u>In</u> *Prize stories of 1920* (1921), **P-618.**

S-631   The pagan / by Gordon Arthur Smith. New York: Charles Scribner's Sons, 1920. 364 p.
Contents: The pagan -- Tropic madness -- Jeanne, the maid -- Every move -- Letitia -- A young man's fancy -- The return.
LC: Mr 25, '20.
PW: Mr 20, '20.

S-632   There goes the groom / by Gordon Arthur Smith . . . New York: E. P. Dutton & Company, [c1922]. 237 p.
PW: Je 3, '22.

S-633   Smith, Harriet Lummis. Agatha's aunt / by Harriet Lummis Smith. Indianapolis: The Bobbs-Merrill Company, [c1920]. 340 p.
LC: Ag 30, '20.
PW: S 25, '20.

S-634   Other people's business: the romantic career of the practical Miss Dale / by Harriet Lummis Smith. Indianapolis: The Bobbs-Merrill Company, [c1916]. 367 p.
LC: O 25, '16.
PW: S 23, '16.

S-635   Pollyanna of the orange blossoms / by Harriet Lummis Smith . . . ; illustrated by H. Weston Taylor. Boston: L. C. Page & Company (Inc.), 1924. 313 p., front., [5] leaves of plates.
At head of title: The third glad book.
LC: My 31, '24.
PW: My 24, '24.

S-636   Pollyanna's jewels / by Harriet Lummis Smith . . . ; illustrated by H. Weston Taylor. Boston: L. C. Page & Company, [c1925]. 328 p., front., [5] leaves of plates.
At head of title: The fourth glad book.
LC: S 2, '25.
PW: D 12, '25.

S-637   Smith, Harry James, 1880-1918. Amédée's son / by Harry James Smith. Boston; New York: Houghton Mifflin Company, 1908. (Cambridge: The Riverside Press). 335, [1] p.
LC: Ag 19, '08.
PW: O 3, '08.

S-638   Cape Breton tales / by Harry James Smith . . . ; with illustrations by Oliver M. Wiard. Boston: The Atlantic Monthly Press, [c1920]. 140 p., front., [4] leaves of plates. Reprinted from various sources.
Contents: On the French shore of Cape Breton -- La Rose witnesseth -- At a Breton calvaire -- The privilege -- Their true love -- Garlands for Pettipaw -- Fly, my heart.
LC: D 17, '20.

S-639   Enchanted ground: an episode in the life of a young man / by Harry James Smith. Boston; New York: Houghton Mifflin Company, 1910. (Cambridge: The Riverside Press). 345, [1] p.
LC: Ag 25, '10.
BLC: London: Constable, 1910.

S-640   Smith, Henry E. The pride of the rancho / by Henry E. Smith . . . ; a novel founded upon his play of the same name. New York: J. S. Ogilvie Publishing Company, [c1909]. 190 p., front. [Ill. by W. L. Burford.] Designed end papers.
LC: D 21, '09.
PW: Ja 8, '10.

S-641   Smith, Henry Justin, b. 1875. Josslyn: the story of an incorrigible dreamer / by Henry Justin Smith. Chicago: Covici-McGee Co., 1924. 252 p.
LC: My 13, '24.
PW: Je 14, '24.

S-642   The other side of the wall / by Henry Justin Smith; illustrated by Clinton Pettee. Garden City, New York: Doubleday, Page & Company, 1919. 342 p., front., [3] leaves of plates. **OSU, CLU**
LC: O 18, '19.
PW: S 27, '19.

S-643   Smith, Horace Herbert, 1868-1936. The war maker: being the true story of Captain George B. Boynton / by Horace Smith; with portrait. Chicago: A. C. McClurg & Co., 1911. 415 p., photo. front. (port.). [Photo. by Pirie MacDonald.]

S-644   Smith, J. G., Mrs., 1818-1905. Angels and women: a revision of the unique novel Seola / by Mrs. J. G. Smith. New York: Published by A. B. Abac Company, 1924. 268 p.

S-645   Smith, J. H. Maudelle: a novel founded on facts gathered from living witnesses / by J. H. Smith. Boston, Mass.: Mayhew Publishing Company, 1906. 458 p.

S-646   Smith, J. R. (John Randolph). Gladys: the angel of the good / by J. R. Smith . . . Springfield, Mo.: Press of Jewell Publishing Co., 1909. 293 p., photo. front. **DLC**
LC: O 1, '09.

Smith, J. Elwin. "Dad's grave." <u>In</u> *The heart of childhood* (1906), **H-441.**

S-647   Smith, James Cosslett, 1857-1917. Miss Peyton of Virginia: and other stories / by James Cosslett Smith. New York: The Knickerbocker Press, 1921. 77 p.
Contents: Miss Peyton of Virginia -- The law or the lady? -- A Christmas paradox -- Was she a suffragist -- The unseen eye -- Doublets -- The Phoenix -- A good Indian.

S-648   [Smith, Jeanie Oliver], 1836-1925. A forest idyl / by Temple Oliver [pseud.]. Boston: Sherman, French & Company, 1913. 222 p.

S-649   Smith, John Leonard. The merchant of Mount Vernon / by John Leonard Smith. Los Angeles: Published by the author, 1907. 226 p.
LC: O 31, '07.

Smith, John Randolph. <u>See</u> **Smith, J. R.**

S-650   Smith, John Talbot, 1855-1923. The art of disappearing / by John Talbot Smith . . . New York: William H. Young and Company, 1902. 367 p.
Revised edition: *The man who vanished*, (1922).

S-651 ____ The black cardinal: a novel / by John Talbot Smith. New York: The Champlain Press, 1914. 360 p.
LC: Jl 15, '14.

S-652 ____ The man who vanished: a novel / by John Talbot Smith . . . New York: Blase Benziger & Co., Inc., 1922. 357 p. "This book was first published in 1902 under the title of The art of disappearing."
LC: Mr 25, '22. (Copyright is claimed on several chapters rewritten.)
PW: Ap 1, '22.

S-653 [Smith, Juliet C.] Until seventy times seven. New York: T. Whittaker, 1903. 180 p.
Unexamined copy: bibliographic data from OCLC, #26967271.

S-654 Smith, Juliette Gordon. The Wednesday wife / by Juliette Gordon Smith. New York: The Macmillan Company, 1921. 225 p.
LC: S 28, '21.
PW: O 22, '21.
BLC: London: Hutchinson, [1922].

S-655 Smith, Lilla Hall, b. 1860. Down our way / by Lilla Hall Smith; frontispiece by John Rae. New York: Dodd, Mead and Company, 1911. 341 p., front.
LC: S 16, '11.
PW: S 16, '11.

Smith, Lydia Annie (Jocelyn). See **Smith, Annie L. (Annie Lydia), b. 1836.**

Smith, Mabell Shippie (Clarke), Mrs. See **Pelton, Mabell Shippie Clarke, 1864-1942.**

S-656 Smith, Margaret B. The best of people: and other short stories / by Margaret B. Smith; revised by Dorothy Starr Dinsmore. Philadelphia, Pa.: Published by the Westbrook Publishing Company, [c1922]. 22 p., ill. **DLC**
Contents: The best of people -- The return -- Romance and Martha Pennypacker -- Charity -- The clown.

S-657 ____ Safe people: a story of the stage / by Margaret B. Smith. Philadelphia, Pa.: The Westbrook Publishing Company, [c1922]. 22 p.
Unexamined copy: bibliographic data from NUC.

S-658 Smith, Marietta. The better part: a story of love and service / by Marietta Smith; illustrated. [Atchison, Kan.: Burbank Printing Co.], 1918. 84 p., ill. **DLC**
PW: Ag 9, '19.

Smith, Mary Chapin. See **Smith, Chetwood, Mrs.**

S-659 Smith, Mary Elizabeth. In Bethany House: a story of social service / by Mary Elizabeth Smith. New York; Chicago; Toronto; London; Edinburgh: Fleming H. Revell Company, [c1912]. 293 p.

S-660 Smith, Mary O. The autobiography of a tree / by Mary O. Smith. Boston, Massachusetts: B. J. Brimmer Company, [c1923]. 81 p. **FQG**

S-661 Smith, Mattie S. (Mattie Sampson), b. 1840. Miss Claire's pupils / by Mattie S. Smith. Fulton, Kentcky: The National Baptist Publishing House, [c1905]. 311 p. Includes poetry. **CRL**

Smith, Max Everhart, b. 1848. See **Octave.**

S-662 Smith, Myra M. (Myra Malinda). Out of tune / by Myra M. Smith . . . Boston, Mass.: Mayhew Publishing Company, 1906. 249 p.
LC: Ag 21, '06.

Smith, Naomi Gillespie. Laddie. In *Castle stories* **(1908), C-187.**

Smith, P. G. Chilly con carney. In *A bit of old ivory* **(1910), B-626.**

____ Widow Lavelle's lots. In *A bit of old ivory* **(1910), B-626.**

S-663 Smith, Paul Jordan, b. 1885. Cables of cobweb / by Paul Jordan-Smith. New York: Lieber & Lewis, 1923. 369 p. **PAU**
LC: Ap 7, '23.
BLC: London: Brentano's, 1923.

S-664 ____ Nomad / by Paul Jordan-Smith . . ; illustrated by J. D. Laudermilk. New York: Minton, Balch & Company, 1925. 253 p., front., [2] leaves of plates.
LC: Ap 27, '25.
PW: Ap 25, '25.

S-665 Smith, Ruel Perley, 1869-1937. Prisoners of fortune: a tale of the Massachusetts Bay colony / by Ruel Perley Smith; with a frontispiece by Frank T. Merrill. Boston: L. C. Page & Company, 1907. 392 p., col. front.
LC: Ja 28, '07.

S-666 ____ The rival campers, or, The adventures of Henry Burns / by Ruel P. Smith; illustrated by A. B. Shute. Boston: L. C. Page & Company, 1905. 388 p., front., [5] leaves of plates.
LC: S 27, '07.

S-667 Smith, Russell (Russell Duryee), b. 1861. Sea king of Barnegat / by Russell D. Smith. New York: Duffield & Company, 1918. 294 p.
LC: O 1, '18.

S-668 ____ The wild white woods, or, A winter camp on the Canada line / by Russell D. Smith. New York: E. P. Dutton & Company, [c1913]. 354 p., front., [3] leaves of plates. [Ill. by G. A. Harker.]
LC: Ag 11, '13.

S-669 Smith, S. Harper, b. 1855. Circumvented, or, Success despite opposition: a true tale tersely told / by Dr. S. Harper Smith; with twenty-one illustrations. McKeesport, Pa.: Daily News Publishing Company, 1901, [c1900]. 251 p., incl. front., ill. [Ill. by author.]

S-670 Smith, S. Jennie. Madge, a girl in earnest / by S. Jennie Smith; illustrated by James E. McBurney. Boston: Lee and Shepard, 1902. 259 p., front., [3] leaves of plates.

S-671   Smith, Sidney, 1877-1935. Andy Gump: his life story / by Sidney Smith. Chicago: The Reilly & Lee Co., [c1924]. 183 p., ill.
Features characters from the comic strip, "The Gumps" drawn by Sidney Smith.

S-672   Smith, Ted Pauter. Young Dee of Dundee / by Ted Pauter Smith. Chicago: [s. n., c1925]. 95 p. **DLC**

Smith, Titus Keiper, b. 1859. <u>See</u> **Wright, Joshua, pseud.**

S-673   Smith, W. Letterman (William Letterman), b. 1856. William Updick: his philosophy / by W. Letterman Smith. New York; Washington: The Neale Publishing Co., 1908. 111 p.

S-674   Smith, Wallace, 1888-1937. The little tigress: tales out of the dust of Mexico / by Wallace Smith; with drawings from a field sketch book. New York; London: G. P. Putnam's Sons, 1923. 209 p., front., [14] leaves of plates. [Ill. by author.] Illustrated end papers. **OSU, MIA**
Contents: La cucaracha -- The little tigress -- Tradition and a dirty joke -- Judas and the firing squad -- Fierro is sentimental -- Dust of Mexico -- Viva Mexico! -- Political economy -- Words and music -- A desert day -- Our Gods -- Farewell and hail -- Enter your house -- Honor of the family -- Quien vive? -- Nocturne -- No country for a woman -- Greaser and gringo -- Dust of Mexico again.
LC: O 11, '23.

S-675   Smith, Wilfrid Robert b. 1809. Love's crooked path; the romance of a marriage to reform, from real life in the frozen north / by Wilfrid Robert Smith. "Platinum Bill". . . Myrtle Point, Or.: [American Presses], c1921. 264 p.
Unexamined copy: bibliographic data from NUC.
LC: N 25, '21.

S-676   Smith, William Augustus. His pseudoic majesty, or, The knights of the fleece / by William Augustus Smith; illustrated by A. West from original drawings by the author. New York: The Liberty Publishing Company, 1903. 397 p., front., [7] leaves of plates.
BLC: London: Watts & Co., 1903.

S-677   Smith, William Christopher, b. 1861. On Aaron's neck; and, Amos Strong, legislator: two short stories / by William C. Smith. [Hyannis, Mass.: Printed by F. B. & F. P. Goss], 1910. 42 p.
LC: Je 7, '10.

S-678   Smith, William Hawley, 1845-1922. The promoters: a novel without a woman / by William Hawley Smith . . . ; illustrated by John Clitheroe Gilbert. Chicago; New York; London: Rand, McNally & Company, 1904. 367 p., front., [7] leaves of plates.
PW: Je 25, '04.

Smith, William Joan Clarke. <u>See</u> **Smith, Clarke.**

Smith, William Letterman. <u>See</u> **Smith, W. Letterman.**

S-679   [Smith-Tapman, Lillian]. The success of failure / by a wayfarer. New York: Tapman Publishing Company, [c1913]. 299 p.

S-680   Smits, Lee J. The spring flight: a novel / by Lee J. Smits. New York: Alfred A. Knopf, 1925. 350 p.
PW: Ap 4, '25.

S-681   Smyth, Clifford, 1866-1943. The gilded man: a romance of the Andes / by Clifford Smyth; with an introduction by Richard Le Gallienne. New York: Boni and Liveright, 1918. 356 p. Illustrated end papers.

Smyth, P. G. (Patrick Grehan), b. 1857. Chilly con carney. In *A bit of old ivory, and other stories* **(1910), B-626.**

____ Widow Lavelle's lots. In *A bit of old ivory, and other stories* **(1910), B-626.**

S-682   Smythe, James P. Rescuing the Czar: two authentic diaries / arranged and translated by James P. Smythe. San Francisco: California Printing Co., 1920. 269 p.

S-683   Snead, Georgie Tillman. Beneath Virginia skies / by Georgie Tillman Snead. New York: Scott-Thaw Company, 1904. 343 p., photo. front., [5] leaves of photo. plates.

S-684   ____ The story of Agatha Ann / by Georgie Tillman Snead . . . Philadelphia: The John C. Winston Co., 1913. 121 p., photo. front. **OSU, DLC**
Cover title: *Agatha Ann.*
LC: N 15, '13.

S-685   Sneddon, Robert. The call of youth / novelized by Robert Sneddon; from Hugh Ford's Paramount picture "The call of youth", adapted from Henry Arthur Jones' play, "James the fogy". [New York: Prospect Press], c1921. 9 p. **DLC**
Caption title.

____ The little golden shoes. In *Forum stories* **(1914), F-306.**

____ The mute. In *The Bellman book of fiction* **(1921), B-485.**

____ A son of Belgium. In *War stories* **(1919), W-94.**

S-686   Snedeker, Caroline Dale, 1871-1956. The coward of Thermopylae / by Caroline Dale Snedeker. Garden City, New York: Doubleday, Page & Company, 1911. 466 p., col. front., [3] leaves of col. plates. Maps on end papers. [Ill. by Leon V. Solon.]
Reissued in 1912 as *The Spartan.*
LC: Ap 28, '11.
PW: Ap 29, '11.

S-687   ____ The perilous seat / by Caroline Dale Snedeker . . . Garden City, N. Y.: Doubleday, Page & Company, 1923. 314 p.
LC: My 21, '23.
PW: Ap 21, '23.
BLC: London: Methuen, Garden City, N. Y. printed, 1923.

S-688 [_____] Seth Way: a romance of the New Harmony community / by Caroline Dale Owen [pseud.] (Mrs. Charles H. Snedeker); with illustrations by Franklin Booth. Boston; New York: Houghton Mifflin Company, 1917. (Cambridge: The Riverside Press). 413, [2] p., col. front.
LC: N 30, '17.
PW: N 24, '17.

_____ The Spartan (1912). See **Snedeker, Caroline Dale, 1871-1956.** *The coward of Thermopylae* **(1911), S-686.**

S-689 Snider, Denton Jaques, 1841-1925. Freeburg and the Freeburgers: a novel of mid-western town-life before the Civil War / by Denton Jaques Snider. Saint Louis: William Harvey Miner Co., Inc., 1925. 432 p.

S-690 _____ The rise of young Shakespeare: a biographic novel / by Denton Jaques Snider. St. Louis: The William Harvey Miner Co., Inc., 1925. 464 p.
LC: F 28, '25.

S-691 Snow, Ellen, author and reformer. The confession of Seymour Vane / by Ellen Snow . . . New York: R. F. Fenno & Company, [c1908]. 77 p.
LC: D 29, '08.

S-692 _____ The evolution of Rose / by Ellen Snow. Boston: Richard G. Badger, 1907. (Boston: The Gorham Press). 74 p.
LC: D 27, '07.

S-693 Snow, Etta U. (Etta Udora), 1862-1904. When immortals wed / by Etta U. Snow. Concord, New Hampshire: Rumford Printing Company, 1907. 138 p., photo. front. (port).   **HSA**
LC: Ag 28, '07.

S-694 Snow, Francis Haffkine, 1876-1949. Red flowers / by Francis Haffkine Snow. New York: Boni and Liveright, [c1921]. 289 p.
LC: My 18, '21.
PW: My 21, '21.

S-695 Snowden, Elizabeth "Ti": being a rustic local idyl / by Elizabeth Snowden. [Ticonderoga, New York: Press of Sentinel, 1901]. 300 p.

S-696 Snyder, Charles M. (Charles McCoy), b. 1859. The flaw in the sapphire / by Charles M. Snyder . . . New York: The Metropolitan Press, 1909. 311 p.
LC: S 20, '09.

S-697 Snyder, John. The wind trust: a possible prophecy / by John Snyder; with an introducion by Edward Everertt Hale. Boston: James H. West Company, [c1903]. 36 p.

S-698 Soares, Rae. Cupid and the law: a collection of short stories / by Rae Soares. Honolulu: The Hawaiian Gazette Co., 1908. 100 p.   **DLC**
Contents: A deal in opium -- A morern Evangeline -- Cupid and the law -- The new magnetic healer -- In the valley of teeth -- The raid at Punchbowl -- A change of opinion -- A fatal excursion.

S-699 Sohrab, Mirza Ahmad, b. 1891. Heart phantasies / by Mirza Ahmad Sohrab of Esphahan, Persia . . . [Los Angeles, Calif.: Persian-American Publishing Co.], [c1924]. 121 p.
On cover: Injizābāt-i al-qalb.
LC: O 22, '24.

S-700 Solano, Solita, b. 1888. The happy failure / by Solita Solano. New York; London: G. P. Putnam's Sons, 1925. ([New York]: The Knickerbocker Press). 350 p.
LC: Ag 25, '25.
PW: Ag 29, '25.

S-701 _____ The uncertain feast / by Solita Solano. New York; London: G. P. Putnam's Sons, 1924. (New York: The Knickerbocker Press). 336 p.
LC: O 11, '24.
PW: S 20, '24.

Soldier Doctor. See *Gone West* **(1919), G-289.**

S-702 Solis-Cohen, Emily, b. 1886. David the giant killer: and other tales of Grandma Lopez / by Emily Solis-Cohen, Jr.; with illustrations by Alfred Feinberg. Philadelphia: The Jewish Publication Society of America, 1908. 250 p., front., [4] leaves of plates.
Contents: David the Giant Killer: Grandma is coming! -- David the Giant Killer -- Hanukah memories. In Shushan the Capital: Purim in the country -- In Shushan the Capital -- Myrtle-that-was-changed-to-esther. The sacrifice at Modin: Grandma's wedding -- The sacrifice at Modin -- The cleansing of the temple. The hidden Smithy: Sabbath eve -- The hidden Smithy -- The battle of the field of barley. The fall of Michmash: Youth's bright lexicon -- The fall of Michmash. At the fork of the roads: Habdalah -- At the fork of the roads -- The good carpenter. Carmel: Captured by the Indians -- Carmel -- The passing of Elijah. Amid the alien corn: Ruth's story -- Amid the alien corn -- The forgotten sheaf. How Daniel became judge: By the waters of Babylon -- How Daniel became judge -- A nation of teachers. The golden image. Conclusion: The Jack Horner Pie.

S-703 Somerville, Charles, 1876?-1931. The shriek: a satirical burlesque / by Charles Somerville; with illustrations by the author. New York: W. J. Watt & Company, [c1922]. 152 p., incl. front., ill.
LC: Je 21, '22.
PW: Ap 22, '22.

S-704 _____ A woman's way: a novel / by Charles Somerville; from the play by Thompson Buchanan. New York: W. J. Watt and Company, [c1909]. 327 p., col. front. [Ill. by Howard Chandler Christy], [10] leaves of photo. plates.
LC: O 29, '09.
PW: D 4, '09.

S-705 Somerville, Doris. Green chalk / by Doris Somerville. London: John Lane, the Bodley Head; New York: John Lane Company; Toronto: Bell & Cockburn, 1913. 327, [1] p.   **DLM**
BLC: London: John Lane, 1913.

S-706 Somerville, George B., b. 1875. The Boardwalk love letters of Hiram and Ella / by George B. Somerville; illustrations by W. S. Irwin. [Atlantic City, New Jersey: Boardwalk Publishing Company, c1915]. 85 p., front., [3] leaves of plates.   **DLC**

S-707 Somerville, Henry, d. 1915. Jack Racer / by Henry Somerville; decorations by Anne Goldthwaite. New York: McClure, Phillips & Co., 1901. 430 p.
PW: S 14, '01.

S-708 ____ Racer of Illinois / by Henry Somerville . . . New York: McClure, Phillips & Co., 1902. 432 p.
PW: O 4, '02.

Son of the South, A., pseud. See **Allen, F. H.**

S-709 Sonnichsen, Albert, 1878-1931. Confessions of a Macedonian bandit / by Albert Sonnichsen . . . New York: Duffield & Company, 1909. 268 p., photo. front., [15] leaves of photo. plates, folded map. **TMA**
PW: S 4, '09.

S-710 ____ Deep sea vagabonds / by Albert Sonnichsen . . . New York: McClure, Phillips & Co., 1903. 336 p.
PW: My 2, '03.
BLC: London: McClure, Phillips & Co., New York, 1903. Another edition: London: Methuen & Co., 1904.

S-711 Sooy, John M. Episodes of a quaint countryside / by John M. Sooy. Philadelphia, Pa.: The Wendell Sooy Publishing Company, [c1915]. 409 p., front., [10] leaves of plates.

S-712 Sorin, Scota, *pseud.* Blackbird: a story of Mackinac Island / by Scota Sorin [pseud.]; illustrations and decorations by Clyde E. Darr. [Detroit, Mich.: Citator Publishing Company, c1907]. 141, [1] p., front., [2] leaves of plates, ill.
LC: O 9, '08.

S-713 ____ The pendulum: a story / by Scota Sorin [pseud.]. New York: Duffield & Company, 1910. 282 p., front. [Ill. by John Rae.]
LC: N 8, '10.

S-714 Sosey, Frank H. (Frank Hanley), b. 1864. Robert Devoy: a tale of the Palmyra massacre / Frank H. Sosey. [Palmyra, Mo.: Press of Sosey Bros., c1903]. 172 p., front., [4] leaves of plates.

S-715 The so-so stories: a series of humorous stories of interest to physicians / illustrated. Jersey City, N. J.: Published by Reed & Carnrick, [c1914]. 104 p., ill. [Ill. by A. B. Butler, Jr. and C. K. Stevens.]
Contents: Casting bread on the waters of imagination / Homer Croy -- The redemption of Jim Tracy / J. A. Terry -- It's all in a name / Homer Croy -- The pink of imagination / Homer Croy -- When a feller needs a friend / Homer Croy -- I'm cured / Roy L. McCardell -- Merely a case / Barton Braley -- The strenuous life / by a physician.

S-716 Sousa, John Philip, 1854-1932. The fifth string / by John Philip Sousa; the illustrations by Howard Chandler Christy. Indianapolis: Bowen-Merrill Company, [c1902]. 124 p., front., [6] leaves of plates.
PW: F 8, '02.
BLC: London: B. F. Stevens & Brown, [1902].

S-717 ____ The transit of Venus / by John Philip Sousa; illustrated by Helen Bell. Boston: Small, Maynard & Company, [c1920]. 250 p., front.
LC: F 14, '20.
PW: Mr 20, '20.

S-718 Southern lights and shadows / edited by William Dean Howells and Henry Mills Alden. New York; London: Harper & Brothers, 1907. 288 p. (Harper's novelettes.)
Contents: The capture of Andy Proudfoot / Grace MacGowan Cooke -- The level of fortune / Abby Meguire Roach -- Pap Overholt / Alice MacGowan -- In the piny woods / Mrs. B. F. Mayhew -- My fifth in Mammy / William L. Sheppard -- An incident / Sarah Barnwell Elliott -- A snipe hunt / M. E. M. Davis -- The courtship of Colonel Bill / J. J. Eakins -- The balance of power / Maurice Thompson.
LC: F 28, '07.
References: BAL 9778; Gibson & Arms 07-A.

Southgate, Richard B. The balance. In *Made to order* (1915), M-352.

S-719 Southwick, E. L. (Emma Lewis), b. 1875. Eyes that see not / by E. L. Southwick. New York: Siebel Publishing Corporation, 1925. 311 p. **ABC**

S-720 [Southworth, Horatio Woodburn, b. 1839]. To Nazareth or Tarsus? / by the author of "Not on Calvary," "The First Millennial Faith," etc. New York: J. S. Ogilvie Publishing Company, c1901. 217 p.
Cover title: *Nazareth or Tarsus?*

S-721 Space, M. T., 1858-1919, *pseud.* Thé dansant in the Bowery / by M. T. Space [pseud.]. Portland, Maine: The Mosher Press, 1915. 5, [1] p.

S-722 ____ Playing the tank towns and other sketches / by M. T. Space [pseud.]. Portland, Maine: The Mosher Press, 1916. 39, [1] p.
Contents: Playing the tank towns -- The new orderly -- Inside stuff -- Lines to the Ostheimer Tavern -- Little Dugey and the perfect ass -- How Casey became an officer -- The call of the Landsturm.

S-723 Spadoni, Adriana. Mrs. Phelps' husband / by Adriana Spadoni . . . Indianapolis: The Bobbs-Merrill Company, [c1924]. 428 p.
LC: Mr 24, '24.
PW: Mr 29, '24.
BLC: London: Brentano's, 1924.

S-724 ____ The noise of the world / by Adriana Spadoni . . . New York: Boni and Liveright, [c1921]. 256 p.
LC: Mr 18, '21.
PW: Mr 26, '21.
BLC: London: Bentano's, 1923.

S-725 ____ The swing of the pendulum / Adriana Spadoni. New York: Boni and Liveright, [c1919]. 462 p. **OSU, TXU**
LC: Ja 9, '20.
PW: Ja 17, '20.
BLC: London: Hutchinson & Co., [1921].

S-726 Spalding, Arthur Whitefield, 1877-1953. A man of valor: a story of the life of Jonathan, son of Saul / by Arthur W. Spaulding. Washington, D. C.: Review and Herald Publishing Assn., c1908. 247 p., front., [11] leaves of plates. Decorated end papers.

S-727 Spalding, Phebe Estelle, 1859-1937. The Tahquitch maiden: a tale of the San Jacintos / by Phebe Estelle Spalding; illustrated. San Francisco: Paul Elder & Company, [c1911]. 26 p., ills. mounted on front and [2] leaves of plates.

S-728 Sparhawk, Frances Campbell, b. 1847. Honor Dalton: a novel / by Frances Campbell Sparhawk. New York; Chicago; Toronto; London; Edinburgh: Fleming H. Revell Company, [c1903]. 419 p.

S-729 Sparling, E. Earl (Edward Earl), 1897-1951. Under the levee / by E. Earl Sparling. New York; London: Charles Scribner's Sons, 1925. 290 p.
PW: F 21, '25.

S-730 Sparrow, M. Dunton (Maria Dunton). Hereford: a story / by M. Dunton Sparrow . . . Boston: Richard G. Badger, 1910. (Boston: The Gorham Press). 183 p., photo. front., [4] leaves of photo. plates.
LC: F 26, '10.

S-731 Speake, Cornelia. Reminiscences / by Cornelia Speake. Baltimore: Cushing & Company, 1901. 113 p., photo. front. (port.).   SMI

S-732 Speakman, Harold, b. 1888. This above all / by Harold Speakman. Indianapolis: The Bobbs-Merrill Company, [c1924]. 374 p.
LC: S 15, '24.

S-733 Speare, Dorothy, 1898-1951. Dancers in the dark / Dorothy Speare. New York: George H. Doran Company, [c1922]. 290 p.
LC: Ap 18, '22.
PW: Mr 25, '22.

S-734 ____ The gay year / Dorothy Speare. New York: George H. Doran Company, [c1923]. 314 p.
LC: S 28, '23.
PW: N 3, '23.

S-735 ____ The girl who cast out fear / Dorothy Speare. New York: George H. Doran Company, [c1925]. 324 p.
LC: N 14, '25.
PW: N 14, '25.

S-736 Spearman, Frank H. (Frank Hamilton), 1859-1937. The close of the day / by Frank H. Spearman. New York: D. Appleton and Company, 1904, [c1903]. 224 p.
PW: F 6, '04.

____ Conductor Pat Francis. In *The railroad* (1901), R-6.

S-737 ____ The daughter of a magnate / by Frank H. Spearman; illustrated by T. [i. e. F.] R. Gruger. New York: Charles Scribner's Sons, 1903. 273 p., front., [7] leaves of plates.
PW: O 31, '03.

S-738 ____ Doctor Bryson: a novel / by Frank H. Spearman. New York: Charles Scribner's Sons, 1902. 308 p.
PW: O 11, '02.

S-739 ____ Held for orders: being stories of railroad life / by Frank H. Spearman. New York: McClure, Phillips & Company, 1901. 359 p., front., [7] leaves of plates. [Ill. by Jay Hambridge.]
Contents: The switchman's story: Shockley -- The wiper's story: How McGrath got an engine -- The roadmaster's story: The Spider Water -- The striker's story: McTerza -- The despatcher's story: The last order -- The nightman's story: Bullhead -- The master mechanic's story: Delaroo -- The operator's story: De Molay four -- The trainmaster's story: Of the old guard -- The yellow mail story: Jimmie the wind.
PW: N 2, '01.
BLC: London: McClure, Phillips & Company, 1901.

S-740 ____ Laramie holds the range / by Frank H. Spearman; illustrated by James Reynolds. New York: Charles Scribner's Sons, 1921. 374 p., front., [3] leaves of plates.
LC: Ag 30, '21.
PW: S 3, '21.
BLC: London: Hodder & Stoughton, [1921].

____ The lost voice. In *The battle for the Pacific* (1908), B-357.

S-741 ____ The marriage verdict: a novel / by Frank H. Spearman. New York: Charles Scribner's Sons, 1923. 321 p.
LC: Mr 26, '23.
PW: Ap 7, '23.
BLC: London: Hodder & Stoughton, [1923].

S-742 ____ Merrilie Dawes / by Frank H. Spearman; illustrated by Arthur E. Becher. New York: Charles Scribner's Sons, 1913. 382 p., col. front., [3] leaves of col. plates.
LC: S 9, '13.
PW: S 13, '13.

____ A million dollar freight train. In *The railroad* (1901), R-6.

S-743 ____ The mountain divide / by Frank H. Spearman; illustrated by Armand Both. New York: Charles Scribner's Sons, 1912. 319 p., front., [3] leaves of plates.
LC: S 17, '12.
PW: S 21, '12.

S-744 ____ Nan of Music Mountain / by Frank H. Spearman; illustrated by N. C. Wyeth. New York: Charles Scribner's Sons, 1916. 430 p., col. front., [3] leaves of col. plates.
LC: Ap 13, '16.
PW: Ap 15, '16.
BLC: London: Hodder & Stoughton, New York printed, 1916.

S-745 ____ Robert Kimberly / by Frank H. Spearman; illustrated by James Montgomery Flagg. New York: Charles Scribner's Sons, 1911. 437, [1] p., col. front., [3] leaves of col. plates.
LC: Mr 2, '11.
PW: Mr 4, '11.

S-746 ____ Selwood of Sleepy Cat / by Frank H. Spearman. New York: Charles Scribner's Sons,

1925. 326 p., front. [Ill. by James Reynolds.]
LC: Mr 13, '25.
PW: Mr 14, '25.
BLC: London: Hodder & Stoughton, [1925].

S-747   ____ Whispering Smith / by Frank H. Spearman; illustrated by N. C. Wyeth. New York: Charles Scribner's Sons, 1906. 421 p., col. front., [3] leaves of col. plates.
LC: S 1, '06.
PW: N 17, '06.
BLC: London: Hodder & Stoughton, New York printed, 1906.

S-748   Spears, Raymond S. (Raymond Smiley), 1876-1950. Diamond tolls / by Raymond S. Spears; frontispiece by Ralph Pallen Coleman. Garden City, New York: Doubleday, Page & Company, 1920. 249, [1] p., col. front.
LC: Mr 23, '20.
PW: Mr 6, '20.

    ____ A river combine-professional. In *Prize stories of 1924* (1925), P-622.

S-749   ____ The river prophet / by Raymond S. Spears; frontispiece by Ralph Pallen Coleman. Garden City, New York: Doubleday, Page & Company, 1920. 246 p., col. front.
LC: Je 21, '20.
PW: Je 26, '20.

    ____ The Silver Lake panic. In *Greatest short stories* (1915), G-424.

Spektor, Mordecai. A gloomy wedding. In *Yiddish tales* (1912), Y-20.

Spektor, Mordecai. An original strike. In *Yiddish tales* (1912), Y-20.

Spektor, Mordecai. Poverty. In *Yiddish tales* (1912), Y-20.

Spencer, H. H. Hard on the manager. In *Second suds sayings* (1919), S-266.

S-750   Spencer, Katharine S. (Katharine Smith), b. 1855. Nurse Lee / by Katharine S. Spencer; illustration by Bertha L. Corbett. Racine, Wisconsin: The Journal Printing Company, 1909. 46 p., front.

S-751   Spencer, Mary Etta. The resentment / by Mary Etta Spencer. [Philadelphia: Printed by A. M. E. book concern 1921]. 216 p.
Unexamined copy: bibliographic data from OCLC #28370494.
LC: D 5, '21.
PW: Ap 22, '22.

S-752   Spencer, May. The spray of honeysuckle, or, Cast up by the waves / by Miss May Spencer. Leithchfiels, Ky.: Gazette Publishing Company, 1903. 93 p.
DLC (microfilm)
LC: F 21, '03.
PW: Je 20,' 03.

S-753   Sperow, Everett H. (Everett Hollingsworth). The Rose of Sharon: the story of the Shulammite maiden / by Everett H. Sperow . . . Boston: The Gorham Press; Toronto: The Copp Clark Co., [c1918].
262 p.   **DLC**
(Library of religious thought.)

S-754   Spiers, A. M. (Augustus Mansfield), b. 1871. Nell of Narragansett Bay / by A. M. Spiers. Boston, Massachusetts: The Stratford Co., 1925. 294 p.
PW: Ag 8, '25.

S-755   Spindler, Will H. (Will Henry), b. 1899. Comrades of the Lone Star / by Will Henry Spindler. Boston: The Roxburgh Publishing Company, [c1921].
259 p.   **DLC**
LC: My 9, '21.

S-756   The Spinners' book of fiction / by Gertrude Atherton, Mary Austin, . . . [et al.]; with a dedicatory poem by George Sterling; collected by the Book Committee of the Spinners' Club; illustrated by Lillie V. O'Ryan, Maynard Dixon, Albertine Randall Wheelan, Merle Johnson, E. Almond Withrow and Gordon Ross; initials and decorations by Spencer Wright. San Francisco; New York: P. Elder and Company, [c1907]. 367 p., col. front., [5] leaves of col. plates. Designed end papers.
Contents: Concha Arguello, Sister Dominica / by Gertrude Atherton -- The ford of Crevecour / by Mary Austin -- A Californian / by Geraldine Bonner -- Gideon's knock / by Mary Halleck Foote -- A yellow man and a white / by Eleanor Gates -- The judgment of man / by James Hopper -- The league of the old men / by Jack London -- Down the flume with the sneath piano / by Bailey Millard -- The contumacy of Sarah L. Walker / by Miriam Michelson -- Breaking through / by W. C. Morrow -- A lost story / by Frank Norris -- Hantu / by Henry Milner Rideout -- Miss Juno / by Charles Warren Stoddard -- A little savage gentleman / by Isabel Strong -- Love and advertising / by Richard Walton Tully -- The Tewana / by Herman Whitaker.
References: BAL 11999.

S-757   Spitzer, Marian. Who would be free / by Marian Spitzer. New York: Boni and Liveright, 1924.
319 p.

S-758   Spivey, Thomas Sawyer, 1856-1938. Autobiography of a Johnny: edited by one who knew him well / Thomas Sawyer Spivey; illustrations by Tula Tanner. New York; Washington: Neale Publishing Company, 1905. 207 p., front., ill.
PW: Je 3, '05.

S-759   ____ The caverns of Crail: a novel / by Thomas Sawyer Spivey. New York: The Cosmopolitan Press, 1912. 307 p.
LC: S 16, '12.
PW: N 16, '12.

S-760   ____ Dr. Paul McKim / by Thomas Sawyer Spivey . . . ; illustrated by Glen Tracy. New York; Washington: The Neale Publishing Company, 1908. 401 p., front., [6] leaves of plates.
LC: F 8, '08.
PW: F 15, '08.

S-761   ____ The Hoosier widow / by Thomas Sawyer Spivey . . . ; illustrated by Glen Tracy. New York; Washington: The Neale Publishing Company, 1908.

294 p., front., [6] leaves of plates.
LC: F 8, '08.
PW: Ap 4, '08.

S-762 _____ Jane and I / by Thomas Sawyer Spivey . . . ; illustrated by Tula Tanner. New York; Washington: The Neale Publishing Company, 1904. 125 p., ill.
                                                                CWR

S-763 _____ The seven sons of Ballyhack / by Thomas Sawyer Spivey; with illustrations adapted from pictures by the old masters. New York: The Cosmopolitan Press, 1911. 317 p., front., [13] leaves of plates.
LC: D 18, '11.
PW: Ja 13, '12.

S-764 Spofford, Harriet Elizabeth Prescott, 1835-1921. The elder's people / by Harriet Prescott Spofford. Boston; New York: Houghton Mifflin Company, 1920. 334 p., front. [Ill. by Elizabeth Shippen Green.]
Contents: The deacon's whistle -- A change of heart -- A rural telephone -- The step-father -- John-a-dreams -- Miss Mahala's miracle -- An old fiddler -- The blessing called peace -- Father James -- The impossible choice -- A village dressmaker -- Miss Mahala's will -- A life in a night -- Miss Mahala and Johnny.
LC: Mr 29, '20.
PW: Mr 27, '20.
References: BAL 18561.

S-765 _____ The king's Easter / by Harriet Prescott Spofford. Boston: World Peace Foundation, 1912. 16 p.   **NYP**
Reprinted: Harper's magazine, January, 1910.
References: BAL 18559.

S-766 _____ The making of a fortune: a romance / by Harriet Prescott Spofford; with illustrations by Alice Barber Stephens. New York; London: Harper & Brothers, 1911. 113, [1] p., front., [3] leaves of plates.
LC: Mr 18, '11.
PW: Mr 25, '11.
References: BAL 18555.

S-767 _____ Old Washington / by Harriet Prescott Spofford; with a frontispiece from a drawing by George Alfred Williams. Boston: Little, Brown and Company, 1906. 279 p., col. front.
Contents: A Thanksgiving breakfast -- A guardian angel -- In a conspiracy -- A little old woman -- The colonel's Christmas.
LC: Mr 20, '06.
PW: Mr 31, '06.
References: BAL 18547.

S-768 _____ That Betty / by Harriet Prescott Spofford. New York; Chicago; Toronto; London; Edinburgh: Fleming H. Revell Company, [1903]. 200 p.
PW: S 19, '03.
References: BAL 18542.

S-769 Spooner, Arthur Willis. Pauline: a romance of the Civil War / by Arthur Willis Spooner . . . Boston: Sherman, French & Company, 1915. 278 p., photo. front.

S-770 Spooner, Cecil. The fortunes of Betty: a sweet and tender romance of an old soldier's daughter / novelized from the successful play of the same name by Cecil Spooner. New York: J. S. Ogilvie Publishing Company, [c1910]. 218 p., photo. front., [7] leaves of photo. plates. [Some photo. by N. Y. Hall.]
LC: N 7, '10.

S-771 The Sporting spirit: an anthology / compiled by Charles Wright Gray. New York: Henry Holt and Company, 1925. 319 p.   **IND**
Contents: Too much speed / by Byron Morgan -- Mister Conley / by Charles E. Van Loan -- Grandson / by Earl Reed Silvers -- Two stones with one bird / by H. C. Witwer -- Highboy rings down the curtain / by George Agnew Chamberlain -- The captain / by William Almon Wolff -- Byme-by-tarpon / by Zane Grey -- Goliath / by Dana Burnet -- Out of the bunker / by Frances Ouimet -- Soft ice / by Ralph Henry Barbour -- The Christmas handicap / by Gerald Beaumont -- The men who climbed / by M. L. C. Pickthall --The one-goal man / by Charles Neville Buck -- His father's son / by Charles Wright Gray -- Dick takes the chair / by William T. Tilden, 2nd -- The man on the mark / by Charles W. Paddock -- Champions all / by Richard Connell.
PW: My 16, '25.

S-772 Spoth, John C. (John Charles). Between train-time tales / by John Charles Spoth . . . [New York: Monotyped and printed by Clarence S. Nathan . . . , c1910]. 84 p.
Contents: The ten-thirty's freight -- An automobile tragedy -- The name on the medal -- "T. W. H." -- The passing of Fingelman's delicatessen store -- Mr. Isaac Cohen -- A tale of the rabbit's foot -- The bribing of Bridget -- "Razor Pete's" Waterloo -- From the hometown paper.

S-773 _____ A knight in homespun / by John Charles Spoth. Boston, Massachusetts: The C. M. Clark Publishing Company, 1909. 328 p., front., [7] leaves of plates. [Ill. by D. S. Ross.]
LC: Mr 8, '09.
PW: Ap 3, '09.

Spotswood, Dillon Jordan. See **Nuverbis, pseud.**

S-774 Sprague, Roger, 1869-1935? The flamingo's nest: a Honolulu story / by Roger Sprague. Berkeley, Cal.: Lederer, Street and Zeus, 1917. 369, [1] p., ill. (map).
LC: D 27, '17.
PW: Ja 12, '18.

S-775 Sprague, William C. (William Cyrus), 1860-1922. Felice Constant, or, The master passion: a romance / by William C. Sprague. New York: Frederick A. Stokes Company, 1904. 322 p., col. front. [Ill. by Frank T. Merrill.]
PW: My 14, '04.

S-776 _____ Tad: the story of a boy who had no chance / by William C. Sprague . . . Detroit, Mich.: The Sprague Publishing Company, 1907. 216 p., front., [15] leaves of plates. [Some ill. by W. Darr.]

S-777 Springer, Fleta Campbell. Gregg: a novel / by Fleta Campbell Springer. New York; London: Harper & Brothers, [1919]. 309, [1] p.
LC: F 21, '19.
PW: Mr 1, '19.

_____ Legend. In *The Harper prize short stories (1925)*, **H-233.**

_____ The rotter. In *The best short stories of 1920 and the yearbook of the American short story (1921)*, **B-565.**

_____ Solitaire. In *The best short stories of 1918 and the yearbook of the American short story (1919)*, **B-563.**

S-778 Springer, Mary Elizabeth. Dolly Madison: a story of the War of 1812 / by Mary Elizabeth Springer. New York: Bonnell Silver & Co., 1906. 244 p.

S-779 _____ Elizabeth Schuyler: a story of old New York / by Mary Elizabeth Springer . . . New York: Press of Isaac H. Blanchard Co., [c1903]. 256 p.
PW: My 2, '03.

S-780 Springer, Rebecca Ruter, 1832-1904. Marcus and Miriam: a story of Jesus / by Rebecca Ruter Springer . . . Elgin, Illinois: Published by David C. Cook Publishing Company, [c1908]. 94 p., incl. front. ill., ill. Printed in two colunms.

Springer, Thomas Grant, b. 1873. The blood of the dragon. In *Prize stories of 1919 (1920)*, **P-617.**

S-781 _____ The red cord: a romance of China / by Thomas Grant Springer; with an introduction by John Luther Long; illustrations by S. Y. Pang. New York: Brentano's, [c1925]. 302 p., ill.
LC: S 9, '25.

S-782 Sproul, Albert C. (Albert Cliff). Spies / by Albert C. Sproul. Elgin; Chicago; New York; Boston: Published by David C. Cook Publishing Company, [c1918]. 37 p., ill. [Ill. by L. E. Dugger.] **DLC**

S-783 Spurgeon, Otis L. (Otis Lee), b. 1880. 10,132 / by Otis L. Spurgeon. Boston: Richard G. Badger, [c1920]. ([Boston]: The Gorham Press). 218 p.
PW: My 8, '20.

S-784 The Squaw book. The squaws of the Onondagas made this book that the great chiefs might give them wampum for it, so that the squaws, having wampum, might bribe the medicine men to cure with weird charms those who have been wounded in the long battle and cannot fight for themselves . . . Syracuse, N. Y.: Published for the benefit of the Free Dispensary, [c1909]. 99 p.
"Copyright, 1909, by Gertrude Van Duyn Southworth."
Unexamined copy: bibliographic data from OCLC, #21696636.

S-785 Squier, Emma-Lindsay, b. 1892. On autumn trails: and adventures in captivity / by Emma-Lindsay Squier . . . ; illustrated by Paul Bransom. New York: Cosmopolitan Book Corporation, 1923. 239 p., front., [3] leaves of plates.
Contents: At sunset in the meadow -- Where the death plant grew -- Held in trust -- Friends of a quill -- The last moose -- In memory of the loon -- The friend who was hurt -- The third day of the moon -- Joe Martin, gentleman -- The white wish -- Luigi, servant of fate.

LC: S 26, '23.
PW: O 6, '23.
BLC: London: T. Fisher Unwin, 1925.

_____ The soul of Caliban. In *"Dawgs!": an anthology of stories about them (1925)*, **D-184.**

S-786 _____ The wild heart / by Emma-Lindsay Squier; with an introduction by Gene Stratton-Porter; illustrations and decorations by Paul Bransom. New York: Cosmopolitan Book Corporation, 1922. 220 p., ill.
LC: Ap 3, '22.
PW: Ap 29, '22.

S-787 Squier, Lee Welling. b. 1859. A lamb to the slaughter; an Americn girl's experience in the Orient from the China-Japan war to the relief of Peking / Lee Welling Squier. Greensburg, Pa., The Patriot Publishing Co., [c1901]. 402 p. **MUS**

S-788 Squire, Frances 1867-1914. The Ballingtons: a novel / by Frances Squire. Boston: Little, Brown and Company, 1905. 445 p.
PW: O 7, '05.

S-789 Stabb, William J. B. A story of many colors, or, Romance in a lodging-house / by W. J. B. Stabb. Boston; New York: Dickerman Publishing Co., [c1903]. 59 p., photo. front. (port.), [3] leaves of photo. plates.

S-790 Stafford, J. R. (John Richard), 1874-1966. When cattle kingdom fell / by J. R. Stafford. New York: B. W. Dodge & Company, 1910. 374 p.
LC: N 29, '10.
PW: D 17, '10.

S-791 Stagg, Clinton Holland, 1890-1916. High speed / by Clinton H. Stagg. New York: W. J. Watt & Company, [c1916]. 297, [2] p., front., [1] leaf of plates.
LC: O 19, '16.
PW: N 25, '16.
BLC: London: Grant Richards, 1920.

S-792 _____ Silver sandals / by Clinton H. Stagg; illustrations by Will Foster. New York: W. J. Watt & Company, [c1916]. 305 p., front., [1] leaf of plates, ill. (cryptogram).
LC: Je 8, '16.
PW: Ag 5, '16.

S-793 _____ Thornley Colton: blind detective / by Clinton H. Stagg . . . New York: G. Howard Watt, 1923. 343 p.
LC: Ag 21, '24.
BLC: London: Simpkin, Marshall & Co., 1915.
British title: *Thornley Colton: blind reader of hearts.*

S-794 Stahl, John M. (John Meloy), 1860-1944. Just stories / by John M. Stahl. Chicago: M. A. Donohue & Co., [c1916]. 156 p. **IAT**
Contents: Dolly's bargain cigars -- The traveling man's wife -- Gustavus Adolphus -- How Joe helped Harry in his courting -- The mysterious woman -- Butchering time -- The three women -- Utilizing the bath tub -- The moral of the six cylinder -- Robert's daughter --

630

Common cheats -- The three wise men of Chicago -- Her black curls -- The spelling bee at Froggy corners.
LC: Mr 25, '16.
PW: Ap 22, '16.

S-795   Stair, Grace. A bird of passage / by Grace Stair.
Boston: Richard G. Badger, [c1921]. ([Boston]:
The Gorham Press). 349 p., col. front.

S-796   Staley, Byron E. Oram of the forest / by Byron E.
Staley . . . Author's edition. Hagerstown, Md.: The
Tower, 1907. 104 p.
Unexamined copy: bibliographic data from NUC.

S-797   Stallings, Laurence, 1894-1968. Plumes / by
Laurence Stallings. New York: Harcourt, Brace and
Company, [c1924]. 348 p.
BLC: London: Jonathan Cape, printed in U. S. A.,
1924.

Stamey, DeKeller. See Alein, Niela, pseud.

S-798   Stanard, Mary Newton, 1865-1929. The dreamer: a
romantic rendering of the life-story of Edgar Allan
Poe / by Mary Newton Stanard . . . Richmond,
Virginia: The Bell Book and Stationery Company,
1909. 375 p.   CWR
PW: Jl 3, '09.

Stand-by, Timothy, pseud. See Clark, Joseph,
b. 1854.

S-799   Standerson, Grantly. The hundredth wave: a novel
written to accomplish two strongly interlinked
purposes / by Grantly Standerson. Chicago: Charles
H. Kerr & Company, 1916. 538 p.

S-800   Stanford, Alfred B. (Alfred Boller), b. 1900. A city
out of the sea / by Alfred Stanford. New York;
London: D. Appleton and Company, 1924. 342,
[1] p.
LC: My 27, '24.
PW: Je 7, '24.

S-801   _____ The ground swell / by Alfred B. Stanford.
New York; London: D. Appleton and Company,
1923. 300, [1] p.
LC: Ja 29, '23.
PW: F 10, '23.

S-802   Stanger, Theophil, b. 1875. Mr. Pickett of Detroit /
by Theophil Stanger. [Ann Arbor, Mich.: Millard
Press, c1916]. 143 p.

S-803   Stanger, Wesley Allen, b. 1880. Rescued from fiery
death: a powerful narrative of the Iroquois Theater
disaster: mighty flames graphically portrayed . . . /
by Wesley A. Stanger; thirty-five full page pictures,
half-tones from actual photographs and pen drawings
-- true to life. Chicago: Laird & Lee, [c1904].
317 p., incl. front., [23] p. of plates, ill. (some
photo.).   MNU

S-804   Stanley, Caroline Abbot, 1849-1919. Dr. Llewellyn
and his friends / by Caroline Abbot Stanley;

illustrated. New York; Chicago; Toronto; London;
Edinburgh: Fleming H. Revell Company, [c1914].
320 p., front., [2] leaves of plates. [Ill. by Victor
Pérard & A. B. Frost.]
LC: S 21, '14.
PW: S 5, '14.

S-805   _____ The First Church's Christmas barrel / by
Caroline Abbot Stanley . . . ; illustrations by Gayle
Porter Hoskins. New York: Thomas Y. Crowell
Company, [1912]. 71 p., front., [2] leaves of plates.
LC: S 10, '12.
PW: O 5, '12.

S-806   _____ The keeper of the vineyard: a tale of the
Ozarks / by Caroline Abbot Stanley . . . ; illustrated.
New York; Chicago; Toronto; London; Edinburgh:
Fleming H. Revell Company, [c1913]. 344, [1] p.,
col. front., [3] leaves of col. plates. [Ill. by Samuel
M. Palmer.]
LC: Ja 24, '14.
PW: N 15, '13.

_____ Margaret Sloan's career. In Stockman stories
(1913), S-956.

_____ Margaret's summer boarders. In Stockman
stories (1913), S-956.

S-807   _____ The master of "The Oaks": a novel / by
Caroline Abbot Stanley. New York; Chicago;
Toronto; London; Edinburgh: Fleming H. Revell
Company, [c1912]. 389 p., front., [3] leaves of
plates. [Ill. by S. M. Palmer.]
LC: Ja 2, '13.
PW: S 14, '12.
BLC: London: Andrew Melrose, printed in U. S.
A., [1912].

S-808   _____ A modern Madonna / by Caroline Abbot
Stanley . . . New York: The Century Co., 1906.
401 p.
LC: S 1 '06.
PW: O 6, '06.

S-809   _____ Order no. 11: a tale of the border / by
Caroline Abbot Stanley; with illustrations by Harry C.
Edwards. New York: The Century Co., 1904.
420 p., front., [4] leaves of plates.
PW: Ap 2, '04.

S-810   Stanley, Caroline Abbot, 1849-1919. Their
Christmas golden wedding / by Caroline Abbot
Stanley . . . ; illustrations by Emlen McConnell.
New York: Thomas Y. Crowell Company, 1913.
63 p., col. front., [2] leaves of col. plates.
LC: S 5, '13.
PW: S 13, '13.

S-811   Stanley, Frederic Arthur. The third party / by
Frederic Arthur Stanley. New York: The Macaulay
Company, 1915. 286 p., photo. front., [5] leaves of
photo. plates.
LC: Ag 16, '15.
PW: Ag 14, '15.

S-812 Stanley, H. A. (Hiram Alonzo), b. 1859. The backwoodsman: the autobiography of a Continental on the New York frontier during the Revolution / by H. A. Stanley. New York: Doubleday, Page & Company, 1901. 371 p. Designed end papers.
LC: Ag 12, '01.
BLC: London: Doubleday, Page & Company, New York printed, 1901.

S-813 Stanley, Martha M. (Martha Melean Burgess), b. 1872. The souls of men / by Martha M. Stanley; illustrations by Joseph Cummings Chase. New York: G. W. Dillingham Company, [c1913]. 353 p., incl. front., [3] leaves of plates.
LC: F 28, '13.
PW: Mr 1, '13.

Stanley, Mary Valentine. The old pearl necklace. In *Short stories for class reading* (1925), S-461.

S-814 Stanton, E. Brandon (Elizabeth Brandon). "Fata morgana": a vision of empire-- the Burr conspiracy in Mississippi Territory and the great Southwest--Natchez love story of ex-Vice President Aaron Burr: a historical novel / by Elizabeth Brandon Stanton . . . [Crowley, La.: Printed by the Signal Publishing Co., c1917]. 348 p.
LC: N 20, '17.

S-815 ____ Grant Vernon: a Boston boy's adventures in Louisiana / by E. Brandon Stanton; illustrated. Boston: Roxburgh Publishing Company, Incorporated, [c1909]. 172 p., incl. [5] leaves of photo. plates, photo. front.
LC: Mr 30, '09.

Stanton, Teresa. From over the sea. In *The Senior lieutenant's wager: and other stories* (1905), S-312.

S-816 Stanwood, Alida. Memories, or, How Sara Winters found fullness of joy / by Alida Stanwood. New York: Eaton & Mains, 1904. 126 p.   **NYP**

S-817 Stanzel, Lula Vinette, b. 1872. The Darkwood tragedy / by Lula V. Stanzel. Washington, D. C.: Neale Publishing Company, 1902. 182 p. Unexamined copy: bibliographic data from OCLC, #26968304.
PW: Je 14, '02.

S-818 Stapleford, Julia M. Baker. Wah-see-ola, the light of the tribes at the meeting waters / by Julia M. Baker Stapleford. Fort Wayne, Indiana: Fort Wayne Paper & Blank Book Co., 1905. 326 p.

S-819 Stapleton, Patience Tucker, 1861-1893. Trailing yew: a story of Monhegan. Boston: Hudson Printing Co., 1921. 122 p., ill.

Starbuck, A., jt. ed. See *War stories* (1919), W-94.

S-820 Starbuck, F. Lewis. Dan: an allegory in three parts in which the subjects of birth, life and death are represented in the story of Dan Mannering / by F. Lewis Starbuck. [Bloomington, Ill.: Pantagraph Printing and Stationery Co., c1916]. 59 p., [3] leaves of plates. [Ill. by H. Gates.]   **DLC**

S-821 Stark, William Weldon. Guy Hunter: a novel / by William Weldon Stark. New York: Cochrane Publishing Co., 1908. 276 p.   **GPM**
LC: Ag 10, '08.
PW: Ag 29, '08.

S-822 Starkey, Helen. Plato paved the way / by Helen Starkey; frontispiece by Hermann Heyer. New York: The Neale Publishing Company, 1913. 141 p., front.

Starr, E. The clearer sight. In *Atlantic narratives*; first series (1918), A-360.

S-823 Starrett, Vincent, 1886-1974. Coffins for two / by Vincent Starrett. Chicago: Covici-McGee Co., 1924. 242 p.
Contents: The fugitive -- The elixir of death -- Exeunt omnes -- Four friends of Mavis -- The head of Cromwell -- The widow of Maltrata -- The Princess Antimacassar -- Decadence and John Fenderson -- Coffins for two -- The truth about Delbridge -- The end of the story -- The pleasant madness of the faculty -- Thirty pieces of silver -- The episode of the plugged dime -- The man who loved leopards -- Request of the dying -- Eighteen steps -- The artistic temperament.
LC: F 18, '24.
PW: Mr 8, '24.

S-824 ____ The unique Hamlet: a hitherto unchronicled adventure of Mr. Sherlock Holmes / by Vincent Starrett. Chicago, Illinois: Privately printed for the friends of Walter M. Hill, at Christmas 1920. 39 p.   **ALL**
LC: D 6, '20.

S-825 Stauffer, Mack. Humanity and the mysterious knight / by Mack Stauffer. Boston: Roxburgh Publishing Company, [c1914]. 295 p.
PW: My 29, '15.

Staunton, Schuyler, pseud. See **Baum, Lyman Frank, 1856-1919.**

Stearns, Edgar Franklin. See **Franklin, Edgar.**

Stearns, Lincoln M. Stover, the resourceful. In *Clever business sketches* (1909), C-490.

S-826 Stebbins, Harry Andrew, b. 1893. The house of a thousand cobwebs: and nine other fables / by H. A. Stebbins . . . ; illustrated by Ray Winters. San Francisco: The Abbott Press, 1920. 164 p., col. ill. (port.).
Contents: The house of a thousand cobwebs -- All to the mustache -- The late Mr. Jazz -- Go thou and sin some more -- The fiasco of Flavius Flivver -- All is not bird that twitters -- Hewers of wood and drawers of water -- The pot of gold at the end of the payroll -- The boss who listened to treason -- All fuzz and a yard wide.
PW: Ap 17, '20.

Steel, Francis. Steve. In *California story book* (1909), C-40.

Steele, Carol, jt. aut. *Her caveman's letters and her's in reply* (1908). See **Swift, Lance, jt. aut., S-1155.**

S-827 Steele, Charles Homer. Helen Parker / by Charles Homer Steele. Chicago; New York: The Henneberry Company, [c1901]. 357 p.   **DLC**

Steele, Chester K., pseud. <u>See</u> **Stratemeyer, Edward, 1862-1930.**

S-828   Steele, Jack. The house of iron men / by Jack Steele; frontispiece in color by Clara M. Burd. New York: Published by Desmond Fitzgerald, [c1911]. 344 p., col. front.
LC: S 1, '11.

S-829   _____ A husband by proxy / by Jack Steele. New York: Desmond FitzGerald, Inc., [c1909]. 345 p.
LC: Ap 27, '09.
BLC: London: Ward, Lock, & Co., 1910.

S-830   Steele, L. M. Dr. Nick / by L. M. Steele; with a fronstispiece by Ronald Anderson. Boston: Small, Maynard & Company, [c1916]. 435 p., col. front.

S-831   Steele, Robert, b. 1880. One man: a novel / by Robert Steele. New York: Mitchell Kennerly, 1915. 394 p.
PW: My 29, '15.

S-832   Steele, Rufus, b. 1877. Aces for industry / by Rufus Steele. Boston; New York: Houghton Miffin Company, 1919. (Cambridge: The Riverside Press). 93 p.

Steele, Wilbur Daniel, 1886-1970. The anglo-saxon. <u>In</u> *Prize stories of 1922 (1923)*, **P-620.**

_____ Ching, Ching, Chinaman. <u>In</u> *The best short stories of 1917 and the yearbook of the American short story* **(1918), B-562.**

_____ The dark hour. <u>In</u> *The best short stories of 1918 and the yearbook of the American short story* **(1919), B-563.**

_____ Down on their knees. <u>In</u> *The best short stories of 1916 and the yearbook of the American short story* **(1917), B-561.**

_____ Footfalls. <u>In</u> *Prize stories of 1920* **(1921), P-618.**

_____ For they know not what they do. <u>In</u> *Prize stories of 1919 (1920)*, **P-617.**

_____ From the other side of the south. <u>In</u> *The best short stories of 1922 and the yearbook of the American short story* **(1923), B-567.**

S-833   _____ Isles of the blest / by Wilbur Daniel Steele . . . New York; London: Harper & Brothers, 1924. 403 p.
LC: N 1, '24.
BLC: London: T. Fisher Unwin, 1925.

S-834   _____ Land's end: and other stories / by Wilbur Daniel Steele . . . New York; London: Harper & Brothers, [1918]. 303, [1] p., front. [Ill. by P. E. Cowen.]
Contents: Land's end -- The woman at Seven Brothers -- White horse winter -- Down on their knees -- The killer's son -- A devil of a fellow -- The yellow cat -- A man's fool -- Ked's hand -- "Romance."
LC: Ag 27, '18.

_____ The marriage in Kairwan. <u>In</u> *Prize stories of 1921* (1922), **P-619.**

_____ Out of exile. <u>In</u> *The best short stories of 1920 and the yearbook of the American short story* (1921), **B-565.**

S-835   _____ The shame dance: and other stories / by Wilbur Daniel Steele. New York; London: Harper & Brothers Publishers, [c1923]. 392 p.
Contents: The shame dance -- The white man -- "La Guiablesse" -- Both judge and jury -- Always summer -- At Two-in-the-bush -- The Anglo-Saxon -- The marriage in Kairwan -- "He that hideth his secret" -- From the other side of the South -- "Arab stuff" -- The man who sat.
LC: My 19, '23.
BLC: London: T. Fisher Unwin, 1924.

S-836   _____ Storm / by Wilbur Daniel Steele. New York; London: Harper & Brothers, 1914. 329, [1] p., front.
LC: Mr 18, '14.

S-837   _____ Taboo / by Wilbur Daniel Steele. New York: Harcourt, Brace and Company, [c1925]. 260 p.
LC: Ag 24, '25.
PW: Ag 22, '25.
BLC: London: Hutchinson & Co., [1927].

_____ What do you mean-Americans? <u>In</u> *Prize stories of 1924 (1925)*, **P-622.**

_____ When Hell froze. <u>In</u> *The Harper prize short stories* **(1925), H-233.**

_____ White horse winter. <u>In</u> *Representative short stories* **(1917), R-176.**

_____ The yellow cat. <u>In</u> *The best short stories of 1915 and the yearbook of the American short story* **(1916), B-560.**

S-838   Steely, Guy. Wally: a story of the West / by Guy Steely; frontispiece by W. W. Fawcett. New York: Dodd, Mead and Company, 1911. 372 p., front.
LC: S 30, '11.
PW: O 7, '11.

S-839   Steere, C. A. (Charles Allen), b. 1860. When things were doing / by C. A. Steere. Chicago: Charles H. Kerr & Company, 1908. 282 p.   **OSU, CRL**
PW: Ja 4, '08.

Steffens, Lincoln. Collusion. <u>In</u> *Short stories from Life* **(1916), S-463.**

_____ A Po-lice-man. <u>In</u> *Short stories from Life* **(1916), S-463.**

_____ Strictly business. <u>In</u> *Short stories from Life* **(1916), S-463.**

S-840   Stein, Evaleen. Troubadour tales / by Evaleen Stein; with illustrations by Virginia Keep, Maxfield Parrish, B. Rosenmeyer & Edward Edwards. Indianapolis: The Bobbs-Merrill Company, [c1903]. 165 p., col. front., [8] leaves of col. plates, ill.
Contents: The page of Count Reynaurd -- The lost rune --Count Hugo's sword -- Felix.

S-841 Stein, Gertrude, 1874-1946. Geography and plays / by Gertrude Stein. Boston: The Four Seas Company, [c1922]. 419 p.
Contents: Susie Asado [poem] -- Ada -- Miss Furr and Miss Skeene -- A collection -- France -- Americans -- Italians -- A sweet tail (gypsies) -- The history of Belmonte -- In the grass (on Spain) -- England -- Mallorcan stories [poem] -- Scenes. Actions and dispositions of relations and positions -- The king or something (The public is invited to dance) -- Publishers, the portrait gallery, and the manuscripts of the British museum -- Roche -- Braque -- Portrait of Prince B. D. -- Mrs. Whitehead [poem] -- Portrait of Constance Fletcher -- A poem about Walberg [poem] -- Johnny Grey [poem] -- A portrait of F. B. -- Sacred Emily -- IIIIIIIII [poem] -- One (Van Vechten) [poem] -- One. Harry Phelan Gibb -- A curtain raiser [poem] -- Ladies voices (curtain raiser) [play] -- What happened. A play in five acts. -- White wines. Three acts. [play] -- Do let us go away. A play. -- For the country entirely. A play in letters. -- Turkey bones and eating and we liked it. A play. -- Every afternoon. A dialogue. -- Captain Walter Arnold. A play. -- Please do not suffer. A play. -- He said it. Monologue. -- Counting her dresses. A play. -- I like it to be a play. A play. -- Not sightly. A play. -- Bonne Annee. A play. -- Mexico. A play. -- A family of perhaps three -- Advertisements -- Pink melon joy -- If you had three husbands -- Work again -- Tourty or tourtebattre. A story of the great war -- Next. (Life and letters of Marcel Duchamp) -- Land of nations (sub title: And ask Asia) -- Accents in Alsace. A reasonable tragedy. [play] -- The psychology of Nations or What are you looking at.
LC: Ja 24, '23.
PW: S 8, '23.
References: Haas & Gallup VI; Sawyer, p. 42-44; Wilson A5.

S-842 _____ Three lives; stories of the good Anna, Melanctha, and the gentle Lena / by Gertrude Stein. New York: The Grafton Press, 1909. 279 p. Unexamined copy: bibliographic data from OCLC, #556608.
LC: Jl 30, '09.
PW: D 4, '09.
References: Haas & Gallup II; Sawyer, p. 33-35; Wilson A1.

S-843 Stein, Max. William Bright, captain of commerce: a story of commercial progress / by Max Stein. Chicago: United States Publishing House, [c1912]. 195 p.
LC: Ja 22, '13.

Steinberg, Judah. At the matzes. In *Yiddish tales* (1912), Y-20.

_____ A livelihood. In *Yiddish tales* (1912), Y-20.

S-844 Steiner, Edward Alfred, 1866-1956. The broken wall: stories of the mingling folk / by Edward A. Steiner . . . New York; Chicago; Toronto; Edinburgh: Fleming H. Revell Company, [c1911]. 219 p., front., [7] leaves of plates.
Contents: The lady of the Good Will mines -- Committing a matrimony -- "Hisn, mine and ourn" -- A slavic Oklahoman -- Mules and the Tolstoy doctrine -- When Miss Mary passes -- Dobra Bridget -- Hot, through many generations -- The fellowship of suffering -- When the sun stands still -- The dark people -- "Will he let me in?" -- Americanus sum.
LC: N 10, '11.

S-845 _____ The cup of Elijah / by Edward A. Steiner . . . New York; Chicago; Toronto; London; Edinburgh: Fleming H. Revell Company [c1910]. 39 p. Ornamental borders. **CBC**
LC: F 26, '10.

S-846 _____ The mediator: a tale of the Old world and the New / by Edward A. Steiner. New York; Chicago; Toronto; London; Edinburgh: Fleming H. Revell Company, [c1907]. 356 p.
LC: S 13, '07.

S-847 _____ The parable of the cherries / by Edward A. Steiner . . . New York; Chicago; Toronto; London; Edinburgh: Fleming H. Revell Company, [c1913]. 64 p., col. front., [1] leaf of col. plates.
Contents: The doctor -- The rabbi -- The priest -- The pastor -- The market.
LC: N 15, '13.

S-848 _____ Sanctus Spiritus and company / by Edward A. Steiner . . . New York: George H. Doran Company, [c1919]. 320 p.
LC: N 12, '19.

S-849 Stellman, Louis John, b. 1877. Port o'gold: a history-romance of the San Francisco Argonauts / Louis J. Stellman. Boston: Richard G. Badger, [c1922]. ([Boston]: The Gorham Press). 416 p., photo. front., [15] leaves of plates.
LC: F 12, '23.
PW: Mr 10, '23.

S-850 _____ Said the observer / by Louis J. Stellmann; illustrations by J. P. Burnham and V. C. Forsythe. San Francisco: The Whitaker & Ray Co., Incorporated, 1903. 72 p., incl. front., ill.

S-851 [Stendel, Harry Henry]. "Verdum Belle"; The best "dog story" of the World War . . . ; Containing Senator Vest's "Tribute to the dog;" Eugene Field's Indictment of dog laws; poems eulogizing our canine friend, the dog, by Byron, Longfellow, Guest, Ghey, Miss Ashley, and Miss Bernard. St. Louis, Missouri: H. H. Stendel & Company, [n. d.]. 16 p., ill.
SNN
LC: Ja 2, '19.

S-852 Stephens, Dan Voorhees, 1868-1939. Phelps and his teachers . . . / by Dan V. Stephens . . . ; Decorations by Nina E. Lumbard. Fremont, Nebraska: Hammond & Stephens Co., c1901. 118 p. **NYP**

S-853 _____ Silas Cobb: a story of supervision / by Dan V. Stephens. Fremont, Nebraska: Hammond Bros. & Stephens, [c1901]. 363 p., ill.
PW: Ag 10, '01.

S-854 [Stephens, Kate], 1853-1938. A woman's heart: manuscripts found in the papers of Katherine Peshconet and edited by her executor Olive Ransom [pseud.]. New York: Doubleday, Page & Company, 1906. 252 p. **DLC**

Stephens, Louise G., b. 1843. See **Katharine, pseud.**

S-855 Stephens, Robert Neilson, 1867-1906. The bright face of danger: being an account of some adventures of Henri de Launay, son of the Sieur de la Tournoire / Freely translated into modern English by Robert Neilson Stephens . . . ; illustrated by H. C. Edwards. Boston: L. C. Page & Company, 1904. 322 p., incl.

front., [5] leaves of plates.
"The bright face of danger is, in a distant way, a sequel to `An enemy to the king'."
PW: My 14, '04.
BLC: London: Eveleigh Nash, 1904.

S-856 ____ Captain Ravenshaw, or, The maid of Cheapside a romance of Elizabethan London / by Robert Neilson Stephens . . . ; illustrated by Howard Pyle and others. Boston: L. C. Page & Company, 1901. 369 p., front., [6] leaves of plates. [Some ill. by Philip R. Goodwin & Ethel Franklin Betts.]
PW: S 14, '01.
BLC: London: Ward, Lock, & Co., [1901].

S-857 ____ Clementina's highwayman: a romance / by Robert Neilson Stephens . . . and George Hembert Westley . . . ; illustrated by Adelaide Everhart. Boston: L. C. Page & Company, 1907. 335 p., front., [5] leaves of plates.
LC: Ag 30, '07.

S-858 ____ The flight of Georgiana: a story of love and peril in England in 1746 / by Robert Neilson Stephens; illustrated by H. C. Edwards. Boston: L. C. Page & Company, 1905. 339 p., col. front., [5] leaves of plates.
BLC: London: Eveleigh Nash, 1905.

S-859 ____ The mystery of Murray Davenport: a story of New York at the present day / by Robert Neilson Stephens; illustrated by H. C. Edwards. Boston: L. C. Page & Company, 1903. 312 p., incl. front., [5] leaves of plates.
PW: Ap 25, '03.
BLC: London: Eveleigh Nash, 1903.

S-860 ____ A soldier of Valley Forge: a romance of the American Revolution / by Robert Neilson Stephens . . . and G. E. Theodore Roberts . . . ; with a frontispiece in full colour from a painting by Frank T. Merrill. Boston: L. C. Page & Company, 1911. 328 p., col. front.
LC: Ap 12, '11.
PW: Ap 22, '11.

S-861 ____ The sword of Bussy, or, The word of a gentleman: a romance of the time of Henry III / by Robert Neilson Stephens and Herman Nickerson; with a frontispiece in full colour from a painting by Edmund H. Garrett. Boston: L. C. Page & Company, 1912. 315 p., col. front.
LC: N 7, '12.
PW: N 30, '12.

S-862 ____ Tales from Bohemia / by Robert Neilson Stephens . . . ; illustrated by Wallace Goldsmith. Boston: L. C. Page & Company, 1908. 341 p., front., [7] leaves of plates. Illustrated end papers.
Contents: The only girl he ever loved -- A bit of melody -- On the bridge -- The triumph of Mogley -- Out of his past -- The new side partner -- The needy outsider -- Time and the Tombstone -- He believed them -- A vagrant -- Under an awning -- Shandy's revenge -- The whistle -- Whiskers -- The bad break of Tobit McStenger -- The scars -- "La Gitana" -- Transition -- A Man who was no good -- Mr. Thornberry's eldorado -- At the stage door -- "Poor Yorick" -- Coincidence -- Newgag the comedian -- An operatic evening.
LC: S 14, '08.
PW: O 3, '08.

S-863 Stephenson, Cora Bennett. The hand of God / by Cora Bennett Stephenson. Boston: The Ball Publishing Co., 1909. 317 p., photo. front.
LC: Ap 19, '09.

S-864 Stephenson, Henry Thew, 1870-1957. Christie Bell of Goldenrod Valley: a tale of southern Indians and of Cincinnati in the olden time / by Henry Thew Stephenson. Indianapolis: Federal Publishing Company, 1918. 378 p., col. front., [5] leaves of plates. [Ill. by Winifred Austin Shick.]
LC: Ap 15, '18.

S-865 ____ The fickle wheel: a tale of Elizabethan London / by Henry Thew Stephenson; illustrated by C. M. Relyea. Indianapolis: The Bowen-Merrill Company, [c1901]. 380 p., front., [5] leaves of plates.
PW: O 5, '01.
BLC: London: B. F. Stevens & Brown, [1901].

S-866 Stephenson, Nathaniel Wright, 1867-1935. The beautiful Mrs. Moulton / by Nathaniel Stephenson. London; New York: John Lane, The Bodley Head, 1902. 326 p., front.
PW: O 4, '02.

S-867 ____ Eleanor Dayton / by Nathaniel Stephenson. New York; London: John Lane, 1903. 315 p.
PW: S 12, '03.

S-868 ____ They that took the sword / by Nathaniel Stevenson. London; New York: John Lane, The Bodley Head, 1901. 301 p.
PW: Je 22, '01.

S-869 Sterling, Sara Hawks. A lady of King Arthur's court: being a romance of the Holy Grail / by Sara Hawks Sterling . . . ; pictured by Clara Elsene Peck. Philadelphia: Published by George W. Jacobs & Co., 1907. 261, [1] p., incl. col. front., [4] leaves of col. plates. Decorated end papers.
LC: O 10, '07.
BLC: London: Chatto & Windus, printed in U. S. A., 1909.

S-870 ____ Shake-speares sweetheart / by Sara Hawks Sterling; pictured by Clara Elsene Peck. Published at Philadelphia: George W. Jacobs & Co., 1905. 281, [1] p., col. front., [4] leaves of col. plates. Decorated end papers.
BLC: London: Chatto & Windus, 1907.

Stern, Elizabeth Gertrude Levin, 1890-1954, jt. aut. *A friend at court* (1923). See **Stern, Leon, 1887-1980, jt. aut., S-870.**

Stern, G. B. "The eleventh hat." In *Aces* (1924), **A-42.**

____ "The beloved." In *More aces* (1925), **M-962.**

S-871 Stern, Leon, 1887-1980. A friend at court / by Leon Stern and Elizabeth Gertrude Stern. New York: The Macmillan Company, 1923. 335 p.
LC: My 9, '23.

Sterne, Elaine, b. 1894. Mirage. In *As we are* (1923), A-325.

S-872 ____ The road of ambition / by Elaine Sterne; illustrated by Ray N. Jackson. New York: Britton Publishing Company, [c1917]. 496 p., col. front., [3] leaves of col. plates.
PW: Ap 28, '17.

S-873 Sterner, Lawrence. The un-Christian Jew / by Lawrence Sterner. New York: The Neale Publishing Company, 1917. 307 p. OSU copy has paper label over Neale imprint: Published by the author, New York, 1919.

S-874 Sterns, Justin. Osru: a tale of many incarnations: the history of a soul / by Justin Sterns. New York: Lenox Publishing Company, [c1910]. 197 p., front.
LC: Ap 14, '10.
Another edition: New York: Theosophical Publishing Company, 1911, [c1910].

S-875 Sterrett, Frances Roberta, b. 1869. The amazing inheritance / by Frances R. Sterrett . . . New York; London: D. Appleton and Company, 1922. 323 p.
LC: S 6, '22.
PW: S 30, '22.

S-876 ____ The jam girl / by Frances R. Sterrett; illustrated. New York; London: D. Appleton and Company, 1914. 308 p., front., [3] leaves of plates. [Ill. by C. H. Taffs.]
LC: Ja 29, '14.
PW: Ja 31, '14.

S-877 ____ Jimmie the sixth / by Frances R. Sterrett . . . ; illustrated. New York; London: D. Appleton and Company, 1918. 322 p., front., [5] leaves of plates. [Ill. by May Wilson Preston.]
LC: O 30, '18.
PW: N 9, '18.

S-878 ____ Mary Rose of Mifflin / by Frances R. Sterrett; illustrated by Maginel Wright Enright. New York: D. Appleton and Company, 1916. 315 p., front., ill.
LC: Mr 4, '16.
PW: Mr 25, '16.

S-879 ____ Nancy goes to town / by Frances R. Sterrett . . . New York; London: D. Appleton and Company, 1920. 298, [1] p.   **NYP**
LC: O 25, '20.
PW: N 13, '20.

S-880 ____ Rebecca's promise / by Frances R. Sterrett; illustrated by E. C. Caswell. New York; London: D. Appleton and Company, 1919. 329 p., front., [3] leaves of plates.
LC: Jl 21, '19.
PW: Jl 26, '19.

S-881 ____ These young rebels / by Frances R. Sterrett. New York; London: D. Appleton and Company, 1921. 304, [1] p., front.
LC: Ag 3, '21.
PW: Ag 20, '21.

S-882 ____ Up the road with Sallie / by Frances R. Sterrett; illustrated by C. H. Taffs. New York; London: D. Appleton and Company, 1915. 314, [1] p., front., [3] leaves of plates.
LC: S 15, '15.
PW: S 25, '15.

S-883 ____ William and Williamina / by Frances R. Sterrett; illustrated by Maginel Wright Enright. New York; London: D. Appleton and Company, 1917. 346, [1] p., front., [7] leaves of plates.
LC: O 15, '17.
PW: O 27, '17.

Stettheimer, Ettie. See Waste, Henrie, pseud.

S-884 Stevens, Charles McClellan, b. 1861. Uncle Jeremiah and his neighbors at the St. Louis exposition / by C. M. Stevens . . . ; profusely illustrated with eighty humorous sketches by R. W. Taylor. Chicago: Thompson & Thomas, 1904. 332 p., front., ill.

S-885 ____ Uncle Jeremiah at the Panama-Pacific exposition: strange, startling and amazing adventures of the famous farmer philosopher and his friends amid the gorgeous scenes at the Golden Gate. By C. M. Stevens . . . ; illustrated by Harold F. Colson. Chicago: The Hamming-Whitman Company, [c1915]. 319 p., ill.   **DLC**
LC: Jl 1, '15.

S-886 Stevens, Grant Eugene. Wicked city / by Grant Eugene Stevens. Chicago: [s. n.], 1906. 340 p., ill.   **CLU**
LC: Je 4, '06.

S-887 Stevens, Isaac Newton, 1858-1920. An American suffragette: a novel / by Isaac N. Stevens . . New York: William Rickey & Company, 1911. 248 p.
LC: S 11, '11.
PW: S 30, '11.

S-888 ____ The liberators: a story of future American politics / by Isaac N. Stevens; illustrations by Nella Fountain Binkley [sic]. New York: B. W. Dodge & Company, 1908. 352 p., front.
PW: My 9, '08.

S-889 ____ What is love? / by Isaac Newton Stevens . . . New York: Duffield & Company, 1918. 216 p.   **DLC**
LC: S 13, '18.
PW: S 28, '18.

S-890 Stevens, Myrtle Gest. The highways and the hedges / by Myrtle Gest Stevens; illustrated by Frederic Mussey. [Phoenix: Arizona State Press, c1911]. 50 p., [2] leaves of photo. plates.   **DLC**

S-891 Stevens, Nettie. Tompkinsville folks: a story of the Central States' village life / by Nettie Stevens. Boston, Mass.: The C. M. Clark Publishing Company, 1909. 377 p., front., [5] leaves of plates. [Ill. by Grace Perry.]
LC: O 30, '09.
PW: D 18, '09.

Stevens, Rowan. The battle for the Pacific. In *The battle for the Pacific* (1908), B-357.

S-892   Stevens, Sheppard, 1862-1909. In the eagle's talon: a romance of the Louisiana Purchase / by Sheppard Stevens [i. e. Mrs. S. Stevens]; illustrated by A. Russell. Boston: Little, Brown, and Company, 1902. 475 p., front., [5] leaves of plates.
PW: Je 14, '02.

S-893   ____ The sign of triumph: a romance of the Children's Crusade / by Sheppard Stevens . . . ; illustrated by Harry C. Edwards. Boston: L. C. Page & Company, 1904. 337 p., front., [3] leaves of plates.
PW: Mr 12, '04.
BLC: London: Chapman Hall, 1904.

S-894   Stevens, Thomas Wood, 1880-1942. Hold Redmere: a tale / by Thomas Wood Stevens and Alden Charles Noble. Ridgewood, New Jersey: Alwil Shop, 1901. [42] p.   **VIC**

S-895   ____ The parchment in the hollow hilt / Thomas Wood Stevens & Alden Charles Noble. Chicago: The Blue Sky Press, [c1904]. [33] p.   **BKL**
PW: Je 4, '04.

S-896   Stevenson, Burton Egbert, 1872-1962. Affairs of state: being an account of certain surprising adventures which befell an American family in the land of windmills / by Burton E. Stevenson; with illustrations by F. Vaux Wilson. New York: Henry Holt and Company, 1906. 335 p., front., [3] leaves of plates.
PW: O 6, '06.
BLC: London: Chatto & Windus, 1907.

S-897   ____ At odds with the Regent: a story of the Cellamare conspiracy / by Burton Egbert Stevenson; with a frontispiece by Anna Whelan Betts. Philadelphia; London: J. B. Lippincott Company, 1901, [c1900]. 365 p., front.

S-898   ____ Cadets of Gascony: two stories of old France / by Burton E. Stevenson; illustrated by Anna Whelen Betts. Philadelphia; London: J. B. Lippincott Company, 1904. 378 p., front., [4] leaves of plates.
Contents: Marsan -- A child of the night.
PW: Ap 2, '04.

         ____ The case of Mrs. Magnus. In *Master tales of mystery* (1915), M-588.5.

S-899   ____ The destroyer: a tale of international intrigue / by Burton E. Stevenson . . . ; illustrated by Thomas Fogarty. New York: Dodd, Mead and Company, 1913. 434 p., front.
LC: O 2, '13.
PW: O 11, '13.

S-900   ____ The girl with the blue sailor / by Burton E. Stevenson . . . New York: Dodd, Mead & Company, 1906. 310 p., front., [4] leaves of plates.
[Ill. by Charlotte Weber-Ditzler.]
PW: My 5, '06.

S-901   ____ The gloved hand: a detective story / by Burton E. Stevenson . . . ; with illustrations by Thomas Fogarty. New York: Dodd, Mead and Company, 1913. 343 p., front., [3] leaves of plates.
"This story was published in the Popular magazine under the title of The mind master."
LC: Mr 24, '13.
PW: Mr 29, '13.

S-902   ____ The heritage: a story of defeat and victory / by Burton Egbert Stevenson. Boston; New York: Houghton, Mifflin and Company, 1902. (Cambridge: The Riverside Press). 324 p.
PW: N 1, '02.
BLC: London: A. P. Watt & Son, Cambridge, Mass. printed, 1902.

S-903   ____ The Holladay case: a tale / by Burton E. Stevenson. New York: Henry Holt and Company, 1903. 298 p., front.
PW: D 5, '03.
BLC: London: William Heinemann, 1903.

S-904   ____ A king in Babylon / by Burton E. Stevenson . . . ; with illustrations by W. H. D. Koerner. Boston: Small, Maynard & Company, [c1917]. 391 p., col. front., [4] leaves of plates.
LC: S 22, '17.
PW: S 15, '17.
BLC: London: Hutchinson & Co., 1918.

S-905   ____ The kingmakers / by Burton E. Stevenson . . . ; frontispiece by E. C. Caswell. New York: Dodd, Mead and Company, 1922. 314 p., front.
LC: N 1, '22.
PW: N 11, '22.
BLC: London: Hutchinson & Co., [1922].

S-906   ____ Little comrade: a tale of the great war / by Burton E. Stevenson. New York: Henry Holt and Company, 1915. 315 p.
LC: Mr 11, '15.
PW: Mr 13, '15.
BLC: London: Hutchinson & Co., 1915.

S-907   ____ The Marathon mystery: a story of Manhattan / by Burton E. Stevenson . . . ; with five scenes in colour by Eliot Keen. New York: Henry Holt and Company, 1904. 323 p., col. front., [4] leaves of col. plates.   **CLE**
PW: D 10, '04.
BLC: London & New York: Harper & Bros, 1904.

S-908   ____ The mystery of the Boule cabinet: a detective story / by Burton E. Stevenson . . . ; with illustrations by Thomas Fogarty. New York: Dodd, Mead & Company, 1912. 362 p., front., [3] leaves of plates.
LC: Mr 26, '12.
PW: Mr 30, '12.
BLC: London: Eveleigh Nash, 1915.

S-909   ____ The path of honor: a tale of the war in the Bocage / by Burton E. Stevenson . . . ; with illustrations by Olive Rush and Ethel Pennewill Brown. Philadelphia: London: J. B. Lippincott Company, 1910. 312 p., front., [3] leaves of plates.
LC: O 4, '10.
PW: N 12, '10.

S-910   ____ The quest for the rose of Sharon / by Burton E. Stevenson; illustrated. Boston: L. C. Page & Company, 1909. 207 p., front., [5] leaves of plates. [Ill. by Thomas Fogarty.]
LC: Ap 30, '09.
PW: My 15, '09.

____ Rah, rah, rah, Murray. In *Stories of the colleges* (1901), S-985.

S-911   ____ A soldier of Virginia: a tale of Colonel Washington and Braddock's defeat / by Burton Egbert Stevenson. Boston; New York: Houghton, Mifflin and Company, 1901. (Cambridge, Mass.: The Riverside Press). 325, [1] p., front., [3] leaves of plates, map. [Ill. by Philip R. Goodwin.]
PW: Mr 30, '01.
BLC: London: A. P. Watt & Son, Cambridge, Mass., printed, [1901]. Another edition: London: Duckworth & Co., Cambridge, Mass., printed, 1901.

S-912   ____ The storm-center: a romance / by Burton E. Stevenson; frontispiece by Edward C. Caswell. New York: Dodd, Mead and Company, 1924. 327 p., front.
LC: Ja 15, '24.
PW: Ja 19, '24.
BLC: London: Hutchinson & Co., [1924].

S-913   ____ That affair at Elizabeth / by Burton E. Stevenson . . . New York: Henry Holt and Company, 1907. 307 p.
LC: O 26, '07.
PW: N 23, '07.

Stevenson, John, b. 1853. See **Jackson, Stephen, pseud.**

S-914   Stevenson, Louis Lacy. Big game / by Louis Lacy Stevenson. New York: Brentano's, 1924. 332 p.
PW: Ap 5, '24.

Stevenson, Myra E. McDermott. See **McDermott-Stevenson, Myra E.**

S-915   Steventon, John, *pseud.* The auto-orphan / by John Steventon [pseud.]. Boston: Richard G. Badger, [c1913]. (Boston: The Gorham Press). 122 p.
Contents: The auto-orphan -- The boy on horseback -- A boy's suspicions -- Scenes of my childhood -- At grandfather's -- The preacher -- Identification -- "If a body kiss a body need a body cry" -- The sick tell no tales -- The schoolmaster -- Boy and dog -- Spare the rod and spoil the child -- As a father pitieth his child -- The priest -- Home with my father -- The manhunt -- Curtain.

S-916   Stewart, b. 1879, *pseud.* Silence: a compound problem novel / by Stewart [pseud.]. Jersey City: Connoisseur's Press, 1908. 435 p.   **NDD**
LC: Ag 28, '08.
PW: Jl 18, '08.

S-917   Stewart, Cal, 1856-1919. Uncle Josh stories; including readings, humorous poems, and sketches / by Cal Stewart (Your Uncle Josh). Boston: Walter H. Baker Company, 1924. 113 p.
Contents: The opera at Punkin Center -- Moving pictures at Punkin Center -- Uncle Josh takes the census -- Uncle Josh buys a talking machine -- The Chautauqua at Punkin Center -- Uncle Josh and the honey bees -- Uncle Josh and the soldier -- Uncle Josh in the cafeteria -- Moving day at Punkin Center -- Uncle Josh and Aunt Nancy on a visit to New York -- Uncle Josh keeps house -- Uncle Josh joins the Grangers -- Uncle Josh has his photo taken -- Automobile -- Fourth of July at Punkin Center -- Uncle Josh and the Labor Union -- Show troupe at Punkin Center [play] -- Uncle Josh and the sailor -- Uncle Josh in the barber shop -- Uncle Josh and the insurance company -- The county fair at Punkin Center -- Uncle Josh at the Bug House -- The photoplay of life [play] -- Uncle Josh's troubles in a hotel -- Fiddled out of house and home [play] -- The village gossips [play] -- A busy week at Punkin Center -- Uncle Josh's rheumatism -- Revival meeting at Punkin Center -- Uncle Josh's second trip to the metropolis -- Uncle Josh and the Billikin -- Uncle Josh at the dentist [play] -- Uncle Josh in an automobile -- And then I laughed [poem] -- Uncle Josh at the skating rink -- Train time at Punkin Center [play] -- Gassed [poem].

S-918   ____ Uncle Josh Weathersby's "Punkin Centre" stories / by Cal Stewart. [Chicago: Regan Printing House, c1903]. 170 p., ill.   **IPL**
Contents: My old yaller almanac -- Arrival in New York -- Uncle Josh in society -- Uncle Josh in a Chinese laundry -- Uncle Josh in a museum -- Uncle Josh in Wall Street -- Uncle Josh and the fire department -- Uncle Josh in an auction room -- Uncle Josh on a Fifth Avenue 'bus -- Uncle Josh in a department store -- Uncle Josh's comments on the signs seen in New York -- Uncle Josh on a street car -- My first pair of copper toed boots -- Uncle Josh in police court -- Uncle Josh at Coney Island -- Uncle Josh at the opera -- Uncle Josh at Delmonico's -- It is fall -- Si Pettingill's brooms -- Uncle Josh plays golf -- Jim Lawson's hogs -- Uncle Josh and the lightning rod agent -- A meeting of the Annanias club -- Jim Lawson's hoss trade -- A meeting of the school directors -- The weekly paper at Punkin Centre -- Uncle Josh at a camp meeting -- The unveiling of the organ -- Uncle Josh plays a game of base ball -- The Punkin Centre and Paw Paw Valley Railroad -- Uncle Josh on a bicycle -- A baptisin' at the Hickory Corners Church -- A reminiscence of my railroad days -- Uncle Josh at a circus -- Uncle Josh invites the city folks to visit him -- Yosemite Jim, or a tale of the great white death -- Uncle Josh Weathersby's trip to Boston -- Who marched in sixty-one.
Another edition: Chicago: Stanton and Van Vliet Co., c1905.

S-919   Stewart, Charles David, b. 1868. Buck: being some account of his rise in the great city of Chicago / by Charles D. Stewart; with illustrations by R. M. Brinkerhoff. Boston; New York: Houghton Mifflin Company, 1919. (Cambridge [Mass.]: The Riverside Press). 298 p., front., [10] leaves of plates.
LC: F 10, '19.

S-920   ____ Finerty of the sand-house / by Charles D. Stewart . . . New York: The Century Co., 1913. 156 p.
LC: Ap 3, '13.

S-921   ____ The fugitive blacksmith / by Charles D. Stewart. New York: The Century Co., 1905. 321 p., front.
PW: F 18, '05.
BLC: London: Hodder & Stoughton, [New York printed], 1905.

S-922   ____ Partners of Providence / by Charles D. Stewart; illustrated by C. J. Taylor. New York: The Century Company, 1907. 538 p., incl. front., ill.
PW: Mr 30, '07.
BLC: London: Duckworth & Co., printed in U. S. A., 1907.

S-923   ____ Valley waters / by Charles D. Stewart. New York: E. P. Dutton & Company, [c1922]. 370 p.
LC: O 30, '22.
PW: N 25, '22.

S-924 _____ The wrong woman / by Charles D. Stewart. Boston; New York: Houghton Mifflin Company, 1912. (Cambridge [Mass.]: The Riverside Press). 285, [1] p., col. front., [3] leaves of col. plates. [Ill. by Harold M. Brett.]
LC: Ja 17, '12.
PW: Ja 6, '12.

S-925 Stewart, Donald Ogden, b. 1894. Aunt Polly's story of mankind / by Donald Ogden Stewart. New York: George H. Doran Company, [c1923]. 281 p., front. [Ill. by Herb Roth.] Illustrated end papers.
LC: N 30, '23.
PW: D 8, '23.

S-926 _____ The crazy fool / by Donald Ogden Stewart; decorations by Herb Roth. New York: Albert & Charles Boni, 1925. 246 p.
LC: Je 19, '25.
PW: Je 20, '25.

S-927 _____ Mr. and Mrs. Haddock abroad / by Donald Ogden Stewart; illustrations by Herb Roth. New York: George H. Doran Company, [c1924]. 267 p., incl. front., ill. Colored, illustrated end papers.
LC: N 13, '24.
PW: N 8, '24.
BLC: New York & London: Harper & Bros, 1926.

S-928 _____ A parody outline of history / by Donald Ogden Stewart. New York: George H. Doran Company, 1921. 230 p., ill.
Title continues: " . . . wherein may be found a curiously irreverent treatment of American historical events, imagining them as they would be narrated by America's most characteristic contemporary authors, together with divers delightful, droll drawings, penciled by Herb Roth, the whole forming an amusing and satirical picture of American letters of today.
LC: D 2, '21.
PW: D 10, '21.

S-929 Stewart, John R. (John Rogers), b. 1854. The Fraters / by John R. Stewart. Nashville, Tenn.; Dallas, Tex.; Richmond, Va.: Publishing House of the M. E. Church, South; Smith & Lamar, agents, 1916. 140 p.

Stewart, Lula Shortridge. Old Jud Watkins. In *Club stories* (1915), C-502.

Stewart, Mary. Really married. In *Marriage* (1923), M-457.

Stewart, Solon K. The contract of Corporal Twing. In *The best short stories of 1923 and the yearbook of the American short story* (1924), B-568.

S-930 Stickney, Mary E. (Mary Etta), b. 1853. Ouray Jim: and other stories / by Mary E. Stickney . . . Longmont, Colorado: The Ledger Publishing Company, 1904. 86 p.
Contents: Ouray Jim -- "A star route" case -- An Arizona speculation -- The Jack pot mine.

S-931 Stiefel, H. C. Slices from a long loaf: log-book of an eventful voyage by five Pittsburg tourists down the beautiful Allegheny River, from Oil City to Pittsburg, with a few extra chips thrown in that may help to serve as a diversion; a memorable cruise amid unrivalled natural scenery, through a historical country that has now become the World's Industrial Center-facts and figures about Pittsburg's greatness-- many things that happened en route, humorous and otherwise, and a few that are supposed to have happened in other days gone by / by H. C. Stiefel. Pittsburg, Pa: Bissell Block Publishing Company, [c1905]. 221 p., front., [15] leaves of plates. [Ill. by Covert, Bragdon, Sid Smith, Dalrymple, or F. E. Johnson.]   **GJG**

Stienback, Leroy Lindley, b. 1837. See **Homer, N. Y., pseud.**

S-932 Stiles, George Kean, b. 1873. The dragoman: a novel / by George K. Stiles. New York; London: Harper & Brothers, 1913. 311, [1] p., front.

Stillman, Albert Leeds. The twins in college. In *A little book of Rutgers tales* (1905), L-378.

S-933 Stillman, Annie Raymond, b. 1855. Fool's gold: a study in values: a novel / by Annie Raymond Stillman. Chicago; New York; Toronto; London; Edinburgh: Fleming H. Revell Company, 1902. 324 p.
PW: O 4, '02.

S-934 Stilson, Charles B. (Charles Billings). The ace of blades / by Charles B. Stilson. New York: G. Howard Watt, 1924. 293 p.
LC: Ag 21, '24.
BLC: London: Hutchinson & Co., 1925.

S-935 _____ A cavalier of Navarre: a tale of pikemen and musketeers / by Charles B. Stilson . . . New York: G. Howard Watt, 1925. 304 p.
LC: Je 16, '25.
PW: My 9, '25.
BLC: London: Hutchinson & Co., [1925].

S-936 _____ The island God forgot / by Charles B. Stilson and Charles Beahan. New York: H. Holt and Company, 1922. 319 p.
LC: Ag 26, '22.

Stimson, Frederic Jesup, 1855-1943. By due process of law. In *The best short stories of 1923 and the yearbook of the American short story* (1924), B-568.

S-937 _____ In cure of her soul / by Frederic Jesup Stimson. New York: D. Appleton and Company, 1906. 612 p., front., [8] leaves of plates. [Ill. by Arthur E. Becher & A. B. Wenzell.]
PW: Je 23, '06.

S-938 _____ Jethro Bacon of Sandwich; The weaker sex / by F. J. Stimson. New York: Charles Scribner's Sons, 1902. 222 p.
Jethro Bacon was first published in Scribner's magazine, Nov. 1902; *The weaker sex* in the Atlantic monthly, April, 1901.
PW: N 8, '02.

S-939   ____ My story: being the memoirs of Benedict Arnold: late Major-General in the Continental Army and Brigadier-General in that of His Britannic Majesty / by F. J. Stimson (J. S. of Dale); with portraits and a map. New York: Charles Scribner's Sons, 1917. 622 p., front., [2] leaves of plates (port., map).
LC: O 31, '17.

S-940   [Stine, Milton H. (Milton Henry)], 1853-1940. The autobiography of Mary Jane / by Mary Jane [pseud.]. Boston: The Christopher Publishing House, [c1924]. 117 p.
LC: F 4, '24.

S-941   ____ Baron Stiegel / by Rev. M. H. Stine, Ph. D. Philadelphia: Lutheran Publication Society, [c1903]. 331 p.
On spine: The John Rung Prize Series.
PW: Je 6, '03.

S-942   ____ The devil's bride: a present day arraignment of formalism and doubt in the church and in society, in the light of the Holy Scriptures: given in the form of a pleasing story / by Rev. Milton H. Stine . . . ; illustrated by Paul Krafft. Harrisburg, Pa.: Published by the Minter Company, [c1910]. 303 p., [8] leaves of plates.   **CDC**
T. p. printed on a leaf which is not an integral part of a gathering.
LC: O 17, '10.

S-943   Stine, Wilbur M. (Wilbur Morris), b. 1863. Amos Meakin's ghost / by Wilbur Morris Stine. Philadelphia: The Acorn Press, 1924. 327 p.
LC: Jl 17, '24.
PW: Ag 2, '24.

S-944   ____ Ariel: and other writings / by Wilbur Morris Stine. Swarthmore, Pennsylvania: The Acorn Press, 1906. 82 p.   **BBH**
Contents: Ariel -- The tree and the vine -- The moan of the sea.
LC: Je 4, '06.

S-945   Stinson, Hunter. Fingerprints / Hunter Stinson. New York: Henry Holt and Company, 1925. 269 p.
LC: Ap 17, '25.
PW: Ap 25, '25.

Stirling, Yates, Jr. The battle off the hook. In *The battle for the Pacific* (1908), B-357.

____ The bombardment of the Golden gate. In *The battle for the Pacific* (1908), B-357.

____ The cruise of a commerce destroyer. In *The battle for the Pacific* (1908), B-357.

____ A fight in the fog. In *The battle for the Pacific* (1908), B-357.

S-946   Stitzer, Daniel Ahrens, b. 1869. My escape from the gallows / by Dan A. Stitzer. Baltimore, Md.: The McLean Company [c1916]. 36 p.
Unexamined copy: bibliographic data from NUC.
LC: Ja 3, '17.

S-947   ____ Stories of the occult / by Dan A. Stitzer. Boston: Richard G. Badger; Toronto: The Copp Clark Co., Limited, [c1917]. 216 p.
Contents: Dual personality -- The occult hand -- The resurrection.
LC: Ap 19, '17.

S-948   Stock, Etta Florence. The redemption of Charley Phillips / by Etta Florence Stock. Boston: The Four Seas Company, 1919. 221 p., front.
LC: Ap 5, '19.

S-949   ____ To every man his work / by Etta Florence Stock. Boston: The Four Seas Company, 1919. 134 p., front.   **DLC**
LC: Ap 5, '19.

S-950   Stocking, Charles Francis, b. 1873. Andean days / by Charles Francis Stocking . . . Chicago: The Maestro Co., 1917. 46 p., ill.   **DLC**
Contents: El Toro -- The devil's fangs -- The quality of manhood -- Sunbeams. Adapted from the story by Verna Olive Ward -- The miracle -- In the shadows.

S-951   ____ Carmen Ariza / by Charles Francis Stocking . . . Chicago: The Maestro Co., 1916. 149, 380, 187, 269, 4 p., col. photo. front.   **KSU**
LC: D 27, '15.

S-952   ____ The diary of Jean Evarts / by Charles Francis Stocking . . . Freeport, Ill.: The Standard Publishing Company, 1912. 352 p.
Unexamined copy: bibliographic data from OCLC, #1572308.

S-953   ____ The mayor of Filbert / by Charles Francis Stocking . . . Chicago: The Maestro Co., 1916. 299 p., front., [2] leaves of plates. [Ill. by Brown-Gossett Studio.]
LC: D 9, '16.
PW: D 23, '16.

S-954   ____ Thou Israel / by Charles Francis Stocking. Chicago: The Maestro Co., 1921. 35, 156, 184, 182, 220 p., col. front.
LC: D 19, '21.

S-955   Stocking, Jane. Via P. & O. / by Jane Stocking. New York: Dodd, Mead and Company, 1914. 257 p.

S-956   Stockman stories. Pittsburgh, Pennsylvania: The Stockman-Farmer Publishing Co., [c1913]. 186 p.   **IAT**
Contents: Margaret Sloan's career / Caroline Abbot Stanley -- Pennsylvania! [poem] / Lydia M. D. O'Neil -- Margaret's summer boarders / Caroline Abbott Stanley -- Thanksgiving Eve [poem] / J. M. Cochran -- One Thanksgiving / Hepsy Neff -- He visited his old home -- A night in a log / Lewis B. Miller -- Christmas Eve [poem] / J. M. Cochran -- The right Mr. Brown / C. A. Parker -- The best decorator in the city / Hepsy Neff -- The shout fiscal's prisoner / Alice Louise Lee -- The corn song [poem] / John G. Whittier -- Patsey's progress / Annabelle Williams.
LC: N 28, '13.

Stockton, Frank Richard, 1834-1902. Aunt Nancy's annuity. In *A house party* (1901), H-903.

S-957   ____ The captain's toll-gate / by Frank R. Stockton; with a memorial sketch by Mrs. Stockton and a bibliography; illustrated. New York: D. Appleton &

Company, 1903. 359 p., front., [4] leaves of plates (some photo.). [Ill. by Jacques Reich and S. Schneider.]
LC: My 29, '03.
PW: Je 6, '03.
BLC: London: Cassell & Co., 1903.
References: BAL 18945.

S-958 ____ John Gayther's garden and the stories told therein / by Frank R. Stockton; illustrated. New York: Charles Scribner's Sons, 1902. 365 p., front., [7] leaves of plates. [Ill. by V. A. Svoboda, Fletcher C. Ransom, Rose Cecil O'Neill, and George B. Waldon.]
Contents: John Gayther's garden -- What I found in the sea / Told by John Gayther -- The bushwhacker nurse / Told by the daughter of the house --The lady in the box / Told by John Gayther -- The cot and the rill / Told by the mistress of the house -- The gilded idol and the king conch-shell / Told by the master of the house -- My balloon hunt / Told by the Frenchman -- The foreign prince and the hermit's daughter / Told by Pomona and Jonas -- The conscious Amanda / Told by the daughter of the house -- My translatophone / Told by the old professor -- The vice-consort / Told by the next neighbor -- Blackgum ag'in' thunder / told by John Gauther.
LC: N 11, '02.
PW: N 22, '02.
BLC: London: Cassell & Co., 1903.
References: BAL 18944.

S-959 ____ Kate Bonnet: the romance of a pirate's daughter / by Frank R. Stockton; illustrated by A. I. Keller and H. S. Potter. New York: D. Appleton and Company, 1902. 420 p., front., [7] leaves of plates.
LC: F 8, '02.
PW: Mr 1, '02.
BLC: London: Cassell & Co., 1902.
References: BAL 18943.

S-960 Stoddard, Cal, b. 1866, *pseud.* The home that was built by hens / by "Uncle Cal" Stoddard [pseud.]; illustrated by L. Stahmer, Jr. Chicago, Ill.: Published by American Poultry Journal Publishing Company, 1913. 70, [5] p.

S-961 [____] The tale of the golden egg: a story founded on facts. Buffalo, N. Y.: Published by Golden Egg Publishing Company, [c1910]. 69 p.   DLC
LC: D 22, '10.

S-962 Stoddard, Charles Warren, 1843-1909. For the pleasure of his company: an affair of the misty city, thrice told / by Charles Warren Stoddard; designs by Marshall Douglass. San Francisco: A. M. Robertson, 1903. 257 p., [2] leaves of plates (1 double leaf).
LC: My 25, '03.
PW: Je 6, '03.
References: BAL 19013.

____ Miss Juno. In *Spinners' book of fiction* (1907), S-755.

____ A prodigal in Tahiti. See *The Great modern American stories* (1920), G-422.

S-963 Stoddard, Janie E. Tempests of the play gods: a novel / by Janie E. Stoddard. New York;

Washington: The Neale Publishing Company, 1904. 268 p.   DLC
PW: Jl 16, '04.

S-964 Stoddard, Willim Bliss. A lovable degenerate / by William B. Stoddard. New York: Cochrane Publishing Co., 1908. 162 p.
Unexamined copy: bibliographic data from OCLC, #30089151.
LC: N 18, '08.

S-965 Stoddard, William Osborn, 1835-1925. Montanye, or, The slavers of old New York: a historical romance / by William O. Stoddard. Philadelphia: Henry Altemus Company, [c1901]. 356 p.
PW: Mr 23, '01.

S-966 Stokely, Edith Keeley. A man mine equal / by E. K. Stokely. Boston: Atlantic Printing Company, 1912. 49 p.   micro.

S-966.5 ____ Miss Billy: a neighborhood story / by Edith Keeley Stokely and Marian Kent Hurd; illustrated by Charles Copeland. Boston: Lothrop Publishing Company, [1905]. 349 p., front., [5] leaves of plates.

Stoll, Albert, comp. See *Clever business sketches* (1909), C-490.

S-967 Stollnitz, H. S. (Henry Sandé), b. 1865. The Baal Magiha, proof reader: taken from life / by H. S. Stollnitz. [S. l.: s. n., 191-?]. 16 p.   NYP

S-968 ____ The geshtippelte shtippler: an odd love message / by H. S. Stollnitz. [S. l.: s. n., 191-?] 20 p.   NYP

S-969 ____ Glimpses of a strange world / by H. S. Stollnitz . . . Cambridge, Mass.: Printed for the author [The University Press], 1908. 202 p.
Contents: Alter the "'ayker" -- M'abdooth L'cherooth -- The "Baskol" -- The Shimanowski family in New York -- Between duties -- Zalmen the Sh'leeach -- Sheeka Klezmer.

S-970 Stone, A. American pep: a tale of America's efficiency / by A. Stone . . . ; illustrated by Frank Keane. New York: The Robert J. Shores Corporation, 1918. 336 p., front., [3] leaves of plates.
LC: S 28, '18.
PW: S 28, '18.

S-971 ____ Fighting Byng: a novel of mystery, intrigue and adventure / by A. Stone; illustrations by L. Pern Bird. New York: Britton Publishing Co., 1919. 351 p., front., [3] leaves of plates.
LC: F 18, '19.
PW: Mr 29, '19.

S-972 ____ The whirlwind / by A. Stone. Milton-On-The-Hudson, N. Y.: The A. Stone Foundation, 1923. 312 p.
LC: N 20, '23.
PW: D 1, '23.

Stone, Amy W. Possessing Prudence. In *Atlantic narratives*; first series (1918), A-360.

Stone, Elinore Cowan. One uses the handerchief. In *Prize stories of 1924 (1925), P-622.*

S-973   Stone, Ella Blake. O-So-Ge-To, the Hopi maiden, and other stories / by Ella Blake Stone; decorated and illustrated by Laura A. Humphreys. Chicago: W. B. Conkey Company, 1907. 97 p., incl. front., plates. Ornamental borders.
Unexamined copy: bibliographic data from OCLC, #1684207.
Contents: O-So-Ge-To, the Hopi maiden -- A water waif -- My burglar -- How we fooled Miss Polly -- "Into each life some rain must fall" -- Old Ben -- Nan, a Florida cracker -- Darkey logic.
LC: O 14, '07.

S-974   Stone, Grace Zaring, b. 1891. Letters to a djinn / by Grace Zaring Stone. New York: The Century Co., 1922. 258 p.

S-975   Stone, Jane, *pseud.* The new man / by Jane Stone [pseud.]. New York: Thomas Y. Crowell Company, [1913]. 123 p., col. front.
Unexamined copy: bibliographic data from NUC.
PW: O 11, '13.

S-976   Stone, Matilda Woods. Every man his chance / by Matilda Woods Stone. Boston: Richard G. Badger, 1909, [c1908]. ([Boston]: The Gorham Press).
202 p.
LC: D 15, '08.
PW: Ja 16, '09.

S-977   Stone, Pattie, 1853-1931. As ye sow: a romance of Coosa Valley / by Pattie Stone. New York; Washington: The Neale Publishing Company, 1906.
159 p.   **OSU, SUC**
LC: Jl 2, '06.

S-978   _____ The tale of a hundred years: the story of four generations, Marchand, his daughter, granddaughter and great grandson, the hero of this tale / by Pattie Stone. Montgomery, Ala.: The Brown Printing Company, 1922. 126 p.   **DLC**

S-979   Stoothoff, Ellenor, b. 1873, *pseud.* The nightingale: a lark / by Ellenor Stoothoff [pseud.]. Boston; New York: Houghton Mifflin Company, 1914. (Cambridge: The Riverside Press). 337, [1] p.

S-980   Storer, Maria Longworth, 1849-1932. The Borodino mystery / by Maria Longworth Storer. St. Louis, Mo.; London: B. Herder, [c1916]. 258 p.
LC: S 8, '16.

S-981   _____ Probation / by Maria Longworth Storer . . . St. Louis, Mo.: Published by B. Herder, 1916.
386 p.
LC: F 7, '16.

S-982   _____ Sir Christopher Leighton, or, The Marquis de Vaudreuil's story / by Maria Longworth Storer. St. Louis, Mo.; Freiburg (Baden) Germany; London . . . : Published by B. Herder . . . , [c1915]. 325 p.
                                          HCD
LC: S 30, '15.

S-983   _____ The villa Rossignol, or, The advance of Islam / by Maria Longworth Storer. St. Louis; London: B. Herder Book Co., 1918. 384 p.
LC: Ap 1, '18.

S-984   Stories from the Midland / selected and edited by John T. Frederick. New York: Alfred A. Knopf, 1924. 319 p.
Contents: Wasted / by Mary Arbuckle -- Doc Greer's practice / by Agnes Mary Brownell -- The scarlet one / by George Carver -- Thomas / by Henry Goodman -- The mixing / by Don Harrison -- Mist-green oats / by Raymond Knister -- Knowing dad / by Ival McPeak -- The man with the good face / by Frank Luther Muilenburg -- The prairie / by Walter J. Muilenburg -- Heart of youth / by Walter J. Muilenburg -- Glare of circumstance / by Roger L. Sergel -- In the uplands / by Walter L. Myers -- A rural community / by Ruth Suckow -- Uprooted / by Ruth Suckow -- Arkansas / by Raymond Weeks.
LC: Mr 12, '24.
PW: Mr 15, '24.

S-985   Stories of the colleges: being tales of life at the great American universities / told by noted graduates. Philadelphia; London: J. B. Lippincott Company, 1901. 353 p.
Contents: Philosophy 4 / by Owen Wister -- A bachelor of arts / by Richard Holbrook -- Rah, rah, rah, Murray / by Burton Egbert Stevenson -- Smith of "Pennsylvania" / by Francis Churchill Williams -- A lightning change / by Albert Payson Terhune -- The code of the corps / by General Charles King -- A hazing interregnum / by Cyrus Townsend Brady -- The personal equation / by James Gardner Sanderson -- The head marshal of the University of Chicago / by James Weber Linn.

Storm, Ethel. The three telegrams. In *The best short stories of 1920 and the yearbook of the American short story (1921), B-565.*

S-986   The story of Alice. Morgan, Utah: [Chimes Press, Ogden, Utah], December twenty-fifth, 1925. 36 p., photo. front.   **PUL**
OCLC attributes to Anderson, James A.

S-987   Stout, J. F. (James Frank), b. 1850. Lucanus: a friend of the Christ / by J. F. Stout. Cincinnati: Jennings and Graham; New York: Eaton and Mains, [c1904]. 309 p.

S-988   Stovall, Dennis H., d. 1941. The gold bug story book: mining camp tales by a western writer / Dennis H. Stovall. [Denver, Colo.: Printed by the Reinert Publishing Company, 1906?] 151 p., front., ill.
Contents: Millie and the thoroughbred -- Because of Fannie -- On and off the water wagon -- The tin horn of gold bug -- When the plunger quit -- The gold bug kid -- An ill wind -- The "dare devil" -- The silver candlestick -- A confusion of goods -- When the red jacket paid -- Joe Kelly's burro -- For the love of Sadie.

S-989   _____ Suzanne of Kerbyville / by Dennis H. Stovall. New York: The Editor Publishing Co., 1904. 209 p., front., [4] leaves of plates.

S-990   Stovall, Eugenia Orchard, b. 1872? A son of Carolina / by Genie Orchard Stovall. New York; Washington: The Neale Publishing Company, 1909. 369 p.   **KUK**
LC: N 19, '09.
PW: N 13, '09.

Stover, Mary S. The Red cross lady. In *Called to the colors and other stories (1915), C-50.*

S-991　Stow, Edith, b. 1875. Nancy the joyous / by Edith Stow; frontispiece by James McCracken; decorations by Joseph Pierre Nuyttens. Chicago: The Reilly & Britton Company, [c1914]. 253 p., col. front.
LC: Je 15, '14.

S-992　Stowell, Jay S. (Jay Samuel), 1883-1966. J. W. thinks black: volume number two in the John Wesley, Jr., series / by Jay S. Stowell. New York; Cincinnati: The Methodist Book Concern, [c1922]. 179 p., incl. photo. front., [7] leaves of photo. plates. **MTU**

S-993　[Stowell, John], b. 1850. Don Coronado through Kansas, 1541, then known as Quivira: a story of the Kansas, Osage, and Pawnee Indians. [Seneca, Kansas: Set up, stereotyped, printed and bound by the Don Coronado Company, c1908]. 384 p., photo. front., [3] leaves of photo. plates. **CWR**

S-994　Stowell, William Averill, b. 1882. The mystery of the singing walls / by William Averill Stowell . . . New York; London: D. Appleton and Company, 1925. 292, [1] p., front. [Ill. by William Fisher.]
LC: Ap 6, '25.
PW: Ap 18, '25.

S-995　＿＿＿ The wake of the setting sun / by William Averill Stowell. New York; London: D. Appleton and Company, 1923. 303, [1] p., front.
LC: Ap 11, '23.
PW: My 5, '23.

S-996　Strahan, Kay Cleaver, 1888-1941. Peggy-Mary / by Kay Cleaver Strahan. New York: Duffield & Company, 1915. 153 p., col. front. (port.). **DLC**
LC: Ag 21, '15.

S-997　＿＿＿ Something that begins with "T" / by Kay Cleaver Strahan; illustrated by William A. Kirkpatrick. Boston: Small, Maynard and Company, [c1918]. 312 p., col. front., [2] leaves of plates.
LC: My 6, '18.
BLC: London: Jarrolds, printed in U. S. A., [1921].

S-998　Stranathan, May, b. 1865. The Huff case / May Stranathan. Boston: Richard G. Badger, 1912. ([Boston, U. S. A.]: The Gorham Press). 69 p. **AVL**
PW: F 24, '12.

S-999　[Stratemeyer, Edward], 1862-1930. Belinda of the Red Cross / by Robert W. Hamilton [pseud.]; frontispiece by A. O. Scott. New York: Sully and Kleinteich, [c1917]. 342 p., col. front.
PW: S 15, '17.

S-1000　[＿＿＿] The diamond cross mystery: being a somewhat different detective story / by Chester K. Steele [pseud.]; illustrated by Frances Edwina Dumm. New York: George Sully & Company, [c1918]. 295 p., front., [3] leaves of plates.
LC: Ap 11, '18.
PW: Ap 27, '18.

S-1001　[＿＿＿] The golf course mystery: being a somewhat different detective story / by Chester K. Steele [pseud.]; illustrated by A. O. Scott. New York: George Sully and Company, [c1919]. 303 p., front., [3] leaves of plates.
LC: Ja 2, '19.
PW: Ja 25, '19.

S-1002　[＿＿＿] Making good with Margaret / by E. Ward Strayer [pseud.]; illustrated by A. O. Scott. New York: George Sully & Company, [c1918]. 268 p., front., [1] leaf of plates.

S-1003　[＿＿＿] The mansion of mystery: being a certain case of importance, taken from the note-book of Adam Adams, investigator and detective / by Chester K. Steele [pseud.] . . . New York: Cupples & Leon Company, [c1911]. 310 p., front., [3] leaves of plates. [Ill. by H. Richard Boehm.]
LC: Mr 21, '11.
PW: Ap 22, '11.

Stratton, George Frederick, b. 1852. <u>See</u> **Carling, George, pseud.**

S-1004　Stratton, Lilyan. Homing / by Lilyan Stratton; frontispiece by J. V. Ranck. [Newark, N. J.: Colyer Printing Co., c1923.] 359 p., col. front., [1] leaf of plates. (port.).
LC: O 8, '23.

S-1005　＿＿＿ Reno: a book of short stories and information / by Lilyan Stratton . . . ; scenic views by Van-Noy Interstate Company of San Francisco. Newark: Colyer Printing Company, [c1921]. 268 p., photo. front. [Ill. by Bushnell Studios], [31] leaves of plates (chiefly photo.).
Contents: Social and industrial life -- Reno tragedies -- Reno romance -- Reno comedies -- Reno and its people -- Nevada divorce laws -- Sons of the Sagebrush.
LC: D 15, '21.
PW: Ja 28, '22.

S-1006　Stratton-Porter, Gene, 1863-1924. At the foot of the rainbow / Gene Stratton-Porter . . . ; four paintings in color by Oliver Kemp; designs and decorations by Ralph Fletcher Seymour. New York: The Outing Publishing Company, 1907. 258 p., col. front., [3] leaves of col. plates, ill. Illustrated end papers. **IPL**
LC: Ja 2, '08.
PW: D 28, '07.
BLC: London: Hodder & Stoughton, [1913].

S-1007　＿＿＿ A daughter of the land / by Gene Stratton-Porter; frontispiece by Frances Rogers. Garden City, New York: Doubleday, Page & Company, 1918. 475, [1] p., col. front. Illustrated end papers.
PW: Ag 3, '18.
BLC: London: John Murray, 1918.

S-1008　＿＿＿ Freckles / by Gene Stratton-Porter . . . ; decorations by E. Stetson Crawford. New York: Doubleday, Page & Company, 1904. 433 p., front., ill.
PW: D 17, '04
BLC: London: John Murray, 1905.

S-1009 ____ A girl of the Limberlost / by Gene Stratton Porter; illustrations by Wladyslaw T. Benda. New York: Doubleday, Page & Company, 1909. 485 p., col. front., [3] leaves of col. plates.
LC: Ag 17, '09.
PW: Ag 28, '09.
BLC: London: Doubleday, Page, & Co., New York printed, 1909.

S-1010 ____ The harvester / by Gene Stratton-Porter; illustrations by W. L. Jacobs. Garden City, New York: Doubleday, Page & Company, 1911. 564 p., col. front., [3] leaves of col. plates.
LC: S 9, '11.
PW: Ag 26, '11.
BLC: London: Hodder & Stoughton, Garden City, N. Y. printed, 1911.

S-1011 ____ Her father's daughter / by Gene Stratton-Porter; frontispiece by Dudley Gloyne Summers. Garden City, N. Y.; Toronto: Doubleday, Page & Company, 1921. 486 p., col. front. Illustrated end papers.
LC: Ag 25, '21.
PW: Ag 13, '21.
BLC: London: John Murray, 1921.

S-1012 ____ The keeper of the bees / by Gene Stratton-Porter; decorations by Lee Thayer; illustrations by Gordon Grant. Garden City, New York: Doubleday, Page & Company, 1925. 515 p., col. front., [3] leaves of col. plates, ill.
LC: Ag 28, '25.
PW: Ag 15, '25.
BLC: London: Hutchinson & Co.; printed in U. S. A., 1925.

S-1013 ____ Laddie: a true blue story / by Gene Stratton-Porter; illustrations by Herman Pfeifer. Garden City, N. Y.: Doubleday, Page & Company, 1913. 602 p., col. front., [3] leaves of col. plates. Illustrated end papers.
LC: Ag 19, '13.
PW: Ag 30, '13.
BLC: London: John Murray, 1915.

S-1014 ____ Michael O'Halloran / by Gene Stratton-Porter . . . ; illustrations by Frances Rogers. Garden City, New York: Doubleday, Page & Company, 1915. 560 p., col. front., [3] leaves of col. plates. Illustrated end papers.
LC: Ag 19, '15.
PW: Ag 21, '15.
BLC: London: John Murray, 1915.

S-1015 ____ The song of the cardinal: a love story / by Gene Stratton-Porter; the illustrations being camera studies from life by the author. Indianapolis: The Bobbs-Merrill Company, [1903]. 162, [1] p., incl. photo. front., ill.
PW: Jl 18, '03.

S-1016 ____ The white flag / by Gene Stratton-Porter; frontispiece by Lester Ralph. Garden City, N. Y.: Doubleday, Page & Company, 1923. 483 p., col. front. Designed end papers.

LC: S 12, '23.
PW: Ag 18, '23.
BLC: London: John Murray, 1923.

S-1017 ____ Wings / by Gene Stratton-Porter. Garden City, N. Y.: Garden City Publishing Company, 1925. 116 p., ill.
Unexamined copy: bibliographic data from OCLC, #8984513.

S-1018 Strauss, L. F. (Leopold Frederick). A tale of West and East / by L. F. Strauss. Boston: The Four Seas Company, 1914. 355 p., incl. photo. front. (port.), [8] leaves of photo. plates.

Strayer, E. Ward, pseud. See **Stratemeyer, Edward L.**

S-1019 Street, Julian, 1879-1947. After thirty / by Julian Street . . . New York: The Century Co., 1919. 273 p., front. [Ill. by Arthur William Brown.] **EEM**
LC: Ag 19, '19.
PW: Ag 16, '19.

____ The bird of Serbia. In *The best short stories of 1918 and the yearbook of the American short story* **(1919), B-563.**

S-1020 ____ A bride and a bridle / by Julian Street and Frank Finney. Portsmouth, Virginia: The Seaboard Airline Railway, Passenger Department, [c1903]. 30 p., front., [7] leaves of plates.

S-1021 ____ Cross-sections / by Julian Street. -- 1st ed. -- Garden City, New York: Doubleday, Page & Company, 1923. 314 p.
Contents: Living up to Letchwood --A voice in the hall -- The bride of Boreas -- The Englishman -- The silk hat -- The bird of Serbia -- The lost Columbine -- Hands -- The jazz baby.
LC: S 25, '23.
PW: S 15, '23.

S-1022 ____ The goldfish: a Christmas story for children between six and sixty / by Julian Street . . . ; illustrations by Eugénie Wireman. New York; London: John Lane Co.; Toronto: Bell & Cockburn, 1912. 58 p., col. front., [4] leaves of plates (some col.). **BRL**
LC: O 15, '12.
PW: O 19, '12.

S-1023 ____ A harmony in two flats / by Julian L. Street; illustrated by C. D. Williams. New York; Chicago: Regina Music Box Company, 1902. [24] p., col. ill. **NYP**

S-1024 ____ A limited engagement / by Street & Finney. Portsmouth, Virginia: Seaboard Air-Line Railway, Passenger Department, [c1905]. 31 p., front., [5] leaves of plates. [Ill. by Henry Holt.] Designed end papers. Printed on double leaves.

____ The lost columbine. In *Marriage* **(1923), M-457.**

S-1025 ____ Merely a matter of matrimony: a short story of love and society in New York / by Julian Street and Frank Finney. New York: Hackett, Carhart & Co., [c1904]. 23 p., ill. [Ill. by the authors.]

S-1026 _____ Mr. Bisbee's princess: and other stories / by
Julian Street. Garden City, N. Y.: Doubleday, Page
& Company, 1925. 203 p.
Contents: Mr. Bisbee's princess -- A speaking likeness -- Syringas.
LC: Je 1, '25.
PW: My 23, '25.
BLC: London: William Heinemann, printed in U. S.
A., 1925.

S-1027 _____ My enemy the motor: a tale in eight honks and
one crash / by Julian Street; illustrations by Horace
Taylor. New York: John Lane Company, 1908.
123 p., incl. front., ill.
LC: F 26, '08.
PW: Mr 7, '08.

S-1028 _____ The need of change / by Julian Street . . .
New York: John Lane Company, 1909. 79 p., front,
ill. [Ill. by Horace Taylor.]
LC: Ag 3, '09.
PW: Ag 14, '09.

S-1029 _____ Rita Coventry / by Julian Street. -- 1st ed. --
Garden City, New York: Doubleday, Page &
Company, 1922. 306 p.
LC: O 13, '22.
PW: S 16, '22.
BLC: London: Mills & Boon, printed in U. S. A.,
[1923].

S-1030 _____ The sharpness of Steele: a story with a point /
by Julian Street. New York; Newark, N. J.;
Brooklyn, N. Y.: Sorosis Shoe Department, Arnold
Constable & Co., [191-?]. 31 p., ill.   **NYP**

S-1031 _____ Sunbeams, Inc. / by Julian Street; frontispiece
by Arthur William Brown. Garden City, New York:
Doubleday, Page & Company, 1920. 120 p., front.
LC: S 22, '20.
PW: S 18, '20.

S-1032 _____ The treasure on the beach / by Street &
Finney. Portsmouth, Va.: The Seaboard Air Line
Railway, Passenger Department, [c1906]. 36 p., col.
front., [5] leaves of col. plates. [Front. by Avery
Giulford Wullys, ill. by Harrison Fisher, Sewell
Collins, Leon de Bernebruchs, Will Grefé and C. D.
Williams.]

S-1033 _____ Violets and vexation / by Julian Street and
Frank Finney. Troy, N. Y.: United Shirt and Collar
Company, 1904. 24 p., ill.
Unexamined copy: bibliographic data from OCLC,
#26986010.

S-1034 Streeter, Edward, b. 1891. "As you were, Bill!" / by
Edward Streeter . . . with 42 illustrations in
black-and-white by G. William Breck ("Bill Breck").
New York: Frederick A. Stokes Company, [c1920].
154 p., ill.
LC: My 3, '20.
PW: My 1, '20.
BLC: London: C. A. Pearson, 1920.

S-1035 _____ Beany, Gangleshanks, and the Tub / by
Edward Streeter. New York; London: G. P.
Putnam's Sons, 1921. ([New York]: The

Knickerbocker Press). 335 p.
LC: O 31, '21.
PW: O 8, '21.

_____, contributor. See *Bobbed hair* **(1925), B-700.**

S-1036 _____ Dere Mable: love letters of a rookie / by
Edward Streeter . . . ; with 35 illustrations in
black-and-white by G. William Breck ("Bill Breck")
. . . New York: Frederick A. Stokes Company,
[c1918]. 61, [1] p., front., [28] leaves of plates
(some double-sided).
LC: My 2, '18.
PW: My 11, '18.
BLC: London: Jarrolds, [1919].

S-1037 _____ "Same old Bill, eh Mable!" / by Edward
Streeter . . . ; with 27 illustrations in black-and-white
by G. William Breck ("Bill Breck") . . . New York:
Frederick A. Stokes Company, [c1919]. 120 p.,
front., ill.
LC: Jl 18, '19.
PW: Jl 19, '19.
BLC: London: Jarrolds, [1919].

S-1038 _____ "Thats me all over, Mable" / by Lieut. Edward
Streeter. . . ; with 25 illustrations in black-and-white
by Corp. G. William Breck ("Bill Breck") . . . New
York: Frederick A. Stokes Company, [c1919].
69 p., front., [24] leaves of plates.
LC: Ja 18, '19.
PW: Ja 25, '19.

S-1039 Streeter, John Williams, 1841-1905. Doctor Tom:
the coroner of Brett / by John Williams Streeter . . .
New York: The Macmillan Company; London:
Macmillan & Co., Ltd., 1904. 271 p.
PW: O 8, '04.

S-1040 Stretch, Minnie Curry. Snap shots / by Minnie Curry
Stretch. Christy, Mo.: Published by Curry & Son,
1901. 48 p.   **DLC**

S-1041 Stribling, T. S. (Thomas Sigismund), 1881-1965.
Birthright: a novel / by T. S. Stribling; illustrated by
F. Luis Mora. New York: The Century Co., 1922.
309 p., front., [7] leaves of plates.
LC: Mr 27, '22.
PW: Ap 1, '22.
BLC: London: W. Collins Sons & Co., [1925].

S-1042 _____ The cruise of the dry dock / by T. S. Stribling;
illustrated by Herbert Morton Stoops. Chicago: The
Reilly & Britton Co., [c1917]. 345 p., col. front., [3]
leaves of col. plates.
LC: Ag 13, '17.
PW: S 1, '17.

S-1043 _____ Fombombo / by T. S. Stribling . . . New
York; London: The Century Co., 1923. 311 p.,
front. [Ill. by J. Clinton Shepherd.]
LC: S 18, '23.
PW: S 29, '23.
BLC: London: Nisbet, 1923.

S-1044 ____ Red sand / by T. S. Stribling. New York: Harcourt, Brace and Company, [c1924]. 325 p.
LC: Ap 17, '24.
PW: Ap 19, '24.
BLC: London: Nisbet & Co., 1924.

S-1045 ____ The city of peril / by Arthur Stringer. New York: Alfred A. Knopf, 1923. 317 p.
LC: Ja 29, '23.
PW: F 10, '23.

S-1046 ____ The diamond thieves / by Arthur Stringer; frontispiece by W. B. King. Indianapolis: Bobbs-Merrill Company, [c1923]. 416 p., front.
LC: N 5, '23.
PW: N 24, '23.
BLC: London: Hodder & Stoughton, [1925].

S-1047 ____ The door of dread: a secret service romance / by Arthur Stringer . . . ; illustrated by M. Leone Bracker. Indianapolis: The Bobbs-Merrill Company, [c1916]. 375 p., front., [3] leaves of plates.
LC: Je 2, '16.
PW: Je 3, '16.

S-1048 ____ Empty hands / by Arthur Stringer; illustrated by Herbert M. Stoops. Indianapolis: The Bobbs-Merrill Company, [c1924]. 360 p., front., [3] leaves of plates.
LC: Ap 2, '24.
PW: Ap 12, '24.
BLC: London: Hodder & Stoughton, [1924].

S-1049 ____ The gun-runner: a novel / by Arthur Stringer . . . New York: B. W. Dodge & Company, 1909. 370 p.
"A portion of this novel was printed in the January, 1909 number of The Popular magazine."
LC: My 31, '09.
PW: Ap 17, '09.
Another edition: Indianapolis: The Bobbs-Merrill Company, [1923]. 316 p., front.
Unexamined copy: bibliographic data from LC.
LC: Ap 19, '23 [revision throughout text].

S-1050 ____ The hand of peril: a novel of adventure / by Arthur Stringer . . . New York: The Macmillan Company, 1915. 331 p., col. front. [Ill. by George W. Hood.]
LC: Ap 22, '15.
PW: My 1, '15.

S-1051 ____ The house of intrigue / by Arthur Stringer; illustrated by Armand Both. Indianapolis: The Bobbs-Merrill Company, [c1918]. 363 p., front., [5] leaves of plates.
LC: Mr 26, '18.
PW: Ap 20, '18.

S-1052 ____ The man who couldn't sleep: being a relation of the divers strange adventures which befell one Witter Kerfoot when, sorely troubled with sleeplessness, he ventured forth at midnight along the highways and byways of Manhattan / by Arthur Stringer; frontispiece by Frank Snapp. Indianapolis: The Bobbs-Merrill Company, [c1919].

351 p., front.
LC: Mr 17, '19.
PW: Mr 1, '19.

S-1053 ____ Manhandled / by Arthur Stringer and Russell Holman; illustrated with scenes from the photoplay, a Paramount picture starring Gloria Swanson. New York: Grosset & Dunlap, [c1924]. 312 p., photo. front., [7] leaves of photo. plates.
LC: Ag 18, '24.
PW: Ag 16, '24.

S-1054 ____ Phantom wires: a novel / by Arthur Stringer; illustrated by Arthur William Brown. Boston: Little, Brown, and Company, 1907. 295 p., front., [3] leaves of plates.
LC: Mr 21, '07.
PW: Mr 30, '07.
Another edition: Indianapolis: The Bobbs-Merrill Company, [1923].
Unexamined copy: bibliographic data from LC.
LC: Mr 16, '23 [revision throughout text].

S-1055 ____ Power / by Arthur Stringer. Indianapolis: The Bobbs-Merrill Company, [c1925]. 308 p.
LC; Ap 20, '25.
PW: My 23, '25.
BLC: Toronto: McClelland & Stewart, printed in U. S. A., [1925].

S-1056 ____ The prairie child / by Arthur Stringer; illustrated by E. F. Ward. Indianapolis: The Bobbs-Merrill Company, [c1922]. 382 p., front., [4] leaves of plates.
LC: Ap 24, '22.
PW: Ap 22, '22.
BLC: London: Hodder & Stoughton, [1923].

S-1057 ____ The prairie mother / by Arthur Stringer; illustrated by Arthur E. Becher. Indianapolis: The Bobbs-Merrill Company, [c1920]. 359 p., front., [5] leaves of plates.
LC: Je 30, '20.
PW: Jl 17, '20.
BLC: London: Hodder & Stoughton, [1920].

S-1058 ____ The prairie wife: a novel / by Arthur Stringer . . . ; with illustrations by H. T. Dunn. Indianapolis: The Bobbs-Merrill Company, [c1915]. 316, [1] p., col. front., [5] leaves of col. plates.
LC: S 23, '15.
PW: S 18, '15.

S-1059 ____ The shadow / by Arthur Stringer. New York: The Century Co., 1913. 302 p.
LC: F 3, '13.
PW: F 1, '13.

S-1060 ____ The silver poppy: a novel / by Arthur Stringer. New York: D. Appleton and Company, 1903. 291 p.
PW: Ag 22, '03.

S-1061 ____ The story without a name / by Arthur Stringer and Russell Holman; illustrated with scenes from the photoplay, a Parmount Picture. New York: Grosset

& Dunlap, [c1924]. 316 p., photo. front., [7] leaves of photo. plates.
LC: N 24, '24.
PW: Ja 17, '25.

S-1062 ____ Twin tales: Are all men alike, and, The lost Titian / by Arthur Stringer. Indianapolis: The Bobbs-Merrill Company, [c1921]. 288 p.
LC: N 10, '21.

S-1063 ____ The under groove: a novel / by Arthur Stringer. New York: The McClure Company, 1908. 335 p., front., [5] leaves of plates. [Ill. by Emlen McConnell.]
LC: Ap 18, '08.
PW: Ap 25, '08.

S-1064 ____ The wine of life / by Arthur Stringer. New York: Alfred A. Knopf, 1921. 389 p.
LC: Ag 9, '21.
PW: Ap 16, '21.

S-1065 ____ The wire tappers / by Arthur Stringer . . . ; illustrated by Arthur William Brown. Boston: Little, Brown, and Company, 1906. 324 p., front., [5] leaves of plates.
PW: My 19, '06.
Another edition: Indianapolis: The Bobbs-Merrill Company, [1922].
LC: D 7, '22 [revision throughout text].

Stringer, Eliza C. Walker, jt. aut. *The king and the cross* (1901). See **Stringer, George Alfred, jt. aut., S-1066.**

S-1066 Stringer, George Alfred. The king and the cross: a tale of old and new France / by George Alfred Stringer and Eliza C. Walker Stringer. Boston: Eastern Publishing Company, 1901. 345 p.

S-1067 Strobridge, Idah (Idah Meacham), 1855-1932. In miners' mirage-land / by Idah Meacham Strobridge. Los Angeles, California: [Printed by the Baumgardt Publishing Company], 1904. 129 p., front., ill. [Ill. by J. Duncan Gleason.]   **MNU**
Many of these sketches originally appeared in the Los Angeles "Times" and the San Francisco "Chronicle".
Contents: Mirages of the desert -- The myths of the desert -- The secret mine of the brown men -- The charm of the desert -- The quest of Old Man Berry -- The lovers of the desert -- Forman's find -- The lessons of the desert -- The marvelous Hardin Silver -- The lure of the desert -- The rise and fall of Hardin City -- The men of the desert -- Three little lakes of gold -- The beauty of the desert -- The lost blue bucket mines -- A memory of the desert -- A desert mystery -- The toll of the desert -- Graves of the desert.
PW: D 10, '04.

S-1068 ____ The land of purple shadows / by Idah Meacham Strobridge. Los Angeles: The Artemisia Bindery, 1909. 133, [1] p., front., [2] leaves of plates. [Ill. by Maynard Dixon.]   Partly reprinted from various periodicals.
LC: D 11, '09.
PW: D 18, '09.

S-1069 ____ The loom of the desert / by Idah Meacham Strobridge. Los Angeles: [Artemisia Bindery], 1907. 141, [1] p., [2] leaves of plates. [Ill. by Maynard Dixon.]   **NYP**
Partly reprinted from various periodicals.

S-1070 Strode, C. D. (Charles Darwin), b. 1861. Cornfield philosophy / by C. D. Strode; illustrated. Chicago: The Blakely Printing Co., 1902. 224 p., front., ill. [Ill. by Percy Anderson.]   **DLC**

S-1071 Strong, Clara Lathrop. Forfeit: a novel / by Clara Lathrop Strong. Boston; New York: Houghton Mifflin Company, 1912. (Cambridge: The Riverside Press). 313, [1] p., front. [Ill. by S. M. Chase.]
LC: O 12, '12.

Strong, Harrington, pseud. See **McCulley, Johnston.**

S-1072 Strong, Isobel, b. 1858. The girl from home; a story of Honolulu / by Isobel Strong. New York: McClure, Phillips & Co., 1905. 206, [1] p.   **DLC**
PW: Ap 29, '05.

____ A little savage gentleman. In *Spinners' book of fiction* (1907), S-755.

S-1073 Strong, Jason Rolfe. The starlight of the hills: a romance of the Kentucky mountains / by Jason Rolfe Strong. New York; Cincinnati: Frederick Pustet Co., (Inc.); London: B. Herder, 1923. 386 p., front., [2] leaves of plates.   **KUK**
LC: Jl 25, '23.
PW: S 22, '23.

S-1074 Strong, Louise Jackson. The swoop of the Week, or, The treasure at "Ma's Legacy" / by Louise Jackson Strong. Cincinnati: Jennings and Graham; New York: Eaton and Mains, [c1913]. 312 p.   **DLC**

S-1075 Strong, Marian. The greatest thing in the world / by Marian Strong. Baltimore, Md.: Saulsbury Publishing Company, [c1919]. 24 p., front., [1] leaf of plates.   **DLC**

S-1076 Strother, Emily Vielé, b. 1865. Eve Dorre: the story of her precarious youth / by Emily Vielé Strother; with a frontispiece in colors by Grace Cochrane Sanger. New York: E. P. Dutton & Company, [c1915]. 256 p., col. front.
PW: O 16, '15.
BLC: London & Toronto: J. M. Dent & Sons, 1916.

S-1077 Strouse, George H., Mrs. Asendi: a West African tale / by Mrs. George H. Strouse. Easton, PA: Chemical Publishing Company, 1907. 95 p., front., plates.
Unexamined copy: bibliographic data from OCLC, #30981549.

S-1078 Strouse, Martyn W. Judge Fritznoodle / by Martyn W. Strouse; illustrated. Boston: The Roxburgh Publishing Company, [c1909]. 282 p., front., [5] leaves of plates. [Ill. by P. H. Shea.]
Title continues: "A correct chronicle of the doings in the German-American settlement of Prairiestadt, Cabbage Township, Richsoil County, `Out-West,' during the Free Soil Period."
LC: Ag 17, '09.

S-1079 Struly, Ewer, b. 1884, *pseud*. My three years at Andover / by Ewer Struly [pseud.]. Boston: Mayhew Publishing Company, 1908. 137 p.   **RBN**

Strunsky, Anna, jt. aut. *The Kempton-Wace letters* (1903). See **London, Jack, 1876-1916, jt. aut., L-446.**

Strunsky, Rose. "Little darling". In *Forum stories* **(1914), F-306.**

S-1080 Strunsky, Simeon, 1879-1948. The patient observer and his friends / by Simeon Strunsky. New York: Dodd, Mead and Company, 1911. 348 p.
Reprinted from the New York Evening post for 1910 and various periodicals.
LC: Mr 18, '11.
PW: Mr 25, '11.

S-1081 [____] Professor Latimer's progress: a novel of contemporaneous adventure / with illustrations by J. Ormsbee. New York: Henry Holt and Company, 1918. 347 p., front., [5] leaves of plates.
PW: Ap 27, '18.

S-1082 ____ Sinbad and his friends / by Simeon Strunsky. New York: H. Holt and Company, 1921. 261 p.
LC: O 29, '21.
PW: N 19, '21.

S-1083 ____ Through the outlooking glass: being the curious adventures of Theodore the Red Knight in his quest of the third cup, of his faithful companion Alice . . . and divers quaint . . . persons . . . a veritable Theodyssey of incindents, set down in simple third terms / by Simeon Strunsky. [New York: s.n., 1912?]. 24 p.

S-1084 Stuart, Charles Duff. Casa Grande: a California pastoral / by Charles Duff Stuart. New York: Henry Holt and Company, 1906. 367 p.
LC: S 22, '06.
PW: O 6, '06.

S-1085 Stuart, Eleanor, b. 1876. The postscript / by Eleanor Stuart. New York: The McClure Company, 1908. 194 p.
LC: Ap 25, '08.
PW: My 2, '08.

S-1086 ____ The romance of Ali / by Eleanor Stuart. New York; London: Harper & Brothers Publishers, 1913. 333, [1] p., col. front. [Ill. by Frank T. Merrill.]
LC: Jl 19, '13.
PW: Ag 9, '13.

Stuart, F. W., Jr. A page from the doctor's life. In *A book of narratives* **(1917), B-734.**

S-1087 Stuart, Henry Longan, 1875-1928. Fenella: a novel / by Henry Longan Stuart . . . Garden City, New York: Doubleday, Page & Company, 1911. 400 p.
LC: My 1, '11.
PW: My 6, '11.
BLC: London: Chatto & Windus, 1911.

S-1088 ____ Weeping cross: an unworldly story / by Henry Longan Stuart. New York: Doubleday, Page & Company, 1908. 497 p.
LC: Ag 14, '08.

PW: Ag 29, '08.
BLC: London: Chatto & Windus, 1908.

S-1089 Stuart, Ruth McEnery, 1856-1917. Aunt Amity's silver wedding: and other stories / by Ruth McEnery Stuart; illustrated. New York: The Century Co., 1909. 228 p., incl. 13 leaves of plates, front. [Ill. by Harry C. Edwards, Frederic D. Steele, & A. B. Frost.]
Contents: Aunt Amity's silver wedding -- "Petty larceny" -- The hair of the dog -- Thanksgiving on Crawfish Bayou.
LC: O 13, '09.
PW: O 9, '09.

____ The broken story. In *A house party: an account of stories told at a gathering of famous American authors* **(1901), H-903.**

S-1090 ____ The cocoon: a rest-cure comedy / by Ruth McEnery Stuart. New York: Hearst's International Library Co., [c1915]. 190 p., front.
LC: Ap 7, '15.
PW: Ap 24, '15.

S-1091 ____ George Washington Jones: a Christmas gift that went a-begging / by Ruth McEnery Stuart . . . ; with pictures by Edward Potthast. Philadelphia: Henry Altemus Company, [c1903]. 147 p., front. and t. p. on double-leaf plate, [4] leaves of plates.
PW: D 5, '03.
BLC: London: Charles H. Kelly, [1904].

S-1092 ____ The haunted photograph; Whence and whither; A case in diplomacy; The afterglow / by Ruth McEnery Stuart; illustrated by Wm. L. Jacobs, Peter Newell, Ethel Pennewill Brown and Wilson C. Dexter. New York: The Century Co., 1911. 170 p., front., [9] leaves of plates.
LC: N 7, '11.
PW: N 4, '11.

S-1093 ____ Napoleon Jackson: the gentleman of the plush rocker / by Ruth McEnery Stuart . . . ; with pictures by Edward Potthast. New York: The Century Co., 1902. 132 p., incl. 7 plates, front.
PW: O 25, '02.

S-1094 ____ The river's children: an idyl of the Mississippi / by Ruth McEnery Stuart . . . ; with pictures by Harry C. Edwards. New York: The Century Co., 1904. 179 p., incl. 4 plates, front.
PW: O 22, '04.

S-1095 ____ The second wooing of Salina Sue: and other stories / by Ruth McEnery Stuart; illustrations by Kemble and Frost. New York; London: Harper & Brothers, 1905. 236, [1] p., front., [11] leaves of plates. [Ill. by Clifford Carleton, Thomas Fogarty, A. B. Frost, & E. W. Kemble.]
Contents: The second wooing of Salina Sue -- Minervy's valentines -- Tobe Taylor's April foolishness -- Egypt -- Milady -- The romance of Chinkapin castle.
PW: Ap 15, '05.

S-1096 ____ Sonny's father: in which the father, now become grandfather, a kindly observer of life and a genial philosopher, in his desultory talks with the

family doctor, carries along the story of Sonny / by Ruth McEnery Stuart . . . ; illustrated. New York: The Century Co., 1910. 240 p., front., [10] leaves of plates. [Ill. by Jessie W. Smith, Peter Newell and others.]
LC: O 27, '10.
PW: O 29, '10.

Stuart, Ruth McEnery. Sonny's schoolin'. In *Modern short stories* (1918), M-878.

S-1097   ____ The unlived life of little Mary Ellen / by Ruth McEnery Stuart; with decorations by Ruth Sypherd Clements. [Indianapolis]: The Bobbs-Merrill Company, [c1910]. 90 p., incl. front.
LC: N 28, '10.
PW: D 17, '10.

S-1098   Stubbins, Thomas Alva. The patriot / by Thomas Alva Stubbins. Chicago: M. A. Donohue & Company, 1908. 287 p., front., [3] leaves of plates. [Ill. by B. M. French.]   **LWA**
LC: Mr 6, '08.

S-1099   Stubbs, Charles E. His Majesty's guest / by Charles E. Stubbs. New York: Moffat, Yard and Company, 1923. 359 p., front.
LC: D 10, '23.

S-1100   Stump, David Leroy. The love of Meltha Laone; or, Beyond the sun; a novel / by David Leroy Stump. Boston: The Roxburgh Publishing Company, Inc., [c1913]. 262 p.
Unexamined copy: bibliographic data from NUC.
PW: Ag 23, '13.

Stuntz, Stephen Conrad. See **Conrad, Stephen, 1875-1918.**

S-1101   The sturdy oak: a composite novel of American politics / by fourteen American authors: Samuel Merwin, Harry Leon Wilson, Fannie Hurst, Dorothy Canfield, Kathleen Norris, Henry Kitchell Webster, Anne O'Hagan, Mary Heaton Vorse, Alice Duer Miller, Ethel Watts Mumford, Marjorie Benton Cooke, William Allen White, Mary Austin, Leroy Scott; theme by Mary Austin; the chapters collected and (very cautiously) edited Elizabeth Jordan; illustrations by Henry Raleigh. New York: Henry Holt and Company, 1917. 346 p., front., [3] leaves of plates.

S-1102   Sturdy, W. A., b. 1840. The open door / by W. A. Sturdy. Boston: The author, J. D. Bonnell & Son, printers, 1905. 394 p.   **DLC** (microfilm)
LC: O 24, '05.

S-1103   Sturgess, Ethlyn P. Cooke. A chime of wedding bells / by Ethlyn P. Cooke Sturgess. Philadelphia, Pennsylvania: The Bell Publishing Company, [c1906]. 64 p.
LC: O 26, '06.

S-1104   [Sturgis, Granville Forbes], b. 1880. Mildmay park: episodes of a doughboy in a London hospital / by My Sergeant [pseud.]. Boston: Ricard G. Badger,

[c1920]. ([Boston, U. S. A.]: The Gorham Press). 149 p.   **ORU**

S-1105   Sturrock, Dudley. The distant drum: by Dudley Sturrock. New York: John Lane Company; London: John Lane, The Bodley Head; Toronto: Bell & Cockburn, 1913. 310 p.   **DLC**
LC: Je 10, '13.
BLC: London: John Lane, 1913.

Sturtzel, H. A. Back o' the yards. In *The Grim thirteen* (1917), **G-537.**

Stuttle, L. D. Avery, Mrs. See **Avery-Stuttle, Lilla Dale.**

S-1106   Stuyvesant, Peter. The great adventure / by Peter Stuyvesant. Cincinnati: The Standard Publishing Company, [c1918]. 340 p., front., ill.

S-1107   Sub Rosa. Drifting, or, The romance of an octopus: a novel of love, politics and newspaper life under the rule of the commercial trusts / by Sub Rosa. [Chicago: The Elysian Fields Publishing Co., c1904]. 471, [1] p., front. Designed end papers.
PW: Ja 21, '05.

S-1108   Sublette, C. M. (Clifford MacClellan), 1887-1939. The Scarlet Cockerel: a tale wherein is set down a record of the strange and exceptional adventures of Blaise de Breault and Martin Belcastel in the New World, as members of expeditions sent out by the great Coligny / by C. M. Sublette; with a frontispiece by Frank M. Rines. Boston: The Atlantic Monthly Press, [c1925]. 293 p., front.
BLC: London: Hodder & Stoughton, [1926].

S-1109   Suckow, Ruth, 1892-1960. Country people / Ruth Suckow. New York: Alfred A. Knopf, 1924.
213 p. Designed end papers.
LC: My 31, '24.
PW: My 31, '24.
BLC: London: Jonathan Cape, 1926.

____ Four generations. In *The best short stories of 1924 and the yearbook of the American short story* (1925), **B-569.**

S-1110   ____ The odyssey of a nice girl / Ruth Suckow. New York: Alfred A. Knopf, 1925. 364 p. Designed end papers.
LC: O 30, '25.
PW: O 31, '25.
BLC: London: Jonathan Cape, 1926.

____ Renters. In *The best short stories of 1923 and the yearbook of the American short story* (1924), **B-568.**

____ A rural community. In *Stories from the Midland* (1924), **S-984.**

____ Uprooted. In *Stories from the Midland* (1924), **S-984.**

S-1111 Sulek, O. Bohumil (Oldroch Bohumil). Years in waiting / by O. Bohumil Sulek. [Cedar Rapids, Iowa: printed by Laurance Press Company, c1913]. 56 p.
DLC

Sullivan, Elizabeth Higgins. <u>See</u> **Higgins, Elizabeth.**

Sullivan, Flavel Woodruff. <u>See</u> **Navillus, W. F., pseud.**

Sullivan, Francis Paul, b. 1885. <u>See</u> **Ó Súilleabháin, Pronnséas.**

S-1112 Sullivan, Francis William, b. 1887. Alloy of gold / by Francis William Sullivan . . . New York: Robert M. McBride & Company, 1915. 336 p.
LC: Ag 31, '15.
PW: S 4, '15.
BLC: London: McBride, Mast & Co., [1916].

S-1113 ____ Children of Banishment / by Francis William Sullivan. New York; London: G. P. Putnam's Sons, 1914. ([New York]: The Knickerbocker Press). 370 p., col. front. [Ill. by Robert Edwards.] Originally brought into print in a magazine . . . under the title of "The Forest of Eden."
LC: S 5, '14.
PW: Ag 22, '14.

S-1114 [____] The free range / by Elwell Lawrence [pseud.]; illustrations by Douglas Duer. New York: W. J. Watt & Company, [c1913]. 311 p., front., [4] leaves of plates (1 double-leaf plate).
LC: Ag 18, '13.

S-1115 [____] The harbor of doubt / by Frank Williams [pseud.] . . . ; illustrations by G. W. Gage. New York: W. J. Watt & Company, [c1915]. 307 p., front., [1] leaf of plates.
LC: N 20, '15.
PW: Ja 22, '16.

S-1116 ____ Star of the north / by Francis William Sullivan. New York; London: G. P. Putnam's Sons, 1916. (New York: The Knickerbocker Press). 379 p., col. front. [Ill. by D. C. Hutchison.]
LC: My 31, '16.
PW: Je 3, '16.

S-1117 [____] The wilderness trail / by Frank Williams [pseud.]; illustrations by Douglas Duer. New York: W. J. Watt & Company, [c1913]. 296 p., front., [3] leaves of plates.
LC: Je 23, '13.

S-1118 Sullivan, Frank S. (Frank Seymour), b. 1873. The governor's reverie: and other stories / by Frank S. Sullivan. Topeka, Kan.: Crane & Company, 1916. 128 p.
Contents: The governor's reverie -- An Indian story -- Stung -- His reward; an epitaph -- The old calaboose -- A joy-ride with a schoolma'am -- The struggle with Dead-shot Dick -- Fishing -- A knight of the golden eagle -- The old home town -- A five-hundred dollar race.
LC: D 16, '16.

S-1119 Sullivan, Josephine Byrne. Father Joseph and other stories / by Josephine Byrne Sullivan (Aunt Rowena). Detroit, Michigan: The Michigan Catholic publishers, [c1905]. 175 p.
OSU, EEX
Contents: Father Joseph -- Granny's story -- The matchmaker's daughter -- The rebel's progeny -- The Bishop's Christmas -- Leoni's unhappy quest -- Tom Breen's return -- The vocation of Zelie -- Sister Angelique -- The hermit of Grandville -- Mollie Doyle's experience.

S-1120 Sullivan, Margaret Davies. Goddess of the dawn: a romance / by Margaret Davies Sullivan; illustrations by George Bridgman. New York: G. W. Dillingham Company, [c1914]. 341 p., col. front., [2] leaves of plates.
PW: F 7, '14.

Sullivan, Mary Agnes, b. 1871. <u>See</u> **Ferraro, Agnese, pseud.**

S-1121 Sullivan, May Kellogg. The trail of a sourdough: life in Alaska / by May Kellogg Sullivan . . . Boston: Richard G. Badger: The Gorham Press, [c1910]. 258 p., incl. 2 plates, front., ill. [Ill. by C. A. McArthur.]
LC: O 7, '10.
PW: S 3, '10.

S-1122 Sullivan, T. R. (Thomas Russell), 1849-1916. The courage of conviction: a novel / by T. R. Sullivan. New York: Charles Scribner's Sons, 1902. 257 p.
PW: Je 7, '02.

S-1123 ____ The hand of Petrarch: and other stories / by T. R. Sullivan. Boston; New York: Houghton Mifflin Company, 1913. ([Cambridge]: The Riverside Press). 340 p.
Title within ornamental borders.
Contents: The hand of Petrarch -- Winter island -- Our actress -- Credit at Dunstan's -- The penguin -- The chanza -- A Roman cabman.
LC: Jl 2, '13.
PW: Jl 5, '13.

S-1124 ____ The heart of us: a novel / by T. R. Sullivan. Boston; New York: Houghton Mifflin Company, 1912. (Cambridge: The Riverside Press). 333, [1] p.
LC: F 21, '12.
PW: F 24, '12.

S-1125 [Sullivan, William Laurence], 1872-1935. The priest: a tale of modernism in New England / by the author of "Letters to his holiness, Pope Pius X". Boston: Sherman, French & Company, 1911. 269 p.

S-1126 Sumerwell, Florida Pope. Four in family: the story of how we look from where the dog sits / by Florida Pope Sumerwell; with illustrations and decorations by George Kerr. Indianapolis, Ind.: The Bobbs-Merrill Company Publishers, [c1911]. 181, [1] p., col. front., [11] leaves of col. plates.
LC: Mr 8, '11.
PW: Mr 11, '11.

S-1127   Summers, Charles. The nomads: a socio-economic
          novel / by Charles Summers; illustrated by G. Pearse
          Ennis. St. Louis, Mo.: Cosmos Publishing
          Company, [c1903]. 169 p., incl. 4 leaves of plates,
          photo. front. (port.), [1] leaf of plates.

S-1128   Summers, Elizabeth Montgomery. A girl of the
          Ozarks / by Elizabeth Montgomery Summers.
          Boston, Massachusetts: The C. M. Clark Publishing
          Co., [c1911]. 247 p., col. front., [5] leaves of plates.
          [Ill. by R. I. Conklin.]   **OSU, NDD**
          LC: My 1, '13.

S-1129   Summers, Florence Elizabeth. Dere Bill: Mabel's
          love letters to her rookie / by Florence Elizabeth
          Summers; with 43 illustrations in black and white by
          Natalie Stokes. New York: Frederick A. Stokes
          Company, [c1919]. 119, [1] p., ill.
          LC: Mr 3, '19.

          Sumner, Allene M. "The little white fool". _In The_
          best college short stories, 1917-18 **(1919), B-557.**

S-1130   Surat, George. An East Coast affair / by George
          Surat. n. p., n. d. (1924?). 148 p.   **FDA**

S-1131   Surbridge, Agnes. The confessions of a club woman
          / by Agnes Surbridge; illustrated by A. J. Keller.
          New York: Doubleday, Page & Company, 1904.
          241 p., front., [3] leaves of plates.

S-1132   Surev, _pseud._ Uncle Carl / by Surev [pseud.]. New
          York; Washington: The Neale Publishing Company,
          1908. 429 p.

S-1133   Surrender!: the romance of a woman's soul /
          Anonymous; frontispiece by Delos Palmer, Jr. New
          York: The Macaulay Company, [c1924]. 317 p.,
          front.
          PW: O 25, '24.

S-1134   Sutherland, Jerusha Melissa. Childhood home and
          scenes on the farm / by Jerusha Melissa Sutherland.
          Paris, Illinois: [s. n.], 1903. 68 p.   **KSU**

S-1135   Sutherland, John MacLeod. Then cometh the devil:
          a story of life and love in the sportiest town on the
          river / by John MacLeod Sutherland . . . ; illustrated.
          Butler, Indiana, U. S. A.: Luther H. Higley,
          Publisher, [c1907]. 408 p., front., [3] leaves of
          plates. [Ill. by F. Brown.]

S-1136   Sutphen, Van Tassel, 1861-1945. The doomsman /
          by Van Tassel Sutphen; illustrated. New York;
          London: Harper & Brothers, 1906. 294 p., front.,
          [7] leaves of plates. [Ill. by Fletcher C. Ransom &
          H. C. Wall.]
          PW: Je 16, '06.

S-1137   ____ The gates of chance / by Van Tassel Sutphen.
          New York; London: Harper & Brothers, 1904.
          302 p., front. [Ill. by Charles J. Post.]
          PW: My 14, '04.
          BLC: London: Ward, Lock & Co., 1908.

S-1138   ____ In jeopardy / by Van Tassel Sutphen . . . -- 1st
          ed. -- New York; London: Harper & Brothers

Publishers, [c1922]. 299, [1] p.
LC: S 23, '22.
PW: S 30, '22.

S-1139   ____ The nineteenth hole: being tales of the fair
          green / by Van Tassel Sutphen; illustrated. -- Second
          series. -- New York; London: Harper & Brothers,
          1901. 190 p., col. front. (port.), [8] leaves of plates.
          [Ill. by A. B. Frost, Howard Chandler Christy, and
          Edward Penfield.] Designed end papers.
          Contents: The teleautomaton -- The car of Juggernaut -- The
          Tantalus loving-cup -- The love chase -- The greatest thing in the
          world -- The round robin championship -- The mixed-up foursome --
          First aid to the injured.
          PW: Ag 3, '01.

          Sutton, Anne. The dream beautiful. _In The best_
          college short stories, 1924-1925 **(1925), B-558.**

          Sutton, Eli Ransome. _See_ **Sutton, Ransom.**

S-1140   Sutton, Elisabeth. Dead fingers / by Elisabeth Sutton;
          illustrated by George Baker. New York: The H. K.
          Fly Company, [c1918]. 295 p., front.

S-1141   Sutton, H. S. (Henry Sidney). Rhoda Roland: a
          woman from the West in Washington / by H. S.
          Sutton. Washington, D. C.: Henry E. Wilkens
          Printing Co., [c1902]. 300 p.
          PW: Ag 8, '08.

S-1142   Sutton, Ransom, 1869-1934. The passing of the
          fourteen: life, love and war among the brigands and
          guerillas of Mexico / by Ransom Sutton. New York:
          The Devin-Adair Company, 1914. 313 p., front., [4]
          leaves of photo. plates. [Ill. by F. Luis Mora.]
          LC: Je 30, '14.

S-1143   Swafford, Charles Carroll. The silent conflict: a
          story of industrial warfare / by Charles Carroll
          Swafford. Boston: Roxburgh Publishing Company,
          Inc., [c1916]. 347 p., front. (port.).   **OSU, UUM**

S-1144   Swales, Susan Matilda Bradshaw, b. 1843. Tweed:
          a story of the Old South / by S. M. Swales. New
          York: Broadway Publishing Co., [c1911]. 419 p.,
          front.
          LC: O 21, '11.

S-1145   Swallow, Jane Frances. A romance of the Siege of
          Vicksburg / by Jane Frances Swallow. Boston,
          Massachusetts: Chapple Publishing Company, Ltd.,
          1925. 126 p., photo. front. (port.).

S-1146   Swan, E. W. Along the line, --or--, Western railroad
          stories / --by-- E. W. Swan. New York: Broadway
          Publishing Company . . . , [c1905]. 121 p.   **MUS**
          Contents: The passing of fireman O'Leary -- When the Texan was
          yardmaster -- The dumb luck of "Wide-open Jim" -- The fate of the
          368 -- The golden rule trainmaster -- The lap-order at Kenton -- That
          "spotter" deal -- The foreman's order.
          PW: Je 10, '05.

S-1147   Swann, R. W. Michael Bartmore / by R. W. Swann.
          [Washington, D. C.: Printed and published by the
          Columbia Polytechnic Institute for the Blind . . . ,
          c1913]. 47 p.   **DLC**

S-1148 Swayze, George B. H. (George Banghart Henry), b. 1833. Yarb and Cretine, or, Rising from bonds / by George B. H. Swayze. Boston: The C. M. Clark Publishing Co., 1906. 414 p., front., [9] leaves of plates. [Ill. by F. Gilbert Edge.]
LC: D 21, '06.

Sweeney, M. J. The new rules. In *Allegheny stories (1902)*, **A-142**.

Sweet, Frank H. In Skeleton Pool, the story of a raftsman. In *Golden stories (1909)*, **G-285**.

S-1149 Sweet, Louis Matthews, 1869-1950. The makin' o' Joe / by Louis Matthews Sweet. New York: George H. Doran Company, [c1919]. 308 p.
LC: O 30, '19.
PW: N 8, '19.

Sweetland, Charles A. The phantom bookkeeper. In *Clever business sketches (1909)*, **C-490**.

S-1150 Sweny, Harry Roy. Through the tall pine's top: a vision of the old school / by Harry Roy Sweny . . . [Albany, N. Y.]: Privately printed [J. B. Lyon Co.], Christmas, 1910. 24 numbered leaves, printed on one side of leaf only.

S-1151 Swetnam, Flora. Miss Phena / by Flora Swetnam; illustrated. New York City: American Tract Society, [c1916]. 182 p., front., [2] leaves of plates. [Ill. by Albert Matzke.]   **DLC**
LC: O 30, '16.

S-1152 Swift, F. R. (Frederick R.). Florida fancies / by F. R. Swift; with drawings by Albert E. Smith. New York; London: G. P. Putnam's Sons, 1903. ([New York]: The Knickerbocker Press). 120 p., photo. front., [10] leaves of photo. plates, ill.   **KSU**

S-1153 Swift, Helen, b. 1869. Where green lanes end / by Helen Swift. New York: B. W. Huebsch, Inc., 1924. 84 p.
LC: Je 6, '24.
BLC: London: Chapman Hall, printed in U. S. A., 1927.

S-1154 Swift, Ike. Sketches of Gotham / by Ike Swift; a collection of unusual stories told in an unusual way. New York: R. K. Fox [c1906]. 286 p., incl. front. (port.)., ill.
Unexamined copy: bibliographic data from OCLC, #30095162.

S-1155 Swift, John Newton, b. 1854. No surrender: the story of a strange voyage in strange company / by John N. Swift and W. S. Birge. New York: Broadway Publishing Company, [c1905]. 376 p., front.
PW: S 2, '05.

S-1156 Swift, Lance. Her caveman's letters and her's in reply / by Lance Swift and Carol Steele. Philadelphia: Gilliam's Sons Company, 1908. 183 p., [1] leaf of col. plates.

S-1157 Swift, Morrison I. (Morrison Isaac), b. 1856. The damask girl: and other stories / by Morrison I. Swift. New York: The Morrison I. Swift Press, 1906. 144 p.   **OSU, CWR**
Contents: The myth of Pelican Dome -- A very rash doctor -- Caton's daughter -- Call again -- The scientist's wife -- The damask girl -- Mighty Lionel -- Changing the climate of Tulip Valley -- Urgent.
PW: S 22, '06.

S-1158 ____ The horroboos / by Morrison I. Swift. Boston: The Liberty Press, 1911. 241 p.
PW: Jl 29, '11.

S-1159 ____ The monarch billionaire, by Morrison I. Swift . . . New York: J. S. Ogilvie Publishing Company, [c1903]. 317 p.   **CWR**
PW: Ag 29, '03.

Swift, Otis Peabody. Paradise lost. In *The best college short stories, 1917-18 (1919)*, **B-557**.

S-1160 Swigart, Frank, 1840-1912. Mary Lawson / by Frank Swigart. Boston: Roxburgh Publishing Company Incorporated, [c1909]. 280 p.
LC: D 16, '09.

S-1161 Switzer, Maurice, 1870-1929. Bedtime business stories: a collection of short business stories reprinted from Motor Chat, the house organ of the Kelly-Springfield Tire Company / by Maurice Switzer. New York: Kelly-Springfield, 1925. 114 p.   **NYP**
Contents: The K. O. Kid -- The benign infection -- The man who could take it or leave it -- When it's easier said than done -- The man who got next-to himself -- The good mixer -- Personality, minus -- How not to get rich -- Old Timer makes a few remarks -- Napoleon Grubb -- Concerning speed -- Bill and the snowplow -- Making the world pay up -- Substance and shadows -- The courtship of David -- Both sides of the fence -- Hard shell -- A matter of comparison -- Mr. Gabbler's Christmas Eve -- The unexpected guest -- You never can tell -- Clothes and the man.

S-1162 ____ Trying it on the dog / by Maurice Switzer . . . ; illustrated by Frank Godwin. Indianapolis: The Bobbs-Merrill Company, [c1921]. 282 p., front., [5] leaves of plates.   **CLE**
LC: My 25, '21.

Sykes, A. L., jt. aut. *Banduk jaldi banduk!* (1907). See **Jones, Claude P. (Claude Perry), jt. aut., J-177**.

Synon, Mary. The bounty-jumper. In *The best short stories of 1915 and the yearbook of the American short story (1916)*, **B-560**.

S-1163 ____ The fleet goes by / by Mary Synon. New York: Charles Scribner's Sons, 1914. 44 p.
LC: S 1, '14.

____ None so blind. In *The best short stories of 1917 and the yearbook of the American short story (1918)*, **B-562**.

____ Shadowed. In *Prize stories of 1923 (1924)*, **P-621**.

S-1164 Szymanowski, Stephen Korwin, b. 1854. The searchers / by Stephen K. Szymanowski; illustrated. Los Angeles: Southern California Printing Co., 1908. 300 p., [9] leaves of photo. plates.
LC: My 2, '08.

T

T-1   Taber, Clarence Wilbur, b. 1870. Anya Kovalchuk /
by Clarence Wilbur Taber. Chicago: Covici-McGee
Co., 1923. 399 p.
LC: O 16, '23.
PW: O 27, '23.

T-2   _____ Breaking sod on the prairies: a story of early
days in Dakota / by Clarence W. Taber; illustrated by
Edward J. Boecher. Yonkers-on-Hudson, New York:
World Book Company, 1924. 292 p., ill.
                                          OSU, MNU
(Pioneer life series / edited by Howard R. Driggs).
LC: F 27, '24.
PW: Mr 15, '24.

Taber, Harry Persons, b. 1865, jt. aut. *The Gordon
elopement* (1904). <u>See</u> **Wells, Carolyn, d. 1942, jt.
aut., W-330.**

Taber, Harry Persons, b. 1865, jt. aut. *The
matrimonial bureau* (1905). <u>See</u> **Wells, Carolyn, d.
1942, jt. aut., W-335.**

T-3   Taber, Louise E. (Louise Edgar), b. 1890. The flame
/ by Louise E. Taber. New York: The Alice
Harriman Company, 1911. 313 p.
LC: O 2, '11.
PW: O 14, '11.

T-4   Taber, Mary J. (Mary Jane), b. 1834. Bathsheba's
letters to her cousin Deborah 1831-1861 / by Mary J.
Taber . . . Philadelphia: The John C. Winston
Company, 1913. 253 p.

T-5   _____ A honeymoon soliloquy / by Mary J. Taber
. . . Philadelphia: The John C. Winston Company,
1914. 42 p.   **DLC**
LC: Je 8, '14.

T-6   Taber, Ralph Graham. Chained lightning: a story of
adventure in Mexico / by Ralph Graham Taber . . . ;
illustrated from photographs by the author and his
friend M. Ravelle. New York: The Macmillan
Company, 1915. 273 p., photo. front., [7] leaves of
photo. plates.

T-7   Taber, Susan. Country neighbors: a Long Island
pastoral / by Susan Taber; frontispiece by John Rae.
New York: Duffield & Company, 1912. 323 p.,
front.
LC: F 1, '12.
PW: F 10, '12.

T-8   _____ The jewel of their souls / by Susan Taber.
New York: Duffield & Company, 1914. 346 p.,
front.
LC: O 24, '14.

T-9   _____ The optimist / by Susan Taber. New York:
Duffield & Company, 1917. 270 p., front.
Contents: The optimist -- Two feminists -- The spoiled child -- The
sword -- His brother's story -- The winter of her discontent -- The
patriot -- Alethia -- The wedding veil -- A legacy -- Easter morning --
Alice in Wonderland.
LC: Ag 25, '17.
PW: O 20, '17.

T-10   Taber, Susan. Unexpected affinities; a serio-comedy
/ by Susan Taber . . . New York: Duffield &
Company, 1913. 397 p., front.
Unexamined copy: bibliographic data from NUC.
LC: Ap 1, '13.
PW: Ap 5, '13.

Taft, Israel Plummer, b. 1857. <u>See</u> **Yeld, Thomas,
Sir, pseud.**

T-11   Taft, William Nelson. On secret service:
detective-mystery stories based on real cases solved
by government agents / by William Nelson Taft.
New York; London: Harper & Brothers, [c1921].
356, [1] p.
Contents: A flash in the night -- The mint mystery -- The Ypiranga
case -- The clue on shelf 45 -- Phyllis Dodge, smuggler extraordinary
-- A matter of record -- The secret still -- The taxicab tangle -- A
match for the government -- The girl at the switchboard -- Lost-
$100,000 -- The double code -- The trail of the white mice -- Wah
Lee and the flower of heaven -- The man with three wives -- After
seven years -- The poison-pen puzzle -- Thirty thousand yards of silk
-- The clue in the classified column -- In the shadow of the capitol --
A million-dollar quarter -- "The looting of the C.T.C." -- The case of
Mrs. Armitage -- Five inches of death.

T-12   Taggart, Marion Ames, 1866-1945. The Annes / by
Marion Ames Taggart; frontispiece by W. C. Nims.
Garden City, N. Y.; Toronto: Doubleday, Page &
Company, 1921. 271, [1] p., front.   **BRL**
LC: Je 14, '21.
PW: My 21, '21.

_____ Bricks and mortar. <u>In</u> *A bit of old ivory, and
other stories* (1910), **B-626.**

T-13   _____ The cable: a novel / by Marion Ames Taggart
. . . New York; Cincinnati; Chicago: Benziger
Brothers, 1923. 407 p.
LC: Ap 12, '23; Jl 24, '23.
PW: S 15, '23.

T-14   _____ The elder Miss Ainsborough / by Marion Ames
Taggart. New York; Cincinnati; Chicago: Benziger
Brothers, 1915. 237 p., col. front. [Ill. by Cyrus
Cuneo.]
LC: F 11, '15.
PW: F 27, '15.

_____ The fall of the year. <u>In</u> *The friendly little
house: and other stories* (1910), **F-432.**

_____ The friendly little house. <u>In</u> *The friendly little
house: and other stories* (1910), **F-432.**

_____ The habit of Jerry. <u>In</u> *A bit of old ivory, and
other stories* (1910), **B-626.**

_____ In passing. <u>In</u> *The Senior lieutenant's wager:
and other stories* (1905), **S-312.**

_____ The light fantastic. <u>In</u> *The lady of the tower*
(1909), **L-13.**

_____ Major Bobby, peacemaker. <u>In</u> *The lady of the
tower* (1909), **L-13.**

653

T-15   ____ No handicap: a novel / by Marion Ames Taggart . . . New York; Cincinnati; Chicago: Benziger Brothers, [c1922]. 348 p.
LC: O 30, '22.
PW: D 30, '22.

T-16   ____ One afternoon: and other stories / by Marion Ames Taggart . . . New York; Cincinnati; Chicago: Benziger Brothers, 1905. 182 p., ill. **ABC**
Contents: One afternoon -- The hopes of spring -- The professor's Christmas gift -- A touch of spring -- "Only Emmaline" -- The onlooker -- Professional services -- St. Martin's summer -- King Cophetua -- A surrender -- Her daughter's mother -- The clear vision of Niddy Longears -- The king's toast -- The hope of the Kerners -- The madonna of the falling leaves -- Elizabeth -- Her thirds -- The constancy of Michael Connors -- The day of small things -- The fall of a castle -- The passing of Pippa.

    ____ Pro Patria. In *The friendly little house: and other stories* (1910), **F-432.**

T-17   ____ The unraveling of a tangle / by Marion Ames Taggert . . . New York; Cincinnati; Chicago: Benziger Brothers, 1903. 146 p., front., ill. **DLC**
PW: Mr 14, '03.

    ____ The war of the roses. In *The lady of the tower* (1909), **L-13.**

    ____ When the dumb speak. In *A bit of old ivory, and other stories* (1910), **B-626.**

T-18   ____ "Who is Sylvia ?" / by Marion Ames Taggart; illustrated by Vera Clere. Garden City, N. Y.: Doubleday, Page & Company, 1922. 285 p., front., [3] leaves of plates.
LC: O 30, '22.
PW: O 14, '22.
    ____ A woman's way. In *The lady of the tower* (1909), **L-13.**

T-19   Taine, John, 1883-1960, *pseud.* The purple sapphire / by John Taine [pseud.]. New York: E. P. Dutton & Company, [c1924]. 325 p.
LC: O 4, '24.
PW: N 1, '24.

T-20   Talbot, Ellen V. The courtship of Sweet Anne Page / by Ellen V. Talbot; illustrations by Sewell Collins. New York; London: Funk & Wagnalls Company, 1902. 91 p., ill.
PW: Mr 8, '02.

T-21   Talbot, Grace. Much-married saints and some sinners: sketches from life among Mormons and Gentiles in Utah / by Grace Talbot. New York: The Grafton Press, [c1902]. 130 p. **UUA**
Contents: Story of a five-wived saint -- A Mormon missionary -- The vicissitudes of a small saint -- The pearl of great price -- Roskin's roost -- The burden of a bride -- The order of enoch -- Faith and wrinkles -- A modern mormon -- Brahmo Somaj -- How the saints buttered the bread of the sinners on both sides.
PW: F 7, '03.

T-22   Talbot, Marjorie. Merrill / by Marjorie Talbot. Boston: Mayhew Publishing Co., 1906. 78 p., [1] leaf of plates (port.). **DLC**

T-23   Talbot, Richard J. (Richard James), b. 1874. The chainbreakers / by Richard J. Talbot. Boston: The Roxburgh Publishing Company, Inc., [c1914].

509 p., incl. front., [4] leaves of plates. [Ill. by Warren Y. Cluff.] **NDD**
LC: Jl 14, '14.

T-24   Talkington, Lola Callie, b. 1890. Merle Maxwell; a novel / by Lola C. Talkington. McKinney, Tex.: O. M. Goddard, 1918. 308 p., front.
Unexamined copy: bibliographic data from OCLC, #26790191.
PW: Jl 6, '18.

Tapman, Lillian Smith. See **Smith-Tapman, Lillian.**

T-25   Tapp, Sidney C. (Sidney Calhoun), b. 1870. The struggle / by Sidney C. Tapp . . . New York: A. Wessels Company, 1906. 324 p.
PW: F 10, '06.

T-26   Tappan, Eva March, 1854-1930. In the days of Queen Elizabeth / by Eva March Tappan; illustrated from famous paintings. Boston: Lee and Shepard, 1902. 294 p., front., [7] leaves of plates. (Makers of England series).
PW: S 13, '02.
BLC: London: Hutchinson & Co., 1905.

T-27   ____ In the days of Queen Victoria / by Eva March Tappan . . . ; illustrated from famous paintings and engravings and from photographs. Boston: Lothrop, Lee & Shepard Co., 1903. 354 p., front., [11] leaves of plates. [Ill. by Alfred E. Chalon, Sir W. Beechey, Sir George Hayter, John Partridge, F. Winterhalter, or A. Bassano.] **WAU**
(Makers of England series).
PW: Ag 29, '03.
BLC: London: Hutchinson & Co., 1905.

T-28   ____ In the days of William the Conqueror / by Eva March Tappan . . . ; illustrated by J. W. Kennedy. Boston; Lothrop, Lee & Shepard Co., [c1901]. 298 p., front., [7] leaves of plates. **MIA**
PW: S 14, '01.
BLC: London: Hutchinson & Co., 1905.

T-29   ____ Old ballads in prose / by Eva March Tappan; illustrated by Fanny Y. Cory. Boston; New York: Houghton, Mifflin and Co., 1901. 228 p., front., [3] leaves of plates.
Contents: Saddle to rags -- Willie Wallace -- Catskin -- Robin Hood rescues the lady's three sons -- King John and the Abbot -- Forester Etin -- False Foodrage -- The proud sheriff visits Robin Hood -- The hireman chiel -- The demon lover -- Robin Hood's rueful guest -- One who would harm -- The barring of the door -- Tamlane -- Patient Annie -- How Robin Hood served the King -- The false knight -- Earl Mar's daughter -- The water of Wearie's Well -- The Queen's champions -- Lizzie Lindsay -- The King and the Miller of Mansfield.
PW: O 12, '01.
BLC: London: Longman's Co., 1901.

T-30   Tarbell, Ida M. (Ida Minerva), 1857-1944. Father Abraham / by Ida M. Tarbell . . . ; with illustrations by Blendon Campbell. New York: Moffat, Yard and Company, 1909. 39 p., col. front., [5] leaves of plates.
LC: Ap 2, '09.
PW: My 1, '09.

T-31   ____ He knew Lincoln / by Ida M. Tarbell . . . New York: McClure, Phillips & Co., 1907. 39 p., col. front., [6] leaves of plates. [Front. by Blendon

Campbell; ill. by Jay Hambidge.]
PW: Ap 6, '07.

T-32   _____ In Lincoln's chair / by Ida M. Tarbell. New
York: The Macmillan Company, 1920. 55 p.
PW: Ap 24, '20.

T-33   _____ The rising of the tide: the story of Sabinsport /
by Ida M. Tarbell. New York: The Macmillan
Company, 1919. 277 p.
LC: Ap 2, '19.
PW: Ap 12, '19.
BLC: London: Macmillan & Co.; printed in U. S.
A., 1919.

T-34   Tarkington, Booth, 1869-1946. Alice Adams / by
Booth Tarkington; illustrated by Arthur William
Brown. Garden City, N. Y.; Toronto: Doubleday,
Page & Company, 1921. 434 p., front., [3] leaves of
plates.
LC: Je 22, '21.
PW: Je 4, '21.
BLC: London: Hodder & Stoughton, [1921].
References:References: Currie, p. 71-72; Russo &
Sullivan, *Tarkington*, p. 53-55.

T-35   _____ Beasley's Christmas party / by Booth
Tarkington; illustrated by Ruth Sypherd Clements.
New York; London: Harper & Brothers, 1909. 99,
[1] p., col. front., col. ill.
Title page printed in black, green, and red.
LC: O 29, '09.
PW: O 21, '11.
References: Currie, p. 58-59; Russo & Sullivan,
Tarkington, p. 24-26.

T-36   _____ The beautiful lady / Booth Tarkington. New
York: McClure, Phillips & Co., 1905. 143, [1] p.,
front., [6] leaves of plates. [Ill. by Blendon
Campbell; title vignettes, initials, and other ills. by
W. J. (William James Jordan).] Illustrated end
papers.
PW: Je 3, '05.
BLC: London: John Murray, 1905.
References: Currie, p. 54-55; Russo & Sullivan,
Tarkington, p. 16-17.

        _____ Captain Schlotterwerz. In *War stories* (1919),
W-94.

T-37   _____ Cherry / by Booth Tarkington; illustrated.
New York; London: Harper & Brothers, 1903. 178,
[1] p., col. front., [2] leaves of col. plates. [Ill. by
C. D. Williams & A. I. Keller; decorations by Robert
Murray Wright.] Designed end papers.
LC: O 19, '03.
PW: O 24, '03.
References: Currie, p. 51-52; Russo & Sullivan,
Tarkington, p. 12-13.

        _____ City smoke. In *A book of narratives* (1917),
B-734.

T-38   _____ The conquest of Canaan: a novel / by Booth
Tarkington . . . ; illustrations by Lucius W.
Hitchcock. New York; London: Harper & Brothers,

1905. 388, [1] p., front., [7] leaves of plates.
Ornamental initials.
LC: O 26, '05.
PW: N 11, '05.
References: Currie, p. 55-56; Russo & Sullivan,
Tarkington, p. 17-18.

        _____ The destroyers of Nuremberg. In *For France*
(1917), **F-235.**

T-39   _____ The fascinating stranger: and other stories / by
Booth Tarkington. Garden City, N. Y.: Doubleday,
Page & Company, 1923. 492 p. Currie lists entry
for Limited Edition.
Contents: The fascinating stranger -- The party -- The one-hundred
dollar bill -- Jeannette -- The spring concert -- Willamilla -- The only
child -- Ladies' ways -- Maytime in Marlow -- "You" -- "Us" -- The
tiger -- Mary Smith.
LC: My 21, '23.
PW: Ap 28, '23.
BLC: London: Curtis Brown, printed in U. S. A.,
1925.
References: Currie, p. 75-77; Russo & Sullivan,
Tarkington, p. 67-69.

T-40   _____ The flirt / by Booth Tarkington . . . ;
illustrations by Clarence F. Underwood. Garden
City, New York: Doubleday, Page & Company,
1913. 378 p., front., [7] leaves of plates. Illustrated
t. p.
LC: Mr 11, '13.
PW: Mr 22, '13.
BLC: London: Hodder & Stoughton, Garden City,
N. Y., printed, 1913.
References: Currie, p. 61-62; Russo & Sullivan,
Tarkington, p. 27-28.

        _____ Fox terrier or something. In *"Dawgs!"* (1925),
D-184.

T-41   _____ Gentle Julia / by Booth Tarkington; illustrated
by C. Allan Gilbert and Worth Brehm. Garden City,
N. Y.: Doubleday, Page & Company, 1922. 375 p.,
col. front., [3] leaves of plates.
LC: My 11, '22.
PW: Ap 29, '22.
BLC: London: Hodder & Stoughton, [1922].
References:References: Currie, p. 73-74; Russo &
Sullivan, *Tarkington*, p. 61-63.

        _____ A great man's wife. See *Anthony, the joker*
(1924), **A-286.**

T-42   _____ The guest of Quesnay / by Booth Tarkington
. . . ; illustrations by W. J. Duncan. New York: The
McClure Company, 1908. 335 p., col. front., [4]
leaves of plates.
LC: S 26, '08.
PW: O 17, '08.
BLC: London & New York: McClure Company;
printed in U. S. A., 1908. Another edition: London:
William Heinemann, 1908.
References: Currie, p. 57-58; Russo & Sullivan,
Tarkington, p. 21-22.

T-43   _____ Harlequin and Columbine: and other stories.
Garden City, New York: Doubleday, Page &

Company, 1918. 403 p., front. [Ill. by author.]
WVA
(The works of Booth Tarkington; v. 8). Russo &
Sullivan: "All the stories in this volume are here first
collected."
Contents: Harlequin and Columbine -- Mary Smith -- Truth is
stranger than fiction -- Marjorie Jones' picnic -- Penrod-zöologist --
The fairy coronet -- The second name -- Brudie's pickle.
References: Currie, p. 145-146; Russo & Sullivan,
Tarkington, p. 45-46.

T-44   Harlequin and Columbine / by Booth
Tarkington; frontispiece by E. Stetson Crawford.
Garden City, N. Y.; Toronto: Doubleday, Page &
Company, 1921. 188 p., front.
First separate printing.
LC: D 22, '21.
PW: D 10, '21.
BLC: London: Curtis Brown, 1921.
References: Currie, p. 72-73; Russo & Sullivan,
Tarkington, p. 59-60.

T-45   His own people, by Booth Tarkington;
illustrated by Lawrence Mazzanovich and F. R.
Gruger, decorated by Wm. St. John Harper. New
York: Doubleday, Page & Co., 1907. 150 p., col.
front., [5] leaves of plates (1 col.). Illustrated end
papers.
LC: S 25, '07.
PW: O 5, '07.
BLC: London: Doubleday, Page & Co., New York
printed, 1907.
Another edition: London: John Murray; New York
printed, 1907.
References: Currie, p. 56-57; Russo & Sullivan,
Tarkington, p. 19-20.

T-46   In the arena: stories of political life / Booth
Tarkington; illustrated by A. I. Keller, Power
O'Malley and J. J. Gould. New York: McClure,
Phillips & Co., 1905. 276 p., front., [7] leaves of
plates.
Contents: "In the first place" -- Boss Gorgett -- The aliens -- The
need of money -- Hector -- Mrs. Protheroe -- Great men's sons.
PW: F 4, '05.
BLC: London: John Murray, New York [printed],
1905.
References: Curie, p. 52-53; Russo & Sullivan,
Tarkington, p. 14-15.

T-47   The magnificent Ambersons / by Booth
Tarkington; illustrated by Arthur William Brown.
Garden City, New York: Doubleday, Page &
Company, 1918. 516 p., front., [7] leaves of plates.
LC: O 28, '18.
PW: O 26, '18.
BLC: London: Hodder & Stoughton, [1918].
References:References: Currie, p. 69-70; Russo &
Sullivan, *Tarkington*, p. 48-50.

T-48   The midlander / by Booth Tarkington. Garden
City, New York: Doubleday, Page & Company,
1924. 493 p.
Preceded by limited edition, 1923; Currie lists entry
for limited edition.
LC: D 29, '23.
PW: Ja 5, '24.
BLC: London: William Heinemann, printed in U. S.

A., 1924.
References: Currie, p. 77-79; Russo & Sullivan,
Tarkington, p. 71-73.

T-49   Monsieur Beaucaire; The beautiful lady; His
own people; and other stories. Garden City, New
York: Doubleday, Page and Company, 1918.
427 p., front.
Unexamined copy: bibliographic data from
references.
(The works of Booth Tarkington; v. 9). Russo &
Sullivan: "Five of the seven stories in this volume
had previous book appearances; the following are
here first collected: *Mr. Brooke*; *Lord Jerningham*."
BLC: London: John Murray, 1901.
References: Currie, p. 145-146; Russo & Sullivan,
Tarkington, p. 46-47.

     The one hundred dollar bill. In *Prize stories of
1923* (1924), P-621.

T-50   Penrod / by Booth Tarkington; illustrated by
Gordon Grant. Garden City, New York: Doubleday,
Page & Company, 1914. 345 p., incl. front., ill.
LC: Mr 28, '14.
BLC: London: Hodder & Stoughton, [1914].
References; Currie, p. 62-64; Russo & Sullivan,
Tarkington, p. 29-33.

T-51   Penrod and Sam / by Booth Tarkington . . . ;
illustrated by Worth Brehm. Garden City, New
York: Doubleday, Page & Company, 1916. 356 p.,
front., [7] leaves of plates.
LC: O 30, '16.
PW: N 4, '16.
BLC: London: Hodder & Stoughton, 1917.
References: Currie, p. 67-68; Russo & Sullivan,
Tarkington, p. 41-44.

T-52   Ramsey Milholland / by Booth Tarkington;
illustrated by Gordon Grant. Garden City, New
York: Doubleday, Page & Company, 1919. 218 p.,
front., [4] leaves of plates, ill.
LC: Ag 23, '19.
BLC: London: Hodder & Stoughton, [1919].
References:References: Currie, p. 70-71; Russo &
Sullivan, *Tarkington*, p. 50-51.

     Renfrew and the new generation. In *Short
stories for class reading* (1925), S-461.

T-53   Seventeen: a tale of youth and summer time
and the Baxter family especially William / by Booth
Tarkington; illustrated. New York; London: Harper
& Brothers, 1916. 328, [1] p., front., [15] leaves of
plates (some double-leaf). [Ill. by Arthur W. Brown.]
PW: Mr 11, '16.
BLC: London: Hodder & Stoughton, 1916.
References: Currie, p. 66-67; Russo & Sullivan,
Tarkington, p. 36-40.

T-54   The Spring concert / Booth Tarkington. New
York: The Ridgway Company, [c1916]. 31 p.
AZS
Russo & Sullivan note: "Probably distributed gratis
as advertising matter . . . Previously published in
Everybody's Magazine, October, 1916."
References: Currie, p. 50; Russo & Sullivan,
Tarkington, p. 128.

T-55   ____ The turmoil: a novel / by Booth Tarkington
. . . ; illustrated by C. E. Chambers. New York;
London: Harper & Brothers, 1915. 348, [1] p., col.
front., [8] leaves of plates.
PW: F 13, '15.
BLC: London: Hodder & Stoughton, 1915.
References: Currie, p. 64-65; Russo & Sullivan,
Tarkington, p. 34-36.

T-56   ____ The two Vanrevels / by Booth Tarkington
. . . ; illustrations by Henry Hutt. New York:
McClure, Phillips & Co., 1902. 351 p., front., [6]
leaves of col. plates.
Currie lists entry for limited signed edition.
PW: O 4, '02.
BLC: London: Grant Richards, 1902.
References: Currie, p. 49-50; Russo & Sullivan,
Tarkington, p. 9-12.

____ "Us." In *Marriage* (1923), M-457.

T-57   ____ Women / by Booth Tarkington. Garden City,
N. Y.: Doubleday, Page & Company, 1925. 415 p.
LC: D 17, '25.
PW: N 28, '25.
BLC: London: William Heinemann, printed in U. S.
A., 1925.
References: Currie, p. 80-81; Russo & Sullivan,
Tarkington, p. 74-77.

T-58   ____ The works of Booth Tarkington. 12 vols.
Unexamined copy: bibliographic data from
references.
Reprints save for:
        Vol. 8: Harlequin and Columbine and
        other stories. See separate entry above,
        T-44.
        Vol. 9: Monsieur Beaucaire; The beautiful
        lady; His own people; and other
        stories. See separate entry above, T-49.

Tarkington, John Stevenson, 1832-1928. See
Steventon, John, pseud.

Tarleau, Lisa Ysaye. Loutré. In *The Harper prize
short stories* (1925), H-233.

Tashrak, pseud. See **Zevin, Israel J. (Israel
Joseph), 1872-1926.**

T-59   Tate, Henry. Aaron Crane / by Henry Tate . . .
New York; London; Montreal: The Abbey Press,
[c1901]. 248 p., front., [2] leaves of plates.
PW: Ap 26, '02.

T-60   Tatlow, Richard H. Orpah: a religious and historical
novel with the principal scenes in Missouri,
immediately proceeding, during and following the
great Civil War / by Richard H. Tatlow and John D.
Crisp. Chicago: Scroll Publishing Company,
[c1902]. 573 p.

T-61   Tatum, Edith. When the bugle called / by Edith
Tatum. New York; Washington: The Neale
Publishing Company, 1908. 132 p.   **SLG**
LC: Mr 28, '08.

T-62   Taulman, Francis Asbury, b. 1841. The poplars, or,
The good results of an evil deed / by Francis Asbury
Taulman . . . New York: Cochrane Publishing
Company . . . , 1909. 376 p.
LC: N 19, '09.

T-63   Tavenner, James W. Fernwood Community Center /
by James W. Tavenner; illustrated with twelve full
page drawings. Boston: The Roxburgh Publishing
Company, Inc., [c1921]. 223 p., ill.   **EYP**

T-64   Taylor, Ada White. The mystic spell: a
metaphysical romance / by Ada White Taylor. Los
Angeles, California: Published by The Austin
Publishing Company, [c1923]. 276 p.
LC: Ap 10, '23.

Taylor, Arthur Russell. Mr. Squem. In *Atlantic
narratives*; first series (1918), A-360.

T-65   ____ Mr. Squem and Some male triangles / by
Arthur Russell Taylor . . . New York: George H.
Doran Company, [c1918]. 160 p.

Taylor, Bayard. The chiropodist. In *International
short stories* (1910), I-29.

T-66   Taylor, Bert Leston, 1866-1921. The charlatans / by
Bert Leston Taylor; with illustrations by George
Brehm. Indianapolis: The Bobbs-Merrill Company,
[c1906]. 390, [1] p., col. front., [9] leaves of plates,
ill.
LC: Ag 30, '06.
PW: N 3, '06.

T-67   ____ The log of the water wagon, or, The cruise of
the good ship "Lithia" / by Bert Leston Taylor and
W. C. Gibson; illustrations by L. M. Glackens.
Boston: Published by H. M. Caldwell Co., [c1905].
128 p., ill.
PW: Ag 12, '05.

T-68   ____ Monsieur d'En Brochette: being an historical
account of some of the adventures of Huevos Pasada
par Agua, Marquis of Pollio Grille, Count of Pate de
Foie Gras, and much else besides / by Bert Leston
Taylor, Arthur Hamilton Folwell and John Kendrick
Bangs; illustrated by Frank A. NanKivell. New
York: Keppler & Schwarzmann, 1905. 179 p.,
front. ill., ill.
LC: Ag 16, '05.
PW: Ag 5, '05.
References: BAL 767

T-69   Taylor, C. Bryson, b. 1880. In the dwellings of the
wilderness / by C. Bryson Taylor; with decorations in
colour. New York: Henry Holt and Company, 1904.
184 p., col. front., [1] leaf of col. plates. [Ill. by
Decorative Designers.]
PW: My 14, '04.

T-70   Taylor, C. Bryson, b. 1880. Nicanor, teller of tales:
a story of Roman Britain / by C. Bryson Taylor;
having pictures and designs by Troy and Margaret
West Kinney. Chicago: A. C. McClurg & Co.,
1906. 421, [1] p., col. front., [4] leaves of col.
plates. Ornamental borders in green.
PW: Ap 28, '06.

Taylor, Charles A., jt. aut. *Over the Rhine* (1918). See **Balshofer, Fred J., jt. aut., B-135.**

T-71   Taylor, Charles Maus, b. 1849. Only a grain of sand / by Charles Maus Taylor; illustrations by Clare Victor Dwiggins. Philadelphia: The John C. Winston Co., 1905. 40 l. (first and last leaves blank). **PAU**

T-72   Taylor, Charles Tracy, Mrs. A daughter of the manse: a novel / by Mrs. Charles Tracy Taylor; illustration by Alice Barber Stephens. Philadelphia: The John C. Winston Company, 1909. 402 p., front.
LC: Ap 6, '10.
PW: Mr 5, '10.

T-73   Taylor, Emerson Gifford, 1874-1932. A daughter of Dale / by Emerson Gifford Taylor. New York: The Century Co., 1904. 352 p., col. front. **VA@**
PW: Je 4, '04.

T-74   _____ The day after dark / by Emerson Gifford Taylor . . . Boston: Small, Maynard & Company, [c1922]. 300 p.
LC: S 21, '22.
BLC: London: Mills & Boon, 1923.

T-75   _____ The long way round / by Emerson Gifford Taylor. Boston: Small, Maynard & Company, [c1921]. 370 p.
LC: Mr 25, '21.
PW: Ap 2, '21.

T-76   _____ The upper hand / by Emerson Gifford Taylor . . . New York: A. S. Barnes & Company, 1906. 325 p.
LC: Jl 10, '06.
PW: S 8, '06.

Taylor, Hobart C. Chatfield. See **Chatfield-Taylor, Hobart.**

T-77   Taylor, Job. Broken links / by Job Taylor; illustrations by John Goss. Boston, Mass., U. S. A.: The C. M. Clark Publishing Co., 1908. 322 p., front., [9] leaves of plates.

T-78   Taylor, John Edwin. Cy Hains's sermo-phone and other stories / by John Edwin Taylor. Augusta, Maine: Kennebec Journal Press, 1909. 62 p., photo. front. (port.).
Contents: Cy Hains's sermo-phone -- Dr. Lunt and his telebird system -- The cow that gave eighteen quarts of milk -- Cupid and the cat's tail -- Capturing a bear with two bushels of beans -- Dixie, the foster-mother.

Taylor, John M., b. 1888, jt. aut. *The chronicles of Quincy Adams* (1912). See **Pidgin, Charles Felton, 1844-1923, jt. aut., P-390.**

T-79   Taylor, Katharine Haviland. Barbara of Baltimore / by Katharine Haviland Taylor . . . ; illustrated by Frances Rogers. New York: George H. Doran Company, [c1919]. 278 p., front., [3] leaves of plates. **OSU, MDS**
LC: S 19, '19.
PW: S 6, '19.

T-80   _____ Cecilia of the pink roses / by Katharine Haviland Taylor; illustrated by May Wilson Preston. New York: George H. Doran Company, [c1917].

271 p., col. front., [5] leaves of col. plates.
LC: My 24, '17.
PW: My 5, '17.

T-81   _____ Cross currents / by Katharine Haviland Taylor. Philadelphia: George W. Jacobs & Company, [c1922]. 303 p.
LC: Ap 27, '22.
PW: Je 3, '22.
BLC: London: Methuen & Co., 1923.

T-82   _____ A modern trio in an old town / by Katharine Haviland Taylor . . . ; illustrated by Morgan Dennis. New York: Harcourt, Brace and Company, [c1922]. 268 p., front., [3] leaves of plates. **DLC**
LC: Ag 19, '22.
PW: S 2, '22.

T-83   _____ Natalie Page / by Katharine Haviland Taylor . . . Philadelphia: George W. Jacobs & Company Publishers, [c1921]. 301 p.
LC: Ap 25, '21.
PW: Ap 30, '21.

T-84   _____ Real stuff / by Katharine Haviland Taylor; illustrations by Ada C. Williamson. New York: Harcourt, Brace and Company, 1921. 243 p., front., [3] leaves of plates.
LC: S 29, '22.
PW: O 22, '21.
BLC: London: Methuen & Co., 1924.

T-85   _____ The second Mrs. Clay / by Katharine Haviland Taylor. Garden City, N. Y.; Toronto: Doubleday, Page & Company, 1921. 281, [1] p.
LC: My 20, '21.
BLC: London: Methuen & Co., 1924.

T-86   _____ Tony from America / by Katharine Haviland Taylor; with illustrations by Dennis Morgan. New York: Harcourt, Brace and Company, [c1924]. 286 p., front., [3] leaves of plates.
LC: F 19, '24.
PW: F 16, '24.
BLC: London: Hodder & Stoughton, 1926.

T-87   _____ Yellow soap / by Katharine Haviland Taylor. Garden City, N. Y.: Doubleday, Page & Company, 1920. 306 p., front. [Ill. by Decorative Designers: Botkin.]
LC: Je 21, '20.
PW: Mr 6, '20.

T-88   Taylor, Lee Mays, b. 1865. The Texan: a tale of Texas / by Lee M. Taylor. [Georgetown, Tex.: s. n.], 1908. 196 p., front., [4] leaves of plates. [Some ill. by Froebel.] **TXS**
LC: D 24, '08.

T-89   Taylor, Mary Colliver. Bachelor Bob: a story of the South / by Mary Colliver Taylor . . . Columbus, Ohio: The Evans Printing Company, 1903. 208 p.

T-90   _____ Nobody yet somebody: a story founded upon fact / by Mary Colliver Taylor . . . Columbus, Ohio: Printed by the New Franklin Printing Co., 1913. 132 p.

T-91 _____ Try to win / by Mary Colliver Taylor. Columbus, O.: The Ohio Co., c1905. 155 p. Unexamined copy: bibliographic data from OCLC, #11963311.

T-92 Taylor, Mary Imlay, 1878-1938. Anne Scarlett / by M. Imlay Taylor. Chicago: A. C. McClurg & Co., 1901. 350 p.
PW: O 12, '01.

T-93 _____ Caleb Trench / by Mary Imlay Taylor . . . ; with frontispiece by Emlen McConnell. Boston: Little, Brown and Company, 1910. 300 p., col. front.
LC: Mr 22, '10.
PW: Mr 26, '10.

T-94 _____ A candle in the wind / by Mary Imlay Taylor . . . New York: Moffat, Yard and Company, 1919. 365 p.
LC: Ag 20, '19.
PW: Ag 23, '19.

T-95 _____ The impersonator / by Mary Imlay Taylor; illustrated by Ch. Grunwald. Boston: Little, Brown and Company, 1906. 392 p., front., [5] leaves of plates.
LC: O 15, '06.
PW: Ja 26, '07.
BLC: London: Gay & Bird; Boston, U. S. A. [printed], 1906.

T-96 _____ The long way / by Mary Imlay Taylor. Boston: Little, Brown and Company, 1913. 292 p.
LC: My 26, '13.
PW: My 10, '13.

T-97 _____ The lotus lantern / by Mary Imlay Taylor and Martin Sabine; with illustrations by F. Vaux Wilson. Boston: Little, Brown & Company, 1911. 308 p., front., [3] leaves of plates.
LC: S 28, '11.
PW: O 7, '11.

T-98 _____ My Lady Clancarty: being the true story of the Earl of Clancarty and Lady Elizabeth Spencer / by Mary Imlay Taylor. Boston: Little, Brown and Company, 1905. 298 p., col. front., [3] leaves of col. plates. [Ill. by Alice B. Stephens.]
PW: Mr 25, '05.

T-99 _____ The reaping / by Mary Imlay Taylor; with a frontispiece in color by George Alfred Williams. Boston: Little, Brown and Company, 1908. 334 p., col. front.
LC: Ja 9, '08.
PW: F 29, '08.
BLC: London: Hutchinson & Co.; Boston, Mass. [printed], 1909.

T-100 _____ The rebellion of the Princess / by M. Imlay Taylor. New York: McClure, Phillips & Co., 1903. 326 p.
PW: Mr 28, '03.

T-101 _____ The wild fawn / by Mary Imlay Taylor. New York: Moffat, Yard and Company, 1920. 388 p.

LC: My 3, '20.
PW: My 8, '20.

Taylor, Sophie C. See **Taylor, Charles Tracy, Mrs.**

T-102 Taylor, William A. (William Alexander), 1837-1912. Intermere / by William Alexander Taylor. Columbus, Ohio: The XX. Century Pub. Co., 1901-1902, [c1901]. 148 p., photo. front. (port.).
PW: Ja 11, '02.

Teall, Edward Nelson, 1880-1947, jt. aut. *The unknown quantity*, 1919. See **Achorn, Edgar O. (Edgar Oakes), jt. aut., A-43.**

T-103 Teall, Gardner Callahan, 1878-1956. The contessa's sister: a novel / by Gardner Teall. Boston; New York: Houghton Mifflin Company, 1911. (Cambridge: The Riverside Press). 243, [1] p.
LC: Ap 7, '11.
PW: Ap 1, '11.

Teasdale, Minnie, b. 1880. See **Skinner, Gertrude, pseud.**

T-104 Tedford, Sarah J. Arizona, or, The arrivals / by Sarah J. Tedford. Los Angeles: Hollywood Publishing Company, [1908?], c1899. 102 p., [1] leaf of plates (port.).
Unexamined copy: bibliographic data from OCLC, #12141649.
Teed, Cyrus Reed, 1839-1908. See **Chester, Lord, pseud.**

T-105 Teller, Charlotte, b. 1876. The cage / by Charlotte Teller. New York: D. Appleton and Company, 1907. 340 p.
LC: Mr 2, '07.

Temple, Ronald, jt. aut. *The lords of dawn* (1916). See **Marsh, George Turner, b. 1857, jt. aut., M-472.**

Templer, Will. See **Becker, William Templer.**

T-106 Templeton, Frank. Margaret Ballentine, or, The fall of the Alamo: a romance of the Texas revolution / by Frank Templeton. Houston, Texas: State Printing Company, 1907. 244 p., front. (prot.), [8] leaves of plates. **IAU**
LC: Mr 4, '07.

T-107 Templeton, Herminie. Darby O'Gill and the good people / by Herminie Templeton. New York: McClure, Phillips & Co., 1903. 294 p. **IUL**
Contents: Darby O'Gill and the good people -- Darby O'Gill and the leprechaun -- The convarsion of Father Cassidy -- How the fairies came to Ireland -- The adventures of King Brian Connors -- The banshee's comb.
PW: My 2, '03.

T-108 The ten-foot chain, or, Can love survive the shackles? : a unique symposium / by Achmed Abdullah . . . [et al.]. New York: Reynolds Publishing Company, Inc., 1920. 159 p., front., ill. [Ill. by Herbert Morton Stoops.]
Contents: An Indian jataka / by Achmed Abdullah -- Out of the dark

/ by Max Brand -- Plumb nauseated / by E. K. Means -- Princess or Percheron / by Perley Poore Sheehan.
LC: O 1, '20.

T-109   Tenney, E. P. (Edward Payson), 1835-1916. The dream of my youth / by E. P. Tenney. Boston: Lothrop Publishing Company, [c1901]. 336 p.
LC: Ap 25, '01.
PW: My 4, '01.
BLC: London: C. H. Kelly, 1901.

T-110   Tequay, Anne, *pseud*. Making an American gentleman / by Anne Tequay [pseud.]. Boston: The Roxburgh Publishing Co., Inc., [c1920]. 162 p.
PW: O 23, '20.

T-111   Terhune, Albert Payson, 1872-1942. The amateur inn / by Albert Payson Terhune. New York: George H. Doran Company, [c1923]. 287 p.
LC: N 1, '23.
PW: N 3, '23.
BLC: London: Hodder & Stoughton, printed in U. S. A., [1924].

T-112   ____ Black Caesar's clan: a Florida mystery story / by Albert Payson Terhune . . . New York: George H. Doran Company, [c1922]. 281 p.
LC: O 5, '22.
PW: S 30, '22.
BLC: London: Hodder & Stoughton, printed in U. S. A., [1924].

T-113   ____ Black gold / by Albert Payson Terhune . . . New York: George H. Doran Company, [c1922]. 297 p.
LC: Mr 29, '22.
PW: F 11, '22.
BLC: London: Hodder & Stoughton, printed in U. S. A., [1922].

T-114   ____ Bruce / by Albert Payson Terhune . . . New York: E. P. Dutton & Company, [c1920]. 204 p.
LC: Ap 24, '20.
PW: My 8, '20.

T-115   ____ Buff: a collie: and other dog-stories / by Albert Payson Terhune . . . New York: George H. Doran Company, [c1921]. 341 p., photo. front. [Ill. by Jack Sussman.]
Contents: Buff: A Collie -- Something -- Chums -- Human-interest stuff -- "One minute longer" -- The foul fancier -- The grudge -- The Sunnybank Collies.
LC: Ag 30, '21.
PW: Jl 2, '21.
BLC: London: Hodder & Stoughton, 1921.

T-116   ____ Caleb Conover, railroader / by Albert Payson Terhune; illustrated in water-colors by Frank Parker. New York; London: The Authors and Newspapers Association, 1907. 322 p., front., [4] leaves of plates (some col.; 1 facsim.).
LC: F 28, '07.
PW: Ap 20, '07.
BLC: London: Cassell, 1907.

T-117   ____ Dad / by Albert Payson Terhune; frontispiece by W. D. Goldbeck. New York: W. J. Watt &

Company, [c1914]. 307 p., front.
LC: N 10, '14.
PW: Ja 30, '14.
BLC: London: Methuen & Co., 1920.

T-118   ____ Dollars and cents / by Albert Payson Terhune . . . New York: Robert J. Shores, 1917. 281 p., front., [2] leaves of plates.
LC: My 4, '17.

T-119   ____ The fighter / by Albert Payson Terhune. New York: Frank F. Lovell Company, [c1909]. 358 p.
LC: D 20, '09.
PW: Ja 22, '10.
BLC: London: Methuen & Co., 1919.

T-120   ____ Fortune / by Albert Payson Terhune; illustrated by W. Clinton Pette [i. e., Pettee]. Garden City, New York: Doubleday, Page & Company, 1918. 360 p., front., [3] leaves of plates.   **CSL**
LC: O 2, '18.
PW: N 9, '18.

T-121   ____ Further adventures of Lad / by Albert Payson Terhune . . . ; with frontispiece by Charles Livingston Bull. New York: George H. Doran Company, [c1922]. 341 p., front.
LC: O 5, '22.
PW: Ag 5, '22.
BLC: London: Hodder & Stoughton, printed in U. S. A., [1922].

T-122   ____ His dog / by Albert Payson Terhune . . . New York: E. P. Dutton & Company, [c1922]. 183 p., photo. front. [Ill. by Lejaren Hiller.]
PW: Mr 18, '22.
BLC: London & Toronto: J. M. Dent & Sons, 1922.

T-123   ____ Lad: a dog / by Albert Payson Terhune. New York: E. P. Dutton & Company, [c1919]. 349 p., photo. front.
Stories reprinted in part from various periodicals.
LC: My 5, '19.
PW: My 10, '19.
BLC: London & Toronto: J. M. Dent, 1920.

____ A lightning change. In *Stories of the colleges* **(1901), S-985.**

T-124   ____ Lochinvar luck / by Albert Payson Terhune . . . ; with a frontispiece by Morgan Stinemetz. New York: George H. Doran Company, [c1923]. 309 p., col. front.
LC: F 8, '23.
PW: F 3, '23.
BLC: London: Hodder & Stoughton, printed in U. S. A., [1924].

T-125   ____ The man in the dark / by Albert Payson Terhune. New York: E. P. Dutton & Company, [1921]. 311 p.
PW: Mr 26, '21.

T-126   ____ Najib / by Albert Payson Terhune. New York: George H. Doran Company, [c1925]. 311 p.
LC: Ap 11, '25.

PW: F 28, '25.
BLC: London: Hodder & Stoughton, [1926].

T-127 ____ The new mayor / by Albert Payson Terhune.
New York: J. S. Ogilvie Publishing Company,
c1907. 232 p., photo. front., [11] leaves of photo.
plates.
"Founded upon George Broadhurst's successful play
The man of the hour, under the direction of Wm. A.
Brady and Jos. R. Grismer."
PW: F 1, '08.

____ On strike. In *Prize stories of 1919* (1920),
P-617.

T-128 ____ The pest / by Albert Payson Terhune . . . New
York: E. P. Dutton & Company, [c1923]. 327 p.
                  CLE
LC: Ja 27, '23.
PW: Ja 27, '23.

T-129 ____ The runaway bag / by Albert Payson Terhune.
New York: George H. Doran Company, [c1925].
307 p.
LC: O 27, '25.
PW: O 31, '25.

T-130 ____ The story of Damon and Pythias / by Albert
Payson Terhune; adapted and illustrated from the
photo-play conceived and produced by the Universal
Film Manufacturing Company. New York: Grosset
and Dunlap, [c1915]. 307 p., photo. front., [13]
double-sided leaves of photo. plates and 1 double-leaf
with 2 photo. images.

T-131 ____ The tiger's claw / by Albert Payson Terhune.
New York: George H. Doran Company, [c1924].
262 p.
LC: S 23, '24.
BLC: London: Hodder & Stoughton, [1925].

T-132 ____ The woman: a novel / by Albert Payson
Terhune; founded on William C. DeMille's play of
the same name; illustrations by W. B. King.
Indianapolis: The Bobbs-Merrill Company, [c1912].
341, [1] p., front., [4] leaves of plates.
LC: S 11, '12.
PW: S 7, '12.

____ "The writer-upward." In *Prize stories of 1922*
(1923), P-620.

T-133 ____ The years of the locust / by Albert Payson
Terhune . . . ; frontispiece by Eleanor Howard. New
York: Robert J. Shores, [c1917]. 342 p., col. front.
(port.).   **DLC**
LC: Mr 18, '18.
PW: My 4, '18.

T-134 Terhune, Anice Morris (Stockton). The boarder up at
Em's: a story of New England folks / by Anice
Terhune; frontispiece by E. F. Ward. New York:
The Macaulay Company, [c1925]. 313 p., front.
LC: Ap 15, '25.
PW: Ap 4, '25.

T-135 ____ The eyes of the village / by Anice Terhune;
frontispiece by John Ellison Brown. New York: The
Macaulay Company, [c1922]. 315 p., front.
LC: Mr 11, '22.
BLC: London: J. Bale & Co., 1922.

T-136 Terhune, Everit Bogert. Michel Gulpe / by Everit
Bogert Terhune; illustrations by Sidney Marsh Chase.
New York: G. W. Dillingham Company, 1902. 181,
[1] p., incl. front., [3] leaves of plates.

Terhune, Mary Virginia Hawes, 1830-1922. <u>See</u>
Harland, Marion, pseud.

T-137 Terreve, Retsel, *pseud.* A man without principle? /
by Retsel Terreve [pseud.]. [Baltimore: Hocking
Publishing Co., c1908]. 345 p.
LC: D 4, '08.
Another edition: Norfolk, Va.: The Hocking
Publishing Co., [1908]. 348 p., front. plates.
Unexamined copy: bibliographic data from NUC.

T-138 Terrill, Lucy Stone. A thing apart / by Lucy Stone
Terrill. Indianapolis: The Bobbs-Merrill Company,
[c1921]. 299 p.   **CLU**

Terry, Gibert Cunyngham. The jewels of Bendita.
In *Argonaut stories* (1906), **A-298.**

T-139 Terry, Howard L. (Howard Leslie), 1877-1964. A
voice from the silence: a story of the Ozarks / by
Howard L. Terry; illustrated by J. B. Bumgardner.
Santa Monica, California: The Palisades Press,
[1914]. 355 p., front., [2] leaves of plates.

Terry, J. A. The redemption of Jim Tracy. In *The
so-so stories* (1903), **S-715.**

T-140 Terwilliger, R. L. (Roy Lawrence), b. 1875. The
Way of the Little King: stories told at the Carmen de
Beas, by the Way of the Little King in Granada, 1908
/ composed and illustrated by R. L. Terwilliger.
[Chicago: Printed by J. C. Veeder Company, c1910].
60 l., front., [6] leaves of plates. Leaves printed on
one side only.   **DLC**
Contents: The Way of the Little King -- The story of the three trees
-- A story of Kaseem -- The story of the builder -- The wisdom of the
sword -- The tower of the luminary -- Mohammed and Nadia.
LC: Ja 25, '11.

T-141 Thacker, May Dixon. The strength of the weak /
May Dixon Thacker. New York: Broadway
Publishing Co., 1910. 450 p.
LC: D 12, '10.

T-142 Thanet, Octave, 1850-1934, *pseud.* And the captain
answered / by Octave Thanet [pseud.] . . .
Indianapolis: The Bobbs-Merrill Company, [c1917].
84, [1] p.
LC: O 27, '17.
PW: N 24, '17.

T-143 ____ By inheritance / by Octave Thanet [pseud.];
with illustrations by Thomas Fogarty. Indianapolis:
The Bobbs-Merrill Company, [c1910]. 394 p.,
front., [3] leaves of plates.
LC: Mr 30, '10.
PW: Ap 2, '10.

_____ The labor question at Glasscock's. In *The Miller's holiday* (1920), **M-817.**

T-144 _____ The lion's share / by Octave Thanet [pseud.]; with illustrations by E. M. Ashe. Indianapolis: Bobbs-Merrill Company, [1907]. 376 p., front., [5] leaves of plates.
LC: S 30, '07.
PW: O 12, '07.

T-145 _____ The man of the hour / by Octave Thanet [pseud.]; with illustrations by Lucius Wolcott Hitchcock. Indianapolis: The Bobbs-Merrill Company, [c1905]. 477 p., front., [6] leaves of plates.
PW: Ag 12, '05.

_____ A matter of rivalry. In *Life at high tide* (1907), **L-281.**

_____ The messenger. In *A house party* (1901), **H-903.**

_____ The miller's seal. In *The Miller's holiday* (1920), **M-817.**

T-146 _____ A step on the stair / by Octave Thanet [pseud.]. Indianapolis: The Bobbs-Merrill Company, [c1913]. 43, [1] p.
LC: Mr 22, '13.
PW: Mr 29, '13.

T-147 _____ Stories that end well / by Octave Thanet [pseud.]. Indianapolis: The Bobbs-Merrill Company, [c1911]. 340 p.
Republished from various periodicals.
Contents: An adventure in Altruria -- Through the terrors of the law -- The real thing -- The old partisan -- Max-or his picture -- The stout Miss Hopkins' bicycle -- The spellbinder -- The object of the federation -- The lonely little girl -- The hero of company G -- A miracle play.
LC: S 8, '11.

_____ The stout Miss Hopkins's bicycle. In *Different girls* (1906), **D-383.**

_____ The wild western way. In *The Miller's holiday* (1920), **M-817.**

T-148 Thaumazo, Fred, *pseud.* Voices in the hills / by Fred Thaumazo [pseud.]. New York: Broadway Publishing Co., 1913. 110 p., photo. front. (port.).
DLC

T-149 Thaxton, Jesse B. Cain, or, the vagabond of Nod / by Jesse B. Thaxton. New York: Broadway Publishing Company, [c1905]. 483 p., front. (port.). **DLC**
PW: Mr 10, '06.

T-150 Thayer, Alford Finley. The forest empire: a story of the land frauds in the west / by Alford Finley Thayer and Eliene Finley Thayer. New York; Chicago; San Francisco: The International Company, 1909. 216 p., [8] leaves of photo. plates. **CBA**

Thayer, Eliene Finley, jt. aut. *The forest empire* (1909). See **Thayer, Alford Finley, jt. aut., T-150.**

Thayer, Emma Redington Lee, b. 1874. See **Thayer, Lee.**

Thayer, Harriet Maxon, b. 1889. Kindred. In *The best short stories of 1921 and the yearbook of the American short story* (1922), **B-566.**

T-151 Thayer, Lee, b. 1874. Doctor S. O. S. / by Lee Thayer. Garden City, N. Y.: Doubleday, Page & Company, 1925. 305 p.
LC: My 4, '25.
PW: Ap 25, '25.
BLC: London: Hurst & Blackett, [1925]. Another edition: London: William Heinemann, printed in U.S. A., 1925.

T-152 _____ The key / by Lee Thayer. Garden City, New York: Doubleday, Page & Company, 1924. 262 p.
LC: N 25, '24.
PW: N 15, '24.
BLC: London: Curtis Brown, printed in U. S. A., 1924.
Another edition: London: Hurst & Blackett, [1924].

T-153 _____ The mystery of the thirteenth floor / by Lee Thayer. New York: The Century Co., 1919. 396 p., front. [Ill. by Gordon H. Grant.]
LC: F 26, '19.
PW: F 22, '19.

T-154 _____ Q. E. D. / by Lee Thayer; frontispiece by the author. Garden City, N. Y.; Toronto: Doubleday, Page & Company, 1922. 278 p., col. front.
LC: Ap 3, '22.

T-155 _____ The sinister mark / by Lee Thayer. Garden City, New York: Doubleday, Page & Company, 1923. 304 p.
LC: Je 18, '23.
PW: Je 16, '23.
BLC: London: Hurst & Blackett, 1923.

T-156 _____ That affair at "The Cedars" / by Lee Thayer; frontispiece by Clarence Rowe. Garden City, N. Y.; Toronto: Doubleday, Page & Company, 1921. 303, [1] p., col. front.
LC: F 5, '21.
BLC: London: Curtis Brown, Garden City, N. Y., printed, 1921.

T-157 _____ The unlatched door / by Lee Thayer. New York: The Century Co., 1920. 317 p., front. [Ill. by John A. Coughlin.]
LC: Je 1, '20.
PW: Je 12 '20.

T-158 Thayer, Harriet Maxon. The genial sultan; The princess who could not see; Late for the coronation / by Harriet Maxon Thayer. Philadelphia: Dorrance, [c1923]. 80 p., col. front., ill.
Half title: *The genial sultan and other stories.*

T-159 Thayer, Stephen Henry, 1839-1919. Daughters of the Revolution / by Stephen Henry Thayer . . . New York; London; Montreal: The Abbey Press, [c1901]. 244 p. Designed end papers.
PW: F 8, '02.

T-160 Theadorer. The finest baby in the world: being letters from a man to himself about his child / by Theadorer. New York; Chicago; Toronto: Fleming H. Revell Company, [c1904]. 63 p.
Contents: Letter no. one: The finest baby in the world -- Letter no. two: The mystery of the dawn -- Letter no. three: The unexpressed fear -- Letter no. four: My invisible spears -- Letter no. five: A haunted house -- Letter no. six: The conclusion of the whole matter.

T-161 Their husbands' wives / edited by William Dean Howells and Henry Mills Alden. New York; London: Harper & Brothers Publishers, c1906. 181 p. **VA@**
(Harper's novelettes).
Contents: Eve's diary / S. L. Clemens -- Covered embers / E. S. Phelps -- Life's accolade / A. M. Roach -- The bond / E. Pottle -- The eyes of affection / G. Hibbard -- "The marriage question" / G. E. Channing.
LC: Mr 8, '06.
PW: Mr 24, '06.
References: BAL 9769; Gibson & Arms 06-B.

T-162 Theiss-Whaley, M. L. (Maria Louise), b. 1854. By earthquake and fire, or, The checkered romance of two generations. San Francisco: Brunt's, 1914. 489, [1] p.

T-163 [Thetford, A. Thomas]. Mr. Smith, the personnel officer: a novel / by a soldier who was in the United States Army 19 months and was prevented from seeing foreign service by a personnel officer. Gainesville, Fla.: Printed for the author by Pepper Printing Company, 1920. 140 p. **DLC**

T-164 Thierry, James Francis. The adventure of the eleven cuff-buttons: being one of the exciting episodes in the career of the famous detective Hemlock Holmes, as recorded by his friend Dr. Watson / by James Francis Thierry. New York: The Neale Publishing Company, 1918. 190 p. **KSU**
LC: N 18, '18.

Thiery, Marie. My strange neighbors, the story of an old house. In *Golden stories* (1909), G-285.

Thivars, Michael. The plucking of the pears, the story of a suburban villa. In *Golden stories* (1909), G-285.

"Thomas," pseud. See **Upham, Francis Bourne, 1862-1941.**

T-165 Thomas, A. E. (Albert Ellsworth), 1872-1947. Cynthia's rebellion / by A. E. Thomas. New York: Charles Scribner's Sons, 1904. 277 p.
PW: My 7, '04.

T-166 ____ The double cross / by A. E. Thomas. New York: Dodd, Mead and Company, 1924. 284 p.
LC: S 4, '24.
BLC: London: Methuen & Co., 1925.

T-167 Thomas, Arthur, b. 1884, *pseud*. In the days of Brigham Young / by Arthur Thomas [pseud.]. New York: Broadway Publishing Co., [c1914]. 109 p.
LC: N 2, '14.

T-168 Thomas, Augustus, 1857-1934. The witching hour / by Augustus Thomas; illustrated from scenes in the play. New York; London: Harper & Brothers, 1908. 248 p., photo. front., [7] leaves of photo. plates.
LC: O 15, '08.

Thomas, Charles Swain, ed. See *Atlantic narratives* **(1918), A-360, A-361.**

Thomas, Chauncey. Ruggles' first case, the story of a mine. In *Golden stories* **(1909), G-285.**

____ Sheriff of Elbert. In *Comedy* **(1901), C-614.**

T-169 Thomas, Edwin M. Negotiable / by Edwin M. Thomas; frontispiece drawing by C. A. Morrisette. New York, N. Y.: [s. n., c1908]. 93 p., front.
DLC

T-170 Thomas, Elisabeth R. Tales of Palm Beach and Florida / by Elisabeth R. Thomas. [S. l.: s. n., 192-?]. 236 p.
Contents: The climber -- The rise of Susie Marvin -- The fish charmer -- Jeunesse a la mode -- The clue -- A sinister romance -- The Marquise de Hautcoeur -- Sweet charity -- A sketch in vaudeville.

T-171 Thomas, Ethel. The better way / by Ethel Thomas. Charlotte, N. C.: Clark Publishing Company, [19--]. 240 p.
Unexamined copy: bibliographic data from OCLC, #9816270.
"A story founded on facts, showing the happy results of cooperation between labor and capital, and the reward of faithful and loyal service of mill operatives."

T-172 ____ Only a factory boy: and From ball room to weave room / by Ethel Thomas. Charlotte, N. C.: Mill News Company, c1914. 224 p., [1] leaf of plates (port.).
Unexamined copy: bibliographic data from OCLC, #3899100.

T-173 Thomas, Frederick. The mill on the creek: a romance of the Hudson / by Frederick Thomas. New York: Broadway Publishing Co., 1913. 213 p.
OSU, DLC

T-174 Thomas, Henry Wilton, b. 1867. The sword of wealth / by Henry Wilton Thomas. New York; London: G. P. Putnam's Sons, 1906. ([New York]: The Knickerbocker Press). 318 p.
PW: D 8, '06.

T-175 Thomas, J. S. (John Singleton), b. 1849. In after years / by J. S. Thomas . . . Parsons, Kansas: The Foley Railway Printing Company, 1913. 303 p., photo. front. (port.). **MNU**
LC: Jl 23, '13.

T-176 ____ Two old letters / by J. S. Thomas. Parsons, Kansas: The Foley Railway Printing Company, 1904. 288 p., photo. front. (port.), [6] leaves of photo. plates. **TSW**
"A true history that reads like fiction."

T-177　　Thomas, Robert James, b. 1884. The whistling lady,
A sheep's sense of fair play, "Number six", / by
Robert Thomas. . . Binghamton, N. Y.: Printed by
Kennedy-Morris Corp., 1923. 80 p.
Unexamined copy: bibliographic data from OCLC,
#8413553.

T-178　　Thomas, Rowland. Fatima, or, Always pick a fool
for your husband: being the strange adventures of a
woman who was the most beautiful creature, and
quite, quite the cleverest creature ever was, and knew
it / by Rowland Thomas; with illustrations by J.
Duncan [i. e. Michael] Gleeson. Boston: Little,
Brown, and Company, 1913. 353 p., col. front., [5]
leaves of col. plates.
LC: S 24, '13.
BLC: Toronto: McClelland & Goodchild; Boston,
U. S. A. [printed], 1913.

T-179　　____ Felicidad: the romantic adventures of an
enthusiastic young pessimist / by Rowland Thomas;
with illustrations by Henry Roth. Boston: Little,
Brown, and Company, 1914. 313 p., col. front.
Illustrated t. p. and end papers.
LC: Ap 2, '14.
PW: Ap 4, '14.

T-180　　____ The little gods: a masque of the Far East / by
Rowland Thomas; illustrated by Charles Sarka.
Boston: Little, Brown, and Company, 1909. 304 p.,
front., [6] leaves of plates.
Stories partly reprinted from Collier's and
Everybody's magazine.
Contents: Prologue -- The little Gods -- Fagan -- God's little devils --
The little man -- A little ripple of patriotism -- The superfalous man --
The valley of sunshine and shadow -- What Okimi learned -- Where
there is no turning -- An optimist -- The fortune -- McGennis's
promotion -- Epilogue.
LC: Mr 10, '09.
PW: Mr 27, '09.
BLC: London: Stanley Paul & Co., [1910].

Thomas, W. I., jt. ed. See *Minnesota stories*
(1903), M-842.

T-181　　Thompson, Charles Miner, b. 1864. An army mule /
by Charles Miner Thompson; with illustrations by F.
R. Gruger. Boston; New York: Houghton Mifflin
Company, 1910. (Cambridge: The Riverside Press).
193, [1] p., front., [6] leaves of plates.
First published in the Youth's companion.
LC: My 16, '10.
PW: Ap 30, '10.

T-182　　____ The calico cat / by Charles Miner Thompson;
with illustrations by F. R. Gruger. Boston; New
York: Houghton Mifflin Company, 1908.
(Cambridge: The Riverside Press). 227, [1] p.,
front., [7] leaves of plates, ill.　　Originally
published in the Youth's companion.
LC: O 10, '08.
PW: N 14, '08.

Thompson, Charles Vance, 1863-1925. See
Thompson, Vance.

T-183　　Thompson, E. S. L. (Elizabeth Shepherd Lamb), b.

1848. The raising of the sons of Wooley / by E. S.
L. Thompson; handsomely illustrated. Chicago:
Rhodes & McClure Publishing Company, 1903.
303 p., incl. 19 leaves of plates. [Some ill. by H. S.
De Lay.] Designed end papers.

T-184　　Thompson, Edith Chetwood. Hearts atour: a novel /
by Edith Chetwood and Edward P. Thompson. New
York: Published by The Evening Post Job Printing
Office; Chester, Eng.: Alfred W. Lucas, [c1910].
331 p., front., [6] leaves of plates. [Ill. by C. L.
Wrenn.]
LC: S 8, '10.
PW: S 17, '10.

Thompson, Edward P., jt. aut. *Hearts atour* (1910).
See **Thompson, Edith Chetwood, jt. aut., T-184.**

Thompson, Elizabeth Shepherd Lamb. See
Thompson, E. S. L.

T-185　　Thompson, Florence Seyler. A thousand faces / by
Florence Seyler Thompson and George W. Galvin.
Boston: Richard G. Badger; Toronto: The Copp
Clark Co., Limited, [c1915]. 308 p.　　　　**CLU**
LC: O 19, '15.
PW: Ja 15, '16.

Thompson, Frances. Adeste fidelis. In *The rejected
apostle* (1924), R-164.

____ The ebony cross. In *The rejected apostle*
(1924), R-164.

____ Madonna and child. In *The rejected apostle*
(1924), R-164.

T-186　　Thompson, Frank. The transgressor / by Frank
Thompson . . . Boston: Richard G. Badger, [c1920].
([Boston]: The Gorham Press). 193 p.
PW: Mr 20, '20.

T-187　　Thompson, Garrett W. (Garrett William), b. 1867.
Threads: a story / by Garrett W. Thompson.
Philadelphia: The John C. Winston Company, 1905.
344 p.
PW: Je 17, '05.

T-188　　Thompson, Hamilton. The river road: a novel of
New England seacoast folk / by Hamilton Thompson;
frontispiece by George W. Gage. New York: W. J.
Watt & Company, [c1923]. 316 p., front.
LC: Je 15, '23.
PW: Ag 18, '23.

T-189　　[Thompson, Harriet Alfarata], d. 1922. Idealia, a
Utopian dream, or, Resthaven. [Albany, N. Y.: J.
B. Lyon Company, c1923]. 84 p., photo. front.
(port.), [1] leaf of photo. plates.　　　　**NYP**

T-190　　Thompson, I. Owen. Adventures and day dreams /
by I. Owen Thompson; illustrated. Long Beach,
California: [s. n.], 1913. 100 [i.e. 120] p., photo.
ill.
Irregularly paged. Rectos only of leaves bearing
illustrations are counted in pagination.

Contents: Bix, his own master, or, The dawn of day -- The wolf --
On the trail -- The valley of the mirror lake -- Uncle Billy's kid --
From the life of May we pass to December's gray -- True to his
promise -- Nell -- In the mountains -- Christmas in the frozen North
or sunny South -- Forest and stream, or, A dream.

T-191 Thompson, J. Washington (Joseph Washington).
Alice Mansfield's sin, or, The Power of a woman's
love / by J. Washington Thompson . . . Philadelphia,
Pa.: Thompson Publishing Company, 1908. 212 p.,
photo. front. (port.). [Photo. by Balto. Eng. Co.]
PW: Ag 8, '08.

Thompson, Kathleen. The Colonel and "The Lady".
In *Argonaut stories* (1906), A-298.

Thompson, Lillian Bennet. See **Bennet-Thompson,
Lillian.**

T-192 Thompson, Mable N. H. (Mable Naomi Harriet), b.
1890. A life's tragedy / by Mable N. H. Thompson.
Boston: Chapple Publishing Company, Ltd., 1913.
375 p.   **GZW**

T-193 Thompson, Maravene. Persuasive Peggy / by
Maravene Thompson; with four illustrations by
Clarence F. Underwood. New York: Frederick A.
Stokes Company, [c1916]. 308 p., front., [3] leaves
of plates.
LC: Ja 12, '16.
PW: Ja 8, '16.
BLC: London: Hutchinson & Co., 1916.

T-194 _____ The woman's law / by Maravene Thompson;
with eight illustrations by W. D. Goldbeck. New
York: Frederick A. Stokes Company, [c1914].
299 p., front., [7] leaves of plates (1 double-leaf).
LC: Ap 1, '14.
PW: Mr 28, '14.
BLC: London: Eveleigh Nash, 1914.

T-195 Thompson, Marshall Putnam, b. 1869. The
lieutenant, the girl and the viceroy: the story of the
adventurers of these three with Il liberator in South
America / by Marshall Putnam Thompson. Boston:
The C. M. Clark Publishing Co., 1907. 272 p., col.
front., [9] leaves of plates. [Ill. by W. Kirkpatrick.]
LC: Mr 14, '07.

Thompson, Maurice, 1844-1901. The balance of
power. In *Southern lights and shadows* (1907),
S-718.

T-196 _____ Rosalynde's lovers / by Maurice Thompson;
with drawings by G. Alden Peirson. Indianapolis:
The Bowen-Merrill Company, [c1901]. 246, [1] p.,
front., [10] leaves of plates, ill.
LC: F 26, '01.
PW: O 5, '01.
BLC: London: B. F. Stevens & Brown,
1901.
References:References: BAL 20058; Russo &
Sullivan, *Seven Authors*, p. 227-228.

T-197 _____ Sweetheart Manette / by Maurice Thompson
. . . with a frontispiece by Emlen McConnell.
Philadelphia; London: J. B. Lippincott Company,
1901. 259 p., front.   **OCP**

LC: F 26, '01.
PW: Mr 9, '01.
BLC: London: John Macqueen, 1901.
References: BAL 20056; Russo & Sullivan, *Seven
Authors*, p. 226-227.

Thompson, Oella Azuba. See **Slater, S., Jr., pseud.**

T-198 Thompson, Vance, 1863-1925. The carnival of
destiny / by Vance Thompson. New York: Moffat,
Yard & Company, 1916. 314 p., col. front. [Ill. by
G. W. Gage.]
Contents: The passing of the herds -- The Lady of Magdala -- "Make
the bed for Attila" -- The soul of Messer Guido -- The King of
Scotland's daughter -- My Lady Greensleeves -- The emperor's gift --
A tenement of black fumes.
LC: Ap 17, '16.
PW: Ap 8, '16.

_____ The day of Daheimus. In *The Grim thirteen*
(1917), G-537.

T-199 _____ Diplomatic mysteries / by Vance Thompson;
illustrated. Philadelphia; London: J. B. Lippincott
Company, 1905. 379 p., front., [7] leaves of plates.
[Ill. by Arthur E. Jameson, H. McCormick, H. G.
Williamson, and Gordon Grant.]
Contents: The undoing of a king -- The great Austrian conspiracy --
The sultan's secret agents -- A crown prince's escapade -- The fight
between France and the Vatican -- The truth about President Faure --
The lady of the opals -- Tolstoi, the one free man in Russia -- "Made
in England " -- How revolutions are made in Russia.
PW: Je 3, '05.

T-200 _____ The green ray / by Vance Thompson.
Indianapolis: The Bobbs-Merrill Company, [c1924].
310 p.
LC: O 10, '24.
BLC: London: Hutchinson & Co., [1925].

T-201 _____ Mr. Guelpa: the famous French detective
visits America and finds the most baffling mystery of
his career awaiting him / by Vance Thompson.
Indianapolis: The Bobbs-Merrill Company, [c1925].
339 p.
LC: N 30, '25.
BLC: London: Hutchinson & Co., 1926.

T-202 _____ The pointed tower: a novel / by Vance
Thompson; illustrated by Gerald Leake. Indianapolis:
The Bobbs-Merrill Company, [c1923]. 329 p.,
front., [3] leaves of plates.
LC: F 1, '23.
PW: Ja 20, '23.
BLC: London: Hutchinson & Co., [1923].

T-203 _____ The scarlet iris / by Vance Thompson . . . ;
illustrated by A. D. Rahn. Indianapolis: The
Bobbs-Merrill Company, [c1924]. 312 p., front., [3]
leaves of plates.
LC: F 28, '24.
PW: Mr 15, '24.

T-204 _____ Spinners of life / by Vance Thompson;
illustrated by E. M. Ashe and Rollin Kirby.
Philadelphia; London: J. B. Lippincott Company,
1903. 294 p., front., [3] leaves of plates.
PW: My 9, '03.
BLC: London: Methuen & Co., 1904.

T-205   Thomson, Charles Goff. Terry: a tale of the hill people / by Charles Goff Thomson. New York: The Macmillan Company, 1921. 275 p.
LC: Ap 6, '21.
BLC: London & New York: Andrew Melrose, 1923.

T-206   Thomson, Edith. Afterglow / by Edith Thomson. New York: E. P. Dutton & Company, [c1922]. 273 p.
PW: My 20, '22.
BLC: London: J. Bale & Co., printed in U. S. A., 1922.

Thomson, Margaret. In the firelight. In *A book of narratives* (1917), **B-734.**

Thomson, Priscilla Norton, Mrs. See **Norton-Thomson, L., Mrs.**

T-207   Thorndyke, George Howard. The witch's castle / by George Howard Thorndyke. Knoxville, Tennessee: Published by Life & Letters Co., [c1903]. 300 p., photo. front., photo. ill., music, plan.

T-208   Thorne, Grace Evelyn. Montana, a romance of the western plains / by Grace Evelyn Thorne. Founded on the phenomenally successful play of the same name by Harry D. Carey . . . New York City: The Harry D. Carey Amusement Co., c1906. 150 p., incl. front., ill. (incl. ports.).
Unexamined copy: bibliographic data from NUC.

T-209   Thorne, Jack, b. 1863, *pseud.* Hanover, or, The persecution of the lowly: a story of the Wilmington massacre / by Jack Thorne [pseud.]. [S. l.]: Published by M. C. L. Hill, [1901]. 136 p.
Unexamined copy: bibliographic data from OCLC, #1472851.

Thorne, Mabel, jt. aut. *The secret toll* (1922). See **Thorne, Paul, jt. aut., T-210.**

____, jt. aut. *The Sheridan Road mystery* (1921). See **Thorne, Paul, jt. aut., T-211.**

T-210   Thorne, Paul. The secret toll / by Paul and Mabel Thorne. New York: Dodd, Mead and Company, 1922. 268 p.
LC: Je 20, '22.

T-211   ____ The Sheridan Road mystery / by Paul and Mabel Thorne. New York: Dodd, Mead and Company, 1921. 291 p.
LC: N 2, '21.
PW: D 10, '21.

Thorne, Victor, pseud. See **Jackson, Frederick, b. 1886.**

T-212   Thornton, A. G. An astronomer at large / by A. G. Thornton. New York; London; G. P. Putnam's Sons, 1924. ([New York]: The Knickerbocker Press). 374 p.
BLC: London & New York: Andrew Melrose, 1924.

T-213   Thornton, Amasa. An old-fashioned woman / by Amasa Thornton. New York City: The Sherwood Company, 1913. 145 p.   **DLC**
Imprint from label. Imprint under label reads: New York, Printed for the author by Burr Printing House.

T-214   Thornton, Marcellus Eugene, 1846-1924. The lady of New Orleans: a novel of the present / by Marcellus Eugene Thornton. London; New York; Montreal: The Abbey Press . . . , [c1901]. 330 p., photo. front.
PW: Mr 29, '02.

T-215   Thornton, Mary Taylor. When Pan pipes: a fantastic romance / by Mary Taylor Thornton. New York: George H. Doran Company, [1916]. 408 p.
Illustrated lining papers signed by F. Rogers.
PW: Je 17, '16.
BLC: London: Sampson Low & Co., [1915].

T-216   Thorpe, Betty. Fioretta, or, O cessate di piagarmi / by Betty Thorpe; illustrated by Don Blanding. Honolulu: Advertising Publishing Co., 1922. 63 p., photo. front. (port.), ill.   **NYP**

T-217   Thorpe, Francis Newton, 1857-1926. The divining rod: a story of the oil regions / by Francis Newton Thorpe . . . Boston: Little, Brown, and Company, 1905. 356 p.
PW: N 4, '05.

T-218   ____ The spoils of empire: a romance of the Old World and the New / by Francis Newton Thorpe; illustrated by Frank B. Masters. Boston: Little, Brown, 1903. 421 p., front., [5] leaves of plates.
PW: My 9, '03.

Thrice, Luke, pseud. See **Russell, John, 1885-1956.**

T-219   Thrice told tales: thirteen re-prints of stories: written for the advanced course in story writing, Columbia University (Extension Division) / with an introduction by Blanche Colton Williams . . . New York: Dodd, Mead and Company, 1924. 315 p.
Contents: Fifty-two weeks for Florette / Elizabeth Alexander -- Wasted / Mary Arbuckle -- Natalka's portion / Rose Cohen -- The kiss of the accolade / James W. Bennett -- The destiny of Dan IV / Samuel A. Derieux -- The cat of the cane-brake / Frederick Stuart Greene -- "Contact!" / Frances Noyes Hart -- Per contra / Harry Anable Kniffin -- Butterflies / Rose Sidney -- The wall / Harriet Welles -- Turkey red / Frances Gilchrist Wood.

T-220   Throckmorton, Josephine Holt. Donald MacDonald / by Josephine Holt Throckmorton. Washington, D. C.: The Neale Publishing Co., c1907. 142 p. **DLC**
LC: Je 3, '07.
Another edition: Murdock McPhee & Co., [c1907].

T-221   ____ Sergeant Jimmy. Washington, D. C.: Judd & Detweiler, Inc., [c1911]. 170 p., plates.
Unexamined copy: bibliographic data from OCLC, #23876058.
LC: Je 12, '11.

T-222   Through the forbidden gates: and other stories. Boston, U. S. A.: The Shortstory Publishing Co., [c1903]. 248 p.   **NOC**
Contents: Through the forbidden gates / Carroll Carrington --

Margaret Kelly's wake / S. C. Brean -- A celestial crime / Charles
Stuart Pratt -- For the sake of Lize / C. B. Lewis -- The music of
money / Newt. Newkirk -- The diamond drill and Mary / H. J. W.
Dam -- Hans Kremler's anniversary / Elisabeth F. Dye -- The vase of
the Mikado / A. Earnest B. Lane -- On pigeon river / Jeanie Drake --
The smile of Joss / William J. Neidig -- The king of the subdivision /
James O'Shaughnessy -- The pillow of justice / E. S. Innet -- The lost
jurisdiction / Ellis Meredith -- The diary of a white kaffir / James O.
Fagan -- The statement of Jared Johnson / Geraldine Bonner -- The
levitation of Jacob / Clifford Howard -- The white brick / F. E.
Chase -- When time turned / Ethel Watts Mumford -- The family
skeleton's wedding journey / Annie F. Johnston -- Missing / Mary
Boardman Sheldon.

T-223   Thruston, Lucy Meacham Kidd, b. 1862. Called to
         the field: a story of Virginia in the Civil War / by
         Lucy Meacham Thruston. Boston: Little, Brown and
         Company, 1906. 340 p.
         PW: Mr 3, '06.

T-224   ____ A girl of Virginia / by Lucy M. Thruston . . . ;
         with a frontispiece by Ch. Grunwald. Boston: Little,
         Brown, and Company, 1902. 306 p., front.   **CLE**
         PW: Je 14, '02.

T-225   ____ Jenifer / by Lucy Meacham Thruston; with a
         frontispiece by J. W. Kennedy. Boston: Little,
         Brown, and Company, 1907. 298 p., front., [3]
         leaves of plates.
         LC: My 1, '07.

T-226   ____ Mistress Brent: a story of Lord Baltimore's
         colony in 1638 / by Lucy Meacham Thruston;
         illustrated by Charles Grunwald. Boston: Little,
         Brown and Company, 1901. 352 p., front., [4]
         leaves of plates.
         PW: O 12, '01.

T-227   ____ Where the tide comes in / by Lucy Meacham
         Thruston; illustrated by Ch. Grunwald. Boston:
         Little, Brown, and Company, 1904. 391 p., front.,
         [5] leaves of plates.
         PW: Ap 9, '04.

T-228   Thurber, Robert Bruce, 1882-1947. Mr. Ingle comes
         through / by Robert Bruce Thurber . . . Nashville,
         Tennessee: Southern Publishing Association,
         [c1924]. 128 p., photo. ill.   **NCU**

T-229   Thurman, Mary Cochran. Sketches in ebony and
         gold / by Mary Cochran Thurman. Montreal; New
         York; London: Broadway Publishing Company,
         [c1902]. 148 p., front. (port.).
         PW: D 19, '03.

T-230   Thurston, Mabel Nelson, b. 1869. On the road to
         Arcady / By Mabel Nelson Thurston; illustrated by
         Samuel M. Palmer. New York; Chicago; Toronto,
         [etc.]: Fleming H. Revell Company, [c1903].
         232 p., col. front. Illustrated end papers.
         PW: O 31, '03.

T-231   ____ Sarah Ann / by Mabel Nelson Thurston; with
         illustrations by E. C. Caswell. New York: Dodd,
         Mead and Company, 1917. 230 p., front., [3] leaves
         of plates.   **ABC**
         LC: S 11, '17.
         PW: S 8, '17.

T-232   Thwing, Eugene, 1866-1936. The man from Red
         Keg / by Eugene Thwing . . . ; illustrations by Walter
         H. Everett. New York: Dodd, Mead and Company,
         1905. 431 p., front., [5] leaves of plates.
         PW: N 4, '05.

T-233   ____ The Red-Keggers / by Eugene Thwing;
         illustrations by W. Herbert Dunton. New York: The
         Book-Lover Press, 1903. 429 p., front., [9] leaves of
         plates.
         BLC: London: Hodder & Stoughton, 1904.
         PW: S 5, '03.

T-234   Tibbals, Seymour Selden, b. 1869. When Monty
         came home from the Marne; a monolog . . .
         Franklin, Ohio: Eldridge Entertainment House,
         c1918. [8] p.
         Unexamined copy: bibliographic data from OCLC,
         #20219811.

         Tibbetts, Edgar Alfred, 1848-1908. See **Jonsson,
         Ivar, pseud.**

T-235   Tibbitts, George F. (George Franklin), b. 1864. The
         mystery of Kun-Ja-Muck cave / by George F.
         Tibbitts; frontispiece by Frank R. Southard. New
         York: Published by Brieger Press, Inc., [c1924].
         319 p., col. front.

         Tichborne, Josephine Caroline. See **Sawyer,
         Josephine.**

         Tiernan, Francis Christine (Fisher), Mrs., 1846-1920.
         See **Reid, Christian, pseud.**

T-236   Tietjens, Eunice Hammond, 1884-1944. Jake / by
         Eunice Tietjens. New York: Boni and Liveright,
         [c1921]. 221 p.
         LC: Ap 8, '21.

T-237   Tilden, Freeman, b. 1883. Khaki: how Tredick got
         into the war / by Freeman Tilden; frontispiece by J.
         Henry. New York: The Macmillan Company, 1918.
         220 p., front.
         LC: Jl 10, '18.

T-238   ____ Mr. Podd / by Freeman Tilden. New York:
         The Macmillan Company, 1923. 288 p.
         LC: Je 13, '23.
         PW: Jl 7, '23.

T-239   ____ That night: and other satires / by Freeman
         Tilden. New York: Hearst's International Library
         Co., 1915. 324 p., front. Reprinted in part from
         various periodicals.
         Contents: That night -- The defective -- The good influence --
         Artistic temperament -- O perfect love -- The optimist -- Prison-made
         -- Wildcats -- The lesser fleas -- The hero -- The necessity for
         remaining dead -- The man with a country -- L'envoi: no-time.
         LC: S 27, '15.
         PW: O 23, '15.

T-240   ____ The virtuous husband / by Freeman Tilden.
         New York: The Macmillan Company, 1925. 492 p.
         LC: Jl 8, '25.
         PW: S 12, '25.

T-241   Tilden, William T., 1893-1953. It's all in the game: and other tennis tales / by William T. Tilden, 2nd; illustrated by Arthur Schwieder. Garden City, N. Y.; Toronto: Doubleday, Page & Company, 1922. 245 p., front., [3] leaves of plates.
Contents: It's all in the game -- Dick takes the chair -- The come-back of Dick Thomas -- Food for thought -- Two up, luck, and three to play -- The hole in the pinch -- On a line with the net -- Mine! -- The ghost of Wimbledon -- They also serve -- "The hour-glass" -- The double cross -- The alibi-buster -- Bye-bye, alibi -- Mixed troubles.
LC: Mr 18, '22.
BLC: London: Methuen & Co., 1922.

T-242   ____ The phantom drive: and other tennis stories / by William T. Tilden. New York: American Lawn Tennis, 1924. 235 p., photo. front., [9] leaves of photo. plates. **YQR**
Contents: The phantom drive -- The drive from the sideline -- The double comeback -- The double cross -- The amateur -- The ghost of Wimbledon -- "Ito" -- They also serve -- On a line with the net -- "Mine!" -- Food for thought -- Mixed troubles.

T-243   ____ The pinch quitter: and other tennis stories for junior players / by William T. Tilden. New York: American Lawn Tennis, 1924. 202 p., photo. front. (port.), [4] leaves of photo. plates. **KSU**
Contents: The pinch quitter -- The love game -- Brickie's game point -- Brickie gets a goat -- It's all in the game -- Dick takes the chair -- The come-back of Dick Thomas -- Two up, luck, and three to play -- The hole in the pinch -- The alibi buster -- Bye-bye, alibi.

Tildesley, Alice L. Half-past ten. In *The best short stories of 1916 and the yearbook of the American short story* (1917), **B-561**.

T-244   Tileston, Merrill. Chiquita: an American novel: the romance of a Ute Chief's daughter / by Merrill Tileston. Chicago, U. S. A.: Published by the Merrill Company, 1902. 306 p., col. front., [7] leaves of col. plates.
PW: Jl 12, '02.

T-245   Tilford, Tilden, 1876-1926. Butternut Jones: a lambkin of the West / by Tilden Tilford. New York: D. Appleton and Company, 1903. 370 p., front.
PW: N 21, '03.

T-246   Tilghman, Zoe A. (Zoe Agnes), b. 1880. The dugout / by Zoe A. Tilghman. Oklahoma City: Harlow Publishing Company, 1925. 107 p. **OKU**

T-247   Tillinghast, Ada Whitton. Cobble Valley golf yarns and other sketches / by A. W. Tillinghast. Philadelphia, Pa.: Philadelphia Printing and Publishing Co., [c1915]. 295 p., ill. **MNU**
Contents: The outcasts -- One every minute -- The home hole -- A woman's way -- The Jonah Breakers -- Once to every man -- Putting it over Matthew -- The yellow streak -- The philanthropist -- The spur -- From the shoulder -- The Wellington emerald -- Tess and company -- On Hallowe'en -- King's men -- By speedometer -- Christmas Eve -- In the bag -- The runner-up.

T-248   Tilton, Dwight, *jt. pseud.* The golden greyhound: a novel / by Dwight Tilton [jt. pseud.] . . . ; illustrated by E. Pollak. Boston: Lothrop, Lee & Shepard Co., [1906]. 366 p., incl. front., [4] leaves of plates.
PW: Mr 24, '06.
BLC: London: Dean & Son, 1906.

T-249   [____] Letters from a son to his self-made father:

being the replies to letters from a self-made merchant to his son / by Charles Eustace Merriman [jt. pseud.]; illustrations by Fred Kulz. Boston, Mass.: New Hampshire Publishing Corporation, 1903. 289 p., front., [5] leaves of plates.
PW: D 12, '03.

T-250   ____ Meyer & Son: a novel / by Dwight Tilton [jt. pseud.] . . . Boston, Massachusetts: C. M. Clark Publishing Company, 1908. 323 p., front., [7] leaves of plates. [Ill. by John Goss.]
"Based upon the three-act play of the same name by Thomas Addison."
PW: D 12, '08.

T-251   ____ Miss Petticoats / by Dwight Tilton [jt. pseud.]; with illustrations by Charles H. Stephens. Boston: C. M. Clark Publishing Company, 1902. 377 p., col. front., [6] leaves of col. plates.
PW: My 24, '02.
BLC: London: Ward, Lock & Co., printed in U. S. A., 1903.

T-252   ____ My Lady Laughter: a romance of Boston town in the days of the great siege / by Dwight Tilton [jt. pseud.] . . . ; illustrations by Charles H. Stephens. Boston, Mass.: C. M. Clark Publishing Co. (Inc.), [c1904]. 442 p., col. front., [9] leaves of col. plates.
PW: D 3, '04.
BLC: London: Dean & Son, [U. S. A. printed], 1905.

T-253   ____ On Satan's mount / by Dwight Tilton [jt. pseud.] . . . ; illustrations by Charles H. Stephens. Boston: C. M. Clark Publishing Company, 1903. 459 p., front.
PW: Mr 7, '03.
BLC: London: Ward, Lock & Co., printed in the United States of America, 1904.

T-254   [____] A self-made man's wife: her letters to her son, being the woman's view of certain famous correspondence / by Charles Eustace Merriman [jt. pseud.]. . . ; illustrated by F. T. Richards. New York; London: G. P. Putnam's Sons, 1905. ([New York]: The Knickerbocker Press). 249 p., front., [5] leaves of plates.
PW: Mr 25, '05.

T-255   Tincker, M. A. (Mary Agnes), 1831-1907. Grapes and thorns, or, A priest's sacrifice / by M. A. Tincker . . . New York: Copyright . . . by Christian Press Association Publishing Co. . . , 1909. 286 p.

T-256   Tingle, Anna Adams. The Barleyville sewin' circle: discuss "syance what ain't syance" / by Anna Adams Tingle; illustrated by C. S. Hammock. [Moville, Iowa?: s. n., 1903?]. 168 p., [5] leaves of plates (incl. photo. port.). **CNO**

T-257   Tinley, J. W. (James Walter), b. 1866. The influence of a single life / by Rev. J. W. Tinley . . . Atlanta, Ga.: The Franklin Printing and Publishing Co., 1902. 204 p., photo. front. (port.). Designed end papers. **GPM**

T-258   Tinsley, Lelia M. (Lelia Mary). Setting the golden egg: being the prayer of a woman for the union and growth of science and art in this day of human upheaval / Lelia M. Tinsley . . . New York: The Tinsley Company, [c1916]. 128 p.   **DLC**

Tisdale, Lieu. See **L. G. T.**

T-259   Titterington, Sophie Bronson. The voice of a child / by Sophie Bronson Titterington. New York: American Tract Society, [c1912]. 58 p.   **DLC**

T-260   Titus, Charles Buttz, b. 1863. Sam Wang's college; or, China won / by Charles Buttz Titus, A. B. . . . Boston, U. S. A.: The Christopher Publishing House, [c1925]. 120 p.   **BSC**
PW: Ap 18, '25.
Another edition: New Castle, IN.: The author, 1921. 29 p.
Unexamined copy: bibliographic data from OCLC, #20792709.

T-261   Titus, Harold, b. 1888. The beloved pawn / by Harold Titus. -- 1st ed. -- Garden City, New York: Doubleday, Page & Company, 1923. 316 p.
LC: N 3, '23.
PW: N 3, '23.
BLC: London: Hodder & Stoughton, [1924].

T-262   ____ Bruce of the Circle A / by Harold Titus . . . ; illustrated. Boston; Small, Maynard & Company, [c1918]. 294 p., front., [2] leaves of plates. [Front. by G. W. Gage; ill. by Stanley L. Wood.]
LC: My 6, '18.
PW: Je 1, '18.
BLC: London: Hodder & Stoughton, [1922].

T-263   ____ "--I conquered" / by Harold Titus; with a frontispiece in color by Charles M. Russell. Chicago: Rand, McNally & Company, [c1916]. 302 p., col. front.
LC: Mr 20, '16.
PW: Mr 18, '16.

T-264   ____ The last straw / by Harold Titus; illustrated by George W. Gage. Boston: Small, Maynard & Company, [c1920]. 288 p.
LC: Mr 17, '20.
PW: Ap 3, '20.
BLC: London: Hodder & Stoughton, [1921].

T-265   ____ Spindrift: a novel of the Great Lakes / by Harold Titus. Garden City, New York: Doubleday, Page & Company, 1925. 326 p.   **CLE**
LC: Ja 29, '25.
BLC: London: Hodder & Stoughton, [1924].

T-266   ____ "Timber" / by Harold Titus . . . Boston: Small, Maynard & Company, [c1922]. 379 p.
LC: Ap 8, '22.
PW: Ap 29, '22.
BLC: London: Hodder & Stoughton, [1923].

T-267   Tobenkin, Elias, 1882-1963. God of might / by Elias Tobenkin . . . New York: Minton, Balch & Company, 1925. 272 p.
LC: Mr 18, '25.
PW: F 28, '25.

T-268   ____ The house of Conrad / by Elias Tobenkin. New York: Frederick A. Stokes Company, [c1918]. 375 p., front. [Ill. by J. Henry.]
LC: Mr 11, '18.
PW: Mr 16, '18.

T-269   ____ The road / by Elias Tobenkin. New York: Harcourt, Brace and Company, [c1922]. 316 p.
LC: F 3, '22.
PW: Ja 28, '22.

T-270   ____ Witte arrives: a novel / by Elias Tobenkin; with a frontispiece by J. Henry. New York: Frederick A. Stokes Company, [c1916]. 304 p., front.
LC: Ag 28, '16.
PW: Ag 26, '16.

T-271   Todd, Harry Coulter. The white slave: a novel / by Harry Coulter Todd . . . New York: The Neale Publishing Company, 1913. 274 p.
LC: S 4, '13.
PW: Ja 17, '14.

T-272   Todd, Mary Ives, b. 1849. An American Abelard & Heloise: a love story / by Mary Ives Todd. New York: The Grafton Press, [c1904]. 337 p.

T-273   ____ An American madonna: a story of love / by Mary Ives Todd. New York: The Binghamton Book Mfg. Co., 1908. 264 p., front., [2] leaves of plates.   **DLC**
LC: Ja 5, '08.

T-274   ____ Just friends: a common sense story / by Mary Ives Todd . . . New York: Calkins and Company, 1908. 150 p., incl. front., ill. (ports.).   **DLC**
LC: Je 2, '08.

T-275   ____ Violina, or, Poland and liberty: a romance / by Mary Ives Todd. New York: Published by John L. Strus, [c1904]. 268 p., front., [10] leaves of plates. [Front. signed by Winterhalter.]
PW: Ag 20, '04.

Togo, Hashimura, pseud. See **Irwin, Wallace.**

T-276   Tokalon, Zeteo. The pale youth and other stories / Zeteo Tokalon . . . Boston: The Montmartre Publishers, [1925]. 94 p.   **CRB**
Contents: The story of the pale youth -- A recollection -- The five is out -- Coincidence -- A week without Sunday -- Forced inebriation -- Elizabeth -- Love [poem] -- My pilgrimage -- Free love -- Yellow versus blue -- Honi soit qui mal y pense -- The usual thing -- Contrasting types -- Squalor inter nos provenit.

T-277   Toldridge, Elizabeth. The soul of love / by Elizabeth Toldridge. New York: Broadway Publishing Co., [c1910]. 104 p.
Contents: The greeting -- The parting -- Memory glow -- The rock of vision -- Love's highest note.
LC: D 24, '10.

T-278   Tomlinson, Everett T. (Everett Titsworth),
1859-1931. Captain Dan Richards / by Evertt T.
Tomlinson . . . ; illustrated. New York, N. Y.;
Newark, N. J.: Barse & Hopkins, [c1912]. 300 p.,
front.
Copyright records: Philadelphia, Boston, [etc.]: The
Griffith & Rowland Press, [1914]; 2 c. Ap 6, '14.

T-279   _____ Elder Boise: a novel / by Everett Tomlinson.
New York: Doubleday, Page & Co., 1901. 403 p.
PW: Je 22, '01.

T-280   _____ The fruit of the desert / by Everett T.
Tomlinson. Philadelphia: The Griffith & Rowland
Press, 1907. 324 p., front., [3] leaves of plates. [Ill.
by Frank McKernan.]
LC: S 25, '07.

T-281   _____ The self-effacement of Malachi Joseph / by
Everett T. Tomlinson . . . Philadelphia: The Griffith
& Rowland Press, 1906. 236 p., front., [3] leaves of
plates. [Ill. by Frank McKernan.]
LC: Ag 2, '07.

T-282   _____ The sifting of Philip / by Everett T. Tomlinson
. . . Philadelphia; Boston; New York; Chicago; St.
Louis; Atlanta; Dallas: American Baptist Publication
Society, [1908]. 297 p., front., [3] leaves of plates.
[Ill. by Frank McKernan.]   **DLC**
LC: O 16, '08.

T-283   _____ The winner / by Everett T. Tomlinson . . .
Philadelphia: The Griffith & Rowland Press, 1903.
308 p., front., [11] leaves of plates. [Ill. by F.
McKernan.]
PW: O 31, '03.

T-284   Tompkins, Ellen Wilkins. The egotistical I / by Ellen
Wilkins Tompkins. New York: E. P. Dutton &
Company, [c1913]. 172 p.   **OSO**

T-285   _____ The enlightenment of Paulina: a novel / by
Ellen Wilkins Tompkins . . . New York: E. P.
Dutton & Co., [c1917]. 335 p.
LC: O 19, '17.
PW: O 27, '17.

Tompkins, Florence. <u>See</u> **Dendron, Bertram,
pseud.**

T-286   Tompkins, Juliet Wilbor, 1871-1956. At the sign of
the oldest house: a modern romance / by Juliet
Wilbor Tompkins; illustrated by Edward L. Chase.
Indianapolis: The Bobbs-Merrill Company, [c1917].
217, [1] p., front., [15] leaves of plates.
LC: N 21, '17.
PW: D 1, '17.

T-287   _____ Diantha / Juliet Wilbor Tompkins. New York:
The Century Co., 1915. 262 p., front. [Ill. by P. D.
Johnson.]
LC: Je 2, '15.

T-288   _____ Dr. Ellen / by Juliet Wilbor Tompkins. New
York: The Baker & Taylor Company, [1908].
280 p., col. front.

Cover title: Doctor Ellen.
LC: Ja 16, '08.
PW: F 1, '08.

T-289   _____ Ever after / by Juliet Wilbor Tompkins;
frontispiece. Garden City, N. Y.: Doubleday, Page
& Company, 1913. 287, [1] p., col. front.
LC: My 19, '13.
PW: My 31, '13.

T-290   _____ A girl named Mary / by Juliet Wilbor
Tompkins; with illustrations by Frederic R. Gruger.
Indianapolis: The Bobbs-Merrill Company, [c1918].
256 p., front., [4] leaves of plates.
LC: Jl 29, '18.
PW: Jl 27, '18.

T-291   _____ Joanna builds a nest / by Juliet Wilbor
Tompkins; illustrated by Ethel C. Taylor.
Indianapolis: The Bobbs-Merrill Company, [c1920].
256, [1] p., front., [3] leaves of plates. Illustrated
end papers.
LC: O 9, '20.
PW: O 9, '20.

T-292   _____ A line a day / by Juliet Wilbor Tompkins;
illustrated by John Alonzo Williams. Indianapolis:
The Bobbs-Merrill Company, [c1923]. 302 p.,
front., [3] leaves of plates.
LC: O 19, '23.
PW: N 3, '23.

T-293   _____ Mothers and fathers / by Juliet Wilbor
Tompkins. New York: The Baker & Taylor Co.,
1910. 373 p., col. front. [Ill. by Alice B. Stephens.]
Contents: Weatherby's mother -- Elsie's return -- The real tragedy --
The house to themselves -- Constance Dorothes -- The lady from
California -- Telling Kate -- Something -- A mother of four -- The
riper years -- Nature -- The viper -- The house beautiful -- The
modern way -- My mother's diary -- A spoiled old lady -- The rule of
the magnificent -- The thrifty Sarah.
LC: O 17, '10.

T-294   _____ Open house / by Juliet Wilbor Tompkins . . .
New York: The Baker & Taylor Company, [1909].
276 p., front. [Ill. by F. Graham Cootes.]
LC: Ja 18, '09.
PW: Ja 30, '09.

T-295   _____ Pleasures and palaces: being the home-making
adventures of Marie Rose / by Juliet Wilbor
Tompkins; illustrated by Howard Chandler Christy.
Garden City, New York: Doubleday, Page &
Company, 1912. 236 p., front., [12] leaves of plates
(2 double-leaf).
LC: Mr 30, '12.
PW: Ap 6, '12.
BLC: London: Hodder & Stoughton, Garden City,
N. Y. printed, 1912.

T-296   _____ The seed of the righteous / by Juliet Wilbor
Tompkins; illustrated by Lucius W. Hitchcock.
Indianapolis: The Bobbs-Merrill Company, [c1916].
270 p., front., [4] leaves of plates.
LC: Ap 27, '16.
PW: Ap 15, '16.

T-297   _____ The starling / by Juliet Wilbor Tompkins . . . ;

illustrated by John Alonzo Williams. Indianapolis: The Bobbs-Merrill Company, [c1919]. 267 p., front., [3] leaves of plates.
LC: Jl 5, '19.

T-298 _____ The top of the morning / by Juliet Wilbor Tompkins . . . New York: The Baker & Taylor Company, 1910. 342 p., col. front. [Ill. by Z. P. Nikolaki.]　　　　　　　　　　　　**CLU**
LC: Ja 31, '10.
PW: F 19, '10.

T-299 Toohey, John Peter, b. 1880. Fresh every hour: detailing the adventures, comic and pathetic of one Jimmy Martin, purveyor of publicity, a young gentleman possessing sublime nerve, whimsical imagination, colossal impudence, and, withal, the heart of a child / by John Peter Toohey. New York: Boni and Liveright, [c1922]. 256 p.

Tooker, Gertrude Fulton. Her birthright. In *Club stories* (1915), C-502.

T-300 Tooker, L. Frank (Lewis Frank), 1855-1925. The middle passage / by L. Frank Tooker . . . New York: The Century Co., 1920. 272 p.
LC: S 21, '20.
PW: S 25, '20.

T-301 _____ Under rocking skies / by L. Frank Tooker . . . New York: The Century Co., 1905. 282 p., incl. [5] leaves of plates, front.
PW: O 7, '05.

Toomer, Jean. Blood-burning moon. In *The best short stories of 1923 and the yearbook of the American short story* (1924), B-568.

T-302 _____ Cane / by Jean Toomer; with a foreword by Waldo Frank . . . New York: Boni and Liveright, [c1923]. 239 p.
LC: S 13, '23.
PW: O 20, '23.

T-303 Tootle, Harry King. The daughter of David Kerr / by Harry King Tootle; with illustrations by M. Leone Bracker. Chicago: A. C. McClurg & Co., 1912. 343 p., col. front., [4] leaves of plates.
LC: S 9, '12.

Tope, J. Leroy. See *The Blood of Venus,* (1910), B-682.

T-304 Torbett, D. Common clay: a novelization of Cleves Kinkead's drama / by D. Torbett; illustrated from photographs of the play. New York: Edward J. Clode, [c1916]. 354 p., photo. front., [7] leaves of photo. plates.
LC: Mr 21, '16.
PW: Ap 1, '16.

T-305 _____ Kick-in: a novelization of Willard Mack's play / by D. Torbett; illustrated from photographs of the play. New York: Edward J. Clode, [c1915]. 279 p., photo. front., [7] leaves of photo. plates.
LC: S 15, '15.
PW: O 16, '15.

T-306 _____ The land of promise: a novelization of W. Somerset Maugham's play / by D. Torbett; illustrated from photographs of the play. New York: Edward J. Clode Publisher, [c1914]. 312 p., photo. front., [5] leaves of photo. plates.
LC: Ap 1, '14.

T-307 _____ Life: a novelization of Thompson Buchanan's play / by D. Torbett; illustrated from photographs of the play. New York: E. J. Clode, [c1915]. 343 p., photo. front. (port.), photo. plates.
Unexamined copy: bibliographic data from OCLC, #6339075.
LC: F 25, '15.
PW: Mr 13, '15.

T-308 _____ On trial: the story of a woman at bay / by Elmer L. Reizenstein; made into a book from the play of the same name by D. Torbett; illustrated. New York: Dodd, Mead & Company, 1915. 328 p., photo. front., [7] leaves of photo. plates. [Photo. by White, New York.]
LC: S 22, '15.

T-309 _____ The schemers / by D. Torbett. New York: C. H. Doscher & Co., [c1908]. 157 p.
LC: Mr 2, '08.
PW: Mr 21, '08.

T-310 _____ Sinners: a novelization of Owen Davis's play / by D. Torbett; illustrated from photographs of the play. New York: Edward J. Clode, [c1915]. 302 p., front., [7] leaves of plates.
LC: Je 22, '15.
PW: Jl 10, '15.

Torrey, Grace. The record quarter. In *California story book* (1909), C-40.

T-311 Torrey, Jane Anne, b. 1868. Alice in Sunderland / by Jane Anne Torrey. New York: Cochrane Publishing Co., 1909. 153 p.　　**AZS**
LC: O 6, '09.

Torrey, Marian (Richards). See **Richards, Marian Edwards.**

T-312 Totten, Joseph Byron, b. 1875. The cowboy and the squaw: a novel founded upon the play of the same title / by Joseph Byron Totten. Baltimore, Md.: I. & M. Ottenheimer, 1908. 94 p.

T-313 Totten, Martha Barr. Lew Ott / by Martha Barr Totten. [S. l.: s. n., c1909]. 181 p.　　**DLC**

T-314 Towndrow, Grace Eleanore. The career of joy / by Grace Eleanore Towndrow; frontispiece by Isabella Morton. Boston, Massachusetts: The C. M. Clark Publishing Company, 1909. 231 p., front.
LC: O 8, '09.

T-315 Towne, Belle Kellogg. Snowflakes and heartaches / by Belle Kellogg Towne. Elgin, Illinois: David C. Cook Publishing Co., [c1912]. 64 p., ill. [Ill. by E. C. Caswell.]

T-316　　Towne, Charles Hanson, 1877-1949. The bad man: a novel / by Charles Hanson Towne; based on the play by Porter Emerson Browne. New York; London: G. P. Putnam's Sons, 1921. (New York: The Knickerbocker Press). 279 p., photo. front. (port.).
LC: F 7, '21.
PW: Ja 29, '21.

T-317　　____ The chain: a novel / by Charles Hanson Towne. New York; London: G. P. Putnam's Sons, 1922. (New York: The Knickerbocker Press). 364 p.
LC: S 14, '22.
PW: S 9, '22.

T-318　　____ The gay ones / by Charles Hanson Towne . . . New York; London: Published by The Century Co., [c1924]. 323 p.
LC: Mr 24, '24.
PW: Ap 5, '24.

____ Shelby. In *The best short stories of 1921 and the yearbook of the American short story* (1922), B-566.

T-319　　Townes, William Tunstall, b. 1854. With hooks of steel: a tale of old-time Virginia / by William T. Townes. New York: The Neale Publishing Company, 1913. 216 p.

Townsend, C. H. Gregory and the scuttle. In *Atlantic narratives*; 2nd series (1918), A-361.

T-320　　Townsend, Charles, b. 1857. The Mahoney million / by Charles Townsend; with illustrations by Clare Angell. New York: New Amsterdam Book Company, 1903. 215 p., col. front., [3] leaves of plates.
PW: Ap 26, '02.

T-321　　Townsend, Edward W. (Edward Waterman), 1855-1942. Chimmie Fadden and Mr. Paul / by Edward W. Townsend; illustrated by Albert Levering. New York: Printed by The Century Co., 1902. 382 p., ill.
PW: My 10, '02.
BLC: Toronto: Copp Clark Co., 1902.

T-322　　____ The climbing Courvatels / by Edward W. Townsend . . . ; with eight full-page illustrations in colour by J. V. McFall. New York: Frederick A. Stokes Company, [1909]. 290 p., col. front., [7] leaves of col. plates.
LC: F 5, '09.

T-323　　____ Days like these: a novel / by Edward W. Townsend. New York; London: Harper & Brothers, 1901. 443, [1] p.
PW: Je 1, '01.

T-324　　____ Fort Birkett: a story of mountain adventure / by Edward W. Townsend. New York: W. J. Ritchie, 1903. 277 p., front. [Ill. by Albert Levering.]
PW: Jl 4, '03.

T-325　　____ Lees & leaven: a New York story of to-day / by Edward W. Townsend. New York: McClure, Phillips & Co., 1903. 299 p.
PW: Mr 7, '03.
BLC: London: McClure, Phillips & Co., 1903.

T-326　　____ Reuben Larkmead: a story of worldlings / by Edward W. Townsend; illustrations by Wallace Morgan. New York: G. W. Dillingham Company, [1905]. 205 p., front., [10] leaves of plates.
PW: Ap 1, '05.
BLC: London: T. Fisher Unwin, New York [printed], 1905.

T-327　　____ A summer in New York: a love story told in letters / by Edward W. Townsend . . . New York: Henry Holt and Company, 1903. 196 p., ill.
PW: Mr 21, '03.

T-328　　____ "Sure": new "Chimmie Fadden" stories / by Edward W. Townsend. New York: Dodd, Mead & Company, 1904. 188 p., front., [7] leaves of plates.
PW: Mr 26, '04.

Townsend, F. L., Mrs. See **Townsend, Metta Folger.**

T-329　　Townsend, Frank Sumner. Hugh Graham: a tale of the pioneers / by Frank Sumner Townsend. New York; Cincinnati: The Abingdon Press, [c1916]. 368 p., front., [3] leaves of plates. [Ill. by George T. Tobin.]

T-330　　Townsend, Horace, 1859-1922. A handful of silver: six stories of silversmiths / written by Horace Townsend; pictured by Alex. M. McLellan. New York: The Gorham Company, 1902. 146 p., col. front., [5] leaves of col. plates. Decorative end papers.
Contents: In distant ages born. How the blind singer opened the eyes of the silversmith to all the beauties of the common life -- The girdle of Cleopatra. Which to his sorrow Neku the silversmith wrought for her in her glorious city of Alexandria -- In old Nuremberg. A story of youth and age, showing how the emperor's prize was lost and afterwards was won again -- The silver crucifix. Chapter CXXIX book first of his life translated from the Italian of Messer Benvenuto Cellini -- A prince of silversmiths. How Maxtla the High Priest asked of Montezuma his best and his dearest as a gift to the gods -- In the northern woods. Which was where Lieutenant Revere engraved the pair of silver buckles lost by Céline Paret.
BLC: London: John Hogg, 1903.

T-331　　Townsend, John Wilson. Kentucky in American letters, 1784-1912 / by John Wilson Townsend; with an introduction by James Lane Allen. Cedar Rapids, Iowa: The Torch Press, 1913. 2 Vols.: V. I: 368 p.
BAL 479 notes: "*The Last Christmas tree*, Vol. II, pp. 13-17; reprinted from The Saturday Evening Post, Dec. 5, 1908." See also Allen, *The last Christmas tree*, A-171.
BAL 6260 notes: "*The Christmas Tree on Pigeon*, Vol. II, pp. 176-181. Originally in *Collier's Weekly*, Dec. 11, 1909. Collected in *In Happy Valley*, 1917."
LC: O 28, '13.
PW: D 20, '13.

T-332　　[Townsend, Metta Folger], b. 1862. In the Nantahalas: a novel / by Mrs. F. L. Townsend.

New York: Broadway Publishing Co., [c1910].
186 p.
LC: D 24, '10.

T-333   ____ On golden hinges / by Metta Folger Townsend.
New York: Broadway Publishing Co., [c1915]. 320,
[1] p.

T-334   Townsend, William Capron. Love and liberty: a
romance of anti-slavery days / by William Capron
Townsend. New York; London; Montreal: The
Abbey Press, [c1901]. 502 p.
PW: S 14, '01.

T-335   Toy, Mary F. S. (Florilla Seymour), 1852-1934.
When summer goes: a novel / by Mary F. S. Toy.
Hartford, Conn.: The S. S. Scranton Company,
1925. 306 p.
LC: Je 17, '25.

T-336   Tozier, Josephine, b. 1863. A spring fortnight in
France / by Josephine Tozier . . . ; numerous
illustrations. New York: Dodd, Mead and Company,
1907. 352 p., front., [35] leaves of plates (mostly
photo., 3 maps).   **KSU**
LC: S 25, '07.
BLC: London: Curtis Brown, printed in U. S. A.,
1907.

T-337   Trace, Granville, b. 1878. The rescuers / by
Granville Trace. St. Paul: The Sentinel Company,
1909. 137 p.
LC: Je 25, '09.

T-338   [Tracy, Edith Bronson]. Lydia of old Cape Cod.
[Waterbury, Conn.: The Mattatuck Press Inc.,
1912]. 53 p.
Unexamined copy: bibliographic data from NUC.
LC: Ja 28, '13.

Tracy, F. B. The farmer's railroad. In *The railroad*
(1901), R-6.

T-339   Tracy, Felix, Mrs. Azubah / by Mrs. Felix Tracy.
[S. l.: s. n., not after 1905]. 172 p., front., [1] leaf
of photo. plates. Designed end papers.

Tracy, Martha Desire. See **Tracy, Felix, Mrs.**

T-340   Tracy, R. Archer (Robert Archer), b. 1878. The
sword of Nemesis / by R. Archer Tracy. New York:
The Neale Publishing Company, 1919. 327 p.
PW: Ja 24, '20.

Tracy, Roger Sherman, 1871-1926. See **Hodge, T.
Shirby, pseud.**

Tracy, Virginia. The lotus eaters. In *Short story
classics* **(1905), S-466.**

T-341   ____ Merely players: stories of stage life / by
Virginia Tracy. New York: The Century Co., 1909.
336 p. Reprinted from Collier's weekly, Scribner's
magazine and Munsey's magazine.
Contents: The lotus eaters -- A votary in motley -- The tameless team
-- In August -- The Princess Rosalba -- The interpretress -- A danger
of delay -- Nobility obliges -- Above rubies -- An indiscretion of His

Majesty -- The candle's flame -- The professionals.
LC: Mr 27, '09.
PW: Ap 24, '09.

T-342   ____ "Persons unknown" / by Virginia Tracy;
illustrations by Henry Raleigh. New York: The
Century Co., 1914. 486 p., front., [7] leaves of
plates.
LC: O 31, '14.
PW: O 24, '14.

T-343   The Tragedy that wins and other short stories.
Philadelphia, Pa.: John Joseph McVey, 1905.
206 p.   **TXA**
"These short stories were written by the seniors and
juniors of St. Joseph's College, Philadelphia. They
are the work of one class, the English class."
Contents: The two red lights / Francis J. Hardart -- The dead Indian
/ Denis E. Kelly -- The lawyer's story / Arthur E. McCarron -- The
drama that won the prize / Thomas A. Healy -- The mysterious
apparitions / Edward J. Lyng -- The doctorine of pre-established
harmony / Nelson Rowland -- The romance of an inventor / Stephen
J. McTague -- Lost and found / Francis J. McDermott -- A sad
ending / Arthur E. McCarron -- The houses of Husse and Montefort /
Lawrence F. Flick -- Boschovich's stratagem / Denis E. Kelly -- A
close shave / Denis E. Kelly -- A war-time tragedy / Arthur E.
McCarron -- A Japanese hero / Francis J. McDermott -- The unlucky
toreador / Edward J. Lyng -- The escape of Captain Neville / Francis
X. Byrnes --The game in the cars / Nelson F. Rowland -- "Teddy" /
Denis E. Kelly -- A brief reunion / Francis X. Byrnes -- The tragedy
that wins.

T-344   Train, Arthur Cheney, 1875-1945. As it was in the
beginning / by Arthur Train. New York: The
Macmillan Company, 1921. 145 p.
LC: F 24, '21.
PW: Mr 5, '21.

T-345   ____ The butler's story: being the reflections,
observations and experiences of Mr. Peter Ridges, of
Wapping-on-Velly, Devon, sometime in the service of
Samuel Carter, Esquire, of New York / written by
himself and edited by Arthur Train . . . ; with
illustrations by F. C. Yohn. New York: Charles
Scribner's Sons, 1909. 242 p., front., [3] leaves of
plates.
LC: Mr 12, '09.
PW: Mr 20, '09.
BLC: London: T. Werner Laurie, [1909].

T-346   ____ By advice of counsel: being adventures of the
celebrated firm of Tutt & Tutt, attorneys &
counsellors at law / by Arthur Train; with frontispiece
by Arthur William Brown. New York: Charles
Scribner's Sons, 1921. 267 p., front.   **ODL**
Contents: The shyster -- The kid and the camel -- Contempt of court
-- By advice of counsel -- "That sort of woman" -- You're another! --
Beyond a reasonable doubt.
LC: Mr 18, '21.

T-347   ____ "C Q", or, In the wireless house / by Arthur
Train . . . ; with illustrations by R. M. Crosby. New
York: The Century Co., 1912. 301 p., ill.
LC: Ag 27, '12.

T-348   ____ The confessions of Artemas Quibble: being the
ingenuous and unvarnished history of Artemas
Quibble, Esquire, one-time practitioner in the New
York criminal courts, together with an account of the
divers wiles, tricks, sophistries, technicalities and

sundry artifices of himself and others of the fraternity, commonly yclept "shysters" or "shyster lawyers" / as edited by Arthur Train; illustrated. New York: Charles Scribner's Sons, 1911. 227 p., front., [7] leaves of plates. [Ill. by F. R. Gruger.]
LC: S 27, '11.
PW: O 7, '11.

T-349 ____ The earthquake / by Arthur Train. New York: Charles Scribner's Sons, 1918. 307 p.
LC: Mr 19, '18.
PW: Mr 23, '18.

T-350 ____ The "goldfish": being the confessions of a successful man. New York: The Century Co., 1914. 340 p.

T-351 Train, Arthur Cheney, 1875-1945. The hermit of Turkey Hollow: the story of an alibi, being an exploit of Ephraim Tutt, attorney & counselor at law / by Arthur Train. New York: Charles Scribner's Sons, 1921. 207 p.
LC: O 8, '21.
PW: O 15, '21.

T-352 ____ His children's children / by Arthur Train. New York: Charles Scribner's Sons, 1923. 391 p.
LC: F 24, '23.
BLC: London: Eveleigh Nash & Grayson, printed in U. S. A., 1923.

T-353 ____ The lost gospel / by Arthur Train; with a frontispiece by James Dougherty. New York: Charles Scribner's Sons, 1925. 77 p., col. front.
LC: S 9, '25.
PW: S 12, '25.

T-354 ____ McAllister and his double / by Arthur Train; illustrated. New York: Charles Scribner's Sons, 1905. 341 p., front., [11] leaves of plates. [Ill. by Alonzo Kimball & F. C. Yohn.]
PW: S 30, '05.
BLC: London: George Newnes, New York printed, 1905.

T-355 ____ The man who rocked the earth / by Arthur Train and Robert Williams Wood; frontispiece. Garden City, New York: Doubleday, Page & Company, 1915. 228 p., col. front. [Ill. by Walter L. Greene.] Illustrated end papers signed by R. W. Wood.
LC: My 18, '15.

T-356 ____ Mortmain / by Arthur Train. New York: D. Appleton and Company, 1907. 314 p., front., [7] leaves of plates. [Ill. by J. C. Leyendecker, James Montgomery Flagg, and William Oberhardt.]
Contents: Mortmain -- The rescue of Theophilus Newbegin -- The vagabond -- The man hunt -- Not at home -- A study in sociology -- The little feller -- Randolph '64.
LC: O 18, '07.
PW: O 19, '07.

T-357 ____ The needle's eye / by Arthur Train. New York: Charles Scribner's Sons, 1924. 416 p.
LC: O 3, '24.
PW: S 20, '24.

____ Old Duke. In *"Dawgs!"* (1925), D-184.

T-358 ____ Tut, tut! Mr. Tutt / by Arthur Train. New York: Charles Scribner's Sons, 1923. 315 p., front.
Contents: The bloodhound -- Tut, tut! Mr. Tutt -- The liberty of the jail -- Hocus-pocus -- Saving his face -- In witness whereof -- The twelve little husbands -- The cloak of St. Martin.
LC: S 17, '23.
PW: O 6, '23.
BLC: London: Eveleigh Nash & Grayson, New York printed, [1924].

T-359 ____ Tutt and Mr. Tutt / by Arthur Train. New York: Charles Scribner's Sons, 1920. 348 p., front., [3] leaves of plates. [Ill. by Arthur W. Brown.]
LC: Ap 13, '20.
PW: Ap 10, '20.

T-360 ____ The world and Thomas Kelly / by Arthur Train . . . New York: Charles Scribner's Sons, 1917. 434 p.
LC: N 16, '17.
PW: N 24, '17.

T-361 Train, Ethel Kissam, 1875-1923. Bringing out Barbara / by Ethel Train. New York: Charles Scribner's Sons, 1917. 232 p.
LC: Ap 4, '17.
PW: Ap 7, '17.

T-362 ____ "Son" / by Ethel Train. New York: Charles Scribner's Sons, 1911. 289, [1] p.
LC: S 20, '11.

T-363 ____ "Son": and other stories of childhood and age / by Ethel Train. New York: Charles Scribner's Sons, 1923. 546 p.
Contents: "Son" -- Jim -- The little clown -- Tom -- Nils -- Bill -- The outlaw -- Cousin Lemuel -- The reflex -- The little pink girl -- The old cock -- The ugly duckling -- The reformation of Rhoda -- In the garden -- The rule of three -- Angels unawares.
LC: D 11, '23.
PW: F 9, '24.

Trainor, Ursula Margaret. "Just a story." In *The lady of the tower* (1909), L-13.

T-364 Traprock, Walter E., 1877-1946, *pseud.* The cruise of the Kawa: wanderings in the South seas / by Walter E. Traprock [pseud.] . . . ; with seventeen illustrations and a map. New York; London: G. P. Putnam's Sons, [c1921]. 146 p., photo. front., [16] leaves of photo. plates.
LC: O 27, '21.

T-365 ____ My northern exposure: the Kawa at the Pole / by Walter E. Traprock [pseud.] . . . ; with twenty-one full page illustrations. New York; London: G. P. Putnam's Sons, 1922. ([New York]: The Knickerbocker Press). 245 p., front., ill. [Ill. by N. Courtney Owen.] Illustrated end papers. **KSU**
LC: O 10, '22.
PW: S 23, '22.

T-366 ____ Sarah of the Sahara: a romance of nomads land / by Walter E. Traprock [pseud.] . . . ; with seventeen full page illustrations. New York; London: G. P. Putnam's Sons, 1923. ([New York]: The

Knickerbocker Press). 224 p., photo. front., photo. ill. Colored, illustrated end papers.   **SPP**
LC: O 11, '23.
PW: O 13, '23.

Trask, Kate Nichols. See **Trask, Katrina.**

T-367   Trask, Katrina, 1853-1922. Free not bound / by Katrina Trask. New York; London: G. P. Putnam's Sons, 1903. ([New York]: The Knickerbocker Press). 268 p.
PW: O 31, '03.

T-368   ____ In my lady's garden: pages from the diary of Sir John Elwynne / by Katrina Trask . . . London: John Lane, The Bodley Head; New York: John Lane Company, 1907. 60 p. Text within ornamental borders. Reproduced from the Atlantic monthly.
PW: Mr 23, '07.

T-369   ____ The invisible balance sheet / by Katrina Trask . . . New York: John Lane Company; London: John Lane, The Bodley Head; Toronto: S. B. Gundy, 1916. 375 p.
LC: N 13, '16.
PW: N 25, '16.

T-370   Trautmann, W. E. (William Ernst), b. 1869. Hammers of hell / by W. E. Trautmann and Peter Hagboldt. Chicago, Ill.: The New World Pub. Co., c1921. 338 p.   **DLC**

T-371   ____ Riot / by W. E. Trautmann and Peter Hagboldt. Chicago, Ill.: Published by Chicago Labor Printing Co . . . , [ca. 1920]. 338 p.   **IAY**
LC reports: [1922].

T-372   Travers, Libbie Miller. The honor of a Lee / by Libbie Miller Travers. New York: Cochrane Publishing Co., 1908. 383 p.
Unexamined copy: bibliographic data from OCLC, #15866202.
LC: S 15, '08.

T-373   Travis, Elma A. (Elma Allen), 1861-1917. The cobbler / by Elma A. Travis . . . New York: The Outing Publishing Company, 1908. 287, [1] p.
LC: Je 6, '08.
PW: Je 13, '08.

T-374   ____ The Pang-Yanger / by Elma A. Travis, M. D. New York: McClure, Phillips & Co., 1905. 336 p.
PW: N 11, '05.

T-375   The tree of knowledge: a document / by a woman. New York: The Stuyvesant Press, 1908. 306 p.

Trego, Benjamin Thomas. See **Trego, Brooke.**

T-376   Trego, Brooke. 1861-1933. The god-bearer / by Brooke Trego. Boston: The Gorham Press; Toronto: The Copp Clark Co., Limited, [c1914]. 314 p., front. [Ill. by Sears Gallagher.]

T-377   Tremaine, Bobbie. Confessions of a dancer / Bobbie Tremaine. New York: Macfadden Publications, Inc., [1923]. 249 p., ill.
Unexamined copy: bibliographic data from NUC.
(True Story Series; no. 4)

T-378   Trent, Hilary. Mr. Claghorn's daughter / by Hilary Trent. New York: J. S. Ogilvie Publishing Company, c1903. 277 p.
PW: My 2, '03.

T-379   Trepoff, Ivan, 1867-1931, *pseud.* The forsaken / by Ivan Trepoff. New York: Cochrane Publishing Co., 1910. 179 p., front.
Unexamined copy: bibliographic data from OCLC, #18231735.

T-380   ____ He that is without sin / by Ivan Trepoff [pseud.]. New York: The Cosmopolitan Press, 1911. 355 p.   **DLC**
LC: D 18, '11.

T-381   ____ Spiritmist / by Ivan Trepoff [pseud.]. New York: Donald W. Newton, [c1909]. 288 p., front. [Ill. by The Decorative Designers.]
LC: My 3, '09.

T-382   Treynor, Albert M. Rogues of the north / by Albert M. Treynor; frontispiece by Anton Otto Fischer. New York: Chelsea House, 1922. 308 p., front.
LC: Ap 18, '22.
PW: Jl 29, '22.
BLC: London: Hutchinson & Co., [1924].

Trimble, Jessie, b. 1873. See **Stone, Jane, pseud.**

T-383   Tripp, Howland. In whaling days / by Howland Tripp. Boston: Little, Brown and Company, 1909. 371 p.
Contents: About the author -- A town meeting episode -- A tribute to women -- Peanut Jim -- A skim-milk incident -- The first tale of Phineas Foodle -- The second tale of Phineas Foodle -- The longtrades and blindstays -- Jerry -- How Jerry went to Boston -- The Quakers outwitted -- Jury duty -- One of the Cheeryble Brothers -- Thee keeps all my business -- Henry Vallis and Margaret Dane -- A wild goose story -- A few poems of the author.
LC: My 27, '09.

T-384   Trombley, D. T. (Daniel T.), 1849-1940. Batiste of Isle La Motte: his "trubbles" / by D. T. Trombley. Burlington: Free Press Printing Company, 1915. 85 p., ill.

T-385   Trombly, Della. The hermit of the Adirondacks / by Della Trombly. Boston: Sherman, French & Company, 1915. 264 p.   **YPM**
LC: D 17, '15.
PW: D 4, '15.

Troop, Edna Willa Sullivan, Mrs. See **Sorin, Scota, pseud.**

T-386   Trotter, Melvin E. (Melvin Earnest), 1870-1940. Jimmie Moore of Bucktown / by Melvin E. Trotter. Chicago: The Winona Publishing Company, 1904. 231 p.   **SVP**
PW: D 17, '04.
BLC: London: Fleming H. Revell Co., [1904].

T-387   Troubetzkoy, Pierre, 1864-1936. The passer-by: an episode / by Prince Pierre Troubetzkoy. New York: Doubleday, Page & Company, 1908. 330 p., col. front. [Ill. by Amélie Rives.]
PW: D 5, '08.
BLC: London: Grant Richards, 1908.

Troubetzkoy, Princess Amelie, pseud. See **Rives, Amelie.**

T-388 Truax, Lincoln. The king of the money kings / by Lincoln Truax; illustrations by Frederick Ward Studio. Chicago: The Money Kings Pub. Co., 1916. 288 p., front., plates. Unexamined copy: bibliographic data from NUC. PW: Ap 22, '16.

True, C. E. See **Surev, pseud.**

T-389 Truman, Orson Harold, b. 1850. The conquest: a story of the past, present, and future, real and ideal / by O. H. Truman. La Crosse, Kan.: O. H. Truman, [1909], c1884. 45 p., port. Unexamined copy: bibliographic data from OCLC, #15551682. "This work was begun in 1883; it was published under copyright in 1884. After waiting a quarter of a century it is re-published with a few alterations."

T-390 Trumbull, Annie Eliot, 1857-1949. Life's common way / by Annie Eliot Trumbull. New York: A. S. Barnes and Company, 1903. 420 p. PW: My 9, '03.

T-391 Tsanoff, Corrinne S. (Corrinne Stephenson), b. 1888. Pawns of liberty: a story of fighting yesterdays in the Balkans / by Corrinne S. and R. A. Tsanoff. New York: Outing Publishing Company, 1914. 424 p.

Tsanoff, Radoslav Andrea, b. 1887, jt. aut. *Pawns of liberty* (1914). See **Tsanoff, Corrinne S. (Corrinne Stephenson), b. 1888, jt. aut., T-391.**

T-392 Tubbs, Ella Embery. The golden sunset / Ella Embery Tubbs . . . Binghamton, N. Y.: Kennedy-Morris Corporation, printer-publishers, 1916. 187 p. **OSU, IGR** Contents: Pride goeth before a fall -- Melindie's one extravagance -- A belated wedding trip -- The training of children -- Hope deferred -- Christmas giving -- The new minister -- A trip to the Canal Zone -- The boy that was a problem -- A trip around the world.

T-393 Tuck, Clyde Edwin. The Bald Knobbers: a romantic and historical novel / by Clyde Edwin Tuck . . . ; with illustrations by Will Water. Indianapolis: B. F. Bowen & Company, 1910. 325 p., front., [4] leaves of plates. **DLC** LC: O 17, '10.

T-394 Tucker, George Fox, 1852-1929. Mrs. Bobble's trained nurse / by George Fox Tucker . . . New York: Robert J. Shores, 1916. 101 p., front. **DLC**

T-395 Tucker, Prentiss, b. 1875. In the land of the living dead: an occult story / by Prentiss Tucker. Oceanside, California: Published by The Rosicrucian Fellowship, International Headquarters; London: L. M. Fowler & Co., [c1921]. 168 p. LC: Ap 26, '21.

T-396 Tuckerman, Arthur. Breath of life: a story of youth / by Arthur Tuckerman. New York; London: G. P. Putnam's Sons, 1922. ([New York]: The Knickerbocker Press). 347 p. **CLE** LC: O 10, '22.

T-397 _____ Galloping dawns / by Arthur Tuckerman. Garden City, N. Y.: Doubleday, Page & Company, 1924. 271 p. "First edition." PW: My 31, '24.

T-398 Tudor, Anthony. The case of Paul Breen / by Anthony Tudor . . . ; illustrated by Henry Roth. Boston: L. C. Page & Company, 1911. 460 p., front., [5] leaves of plates. LC: Je 22, '11.

T-399 Tufts, Drew. Hiram Blair / by Drew Tufts; with four illustrations by H. S. De Lay. Chicago: A. C. McClurg & Co., 1912. 443, [1] p., front., [3] leaves of plates. PW: My 11, '12.

T-400 Tull, Jewell Bothwell. Sylvia of the Stubbles / by Jewell Bothwell Tull. Chicago: The Reilly & Lee Co., [c1923]. 249 p. LC: S 7, '23. PW: O 13, '23.

Tulloch, Eliza E. See **Tulloch, Lida C., pseud.**

T-401 Tulloch, Lida C., *pseud.* Alicia's ambition / by Lida C. Tulloch [pseud.]. Washington [D. C.]: The Neale Publishing Company, 1901. 147 p.

T-402 Tully, Jim. Emmett Lawler / by Jim Tully. New York: Harcourt, Brace and Company, [c1922]. 315 p. LC: F 27, '22. BLC: London & New York: Andrew Melrose, Rahway printed, [1922].

Tully, Richard Walton. All in the play. In *California story book* (1909), C-40.

_____ Love and advertising. In *Spinners' book of fiction* (1907), S-755.

_____ A matter of state. In *Under Berkeley Oaks* (1901), U-8.

T-403 Tupper, Edith Sessions. Hearts triumphant / by Edith Sessions Tupper. New York: D. Appleton and Company, 1906. 285 p., front., [3] leaves of plates. [Ill. by G. Patrick Nelson.] LC: S 21, '06. PW: O 6, '06.

T-404 _____ The stuff of dreams / by Edith Sessions Tupper. New York: B. W. Dodge & Company, 1908. 292 p., front., [3] leaves of plates. [Ill. by O. T. Jackman.] LC: N 12, '08. PW: D 5, '08.

T-405 Tupper, Tristram. Adventuring / by Tristram Tupper . . . New York: George H. Doran Company, [c1923]. 214 p. LC: Ag 31, '23.

_____ Grit. In *Prize stories of 1921* (1922), **P-619.**

T-406 _____ The house of five swords: a romance / by Tristram Tupper. New York: George H. Doran Company, [c1922]. 317 p.
LC: O 25, '22.
BLC: London: Hodder & Stoughton, printed in U. S. A., [1923].

Turnbull, Francese Hubbard Litchfield. See **Turnbull, Lawrence, Mrs.**

T-407 Turnbull, Lawrence, Mrs., d. 1927. The royal pawn of Venice: a romance of Cyprus / by Mrs. Lawrence Turnbull. Philadelphia; London: J. B. Lippincott Company, 1911. 360 p., front. (port.).
LC: My 24, '11.

T-408 Turnbull, Margaret, d. 1942. Alabaster lamps / by Margaret Turnbull . . . Chicago: The Reilly & Lee Co., [c1925]. 340 p. Illustrated end papers.
LC: S 14, '25.
PW: S 12, '25.
BLC: London: Herbert Jenkins, 1925.

T-409 _____ The close-up / Margaret Turnbull. New York; London: Harper & Brothers, [1918]. 350, [1] p., col. front. [Ill. by George W. Gage.]
LC: O 29, '18.
PW: N 9, '18.

T-410 Turnbull, Margaret, d. 1942. Handle with care: a novel / by Margaret Turnbull . . . New York; London: Harper & Brothers, [1916]. 337, [1] p., front. **DLC**
LC: Ja 8, '16.
PW: Ja 15, '16.

T-411 _____ W. A. G.'s tale / edited by Margaret Turnbull; with Zobzee illustrations by the author. Boston; New York: Houghton Mifflin, 1913. ([Cambridge, Mass.]: The Riverside Press). 169 p., col. front., ill. [Ill. by M. L. Kirk.] **NYP**
LC: F 28, '13.
PW: F 22, '13.

T-412 Turner, George Kibbe, 1869-1952. The biography of a million dollars / by George Kibbe Turner; with illustrations by F. R. Gruger. Boston: Little, Brown, and Company, 1918. 356 p., front., [3] leaves of plates.
LC: F 25, '18.

_____ Birth stones. In *Marriage* (1923), **M-457.**

T-413 _____ Hagar's hoard / George Kibbe Turner. New York: Alfred A. Knopf, 1920. 311 p.
LC: O 1, '20.
PW: O 2, '20.
BLC: London: William Heinemann, 1921.

T-414 _____ The last Christian / by George Kibbe Turner; with frontispiece in color. New York: Hearst's International Library Co., 1914. 281 p., incl. col. front. [Ill. by W. H. D. Koerner.]
LC: O 1, '14.

T-415 _____ Red Friday / by George Kibbe Turner. Boston: Little, Brown and Company, 1919. 253 p.
LC: Je 7, '19.
PW: Je 7, '19.

T-416 _____ The taskmasters / by George Kibbe Turner. New York: McClure, Phillips & Co., 1902. 316 p. (First novel series).
PW: N 8, '02.

_____ A temperance campaign. In *Politics* (1901), **P-461.**

_____ A white sheep. In *Youth* (1901), **Y-51.**

T-417 _____ White shoulders / George Kibbe Turner. New York: Alfred A. Knopf, 1921. 283 p.
LC: Ag 8, '21.
BLC: London: Mills & Boon, 1921.

Turner, Madge. Michael of the mists. In *The best college short stories, 1924-1925* (1925), **B-558.**

T-418 Turpin, Edna Henry Lee, 1869-1952. Abram's freedom / by Edna Turpin. Boston; New York; Chicago: The Pilgrim Press, [c1913]. 32 p., front. "Reprinted from the Atlantic Monthly."
LC: O 13, '13.

T-419 _____ Happy Acres / by Edna H. L. Turpin . . . ; illustrated by Mary Lane McMillan. New York: The Macmillan Company, 1913. 363 p., front., ill.
                                                              NOC
LC: S 8, '13.

Tuttle, Emma Rood, 1839-1916, jt. aut. *Stories from beyond the borderland* (1910). See **Tuttle, Hudson, 1836-1910, jt. aut., T-422.**

T-420 Tuttle, Ervilla Goodrich, b. 1869. Jan Tanner-- soldier for the starry flag / Ervilla Goodrich Tuttle. [New York: Printed by Wynkoop-Hallenbeck-Crawford Co., c1919]. 45, [1] p. **DLC**
LC: My 16, '19.

T-421 Tuttle, Florence Guertin, b. 1869. Give my love to Maria / by Florence Guertin Tuttle. New York; Cincinnati: The Abingdon Press, [c1917]. 262 p., front.
Reprinted in part from various periodicals.
Contents: The story of the stories -- Give my love to Maria -- The French doll's dowry -- Idols of gold -- As shown by the tape -- Cupid at forty -- A wingless victory -- A successful failure -- What doth it profit a man? -- Mademoiselle -- Gentlemen unafraid -- "Unto them a child".
LC: Ap 25, '17.

T-422 Tuttle, Hudson, 1836-1910. Stories from beyond the borderland / by Hudson Tuttle and Emma Rood Tuttle. Berlin Heights, Ohio: The Tuttle Publishing Company, 1910. 314 p., photo. front. (port.).
Contents: The Border land -- An angel or the dear Christ -- Take my lyre -- Over the great divide -- Little Tim, the newsboy -- Fable of the stork -- A dream that was true -- The king bumblebee -- The Sefton children -- False pretensions -- Your writing book -- A wasted life -- Budding rose -- Shall we be new angels -- Legend of the witch-hazel -- Our sacred Thanksgiving -- The cruel boy and the angel -- The sunbeams' task -- The hand of toil -- A story of the Danube -- Gold digging in the garden -- Where are the yesterdays gone? -- Fate of the moon eaters -- Hial's perpetual motion -- The history of a heart -- Paul Felden -- Pimmon, the idiot slave -- Clem -- Kindness -- The

recording mirror -- A Christmas story -- The divine child -- The canary's world -- From life to death -- The legend of Minehonto -- Nutting years ago -- A New Year's story -- A spirit's revenge -- How an acorn becomes an oak -- The good little girl -- The water-lily -- The rival musicians -- Origin of the mushroom -- The two angels -- The farmer -- Return of the song thrush -- The wainscot rat -- Missionary effort on Osman Island -- The hoarding squirrel -- The swan-maidens -- Cherokee Charley -- The snow-owl -- A story of Easter -- The boy and the river -- Decoration Day -- Think before you strike -- Bob's thoughts came home -- The discontented chickens -- St. Valentine -- Abe, the dwarf -- Sorrows of angels -- The Christ of the Andes.
LC: Ja 22, '10.
PW: Mr 5, '10.

T-423   Tuttle, Margaretta Muhlenberg Perkins, b. 1880. The cobweb / by Margaretta Tuttle. Boston: Little, Brown, and Company, 1925. 330 p.
LC: Ap 11, '25.
PW: Ap 18, '25.
BLC: London: Hodder & Stoughton, [1925].

T-424   _____ Feet of clay / by Margaretta Tuttle; with illustrations by H. R. Ballinger. Boston: Little, Brown, and Company, 1923. 368 p., front., [3] leaves of plates.
LC: S 15, '23.
PW: S 8, '23.
BLC: London: Hodder & Stoughton, 1923.

T-425   _____ His worldly goods / by Margaretta Tuttle; with frontispiece in color by Paul Meylan. Indianapolis: The Bobbs-Merrill Company Publishers, [c1912]. 410 p., col. front.
LC: My 27, '12.
PW: Je 1, '12.

T-426   Tuttle, Mary McArthur, 1849-1916. International ties / by Mary McArthur Tuttle; a historical novel. [Washington, D. C.]: The Crane Press, [c1915]. 2 v.   **DLC**

T-427   _____ Types of men and women (as studied through ideality) / Mary McArthur T. Tuttle (Mrs. Herbert Tuttle). [S. l.: s. n., c1907]. 102 p.   **DLC**
LC: N 14, '07.

T-428   Tuttle, W. C. (Wilbur C.), b. 1883. The devil's payday / by W. C. Tuttle. -- 1st ed. -- Garden City, New York: Garden City Publishing Co., Inc., 1923, [c1922]. 115 p.   **OSU, UBY**

Tuttle, Worth. The mask. In *As we are* (1923), **A-325.**

T-429   [Twain, Mark], *pseud.* The curious republic of Gondour: and other whimsical sketches / by Samuel L. Clemens . . . New York: Boni and Liveright, 1919. 140 p.
Contents: The curious republic of Gondour -- A memory -- Introductory to "Memoranda" -- About smells -- A couple of sad experiences -- Dan Murphy -- The "Tournament" in A. D. 1870 -- Curious relic for sale -- A reminiscence of the back settlements -- A royal compliment -- The approaching epidemic -- The tone-imparting committee -- Goldsmith's friend abroad again -- Our precious lunatic -- The European War -- The wild man interviewed -- Last words of great men.
PW: Je 21, '19.
References: BAL 3527; Johnson, p. 96-97.

T-430   _____ A dog's tale / by Mark Twain [pseud.]; illustrated by W. T. Smedley. New York; London: Harper & Brothers, 1904. 35, [1] p., col. front., [3] leaves of col. plates.
LC: S 15, '04.
PW: O 1, '04.
References: BAL 3483; Johnson, p. 78-79. BAL 3479: Another edition printed from plates of Harper's Magazine, Dec. 1903.

T-431   _____ A double barrelled detective story / by Mark Twain [pseud.] . . . ; illustrated by Lucius Hitchcock. New York; London: Harper & Brothers, 1902. 179 p., front., [6] leaves of plates.
LC: Ap 10, '02.
PW: Ap 19, '02.
BLC: London: Chatto & Windus, 1902.
References: BAL 3471; Johnson, p. 75-76.

T-432   _____ Eve's diary: translated from the original ms. / by Mark Twain [pseud.]; illustrated by Lester Ralph. London; New York: Harper & Brothers, 1906. 109 p., front., ill. on even numbered pages.
PW: Je 16, '06.
References: BAL 3489; Johnson, p. 84-85.

T-433   _____ Extract from Captain Stormfield's visit to heaven / by Mark Twain [pseud.]. New York; London: Harper & Brothers, 1909. 120, [1] p., front. [Ill. by Albert Levering.]
LC: O 16, '09.
PW: O 23, '09.
References: BAL 3511; Johnson, p. 91-92.

T-434   _____ Extracts from Adam's diary: translated from the original ms. / by Mark Twain [pseud.]; illustrated by F. Strothmann. New York; London: Harper & Brothers, 1904. 89 p., front., ill. on even-numbered pages.
LC: Ap 7, '04.
PW: Ap 16, '04.
References; BAL 3480; Johnson, p. 80-81.

T-435   _____ A horse's tale / by Mark Twain [pseud.]; illustrated by Lucius Hitchcock. New York; London: Harper & Brothers, 1907. 152, [1] p., front., [4] leaves of plates.
LC: O 24, '07.
PW: N 9, '07.
References: BAL 3500; Johnson, p. 89-90.

T-436   _____ The mysterious stranger: a romance / by Mark Twain [pseud.]; with illustrations by N. C. Wyeth. New York; London: Harper & Brothers, [c1916]. 150, [1] p., col. front., [6] leaves of col. plates.
                                                CIN
LC: O 27, '16.
PW: N 4, '16.
References: BAL 3520; Johnson, p. 94-95.

T-437   _____ The mysterious stranger: and other stories / by Mark Twain [pseud.]. -- 1st ed. -- New York; London: Harper & Brothers, 1922. 323, [1] p., front.
Contents: The mysterious stranger -- A horse's tale -- Extract from Captain Stormfield's visit to heaven -- A fable -- My platonic sweetheart -- Hunting the deceitful turkey -- The McWilliamses and

the burglar alarm.
LC: My 10, '22.
PW: My 20, '22.
References: BAL 3534; Johnson, p. 99-100.

T-438 ____ The suppressed chapter of "Life on the Mississippi". [S. l.: s. n., 1913?]. [4] p.
Unexamined copy: bibliographic data from OCLC, #2918317.
References: BAL 3519.

T-439 ____ The $30,000 bequest: and other stories / by Mark Twain [pseud.]; illustrated. New York; London: Harper & Brothers, 1906. 522, [1] p., photo. front., [7] leaves of plates, ill. [Ill. by W. T. Smedley, C. D. Weldon, F. Luis Mora, and Albert Levering.]
Contents: The $30,000 bequest -- A dog's tale -- Was it heaven? or hell? -- The Californian's tale -- A helpless situation -- A telephonic conversation -- Edward Mills and George Benton: a tale --Saint Joan of Arc -- The five boons of life -- The first writing-machines -- Italian without a master -- Italian with grammar -- A burlesque biography -- General Washington's negro body-servant -- Wit inspirations of the "two-year-olds" -- An entertaining article -- A letter to the secretary of the treasury -- Amended obituaries -- A monument to Adam -- A humane word from Satan -- Introduction to "The new guide of The conversation in Portuguese and English" -- Advice to little girls -- Post-mortem poetry -- A deception -- The danger of lying in bed -- Portrait of King William III -- Does the race of man love a lord? -- Eve's diary -- The invalid's story -- The captain's story -- Mark Twain: a biographical sketch -- In memoriam -- The belated Russian passport -- Two little tales -- Diplomatic pay and clothes -- Extracts from Adam's diary -- The death disk -- A double-barrelled detective story.
LC: S 27, '06.
PW: O 13, '06.
References: BAL 3492; Johnson, p. 85-86.

T-440 Tweedy, Frank, 1854-1937. The discarded confidante: and other stories / by Frank Tweedy. New York: The Neale Publishing Company, 1918. 258 p., front.   **DLC**
Contents: The discarded confidante -- Bobbie -- A red-headed girl -- Three months -- Money -- The subliminal brute -- Prisoners of fate -- The doormat.

T-441 Twells, J. H. (Julia Helen). By the higher law / by Julia H. Twells, Jr. . . . Philadelphia: Henry T. Coates and Company, [c1901]. 285 p., front., [4] leaves of plates. [Ill. by PAL, i.e. Jean de Paleologue.]

T-442 Twenty miles out: indiscretions of a commuter's wife / by herself; sketches by Beatrice Stevens. Boston: Little, Brown and Company, 1925. 156 p., front., ill.   **OSU, CLE**

T-443 Twenty tales by twenty women: from real life in Chicago / Anonymous. Chicago, Ill.: Novelty Publishing Co., [c1903]. 316 p.
Contents: A woman's anguish -- The diary of a Chicago girl -- The life story of a Southern widow -- A story of the Chicago ghetto -- A woman of thirty-eight -- A forecast -- A daughter of proud Kentucky -- My lover's bequest -- The victim of a drug -- What happened to a girl who flirted -- Sold at a fixed price -- A story of suicide bridge -- Two babes and two mothers -- Not guilty -- My lover's daughter -- As told to a clergyman -- A story of stage life -- A trip across the lake -- One woman's way -- A story of the levee -- A scientific phenomenon.
PW: Je 20, '03.

T-444 Twenty-five ghost stories / compiled and edited by W. Bob Holland. New York: J. S. Ogilvie

Publishing Company . . . , [c1904]. 255 p., ill.
Contents: The black cat -- The flayed hand -- The vengeance of a tree -- The parlor-car ghost -- Ghost of Buckstown Inn -- The burglar's ghost -- A phantom toe -- Mrs. Davenport's ghost -- The phantom woman -- The phantom hag -- From the tomb -- Sandy's ghost -- The ghosts of Red Creek -- The spectre bride -- How he caught the ghost -- Grand-dame's ghost story -- A fight with a ghost -- Colonel Halifax's ghost story -- The ghost of the count -- The old mansion -- A misfit ghost -- An unbidden guest -- The dead woman's photograph -- The ghost of a live man -- The ghost of Washington.
PW: O 15, '04.

T-445 Twenty-three stories / by twenty and three authors. New York: D. Appleton and Company, 1924. 349, [1] p.   **OUN**
Contents: Kerfol / Edith Wharton -- The Chink and the child / Thomas Burke -- The nomad / Robert Hichens -- The crucifixion of the outcast / W. B. Yeats -- The drums of Kairwan / the Marquess Curzon of Kedleston -- A life - a bowl of rice / L. De Bra -- Hodge / Elinor Mordaunt -- Hatteras / A. W. Mason -- The ransom / Cutliffe Hyne -- The other twin / Edwin Pugh -- The narrow way / R. Ellis Roberts -- Davey Jone's gift / John Masefield -- The call of the hand / Louis Golding -- The sentimental mortgage / Arthur Lynch -- Captain Sharkey / A. Conan Doyle -- Violence / Algernon Blackwood -- The reward of enterprise / Ward Muir -- Grear's dam / Morley Roberts -- The king of Maleka / H. De Vere Stacpoole -- Alleluia / T. F. Powys -- The monkey's paw / W. W. Jacobs -- The creatures / Walter de la Mare -- The taipan / W. Somerset Maugham.
LC: N 8, '24.

T-446 Twing, Carolinn Edna Skinner, b. 1844. Henry Drummond in spirit life / <Mrs. Carolinn E. S. Twing, Medium>. Springfield, Mass.: Star Publishing Co., 1902. 46 p.
Unexamined copy: bibliographic data from NUC.

T-447 ____ Jim, or, The touch of an angel mother / by Carrie E. S. Twing. Lily Dale, N. Y.: Sunflower Pub. Co., 1901. 358 p., front. (port.).

T-448 Tybout, Ella Middleton. Poketown people, or, parables in black / by Ella Middleton Tybout; with illustrations in color by Frank Verbeck and Beulah S. Moore. Philadelphia; London: J. B. Lippincott Company, 1904. 356 p., incl. col. front., [5] leaves of col. plates
Contents: The offending eye -- Brother Johnsing's sperience -- An unwilling Delilah -- The ass that vanquished Balaam -- Ananias of Poketown -- The feast of locusts -- The regeneration of Isaiah -- The return of sister Juliana -- A very wise virgin -- Moses, Jr. -- The blast of the trumpet -- The intervention of Gran'pap -- At Fiddler's Bridge.
PW: D 17, '04.

T-449 ____ The smuggler / by Ella Middleton Tybout; with illustrations in color by Howard Everett Smith. Philadelphia; London: J. B. Lippincott Company, 1907. 282 p., col. front., [2] leaves of col. plates.
LC: S 28, '07.
PW: O 9, '07.

T-450 ____ The wife of the Secretary of State / by Ella Middleton Tybout . . . Philadelphia; London: J. B. Lippincott Company, 1905. 359 p., front. [Ill. by Clyde O. De Land.]
PW: N 11, '05.

T-451 Tyler, Charles Waller, b. 1841. The K. K. K. / by C. W. Tyler. New York; London; Montreal: The Abbey Press, [c1902]. 359 p.

T-452 ____ Quality Bill's girl: a detective story / by Charles W. Tyler. New York: Chelsea House, [c1925]. 256 p.
PW: My 23, '25.
BLC: London: Hutchinson & Co., [1926].

T-453   The scout: a tale of the Civil War / by C. W. Tyler . . . Nashville, Tenn.: Printed for the author [by] Publishing House, M. E. Church, South, 1912, [c1911]. 345 p., photo. front., [1] leaf of col. plates.
LC: D 22, '11.
LC reports: Nashville, Tenn.: The Cumberland Press, 1911.

T-454   Tyler, G. Vere (Georgie Vere). Children of transgression / by G. Vere Tyler. New York: Henry Holt and Company, 1922. 316 p.
LC: Mr 29, '22.

T-455   The daughter of a Rebel: a novel / by G. Vere Tyler. New York: Duffield & Company, 1913. 323 p.
LC: Mr 1, '13.

T-456   Tyler, Therese, b. 1884. The dusty road / by Therese Tyler; with a frontispiece by H. Weston Taylor. Philadelphia; London: J. B. Lippincott Company, 1915. 326 p., front.
PW: F 13, '15.

T-457   Tynan, James J. The great divide / by James J. Tynan; a novelized version of the photoplay; illustrated with scenes from the photoplay, a Metro-Goldwyn picture. New York: Grosset & Dunlap, [c1925]. 293 p., photo. front., [7] leaves of photo. plates.
LC: Mr 5, '25.
PW: Mr 14, '25.

T-458   The shooting of Dan McGrew / by James J. Tynan; based on the famous poem of Robert W. Service; illustrated with scenes from the photoplay, a Metro-Sawyer-Lubin production. New York: Grosset & Dunlap, [c1924]. 283 p., photo. front., [7] leaves of photo. plates.
LC: Jl 3, '24.

T-459   Tyrrell, Henry, 1865-1933. Shenandoah: love and war in the valley of Virginia 1861-5: based upon the famous play by Bronson Howard / by Henry Tyrrell; illustrated by Harry A. Ogden, John H. Cassel and others. New York; London: G. P. Putnam's Sons, 1912. (New York: The Knickerbocker Press). 389 p., col. front., [14] leaves of plates. [Ill. by Harry A. Ogden, John H. Cassel, and John W. Ehninger.]

T-460   Tyrrell, Ross. The pathway of adventure / by Ross Tyrrell. New York: Alfred A. Knopf, 1920. 310 p.   **DPL**
(Borzoi mystery stories; 6).
LC: My 20, '20.
PW: Je 12, '20.

T-461   Tyson, Anne Arrington. Dramana: a romance of the stage / by Annie Arrington Tyson. New York; Washington: The Neale Publishing Company, 1903. 271 p.
PW: D 19, '03.

T-462   Tyson, Anne Arrington. The price of honor / by Anne Arrington Tyson. Boston: The Four Seas Company, 1921. 253 p., front., [2] leaves of plates.
LC: N 18, '21.

T-463   Tyson, John Aubrey, b. 1870. The barge of haunted lives / by J. Aubrey Tyson . . . New York: The Macmillan Company, 1923. 333 p.
LC: F 28, '23.
PW: Mr 17, '23.

T-464   The Scarlet Tanager / by J. Aubrey Tyson. New York: The Macmillan Company, 1922. 340 p.
LC: Mr 16, '22.
PW: Ja 3, '25.

T-465   The stirrup cup / by J. Aubrey Tyson. New York: D. Appleton & Co., 1903. 208 p.
(Novelettes de luxe).
PW: Ap 11, '03.

U

Uhlrich, Eugenie. Breaking the news. In *The Senior lieutenant's wager: and other stories* **(1905), S-312.**

U-1   Ullman, Albert Edward. "The line's busy" / by Albert Edward Ullman; with 21 illustrations in black-and-white by C. A. Voight . . . New York: Frederick A. Stokes Company, [c1920]. 122 p., front., ill.
BLC: London: Jarrolds, 1920.

Ullmann, Alice Woods. See **Woods, Alice, 1871-1959.**

U-2   Ulrich, A. E. (Alois Ernest), b. 1860. Money mad: an American novel by an American citizen / A. E. Ulrich; with frontispiece by Samuel Gfroerer. Louisville, Kentucky: Press of C. T. Dearing Printing Company, 1924. 390 p., front.
LC: Je 13, '24.

U-3   Ulrich, Charles Kenmore, 1861-1941. Fires of faith: the romance of a Salvation Army lassie / by Charles Kenmore Ulrich; illustrated with scenes from the photoplay produced and copyrighted by the Famous Players-Laskey Corporation. New York: Grosset & Dunlap, [c1919]. 270 p., photo. front., [7] leaves of photo. plates.   **CPT**
LC: My 6, '19.

U-4   The wolf of Purple Canyon: a romance of the Southwest / by Charles Kenmore Ulrich . . . New York: The James A. McCann Company, 1921. 309 p., front., [3] leaves of plates. [Ill. by W. Bournazel.]
LC: F 28, '21.
BLC: London: Hutchinson, [1922].

Uhlich, Eugenie, contributor. See *A double knot* **(1905), D-499.**

U-5   Ulrich, Roy. Wanda of the white sage: a love story / by Roy Ulrich. New York: Chelsea House, [c1925]. 256 p.
BLC: London: T. Nelson & Sons, [1928].

U-6   Umbstaetter, H. D. (Herman Daniel), b. 1851. The

red-hot dollar: and other stories from the Black Cat /
by H. D. Umbstaetter; with an introd. by Jack
London. Boston: L. C. Page & Company, 1911.
239 p.

Contents: The red-hot dollar -- The unturned trump -- The real thing
-- When the cuckoo called -- One chance in a million -- Doodle's
discovery -- Kootchie -- Her eyes, your honor -- For the sake of
Toodleums -- In Hell's cañon -- The mystery of the thirty millions --
Asleep at Lone Mountain.

PW: Ag 5, '11.

U-7   Unconventional Joan. Chicago, Illinois: Bungalow
Book Company, [c1922]. 300 p.

U-8   Under the Berkeley Oaks: stories / by students of the
University of California; selected and edited by the
editorial staff of the University of California
Magazine. San Francisco: A. M. Robertson, 1901.
227 p., front.

Contents: Travis Hallett's half-back / Frank Norris, '94 -- The proud
dig and the lazy student / James Hopper, '98 -- The legend of the
River Wayste / Ida H. Ballard, '94 -- The singular experience of the
gilstraps / Gertrude Henderson, '95 -- The confraternity of the holy
agony / Harley M. Leete, '01 -- The little maid's tragedy / Mary
Bell, '98 -- The fate of the four / Centennia Barto, '98 (Mrs. Leslie
Mott) -- A matter of state / Richard Walton Tully, '01 -- Shadows /
Ralph E. Gibbs, '98 -- The second edition / Agnes Crary, '92 (Mrs.
P. L. Weaver).

LC: D 19, '00.
PW: Mr 23, '01.
References: BAL 15035.

U-9   Under the sunset / edited by William Dean Howells
and Henry Mills Alden. New York; London: Harper
& Brothers Publishers, 1906. 264 p.
(Harper's novelettes).

Contents: The end of the journey / Grace Ellery Channing -- The
sage-brush hen / Thomas A. Janvier -- A madonna of the desert / Elia
W. Peattie -- The prophetess of the Land of No-Smoke / Marie
Manning -- A little pioneer / Phillip Verrill Mighels -- Back to
Indiana / Elmore Elliott Peake -- The Gray Chieftain / Charles A.
Eastman, M. D. -- The inn of San Jacinto / Zoe Dana Underhill --
Tio Juan / Maurice Kingsley -- Jamie the Kid / Josiah Flynt.

LC: My 11, '06.
PW: My 19, '06.
References: BAL 9770.

Underhill, Elise Morris, jt. aut. *The runaway place
(1909)*. See **Eaton, Walter Prichard, 1878-1957, jt.
aut., E-23.**

U-10   Underhill, Ruth Murray, b. 1884. The white moth /
by Ruth Murray Underhill. New York: Moffat,
Yard and Company, 1920. 307 p.
LC: N 6, '20.
PW: Ja 15, '21.

Underhill, Zoe Dana. The inn of San Jacinto. In
Under the Sunset (1906), U-9.

U-11   Underwood, Earl, b. 1870. Representing John
Marshall & Co.: being confessions of Edward R.
Ward, a drummer / by Earl Underwood; illustrated
by Gordon H. Grant. New York: G. W. Dillingham
Company, 1905. 171 p., front., [5] leaves of plates.

U-12   Underwood, Edna Worthley, 1873-1961. A book of
dear dead women / by Edna Worthley Underwood.
Boston: Little, Brown, and Company, 1911. 327 p.
"The painter of dead women" reprinted from the
Smart set for January, 1910.

Contents: One of Napoleon's loves -- The painter of dead women --
The mirror of La Granja -- Liszt's Concerto Pathétique -- Sister
Seraphine -- The sacred relics of Saint Euthymius -- The Opal isles --
The house of gauze -- The king.

LC: Mr 28, '11.
BLC: London: Andrew Melrose, Cambridge [Mass.
printed], 1912.

U-13   ____ The passion flower / by Edna Worthley
Underwood . . . Boston; New York: Houghton
Mifflin Company, 1924. (Cambridge [Mass.]: The
Riverside Press). 303 p.
"The passion flower is volume two of The new world
trilogy. The others are: The pentitent and the
pageant-maker."
LC: Mr 31, '24.

U-14   ____ The penitent / by Edna Worthley Underwood.
Boston; New York: Houghton Mifflin Company,
1922. (Cambridge: The Riverside Press). 367 p.
"The penitent is volume one of The new world
trilogy."
LC: O 13, '22.

U-15   ____ The whirlwind / by Edna Worthley
Underwood; with a frontispiece by William A.
Kirkpatrick. Boston: Small, Maynard and Company,
[c1918]. 298 p., col. front.
LC: S 26, 18.
BLC: London: Hurst & Blackett, 1919.

U-16   Underwood, J. Cabaniss. Gilbert, or, Then and now:
a thrilling story of the life and achievements of a
Virginia negro / by J. Cabaniss Underwood.
Philadelphia: H. D. Shaiffer, [c1902]. 309 p.,
front., [5] leaves of plates.

U-17   Underwood, Matilda Downing. Blue Belle of the
forest: a story of the olden time, in the middle West /
by Matilda Downing Underwood. [Wilmington,
Ohio: Journal-Republican Print, c1919]. 134 p., [4]
leaves of photo. plates.   **MIA**
LC: My 13, '21.

U-18   Underwood, Ruth. A living legacy / by Ruth
Underwood; illustrated by George Gibbs.
Philadelphia: The John C. Winston Company, 1912.
438 p., col. front.

U-19   An unwedded wife. Chicago: W. B. Conkey
Company, [c1908]. 320 p.
On spine: Unwedded wife--Calhoun.

U-20   Upchurch, James T., b. 1870. Behind the scarlet
mask / by J. T. Upchurch . . . Fort Worth: World
Printers, [c1924]. 288 p., ill.
LC: My 19, '24.

U-21   Updegraff, Allan, 1883-1965. Dancers in the wind /
by Allan Updegraff. New York: Boni and Liveright,
1925. 368 p.
LC: O 14, '25.
PW: O 17, '25.

U-22   ____ Second youth: being, in the main, some
account of the middle comedy in the life of a New
York bachelor; a novel / by Allan Updegraff. New

York; London: Harper & Brothers, [1917]. 327 p.,
front. [Ill. by Frederic A. Anderson.]
LC: Ap 21, '17.
PW: My 5, 17.

U-23   ____ Strayed revellers: a novel of modernistic truth
and intruding war / by Allan Updegraff. New York:
Henry Holt and Company, 1918. 390 p.
LC: Ag 29, '18.
PW: Ag 31, '18.

U-24   Updegraff, Robert R. (Robert Rawls), b. 1889.
Obvious Adams: the story of a successful
businessman / by Robert R. Updegraff. New York;
London: Harper & Brothers, [c1916]. 56 p.
LC: S 9, '16.
PW: S 16, '16.

U-25   [Upham, Francis Bourne], b. 1862. Simon Peter,
fisherman / by "Thomas" [pseud.]. New York:
Eaton & Mains; Cincinnati: Jennings & Pye,
[c1904]. 189 p.   **DRU**
PW: Mr 26, '04.

U-26   ____ Simon Peter, shepherd / by Francis Bourne
Upham ("Thomas"). New York: Eaton & Mains;
Cincinnati: Jennings & Graham, [c1910]. 239 p.
                                              IMC
LC: Mr 8, '10.
PW: Mr 26, '10.

U-27   Upright, Blanche. The losing gain / by Blanche
Upright. New York: W. J. Watt & Company,
[c1922]. 309 p.
LC: Mr 12, '23.
PW: S 1, '23.

U-28   ____ The valley of content / by Blanche Upright.
New York: W. J. Watt & Company, [c1922]. 315 p.
LC: Je 21, '22.
PW: Ag 5, '22.

U-29   Upton, Charles Elmer, b. 1872. Down Wild Goose
Canyon / by Charles Elmer Upton . . . Placerville,
Cal.: Charles Elmer Upton, 1910. 52 p., photo.
front., [1] leaf of photo. plates. "The story `Down
Wild Goose Canyon,' originally appeared in the
Argosy . . . while the quatrain, `Endeavor,' was first
published in Youth's companion . . ."
Contents: Stories: Down Wild Goose Canyon -- An unpopular boy
-- In darkness -- When Minnie went to school -- A girl of the Sierras
-- Verses.
LC: N 21, 10.

U-30   Upton, Uno. The strugglers: a story / by Uno
Upton. Chicago: Dearborn Publishing Co., [c1911].
257 p.
LC: Ag 7, '11.
PW: Ag 26, '11.

U-31   Urner, Mabel Herbert, 1881-1957. The journal of a
neglected wife / by Mabel Herbert Urner. New
York: B. W. Dodge & Company, 1909. 253 p.
LC: F 17, '09.
PW: Mr 6, '09.

U-32   ____ The married life of Helen and Warren / by

Mabel Herbert Urner. Boston: Small, Maynard &
Company, [c1925]. 404 p.
LC: S 21, '25.
PW: O 31, '25.

U-33   ____ The woman alone / by Mabel Herbert Urner.
New York: Hearst's International Library Co., 1914.
286 p.
LC: S 30, '14.

V

Vail, Clara Warren. A reminiscence. In *A book of
Bryn Mawr stories* (1901), B-732.

V-1   Vail, Laurence, b. 1891. Piri and I / by Lawrence
Vail. New York: Lieber & Lewis, 1923. 245 p.
LC: D 6, '23.

V-2   Vaile, William N. (William Newell), 1876-1927. The
mystery of the Golconda / by William N. Vaile.
Garden City, N. Y.: Doubleday, Page & Company,
1925. 301 p.
PW: S 5, '25.
BLC: London: William Heinemann, printed in U. S.
A., 1925.

V-3   Vaka, Demetra, 1877-1946. A child of the Orient /
by Demetra Vaka (Mrs. Kenneth-Brown). Boston;
New York: Houghton Mifflin Company, 1914.
(Cambridge: The Riverside Press). 297, [1] p.
PW: My 9, '14.
BLC: London: John Lane, 1914.

V-4   ____ The duke's price / by Demetra and Kenneth
Brown; with illustrations by A. G. Learned. Boston;
New York: Houghton Mifflin Company, 1910.
(Cambridge: The Riverside Press). 292 p., col.
front., [1] leaf of col. plates.
LC: Mr 19, '10.
PW: Mr 5, '10.

V-5   ____ The first secretary: a novel /by Demetra and
Kenneth Brown; . . . drawings by Sydney Adamson.
New York: B. W. Dodge & Company, 1907.
350 p., col. front., [4] leaves of plates. **OSU, AUM**
LC: N 1, '07.
PW: N 23, '07.

V-6   [____] The grasp of the Sultan / with illustrations by
W. T. Benda. Boston; New York: Houghton Mifflin
Company, 1916. (Cambridge: The Riverside Press).
302, [2] p., front. (double-leaf), [3] plates (double-
leaf).
BLC: London: Cassell & Co., 1917.

V-7   ____ The heart of the Balkans / by Demetra Vaka
(Mrs. Kenneth-Brown). Boston; New York:
Houghton Mifflin Company, 1917. 247 p.
LC: My 21, '17.
PW: My 26, '17.

V-8   ____ In pawn to a throne / by Demetra Vaka and
Kenneth Brown . . . New York: John Lane
Company; London: John Lane, The Bodley Head,
1919. 326 p.
LC: O 25, '19.
BLC: London: John Lane, 1920.

V-9   In the shadow of Islam / by Demetra Vaka (Mrs. Kenneth-Brown); with illustrations by E. Pollak-Ottendorff. Boston; New York: Houghton Mifflin Company, 1911. (Cambridge: The Riverside Press). 315, [1] p., front., [3] leaves of plates.
LC: O 12, '11.
BLC: London: Constable & Co., Cambridge, Mass. [printed], 1911.

V-10 Vale, Charles, 1875-1928. John Ward, M. D. / by Charles Vale. New York: Mitchell Kennerley, 1913. 320 p.

Vale, Charles, comp. See *Forum stories* **(1914), F-306.**

V-11 Vale, Robert B. Efficiency in Hades: the romantic adventures of an enterprising expert in the lower world / by Robert B. Vale; illustrated by Stuart Hay. New York: Frederick A. Stokes Company, 1923. 148 p., front., ill.
LC: Ag 28, '23.

V-12 Valentine, Edward Abram Uffington, b. 1870. Hecla Sandwith / by Edward Uffington Valentine. Indianapolis: The Bobbs-Merrill Company, [1905]. 433 p.
PW: Mr 25, '05.
BLC: London: Harper & Bros., [printed in U. S. A.], 1905.

V-13   The labyrinth of life / by E. A. U. Valentine. New York: E. P. Dutton & Company, 1912. 385, [1] p.
Printed in Great Britain.
BLC: London: J. M. Dent & Sons, 1912.

V-14 Valentine, Jane, *pseud.* In the market place / by Jane Valentine [pseud.] . . . New York; London; Montreal: The Abbey Press, [c1902]. 618 p. **DLC**
PW: Ja 10, '03.

V-15   Jonas Brand, or, Living within the law / by Jane Valentine [pseud.] . . . New York; London; Montreal: The Abbey Press, [c1901]. 263 p. **NYP**
PW: S 7, '01.

Valentine, Mary. The old pearl necklace. In *Short stories for class reading* **(1925), S-461.**

V-16 Valerga, Susan L. Esperanza / by Susan L. Valerga. [San Francisco, Cal., Press of Brown & Power Stationery Co., c1911]. 174 p. Decorative end papers.

V-17 Van, Jennie E., *pseud.* Wise old Deacon: the story of a dog / by Jennie E. Van [pseud.]. New York: Broadway Publishing Company, 1903. 68 p., front. (port.), [5] leaves of plates.
Unexamined copy: bibliographic data from OCLC, #26960866.

Van Allen, William Harman. See **Van Helmont, Richard, 1870-1931.**

Van Amringe, Jennie Elizabeth Wilmuth, Mrs. See **Van, Jennie, pseud.**

V-18 Van-Anderson, Helen, b. 1859. Carrol's conversion: a story of life / by Helen Van-Anderson . . . New York City: Published by The New York Magazine of Mysteries, [c1904]. 342 p.   **ORU**

V-19 Vanardy, Varick, 1865-1922, *pseud.* Alias "the Night Wind": the story of an all-sweeping revenge against false witnesses / by Varick Vanardy [pseud.]. New York: G. W. Dillingham Company, [c1913]. 316 p., front., [2] leaves of plates. [Ill. by J. Hodson Redman.]
LC: O 18, '13.
PW: N 8, '13.

V-20 [____] A gentleman of quality / by Frederic Van Rensselaer Dey . . . ; with a frontispiece in color by Frank P. Fairbanks. Boston: L. C. Page & Company, 1909. 350 p., col. front.
LC: Mr 19, '09.
PW: Ap 3, '09.
BLC: London: Cassell & Co., 1910.

V-21   The girl by the roadside / by Varick Vanardy [pseud.]. New York: The Macaulay Company, 1917. 314 p., front., [3] leaves of plates. [Ill. by Albert Matzke.]
LC: Je 16, '17.
PW: Je 9, '17.

V-22   The lady of the night wind / by Varick Vanardy [pseud.]. New York: The Macaulay Company, [c1919]. 315 p., front. [Ill. by George W. Gage.]
LC: Ap 10, '19.
PW: Ap 12, '19.

V-23 [____] The magic story / by Frederic Van Rensselaer Dey. New York: The Success Company, 1903. 67 p., front.

V-24   The Night Wind's promise / by Varrick Vanardy [pseud.] . . . New York: G. W. Dillingham Company, [c1914]. 320 p.
LC: O 30, '14.
PW: O 24, '14.

V-25   The return of the Night Wind / by Varick Vanardy [pseud.]. New York: G. W. Dillingham Company, [c1914]. 326 p.
LC: F 5, '14.
PW: F 14, '14.
"A sequel to *Alias the Night Wind.*"

V-26   Something doing / by Varick Vanardy [pseud.] . . . New York: The Macaulay Company, [c1919]. 309 p., front. [Ill. by George W. Gage.]
LC: S 23, '19.
PW: S 13, '19.

V-27 [____] The three keys / by Frederic Ormond [pseud.]; frontispiece by Harrison Fisher. New York: W. J. Watt & Company, [1909]. 301 p., col. front., [2] leaves of plates. [Ill. by Harrison Fisher & George T. Knight.]
LC: Je 14, '09.
PW: Je 26, '09.

V-28 _____ The two-faced man / by Varick Vanardy [pseud.] . . . New York: The Macaulay Company, 1918. 338 p., front. [Ill. by H. J. Peck.]
LC: My 7, '18.
PW: Je 8, '18.

V-29 _____ Up against it / by Varick Vanardy [pseud.]. New York: The Macaulay Company, [c1920]. 369 p., front. [Ill. by George W. Gage.]
LC: S 3, '20.
PW: Ag 14, '20.

V-30 Van Bergen, Robert. A boy of old Japan / by R. Van Bergen . . . ; illustrated with original Japanese color pictures. Boston: Lee and Shepard, 1901. 246 p., col. photo. front., [7] leaves of col. photo. plates. [Photo. by Heliotype Co., Boston.]   WAU

V-31 Van Beverhoudt, O. (Octavius). Melzar: a tale of the Jericho Road / by O. Van Beverhoudt. New York: Broadway Publishing Co., 1913. 319 p.
LC: Jl 10, '13.

V-32 Van Buren, Evelyn. Pippin / by Evelyn Van Buren; with illustrations by Reginald B. Birch. New York: The Century Co., 1913. 316 p., incl. [7] leaves of plates, front.
LC: F 26, '13.
PW: Mr 1, '13.

V-33 _____ Zizi's career / by Evelyn Van Buren. Indianapolis: The Bobbs-Merrill Company, [c1921]. 348 p.
LC: F 7, '21.
PW: Mr 12, '21.

V-34 Van Buren, Sara. The major's niece / by Sara Van Buren Brugière and Adeline Brady. New York; London; Montreal: The Abbey Press, [c1902]. 265 p.

V-35 Vance, Louis Joseph, 1879-1933. Alias the Lone Wolf / by Louis Joseph Vance. Garden City, N. Y.; Toronto: Doubleday, Page & Company, 1921. 348 p., col. front.
LC: N 12, '21.
PW: N 12, '21.
BLC: London: Hodder & Stoughton, [1921].

V-36 _____ The bandbox / by Louis Joseph Vance; with illustrations by Arthur I. Keller. Boston: Little, Brown, and Company, 1912. 319 p., front., [4] leaves of plates (some col.).
LC: Ap 5, '12.
PW: Ap 13, '12.
BLC: London: Grant Richards, [1912].

V-37 _____ Baroque: a mystery / by Louis Joseph Vance. New York: E. P. Dutton & Company, [c1923]. 204 p.
"Under the editorial title of Double doom, this story has appeared serially in McCall's magazine."
LC: My 25, '23.
PW: Je 9, '23.
BLC: London: Hodder & Stoughton, [1923].

V-38 _____ The black bag / by Louis Joseph Vance; with illustrations by Thomas Fogarty. Indianapolis: The Bobbs-Merrill Company, [c1908]. 441 p., front., [9] leaves of plates.
LC: Ja 6, '08.
PW: F 8, '08.
BLC: London: Grant Richards, 1908.

V-39 _____ The brass bowl / by Louis Joseph Vance; with illustrations by Orson Lowell. Indianapolis: The Bobbs-Merrill Company, [1907]. 379, [1] p., front., [6] leaves of plates.
LC: Jl 31, '08.
PW: Mr 30, '07.
BLC: London: Grant Richards, printed in U. S. A., 1907.

V-40 _____ The bronze bell / by Louis Joseph Vance; with illustrations by Harrison Fisher. New York: Dodd, Mead and Company, 1909. 361 p., col. front., [3] leaves of col. plates.
LC: Mr 15, '09.
PW: Mr 27, '09.
BLC: London: Grant Richards, 1909.

V-41 _____ Cynthia-of-the-minute: a romance / by Louis Joseph Vance; illustrations by Arthur I. Keller. New York: Dodd, Mead and Company, 1911. 349 p., front., [3] leaves of plates. "Copyright, 1911 by Louis Joseph Vance as `The crimson rambler.'"
LC: Ap 3, '11.
PW: Ap 8, '11.
BLC: London: B. F. Stevens & Brown, printed in U. S. A., 1911.
Another edition: London: Grant Richards, 1911.

V-42 _____ The dark mirror / by Louis Joseph Vance; illustrated by Rudolph Tandler. Garden City, N. Y.; London: Doubleday, Page and Company, 1920. 368 p., front., [3] leaves of plates.
LC: Ap 5, '20.
PW: Mr 27, '20.
BLC: London: Curtis Brown, Garden City, N. Y. printed, 1920.

V-43 _____ The day of days: an extravaganza / by Louis Joseph Vance . . . ; with illustrations by Arthur William Brown. Boston: Little, Brown and Company, 1913. 300 p., front., [3] leaves of plates.
LC: F 18, '13.
PW: F 15, '13.
BLC: London: Grant Richards, 1914.

V-44 _____ The destroying angel / by Louis Joseph Vance; with illustrations by Arthur I. Keller. Boston: Little, Brown and Company, 1912. 325 p., front., [3] leaves of plates.
LC: O 8, '12.
PW: O 12, '12.
BLC: London: Grant Richards, 1913.

V-45 _____ The false faces: further adventures from the history of the Lone Wolf / by Louis Joseph Vance; frontispiece. Garden City, New York: Doubleday, Page & Company, 1918. 331 p., col. front. [Ill. by Clarence Rowe.]

LC: Ja 30, '18.
PW: Ja 19, '18.
BLC: London: Skeffington & Son, [1920].

V-46 ____ The fortune hunter / by Louis Joseph Vance . . . ; with illustrations by Arthur William Brown. New York: Dodd, Mead and Company, 1910. 338 p., front., [5] leaves of plates. "The plot of the story is taken from the comedy of the same title by Mr. Winchell Smith."
LC: F 12, '10.
PW: F 19, '10.
BLC: London: B. F. Stevens & Brown, printed in U. S. A., 1910.

V-47 ____ Joan Thursday: a novel / by Louis Joseph Vance; with illustrations by Oscar Cesare. Boston: Little, Brown and Company, 1913. 385 p., front., [3] leaves of plates.
LC: S 24, '13.
PW: S 27, '13.
BLC: London: Grant Richards, [1913].

V-48 ____ Linda Lee, incorporated: a novel / by Louis Joseph Vance. New York: E. P. Dutton & Company, [c1922]. 389 p. "Under the title of `The coast of Cockaigne', an abridged version of this story was published serially during the winter of 1921-22 in McCall's magazine."
LC: Ap 18, '22.
PW: Ap 29, '22.

V-49 ____ The Lone Wolf: a melodrama / by Louis Joseph Vance; with illustrations by R. F. Schabelitz. Boston: Little, Brown, and Company, 1914. 315 p., front., [3] leaves of plates.
LC: O 14, '14.
PW: O 17, '14.
BLC: London: E. Nash, 1915.

V-50 ____ The Lone Wolf returns / by Louis Joseph Vance. New York: E. P. Dutton & Co., [c1923]. 367 p.
PW: S 29, '23.
BLC: London: Hodder & Stoughton, [1924].

V-51 ____ Mrs. Paramor / by Louis Joseph Vance. New York: E. P. Dutton & Company, [c1924]. 283 p.
LC: Jl 19, '24.
PW: Jl 19, '24.

____ The mystery of seven minutes. In *Master tales of mystery* (1915), M-588.5.

V-52 ____ No man's land: a romance / by Louis Joseph Vance. New York: Dodd, Mead and Company, 1910. 356 p., col. front., [3] leaves of plates. [Ill. by Thomas Fogarty.]
LC: O 15, '10.
PW: O 22, '10.
BLC: London: B. F. Stevens & Brown, 1910.

V-53 ____ Nobody / by Louis Joseph Vance; illustrated by W. L. Jacobs. New York: George H. Doran Company, [c1915]. 352 p., front., [3] leaves of plates. Illustrated end papers.

This novel was originally published serially under the title of "An Outsider."
LC: O 14, '15.
PW: O 9, '15.
BLC: London: Hodder & Stoughton, printed in U. S. A., 1916.

V-54 ____ The pool of flame / by Louis Joseph Vance . . . ; illustrations by John Rae. New York: Dodd, Mead and Company, 1909. 350 p., front., [3] leaves of plates.
LC: N 5, '09.
PW: D 4, '09.
BLC: London: Grant Richards, 1910.

V-55 ____ The private war: being the truth about Gordon Traill: his personal statement / by Louis Joseph Vance. New York: D. Appleton and Company, 1906. 315 p., front., [3] leaves of plates. [Ill. by H. C. Edwards.] **VPI**
BLC: London: E. Grant Richards, 1906.

V-56 ____ Red masquerade: being the story of the Lone Wolf's daughter / by Louis Joseph Vance; frontispiece by Douglas Duer. Garden City, N. Y.: Doubleday, Page & Company, 1921. 311, [1] p., front.
LC: Je 14, '21.
PW: Je 4, '21.
BLC: London: Hodder & Stoughton, [1921].

V-57 ____ The road to En-Dor: a novel / by Louis Joseph Vance. New York: E. P. Dutton & Company, [c1923-1924]. 396 p.
PW: F 28, '25.

V-58 ____ Sheep's clothing / by Louis Joseph Vance; with illustrations by James Montgomery Flagg. Boston: Little, Brown, and Company, 1915. 279 p., front., [4] leaves of plates.
LC: F 20, '15.
PW: F 13, '15.

V-59 ____ Terence O'Rourke: gentleman adventurer / by Louis Joseph Vance . . . New York: A. Wessels Company, 1905. 393 p., col. front. [Ill. by W. V. Cahill.]
Cover title: *The romance of Terence O'Rourke.*
PW: Je 24, '05.
BLC: London: E. Grant Richards, printed in U. S. A., 1906.

V-60 ____ The trey o' hearts: a motion-picture melodrama / by Louis Joseph Vance . . . ; illustrated with photographs from the picture-play production by the Universal Film Manufacturing Company. New York: Grosset & Dunlap, [c1914]. 283, [1] p., photo. front., [15] leaves of double-sided photo. plates.
LC: N 28, '14.
PW: Ja 2, '15.

V-61 Vance, Thomas L. Yahweh: a god of blood and fire / by Thomas L. Vance. Seattle, Washington: The Crucible Publishing Company, 1924, [c1923]. 296 p.
LC: D 7, '23.

V-62 Vance, Wilson J., 1846-1911. Big John Baldwin: extracts from the journal of an officer of Cromwell's army recording some of his experiences at the court of Charles I and subsequently at that of the Lord Protector and on the fields of love and war, and finally in the colony of Virginia / edited with sparing hand by Wilson Vance. New York: Henry Holt and Company, 1909. 375 p.
LC: S 14, '09.

V-63 Van Coover, A. J. The slow-grinding mills / by A. J. Van Coover . . . New York: The Abbey Press, [c1903]. 234 p.

V-64 Van Curen, C. M. (Charles Melvin). The waif of the wreck and Joe Gains / by C. M. Van Curen. Bolivar, N. Y.: Van Publishing Company, [c1919]. (Baltimore, Md.: George W. King Printing Co.) 248 p.
LC: Ap 12, '20.
PW: Je 12, '20.

V-65 Vandeburg, Millie Bird, b. 1886. The door to the moor / by Millie Bird Vandeburg. Philadelphia: Dorrance and Company, 1925. 264 p.
PW: My 30, '25.
BLC: London: Cassell & Co., 1927.

V-66 Vandegriff, Margaret, 1845-1913, *pseud.* Umbrellas to mend / by Margaret Vandegrift [pseud.] . . . Boston: Richard G. Badger, 1905. (Boston: The Gorham Press). 176 p.
PW: F 24, '06.

Van den Bark, Melvin. Two women and Hog-back Ridge. In *The best short stories of 1924 and the yearbook of the American short story* (1925), B-569.

V-67 Van Denburg, Frank A. Hezekiah's kortship / by Hezekiah Jones' wife; Frank A. Van Denburg. Boston: Richard G. Badger, 1904. (Boston, U. S. A.: The Gorham Press). 183 p.

V-68 Van Denburgh, Mary T. (Mary Turrill). Ye On's ten hundred sorrows: and other stories / by Mary T. Van Denburgh. San Francisco: The Murdock Press, 1907. 50 p., ill.
Partly reprinted from various periodicals.
Contents: Ye On's ten hundred sorrows -- The doll of the white devils -- The exiles -- See Wah's New Year.

V-69 Vandercook, Margaret, b. 1876. The loves of Ambrose / by Margaret Vandercook; illustrated by Gordon Grant. Garden City, N. Y.: Doubleday, Page & Company, 1914. 233 p., front. Illustrated t. p. and end papers.

V-70 Van der Naillen, A. (Albert), 1830-1928. Balthazar the Magus / by A. Van der Naillen . . . New York: R. F. Fenno & Company, 1904. 270 p., photo. front. (port.)., [2] leaves of plates, ill.
PW: Ag 27, '04.

Van Deventer, Emma M. See **Lynch, Lawrence L., pseud.**

V-71 Van de Water, Virginia Terhune, 1865-1945. In the web of life / by Virginia Terhune Van de Water . . . ; illustrated. New York: Hearst's International Library Co., [c1914]. 345 p., front., [3] leaves of plates.
PW: D 5, '14.

V-72 ____ The shears of Delilah: stories of married life / by Virginia Terhune Van de Water. New York; London: G. P. Putnam's Sons, 1914. (The Knickerbocker Press). 312 p., col. front. [Ill. by Robert Edwards.]
Reprinted in part from various periodicals.
Contents: The shears of Delilah -- Good for the soul? -- Passing the love of women -- A biological factor -- The liar -- The outsider -- New wine in old bottles -- The first stone -- Confessions of a "successful" mother -- The nagger.
LC: F 17, '14.
PW: F 21, '14.

V-73 ____ The two sisters / by Virginia Terhune Van de Water . . . ; illustrated. New York: Hearst's International Library Co., 1914. 332 p., front., [4] leaves of plates. [Ill. by H. C. Wall & A. I. Keller.]
LC: My 12, '14.
PW: My 30, '14.

V-74 ____ Why I left my husband: and other human documents of married life / by Virginia Terhune Van de Water. New York: Moffat, Yard and Company, 1912. 261 p.
Reprinted from the Cosmopolitan and Good housekeeping.
Contents: Why I left my husband -- Why I left my wife -- Why we are living together -- Whom God hath joined -- Why I left home -- Why I married again -- The tie that binds.
LC: O 11, '12.
PW: O 12, '12.

V-75 [Van Dine, S. S.], *pseud.* The man of promise / by Willard Huntington Wright. New York: John Lane Company; London: John Lane, The Bodley Head, 1916. 351 p.
PW: F 26, '16.

Van Dine, Warren L., b.1902. The poet. In *The best short stories of 1924 and the yearbook of the American short story* (1925), B-569.

V-76 Van Doren, Carl, 1885-1950. Other provinces / Carl Van Doren. New York: Alfred A. Knopf, 1925. 149 p.

V-77 Van Dresser, Jasmine Stone, b. 1875. Gibby of Clamshell Alley / by Jasmine Stone Van Dresser; illustrations by William Van Dresser. New York: Dodd, Mead and Company, 1916. 378 p., front., [7] leaves of plates. Illustrated end papers.
LC: Mr 21, '16.

V-78 Van Duesen, Rebecca. Sea breezes and sand dunes / by Rebecca Van Duesen. New York; London; Montreal: The Abbey Press, [c1902]. 192 p.

V-79 Van Dyke, Henry, 1852-1933. The blue flower / by Henry Van Dyke; illustrated. New York: Charles Scribner's Sons, 1902. 298, [1] p., col. front., [7] leaves of col. plates. [Ill. by Howard Pyle, C. K. Linson, J. R. Weguelin, Arthur Heming, and F. V. DuMond.]

Contents: The blue flower -- The souce -- The mill -- Spy rock -- Wood-magic -- The other wise man -- A handful of clay -- The lost word -- The first Christmas-tree.
PW: N 8, '02.
BLC: London: George Newnes, New York printed, 1902.

V-80 _____ The broken soldier and the maid of France / by Henry Van Dyke; with illustrations by Frank E. Schoonover. New York; London: Harper & Brothers, 1919. 65, [1] p.
LC: S 9, '19.
PW: S 20, '19.

V-81 _____ Half-told tales / by Henry Van Dyke. New York: Charles Scribner's Sons, 1925. 150 p., ill. [Ill. by Garth Jones.]
Contents: A tale of travel -- Tale of the two runners --Tale of the cursing of capital -- Tale of the jewels -- Tale of a habitation forfeited -- A parable of wedlock -- Tale of learning by experience -- Tale of the embankment -- Tale of the two wolves -- The Jericho road -- Tale of the hitching-post -- Tale of the only infallible soap -- A man praying -- Tale of the shaky bridge -- Tale of the prisoner --Tale of the philosophic husband -- A tale of peace -- A tale of man and the machine -- A tale of friends -- The key of the tower -- The king's jewel -- The ripening of the fruit -- An old game -- A change of air -- Beggars under the bush -- Stronghold -- The return of the charm --In the odor of sanctity -- The primitive and his sandals -- The hero and tin soldiers.
LC: O 14, '25.
PW: O 3, '25.

V-82 _____ The lost boy / by Henry Van Dyke; illustrated. New York; London: Harper & Brothers, 1914. 68, [1] p., front., [2] leaves of plates. [Ill. by N. C. Wyeth.]
LC: S 14, '14.
PW: S 26, '14.

V-83 _____ The mansion / by Henry Van Dyke; with illustrations by Elizabeth Shippen Green. New York; London: Harper & Brothers, 1911. 60, [1] p., front. Inserted t. p. counted in pagination.
LC: O 16, '11.
PW: O 21, '11.
Holiday edition: 44, [1] p., col. ill. and ill. end papers.

V-84 _____ The ruling passion: tales of nature and human nature / by Henry Van Dyke; with illustrations by W. Appleton Clark. New York: Charles Scribner's Sons, 1901. 295, [1] p., col. front., [7] leaves of col. plates.
Contents: A lover of music -- The reward of virtue -- A brave heart -- The gentle life -- A friend of justice -- The white blot -- A year of nobility -- The keeper of the light.
PW: O 19, '01.
BLC: Toronto: Copp, Clark Co., 1901.

V-85 _____ The sad shepherd: a Christmas story / by Henry Van Dyke. New York: Charles Scribner's Sons, 1911. 56 p., front.
LC: S 13, '11.
PW: S 16, '11.
BLC: London & New York: Harper & Bros., 1912.

V-86 _____ The spirit of Christmas / by Henry Van Dyke. New York: Charles Scribner's Sons, 1905. 59 p., front.
Contents: A dream-story: The Christmas angel -- A little essay: Christmas-giving and Christmas-living -- A short Christmas sermon: Keeping Christmas -- Two Christmas prayers: A Christmas prayer for the home -- A Christmas prayer for lonely folks.
PW: N 18, '05.

V-87 _____ The unknown quantity: a book of romance and some half-told tales / by Henry Van Dyke. New York: Charles Scribner's Sons, 1912. 370 p., col. front. [6] leaves of plates (some col.). [Ill. by Charles S. Chapman, Garth Jones, Sigismond [sic] de Ivanowski, Paul Julien Meylan, and Blendon Campbell.]
Contents: The wedding-ring -- Messengers at the window -- The countersign of the cradle -- The key of the tower -- The ripening of the fruit -- The king's jewel -- The music-lover -- Humoreske -- An old game -- The unruly sprite -- A change of air -- The night call -- The effectual fervent prayer -- The return of the charm -- Beggars under the bush -- Stronghold -- In the odour of sanctity -- The sad shepherd -- The mansion.
LC: O 15, '12.
PW: O 19, '12.

V-88 _____ The valley of vision; a book of romance, and some half-told tales / by Henry Van Dyke . . . New York: Charles Scribner's Sons, 1919. 306 p., front., [7] leaves of plates. [Ill. by Franklin Booth, E. Hopper, and Holman Hunt.] **YNG**
Contents: A remembered dream -- Antwerp road -- A city of refuge -- A sanctuary of trees -- The king's high way -- The traitor in the house -- Justice of the elements -- Ashes of vengeance -- The broken soldier and the maid of France -- The hearing ear -- Sketches of Quebec -- A classic instance -- The new era and carry on -- The primitive and his sandals -- Diana and the lions -- The hero and the tin soldiers -- Salvage point -- The boy of Nazareth dreams.
LC: Mr 20, '19.

_____, contributor. See *The whole family* (1908), **W-578.**

V-89 Van Dyne, Anna Lyle. On the Indian trail / by A. Lyle Van Dyne. Chicago: Printed for the author by the Abingdon Press, [c1921]. 120 p. **IMN**

Van Dyne, Edith, pseud. See **Baum, Lyman Frank, 1856-1919.**

Vane, Isabella Cornelia de. See **De Vane, I. C. (Isabella Cornelia).**

V-90 Van Fossen, Loo B. The romance of the Hamilton estate: a novel / by Loo B. Van Fossen; illustrated by H. E. Crawford. Kansas City, Mo.: Burton Publishing Company, [c1915]. 167 p., incl. front., [1] leaf of plates.

V-91 Van Gorden, Scott. The frontiersman's vengeance / by Scott Van Gorden. Chicago: Rhodes & McClure Publishing Company, 1904. 289 p., [1] leaf of plates, ill.

V-92 _____ The pioneer's hoard: a thrilling romance of the Ozarks / by Scott Van Gorden; handsomely illustrated. Chicago: Rhodes & McClure Publishing Company, 1902, [c1903]. 530 p., front., ill. [Some ill. by H. S. De Lay.] Decorative end papers.
PW: F 28, '03.

V-93 _____ Rough life on the frontier / by Scott Van Gorden; handsomely illustrated. Chicago: Rhodes & McClure Publishing Company, [1903]. 530 p., front., ill. [Ill. by H. S. De Lay.] **EEM**
Another edition: Chicago: Thos. W. Jackson Publishing Company, [c1903]. **KSU**

V-94 Van Helmont, Richard, 1870-1931. The legend of the Monk Lawrence / by Richard Van Helmont. Boston: Privately printed, 1905. 22 p. **NYP** Caption title.

V-95 Van Houtte, Albert Leon, b. 1888. The bells of El Carmelo: a romance of California of today / by Albert Leon Van Houtte; photographic illustrations by L. S. Slevin, Carmel, Calif. Los Angeles: Times-Mirror Press, 1923. 141 p., photo. front. (port.), photo. ill.

V-96 Van Leer, Marshall Benjamin. The call of the hills / Marshall Benjamin Van Leer. Cincinnati: Jennings and Graham; New York: Eaton and Mains, [c1913]. 236 p., col. front. **DLC**

V-97 Van Loan, Charles E. (Charles Emmett), 1876-1919. The big league / by Charles E. Van Loan. Boston: Small, Maynard and Company, [c1911]. 252 p., incl. front. [Ill. by Arthur Carey.] **FUG**
Contents: The Crab -- The low brow -- The fresh guy -- The quitter -- The bush league demon -- The cast-off -- The busher -- A job for the pitcher -- The golden ball of the Argonauts.
LC: Jl 29, '11.
PW: Jl 1, '11.

V-98 ____ Buck Parvin and the movies / by Charles E. Van Loan; illustrated by Arthur William Brown. New York: George H. Doran Company, [c1915]. 366 p., front., [7] leaves of plates. Illustrated end papers.
Contents: The extra man and the milkfed lion -- The international cup -- Man-afraid-of-his wardrobe -- Water stuff -- Buck's lady friend -- Desert stuff -- Author! Author! -- Snow stuff -- This is the life.
LC: O 5, '15.
PW: S 18, '15.

V-99 ____ Fore! / by Charles E. Van Loan. New York: George H. Doran Company, [c1918]. 328 p.
Contents: Gentlemen, you can't go through -- Little Poison Ivy -- The Major, D. O. S. -- A mixed foursome -- "Similia similibus curantur" -- A cure for lumbago -- The man who quit -- The Ooley-cow -- Adolphus and the rough diamond.
LC: My 20, '18.
PW: My 25, '18.

V-100 ____ Inside the ropes / by Charles E. Van Loan; illustrated by Arthur Hutchins. Boston: Small, Maynard and Company, [c1913]. 411 p., front., [2] leaves of plates.
LC: Ap 1, '13.
PW: My 3, '13.

V-101 ____ The lucky seventh: tales of the big league / by Charles E. Van Loan . . . ; illustrated by Hibberd V. B. Kline. Boston: Small, Maynard and Company, [c1913]. 337 p., front.
Contents: The Mexican marvel -- The good old wagon -- For revenue -- The bachelor Benedict -- "Butterfly" Boggs: pitcher -- Will a duck swim? -- Crossed "signs" -- Won off diamond -- The pitch-out.
LC: My 2, '13.
PW: My 3, '13.

____ Mister Conley. In *The Sporting spirit* (1925), **S-771.**

V-102 ____ Old man Curry: race track stories / by Charles E. Van Loan; introduction by L. B. Yates. New York: George H. Doran Company, [c1917]. 276 p.
Contents: Levelling with Elisha -- Playing even for Obadiah -- By a hair -- The last chance -- Sanguinary Jeremiah -- Eliphaz, late Fairfax -- The redemption handicap -- A morning workout -- Egyptian corn -- The modern judgment of Solomon.
LC: O 9, '17.
PW: S 29, '17.

V-103 ____ Score by innings: baseball stories / by Charles E. Van Loan; introduction by Grantland Rice. New York: George H. Doran Company, 1919. 349 p., photo. front. (port.).
Contents: The National Commission decides -- Piute vs. Piute -- Chivalry in Carbon County -- The squirrel -- IOU -- The bone doctor -- His own stuff -- Excess baggage -- Nine assists and two errors -- Mister Conley.
LC: Mr 29, '19.
PW: F 15, '19.

V-104 ____ Taking the count: prize ring stories / by Charles E. Van Loan; foreword by Irvin S. Cobb. New York: George H. Doran Company, [c1915]. 354 p.
Contents: The sporting doctor -- One thirty-three -- Ringside -- The spotted sheep -- On account of a lady -- No business -- Out of his class -- Scrap iron -- The pearl brooch -- The revenge of Kid Morales -- Easy picking -- For the pictures.
LC: S 19, '19.
PW: S 20, '19.

V-105 ____ The ten-thousand-dollar arm: and other tales of the big league / by Charles E. Van Loan . . . ; illustrated by Wallace Goldsmith. Boston: Small, Maynard and Company, [c1912]. 336 p., front., [13] leaves of plates.
Contents: The ten-thousand-dollar arm -- Sweeney to Sanguinetti to Schultz -- Little Sunset -- The loosening up of Hogan -- The Phantom league -- The comeback -- Behind the mask -- McCluskey's prodigal -- A rain check.
LC: My 16, '12.
PW: My 11, '12.

V-106 Van Loan, Philip. The soul of the violin: a dramatic musical inspiration / by Philip Van Loan. New York, N. Y.: Published by Dramus Producing and Releasing Co., Inc., [c1919-1924]. 180 p., [8] leaves of plates. [Some ill. by the author.]

V-107 Van Loon, Hendrik Willem, 1882-1944. The story of Wilbur the Hat: being a true account of the strange things which sometimes happen in a part of the world which does not exist / written and drawn for the fun of it by Hendrik Willem Van Loon. New York: Horace B. Liveright, [c1925]. 110 p., col. ill. Designed end papers.
LC: Mr 27, '25.
PW: Mr 28, '25.

V-108 Van Norden, Charles, 1843-1913. Yoland of Idle Isle / Charles Van Norden. New York: D. Appleton and Company, 1907. 306 p.
LC: S 6, '07.
PW: S 14, '07.

V-109 Van Ogle, A. Nobody's cousin / by A. Van Ogle. New York: Cochrane Publishing Company, 1910. 108 p. **DLC**
LC: Ap 28, '10.

V-110 Van Praag, Francis Wells. Clayton Halowell / by Francis W. van Praag; illustrations by Winthrop Earle. New York: R. F. Fenno & Company, [c1901]. 304 p., front., [8] leaves of plates.
PW: Mr 23, '01.

V-111 _____ The weaving of webs / by F. W. Van Praag . . . New York: R. F. Fenno & Company, 1902. 366 p.
PW: N 22, '02.

Van Saanen, Marie Louise, pseud. See **Rutledge, Maryse, pseud.**

V-112 Van Santvoord, Seymour, 1858-1938. Octavia: a tale of ancient Rome / by Seymour Van Santvoord . . . New York: E. P. Dutton & Company, [c1923]. 458 p., front., [2] leaves of plates.
LC: Jl 6, '23.

V-113 Van Schaick, George, 1861-1924. The girl at Big Loon post / by George Van Schaick . . . ; illustrated by I. D. Sisson. Boston: Small, Maynard & Company, [c1916]. 413 p., col. front., [3] leaves of plates.
LC: S 18, '16.
PW: S 2, '16.

V-114 _____ The peace of Roaring River / by George Van Schaick . . . with illustrations by W. H. D. Koerner. Boston: Small, Maynard & Company, [c1918]. 313 p., incl. front., [3] leaves of plates.
LC: D 30, '18.
PW: N 9, '18.
BLC: London: Hurst & Blackett, [1918].

V-115 _____ The son of the otter / by George Van Schaick . . . Boston: Small, Maynard & Company, [c1915]. 345 p., col. front.
LC: N 29, '15.
PW: N 27, '15.

V-116 _____ Sweetapple Cove / by George Van Schaick; with a frontispiece by George W. Gage. Boston: Small, Maynard & Company, [c1914]. 386 p., col. front.
LC: My 20, '14.
PW: My 2, '14.

V-117 _____ A top-floor idyl / by George Van Schaick; illustrated by Chase Emerson. Boston: Small, Maynard & Company, [c1917]. 433 p., col. front., [2] leaves of plates.
LC: S 7, '17.
PW: Ag 25, '17.
BLC: London: Skeffington & Son, [1919].

Van Shierbrand, Wolf. Ahead of the world. In *Second suds sayings* (1919), S-266.

V-118 Van Slingerland, Nellie Bingham, b. 1850. Cupid the devil's stoker: a romance of heredity in Argentina and Old Spain / by Nellie Bingham Van Slingerland (Neile Bevans); eighteen illustrations by Charles Dalton Cathcart. New York: Guarantee Publishing Co., 1905. 264 p., photo. front. (port.), [14] leaves of plates, ill.
PW: D 16, '05.

LC records another edition: New York: Fifth Avenue Publishing Co., 1905.

V-119 Van Slyke, Lucille, b. 1880. Eve's other children / by Lucille Baldwin Van Slyke; with four illustrations by Wladislaw T. Benda. New York: Frederick A. Stokes Company, 1912. 275 p., front., [3] leaves of plates. **OSU, CWR**
LC: S 16, '12.
PW: S 21, '12.

V-120 _____ Little miss by-the-day / by Lucille Van Slyke . . . ; with a frontispiece in color by Mabel Hatt. New York: Frederick A. Stokes Company, [c1919]. 304 p., col. front.
LC: O 3, '19.
BLC: London: Nisbet & Co., 1920.

V-121 _____ Nora pays / by Lucille Van Slyke . . . . New York: Frederick A. Stokes Company, 1925. 309 p.
LC: Ja 24, '25.
PW: Ja 24, '25.
BLC: London: Methuen & Co., 1925.

V-122 Van Steinburg, Dora F. Aunt Tirzah: a novel / by Dora F. Van Steinburg. New York: Broadway Publishing Co., [c1910]. 253 p.
LC: N 18, '10; D 24, 10.

V-123 Van Vechten, Carl, 1880-1964. The blind bow-boy / Carl Van Vechten; with a decoration by Robert E. Locher. New York: Alfred A. Knopf, 1923. 261 p., col. front.
Cunningham and Kellner note tall paper edition.
LC: Ag 21, '23.
PW: Ag 18, '23.
BLC: London: Grant Richards, 1923.
References: Kellner, A 13; Cunningham, 15.

V-124 _____ Firecrackers: a realistic novel / by Carl Van Vechten. New York: Alfred A. Knopf, 1925. 246 p.
Kellner notes tall paper edition.
LC: Ag 28, '25.
PW: Ag 8, '25.
References: Kellner, A 16.

V-125 _____ Peter Whiffle: his life and works / Carl Van Vechten. New York: Alfred A. Knopf, 1922. 247 p.
Cunningham and Kellner note private edition.
LC: Ap 26, '22.
PW: Ap 15, '22.
BLC: London: Grant Richards, 1923.
References: Kellner, A 12; Cunningham 14.

V-126 _____ The tattooed countess: a romantic novel with a happy ending / Carl Van Vechten. New York: Alfred A. Knopf, 1924. 286 p.
Cunningham and Kellner note tall paper edition.
LC: Ag 26, '24.
PW: Ag 16, '24.
References: Kellner, A 14; Cunningham 16.

V-127 Van Vorst, John, Mrs., 1873-1928. Bagsby's daughter / by Bessie & Marie Van Vorst . . . New York; London: Harper & Brothers, 1901. 337,

[1] p., front., [10] leaves of plates. [Ill. by C. Carleton.]
PW: O 12, '01.

V-128 ____ The issues of life: a novel of the American woman of today / by Mrs. John Van Vorst. New York: Doubleday, Page & Company, 1904. 343 p.
PW: Ap 16, '04.
BLC: London: Doubleday, Page & Co., New York printed, 1904.

V-129 ____ Letters to women in love / by Mrs. John Van Vorst. New York: D. Appleton and Company, 1906. 309 p., front. (port.).
Contents: Foreword -- To Miss Beatrice Thayer -- To Mrs. Elizabeth Aiken -- To Mrs. Jack Burnside -- To Mrs. Mortimer Cairesbrooke.
PW: O 13, '06.

V-130 Van Vorst, Marie, 1867-1936. Amanda of the mill: a novel / by Marie Van Vorst. New York: Dodd, Mead & Company, 1905. 340 p.
PW: Ap 8, '05.
BLC: London: William Heinemann, 1904.

____, jt. aut. *Bagsby's daughter* (1901). <u>See</u> **Van Vorst, John, Mrs., 1873-1928, jt. aut., V-127.**

V-131 ____ Big Tremaine: a novel / by Marie Van Vorst; with frontispiece by W. B. King. Boston: Little, Brown, and Company, 1914. 373 p., front.
LC: O 6, '14.
PW: O 10, '14.

V-132 ____ The broken bell / by Marie Van Vorst; illustrated by Frank Craig. Indianapolis: The Bobbs-Merrill Company, [c1912]. 276, [1] p., front., [3] leaves of plates.
LC: My 8, '12.
PW: My 4, '12.
BLC: London: Constable & Co., 1913.

V-133 ____ Fairfax and his pride: a novel / by Marie Van Vorst. Boston: Small, Maynard & Company, [c1920]. 352 p.
LC: Mr 8, '20.
PW: Mr 13, '20.
BLC: London: Chatto & Windus, 1913.

V-134 ____ First love / by Marie Van Vorst . . . ; with illustrations by F. Graham Cootes. Indianapolis: The Bobbs-Merrill Company, [c1910]. 330 p., front., [4] leaves of plates.
LC: O 12, '10.
PW: O 15, '10.
BLC: London: Mills & Boon, 1910.

V-135 ____ The girl from his town / by Marie Van Vorst; with illustrations by F. Graham Cootes. Indianapolis: The Bobbs-Merrill Company, [c1910]. 327, [1] p., front., [3] leaves of plates.
LC: Mr 23, '10.
PW: Mr 26, '10.
BLC: London: Mills & Boon, 1910.

V-136 ____ His love story / by Marie Van Vorst . . . ; illustrations by Howard Chandler Christy. Indianapolis: The Bobbs-Merrill Company, [c1913]. 284, [1] p., col. front., [5] leaves of col. plates. Illustrated end papers.

LC: My 26, '13.
PW: My 31, '13.
BLC: London: Mills & Boon, 1914.

V-137 ____ In ambush / by Marie Van Vorst . . . Philadelphia: J. B. Lippincott Company, 1909. 303 p.
LC: O 29, '09.
PW: N 13, '09.
BLC: London: Methuen & Co., 1909.

V-138 ____ Mary Moreland: a novel / by Marie Van Vorst . . . ; with frontispiece by C. H. Taffs. Boston: Little, Brown and Company, 1915. 359 p., front.
LC: My 24, '15.
PW: My 29, '15.
BLC: London: Mills & Boon, [1915].

V-139 ____ Miss Desmond: an impression / by Marie Van Vorst. New York: The Macmillan Company; London: Macmillan & Co., Ltd., 1905. 268 p.
PW: N 18, '05.
London: William Heinemann, Norwood, Mass. [printed], 1905.

V-140 ____ Philip Longstreth: a novel / by Marie van Vorst. New York; London: Harper & Brothers, 1902. 395, [1] p.
PW: Ap 19, '02.

V-141 ____ The queen of Karmania / by Marie Van Vorst. Boston: Small, Maynard & Company, [c1922]. 358 p.
LC: Ap 8, '22.
PW: Ap 29, '22.
BLC: London: Mills & Boon, 1922.

V-142 ____ The sentimental adventures of Jimmy Bulstrode / by Marie Van Vorst; with illustrations by Alonzo Kimball. New York: Charles Scribner's Sons, 1908. 374 p., front., [3] leaves of plates.
PW: Mr 28, '08.
BLC: London: Methuen & Co., 1908.

V-143 ____ The sin of George Warrener / by Marie Van Vorst . . . New York; London: The Macmillan Company, 1906. 316 p.
PW: Je 23, '06.
BLC: London: William Heinemann, 1906.

V-144 ____ Sunrise / by Marie Van Vorst. New York: Dodd, Mead and Company, 1924. 243 p.
LC: S 4, '24.
PW: Ag 30, '24.
BLC: London: Mills & Boon, 1924.

V-145 ____ Tradition / by Marie Van Vorst. Boston: Small, Maynard & Company, [c1921]. 277 p.
LC: O 4, '21.
PW: S 24, '21.
BLC: London: Mills & Boon, 1921.

V-146 Van Zandt, Earl C. (Earl Christian), b. 1894. Yank-the Crusader / by Earl C. Van Zandt. Denver, Colorado: The Wahlgreen Publishing Company, 1919. 242 p., plates. **DLC**

LC: Ag 25, '19.
Another edition: Denver, Colorado: [Published by Walter C. Erickson], August 1919. 242 p., [8] leaves of photo. plates.

V-147   Van Zile, Edward S. (Edward Sims), 1863-1931. A duke and his double / by Edward S. Van Zile; with frontispiece by Florence Scovel Shinn. New York: Henry Holt and Company, 1903. 187 p., front.
PW: Ag 1, '03.
BLC: London: William Heinemann, 1903.

V-148   ____ Perkins, the fakeer: a travesty on reincarnation; his wonderful workings in the cases of "When Reginald was Caroline", "How Chopin came to Remsen", and "Clarissa's troublesome baby" / by Edward S. Van Zile; illustrated by Hy Mayer. New York; London: The Smart Set Publishing Co., 1903. 377 p., incl. front., [3] leaves of plates.
PW: My 9, '03.

V-149   Vargo, Rose. Their broken promise / by Rose (Kiss) Vargo . . . [Wilkes-Barre, Pa. ?]: Sold only by the author, [c1918]. 187 p. Designed end papers. **DLC**
LC: Ag 15, '19.

V-150   Varney, George R. Out of the depths: a story of Western love, religion and reform / by George R. Varney. Philadelphia; Boston; Chicago; St. Louis; Atlanta; Dallas: The Griffith & Rowland Press, [c1909]. 429 p., col. photo. front., [3] leaves of photo. plates.
LC: Je 5, '09.
PW: Je 19, '09.

V-151   Varney, Harold Lord. Revolt / Harold Lord Varney. New York: Irving Kaye Davis & Co., 1919. 416 p., ill.
Unexamined copy: bibliographic data from PW.
PW: Ag 16, '19.

V-152   Vassall, William F. Under the skin / by William F. Vassall. Brooklyn, N. Y.: F. Stone Williams Co., [c1923]. 309 p.   **DLC**

V-153   Vaughn, Emma Upton. The Cresap pension: a story of a perculiar [sic] pension fraud / by Emma Upton Vaughn . . . ; illustrated by H. E. Crawford. Kansas City, Mo.: Burton Publishing Company, 1915. 338 p., incl. col. front., [4] leaves of plates.   **DLC**
LC: D 20, '15.

V-154   ____ The lower bureau drawer / by Emma Upton Vaughn. New York: The Editor Company, [c1903]. 180 p.

V-155   Veatch, Byron E. (Byron Elbert), 1858-1930. Men who dared / by Byron E. Veatch. Chicago, Ill.: Homer Harisun & Co., [c1908]. 346 p.
Contents: The fiddlin' kid -- The two samurai -- The silent friend -- Old Rogers -- A delayed verdict -- The king of Calaveras -- Next Christmas.
LC: D 28, '08.
PW: Ap 3, '09.

V-156   ____ Next Christmas / by Byron E. Veatch . . . Chicago: Browne & Howell Co., 1913. 63 p.
LC: O 6, '13.
PW: O 25, '13.

V-157   ____ The two Samurai / by Byron E. Veatch . . . Chicago: F. G. Browne & Co., 1913. 43 p., col. front. Illustrted end papers.
LC: Mr 5, '13.
PW: Mr 8, '13.

Venable, Edward C. (Edward Carrington), 1884-1936. At Isham's. In *The best short stories of 1918 and the yearbook of the American short story (1919), B-563.*

V-158   ____ Pierre Vinton: the adventures of a superfluous husband / by Edward C. Venable. New York: Charles Scribner's Sons, 1914. 256 p.
LC: O 14, '14.

V-159   Venable, William Henry, 1836-1920. A dream of empire, or, The house of Blennerhassett / by William Henry Venable. New York: Dodd, Mead and Company, 1901. 344 p.
PW: My 18, '01.

VerBeck, Hanna Rion. See **Rion, Hanna.**

Vermilye, Frederick M., Mrs. See **Jordan, Kate.**

V-160   Vernon, Thomas R., b. 1854. Rob Baxter: romance of a country boy / by Thomas R. Vernon . . . ; illustrated by William Redheffer. Harleysville, PA: I. R. Haldeman, 1904. 139 p., photo. front. (port.), [4] leaves of plates.
Cover title: *Rob Baxter: a story of a country bred boy.*
LC records: Media, Pa.: T. V. Cooper & Sons, 1904.

V-161   Verrall, Anthony. The new commandment / by Anthony Verrall. New York: Edward J. Clode, [c1909]. 240 p.
LC: Ag 24, '09.
BLC: London: T. Werner Laurie, [1910].

V-162   Vesey, Arthur Henry. The castle of lies / by Arthur Henry Vesey. New York: D. Appleton and Company, 1906. 363 p.
PW: My 5, '06.

V-163   ____ The clock and the key / by Arthur Henry Vesey . . . New York: D. Appleton and Company, 1905. 303 p.   **NYP**
PW: F 11, '05.
BLC: London: Sidney Appleton, 1905.

V-164   Veterans all / Anonymous. New York: American Library Service, 1925, [c1924]. 200 p.
PW: F 14, '25.

V-165   Viclare, Julien, *pseud.* Amethyst Gray: the evangelist's temptation / by Julien Viclare [pseud.]. [Buffalo, N. Y.]: Press of A. H. Morey Printing Company, 1902]. 272 p.
Unexamined copy: bibliographic data from NUC.

V-166   Viélé, Herman Knickerbocker, 1856-1908. Heartbreak Hill: a comedy romance / by Herman Knickerbocker Viélé . . . ; illustrations by John Rae. New York: Duffield & Company, 1908. 330 p., col. front., [5] leaves of col. plates, ill.
LC: S 10, '08.

V-167   ____ The last of the Knickerbockers: a comedy romance / by Herman Knickerbocker Vielé . . . Eldridge Court, Chicago: Herbert S. Stone & Company, 1901. 354 p.
PW: N 9, '01.

V-168   ____ Myra of the pines / by Herman Knickerbocker Vielé. New York: McClure, Phillips & Co., 1902. 326 p.
PW: Je 14, '02.
BLC: London: T. Fisher Unwin, 1904.

V-169   ____ On the lightship / by Herman Knickerbocker Vielé; introduction by Thomas A. Janvier. New York: Duffield & Company, 1909. 312 p.
Contents: Introduction -- The story of Ignatius, the Almoner -- The dead man's chest -- The Carhart mystery -- The monstrosity -- The priestess of Amen Ra -- The girl from Mercury -- The unexpected letter -- The money meter -- The guest of honor -- The man without a pension.
LC: S 21, '09.

V-170   Viereck, George Sylvester, 1884-1962. The house of the vampire / by George Sylvester Viereck . . . New York: Moffat, Yard & Company, 1907. 190 p.
LC: S 7, '07.
PW: O 5, '07.

V-171   Vila, Annie Fields, b. 1844. The former countess: a romance of the French revolution / by Annie Fields Vila. Boston: Sherman, French & Company, 1912. 227 p., incl. [3] leaves of plates, front. [Ill. by Elizabeth Train & Frank T. Merrill.]
LC: Ja 8, '13.
PW: Ja 11, '13.

V-172   [____] Inherited freedom: dedicated to the daughters of the revolution in America, the D. R. and the D. A. R. / written by a daughter. Boston: Published by the W. B. Clarke Company, [c1905]. 260 p., photo. front. (port.).   **DLC**

V-173   Villa, Silvio. The unbidden guest / by Silvio Villa, with four illustrations by Carlo Beuf. New York: The Macmillan Company, 1922. 284 p., [4] leaves of plates.   **KSU**

V-174   Villars, Isaiah, 1839-1915. Ministerial misfit, or, The biography of Rev. Timothy Tanglefoot / by Isaiah Villars. . . Springfield, Ill.: Press of Illinois State Register, 1901. 250 p.
PW: S 7, '01.

V-175   Vilsack, Gladys Brace. The unpardonable sin / by Gladys Brace Vilsack. New York: Broadway Publishing Co., [c1915]. 186 p.   **DLC**
LC: Mr 29, '16.

V-176   Vincent, Clarence Augustus. Night and the stars: a tale of the Western Reserve / by Clarence Augustus Vincent. Chicago, Illinois: The Winona Publishing Company, [c1906]. 360 p.

V-177   Vincent, Edgar L. (Edgar La Verne), 1851-1936. Hot coals: a story of today / by Edgar L. Vincent . . . Boston, Massachusetts: The C. M. Clark Publishing Company, [c1910]. 465 p., front.
LC: F 11, '11.

V-178   ____ Margaret Bowlby: a love story / by Edgar L. Vincent. Boston: Lothrop Publishing Company, [1902]. 436 p.
PW: My 17, '02.

V-179   Vincent, J. W. Tales of the Ozarks / by J. W. Vincent. Linn Creek, Mo.: Reveille Printing House, 1913. [36] p.   **NYP**
Contents: The lovers' leap -- What Jack Carrender found -- A game of cross purposes -- A hunter hunted -- The rise of '37 -- The unofficial quarantine -- A backwoods Christmas dinner.

Vinson, Elmer Ellsworth, b. 1872. <u>See</u> **Evinson, Elmer, pseud.**

V-180   Virtue, Ephie Gladys. Helen Dale: Christian science story / by Ephie Gladys Virtue . . . St. Paul: Virtue Printing Co., 1912. 177 p.

V-181   Visscher, William Lightfoot, 1842-1924. Amos Hudson's motto: a story / by Col. William Lightfoot Visscher. [Chicago]: Published by Estate of P. D. Beckwith, [c1905]. 152 p.   **DLC**
LC: Ja 19, '06.

V-182   ____ Fetch over the canoe: a story of a song / by William Lightfoot Visscher. Chicago, Ill.: Atwell Printing and Binding Co., 1908. 114 p., front., ill. (some photo.). [Ill. by A. Van Leshout.]   **JFS**

____ A thrifty woman. <u>In</u> *Second suds sayings* **(1919), S-266.**

Vogt, August, jt. aut. Breathing driftwood (1925). <u>See</u> Cloninger, Margaret D., C-497.

Von Claussen, Ida. <u>See</u> **Claussen, Ida von.**

V-183   Von der Lin, Katherin, b. 1878. The way of the world / by Katherin von der Lin. Los Angeles, California: [Times Mirror Printing & Binding House], 1921. 326 p., photo. front., [15] leaves of photo. plates.

Von Eichen, Augusta Friedrich. Rachelle. <u>In</u> **Pacific Coast Women's Press Association.** *La copa de oro* **(1905), P-2.**

V-184   Von Hutten, Baroness, 1874-1957. Araby / by Baroness von Hutten; illustrated by C. J. Budd. New York; London: The Smart Set Publishing Co., 1904. 213, [1] p., incl. front., [5] leaves of plates.
PW: Mr 26, '04.

V-185   ____ The bag of saffron / by Bettina von Hutten . . . ; illustrated by Stockton Mulford. New York: D. Appleton and Company, 1918. 450 p., col. front., [3] leaves of col. plates.
LC: F 18, '18.
PW: Mr 2, '18.
BLC: London: Hutchinson & Co., 1917.

V-186   ____ Beechy, or, The lordship of love / by Bettina von Hutten; with colored frontispiece by A. G. Learned. New York: Frederick A. Stokes Company, [1909]. 381 p., col. front.
LC: S 29, '09.
PW: Ap 3, '09.

V-187   ____ Bird's fountain / by Bettina von Hutten. New York: D. Appleton and Company, 1915. 347 p.
LC: D 3, '15.
PW: D 4, '15.
BLC: London: Hutchinson & Co., 1915.

V-188   ____ The green patch / by Bettina von Hutten . . . New York: Frederick A. Stokes Company, [c1910]. 366 p.
LC: O 14, '10.
PW: O 22, '10.
BLC: London: Hutchinson & Co., 1910.

V-189   ____ The halo / by Bettina von Hutten; with frontispiece by B. Martin Justice. New York: Dodd, Mead and Company, 1907. 340 p., col. front.
LC: N 9, '07.
PW: N 23, '07.
BLC: London: Methuen & Co., 1907.

V-190   ____ Happy house / by the Baroness von Hutten. New York: George H. Doran Company, [c1920]. 308 p.
LC: Ja 17, '20.
PW: Mr 6, '20.
BLC: London: Hutchinson & Co., [1919].

V-191   ____ He and Hecuba: a novel / by Baroness von Hutten . . . New York: D. Appleton and Company, 1905. 299 p.
PW: O 7, '05.

V-192   ____ Helping Hersey / by the Baroness von Hutten . . . New York: George H. Doran Company, [c1914]. 256 p.
Contents: Peterl in the Black Forest -- In loving memory -- Helping Hersey -- Ker Kel -- Mrs. Hornbeam's headdress -- The common man's story -- The iron shutter -- Two Apaches -- The principino -- Three times -- A Berlin adventure.
PW: Jl 3, '20.
BLC: London: Skeffington & Son, 1918.

V-193   ____ Julia / by the Baroness von Hutten. New York: George H. Doran Company, [c1924]. 281 p.
LC: D 10, '24.
BLC: London: Hutchinson, [1924].

V-194   ____ Kingsmead: a novel / by Bettina von Hutten; with frontispiece by Will Foster. New York: Dodd, Mead and Company, 1909. 329 p., col. front.
LC: F 18, '09.
PW: Ap 3, '09.
BLC: London: Hutchinson, 1909.

V-195   ____ Mag Pye / by Bettina von Hutten . . . New York: D. Appleton and Company, 1917. 256, [1] p.   **CLE**
PW: Mr 3, '17.
BLC: London: Hutchinson & Co., 1917.

V-196   ____ Maria / by Bettina von Hutten. New York: D. Appleton and Company, 1914. 358, [1] p.
LC: Jl 2, '14.
PW: Jl 11, '14.
BLC: London: Hutchinson & Co., 1914.

V-197   ____ "Marr'd in making" / by Baroness von Hutten

. . . ; with a frontispiece by E. Plaisted Abbott. Philadelphia; London: J. B. Lippincott Company, 1901. 305 p., front.
BLC: Westminster: Archibald Constable & Co., 1901.

V-198   ____ Mothers-in-law / by the Baroness von Hutten. New York: George H. Doran Company, [c1922]. 296 p.
LC: Ap 15, '22.
PW: Mr 18, '22.
BLC: London: Cassell & Co., 1922.

V-199   ____ The one way out / by Bettina von Hutten; with illustrations by Harrison Fisher. New York: Dodd, Mead and Company, 1906. 99, [1] p., col. front., [4] leaves of col. plates. Ornamental borders.
PW: N 10, '06.

V-200   ____ Our lady of the beeches / by the Baroness von Hutten. Boston; New York: Houghton, Mifflin & Co., 1902. (Cambridge: The Riverside Press). 259, [1] p.
PW: N 1, '02.

V-201   ____ Pam / by Bettina von Hutten . . . ; with illustrations by B. Martin Justice. New York: Dodd, Mead and Company, 1905. 391 p., col. front., [4] leaves of plates.
PW: Mr 11, '05.
BLC: London: William Heinemann, 1904.

V-202   ____ Pam at fifty / by the Baroness von Hutten. New York: George H. Doran Company, [c1924]. 317 p.
BLC: London: Cassell & Co., 1923.
LC: Mr 18, '24.
PW: Ap 26, '24.

V-203   ____ Pam decides: a sequel to "Pam" / by Bettina von Hutten . . . ; with illustrations by B. Martin Justice. New York: Dodd, Mead and Company, 1906. 340 p., col. front., [5] leaves of plates.
PW: My 5, '06.

V-204   ____ Sharrow / by Bettina von Hutten. New York: D. Appleton and Company, 1912. 458 p.
PW: Je 1, '12.
BLC: London: Hutchinson & Co., 1912.

V-205   ____ Violett: a chronicle / by Baroness von Hutten. Boston; New York: Houghton, Mifflin and Company, 1904. (Cambridge: The Riverside Press). 285, [1] p.
PW: F 20, '04.

V-206   [Von Ravn, Clara], b. 1870. The scribe of a soul / by Clara Iza Price [pseud.]; introduction by Professor A. Van der Naillen . . . Seattle, Washington: Denny-Coryell Company, 1901. 201 p.

V-207   Von Schriltz, Guy W. (Guy White), b. 1885. He who laughs last / by Guy W. Von Schriltz. Topeka: Crane & Company, 1914. 96 p., ill. [Ill. by Ward Lockwood.]   **NYP**

Von Scyler, Catherine, pseud. See **Smith, Annie Laura, b. 1873.**

V-208 Von Ziekursch, Theodore. White trails's end / by Theodore Von Ziekursch. Philadelphia: Macrae Smith Company, 1925. 285 p.
PW: Ap 25, '25.

V-209 Voorhees, James Paxton. The caverns of dawn / by James Paxton Voorhees . . . Plainfield, Indiana: The Raidabaugh-Voorhees Company, 1910. 519 p.
LC: Je 4, '10.

V-210 ____ "Flaws" / by James Paxton Voorhees . . . Plainfield, Ind.: The Caverns of Dawn Medium, 1925. 76 p.   **DLC**
LC: F 18, '25.

V-211 Voorhies, Frank C. (Frank Corey), b. 1877. The love letters of an Irishwoman / F. C. Voorhies. Boston, Massachusetts: The Mutual Book Company, [c1901]. 32 p.

V-212 ____ Mrs. McPiggs' of the Very Old Scratch: a half grown novel / by Frank C. Voorhies . . . Boston, Massachusetts: The Mutual Book Company, c1003 [i. e. c1903]. 29 p.
PW: F 28, '03.

V-213 ____ Reflections of Bridget McNulty / by Frank C. Voorhies . . . Boston; New York: Dickerman Publishing Company, 1903, [c1902]. 28 p.
PW: Mr 28, '03.

V-214 [____] The story of Lizzie McGuire / by herself. Boston; New York: Henry A. Dickerman & Son, [c1902]. 84 p., front.

V-215 ____ Twisted history / by Frank C. Voorhies . . . ; illustrations by T. Cromwell Lawrence. New York: G. W. Dillingham Company, [c1904]. 208 p., ill.
PW: Ap 2, '04.

____ Vorpé, Florence. A colonial valentine. In *Castle stories (1908)*, **C-187.**

____ Hotspur. In *Castle stories (1908)*, **C-187.**

____ The soul of a musician. In *Castle stories (1908)*, **C-187.**

V-216 Vorse, Mary Heaton, 1874-1966. The breaking in of a yachtsman's wife / by Mary Heaton Vorse; with illustrations by Reginald B. Birch. Boston; New York: Houghton, Mifflin and Company, 1908. (Cambridge: The Riverside Press). 275, [1] p., front., [21] leaves of plates.
PW: My 16, '08.

____ De Vilmarte's luck. In *The best short stories of 1918 and the yearbook of the American short story (1919)*, **B-563.**

V-217 ____ Fraycar's fist / by Mary Heaton Vorse. New York: Boni and Liveright, [c1924]. 401 p.
LC: Ap 25, '24.
PW: My 3, '24.

V-218 ____ Growing up / by Mary Heaton Vorse . . . New York: Boni and Liveright, [c1920]. 237 p.
LC: Je 25, '20.
PW: Jl 3, '20.
BLC: London: Brentano's; printed in U. S. A., 1923.

V-219 ____ The heart's country / by Mary Heaton Vorse; with illustrations by Alice Barber Stephens. Boston; New York: Houghton Mifflin Company, 1914. (Cambridge: The Riverside Press). 291, [1] p., col. front., [3] leaves of col. plates.
LC: Ap 30, '14.
PW: My 2, '14.

V-220 ____ I've come to stay: a love comedy of Bohemia / by Mary Heaton Vorse. New York: The Century Co., 1918, [c1919]. 190 p., front. [Ill. by A. W. B., i.e. Arthur W. Brown.]
LC: Ap 22, '19.
PW: Ap 19, '19.

V-221 ____ The ninth man: a story / by Mary Heaton Vorse; with illustrations by Frank Craig. New York; London: Harper & Brothers, 1920. 80, [1] p., col. front., [3] leaves of plates (1 col.).
LC: S 2, '20.
PW: S 18, '20.

____ The other room. In *The best short stories of 1919 and the yearbook of the American short story (1920)*, **B-564.**

V-222 ____ The Prestons / by Mary Heaton Vorse . . . New York: Boni and Liveright, 1918. 427 p.
LC: Ja 3, '19.
PW: D 7, '18.

____ The promise. In *The best short stories of 1923 and the yearbook of the American short story (1924)*, **B-568.**

____, contributor. See *The sturdy oak (1917)*, **S-1101.**

____ Twilight of the God. In *Prize stories of 1922 (1923)*, **P-620.**

V-223 ____ The very little person / by Mary Heaton Vorse; with illustrations by Rose O'Neill. Boston; New York: Houghton Mifflin Company, 1911. (Cambridge: The Riverside Press). 163, [1] p., front., [7] leaves of plates.
LC: My 12, '11.
PW: Ap 29, '11.

____ The wallow of the sea. In *The best short stories of 1921 and the yearbook of the American short story (1922)*, **B-566.**

____, contributor. See *The whole family (1908)*, **W-578.**

V-224 Vorys, George W. Billikin and others: being a collection of express stories / written and illustrated by George W. Vorys. Ann Arbor, Michigan: [The

Ann Arbor Press], 1910. [44] p., front., [1] leaf of plates.

Contents: The deadly viverrae mangustae -- Fraternal love -- A misdeal -- The tale of a parrot -- Lannigan's goal -- Celery, salary or sea-fish -- Circumstantial evidence -- Billikin, an olden time express man.

V-225   Votaw, Clarence E., 1853-1948. Jasper Hunnicutt of Jimpsonhurst / Clarence E. Votaw . . . Chicago, Illinois: Published by Union Book and Publishing Co., [c1907]. 194 p., [1] leaf of photo.

V-226   Voûte, Emile. The passport / by Emile Voûte. New York: Mitchell Kennerley, 1915. 362 p.
PW: O 2, '15.

V-227   Vrooman, Julia Scott. The high road to honor / by Julia Scott Vrooman. New York: Minton, Balch & Company, 1924. 299 p.
LC: S 26, '24.
PW: S 27, '24.

W

W-1   Waddell, Charles Carey, 1868-1930. The girl of the guard line / by Charles Carey Waddell. New York: Moffat, Yard and Company, 1915. 292 p.
LC: O 20, '15.

W-2   [____] The Van Suyden sapphires / by Charles Carey. New York: Dodd, Mead and Company, 1905. 333 p., col. front. [Ill. by C. B. Falls.]
PW: Ap 29, '05.

W-3   Wade, Blanche Elizabeth. Anne, princess of everything / by Blanche Elizabeth Wade . . . New York: Sully & Kleinteich, [c1916]. 207 p., front., [3] leaves of plates. [Ill. by R. Emmett Owen.]
LC: O 24, '16.
PW: N 4, '16.

W-4   ____ A garden in pink / by Blanche Elizabeth Wade; with numerous drawings and decorations in color by Lucy Fitch Perkins; and twelve illustrations from photographs. Chicago: A. C. McClurg and Company, 1905. 201 p., front., ill. (some col.).
PW: N 18, '05.

W-5   ____ The stained glass lady: an idyl / by Blanche Elizabeth Wade . . . ; with frontispiece and other drawings by Blanche Ostertag. Chicago: A. C. McClurg & Co., 1906. 228, [1] p., col. front. Colored, illustrated end papers; ornamental borders.   **OSU, IGA**
LC: O 13, '06.
PW: O 20, '06.

W-6   Wade, Francis Henry. God's scarlet law / by . . . Francis Henry Wade; with eleven full page illustrations by Landerholm. Providence, R. I.: The Oxford Press, [c1925]. 413 p., front., [10] leaves of plates.

Waggaman, Mary T. (Mary Teresa), 1846-1931. At the turn of the tide. In *A bit of old ivory, and other stories* (1910), **B-626**.

____ A belated planet. In *A bit of old ivory, and other stories* (1910), **B-626**.

____ The Bretherton bowl. In *The Senior lieutenant's wager: and other stories* (1905), **S-312**.

W-7   ____ Carroll Dare / by Mary T. Waggaman . . . New York; Cincinnati; Chicago: Benziger Brothers, [c1903]. 161 p., incl. col. front., incl. [11] col. leaves of plates.
PW: N 21, '03.

W-8   ____ Corinne's vow / by Mary T. Waggaman. New York; Cincinnati; Chicago: Benziger Brothers, 1902. 144 p., incl. front., incl. 15 leaves of plates.
PW: F 15, '02.

____, contributor. See *A double knot* (1905), **D-499**.

W-9   ____ Eric, or, The black finger / by Mary T. Waggaman . . . Philadelphia: H. L. Kilner & Co., [c1910]. 183 p., [6] leaves of plates. [Ill. by O. C. Wigand.]
"Reprinted from The messenger."
LC: N 10, '10.

____ An expiation. In *The friendly little house: and other stories* (1910), **F-432**.

W-10   ____ Grapes of thorns: a novel / by Mary T. Waggaman. New York; Cincinnati; Chicago: Benziger Brothers, Publishers of Benziger magazine, 1917. 340 p., front., [2] leaves of plates.
LC: Ap 7, '17.
PW: Ap 21, '17.

W-11   ____ Lisbeth: the story of a first communion / by Mary T. Waggaman. New York: P. J. Kenedy & Sons, [c1914]. 187 p.
LC: N 27, '14.

____ The Rokeby ghost. In *A bit of old ivory, and other stories* (1910), **B-626**.

W-12   ____ The secret of Pocomoke / by Mary T. Waggaman . . . Notre Dame, Indiana, U. S. A.: The Ave Maria, [c1914]. 265 p., photo. front.
LC: Ap 23, '14.

W-13   ____ Sergeant Tim / by Mary T. Waggaman . . . Notre Dame, Indiana, U. S. A.: The Ave Maria, [c1918]. 335 p.

____ Sister Angela's patient. In *The friendly little house: and other stories* (1910), **F-432**.

W-14   ____ Strong arm of Avalon / by Mary T. Waggaman. New York; Cincinnati; Chicago: Benziger Brothers, [c1904]. 149 p.   **OSU, RMC**
PW: Ap 9, '04.

____ The Tomkyns' telephone. In *A bit of old ivory, and other stories* (1910), **B-626**.

W-15   ____ White eagle / by Mary T. Waggaman. Notre Dame, Ind.: Ave Maria, 1915. 208 p., front. Unexamined copy: bibliographic data from OCLC, #29407280.

W-16   Waggoner, George Andrew, b. 1842. Stories of old Oregon / by George A. Waggoner. Salem, Oregon: Statesman Publishing Co., 1905. 292 p., photo. front., [18] leaves of photo. plates.
Contents: Oregon's pioneers -- Stories of old Oregon -- A test of courage -- Adventures in the mines -- How Captain Dobbins was promoted -- A legend of Wallowa Lake -- Ned Leach's story -- Jack Hart's encounter with road agents -- Was it luck or providence -- Buckskin's fight with the wolves -- A chance meeting of old friends -- Dandy Jim.

W-17   Wagnalls, Mabel, b. 1871. Miserere: (a musical story) / by Mabel Wagnalls . . . -- Rev. 3rd ed. -- New York; London: Funk & Wagnalls Company, 1906. 80 p., front., [2] leaves of plates.
PW: O 20, '06.
First printing: 1892, 63 p. (Lyle Wright, 1876-1900, #5708.)

W-18   ____ The palace of danger: a story of La Pompadour / by Mabel Wagnalls . . . ; illustrated by John Ward Dunsmore. New York; London: Funk & Wagnalls Company, 1908. 311 p., front., [3] leaves of plates.
PW: O 10, '08.
BLC: London: John Long, [1909].

W-19   ____ The rose-bush of a thousand years / by Mabel Wagnalls . . . illustrated with eight full page reproductions from the motion-picture drama, Revelation, featuring Madame Nazimova. New York; London: Funk & Wagnalls Company, 1918. 77 p., photo. front., [7] leaves of photo. plates.
LC: My 23, '18.

W-20   Wagner, Clara Eleanor. Cupid in hell / by Clara Eleanor Wagner . . . ; illustrated by the Terry Engraving Company. Columbus, Ohio: Published by Nitschke Brothers, 1910. 193 p., photo. front. (port.). Designed end papers.
LC: D 3, '10.

    Wagner, Ellasue Canter. Kim Hong Til and the first "bike". In When God walks the road and other stories (1924), W-445.

W-21   ____ Kim Su Bang: and other stories of Korea / by Ellasue Canter Wagner. Nashville, Tenn.: Woman's Board of Foreign Missions M. E. Church, South, [c1909]. 99 p., photo. front., [7] leaves of photo. plates.   **VXW**
Contents: Kim Su Bang -- Toksunie -- Mittome -- Come unto me.
LC: N 15, '09.
PW: D 11, '09.

W-22   ____ Kumokie, a bride of old Korea: a love story of the Orient / by Ellasue Canter Wagner. Nashville, Tenn.; Dallas, Tex.; Richmond, Va.: Publishing House M. E. Church, South, Lamar & Burton, agents, 1922. 230 p., front., [5] leaves of plates. [Ill. by L. Pearl Saunders.]

    ____ Mongoonie the brave. In When God walks the road and other stories (1924), W-445.

W-23   ____ Pokjumie: a story from the land of Morning Calm / by Ellasue Canter Wagner . . . Nashville, Tenn.; Dallas, Tex.: Publishing House of the M. E. Church, South: Smith & Lamar, agents, 1911. 115 p., photo. front.   **TJC**
LC: D 15, '11.
PW: D 23, '11.

W-24   Wagner, Frank, b. 1853. Battle with fate: the trials and adventures of an orphan boy. A demonstration of caste, rank and society as created by riches and position / by Frank Wagner . . . ; illustrated by Paul Wilde. [Vancouver, Wash.: Duncan Printing Co.], c1921. 186 p.
LC: Ap 7, '21.

    Wainwright, Helen. The rejected apostle. In The rejected apostle (1924), R-164.

W-25   Wainwright, Virginia. A Boston artist in Quebec: and other love stories / by Virginia Wainwright . . . Brookline, MA: V. Wainwright, [c1922]. 35 p. Unexamined copy: bibliographic data from OCLC, #29274961.
Contents: A Boston artist in Quebec -- A romance of Montreal -- Wanted: a poetry reader -- The lure of the Russian ballet.
LC: O 4, '22.

W-26   Wait, Frona Eunice, 1859-1946. The stories of El Dorado / by Frona Eunice Wait. San Francisco, California: Sunset Press, [c1904]. 270 p., ill. [Ill. by John W. Clawson, Amadee Joullin, & X. Martinez.]   **VA@**
Contents: The happy island -- Zamna, the eye of the sun -- Votan, the people's heart -- Lord of the sacred tunkel -- The stars' ball -- The National Book -- Manco-Capac, the powerful one -- Bochica and the zipa -- The song of Hiawatha -- Michabo, the great white hare -- The birth of corn -- The wrathy chieftain -- Quetzalcoatl, the plumed serpent -- Cholula, the sacred city -- Tulla, the hiding nook of the snake -- Departure of the golden hearted -- El Dorado, the golden -- Bimini, the fountain of youth -- Montezuma and the paba -- The child of the sun -- The gilded man -- The white seas of the Manoas -- The mountain of gold -- The Amazon queens -- The seven cities of Cibola -- The kingdom of Quivera -- The land of gold -- The new El Dorado -- Appendix.

W-27   Wakefield, Frank H. Marriage-limited: a novel / by Frank H. Wakefield. New York; Washington: The Neale Publishing Company, 1904. 327 p.
PW: D 10, '04.

W-28   Wakeman, Annie. A gentlewoman of the slums: being the autobiography of a charwoman / as chronicled by Annie Wakeman; illustrations by `Rip'. Boston: L. C. Page & Company, 1901. 303 p., front., [5] leaves of plates. Unexamined copy: bibliographic data from OCLC, #28566727.
LC: S 30, '01.

W-29   Walcott, Earle Ashley, 1859-1931. The apple of discord / by Earle Ashley Walcott . . . ; with illustrations by Alice Barber Stephens. Indianapolis: The Bobbs-Merrill Company, [c1907]. 436 p., front., [5] leaves of plates.
LC: S 30, '07.

W-30   ____ Blindfolded / by Earle Ashley Walcott; with illustrations by Alice Barber Stephens. Indianapolis:

The Bobbs-Merrill Company, [c1906]. 400 p., front., [7] leaves of plates.
PW: S 15, '06.

W-31   ____ The open door: a romance of mystery--Time, 1905 / by Earle Ashley Walcott; illustrated by Arthur William Brown. New York: Dodd, Mead and Company, 1910. 341 p., front., [3] leaves of plates.
LC: S 17, '10.

Walden, A. M. On the edge of Death Valley. In **Seattle Writer's Club. *Tillicum tales* (1907), S-248.**

W-32   Waldo, Harold. The magic midland / by Harold Waldo . . . New York: George H. Doran Company, [c1923]. 305 p.
LC: N 1, '23.
PW: N 3, '23.

W-33   ____ Stash of the marsh country / by Harold Waldo. New York: George H. Doran Company, [c1921]. 347 p.
LC: Je 10, '21.
PW: Je 11, '21.

W-34   Waldo, Nigel. Wallflowers / by Nigel Waldo; illustrated by Arthur Litle. New York: The Hannis Jordan Company, [c1918]. 60 p., front.
PW: Je 22, '18.

W-35   Waldron, Webb, b. 1882. The road to the world / by Webb Waldron. New York: The Century Co., 1922. 416 p.
LC: Mr 27, '22.

W-36   ____ Shanklin / by Webb Waldron . . . Indianapolis: The Bobbs-Merrill Company, [c1925]. 334 p.
LC: O 16, '25.
PW: S 26, '25.

W-37   Walk, Charles Edmonds, b. 1875. The crimson cross / by Charles Edmonds Walk . . . and Millard Lynch . . . ; illustrations by Will Grefé. Chicago: A. C. McClurg & Co., 1913. 275 p., col. front., [2] leaves of col. plates.
LC: Ap 2, '13.
PW: Ap 19, '13.
BLC: London: A. C. McClurg & Co., Chicago [printed], 1913.

W-38   ____ The green seal / by Charles Edmonds Walk . . . ; with illustrations by Will Grefé. Chicago: A. C. McClurg & Co., 1914. 403, [1] p., front., [3] leaves of plates.
LC: Mr 28, '14.
PW: Ap 11, '14.

W-39   ____ The Paternoster ruby / by Charles Edmonds Walk; with five illustrations by J. V. McFall. Chicago: A. C. McClurg & Co., 1910. 374 p., col. front., [4] leaves of col. plates, plan.
LC: O 26, '10.
PW: N 12, '10.

W-40   ____ The silver blade: the true chronicle of a double mystery / by Charles Edmonds Walk; with five illustrations in color by A. B. Wenzell. Chicago: A.

C. McClurg & Co., 1908. 406 p., col. front., [4] leaves of col. plates.
LC: Mr 16, '08.
PW: Mr 21, '08.

W-41   ____ The time lock / by Charles Edmonds Walk . . . ; with illustrations by Will Grefé. Chicago: A. C. McClurg & Co., 1912. 419 p., col. front., [3] leaves of col. plates.
LC: O 7, '12.
PW: O 12, '12.

W-42   ____ The yellow circle / by Charles Edmonds Walk . . . ; with four illustrations by Will Grefé. Chicago: A. C. McClurg & Co., 1909. 390 p., col. front., [3] leaves of col. plates.   **NYP**
LC: S 20, '09.
PW: O 2, '09.

Walker, Beatrice. Greater love hath no man. In *The best college short stories, 1917-18 (1919), B-557.*

W-43   Walker, Dugald Stewart, 1883-1937. The dust of seven days / by Dugald Stewart Walker. Kansas City: Alfred Fowler, 1924. [28] p., ill.   **NYP**

W-44   Walker, E. M. Bunny's house: a novel / by E. M. Walker. New York; Cincinnati; Chicago: Benziger Brothers, 1922. 270 p.
LC: F 17, '22.
PW: My 20, '22.

W-45   Walker, Guy Morrison, b. 1870. Skeletons: (a claim agent's stories) / by Guy M. Walker. Boston: The Stratford Co., 1921. 134 p.
Contents: Hoyt's wife -- Doctor X -- Little old New York -- Bob Barnett -- The lifer's story -- The paternal instinct -- The man who came back -- Charles Morris, Dedham case.

W-46   Walker, J. Bernard (John Bernard), b. 1858. America fallen!: the sequel to the European War / by J. Bernard Walker . . . New York: Dodd, Mead and Company, 1915. 203 p., maps.
BLC: London: G. P. Putnam's Sons, 1915.

W-47   Walker, Marie Winchell, b. 1875. A lover of truth: a health novel / by Marie Winchell Walker . . . Chicago: Stanley Merritt, Publisher, [c1923]. 198 p.
LC: Je 22, '23.
LC reports: front., plate.

W-48   Walker, Thos. H. B. (Thomas Hamilton Beb), b. 1873. Bebbly; or, The victorious preacher / by Thos. H. B. Walker . . . Gainesville, Fla.: Pepper Publishing and Printing Co., [c1910]. 221 p., incl. front. (port.), ill.
Unexamined copy: bibliographic data from OCLC, #19999662.
LC: J 24, '10.

W-49   ____ J. Johnson, or, "The unknown man": an answer to Mr. Thos. Dixon's "Sins of the fathers" / by Thos. H. B. Walker . . . De Land, Fla.: The E. O. Painter Printing Co., [c1915]. 192 p., front., [4] leaves of plates. [Some ill. by John Henry Adams.]   **IAY**
LC: Ag 14, '15.

W-50　[Walker, William Hall]. Sir Charlton Richards' last kiss . . . Brookside, Great Barrington, Massachusetts: [s. n.], 1916. 24 p.　　**NYP**

W-51　Wall, Ida Blanche, b. 1866. Comedy of a petty conflicts / by Ida Blanche Wall . . . New York: Broadway Publishing Co., [c1908]. 236 p., front., [2] leaves of plates. [Ill. by Wm. L. Hudson.] **DLC**
PW: Ag 8, '08.

W-52　____　Romance and tragedy of a summer / by Mrs. D. H. Wall; with an introduction by Joseph Tyler Butts. New York; London: F. Tennyson Neely, [c1903]. 171 p., photo. front. (port.).　　**TJC**
PW: D 19, '03.

W-53　____　Sister in name only / by Mrs. D. H. Wall. New York; London: F. Tennyson Neely, [c1902]. 85 p.　　**GUA**
PW: Ap 26, '02.

W-54　Wall, Mary Virginia. The daughter of Virginia Dare / by Mary Virginia Wall. New York; Washington: The Neale Publishing Company, 1908. 194 p.
LC: My 22, '08.

Wall, Louise Herrick. The accolade. In *Youth* **(1901), Y-51.**

W-55　Wallace, Dillon, 1863-1939. Grit-a-plenty: a tale of the Labrador wild / by Dillon Wallace . . . ; illustrated. New York; Chicago; London; Edinburgh: Fleming H. Revell Co., [c1918]. 252 p., front., [5] leaves of plates. [Ill. by Charles S. Corson.]
PW: Ag 24, '18.
BLC: London & Edinburgh: Oliphants, printed in U. S. A., [1919].

W-56　Wallace, Edna Kingsley. The quest of the dream / by Edna Kingsley Wallace. New York; London: G. P. Putnam's Sons, 1913. ([New York]: The Knickerbocker Press). 292 p.
LC: O 3, '13.

W-57　____　The stars in the pool: a prose poem for lovers / by Edna Kingsley Wallace. New York: E. P. Dutton & Company, [c1920]. 111 p.
LC: N 15, '20.

W-58　Wallace, John H., Jr. The senator from Alabama: a romance treating of the disfranchisement of the Negro and including a scathing arraignment of the White House social-equality policy / by John H. Wallace, Jr. New York; Washington: The Neale Publishing Company, 1904. 283 p.

W-59　Wallace, L. M., b. 1884. The lure of the West / by L. M. Wallace. Chicago: Joseph H. Meier, [c1924]. 288 p., front., [1] leaf of plates. [Ill. by J. T. Armbrust.]
LC: N 17, '24.

W-60　____　The outlaws of Ravenhurst / by L. M. Wallace; illustrations and initials by the author. Chicago, Ill.: Franciscan Herald Press, [c1923]. 327 p., front., [3] leaves of plates, ill.
LC: My 9, '23.

Wallace, Mary. <u>See</u> **Keon, Grace, pseud.**

Wallace, Mary Imelda, Sister. <u>See</u> **Wallace, L. M.**

W-61　Wallace, Susan Arnold Elston, 1830-1907. The city of the King: what the child Jesus saw and heard / by Mrs. Lew Wallace . . . ; with illustrations. Indianapolis: The Bobbs-Merrill Company, [c1903]. 97 p., photo. front., [11] leaves of plates (all photo. but 1).
PW: D 5, '03.
References: Russo & Sullivan, *Seven Authors*, p. 435-436.

W-62　Waller, Mary E. (Mary Ella), 1855-1938. A cry in the wilderness / by Mary E. Waller . . . ; with frontispiece in color by Arthur I. Keller. Boston: Little, Brown and Company, 1912. 428 p., col. front.
LC: O 30, '12.
PW: O 19, '12.
BLC: London: Andrew Melrose, 1912.

W-63　____　A daughter of the rich / by M. E. Waller; illustrated by Ellen Bernard Thompson. Boston: Little, Brown, and Company, 1903. 349 p., front., [5] leaves of plates.
PW: O 24, '03.
BLC: London: Ward, Lock & Co., 1904. [Printed from American plates.]

W-64　____　Deep in the hearts of men / by Mary E. Waller. Boston: Little, Brown and Company, 1924. 459 p.
LC: My 3, '24.
PW: My 17, '24.

W-65　____　Flamsted quarries / by Mary E. Waller . . . ; with illustrations by G. Patrick Nelson. Boston: Little, Brown and Company, 1910. 493 p., front., [3] leaves of plates.
LC: S 21, '10.
PW: S 17, '10.
BLC: London: Andrew Melrose, 1911.

W-66　____　My ragpicker / by Mary E. Waller. Boston: Little, Brown, and Company, 1911. 112, [1] p.
LC: O 28, '11.
PW: O 28, '11.
BLC: London: Andrew Melrose, 1911.

W-67　____　Out of the silences / by Mary E. Waller. Boston: Little, Brown, and Company, 1918. 354 p.
LC: N 1, '18.
PW: N 9, '18.
BLC: London: Andrew Melrose, 1919. (Second edition).

W-68　____　Sanna: a novel / by M. E. Waller . . . New York; London: Harper & Brothers, 1905. 398, [1] p.
PW: Ap 29, '05.
Reissue: Sanna of the island town. Boston: Little, Brown and Company, 1912. 398, [1] p.
LC: Ap 10, '12.
PW: Ap 13, '12.

BLC: London: Andrew Melrose; Boston [Mass. printed], 1912.

_____ The thought and the stone. In *The joy in work* (1920), **J-229.**

W-69 _____ The wood-carver of 'Lympus / by M. E. Waller; with a frontispiece from a drawing by C. C. Emerson. Boston: Little, Brown, 1904. 311 p., front.
BLC: London: Andrew Melrose, 1909.

W-70 _____ A year out of life / by Mary E. Waller. New York: D. Appleton and Company, 1909. 305, [1] p.
LC: Mr 26, '09.
PW: Ap 17, '09.
BLC: New York: D. Appleton & Co.; London: Andrew Melrose, 1909.

W-71 Wallin, Clarence Monroe. Gena of the Appalachians / by Clarence Monroe Wallin. New York: Cochrane Publishing Company, 1910. 109 p.   **TNS**
LC: Ja 28, '11.

W-72 Walling, Anna Strunsky, b. 1879. Violette of Père Lachaise / by Anna Strunsky Walling. New York: Frederick A. Stokes Company, [1915]. 198 p.

W-73 Walsh, George Ethelbert, 1865-1914. Allin Winfield: a romance / by George Ethelbert Walsh . . . ; illustrated. New York: F. M. Buckles & Company, 1902. 326 p., front., [3] leaves of plates. [Ill. by F. A. Carter.]
PW: F 8, '02.

_____ Captain Sampson's queer cargo. In *The battle for the Pacific* (1908), **B-357.**

W-74 _____ A friend of the Seminole / by George Ethelbert Walsh . . . Elgin, Illinois: Published by the David C. Cook Publishing Co., [c1911]. 96 p., ill. [Ill. by E. C. Caswell.] Text is in two columns.
LC: D 1, '11.

W-75 _____ The mysterious burglar / by George E. Walsh. New York: F. M. Buckles & Company, 1901. 247 p.
PW: Je 8, '01.
BLC: London: Ward, Lock & Co., 1903.

_____ Private or privateer. In *The battle for the Pacific* (1908), **B-357.**

W-76 _____ The strange cargo of the Southern Belle / by George Ethelbert Walsh. Elgin; Chicago; New York; Boston: Published by David C. Cook Publishing Company, [c1906]. 59 p., ill.
LC: N 7, '06.
PW: D 22, '06.

W-77 Walsh, John H. (John Henry), b. 1879. Cam Clarke / by John H. Walsh; with frontispiece by William Van Dresser. New York: The Macmillan Company, 1916. 309 p., col. front.
LC: F 24, '16.

W-78 _____ Glenwood of Shipbay / by John H. Walsh . . . New York: The Macmillan Company, 1921. 303 p.
LC: O 12, '21.

Walsh, Julia, contributor. See *A double knot* (1905), **D-499.**

W-79 Walsh, Lavinia. When the dead walk: a novel / by Lavinia Walsh. New York: Mutual Publishing Company, [c1902]. 386 p., front.

Walsh, Mary Catherine Frances. See **Law, Hyran S., pseud.**

Walsh, William F. A portrait in two panels. In *The best college short stories, 1924-1925* (1925), **B-558.**

W-80 Walsh, William Thomas. The mirage of the many / by William Thomas Walsh. New York: Henry Holt and Company, 1910. 326 p.
LC: Ag 29, '10.
PW: S 10, '10.

W-81 Walter, Eugene, 1874-1941. The easiest way: a story of metropolitan life / by Eugene Walter and Arthur Hornblow; illustrations by Archie Gunn and Joseph Byron. New York: G. W. Dillingham Company, [c1911]. 347 p., front., [6] leaves of plates.
LC: Mr 10, '11.
PW: Mr 4, '11.
BLC: London: T. Fisher Unwin, 1911.

W-82 _____ The great issue, or, The undertow / by Eugene Walter. New York: C. H. Doscher & Co., [c1908]. 346 p.
PW: Ap 11, '08.

_____, jt. aut. *Paid in full* (1908). See **Harding, John W. (John William), b. 1864, jt. aut, H-197.**

W-83 _____ The wolf / by Eugene Walter . . . ; founded on the play by Charles Somerville; illustrated from flashlights taken of Sam S. and Lee Shubert's, Inc.'s production of "The wolf". New York: G. W. Dillingham Company, [c1908]. 325 p., photo. front., [7] leaves of photo. plates.

W-84 Walter, William W. (William Wilfred), b. 1869. The arbiter of your fate: sequel to The pastor's son and The doctor's daughter / by William W. Walter. Aurora, Ill.: William W. Walter . . . , [c1911]. 249 p.
LC: O 18, '11.

W-85 _____ The doctor's daughter; sequal to The pastor's son / by William W. Walter. Aurora, Ill.: W. W. Walter, [c1908]. 253 p.
Unexamined copy: bibliographic data from OCLC, #28876914.
LC: N 5, '08.
Revised edition: [c1909], 231, [1] p.   **OSU**

W-86 _____ The healing of Pierpont Whitney / by William W. Walter . . . Aurora, Illinois: Published and for sale by William W. Walter, [c1913]. 231 p.
LC: D 15, '13.

W-87   ____ The pastor's son / by William W. Walter. Aurora, Illinois: Published and for sale by William W. Walter . . . , [c1907]. 198 p.
LC: Ag 21, '07.

W-88   ____ The unfoldment / by William W. Walter. Aurora, Illinois: Published and for sale by William W. Walter, [c1921]. 206 p.
LC: F 4, '21.

W-89   Walther, Adelaide. A vision of truth: the soul's awakening: a story / Adelaide Walther. Grand Rapids, Michigan: Published by the author Adelaide Walther, 1915. 303, [1] p., photo. port., [2] leaves of plates. [Ill. by H. S. De Lay.]
Addenda p. [1]-[5] at end.

W-90   Walton, Esmeé, b. 1876. Aurora of Poverty hill / by Esmeé Walton; illustrated by Hudson. New York: Broadway Publishing Co., 1908. 305 p., front., plates.
Unexamined copy: bibliographic data from OCLC, #30152453.

W-91   Walton, George Lincoln, 1854-1941. Oscar Montague--paranoiac / by George Lincoln Walton . . . ; with a frontispiece by H. Weston Taylor. Philadelphia; London: J. B. Lippincott Company, 1919. 303 p., front.

Walton, Louise Monroe. Deserted. In *Club stories* **(1915), C-502.**

W-92   Waltz, Elizabeth Cherry, 1866-1903. The ancient landmark: a Kentucky romance / by Elizabeth Cherry Waltz. New York: McClure, Phillips & Co., 1905. 269 p.
PW: S 23, '05.
BLC: London: McClure, Phillips & Co., New York [printed], 1905.
Another edition: London: Methuen & Co., 1906.

W-93   ____ Pa Gladden: the story of a common man / by Elizabeth Cherry Waltz. New York: The Century Co., 1903. 338 p., incl. 7 leaves of plates, front. [Ill. by William L. Jacobs and C. Harding.]
PW: O 24, '03.
BLC: London: Hodder & Stoughton, 1904.

Walworth, Dorothy. <u>See</u> **Carman, Dorothy Walworth.**

W-94   War stories / selected and edited by Roy J. Holmes . . . and A. Starbuck . . . New York: Thomas Y. Crowell Company, [c1919]. 329 p.
Reprinted in part from various periodicals.
Contents: Absent without leave / T. Beer -- Out of the sky / A. Brooks -- The Christmas fight of X 157 / D. Burnet -- "Red, white and blue" / D. Burnet -- Underseaboat F-33 / D. Byrne -- The little man in the smoker / J. F. Dwyer -- "Squads right" / G. Emery -- One hundred per cent / Edna Ferber -- Blind vision / Mary M. Freedly -- The flag factory / Margarita S. Gerry -- Bill / D. H. Haines -- Behind the door / G. Morris -- The unsent letter / G. Morris -- Infamous inoculation / W. H. Osborne -- His escape / W. Payne -- The boy's mother / Laura S. Porter -- The sixth man / G. P. Putnam -- The godson of Jeanette Gontreau / F. W. Sullivan --A son of Belgium / R. W. Sneddon -- Captain Schlotterwerz / B. Tarkington -- The feminine touch / G. Weston -- Appendix: Short biographical sketches of the contributors to this volume.

W-95   Ward, A. B., b. 1857. The sage brush parson / by A. B. Ward. Boston: Little, Brown, & Company, 1906. 390 p.

W-96   Ward, Christopher, 1868-1943. Foolish fiction / by Christopher Ward . . . New York: Henry Holt and Company, 1925. 194 p., front., ill.
"Acknowledgement is . . . made to the Saturday review of literature, in whose columns some of the parodies in this book originally appeared in condensed form and under other titles."
Contents: Robinson Crusoe -- Hard Sarker / by John M-sef-eld -- Barrels and-barrels / by J-s-ph H-rg-sh-im-r -- Country people / by R-th S-ck-w -- The tittattoed Countess -- So little / by Edna Fervor -- Wings / by Eth-l K-ll-y -- The greener hat -- Mockbeggar / by L-ur-nce W. M-yn-ll -- The older gentlemen / by Hugh Tophole -- Jenny forlorn / with apologies and regards to Elinor Wylie -- Rose of the New York journal / by K-thl-n N-rr-s -- The rougherneck / by Robert W. Surface -- Misdeal / by D-le C-ll-ns -- Wouldn't smoke / by F. Br-tt Y-ung -- The enchanted hell / by Peter Be Kind.
LC: O 10, '25.
PW: O 17, '25.

W-97   ____ Gentleman into goose: being the exact and true account of Mr. Timothy Teapot, Gent., of Puddleditch, in Dorset, that was changed to a great grey gander at the wish of his wife. How, though a gander, he did wear breeches, and smoak a pipe. How he near lost his life to his dog Tiger . . . / by Christopher Ward; with wooden engravings by C. W. and C. W., Jr. [New York]: Published and sold . . . in ye Citie of New Yorke, by Henry Holt and Companie, [1924?]. 40 p., front., ill. [Ill. by Christopher Ward and Christopher Ward, Jr.] **KUK**
PW: Jl 19, '24.
BLC: London: T. W. Laurie, 1924.

W-98   ____ The triumph of the nut: and other parodies / by Christopher Ward. New York: Henry Holt and Company, 1923. 178 p.   **AKR**
Contents: The triumph of the nut or Too many marriages -- The flame that failed - réchauffé from "The vehement flame" -- Blacker oxen by Gertrude Otherton -- Glimpsing the moon - with an obeisance to Edith Wharton -- The vanishing point - with apologies to "The breaking point" -- Babbit - on Sinclair Lewis -- Joseph and the bright shawl -- The judge or Turning the tables - Illustrating the influence of Henry James upon an otherwise perfectly good novelist, Rebecca West -- The perils of peregrine - á la Jeffrey Farnol -- One of hers - Long after Willa Cather -- Paradise be damned! by F. Scott Fitzjazzer -- The trials of Triona - in Locke step -- Captain Bloodless - an episode -far from Sabatini -- Some Freedom! - "With a great price ($2.00) obtained I this freedom!" -- Certain people of no importance - not by Kathleen Norris -- The blunderer of the wasteland by Jane Grey -- The dry land - another kind of "Waste Land" inspired by T. S. Eliot.
LC: O 12, '23.
PW: O 20, '23.

W-99   ____ Twisted tales / by Christopher Ward . . . New York: Henry Holt and Company, 1924. 217 p.
Contents: Stummox / by Fannie Wurst -- The nightmare / by H. Jeewells -- The woman of Knockemout / by Call Hain -- A baked Alaskan / by James Oliver Dogwood -- The wife of the five-centaur / by Cyril Whom -- Blatherstones / by Hethel Hem Dell -- The blind booby / by Carl Far Fetchten -- A loose lady / by Calla Wither -- The inlander / by Tooth Barkington -- The mine with the open door / by our own special haroldbell-writer -- A cure of soups / by Miss Eclair -- Michael's awful deeds / by E. Philip Soppenheim -- Six authors in search of a character -- Defeat / by the author of V-ct-ry -- Antony and Cytherea / by Joseph H-rg-sh-m-r -- Romeo, and the faint perfume / by Z-na G-le -- The Polonius problem / by J. S. Fl-tch-r -- The Lears of the Limberlost / by Gene Hadden Order -- An imminent American: William Jinglings Brine / by Lytton Starchey -- Letters from Elysium, or, extending diagonally over half of cover.
LC: O 4, '24.

W-100 Ward, Duren James Henderson, 1851-1942. Fundamentalism and modernism: a seaside episode. Denver (Colo.): Up the Divide Publishing Company, 1925. 30 p. **DPL** (photocopy)

Ward, Elizabeth Stuart, Mrs. See **Phelps, Elizabeth Stuart, 1844-1911.**

Ward, Florence Gannon Hanfield. See **Ward, J. Carlton, Mrs.**

W-101 Ward, Florence Jeannette Baier, 1886-1959. The flame of happiness / by Florence Ward. Philadelphia: George W. Jacobs & Company, [c1924]. 357 p.
LC: D 1, '24.
PW: D 20, '24.

W-102 ____ Phyllis Anne / by Florence Ward. New York: The James A. McCann Company, [c1921]. 245 p.
LC: N 9, '21.

W-103 ____ The singing heart / by Florence Ward. New York: The James A. McCann Company, 1919. 308 p.
LC: N 28, '19.

W-104 Ward, Gus. Dale King, the apostle of sunshine / by Gus Ward. Crisfield, Md., [c1925]. 122 p., front. (port.).
Unexamined copy: bibliographic data from NUC.

W-105 [Ward, Herbert D. (Herbert Dickinson)], 1861-1932. Lauriel: the love letters of an American girl / edited by A. H.; with a portrait frontispiece in photogravure. Boston: L. C. Page & Company, 1902. 301 p., front. [Ill. by Carle J. Blenner.] **SUC**

W-106 ____ The light of the world / by Herbert D. Ward. Boston; New York: Houghton, Mifflin and Company, 1901. (Cambridge: The Riverside Press). 57, [1] p., front.
PW: Mr 23, '01.

W-107 Ward, Hilda. The girl and the motor / by Hilda Ward; illustrated by the author. Cincinnati: The Gas Engine Publishing Co., 1908. 111 p., front., [4] leaves of plates. Designed end papers.
LC: D 11, '08.

W-108 Ward, J. Carlton, Mrs., b. 1860. Under the northern lights / by Mrs. J. Carlton Ward. New York: A. Wessels, 1909. 272 p., col. front., [2] col. plates. [Ill. by Z. P. Nikolai.]
LC: S 15, '09.
PW: S 18, '09.

W-109 Ward, J. Olive Patricia (Jane Olive Patricia). The herd / by J. Olive Patricia Ward. New York: Cochrane Publishing Co., 1908. 218 p., photo. front. (port.).
LC: S 4, '08.
PW: O 3, '08.

W-110 Ward, Jessie Jane, b. 1885. The call at evening / by Jessie Ward. Lamoni, Ia.: Herald Publishing House, [c1920]. 433 p., ill.

Unexamined copy: bibliographic data from OCLC, #16705790.
LC: Ja 13, '21.

W-111 Ward, Josiah M. (Josiah Mason), b. 1859. Come with me into Babylon: a story of the fall of Nineveh / by Josiah M. Ward; illustrated by James E. McBurney and W. B. Gilbert. New York: Frederick A. Stokes Company, [1902]. 439 p., front., [7] leaves of plates.

W-112 Wardall, Marie. The kingdom of infancy / by Marie Wardall. Philadelphia; London: The Nunc Licet Press, [c1905]. 194 p. **EXS**

W-113 [Warde, Reginald], b. 1878. A daughter of Indra / presented by F. Z. E. San Francisco: The Essene Publishing Co., [c1925]. 255 p.
LC: D 22, '25.

W-114 Warder, Geo. W. (George Woodward), b. 1848. The stairway to the stars, or, Enola Reverof: a novel of psychic and electric study and biography / by George Woodward Warder . . . New York: [s. n.], 1903. 166 p., photo. front. (port.). **NYP**

W-115 Wardman, Ervin, 1865-1923. The Princess Olga / by Ervin Wardman. New York; London: Harper & Brothers, 1906. 314, [1] p.
PW: Ap 21, '06.

W-116 Warfield, David. Ghetto silhouettes / by David Warfield & Margherita Arlina Hamm. New York: James Pott & Company, 1902. 189 p., photo. front. (port.), [4] leaves of photo. plates.
Contents: The end of the dream -- The romance of a minder -- Revenge is mine -- The story of Philip -- The run on Jobblelousky's -- A bird of prey -- Solomon and Santa Claus -- The God of his fathers -- The ruin of a schatchen -- A monument of patience.
PW: N 8, '02.

W-117 Waring, Eleanor Howard. The white path: a novel / by Eleanor Howard Waring; with frontispiece by James Crichton. New York; Washington: The Neale Publishing Company, 1907. 347 p., front.
LC: D 14, '07.
PW: Ja 4, '08.

W-118 Waring, Malvina Sarah, 1842-1930. That Sandhiller: a novel / by Malvina Sarah Waring . . . ; illustrations by James Crichton. New York; Washington: The Neale Publishing Company, 1904. 412 p., front., [2] leaves of plates.

W-119 Waring, Robert L. (Robert Lewis), b. 1863. As we see it / by Robert L. Waring. Washington, D. C.: Press of C. F. Sudwarth, 1910. 233 p., photo. front. (port.).
LC: F 15, '10.
PW: Ap 9, '10.

W-120 Warman, Cy, 1855-1914. The last spike: and other railroad stories / by Cy Warman. New York: Charles Scribner's Sons, 1906. 286 p.
Contents: The last spike -- The belle of Athabasca -- Pathfinding in the Northwest -- The curé's Christmas gift -- The mysterious signal -- Chasing the white mail -- Oppressing the oppressor -- The iron horse and the trolley -- In the Black Cañon -- Jack Ramsey's reason -- The great wreck on the Père Marquette -- The story of an Englishamn -- On the limited -- The conquest of Alaska -- Number three -- The stuff that stands -- The Milwaukee run.
PW: F 10, '06.

W-121   Weiga of Temagami: and other Indian tales / by Cy Warman. New York; Boston: H. M. Caldwell Co., [c1908]. 206 p., front., [15] leaves of plates. Ornamental borders.

Contents: Gitche Manito -- Weiga of Temagami -- A universal love song -- "The Welcome of the Wild" -- Little papoose -- The cross of the Cree -- An Ojibway mother's cradle song -- Fannie -- Sawing wood -- The little bird and the blacksmith -- Back to the wild -- Sabo -- The slaughter -- The heathen -- Red and white -- How God made Temagami -- Hoskaninni's ghost -- The belle of Athabasca -- The search for gold -- Chekko and Uncle Ben -- When Manuelito died -- Eleven hours of afternoon - The woes of huntin'-trouble -- Lanuna.
LC: Je 6, '08.
PW: N 7, '08.

W-122 Warner, Adam Dixon. Folcarinia: a political love story / by Adam Dixon Warner . . . Denver, Colo.: Smith-Brooks Printing Co., 1908. 279 p.

W-123 Warner, Anna Bartlett, 1827-1915. West Point colors / by Anna B. Warner. New York; Chicago; Toronto; London; Edinburgh: Fleming H. Revell Company, [c1903]. 428 p., front., [7] leaves of plates.
LC: O 31, '03.
BLC: London: James Nisbet & Co., 1903.
References: BAL 21111.

W-124 Warner, Anne, 1869-1913. The gay and festive Claverhouse: an extravaganza / by Anne Warner; with illustrations by Clarence F. Underwood. Boston: Little, Brown, and Company, 1914. 216 p., front., [5] leaves of plates.
PW: O 3, '14.

W-125 [____] His story, their letters: a prologue / by F. D. B. [pseud.]. Chicago: Frederick J. Drake & Company, [1902]. 141 p., front. [Ill. by Victor Dyfyerman.] **UOK**

W-126   How Leslie loved / by Anne Warner . . . ; with illustrations by A. B. Wenzell. Boston: Little, Brown, and Company, 1911. 292 p., col. front., [2] leaves of col. plates.
LC: F 21, '11.
PW: F 25, '11.

W-127   In a mysterious way / by Anne Warner; illustrated by J. V. McFall. Boston: Little, Brown and Company, 1909. 290 p., front., [4] leaves of plates.
LC: Ap 16, '09.
PW: My 8, '09.

W-128   Just between themselves: a book about Dichtenberg / by Anne Warner . . . ; frontispiece in color by Will Grefé. Boston: Little, Brown, and Company, 1910. 275 p., col. front. **CLU**
LC: Ap 21, '10.
PW: Ap 30, '10.
BLC: London: T. Fisher Unwin, 1910.

W-129   An original gentleman / by Anne Warner; with a frontispiece by Alice Barber Stephens. Boston: Little, Brown, and Company, 1908. 339 p., front.
PW: O 3, '08.

W-130   The panther: a tale of temptation / by Anne Warner; with illustrations by Paul K. M. Thomas.

Boston: Small, Maynard & Company, 1908. 91 p., col. front., [3] leaves of plates. Ornamental borders throughout.
PW: O 24, '08.

W-131   The rejuvenation of Aunt Mary / by Anne Warner . . . ; illustrated with four full-page illustrations. Boston: Little, Brown, and Company, 1905. 323 p., front.,[3] leaves of plates. [Ill. by Decorative Designers.]
PW: O 14, '05.
BLC: London: Gay & Bird, 1907.

W-132   Seeing England with Uncle John / by Anne Warner . . . ; with illustrations by Frederic R. Gruger. New York: The Century Co., 1908. 492 p., front., ill., map.
PW: Mr 21, '08.
BLC: London: Gay & Hancock, 1908.

W-133   Seeing France with Uncle John / by Anne Warner; with illustrations by May Wilson Preston. New York: The Century Co., 1906. 322 p., front., ill.
LC: S 28, '06.
PW: O 20, '06.
BLC: London: Gay & Bird, 1906.

W-134   Sunshine Jane / by Anne Warner . . . ; with frontispiece by Harriet Roosevelt Richards. Boston: Little, Brown, and Company, 1914. 279 p., front.
                              EZA
PW: F 14, '14.
BLC: London: Releigous Tract Society, 1914.

W-135   Susan Clegg: her friend and her neighbors / by Anne Warner; illustrated. Boston: Little, Brown, and Company, 1910. 397 p., front., [1] leaf of plates. [Ill. by Walter J. Enright & Decorative Designers.]
LC: S 16, '10.
PW: S 10, '10.

W-136   Susan Clegg and a man in the house / by Anne Warner; illustrated from drawings by Alice Barber Stephens. Boston: Little, Brown, and Company, 1907. 279 p., front., [3] leaves of plates.
LC: O 3, '07.
PW: O 12, '07.

W-137   Susan Clegg and her friend Mrs. Lathrop / by Anne Warner . . . Boston: Little, Brown and Company, 1904. 227 p., front. [Ill. by W. J. Enright.]
"The first four chapters of `Susan Clegg and her friend Mrs. Lathrop' appeared in the `Century magazine' as separate stories during the past year." Contents: The marrying of Susan Clegg -- Miss Clegg's adopted -- Jathrop Lathrop's cow -- Susan Clegg's cousin Marion -- The minister's vacation.
PW: O 8, '04.
BLC: London: Dean & Son, Cambridge, U. S. A. [printed 1904].

W-138   Susan Clegg and her love affairs / by Anne Warner; with frontispiece by H. M. Brett. Boston: Little, Brown and Company, 1916. 320 p., front.
LC: My 11, '16.
PW: My 13, '16.

W-139 ____ Susan Clegg and her neighbors' affairs / by Anne Warner. Boston: Little, Brown, and Company, 1906. 220 p., front. [Ill. by Decorative Designers.]
Contents: Mrs. Lathrop's love affair -- Old man Ely's proposal -- The wolf at Susan's door -- A very superior man.
LC: Je 7, '06.
PW: Je 23, '06.
BLC: London: Gay & Bird, 1906.

W-140 ____ The taming of Amorette: a comedy of manners / by Anne Warner . . . ; with illustrations by Clarence F. Underwood. Boston: Little, Brown, and Company, 1915. 210 p., front., [5] leaves of plates.   **OSU, KLG**
LC: Mr 15, '15.
PW: Mr 13, '15.

W-141 ____ The tigress / by Anne Warner . . . ; frontispiece by R. F. Schabelitz. New York: W. J. Watt & Company, [c1916]. 310 p., front.
LC: Je 8, '16.
PW: Je 3, '16.

W-142 ____ When woman proposes / by Anne Warner . . . ; with illustrations by Charlotte Weber Ditzler and decorations by Theodore B. Hapgood. Boston: Little, Brown & Company, 1911. 158 p., col. front., [3] leaves of col. plates. Ornamental borders.
LC: S 23, '11.
PW: S 23, '11.

W-143 ____ A woman's will / by Anne Warner, illustrated by J. H. Caliga [sic]. Boston: Little, Brown, and Company, 1904. 359 p., front., [3] leaves of plates.   **MNL**

W-144 ____ Your child and mine / by Anne Warner . . . ; illustrated. Boston: Little, Brown and Company, 1909. 314 p., front., [7] leaves of plates. [Ill. by Paul Julien Meylan, Ethel Farnsworth, A. E. Jackson, A. Ball, W. H. Margedson, Cyrus Fosmire, and E. Tattersal.]
Contents: The surrenders of Cornwallis -- The practical care of a fairy -- The parting of the clouds -- A Christmas devotee -- Who is she? -- A true woman -- The mysterious man -- "Le Petit" -- The captain's charm -- The old witch and the black cats -- Himself reborn -- Little sister and baby -- An old-fashioned school -- The German Easter and the Easter Rabbit -- Trading his mother -- The very bottom of her purse -- The Steinhard pride -- Through the eyes of a dog -- His Majesty and the fairies -- The closing of Santa Claus' door -- The soul of a tree.
LC: S 28, '09.
PW: O 9, '09.

W-145 Warner, Frances Lester, b. 1888. Endicott and I / by Frances Lester Warner. Boston; New York: Houghton Mifflin Company, 1919. (Cambridge: The Riverside Press). 213 p., front. Reprinted in part from various periodicals.
LC: O 16, '19.

W-146 Warner, William Henry. The bridge of time / by William Henry Warner . . . New York: Scott & Seltzer, 1919. 372 p., col. front.
LC: D 22, '19.
PW: D 6, '19.
BLC: London: Eveleigh Nash Co., 1920.

W-147 ____ Mothers of men / by William Henry Warner

and De Witte Kaplan; with frontispiece by E. L. Blumenschein. New York: Temple Scott, 1919. 317 p., col. front.
LC: Mr 7, '19.
PW: Mr 15, '19.

W-148 ____ Sacrilegious hands / by William Henry Warner . . . New York: Greenberg, Publisher, Inc., 1925. 305 p.
LC: Mr 19, '25.
PW: Ap 11, '25.

W-149 Warnock, T. B., b. 1859. Richard Hume / by T. B. Warnock. New York: R. F. Fenno & Company, 1902. 251 p.   **DLC**

W-150 Warren, Benjamin Clark. The Christian pirate, or, Romance and realities of a sunny shore / by "Ben and Bob", Benjamin Clark Warren, Robert Lincoln Parkinson. Philadelphia, Penna., U. S. A.: The Ben and Bob Publishing Company, [Press of Alfred M. Sloccum Co.] [c1911]. 318 p., front., [5] leaves of plates.   **DLC**
LC: D 1, '11.

W-151 ____ In the land of the Romburg: a society story / by Benjamin Clark Warren; illustrated. New York: Broadway Publishing Co., [c1906]. 281 p., front., [3] leaves of plates. [Ill. by Sydney K. Hartman.]
LC: D 27, '06.
PW: F 9, '07.

Warren, Charles, 1868-1954. A manufacturer of history. In *Politics* **(1901), P-461.**

W-152 Warren, Constance M. (Constance Martha), b. 1877. Pearls astray: a romantic episode of the last democracy / by Constance M. Warren; illustrations by J. Harleston Parker. Boston: Small, Maynard and Company, [c1920]. 158 p., ill.   **UAI**
LC: O 26, '20.

W-153 ____ The Phoenix / by Constance M. Warren; with frontispiece by Christine Tucke Curtiss. Boston; New York: Houghton Mifflin Company, 1917. (Cambridge, Mass.: The Riverside Press). 355, [1] p., col. front.
LC: Mr 17, '17.

W-154 Warren, Garnet. An old fashioned Christmas story / by Garnet Warren. Cincinnati, Ohio: Published by the Fleuron Press, [c1924]. 82 p.

W-155 Warren, Maude Lavinia Radford, 1875-1934. Barbara's marriages: a novel / by Maude Radford Warren. New York; London: Harper & Brothers Publishers, 1915. 350, [1] p., front.
LC: Mr 29, '15.
PW: Ap 3, '15.

W-156 ____ Carnival colors / by Maude Radford Warren . . . Indianapolis: The Bobbs-Merrill Company, [c1925]. 354 p.
LC: Mr 9, '25.
PW: Mr 14, '25.

W-157 ____ The house of youth / by Maude Radford Warren. Indianapolis: The Bobbs-Merrill Company, [c1923]. 376 p.
LC: O 11, '23.
PW: O 6, '23.

W-158 ____ The land of the living: a novel / by Maude Radford Warren. New York; London: Harper & Brothers, 1908. 313, [1] p., front., [1] leaf of plates.
LC: Jl 16, '08.
PW: Ag 8, '08.

W-159 ____ The main road: a novel / by Maude Radford Warren . . . New York; London: Harper & Brothers, 1913. 390, [1] p., col. front.   **AZU**
LC: O 4, '13.
PW: O 11, '13.

W-160 ____ Peter-Peter: a romance out of town / by Maude Radford Warren; illustrated by Rose O'Neill. New York; London: Harper & Brothers, 1909. 306 p., incl. 30 leaves of plates, front., ill.
LC: My 14, '09.
PW: Je 5, '09.

Warren, Patience, pseud. <u>See</u> **Kelsey, Jeannette Garr (Washburn), Mrs., b. 1850.**

W-161 Warren, Rose Harlow. A Southern home in war times / Rose Harlow Warren. New York: Broadway Publishing Company, [c1914]. 93 p.   **KSU**

W-162 Warren, Stanley, b. 1871. In defense of His Excellency: an incident of political Washington / by Stanley Warren. New York: Broadway Publishing Company . . . , [c1904]. 118 p., photo. front. (port.).

Warrington, Maris, pseud. <u>See</u> **Billings, Maris, pseud.**

W-163 [Warwick, Anne, *pseud.*]. Ashes of incense: a novel / by the author of Mastering Flame. New York; London: Mitchell Kennerley, 1912. 315 p.   **NYP**
BLC: London: Mills & Boon, 1912.

W-164 ____ The best people / by Anne Warwick [pseud.]. New York: John Lane Company; Toronto: S. B. Gundy, [c1918]. 345 p.   **TLM**
LC: Ap 5, '18.
PW: Mr 30, '18.

W-165 ____ The Chalk line / by Anne Warwick [pseud.]. New York: John Lane Company, 1915. 278 p.
LC: Mr 2, '15.
PW: Mr 6, '15.

W-166 ____ Compensation / by Anne Warwick [pseud.]. New York: John Lane Company, 1911. 332, [1] p.   **ABC**
LC: F 28, '11.
PW: Mr 4, '11.

W-167 [____] Mastering flame: a novel. New York; London: Mitchell Kennerley, 1912. 350 p.   **NBU**

W-168 ____ The unknown woman / by Anne Warwick [pseud.]; with frontispiece in color by Will Grefé. New York: John Lane Company, 1912. 345 p., col. front.
LC: Mr 25, '12.
PW: Mr 30, '12.

W-169 ____ The unpretenders / by Anne Warwick [pseud.] . . . New York: John Lane Company, 1916. 248 p.   **ABC**
LC: F 26, '16.
PW: F 26, '16.

W-170 ____ Victory Law / by Anne Warwick [pseud.]. New York: John Lane Co.; Toronto: Bell and Cockburn, 1914. 316 p.   **OSU, CLE**
LC: Mr 17, '14.
PW: Mr 14, '14.

W-171 Warwick, Bessie B. A romance of the Jersey Pines / by Bessie B. Warwick. Boston: Richard G. Badger, [c1922]. ([Boston, U. S. A.]: The Gorham Press). 240 p.   **CKM**
LC: N 25, '22.

W-172 Washburn, Claude C. (Claude Carlos), 1883-1926. Gerald Northrop: a novel / by Claude C. Washburn. New York: Duffield & Company, 1914. 521 p., front. [Ill. by Howard Heath.]
LC: O 3, '14.

W-173 ____ The green arch / by Claude C. Washburn. New York: Albert & Charles Boni, 1925. 147 p.
LC: N 11, '25.
PW: N 14, '25.

W-174 ____ The lonely warrior / by Claude C. Washburn. New York: Harcourt, Brace and Company, [c1922]. 345 p.
LC: F 3, '22.
PW: Ja 28, '22.
BLC: London: Mills & Boon, Rahway printed, [1922].

W-175 ____ Order / by Claude C. Washburn. New York: Duffield and Company, 1920. 339 p.
LC: Mr 6, '20.
PW: My 1, '20.

W-176 ____ The prince and the princess / by Claude C. Washburn. New York: Albert & Charles Boni, 1925. 312 p.
LC: F 12, '25.
PW: F 7, '25.

W-177 Washburn, Eva Jane. Eureka / by Eva Jane Washburn. Paducah, Kentucky: Sun Publishing Co., 1910. 106 p., photo. front. (port.), [6] leaves of photo. plates.   **KSL**
LC: Mr 11, '10.

W-178 Washburn, Hannah Blaney. A winter in retirement, or, Scattered leaves / by Hannah Blaney Washburn. New York: Frank Allaben Genealogical Company, [c1914]. 113 p.   **VSL**

W-179 [Washburn, W. T. (William Tucker)], 1841-1916.
The deuce of hearts. New York: R. F. Fenno &
Company, [c1901]. 503 p.   **DLC**
PW: Ap 20, '01.

W-180 _____ The first stone: and other stories / by W. T.
Washburn . . . New York: R. F. Fenno &
Company, 1904. 217 p.
Contents: The first stone -- Madagascar -- Perplexed -- The jaundice
-- The boss -- More truth than tale -- A Mormon maiden -- Tolnuk
and Ima -- Sleuth -- Hero or fool? -- A lucky watch -- Mrs.
O'Rafferty -- Half-moon club -- Half a dozen raw -- Ildra.
LC: O 29, '04.
PW: D 24, '04.

W-181 Washburne, Marion Foster, b. 1863. The house on
the north shore / by Marion Foster Washburne . . . ;
illustrated by Walter J. & Maginal Wright Enright.
Chicago: A. C. McClurg & Co., 1909. 287 p.,
front., [4] leaves of plates.   **TJC**
LC: S 13, '09.
PW: O 9, '09.

W-182 _____ A little fountain of life / by Marion Foster
Washburne. Chicago; New York; London: Rand,
McNally & Company, [c1904]. 232 p.   **DLC**
PW: S 17, '04.

W-183 Wason, Robert Alexander, 1874-1955. And then
came Jean: a novel / by Robert Alexander Wason
. . . ; with a frontispiece by Philip L. Hale. Boston:
Small, Maynard & Company, [c1913]. 449 p., col.
front.
LC: N 26, '13.
PW: N 8, '13.

W-184 _____ The dog and the child and the ancient sailor
man / by Robert Alexander Wason. Indianapolis:
The Bobbs-Merrill Co., [c1911]. 96 p.
LC: Ja 2, '14.
Expanded version: . . . with a frontispiece by Arthur
Hutchins. Boston: Small, Maynard and Company,
[c1913]. 209 p., front.

W-185 _____ Friar Tuck: being the chronicles of the
Reverend John Carmichael, of Wyoming, U. S. A.:
as set forth and embellished by his friend and admirer
Happy Hawkins / and here recorded by Robert
Alexander Wason . . . ; illustrated by Stanley L.
Wood. Boston: Small, Maynard and Company,
[1912]. 448 p., front., [3] leaves of plates.
LC: S 10, '12.
BLC: London: Grant Richards, Cambridge, Mass.
printed, 1913.

W-186 _____ Happy Hawkins / by Robert Alexander Wason;
illustrated by Howard Giles. Boston: Small,
Maynard and Company, [c1909]. 352 p., front., [15]
leaves of plates.
LC: S 4, '09.
PW: Ag 28, '09.
BLC: London: Grant Richards, New York printed,
1912.

W-187 _____ Happy Hawkins in the Panhandle / by Robert
Alexander Wason . . . ; with a frontispiece by George
W. Gage. Boston: Small, Maynard and Company,

[c1914]. 492 p., col. front.
LC: O 31, '14.
PW: O 31, '14.
BLC: London: Grant Richards, [1914].

W-188 _____ The knight-errant: a novel of to-day / by
Robert Alexander Wason; illustrated by Hanson
Booth. Boston: Small, Maynard & Company,
[c1911]. 398 p., col. front., [4] leaves of plates.
LC: S 13, '11.
PW: O 7, '11.
BLC: London: Grant Richards, Cambridge, U. S.
A. printed, 1912.

_____ Knute Ericson's celebration. In *The Grim
thirteen* (1917), G-537.

_____, jt. aut. *Nachette* (1909). See **Nye, Ned,
b. 1876, jt. aut., N-188.**

W-189 _____ The steering wheel / by Robert Alexander
Wason; illustrated by Paul J. Meylan. Indianapolis:
The Bobbs-Merrill Company, [c1910]. 399 p.,
front., [4] leaves of plates.
LC: O 5, '10.
PW: O 8, '10.

W-190 _____ The wolves; a fable with a purpose / by Robert
Alexander Wason; illustrated by G. Weiser.
Chicago: C. H. Kerr & Company, 1908. 31 p.,
ill.   **UUM**
LC: S 3, '08.

W-191 Wasson, George S. (George Savary), 1855-1931?
Cap'n Simeon's store / by George S. Wasson.
Boston; New York: Houghton, Mifflin and
Company, 1903. (Cambridge: The Riverside Press).
287 p., front. [Ill. by Marcia O. Woodbury.] A
collection of stories, some of which appeared
originally in the Atlantic monthly, Scribner's
magazine, the Century, and Harper's weekly.
Contents: Killick Cove and Simeon's store -- Hoss sense vs. book
learning -- The dayspring breeze -- Superstitions of the cove -- The
witch-bridle -- Who fell from aloft? -- The "works" on the schooner
Harvester -- Rusticators at the Cove -- The Wreck Island ructions --
Doctors, both human and veteran -- Deacon Spurshoe's Jonah -- The
"teching" of the Vesper -- The Oakum Hill Ground.
PW: My 2, '03.

W-192 _____ The green shay / by George S. Wasson . . . ;
with frontispiece by the author. Boston; New York:
Houghton, Mifflin and Company, 1905. (Cambridge
[Mass.]: The Riverside Press). 304, [2] p., front.
"Portions of chapters I and XIII have appeared in the
Youth's Companion, and of chapter III in the
Outlook."
PW: O 14, '05.
BLC: London: Archibald, Constable & Co.,
Cambridge, Mass. printed, 1905.

W-193 _____ Home from sea / by George S. Wasson; with
illustrations by the author. Boston; New York:
Houghton, Mifflin and Company, 1908. (Cambridge:
The Riverside Press). 333, [1] p., front., [5] leaves
of plates.
"Partly reprinted from the Atlantic monthly and
Century magazine."
Contents: The rote -- The two chanty-men -- The sea-glin -- Keeping

tally -- Skipper Haultaut's wooing -- The voyage of the brig
December -- Overhauling the politicianers -- The nerve of Skipper
Fairway -- Heavin' the project -- The brazen-face.
PW: Ap 18, '08.

W-194   Waste, Henrie, *pseud.* Love days: (Susanna More's)
/ by Henrie Waste [pseud.]. New York: Alfred A.
Knopf, 1923. 426 p.
LC: O 16, '23.

W-195   _____ Philosophy: an autobiographical fragment / by
Henrie Waste [pseud.]. New York; London;
Bombay; Calcutta; Madras: Longmans, Green and
Co., 1917. 274 p.   **MNU**
LC: Ja 19, '17.
BLC: London: Longman's Co.; U. S. A. [printed],
1917.

W-196   Watanna, Onoto, b. 1879, *pseud.* Cattle / by
Winnifred Eaton (Onota Watanna [pseud.]);
frontispiece by George W. Gage. New York: W. J.
Watt & Co., [c1924]. 294 p., front.
LC: Ap 11, '24.
PW: Ap 26, '24.
BLC: London: Hutchinson & co., [1923].

W-197   _____ Daughters of Nijo: a romance of Japan / by
Onoto Watanna [pseud.] . . . ; with illustrations and
decorations by Kiyokichi Sano. New York: The
Macmillan Company; London: Macmillan & Co.,
ltd., 1904. 397 p., incl. col. front., incl. 7 col.
leaves of plates, ill.
PW: My 14, '04; Je 4, '04.

W-198   _____ The diary of Delia: being a veracious
chronicle of the kitchen, with some side-lights on the
parlour / by Onoto Watanna [pseud.]; illustrated by
May Wilson Preston. New York: Doubleday, Page
& Company, 1907. 229 p., front., [7] leaves of
plates.
PW: Je 1, '07.
BLC: London: Doubleday, Page & Company; New
York printed, 1907.

W-199   _____ The heart of Hyacinth / by Onoto Watanna
[pseud.]; illustrated; decorations by Kiyokichi Sano.
New York; London: Harper & Brothers, 1903. 250,
[1] p., col. front., [3] leaves of col. plates.
PW: S 19, '03.

W-200   [_____] His royal nibs / by Winifred Eaton Reeve . . .
New York: W. J. Watt & Co., [c1925]. 318 p.
             OSU, NYP

W-201   _____ The honorable Miss Moonlight / by Onoto
Watanna [pseud.] . . . New York; London: Harper
& Brothers, 1912. 174, [1] p., col. front. [Ill. by K.
Kato.]   **AZU**
LC: S 27, '12.
PW: O 12, '12.

W-202   _____ A Japanese blossom / by Onoto Watanna
[pseud.]; illustrated by L. W. Ziegler [sic]. New
York; London: Harper & Brothers, 1906. 263,
[1] p., col. front., [3] leaves of col. plates.
PW: O 20, '06.

W-203   _____ A Japanese nightingale / by Onoto Watanna
[pseud.]; illustrated by Genjiro Yeto. New York;
London: Harper & Brothers, 1901. 225, [1] p., col.
front., [2] leaves of col. plates. Illustrated end
papers.
PW: O 19, '01.
BLC: London: Archibald Constable & Co., 1904.

W-204   _____ The love of Azalea / by Onoto Watanna
[pseud.]; illustrated by Gazo Foudji. New York:
Dodd, Mead & Company, 1904. 239 p., col. front.,
[5] leaves of col. plates.
PW: O 15, '04.
BLC: London: B. F. Steven & Brown, printed in the
U. S. A., 1904.

W-205   [_____] Marion: the story of an artist's model / by
herself and the author of "Me"; illustrations by Henry
Hutt. New York: W. J. Watt & Company, [c1916].
307 p., front., [23] leaves of plates.

W-206   [_____] Me: a book of remembrance. New York:
The Century Co., 1915. 356 p.

W-207   _____ Sunny-San / by Onoto Watanna [pseud.] . . .
New York: George H. Doran Company, [c1922].
311 p.
LC: Ap 28, '22.
PW: My 6, '22.
BLC: London: Hutchinson & Co., [1922].

W-208   _____ Tama / by Onoto Watanna [pseud.]; illustrated
by Genjiro Kataoka. New York; London: Harper &
Brothers, 1910. 243, [1] p., col. front., [3] leaves of
col. plates. Illustrated end papers.
LC: O 15, '10.
PW: O 22, '10.

W-209   _____ The wooing of Wistaria / by Onoto Watanna
[pseud.]. New York; London: Harper & Brothers,
1902. 388 p., col. front., (port.).
PW: S 20, '02.

W-210   Waterloo, Stanley, 1846-1913. The Cassowary:
what chanced in the Cleft Mountains / by Stanley
Waterloo . . . Chicago: Monarch Book Company,
[c1906]. 402 p., front., [12] leaves of plates, music.
[Ill. by Samuel J. Kennedy.]
PW: Mr 2, '07.

W-211   _____ A son of the ages: the reincarnations and
adventures of Scar, the link: a story of man from the
beginning / by Stanley Waterloo . . . ; illustrated by
Craig Johns. Garden City, New York: Doubleday,
Page & Company, 1914. 334 p., front., [3] leaves of
plates.
LC: Mr 28, '14.
BLC: London: Curtis Brown; Garden City, N.Y.
[printed], 1914.

Waterman, Abby L. Billy-Too. *In California story
book* (1909), C-40.

W-212   Waters, Patrick H. A scheme for millions / by
Patrick H. Waters. New York: Broadway Publishing
Company, [c1905]. 141 p.   **DLC**

W-213 Waters, Russell Judson. El estranjero: the stranger: a story of Southern California / by Russell Judson Waters . . . ; illustrated by Will E. Chapin. Chicago; New York: Rand McNally & Company, 1910. 298 p., front., [25] leaves of plates. Illustrated margins.
LC: O 21, '10.

W-214 Watkins, Mary Lindsey. My Lady Primrose; a love story / by Mary Lindsey Watkins. New York; Washington: The Neale Publishing Company, 1903. 134 p. **DLC**
LC: Ag 8, '03.
PW: Ag 22, '03.

W-215 Watrous, A. E. (Andrew Edward), d. 1902. Young Howson's wife / by A. E. Watrous. New York: Quail & Warner, 1902. 300 p.
Contents: The married women: Young Howson's wife -- Oliver Mendwell's wife -- The murder in our flat -- A holiday with Camilla -- A pug's Christmas dream -- Fin de siècle. The unmarried: My niece Cicely -- Mr. Draper's diary -- The two cornets of Monmouth -- Old coaching days -- The mad poet's quest -- The appearance of evil -- The woman who sang -- The life of Tommy Tremaine -- A Clito to the ring -- The case of Barbara Babarant -- Two little match girls --The hat that Jim bought.
PW: Mr 29, '02.

W-216 Watrous, Elizabeth Snowden Nichols. It: being our individual magneto / by Elizabeth Snowden Nichols Watrous. New York: Cochrane Publishing Company, 1910. 362 p. **DLC**
LC: N 17, '10.
PW: F 4, '11.

W-217 Watrous, Jerome A. (Jerome Anthony), b. 1840. Richard Epps: and other stories / by J. A. Watrous . . . Milwaukee, Wis.: Printed by the Evening Wisconsin Company, [c1906]. 175 p., photo. front. (port.). **JFK**
Contents: Richard Epps -- Two mason stories -- Just before Christmas -- Three pathetic scenes -- An army four hundred -- About two army camps -- A busy day for McKinley -- Fourth of July, 1863 -- This day of memories -- Christmas in camp -- The mellowing days -- McKinley's Washington trips -- Bravery of young women -- Sons of fighters -- Sidelight on a great event in American history -- "Old Man, are you hurt?" -- Unrecorded army tragedies -- Secret service stories -- That applejack raid -- An American's part in giving Japan a famous army -- A reporter's advance -- The minister's boys-The Underwoods -- Some Grant stories -- He and his son -- Stories about army horses -- Billy Hockabout -- The colonel's little doctor.

W-218 Watson, Evelyn. The house by the red pump: a story / by Evelyn Watson. Saint Louis, Mo.: Becktold Printing and Book Mfg. Co., [c1904]. 153 p. **DLC**

W-219 Watson, Jeannette Grace Watkins. Ole Ann: and other stories / by Jeannette Grace Watson; illustrated by Bertha Rockwell. Akron, O.; New York; Chicago: The Saalfield Publishing Company, [c1905]. 126 p., incl. front., ill.
Contents: Ole Ann -- Monon -- The day before yesterday -- After freedom came -- Uncle Davie and the telephone -- Polly -- Cupid and Rose -- Pauliny -- Julie -- From the kingdom o'Calloway.

W-220 Watson, Margery, b. 1864. The responsibility of Ruffles / by Margery Watson. Boston; New York; Chicago: The Pilgrim Press, [c1913]. 184 p., col. front., [1] leaf of plates. [Ill. by Frank T. Merrill.]
LC: O 10, '13.
PW: N 8, '13.

W-221 Watson, Thomas E. (Thomas Edward), 1856-1922. Bethany: a story of the old South / by Thomas E. Watson; illustrated. New York: D. Appleton and Company, 1904. 383 p., front., [5] leaves of plates.
PW: O 22, '04.

W-222 [Watson, Virginia Cruse]. Midshipman days / by Roger West [pseud.]; with illustrations. Boston; New York: Houghton Mifflin Company, 1913. (Cambridge: The Riverside Press). 241, [1] p., front., [5] leaves of plates. [Ill. by W. L. Cattrey, C. T. Clement, George F. Gray, & R. L. Hilton.] **DLC**

W-223 Watt, Marion Frances. Maurice, and other stories / by Marion Frances Watt. Seattle: The Ivy Press, 1902. 313 p.
Unexamined copy: bibliographic data from OCLC, #8679479.
Contents: Maurice -- Miss Williams -- Ulrica -- 'Lisabeth -- Doris.
PW: N 1, '02.

W-224 Wattles, Wallace Delois, 1860-1911. Hell-fire Harrison / by W. D. Wattles; illustrated and decorated in colors by Frank T. Merrill. Boston: L. C. Page & Company, 1910. 100 p., col. front., [5] leaves of plates. Ornamental margins.

W-225 Watts, Mary Stanbery, b. 1868. The Boardman family / by Mary S. Watts . . . New York: The Macmillan Company, 1918. 352 p.
LC: Ap 10, '18.
PW: Ap 20, '18.

_____ The dove 'o peace, the story of a highwayman. In *Golden stories* (1909), G-285.

W-226 _____ The fabric of the loom / by Mary S. Watts. New York: The Macmillan Company, 1924. 268 p.
LC: O 15, '24.
PW: O 25, '24.

W-227 _____ From father to son / by Mary S. Watts. New York: The Macmillan Company, 1919. 310 p.
LC: Jl 9, '19.
PW: Jl 19, '19.

W-228 _____ The house of Rimmon / by Mary S. Watts. New York: The Macmillan Company, 1922. 378 p.
LC: Mr 8, '22.
PW: Ap 1, '22.

W-229 _____ The legacy: a story of a woman / by Mary S. Watts. New York: The Macmillan Company, 1911. 394 p.
LC: My 4, '11.
PW: My 13, '11.
BLC: London: Macmillan: Norwood, Mass. [printed], 1911.

W-230 _____ Luther Nichols / by Mary S. Watts. New York: The Macmillan Company, 1923. 362 p.
LC: O 3, '23.
PW: O 13, '23.

W-231 _____ Nathan Burke / by Mary S. Watts. New York: The Macmillan Company, 1910. 628 p.
LC: Ap 18, '10.
PW: Ap 30, '10.

_____ Nice neighbours. In *Prize stories of 1923* **(1924), P-621.**

W-232   _____ The noon-mark / by Mary S. Watts. New York: The Macmillan Company, 1920. 336 p.
LC: O 27, '20.
PW: Ja 22, '21.

W-233   _____ The rise of Jennie Cushing / by Mary S. Watts. New York: The Macmillan Company, 1914. 487 p.
LC: O 8, '14.
PW: O 24, '14.

W-234   _____ The rudder: a novel with several heroes / by Mary S. Watts . . . New York: The Macmillan Company, 1916. 453, [1] p., front. [Ill. by J. Henry.]
LC: Mr 23, '16.
PW: Ap 1, '16.
BLC: London: Macmillan, printed in U. S. A., 1916.

W-235   _____ The tenants: an episode of the '80s / by Mary S. Watts. New York: The McClure Company, 1908. 313 p.
PW: Ap 4, '08.

W-236   _____ Van Cleve / by Mary S. Watts. New York: The Macmillan Company, 1913. 396 p.
LC: O 16, '13.
PW: D 27, '13.

W-237   Way, L. N. The call of the heart / by L. N. Way; frontispiece illustrated by Ch. Weber Ditzler. New York: G. W. Dillingham Company, [c1909.] 332 p., col. front.   **DLC**
LC: O 23, '09.

W-238   Way, Norman. Captains three / by Norman Way; illustrations by Armand Both. New York: Edward J. Clode Publisher, [c1912]. 285 p., front., [7] leaves of plates. Illustrated end papers.
LC: Ap 22, '12.

W-239   _____ Mary Janes's pa / by Norman Way; illustrated. New York: The H. K. Fly Company, [c1909]. 314 p., col. front., [5] leaves of col. plates. "From the play of the smae name by Edith Ellis."
LC: Ag 13, '09.

W-240   _____ The moccasins of gold / by Norman Way; illustrated by A. W. Parsons. New York: Edward J. Clode Publisher, [c1912]. 302 p., front., [5] leaves of plates.
LC: O 16, '12.

Wayfarer, A., pseud. See **Smith-Tapman, Lillian.**

W-241   [Wayne, Charles Stokes], b. 1858. The city of encounters / by Horace Hazeltine [pseud.]; illustrations by Harry Stacey Benton. New York: Mitchell Kennerley, [c1908]. 384 p., front., [6] leaves of plates.
LC: O 1, '08.

W-242   _____ The marriage of Mrs. Merlin / by Charles Stokes Wayne; illustrated by Louis F. Grant. New York: G. W. Dillingham Company, [1907]. 262 p.,

front., [3] leaves of plates.
LC: Ag 23, '07.
PW: O 5, '07.
BLC: London: T. Fisher Unwin, New York [printed], 1907.

W-243   _____ A prince to order: a novel / by Charles Stokes Wayne. New York; London: John Lane, The Bodley Head, 1905. 317 p.
PW: Ap 1, '05.

W-244   [_____] The sable lorcha / by Horace Hazeltine [pseud.]; with eight illustrations by J. J. Gould. Chicago: A. C. McClurg & Co., 1912. 387 p., front., [7] leaves of plates.

W-245   [_____] The snapdragon / by Horace Hazeltine [pseud.]. New York: Desmond FitzGerald, Inc., [c1913]. 355 p., front.
PW: Mr 29, '13.

Wayne, Winifred. Conformity. In *The best college short stories, 1924-1925* **(1925), B-558.**

W-246   Weatherly, Josephine. After strange gods / by Josephine Weatherly. New York: Broadway Publishing Co., 1913. 162 p., photo. front. (port.).
LC: N 6, '13.

W-247   Weaver, Henrietta. Flame and the shadow-eater / by Henrietta Weaver. New York: Henry Holt and Company, 1917. 330 p.
Contents: The seller of dreams -- The wonder-bubble of the world -- Mirage in the desert -- Dust in the wind -- Caprice -- The marvelous year -- The understanding dream -- Fetters -- The Phoenix car -- Three visions -- The enwrapped -- The sundering veil -- The glittering stone -- Despoilers -- The night-comer.
LC: My 26, '17.
PW: My 26, '17.

Weaver, John V. A.(John Van Alstyne), 1893-1938, contributor. See *Bobbed hair* **(1925), B-700.**

W-248   _____ Margey wins the game / John V. A. Weaver. New York: Alfred A. Knopf, 1922. 110 p.
LC: My 12, '22.
PW: My 6, '22.

Webb, Anna Spanuth, Mrs. See **Bute, Currer, pseud.**

W-249   Webb, Aquilla, b. 1870. The Christian athlete: a sermon story / by Aquilla Webb . . . Los Angeles, Cal.: Commercial Printing House, 1902. 178 p.

W-250   Webb, Eliza Ann. The mystery of the old mill / by Eliza Ann Webb. [Morgantown, W. Va.: The Morgantown Printing and Binding Co., 1924.] 317 p., front., [4] leaves of plates. [Ill. by Kay H. Paisley.]   **WVU**
LC: D 20, '24.
PW: F 14, '25.

W-251   Webb, Richard. Me and Lawson: "Humpty" Hotfoots little run in with Frenzied Copper, Amalgamated Gas and Scrambled Oil / by Richard Webb; illustrations by W. W. Denslow. New York:

G. W. Dillingham Company, [c1905]. 78 p., incl. front., incl. 3 plates, ill. **IPL**
Contents: Humpty and the boss -- Scrambled Oil -- Amalgamated Gas -- The lamb chance.

W-252   Webb, Virginia, *pseud.* One American girl / by Virginia Webb [pseud.] . . . New York: G. W. Dillingham Company, [c1901]. 402 p.   **DLC**
(On cover: Dillingham's American authors library, no. 70).
PW: Mr 2, '01.

Webster, Annie. A love story. <u>In</u> *Youth* **(1901), Y-51.**

W-253   Weber, Adele. The fortunes of the Van der Bergs / by Adele Weber. New York: J. S. Ogilvie Publishing Company, [c1902]. 147 p., front., [6] leaves of plates.

W-254   Webster, Doris. Uncle James' shoes / by Doris and Samuel Webster. New York; London: Published by the Century Co., 1923. 284 p.
PW: S 8, '23.
BLC: London: Hodder & Stoughton, [1924].

W-255   Webster, Edwin J. Strenuous animals: veracious tales / by Edwin J. Webster; illustrated by E. W. Kemble & Bob Addams. New York: Frederick A. Stokes Company, [1904]. 157 p., incl. front., ill.   **KSU**
Content: The imported grizzly -- The return of the prodigal -- The fate of the balloonist dog -- The spectacled eagle -- The cable-laying ferret -- The downfall of the pet frog -- The oil-loving dogfish -- An ursine checker-player.
PW: O 22, '04.

W-256   Webster, Henry Kitchell, 1875-1932. An American family: a novel of to-day / by Henry Kitchell Webster . . . Indianapolis: The Bobbs-Merrill Company, [c1918]. 452 p.
"This novel appeared serially in Everybody's magazine under the title The white arc."
PW: O 5, '18.

W-257   ____ The butterfly / by Henry Kitchell Webster . . . ; illustrated. New York; London: D. Appleton and Company, 1914. 310, [1] p., front., [5] leaves of plates. [Ill. by Clarence F. Underwood.]
LC: Ja 19, '14.
PW: Ja 31, '14.

W-258   ____ The Duke of Cameron Avenue / by Henry Kitchell Webster . . . New York: The Macmillan Company; London: Macmillan & Co., 1904. 133 p., photo. front. (port.), [2] leaves of plates. [Ill. by Arthur E. Jameson.] Designed end papers.
(Little novels by favourite authors.)
PW: Mr 5, '04.

W-259   ____ The ghost girl / by Henry Kitchell Webster . . . New York; London: D. Appleton and Company, 1913. 322, [1] p., front.   **IUA**
LC: F 4, '13.
PW: F 8, '13.

W-260   ____ The girl in the other seat / by Henry Kitchell Webster . . . ; illustrated. New York; London: D. Appleton and Company, 1911. 341, [1] p., front., [3]

leaves of plates. [Ill. by Howard Heath and A. C. Machefert.]
LC: My 9, '11.
PW: My 13, '11.

____ His wife's visitor. <u>In</u> *Marriage* **(1923), M-457.**

W-261   ____ The innocents: a novel / by Henry Kitchell Webster. Indianapolis: The Bobbs-Merrill Company, [c1924]. 345 p.
LC: Ag 30, '24.
PW: Ag 30, '24.
BLC: London: E. Nash & Grayson, 1925.

W-262   ____ Joseph Greer and his daughter: a novel / by Henry Kitchell Webster. Indianapolis: The Bobbs-Merrill Company, [c1922]. 489 p.
LC: N 13, '22.
PW: N 11, '22.
BLC: London: Eveleigh Nash Co., 1923.

W-263   ____ A king in khaki / by Henry Kitchell Webster . . . ; illustrated. New York: D. Appleton and Company, 1909. 319, [1] p., front., [3] leaves of plates. [Ill. by Rose C. O'Neill.]
LC: Ap 8, '09.
PW: Ap 17, '09.
BLC: London: Ward, Lock & Co., 1910.

W-264   ____ Mary Wollaston / by Henry Kitchell Webster. Indianapolis: The Bobbs-Merrill Company, [c1920]. 372 p.
LC: S 27, '20.
PW: O 30, '20.
BLC: London: Eveleigh Nash & Grayson; printed in the U. S. A., 1922.

W-265   ____ The other story: and other stories / by Henry Kitchell Webster. Indianapolis: The Bobbs-Merrill Company, [c1923]. 366 p.
Contents: The other story -- Inside and out -- The Honorable Sylvia -- Bill came back -- The grafter -- The shower -- Giving Cynthia a rest -- The ingredients -- The good angel -- Strictly vicarious -- The new technique -- Transmutation.
LC: O 19, '23.
PW: N 3, '23.

W-266   ____ The painted scene: and other stories of the theater / by Henry Kitchell Webster . . . ; illustrations by Arthur William Brown and Herman Pfeifer. Indianapolis: The Bobbs-Merrill Company, [c1916]. 400 p., front., [9] leaves of plates.
"The stories collected here appeared, severally, in the Saturday evening post, McClure's and Colliers."
Contents: The painted scene -- The spoon tune --Brunette medium -- The spring of the year -- The high-brow lady -- Heart of gold -- The redeemer -- The only girl -- The real dope -- How to appreciate Henry.
LC: O 4, ' 16.
PW: S 30, '16.
BLC: London: Constable & Co., 1917.

W-267   ____ The real adventure: a novel / by Henry Kitchell Webster; illustrated by R. M. Crosby. Indianapolis: The Bobbs-Merrill Company, [c1916]. 574 p., front., [8] leaves of plates.
LC: F 3, '16.
PW: Ja 29, '16.

W-268   Real life: into which Miss Leda Swan of Hollywood makes an adventurous excursion / by Henry Kitchell Webster; illustrated by Everett Shinn. Indianapolis: The Bobbs-Merrill Company, [c1921]. 315 p., front., [4] leaves of plates. Plates (except front.) printed on both sides.
LC: Ag 8, '21.
PW: Jl 30, '21.

W-269   Roger Drake: captain of industry / by Henry Kitchell Webster . . . New York: The Macmillan Company; London: Macmillan and Co., Ltd., 1902. 306 p., front., [16] leaves of plates. [Ill. by Howard Giles.]
PW: N 8, '02.

W-270   The sky-man / by Henry Kitchell Webster. New York: The Century Co., 1910. 344 p., front., [7] leaves of plates. [Ill. by Dan Smith.]
LC: Ap 18, '10.
PW: Ap 16, '10.

    , contributor. <u>See</u> *The sturdy oak* (1917), **S-1101.**

W-271   The thoroughbred / by Henry Kitchell Webster . . . ; with illustrations by W. B. King. Indianapolis: The Bobbs-Merrill Company, [c1917]. 257, [1] p., front., [10] leaves of plates.
LC: Ja 31, '17.
PW: F 3, '17.

W-272   Traitor and loyalist, or, The man who found his country / by Henry Kitchell Webster . . . New York: The Macmillan Company; London: Macmillan & Co., Ltd., 1904. 318 p., front., [6] leaves of plates.
PW: O 8, '04.

W-273   The whispering man / by Henry Kitchell Webster . . . New York: D. Appleton and Company, 1908. 336 p., front. [Ill. by Howard Heath.]
LC: S 25, '08.
PW: O 10, '08.
BLC: London: Eveleigh Nash Co., 1908.

W-274 Webster, Jean, 1876-1916. Daddy-Long-Legs / by Jean Webster; with illustrations by the author. New York: The Century Co., 1912. 304 p., ill.
LC: O 1, '12.
PW: O 5, '12.
BLC: London: Hodder & Stoughton, 1913.

W-275   Dear enemy / by Jean Webster; illustrated by the author. New York: Century Co., 1915. 350 p., ill.
LC: N 8, '15.
PW: O 30, '15.
BLC: London: Hodder & Stoughton, [1915].

W-276 [   ] The four-pools mystery. New York: The Century Co., 1908. 336 p., front. [Ill. by G. Varian.]
LC: Mr 5, '08.
PW: Mr 28, '08.
BLC: London: Hodder & Stoughton, 1916.

W-277   Jerry Junior / by Jean Webster . . . ; with illustrations by Orson Lowell. New York: The Century Co., 1907. 282 p., incl. 14 plates, front.
PW: Ap 27, '07.

W-278   Just Patty / by Jean Webster . . . ; illustrated by C. M. Relyea. New York: The Century Co., 1911. 342 p., front., [3] leaves of plates.   **KBE**
LC: O 31, '11.
PW: O 14, '11.
BLC: London: Hodder & Stoughton, 1915.

W-279   Much ado about Peter / by Jean Webster; illustrated by Charlotte Harding and Harry Linnell. New York: Doubleday, Page & Company, 1909. 300 p., front., [7] leaves of plates.
LC: Mr 11, '09.
PW: Mr 27, '09.
BLC: London: Doubleday, Page, & Co., New York printed, 1909.

W-280   The wheat princess / by Jean Webster . . . New York: The Century Co., 1905. 340 p.
PW: O 28, '05.

W-281   When Patty went to college / by Jean Webster; with illustrations by C. D. Williams. New York: The Century Co., 1903. 280 p., front., [5] leaves of plates.
PW: Ap 4, '03.

Webster, Samuel, jt. aut. *Uncle James' shoes* (1923). <u>See</u> **Webster, Doris, jt. aut., W-254.**

W-282 Wedge, Frederick R. (Frederick Rhinaldo). The fighting parson of Barbary Coast / by Frederick R. Wedge; illustrations by C. E. Shaw. Columbus, Nebraska: Tribune Printing Company, 1912. 155 p., front., [5] leaves of plates.   **CSH**

Weed, Truman Andrew Wellington, b. 1841. See **Wellington, Andrew, A. M., pseud.**

W-283 Weeks, Herbert. Romance of the Caribbean Sea / by Herbert Weeks. New York: [Printed by J. J. Little and Ives Company], 1925. 207 p., incl. front. (map).   **DLC**

Weeks, Raymond. Arkansas. In *Stories from the Midland* (1924), **S-984.**

W-284 Weiman, Rita, 1889-1954. Footlights / by Rita Weiman. New York: Dodd, Mead and Company, 1923. 341 p.
Contents: The curtain rises -- Footlights -- Madam Peacock -- Greasepaint -- The back drop -- Two masters -- Up stage -- Curtain! -- The curtain falls.
LC: Ap 3, '23.

W-285   Playing the game: a story of a society girl / by Rita Weiman. New York: Cupples & Leon Company, [c1910]. 270 p., front., [5] leaves of plates. [Some ill. by Modest Stein and W. H. Loomis.]
LC: Jl 13, '10.

     The stage door. In *More aces* (1925), **M-962.**

W-286 Weir, F. Roney (Florence Roney), 1861-1932. The green eyed one / by F. Roney Weir . . . Boston: Small, Maynard & Company, [c1923]. 341 p. **AZU**
LC: S 29, '23.
PW: N 3, '23.

W-287 ____ The hired man: his sayings, doings and experiences / by F. Roney Weir. Minneapolis, Minn.: Farm, Stock & Home Pub. Co., [c1903]. 225 p., [11] leaves of plates.
"Illustrated by Miss Ethel Palmer."

____ A matrimonial epidemic at Skookum. In **Seattle Writer's Club.** *Tillicum tales* **(1907), S-248.**

W-288 ____ Merry Andrew / by F. Roney Weir; illustrated by Ralph G. Heard. Boston: Small, Maynard and Company, [c1918]. 361 p., col. front., [2] leaves of plates.
LC: My 21, '18.
PW: My 4, '18.

W-289 Weir, Hugh C. (Hugh Cosgro), b. 1884. Miss Madelyn Mack, detective / by Hugh C. Weir; illustrated. Boston: The Page Company, 1914. 328 p., col. front., [4] leaves of plates.
LC: Je 1, '14.
PW: Je 20, '14.

W-290 ____ With the flag at Panama: a story of the building of the Panama Canal / by Hugh C. Weir; illustrated by W. F. Stecher. Boston; Chicago: W. A. Wilde Company, [c1911]. 322 p., front., [4] leaves of plates.
LC: N 22, '11.
PW: N 4, '11.

W-291 Weishaar, J. A. The tabernacle on the Wissahickon: a tale of the early days of Pennsylvania / by J. A. Weishaar. St. Louis, Mo.; Chicago, Ill.: Eden Publishing House, 1921. 288 p., photo. front.

W-292 Weiss, Leah. I object / by Leah Weiss. Cincinnati: Printed for the author by the Caxton Press, [c1923]. 172 p., front. (port.), [4] leaves of plates.
LC: D 8, '23.

W-293 ____ "Sin-o'-Man" / by Leah Weiss . . . Cincinnati, Ohio: Monfort & Company Press, 1924. 330 p., music.

W-294 Weiss, Sara. Decimon Hûŷdas: a romance of Mars: a story of actual experiences in Ento (Mars) many centuries ago / given to the psychic Sara Weiss and by her transcribed automatically under the editorial direction of spirit Carl Del'Ester; illustrated with six original drawings. Rochester, New York: Austin Publishing Company, 1906. 207 p., photo. front. (port.), [6] leaves of plates.

W-295 ____ Journeys to the planet Mars, or, "Our mission to Ento" / by Sara Weiss . . . New York: The Bradford Press . . . , [c1903]. 548 p., [13] leaves of plates.

W-296 Weitbrec, Blanche. The men on horseback / by Blanche Weitbrec; illustrations by Corinne Turner. New York: Desmond FitzGerald, Inc., [c1911]. 236 p., front., ill. Illustrated end papers.
LC: O 3, '11.

W-297 Welch, Alden W. (Alden Walling), b. 1887. Wolves / Alden W. Welch. New York: Alfred A. Knopf, 1919. 236 p.
LC: Je 11, '19.
PW: Je 21, '19.

Welch, Kathleen. Thy kingdom come. In *The rejected apostle* **(1924), R-164.**

W-298 Welcker, Adair. For people who laugh: showing how, through woman, came laughter into the world / by Adair Welcker. San Francisco, California: Adair Weicker, 1904. 107 p. **EYM**

W-299 ____ People: (thither coming out of a region wherein disasters are met as if they were a jest) whom you may meet at the fair / by Adair Welcker. Berkeley, Cal.: Printed by Lederer, Street & Zeus Company . . . , [c1913]. 160 p. **MNU**
Contents: The lunatic; The stern parent; the romantic daughter; The lover -- An ancient mariner, apparently much married, who will be seen at the fair -- The Los Angeles County poet (said to be about to start a new cult at Long Beach), who will be at the fair -- A dog that can teach some U. S. universities that in which they have proved to be lacking -- No boudoir (his own private dictionary would give the pronunciation "bood-wah") writer, who, surrounded by clouds as he comes, will descend from Tamalpais, to be at the fair -- An "Ancient Adonis," who will not fail to be seen on parade -- A physiognomist, who knew not what others were going to think of his own face and in consequence do to him -- Two, who following the advice of Greeley, will be seen at the fair -- One, who will not be at the fair -- A dentist who, with the wife that his instruments helped to win---will be at the fair -- How, according to the Colonel, women can certainly be won -- The human feminine tortoise, who, in a race, outran the hare -- The man of an accomplished ambition who will be at the fair --The night of misadventures of a man who will be at the fair -- What of a city at one time, (and at no great distance away from its center), was its inferno -- Afterward.

W-300 Welles, Charles Stuart, 1848-1927. The Ellwoods / by Charles Stuart Welles, M. D. London: Simpkin, Marshall, Hamilton, Kent & Co., Ltd.; New York: Morgan M. Renner, [1904]. 351 p. (p. 345-351 advertising matter). **CIN**

W-301 ____ Lady Corrigan's love match / by Charles Stuart Welles . . . New York: The Selb Press, 1917. 67 p. Unexamined copy: bibliographic data from NUC.
LC: Ag 16, '17.

W-302 ____ The princess of hearts / by Charles Stuart Welles . . . Mursley, Bucks, England: C. S. Welles; New York: The Selb Press, 1917. 39 p., front. (port.). **DLC**
LC: O 26, '16.

W-303 Welles, Harriet. Anchors aweigh / by Harriet Welles; with an introduction by Hon. Josephus Daniels, Secretary of the Navy. New York: Charles Scribner's Sons, 1919. 275 p., front., [6] leaves of plates. [Ill. by Henry Peck.]
LC: Mr 3, '19.
PW: Mr 1, '19.

_____ Progress. In *Prize stories of 1924* (1925), **P-622.**

_____ The wall. In *Thrice told tales* (1924), **T-219.**

W-304   Wellington, Andrew, 1841-1927, *pseud.* Deborah Moses, or, Pen pictures of colonial life in New England / by Andrew Wellington [pseud.] . . . Concord, N. H.: Published by the Good Will Publishing Co., [c1915]. 550 p., front., [15] leaves of plates, ill. [Ill. by W. L. Williams; photos. by A. S. Burbank, Plymouth, Mass.]

Wellington, Catharine N. Invalid home. In *The best college short stories, 1917-18* (1919), **B-557.**

W-305   Wellman, Rita, 1890-1965. The house of hate: a novel / by Rita Wellman. New York: Robert M. McBride & Company, 1924. 276 p.
LC: N 17, '24.
PW: O 18, '24.

W-306   _____ The wings of desire / by Rita Wellman . . . New York: Moffat, Yard & Company, 1919. 343 p.
LC: S 26, '19.
PW: S 20, '19.

W-307   Wells, Amos R. (Amos Russel), 1862-1933. Tuxedo avenue to Water street: being the story of a transplanted church / by Amos R. Wells; illustrated by Josephine Bruce. New York; London: Funk and Wagnalls Company, 1906. 259 p., front., [7] leaves of plates.

W-308   Wells, Carolyn, d. 1942. Abeniki Caldwell: a burlesque historical novel / by Carolyn Wells; illustrated with numerous engravings printed from the original wood blocks. New York: R. H. Russell, 1902. 289 p., ill.
PW: D 20, '02.

W-309   _____ The affair at Flower Acres / by Carolyn Wells. New York: George H. Doran Company, [c1923]. 284 p.
LC: My 3, '23.
PW: Ap 28, '23.

W-310   _____ Anybody but Anne / by Carolyn Wells . . . ; with a frontispiece in color by Robert McCaig. Philadelphia; London: J. B. Lippincott Company, 1914. 309 p., col. front., [1] leaf of plates.
LC: Ap 21, '14.
PW: Ap 4, '14.

W-311   _____ Anything but the truth: a Fleming Stone story / by Carolyn Wells . . . Philadelphia; London: J. B. Lippincott Company, 1925. 319 p.
LC: Mr 7, '25.
PW: F 21, '25.

W-312   _____ Betty's happy year / by Carolyn Wells . . . ; with illustrations by Reginald B. Birch. New York: The Century Co., 1910. 295 p., front., ill.
LC: S 29, '10.
PW: O 1, '10.

_____, contributor. See *Bobbed hair* (1925), **B-700.**

W-313   _____ The bride of a moment / by Carolyn Wells. New York: George H. Doran Company, [c1916]. 307 p.
LC: Ag 21, '16.
PW: Ag 19, '16.
BLC: London: Hodder & Stoughton, [1920].

W-314   _____ A chain of evidence / by Carolyn Wells . . . ; with illustrations in color by Gayle Hoskins. Philadelphia; London: J. B. Lippincott Company, 1912. 324 p., col. front., [1] leaf of col. plates.
LC: Ap 30, '12.
PW: My 4, '12.

W-315   _____ The clue / by Carolyn Wells. Philadelphia; London: J. B. Lippincott Company, 1909. 341 p., incl. col. front.   **GZM**
LC: S 29, '09.
PW: O 23, '09.

W-316   _____ The come back / by Carolyn Wells . . . New York: George H. Doran Company, [c1921]. 286 p.
LC: Je 10, '21.
PW: Je 4, '21.
BLC: London: Hodder & Stoughton, printed in U. S. A., [1921].

W-317   _____ The curved blades / by Carolyn Wells; with a frontispiece in color by Gayle Hoskins. Philadelphia; London: J. B. Lippincott Company, 1916. 333 p., col. front.
LC: Mr 2, '16.
PW: Mr 11, '16.

W-318   _____ The daughter of the house: a Fleming Stone story / by Carolyn Wells. Philadelphia; London: J. B. Lippincott Company, 1925. 317 p.
LC: O 24, '25.
PW: O 10, '25.

W-319   _____ The diamond pin / by Carolyn Wells . . . ; with a frontispiece in color by Gayle Hoskins. Philadelphia; London: J. B. Lippincott Company, 1919. 300 p., col. front.
LC: Ap 3,'19.
PW: Mr 22, '19.

W-320   [_____] The disappearance of Kimball Webb / by Rowland Wright [pseud.]. New York: Dodd, Mead and Company, 1920. 304 p.

W-321   _____ Doris of Dobbs Ferry / by Carolyn Wells . . . ; illustrated by Frances Rogers. New York: George H. Doran Company, [c1917]. 290 p., front., [3] leaves of plates.   **MNL**
LC: N 2, '17.
PW: D 8, '17.

W-322   _____ The Emily Emmins papers / by Carolyn Wells; with illustrations by Josephine A. Meyer. New York; London: G. P. Putnam's Sons, 1907. ([New York]: The Knickerbocker Press). 273 p., ill.
LC: N 22, '07.
PW: N 23, '07.

W-323 ____ The eternal feminine / by Carolyn Wells. New York: Franklin Bigelow Corporation: The Morningside Press, [c1913]. 58 p. (Onyx series.)
LC: S 29, '13.

W-324 ____ Face cards / by Carolyn Wells . . . New York; London: G. P. Putnam's Sons, 1925. ([New York]: The Knickerbocker Press). 334 p.
LC: Ap 29, '25.
PW: My 2, '25.

W-325 ____ Faulkner's folly / by Carolyn Wells . . . New York: George H. Doran Company, [c1917]. 294 p., front. (plan.).
LC: O 25, '17.
PW: O 20, '17.

W-326 ____ Feathers left around / by Carolyn Wells . . . Philadelphia; London: J. B. Lippincott Company, 1923. 348 p.
LC: Mr 6, '23.
PW: F 24, '23.

W-327 ____ The fourteenth key / by Carolyn Wells . . . New York; London: G. P. Putnam's Sons, 1924. (Knickerbocker Press). 334 p.
LC: Ag 28, '24.
PW: Ag 16, '24.

W-328 ____ The furthest fury: a Fleming Stone story / by Carolyn Wells . . . Philadelphia; London: J. B. Lippincott Company, 1924. 320 p.
LC: Mr 20, '24.
PW: F 2, '24.

W-329 ____ The gold bag / by Carolyn Wells . . . ; with a frontispiece by George W. Barratt. Philadelphia; London: J. B. Lippincott Comapny, 1911. 333 p., col. front.
LC: F 23, '11.
PW: Mr 4, '11.

W-330 ____ The Gordon elopement: the story of a short vacation / by Carolyn Wells and Harry Persons Taber; illustrated by Frederic Dorr Steele. New York: Doubleday, Page & Company, 1904. 235 p., col. front. (double leaf), music.
PW: Mr 19, '04.

W-331 ____ In the onyx lobby / by Carolyn Wells. New York: George H. Doran Company, [c1920]. 288 p.
LC: S 17, '20.
PW: S 4, '20.
BLC: London: Hodder & Stoughton, printed in U. S. A., [1920].

W-332 ____ The luminous face / by Carolyn Wells . . . New York: George H. Doran Company, [c1921]. 270 p.
LC: S 16, '21.
PW: S 17, '21.

W-333 ____ The man who fell through the earth / by Carolyn Wells . . . New York: George H. Doran Company, [c1919]. 299 p.
LC: O 21, '19.
PW: N 1, '19.

W-334 ____ The mark of Cain / by Carolyn Wells . . . ; with a frontispiece in color by Gayle Hoskins. Philadelphia; London: J. B. Lippincott Company, 1917. 307 p., col. front.
LC: Mr 12, '17.
PW: Mr 3, '17.
BLC: London: Hodder & Stoughton, [1920].

W-335 ____ The matrimonial bureau / by Carolyn Wells and Harry Persons Taber. Boston; New York: Houghton, Mifflin & Company, 1905. (Cambridge: The Riverside Press). 281, [1] p., col. front., [3] leaves of col. plates. Illustrated end papers.
PW: Ap 8, '05.

W-336 ____ The Maxwell mystery / by Carolyn Wells . . . ; with a frontispiece in color by Gayle Hoskins. Philadelphia; London: J. B. Lippincott Company, 1913. 302 p., incl. col. front.
LC: Ap 2, '13.
PW: Mr 22, '13.

W-337 ____ More lives than one / by Carolyn Wells. New York: Boni and Liveright, [c1923]. 241 p.
LC: O 16, '23.
PW: O 27, '23.
BLC: London: Hodder & Stoughton, [1924].

W-338 ____ The Moss mystery / by Carolyn Wells. -- 1st ed. -- Garden City, New York: Garden City Publishing Co., Inc., 1924. 119 p.   MNU (Famous authors series; no. 43).
LC: Ap 2, '24.

W-339 ____ The mystery girl / by Carolyn Wells . . . Philadelphia; London: J. B. Lippincott Company, 1922. 349 p.
LC: Mr 23, '22.
PW: F 18, '22.

W-340 ____ The mystery of the sycamore / by Carolyn Wells . . . ; with a frontispiece in color by Frank McKernan. Philadelphia: J. B. Lippincott Company, 1921. 336 p., col. front.
"Copyright 1920 by Street & Smith Corporation, under title: The parden tree."
LC: Ap 18, '21.
PW: Mr 12, '21.

W-341 ____ Prillilgirl: a Fleming Stone story / by Carolyn Wells . . . Philadelphia; London: J. B. Lippincott Company, 1924. 332 p.
LC: S 13, '24.
PW: O 11, '24.

W-342 ____ Ptomaine Street: the tale of Warble Petticoat / by Carolyn Wells. Philadelphia; London: J. B. Lippincott Company, 1921. 124, [1] p.
LC: D 15, '21.
PW: D 3, '21.

W-343 ____ Raspberry jam / by Carolyn Wells; with a frontispiece in color by Gayle Hoskins. Philadelphia; London: J. B. Lippincott Company, 1920. 314 p., col. front.
LC: My 5, '20.
PW: Ja 31, '20.

W-344   ____ The room with the tassels / by Carolyn Wells. New York: George H. Doran Company, [c1918]. 283 p.
LC: S 30, '18.
PW: S 28,' 18.

W-345   ____ Spooky Hollow: a Fleming Stone story / by Carolyn Wells. Philadelphia; London: J. B. Lippincott Company, 1923. 368 p.
LC: O 25, '23.
PW: Ag 25, '23.

W-346   ____ Two little women on a holiday / by Carolyn Wells . . . ; with frontispiece by E. C. Caswell. New York: Dodd, Mead and Company, 1917. 300 p., front.   **PSC**
LC: S 25, '17.
PW: S 29, '17.

W-347   ____ The vanishing of Betty Varian / by Carolyn Wells . . . New York: George H. Doran Company, [c1922]. 282 p.
LC: Ag 3, '22.
PW: Je 24, '22.
BLC: London: W. Collins Sons & Co., [1924].

W-348   ____ Vicky Van / by Carolyn Wells; with frontispiece in color by Gayle Hoskins. Philadelphia; London: J. B. Lippincott Company, 1918. 304 p., col. front.
LC: Mr 14, '18.
PW: Mr 23, '18.
BLC: London: Hodder & Stoughton, [1920].

W-349   ____ Wheels within wheels / by Carolyn Wells. New York: George H. Doran Company, [c1923]. 267 p.
LC: O 1, '23.
PW: N 3, '23.

W-350   ____ The white alley / by Carolyn Wells; with a frontispiece in color by Gale Hoskins. Philadelphia; London: J. B. Lippincott Company, 1915. 300 p., col. front.
LC: My 20, '15.
PW: My 1, '15.

W-351 Wells, Elizabeth Adams. My dog days: and other animal stories / by Elizabeth Adams Wells. [Battle Creek, Mich.: Review and Herald Pub. Co., c1901.] 170 p., front., [1] leaf of plates, ill.
Contents: My dog days -- Bunny -- Canary songs -- Cat tales -- The miller's horse.

Wells, Helen Weston. See **Blake, Forest, pseud.**

W-352 Wells, Morris B. (Morris Benjamin), b. 1867. Five gallons of gasoline / by Morris B. Wells; illustrations by Harrison Fisher. New York: Dodd, Mead & Company, 1911. 351 p., col. front. "Five gallons of gasoline was written by the author whose name appears on the title page in collaboration with a well-known writer, who . . . did not wish to have his name appear in the present volume."
PW: My 13, '11.
BLC: London: David Nutt. 1911.

W-353 Wells, Paul. The man with an honest face: being the personal experiences of a gentleman who signs the name of Howard Dana, at a critical time in his career / by Paul Wells; illustrated. New York; London: D. Appleton and Company, 1911. 322 p., front., [3] leaves of plates. [Ill. by John Cassel.]

W-354 Wells, Percival W., b. 1883, *pseud.* The great corrector: more or less a vital satire / by Percival W. Wells [pseud.] . . . Wantagh, New York: Bartlett Publishing Company, 1916. 219 p.   **NYP**
LC: S 9, '16.

W-355 Wells, Rebecca. The old home / by Rebecca Wells. Boston: Roxburgh Publishing Company, Inc., [c1913]. 98 p., photo. front., [5] leaves of photo. plates.

Welsh, Charles, 1850-1914, ed. <u>See</u> *Chauffeur chaff, or, Automobilia* **(1905), C-330.**

W-356 Welty, Cora Gottschalk, 1876-1951. The masquerading of Margaret / by Cora Cottschalk Welty. Boston: C. M. Clark Publishing Co., 1908. 222 p., front., [5] leaves of plates. [Ill. by William Kirkpatrick.]
LC: D 30, '08.
PW: Ap 3, '09.

W-357 Wemyss, George. The secret book / by George Wemyss; with a frontispiece by Clinton Balmer. New York: Sturgis & Walton Company, 1911. 356 p., col. front.
BLC: London: W. J. Ham-Smith, printed in U. S. A., 1912.

W-358 [Wende, Leo C. (Leo Conrad)], b. 1883. The will and the way: a guide to self help and self development. [Los Angeles: Wm. B. Straube Print, c1914]. 90 p.   **DLC**

W-359 Wentworth, Edward Chichester. The education of Ernest Wilmerding: a story of opening flowers / by Edward Chichester Wentworth. Chicago: Covici-McGee Co., 1924. 268 p.
LC: Ja 31, '24.

Wentz, Albert Edwin, b. 1863. <u>See</u> **King, Kenneth Kenelm, pseud.**

W-360 Werner, Carl, 1873-1945. The law of life: a novel / by Carl Werner; illustrations by Robert W. Amick. New York: Dodd, Mead and Company, 1914. 327 p., front., [3] leaves of plates.
PW: Ja 31, '14.

W-361 Werner, Orilla. Helen Custer / by Orilla Werner. Franklin, Ohio: Published by the Franklin Press, 1902. 152 p.   **NYP**

W-362 Wertheim, Alexander. Humorous tales and ghost stories / by Alexander Wertheim. Montreal; New York; London: Broadway Publishing Co., [c1904]. 246 p., photo. front. (port.).   **TXI**
Contents: The piano prince -- Professor Chimborazo's lectures -- Judge Slowbagger -- Sylvester Stromeyer -- Franz Kinkelbach -- The fatal post card -- A New Orleans auction room -- A provoking

calamity -- The Italian bandit chief -- Giuseppo Caramboli -- The maiden grandmother -- Bill Fogey -- A practical course in law -- Casper Langnas -- Hans Schnabelwitz -- Alfred Buchfink -- The white calf -- A dancing ghost -- An obliging ghost.

W-363   Wescott, Glenway, b. 1901. The apple of the eye / by Glenway Wescott. New York: Lincoln MacVeagh, The Dial Press, 1924. 292 p.
LC: O 8, '24.
PW: D 27, '24.
BLC: London: Thornton Butterworth, 1926.

_____ In a thicket. *In The best short stories of 1924 and the yearbook of the American short story* **(1925), B-569.**

West, Alwin. Rowan Island, the story of a poet's secretary. In *Golden stories* **(1909), G-285.**

W-364   West, Emery, *pseud.* Country sketches / by Emery West [pseud.]. New York: Cochrane Publishing Company . . . , 1910. 79 p.
Contents: An earnest soul -- The pretty girl -- Her beaux -- A merry widow -- Neighbors -- The candidate.
LC: Mr 7, '10.

W-365   West, Kenneth. The valley of judgment / by Kenneth West. Boston: The Roxburgh Publishing Company Incorporated, [c1925]. 284 p., incl. front.   **DLC**
LC: F 19, '25.
PW: F 28, '25.

W-366   West, Kenyon. Cliveden / by Kenyon West. Boston: Lothrop Publishing Company, [1903]. 473 p.
PW: Mr 21, '03.

W-367   West, Lillian Clarkson, b. 1869. Aunt Hope's kitchen stove and the girls around it / by Lillian Clarkson West; cover design by Dixie Selden. Cincinnati: Stewart & Kidd Company, 1911. 324 p.

West, Paul Clarendon, 1871-1918, jt. aut. *The innocent murderers* (1910). See **Johnston, William, 1871-1929, jt. aut., J-168.**

West, Roger, pseud. See **Watson, Virginia Cruse, b. 1872.**

W-368   West winds: California's book of fiction / written by California authors and illustrated by California artists; edited by Herman Whitaker. San Francisco: Paul Elder and Company, [c1914]. 219 p., front., [7] leaves of plates. [Ill. by Perham W. Nahl, J. A. Cahill, George W. Kegg, Will Crawford, Ruth Aikins, Maynard Dixon, and Alice Best.]
Contents: The bandit's better half / Herman Whitaker -- Bufo, the mascot / Elizabeth Abbey Everett -- Shovelnose Kelly, master and owner / Shirley A. Mansfield -- The mother / Sarah Thurston Nott -- The greatest of these / Agnes Morley Cleaveland -- The corner table / Rebecca N. Porter -- Pals / Julia B. Foster -- The enchanted mesa / Charles F. Lummis -- The son of the wolf / Jack London -- The phantom coach / Hester A. Dickinson -- The crooked pine / Elizabeth Griswold Rowe -- The Kis Khilim / Frances Orr Allen -- Jane Ann, A ward of the state / Mrs. Carl Bank -- The temptation of Ann O'Brien / Harriet Holmes Haslett -- The quest / Torrey Connor.

W-369   Westcott, Edward Noyes, 1847-1898. The teller: a story / by Edward Noyes Westcott; with the letters of Edward Noyes Westcott, edited by Margaret Westcott Muzzey; and an account of his life by Forbes Heermans. New York: D. Appleton and Company, 1901. 113 p., photo. front. (port.), [3] leaves of photo. plates (2 ports.).
LC: S 25, '01.
PW: O 12, '01.
BLC: London: C. Arthur Pearson, New York printed, 1901.
References: BAL 21316.

W-370   Westcott, Frank Noyes. Dabney Todd / by Frank N. Westcott; illustrated by M. V. Hunter. New York: The H. K. Fly Co., [c1916]. 311 p., incl. front., [3] leaves of plates.
LC: Ja 24, '17.
PW: Ja 27, '17.

W-371   _____ Hepsey Burke / by Frank N. Westcott; illustrated by Frederick [sic] R. Gruger. New York: The H. K. Fly Company, [c1915]. 314 p., incl. front., [7] leaves of plates.
LC: S 1, '15.

Westerfield, E. W. See **Westphal, Polhemus, pseud.**

W-372   Westermayr, Arthur J. Power of innocence / by Arthur J. Westermayr; illustrated by Lillian Adams. New York: R. F. Fenno & Company . . . , [c1909]. 410 p., incl. front., [4] leaves of plates.
LC: N 17, '09.
PW: N 20, '09.

W-373   _____ Rudra: a romance of ancient India / by Arthur J. Westermayr . . . ; annotated and furnished with comprehensive glossary. New York: G. W. Dillingham Company, [c1912]. 447 p., col. front.
LC: Mr 30, '12.
PW: Ap 13, '12.

W-374   _____ Udara, prince of Bidur: a romance of ancient India / by Arthur J. Westermayr . . . ; footnoted and furnished with exhaustive alphabetical glossary; illustrations by F. T. Chapman. New York: G. W. Dillingham Company, [c1913]. 408 p., col. front., [2] leaves of col. plates.
LC: Ap 25, '13.
PW: Ap 26, '13.

W-375   Westervelt, Josephine Hope. Dragon's end / by Josephine Hope Westervelt . . . Philadelphia: Sunday School Times Company, 1923. 184 p., photo. front.
LC: D 28, 23.

W-376   _____ Fine gold, or, The pearl of great price: a missionary romance of South America / by Josephine Hope Westervelt. Los Angeles, Calif.: The Biola Book Room, Bible Institute of Los Angeles . . . , [c1924]. 141 p., photo. front., [19] leaves of photo. plates.
PW: Ap 11, '25.

W-377   _____ The lure of the leopard skin: a story of the African wilds / by Josephine Hope Westervelt. New

York; Chicago; London; Edinburgh: Fleming H. Revell Company, [c1921]. 240 p., front.
LC: D 12, '21.

W-378   ____ The quest of the hidden ivory: a story of adventure in tropical Africa / by Josephine Hope Westervelt . . . New York; Chicago; London; Edinburgh: Fleming H. Revell Company, [c1924]. 226 p., front., [5] leaves of plates. [Ill. by William James.]
LC: O 9, '24.
PW: O 18, '24.

Westley, G. Hembert (George Hembert), 1865-1936, jt. aut. *Clementina's highwayman* (1907). <u>See</u> **Stephens, Robert Neilson, 1867-1906, jt. aut., S-857.**

W-379   ____ The maid and the miscreant / by G. Hembert Westley. Boston: Mayhew Publishing Co. . . . , 1906. 217 p.
LC: Ja 11, '07.
PW: F 16, '07.

W-380   Weston, George, b. 1880. The apple-tree girl: the story of little Miss Moses, who led herself into the promised land / by George Weston; with illustrations by F. R. Gruger. Philadelphia; London: J. B. Lippincott Company, 1918. 157 p., col. front., [5] leaves of plates.
LC: Mr 14, '18.
PW: Mr 23, '18.

W-381   ____ The beauty prize / by George Weston . . . New York: Dodd, Mead and Company, 1925. 275 p.
LC: Jl 1, '25.
PW: Je 27, '25.

    ____ The feminine touch. <u>In</u> *War stories* **(1919), W-94.**

W-382   ____ Mary minds her business / by George Weston . . . ; with frontispiece by John Alonzo Williams. New York: Dodd, Mead and Company, 1920. 323 p., front.
LC: Mr 23, '20.
PW: Ap 3, '20.

W-383   ____ Oh, Mary, be careful! / by George Weston; with seven illustrations by R. M. Crosby. Philadelphia; London: J. B. Lippincott Company, 1917. 177, [1] p., col. front., [6] leaves of plates.
LC: Mr 12, '17.
PW: Mr 3, '17.
BLC: London: George Newnes, [1919].

W-384   ____ Queen of the world / by George Weston . . . New York: Dodd, Mead & Company, 1923, [c1922]. 259 p.
LC: Mr 7, '23.
PW: Mr 17, '23.
BLC: London: Hodder & Stoughton, [1924].

W-385   ____ You never saw such a girl / by George Weston . . . New York: Dodd, Mead and Company, 1919.

240 p.
LC: Je 24, '19.
PW: Je 28, '19.

W-386   Westover, Clyde C. The dragon's daughter / by Clyde C. Westover . . . New York: The Neale Publishing Company, 1912. 180 p.
LC: D 4, '12.
PW: N 30, '12.

W-387   ____ The romance of gentle Will: a hitherto unpublished chapter in the story of the love of the immortal bard / by Clyde C. Westover. New York; Washington: The Neale Publishing Company, 1905. 297 p.
PW: S 2, '05.

W-388   ____ The scuttlers / by Clyde C. Westover . . . New York: The Neale Publishing Company, 1914. 315 p.
Unexamined copy: bibliographic data from NUC.

W-389   Westphal, Polhemus, *pseud*. The resurrection of a heart / by Polhemus Westphal [pseud.]. New York: Broadway Publishing Company, 1913. 83 p., front.
Unexamined copy: bibliographic data from NUC.

W-390   Wetherill, J. K. (Julia Keim), b. 1858. The wandering joy / by J. K. Wetherill. New York; Baltimore; Atlanta: Broadway Publishing Co., 1910. 172 p.   **IXA**

W-391   Wetjen, Albert Richard, 1900-1948. Captains all / Albert Richard Wetjen. New York: Alfred A. Knopf, 1924. 217 p.

W-392   Wetmore, Amy D'Arcy. The climber / by Amy D'Arcy Wetmore; with six illustrations by George R. Brill. Baltimore: The Norman, Remington Co., [1914]. 92 p., front., [5] leaves of plates.
LC: O 23, '14.

W-393   Wetmore, Claude Hazeltine, 1862-1944. Fighting under the Southern cross: a story of the Chile-Peruvian war / by Claude H. Wetmore, containing pronouncing vocabulary and map of Callao bay; with illustratons by H. Burgess. Boston; Chicago: W. A. Wilde Company, [c1901]. 335 p., front., [4] leaves of plates, map.
PW: O 5, '01.

W-394   ____ In a Brazilian jungle: being a story of adventure, with an insight into Brazilian life and industries / by Claude H. Wetmore; with illustrations by H. Burgess. Boston; Chicago: W. A. Wilde Company, [1903]. 315 p., front., [4] leaves of plates.
PW: O 31, '03.

W-395   ____ Incaland: a story of adventure in the interior of Peru and the closing chapter of the war with Chile / by Claude H. Wetmore . . . ; with illustrations by H. Burgess. Boston; Chicago: W. A. Wilde Company, [c1902]. 309 p., front., [4] leaves of plates.
PW: O 11, '02.

W-396   ____ Out of a fleur-de-lis: the history, romance, and biography of the Louisiana purchase exposition / by Claude H. Wetmore; with a forward by Hon. David R. Francis; illustrated and containing a map of the exposition grounds and buildings. Boston; Chicago: W. A. Wilde Company, [c1903]. 432 p., front., [10] leaves of plates, map. [Ill. by W. F. Stecher, et al.]
PW: D 5, '03.

Wetmore, Elizabeth Bisland. See **Bisland, Elizabeth.**

Wetmouth, John. See **Prune, Nat, pseud.**

W-397   Weyl, Maurice. The choice / by Maurice Weyl. New York: Mitchell Kennerley, 1919. 356 p.
LC: Jl 11, '19.
PW: Jl 19,' 19.

W-398   ____ The happy woman / by Maurice Weyl . . . New York: Mitchell Kennerley, 1920. 325 p.
LC: Ap 7, '20.
PW: Mr 13, '20.

W-399   Whalen, Will W. (William Wilfrid), b. 1886. Bridget, or, What's in a name? / by Will W. Whalen. Boston: Mayhew Publishing Company, [c1906]. 135 p., photo. front., [3] leaves of photo. plates.
                                     UUM
PW: Mr 23, '07.

W-400   ____ Ill-starred Babbie / by Will W. Whalen . . . Boston, Mass.: Mayhew Pub. Co. . . . , [c1912]. 212 p., front., [2] leaves of plates.
LC: O 3, '12.

W-401   ____ The lily of the coal fields / by Will W. Whalen. -- 2nd. ed. -- Boston: Mayhew Publishing Company, [c1910]. 208 p., [1] leaf of plates. [Ill. by F. S. Brunner.]   **DLC**
Revised edition of *Bridget, or, What's in a name?* (1906).
LC: D 29, '10.

W-402   ____ The Red Lily of Buchanan Valley / by Will W. Whalen. Orrtanna, Adams County, Pa.: The White Squaw Publishing Company, [c1923]. 48 p.   **SMI**
"A romance founded on the life of the Irish girl stolen by the Indians from Buchanan Valley, Adams County, Pennsylvania, in 1758. A story too strange and grim not to be true."

Whaley, Maria Louise (Theiss), Mrs. See **Theiss-Whaley, M. L.**

W-403   Wharton, Anne Hollingsworth, 1845-1928. A rose of old Quebec / by Anne Hollingsworth Wharton . . . ; with eight illustrations. Philadelphia; London: J. B. Lippincott Company, 1913. 196,[1] p., front., [7] leaves of plates. [Ill. by Spero and P. Naumann; some photo.]

W-404   Wharton, Edith, 1862-1937. The age of innocence / by Edith Wharton . . . New York; London: D. Appleton and Company, 1920. 364, [1] p.
LC: O 25, '20.
PW: O 30, '20.
References: Davis, p. 21; Melish, p. 61-62; Garrison A30.

W-405   ____ Crucial instances / by Edith Wharton . . . New York: Charles Scribner's Sons, 1901. 241, [1] p.
Contents: The duchess at prayer -- The angel at the grave -- The recovery -- "Copy": a dialogue -- The Rembrandt -- The moving finger -- The confessional.
LC: Mr 23, '01.
PW: Ap 6, '01.
BLC: London: John Murray, 1901.
References: Davis, p. 5; Melish, p. 8-10; Garrison A5.

W-406   ____ The custom of the country / by Edith Wharton. New York: Charles Scribner's Sons, 1913. 594 p.
LC: O 21, '13.
PW: N 1, '13.
BLC: London: Macmillan & Co., 1913.
References: Davis, p. 16; Melish, p. 48-49; Garrison A21.

W-407   ____ The descent of man: and other stories / by Edith Wharton. New York: Charles Scribner's Sons, 1904. 312 p.
Contents: The descent of man -- The mission of Jane -- The other two -- The quicksand -- The dilettante -- The reckoning -- Expiation -- The lady's maid's bell -- A Venetian night's entertainment.
LC: Ap 29, '04.
PW: My 7, '04.
BLC: London: Macmillan & Co., 1904.
References: Davis, p. 8-9; Melish, p. 20-22.

W-408   ____ Ethan Frome / by Edith Wharton. New York: Charles Scribner's Sons, 1911. 195 p.
LC: O 5, '11.
PW: O 7, '11.
BLC: London: Macmillan & Co., New York printed, 1911.
References: Davis, p. 14-15; Melish, p. 42-44; Garrison A19.

W-409   ____ The fruit of the tree / by Edith Wharton; with illustrations by Alonzo Kimball. New York: Charles Scribner's Sons, 1907. 633 p., front.,[2] leaves of plates.
LC: O 12, '07.
PW: O 26, '07.
BLC: London: Macmillan & Co., 1907.
References: Davis, p. 10-11; Melish, p. 30-31; Garrison A14.

W-410   ____ The glimpses of the moon / by Edith Wharton . . . New York; London: D. Appleton and Company, 1922. 364 p.
LC: Jl 25, '22.
PW: Jl 29, '22.
References: Davis, p. 22; Melish, p. 67-68; Garrison A31.

W-411   ____ The hermit and the wild woman: and other stories / by Edith Wharton. New York: Charles Scribner's Sons, 1908. 279 p.
Contents: The hermit and the wild woman -- The last asset -- In trust -- The pretext -- The verdict -- The pot-boiler -- The best man.
LC: S 23, '08.
PW: O 3, '08.
BLC: London: Macmillan & Co., 1908.
References: Davis, p. 12; Melish, p. 34-36; Garrison A15.

W-412   ____ The house of mirth / by Edith Wharton; with illustrations by A. B. Wenzell. New York: Charles Scribner's Sons, 1905. 532, [1] p., front., [7] leaves

of plates.
LC: O 13, '05.
PW: O 28, '05.
BLC: London: Macmillan & Co., 1905.
References: Davis, p. 10; Melish, p. 26-27; Garrison A12.

W-413 _____ Madame de Treymes / by Edith Wharton; with illustrations. New York: Charles Scribner's Sons, 1907. 146, [1] p., col. front., [1] leaf of col. plates. [Ill. by Alonzo Kimball.]
LC: F 23, '07.
PW: Mr 16, '07.
BLC: London: Macmillan & Co., 1907.
References: Davis, p. 11; Melish, p. 28-29; Garrison A13.

W-414 _____ The Marne / by Edith Wharton . . . New York: D. Appleton and Company, 1918. 128 p.
LC: D 13, '18.
PW: D 21, '18.
BLC: London: Macmillan & Co., 1918.
References: Davis, p. 19; Melish, p. 57-58; Garrison A27.

W-415 _____ The mother's recompense / by Edith Wharton . . . New York; London: D. Appleton and Company, 1925. 341, [1] p.
LC: Ap 27, '25.
PW: My 2, '25.
References: Davis, p. 26-27; Melish, p. 80-81; Garrison A37.

W-416 _____ Old New York / by Edith Wharton . . . ; decorations by E. C. Caswell. New York; London: D. Appleton and Company, 1924. 4v.
False dawn (The 'forties). 142, [1] p.
The old maid (The 'fifties). 190, [1] p.
The spark (The 'sixties). 108, [1] p.
New Year's day (The 'seventies). 159, [1] p.
LC: My 22, '24.
PW: My 31, '24.
References: Davis, p. 23-26; Melish, p. 72-79; Garrison A36.

W-417 _____ The reef: a novel / by Edith Wharton . . . New York: D. Appleton and Company, 1912. 366, [1] p.
LC: N 22, '12.
PW: N 30, '12.
BLC: London: Macmillan & Co., 1912.
References: Davis, p. 15-16; Melish, p. 45-47; Garrison A20.

W-418 _____ Sanctuary / by Edith Wharton; with illustrations by Walter Appleton Clark. New York: Charles Scribner's Sons, 1903. 183, [1] p., col. front., [10] leaves of plates.
LC: O 22, '03.
PW: N 14, '03.
BLC: London: Macmillan & Co., 1913.
References: Davis, p. 7; Melish, p. 14-15; Garrison A8.

W-419 _____ A son at the front / by Edith Wharton . . . New York: Charles Scribner's Sons, 1923. 426 p.
LC: S 10, '23.
PW: S 8, '23.

BLC: London: Macmillan & Co., 1923.
References: Davis, p. 22-23; Melish, p. 69-71; Garrison A32.

W-420 _____ Summer: a novel / by Edith Wharton . . . New York: D. Appleton and Company, 1917. 290, [1] p.
LC: Jl 5, '17.
PW: Jl 14, '17.
BLC: London: Macmillan & Co., 1917.
References: Davis, p. 18; Melish, p. 55-56; Garrison A26.

W-421 _____ Tales of men and ghosts / by Edith Wharton. New York: Charles Scribner's Sons, 1910. 438 p.
Contents: The bolted door -- His father's son -- The daunt Diana -- The debt -- Full circle -- The legend -- The eyes -- The blond beast -- Afterward -- The letters.
LC: O 25, '10.
PW: O 29, '10.
BLC: London: Macmillan & Co., 1910.
References: Davis, p. 13-14; Melish, p. 39-41; Garrison A18.

_____ Triumph of the night. In *Short stories for high schools* (1915), S-462.

W-422 _____ The valley of decision: a novel / by Edith Wharton. New York: Charles Scribner's Sons, 1902. 2 v.: 342, [1] p.; 311, [1] p.
Contents: Contents of volume first: Book I: The old order -- Book II: The new light. Contents of volume second: Book III: The choice -- Book IV: The reward.
LC: F 21, '02.
PW: Mr 1, '02.
BLC: London: John Murray, 1902.
References: Davis, p. 6; Melish, p. 11-13; Garrison A6.

W-423 _____ Xingu: and other stories / by Edith Wharton. New York: Charles Scribner's Sons, 1916. 436 p.
Contents: Xingu -- Coming home -- Autres temps ... -- Kerfol -- The long run -- The triumph of night -- The choice -- Bunner sisters.
LC: O 25, '16.
PW: N 4, '16.
BLC: London: Macmillan & Co.; New York printed, 1916.
References: Davis, p. 17-18; Melish, p. 52-54; Garrison A24.

Wharton, Francis Willing. The wrong door. In *Quaint courtships* (1906), Q-3.

W-424 Wharton, Henry M. (Henry Marvin), 1848-1928. Stories short and sweet / by Henry M. Wharton . . . New York; Washington: The Neale Publishing Company, 1910. 253 p.
Contents: Little Emily -- Falling from grace -- He died for me -- We never know -- The dying soldier boy -- Good cheer -- Jim -- Saved from drink -- A Florida cracker and a razor-back hog -- Forgiveness -- Morality alone will not do -- "Come" -- Waiting for the second table -- An experience of the war -- Sam Jones -- Should women vote? -- Saved by mistake -- Fond of a joke -- He got his man -- Sympathy -- A latter day prodigal -- My first convert -- In the arms of angels -- Responsibility -- A drunkard's home -- The other shore -- Sir George Williams -- Victory -- A story of two young men -- A mountain gem -- Another chance -- A boy scout -- He came to himself -- The power of song -- She cried her eyes out -- The tables turned -- Railroad men -- Perfection -- Receptions -- The worst of sinners -- Perseverance -- The courage of conviction -- Saved by his boy -- A

wedding in Nazareth -- Mother Love -- An infidel converted -- Borrowed trouble -- Does the wife rule? -- His priceless hope -- True courage -- Todd Hall, detective -- Ups and downs -- Psychology and prayer -- The new world -- Higher up -- Safe at home -- Providence -- Self-control -- Saved by grace -- A remarkable run on a bank -- Capture of a desperado -- Death of Edgar Allan Poe -- Repartee -- "Bright Eyes".

W-425   ____ White blood: a story of the South / by Rev. Henry M. Wharton . . . New York; Washington: The Neale Publishing Company, 1906. 365 p. **KTS**
LC: Jl 2, '06.
PW: Ag 11, '06.

W-426   Wharton, Sydney. The wife decides: a novel / by Sydney Wharton; illustrations by Joseph Cummings Chase; frontispiece by J. Knowles Hare, Jr. New York: G. W. Dillingham Company, [c1911]. 312 p., col. front., [3] leaves of plates.
LC: Mr 29, '11.
PW: Ap 1, '11.

W-427   What would one have?: a woman's confessions. Boston: James H. West Company, [c1906]. 260 p.
NDD

W-428   Wheat, Lu. Ah Moy: the story of a Chinese girl / by Lu Wheat; illustrated by Mary E. Curran. New York; Boston: The Grafton Press, [c1908]. 154 p., incl. front.
LC: Jl 3, '08.
PW: S 5, '08.

W-429   ____ Helen: a story of things to be / by Lu Wheat . . . New York: The Grafton Press, [c1908]. 207 p., front. (port.).
LC: My 14, '08.
PW: O 10, '08.

W-430   ____ The third daughter: a story of Chinese home life / by Mrs. Lu. Wheat. Los Angeles, California: Published by Oriental Publishing Co., [c1906]. 318 p., front.
PW: F 24, '06.

W-431   Wheaton, Emily. The Russells in Chicago / by Emily Wheaton; illustrated by Fletcher C. Ransom. Boston: L. C. Page & Company, 1902. 257 p., front., [15] leaves of plates.
(Page's commonwealth series, no. 5).

Wheeler, Andrew Carpenter, 1835-1903. See **Mowbray, J. P. ("J. P. M."), pseud.**

W-432   Wheeler, Griswold. The return: and other stories / by Griswold Wheeler. [S. l.]: Privately printed, [c1922]. 240, [1] p.   **DLC**
Contents: The return -- What would you expect? -- The unconscious mutt -- Still unafraid -- As yesterday -- A race of tricksters -- The man he might have been -- Next -- The greater joy -- Another light that failed.
LC: O 5, '22.

W-433   Wheeler, Harriet, b. 1858. Cub's career / by Harriet Wheeler. London; New York; Montreal: The Abbey Press, [c1902]. 173 p., photo. front., [4] leaves of photo. plates.
PW: My 3, '02.

W-434   ____ The woman in stone; a novel / by Harriet Wheeler . . . ; illustrated. New York: Broadway Publishing Company, 1903. 168 p., photo. front.
WII
PW: D 19, '03.

W-435   Wheeler, Helen Maude. An up-to-date pauper / by Helen Maude Wheeler. Boston, Massachusetts: The C. M. Clark Publishing Company, 1907. 521 p., col. front. [Ill. by John Goss.]

W-436   Wheeler, James Cooper, b. 1849. Captain Pete in Alaska / by James Cooper Wheeler . . . New York: E. P. Dutton & Company . . . , [c1910]. 302 p., front., [4] leaves of plates. [Ill. by G. A. Harker.]
ALK
LC: S 3, '10.
PW: O 8, '10.

W-437   ____ Captain Pete of Cortesana / by James Cooper Wheeler. New York: E. P. Dutton & Company, [c1909]. 292 p., front., [4] leaves of plates. [Ill. by D. C. Hutchison.]
LC: S 10, '09.
PW: O 2, '09.

W-438   ____ Captain Pete of Puget Sound / by James Cooper Wheeler. New York: E. P. Dutton & Company, [c1909]. 275 p., front., [4] leaves of plates.
Unexamined copy: bibliographic data from OCLC, #2758407.
LC: S 10, '09.
BLC: London; Edinburgh: W. & R. Chambers, 1911.

W-439   ____ There she blows!: a whaling yarn / by James Cooper Wheeler . . . New York: E. P. Dutton & Company, [c1909]. 287 p., col. front., [4] leaves of plates, ill. [Ill. by George A. Traver.]   **IAK**
LC: Jl 10, '09.
PW: Ag 7, '09.

W-440   [Wheeler, Mary Sparkes], 1835-1919. As it is in Heaven / by One of the Redeemed [pseud.]. Philadelphia: P. W. Ziegler Co., [c1906]. 408 p., incl. 11 leaves of plates, front.

Wheeler, Post, Mrs. See **Rives, Hallie Erminie, 1876-1956.**

W-441   Wheeler, Van Zandt. The creed of her father: a novel / by Van Zandt Wheeler; frontispiece by Harold A. Van Buren. New York: Britton Publishing Co., [c1919]. 335 p., front.

W-442   Wheeler-Cooper, Jeanette. The hidden treasure of Mokoloho / written by Jeanette Wheeler-Cooper, 1916. [Chicago: J. Cremer], c1919. 49 p.   **DLC**
"The story is written from the time Dr. Livingston and H. Stanly explored North Africa."

Wheelwright, John T. The Roman bath. In *The best short stories of 1920 and the yearbook of the American short story* (1921), **B-565.**

W-443 Whelan, Charles Elbert, 1862-1928. Bascom Clarke: the story of a southern refugee / by Charles E. Whelan; frontispiece by George W. French. Madison, Wis.: The American Thresherman, [c1913]. 216 p., front., [5] leaves of plates.

W-444 Whelen, Christine C. (Christine Crosby). The jolts and jars of Amanda Hunter, and, A family jar / by Christine C. Whelen . . . Baltimore, Md.: Saulsbury Publishing Company, [c1919]. 55 p. **DLC**

W-445 When God walks the road, and other missionary stories / edited by Sara Estelle Haskin. Nashville, Tenn.; Dallas, Tex.; Richmond, Va.; San Francisco, Calif.: Publishing House of the M. E. Church, South, Lamar & Barton, Agents, 1924. 55 p. **KAT**
Contents: When God walks the road / Alliene Fridy -- The ten wishes / Helen Burr -- Nance's dream doll / Emma K. Olmstead -- Mongoonie the brave / Ellasue Wagner -- Little foe of all the world / Grace Bigelow House -- The story of a great choice / Mary De Bardeleben -- How Miung Ja found her name / Lillian Nichols --Kim Hong Til and the first "bike" / Ellasue Wagner -- The story of a slave boy who became great / Sara Estelle Haskin -- Dorothy finds a way / Etta Fulkerson -- The whitest gift of all / Harriet T. Comstock.

W-446 Wherry, Edith, *pseud*. The red lantern: being the story of the goddess of the red lantern light / by Edith Wherry [pseud.]. New York: John Lane Company, 1911. 306 p.
LC: My 2, '11.
PW: Ap 1, '11.
BLC: London: John Lane, 1911.

W-447 _____ The wanderer on a thousand hills / by Edith Wherry [pseud.]. New York: John Lane Company; London: John Lane; Toronto: S. B. Gundy, 1917. 305 p.
LC: Ap 17, '17.
PW: Ap 14, '17.

Whinnery, James Everhart, b. 1860. See **Blair, Uncle, pseud.**

W-448 Whipple, S. A. D. Arthur St. Clair of Old Fort Recovery / by S. A. D. Whipple. New York: Broadway Publishing Co., [c1911]. 201 p., col. front., [8] leaves of plates.

Whitaker, Herman, 1867-1919. The bandit's better half. In *West winds* (1914), W-368.

W-449 _____ Cross trails: the story of one woman in the North Whitaker / by Herman Whitaker . . . ; illustrated. New York; London: Harper & Brothers, 1914. 263, [1] p., front., [7] leaves of plates. [Ill. by Edward C. Caswell.]
LC: O 24, '14.
PW: Je 20, '14.

W-450 _____ The mystery of the Barranca / by Herman Whitaker . . . New York; London: Harper & Brothers, 1913. 280, [1] p., col. front. [Ill. by Maynard Dixon.]
LC: F 8, '13.

W-451 _____ Over the border: a novel / by Herman Whitaker. New York; London: Harper & Brothers Publishers, [1917]. 415, [1] p., front.
LC: My 22, '17.
PW: My 26, '17.

W-452 _____ The planter: a novel / by Herman Whitaker . . . New York; London: Harper & Brothers, [c1909]. 535 p., front. and t.p. on double-leaf plate. (Tales of the frontier).
LC: Mr 11, '09.
PW: Mr 20, '09.

W-453 _____ The probationer: and other stories / by Herman Whitaker. New York; London: Harper & Brothers, 1905. 328, [1] p.
Contents: The probationer -- A son of Anak -- The mercy of the frost -- A drummer of the queen -- The freckled fool -- A son of copper sin -- A saga of 540 -- The Black Factor -- An Iliad of the snows -- The devil's muskeg -- A slip of the noose -- A tale of the Pasquia Post -- Matty's Christmas present.
PW: Mr 11, '05.

W-454 _____ The settler: a novel / by Herman Whitaker . . . New York; London: Harper & Brothers, 1907. 368 p., front. [Ill. by Mac M. Pease.]
LC: O 10, '07.
PW: O 19, '07.

_____ The stiff condition. In *Quaint courtships* (1906), Q-3.

_____ The Tewana. In *Spinners' book of fiction* (1907), S-755.

_____, ed. See *West winds* (1914), W-368.

W-455 Whitaker, Lydia. The prophet of Martinique: a love story: embracing a vivid account of the historic destruction by Mont Pelee / by Lydia Whitaker; illustrated. New York: J. S. Barcus Company, [c1906]. 306 p., photo. front., [9] leaves of plates. (Some photo. by Underwood & Underwood.)

W-456 Whitaker, O. B. (Olivar Barr), b. 1869. Dick Haley: a thrilling story of poverty, heroism and suffering, dealing with real life and a vital problem of our public schools / by O. B. Whitaker . . . Dayton, Ohio: Christian Publishing Association, 1910. 230 p., photo. front., [8] leaves of photo. plates. **BGU**
LC: My 12, '10.

W-457 _____ Herbert Brown: a thrilling religious and moral story / by O. B. Whitaker . . . Chicago: M. A. Donohue & Company, [c1905]. 314 p., [6] leaves of photo. plates. **MUU**
PW: N 18, '05.

W-458 Whitcomb, Russell. Hounded by a shadow / by Russell Whitcomb. New York: Post Card Fiction, [c1905]. 11 p. **NYP**

W-459 White, Ansley DeForest, b. 1886. The transgressor (published anonymously) and other stories, showing the effects of liquor upon society; and its coalition of evil sequalae [!] / by A. DeForest White, Jr.; with illustrations by Louis A. Plogsted. [Buffalo?, N. Y.]: The Inter-State Prohibition Publishing Association, 1909. 112 p., front., ill. (map)., [4] leaves of plates. Unexamined copy: bibliographic data from NUC.

W-460 White, Bouck, b. 1874. The mixing: what the Hillport neighbors did / by Bouck, White. Garden City, N. Y.: Doubleday, Page & Company, 1913. 344 p., ill. t.p. an double leaves, ill. [Ill. by Decorative Designers.]

W-461 White, Buchanan. The rural school-teacher, or, A double West Virginia love story / by Buchanan White . . . ; illustrated by photos & drawings. New York: Broadway Publishing Company . . . , [c1909]. 120 p., photo. front. (port.), [3] leaves of plates (2 photo.). [Ill. by Wm. L. Hudson.] **WVU**

W-462 White, Caroline Earle, 1833-1916. An ocean mystery / by Caroline Earle White . . . Philadelphia; London: J. B. Lippincott Company, 1903. 260 p.
OSU, DLC

W-463 White, Edward J. (Edward Joseph), 1869-1935. William and Matilda: a mediaeval historical romance of William the Conqueror and his wife, Matilda / by Edw. J. White. Boston, Mass.: The Stratford Company, 1925. 315 p., front., [12] leaves of plates. PW: Ag 8, '25.

White, Edward Lucas, 1866-1934. Amina. In *The Bellman book of fiction* (1921), B-485.

W-464 ____ Andivius Hedulio: adventures of a Roman nobleman in the days of the Empire / by Edward Lucas White . . . New York: E. P. Dutton & Company . . . , [1921]. 613 p. Maps on end papers. LC: O 27, '21.

W-465 ____ El Supremo: a romance of the great dictator of Paraguay / by Edward Lucas White. New York: E. P. Dutton & Company . . . , [c1916]. 700 p. LC: O 26, '16.

W-466 ____ Helen: the story of the romance of Helen of Troy, born Helen of Sparta, and of Aithre, mother of King Theseus of Attica, who became Helen's bondslave, handmaid and foster-mother / by Edward Lucas White; decorated by Theodore Nadejen. New York: George H. Doran Company, [c1925]. 250 p., ill. LC: Je 1, '25. PW: My 30, '25. BLC: London: Johnathan Cope, 1925.

W-467 ____ The song of the sirens: and other stories / by Edward Lucas White . . . New York: E. P. Dutton & Company . . . , [c1919]. 348 p. Contents: The song of the sirens -- Iarbas -- The right man -- Dodona -- The elephant's ear -- The fasces -- The swimmers -- The skewbald panther -- Disvola -- The flambeau bracket. LC: Mr 1, '19.

W-468 ____ The unwilling vestal: a tale of Rome under the Cæsars / by Edward Lucas White. New York: E. P. Dutton & Company, [c1918]. 317 p., plan. LC: Ap 3, '18. PW: Ap 13, '18.

W-469 White, Eliza Orne, b. 1856. The first step: a novel / by Eliza Orne White. Boston; New York: Houghton Mifflin Company, 1914. (Cambridge: The Riverside Press). 194, [2] p. LC: Mr 23, '14. PW: Ap 4, '14.

W-470 ____ John Forsyth's aunts / by Eliza Orne White. New York: McClure, Phillips & Company, 1901. 269 p. PW: D 7, '01. BLC: London: McClure, Phillips & Co., 1901.

W-471 ____ Lesley Chilton / by Eliza Orne White. Boston; New York: Houghton, Mifflin and Company, 1903. (Cambridge: The Riverside Press). 356 p. PW: O 3, '03.

W-472 ____ The Wares of Edgefield / by Eliza Orne White. Boston; New York: Houghton Mifflin Company, 1909. (Cambridge: The Riverside Press). 439, [1] p. LC: O 7, '09. PW: O 9, '09.

W-473 White, George M. (George Miles). From Boniface to bank burglar, or, The price of persecution: how a successful business man, through the miscarriage of justice, became a notorious bank looter / by George M. White, alias George Bliss. Bellows Falls, Vt.: Truax Printing Company, 1905. 495 p., incl. 1 leaf of plates, front. (port.). Another edition: New York: The Seaboard Publishing Company, 1907. Photo. front., [13] leaves of photo. plates. [Photo. by Boyd Photo, Rockwood Photo, and Brown Bros. Photo.] **KSU**

W-474 White, Grace Miller. From the valley of the missing / by Grace Miller White . . . ; frontispiece by Penrhyn Stanlaws. New York: W. J. Watt & Company, [1911]. 342 p., col. front. LC: Ag 15, '11. PW: N 18, '11.

W-475 ____ The ghost of Glen Gorge / by Grace Miller White; frontispiece by William Leipse [sic]. New York: The Macaulay Company, [c1925]. 319 p., front. LC: Mr 7, '25. PW: F 28, '25.

W-476 ____ Judy of Rogues' Harbor / by Grace Miller White; frontispiece by Howard Chandler Christy. New York: The H. K. Fly Company, [c1918]. 357 p., front. and t. p. on double leaves. BLC: London: Hodder & Stoughton, [1925].

W-477 ____ The marriage of Patricia Pepperday / by Grace Miller White; with frontispiece by Ralph P. Coleman. Boston: Little, Brown and Company, 1922. 347 p., front. LC: Mr 2, '22. PW: Mr 18, '22. BLC: London: Hodder & Stoughton, [1925].

W-478 ____ Rose o' paradise / by Grace Miller White . . . ; illustrated by W. J. Shettsline. New York: The H. K. Fly Company, [c1915]. 352 p., front., [3] leaves of plates. LC: O 11, '15. PW: N 13, '15. BLC: London: Mills & Boon, 1918.

W-479 ____ The secret of the storm country / by Grace Miller White . . . ; illustrated by Lucius W. Hitchcock. New York: The H. K. Fly Company, [c1917]. 352 p., front., [3] leaves of plates. Sequel to *Tess of the storm country*. PW: Je 30, '17. BLC: London: Hutchinson & Co., [1924].

W-480   _____ The shadow of the sheltering pines: a new romance of the storm country / by Grace Miller White . . . New York: The H. K. Fly Company, [c1919]. 314 p., front.

W-481   _____ Storm country Polly / by Grace Miller White; with frontispiece by Frank Tenney Johnson. Boston: Little, Brown and Company, 1920. 309 p., front.
LC: My 15, '20.
PW: My 8, '20.
BLC: London: Hudder & Stoughton, [1924].

W-482   _____ Tess of the storm country / Grace Miller White; illustrations by Howard Chandler Christy. New York: W. J. Watt & Company, [c1909]. 365 p., front., [2] leaves of plates.
LC: N 15, '09.
PW: Mr 19, '10.

W-483   _____ When tragedy grins / by Grace Miller White; illustrations by R. F. Schabelitz. New York: W. J. Watt & Company, [c1912]. 327 p., front., [5] leaves of plates (2 double leaves).
LC: F 19, '12.
PW: Ap 13, '12.
BLC: London: C. Palmer & Hayward, 1916.

White, Henry, b. 1876. <u>See</u> **Oliver, Roland, pseud.**

W-484   White, Hervey, b. 1866. The house in the road: a fantasy of truth / by Hervey White. Woodstock, New York: The Maverick Press, c1913. 157 p.
LC: D 2, '13.

W-485   _____ Man overboard!: a naughty novel / by Hervey White. Woodstock, N. Y.: Published by the Maverick Press, [c1922]. 308, [1] p.   **DLC**

W-486   _____ When Eve was not created: and other stories / by Hervey White. Boston: Small, Maynard & Company, 1901. 220 p.
Contents: When Eve was not created -- The man and the lake -- A monochrome -- The history of a paradox.
PW: My 18, '01.

W-487   White, Ida Belle. Spirits do return / by Ida Belle White. Kansas City, Missouri: The White Publishing Co. . . , [c1915]. 251 p., photo. front. (port.), ill.

W-488   White, Mary Josephine. Raggety: his life and adventures / by Mary Josephine White; with drawing by Clifford K. Berryman. Washington, D. C.: Privately printed for the author by H. L. & J. B. McQueen, Inc., 1913. 71 p., incl. front., ill.

W-489   White, Mary K. Twice loyal: a novel / by Mary K. White. New York: The Neale Publishing Company, 1917. 265 p.   **DLC**
PW: S 15, '17.

W-490   White, Matthew, 1857-1940. Guy Hammersley, or, Clearing his name / by Matthew White, Jr. . . . New York: Street & Smith, [c1901]. 243 p., front., [3] leaves of plates.   **CGU**

W-491   White, Michael, b. 1866. The garden of Indra / by Michael White; pictures by Wladyslaw T. Benda. New York: Duffield & Company, 1912. 274 p.,

front., [7] leaves of plates.
Contents: The black magic -- His caste -- The gods of Simla -- Under the sacred bo-tree -- Miss Bayard's yogi -- The soul of a crow -- The Lord alligators -- The treasure of the mosque -- Eternum X -- The white lord of Krishnabad -- Force mercurial -- Jackson's monkeys -- The light of the palace -- The tiger's claw -- The black panther.
LC: F 1, '12.

W-492   _____ Lachmi Bai, Rani of Jhansi: the Jeanne D'Arc of India / by Michael White. New York: J. F. Taylor & Company, 1901. 297 p., front., [5] leaves of plates. [Ill. by Margaret L. White.]
PW: D 14, '01.

W-493   White, Owen. Out of the desert: the historical romance of El Paso / by Owen White. El Paso, Texas: The McMath Company, 1923. 442 p., [8] leaves of photo. plates, photo. ill.   **DMM**

W-494   White, Stewart Edward, 1873-1946. Arizona nights / by Stewart Edward White; illustrations by N. C. Wyeth. New York: The McClure Company, 1907. 351 p., col. front., [6] leaves of col. plates.
Contents: Pt. 1: Arizona nights -- Pt. 2: The two-gun man -- Pt. 3: The rawhide.
LC: O 31, '07.
PW: N 16, '07.
BLC: London: Hodder & Stoughton, 1907.

W-495   _____ The blazed trail / by Stewart Edward White . . . illustrated by Thomas Fogarty. New York: McClure, Phillips & Co., 1902. 413 p., front., [6] leaves of plates.   **KSU**
"Part II of this book appeared in McClure's magazine for December, 1901 and January and February, 1902 under the title of `The forest runner.'"
PW: My 24, '02.
BLC: Westminster: Archibald Constable & Co., printed in the United States, 1902.

W-496   _____ Blazed trail stories: and Stories of the wild life / by Stewart Edward White. New York: McClure, Phillips & Co., 1904. 260 p., col. front. [Ill. by Thomas Fogarty.]
Contents: Blazed trail stories: The riverman -- The foreman -- The scaler -- The river-boss -- The fifth way -- The life of the winds of heaven. Stories of the wild life: The girl who got rattled -- Billy's tenderfoot -- The two cartridges -- The race -- The saving grace -- The prospector -- The girl in red.
PW: O 1, '04.
BLC: London: McClure, Phillips Y Co., New York [printed], 1904.

W-497   _____ The claim jumpers: a romance / by Stewart Edward White. New York: D. Appleton and Company, 1901. 284 p.   **COD**
(Appleton's town and country library; no. 197).
PW: My 18, '01.
BLC: London: Hodder & Stoughton, printed in U. S. A., 1905.

W-498   _____ Conjuror's house: a romance of the free forest / by Stewart Edward White . . . New York: McClure, Phillips & Co., 1903. 260 p., front., [5] leaves of plates. [Ill. by Charles S. Chapman.]
PW: Mr 28, '03.
BLC: London & New York: McClure, Phillips, and Co., 1903.
Another edition: London: Methuen & Co., 1903.

_____ A double shot. In *Argonaut stories* (1906), **A-298.**

W-499　_____ The glory hole / by Stewart Edward White. Garden City, N. Y.: Doubleday, Page & Company, 1924. 495 p.
LC: N 13, '24.
PW: N 1, '24.
BLC: London: Hodder & Stoughton, [1924].

W-500　_____ Gold / by Stewart Edward White; illustrated by Thomas Fogarty. Garden City, New York: Doubleday, Page & Co., 1913. 437 p., col. front., [3] leaves of col. plates, ill. Illustrated end papers. "Stewart Edward White who has brought the East and South and North to understand the West. A little chat about the man and his books, by Eugene F. Saxton": 12, [1] p. at end.
LC: O 8, '13.
PW: O 11, '13.
BLC: London: Hodder & Stoughton, 1914.

W-501　_____ The gray dawn / by Stewart Edward White; illustrated by Thomas Fogarty. Garden City, New York: Doubleday, Page & Co., [c1915]. 395, [1] p., col. front., [3] leaves of col. plates. Illustrated end papers.
LC: O 27, '15.
PW: N 6, '15.
BLC: London: Hodder & Stoughton, [1915].

W-502　_____ The killer / by Stewart Edward White. Garden City, New York: Doubleday, Page & Company, 1920. 346 p., col. front. [Ill. by D. D. Pettee.]
LC: Je 7, '20.
PW: My 29, '20.
BLC: London : Hodder & Stoughton, 1920. Merle Johnson: "A few copies were issued in advance of trade issue." 1919, 134 p.
LC: S 30, '19.

W-503　_____ The Leopard Woman / by Stewart Edward White; illustrated by W. H. D. Koerner. Garden City, New York: Doubleday, Page & Company, 1916. 313 p., front., [7] leaves of plates.
LC: O 18, '16.
PW: O 21, '16.
BLC: London: Hodder & Stoughton, 1918.

W-504　_____ The mystery / by Stewart Edward White and Samuel Hopkins Adams; illustrations by Will Crawford. New York: McClure, Phillips & Co., 1907. 286 p., front., [15] leaves of plates.
LC: Ja 3, '07.
PW: Ja 26, '07.

W-505　_____ On tiptoe: a romance of the redwoods / by Stewart Edward White; with a frontispiece by Thomas Fogarty. New York: George H. Doran Company, [c1922]. 264, [1] p., col. front.
LC: O 6, '22.
PW: S 9, '22.
BLC: London: Hodder & Stoughton, [1922].

W-506　_____ The riverman / by Stewart Edward White; illustrations by N. C. Wyeth and Clarence F. Underwood. New York: The McClure Company, 1908. 368 p., col. front., [13] leaves of col. plates.

LC: Ag 19, '08.
PW: Ag 29, '08.
BLC: London: Hodder & Stoughton, 1908.

W-507　_____ The rose dawn / by Stewart Edward White. Garden City, New York: Doubleday, Page & Company, 1920. 369, [1] p.
LC: N 26, '20.
PW: N 20, '20.
BLC: London: Hodder & Stoughton, [1921].

W-508　_____ The rules of the game / by Stewart Edward White; illustrated by Lejaren A. Hiller. New York: Doubleday, Page & Company, 1910. 644 p., col. front., [3] leaves of col. plates.
LC: Ap 29, '10.
PW: N 19, '10.
BLC: London: Thomas Melson & Sons, 1911.

_____ The saving grace. In *Comedy* (1901), **C-614.**

W-509　_____ The sign at six / by Stewart Edward White; illustrated by M. Leone Bracker. Indianapolis: The Bobbs-Merrill Company, [c1912]. 264, [1] p., front., [5] leaves of plates.
LC: Ag 21, '12.
BLC: London: Hodder & Stoughton, [1912].

W-510　_____ The silent places / by Stewart Edward White; illustrated by Philip R. Goodwin. New York: McClure, Phillips & Co., 1904. 304 p., col. front., [6] leaves of col. plates.
PW: Ap 23, '04.
BLC: London: McClure, Phillips & Co., printed in U. S. A., 1904. Another edition: London: Hodder & Stoughton, 1904.

W-511　_____ Simba / by Stewart Edward White. Garden City, N. Y.: Doubleday, Page & Company, 1918. 332 p.
LC: Mr 13, '18.
PW: Mr 9, '18.

W-512　_____ Skookum Chuck: a novel / by Stewart Edward White. Garden City, N. Y.: Doubleday, Page & Company, 1925. 296 p.
LC: O 16, '25.
BLC: London: William Heinemann, printed in U. S. A., 1925.

W-513　_____ The westerners / by Stewart Edward White. New York: McClure, Phillips & Co., 1901. 344 p.
PW: S 14, '01.
BLC: London: Archibald Constable & Co., 1901.

W-514　White, Walter Francis, 1893-1955. The fire in the flint / Walter F. White. New York: Alfred A. Knopf, 1924. 300 p.
BLC: London: Williams & Norgate, 1925.

W-515　White, William Allen, 1868-1944. A certain rich man / by William Allen White. New York: The Macmillan Company, 1909. 434 p.
LC: Jl 9, '09.
PW: Ag 7, '09.

W-516 _____ God's puppets / by William Allen White . . .
New York: The Macmillan Company, 1916. 309 p.,
col. front. (port.).
Contents: A social rectangle -- "The one a Pharisee" -- "A
prosperous gentleman" -- The gods arrive -- The strange boy.
LC: Mr 16, '16.
PW: Mr 25, '16.
BLC: London: Macmillan, printed in U. S. A.,
1916.

W-517 _____ In our town / by William Allen White;
illustrations by F. R. Gruger and W. Glackens. New
York: McClure, Phillips & Co., 1906. 369 p., [15]
leaves of plates.
PW: Ap 21, '06.

W-518 _____ In the heart of a fool / by William Allen White.
New York: The Macmillan Company, 1918. 615 p.
LC: N 7, '18.
PW: N 16, '18.

W-519 _____ The martial adventures of Henry and me / by
William Allen White . . . ; with illustrations by Tony
Sarg. New York: The Macmillan Company, 1918.
338 p., front., ill., music.
LC: Ap 10, '18.
PW: Ap 20, '18.

W-520 _____ Stratagems and spoils: stories of love and
politics / by William Allen White . . . ; illustrated.
New York: Charles Scribner's Sons, 1901. 291 p.,
front., [5] leaves of plates. [Ill. by A. I. Keller, W.
R. Leigh, and Harrison Fisher.]
Contents: The man on horseback -- A victory for the people -- "A
triumph 's evidence" -- The mercy of death -- A most lamentable
comedy.
PW: N 2, '01.

_____, contributor. See *The sturdy oak* (1917),
S-1101.

W-521 White, William Patterson, b. 1884. The heart of the
range / by William Patterson White; frontispiece by
George W. Gage. Garden City, N. Y.; Toronto:
Doubleday, Page & Company, 1921. 313, [1] p.,
front.
LC: Je 17, '21.
BLC: London: Hodder & Stoughton, [1921].

W-522 _____ Hidden trails / by William Patterson White;
frontispiece by Ralph Pallen Coleman. Garden City,
New York: Doubleday, Page & Company, 1920.
335, [1] p., col. front.
LC: Jl 17, '20.
PW: Jl 17, '20.
BLC: London: Hodder & Stoughton, [1921].

W-523 _____ Lynch lawyers / by William Patterson White;
with frontispiece by Anton Otto Fischer. Boston:
Little, Brown, and Company, 1920. 387 p., front.
PW: Ja 17, '20.
BLC: London: Hodder & Stoughton, [1923].

W-524 _____ The owner of the Lazy D / by William
Patterson White; with frontispiece by Anton Otto
Fischer. Boston: Little, Brown, and Company,
1919. 324 p., front.   **CLE**

LC: Ag 21, '19.
PW: Ag 16, '19.

W-525 _____ Paradise Bend / by William Patterson White;
frontispiece by Ralph Pallen Coleman. Garden City,
N. Y.: Doubleday, Page & Company, 1920. 287,
[1] p., col. front.
LC: O 21, '20.
PW: O 23, '20.
BLC: London: Hodder & Stoughton, [1921].

W-526 _____ The rider of Golden Bar / by William Patterson
White; with frontispiece by Remington Schuyler.
Boston: Little, Brown, and Company, 1922. 391 p.,
front.
LC: Ja 11, '22.
PW: Ja 14, '22.
BLC: London: Hodder & Stoughton, 1922.

W-527 _____ The twisted foot / by William Patterson White;
with frontispiece by George W. Gage. Boston:
Little, Brown and Company, 1924. 329 p., front.
LC: Ag 18, '24.
PW: Ag 16, '24.
BLC: London: Hodder & Stoughton, [1925].

W-528 _____ The wagon wheel / by William Patterson
White; with frontispiece by Remington Schuyler.
Boston: Little, Brown, and Company, 1923. 320 p.,
front.
LC: Mr 15, '23.
PW: Mr 17, '23.

W-529 Whitefield, Charles T. A plain American in England
/ by Charles T. Whitefield. New York: Doubleday,
Page & Company, 1910. 41 p.   **MNU**
BLC: London: Grant Richards; Garden City, N. Y.
printed, 1912.

W-530 Whitehead, A. C. (Albert Carlton), b. 1875. The
standard bearer: a story of army life in the time of
Caesar / by A. C. Whitehead . . . New York;
Cincinnati; Chicago: American Book Company,
[c1915]. 305 p., col. front., ill. [Ill. by Varian.]
                                              RBN

W-531 Whitehead, Harold, b. 1880. The business career of
Peter Flint / by Harold Whitehead . . . ; illustrated by
John Goss. Boston: The Page Company, 1919.
365 p., col. front., [4] leaves of plates.
LC: S 27, '19.

W-532 _____ Dawson Black: retail merchant / by Harold
Whitehead . . . ; illustrated by John Goss. Boston:
The Page Company, 1918. 357 p., col. front., [4]
leaves of plates.
LC: Jl 11, '18.
PW: Ag 3, '18.

Whitehill, Buell B., jt. ed. See *Allegheny stories*
(1902), A-142.

W-533 Whitehouse, Florence Brooks. The effendi: a
romance of the Soudan / by Florence Brooks
Whitehouse . . . ; illustrated by I. H. Caliga. Boston:
Little, Brown, and Company, 1904. 414 p., front.,
[3] leaves of plates.
PW: My 7, '04.

W-534 Whitehouse, Florence Brooks. The god of things: a novel of modern Egypt / by Florence Brooks Whitehouse; ... with illustrations from drawings by the author. Boston: Little, Brown, and Company, 1902. 288 p., front., [4] leaves of plates.
Unexamined copy: bibliographic data from OCLC, #24424640.
PW: My 3, '02.

W-535 Whiteley, Isabel Nixon, b. 1859. Wanted--a situation: and other stories / by Isabel Nixon Whiteley ... St. Louis, Mo.: Published by B. Herder, 1904. 191 p. **DLC**
Contents: Wanted--a situation -- Her novel -- Two chorus girls -- Mrs. Golobiewsky's first good time -- A victory of Our Lady -- In the shadow of the Creizker -- How the phonograph made a match -- A momentary madness -- A criminal type -- Our Lady's roses -- A box of chocolates -- Nora's blockade running.

W-536 Whitell, Evelyn. The builder's crown of jewels / by Evelyn Whitell ... Los Angeles: The Master Press ..., 1925. 142 p.
LC: Jl 20, 25.

W-537 ____ A California poppy: the story of a child healer / by C. Evelyn Whitell. San Francisco, Cal.: Mission Center for Universal Light, [c1916]. 24 p. Cover title.

W-538 ____ Extraordinary Mary / by Evelyn Whitell. Los Angeles, California: Master Mind Publishing Company, [c1920]. 72 p. **DLC**

W-539 ____ The healing of the Hawaiian: a story of the Hawaiian Islands / by Evelyn Whitell ... Los Angeles: Published by the Master Press ..., [c1923]. 155 p.
LC: Jl 16, '23.

W-540 ____ The woman healer / by Evelyn Whitell. Los Angeles, Cal.: The Master Mind Publishing Co., [c1920]. 88 p. **DLC**
LC: Je 1, '20.
PW: Ag 28, '20.

W-541 Whitelock, William Wallace, 1869-1940. When kings go forth to battle: a novel / by William Wallace Whitelock; with illustrations in color by Frank H. Desch. Philadelphia; London: J. B. Lippincott Company, 1907. 311 p., incl. col. front., [2] leaves of col. plates.
LC: S 6, '07.
BLC: London: Grant Richards, 1908.

W-542 [Whiteside, Guy Kenneth], b. 1879. Her wedding night / by John Ferriss St. John [pseud.]. ... White Hall, Ill.: Printed by G. K. Whiteside, 1909. 244 p. **DLC**
LC: S 22, '09.
PW: Ja 22, '10.

W-543 Whiteside, Mary Brent. Bill Possum: his book / by Mary Brent Whiteside; illustrated by G. P. Haynes. [Atlanta, Ga.: s. n., c1909.] 104 p., ill.
PW: Ap 10, '09.

Whiteside, Norman. The voice of wilderness. In *The friendly little house: and other stories* (1910), **F-432.**

W-544 [Whitford, Daniel]. Hank Long's first voyage; a Wall Street incident. [New York: Printed under supervision of Jos. J. Rafter, c1908]. 128 p.

W-545 Whiting, Anna Katharine. Glenwood / by Anna Katharine Whiting. Boston, Mass.: The C. M. Clark Publishing Co., 1907. 387 p., incl. front., [7] leaves of plates.
Unexamined copy: bibliographic data from NUC.
LC: N 12, '07.
PW: D 14, '07.

W-546 Whiting, Robert Rudd, b. 1877. A ball of yarn: its unwinding / by Robert Rudd Whiting; the illustrations by Merle Johnson. San Francisco; New York: Paul Elder & Company, [c1907]. 79 p., col. front., [4] leaves of col. plates.
"Many of these yarns were first printed in the New York Sun."
Contents: The first skein: The yarn of the breath bound village -- The yarn of the inventive vamp -- The yarn of the blind ball-tosser. The second skein: The yarn of the two-tailed pointer -- The yarn of the human louvre -- The yarn of suggested senility. The third skein: The yarn of the football fantastic -- The yarn of the brawny batsman -- The yarn of the certain system. The fourth skein: The yarn of the fleet-footed fielder -- The yarn of the thespian triumphant -- The yarn of the sinner stung.
LC: O 1, '07.
PW: O 19, '07.

W-547 ____ The judgement of Jane / by Robert Rudd Whiting ... New York: Moffat, Yard and Company, 1915. 190 p. **DLC**
LC: O 12, '15.
PW: O 9, '15.

W-548 Whitlock, Brand, 1869-1934. The fall guy / by Brand Whitlock. Indianapolis: The Bobbs-Merrill Company, [c1912]. 382 p. Partly reprinted from various periodicals.
Contents: The fall guy -- The field of honor -- The sleeping column -- The orator of the day -- Fowler Brunton, attorney at law -- The last chance -- The old house across the street -- The girl that's down -- The preacher's son -- The finals and Alice Gray -- Their quest -- In the fall -- The question -- Lead us not into temptation.
LC: My 15, '12.
PW: My 4, '12.

W-549 ____ The gold brick / by Brand Whitlock. Indianapolis: The Bobbs-Merrill Company, [c1910]. 342 p. Partly reprinted from various periodicals.
Contents: The gold brick -- The has-been -- What will become of Annie? -- The vindication of Henderson of Greene -- Senate bill 578 -- Macochee's first campaign fund -- A secret of state -- The colonel's last campaign -- Reform in the first -- Malachi Nolan -- The pardon of Thomas Whalen -- That boy.
LC: O 19, '10.
PW: O 22, '10.

W-550 ____ The happy average / by Brand Whitlock. Indianapolis: The Bobbs-Merrill Company, [c1904]. 347 p.
PW: O 15, '04.

W-551 ____ Her infinite variety / by Brand Whitlock ... ; with illustrations by Howard Chandler Christy; decorations by Ralph Fletcher Seymour. Indianapolis: The Bobbs-Merrill Company, [1904]. 167, [1] p., front., [11] leaves of plates, ill.
PW: F 27, '04.

W-552   ____ J. Hardin & son: a novel / by Brand Whitlock. New York; London: D. Appleton and Company, 1923. 451 p.
LC: O 17, '23.
PW: O 27, '23.

W-553   ____ The 13th District: a story of a candidate / by Brand Whitlock. Indianapolis: The Bowen-Merrill Company, [c1902]. 490 p.
PW: Ap 5, '02.

W-554   ____ The turn of the balance / by Brand Whitlock; with illustrations by Jay Hambidge. Indianapolis: The Bobbs-Merrill Company, [c1907]. 622 p., front., [6] leaves of plates.
PW: Mr 16, '07.
BLC: London: Alston Rivers, 1907.

W-555   Whitman, H. E. O. (Henry Esmond Oram), b. 1900. The Pirate of Pittsburgh / by H. E. O. Whitman. Boston; New York: Houghton Mifflin Company, 1925. (Cambridge: The Riverside Press). 258, [1] p.
PW: F 28, '25.

Whitman, Stephen French. Amazement. *In The best short stories of 1920 and the yearbook of the American short story* (1921), **B-565.**

W-556   ____ Children of hope: a novel / by Stephen Whitman; with illustrations by F. R. Gruger. New York: The Century Co., 1916. 508 p., front., [5] leaves of plates.
LC: Ap 28, '16.
PW: Ap 15, '16.

W-557   ____ The happy-ship: setting forth the adventures of Shorty and Patrick, U. S. S. Oklahoma / by Stephen French Whitman; illustrations by F. C. Yohn. New York: McBride, Nast & Company, 1913. 262 p., front., [5] leaves of plates.
LC: Ja 28, '14.

W-558   ____ The isle of life: a romance / by Stephen French Whitman. New York: Charles Scribner's Sons, 1913. 498 p.
LC: Mr 6, '13.
PW: Mr 1, '13.
BLC: London: Constable & Co.; New York [printed], 1914.

____ The last room of all. *In Prize stories of 1920* **(1921), P-618.**

W-559   ____ Predestined: a novel of New York life / by Stephen French Whitman. New York: Charles Scribner's Sons, 1910. 464 p.
LC: Mr 7, '10.
PW: Mr 5, '10.

W-560   ____ Sacrifice / by Stephen French Whitman. New York; London: D. Appleton and Company, 1922. 337, [1] p., front.
LC: Mr 2, '22.
PW: Mr 18, '22.

W-561   ____ Shorty & Patrick: U. S. S. Oklahoma / by Stephen French Whitman . . . ; illustrations by F. C.

Yohn. New York: P. F. Collier & Son, [c1910]. 169 p., front., [4] leaves of plates.
LC: D 22, '10.
PW: D 3, '10.

W-562   Whitney, A. D. T. (Adeline Dutton Train), 1824-1906. Biddy's episodes / by Mrs. A. D. T. Whitney. Boston; New York: Houghton, Mifflin and Company, 1904. (Cambridge: The Riverside Press). 327 p.

Whitney, George Erastus, Mrs. See **Whitney, Gertrude Copen.**

W-563   Whitney, Gertrude Capen, 1861-1941. Above the shame of circumstance / by Gertrude Capen Whitney . . . Boston: Sherman, French & Company, 1913. 307 p., front., [5] leaves of plates. Marginal illustrations and decorations.
LC: D 15, '13.
PW: D 20, '13.

W-564   ____ The house of Landell, or, Follow and find / by Gertrude Capen Whitney (Mrs. George Erastus Whitney) . . . New York: R. F. Fenno & Company, [c1917]. 468 p.
LC: Ag 1, '17.
PW: Ag 11, '17.

W-565   ____ I choose / by Gertrude Capen Whitney. Boston: Sherman, French & Company, 1910. 90 p.
LC: Ap 11, '10.
PW: Ap 11, '10.

W-566   ____ The interpreter: a novel / by Gertrude Capen Whitney. Boston: The Four Seas Company, [c1925]. 212 p.   **CLU**

W-567   ____ On the other side of the bridge / by Gertrude Capen Whitney. Boston: The Four Seas Company, 1922. 204 p.   **KGG**
LC: N 3, '22.

W-568   ____ Where the sun shines / by Gertrude Capen Whitney . . . Boston: Christopher Publishing House, [c1920]. 121 p.   **OBE**
LC: Jl 15, '20.
PW: Jl 24, '20.

W-569   ____ Yet speaketh he / by Gertrude Capen Whitney. Boston: Sherman, French & Company, 1910. 85 p.
LC: Ap 11, '10.
PW: Je 4, '10.

W-570   Whitney, Louisa M. (Louisa Maretta Bailey), b. 1844. Goldie's inheritance: a story of the siege of Atlanta / by Louisa M. Whitney. Burlington, Vt.: Free Press Association, 1903. 263 p.

W-571   Whitson, John Harvey, b. 1854. Barbara, a woman of the West / by John H. Whitson; illustrated by Chase Emerson. Boston: Little, Brown, and Company, 1903. 314 p., front., [4] leaves of plates.
PW: Ap 25, '03.

W-572   ____ The castle of doubt / by John H. Whitson; with a frontispiece in color from a drawing by I. H. Caliga. Boston: Little, Brown, and Company, 1907. 283 p., col. front.
LC: My 1, '07.
PW: My 11, '07.

W-573   ____ Justin Wingate, ranchman / by John H. Whitson; with illustrations from drawings by Arthur E. Becher. Boston: Little, Brown and Company, 1905. 312 p., front., [3] leaves of plates.
PW: Ap 29, '05.

W-574   ____ The rainbow chasers: a story of the plains / by John H. Whitson; with illustrations from drawings by Arthur E. Becher. Boston: Little, Brown, and Company, 1904. 393 p., front., [5] leaves of plates.
PW: My 4, '07
BLC: London: Ward, Lock, & Co., printed from American plates, 1905.

W-575   Whittles, Thomas Davis, b. 1873. The lad who heard the angel's song / by Thos. D. Whittles. Printed but not published. [Fergus Falls, Minn.] Fergus Falls Free Press Print, [c1908]. 24 p.
Unexamined copy: bibliographic data from NUC.

W-576   ____ The lumberjack sky pilot / by Thomas D. Whittles. Chicago: The Winona Publishing Company, 1908. 233 p., photo. front., [14] leaves of photo. plates.

W-577   ____ The parish of the pines: the story of Frank Higgins, the lumberjacks' sky pilot / by Thomas D. Whittles; illustrated. New York; Chicago; Toronto; London; Edinburgh: Fleming H. Revell Company, [c1912]. 247 p., photo. front., [7] leaves of photo. plates.
LC: Ja 2, '13.

W-578   The whole family: a novel / by twelve authors: William Dean Howells, Mary E. Wilkins Freeman, Mary Heaton Vorse, Mary Stewart Cutting, Elizabeth Jordan, John Kendrick Bangs, Henry James, Elizabeth Stuart Phelps, Edith Wyatt, Mary R. Shipman Andrews, Alice Brown, Henry Van Dyke. New York; London: Harper & Brothers, 1908. 314 p., front., [11] leaves of plates. [Ill. by Alice Barber Stephens.]
LC: O 15, '08.
PW: O 24, '08.
References: Gibson & Arms 08-C.

W-579   Wicker, Frederick William, b. 1878. Blinded by love: a romance of life / by F. W. Wicker. Baltimore, Md.: Saulsbury Publishing Company, [c1919]. 111 p.   **SOI**
LC: S 5, '19.

W-580   Wickham, Harvey. The Boncocur affair / by Harvey Wickham. New York: Edward J. Clode, [c1923]. 310 p.
LC: Ap 24, '23.
BLC: London: Skeffington & Son, [1925].

W-581   ____ The clue of the primrose petal / by Harvey Wickham. New York: Edward J. Clode, [c1921]. 313 p.

LC: D 28, '21.
BLC: London: Brentano's, printed in U. S. A., [1923].

W-582   ____ Jungle terror / by Harvey Wickham; frontispiece by Ralph Pallen Coleman. Garden City, New York; London: Doubleday, Page & Company, 1920. 244 p., col. front.
LC: Ap 26, '20.
PW: Jl 3, '20.

W-583   ____ The scarlet X / by Harvey Wickham . . . New York: Edward J. Clode, [c1922]. 315 p.
LC: Mr 22, '23.
PW: Ap 1, '22.
BLC: London: Brentano's; printed in U. S. A., 1923.

W-584   ____ The trail of the squid / by Harvey Wickham. New York: Edward J. Clode, [c1924]. 320 p.
LC: F 12, '24.
PW: Mr 8, '24.

W-585   Widdemer, Margaret. The boardwalk / Margaret Widdemer . . . New York: Harcourt, Brace and Howe, 1920. 241 p.
Contents: Changeling -- Rosabel Paradise -- Don Andrews' girl -- Black magic -- The congregation -- The fairyland heart -- Good times -- Oh, Mr. Dream-man -- Devil's hall.

W-586   ____ Charis sees it through, by Margaret Widdemer. New York, Harcourt, Brace and Company, [c1924]. 272 p.
LC: S 15 '24.
PW: S 20, '24.

W-587   ____ Graven image / by Margaret Widdemer . . . New York: Harcourt, Brace and Company, [c1923]. 319 p.
LC: O 19, '23.
PW: O 13, '23.
BLC: London: G. G. Harrup & Co., 1924.

    ____ Her child. In *Forum stories* **(1914), F-306.**

W-588   ____ I've married Marjorie / by Margaret Widdemer . . . New York: Harcourt, Brace and Howe, 1920. 258 p.
LC: Ag 14, '20.
PW: Ag 21, '20.

W-589   ____ A minister of grace / by Margaret Widdemer. New York: Harcourt, Brace and Company, [c1922]. 286 p.
Contents: Of the clan of God -- As one having authority -- Wild woodland -- A moment of revolt -- "Noblesse oblige" -- That other Eileen -- Adjustment -- The little queens of death -- Powers of darkness.
LC: Ag 26, '22.

W-590   ____ The rose-garden husband / by Margaret Widdemer; with illustrations by Walter Biggs. Philadelphia; London: J. B. Lippincott Company, 1915. 207, [1] p.
LC: F 27, '15.
BLC: London: Hodder & Stoughton, 1915.

W-591   ____ Why not? / by Margaret Widdemer . . . ; illustrated. New York: Hearst's International Library Co., 1915. 338 p., col. front., [2] leaves of plates. [Ill. by G. W. Hood.]

LC: S 17, '15.
PW: S 25, '15.
BLC: London: Hodder & Stoughton, 1916.

W-592   _____ The wishing-ring man / by Margaret Widdemer; frontispiece by Willy Pogany. New York: Henry Holt and Company, 1917. 302 p., col. front.
LC: O 2, '17.
PW: O 13, '17.
BLC: London: Hodder & Stoughton, [1918].

W-593   _____ The year of delight / by Margaret Widdemer. New York: Harcourt, Brace and Company, 1921. 311 p.
LC: S 1, '21.
PW: My 30, '25.

W-594   _____ You're only young once / by Margaret Widdemer . . . New York: Henry Holt and Company, 1918. 313 p.
LC: S 14, '18.
PW: S 14, '18.
BLC: London: Hodder & Stoughton, [1919].

Wiechmann, Ferdinand Gerhard, 1858-1919. See Monroe, Forest, pseud.

W-595   Wiggin, Kate Douglas Smith, 1856-1923. The affair at the inn / by Kate Douglas Wiggin, Mary Findlater, Jane Findlater, Allan McAulay. Boston; New York: Houghton, Mifflin and Company, 1904. (Cambridge: The Riverside Press). 220 p., col. front., [5] leaves of col. plates. [Ill. by Martin Justice.]
PW: S 24, '04.
References: BAL 22633.

W-596   _____ Creeping Jenny: and other New England stories / by Kate Douglas Wiggin; with a frontispiece by Helen Mason Grose. Boston; New York: Houghton Mifflin Company, 1924. (Cambridge [Mass.]: The Riverside Press). 164 p., col. front.
Contents: Creeping Jenny -- The author's reading at Bixby centre -- The quilt of happiness -- Matt Milliken's improvements.
LC: S 19, '24.
PW: S 27, '24.
References: BAL 22699.

W-597   _____ The diary of a goose girl / by Kate Douglas Wiggin; with illustrations by Claude A. Shepperson. Boston; New York: Houghton, Mifflin and Company, 1902. (Cambridge, [Mass.]: The Riverside Press). 117 p., front., ill.
LC: Ap 29, '02.
PW: My 17, '02.
BLC: London: Gay & Bird, Cambridge, Mass. printed, 1902.
References: BAL 22627.

W-598   _____ Ladies-in-waiting / by Kate Douglas Wiggin; with frontispiece by Christine Tucke Curtiss. Boston; New York: Houghton Mifflin Company, 1919. (Cambridge [Mass.]: The Riverside Press). 322, [1] p., col. front.
LC: O 16, '19.
PW: N 1, '19.
BLC: London: Hodder & Stoughton, 1919.
References: BAL 22680.

W-599   _____ Love by express: a novel of California / by Kate Douglas Wiggin. [Buxton, Me.]: Privately printed by the Dorcas society of Hollis and Buxton, Maine, 1924. 120 p., photo. front. (port.).
LC: Ag 4, '24.
PW: Ag 23, '24.
References: BAL 22698.

W-600   _____ The old Peabody pew: a Christmas romance of a country church / by Kate Douglas Wiggin; with illustrations by Alice Barber Stephens. Boston; New York: Houghton, Mifflin and Company, 1907. 143 p., col. front., [5] leaves of col. plates. Designed end papers.
LC: O 12, '07.
PW: O 26, '07.
BLC: London: Archibald Constable & Co., 1907.
References:References: BAL 22644.

W-601   _____ Penelope's Irish experiences / by Kate Douglas Wiggin. Boston; New York: Houghton, Mifflin and Company, 1901. (Cambridge [Mass]: The Riverside Press). 329 p.
A sequel to *Penelope's progress*.
OSU copy is apparent later issue as BAL notes printing 1, issue 1 with 327 p. Later issues corrected omissions from final chapter.
LC: Ap 11, '01; O 30, '01.
PW: Ap 27, '01; N 16, '01.
BLC: London: Gay & Bird, 1901.
References: BAL 22625; BAL 22628 notes "Holiday Edition," 1902.

W-602   _____ Penelope's postscripts: Switzerland: Venice: Wales: Devon: home / by Kate Douglas Wiggin. Boston; New York: Houghton Mifflin Company, 1915. (Cambridge: The Riverside Press). 216, [1] p., col. front.
LC: Ag 9, '15.
PW: Ag 14, '15.
BLC: London: Hodder & Stoughton, 1915.
References: BAL 22672.

W-603   _____ Robinetta / by Kate Douglas Wiggin, Mary Findlater, Jane Findlater, Alan McAulay. Boston; New York: Houghton Mifflin Company, [1911]. (Cambridge: The Riverside Press). 330 p., col. front.
LC: Mr 17, '11.
PW: Mr 4, '11.
BLC: London: Gay & Hancock, 1911.
References: BAL 22655.

W-604   _____ The romance of a Christmas card / by Kate Douglas Wiggin; illustrated by Alice Ercle Hunt. Boston; New York: Houghton Mifflin Company, 1916. (Cambridge: The Riverside Press). 123, [1] p., col. front., [3] leaves of col. plates. Illustrated end papers.
LC: O 18, '16.
PW: O 21, '16.
BLC: London: Hodder & Stoughton, 1916.
References: BAL 22675.

W-605   _____ Rose o' the river / by Kate Douglas Wiggin; illustrated by George Wright. Boston; New York: Houghton Mifflin & Company, 1905. (Cambridge:

The Riverside Press). 176, [1] p., col. front., [9] leaves of col. plates.
LC: Je 26, '05.
PW: O 7, '05.
BLC: London: Archibald Constable & Co., 1905.
References: BAL 22636.

W-606 ____ The story of Waitstill Baxter / by Kate Douglas Wiggin; with illustrations by H. M. Brett. Boston; New York: Houghton Mifflin Company, 1913. (Cambridge, [Mass.]: The Riverside Press). 372, [1] p., col. front., [3] leaves of col. plates.
LC: O 8, '13.
PW: O 11, '13.
BLC: London: Hodder & Stoughton, 1913.
References: BAL 22668.

W-607 ____ Susanna and Sue / by Kate Douglas Wiggin; with illustrations by Alice Barber Stephens and N. C. Wyeth. Boston; New York: Houghton Mifflin Company, 1909. (Cambridge: The Riverside Press). 225, [1] p., col. front., [3] leaves of col. plates.
LC: O 15, '09.
PW: O 9, '09.
BLC: London: Hodder & Stoughton, 1909.
References: BAL 22652.

W-608 Wight, Estella. In the shelter of the little brown cottage / by Estella Wight. Lamoni, Iowa: Board of Publication of The Reorganized Church of Jesus Christ of Latter Day Saints, 1915. 320 p.
Unexamined copy: bibliographic data from OCLC, #30884767.

W-609 ____ A vineyard story / by Estella Wight. Independence, Missouri: Board of Publication of the Reorganized Church of Jesus Christ of Latter Day Saints, 1921. 384 p., [10] leaves of plates, ill.
Unexamined copy: bibliographic data from OCLC, #22011134.

W-610 Wightman, Richard, b. 1867. Soul-spur / by Richard Wightman. New York, The Century co., 1914. 204 p., photo. front.
LC: O 19, '14.

W-611 ____ The things he wrote to her / by Richard Wightman. New York: The Century Co., 1914. 108 p.
PW: Ap 4, '14.

Wilby, Agnes A. (Agnes Andrews), jt. aut. *On the trail to sunset (1912).* See **Wilby, Thomas W. (Thomas William), b. 1870, jt. aut., W-612.**

W-612 Wilby, Thomas W. (Thomas William), b. 1870. On the trail to sunset / by Thomas W. and Agnes A. Wilby; illustrated from photographs. New York: Moffat, Yard and Company, 1912. 544 p., photo. front., [15] leaves of photo. plates.

W-613 Wilcox, Ella Wheeler, 1850-1919. Kingdom of love, and, How Salvator won / by Ella Wheeler Wilcox. Chicago: W. B. Conkey Company, [c1902]. 160 p., incl. photo. front. (port.).
CWR Poems and one short story, "Dick's family," p. 147-160.
BLC: London: Gay & Bird, 1906.

W-614 Wilcox, Henry S. A strange flaw / by Henry S. Wilcox. Chicago: Thompson & Thomas, 1906. 270 p.
LC: Ag 16, '06.
Another edition: Wilcox Books Concern, 1906.

W-615 Wild, Payson S. (Payson Sibley), b. 1869. Megistotheos and my "animula vagula" / by Payson S. Wild. [Chicago]: The Chicago Literary Club, 1923. 32 p.

W-616 Wilder, Nat (Nathaniel Parker), b. 1858. A royal tragedy: when kings and savages ruled / by Nat Wilder, Jr.; illustrations by J. Hodson Redman. New York: From the Press of the Fireside Publishing Co., [c1910]. 235, [1] p., front. (map), ill. (some ports.).
LC: O 13, '10.

W-617 Wiley, George Ephraim. Southern plantation stories and sketches / by George E. Wiley; illustrations by Frank S. Dixon . . . New York: [Press of J. J. Little & Company], 1905. 127 p., front., plates.
Unexamined copy: bibliographic data from OCLC, #12417731.

W-618 Wiley, Hugh, b. 1884. Jade: and other stories / by Hugh Wiley. New York: Alfred A. Knopf, 1921. 245 p.
Contents: Jade -- Joss -- Hop -- Junk -- Tong -- Yellow dawn -- The release.
LC: N 25, '21.
BLC: London: William Heinemann, 1922.

W-619 ____ Lady Luck / by Hugh Wiley. New York: Alfred A. Knopf, 1921. 223 p.
LC: N 25, '21.

W-620 ____ Lily / by Hugh Wiley. New York: Alfred A. Knopf, 1922. 278 p.
LC: N 10, '22.

W-621 ____ The prowler / by Hugh Wiley. New York: Alfred A. Knopf, 1924. 272 p.
LC: O 24, '24.

W-622 ____ The Wildcat / by Hugh Wiley. New York: George H. Doran Company, [c1920]. 278 p.
LC: S 17, '20.
PW: S 4, '20.

W-623 Wiley, John, b. 1899. The education of Peter: a novel of the younger generation / by John Wiley. New York: Frederick A. Stokes Company, 1924. 313 p.

W-624 Wiley, Richard Taylor, b. 1856. Sim Greene: a narrative of the Whisky Insurrection: being a setting forth of the memoirs of the late David Froman, Esq. / by Richard T. Wiley. Philadelphia: The John C. Winston Company, 1906. 380 p., front., [3] leaves of plates.

Wilkins, Mary E. See **Freeman, Mary E. (Wilkins).**

W-625 Wilkins, Zora Putnam. Letters of a business woman to her daughter; and Letters of a business girl to her mother / by Zora Putnam Wilkins. Boston, Massachusetts: Marshall Jones Company, [c1923]. 151 p.

W-626 Wilkinson, Cary H. (Cary Hamilton), b. 1844. The tragedy of Baden / by Cary H. Wilkinson. New York; Washington: The Neale Publishing Company, c1906. 195 p. **AJB**

W-627 Wilkinson, Florence. The silent door / by Florence Wilkinson. New York: McClure, Phillips & Co., 1907. 436 p.
LC: Mr 9, '07.
PW: Mr 23, '07.

W-628 _____ The strength of the hills: a novel / by Florence Wilkinson. New York; London: Harper & Brothers, 1901. 395, [1] p.
PW: O 5, '01.

W-629 Will, John McArthur. Out of darkness into light: a story of the pioneer West / by John McArthur Will. Boston: The Roxburgh Publishing Company, Inc., [c1918]. 192 p., photo. front.
LC: O 1, '18.
PW: O 26, '18.

W-630 _____ The pages of life / by John McArthur Will . . . Boston: The Roxburgh Publishing Company, Inc., [c1919]. 256 p. **DLC**
LC: Ja 16, '20.
PW: Ja 31, '20.

W-631 Willacy, John G. Hidden power / by John G. Willacy. San Antonio: Passing Show Printing Co., [c1917]. 330 p. **DLC**

W-632 Willard, Charles Dwight, 1866-1914. The fall of Ulysses: an elephant story / by Charles Dwight Willard; illustrations by Frank Ver Beck. New York: George H. Doran Company, 1912. 80 p., col. front., [3] leaves of col. plates. **AZU**
PW: O 26, '12.

_____ The jack-pot. In *Argonaut stories* (1906), **A-298.**

Willard, Josiah Flynt, 1869-1907. See **Flynt, Josiah.**

W-633 Willard, Madeline Deaderick. The King's Highway: a romance of the Franciscan Order in Alta California / by Madeline Deaderick Willard. Los Angeles: Grafton Publishing Corporation, 1913. 199 p., photo. front. (port.), [1] leaf of photo. plates.

W-634 Willard, Rosseter. The senator's sweetheart / by Rosseter Willard; with an introduction by Mrs. Cushman K. Davis; illustrated by Felix Mahoney. New York: The Grafton Press, [c1903]. 266 p., col. front., [6] leaves of plates.

W-635 Willets, Gilson, b. 1869. The double cross: a romance of mystery and adventure in Mexico of to-day / by Gilson Willets; illustrations by Joseph Cummings Chase. New York: G. W. Dillingham Company, [c1910]. 370 p., col. front., [5] leaves of plates, ill.
LC: O 10, '10.
BLC: London: T. Fisher Unwin, 1910.

W-636 _____ The first law: a romance / by Gilson Willets; illustrations by Robert A. Graef. New York: G. W. Dillingham Company, [c1911]. 352 p., col. front., [3] leaves of plates.
LC: Je 13, '11.
BLC: London: T. Fisher Unwin, New York [printed], 1911.

W-637 Willett, George Henry. Trempealeau Mountain / by George Henry Willett; photographic illustrations by Dr. Eben D. Pierce. New York; Cincinnati: The Abingdon Press, [c1914]. 189 p., photo. front., [6] leaves of photo. plates.

W-638 Willey, George Franklyn, b. 1869. Soltaire: a romance of the Willey slide and the White Mountains / by George Franklyn Willey; illustrated by Hiram P. Barnes. Manchester, N. H.: New Hampshire Publishing Corporation, 1902. 143 p., front., [10] leaves of plates.
PW: F 7, '03.

W-639 Willey, Mary B. The poorhouse lark / by Mary B. Willey. New York; London: F. Tennyson Neely . . . , [1902]. 222 p. **VIC**
PW: F 7, '03.

William, William Orson. See **William, W. O.**

Williams, Alyn, Mrs. See **Williams, Anna Vernon Dorsey.**

W-640 Williams, Anna Vernon Dorsey. The spirit of the house / by Anna Dorsey Williams (Mrs. Alyn Williams). New York; London: D. Appleton and Company, 1924. 328 p.

Williams, Annabelle. Patsey's progress. In *Stockman stories* (1913), **S-956.**

W-641 Williams, B. C. (Blanche Catherine), b. 1880. Variety tales: examples of kinds of short stories / by B. C. Williams. Cincinnati: Press of Jennings and Graham, 1905. 135 p., col. front. **DLC**
Contents: Slumber song-a poem -- A nest-a story of children and birds -- A land of content-a moral story -- The disappearance of Elfinnis-a detective story -- The ghost of the marble face-a ghost story -- Something missing-a humorous New England story -- Miraculous happenings-a cyclone story -- Tony and Fluffy-a fable -- Fate or prophecy-a horror story -- A colonial fairy story -- A child of music-a boarding school story -- A trial at entertaining-a dramatic story -- Mrs. Asborn the village gossip- a dialect and burlesque story -- When the ways are three-an allegory -- Shuffling along-a character sketch -- Caught by the sea-a love story -- The adventures of Zim-an adventure story -- Double editing-a decided plot -- Only an Easter egg-a religious story -- A business enterprise-a true commercial story -- Slumber-land-a description.

W-642 Williams, Ben Ames, 1889-1953. All the brothers were valiant / by Ben Ames Williams. New York: The Macmillan Company, 1919. 204 p.
LC: My 21, '19.
BLC: London: Mills & Boon, 1920.

W-643 _____ Audacity / by Ben Ames Williams. New York: E. P. Dutton & Company, [c1924]. 205 p. "Copyright, 1920 (under the title `Toujours de l'audace')."
PW: Mr 15, '24.

W-644   Black pawl / by Ben Ames Williams. New York: E. P. Dutton & Company, [c1922]. 177 p.
LC: O 30, '22.
BLC: London: Mills & Boon, 1922.

W-645   Evered / by Ben Ames Williams. New York: E. P. Dutton & Company . . . , [c1921]. 217 p.
PW: Je 18, '21.
BLC: London: Mills & Boon, 1921.

W-646   The great accident / by Ben Ames Williams . . . New York: The Macmillan Company, 1920. 405 p.
LC: Mr 25, '20.
PW: Ap 24, '20.
BLC: London: Macmillan, 1920.

W-647   The rational hind / by Ben Ames Williams . . . New York: E. P. Dutton & Company . . . , [c1925]. 242 p.
PW: Je 13, '25.
BLC: London: Mills & Boon, 1925.

     The right whale's flukes. In *The Bellman book of fiction* (1921), **B-485.**

W-648   The sea bride / by Ben Ames Williams. New York: The Macmillan Company, 1919. 305 p.   **GZM**
LC: O 8, '19.
PW: N 1, '19.
BLC: London: Mills & Boon, 1920.

     Sheener. In *The best short stories of 1920 and the yearbook of the American short story* (1921), **B-565.**

     They grind exceeding small. In *Prize stories of 1919* (1920), **P-617.**

W-649   Thrifty stock: and other stories / by Ben Ames Williams . . . New York: E. P. Dutton & Company, [c1923]. 351 p.
Contents: Thrifty stock -- They grind exceeding small -- Old Tantrybogus -- One crowded hour -- Mine enemy's dog -- "Jeshurun waxed fat" -- Epitome -- A dream -- His honor -- The coward -- Not a drum was heard -- The man who looked like Edison -- Success -- Sheener -- The field of honor -- The unconquered -- The right whale's flukes -- Note.
LC: Jl 2, '23.
PW: Jl 21, '23.

     A use for clods. In *Short stories for class reading* (1925), **S-461.**

Williams, Blanche Colton, 1879-1944, ed. See *A book of short stories* (1918), **B-735.**

    , ed. See *Thrice told tales* (1924), **T-219.**

Williams, Caroline Field. The other kind. In *Club stories* (1915), **C-502.**

Williams, Churchill. See **Williams, Francis Churchill.**

W-650 Williams, Cora Lenore, 1865-1937. As if: a philosophical phantasy / by Cora Lenore Williams. San Francisco: Paul Elder and Company, [1914]. 64 p.

W-651 Williams, Earl Willoughby, b. 1885. The court of Belshazzar: a romance of the great captivity / by Earl Williams. Indianapolis: The Bobbs-Merrill Company, [c1918]. 352 p.

W-652 Williams, Egerton R. (Egerton Ryerson), 1873-1925. Ridolfo: the coming of the dawn: a tale of the Renaissance / by Egerton R. Williams, Jr.; with illustrations in color by Joseph C. Leyendecker. Chicago: A. C. McClurg & Co., 1906. 406 p., col. front., [3] leaves of col. plates.
LC: O 13, '06.
BLC: London: C. F. Cazenove & Son; Chicago: A. C. McClurg & Co.; Cambridge, U. S. A. [printed], 1906.

W-653 Williams, Flora (McDonald), Mrs., b. 1842. The blue cockade: a story of the confederacy / by Flora McDonald Williams. New York; Washington: The Neale Publishing Company, 1905. 381 p.
Unexamined copy: bibliographic data from OCLC, #14163165.

W-654 Williams, Francis Churchill, 1869-1945. The captain / by Churchill Williams; illustrated by Arthur I. Keller. Boston: Lothrop Publishing Company . . . , 1903. 439 p., front., [3] leaves of plates.
PW: F 14, '03.

W-655   J. Devlin-- boss: a romance of American politics / by Francis Churchill Williams; illustrated by Clifford Carlton. Boston: Lothrop Publishing Company, [c1901]. 520 p., front.
PW: Ag 10, '01.
BLC: London: Charles H. Kolly, 1901.

     Smith of "Pennsylvania." In *Stories of the colleges* (1901), **S-985.**

Williams, Frank, pseud. See **Sullivan, Francis William.**

W-656 Williams, Harper. The thing in the woods / by Harper Williams. New York: Robert McBride & Company, 1924. 291 p.   **KLG**
PW: O 18, '24.

W-657 Williams, Henry Smith, 1863-1943. The witness of the sun / by Henry Smith Williams; frontispiece by C. Lotave. Garden City, New York: Doubleday, Page & Company, 1920. 305, [1] p., col. front. (port.).
LC: S 22, '20.
PW: S 18, '20.

W-658 Williams, Herschel, b. 1874. Uncle Bob and Aunt Becky's strange adventures at the world's great exposition . . . / by Herschel Williams; 105 striking pen and ink sketches especially drawn for this work. Chicago: Laird & Lee, [c1904]. 358 p., front., ill. [Ill. by John C. Gilbert.]

W-659 Williams, Isabel Cecilia. The alchemist's secret / by Isabel Cecilia Williams. New York: P. J. Kenedy & Sons, [c1910]. 183 p.
LC: Ap 27, '10.

W-660   "Deer Jane" / by Isabel Cecilia Williams. New York: P. J. Kenedy & Sons, [c1911]. 160 p., front. [Ill. by Jos. S. Loman.]
LC: Jl 10, '11.

W-661 _____ In the crucible: tales from real life / by Isabel Cecilia Williams. New York: P. J. Kenedy & Sons . . . , [c1909]. 177 p.
Contents: Black beauty -- On the country road -- Little James -- And a little child shall lead them -- One Thanksgiving eve -- Terry -- Greater love no man hath -- Tatters -- Out of the depths -- Granny -- Their victory -- My friend the rag-picker -- Faithful Alan -- What doth it profit?
LC: My 17, '09.

W-662 Williams, Jesse Lynch, 1871-1929. The day-dreamer: being the full narrative of "The stolen story" / by Jesse Lynch Williams. New York: Charles Scribner's Sons, 1906. 326 p.
"This is a novelization of the play called the stolen story . . . In magazine form The day dreamer was called news and the man."
PW: Mr 17, '06.

W-663 _____ The girl and the game: and other college stories / by Jesse Lynch Williams . . . ; illustrated. New York: Charles Scribner's Sons, [1908]. 343 p., front., [5] leaves of plates. [Ill. by H. C. Edwards, Henry Hutt, and W. T. Smedley.] **ANC**
Contents: The girl and the game -- The college and the circus -- At the corner of Lover's Lane -- Leg pull -- Reddy Armstrong's reformation -- The advantages of a college education -- The man in the window -- What the old graduate learned -- Talks with a kid brother.
LC: My 23, '08.
PW: Je 6, '08.

W-664 _____ The married life of the Frederic Carrolls / by Jesse Lynch Williams; illustrated. New York: Charles Scribner's Sons, [1910]. 602 p., front., [7] leaves of plates. [Ill. by F. R. Gruger and William Potts.]
LC: N 30, '10.
PW: D 10, '10.

W-665 _____ My lost duchess: an idyl of the town / by Jesse Lynch Williams . . . ; with illustrations by Wallace Morgan. New York: The Century Co., 1908. 311 p., incl. 5 col. plates, front.
PW: Ap 18, '08.

W-666 _____ Not wanted / by Jesse Lynch Williams. New York: Charles Scribner's Sons, 1923. 83 p.
LC: D 4, '23.
PW: D 22, '23.

W-667 _____ Remating time / by Jesse Lynch Williams; with illustrations by Henry Raleigh. New York: Charles Scribner's Sons, 1916. 111 p., front., ill.
LC: My 3, '16.
PW: My 6, '16.

W-668 Williams, John S. (John Silas), b. 1865. The siege: a novel of love and war / by John S. Williams. New York: The Cosmopolitan Press, 1912. 410 p.
LC: N 29, '12.
PW: N 16, '12.

Williams, Margery. See **Bianco, Margery Williams, 1880-1944.**

W-669 Williams, Mary Gertrude. Alias Kitty Casey: a novel / by Mary Gertrude Williams. New York: P. J. Kenedy & Sons, [c1911]. 178 p.
LC: D 15, '11.

W-670 Williams, Michael, 1878-1950. The book of the high romance: a spiritual autobiography / by Michael Williams. New York: The Macmillan Company, 1918. 350 p. **ATO**
PW: Ap 27, '18.
New edition with new material: 1924, 406 p. Cover title: *The high romance.* **BGU**

Williams, Nathan Winslow, 1860-1925. See **Dallas, Richard, pseud.**

W-671 Williams, Neil Wynn. The electric theft / by Neil Wynn Williams. Boston: Small, Maynard & Company, 1906. 311 p.
BLC: London: Greening & Co., 1906.

W-672 Williams, Sarah Stone, *pseud.* The man from London town / by Sarah Stone Williams (Hester E. Shipley). New York; Washington: The Neale Publishing Company, 1906. 288 p.
LC: Jl 30, '06.

W-673 Williams, Sidney, 1878-1949. The body in the blue room / by Sidney Williams; frontispiece by J. Clinton Shepherd. Philadelphia: The Penn Publishing Company, 1922. 318 p., front.
LC: F 24, '22.
BLC: London: Hurst & Blackett, [1924].

W-674 _____ The eastern window / by Sidney Williams. Boston: Marshall Jones Company, 1918. 103 p.
LC: Ag 15, '18.
PW: Jl 13, '18.

W-675 _____ In the tenth moon / by Sidney Williams; illustrated by Henry Pitz. Philadelphia: The Penn Publishing Company, 1923. 325 p., front.
LC: Je 20, '23.
BLC: Hurst & Blakett, [1924].

W-676 _____ Mystery in red / by Sidney Williams. Philadelphia: The Penn Publishing Company, 1925. 320 p.
LC: Mr 13, '25.
PW: Mr 21, '25.
BLC: London: Hurst & Blackett, [1925].

W-677 _____ A reluctant Adam / by Sidney Williams. Boston; New York: Houghton Mifflin Company, 1915. (Cambridge: The Riverside Press). 316 p., front. [Ill. by R. M. Crosby.]
LC: Mr 1,'15.
PW: Mr 6, '15.

W-678 _____ An unconscious crusader / by Sidney Williams . . . Boston: Small, Maynard & Company, [c1920]. 290 p.
LC: Mr 17, '20.
PW: Ap 3, '20.

Williams, Wilbur Herschel. See **Williams, Herschel.**

W-679 [Williams, William Orson]. An old dusty's story. New York; London; [etc.]: The Abbey Press, [1901]. 272 p.
Unexamined copy: bibliographic data from NUC.
PW: D 14, '01.

W-680　Williams, Wayland Wells, 1888-1945. Family: a novel / by Wayland Wells Williams . . . New York: Frederick A. Stokes Company, 1923. 307 p., ill. (genealogy table).
LC: Mr 31, '23.
PW: Mr 31, '23.
BLC: London & New York: Andrew Melrose, [1923].

W-681　____ Goshen street: a novel / by Wayland Wells Williams . . . New York: Frederick A. Stokes Company Publishers, [c1920]. 323 p.
LC: O 1, '20.
PW: O 2, '20.

W-682　____ I, the king: the story of a rich young man / by Wayland Wells Williams. New York: Frederick A. Stokes Company, 1924. 340 p.
LC: Mr 17, '24.

W-683　____ The whirligig of time / by Wayland Wells Williams; with a frontispiece by J. Henry. New York: Frederick A. Stokes Company, [c1916]. 383 p., front.
LC: Ap 25, '16.
PW: Ap 15, '16.

W-684　Williams, Wm. Carver (William Carver). The old couple: a Christmas story / by Wm. Carver Williams. Boston: The Pinkham Press, 1921. 18 p., ill.

W-685　Williamson, Clara M. (Clara Marion Young), b. 1860. 'Neath sunny southern skies / by Clara M. Williamson. [New Orleans, La.: Press of Palfrey-Rodd-Pursell Co., Ltd.], 1908. 139 p., incl. front. [Ill. by Mrs. C. Schaeffer.]　**FDA**

W-686　Williamson, Corolin Crawford. Mary Starkweather / by Corolin Crawford Williamson. New York; London; Montreal: The Abbey Press . . . , [c1901]. 603 p., [3] leaves of plates (1 photo. port.).
PW: F 22, '02.

W-687　Williamson, N. B. (Nancy Blasdel Graves), b. 1838. Lamech / by Mrs. N. B. Williamson. San Francisco: The Whitaker & Ray Company (Incorporated) . . . , 1904. 231 p.

W-688　Williamson, Roland. The Star well: and other stories / by Roland Williamson; illustrated by the author. New York: The Knickerbocker Press, 1916. 71 p., front., [2] leaves of plates. "Reprinted through the courtesy of Maury's Magazine, The Churchman and The Christian Herald."
Contents: The Star well -- "Uncle Phil," a story from the yellow fever field -- Only a snipe.

W-689　Williamson, Thames Ross, b. 1894. Run sheep run / by Thames Williamson. Boston: Small, Maynard & Company, [c1925]. 277 p. Illustrated end papers.
PW: N 14, '25.

W-690　Willing, Clara Hunter. Gibbon's millions / by Clara Hunter Willing. [S. l.: s. n.], c1903. 112 p. **DLC**
Contents: Gibbons' millions -- The artist's cat -- A spring fancy -- A sketch in black and white / [by A. G. Willing] -- Laffin' in church / [poem by M. A. Willing].

W-691　Willoughby, Barrett. Rocking moon: a romance of Alaska / by Barrett Willoughby . . . New York; London: G. P. Putnam's Sons, 1925. ([New York]: The Knickerbocker Press). 360 p., front.
LC: Ap 4, '25.
PW: Ap 18, '25.

W-692　____ Where the sun swings north / by Barrett Willoughby. New York; London: G. P. Putnam's Sons, 1922. ([New York]: The Knickerbocker Press). 355 p.
LC: O 21, '22.

Willoughby, Florence (Barrett), Mrs. See **Willoughby, Barrett.**

W-693　Willoughby, Frank, b. 1866. For Zion's sake: a tale of real life / by Frank Willoughby. New York; Washington; Baltimore; Indianapolis; Norfolk; Des Moines: Broadway Publishing Co., [c1911]. 257 p.　**DLC**
LC: O 21, '11.
PW: D 9, 11.

W-694　____ The superman / by Frank Willoughby. New York: Authors & Publishers Corporation, 1922. 275 p.
LC: Mr 24, '23.

W-695　____ Through the needle's eye: a narrative of the restoration of the Davidic Kingdom of Israel in Palestine with Jesus Christ as King / by Frank Willoughby; based upon The bride of Christ by Emry Davis. New York: Published by the Palestine Press, 1925. 154 p.　**CBC**
LC: Ap 17, '25.

W-696　Wills, Anthony E., b. 1880. Monsieur Paul De Fere / by Anthony E. Wills. New York; London; Montreal: The Abbey Press, [c1901]. 211 p., front. (port.).
PW: S 7, '01.

W-697　Wills, Ridley. Harvey Landrum: a novel / by Ridley Wills. New York: Simon and Schuster, 1924. 271 p.　**MNU**
LC: N 25, '24.
PW: N 8, '24.

W-698　[____] Hoax. New York: George H. Doran Company, [c1922]. 297 p.

Willsie, Honoré. See **Morrow, Honoré (McCue) Willsie.**

W-699　Wilson, A. F. (Anne Florence), b. 1873. The wars of peace / by A. F. Wilson; illustrated by H. C. Ireland. Boston: Little, Brown and Company, 1903. 392 p., front., [4] leaves of plates.
PW: My 16, '03.

W-700　Wilson, Annie E. Webs of war: in white and black / by Annie E. Wilson. New York: Broadway Publishing Co., 1913. 272 p.　**LUU**
LC: O 29, '13.

W-701 Wilson, Augusta J. (Augusta Jane) Evans, 1835-1909. Devota: "J'y suis, j'y reste" / by Augusta Evans Wilson . . . ; illustrations by Stuart Travis. New York: G. W. Dillingham Co., [1907]. 122 p., front., [3] leaves of plates. Ornamental borders.
LC: Je 8, '07.
PW: Jl 13, '07.
BLC: London: T. Fisher Unwin; New York [printed], 1907.
References: BAL 22992.

W-702 _____ A speckled bird / by Augusta Evans Wilson . . . New York: G. W. Dillingham Company, [1902]. 426 p.
LC: Jl 3, '02.
PW: Ag 16, '02.
BLC: London: Hutchinson & Co., 1902. Another edition: London: T. Fisher Unwin; New York [printed], 1902.
References: BAL 22991.

Wilson, Bourdon, jt. aut. *In quest of Aztec treasure* (1911). See **Noll, Arthur Howard, 1855-1930, jt. aut., N-110.**

W-703 Wilson, C. R. (Charles Robert), b. 1852. Bear Wallow belles: a love story of the Civil War / by C. R. Wilson . . . Louisville, Ky.: R. H. Carothers, printer, [c1903]. 240 p.

W-704 Wilson, Charles Newton. Thro' the buhrs / by Charles Newton Wilson. Boston, Massachusetts: The C. M. Clark Publishing Company, [c1910]. 423 p., col. front., [8] leaves of plates. [Ill. by Edward Mason; 1 photo. by Leslie-Judge Co.]

Wilson, Charles Robert. See **Wilson, C. R.**

Wilson, Cochran. A question of bars, the story of a delayed letter. *In Golden stories* **(1909), G-285.**

W-705 Wilson, David Joshua. The New York girl in Virginia / by David J. Wilson. [Aberdeen, Md.; Bel Air, Md.: Harford Printing and Publishing Company, c1921]. 255 p., photo. ill.

Wilson, Edmund, Jr. jt. aut. *The undertaker's garland,* (1922). See **Bishop, John Peale, 1892-1944, jt. aut., B-620.**

W-706 Wilson, Grove, 1883-1954. Man of strife / by Grove Wilson. New York: Frank- Maurice, Inc., 1925. 348 p.
LC: O 22, '25.
PW: N 7, '25.

W-707 Wilson, Guy H. His beautiful life / by Guy H. Wilson. Dallas, Texas: Johnston Printing Co., 1910. 242 p., photo. front. (port.). **DLC**
LC: Mr 8, '11.

W-708 Wilson, Harmon D., 1872-1903. Troubles of a worried man, and other sketches, including a "take" of verse / by Harmon D. Wilson. Introduction by William Allen White and a biographical sketch by J. E. House. Illustrated by Albert T. Reid. Topeka, Kan.: Published by his newspaper associates [printed by Geo. A. Clark], 1903. 186 p., front., [3] leaves of plates, ill.
Contents: Preface -- Biography -- Introduction -- Troubles of a worried man -- Sketches of the ornery boy -- The observations of Knute Olafson -- The Hon. Timothy Tugbutton and his remarks -- Little "takes" of every-day verse [poems] -- In shorter meter [poems].

W-709 Wilson, Harry Leon, 1867-1939. The boss of Little Arcady / by Harry Leon Wilson . . . ; illustrated by Rose Cecil O'Neill. Boston: Lothrop Publishing Company, [1905]. 371 p., front., [3] leaves of plates.
PW: Ag 12, '05.
BLC: London: Kegan Paul & Co., 1905.

W-710 _____ Bunker Bean / by Harry Leon Wilson . . . ; illustrated by F. R. Gruger. Garden City, New York: Doubleday, Page & Company, 1913. 307, [1] p., front., [7] leaves of plates.
LC: Ja 17, '13.
PW: Ja 18, '13.
BLC: London: John Lane, 1919.

W-711 _____ Cousin Jane / by Harry Leon Wilson . . . New York: Cosmopolitan Book Corporation, 1925. 388 p.
LC: O 31, '25.
PW: N 21, '25.
BLC: London: Hodder & Stoughton, [1926].

W-712 _____ Ewing's lady / by Harry Leon Wilson . . . New York: D. Appleton and Company, 1907. 316 p. **GZM**
LC: N 22, '07.
PW: N 23, '07.

_____ Flora and Fauna. *In The best short stories of 1923 and the yearbook of the American short story* **(1924), B-568.**

W-713 _____ The lions of the Lord: a tale of the old West / by Harry Leon Wilson; illustrated by Rose Cecil O'Neill. Boston: Lothrop Publishing Company, [1903]. 520 p., front., [5] leaves of plates.
PW: Je 13, '03.

W-714 _____ Ma Pettengill / by Harry Leon Wilson. Garden City, N. Y.: Doubleday, Page & Company, 1919. 324 p.
LC: Ap 10, '19.
PW: Ap 5, '19.
BLC: London: John Lane, [1919].

W-715 _____ Ma Pettengill talks / by Harry Leon Wilson. Garden City, New York: Garden City Publishing Co., Inc., 1923. 118 p.
(Famous authors series).

W-716 _____ The man from home: a novel / by Harry Leon Wilson . . . ; illustrated by C. H. Taffs. New York; London: D. Appleton and Company, 1915. 307, [1] p., front., [3] leaves of plates.
"Founded upon the play by N. Booth Tarkington and Harry Leon Wilson."
LC: Ap 30, '15.
PW: My 1, '15.

W-717 _____ Merton of the movies / by Harry Leon Wilson. Garden City, N. Y.; Toronto: Doubleday, Page & Company, 1922. 335 p.
LC: My 11, '22.
PW: Ap 15, '22.
BLC: London: John Lane, [1922]. Deluxe theatre edition: containing six full-page illustrations from the play, 1923, [c1922].

W-718 _____ Oh, doctor!: a novel / by Harry Leon Wilson . . . ; with illustrations by Henry Raleigh. New York: Cosmopolitan Book Corporation, 1923. 384 p., front., [3] leaves of plates.
LC: S 26, '23.
PW: O 13, '23. .
BLC: London: John Lane, 1923.

W-719 _____ Professor how could you!: a novel / by Harry Leon Wilson . . . New York: Cosmopolitan Book Corporation, 1924. 340 p.
LC: O 9, '24.
PW: O 11, '24.
BLC: London: John Lane, 1925.

W-720 _____ Ruggles of Red Gap / by Harry Leon Wilson; illustrated by F. R. Gruger. Garden City, New York: Doubleday, Page & Company, 1915. 371 p., front., [7] leaves of plates.
LC Mr 30, '15.
PW: Ap 3, '15.
BLC: London: John Lane, Garden City, N. Y. printed, 1917.

W-721 _____ The seeker / by Harry Leon Wilson . . . ; illustrated by Rose Cecil O'Neill. New York: Doubleday, Page & Company, 1904. 341 p., front., [3] leaves of plates, ill.
PW: Ag 27, '04.
BLC: London: William Heinemann, New York printed, 1905.

W-722 _____ Somewhere in Red Gap / by Harry Leon Wilson; illustrated by John R. Neill, F. R. Gruger and Henry Raleigh. Garden City, New York: Doubleday, Page & Company, 1916. 408 p., front., [7] leaves of plates.
LC: S 30, '16.
PW: S 30, '16.
BLC: London: Curtis Brown, New York printed, 1916.

W-723 _____ The spenders: a tale of the third generation / by Harry Leon Wilson; illustrated by O'Neill Latham. Boston: Lothrop Publishing Company, [1902]. 512 p., front., [5] leaves of plates.
PW: Je 14, '02.
BLC: London: Charles H. Kelly, 1902.

_____, contributor. See The sturdy oak (1917), S-1101.

W-724 _____ The wrong twin / by Harry Leon Wilson; illustrated by Frederic R. Gruger. Garden City, New York; Toronto: Doubleday, Page & Company, 1921. 361, [1] p., front., [3] leaves of plates.
LC: Ap 28, '21.
PW: Ap 2, '21.
BLC: London: John Lane, [1921].

W-725 Wilson, John Fleming, 1877-1922. Across the latitudes / by John Fleming Wilson; illustrated. Boston: Little, Brown and Company, 1911. 376 p., front., [6] leaves of plates. [Ill. by S. M. Chase, Anton Fischer, Charles Sarka, Henry Reuterdahl, and Gerrit A. Beneker.]
Contents: Chief Engineer Michael O'Rourke -- The unwilling war correspondent -- The bad egg -- Neighbors -- The schooner Mary E. Foster: guardian -- T. Haldane's bequest -- The oldest journalist in the South seas -- Strange ports -- James Galbraith, able-bodied seaman -- The voice of authority -- The dog -- A periodical proselyte.
LC: O 3, '11.
PW: O 14, '11.

_____ The amateur revolutionist. In Argonaut stories (1906), A-298.

W-726 _____ The land claimers / by John Fleming Wilson; with illustrations by Arthur E. Becher. Boston: Little, Brown and Company, 1911. 291 p., front., [3] leaves of plates.
LC: Ap 26, '11.
PW: Ap 15, '11.

W-727 _____ The man who came back / by John Fleming Wilson. New York: Sturgis & Walton Company, 1912. 152 p., front. [Ill. by M. L. Bracker.]
LC: O 31, '12.
PW: N 16, '12.

W-728 _____ The master key / by John Fleming Wilson; illustrated with scenes from the photo play produced and copyrighted by the Universal Film Manufacturing Company. New York: Grosset & Dunlap, [c1915]. 312 p., photo. front., [7] leaves of photo. plates. Plates (except frontispiece) printed on both sides.
LC: Ap 17, '15.
PW: Je 5, '15.

W-729 _____ The princess of Sorry Valley / by John Fleming Wilson . . . New York: Sturgis & Walton Company, 1913. 302 p.
LC: Je 23, '13.

W-730 _____ Somewhere at sea: and other tales / by John Fleming Wilson; with an introduction by Robert H. Davis; and an appreciation by Raymond Blathwayt. New York: E. P. Dutton & Company, [c1923]. 423 p.
Contents: Somewhere at sea -- The admiral of the Ooze -- The great Arctic handicap -- The story of Gunderson -- The saving sense -- Ninety days -- Junk -- The business of going to sea -- Number 1100 -- Creation reef -- David Mackleby -- Commodore Erroll's subscription.
LC: Ja 7, '24.
BLC: London: J.M. Dent & Sons, 1924.

_____ Tad Sheldon, second-class scout. In A book of narratives (1917), B-734.

W-731 Wilson, Joseph Erwin. The servers, or, "In business for Christ, why not?" / by Joseph Erwin Wilson . . . . [Houston, Tex., Mercules Printing & Book Co., c1919.] 397 p.　　　　　　**NYP**

W-732 Wilson, Joseph Kennard, 1852-1923. Longcove doings / by Joseph Kennard Wilson. Boston; Chicago: United Society Christian Endeavor, [c1917]. 185 p.

Wilson, K. A maker of violins. In Seattle Writers' Club. Tillicum tales (1907), S-248.

W-733 Wilson, Margaret, b. 1882. The able McLaughlins / by Margaret Wilson. New York; London: Harper & Brothers, publishers, [c1923]. 262, [1] p.
LC: S 27, '23.
PW: O 13, '23.
BLC: London: John Long, 1923.

W-734 _____ The Kenworthys / by Margaret Wilson. New York; London: Harper & Brothers, 1925. 385 p.
LC: Ag 17, '25.
PW: Ag 22, '25.

Wilson, Margaret Adelaide. The perfect interval. In *The Bellman book of fiction* (1921), **B-485.**

W-735 Wilson, Olivia Lovell. Janita's dower / by Olivia Lovell Wilson. New York: The Abbey Press, [1902]. 210 p.
Unexamined copy: bibliographic data from OCLC, #26883152.
PW: F 7, '03.

Wilson, Richard Henry, 1870-1948. See **Fisguill, Richard, pseud.**

W-736 Wilson, Samuel Graham, 1858-1916. Mariam: a romance of Persia / by Samuel Graham Wilson. New York; Boston; Chicago: American Tract Society, [c1906]. 122 p., front., [13] leaves of plates.
PW: O 20, '06.

W-737 Wilson, Thos. H. (Thomas Herod), b. 1876. From the throttle to the throne: a railroad, hunting, love and religious romance / by Thos. H. Wilson. Springfield, Mo.: The Inland Printing and Binding Co., 1908. 281 p., photo. front.

W-738 Wilson, William R. A. (William Robert Anthony), 1870-1911. A knot of blue / by William R. A. Wilson . . . ; with illustrations by Charles Grunwald. Boston: Little, Brown and Company, 1905. 355 p., front., [3] leaves of plates.
PW: My 4, '07.

W-739 _____ A rose of Normandy / by William R. A. Wilson; illustrated by Ch. Grunwald. Boston: Little, Brown and Company, 1903. 378 p., front., [5] leaves of plates.
PW: Ap 25, '03.

W-740 Wilson, William Thomas. For the love of Lady Margaret: a romance of the lost colony / by William Thomas Wilson. Charlotte, N. C.: Stone & Barringer Company, 1908. 305 p., front., [4] leaves of plates. [Ill. by Rita Carter.]

W-741 Wilson, Wood Levette. The end of dreams / by Wood Levette Wilson; illustrations by A. G. Learned. New York: Mitchell Kennerley, [c1909]. 348 p., front., [4] leaves of plates.
LC: D 15, '09.

W-742 Wilt, A. M. Sinclair. Head winds / A. M. Sinclair Wilt. New York: Duffield and Company, 1923. 233 p.
LC: N 22, '23.

W-743 Wimberly, C. F. (Charles Franklin), 1866-1946. The vulture's claw: a tale of rural life / by C. F. Wimberly . . . New York: R. F. Fenno & Company, [c1910]. 356 p., front., [5] leaves of photo. plates.
LC: N 17, '10.

W-744 Winchester, Paul, 1851-1932. Around the throne: sketches of Washington society during a recent administration / reported by Paul Winchester. Baltimore: B. G. Eichelberger, 1902. 187 p. **NYP**

W-745 Winchevsky, Morris, 1856-1932, *pseud.* Stories of the struggle / by Morris Winchevsky [pseud.]. Chicago: Charles H. Kerr & Company, 1908. 170 p.
Partly reprinted from various periodicals.
Contents: Why he did it -- Grishka's romance -- Martinelli's marriage -- He, she and it -- Communism a failure -- The growling editor -- The knout and the fog -- Malek's friend -- Cranky old Ike -- The prince of freedom -- The man lazy on principle -- Eck-ke -- Eliakum Zunser -- The blues versus the reds -- A persevering woman.

W-746 Wind, G. L. (Gerhard Lewis), b. 1896. Natalie / by G. L. Wind . . . ; with frontispiece by the author. Milwaukee: Northwestern Publishing House Print, 1925. 210 p., front.
LC: D 1, '25.

Windle, Louise F. Verdict rendered. In *The best college short stories, 1917-18* (1919), **B-557.**

W-747 Wing, George Clary, b. 1848. The pharos, or, John Bubb's jour / by George Clary Wing. Cleveland, Ohio: [George Clary Wing, c1919]. 80 p. **CWR**

W-748 Wing, J. Thurber (Jefferson Thurber), b. 1892. Taliput leaves in the path of the sunrise / by J. Thurber Wing, Jr.; illustrated with photographs by the author. New York: Mitchell Kennerley, 1921. 191 p., photo. front., [23] leaves of photo. plates.

W-749 Winger, F. S. (Frank Stover), b. 1865. The wizard of the island, or, The vindication of Prof. Waldinger / by F. S. Winger. -- 1st ed. -- Chicago, Illinois: Winger Publishing Company, 1917. 160 p., front., ill.
LC: Je 15, '17.

W-750 Winget, D. H. (De Witt Harris), b. 1850. Love and a limosene: a romance of today / by D. H. Winget . . . Clinton, Iowa: [Press of the Merry War], December, 1911. 128 p., [1] leaf of photo. plates (port.).
Cover title: Love and a limousine.

W-751 Winn, Mary Polk. The law and the letter: a story of the province of Louisiana / by Mary Polk Winn and Margaret Hannis. New York; Washington: The Neale Publishing Company, 1907. 184 p., front., [4] leaves of plates. [Ill. by Geo. E. Hausmann.]

W-752 _____ A master of the inner court / by Mary Polk Winn . . . New York City: Broadway Publishing Co., [c1915]. 182 p., front. [Ill. by Benjamin L. Robinson.] **DLC**
LC: Ja 24, '16.

W-753　Winship, Glen B. (Glen Brion). Volonor / by Glen
B. Winship. New York: Thomas Seltzer, 1925.
313 p. Illustrated end papers.
PW: S 19, '25.

W-754　Winslow, Belle Hagen, 1871-1956. Where man is
king / by Belle Hagen Winslow . . . Minneapolis,
Minn.: Augsburg Publishing House, 1921. 266 p.

W-755　____ The white dawn / Belle Hagen Winslow.
Minneapolis, Minn.: Augsburg Publishing House,
1920. 261 p.　　　　　　　　　　　　　　**BSF**
LC: F 1, '21.

W-756　Winslow, Elizabeth Bruce R. Rosamond of
Monterre: a Canadian pastoral / by Elizabeth Bruce
R. Winslow. Boston: The Four Seas Company,
1923. 102 p., front.
LC: Ag 6, '23.

W-757　Winslow, Helen M. (Helen Maria), 1851-1938.
Concerning Polly and some others / by Helen M.
Winslow . . . ; illustrated by Charles Copeland.
Boston: Lee and Shepard, 1902. 359 p., front., [5]
leaves of plates.
PW: S 13, '02.

____ Peggy at Spinster Farm. See **Winslow, Helen
M. (Helen Maria), 1851-1938.** *Spinster farm*
(1908), W-760.

W-758　____ The pleasuring of Susan Smith / by Helen M.
Winslow . . . ; illustrated by Jessie Gillespie. Boston:
L. C. Page & Company, 1912. 203 p., front., [7]
leaves of plates.　　　　　　　　　　　　**CLE**
LC: Je 20, '12.
PW: Jl 6, '12.
BLC: London: Sir Isaac Pitman & Sons, Boston, U.
S. A. [printed], 1912.

W-759　____ The president of Quex: a woman's club story /
by Helen M. Winslow . . . ; illustrated by W. L.
Jacobs. Boston: Lothrop, Lee & Shepard Co.,
[1906]. 306 p., front., [15] leaves of plates.
LC: O 8, '06.
PW: O 20, '06.

W-760　____ Spinster Farm / by Helen M. Winslow . . . ;
illustrated from photographs by Mary G. Huntsman.
Boston: L. C. Page & Company, 1908. 277 p.,
front., [15] leaves of plates.
First impression issued with variant title page: *Peggy
at Spinster farm.*
LC: My 8, '08.
PW: My 23, '08.

W-761　____ A woman for mayor: a novel of to-day / by
Helen M. Winslow . . . ; frontispiece by Walter Dean
Goldbeck. Chicago: The Reilly & Britton Co., 1909.
342 p., col. front.
LC: Je 14, '09.
PW: Jl 3, '09.

Winslow, Rose Guggenheim. See **Burr, Jane,
pseud.**

W-762　Winslow, Stanton. A southern girl / by Stanton
Winslow. San Francisco: The Whitaker & Ray
Company, Incorporated, 1903. 247 p.
PW: F 13, '04.

Winslow, Thyra Samter, 1893-1961. Her own room.
In *More aces* **(1925), M-962.**

____ A love affair. **In** *Aces* **(1924), A-42.**

W-763　____ Picture frames / Thyra Samter Winslow. New
York: Alfred A. Knopf, 1923. 324 p. Designed end
papers.
Contents: Little Emma -- Grandma -- Mamie Carpenter -- A cycle of
Manhattan -- Amy's story -- City folks -- Indian summer -- A love
affair -- Birthday -- Corinna and her man -- The end of Anna.
LC: Ap 25, '22.
BLC: London: Constable & Co.; printed in U. S.
A., 1924.

W-764　Winslow, William Henry, 1840-1917. Naval lads and
lassies in war with Dixie / by William Henry
Winslow . . . Boston, Massachusetts: The C. M.
Clark Publishing Co., [c1911]. 226 p., col. front.
[Ill. by D. S. Ross.]　　　　　　　　　　　**BRL**
LC: Mr 28, '12.

W-765　____ The sea letter: a mystery of Martha's
Vineyard / by William Henry Winslow; illustrated.
Boston: Henry A. Dickerman & Son, [c1901].
336 p., front., [17] leaves of plates. [Ill. by H. S.
Clark.]
LC: O 16, '01.
PW: O 12, '01; D 7, '01.

W-766　____ Southern buds and sons of war / by William
Henry Winslow . . . Boston, Mass., U. S. A.: The
C. M. Clark Publishing Co., 1907. 279 p., front.,
[9] leaves of plates. [Ill. by John Goss.]
PW: D 21, '07.

W-767　Winston, Annie Steger. Memoirs of a child / by
Annie Steger Winston. New York; London; Bombay:
Longmans, Green, and Co., 1903. 169 p.　　**EYP**

W-768　Winston, Caddie, b. 1863. The little house by the
way / by Caddie Winston; illustrated by Mary
McNaughton. [Palestine, Texas: Press of the
Evening Record, c1912]. 36 p., front., [5] leaves of
plates.　　　　　　　　　　　　　　　　　**DLC**

W-769　Winston, N. B. (Nannie B.) The grace of orders / by
N. B. Winston. New York; London; Montreal: The
Abbey Press, [c1901]. 334 p.

W-770　Winter, Alice Ames, 1865-1944. Jewel weed / by
Alice Ames Winter . . . ; with illustrations by
Harrison Fisher. Indianapolis: The Bobbs-Merrill
Company, [c1906]. 434 p., front., [5] leaves of
plates.
LC: O 8, '06.
PW: N 3, '06.

W-771　____ The prize to the hardy / by Alice Winter; with
drawings by R. M. Crosby. Indianapolis:
Bobbs-Merrill Company, [c1905]. 347 p., front., [3]
leaves of plates.
PW: Mr 4, '05.

W-772 Winter, Charles E. (Charles Edward), 1870-1948.
Ben Warman / by Charles E. Winter. [New York]:
Printed for the author by J. J. Little & Ives Company,
1917. 331 p.
LC: Ag 29, '17.

W-773 ____ Grandon of Sierra / Charles E. Winter;
illustrated by Hudson. N. Y.: Broadway Publishing
Co., [c1907]. 458 p.
OSU copy lacks ills.; LC reports: front., plates.
LC: Je 8, '07.
Another edition: New York: printed by J. J. Little &
Ives Co., [c1907]. OSU copy lacks ills.; LC reports:
imperfect: lacking illustrations.
Cover title: Grandon of Sierra: a story of the new
West.

W-774 Winter, Louise. Hearts aflame / by Louise Winter;
illustrated by Archie Gunn. New York; London:
The Smart Set Publishing Co., 1903. 230 p., incl.
front., [5] leaves of plates.
PW: S 5, '03.

W-775 Winter, William West, 1881-1940. The boss of
Eagle's Nest: a western story / by William West
Winter. New York: Chelsea House, [c1925]. 319 p.
LC: F 18, '25.
PW: F 21, '25.

W-776 ____ Louisiana Lou: a western story / by William
West Winter . . . New York City: Chelsea House,
[c1922]. 312 p., incl. front. [Ill. by Edgar F.
Wittmack.]
LC: N 10, '22.
PW: F 24, '23.
BLC: London: Hutchinson & Co., [1924].

W-777 ____ Millions in motors: a big business story / by
William West Winter . . . New York City: Chelsea
House, [c1924]. 312 p.
LC: Ja 21, '24.
PW: Ja 26, '24.

W-778 ____ Quemado: a western story / by William West
Winter . . . New York City: Chelsea House,
[c1923]. 307 p.
LC: Jl 5, '23.
BLC: London: Hutchinson & Co., [1925].

W-779 ____ The winner / by William Winter. Indianapolis:
The Bobbs-Merrill Company, [c1915]. 295 p., front.
LC: Ag 30, '15.
PW: S 4, '15.

Winter Evening Reading Club. See The Secret of
Table Rock (1904), S-267.

W-780 Winthrop, Theodore, 1828-1861. Mr. Waddy's
return / by Theodore Winthrop; edited by Burton E.
Stevenson. New York: Henry Holt and Company,
1904. 278 p.
LC: O 21, '04.
PW: N 5, '04.
References: BAL 23174.

W-781 Wise, John S. (John Sergeant), 1846-1913. The
lion's skin: a historical novel and a novel history / by
John S. Wise . . . New York: Doubleday, Page &
Company, 1905. 404 p.
PW: Mr 11, '05.

W-782 [Wise, Thomas A. (Thomas Alfred)], 1865-1928. A
gentleman from Mississippi: a novel / founded on the
popular play of the same title produced under the
management of Wm. A. Brady and Jos. R. Grismer.
New York: J. S. Ogilvie Publishing Company,
[c1909]. 189 p., front., [7] leaves of plates. First
published in the Question, 1909, under title: A
gentleman from Mississippi, by Thomas A. Wise;
novelized from the play by Frederick R. Toombs.

W-783 Wishar, John Herman. The transformation / by John
Herman Wishar; photographic studies by X. O.
Howe. San Francisco, Cal.: The Reynard Press,
July, 1911. 129 p., incl. 2 photo. plates.

Wister, Owen, 1860-1938. Extra dry. In
Representative American short stories (1923), R-175.

W-784 ____ How doth the simple spelling bee / by Owen
Wister; with illustrations by F. R. Gruger. New
York: The Macmillan Company; London: The
Macmillan Co., Ltd., 1907. 99 p., front., [6] leaves
of plates.
PW: Mr 9, '07.

W-785 ____ Lady Baltimore / by Owen Wister . . . ; with
illustrations by Vernon Howe Bailey and Lester
Ralph. New York; London: The Macmillan
Company, 1906. 406 p., incl. 12 plates, front., ill.
PW: Ap 14, '06.

W-786 ____ Members of the family / by Owen Wister; with
illustrations by H. T. Dunn. New York: The
Macmillan Company, 1911. 317 p., front., [11]
leaves of plates, music.
LC: My 11, '11.
BLC: London: Macmillan, 1911.

____ Mother. In A house party (1901), H-903.

W-787 ____ Mother / by Owen Wister . . . ; illustrations &
decorations by John Rae. New York: Dodd, Mead
& Company, 1907. 95 p., incl. col. front., incl. 6
plates (some col.), ill.
"In 1901, this story appeared anonymously as the
ninth of a sequence of short stories by various
authors, in a volume entitled A house party. It has
been slightly remodelled for separate publication."
LC: O 10, '07.

____ Philosophy 4. In Stories of the colleges
(1901), S-985.

W-788 ____ Philosophy 4: a story of Harvard University /
by Owen Wister . . . New York: The Macmillan
Company; London: Macmillan & Co., Ltd., 1903.
95 p., photo. front. (port.), [2] leaves of plates. [Ill.
by Seymour M. Stone.] Designed end papers.
(Little novels by favourite authors).
PW: My 23, '03.

W-789   ____ The Virginian: a horseman of the plains / by Owen Wister . . . ; with illustrations by Arthur I. Keller. New York: The Macmillan Company; London: Macmillan Co., Ltd., 1902. 504 p., front., [7] leaves of plates.
PW: Je 21, '02.

W-790   Witherspoon, Halliday, *pseud.* Liverpool Jarge / Halliday Witherspoon [pseud.]. [Boston: Square Rigger Co., c1922.] [120] p.   **BUF**

W-791   Wittigschlager, Wilhelmina. Minna: wife of the young rabbi: a novel / by Wilhelmina Wittigschlager; drawings by W. Herbert Dunton. New York: Consolidated Retail Booksellers, 1905. 345 p., front., [3] leaves of plates.
PW: D 9, '05.

W-792   Witwer, H. C. (Harry Charles), 1890-1929. Alex the great / by H. C. Witwer . . . ; illustrated by Arthur William Brown. Boston: Small, Maynard & Company, [c1919]. 313 p., front., [6] leaves of plates.
LC: O 3, '19.

____, contributor. See *Bobbed hair* (1925), B-700.

W-793   ____ Fighting back: a sequel to "The leather pushers" / by H. C. Witwer . . . ; illustrated with scenes from the photoplay The Universal-Jewel series. New York: Grosset & Dunlap, [c1924]. 339 p., photo. front., [7] leaves of photo. plates.
LC: O 16, '24.

W-794   ____ Fighting blood / by H. C. Witwer. New York; London: G. P. Putnam's Sons, 1923. (New York: The Knickerbocker Press). 377 p.
LC: Mr 27, '23.
PW: Mr 31, '23.

W-795   ____ From baseball to Boches / by H. C. Witwer; illustrated from drawings by F. R. Gruger and Arthur William Brown. Boston: Small, Maynard & Company, [1918]. 366 p., front., [3] leaves of plates.
LC: S 26, '18.

W-796   ____ Kid Scanlan / by H. C. Witwer . . . Boston: Small, Maynard & Company, [c1920]. 394 p.
LC: Je 24, '20.
PW: Je 12, '20.

W-797   ____ The leather pushers / by H. C. Witwer. New York; London: G. P. Putnam's Sons, [c1921]. ([New York]: The Knickerbocker Press). 341 p.
LC: O 27, '21.

W-798   ____ Love and learn: the story of a telephone girl who loved not too well but wisely / by H. C. Witwer . . . New York; London: G. P. Putnam's Sons, 1924. 332 p.
Unexamined copy: bibliographic data from OCLC, #368249.
LC: N 22, '24.
PW: Ja 31, '25.

W-799   ____ The rubyiat of a freshman / by H. C. Witwer. Chicago: The Collegiate World Publishing Company, [c1921]. 62 p., ill.   **MNU**

W-800   ____ "A smile a minute" / by H. C. Witwer; illustrated from drawings by F. R. Gruger and Arthur W. Brown. Boston: Small, Maynard & Company, [c1919]. 378 p., front., [8] leaves of plates.
LC: Je 23, '19.

W-801   ____ There's no base like home / by H. C. Witwer; illustrated by Arthur William Brown. Garden City, N. Y.: Doubleday, Page & Company, 1920. 284 p., front., [7] leaves of plates.
LC: Je 11, '20.
PW: My 29, '20.

____ Two stones with one bird. In *The Sporting spirit* (1925), S-771.

W-802   Wolcott, Geneva V. Rings of smoke / by Geneva V. Wolcott. Wilmington, Del.: The Electric Press, 1902. 69 p., front. [Ill. by Heisler.]   **DLC**

W-803   Wolcott, Laura, d. 1916. A gray dream and other stories of New England life: two volumes in one / by Laura Wolcott. New Haven: Yale University Press; London: Humphrey Mulford: Oxford University Press, 1918. 288 p. Paged continuously. Each volume with added t. p.; first added t. p. reads: A gray dream; second added t. p. reads: The heart of a child. Reprinted in part from various periodicals.
Contents: V. 1. A gray dream: The embarrassment of years -- Rachel Eliot -- Emilia -- Grandmother -- A gray dream -- A New England lady -- The story of the two Betsys -- A dominant mother -- Miss "Dassah's philosophy -- The wooing of Dangerfield Clay -- A New England festival. V. 2. The heart of a child: The child's Christmas Eve -- The child's Christmas -- The child's two mysteries -- The child's Eden -- How Dickon climbed with a hoe -- How Dickon made a bird's nest -- Dickon goes a-fishing -- Grandmother's cosset-lamb story.
LC: D 23, '18.

W-804   ____ Maddalena's day: and other sketches / by Laura Wolcott. New Haven: Yale University Press; London: Humphrey Milford: Oxford University Press, 1920. 134 p.
"Six of the sketches in this volume appeared formerly in the columns of the New York evening post and the Springfield republican."
Contents: Out of the present: Maddalena's day -- Our knight of the lagoons -- A corner of Venice -- The old custode at Lucca -- The spell of Pisa -- A footpath in Provence -- November by the North Sea -- Across the Centuries --   On donkey-back to Cape Spartel. Out of the past: The abbey's legend -- The priest's dilemma -- The iniquity of Midas -- A brief for Mistress Socrates -- Cophetua and the beggar-maid.
LC: D 21, '20.

W-805   Wolf, Emma, 1865-1932. Fulfillment: a California novel / by Emma Wolf. New York: Henry Holt and Company, 1916. 397 p.
PW: Ap 1, '16.

Wolfe, E. D., jt. aut. *The redemption of Cardus* (1914). See **Wolfe, W. F., jt. aut., W-807.**

W-806   Wolfe, J. M. (John Marion). Bessie of Brandenburg / by J. M. Wolfe. Boston: The Roxburgh Publishing Company, 1917. 180 p., photo. front.   **DLC**

W-807   Wolfe, W. F. The redemption of Cardus / by W. F. and E. D. Wolfe. Columbus, Ohio: F. J. Heer Printing Co., 1914. 317 p. Designed end papers.

W-808   Wolfenstein, Martha, 1869-1906. Idyls of the Gass / by Martha Wolfenstein. Philadelphia: The Jewish Publication Society of America, 1901. 295 p.
PW: D 14, '01.

W-809   ____ A renegade: and other tales / by Martha Wolfenstein . . . Philadelphia: The Jewish Publication Society of America, 1905. 322 p. Partly reprinted from various periodicals.
Contents: I. A renegade -- II. Dovid and Resel -- III. Lobelè Shlemiel -- IV. A sinner in Isreal -- V. Nittel-nacht -- VI. A judgment of Solomon -- VII. A goy in the good place -- VIII. Genendel the pious -- IX. A monk from the ghetto -- X. Grandmother speaks: Chayah -- XI. Grandmother speaks: Our friend -- XII. Babette -- XIII. The beast.
PW: D 23, '05.

W-810   Wolff, Perlita. Ezra / by Perlita Wolff. Boston: Reid Publishing Company, 1911. 240 p.   **DLC**

W-811   Wolff, William Almon, 1885-1933. Behind the screen: hero--Robert Lansing: the girl--Mary Brewster: the villain--Jim Hazzard: with an exceptionally strong company / by William Almon Wolff; illustrations by Fred J. Arting. Chicago: A. C. McClurg & Co., 1916. 320, [1] p., front., ill.   **EEM**
LC: Ap 28, '16.
PW: My 13, '16.

   ____ The captain. In *The Sporting spirit* (1925), **S-771.**

W-812   ____ The path of gold / by William Almon Wolff; illustrations by C. B. Falls. New York: Reynolds Publishing Company, Inc., 1920. 302 p., front., ill.
LC: D 4, '20.
PW: Ap 30, '21.

W-813   ____ The show-off: a novel / by William Almon Wolff; from the play by George Kelly. Boston: Little, Brown and Company, 1924. 308 p.
LC: O 21, '24.
PW: O 25, '24.

W-814   ____ Sold south / by William Almon Wolff. New York; London: G. P. Putnam's Sons, 1921. ([New York]: The Knickerbocker Press). 330 p.
LC: O 31, '21.
PW: O 22, '21.

W-815   Wolfrom, Anna. A romance of Wolf Hollow / by Anna Wolfrom. Boston: The Gorham Press, 1902. 63 p., front., [5] leaves of plates.   **DLC**

W-816   Wonder, William, 1829-1911. Reciprocity: (social and economic): in the thirtieth century, the coming co-operative age: a forecast of the world's future / by William Wonder. New York: The Cochrane Publishing Company . . . , 1909. 217 p., front.
At head of title: For thinking people.

W-817   Wonderly, W. Carey (William Carey), b. 1885. The world to live in / by W. Carey Wonderly. New

York: Moffat, Yard & Company, 1918. 361 p.   **PUL**

W-818   Wood, Charles S. (Charles Seely), 1845-1912. Christmas at Big Moose Falls / by Charles S. Wood. Boston: Richard G. Badger, [c1911]. ([Boston, U. S. A.]: The Gorham Press). 63 p.   **OSU, BRL**
LC: O 20, '11.
PW: O 28, '11.

W-819   ____ "Don't give up the ship!" / by Charles S. Wood; illustrated by Frank T. Merrill. New York: The Macmillan Company, 1912. 314 p., col. front., [7] leaves of plates.
LC: S 12, '12.

   Wood, Clement, 1888-1950. The case of Doctor Ford. In *As we are* (1923), A-325.

   ____ The coffin. In *The best short stories of 1922 and the yearbook of the American short story* (1923), **B-567.**

W-820   ____ Folly / by Clement Wood . . . Boston: Small, Maynard & Company, [c1925]. 300 p.
LC: O 1, '25.
PW: O 24, '25.

W-821   ____ Mountain: a novel / by Clement Wood . . . New York: E. P. Dutton & Company . . . , [c1920]. 355 p.
LC: My 20, '20.
PW: Je 26, '20.

W-822   ____ Nigger: a novel / by Clement Wood . . . New York: E. P. Dutton & Company . . . , [c1922]. 232 p.
LC: O 30, '22.
PW: O 21, '22.

W-823   Wood, Edith Elmer, 1871-1945. Shoulder-straps and sun-bonnets / by Edith Elmer Wood. New York: Henry Holt and Company, 1901. 317 p.
Most of the stories originally published in various magazines.
Contents: The real Raleigh Kent -- What woman mars woman mends -- Martha Ellen at the Chicago exposition --The angel of the Mizzentop -- When Greek meets Greek -- Mam'selle Célestine's visitors -- Seesaw: a romance in relays -- Waiting orders -- The other point of view -- Geraldine -- A sentimental strategist -- Payment in full -- That cranberry crop -- The defection of Dorothy -- Not in the signal code: a fable for captains.

W-824   ____ The spirit of the service / by Edith Elmer Wood; illustrated by Rufus F. Zogbaum. New York: The Macmillan Company; London: Macmillan & Co. Ltd., 1903. 334 p., front., [5] leaves of plates.   **LUU**

   Wood, Emma Amanda Tanner. See **Cunningham, Caroline.**

W-825   Wood, Eric. The Flaming Cross of Santa Marta / by Eric Wood. New York; London: D. Appleton and Company, 1923. 256 p., front. [Ill. by A. D. Rahn.]
LC: My 2, '23.
PW: Je 9, '23.

W-826   Wood, Eugene, 1860-1923. Back home / by Eugene Wood; illustrated by A. B. Frost. New York:

McClure, Phillips & Co., 1905. 286 p., front., [7] leaves of plates.
Contents: Introduction -- The old red school-house -- The Sabbath-school -- The revolving year -- The swimming-hole -- The firemen's tournament -- The devouring element -- Circus day -- The county fair -- Christmas back home.
PW: S 30, '05.

W-827 ____ Folks back home / by Eugene Wood. New York: The McClure Company, 1908. 328 p.
Contents: The seal of the covenant -- The lost day -- An Indian summer love story -- The seventh trumpet -- M'Ree Hutchins' husband -- The warning -- The elopement -- The fictional mind -- The makin's of Abel Horn -- The love story of Robert Prouty -- The days of his separation -- That about Laura Hornbaker -- Stars in his crown.
PW: Mr 14, '08.

W-828 ____ Our town / by Eugene Wood . . . ; illustrated by J. R. Shaver and Horace Taylor. Boston: Richard G. Badger, [c1913]. ([Boston]: The Gorham Press). 201 p., front., ill.   **AUM**
LC: S 29, '13.

Wood, Frances Gilchrist. Shoes. _In The best short stories of 1924 and the yearbook of the American short story (1925), B-569._

____ Turkey red. _In Prize stories of 1919 (1920), P-617._

____ The white battalion. _In The best short stories of 1918 and the yearbook of the American short story (1919), B-563._

W-829 Wood, Henry Cleveland, b. 1855. The night riders: a thrilling story of love, hate and adventure, graphically depicting the tobacco uprising in Kentucky / by Henry C. Wood . . . Chicago: Laird & Lee, [c1908]. 301 p., incl. front., incl. 1 leaf of plates, ill. [Ill. by M. L. McComb.]
LC: Ap 8, '08.

W-830 Wood, Jonathan. Hiram Gray: the rebel Christian / by Jonathan Wood. [Hammond, Ind.: Printed by W. B. Conkey Co., c1915]. 180 p., incl. photo. front.
LC: My 8, '15.

W-831 Wood, Julia Francis. A parable for fathers / by Julia Francis Wood; a loyal daughter's story of a Loyal Legion man; reprinted from the Atlantic monthly, January, 1918, for the Commandery of the state of Massachusetts, Military Order of the Loyal Legion of the United States. [Boston], 1918. 8 p.
DLC (photocopy)
DLC copy third printing.

W-832 Wood, L. C. (Lydia Cope), b. 1845. For a free conscience / by L. C. Wood . . . New York; Chicago; Toronto; London; Edinburgh: Fleming H. Revell Company, [c1905]. 414 p.
BLC: London: Headley Bros., [1905].

Wood, Leonard, Jr. The grip of the tropics. _In Made to order (1915), M-352._

____ Until tomorrow. _In The best college short stories, 1917-18 (1919), B-557._

W-833 Wood, Lillian E. Let my people go / by Lillian E.

Wood. [Philadelphia, Pa.: A. M. E. Book Concern Printers, n. d.]. 132 p.
Unexamined copy: bibliographic data from OCLC, #28441543.

W-834 Wood, Mary Rosalie Alling. The turn of the current: a study of the new consciousness / by Mary Rosalie Alling Wood . . . New York; Washington: The Neale Publishing Company, 1904. 244 p. Pasted down manuscript slip over imprint reads, "Washington, published by the author."

Wood, Robert Williams, 1868-1955, jt. aut. _The man who rocked the earth_ (1915). _See_ **Train, Arthur Cheney, 1875-1945, jt. aut., T-355.**

Wood, Sabine W. _See_ **Fisher, Jacob, pseud.**

W-835 Wood, Sam H. (Samuel Harry), b. 1856. Universal peace, or, The crowning work of two lives / by Sam H. Wood. Salt Lake City, Utah: Uintaland Publishing Company, 1914. 248 p., photo. front. (port.).   **CRL**
A sequel to Barriers burned away by E. P. Roe.

W-836 Wood, Warren. The tragedy of the deserted isle: a chronicle of the Burr and Blennerhassett conspiracy / by Warren Wood. Boston, Massachusetts: C. M. Clark Publishing Company, 1909. 393 p., photo. front., [7] leaves of plates (some photo., some ports.).
LC: Ap 16, '09.

W-837 ____ When Virginia was rent in twain: a romance of love and war and statecraft / by Warren Wood . . . New York: Broadway Publishing Company, [c1913]. 358 p., col. front., [5] leaves of plates.
LC: D 24, '13.

W-838 Wood-Seys, Roland A. (Roland Alexander), 1854-1919. Adrian Scroop / by Roland A. Wood-Seys (Paul Cushing) . . . New York: Dodd, Mead and Company, 1912. 349 p.

W-839 [____] Sappho in Boston / illustrated. New York: Moffat, Yard & Company, 1908. 257 p., front., [1] leaves of plates. [Ill. by James M. Flagg.]
LC: S 24, '08.
PW: N 14, '08.

W-840 Woodbridge, Elisabeth, 1870-1964. Isaiah incorporated / by Elisabeth Woodbridge. New Haven: Yale University Press, 1920. [38] p.   **MNU**
PW: D 11, '20.

W-841 ____ The Jonathan papers / by Elisabeth Woodbridge. Boston; New York: Houghton Mifflin Company, 1912. (Cambridge: The Riverside Press). 233 p.
"The papers in this volume first appeared in the Outlook, the Atlantic, and Scribner's."
Contents: A placid runaway -- An unprogressive farm -- A desultory pilgrimage -- The yellow valley -- Larkspurs and hollyhocks -- The farm sunday -- The grooming of the farm -- "Escaped from old gardens" -- The country road -- The lure of the berry -- In the rain -- As the bee flies -- A dawn experiment -- In the wake of the partridge -- Beyond the realm of weather -- Comfortable books -- In the firelight.

W-842   _____ More Jonathan papers / by Elisabeth
Woodbridge. Boston; New York: Houghton Mifflin
Company, 1915. (Cambridge: The Riverside Press).
216 p.
Contents: The searchings of Jonathan -- Sap-time -- Evenings on the
farm -- After frost -- The joys of garden stewardship -- Trout and
arbutus -- Without the time of day -- The ways of Griselda -- A row-
boat pilgrimage.
LC: N 18, '15.
PW: D 4, '15.

Woodbridge, William W. (William Witherspoon), b.
1883. The best policy after all. In *Clever business
sketches* (1909), **C-490.**

W-843   _____ "Bradford, you're fired!": a story of the
super-self / by William W. Woodbridge. Tacoma,
Washington: Published by Smith-Digby Company,
1917. 54 p., ill.
LC: Ag 18, '17.

W-844   _____ Skooting skyward: a novel / by Mr. Woodrow
Bridges; edited and revised by William W.
Woodbridge. Tacoma: Smith-Kinney Co., 1912.
63 p., front., [7] leaves of plates.
LC: N 5, '12.

W-845   Woodbury, Charles J., Mrs., 1848-1927. The potato
child: & others / by Mrs. Charles J. Woodbury;
frontispiece after a bas-relief by Elizabeth Ferrea.
San Francisco: Paul Elder and Company, [c1910].
27 p., front.
Contents: The potato child -- A story that never ends -- A Nazareth
Christmas.
LC: Je 9, '10.
PW: Ag 13, '10.

W-846   Woodbury, Helen, b. 1894. The misty flats / by
Helen Woodbury. Boston: Little, Brown and
Company, 1925. 342 p.
PW: S 5, '25.

Woodbury, Lucia Purdence Hall. See **Woodbury,
Charles J., Mrs.**

W-847   Woodcock-Savage, Charles. A lady in waiting:
being extracts from the diary of Julie de Chesnil,
sometimes lady in waiting to her Majesty, Queen
Marie Antoinette / by Charles Woodcock-Savage.
New York: D. Appleton and Company, 1906.
330 p., front.   **SEA**
PW: Mr 3, '06.

W-848   Woodling, M. E. (Marvin E.). After many years,
--or--, Man's inhumanity to man / by M. E. Woodling
. . . New York; London; Montreal: The Abbey
Press . . . , [c1902]. 226 p.

W-849   Woodman, H. Rae (Hannah Rea), b. 1870. The
Noahs afloat: a historical romance / by H. Rea
Woodman. New York; Washington: The Neale
Publishing Company, 1905. 323 p.

W-850   Woodman, Mary. A touch of New England
charming: an old-fashioned story for young and old
hearts / by Mary Woodman; profusely illustrated.
New York: Cupples & Leon, 1904, [c1903]. 313 p.,

ill.   LC records: Boston: J. G. Cupples, 1903.
PW (Je 27, '03) reports Cupples & Leon relocated in
New York.
PW: O 10, '03.

W-851   _____ A touch of Portugal, or, The little Count of
Villa Moncão / by Mary Woodman. Boston:
Atlantic Printing Company, 1910. 132 p., photo.
front., [13] leaves of plates (all photo. save one).
                                                  MUS
LC: Ja 23, '11.

W-852   Woodrow, Wilson, Mrs., 1875?-1935. The beauty /
by Mrs. Wilson Woodrow . . . ; with illstrations by
Will Grefé. Indianapolis: The Bobbs-Merrill
Company, [c1910]. 321, [1] p., front., [5] leaves of
plates.
LC: Mr 12, '10.
PW: Mr 26, '10.

W-853   _____ The bird of time: being conversations with
Egeria / by Mrs. Wilson Woodrow. New York:
McClure, Phillips & Co., 1907. 276 p.

W-854   _____ The Black Pearl / by Mrs. Wilson Woodrow
. . . ; illustrated. New York; London: D. Appleton
and Company, 1912. 323, [1] p., [3] leaves of plates.
[Ill. by G. H. Hilder.]
LC: S 16, '12.
PW: S 7, '12.

W-855   _____ Building the Union / by Mrs. Wilson Woodrow
and Archibald Sessions. New York: Brandt and
Kirkpatrick, Inc., 1917. 61 p.
Unexamined copy: bibliographic data from LC.
LC: Ap 4, 1917.

W-856   _____ Burned evidence / by Mrs. Wilson Woodrow.
New York; London: G. P. Putnam's Sons, 1925.
([New York]: The Knickerbocker Press). 329 p.
LC: Ap 15, '25.
PW: Ap 25, '25.

W-857   _____ The hornet's nest / by Mrs. Wilson Woodrow;
with illustrations by Paul Stahr. Boston: Little,
Brown and Company, 1917. 313 p., front., [3]
leaves of plates.   **OSU, LUU**
LC: Mr 26, '17.
PW: Mr 24, '17.

_____ The new earth. In **Conrad, Joseph.** *Il conte*
(1925), C-697.

W-858   _____ The new missioner / by Mrs. Wilson Woodrow
. . . New York: The McClure Company, 1907.
309 p., front., [7] leaves of plates. [Ill. by J. W.
Taylor.]
LC: O 16, '07.
PW: O 26, '07.

W-859   _____ Sally Salt / by Mrs. Wilson Woodrow . . . ;
with illustrations by David Robinson. Indianapolis:
The Bobbs-Merrill Company, [c1912]. 349 p., col.
front., [4] leaves of col. plates.
PW: Mr 16, '12.

W-860 ____ The second chance / by Mrs. Wilson
Woodrow; frontispiece by Howard Chandler Christy.
New York: W. J. Watt & Co., [c1924]. 365 p.,
front.
LC: Ap 11, '14.
BLC: London: W. Collins Sons & Co., [1925].

W-861 ____ The silver butterfly / by Mrs. Wilson
Woodrow; with illustrations by Howard Chandler
Christy. Indianapolis: The Bobbs-Merrill Company,
[c1908]. 341, [1] p., col. front., [5] leaves of col.
plates.
LC: O 15, '08.
PW: O 17, '08.

W-862 ____ Swallowed up / by Mrs. Wilson Woodrow.
New York: Brentano's, [c1922]. 320 p.
LC: N 9, '22.
PW: N 18, '22.
BLC: London: Brentano's; Binghampton [sic]
[printed], 1923.

W-863 Woodruff, Helen S. (Helen Smith). The imprisoned
freeman / by Helen S. Woodruff. New York:
George Sully & Company, [1918]. 411 p.
LC: Ap 15, '18.
PW: Ap 27, '18.

W-864 ____ The lady of the lighthouse / by Helen S.
Woodruff; with decorations by Griselda M. McClure.
New York: George H. Doran Company, [c1913].
89 p., col. front., ill. Illustrated end papers.
LC: N 11, '13.
PW: Ja 31, '14.

W-865 ____ The little house / by Helen S. Woodruff . . .
New York: George H. Doran Company, [c1914].
270 p.   **OSU, DLC**
LC: S 28, '14.

W-866 ____ Mis' Beauty / by Helen S. Woodruff;
illustrated by the author. New York: The Alice
Harriman Company, 1911. 163 p., col. front., [4]
leaves of col. plates.
LC: N 22, '11.
PW: D 16, '11.
BLC: London: Hodder & Stoughton, 1913.

W-867 ____ Mr. Doctor-Man / by Helen S. Woodruff . . .
New York: George H. Doran Company, [c1915].
96 p., photo. front. (port.).
PW: D 18, '15.

W-868 ____ What David did: love letters of two babies /
written and illustrated by Helen S. Woodruff . . .
New York: Boni and Liveright, [c1921]. 125 p.,
ill.   **DLC**
LC: Mr 18, '21.
PW: Mr 19, '21.

W-869 Woods, Alice, 1871-1959. Edges / by Alice Woods;
with illustrations by the author. Indianapolis: The
Bowen-Merrill Company, [c1902]. 207 p., front., [5]
leaves of plates, ill.

PW: N 22, '02.
BLC: London: B. F. Stevens & Brown, [1902].

W-870 ____ Fame-seekers / by Alice Woods . . . ; with
illustrations by May Wilson Preston. New York:
George H. Doran Company, [c1912]. 253 p., col.
front., [3] leaves of col. plates.
LC: Ap 12, '12.
PW: Ap 27, '12.

W-871 [____] A gingham rose / by Alice Woods Ullman;
with a frontispiece by the author. Indianapolis: The
Bobbs-Merrill Company, [c1904]. 381 p., front.

W-872 ____ The hairpin duchess / by Alice Woods. New
York: Duffield and Company, 1924. 224 p.
LC: O 31, '24.
PW: N 15, '24.

W-873 ____ The thicket: a novel / by Alice Woods. New
York: Mitchell Kennerley, 1913. 251 p.

W-874 Woodward, W. E. (William E., 1874-1950. Bread &
circuses / by W. E. Woodward. New York; London:

Harper & Brothers, 1925. 353 p.
LC: N 12, '25.
PW: N 21, '25.

W-875 ____ Bunk / by W. E. Woodward. New York;
London: Harper & Brothers, 1923. 370 p.
LC: S 14, '23.

W-876 ____ Lottery / by W. E. Woodward . . . New
York; London: Harper & Brothers, 1924. 424 p.
LC: O 16, '24.
PW: O 25, '24.

W-877 Woodworth, Herbert Grafton, b. 1860. In the
shadow of Lantern Street / by Herbert G.
Woodworth. Boston: Small, Maynard & Company,
[c1920]. 312 p.   **CLU**
LC: F 14, '20.
PW: Mr 13, '20.
BLC: London: Hutchinson & Co., [1922].

W-878 ____ Where the twain met / by Herbert G.
Woodworth . . . Boston: Small, Maynard &
Company, [c1925]. 334 p.
LC: Mr 2, '25.
PW: Mr 28, '25.
BLC: London: Hutchinson & Co., 1926.

Woodworth, Marguerite A. Somewhere in France.
In *The best college short stories, 1917-18* **(1919),
B-557.**

W-879 Wooldridge, C. W. (Charles William, b. 1847.
Perfecting the earth: a piece of possible history / by
C. W. Wooldridge . . . Cleveland, Ohio: The
Utopia Publishing Company, [c1902]. 326 p., photo.
front. (port.), ill. (maps, plans, and diagrams).
PW: O 11, '02.

Woolf, Paul. The blue spider. In *The best college short stories, 1924-1925* (1925), B-558.

Woollcott, Alexander, contributor. See *Bobbed hair* (1925), B-700.

W-880 Woolley, Edward Mott, 1867-1947. Addison Broadhurst, master merchant: the intimate history of a man who came up from failure / by Edward Mott Woolley. Garden City, New York: Doubleday, Page & Company, 1913. 278 p.
LC: Ap 24, '13.
PW: Ap 26, '13.

W-881 ____ The cub reporter / by Edward Mott Woolley; with illustrations by Arthur Hutchins. New York: Frederick A. Stokes Company, [1913]. 255 p., front., [3] leaves of plates.
LC: S 8, '13.
PW: S 13, '13.

W-882 ____ The junior partner: the inner secrets of seven men who won success / by Edward Mott Woolley. New York: E. P. Dutton & Company, [c1912]. 323, [1] p., front., [8] leaves of plates. [Ill. by Hy S. Watson.]
LC: Ag 29, '12.
PW: S 14, '12.

W-883 ____ Roland of Altenburg / by Edward Mott Woolley. Chicago: Herbert S. Stone & Company, 1904. 350 p.

W-884 Woolwine, Thomas Lee, 1874-1925. In the valley of the shadows / by Thomas Lee Woolwine; illustrated by Charles M. Relyea. New York: Doubleday, Page & Company, 1909. 115 leaves, col. front., [3] leaves of col. plates.
Leaves of text printed and numbered on one side only.
LC: F 9, '09.
PW: F 20, '09.
BLC: London: Doubleday, Page & Company; New York printed, 1909.

W-885 Woolworth, Solomon. The life of Gus Davis Trifler, a story founded on facts / by Solomon Woolworth, in his eighty-sixth year. Newark, N. J., 1905. 76 p., front. (port.). **DLC**

W-886 Worden, Hattie Weller. Eva: a novel / by Hattie Weller Worden . . . Lily Dale, N. Y.: Sunflower Publishing Co., 1906. 359 p., front. (port.). **DLC**
LC: Jl 23, '06.

W-887 Work, Edgar Whitaker, b. 1861. By the roadside / Edgar Whitaker Work. New York: American Tract Society, [c1912]. 24 p., ill. **NYP**

W-888 ____ The folly of the Three Wise Men / by Edgar Whitaker Work; decorations by C. B. Falls. New York: George H. Doran Company, [c1915]. 80 p., front., ill.
LC: O 25, '15.

W-889 ____ "Moses": a Rocky Mountain sketch / Edgar W. Work. Dayton, Ohio: Press of United Brethren Publishing House, 1901. 42 p.

W-890 Workman, Hanson, Mrs., 1859-1926. An American singer in Paris: a novel / by Mrs. Hanson Workman; illustrated by Glen Tracy. Cincinnati: The Tribune Printing Co., 1908. 396 p., front., [2] leaves of plates.

Workman, Mary Christiana Sheedy. See **Workman, Hanson, Mrs.**

W-891 Wormington, Alma Lillian. The soul of a young girl / by Alma Lillian Wormington. Kansas City, Mo.: Franklin Hudson Publishing Co., 1921. 160 p., front. (port.). **DLC**
LC: F 10, '22.

W-892 Wormser, Gwendolyn Ranger, b. 1893. Abraham Goode / by Ranger Wormser. New York: J. R. Wells, 1924. 32 p.
Unexamined copy: bibliographic data from OCLC, #6673883.

W-893 ____ The scarecrow: and other stories / by G. Ranger Wormser. New York: E. P. Dutton & Company, [c1918]. 243 p. **OSU, CCT**
Contents: The scarecrow -- Mutter Schwegel -- Haunted -- Flowers -- The shadow -- The effigy -- The faith -- Yellow -- China-Ching -- The wood of living trees -- Before the dawn -- The stillness.
PW: N 9, '18.

W-894 Worth, Marc, *pseud.* Walls of fire / by Marc Worth [pseud.]. New York: Cosmopolitan Publishing Co., 1925. 272 p.

W-895 Worth, Nicholas, 1855-1918, *pseud.* The southerner: a novel / being the autobiography of Nicholas Worth [pseud.]. New York: Doubleday, Page & Company, 1909. 424 p.
LC: S 28, '09.

W-896 Worth, Patience (Spirit). Hope Trueblood / by Patience Worth; communicated through Mrs. John H. Curran, edited by Casper S. Yost. New York: Henry Holt and Company, 1918. 363 p.
LC: My 18, '18.
BLC: London: Skeffington & Son, [1919].

W-897 ____ The sorry tale: a story of the time of Christ / by Patience Worth, communicated through Mrs. John H. Curran; edited by Casper S. Yost. New York: Henry Holt and Company, 1917. 644 p.
LC: Jl 25, '17.

W-898 Worth, Pauline Wilson. Death Valley Slim, and other stories / by Pauline Wilson Worth; illustrations by C. A. Friedmann. Los Angeles: Segnogram Press, 1909. [48] p., ill. **KCC**
Partly reprinted from "Out West magazine" and "The Western world."
Contents: Death Valley Slim -- The princess -- The race for the sun beam -- Fourth of July consolidated -- Slippy's salute -- The winning of Benjamin Senior.
LC: Mr 29, '09.

W-899 Worthington, D. The broken sword, or, a pictorial page in Reconstruction / by D. Worthington. Wilson,

N. C.: P. D. Gold & Sons, 1901. 326 p., front., ill.
[Ill. by J. D. Bullock.]   **KUK**

W-900   Worthington, Elizabeth Strong. Twenty-eight seconds
and after, a tale of the San Francisco earthquake and
fire / by Elizabeth Strong Worthington; illustrated by
Charles L. Wrenn. [Oakland?, Calif.], 1906. 56 p.,
ill.
Unexamined copy: bibliographic data from OCLC,
#16509207.

W-901   Worts, George F. (George Frank), b. 1892. Peter the
brazen: a mystery story of modern China / by
George F. Worts; with a frontispiece by Gayle
Hoskins. Philadelphia; London: J. B. Lippincott
Company, 1919. 379 p., col. front.
LC: O 13, '19.

W-902   [Worts, Sara E.] Confessions of an innocent widow /
by the widow herself. New York: Broadway
Publishing Company, 1912. 119 p.
Unexamined copy: bibliographic data from OCLC,
#26000941.
LC: O 3, '12.

W-903   Wright, Alfred Askin, b. 1869. Pearl summers / by
Alfred Askin Wright . . . Boston: Christopher
Publishing House, [c1919]. 240 p.
LC: O 21, '19.
PW: Jl 19, '19.

W-904   Wright, Allen Kendrick. Dalleszona and the seventh
treasure / by Allen Kendrick Wright. Boston: The
Roxburgh Publishing Co., Inc., [c1922]. 234 p.
(Taw-no-ker series).
LC: D 20, '22.

W-905   ____ To the poles by airship, or, Around the world
endways / by Allen Kendrick Wright. Los Angeles,
Cal.: Baumgardt Publishing Co., 1909. 108 p.,
photo. front., ill.
LC: S 16, '09.

W-906   Wright, Anna Potter. Burton Street folks / by Anna
Potter Wright . . . Chicago: The Bible Institute
Colportage Association, [c1913]. 123 p., ill.

         Wright, Caroline. See **Germaine, Quincy, pseud.**

W-907   Wright, Carrie Douglas, b. 1862. Lincoln's first
love: a true story / by Carrie Douglas Wright.
Chicago: A. C. McClurg & Co., 1901. 51, [1] p.,
photo. front.

         Wright, Clara (Parrish), Mrs., b. 1861. See **Parrish-
Wright, Clara.**

W-908   Wright, Emily Dudley, b. 1860. Paddie / by Emily
Dudley Wright . . . Boston, Massachusetts: The
Stratford Co., 1920. 261 p.
LC: Mr 20, '20.
PW: AP 17, '20.

         Wright, Emma Howard. A piece of pink ribbon. In
The Senior lieutenant's wager: and other stories
(1905), S-312.

W-909   Wright, Gene. Pandora La Croix: a novel / by Gene
Wright. Philadelphia; London: J. B. Lippincott
Company, 1924. 302 p.
LC: My 16, '24.
PW: My 3, '24.

W-910   ____ Yellow fingers: a novel / by Gene Wright.
Philadelphia; London: J. B. Lippincott Company,
1925. 332 p.
LC: O 27, '25.
PW: O 10, '25.

W-911   Wright, Harold Bell, 1872-1944. The calling of Dan
Matthews / by Harold Bell Wright . . . ; with
illustrations by Arthur I. Keller. Chicago: The Book
Supply Company, 1909. 363, [1] p., col. front., [3]
leaves of col. plates.
LC: My 19, '09; Ag 7, '09.
PW: Ag 28, '09.
BLC: London: Hodder & Stoughton, 1910.

W-912   ____ The eyes of the world: a novel / by Harold
Bell Wright . . . ; with illustrations by F. Graham
Cootes. Chicago: The Book Supply Company,
[c1914]. 464 p., col. front., [3] leaves of col. plates.
LC: Ag 12, '14.
PW: S 5, '14.

W-913   ____ Helen of the old house / by Harold Bell
Wright. New York; London: D. Appleton and
Company, 1921. 371, [1] p.
LC: S 2, '21.

W-914   ____ The mine with the iron door: a romance / by
Harold Bell Wright. New York; London: D.
Appleton and Company, 1923. 338, [1] p., col.
front.
LC: Jl 24, '23.
PW: Ag 4, '23.

W-915   ____ The re-creation of Brian Kent: a novel / by
Harold Bell Wright . . . ; illustrations by J. Allen St.
John. Chicago: The Book Supply Company, [1919].
352 p., col. front., [3] leaves of col. plates.
LC: Ag 25, '19.
PW: Ag 23, '19.

W-916   ____ The shepherd of the hills: a novel / by Harold
Bell Wright . . . ; with illustrations by John H.
Weddell. Chicago: The Book Supply Company,
1907. 351, [1] p., [9] leaves of plates. [One ill. by
F. Graham Cootes.]
LC: Ag 12, '07.
PW: S 14, '07.
BLC: London: Hodder & Stoughton, 1909.

W-917   ____ A son of his father / by Harold Bell Wright
. . . New York; London: D. Appleton and
Company, 1925. 354, [1] p., col. front.
LC: Jl 27, '25.
PW: Ag 8, '25.

W-918   ____ That printer of Udell's: a story of the middle
West / by Harold Bell Wright; illustrated by John
Clitheroe Gilbert. Chicago: The Book Supply
Company, 1903. 467, [1] p., incl. front., [8] leaves
of plates.
PW: My 2, '03.

W-919 _____ Their yesterdays / by Harold Bell Wright; with illustrations by F. Graham Cootes. Chicago: The Book Supply Company, [1912]. 310, [1] p., col. front., [3] leaves of col. plates.
LC: S 11, '12.
PW: N 2, '12.

W-920 _____ The uncrowned king / by Harold Bell Wright . . . ; illustrations by John Rea Neill. Chicago: The Book Supply Company, [1910]. 118 p., incl. col. front., col. ill.
LC: O 8, '10.
PW: O 15, '10.

W-921 _____ When a man's a man: a novel / by Harold Bell Wright . . . ; illustrations and decorations by the author. Chicago: The Book Supply Company, [1916]. 348 p., incl. front., ill.
LC: Ag 11, '16.
PW: Ag 12, '16.

W-922 _____ The winning of Barbara Worth / by Harold Bell Wright . . . ; with illustrations by F. Graham Cootes. Chicago: The Book Supply Company, [1911]. 511 p., front., [5] leaves of plates, maps.
LC: Ag 23, '11.
PW: S 30, '11.
BLC: London: Hodder & Stoughton, [1923].

W-923 Wright, Helen S. (Helen Saunders), b. 1874. The valley of Lebanon / by Helen S. Wright . . . New York: Robert J. Shores, 1916. 151 p., front.
PW: Je 3, '16.

W-924 Wright, J. W. (Jacob William), b. 1871. Memory trails: a little book of prose & verse / by J. W. Wright. Carmel-by-the-Sea, California: The Press in the Forest, publishers, [c1925]. [28] p. Decorations.
Contents: The whim horse -- The voice of the woods -- No matter what folks say.

W-925 _____ No gifts; &, The doves of December: also some verses and comments / written by J. W. Wright. Carmel-by-the-sea, Calif.: The Press in the Forest, 1924. 32 p., ill.   **OSU, COF**
Cover title. In this book may be found two stories for reading when the yule log is lighted or at other time: *No gifts* and *The doves of December*, also some verses and comments written by J. W. Wright and the types handset by the author, likewise printed and bound into a book by him in his shop and signed this first day of December A. D. 1924 . . . Carmel-by-the-sea, Calif.: The Press in the Forest, 1924.
LC: D 11, '24.

W-926 _____ The whim horse; and, a song of freedom entitled Five thousand more / by J. W. Wright . . . Carmel-by-the-sea, California: The Press in the Forest, 1925. 29 p., ill. [Ill. by Ralph F. Mocine.]
LC: F 24, '25.

W-927 Wright, James North, 1838-1910. Where copper was king: a tale of the early mining days on Lake Superior / by James North Wright. Boston: Small, Maynard & Company, 1905. 352 p.

W-928 Wright, John C. (John Couchois), b. 1874. Ella: a story of the white slave traffic / by John C. Wright. Harbor Springs, Mich.: Published by John C. Wright, [c1911]. 132 p.
LC: O 16, '11.

W-929 _____ The great myth / by John C. Wright. Lansing, Michigan: The Michigan Education Co., [c1922]. 170 p.   **NYP**
LC: My 31, '22.

W-930 Wright, Joshua, b. 1859, *pseud.* The book agent: his book / by Joshua Wright [pseud.]. New York: Thomson and Smith, 1904. 200 p., front.   **KSU**

W-931 [Wright, Mabel Osgood], 1859-1934. At the sign of the fox: a romance / by Barbara [pseud.]. . . New York; London: The Macmillan Company, 1905. 372 p., col. front. [Ill. by Gleeson.]
PW: Jl 15, '05.

W-932 _____ Aunt Jimmy's will / by Mabel Osgood Wright . . . ; illustrated by Florence Scovell Shinn. New York: The Macmillan Company; London: Macmillan & Co., 1903. 272 p., front., [7] leaves of plates.
PW: O 31, '03.

W-933 [_____] The garden of a commuter's wife / recorded by the gardener [pseud.]; with eight illustrations in photogravure. New York: The Macmillan Company; London: Macmillan & Co., ltd., 1901. 354 p., front., [7] leaves of plates.   **KSU**

W-934 [_____] The garden, you and I / by Barbara [pseud.] . . . New York: The Macmillan Company; London: Macmillan & Co., Ltd., 1906. 397 p., col. front., [26] leaves of photo. plates, (1 double leaf), ill. (plan).   **BGU**
PW: Je 16, '06.

W-935 _____ The love that lives / by Mabel Osgood Wright . . . ; frontispiece in colour, by Hermann C. Wall. New York: The Macmillan Company, 1911. 406 p., col. front.   **OSU, CLE**
LC: O 26, '11.

W-936 [_____] The open window: tales of the months / told by Barbara [pseud.]. . . New York: The Macmillan Company, 1908. 381 p., front.   **TMA**
Contents: The Markis and the Major -- The stalled train -- The vandoo -- The immigrants -- Tree of life -- Wind in the grass -- The simple life -- The adoption of Albert and Victoria -- Groundsel-tree -- The open window -- The rat-catcher -- Transition.
LC: Je 17, '08.
PW: Je 27, '08.

W-937 [_____] People of the whirlpool: from the experience book of a commuter's wife; with eight full-page illustrations. New York: The Macmillan Company; London: Macmillan & Co., Ltd., 1903. 365 p., front., [7] leaves of plates.

W-938 _____ Poppea of the post-office / by Mabel Osgood Wright (Barbara) . . . ; with frontispiece by the Kinneys. New York: The Macmillan Company,

1909. 347 p., front.
LC: Jl 6, '09.
PW: Jl 17, '09.

W-939   ____ Princess Flower Hat: a comedy from the
perplexity book of Barbara the commuter's wife / by
Mabel Osgood Wright . . . New York: The
Macmillan Company, 1910. 283 p., front.
LC: O 20, '10.
PW: N 5, '10.
BLC: London: Macmillan, 1910.

W-940   ____ The stranger at the gate: a story of Christmas /
by Mabel Osgood Wright; with a frontispiece by
Herman C. Wall; and decorations by Bertha Stuart.
New York: The Macmillan Company, 1913. 305 p.,
col. front., ill. Illustrated end papers.   **CWR**
LC: N 13, '13.
PW: D 6, '13.

W-941   [____] The woman errant: being some chapters
from the wonder book of Barbara, the commuter's
wife; with illustrations by Will Grefé. New York:
The Macmillan Company; London: Macmillan &
Co., Ltd., 1904. 376 p., front., [5] leaves of plates.

W-942   Wright, Mary Tappan, 1851-1917. Aliens / by Mary
Tappan Wright. New York: Charles Scribner's
Sons, 1902. 423, [1] p.
PW: Mr 22, '02.

W-943   ____ The charioteers / by Mary Tappan Wright.
New York; London: D. Appleton and Company,
1912. 345, [1] p.
LC: My 17, '12.
PW: Je 8, '12.

W-944   ____ The test / by Mary Tappan Wright. New
York: Charles Scribner's Sons, 1904. 360 p.
PW: Mr 26, '04.

W-945   ____ The tower: a novel / by Mary Tappan Wright.
New York: Charles Scribner's Sons, 1906. 422 p.

W-946   Wright, Richardson Little, 1887-1961. The open
door / by Richardson Wright. New York: McBride,
Nast & Company, 1914. 406 p.
PW: O 24, '14.

Wright, Rowland, pseud. <u>See</u> **Wells, Carolyn, 1862-
1942.**

Wright, Willard Huntington, 1888-1939. <u>See</u> **Van
Dine, S. S, pseud.**

W-947   Wright, Zara. Black and white tangled threads / by
Zara Wright . . . [Chicago: Barnard & Miller,
c1920]. 340 p., photo. front. (port.).   **NYP**

W-948   Wulff, Mary Virginia. The scarlet thread / by Mary
Virginia Wulff. Louisville: John P. Morton &
Company Incorporated, 1924. 221 p., photo. front.
PW: Ja 17, '25.

W-949   Wyatt, Edith Franklin, 1873-1958. Every one his
own way / by Edith Wyatt. New York: McClure,

Phillips and Company, 1901. 290 p., ill. [Ill. by
William James Jordan.]   **MIA**
PW: My 11, '01.
BLC: London: McClure, Phillips, and Company,
1901.

____ In November. <u>In</u> *Atlantic narratives*; **2nd
series (1918), A-361.**

W-950   ____ The invisible gods: a novel / by Edith Franklin
Wyatt . . . -- 1st ed. -- New York; London: Harper
& Brothers, 1923. 432 p.
LC: F 16, '23.
PW: Mr 3, '23.

W-951   ____ True love: a comedy of the affections / by
Edith Wyatt. New York: McClure, Phillips & Co.,
1903. 288 p.
PW: Mr 7, '03.

____, contributor. <u>See</u> *The whole family* **(1908),
W-578.**

W-952   Wyatt, Horace, b. 1876. Malice in Kulturland / by
Horace Wyatt; with illustrations by W. Tell. New
York: E. P. Dutton & Co., 1917. 84 p., ill.
BLC: London: The Car Illustrated, 1914.

W-953   Wyatt, Lucy May Linsley. Constance Hamilton / by
Lucy May Linsley Wyatt. New York; London;
Montreal: The Abbey Press, [c1901]. 183 p.
PW: Ap 26, '02.

Wycliffe, John, pseud. <u>See</u> **Bedford-Jones, H.
(Henry), 1887-1949.**

W-954   Wylie, Edna Edwards. The ward of the sewing-circle
/ by Edna Edwards Wylie. Boston: Little, Brown
and Company, 1905. 202 p., front. [Ill. by Beatrice
Baxter.]   **DLC**

W-955   Wylie, Elinor, 1885-1928. Jennifer Lorn, a sedate
extravaganza / by Elinor Wylie; illuminating episodes
in the lives of the Hon. Gerald Poynyard and his
bride. New York: Printed for George H. Doran
Company, 1923. 302 p., ill.
LC: N 30, '23.
PW: N 24, '23.
BLC: London: Grant Richards, printed in U. S. A.,
1924.
References: BAL 23495. BAL notes `Poyngard'
[sic].

W-956   ____ The Venetian glass nephew / by Elinor Wylie.
New York: George H. Doran Company, 1925.
182 p.
LC: S 15, '25.
PW: S 19, '25.
BLC: London: William Heinemann, printed in U. S.
A., 1926.
References: BAL 23505. BAL also notes limited
edition.

W-957   Wyman, Lillie Buffum Chace, 1847-1929. Gertrude
of Denmark: an interpretative romance / by Lillie
Buffum Chace Wyman; introduction by Courtney
Langdon. Boston, Massachusetts: Marshall Jones
Company, [c1924]. 260 p., front.

W-958   Wyneken, Leopold Ernest, b. 1838. Chronicles of Manuel Alanus: a true story of old San Francisco / by L. Ernest Wyneken. New York: Cochrane Publishing Co., 1908. 445 p., col. front. [Ill. by Leopold E. Wyneken.]

W-959   Wynne, Joseph F., d. 1929, *pseud.* A blighted rose / by Joseph F. Wynne [pseud.]. Detroit, Mich.: The Angelus Publishing Co., 1902. 425 p.
PW: My 24, '02.

W-960   ____ Izamal / by Joseph F. Wynne [pseud.] . . . Detroit, Mich.: The Angelus Publishing Company, [c1911]. 279, [1] p.
PW: Mr 11, '11.

W-961   ____ Paul's offering; and Gates ajar: stories / by Joseph F. Wynne [pseud.]. Detroit, Michigan: The Angelus Publishing Company, [c1906]. 167 p.
DLC

W-962   Wynne, Madeline Yale, 1847-1918. An ancestral invasion: and other stories / by Madeline Yale Wynne; selected by Annie Cabot Putnam. Garden City, New York: The Country Life Press, 1920. 164 p. **MIA**
Contents: A master-hand at bees -- An ancestral invasion -- The undoing of the burglar -- Sabriny, Dad and Co. -- A drove of facts and a flock of fancies -- A chip of the old block -- A study in hands -- A flight of feathers -- An experiment in time -- A game of solitaire -- The house that Stephen built -- In nether spaces.
LC: Ag 18, '20.

____ The little room. In *Shapes that haunt the dusk* **(1907), S-339.**

X

X-1   X. Wolfine: a romance in which a dog plays an honorable part / by X. New York: Sturgis & Walton Company, 1915. 345 p. **NYP**

X-2   X, Mr. 1943 / by Mr. X. Philadelphia: Dorrance, [c1922]. 372 p.
PW: S 30, '22.

Y

Y-1   Yale tales / compiled and edited by Boeder Van Harlan. New Haven, Conn.: [s. n.], 1901. 98 p.
Contents: The first night / Roi M. Mason -- The prom. concert / Roi M. Mason -- Bill Wayne, Esq. / B. Q. Meyer -- Henrico Samuel-Smith, freshman / B. Q. Meyer -- The squaring up of Hoppy the roustabout / E. Lyttleton Fox -- Just a story / W. R. Kinney.

Y-2   Yarbrough, J. C. (John Coffee), b. 1874. A tale of exiles / by J. C. Yarbrough. Boston: The Roxburgh Publishing Company, Inc., 1921. 130 p., front. (map). **OSU, KSU**
LC: My 14, '21.

Y-3   Yates, Elizabeth Hall. Masques / by Elizabeth Hall Yates; illustrated by Ralph P. Coleman. Philadelphia: The Penn Publishing Company, 1923. 319 p., front.
LC: Je 20, '23.

Y-4   Yates, Frederick Benjamin, b. 1848. Muzetta: a story of the '60s / by Frederick Benjamin Yates. New York: Published by the Shakespeare Press . . . , [c1911]. 241 p.

Y-5   Yates, Katherine M. (Katherine Merritte), b. 1865. Along the trail: in which Marjorie finds that everyone does not hurry past the rough places on the rail [sic], --and why / by Katherine M. Yates . . . Boston: Davis & Bond, 1912. 62 p.
LC: Mr 11, '14.

Y-6   ____ At the door: a tale to read both on the lines and between / by Katherine M. Yates . . . Chicago: K. M. Yates & Company, 1905. 32 p.
PW: O 14, '05.
Another edition: Boston, Mass.: Davis & Bond, [1905].

Y-7   ____ On the hill-top / by Katherine M. Yates . . . Boston: The Harmony Shop . . . , [c1919]. 45 p.
LC: Ag 4, '19.

Y-8   ____ A tale from the rainbow land / by Katherine M. Yates; illustrated by Audley B. Wells. San Francisco: Paul Elder and Company, [1914]. 30 p.
LC: D 23, '14.

Y-9   Yates, L. B. The autobiography of a race horse / by L. B. Yates. New York: George H. Doran Company, [c1920]. 234 p.
LC: My 29, '20.
PW: My 29, '20.

Y-10   ____ Picking winners with Major Miles / by L. B. Yates. Indianapolis: The Bobbs-Merrill Company, [c1922]. 331 p.
LC: Ag 31, '22.
PW: S 2, '22.

Y-11   Yechton, Barbara, 1864-1939, *pseud.* Honor D'Everel / by Barbara Yechton [pseud.]. New York: Dodd, Mead & Company, 1903. 362 p., front.
PW: O 10, '03.

Y-12   ____ Young Mrs. Teddy / by Barbara Yechton [pseud.]. New York: Dodd, Mead & Company, 1901. 309 p.
PW: O 19, '01.

Y-13   Yeld, Thomas, Sir, b. 1857, *pseud.* The maid of the Combahee; a romance of the South / from the manuscript of Sir Thomas Yeld, bart. [pseud.]. Baltimore, Md.: Saulsbury Publishing Co., [c1918]. 325 p., front.
Unexamined copy: bibliographic data from OCLC, #5418966.

Y-14   Yerf, Christopher. Emily Bellefontaine / by Christopher Yerf. Chicago: W. B. Conkey Company, 1908. 237 p., front., [7] leaves of plates. [Ill. by F. J. Saunders.] **DLC**

Y-15   Yerington, C. W. (Charles William), b. 1856. Simple Simon / by C. W. Yerington; illustrated. New York: Broadway Publishing Company, [c1905]. 213 p., front. (port.), [4] leaves of plates. [Ill. by R. H. Lance.] **DLC**
PW: D 16, '05.

Yeslah, M. D. See **Halsey, Mina Deane, b. 1873.**

Y-16   Yezierska, Anzia, 1885-1970. Bread givers: a novel: a struggle between a father of the Old World and a daughter of the New / by Anzia Yezierska. Garden City, New York: Doubleday, Page & Company, 1925. 297 p.
LC: S 21, '25.
PW: S 12, '25.
BLC: London: William Heinemann, printed in U. S. A., 1925.

Y-17   _____ Children of loneliness: stories of immigrant life in America / by Anzia Yezierska. New York; London: Funk & Wagnalls Company, 1923. 270 p., front. (port.).
Contents: Mostly about myself -- America and I -- An immigrant among the editors -- To the stars -- Children of loneliness -- Brothers -- A bed for the night -- Dreams and dollars -- The lord giveth -- The song triumphant -- An interview with Anzia Yezierska: "You can't be an immigrant twice" / by R. Duffy.
LC: N 3, '23.
BLC: London: Cassell & Co., 1923.

        _____ "The fat of the land". In *The best short stories of 1919 and the yearbook of the American short story* (1920), B-564.

Y-18   _____ Hungry hearts / by Anzia Yezierska. Boston; New York: Houghton Mifflin Company, 1920. (Cambridge: The Riverside Press). 297, [1] p.
LC: O 29, '20.
PW: N 13, '20.
BLC: London: T. Fisher Unwin; Cambridge Mass. printed, 1922.

Y-19   _____ Salome of the tenements / by Anzia Yezierska . . . New York: Boni and Liveright, [c1923]. 290 p.
LC: Ja 15, '23.
PW: D 30, '22.
BLC: London: T. Fisher Unwin, 1923.

Y-20   Yiddish tales / translated by Helena Frank. Philadelphia: The Jewish Publication Society of America, 1912. 599 p.   **CWR**
Contents: The misfortune / Reuben Asher Braudes -- Earth of Palestine / Jehalel (Judah Löb Lewin) -- A woman's wrath / Isaac Löb Perez -- The treasure / Isaac Löb Perez -- It is well / Isaac Löb Perez -- Whence a proverb / Isaac Löb Perez -- An original strike / Mordecai Spektor -- A gloomy wedding / Mordecai Spektor -- Poverty / Mordecai Spektor -- The clock / Sholom-Alechem (Shalom Rabinovitz) -- Fishel the teacher / Sholom-Alechem (Shalom Rabinovitz) -- An easy fast / Sholom-Alechem (Shalom Rabinovitz) -- The passover guest / Sholom-Alechem (Shalom Rabinovitz) -- Gymnasiye / Sholom-Alechem (Shalom Rabinovitz) -- Sabbath / Eliezer David Rosenthal -- Yom Kippur / Eliezer David Rosenthal -- Bertzi Wasserführer / Isaiah Lerner -- Ezrielk the scribe / Isaiah Lerner -- Yitzchok-Yossel Broitgeber / Isaiah Lerner -- A livelihood / Judah Steinberg -- At the matzes / Judah Steinberg -- Three who ate / David Frischmann -- Military service / Micha Joseph Berdyczewski -- Forlorn and forsaken / Isaiah Berschadski -- The hole in a beigel / Tashrak (Israel Joseph Zevin) -- As the years roll on / Tashrak (Isreal Joseph Zevin) -- Reb Shloimeh / David Pinski -- A picnic / S. Libin (Israel Hurewitz) -- Manasseh / S. Libin (Israel Hurewitz) -- Yohrzeit for mother / S. Libin (Israel Hurewitz) -- Slack times they sleep / S. Libin (Israel Hurewitz) -- Shut in / Abraham Raisin -- The charitable loan / Abraham Raisin -- The two brothers / Abraham Raisin -- Lost his voice / Abraham Raisin -- Late / Abraham Raisin -- The Kaddish / Abraham Raisin -- Avròhom the orchard-keeper / Abraham Raisin -- The Rav and the Rav's son / Hirsh David Naumberg -- Women / Meyer Blinkin -- If it was a dream / Löb Schapiro -- A simple story / Shalom Asch -- A Jewish child / Shalom Asch -- A scholar's mother / Shalom Asch -- The sinner / Shalom Asch -- Country Folk / Isaac Dob Berkowitz -- The last of them / Isaac Dob Berkowitz -- A folk tale: The clever rabbi.

Y-21   Yoes, John W. (John Wesley), b. 1870. Jack Brainard: a romance of the Cherokee hills / by John W. Yoes; photograph illustrations by Mrs. Forester and Geo. R. Micheal. Boston: Eastern Publishing Company, 1904. 322 p. photo. front., [6] leaves of photo. plates.

Y-22   Yopp, William Isaac. A dual role: a romance of the Civil War / by William Isaac Yopp. [Dallas, Texas: John F. Worley, publisher, c1902]. 169 p., photo. front. (port.), [11] leaves of plates.

Y-23   York, Chauncey F. Overlook Farm: thrilling pioneer stories: the most natural, interesting, informing account and concise description of the frontiersmen's lives and activities ever published . . . / by Chauncey F. York . . . ; illustrated. Detroit, Michigan: Published by Chauncey F. York . . . , [c1915]. 2 vol. in 1; 88, 88 p., ill. (1 port., some photo.). [Ill. by Chas. H. Spencer.]   **EYW**
Contents: Vol. I: Sam Peters -- Vol. II: Mick.
LC: Ap 17, '16.

Y-24   York, Wealthy Ann. Some adventures of two vagabonds / by one of 'em, by Wealthy Ann York. New York: Broadway Publishing Co. . . . , [c1908]. 173 p.   **UCW**
Contents: A point of etiquette -- The coming of Hannah Jane -- The unknown sailor's chief mourner -- The mystery of the red house -- The waking of the salt marsh and the blooming of the dunes -- An'rew T. and how he met the great man -- Cap'n Ame'sy's business proposition -- Carmelita's Mary Magdalen -- La P'tit Angelo -- Accepted with a number one.

        Yost, Casper Salathiel, 1864-1941, ed. See **Worth, Patience, (Spirit)**.

Y-25   Yost, Robert Morris. The stage driver's romance. [Farmington, MO., 1903].
Unexamined copy: bibliographic data from NUC.

Y-26   Young, Annie McKnight. The quest of a pearl / by Annie McKnight Young . . . Cincinnati, O.: F. L. Rowe, 1925. 305 p.   **DLC**
LC: Ja 8, '26.

Y-27   Young, Anthony Gascoyne, b. 1892. Kathleen's love: a story of a woman's love / by Anthony Gascoyne Young . . . New York: Charles Watson Russell, 1925. 254 p.   **DLC**
LC: Ag 1, '25.

        Young, Elizabeth F. Bernice, Patrice and Clarice. In *California story book* (1909), C-40.

Y-28   Young, Elizabeth G. Homestead ranch / by Elizabeth G. Young. New York; London: D. Appleton and Company, 1922. 295, [1] p., front. [Ill. by Arthur E. Becher.]
PW: Ap 8, '22.

Y-29   Young, Everett. A gentleman of sorts / by Everett Young. New York: Henry Holt and Company, 1923. 382 p.
LC: My 31, '23.
PW: Je 9, '23.

Y-30   Young, G. Bayard. The strangers at the door: a Christmas story / by G. Baynard Young. Philadelphia: The Castle Press, 1919. 49 p., front., ill. [Ill. by Ehrhart.]
LC: D 22, '19.

Y-31   Young, Gordon Ray, 1886-1948. Crooked shadows / by Gordon Young. Garden City, N. Y.: Garden City Publishing Co., Inc., 1924. 120 p.
Unexamined copy: bibliographic data from OCLC, #12203228.
(Famous authors series; no.44).
LC: Ap 2, '24.

Y-32   _____ Days of '49 / by Gordon Young. New York: George H. Doran Company, [c1925]. 425 p.
PW: N 14, '25.
BLC: London: Hodder & Stoughton, [1926].

Y-33   _____ Hurricane Williams / by Gordon Young. Indianapolis: The Bobbs-Merrill Company, [c1922]. 342 p.
LC: Ap 14, '22.
PW: Ap 15, '22.
BLC: London: T. Fisher Unwin, 1924.

Y-34   _____ Savages / by Gordon Ray Young; frontispiece by Rudolph Tandler. Garden City, N. Y.; Toronto: Doubleday, Page & Co., 1921. 327 p., front. **UMC**
LC: My 27, '21.
PW: Ap 30, '21.
BLC: London: Jonathan Cape, printed in U. S. A., 1922.

Y-35   _____ Seibert of the island / by Gordon Young. New York: George H. Doran Company, [1925?]. 313 p.
BLC: London: T. Fisher Unwin, 1924.

Y-36   _____ The vengeance of Hurricane Williams / by Gordon Young. New York: George H. Doran Company, [c1925]. 281 p.
LC: N 2, '25.

Y-37   _____ Wild blood / by Gordon Young . . . Indianapolis: The Bobbs-Merrill Company, [c1921]. 344 p.   **AZU**
LC: O 17, '21.
PW: O 29, '21.
BLC: London: T. Fisher Unwin, 1923.

Y-38   Young, Laurence Ditto. The climbing doom / by Laurence Ditto Young; illustrations by Albert M. Sterling. New York: G. W. Dillingham Co., [c1909]. 326 p., front., [5] leaves of plates.
Unexamined copy: bibliographic data from OCLC, #7396058.
LC: Mr 29, '09.

Y-39   Young, Mary Stuart. The Griffins: a colonial tale / by Mary Stuart Young (Mrs. Louis G. Young). New York; Washington: The Neale Publishing Company, 1904. 182 p.
PW: Ja 28, '05.

Y-40   Young, Rida Johnson. Brown of Harvard / by Rida Johnson Young and Gilbert P. Coleman; illustrated. New York; London: G. P. Putnam's Sons, 1907. ([New York]: The Knickerbocker Press). 319 p., front., [7] leaves of photo. plates.
LC: My 17, '07.

Y-41   _____ Little old New York / by Rida Johnson Young; profusely illustrated with scenes from the

Cosmopolitan photoplay, starring Marion Davies. New York: Grosset & Dunlap, [c1923]. 307 p., photo. front., [11] leaves of photo. plates.
LC: Je 11, '23.
PW: S 22, '23.

Y-42   _____ Out of the night / by Rida Johnson Young. New York: W. J. Watt & Co., [c1925]. 314 p.
LC: O 15, '25.
PW: S 26, '25.

Y-43   _____ The story of Mother Machree: a story of a mother's love / by Rida Johnson Young; illustrated with scenes from the photoplay, a William Fox production. New York: Grosset & Dunlap, [c1924]. 159 p., photo. front., [7] leaves of photo. plates.
PQA

Y-44   Young, Rose E. (Rose Emmet), 1869-1941. Henderson / by Rose E. Young . . . Boston; New York: Houghton, Mifflin and Company, 1904. (Cambridge: The Riverside Press). 189, [1] p.
PW: F 20, 04.
BLC: London: Gay & Bird; Cambridge, Mass. printed, 1984.

Y-45   _____ Sally of Missouri / by R. E. Young. New York: McClure, Phillips & Co., 1903. 292 p.
PW: O 24, '03.
BLC: London: William Heinemann, printed in U. S. A., 1904.

Y-46   Young, S. Hall (Samuel Hall), 1847-1927. The Klondike clan: a tale of the great stampede / by S. Hall Young; illustrated. New York; Chicago; Toronto; London; Edinburgh: Fleming H. Revell Company, [c1916]. 393 p., front., [7] leaves of plates. Illustrated end papers.
LC: D 21, '16.
PW: N 25, '16.

Young, Sara Lee, b. 1847. <u>See</u> **Younge, Leigh, pseud.**

Y-47   Young, Virginia Durant. One of the blue hen's chickens / by Virginia Durant Young . . . Bangor, Maine: C. W. Close, Publisher, 1901. 176 p.
PW: Mr 30, '01.

Y-48   Younge, Leigh, b. 1847. Golden grain / by Leigh Younge. Cincinnati: Monfort & Company, 1915. 220 p.
PW: S 23, '16.

Y-49   _____ A seed thought / by Leigh Younge. Cincinnati: Monfort & Company, 1913. 176 p.   **KCC**
LC: N 19, '13.

Y-50   Yourie Gardenin: a Russian character study / Anonymous. New York; Washington: The Neale Publishing Company, 1905. 280 p.   **KLG**

Y-51   Youth. New York: McClure, Phillips & Co., 1901. 164 p., front. (Stories from McClure).   **SOI**
Contents: The star spangled banner and A tune in court / by Marion Hill -- A little feminine Casabianca / by G. Madden Martin -- A white sheep / by G. K. Turner -- The little boy and his pa / by Ellsworth

Kelley -- The accolade / by Louise Herrick Wall -- A love story / by Annie Webster.
LC: O 2, '01.
PW: O 26, '01.

Y-52   Ysaye, Lisa, b. 1885. The inn of disenchantment / by Lisa Ysaye. Boston; New York: Houghton Mifflin Company, 1917. (Cambridge: The Riverside Press). 156, [2] p.   **SPP**

Y-53   Yulee, C. Wickliffe (Charles Wickliffe), b. 1849. The awakening: a novel of Washington life / by C. Wickliffe Yulee. New York; Washington: The Neale Publishing Company, 1905. 379 p., [5] leaves of plates.
PW: Ja 6, '06.

Z

Z-1   Zalk, Louis. The lady Wiladera and the hermit Edgar: a prose poem / by Louis Zalk. Saint Paul, Minnesota: Privately printed by the Pioneer Company, [c1910]. 87 p.   **DLC**
LC: D 30, '10.

        Zangwill, Israel. Noah's ark. In *Aces* (1924), A-42.

Z-2   Zanuck, Darryl Francis, b. 1902. Habit: and other short stories / by Darryl Francis Zanuck . . . ; cover design and sketches by E. A. Scram. Los Angeles, Calif.: Times-Mirror Press, 1923. 311 p.
Contents: Habit -- The scarlet ladder -- Say it with dreams -- The forgotten city.
LC: Ap 24, '23.

Z-3   Zeller, George Anthony, 1858-1938. The bereft: a series of asylum romances / by George Anthony Zeller . . . [Springfield? Ill.]: Department of Public Welfare, [1919?]. 114 p.   **NYP**
"Editorial comment, Institution Quarterly, 1919."

Z-4   Zeman, Josephine. My crime: a novel / by Josephine Zeman. New York: J. S. Ogilvie Publishing Company, [c1907]. 323 p.
LC: Ap 17, '07.
PW: Mr 30, '07.

Z-5   ____ The victim's triumph: a panorama of modern society / by Josephine Zeman. New York: G. W. Dillingham Company . . . , [c1903]. 244 p., front.
PW: My 23, '03.
BLC: London: T. Fisher Unwin, New York [printed], 1903.

Z-6   Zern, Frank W. Cornelius / by Frank W. Zern . . . Boston: The Christopher Publishing House, [c1922]. 162 p.   **NYP**
LC: Ja 26, '23.
PW: D 9, '22.

        Zevin, Isreal J. (Israel Joseph), 1872-1926. As the years roll on. In *Yiddish tales* (1912), **Y-20.**

        ____ The hole in a beigel. In *Yiddish tales* (1912), **Y-20.**

Z-7   ____ Shulem the Shadchen / by Tashrak [pseud.] (Israel J. Zevin). Chicago: H. L. Meites and Sons, 1925. 325 p.

Z-8   [Zimmerman, Jacob]. Black and white / anonymous; with illustrations by Joseph Rodgers. Philadelphia: The Literary Bureau, Inc., [c1911]. 167 p., front., [4] leaves of plates.

Z-9   Zimmerman, L. M. (Leander M.), b. 1860. Cordelia: a story for the homemaker and the breadwinner / by L. M. Zimmerman . . . Baltimore, Maryland: [Meyer & Thalheimer, printers, c1914]. 254 p., col. front.
PW: Ap 3, '15.

Z-10   ____ "Dot": "a novel of to-day" / by L. M. Zimmerman; illustrated. Baltimore, Md.: Press of Meyer & Thalheimer, [c1909]. 236 p., front. (port.), [13] leaves of plates.

Z-11   Zitkala-Sa, 1876-1938. American Indian stories / by Zitkala-Sa (Gertrude Bonnin) . . . Washington: Hayworth Publishing House, 1921. 195 p., photo. front. (port.).   **OSU, SDL**
Contents: Impressions of an Indian childhood -- The school days of an Indian girl -- An Indian teacher among Indians -- The Great Spirit -- The soft-hearted Sioux -- The trail path -- A warrior's daughter -- A dream of her grandfather -- The widespread enigma of Blue-Star Woman -- America's Indian problem.

Z-12   Zogbaum, Rufus Fairchild, 1849-1925. The junior officer of the watch / by Rufus Fairchild Zogbaum; illustrated by the author. New York: D. Appleton and Company, 1908. 311 p., front., [3] leaves of plates.

Z-13   Zollinger, Gulielma, 1856-1917. The rout of the foreigner / by Gulielma Zollinger . . . Chicago: A. C. McClurg & Co., 1910. 326 p., front., [9] leaves of plates. [Ill. by F. M. Chambers.]
LC: O 19, '10.

Z-14   Zurcher, Otto. Life or death: a true story / by Otto Zurcher. New York: The Knickerbocker Press, 1916.
60 p.
LC: Mr 4, '16.

Z-15   Zuss, X. Q. The pinkled frinft: (don't wrinkle your nose when you pronounce it): a strange story of mystery and wrath / by X. Q. Zuss. Chicago: Unusual Publishing Company, 1917. 95 p., ill.
LC: Ag 20, '17.

Title Index

TITLE INDEX

Quotation marks denote short stories.
An asterisk denotes cover title or British title.

"A as in father." H-987
Aaron Crane. T-59
"Aaron Hall." S-446
"Aaron Harwood." R-219
Abandoned farm. H-771
Abandoned farmers. C-516
Abandoned room. C-64
"Abaza." N-5
Abbé Pierre. H-958
"Abbey's legend." W-804
"Abdhil Rahman." C-299
"Abduction of Red Kelly." D-651
Abe and Mawruss. G-252
"Abe Lincoln, foundling." S-121
"Abe, the dwarf." T-422
Abel Griscoms' letters. A-39
Abeniki Caldwell. W-308
"Abe's game of jacks." R-319
"Abijah's bubble." S-618
Able McLaughlins. W-733
Abner Daniel. H-169
 Abner Grimes. L-27.5
"About bluffing." E-40
"About hands and feet." S-80
"About ideals." S-75
About Miss Mattie Morningglory. B-460
"About smells." T-429
"About two army camps." W-217
About us and the deacon. S-599
Above par. H-1053
"Above rubies." T-341
Above suspicion. O-149
Above the clouds. S-575
Above the shame of circumstance. W-563
"Above their fellows." D-149
Abraham Goode. W-892
Abraham's bosom. K-189
Abram's freedom. T-418
Abroad with the Jimmies. B-461
"Absence of Bill." E-146
"Absolute faith." M-854
Abundant harvest. D-64
Abysmal brute. L-430
Abyss. K-418
"Academic question." C-96
Acadian exile. G-358
"Accad the swordmaker." B-1276
"Accepted with a number one." Y-24
Accessory after the fact. H-706
Accidental honeymoon. P-554
Accidentals. M-266
"Accidents to others." P-176
Accolade. P-303
Accomplice. H-616
Accomplished through sacrifice. E-252
According to her light. D-38
"According to the code." C-526, P-633
According to the pattern. H-622
"According to their lights." H-517
Accurséd Roccos. J-95
"Accusation." S-593

Accused. E-118
Ace of blades. S-934
Aces for industry. S-832
Aces. A-42
Achievements of Luther Trant. B-125
Achsah, the sister of Jairus. J-190
Ackroyd of the faculty. R-63
Acolhuans. B-403
"Across a picket fence." F-272
Across the arid zone. C-885
"Across the border." B-1001
"Across the Centuries." W-804
Across the latitudes. W-725
Across the mesa. H-79
Across the threshold. F-86
"Across the waters." L-223
"Across the way." G-373
Across the years. P-507
"Action, reaction." H-510
"Actor." M-1155
"Actors all." C-9
Actress. H-31, O-204
"Actress." O-204
Actress and clerk. D-216
"Ada." S-841
Adam Clarke. M-406
"Adam condemns present fashions." J-197
Adam Rush. M-661
Adam Shuffler. B-393
Adam's garden. P-648
"Adapa the fisherman." B-1276
"Added amendment." K-372
Added upon. A-222
Addison Broadhurst, master merchant. W-880
"Addolorata's intervention." F-464
"Adeline Thurston, poetess." J-210
"Ades' "ad" for aid." R-382
Ade's fables. A-86
Adele Hamilton. E-107
Adell Waltby. S-31
"Adina." J-47
"Adjustable lunatic." R-325, R-326
"Adjustment." W-589
"Adjustment of nature." H-503
"Admirable." A-215
"Admirable Whoople." L-403
"Admiral." H-499
"Admiral of the Ooze." W-730
Admiral's light. R-300
Adnah. E-125
"Adobe walls." B-410
"Adolphus and the rough diamond." V-99
"Adopted." D-470
Adoption. C-298
"Adoption." C-298, C-679, G-20
"Adoption of Albert and Victoria." W-936
"Adorable uncle." E-146
"Adorers of Anne." B-651
Adrian Scroop. W-838
Adrienne. H-943
"Adrienne." F-452

Barbara. C-496
Barbara, a woman of the West. W-571
"Barbara Carlyle." O-205
"Barbara Graham." S-82
Barbara of Baltimore. T-79
Barbara of the snows. G-454
Barbara picks a husband. H-10
"Barbara's lawn party." S-80
Barbara's marriage and the Bishop. N-36
Barbara's marriages. W-155
Barbarian. C-65
Barbarians. C-238
"Barbed wire." G-213
Barbry. R-301
"Barclay lawn party." A-92
"Bard." C-401
Baree, son of Kazan. C-1036
"Barely civil engineer." F-175
Barent Creighton. S-334
"Bargain of bargains." O-14
Bargain true. B-305
"Bargain with Pegleg." N-124
Barge of haunted lives. T-463
Barleyville sewin' circle. T-256
"Barn-door outlook." P-624
Barnabetta. M-513
Barnaby Lee. B-521
"Barnacle goose." B-1371
"Barnacles." F-255
"Barnegat Bell." L-542
"Barnegat romance." L-542
"Barnegat sleuth." L-542
Barnegat yarns. L-542
Barnes family. C-877
Barney. H-1063
"Barney Mulligan, the far-down linen peddler, on..." M-280
"Barnum's lady." M-826
Baron of Diamond Tail. O-34
Baron of the Barrens. B-684
"Baron Starkheim." P-546
Baron Stiegel. S-941
Baronet rag-picker. C-771
Baroque. V-37
Barrel mystery. F-198
"Barrel was not empty." K-106
Barren ground. G-234
Barrier. B-375, F-407
"Barring of the door." T-29
Barry Gordon. P-196
Barry Wynn. B-319
Barselma's kiss. L-177
"Barstow lynching." H-464
"Bart Harrington, genius." J-209
Bart of Kane County. M-688
"Bart of Kane County." M-688
"Bart Wherry." H-921
"Barter." M-587
"Bartlem." L-356
"Bartolo's return." M-800
Bascom Clarke. W-443
"Base ball and other college fiends." H-735
"Bashful one." R-467
Basil Everman. S-528

Basket of fate. P-383
"Baskol." S-969
"Bass drums." M-928
Bat. M-488
"Bat and the star." A-219
Bat Wing Bowles. C-754
"Batallion days." S-445
"Bâtard." L-438
"Batch of letters, or one day ..." A-94
Batch of smiles. C-173
"Bathers." D-671
"Bathing booty." C-552
Bathsheba's letters to her cousin Deborah. T-4
Batiste of Isle La Motte. T-384
Battle. M-886
"Battle and a quarrel." P-57
Battle cry of peace. B-644
Battle cry. B-1155
"Battle for Teeka." B-1295
Battle for the Pacific. B-357
Battle invisible. R-110
"Battle invisible." R-110
Battle months of George Daurella. D-399
"Battle of Aiken." M-1013
Battle of Booby's Bluffs. L-369
"Battle of manila envelopes." M-981
"Battle of Perryville." E-146
"Battle of sedan." C-564
"Battle of Sentaro." H-893
"Battle of the field of barley." S-702
"Battle of Washington square." C-671
Battle with fate. W-24
"Battle-cruise of the Svend Foyn." C-688
Battle-ground. G-235
"Battle-prayer of Parson Small." F-347
"Battleground." S-533
"Battler." H-463
Battles royal down North. D-604
"Battling with love and fate." A-174
Battling with love and fate. A-174
Bauble. B-287
Bawlerout. H-98
"Bayard of Broadway." B-68
Bayard's courier. B-527
Bayou triste. N-72
"Baytop." G-322
Be ye beggar or king. M-822
Beached keels. R-302
"Beaded pouch." F-309
Beany, Gangleshanks, and the Tub. S-1035
Bear and the lamb. H-553
"Bear tamer's daughter." B-537
Bear Wallow belles. W-703
"Bear who found nothing in economy." D-412
"Bear who loved the tigress." D-412
"Bear who travelled on his nerve." D-412
"Bear who tried to be truthful." D-412
"Bear who was happy though married." D-412
"Bear whose name was Willie Wisdom." D-412
"Bearcat Bob butts in." B-73
"Bearded grain." M-1155
"Bearess who had money." D-412
"Bearess who wanted a career." D-412

"Free love." T-276
Free lovers. K-16
Free not bound. T-367
Free range. S-1114
Free Range Lanning. B-932
Free soil. L-612
Freeburg and the Freeburgers. S-689
"Freedom." F-9
"Freedom of the seas." M-854
"Freedom's faults." C-925
"Freedom's shriek." C-925
Freighter. R-610
"French doll's dowry." T-421
"Frenches first." O-132
"Frenchman." J-148
Frenchy. S-22
"Frenigike." P-386
Frenological finance. D-134
Frescati. D-11
Fresh air child. H-380
"Fresh air kids." H-663
Fresh every hour. T-299
Fresh from the Barrens. S-592
"Fresh guy." V-97
"Fresh waters." C-373
Fresh waters and other stories. C-373
Freshman. H-764
"Freshman full-back." P-30
"Freshman's diary." B-351
"Freshman's first return home." J-181
Friar of Wittenberg. D-177
Friar Tuck. W-185
Friar's daughter. P-328
"Frictional electricity." C-429
"Friday afternoon in the old-time school." H-572
Friday in the basement. H-30
Friday, the thirteenth. L-120
"Friday, the thirteenth." H-284
"Friend." C-573, M-1155
Friend at court. M-883, S-871
"Friend in court." S-593
"Friend of justice." V-84
"Friend of Napoleon." C-671
"Friend of the married." C-1068
Friend of the Seminole. W-74
"Friend that saved the ship." M-1107
"Friend who was hurt." S-785
Friend with the countersign. B-528
"Friendly call." H-514
"Friendly enemies." K-372
Friendly little house. F-432
Friendly road. G-418
"Friendly sentinel." E-146
"Friends." K-90, M-200, M-1074
"Friends in San Rosario." H-513
"Friends in waiting." H-60
Friends o' mine. S-75
"Friends of a quill." S-785
Friends of Mr. Sweeney. D-122
"Friends of the friends." J-43
"Friendship of Alanna." N-141
Friendship Village. G-19
Friendship Village love stories. G-20

Frigate's namesake. A-5
"Frills and Ednaferberlows." F-175
"Frog and the puddle." F-62
"Frog that played the trombone." M-621
From a bench in our square. A-74
"From a far country." B-886
"From a human standpoint." R-122
From a thatched cottage. H-399
"From A to Z." G-247
"From across the hall." C-96
From an Oregon Ranch. K-13
From baseball to Boches. W-795
From behind the veil. A-323
From Berlin to Bagdad. M-191
From Boniface to bank burglar. W-473
"From cellar to garret." M-900
"From Christmas to Easter." G-569
"From Dan to Beersheba." M-329
From death to life. M-464
"From Dolly to Dick." M-83
"From each according to his ability." H-519
From far Dakota, and otherwhere. R-543
From father to son. W-227
From Four Corners to Washington. C-577
From Hawthorne Hall. J-132
"From land to land." I-77
"From life to death." T-422
"From Mars." P-629
"From my notebook." G-318
From out of the flame. B-1285
"From out of the old life." J-215
From out of the West. H-670
From pit to palace. L-108
From place to place. C-521
"From Reykjavik to Gloucester." C-685
From sunup to sundown. H-257
From Superman to man. R-506
From tenement house to farm colony. G-201
"From tenement walls." O-205
From the Alamo to San Jacinto. L-609
"From the cabby's seat." H-503
From the car behind. I-18
"From the diary of a modern minister." R-190
From the heart of Israel. D-530
"From the hometown paper." S-772
From the housetops. M-120
"From the kingdom o'Calloway." W-219
From the life. O-53
"From the life of May we pass to December's gray." T-190
From the Marais des Cygnes. A-354
From the melting pot into the mold. D-561
From the old pueblo and other tales. F-434
"From the other side of the South." S-835
From the ranks. K-215
"From the shoulder." T-247
From the south of France. J-57
From the throttle to the throne. W-737
"From the tomb." T-444
From the unvarying star. L-118
From the valley of the missing. W-474
From the West to the West. D-623
"From tide to tide." M-1107
"From twelve to one." S-75

TITLE INDEX

Gilded rose. C-399
Gilded way. M-425
* Gillette's marriage. B-821
"Gimil the scribe." B-1276
Ginger cure. R-530
"Ginger snap." D-619
"Ginggob and Gumalub the wicked Jins." O-88
Gingham rose. W-871
"Giovanna as the wrong princess." M-597
"Giovanna first remembers." M-597
"Giovanna's commencement." M-597
"Giovanna's Italian renaissance." M-597
"Gipsies of the glen." H-143
"Gipsy camp." P-176
"Gipsy spirit." S-75
"Gipsy's story." H-435
"Girdle of Cleopatra." T-330
Girdle of the great. D-516
Girl. K-49
"Girl." H-521
Girl, a horse and a dog. L-594
Girl against odds. M-920
"Girl and a nudibranc." F-411
Girl and the bill. M-701
Girl and the deal. H-241
Girl and the devil. E-52
Girl and the game. W-663
"Girl and the game." W-663
"Girl and the graft." H-516
"Girl and the habit." H-516
Girl and the Kaiser. H-820
Girl and the motor. W-107
"Girl and the panther." S-446
Girl at Big Loon post. V-113
Girl at central. B-722
"Girl at the switchboard." T-11
Girl by the roadside. V-21
"Girl farmers." P-572
Girl from Four Corners. P-531
"Girl from Galacia." P-546
Girl from Girton. B-201
"Girl from Girton." B-201
Girl from his town. V-135
Girl from Hollywood. B-1293
Girl from home. S-1072
"Girl from Mercury." V-169
Girl from Montana. H-635
Girl from no. 13. P-167
Girl from the Big Horn country. C-323
Girl from Tim's place. M-1141
Girl from Vermont. S-92
Girl he left behind. L-471
Girl I left behind me. M-825
"Girl in garnet." B-1187
Girl in his house. M-220
Girl in question. H-899
"Girl in red." W-496
Girl in the fog. G-288
Girl in the golden atom. C-981
Girl in the mirror. J-206
Girl in the other seat. W-260
Girl in the slumber-boots. S-238
"Girl in the villa." P-546

Girl in this century. D-75
Girl in waiting. E-261
Girl named Mary. T-290
Girl next door. D-444
Girl of Chicago. P-90
Girl of Ghost Mountain. D-628
Girl of ideas. F-187
Girl of La Gloria. D-559
Girl of the Blue Ridge. E-216
Girl of the Golden Gate. M-669
Girl of the golden West. B-447
Girl of the guard line. W-1
Girl of the Limberlost. S-1009
Girl of the Ozarks. S-1128
"Girl of the Sierras." U-29
"Girl of the star-bright eyes." D-349
Girl of the West. B-489
Girl of Virginia. T-224
Girl on the hilltop. G-40
Girl out there. H-242
Girl Philippa. C-253
Girl proposition. A-89
Girl question. H-196
Girl rough riders. I-16
"Girl that's down." W-548
"Girl tourist." B-820
"Girl who came back." S-81
Girl who cast out fear. S-735
Girl who disappeared. R-488
"Girl who does not want to marry." S-80
"Girl who got rattled." W-496
Girl who kept up. C-971
Girl who lived in the woods. C-741
"Girl who loved Herbert." J-208
Girl who loved the land. M-583
"Girl who took notes and got wise ..." A-94
Girl who walked without fear. R-228
"Girl who was." J-215
"Girl who was the ring." G-541
"Girl who went right." F-63
"Girl who wouldn't marry." L-615
Girl who wrote. D-15
"Girl with the beautiful shoulders." H-384
Girl with the blue sailor. S-900
"Girl with the green toque." D-115
"Girl with the red feather." N-74
Girl with the rosewood crutches. G-228
Girl with two selves. C-828
"Girl without booking." G-444
"Girl worth while." D-547
Girls. F-68
"Girls and girls." G-569
"Girl's heart." F-363
Girls of '64. K-362
"Girls who pet." M-928
"Gitche Manito." W-121
"Giuseppo Caramboli." W-362
Give my love to Maria. T-421
"Give my love to Maria." T-421
Givers. F-394
"Givers." F-394
"Givin' hand." E-146
"Giving Cynthia a rest." W-265

821

Kazan. C-1051
"Keala." G-348
"Keats Shadd." C-373
Kedar Kross. S-473
"Ked's hand." S-834
Keeban. B-128
Keep off the grass. E-198
"Keep out, or you'll be hurt." Q-4
"Keep the law." M-854
Keeper of the bees. S-1012
"Keeper of the bridge." B-1371
"Keeper of the fairy gold." M-372
"Keeper of the light." V-84
Keeper of the vineyard. S-806
"Keeping a seat at the benefit." F-152
"Keeping expenses down." G-260
"Keeping tally." W-193
Keeping the peace. M-1014
Keeping up appearances. F-324
Keeping up with Harry. B-13
Keeping up with Lizzie. B-20
"Keeping up with neighbors." K-177
Keeping up with William. B-21
"Keesh, the son of Keesh." L-435
"Keidansky decides to leave the social problem..." R-232
Keith of the border. P-116
Kelly. S-217
Kempton-Wace letters. L-446
"Kendrick's Sunday." P-527
Kenelm's desire. C-816
Kennedy Square. S-619
Kenny. D-29
"Kenny's debt." D-618
"Kenny's royal flush." C-1012
"Keno." F-258
Kent Fort Manor. B-11
Kent Knowles. L-312
Kentons. H-929
Kentuckian. N-21, P-6
"Kentucky boy." B-831
Kentucky chronicle. G-403
"Kentucky Colonel has a grievance." N-155
"Kentucky Colonel tells of the feud two women started." N-155
Kentucky girl. S-236
Kentucky in American letters. T-331
"Kentucky mountaineer." F-343
Kentucky of Kentucky. K-342
Kentucky ranger. C-1002
Kentucky warbler. A-169
Kenworthys. W-734
"Keour, a story of Kalawao." G-348
"Ker Kel." V-192
"Kerfol." W-423
"Kerrigan." D-117
"Kerrigan's kid." B-406
"Kesiah's independence." P-413
"Ketchin' a chicken." M-942
Kettle of coin. G-538
"Keturah's gumption." P-413
Key. T-152
"Key." B-64
Key note. B-1249
Key of paradise. P-384

Key of the fields. R-308
"Key of the tower." V-81, V-87
Key to yesterday. B-1160
Keys of heaven. L-99
Keys of the city. D-124, G-352
Keziah Coffin. L-313
Khaki. T-237
"Khama." B-1179
"Khizr." A-38
Kick-in. T-305
"Kid." R-319
"Kid and the camel." T-346
"Kid and the cowboys." S-302
"Kid hangs up his stocking." R-319, R-320
"Kid of Apache Teju." K-82
Kid Scanlan. W-796
Kidder. M-320
"Kidder." M-320
Kidnaping Syndicate. B-741
Kidnapped colony. A-260
Kidnapped damozel. F-312
Kidnapped millionaires. A-62
"Kidnappers." D-117, D-166
"Kidnapping of Maria Luisa." M-598
"Kidnapping." H-240
Kildares of Storm. M-674
Killer. W-502
"Killer's son." S-834
"Killick Cove and Simeon's store." W-191
"Killorin's Caribbean days." C-688
"Killy, Killy, Killy." S-451
Kilo. B-1352
"Kilted German." K-372
Kim Su Bang. W-21
"Kim Su Bang." W-21
"Kin." R-322
Kincaid's battery. C-20
"Kind conductor." S-81
"Kind grief." M-271
Kind hearts and coronets. H-307
"Kind of a time." E-86
"Kind of music that is too good ..." A-94
"Kindergarten experiment." E-204
Kindling. H-845
Kindly light. K-250
"Kindly light." K-250
"Kindly old gentleman." B-843
"Kindness." T-422
Kindred. S-576
Kindred of the dust. K-427
King. K-293
"King." U-12
"King Albicore." H-21
King and the cross. S-1066
"King and the Miller of Mansfield." T-29
"King bumblebee." T-422
King Charlie's Raiders. B-935
King Coal. S-510
"King Cophetua." T-16
"King Edward's coronation." D-644
"King gander of Sea Dog shoal." F-272
"King Henry." S-448
"King Henry VIII admits some matrimonial mistakes." J-197

King in Babylon. S-904
"King in his shirt-sleeves." D-639
King in khaki. W-263
King in rags. M-890
King John. S-436
"King John and the Abbot." T-29
King Kavanaugh. K-178
King of Andorra. H-273
King of Arcadia. L-597
"King of Calaveras." V-155
"King of Cherokee." R-621
"King of Goulnaspurra." O-14
King--of Kearsarge. F-423
King of Kor. M-498
"King of Montobewlo." O-14
King of No Man's Land. F-424
King of Nobody's Island. E-203
"King of Scotland's daughter." T-198
"King of the also-rans." B-407
King--of the Khyber rifles. M-1132
"King of the Malamutes." H-674
King of the money kings. T-388
"King of the northern slopes." L-377
King of Thomond. B-266
King of Unadilla. G-53
"King or something." S-841
King Philip of Primrose Street. F-188
"King Solomon Nebuchadnezzar Joy." P-599
"King Solomon's family vacation trip." J-197
King Spruce. D-228
King Tut-ankh-Ámen. B-454
King who came. S-350
"King Widaagh's spell." S-452
Kingdom of evil. H-452
Kingdom of gold. C-127
Kingdom of infancy. W-112
Kingdom of love. W-613
"Kingdom of Quivera." W-26
Kingdom of slender swords. R-373
Kingdom of two. A-111
Kingdom round the corner. D-188
Kingmakers. S-905
"Kings and commoners." O-14
"King's caprice." H-839
King's coming. D-257
King's divinity. B-42
King's Easter. S-765
King's End. B-1047
"King's harnt." G-322
"King's high way." V-88
King's Highway. W-633
"King's jewel." V-81, V-87
King's mark. B-139
"King's men." T-247
King's messenger. A-287
"Kings of Curlew Island." R-621
Kings of the Missouri. P-234
"King's shoes." C-832
"King's toast." T-16
"King's touch." C-401
"King's whirr." H-419
Kingsmead. V-194
Kirk Ward's ghost. C-960

Kirstie. F-143
"Kiss." I-28, M-587
Kiss and the queue. A-219
"Kiss and the queue." A-219
"Kiss fantastical." H-435
Kiss of Apollo. B-581
Kiss of glory. B-837
"Kiss of the bullet." H-952
"Kissing by favor." C-933
"Kitchen side of the door." F-62
"Kitsuné yashiki." B-38
"Kittenish superanns and the ..." A-90
"Kittie's sister Josephine." J-210
"Kittiwake gull." L-542
Kitty Canary. B-762
Kitty Dixon, belle of the South Anna. B-1147
Kitty Knight. C-665
Kitty of the roses. B-185
"Kleptomaniac." B-1362
Klondike clan. Y-46
"Knave of keys." P-25
"Knee length dramas." C-925
"Knee-deep in June." S-75
"Knee-deep in knickers." F-71
"Knifin' de dough." H-413
"Knight at the portal." B-820
Knight in denim. B-530
Knight in grey. R-231
Knight in homespun. S-773
"Knight of Avenue A." S-80
Knight of Columbia. K-218
Knight of lonely land. C-76
Knight of the Cumberland. F-348
Knight of the golden circle. L-206
"Knight of the golden eagle." S-1118
Knight of the highway. S-177
Knight of the toilers. N-55
Knight of the XX. century. C-837
Knight of the wilderness. G-14
"Knight of the wire." L-152
Knight of today. H-920
Knight Vale of the K. K. K. S-120
Knight-errant. W-188
"Knighthood of Tony." R-122
"Knight's gambit." C-559
"Knight's move." G-121
Knights of the fleece. S-676
"Knitters in the sun." B-343
Knitting of the souls. G-100
Knock on the door. H-769
"Knock wood." M-773
"Knocker." G-510
Knockers' club. F-335
Knocking the neighbors. A-93
Knot of blue. W-738
"Knout and the fog." W-745
"Koolau the leper." L-442
"Kootchie." U-6
"Kotchin' de nines." C-832
Kottō. H-438
Kranbach Nocturne. K-300
"Krishmarao, who fought the disease devil out of Manglewari." M-1168

Little angel of Canyon Creek. B-885
Little apostle on crutches. D-281
Little back room. C-229
"Little bear tale." H-113
"Little bear who grew." P-366
"Little bells." M-271
"Little Bill's bandit." R-467
"Little bird and the blacksmith." W-121
"Little bisque dog." R-189
Little black men. H-496
"Little blue cat from Malta." M-605
"Little blue overalls." D-470
"Little Bo-peep." K-94
Little Bok. B-203
"Little Bok." B-203
Little book. C-919
Little book for Christmas. B-886
"Little book of Christmas." B-146
Little book of Rutgers tales. L-378
Little Boom No. 1. L-149
"Little boy." S-593
"Little boy and Mister Dark." C-832
"Little boy that was." L-553
Little brother. F-199
Little Brother o' Dreams. E-12
"Little brother of the books." B-68
Little brother of the rich. P-161
"Little brothers." P-101
Little brown jug at Kildare. N-81
Little Burr, the Warwick of America. P-398
"Little Byron." E-204
Little candle. P-570
"Little Chajim at the Melamed." C-565
Little chap. A-234
"Little Cherry and Uncle Joel." J-4
Little chevalier. D-137
Little child. C-987
"Little child shall feed them." C-552
Little child shall lead them. H-5
"Little child shall lead them." C-1015
"Little Christmas story." G-286
"Little Christopher." D-10
Little church around the corner. R-617
Little citizens. K-91
Little city of hope. C-910
"Little clown." M-161, T-363
Little Codfish Cabot at Harvard. O-113
Little comrade. S-906
Little conscript. B-1130
"Little convent girl." K-231
Little Corky. H-1032
"Little corner." S-82
Little Count of Villa Moncão. W-851
"Little cousin of No. 12." M-267
Little dark man. P-481
"Little dark man." P-481
"Little daughter of Eve." G-213
"Little Dave." D-352
"Little death." M-478
"Little dinner." B-622
"Little dollar's Christmas journey." R-319, R-320
"Little dramas of the curbstone." N-128
"Little Dugey and the perfect ass." S-722

"Little Emily." W-424
"Little Emma." W-763
Little eohippus. R-193
"Little essay on books." D-644
"Little Esther." P-226
Little Eve Edgarton. A-10
"Little feller." T-356
Little fiddler of the Ozarks. E-134
"Little fifer." R-251
"Little fop." H-454
Little fortune. K-406
Little fountain of life. W-182
* Little France. B-892
Little French girl. S-275
"Little friend coyote." G-541
"Little gall." B-831
Little gentleman across the road. A-6
"Little-girl-afraid-of-a-dog." F-402
Little girl and her doll. B-781
"Little girl at home." S-81
"Little girl up Damascus way." H-60
Little girl who couldn't-get-over-it. B-282
"Little girl who should have been a boy." D-470
"Little god and Dicky." B-57
"Little god and the machine." B-917
Little god Ebisu. D-407
Little gods. T-180
"Little Gods." T-180
Little gods laugh. F-105
"Little gray lady." S-618
"Little gray street." M-271
Little green door. B-330
Little green god. M-567
Little grey lady. M-273
"Little heiress." M-1008
Little hills. B-161
"Little horseradish woman." D-530
"Little hour." M-271
Little house. D-189, W-865
Little house by the way. W-768
Little house in the little street where the sun never came. L-481
"Little house of devotion." H-372
Little hunchback Zia. B-1230
Little James. W-661
"Little jaunt." S-80
"Little Juda." N-102
"Little Kansas leaven." C-93
Little knight of the X Bar B. M-626
Little Lady Bertha. S-471
Little lady of the big house. L-447
Little lady of the Hall. R-645
Little leaven. G-494
"Little life-tragedy in brown." O-140
"Little local colour." H-521
"Little lost love." H-372
Little lost sister. B-1026
Little love stories of Manhattan. C-326
"Little lover." D-470
"Little Lucy Rose." F-389
Little maid of Boston town. S-487
"Little man." T-180
"Little man of Twenty-eighth Street." B-536
"Little Marcus." A-255

"Mabel's mistake." H-284
Mac of Placid. L-487
"Mac of the island." K-75
McAllister and his double. T-354
McAllister's grove. H-656
"Macbeth sees himself." R-427
McCarty incog. O-168
"McCluskey's prodigal." V-105
McCrohan and Slammin- guides. N-180
"McDermott." M-448
McDonald of Oregon. D-676
"McElhattan and his springs." S-447
"McEwen of the shining slave makers." D-550
"McGennis's promotion." T-180
"McGill." B-377
"MacGregor and the button." H-143
"MacGregor and the minister's coat." H-143
"MacGregor and the white cow." H-143
"MacGregor attends a fire." H-143
"MacGregor on humor." H-143
"MacGregor on writing a book." H-143
MacGregors. H-789, M-29
"McGuffey and his pupils." M-730
"MacHassan Ah." M-1136
"Machinery." D-644
"McIntosh of Vergennes." R-462
MacIvor's folly. K-4
Mack. A-53
"McKenna in reminiscences of the Chicago fire of 1871." M-280
"McKenna's candidacy for chaplain." M-280
"McKeon's graft." R-614
"McKinley's Washington trips." W-217
"McLarty's new saloon." D-619
McLean. B-404
"McLeod at the log-rolling." P-329
"Macochee's first campaign fund." W-549
"MacRoman." K-285
"McTavish." M-1019
"McWilliamses and the burglar alarm." T-437
"Mad artist." R-112
Mad marriage. G-146
"Mad master." S-140
"Mad Meg." L-542
"Mad poet's quest." W-215
Mad? Which? Neither? M-574
"Madagascar." W-180
"Madam Marcot, milliner." D-61
"Madam Peacock." W-284
"Madam President." R-427
"Madame a Tort!" M-773
"Madame Anna." M-267
"Madame Bo-Peep, of the ranches." H-521
Madame Bohemia. N-38
"Madame Brimborion." H-326
"Madame de Benoit." B-911
Madame de Treymes. W-413
"Madame la Marquise." B-911
"Madame La Vergne smiles." C-52
Madame Margot. B-522
Madame Mésange. S-609
"Madame Naida." M-723
Madame Valcour's lodger. O-81
Madame X. M-67

Madcap. G-147
Madcap cruise. B-349
"Madcaps." D-19
Maddalena's day. W-804
"Maddalena's day." W-804
"Made an odd clean-up." K-106
"Made in England." T-199
"Made in Germany." B-197
Made to order. M-352
Madeline. F-110
Madeline: the island girl. D-69
Madelon passes. E-49
"Mademoiselle." T-421
Mademoiselle Celeste. K-344
Mademoiselle of Cambrai. F-314
"Mademoiselle Prune." H-949
"Mademoiselle's holiday." S-597
Madge, a girl in earnest. S-670
Madigans. M-747
Madison Hood. D-545
"Madison Square Arabian Night." H-517
"Madman's funeral." B-620
"Madman's luck." D-613
"Madness of Antony Spatola." D-678
"Madness of Bald Eagle." E-9
Madness of John Harned. L-454
Madness of May. N-83
Madness of Philip. B-57
"Madness of Philip." B-57
"Madonna of Devil's Creek." H-456
"Madonna of our square." B-1141
Madonna of sacrifice. O-108
"Madonna of the brush." P-583
"Madonna of the Casa Grande." C-1015
Madonna of the curb. M-1175
"Madonna of the falling leaves." T-16
Madonna of the hills. E-185
Madonna of the slate. R-227
"Madonna of the slate." R-227
"Madonna of the tambourine." R-122
"Madonna of the toys." C-1067
"Madonna of Tinkle Tickle." D-613
"Maestro of Balangilang." H-835
Mag Pye. V-195
Magdalene of old. C-819
Maggie of Virginsburg. M-522
Maggie Pepper. K-313
Magi in the west and their search for the Christ. D-368
"Magic." F-9, H-570
Magic and Mary Rose. B-110
Magic box. F-87
"Magic box." F-87
"Magic cape." K-90
"Magic casket." A-277
"Magic cloak." D-349
Magic mantle. J-25
"Magic mantle." J-25
"Magic mashie." S-8
Magic mashie and other golfish stories. S-8
Magic midland. W-32
"Magic of a voice." H-935
"Magic of sourness." E-226
Magic of the sea. C-676

Miss Petticoats. T-251
Miss Peyton of Virginia. S-647
"Miss Peyton of Virginia." S-647
Miss Phena. S-1151
Miss Philura's wedding gown. K-251
Miss Primrose. G-223
"Miss Prissy's diamond rings." O-21
Miss Prissy's diamond rings and other tales. O-21
Miss Pritchard's wedding trip. B-1252
"Miss Puss's parasol." H-277
"Miss Queroot." B-209
"Miss Ripley's point of view." B-196
"Miss Rose." S-80
Miss Santa Claus of the Pullman. J-139
"Miss Scarborough's point of view." B-470
Miss Schuyler's alias. H-856
"Miss Scruggs." S-109
Miss Selina Lue and the soap-box babies. D-103
"Miss Sticky-Moufie-Kiss." F-175
Miss Sylvester's marriage. C-310
"Miss Thankful's relations." A-215
Miss Theodosia's heartstrings. D-468
Miss 318. H-991
Miss 318 and Mr. 37. H-992
"Miss Tilly an' Marse Jeems." R-413
"Miss Toodles and the burglar." G-163
"Miss Trumbull's triumph." B-199
"Miss Tyndall's picture." A-92
"Miss Underhill's lesson." J-214
Miss Varney's experience. D-472
"Miss Varney's experience." D-472
Miss Wealthy, deputy sheriff. N-30
"Miss Williams." W-223
"Miss Windermere's country house." G-561
"Missed a few." E-146
"Missile." P-281
"Missing bride." B-1362
"Missing chord." H-506
"Missing daughter of Chee Tong." B-34
Missing empire. G-130
Missing initial. L-333
Missing link. K-301
Missing links in the story. D-53
"Missing match." C-467
"Missing Mr. Master." B-1356
"Missing: page thirteen." G-430
"Missing St. Michael." M-596
"Mission of a bookmark." B-533
"Mission of Jane." W-407
Mission of Victoria Wilhelmenia. M-360
Mission tales in the days of the dons. F-236
Mission to hell. E-56
"Missionary effort on Osman Island." T-422
Mississippi Argonauts. C-164
Mississippi bubble. H-884
Mississippi stories. C-137
"Missouri appleblossom." H-372
"Missouri spree." C-925
Missouri yesterdays. H-372
Missourian. L-575
Missourian's honor. A-319
Missy. G-93
"Missy and I." G-87

"Mistake." R-420
Mr. Achilles. L-162
"Mr. Alberg's worry." R-190
"Mr. Ambassador." D-61
"Mr. and Mrs. Elliot." H-463
Mr. and Mrs. Haddock abroad. S-927
Mr. and Mrs. Pierce. M-283
Mr. & Mrs. Sên. M-834
Mr. Arnold. L-600
Mr. Barnes, American. G-584
"Mr. Ben Gordon." J-142
Mister Bill. L-617
"Mr. Billing's pockets." B-1361
Mr. Bingle. M-130
Mr. Bisbee's princess. S-1026
"Mr. Bisbee's princess." S-1026
"Mr. Bishop." O-142
"Mr. Bob." O-138
"Mr. Bolster." G-322
"Mr. Boozer." E-224
"Mr. Bosco." A-219
"Mr. Braddy's bottle." C-672
"Mr. Bridge's nightmare." J-96
"Mr. Brinkley to the rescue." J-208
"Mr. Brooke." T-49
"Mr. Carnegie's gift." D-643
"Mr. Carnegie's hero fund." D-639
"Mr. Carteret and his fellow Americans abroad." G-396
Mr. Carteret and others. G-396
"Mr. Carteret's adventure with a locket." G-396
Mr. Claghorn's daughter. T-378
"Mr. Comstock's arrival." S-121
"Mister Conley." V-103
"Mr. Crane's last wife." O-142
Mr. Crewe's career. C-417
Mr. Cushing and Mlle. du Chastel. R-602
"Mr. De Shine wins out." G-443
"Mr. De Shine's return." G-443
Mr. Dimock. O-182
Mr. Doctor-Man. W-867
"Mr. Dombledon." G-25
Mr. Dooley on making a will and other necessary evils. D-640
Mr. Dooley on timely topics of the day. D-641
Mr. Dooley says. D-642
Mr. Dooley's opinions. D-643
"Mr. Draper's diary." W-215
Mr. Durbar's toast. M-84
"Mr. Durbar's toast." M-83
"Mr. Feeney's social experiment." K-162
Mister Fish Kelly. M-14
Mr. Foley of Salmon. C-1005
Mister 44. R-54
"Mr. Gabbler's Christmas Eve." S-1161
Mr. Goggles. B-1078
"Mr. Green's promise." D-327
"Mr. Groby's slippery gift." D-597
"Mr. Grossnickle's ghost." H-168
Mr. Guelpa. T-201
Mr. Hawkins' humorous adventures. F-365
"Mr. Henry Shelfords' advice." P-380
Mr. Hobby. K-76
"Mr. Holiday." M-1019
"Mr. Icky." F-165

Mr. Ingle comes through. T-228
"Mr. Isaac Cohen." S-772
Mr. Jackson. G-445
"Mr. Jeckel's wife." P-380
Mr. Keegan's elopement. C-418
Mr. Langdon's mistake. H-400
"Mr. Leffington feels inspired." H-592
"Mr. Lindsay on `San Jewan'." A-92
"Mr. Lobel's apoplexy." C-531
"Mr. MacGlowrie's widow." H-329
Mr. Man. K-399
"Mr. Mangle sidesteps trouble." G-444
Mr. Munchausen. B-148
Mr. Opp. R-214
"Mr. Payson's satirical Christmas." A-92
Mr. Perryman's Christmas eve. P-501
Mr. Pickett of Detroit. S-802
Mr. Podd. T-238
"Mr. Pottle and culture." C-672
"Mr. Pottle and pageantry." C-672
"Mr. Pottle and the one man dog." C-672
"Mr. Pottle and the South-Sea cannibals." C-672
Mr. Pratt. L-315
Mr. Pratt's patients. L-316
"Mr. Punkin dilates on wireless telegraphy." P-633
"Mr. Punkin talks on football." P-633
"Mr. Rabbit's home brew." P-25
"Mr. Ruth and Mr. Dempsey." C-925
Mr. Salt. P-190
Mr. Scraggs. P-362
"Mr. Skinner's night in the underworld." C-429
"Mr. Slate." O-64
Mr. Smith, the personnel officer. T-163
"Mr. Snively's vacation." J-198
Mr. Squem and Some male triangles. T-65
"Mr. Thornberry's eldorado." S-862
Mr. Togo maid of all work. I-60
Mr. Waddy's return. W-780
"Mr. Waldo amuses the baby." J-208
"Mr. Warriner's transformation." S-82
Mr. Whitman. P-638
"Mr. Wilson: That's all." G-259
"Mr. Wimberley's trousers." A-92
"Mr. Winkelberg." H-454
Mr. World and Miss Church-Member. H-287
Mr. Wu. M-835
Mrs. Alderman Casey. C-107
"Mrs. Animule." O-64
"Mrs. Anthony." S-80
"Mrs. Asborn the village gossip." W-641
"Mrs. Atwood's outer raiment." C-1065
Mrs. Balfame. A-343
"Mrs. Beatty takes offense." M-971
"Mrs. Bidwell's tea." L-496
"Mrs. Bill's protectorate." L-243
"Mrs. Billy's baby and the professor." M-83
"Mrs. Blenker's windfall." H-952
Mrs. Bobble's trained nurse. T-394
Mrs. Brand. K-43
"Mrs. Brown." S-109
Mrs. Budlong's Christmas presents. H-994
"Mrs. Carment's new prayer." M-243
"Mrs. Christy's beginnings." S-82

Mrs. Clyde. G-330
"Mrs. Copeland's convalescents." C-586
"Mrs. Crumpey's boarders." J-198
Mrs. Darrell. S-260
"Mrs. Davenport's ghost." T-444
"Mrs. Derwall and the higher life." D-671
"Mrs. Dud's sister." B-60
"Mrs. Dummerford's niece." E-32
Mrs. Eli and Policy Ann. O-82
Mrs. Essington. C-213
Mrs. Farrell. H-933
Mrs. Featherweight's musical moments. B-910
"Mrs. Garrigan's new carpet." M-971
"Mrs. Gerlison's own story." P-57
"Mrs. Golobiewsky's first good time." W-535
"Mrs. Hannah Smith, nurse." K-34
"Mrs. Henry Nesbit." M-723
"Mrs. Holzapple's convictions." M-514
"Mrs. Hornbeam's headdress." V-192
Mrs. Hope's husband. B-1206
* Mrs. J. Worthington Woodward. B-438
"Mrs. Jeff." M-290
Mrs. Jim and Mrs. Jimmie. C-699
"Mrs. Jim Kennedy attends a meeting at Baker's Hall..." M-280
"Mrs. Jimmy goes camping." G-443
"Mrs. Joe Buey." H-921
"Mrs. John Hart." H-921
Mrs. John Vernon. A-84
"Mrs. Lathrop's love affair." W-139
Mrs. Lemon's neighbors. O-68
"Mrs. Lewis "sees" a ball game." K-177
Mrs. Linthicum and Mary Jane. M-679
"Mrs. McGovern prisints her daughter." B-820
"Mrs. McMurtrie's rooster." P-218
Mrs. McPiggs' of the Very Old Scratch. V-212
"Mrs. Maecenas." B-1218
Mrs. Mahoney of the tenement. M-924
"Mrs. Mainwaring's second marriage." S-140
Mrs. Marden's ordeal. H-394
"Mrs. Mark Thompson." H-921
Mrs. Mason's daughters. E-83
"Mrs. Medwin Flickerbridge." J-35
"Mrs. Meekey explains the higher thought." F-153
"Mrs. Murchison." O-59
"Mrs. O'Rafferty." W-180
Mrs. Paramor. V-51
"Mrs. Partridge presents." K-33
"Mrs. Pearl Prunepincher's page in every lady's magazine." F-175
Mrs. Pendleton's four-in-hand. A-344
"Mrs. Pepper in Paris." G-347
Mrs. Phelps' husband. S-723
"Mrs. Pinkney's spring spell." M-942
"Mrs. Porter's April story." H-663
"Mrs. Protheroe." T-46
Mrs. Radigan. L-401
Mrs. Raffles. B-149
"Mrs. Randolph's nerve." S-195
Mrs. Red Pepper. R-278
"Mrs. Rensling takes a rest." H-350
"Mrs. Rodjezke's last job." H-454
"Mrs. Sardotopolis' evening off." H-454
"Mrs. Shelly." L-356
"Mrs. Sinkers has the clocks." G-309

"Mrs. Smith's husband." L-496
Mrs. Strangeways. M-972
"Mrs. Strangeways." M-972
Mrs. Tree. R-241
"Mrs. Tremley." C-1070
Mrs. Tree's will. R-242
"Mrs. Trippit gets back at Johnny." G-444
"Mrs. Truckles' broad jump." F-260
"Mrs. Tumulty's hat." P-25
"Mrs. Turner." O-185
Mrs. Van Twiller's salon. F-414
"Mrs. Vietch." H-917
"Mrs. Von Dorn, Aunt Betty Caslin and ..." B-369
Mrs. Wiggs of the cabbage patch. R-215
Mrs. William Horton speaking. K-173
"Mrs. Winn's way." G-569
"Mrs. With's affinity." S-121
"Mrs. Worthley's secret." B-1362
Mistress Anne. B-79
Mistress Brent. T-226
"Mistress Carrington of Virginia." C-974
Mistress Dorothy of Haddon Hall. H-356
Mistress Dorothy. B-295
Mistress Hetty. H-868
Mistress Joy. C-727
"Mistress Mackie and the powders." H-143
Mistress Nell. H-429
"Mistress of art." R-122
"Mistuh Macbeth." C-557
Misty flats. W-846
"Misunderstanding." L-28
"Misunderstood by the world." S-571
Misunderstood hero. B-395
"Misunderstood man." C-139
Mitch Miller. M-593
"Mittome." W-21
Mixed dates. B-238
Mixed faces. N-169
"Mixed foursome." S-8, V-99
"Mixed troubles." T-241, T-242
"Mixed-up foursome." S-1139
Mixing. W-460
"Mizpeh." R-538
Mlle. Fouchette. M-1162
Mlle. L'Inconnue. G-230
M'lord o' the white road. F-366
Mme. Maimee. B-923
"Moan of the sea." S-944
Moan of the Tiber. P-323
"Mobile, the heart of the storied south." C-52
"Mobile's quest." R-621
Moccasin Ranch. G-61
Moccasins of gold. W-240
"Mock Don Yuen and the Tongs." D-255
"Mock Don Yuen meditates." D-255
"Mock husband." D-413
"Mock sun." H-1029
Mocking bird's breed. M-323
"Mode." R-427
"Model girl." A-215
Modern Apollos. M-257
Modern arms and a feudal throne. H-310
Modern Becky Sharp. B-1029

Modern blessing fire. C-750
"Modern Bluebeard." H-284
"Modern buccaneer." K-372
Modern chronicle. C-416
"Modern Cleopatra." D-117
"Modern conversation." M-587
"Modern courtships." P-183
"Modern Cœur-de-lion." B-1001
"Modern daughter." G-332
"Modern Evangeline." S-698
Modern evil. B-1368
Modern ghost stories. B-1174
Modern Hamilton. E-106
"Modern horse jock." E-224
"Modern judgment of Solomon." V-102
Modern knight. H-731, N-163
"Modern knight and lady fair." B-691
Modern love chase. A-366
Modern Madonna. S-808
"Modern Mercury." H-240
"Modern Methuselah." P-633
Modern miracle. C-960
"Modern Mobile." C-52
"Modern mormon." T-21
"Modern mother." G-332
Modern obstacle. M-786
Modern pagans. S-391
Modern paradise. O-66
"Modern paradise." M-1189
Modern patrician. M-925
"Modern Petrarach." S-444
Modern Prometheus. B-582
Modern revolt from Rome. B-543
"Modern rural sports." H-504
Modern short stories. M-879
Modern Socrates. B-755
Modern tragedy. D-563
Modern trio in an old town. T-82
"Modern utopia." C-1015
"Modern way." T-293
"Modern wedding." P-183
Modern women. K-378
Modernist. H-946
Moderns. D-88
"Modest Jones." P-101
"Modest man." L-403
"Mohammed and Nadia." T-140
Mohawk Peter. D-482
"Mold of heroines." S-81
"Mole's path." R-462
Mollie and the unwiseman. B-147
"Mollie darling." K-162
"Mollie Doyle's experience." S-1119
Mollie's substitute husband. M-69
Molly. D-262
"Molly." B-826
"Molly, a range cow." P-171
Molly and I. A-58
"Molly Jenner's way." S-80
Molly McDonald. P-120
Molly Make-Believe. A-11
Mollyjoggers. D-619
"Molly's change of scene." S-80

My friend Prospero. H-214
"My friend the elephant." E-204
"My friend the rag-picker." W-661
"My friend the undertaker." L-571
My friend Will. L-553
"My friend Zahn." H-312
"My friend's wife and I." L-230
"My garden." O-64
My garden doctor. D-600
My garden of hearts. S-80
"My gipsey sweetheart." S-445
"My golf." L-496
"My grandame's secret." G-52
My grandfather's best brand. H-420
"My grandfather's ghost stories." D-313
My guardian. C-597
My heart and Stephanie. K-23
"My hearth." H-510
"My host the enemy." C-41
My host the enemy and other tales. C-41
"My invisible spears." T-160
My Japanese prince. G-585
"My kindergarten of fifty years." B-1197
"My kingdom is not of this world." C-474
"My lady." S-195
"My Lady and lovingkindness." A-157
My lady Beatrice. C-720
My Lady Clancarty. T-98
"My lady fair." I-28
"My Lady Greensleeves." T-198
"My Lady Hope." K-148
My Lady Laughter. T-252
My Lady Lee. P-604
"My Lady o'roses." A-157
My lady of doubt. P-121
My lady of the chimney corner. I-36
My lady of the fog. B-190
"My Lady of the Gondola." G-318
My lady of the North. P-122
My lady of the South. P-123
My lady Peggy goes to town. M-607
My Lady Peggy leaves town. M-608
My Lady Primrose. W-214
My Lady Valentine. R-409
My lady's fortune hunt. K-267
My lady's garter. F-483
My lady's kiss. I-27
My lady's slipper. B-890
My land. My country. My home. A-116
"My last shrubbery." S-85
My Li'l' Angelo. C-657
My life in two worlds. H-528
My little kingdom. M-52
My little sister. R-436
"My little sister." H-904
My Lord Farquhar. M-951
My lost duchess. W-665
My love and I. B-1050
"My lover's bequest." T-443
"My lover's daughter." T-443
"My master goes to jail." P-176
"My master makes a mistake." P-176
"My maussuh." G-290

"My metamorphosis." H-326
"My mother." M-1155
"My mother's diary." T-293
"My next-door neighbor." O-64
"My niece Cicely." W-215
"My niece, Mrs. Dove." D-585
My northern exposure. T-365
My old field. R-171
"My old log fire." M-942
My old maid's corner. F-415
"My old man." H-463
"My old yaller almanac." S-918
"My ole colored mammy." H-904
"My otherself." H-326
"My own early home." D-352
My own Main Street. J-169
"My pastor." B-231
"My pickaninny." B-134
"My pilgrimage." T-276
"My platonic sweetheart." T-437
My Quaker maid. R-640
"My race for Justice of the Peace in precinct 5." S-85
My ragpicker. W-66
"My roomy." L-67
"My sister Madge." O-205
My soldier lady. D-653
My son. H-262
"My song." I-28
"My southern mother." H-904
"My stomach and I." I-28
My story. S-939
My strange life. M-1172
"My strange wanderings." A-219
"My study." O-64
"My summer girl." P-633
"My teeth and toothache experiences." S-85
My three years at Andover. S-1079
"My translatophone." S-958
My tussle with the devil. H-510
"My tussle with the devil." H-510
"My uncaged mockingbird." M-942
"My vacation on the east side." R-232
"My violet." B-1187
"My visit to a great art gallery." S-85
"My visit to the Shakers." S-80
"My whiskey-flask." I-28
My wife's wedding presents. J-116
"My Wild Rose." H-51
My wondrous dream. B-119
Myra of the pines. V-168
Myriam and the mystic brotherhood. H-916
"Myron Daw." M-723
Myrta. C-890
Myrtle Baldwin. M-1144
"Myrtle-that-was-changed-to-Esther." S-702
"Myrtle's treasure." S-80
Mysteries of Ann. B-1051
Mysteries of the Zímniy dvóretz. P-5
"Mysterious birthday box." G-163
Mysterious burglar. W-75
Mysterious card. M-892
"Mysterious disappearance of Old Mayhew." J-4
"Mysterious guests." H-168

Noble criminal. R-192
Noble Earl of Fleetwood. A-276
Noble fool. E-251
Noble girl. B-947
"Noble nuns." M-200
"Noblesse." F-389
"Noblesse oblige." A-144, G-290, M-1159, W-589
"Noblesse obliged." C-551
Noblest Roman. M-964
Nobody. V-53
"Nobody knows." A-243
Nobody yet somebody. T-90
Nobody's. D-324
Nobody's child. D-271
Nobody's cousin. V-109
"Nocturne." H-240, H-453, S-674
"Noel of 1864." A-98
Noise of the world. S-724
Nomad. S-664
Nomads. S-1127
Nomads of the North. C-1052
Nonchalante. O-87
None but the brave. S-246
"None but the brave." H-952
None so blind. D-248, F-155
"Noodle factory story." D-619
"Noodle's flat." G-443
Noon. M-554
"Noon." S-10
Noon-mark. W-232
Noonday night. S-381
"Noose matrimonial." S-41
"Nor iron bars on a cage." B-48
"Nor' Neilan's daughter." M-971
Nora pays. V-121
"Nora's blockade running." W-535
Norkoma. G-531
Norma Lane. C-714
Norman Holt. K-221
"Norman's courtship." G-489
Norroy, diplomatic agent. B-1008
"Norry Donlan, benefactress." E-5
North. H-480
"North bastion." S-450
North land. M-334
North Mountain mementos. S-448
North of fifty-three. S-502
North of 36. H-886
North Pacific. A-179
"North Pole." S-593
North Star. H-523, K-237
"North wind's malice." B-383
Northerner. D-141
"Northwest by north." P-25
Norton Hardin. C-837
"Nose for it." E-146
"Nose for the king." L-468
"Nostalgia." M-267
"Not a day over twenty-one." F-67
"Not a drum was heard." W-649
"Not a Gregory." D-19
Not a judgement-. K-146
"Not a sad story." C-1065

"Not agreeable." E-146
Not all the king's horses. C-221
"Not at home." T-356
"Not before the footlights." E-146
"Not down in the log." C-690
"Not guilty." C-1021, T-443
Not in His steps. H-804
"Not in the signal code." W-823
Not included in a sheepskin. F-411
"Not interested." E-146
"Not much respect for jestice." E-146
Not of her race. F-329
Not on the chart. M-466
"Not superstitious." E-146
Not taps, but reveille. A-235
Not to have and to hold. N-175
"Not to the flesh." A-182
Not under the law. H-641
"Not vague but striking." E-146
Not wanted. W-666
"Not wisely but too well." C-562
"Not with his boots on." R-97
"Notable war-time dance and oyster supper." B-1286
Notary of Grand Pré. M-308
"Note." D-288
Note of discord. C-1022
"Note to a chapter on journalism." M-453
"Noted people." P-176
"Notes for a tragedy." H-454
"Notes from a French village in the war zone." C-93
"Notes on the utilization of human remains." H-433
"Nothin' but the truth." E-146
Nothing a year. D-116
Nothing but the truth. I-87
"Nothing Child." G-541
"Nothing doing." E-146
Nothing else matters. J-134
"Nothing to do." N-157
Notturno. C-141
Novels and stories of Richard Harding Davis. D-161
Novels and tales of Henry James. J-43
"November." C-974
"November afternoon." S-8
"November by the North Sea." W-804
"November second." M-271
"Novena." N-60
Nowhere else in the world. H-960
"Nth commandment." H-1056
"Nubta and Ardi, builders." B-1276
"Nude in literature." C-925
"Nugget." C-921
Nuisance. G-342
"Nuisance." R-423
Number six. T-177
"Number 52 Rue Nationale." D-349
"Number four, Balzac Street." P-527
"Number 1100." W-730
"Number seven." C-239
"Number 13." E-146
No. 13, rue du Bon Diable. H-207
No. 13 Toroni. R-151
No. 13 Washington Square. S-210
Number thirty. J-175

Old-fashioned romance. N-65
"Old-fashioned school." W-144
"Old-fashioned wife." K-156
Old-fashioned woman. T-213
"Old-time March meeting." R-462
"Old-time "turkey shoot" on the Kankakee." B-1286
"Old-time wiregrass frolic." H-572
"Old-timer." E-146
Older, the newer. D-603
"Oldest journalist in the South seas." W-725
Oldfield. B-162
Ole Ann. W-219
"Ole Ann." W-219
"Ole bline Hannah." G-166
"Ole Bull's castle." S-449
"Ole Hawg." C-239
"Ole Joe an' de yaller mule." C-382
"Ole 'Lijah's weddin'-a plantation episode." C-382
"Ole Mis' Freshours." M-942
Ole watah mill deserted by man ... E-173
Olea. G-261
Oliver Langton. P-587
"Oliver Mendwell's wife." W-215
Oliver October. M-132
"Olivia's pottage." C-3
"Olivia's sun-dial." F-453
Ollivant orphans. I-49
Olympian. O-99
Olympian nights. B-150
"Olympians." B-1218
Olympic victor. C-682
Om. M-1134
"Omaha Slim." L-18
"Ommirandy." G-322
Ommirandy: plantation life at Kingsmill. G-322
"Omna vincit amor." M-974
"On a bridge." H-436
"On a brief text from Isiah." B-1089
"On 'count ob Miss Win'fred." P-599
"On a day like this." H-454
On a lark to the planets. M-923
"On a lee shore." P-38
"On a line with the net." T-241, T-242
"On a park bench." D-544
On a passing frontier. L-345
"On a pedestal." B-208
"On a pretty girl at the opera." H-326
On Aaron's neck. S-677
"On account of a lady." V-104
"On an errand of mercy." M-621
On and off the breadwagon. D-572
"On and off the water wagon." S-988
"On art collecting." M-596
"On athletics." D-643
On autumn trails. S-785
"On behalf of the management." H-513
"On Black Moshannon." S-445
On board a whaler. H-124
"On board the Athol." R-420
On board the Beatic. R-69
On board the Mary Sands. R-243
On Christmas Day in the evening. R-279
On Christmas Day in the morning. R-280

"On Christmas Eve." G-286
"On Christmas giving." B-886
"On counting chickens." S-81
"On criminal trials." D-640
"On donkey-back to Cape Spartel." W-804
"On Easter morning." P-413
"On Edom Hill." C-606
"On enjoying one's own writings." R-232
"On food in war." D-640
On fortune's road. P-191
On furlough. O-83
"On Georges Shoals." C-678
"On Gittings' farm." M-320
"On going to sea." H-23
"On going to see the doctor." D-640
On golden hinges. T-333
"On golf." D-640
"On Hallowe'en." T-247
"On hand just once." C-1012
"On heroes and history." D-640
"On his majesty's service." H-952
On his toes! M-158
"On home life." D-640
"On James Creek." H-389
"On jay towns." E-7
"On losing friends." S-80
"On lying." D-643
"On making a will." D-640
"On matrimony." G-296
"On medical conservation." B-144
"On my journey home." G-166
"On old age." D-640
On our hill. B-61
"On past glories." D-640
"On St. Patrick's Day." D-640
On Satan's mount. T-253
On secret service. T-11
"On Slater circuit." N-41
"On some fortunate yet thrice blasted shore." L-124
On Taku Bar. M-715
"On the Amazon." P-471
"On the Banks of the Shrewsbury." G-384
"On the bottom of the dory." C-677
"On the bridge." S-862
"On the country road." W-661
"On the crest of the range." S-575
"On the descent of man." D-640
"On the dock." C-810
"On the echo o' the morn." C-685
"On the edge." C-90
* On the fighting line. R-70
On the firing line. R-70
"On the forecastle deck." R-423
"On the French shore of Cape Breton." S-638
"On the game of cards." D-640
"On the gift of oratory." D-640
"On the god's knees." C-996
"On the graces and anxieties of pig driving." P-624
"On the heights." L-28
"On the high seas." P-288
"On the higher baseball." D-640
On the hill-top. Y-7
On the Indian trail. V-89

"Our mammy." D-10
Our mammy: and other stories. D-10
"Our mantua-maker." R-534
Our Miss York. M-1001
Our mission to Ento. W-295
Our Mr. Wrenn. L-267
"Our mother's passion." C-539
Our nation's altar. C-751
Our nation's curse. B-818
Our Natupski neighbors. M-841
Our next-door neighbors. M-399
"Our Paris letter." J-96
"Our pilgrim fathers." B-950
"Our political equality cranks." B-231
"Our precious lunatic." T-429
"Our private romance." A-92
"Our representatives abroad." D-639
Our right to love. D-338
"Our rivals in fiction." R-232
"Our roof garden among the tenements." R-322
"Our sacred Thanksgiving." T-422
"Our Saturday at home." D-313
Our search for the missing millions. C-367
Our sister republic. O-189
Our square and the people in it. A-76
Our story of Atlantis. P-302
Our town. W-828
"Our town." B-231
"Our uncle George." S-121
Our Uncle William. F-316
"Our uninvited guest." C-41
"Our yard." G-220
Ouray Jim. S-930
"Ouray Jim." S-930
"Ourselves." R-427
Out for the coin. H-699
Out nation's peril. R-596
Out of a clear sky. D-104
Out of a fleur-de-lis. W-396
Out of Africa. C-167
Out of bondage. R-462, R-546
"Out of bondage." R-462
"Out of class b into the king row." A-93
"Out of darkness." R-220
Out of darkness into light. W-629
"Out of Egypt." B-1375
Out of Gloucester. C-685
"Out of his class." V-104
"Out of his orbit." L-210
"Out of his past." S-862
"Out of Nazareth." H-520
"Out of nowhere into nothing." A-241
"Out of reach of the baby." M-773
Out of Russia. M-459
"Out of season." H-463
"Out of sympathy." K-82
Out of the air. I-50
Out of the ashes. M-1121, R-173
Out of the beaten track. N-183
Out of the darkness. D-659, G-367
Out of the depths. B-504, P-87, V-150
"Out of the depths." C-275, G-286, W-661
Out of the desert. W-493

"Out of the Dope Book." F-470
Out of the dump. M-432
"Out of the jaws of a black man-eating panther." M-1168
Out of the lion's mouth. C-450
Out of the Middle West. B-1331
Out of the mire. G-392
Out of the mist. D-62
"Out of the mist." M-469
"Out of the mouth of babes." K-82
Out of the night. Y-42
"Out of the night." B-383
Out of the Ozarks. R-598
"Out of the past." N-68
Out of the primitive. B-505
Out of the ruts. K-107
Out of the silences. W-67
Out of the silent North. D-533
Out of the West. H-601
Out of tune. S-662
"Out of work." L-615
"Out on bail." G-296
"Out there." G-247
Out where the world begins. C-821
"Out with the big top." G-443
"Out with the church." S-593
"Out-Heroding Herod." F-372
Outbound road. M-1085
Outcast. H-587
"Outcast." H-21, M-320, P-11
Outcast manufacturers. F-304
"Outcasts." T-247
Outcry. J-44
Outland. A-376
Outlaw. G-480
"Outlaw." C-582, G-65, T-363
"Outlaw, a steer." P-171
"Outlaw and suffrajet." M-382
Outlaws. A-311
"Outlaws and opera." R-427
Outlaws of Ravenhurst. W-60
Outlet. A-49
Outlines. B-286
"Outliving a shroud." B-1286
Outrageous Miss Dawn-Dream. L-481
Outside a city wall. K-352
Outside Inn. K-70
Outside the law. B-229
Outsider. S-53
"Outsider." V-72
"Outside of the house." F-392
"Outward bound." C-573
Oval diamond. F-312
Over against Green Peak. H-1021
Over here stories. R-517
Over here. K-71
Over Paradise ridge. D-105
"Over plate 16,903 of beef-and." G-309
Over the border. R-422, W-451
"Over the great divide." T-422
"Over the hill to the rich house." R-293
"Over the mountains." C-594
Over the pass. P-55
Over the plum-pudding. B-151

898

Picked company. F-217
"Picked seven at Hat-Band." C-41
"Picker's relief." R-505
Picking winners with Major Miles. Y-10
"Pickled pansy." H-663
"Pickpockets." G-592
Pickwick ladle. M-931
"Pickwick ladle." M-931
"Picnic." F-175
"Picnic in Turkey." P-101
Pictorial page in Reconstruction. W-899
"Picture." D-544
Picture frames. W-763
"Picture in the locket." L-424
"Picture of the plains." M-92
Picture on the wall. E-135
Pictureland of the heart. K-354
Pictures of Polly. C-845
Pidgin island. M-233
Pie and the pirate. L-143
Piebald. H-381
"Piece of steak." L-468
"Piece of string." P-624
"Piece of wreckage." K-82
"Pieces of silver." C-673
Pieces of the game. C-281
"Pierre Ranco, madman." M-320
Pierre Vinton. V-158
"Pierre's part." R-46
"Pierrot." M-271
Pierrot, dog of Belgium. D-679
"Pies." L-18
"Pig." H-454
"Pig and the man." M-688
Pig iron. P-82
"Pig or pup?" E-146
"Pigeon-blood ruby." B-470
"Pigeons-migration of birds." C-1000
Pigs is pigs. B-1357
Pigs to market. C-222
"Pike's Peak by moonlight." C-82
"Pike's Peak or bust." D-313, L-188
"Pilgrim." C-277
Pilgrim and the pioneer. B-458
"Pilgrim chamber." B-1040
Pilgrim stories. P-641
"Pilgrimage to Cranbrook." B-743
Pilgrims' first Christmas. S-222
Pilgrims into folly. I-61
Pilgrims of the plains. A-288
Pilgrim's progress in other worlds. M-543
"Pilgrims to Mecca." F-219
Pillar of salt. L-165
Pillar of sand. C-189
Pillars of Eden. M-762
Pillars of Rehoboth Church. R-458
Pillars of smoke. P-420
"Pilson Blair." H-921
"Pimienta pancakes." H-506
"Pimmon, the idiot slave." T-422
"Pinafore and "The Duke" skin a corporation." G-443
Pinch quitter. T-243
"Pinch quitter." T-243

Pincus Hood. H-720
"Pinderina Scribblerus, an American Montagu." M-827
Pine Grove house. H-87
Pine Ridge plantation. D-575
Pines of Lory. M-859
"Pineville Woman's Club." P-413
Piney Home. K-184
"Piney on a rampage." J-174
Piney Ridge cottage. A-227
"Pink bait." C-559
"Pink cravat." C-306
"Pink foxgloves." S-271
"Pink ghost of Franklin square." B-1188
"Pink melon joy." S-841
"Pink party at Pathacket." P-633
Pink sash. A-16
"Pink shawls." F-393
"Pink tights and ginghams." F-71
Pink typhoon. R-417
Pinkled frinft. Z-15
Pinto Ben. H-321
Pioneer. B-724
Pioneer doctor. G-345
"Pioneer life on the Kankakee eighty years ago." B-1286
"Pioneer woman's peril." C-41
Pioneer's hoard. V-92
"Pioneers of Forty-Nine." H-326
"Pioneers three and a horse trade." B-1286
Pipe dreams & twilight tales. J-4
"Piper of Hamelin." H-433
"Pipes o' Pan." C-62
"Pipes of Pod Fogarty." M-971
Pipes of yesterday. K-411
Pippin. R-244, V-32
"Pipsisseway's pine." S-444
"Pirate Joe." F-236
Pirate of Panama. R-22
Pirate of parts. N-49
Pirate of Pittsburgh. W-555
"Pirate Wilson-deserter." C-996
"Pirates." B-1021, M-974
Pirates' hope. L-601
Pirates of the sky. G-7
"Pirates twain." H-23
Piri and I. V-1
Pit. N-127
"Pitch-out." V-101
"Pitcher plant." S-447
Pitcher Pollock. M-615
"Pitchers and lamps." R-538
"Pitiful man." M-854
"Pity of it." C-167
"Pity 'tis, 'tis true." O-63
"Pitzela's son." H-454
"Piute vs. Piute." V-103
"Place aux dames!" G-291
Place beyond the winds. C-644
Place in the sun. B-36
"Place in the sun." C-570
"Place of abandoned gods." C-604
Place of honeymoons. M-234
"Place of martyrs." D-672
"Place of purgatory." E-5

914

Rose of the world. M-539, N-143
"Rose of Wolfville." L-243
Rose parlor. C-75
"Rose petals." R-112
Rose-bush of a thousand years. W-19
Rose-garden husband. W-590
"Roseback plate." M-931
Roselin. M-734
Rosemary. H-30
Rosemary for remembrance. C-152, G-527
Rosemary Leigh. S-580
"Rosemary Roselle." H-544
"Rosemary's stepmother." N-141
"Rosenthal the Jew." R-576
"Roses and the song." R-122
"Roses of today." M-972
"Roses, ruses and romance." H-519
"Rose's thorns." L-243
"Rosh Hashonah." L-222
Rosie world. F-122
Rosine. S-581
"Rosita." M-290
"Roskin's roost." T-21
Rosnah. K-93
Rosy. D-459
"Rosy balm." B-1040
"Rote." W-193
"Rouge et noir." H-499
Rough life on the frontier. V-93
Rough rider. B-507
Rough-hewn. C-97
"Roulette." H-1062
Round Anvil Rock. B-163
Round Hill farm. M-839
"Round of visits." J-36
"Round robin championship." S-1139
Round the circle. D-218
"Round the circle." H-520
Round the corner in Gay street. R-285
"Round Valley." H-312
Round-up. F-431, M-1164
"Rounded with a sleep." B-1197
"Roundhouse Tom." A-45
"Rounding up spies." E-186
Rout of the foreigner. Z-13
Routledge rides alone. C-625
"Rover's last fight." R-319
Rovin' Redden. R-404
Roving red rangers. R-443
Roving river. P-265
"Row of old shoes." L-17
"Row-boat pilgrimage." W-842
Rowdy of the "Cross L." B-796
Roxy's good angel. O-23
"Roxy's good angel." O-23
Royal Americans. F-218
"Royal compliment." T-429
"Royal doings." D-639
Royal end. H-215
Royal good fellow. H-410
Royal knight. M-174
Royal outlaw. H-955
Royal pawn of Venice. T-407

Royal rogues. B-137
Royal tragedy. W-616
"Roy's awakening." D-547
"Roystering blades." A-93
"Ru of the reserves." B-63
"Rub of the green." S-8
"Rubaiyat of a Scotch highball." H-517
"Rubber hunter." G-514
"Rubber plant's story." H-520
"Rubber stamp." P-65
"Rube." G-510
Ruben and Ivy Sên. M-837
"Rube's honeymoon." G-510
"Rube's pennant." G-510
"Rube's Waterloo." G-510
"Ruby and the caldron." G-431
Ruby cross. K-147
Ruby Floyd's temptation. B-204
"Ruby Floyd's temptation." B-204
Ruby necklace. M-734
Ruby necklace and other stories. J-188
Ruby of Kishmoor. P-661
"Ruby of Kishmoor." P-659
Rubyiat of a freshman. W-799
Rudder. W-234
"Rudolph where have you been." G-253
Rudra. W-373
Rue with a difference. R-103
Ruel Durke. B-1107
Rufus. R-286
Rugged water. L-323
Rugged way. K-392
Ruggles of Red Gap. W-720
"Ruin of a schatchen." W-116
"Rule of the magnificent." T-293
Rule of three. E-225
"Rule of three." T-363
"Ruler of men." H-514
Ruler of the kingdom. K-148
"Ruler of the kingdom." K-148
Rulers of kings. A-347
"Rulers of the realm." F-411
Rulers of the surf. M-1106
Rules of the game. W-508
Ruling passion. V-84
"Rummage barrel." G-569
"Rummage sale." B-1281
"Rummage sale at Pineville." P-413
Rummyniscences. K-1
"Rumours." D-585
"Run on Jobblelousky's." W-116
Run sheep run. W-689
Runaway. D-318
Runaway bag. T-129
Runaway June. C-359
"Runaway match." B-1043
Runaway place. E-23
Runaway woman. D-460
Rung ho! M-1135
"Runner-up." H-68, T-247
"Running Elk." B-383
Running fight. O-128
Running free. C-686

"Saved by his boy." W-424
"Saved by mistake." W-424
"Saved from drink." W-424
Saved for a purpose. C-396
Saved from the jaws of hell. I-74
"Saved places." R-461
"Savers." E-226
"Saving Grace." E-146, W-496
"Saving grace." W-496
"Saving his face." T-358
"Saving of Benjamin Ray." S-82
"Saving of dad." P-522
"Saving sense." W-730
"Saving the long house." K-152
"Saviour of Mont César." H-1034
"Savonarola Finnerty." H-923
"Sawing wood." W-121
"Sax, the first musician." B-1272
"Say it with dreams." Z-2
Say it with bricks. L-71
Say it with oil. L-71
Scalawags. N-24
"Scale." P-569
"Scaler." W-496
Scales of justice. K-328
"Scallop Island." S-597
"Scalp bounty." S-450
Scalp-lock. C-762
"Scandal." C-199
"Scapa flow." B-481
"Scape of the snipe." H-113
"Scapegoat." A-92
Scapegoats. C-9
Scar. D-205, R-470
Scar that tripled. S-409
"Scar-face." H-674
Scarecrow. W-893
"Scarecrow." W-893
Scarlet and black. G-440
Scarlet car. D-166
Scarlet Cockerel. S-1108
Scarlet empire. P-133
"Scarlet hunter." B-1317
"Scarlet ibis." A-255
Scarlet iris. T-203
"Scarlet ladder." Z-2
Scarlet line. R-538
"Scarlet line." R-538
Scarlet macaw. L-410
Scarlet plague. L-458
Scarlet repentance. B-456
Scarlet rider. R-605
Scarlet Scourge. M-102
Scarlet shadow. H-1065
Scarlet Tanager. T-464
Scarlet thread. W-948
Scarlet wagon. G-227
Scarlet X. W-583
Scarlett of the Mounted. M-685
Scarred chin. P-193
"Scarred rifle." M-320
"Scars." N-35, S-862
Scars and stripes. B-1111

Scars on the southern seas. B-1009
"Scat!" C-428
Scattered leaves. W-178
Scattergood Baines. K-59
"Scavenger." J-4
"Scene in Yamacraw." S-593
"Scenes, actions and dispositions of relations and positions." S-841
"Scenes of Cable's romances." H-433
"Scenes of my childhood." S-915
"Scented letters." G-444
"Scheme for a national jack pot." E-40
Scheme for millions. W-212
Schemers. H-211, T-309
"Scherzando." B-1218
"Schlosser's wife." G-124
Schmidt. O-135
"School days." B-950
"School days of an Indian girl." Z-11
School for John and Mary. B-160
"School ma'am bred in old Kentucky." N-155
"School teacher." M-1155
Schoolma'ams of District 91. M-646
"Schoolmaster." S-915
Schoolmaster of Hessville. M-528
"Schools and schools." H-512
"Schooner Mary E. Foster: guardian." W-725
"Schopenhauer's son." H-454
"Scientific cracksman." R-143
"Scientific phenomenon." T-443
"Scientific spirit." B-203
Scientific Sprague. L-605
"Scientific value of Creole." H-433
"Scientist's wife." S-1157
"Scipio makes a shot." R-622, R-623
"Scissors-grinder." D-530
Score by innings. V-103
"Scorn of women." L-440
Scot. M-1177
"Scotch express." C-896
"Scotch precautions." F-372
"Scotch-Irishman." D-149
"Scotchy and I." C-1
Scott who was nine. N-103
Scottie and his lady. M-1047
Scourge. D-206
Scout. T-453
Scout of the Buckhannon. M-348
"Scrambled brains." D-413
Scrambled eggs. M-265
"Scrambled Oil." W-251
"Scrap." O-88
"Scrap iron." V-104
"Screaming skull." C-916, S-443
"Screen." C-373
"Scribe." M-1155
Scribe of a soul. V-206
Scroggins. L-394
Scudders. B-27
Scuffles. R-440
"Sculptor's funeral." C-198, C-199
Scuttlers. W-388
Sea breezes and sand dunes. V-78
Sea bride. W-648

"Sinkers on a hunting trip." G-309
"Sinker's opinion of horses." G-309
"Sinkers photographs Lena." G-309
"Sinkers saw the feetball." G-309
"Sinkers sees baseball." G-309
"Sinkers sends a telegram." G-309
"Sinkers thinks of his mind." G-309
"Sinkers turned sailorman." G-309
"Sinkers was a cit, but quit." G-309
"Sinkers works the Raines' law." G-309
"Sinner in Isreal." W-809
Sinners. T-310
"Sinners." B-548
"Sinning of Jessie MacLean." M-933
Sins of--. G-366
Sins of Saint Anthony. C-593
"Sins of Saint Anthony." C-593
Sins of the father. D-432
Sins of the fathers. H-1084
"Sins of the fathers." M-872
Sir Charlton Richards' last kiss. W-50
Sir Christopher. G-312
Sir Christopher Leighton. S-982
Sir Galahad of New France. J-131
"Sir George Williams." W-424
Sir Guy of Warwick. G-114
Sir Henry Morgan. B-897
Sir John and the American girl. B-470
"Sir John and the American girl." B-470
Sir John Hawkwood. A-273
Sir Mortimer. J-160
Sir Raoul. L-546
"Sir Toby's career." C-709
Sir Walter of Kent. L-260
"Sir Watson Tyler." O-53
Siren. L-477
"Siren." S-452
"Siren of Scalawag Run." D-613
"Siren of the boches." E-186
Siren of the snows. S-358
Sirocco. B-1092
Sis. C-544, L-477
"Sis Fluridy's cakewalk." M-329
"Sis Lindy's busy day." M-942
Sis within. H-710
"Sissies." H-350
"Sister Angelique." S-1119
"Sister Benizia's début." B-533
"Sister Ca'line's enticement." M-947
Sister Clementia. L-106
"Sister Dolores." M-800
"Sister Estelle to the rescue." J-210
"Sister Genevieve." D-560
"Sister Hannah." S-82
Sister in name only. W-53
"Sister Liza's boy." J-4
Sister of a certain soldier. M-371
"Sister Seraphine." U-12
Sister Sue. P-520
"Sister Taylor's registered letter." P-218
Sister-in-law. M-1165
Sisters. N-145
"Sisters." R-382

"Sisters of the Golden Circle." H-503
"Sisters under their skin." F-65
"Sisters under their skins." M-621
Sisters-in law. A-348
Sita. B-116
"Situation in the Transvall." P-633
"Siwash." L-440
"Six bachelor maids." G-163
Six best cellars. H-76
Six breeds. K-285
Six feet four. G-482
646 and the troubleman. O-69
"Six lines of news." B-686
Six mad men. F-5
"Six reasons why." C-673
Six seconds of darkness. C-563
"Six soldiers with seven legs off." M-794
Six stars. L-403
Six trees. F-399
Six-cylinder courtship. F-99
"Six-fingered man." B-1197
Six-pointed cross in the dust. O-73
Sixes and sevens. H-515
"Sixteenth man." S-302
"Sixth McNally." G-260
Sixth speed. R-57
Sixty Jane and The strike on the Schlafeplatz railroad. L-481
Sixty-first second. J-118
Sixty-five on time. B-93
"Sixty years after." M-508
"Sizing up a boss." H-350
"Skanando, the geomancer." S-448
"Skating at Grandpa's." G-592
"Skating carnival." C-1
Skeeters Kirby. M-595
"Skeleton in the closet." S-593
Skeletons. W-45
Sketch book of a cadet from Gascony. B-481
"Sketch in black and white." W-690
"Sketch in charcoal." G-286
"Sketch in vaudeville." T-170
"Sketch of the Creole patois." H-433
Sketches in ebony and gold. T-229
Sketches of Gotham. S-1154
"Sketches of Quebec." V-88
"Sketches of the ornery boy." W-708
"Skewbald panther." W-467
Skid Puffer. F-412
Skidoo! H-700
"Skiing." C-1
"Skim-milk incident." T-383
"Skin of the bear." H-312
Skinner makes it fashionable. D-451
Skinner's baby. D-452
Skinner's big idea. D-453
Skinner's dress suit. D-454
"Skinny and Freckles." O-88
"Skipper." F-255
Skipper and the skipped. D-235
"Skipper Haultaut's wooing." W-193
Skipper John of the Nimbus. M-170
Skippy Bedelle. J-119
"Skippy of Scrabble Alley." R-319

"Sorrow of the little violet." B-1139
Sorrows of a show girl. M-190
"Sorrows of a stenographer." J-103
"Sorrows of angels." T-422
"Sorrows of George Morgan." J-103
"Sorrows of Seiden." G-253
Sorrows of Sap'ed. R-481
Sorry tale. W-897
"Soul above buttons." K-94
Soul and symbol. P-388
"Soul merchant." R-129
Soul of a child. B-629
"Soul of a crow." W-491
Soul of a mummy. S-140
"Soul of a mummy." S-140
Soul of a serf. E-138
"Soul of a singer." L-152
Soul of a tenor. H-474
"Soul of a tree." W-144
"Soul of a Turk." A-25
Soul of a young girl. W-891
Soul of Abe Lincoln. B-6
Soul of an organ. S-401
Soul of Ann Rutledge. B-7
Soul of China. M-838
"Soul of Henry Harrington." B-1193
Soul of Henry Harrington and other stories. B-1193
Soul of love. T-277
Soul of Melicent. C-15
"Soul of Messer Guido." T-198
"Soul of O Sana San." R-213
"Soul of Sing Lee." H-454
Soul of the 'sixties. M-686
Soul of the violin. V-106
Soul of the world. B-31
Soul scar. R-145
Soul toys. H-573
Soul-spur. W-610
"Soul's destiny." C-565
Souls for sale. H-997
Souls in hell. O-91
"Souls in intaglio." O-142
Soul's love letter. M-1
Souls of men. S-813
Souls of passage. B-262
Souls of the infinite. G-532
Soul's redemption. M-423
Souls resurgent. C-165
"Sound adjutant's call." B-831
Sound and fury. H-488
"Sound and fury." H-514
"Sound in the night." S-530
Sound of the hammer. H-110
Sound of water. G-126
Soundings. G-135
"Sour sweetings." F-392
Source. K-60
"Source." V-79
Souter's lamp. M-243
"Souter's lamp." M-243
"South bosque tragedy." S-600
South Mountain sketches. S-450
"South of the Slot." L-465

South Sea tales. L-462
"Southern belle." H-904
Southern buds and sons of war. W-766
Southern girl. W-762
Southern home in war times. W-161
Southern lights and shadows. S-718
"Southern mountaineer." F-343
"Southern pine." I-28
Southern plantation stories and sketches. W-617
Southerner. D-433, W-895
Southerners. B-898
Southland before and after the civil war. G-181
Southland stories. H-722
"Southwest chamber." F-401
"Southwestern justice." R-467
"Souvenir." C-14
Sovereign good. H-1047
Sovereign power. L-568
Sowing and reaping. M-244
Sowing and waiting. B-1257
Sowing of Alderson Cree. M-918
Sowing of swords. M-686
"Space annihilator." C-985
"Span of a minute." M-200
"Spaniel and the cops." B-1145
Spanish acres. E-247
Spanish doubloons. K-139
"Spanish tale." M-202
Spare room. F-54
"Spare the rod and spoil the child." S-915
Spark. W-416
"Sparrows in Madison Square." H-520
Spartan. S-686
"Speaking likeness." S-1026
"Speaking of angels." A-46
Speaking of operations. C-530
"Speaking of tenacity." E-146
Spears of destiny. S-589
Special messenger. C-271
"Special messenger." S-306
Special orders for Commander Leigh. S-102
"Special type." J-35
Speckled bird. C-1059, W-702
"Speck's idol." M-688
"Spectacled eagle." W-255
Spectacular kid. R-405
"Spectral hound." B-1174
"Spectral illusions." B-1174
"Spectre bride." T-444
"Spectre in the cart." P-8
Spectre of power. C-871
"Spectre of the links." S-8
"Speculation in Mrs. Catling." O-185
"Speech delivered by old man Anthony Devlin..." M-280
"Speed." K-378
"Speed pill." B-406
Spell. O-111
"Spell of Pisa." W-804
"Spell of the evil eye." H-51
"Spell-bound." E-146
"Spellbinder." T-147
Spellbinders. B-167
"Spellin' match at the Ridge." B-966

"White man." S-835
"White man and the red man." J-4
White man's burden. H-715
"White man's errand." E-9
"White man's way." L-449
White mice. D-169
White Monarch and the gas-house pup. K-286
"White Monarch and the gas-house pup." K-285
White morning. A-353
White moth. U-10
"White moths." H-890
"White mountains." G-592
"White muscats of Alexandria." M-1019
"White night." B-1021
White oxen: and other stories. B-1218
"White oxen." B-1218
White pagoda. S-276
White path. W-117
"White peacock." M-271
White pearl. F-114
"White pebbles." B-1044
White people. B-1237
"White petal." P-82
White quiver. S-68
White ribboner. M-157
White River raft. M-813
White rock. N-102
White rose. P-527
"White rose." P-523, P-527
White Rose of the Miami. A-211
White roses. B-1090
"White saint." A-219
White sapphire. H-334
"White seas of the Manoas." W-26
White shield. M-570, R-122
"White shield." R-122
White shoulders. T-417
White sister. C-917
White slave. T-271
"White stag's tryst." R-621
"White star." M-708
White stone. M-865
White streak. G-270
White supremacy. C-63
White terror and the red. C-29
White tiger. R-313
White trails's end. V-208
"White Wakunda." N-35
"White water." D-604
"White wild goose." M-271
"White wish." S-785
White witch of a salem town. F-92
White-blood. M-373
"Whitehorn buck." R-622, R-623
Whiter than snow. R-620
Whitest man. M-383
"Whitest man in Leadville." B-1179
Whitewash. M-1123
Whitewing. C-230
Whither. P-576
"Whither are we drifting." S-85
"Whither thou goest." B-984
Who? K-133

Who and what am I? H-529
Who builds? M-575
"Who crosses Storm Mountain?" C-870
"Who fell from aloft?" W-191
Who follows in their train? H-770
Who goes there! C-276
"Who hit Billy Patterson?" E-224
Who is my neighbor? B-671
"Who is she?" W-144
Who is Sylvia? T-18
"Who is Sylvia?" K-92
Who is the heir? H-210
"Who killed Cock Robin?" C-62
Who killed William Drew? M-104
"Who laughs last." C-62
"Who loves gives." R-46
"Who marched in sixty-one." S-918
"Who only stand and wait." S-597
"Who rode La Sylphide?" C-474
Who shall command thy heart? S-354
"Who stand for the Gods." D-597
"Who wants a green bottle?" R-388
Who was responsible? S-360
"Who was scared the most." S-593
"Who was she?" B-1174
"Who won? or, The double courtship." G-489
"Who won the pretty widow?" H-223
Who would be free. S-757
"Who would not vote for a brewer?" D-619
Whoa. G-592
Whole family. W-578
"Whom God hath joined." M-162, V-74
Whom the gods destroyed. B-68
"Whom the gods destroyed." B-68
Whom the Romans call Mercury. R-255
"Who's a piker?" C-320
"Who's it?" L-74
"Who's who." L-74
"Whose business is to live." L-437
Whose fault? B-358
Whose love was the greater? B-415
"Whose petard was it?" M-775
"Whose picture?" C-306
Whoso findeth a wife. D-539
Whosoever shall offend. C-918
"Whosoever shall receive this child." P-101
Why? C-812
"Why." P-629
"Why authors?" L-74
Why Doctor Dobson became a quack. N-182
"Why Doctor Dobson became a quack." N-1821
"Why Dopey McKnight is still in jail for alimony." M-35
"Why "Gondola" was put away." A-92
"Why he did it." W-745
"Why her name is Marguerite V. L. F. Clement." B-536
"Why I left home." V-74
Why I left my husband. V-74
"Why I left my husband." V-74
"Why I left my wife." V-74
"Why I married again." V-74
"Why I remained a bachelor." G-332
"Why it was W-on-the-eyes." M-908
Why, Jimmy. H-740

Illustrator Index

Lantz, Walter. K-1
Lappen, Frank A. P-401
Larcrest, Carl E. C-583
Lasky, Jesse L. L-84
Lassell, Charles. H-119
Latham, O'Neill. W-723
Laub, J. E. D-175
Laudermilk, J.D. S-664
Lawrence, T. Cromwell. I-10, L-439, V-215
Lawrence, William Hurd. C-4, D-611, F-393, F-394, P-306
Lawson, Ernest. F-235
Leaf, Reuben. L-136
Leake, Gerald, b. 1885. H-62, L-562, T-202
Learned, Arthur Garfield, 1872-1959. K-23, M-343, M-1123, R-121, V-4, V-186, W-741
Leary, J. F. M-576
Lederer, Charles, 1856-1925. M-590
Lee, E. M. S-248
Leigh, W. K. C-844
Leigh, William Robinson, 1866-1955. C-429, L-182, L-468, P-461, Q-14, W-520
Lemon, J. A. B-1211, B-1213, F-17, H-427
Lenski, Lois Lenore. G-192
Leonard, Haygarth. C-543, M-488, M-548
Leslie-Judge Co. W-704
Lesser, Elizabeth. L-209
Lessey, May. K-6
Lester, Charles F. B-909
Letcher, Blanche. E-14
Leu, August. N-63
Levering, Albert, 1869-1929. A-93, B-140, B-147, B-149, B-150, B-1347, G-257, L-403, P-25, P-239, T-321, T-324, T-433, T-439
Levy, Alex O. A-59, G-465, H-290
Lewis, George K. M-688
Leyendecker, Frank X., 1877-1924. B-908, M-796, M-817
Leyendecker, J. C. (Joseph Christian), 1874-1951. B-837, C-258, C-914, H-956, I-26, L-507, M-1021, N-124, P-37, T-356, W-652
Li, Chu-t'ang. P-442
Liepse, William. W-475
Liesmann, Frederick J. L-280
Lincoln, F. Foster (Frederic Foster). B-176, F-261, F-270, F-273
Linnell, Harry. W-279
Linson, Corwin Knapp, b. 1864. M-300, V-79
Litchfield, J. H. M-463
Litle, Arthur. B-482, H-68, H-512, W-34
Little, J. Wesley (John Wesley), 1867-1923. S-448
Little, Nat. B-78, M-1000
Livingston, G. B-608
Locher, Robert Evans, 1888?-1956. V-123
Lockman, DeWitt McClellan, 1870-1957. A-220
Lockwood, Ward. V-207
Loeb, Louis, 1866-1909. H-214
Logan and Stockton Photo-Engraving Co. M-622
Loman, Jos. S. W-660
Longabaugh, C. O. H-904, M-1030
Loomis, Charles Battell, 1861-1911. L-492, L-494
Loomis, M. C. H-904
Loomis, W. H. H-384, K-79, R-616, W-285
Loose, Albert. M-83
Lord, Caroline A., 1860-1928. B-1220
Lorenz, L. F. A. H-237, O-103
Lotave, Carl G., 1872-1924. W-657
Louderback, Walt. C-1033, C-1034, C-1037, C-1041, D-604,

L-309, M-89, M-181, M-709, R-488
Loughridge, George. C-646
Lowell, James H., Jr. H-143
Lowell, Orson. B-635, B-1245, D-192, H-292, K-205, L-143, M-747, P-588, Q-9, V-39, W-277
Lowenheim, F. B-548
Lubell, D. D-512
Lucas, J. M-947
Lukens, Winfield S. C-402, E-2, H-1006, M-873
Luks, George Benjamin, 1867-1933. S-593
Lumbard, Nina E. S-852
Lyford, Philip. M-400
Lynch, Vincent. D-229
McAnglly, F. M-522
McArthur, C. A. S-1121
Macauley, Charles Raymond, 1871-1934. A-73, B-142, B-554, B-1213, H-232, R-576
McBurney, James E. G-312, H-190, P-241, S-670, W-111
McCaig, Robert. C-64, O-14, W-310
McCall, Annetta Gibson. B-589
McClure, Griselda Marshall. C-932, F-108, F-109, H-380, K-290, S-77, W-864
McClure, Louise Charles, 1867-1957. C-514
McComb, M. L. W-829
McConnell, Emlen. B-262, D-376, K-152, L-240, M-699, R-90, S-246, S-810, S-1063, T-93, T-197
McCord, P. B. (Peter B.), d. 1908. M-81
McCormick, Howard, 1875-1943. F-439, T-199
McCormick, Katherine H. (Katherine Hood), 1882-1960. S-443, S-448, S-451, S-452
McCouch, Gordon Mallet, 1885-1962. C-692
McCracken, James. S-991
McCullough, W. A. (William A.). C-41, I-10
McCutcheon, John T. (John Tinney), 1870-1949. A-86, A-87, A-89, A-90, A-91, A-94, A-96, C-933, M-107, M-146, M-147, M-148, M-149, M-590
McDaniel, Gertrude. M-23
MacDonald, Harold L., b. 1861. P-386, P-387
MacDonald, Pirie. S-643
MacDonall, Angus. C-39, M-856
McDougall, Walt. K-79
McFall, J. V. B-514, D-503, H-56, O-187, P-256, P-269, P-271, T-322, W-39, W-127
Machefert, Adrien Claude, b. 1881. A-320, C-946, W-260
McIlvaine, Thomas. H-231
McKernan, Frank. B-1011, B-1106, E-3, F-240, F-437, J-2, K-219, M-365, M-458, M-459, M-462, T-280, T-281, T-282, T-283, W-340
McKew, Geo. A. B-661
Mackey, Hugh. M-197
MacIlvain, A. C. H-209
McLellan, Alex. M. T-330
McLintock, Robert A. M-313
McManus, George, 1884-1954. H-384
McMein, Neysa. P-640
McMillan, Mary Lane. F-475, F-477, T-419
MacNamara, Esther. M-1055
McNaughton, Mary. W-768
McPherson, Carol. H-707
McQuinn, Robert. L-475
McVickar, Harry Whitney, b. 1860. M-345
Macy, Harriet. P-588
Madan, F. B. E-207, L-609

Shepherd, J. G. G-479

Shepherd, Joy Clinton, b. 1888. K-74, S-4, S-9, S-1043, W-673

Sheppard, J. Warren. D-240

Sheppard, William Ludwell, 1833-1912. O-63

Shepperson, Claude, b. 1867. W-597

Sheridan, John E. D-260

Sherman-Kidd, R. D-85

Shettsline, W. J. W-478

Shick, Winifred Austin. S-864

Shilrock, Walter H. H-554

Shinn, Everett, 1876-1953. C-733, D-665, H-493, J-117, W-268

Shinn, Florence Scovel. B-65, B-969, C-409, G-184, K-348, L-400, L-491, L-496, M-531, M-924, P-19, P-21, P-27, R-212, V-147, W-932

Sholl, W. W. S-444

Shrader, E. Roscoe. D-228, L-605

Shriner, H. M-65

Shute, A. B. C-231, G-524, K-105, L-149, M-1143, N-21, S-583, S-666

Sichel, Harold M., b. 1881. B-1137, G-491, R-347

Simons, O. W. S-361

Simont, Joseph. R-286

Sindell, Martin, b. 1867. S-526

Sisson, I. D. V-113

Skene, Martha Fenner. S-381

Skidmore, T. D. B-390, B-1375, C-206, H-1057, K-423

Slevin, L. S. V-95

Sloan, John, 1871-1951. B-541, E-53, E-191, E-197, F-235, M-593

Sloneker, Geo. O. M-561

Smedley, W. T. (William Thomas), 1858-1920. B-869, B-1046, C-277, J-40, J-56, M-573, P-310, T-430, T-439, W-663

Smith, Albert E. S-1152

Smith, Albert H. S-592

Smith, Brantley. M-31

Smith, Carolyn. M-645

Smith, Dan, d. 1934. E-167, H-8, W-270

Smith, E. Bert. S-172

Smith, E. Boyd (Elmer Boyd), 1860-1943. A-48, A-49, A-51, A-369, C-587, K-339

Smith, Erwin E. A-52

Smith, F. Berkeley (Frank Berkeley), b. 1869. S-610, S-611

Smith, F. Hopkinson (Francis Hopkinson), 1838-1915. S-611, S-612

Smith, Frank. S-630

Smith, Granville. See Smith, Walter Granville.

Smith, Harry. A-87, A-96

Smith, Howard E. (Howard Everett), 1885-1970. C-627, P-217, P-307, T-449

Smith, Jessie Willcox, 1863-1935. B-65, B-1228, C-854, L-475, S-1096

Smith, Langdon. B-710, F-236

Smith, Lewis E. P-519

Smith, Marshall D. B-1118, C-507, C-508, C-509, C-510, C-511, C-512

Smith, S. Harper, b. 1855. S-669

Smith, S. W. S-444

Smith, Sidney, 1877-1935. S-671, S-931

Smith, Wallace, 1888-1937. B-703, H-448, H-449, S-674

Smith, Walter Granville, b. 1870. G-235, H-89, P-308, S-613

Snapp, Frank. B-599, B-600, B-1164, F-274, F-488, H-1002, K-402, L-549, M-342, M-721, M-808, M-1023, R-73, S-1052

Snyder, W. P. C-1010

Solon, Leon V. G-16, S-221, S-686

Somerville, Charles, 1876?-1931. S-703

Somerville, Howard. C-116

Soper, J. H. Gardner. C-416, P-539

Soule Art Company. D-466

Soulen, Henry James, 1888-1965. S-251

Southard, Frank R. C-38, P-273, T-235

Spaenkuch, August. H-147, P-170

Speakman, Anna W. C-982, H-640

Spearman, Frank H. F-319

Speed, Lancelot, 1860-1931. D-80

Spencer, Chas H. Y-23

Spencer, Hugh, 1887-1975. M-332

Spero, Max J. H-782, I-86, P-559, W-403

Spiegle, F. M. B-24

Spink, Henry. O-18

Spradling, Frank L., 1885-1972. G-516, K-144, R-361

Sprout, Donald A. F-372

Staal, G. A-331

Stacey, Walter S., 1846-1929. G-229

Staggs, S. E. G-182

Stahmer, L., Jr. S-960

Stahr, Paul. B-87, B-317, B-1004, B-1169, F-364, H-846, H-850, I-39, K-134, K-135, K-314, M-100, O-151, O-157, R-52, R-58, S-374, W-857

Staib, G. A-299

Stanlaws, Penrhyn. B-916, E-260, R-202, W-474

Starkweather, William Edward Bloomfield, 1879-1969. D-84, H-310, K-211, M-554, P-63

Stearns, Robert L. H-795

Stebbins, R. B-347, P-431

Stebbins, Roland S. B-280

Stecher, William F. (William Frederick), b. 1864. B-325, B-669, B-670, C-41, G-523, O-3, R-622, W-290, W-396

Steele, Frederic Dorr, 1873-1944. A-82, B-229, B-718, B-1348, C-1064, D-152, D-155, D-158, D-160, D-163, D-166, D-168, F-193, F-255, H-77, H-1052, J-111, K-90, K-94, M-510, N-83, P-592, S-10, S-135, S-254, S-533, S-1089, W-330

Steele, Wilbur Daniel, 1886-1970. R-47

Stein, Modest. B-1288, C-929, D-633, E-192, E-193, F-138, F-154, G-329, R-616, S-294, W-285

Steinberger, D. Orrin. R-225

Steinbruegge, H. E. H-599

Stella, Joseph, 1877-1946. P-483

Stephens, Alice Barber, 1858-1932. B-83, B-613, B-1057, C-866, C-1065, C-1067, C-1070, C-1072, D-286, D-289, D-300, D-301, D-324, E-171, F-393, F-442, G-220, G-221, G-224, G-434, H-517, K-246, L-94, L-372, L-477, M-514, M-521, P-66, P-288, R-66, R-68, R-70, R-289, R-377, S-766, T-72, T-98, T-293, V-219, W-29, W-30, W-129, W-136, W-578, W-600, W-607

Stephens, Charles H. C-157, C-158, L-418, P-389, S-556, S-558, T-251, T-252, T-253

Sterling, Albert M. Y-38

Sterner, Albert, 1863-1946. D-117, F-235, K-231, L-481

Stevens, Beatrice. P-262, T-442

Stevens, C. K. S-715

Stevens, Dalton. A-64, B-745, G-200, J-209, R-122, S-209, S-211

Stevens, F. A. E-222

Stevens, W. D. (William Dodge), b. 1870. A-70, A-254, B-464, C-56, C-57, C-62, C-247, C-268, D-188, E-238, E-257, F-374, F-390, G-126, K-91, P-312, P-409

Stevens, Walter Craft. C-380

Stevenson, Gordon. D-51

Stewart, Chelsea S. B-238
Stewart, Robert W. C-1043
Stick, Frank. K-229
Stillwell, Sarah S. S-427, S-428
Stinemetz, Morgan. D-184, M-1168, T-124
Stokes, Natalie. S-1129
Stone, Eugene E. Q-18
Stone, Seymour M. A-138, C-708, D-378, F-118, H-568, K-221, L-239, R-362, W-788
Stone, Walter King, b. 1875. E-22
Stoner, Harrie A. B-720, R-557
Stoops, Herbert Morton. C-1057, L-570, S-1042, S-1048, T-108
Storer, Florence. D-303, D-304, P-215, R-287
Stout, George L. (George Leslie). F-377
Stowe, Helen. C-1062
Strang, Ray C. B-571
Stratton-Porter, Gene. S-1015
Strauss, Malcolm A. L-613, P-392
Street, Frank, 1893-1944. G-514, N-145
Street, Julian 1879-1947. S-1025
Strehlau, Carl. B-223
Strong, Beulah. H-52, H-54
Strong, C. A. H-5
Strong, Joseph Dwight, 1852-1900. H-317
Strothmann, Fred, 1879-1958. B-1120, H-802, L-477, P-25, T-434
Stuart, Bertha. C-57, I-17, M-1021, W-940
Success. O-114
Sully. P-387.
Summers, Dudley Gloyne. H-965, L-416, S-1011
Sussman, Jack. T-115
Svoboda, Vincent A., 1877-1961. S-958
Swift, E. Ellis. E-39
Swinnerton, Jimmy, 1875-1974. B-1211, B-1213, D-412
Swope, H. W. S-451, S-452
Sykes, C. H. M-947
Sykes, Charles. R-619
Taber, Ralph Graham. T-6
Tadd-Little, Edith. L-384
Taffs, C. H. B-265, D-125, D-306, D-606, H-68, H-259, J-122, M-20, M-236, N-88, R-3, S-876, S-882, V-138, W-716
Takénouche, Keichū. H-439
Talbert, John Randolph. E-89
Tandler, Rudolph F. A-186, L-216, L-217, R-271, V-42, Y-34
Tanner, Tula. S-758, S-762
Tarbell, Harlan, 1890-1960. S-144
Tarkinton, Booth, 1869-1946. T-43
Tattersal, E. W-144
Tavernier, Jules, 1844-1899. H-317
Taylor, Charles Jay, 1855-1929. S-74, S-922
Taylor, Ethel C. T-291
Taylor, F. Walter. B-1084, D-291, D-293, D-297, F-272, F-235, L-169, R-369, S-533
Taylor, H. Weston. A-21, B-180, B-802, C-179, C-553, C-557, C-562, C-803, C-804, F-140, H-630, H-633, H-1001, J-68, K-337, O-104, P-518, P-648, R-448, R-451, S-90, S-194, S-635, S-636, T-456, W-91
Taylor, Harold A. R-636
Taylor, Horace. A-60, H-512, L-315, S-1027, S-1028, W-828
Taylor, J. Walter. W-858
Taylor, R. W. S-884
Taylor, W. L. G-68
Taylor, William F. B-1072, H-845, J-85
Tell, W. W-952

Terry Engraving Company. W-20
Terry, J. C. D-345
Terwilliger, R. L. T-140
Thayer, Albert R. M-568
Thayer, E. R. Lee (Emma Redington Lee), b. 1874. B-118, M-524, R-276, S-1012, T-154
Thayer, Raymond L. C-809, J-74, M-1060
Thomas, Paul K. M. W-130
Thompson, Ellen Bernard. W-63
Thompson, Mills. B-881
Thompson, Nellie L. D-482, L-409
Thompson, Paul. H-836
Thompson, Th. B. J-183
Thomson, Carman. E-110
Thomson, David F. Q-2
Thomson, Rodney. H-280, L-231
Thorndike, Willis H. A-98
Thulstrup, Thure de. S-20
Thurston, Maud. R-285
Tice, Clara. B-1139
Tillotson, C. E. A-224
Timan, W. G-229
Tinker, Edward Larocque, 1881-1968. K-119
Tittle, Walter, b. 1883. A-11, B-385, B-883, D-426
Toaspern, Otto, 1863-ca. 1925. G-301
Tobin, George Timothy, 1864-1956. B-41, C-340, C-444, P-324, T-329
Tolson, Norman. P-207
Tornrose, A. T. M-411
Tousey, Maud. B-67
Towles, Beverly. N-171
Townsend, Harry E. C-314, O-100, P-196, P-212
Tracy, Glen. S-760, S-761, W-890
Train, Elizabeth. V-171
Traver, George A., 1864-1928. A-179, W-439
Travis, Stuart. K-213, K-312, M-1151, R-11, W-701
Trego, William T. K-216, K-222
Trudeau, Hazel Martyn. P-161
True, Allen T. B-503, B-505, G-85, M-1099, O-135, P-117
True, Lilian Crawford. D-75
Trueman, A. S. O-102
Truesdell, Eva M. H-199
Turnbull, Margaret, d. 1942. T-411
Turner, Corinne. L-473, W-296
Turner, H. J. M-180
Tyng, Griswold. B-850, C-472, D-138, H-376, H-817, H-1055, K-104, P-39, P-512
Underwood & Underwood. B-689, B-1136, M-507, W-455
Underwood, Clarence F., b. 1871. B-178, B-184, B-188, B-190, B-237, B-389, B-872, B-1112, B-1235, C-194, C-212, F-99, H-72, K-171, K-344, K-345, M-466, N-87, P-105, P-314, P-316, P-355, P-557, R-34, R-574, S-191, S-193, S-196, S-197, S-198, S-200, S-202, S-203, T-40, T-193, W-124, W-140, W-257, W-506
Upjohn, Anna Milo. S-176
Van Benscoten, L. C. K-381
Van Buren, Harold A. D-569, W-441
Van Buren, Raeburn, b. 1891. B-361
Van Buskirk, Kate. E-231
Van Dresser, William. B-35, B-36, D-113, D-468, H-682, I-82, K-377, L-447, M-25, M-27, M-395, M-398, P-24, R-449, R-606, S-192, V-77, W-77
Van Leshout, Alexander J., b. 1868. C-793, V-182
Van Loan, Philip. V-106

D-454, F-254, F-260, F-262, F-264, F-265, F-266, H-532, K-322,
K-392, M-578, M-853, R-350, S-896, T-97

Wilson, Grace. E-168

Wilson, Latimer F. M-424

Wilson, Latimer J. D-579

Wilson, W. O. H-668

Wilson, William J. F-456

Wind, G. L. (Gerhard Lewis), b. 1896. W-746

Wing, Frank. P-588

Wing, J. Thurber (Jefferson Thurber), b. 1892. W-748

Winn, Ed. R-42

Winslow, Eleanor. B-294

Winter, Milo, 1886-1956. A-378

Winterhalter, Franz Xaver, 1805-1873. T-27, T-275

Winters, Ray. S-826

Wireman, Eugenie M., d. 1934. K-251, P-242, S-1022

Witherbee, Frank I. S-25

Withington, Elizabeth. P-69, P-70

Withrow, E. Almond. S-756

Wittmack, Edgar Franklin, 1894-1956. B-932, M-93, W-776

Wm. S. Scott Studio. J-225

Wolcott, Lucius. See Hitchcock, Lucius Wolcott.

Wolf, George A. (George Anderson), b. 1893. H-941

Wolfe, George Ellis. A-81, B-302, B-303, R-32, R-570

Wolfson, A. A-297

Wood, Franklin T., 1887-1945. B-1180

Wood, H. P-134

Wood, Harry. K-177

Wood, James L. B-174

Wood, Louise. C-810

Wood, Robert Williams, 1868-1955. T-355

Wood, Stanley Llewellyn. B-799, B-838, K-82, K-336, L-277,
S-366, T-262, W-185

Wood, Virginia Hargraves. C-961

Woodburn, Thomas B. J-78

Woodbury, Charles H. (Charles Herbert), 1864-1940. J-83, R-300

Woodbury, Marcia Oakes, 1865-1914. J-83, W-191

Woodruff, Claude Wallace, b. 1884. H-1064

Woodruff, Helen S. (Helen Smith). W-866, W-868

Woods, Alice, 1871-1959. W-869, W-871

Woodville, Richard Caton, 1856-1927. M-817

Woolfolk, E. M. P-163

Woolrych, F. Humphrey. R-591

Woolston, Florence J. F-367

Worden, W. E. F-93

Worrall, W. H. C-156

Wrenn, Charles L. D-33, D-425, D-500, G-163, G-198, H-977,
J-52, L-327, L-329, L-330, L-331, L-334, L-337, L-339, M-887,
R-644, T-184, W-900

Wright, Blanche Fisher. P-278

Wright, George. A-133, B-329, B-898, D-158, D-160, D-431,
D-460, D-651, H-891, M-203, N-28, P-9, P-32, R-217, S-468,
S-616, S-622, W-605

Wright, Harold Bell, 1872-1944. W-921

Wright, Holland. R-505

Wright, Robert Murray. T-37

Wright, Spencer. S-756

Wullys, Avery Giulford. S-1032

Wyeth, N. C. (Newell Convers), 1882-1945. B-292, B-611,
B-1317, C-343, C-677, C-679, C-680, C-692, J-150, J-157, L-241,
L-482, M-460, M-719, M-1087, P-11, P-15, P-106, P-362, Q-13,
S-744, S-747, T-436, V-82, W-494, W-506, W-607

Wykoff, Joseph. C-788

Wyneken, Leopold Ernest, b. 1838. W-958

Yenwood, Francis. G-110

Yeto, Genjiro. B-699, H-438, W-203

Yohn, F. C. (Frederick Coffay), 1875-1933. A-251, A-268, B-15,
B-880, B-1226, C-16, C-18, C-19, C-376, C-679, C-684, C-686,
C-882, D-32, D-144, D-268, F-343, F-345, F-346, F-347, F-348,
F-349, F-350, G-375, I-68, J-149, J-156, J-160, L-402, L-436,
N-77, P-8, P-39, P-50, P-129, S-613, S-614, T-345, T-354, W-557,
W-561

Young, F. Liley. G-411, H-1079

Zeigler, Lee Woodward, b. 1868. B-251, B-264, D-175, D-348,
W-202

Zogbaum, Rufus Fairchild, 1849-1925. K-217, W-824, Z-12

Publisher Index

A. Abbott (Firm). L-385

A. B. Abac Company. S-644

A. C. Graw (Firm). B-1115

A. C. McClurg & Company. A-206, A-208, A-247, B-5, B-130, B-422, B-499, B-500, B-501, B-503, B-504, B-505, B-507, B-508, B-510, B-511, B-512, B-514, B-609, B-610, B-611, B-612, B-653, B-776, B-866, B-871, B-872, B-874, B-883, B-884, B-888, B-903, B-905, B-964, B-1001, B-1287, B-1288, B-1289, B-1290, B-1291, B-1292, B-1294, B-1295, B-1296, B-1297, B-1298, B-1299, B-1300, B-1301, B-1302, B-1303, B-1304, B-1305, B-1306, B-1307, B-1308, B-1309, C-86, C-134, C-135, C-305, C-739, C-741, C-757, Ç-765, C-770, C-828, C-830, C-976, D-39, D-41, D-77, D-331, D-578, D-623, D-675, D-676, E-31, E-130, E-132, E-137, E-163, E-195, E-204, F-55, F-141, F-236, F-429, F-430, F-431, G-128, G-356, G-357, G-512, H-163, H-164, H-165, H-295, H-296, H-297, H-318, H-729, H-858, H-956, H-1032, J-135, J-232, K-13, K-80, K-82, K-85, K-347, L-86, L-111, L-290, L-291, L-293, L-294, L-296, L-500, L-553, M-36, M-37, M-40, M-43, M-45, M-46, M-49, M-51, M-55, M-314, M-333, M-408, M-571, M-572, M-573, M-577, M-903, M-1054, M-1083, M-1084, M-1088, M-1089, M-1091, M-1092, M-1093, M-1095, M-1097, M-1098, M-1101, O-6, O-10, O-34, O-35, O-36, O-38, O-39, O-41, O-43, O-44, O-47, O-106, O-110, P-105, P-106, P-107, P-108, P-110, P-111, P-112, P-113, P-114, P-115, P-116, P-117, P-118, P-119, P-120, P-121, P-122, P-123, P-125, P-126, P-127, P-129, P-130, P-131, P-191, P-218, P-260, P-269, P-270, P-271, P-304, P-560, R-110, R-633, R-634, R-636, R-637, R-638, R-642, R-643, S-292, S-293, S-297, S-298, S-300, S-301, S-303, S-304, S-308, S-643, T-70, T-92, T-303, T-399, W-4, W-5, W-37, W-38, W-39, W-40, W-41, W-42, W-181, W-244, W-652, W-811, W-907, Z-13

A. E. Kern & Co. B-1027

A. Flanagan Company. K-276, M-80

A. Hograve & Co. I-4

A. I. Bradley & Company. B-1257

A. L. Burt Company. F-480, G-504, G-513

A. M. Davis Co. R-409

A. M. E. Book Concern. P-381, S-751, W-833

A. M. Robertson (Firm). F-93, G-109, J-227, L-278, R-427, S-962, U-8

A. R. De Beer (Firm). F-470, F-471

A. R. Furbush (Firm). M-795

A. S. Barnes & Co. B-840, C-29, C-683, C-733, C-734, D-236, E-66, G-48, H-491, H-493, H-494, J-128, J-129, L-233, L-234, L-238, L-240, L-304, L-315, L-317, L-318, L-374, L-495, M-710, M-1015, N-72, O-45, P-483, R-576, R-583, R-584, S-240, S-404, T-76, T-390

A. V. Haight Company. I-14

A. W. Shaw Company. H-162

A. Wessels Company. B-547, C-666, S-8, S-40, S-104, T-25, V-59, W-108

Abbey Press. A-144, A-174, A-367, B-84, B-231, B-233, B-753, B-945, B-959, B-1114, B-1238, B-1240, B-1365, C-141, C-407, C-467, C-473, C-750, C-878, C-899, C-970, D-35, D-135, D-311, D-312, D-313, D-350, D-471, D-481, D-668, E-55, E-84, E-93, E-229, F-101, F-117, F-125, F-466, F-473, G-213, G-469, G-556, G-593, H-50, H-142, H-273, H-311, H-467, H-554, H-591, H-788, H-795, H-975, H-1083, I-9, I-12, J-142, J-195, K-8, K-46, K-86, K-131, K-320, K-375, L-109, L-133, L-142, L-153, L-178, L-415, M-86, M-391, M-434, M-455, M-464, M-561, M-951, M-1049, M-1147, M-1170, M-1189, N-70, N-102, N-183, O-25, O-64, O-67, P-7, P-138, P-168, P-184, P-247, P-600, P-633, R-45,

R-172, R-294, R-501, R-505, R-597, S-109, S-110, S-470, S-540, S-571, T-59, T-159, T-214, T-334, T-451, V-14, V-15, V-34, V-63, V-78, W-433, W-679, W-686, W-696, W-735, W-769, W-848, W-953

Abbott Press. S-826

Aberdeen Publishing Company. D-18, D-252, F-146, M-654, M-750

Abingdon Press. B-754, B-1183, C-38, C-45, C-337, C-340, C-964, C-992, F-128, G-390, H-586, H-893, H-894, K-330, P-1, P-225, P-273, P-274, P-275, P-324, S-360, T-329, T-421, V-89, W-637

Acme Publishing Company. M-630, M-1057, P-466

Acorn Press. S-943, S-944

Address the Hornet. C-81

Advance Press. P-60

Advance Publishing Company. B-324, S-388, S-392, S-394, S-395

Advent Christian Publication Society. G-349

Advertising Publishing Co. T-216

Advocate Publishing Co. M-822

Ainslee Publishing Company. S-41

Albert & Charles Boni. B-1218, C-861, D-219, K-119, K-395, M-168, M-169, S-926, W-173, W-176

Albert H. King (Firm). H-212

Alfred A. Knopf, Inc. A-307, A-310, B-273, B-439, B-440, B-481, B-620, B-628, B-629, B-733, B-828, C-192, C-195, C-196, C-199, C-884, C-920, C-983, C-984, D-24, D-217, D-315, D-316, D-317, D-319, E-243, E-244, F-80, F-81, F-82, F-376, F-377, G-289, H-339, H-488, H-539, H-540, H-541, H-542, H-543, H-544, H-545, H-547, H-548, H-549, H-550, H-551, H-552, H-797, H-921, H-1073, I-73, J-79, J-80, J-81, K-69, K-73, K-285, K-287, L-269, N-187, P-109, P-172, P-173, P-281, R-508, R-614, R-615, S-285, S-334, S-680, S-984, S-1045, S-1064, S-1109, S-1110, T-413, T-417, T-460, V-76, V-123, V-124, V-125, V-126, W-194, W-248, W-297, W-391, W-514, W-618, W-619, W-620, W-621, W-763

Alfred M. Slocum Co. P-222, W-150

Alice Harriman Company. A-177, B-996, E-14, G-546, H-239, N-45, P-598, R-102, R-440, T-3, W-866

Allen Publishing Company (Jackson, Mich.). P-419

Allen, Lane & Scott. A-301

Alliance Publishing Co. B-672, D-13

Allied Printing Trades Council (Boston, Mass.). F-318

Allyn and Bacon. R-175

Alpert Press. L-230

Alwil Shop. S-894

Alwood Company. B-991

American Baptist Publication Society. B-638, B-1011, G-528, H-623, H-650, H-950, J-91, T-282

American Book Company. W-530

American Bureau of Moral Education. R-488

American Humane Education Society. C-500, P-176

American Issue Publishing Company. D-437, H-100, P-246

American Lawn Tennis. T-242, T-243

American Library Service. C-180, H-126, V-164

American Lumberman. M-389

American News Company. H-773

American Poultry Journal Publishing Company. S-960

American Presses. S-675

American Printing Co. C-315

American Publishing Company. B-356

American Publishing House. P-317

American Sabbath Tract Society (Plainfield, N. J.). C-469

R-341, R-342, R-343, R-345, R-347, R-348, R-356, R-472, R-478,
S-152, S-180, S-328, S-372, S-375, S-377, S-378, S-384, S-385,
S-387, S-389, S-390, S-459, S-585, S-589, S-733, S-734, S-735,
S-848, S-925, S-927, S-928, S-1149, T-65, T-79, T-80, T-111,
T-112, T-113, T-115, T-121, T-124, T-126, T-129, T-131, T-215,
T-405, T-406, V-53, V-98, V-99, V-102, V-103, V-104, V-190,
V-192, V-193, V-198, V-202, W-32, W-33, W-207, W-309,
W-313, W-316, W-321, W-325, W-331, W-332, W-333, W-344,
W-347, W-349, W-466, W-505, W-622, W-632, W-698, W-864,
W-865, W-867, W-870, W-888, W-955, W-956, Y-9, Y-32, Y-35,
Y-36

George Sully and Company. C-786, C-787, C-788, F-239, G-88,
H-49, H-779, H-780, K-125, L-471, S-1000, S-1001, S-1002,
W-863

George Thiell Long (Firm). E-255, O-115

George W. Jacobs & Company. A-139, A-152, B-636, B-648,
B-732, B-969, B-983, C-27, C-34, C-128, C-129, C-431, C-637,
C-815, D-421, E-125, F-300, G-456, G-458, H-43, H-45, H-240,
H-241, H-242, H-243, H-381, H-710, H-746, H-748, H-749,
H-752, H-753, H-980, I-26, J-17, K-344, K-345, M-79, M-155,
M-320, M-875, M-1174, M-1175, M-1176, N-93, P-159, S-3, S-4,
S-9, S-11, S-869, S-870, T-81, T-83, W-101

George Wahr (Firm). S-353, S-354

George Wharton James. M-92

Germania Publishing Co. G-539

Gertreva Publishing Company. S-86

Gibson Publishing Company. E-203

Gillett Service League. C-1060

Gilliam's Sons Company. S-1156

Gillis Press. B-781

Gilloa Book Company. B-627

Gilmartin Company. F-73

Glad Tidings Publishing Co. J-108, J-200

Glass & Prudhomme Co. R-209

Glen Falls Publishing Company. H-680, H-681

Gnostic Press. H-603, M-1102, M-1103

Goddard, O. M. T-24

Godfrey A. S. Wieners (Firm). B-314

Goerck Art Press. B-910

Golden Egg Publishing Company. S-961

Golden Press. I-11

Golden Rule Co. H-625, H-626, H-635, H-647

Goldsmith-Woolard Publishing Co. C-634

Good Thoughts Press. G-38

Good Will Publishing Co. W-304

Goodhue Company. S-346

Goodman's Sons & Co. C-2

Goodspeed Press. G-376

Goodyear Book Concern. D-3, H-602

Gorham Company. T-330

Gorham Press. B-157, B-170, B-1182, D-74, E-57, G-286, H-572,
H-715, H-1039, R-411, R-460, S-753, T-376, W-815

Gorham, Edwin S. M-273, M-687

Gospel Publishing House. H-683

Gospel Trumpet Company. B-553, H-36, H-37, M-1031, N-17

Gowdy-Simmons Publishing Co. M-338, M-958

Grafton Press. B-534, B-544, B-546, B-1180, C-326, C-961, D-83,
H-444, J-97, J-179, J-185, L-299, L-504, M-195, M-319, M-700,
M-1187, O-103, P-158, P-244, P-297, P-362, P-599, R-543, S-187,
S-606, S-842, T-21, T-272, W-428, W-429, W-634

Grafton Publishing Corporation. C-159, M-900, W-633

Gramercy Publishing Company. F-438

Great Divide Publisher. P-231

Greaves Publishing Company. H-51

Greenberg, Publisher. P-604, S-436, W-148

Greenwood Printing Co. L-36

Greyfriars' shop publishers, The. A-160

Griffith & Rowland Press. B-951, C-462, C-463, C-464, C-669,
D-65, D-243, D-592, F-437, H-622, H-709, J-2, M-566, M-570,
S-92, T-278, T-280, T-281, T-283, V-150

Griffith-Stillings Press. F-12, F-13

Grosset & Dunlap. B-339, B-1094, B-1320, C-114, C-235, C-400,
C-1035, C-1046, D-43, D-147, E-26, E-27, E-237, F-281, G-399,
G-510, H-613, H-763, H-764, J-9, M-99, M-230, M-315, M-316,
M-664, M-665, P-144, P-400, P-468, R-138, R-139, R-183, R-196,
R-198, S-439, S-1053, S-1061, T-130, T-457, T-458, U-3, V-60,
W-728, W-793, Y-41, Y-43

Grove Publishing House. P-613

Guarantee Publishing Co. D-50, D-121, D-337, V-118

Guiding Star Publishing House. C-366

Gulf Publishing Company. M-358

Gustin's Printery. A-323

H. A. Simmons & Co. R-315

H. B. Wiggin's Sons Company. E-220, E-221, E-222

H. D. Shaiffer (Firm). U-16

H. H. Stendel & Company. S-851

H. J. Smith & Devereaux Co. H-600

H. K. Fly Company. A-36, B-616, B-839, B-939, B-1109, C-131,
C-132, C-176, C-389, C-807, C-808, C-809, C-1006, D-40, D-44,
D-91, D-332, E-197, E-235, E-236, E-238, E-239, G-283, H-405,
H-905, H-984, I-81, J-72, J-73, J-74, K-313, K-422, K-428, M-66,
M-67, M-68, M-91, M-1060, R-200, S-87, S-374, S-1140, W-239,
W-370, W-371, W-476, W-478, W-479, W-480

H. L. & J. B. McQueen, Inc. W-488

H. L. Kilner & Co. D-278, D-279, D-280, D-282, D-283, D-472,
E-59, K-179, L-134, O-144, W-9

H. L. Meites and Sons. Z-7

H. M. Caldwell Co. C-330, T-67, W-121

H. S. Crocker & Co. K-102

H. S. Jewell. D-619

H. S. Stone & Company. L-117

H. W. Wilson Company. M-842

Haber Printing Co. P-226

Hackett, Carhart & Co. S-1025

Hadley Press. P-439

Haldeman-Julius Company. H-25, H-27, H-445, H-453, S-514

Hall Publishing Co. H-83

Hallowell Co. M-465

Hamilton Brothers. I-13

Hamilton Printing Co. (Chatanooga, Tenn.). R-107

Hamming Publishing Co. D-545

Hamming-Whitman Company. S-885

Hammond Bros. & Stephens. S-852, S-853

Hammond Publishing Company. P-267

Hampton Institute Press. A-248

Hannis Jordan Company. W-34

Harcourt, Brace & Howe. D-591, G-50, J-89, L-263, L-266,
L-368, O-201, W-585, W-588

Harcourt, Brace and Company. A-182, A-325, A-326, B-704,
C-89, C-94, C-95, C-97, C-894, C-903, F-177, F-179, H-562,
H-570, H-571, H-609, H-1035, I-50, J-127, K-67, L-261, L-262,
M-621, O-142, O-192, P-81, S-184, S-338, S-442, S-460, S-797,
S-837, S-1044, T-82, T-84, T-86, T-269, T-402, W-174, W-586,
W-587, W-589, W-593

Harford Printing and Publishing Company. W-705

Harlow Publishing Company. T-246

B-813, B-814, B-815, B-816, B-1018, B-1176, B-1224, B-1327,
C-76, C-79, C-116, C-118, C-119, C-120, C-179, C-297, C-311,
C-312, C-313, C-314, C-505, C-552, C-558, C-639, C-645, C-774,
C-776, C-777, C-816, C-891, C-929, C-948, C-949, C-950, C-951,
C-1009, D-133, D-353, D-354, D-440, D-468, D-501, D-502,
D-503, D-558, E-108, E-215, E-216, E-217, E-218, E-219, E-245,
E-246, E-247, E-248, E-249, E-263, F-105, F-157, F-159, F-160,
F-277, F-278, F-280, F-361, F-474, G-135, G-178, G-275, G-312,
G-313, G-315, G-354, G-453, H-52, H-53, H-54, H-55, H-56, H-
281, H-386, H-394, H-436, H-458, H-462, H-523, H-733, H-852,
H-923, H-951, H-1006, I-39, J-110, J-119, J-122, J-123, J-124,
J-151, J-154, J-159, J-161, J-166, J-167, J-170, J-171, J-217, J-218,
J-219, J-221, K-273, K-274, K-286, K-322, K-329, L-112, L-125,
L-372, L-377, L-565, L-567, M-20, M-21, M-23, M-24, M-25,
M-27, M-28, M-62, M-177, M-178, M-245, M-246, M-301,
M-302, M-305, M-311, M-342, M-395, M-396, M-398, M-399,
M-478, M-479, M-480, M-481, M-482, M-483, M-485, M-486,
M-487, M-507, M-548, M-552, M-617, M-681, M-682, M-944,
M-986, M-1069, N-9, O-8, O-11, O-14, O-187, P-140, P-227,
P-228, P-229, P-377, R-63, R-64, R-65, R-66, R-67, R-68, R-69,
R-70, R-71, R-72, R-73, R-182, R-202, R-245, R-252, R-361,
R-471, R-561, S-6, S-19, S-21, S-60, S-105, S-106, S-358, S-429,
S-430, S-497, S-498, S-499, S-500, S-502, S-503, S-767, S-788,
S-892, S-1054, S-1065, T-93, T-95, T-96, T-97, T-98, T-99,
T-178, T-179, T-180, T-217, T-218, T-223, T-224, T-225, T-226,
T-227, T-383, T-412, T-415, T-423, T-424, T-442, U-12, V-36,
V-43, V-44, V-47, V-49, V-58, V-131, V-138, W-62, W-63, W-64,
W-65, W-66, W-67, W-68, W-69, W-95, W-124, W-126, W-127,
W-128, W-129, W-131, W-134, W-135, W-136, W-137, W-138,
W-139, W-140, W-142, W-143, W-144, W-477, W-481, W-523,
W-524, W-526, W-527, W-528, W-533, W-534, W-571, W-572,
W-573, W-574, W-699, W-725, W-726, W-738, W-739, W-813,
W-846, W-857, W-954

Liveright, Horace B. V-107

Lloyd, Adams, Noble (Firm). M-352

Longmans, Green & Company. C-393, D-80, H-582, H-944,
P-383, W-195, W-767

L'Ora Queta Publishing Company. M-726

Lord Baltimore Press. B-1328

Loring-Axtell Company. D-372

Los Angeles Printing Company. G-400

Lothrop Publishing Company. A-62, B-14, B-15, B-329, B-330,
B-632, C-926, E-67, E-68, E-69, E-70, E-74, E-94, E-153, H-4,
H-89, H-195, H-220, H-292, H-383, H-1003, L-282, L-405,
M-300, M-303, N-71, O-93, P-71, P-73, P-290, P-638, R-34,
S-488, S-966.5, T-109, V-178, W-366, W-654, W-655, W-709,
W-713, W-723

Lothrop, Lee & Shepard Co. B-331, B-668, B-838, B-1015,
B-1067, B-1068, B-1179, C-783, E-65, E-71, E-72, E-73, E-75,
E-77, E-78, F-61, G-8, G-173, H-895, K-152, K-388, K-389,
K-390, K-391, K-392, M-346, M-626, M-627, M-853, M-1064,
M-1139, M-1140, M-1141, M-1142, M-1144, P-48, P-67, P-68,
P-69, P-70, P-72, P-288, P-291, R-516, R-518, S-487, T-27, T-28,
T-248, W-759

Louis Lange Publishing Company. S-141

Louis V. Harvey (Firm). C-436

Louisiana Printing Company. O-50

Louisville and Nashville Railroad Company. C-52

Lowman & Hanford Co. A-296, C-502, S-248

Lubin Manufacturing Company. H-57

Lucas Brothers. H-375

Lucas-Lincoln Company. M-407

Lumber Review Company. C-506

Lunar Publishing Company. B-1082

Luther H. Higley (Firm). S-1135

Lutheran Book Concern. C-448, C-449, C-450, G-279, G-280,
G-350, L-515, M-819, S-158

Lutheran Literary Board. R-235

Lutheran Publication Society. C-791, S-282, S-941

M. A. Donohue & Co. A-137, C-851, D-420, D-518, D-626,
G-361, H-97, K-398, M-65, M-353, M-679, Q-21, R-506, S-27, S-
56, S-794, S-1098, W-457

M. A. Long Book and Publishing House. F-182

M. H. Wiltzius & Co. C-793

M. J. Roth (Firm). P-462

M. P. Publishing Co. B-644

M. S. Boyce (Firm). B-823

M. S. Greene & Company. J-25

M. W. Hazen Company. E-120, G-163, J-52, R-644

M. Witmark & Sons. K-372

M'Cord & M'Cord. M-80

Macaulay Company. A-285, B-1293, C-504, C-561, C-592, C-880,
D-92, D-146, D-332, D-484, D-485, D-486, D-487, D-489, D-491,
D-531, D-532, D-533, D-534, D-535, D-536, D-537, D-539,
D-540, E-126, E-131, F-44, F-204, G-87, G-168, H-133, H-236,
H-535, J-99, K-14, K-16, K-20, K-412, L-527, M-152, M-264,
M-582, M-659, M-986, M-987, O-190, O-191, P-93, P-94, P-95,
P-96, P-97, P-166, P-167, P-258, P-259, P-261, P-331, P-332,
P-333, R-483, R-484, R-485, S-357, S-359, S-365, S-367, S-370,
S-371, S-811, S-1133, T-134, T-135, V-21, V-22, V-26, V-28,
V-29, W-475

McBride, Nast & Company. B-635, C-1066, D-27, D-31, D-32,
D-33, E-22, F-202, F-276, G-228, H-747, H-1031, J-19, O-124,
S-316, W-557, W-946

McClelland & Company. B-403

McClure Company. See S. S. McClure Company.

McClure Publishing Co. R-551

McClure, Phillips & Co. A-92, A-256, B-57, B-386, B-699,
B-1020, B-1207, B-1208, B-1228, B-1348, B-1357, C-148, C-198,
C-614, C-952, C-1064, C-1065, C-1067, D-617, F-374, F-419,
G-89, H-20, H-214, H-275, H-276, H-277, H-492, H-499, H-503,
H-517, H-657, H-821, H-835, K-40, K-45, K-91, K-161, L-182,
L-188, L-210, L-354, L-440, L-525, M-255, M-509, M-521,
M-680, M-684, N-7, O-132, P-197, P-342, P-349, P-363, P-365,
P-366, P-409, P-461, R-6, R-310, R-533, R-581, S-253, S-707,
S-708, S-710, S-739, S-1072, T-31, T-36, T-46, T-56, T-100,
T-107, T-325, T-374, T-416, V-168, W-92, W-470, W-495,
W-496, W-498, W-504, W-510, W-513, W-517, W-627, W-826,
W-853, W-949, W-951, Y-45, Y-51

McClure's Magazine. R-419, R-422, R-425, R-426

McCombs Print. S-569

McCowat-Mercer Printing Company. L-62

McCoy & Calvin. A-142

MacDaniel Publishing Company. G-470

McDevitt-Wilson's (Firm). S-137

McDowell Press. M-349

McElroy Publishing Company. F-308

Macfarlane Company. M-172

McGirt Publishing Co. M-198

McGrath-Sherrill Press. N-112

McLean Company. C-790, C-979, G-307, H-201, M-351, M-1165,
P-373, R-178, S-946

Maclear & Marcus. G-231

McMath Company. W-493

Macmillan Company. A-111, A-164, A-166, A-168, A-170,

Powell & White (Firm). F-40, M-803
Prairie Press. F-110

Pratt & Peck Co. B-411
Presbyterian Committee of Publication. B-782, D-12, D-381, H-382, O-77
Press in the Forest. W-924, W-925, W-926
Press of "The Rose-Jar." L-115
Press of Bolte and Braden Co. F-363
Press of Geo. Spaulding & Company. P-2
Press of Gibson Bros. B-911
Press of Illinois State Register. V-174
Press of Lefavor-Tower Company. M-800
Press of Palfrey-Rodd-Pursell Co. W-685
Press of Sentinel. S-695
Press of the Dept. of Journalism, University of Washington. M-388
Press of the Enterprise. C-856
Press of the Merry War. W-750
Press of the Reliance Trading Company. L-552
Press of W. S. Van Cott. J-226
Press Parisian. R-519
Press Printing Co. R-61
Princeton University Press. M-671
Probono Publishing Company. M-729
Professional Publishing Company. P-78
Progressive Thinker Publishing House. L-485, R-270
Progressive Woman Publishing Co. K-9
Prospect Press. C-775, S-685
Public Publishing Company. H-922
Publishers' Printing Co. K-279, L-276
Publishing House of the Pentecostal Church of the Nazarene. L-194, M-70, M-73
Pueblo Publishing Co. A-312
Pulitzer Publishing Company. S-38
Punton-Clark Pub. Co. R-62
Purdy Publishing Company. C-600
Purnell's (Firm). H-464
Purvis, W. S. S-73
Q and C Company. B-1347
Quail & Warner. D-15, K-110, M-1107, Q-2, W-215
Queen's Shop. K-116
Quinn and Boden Company. A-365
R. E. Lee Company. N-69
R. F. Fenno & Company. A-273, B-711, C-102, C-105, C-107, C-155, D-84, D-85, D-412, E-18, F-298, G-468, G-542, G-543, G-544, H-143, H-310, H-356, H-703, H-911, J-53, K-211, K-384, L-106, L-389, L-609, M-5, M-390, M-554, M-757, M-766, M-969, M-970, N-153, P-63, P-587, S-551, S-691, V-70, V-110, V-111, W-149, W-179, W-180, W-372, W-564, W-743
R. H. Carothers (Firm). W-703
R. H. Carothers & Son. A-314
R. H. Russell (Firm). A-88, A-89, A-94, B-142, D-155, D-643, D-644, G-166, K-379, L-63, L-232, W-308
R. I. Palmer (Firm). M-646
R. R. Donnelley and Sons Company. A-2, P-583, S-157
Radiant Life Press. P-454
Raeder Press. A-387
Rafter, Jos. J. (Joseph J.). W-544
Raidabaugh-Voorhees Company. V-209
Ralph Fletcher Seymour Co. F-45, F-461, P-209
Rand McNally and Company. B-460, C-147, D-524, E-80, F-483, G-7, G-114, I-27, K-227, M-397, N-48, O-69, P-186, P-187, P-526, P-641, R-92, R-520, R-639, R-640, R-641, S-678, T-263,

W-182, W-213
Randolph, Sterling & Van Ess. B-1241
Ransom, Will, 1878-1955. P-380
Raven Press. M-544
Raven Publishing Company. L-26
Raymond Publishing Company. N-56
Reading Eagle (Firm). R-378
Real American Syndicate. S-13
Record (Burlington, Colo.). P-318
Redfield Brothers (Firm). H-851
Reed & Carnrick. S-715
Reed Publishing Company (Denver, Colo.). D-356, E-92, F-373
Reflex Publishing Company. B-1239
Regan Printing House. B-1286, S-918
Regina Music Box Company (New York, N. Y.). S-1023
Reid Publishing Company. D-248, H-367, H-406, H-407, P-87, S-526, W-810
Reilly & Britton Co. B-227, B-363, B-364, B-365, B-497, B-1034, C-39, C-1057, D-25, D-29, D-30, D-97, D-100, D-572, E-110, E-159, G-14, H-332, H-912, I-79, I-80, K-74, L-570, O-82, P-161, P-162, P-210, P-501, P-588, R-95, S-46, S-991, S-1042, W-761
Reilly & Lee Co. C-1013, M-247, M-400, M-401, M-790, P-293, P-427, P-428, S-47, S-48, S-49, S-50, S-51, S-671, T-400, T-408
Reilly Publishing Co. C-497
Reinert Publishing Company. S-988
Remington Press. R-527
Renner, Morgan M. W-300
Reporter-Star Publishing Co. R-180
Republican Printing Company. C-574
Republican Publishing Co. L-425
Reveille Printing House. V-179
Revere Publishing Company. H-338
Review and Herald Pub. Co. W-351
Review and Herald Publishing Association. S-726
Review of Reviews Co. (New York, N.Y.). L-277
Review Press. E-252
Reynard Press. W-783
Reynolds, John N. P-530
Reynolds Publishing Company. C-925, T-108, W-812
Rhodes & McClure Publishing Company. H-679, T-183, V-91, V-92, V-93
Richard G. Badger (Firm). A-6, A-84, A-189, A-384, B-169, B-176, B-240, B-327, B-518, B-647, B-671, B-757, B-954, B-1024, B-1029, B-1079, B-1102, B-1107, B-1143, B-1210, C-51, C-108, C-143, C-428, C-442, C-709, C-887, C-889, C-890, C-892, C-977, D-5, D-48, D-284, D-333, D-335, D-504, E-140, F-14, F-22, F-38, F-180, F-181, F-188, F-205, F-329, G-39, G-232, G-306, G-308, G-345, G-358, G-439, G-529, G-550, G-562, H-39, H-95, H-222, H-223, H-366, H-533, H-573, H-592, H-593, H-725, H-781, H-799, H-823, H-856, H-918, H-954, H-1049, H-1053, H-1085, J-100, J-126, J-177, J-202, K-99, K-245, K-324, K-400, L-206, L-252, L-474, L-517, L-578, L-579, L-617, M-288, M-383, M-436, M-501, M-663, M-851, M-960, M-1028, M-1178, M-1190, N-152, N-189, O-1, P-4, P-100, P-188, P-446, P-448, P-584, P-589, P-610, Q-1, R-46, R-224, R-226, R-385, R-413, R-503, R-560, S-178, S-243, S-247, S-311, S-337, S-432, S-473, S-474, S-594, S-597, S-692, S-730, S-783, S-795, S-849, S-915, S-947, S-976, S-998, S-1104, S-1121, T-185, T-186, V-66, V-67, W-171, W-818, W-828
Ridgway Company. H-507, M-715, M-1005, T-54
Riverdale Press. C-515
Riverside Press. C-591, D-352
Riverton Press. M-393

Pseudonym Index

Abbath.
Abbott, Aaron, b. 1867.
Adams, James Alonzo, 1842-1925.
Adams, Mary.
Adams, Samuel Hopkins, 1871-1958.
Adeler, Max.
Ager, Carolus.
Aikman, Henry G.
Ailenrock, M. R.
Aix.
Alberg, Albert.
Alberton, Edwin.
Alden, Isabella Macdonald, 1841-1930.
Aldrich, Clara Chapline (Thomas).
Aldrich, Darragh, 1884-1967.
Alein, Niela.
Alien.
Alla, Ogal.
Allen, Edward.
Allen, F. H.
Allen Robert.
Allen, Will.
Alter, John E.
Althouse, Daniel Whitman.
Amber, Miles.
Ames, Eleanor Maria (Eastbrook), 1831-1908.
Ames, Joseph Bushnell, 1878-1928.
Angell, Bryan Mary, b. 1877.
Anna May.
Anthony, H.
Applegate, William Edward.
Armstrong, Harold H. (Harold Hunter), b. 1884.
Armstrong, Willimina Leonora, 1866-1947.
Arnold, Faith Stewart.
Atkinson, Grace Lucie, Mrs.

Atwater, Caroline, 1853-1939.
Augustine, William Azariah, b. 1885.
Aumerle, Richard.
Aunt Rowena.
Austin, Benjamin Fish, b. 1850.
Austin, Mary.
Babcock, Winnifred (Eaton), b. 1879.
Bacon, Dolores.
Bacon, Edward.
Bacon, Josephine Dodge Daskam, 1876-1961.
Bacon, Mary D., b. 1866.
Bacon, Mary Schell Hoke, 1870-1936.
Bagg, Helen F.
Baker, Emma Eugene Hall.
Baker, Mrs. Louise, b. 1858.
Baker, Ray Stannard, 1870-1946.
Ballard, Robert.
Barbara.
Barbour, A. Maynard.
Barbour, Anna May.
Barker, Bruce.
Baron.
Barr, J., Mrs.
Barron, Edward.

Keizer, Genet.
Littleheart, Oleta.
Grapho.
Phelps, Elizabeth Stuart, 1844-1911.
Fabian, Warner.
Clark, Charles Heber, 1841-1915.
Field, Charles K. (Charles Kellogg), b. 1873.
Armstrong, Harold H. (Harold Hunter), b. 1884.
Murrell, Cornelia Randolph.
Bausman, Frederick.
Eaves, Catherine.
Philips, A. E. (Albert Edwin), b. 1845.
Pansy.
Aldrich, Darragh, 1884-1967.
Aldrich, Clara Chapline (Thomas).
Stamey, DeKeller.
Baker, Mrs. Louise, b. 1858.
Mock, Fred, b. 1861.
Hall, Edward Allen, b. 1854.
Son of the South, A.
Dodd, Robert Allen, b. 1887.
Dromgoole, Will Allen, 1860-1934.
Bat, Bill.
Daniel.
Cobden, Ellen Melicent, 1848-1914.
Kirk, Eleanor.
Gunnison, Lynn.
Cromarsh, H. Ripley.
Smith, Anna May.
Shands, Hubert Anthony, b. 1872.
Edward, William.
Aikman, Henry G.

Dost, Zamin Ki.
Miles, Mrs. Gertrude Elizabeth (Wilder), b. 1860.
Kimball, Atkinson, jt. pseud. of Kimball, Richard Bowland and Atkinson, Grace Lucia.
Brooke, Alison.
Frejolity, Azariah.
Maher, Richard Aumerle.
Sullivan, Josephine Byrne.
Nitsua, Benjamin.
Martin, Mary.
Watanna, Onoto.
Bacon, Mary Schell Hoke, 1870-1936.
Bacon, Mary D, b. 1866.
Lovell, Ingraham.
Bacon, Edward.
Bacon, Dolores.
Hall, Jarvis.
Hall, Eugene.
Alien.
Grayson, David.
Sabina, Poppaea.
Wright, Mabel Osgood, 1859-1934.
Barbour, Anna May (Anna Maynard).
Barbour, A. Maynard (Anna Maynard).
Lincoln, J. W. (John Willard), b. 1875.
Ronzone, Benjamin Anthony, b. 1848.
Renfrew, Garroway.
Potter, David, b. 1874.

Brown Paula.
Brown, Philetus.
Broyles, Lester Everret.
Bruce, Kenneth.
Bryce, Ronald.
Buck, Charles Neville, b. 1879.
Budgett, Frances Elizabeth Janes, 1873-1928.
Bullard, Arthur, 1879-1929.
Burgundy, Billy.
Burmeister, José Bergin (King), Mrs., b. 1882.
Burns, Ella, b. 1861.
Burr, Jane.
Bute, Currer.
Byrne, Donn.
Cadmus.
Campbell, Scott.
Cannon, Alanson B.
Carden, W. Thomas.
Carew, Roger M.
Carleton, William.
Carling, George.
Carroll, George S.
Cavazza, Elisabeth.
Chambers, Rosa, Mrs., b. 1886.
Chappell, George Shepard, 1877-1946.
Charlesworth, M. E.
Chenery, Susan.
Cheney, Walter Thomas.
Cher, Marie.
Chester, Lord.
Childe, Crispin.
Chilton, Leila O.
Chipperfield, Robert Orr.
Clare, W. H.
Clark, Arthur March, b. 1853.
Clark, Charles Heber, 1841-1915.
Clark, Hugh A.
Clark, Joseph, b. 1854.
Clemens, Samuel Langhorn, 1835-1910.
Clementia.
Clifton, Wallace.
Clinton, Major.
Cobb, Percival Bartlett, b. 1883.
Cobden, Ellen Melicent, 1848-1914.
Cody, Sherwin, 1868-1959.
Coggs, Dr.
Cohen, Alfred J., 1861-1928.
Coleman, McAlister.

Collier, Nick Sherlock.
Collingwood, Herbert W. (Herbert Winslow), 1857-1927.
Collins, Frederick Lewis, b. 1882.
Colvin, Addison Beecher, b. 1858.
Commodore.
Comstock, Anna Botsford, 1854-1930.
Cone, Andrew Jackson.
Conkley, Ralph.
Cook, William Wallace, 1867-1933.
Cooke, John Estes.

Dykes, Pauline Browning.
Cody, Sherwin, 1868-1959.
Terreve, Retsel.
Crayon, Diedrick, 1876-1916.
Rockey, Howard, 1886-1934.
Lundsford, Hugh.
Dejeans, Elizabeth.

Edwards, Albert.
Limerick, Oliver Victor.
Crane, Mary.

Desmond, Dionne.
Winslow, Rose Guggenheim.
Webb, Anna Spanuth, Mrs.
Donn-Byrne, Brian Oswald, 1889-1928.
Real name unknown.
Davis, Frederick William, 1858-1933.
Fontaine, Felix.
Noodle, Major Tom.
Maloy, Charles Raymond, b. 1873.
Bartlett, Frederick Orin, b. 1876.
Stratton, George Frederick, b. 1852.
Schmidt, Carl George, b. 1862.
Pullen, Elisabeth.
Hayward, Rachel.
Traprock, Walter E.
Booth, Maud Ballington, 1865-1948.
Gore, Susan Frances Richards.
Don Jon.
Scherr, Marie.
Teed, Cyrus Reed, 1839-1908.
Schieren, Harrie Victor, b. 1881.
Ollie.
Ostrander, Isabel Egenton, 1883-1924.
Hanscombe, Walter Clarence.
Duncan, James A.
Adeler, Max.
Boggs, Robert.
Stand-by, Timothy.
Twain, Mark.
Feehan, (Sister) Mary Edward, b. 1878.
Quinby, Laurie J.
Culley, Frank Clinton.
Wells, Percival W.
Amber, Miles.
Brown, Philetus.
Giberga, Ovidio.
Dale, Alan.
McAlister, Frank A, jt. pseud. of McAlister Coleman and Frank Davis Halsey.
Davis, J. Frank (James Francis), 1870-1942.
"The Hope Farm Man."

Lewis, Frederick.
Hiram, Harvester.
Davidson, Charles Lock, b. 1859.
Lee, Marian.
Rebel, A.
Eggleston, Richard Beverley, b. 1867.
Edwards, John Milton.
Baum, L. Frank (Lyman Frank), 1856-1919.

Galpin, J. A.
Gambier, Kenyon.
Gardener, The.
Garnett, Captain Mayn Clew.
Garrett, Edward Peter, 1878-1954.
Garrett, Garet.
Gattle, Caroline A., b. 1871.
Gaul, Avery.
Gaul, Hariette Lester (Avery), Mrs.,
b. 1886.
Germaine, Quincy.
Giberga, Ovidio.
Gibson, Peter.
Gifford, Franklin Kent, 1861-1948.
Gill, Mary (Gill).
Gillis, Adolph.
Gilmer, Elizabeth Merriwether, 1861-1951.
Gladden, Hope.
Gloria, F. M.
Goetchius, Marie Louise.
Gold, Michael.
Goldberg, Israel, 1887-1964.
Golden Light.
Gollmar, Arthur Howard, b. 1871.
Gordon, Carol.
Gordon, John.
Gordon, Julien.
Gore, Susan Frances Richards.
Graham, John.
Granich, Irving, 1894-1967.
Grant, Douglas.
Grant, Margaret.
Granville-Barker, Helen Manchester.
Grapho.
Graves, Charlotte F., b. 1846.
Gray, Carl.
Graye, Dawn.
Grayson, David.
Greaves, Richard.
Greenslet, Mrs. Ella (Holst), b. 1873.
Guest, Gilbert.
Guilbeault, Zephirin J.
Gummere, Francis B.
Gunnison, Lynn.
Hains, Thornton Jenkins, b. 1866.
Hale, Marice Rutledge (Gibson), b.1884.

Hall, Asa Zadel.
Hall, Edward Allen, b. 1854.
Hall, Helene.
Hall, Holworthy.
Hall, Jarvis.
Halsey, Frank Davis.

Halsted, Leonora B.
Hamilton, Robert W.
Hankins, Arthur Preston.
Hannett, Arthur Thomas, b. 1884.
Hanscombe, Walter Clarence.
Harlan, M. R., Mrs., b. 1879.
Harland, Marion.

Blackstone, Valerius D.
Lathrop, Lorin Andrews, 1858-1929.
Wright, Mabel Osgood, 1859-1934.
Hains, Thornton Jenkins, b. 1866.
Garrett, Garet.
Garrett, Edward Peter, 1878-1954.
Gordon, Carol, pseud.
Gaul, Hariette Lester (Avery), Mrs., b. 1886.
Gaul, Avery.

Wright, Caroline.
Coggs, Dr.
Malanotte, Mario.
Newman, Richard Brinsley.
Houmas, Mount.
Worth, Marc.
Dix, Dorothy.
Robertson, Anna Adelia, b. 1875.
Kubinyi, Mrs. Florence Marie (Telmany) von, b. 1895.
Hale, Marice Rutledge (Gibson), b. 1884.
Granich, Irving, 1894-1967.
Learsi, Rufus.
Hicks, William Watkin, 1837-1915.
Julier, Arthur H. G.
Gattle, Caroline A., b. 1871.
Munson, Gorham Bert, 1896-1969.
Cruger, Van Rensselaer, Mrs.
Chenery, Susan.
Phillips, David Graham, 1867-1911.
Gold, Michael.
Ostrander, Isabel Egenton, 1883-1924.
Coryell, John Russell, 1851-1924.
Huntington, Helen.
Adams, James Alonzo, 1842-1925.
Jemimy, Aunt.
Park, Charles Caldwell, 1860-1931.
Oeston, Agata Dolores Mercedes.
Baker, Ray Stannard, 1870-1946.
McCutcheon, George Barr, 1866-1928.
Stoothoff, Ellenor.
Brenan, Florence McCarthy, b. 1854.
Bates, Jimmie.
Heigh, John.
Ames, Joseph Bushnell, 1878-1928.
Garnett, Captain Mayn Clew.
Goetchius, Marie Louise.
Rutledge, Maryse.
Van Saanen, Marie Louise.
Edson, Harold.
Allen, Edward.
Boynton, Helen (Mason), Mrs., b. 1841.
Porter, Harold Everett, 1887-1936.
Bagg, Helen F.
**McAlister, Frank A., jt. pseud. of McAlister Coleman
and Frank Davis Halsey.**
Elbon, Barbara.
Stratemeyer, Edward, 1862-1930.
Kinsburn, Emart.
Thomas, Arthur.
Clare, W. H.
Cottrell, Marie.
Terhune, Mary Virginia Hawes.

Harmonia.
Harper, Olive.
Harper, Sarah Jane, b. 1863.
Harrington, Eugune W., b. 1866.
Harrison, Henry Sydnor, 1880-1930.
Hassan, Abdul.
Haubold, Herman Arthur, 1867-1931.
Hawkins, Nehemiah, 1833-1928.
Hawser, A. B.
Hawser, Cap'n.
Hay, Timothy.
Hayward, Rachel.
Hazeltine, Horace.
Heigh, John.
Henry, O.
Hicks, William Watkin, 1837-1915.
Hidden, William Buffett.
Highland, Lawrence.
Hiram, Harvester.
Hobart, George Vere, 1867-1926.

Hodge, T. Shirby.
Holden, Marietta, b. 1845.
Holley, Marietta, 1844-1926.
Homer, N. Y.
Hood, Archer Leslie.

Hope Farm Man, The.

Hoskins, Jesse.
Houmas, Mount.
Hulsbuck, Solly.
Hume, Jean B.
Humphreys, Dean.
Huntington, Faye.
Huntington, Helen.
Illinois Girl, An.
Ingraham, Frances C.
Ink, Evangeline, 1883-1923.
Irwin, Wallace.
J. P. M.
Jabez, Brother.
Jackson, Frederick, b. 1886.
Jackson, Stephen.
Jaisohn, Philip, 1866-1951.
James, Martha.
Jane, Mary.
Janvier, Margaret Thompson, 1845-1913.
Jemimy, Aunt.
Jett, Ann Searcy, b. 1843.
Johnson, Anna, b. 1860.
Johnson, Wolcott.
Jones, Richard Morgan.
Jonsson, Ivar.
Josiah.
Josiah Allen's Wife.
Julier, Arthur H. G.
Juneau, May.
Justis Henry G. D.
Kain, Kress.
Karl.
Katharine.

Real name unknown.
D'Apery, Helen (Burrell), Mrs., 1842-1915.
Humphreys, Dean.
Stoddard, Cal.
Second, Henry.
Seymour, George Steele, b. 1878.
Trepoff, Ivan.
Knight of Chillon of Switzerland and associates.
Muller, J. (Julius Washington), 1867-1930.
Muller, J. (Julius Washington), 1867-1930.
Rollins, Montgomery, 1867-1918.
Chambers, Rosa, Mrs., b. 1886.
Wayne, Charles Stokes, b. 1858.
Gummere, Francis B.
Porter, William Sydney, 1862-1910.
Golden Light.
Physiopath, A.
Linfield, Mary Barrow, b. 1891.
Colvin, Addison Beecher, b. 1858.
Bauer, Wright.
McHugh, Hugh.
Tracy, Roger Sherman, 1871-1926.
"Princess, The."
Josiah Allen's Wife.
Stienback, Leroy Lindley, b. 1837.
Leslie, Lilian, jt. pseud. of Perkins, Violet Lilian
and Hood, Archer Leslie.
Collingwood, Herbert W. (Herbert Winslow),
1857-1927.
Fones, Warren.
Gill, Mary.
Miller, Harvey Monroe, b. 1871.
Viclare, Julien.
Harper, Sarah Jane, b. 1863.
Foster, Theodosia Maria, 1838-1923.
Granville-Barker, Helen Manchester.
Owen, Belle, b. 1866.
Bell, Clara Ingraham.
Evangeline.
Togo, Hashimura.
Wheeler, Andrew Carpenter, 1835-1903.
Koons, Ulysses Sidney.
Thorne, Victor.
Stevenson, John, b. 1853.
Osia, N. H.
Doyle, Martha Claire (MacGowan), Mrs., b. 1868.
Stine, Milton Henry, 1853-1940.
Vandegrift, Margaret.
Graves, Charlotte F., b. 1846.
Se Arcy, Ann.
Daring, Hope.
Brigham, Johnson, 1846-1936.
Brinley, Jay.
Tibbetts, Edgar Alfred, 1848-1908.
Emerson, W. H. (William H.), b. 1833.
Holley, Marietta, 1844-1926.
Gollmar, Arthur Howard, b. 1871.
Fisler, May Lewis, Mrs., b. 1866.
Donnelly, H. Grattan (Henry Grattan), 1850-1931.
Parrack, J. B.
Bloomingdale, Charles, Jr., 1868-1942.
Stephens, Louise G.

Kayamar.
Keating, Mrs. Anne.
Keizer, Genet.
Kelley, Francis Clement, bishop, 1870-1948.
Kelsey, Jeannette Garr (Washburn),
Mrs., b. 1850.
Kemp, Leonora (Valdez).
Kennedy, Kathleen.
Keon, Grace.
Kernodle, Louise Wellons Nurney, b. 1866.
Kimball, Atkinson.
Kimball, Richard Bowland.
Richard Bowland Kimball.
King, Kenneth Kenelm.
King, Scobe.
Kinsburn, Emart.
Kirk, Eleanor.
Knight of Chillon of
Switzerland and associates.
Knoppe, A. D.
Koons, Ulysses Sidney.
Krause, Lyda Farrington, 1864-1939.
Krout, Caroline Virginia, 1852-1931.
Kubinyi, Mrs. Florence Marie (Telmany) von,
b. 1895.
Kummer, Frederic Arnold, 1873-1943.
Lacey, Joseph Berry, b. 1842.
La Coste, Guy Robert.

Lamity, K.
Lathrop, Lorin Andrews, 1858-1929.
Law, Hyran S.
Lawrence, Albert.
Lawrence, Alberta (Chamberlin),
b. 1875.
Lawrence, Elwell.
Learsi, Rufus.
Lee, Charles C.
Lee, Marian.
Leo, Brother Zachary, b. 1881.
Leslie, Lilian.
Lessing, Bruno.
Lewis, Frederick.
Lewis, George Edward, b. 1870.
Limerick, Oliver Victor.
Lincoln, J. W. (John Willard), b. 1875.
Lincoln, May.
Linden, Edmund.
Linebarger, Paul Myron Wentworth, b. 1871.
Linfield, Mary Barrow, b. 1891.
Little, Frances.
Littleheart, Oleta.
Lloyd, John.
Loevius, Frederick.
Long, Lily A. (Lily Augusta), 1862-1927.
Loomis, Annie Elisabeth, 1850-1940.
Loose, Katharine Riegel, b. 1877.
Lothrop, Harriet Mulford Stone, 1844-1924.
Lovell, Ingraham.
Lundsford, Hugh.
Lynch, Jerome Morley, Mrs., 1864-1943.
Lynch, Lawrence L.

Robinson, Katharine.
Tequay, Anne.
Abbath.
Muredach, Myles.
Warren, Patience.

Davis, Mary L. K.
Richards, Annie Louise.
Doonan, Grace Wallace, Mrs.
Eldonrek, Louise.
Kimball, Richard Bowland and Atkinson, Grace Lucia.
Kimball, Atkinson, jt. pseud. of Mrs. Grace Lucie Atkinson and

Wentz, Albert Edwin, b. 1863.
McCue, Thomas F., b. 1866.
Hankins, Arthur Preston.
Ames, Eleanor Maria (Eastbrook), 1831-1908.
Hawkins, Nehemiah, 1833-1928.

Lacey, Joseph Berry, b. 1842.
Jabez, Brother.
Yechton, Barbara.
Brown, Caroline.
Gloria, F. M.

Fredericks, Arnold.
Knoppe, A. D.
Berton, Guy, jt. pseud. of Guy Robert La Coste
and Eadfrid A. Bingham.
Bonner, John Sturgis.
Gambier, Kenyon.
Walsh, Mary Catherine Frances.
Lawrence, Mrs. Alberta (Chamberlin), b. 1875.
Lawrence, Albert.

Sullivan, Francis William, b. 1887.
Goldberg, Israel, 1887-1964.
Rose, Martha Emily (Parmelee), b. 1834.
Comstock, Anna Botsford, 1854-1930.
Scarlet, Will.
Perkins, Violet Lilian and Hood, Archer Leslie.
Block, Rudolph Edgar.
Collins, Frederick Lewis, b. 1882.
Blacklock, Alaska.
Burgundy, Billy.
Barker, Bruce.
Broughton, Ida May, b. 1863.
Bliss, Alfonso.
Myron, Paul.
Highland, Lawrence.
Macaulay, Fannie Caldwell, 1863-1941.
Abbott, Aaron, b. 1867.
Morgan, Jacque Lloyd, b. 1873.
Thaumazo, Fred.
Doubleday, Roman.
Olmis, Elisabeth.
Schock, Georg.
Sidney, Margaret.
Bacon, Josephine Dodge Daskam, 1876-1961.
Buck, Charles Neville, b. 1879.
St. Felix, Marie.
Van Deventer, Emma M.

Pullen, Elisabeth.
Purdy, Jennie Bouton.
Putnam, George Palmer, 1887-1950.
Putnam, J. Wesley.
Quarles, M. D., Mrs.
Quillin, Horace Stewart, b. 1863.
Quinby, Laurie J.
Quint, Wilder Dwight, 1863-1936.

Raimond, C. E.
Ransom, Olive.
Rath, E. J.
Rebel, A.
Reeve, Winnifred Eaton.
Reid, Christian.

Rekrap.
Renfrew, Garroway.
Rhodes, Hattie, H.
Richards, Annie Louise.
Richardson, George Tilton.

Richardson, Robert.
Ritchie, Lily M., b. 1867.
Rives, Amelie.
Robertson, Alice Alberthe.

Robertson, Anna Adelia, b. 1875.
Robinet, Lee.
Robins, Elizabeth, 1862-1952.
Robinson, Katharine.
Rock, James.
Rockey, Howard, 1886-1934.
Roland, John.
Rollins, Montgomery, 1867-1918.
Ronzone, Benjamin Anthony, b. 1848.
Rose, Martha Emily (Parmelee), b. 1834.
Rosewater, Frank, b. 1856.

Ross, Betsey.
Rosso, Harley.
Russell, John, 1885-1956.
Rutledge, Maryse.
Sabina, Poppaea.
St. Felix, Marie.
St. John, John Ferris.
St. Luz, Berthe.
Scala, Guglielmo.
Scarlet, Will.
Schem, Lida C., 1875-1923.
Scherr, Marie.
Schieren, Harrie Victor, b. 1881.
Schmidt, Carl George, b. 1862.
Schock, Georg.
Schroeder, Reginald.

Schuyler, William, 1855-1914.
Sealis, Hatherly.
Se Arcy, Ann.
Searles, Jean Randolph.
Seawell, Molly Elliot, 1860-1916.
Second, Henry.

Cavazza, Elisabeth.
Shubael.
Bend, Palmer.
Drago, Harry Sinclair, 1888-1979.
Powel(l), Elizabeth.
Eskew, Harry.
Clifton, Wallace.
Merriman, Charles Eustace, jt. pseud.
Tilton, Dwight, jt. pseud.
Robins, Elizabeth, 1862-1952.
Stephens, Kate, 1853-1938.
Brainerd, Chauncey Cory and Brainerd, Edith Rathbone   (Jacobs).
Cone, Andrew Jackson.
Watanna, Onoto.
Tiernan, Francis Christine (Fisher), Mrs.,
1846-1920.
Parker, William Hendrix.
Barr, J., Mrs.
Webb, Virginia.
Kennedy, Kathleen.
Merriman, Charles Eustace, jt. pseud.
Tilton, Dwight, jt. pseud.
Perkins, Margaret Mower.
Briarly, Mary.
Troubetzkoy, Princess Amelie.
David, K.
St. Luz, Berthe.
Gladden, Hope.
Bennet, Robert Ames, 1870-1954.
Raimond, C. E.
Kayamar.
Patten, Clinton A.
Bryce, Ronald.
Oliver, John Rathbone, 1872-1943.
Hay, Timothy.
Baron.
Lee, Charles C.
Mayoe, Franklin.
Mayoe, Marian.
Braden, Jenness Mae.
McClure, Harvey Ross, b. 1886.
Thrice, Luke.
Hale, Marice Rutledge (Gibson), b. 1884.
Ballard, Robert.
Lynch, Jerome Morley, Mrs., 1864-1943.
Whiteside, Guy Kenneth, b. 1879.
David, K.
Schuyler, William, 1855-1914.
Leo, Brother Zachary, b. 1881.
Blake, Margaret.
Cher, Marie.
Childe, Crispin.
Carroll, George S.
Loose, Katharine Riegel, b. 1877.
**Davis, Schroeder, jt. pseud. of Oscar King Davis
and Reginald Schroeder.**
Scala, Guglielmo.
Foster, Charles Freeman, 1830-1912.
Jett, Ann Searcy, b. 1843.
Bienz, Mrs. Adah Viola (Rohrer), b. 1872.
Davis, Foxcroft.
Harrison, Henry Sydnor, 1880-1930.

Wentz, Albert Edwin, b. 1863.
West, Emery.
West, Roger.
Westerfield, E. W.
Westphal, Polhemus.
Wetmouth, John.
Wheeler, Andrew Carpenter, 1835-1903.
Wheeler, Mary Sparkes, Mrs., 1835-1919.
Wherry, Edith.
Whinnery, James Everhart.
White, Henry, b. 1876.
Whiteside, Guy Kenneth, b. 1879.
Wiechmann, Ferdinand Gerhard, 1858-1919.
Williams, Nathan Winslow.
Wilson, Richard Henry.
Winchevsky, Morris.
Winslow, Rose Guggenheim.
Witherspoon, Halliday.
Wood, Sabine W.
Wood-Seys, Roland A. (Roland Alexander), 1854-1919.
Worth, Marc.
Worth, Nicholas.
Worthington, Elizabeth Strong.
Wright, Caroline.
Wright, Joshua.
Wright, Mabel Osgood, 1859-1934.

Wright, Rowland.
Wright, Willard Huntington, 1888-1939.
Wycliffe, John.
Wynne, Joseph F.
Yechton, Barbara.
Yeld, Thomas, Sir.
Young, Sara Lee, b. 1847.
Younge, Leigh.
Zevin, Israel J. (Israel Joseph), 1872-1926.

King, Kenneth Kenelm.
Pollock, M. I.
Watson, Virginia Cruse, b. 1872.
Westphal, Polhemus.
Westerfield, E. W.
Prune, Nat.
Mowbray, J. P. ("J. P. M.").
One of the Redeemed.
Muckleston, Harold Struun, Mrs.
Blair, Uncle.
Oliver, Poland.
St. John, John Ferris.
Monroe, Forest.
Dallas, Richard.
Fisguill, Richard.
Benedict, Leopold, b.1856.
Burr, Jane.
Nutter, William Herbert, b. 1874.
Fisher, Jacob.
Cushing, Paul.

Gillis, Adolph.
Page, Walter Hines, 1855-1918.
Nicholas, Griffith A.
Germaine, Quincy.
Smith, Titus Keiper, b. 1859.
Barbara.
Gardener, The.
Wells, Carolyn, 1862-1942.
Van Dine, S. S.
Bedford-Jones, H. (Henry), 1887-1949.
O'Loan, Charlotte A.
Krause, Lyda Farrington, 1864-1939.
Taft, Israel Plummer, b. 1857.
Younge, Leigh.
Young, Sara Lee, b. 1847.
Tashrak.